ATHLI
20

THE INTERNATIONAL TRACK AND FIELD ANNUAL

BY PETER MATTHEWS
ASSOCIATION OF TRACK & FIELD STATISTICIANS

SPORTS BOOKS

Published by SportsBooks Ltd

Copyright: SportsBooks Limited and Peter Matthews 2017

SportsBooks Limited
9 St Aubyns Place
York
YO24 1EQ
United Kingdom
Tel: 01904 613475
e-mail   randall@sportsbooks.ltd.uk
Website   www.sportsbooks.ltd.uk

All rights reserved. No part of this publication may be produced or transmitted in any form or by any means, including photocopying and recording, without written permission of the publishers. Such written permission must also be obtained before any part of the publication is stored in any retrieval system of any nature.

This publication incorporates the ATFS Annual.

Front page photograph supplied by Mark Shearman, 22 Grovelands Road, Purley, Surrey, CR8 4LA. Tel: 0208 660 0156: mark@athleticsimages.com

British Library Cataloguing in Publication Data

Athletics: the international track and
field annual – 2017
1. Athletics. Track & Field events –
Serials
1. International athletics annual (London)
796.4'2'05

ISBN 9781907524530

Cover design: Kath Grimshaw

Printed arranged by Jellyfish Solutions, UK

CONTENTS

Introduction	5
Abbreviations	6
Acknowledgements	9
ATFS & Web Sites	10

Review of 2016

Diary of the year by *Peter Matthews*	11
Athletes of the year – Men by *Peter Matthews*	21
Athletes of the year – Women by *Peter Matthews*	30

Cross-country

	40
Road race review by *Marty Post*	42
Marathon review by *Marty Post*	45
Marathon Majors	49
Ultramarathon review by *Andy Milroy*	49

Major Championships 2016

Olympic Games	51
European Youth Championships	63
European Championships	64
IAAF World Indoor Tour	71
IAAF World Race Walking Team Championships	71
IAAF World Race Walking Challenge	72
IAAF World Combined Events Challenge	72
IAAF Hammer Throw Challenge	72
World Marathon Majors 2015-16	72
African Championships	73
Asian Junior Championships	74
Balkan Championships	74
European Cup Winter Throwing	74
European Cup 10,000m	74
Ibero-American Championships	75
NACAC (U23) Championships & Oceania Walks Championships	75
Pan-American Combined Events Cup	75
Championships of the Small States of Europe	75
South American HMar, 50kW and U23 Championships	75
South Asian Games	76
IAU 100km World Championships	76
IAU 24 Hour European Championships	76
European and World Mountain Running Championships	76
IAAF Diamond League	77

Early 2017 Championships

European Indoor Championships	79
IAAF World Cross-country Championships	81

Preview of 2017 World Championships

	82
World Youth Championships	84
Commonwealth Games 2018	85

IAAF World Athletics Tour – Major Meetings 2016-2017	86
Major international events 2017-2021	87
Drugs bans	89
Obituary	91
World Lists Trends – 10th and 100th bests on world lists	104
Memories of the half-milers that time forgot *by Bob Phillips*	106
Corrections to *Athletics 2016* (year lists 2015) - and earlier years	109
Reference Books 2016–2017	111
Tribute to Ashton Eaton & Yelena Isinbayeva	115
Hall of Fame	118

National champions and Biographies

National champions 2016 and biographies of leading athletes	119
Introduction to World lists and indexes	231

Records

World and Continental records - men	233
World and Continental records - women	238
World bests - non-standard events	244
World long distance bests	245
World Indoor Records	246
World indoor junior records	247
World Veterans/Masters records	248
World and Continental Records set in 2016	250
World and Continental Records set in Jan-Mar 2017	252
World Records superlatives and split times	253

All-time Lists

Men	254
Women	292
Junior men	325
Junior women	330
Ultra (100k and 24 hours)	54
Indoor sprints	507

2016 World Lists

Men	336
Women	422
Men's Index	509
Women's Index	543

2017 World Indoor lists	576

Miscellany

Retirements announced, top women athletes giving birth in 2016	39
Marriages of athletes in 2016	39
Transfer of national allegiance	39
Women's name changes	39
Late Amendments	592

INTRODUCTION

THE PAST YEAR has been a turbulent one for athletics with the suspension of the Russian Federation and an overhaul of procedures at the sport's international governing body, the IAAF, following the arrest of its former President, Lamine Diack and investigations into the actions of his team. During 2016 a new IAAF President (Lord) Sebastian Coe introduced fundamental changes in the governance of the IAAF and a new CEO, Olivier Gers, was appointed in August.

For several years an increasing number of Russian athletes have been found positive for the use of performance-enhancing substances and barred from international competition. Media investigations into this were led by the German TV station ARD, who aired a documentary "Top Secret Doping: How Russia Makes it Winners" on 3 December 2014. Following the broadcast, WADA set up an Independent Commission "to conduct an independent investigation into doping practices; corrupt practices around sample collection and results management; and other ineffective administration of anti-doping processes that implicate Russia, the IAAF, athletes, coaches, trainers, doctors and other members of athletes' entourages; as well as the accredited laboratory based in Moscow and the Russian Anti-Doping Agency (RUSADA)." The WADA investigation led to suspension of the Russian Federation (ARAF) by the IAAF after the exposing of a deeply rooted culture of cheating and exploitation of athletes. WADA Commission reports were presented by Richard McLaren in July 2016 and in December 2016 – and these gave a damning indictment into the widespread use of doping in Russian sport.

The suspension of the Russian federation meant that Russian athletes were banned from international competition including the Olympic Games and that ban remains in force at the time of going to press. Darya Klishina was permitted to compete at the Games, having shown that she was subject by proper testing procedures and in February 2017 three other Russians were accepted by the IAAF Doping Review Board as having met the exceptional eligibility criteria to compete in international competition as neutral athletes. This has been followed by applications from scores more athletes, and it remains to be seen how many will be allowed to compete while work continues to address the core problems in Russia. It should not, however, be thought that doping is only a problem in Russia,

The main competitive focus for athletics in 2016 was, of course, the Olympic Games and the conditions in Rio de Janeiro helped to ensure very high standards. Half a century ago world records were improved very regularly, but in the modern era we have become accustomed to just a handful each year after a levelling out in standards after huge changes in universal participation, medical and scientific knowledge, intensive preparation and coaching and professionalism. So the world records set in Rio were all the more remarkable. Few would have expected the records set by Michael Johnson at 400m and Wang Junxia at 10,000m in the 1990s, to go, but in Rio they were not just beaten, but smashed by the superlative achievements of Wayde van Niekerk and Almaz Ayana, while Anita Wlodarczyk added to her series of world hammer records in a year in which she established a dominance of an event very rarely seen in the history of our sport. These athletes at the pinnacle of achievement were joined by Usain Bolt, who completed his triple triple and remains the athletics super-star, also gaining many athlete of the year awards. As often happens with Olympic years standards of performance in depth reached record levels and this is reflected in the year lists that comprise a substantial part of this Annual. Now we look forward to another fascinating year of competition, headed by the World Championships in London, where we can expect massive crowd enthusiasm, just as we had at the Olympic Games there in 2012.

Peter Matthews, April 2017.

ABBREVIATIONS

The following abbreviations have been used for meetings with, in parentheses, the first year that they were held.

AAU	(USA) Amateur Athletic Union Championships (1888) (later TAC)
Af-AsG	Afro-Asian Games (2003)
AfCh	African Championships (1979)
AfG	African Games (1965)
Af-J	African Junior Championships (1994)
AmCp	America's Cup (World Cup Trial) (1977)
APM	Adriaan Paulen Memorial, Hengelo
AsiC	Asian Championships (1973)
AsiG	Asian Games (1951)
Asi-J	Asian Junior Championships (1990)
ASV	Weltklasse in Köln, ASV club meeting (1934)
Athl	Athletissima, Lausanne (1976)
Balk	Balkan Games (1929), C - Championships
Barr	(Cuba) Barrientos Memorial (1946)
BGP	Budapest Grand Prix (1978)
Bisl	Bislett Games, Oslo (1965) (Bergen 2004)
Bol G	Bolivar Games (1938)
BrGP	British Grand Prix
CAC	Central American and Caribbean Championships (1967)
CAG	Central American and Caribbean Games (1926)
C.Asian	Central Asian Championships
CAU	Inter-counties, GBR (1934)
CG	Commonwealth Games (1930)
C.Cup	Continental Cup (2010)
Déca	Décanation, Paris (C) (2005)
DL	Diamond League (2010)
DNG	DN Galan, Stockholm (1966)
Drake	Drake Relays (1910)
EAF	European Athletics Festival, Bydgoszcz (2001)
EAsG	East Asian Games (1993)
EC	European Championships (1934)
ECCp	European Clubs Cup (1975)
EChall	European Challenge (10,000m 1997, Throws 2001); see ET
ECp	European Cup - track & field (1965), multi-events (1973)
EI	European Indoor Championships (1970, Games 1966-9)
EICp	European Indoor Cup (2003)
EJ	European Junior Championships (1970)
ET	European Team Championships (replaced European Cup, 2009)
EU23	European Under-23 Championships (1997) and European Under-23 Cup (1992-4)
FBK	Fanny Blankers-Koen Games, Hengelo (formerly APM) (1981)
FlaR	Florida Relays (1939)
FOT	(USA) Final Olympic Trials (1920)
Franc	Francophone Games (1989)
Gaz	Gaz de France meeting, FRA (was BNP) (1968)
GGala	Golden Gala, Roma (from 1980), Verona (1988), Pescara (1989), Bologna (1990)
GL	Golden League (1998-2009)
GNR	Great North Run – Newcastle to South Shields, GBR (1981)
GP	Grand Prix
GPF	IAAF Grand Prix Final (1985)
GS	Golden Spike, Ostrava (1969)
Gugl	Zipfer Gugl Grand Prix, Linz (1988)
GWG	Goodwill Games (1986)
Gyulai	István Gyulai Memorial, Budapest (2011-13), Székesfehérvár (2014-16)
Hanz	Hanzekovic Memorial, Zagreb (1958)
Herc	Herculis, Monte Carlo, Monaco (1987)
IAAF	International Association of Athletics Federations
IAC	IAC meeting (1968), formerly Coca-Cola
IAU	International Association of Ultrarunners
IbAm	Ibero-American Championships (1983)
ISTAF	Internationales Stadionfest, Berlin (1921)
Jenner	Bruce Jenner Classic, San Jose (1979)
Jerome	Harry Jerome Track Classic (1984)
Jordan	Payton Jordan U.S. Track & Field Open, Stanford (2004)
JUCO	Junior Colleges Championships, USA
KansR	Kansas Relays, Lawrence (1923)
Kuso	Janusz Kusocinski Memorial (1954)
Kuts	Vladimir Kuts Memorial (1978)
LGP	London Grand Prix, Crystal Palace
LI	Loughborough International (1958)
MAI	Malmö Al Galan, Sweden (1958)
Mast	Masters pole vault, Grenoble (1987), Donetsk
MedG	Mediterranean Games (1951)
Mill	Millrose Games, New York indoors (1908)
ModR	Modesto Relays (1942)
MSR	Mt. San Antonio College Relays (1959)
NA	Night of Athletics, Heusden (2000) formerly Hechtel
NACAC	North American, Central American & Caribbean Ch (2003)
NC	National Championships
NC-w	National Winter Championships
NCAA	National Collegiate Athletic Association Championships, USA (1921)
NCAA-r	NCAA Regional Championships (2003)
NCp	National Cup
Nebiolo	Memorial Primo Nebiolo, Torino (2000, originally 1963)
NG	National Games
Nik	Nikaïa, Nice (1976)
NM	Narodna Mladezhe, Sofia (1955)
N.Sch	National Schools
Nurmi	Paavo Nurmi Games (1957)
NYG	New York Games (1989)
OD	Olympischer Tag (Olympic Day) (1963)
Oda	Mikio Oda Memorial Meeting, Hiroshima (1967)
Odlozil	Josef Odlozil Memorial, Prague (1994)
OG	Olympic Games (1896)
OT	Olympic Trials
Owens	Jesse Owens Memorial (1981)
PAm	Pan American Games (1951)
PArab	Pan Arab Championships (1977) (G-Games 1953)
Pedro	Pedro's Cup, Poland (2005)
PennR	Pennsylvania Relays (1895)
PTS	Pravda Televízia Slovnaft, Bratislava (1957) (later GPB)
Pre	Steve Prefontaine Memorial (1976)

RdVin	Route du Vin Half Marathon, Luxembourg (1962)	Dec	decathlon
RomIC	Romanian International Championships (1948)	DT	discus
		h	hurdles
RWC	Race Walking Challenge Final (2007)	Hep	heptathlon
SACh	South American Championships (1919)	HJ	high jump
SAsG	South Asian Games (1984)	HMar	half marathon
SEAG	South East Asia Games (1959)	HT	hammer
SEC	Southeastern Conference Championships	JT	javelin
SGP	IAAF Super Grand Prix	LJ	long jump
Skol	Skolimowska Memorial (2010)	Mar	marathon
Slovn	Slovnaft, Bratislava (formerly PTS) (1990)	Pen	pentathlon
Spark	Sparkassen Cup, Stuttgart (indoor) (1987)	PV	pole vault
Spart	(URS) Spartakiad (1956)	R	relay
Spitzen	Spitzen Leichtathletik Luzern (1987)	SP	shot
Stra	Stramilano Half marathon, Milan (1972)	St	steeplechase
Super	Super Meet, Japan (Tokyo, Shizuoka, Yokohama, Kawasaki)	TJ	triple jump
		W	walk
		Wt	weight

Miscellaneous abbreviations

TexR	Texas Relays (1925)
Tsik	Athens Grand Prix Tsiklitiria (1998)
USOF	US Olympic Festival (1978)
VD	Ivo Van Damme Memorial, Brussels (1977)
Veniz	Venizélia, Haniá, Crete (1936)
WAC	Western Athletic Conference Championships (1962)
WAF	World Athletics Finals (2003)
WCh	World Championships (1983)
WCM	World Challenge Meeting (2010)
WCp	World Cup - track & field (1977), marathon (1985) Walking – Lugano Trophy – men (1961), Eschborn Cup – women (1979)
WCT	World Championships Trial
WG	World Games, Helsinki (1961)
WI	World Indoor Championships (1987), World Indoor Games (1985)
WJ	World Junior Championships (1986)
WK	Weltklasse, Zürich (1962)
WMilG	World Military Games
WRly	World Relays (2014)
WUG	World University Games (1923)
WY	World Youth Championships (1999)
Zat	Emil Zátopek Classic, Melbourne
Znam	Znamenskiy Brothers Memorial (1958)

-j, -y, -23 Junior, Youth or under-23
Dual and triangular matches are indicated by "v" (versus) followed by the name(s) of the opposition. Quadrangular and larger inter-nation matches are denoted by the number of nations and -N; viz 8-N designates an 8-nation meeting.

+	Intermediate time in longer race
=	Tie (ex-aequo)
A	Made at an altitude of 1000m or higher
b	date of birth
D	Made in decathlon competition
dnf	did not finish
dnq	did not qualify
dns	did not start
exh	exhibition
h	heat
H	Made in heptathlon competition
hr	hour
i	indoors
kg	kilograms
km	kilometres
m	metres
M	mile
m/s	metres per second
mx	Made in mixed men's and women's race
nh	no height
O	Made in octathlon competition
P	Made in pentathlon competition
pb	personal best
Q	Made in qualifying round
qf	quarter final (or q in lists)
r	Race number in a series of races
sf	semi final (or s in lists)
w	wind assisted
WIR	world indoor record
WR	world record or best
y	yards
*	Converted time from yards to metres: For 200m: 220 yards less 0.11 second For 400m: 440 yards less 0.26 second For 110mh: 120yh plus 0.03 second

Events
CC   cross-country

Countries

(IAAF membership now stands at 214). IAAF and IOC abbreviations are now identical.

AFG	Afghanistan	AND	Andorra	BAR	Barbados
AHO	Netherlands Antilles #	ANG	Angola	BDI	Burundi
AIA	Anguilla	ANT	Antigua & Barbuda	BEL	Belgium
ALB	Albania	ARG	Argentina	BEN	Benin
ALG	Algeria	ARM	Armenia	BER	Bermuda
		ARU	Aruba	BHU	Bhutan
		ASA	American Samoa	BIH	Bosnia Herzegovina
		AUS	Australia	BIZ	Belize
		AUT	Austria	BLR	Belarus
		AZE	Azerbaijan	BOL	Bolivia
		BAH	Bahamas	BOT	Botswana
		BAN	Bangladesh	BRA	Brazil

Code	Country	Code	Country	Code	Country
BRN	Bahrain	IRI	Iran	PLW	Palau
BRU	Brunei	IRL	Ireland	PNG	Papua New Guinea
BUL	Bulgaria	IRQ	Iraq	POL	Poland
BUR	Burkina Faso	ISL	Iceland	POR	Portugal
CAF	Central African Republic	ISR	Israel	PRK	North Korea (DPR Korea)
		ISV	US Virgin Islands		
CAM	Cambodia	ITA	Italy	PUR	Puerto Rico
CAN	Canada	IVB	British Virgin Islands	PYF	French Polynesia
CAY	Cayman Islands	JAM	Jamaica	QAT	Qatar
CGO	Congo	JOR	Jordan	ROU	Romania
CHA	Chad	JPN	Japan	RSA	South Africa
CHI	Chile	KAZ	Kazakhstan	RUS	Russia
CHN	People's Republic of China	KEN	Kenya	RWA	Rwanda
		KGZ	Kyrgyzstan	SAM	Samoa
CIV	Côte d'Ivoire (Ivory Coast)	KIR	Kiribati	SCG	Serbia & Montenegro (to 2006)
CMR	Cameroon	KOR	Korea		
COD	Democratic Republic of Congo	KOS	Kosovo	SCO	Scotland
		KSA	Saudi Arabia	SEN	Sénégal
COK	Cook Islands	KUW	Kuwait	SEY	Seychelles
COL	Colombia	LAO	Laos	SIN	Singapore
COM	Comoros	LAT	Latvia	SKN	St Kitts & Nevis
CPV	Cape Verde Islands	LBA	Libya	SLE	Sierra Leone
CRC	Costa Rica	LBR	Liberia	SLO	Slovenia
CRO	Croatia	LCA	St Lucia	SMR	San Marino
CUB	Cuba	LES	Lesotho	SOL	Solomon Islands
CUR	Curaçao	LIB	Lebanon	SOM	Somalia
CYP	Cyprus	LIE	Liechtenstein	SRB	Serbia
CZE	Czech Republic	LTU	Lithuania	SRI	Sri Lanka
DEN	Denmark	LUX	Luxembourg	SSD	South Sudan
DJI	Djibouti	MAC	Macao	STP	São Tomé & Príncipe
DMA	Dominica	MAD	Madagascar	SUD	Sudan
DOM	Dominican Republic	MAR	Morocco	SUI	Switzerland
ECU	Ecuador	MAS	Malaysia	SUR	Surinam
EGY	Egypt	MAW	Malawi	SVK	Slovakia
ENG	England	MDA	Moldova	SWE	Sweden
ERI	Eritrea	MDV	Maldives	SWZ	Swaziland
ESA	El Salvador	MEX	Mexico	SYR	Syria
ESP	Spain	MGL	Mongolia	TAN	Tanzania
EST	Estonia	MKD	Former Yugoslav Republic of Macedonia	TCH	Czechoslovakia (to 1991)
ETH	Ethiopia			TGA	Tonga
FIJ	Fiji	MLI	Mali	THA	Thailand
FIN	Finland	MLT	Malta	TJK	Tadjikistan
FRA	France	MNE	Montenegro	TKM	Turkmenistan
FRG	Federal Republic of Germany (1948-90)	MNT	Montserrat	TKS	Turks & Caicos Islands
		MON	Monaco	TLS	East Timor
FSM	Micronesia	MOZ	Mozambique	TOG	Togo
GAB	Gabon	MRI	Mauritius	TPE	Taiwan (Chinese Taipei)
GAM	The Gambia	MSH	Marshall Islands	TTO	Trinidad & Tobago
GBR	United Kingdom of Great Britain & Northern Ireland	MTN	Mauritania	TUN	Tunisia
		MYA	Myanmar	TUR	Turkey
GBS	Guinea-Bissau	NAM	Namibia	TUV	Tuvalu
GDR	German Democratic Republic (1948-90)	NCA	Nicaragua	UAE	United Arab Emirates
		NED	Netherlands	UGA	Uganda
GEO	Georgia	NEP	Nepal	UKR	Ukraine
GEQ	Equatorial Guinea	NFI	Norfolk Islands	URS	Soviet Union (to 1991)
GER	Germany (pre 1948 and from 1991)	NGR	Nigeria	URU	Uruguay
		NGU	Papua New Guinea	USA	United States
GHA	Ghana	NI	Northern Ireland	UZB	Uzbekistan
GIB	Gibraltar	NIG	Niger	VAN	Vanuatu
GRE	Greece	NMA	Northern Marianas Islands	VEN	Venezuela
GRN	Grenada			VIE	Vietnam
GUA	Guatemala	NOR	Norway	VIN	St Vincent & the Grenadines
GUI	Guinea	NRU	Nauru		
GUM	Guam	NZL	New Zealand	WAL	Wales
GUY	Guyana	OMA	Oman	YEM	Republic of Yemen
HAI	Haiti	PAK	Pakistan	YUG	Yugoslavia (to 2002)
HKG	Hong Kong, China	PAN	Panama	ZAM	Zambia
HON	Honduras	PAR	Paraguay	ZIM	Zimbabwe
HUN	Hungary	PER	Peru		# ceased to exist as a separate territory in 2010, and absorbed into the Netherlands.
INA	Indonesia	PHI	Philippines		
IND	India	PLE	Palestine		

ACKNOWLEDGEMENTS

MY THANKS TO all those who have helped me to compile this Annual with lists or other information information. My valued correspondents remain much the same year on year, but the number tends to decline as we statisticians get older and there no longer seem to be many younger enthusiasts. Perhaps many take for granted that information will be available via the Internet and surely that has transformed the collation of data, but there remains to need to check, correct an collate this. So a warm welcome to any newcomers who can help us in our work in producing definitive reference sources.

As usual I have worked up the world year lists in this annual from original compilations by Richard Hymans and Mirko Jalava with reference to those of many other experts. Mirko's superb web site www.tilastopaja.net provides great depth of worldwide results I am indebted to Pino Mappa for work on men's lists, Carlos Fernández for his expertise on the road lists and to Ray Herdt for the walks. I circulate draft lists to a number of ATFS experts and receive much valuable information from a worldwide circle of correspondents, most of whom have helped with information from their nations for many years. Of the great Spanish group Juan Mari Iriondo and Miguel Villaseñor checked the biographies and obituaries. Børre Lilloe provided much index data and Ken Nakamura checked distance lists. Bob Phillips has again provided an article, keeping up his long association with the Annual.

Both for this annual and throughout the year with *Athletics International* that I produce with Mel Watman, Winfried Kramer helps with widespread probing for results as do the area experts: *Africa*: Yves Pinaud, *Asia*: Heinrich Hubbeling, *Central and South America*: Eduardo Biscayart and Luis Vinker, and specialists: *Records* György Csiki, *Road racing*: Marty Post, *Ultrarunning* Andy Milroy, *Indoors* Ed Gordon, *Multi events*: Hans van Kuijen and Enn Endjärv, *Pole vault* Kenneth Lindqvist, *800m:* Nejat Kök.

Australia: Paul Jenes; *Austria*: Dr Karl Graf; *Belgium*: André de Hooghe and Alain Monet; *Bulgaria*: Aleksandar Vangelov; *China*: Mirko Jalava; *Cuba*: Alfredo Sánchez; *Czech Republic*: Milan Urban; *Denmark*: Erik Laursen; *Dominican Republic*: Arisnel Rodríguez; *Estonia*: Erlend Teemägi and Enn Endjärv; *Finland*: Juhani Jalava, Mirko Jalava, Mikko Nieminen and Matti Hannus; *France*: Alain Bouillé, Carles Baronet and Patricia Doilin; *Germany:* Klaus Amrhein; *Greece*: Thomas Konstas and Nikos Kriezis; *Hungary*: György Csiki; *India*: Ram. Murali Krishnan; *Ireland*: Pierce O'Callaghan and Liam Hennessy; *Israel*: David Eiger; *Italy*: Raul Leoni; *Japan*: Yoshimasa Noguchi, Akihiro Onishi, Tatsumi Senda and Ken Nakamura; *Latvia*: Andris Stagis; *Lithuania*: Stepas Misiunas; *Luxembourg*: Georges Klepper; *Malaysia*: Jad Adrian, *Montenegro*: Ivan Popovic; *New Zealand*: Murray McKinnon and Steve Hollings; *Norway*: Børre Lilloe; *Poland*: Zbigniew Jonik and Janusz Rozum; *Portugal*: Arons Carvalho; *Puerto Rico*: Pedro Anibal Diaz; *Russia*: Sergey Tikhonov; *Serbia*: Ozren Karamata and Olga Acic; *Slovakia*: Alfons Juck; *Slovenia*: Zdravko Peternelj; *South Africa:* Danie Cornelius, Clyde Kinloch, Richard Meyer and Riël Hauman; *Spain*: José Luis Hernández, Miguel Villaseñor, Carles Baronet and the AEEA team; *Sweden*: Jonas Hedman, Lennart Julin and Peter Larsson; *Switzerland*: Alberto Bordoli and Antonin Hejda; *Trinidad:* Bernard Linley, *Turkey*: Nejat Kök, *Ukraine*: Ivan Kachkivskiy; *UK*: Tony Miller and Ian Hodge; *USA*: Tom Casacky, Garry Hill, Mike Kennedy, Sieg Lindstrom, Glen McMicken, Marty Post, Jack Shepherd and *Track Newsletter*. Also various national federation lists and to those who post results or ranking lists to various web sites.

Also to Marco Buccellato, Mark Butler, Carole Fuchs, José Maria García, Grzegorz Gladzikowski, Stan Greenberg, Alan Lindop, Rooney Magnusson (obituaries), Bill Mallon, David Monti, Jiri Ondrácek (European U23), Zdenek Procházka (hammer), Miguel Villaseñor and Rob Whittingham.

My apologies to anybody whose name I may have missed or who have corresponded with other key ATFS personnel, but all help, however small is deeply appreciated.

Keep the results flowing

During the year Mel Watman and I publish marks to ATFS standards (150-200 deep on world lists) in *Athletics International*, of which there are over 35 issues per year by email. This serves as a base from which the lists in this book can be compiled, together with information from web sites, especially Mirko Jalava's *Tilastopaja*, *Track & Field News* (USA) with its email results spin-off *Track Newsletter* and newsletters, especially Alfons Juck's *EME News* and Carles Baronet's *Track in Sun*.

In order to ensure that the record of 2017 is as complete as possible I urge results contribution worldwide to AI, and then in turn our lists in *Athletics 2018* (if there is one) will be as comprehensive as we can make them.

Peter Matthews

THE ASSOCIATION OF TRACK & FIELD STATISTICIANS

The ATFS was founded in Brussels (at the European Championships) in 1950 and ever since has built upon the work of such key founding members as Roberto Quercetani, Don Potts and Fulvio Regli to produce authoritative ranking lists in the International Athletics Annual and elsewhere.

Current Executive Committee
President: Paul Jenes AUS
Vice-President: A.Lennart Julin SWE
Treasurer: Tom Casacky USA
Secretary: Michael J McLaughlin AUS
Past Presidents: Rooney Magnusson SWE, Dr Roberto Quercetani ITA
Committee: Eduardo Biscayart ARG/USA, Riël Hauman RSA, Nejat Kök TUR, Bernard Linley TRI, Giuseppa Mappa ITA, Peter J Matthews GBR, Yoshimasa Noguchi JPN, Yves Pinaud FRA

Website: www.atfs.org

Internet – Websites

IAAF	www.iaaf.org
IAU	www.iau-ultramarathon.org
Africa (CAA)	www.webcaa.org
Asian AA	athleticsasia.org
CAC Confederation	www.cacacathletics.org
European AA	www.european-athletics.org
NACAC	www.athleticsnacac.org
Oceania AA	www.athletics-oceania.com
South American Fed.	www.consudatle.org
WMRA	www.wmra.info
World Masters	www.world-masters-athletics.org
Marathon Majors	www.worldmarathonmajors.com
Africa	www.africathle.com
Andorra	www.faa.ad
Argentina	www.cada-atletismo.org
Australia	www.athletics.com.au
Austria	www.oelv.at
Bahamas	www.bahamastrack.com
Belarus	www.bfla.eu
Belgium	www.val.be
Bermuda	www.btfa.bm
Bosnia Hercegovina	www.asbih.org
Brazil	www.cbat.org.br
Bulgaria	www.bfla.org
Canada	www.athletics.ca
Chile	www.fedachi.cl
China	www.athletics.org.cn
Costa Rica	www.fecoa.org
Croatia	www.has.hr
Cyprus	www.koeas.org.cy
Czech Republic	www.atletika.cz
Denmark	www.dansk-atletik.dk
Dominican Republic	www.fedomatle.org
England	www.englandathletics.org
Estonia	www.ekjl.ee
Finland	www.sul.fi
France	www.athle.com
Germany	www.leichtathletik.de
Great Britain	www.britishathletics.org.uk
deep statistics	www.topsinathletics.info
	www.thepowerof10.info
Greece	www.segas.gr
Hong Kong	www.hkaaa.com
Hungary	www.masz.hu
Iceland	www.fri.is
India	www.indianathletics.org
Indonesia	www.indonesia-athletics.org
Ireland	www.athleticsireland.ie
Israel	www.iaa.co.il
Italy	www.fidal.it
Jamaica	www.trackandfieldja.com
Japan	www.jaaf.or.jp
running news	japanrunningnews.blogspot.co.uk
Kazakhstan	www.kazathletics.kz
Kenya	www.athleticskenya.or.ke
Latvia	www.lat-athletics.lv
Lithuania	www.lengvoji.lt
Luxembourg	www.fla.lu
Macedonia	www.afm.org.mk
Malaysia	www.maf.org.my
results	www.adriansprints.com
Mexico	www.fmaa.mx
Moldova	www.fam.com.md
Monaco	www.fma.mc
Montenegro	www.ascg.co.me
Morocco	www.moroccanathletics.com
Netherlands	www.atletiekunie.nl
New Zealand	www.athletics.org.nz
Northern Ireland	www.niathletics.org
Norway	www.friidrett.no
Peru	www.fedepeatle.org
Poland	www.pzla.pl
Portugal	www.fpatletismo.pt
	www.atletismo-estatistica.pt
Puerto Rico	www.atletismofapur.com
	www.pedroanibaldiaz.com
Romania	www.fra.ro
Russia	www.rusathletics.com
Scotland	www.scottishathletics.org.uk
	www.scotstats.net
Serbia	www.ass.org.rs
Singapore	www.singaporeathletics.org.sg
Slovakia	www.atletikasvk.sk
Slovenia	www.atletska-zveza.si
South Africa	www.athletics.org.za
Spain	www.rfea.es
Sweden	www.friidrott.se
Switzerland	www.swiss-athletics.ch
Taiwan	www.cttfa.org.tw
Trinidad & Tobago	www.ttnaaa.org
Turkey	www.taf.org.tr
Ukraine	www.uaf.org.ua
Uruguay	www.atlecau.org.uy
USA	www.usatf.org
collegiate results	www.ustfccca.org
Wales	www.welshathletics.org
	athleticsstatswales.webeden.co.uk

Other recommended sites for statistics and results

AIMS	www.aimsworldrunning.org
ARRS	www.arrs.net
British historical	www.gbrathletics.com
	www.athlos.co.uk
DGLD (German stats)	www.ladgld.de
French history etc.	http://cdm.athle.com
Marathons	www.marathonguide.com
Masters Track & Field	www.mastersathletics.net
Mirko Jalava	www.tilastopaja.org
NUTS/Track Stats	www.nuts.org.uk
Rankings etc	www.all-athletics.com
Runners World	www.runnersworld.com
Tracklion (NED/BEL)	sportslion.net/tracklion.html
Track & Field News	www.trackandfieldnews.com
Track in Sun results	trackinsun.blogspot.co.uk
Ultra marathon stats	statistik.d-u-v.org/index.php
World juniors	www.worldjuniorathleticsnewsnzl.co.nz
Olympic Games	www.aafla.org
	www.sports-reference.com

DIARY OF 2016
by Peter Matthews

A chronological survey of highlights in major events in the world of track and field athletics.
See Championships or National sections for more details. DL = Diamond League, WCM = World Challenge Meeting, WIT = World Indoor Tour.

January

7   A panel of the IAAF Ethics Board (formerly Commission), chaired by Michael Beloff QC, announced that Papa Massata Diack, former marketing consultant to the IAAF, Valentin Balakhnichev, former President of the All-Russia Athletic Federation (ARAF) and former IAAF Treasurer, and Alexei Melnikov, former Chief ARAF Coach for long distance walkers and runners, were banned from any involvement in athletics for life, while Gabriel Dollé, former Director of the IAAF's Anti-Doping Department, was banned for five years.

22   **Dubai**, United Arab Emirates. 17th Standard Chartered Marathon. Ethiopians dominated the race with the first 6 men, headed by Tesfaye Abera 2:04:24 from a previous best of 2:09:46, and the first 11 women if one includes Ethiopian born Shitaye Eshete of Bahrain 6th. The women's winner was Tirfi Tsegaye in 2:19:41 from Amane Beriso, 2:20:48 for the fifth fastest ever women's marathon debut, and Meselech Melkamu 2:22:29.

30   **Brockport**, NY, USA. Jenn Suhr added 1cm to the world indoor record that she had set in 2013 with 5.03.

31   **Osaka**, Japan. 35th Women's Marathon. Kayoko Fukushi won in a course record 2:22:17.

February

3   **Düsseldorf**, Germany. PSD Bank meeting. Kim Collins set a world age-39 best of 6.53 and Orlando Ortega a Spanish record 6.49 for 60m hurdles.

6   **Karlsruhe**, Germany. The first meeting in the IAAF World Indoor Tour. Mike Rodgers twice ran a world leading 6.52 60m, from Kim Collins 6.54, his first 60m defeat after 14 consecutive victories. Other world leading marks included Dafne Schippers, 7.07 in her heat and 7.08 in the final of the women's 60m from Barbara Pierre 7.09, and Kendra Harrison, 7.82 in her 60mh heat prior to 7.86 after a poor start in the final.

9-12   **South Asian Games**, Guwahati, India. The host nation comfortably headed the medal table.

12   **Fayetteville**, USA, Tyson Invitational. Top mark was 8.38 long jump by Marquis Dendy.

12   **Torun**, Poland. EA Permit. Ewa Swoboda set a world indoor junior record for 60m at 7.07.

12   **Ra's Al Khaymah**, United Arab Emirates. Cynthia Limo was the winner of the annual half marathon in 66:04 from Gladys Cherono 66:07 and Genet Ayalew, Ethiopian record 66:26, as a record six women broke 67 minutes. Men's winner was Birhanu Legesse 60:40.

13   **Berlin**, Germany, ISTAF meeting. Dimitri Bascou's 7.41 for 60m hurdles was a French record and the world's fastest for four years. Alexandra Wester long jumped 6.95, having started the year with an outdoor best of 6.59 and improving to 6.72 on 3 February. Thiago Braz da Silva improved the South American pole vault record to 5.93 and beat Renaud Lavillenie 5.85. Dafne Schippers won the 60m in a pb 7.00.

13   **Hustopece**, Czech Republic, Gianmarco Tamberi won the high jump with an Italian record 2.38, with Chris Baker 2nd at 2.36, improving his best from 2.28.

13   **Los Angeles**, USA. Galen Rupp had a winning marathon debut as he won the US Olympic Trial in 2:11:13.

14   **Boston (Roxbury)**, USA. New Balance GP (WIT). Meseret Defar won the 3000m in 8:30.05, her first track race since 2013, and other middle distance world leading marks were set by Nick Willis, 1M 3:53.27, and Dawit Seyaum, 1500m 4:01.86.

17   **Stockholm**, Sweden. Globen Galan (WIT). Three world indoor records/bests were set in a great meeting: 59.83 by 18 year-old Abdelilah Haroun at 500m, 2:14.20 for 1000m by Ayanleh Souleiman (200m splits 25.61, 52.29, 1:19.44), and 4:13.31 by Genzebe Dibaba at 1 mile to take 3.83 off Doina Melinte's 1990 mark. The mile was paced to 800m in 2:05.69 by Joanna Józwik, before Dibaba took over, passing 1500m in 3:56.46; her 440y splits were 62.7, 2:06.1 and 3:10.4.

19-21   **Asian Indoor Championships**, Doha, Qatar. Mutaz Essa Barshim won his fourth successive gold medal at this biennial event by clearing 2.35 in the high jump. Double wins at 1500m and 3000m were achieved by Mohamed Al-Garni who retained both titles from 2014 in 3:36.35 and 7:39.23, both championship records, and Betlhem Desalegn with the women's races.

20 **Glasgow**, GBR. In his one track race of the winter Mo Farah won the 3000m in 7:39.55. This was the final meet of the World Indoor Tour, in which event winners earned $20,000. The biggest payout went to Adam Kszczot, who followed up his 800m victories in Karlsruhe (1:45.96) and Stockholm (1:45.63) with another assured win in 1:46.23. With $3000 for first place in each race he took a total of $29,000. Sifan Hassan won the 1500m in 4:01.40 from Gudaf Tsegay, whose 4:01.81 was a world indoor junior record. Li Ling set an Asian women's pole vault record of 4.70 for her third title and Abdelaati Iguider won the 1500m in 3:34.94, the fastest of the indoor season, well ahead of Ayanleh Suleiman 3:36.30.

20 **New York (Armory)**, USA. 109th Millrose Games. Ekateríni Stefanídi won the pole vault on count-back from Demi Payne, whose 4.90 was the best ever second place mark. The famed Wanamaker Mile went to Matthew Centrowitz for a third time, his 3:50.63 a race record.

21 **Clermont-Ferrand**, France. Renaud Lavillenie pole vaulted 6.02 to beat a top field with Shaunacy Barber 2nd at 5.01 and five over 5.84 or higher. He improved this world best to 6.03 at Jablonec on 5 March.

26-27 **SEC Championships**, Fayetteville, USA. Felicia Brown won the 200m in 22.45, a time that remained the women's indoor best for 2017.

27-28 **French Indoor Championships**, Clermont-Ferrand. Highlights included Pascal Martinot Lagarde, 7.47 for 60mh, and Renaud Lavillenie 5.93 pole vault.

27-28 **German Indoor Championships**, Leipzig. Julian Reus improved the German 60m record to 6.52 and also won the 200m in 20.55 and Tatjana Pinto iimproved her best from 7.29 to 7.19 heat, 7.12 semi and 7.07 in the 60m final. Another big improver was Max Hess from 16.55 to 17.00 in the triple jump.

27-28 **Russian Winter Walks Championships**, Sochi. Several walkers returned from their drugs bans to feature well here, notably the winners of the 35k, Sergey Bakulin 2:28:20, and women's 20k Olga Kaniskina 1:25:54.

27-28 **UK Indoor Championships**, Sheffield. Asha Philip beat Dina Asher-Smith 7.10 to 7.15 at 60m and Tom Bosworth took his national 3000m walk record from 11:15.81 to 10:58.21.

28 **Tokyo Marathon**, Japan. Feyisa Lilesa had a clear win in the last race in the 2015/16 World Marathon Majors series, pulling away from Dickson Chumba over the last kilometre to record the third win of his marathon career (previous wins were in 2009 and 2010), in 2:06:56. Helah Kiprop ran even splits of 70:41 and 70:46 to win the women's race in 2:21:27 by 24secs from Amane Gobena. There were 34,694 finishers (27.126 men and 7568 women).

March

4-6 **New Zealand Championships**, Dunedin. Tom Walsh won his seventh successive shot title with 21.11 and 19 year-old Eliza McCartney set an Oceania pole vault record at 4.80.

5 **Melbourne**, Australia (WCM). David Rudisha, who likes to start his campaign here, won the 800m again in 1:44.78 and Dane Bird-Smith set an Oceania 3000m walk record with 18:38.97.

5 **Jablonec nad Nisou, Czech Republic**. Renaud Lavillenie achieved the best pole vault of 2016 with 6.03 and Richard Kilty made up for a false start in the UK Champs by winning the 60m in 6.50.

5-6 **Spanish Indoor Championships**, Madrid. Ruth Beitia cleared 1.98 in the high jump for her 15th successive national indoor title.

11-12 **US Indoor Championships**, Portland. World leading marks by two men: Marquis Dendy, 8.41 long jump, and Colin Dunbar, 23.96 weight, and four women: Barbara Pierre (=), 7.00 60m, Brianna Rollins, 7.76 60mh, Michelle Carter, 19.49 shot and Vashti Cunningham, 1.99 high jump, also a world junior indoor record, headed performances at a top quality meeting. Pole vault winners also excelled: Sam Kendricks 5.90 and Sandi Morris 4.95 from Jenn Suhr 4.90 and Demi Payne 4.85, the best ever third place mark.

11-12 **NCAA Indoor Championships**, Birmingham AL, USA. Oregon won both men's and women's team titles. Edward Cheserek won the 3000m and 5000m and anchored the Oregon team to victory in the distance medley relay. Sprinters were to the fore with world leads from Ronnie Baker, 60m 6.47, and Courtney Okolo, 400m 50.69, and Felicia Brown winning the 200m in 22.47. Kendell Williams added 25 points to her collegiate record for women's pentathlon with 4703.

12 **African Cross-Country Championships**, Yaoundé, Cameroon. Kenyans dominated as they won all four races (taking 10 of the 12 podium places) and all four team titles. James Rungaru and Alice Aprot Nawowuna were the senior individual champions.

12 **Perth**, Australia. Brooke Stratton set an Oceania long jump record of 7.05.

12 **Nagoya**, Japan. The favourite Eunice Jepkirui Kirwa successfully defended her women's marathon title with 2:22:40. This was her fifth win in her last six marathons, her fastest time and fifth under 2:24. The next seven finishers, all Japanese, set pbs.

12 **Bloemfontein**, South Africa. Wayde van Niekerk benefitted from high altitude to

run 100m in 9.98, making him the first man to run sub-10, sub-20 and sub-44.

12-13 16th **European Cup Winter Throwing**, Arad, Romania. The best marks included 20.68 shot by Andrei Gag and 72.58 in the women's hammer by Zalina Marghieva.

13 **Rome-Ostia**, Italy. Solomon Kirwa Yego ran the year's fastest half marathon, his 58:44 on this 20m downhill point-to-point course 43 secs faster than runner-up Leonard Langat.

17-20 **IAAF World Indoor Championships**, Portland, USA. Championship records both came at pole vault: Renaud Lavillenie, 6.02 and Jenn Suhr 4.90. Ashton Eaton (heptathlon 6479) and Brianne Theisen-Eaton (pentathlon 4881) became the first husband and wife gold medallists, and other top marks by winners included Brittany Reese, long jump 7.22, Omar McLeod, 60mh 7.41, and Tom Walsh, who set three Oceania shot records, 21.60, 21.64 and 21.78. The US was clearly dominant with 13 gold, 6 silver and 4 bronze medals, and Ethiopia with 2 golds was the only other nation to win more than one event. *For report and leading results see Athletics 2016 p. 93-94.*

19 **Dudince**, Slovakia. Tom Bosworth in a British record 1:20:41 and Eleanor Giorgi 1:28:05 won the 20k races, and Rafal Augustyn the 50k in 3:43:22 in the 35th edition of this walks meeting.

20 **Asian Walks Championships**, Nomi, Japan. 20 men bettered 1:22 in the 20k won by Daisuke Matsunaga 1:18:53 and the women's 20k was won by Wang Na 1:28:21.

26 **World Half Marathon Championship**, Cardiff. GBR, Despite falling at the start Geoffrey Kamworor was a decisive winner in 59:10 from team-mate Bidan Karoki and Mo Farah, and Peres Jepchirchir headed a Kenyan 1-2-3 in 67:31 in the women's race to ensure two Kenyan team victories.

30-2 Apr 89th **Texas Relays**, Austin, USA. Top performance was an outdoor world leading pole vault mark of 5.91 by Shawnacy Barber.

31- 2 Apr **Florida Relays**, Gainesville, USA. LA Shawn Merritt ran the 200m in 20.23, his fastest for four year, and there were plenty more top sprint performances.

April

2 **Prague**, Czech Republic. There were fast times in windless conditions, with winners Daniel Wanjiru 59:20 and Violah Jepchumba 65:51. The last remained the world's fastest of 2016 and behind her Worknesh Degefa ran an Ethiopian record 66:14.

3 **Paris Marathon**, France. Cyprian Kotut 2:07:11 and Visiline Jepkeshko 2:25:53 were the winners in sunny but cool weather. There was a race record 41,708 finishers (31,624 men and 10.084 women).

6-7 **Athens**, Georgia, USA. In her first outdoor race of the year Kendra 'Keni' Harrison, sped to 12.36 100m hurdles at the 'Spec' Towns Invitational.

10 **Rotterdam Marathon**, Netherlands. Marius Kipserem took 3:10 off his pb as he won in 2:06:11. He was followed by two marathon debutants Solomon Deksisa 2:06:22 and Geoffrey Kirui 2:07:23. The women's winner was Letebrhan Gebreslasea in 2:26:15.

14-16 58th **Mt SAC Relays**, Norwalk, California, USA. Held this year at Cerritos College rather than in Walnut, as the stadium there is being renovated in preparation for a bid for the 2020 Olympic Trials. Ameer Webb had a notable sprint double in 9.90w and 19.91. The latter was a world-leading time, as was the 10.95 for 100m by Jenna Prandini.

15-16 **South African Championships**, Stellenbosch. Caster Semenya won an amazing and unique triple on the second day. At 13:10 local time she ran a pb 50.74 for 400m, at 14:15 1:58.45 for 800m (her fastest since the 2012 Olympics) and at 17:40 4:10.91 for 1500m. Chris Harmse won his 21st successive RSA title at hammer to tie the all-time record for any nation.

16 **Kingston**, Jamaica. With 9.95 Yohan Blake ran his fastest 100m since 2012.

16 **Nassau**, Bahamas. Chris Brown is still a leading 400m runner but there was sharp sprinting at the Invitational meeting named in his honour. 200m times of 19.78 by LaShawn Merritt and 22.26 by Torie Bowie and 400m times of 44.36 by Kirani James and 49.69 by Shaunae Miller led the way.

17 **Hamburg Marathon**, Germany. Winners were Tesfaye Abera 2:06:58 and Meselech Melkamu 2:21:54.

18 120th **Boston Marathon**, USA. Ethiopian runners dominated, taking the first three places for the first time in the men's race won by Hayle Lemi in 2:12:45, and top two in the women's won by Atsede Baysa 2:29:19, but times were slow as the temperature rose from 17°C at the start to 22°C and there were strong headwinds.

22 **Gainesville, USA**. At the Tom Jones Memorial meeting Femi Ogunode equalled the Asian record for 100m that he had set at 9.91 last year. This was a world leading mark, as was the 22.25 run by Dafne Schippers for 200m and the 42.22 for 4x100m run by a multi-nation women's team.

23 **Fayetteville**, USA. By winning the 100m in 9.99 at the John McDonnell Invitational Omar McLeod became the first man ever to run under 10 secs for 100m and 13 secs for 110m hurdles.

24 Virgin **London Marathon**, GBR. Eliud Kipchoge ran the second fastest ever marathon on a standard course as he won for the second successive year in 2:03:05 with halves of 61:24

and 61:41 to earn a total of $180,000. He finished so strongly as he pulled away from Stanley Biwott (2nd in 2:03:51) that he covered the 5k to 40k in 14:42 and took just 6:16 for the final 2.195k as against Biwott's 14:51 and 6:53. They went through 30k in a world record 1:27:13. Kenenisa Bekele was an isolated third in 2:06:36. Mary Keitany was the women's favourite, but disaster struck shortly before 35k when she, Jemima Sumgong and Aselefech Mergia got tangled up and fell heavily. Keitany was the worst affected and she struggled from there to the finish for 9th in 2:28:30 while Sumgong won in 2:22:58 from Tigist Tufa 2:23:03 and Florence Kiplagat 2:23:39. There were a record 39,140 finishers from 39,523 starters.

27-30 107th **Drake Relays**, Des Moines, USA. Kirani James beat LaShawn Merritt 44.08 to 44.22 to take their career record to 11-7 to James. Omar McLeod ran the second fastest time of his career with 13.08 in rainy conditions, way ahead of David Oliver 13.31 and the women's 100m hurdles was fast too as Keni Harrison won in 12.56.

28-30 122nd **Penn Relays**, Philadelphia, USA. The USA had five wins and Jamaica one in the annual relays match.

May

1 **Stanford**, USA. Payton Jordan Invitational. As usual there was excellent depth of distance times such as the best ever times for places 23-27 (under 33 mins) for women's 10,000m races. Bernard Lagat took over 40 seconds off the world M40 record as he won the 10,000m with 27:49.35 in his track debut at the distance with a 58.8 last lap.

6 **Doha**, Qatar. Once again this was a high-class meeting, the first and one of the best of the 2016 IAAF Diamond League meetings. Athletes had perfect conditions, 32°C and 46% humidity at the start to 30°C and 58% at the end with a light breeze down the home straight, and unsurprisingly at this time of year there were a mass of world-leading marks, as these came in 12 of the 16 main events. The world's top two women triple jumper had a great duel, with Caterine Ibargüen beating Yulimar Rojas 15.04 to 14.92w. This was a meeting record as were Ameer Webb 200m 19.95, Sandi Morris another outdoor PV best 4.83 and Tori Bowie 100m 10.80 from fast-finishing Dafne Schippers 10.83. Piotr Malachowski won the discus with 68.03 from Philip Milanov's Belgian record 67.26 and on the track stars included Almaz Ayana with a 3000m win in 8:23.11 win over Mercy Cherono 8:26.11 and Omar McLeod ran 13.05 for 110m hurdles in beating Orlando Ortega, Spanish record 13.12.

7 **Kingston**, Jamaica Invitational (WCM). Top mark was Elaine Thompson's 10.71w for 100m. More top windy wins were by Shaunae Miller 22.14w 200m and Brianna Rollins 100mh 12.52w. Kim Collins smashed the world over-40 record at the first opportunity when he was 5th in 10.08 in the 100m won by Kemar Bailey-Cole 10.01.

7-8 **World Race Walking Cup**, Rome, Italy. Chinese athletes won the four races (and also took three sets of team gold medals) on the first day, but next day first across the line in the 50k on the second day was Alex Schwazer in 3:39:00 in his first big race and just ten days after finishing his three and a half year drugs ban. However, he later lost this with an 8-year ban for a further transgression and the win went to Jared Tallent 3:42:36. The American Erin Talcott made history when she became the first woman to contest the 50k; she recorded 4:51:08 as the last finisher. Liu Hong also lost her 20k win in 1:25:59, but that was for a stimulant warning. There were excellent standards in depth.

12-14 **Collegiate Conference Championships**, USA. Nethaneel Mitchell-Blake had a brilliant sprint triple for LSU with 10.16, 19.95 and 38.33 relay in the Southeastern Conference (SEC) in Tuscaloosa, where Felicia Brown ran 22.19w and 22.26 for 200m and Lindon Victor made sensational improvement at an 8446 decathlon from a previous best of 7453.

14 **Shanghai**, China (DL). Sandra Perkovic set a DL record of 70.88, and that remained the best discus throw of 2016. Faith Kipyegon set a Commonwealth record of 3:56.82 to win the 1500m with Hellen Obiri and Dawit Seyaum just under 4 mins, and Muktar Edris won the 5000m in 12:59.96 from Joshua Cheptegei and Thomas Longosiwa, just over 13 mins. Omar McLeod ran a world-leading 12.98 for 110mh despite the distraction of false start disqualifications of Orlando Ortega and Aries Merritt.

14 **George Town**, Cayman Islands. Usain Bolt made his seasonal debut with a 10.05 win at 100m in the 5th Cayman Invitational.

14-16 **Ibero-American Championships**, Rio de Janeiro, Brazil, The home nation was easily the most successful in an event that proved a good trial for the Olympic athletics.

18 **Beijing**, China (WCM). Majed El Dein Ghazal, with a previous best of 2.31, successively cleared 2.32, 2.34 and 2.36 in the high jump and another outdoor lead came with 5.92 by Sam Kendricks in the pole vault.

20 **Ostrava**, Czech Republic. 54th Golden Spike (WCM). At a meeting at which Jan Zelezny is the meeting director, the javelin took the headlines as Thomas Röhler headed a top field with a final round 87.37. Usain Bolt won the 100m in 9.98 into a 0.4 wind and Konrad Bukowiecki improved his world junior shot record to 21.01.

21 **Halle**, Germany. 42nd Werfertage. Julia Fischer, discus 68.49, Gong Lijiao, shot 20.43,

and hammer throwers Pawel Fajdek 80.39 and Anita Wlodarczyk 79.48 had the best marks.

22 **Hengelo**, Netherlands. 33rd Fanny Blankers-Koen Games (WCM). Dafne Schippers clocked a world leading 200m time of 22.02 into a 0.3 wind.

22 **Rabat**, Morocco (DL). Raised this year to DL status, Almaz Ayana again ran fast for 5000m with 14:16.31, but still 5.16 short of Tirunesh Dibaba's WR from 2009 although at 3000m in 8:32.33 she was well ahead of Dibaba's schedule (8:38.83). This was a world-leading mark as were 800m in 1:56.64 by Caster Semenya, 8:02.77 for steeplechase by Conseslus Kipruto and 7:35.85 for 3000m by Abdelaati Iguider. Top field event mark was 8.38 long jump by Ruswal Samaai to equal his pb.

25 **Dakar**, Sénégal (WCM). Frank Elemba made a notable improvement on the Congo shot record from 20.25/20.53i to 21.01.

26-28 **NCAA Qualifying**, USA. Preliminary rounds for the NCAA Championships were held in Eastern and Western sections at Jacksonville and Lawrence, the latter condensed into two days as the first day's proceedings were washed out by four inches of rain and lightning.

27-28 **Eugene**, USA. 42nd Prefontaine Classic (DL). Another splendid meeting included an American record 12.24 for 100m hurdles by Keni Harrison, a superb run that meant that she finished 0.31 clear of the previous record holder Brianna Rollins. Also close to a world record was Ruth Jebet, who won the 3000m steeplechase in 8:59.97 from Hyvin Jepkemoi, an African and Commonwealth record 9:00.01, and Emma Coburn, a North American record 9:10.76. Torie Bowie 21.99 beat both Dafne Schippers 22.11 and Elaine Thompson 22.16 at 200m, and 100m wins went to Justin Gatlin 9.88w and English Gardner 10.81. More world-leading marks were set by Faith Kipyegon 1500m 3:56.41, Muktar Edris, 5000m 12:59.43, Christian Taylor, TJ 17.76 and Ihab Abdelrahman, JT (=) 87.37 – and on the first day of the meeting Mo Farah, 10,000m 26:53.71, and Joe Kovacs, shot 22.13.

28 **La Coruña**, Spain. The Chinese walkers Wang Zhen and Liu Hong both made it three wins in three 20k races in 2016 when they won here in 1:20:17 and 1:27:43 respectively

28 **Oordegem**, Belgium. This has become a huge meeting and the distance races, as usual, provided huge depth with, for instance, 19 races at 800m and 11 at 1500m for men and 12 at 800m and 6 at 1500m for women, with large fields. With the disintegration of the domestic programme in Britain, 86 British athletes took part here.

28-29 **Götzis**, Austria. Damian Warner 8523 decathlon and Brianne Theisen-Eaton 6765 were the winners at the 43rd Hypo Meeting in Götzis. Warner ran 10.15 for the 100m, the fastest ever in a decathlon. There were pbs for the heptathlon 2-3: Laura Ikaunice-Admidina raised her national record from 6516 to 6622 and Carolin Schäfer scored 6557.

28-29 **European Clubs Cup**, Mersin, Turkey. Enka of Turkey were the men's champions and Sporting Clube de Portugal the women's.

29 **Bottrop**, Germany. Kim Collins found ideal conditions as, with the wind reading +1.9, he ran a lifetime best of 9.93 for 100m. That achieved his aim of being the first to break 10 seconds for the world age 40 record, and, most remarkably for the world champion of 2003, took 0.03 off his national record.

June

2 **Rome**, Italy. Golden Gala Pietro Mennea (DL). In another attempt at the world 5000m record Almaz Ayana missed by just 1.44 sec. after being well ahead of schedule at 3000m in 8:30.43. Other world-leading marks were set by Conseslus Kipruto, 8:01.41 3000m steeplechase, 1:56.64 Caster Semenya 800m (=), and Janeive Russell, 53.96 400mh. Wayde van Niekerk won the 400m in 44.19 and Greg Rutherford the long jump with 8.31.

3-6 **Asian Junior Championships**, Ho Chih Minh, Vietnam.

4.5 **Zhukovskiy**, Russia. 58th Znamenskiy Memorial. Vera Rebrik's 66.77 javelin was perhaps the best performance.

5 **Birmingham**, GBR (DL). Mo Farah sent the crowd home happy with 7:32.62 for 3000m in the last event to take 0.17 off the 34 year-old British record by David Moorcroft. David Rudisha won the 600m in 1:13.10, the second fastest ever for the distance but missing the WR of 1:12.81; he was timed at 23.31 for 200m and 47.17 for 400m; Pierre-Ambroise Bosse was close with a European best 1:13.21. The year's best times came in the 1500m when Asbel Kiprop ran the year's one sub-3:30 time with 3:29.33 and in the 3000m steeplechase from Conseslus Kipruto who ran a pb 8:00.12. Caterine Ibargüen's triple jump win streak of 34 competitions was ended as Olga Rypakova beat her 14.61 to 14.56.

5 **European Cup 10,000m**, Mersin, Turkey.

7 **Montreuil-sous-Bois**, France. Jimmy Vicaut tied the European 100m record with 9.86.

8-11 **NCAA Championships**, Eugene, USA. Donavan Brazier smashed Jim Ryun's 50 year-old meeting record of 1:44.3 in setting a US junior record of 1:43.55 and Jarrion Lawson emulated Jesse Owens in a winning triple, 100m 10.22 (-2.3), 200m 20.19 and LJ 8.15. Arianna Washington won the 100m in 10.95w and 200m in 22.21 and there were 5000m/10,000m doubles from Dominique Scott and Edward Chesarek, who took his total of NCAA titles to 15. There was also a world-leading mark in the women's 400m hurdles where Shamier Little lowered her 53.74 pb to 53.51 and Courtney Okolo sealed a brilliant collegiate season with wins at 400m and 4x400m. Florida 62 won the men's title from Arkansas 56 and Texas A&M 50, and Arkansas 72 the women's from Oregon 62 and Georgia 41.

9 **Oslo**, Norway (DL). 51st Bislett Games. Despite wet, windy and chilly conditions Dafne Schippers ran a scintillating DL record 21.93 for 200m. Dream Mile wins went to Asbel Kiprop in 3:51.48 and Faith Kipyegon 4:18.60, with Laura Muir 2nd in a Scottish record 4:19.12. In the javelin Thomas Röhler threw a world-leading 89.30 and in the shot Joe Kovacs 22.01 went over 22m for the second time in the season while in second place Konrad Bukowiecki set a world junior record with 21.14.

11 **Kingston**, Jamaica. Despite what he described as a "horrible" start, Usain Bolt ran 9.88 for 100m, Wade van Niekerk ran the third quickest ever 300m, 31.03, with LA Shawn Merritt 2nd in 31.23, and Shaunae Miller ran a Bahamas record 22.05 for 200m.

11 **Championships of Small States of Europe**. Marsa, Malta.

14 **Luzern**, Switzerland. The level of performance at the 30th Spitzen Leichtathletik meeting was considerably affected by the cold conditions.

16 **Stockholm**, Sweden. Bauhaus Meeting (DL). Continuous rain throughout the day left the track awash in places. Top performances included 17.59 triple jump by Christian Taylor and 9:08.37 steeplechase by Ruth Jebet. Ethiopians took the first six places in the men's 5000m, won by Ibrahim Jeylan in 13:03.22. There was a warm welcome for Susanna Kallur who was 5th in 13.00 in her first 100m hurdles race in six years.

17-19 **Greensboro, NC**. 16 year-old Sydney McLaughlin smashed many records at 400mh in the New Balance Nationals. Her time of 54.45 was not inly a US high school and American Junior record but also took both World Youth and Junior marks.

18 13th **WMRA Long Distance World Mountain Running Championships**, Podbrodo, Slovenia.

18 **Szczecin**, Poland. The 62nd Kusocinski Memorial included a Polish record high jump of 1.99 by Kamila Licwinko and top hammer throws by Pawel Fajdek 80.10 and Anita Wlodarczyk 79.61.

18 **Boston**, USA. The inaugural adidas Boost Boston Games was the first competitive street track and field meeting in America.

18-19 **German Championships**, Kassel. After missing the 2015 championships, Robert Harting returned to win his ninth discus title in ten years with a fine throw of 68.04 and Betty Heidler threw the hammer 75.32 for an eleventh hammer title.

20-23 **Russian Championships**, Cheboksary. Competing for the first time for nearly three years (she gave birth to a daughter in June 2014) Yelena Isinbayeva cleared 4.50 in qualification and next day in the final not only raised the leading world outdoor mark of the year to 4.90 but even had a crack at the world record height of 5.07! Anzhelika Sidorova was second with a pb 4.85.

22-26 **African Championships**, Durban, South Africa. Caster Semenya starred as on successive days she won the 1500m in 4:01.99, clocked 2:02.01 in her 800m heat, and won the final in 1:58.20 followed less than an hour later with the anchor leg, in which she moved from 3rd to 1st with an estimated 49.6 leg, in the 4x400m won by South Africa in a national record of 3:28.49. South Africans dominated the meeting, with other winners including Wayde van Niekerk, 200m in 20.02 (after 20.03 in his semi), Rushwal Samaai, LJ 8.40, Wenda Nel, 400mh 54.86, and Sunette Viljoen, JT 64.08. Best distance mark was a world-leading 30:26.94 in the 10,000m by Alice Aprot Nawowuna. Sirine Ebondo (née Balti) won her seventh African Championships title in the pole vault (from 2000), tying the individual event record, Grace Njue (née Wanjiru) her sixth at 20k walk, and Viljoen her fifth at javelin.

23 **Madrid**, Spain (WCM). Yulimar Rojas became the youngest woman ever to triple jump 15m as at 20 years 246 days she set a Venezuelan record at 15.02. Nery Brenes took 0.05 off his five year-old Costa Rican 400m record with 44.60.

23-25 **Belarus Championships**, Grodno. Ivan Tikhon threw the hammer 80.04 for his first throw over 80m since 2012.

24-26 **French Championships**, Angers. Renaud Lavillenie improved the world outdoor best pole vault of 2016 to 5.95 and Jimmy Vicaut reinforced his status as top European sprinter with 9.94 in his heat and 9.88 in the final. Teddy Tamgho, in winning the triple jump with a last round 17.15, fractured his left femur

24-26 **Italian Championships**, Rieti. Gianmarco Tamberi high jumped 2.35, and Chiara Rosa won her 12th successive shot title.

24-26 **Polish Championships**, Bydgoszcz. Pawel Fajdek improved his world-leading hammer mark to 81.67, Anita Wlodarczyk won the women's hammer with 78.69 and Piotr Malachowski won his 11th discus title in 12 years with 68.10.

24-26 **UK Championships**, Birmingham. For the first time ever, three Britons broke 10.00 in the same 100m race; winner was James Dasaolu 9.93w (+3.0).

25 **Kuortane**, Finland. Four men, headed by Johannes Vetter pb 88.23, threw the javelin over 85m.

25-26 75th **Balkan Championships**, Pitesti, Romania. Turkey topped the points table.

25-26 **Ratingen**, Germany. Arthur Abele went to the head of the decathlon world rankings with 8605 points, an improvement of 128 on his best, and Jessica Ennis-Hill won the heptathlon with 6733 points, her best since the 2012 Olympic Games, including a long jump pb of 6.63.

29 **Hengelo**, Netherlands. The Ethiopian 10,000m trials for the Worlds were again held here. There was superb depth behind winners Yigrem Demelesh 26:51.11 (3 men under 27 mins) and Almaz Ayana 30:07.00 (the world's fastest for seven years) on her track debut at the distance (9 women under 31 mins). Tirunesh Dibaba was 3rd in 30:28.53, but this was her first ever loss (after 11 wins from 2005) in a track 10,000m race.

29 **Turku**, Finland. 54th Paavo Nurmi Games. Thomas Röhler had throws of 89.34, 91.28 and 91.04 in the javelin.

30- Jul 1 **Kenyan Trials**, Nairobi. Vivian Cheruiyot won the 5000m in 15:01.60 and 10,000m in 31:36.37, both by big margins and in impressive times at high altitude. David Rudisha ran 1:43.4 for 800m in his heat but in the final was content to do enough to qualify with 3rd in 1:44.23 as Alfred Kipketer won in 1:43.73.

30-Jul 3 **Brazilian Championships**, São Bernardo do Campo. Fabiana Murer set her 14th outdoor South American pole vault record with 4.87.

30-Jul 3 **Jamaican Championships**, Kingston. As usual there was terrific sprinting. In the men's 100m Yohan Blake returned to top form to win from Nickel Ashmeade, both given 9.95, but Usain Bolt was a non-starter, citing a hamstring injury sustained in warm-up before the heats; nonetheless he won his semi in 10.04 after which a Grade 1 tear was diagnosed. Blake added the 200m title in 20.29. Elaine Thompson was a brilliant women's 100m winner in 10.70, but withdrew from the 200m due to a tightened hamstring, and Omar McLeod won the 110mh in 13.01.

July

1-10 **US Olympic Trials/Championships**, Eugene. Great performances abounded and world best marks for 2016 were set in nine events. LaShawn Merritt won the 400m in 43.97 with another world best in the 200m at 19.74 in his 200m semi, but was beaten 19.75 to 19.79 in the final by Justin Gatlin, who had earlier won the 100m in 9.80. Other performances that remained the best of the year came in the long jumps in which Jeff Henderson beat Jarrion Lawson 8.59w to 8.58 and Brittney Reese jumped 7.31 for her 7th US outdoor title, high jump, Chaunté Lowe 2.01, and 400mh, Dalilah Muhammad 52.88. After an ankle injury in April Alyson Felix came to the meeting with only two low-key 400m races behind her, but she won in 49.68. However, she was unable to make the OG team at 200m as she came 4th in 22.54. Bernard Lagat earned his fifth Olympic berth by winning the 5000m and Molly Huddle won both 5000m and 10,000m. Biggest shock was that Keni Harrison managed only 6th in the women's 100m hurdles, She ran 12.62 but winner Brianna Rollins ran 12.34 from Kristi Castlin 12.50 and Nia Ali 12.54. 16 year-old Sydney McLaughlin ran 54.15 for a world junior and youth record in 3rd place in the 400mh and became the youngest US Olympic for 44 years.

2 **European Mountain Running Championships**, Arco, Italy, The host nation achieved their 21st men's team win in the 22 years of the event (20th successive) with Martin DeMatteis taking his third men's individual title.

6-10 **European Championships**, Amsterdam, Netherlands. There was just one new championships record – Ekateríni Stefanídi 4.81 in the women's pole vault, and gold medals were spread amongst 19 nations, headed by Poland 6, Britain and Germany 5 and Netherlands and Turkey 4. Turkey, with stars imported from all over the world, increased their points tally (for first eight) from 19 to 93; for them Yasemin Can won the 5000m and 10.000m double. Dafne Schippers, 100m and 2000m, was another double winner. Ten athletes retained titles won in 2014 with three other winners adding to previous gold medals.

12 **Cetniewo**, Poland, Anita Wlodarczyk exceeded 80m with the hammer for the first time in 2016 with 80.26.

14-17 **European Youth Championships**, Tbilisi, Georgia. Britain with 5 and Germany with 4 winners were the most successful nations with Germany just ahead on points for top eight. Alina Shukh set a world youth record for her 6186 heptathlon score.

15 **Herculis, Monaco (DL)**. Caster Semenya broke her South African record and ran a Diamond League best of 1:55.33 for 800m, with Francine Niyonsaba 2nd in 1:56.24; Margaret Wambui came in 3rd in 1:56.64 but was disqualified for a lane infringement, and there were three more pbs as eight women broke 2 minutes. Gianmarco Tamberi high jumped 2.39 on his third attempt for an Italian record, but suffered a season-ending injury to his left ankle when he crashed through the bar on his second attempt at 2.41. Valerie Adams won the shot with 20.08 for her best distance since September 2014 and Ekateríni Stefanídi pole vaulted 4.81 for her fourth consecutive meeting over 4.80. As usual at this meeting there were great performances across the range of attempts such as wins for Wayde van Niekerk, 400m 44.12, Hellen Obiri, 3000m 8:24.27, Orlan-

do Ortega, 110mh 13.04 Spanish record, and Caterine Ibargüen, triple jump 14.96.

15 **Edmonton**, Canada. Melissa Bishop improved her Canadian record to 1:57.43.

15-17 **Eberstadt**, Germany. There were second successive wins at the annual high jump competition from Derek Drouin, 2.38 from Mutaz Essa Barshim 2.34, and Marie-Laurence Jungfleisch 2.00 from Kamila Licwinko 1.96.

15-17 9th **NACAC U23 Championships**, San Salvador, El Salvador. 15 nations won medals but the USA was dominant with 25 golds, 26 silvers and 11 bronze to four golds by Jamaica and Canada.

16 **Heusden-Zolder**, Belgium. KBC Night of Athletics. Ayanleh Souleiman had the top mark with 3:31.68 for 1500m.

17-18 **Székesfehérvár**, Hungary. 6th István Gyulai Memorial Meeting. David Rudisha ran a world-leading 1:43.35 for 800m, Akani Simbine a South African record 9.89 for 100m, and Valerie Adams continued her return with 20.19 to win the shot from Christine Schwanitz 20.14. Donald cleared 2.37 on his third attempt beating the pb that he had set in his second year of high jumping, 2.35 in 2007 when he was world champion. Bohdan Bondarenko was 2nd with 2.35.

19-24 **World Junior Championships**, Bydgoszcz, Poland. Three champions from the World Juniors at Eugene 2014 defended their titles: Jaheel Hyde in the 400m hurdles, Lázaro Martínez in the triple jump and Konrad Bukowiecki in the shot, and the last smashed the world junior record for the 6kg shot with his mighty 23.34. Also setting a world junior record was the surprising Neeraj Chopra, with 86.48 for javelin and championship records were set in ten events. The USA with 11 gold (including all four relays), 6 silver and 4 bronze medals wa easily the most successful nation. Then Kenya won five and Ethiopia four gold medals. Unfortunately the horizontal jumpers and the throwers were restricted to just four attempts in their finals – yet another attack on the field events and totally unnecessary.

20-21 **Zhukovskiy**, Russia. Russia Cup. High jumpers starred with wins from Ivan Ukhov 2.34 and Mariya Kuchina 2.00.

21 The Court of Arbitration for Sport rejected an appeal by 68 Russian athletes and the Russian Olympic Committee to overturn the IAAF's blanket ban on the Russian team competing at the Rio Olympic Games.

22-23 **London (Olympic Stadium)**, GBR. Sainsbury's Anniversary Games (DL). Keni Harrison had shown terrific form all year, and that was topped with her world record 12.20 (12.194 precisely) for 100m hurdles, to take 0.01 off the world record set by Yordanka Donkova in 1988. Further world-leading marks on the first day were recorded by Christian Taylor, triple jump 17.78, Shaunae Miller, 400m 49.55, and the British women's record 4x100m of 41.81. The most keenly awaited event of that first day was, however, the appearance of Usain Bolt and he ran his 32nd sub-20 time for 200m with 19.89, and a second British record went to Laura Muir, 1500m in 3:57.49. On the second day Mo Farah won the 5000m in 12:59.29, his fastest for four years, and UK teams ran 37.73 and 37.81 for a 1-2 at 4x100m, while top field marks came from Sandra Perkovic, discus 69.94, and Ekateríni Stefanídi, pole vault 4.80.

23-24 **Spanish Championships**, Gijón. Ruth Beitia won her eleventh successive (and twelfth in all) Spanish outdoor high jump title and Berta Castells her 13th at hammer.

28 **Moscow**, Russia. Most of the Russian athletes who were denied competition at the Olympic Games took part in a meeting "2016 Stars". Top marks came from Sergey Shubenkov, 110mh 13.23, Vera Rebrik, javelin 66.03, and Marina Pandakova, 3000m walk 11:50.30.

August

12-21 **Olympic Games**, Rio de Janeiro. *See Olympics section*

25 **Lausanne**, Switzerland. Athletissima (DL). Just three of the individual Olympic champions in action here won their events. Best was Elaine Thompson, who won the 100m by some 3m in 10.78; also Dalilah Muhammad won the 400mh in 53.78 and Caterine Ibargüen the triple jump with 14.76. Orlando Ortega beat Omar McLeod 13.11 to 13.12 and Valerie Adams 19.94 beat Michelle Carter 19.49 in the shot. There were the best ever place 3-5 times in the 1000m behind Ayanleh Souleiman 2:13.49 and Robert Biwott 2:13.89 and the top eight finishers (under 2:17) set pbs.

26 **Warsaw**, Poland. Anita Wlodarczyk set her sixth world hammer record with a fourth round 82.98, fittingly at the Kamila Skolimowska Memorial meeting. In the men's event Pawel Fajdek put aside his extraordinary failure in Rio with all his six throws over 78.50 (three over 80m), topped by 82.47, adding 60cm to his world-leading throw of 2016.

26-28 **Swedish Championships**, Sollentuna. Daniel Ståhl produced the world's best discus throw of the year – 68.72.

27 **Saint-Denis**, France. Meeting de Paris (DL). Ruth Jebet, having threatened all season, smashed the world record for 3000m steeplechase, as she followed pacemaker Caroline Chepkurui at 1000m in 2:56.36 and then reached 2000m in 5:54.16 (fastest ever split) and ended with 8:52.78 compared with the old record of 8:58.81 by Gulnara Galkina. Tenth place in 9:21.49 was an all-time record. Laura Muir took 2.27 off her 1500m UK record with 3:55.22 for the Commonwealth record, a last lap in 59.99 bringing her home ahead of six

other women who broke 4 minutes, 7 of the top 11 running pbs, and 12th place being a record 4:03.24. 19 year-old Yomif Kejelcha won the 3000m in a world junior record 7:28.19 from Abdelaati Iguider 7:30.09, Hagos Gebrihiwet 7:30.45, Ryan Hill 7:30.93, Albert Rop 7:32.02 and Bethwel Birgen 7:32.48, times that remained the six fastest of 2016. Another 19 year-old made a major advance as Alfred Kipketer won the 800m in 1:42.87 and Tom Walsh took his Oceania shot record to 21.81 and 22.00.

September

1 **Zürich**, Switzerland. Weltklasse. The first of the two final meetings meant that 16 Diamond Race titles were decided here. Top men's performance was Tom Walsh's Oceania shot record of 22.20 as Ryan Crouser threw 22.00 and yet lost. Asafa Powell won the 100m in 9.94 for his 97th wind-legal sub-10.00 time and Christian Taylor's 17.80 triple jump broke Jonathan Edwards' 20 year-old meeting record by 1cm. On the women's side there was a close and exciting rematch in the 200m between Olympic gold and silver medallists Elaine Thompson 21.85 and Dafne Schippers 21.86 with Allyson Felix 3rd 22.02, while Sandra Perkovic had her seventh discus win (68.44) out of seven DL meetings for a perfect score of 80 points. Six women beat 4 minutes in the 1500m with Shannon Rowbury edging Laura Muir 3:57.78 to 3:57.85 and Faith Kipyegon only 7th.

3 **Berlin**, Germany. 75th ISTAF (WCM). German javelin throwers took places 1-4; Johannes Vetter winning with 89.57 from Julian Weber 88.29, both pbs, while Christina Obergföll ended her career with the women's victory at 64.28. Caster Semenya and Francine Niyonsaba completed their season-long dominance at 800m, 1:55.68 to 1:57.58. Bernard Lagat's last track race of his wonderful career resulted in a loss at 3000m to Augustine Choge 7:43.63 to 7:43.00.

3 **New York. 5th Avenue Mile**. Eric Jenkins surprised with a narrow win over Matthew Centrowitz 3:49.4 to 3:49.5 and Jenny Simpson won for the 5th time in 6 years, beating Laure Muir 4:18.4 to 4:18.5 on the slightly downhill road course.

3-4 **Finland v Sweden**, Tampere. Double victory for Sweden over Finland 210-200 for men and 213-197 for women in the annual Finnkampen.

5 **Zagreb**, Croatia. 67th Boris Hanzekovic Memorial (WCM). Another great clash between shot putters Ryan Crouser and Tom Walsh was won by the former 22.28 to 22.21, the fourth Oceania record in two weeks by Walsh.

6 **Rovereto**, Italy. Genzebe Dibaba provided the highlight of the 52nd Palio Citta di Quercia meeting with 4:14.30 for 1 mile, the second fastest ever outdoors.

9 **Brussels**, Belgium. 40th Van Damme Memorial. This was again half of the DL final and the star was Sandi Morris who became only the third woman (second outdoors) to clear five metres in the pole vault. Conseslus Kipruto ran 8:03.74 for 3000m steeplechase, completing winning all five DL races that he ran in 2016. Elaine Thompson won the 100m in 10.72 by a huge margin from Dafne Schippers 10.97, Caster Semenya dropped down in distance but still impressed to win the 400m in 50.40, and Almaz Ayana ran another fast 5000m, 14:18.89. The hugely talented Luvo Manyonga produced a pb 8.48 in the long jump

11 35th **Great North Run, Newcastle to South Shields**, GBR. Mo Farah became the first man to win this race three years running with 60:04 and Vivian Cheruiyot celebrated her 33rd birthday by beating Priscah Jeptoo 67:54 to 67:55 to win the women's race; Tirunesh Dibaba was third in 68:04.

11 32nd **WMRA World Mountain Running Championships**, Sapareva Banya, Bulgaria. Andrea Mayr recorded a record sixth win in the women's race.

13 **Marseille** France. The French team had a first win in the annual meeting with 115 points from Americas 109 and Ukraine 102.

23-25 **South American U23 Championships**, Lima, Peru

25 BMW **Berlin Marathon**, Germany. In a great race Kenenisa Bekele, Ethiopian record 2:03:03, and Wilson Kipsang 2:03.13 ran the second and fourth equal fastest times on a record-eligible course; they ran the first half in 61:11. Aberu Kebede was a commanding women's winner in 2:20:45 to come home 3:13 clear of Birhane Dibaba. There were 36,054 finishers (26,807 men and 9247 women).

25-28 **Suzhou**, Chia. Many of the world's top walkers took part in a 4-day tour with races at 10k, 20k, 10.5k and 10k. Overall winners were (men) Dane Bird-Smith 3:27:59 and (women) Qieyang Shenjie 3:49:23.

October

9 39th **Chicago Marathon**, USA. Florence Kiplagat won as she had in 2016. With a fast 2:21:32 she finished 1:56 ahead of Edna Kiplagat and Valentine Kipketer was 3rd in 2:23:41. With no pacemakers or time bonuses the men's race was unusually slow, Abel Kirui winning in 2:11:23, 3 secs ahead of Dickson Chumba. There were 40,350 finishers from 41,350 starters.

16 **Amsterdam Marathon**, Netherlands. In perfect conditions Daniel Wanjiru improved his pb from 2:08:18 to 2:05:21 followed by Sammy Kitwara 2:05:45 and Marius Kimutai 2:05:47 (3:27 off his best). Eight men (all Kenyans) bettered 2:07 with 12 at 2:08:19 or better for the second highest ever number of men under 2:07 and 2:08 in one race. Women's

winner Meselech Melkamu had her second marathon victory of the year (after Hamburg in April) and fourth of her career; 2:23:31 was her seventh sub-2-26 time in 12 marathons.

22-23 IAU 24 Hours European Championships, Albi, France. Maria Jansson recorded the second greatest ever distance by a woman with a European record 250.647k and Dan Lawson was the men's winner in 261,843k.

23 Valencia, Spain. As usual there were fast times in this half marathon with the winners Stephen Kibet 59:27 and Peres Jepchirchir 67:09.

30 Frankfurt-am-Main, Germany. Mark Korir won the 35th Mainova Frankfurt Marathon in 2:06:48 and Mamitu Daska was the women's winner in 2:25:27.

November

6 46th **New York City Marathon**, USA. This year's race won by Ghirmay Ghebreslassie in 2:07:51, with Mary Keitany winning the women's race for the third successive year in 2:24:26, attracted the largest ever field as there were 51,394 finishers (29,930 men and 21,464 women) from 51,999 starters.

11 IAU World 50k Champs, Doha, Qatar.

20 New Delhi, India. Strong fields were attracted to the 12th Airtel Delhi Half Marathon and winners were Eliud Kipchoge 59:44 and Worknesh Degefa 67:42.

27 IAU World 100k Champs, Los Alcazares, Spain. Hideaki Yamauchi was the men's winner in 6:18:22 from Bongmusa Mthembu 6:24:05 African record, and the women's title was won in an Oceania record 7:34:35 by Kirsten Bull. Team titles went to South Africa and Japan.

December

4 Fukuoka, Japan. Yemane Tsegay was the winner in 2:08:48 from Patrick Makau 2:08:57 and the amazing Yuki Kawauchi who was 3rd in 2:09:11 in his 62nd marathon, all but two under 2:20.

11 European Cross-Country Championships, Chia, Sardinia, Italy. Transferees from Kenya to Turkey went 1-2 in both the senior races: Aras Kaya and Polat Kemboi Arikan in the mens's and Yasemin Can and Meryem Akdag in the women's. Turkey won the women's team title in the latter but Great Britain had the greatest overall success, with team wins in the senior men, and U23 and U20 women and team medals in all six races. Jakob Ingebrigtsen, just 16 in September, added to the success of his brothers by winning the men's U20 race.

Impact on All-time Lists by 2016 performances

THE GREATEST IMPACT made on junior all-time lists in 2016 was undoubtedly that by Konrad Bukowiecki at shot. He set world junior records with the 7.26kg shot: 21.14 at Oslo on 9 June and with the 6kg shot 23.34 to win the World Junior title at Bydgoszcz on 19 July. After his two years as a junior in 2015 and 2016 he had at 7.26kg – 8 of the top ten performances, 15/20 and 24/34 over 20.36m, plus at 6kg – 7 of the top 10 and 11 of the 20 over 22m (Jacko Gill has 7). In contrast, Yomif Kejelcha set a world junior record at 3000m but that was the only change in the top ten performers at the men's distance events.

There was remarkably little change in some of the men's all-time performer lists. The first change at 1500m came from Timothy Cheruiyot 3:31.34 to rank 71st and the first at 1 mile from Elijah Manangoi 3:52.04 to rank 139th. At 3000m steeplechase Conseslus Kipruto moved up one place with his 8:00.12 , but that was the only change in the top 60 performers. Even more remarkable was the lack of top times at 5000m. Mo Farah headed the world list with 12:59.29 but that ranked, at the end of 2016, as 292nd on the all-time performances list! Also the top performer to move up was Geoffrey Kamworer, 91st with his 12:59.98. Top new mark in the 20k walk was 1:18:45 by Isamu Fujiwara for 60th place. In the hammer Pavel Fajdek dominated 2016 lists, but the all-time performances list has 160 marks over 82.50 and Fajdek's best was 82.47, and the top new mark in the all-time performers was 78.87 by Wagner Domingos for 152nd.

The greatest dominance at any event in 2016 was that by Anita Wlodarczyk in the women's hammer and her effect on the all-time list was huge. Now she has the top 9 performances of all-time, 17 of the top 21 and 21 of the top 30. Taking all throws in a series into account, she has 47 of the top 57 over 78m. The Olympic 10,000m with Almaz Ayana's fantastic world record means that that race has 4 of the top 5 performances of all-time, and 6 of the top 10 of all-time at 3000m steeplechase were run in 2016 – 4 by Ruth Jebet and 2 by Hyvin Jepkemoi.

The women's junior all-time lists were most changed at the top at 100m hurdles with 4 women in the top 7 and at 400m hurdles Sydney McLaughlin's 2016 times are now 1st, 3rd and 4th.

ATHLETES OF 2016
By Peter Matthews

WHILE USAIN BOLT continued to attract great attention for the sporting public around the world and figured prominently in sportsman of the year awards, most athletics pundits made their choice as World Athlete of the Year the man who thrilled all with what was surely THE performance of the year: Wayde van Niekerk's magnificent world record for 400 metres at the Olympic Games. The 24 year-old South African had been a surprise World Champion in 2015, but was clearly the world number one. In 2016 he really came into his own as he was undefeated at all distances: two races at 100m (9.98A and 10.03A), three finals at 200m, 20.97A, 20.35A and 20.02 to win the African title, one at 300m, 31.03 for third world all-time, and five finals at 400m (44.98, 44.19, 44.28, 44.12, 43.03 plus sub-45 heat times of 44.11A and 44.45). With a 200m best of 19.94 in 2015, he became the first man ever to run sub-10.00, 20.00 and 44.00 for 400m.

Other Olympic champions to have been unbeaten in 2016 were Usain Bolt, five finals at 100m and two at 200m. Mo Farah won his two finals at 5000m and his two races at 10,000m, although beaten in races at 1500m, 3000m and half marathon. Wang Zhen won all his four 20k walk races, while unbeaten in limited competitions were Ashton Eaton, his two decathlons, Eliud Kipchoge, his two marathons and his one half marathon, and Matej Tóth in his only 50k race walk. Conseslus Kipruto won 7/8 at 3000m steeplechase and Christian Taylor 7/8 at triple jump.

Just three Olympic champions were also Diamond Race winners: Kipruto, Taylor and Kerron Clement and most DL wins (maximum 7) were achieved by Kipruto 6, Taylor 5, LaShawn Merritt, Orlando Ortega, Renaud Lavillenie and Piotr Malachowski 4.

Selections for World Top Ten

	PJM	TFN	AI
Wayde van Niekerk*	1	1	1
Mo Farah*	2	2	2
Eliud Kipchoge	3	4	5
Usain Bolt*	4	3	3
Ashton Eaton	5	5	4
Christian Taylor	6	7	7=
Conseslus Kipruto	7	6	7=
Ryan Crouser	8	8	9
Omar McLeod	9	9	10
David Rudisha	10	10	6

*IAAF finalists, Bolt was their athlete of the year. Andre de Grasse was IAAF Rising Star of the Year.

100 Metres

THE INCOMPARABLE Usain Bolt is top for the sixth time at 100m. He again had more limited preparation than he would have liked, but while he had just 0.013 to spare over Justin Gatlin at the 2015 Worlds, this year he had a 0.08 margin at the Olympic Games and he was unbeaten in his four finals. Gatlin's 9.80 at the US Champs was the year's fastest, 0.01 better than Bolt in Rio, and pre Rio Gatlin won his eight finals. His times were, however, not as good as in 2015. The top two each had three wind-legal sub 9.90 times, and were joined in this by Jimmy Vicaut with two and by Trayvon Bromell and Akani Simbine, one each. These three men were 7th, 8th and 5th respectively in the Olympic final, behind Andre De Grasse and Yohan Blake. De Grasse lacked the range of top times of his rivals with a 9.99 and 9.99w but won 5 of his 8 finals including in Oslo. Blake, however, even with a limited racing schedule, had a better set of times and was 3-0 v Simbine and 2-0 v Asafa Powell, who closed further on his target of 100 sub-10 times with another four to take him to 97 (plus 8w and 1 while banned). He won 6 of his 11 finals, but 4th in the Jamaican Champs behind Blake, Nickel Ashmeade (5s1 OG) and Jevaughn Minzie meant that he missed the Olympics. Powell was, however 2-1 v Simbine and 2-0 v OG 6th and African champion Ben Youssef Meité, beating both in Zürich. Meité finished the year well with 2nd to Powell in Lausanne and a win in Saint-Denis over Simbine (Vicaut 5th). Vicaut had fast times and a DL win in London, but was only 3rd at the Europeans, while Bromell raced in only five meetings, although he was the world's third fastest with 9.84 for US Champs, 2nd when Marvin Bracy (6sf OG) and Mike Rodgers were 3rd and 4th. Femi Ogunode had fast times in good company but went out in his heat in Rio. Three men ran sub-10 with wind assistance at the British Champs: James Dasaolu, James Ellington and Chijindu Ujah, but at the end of the year bobsledder Joel Fearon emerged as top UK 100 man with a 9.96 best and 3rd in Lausanne. In all 25 men ran legal sub-10 times compared to a record 27 in 2015 and 16 in 2014.

Kim Collins (40 in April) improved his national record with a world M40 best of 9.93 in Bottrop, but his next best was 10.07 (and 10.10w).

Most times at 10.00/10.05 or faster: Gatlin 7+2w/10+2w, Vicaut 6/9, Simbine 6/8+1w, Meité 5+1w/8+3w, Blake 5/7, Powell 4+1w/10+1w, Bolt 4/6, De Grasse 3+1w/5+3w, Bromell 3+1w/5+1w, Rodgers 2+2w/4+2w, Ashmeade 2/6, Gay 1+2w/5+2w, Ogunode 1+1w/2+2w, J Fearon 1/5+1w, K Bailey-Cole 1/4.

Asafa Powell topped the world indoor 60m list, twice running a CAC record 6.44 – in heat and semi-final at the World Indoors, but in the final he was beaten, 6.47 to 6.50 by Trayvon Bromell. Ronnie Baker also ran 6.47, to win the NCAA title to cap an unbeaten season.

1. Bolt, 2. Gatlin, 3. Blake, 4. De Grasse,
5. Powell, 6. Simbine, 7. Meité, 8. Vicaut,
9. Bromell, 10. Ashmeade

200 Metres

USAIN BOLT ran the 200m in just two meetings: 19.89 in London and 19.78 in the Olympic final (19.78 also in his semi), but that was enough for his eighth top ranking. The year's fastest times came at the US Champs as LaShawn Merritt ran 19.74 in his semi and 19.79 for 2nd in the final behind Justin Gatlin 19.75. Ameer Webb was 3rd in 20.00 after 19.97 in his semi. There were 20 wind-legal sub-20 times in 2016, with Merritt running 4 and Bolt and Webb 2 each. Merritt had three wins (including 19.78 in Nassau) but his ranking suffers with 6th at the Olympics after he had run the 400m. Although only 3rd at the Canadian Champs Andre De Grasse had a solid season and was 2nd at the Olympics, where 3rd to 5th were Christophe Lemaitre, Adam Gemili and Churandy Martina. Alonso Edward had the busiest season of the top men including a win, three 2nds and a 3rd in DL meetings, but was only 7th in Rio and 6th at the DL final in Brussels, when Julian Forte, Gemili and Martina were 1-2-3, all under 20 secs, Lemaitre 4th and Ramil Guliyev (OG 8th) 5th. Gatlin's only 200m competition apart from that brilliant US win came at the Olympics, but he did not make the final as he was 3rd in his semi. Overall Martina was 3-3 v Edward. Webb started well with wins at Mt. SAC 19.91, Doha 19.85 and Rome 20.04, but was 5th in Birmingham and 4th in Luzern plus 6th in his Rio semi. Forte, 3rd Jamaican Champs, did not have enough to support his Brussels win. Bruno Hortelano was the surprise European champion with Guliyev 2nd and Martina disqualified after crossing the line a metre ahead, and Wayde van Niekerk was African champion in 20.02. Michael Norman showed great promise with 5th at the US Champs as well as wins in all his junior races including US and World titles, and before injury Miguel Francis ran 19.88 and a probably irregular 19.67.

Most times at 20.10/20.30 or better: Edward 5+1w/11+1w, Webb 5/6, Merritt 4+1w/8+1w, Martina 3/8, De Grasse 3/6, Gemili 3/5, Bolt 3/4, Lemaitre 1/8, Mitchell-Blake 1+1w/4+2w; M Francis 1+1?/3+1?, N Lyles & Rodney 1+1w/3+1w, A Brown & Forte 1/4, Gatlin & Guliyev 1/3, Norman 1w/5+1w, Hortelano, Lawson & Talbot 0/3.

1. Bolt, 2. De Grasse, 3. Merritt, 4. Gemili,
5. Martina, 6. Edward, 7. Lemaitre, 8. Gatlin,
9. Webb, 10. Forte

400 Metres

WAYDE VAN NIEKERK had won the 2015 World title in 43.48 but even so few expected that he would take Michael Johnson's world record of 43.18 in 2016. However, he did, in superb style with his 43.03 at the Olympic Games, running blind in the outside lane, finding perfect conditions just as Johnson had in Seville 1999. This concluded an unbeaten year in six competitions at 400m. Well beaten, 2nd and 3rd in Rio were Kirani James 43.76 (easily his fastest of the year) and LaShawn Merritt 43.85. James beat Merritt 3-0 so that his record was 7 wins out of 8 and Merritt's 5 out of 8; James and Merritt were 1-2 at the Drake Relays and Pre Classic. The top three ran 14 of the 16 fastest times of the year to 44.23, joined by Machel Cedenio, 4th in Rio in 44.01 and Baboloki Thebe 44.22 at altitude in Gaborone. 20 year-old Cedenio had five times sub 44.50, as did the Olympic 7th placer Braion Taplin, whom he beat 3-0. 19 year-old Thebe confirmed his huge potential by winning the African title but was disqualified at the World Juniors, got injured and was unable to start in his Olympic semi. His even younger Botswana compatriot Karabo Sibanda (2nd African Champs) was 5th and Ali Khamis Abbas 6th in Rio, but both had thin racing programmes, with no DL competition, and the other OG finalist Matthew Hudson-Smith also had a light season after injury, although he won at the London DL. Taplin was 2nd in Rome and 3rd in Monaco, before 2nd in the DL final in Zürich behind Merritt and ahead of Nery Brenes, Martyn Rooney, Steve Gardiner and Isaac Makwala (Rooney going out in his heat and the other three in the semis in Rio). Gil Roberts was 2nd in the US Champs and had four sub-45 including 4th in his Rio semi, and Javon Francis was Jamaican champion and 6th in his Olympic semi with six sub-45s but 86 such times (by 24 men) were much scarcer than in 2015 when there 125 (by 33 men) Abdelilah Haroun won the World Junior title with Sibanda 3rd, and Gardiner beat Makwala 3-2 as both raced extensively in DL races.

Most sub-45.00 times: James, Merritt, Cedenio, Taplin 9; van Niekerk 7, Francis 6, Gardiner, Roberts 4; Abbas, Hudson-Smith, Makwala 3.

1. van Niekerk, 2. James, 3. Merritt, 4. Cedenio,
5. Taplin, 6. Sibanda, 7. Abbas, 8. Hudson-Smith,
9. Roberts, 10. Gardiner

800 Metres

DAVID RUDISHA may never quite recapture his 2012 form, but confirmed his status as the greatest of all-time at the event by running superbly to retain his Olympic title; he is top for the sixth time. His 1:42.15 in that race and four of the fastest eleven times of the year making superfluous his three earlier season losses in his eight 800m competitions of 2016. He also ran the second fastest ever time for 600m with 1:13.10 in Birmingham. Taoufik Makhloufi 1:42.61 and Clayton Murphy 1:42.93 ran to 2nd and 4th on the world lists when they took the other Olympic medals, and 4 Pierre-Ambroise Bosse, 5 Ferguson Cheruiyot and 6 Marcin Lewandowski also ran fast in Rio. Makhloufi had two firsts and two seconds in his other 800m races, all under 1:45 and Murphy was the revelation of the year as he also won the US title and improved his pb by 2.66, but his only DL race was 7th in the final in Brussels. That was won by Adam Kszczot, who most surprisingly missed the OG final, not quick enough when 3rd behind Rudisha and Murphy in his semi; he was 3-2 v Lewandowski overall including when they were 1st and 2nd at the European Champs (4 Tuka, 5 Bosse). The World Junior champion Kipyegon Bett had three wins and three seconds, including in Brussels, where followed 3 Amel Tuka (4sf OG), 4 Cheruiyot, 5 Kipketer, 6 Bosse with another strong Kenyan Jonathan Kitilit 8th. Cheruiyot beat both Bosse and Alfred Kipketer 3-2, but Kipketer, 7th in Rio, had a positive record against most others and won in Monaco and Saint-Denis, running 1:42.87 there, 0.11 ahead of Makhloufi and there was little between most of those ranked from 3rd to 12th. Nicholas Kipkoech beat Kitilit 5-4; they were 4th and 6th at the Kenyan Trials, won by Kipketer from Cheruiyot and Rudisha. Boris Berian was an impressive winner of the World Indoor title and started outdoors with a big win at the Pre Classic, but had a very limited season after that, although 2nd US Champs and 8th in Rio. Most times sub-1:45.0: Rudisha 8, Cheruiyot, Bosse 7; Makhloufi, Kipkoech, Kitilit 6; Kszczot, Lewandowski, Kipketer, McBride 5; K Bett 4, Berian 3.

1. Rudisha, 2. Makhloufi, 3. Cheruiyot,
4. Kipketer, 5. Bosse, 6. Kszczot,
7. Lewandowski, 8. Murphy, 9. Bett, 10. Berian

1500 Metres

AT HIS best, as for instance when he ran the year's one sub-3:30 1500m time, 3:29.33 in the Birmingham DL race, Asbel Kiprop remained the top miler and he ranked first at this event for the sixth time with four of the 13 fastest 1500m times of the year. But after six wins, including further DL wins in Doha, Eugene and Oslo (year's best mile of 3:51.48), he was 6th in Monaco, the race that had the greatest depth of top times, and in the Olympics, finishing with 3rd in the DL final in Brussels. The Olympic final was ridiculously slow, but all credit to Matthew Centrowitz who controlled the race beautifully before sprinting home to win in 3:50.00. However he had a very limited season as his other outdoor 1500m races were a 9th and 1st in warm-up races in Portland and 3:34.09 to win the US title, but he also won the World Indoor title with a fast finish after a slow start. Ronald Kwemoi won in Monaco in 3:30.49 followed by Elijah Manangoi, Taoufik Makhloufi, and Abdelaati Iguider. Mo Farah, Kiprop, Ryan Gregson, Jakub Holusa, Charlie Grice and Henrik Ingebrigtsen to make ten men under 3:34. Also there were seven men at this level in Brussels, where the order was Timothy Cheruiyot 3:31.34, Iguider, Kiprop, Makhloufi, Ingebrigtsen, Robert Biwott and Vincent Kibet. Makhloufi and Nick Willis took Olympic silver and bronze, followed by Ayanleh Souleiman and Iguider. The last was most consistent, with 2nd places in Eugene, Birmingham and was 2-2 v Makhloufi and 3-2 v Kiprop. Manangoi withdrew from his semi at the Olympics due to injury and was 10th in Brussels, but had a win (Rome), three 2nds and a 3rd in the DL and was 3-1 v Makhloufi. Fouad El Kaam won the African title from Cheruiyot, who missed out on the Olympics as he was 4th at the Kenyan Trials, a place behind Kwemoi (13th OG). Souleiman had just one non-Olympic 1500m, a win in Heusden. Gregson was the most prolific racer, but was beaten 3-0 by Willis and 4-1 by Biwott; he was 2-2 v Silas Kiplagat, who had a DL win in London.

Most times sub-3:35.0 or 3:52.0M: Kiprop 6, Iguider, Manangoi, Gregson 4; Kiplagat, Biwott, Kibet 3.

1. Kiprop, 2. Iguider, 3. Makhloufi, 4. Manangoi,
5. Cheruiyot, 6. Centrowitz, 7. Willis, 8. Kwemoi,
9. Souleiman, 10. Kiplagat

3000 Metres/2 Miles

HE MISSED Olympic selection for Ethiopia at 5000m, but Yomif Kejelcha ran the year's fastest 3000m time. a world junior record 7:28.19 at Saint-Denis, a race in which the six best times of the year were set, as Abdelaati Iguider, Hagos Gebrhiwet, Ryan Hill, Albert Rop and Bethwel Birgen followed under 7:33. Mo Farah was next on the list with his British record 7:32.62 in Birmingham. Kejelcha won the World Indoor title from Hill, Augustine Choge and Iguider with awesome final pace after a slowly-run race.

5000 Metres

MO FARAH once again showed that he is the consummate racer as he competed his fourth successive global double to won the Olympic title in 13:03.30, having won at the London DL in 12:59.29. That was the year's fastest and there were four more sub-13 minute times: from Muktar Edris, when he won in Eugene and Shanghai, Dejen Gebremeskel in Boston, and Geoffrey Kamworor, 2nd in Eugene in his only 5000m of 2016. Edris was disqualified in Rio after finishing 4th and was beaten 3-1 by compatriot Hagos Gebrhiwet, 3rd in Rio, including at the DL final in Zürich. There Edris was only 10th as Gebrhiwet won from Paul Chelimo, who, after 13th in Eugene and 3rd in the US Champs behind Bernard Lagat and Hassan Mead, was a surprise Olympic silver medallist. Dejen Gebremeskel, after fast wins in Hengelo and Boston, was the third Ethiopian representative in Rio, but was 12th, and Yomif Kejelcha had a better overall record with four times under 13:10. Very surprisingly no Kenyan made the Olympic final; their best of the year was Thomas Longosiwa, 4th in their Trials but with 13:01.69 for 3rd Shanghai and 13:02.91 4th Eugene. Further top Olympic placings were 4th Mohammed Ahmed (also 3rd Eugene, 8th Zürich), 5th Bernard Lagat (world age-40 record 13:06.78 at 41, 6th Zürich), 6th Andrew Butchart (the Scot who made a big breakthrough including 2nd at London), 7th Albert Rop (1st Heusden, 4th Zürich), 8th Joshua Cheptegei (2nd Shanghai, 8th Eugene).

Most times under 13:15: Gebrhiwet 5, Edris 4+1dq, Kejelcha 4, Cheptegei, Longosiwa, Rop 3.

1. Farah, 2. Gebrhiwet, 3. Chelimo, 4. Edris, 5. Kejelcha, 6. Ahmed, 7. Cheptegei, 8. Longosiwa, 9. Rop, 10. Gebremeskel

10,000 Metres

MO FARAH is top at this event for the fourth time and he won the Olympic title from Paul Tanui, who had been 3rd in the 2013 and 2015 Worlds, and the Ethiopians Tamirat Tola and Yigrem Demelash. as once again the East Africans were unable to handle Farah's finish, short or sustained, and the man expected to be the main challenger, Geoffrey Kamworor, faded to 11th. The year's best time was 26:51.11 by Demelash, who won the Ethiopian Trial race at Hengelo, from Tola and Abadi Embaye (15th OG, ETH champion), and the remaining seven of the year's top ten times came at Eugene, where Farah won in 26:53.71 from William Sitonik, Tola, Stephen Sambu, Ibrahim Jeylan (dnf ETH Trial), Zersenay Tadese and Nicholas Kosimbei. Tanui won three Japanese races and the Kenyan Trials in an outstanding high altitude time of 27:46.15 with Sitonik 4th. The rankings substantially follow the Olympic order 5th to 8th.

1. Farah, 2. Tanui, 3. Tola, 4. Demelash, 5. Rupp, 6. Cheptegei, 7. Karoki, 8. Sitonik, 9. Embaye, 10. Sambu

Half Marathon

GEOFFREY KAMWOROR ran just one half marathon in 2016 but that was a brilliant win in the World Championship race, 25 secs ahead of Bidan Karoki and Mo Farah a further 23 secs back in third just ahead of Abayneh Ayele. This was despite Kamworor falling heavily at the start, grazing both knees in the process and only narrowly avoiding being trampled by the hordes of surrounding runners. There was just one sub-59 min time this year – 58:44 by Solomon Yego in the Rome-Ostia race – but the greatest depth of times came at Copenhagen, James Wangari winning in 59:07 from Stephen Kibet and Albert Kangogo. Karoki, 5th, was one of six men at 59:36 or better. Wangari had another fast win, 59:12 in Milan, and Kibet also won at Valencia in 59:29 with five men under the hour and Yego 6th.

Marathon

ELIUD KIPCHOGE cemented his place as very much the world's top marathoner. After a 1st and a 2nd in his first year at the distance in 2013, he won both his races in 2014, 2015 and now 2016. He beat by far the most competitive field in London and then took the Olympic title. It was hot in Rio, so times were slowed, but the quality of the competitors, attracted by the Olympics, was higher than for most global championship summer marathons. While Kenyans continued to dominate marathons around the world, the big surprise in Rio was that Kipchoge's compatriots, Stanley Biwott and Wesley Korir failed to finish. Kenenisa Bekele was most disappointed not to get Olympic selection, but after 3rd in London, he ran the year's fastest in Berlin, at 2:03:03 just 8 seconds ahead of Wilson Kipsang and just 2 secs better than Kipchoge in London. Biwott had been 2nd in London, but also failed to finish in New York, and another non-finisher in Rio was Tesfaye Abera, but he was the one man other than Kipchoge to win two fast marathons: Dubai and Hamburg. Fayisa Lelisa, who had earlier won in Tokyo, was the Olympic silver medallist and Galen Rupp the bronze after winning the US Olympic Trial on his marathon debut. Rupp, however, did not break 2:10. whereas Evans Chebet had two times in the 2:05s – 2nd in Seoul behind Wilson Loyanae and 3rd in Berlin. The US Majors races were Boston, won in a slow time by Hayle Lemi Berhanu (but who was 2nd in Dubai in 2:04:33 before OG 13th), Chicago, also slow, by Abel Kirui, and New York, won, without pacemakers, by Ghirmay Ghebreslassie in 2:07:51, 5 secs slower than his 4th in London (when Kipsang was 5th) and he was also 4th OG. Another consistent man was Sisay Lemma, 4th Dubai and Berlin and 7th London.

1. Kipchoge, 2. Bekele, 3. Lilesa, 4. Ghebreslassie, 5. Kipsang, 6. Abera, 7. Chebet, 8. Lemi Berhanu, 9. Lemma, 10. Rupp

3000 Metres Steeplechase

CONSESLUS KIPRUTO was ranked as world number one at the age of 18 in 2013 and it was surprising that he slipped a little to 5th in 2014 and 3rd in 2015, but in 2016 he showed that he was clearly the top man. He won 7 of his 8 competitions, his one loss being when he was 2nd at the Kenyan Trials to Brimin Kipruto. He broke the Olympic record to win in Rio and won his five DL races, although disappointed that he could not quite get the pace right to break 8 minutes, coming closest with 8:00.12 in Birmingham with the next four best times. Second fastest was Julius Birech, the top man of 2014 and 2015, at 8:03.90 for 2nd in Rabat. He was also 2nd in Doha and Rome, but failed to finish at the Kenyan Trials, at which Ezekiel Kemboi was 3rd to make his 11th successive global championship team. Kemboi was unfortunately disqualified in Rio after finishing third, but his actual racing there surely qualified him for a ranking, although he was only 12th in Rome and 11th in Rome (with a win in Beijing). That meant only one Kenyan medal at the Olympics, as Brimin K was 6th with Evan Jager and Mahiedine Mekhissi-Benabbad taking silver and bronze, Soufiane El Bakkali 4th and Yoann Kowal 5th. Jager had two wins in the US and was then 2nd to Conseslus K in the DL final in Brussels in his best time of the year, 8:04.01, followed by Mekhissi (also European champion), Nicholas Bett, Abraham Kibiwot, Hilary Bor, Andy Bayer and Kowal with El Bakkali 9th and Paul Kipsiele Koech 14th. Kibiwot won the Kenyan Championship, was 3rd in the African Champs behind the Ethiopians Chala Beyo and Jigisa Tolosa, and had a 3-1 win-loss advantage over P K Koech and Bett and 2-0 over Brimin K. As ever Koech had problems handing altitude and was 6th at the Kenyan Trials but he was 2-1 v Kemboi and El Bakkali and 4-1 v Barnabas Kipyego.

Most times under 8:15: C Kipruto 7, Kibiwot 5, P Koech 4, Jager, Birech, Bett, Kipyego 3.

1. C Kipruto, 2. Jager, 3. Birech, 4. Mekhissi-Benabbad, 5. Kibiwot, 6. Koech, 7. Kemboi, 8. El Bakkali, 9. Bett, 10. Kowal

110 Metres Hurdles

OMAR MCLEOD had run 12.97 in 2015 but was only 6th in the World Champs. In 2016 he was clearly the world's best, winning 6 of his 9 finals at 110m hurdles and also running 100m on the flat in 9.99, for the first man sub-10 and sub-13. His first five wins came in succession, including the two fastest times of the year, 12.98 in Shanghai and 13.01 at the Jamaican Champs. Then he fell in Monaco and was disqualified in Székesfehérvár before a commanding victory in the Olympic final in 13.05 and ending with 2nd in Lausanne to Orlando Ortega. The Olympic silver and bronze medallists Ortega and Dimitri Bascou joined McLeod as the men with the most top times. Ortega, newly qualified for Spain, had an excellent season with 7 wins in 11 finals, also with DL wins in Rome, Monaco and the final in Brussels when he was followed by three Frenchmen: Pascal Martinot-Lagarde (OG 4th, beaten 4-2 overall by Bascou), Wilhem Belocian (dq heat OG) and Bascou. American footballer Devon Allen did not run in Europe, but followed an unbeaten US season that included NCAA and US titles with 5th in the Olympics. The 2015 number one David Oliver started fairly well and had three sub-13.20 times to a win in Kingston in 13.09 prior to the US Championships, but there a left hamstring injury meant that he was unable to finish his semi-final. After the Olympics he had a couple of modest runs in Europe, beaten in both by Belocian. And 2015's no. 2 Sergey Shubenkov was restricted to running only in Russia where he was unbeaten and consistent in the 13.2-13.3 range. Aries Merritt made a marvellous return from a kidney transplant for 4th in 13.22 in the US Champs, where Ronnie Ash was 2nd and Jeff Porter 3rd, but they fared less well in the Olympics, dq last and 3rd semi respectively. Hansle Parchment beat both Bascou and Oliver 2-0 when he was 2nd in Doha and Shanghai, but his season was ended early by injury. Bascou won the European title from Balázs Baji and Belocian.

Most times under 13.30: Bascou 10+1w, Ortega 9+1w, McLeod 9, Martinot-Lagarde 6+1w, Shubenkov 5, Oliver 3, Belocian 2+1w.

At 60m hurdles indoors McLeod won the World Indoor title from Martinot-Lagarde, Bascou and Jarret Eaton. McLeod's 7.41 was a national record that tied the world best for the year run a month earlier by Bascou. Ortega, not qualified to run for Spain at the Worlds, set a Spanish record of 7.49 ahead of Bascou in Düsseldorf.

1. McLeod, 2. Ortega, 3. Bascou, 4. Martinot-Lagarde, 5. Allen. 6. Oliver, 7. Shubenkov, 8. Belocian, 9. Ash, 10. Parchment

400 Metres Hurdles

PRIOR TO Rio the world's fastest of 2015 was 48.10 by Johnny Dutch in Kingston. But at the Olympics the first five bettered that in the final, Kerron Clement winning in 47.73 from national records by Boniface Muchuru Tumuti, Yasmani Copello and Thomas Barr all sub-48, and Annsert Whyte. Tumuti had won the African title and the Kenyan Trials, and Copello the European title, while Barr made astonishing improvement. He had set Irish records at 48.90 in 2014 and 48.65 in 2015, but his best in 2016 was 50.09 before 48.93 heat, 48.39 semi and 47.97 final in Rio, where the remaining finalists were Rasmus Mägi, Haron Koech and Javier Culson (dq false start). Clement won only one of his first six races of the year but then came to form in winning the US title in 48.50 from Byron Robinson and Michael Tinsley with Dutch 5th. Clement, who was previously top ranked in 2007 and 2009, also won in London and at the DL final in Zürich with 2nd place in 48.19 in Saint-Denis. There Nicholas Bett won in 48.01 with Copello 3rd and Culson 4th. World champion Bett was way below par in placing 5th to 8th in his four DL races and then dq in his Olympic hear, but he had showed a return to form with 48.68 for 2nd in Lausanne. Tumuti was unsuccessful in the Diamond League – 9th in Shanghai, 7th at Lausanne and dnf Zürich – but Culson fared well with a win in Stockholm and 2nd places in Oslo, London and Zürich. Mägi was only 3rd in his semi at the Europeans but ended well with a win in Lausanne, 5th Saint-Denis, 4th Zürich (5. Kariem Hussein, 6. Barr), and 1st Rovereto. Other than his Olympic 5th, Whyte ran only in Jamaica. Dutch beat Robinson (3rd sf OG) 2-1 and was 1-1 v Tinsley (6ht OG). Tinsley, however won in Shanghai and Eugene and was 4-4 v Clement. 3-2 v Bett etc. L.J. van Zyl was 4th in the Africans and 5th OG sf, but had three DL fourth places and 3rd in Zürich; he was 3-0 v Bett, 2-1 v Tinsley, 2-0 v Dutch, 3-1 v Mägi.

Most times to 49.00: Clement, Copello 7; Mägi, Culson 6; Whyte, Nozawa 4; Barr, Koech, Warholm, Dutch, Robinson, Cato, van Zyl, Anderson, Chalyy, Hussein, Tinsley 3.

1. Clement, 2. Copello, 3. Culson, 4. Tumuti, 5. Mägi, 6. Barr, 7. Whyte, 8. van Zyl, 9. Tinsley, 10. Bett

High Jump

THE PROMISE for men's high jumping of 2014 was not quite maintained and, as in 2015, Mutaz Essa Barshim was the only one to clear 2.40. He did this at Opole in June and had much the best series of marks. He started with four indoor wins but then was 4th at the World Indoors behind Gianmarco Tamberi, Robbie Grabarz and Erik Kynard. He started outdoors with 7th Doha 2.26 and 6th Rome 2.27 but was over at least 2.30 in his remaining eight outdoor events and beat his great rival Bohdan Bondarenko 3-2. But they were 2nd at 2.36 and 3rd at 2.33 at the Olympics where Derek Drouin won by clearing 2.38. Drouin also won at Eberstadt with 2.38 (2 Barshim 2.34) but otherwise only cleared 2.30 once and had five competitions below this due to suffering from a stress fracture in his back for much of the year. Nonetheless he beat Barshim 3-1 and was 1-1 v Bondarenko, who had problems with sinusitis in Rio. Tamberi had a brilliant indoor season winning all five competitions at 2.33 or more, headed by Italian records at 2.35 and 2.38, plus two 2.36s. Outdoors he was beaten 2-0 by Kynard, but then rounded into form, winning the European title and setting brilliant Italian records of 2.37 and 2.39 at Monaco before suffering a season-ending injury while trying higher; he would clearly have been favourite for the Olympic title. He was 2-1 v Bashim outdoors and 1-0 indoors. Grabarz and Andriy Protsenko (who had back and Achilles problems in 2016) were 4= in Rio with Kynard 6th, all at 2.33 and Majed El Dein Ghazal and Donald Thomas 7= at 2.29. Kynard beat Grabarz 4-2 outdoors and had better marks, but Protsenko had a next best outdoors of 2.29 and was 9= at the Europeans (Grabarz 2nd), although he beat Ghazal (who had big progress to 2.36) 2-0. Meanwhile in Russia Ivan Ukhov jumped 2.35 and 2.34. Thomas had 2.33 indoors and a couple of 2.31s outdoors before a sudden improvement to 2.37 at Székesfehérvár, but overall he lost 3-1 (1t) to Marco Fassinotti, another who was best indoors.

Most competitions over 2.35/2.30m (outdoors+in): Barshim 5+2i/7+3i, Bondarenko 2/6, Tamberi 2+4i/3+5i, Drouin 2/3, Kynard 1/5+2i, Ghazal, Ukhov 1/4; Thomas 1/3+1i, Grabarz 5+2i, Zhang 4+1i, Onnen 3, Baniótis 3i.

1. Barshim (2), 2. Drouin (3), 3. Bondarenko (4), 4. Kynard, 5. Tamberi (1), 6. Grabarz, 7. Ghazal, 8. Ukhov, 9. Protsenko, 10. Thomas (-), - Fassinotti (10). (Including indoors).

Pole Vault

ALTHOUGH Thiago Braz da Silva beat him 6.03 to 5.98 for the Olympic title Renaud Lavillenie was top for the seventh successive year. He was at his best indoors with 6.03 and 6.02 twice, including to win the World Indoor title, but also had the 2nd to 5th best marks outdoors, and won 5/7 indoors and 11/15 outdoors, although no height at the Europeans. Sam Kendricks was 2nd at the World Indoors and 3rd OG; he had slightly better marks than Braz with 1 indoor and 6 outdoor competitions over 5.85 to 1 and 3 by the Brazilian and also had the edge on win-loss 1-0 in and 3-2 out, but the latter's Olympic feat gives him the ranking edge although he was only 12= at the World Indoors. Shawnacy Barber was the most prolific competitor with 13 indoor and 22 outdoor competitions, and he set a North American indoor record at 6.00 in Reno and had 5.91 and 5.90 outdoors but he had a cocaine ban mid-season and his form dipped, including when 10th at the Olympics. Robert Sobera was the European champion with a modest 5.60 in windy, tricky conditions at the Europeans from Jan Kudlicka and Robert Renner, but well down on win-loss to Piotr Lisek (4= EC) although 5-5 to another Pole Pawel Wojciechowski (7 EC, dnq 16= OG). Kudlicka and Lisek were 4= in Rio and at the World Indoors jumped 5.75 as did Barber when these three were 4=, 3rd, 4=. Raphael Holzdeppe had five events at 5.70 or higher indoors but only one outdoors. Konstadínos Filippídis (7 WI, 7= EC, 7= OG) was 3-2 v Lisek indoors but 3-5 outdoors and Xue Changrui, although with less impressive heights, was 4-0 v Sobera.

Most competitions over 5.70m (outdoors+in): Lavillenie 15+7i, Kendricks 12+7i, Braz da Silva 11+1i, Barber 8+11i, Kudlicka 7+2i, Lisek 6+4i, Filippídis 5+3i, Xue, Scherbarth 4; Wojciechowski 3+3i, Cunningham 3, Menaldo 2+1i, Holzdeppe 1+5i, Sobera 1+3i.
1. Lavillenie, 2. Braz da Silva, 3. Kendricks, 4. Kudlicka (6), 5. Barber (4), 6. Lisek (5), 7. Filippídis, 8. Xue Changrui, 9. Sobera, 10. Wojciechowski. (Including indoors)

Long Jump

GREG RUTHERFORD and Jeffrey Henderson have contested top ranking for three years. In 2016 they were only 10= and 7= on the world list for wind-legal marks, yet still vied for top ranking. Henderson had a moderate start to the year: indoors 2nd at the US Champs and 4th World Indoors at 8.19, then four non-winning outdoor events with a best of 8.19. But then came the wind-aided top quality marks at the US Champs (7 men at 8.25 plus): 1 Henderson 8.59w, 2 Jarrion Lawson 8.58 (year's best wind-legal mark), 3 Will Claye 8.42w, 4 Marquis Dendy 8.42w, 5 Mike Hartfield 8.39w, and Henderson won the Olympic title with 8.38. Rutherford in contrast had consistently good marks, 8.26A indoors and then seven outdoor wins (5 at 8.20 or better) and a 5th before 3rd at the Olympics with 8.29. Lawson won the NCAA title indoors and out and went on to OG 4th, but that was Claye's only LJ of the year while Dendy had only one other outdoor LJ (3rd Baie Mahault behind Marquise Goodwin 8.45 and Hartfield) after an excellent indoor season, winning US (8.41) and World (8.26) titles plus wins at 8.38 and 8.13. Luvo Manyonga excelled with 8.37 for Olympic silver and 8.48 to win the DL final in Brussels from Fabrice Lapierre (OG 10th, 2nd WI) and Lawson, and that may be enough to rank him ahead of Rushwal Samaai, who had beaten him three times including when they were 1st and 2nd at the African Champs but who was held back to 9th in Rio by a hamstring injury. Top Chinese men had good competitions although without top marks: Gao Xinglong had DL wins in Shanghai and London and 4th in Brussels; he was 3-2 v Wang Jianan, but while Wang was 5th at the Olympics, Gao had three no jumps. Marquise Goodwin concentrated on long jump even though he had a year left on his NFL contract with the Buffalo Bills and beat Hartfield 3-1, although 7th at the US Champs (8.25w). Just missing ranking was Emiliano Lasa (6th OG), who beat Damar Forbes (12th OG) 4-1. Michal Tornéus jumped 8.44A at Monachil and was 2nd to Rutherford at the Europeans, but was dnq 26 in Rio.,

Most competitions over 8.10m: Rutherford, Lapierre 6+1i; Manyonga 5+1w, Henderson 5+1i, Goodwin 4+1w, Lawson 3+2i, Hartfield 3+1w, Gao, Lasa, Kopeykin 3; Dendy 2+4i, Forbes 2+2w, Wang 2+1i, Gotch, Tornéus 1+2w.

1. Rutherford, 2. Henderson, 3. Manyonga, 4. Samaai, 5. Lawson, 6. Lapierre, 7. Gao, 8. Wang, 9. Goodwin, 10. Hartfield. – Dendy (6). (Including indoors).

Triple Jump

CHRISTIAN TAYLOR had an outstanding season with seven wins and a second for his fourth top ranking in six years. He had the top three marks, 17.86 OG, 17.80 DL final and 17.78 London. The one loss was when Will Claye beat him 17.65 to 17.39 at the US Champs. Claye took Olympic silver and Dong Din the bronze and these three had the best 17 marks of the year: Taylor 8, Dong 5 (3 indoors), Claye 4. Of Taylor's great rivals, Pedro Pichardo did not compete in 2016, and Teddy Tamgho's steady progress to regain form ended with a broken leg sustained at the French Championships, where he won with 17.15. After the top three, who were far ahead, the Olympic 4th to 8th were Cao Shuo, Jhon Murillo, Nelson Évora, Troy Doris and Omar Craddock. It was their only 17m mark of the year for Cao, Murillo and Évora. Although he was dnq 16th in Rio, Max Hess won the European title with 17.20 from Karol Hoffmann and was 2nd at the World Indoors with 17.14 behind Dong 17.33. Chris Carter was the second best US jumper; he won the US title indoors but was 6th outdoors; however, he was 3-2 (1-1 indoors) v Craddock (2nd and 4th at those US Champs) and 5-2 v Chris Benard (US 3rd in and out, dnq 16 OG, 11 WI). Consistently good were Troy Doris, 7th OG and 2nd in Zürich, 2-1 v Hess and 2 v Carter, and ex-Cuban Alexis Copello, best six competitions 16.98 to 16.90 and 5-1 v Craddock, 2-0 v Hess and Murillo, but 2-4 v Carter. Cao was 2nd and Copello 3rd in Beijing. Craddock beat Benard 2-0 indoors, but Benard was ahead in all their six outdoor meetings. Lyukman Adams had similar marks to those ranked 4th to 10th but was unable to compete outside Russia.

Most competitions over 17.00: Taylor 10, Claye 5, Dong Bin 4+3i, Carter 3+1i, Craddock 3, Doris 2+2w, Hess 2+1w+2i

1. Taylor, 2. Claye, 3. Dong, 4. Carter, 5. Copello, 6. Doris, 7. Cao Shuo (8), 8. Hess (7), 9. Murillo, 10. Benard. (Including indoors)

Shot

RYAN CROUSER had not ranked in the top ten before, just missing out in 2015, but he stormed to the top in 2016 as he won his five indoor competitions and 6 of 9 outdoors. These included the top marks of the year, 22.52 to win the Olympic title and 22.28 in Zagreb after a slight blip when he was 6th in Eugene in May. He also lost narrowly in two mighty contests as Tom Walsh beat him with Oceania records 22.00 to 21.99 in Saint-Denis and 22.20 to 22.00 in Zürich. Joe Kovacs was the third man over 22m and was 2nd with Walsh 3rd at the Olympics, but Walsh was ahead on win-loss, 3-2 v Crouser and 4-3 v Kovacs, and also won the World Indoor title with 21.78. Walsh won 8 of his 14 outdoor competitions and improved his Oceania record to 22.21 for 2nd in Zagreb. The big three were well ahead of the rest with Darrell Hill and David Storl having the next best set of marks, each four over 21m. Hill was 3rd behind Crouser and Kovacs at the US Champs, but only dnq 23 at the Olympics; he was 2-2 v Storl, who was 7th at the Olympics behind 4 Frank Elemba, 5 Darlan Romero, 6 Tomasz Majewski with O'Dayne Richards 8th. Kurt Roberts won the US Indoor title and had a positive win-loss record against top men, including 3-2 v Hill and 3-0 v Elemba, but was dnq 19th at the World Indoors and dnq 13th at the US Champs. Against that he won in Stockholm and was 3rd at Saint-Denis and 4th in the DL final in Zürich behind the big three and ahead of Elemba, Hill, Konrad Bukowiecki, Romani, Storl and Majewski when all the top men met. Elemba was 4-1 v Majewski, 3-0 v Storl, 3-2 v Hill and Bukowiecki. The 19 year-old Bukowiecki set world junior records at 21.01 and 21.15 with the senior shot and 23.34 with the 6kg shot when he won the World Junior title; he beat compatriot Majewski 7-2. Storl won the European title from Michel Haratyk (dnq 18 OG), Tsanko Arnaudov and Bukowiecki. Indoor form takes Tim Nedow (7 WI, dnq 16 OG) ahead of Haratyyk.

Most competitions over 20.80: Walsh 15+1i, Crouser 9+3i, Kovacs 9, Storl 7, Hill 5, Haratyk 3+2i, Roberts 3+1i, Elemba 3, Nedow 1+5i, Stanek 1+3i.

1. Crouser, 2. Walsh. 3. Kovacs, 4. Elemba, 5. Hill, 6. Storl, 7. Roberts, 8. Bukowiecki, 9. Majewski, 10. Haratyk (-), - Nedow (10).

Discus

ALTHOUGH HE was beaten by Christoph Harting to the Olympic title, Piotr Malachowski had, as in 2015, easily the best depth of top marks. In all he had 12 wins in 19 competitions including the European title and three DLs. Robert Harting beat younger brother Christoph to the German title (with Daniel Jasinski 3rd and Martin Wierig 4th), but was dnq 15 at the Olympics. Christoph beat Malachowski and was 4th at the Europeans but did not contest any DL meetings. Robert did (2nd, 3rd, and 4th) and was 3-2 v Philip Milanov and 4-1 v Daniel Ståhl. Other top men at Europeans & Olympics: Jasinski 8th/3rd, Martin Kupper 4th/7th, Gerd Kanter 5th/3rd, Zoltán Kövágó 7th/6th, Milanov 9th/2nd, Ståhl dnq 14/5th. Jasinski's form fell away, with three top meetings under 61m post-Rio, while Weisshaidinger (6th OG) excelled with a win in Berlin, 2nd in Lausanne and 3rd in the DL final in Brussels, behind Ståhl and Malachowski, and ahead of Kupper, Milanov, Apostolos Parellis (8 OG, dnq 18 Eur) and Robert Urbanek (dnq 17 OG, 9 Eur). Weisshaidinger was 2-1 v Milanov and 3-0 v R Harting, who was 3-2 v Milanov and 4-1 v Ståhl. Milanov was 6-2 v Ståhl, 4-1 v Kanter and 2-1 v Jasinski, and Ståhl 5-2 v Kanter, who beat his Estonian compatriot Kupper 9-5 and Jasinski 4-1.

Most competitions over 65m: Malachowski 17, C Harting, Ståhl 7; R Harting, Urbanek 6; Milanov, L M Martínez 5; Jasinski, Kanter, Kövágó, Weisshaidinger, Finley 4; Dacres 3.

1. Malachowski, 2. C Harting, 3. Weisshaidinger, 4. R Harting, 5. Milanov, 6. Ståhl, 7. Kanter, 8. Kupper, 9. Kövágó, 10. Jasinski

Hammer

PERHAPS THE most amazing result of 2016 was that Pavel Fajdek threw only 72.00 for 17th in the Olympic qualifying competition. Other than that he won all his 12 competitions, all at least 79.12 and he had the 12 best performances of the year (80.10 or better). Ivan Tikhon had the only other 80m throw, 80.04 to win the Belarus title, one of his four events, that also included European and Olympic silvers. Fajdek, of course, won at the Europeans, and Dilshod Nazarov became the Olympic champion with Wojciech Nowicki 3rd in both and Marcel Lomnicky 5th in both. The surprise Olympic 4th placer was Diego Del Real, followed by Lomnicky and Ashraf Amjad El-Seify, who was 2-1 v Lomnicky. Del Real was NACAC champion but did not get to compete in the DL and lacked the depth of throws of other top ten men. The top three men had the best 19 performances and then came, at 78.63, Wagner Domingos, who was unbeaten in a busy season to the end of June, but without meeting major rivals and was then 7th at Székesfehérvár and 12th at the Olympics. Without the ability to compete outside Russia, Sergey Litvinov and Aleksey Sokirskiy had the next best marks, and the rankings are completed by the Olympic 7th and 8th placers Krisztián Pars and David Söderberg.

Most competitions over 80m/78m: Fajdek 12/14, Tikhon 1/4, Nazarov 7, Nowicki 6.

1. Fajdek, 2. Nazarov, 3. Tikhon, 4. Nowicki, 5. El-Seify, 6. Lomnicky, 7. Litvinov, 8. Sokirskiy, 9. Söderberg, 10. Pars

Javelin

THOMAS RÖHLER went to the European Championships as clear favourite with the two best throws of the year, 91.28 in Turku and 89.30 in Oslo, but came a disappointing 5th in Amsterdam. However, he put that behind him by winning the Olympic title with 90.30 and he had a positive win-loss record against all, including 4-1 v Julius Yego, 6-0 v Keshorn Walcott as these two men took Olympic silver and bronze, and 7-2 against both Johannes Vetter and Jakub Vadlejch. Apart from Röhler, form amongst the top men was very mixed. Yego threw 88.24 in Rio, and beat Walcott 3-1, Vadlejch 4-1 and Vetter 2-1, but, troubled by an injured ankle, his next best was 84.68 for 2nd in Eugene, where Ihab Abdelrahman was the winner and Röhler third. Abdelrahman also won in Stockholm and beat Yego 4-0 but did not compete after June having failed a drugs test in April, for which he eventually received a 2-year ban that he is appealing. Zürich concluded the DL season and there Vadlejch (8th OG) won from Röhler, Julian Weber (9th OG), Antti Ruuskanen (6th OG), Tero Pitkämäki dnq 21 OG), Vitezslav Vesely (7th OG), Kim Amb (dnq 16 OG, 7 Eur) and Sigismunds Sirmais (dnq 14th OG), who had been the surprise European Champion from Vesely and Ruuskanen, but who could not get near his 86.66 otherwise; Walcott had no throws. Vadlejch had a mid-season dip and was only 8th at the Europeans but he also had DL wins in London and Saint-Denis and the best set of marks other than Röhler; he was 4-3 v Walcott, who was 3-2 v Vetter and 3-1 v Vesely. Röhler won the German title from Weber, Andreas Hofmann, Vetter and Lars Hamann (dnq 20 Eur). Vetter and Weber were 4-4 and Vesely 4-3 v Vadlejch. Dmytro Kosynskyy was 5th at the Olympics and 4th at Saint-Denis, but dnq EC, and Hamish Peacock (dnq 25 OG) and Ryohei Arai (11th OG) had slightly better marks.

Most competitions over 84m/82.50m: Röhler 11/15, Vadlejch 9/11, Vetter, Weber 6/9; Walcott 3/6, Hamann 3/5, Abdelrahman, Pitkämäki 3/4; Arai 3/1, Peacock 2/8, Ruuskanen 2/7, Yego, Amb 2/4; Hofmann 2/3, Vesely 1/5, Kosynskyy 1/4.

1. Röhler, 2. Yego, 3. Vetter, 4. Vadlejch, 5. Walcott, 6. Weber, 7. Ruuskanen, 8. Vesely, 9. Kosynskyy, 10. Peacock . If eligible: 8. Abdelrahman.

Decathlon

ASHTON EATON remained the decathlon supremo as he won the US title with 8750 and retained his Olympic title with 8893, his third highest ever score. But he had a winning margin of just 59 points in Rio as Kevin Meyer excelled to add 313 to his previous best with a French record 8834 for the silver medal. Meyer had 'dnfs' in Florence and Talence, but was also 2nd in Götzis with 8425. Damien Warner was the Götzis winner with 8523 and Olympic 3rd with 8666. Unlike the top three, Kai Kazmirek had three completed decathlons and took the IAAF Challenge with 3rd Götzis, 2nd Ratingen and 4th Olympics from Jeremy Taiwo (4 Götzis, 2 US, 11 OG) and Adam Sebastian Helcelet (11 Götzis, 2 EC, 12 OG, 9 Talence). Arthur Abele had won at Ratingen with 8604 for 4th on the world list, but did not finish at Götzis and was 15th in Rio, where 10 of the top 12 (8291 or more) set season's bests and further top placings were 5 Larbi Bouraada (only decathlon). 6 Leonel Suárez, 7 Zach Ziemek (2 NCAA, 3 US), 8 Thomas Van Der Plaetsen (1 EC), 9 Kurt Felix. Lindon Victor was 16th and Maicel Uibo 24th, after top scores in the US, where Victor won the SEC title with 8446 from Felix 8315, and the NCAA title with 8379 and Uibo 3rd.

Eaton won the World Indoor heptathlon title with 6470 points, far ahead of Oleksiy Kasyanov, whose 6182 was nonetheless the season's second best score.

1. Eaton, 2. Meyer, 3. Warner, 4. Kazmirek, 5. Bouraada, 6. Suárez, 7. Ziemek, 8. Taiwo, 9. Abele, 10. Victor

20 Kilometres Walk

WANG ZHEN won the IAAF Walks Challenge and was clearly the top man at 20k, winning all his four races: Chinese Trials, World Cup, La Coruña and Olympics. Cai Zelin was 3rd, 2nd, dnf and 2nd in those races, while others to feature in both World Cup and Olympics were Dane Bird-Smith 4/3, Caio Bonfim 8/4, Christopher Linke 10/5 and Iñaki Gómez 7/12. The World Cup 3/5/6 fell back at the Olympics: Álvaro Martín 22nd, Benjamin Thorne 27th and Andrés Chocho dq. The three fastest times of the year were by Japanese as Eiki Takahashi 1:18:26 and Isamu Fujisawa 1:18:45 were 1-2 in their championships but these men were respectively 12/42 and 69/21 at World Cup/OG. Daisuke Matsunaga had been disqualified in the Japanese Champs but won in Nomi in 1:18:53 from Gómez and was 7th at the Olympics. Tom Bosworth was 6th OG, after winning in Dudince and 34th World Cup. He was also disqualified in Podĕbrady, where Perseus Karlström (dnf OG) won from Linke.

1. Wang Zhen, 2. Cai Zelin, 3. Bird-Smith, 4. Bonfim, 5. Linke, 6. Bosworth, 7. Matsunaga, 8. Gómez, 9. Karlström, 10. Martín

50 Kilometres Walk

AS USUAL the top race of the year, in this case at the Olympics, was pre-eminent in determining the rankings. The order in Rio was: 1 Matej Tóth (only race), 2 Jared Tallent (also won World Cup), 3 Hirooki Arai (2 JPN Ch), 4 Evan Dunfee, 5. Yu Wei, 6. Robert Heffernan, 7 Håvard Haukenes, 8 Yohann Diniz, who I move up as he set the year's fastest time, 3:37:48 to win the French title. Yu was also 3rd in a fast race at the Chinese Trial behind Wang Zhendong (11 OG) and Han Yucheng (47 OG, dnf WCp). Takayuki Tanii (14th OG) won the Japanese title in 3:44:12 and Andrés Chocho was disqualified in Rio, but had won at altitude in Juárez in 3:42:57. Another IAAF Challenge race winner was Rafal Augustyn (22 OG) at Dudince in 3:43:22 with Haukenes 4th. Ihor Hlavan and Marco De Luca were 2nd and 3rd at the World Cup, before dnf and 21st at the Olympics.

1. Tóth, 2. Tallent, 3. Arai, 4. Diniz, 5. Dunfee, 6. Yu Wei, 7. Heffernan, 8. Wang Zhendong, 9. Haukenes, 10. Tanii

WOMEN

ANITA WLODARCZYK has reached a level of dominance at her event that has been very rare throughout athletics history. In 2016 she won all her 12 competitions and twice improved her world record, with 82.29 at the Olympic Games and 82.98 at the Karolina Skolimowska Memorial meeting in Warsaw. She had the 12 best performances of the year and indeed if we take all throws in her series she had 42 better than the best anybody else achieved in 2016 – 76.85 by Zhang Wenxiu. Wlodarczyk's success this year follows winning all 11 competitions in 2017 and 7/8 in 2015 (7 successive wins after her last loss, 76.41 to 78.00 by Betty Heidler in Ostrava). Heidler remains the world's second best ever with her last world record, 79.42 in 2011, and Wlodarczyk now has the top seven performances of all-time and the best 21 throws ever (17 in 2016). All that makes the Polish star, who turned 31 in August 2016, as the obvious selection for the top woman athlete of 2016, despite the brilliant achievements of Almaz Ayana, Elaine Thompson, Ruth Jebet, Sandra Perkovic and Keni Harrison, all of whom did enough to have ranked top in many years.

Seven women Olympic champions were unbeaten at their events in 2016. Wlodarczyk at hammer, Sandra Perkovic all 11 at discus and Caster Semenya not only won all 11 finals and five prelims at 800m but also her one race at 200m, and her four at 1500m; she did, however, lose one of her seven finals at 200m. Then Elaine Thompson won her eight finals and four prelims at 100m (although with losses at 60m and 200m), and Shaunae Miller won her six finals at 400m and three at 200m (2nd in her one 100m race). In more limited competition Almaz Ayana won her two 10,000m races (and her one at 3000m but 3/4 at 5000m) and Jemima Sumgong both marathons. Liu Hong finished first in all her four 20k walk races, but lost two of these through a 1-month stimulant ban. Kendra Harrison won 10/11 at 100m hurdles (that 6th place in the US Champs being very costly!), Caterine Ibarguën 9/10 at triple jump and Ruth Jebet 5/6 at 3000m steeplechase. Without the opportunity to compete outside Russia, Vera Rebrik at javelin won all the eight top competitions at home.

Seven women were both Olympic champions and Diamond Race winners. These were headed by Perkovic, who won all seven DL competition at discus. Then six wins were achieved by Ibarguën at triple jump, five wins by Caster Semenya at 800m and Ruth Beitia at high jump, four wins by Elaine Thompson at 100m (and one at 200m), Ruth Jebet at steeplechase, and Ekateríni Stefanídi at pole vault. Also Kendra Harrison had six wins at 100m hurdles, Ivana Spanovic five at long jump. and Valerie Adams at shot and Madara Palameika at javelin both had four wins. Almaz Ayana had three wins at 5000m and one at 3000m, and Dafne Schippers three at 200m and one at 100m.

100 Metres

AFTER SHELLY-ANN FRASER-PRYCE had been top ranked four times in seven years, another Jamaican took over in 2016. Elaine Thompson was undefeated in eight 100m competitions and ran the three fastest times of the year: 10.70 to win the Jamaican title from Fraser-Pryce, Christania Williams and Veronica Campbell-Brown, the Olympic title in 10.71 and, after earlier DL wins in Rome and Lausanne, the DL final in Brussels 10.72 from Dafne Schippers and Williams. The first seven in the brilliant Olympic final ran 10.94 or faster, as Thompson was followed by Torie Bowie, Fraser-Pryce, Marie-Josée Ta Lou, Schippers (European champion and winner in Monaco), Michelle-Lee Ahye and English Gardner, with Williams trailing in last. Gardner was the year's second fastest with the 10.74 that she ran to win at the US Champs, from Tianna Bartoletta, Bowie, Morolake Akinosun and Jenna Prandini. Bowie was 2-0 v Schippers, who was 3-1 v Ta Lou. Gardner had DL wins in Eugene and Birmingham and Ta Lou won in London. Ahye ran a consistent series of fast times and beat her compatriot Murielle Ahouré 2-0 and was 3-0 v Williams. Bartoletta was 2nd and Ahouré 3rd in Eugene in their only clash, and both were 4th in their Olympic semis. Without super-fast times, as she concentrated on the 200m, Dina Asher-Smith was nonetheless 2-0 v Akinosun, Simone Facey and compatriot Desiree Henry. Overall standards were again very high with 51 sub-11.00 times by 14 women (plus 8 wind-assisted times).

Most times under 11.00/11.10: Thompson 7+1w/9+1w, Gardner 6+2w/10+2w, Bowie 6+1w/8+1w, Schippers 7+1w/8+1w, Ahye 4+2w/8+2w, Ta Lou 4+1w/6+1w, Fraser-Pryce 4/7, Prandini 2+2w/2+3w, Ahouré 2+1w/8+1w; Bartoletta 2+1w/5+2w, Camp-

Selections for World Top Ten			
	PJM	TFN	AI
Anita Wlodarczyk*	1	1	1
Almaz Ayana*	2	2	2
Elaine Thompson*	3	3	3
Ruth Jebet	4	4	4
Sandra Perkovic	5	6	5
Kendra Harrison	6	5	6
Vivian Cheruiyot	7	9	
Caterine Ibargüen	8	10	7
Shaunae Miller	9	8	9
Faith Kipyegon	10		
Nafissatou Thiam			10
Caster Semenya	-	7	8
*IAAF finalists, Wlodarczyk was their athlete of the year.			
Thiam was IAAF Rising Star of the Year.			

bell-Brown 2+1w/2+1w, C Williams 2/7, A Washington 2w/2+2w, Cunliffe 1/3, Okagbare 1w/3+1w, D Henry 0/6, Facey 0/4, Asher-Smith 0/3.
1. Thompson, 2. Bowie, 3. Schippers, 4. Gardner, 5. Fraser-Pryce, 6. Ta Lou, 7. Ahye, 8. Bartoletta, 9. Ahouré, 10. Williams

At 60m indoors Barbara Pierre beat Schippers 7.02 to 7.04 for the World title, and both ran 7.00 to head the year list. 3rd to 7th at the World Indoors were Thompson, Ahye, Asha Philip, Tori Bowie, and Ta Lou. Schippers had 7, Pierre 5, Thompson and Ta Lou 3 and Ahye 2 times at 7.10 or better.

200 Metres

AFTER THEIR extremely close battle in the 2015 Worlds, Elaine Thompson beat Dafne Schippers 21.78 to 21.86 at the Olympics. Thompson then won the DL final in Zürich, but this was much closer, 21.85 to 21.86 by Schippers, who had four times in all under 22 secs (and 8 of the world's fastest 15 times of 2016) to two by Thompson and one by Tori Bowie (21.99 at Eugene). Bowie was 3rd at the Olympics after taking the US title from Deajah Stevens, Jenna Prandini and Allyson Felix who, after a April ankle injury, thus lost her chance to bid for the 200/400 double at the Olympics. African champion Marie-Josée Ta Lou was 4th and European champion Dina Asher-Smith 5th, with Michelle-Lee Ahye 6th, Stevens 7th and European runner-up Ivet Lalova-Collio 8th in the Olympic final. Stevens had made massive progress, from a best in 2015 of 23.18 to 22.25 for 2nd at the NCAAs, won by Ariana Washington (5th US) in 22.21. Felix had just one more 200m competition, but that was 3rd in 22.02 in Zürich, a place ahead of Asher-Smith with Ahye 7th. Simone Facey won at the Jamaican Champs from Veronica Campbell-Brown, and this pair were 3rd semi and 3rd heat at the Olympics. Shaunae Miller was the year's fifth fastest with 22.05, but did not contest the major races, and Joanna Atkins had an impressive series of times but did not make the US final.

Felicia Brown ran the three fastest times indoors, headed by 22.45 and also won the NCAA title.

Most times under 22.70: Schippers, Stevens 10; Prandini 9, Bowie 7, Thompson, Atkins 6; F Brown 5+3w+3i, Asher-Smith, Lalova-Collio 5; Campbell-Brown 4+1w, Facey, E Nelson 4; Townsend 3+1w, Felix, Washington 3; Solomon 2+2w, Miller, Ellis-Watson 2+1w.
1. Thompson, 2. Schippers, 3. Bowie. 4. Asher-Smith, 5. Ta Lou, 6. Stevens, 7. Prandini, 8. Felix, 9. Ahye, 10. Lalova-Collio

400 Metres

SHAUNAE MILLER and Allyson Felix came to Rio undefeated at 400m in 2016, and there Miller hurled herself to the title in 49.44 from Felix 49.51, the two fastest times of the year (and the pair shared the top six times). Shericka Jackson twice ran under 50 secs and took the Olympic silver medal but she was beaten 7-1 by Stephenie Ann McPherson, who was 6th in Rio and 3rd in the Brussels DL final behind Caster Semenya (her only 400m against top women) and Courtney Okolo. Phyllis Francis had been 2nd to Felix at the US Trials with Natasha Hastings 3rd, but these positions were reversed in Rio as Hastings was 4th and Francis 5th, the final completed by Olha Zemlyak 7th and Libania Grenot 8th. The US Trials was highly competitive as 4th to 6th were Taylor Ellis-Watson, Francena McCorory, and Okolo. The other nation with such strength in depth was Jamaica, and at their Champs the order was McPherson, Christine Day (4sf OG), Jackson, and Novlene Williams-Mills. Helping to sort out the rankings, win-loss showed McPherson 4-3 v Hastings, who was 2-1 v McCorory and 1-1 v Francis. Okolo, also NCAA champion from Ellis-Watson, was 2-1 v Hastings and 1-1 v McCorory. European champion Grenot was well ahead of Day in the Olympic semi that eliminated the Jamaican, although Williams-Mills beat Grenot 2-0.

Most times under 50.80: Okolo 9+1i, McPherson 8, McCorory 7, Miller 6, Hastings, Jackson, Francis 5; Felix, Day 4; Ellis-Watson, Grenot 3.
1. Miller, 2. Felix, 3. McPherson, 4. Jackson, 5. Hastings, 6. Francis, 7. Okolo, 8. McCorory, 9. Grenot, 10. Day

800 Metres

CASTER SEMENYA, Francine Niyonsaba and Margaret Wambui were in a different league from the rest, both medically it seems (released from testosterone control) and athletically. They were 1-2-3 at the Olympics and in Zürich as Semenya was undefeated, indeed unapproachable, with three 1:55 plus times without I think running all out for a fast time, and this trio ran the eleven sub-1:57 times of the year. Melissa Bishop was the next fastest with 1:57.04 for Olympic 4th, when Joanna Józwik, Lynsey Sharp, Maryna Arzamasova and Kate Grace followed her home in the final. Eunice Sum, world number one in the previous three years, was a surprising elimination in the Olympics semis, but bounced back with 2nd to Niyonsaba in Lausanne, ahead of Sharp, Bishop, Selina Büchel, Habitam Alemu and Nataliya Pryshchepa. At the DL final in Zürich, Józwik was 4th, Grace 5th, Arzamasova 6th, Pryshchepa 7th and Bishop 8th, all under 1:59. Sum was 5-1 v Sharp, who was 4-3 v Józwik and 5-1 v Arzamasova. Pryshchepa (4sf OG) was a surprise winner of the European title from Rénelle Lamote, Lovisa Lindh and Büchel, but beaten 2-0 by Arzamasova. Ajee' Wilson was 2nd in the US champs to Grace and 3rd in her Rio semi.

Indoors Niyonsaba won the World title from Wilson and Wambui.

Most times under 1:59.8: Semenya, Bishop 11; Niyonsaba, Sharp 9; Wambui, Sum 8; Arzamasova 6, Alemu 5, Józwik, Grace, Pryshchepa, Büchel, Wilson 4; Lamote, Ludlow, Oskan-Clarke 3.

1. Semenya, 2. Niyonsaba, 3. Wambui, 4. Bishop, 5. Józwik. 6. Sum, 7. Sharp, 8. Lamote. 9. Arzamasova, 10. Grace

1500 Metres

GENZEBE DIBABA set another world indoor record, with 4:13.31 for 1 mile at Stockholm, but outdoors had just three competitions; wins in Barcelona and Rovereto and 2nd in the Olympic final that was very slow for the first two laps before a dynamic finish. There she had to yield to Faith Kipyegon, who had started with fast wins in Shanghai 3:56.82 and Eugene 3:56.41 at 1500m and 4:18.60 for 1 mile at Oslo and then won the Kenyan Trials. That unbeaten run was ended in much the year's fastest race in depth – in Saint-Denis when Laura Muir (7 OG) set her second British record of the year (after 3:57.49 in London) by speeding to the year's best of 3:55.22. Kipyegon was 2nd in 3:56.41 and then came Sifan Hassan (5 OG), Shannon Rowbury (4 OG), Dawit Seyaum (8 OG, Jenny Simpson (3 OG) and Besu Sado (9 OG), all under 4 minutes with four more under 4:03.3. Kipyegon ended her year with 7th in Zürich, where six beat 4 minutes: Rowbury, Muir, Hassan, Simpson, Seyaum and Sado. Hassan was 2nd and Meraf Bahta 3rd in London and Bahta 6th OG before 12th in Saint-Denis and 8th in Zürich with Gudaf Tsegay 13th and 9th in these races. Although in a different order, the top seven are the same as in 2015. In addition to those mentioned, Hellen Obiri made it nine women under 4 minutes with 3:59.34 for 2nd in Shanghai; she was 11th in Zürich.

Fastest indoors at 1500m was Dibaba at 3:56.46 en route to her mile record and the medallists at the World Indoors were Hassan, Seyaum and Tsegay.

Most times under 4:04 (or 4:23.6M): Kipyegon 6, Seyaum 4+2i, Hassan 4+1i, Muir 4, Dibaba 3+1i, Simpson, Sado, Bahta 3, Tsegay 2+1i

1. Kipyegon, 2. Dibaba, 3. Muir, 4. Hassan, 5. Simpson, 6. Rowbury, 7. Seyaum, 8. Sado, 9. Bahta, 10. Tsegay

3000 Metres

GENZEBE DIBABA ran the fastest time of 2016, with 8:22.50 indoors and won her other races at the distance, taking the World Indoor title and running 8:31.84 outdoors in Lausanne. The top race outdoors, however, was the DL race in Doha won by Almaz Ayana in 8:23.11, with Mercy Cherono and Gelete Burka under 8:30, followed by Vivian Cheruiyot, Janet Kisa and Viola Kibiwot, with ten women at 8:43.27 or better. Cherono was also under 8:30 on Monaco, where Hellen Obiri won in 8:24.27 and Kisa was 3rd in 8:28.49. Meseret Defar made a splendid return after three years out with 8:30.83 indoors at Boston and then won the World Indoor silver, but outdoors had only one track race, a win in 15:06.96 for 5000m at Boston.

5000 Metres

SHE COULD not quite get the world record, but Almaz Ayana showed terrific form with the three fastest times of the year, 14:12.59 in Rome, 14:16.31 in Rabat and 14:18.89 in the DL final in Brussels. The last came after the Olympic Games, in which, after her 10,000m win and a fast 5000m heat, she faded to third. Genzebe Dibaba passed the event to concentrate on the 1500m, and Vivian Cheruiyot came back from her 10,000m silver to win the Olympic title from Hellen Obiri. Earlier Cheruiyot had been 3rd in Eugene behind Obiri and Viola Kibiwot, and won in Birmingham and at the Kenyan Trials, while Obiri had three wins and three second places, also at the Kenyan Trials and in Brussels. Mercy Cherono was 4th and Senbere Teferi 5th at the Olympics, with the former 2-0 up on win-loss. Teferi was 3rd in Brussels, followed by 4 Etenesh Diro, 5 Shannon Rowbury, 6 Alice Aprot Nawowuna, 7 Kibiwot, 8 Margaret Chelimo. Yasemin Can was European champion and 6th at the Olympics and another significant race was in Rome when Ayana was followed by Cherono, Kibiwot, Teferi, Diro, Can and Kisa.

Most times under 15:00: Ayana, Teferi 5; Kibiwot 4, Obiri, Cherono, Cheruiyot, Can, Burka 3.

1. Ayana, 2. Cheruiyot, 3. Obiri, 4. M Cherono, 5. Teferi, 6. Kibiwot, 7. Diro, 8. Can, 9. Kisa, 10. Rowbury

10,000 Metres

WANG JUNXIA'S 29:31.78 in 1993 was not believed by some, dismissed as drug-assisted by others, and nobody got within 22 secs of it in the ensuing 23 years. Then at Rio in the Olympic Games Almaz Ayana smashed that world record with an amazing 29:17.45 and behind her Vivian Cheruiyot 29:32.53, Tirunesh Dibaba 29:42.56 and Alice Aprot Nawowuna 29:53.51 went to 3rd, 4th and 5th on the world all-time list. Tirunesh had returned this year after no track races in 2014 and 2015 as arguably the greatest ever woman 10,000m runner, having won all her 11 previous races at the distance, including two World and two Olympic titles. She was third behind Ayana and Gelete Burka in the European Trial race in Hengelo, a race in which nine women broke 31 minutes and were in the top 14 in the world, and then improved her pb by 12.2 secs for that Olympic bronze. 5th to 8th in the Olympics all bettered 30:30: Betsy Saina (2nd KEN Trial), Molly Huddle (US champion), Yasemin Can and Burka before a gap back to Karoline Bjerkeli Grøvdal 31:14.07.

Ranking after the Olympic top eight were 4th to 7th in the Ethiopian Trial: Netsanet Gudeta, Genet Yalew, Senbere Tefere and Belaynesh Oljira. Can, Dulce Félix and Grøvdal took the medals at the European Championships.

1. Ayana, 2. Cheruiyot, 3. Dibaba, 4. Aprot Nawowuna, 5. Saina, 6. Huddle, 7. Can, 8. Burka, 9. Gudeta, 10. Yalew

Half Marathon

Violah Jepchumba ran the year's fastest time, 65:51 at Prague, and had three more races in 68+ minutes, two wins and second in Valencia to Peres Jepchirchir, who was much the most prolific producer of fast times, six under 68:30. She won the World title from Cynthia Limo, Mercy Wacera Ngugi and Netsanet Gudeta and also won at Yangzhou, Ustí and Eldoret. She was, however, 4th in the race that had six of the year's top ten times (under 67 mins) − at Ra's Al-Khaymah, won by Limo from Gladys Cherono and Genet Yalew (5th Worlds), with Gladys Chesire 5th and Jemima Jelagat Sumgong 6th, with record place times from 2nd to 10th. In another race featuring many of the world's best Jepchirchir was 5th in New Delhi behind Worknesh Degefa, Yeshaneh Ababel, Hellah Kiprop and Chesire, with Wacera Ngugi, Gelete Burka and Gudeta 6th to 8th. Other top ten times came come Degefa, 2nd in Prague, and in Houston from Wacera Ngugi and Limo, and Degefa had another big win, Rome to Ostia. As usual there were also big names in the Great North Run, won by Vivian Cheruiyot on her half marathon debut from Priscah Jeptoo (8th RAK), Tirunesh Dibaba and Joyce Chepkirui (2nd to Molly Huddle in New York).

Marathon

JUST LIKE Eliud Kipchoge so the women's number one went to the winner in London and at the Olympic Games – Jemima Sumgong Jelagat. The year's fastest came, however, in Dubai: Tirfe Tsegaye 2:19:41 from Amane Beriso 2:20:48. There were also fast winners in Majors races: Aberu Kebede, 2:20:45 in Berlin, Helah Kiprop, 2:21:27 in Tokyo, and Florence Kiplagat, 2:21:32 Chicago. Two of these women ran at the Olympics: Tsegaye 4th (also 2nd Boston) and Kiprop dnf. Second and third at the Olympics were Eunice Jepkirui (also 1st Nagoya) and Mare Dibaba (6th London) and further top places in London were 2 Tigist Tufa (dnf OG), 3 F Kiplagat, 4 Olga Mazuronak (5th OG). Edna Kiplagat was 2nd in Chicago after 3rd in Tokyo, where 2nd was Amane Gobena (2nd Saitama), 4th Kebede and 5th Birhane Dibaba (2nd Berlin). Meselech Melkamu followed 3rd in Dubai with wins at Hamburg and Amsterdam.

1. Sumgong, 2. Jepkirui, 3. F Kiplagat, 4. Tsegaye, 5. E Kiplagat, 6. M Dibaba, 7. Kebede, 8. Melkamu, 9. Mazuronak, 10. B Dibaba

3000 Metres Steeplechase

THE ABILITY of Ruth Jebet has been evident since she won the World Junior title in 2014, but she stepped up from her 9:20.55 best that year to a new dimension in 2016. Jebet (she told us that she preferred that spelling rather than Chebet as used previously) ran a pb 9:15.98 for 2nd to Shanghai. She was well behind Hyvin Jepkemoi on that occasion but then came six successive victories. In Eugene, with 8:59.97, she became the second woman to better 9 minutes and she ran 8:59.75 to win the Olympic final. There was some surprise that she had not pushed harder to beat Gulnara Galkina's eight year-old world record of 8:58.81, but she reserved that for the next DL race when she ran a marvellous 8:52.78 in Saint-Denis, following pacemaker Caroline Chepkurui, 1000m 2:56.36, and clear from 2000m in 5:54.16 (compared to Galkina's 6:01.20). Jepkemoi had five wins and four second places (all to Jebet) as both Olympics and DL final in Zürich had the same first four: Jebet, Jepkemoi, Emma Coburn and Beatrice Chepkoech with Sofia Assefa 5th and 6th, Etenesh Diro was only 15th in Rio but was 5th in Zürich. Gesa-Felicitas Krause was European champion and 6th at the Olympics where the Australians Madeline Hills and Genevieve LaCaze came 7th and 9th, with the former having a 4-2 win-loss advantage although slower times. The 2015 number one Habiba Ghribi had only three competitions, winning the London DL before 12th in Rio, and the number three Virginia Nyambura was 7th in Saint-Denis and Zürich, went 1-1 v Diro and LaCaze and 2-0 v Hills (12th Saint-Denis) and Colleen Quigley (8th OG).

Most times under 9:30: Jebet, Jepkemoi, Assefa 7; Coburn, Chepkoech 6; Krause, Diro, Quigley 4; LaCaze, Hills, Frerichs 3.

1. Jebet, 2. Jepkemoi, 3. Coburn, 4. Chepkoech, 5. Assefa, 6. Krause, 7. Hills, 8. LaCaze, 9. Diro, 10. Nyambura

100 Metres Hurdles

THERE WAS, as expected, a great standard in the US Trials as Brianna Rollins won in 12.34 from Kristi Castlin, Nia Ali, Queen Harrison, Sharika Nelvis and Kendra Harrison, who ran 12.62. But while Rollins had a fine year, almost back to her great 2013 season, with 5 of the year's 14 times at 12.54 or better and went on to win the Olympic title from Ali and Castlin in a US clean sweep, there was not the slightest doubt that Keni Harrison was the year's number one. She moved to number two on the world all-time list with 12.24 in the Pre Classic in Eugene and came back from her Trials disappointment with a brilliant 12.20 in the London DL, taking 0.01 off Yordanka Donkova's WR that had stood since 1988. She had 10 wins in 11 finals and had 8 of the top 9 times (12.46 or better). Castlin ranks third, beating Ali 4-2 and then the next US hurdlers are in close contention with the Olympic 4th Cindy Ofili and 5th Cindy Roleder. Queen Harrison beat Nelvis and Jasmin Stowers 4-1 but did not meet those two Europeans. Ofili beat Roleder 3-0 and was 2-2 v Stowers and Dawn Harper Nelson (3sf US Trials, but, like Stowers, with excellent DL results). Nelvis beat Stowers 3-2 and was 1-1 v Harper Nelson, and Stowers beat Roleder 5-2 and Alina Talay 2-1. Roleder beat Talay (crashed in OG semi) and Tiffany Porter (OG 7th) for the European title. Pedrya Seymour made a great breakthrough from 13.50 in her first 100mh race in April with five Bahamas records to 12.64 for Olympic 6th.

At 60m indoors, Ali won the World title from Rollins and Porter with K Harrison 8th after Rollins had run the year's fastest time of 7.76 to win the US title from K Harrison and Q Harrison. Of the ten times at 7.84 or faster Rollins and K Harrison each had four with Ali and Q Harrison one each.

Most times at 12.70 or faster: K Harrison 13, Rollins 11+1w, Castlin 9, Ali 7, Roleder, Ofili, Stowers, Talay 3; Nelvis 2+1w, Q Harrison 1+3w.

1. K Harrison, 2. Rollins, 3. Castlin, 4. Ali, 5. Ofili, 6. Harper Nelson, 7. Stowers. 8. Q Harrison, 9. Roleder, 10. Nelvis.

400 Metres Hurdles

AFTER A difficult couple of years following her World silver in 2013, Dalilah Muhammad had a splendid season. Three early season losses were followed by five successive wins, including the fastest times of the year, 52.88 for the US title and 53.13 at the Olympics. Shamier Little was the 2016 second fastest with 53.51 to win the NCAA title, but after her undefeated collegiate season was only 5th in her US Trials semi and had 6th, 6th and 5th in DL races before recovering her form to win in Zürich in 53.97. She was beaten 3-1 by Sara Slott Peterson, who had another consistently excellent year, topped by the European title and Olympic 2nd. The Olympic 3rd Ashley Spencer and 4th Zuzana Hejnová had very little on the DL circuit, Spencer (2nd US Trials) an 8th and a 6th, and Hejnová 4th in the DL final in Brussels, but their Olympic times put them 4th and 5th on the year list. Muhammad had two DL wins as did Elidh Doyle and Cassandra Tate, whose fastest times out them 8th and 12= on the year list. Doyle was 8th at the Olympics, but was 4-2 v Tate, 3-1 v Little and 2-1 v Spencer (and 0-2 v Hejnová), and Tate had win-loss advantage over Little, Spencer and Slott Petersen, so ranking is hard. Janeive Russell was Olympic 7th, won in Rome and was 2-0 v Doyle and Tate in limited competition. Ristananna Tracey was 5th in Rio, won the Jamaican title from Leah Nugent (6th OG) and Kaliese Spencer, and was 1-1 v Russell. Wenda Nel won the African title and was 2-1 v Little but 6th in her Olympic semi. Sydney McLaughlin (17 in August) set world youth records at 54.46 and 54.15 (3rd US Trials) but could not hold this form at the Olympics (5th semi).

Most times under 54.0/55.0: Muhammad 5/9, Little 2/3, Petersen 1/7, A Spencer, Russell 1/5; Hejnová, Georganne Moline 1/2; Doyle 10, Nel 6, Tate 5, Tracey 4, McLaughlin 3.

1. Muhammad, 2. Petersen, 3. A Spencer, 4. Hejnová, 5. Russell, 6. Doyle, 7. Tate, 8. Little, 9. Tracey, 10. Nel

High Jump

STANDARDS WERE down and for some there was quite a marked difference between indoor and outdoor form. The 'magic' 2m barrier was met by three women: Chaunté Lowe, US title with 2.01, Marie-Laurence Jungfleisch, 2.00 at Eberstadt, and Mariya Kuchina at the Russian Cup. Lowe's next best was 1.97 for 4th at the Olympics after being undefeated in six outdoor events, headed by 1.96 to win the Ibero-American title. Jungfleisch cleared 1.95 to win the German Indoor title and 1.94 was her next best outdoors – in Olympic qualifying before 1.93 for 7= in the final. Kuchina did 1.98 indoors but her only other result more than 1.91 was 1.96 for 2nd at the Russian Champs won at 1.98 by Anna Chicherova, whose only other competition was 1.94 to win the Russian Cup; both would surely have ranked if they had international opportunities. The top four jumped 1.97 in Rio, with Ruth Beitia taking the Olympic title from Mirela Demireva, Blanka Vlasic and Lowe on count-back. That was Vlasic's only outdoor competition after one indoors (1.95) and right Achilles problems, so there was remarkably little action from many of the leading women. Beitia, however, was clear for top ranking as the remarkable 37 year-old had two wins and four second places indoors, including 2nd at the World Indoors, where four women cleared 1.96: in order Vashti Cunningham, Beitia, Kamila Licwinko and Airine Palsyte. Then Beitia won 10 of 11 outdoor competitions, her one loss being 6th at Eugene and her best was 1.98 three times. 18 year-old Cunningham had only six outdoor events, but was USA 2nd with 1.97 before 13= OG. Demireva had a consistent season and was 2= at the Europeans with Palsyte behind Beitia and was 2-2 v Licwinko (2nd Eberstadt, 9th OG). Beitia won the DL final in Zürich from 2= Sofie Skoog (9= EC. 7= OG) and Inika McPherson (10= OG), 4 Licwinko, 5= Palsyte (13= OG) & Demireva. The best height cleared at the Olympics was 1.98 by Nafissatou Thiam and Katarina Johnson-Thompson in the heptathlon. They had limited competition, but Thiam (next best 1.94) won in Brussels 1.94 and was 4th at the Europeans, and KJT was 3rd in a top competition in London at 1.95. Levern

Spencer, 2nd in Brussels, (5= WI, 6 OG) was the busiest jumper with 23 competitions and was 3-2 (1 tie) v Alessia Trost (6= EC, 5 OG) and 4-3 v Svetlana Radvizil (13= OG). All very tricky!

Most competitions over 2.00/1.96m outdoors (+indoors): Lowe 1/3, Kuchina 1/2 +1i, Beitia 5+2i, Demireva 3, Licwinko 2+2i, Palsyte 1+2i.
1. Beitia, 2. Lowe, 3. Demireva, 4. Vlasic (8), 5. Licwinko (4), 6. Thiam (-), 7. Johnson-Thompson (-), 8. Spencer (6), 9. Trost (7), 10. Jungfleisch (9). - Cunningham (5), Palsyte (10). (Including indoors)

Pole Vault

MOST OF the world's best competed intensively in the indoor season, and Jenn Suhr was the star as she improved her world indoor record to 5.03 and had further competitions at 4.91, 4.90 for 2nd at the US Champs to Sandi Morris 4.95, and 4.90 to win the World Indoor title with Morris 2nd at 4.85. Although she won the US title at 4.80, 5cm ahead of Morris, Suhr struggled outdoors with injuries and then illness that held her back to 4.60 for 7= at the Olympics; she was back at the end of the year with 4.88 and 5.01 in minor meetings. Morris, however, who had made rapid progress from 4.55 in 2014 and 4.76 in 2015, went on to end the year with North American outdoor records at 4.93 in Houston and 4.94 and 5.00 in the DL final in Brussels. Ekateríni Stefanídi (3rd WI, best of 4.90 indoors, 4.86 out) beat her on count-back at 4.85 at the Olympics, but Morris was 5-1 up outdoors and 2-0 indoors. Yelena Isinbayeva, in her first competition since winning the World title in August 2003, was superb in clearing 4.90 to take the Russian title from Anzhelika Sidorova 4.85, but that was her only (and probably last) competition. Demi Payne was over 4.80 three times indoors including when 2nd to Suhr at the Millrose Games, where both went over 4.90, and 3rd 4.85 at the US Champs, but competed only three times outdoors (4.45, 4.43 and 4.25 US Trials) due to a wrist injury. Also over 4.80 were Nikoléta Kiriakopoúlou (4.81) and Nicole Büchler (4.80, 4th WI) indoors and five more women outdoors: Sidorova, Alana Boyd and Eliza McCartney (5th WI) each twice, plus Fabiana Murer (4.87) and Yarisley Silva (4.84). McCartney and Boyd did so for 3rd and 4th at the Olympics, where Büchler was 6th, Silva 7= and Murer no height in qualifying. Boyd did not otherwise compete outside Oceania and was 3-3 v the 19-year old McCartney, while Silva had a good win-loss record: 2-1 v McCartney, 2-2 v Büchler and 3-1 v Holly Bradshaw (5th OG and winner in Zürich). There is little between this group. Lisa Ryzih was 2nd to Stefanídi with Angelica Bengtsson 3rd at the European Championships.

Most competitions over 4.60m (outdoors + in): Stefanídi 13+9i, Silva 9, Morris 7+9i, Suhr 7+7i, Büchler 6+3i, Hutson 6+1i Boyd 5, Sidorova 4+4i, Bradshaw 4+1i, Ryzih, Strutz 4; McCartney 3+1i, Murer, Bengtsson, L Weeks 2+2i; Ptácníková, Clark 2+1i; Kiriakopoúlou 1+3i, Payne 0+4i.
1. Morris, 2. Stefanídi, 3. McCartney (6), 4. Büchler (5), 5. Boyd (8), 6. Silva (9), 7. Sidorova (7), 8. Bradshaw (10), 9. Suhr (3), 10. Murer (-). - Payne (4). (Including indoors)

Long Jump

BRITTNEY REESE jumped 7.31 at the US Champs, the best in the world for 12 years, but despite jumping 7.15 at the Olympics (7.26 from take-off) that was 2cm short of the winning mark by Tianna Bartoletta with Ivana Spanovic setting a Serbian record 7.08 for 3rd. Reese also won the World Indoor title, returning from injury with 7.22 from Spanovic 7.07 and returns to the top ranking she had each year 2009-13 as she beat Bartoletta 4-2 and Spanovic 3-1 outdoors. Reese won 6/9 outdoors and all her four competitions indoors. Spanovic improved her national record to 7.10 in her final event of a splendid season in Belgrade and beat Bartoletta 7-1 in her 8 wins in 11 events outdoors and 3/5 indoors. Joining the top three by exceeding 7m were Sosthene Moguenara, 7.15 in Weinheim but with a next best of 6.74 and 10th OG, and Brooke Stratton, an Oceania record 7.05 in Perth with a 6.94 before that, but afterwards her best was 6.74 for 7th OG. German champion Malaika Mihambo was 3rd Europeans and 4th OG, where African champion Ese Brume was 5th and Ksenija Balta 6th. Brume had limited competition with no DL ventures and Balta was 7th WI. Lorraine Ugen was the top British jumper if one includes indoor form (3rd World Indoors 6.93), but outdoors Jazmin Sawyers had the advantage with 2nd Europeans and 8th OG to dnq 18 and 11th for Ugen. Balta was 4th EC and also in the DL final in Zürich, well behind Reese and Spanovic and beaten on second best by Darya Klishina (9th OG), the one Russian permitted to compete internationally, with Ugen 5th, Bartoletta 6th, Sawyers 8th and Moguenara 10th. Janay DeLoach had a mixed year, 4th at the World Indoors, 6.93 for 3rd at the US Champs but dnq 13th at the Olympics and poor DL results. Alexandra Wester promised much with 6.95 indoors and 6th WI, and then 7.00w for 2nd at Weinheim, but her form fell away for 7th EC and dnq 34 OG.

Most competitions over 6.70m (outdoors+in): Spanovic 13+4i, Reese 11, Bartoletta 5+1w, Stratton 4, Wester 3+3i, Burks 3+2w+3i, Ugen 3+1w+3i, Mihambo 3+1w, Balta 3+2i, Moguenara 3, Klishina 2+1w, Proctor, A Jones 2+2i; De Loach 1+2i.
1. Reese, 2. Spanovic, 3. Bartoletta, 4. Mihambo, 5. Stratton, 6. Balta, 7. Sawyers (8), 8. Ugen (7), 9. Brume, 10. Klishina. (Including indoors)

Triple Jump

CATERINE IBARGÜEN completed four years at number one, with nine wins in ten competitions, but she had a new challenger in Yulimar Rojas and Olga Rypakova beat her in the Birmingham DL so that Ibargüen's win streak ended at 34 from 2012. These three women were 1-2-3 at the Olympic Games. Of the 8 performances at over 14.75, Ibargüen had 5, topped by 15.17 in Rio and 15.04 in Doha, and Rojas 3. Rojas emerged with five Venezuelan indoor records from 13.93 to a new South American mark at 14.69 and won the World Indoors from Kristin Gierisch, Paraskeví Papahrístou and Keturah Orji. Outdoors Rojas improved her 2015 best of 14.20 to 15.02 in Madrid via national records 14.61 and 14.79 before 14.92w when 2nd in Doha; she jumped 14.98 in Rio. Rypakova was a clear third, ending with 2nd to Ibargüen in the DL final in Brussels, when followed by Patricia Mamona, Papahrístou and Kimberley Williams, who had been respectively 6th, 8th and 7th at the Olympics. There the 20-year old Orji followed her US and NCAA (indoors and out) titles with 4th place and Hanna Minenko was 5th. Mamona was the European champion from Minenko, Papahrístou, Anna Jagaciak Michalska (10th OG) and Susana Costa (9th OG). Minenko was 2-0 v Papahrístou and 3-1 v Williams, who was 4-2 v Papahrístou. Shaneika Thomas was 2nd to Williams at the Jamaican Champs and dnq 14th at the Olympics. Yekaterina Koneva was the top Russian with 14.42, although beaten to the national title by Viktoriya Prokopenko, and Liadagmis Povea had good marks in Cuba, but was dnq 25th in Rio. With 8th European and 11th OG, Gierisch did not quite match her indoor form.

Most competitions over 14.30m: Ibargüen 11, Rypakova 8+1i, Rojas 4+4i, Mamona, Orji 3+1w; Papahrístou 3, Povea 2+2w, S Costa, Elbe 2+1w.

1. Ibargüen, 2. Rojas, 3. Rypakova, 4. Orji, 5. Mamona, 6. Minenko, 7. Williams, 8. Papahrístou, 9. Thomas (10), 10. Jagaciak Michalska (-). - Koneva (9) (Including indoors)

Shot

THE THREE women who exceeded 20m in 2015 were rejoined by Valerie Adams, who did this in three competitions to 2 by Christina Schwanitz, 1 indoors and 1 out by Michelle Carter and 1 by Gong Lijiao. Carter, who lost weight after controlling a thyroid problem, won the World Indoor title with a North American indoor record of 20.21, Anita Márton 2nd and Adams 3rd, and also set a North American outdoor record when she took the Olympic title at 20.63 on her last throw. That overtook Adams, whose 20.42 was her best since surgery, and Márton once again set a pb at a major event, a Hungarian record 19.87 for the bronze medal with Gong 4th and Schwanitz a disappointing 6th. Carter also won the DL final in Brussels from Adams, Márton, and Brittany Smith. Carter and Adams, substantially ahead of the rest, went 3-3 outdoors, while Gong, who did not contest any DL meets, lost only at the Olympics, and Schwanitz beat Márton 5-2, including when they were 1-2 at the European Champs. Americans feature strongly after the top five. Raven Saunders (20 in May) was undefeated in the collegiate season outdoors, taking the NCAA title, was 2nd to Carter at the US Champs and 5th at the Olympics. Felisha Johnson was 3rd, Tia Brooks 4th, Jill Camarena-Williams 5th and Smith 6th at the US Champs, but Johnson was dnq 14th at the Olympics and was beaten 4-1 by Brooks and 2-1 by Smith (& 1-0 indoors). Of this group, Brooks had the best marks and was 3-2 v Márton and 3-1 v Cleopatra Borel (OG 7th, WI 4th). Johnson owes her 8th ranking to having better marks than Borel and Alyona Dubitskaya (OG 8th).

Most competitions over 20m/19m: Adams 3/14+1i, Schwanitz 2/14, Carter 1+1i/8+2i, Gong 1/6+1i, Márton 4+1i.

1. Carter, 2. Adams, 3. Schwanitz, 4. Márton, 5. Gong, 6. Saunders, 7. Brooks, 8. Smith. 9. Johnson (10), 10. Borel (9). (Including indoors).

Discus

SANDRA PERKOVIC ranks as number one and was the Diamond League discus winner for the fifth successive year. She won all her 11 competitions (at 67.10 or better) for 11 of the best 20 performances of the year, including the European and Olympic titles and all seven DL meetings, so was even more dominant than usual. She had the best five marks headed by 70.88 and 70.59 Yaimí Pérez was second on the world list, and had the next best set of top marks but was 4th, 5th and 5th in her three DL competitions and had three no throws in the Olympic final. She was also beaten on win-loss by all the top women including 4-2 by her Cuban compatriot Denia Cabellero, who had a consistent year including six 3rd places – five at DL meetings and at the Olympics. There Mélina Robert-Michon again excelled on the big occasion, improving her 3 year-old French record with 66.73 for the Olympic silver, and she beat Cabellero 4-0, Pérez 2-0 and Dani Samuels (4th OG) 1-0. Chinese athletes trained and competed in Germany as well as China and fared well at the Olympics: Su Xinyue 5th, Chen Yang 7th and Feng Bin 8th, and as usual there was a strong German group: Nadine Müller won the German title from Julia Fischer and Shanice Craft and this trio were 2nd/9th, 4th/6th and 3rd/11th at Europeans/Olympics, all ahead of Robert-Michon 5th at the Europeans. Overall Fischer beat Müller 5-4. Just missing rankings were Yekaterina Strokova, winner of 6/8 top Russian events, and Jade Lally, who started the year well in Australia and the USA, including a pb of 65.10, but who was 7th Europeans and dnq 28th Olympics.

Most competitions over 63m: Perkovic 13, Samuels 11, Pérez, Caballero 10; Müller 9, Fischer 8, Robert-Michon 7, Craft, Su 6; Lally, Strokova 4; Chen, Feng 3.
1. Perkovic, 2. Robert-Michon, 3. Caballero, 4. Samuels, 5. Su Xinyue, 6. Fischer, 7. Müller, 8. Pérez, 9. Chen Yang, 10. Feng Bin

Hammer

ANITA WLODARCZYK ranks top for the fifth time and fourth in succession and was far superior to the rest of the world. She set world records with 82.29 at the Olympic Games and 82.98 in Warsaw, a throw that was 6.23m better than anybody else, Zhang Wenxiu when she won Olympic silver. Wlodarczyk won all her 12 competitions and had the 12 best performances of the year. Zhang won 3 of her 7 competitions, but lost three times to her compatriot Wang Zheng, who had three no throws in the Olympic final. German champion Betty Heidler was 4th at the Olympics and ranks in the top three for the 10th time in 13 years in the rankings. Sophie Hitchon excelled in Rio with 74.54, her 13th British record, to take the bronze medal, but Heidler had a far superior set of marks. Zalina Marghieva beat Amber Campbell 2-1 and they were 5th and 6th in Rio with a similar set of performances. DeAnna Price was undefeated in the collegiate season up to winning the NCAA title, was 3rd in the US Champs behind Campbell and Gwen Berry, and then 8th at the Olympics, a place behind Hanna Malyshik. Berry failed a test for a stimulant and lost what would have been a North American record of 76.31. although she returned for dnq 14th at the Olympics. Hanna Skydan was 3rd at the Europeans behind Wlodarczyk and Heidler, ahead of Hitchon, Marghieva and Malwina Kopron (Malyshik dnq 26), but just missed a place in the Olympic final. Joanna Fiodorow completes the rankings; she was 10th at the Europeans and 9th at the Olympics and beat Kopron (dnq 15 OG) 6-4.

Most competitions over 72.50m: Wlodarczyk 15, Heidler 7, Zhang 4, Wang. Campbell, Marghieva, Skydan 3.
1. Wlodarczyk, 2. Zhang, 3. Heidler, 4. Hitchon, 5. Wang, 6. Marghieva, 7. Campbell, 8. Price, 9. Skydan, 10. Fiodorow

Javelin

THIS WAS an extremely difficult event to rank, not least because the top mark of the year 67.30 was by Vera Rebrik, the Russian who used to compete for Ukraine. She had two further marks in the top ten performances, 66.77 and 66.03 and was undefeated, winning all the top Russian competitions. But how to rate her given that she could not compete against the rest of the world because of the ban on Russia? Sara Kolak made a huge improvement from Croatian records of 57.79 in 2013 and 2014 to 60.24, 62.75, 63.50 for 3rd at the Europeans, and 64.30 in qualifying and 66.16 to win the Olympic title. She was 2-2 with Barbora Spotáková (who had broken a bone in her right foot early in the year) and Tatyana Kholodovich, who were 5th/3rd and 1st/5th at Europeans/Olympics, but while Kolak was 6th at Monaco in her only DL opportunity, Spotáková had two 2nds and a 3rd and Kholodovich a win (Monaco) and a 3rd in DL events, with the former 4-3 ahead on win-loss. Madara Palameika also comes into the picture as she won the DL final in Brussels from Spotáková, Kara Winger, Martina Ratej and Kholodovich and also won in Birmingham and Lausanne, but she was 7th Europeans and 10th OG. Kathryn Mitchell, 6th OG and 7th Brussels, was the most prolific 62m plus thrower and was 3-1 on win-loss over Sunette Viljoen and Christina Obergföll (8th OG). Viljoen, however, was the African champion and 2nd at the Olympics and won in Doha and Rome but was 5th in Monaco and Lausanne. Maria Andrejczyk improved exactly 5m in the year to 67.11 for 2nd on the world list and after dnq 13th at the Europeans was 4th at the Olympics, where Lu Huihui was 7th. As usual there was close rivalry between the top Germans and at their championships the order was Christin Hussing (dnq 17 Eur, 12 OG), Katharina Molitor (4th Eur), Linda Stahl (2nd Eur, 11th OG) and Obergföll.

Most competitions over 62m: Mitchell 12, Spotáková 10, Kholodovich 8, Palameika 7, Rebrik, Obergföll 6; Kolak, Andrejczyk, Lu 5; Liu Shiying, Molitor 4; Stahl, Ruíz 3.
1. Rebrik, 2. Kolak, 3. Spotáková, 4. Kholodovich, 5. Palameika, 6. Mitchell, 7. Viljoen, 8. Andrejczyk, 9. Obergföll, 10. Lu Huihui

Heptathlon

JESSICA ENNIS-HILL sealed a marvellous career with 6775 for Olympic silver after 6733 at Ratingen. The latter included her one pb of the year, 6.63 in the long jump, and both included very solid performances throughout, but she was beaten to the Olympic title by a brilliant showing from 21 year-old Nafissatou Thiam, who in true Ennis style set pbs in five of the seven events for a 6810 total. Brianne Theisen-Eaton had the third and fifth highest scores with 6765 at Götzis and 6653 for Olympic bronze. The next best scores were 6626 by Anouk Vetter to win the European title, 6622 and 6617 by Laura Ikauniece-Admidina for 2nd at Götzis and 4th Olympics, with Carolin Schäfer 3rd 6557 and 5th 6540 in those major events. The top 25 scores of the year included those for the first 11 in Rio. Thiam had been 4th in Götzis with 6491, while other Götzis/Olympic placings were: Katarina

Johnson-Thomson 6th at each, Yorgelis Rodríguez 9th/7th, Vetter 8th/10th, Barbara Nwaba 5th/12th, Claudia Rath 7th/14th, Jennifer Oeser 12th/9th, Antoinette Nana Djimou 13th/11th. Many of the top women did not contest three or more heptathlons to qualify for the IAAF Challenge, and that was won by Schäfer, also 2nd at Ratingen, from Vetter, Nwaba (US champion), Rodríguez and Nana Djimou (2nd Europeans). Györgyi Zsivoczky-Farkas was 8th in Rio plus 5th at the Europeans and 4th in Talence, won by Nadine Broersen (13th OG) with Rath 3rd.

The best indoor pentathlon scores were for the first three at the World Indoors: Brianne Theisen-Eaton 4881, Anastasiya Mokhnyuk 4847 and Alina Fyodorova 4770.

1. Thiam, 2. Ennis-Hill, 3. Theisen-Eaton, 4. Ikauniece-Admidina, 5. Schäfer, 6. Johnson-Thompson, 7. Vetter, 8. Rodríguez, 9. Nwaba, 10. Zsivoczky-Farkas

20 Kilometres Walk

THE FASTEST times of the year were set by Russian walkers – Yelena Lashmanova 1:24:58 to win the Russian title and Olga Kaniskina 1:25:54 at their winter championship. Both were retuning from drugs bans, but such has been the appalling record by this group for many years that I am not including them in my rankings. There were fast times aplenty in these races, each with five women under 1:28, but it is in any case very difficult to compare the walkers without international competition. Yekaterina Medvedyeva was 2nd in both, Marina Pandakova 3rd and 5th, Klavdiya Afanasyeva 5th and 4th, with Mariya Pomomaryova 3rd at the Champs and Svetlana Vasilyeva 4th in the Winter Champs.

Liu Hong finished first in all her races starting with the Chinese Trial in 1:25:56, but then had a 1 month ban for inadvertently using an anti-asthmatic lotion and lost her 1st places at the World Cup and La Coruña. She was back, however, for the Olympics and won there from María Guadeloupe González, who had earlier won in Juárez and at the World Cup (after Liu dq). Further top OG places (with World Cup in brackets) were: 3 Lu Xiuzhi (5th), 4 Antonella Palmisano (only other race 1st at Alytus), 5 Qieyang Shenjie (2), 6 Ana Cabecinha (6), 7 Érica de Sena (3), 8 Beatriz Pascual (dnf), 9 Regan Lamble (12), 10 Anezka Drahotová (10), 11 Elisa Rigaudo (4), 12 Inês Henriques (8). Eleanor Giorgi was disqualified in both the big races but won in Dudince (2 de Sena, 3 Cabecinha), was 2nd at Rio Maior (1 Qieyang, 3 Rigaudo, 4 de Sena, 5 Henriques), and 3rd at La Coruna (2 Qieyang, 4 Henriques). Yang Jiayu was 3rd at the Chinese Trial behind Liu and Lu and ahead of Qieyang, before 7th at the World Cup.

1. Liu Hong, 2. González, 3. Lu Xiuzhi, 4. Qieyang Shenjie, 5. de Sena, 6. Rigaudo, 7. Palmisano, 8. Cabecinha, 9. Giorgi, 10. Lamble

Athletes ranked in 2016 top 10s who have had most years ranked in my World top 10s at one event

Men

15	3kmSt	Ezekiel Kemboi
15	3kmSt	Paul Kipsiele Koech
14	DT	Gerd Kanter
13	HT	Krisztián Pars
12	200m	Usain Bolt
11	SP	Tomasz Majewski
11	DT	Piotr Malachowski
10	400m	LaShawn Merritt
10	800m	David Rudisha
10	1500m	Asbel Kiprop
10	400mh	Kerron Clement
10	DT	Zoltán Kövágó

Women

14	SP	Valerie Adams
14	HJ	Blanka Vlasic
13	200m	Allyson Felix
13	HT	Berry Heidler
13	HT	Zhang Wenxiu
12	HJ	Ruth Beitia
11	PV	Fabiana Murer
10	PV	Jenn Suhr
10	SP	Gong Lijiao

Most years at number one

Men

8	200m	Usain Bolt
7	PV	Renaud Lavillenie
6	100m	Usain Bolt
6	800m	David Rudisha
6	1500m	Asbel Kiprop
6	DT	Robert Harting

Women

8	SP	Valerie Adams
7	JT	Barbora Spotáková
6	10,000m	Tirunesh Dibaba
6	LJ	Brittany Reese

Multiple events number one rankings

Men

14	Usain Bolt 8 200m, 6 100m
9	Mo Farah 5 5000m, 4 10,000m

Women

7	Allyson Felix 5 200m, 2 400m

CHANGES OF NAMES AND NATIONALITIES

Some Recent Marriages

Female	Male	
Abeba Aregawi SWE	Yemane Tsegay ETH	.1.17
Aleksandra Butkina RUS	Sergey Timshin RUS	.6.15
Julia Fischer GER	Robert Harting GER	17.9.16
Sofia Hellberg-Jonsén SWE	Evan Jager USA	8.10.16
Yekaterina Koneva RUS	Sergey Polyanskiy RUS	.10.16
Susan Kuijken NED	Andrew Krumins AUS	.9.16
Shaunae Miller BAH	Maicel Uibo EST	4.2.17
isha Praught JAM	Will Leer USA	15..10.16
Iveta Smková SVK	Jozef Repcík SVK	.9.16
Dani Samuels AUS	Joe Stevens AUS	.10.16
Oksana Spasovkhodskaya RUS	Aleksandr Skorobogatko RUS	.12.16

Further recent women's name changes

Original	Married name
Xenia Achkinadze GER	Stolz
Jessica Andrews GBR	Martin
Anastasiya Bessoltseva RUS	Podolskaya
Jasmine Chaney USA	Hyder
Tara Erdman USA	Welling
Tetyana Fetiskina UKR	Nychyporchuk
Christie Gordon CAN	Moerman
Lauren Hagens USA	Paquette
Nia Henderson USA	Gailliard
Yekaterina Kuntsevich AUT	Krasovskiy
Zalina Marghieva MDA	Petrivskaya
Sinta Ozolina LAT	Sprudzane
Bianca Perie ROU	Ghelber
Chelsea Reilly USA	Sudaro
Regina Sarsekova KAZ	Kaysarova
Mariya Shumilova RUS	Gromysheva
Morgan Snow USA	Goodwin
Tamara Stasyuk UKR	Havrylyuk
Lucy Van Dalen NZL	Oliver
Anna Yermakova UKR	Lunyova
Jessica Young USA	Young-Warren
Hanna Zinchuk BLR	Malyshik

Retired in 2016–17

Men: Ladji Doucouré FRA, Ashton Eaton USA, Kamghe Gaba GER, Juan Carlos Higuero ESP, Johannes Hock GER, Reese Hoffa USA, Paul Kipsiele Koech KEN, Tomasz Majewski POL, Stanislav Melnikov UKR, Koji Murofushi JPN, Carl Myerscough GBR, Mikel Odriozola ESP, Björn Otto GER, Mario Pestano ESP, André Pollmacher GER, Antonio Reina ESP, Félix Sánchez DOM, Aleksandr Shustov RUS, Chris Solinsky USA, Raul Spank GER, Jesse Stroobants BEL, Andreas Thorkildsen NOR, Chris Tomlinson GBR, Hans Van Alphen BEL.

Women: Natalya Antyukh RUS, Alana Boyd AUS, Stephanie Brown Trafton USA, Jill Camarena-Williams USA, Esther Cramer GER, Virginia Crawford USA, Carolin Dietrich (née Nuyra) GER, Céline Distel-Bonnet FRA, Jessica Ennis-Hill GBR, Lauren Fleshman USA, Kristina Gadschiew GER, Mabel Gay CUB, Yelena Isinbayeva RUS, Wioletta Frankiewicz POL, Julia Labonté CAN, Marissa Lavanchi SUI, Priscilla Lopes-Schliep CAN, Jennifer Meadows GBR, Fabiana Murer BRA, Natalya Nazarova RUS, Mizuki Noguchi JPN, Christina Obergföll GER, Lucy Oliver (née Van Dalen) NZL, Marie Polli SUI, Sanya Richards-Ross USA, Elisa Rigaudo ITA, Jessica Samuelsson SWE, Goldie Sayers GBR, Liliya Shobukhova RUS, Melanie Skotnik FRA, Kim Smith NZL, Brianne Theisen-Eaton CAN, Morgan Uceny USA, Lisa Urech SUI, Yuliya Zaripova RUS, Michelle Zeltner SUI, Linda Züblin SUI

Transfer of Nationality/Allegiance

Name	From	To	Noted	Eligible
Men				
Jahvid Best	USA	LCA	15.6.16	
Kemarly Brown	JAM	BRN	19.8.15	10.8.16
Peter Callahan	USA	BEL	20.5.16	
Maurys Surel Castillo	CUB	ESP	9.12.15	3.3.16
Mohamed Reda Chahboun		MAR	ITA	2.3.16
Samuel Chelanga	KEN	USA	14.8.15	2.3.16
Abraham Cheroben	KEN	BRN	19.8.15	1.8.16
Oleksabdr Dryhol	UKR	ISR	25.6.14	23.6.16
Peter Emelieze	NGR	GER	26.1.16	23.4.16
Andrew Fisher	JAM	BRN	19.8.15	9.8.16
Gianni Frankis	GBR	ITA	2.3.16	
Antwon Hicks	USA	NGR	24.4.14	17.7.16
Antonio Infantino	GBR	ITA	.3.16	11.6.16
Evans Kiplagat	KEN	AZE	26.4.16	9.6.16
Leonard Korir	KEN	USA	3.5.16	23.5.16
Ahmed Bader Magour	EGY	QAT	14.4.16	23.4.16
Emmanuel Matadi	USA	LBR	11.6.16	
Raihau Maiau	PYF	FRA	4.3.16	
Alsadik Mikhou	MAR	BRN	17.9.15	17.9.16
Chidi Okezie	USA	NGR	15.3.16	
Orlando Ortega	CUB	ESP	8.9.15	5.11.16
Sean Safo-Antwi	GBR	GHA	8.3.16	
Aubrey Smith	CAN	JAM	11.7.15	11.7.16
David Smith	USA	PUR	29.6.16	
Dame Tasama	ETH	BEL	.1.17	
David Torrence	USA	PER	19.5.16	25.7.16
Juan Carlos Trujillo	USA	GUA	2.7.16	
Aaron Unterberger	USA	CAN	30.6.16	
Women				
Lorène Bazolo	CGO	POR	3.5.16	23.5.16
Julia Bleasdale	GBR	GER		8.3.16
Rose Chelimo	KEN	BRN	19.8.15	1.8.16
Elizeba Cherono	KEN	NED	26.1.16	25.6.16
Kali Davis-White	USA	JAM	22.7.16	
Olivia Ekponé	USA	NGR	3.10.15	
Merima Hasen	ETH	BRN	22.9.13	22.9.16
Jessica Inchude	POR	GBS	26.7.16	
Mulem Jean	USA	HAI	21.7.16	
Sally Kipyego	KEN	USA	.1.17	
Yekaterina Kuntsevich	RUS	AUT	11.4.16	27.6.16
Daina Levy	CAN	JAM	23.7.16	
Jennifer Madu	USA	NGR	17.7.16	
Tigist Mekonen	ETH	BRN	9.9.14	9.9.15
Aisha Naibe-Way	GBR	SLE	.3.16	
Leah Nugent	USA	JAM	22.7.16	
Efonime Odiong	NGR	BRN	12.3.15	11.6.16
Alexi Pappas	USA	GRE	3.3.16	
Jasmine (Camacho-)Quinn		USA	PUR	29.6.16
Yusneysi Santiusti	CUB	ITA	31.12.15	2.3.16
Gelete Tola	ETH	GER	16.6.16	27.6.16
Aliphine Tuliamuk-Bolton	KEN	USA	29.4.16	23.5.16
Judit Varga	ITA	HUN	5.1.16	
Carole Zahi	CIV	FRA	10.11.15	2.3.16
Valeria Zavyalova	RUS	AUS	15.5.16	
Belaynesh Zemedkun	ETH	USA	29.10.13	3.3.16

Change of name and nationality

Men

Winston Barnes JAM	Emre Zafer Barnes TUR
Lloyd Gumbs GBR	Lloyd Hanley-Byron SKN
Amos Kibitok KEN	Aras Kaya TUR

Women

Vivian Jemutai KEN	Yasemin Can TUR
Miriam Maiyo KEN	Meryem Akda TUR
Misiker Mekonnin ETH	Misiker Demissie USA

CROSS-COUNTRY – NATIONAL CHAMPIONS 2016

Country	Men (long distance)	Women (long distance)
Argentina	Martin Méndez	Sandra Amarillo
Australia	Stewart McSweyn	Kate Spencer
Austria	Christian Steinhammer	Nada Pauer
Belarus	Sergey Platonov	Nina Savina
Belgium	Jeroen D'Hoedt	Louise Carton
Brazil	Gilberto Lopes	Juliana dos Santos
Bulgaria	Ivan Popov	Silvia Danekova
Canada (Nov)	Ross Proudfoot	Sarah Gollish
Chile	Mauricio Valdivia	Geraldine Beccera
China	Zhu Renxue	Zhang Deshun
Colombia	Javier Peña	Sandra Rosas
Croatia (Nov)	Antun Rudolf Pavelic	Matea Parlov
Cuba	Yuleidys La O	Yudileyvis Castillo
Czech Republic (Nov)	Jirí Homolac	Simona Vrzalová
Ecuador	Miguel Almachi	Diana Landi
England	Jonathan Hay	Lily Partridge
France	Hassan Chahdi	Clémence Calvin
Germany	Richard Ringer	Maya Rehberg
Greece	Dímos Maggínas	Ourania Reboúli
Hungary	Lászlo Gregor	Zita Kácser
India	Man Singh	Swathi Gadhave
Ireland (Nov)	Mark Christie	Shona Heaslip
Israel	Demeke Teshala	Chemtai Korlima
Italy	Yemenebrehan Crippa	Silvia La Bambera
Japan	Takashi Ichida	Yukari Abe
Kazakhstan	Mikhail Krasilov	Zhanna Mamazhanova
Kenya	Geoffrey Kamworor	Alice Aprot
Netherlands	Tom Wiggers	Ruth van der Meijden
New Zealand	Jonathan Jackson	Laura Nagel
Northern Ireland	Aaron Doherty	Shalane McMurray
Norway (Oct)	Senay Amlesom ERI	Maria Sagnes Wågan
Poland	Tomasz Grycko	Angelika Cichocka
Portugal	Nelson Cruz	Salome Rocha
Romania (Oct)	Marius Ionescu	Ancuta Bobocel
Russia	Mikhail Strelkov	Natalya Vlasova
"" (October)	Mikhail Strelkov	Lyudmila Lebedeva
Scotland	Andrew Butchart	Beth Potter
Serbia	Nemenja Cerovac	Biljana Cvijanovic
Slovakia (Nov)	Peter Durec	Lucia Janecková
Slovenia	Rok Puhar	Patricija Plazar
South Africa	David Manja	Kesa Molotsane
Spain	Antonio Abadia	Trihas Gebre
Sweden (Oct)	Abraham Adhanom ERI	Charlotta Fougberg
Switzerland	Marcel Berni	Fabienne Schlumpf
Trinidad & Tobago	Matthew Hagley	Samantha Shukla
Uganda	Phillip Kipyeko	Stella Chesang
Ukraine	Oleksandr Matviychuk	Nataliya Batrak
"" (October)	Dmytro Struk	Yuliya Shmatenko
USA	Craig Lutz	Mattie Suver
Venezuela	Alexis Peña	Mirena Goncalvez
Wales	Dewi Griffiths	Caryl Jones
Arab	Aweke Ayalew BRN	Alia Mohamed Saeed UAE
Asia	Albert Rop BRN	Eunice Chumba BRN
Balkan (Nov)	Ramazan Özdemir TUR	Ancuta Bobocel ROU
European Clubs	Bekir Karayel TUR	Irene Cheptai KEN/TUR
Team	Alès Cévannes Athlétisme FRA	Üsküdar Belediye TUR
NCAA (USA)	Patrick Tiernan AUS	Karissa Schweizer
Nordic	Ørjan Grønnevig NOR	Charlotta Fougberg SWE
Oceania	Nicholas Wightman AUS	Laura Nagel NZL
Pan-American	Donald Cowart USA	Alison Grace Morgan USA
World University	Hicham Amghar MAR	Sevilay Eytemis TUR

Short

Country	Men	Women
Austria	Christian Steinhammer	
China	Dong Guojian	Zhang Deshun

France	Bryan Cantero	Johanna Gayer Carles
Germany	Florian Orth	
Norway	Hans Kristian Fløystad	Eli Anne Dvergsdal
Poland	Mateusz Demczyszak	
Portugal	André Pereira	Daniela Cunha
Russia	Aleksey Gushchin	Lyudmila Ledebeva
Sweden	Abraham Adhanom ERI	Sarah Lahti
Switzerland	Mario Bachtiger	Fabienne Schlumpf
Ukraine	Serhiy Rybak	Nataliya Batrak
"" (October)	Volodomyr Kyts	Nataliya Batrak

Winners Major Cross-Country Races 2016

6 Jan	San Giorgio su Legnano (IAAF)	Imane Merga ETH	Alice Aprot KEN
9 Jan	Edinburgh (EA)	Garrett Heath USA	Kate Avery GBR
10 Jan	Amorebieta	Thomas Ayeko UGA	Mercy Cherono KEN
16 Jan	Antrim (IAAF)	Aweke Ayalew BRN	Alice Aprot KEN
17 Jan	Santiponce, Seville (IAAF)	Tamirat Tola ETH	Faith Kipyegon KEN
24 Jan	Elgóibar (IAAF)	Aweke Ayalew BRN	Irene Cheptai KEN
24 Jan	Villa Lagarina, Rovereto (EA)	Rodgers Maiyo KEN	Alemitu =Hawi ETH
24 Jan	Hannut (EA)	Dame Tasame ETH	Birtukan Fente ETH
31 Jan	San Vittore Olana (IAAF)	Joseph Birech KEN	Faith Kipyegon KEN
13 Feb	Nairobi (IAAF)	Geoffrey Kamworor KEN	Alice Aprot KEN
13 Mar	Albufeira (IAAF)	Nelson Cruz POR	Carla Salomé Rocha POR
24 Sep	Lidingöloppet (EA) 30k	Japhet Kipkorir KEN	Maria Larsson SWE
9 Oct	Middlefart (EA)	David Nilsson SWE	Anna Emilie Møller DEN
13 Nov	Burgos (Atapuerca) (IAAF)	Aweke Ayalew BRN	Senbere Teferi ETH
20 Nov	Darmstadt (EA)	Daniel Komoi KEN	Caterina Granz GER
20 Nov	Soria (EA)	Timothy Toroitich UGA	Alice Aprot KEN
27 Nov	Tilburg (EA)	Sondre Nordstad Moen NOR	Fabienne Schlumpf SUI
27 Nov	Alcobendas (IAAF)	Timothy Toroitich UGA	Fionnuala McCormack IRL
28 Nov	Leffinckroucke (EA)	Shiretagaseleon Barega ETH	Worknesh Degefa ETH
18 Dec	Brussels (IAAF)	Isaac Kimeli BEL	Fionnuala McCormack IRL

IAAF – IAAF permit races, EA – European Athletics permit races

African Cross-Country Championships 2016

At Yaoundé, Cameroon, March 12
Senior Men (10k)
1. James Rungaru KEN 26:34
2. Phillip Kipyeko UGA 26:35
3. Charles Muneria KEN 26:46
4. Cleophas Ngetich KEN 26:52
5. Geoffrey Koech KEN 27:09
6. Getaneh Tamire ETH 27:13
7. Philip Langat KEN 27:13
8. Abdallah Mande UGA 27:15
9. Daniel Rotich UGA 27:38
10. Birhan Nebebew ETH 27:48
Team: 1. KEN 13, 2. UGA 30, 3. ETH 41, 4. RSA 69, 5. SUD 109, 6. CMRE 145, 7. NGR 173
Junior Men (8k)
1. Isaac Kipsang KEN 21:33
2. Ronald Kiprotich KEN 21:44
3. Aron Kifle ERI 21:48
4. Anthony Kiptoo KEN 21:56
5. Andrew Lorot KEN 21:59
6. Nickson Kiplagat KEN 22:11
Team: 1. KEN 12, 2. ETH 38, 3. RSA 80
Senior Women (10k)
1. Alice Aprot Nawawuna KEN 29:52
2. Sheila Chepkirui KEN 30:44
3. Beatrice Mutai KEN 31:08
4. Dera Dira ETH 31:13
5. Daisy Jepkemei KEN 31:29
6. Nancy Nzisa KEN 31:30
7. Pauline Kaveke KEN 31:43
8. Kidsan Alema ETH 31:51
9. Alamirew Tirusew ETH 32:10
10. Stella Chesang UGA 32:42
Team: 1. KEN 26, 2. ETH 32, 3. RSA 73, 4. SUD 90, 5. CMR 112
Junior Women (6k)
1. Miriam Cherop KEN 18:31
2. Gloria Kite KEN 18:39
3. WInfredah Mbithe KEN 18:40
4. Lucy Cheruiyot KEN 18:42
5. Muliye Dekobo ETH 18:52
6. Tersit Desalegn ETH 19:02
Team: 1. KEN 10, 2. ETH 26, 3. MAR 72.

European Cross-Country Championships 2016

At Chia, Italy, December 15
Senior Men (10.15k)
1. Aras Kaya TUR 27:39
2. Polat Kemboi Arikan TUR 27:42
3. Callum Hawkins GBR 27:49
4. Andrew Butchart GBR 28:01
5. Andy Vernon GBR 28:11
6. Ilias Fifa ESP 28:19
7. Ayad Lamdassem ESP 28:22.
8. Adel Mechaal ESP 28:26
9. Marouan Razine ITA 28:27.
10. Kaan Kigen Özbilen TUR 28:30
11. Antonio Abadía ESP 28:33.
12. Abdi Hakin Ulad DEN 28:37
13. Sondre Nordstad Moen NOR 28:46
14. Soufiane Bouchikhi BEL 28:47
15. Marco Najibe Salami ITA 28:48
74 of 78 finished.
Teams: 1. GBR 28, 2. ESP 32, 3. TUR 38, 4. FRA 79, 5. ITA 82, 6. NED 137, 7. UKR 146, 8. NOR 153, 9. DEN 159, 10. IRL 197, 11. AUT 204.
Under-23 Men (8.15k)
1. Isaac Kimeli BEL 22:48
2. Carlos Mayo ESP 22:53
3. Yemaneberhan Crippa ITA 22:54
4. Amanal Petros GER 23:01
5. Jonathan Davies GBR 23:01
6. Napoleon Solomon SWE 23:03
7. Jesus Ramos ESP 23:08
8. Simon Debognies BEL 23:14
69 of 73 finished.
Teams: 1. ITA 35, 2. BEL 53, 3. GBR 58, 4. ESP 64, 5. GER 81, 6. FRA 83, 7. SWE 129, 8. UKR 164, 9. POR 202, 10. ISR 214.
U20 Men (6.15k)
1. Jakob Ingebrigtsen NOR 17:06
2. Yohanes Chiappinelli ITA 17:14
3. Mahamed Mahamed GBR 17:16
4. Jimmy Gressier FRA 17:19
5. Mohamed-Amine El Bouajaji FRA 17:20
85 of 87 finished.
Teams: 1. FRA 26, 2. ESP 42, 3. GBR 43, 4. ITA 91, 5. ISR 92; 14 completed.
Senior Women (8.15k)
1. Yasemin Can TUR 24:46
2. Meryem Akdag TUR 24:56
3. Karoline Bjerkeli Grøvdal NOR 25:26
4. Ancuta Bobocel ROU 25:27
5. Fionnuala McCormack IRL 25:28
6. Stephanie Twell GBR 25:40
7. Trihas Gebre ESP 25:41
8. Fabienne Schlumpf SUI 25:46
9. Liv Westphal FRA 25:47
10. Elizeba Cherono NED 25:57

11. Roxana Bârca ROU 26:01
12. Gemma Steel GBR 26:06
13. Özlem Kaya TUR 26:12
14. Charlotta Fougberg SWE 26:12
15. Eva Vrabcová-Nyvltová CZE 26:13
71 of 73 finished.
Teams: 1. TUR 35, 2. GBR 51, 3. ROU 79, 4. FRA 101, 5. ESP 117, 6. IRL 123, 7. GER 127, 8. CZE 135, 9. POR 151, 10. ITA 162, 11. SUI 164, 12. UKR 207.

Under-23 Women (6.15k)
1. Sofia Ennaoui POL 19:21
2. Anna Gehring GER 19:24
3. Alice Wright GBR 19:42
4. Charlotte Taylor GBR 19:44
5. Katarzyna Rutkowska POL 19:49
6. Caterina Granz GER 19:50
7. Rebecca Murray GBR 19:52
8. Viktoriya Kalyuzhina UKR 19:54
53 of 53 finished.
Teams: 1. GBR 26, 2. GER 33, 3. ITA 67, 4. UKR 69, 5. TUR 104, 6. FRA 111, 7. ESP 130, 8. SVK 180.

U20 Women (4.157k)
1. Konstanze Klosterhalfen GER 12:26
2. Anna Emilie Møller DEN 12:43
3. Harriet Knowles-Jones GBR 12:52
4. Alina Reh GER 12:53
5. Jasmijn Lau NED 12:57
80 of 81 finished.
Teams: 1. GBR 33, 2. GER 57, 3. NED 71, 4. FRA 89, 5. ESP 99, 14 completed.

2016 WORLD ROAD RACE REVIEW
By Marty Post

THERE WAS unprecedented quality by women road racers at half marathons in 2016. Single year records for number of performances at sub-69 minutes and sub-68 minutes were set at 60 and 31 respectively, smashing the former marks of 45 in 2012 and 17 in 2013. (Numbers exclude the 86.5m net downhill course in San Diego where there was a 67:51 in 2016).

Violah Jepchumba had the top performance of the year, 65:51 at Prague on April 2 as she became just the sixth woman to break 66 minutes with the eighth fastest time ever. The 25-year-old Kenyan went out at blistering pace, as she covered the four 5k segments in 15:05, 15:24 (30:29), 15:52 (46:21) and 16:03 (1:02:24) . Her 15k split was not only a 2016 world lead but the second fastest ever, seven seconds off of Florence Kiplagat's world record at Barcelona in 2015. Worknesh Degefa's 46:34, en route to finishing in an Ethiopian record 66:14, was number six all time.

Ra's Al Khaymah was responsible for four of the top seven yearly times while Mary Wacera's 66:29 at Houston on January 27 was a North American all-comer's record. Peres Jepchirchir was arguably the top half-marathoner of the year as she won the IAAF world championships in 67:31 and had three more sub-68 wins at Yangzhou, Valencia and Ústí nad Ladem. Mary Keitany won at Olomouc in 68:53 giving her a 14-1 lifetime half-marathon record (with one second place) and her 13th consecutive win since October 2007. All of her times have been faster than 69 minutes with 8 sub-67s and 12 sub-68s (excluding two splits in longer distance races.)

Prague was the site of another sensational Jepchumba performance on September 10 at the Birell Grand Prix 10k. Her 30:24 there was an African record, just three seconds off the world record and gave her the two fastest times of the year. She had a noteworthy halfway split of 14:46, equal to the best performance in history for 5k. (The IAAF does not recognize that distance for official world records.)

While there were no IAAF road world records for women in 2016, two men became record holders. Not only did this take place in the same race, but it was at a distance far short of the finish line. The pace at the Virgin Money London Marathon on April 24 was so rapid that both Eliud Kipchoge – who would go on to win in 2:03:05 – and Stanley Biwott passed 30k in 1:27:13. Race officials had certified that distance and provided official timing to ensure it would meet requirements for world record ratification. Earlier in the year at Dubai on January 22, Sisay Lemma was timed in 1:27:20, although that mark was not submitted for ratification; two other non-finisher pace-makers were given the same time but not record-eligible. The pre-2016 WR stood at 1:27:37 and all told there 16 faster times among Dubai (8), London (3) and Berlin (5, led by 1:27:26).

Solomon Kirwa Yego had the only sub-59 minute half marathon of the year, 58:44 on the point-to-point Rome to Ostia course. James Mwangi had the second (59:07, Copenhagen) and fourth (59:12, Milano) performances in 2016. In between was a 59:10 by Geoffrey Kamworor when he won the gold medal at the IAAF World Championships. Kenyan men had all 20 of the year's fastest times.

In an unprecedented circumstance, the fastest 10k of the year, 27:15, was a split by Mwangi at Copenhagen, and there were four 27:28s tied for second fastest of the year. Zane Robertson set a New Zealand national record of 27:28 when he won at Berlin on October 9. Mwangi also recorded a 41:32 for 15k at Copenhagen to top the 2016 rankings with the tenth fastest time in history.

Claimed as the largest fully-timed road race in the world was the City to Surf 14k in Sydney, Australia with 67,629 finishers (33,076 men and 34,553 women).

WINNERS OF LEADING 2016 ROAD RACES

Date	Race	Men	Women
3 Jan	Adana HMar	Barselius Kipyego KEN 60:46	Yeshaneh Ababel ETH 69:36
17 Jan	Houston HMar	Lelisa Desisa ETH 60:37	Mary Wacera KEN 66:29*
24 Jan	Alicante HMar	Morris Gachaga KEN 61:02	Polline Wanjiku KEN 70:25
31 Jan	Marrakech HMar	Mustapha El Aziz MAR 60:39	Keltoum Bouaasariya MAR 72:29
7 Feb	Granollers HMar	Alex Oleitiptip KEN 61:01	Nancy Kiprop KEN 71:30
7 Feb	Marugame HMar	Goitom Kifle ERI 60:49	Eunice Kirwa BRN 68:06
12 Feb	Ra's Al Khaymah HMar	Birhanu Legesse ETH 60:40	Cynthia Limo KEN 66:04
14 Feb	Barcelona HMar	Vincent Kipruto KEN 62:54	Florence Kiplagat KEN 69:19
14 Feb	Yamaguchi HMar	Charles Ndirangu KEN 61:00	Miho Shimuzo JPN 69:41
28 Feb	San Juan 10k	Bidan Karoki KEN 27:42	Mary Wacera KEN 31:49
6 Mar	Casablanca 10k (short?)	Hassan El Abbassi MAR 27:26	Pascalia Kipkoech KEN 31:14
6 Mar	Den Haag HMar	Edwin Kipyego KEN 60:27	Minna Lamminen FIN 74:15
6 Mar	Nairobi (A) HMar (400m sh)	Wilfred Kimitei KEN 60:38	Valentine Kipketer KEN 69:05
6 Mar	Paris HMar	Cyprian Kotut KEN 61:00	Dibaba Kuma ETH 69:21
6 Mar	Verbania HMar	Abayneh Tsehay ETH 61:43	Hellen Musyoka KEN 73:04
13 Mar	Bath HMar	Robert Mbithi KEN 61:45*	Lenah Jerotich KEN 72:24
13 Mar	New Orleans 8k	Toloss Gedefa ETH 22:40	Buze Diriba ETH 25:56
13 Mar	Rome-Ostia HMar	Solomon Kirwa Yego KEN 58:44*	Worknesh Degefa ETH 67:08
19 Mar	Laredo 10k	Joshua Cheptegei UGA 27:46	Zulema Fuentes Pila ESP 33:33
20 Mar	Lisboa HMar	Sammy Kitwara KEN 59:47	Ruti Aga ETH 69:16
20 Mar	Milano HMar	James Wangari KEN 59:12*	Rael Kiyara KEN 70:19
20 Mar	Mobile 10k	Dominic Ondoro KEN 28:25	Carol Kipkirui KEN 31:58
20 Mar	New York City HMar	Stephen Sambu KEN 61:16	Molly Huddle USA 67:41*
20 Mar	Venlo HMar	Geoffrey Yegon KEN 59:44*	Perendis Lekapana KEN 70:34
26 Mar	New Orleans 10k	John Muritu KEN 28:02	Buze Diraba ETH 31:57
26 Mar	Paderborn 10k	Geoffrey Yegon KEN 28:22	Karoline Bjerkeli Grøvdal NOR 31:36
26 Mar	Paderborn HMar	Nicholas Korir KEN 61:44	Fate Tola ETH 69:51
2 Apr	Charleston 10k	Dominic Ondoro KEN 29:01	Monicah Wanjuhi Ngige KEN 32:57
2 Apr	Praha HMar	Daniel Wanjiru KEN 59:20	Violah Jepchumba KEN 65:51*
3 Apr	Berlin HMar	Richard Mengich KEN 59:48	Elizeba Cherono NED 70:43
3 Apr	Brunssum 10k	Wilfred Kimitei KEN 28:02	Edith Chelimo KEN 31:07
3 Apr	Carlsbad 5k	Joshua Cheptegei UGA 13:24	Meseret Defar ETH 15:02
3 Apr	Chicago 8k	Stephen Sambu KEN 22:45	Alexi Pappas GRE 26:17
3 Apr	Warszawa HMar	Daniel Muteti KEN 62:14	Perendis Lekapana KEN 70:41
3 Apr	Washington DC 10M	Sam Chelanga USA 48:26	Veronicah Nyaruai KEN 53:12
16 Apr	Azpeitia HMar	Emmanuel Bett KEN 61:47	Zulema Fuentes Pila ESP 76:32
16 Apr	Boston 5k	Dejen Gebrmeskel ETH 13:39	Molly Huddle USA 15:14
17 Apr	Annecy HMar	Stephen Ogari KEN 63:23	Edith Chelimo KEN 70:38
24 Apr	Istanbul HMar	Ali Kaya TUR 60:16	Violah Jepchumba KEN 68:18
24 Apr	Nice HMar	Kennedy Kipyego KEN 61:46	Muliye Dekobo ETH 71:08
24 Apr	Würzburg 10k	Isaac Temoi KEN 29:11	Alice Aprot Nawawuma KEN 32:14
24 Apr	Yangzhou HMar	Mosinet Geremew ETH 60:43	Peres Jepchirchir KEN 67:21
30 Apr	Columbus HMar (US Ch)	Christo Landry USA 62:52	Tara Welling USA 70:25
1 May	Puy-en-Velay 15k	Birhanu Yemataw ETH 43:19	Dibaba Kuma ETH 49:46
1 May	Spokane 12k	Philip Langat KEN 34:26	Cynthia Limo KEN 38:03*
8 May	Piacenza HMar	James Lokomwa KEN 60:56	Viola Jelagat KEN 71:10
14 May	Grand Rapids 25k (US Ch)	Christo Landry USA 1:15:32	Aliphine Tuliamuk USA 1:25:36
14 May	New York City 10k	Lucas Rotich KEN 28:29	Cynthia Limo KEN 31:39
15 May	Bengaluru 10k	Mosinet Geremew ETH 28:36	Peres Jepchirchir KEN 32:15
15 May	Berlin 25k	Bernard Bett KEN 1:15:51	Viola Jelagat KEN 1:26:00
15 May	Cape Town 12k	Stephen Mokoka RSA 33:34	Irvette van Zyl RSA 39:40
15 May	Casablanca HMar	Abraham Kiptum KEN 61:26	Lucy Cheruiyot KEN 71:17
15 May	Gifu HMar	Patrick Mwaka KEN 61:51	Eunice Kirwa BRN 68:55*
15 May	Lisboa 5k	*women only*	Purity Rionoripo KEN 15:16
15 May	San Francisco 12k	Isaac Mukundi KEN 35:23	Caroline Chepkoech KEN 40:36
21 May	Göteborg HMar	Richard Mengich KEN 59:35*	Violah Jepchumba KEN 68:01*
21 May	Karlovy Vary HMar	Abraham Kasongor KEN 62:08	Joyciline Jepkosgei KEN 69:07*

Date	Race	Men	Women
22 May	Lugano HMar	Cosmas Kipchoge KEN 61:02	Muliye Dekebo ETH 69:46
22 May	Manchester 10k	Kenenisa Bekele ETH 28:08	Tirunesh Dibaba ETH 31:16
28 May	Ottawa 10k	Mohammed Ziani MAR 28:37	Peres Jepchirchir KEN 31:29
30 May	Boulder (A) 10k	Isaac Mukundi KEN 29:13	Amane Gobena ETH 33:40
4 Jun	Albany 5k	women only	Brianne Nelson USA 15:46
4 Jun	Ceske Budejovice HMar	Barselius Kipyego KEN 60:30	Ashete Bekere ETH 70:40*
5 Jun	San Diego HMar (dh 86.5m)	Scott Smith USA 62:34	Shalane Flanagan USA 67:51*
11 Jun	New York City 10k	women only	Jemima Sumgong KEN 31:26
11 Jun	Oelde 10k	Geoffrey Yegon KEN 28:15	Edith Chelimo KEN 31:36
11 Jun	Zwolle HMar	Richard Mengich KEN 60:37*	Helah Kiprop KEN 68:36
18 Jun	Langueux 10k	Robert Kaptingei KEN 28:15	Meskerem Amare ETH 32:31
25 Jun	Appingedam 10k	John Langat KEN 27:59	Dibaba Kuma ETH 32:30
25 Jun	Olomouc HMar	Stanley Biwott KEN 60:46	Mary Keitany KEN 68:53
26 Jun	Boston 10k	Daniel Chebii KEN 27:55	Shalane Flanagan USA 30:52*
4 Jul	Atlanta 10k (34m dh)	Gabriel Geay TAN 28:49	Edna Kiplagat KEN 32:24
11 Jul	Utica 15k	Teshome Mekonen ETH 43:58	Cynthia Limo KEN 48:50
15 Jul	Buffalo 4M	Silas Kipruto KEN 18:13	Monica Ngige KEN 20:37
16 Jul	Kingsport 8k	Yitayal Atnafu ETH 22:31	Emily Boles USA 31:06
24 Jul	Capitola 6M	Isaac Mukundi KEN 27:31	Risper Gesabwa KEN 31:34
30 Jul	Davenport 7M	Silas Kipruto KEN 33:03	Mary Keitany KEN 35:20*
30 Jul	Port Elizabeth HMar	Edwin Koech KEN 61:16	Sheila Chesang KEN 70:58
31 Jul	Bogota (A) HMar	Tadese Tola ETH 65:16	Purity Rionoripo KEN 71:56
6 Aug	Cape Elizabeth 10k	Ben True USA 28:17	Mary Keitany KEN 30:45*
14 Aug	Sydney 14k	Harry Summers AUS 41:43	Cassie Fien AUS 47:21
21 Aug	Falmouth 7M	Stephen Sambu KEN 32:10	Caroline Chepkoech KEN 36:25
21 Aug	Klagenfurt HMar	Peter Kirui KEN 60:48	Viola Jelagat KEN 72:25
27 Aug	Flint 10M	Dathan Ritzenhein USA 47:24	Joan Ayabei KEN 55:37
4 Sep	Tilburg 10M/10k	Rodgers Kwemoi KEN 46:04	Alice Aprot Nawowuna KEN 31:34
5 Sep	New Haven 20k (US Ch)	Leonard Korir USA 59:15	Aliphine Tuliamuk USA 65:47
10 Sep	S.Shields HMar (dh 30m)	Mo Farah GBR 60:04	Vivian Cheruiyot KEN 67:54
10 Sep	Praha 10k	Abraham Kipyatich KEN 27:40	Violah Jepchumba KEN 30:24
11 Sep	Hamburg 10k	Kalipus Lomwai KEN 28:15*	Antonina Kwambai KEN 31:52*
17 Sep	Ústí nad Labem HMar	Barselius Kipyego KEN 59:15*	Peres Jepchirchir KEN 67:24
18 Sep	Amsterdam/Zaandam 10M	Edwin Kiptoo KEN 45:25	Alice Aprot Nawowuna KEN 51:59
18 Sep	Copenhagen HMar	James Wangari KEN 59:07*	Hiwot Gebrekidan ETH 68:00*
18 Sep	Krems HMar	Peter Kirui KEN 59:53	Parendis Lekapana KEN 69:49
18 Sep	Philadelphia HMar	Augustine Chogo KEN 63:25	Buze Diriba ETH 71:49
18 Sep	Providence 5k (US Ch)	Ryan Hill USA 13:57	Aliphine Tuliamuk USA 15:22
25 Sep	Paris/Versailles 16.3k	Stephen Ogari KEN 49:58	Etagegne Woldu ETH 55:19
25 Sep	Remich HMar	Kalipus Lomwai KEN 63:57	Nancy Arusei KEN 72:31
2 Oct	Breda HMar	Nicholas Korir KEN 59:50*	Ivy Kibet KEN 71:24
2 Oct	Cardiff HMar	Shadrack Korir KEN 60:53	Violah Jepchumba KEN 68:13
2 Oct	Glasgow HMar (150m short)	Callum Hawkins GBR 60:24	Betsy Saina KEN 67:22
2 Oct	Lisboa HMar	Nguse Amlosom ERI 62:39	Genet Yalew ETH 70:25
2 Oct	San Jose HMar	Shadrack Biwott USA 61:55	Sally Kipyego KEN 69:53
2 Oct	Trento HMar	Victor Chumo KEN 62:14*	Angela Tanui KEN 69:27*
9 Oct	Berlin 10k	Zane Robertson NZL 27:28*	Sarah Lahti SWE 31:57
9 Oct	Boston HMar	Daniel Salel KEN 63:13	Mary Wacera KEN 70:19
9 Oct	Groningen 4M	Tamirat Tola ETH 17:38	Viola Kibiwott KEN 20:02
9 Oct	Paris 20k	Mourad Amdouni FRA 59:18	Mamo Woldu ETH 66:24
9 Oct	St. Paul 10M (US Ch)	Sam Chelanga USA 47:25	Jordan Hasay USA 52:49
10 Oct	Boston 10k (US Ch)	women only	Emily Sisson USA 31:47
16 Oct	Pettinengo 9.6km/W 4k	Jacob Kiplimo UGA 28:08	Viola Kibiwott KEN 12:26
22 Oct	Valencia HMar	Stephen Kosgei KEN 59:27	Peres Jepchirchir KEN 67:09*
23 Oct	Portsmouth 10M	Chris Thompson GBR 47:23	Tirunesh Dibaba ETH 51:49
30 Oct	Arezzo HMar	Josh Koech KEN 62:13	Ruth Chebitok KEN 74:11
30 Oct	Marseille/Cassis 20k	Henry Kiplagat KEN 59:28	Joyceline Jepkosgei KEN 67:02*
5 Nov	New York City 5k uphill	Donn Cabral USA 14:18	Karoline Bjerkeli Grøvdal NOR 15:40
6 Nov	Pittsburg 10M	Leonard Korir USA 47:13	Buze Diriba ETH 51:38*

13 Nov	Cueno 10km/W 6k	Jacob Kiplimo UGA 28:26	Ruth Chebitok KEN 19:49
13 Nov	Istanbul 15k	Jemal Yimer Mekonnen ETH 44:14	Yasemin Can TUR 48:40
13 Nov	Njabini (A) HMar	Nicodemus Kimutai KEN 61:56	Edith Chelimo KEN 69:45
20 Nov	Addis Ababa (A) 10k	Abe Gashahun ETH 28:54	Fotyen Tesfay ETH 33:10
20 Nov	Boulogne-Billancourt HMar	Morris Gachaga KEN 62:04	Gebeyanesh Ayele ETH 70:21
20 Nov	New Delhi HMar	Eliud Kipchoge KEN 59:44	Worknesh Degefa ETH 67:42
20 Nov	Nijmegen 15k	Joshua Cheptegei UGA 42:08	Susan Krumins NED 49:30
24 Nov	Manchester USA 4.75M	Ben True USA 21:31	Emily Sisson USA 24:08
24 Nov	San Jose 5k	Morgan Pearson USA 13:32	Caroline Chepkoech KEN 15:18*
26 Nov	Basel 7.55k/W 5.9k	Tadesse Abraham SUI 21:44	Helen Bekele ETH 19:26
27 Nov	Barcelona 9.9k	Yemane Haileselassie ERI 30:24	Inês Monteiro ESP 22:59
3 Dec	Genève 7.32k	Tadesse Abraham SUI 21:01	Helen Bekele ETH 24:16
3 Dec	Nanning HMar	Mosinet Geremew ETH 62:25	Etalemahu Zeleke ETH 72:32
4 Dec	's-Heerenberg 15k	Herpasa Negasa ETH 43:02	Eunice Kirwa BRN 48:37
10 Dec	Haicang HMar	Joshua Kipkorir KEN 60:24	Sarah Chepchirchir KEN 67:52*
18 Dec	Houilles 10k	Cornelius Kangogo KEN 28:19	Viola Kibiwott KEN 31:14*
23 Dec	Okayama 10k	women only	Rosemary Wanjiru KEN 32:04
31 Dec	Bolzano 10.05k/W 5.05k	Muktar Edris ETH 28:52	Agnes Tirop KEN 15:44
31 Dec	Madrid 10k (dh 55m)	Nguse Amsolom ERI 28:09	Brigid Kosgei KEN 32:07
31 Dec	São Paulo 15k	Leul Gebreselassie ETH 44:53	Jemima Sumgong KEN 48:35*

* = course record

MARATHON REVIEW 2016
By Marty Post

ELIUD KIPCHOGE moved to the very top of the list ranking the greatest marathoners of all-time with two sterling efforts in 2016. At London in April a host of top competitors, including Kipchoge and Stanley Biwott, set out at a frenetic pace. They passed the halfway point in 1:01:24, 25k in 1:12:39 and 30k in 1:27:13, all the fastest splits ever recorded. Kipchoge covered the subsequent 10k in 29:36 and reached the finish line in 2:03:05, missing the world record by only eight seconds. Biwott fell back, but still posted a 2:03:51, making him the seventh man to break two hours four minutes on a record quality course. Four months later Kipchoge stood at the Olympic Games starting line in the role of heavy favorite, often a curse as an unheralded competitor has generally prevailed. Not on this day. He was always near the front, in control. After a rather pedestrian 1:05:55 opening half, he put the pressure on with an uncontested 14:44 between 35 and 40k to easily dispose of his last two challengers. His second half of 1:02:49 was more than a minute faster than anyone else. At year's end Kipchoge's career record read seven victories in eight marathon races with a lone defeat behind a Wilson Kipsang world record at Berlin in 2013.

Feyisa Lelisa became the eighth fastest Olympic marathoner at 2:09:54 for the silver medal. In something of a shocker, the rather inexperienced Galen Rupp took the bronze medal; despite worthy track credentials (26:44.36 10,000m pb), his only previous marathon was a 2:11:13 win at the USA Trials in February.

A month later an historic streak was in jeopardy at the BMW Berlin Marathon. Since 2011 the German capital had been the site of the annual world-leading time (discounting the wind-aided 2011 Boston Marathon) but now there was that 2:03:05 at London. No problem. A dramatic showdown between Kenenisa Bekele and Wilson Kipsang resulted in the former claiming a ten second victory in 2:03:03. Bekele, whose last two marathons were a DNF at Dubai in 2015 and a third place 2:06:36 at London five months earlier – when he claimed he was only "80 per cent fit" – fell behind Kipsang several times late in the race, yet he ran the final 2.2k in just 6:08 to prevail over the former world record holder. His time also displaced Haile Gebreselassie's former WR 2:03:59 there in 2008 as the Ethiopian national record. The field, including Bekele and Kipsang, had gone out in a blistering 1:01:11, the fastest first half ever, toppling London's short-lived claim to this distinction. The pace setters fell by the wayside early; Evans Chebet, among the elite, finished a far-back third with a two-second personal best 2:05:31. Ironically Kipsang ran 10 seconds faster than 2013 only to equal the fastest non-winning time on a record eligible course. It was an unprecedented third sub-2:04 for him and a record seventh lifetime sub-2:05. Kipsang has a top five average of 2:03:54 and he has broken 2:05 seven years in a row.

Two of the leading finishers at the Seoul Marathon on March 20, produced record-breaking results. The 2:05:13 winning time of Wilson Loyanae was the fastest ever for the month of March. The third finisher, Kaan Kigen Özbilen, was formerly Mike Kipruto Kigen of Kenya but he switched national allegiance to Turkey thus making his time of 2:06:10 a new European record (although yet to be ratified). Another former African, Tadesse Abraham, lowered the Swiss national record to 2:06:49.

Kenneth Mungara picked up his third consecutive veteran's marathon record with a 2:08:38 at Milan on April 3, but the most publicized age group world record came at Toronto on October 16. Ed Whitlock, already owning the AGWRs for 70-74 (2:54:49), 75-79 (3:04:54) and 80-84 (3:15:54), averaged just over nine minutes per mile to obliterate the former 85+ mark with a 3:56:34.

Japan's Yuki Kawauchi continued to augment his record totals of quality marathon performances. At year's end he owned the most sub-2:13s (34), sub-2:14s (40), sub-2:15s (44), sub-2:16s (50), sub-2:17s (55), sub-2:18s (59) and sub-2:19s (62). Tsegay Kebede ran a record 20th sub-2:11.

Kenyan women had competed in every Olympic marathon since the inaugural event in 1984 but the best this East African powerhouse had to show was a silver medal in 2004. In 2016 frustration ended when Jemima Jelagat Sumgong strode to a nine second victory, as she ran 16:30 between 35 and 40k, the fastest split of the race, and then surged over the final mile. In fact Kenya might have earned gold and silver if Eunice Jepkirui Kirwa had not changed her national allegiance to Bahrain in 2014 making her the first Olympic medalist from that country. Mare Dibaba, highly touted off her 2015 World Championships victory, was third.

Tirfi Tsegaye had the year's only sub-2:20 (2:19:41, Dubai) while Aberu Kebede won her second Berlin Marathon in 2:20:45. She is the most prolific high quality marathoner ever in times under 2:24 (10), 2:25 (13) and 2:26 (15). In a footnote at Berlin, Katharina Heinig finished in 2:28:34 which along with Katrin Dörre's 1999 PR of 2:24:35 set a new mother-daughter record of 4:53:09. Gideon and Valentine Kipketer, with lifetime PRs of 2:08:35 and 2:23:02 in different races, set a same race record of 4:36:01 (2:12:20/2:23:41) at Chicago.

The marathon often draws a variety of unique challenges to complete the distance in the fastest time possible. One such category involves running it on an indoor track, and at the Armory Track & Field Center at New York City on April 9, both the male and female world best fell respectively to Malcolm Richards (2:21:56) and Allie Kieffer (2:44:44), a dizzying 200-meter grind for 211 laps.

World Marathon Majors

SERIES X of the Abbott World Marathon Majors competition spanned the 2016 Boston Marathon through the 2017 Boston Marathon. For all intents and purposes, however, it was over in August at Rio de Janeiro when London Marathon champions, Eliud Kipchoge and Jemima Jelagat both won the Olympic Games gold medals there. Kipchoge defended his Series IX title and became the first man in the Majors era, which began in 2006, with five victories, having previously won in Chicago (2014), London (2015) and Berlin (2015). Mary Keitany won her third New York City Marathon and with two London wins, was the first woman with five lifetime Majors. Ghirmay Ghebreselassie's victory at New York City seven days before his 21st birthday made the 2015 World Champion the youngest ever with two Major titles.

After 67 Majors events, Kenyan woman are just one victory ahead of the Ethiopians, 28 to 26; at year's end African women had won 44 consecutive Majors. Kenyans dominate the Ethiopians among the men, 44-15.

Top Men, Series X: 1. Eliud Kipchoge KEN, 50 points; 2. Wilson Kipsang KEN 41, 3. Kenenisa Bekele ETH 34

Top Women, Series X: 1. Jemima Jelagat KEN 50, 2. Florence Kiplagat KEN 34, 3. Birhane Dibaba ETH 32 (prior to Boston 2017).

WINNERS OF 2016 INTERNATIONAL MARATHONS

Date	Location	Men's Winner	Time	Women's Winner	Time
2 Jan	Xiamen	Vincent Kipruto KEN	2:10:18	Worknesh Edesa ETH	2:24:04
8 Jan	Tiberias	Teferi Kebede ETH	2:15:31	Edinah Kwambai KEN	2:51:16
17 Jan	Hong Kong	Mike Mutai KEN	2:12:12	Letebrhan Gebreslasea ETH	2:36:51
17 Jan	Houston	Birhanu Gedefa ETH #	2:11:53	Biruktayit Degefa ETH	2:26:07
17 Jan	Mumbai	Gideon Kipketer KEN	2:08:35*	Shuko Genemo ETH	2:27:50
22 Jan	Dubai	Tesfaye Abera ETH	2:04:24	Tirfi Tsegaye ETH	2:19:41

MARATHON 2015

Date	City	Men's Winner	Time	Women's Winner	Time
31 Jan	Marrakech	Moses Mbugua KEN	2:11:41	Shasho Insermu ETH	2:32:42
31 Jan	Osaka	women only		Kayoko Fukushi JPN	2:22:17
6 Feb	Lagos	Abraham Kiptum KEN	2:16:19*	Halima Hussein ETH	2:38:36*
7 Feb	Oita	Melaku Abera ETH	2:09:27	Hiroko Yoshitomi JPN	2:45:07
14 Feb	Santa Monica (122m dh)	Weldon Kirui KEN	2:13:06	Nataliya Lehonkova UKR	2:30:40
21 Feb	Sevilla	Cosmas Lagat KEN	2:08:14*	Paula González ESP	2:31:18
26 Feb	Tel Aviv	William Kiprono KEN	2:10:51	Korlena Chemtai KEN	2:40:17
28 Feb	Tokyo	Feyisa Lilesa ETH	2:06:56	Helah Kiprop KEN	2:21:27*
6 Mar	Otsu	Lucas Rotich KEN	2:09:11	men only	
13 Mar	Barcelona	Dino Sefir ETH	2:09:31	Valerie Aiyabei KEN	2:25:26*
13 Mar	Brescia	Reuben Kerio KEN	2:09:05*	Abebu Gelan ETH	2:37:31
13 Mar	Nagoya	women only		Eunice Jepkirui Kirwa BRN	2:22:40
13 Mar	Rabat	Sammy Kigen Korir KEN	2:09:23	Pamela Rotich KEN	2:28:06
20 Mar	Chongqing	Kelkile Gezahegn ETH	2:10:54	Liu Ruihuan CHN	2:26:13
20 Mar	Taipei City	William Chebor KEN	2:13:05	Olga Kotovska UKR	2:36:38
20 Mar	Seoul	Wilson Loyanae KEN	2:05:13*	Rose Chelimo KEN	2:24:14
27 Mar	Dongguan	Kenneth Limo KEN	2:11:18	Chemutai Rionotukei KEN	2:34:38
27 Mar	Zhengzhou	Bejiga Regasa ETH	2:11:21	Leah Kiprono KEN	2:27:39
3 Apr	Daegu	James Kwambai KEN	2:10:46	Caroline Kilel KEN	2:27:39
3 Apr	Debno	Cosmas Kyeva KEN	2:11:56	Stellah Barsosio KEN	2:33:13
3 Apr	Linz	Edwin Koech KEN	2:09:06	Halima Hassen ETH	2:38:13
3 Apr	Milano	Ernest Ngeno KEN	2:08:15	Brigid Kosgei KEN	2:27:45
3 Apr	Paris	Cyprian Kotut KEN	2:07:11	Visiline Jepkesho KEN	2:25:53
3 Apr	Santiago	Victor Kipchirchir KEN	2:11:01*	Olga Kimaiyo KEN	2:35:24
10 Apr	Gunsan	Chala Damessa ETH	2:11:45	Lim Ye-jin KOR	2:36:09
10 Apr	Hannover	Lusapho April RSA	2:11:27	Anna Hahner GER #	2:30:35
10 Apr	Pyongyang	Pak Chol PRK	2:14:10	Kim Ji-hyang PRK	2:28:06
10 Apr	Roma	Amos Kipruto KEN	2:08:12	Rahma Tusa ETH	2:28:49
10 Apr	Rotterdam	Marius Kipserem KEN	2:06:11	Letebrhan Gebreslasea ETH	2:26:15
10 Apr	Wien	Robert Chemosin KEN	2:09:48	Shuko Genemo ETH	2:24:31
10 Apr	Wuhan	Johnstone Maiyo KEN	2:11:15*	Meseret Legesse ETH	2:26:08*
16 Apr	Bloemfontein (A short?)	Asefa Mengistu ETH	2:11:16	Shitaye Gemechu ETH	2:43:05
17 Apr	Annecy	Isaac Birir Kipkosgei KEN #	2:14:28	Helen Bekele Tola ETH	2:29:21*
17 Apr	Brighton	Duncan Maiyo KEN	2:09:56	Grace Momanyi KEN	2:34:15
17 Apr	Enschede	elite women only		Sarah Jebet KEN	2:27:59*
17 Apr	Hamburg	Tesfaye Abera ETH	2:06:58	Meselech Melkamu ETH	2:21:54*
17 Apr	Lódz	Abraw Misganaw ETH	2:13:24	Racheal Mutgaa KEN	2:31:41
17 Apr	Nagano	Jairus Chanchima KEN	2:15:31	Shasho Insermu ETH	2:34:19
18 Apr	Boston (136.3m dh)	Lemi Berhanu Hayle ETH	2:12:45	Atsede Baysa ETH	2:29:19
24 Apr	Düsseldorf	Japhet Kosgei KEN	2:10:46	Zsofia Erdelyi HUN	2:35:37
24 Apr	London	Eliud Kipchoge KEN	2:03:05*	Jemima Sumgong KEN	2:22:58
24 Apr	Madrid	Peter Kiplagat KEN	2:11:44	Askale Alemayehu ETH	2:33:08
24 Apr	Warsaw	Artur Kozlowski POL	2:11:54	Kumeshi Sichala ETH	2:28:43
24 Apr	Zürich	Yuki Kawauchi JPN	2:12:04	Daniela Aeschbacher SUI	2:47:49
1 May	Volgograd	Fyodor Shutov RUS	2:11:26	Tatyana Arkhipova RUS	2:28:34
8 May	Dongying	Dickson Tuwei KEN	2:09:27	Eunice Chumba BRN	2:31:13
8 May	Geneva (dh 46m)	Julius Rotich KEN	2:11:11	Jane Kiptoo KEN	2:35:04
8 May	Praha	Lawrence Cherono KEN	2:07:24	Lucy Karimi KEN	2:24:46
15 May	Kraków	Cosmas Kyeva KEN	2:11:58	Gladys Chemwono KEN	2:30:30
15 May	Lima	Nicholas Manza Kamakya KEN	2:13:57	Caroline Jebiwot Kiptoo KEN	2:39:15*
15 May	Riga	Dominic Kimwetich KEN	2:11:45*	Shitaye Gemechu ETH	2:38:41
28 May	Luxembourg	John Komen KEN	2:12:59	Belaynesh Yigezu ETH	2:42:35
29 May	Ottawa	Dino Sefir ETH	2:08:14	Koren Jelila ETH	2:27:06
4 Jun	Stockholm	Stanley Koech KEN	2:10:58*	Jane Moraa Onyangi KEN	2:31:46
11 Jun	Lanzhou (A)	Robert Kwambai KEN	2:13:20	Tsehay Desalegn ETH	2:32:16
18 Jun	Duluth	Elisha Barno KEN	2:11:26	Sarah Kiptoo KEN	2:33:29
3 Jul	Southport	Kenneth Mungara KEN	2:09:00	Misato Horie JPN	2:26:40*

MARATHON 2015

Date	City	Men's Winner	Time	Women's Winner	Time
28 Aug	Sapporo	Ryo Kiname JPN	2:13:16	Kaori Yoshida JPN	2:32:33
11 Sep	Medellin (A)	Amos Kiplagat KEN	2:17:52	Caroline Chemutai KEN	2:37:32
11 Sep	Münster	Duncan Koech KEN	2:12:59	Elizabeth Rumokol KEN	2:33:01
11 Sep	Wroclaw	Cosmas Mutuku Kyeva KEN	2:14:38	Stellah Barsosio KEN	2:34:09*
17 Sep	Beijing	Mekuant Ayenew ETH	2:11:09	Meseret Mengistu ETH	2:25:56
18 Sep	Cape Town	Asefa Mengistu ETH	2:08:41	Tish Jones GBR	2:36:13
18 Sep	Sydney	Tomohiro Tanigawa JPN	2:12:13	Makda Harun ETH	2:32:22
24 Sep	Hengshui	Kelkile Gezahegn ETH	2:11:11	Meseret Legesse ETH	2:28:04
25 Sep	Berlin	Kenenisa Bekele ETH	2:03:03	Aberu Kebede ETH	2:20:45
25 Sep	Mombasa	Paul Maina KEN	2:12:13	Nancy Koech KEN	2:40:01
25 Sep	Moscow	Artyom Alekseyev RUS	2:13:40	Tatyana Aryasova RUS	2:32:34
25 Sep	Warszawa	Ezekiel Omullo KEN	2:08:55	Gladys Kibiwott BRN	2:36:34
2 Oct	Bruxelles	Eric Kering KEN	2:16:52	Virginie Van Droogenbroeck BEL	2:53:45
2 Oct	Köln	Raymond Choge KEN	2:08:39	Bornes Kitur KEN	2:32:16
2 Oct	Kosice	David Kiyeng KEN	2:08:58	Chaltu Tafa ETH	2:32:20
2 Oct	Lisboa	Alfred Kering KEN	2:10:27	Sarah Chepchirchir KEN	2:24:13*
2 Oct	Lyon	Alex Saekwo KEN	2:10:49	Joan Kigen KEN	2:33:27
9 Oct	Chicago	Abel Kirui KEN	2:11:23	Florence Kiplagat KEN	2:21:32
9 Oct	Eindhoven	Festus Talam KEN	2:06:26	Truphena Chepchirchir KEN	2:30:32
9 Oct	Metz	Eliud Magut KEN	2:11:43	elite men only	
9 Oct	St. Paul	Dominic Ondoro KEN	2:08:51*	Jane Kibii KEN	2:30:01
9 Oct	Zagreb	Wycliffe Kipkorir Biwott KEN	2:14:17	Stellah Barsosio KEN	2:33:46*
16 Oct	Amsterdam	Daniel Wanjiru KEN	2:05:21*	Meselech Melkamu ETH	2:23:21
16 Oct	Gyeongju	Filex Kiprotich KEN	2:06:58	Kang Su-jung KOR	2:45:57
16 Oct	Toronto	Philemon Rono KEN	2:08:27	Shure Demise ETH	2:25:18
23 Oct	Chunchon	Luka Kanda KEN	2:07:21	Kim Ji-eun KOR	2:34:39
23 Oct	Dresden	Joseph Munywoki KEN	2:10:21	Gladys Kiprotich KEN	2:40:26
23 Oct	Rennes (dh 65m)	Justus Kipkosgei KEN	2:09:29	Helen Jepkurgat KEN	2:31:07
23 Oct	Venezia	Julius Rotich KEN	2:10:22	Priscah Cherono KEN	2:27:41
30 Oct	Dublin	Dereje Debele ETH	2:12:18	Helalia Johannes NAM	2:32:32
30 Oct	Frankfurt	Mark Korir KEN	2:06:48	Mamitu Daska ETH	2:25:27
30 Oct	Ljubljana	Laban Mutai KEN	2:09:16	Purity Changwony KEN	2:29:32
30 Oct	Nairobi (A)	Robert Kipkemboi KEN	2:13:27	Jane Jelagat KEN	2:34:18
30 Oct	Osaka	Benjamin Ngandu KEN	2:12:47	Yoshiko Sakamoto JPN	2:36:02
30 Oct	Podgorica	Abel Rop KEN	2:19:17	Gladys Biwott KEN	2:42:18
30 Oct	Shanghai	Stephen Mokoka RSA	2:10:18	Roza Dereje ETH	2:26:18
6 Nov	Hangzhou	Bejiga Regasa ETH	2:11:21	Anne Cheptanui KEN	2:31:20
6 Nov	New York City	Ghirmay Ghebreslassie ERI	2:07:51	Mary Keitany KEN	2:24:26
6 Nov	Porto	Samuel Theuri Mwaniki KEN	2:11:48	Loice Jebet Kiptoo KEN	2:29:13
6 Nov	Seoul	Joel Kimurer KEN	2:08:07	Kim Sun-ae KOR	2:44:13
12 Nov	Hefei	Gezahegn Kelkilew Dejene ETH	2:08:56	Grace Momanyi KEN	2:28:28
13 Nov	Athína	Luka Lobuwan KEN	2:12:49	Nancy Arusei KEN	2:38:13
13 Nov	Beirut	Edwin Kiptoo KEN	2:13:19	Tigist Girma ETH	2:32:48
13 Nov	Cannes	Elisha Kipchirchir KEN	2:10:45	Konjit Tilahun ETH	2:37:55
13 Nov	Istanbul	Evans Kiplagat AZE	2:13:30	Agnes Barsosio KEN	2:28:25
13 Nov	Saitama	women only		Flomena Cheyech KEN	2:23:18*
20 Nov	Valencia	Victor Kipchirchir KEN	2:07:39	Valerie Aiyabei KEN	2:24:48*
20 Nov	Verona	Edward Koech KEN	2:10:52	Tunde Szabó HUN	2:44:19
27 Nov	Firenze	Teshome Shumi ETH	2:11:57	Winnie Jepkorir KEN	2:28:46
27 Nov	La Rochelle	Emmanuel Ngatuny KEN	2:10:46	Jane Moraa Onyangi KEN	2:30:51
27 Nov	San Sebastián	Hosea Kiprono Maiyo KEN	2:11:51	Maria Casanueva ESP	2:35:32
4 Dec	Fukuoka	Yemane Tsegay ETH	2:08:48	men only	
4 Dec	Macau	Peter Some KEN	2:12:52	Kim Ji-hyang PRK	2:36:16
4 Dec	Sacramento (105m dh)	Nelson Oyugi KEN	2:11:41	Sarah Kiptoo KEN	2:31:20
4 Dec	Singapore	Felix Kirwa KEN	2:17:17	Rebecca Chesir KEN	2:43:03
11 Dec	Guangzhou	Salah Bounasr MAR	2:11:09	Aynalem Kassahun ETH	2:31:52
11 Dec	Honolulu	Lawrence Cherono KEN	2:09:39*	Brigid Koskei KEN	2:31:11
18 Dec	Hofu	Ryo Hashimoto JPN	2:11:20	Hisae Yoshimatsu JPN	2:40:21
18 Dec	Taipei	Sammy Kitwara KEN	2:09:59	Mercy Kibarus KEN	2:36:33

* course record; # race day winner subsequently disqualified; dh = downhill course; A = altitude over 1000m

REVIEW OF ULTRARUNNING 2016
by Andy Milroy

2016 WAS A very interesting year for Ultrarunning as there was a world-wide reach to an extent not seen before with an Australian woman taking the World 100k title, a Japanese the men's and the South Africans the men's team title. Also an American woman set a new world record for the track 100 miles, a Chinese woman ran the greatest 2016 24 hour distance on the track whilst a German woman ran the fastest 100k and a Swedish woman the two longest road 24 hour distances of the year. To finish the year, a Japanese man surpassed the previous best 2016 24 hour mark set by a Briton in winning the European 24 Hour championships.

The World 100k was held, with keen anticipation, in Los Alcazares in south eastern Spain on a flat 10k loop. For the first time for many years a very strong team of top South Africans were entered. They included the first three in the 2016 Comrades in May: David Gatebe, Ludwick Mamabolo and Bongmusa Mthembu plus the 2015 winner Gift Kelehe. Unfortunately their inexperience in this hothouse showed and they went off too fast, running at world record pace, but the tight turns on the course put paid to any hopes of record breaking. Despite this, such was the talent of the RSA team that it took an outstanding, well judged performance from the little known Japanese runner Hideaki Yamauchi, second at Yubetsu earlier in the year, to deny them individual victory. His 6:18:22 was some five minutes ahead of Mthembu 6:24:06 with the leading American Patrick Reagan third 6:35:42. With a European, the Pole Tomasz Walerowicz in fourth, four continents were represented in the first four places!

The World team title was taken by South Africa 19:51:40 by four minutes from Japan 19:55:46 and the USA 20:03:04 with Norway fourth 20:39:06 and Australia fifth 20:55:44 – so five different continents. Yamauchi's time was the year's fastest and he is a clear No.1 in the event.

In the women's race there was a group that was together for much of the race. Kirstin Bull took the lead at 55k while Nikolina Sustic CRO and Joasia Zakrzewski GBR battled for second and third places. Bull won in 7:34:25 from Sustic 7:36:10 who had moved away at 80k from Zakrzewski, third in 7:41:38. Japan took the team title in 23:23:14 from Croatia 23:48:19 and the USA 24:05:33, although their first woman Mikiko Ota 7:47:38 was only fifth.

Bull's mark was not the fastest 100k of the year as Nele Alder-Baerens GER ran 7:29:04 at Leipzig in August. She is new to the 100k, but ran 3:20:33 for 50k in 2016 and has a 2:47:07 marathon pb. She has competed in the Deaflympics (previously called World Games for the Deaf), winning at 5000m and has great potential at 100k but chose not to run the World event in her first year at the distance.

There was no World 24 hour Championships; the intention being that there would be area championships. This happened for Asia and Oceania where the championship race was held in Kaohsiung TPE and won by Barry Loveday AUS with 235.868k and Nikki Wynd AUS 209.497k. The European race in Albi FRA was won by Dan Lawson GBR with 261.843k. Official splits for 100 miles and 200k are not available, but times at the end of the laps in which these distances were passed reveal a remarkable picture. Aleksandr Sorokin LTU went into the race with the greatest 24 hour distance until then in 2016 and set out to win the race decisively. A 6:50:34 100k runner, he stamped his authority on the race and reached 100 miles in 12:36:39, the fastest split in any such championships. Don Ritchie, in winning the 24 hour race at Milton Keynes in 1990, was quick at 200k, but Sorokin was quicker 16:26:15 to Don's 16:31:08. Only a handful of elite performers have run faster, but Sorokin was to pay for this fast early pace and ended up fifth. Stéphane Ruel FRA 257.296k and Tamás Rudolf HUN 255.250k were second and third while France won the team title.

The year's greatest distance was 263.127k by Yoshihiko Ishikawa in Tokyo in December. However, as winner of the most competitive race of the year, Dan Lawson has to be World No 1 at 24 hours. Maria Jansson SWE ranks as the world no. 1 woman. She produced the best performance in winning the European title with 250.647k, a new European record, breaking Lizzie Hawker's former world best. Only Mami Kudo has gone further in 24 hours. Two Poles took second and third, Patrycja Bereznowska 241.633k and Agata Matejczuk 232.285k as the Polish team took the European title.

There was no North American championships, which had interesting ramifications. Two of the former US World 24 hour team qualified for the World 100k, and one of those Pam Smith set US track records at 14:09:44 for 100 miles and 18:47:04 for 200k. In her remarkable 24 hour run, Jansson went through just over 200k in 19:12:10. Seven months after Smith's run another American Gina Slaby, aiming to make the US 24 hour team for 2017, targeted her 100 mile mark and excelled by breaking the world mark with 13:45:49.

The best marks for 2016 at 48 hours came at Bruce ACT Australia, with Michael Thwaites running the greatest male distance of 413.059k and Wynd setting the greatest female distance of 343.044k. In the 6 day event Joe Fejes confirmed his world dominance, running 887.509k at Balatonfüred HUN well clear of his main rival Wolfgang Schwerk 874.294k. Also there were the two women's marks of the year: Luisa Zecchino ITA 732.162k ahead of Sumie Inagaki JPN 713.530k.

The fastest 1000 mile marks of the year came in the 3100 mile race in New York as Nikolay Duzhiy RUS ran 13:14:36:35 and Paula Mairer AUT 15:06:43:30. Called 'The Mount Everest of Ultramarathons' by the *New York Times*, this is the longest certified footrace in the world and in 2016 it was won by Yuri Trostenyuk UKR 46 days 01:10:25 with Pekka Aalto FIN just over an hour and forty minutes behind him (46 days 02:54:22). The first woman was Theresa Janaková SVK 51 days 07:31:07. Trostenyuk did not go on to 5000k and the 2016 fastest time was 47:07:35:21 by Aalto (his best ever is 40:12:30:26!) with 51:10:45:13 by Janaková the best women's mark.

Of the traditional point-to-point races, the Comrades was dominated by South Africans at home. Gatebe set a new Down record from Pietermaritzburg to Durban in 5:18:19 well clear of Mamabolo 5:24:05 and Mthembu 5:26:39. The first two women were also South Africans, Charne Bosman 6:25:55 and Caroline Wostmann 6:30:44, with Kajsa Berg SWE, second in the 2015 World 100k, third in 6:39:04. The Spartathlon from Athens to Sparta was won by Andrzej Radzikowski POL in 23:02:23 from Marco Bonfiglio ITA 23:36:58 and Radek Brunner CZE 24:07:29. Without a Continental 24 Hour championships it is not surprising that two American women dominated the female race. Katalin Nagy won with 25:23:52 from Smith 27:13:31 and Zsuzsanna Maraz HUN 27:45:42.

The longest stage race was the French Trans-Gaule on 19 stages covering 1190k. It was won by David Le Broch FRA with an elapsed time of 105:26:58, over five hours ahead of his fellow-countrymen Patrick Poivet 111:01:26 and Jean-Louis Vidal 112:12:55. The first woman was Jennifer Bradley GBR with 134:56:09 from Marie-Jeanne Simons FRA 144:41:34 and the veteran Jannet Lange NED 145:59:31.

There are still areas of the world where ultras are rarely held or where the sport is still emerging, but it is the challenge and demands of covering extreme distances on foot which offer an accessibility, a camaraderie of people competing, not against each other but against a distance or a time limit, which has increasing appeal.

ULTRA ALL-TIME LISTS

MEN'S 100 KILOMETRES

6:10:20t	Don Ritchie	GBR	1978
6:13:33	Takahiro Sunada	JPN	1998
6:15:30	Jean-Paul Praet #	BEL	1989
6:18:09	Valmir Nunes	BRA	1995
6:18:22	Hideaki Yamauchi	JPN	2016
6:18:24	Mario Ardemagni	ITA	2004
6:18:26	Vasiliy Larkin	RUS	2013
6:19:20	Steven Way	GBR	2014

24 HOURS Km

303.506t	Yiannis Kouros	GRE/AUS	1997
285.366t	Yoshikazu Hara	JPN	2014
282.282	Denis Zhalybin	RUS	2006
277.543	Michael Morton	USA	2012
276.209	Wolfgang Schwerk	FRG	1987
275.982t	Anatoliy Kruglikov	RUS	1995
274.884	Ryoichi Sekiya	JPN	2007
274.715	Bernard Gaudin	FRA	1982
Indoors: 275.576 Nikolay Safin ¶		RUS	1993

WOMEN'S 100 KILOMETRES

6:33:11	Tomoe Abe	JPN	2000
7:00:27	Norimi Sakurai	JPN	2007
7:00:48	Ann Trason	USA	1995
7:08:35	Camille Herron	USA	2015
7:10:32	Tatyana Zhyrkova	RUS	2004
7:11:42	Nariko Kawaguchi	JPN	1996
7:18:57	Birgit Lennartz	GER	1990
7:20:22	María Venâncio	BRA	1998

WOMEN'S 24 HOURS

255.303t	Mami Kudo	JPN	2011
250.647	Maria Jansson	SWE	2016
250.106t	Edit Bérces	HUN	2002
247.076	Elizabeth Hawker	GBR	2011
244.669	Sabrina Moran/Little	USA	2013
244.495	Katalin Nagy	USA	2015
244.232	Michaela Dimitriadu	CZE	2012
243.657	Sigrid Lomsky	GER	1993
Indoor track			
248.901	Yelena Sidorenkova	RUS	1996

OLYMPIC GAMES 2016

August 12-21, Rio de Janeiro (Brazil)

THE GAMES OF the 31st Olympiad were held in conditions that were pretty much ideal throughout. There was some rain: at the start of the first morning session on 12 August, then heavy rain early on the evening of 15 August that caused a half-hour cessation of action and marred the first two heats of the 110m hurdles, at the end of the evening on 18 August (women's 400mH and men's 200m) and (welcome) for the start of the men's marathon on 20 August. But temperatures were often in the 30-34°C range. In such conditions the level of performance were generally high and world leads for 2016 (at the time) were set in 19 events. The IAAF claimed that a record 2283 athletes from 199 federations competed.

There were three terrific world records, the first, and most remarkable, coming in the morning session of the opening day as Almaz Ayana took 14.33 seconds off the mark that had seemed untouchable until now by Wang Junxia in the year of the Chinese distance runners, 1993, with 10,000m in 29:17.45. Then came another surprising record as Wayde van Niekerk sped away from previous champions Kirani James and LaShawn Merritt to clock 43.03 for 400m, taking 0.15 off Michael Johnson's 1999 mark. In contrast almost expected was the 82.29 hammer throw by Anita Wlodarczyk, the best of her four throws over the old Olympic record. There were nine Olympic records in all – also from Thiago Braz da Silva, giving a huge thrill to the locals with 6.03 in the pole vault after Renaud Lavillenie had added 1cm to his previous Olympic record with 5.98, Conseslus Kipruto, 8:03.28 steeplechase, Ryan Crouser 22.52 shot, and Vivian Cheruiyot, 14:26.17 5000m. Ashton Eaton equalled the decathlon record with 8893 points. IAAF President Sebastian Coe said at the closing press conference that there has been 10 area and 95 national records set.

Naturally Usain Bolt took worldwide headlines as once again he transcended our sport as his 100m, 200m and 4x100m wins made for a unique treble treble (Nesta Carter's positive drugs test from Beijing 2008 notwithstanding). Also winning two individual gold medals were Elaine Thompson, who was a metre clear in both 100m and 200m, and the marvellous Mo Farah who doubled at 5000m and 10,000m as in London 2012. No matter what the rest of the world may try, nobody can match Farah's finish, last laps of 55.36 in the 10,000m and 52.83 in the 5000m after a good pace in both.

There were as ever surprises and disasters.

The greatest shock came as Pawel Fajdek failed to qualify for the men's hammer final. He had been the cast-iron favourite, yet managed only 72.00, easily his worst performance since 2011. He had been over 80m in 10 of his competitions in 2016 plus 79.12 in his first event and 78.82 in qualifying at the Europeans. One defending champion, Robert Harting, failed to qualify for the discus final. The biggest surprise winner was Sara Kolak, who set Croatian records in both qualifying (64.30) and final (66.18) of the javelin, but there were also more wins for clear favourites such as Omar McLeod 110mh, Christian Taylor triple jump, and for women: Caster Semenya 800m, Brianna Rollins 100mh, Dalilah Muhammad 400mh, Caterine Ibargüen triple jump and Liu Hong 20k walk.

The USA were, as usual, easily the most successful nation with 32 medals including 13 gold (their most since 1996). They had the one clean sweep of the medals – in the women's 100m hurdles. Once again, however, they met with disaster in the 4x100m, but were supreme at the other relays and, in addition to their traditional areas, had great results from men's and women's distance races. Kenya and Jamaica each won six golds and Britain headed five nations that each won two, but in a sensationally successful Games across all sports actually increased their points total from London 2012 and were the top European nation. Overall the top nations in the points table were very similar to those of the 2015 World Championships, although here a big gap opened between the USA and Kenya. Canada, headed by Derek Drouin's high jump success, South Africa, with van Niekerk and Semenya, and Croatia, with wins by Sandra Perkovic and Kolak, continued their major advance from previous Olympics, but Cuba continued to decline.

Jesús Ángel García ESP, at 50k walk, tied the record of Merlene Ottey by competing at a seventh Games.

A novel venture was having some finals in the morning sessions. There was disappointment, however, in that there were all too many empty seats for most sessions and the booing of Renaud Lavillenie, both when he battled local favourite Braz da Silva and on the medal podium, was unforgiveable.

Men

100 Metres *(prelim, h 13th, sf, F (+0.2) 14th*
1. Usain Bolt JAM 9.81
2. Justin Gatlin USA 9.89
3. Andre De Grasse CAN 9.91

Medals and Points Table

Medals and Points Table
Points: 8 for 1st to 1 for 8th place. 70 nations placed athletes in top eight, 42 won medals, and 23 won gold.

Nation	G	S	B	Points	2012*	2008*
USA	13	10	9	309.5	305	207
KEN	6	6	1	131	113	136
JAM	6	3	2	106	107	120
GBR	2	1	4	92.5	83.5	72
CHN	2	2	2	81	75	39
GER	2	-	1	72.5	95	43.5
ETH	1	2	5	72	90	76
CAN	1	1	4	65	22.5	23
FRA	-	3	3	57	41	37
POL	1	1	1	44.5	21	43
RSA	2	2	-	34	17	14
AUS	-	1	1	33	27	40
NZL	-	1	3	25	8	15
UKR	-	-	1	23.5	42	50
BRA	1	-	-	23	11	21
TTO	-	-	1	23	35	18
CRO	2	-	1	22	8	7
BRN	1	1	-	21	9	10
NED	-	1	-	20	13	3
BLR	-	1	-	20	6	65
CZE	-	-	1	19.5	29	23
ESP	1	1	-	18	12	31.5
BAH	1	-	1	18	19	22
ALG	-	2	-	18	8	3
CUB	-	-	1	16.5	26	61
JPN	-	1	1	16	13	12
EST	-	-	-	15	6	8
BEL	1	-	-	14	19	19
ITA	-	-	-	14	15	20
CIV	-	-	-	13	-	5
SVK	1	-	-	12	3	2
COL	1	-	-	12	7	-
MEX	-	1	-	12	4	5
TUR	-	-	1	12	20	16
HUN	-	-	1	11	8	6
QAT	-	1	-	10	5.5	3
GRE	1	-	-	10	4	7
Note RUS				-	169.5	200

POR, MAR, GRN (1S) 9; TJK (1G), BOT, BUL (1S), IRL 8; BDI, DEN, VEN (all 1S) 7; KAZ (1B), SRB (1B), ERI 6; CGO, DJI, LAT, SUI, NGR, UGA 5; SWE 4.5; CYP, FIN, ISR, MDA, NOR, TAN; 3 AUT, LCA, URU 3; GUY, PAN 2; SYR 1. 42 nations won medals, 67 placed athletes in the top eight.

* Not yet adjusted for all the changes due to recent positive drugs findings

4. Yohan Blake JAM		9.93
5. Akani Simbine RSA		9.94
6. Ben Youssef Meité CIV		9.96
7. Jimmy Vicaut FRA		10.04
8. Trayvon Bromell USA		10.06

BOLT BECAME the first athlete to win the Olympic 100m three times; indeed the first to complete an Olympic treble in any track event. After winning his heat in 10.07 (Gatlin fastest at 10.01), he ran a season's best of 9.86 in his semi with the other semis won by Gatlin 9.94 and Vicaut 9.95. Unlike the 2015 Worlds Bolt, after a slowish start, poured on the pace in the second half and sped to a 0.08 advantage over Gatlin, at 34 the oldest ever medallist in the event and who now has a complete set of 100m medals, in the final run just over an hour after the semis. A close battle for the bronze was won by De Grasse in a pb 9.91 (after pb 9.92 in the semi) from Blake, who ran his fastest time for four years.

200 Metres (h 16th, sf 17th, F (-0.5) 18th

1. Usain Bolt JAM	19.78
2. Andre De Grasse CAN	20.02
3. Christophe Lemaitre FRA	20.12
4. Adam Gemili GBR	20.12
5. Churandy Martina NED	20.13
6. LaShawn Merritt USA	20.19
7. Alonso Edward PAN	20.23
8. Ramil Guliyev TUR	20.43

DE GRASSE'S 20.09 was the fastest heat and he improved to a Canadian record 19.80 behind Bolt's 19.78 in their semi, while Merritt 19.94 and Edward 20.07 won the other semis, but Justin Gatlin was 3rd in the last in 20.13 and eliminated. Bolt was the only man to run faster in the final than in the semis and he ran such a strong turn in lane 6 that he was some 3m clear entering the straight and, visibly gritting his teeth, held most of that advantage to cross the line ahead of De Grasse in lane 4. It was very close for 3-4-5 as they ran 20.116, 20.119 and 20.122, but Merritt tired in his sixth race of the Games.

400 Metres (h 12th, sf 13th, F 14th)

1. Wayde van Niekerk RSA	43.03*
2. Kirani James GRN	43.76
3. LaShawn Merritt USA	43.85
4. Machel Cedenio TTO	44.01
5. Karabo Sibanda BOT-J	44.25
6. Ali Khamis Abbas BRN	44.36
7. Bralon Taplin GRN	44.45
8. Matthew Hudson-Smith GBR	44.61

VAN NIEKERK'S marvellous world record was later voted men's performance of 2016. His unofficial 100m splits were 10.7, 20.5 (behind Merritt 20.4) and 31.0 as he finished well clear of the two men who had disputed supremacy at the event in recent years, James and Merritt (both 31.2 at 300m). National records were also set by Cedenio and Abbas as there were the quickest ever times for places four to eight. Van Niekerk ran in lane 8, having not seemed bothered to win his semi, in which he ran 44.45 behind Cedenio 44.39. The other semis were won by Taplin 44.44 and James 44.02 from Merritt 44.21; all eight qualifiers ran faster then 44.5.

800 Metres (h 12th, sf 13th, F 14th)

1. David Rudisha KEN	1:42.15
2. Taoufik Makhloufi ALG	1:42.61
3. Clayton Murphy USA	1:42.93

4. Pierre-Ambroise Bosse FRA 1:43.41
5. Ferguson Cheruiyot KEN 1:43.55
6. Marcin Lewandowski POL 1:44.20
7. Alfred Kipketer KEN 1:46.02
8. Boris Berian USA 1:46.15

RUDISHA RETAINED his title. This time he did not lead all the way as 19 year-old compatriot Kipketer stormed through 200m in 23.2 and 400m in 49.23 (Rudisha 23.4 and 49.8). Then Rudisha strode magnificently along the back straight, and held a 3m lead over Bosse and Makhloufi at 600m in 1:16.04. He led into the final straight by around 4m and never faltered, winning by that margin in 1:42.15, the world's fastest since the 2012 Olympic final but one that he has bettered ten times. Rudisha had been fastest in the heats with 1:45.09 and won his semi in 1:43.88 after Bosse and Makhloufi had run 1:42.85 in semi 1 and Kipketer had won semi 2 in 1:44.38. Makhloufi set an Algerian record and Murphy's long drive for home took him past Bosse in the last 30m; his pb 1:42.93 improved his pb from 1:44.30 in his semi and 1:44.76 pre-Rio.

1500 Metres (h 16th, sf 18th, F 20th)

1. Matthew Centrowitz USA 3:50.00
2. Taoufik Makhloufi ALG 3:50.11
3. Nick Willis NZL 3:50.24
4. Ayanleh Souleiman DJI 3:50.29
5. Abdelaati Iguider MAR 3:50.58
6. Asbel Kiprop KEN 3:50.87
7. David Bustos ESP 3:51.06
8. Ben Blankenship USA 3:51.09
9. Ryan Gregson AUS 3:51.39
10. Nate Brannen CAN 3:51.45
11. Ronald Musagala UGA 3:51.68
12. Charlie Grice GBR 3:51.73
13. Ronald Kwemoi KEN 3:56.76

CENTROWITZ RAN a masterly race as he controlled the final though painfully slow opening laps of 66.83 and 69.75, but with the speed to run the next in 55.41 and 38.0 for the final 300m. His last 600m was 1:17.8 and 800m 1:49.8. The favourite Kiprop joined him with 200m to go but soon faltered and most of the field can take little comfort from the way they ran the race, which had the slowest winning Olympic time since 1932. Defending champion Makhloufi took his second silver medal of the Games. 17 men broke 3:40 in the heats, fastest 3:38.31 by Jakub Holusa, and 7 in the semis, fastest 3:39.42 by Kwemoi.

5000 Metres (h 17th, F 20th)

1. Mo Farah GBR 13:03.30
2. Paul Chelimo USA 13:03.90
3. Hagos Gebrhiwet ETH 13:04.35
4. Mohammed Ahmed CAN 13:05.94
5. Bernard Lagat USA 13:06.78
6. Andrew Butchart GBR 13:08.61
7. Albert Rop BRN 13:08.79
8. Joshua Cheptegei UGA 13:09.17
9. Birhanu Yemataw BRN 13:09.26
10. Abrar Osman ERI 13:09.56
11. Hassan Mead USA 13:09.81
12. Dejen Gebremeskel ETH 13:15.91
13. Elroy Gelant RSA 13:17.47
14. Brett Robinson AUS 13:32.20
15. David Torrence PER 13:43.12
dq. Muktar Edris ETH (13:04.79)

FARAH HAS not lost a championship 5000m since 2009 and, despite tired legs from his 10,000m triumph, went ahead at 3100m in the final and, after 4000m in 10:39.38, ran 4:00.9 for the final 1600m, 2:23.92 for the last 1000m and a last lap in 52.83 racing away from Gebrhiwet, who had been with him at the bell, The surprising Chelimo passed the Ethiopian for the silver, improving his pb from 13.21.61 to 13:19.54 the fastest time of the heats and 13:03.90 in the final; he was initially disqualified but later reinstated while Edris remained dqed for running inside the track. The early pace in the final was steady: Gebremeskel leading at 1000m 2:37.40 and 3000m 7:57.15 and Gebrhiwet at 2000m 5:15.96, but it was not fast enough to drop Farah, whose double double emulated that of Lasse Viren in 1972 and 1976 and was his sixth at a major championship.

10,000 Metres (13th)

1. Mo Farah GBR 27:05.17
2. Paul Tanui KEN 27:05.64
3. Tamirat Tola ETH 27:06.26
4. Yigrem Demelash ETH 27:06.27
5. Galen Rupp USA 27:08.92
6. Joshua Cheptegei UGA 27:10.06
7. Bidan Karoki KEN 27:22.93
8. Zersenay Tadese ERI 27:23.86
9. Nguse Tesfaldet ERI 27:30.71
10. Abraham Cheroben BRN 27:31.86
11. Geoffrey Kamworor KEN 27:31.94
12. Zane Robertson NZL 27:33.67

FARAH BECAME the sixth man to be double Olympic champions at 10,000m and again no one was prepared to cut out a savage pace which might just blunt his finishing speed. The first 5000m took 13:53.11 but the second 13:12.06. From 8000m onwards the pace was relentless as the eventual top five broke clear. The ninth kilometre was run in 2:36.12 and at 9000m (24:36.95) Farah went ahead for the first time. Following a penultimate lap of 61.24 Farah led at the bell but along the back straight Tanui hit the front and was still just ahead entering the final straight. It was a brave attempt, but Farah found another gear to pull away for victory in 27:05.17. The last 400m had taken 55.36, the last kilometre 2:28.22, the final mile around 4:03; this despite Farah tripping over Rupp's heel approaching 4000m and coming close to being trampled before he regained his feet and chased after the leaders.

Marathon *(21st)*

1. Eliud Kipchoge KEN — 2:08:44
2. Feyisa Lilesa ETH — 2:09:55
3. Galen Rupp USA — 2:10:05
4. Ghirmay Ghebreslassie ERI — 2:11:04
5. Alphonce Simbu Felix TAN — 2:11:15
6. Jared Ward USA — 2:11:30
7. Tadesse Abraham SUI — 2:11:42
8. Solomon Mutai UGA — 2:11:49
9. Callum Hawkins GBR — 2:11:52
10. Eric Gillis CAN — 2:12:29
11. Abdi Nageeye NED — 2:13:01
12. Mumin Gala DJI — 2:13:04
13. Lemi Berhanu ETH — 2:13:29
14. Stephen Kiprotich UGA — 2:13:32
15. Paulo Paula BRA — 2:13:56

KIPCHOGE, WORLD champion at 5000m in 2003, was the favourite, and duly won the seventh of his eight marathons. Run at first in rain and throughout in humid conditions, the first half was covered in a steady 1:05:55 before the fastest 5k so far, 15:03 to 30k (1:33:15) at which point the large pack had shrunk to nine. A decisive move came at 32k when Kipchoge, Lilesa, Berhanu and Rupp broke clear. Berhanu dropped back as the next 5k was run in 14:24 and Kipchoge maintained a fast pace with 14:44 to 40k as the other two could not match that and the winner ran the rest of the way in 6:20 compared to 6:53-6:54 for the next three so that his 70 sec was the biggest winning margin since 1972. 140 of 155 runners finished

3000 Metres Steeplechase *(h 15th, F 17th)*

1. Conseslus Kipruto KEN — 8:03.28*
2. Evan Jager USA — 8:04.28
3. Mahiedine Mekhissi-Benabbad FRA — 8:11.52
4. Soufiane El Bakkali MAR — 8:14.35
5. Yoann Kowal FRA — 8:16.75
6. Brimin Kipruto KEN — 8:18.79
7. Hillary Bor USA — 8:22.74
8. Donn Cabral USA — 8:25.81
9. Altobelli da Silva BRA — 8:26.30
10. Matthew Hughes CAN — 8:36.83
11. Yemane Haileselassie ERI-J — 8:40.68
dq (3). Ezekiel Kemboi KEN — (8:08.47)
dq (8). Amor Benyahia TUN — (8:21.67)
dnf. Hamid Ezzine MAR, Jacob Araptany UGA

KENYA WON only one medal for the first time since 1984, but that was clear-cut as Kipruto raced away from Jager with a 60.2 last lap in 36°C heat. Actually Kemboi, four times World and twice Olympic champion finished third, but he was very harshly disqualified after a French protest for his having briefly stepped off the track after a water jump early in the race.

110 Metres Hurdles *(h 15th, sf, F (+0.2) 16th)*

1. Omar McLeod JAM — 13.05
2. Orlando Ortega ESP — 13.17
3. Dmitri Bascou FRA — 13.24
4. Pascal Martinot-Lagarde FRA — 13.29
5. Devon Allen USA — 13.31
6. Johnathan Cabral CAN — 13.40
7. Milan Trajkovic CYP — 13.41
dq. Ronnie Ash USA — (13.45)

FOR THE first time, barring the boycotted 1980 Games, the USA did not provide an Olympic medallist at the 110mh, while there was the first ever Jamaican champion in McLeod, who was fastest in each round – 13.27, 13.15 and 13.05. Silver went to Ortega, allowed to run for Spain after his switch from Cuba only days before the Games. The first two heats were lashed by torrential rain and a special extra race was run two hours later to offer athletes from those a chance to make the semis, Jamaican Deuce Carter taking advantage.

400 Metres Hurdles *(h 15th, sf 16th, F 17th)*

1. Kerron Clement USA — 47.73
2. Boniface Mucheru Tumuti KEN — 47.78
3. Yasmani Copello TUR — 47.92
4. Thomas Barr IRL — 47.97
5. Annsert Whyte JAM — 48.07
6. Rasmus Mägi EST — 48.40
7. Haron Koech KEN — 49.09
dq (fs). Javier Culson PUR — –

PRIOR TO the Games only Clement (48.40) and Copello (48.42) had broken 48.5 in 2016, but the year lists were transformed here, as Whyte won his heat in 48.37 and semi in 48.32, with the other semi winners Clement in 48.26 and Barr 48.39 Irish record. Karsten Warholm smashed the Norwegian record with 48.49 in his heat. In the final Whyte improved further to 48.06 but ahead of him four men broke 48 secs, national records by 2-3-4 as Clement, World champion in 2007 and 2009, at last won Olympic gold having won silver in 2008, and Tumuti improved his best from 48.29 to 47.78 and Copello from 48.42 to 47.92. Reigning World champion Nicholas Bett was disqualified for deliberately knocking down the last hurdle in his heat.

High Jump *(Q 2.31 14th, F 16th)*

1. Derek Drouin CAN — 2.38
2. Mutaz Essa Barshim QAT — 2.36
3. Bohdan Bondarenko UKR — 2.33
4= Robbie Grabarz GBR — 2.33
4= Andrey Protsenko UKR — 2.33
6. Erik Kynard USA — 2.33
7= Kyriakos Ioannou CYP — 2.29
7= Donald Thomas BAH — 2.29
7= Majed El Dein Ghazal SYR — 2.29
10. Tihomir Ivanov BUL — 2.29
11. Trevor Barry BAH — 2.25
12. Dimitrios Hondrokoukis CYP — 2.25
13. Joel Castro PUR — 2.25
14. Jaroslav Bába CZE — 2.20
15. Brandon Starc AUS — 2.20

WORLD CHAMPION Drouin had a modest record through injury in 2016, but came good when it mattered to clear 2.38 with plenty to spare on his first attempt. That height was too much for Barshim, who had a clean card up to 2.36, and for Bondarenko, who passed 2.36 and had two failures at 2.38 and one at 2.40. The qualifying standard had been set at 2.31, but 11 men cleared 2.29 and advanced with the 4 first-time clearers of 2.26.

Pole Vault (Q 5.75m 13th, F 15th)

1.	Thiago Braz da Silva BRA	6.03*
2.	Renaud Lavillenie FRA	5.98
3.	Sam Kendricks USA	5.85
4=	Jan Kudlicka CZE	5.75
4=	Piotr Lisek POL	5.75
6.	Xue Changrui CHN	5.65
7=	Michal Balner CZE	5.50
7=	Konstadínos Filippídis GRE	5.50
7=	Daichi Sawano JPN	5.50
10.	Shawnacy Barber CAN	5.50
11.	Germán Chiaraviglio ARG	5.50
nh.	Pauls Pujats LAT	–

LAVILLENIE CLEARED every height in the final from 5.75 to an Olympic record 5.98 first-time and seemed sure to retain his title, but Braz da Silva, who had set a South American record with his second attempt at 5.93, having passed 5.98, cleared, on another second attempt at close to midnight, 6.03 by a huge margin; Lavillenie's two tries at this height were close failures and he then managed just a half-hearted attempt at 6.08. A great competition – but severely marred by the appalling behaviour of the local fans, thrilled of course by the Brazilian success but behaving like the worst football fans in booing the Frenchman. Nine men cleared 5.70 and three 5.60 in qualifying for the final, former World champions Pawel Wojciechowski and Raphael Holzdeppe managed only 5.45.

Long Jump (Q 8.15m 12th, F 13th)

1.	Jeffrey Henderson USA	8.38/0.2
2.	Luvo Manyonga RSA	8.37/-0.3
3.	Greg Rutherford GBR	8.29/0.3
4.	Jarrion Lawson USA	8.25/-0.5
5.	Wang Jianan CHN	8.17/-0.5
6.	Emiliano Lasa URU	8.10/-0.6
7.	Henry Frayne AUS	8.06/-0.5
8.	Kafétien Gomis FRA	8.05/0.0
9.	Rushwal Samaai RSA	7.97/-0.4
10.	Fabrice Lapierre AUS	7.87/-0.9
11.	Huang Changzhou CHN	7.86/-0.5
12.	Damar Forbes JAM	7.82/-0.8

AFTER JUST two men, Wang 8.24 and Henderson 8.20, managed the automatic qualifying standard of 8.15, the lead changed regularly in the final. Rutherford started with 8.18, only to be passed by Henderson 8.20 and Lawson 8.19, but in the third round he regained the lead with 8.22 before Lawson ended that round with 8.25. In the fourth round Manyonga took over with 8.28 as Rutherford improved to 8.26. Then the exciting Manyonga went out to 8.37 only for the gold to be snatched by Henderson (8.22 at that point) going 1 cm better with his last jump. However, ending the competition Lawson looked to have touched down at over 8.40 only to be amazed as the distance came up as 7.78 – replays confirming that his left-hand touched the sand far behind his feet.

Triple Jump (Q 16.95m 15th, F 16th)

1.	Christian Taylor USA	17.86/0.7
2.	Will Claye USA	17.76/0.4
3.	Dong Bin CHN	17.58/-0.2
4.	Cao Shuo CHN	17.13/-0.2
5.	Jhon Murillo COL	17.09/0.0
6.	Nelson Évora POR	17.03/0.1
7.	Troy Doris GUY	16.90/-0.2
8.	Lázaro Martínez CUB-J	16.68/-0.5
9.	Alberto Álvarez MEX	16.56/0.3
10.	Benjamin Compaoré FRA	16.54/0.6
11.	Xu Xiaolong CHN	16.41/0.0
12.	Karol Hoffmann POL	16.31/0.7

THE THREE medallists were a class apart from the rest. Each went over 17m in qualifying: Taylor 17.24, Dong 17.10, Claye 17.05 and each were over 17.50 in the first round of the final, in order Dong 17.58, Taylor 17.86, a distance that remained the world's best of 2016, and Claye 17.76. None improved, although Taylor had further jumps at 17.77 twice and Claye 17.61 and 17.55, while Dong retired with an ankle injury after two fouls. Cao was the best of the rest with Murillo setting a Colombian record. Immediately the competition ended Claye bounded into the stands and proposed to long-time girl friend Queen Harrison.

Shot (Q 20.65m & F 18th)

1.	Ryan Crouser USA	22.52*
2,	Joe Kovacs USA	21.78
3.	Tomas Walsh NZL	21.36
4.	Frank Elemba CGO	21.20
5.	Darian Romani BRA	21.02
6.	Tomasz Majewski POL	20.72
7.	David Storl GER	20.64
8.	O'Dayne Richards JAM	20.64
9.	Jacko Gill NZL	20.50
10.	Damien Birkinhead AUS	20.45
11.	Stipe Zunic CRO	20.04
nt.	Konrad Bukowiecki POL-J	–

CROUSER'S 21.59 in qualifying was far ahead of the next best, Walsh 21.02, and he dominated with the four best throws of the final. Kovacs took the first round lead with 21.78 from the national record 21.20 by Elemba, but then it was all Crouser with 22.22, 22.26, 21.93, 22.52 (to break the Olympic record of 22.47 by Ulf Timmermann in 1988) and 21.74. The consistent Walsh took bronze with three throws at 21.20 or better, and also setting a national record was Brazilian Romani.

Discus

(Q 65.50m 12th, F 13th)

1.	Christoph Harting GER	68.37
2.	Piotr Malachowski POL	67.55
3.	Daniel Jasinski GER	67.05
4.	Martin Kupper EST	66.58
5.	Gerd Kanter EST	65.10
6.	Lukas Weisshaidinger AUT	64.95
7.	Zoltán Kövágó HUN	64.50
8.	Apostolos Parellis CYP	63.72
9.	Philip Milanov BEL	62.22
10.	Axel Härstedt SWE	62.12
11.	Mason Finley USA	62.05
12.	Andrius Gudzius LTU	60.66

DEFENDING CHAMPION Robert Harting was only 15th in qualifying with 62.21, but his younger brother Christoph came from second place at 66.34 to take the gold in the final round with 68.37 to pass Malachowksi, who had opened the final with 67.32, 67.06 and 67.55. Third and fourth places were also determined in the final round as first Kupper went from 6th (64.47) to 2nd with 66.58 and then Jasinski improved from 66.08 to 67.05. Four men had been over 65m in qualifying: Malachowski 65.89, Weisshaidinger 65.86, C Harting 65.41 and Gudzius 65.18.

Hammer *(Q 76.50m 17th, F 19th)*

1.	Dilshod Nazarov TJK	78.68
2.	Ivan Tikhon BLR	77.79
3.	Wojciech Nowicki POL	77.73
4.	Diego Del Real MEX	76.05
5.	Marcel Lomnicky SVK	75.97
6.	Ashraf Amjad El-Seify QAT	75.46
7.	Krisztián Pars HUN	75.28
8.	David Söderberg FIN	74.61
9.	Sergey Kolomoyets BLR	74.22
10.	Serghei Marghiev MDA	74.14
11.	Yevhen Vynohradov UKR	74.11
12.	Wagner Domingos BRA	72.28

THE BIGGEST shock of the Games came when clear favourite Pavel Fajdek managed only 72.00 for 17th in the qualifying after 29 successive wins from March 2015, when a mere 73.95 made the top 12 and the best throw was 77.64 by Nowicki. Tikhon, who had lost his 2004 silver medal and also served a drugs bans in 2010-12, opened the final with 76.13, to be passed by Nazarov 76.16. Then these two improved to 77.43 and 77.27 in the second round, before Nazarov went on to 78.07 in round 3 and 78.68 in round 5 for Tajikistan's first Olympic gold at any sport. Del Real surprised by going into third place with a third-round 76.05 but was passed for the bronze by Nowicki's last-round 77.73.

Javelin *(Q 83.00m 17th, F 20th)*

1.	Thomas Röhler GER	90.30
2.	Julius Yego KEN	88.24
3.	Keshorn Walcott TTO	85.38
4.	Johannes Vetter GER	85.32
5.	Dmytro Kosynskyy UKR	83.95
6.	Antti Ruuskanen FIN	83.05
7.	Vitezslav Vesely CZE	82.51
8.	Jakub Vadlejch CZE	82.42
9.	Julian Weber GER	81.36
10.	Braian Toledo ARG	79.81
11.	Ryohei Arai JPN	79.47
12.	Petr Frydrych CZE	79.12

DEFENDING CHAMPION Walcott improved his season's best from 86.35 to 88.68 in qualifying with Vetter next best at 85.96. European champion Zigismunds Sirmais was only 14th with 80.65 and former World Champion Tero Pitkämäki 21st with 79.56. Yego, with a season's best of 84.68, threw 88.23 in the first round. This remained his only valid throw as he passed his final two throws due to an ankle injury and he held on to the lead until Röhler, who had opened with 87.40, threw 90.30 for gold in round five. Walcott could not get near his qualifying throw, but his 85.38 in round two was enough for the bronze.

Decathlon *(17th-18th)*

1.	Ashton Eaton USA	8893*
2.	Kevin Mayer FRA	8834
3.	Damian Warner CAN	8666
4.	Kai Kazmirek GER	8580
5.	Larbi Bouraada ALG	8521
6.	Leonel Suárez CUB	8460
7.	Zach Ziemek USA	8392
8.	Thomas Van Der Plaetsen BEL	8332
9.	Kurt Felix GRN	8323
10.	Luiz Aberto de Araújo BRA	8315
11.	Jeremy Taiwo USA	8300
12.	Adam Sebastian Helcelet CZE	8291
13.	Bastien Auzeil FRA	8064
14.	Cedric Dubler AUS	8024
15.	Arthur Abele GER	8013

EATON HAD a somewhat mixed competition, but equalled Roman Sebrle's Olympic record of 8893 points. He was, however, run unexpectedly close by Meyer, who set four individual event pbs including 5.40 pole vault and added 313 to his previous best of 8521, smashing Christian Plaziat's 1990 French record of 8574 with 8834 to rank sixth all-time with the fastest ever non-winning score. Warner, who out-ran Eaton 10.30 to 10.46 at 100m and 13.58 to 13.80 at 110mh, took the bronze medal.

4 x 100 Metres Relay *(h 18th, F 19th)*

1. JAM	37.27	Powell, Blake, Ashmeade, Bolt (ht: Minzie, Powell, Ashmeade, Bailey-Cole)
2. JPN	37.60	Yamagata, Iizuka, Kiryu, Cambridge
3. CAN	37.64	Haynes, Brown, Rodney, De Grasse (ht: 4 Ajomale)
4. CHN	37.90	Tang Xingqiang, Xie Zhenye, Su Bingtian, Zhang Peimeng
5. GBR	37.98	Kilty, Aikines-Aryeetey, Ellington, Gemili (ht: 4 Ujah)

6. BRA	38.41	R de Souza, V dos Santos, de Barros, Vides
dq. USA	(37.62)	Rodgers, Gatlin, Gay, Bromell (ht: 2 C Coleman, 4 Lawson)
dq. TTO	(38.09)	Bledman, Sorrillo, Callender, Thompson

USAIN BOLT anchored the Jamaican team to their and world's fourth fastest ever time and their seventh global 4x100m title in the period 2008-16. There were heat wins from the USA in 37.65 (from Canada' national record 37.82) and Japan national record 37.68 from 37.94 by Jamaica. In the final the brilliantly slick baton passing of the Japanese enabled them to be slightly ahead of Jamaica at the final change with anchor-man Asuka Cambridge (born in Jamaica of a Japanese mother and Jamaican father) being overhauled by Bolt but remaining ahead of the USA's Bromell and improving the Asian record to 37.60. The Americans crossed the line third but they were disqualified because at the first change Justin Gatlin took the baton from Mike Rodgers before the start of the exchange zone. That enabled Canada, anchored by Andre De Grasse to a national record of 37.64, to be upgraded to third place.

4 x 400 Metres Relay *(h 19th, F 20th)*

1. USA	2:57.30	Hall 45.3, McQuay 43.2, Roberts 44.79, Merritt 43.97
2. JAM	2:58.16	Matthews 45.5, Allen 44.0, Dunkley 44.82, Francis 43.78
3. BAH	2:58.49	Russell 45.3, Mathieu 45.1, Gardiner 43.79, Brown 44.20
4. BEL	2:58.52	Watrin 46.0, J Borlée 44.1, D Borlée 44.71, K Borlée 43.67
5. BOT	2:59.06	Makwala 44.8, Sibanda 43.9, Nkobolo 44.94, Maotoanong 45.28
6. CUB	2:59.53	Collazo 45.8, Chacón 44.7, Pellicier 45.33, Lescay 43.60
7. POL	3:00.50	Krawczuk 45.9, Pietrzak 44.9, Krzewina 44.94, Omelko 44.59
8. BRA	3:03.28	P de Oliveira 45.5, Russo 45.4, P dos Santos 46.18, H Souza 46.10

THE USA regained the Olympic 4x400m title but the quality was high with a record six teams breaking 3 minutes in the heats and in the final. Fastest heat times came from Jamaica 2:58.29 and USA 2:58.38 with Trinidad & Tobago disqualified for a lane violation after coming 3rd in 2:58.84 in heat 1 with Belgian winning heat 2 in a national record 2:59.25 when Britain were unfortunately disqualified for a marginal and disputed minor exchange-zone infraction after Martyn Rooney's final leg 43.75 took them to 2:58.88. Isaac Makwala's opening 44.8 leg gave Botswana a lead in the final, but Tony McQuay then took the US into a lead they never yielded with a 43.4 split. Javon Francis with 43.78 took Jamaica from 4th to 2nd on the final leg.

20 Kilometres Walk *(12th)*

1. Wang Zhen CHN	1:19:14
2. Cai Zelin CHN	1:19:26
3. Dane Bird-Smith AUS	1:19:37
4. Caio Bonfim BRA	1:19:42
5. Christopher Linke GER	1:20:00
6. Tom Bosworth GBR	1:20:13
7. Daisuke Matsunaga JPN	1:20:22
8. Matteo Giupponi ITA	1:20:27
9. Manuel Esteban Soto COL	1:20:36
10. Evan Dunfee CAN	1:20:49
11. Miguel Angel López ESP	1:20:58
12. Iñaki Gómez CAN	1:21:12
13. Manish Singh IND	1:21:21
14. Ever Palma MEX	1:21:24
15. Eider Arévalo COL	1:21:36

ALTHOUGH DEFENDING champion Chen Ding was only 39th in 1:23:54, there was a Chinese 1-2. Bosworth led at 10k in 40:10, 5 sec ahead of Matsunaga with a pack at 40:22. Bosworth still led to 13k, but the leaders increased the tempo with second half 2k splits of 7:55, 7:53, 7:56, 7:42 and 7:26 so that Wang covered the second half in 38:52. There were national records from Bonfim and Bosworth.

50 Kilometres Walk *(19th)*

1. Matej Tóth SVK	3:40:58
2. Jared Tallent AUS	3:41:16
3. Hirooki Arai JPN	3:41:24
4. Evan Dunfee CAN	3:41:38
5. Yu Wei CHN	3:43:00
6. Robert Heffernan IRL	3:43:55
7. Håvard Haukenes NOR	3:46:33
8. Yohann Diniz FRA	3:46:43
9. Caio Bonfim BRA	3:47:02
10. Chris Erickson AUS	3:48:40
11. Wang Zhendong CHN	3:48:50
12. Quentin Rew NZL	3:49:32
13. Horacio Nava MEX	3:50:53
14. Takayuki Tanii JPN	3:51:00
15. Adrian Blocki POL	3:51:31

DINIZ HELD a 28 sec lead over Tóth and Tallent at 5k (22:10) and 30 sec at 10k (44:18), the chasing pack numbering nine. He then blasted through the next 5ks in 21:40, 21:43 and 21:50 so that his lead over Tóth stretched to 53 sec at 15k, to 1:23 sec at 20k (1:27:41) and 1:40 at 25k (1:49:31). Diniz began to slow to 30k (2:11:29) and stomach problems caused him to stop at around 32k. He began walking again when Dunfee caught up with him and by 35k Dunfee, who had covered his 5k segment in 21:50, was 8 sec ahead of Diniz (2:34:39 to 2:34:47). At 40k it was Tallent (22:01) in a 4 sec lead over Arai with Tóth and Dunfee another 3 sec back and Diniz a distant seventh. Tallent clocked 21:53 for the penultimate 5k, giving him a 22 sec margin over Tóth with Arai next, but Tóth zipped through the final 5k in 21:49, overtaking the Australian around 2k before the finish to win by 18 sec with Arai another 8 sec behind. Arai was disqualified for impeding Dunfee, who set a North American record, but was later reinstated.

Women

100 Metres (prelim, h 12th, sf & F (0.5) 13th)

1.	Elaine Thompson JAM	10.71
2.	Tori Bowie USA	10.83
3.	Shelly-Ann Fraser-Pryce JAM	10.86
4.	Marie-Josée Ta Lou CIV	10.86
5.	Dafne Schippers NED	10.90
6.	Michelle-Lee Ahye TTO	10.92
7.	English Gardner USA	10.94
8.	Christania Williams JAM	11.80

THOMPSON WAS a brilliant winner in 10.71 with a winning margin of 0.12 and the second fastest time at the event in Olympic history (to FloJo in 1988). She had the second slowest reaction time but was leading by 20m. Bowie took the silver and it was close for bronze with Fraser-Pryce 10.852 to Ta Lou 10.859. For the first time six women bettered 11 secs. Fraser-Pryce was fastest in the heats with 10.96 and all eight finalists beat 11 secs in the semis, the winners being Bowie 10.90, Fraser-Pryce and Thompson 10.88, with second-placers Ahye, Schippers and Gardner also running 10.90.

200 Metres (h 15th, sf 16th, F (-0.1) 17th)

1.	Elaine Thompson JAM	21.78
2.	Dafne Schippers NED	21.88
3.	Tori Bowie USA	22.15
4.	Marie-Josée Ta Lou CIV	22.21
5.	Dina Asher-Smith GBR	22.31
6.	Michelle-Lee Ahye TTO	22.34
7.	Deajah Stevens USA	22.65
8.	Ivet Lalova-Collio BUL	22.69

THOMPSON BECAME the sixth women to complete the Olympic 100m/200m double. After Ta Lou ran the fastest heat time with 22.31, the 1-2 in the first semi was a repeat of the 2015 Worlds as Schippers beat Thompson 21.96 to 22.13, with Bowie 22.13 and Ta Lou 22.28 winning the other semis. In the final, however, Thompson ran a great first 100m and entered the straight 3m clear of Schippers, holding on to win by a metre, with Bowie coming through late for the bronze from Ta Lou, whose 22.21 was an Ivorian record. The great Veronica Campbell-Brown was only third in her heat in 22.97 and drifted into the lane outside her, but did not advance.

400 Metres (h 13th, sf 14th, F 15th)

1.	Shaunae Miller BAH	49.44
2.	Allyson Felix USA	49.51
3.	Shericka Jackson JAM	49.85
4.	Natasha Hastings USA	50.34
5.	Phyllis Francis USA	50.41
6.	Stephenie Ann McPherson JAM	50.97
7.	Olha Zemlyak UKR	51.24
8.	Libania Grenot ITA	51.25

THE FINAL provided one of the moments of the Games as Miler dived across the line as her legs gave out. She had done enough, however, to beat Felix, three lanes inside her by 0.07, with Jackson a clear-cut third. Hastings had taken a early lead with 11.5 at 100m (Miller 11.8) and these two were level at 200m in 22.9 from Felix 23.2. Miller moved clear around the end to reach 300m in 35.3 from Hastings 35.7 and Felix 35.8 only for Felix to wear her down and draw level with 10m to go, before that dramatic ending. Francis ran the fastest heat with 50.58 and four women broke 50 in the semis, Felix beating Miller 49.67 to 49.91 in the third and Jackson beating Hastings 49.83 to 49.90 in the second.

800 Metres (h 17th, sf 18th, F 20th)

1.	Caster Semenya RSA	1:55.28
2.	Francine Niyonsaba BDI	1:56.49
3.	Margaret Wambui KEN	1:56.89
4.	Melissa Bishop CAN	1:57.02
5.	Joanna Józwik POL	1:57.37
6.	Lynsey Sharp GBR	1:57.69
7.	Marina Arzamasova BLR	1:59.10
8.	Kate Grace USA	1:59.57

THERE WAS little doubt that Semenya would win and she duly did, leading through 400m in 57.59, settling behind Wambui who led by 3m at 600m in 1:26.72, and striding clear to easily by some 10m in a South African record 1:55.28. The issue of hyperandrogenism dominated this event as not only Semenya but also the other two medallists, Niyonsaba and Wambui, have been the subject of speculation over their levels of testosterone. Currently, due to a Court of Arbitration for Sport ruling, runners suspected of naturally elevated testosterone levels no longer have to take inhibitor medication (testosterone-suppressants) if they wish to race, a situation the IAAF is challenging. The other finalists were surely at a severe disadvantage and Bishop excelled for 4th in a Canadian record 1:57.02. There were fast times throughout with 16 beating 2 minutes in the heats, headed by Bishop 1:58.38 and Arzamasova 1:58.44, and 14 doing so in the semis, headed by Semenya 1:58.15.

1500 Metres (h 12th, sf 14th, F 16th)

1.	Faith Kipyegon KEN	4:08.92
2.	Genzebe Dibaba ETH	4:10.27
3.	Jennifer Simpson USA	4:10.53
4.	Shannon Rowbury USA	4:11.05
5.	Sifan Hassan NED	4:11.23
6.	Meraf Bahta SWE	4:12.59
7.	Laura Muir GBR	4:12.88
8.	Dawit Seyaum ETH	4:13.14
9.	Besu Sado ETH	4:13.58
10.	Sofia Ennaoui POL	4:14.72
11.	Laura Weightman GBR	4:14.95
12.	Rabab Arrafi MAR	4:15.16

THE WINNING time was the second slowest in Olympic history as the final started excruciatingly slowly with a 76.57 first lap and the second taking 70.54 so that 800m was reached in 2:27.11. G Dibaba led at the point, charged around the third lap in 56.79 and led at the bell led from Kipyegon and Muir in 3:10.2 with Hassan 3m behind. With 200m to go Kipyegon overtook Dibaba and carried on for a convincing victory as Muir was swallowed up and finished seventh. Hassan was third until the very last stages when Simpson (winning the USA's first ever Olympic medal in this event) and Rowbury overtook her. The times for the last 400m and 800m: were extraordinary: Kipyegon 58.6 & 1:57.2, Dibaba 60.1 & 1:58.5, Simpson 59.1 & 1:58.9, Rowbury 59.4 & 1:59.2, Hassan 60.1 & 1:59.2. The fastest time in the heats was 4:05.33 by Seyaum and winners of the semi-finals were Dibaba 4:03.06 and Kipyegon 4:03.95.

5000 Metres (h 7th, F 10th)

1. Vivian Cheruiyot KEN		14:26.17*
2. Hellen Obiri KEN		14:29.77
3. Almaz Ayana ETH		14:33.59
4. Mercy Cherono KEN		14:42.89
5. Senbere Teferi ETH		14:43.75
6. Yasemin Can TUR		14:56.96
7. Karoline Bjerkeli Grøvdal NOR		14:57.53
8. Susan Kuijken NED		15:00.69
9. Eloise Wellings AUS		15:01.59
10. Madeline Hills AUS		15:04.05
11. Shelby Houlihan USA		15:08.89
12. Genevieve LaCaze AUS		15:10.35
13. Eilish McColgan GBR		15:12.09
14. Yeshaneh Ababel ETH		15:18.26
15. Miyuki Uehara JPN		15:34.97

HAVING RUN a brilliant world record in the 10,000m Ayana surely ran unnecessarily fast to win her 5000m heat by 13 sec in 15:04.35, with Cheruiyot easing through in 3rd place 15:17.74. There was a touching example of sportsmanship in this race as at c.3200m Nikki Hamblin tripped and fell, inadvertently bringing down Abbey D'Agostino, who quickly got up but stopped to help Hamblin to her feet. Both completed the race far behind the rest and compassionate officials advanced them to the final but D'Agostino had sustained an ankle injury that caused her to withdraw. Both subsequently received awards from the International Fair Play Committee. Obiri won the other heat in 15:19.38. In the final Ayana led by 25m at 3000m in 8:47.80, but by 4000m in 14:39.75 was being reeled in, and her hard programme told so that she had no response when Cheruiyot and Obiri passed her. Cheruiyot led Obiri by 3m at the bell and swept on to her sixth global title.

10,000 Metres (12th)

1. Almaz Ayana ETH		29:17.45*
2. Vivian Cheruiyot KEN		29:32.53
3. Tirunesh Dibaba ETH		29:42.56
4. Alice Aprot Nawowuna KEN		29:53.51
5. Betsy Saina KEN		30:07.78
6. Molly Huddle USA		30:13.17
7. Yasemin Can TUR		30:26.41
8. Gelete Burka ETH		30:26.66
9. Karoline Bjerkeli Grøvdal NOR		31:14.07
10. Eloise Wellings AUS		31:14.94
11. Emily Infeld USA		31:26.94
12. Sarah Lahti SWE		31:28.43
13. Diane Nukuri BDI		31:28.69
14. Susan Kuijken NED		31:32.43
15. Joanne Pavey GBR		31:33.44

THE WORLD record of 29:31.78 by Wang Junxia in 1993 had looked out of reach, indeed 29:53.80 was the nearest that any woman had come to it, yet Ayana, in just her second race ever at the event, improved the record by an amazing 14.33 secs and Cheruiyot, Tirunesh Dibaba and Aprot Nawowuna went to 3rd, 4th and 5th on the world all-time list. Dibaba had won all her eleven track 10,000m races, including two Olympic and three World titles, prior to 2017 and here she improved her best by 12.1 secs yet was well behind the winner. The first 5000m of the race, which started at 11:10 am, with Nawowuna the leader was covered in 14:46.81, the second half – with Ayana ahead from 5200m – took just 14:30.64! The kilometre splits were 3:01.53, 2:54.26, 2:56.91 (8:52.70) , 2:57.09, 2:57.02, 2:49.93, 2:53.24, 2:55.39, 2:57.53 and 2:54.57 with a last lap of 68.07. Ayana's breakaway lap was 66.67, followed by 67.79, 67.35 and 68.80 – amazing, courageous running. Cheruiyot, twice World champion with a pb of 30:30.44, was a detached second for most of the second half and finished in 29:32.53, a Kenyan record and time that broke Paula Radcliffe's Commonwealth record of 30:01.09.

There were record times for places 1-8 and 18-34, with five under 30 minutes comparing to a previous record of two, 24 under 32 mins comparing with the previous record of 20 (Worlds 2005), and 33 under 33 mins, previous 29 at Stanford 2014. All the first 13 finishers set pbs with 7 national records in all.

Marathon (14th)

1. Jemima Sumgong Jelagat KEN		2:24:04
2. Eunice Jepkirui BRN		2:24:13
3. Mare Dibaba ETH		2:24:30
4. Tirfi Tsegaye ETH		2:24:47
5. Olga Mazuronak BLR		2:24:48
6. Shalane Flanagan USA		2:25:26
7. Desiree Linden USA		2:26:08
8. Rose Chelimo BRN		2:27:36
9. Amy Cragg USA		2:28:25
10. Kim Hye-song PRK		2:28:36
11. Kim Hye-gyong PRK		2:28:36
12. Jelena Prokopcuka LAT		2:29:32
13. Valeria Straneo ITA		2:29:44
14. Kayoko Fukushi JPN		2:29:53
15. Gladys Tejeda PER		2:29:55

HAVING WON at London earlier in the year, Sumgong, with negative splits of 72:57 and 71:07, became the first Kenyan female Olympic marathon champion. In second place Kenyan-born Jepkirui claimed Bahrain's first Olympic medal; she was followed by two Ethiopians. Mazuronak led at halfway in 72:56 and by 30k (1:32:14) the lead pack was down to seven. The first decisive move came at 36k from Jepkirui, who was followed by Dibaba and Sumgong who quickly broke away from the others. Dibaba began to fall back in the 40th kilometre, but with a kilometre to go, Sumgong held a 15m lead that extended to around 50m by the finish. 133 of 156 runners finished. The North Korean Kim twins came in together, holding hands, in 2:28:36 and the Estonian Luik triplets placed 97th, 114th and dnf.

3000 Metres Steeplechase *(h 13th, F 17th)*

1.	Ruth Jebet BRN	8:59.75
2.	Hyvin Jepkemoi KEN	9:07.12
3.	Emma Coburn USA	9:07.63
4.	Beatrice Chepkoech KEN	9:16.05
5.	Sofia Assefa ETH	9:17.15
6.	Gesa Felicitas Krause GER	9:18.41
7.	Madeline Hills AUS	9:20.38
8.	Colleen Quigley USA	9:21.10
9.	Genevieve LaCaze AUS	9:21.21
10.	Lalita Babar IND	9:22.74
11.	Courtney Frerichs USA	9:22.87
12.	Habiba Ghribi TUN	9:28.75
13.	Lydia Rotich KEN	9:29.90
14.	Aisha Praught JAM	9:34.20
15.	Etenesh Diro ETH	9:38.77

THIS WAS another morning final and run in very hot (34°C) weather. It started at a modest pace with a first kilometre in 3:05.93 but then Jebet kicked hard and ran clear of the field with laps of 68.2 and 69.2 for her second kilometre in 2:54.13. She could surely have taken the world record had she pushed for it, but was content to run the final kilometre in 2:59.69 and an Asian record, leaving the WR to be smashed after Rio. Jepkemoi and Chepkoech looked set for silver and gold, but the latter faded and Coburn produced a decisive last lap to the bronze and a North American record. 13 women under 9:30 beats the previous record of 11 at the 2009 Worlds. The heats, headed by Jebet 9:12.62, had been fast with 12 under 9:30 and 18, instead of the scheduled 15 made the final as three runners who fell in heat 3, Diro, Praught and Sara Treacy, were advanced.

100 Metres Hurdles *(h 16th, sf, F (0.0) 17th)*

1.	Brianna Rollins USA	12.48
2.	Nia Ali USA	12.59
3.	Kristi Castlin USA	12.61
4.	Cindy Ofili GBR	12.63
5.	Cindy Roleder GER	12.74
6.	Pedrya Seymour BAH	12.76
7.	Tiffany Porter GBR	12.76
8.	Phylicia George CAN	12.89

EVEN WITHOUT world record holder Keni Harrison, the US achieved a unique clean sweep. Rollins was fastest in each round, 12.54 heat and 12.47 semi before taking the gold medal by a 0.11 winning margin from Ali and Castlin, who had both won their semis, 12.65 and 12.63 respectively. Also in the semi Seymour, who started the season with a pb 13.50, took 0.19 off her Bahamas record with 12.64. Ofili and Porter took 4th and 7th places, the first time that Ofili had beaten her elder sister.

400 Metres Hurdles *(h 15th, sf 16th, F 19th)*

1.	Dalilah Muhammad USA	53.13
2.	Sara Slott Petersen DEN	53.55
3.	Ashley Spencer USA	53.72
4.	Zuzana Hejnová CZE	53.92
5.	Ristanna Tracey JAM	54.15
6.	Leah Nugent JAM	54.45
7.	Janeive Russell JAM	54.56
8.	Eilidh Doyle GBR	54.61

THERE WAS a US winner of this event for the first time since it was introduced to the Olympics in 1984 as Muhammad, who had been easily the fastest in the semis (53.89 to 54.55 by Hejnová and Slott Petersen) won by 0.42 from Petersen, whose 53.55 took 0.44 off her Danish record. Spencer overtook Hejnová after the final hurdle and then three Jamaicans took places 5-7 with Tracey (who had run the fastest heat with 54.88) setting a pb. 17 year-old Sydney McLaughlin, who had been suffering from a cold, was 5th in her semi in 56.22.

High Jump *(Q 1.94 18th, F 20th)*

1.	Ruth Beitia ESP	1.97
2.	Mirela Demireva BUL	1.97
3.	Blanka Vlasic CRO	1.97
4.	Chaunté Lowe USA	1.97
5.	Alessia Trost ITA	1.93
6.	Levern Spencer LCA	1.93
7=	Marie-Laurence Jungfleisch GER	1.93
7=	Sofie Skoog SWE	1.93
9.	Kamila Licwinko POL	1.93
10=	Inika McPherson USA	1.93
10=	Iryna Herashchenko UKR	1.93
10=	Morgan Lake GBR-J	1.93
13=	Airine Palsyte LTU	1.88
13=	Svetlana Radzivil UZB	1.88
13=	Vashti Cunningham USA-J	1.88
16.	Desiree Rossit ITA	1.88
17.	Alyxandra Treasure CAN	1.88

AT THE age of 37, easily the oldest ever winner of the event, Beitia won her first global title, with first attempts at 1.88, 1.93 and 1.97, whereas Demireva had one failure at 1.88, Vlasic cleared each height on her second attempt and Lowe cleared 1.97 on her third try. All failed three times at 2.00. Thiam and Johnson-Thompson cleared 1.98 in the heptathlon high jump. A record 17 women cleared 1.94 in the qualifying round to make the final.

Pole Vault (Q 4.60m 16th, F 19th)

1. Ekateríni Stefanídi	GRE	4.85
2. Sandi Morris	USA	4.85
3. Eliza McCartney	NZL	4.80
4. Alana Boyd	AUS	4.80
5. Holly Bradshaw	GBR	4.70
6. Nicole Büchler	SUI	4.70
7= Yarisley Silva	CUB	4.60
7= Jennifer Suhr	USA	4.60
9. Martina Strutz	GER	4.60
10. Lisa Ryzih	GER	4.50
11. Tina Sutej	SLO	4.50
12. Kelsie Ahbe	CAN	4.50

SEVEN WOMEN qualified for the final by clearing the stipulated 4.60 and were joined by five others on count-back at 4.55, but Fabiana Murer disappointed home fans by failing to clear her opening height of 4.55. An exciting final resulted in a narrow win for Stefanídi over Morris, as both cleared both 4.80 and 4.85 on their second attempts, but Morris also had one failure at 4.70; both failed at 4.90. 19 year-old McCartney tied her NZ record at 4.80 and took the bronze by going over on her first try while Boyd needed two attempts. Both Suhr, who was unwell, and World champion Silva went out at 4.70.

Long Jump (Q 6.75m 16th, F 17th)

1. Tianna Bartoletta	USA	7.17/0.6
2. Brittany Reese	USA	7.15/0.6
3. Ivana Spanovic	SRB	7.08/0.6
4. Malaika Mlhambo	GER	6.95/0.6
5. Ese Brume	NGR	6.81/0.5
6. Ksenija Balta	EST	6.79/-0.2
7. Brooke Stratton	AUS	6.74/0.7
8. Jasmin Sawyers	GBR	6.69/0.5
9. Darya Klishina	RUS	6.63/0.0
10. Sosthene Moguenara	GER	6.61/0.0
11. Lorraine Ugen	GBR	6.58/-0.1
nj. Maryna Bekh	UKR	–

SPANOVIC 6.87 and Mlhambo 6.82 led the qualifiers and these two were the first round leaders with 6.95 and 6.83 respectively. In the second round Bartoletta jumped 6.94 and Reece 6.79, and Bartoletta added 1cm in round three. The decisive round was the fifth. Vigorously chewing gum, Reese swept into the lead with 7.09, followed by a Serbian record 7.08 (7.18 from take-off) by Spanovic. Reese's lead was brief, for, after Mohambo had improved to 6.95, Bartoletta harnessed her great speed to clear 7.17. That remained the best although the top three all exceeded 7m in the final round: 7.05 by Spanovic, 7.15 by Reese (7.26 from take-off with a trailing hand in the sand) and 7.13 from Bartoletta.

Triple Jump (Q 14.40m 13th, F 14th)

1. Caterine Ibargüen	COL	15.17/0.4
2. Yulimar Rojas	VEN	14.98/0.8
3. Olga Rypakova	KAZ	14.74/0.3
4. Keturah Orji	USA	14.71/0.0
5. Hanna Minenko	ISR	14.68/0.5
6. Patricia Mamona	POR	14.65/0.1
7. Kimberly Williams	JAM	14.53/0.4
8. Paraskeví Papahrístou	GRE	14.26/0.4
9. Susana Costa	POR	14.12/0.6
10. Anna Jagaciak Michalska	POL	14.07/0.9
11. Kristin Gierisch	GER	13.96/-0.2
12. Kristiina Mäkelä	FIN	13.95/0.1

IBARGÜEN MOVED up from silver in 2012 to gold here (the first ever for Colombia in athletics) with 15.03 in round 2 and 15.17 (hop 5.48, step 4.57 and jump 5.12) in round 4. Rojas, whose last four jumps were 14.87, 14.98, 14,66 and 14.98, was her closest challenger. Defending champion Rypakova had a solid series, opening with 14.73 and improving with 14.74 in round five and Orji started by adding 18cm to her North American record with 14.71. 16 women had exceeded 14m in qualifying, Orji scraping through with 14.08 and best being 14.52 by Ibargüen.

Shot (Q 18.40m & F 12th)

1. Michelle Carter	USA	20.63
2. Valerie Adams	NZL	20.42
3. Anita Márton	HUN	19.87
4. Gong Lijiao	CHN	19.39
5. Raven Saunders	USA	19.35
6. Christina Schwanitz	GER	19.03
7. Cleopatra Borel	TTO	18.37
8. Alyona Dubitskaya	BLR	18.23
9. Geisa Arcanjo	BRA	18.16
10. Natalia Ducó	CHI	18.07
11. Yelena Abramchuk	BLR	17.37
12. Auriole Dongmo	CMR	16.99

ADAMS LED the qualifiers with 19.74 to the next best by Schwanitz 19.18 and looked set for her third successive Olympic gold as she opened with 19.79 and then a season's best of 20.42. Coming into the final round Carter was second with 19.87 (and two more puts over 19.80) and Martón third over Gong, both with 19.39. Then Márton smashed her best with 19.87 before Carter produced a mighty throw, taking her North American record from 20.24 to 20.63. Just one throw was left and Adams responded well, but 20.39 was short and she had to settle for silver this time, while Carter went one step further than her father and coach Michael, silver medallist in 1984.

Discus (Q 62.00m 15th, F 16th)

1. Sandra Perkovic	CRO	69.21
2. Mélina Robert-Michon	FRA	66.73
3. Denia Caballero	CUB	65.34
4. Dani Samuels	AUS	64.90
5. Su Xinyue	CHN	64.37
6. Nadine Müller	GER	63.13
7. Chen Yang	CHN	63.11
8. Feng Bin	CHN	63.06
9. Julia Fischer	GER	62.67
10. Zinaida Sendriute	LTU	61.89

11. Shanice Craft GER	59.85	
nt. Yaimí Pérez CUB	–	

PERKOVIC HAD two fouls in torrential rain in qualifying before a final effort of 64.81, second best of the day to Su's 65.14, and had only one valid throw in the final. But her third round throw was 69.21 and this gave her a clear win over 37 year-old Robert-Michon, who had taken an early lead with 65.52 and improved her French record to 66.73 in round five. Caballero had also had two fouls in qualifying before 62.94 but had a solid series in the final, topped by 65.34 for bronze.

Hammer (Q 72.00m 12th, F 15th)

1. Anita Wlodarczyk POL	82.29*	
2. Zhang Wenxiu CHN	76.75	
3. Sophie Hitchon GBR	74.54	
4. Betty Heidler GER	73.71	
5. Zalina Marghieva MDA	73.50	
6. Amber Campbell USA	72.74	
7. Hanna Malyshik BLR	71.90	
8. DeAnna Price USA	70.95	
9. Joanna Fiodorow POL	69.87	
10. Rosa Rodríguez VEN	69.26	
11. Alexandra Tavernier FRA	65.18	
nt. Wang Zheng CHN	–	

WLODARCZYK CONFIRMED her status as very clearly the world's best woman hammer thrower. She led the qualifiers with 76.93 from Zhang 73.58, and had a series in the final of 76.35, 80.40, 82.29, x, 81.74, 79.60. Her second round throw was an Olympic record and her third throw added 1.21m to her 2015 world record. Ever-consistent Zhang won her sixth global silver or bronze medal, starting with 75.08 and improving to 76.19 in R3 and 76.75 in R5, and on her final throw Hitchon set her 13th British record and took Britain's first hammer medal since Malcolm Nokes in 1924.

Javelin (Q 63.00m 16th, F 18th)

1. Sara Kolak CRO	66.18
2. Sunette Viljoen RSA	64.92
3. Barbora Spotáková CZE	64.80
4. Maria Andrejczyk POL	64.78
5. Tatyana Kholodovich BLR	64.60
6. Kathryn Mitchell AUS	64.36
7. Lu Huihui CHN	64.04
8. Christina Obergföll GER	62.92
9. Flor Dennis Ruíz COL	61.54
10. Madara Palameika LAT	60.14
11. Linda Stahl GER	59.71
12. Christin Hussong GER	57.70

THE WINNER of this event was a big surprise as Kolak made a superb breakthrough. The 21 year-old Croatian had made extraordinary progress as her best was 57.79 before starting 2016 with 60.24, improving to 62.75 and 63.50 when 3rd in the Europeans. Here she had a couple of 55m throws in qualifying before a national record of 64.30 that she improved to 66.18 in round 4 of the final. Andrejczyk had led the qualifying with a Polish record 67.11 but her best in the final was 64.78 for 4th as Viljoen took silver with her opening 64.92 and Spotáková bronze with a fifth round 64.80 as seven women exceeded 64m.

Heptathlon (12/13th)

1. Nafissatou Thiam BEL	6810
2. Jessica Ennis-Hill GBR	6775
3. Brianne Theisen-Eaton CAN	6653
4. Laura Ikauniece-Admidina LAT	6617
5. Carolin Schäfer GER	6540
6. Katarina Johnson-Thompson GBR	6523
7. Yorgelis Rodríguez CUB	6481
8. Györgyi Zsivoczky-Farkas HUN	6442
9. Jennifer Oeser GER	6401
10. Anouk Vetter NED	6394
11. Antoinette Nana Djimou FRA	6383
12. Barbara Nwaba USA	6309
13. Nadine Broersen NED	6300
14. Claudia Rath GER	6270
15. Evelin Aguilar COL	6263

ENNIS-HILL DEFENDED her title with a solid set of performances, but had to yield by 35 points to an inspired Thiam, who produced pbs in five of the seven events and added 302 points to her two year-old pb with a national record 6810. High spot was her high jump of 1.98, matched by Johnson-Thompson, but the Briton could place only 6th overall after dismal throws. Ennis-Hill led in the first event with 12.84 for 100mh and at the end of the first day with 4057 from Thiam 3985, Akela Jones 3964 and KJT 3957, but Jones had a bad second day to finish 20th with 6173, and Theisen-Eaton moved up from 6th to 3rd as Thiam took a clear lead with brilliant marks of 6.58 long jump and 53.13 javelin, so that even 2:16.03 to Ennis-Hill's 2:09.07 was enough to secure gold. Ikaunice-Admidina moved from 12th to 5th with her 55.93 javelin.

4 x 100 Metres Relay (h 18th, F 19th)

1. USA	41.01	Bartoletta, Felix, Gardner, Bowie (ht: 4 Akinosun)
2. JAM	41.36	C Williams, Thompson, Campbell-Brown, Fraser-Pryce (ht: 1 Facey, 2 Forbes)
3. GBR	41.77	Philip, Henry, Asher-Smith, Neita
4. GER	42.10	Pinto, Mayer, Lückenkemper, Haase
5. TTO	42.12	Hackett, Ahye, Baptiste, St. Fort
6. UKR	42.36	Povh, Pohrebnyak, Ryemyen, Bryzgina
7. CAN	43.15	Jacques, Emmanuel, George, Bingham
8. NGR	43.21	Asumnu, Okagbare, Madu, Osazuwa

THE USA team won in a time bettered only by their 40.82 WR in London 2012. Behind them Jamaica, with Thompson adding a silver to her two golds, and Britain were clear in their medal places. But the US had dropped the baton at the second change between Felix and Gardner in their heat, carrying on to finish in 66.71 but disqualified, the heat winner being Germany 42.18. The Americans lodged an appeal, claiming that the baton was knocked out of Felix's hand because the Brazilian runner had obstructed her (after that Felix attempted to get the baton to Gardner by throwing it!). The referee allowed the USA team a possible reprieve – running solo in the same lane as in the heat, the team would qualify for the final if they bettered the fastest loser time of 42.70 from the other heat won by Jamaica in 41.79, and they did that, in 41.77.

4 x 400 Metres Relay (h 19th, F 20th)

1. USA 3:19.06   Okolo 50.3, Hastings 49.2, Francis 49.82, Felix 49.66
2. JAM 3:20.34   McPherson 50.6, McLaughlin-Whilby 49.6, Jackson 49.47, Williams-Mills 50.52
3. GBR 3:25.88   Doyle 52.5, Onuora 51.4, Diamond 51.15, Ohuruogu 50.72
4. CAN 3:26.43   Muir 52.0, Brown 51.1, Montcalm 52.74, Watson 50.56
5. UKR 3:26.64   Logvynenko 53.3, Bibik 51.5, Melnyk 51.49, Zemlyak 50.30
6. ITA 3:27.05   Chigbolu 52.6, Spacca 51.8, Folorunso 51.68, Grenot 50.88
7. POL 3:27.28   Holub 52.3, Wyciszkiewicz 51.2, Baumgart 52.63, Kielbasinska 51.08
8. AUS 3:27.45   Thornton 52.8, Rubie 51.2, Sargent-Jones 52.86, Mitchell 50.52

THERE WERE impressive heat wins by the USA 3:21.42 (with McCorory fastest on the third leg at 49.68) and Jamaica 3:22.28. Floria Guei anchored the French team in 49.76, but they missed qualifying with their 3:26.18. In the final Okolo gave the USA a lead they would never relinquish and the trio who followed her all broke 50 secs as did the second and third leg Jamaicans. Felix brought the US home some 10m ahead and took her Olympic collection to a women's record six golds and nine in all to tie the record.

20 Kilometres Walk (19th)

1. Liu Hong CHN   1:28:35
2. María Guadalupe González MEX   1:28:37
3. Lu Xiuzhi CHN   1:28:42
4. Antonella Palmisano ITA   1:29:03
5. Qieyang Shenjie CHN   1:20:04
6. Ana Cabecinha POR   1:29:23
7. Érica de Sena BRA   1:29:29
8. Beatriz Pascual ESP   1:30:24
9. Regan Lamble AUS   1:30:28
10. Anezka Drahotová CZE   1:30:43
11. Elisa Rigaudo ITA   1:31:04
12. Inês Henriques POR   1:31:28
13. Emilie Menuet FRA   1:32:04
14. Kimberley García PER   1:32:09
15. Antigóni Drisbióti GRE   1:32:32

LIU HAD twice finished fourth at the Olympics, but won this time – by just two seconds from González as she covered the last 2k lap in 8:11 and making a decisive burst just 40m from the finish. The previous 2ks had been walked in 9:15, 9:13, 8:58, 8:59 and 8:59 to a 10k time of 45:24 with 15 athletes in the lead pack and then 8:47, 8:50, 8:42 and 8:41 as that pack steadily whittled down. 63 of 74 finished (5 dnf, 6 dq).

Best ever times by place

TESTIMONY TO the marvellous competition and generally superb conditions there were the best marks ever recorded for these places:
Men – 200m: 7; **400m:** 1, 4-8; **SP (qual)** 12-14+; **Dec:** 2, 4x100: 3-5, **4x400:** 5-6. **Women – 100m:** 6-7; **10,000m:** 1-8, 18-34; **3000SC:** 3, 11-13, 16, 18; **HJ (qual):** 13-17; **PV:** 4, 5=; (qual): 13-17 (=), 18-23; **Hep:** 7, 10, 11 (=), 16-23; **4x100:** 2-6 (4 was =)

Best ever in preliminary rounds

Heat W 3000SC: 9:12.62 Ruth Jebet
Qual W PV: 4.60 seven women; **HT:** 76.93 Anita Wlodarczyk.

Best ever non-qualifying marks at any Games/ Championships

Men – 200: 20.13 Justin Gatlin; **800:** 1:44.70 Adam Kszczot; **SP:** 20.40 Andrej Gag; **4x100:** GER 38.26; **Women - PV:** 4.55 four women; **HT:** 70.09 Hanna Skydan; 4x100: 42.70 CHN, **4x400:** 3:26.02 GER

European Youth Championships

July 14-17, Tbilisi (Georgia)

Men: 100m: Marvin Schulte GER 10.56, **200m:** John Efoloko GBR 21.15, **400m:** Igor Zubko BLR 47.16, **800m:** George Mils GBR 1:48.82, **1500m:** Jake Heyward GBR 4:00.64, **3000m:** Elzan Bibic SRB 8:09.06, **2000mSt:** Tim Van De Velde 5:53.77, 91.4 cm **110mh:** Dániel Eszes HUN 13.39, **400mh:** Alessandro Sibilio ITA 51.46, **HJ:** Lukas Mihota GER 2.18, **PV:** Emmanouíl Karális GRE 5.40, **LJ:** Panayiótis Mantzouroyiánnis GRE 7.60, **TJ:** Martin Lamou FRA 16.02, **5kg SP:** Odisséfs Mouzenídis GRE 21.51, **1,5kg DT:** Georgios Koniarakis CYP 62.16, **5kg HT:** Myhaylo Havrylyuk UKR 82.26, **700g JT:** Kristaps Jaunpujens LAT 77.01, **Yth Dec:** Manuel Wagner GER 7382, **10,000mW:** Lukasz Niedzielek POL 44:06.49, **Medley R:** ITA 1:52.78. **Women: 100m:** Keshia Kwadwo GER 11.76, **200m:** Marine Mignon FRA 23.35, **400m:** Andrea Miklos ROU 52.70, **800m:** Isabelle Boffey GBR 2:07.19, **1500m/3000m:** Delia Sclabas SUI 4:21.52/9:23.44, **2000mSt:** Anna Mark Helwigh DEN 6:34.52, **76.2 cm 100mh:** Desola Oki ITA 13.30, **400mh:** Viivi Lehikoinen 58.28, **HJ:** Maja Nilsson SWE 1.82, **PV:** Alina Strömberg FIN 4.15, **LJ:** Holly Mills GBR 6.19, **TJ:** Georgina Anitei ROU 13.19, **3kg SP/DT:** Alexandra Emilianov MDA 18.50/58.09, **3kg HT:** Katerina Skypalová CZE 66.58, **500g JT:** Arianne Morais Duarte NOR 60.89, **Yth Hep:** Alina Shukh UKR 6186, **5000mW:** Meryem Bezmek TUR 22:50.22, **Medley R:** FRA 2:08.48

EUROPEAN CHAMPIONSHIPS 2016

Jul 6-10, Amsterdam (Netherlands)

The 23rd edition of the event was the second time it has been held in an Olympic year. It was the most significant athletics to be staged in Amsterdam since the 1928 Olympic Games and the Olympic Stadium, of c.17.000 capacity, was used this time. European Athletics President Sven Arne Hansen described the Championships as being a great success.

There was one championship record – from Ekateríni Stefanídi in the women's pole vault. and while the overall level of performances was not as good as some previous Championships, it was significantly up on the pre-Olympic Europeans of 2012 and many fewer of Europe's best passed up the opportunity of competing. Although Britain was again the chief defaulter, at least they sent a proper team this time, and were at the top of the placing table from Germany and Poland. Six gold medals meant that Poland topped the medal table for the first time ever. With their recruits from all over the world, Turkey won four gold medals and increased their points score from 19 to 93! Home nation the Netherlands made a major advance and Switzerland also had their best ever European Championships with 5 medals and 13 top 8 positions.

Even more than Stefanídi's pole vault, the performance of the meeting was surely the astonishing 42.04 run by the women's 4x100m team from the Netherlands, and that followed the gold medal 100m run of 10.90 by Dafne Schippers and Anouk Vetter's 6626 Dutch record in the heptathlon. First Churandy Martina had thrilled all with his 100m victory, only to lose his 200m 'win' through disqualification. Joining Schippers in winning two gold medals was Yasemin Can of Turkey in the 5000m and 10,000m. The biggest shock was Renaud Lavillenie's no heighting in the pole vault as his opening height, crazy given the conditions, was 5.75m. Sandra Perkovic won her fourth successive European discus title, Mahiedine Mekhissi-Benabbad (3000mSC), David Storl (SP), Ruth Beitia (HJ) and Anita Wlodarcyk (HT) their third, as in all 10 athletes (4 men and 6 women) retained their individual titles from 2014, with second titles going to Martin Rooney (400m), Adam Kszczot (800m), Greg Rutherford (LJ), Schippers (100m), Libania Grenot (400m) and Christina Schwanitz (SP). Polat Kemboi Arikan (10,000m) regained the title he won in 2012 and Piotr Malachowski (DT) won as he had in 2010, while Martina had won at 200m in 2012.

The collapse of European distance running was again emphasised by the fact that gold and silver in the men's 5000m, 10,000m and half marathon and in the women's 5000m, plus the winner at 10,000m were all African-born and there was considerable concern about the number of transferees taking part.

Medals and Points Table

Points: 8 for 1st to 1 for 8th place.

Nation	G	S	B	Total	Points	2014
GBR	5	3	8	16	169.5	196
GER	5	4	7	16	161.25	167
POL	6	5	1	12	147.25	132
FRA	2	5	3	10	105	191.5
NED	4	1	2	7	98	73
TUR	4	5	2	12	93	19
ESP	3	4	1	8	75	86
ITA	2	1	2	5	67	69
UKR	1	-	-	1	52	82
SUI	2	-	3	5	49.5	26
CZE	-	4	-	4	48.5	47.5
BLR	1	2	-	3	45	43
BEL	2	1	-	3	44.5	22
POR	2	1	2	6	43	24
SWE	-	2	2	4	40	34
NOR	1	-	2	3	39	10
BUL	-	2	1	3	35.5	13
GRE	1	-	1	2	34.75	19
HUN	-	2	-	2	26	19
EST	-	-	1	1	20	19
SRB	1	-	1	2	20	23
FIN	-	-	1	1	18.5	29
IRL	-	-	1	1	17	16
CRO	1	-	1	2	14.75	24
DEN	1	-	-	1	14	6
LAT	1	-	-	1	13	12
SLO	-	-	1	1	13	9

More points (medals): LTU (1S) 11.5, AZE (1B) 9, AUT (1B) 8, SVK 8, ISR (1S) 7, ALB (1S) 7, ROU 6, CYP 5.5, MDA 5, BIH 5, ISL 2.

Men

100 Metres *(q 6th, sf & F (0.0) 7th)*

1. Churandy Martina NED		10.07
2. Jak Ali Harvey TUR		10.07
3. Jimmy Vicaut FRA		10.08
4. Bruno Hortelano ESP		10.12
5. James Ellington GBR		10.19
6. Ramil Guliyev TUR		10.23
7. Solomon Bockarie NED		10.25
dq (fs) Richard Kilty GBR		–

AS IN the other sprints a qualifying round was introduced, from which 16 advanced to join eight seeds. Fastest in the semi were Vicaut 10.03, Harvey and Ellington 10.04, but favourite Vicaut disappointed in the final in which Martina beat Harvey by 0.005.

200 Metres (q 7th sf & F (-0.9) 8th)

1. Bruno Hortelano ESP   20.45
2. Ramil Guliyev TUR   20.51
3. Daniel Talbot GBR   20.56
4. Solomon Bockarie NED   20.56
5. Nethaneel Mitchell-Blake GBR 20.60
6. Davide Manenti ITA   20.66
7. Alex Wilson SUI   20.70
dq (1) Churandy Martina NED   (20.37)

AFTER TALBOT 20.37 and Hortelano and Bockarie 20.39 had been fastest in the semis, the favourite Martina finished 0.08 clear of Hortelano in the final with a strong finish from the outside lane. However, he was disqualified for stepping on the line soon after the start.

400 Metres (q 6th, sf 7th, F 8th)

1. Martyn Rooney GBR   45.29
2. Pavel Maslák CZE   45.36
3. Liemarvin Bonevacia NED   45.41
4. Kevin Borlée BEL   45.60
5. Luka Janezic SLO   45.65
6. Rafal Omelko POL   45.67
7. Mame-Ibra Anne FRA   45.75
8. Matteo Galvan ITA   45.80

HAVING A best of only 45.78 in 2016 prior to the event, Rooney was the fastest in the semis in 45.04 from Galvan, who ran an Italian record 45.12, and Omelko 45.14, and then retained his title in poorer weather conditions.

800 Metres (h 7th, sf 8th, F 10th)

1. Adam Kszczot POL   1:45.18
2. Marcin Lewandowski POL   1:45.54
3. Elliot Giles GBR   1:45.54
4. Amel Tuka BIH   1:45.74
5. Pierre-Ambroise Bosse FRA   1:45.79
6. Thijmen Kupers NED   1:46.67
7. Álvaro de Arriba ESP   1:47.58
8. Giordano Benedetti ITA   1:47.64

KSZCZOT RETAINED his title and as in 2014 there was a Polish 1-2 while Giles improved his best from 1:47.21 to 1:45.54. Kupers led through 400m 52.51 and 600m 1:19.12. Fastest in the heats was Kupers 1:46.48 and in the semis Kszczot 1:46.32.

1500 Metres (h 7th, F 8th)

1. Filip Ingebrigtsen NOR   3:46.65
2. David Bustos ESP   3:46.90
3. Henrik Ingebrigtsen NOR   3:47.18
4. Richard Douma NED   3:47.32
5. Florian Carvalho FRA   3:47.32
6. Lee Emanuel GBR   3:47.57
7. Jake Wightman GBR   3:47.68
8. Filip Sasínek CZE   3:47.76

FIVE MEN broke 3:40 in the heats, headed by Wightman 3:39.32, but there was one of those tediously slow starts to the final so that the winning time was the slowest since 1950. Henrik Ingebrigtsen had won in 2012 and come 3rd in 2014, a position he retained here, as his 23 year-old younger brother Filip sped the last lap in 51.5 to take the gold. Wightman faded in the frantic finish after leading into the finishing straight.

5000 Metres (10th)

1. Ilias Fifa ESP   13:40.85
2. Adel Mechaal ESP   13:40.85
3. Robert Ringer GER   13:40.85
4. Henrik Ingebrigtsen NOR   13:40.86
5. Mourad Amdouni FRA   13:40.94
6. Hayle Ibrahimov AZE   13:42.20
7. Florian Orth GER   13:45.40
8. Yemaneberhan Crippa ITA   13:46.30

JUST 0.01 covered the first four, surely the closest mass finish in a championship distance race. The times to a thousandth were 13:40.844, 13:40.847, 13:40.850 and 13:40.85. Ibrahimov, second to Mo Farah in 2014, led most of the way with kilometre splits of 2:51.69, 2:44.54, 2:48.94 and 2:46.78 before the 2:28.90 final kilometre.

10,000 Metres (8th)

1. Polat Kemboi Arikan TUR   28:18.52
2. Ali Kaya TUR   28:21.42
3. Antonio Abadía ESP   28:26.07
4. Dmytro Lashyn UKR   28:27.90
5. Dewi Griffiths GBR   28:28.55
6. Juán Pérez ESP   28:37.42
7. Daniel Mateo ESP   28:43.03
8. Soufiane Bouchikhi BEL   29:03.74

THE TWO former Kenyans running for Turkey were well ahead of the rest of a very moderate field of just 11 runners and Arikan regained the title he won in 2012.

Half Marathon (10th)

1. Tadesse Abraham SUI   62:03
2. Kaan Kigen Özbilen TUR   62:27
3. Daniele Meucci ITA   62:38
4. Marcin Chabowski POL   62:54
5. Abdi Hakin Ulad DEN   63:22
6. Abdi Nageeye NED   63:43
7. Hassan Chahdi FRA   63:43
8. Carles Castillejo ESP   63:52

THE INAUGURAL European men's half marathon champion was Abraham, originally from Eritrea but a Swiss resident since 2004 and he led Switzerland to the team victory.

Half Marathon Cup (up to 5 per team, 3 to score):
1. SUI 3;12:04, 2. ESP 3:12:06, 3. ITA 3:12:41, 4. TUR 3:14:34, 5. SWE 3:14:55, 6. NED 3:15:36, 7. IRL 3:17:18, 8. UKR 3:17:49, 9. GBR 3:18:26, 10. GER 3:18:41, 11. FRA 3:19:57, 12. NOR 3:20:31, 13. POR 3:22:15, 14. AUT 3:22:35, 15. ISR 3:23:53, 16. CZE 3:27:29

3000 Metres Steeplechase (h 6th, F 8th)

1. Mahiedine Mekhissi-Benabbad FRA 8:25.63
2. Aras Kaya TUR   8:29.91
3. Yoann Kowal FRA   8:30.79
4. Sebastián Martos ESP   8:31.93

5. Jamel Chatbi ITA 8:32.43
6. Rob Mullett GBR 8:33.29
7. Kaur Kivistik EST 8:33.75
8. Abdoullah Bamoussa ITA 8:35.45

HAD HE not celebrated too enthusiastically in 2014 by finishing bare-chested and consequently disqualified, Mekhissi-Benabbad would now be a four-time European steeplechase champion. Splits of 2:56.99, 2:47.47 and 2:41.17 show how he won clearly after also being fastest in the heats with 8:31.42 from 8:31.50 by Krystian Zalewski, a non-starter in the final.

110 Metres Hurdles (q 8th, sf & F (0.0) 9th)

1. Dimitri Bascou FRA 13.25
2. Balázs Baji HUN 13.28
3. Wlhem Belocian FRA 13.33
4. Damian Czykier POL 13.40
5. Milan Trajkovic CYP 13.44
6. Aurel Manga FRA 13.47
7. Yidiel Contreras ESP 13.54
dns. Andrew Pozzi GBR –

IN THE preliminary round Trajkovic improved his Cypriot record from 13.55 to 13.39, then the semis were won by Pozzi 13.31, Belocian 13.28 (from Kiss equal HUN record 13.29) and Bascou 13.20. Kiss improved that record in the final behind the favourite Bascou. Pozzi was a last minute withdrawal as a precaution when he felt his calf cramping.

400 Metres Hurdles (h 6th, sf 7th, F 8th)

1. Yasmani Copello TUR 48.98
2. Sergio Fernández ESP 49.06
3. Kariem Hussein SUI 49.10
4. Oskari Mörö FIN 49.24
5. Rhys Williams GBR 49.63
6. Karsten Warholm NOR 49.82
7. Martin Kucera SVK 49.82
dnf. Jack Green GBR –

THERE WERE national records in the semis with 48.42 by Copello, who moved from Cuba to Turkey, and Warholm 48.84, and Copello won a hard-fought final in windy conditions. Fifth placed Williams had been 3-2-1 in the Championships from 2006 to 2012.

High Jump (Q 2.25 9th, F 10th)

1. Gianmarco Tamberi ITA 2.32
2. Robbie Grabarz GBR 2.29
3= Chris Baker GBR 2.29
3= Eike Onnen GER 2.29
5. Tihomir Ivanov BUL 2.24
6. Konstadínos Baniótis GRE 2.24
7= Jaroslav Bába CZE 2.24
7= Dimítrios Hondrokoukis CYP 2.24

TWELVE MEN qualified by clearing 2.25, but only four went higher in the final, when there was a big gap from 2.24 to 2.29. Tamberi was flawless at 2.19, 2.24, 2.29 and 2.32 before trying 2.40 three times.

Pole Vault (Q 5.65m 6th, F 8th)

1. Robert Sobera POL 5.60
2. Jan Kudlicka CZE 5.60
3. Robert Renner SLO 5.50
4= Ben Broeders BEL 5.50
4= Piotr Lisek POL 5.50
6. Mareks Arents LAT 5.50
7= Pawel Wojciechowski POL 5.30
7= Konstadínos Filippídis GRE 5.30
7= Karsten Dilla GER 5.30
7= Ivan Horvat CRO 5.30

NINE MEN made a 15-string final by clearing 5.50 in qualifying and five did so by clearing a mere 5.35, but Lavillenie chose not to start until 5.60. He made that, but in very tricky windy conditions for the final he elected to wait until everyone else had been eliminated and the bar raised to 5.75. But he could not manage that! So Sobera took gold and Kudlicka silver by dint of clearing 5.60 on first and second attempts.

Long Jump (Q 8.00m 6th, F 7th)

1. Greg Rutherford GBR 8.25/0.5
2. Michel Tornéus SWE 8.21w/2.1
3. Ignisious Gaisah NED 7.93/0.0
4. Radek Juska CZE 7.93w/2.1
5. Kristian Bäck FIN 7.91w/2.5
6. Fabian Heinle GER 7.87/1.7
7. Kafétien Gomis FRA 7.84/0.0
8. Konstantin Borichevskiy BLR 7.75/0.0

RUTHERFORD JUMPED a modest 7.93 in qualifying, in which Tornéus 8.19w, Juska 8.11, Heinle 8.11w and Borichevskiy 8.08 went over 8m, but retained his title with a fifth round 8.25 after earlier 8.12 and 8.13. Tornéus had taken a first-round lead with 8.21w.

Triple Jump (Q 16.65m 7th, F 9th)

1. Max Hess GER 17.20/0.5
2. Karol Hoffmann POL 17.16/0.1
3. Julian Reid GBR 16.76/0.5
4. Momchil Karailiev BUL 16.65/0.1
5. Maksim Nesterenko BLR 16.63/0.4
6. Seref Osmanoglou TUR 16.55/-1.4
7. George Tsonov BUL 16.53/0.7
8. Pablo Torrijos ESP 16.34/0.7

HESS PRODUCED a pb 17.20 in round two for his only valid jump in the final, but that earned him the gold four days before his 20th birthday. Hoffmann improved his year's best from 16.67 to 16.93w in qualifying (same as Hess) and after 16.96 in round two improved his 4 year-old pb by 7cm to 17.16 in round 3.

Shot (Q 20.00m 9th, F 10th)

1. David Storl GER 21.31
2. Michal Haratyk POL 21.19
3. Tsanko Arnaudov POR 20.59
4. Konrad Bukowiecki POL-J 20.58
5. Asmir Kolasinac SRB 20.43
6. Andrei Toader ROU-J 20.26

7. Tobias Dahm GER 20.25
8. Borja Vivas ESP 20.16

STORL WON his third title after being given a fight by Haratyk, who led with 20.77 in the first round when Storl fouled. Storl took over with 21.03 in R2, then Haratyk 21.19 in R4 before Storl sealed it with 21.31 in R5. Armaudov's opening 20.59 held on for bronze although 19 year-old Bukowiecki had three throws over 20.50, having thrown 20.,65 in qualifying behind Storl 20.84 with 11 men over 20m.

Discus (Q 64.00m 7th, F 9th)

1. Piotr Malachowski POL 67.06
2. Philip Milanov BEL 65.71
3. Gerd Kanter EST 65.27
4. Christoph Harting GER 65.13
5. Daniel Ståhl SWE 64.77
6. Zoltán Kövágó HUN 64.66
7. Martin Kupper EST 63.55
8. Daniel Jasinski GER 63.35

TOP THROW in qualifying, in which there was a high standard with 12th place going at 63.74 and three men failing to make it although over 63m, was 66.00 by Lois Maikel Martínez, but he managed only 59.27 for last (12th) in the final. There Malachowski started tentatively with 62.73 but took the lead with his second throw of 65.96 and drew further ahead with 66.15 and 67.06, reclaiming the title he won in 2010. Milanov moved into second place with his third round 65.71, overtaking the second round season's best of 65.27 by Gerd Kanter who won his fourth European medal.

Hammer (Q 75.00m 8th, F 10th)

1. Pawel Fajdek POL 80.93
2. Ivan Tikhon BLR 78.84
3. Wojciech Nowicki POL 77.53
4. Mihaíl Anastasákis GRE 75.89
5. Marcel Lomnicky SVK 75.84
6. Sergey Kolomoyets BLR 74.65
7. David Söderberg FIN 74.22
8. Serghei Marghiev MDA 73.21

FAJDEK, THE clear favourite, had two fouls before calmly throwing 78.82 to lead the 12 qualifiers with Tikhon 76.00 and Nowicki 75.85 next best. The order was the same in the final as Fajdek's series was 80.46, 78.85, 79.09, 80.37, 80.93, 79.69. Nowicki had three throws over 77m but was passed by Tikhon (76.60 until then) with 78.84 on his final throw.

Javelin (Q 81.50m 6th, F 7th)

1. Zigismunds Sirmais LAT 86.66
2. Vitezslav Vesely CZE 83.59
3. Antti Ruuskanen FIN 82.44
4. Risto Mätas EST 82.03
5. Thomas Röhler GER 80.78
6. Marcin Krukowski POL 79.49
7. Kim Amb SWE 79.36
8. Kacper Oleszczuk POL 79.34

RUUSKANEN PRODUCED a mighty 88.23 in qualifying with Jakub Vadljech 85.06 and Vesely 84.82 next best, but there were surprise eliminations in Tero Pitkämäki 14th 80.52 and Johannes Vetter 16th 79.98. However, only one man threw further in the final – Sirmais, the 2011 European Junior and 2013 U23 champion, whose pb of 86.66 in the fifth round overhauled Vesely's third round 83.59.

Decathlon (6th-7th)

1. Thomas Van Der Plaetsen BEL 8218
2. Adam Helcelet CZE 8157
3. Mihail Dudas SRB 8153
4. Oleksiy Kasyanov UKR 8072
5. Ashley Bryant GBR 8040
6. Romain Barras FRA 8002
7. Pieter Braun NED 7945
8. Marcus Nilsson SWE 7942

WITH MOST of the top Europeans opting to concentrate on the Olympics, Kasyanov, the 2012 silver medallist, led after the first day with 4234 from Dudas 4199, Jorge Ureña 4152, and Van Der Plaetsen 4146. Urea dropped out of contention with no mark in the discus and Kasyanov had poor throws, but Van Der Plaetsen piled up the points with a 5.40 pole vault and Helcelet set a javelin pb with 67.24.

4 x 100 Metres Relay (h 9th, F 10th)

1. GBR 38.17 Dasaolu, Gemili. Ellington, Ujah
2. FRA 38.38 René, Dutamby, Zeze, Vicaut
3. GER 38.47 Reus, Knipphals, R Schmidt, Jakubczyk (ht: 3 Hering)
4. NED 38.57
5. ITA 38.69 7. SUI 39.11
6. POL 38.69 8. UKR 39.46

THE FAVOURED British team ran 38.12 in their heat (from Germany 38.25) and won the final clearly although Jimmy Vicaut ran a spectacular anchor leg for France.

4 x 400 Metres Relay (h 9th, F 10th)

1. BEL 3:01.10 Watrin 45.8e, J Borlée 44.7e, D Borlée 46.02, K Borlée 44.46
2. POL 3:01.18 Krawczuk 45.8e, Kozlowski 45.1,e Krzewina 45.68, Omelko 44.51
3. GBR 3:01.44 Yousif 45.6e, D Williams 44.8e, J Green 45.64, Hudson-Smith 45.32
4. CZE 3:03.86
5. IRL 3:04.32 7. NED 3:04.52
6. UKR 3:04.45 8. GER 3:05.67

BRITAIN, WHO did not run the 400m champion Martyn Rooney, was fastest in the heats with 3:01.44 and in the final had a 5m lead when Matthew Hudson-Smith took over for the anchor leg. But he stumbled when under pressure some 30m from the finish and brilliant running by his Belgian and Polish opponents took them to gold and silver. Pavel Maslák for the CZE team had the fastest leg in the heats with 44.1 and ran 44.4 in the final.

Women

100 Metres (q 7th, sf & F (-0.2) 8th)

1. Dafne Schippers NED		10.90
2. Ivet Lalova-Collio BUL		11.20
3. Mujinga Kambundji SUI		11.25
4. Asha Philip GBR		11.27
5. Nataliya Pohrebnyak UKR		11.28
6. Tatjana Pinto GER		11.33
7. Floriane Gnafoua FRA		11.36
dnf. Desiree Henry GBR		–

SCHIPPERS WAS a class apart with 10.96 in her semi and 10.90 in far from ideal conditions in the final when she won by 3m, the widest margin since Fanny Blankers-Koen in 1950. Lalova-Collio made it double silver after her 200m the previous day although Henry, after 11.09 in her semi, had looked likely to come second before breaking down halfway through the final.

200 Metres (q & sf 6th, F (-0.4) 7th)

1. Dina Asher-Smith GBR	22.37
2. Ivet Lalova-Collio BUL	22.52
3. Gina Lückenkemper GER	22.74
4. Jamile Samuel NED	22.83
5. Nataliya Pohrebnyak UKR	22.84
6. Jodie Williams GBR	22.96
7. Tessa van Schagen NED	23.03
8. Lisa Mayer GER	23.10

SCHIPPERS DID not contest this event, but Asher-Smith was a convincing champion. Both she and Lalova-Collio had won their semis in 22.57, and in the final the 20 year-old Briton ran a storming bend to win by a metre and a half.

400 Metres (h 6th, sf 7th, F 8th)

1. Libania Grenot ITA	50.73
2. Floria Guei FRA	51.21
3. Anyika Onuora GBR	51.47
4. Christine Ohuruogu GBR	51.55
5. Malgorzata Holub POL	51.89
6. Justyna Swiety POL	51.96
7. Tamara Salaski SRB	52.23
8. Nicki van Leuveren NED	52.76

GRENOT WON her semi in 50.43, her fastest for six years, and went on to dominate the final in 50.73 to retain her title. The other semi-final winners, Guei 51.01 and Onuora 51.84, took the other medals.

800 Metres (h 6th, sf 7th, F 9th)

1. Nataliya Pryshchepa UKR	1:59.70
2. Renelle Lamote FRA	2:00.19
3. Lovisa Lindh SWE	2:00.37
4. Selina Büchel SUI	2:00.47
5. Yusneysi Santiusti ITA	2:00.53
6. Joanna Józwik POL	2:00.57
7. Hedda Hynne NOR	2:00.94
8. Anita Hinriksdótttir ISL	2:02.55

LAMOTE, EUROPE'S fastest this year with 1:58.01, was quickest with a 2:01.60 heat and 1:59.87 semi, and was leading into the straight in the final, but had to settle for silver when Pryshchepa, who had been blocked, produced an astonishing burst of acceleration to win in 1:59.70; she tapped on the shoulders of the front two several times until amazingly they parted and she shot through. Lindh had only made the final as a fastest loser, but snatched the bronze medal in a pb of 2:00.37 on her 25th birthday

1500 Metres (h 8th, F 10th)

1. Angelika Cichocka POL	4:33.00
2. Sifan Hassan NED	4:33.76
3. Ciara Mageean IRL	4:33.78
4. Ingvill Måkestad Bovim NOR	4:34.15
5. Marta Pen POR	4:34.41
6. Maren Kock GER	4:34.54
7. Sofia Ennaoui POL	4:34.84
8. Solange Andreia Pereira ESP	4:34.88

THIS WAS another disgracefully slow race; previously the slowest winning time since the event was introduced in 1969 was 4:18.93. The first two laps in the final were 83.15 and 82.90 before the third was run in 63.47 and Cichocka kicked to victory with 43.48 for the final 300m. The fastest heat was won in 4:09.71 by Amela Terzic (12th and last in the final).

5000 Metres (9th)

1. Yasemin Can TUR	15:18.15
2. Meraf Bahta SWE	15:20.54
3. Stephanie Twell GBR	15:20.70
4. Susan Kuijken NED	15:23.87
5. Laura Whittle GBR	15:24.18
6. Eilish McColgan GBR	15:28.53
7. Louise Carton BEL	15;42.79
8. Gelete Tola GER	15:43.30

AFTER A very slow first kilometre of 3:19.48 Can ran successive splits of 2:57.04, 2:58.14 (3000m 9:14.66), 3:02.04 and 3:01.45 to ensure her distance double. Behind her Bahta and Twell battled for the other medals. 12 runners.

10,000 Metres (6th)

1. Yasemin Can TUR	31:12.86
2. Dulce Félix POR	31:19.03
3. Karoline Bjørkeli Grøvdal NOR	31:23.45
4. Fionnuala McCormack IRL	31:30.74
5. Jo Pavey GBR	31:34.61
6. Veronica Inglese ITA	31:37.43
7. Jessica Andrews GBR	31:38.02
8. Jip Vastenburg NED	32:04.00

YASEMIN CAN (19), the former Vivian Jemutai of Kenya who received Turkish nationality in May 2015 but was cleared to represent her new country only in March 2016, front-ran splendidly, after Pavey had led for 2k, taking her pb from 31:39.58 to a European U23 record of 31:12.86 and led by 80m at one stage.

The medallists and 6th and 7th set pbs. Sara Moreira was second at 5k, but did not finish. 18 runners.

Half Marathon (10th)

1.	Sara Moreira POR	70:19
2.	Veronica Inglese ITA	70:35
3.	Jéssica Augusto POR	70:55
4.	Rasa Drazdauskaite LTU	71:47
5.	Esma Aydemir TUR	71:49
6.	Ouranía Reboúli GRE	71:52
7.	Monica Florea ROU	71:56
8.	Eva Vrabcová-Nyvltová CZE	72:01

MOREIRA WENT away from her rivals at 15k to become the inaugural European women's half marathon champion and led Portugal (1st, 3rd and 12th Félix) to a clear team victory.

Half Marathon Cup (up to 5 per team, 3 to score): 1. POR 3:33:53, 2. ITA 3:36:38, 3. TUR 3:39:59, 4. BLR 3:40:31, 5. ROU 3:40:59, 6. SUI 3:41:21, 7. GBR 3:42:03, 8. LTU 3:43:32, 9. NED 3:43:50, 10. FRA 3:44:23, 11. ESP 3:45:05, 12. FIN 3:45:17, 13. UKR 3:46:50, 14. GER 3:46:50, 15. NOR 3:54:04, 16. SWE 3:54:39

3000 Metres Steeplechase (h 8th, F 10th)

1.	Gesa-Felicitas Krause GER	9:18.85
2.	Luiza Gega ALB	9:28.52
3.	Özlem Kaya TUR	9:35.05
4.	Mariya Shatalova UKR	9:38.17
5.	Fabienne Schlumpf SUI	9:40.01
6.	Anastasiya Puzakova BLR	9:42.91
7.	Michelle Finn IRL	9:43.19
8.	Diana Martín ESP	9:43.65

KRAUSE RAN a pb, just missing the German record in winning very clearly with kilometre splits of 3:09.19, 3:10.00 and 2:59.66. Gega, who had run the fastest heat, in 9:38.87, won Albania's first medal at a major championship and broke the national record.

100 Metres Hurdles (q 6th, sf & F (-0.7) 7th)

1.	Cindy Roleder GER	12.62
2.	Alina Talay BLR	12.68
3.	Tiffany Porter GBR	12.76
4.	Clélia Rard-Reuse SUI	12.96
5.	Anne Zagré BEL	12.97
6.	Elisávet Pesirídou GRE	13.05
7.	Cindy Billaud FRA	13.29
dnf.	Pamela Dutkiewicz GER	–

THE FIRST TWO were Roleder and Talay, silver and bronze medallists from the 2015 Worlds, who had run fastest in the semis, each 12.76, while defending champion Porter won her eighth major championship medal.

400 Metres Hurdles (h 8th, sf 9th, F 10th)

1.	Sara Slott Petersen DEN	55.12
2.	Joanna Linkiewicz POL	55.33
3.	Léa Sprunger SUI	55.41
4.	Ayomide Folorunso ITA	55.50
5.	Yekaterina Belanovich BLR	56.10
6.	Amalie Iuel NOR	56.24
7.	Stine Troest DEN	56.34
8.	Emilia Ankiewicz POL	57.31

SLOTT PETERSEN won as expected although her time was the slowest winning time in European Champs history. She had also been fastest in the semis with 55.59.

High Jump (Q 1.92 6th, F 7th)

1.	Ruth Beitia ESP	1.98
2=	Airine Palsyte LTU	1.96
2=	Mirela Demireva BUL	1.96
4.	Nafassatou Thiam BEL	1.93
5.	Marie-Laurence Jungfleisch GER	1.93
6=	Alessia Trost ITA	1.89
6=	Oksana Okuneva UKR	1.89
6=	Desirée Rossit ITA	1.89

BEITIA HAD just one miss (at 1.93) all the way up to 1.98 before failing at 2.00 and won her third European title. Palsyte and Demireva had clear cards from 1.84, 1.89, 1.93 and 1.96, but could not manage 1.98. The top three and Michaela Hrubá cleared 1.92 in qualifying, being joined by 8 of the 10 women who went over 1.89.

Pole Vault (Q 4.65m 7th, F 9th)

1.	Ekateríni Stefanidi GRE	4.81*
2.	Lisa Ryzih GER	4.70
3.	Angelica Bengtsson SWE	4.65
4.	Nikolia Kiriakopoúlou GRE	4.55
5.	Michaela Meijer SWE	4.55
6.	Femke Pluim NED	4.45
7=	Wilma Murto FIN-J	4.45
7=	Angelica Moser SUI	4.45

STEFANÍDI WAS the only women to enter qualifying at 4.50 when most went through with 4.45 and four with 4.35 and was in superb form in the final, 4.55, 4.65 and 4.70 on her first attempts and then the third time at 4.81 to add 1cm to Yelena Isinbayeva's championship record. Ryzih took just four jumps, clearing 4.55 and 4.760 on second attempts before retiring. with a hamstring problem.

Long Jump (Q 6.60m 6th, F 9th)

1.	Ivana Spanovic SRB	6.94/0.9
2.	Jazmin Sawyers GBR	6.86w/2.8
3.	Malaika Mihambo GER	6.65/2.0
4.	Ksenija Balta EST	6.65/1.4
5.	Karin Melis Mey TUR	6.62/1.1
6.	Khaddi Sagnia SWE	6.59/1.0
7.	Alexandra Wester GER	6.51/0.4
8.	Nadia Akpana Assa NOR	6.51/1.1

SPANOVIC HEADED the qualifiers with 6.90 from Mlhambo 6.76 and improved anther 4cm in round two of the final, There Sawyers produced a lifetime best of 6.86w in round three. Mlhambo beat Balta on a second best of 6.63 to 6.61.

Triple Jump (Q 14.00m 8th, F 10th)

1.	Patricia Mamona POR	14.58/0.8

2. Hanna Minenko ISR 14.51w/2.9
3. Paraskeví Papahrístou GRE 14.47/-1.0
4. Anna Jagaciak Michalska POL 14.40w/3.2
5. Susana Costa POR 14.34/0.0
6. Olga Saladukha UKR 14.23/-0.6
7. Jenny Elbe GER 14.08/1.7
8. Kristin Gierisch GER 14.03/-2.0

THREE-TIMES CHAMPION Saladukha was sixth as Mamona produced a Portuguese record in the final round, having been 4th at that point behind Minenko 14.51w in the third round, her only valid jump of the final. Papahrístou also produced her best at the last, improving from 14.45 to 14.47. Jagaciak Michalska had been best in qualifying with 14.33.

Shot (Q 17.30m 6th, F 7th)

1. Christina Schwanitz GER 20.17
2. Anita Márton HUN 18.72
3. Emel Dereli TUR 18.22
4. Yuliya Leontyuk BLR 18.20
5. Radoslava Mavrodieva BUL 18.10
6. Alyona Dubitskaya BLR 18.03
7. Sara Gambetta GER 17.95
8. Melissa Boekelman NED 17.92

SCHWANITZ WAS far ahead of the rest as she threw 19.02 in qualifying, next best Dereli 17.88, and retained her title with 20.17 in the final.

Discus (Q 58.00m 6th, F 8th)

1. Sandra Perkovic CRO 69.97
2. Julia Fischer GER 65.77
3. Shanice Craft GER 63.89
4. Nadine Müller GER 62.63
5. Mélina Robert-Michon FRA 62.47
6. Nataliya Semenova UKR 62.21
7. Jade Lally GBR 60.29
8. Pauline Pousse FRA 59.62

PERKOVIC TOOK her fourth consecutive European title but encountered a significant challenge from Fischer, who led the qualifiers with 66.20 to the Croatian's 65.25 and led in the final with opening throws of 65.25 and 66.77, before Perkovic, 63.09 at halfway produced 66.03 and 69.97 in rounds 4&5. 15 women achieved the overly easy qualifying standard of 58m.

Hammer (Q 70.00m 6th, F 8th)

1. Anita Wlodarczyk POL 78.14
2. Betty Heidler GER 75.77
3. Hanna Skydan AZE 73.83
4. Sophie Hitchon GBR 71.74
5. Zalina Marghieva MDA 71.73
6. Malwina Kopron POL 70.91
7. Martina Hrasnová SVK 70.62
8. Iryna Novozhylova UKR 70.18

WLODARCZYK WAS best in qualifying with 83.94 from Heidler 71.46, and led throughout the final, improving with every throw: 72.82, 75.73, 77.11, 77.65, 78.12, 78.14 as Heidler, who won the title in 2010 before the Pole's three victories, threw a season's best for the silver, and Skydan had a couple of throws over 73m.

Javelin (Q 58.00m 7th, F 9th)

1. Tatyana Kholodovich BLR 66.34
2. Linda Stahl GER 65.25
3. Sara Kolak CRO 63.50
4. Katharina Molitor GER 63.20
5. Barbora Spotáková CZE 62.66
6. Marina Ratej SLO 60.65
7. Madara Palameika LAT 60.39
8. Asdis Hjálmsdóttir ISL 60.37

KHOLODOVICH MANAGED only 59.37 in the qualifying, led by Spotáková 63.73, but had the two best throws of the final, a BLR record 66.34 in r2 and 65.79 in r4. Stahl, who won in 2019 and been 3rd in 2012 and 2014, took the silver as she improved from 60.80 to 65.25 in the last round to pass Kolak, who had set a Croatian record 63.50 in r2 and Molitor, 63.20 in r2.

Heptathlon (8/9th)

1. Anouk Vetter NED 6626
2. Antoinette Nana Djimou FRA 6458
3. Ivona Dadic AUT 6408
4. Xénia Krizsán HUN 6266
5. Györgyi Zsivoczky-Farkas HUN 6144
6. Katerina Cachová CZE 6051
7. Verena Preiner AUT 6050
8. Sofia Ifantídou GRE 6025

VETTER, WHO set pbs at 100mh, SP and JT, added 81 points to the Dutch record set by Dafne Schippers in 2014 and there was a massive improvement from Dadic who improved her Austrian record from 6196 to 6408 to take silver, 50 points behind Nana Djimou.

4 x 100 Metres Relay (h 9th, F 10th)

1. NED 42.04 Samuel, Schippers, van Schagen, Sedney; (ht: 2 van Hunenstijn)
2. GBR 42.45 Philip, Asher-Smith, B Williams, Neita
3. GER 42.48 Pinto, Mayer, Lückenkemper, Haase
4. UKR 42.87
5. SUI 43.00   7. POL 43.24
6. FRA 43.05   8. ITA 43.57

BRITAIN WERE favourites after winning their heat in 42.59 ahead of a Swiss record-breaking team (42.87), while Germany took the other heat by a wide margin in 42.71. However, the Dutch team – without Dafne Schippers – qualified with 43.34 and in the final, with the 100m champion on the second leg, they ran an inspired race to leave Britain four metres behind in the remarkable time of 42.04, improving their national record by 0.28.

4 x 400 Metres Relay (h 9th, F 10th)

1. GBR 3:25.05 Diamond 51.8e, Onuora 50.7e, Doyle 50.99, Bundy-Davies 51.42
2. FRA 3:25.96 Anacharsis 52.6e, Ntiamoh 51.5e,

3. ITA 3:27.49 Gayot 51.82, Guei 49.92
Chigbolu 52.6e, Spacca 51.6e,
Bazzoni 53.40, Grenot 49.73
4. POL 3:27.60
5. GER 3:27.60 7. NED 3:29.23
6. UKR 3:27.64 8. ROU 3:30.63
EMILY DIAMOND gave Britain a clear lead on the first leg of the final and that was extended by Anyika Onuora and Eilidh Doyle, who did not contest the 400m hurdles, but who ran 51.3 on the opening leg in the heat won by Britain in 3:26.42. There were fast final legs of 49.92 by Floria Guei for France and 49.73 by Libania Grenot, who took Italy from 5th to 3rd.

INTERNATIONAL CHAMPIONSHIPS 2016

IAAF World Indoor Tour Final Standings
(winners granted World Indoor Champs wild card):
Men - 60: 1, Rodgers 27; 2, Collins 17; 3, Safo-Antwi 10; **800:** 1, Kszczot 30; 2=, Kipkoech, Wheating 10; **3000:** 1, Choge 17; 2, Kejelcha 14; 3=, Farah, Gebremeskel, Iguider 10; **PV:** 1, Barber 24; 2=, Kendricks, Lavillenie 10; **TJ:** 1, Craddock 20; 2, Carter 14; 3, Copello 10; **SP:** 1, Nedow 20; 2, Roberts 10; 3=, Gag, Haratyk, Hoffa 7; **Women - 400:** 1, de Witte 15; 2=, Hastings, McPherson 10; **1500:** 1, Embaye 20; 2, Tsegay 14; 3=, G Dibaba, Hassan, Seyaum 10; **60H:** 1, Ali 21; 2, K Harrison 20; 3=, Porter, Rollins 10; **HJ:** 1, Jungfleisch 15; 2, Okuneva 12; 3=, Beitia, Trost, Spencer 10; **LJ:** 1, Ugen 17; 2, Proctor 12; 3=, Balta, DeLoach 10.

27th IAAF World Race Walking Team Championships
May 7-8, Rome (Italy)
Men – 20km (7 May)
1. Wang Zhen CHN 1:19:2
2. Cai Zelin CHN 1:19:34
3. Alvaro Martín ESP 1:19:36
4. Dane Bird-Smith AUS 1:19:38
5. Benjamin Thorne CAN 1:19:55
6. Andrés Chocho ECU 1:20:07
7. Iñaki Gómez CAN 1:20:12
8. Caio Bonfim BRA 1:20:20
9. Ruslan Dmytrenko UKR 1:20:33
10. Christopher Linke GER 1:20:40
11. Mauricio Arteaga ECU 1:21:08
12. Eiki Takahashi JPN 1:21:12
13. Wang Kaihua CHN 1:21:12
14. Nazar Kovalenko UKR 1:21:21
15. Carl Dohmann GER 1:21:26
102 of 122 finished
Teams: 1. CHN 16, 2. CAN 28, 3. ECU 41, 4. GER 45, 5. UKR 55, 6. ESP 55, 7. IND 80, 8. JPN 82, 9. BLR 108, 10. POL 124, 11. BRA 137, 12. AUS 137, 13. COL 154, 14. ITA 160, 15. KOR 168, 16. IRL 186, 17. FRA 201, 18. TUR 207, 19. SVK 208, 20. RSA 225, 21. USA 273.
Men – 50km (8 May)
1. Jared Tallent AUS 3:42:36
2. Ihor Hlavan UKR 3:44:02
3. Marco De Luca ITA 3:44:47
4. Teodorico Caporaso ITA 3:48:29
5. José Ignacio Díaz ESP 3:51:10
6. Ivan Banzeruk UKR 3:51:57
7. Matteo Giupponi ITA 3:52:27
8. José Ignacio Ruiz COL 3:53:53
9. Damian Błocki POL 3:54:26
10. Rolando Saquipay ECU 3:54:32
11. Francisco Arcilla ESP 3:55:06
12. Federico Tontodonati ITA 3:55:17
13. Claudio Villanueva ECU 3:58:56
14. Mikel Odriozola ESP 3:59:58
15. James Rendón COL 4:00:31
drugs dq Alex Schwazer ITA 3:39:00
39 of 65 finished
Teams: 1. ITA 14, 2. UKR 25, 3. ESP 30, 4 ECU 44, 5. COL 47, 6. CHN 78, 7. USA 105 (without correcting for Schwazer dq).
Women – 20km (7 May)
1. María Guadalupe González MEX 1:26:17
2. Qieyang Shenjie CHN 1:26:49
3. Érica de Sena BRA 1:27:18
4. Elisa Rigaudo ITA 1:28:03
5. Lu Xiuzhi CHN 1:28:36
6. Ana Cabecinha POR 1:28:40
7. Yang Jiayu CHN 1:28:56
8. Inês Henriques POR 1:29:00
9. Raquel González ESP 1:29:01
10. Lorena Arenas COL 1:29:31
11. Regan Lamble AUS 1:29:33
12. Kimberly García PER 1:29:38
13. Julia Takacs ESP 1:29:47
14. Beki Smith AUS 1:29:49
15. Tanya Holliday AUS 1:29:56
89 of 104 finished
Teams: 1. CHN 14, 2. AUS 40, 3. COL 58, 4 POR 64, 5. ESP 66, 6. ITA 86, 7. UKR 87, 8. BOL 101, 9. LTU 110, 10. ECU 122, 11. JPN 128, 12. GRE 151, 13. SVK 158, 14. FRA 159, 15. BRA 168, 16. ETH 181, 17. ROU 184, 18. KAZ 193, 19. USA 208 (without correcting for Liu dq)
Prize money: Individual: 1st $30,000, 2nd $15,000, 3rd $10,000, 4th $7000, 5th $5000, 6th $3000, Team: 1st $15,000, 2nd $12,000, 3rd $9,000, 4th $7500, 5th $6000, 6th $3000, Total: $367,500.
Junior Men – 10km (7 May)
1. Zhang Jun CHN 40:23
2. Manuel Bermúdez ESP 40:27
3. Noel Alí Chama MEX 40:29
4. Callum Wilkinson GBR 40:30
5. Andrés Olivas MEX 40:43
6. César Augusto Rodríguez PER 41:08
54 of 57 finished
Teams: 1. MEX 8, 2. PER 13, 3. JPN 17, 4. CHN 17, 5. GBR 23, 6. ESP 23, 7. COL 23, 8. FRA 46, 9. AUS 46, 10. UKR 50, 15 teams scored.

IAAF World Combined Events Challenge

Based on the sum of the best scores achieved in any three of the 13 designated competitions during the year.
Based on the sum of the best scores achieved in any three of the designated competitions during the year.

Men Decathlon
1. Kai Kazmirek GER   25,221   8318 Götzis   8323 Ratingen   8580 OG
2. Jeremy Taiwo USA   24,928   8203 Götzis   8425 USA Ch   8300 OG
3. Adam Sebastian Helcelet CZE 24,498   8050 Götzis   8157 Eur Ch   8291 OG
4. Ashley Bryant GBR   23,811   8056 Götzis   7715 Kladno   8040 Eur Ch
5. Niels Pittomvils BEL   23,652   7665 Firenze   8051 Götzis   7936 Talence
6. Kurt Felix GRN   23,341   7140 P.Am Cup   8323 OG   7878 Talence
7. Martin Roe NOR   23,316   7855 Firenze   7666 Kladno   7795 Eur Ch
8. Lars Rise NOR   23,165   78568 Firenze   7925 Kladno   7372 Talence

Women Heptathlon
1. Carolin Schäfer GER   19,573   6557 Götzis   6476 Ratingen   6540 OG
2. Anouk Vetter NED   19,302   6282 Götzis   6626 Eur Ch   6394 OG
3. Barbara Nwaba USA   19,163   6360 Götzis   6494 USA Ch   6309 OG
4. Yorgelis Rodríguez CUB   19,134   6280 Götzis   6481 OG   6373 Talence
5. Antoinette Nana Djimou FRA   19,021   6458 Eur Ch   6383 OG   6180 Talence
6. Claudia Rath/Salman GER   18,870   6290 Götzis   6270 OG   6310 Talence
7. Györgyi Zsivoczky-Farkas HUN 18,834   6144 Eur Ch   6442 OG   6248 Talence
8. Ivona Dadic AUT   18,759   6196 Götzis   6408 Eur Ch   6155 OG

Prize Money: 1st $30,000, 2nd $20,000, 3rd $15,000, 4th $10,000, 5th $8000, 6th $7000, 7th $6000, 8th $5000.

Best of three scores at qualifying meetings. The women's standard was much higher than the men's as very few of the top men did three decathlons to qualify.

Junior Women – 10km (4 May)
1. Ma Zhenxia 45:25
2. Ma Li CHN 45:25
3. Valeria Ortuño MEX 45:28
4. Noemi Stella ITA 45:55
5. Taika Nummi FIN 46:08
6. Vivian Castillo MEX 46:56

47 of 48 finished

Teams: 1. CHN 3, 2. MEX 9, 3. AUS 21, 4. ITA 24, 5. PER 25, 6. JPN 31, 7. ECU 37, 8. FIN 38, 9. ESP 40, 10. GER 46, 14 scored.

IAAF World Race Walking Challenge

Results of walks at 11 meetings qualified. Walkers needed to compete at three or more of these to qualify and positions were based on the best positions from these races, with a sliding scale of points from three categories. Prize money: 1st $30,000, 2nd $20,000, 3rd $14,000, 4th $9000, 5th $7000, 6th $6000, 7th $4500, 8th $4000, 9th $3000, 10th $2000, 11th $1000, 12th $500.

Final standings: Men: 1. Wang Zhen CHN 36, 2. Jared Tallent AUS 27, 3. Andrés Chocho ECU 26, 4. Lebogang Shange RSA 23, 5. Dane Bird-Smith AUS 21, 6. Pedro Gómez MEX 20, 7. Álvaro Martín ESP 20, 8. Cai Zelin CHN 20, 9. Horacio Nava MEX 18, 10. Julio César Salazar MEX 16. **Women:** 1=. María Guadelupe González MEX & Qieyang Shenjie CHN 34, 3. Eleonora Giorgi ITA 32, 4. Érica de Sena BRA 26, 5. Inês Henriques POR 24, 6. Elisa Rigaudo ITA 21, 7. Mirna Ortíz GUA 19, 8. Ana Cabecinha POR 19, 9. Ángela Castro BOL 12, 10. Viktoria Madarász HUN 12.

IAAF Hammer Throw Challenge

Final standings, top three of the 11 meetings to score. Prize money from $30,000 for 1st to $500 for 12th.

Men: 1. Pawel Fajdek POL 242.89, 2. Dilshod Nazarov TJK 236.37, 3. Wojciech Nowicki POL 232.63, 4. Ashraf Amjad El Seify QAT 229.94, 5. Marcel Lomnicky SVK 229.70, 6. David Söderberg FIN 227.96, 7. Serghei Marghiev MDA 223.87, 8. Marco Lingua ITA 223.21, 9. Krisztián Pars HUN 218.48, 10. Kibwe Johnson USA 215.93.

Women: 1. Anita Wlodarczyk POL 240.44, 2. Sophie Hitchon GBR 218.11, 3. Zalina Marghieva MDA 217.80, 4, Betty Heidler GER 217.52, 5. Amber Campbell USA 215.93, 6. Katerina Safránková CZE 213.14, 7. Hanna Skydan AZE 211.67, 8. Joanna Fiodorow POL 211.36, 9. Kathrin Klaas GER 209.60, 10. Amanda Bingson USA 199.48.

* Championships record throughout this section

Abbott World Marathon Majors 2015–16

Final Standings

Men: 1. Eliud Kipchoge KEN 50, 2= Dickson Chumba KEN, Feyisa Lilisa ETH & Lelisa Desisa ETH 34; 5. Yemane Tsegay ETH 32.

Women: 1. Mary Keitany KEN 41, 2. Mare Dibaba ETH & Helah Kiprop KEN 41 (winner decided by the leaders of the six races), 4= Birhane Dibaba ETH & Tigist Tufa ETH 34.

20th African Championships

June 22-26, Durban (South Africa)

Men:
100m   1. Ben Youssef Meité CIV 9.95w
(2.4)   2. Mosito Lehata LES 10.04

CHAMPIONSHIPS 2016

200m (1.8)	3. Akani Simbine RSA 10.05 1. Wayde van Niekerk RSA 20.02 2. Adama Jammeh GAM 20.45 3. Emmanuel Matadi LBR 20.55	
400	1. Baboloki Thebe BOT-J 44.6 2. Karabo Sibanda BOT-J 45.42 3. Chidi Okezie NGR 45.76	
800m	1. Nijel Amos BOT 1:45.11 2. Jacob Rozani RSA 1:45.38 3. Ryhardt van Rensburg RSA 1:46.15	
1500m	1. Fouad El Kaam MAR 3:39.49 2. Timothy Cheruiyot KEN 3:39.71 3. Vincent Letting KEN 3:40.78	
5000m	1. Douglas Kipserem KEN 13:13.35 2. Elroy Gelant RSA 13:15.13 3. Mangata Ndiwa KEN 13:16.85	
10,000m	1. Stephen Mokoka RSA 28:02.97 2. Wilfred Kimitei KEN 28:03.18 3. Namakoe Nkhasi LES 28:06.33	
3000mSt	1. Chala Beyo ETH 8:21.02 2. Jigisa Tolosa ETH 8:22.79 3. Abraham Kibiwot KEN 8:24.19	
110mh (nwi)	1. Antonio Alkana RSA 13.43* 2. Ty Akins NGR 13.74 3. Mohamed Koussi MAR 13.94	
400mh	1. Boniface Tumuti KEN 49.20 2. Amadou N'Diaye SEN 49.41 3. Haron Koech KEN 49.41	
HJ	1. Mathew Sawe KEN 2.21 2. Keegan Fourie RSA 2.18 3. Fernand Djoumessi CMR 2.15	
PV	1. Hichem Cherabi ALG 5.30 2. Mohamed Romdhana TUN 5.20 3. Jordan Yamoah GHA 5.00	
LJ	1. Rushwal Samaai RSA 8.40w/2.9 2. Luvo Manyonga RSA 8.23w/4.2 3. Ruri Rammokolodi BOT 7.90w/5.5	
TJ	1. Tosin Oke NGR 17.13/1.0 2. Fabrica Zango Hugues BUR 16.81/1.2 3. Khotso Mokoena RSA 16.77/1.7	
SP	1. Jaco Engelbrecht RSA 20.00 2. Frank Elemba CGO 19.89 3. Stephen Mozia NGR 19.84	
DT	1. Russel Tucker RSA 61.44 2. Stephen Mozia NGR 59.16 3. Dewald van Heerden RSA 58.44 drugs dq. (1) Victor Hogan RSA 61.68	
HT	1. Islam Ahmed Taha EGY 68.92 2. Chris Harmse RSA 67.67 3. Tshepang Makhethe RSA 65.54	
JT	1. Phil-Mar van Rensburg RSA 76.04 2. John Ampomah GHA 75.22 3. Alex Kiprotich KEN 74.08	
Dec	1. Friedrich Pretorius RSA 7780 2. Atsu Nyamadi GHA 7501 3. Ali Kamé MAD 6892	
20kW	1. Samuel Gathimba KEN 1:19:24* 2. Hassanine Sbaï TUN 1:20:57 3. Lebogang Shange RSA 1:21:41	
4x100m	1. RSA (Erasmus, van Niekerk, Leotlela, Simbine) 38.84 2. CIV 38.98 3. ZAM 39.77	
4x400m	1. BOT (Sibanda, Thebe, Nkobolo, Maotoanong) 3:02.20	

2. KEN 3:04.25
3. RSA 3:04.73

Women

100m (2.0)	1. Murielle Ahouré CIV 10.99* 2. Carina Horn RSA 11.07 3. Marie Josée Ta Lou CIV 11.15	
200m (1.2)	1. Marie Josée Ta Lou CIV 22.81 2. Alyssa Conley RSA 22.84 3. Gina Bass GAM 22.92	
400m	1. Mupopo Kabange ZAM 51.56 2. Margaret Wambui KEN 52.24 3. Patience George NGR 52.33	
800m	1. Caster Semenya RSA 1:58.20 2. Malika Akkaoui MAR 2:00.24 3. Emily Jerotich KEN 2:00.70	
1500m	1. Caster Semenya RSA 4:01.99* 2. Rabab Arrafi MAR 4:03.95 3. Feyisa Adanech ETH 4:05.22	
5000m	1. Sheila Chepkirui KEN 15:05.45* 2. Margaret Chelimo KEN-J 15:07.56 3. Dera Dida ETH 15:15.26	
10,000m	1. Alice Aprot Nawowuna KEN 30:26.94* 2. Jackline Chepngeno KEN 31:27.73 3. Joyciline Jepkosgei KEN 31:28.28	
3000mSt	1. Norah Tanui KEN 9:25.07* 2. Agnes Chesang KEN 9:27.22 3. Woynshet Ansa ETH 9:39.89	
100mh (1.6)	1. Claudia Heunis RSA 13.35 2. Marthe Yasmine Koala BUR 13.36 3. Maryke Brits RSA 13.47	
400mh	1. Wenda Nel RSA 54.86 2. Maureen Maiyo KEN 56.12 3. Tameka Jameson NGR 57.17	
HJ	1. Lissa Labiche SEY 1.85 2. Doreen Amata NGR 1.82 3. Basant Massad Mohamed EGY 1.79	
PV	1. Sirine Ebondo TUN 4.00 2. Dorra Mahfoudhi TUN 3.80 3. Dinar Nisrine MAR 3.60	
LJ	1. Ese Brume NGR 6.57w/2.8 2. Joëlle Mbumi Nkouindjin CMR 6.39w/2.6 3. Sarah Ngongoa CMR 6.34w/2.7	
TJ	1. Nadia Eke GHA 13.42w/2.8 2. Joëlle Mbumi Nkouindjin CMR 13.37/0.8 3. Patience Ntshingila RSA 13.24/0.8	
SP	1. Auriole Dongmo CMR 17.64 2. Nikki Okwelogu NGR 17.07 3. Chioma Onyekwere NGR 15.71	
DT	1. Nikki Okwelogu NGR 56.75 2. Chinwe Okoro NGR 55.67 3. Chioma Onyekwere NGR 53.91	
HT	1. Amy Sène SEN 68.35 2. Laëtitia Bambara BUR 68.12 3. Sarah Bensaad TUN 62.53	
JT	1. Sunette Viljoen RSA 64.08 2. Jo-Ané van Dyk RSA-J 56.22 3. Pascaline Adanhouegbe BEN 54.88	
Hep	1. Uhunoma Osazuwa NGR 6153 2. Marthe Yasmine Koala BUR 5952 3. Elizabeth Dadzie GHA 5730	
20kW	1. Grace Njue KEN 1:30:43* 2. Yehualye Belete ETH-J 1:31:58 3. Chahineze Nasri TUN 1:34:45	
4x100m	1. RSA (Mamatu, Conley, Thomas, Horn) 43.66	

4x400m
2. GHA 44.05
3. CIV 44.29
1. RSA (Palframan, Griesel, Nel, Semenya) 3:28.49*
2. NGR 3:29.94
3. KEN 3:30.21

Medals
Points: 8 for 1st to 1 for 8th.

	G	S	B
RSA	16	8	9
KEN	8	8	8
NGR	4	6	6
CIV	3	1	2
BOT	3	1	1
GHA	1	3	2
TUN	1	3	2
ETH	1	2	3
MAR	1	2	2
CMR	1	2	2
SEN	1	1	0
EGY	1	0	1
ZAM	1	0	1
ALG	1	0	0
SEY	1	0	0
GAM	0	1	1
LES	0	1	1

1S COD, 1B BEN, LBR, MAD

Asian Junior Championships

June 3-6, Ho Chi Minh (Vietnam)
Men: 100m: Khairul Hafiz Jantan MAS 10.36, **200m:** Yang Chun-Han TPE 20.73, **400m:** Mizuki Obuchi JPN 47.52, **800m:** Amoj Jacob IND 1:51.82, **1500m:** Saroj Ajay Kumar IND 3:57.55, **5000m:** Takato Suzuki JPN 14:16.42, **10,000m:** Sota Watanabe JPN 31:23.93, **3000mSt:** Muhannad Khamis Saifeldin QAT 9:26.79, **110mh** (99cm): Mohd Rizzua Haizad Muhammad MAS 14.00, **400mh:** Yoshiro Watanabe JPN 50.86, **HJ:** Keitaro Fujita JPN 2.16, **PV:** Muntadher Faleh Abdulwahid IRQ 5.25, **LJ:** Zhong Peifeng CHN 7.84/0.2, **TJ:** Sung Jin-syeok KOR 16.19/-0.2, 6kg **SP:** Shin-ichi Yukinaga JPN 18.41, 1.75kg **DT:** Moaaz Mohamed Ibrahim QAT 60.49*, 6kg **HT:** Ashish Jakhar IND 69.00, **JT:** Junya Sado JPN 77.97*, **Dec** (jnr): Yuma Maruyama JPN 6748, **10,000mW:** Zhang Yao CHN 44:33.00, **4x100m:** TPE 39.75, **4x400m:** THA 3:11.59; **Women: 100m:** Liu Qun CHN 11.84, **200m:** Le Tu Chinh VIE 23.94, **400m:** Jisna Mathew IND 53.85, **800m/1500m:** Lili Das IND 2:06.64/4:29.50, **3000m:** Nana Kuraoka JPN 9:31.46, **5000m:** Hana Omori JPN 16:57.39, **3000mSt:** Chika Mukai JPN 10:21.04*, **100mh:** Yu Jiaru CHN 13.79, **400mh:** Haruko Ishizuka JPN 57.91, **HJ:** Chai Yanbo CHN 1.74, **PV:** Chen Qiaoling CHN 4.15, **LJ:** Nguyen Thi Truc Mai VIE 6.34, **TJ:** Kirthana Ramasamy MAS 13.20, **SP:** Nanaka Kori JPN 15.89, **DT:** Yang Huanhuan CHN 51.47, **HT:** Zhao Fan CHN 61.77, **JT:** Su Lingdan CHN 57.32, **Hep:** Du Jiani CHN 5031, **10,000mW:** Wang Wenjing CHN 50:23.89, **4x100m:** THA 45.23, **4x400m:** IND 3:43.57. **Medal winners:** JPN 13G-10S-4B; CHN 11-7-4, IND 7-4-6, MAS 3-3-1, THA & TPE 2-3-4, VIE 2-3-2, QAT 2-2-0, IRQ 1-2-3; 18 nations won medals (10 gold).

75th Balkan Championships

June 25-26, Pitesti (Romania)
Men: 100m/200m: Ramil Guliyev TUR 10.30/20.98, **400m:** Mateo Ruzic CRO 46.31, **800m:** Amel Tuka BIH 1:47.69; **1500m:** Ioan Zaizan ROU 3:42.74, **3000m:** Ramazan Özdemir TUR 8:12.59. **5000m:** Mitko Tsenov BUL 14:29.86, **3000mSt:** Hakan Duvar TUR 8:40.76, **110mh:** Milan Trajkovic CYP 13.73, **400mh:** Rusmir Malkocevic BIH 51.47, **HJ:** Vasilios Konstantinou CYP 2.23, **PV:** Ivan Horvat CRO 5.50, **LJ:** Strahinja Jovancevic SRB 7.92, **TJ:** Levon Aghasyan ARM 16.49, **SP:** Georgi Ivanov BUL 20.62, **DT:** Alin Alexandru Firfirica ROU 60.58, **HT:** Esref Apak TUR 76.45, **JT:** Dejan Mileusnic BIH 77.83, **Dec:** Darko Pesic MNE 78.27, **4x100m/4x400m:** TUR 39.67/3:04.21; **Women: 100m:** Ivet Lalova-Collio BUL 11.57, **200m:** Ekateríni Daláka GRE 24.10, **400m:** Tamara Salaski SRB 52.00, **800m:** Florina Pierdevara ROU 2:04.21, **1500m:** Claudia Bobocea ROU 4:16.94, **3000m:** Roxana Bârca 9:34.62, **5000m:** Teodropra Simovic SRB 16:28.98, **3000mSt:** Ancuta Bobocel ROU 9:46.34, **100mh:** Ivan Loncarek CRO 13.09, **400mh:** Anna Berghii MDA 58.28, **HJ:** Mirela Demireva BUL 1.91, **PV:** Stélla-Iró Ledáki GRE 4.10, **LJ:** Nektaria Panagi CYP 6.49 6.65, **TJ:** Elena Panturoiu ROU 14.33, **SP:** Radoslava Mavrodieva BUL 18.12, **DT:** Hrisoúla Anagnostopoúlou GRE 59.76, **HT:** Zalina Marghieva MDA 73.89, **JT:** Eda Tugsuz TIR 56.47; **Hep:** Beatrice Puiu ROU 5890, **4x100m:** GRE 44.51, **4x400m:** ROU 3:31.26.
Walks *at Florina, Greece 16 April.* **Men 20k:** Adrian Dragomir ROU 1:31:32, **Women 20k:** Panayiota Tsinopoúlou GRE 1:38:29.

15th European Cup Winter Throwing

March 12-13 Arad (Romania)
Men: SP: 1. Andrei Gag ROU 20.68, 2. Tsanko Arnaudov POR 19.85, 3. Sebastiano Bianchetti ITA 19.78; **DT:** 1. Axel Härstedt SWE 62.73, 2. Martin Kupper EST 62.20, 3. Mykyta Nesterenko UKR 62.01; **HT:** 1. Krisztián Pars HUN 75.21, 2. Sergey Kolomoyets BLR 75.17, 3. Marco Lingua ITA 74.51; **JT:** 1. Vladimir Kozlov BLR 79.34, 2. Norbert Bonvecchio ITA 76.66, 3. Zigismunds Sirmais LAT 75.41; B: Jérémy Nicollin FRA 76.77; **Women: SP:** 1. Alena Abramchuk BLR 17.21, 2. Jessica Cérival FRA 17.05, 3. Markéta Cervenková CZE 16.86; **DT:** 1. Mélina Robert-Michon FRA 62.05, 2. Pauline Pousse FRA 58.24, 3. Eliska Stanková CZE 55.55; **HT:** 1. Zalina Marghieva MDA 72.58, 2. Alexandra Tavernier FRA 70.79, 3. Betty Heidler GER 69.83; **JT:** 1. Christin Hussong GER 61.80, 2. Lina Muze LAT 61.26, 3. Asdía Hjalmarsdóttir ISL 59.53.

European Cup 10,000m

June 5, Mersin (Turkey)
Men: 1. Danielle Meucci ITA 28:24.71, 2. Juan Pérez ESP 28:28.93, 3. Jamel Chatbi ITA 28:32.85; Team: 1. ITA 1:25:39.81, 2. ESP 1:27:00.24, 3. UKR 1:27:30.56. **Women:** 1. Esma Aydemir TUR 33:33.38, 2. Rosaria Console ITA 33:44.11, 3. Jenny Nesbitt GBR 33:45.46; Team: 1. GBR 1:42:45.95, 2. TUR 1:42:50.57, 3. ESP 1:42:51.83.

17th Ibero-American Championships

August 1-3, São Paulo (Brazil)
Men: 100m: Stanly del Carmen DOM 10.27, **200m:** Yancarlos Martínez DOM 20.19, **400m:** Yoandys Lescay CUB 45.36, **800m:** Lutimar Paes 1:45.42, **1500m/3000m:** Iván López CHI 3:38.64/7:52.53, **5000m/3000mSt:** Altobeli da Silva 13:53.48/8:33.72, **110mh:** Javier McFarlane PER 13.55, **400mh:** Andrés Silva URU 49.48, **HJ:** Eure Yáñez VEN 2.26, **PV:** Germán Chiaraviglio ARG 5.60, **LJ:** Emiliano Lasa URU 8.01, **TJ:** Mateus de Sá BRA 16.40, **SP:** Darlan Romani BRA 19.67, **DT:** Ronald Julião BRA 59.56, **HT:** Wágner Domingos BRA 72.18, **JT:** Arley Ibargüen COL 80.28, **Dec:** Román Gastaldi ARG 7634, **20,000mW:** Caio Bonfim BRA 1:26:40.7, **4x100m:** DOM 38.52; **4x400m:** COL 3:01.88. **Women: 100m:** Rosângela Santos BRA 11.24, **200m:** Nercely Soto VEN 22.95, **400m:** Jaílma de Lima BRA 51.99, **800m:** Rosibel García COL 2:07.06, **1500m:** Muriel Coneo COL 4:09.35, **3000m:** Juliana dos Santos BRA 9:03.11, **5000m:** Sara Moreira POR 15:40.33, **3000mSt:** Belén Casetta ARG 9:42.93, **100mh:** Fabiana Moraes BRA 12.91, **400mh:** Deborah Rodríguez URU 57.22, **HJ:** Valdileia Martins BRA 1.84 (g, Chaunté Lowe USA 1.96), **PV:** Fabiana Murer BRA 4.60, **LJ:** Eliane Martins 6.52, **TJ:** Keila Costa BRA 14.01, **SP:** Ahymara Espinoza VEN 18.19, **DT:** Karen Gallardo CHI 58.84 (g, Stephanie Brown Trafton USA 61.22), **HT:** Jenny Dahlgren ARG 65.97, **JT:** Flor Dennis Ruiz COL 62.15, **Hep:** Alysbeth Félix PUR 5910, **10,000mW:** Érica de Sena BRA 45:01.32, **4x100m:** PUR 43.55, **4x400m:** BRA 3:32.30. **Medal table:** BRA 18G-17S-21B, COL 5-4-3, ARG 4-4-2, DOM 3-2-0, URU 3-1-2, CHI 3-2-2, VEN 3-0-3, PUR 2-2-2, POR 1-1-1, PER 1-0-2, CUB 1-0-1, ESP 0-7-3, ECU 0-2-1, CRC, PAN 0-1-9, PAR 0-0-1.

NACAC (U23) Championships

July 15-17, San Salvador (El Salvador)
Men: 100m: Kendal Williams USA 10.23, **200m:** Reynier Mena CUB 20.41, **400m:** Nathon Allen JAM 45.39, **800m:** Isaiah Harris USA 1:47.52, **1500m:** Henry Wynne USA 3:51.81, **5000m:** Jayrick Corona USA 15:18.26, **10,000m:** Erik Peterson USA 30:28.74, **3000mSt:** Antoine Thibeault CAN 8:55.96, **110mh:** Will Barnes USA 13.53, **400mh:** Khallifah Rosser USA 49.25, **HJ:** Avion James USA 2.22, **PV:** Devin King USA 5.10, **LJ:** Ifeanyi Otuonye TKS 7.88, **TJ:** Eric Sloan USA 16.15, **SP:** Braheme Days USA 19.36, **DT:** Brian Williams USA 58.00, **HT:** Diego del Real MEX 74.55*, **JT:** Curtis Thompson USA 9.28, **Dec:** Rostam Turner CAN 7601, **20,000mW:** José Alejandro Barrondo GUA 1:34:32.01, **4x100m/4x400m:** USA 38.63/3:00.89*. **Women: 100m:** Sashalee Forbes JAM 11.51, **200m:** Kali Davis-White JAM 22.66w, **400m:** Chris-Ann Gordon JAM 51.02*, **800m:** Lisneidy Veitia CUB 2:02.02*, **1500m:** Jenna Westaway CAN 4:16.03, **5000m:** Lauren LaRocco USA 16:57.27, **10,000m:** Chelsea Blaase USA 35:30.87, **3000mSt:** Regan Yee CAN 10:38.79, **100mh:** Jasmine Camacho-Quinn PUR 12.78*, **400mh:** Kiah Seymour USA 56.19, **HJ:** Akela Jones BAR 1.91*, **PV:** Megan Clark USA 4.40*, **LJ:** Quanesha Burks USA 6.74*, **TJ:** Dannielle Gibson 13.54, **SP:** Raven Saunders USA 18.49*, **DT:** Shelbi Vaughan USA 57.20, **HT:** Becky Famurewa USA 61.03, **JT:** Yulenmis Aguilar CUB 57.09*, **Hep:** Taliyah Brooks USA 5609, **10,000mW:** Yesenia Miranda ESA 49:24.70, **4x100m/4x400m:** USA 42.93*/3:28.45. **Medal table leaders:** USA 25G-26S-11B; JAM 4-4-1, CAN 4-2-9, 15 nations won medals

Oceania Walks Championships.

February 21, Adelaide (Australia)
Men: 20kW: Dane Bird-Smith AUS 1:20:04; **Women:** 20kW: Rachel Tallent AUS 1:31:33.

Pan-American Combined Events Cup

June 17-18, Ottawa (Canada)
Men Dec: 1. Scott Filip USA 7726; 2, James Turner 7565; 3, Michael Morrison USA 7422. **Women Hep:** 1. Quintunya Chapman USA 6035 (w), 2. Alison Reaser USA 5988 (w), 3. Jessica Zelinka 5855 (w).

Championships of the Small States of Europe

June 11, Marsa (Malta)
Men: 100m/200m: Ari Bragi Karason ISL 10.66/21.56, **400m:** Alexandru Babian 47.62, **800m:** Musa Hajdari KOS 1:48.43, **3000m:** Amine Khadiri CYP 8:18.92, **110mh:** Rahib Mammadov AZE 15.01, **HJ:** Vasilios Constantinou CYP 2.16, **PV:** Nikandros Stylianou CYP 5.15, **LJ:** Bachana Khorava GEO 8.02, **SP:** Bob Bertemes LUX 19.99, **DT:** Gudni Valur Gudnason ISL 60.05, **Sprint Medley:** MDA 1:55.50. **Women:** 100m: Alina Cravcenko MDA 12.15w, **200m:** Hrafnhild Eir Hermódsdóttir ISL 24.56, **400m:** Ana Stefanía Gudmindsdóttir ISL 54.02, **800m:** Aníta Hinriksdóttir ISL 2:01.71, **3000m:** Martine Mellina LUX 10:09.56, **100mh:** Natalia Christofi CYP 14.07, **HJ:** Valentina Liashenko GEO 1.90, **LJ:** Hafdís Sigurdardóttir ISL 6.32w, **DT:** Natalia Stratulat MDA 56.01, **HT:** Hanna Skydan AZE 71.41, **Sprint Medley:** ISL 2:08.44. **Combined Points:** 1. MDA 125.5, 2. CYP & ISL 109.5, 4. MLT 70, 5. LUX 54.4, 6. AZE 51.5, 7. ARM 42, 8, BIH 34, 9. MNE 28, 10. GEO 25; 18 nations scored.

South American Championships

Half Marathon
May 29, Asuncion (Paraguay)
Men: Ferdinand Pacheco PER 64:29; **Women:** Joziane da Silva Cardoso BRA 74:38
50kW
February 28, Rio de Janeiro (Brazil)
Claudio Villanueva ECU 4:23:37.

South American U23 Championships

September 23-25, Lima (Peru)
Men: 100m/200m: Rodrigo do Nascimento BRA 10.21*/21.20, **400m:** Alexander Russo BRA 47.07, **800m:** Ramiro Paris ARG 1:48.31, **1500m:** Rafael Loza

ECU 3:56.37; **5000m:** Douglas do Nascimento BRA 14:27.78, **10,000m:** Jordan Ccope PER 30:01.28, **3000mSt:** Daniel do Nascimento BRA 9:05.40, **110mh:** Gabriel Constantino BRA 14.10, **400mh:** Márcio Teles BRA 52.31, **HJ:** Fernando Ferreira BRA 2.20, **PV:** José Rodolfo Pacho ECU 5.10, **LJ:** Higor Alves BRA 7.80, **TJ:** Álvaro Cortez CHI 15.91, **SP:** Willian Dourado BRA 18.99, **DT:** Mauricio Ortega COL 57.60, **HT:** Humberto Mansilla CHI 72.67*, **JT:** Francisco Javier Muse CHI 71.84, **Dec:** Andy Preciado ECU 7162, **20,000mW:** Iván Garrido COL 1:24:41.22; **4x100m/4x400m:** BRA 39.86/3:13.73. **Women: 100m:** Evelin Rivera COL 11.74, **200m:** Vitória Rosa BRA 23.95, **400m:** Astrid Balanta COL 54.45, **800m/1500m:** María Pía Fernández URU 2:08.83/4:24.51, **5000m:** Saida Meneses PER 16:34.66*, **10,000m:** Jéssica Paguay ECU 35:10.63*, **3000mSt:** Belén Casetta ARG 10:05.30*, **100mh:** Diana Bazalar PER 13.52, **400mh:** Melissa González COL 59.26, **HJ:** Lorena Aires URU 1.76, **PV:** Juliana Campos BRA 3.90, **LJ/TJ:** Claudine de Jesus BRA 5.95/13.12, **SP/DT:** Izabela da Silva BRA 16.25/53.94, **HT:** Mayra Gaviria COL 61.55, **JT:** Edivania Araújo BRA 55.94, **Hep:** Fiorella Chiappe ARG 5142, **20,000mW:** Sara Pulido COL 1:39:14.27, **4x100m:** ECU 45.13, **4x400m:** COL 3:42.19.
Medals-Points: BRA 19G-7S-7B-307; ECU 5-6-9-212; COL 8-11-2-178; PER 3-7-9-163; CHI 3-5-7-149; ARG 3-4-4-118; PAR 0-4-0-47; URU 3-0-0-35; BOL 0-1-4-30; 10, PAN 0-0-1-4.

12th South Asian Games

February 9-12, Guwahati (India)
Men: 100m: W.K.Himasha Eashan SRI 10.28, **200m:** Vinoj Suranjaya De Silva SRI 21.00, **400m:** Arokia Rajiv IND 46.23, **800m:** Indunil Herath SRI 1:51.46, **1500m:** Ajay Kumar Saroj IND 3:53.46, **5000m** Man Singh IND 14:02.04*, **10,000m:** Thonakal Gopi IND 29:10.53*, **Mar:** Nitender Singh Rawat IND 2:15:18, **110mh:** Jayakumar Surendhar IND 14.13, **400mh:** Ayyasamy Dharun IND 50.54, **HJ:** Manjula Kumara Wijesekara SRI 2.17, **PV:** M.H.Ishara Sandaruwan SRI 4.90*, **LJ:** Ankit Sharma IND 7.89*, **TJ:** Renjith Maheswary IND 16.45*, **SP:** Om Prakash Singh IND 18.45, **DT:** Arjun Kumar IND 57.21, **HT:** Neeraj Kumar IND 66.14, **JT:** Neeraj Chopra IND 83.23*, **4x100m:** SRI 39.96, **4x400m:** IND 3:06.74. **Women: 100m:** R.M.Rumeshika Kumari Rathnayake SRI 11.71, **200m:** Srabani Nanda IND 23.91, **400m:** Machettira Poovamma IND 54.1, **800m:** W.K.L.A.Nimali SRI 2:09.40, **1500m:** P. Unnikrishnan Chitra IND 4:25.59, **5000m/10,000m:** Surya Loganathan IND 15:45.75*/32:39.86*, **Mar:** Kavita Tungar-Raut IND 2:38:38, **100mh:** Govindaraj Gayathri IND 13.83, **400mh:** Jauna Murmu IND 57.69, **HJ:** Sahana Kumari IND 1.78, **LJ/TJ:** Mayokha Johny IND 6.43*/13.85*, **SP:** Manpreet Kaur IND 17.94*, **JT:** Suman Devi IND 59.45*, **4x100m:** SRI 45.50, **4x400m:** IND 3:35.44.
Medals: IND 28G-22S-8B, SRI 9-11-7, PAK 0-3-8, BAN 0-0-2, NEP 0-0-1.

IAU 100Km World Championships

At Los Alcazares (Spain 27 November.
Men: 1. Hideaki Yamauchi JPN 6:18:22, 2. Bongmusa Mthembu RSA 6:24:05, 3. Patrick Reagan USA 6:35:42, 4. Tomasz Walerowicz POL 6:37:23, 5. Geoffrey Burns USA 6:38:43, 6. José Antonio Requejo ESP 6:41.08, 7. Giorgio Calcaterra ITA 6:41:16, 8. Kaitaro Toike JPN 6:42:30, Team: 1. RSA 19:51:40, 2. JPN 19:55:46, 3. USA 20:03:04, 4. NOR 20:39:06, 5. AUS 20:55:44,, 13 nations scored. **Women** – 1. Kirstin Bull AUS 7:34:35, 2. Nikolina Sustic CRO 7:36:10, 3. Joasia Zakrzewski GBR 7:41:48, 4. Karin Freitag AUT 7:45:58, 5. Mikiko Ota JPN 7:47:38, 6. Aiko Kanematsu JPN 7:47:41, 7. Chiyuki Mochizuki JPN 7:47:55, 8. Mai Fujisawa JPN 7:48:27. Team: 1. JPN 23:23:14, 2. CRO 23:48:19, 3. USA 24:05:33, 4. CAN 24:39:53, 5. FRA 24:46:58; 6 teams scored.

IAU 24 Hour European Championships

October 22-23, Albi (France)
Men: 1. Dan Lawson GBR 261.843k, 2. Ondrej Velicka CZE 258.661, 3. Stéphane Ruel FRA 257.296; Team: 1. FRA 763.291, 2. GBR 743.269, 3. GER 720.006. **Women:** 1. Maria Jannson SWE 250.647k, 2. Patrycja Bereznowska POL 241.633, 3. Agata Matejczuk POL 232.285; Team: 1. POL 701.429, 2. SWE 691.656, 3. FRA 655.332.

15th European Mountain Running Championships

July 2, Arco (Italy)
Men 12.31k: 1. Martin DeMatteis ITA (third win) 53:33, 2, Bernard DeMatteis ITA 53:34, 3, Ahmet Arslam TUR 54:09; Team: 1. ITA 8, 2. CZE 29, 3. GBR 33; **Junior Men** 8.54k: Ferhat Bozkurt TUR 39:00; Team: TUR 10; **Women** 8.54k: 1. Emily Collinge GBR 43:41, 2. Alice Gaggi ITA 44:08, 3. Sara Bottarelli ITA 44:24; Team: 1. ITA 11, 2. GBR 21, 3. CZE 31; **Junior Women** 4.03k: Michaela Stránská CZE 18:03; Team: GBR 18.

World Mountain Running Championships

June 18, Podbrodo (Slovenia)
Marathon distance and 2800m of climbing on a rugged trail course. **Men:** 1. Alessandro Rambaldini ITA 3:44:52, 2. Marco De Gaspari ITA 3:46:12, 3. Mitja Kosovelj SLO 3:46:33; Team: 1. ITA 11:32:19, 2. GBR 11:37:43, 3. GER 11:56:57. **Women:** 1. Annie Conway GBR 4:29:01, 2. Antonella Confortola ITA 4:29:58, 3. Lucija Krkoc SLO 4:30:43; Team: 1. ITA 13:48.18, 2. SLO 13:59:51, 3. GBR 14:04:02.

September 11, Sapareva Banya (Bulgaria)
Men 12.5k (1390m height difference): 1. Joseph Gray USA 1:02:13, 2. Israel Morales MEX 1:03:42, 3. Ahmet Arslan TUR 1:04:49; Team: 1. USA 32, 2. ITA 33, 3. MEX 69; **Junior Men** 7.3k. 700m HD: Joel Ayeko UGA 33:53; Team: UGA 6; **Women** 7.3k. 700m HD: 1. Andrea Mayr AUT (record 6th win) 39:04, 2. Valentina Belotti ITA 40:47, 3. Christel Dewalle FRA 41:05; Team: 1. ITA 17, 2. CZE 32, 3. USA 36; **Junior Women** 3.5k, 500m HD: Sarah Kistner GER 22:48; Team: CZE 19.

IAAF DIAMOND LEAGUE

THE IAAF'S successor to the Golden League, the expanded and more globally widespread Diamond League, was launched in 2010 with 14 meetings spread across Asia, Europe, the Middle East and the USA. The total prize money was increased from $6.63 million (with a $50,000 bonus for any new world record) in 2010 to $8 million from 2011. Winners of each Race receive a Diamond Trophy (4 carats of diamonds) and a $40,000 cash prize.

Winners 2016

D Doha May 6, **Sh** Shanghai May 14, **Ra** Rabat May 22, **E** Eugene May 27-28, **Ro** Rome Jun 2, **Bi** Birmingham Jun 5, **O** Oslo Jun 9, **St** Stockholm Jun 16, **M** Monaco Jul 15, **Lo** London Jul 22-23, **L** Lausanne Aug 25, **P** Paris Saint-Denis Aug 27; Finals: **Z** Zürich Sep 3, **Br** Brussels Sep 11

Men:
100m: Justin Gatlin Sh- 9.94, E- 9.88w; Asafa Powell Z- 9.94; Andre De Grasse O 10.07, Jak Ali Harvey St 10.18, Jimmy Vicaut Lo 10.02, Ben Youssef Meité P 9.96
200m: Alonso Edward Ra- 20.07w, M- 20.10; Ameer Webb D- 19.85, Ro- 20.04; Andre De Grasse Bi- 20.18, Churandy Martina L 19.81, Julian Forte Br- 19.97
400m: LaShawn Merritt D- 44.41, Ra- 44.66, L- 44.50, Z- 44.64; Wayde van Niekerk Ro- 44.19, M- 44.12; Kirani James Bi- 44.23
800m: Ferguson Rotich Cheruiyot Sh 1:45.68, St 1:45.07; Pierre-Ambroise Ra 1:44.51, Lo 1:43.88; Boris Berian E 1:44.20; Alfred Kipketer P- 1:42.87; Adam Ksczot Br 1:44.36
1500m/1M: Asbel Kiprop D- 3:32.15, Bi 3:29.33, O- 3:51.48M; Elijah Manangoi Ro 3:33.96; Ronald Kwemoi M 3:30.49; Ayanleh Souleiman L- 1000m 2:13.49; Timothy Cheruiyot 3:31.34
3000m: Yomif Kejelcha RP 7:28.19
5000m: Muktar Edris SH 12:59.96, E 12:59.43; Hagos Gebrhiwet O 13:07.70, Z 13:14.82; Ibrahim Jeylan St- 13:03.22; Mo Farah L- 12:59.29;
3000mSt: Conseslus Kipruto D- 8:05.13, Ra- 8:02.77, R- 8:01.41, Bi- 8:00.12, M- 8:08.11, Br- 8:03.74; Abraham Kibiwott L- 8:09.58
110mh: Orlando Ortega Ro- 13.22, M- 13.04, L- 13.11, Br- 13.08; Omar McLeod D- 13.05, Sh- 12.98; David Oliver Ra- 13.12
400mh: Kerron Clement Lo- 48.40, Z- 48.72; Michael Tinsley Sh- 48.90, E- 48.74; Yasmani Copello O- 48.79; Javier Culson St- 49.43; Nicholas Bett P- 48.21
HJ: Erik Kynard D- 2.33, BR- 2.32; Mutaz Essa Barshim Bi- 2.37, L- 2.35; Bohdan Bondarenko Ra- 2.31, Ro- 2.33; Gianmarco Tamberi M- 2.39
PV: Renaud Lavillenie E- 5.81, O- 5.80, St- 5.73, P- 5.93; Sam Kendricks Sh- 5.88, L- 5.92, Z- 5.90
LJ: Gao Xinglong Sh- 8.14, Lo- 8.11; Rushwal Samaai Ra- 8.38; Greg Rutherford Ro- 8.31; Marquise Goodwin Bi- 8.42; Damar Forbes M- 8.23; Luvo Manyonga Br- 8.48

TJ: Christian Taylor D- 17.23, E- 17.76, St- 17.59, Lo- 17.79, Z- 17.80; Alexis Copello O- 16.91; Chris Carter P- 16.92
SP: Joe Kovacs E- 22.13, O- 22.01, Lo- 22.04; Tom Walsh St- 21.13, P- 22.00, Z 22.20; Kurt Roberts Sh- 21.40
DT: Piotr Malachowski D- 68.03, Ra- 67.45, Bi- 67.50, M- 65.57; Robert Urbanek Ro- 65.00, Philip Milanov L- 65.61; Daniel Ståhl Br- 65.78
JT: Jakub Vadlejch Lo- 85.72, P- 88.02, Z- 87.28; Thomas Röhler Sh- 85.71, O- 89.30; Ihab Abdelrahman E- 87.37, St- 86.00

Women
100m: Elaine Thompson Ra- 11.02, Ro- 10.87, L- 10.78, Br- 10.72; Tori Bowie D- 10.80, English Gardner Bi- 11.02, Dafne Schippers M- 10.94
200m: Dafne Schippers O- 21.93, Lo- 22.13, P- 22.13; Murielle Ahouré Sh- 22.72; Tori Bowie E- 21.99; Dina Asher-Smith St- 22.72; Elaine Thompson Z- 21.85
400m: Shaunae Miller Sh- 50.45, E- 50.15, Lo- 49.55; Stephenie Ann McPherson O- 51.04; Novlene Williams-Mills St- 52.29; Natasha Hastings P- 50.06; Caster Semenya Br- 50.40
800m: Caster Semenya D- 1:58.26, Ra- 1:56.64, Ro- 1:56.64, M- 1:55.30, Z 1:56.44; Francine Niyonsaba Bi- 1:56.92, L- 1:57.71
1500m: Faith Kipyegon Sh- 3:56.82, E- 3:56.41, O- 4:18.60M; Laura Muir Lo- 3:57.49, P- 3:55.22; Angelika Cichocka St- 4:03.25; Shannon Rowbury Z- 3:57.78
3000m: Almaz Ayana D- 8:23.11; Hellen Obiri M- 8:24.27; Genzebe Dibaba L- 8:31.34
5000m: Almaz Ayana Ra- 14:16.31, Ro- 14:12.59, Br- 14:18.89; Vivian Cheruiyot St 15:12.79
3000mSt: Ruth Jebet E- 8:59.97, St- 9:08.37, P- 8:52.78, Z- 9:07.00; Hyvin Jepkemoi Sh- 9:07.42, O- 9:09.57; Habiba Ghribi Lo- 9:21.35
100mh: Kendra Harrison E- 12.24, Bi- 12.46, St- 12.86, Lo- 12.20, P- 12.44, Z- 12.63; Brianna Rollins O- 12.56
400mh: Eilidh Child D- 54.53, M- 54.08; Janieve Russell Ra- 54.16, Ro 53.96; Cassandra Tate Bi- 54.57, Br- 54.47; Dalilah Muhammad L- 53.78
HJ: Ruth Beitia O- 1.90, St- 1.93, Lo- 1.98, P- 1.98, Z- 1.96; Lavern Spencer Sh- 1.94; Chaunté Lowe E- 1.95
PV: Ekateríni Stefanídi Ra- 4.75, Ro- 4.75, M- 4.81, Lo- 4.80; Sandi Morris D- 4.83, Br- 5.00; Yarisley Silva Bi- 4.84
LJ: Ivana Spanovic Sh- 6.95, O- 6.94, St- 6.90, L- 6.83, P- 6.90; Brittney Reese E- 6.92, Z- 6.95
TJ: Caterine Ibargüen Sh- 14.85, E- 15.18w, O- 14.68, P- 14.87, St- 14.69, Br- 14.60; Olga Rypakova Lo- 14.33
SP: Valerie Adams Ra- 19.68, Ro- 19.69, M- 20.05, L- 19.94; Tia Brooks D- 19.48, Bi- 19.73; Michelle Carter Br- 19.98
DT: Sandra Perkovic Sh- 70.88, E- 68.57, O- 67.10, St- 68.32, Lo- 69.94, P- 67.62, Z- 68.44
JT: Madara Palameika Ra- 64.76, Bi- 64.68, L- 65.29, Br- 66.18; Sunette Viljoen D- 65.14, Ro- 61.95; Tatyana Kholodovich M- 65.62

Final Placings 2016

Men – 100m: 1. Powell 26, 2. Meité 24, 3. Akani Simbine 18; **200m:** 1. Edward 44, 2. Martina 27, 3. Forte 25; **400m:** 1. Merritt 50, 2. Braion Taplin 24, 3. Isaac Makwala 20; **800m: 1.** Cheruiyot 39, 2. Bosse 29, 3. Kszczot 27; **1500m: 1.** Kiprop 42, 2. Manangoi 28, 3. Iguider 21; **5000m:** 1. Gebrhiwet 35, 2. Edris 30, 3. Kejelcha 22; **3000mSt:** 1. C Kipruto 70; 2=, Kibiwott & Paul K.Koech 20; **110mh:** 1. Ortega 60, 2. Pascal Martinot-Lagarde 23, 3. Dimitri Bascou 21; **400mh:** 1. Clement 51, 2. Culson 37, 3. L.J.van Zyl 17; **HJ:** 1. Kynard 46, 2. Barshim 36, 3. Grabarz 31; **PV:** 1. Lavillenie 72, 2. Kendricks 50, 3. Lisek 15; **LJ:** 1. Fabrice Lapierre 36, 2. Gao 30, 3. Manyonga 20; **TJ:** 1. Taylor 60, 2. Copello 32, 3. Carter 28; **SP:** 1. Walsh 58, 2. Kovacs 42, 3. Roberts 22; **DT:** 1. Malachowski 54, 2. Stahl 34, 3. Milanov 26; **JT:** 1. Vadlejch 50, 2. Röhler 46, 3. Julian Weber 15; **Women – 100m:** 1, Thompson 50, 2. Schippers 34, 3. Henry 12; **200m:** 1. Schippers 48, 2. Thompson 30; 3=, Asher-Smith, Facey 16; **400m:** 1. McPherson 39, 2. Hastings 32, 3. Semenya 20; **800m:** 1. Semenya 60, 2. Niyonsaba 50, 3. Sum 17; **1500m:** 1. Muir 40, 2. Kipyegon 36, 3. Rowbury 23; **5000m:** 1. Ayana 50, 2. Obiri 28, 3. Teferi 15; **3000mSt:** 1. Jebet 56, 2. Jepkemoi 44, 3. Sofia Assefa 19; **100mh:** 1. Harrison 70, 2. Dawn Harper Nelson 23, 3. Jasmine Stowers 17; **400mh:** 1. Tate 50, 2. Doyle 40, 3. Petersen 20; **HJ:** 1. Beitia 61, 2. Spencer 25, 3. Sofie Skoog 20; **PV:** 1. Stefanídi 62, 2. Morris 30, 3. Büchler 27; **LJ:** 1. Spanovic 68, 2. Reese 36, 3. Ugen 22; **TJ:** 1. Ibargüen 76, 2. Rypakova 39, 3. Papahrístou 20; **SP:** 1. Adams 58, 2. Márton 33, 3. Carter 32; **DT:** 1. Perkovic 80, 2. Robert-Michon 28, 3. Caballero 24; **JT:** 1. Palameika 59, 2. Kathryn Mitchell 25, 3. Barbora Spotáková 23. Points: 10-6-4-3-2-1 for 1st to 6th, double in finals, in which athletes have to compete in order to qualify.

Changes to Diamond League in 2017

IN A MAJOR restructure, the IAAF Diamond League has adopted a championship-style model with the finalists competing for a prize pool of $3.2 million. Athletes will earn points in the first 12 IAAF Diamond League meetings to qualify for two final meetings where $100,000 will be at stake in each of the 32 Diamond disciplines, including $50,000 for each winner. In previous seasons, athletes accumulated points throughout the IAAF Diamond League season with the overall winner of each of the 32 events being the athlete with the most points, irrespective of whether they won the final.

The season is now a race to reach the finals with the winners crowned as IAAF Diamond League champions. As in a championship, the performance of athletes in the final alone will determine who the champion will be and the prize money won.

In the horizontal jumps and throwing events, there will be a return in 2017 to six attempts for all athletes. This follows last season's disastrous experimental format where all athletes were given three attempts but with only the top four athletes being given three further attempts.

Prize money structure for each of the 32 events at the finals (Zürich Aug 24 & Brussels Sep 1): 1st $50,000, 2nd $20,000, 3rd $10,000, 4th $6000, 5th $5000, 6th $4000, 7th $3000, 8th $2000. Prize money at the 12 qualification meetings: 1st $10,000, 2nd $6000, 3rd $4000, down to $1000 for 8th place.

DIAMOND RACE STATISTICS 2010–2016

Multiple winners
Men

7	Renaud Lavillenie PV 2010-16
5	Christian Taylor TJ 2012-16
4	Piotr Malachowski DT 2010, 2014-16
3	Paul Kipsiele Koech 3k St 2010-12
3	David Oliver 110mh 2010, 2013, 2015
3	Justin Gatlin 100m 2013-15
3	LaShawn Merritt 400m 2013-14, 2016
3	Alonso Edward 200m 2014-16
3	Asbel Kiprop 1500m 2010, 2015-16

Women

5	Valerie Adams SP 2011-14, 2016
5	Sandra Perkovic DT 2012-16
4	Caterine Ibargüen TJ 2013-16
4	Dawn Harper-Nelson 100mh 2012-15
4	Barbora Spotáková JT2010, 2012, 2014-15
4	Kaliese Spencer 400mh 2010-12, 2014
4	Milcah Chemos 3kSt 2010-13
4	Shelley-Ann Fraser-Pryce 100m 2012-13, 2015, 200m 2013
4	Allyson Felix 200m 2010, 2014-15, 400m 2010
3	Vivian Cheruiyot 5000m 2010-12
3	Amantle Montsho 400m 2011-13

3	Silke Spiegelberg PV 2011-13
3	Eunice Sum 800m 2013-15
3	Carmelita Jeter 100m 2010-11, 200m 2011

Most Overall victories
Men

31	Renaud Lavillenie PV
19	Asbel Kiprop 800m/1500m/1M
19	Christian Taylor LJ/TJ
18	Piotr Malachowski DT
15	Usain Bolt 100m/200m
15	LaShawn Merrritt 400m
14	David Rudisha 800m
14	Reese Hoffa SP
14	David Oliver 110mh
14	Justin Gatlin 100m/200m

Women

34	Sandra Perkovic DT
28	Valerie Adams SP
25	Caterine Ibargüen TJ
21	Kaliese Spencer 400mh
18	Allyson Felix 100m/200m/400m
16	Milcah Chemos 3kSt
15	Dawn Harper-Nelson 100mh
15	Barbora Spotáková JT
14	Zuzana Hejnová 400mh
14	Blanka Vlasic HJ

EUROPEAN INDOOR CHAMPIONSHIPS 2017

March 3-5, Kombank Arena, Belgrade (Serbia)
THE MAGNIFICENT VICTORY of Serbia's Ivana Spanovic provided a wonderful finale to a most successful meeting. Her splendid series culminated with 7.24m, the longest indoor women's long jump for 28 years for third on the world-all-time list. Even higher was Kevin Mayer's 6479 heptathlon, a score beaten only by Ashton Eaton. Then there was an incredible 21.97 shot put by 19 year-old Konrad Bukowiecki and completing seven world leading indoor marks for 2017 was the qualifying round TJ 17.52 by Max Hess (when Melvin Raffin set a world junior record 17.20), and performances by women's winners: Ekateríni Stefanídi, PV 4.85, Anita Márton, SP 19.28, and Nafi Thiam, 4870 pentathlon.

Laura Muir's magnificent double involved heats of both events on day 1, then the 1500m final on day 2 and the 3000m final on day 3, so a race more than Lidia Chojecka's similar double in 4:05.13 and 8:43.25 in 2007. Muir broke the British record for 1500m with 4:02.39, taking off in magnificent style after a slow opening lap and maintaining impressive speed to leave the outstanding Konstanze Klosterhalfen, and she came back the next day, following Yasemin Can at a steadily increasing tempo to sprint home in 8:35.67. Both her final times were new championship records and the only other one was Mayer's heptathlon that added 41 points to Roman Šebrle's 2004 European record.

Many field events were at a very high standard, and the horizontal jumpers certainly appreciated the springy track, with the Mondo surface installed on a wood floor some 3m above the ground level of the arena. In contrast the men's track events generally had weak depth, although Andrew Pozzi confirmed his status as the world's premier sprint hurdler of the indoor season, and Pavel Maslák 400 and Adam Kszczot 800m completed unique triple wins in EI history, Richard Kilty convincingly retained his 60m title and Marcin Lewandowski moved up to 1500m success after winning the 800m in 2015. Also winning as they had in 2015 were Nelson Évora TJ, Sabine Büchel 800m, Spanovic and Márton.

The age range of the medallists went from 19 year-old prodigy Bukowiecki to 40 year-old Fabrizio Donato, who set two world M40 records in the triple jump and the amazing 37 year-old Ruth Beitia who relished competing in her 8th European Indoors (a figure matched by Slovakian triple jumper Dana Veldáková) even though she was comprehensively beaten by Airine Palsyte with her brilliant Lithuanian record of 2.01.

Poland were top of the medal table with 7 gold, ending by winning both relays, to Britain's 5, but both shared top position in the points table with 103 ahead of Germany, who took a lrager team, giving expereince to many young talents, as did Sweden who made a big advance and filled all possible team places

The overall spectator experience was excellent – security that was sensible on arrival and friendly within, and, unlike Prague in 2015, there were good sight lines with the cube suspended high over the arena containing excellent information and pictures of the action.

MEN

60 Metres (4-4-4)
1. Richard Kilty GBR 6.54
2. Ján Volko SVK 6.58
3. Austin Hamilton SWE 6.63
4. Odain Rose SWE 6.63
5. Theo Etienne GBR 6.67
6. Pascal Mancini SUI 6.70
7. Sulayman Bah SWE 6.96
dq fs Andrew Robertson GBR –

400 Metres (3-3-4)
1. Pavel Maslák CZE 45.77
2. Rafal Omelko POL 46.08
3. Liemarvin Bonevacia NED 46.26
4. Benjamin Lobo Vedel DEN 46.33
5. Lucas Bua ESP 46.74
6. Samuel García ESP 46.74

800 Metres (3-4-5)
1. Adam Kszczot POL 1:48.87
2. Andreas Bube DEN 1:49.32
3. Álvaro de Arriba ESP 1:49.68
4. Daniel Andújar ESP 1:50.28
5. Thijmen Kupers NED 1:50.47
6. Kevin López ESP 1:54.17

1500 Metres (3-4)
1. Marcin Lewandowski POL 3:44.82
2. Kalle Berglund SWE 3:45.56
3. Filip Sasínek CZE 3:45.89
4. Marc Alcalá ESP 3:46.36
5. Tom Lancashire GBR 3:46.57
6. Sofiane Selmouni FRA 3:46.70
7. Timo Benitz GER 3:46.73
8. Yassin Bouih ITA 3:47.95
9. Llorenç Sales ESP 3:48.56
10. Johan Rogestedt SWE 3:49.91
11. John Travers IRL 3:53.11

3000 Metres (3-5)
1. Adel Mechaal ESP 8:00.60
2. Henrik Ingebrigtsen NOR 8:00.93
3. Richard Ringer GER 8:01.01
4. Hayle Ibrahimov AZE 8:03.19
5. Jonas Leanderson SWE 8:03.91
6. Marouan Razine ITA 8:04.19
7. Yemaneberhan Crippa ITA 8:05.63
8. Carlos Mayo ESP 8:06.15
9. Ali Kaya TUR 8:08.92
10. Andreas Vojta AUT 8:09.18
11. Ramazan Özdemir TUR 8:10.99
12. Aras Kaya TUR 8:16.36

60 Metres Hurdles (3)
1. Andy Pozzi GBR 7.51
2. Pascal Martinot-Lagarde FRA 7.52
3. Petr Svoboda CZE 7.53
4. Garfield Darien FRA 7.54
5. Aurel Manga FRA 7.58
6. Milan Trajkovic CYP 7.60
7. Orlando Ortega ESP 7.64
8. Andreas Martinsen DEN 7.68

High Jump (4-5)
1. Sylwester Bednarek POL 2.32
2. Robbie Grabarz GBR 2.30
3. Pavel Seliverstov BLR 2.27
4. Tihomir Ivanov BUL 2.27
5. Matús Buben̆ík SVK 2.27
6. Silvano Chesani ITA 2.27
7. Mateusz Przybylko GER 2.27
8. Allan Smith GBR 2.18

Pole Vault (3)
1. Piotr Lisek POL 5.85
2. Konstadínos Filippídis GRE 5.85
3. Pawel Wojciechowski POL 5.85
4. Jan Kudlicka CZE 5.80
5. Raphael Holzdeppe GER 5.80
6. Axel Chapelle FRA 5.80
7. Ivan Horvat CRO 5.75
8= Mareks Arents LAT 5.60
8= Stanley Joseph FRA 5.60

EUROPEAN INDOOR CHAMPIONSHIPS 2017

Long Jump (3-4)
1. Izmir Smajlaj ALB 8.08
2. Michel Tornéus SWE 8.08
3, Serhiy Nykyforov UKR 8.07
4. Tomasz Jasczuk POL 7.98
5. Julian Howard GER 7.97
6. Lazar Anic SRB 7.90
7. Filippo Randazzo ITA 7.77
nj, Elvijs Misans LAT –

Triple Jump (3-5)
1. Nelson Évora POR 17.20
2. Fabrizio Donato ITA 17.13
3. Max Hess GER 17.12
4. Elvijs Misans LAT 17.02
5, Melvin Raffin FRA-J 16.92
6. Jean-Marc Pontvianne FRA 16.90
7. Simo Lipsanen FIN 16.84
8. Georgi Tsonov BUL 16.78
9. Pablo Torrijos ESP 16.73

Shot (4)
1. Konrad Bukowiecki POL 21.97
2, Tomáš Staněk CZE 21.43
3. David Storl GER 21.30
4. Tsanko Arnaudov POR 21.08
5. Stipe Zunic CRO 21.04
6. Ladislav Prášil CZE 20.73
7. Mesud Pezer BIH 20.37
8. Mikhail Abramchuk BLR 19.38

Heptathlon (4/5)
1. Kevin Mayer FRA 6479
2. Jorge Ureña ESP 6227
3. Adam Helcelet CZE 6110
4. Dominik Distelberger AUT 6063
5. Fredrik Samuelsson SWE 6015
6. Darko Pesic MNE 5984
7. Niels Pittomvils BEL 5961
8. Matthias Brugger GER 5954
9. Ashley Bryant GBR 5945
10. Jiri Sykora CZE 5902

4 x 400 Metres Relay (5)
1. POL 3:06.99
  Kozlowski, Krawczuk, Wascinski, Omelko
2. BEL 3:07.80
  Vanderbemden, Watrin, K Borlée, D Borlée
3. CZE 3:08.60
  Sorm, Tesar, Kubista, Maslák 45.3
4. FRA 3:08.99
5. UKR 3:09.64
6. TUR 3:15.97

Women

60 Metres (4-5-5)
1. Asha Philip GBR 7.06
2. Olesya Povh UKR 7.10
3. Ewa Swoboda POL 7.10
4. Mujinga Kambundji SUI 7.16
5. Lisa Meyer GER 7.19
6. Alexandra Burghardt GER 7.19
7. Foriane Gnafoua FRA 7.20
8. Rebekka Haase GER 7.21

400 Metres (3-3-4)
1. Floria Guei FRA 51.90
2. Zuzana Hejnová CZE 52.42
3. Justyna Swiety POL 52.52
4. Laviai Nielsen GBR 52.79
5. Léa Sprunger SUI 53.08
6. Malgorzata Holub POL 54.29

800 Metres (3-4-5)
1. Selina Büchel SUI 2:00.38
2, Shelayna Oskan-Clarke GBR 2:00.39
3. Anita Hinriksdóttir ISL 2:01.25
4. Lovisa Lindh SWE 2:01.37
5. Stina Troest DEN 2:02.93
6. Esther Guerrero ESP 2:03.09

1500 Metres (3-4)
1. Laura Muir GBR 4:02.39*
2. Konstanze Klosterhalfen GER 4:04.45
3. Sofia Ennaoui POL 4:06.59
4. Meraf Bahta SWE 4:07.90
5. Luiza Gega ALB 4:11.64
6. Sarah McDonald GBR 4:13.67
7. Darya Borisevich BLR 4:13.81
8. Amela Terzic SRB 4:25.15
dnf. Ciara Mageean IRL –

3000 Metres (3-5)
1. Laura Muir GBR 8:35.67*
2. Yasemin Can TUR 8:43.46
3. Eilish McColgan GBR 8:47.43
4. Maureen Koster NED 8:48.99
5. Stephanie Twell GBR 8:50.40
6. Ana Lozano ESP 8:55.20
7. Giulia Viola ITA 8:56.19
8, Alina Reh GER 8:57.87
9. Hanna Klein GER 8:58.57
10. Nuria Fernández ESP 9:05.17
11. Ancuta Bobocel ROU 9:05.74
12. Charlotta Fougberg SWE 9:09.53

60 Metres Hurdles (3)
1. Cindy Roleder GER 7.88
2. Alina Talay BLR 7.92
3. Pamela Dutkiewicz GER 7.95
4. Hanna Plattsyna UKR 7.96
5. Isabelle Pedersen NOR 8.01
6. Ricarda Lobe GER 8.03
7. Nadine Visser NED 8.04
8. Susanna Kallur SWE 8.14

High Jump (3-4)
1. Airine Palsyte LTU 2.01
2. Ruth Beitia ESP 1.94
3. Yuliya Levchenko UKR 1.94
4. Oksana Okuneva UKR 1.92
5. Jossie Graumann GER 1.92
6. Michaela Hrubá CZE-J 1.92
7. Ana Simic CRO 1.89
8. Morgan Lake GBR 1.85

Pole Vault (4)
1. Ekateríni Stefanídi GRE 4.85
2. Lisa Ryzih GER 4.75
3= Angelica Bengtsson SWE 4.55
3= Maryna Kylypko UKR 4.55
5. Michaela Meijer SWE 4.55
6= Lisa Gunnarsson SWE-J 4.55
6= Minna Nikkanen FIN 4.55
8= Wilma Murto FIN-J 4.40
8= Tina Sutej SLO 4.40

Long Jump (4-5)
1. Ivana Spanovic SRB 7.24
2. Lorraine Ugen GBR 6.97
3. Claudia Salman-Rath GER 6.94
4. Darya Klishina RUS/EA 6.84
5. Ksenija Balta EST 6.79
6. Jazmin Sawyers GBR 6.67
7. Maryna Bekh UKR 6.59
8. Alexandra Wester GER 6.53

Triple Jump (3-4)
1. Kristin Gierisch GER 14.37
2. Patricia Mamona POR 14.32
3. Paraskeví Papahrístou GRE 14.24
4. Anna Jagaciak Michalska POL 14.14
5. Ana Peleteiro ESP 14.13
6. Jenny Elbe GER 14.12
7. Susana Costa POR 13.99
8. Kristiina Mäkelä FIN 13.73

Shot (3)
1. Anita Márton HUN 19.28
2. Radoslava Mavrodieva BUL 18.36
3. Yuliya Leontyuk BLR 18.32
4. Fanny Roos SWE 18.13
5. Claudine Vita GER 18.09
6. Paulina Guba POL 18.00
7. Alyona Dubitskaya BLR 17.85
8. Jessica Cérival FRA 16.84

Pentathlon (3)
1. Nafissatou Thiam BEL 4870
2. Ivona Dadic AUT 4767
3. Györgyi Zsivoczky-Farkas HUN 4723
4. Xénia Krizsán HUN 4631
5. Nadine Broersen NED 4582
6. Verena Preiner AUT 4478
7. Lecabela Quaresma POR 4444
8. Yana Maksimova BLR 4438
9. Lucia Slanícková CZE 4409
10. Bianca Salming SWE-J 4389

4 x 400 Metres Relay (5)
1. POL 3:29.94
  Wyciszkiewicz, Holub, Baumgart, Swiety
2. GBR 3:31.05
  Doyle, Lowe, Iheke, Laviai Nielsen
3. UKR 3:32.10
  Bibik, Melnyk, Bryzhina, Lyakhova
4. ITA 3:32.87
5. FRA 3:33.61
6. GER 3:34.60

Leading Nations – Medals & Points

Nation	G	S	B	Points
POL	7	1	4	103
GBR	5	4	1	103
GER	2	2	5	100
SWE	-	2	2	63
FRA	2	1	-	61.5
ESP	1	2	1	61
CZE	1	2	4	58
UKR	-	1	4	46.5
BLR	-	1	2	25
ITA	-	1	-	25
POR	1	1	-	24
NED	-	-	1	23
GRE	1	1	1	21
SUI	1	-	-	20
HUN	1	-	-	19
DEN	-	-	1	18
BEL	1	1	-	17
AUT	-	1	-	15
BUL	-	1	-	13
ALB	1	-	-	12
SRB	1	-	-	12
NOR	-	1	-	11
SVK	-	1	-	11
TUR	-	1	-	11

14 nations won gold, 26 medals and 36 placed athletes in the top 8s.

The Russian Darya Klishina competed as a neutral athlete.

WORLD CROSS-COUNTRY CHAMPIONSHIPS 2017

March 26, Kampala (Uganda)

THE WORLD CROSS-COUNTRY was dominated even more than usual by the East African nations, who won all the medals bar one – and that was the senior women's team bronze that went to Bahrain whose team comprised three ex-Kenyans and an ex-Ethiopian. In the inaugural mixed relay Kenya won from Ethiopia with third placed Turkey's entire team of two men and two women being transferees from Kenya.

Geoffrey Kamworer retained the senior men's tite that he had won in 2015 and Irene Cheptai led a Kenyan sweep of the top six places in the senior women's race. It looked for a long while as if the host country would have a men's win but Joshua Cheptegei faded badly in the last of the four laps from having a 12 second lead to staggering home in 30th place.

Uganda's Jacob Kiplimo produced a performance of a lifetime to win the junior men's race, the country's first ever gold at a World Cross. Letesenbet Gidey of Ethiopia became the fourth woman to win back-to-back U20 titles.

The decine in distance running in the Western world continued here. The first Europeans to finish in the senior races came in 43rd men and 34th women.

Senior Men 9.858 km
1. Geoffrey Kamworor KEN 28:24
2. Leonard Barsoton KEN 28:36
3. Abadi Hadis ETH 28:43
4. Jemal Yimer ETH 28:46
5. Aron Kifle ERI 28:49
6. Muktar Edris ETH 28:56
7. Vincent Rono KEN 29:00
8. Ibrahim Jeylan ETH 29:07
9. Timothy Toroitich UGA 29:10
10. Bonsa Dida ETH 29:10
11. Samuel Chelanga USA 29:12
12. Leonard Komon KEN 29:16
13. Patrick Tiernan AUS 29:19
14. Ones. Nzikwinkunda BDI 29:21
15. Nicholas Kosimbei KEN 29:23
16. Abdallah Mande UGA 29:25
17. Stephen Klprotich UGA 29:27
18. Getaneh Molla ETH 29:34
19. Afewerki Berhane ERI 29:35
20. Leonard Korir USA 29:43
21. Shadrack Kipchirchir USA 29:44
22. Gabriel Geay TAN 29:47
23. Goitom Kifle ERI 29:56
24. Aweke Ayalew BRN 30:01
25. J-Marie Niyomuzika BDI 30:01
26. Stanley Kebenei USA 30:03
27. Birhanu Balew BRN 30:04
28. Mogos Shumay ERI 30:06
29. Leonard Langat KEN 30:07
30. Joshua Cheptegei UGA 30:08

136 of 143 finished
Team 4 to score, 20 teams completed
1. ETH 21
2. KEN 22
3. UGA 72
4. ERI 75
5. USA 78
6. BDI 119
7. TAN 147
8. AUS 156
9. RSA 162
10. ESP 221
11. RWA 224
12. CAN 315
13. MAW 319
14. PER 321
15. JPN 338
16. DEN 366
17. BOT 403
18. SUD 413
19. NGR 509

Junior Men 7.858 km
1. Jacob Kiplimo UGA 22:40
2. Amdework Walelegn ETH 22:43
3. Richard Yator KEN 22:52
4. Betesfa Getahun ETH 22:58
5. Selemon Barega ETH 23:03
6. Tefera Mosisa ETH 23:04
7. Amos Kirui KEN 23:04
8. Edwin Bett KEN 23:10
9. Yemane Haileselassie ERI 23:18
10. Wesley Ledama KEN 23:25
11. Filmon Ande ERI 23:28
12. Balelign Teshager ETH 23:35
13. Aimen Boulainine ALG 23:36
14. Solomon Berihu ETH 23:38
15. Ronald Kirui KEN 24:00

101 of 105 finished
Team 4 to score. 16 teams completed
1. ETH 17
2. KEN 28
3. ERI 57
4. UGA 59
5. MAR 117
6. TAN 141
7. JPN 161
8. RSA 182
9. USA 193
10. GBR 223
11. ALG 223
12. PER 224
13. AUS 238
14. ESP 247
15. CAN 282
16. SUD 312

Senior Women 9.858 km
1. Irene Cheptai KEN 31:57
2. Alice Aprot Nawowuna KEN 32:01
3. Lilian Rengeruk KEN 32:11
4. Hyvin Jepkemoi KEN 32:32
5. Agnes Tirop KEN 32:32
6. Faith Kipyegon KEN 32:49
7. Ruth Jebet BRN 32:49
8. Belaynesh Oljira ETH 32:53
9. Rose Chelimo BRN 33:01
10. Senebeer Teferi ETH 33:12
11. Eunice Chumba BRN 33:26
12. Mercyline Chelangat UGA 33:29
13. Gebeyanesh Ayele ETH 33:30
14. Sentayehu Lewtegn ETH 33:33
15. Aliphine Tuliamuk USA 33:43
16. Failuna Matanga TAN 33:48
17. Racahael Chebet USA 33:58
18. Stella Chesang UGA 34:27
19. Cavaline Nahimana BDI 34:35
20. Trihas Gebre ESP 34:37
21. Doreen Chemutai UGA 34:41
22. Stephanie Bruce USA 34:42
23. Natosha Rogers USA 34:47
24. Yuka Hori JPN 34:54
25. Doreen Chesang UGA 34:54
26. Zerfie Limeneh ETH 34:59
27. Azucena Díaz ESP 35:06
28. Magdalena Shauri TAN 35:13
29. Emily Chebet UGA 35:17
30. Sarah Pagano USA 35:18

100 of 104 finished
Team 4 to score. 16 teams completed
1. KEN 10
2. ETH 45
3. BRN 59
4. UGA 68
5. USA 90
6. TAN 132
7. ESP 145
8. PER 181
9. CAN 19
10. RSA 20
11. JPN 20
12. ERI 29
13. ALG 22
14. AUS 23
15. ECU 25
16. NGR 38

Junior Women 6.03km
1. Letesenbet Gidey ETH 18:34
2. Hawi Feysa ETH 18:57
3. Celliphine Chespol KEN 19:02
4. Sheila Chelangat KEN 19:12
5. Hellen Lobun KEN 19:16
6. Fatyen Tesfay ETH 19:24
7. Peruth Chemutai UGA 19:29
8. Joyline Cherotich KEN 19:31
9. Emmaculate Chepkirui KEN 19:31
10. Zeineba Yimer ETH 19:32
11. Sandrafelis Tuei KEN 19:59
12. Biri Abera ETH 20:00
13. Wede Kefale ETH 20:04
14. Sarah Chelangat UGA 20:13
15. Tomomi Takamatsu JPN 20:24

97 of 103 finished
Team 4 to score, 16 teams completed
1. ETH 19
2. KEN 20
3. UGA 62
4. JPN 73
5. ERI 134
6. CAN 138
7. BDI 161
8. RSA 181
9. GBR 191
10. MAR 202
11. USA 211
12. PER 211
13. AUS 219
14. ESP 223
15. TAN 249
16. ITA 256

Mixed Relay 7.858 km
1. Kenya (Asbel Kiprop 5:19 2023m, Winfred Mbithe 6:07 2000m, Bernard Koros 5:25 2000m, Beatrice Chepkoech 5:31 1835m) 22:22
2. Ethiopia (Welde Tufa 5:25, Bone Cheluke 6:16, Yomif Kejelcha 5:22, Genzebe Dibaba 5:27) 22:30
3. Turkey (Aras Kaya 5:31, Meryem Akdag 6:13, Ali Kaya 5:24, Yasemin Can 5:29) 22:37
4. BRN 23:20
5. MAR 24:02
6. USA 24:08
7. TAN 24:13
8. ESP 24:29
9. ERI 24:47
10. ITA 25:14
11. SUD 25:53
12. SSD 29:30
dq. Uganda (for changing declared running order)

Britain, the home of cross-country, managed 9th and 10th places in the junior team events, but did not even send a compeitor for the senior men's race.

WORLD CHAMPIONSHIPS 2017

THE 16th IAAF World Championships will be staged in London, GBR on August 5-13 2017 at the London Stadium, Queen Elizabeth Olympic Park.

Previous Championships

ATHLETICS EVENTS AT the Olympic Games have had world championship status, but the first championships for athletics alone were staged in 1983. It should, however, be noted that separate World Championships were held for men's 50 kilometres walk in 1976 and for women's 3000m and 400m hurdles in 1980, as those events were not on the Olympic programme in those years.

Year	Venue	Athletes	Nations
1983	Helsinki, FIN	1572	153
1987	Rome, ITA	1741	157
1991	Tokyo, JPN	1551	164
1993	Stuttgart, GER	1624	187
1995	Göteborg, SWE	1804	191
1997	Athens, GRE	1882	198
1999	Seville, ESP	1821	201
2001	Edmonton, CAN	1677	189
2003	Saint-Denis, FRA	1679	198
2005	Helsinki, FIN	1688	189
2007	Osaka, JPN	1800	197
2009	Berlin GER	1895	200
2011	Daegu KOR	1742	199
2013	Moscow, RUS	1784	203
2015	Beijing, CHN	1761	205

World Championship Records

Men

100m	9.58	Usain Bolt JAM	2009
200m	19.19	Usain Bolt JAM	2009
400m	43.18	Michael Johnson USA	1999
800m	1:43.06	Billy Konchellah KEN	1987
1500m	3:27.65	Hicham El Guerrouj MAR	1999
5000m	12:52.79	Eliud Kipchoge KEN	2003
10,000m	26:46.31	Kenenisa Bekele ETH	2009
Mar	2:06:54	Abel Kirui KEN	2009
3000mSt	8:00.43	Ezekiel Kemboi KEN	2009
110mh	12.91	Colin Jackson GBR	1993
400mh	47.18	Kevin Young USA	1993
HJ	2.41	Bohdan Bondarenko UKR	2013
PV	6.05	Dmitriy Markov AUS	2001
LJ	8.95	Mike Powell USA	1991
TJ	18.29	Jonathan Edwards GBR	1995
SP	22.23	Werner Günthör SUI	1987
DT	70.17	Virgilijus Alekna BLR	2005
HT	83.89	Ivan Tikhon BLR	2005
JT	92.80	Jan Zelezny CZE	2001
Dec	9045	Ashton Eaton USA	2015
4x100m	37.04	Jamaica	2011
4x400m	2:54.29	USA	1993
20kmW	1:17:21	Jefferson Pérez ECU	2003
50kmW	3:36:03	Rob. Korzeniowski POL	2003

Women

100m	10.70	Marion Jones USA	1999
200m	21.74	Silke Gladisch GDR	1987
400m	47.99	Jarmila Kratochvílová TCH	1983
800m	1:54.68	Jarmila Kratochvílová TCH	1983
1500m	3:58.52	Tatyana Tomashova RUS	2003
3000m	8:28.71	Qu Yunxia CHN	1993
5000m	14:26.83	Almaz Ayana ETH	2016
10,000m	30:04.18	Berhane Adere ETH	2003
Mar	2:20:57	Paula Radcliffe GBR	2005
3000mSt	9:06.57	Yekaterina Volkova RUS	2007
100mh	12.28	Sally Pearson AUS	2011
400mh	52.42	Melaine Walker JAM	2009
HJ	2.09	Stefka Kostadinova BUL	1987
PV	5.01	Yelena Isinbayeva RUS	2005
LJ	7.36	Jackie Joyner-Kersee USA	1987
TJ	15.50	Inessa Kravets UKR	1995
SP	21.24	Natalya Lisovskaya URS	1987
	21.24	Valerie Adams NZL	2011
DT	71.62	Martina Hellmann GDR	1987
HT	80.15	Anita Wlodarczyk POL	2015
JT	71.99	Mariya Abakumova RUS	2011
Hep	7128	Jackie Joyner-Kersee USA	1987
4x100m	41.07	Jamaica	2015
4x400m	3:16.71	USA	1993
20kmW	1:25:41	Olimpiada Ivanova RUS	2005

Winners of the most medals

14 Merlene Ottey JAM gold 4x100m 1991, 200m 1993 & 1995; silver 200m 1983, 100m 1993 & 1995, 4x100m 1995; bronze 4x100m 1983, 100m & 200m 1987 & 1991, 4x100m 1993, 200m 1997

13 Usain Bolt JAM gold 100m, 200m & 4x100m 2009, 2013 & 2015; 200m & 4x100m 2011; silver 200m & 4x100m 2007

13 Allyson Felix USA gold 200m 2005, 2007 & 2009, 400m 2015; 4x100m 2007 & 2011; 4x400m 2007, 2009 & 2011; silver 400m 2011, 4x100m & 4x400m 2015; bronze 200m 2011

11 Veronica Campbell-Brown JAM gold 100m 2007, 200m 2011, 4x100m 2015; silver 100m 2005, 2011; 200m 2007, 4x100m 2005, 2007 & 2011, 200m 2009; bronze 200m 2015

11 LaShawn Merritt gold 400m 2009, 2013, 4x400m 2005, 2007, 2009, 2011, 2013, 2015; silver 400m 2007, 2011, 2015

10 Carl Lewis USA gold 100m, LJ & 4x100m 1983; 100m, LJ & 4x100m 1987, 100m & 4x100m 1991; silver LJ 1991; bronze 200m 1993

9 Jearl Miles Clark USA gold 400m 1993, 4x400m 1993, 1995 & 2003; silver 4x400m 1991, 1997, 1999; bronze 400m 1995 & 1997

9 Shelley-Ann Fraser-Pryce JAM gold 100m & 4x100m 2009 & 2015, 100m, 200m & 4x100m 2013; silver 4x100m 2007 & 2011

(8) Michael Johnson USA gold 200m 1991 &

1995, 400m 1993, 1995, 1997 & 1999, 4x400m 1993, 1995 (lost 1999 gold when team dq)

Winners of the most gold medals
11 Usain Bolt
9 Allyson Felix
8 Michael Johnson, Carl Lewis, LaShawn Merritt
7 Shelly-Ann Fraser-Pryce
6 Sergey Bubka PV 1983, 1987, 1991, 1993, 1995, 1997
5 Gail Devers USA 1993-9, Maurice Greene USA 1997-2001, Lars Riedel GER DT 1991-2001, Allen Johnson USA 1995-2003, Jeremy Wariner USA 2003-09, Kenenisa Bekele ETH 2005-09, Tirunesh Dibaba ETH 2003-13

Oldest world champions
Men 37y 258d Venyamin Soldatenko USSR 50kW 1976
Women 40y 268d Ellina Zvereva BLR DT 2001

Oldest medallists
Men 40y 274d Troy Douglas NED 3rd 4x1 2003
       40y 71d John Powell USA 2nd DT 1987
Women 40y 268d Ellina Zvereva BLR 1st DT 2001

Youngest gold medallists
Women 17y 248d Merlene Frazer JAM 4x100m (ran in heat) 1991
Men 18y 177d Ismael Kirui KEN 10,000m 1993

Youngest medallists
M: 16y 305d Darrel Brown TRI 4x100m 2001
W: 15y 153d Sally Barsosio KEN 10,000m 1993

Most wins by event
Men   inc. all with 3 or more
100m   3 Carl Lewis USA 1983-87-91
        3 Maurice Greene USA 1997-99-2001
        3 Usain Bolt JAM 2011-13-15
200m   4 Usain Bolt JAM 2009-11-13-15
400m   4 Michael Johnson 1993-95-97-99
800m   3 Wilson Kipketer DEN 1995-97-99
1500m: 4 Hicham El Guerrouj MAR 1997-99-01-03
        3 Nourredine Morceli ALG 1991-93-95
5000m   3 Mo Farah GBR 2011-13-15
10,000m 4 Haile Gebrselasie ETH 1993-95-97-99
        4 Kenenisa Bekele ETH 2003-05-07-09
Mar   2 Abel Antón ESP 1997-9
        2 Jaouad Gharib MAR 2003-05
        2 Abel Kirui KEN 2009-11
3000mSt 4 Ezekiel Kemboi KEN 2009-11-13-15
        3 Moses Kiptanui KEN 1991-93-95
110mh   4 Allen Johnson USA 1995-97-2001-03
        3 Greg Foster USA 1983-87-91
400mh   2 Edwin Moses 1983-87; Félix Sánchez DOM 2001-03; Kerron Clement USA 2007-09
HJ   2 Javier Sotomayor CUB 1993-97
PV   6 Sergey Bubka UKR 1983-87-91-93-95-97
LJ   4 Iván Pedroso CUB 1995-97-99-2001
        4 Dwght Phillips USA 2003-05-09-11
TJ   2 Jonathan Edwards GBR 1995-2001
        2 Christian Taylor USA 2011-15
SP   3 Werner Günthör SUI 1987-91-93
        3 John Godina USA 1995-97-2001
DT   5 Lars Riedel GER 1991-93-95-97-2001
        3 Robert Harting GER 2009-11-13
HT   3 Ivan Tikhon BLR 2003-05-07
JT   3 Jan Zelezny CZE 1993-95-2001
Dec   3 Dan O'Brien USA 1991-93-95
        3 Tomás Dvorák CZE 1997-99-2001
4x100m 7 USA 1983-87-91-93-99-2003-07
        4 Jamaica 2009-11-13-15
4x400m 9 USA 1987-93-95-2005-07-09-11-13-15
20kmW   3 Jefferson Pérez ECU 2003-05-07
50kmW   3 Rob. Korzeniowski POL 1997-2001-03
Women
100m   3 Shelly-Ann Fraser-Pryce 2009-13-15
200m   3 Allyson Felix USA 2005-07-09
400m   2 Cathy Freeman AUS 1997-99
        2 Christine Ohurogu GBR 2009-13
800m   3 Maria Mutola MOZ 1993-2001-03
1500m   2 Hassiba Boulmerka ALG 1991-95
        2 Tatyana Tomashova RUS 2003-05
        2 Maryam Jamal BRN 2007-09
5000m   2 Gabriela Szabo ROU 1997-99
        2 Tirunesh Dibaba ETH 2003-05
        2 Vivian Cheruiyot KEN 2009-11
        2 Meseret Defar ETH 2007-13
10,000m 3 Tirunesh Dibaba ETH 2005-07-13
Mar   2 Catherine Ndereba KEN 2003-07
        2 Edna Kiplagat KEN 2011-13
3000mSt 1 by six women
100mh   3 Gail Devers USA 1993-95-99
400mh   2 Nezha Bidouane MAR 1997-2001
        2 Zuzana Hejnová CZE 2013-15
HJ   2 Stefka Kostadinova BUL 1987-1995
        2 Hestrie Cloete RSA 2001-03
        2 Blanka Vlasic CRO 2007-09
PV   3 Yelena Isinbayeva RUS 2005-07-13
LJ   3 Brittney Reese USA 2009-11-13
TJ   2 Tatyana Lebedeva RUS 2001-03
        2 Yargelis Savigne CUB 2007-09
        2 Caterine Ibargüen COL 2013-15
SP   4 Valerie Adams NZL 2007-09-11-13
        3 Astrid Kumbernuss GER 1995-97-99
DT   3 Franka Dietzsch GER 1999-2005-07
HT   2 Yipsi Moreno CUB 2001-03
        2 Tatyana Lysenko RUS 2011-13
        2 Anita Wlodarczyk POL 2009-15
JT   2 Trine Hattestad NOR 1993-97
        2 Miréla Manjani GRE 1999-2003
        2 Osleidys Menéndez CUB 2001-05
Hep   3 Carolina Klüft SWE 2003-05-07
        3 Jessica Ennis-Hill GBR 2009-11-15
4x100m 6 USA 1987-95-97-2001-05-07
        3 Jamaica 1991-2009-13-15
4x400m 6 USA 1993-95-2003-07-09-11
        3 Russia 1999-2005-13
        3 Germany: GDR 1983-87, GER 1997
20kmW   3 Olga Kaniskina RUS 2007-09-11

Oldest Competitor
47y 108d Merlene Ottey SLO 100m (1st round) 2007

Qualifying Standards 2017

Event	Men	Women
100m	10.12	11.26
200m	20.44	23.10
400m	45.50	52.10
800m	1:45.90	2:01.00
1500m	3:36.20	4:07.50
(or 1M)	3:53.40	4:26.70
5000m	13:22.60	15:22.00
10,000m	27:45.00	32:15.00
Mar	2:19:00	2:45:00
3000mSt	8:32.00	9:45:00
110/100mh	1.48	12.98
400mh	49.35	56.10
HJ	2.30	1.94
PV	5.70	4.55
LJ	8.15	6.75
TJ	16.80	14.10
SP	20.50	17.75
DT	65.00	61.20
HT	76.00	71.00
JT	83.00	61.40
Dec/Hep	8100	6200
20kmW	1:24:00	1:36:00
50kmW	4:06:00	4:06:00

The qualification system combines entry standards and invitations based on performance lists. As was the case for the 2015 IAAF World Championships and Rio 2016 Olympic Games, the IAAF has established a target number of athletes for each discipline (apart from the 10,000m, marathon and race walks) and extra non-qualifying athletes will be invited to fill the quotas.

There are some special qualification opportunities such as being reigning World champion or winner of the 2016 Diamond League race or Hammer Throw Challenge; and area champions in all individual events except the marathons (for which top 10 finishers in Gold Label Marathons held in the qualification period will qualify). For the 10,000m: the top 15 finishers in 2017 men's and women's World Cross-country Championships. For 20k walks: top three in the 2016 IAAF Challenge, 50kW: top three in the 2016 IAAF Team Championships.

It will still be possible for member federations without any qualified athletes to be represented with one unqualified athlete (subject to certain conditions). Relay teams can qualify by being one of the best ranked teams at the end of the qualification period.

Qualification Period: For the 10,000m, Marathon, Race Walks, Relays and Combined Events: from 1 Jan 2016 to midnight Sunday, 23 Jul 2017 (regardless of time zone).

For all other events: from 1 Oct 2016 to midnight Sunday, 23 Jul 2017 (regardless of the time zone).

For full details download a pdf file from: iaaf-world-championships-london-2017-qualific.pdf

Most World Champs Appearances
Men
12 Jesús Ángel García ESP 1993-2015
10 Virgilijus Alekna LTU 1995-2013
10 Kim Collins SKN 1995-2015
Women
11 Susana Feitor POR 1991-2011
10 Franka Dietzsch GER 1991-2009
10 Nicoleta Grasu ROU 1993-2013

WORLD YOUTH CHAMPIONSHIPS

The 10th (and last) IAAF World Youth (U18) Championships will be in Nairobi, Kenya on 12-16 July 2017.

World U18 Championship Records
Men

100m	10.28A	A H Sani Brown JPN	2015
200m	20.34A	A H Sani Brown JPN	2015
400m	45.24	Kirani James GRN	2009
800m	1:44.08	Leonard Kosencha KEN	2011
1500m	3:36.38A	Kumari Taki KEN	2015
3000m	7:40.10	William Sitonik KEN	2011
2000mSt	5:19.99	Meresa Kassaye ETH	2013
110h *	13.13	Jaheel Hyde JAM	2013
400mh *	49.01	William Wynne USA	2007
HJ	2.27	Huang Haiqiang CHN	2005
PV	5.30A	Armand Duplantis SWE	2015
	5.30A	Vladyslav Malykhin UKR	2015
LJ	8.05A	Maykel Massó CUB	2015
TJ	16.63	Héctor Fuentes CUB	2005
	16.63	Lázaro Martínez CUB	2013
SP 5kg	24.35	Jacko Gill NZL	2011
DT 1.5kg	70.67q	Mykyta Nesterenko UKR	2007
HT 5kg	84.91	Hlib Piskunov UKR	2015
JT 700g	82.96	Reinhardt van Zyl RSA	2011
Decathlon (yth)	8002	Niklas Kaul GER	2015
10000mW	40:51.31	Pavel Parshin RUS	2011

Women

100m	11.08A	Candace Hill USA	2015
200m	22.43A	Candace Hill USA	2015
400m	51.19	Nawal Al-Jack SUD	2005
800m	2:01.13	Anita Henriksdóttir ISL	2013
1500m	4:09.48	Faith Kipyegon KEN	2011
3000m	8:53.94	Mercy Cherono KEN	2007
2000mSt	6:11.83	Korahubish Itaa ETH	2009
100mh *	12.94	Yanique Thompson JAM	2013
400mh	55.94A	Sydney McLaughlin USA	2015
HJ	1.92	Irina Kovalenko UKR	2003
PV	4.35	Vicky Parnov AUS	2007
LJ	6.47	Darya Klishina RUS	2007
TJ	13.86	Cristine Spîtaru ROU	2003
SP 3kg	20.09	Emel Dereli TUR	2013
DT	56.34	Xie Yuchen CHN	2013
HT 3kg	73.20	Réke Gyurátz HUN	2013
JT 500g	60.35	Haruka Kitaguchi JPN	2015
Hep yth	6037	Géraldine Ruckstuhl SUI	2015
5000mW	20:13.91	Olga Shargina RUS	2013
Mixed 4x400m	3:19.54A	USA	2015

* 110mh 91.4cm, 400mh 84cm, W 100mh 84cm

COMMONWEALTH GAMES 2018

THE 21ST COMMONWEALTH GAMES are due to be staged on the Gold Coast in Austrlia on 8-15 April 2018.. These multi-sport competitions are held every four years, and contested by athletes representing the nations of the British Commonwealth. They were first staged as the British Empire Games at Hamilton, Canada in 1930. They became the British Empire and Commonwealth Games in 1954, and the British Commonwealth Games in 1970.

The last Games were held in Glasgow in July - August 2014.

Games Records
Men

100m	9.88	Ato Boldon TRI	1998
200m	19.97	Frank Fredericks NAM	1994
400m	44.24	Kirani James GRN	2014
800m	1:43.22	Steve Cram ENG	1986
1500m	3:32.16	Filbert Bayi TAN	1974
5000m	12:56.41	Augustine Choge KEN	2006
10000m	27:45.39	Wilberforce Talel KEN	2002
Mar	2:09:12	Ian Thompson ENG	1974
3000mSt	8:10.44	Jonathan Ndiku KEN	2014
110mh	13.08	Colin Jackson WAL	1990/94
400mh	48.05	Louis van Zyl RSA	2006
HJ	2.36	Nick Saunders BAH	1990
PV	5.80	Steve Hooker AUS	2006
LJ	8.39w	Yusuf Alli NGR	1990
	8.30	Fabrice Lapierre AUS	2010
TJ	17.86	Jonathan Edwards ENG	2002
SP	21.61	O'Dayne Richards JAM	2014
DT	66.39	Frantz Kruger RSA	2002
HT	77.53	Stuart Rendell AUS	2006
JT	88.75	Marius Corbett RSA	1998
Dec	8663	Daley Thompson ENG	1986
4x100m	37.58	Jamaica	2014
4x400m	2:59.03	Jamaica	1998
20kmW	1:19:55	Nathan Deakes AUS	2006
50kmW	3:42:53	Nathan Deakes AUS	2006

Women

100m	10.85	Blessing Okagbare NGR	2014
200m	22.20	Debbie Ferguson BAH	2002
	22.19w	Merlene Ottey JAM	1982
400m	50.17	Sandie Richards JAM	1998
800m	1:57.35	Maria Mutola MOZ	2002
1500m	4:05.26	Nancy Langat KEN	2010
3000m	8:32.17	Angela Chalmers CAN	1994
500m	14:31.42	Paula Radcliffe GBR	2002
10000m	31:27.83	Salina Kosgei KEN	2002
3000mSt	9:19.51	Dorcus Inzikuru UGA	2006
Mar	2:25:28	Lisa Martin AUS	1990
100mh	12.65	Brigitte Foster-Hylton JAM	2006 (h)
400mh	53.82	Jana Pittman AUS	2006
HJ	1.96	Hestrie Cloete RSA	2002
PV	4.62	Kym Howe-Nadin AUS	2006
LJ	6.97	Bronwyn Thompson AUS	2006
TJ	14.86	Ashia Hansen ENG	2002
SP	20.47	Valerie Adams NZL	2010
DT	65.92	Beatrice Faumuina NZL	1998
HT	71.97	Sultana Frizell CAN	2014
JT	65.96	Kimberley Mickle AUS	2014
Hep	6695	Jane Flemming AUS	1990
4x100m	41.83	Jamaica	2014
4x400m	3:23.82	Jamaica	2014
20kmW	1:32:46	Jane Saville AUS	2006

Most gold medals at all events
Men
6 Don Quarrie JAM 100m 1970-74-78, 200m 1970-74, 4x100mR 1970

Women
7 Marjorie Jackson AUS 100y 1950-54, 220y 1950-54, 4x110yR 1954, 440yR and 660yR 1950

7 Raelene Boyle AUS 100m 1970-74, 200m 1970-74, 400m 1982, 4x100mR 1970-74

6 Pam Kilborn/Ryan AUS 80mh 1962-66-70, LJ 1962, 4x100mR 1966-70

Most Medals – all events
Men: 6 Don Quarrie 1970-78, Harry Hart 1930-34. Allan Wells 1978-82

Women: 9 Raelene Boyle 1970-8. 8 Denise Robertson/Boyd AUS 1974-8; 7 Marjorie Jackson 1950-54, Valerie Young 1958-72, Kathy Cook ENG 1978-86, Angella Issajenko CAN 1982-86, Debbie Flintoff AUS 1982-90

Most Medals at one Games
Men: 4 Keith Gardner 1958 2G, 1S, 1B
Women: 5 Decima Norman 1938 5G; 5 Shirley Strickland 1950 3G, 2S

Oldests (y years, d days)
Men
Winner & Medallist: 42y 335d Jack Holden ENG marathon 1950

Women
Winner   40y 217d Judy Oakes ENG shot 1998
Medallist 40y 252d Rosemary Payne SCO 2nd DT 1974

Youngests
Men
Winner: 16y 263d Sam Richardson CAN LJ 1934
Medallist 16y 260d Sam Richardson CAN 2nd TJ 1934

Women
Winner   17y 137d Debbie Brill CAN HJ 1970
Medallist c.15y Sabine Chebichi KEN 3rd 800m 1974

Most Games Contested
6 Robin Tait NZL 1962-82, successively 4-3-6-1-4-8 at men's discus, Judy Oakes ENG 1978-98, successively 3-1-2-2-1-1 at women's shot.

Record medal-winning span of 20 years by Oakes and by Robert Weir (winner of hammer 1982, and at discus 5-3-1-3 in 1982-94-98-02).

MAJOR MEETINGS 2016-2017

Diamond League, World Challenge and European Athletics Premium Meetings

DL – Diamond League, WC – World Challenge, EAP European Premium Meeting

2016 date		Meeting	2017 date	
5 Mar	WC	Melbourne World Challenge, AUS	–	
6 May	DL	Qatar Super Grand Prix, Doha, QAT	5 May	DL
7 May	WC	Jamaica International, KIngston JAM	20 May	WC
8 May	WC	Golden Grand Prix, Kawasaki, JPN	21 May	WC
14 May	DL	Shanghai Golden Grand Prix, CHN	13 May	DL
18 May	WC	Beijing, CHN	–	
20 May	WC	Golden Spike, Ostrava, CZE	28 Jun	WC
22 May	WC	Fanny Blankers-Koen Games, Hengelo, NED	11 Jun	WC
22 May	WC	Mohammed VI d'Athlétisme, Rabat, MAR	16 Jul	WC
25 May	WC	Dakar, Sénégal	–	
28 May	DL	Prefontaine Classic, Eugene, Oregon, USA	27 May	DL
2 Jun	DL	Golden Gala, Rome, ITA	8 Jun	DL
5 Jun	DL	Müller Grand Prix, Birmingham, GBR	20 Aug	DL
9 Jun	DL	ExxonMobil Bislett Games, Oslo, NOR	15 Jun	DL
16 Jun	DL	Bauhaus, Stockholm, SWE	18 Jun	DL
19 Jun		GP Brasil, São Bernardo 2016, Rio de Janeiro 2017	3 Jun	WC
23 Jun	WC	Meeting Madrid, ESP	14 Jul	WC
29 Jun	EAP	Paavo Nurmi Games, Turku, Finland	13 Jun	WC
15 Jul	DL	Herculis, Monaco, MON	21 Jul	DL
22/23 Jul	DL	Müller Anniversary Games, London (OS)	9 Jul	DL
25 Aug	DL	Athletissima, Lausanne, SUI	6 Jul	DL
27 Aug	DL	Meeting de Paris, Saint-Denis, FRA	1 Jul	DL
1 Sep	DL	Weltklasse, Zürich, SUI	24 Aug	DL
3 Sep	WC	ISTAF, Berlin, GER	27 Aug	WC
5 Sep	WC	Boris Hanzekovic Memorial, Zagreb, CRO	29 Aug	WC
6 Sep	EAP	Palio Citta della Quercia, Rovereto, ITA	29 Aug	EAP
9 Sep	DL	Memorial Van Damme, Brussels, BEL	1 Sep	DL

INDOORS

WIT – IAAF World Indoor Tour; EAA – indoor permit meetings; US USATF series in USA.

2016 date		Meeting	2017 date	
3 Feb	EAA	International PSD Bank, Düsseldorf, GER	1 Feb	WIT
5-6 Feb	US	Armory Track Invitational, New York, USA	4 Feb	US
6 Feb	WIT	BW-Bank Meeting, Karlsruhe, GER	4 Feb	WIT
12 Feb	EAA	Copernicus Cup, Torun, POL	10 Feb	WIT
13 Feb		ISTAF, Berlin	10 Feb	
14 Feb		Russian Winter, Moscow, RUS	4-5 Feb	
14 Feb	WIT	New Balance Indoor GP, Boston (Roxbury), USA	28 Jan	WIT/US
17 Feb	WIT	Globen Galan, Stockholm, SWE	–	
20 Feb	WIT	Glasgow/Birmingham, GBR	18 Feb	WIT
20 Feb		Millrose Games, New York (Armory), USA	11 Feb	US
11/12 Mar	US	USA Indoor Champs. Portland/Albuquerque	4/5 Mar	US

IAAF WORLD COMBINED EVENTS CHALLENGE 2016 & 2017

29/30 Apr	Multistars, Firenze, ITA	28/29 Apr
28/29 May	Hypo-Mehrkampf Meeting, Götzis, AUT	27/28 May
12/13 Jun	TNT Express Meeting, Kladno, CZE	17/18 Jun
27/28 Jun	Stadtwerke Ratingen, GER	24/25 Jun
19/20 Jun	Pan-American CE, Ottawa, CAN	4/5 Jul
19/20 Sep	Decastar, Talence, FRA	16/17 Sep

Plus International Games and Championships
European Athletics Combined Events Permit: Arona, ESP 6-7/4-5 Jun

IAAF WORLD RACE WALKING CHALLENGE 2016 & 2017

21 Feb	Oceania Championships, Adelaide, AUS	19 Feb
6 Mar	Ciudad Juárez MEX	12 Mar
	Monterrey, MEX	19 Mar
20 Mar	Asian Champs, Nomi, JPN	19 Mar
9 Apr	Rio Maior, POR	1 Apr

MAJOR MEETINGS 2016–2021

23 Apr   Taicang, CHN   15 Apr
Pan-American Race Walking Cup, Lima   13/14 May
28 May   Gran Premio Cantones de La Coruña, ESP   28 May
Plus European Cup Race Walking and World Championships
European Athletics Race Walking Permit Meetings 2016 & 2017
Dudince, SVK 19/25 Mar, Podebrady, CZE 9/8 Apr, Alytus, LTU 10/9 Jun,

IAAF HAMMER THROW CHALLENGE 2017
At the following meetings (above): Kawasaki JPN, Rio de Janeiro BRA, Szczecin POL, Ostrava CZE, Székesfehérvár HUN, Madrid ESP.

MARATHON MAJORS 2017
Tokyo 26 Feb, Boston 17 Apr, London 34 Apr, Berlin 24 Sep, Chicago 8 Oct, New York 5 Nov.

ASIAN GRAND PRIX 2017
Jiaxing CHN 24 Apr, Jinhau CHN 27 Apr, Taipei City TPE 30 Apr

EUROPEAN AA CLASSIC MEETINGS 2017 (with 2016 dates of these meetings first)
Montreuil-sous-Bois FRA 7/1 Jun, Bydgoszcz POL (European Athletics Festival) 5/2 Jun, Andújar ESP 16 Jul/2 Jun, Marseille -/3 Jun, Prague, CZE (Josef Odlozil Memorial) 6/5 Jun, Gothenburg SWE 15 Jul/10 Jun, Huelva ESP (Iberoamerican) 3/14 Jun, Szczecin POL (Janusz Kusocinski Memorial) 18/14 Jun, Copenhagen DEN 18/19 Jun, Velenje SLO 14/21 Jun, Tomblaine FRA 14/28 Jun, Sollentuna 28/29 Jun, Székesfehérvár HUN (István Gyulai Memorial) 18/4 Jul, Sotteville-lès-Rouen FRA 18/4 Jul, Luzern SUI (Spitzen) 14 Jun/11 Jul, Padova ITA 17/16 Jul, Heusden-Zolder, BEL 16/22 Jul, Karlstad SWE 27/26 Jul, Malmö SWE -/18 Aug.
Special premium: Jun 1- Athens GRE Street Pole Vault; Aug 22- Warsaw POL

USATF Championship Series 2016/2017 (selection)
Philadelphia (Penn Relays) 28-29/28 Apr, USA v The World at Penn Relays 30/29 Apr, Des Moines (Drake Relays) 30/29 Apr, Prefontaine Classic, adidas Boost Boston Games 18/4 Jun, US Championships Eugene 1-10 Jul, Sacramento 23-25 Jun
Track Town USA Summer Series 2017: Bay Area CAL 28 Jun, Portland 2 Jul, New York 7 Jul l

NORTH AMERICA NACAC MEETINGS 2016/2017 (selection)
George Town CAY 14/13 May, Baie Mahault, Guadeloupe 14/17 May, Kingston, JAM (Racers GP) 21/10 Jun, Vancouver (Harry Jerome Track Classic) CAN 17/11 Jun, Victoria CAN 10/19 Jun, Edmonton CAN (Track Town Classic) 15 Jul/3-4 Jun

MAJOR INTERNATIONAL EVENTS 2017-2021

2017
European Indoor Championships – Belgrade, Serbia (3-5 March)
IAAF World Cross Country Championships – Kampala, Uganda (26 March)
IAAF World Relays – Nassau, Bahamas (22-23 April)
Asian Youth Championships – Bangkok (20-23 May)
European Race Walking Cup, Poděbrady, Czech Republic (21 May)
European Team Championships Super League – Lille, France (24-25 June)
African U20 Championships – Tiemcen, Algeria (29 June-2 July)
IAAF World Youth Championships – Nairobi, Kenya (12-16 Jul)
European U23 Championships – Bydgoszcz, Poland (13-16 Jul)
Commonwealth Youth Games – Nassau, Bahamas (19-23 Jul)
European U20 Championships – Grosseto, Italy (20-23 Jul)
IAAF World Championships – London, GBR (5-13 August)
World University Games – Taipei, Taiwan (20-25 August)
European Cross Country Championships – Samorin, Slovakia (10 Dec)

2018
Asian Indoor Championships – Ranchi, India (February)
IAAF World Indoor Championships – Birmingham, GBR (2-4 March)
IAAF World Cross Country Championships – Aarhus, Denmark (March)
Commonwealth Games – Gold Coast, Australia (8-15 April)
IAAF World Half Marathon Championships – Valencia, Spain (24 March)
IAAF World Race Walking Cup – Taicang, China
African Championships – Lagos, Nigeria
IAAF World Junior Championships – Tampere, Finland (10 July)
European U18 Championships – Györ, Hungary-15
Central American & Caribbean Games – Barranquilla, Colombia (19 Jul – 3 Aug)
European Championships – Berlin, Germany (7-12 August
Asian Games – Jakarta, Indonesia
NACAC Senior Championships, CAN (10-12 August)
IAAF Continental Cup – Ostrava, Czech Republic (8-9 Sep)

MAJOR MEETINGS 2017-2021

Youth Olympic Games – Buenos Aires, Argentina (11-23 Sep)
European Cross Country Championships – Tilburg, Netherlands (x Dec)

2019
European Indoor Championships – Glasgow, GBR (March)
IAAF World Relays – Nassau, Bahamas
Pan-American Games ¬ Lima, Peru (26 Jul – 11 Aug)
World University Games – Brasilia, Brazil
Asian Games – Hanoi, Vietnam
IAAF World Championships – Doha, Qatar (28 Sep – 6 Oct)

2020
European U18 Championships – Rieti, Italy
Olympic Games – Tokyo, Japan (31 July – 9 August)

2021
IAAF World Championships – Eugene, USA

Competition Changes

As from 2017 the **European Team Championships** and **European Combined Events Team Championships** will be staged every two years

The IAAF Council decided to discontinue the **World U18 Championships** after the 2017 edition in Nairobi, Kenya. The IAAF will work with Area Associations to find a more appropriate competition structure for assisting the career development of U18 age group athletes. Mixed relays were added to the **World CC Champs** as new events in Kampala 2017. At the **IAAF World Relays** in Nassau, Bahamas 2017 (which will continue also in 2019 in The Bahamas) Distance Medley Relays will be replaced by a Mixed 4x400 m relay.

A Mile or 5 km road race will be added to the programme for the **World Half Marathon Championships** 2018

For the **IAAF Continental Cup** in Ostrava 2018 the IAAF Council decided to delete the 5000m races for both men and women and replace the men's and women's 4x400m Relay with a Mixed 4x400m Relay composed of two men and two women per team running in any order.

For the **European Cross-country Championships** in Slovakia 2017: There will be two innovations within the competition programme. For first time a mixed relay 4 x 1.5 km will be held, organizers are expecting that up to 20 teams could compete. Two men and women will run for each team. In 2017 (odd year) the order will be W-M-W-M and in even years M-W-M-W. Also in the team scoring only three athletes will be needed instead of current four.

IAAF News

Reform changes agreed in 2017 included reducing the power of the president so that there would be more authority invested in the Congress, Council and Executive Board.

An independent athletics integrity unit was established.

Olivier Gers was hired as the IAAF's first Chief Executive Officer, starting this job on 1 October 2016.

Sponsorship of the IAAF Kids development programme was terminated a year early by Nestlé.

With Darya Klishina already accepted as being able to compete internationally as a neutral athlete, the IAAF Doping Review Board agreed on 23 February 2017 that the applications of three Russians had met the exceptional eligibility criteria to compete in international competition as neutral athletes under competition rule 22.1A(b) while the Russian national federation (RusAF) remains suspended. The Doping Review Board, which is composed of Robert Hersh (chairman), Sylvia Barlag and Antti Pihlakoski, unanimously accepted the applications of Anzhelika Sidorova (2014 European pole vault champion; pb of 4.85), Kristina Sivkova (2015 European Junior 100m bronze medallist; pb of 11.22) and Aleksey Sokirskiy (78.91 hammer thrower). At the time of going to press many other Russian athletes have similarly applied to be able to compete.

The IAAF Council has set up working grops to examine three vexatious issues:
Age Manipulation (chaired by Adille Sumariwalla), in view of athletes competing over-age at Junior and Youth events.
Transfer of Allegiance (chaired by Hiroshi Yokokawa), with new trsanfers frozen for the time being from February 2017.
Performance/Results Manipulation (chaired by Berrnard Amsalem) ,in recognition of faked marks apparently submitted for entry to championships.

ATHLETICS INTERNATIONAL
Edited by Peter Matthews & Mel Watman

The newsletter has, since 1993, been keeping readers in over 60 countries informed of very detailed results (to at least world top 150-200 standards) of track and field, road and cross-country and news items from around the world. It is obtainable by email, with at least 35 issues published annually (weekly in peak season).
Annual subscription 2017: £70 or US $100 or 90 euros. Cash or cheques drawn on a UK bank, payable to Athletics International – or via Paypal or bank transfer.
Athletics International, 13 Garden Court, Stanmore HA7 4TE, UK
Email: mel@gardencourt.fsnet.co.uk

DRUGS BANS 2016

Drugs bans in 2017
As announced by IAAF or national governing bodies.
Suspension: L - life ban, y = years, m = months, W = warning and disqualification, P = pending hearing

Leading athletes

Dawn Harper Nelson USA	8 Feb	3m

Drugs bans in 2016
Leading athletes

Men Name	Date	Ban
Ihab Abdelrahman EGY	17 Apr	2y
Mohamad Al-Garni QAT	15 Jun	4y
Youssef Al-Masrahi KSA	15 Jun	4y
Moukhleb Al-Outaibi KSA	19 Jul & 16 Aug	4y
Shawnacy Barber CAN	9 Jul	W
Béranger Bossé CAF	31 Jan	2y
Konrad Bukowiecki POL		W
Gebo Burka ETH	17 Jan	18m
Fernando Cabada USA	6 Dec	W
Jamel Chatbi ITA	30 Jun	2y 8m
Abdellah Dacha MAR	14 Jul	4y
Mihai Donisan ROU	20 Feb	2y
Girmay Gebre ETH	Jan	
Victor Hogan RSA	15 Apr	9m
Kirill Ikonnikov RUS		L
Trell Kimmons USA	12 Mar	2y
Kennedy Kipyego KEN	17 Apr	4y
Amine Laâlou MAR	9 Apr	8y
Brian Mariano NED	6 Feb	4y
Rimantas Martisauskas LTU	30 Jan	2y
Sentayehu Merga ETH		4y
Gabor Pásztor HUN	7 Jul	4y
Marin Premeru CRO	6 Aor	4y
Alex Schwazer ITA	1 Jan	8y
Dharambir Singh IND	2 Jul	8y
Wang Qin CHN	10 Sep	6m
Women		
Zivile Balciunaite LTU	15 Apr	8y
Gwen Berry USA	11 Mar	3m
Tatyana Chernova* RUS	5 Feb	3y 8m
Jessica Cosby-Torruga USA	12 Sep	6y
Silvia Danekova BUL	Aug	P
Dawn Harper Nelson USA	1 Dec	3m
Olga Kucherenko RUS	18 Dec	2y
and all results annulled from 28 Aug 2011		
Anastasiya Kudinova KAZ	13 Jul	4y
Edinah Kwambai KEN	10 Apr	3m
Abdelhadi Labali MAR	9 Apr	8y
Mirela Lavric ROU	Mar	P
Liu Hong CHN	7 May	1m
Florida Miniyanova KAZ	13 Jul	4y
Anastasiya Mokhnyuk UKR	Mar	P
Hanane Ouhaddou MAR	9 Apr	8y
Mulu Seboka ETH	16 Feb	7m
Ana Claúdia Silva BRA	3 Feb	5m
Anastasiya Soprunova KAZ	31 Jan	4y
Olesya Sviridova RUS	14 Jun	4y

4y: Mohammad Yasseen Al-Hasan KSA (5 Feb), Giorgio Maria Bortolozzi ITA (28 Feb), Moucine Cheaouri MAR (30 Apr), Amandine Guyot FRA (26 Jun), Mohammed Hattouchi MAR (14 Feb), Farkhoiud Kuralov TJK (13 Jun), Kristine Kuznecova LAT (18 Sep), Amin Lotfollahi IRI (11 May), Azwindini Lukhwareni RSA (30 Apr), Maria Magdalena ROU (9 Oct), Neddy Marie SEY (15 Mar), Maria Pizzono ITA (28 Apr), Anton Pototskyi UKR (22 May), Zakaria Rabah MAR (23 Apr), Andrea Ragusa IND (10 Jan), Rohinit Raut IND (28 Apr), Mehdi Rostami Mogaddam IRI (25 Apr), Samarth Sadashiv IND (3 Jan), Kaushal Singh IND (29 Jun), P.N.Soundharya IND (1 Jul & 30 Jul), Gaurav Yadav IND (25 Jun), Jaouad Zain MAR; **3.5y:** Basirah Sharifa Nasir BRN (6 May), Liz Palmer USA (5 Mar), Ronald Silva BRA (10 Jan); **2y:** Mohamed Boufdil MAR (24 Apr), Hirut Beyene ETH (7 Aug); **1.5y:** Girmay Birhanu ETH (14 Jan); **1y:** Yekaterina Generalova RUS (27 May), Rosanna Grufi ITA (26 Feb); 10m: Ryoma Kato JPN (10 Jul); **6m:** Naima El Ayafi MAR, Naima Elaydi MAR (31 Jan), Sabastiano Zappula ITA (10 Jan); **1m:** Vu Thi Ly VIE (25 Sep); **W:** Isabela Silva BRA (20 Sep), Johanna van Schalkwyk RSA (6 Mar)

Coaches: Life ineligibility Quirinon de Moraes BRA from 24 Oct, 10y: Vladimir Mokhnev RUS 2007-14 and from 23 Dec 2016

Add to Drugs Bans 2015
Men

Tim Abeyie GHA	4 Jul	4y
Anis Ananenko BLR	27 May	4y
Roman Avramenko RUS	30 Jul	8y
Maksim Dyldin RUS	22 May	4y
Samson Idiata NGR	17 Sep	4y
Mikhail Idrisov RUS	13 Jun	4y
Robert Kajuga RWA	23 May	4y
German Komarov RUS	16 Jun	4y
Pavel Krivitskiy BLR	11 May	4y
Rohit Kumar IND	17 Sep	8y
Sentayehu Merga ETH	13 Sep	4y
Ángel Mullera ESP	16 Jul	2y
Ivan Noskov RUS	2 Jun	4y
Mikhail Ryzhov RUS	2 Jun	4y
Denis Strelkov RUS	2 Jun	4y
Vadim Vrublevskiy RUS	17 Jun	2y
Aleksandr Yargunkin RUS	13 Aug	4y
Women		
Tosin Adeloye NGR	24 Jul	8y
Elmira Alembekova RUS	2 Jun	4y
Malika Asahssah MAR	15 Nov	4y
Geraldine Duvenage RSA	18 Apr	4y
Veronica Marinescu (Budileanu) ROU	1 Nov	4y
Lyudmila Olyanovska UKR	9 Nov	4y
Sueli Pereira BRA	Dec	4y
Darya Reznichenko UZB	11 Dec	4y
Yekaterina Sharmina RUS	7 Dec	3y
(results annulled 17 Jun 2011 to 5 Aug 2015)		
Vera Sokolova RUS	2 Jun	4y
Olesya Syreva RUS	27 Nov	8y
Kristina Ugarova RUS	7 Sep	2y
Bernice Wilson GBR	12 Feb	10m

8y: Luis Antunes BRA (27 Sep); **4y:** Mohammed Abareghi IRI (11 Jul), Hadisch Ahmadi IRI (9 Oct), A.M. Al Abbody IRQ (10 Oct), Mohammad Ali IRQ (10 Oct), Manuel Isidro Bellorin VEN (26 Apr), Yuriy Bishayev RUS (25 Oct), Denis Berisov BLR (4 Jun), Valeriya Fyodorova RUS (6 Feb), Karthika IND (31 Dec), Benedikt Karus IND (8 Feb), Yevgeniy Khokhlov RUS (11 Aug), Anastasiya Kirhina RUS (8 May), Larisa Kleymenova RUS (9 Sep), Songuel Konak TUR (17 May), Sina Mohammadi IRI (16 Oct), Arishu Patel IND (31 Dec), V Pavan IND (29 Oct), Sueli Silva Pereira BRA (31 Dec), Yevgeniy Rachok BLR (2 Apr), Esmaeel Roomi IRI (16 Apr), Tamara Shchemerova RUS 8 May, V Suresh IND (29 Oct), Taeme Shumye Weldegebriel ETH (23 Sep), Gurmeet Singh IND (19 Sep), Gergana Vitcvheva BUL (14 Feb), Yin Jung CHN (1 Sep), Yogesh IND (24 Nov), Jaouad Zain MAR (29 Nov), Yuliya Zaripova RUS SP/DT (23 Apr); **3y 9m:** Doru Teofilescu ROU (27 Jun); **3y 6m:** Luíz Fernando Matias BRA (19

DRUGS

Sep); **3y:** Martin Pogelschek AUT (Jun); **2y:** Gonzalo Calisto ECU (19 Aug), Christopher Guajardo CHI (17 Jul), Kashish Khanna IND (27 Apr), Tehauraï Ruaroo FRA (14 Jun); 20m: Gregory Pizza USA (25 Jul) **18m:** Delphine Ther FRA (15 Aug); **1y:** Georgi Georgiev BUL (14 Feb), **8m:** Abdrej Bician SVK (9 May), 6m: Margarita Fuentes-Pila ESP (2 Aug), Arianna Toippi ITA (19 Sep); **4m:** Vilmo Luciani ITA (8 Nov); **3m:** Shun Hyon KOR (8 Jun); W: Ines Antunes POR (18 Oct).

Add to Drugs Bans 2014
Men
Nick Mossberg USA   3 Aug   4y
Women
Anastasiya Bazdyreva* RUS   23 Apr   2y
    Results annulled from 23 Apr 14 to 24 Aug 15
Rita Jeptoo KEN (from 2y)   17 Apr & 25 Sep   4y
    Results annulled from April 2014.
6y: Avtar Singh IND (28 Nov); **2y:** Elvira Abdrakhmanova RUS (20 Oct); **9m:** Enrique Sebastien ESP (21 Dec); **8m:** Francisco Iván Filho BRA (12 Oct); **6m:** Cláudia Rodrigues POR (27 Jul

Add to Drugs Bans 2013
Men
Othmane El Goumri MAR   11 Aug   2y
Women
Asli Cakir Alptekin TUR   13 Jan   8y
                reduced to 4y
4y: Cody Bidlow USA (1 Jan); **2y:** Hassan Mahmoud Abdelgawad EGY (31 Jul), Damar Robinson JAM (16 Jun); **1y:** Hélio Fumo MOZ (20 Nov)

Add to Drugs Bans 2012
Men
Nesta Carter JAM   P
Kirill Ikonnikov RUS   3 Aug   L
Pavel Krivitskiy BLR   17 Jul   2y
Abdelhadi Labáli* MAR   9 Jul   2y
Maksim Mazuryk POL   8 Aug
Dmitriy Starodubtsev RUS   8 Aug
Women
Vera Ganeyeva RUS
Yolanda Caballero* COL   24 Oct   4y
Najim El Qady* MAR   19 Nov   2y
Kristina Khaleyeva/Ugarova *RUS   26 Jun   2y
    (results annulled 26 Jun to 25 Dec 2012)
Alena Kudashkina* RUS   9 Jul   2.5y

Add to Drugs Bans 2011
Men
Adil Annani MAR *   4 Nov   4y
Thomas Cawley USA   Jul   4y
Najim El Qady* MAR   19 Mar   2y
Women
Gamze Bulut TUR*   20 Jul   4y
    (results annulled from 20 Jul 2011)
Olga Kucherenko RUS   28 Aug   2y
Yekaterina Sharmina* RUS   17 Jun   3y
    (results annulled 17 Jun 2011 to 5 Aug 2015)

Add to Drugs Bans 2010
Women
Mariya Savinova* RUS   26 Jul   4y
from 24 Aug 15
    (results annulled 26 Jul 2010 to 19 Aug 2013)
2y: Stéphane July SUI (14 Oct)

Add to Drugs Bans 2009
Men
Ildar Minshin RUS *   15 Aug   2y
Women
Tatyana Chernova* RUS   15 Aug   3y 8m
    (results annulled 15 Aug 2009 to 22 Jul 2013)
Lidiya Grigoryeva* RUS   17 Apr   2.5y
    (results annulled 17 Apr 2009 to 14 May 2010)
Irina Timofeyeva* RUS   10 Oct   3y

Add to Drugs Bans 2008
Men
Wilfredo Martínez CUB   16 Aug   1y
Mariya Abakumova RUS   19 Aug   P
Women
Yarelys Barrios CUB   18 Aug   1y
    (results annulled 18 Aug 2008 to 17 Aug 2009)
Anna Chicherova RUS   21 Aug   P
Josephine Onyia ESP   17 Aug
Yekaterina Volkova RUS   15 Aug
2y: Domenico Ruggiero ITA (Aug)

Add to Drugs Bans 2007
Women
Elvan Abeylegesse TUR *   25 Aug   2y
    (results annulled 25 Aug 2007 to 25 Aug 2009
Hrisopiyí Devetzí GRE   31 Aug   4y

Further athletes found positive on retesting of samples, but yet to be fully resolved:
From OG 2008
Nesta Carter JAM 1st 4x100m
Denis Alekseyev RUS 3rd 4x400m
Aleksandr Pogorelov RUS 4th Dec
Ivan Yushkov RUS 10th SP
Yuliya Chermoshanskaya RUS 1st W 4x100m
From OG 2012
Anastasiya Kapachinskaya RUS 2nd W 4x400m
Yevgeniya Kolodko RUS 2nd W SP

Coaches banned: Life: Viktor Chegin RUS, George Skafídas GRE; **4y:** Yevgeniy Yevsyukov RUS
Life: Dr.Sergey Nikolayevich RUS

Russian doping violations
The Court of Arbitration for Sport ruled on April 14 that even though she tested positive for a banned anabolic steroid at the 2005 World Champs, Russia's Tatyana Andrianova will keep her 800m bronze medal because the re-testing of her sample in 2015 was beyond the eight year statute of limitations then in force. The IAAF's sanction of banning the athlete for two years from 22 Sep 2015 and annulling all her results from 9 Aug 2005 (the date of the test) until 8 Aug 2007 has been rescinded.

* Athlete Biological Passport cases

OBITUARY 2016

See ATHLETICS 2016 for obituaries from early 2016: Iolanda Balas, Dick Brown, Lawrie Croxson, Henri Delerue, John Disley, Yuriy Dumchev, Bennie Greyling, Martin Jensen, Arthur Keily, Jim McNamara, Edmund Piatkowski, Dave Sime, Thyge Thòrgerson, Yeóryios Tasníkas, Mirko Vujacic.

Valeriy ABRAMOV (Russia) (b. 22 Aug 1956 Yertsevo near Arkhangelsk) on 14 September in Moscow. His major championships record: 5000m: Olympics 1980- sf; Worlds 1983- 11; Europeans 1982- 6; World Cup 1979- 2, 1981- 4; Eur Cup 1981- 2. At 3000m: Eur Indoors 1982 & 1983- 3. At 1500m: EC: 1978- h; ECp: 1979- 4. At 10000m: ECp: 1983- 3. Russian champion at 1500m 1978, 5000m 1979 (2nd 1980, 1982-3, 3rd 1987), 10000m 1987 (2nd 1985, 3rd 1988). He set Russian records for 5000m of 13:15.6 in 1979 and 13:11.99 at Rieti on 9 Sep 1981 and for 10000m with 27:55.17 in 1984. Other pbs: 800m 1:47.9 (1978), 1500m 3:36.80 (1981), 3000m 7:46.5 (1983).

Michael George Raymond **'Mike' AGOSTINI** (Trinidad & Tobago) (b. 23 Jan 1935 Port of Spain) in Sydney, Australia on 12 May. Ranked in the world's top eight for 100m each year 1953-9 (and at 200m in 1956-7), he was a durable sprinter with considerable championship success: Olympics 6th 100m & 4th 200m 1956; Empire Games: 1st 100y & sf 220y 1954, 3rd 100y & sf 220y 1958 (for Canada); Pan-American Games: 2nd 100m & 3= 200m 1955, 2nd 100m & 3rd 200m and 4x100m 1959 (for British West Indies). He shot to world attention while at Fresno State University with a world indoor 100y record 9.6 on his 19th birthday in 1954 and he went on to win the Empire Games 100y and was ranked 6th in the world by *Track & Field News*. In 1956 he set an unratified world record of 20.1 for 220y straight at Bakersfield on 17 March and tied the world 100y record with 9.3 at Long Beach on 5 May, but the third watch failed so it was not put forward for ratification as there were no approved AAU timers, and no alternate timers. Although he represented Canada after Trinidad, he enjoyed his experience of Melbourne in 1956 so much that he lived in Australia from 1959, becoming an Australian citizen in 1961. He missed the 1960 Olympics as he did not compete in the trials for selecting the British West Indies team, and that summer closed his athletics career at the young age of 25. He worked as a journalist, teacher and coach and for 18 months 1964-6 was Sports Director at Channel Nine. He edited the major athletics magazines in Australia for 25 years and authored nine books. From 1981 to 2006 he was the Honorary Consul and later Consul-General in Australia for Trinidad & Tobago.

Annual progression at 100y/100m, 200m, 220ySt: 1953- 9.4y/10.6, 21.0*; 1954- 9.6y, 21.4*; 1955- 9.4y (CAC record), 10.3A/10.4, 21.3A, 21.2ySt; 1956- 9.3y/10.4, 21.1, 20.1ySt; 1957- 9.5y/9.4yw, 21.0*, 20.4ySt; 1958- 9.5y/10.2, 20.9/20.6 1/2t; 1959- 9.4y/9.3yw/10.3, 21.3/21.2w; 1960- 10.4. Other pbs: 60y 6.1i (1954), 400m 47.4 (1958).

Smart AKRAKA (Nigeria) (b. 13 Apr 1934 Lagos) at his home in Bayelsa State on 8 June. He was president of the Athletics Federation of Nigeria 1993-6, having been a sprinter with a best of 10.4 for 100m, who competed at the 1958 Commonwealth Games (qf 100y and 220y and silver medal at 4x110y) and 1960 Olympic Games (sf 4x100m). His daughter Maria Akraka was a leading runner with Swedish records for 800m 2:00.01 indoors (1998) and 2:00.58 outdoors and 1500m indoors 4:07.74 (1992) and outdoor best 4:08.63 (1994).

Raymond BACHÉ (France) (b. 1 Sep 1947 Estagel) on 18 December. He set a French discus record with 56.54 (1969), pb 59.10 (1972). 7th European Juniors 1966. 16 internationals 1968-73.

Mikhail Mikhaylovich **BARIBAN** (USSR) (b. 25 Feb 1949 Krasnodar) on 8 August in Krasnodar. A triple jumper, he was 9th at the 1972 Olympic Games, won the World Universities title with his pb of 17.20 to top the world list in 1973 and was 3rd in 1973 and 2nd in 1974 at the European Indoors, having won both long jump and triple jump at the 1968 European Juniors. He was USSR champion in 1972.

George **Sam BELL** (USA) (b. 7 Mar 1928 Columbus, Missouri) on 27 June in Bloomington, Indiana. He was head coach at Oregon State 1958-65 and California 1965-9 before his long and successful career at Indiana University 1969-98. He was head coach of the US team against the USSR in 1964 and later coached distance runners on US teams. He was meet director of many meetings including the Pan American Games in 1987 and the US Olympic Trials in 1988. His coaching roster included many Olympians from Dyrol Burleson in the 1950s.

Michael Thomas **'Mike' BLAGROVE** (GBR) (b. 14 Mar 1934) in May in Amersham. He had five internationals for Britain 1958-62, including 7th at 1500m at the 1958 Europeans. That year he was also 7th for England at 1 mile at the

Empire Games and ran the opening leg on the England team that set the world record at 4 x 1 mile (16:30.48) at London (White City) on 27 Sep 1958, 23 days after his 1 mile pb there when he was 5th and Ibbotson 4th, both in exactly 4:00.0 (the world's first four-minute mile!). In 1957 he set the pace through 440y 55.3 and 880y 1:55.6 in Derek Ibbotson's world mile record of 3:57.2. He ran for Ealing Harriers and his other pbs were: 880y 1:51.3 (1959), 1000y 2:10.0 (1958), 1000m 2:21.1 (1958), 1500m 3:42.2 (1958), 2000m 5:17.8 (1958), 3000m 8:15.4 (1957), 2M 8:52.2 (1961), 6M 29:49.0 (1962).

René Joseph **BONINO** (France) (b. 14 Jan 1930 Beausoleil) on 18 August in Autun. He was 2nd at 100m at the European Championships in 1954 and competed at the Olympic Games in 1952 (ht 100m, 5th 4x100m) and 1956 (qf 100m, sf 4x100m). French champion at 100m at 100m 1951-52 and 1954, tied the French record with 10.5 in 1952, and ran on three French 4x100m record teams 1950-6. Pb 200m 21.8 (1952), 30 internationals 1950-6.

Jack BRAUGHTON (GBR) (b. 22 Feb 1921 Grimsby) on 30 October. A member of first Cleethorpes H and then Grimsby H before the War, after that he joined Blackheath Harriers and competed (heat 5000m) at the 1948 Olympic Games. Pbs: 2M 9:10.0 (1953), 3M 13:50.6 (1955), 6M 30:01.0 (1951).

Alfredo CAMPAGNER (Italy) (b. 11 Oct 1920) on 11 October in Schio. At the high jump he set six Italian records from 1.91 in 1936 to 1.98 in 1942, the last staying as the national record for 14 years. He was 6th at the 1946 Europeans; 20 internationals 1939-52, and was Italian champion in 1940-3, 1945-7 and 1951.

Judith Lilian **'Judy' CANTY** (later **WILSON**) (b. 5 Oct 1931 Sydney) on 9 July in Canberra. At long jump she was 7th at the 1948 Olympics and 2nd at the 1950 Empire Games. She was Australian champion in 1948 and 1950 and had a pb of 5.87 in 1951. She was married to Denis Wilson a member of the Australian World 4x1 mile record breaking team in 1959.

Bernard CARABY (France) (b. 21 May 1940 Rouen) on 26 January in Caen. At the marathon he was 24th at the 1971 Europeans, set a French best of 2:19:59 (1971) and had a pb of 2:19:38 (1976). 46th World Cross 1973.

Alex Kapcheromit **CHEROP** (Uganda) (b. 15 Jan 1993) was stabbed to death by a police colleague in his village of Kaworyo on 15 September. At 3000m he was 9th at the World Youths and 7th at the 2010 Youth Olympic Games and also competed at 800m and 1500m at the 2010 World Juniors. He won the Madrid half-marathon in 62:30 in 2015 and ran his 10000m pb of 28:07.55 in June 2016 in Leiden. Other pbs: 800m 1:47.7A (2009), 1500m 3:40.46 (2010), 1M 3:58.45 (2009), 3000m 8:07.65 (2010), 5000m 13:44.79A (2013).

Václav CHUDOMEL (Czech Republic) (b. 27 Sep 1932 Pabenice) on 15 December in Benesov. At the marathon he was 18th at the 1964 Olympic Games, and was 10th in 1962 and 18th in 1966 at the European Championships. National champion 1963, 1966 and 1968-9, and winner at Enschede 1963. He set Czechoslovak records at 2:18:02.6 at Kosice (3rd) in 1963 and 2:15:26 in London (3rd Poly) in 1964. Track pbs: 5000m 14:19.6 (1965) and 10000m 29:39.8 (1962).

William Charles **'Bill' CORNELL** (GBR) (b. 30 Oct 1939 Chelmsford) on 28 March in The Villages. Florida. A member of Chelmsford AC, he had a brief career with just one international for Britain – a heat at 1500m in the 1962 Europeans. That year, while at Southern Illinois University, USA he broke through to 1:50.7 for 880y and 4:00.5 for 2nd in the NCAAs at 1 mile. In 1963 he ran his best times for 880y, 1:48.4 for 2nd at the NCAAs and 1:48.1 for 5th at the AAUs on successive weekends in June. Pb 1500m 3:49.9 (1962). Also in the USA he set British indoor records: 600y 1:11.2 (1962) and 1:11.1 (1964) and unofficial 1:10.8 (1963), 880y 1:50.9 (1964), 1000y 2:10.8 and 2:09.6 (1963). Continuing to live in the USA, he had a highly successful coaching career: at Murray State University from 1967, and then at Southern Illinois from 1982 to 1999.

David CROPPER (GBR) (b. 26 Dec 1945 Birmingham) on 3 December in Solihull. A member of Berry Hill & Mansfield AC and then Birchfield Harriers, he won the AAA Junior and English Schools 880y titles in 1964, then was 4th at the 1967 World University Games, AAA champion in 1969 (2nd 1971-2), CAU champion in 1969 and 1972 and semi-finalist at the 1968 and 1972 Olympics and 1969 Europeans. Known as "the head waiter" due to his sit and kick tactics, he had pbs: 400m 47.8 (1968), 800m 1:46.8 (1973), 1000m 2:22.8 (1970), 1500m 3:49.5 (1970). 12 internationals 1968-73. He was Honorary Treasurer of the AAA in 1985-6 and Chairman of the AAA of England 1991-2004, and a Life Vice-President. A civil engineer (he spent 19 years managing Spaghetti Junction in his native Birmingham), he received the OBE in 2006 for his work as a Highways Agency area manager. In 1971 he married Pat Lowe (silver at 800m 1970 Commonwealth Games and 1971 Europeans and gold in a world record in the 1969 European 4x400m relay title in world record time. She also ran on four other world record teams at 3x800m, 3x880y and 4x800m).

André DE HERTOGHE (Belgium) (b. 19 Jul 1941 Leuven) on 25 August in Leuven. At 1500m he was 11th in 1968 and 1972 at the Olympic Games, 6th in 1966, 5th in 1969 and heat in 1971 at European Championships. He set three Belgian records at 1500m: 3:40.7 (1966, heat Europeans), 3:39.5 (1967) and 3:37.1 (1968) and also 3:56.0 (1968) at 1 mile. Other pbs: 800m 1:46.7 (1967), 1000m 2:19.8 (1971), 2000m 5:05.8 (1970), 3000m 8:07.2 (1969), 5000m 13:54.4 (1971). He was Belgian champion at 800m 1966 and at 1500m 1967 and 1969-71.

Per Axel **ERIKSSON** (Sweden) (b. 11 Apr 1925 Nyhammar, Grangärde) on 6 October at Uppsala. At decathlon he was 7th at the 1948 Olympic Games and dnf 1954 Europeans, representing Sweden on six additional occasions 1947-55. Member of combined team of Nordic countries in the legendary 1949 match v USA. Swedish champion pentathlon 1946-8 and 1951-3 (2nd in 1949-50), Ddcathlon 1948 and 1953-6 (2nd 1949, 1951, 1957). Pbs: Pen 3418 (1946), Dec 6987 (1950) on scoring tables then in use. Board member of the Swedish AA 1964-72.

His brother Hilding Eriksson had 1500m pb 3:50.6 (1945) and Per's son Thomas had pbs: HJ 2.32 (1985), LJ 7.81 (1989), TJ 16.43 (1984), Dec 8025 (1989).

Håkon FIMLAND (Norway) (b. 8 Mar 1942) on 24 July. Norwegian champion at 110mh each year 1971-6, pb 13.9 (1970), 14.26 (1971), 13.7w (1969). Dec 6700 (1969 on '64 tables). He competed at the European Champs of 1969 and 1971, 43 internationals 1966-76.

Claudie FLAMENT (France) (b. 21 Apr 1930 Paris) on 9 February in Paris. She set a French 80mh record with 11.5 (1952). She competed at the Olympics in 1952 (sf) and Europeans 1950 & 1954 (ht). French champion at 80mh 1951 and 1953, pentathlon 1956; 25 internationals 1950-61 and she was also a handball international.

Charles William **'Charlie' FOGG** (GBR) (b. 14 Mar 1934 Congleton, Cheshire) in March. A member of Enfield AC/Borough of Enfield H, he had nine internationals for Britain 1961-75 at 50k walk with a best of 4:22:41 (1975). He was 16th at the 1966 Europeans and was third in the RWA 50k four times as well as 2nd at 20M in a pb 2:42:58 in 1963. Moving from walking, he was a hammer coach at Horsham and Worthing.

Giorgio GANDINI, (Italy) (b. 2 Mar 1935 Brescia) in Bergamo on 15 December. A middle distance runner with pbs: 800m 1:52.2 (1960), 1500m 3:47.0 (1959), he had five internationals 1959-63 and twice won the Campaccio Cross (1959 and 1960). He became a great trainer, especially of Francesco Panetta.

GAO Dianmin (China) on 11 November in Pyeong-chang, Korea at the age of 62. A top sports reporter for the Xinhua News Agency from 1977, he was a member of the IOC press committee and also a member of the IAAF Press Commission until 2011.

Jean GILBERT Touzeau (France) on 5 July committed suicide at the age of 67. A dedicated statistician he was well-known for his work for the French Federation from 1977 to 2007, in particular on their great annual *Athlérama*.

Andrzej GRABARCZYK (Poland) (b. 12 Jan 1964 Poddebice) on 17 July in Lódz. At the triple jump he competed (dnq) at the Olympic Games in 1988 and 1992, and at World Championships was 12th in 1991 and 7th indoors in 1989. He was 6th at the 1990 Europeans and at the 1989 and 1990 European Indoors. Polish champion 1988 and 1990-1, pbs: LJ 7.65 (1990), TJ 17.00 (1991), 17.14w (1990).

Waymond **Earl GRIGGS** (USA) (b. 25 Mar 1936 Barton, Arkansas) on 30 November in Abilene. He ran on the Abilene Christian College teams (anchored by the great Bobby Morrow) that set world records for 4x110y of 39.9 (1957) and 39.7 (1958). pbs: 100y 9.8 (?), 9.6w (1958), 220ySt 20.8w (1958). He had a career in coaching and teaching.

GUU Jin-Shoei (Taiwan) (b. 15 Jan 1960 Hualien) on 25 May in Taipei. He was 16th in the Olympic decathlon in 1984 and had a best of 7714 points in 1985. At Asian Championships he was 2nd in 1983 and 1st in 1985, and was 2nd at the Asian Games in 1990. His best event was the pole vault at which he 3rd at the 1991 Asian Champs and had a best of 5.26 (national record, 1989).

Hubert Georg **HAMACHER** (Germany) (b. 8 Feb 1920 Düsseldorf) on 15 February at home in Düsseldorf. A young sprinter, he had bests of 100m 11.0 and 200m 22.5 in 1939, and was a coach after the War. From 1961 to 1985 he was head of French branches of German steel producing companies in Paris. Working well into his 90s he did invaluable work in researching athletics in the late 19th century. Originally published in German in two editions (Vol. 1 1891-1900 and Vol.2 1880-90), his "Athletics at the end of the 19th Century – History and Statistics" was published in English by the International Athletic Foundation in 2011.

Niilo HANGASVAARA (Finland) (b. 12 Sep 1936 Kittilä) on 19 July in Kittilä. One of the few international athletes to emerge from Northern Lapland, he became a self-coached discus thrower with 19 international matches 1962-9. Finnish champion 1967-8, pb 57.80 (1969).

Roland Thomas **HARDY** (GBR) (b. 11 Jun 1926 Sheepbridge, Derbyshire) in June in Chesterfield. A member of Sheffield United Harriers, he was Britain's fastest walker of the immediate post-war years, setting UK track records at 5M/10000m/7M with 35:24.0/44:37.4/50:11.6 (1950) and 35:15.0/43:42.4/49:28.6 (1952) (5M times also world records); and on the roads at 20k 1:35:37 and 20M 2:35:58 (both 1956). He was disqualified in the 10000m walk at the 1950 Europeans and 1952 Olympics (heat), but was 8th at 20k at the 1956 Olympics. He was AAA champion at 2 miles 1950-2 and 7 miles 1950-3 and 1955, and won the RWA 10 miles each year 1952-6 and 20 miles 1956. He was an engineer with the National Coal Board.

Arthur Harold **'Art' HARNDEN** (USA) (b. 20 May 1924 Yoakum, Texas) on 30 September in Corpus Christi, Texas. In 1948 he ran the opening leg for the US team that won the Olympic 4x400m after a pb of 47.3 when 3rd at the NCAAs for Texas A&M University and matching that (47.47 on auto timing) for 4th at the US Olympic Trials. He had been in the Army Air Force during the War.

Dieter **HOFFMANN** (Germany/GDR) (b. 27 Aug 1941 Danzig (now Gdansk POL) in Luckenwalde on 16 September. He was the first European to put the shot over 20m with European records at 20.06 and 20.10 in 1968, after GDR records at 18.75 in 1966 and 19.54 in 1968, improving his best to 20.60 in 1969, in which year he was European champion and ranked as world number one. He was 12th in 1964 and 4th in 1968 at the Olympics, 8th in 1966 and 7th in 1971 at the Europeans and 2nd in 1966 at the European Indoors. 4th 1965 European Cup and GDR champion in 1968 (2nd 1965-6, 3rd 1961, 1964), indoors 1965-6. 24 internationals 1961-71, pb DT 52.18 (1962).

Annual progress at shot: 1961- 16.98, 1962- 17.67, 1963- 17.10, 1964- 18.36, 1965- 18.50, 1966- 18.75, 1967- 18.88, 1968- 20.10, 1969- 20.60, 1970- 18.91, 1971- 20.52, 1972- 20.39.

John Bryan **HOLT** (GBR) (b. 23 Dec 1938) in York on 17 November. He was the IAAF's first full-time General Secretary from 1976-91, serving under Presidents Adriaan Paulen and Primo Nebiolo during an era of huge change for international athletics. He was AAA Junior 440y champion in 1957, and in 1959 while at Oxford University ran his pb of 1:50.0 for 880y (third in Britain that year), and was 2nd in the 800m and 3rd at 4x400m at the World University Games in Turin. Pb: 440y 48.8 (1959).

Ronald Frederick **'Ron' HOPCROFT** (GBR) (b. 27 February 1918 Chiswick) on 17 March. A notable ultrarunner and later a leading official with Thames Valley Harriers, he set world bests for 100km 7:33:29 and 100 miles 12hr 18:16 on 25 Oct 1958 from Hyde Park Corner to Box in Wiltshire and a British best for 50 miles at Walton on 19 Oct 1957.

Gayle Patrick **HOPKINS** (USA) (b. 7 Nov 1941 Tulsa, Oklahoma) on 20 March in Tucson, Arizona. In 1964 he won the NCAA long jump title with a pb 8.16 and was 2nd in the US Olympic Trials before he had three no jumps in the final at the Olympic Games. His best AAU placing was 3rd in 1965. Pbs: HJ 2.02 (1962), TJ 15.75 (1964). He was a long-time administrator at the University of Arizona, where he had been a student 1962-4 and he received a master's degree from San Francisco State and a Ph.D. from Claremont College.

Stanley Houser **HUNTSMAN** (USA) (b. 20 Mar 1932 Scottdale, Pennsylvania) on 23 November in Austin, Texas. He was coach at Ohio University 1957-70, then at Tennessee 1971-85 and Texas 1985-95, and his athletes achieved considerable national and international success including 41 NCAA champions. He was also US Head Coach at the 1977 World Cup, 1983 World Champs and 1988 Olympic Games. He had a decathlon best of 5575 points ('52 tables) in 1952.

Alfons **IDA** (Germany) (b. 20 Sep 1933 Obersitz, now Obrzycko, Poland) on 24 May in Xanten. He was FRG champion at 3000m steeplechase in 1964 and European Masters M45 champion in 1980. Pbs: 1500m 3:48.8 (1965), 3000m 8:07.8i (1964), 15000m 13:53.6 (1963), 10000m 29:06.8 (1967), Mar 2:24:456.4 (1971), 3000mSt 8:45.2 (1964). 5 internationals 1964-72.

Tony **ISAACS** (GBR) (b. 27 May 1937) on 10 March in Felixstowe. A member of the ATFS, he specialised in statistics for the Pacific Islands with a unique series of 25 annual booklets. and for the javelin, for which he produced six booklets in a History and Statistics series.

Gai Michele **KAPERNICK** (Australia) (b. 20 Sep 1970) on 13 October in Australia. At high jump she was 6th in 1989 and dnq 17= in 1991 at the World Indoor Championships, 6th in 1986 and 5th in 1988 at the World Juniors and 8th at the 1989 World Cup. Pb 1.95 (1991). She was NCAA champion in 1994 for Louisiana State University.

Agata **KARCZMAREK** (née **JAROSZEK**) (Poland) (b. 29 Nov 1963 Warsaw) on 18 July. After competing in gymnastics at the 1980 Games, she took part at three Olympic Games at long jump: 1988- 7th, 1992- 10th, 1996- 6th. She was twice a finalist at five World Championships: 8th 1993 and 7th 1995, also 11th in 1986 and 6th in 1994 at the Europeans. At the World Indoors she was 6th in 1987 and 1989 and 3rd in 1997, and at the European Indoors 5th 1987 and 1989, 6th 1994. She was Polish champion 14 times (1985-9, 1991-7 and 1999-2000), and set the Polish record at 6.97 in 1998. Her former husband Piotr Karczmarek had 400mh pb of 50.57 (1987).

Sagardeep **KAUR** (India) (b. 21 Sep 1981) on 23 November in a road accident near Guhla, Haryana. She ran on the Indian team that won the 4x400m at the 2002 Asian Championships and also at the 2003 Worlds. Pbs: 200m 24.21, 400m 52.50 (both 2004).

Donald Michael **KEANE** (Australia) (b. 12 Nov 1930 Perth) on 10 November. He competed at walks at the Olympic Games of 1952 (10th at

10000m) and 1956 (6th at 20km) and won seven Australian 2 miles walk titles 1950-4 and 1957-8. He set many national records including bests for: 3000m 12:22.6, 2M 13:20.6, 5000m 21:07.07, 10000m 43:38.2, 7M 49:14.2, 15,000m 1:06:09.4, 10M 1:11:07.0, 20,000m 1:30:22.2, 1 Hour 13,649.2k (all in 1956).

Isaiah Fundi **KIPLAGAT** (Kenya) (b.12 Nov 1944 Nandi) in August in Nairobi after a long battle with cancer. He was President of Athletics Kenya after holding various top posts from Vice-Chairman in 1976, and an IAAF Council member from 1999 to 2015, but was suspended by the IAAF in investigations for corruption in November 2015.

Väinö KOSKELA (Finland) (b. 31 Mar 1921 Virolahti) in Virolahti on 10 September. He was 7th at 5000m at the 1948 Olympic Games and in 1949-51 he had some 30 hard races at this his favourite distance. In 1949 he almost beat Emil Zátopek three times in a week, 14:20.8 to 14:20.0 in the Finland-Czechoslovakia match in Helsinki, both ran 14:13.2 (his pb) in Turku just two days later in Turku, then 8:19.4 to 8:19.2 at 3000m two days after that in Pori. In 1950 he improved the Finnish 3000m record to 8:10.4 in Turku and was 3rd in the Finnish 5000m. He did not like a move to 10000m at the Europeans but nevertheless took bronze behind Zátopek and Alain Mimoun. He was 16th in the 1952 Olympic 10000m, had 16 international matches 1947-52 and was Finnish champion at 5000m 1948-9 and cross country 1948. Pb 10000m 30:10.0 (1951).

Lauri Johannes **KOSKI-VÄHÄLÄ** (Sweden) (b. 23 Jun 1945 Ullava, Finland) on 25 August. After living in Sweden for several years he became a Swedish citizen. His best year was 1974 with 8th in the Europeans and pb at javelin of 85.88 (9= in the world). 13 additional internationals 1972-5.

Dr **Woldemeskel KOSTRE** (Ethiopia) on 16 May in Addis Ababa. He coached many of the all-time great Ethiopian runners including Haile Gebrselassie, Kenenisa Bekele, Tirunesh Dibaba, and Derartu Tulu. He was a middle distance runner before studying in Hungary in the 1960s.

Jürgen Wolfgang **KRAEMER** (Germany) (b. 1 Mar 1938) on 4 March in Ahlen. He set an FRG record for 5000m walk with 22:15.0 (1958). Other walks pbs: 3000m 12:57.2 (1959), 20k 1:33:40 (1963), 50k 4:46:51.4 (1961). 3 internationals 1962-6. On IAAF walks committee 1976-87.

Peter Friedrich Wilhelm **KRAUS** (Germany) (b. 17 Jul 1932 Berlin) on 15 January in Straßlach. FRG champion at 200m 1951, he competed at the 1952 Olympic Games (qf 200m, ht 4x200m) and 1954 Europeans (dq ht 4x100m). Pbs: 100m 10.4 (1953), 200m 21.1 (1951), 300m 33.6 (1952), 400m 48.0 (1951). 16 internationals 1951-5.

Pamela Joan **KURRELL** (later ASCARIZ) (USA) (b. 6 Jan 1939 San Francisco) on 14 June in Pacifica, California. Her first AAU medal was 3rd at baseball throw in 1955 and she won that event and discus in 1956. At the discus she was 8th in 1955 and 2nd in 1959 at the Pan-American Games and dnq 18th 1956 and dnq 19th 1960 at the Olympic Games after 2nd and 3rd at the respective Olympic Trials. Pb 48.56 (1960).

Brenda Joyce **LAIDLAW** (née **COX**) (Australia) (b. 17 Apr 1944) on 6 May in Nambour, Queensland. At the 1962 Empire (Commonwealth) Games she won gold at 4x110y relay (third leg) after 3rd at 100y and 4th at 220y. She was then 18 years old and had been 2nd at 100y at the national junior champs and was 3rd at 220y and 4th at 100y at the senior championships. Pbs: 100y 10.5 (1961), 220y 23.9 (1963).

Rolf LAMERS (Germany) (b. 8 Jul 1927 Oberhausen-Hiesfeld) on 17 October in Lahnstein. He was 6th at the 1952 Olympic Games 1500m in a pb 3:46.8/3:47.18 and was FRG champion at 1500m 1950 and 5000m 1956. He set German records for 1500m 3:49.4 (1952) and 4x1500m in 1950 and 1953. Other pbs: 800m 1:50.2 (1954), 1000m 2:24.6 (1952), 1M 4:07.8 (1952), 2000m 5:21.2 (1952), 3000m 8:14.4 (1956), 5000m 14:15.0 (1956). 18 internationals 1951-6.

Karl **Rune LARSSON** (Sweden) (b. 17 Jun 1924 Stockholm) in Järfälla on 17 September. He won bronze medals at 400mh at the 1946 Europeans and 1948 Olympics and at 4x400m at the 1948 Olympics and 1950 Europeans (sf 400mh). 19 further internationals 1943-53, Swedish champion 400m 1947-8, 400mh 1946-51. He set Swedish 400mh records with 52.3 and 51.9 in 1948 with other pbs: 200m 22.3 (1950), 400m 47.9 (1948), 800m 1:51.6 (1948), 200mh 25.0 (1947), LJ 6.95 (1946), Pen 3332 (1951 '34 tables). A schoolmaster and notable speaker, he was an unparalleled inspiration to Swedish junior teams.

Peter LAUFER (Germany) (b. 13 Sep 1936 Wroclaw, Poland) on 4 March. At pole vault he was 8th at the Europeans in 1958, did not qualify for the final at the 1960 Olympic Games and was GDR champion in 1959 and 1961; pb 4.80 (1963), 110mh 14.7 (1963). On 15 Dec 1962 he married Hildrun Claus, who set three world records at long jump 6.36 and 6.40 (1960) and 6.42 (1961) and was Olympic bronze medallist on 1960.

Mervyn George **LINCOLN** (Australia) (b. 22 Nov 1933 Leongartha, Victoria) on 30 April in Melbourne. Although overshadowed by the great Herb Elliott, he ranked second in the world in 1958, when he was 2nd in the Empire/Commonwealth Games 1 Mile, and when Elliott smashed the world record with 3:54.5 in

OBITUARY

Dublin, Lincoln was 2nd in 3:55.9, well inside the previous WR 3:57.2 by Derek Ibbotson in 1957. After 4:00.6 in 1956 before he was 12th in the Olympic 1500m, Lincoln first broke 4 minutes with 3:58.9 in 1957 and ran four such times in 1958. He was Australian champion at 1 mile in 1959 (2nd 1957-8) and had other pbs of: 880y 1:52.3 (1958), 1000m 2:23.8 (1956), 1500m 3:42.0 (1957), 2000m 5:12.5 (1960), 2M 8:52.0 (1958), 3M 13:43.8 (1958).

Thomas James **LOKOMWA** (Kenya) (b. 1987) was killed in a car accident in Kenya on 11 September. From the Turkana tribe, he was a regular figure on the Italian running scene, winning many races in 2015-16. He ran four times below 61 mins for the half-marathon with a personal best of 60:33 to win the Stramilano in 2015. He was a member of the Austrian club Run2gether before joining Italian agent Enrico Dionisi in 2016. Other pbs: 1000m 2:24.54 (2011), 3000m 8:03.99 (2011), 10000m 29:03.7A (2013); road: 10k 28:56 (2016), 15k 42:55 (2015).

Rudolf LÜTTGE (Germany) (b. 19 Dec 1922 Ilsenburg) on 23 September in Bad Schwartau. He set an unratified world record for 30,000m track walk, 2:27:24.8 in 1948 and German walks records with bests of 3000m 12:28.6 (1951), 10000m 46:59.2 (1948), 20,000m 1:38:17.0 (1948) and 50k 4:38:40 (1952). He was 13th in the Olympic 50kW in 1952 and German champion at 10000mW 1947, 1949-53; 25kW 1946, 1948 & 1953; 50kW 1951-2.

Johana Manyim **MAINA** (Kenya) (b. 24 Dec 1990) on 21 July. Based in Japan, where he ran for Fujitsu, he had returned to Kenya in apparently good health and died two days later. He won the Sendai Half Marathon in 2012, 2014 and 2015 and had pbs: 1500m 3:45.0A (2014), 5000m 13:25.24 (2015), 10000m 27:26.92 (2015), HMar 61:19 (2016), 30k 1:29:55 (2014), Mar 2:13:46 (2015).

Ernö MAKÓ (Hungary) (b. 16 Feb 1955, Debrecen) on 17 October in Debrecen. He competed at pole vault at European Indoor Champs in 1980 & 1983 (both 16th) and at World University Games in 1981 (nh in final). He set Hungarian records at 5.30 & 5.36 in 1980, 5.38 in 1981, 5.40 in 1982; indoor: 5.15i, 5.20i & 5.30i in 1980. 30 internationals 1977-86, HUN outdoor champion 1977 & 1985; indoors 1982. Pb Dec 6583 (old score 6755) (1977).

Theresa Altameze **MANUEL** (USA) (b. 7 Jan 1926 Tampa, Florida) on 21 November in Toluca, Illinois. Educated at the Tuskagee Institute, she competed at 80m hurdles (heat), javelin (12th) and 4x100m (heat) at the 1948 Olympic Games. At 80mh she had a best of 11.9 (1948) and was 2nd in 1947 and 1949 and 3rd in 1948 and 1952 at the AAUs. At the Olympic Trials she was 3rd in 1948 and 1952. She was 2nd at the javelin at Trials and AAU in 1948 and 3rd= at the AAU in 1952, and also AAU indoor champion at 50m hurdles in a US indoor record of 7.4 in 1948. She became a notable basketball coach.

Renato MARTINI (Italy) (b. 12 Nov 1949 Tortona/Alessandria) on 27 December in Novi Ligure. 24th in the 1972 Olympic marathon, he was Italian champion at cross-country in 1971 and 1972 and at 30k in 1971. He had 8 internationals for Italy including four at the International/World CC Champs 1970-3. Pbs: Mar 2:19:23, 5000m 14:18.0, 10000m 29:45.8 (all 1972).

Faina Grigoryevna MELNIK (Russia) (b. 9 Jun 1945 Bakota, Ukraine) on 16 December in Moscow. She set a record eleven world records for the women's discus, from 64.22 in 1971 to 70.50 in 1976 and was Olympic champion in 1972 and European in 1971 and 1974. She won 52 successive discus competitions between 1973 and 1976, so it was a major shock when she placed only fourth in the Olympics that year. Suddenly her all-conquering years of success were over, for she was fifth in the 1978 Europeans and failed to qualify for the 1980 Olympic final. She won nine USSR discus titles 1970, 1972-7, 1980-1, the World Student Games 1973, European Cup 1973, 1975 and 1977, and World Cup 1977. Her shot best was 20.03 (1976). She was married to Bulgarian discus thrower Velko Velev 1977-9.

Annual progression: 1965- 48.10, 1966- 49.30, 1967- 48.34, 1968- 50.72, 1969- 54.76, 1970- 61.80, 1971- 64.88, 1972- 66.76, 1973- 69.48, 1974- 69.90, 1975- 70.20, 1976- 70.50, 1977- 68.60, 1978- 70.34, 1979- 69.28, 1980- 69.60, 1981- 66.80, 1982- 63.52.

William Preston **'Bill' MILLER** (USA) (b. 22 Feb 1930 Lawnside, New Jersey) on 27 October in Apache Junction, Arizona. He was the Olympic silver medallist at the javelin in 1952 while serving in the Marine Corps before returning to complete his studies at Arizona State College. That year he was AAU champion (also 2nd 1951 and 1954, 3rd 1953 and 1955), 2nd in the US Olympic Trials. He was world ranked each year 1951-5, with a peak of 3rd in 1952 and 1954, and set an unratified world record of 81.29 at Pasadena on 21 Aug 1954, but his javelin broke on impact and after repair the centre of gravity was outside the permitted area. He was also 4th in the AAU decathlon in 1951 (7114 on tables then in use, 6657 points on 1985 tables) and had a high jump best of 2.03 (1952). He later coached national teams in Indonesia and Malaysia.

Annual progression (position on world list): 1949- 63.48, 1950- 69.11 (14), 1951- 72.49 (6), 1952- 73.95 (4), 1953- 70.77 (14), 1954- 81.29 (1), 1955- 78.65 (4).

Carlo MONTI (Italy) (b. 4 Mar 1920 Milan) on 7 April in Milan. He was a bronze medallist on the Italian 4x100m team at the 1948 Olympic

Games and at 100m at the 1946 Europeans (also sf 200m and ht 4x100m). 14 internationals for Italy 1940-9, he was Italian champion at 100m 1940-1 and 1946-7 and at 200m in 1941-2, 1946 and 1949. Pbs 100m 10.5 and 200m 21.3 (both 1940).

Ian **MUTUKU** (Kenya) (b. 11 May 1997) in Machakos on 24 October. He was 4th at 400m at the 2013 World Youth Champs and the 2014 Youth Olympics; pb 46.67A in 2014.

Fidel **NEGRETE** Gamboa (Mexico) (b. 23 Mar 1932) on 17 November in Toluca. In 1963 he won the Pan-American Games marathon in a Mexican record 2:27:36 and beat that time a year later with 2:26:04 when 21st at the Olympic Games. He had been 2nd in the CAC Games half marathon in 1962.

John Vincent **NEWSOME** (GBR) (b. 2 Oct 1941 Wakefield) on 16 September in Wakefield. He ran a marathon best of 2:16:07.8 (7th best in Britain that year) when he won in Prague in September 1970 after he had run 2:15:39 for 4th in Huddersfield in March on a course that was 833 yards short. Northern marathon champion 1966 and winner of the London to Brighton race in 5:16:07 in 1974. Other pbs: 3M 14:23.0 (1967), 10M: 49:54 (1966), 15M 1:18:13 (1968), 30k 1:37:15 (1968), 20M 1:42:51 (1967), 2 hours track 36.950m (1968). A schoolteacher and member of Wakefield Harriers of whom he became president.

Ezealah **NKAM** (Nigeria) (b. 22 Nov 1994) was killed in a car accident in Nigeria in March. She was 5th at 100m and was one of the Nigerian team that won the 4x100m at the 2013 African Juniors. Pbs: 100m 11.50 (2015), 200m 24.49 (2014), 24.36w (2015).

Pauli **NY** (Finland) (b. 8 Jun 1940 Pieksämäki) on 30 June in Helsinki. An elegantly striding sprinter, he won three Finnish titles (100m 1962-3, 200m 1963) and equalled the Finnish 100m record of 10.5 seven times. 16 international dual matches 1959-64. 100m 10.4w, 200m 21.3 (= Finnish record, both 1963).

Keith **OLLERENSHAW** (Australia) (b. 28 Sep 1928 Lakemba, New South Wales) on 13 March. At the marathon he was 25th at the 1956 Olympic Games, 4th at the 1962 Empire Games and was Australian champion in 1962 (2nd in 1953 and 1956, 3rd 1958). He ran for Western Suburbs in Sydney and had pbs of: 3M 14:16.8 (1954), 5000m 14:31.8 (1959), 6M 29:16.2 (1960) and marathon 2:22:12 (1956).

Olga Eivor Beatrice **OLSON – LAGMAN** (Sweden) (b. 27 Sep 1922 Göteborg) on 2 November in Göteborg. At the shot she was 11th in 1948 and 13th in 1952 at the Olympics and 5th in 1946 and 11th in 1950 (also 13th JT) at the Europeans, and 26 further internationals in 1947-60 (only missing one match in 1959). She won 14 successive Swedish titles 1943-56 and was also javelin champion in 1944 and 1945 and had further top three placings: 6 at shot, 6 at javelin and 5 at discus. Eight Swedish shot records from 11.88 (1943) to 13.29 (1955), with pbs DT 37.22 (1955), JT 39.55 (1949).

Tibor **ORDINA** (Hungary) (b. 17 Mar 1971 Budapest) in Budapest on 12 April. He competed at the Olympic Games in 1996 (dnq 33 TJ), World Champs 1993 (dnq nj LJ) and 1997 (dnq 25 TJ), World Indoors 1997 (8 TJ), European Champs 1994 (dnq 28 LJ) and European Indoors 1992 (21 LJ) and 1994 (11 LJ). 24 internationals 1989-2000, HUN champion LJ 1993, 1995-6, 1998; Indoor LJ 1993-4, 1997, 1999; TJ 1996-7, 1999. Pbs: 60m 6.91i (2000), 100m 10.96 (1992), 200m 21.62 (1993), HJ 2.10i/2.06 (1993), LJ 8.04 (1993), TJ 16.96i (1998), 16.90 (1996).

Mark **OUMA** (Kenya) (b. Uganda) on 10 July in Durban, South Africa, at the age of 55. From 1988 he worked as a freelance journalist and contributed to numerous publications in Africa, Europe and the USA. He was based in South Africa for many years, where he was a correspondent for *Voice of America* and a regular contributor to the IAAF website.

Ferenc **PARAGI** (Hungary) (b. 21 Aug 1953 Budapest) on 21 April in Budapest. He set a world record for the (old) javelin with 96.72 at Tata on 23 Apr 1980. This was one of eight competitions that he had over 90m, from pre-1980 bests of 91.92 in 1977 and 92.14 in 1979 and five such competitions in his best year of 1980. He competed at the Olympic Games in 1976 (dnq 20) and 1980 (10th with 79.52; he had a painful knee after leading the qualifying round with 88.76) and at the European Champs in 1978 (9th). Hungarian champion in 1975-7, 1979 & 1982, 28 internationals 1976-91. Pb new JT 77.32 (1986).

Annual progression: 1967- 41.88, 1968- 50.68, 1969- 67.70, 1970- 70.06, 1971- 74.36, 1972- 80.06, 1973- 81.24, 1974- 82.02, 1975- 89.92, 1976- 87.98, 1977- 91.92, 1978- 86.04, 1979- 92.14, 1980- 96.72, 1981- 88.04, 1982- 86.78, 1984- 73.14, 1985- 84.16; new spec: 1986- 77.32, 1987- 75.28, 1988- 74.96, 1989- 71.08, 1990- 71.90, 1992- 66.94, 1994- 62.72.

André **PARIS** (France) (b. 6 Aug 1925 Thiberville) on 31 March in Rouen. He competed at the Olympic Games in 1948 (2rd 10000m) and 1952 (ht 3000mSt) and four times in the International CC – 6th in 1949 and 5th in 1951. French champion at 10000m 1948; 13 internationals 1948-54. Pbs: 10000m 30:48.0 (1949), 3000mSt 9:05.0 (1952).

Anne **PASHLEY** (married name **IRONS**) (GBR) (b. 13 Jun 1954 Skegness. Lincolnshire) on 7 October. She became a well known opera singer (soprano) after being a leading sprinter. She had 13 internationals for Britain 1953-6, and in 1954 was 3rd at 100m and 4th at 4x100m at the European Championships and 4th at 100y and 2nd at 4x110y at the Empire Games. Then in 1956 she was on the silver-medal winning British 4x100m team after running in the heats of the 100m. She ran on world record teams at 4x100m 1956 and 4x220y in 1953 and set UK records: four for 100y from 11.0 (1953) to 10.8 (1956), three for 100m from 11.9 (1954) to 11.6 (1956), and three each for 4x100m 1956, 4x110y 1954-6. Other pbs: 100y 10.7w (1956), 100m 11.94 (1956), 220y 25.2 (1953), LJ 5.73? (1953). She was WAAA champion at 100y 1953-4 (2nd 1956, 3rd 51), 2nd 220y 1963. Great Yarmouth & Gorleston AC.

Nina Apollonovna **PONOMARYEVA** (USSR/Russia) b. 27 Apr 1929 Smychka, Sverdlovsk) in Moscow on 19 August. She was the Olympic discus champion of 1952 and 1960 and bronze medallist in 1956, European champion in 1954 and won eight Soviet titles between 1951 and 1959. She set a world record at 53.61 in 1952 and her best ever was 56.62 in 1955, but she achieved notoriety for allegedly shop-lifting some hats from C & A Modes in Oxford Street, London, as a result of which the UK v USSR match in 1956 was cancelled. From then she was ranked as world number one each year to 1960 holding on to be 6th in the 1962 Europeans and 11th at her fourth Olympics in 1964. Pb shot 15.04 (1961).

Annual progression (position on world list): 1948- 38.18 (57), 1949- 43.89 (6), 1950- 47.42 (2), 1951- 49.76 (2), 1952- 54.91 (2), 1953- 55.68 (1), 1954- 50.43 (3), 1955- 56.62 (1), 1956- 54.76 (1), 1957- 55.19 (1), 1958- 54.78 (1), 1959- 56.18 (1), 1960- 55.49 (3), 1961- 54.85 (2), 1962- 53.94 (8), 1963- 53.40 (12), 1964- 54.70 (11), 1965- 50.68 (42), 1966- 50.82 (38).

MIGUEL DE LA QUADRA-SALCEDO Gayarre (Spain) (b. 30 Apr 1932 Madrid) on 20 May in Pozuelo de Alarcón. He was Spanish champion at shot in 1955-6, discus in 1953, 1955-6 and 1958-60 and hammer in 1956, and competed at discus at the 1960 Olympics. He set seven Spanish records at discus from 45.91 (1955) to 51.00 to 1960 and nine at hammer from 47.24 (1954) to 49.25 (1956). Pbs: SP 14.37 (1956), JT 48.60 (1958). 18 internationals. He became most famous as a great Spanish TV commentator during the 1960s and 1970s.

Mamie Annette **RALLINS** (USA) (b. 6 Jul 1941 Chicago) on 16 May in a car crash near Fremont, Ohio. Having been at Tennessee State University and running for the Mayor Daley Youth Foundation in Chicago, she competed at two Olympic Games (ht 80mh 1968 and ht 100mh 1972). She was 2nd at 80m hurdles at the 1967 Pan-American Games and was AAU champion indoors at 60yh 1969 and outdoors at 80mh 1967-68 and 100mh 1970 and 1972, winning the US Olympic Trials 80mh in 1968. She became a college track coach at Ohio State and was US head coach at the 1987 World Indoor Championships, assistant coach for the 1996 US Olympic Team and head manager at the 2000 Games. She set world indoor records for 50y hurdles: 7.1 twice and 7.0 in 1969, four US records 100mh 13.5 (1969) to 13.4 (1970), 13.51 (1972). Pbs: 80mh 10.6/10.4w (1968), 100mh 13.3 (1972), 13.1w (1971).

Jean-Louis RAVELOMANANTSOA (Madagascar) (b. 30 Apr 1943 Antananarivo) on 27 September in Lyon, France. His nation's greatest ever athlete, he set an African record with 10.0 for 100m at Helsinki in 1971, after an auto-timed record 10.18A at Mexico City in 1968. He competed at three Olympic Games: 1964 h 100m & 200m, 1968- 8th 100m, h 200m and 1972 sf 100m, and was 3rd at the All-Africa Games 200m in 1965 and the World University Games 100m in 1970. Other national records: 50y 5.1i (1970), 60y 5.9i (1971, tied world record), 100y 9.3 (1971), 9.1w (1975); 200m 20.6 (1972). In 1975 he became the first man to win the Stawell Gift professional race in Australia off scratch for 120m. He studied at Westmont College, USA 1970-2, winning three NAIA titles.

Werner **REIBERT** (Germany) (b. 5 Jan 1948 Biedenkopf) on 21 May in Camon. He competed for the FRG at 400m hurdles at the Europeans in 1971 (sf) and 1974 (h) and in the European Cup was 2nd in 1970 and 4th in 1973. FRG champion 1970, 1973 and 1975; 16 internationals 1970-5, pbs: 110mh 14.7 (1970), 400mh 49.63 (1972).

Diane **ROYLE** (née **WILLIAMS**) (GBR) (b. 24 Nov 1959) in October in Manchester. A member of Sale Harriers, she was Scottish champion at javelin each year 1977-84 and set 15 Scottish records (old javelin) from 47.50 in 1976 to 62.22 in 1985 for third on the UK all-time list behind Fatima Whitbread and Tessa Sanderson. She was 8th for Scotland at the 1978 Commonwealth Games and had two UK internationals 1981-3. UK champion 1980 (3rd 1984) and 2nd WAAA 1985 (3rd 1984). Pb SP 11.99 (1984).

Simone E **SCHALLER** (USA) (later KIRIN) (b. 22 Aug 1912 South Manchester, Connecticut) on 20 October in Arcadia, California at the age of 104. She was the oldest living Olympian, having competed at 80m hurdles in 1932 (4th in a pb 11.8) and 1936 (sf), both after placing 3rd in the US Trials. She was AAU champion in 1933 and represented the Los Angeles AC.

Ernest Earl 'Ernie' **SHELTON** (USA) (b. 28 Oct 1932 Chanute, Kansas) on 9 March in Cambria, California. AAU and NCAA high jump champion 1954-55 and indoor 1955 (tie) and 1956 AAU champion while at the University of Southern California. He ranked as world number one in 1954 and 1955 (pb 2.115, just 1cm behind Walt Davis's world record set in 1953), but slipped to 8th in 1956, when he was 5th in the US Olympic Trials, and 9th in 1957. He won at the Pan-American Games in 1955 and at AAU Champs he was also 2nd in 1953 and 1957-8 and 3rd in 1951. Los Angeles AC. He became a notable sculptor.

Annual progression (position on world list): 1951- 1.96 (49=), 1952- ?, 1953- 2.08 (2=), 1954- 2.11 (1), 1955- 2.115 (1), 1956- 2.08 (6), 1957- 2.055 (12=), 1958- 2.00 (72=). Decathlon pb 6462 ('52 tables) (1955).

István SIMON-BALLA (Hungary) (b. 9 Aug 1958 Sztálinváros) on 12 September in Budapest. At 400m hurdles he competed at the 1982 European Champs (heats), was Hungarian champion 1981-2, 1986 & 1988-9 and set a Hungarian record of 49.62 in 1986. 24 internationals 1979-89 (110mh & 400mh). He later worked as a coach. Pbs: 100m 10.73 (1988), 200m 21.4h (1984), 400m 47.65 (1986), 110mh 13.94 (1984), HJ 2.06 (1977), PV 4.20 (1989), LJ 7.13 (1978), Dec 6950 (1989).

Cecil SMITH (Canada) (b. 22 Apr 1936 Cardiff) on 2 December. Having coached in Essex and been a leading figure in the British Milers Club, he emigrated to Canada in the 1970s, starting coaching there before getting heavily involved with the administration of the sport. He was chairman of the Ontario Coaches Association, and then director of the Ontario Track and Field Association (OTFA) for 25 years. He started *Ontario Athletics* magazine, the predecessor of *Athletics*, the national magazine that he published for many years. He helped organise major meetings in Canada and his huge contribution to the sport also included being a member of the IAAF Technical Committee and being a top statistician, producing many statistical handbooks and national lists. He was a long-time member of the ATFS and was the invaluable contact for Canada for the first 25 years or so of this Annual.

Eva SURANOVÁ (Slovakia) (b. 24 Apr 1946 Ózd) (née Kucmanová) in Bratislava on 31 December. Representing Czechoslovakia, Suranová won the first Olympic medal by a Slovakian woman with 3rd in 1972 at long jump (also a non-qualifier in 1976). She won the European silver medal in 1974 (also 12th 1966, 7th 1969 and dnq 1978), and reached the 100mh semi-final in 1969. TCH champion at LJ 1965-69, 1972 and 1974-75; 100m 1975, 100mh 1968-69, pen 1967; indoor 50m 1976. In all she set 25 TCH records including LJ (6) 6.48 '69 to 6.67 '74, 60m 7.4 '67, 100mh (4) 13.8 '68 to 13.6 '69. Pbs 100m 11.2 (1976), 11.74 (1974); 200m 23.56 (1976), 80mh 11.0 (1967), 100mh 13.5 (1972), LJ also 6.74w (1974); Pen 4550 (1967). 29 internationals 1963-78.

Edward Stanley **TEMPLE** (USA) (b. 20 Sep 1927 Harrisburg, Pennsylvania) on 22 September in Nashville, Tennessee. Having been a sprinter with bests of 9.7 for 100y and 21.5 for 220y, the legendary coach led the Tigerbelles of Tennessee State University, where he was head coach for 44 years, to 34 national team titles, playing a hugely significant part in the development of women's athletics in the USA. His top stars included sprinters Wilma Rudolph, Wyomia Tyus, Edith McGuire, Mae Faggs and Chandra Cheeseborough as well as 800m champion Madeline Manning. He was head coach of the US Olympic women's team of 1960 and 1964 and assistant coach in 1980.

Dr **Alexander THIEME** (GDR) (b. 13 Jan 1954 Karl-Marx Stadt) on 25 November in Chemnitz. He had 20 internationals for the GDR in 1975-9, competing at the 1976 Olympic Games (sf 100m, silver 4x100m), 1977/1979 Worlds (2nd/4th 4x100m), 1978 Europeans (ht 100m, 2 4x100m), 1975 European Indoors (5th 60m). In the European Cup he was 3rd at 100m in 1975, and 1st/1st/2nd at 4x100m 1975/77/79. GDR champion at 60m indoors 1975, 2nd 100m 1977-78, 200m 1976. Pbs: 60m 6.70i (1975), 100m 10.22 (1977), 200m 21.11 (1976).

Prof. Dr. **Günter TIDOW** (Germany) (b. 21 Mar 1943) on 31 January in Bochum. Pbs: SP 17.31 (1968), DT 54.04 (1970), JT 68.65 (1966), Dec 7220 (1966). 3 internationals 1962-6.

Franco TOGNI (Italy) (b. 3 Nov 1960 Alzano Lombardo/ Bergamo) on 29 December in a mountain accident on Monte Grabiasca/ Bergamo. He was Italian marathon champion in Carpi 1996, when he set his pb of 2:12:36. Other pbs: 10000m 29:16.7 (1995), HMar 62:36 (1996). He was a good masters athlete: winning his last NC title in 2016 at Marathon M55 in Ravenna (2:44:07). A mountain runner and mountaineer, he climbed Mont Blanc and Ararat.

Heinrich Otto **'Heinz' ULZHEIMER** (Germany/FRG) (b. 27 Dec 1925 Frankfurt am Main) on 18 December at Bad Sooden-Allendorf. He won Olympic bronze medals at 800m and 4x400m in 1952 and was FRG champion at 800m 1946-49 (2nd 1951-51, 3rd 1950), 400mh 1953 and 400m indoors 1954. Pbs: 400m 47.6 (1954), 800m 1:49.7/1:49.78 (1952), 1000m 2:24.2 (1951), 200mh 25.1 (1954), 400mh 52.6 (1954), and he set European indoor records at 400m 49.4 (1954), 800m 1:52.0 (1953) and 1000y 2:09.4 (1953).

Aleksandar VUCELIC (Yugoslavia) (b. 17 May 1934 Banja Luka, Bosnia) in Zagreb, Croatia, where he lived and competed for AAK Mladost. Overshadowed by Stanko Lorger, he won just one Yugoslav title at 110mh, in 1955 (and also at 400mh in 1958). 5 internationals for Yugoslavia, pbs: 14.6 (1957), 400mh 54.4 (1958).

OBITUARY

Hans WAYNBERG (Germany) (b. 23 Dec 1947) on 22/23 September. He had been a founding member and treasurer of the German statistical group, the DGLD, from 1990.

Anthony James 'Tony' WEEKS-PEARSON (GBR) (b. 12 Oct 1931) on 12 March. A member of Blackheath Harriers, he missed out on being a GB international in a great era for British distance running, but was 2nd at 5000m in the World Student Games in 1953 while at Oxford University and set a British indoor best at 3000m with 8:25.4 in 1954. Track pbs: 2M 9:11.0 (1955), 6M 29:17.2 (1954). His best placings in the National Cross-country were 11th in 1955 and 1958.

George WILLIAMS (GBR) (b. 1935) on 25 December. A member of Belgrave Harriers, he represented Britain in three internationals at 20k walk, including 3rd in the inaugural staging of the Lugano Trophy in 1961. He was also 2nd for England v Russia in 1960 and 3rd in the AAA 2 miles walk in 1955-6 and 1959. Walks pbs: 2M 13:46.8 (1962), 5M 36:50.2 (1959), 7M 53:24.0 (1962), 20k 1:34:02 (1961).

Miruts YIFTER (Ethiopia) (b. 15 May 1944 Adigrat, Tigray) on 22 December in Toronto, Canada. His name in his native language of Beja was Yefter Mururuse. Yifter's age was always shrouded in mystery, but 'Yifter the Shifter' was pretty old when he won a wonderful 5000m and 10000m double at the 1980 Olympics, even if he was not quite as old as he looked. His first international success was third at 10000m in the Eastern and Central African Championships in 1970. A year later, running 5000m for Africa v USA, he miscounted the laps and hared off with two to go but stopped just as the gun went for the last lap! However, he came back the next day to win the 10000m. He won the Olympic bronze at 10000m in 1972 in 27:40.96, which remained his best ever, but was left weeping as the 5000m final got underway, for he could not find the entrance to the track. He would probably have starred in 1976, but was denied the chance of Olympic competition at the very last minute due to the African boycott. Misfortune came again at the end of his career when he was one of the Ethiopian team that misjudged the laps at the 1981 World Cross-country, and put in their burst a lap early. He won gold at 10000m and silver at 5000m at the 1973 African Games, and in both 1977 and 1979 the tiny (1.62m) man won the 5000m and 10000m double at the World Cup, winning each race with his distinctive and devastating finishing kick. That kick came even off the fast pace at which the 5000m was run in 1977, when with 13:13.82 he missed the world record by just 0.9 sec. In 1997 he left Ethiopia and sought political asylum in Canada

Annual progression at 5000m, 10000m: 1971- 13:52.6, 28:53.2; 1972- 13:33.8, 27:40.96; 1973- 13:54.0, 29:04.6; 1974- 29:57.4, 1975- 13:38.93, 28:09.14; 1976- 13:24.4, 28:26.4; 1977- 13:13.81, 27:50.39; 1978- 13:41.6, 28:47.1; 1979- 13:20.8, 27:44.2; 1980- 13:16.34, 27:42.69; 1981- 13:47,07, 28:03.23; 1982- 13:52.2, 28:31.4; 1983- 30:33.0. Pb 3000m 7:51.3i (1979).

Orien Gladwin **YOUNG** (Bermuda/GBR) (b. 14 May 1931) in Portsmouth on 30 September. He was a national champion in Bermuda, for whom he ran at the 1954 Empire Games (heats 100y, 220y) before moving to England as a dockyard apprentice. 3rd AAA 100y 1953. Pbs: 60y 6.4i (1961), 100y 9.8 (1953), 100m 10.7 (1961) 220y 21.6 (1959). He was a stalwart as starter and official in Hampshire athletics and of the Counties Athletics Union (secretary of the Track & Field Committee from 1993). He was president of the City of Portsmouth AC.

Iolanda BALAS – further research by Stuart Mazdon shows that Balas won 15$\underline{4}$ successive high jump competitions 1957-66. The original figure quoted for her was 140, but Stuart's research in 1991 found 150 successive wins, and now he has found four more. It could be that there were more! Year by year tally: 1957- 14, 1958- 22, 1959- 18, 1960- 16, 1961- 18, 1962- 16, 1963- 12, 1964- 10, 1965- 19, 1966- 9.

Died in 2015

Ariane DÖSER/KOLM (Germany) (b. 8 Feb 1937 Reutlingen) on 26 April in Polling. Her 800m pb was 2:08.2 when 4th in the 1958 Europeans, and she was 2nd in 1957 and 8th in 1959 at the World University Games and FRG champion in 1956-58. Pb 400m 57.2 (1958).

Samuel Morse **FELTON** (USA) (b. 26 May 1926 New York) on 24 December in Bar Harbor, Maine. At the hammer he was ranked in the world top ten each year 1948-51, was AAU champion 1949-51 (2nd 1947-8, 1953; 3rd 1952, 1955) and NCAA champion in 1948 for Harvard University. He competed at the Olympic Games in 1948 (4th) and 1952 (11th). He also won the AAU indoor 35lb weight title in 1949. Pbs: DT 49.40 (1948), HT 57.18 (1950), 35lb Wt 17.67i (1949).

Monika Anita **KLEBE - UNGER** (Sweden) (b. 21 Sep 1964 Stora Kil) on 5 October in Frykstra. Ran 400mh at the 1986 (semis) 1990 Europeans (heat) and had 12 further internationals 1985-92. Swedish champion at 400m in 1987 (outdoors) and 1992 (indoors) (also twice 2nd and twice 3rd), and 2nd at 400mh in 1986-7 and 1990. She went to Arkansas State University, USA. Pbs: 400m 53.94 (1990), 400mh 56.47 (1990).

Witold KRUPINSKI (Skierniewice, Poland) (b. 2 Aug 1945) on 16 March. He won the European Junior Games javelin in 1964 and had a pb of 80.26 (1971).

Danuta **MAJEWSKA** (GRAJZAREK)(Poland) (b. 17 Jun 1955 Zlotoryja) on 30 October in Wroclaw. Polish discus champion 1979-81 and 1983, at the European Cup she was 7th 1979, 6th 1981, 7th 1983. Pbs: SP 15.03 (1980), DT 61.06 (1983).

Klaus **ULONSKA** on 13 March in Köln-Lindenthal.

Died in 2013

Nancy Jane **BORWICK** (later JARVIS) (Australia) (b. 20 Mar 1938) on 24 November in Western Australia. She was 8th at long jump at the 1956 Olympic Games, was 2nd in the AUS Champs in 1958 and 1959 (and 3rd at pentathlon in 1959). Pb 6.13 (1956).

Died in early 2017

Horst **ASTROTH** (Germany/GDR) (b. 30 Oct 1923 Naumburg) on 10 January in Naumburg. A member of SV Halle, he was 16th at the 1960 Olympic Games, 8th at the 1962 Europeans and 2nd in the GDR championships in 1956 and 1958-9. 7 internationals 1956-62. Walks pbs: 10000m 46:02.2 (1961), 1Hr 12,833m (1964), 20k 1:34:06.4t (1959), 30k 2:29:42.2t (1959), 50k 4:24:20.8t (1963).

Donald Milton **CAMPBELL** (USA) (b. 9 Apr 1926 Denver) on 3 February. After winning the Purple Heart in Wartime service with the U.S. Army he went to the University of Colorado and in 1948 was 5th in the NCAA 220y and also in the Olympic Trials 100m in 10.58, just missing a team place. At AAU Champs he was 3rd at 200m in 1944 and 1949. In 1951 he ran the lead-off leg for the winning US 4x100m team at the Pan-American Games. Pbs: 100y 9.5A (1947), 100m 10.5/10.58 (1948), 200mt 21.4 (1949), 220y St 21.0 (1947).

Anne-Marie **COLCHEN** (France) (b. 8 Dec 1925 Le Havre) on 26 January. She was captain of the French basketball team and played in 63 internationals 1946-56 with a bronze medal at the 1953 World Championships. As a high jumper she won the European title at a French record 1.60 in 1946 and improved that record to 1.63 in 1949. 14th equal at the 1948 Olympics, 6th Europeans 1950 and French champion 1946 and 1948-50. 11 internationals 1946-55. 1.82m tall.

Angela **CRESSI** (Italy) (b. 3 Sep 1914 Genoa) on 6 March. She was the first Italian woman to throw the javelin over 40m with 40.12 in 1938 and an earlier record at 37.65 in 1936. The war virtually ended a promising career, although she was again in the Italian team in 1947 (5 internationals 1936-47) and competed in age group competition until she was 80.

Pamela **DAVIES** (GBR) (b. 30 May 1934 Clapham) on 24 January. She was 3rd in the International Cross-country in 1968 (5th 1967, 9th 1969) and had an extraordinary record in the English national CC, winning each year 1965-68, 2nd in 1964 and 1969 and 3rd in 1963 after 6th in 1961-2, and was also twice Southern champion. Pbs: 880y 2:19.7 (1963), 1500m 4:43.6 (1968), 1M 5:02.3 (1963), 3000m 10:19.2 (1968), 2M 11:39.0 (1955).

Graham Emmerson **EVERETT** (GBR) (b. 20 Jan 1934) on 30 January. He was Scottish 1 mile champion eight times 1955-61 and 1963 and set native records of 4:07.5 in 1956, 4:06.6 in 1957 and 4:03.9 in 1960. After 3rd place in 1957 he was AAA 1 mile champion in 1958 and had two GB internationals as well as running for Scotland at the 1958 Commonwealth Games (heats 880y and 1M) and four times in the International CC with a best of 18th in 1961. Also Scottish CC champion 1960. Other pbs: 880y 1:51.4 (1960), 1500m 3:45.1 (1960), 1M 4:02.70 (1960), 3000m 8:04.0 (1961), 2M 8:38.2 Scottish record (1961), 3M 13:47.6 (1961).

Roberto **GALLI** (Italy) (b. 19 Jan 1943 Lucca) on 21 February 21 in a car accident at Marina di Carrara. He was Italian high jump champion in 1962-3 and set national records at 2.03 in 1962 and 2.06 and 2.08 in 1963. 5 Internationals 1962-3. Later a coach.

Edward '**Ted**' **HAGGIS** (Canada) (b. 9 Jun 1924 London ON) on 23 January in London, Ontario. He was a quarter-finalist at 100m and 200m at the 1948 Olympic Games and 5th at 4x100m. Canadian champion 100y & 220y 1950. Pbs 100m 10.5 (1948), 220y 21.9 (1951).

Siegfried **HERRMANN** (GDR/Germany) (b.7 Nov 1932) on 14 February in Erfurt. A stylish runner, he set three world records outdoors: 7:46.0 for 3000m at Erfurt on 5 Aug 1965 and on GDR teams at 4x1500m in 1958 and 1963. He also set a series of world bests indoors: 1500m 3:44.6 (1960) and 3:42.0 (1965), 3000m 7:58.7 (1959), 7:58.6 (1964), 7:52.2 (1965) and 7:49.0 (1966), plus European records – one more at 1500m and 3 at 1 mile to 3:58.6 in 1965. His GDR records: 800m (4) 1:52.1 (1953) to 1:48.5 (1956), 1000m (3) 2:28.4 (1953) to 2:23.2 (1955), 1500m (12) 3:57.0 (1952) to 3:41.8 (1956), 1M 4:03.4 (1955), 2000m 5:05.0 (1959), 3000m (3) from 8:12.8 (1955) to 7:51.2 (1963), 5000m (3) 14:11.6 (1955) to 13:30.0 (1965). Other pbs: 400m 50.2 (1954), 1000m 2:18.9 (1965), 1500m 3:39.8 (1963), 1M 3:58.6i/3:59.1 (1963), 10000m 29:11.8 (1967), 3000mSC 8:43.8 (1965).

International Champs record: Olympics: 1956- dnf ht 1500m, 1964- 11 10000m; Europeans: 1958- 6 1500m, 1962- 7 5000m, 1966- ht 5000m; Eur. Indoors: 1966- 2 3000m. GDR titles: 800m 1953, 1500m 1952-4, 1956; 5000m

1956, 1964-66; 10000m 1964; Indoor 3000 1964-6. 38 Internationals 1952-68. He became a top coach, notably of Hartwig Gauder, Olympic 50kW winner in 1980.

Progress at 1500m, 3000m, 5000m: 1950- 4:20.8, 1951- 4:07.6, 9:24.4, 16:19.0; 1952- 3:55.6, 1953- 3:50.0, 8:25.6, 15:20.0; 1954- 3:48.8, 8:50.6, 15:07.8; 1955- 3:42.6, 8:12.8, 14:11.6; 1956- 3:41.8, 7:59.0, 14:08.0; 1958- 3:42.5, 7:59.0, 14:18.4; 1959- 3:40.9, 7:58.7i/8:00.4, 14:11,8; 1960- 3:41.3, 8:03.4; 1961- 3:43.9, 8:01.4, 14:07.4; 1962- 3:42.5, 8:00.8, 13:57.2; 1963- 3:39.8, 7:51.2, 13:46.2; 1964- 3:43.2, 7:P58.6i/7:59.8, 13:55.6; 1965- 3:41.7, 7:46.0, 13:30.0; 1966- 3:43.8,7:49.0i/7:53.0, 13:50.0.

Dr. **Miroslav HORCIC** (Czech Republic) (b. 3 Aug 1921 Nymburk) on 14 January in Karlsruhe, Germany, to where he emigrated in the 1960s and was a coach. He competed at the 1948 Olympic Games (ht 100m, qf 200m, 6th 4x100m). He was Czechoslovak champion at 100m in 1941, 1945, 1948-50 and 1952 and 200m 1949 and set national records at 100m 10.6 (1952) and 200m 21.5 (1949). 21 Internationals 1947-56.

George **Derek IBBOTSON** (GBR) (b. 17 Jun 1932 Huddersfield) on 23 February in Ossett, West Yorkshire. Running for Longwood Harriers (and for South London Harriers 1957-9), after RAF service he shot into world class in 1955, when he was 2nd to Chris Chataway in the AAA 3 miles. A year later he beat Chataway to win that title and later won the Olympic bronze at 5000m. A great favourite of the British public, 'Ibbo' reached the peak of his fame in 1957. In the midst of a hectic programme of some 70 races that year he set a European record for the mile with 3:58.4, then next month retained his AAA 3 miles title in a British record 13:20.8 and six days later, on 19 Jul 1957, took the world mile record with 3:57.2 at the White City; en route he set a British record for 1500m at 3:41.9. He never quite recaptured such form and was 10th in 1958 and 8th in 1962 at 3 miles in the Commonwealth Games. He ran on the England team that set a world record for 4 x 1 mile in 1958. Indoors he set 7 UK records and won AAA titles at 2 miles in 1962 and 1965, when he ran a British indoor record time of 8:42.6. He was also 3rd in the National Cross-country in 1956, followed by 46th in the International CC. 18 UK internationals 1955-65. Other best times: 880y 1:52.2 (1958), 2000m 5:12.8 (1955), 3000m 8:00.0 (1959), 2 miles 8:41.2 (1957), 5000m 13:54.4 (1956), 6 miles 28:52.0 (1955). He was awarded the MBE in the 2008 New Year's Honours. His autobiography was entitled 'Four Minute Smiler'.

His first wife Madeline (née Wooller, b. 31 Dec 1935 Twickenham), who later married squash great Jonah Barrington, was 2nd in the WAAA 1 mile in 1962 and 1963 and won the national cross-country in 1963 and 1964.

Jirí LANSKY (Czech Republic) (b. 17 Sep 1933 Prague) on 14 February at Lázne Tousen. At high jump he was the silver medallist at the Europeans in 1954 and 1958 and was 7= at the 1960 Olympics. In his best year of 1958 he was 4= on the world list with 2.10, the last of his seven Czechoslovak records from 2.01 in 1953. He was national champion in 1954, 1958-60 and 1963-4; 29 internationals 1951-64.

Jean-Paul MARTIN du GARD (France) (b. 3 May 1927 Paris) on 26 February in Paris. He won a European gold medal at 4x400m in 1954 (also sf 400m) after 4th in 1950. At the Olympic Games he was a 400m quarter finalist in 1956 and ran on the 4x400m team in 1952 (6th) and 1956 (heat). He was French champion at 200m in 1955 and ran on three 4x400m teams that set French records 1950-54. Pbs: 200m 21.6 (1954), 400m 47.7 (1952). 35 internationals 1949-56.

Rev. **Philip** Richard Llewellyn **MORGAN** (GBR) (b. 11 Mar 1927) on 14 January in Winslow, Buckinghamshire. An Oxford 'blue' and member of Southend-on-Sea, he had pbs of 1M 4:16.4, 2M 9:06.0, 3M 14:03.8 (3rd AAA Champs), 5000m 14:55.6 and was the Universities AU 3M champion in 1952. He was 2nd to Chris Brasher in the World University Games 5000m in 1951, also had a 2M steeple pb of 10:38.0 (1953) and also ran once in the International CC for Wales – 31st in 1953. His brother Dick ran five times in the International CC.

Frank MURPHY (Ireland) (b. 21 May 1947 Dublin) on 5 January in Dublin. He won European 1500m silver medals outdoors in 1969 (Irish record 3:39.51) (heats 1966 and 1971) and indoors in 1970, and competed at the Olympic Games of 1968 (heat) and 1972 (heat, and sf 800m). He was Irish champion at 800m 1970, 1972 and 1976, 1500m 1967-71 and 1M 1966-7, 1969, 1971-2, and won the AAA 1500m 1969 and junior 880y in 1965. Pbs: 800m 1:47.4 (1969), 1500m 3:38.5 (1972, rec), 1M 3:58.1 (1969). He competed for Clonliffe Harriers and studied at Villanova University, USA, for whom he won the NCAA indoor 880y in 1959.

Nadezhda Fyodorovna **OLIZARENKO** (née Mushta) (USSR/Ukraine) (b. 28 Nov 1953 Bryansk) on 17 February in Kiev. She won the 1980 Olympic title for 800m, when she improved the world record that she had set six weeks earlier of 1:54.85 to 1:53.43 (still the second best of all-time), and was also third at 1500m. An international class athlete for nearly two decades, she was European silver medallist at both 800m and 4 x 400m in 1978 and gold medallist at 800m in 1986. She also won the World Student Games 800m in 1979. After retiring following 1980 she returned to competition in 1984 and was 2nd at the European Indoors in 1985, 7th at the Worlds in 1987, and was USSR 800m champion in 1988 when she was a semi-finalist at the Olympic Games. World Cup: 1979- 2, 1985- 3; European Cup: 1985- 2 (& 1 4x400m). She added another world record at 4 x 800m in 1984. Her only USSR titles were at cross-country 1977 and 4x800m 1979. A sports instructor, she competed for Odessa SA and was married to Sergey Olizarenko (8:24.0 for 3000m steeplechase in 1978). Other pbs: 400m 50.96 (1980), 600m 1:27.3 (1980, world indoor best), 1000m 2:40.59 (1991), 1500m 3:56.8 (1980).

Progress at 800m: 1970- 2:11.4, 1972- 2:08.6, 1974- 2:05.0, 1975- 2:03.3, 1976- 2:05.8, 1977- 1:59.76, 1978- 1:55.82, 1979- 1:57.5, 1980- 1:53.43, 1983- 1:58.16, 1984- 1:56.09, 1985- 1:56.25, 1986- 1:57.15, 1987- 1:58.6, 1988- 1:56.03/1:56.0, 1989- 2:00.56, 1990- 1:58.51, 1991- 2:01.78/

Jean POCZOBUT (France) (b. 20 Jun 1936 Romilly-sur-Seine) on 4 January. He was an IAAF Honorary Life Vice President and an Honorary Member of the International Athletics Foundation, having been a member of the IAAF Council 1995-2011 and treasurer 2003-11. He received the IAAF Golden Order of Merit in 2011 and Veteran Pin in 2003. Previously he had been national coach 1964-77, the national technical director 1977-84, vice-president 1989-93 and president of the French Federation 1993-7.

Ilie POPA (Romania) (b. 9 May 1940) died in March at the age of 76. In 1964 he was 28th in the Olympic 50k walk and was Balkan champion at 20k. Competing for Steaua Bucuresti, he was Romanian champion at 20kW 1961 and 1963-4 and 50kW 1965-6. Pb 50kW 4:27:23 (1966).

Allan H. **STEINFELD** (USA) (b. 7 Jun 1946 Manhattan) on 24 January in Allentown, Pennsylvania. After being technical director of the New York Marathon from 1981 he became the president of the New York Road Runners in 1983 and race director after Fred Lebow's death in 1994, staying in that position until 2005.

István TATÁR (Hungary) (b. 24 Mar 1958 Eger) on 2 January. He set Hungarian records at 60m 6.65i (1986), 100m 10.40 (1980) and 200m 21.8i (1979) as well as ten at relays. Competing in 55 internationals 1976-89, his major championships record was: At 100m/4x100m: OG: 80- h/h, '88- h/8; WCh: '83- qf/sf, '87- 5R; EC: '82 & '86; h/6. Also WI: '89- h 60m; EI: '82- h 200m, '86- h 60m; EJ: '77- 7 100m, sf 200m. He was HUN champion at 100m & 200m 1979 and indoors at 60m 1976, 1986 and 1989, 200m 1981. Pbs: 100m 10.25 (1985), 200m 20.82 (1985). Head coach of Honvéd 2009-15.

Zoran TRIFUNOVIC (Serbia) (b. 22 Nov 1931 Gornji Milanovac) on 8 January in Belgrade. He started with athletics in 1948 at his local club Takovo, but moved to Belgrade in 1954 and competed for AC Partizan until 1961. National champion at 100m in 1955 and 200m in 1955 and 1957; 7 internationals, pbs: 100m 10.6 (1960), 200m 21.8 (1957), 400m 49.5 (1960). He worked as a professor of physical education.

David Michael **'Mike' TURNER** (GBR) (b. 6 May 1939 Liverpool) in January. A member of Liverpool Harriers, he was 11th in 1961 and 6th at 5000m in 1963 and 5th at 10000m in 1967 at the World Student Games and got an 'A' international vest but not a full British one on the track. His greatest success came at cross-country, competing six times for England at the International Cross-country: 1961- 23rd, 1963- 37th, 1964- 20th, 1967 15th, 1969- 13th and 1970- 7th (captain of England's winning team) after finishing 6/8/2/2/4/4 in those years in the National Cross-country. He was 3rd in the AAA 10 miles in 1967 and had pbs: 3000m 8:20.2 (1963), 2M 8:44.0 (1963), 3M 13:23.6 (1967), 5000m 14:09.4 (1964), 6M 27:33.2 (1966), 10000m 28:45.4 (1971), 15000m 45:24.6 (1970), 10M 47:51.4 (1967), 20000m 61:10.8 (1970), 1Hr 20011m (1969), 15M/25000m/30000m: 1:14:39.6/1:17:27.8/1:33:42.6 (1970), 3kSt 8:57.2 (1969. He gained his degree at Cambridge University, going on to get a PhD and becoming a lecturer, then the Bursar of Peterhouse. He served as a British team manager and Treasurer of the BAAB.

Ed WHITLOCK (Canada) (b. 6 Mar 1931 London, England) on 13 March in Toronto. He set an extraordinary set of world age bests for the marathon. In 2000 he became the oldest man to run the distance in under 3 hours with 2:52:47 at the age of 69, going on to a world M70 record of 2:54:48 at age 73, and 2:58:40 at age 74. He set world M80 records with 3:25:54 and 3:15:54 in 2011 (and at half marathon with 1:38:59 in 2012 and 1:38:11 in 2013). Most recently in October 2016, at the age of 85, he became the oldest person to run a marathon in under 4 hours with 3:56:34 in Toronto. He also set many track records from 1500m to 10,000m in M65 to M85 categories to a total of 36 world age records at all events.

He had graduated form the Royal School of Mines, Imperial College, London and ran until then before moving to Canada for an engineering career. He took up running again and ran 2:31:23 at the age of 48, but concentrated on road racing after retiring in his sixties.

Alice Ann Doreen **WHITTY** (Canada) (b. 24 Mar 1934 Vancouver) (later SIMICAK) on 7 January in Richmond. At the high jump she was 3rd at the Empire Games in 1954, and 5th in 1955 and 2nd in 1959 at the Pan-American Games. She also competed at the Olympic Games in 1952 (10th) and 1956 (16=), was Canadian champion in 1951-2, 1956 and 1958-60, and set Canadian records at 1.606 (5'3$\frac{1}{4}$") in 1954 and 1.625 (5'4") in 1956. She took degrees from the University of Oregon and the University of British Columbia.

WORLD LIST TRENDS - MEN

10th Bests	To 2008	2009	2010	2011	2012	2013	2014	2015	2016
100m	9.95- 08	9.97	9.95	**9.89**	9.94	9.96	9.96	9.91	9.93
200m	20.03- 00	20.17	20.11	20.16	20.10	20.10	20.08	19.97	**19.96**
400m	44.51- 96	44.81	44.81	44.78	44.77	44.82	44.71	**44.36**	44.46
800m	1:43.66- 96	1:43.82	1:43.89	1:44.07	1:43.71	1:43.87	1:43.71	1:43.72	**1:43.55**
1500m	3:31.10- 04	3:31.90	3:32.20	3:31.84	3:31.61	3:31.94	3:30.98	**3:30.29**	3:32.30
5000m	**12:54.99- 03**	12:58.16	12:55.95	12:59.15	12:55.99	13:01.64	13:03.85	13:05.30	13:03.22
10000m	**27:00.30- 07**	27:15.94	27:17.61	26:52.84	27:03.49	27:21.50	27:28.27	27:18.86	27:05.64
Half Mar	59:32- 07	59:30	59:40	59:39	**59:15**	59:54	59:21	59:28	59:31
Marathon	2:06:25- 08	2:06:14	2:05:52	2:05:45!	**2:04:54**	2:05:16	2:05:13	2:06:00	2:05:21
3000mSt	**8:08.14- 02**	8:10.63	8:09.87	8:08.43	8:10.20	8:08.83	8:11.86	8:13.37	8:10.65
110mh	13.19- 07	13.21	13.28	13.23	13.13	13.18	13.19	13.13	13.20
400mh	**48.25- 02**	48.30	48.47	48.47	48.41	48.46	48.69	48.44	48.49
HJ	**2.36- 88**	2.33	2.32	2.33	2.32	2.34	2.34	2.33	2.35
PV	**5.90- 98**	5.80	5.80	5.80	5.73	5.80	5.76	5.82	5.80
LJ	**8.35- 97**	8.30	8.25	8.27	8.26	8.29	8.28	8.29	8.31
TJ	**17.48- 85**	17.41	17.29	17.35	17.31	17.26	17.27	17.24	17.16
SP	**21.63- 84**	20.99	21.29	21.16	21.14	21.09	21.37	21.14	21.30
DT	**68.20- 82**	66.19	66.90	67.21	67.50	65.98	66.11	66.40	67.13
HT	**81.88- 88**	79.48	78.73	79.27	79.56	79.16	78.27	78.22	77.78
JT	87.12- 96/97	84.24	85.12	84.81	84.72	84.61	85.92	86.21	86.48
Decathlon	**8526- 98**	8406	8253	8288	8322	8390	8311	8398	8413
20kmW	**1:18:30- 05**	1:19:55	1:20:36	1:19:57	1:19:20	1:19:36	1:19:43	1:19:14	1:19:24
50kmW	**3:41:30- 05**	3:41:55	3:47:54	3:44:03	**3:41:24**	3:43:38	3:43:02	3:44:17	3:42:57

Peak years shown in bold

Men 100th Bests

		2009	2010	2011	2012	2013	2014	2015	2016
100m	10.23- 08	10.22	10.26	10.21	10.20	10.21	10.18	10.16	**10.14**
200m	20.66- 99/00/07	20.68	20.71	20.63	20.57	20.60	20.51	20.51	**20.45**
400m	45.78- 00	45.86	45.92	45.91	45.79	45.87	45.69	**45.61**	45.71
800m	1:46.54- 99	1:46.88	1:46.76	1:46.50	1:46.56	**1:46.44**	1:46.60	1:46.51	**1:46.44**
1500m	3:38.42- 97	3:38.60	3:38.47	3:37.77	**3:36.84**	3:37.77	3:38.47	3:38.13	3:38.20
5000m	13:25.05- 08	13:26.90	13:25.88	13:26.29	**13:23.58**	13:27.29	13:28.60	13:27.10	13:24.13
10000m	**28:04.47- 06**	28:18.00	28:21.00	28:15.79	28:06.74	28:18.68	28:20.77	28:08.4	28:06.33
Half Mar	61:50- 08	61:28	61:38	61:31	61:19	61:25	61:17	**60:58**	61:21
Marathon	2:10:22- 08	2:09:53	2:09:31	2:09:19!	**2:08:32**	2:09:06	2:08:58	2:09:14	2:09:28
3000mSt	**8:31.06- 04**	8:35.21	8:35.29	8:35.45	8:31.2	8:34.42	8:35.05	8:33.69	8:32.63
110mh	13.67- 08	13.71	13.68	13.67	13.66	13.67	13.67	13.62	**13.61**
400mh	50.06- 00	50.35	50.41	50.28	50.15	50.16	50.21	50.06	**49.89**
HJ	2.24- 84/88/89/92/96	2.23	2.23	**2.24**	**2.24**	**2.24**	**2.24**	**2.24**	**2.24**
PV	**5.55- 00**	5.46	5.42	5.45	5.50	5.50	5.50	5.50	5.51
LJ	**7.96- 04**	7.94	7.91	7.94	7.93	7.92	7.89	7.90	7.94
TJ	**16.60- 88**	16.46	16.46	16.53	16.49	16.40	16.38	16.44	16.53
SP	19.48- 84	19.15	19.08	19.18	19.51	19.41	19.47	19.55	**19.56**
DT	60.96- 84	60.00	59.77	59.98	60.95	60.21	60.64	60.36	**61.36**
HT	**73.06- 84**	70.66	70.78	70.44	71.22	70.49	70.48	70.73	71.33
JT	77.14- 91	77.03	76.71	77.38	77.78	77.10	77.16	77.51	**78.29**
Decathlon	**7702- 88**	7623	7526	7678	7648	7586	7559	7594	7620
20kmW	1:22:48- 05	1:23:57	1:24:24	1:23:40	1:23:10	1:22:56	1:23:07	1:23:24	**1:22:25**
50kmW	4:03:49- 99	4:09:24	4:08:08	4:06:15	4:03:04	4:08:33	4:06:22	**4:02:23**	4:02:37

! From 2011 main marathon lists no longer include Boston or other such excessively downhill races

Number of athletes achieving base level standards for world lists:

Men	2011	2012	2013	2014	2015	2016		2011	2012	2013	2014	2015	2016
100m 10.25	133	148	132	163	168	203	HJ 2.20	192	216	197	211	216	212
200m 20.69	122	165	140	187	194	224	PV 5.40	139	177	179	178	168	192
400m 46.19	151	184	177	202	216	228	LJ 7.80	186	183	181	182	182	207
800m 1:47.59	198	220	190	202	208	226	TJ 16.30	142	144	120	124	126	154
1500m 3:39.99	170	201	184	173	171	180	SP 18.70	144	181	180	180	180	196
5000m 13:37.0	193	203	180	169	204	195	DT 58.00	155	177	166	173	171	189
10000m 28:35.0	172	199	168	155	225	202	HT 68.00	149	158	146	149	156	171
HMar 61:59	147	199	171	199	182	179	JT 74.00	173	199	190	187	199	215
Mar 2:10:59	215	233	212	207	191	169	Dec 7400	165	173	143	150	157	145
3000St 8:39.9	147	184	141	138	144	183	20kmW 1:25:00	154	175	175	151	166	192
110mh 13.89	194	214	199	208	215	220	50kmW 4:10:00	110	132	106	113	134	142
400mh 50.79	171	186	177	191	200	224							
							TOTAL	3722	4251	3854	3992	4173	4448

The 2016 numbers compared to those of 2015: for 10th best 13-10, 100th best 16-6 (1 tie), base level 17-6

WORLD LIST TRENDS – WOMEN

This table shows the 10th and 100th bests in the year lists for the last eight years, with previous bests.

10th Bests	To 2007	2009	2010	2011	2012	2013	2014	2015	2016
100m	10.92- 88	11.04	11.08	11.01	10.99	10.93	11.01	10.92	**10.90**
200m	22.24- 88	22.45	22.49	22.55	22.37	22.40	22.46	**22.23**	22.16
400m	**49.74- 84**	50.27	50.43	50.67	50.06	50.19	50.74	50.32	50.25
800m	**1:56.91- 88**	1:58.80	1:58.67	1:58.21	1:57.77	1:58.92	1:58.84	1:58.34	1:58.28
1500m	**3:58.07- 97**	4:00.86	4:00.25	4:01.73	3:59.71	4:01.48	4:00.17	4:01.26	4:00.18
5000m	14:43.87- 05	14:41.62	**14:38.64**	14:39.44	14:50.80	14:47.12	14:52.67	14:47.75	14:38.92
10000m	30:39.86- 08	30:51.92	31:29:03	31:10.02	30:59.19	31:04.85	31:48.6	31:13.29	**30:37.38**
Half Mar	68:23- 00	68:14	67:52	68:07	67:42	67:39	68:13	68:18	**67:16**
Marathon	2:23:22- 06	2:25:06	2:23:44	2:22:43!	**2:20:57**	2:23:00	2:22:30	2:22:51	2:22:40
3000mSt	9:21.76- 08	**9:18.54**	9:24.84	9:25.96	9:23.52	9:27.49	9:23.43	9:20.64	9:18.85
100mh	**12.58- 08**	12.67	12.65	12.73	12.62	12.81	12.71	12.59	12.63
400mh	**53.99- 04**	54.49	54.58	54.69	54.21	54.38	54.74	54.37	54.15
HJ	**2.01- 03**	1.98	1.97	1.96	1.96	1.97	1.97	1.97	1.98
PV	4.70- 07/08	4.65	4.66	4.71	4.70	4.71	4.71	4.72	**4.81**
LJ	**7.07- 88**	6.87	6.89	6.88	6.97	6.91	6.90	6.93	6.93
TJ	**14.84- 08**	14.62	14.48	14.57	14.60	14.50	14.10	14.32	14.56
SP	**20.85- 87**	19.38	19.47	19.26	19.60	18.81	19.03	18.89	19.11
DT	**70.34- 88**	63.89	64.04	63.91	64.45	64.46	65.51	64.79	65.14
HT	**74.40- 08**	73.07	73.40	72.65	75.59	75.02	74.20	73.66	73.09
JT	64.89- 00	63.89	63.36	63.50	64.91	63.55	64.50	65.01	**65.14**
Heptathlon	**6540- 88**	6323	6204	6338	6466	6345	6395	6458	6458
20kmW	1:27:18- 08	1:28:50	1:29:20	1:28:41	**1:27:08**	1:27:53	1:27:54	1:27:09	1:27:18

Peak years shown in bold

Women 100th Bests									
100m	11.36- 00/08	11.41	11.40	11.36	11.34	11.35	11.32	11.31	**11.27**
200m	23.17- 08	23.26	23.27	23.21	23.10	23.19	23.17	23.08	**23.00**
400m	**52.08- 08**	52.44	52.52	52.33	52.36	52.25	52.36	52.25	52.13
800m	2:01.50- 84	2:02.13	2:02.14	2:01.86	**2:01.48**	2:02.05	2:02.05	2:02.06	2:01.80
1500m	4:10.22- 84	4:11.06	4:10.50	4:09.88	**4:09.06**	4:09.98	4:10.09	4:10.24	4:09.28
5000m	15:27.20- 04	15:37.31	15:37.45	15:31.67	15:32.88	15:35.74	15:33.42	15:32.67	**15:26.28**
10000m	32:30.10- 08	32:54.64	32:57.59	32:53.44	32:38.95	32:48.60	32:43.90	32:29.06	**32:21.98**
Half Mar	71:15- 07	70:57	70:59	71:06	70:48	70:44	70:45	70:43	**70:35**
Marathon	2:29:53- 08	2:30:08	2:29:36	2:28:32	**2:28:01**	2:29:10	2:29:17	2:28:24	2:28:49
3000mSt	9:56.48- 08	10:02.94	10:03.50	9:59.44	9:53.79	9:56.50	9:53.19	9:52.62	**9:46.86**
100mh	13.22- 00/08	13.28	13.23	13.16	13.11	13.19	13.14	13.17	**13.07**
400mh	57.21- 07	57.45	57.22	57.26	57.14	57.40	57.34	57.08	**56.85**
HJ	**1.88- 86/87/88/92/93**	1.86	1.87	1.86	1.87	1.87	1.86	1.86	1.87
PV	4.25- 08	4.21	4.25	4.30	4.31	4.30	4.30	4.32	**4.35**
LJ	6.53- 88	6.49	6.51	6.50	**6.55**	6.49	6.45	6.49	6.51
TJ	**13.75- 08**	13.65	13.67	13.70	13.71	13.69	13.60	13.62	13.60
SP	**17.19- 87**	16.43	16.46	16.60	16.82	16.65	16.60	16.84	16.96
DT	**58.50- 92**	56.06	55.05	56.12	56.94	55.70	56.27	56.26	56.83
HT	64.81- 08	63.77	64.12	64.79	**65.78**	64.65	64.79	65.67	65.75
JT	55.55- 00	55.16	54.98	55.34	55.97	55.10	55.78	55.95	**56.19**
Heptathlon	**5741- 88**	5586	5568	5591	5702	5560	5668	5715	5735
20kmW	1:34:11- 05	1:35:54	1:36:32	1:34:52	1:33:43	1:33:48	1:35:20	1:34:16	**1:33:41**

All-time record levels indicated in bold.
! From 2011 main marathon lists no longer include Boston or other such excessively downhill races.

Number of athletes achieving base level standards for world lists:

Women

	2011	2012	2013	2014	2015	2016			2012	2013	2014	2015	2016
100m	11.44	157	173	151	169	179	215	HJ	1.85	172	164	155	148	142	170
200m	23.29	117	152	140	138	174	198	PV	4.25	119	131	123	133	143	169
400m	52.99	187	210	196	190	213	236	LJ	6.35	185	212	171	168	186	189
800m	2:03.50	176	196	166	184	191	211	TJ	13.30	191	199	184	171	169	189
1500m	4:13.5	161	197	167	169	164	195	SP	15.85	163	180	177	189	194	216
5000m	15:45.0	163	201	167	172	192	224	DT	53.65	153	172	159	152	165	180
10000m	33:00.0	117	151	131	133	169	176	HT	61.00	181	205	190	193	205	227
HMar	72:00	174	199	204	193	200	212	JT	53.00	160	177	159	172	176	188
Mar	2:32:00	165	212	170	171	195	196	Hep	5450	146	157	140	156	155	189
3000mSt	10:05.0	136	167	144	161	166	195	20kmW	1:38:00	167	173	194	148	176	198
100mh	13.39	177	198	175	195	191	228	TOTAL		3367	3826	3463	3505	3745	4201
		2011	2012	2013	2014	2015	2016							
400mh	57.99	147	179	143	152	166	192							

The 2016 numbers compared to those of 2015: for 10th best 13-10, 100th best 16-6 (1 tie), base level 17-6

The 2016 numbers compared to those of 2015: for 10th best 17-2 (2 ties), 100th best 20-2, base level 22-0

HALF-MILERS TIME FORGOT
By Bob Phillips

Of all the exceptional achievements I gazed upon with such rapt attention as a youthful fan at the 1960 Rome Olympics it is the men's 800 metres which remains most firmly in my mind. After all, this was the emergence of Peter Snell, winning so unexpectedly his first gold medal when we had all much preferred the chances of the world record-holder, Roger Moens. More than 30 years later – and by then having the good fortune to be a privileged radio commentator rather than a paying spectator – I met Snell, and when I admitted to him that I was surprised by that victory of his he told me that I couldn't have been watching the qualifying rounds closely enough. A shade ungracious a remark, I thought, as I defy anyone, however expert, who was there in Rome to have given Snell any greater chance of gold than I had.

The 800 metres then and now is the event which causes me the greatest delight, and during the summer months of 1960 before setting off by train from London to Rome I had been running half-miles for my club, Watford Harriers. You might say that the half-mile runs in the family – or, rather, that the family runs in the half-mile. My father, who was born in 1910, once claimed to have done a 2:04.8 in his youth, and if that is so then he must have been exceptional for that era. I eventually ran 1:55.8 (statisticians please note: yards, not metres, and cinders, not all-weather). Both my daughters ran 800 metres at county level in the 1980s, and now a grand-daughter has already won a Merseyside title in the same event at 15; and I can see another Kelly Holmes in the making – as, no doubt, in their turn can a thousand other doting grand-fathers the length and breadth of Britain. .

What may surprise the discerning readers of this annual is that I can recall as readily to mind the name of the man who came 5th in that Rome Olympic final. as I can that of Snell's. This 'also ran' was a Swiss named Christian Wägli, who was tall (1.83m) and slim and led the race to beyond 600 metres. Tall, slim front-runners have always had an irresistible appeal to my aesthetic sense, and certainly very much more so than the Snell type, looking more like a rugby-football wing-forward. Wägli's personal best was 1:47.4, which would barely get him into the top 200 in the world nowadays, and I don't suppose that even in Switzerland, where the presiding memory will surely be that of André Bucher's' 2001 World title, Wägli is accorded too much honour.

I would dearly have liked to have seen Rudolf Harbig, but he was already running 1:50.6 when I was six weeks or so old and was to go very much faster the next year which, in an odd way, was to make me even more resentful of Snell's later intrusion. Harbig's seemingly immortal record had at long last been broken by Moens, and the Rome final was as equally marked for me by his downfall as by Snell's defiance. Seeing Mal Whitfield gliding smoothly round the glutinous White City cinders in the early 1950s was some considerable compensation for having been born too late for Harbig, and as Whitfield's fastest half-mile was no better than 1:48.6 I wonder if he, too, was daunted by what Harbig had achieved.

British half-miling had remained self-effacingly in the Olympic shadows in the years after World War II, though we could reasonably claim that the tallest and longest-striding two-lap man of them all, Arthur Wint, was one of ours as he had not taken up the event seriously until after leaving Jamaica and joining the Royal Air Force in 1944, and he did run for Great Britain when not called up for Olympic duty in the service of his native island. After a few glorious years in the 1950s when it was obligatory that your name ended in 'son' to be a leading British half-miler – Hewson, Johnson, Rawson – those Rome Olympics were an ignominious disaster for a country which had once won four Olympic 800 metres titles in succession. None of our three representatives, Hewson included, even reached the semi-finals, and the 1961 AAA Championships 880 yards added to the misery – a Jamaican 1st, an Irishman 2nd, a Finn 3rd and another Irishman 4th. Yet relief was at hand.

My recollections from that year are of a British pair, Bob Piercy and Peter Kilford, racing in tandem from the front with blithe disregard for the opposition and sweeping all before them in the two-a-side international matches which were so popular then, but this is a matter of the memory playing tricks. They did indeed do just that against Poland in September of 1961, though Piercy was controversially disqualified, but that was in Warsaw, and I certainly had neither the money nor the school's permission to have taken time off for that trip. I did see Kilford win for England against the Russian Federal Republic at the White City, but it was one of the visitors who had led for much of the race.

No matter; the point I'm making is that Piercy, at 1.91m in height and weighing 80kg, was habitually another of those big powerful front-runners for whom I had so much admiration, and his imposing presence was even more evident when he was alongside the shorter bespectacled Kilford. Incidentally, Piercy was an insurance claims assessor by occupation, from Hull, in Yorkshire, and Kilford was a clerk at Portsmouth Town Hall, but both found the time to hold down these full-time jobs, train for two hours or so each evening, and produce performances which would still rank very comfortably among the top 20 in Britain these days.

A year or so later came startling news of what was – even by American standards – precocious talent. Steve Haas had run his first half-mile on 7 June 1963 and a fortnight later was 4th in the greatest mass race ever at the distance, as part of the AAU Championships in St Louis. Haas's time of 1:47.6 would have been remarkable by any standards, but what took our breath away was the fact that he had also run 100 yards in 9.4 the year before, and even if that might have been a case of generous timing he had done a credible 20.7 for 220 yards round a turn.

Here, surely, was the man with the blazing basic speed to reduce the 800 metres record – by that date standing to Peter Snell at 1:44.3 – to something under 1:43. Well, we now all know that we had to wait another 16 years for that to happen. Haas came to Europe that summer but was not remotely in the same form, was not selected for the GB-v-USA match at the White City, and never ran anywhere near as fast again. Nor did he even take part in the 1964 US Olympic trials. Too much too soon, perhaps?

In the case of Robbie Brightwerll, it was 'too little' rather than 'too much'. Brightwell had also run very decent times at 100 and 220 yards at the start of his international career and had become one of the world's best quarter-milers – European champion at 400 metres in 1962. His 45.9 for 440 yards on a rain-soaked White City track to win the 1962 AAA title might well have been close to 45 flat had he been racing instead in California on that particular Saturday afternoon, and the world record for 440 yards currently stood at 45.7. Yet what really excited the faithful band of track 'nuts' on the White City terracing in the early summer of 1964 was Brightwell's excursions into half-miling.

His debut had come about more or less unannounced under floodlights on an unfashionable track in London's East End and he won an 800 metres in 1:50.1, which must have been somewhat disheartening for the gaggle of specialists who finished far behind him (2nd place 1:51.9). The race was what he was to describe in his joint autobiography with his future wife, Ann Packer, as 'dipping my toes into a nondescript meeting', and his fiancée's debut at the same distance that night was to have rather greater long-term significance. Her 2:11.1 at Eton Manor would neatly improve to 2:01.1 for gold in Tokyo.

Even so, Brightwell, emboldened by his experimental 'toe dipping', soon took the plunge. Back in what you might call the 'Middle Ages' of British athletics, one of the major fixtures of the season, the Inter-Counties' Championships, was held, bizarrely, in May before even the counties themselves had put on their own meetings. Brightwell's allegiance was to England's largest land-locked county, Shropshire, where he was brought up (though born in India), and despite their limited resources – their only other international athlete was the high hurdler, Mike Parker – the county selectors needed careful persuading of Brightwell's intentions. Their initial 'incredulity', as Brightwell remembered it, was no doubt promptly forgotten as he won the Inter-Counties' title in 1:48.1, beating in the process two instinctive front-runners of international repute, John Boulter and Mike Fleet. The sight of Brightwell majestically moving from 4th place round the final bend and closing relentlessly on Boulter to win in the last few yards remains vividly with me still to this day.

What a pity that he and Ann Packer, after collecting a gold medal and two silvers between them at the Tokyo Olympics, should decide – not unreasonably in that penniless amateur era – to retire from competition and get on with the rest of life. It would be all too easy to extravagantly claim that Robbie Brightwell's premature departure from athletics robbed us of the sort of time that we had nurtured the year before for Steve Haas – suffice it to say that I remain convinced that Brightwell could have run a great deal faster.

However, half-miling seems to have been no more than a passing fancy for him, and he certainly wasn't as expressive about it as one might have hoped. Regarding the 400, he was later to write with graphic candour that 'reaching the three-quarter mark was like being smacked in the face with a shovel'. All he could say, prosaically, of the 800 was that he 'could handle the psychosomatic pressures more easily'. Though there was brief discussion with coach Harry Wilson about running both the 400 and 800 at the Tokyo Olympics, which would have been feasible but would have involved seven races in six days, there was no further mention of the subject after that.

My musings of 'what might have been' at 800 metres now move on a quarter-of-a-century, unapologetically glossing over the era of World records by Ryun, Doubell, Wottle, Wohlhuter, Juantorena and ultimately Coe, to 1989, at which juncture Coe's 1:41.73 had survived longer than any other world record at the event since 1955 (and would do for another eight years to come). In front of me as I type is a copy of the programme for the 1989 Mobil Bislett Games, retrieved from its safe storage alongside so many others from those memorable Oslo meetings over the years, elegantly edited by Stefan Bakke, and in this particular edition containing a wonderful series of photos of Moens running his historic 1:45.7 on the same track 34 years previously.

The list of starters for the men's 800 metres at 10pm excited no especial interest in me that balmy Nordic twilight evening, with the prospect of the 'Dream Mile' still to come 80 minutes later, except for Number 151. He was Robert Kibet, who had languished in obscurity among the phalanx of Kenyan 800 metres runners until the week before when he had run 1:44.2, apparently untroubled by the thin air of Nairobi's 1759-metre altitude permeating his lungs or by the cinders beneath his feet having been churned up by a preceding 10,000 metres race. I doubt that I have ever felt a greater sense of anticipation in any athletics stadium than the few seconds as the leaders in that Oslo 800 metres race passed the clanging bell directly in front of our precarious press-box.

It was not actually Kibet leading but an obliging (and surely well compensated) local 'hare' named Marius Rooth. The time flashed up on the electronic clock – 48.68! – and Kibet was only a couple of metres behind. For an exhilarating further quarter-of-a-minute or so, as Kibet galloped round the curve and on down the back straight – no stylist was he by any description – I honestly thought that I was watching 1 minute 40 seconds about to be broken … then, of course, reality set in and the prolific Johnny Gray closed what had seemed an immeasurable gap and won in 1:43.39. Yet Kibet was still 2nd in 1:43.70 and promised – with the rashness of innocence – to break the world record a fortnight later at the Royal Mail Parcels Games at Crystal Palace

Needless to say, Kibet didn't deliver, finishing a rather distant 2nd to his fellow-Kenyan Olympic champion, Paul Ereng, who broke Coe's track record with 1:43.60. Added to which, Kibet was disqualified for leaving his starting lane too early, Apparently, Kibet had told the press corps in Oslo that he had never heard of Johnny Gray before that race, and Gray had then leaned across and asked Kibet 'Have you heard of Sebastian Coe?', to which the answer again was 'No' Even in 1989 such unworldliness was still refreshing. It is unthinkable that the likes of Kibet could possibly emerge in 2017. But here's hoping.

One record for certain will not be broken. From Robbie Brightwell's Shropshire, with its population of 473,900, there was not a single entry for the senior men's 800 metres at the 2016 county championships. Ironically, it was in Shropshire that the Wenlock Games were first held in 1850, later to be visited by Baron Pierre de Coubertin and directly inspiring him to propose a revival of the Olympic Games.

AMENDMENTS TO ATHLETICS 2016

p.72 **All-Africa Games 2015**: W 4x400m: dq 1. NGR as Adeloye drugs dq, so 1, BOT, 2. KEN, 3. ETH 3:39.99.
p.73 **African Junior Champs 2015**: W 400m: Adeloye dq, replace by Tobi Asamun NGR 55.11.
p.74 **Balkan Champs 2015**: 200m: Ramil Guliyev, SP: Andrei Gag, W DT: Anagnostopoúlou GRE 54.87.
p.93 **World Indoors 2016**: Britney Reese 7.22 long jump was not a championship record.
p.94 **Asian Indoor Champs 2016**: W 60mh: drugs dq Sopronova; replace by Anastasiya Pilipenko KAZ 8.17.
p.107 Obits: Borisav Pisic.
p.110 Obits Iolanda Balas won 154 successive HJ competitions 1957-66.
p.140 AUSTRIA National champions M&W 400H: hurdle misplaced.
p.144 BELGIUM National champions: delete W HT: Sterckendries.
p.146 BULGARIA National champion PV: Piskov 4.50.
p.193 KENYA National champions: delete 800m Kishoyan, 800m: was Kiprop, Women PV: Cherotich (not TJ), TJ Chepchirchir (not SP)
p.205 NETHERLANDS Champs: note LJ: Hertog with prosthetic leg.
p.215 RUSSIA Champs: JT: Tarabin; W DT: Yelena Panova. After drugs dqs: 20kW: Stanislav Yemelyanova 1:20:10, W 800m: Yevgeniya Subbotina 2:02.46, 20kW: Anisya Kirdyapkina 1:26:44.

2015 World Lists

Men
100m: 10.23 Yunier Pérez
200m: 20.52 Bluth 2.2.92, 20.54 Matadi LBR
400m: 45.95 Williams Collazo, 45.99 Washington b. 29.9.93; Best out: 46.02 Dasor 14 Sep; Hand timed: 45.5 Williams Collazo CUB 31.8.86 1 Puebla 17 Apr
800m: 1:46.80 Masilo 5.8.95
1500m: 3:37.08 Ibrahim 1.7.97; 3:38.98A Mark Bett, 3:39.68 Ouladha 31.1.95; Jnr: 3:41.10A Assefa, 3:41.13 Mulugeta Wambui 2.11.96, 3:41.85A Brimin Kiprono; 3:34.29 drugs dq Bensghir
3000m: 7:48.7A C Langat 18.12.91, 7:51.2A Elvis Chirchir KEN 23 May
5000m: 13:11.97 Abadi Hadis (Embaye) 13.11.97
10,000m: 27:25.02 El Abbassi 13.4.84
10k road: 55m downhill: 27:36 Kaan Özbilen (Mike Kigen) TUR 15.1.86 1 Madrid 31 Dec
HMar: 59:15 Kipyatich 10.5.93, 59:59 Mengich 3.4.89, 60:04 S Yego 10.5.87, 60:51 Kipyego 23.7.93, 61:11+ Lemma (61:39+ -14), 61:12 Yator (not 61:52), 61:37 T Komen 6.8.88, 61:44 G Koech 28.8.93, 61:54+ Philemon Rono KEN 8.2.91 27 Sep, 61:56 Ngeny 5.12.88, Juniors: 62:46 Terda Debele ETH .98 7 Istanbul 26 Apr
Mar: 2:08:16 Kangogo 12.12.83, 2:08:53 Shura Kitata 9.6.96, 2:09:57 drugs dq S Merga; 2:10:24 Nageeye NED
3000mSt: 8:24.58 Ibrahim 1.7.97, 8:36.23 Ali Messaoudi ALG 13.10.95 12 Jun
400mh: 47.79 Bett 27.1.90, 49.84A Kosgei .86
HJ: 2.20i Fabrice Saint-Jean FRA 31 Jan
LJ: 8.00w 2.3 Badji 2 Aug, add 7.89 0.1 28 Jun; 7.86 1.8 Guèye 2 Aug, 7.89/8.04w Idiata marked ¶
SP: 20.10i Michal Haratyk; 19.63i Banevicius 20.11.91, 18.69i Jonathan Kalnas 18.4.80 11 Dec, 18.69i Colton Feltes USA 8.4.93 11 Dec, 18.64i Gregori Ott SUI 4.5.94 4 Rochlitz 1 Feb; marks at 20.10, 19.83, 19.65, 19.61, 1953 in May; delete 19.09 Galeta (see best out). 198 men over 18.60. Jnr: 18.47 Demaline 1.3.96
DT: add Malachowski 65.87 1 FBK Hengelo 24 May (x, x, 61.78, 65.87, x, 65.52) for 29/16. Malachowski also had marks at 65.60, 65.59 (twice) for 32/16.
HT: 72.77 Chukwuebuka Enekwechi, 68.65 Noleysis Bicet
JT: 77.18 Osmany Laffita;
4x100m: 39.21A ROU
20kW: 1:23:12A Gathiba 26.10.87, 1:23:45 Wachira 6.5.84; drugs dq: 1:20:04 Strelkov (replace by 1:21:04 4 RUS-w Sochi 27 Feb).
50kW: 4:00:47 Miguel Carvalho POR 2.9.94 1 Leiria 16 Nov

Women
100m: 11.37 Sparling 15.9.97, 11.44 Dulaimi D. Odelin, 11.45 Shelbi White USA-J 3.7.96
200m: 23.32 Gloria Asumnu NGR 22.5.85 28 May
400m: 52.31 Gholston 1.3.95, 52.65 Yaimeisi Borlot; to drugs dq: 51.24 Adeloye ¶ (and all four extra junior performances), replace by 52.31 1 Akure 11 Jul
800m: 2:02.62A Ajok (from 2:03.26A)
1500m: 4:08.15 See b. 9.8.89 (also 2000m 5:43.82i, 3000m 8:55.20i), Jnr: 4:15.02 Lewetegn 9.5.96
1M: Delete 4:31.8 Schneider
3000m: delete repeated 8:41.93 Kibiwot
10000m: 33:01.30A Jepkesho 10.12.89
10k road: 55m downhill Madrid 31 Dec: 1. 31:38 Linet Masai KEN 5.12.89, 3. 32:53 Iwona Lewandowska POL 19.2.85. 4, 32:58 Carla Salomé Rocha POR 25.4.90
HMar: 71:50 Jerotich .87
Mar: 2:23:12 Tollesa 11.9.92, 2:24:44 Jepkesho 31.12.89 (& 10000m 33:01.30A), 2:27:08 Karimi b. 9.10.86 (& HMar 71:33), 2:32:19 Daba ETH
3000mSt: 10:03.4A Tigist Getnet ETH 13 Jun
100mh: 13.25 0.9 Koala 25 Jul (from 13.27)
TJ: 13.77 Daniellys Dutil
JT: 59.86 Flor Denis Ruiz
Hep: 5499 Mrotzek 7.5.90; Jnr 5383 Obermeier 10.7.96
20kW: drugs dq 1:26:17 Sokolova
4x400m: 3:32.16 NGR Ossai, P George 51.83, Mayungbe, Onwumere 52.00 4h1 W.Rly Nassau 2 May, 3:35.68A KEN 11 Jul

Index changes are reflected in this year's Annual.

Amendments to World Indoor Lists 2016

60m: 6.55 Kimmons drugs dq, best earlier 6.58 2h2 Karlsruhe 6 Feb; **200m**: 20.73A Bluth 2.2.92; **400m**: 45.72 Washington 29.9.93, 45.78 Montgomery J 16.8.97, 45.62# I Brown 1.1.97; **1500m**: 3:39.89 drugs dq Bensghir; **Wt**: 21.84 Crayon 15.8.94; **3000mW**: 18:56.87 Perseus Karlström SWE 2.5.90 1 NC Eskilstuna 17 Apr; **W 60mh**: 8.09 Candice Davis-Price 26.10.85; drugs dq 8.07 Sopronova; **Wt**: 21.93 Cooper 10.11.94

Amendments to Previous World Lists

2014 100m: best la 10.27 0.4 Bowens 2 May; **500m**: 59.75 Luguelin Santos DOM 12.11.92 1 Caguas 6 Dec; **PV**: 5.52 Rutger Koppelaar 1 Sittard 18 May (best pre drugs ban, see 5.55); **HT** Krivitskiy drugs dq 79.39 & 79.21 replace by 78.50 4 WK Zürich 16 Aug; **W Mar**: Rita Jeptoo ¶ loses 2:18:57dh win at Boston as well as 2:24:35 win at Chicago.
2014 Indoors: **SP**: delete 19.94 Shapran
2013: **200m**: 20.65 Burkheart USA; **800m**: 1:46.07 Belferrar; **1500m**: 3:37.54 Aman Kedi 16.9.94 so Junior; **HJ**: 2.22i Mihai Anastasiu 16 Dec; **SP**: delete 18.72 Afonin in main list (was best out); **HT**: Krivitskiy drugs dq 79.36.
2012: **SP**: 18.73 Armstead b. 23.7.91, delete 18.88

AMENDMENTS

Christopher Adams (= Alex Adams 19.31); HT: Krivitskiy drugs dq 80.25, 79.37 OK, JT: Pyatnytsa – drugs dq 84.51.
2011: SP: 19.11 Scofield 27.4.87; Jnr 17.98 Boals 14.10.92
2010: SP: 18.95i Smith 5.7.86, delete 18.40 McLachlan; Jnr: 18.00i Davis Fraker USA 26.2.92 2 New York 30 Jan
2009: SP: 19.46 Chad Wesley Smith 5.7.86 (185/131); delete 18.33 Harrison (see 19.60)
2008: W 200: drugs dq 22.57 Chernoshanskaya replace by 22.77 0.0 2s2 NC Kazan 19 Jul.
1997: HJ: 2.28 Juliano Luciano DOM 10.10.77 1 Santo Domingo 31 May

International Championships Changes.

Drugs dqs – move rest up accordingly
2014 European Team: W 5000m (2) Bulut add 3. Jip Vastenberg NED 15:40.74;
2013 World Champs: W LJ: (5) Kucherenko
2013 World University Games: W 1500m: (1) Sharmina, Hep: (1) Chernova
2013 European U23s: W 5000m: (1) Bulut; add 3. Liv Westphal FRA 16:08.85.
2013 European Team: W 800m (2) & 1500m (1) Sharmina
2013 European Indoors: W LJ: (6) Kucherenko
2012 Olympic Games: PV: (4) Starodubtsev; SP: (3) Kolodko; HT: (5) Ikonnikov, (dnq 28) Krivitskiy; JT: (2) Pyatnytsa, so 2. Ruuskanen, 3. Vesely etc.; W 800: (1) Savinova; LJ: (7) Mironchik-Ivanova, HT: (7) Menkova; Hep: (3) Chernova, so 3. Skujyte; 4x400: (2) RUS (Krivoshapka positive), so 2. JAM, 3. UKR
2012 European Champs: W 1500: (2) Bulut, (8) Khaleyeva/Ugarova
2011 World Champs: W 800: (1) Savinova; LJ: (2) Kucherenko; Hep: (1) Chernova
2011 World University Games: 3000mSt: (3) Minshin, replace by 3. Nikolay Chavkin RUS 8:35.10
2011 European Team: W 800m: (1) Savinova; 1500m (2) Martynova.
2010 Continental Cup: W 800m: (3) Savinova
2010 European Champs: W 800m: (1) Savinova; Mar: (9 to 7) Timofeyeva, so. 7. Rosaria Console ITA 2:36:20, 8. Silviya Skvortsova RUS 2:36:31
2009 CAC Championships: W DT: (1) Barrios, title to Yanisley Collado CUB 61.33
2008 World Athletics Final: W DT: (1) Barrios.
2008 Olympic Games: TJ: (5) W Martínez; SP: (11) Yushkov; Dec: (4) Pogorelov; W 400m (5 & 6 Kapachinskaya & Firova; 1500m: (1) Bulut; 5000m (2) & 10000m: (2) Abeylegesse; 3000St: (3) Volkova, so. 3. Petrova... TJ: (3) Devetzí, so 3. Rypakova...; SP: (2) Mikhnevich, (3) Ostapchuk; DT: (2) Barrios, so 2. Antonova...; HT: (4) Pchelnik; W 4x100m: (1) RUS (Chermoshanskaya positive), so 1. BEL, 2. NGR, 3 BRA; 4x400: (2 RUS & 4 BLR), so 2. JAM, 3. GBR
2007 World Championships: 5000 (5) and 10000m (2) Abeylegesse
World Marathon Majors: 2013/14 women's winner: Edna Kiplagat after Rita Jeptoo disqualification.

Appeals Pending

Nesta Carter JAM, Aleksandr Yargunkin RUS, Elvan Abeylegesse TUR (2007 World 10,000m). Tatyana Lebedeva RUS (2008 Olympics LJ/TJ)

Drugs disqualifications and annulled marks – IAAF Biological Passport Cases

Men
Adil Annani: 2012- HMar 61:31, Mar 2:07:43.

Yassine Bensghir: 2014- 1500m 3:34.80
Othmane El Goumri: 2014- 3000m 7:44.73i, 5000m 13:33.82, 2015- 1500m 3:36.21, 3000m 7:36.71, 5000m 13:13.90, 10000m 27:46.34
Abdelhadi Labali: 2013- 800m 1:46.46, 1500m 3:35.95; 2014- 1500m 3:37.52, 3000m 7:45.62i; 2015- 1500m 3:37.89
Ildar Minshin: 3000mSt: 2010- 8:23.18, 2011- 8:17.74 (pb reverts to 8:21.16 '08). 2012- 8:23.07, 2013- 8:34.87, 2015- 8:34.36

Women
Elvan Abeylegesse (25.8.07-25.8.09): 2007- 5000m 15:00.88, 2008- 3000m 8:57.79, 5000m 14:58.79, 10000m 29:56.34; 20009- 8:41.85, 15:30.47, 31:51.98.
Yarelys Barrios (18.8.08- 17.8.09): DT: 2008- perfs 64.98, 64.88, 83.64; 2009- perfs 64.67, 64.57, 63.45, 63.45.
Anastasiya Bazdyreva: 2014- 800m 2:00.90, 2015- 800m 1:58.75 (& 2:02.13i), 1000m 2:40.91i
Gamze Bulut: 2012- 1500m 4:01.18, 3kSt 9:34.88; 2014- 1500m 4:07.79, 5000m 15:37.70.
Yolanda Caballero: 2013- 10k 32:54+, HMar- 70:30; 2014- HMar 70:45
Tatyana Chernova: 2011- 100mh 13.32, LJ 6.82 (& next 6.61), Hep 6880 and others; 2012- 60mh 8.02i, 100mh 13.34, HJ 1.84i, LJ 6.61i/6.54, JT 53.21, Pen (indoors) 4725, Hep 6774 & 6628; 2013- HJ 1.86, LJ 6.57, Hep 6623 & 6284.
Hrisopiyí Devetzí: 2007- LJ 6.69 (best pre-ban 6.57 -0.5 1 Kalamáta 22 Jul), TJ 15.09/15.04/14.75 (best pre ban 14.58 2 ECp München 23 Jun) ; 2008- LJ 6.95i/6.66/6.74w; TJ 15.23; 2009- LJ 6.37, TJ 14.18/14.67w
Lidiya Grigoryeva: Mar: 2009- 2:26:47, 2010- 2:30:31
Olga Kucherenko: LJ: 2012- 7.03, 2013- 7.00i/6.81, 2014- 6.70, 2015- 6.78
Mariya Savinova: 2010 – 800m 1:58.22 & 1:58.64; 2011- 400m 52.71, 600m 1:26.23i, 800m 1:55.87 etc, & 2:01.58i; 2012- 800m 1:56.19
Yekaterina Sharmina (Martynova): 2011- 1500m 4:01.68, 2012- 800m 2:00.24, 1000m 2:38.16, 1500m, 3:59.49; 2013- 800m 1:59.91, 1500m 4:04.55; 2014- 800m 2:01.61, 1500m 4:07.45; 2015- 800m 2:00.14, 1500m 4:05.87.

Note that the full effect of reported drugs re-testing is uncertain for now while appeals are made to CAS etc., in particular as to the period of annulment of results.
2008 OG: Natalya Mikhnevich, Nadezhda Ostapchuk, Oksana Menkova (& 2012), Pavel Lyzhin, Svetlana Usovich
2012 OG: Vera Ganeyeva, Antonina Krivoshapka, Anastasiya Mironchik-Ivanova

Thanks for amendments to year and all-time lists to M. Arons Carvalho, Norbert Heinrich (SP), Yves Pinaud, Alfredo Sánchez

REFERENCE BOOKS 2016-17

World Women's Athletics 100 Best Performers 1911-1962 Vol.5 by John Brant & Janusz Waśko. 492 pages 240 x 170mm. This new edition has yearly rankings for 52 years and has been expanded and revised very considerably since the first edition as a lot of extra results have been found in some marvellous research by historians worldwide. Available from John Brant – john195@john195.karoo.co.uk Cost £20.

Latvijas Vieglatletikas Vesture 1897-1944. This is the first part of a 3-volume history of Latvian athletics by Andris Stagis. The two other parts – covering 1945-91, the period in which Latvia was part of the Soviet Union, and 1992-2015 covering Latvia's second independent period as an athletics nation, will appear in 2017 and 2018 respectively. Stagis, Latvia's principal athletics historian [and an athlete with lifetime bests of 15.62 (TJ) and 55.07 (HT)] has produced a statistically detailed and finely illustrated annual history of Latvian athletics. The 348 page book has over 100 photos, with many of its stars from the 1930's featured. It is available from the author for 25 Euro [+15 Euro postage], at Druvienas 18-80, P/K 62, LV-1079 Riga, LATVIA.

British Athletics 1866-80. By Peter Lovesey and Keith Morbey. National Union of Track Statisticians Historical Series Booklet No. 17. Price £15, but £12 (plus £2.99 postage in the UK) when bought from the printers Lulu.com. http://www.lulu.com/content/paperback-book/british-athletics-1866-80/18571757
There is also an A4 version for £14 plus postage, web address as above but ending: 1866-80-a4-edition/18815372
Full results of the AAC championships, annual year lists by performer and performance, an index of more than 3000 names with birth and death dates where known, a summary of key developments and a copy of the first rules. Twenty-two contemporary illustrations show Victorian athletes in action.

1866 and all that… By Peter Radford gives the story of the 1866 Championships of the Amateur Athletics Club in England, the world's first national athletics championships, with complete results. Available from the author for £6.36 inc p&p., contact president@nuts.org.uk.

Notable biographies include:

Quicksilver: The Mercurial Emil Zátopek by Pat Butcher. 224 pages. Published by Globerunner Productions. £14.99 (UK only). www.globerunner.org/books/

His Own Man is a biography of the great German athlete Otto Peltzer. By Tim Johnston and Donald Macgregor, it was published by Pitch Publishing Ltd at £17.99 on 15 August. Hardcover, 288 pages.

ANNUALS

L'Athlétisme Africain/African Athletics 2016. A5, 152 pages. By Yves Pinaud. Published by Éditions Polymédias with support from the IAAF. The 35th edition in this splendid series has 100 deep men's and women's lists for Africa for 2015, with all-time lists and official continental records, with javelin thrower John Yego on the cover. 20 euro, £18 or US $30 including postage from La Mémoire du Sport, 166 rue de Decize, 03000 Moulins, France. (Also available: booklist with very extensive list of athletics books and magazines for sale).

Asian Athletics 2015 Rankings. A5 100 pages. Heinrich Hubbeling continues his magnificent annual job as this booklet contains top 30 lists for 2015 for athletes from Asian nations, with continuation lists for countries other than China and Japan (up to 4 best per country), national records set in 2015, and full lists of Asian records. Euro 20/US $25 in cash or by International Money Order from the author, Haaksbergener Str 25, 48691 Vreden, Germany. email hhubbeling@t-online.de. Copies also available for 1998, 2004-09, 2011-14 and Asian all-time rankings as at 31.12.2000 at €15/US $20 each.

Athlérama 2015. A5 704pp. The 3nd edition of the French Annual, edited by Patricia Doilin with a strong team of compilers, is again a superb reference book accompanied by a CD containing a pdf of the contents. Packed with information on French athletics – records, profiles of top athletes, results, deep year lists for 2015 for all age groups plus all-time lists and indexes. Maintaining the sequence, there are French top ten lists and reviews for 1915 (limited by WW I) and 1965. 28 euros from the FFA, 33 avenue Pierre de Coubertin, 7540 Paris Cedex 13, France. email Patricia.Doilin@athle.org. See athle.fr.

British Athletics 2016. A5 432 pages. The 57th NUTS Annual, edited by Rob Whittingham, Tony Miller and Peter Matthews. All the usual features are included: deep year lists in all age groups, all-time lists, records, major results, merit rankings, obituaries and index. £20 UK, £23 Europe, £26 outside Europe from Rob Whittingham, 7 Birch Green, Croft Manor,

Glossop, Derbyshire SK13 8PR, UK. Cash or sterling cheques payable to NUTS. Overseas orders may be made using PayPal (add £1) – see the NUTS web site for details, at www.nuts.org.uk

Eesti Kergejõustiku Aastaraamat 2016. 264pp. An attractively produced annual with results and records, and comprehensive Estonian ranking lists indoors and out for 2015. From the Estonian Athletic Federation, Maakri 23, Tallinn 10145, Estonia. ejkl@ejkl.ee

Combined Events Annual 2016 by Hans van Kuijen. The 200 pages contain outdoor and indoor all-time lists, 2016 ranking lists, national records, 50 bests' biographies etc. Cost 35 EUR or 35 GBP or 50 USD. For details contact Hans at j.kuijen4@upcmail.nl. He also has back numbers for each year 2005-15 available

Friidrott 2016. 170x240mm 464p Hardback. This, the 56th edition, features detailed reviews and results of World, Nordic and Swedish meetings and profiles of athletes of the year with top 50 world lists, and top 25 Nordic and Swedish lists. It is most attractively produced with 300 photos. This book and others including "World's Greatest in Athletics" and "Swedish Athletics Championships 1896–2005" are available from Jonas Hedman, Springarvägen 14, 142 61 Trångsund, Sweden.

Friidrott 2016 is available for 495 Swedish crowns (52 EUR) plus postage – the same price as in 2015. E-mail Jonas.hedman@textograf.com. website: www.textograf.com

Israeli Athletics Annual 2016/17. 240 x170mm, 54pp, illustrated. By David Eiger. Records, championship results, 2016 top 20s and all-time lists, with profiles of leading Israeli athletes. 8 euro or US $9 from David Eiger, 10 Ezra Hozsofer Str, Herzliya 46 371, Israel. Past editions from 1986 onwards are also available.

Annuario Atletica 2017 published by FIDAL and edited by Carlo Santi. 644pp, 203 x 200m, packed with features and information and well illustrated. These include various articles starting with a tribute to Adolfo Consolini, world top tens for 1917, then very comprehensive reviews of Italian athletics in 2016 with detailed results and rankings, plus international results and rankings, There are also lists of all Italian internationals and profiles of 115 current top Italian athletes and 118 all-time 'Hall-of-Famers". 20 euro to current account BNL (IBAN 29Z 01005 03309 000 000 010 107) payable to Federazione Italiana di Atletica Leggera for "acquisto Annuario dell'Atletica 2017".

Latvijas Vieglatletikas Gadagramata 2017. A5 344 pp. This is an exemplary example of a national annual. It has been expanded in recent years and now gives most comprehensive coverage of Latvian athletics for 2016, including records, results, athlete profiles and year and all-time lists, compiled by ATFS member Andris Stagis. From the Latvian Athletic Association, Augsiela 1, Riga LV-1009, Latvia. email: lvs@latathletics.lv

Annuaire FLA 2015. A4 272p. The Luxembourg Annual, edited by Georges Klepper, is a magnificent and extraordinarily comprehensive volume, with reviews, results, 2015 and all-time lists, plus many colour photographs. 15 euros locally, by post €18 in Luxembourg, €27 elsewhere to account no. LU32 1111 0200 0321 0000. See www.fla.lu.

2015 Athletics New Zealand Almanac. A5 208pp. Edited by Steve Hollings and Simon Holroyd. Includes deep national ranking lists for 2015 for all ages plus lists for juniors and youths and trends of performance, all-time top 20s, records for the various age groups and results of championships and other major events. For details, see www.athletics.org.nz and go to "Shop". Price: $NZ 24.50 (plus international postage costs).

Ukraine Statistics 2016 by Ivan Kachkivskiy. A5, 504 pages, Cyrillic script. Attractively produced, there are detailed Ukrainian lists for 2016 for all age groups plus statistical profiles for all leading athletes, records and 16 pages of colour photographs. Contact <ivan.work.mail@gmail.com> for details.

Turkish Athletics Annual 2016 compiled and edited by Nejat Kök. A5, 222 pages. Records, results and lists provide detailed information on Turkish athletics in 2016. Contact Nejat Kök <nkok@metu.edu.tr> for details.

2016 USA Track & Field FAST Annual. General editor Tom Casacky. A5 expanded this year from 606 to 670 pages. The 38th FAST Annual, contains records, 50-70 deep US lists for 2015 and all-time, with 15-deep junior and college all-time lists. The final massive index section includes annual progressions and championships details for top American and resident foreign athletes. $25 post paid in the USA or $45 or 40 Euros airmail from Tom Casacky, PO Box 4288, Napa, CA 94558, USA. Payment is easiest by PayPal (to tom@interis.com).

Yleisurheilu 2016. A5 672pp. The Finnish Yearbook, published by Suomen Urheilulitto (Finnish Athletics) and compiled by Juhani and Mirko Jalava, contains every conceivable statistic for Finnish athletics (with results and deep year lists) in 2016 and also world indoor, outdoor and junior lists for the year as known at November. 19 euros plus 10 euros for postage and packaging. Orders by e-mail to juhani@tilastopaja.fi.

Statistical Bulletins

TRACK STATS. The NUTS quarterly journal comes with membership of the NUTS. £25 inc. postage to UK addresses, £30 to Europe, £35 to the rest of the world. Contact Liz Sissons at lizsissons9@gmail.com

May 2016 included 'Babe' Didrikson's account of her 1932 Olympic exploits in Los Angeles; a profile of Reggie Pearman, the American 440y/880y star of the decade after WWII; and an account of when John Disley believed (erroneously) that he had broken the world record for the 3000m steeplechase. There is also an interview by Peter Lovesey with the author of a biography of Walter Knox

July 2016 featured Eric Shirley (still competing at age 87) and a record of his steeplechase races between 1954 and 1963 (he was world ranked 7th in 1955 with 8:47.6); the early years of women's 400m hurdling; the career record of Mike Boit from 1968 to 1977; and articles on two of New Zealand's legendary runners, Dutch-born Dick Quax and Bill Baillie.

October 2016 included editor Bob Phillips' reflections on Rio; a compilation by Tom Hurst of Mike Boit's races from 1978 to 1987; a profile by the late Peter Heidenstrom of the athlete he regarded as New Zealand's greatest – long jumper Yvette Williams; and several book reviews.

The **Spanish group, the AEEA** continues to produce magnificent publications. Membership (four bulletins per year) is 55 euros per year (€61 outside Europe) from AEEA secretary Ignacio Mansilla, C/Encinar del Rey, 18 - 28450 Collado Mediano, Madrid, Spain. email: comunicacion@rfea.es

100 Años De Camp A Través En España (1916-2016). A5 508 pages. This AEEA publication for the Spanish Athletics Federation included illustrations, some in colour. The first 218 pages is the text in Spanish giving the history of cross-country running in Spain and rest contains detailed results of championships. national and international. with indexes of international competitors. Priced at just 15 euros plus postage, email publicacions@rfea.es

Bulletin No. 97 July 2016, a most attractive 264-page A5 production with many colour photographs. It featured the history of Spanish athletes at the Olympic Games both in text (Spanish) and extensive statistical detail, including profiles (some including all career performances) of all medallists. 25 euros including postage for anywhere in the world; alternatively available as a free pdf download from the RFEA Spanish website – see www.rfea.es

Bulletin No. 98 December 2016 is a 444 page A5 book. Main features: a) Deep Spanish lists for 400 metres men compiled by Ignacio Mansilla – 1231 performances by 107 athletes under 47.40 and continuation performer lists to 49.99 (1360 athletes). b) Records for Andalucia by Antonio Muñoz and Alberto Sanchez Traver; c) Deep Spanish all-time lists for U18s, men and women, by Antonio Muñoz.

Also Ignacio Mansilla and Miguel Villaseñor have compiled deep Spanish all-time lists in a 322 page book **Lista Española de todos los tiempos (marcas y atletas)** – complete to 31.10.2016.

The **DGLD** – the **German** statistical group, Deutsche Gesellschaft für Leichtathletik-Dokumentation

Bulletin No. 74 of the **DGLD** – the **German** statistical group, Deutsche Gesellschaft für Leichtathletik-Dokumentation contained 310 pages with, in addition to the usual features, three main sections: 1. Athletics in the time of the Kaiser (1895-1910) Part 1 1895-1905. There are annual German ranking lists, results of championships, German records etc. 2. Jewish athletes in Germany (annual lists 1927-38) and the world, including all-time lists to 1945. 3. Lists of internationals for top German athletes.

No. 75 August 2016. Included results and detailed reports of the German international against France and Switzerland in Basel in 1926, with statistical profiles of all the German team members. Then the first part (A to F) of a listing of all international results for FRG athletes (1951-88); history and statistics of the top GDR club SC Motor Jena 1954-90, women's all-time lists for each age group 14 to 19, and top ten averages for German men's 800m (25 to 1:49.7) etc.

No. 76 November 2016 included the second part (G to Z) of a listing of all international results for FRG athletes (1951-88), and a listing of all German athletes to have competed at Olympic Games and World and European Championships.

Deutsche Bestenliste 2014. A5, 166pp. The 25th edition of the deep Annual German lists was published by the German statistical group, the DGLD. Covering the 2014 season it was very late, but that was due to the sad death in April 2015 of Sven Kuus, who for many years was its chief compiler. The **2015 Bestenliste**, edited by Manfred Grieser, was published in January 2016. The books form part, together with three annual bulletins, of the annual subscription to the DGLD of 55 euro per year. Contact Manfred Holzhausen, Bergheimer Str.33, 41515 Grevenbroich, Germany; manfred.holzhausen@gmx.de. Website: www.ladgld.de

NURMI is the journal of the Finnish Athletics Archive Association (Suomen

Yleisurheiluarkiston), SYUA. Their latest bulletin, No. 19, 76 A4 pages, tells the history (in Finnish) by Petri Maskonen of Joensuun Maraton, a meeting held in Northern Karelia from 1935 to 1963 of which the main event was the 25,000 metres race on a 1000 metres race track. Erkii Tamila set world records at this event in 1939 after one at 15 miles in 1937. Other competitors who competed in the track and field events included such stars as Cornelius Warmerdam at pole vault. For details contact the Chairman of the Board of the society: Mikko Nieminen, mikko.nieminen@dlc.fi.

NURMI has also published **Athletics in the 19th Century, A Statistical Review Volume 1 1881-1884** by Ari Törmä. A4 98 pages. This follows the author's series of publications for specific events and as he explains follows the great works of Hubert Hamacher in covering the years 1881-1900. Here from his vast amount of research he revises HH's lists and expands them. There were a variety of rules and specifications in that period and Ari brings together marks at different weights and distances to provide lists for the modern range of events.

While showing the original mark, he converts performances so that for instance his 1500m lists contain mainly adjusted times for 1 mile marks, but also times in handicap races adjusted for the distance allowed, so converting times from about 1480m to 1610m in the lists. His hammer list contains marks with weights from 6kg to 11kg. Marks by both professional and amateurs are included. See www.aritorma.net.

Hammer Throw Stats History and News Bulletin No. 16. By Zdenek Procházka. pdf of 109 pages. The latest in this series featured deep men's hammer lists for 2015 for seniors, juniors and youths, performers, performance and analysis, plus national records and an all-time list of 2002 US hammer throwers over 56.00). **No. 17** deals with Czech and Slovak hammer stats in great detail in 142 pages. Contact Zdenek at atlet2003@volny.cs.

IAAF Handbooks

The **IAAF Statistics Handbook** for the 2016 Olympic Games, 420 pages, edited by Mark Butler is available as an ebook from the IAAF website (www.iaaf.org). It features full results of all finals from previous Games, with comprehensive facts and figures, best national placings, country index etc..

The **IAAF scoring tables** of athletics have been updated for 2017 and are available to download from the IAAF website.

For details of IAAF Publications see the list at www.iaaf.org

The **European Statistics Yearbook 2015** compiled by Mirko Jalava is available from ther European Athletic Association. Avenue Louis-Ruchonnet 18; CH-1003 Lausanne, Switzerland. Price 25 euros,

The **Sports Archive** collection at Cobham Hall School in Kent, England contains by far the biggest accessible collection of athletics books, magazines, archives etc. in Britain. Steadily built up by the NUTS with collections from the late Bob Sparks, Cliff Temple, Peter Martin, Norris McWhirter, Ron Jewkes, Graham Tanner etc., it needs further organisation, but researchers would find a real treasure trove. Visits by appointment with former 800m international Mike Fleet, who has been in charge of organising the library. He has also prepared a list of duplicates that are available for sale at reasonable prices – these include athlete biographies, British and International Annuals etc. Contact Mike at <mike@mafleet.co.uk> for a list.

GOODBYE TO TWO GREATS
Peter Matthews

TWO OF THE greatest athletes of all-time completed their active careers in 2016 – Yelena Isinbayeva, who is unquestionably the greatest ever female pole vaulter, and Ashton Eaton, the supreme decathlete of recent years.

Isinbayeva had set her first world record in 2003 and at the age of 34 2016 was perhaps a logical time to retire although it was a shame that she was unable to end her stellar career on a high at the Olympic Games. Eaton's career was shorter for he reached world class in 2010 and it was a shock when he announced his retirement in January 2017 after just seven years in the very highest class and this announcement came just days before his 29th birthday. But then he had achieved everything that he needed to in the sport, and, while many regretted that we would not see him go on to further triumphs, the decision, made together with his wife Brianne Theisen-Eaton who also called it a day, was thee result of long deliberation and was fully supported by their coach (since 2009) Harry Marra, agent Paul Doyle and their sponsors. Whatever this highly articulate and intelligent man may turn his hand to in future, one can be sure that he will be most successful.

Ashton James EATON b. 21 January 1988 Portland, Oregon.

Eaton first gave indication of his ability while at Mountain View High School in Bend, Oregon, for whom he won state high school championships at 400m (48.69) and long jump (7.32m) in 2006. Recognising his all-round ability his coach suggested that he consider the decathlon, and the University of Oregon had a strong multi-event program, so he went there at the end of 2006. There he was initially coached by former decathlete Dan Steele and soon developed his talent across the range of individual events,

He first exceeded 8000 points for the decathlon with 8122 in 2008 for fifth at the US Olympic Trials and rose rapidly to be the world's best, setting three world records for the indoor heptathlon – 6499 points in 2010, 6568 in 2011 and 6645 in winning the World title in 2012 – before taking the world record for decathlon with a score of 9039 at the 2012 US Olympic Trials. On that occasion he started with the best ever performances in a decathlon in the first two events, 100m 10.21 and long jump 8.23, and contended heavy rain for the rest of the first day before more personal bests on day two, 5.30 pole vault and 4:14.48 for 1500m. Six weeks later he won the Olympic title with 8869, 198 points ahead of teammate Trey Hardee. In 2013 he won both the US and World decathlon titles. In 2014 he retained his World Indoor heptathlon title with 6632 points, just 13 points short of his world record, but decided not to compete in multi-events outdoors, and made an amazing debut at 400m hurdles, taking his best to 48.69, ninth on the world list for the year. His one decathlon of 2015 came at the World Championships in Beijing when he added six points to his world record with 9045 points, a score set up especially by his astonishing 45.00 for 400m at the end of the first day, easily the fastest time ever run in a multi-event. In 2016 he had two decathlons, winning his third US title with 8750 points and retaining his Olympic title with 8893 points equal the Olympic record set by Roman Sebrle in 2004.

He won five NCAA titles while at the University of Oregon: decathlon 2008-10 and indoor heptathlon 2009 and 2010. He was 18th at his first World Championships decathlon in 2009 before taking the silver medal in 2011.

Individual event bests: 60m 6.66i (2011), 100m 10.21 (2012), 10.19w (2010); 200m 20.76 (2013), 400m 45.00 (2015), 800m 1:55.90i (2010), 1000m 2:32.67i (2010), 1500m 4:14.48 (2012), 60mh 7.51i (2015), 110mh 13.35 (2011), 13.34w (2012); HJ 2.11i (2010), 2.10 (2011); PV 5.40 (2015), LJ 8.23 (2012), SP 15.40 (2013), DT 47.36 (2011), JT 66.64 (2013).

He met the Canadian multi-eventer Brianne Theisen at Oregon and they were married on 15 July 2013. She won the World silver medal in 2013 and 2015 and Commonwealth gold in 2014 at heptathlon, setting Canadian records of 6641 points in 2014 and 6808 in 2015. Then in 2016 she won the Olympic bronze medal.

Ashton Eaton's Decathlons

With junior implements and hurdles

7155	3	NC-j	Indianapolis	21 Jun 2007					
10.58	6.67	12.80	1.87	48.48	14.47	40.63	4.30	35.13	4:58.35

Senior Decathlons

6977	1		Tucson	23 Mar 2007					
10.66/1.5	7.19/0.2	11.97	1.92	48.55	14.92/0.9	37.93	3.75	33.65	4:56.62
7123	2	Pac-10	Stanford	6 May 2007					
10.81/-0.2	7.23/0.1	11.88	1.92	49.19	14.66/1.0	36.57	3.95	36.92	4:39.72

Mark	Pos	Meet	Venue	Date					
7792w	2		Sacramento	28 Mar 2008					
10.82w/3.4		7.64W/5.0	12.21	1.96	47.00	14.21/1.4	35.16	4.50	45.26	4:24.15
7604	1		Pac-10	Tempe		10 May 2008				
10.57/-0.9		6.85/1.0	12.25	1.98	47.68	14.14/-0.6	34.62	4.85	44.29	4:44.48
8055	1		NCAA	Des Moines		12 Jun 2008				
10.64/-1.1		7.68/-2.6	12.79	1.96	47.25	14.27/1.8	39.96	4.60	53.93	4:33.05
8122	5		NC/OT	Eugene		30 Jun 2008				
10.61/-0.4		7.49/0.0	12.28	1.96	47.07	14.26/1.9	39.69	5.10	47.28	4:20.56
8023	1			Eugene		24 Apr 2009				
10.66/1.2		7.58w/3.9	11.61	2.05	47.54	14.08/1.4	38.28	4.55	53.70	4:28.93
8091	1			Eugene		10 May 2009				
10.49w/2.6		7.45/2.0	12.63	2.01	47.12	14.01/1.2	39.80	4.85	49.69	4:36.87
8241w	1		NCAA	Fayetteville		11 Jun 2009				
10.35W/4.1		7.58w/3.5	12.57	1.99	46.85	13.85/-1.3	41.79	4.40	53.62	4:20.75
8075	2		NC	Eugene		26 Jun 2009				
10.34/1.8		7.84/1.4	14.04	2.00	46.30	13.60w/2.1	41.39	5.25	57.84	4:25.15
8061	18		World Champs	Berlin		20 Aug 2009				
10.53/0.2		7.85/0.9	12.26	2.02	47.75	14.28/0.3	37.15	5.00	50.87	4:45.03
8310w	1		Texas Relays	Austin		1 Apr 2010				
10.34w/3.4		7.88w/3.0	13.11	2.02	47.06	13.85w/4.9	43.71	4.60	52.19	4:41.43
8154	1		Pac-10	Berkeley		9 May 2010				
10.59/-0.5		7.43/1.6	12.77	1.94	47.25	13.79/-1.0	42.29	5.15	49.67	4:39.97
8457	1		NCAA	Eugene		11 Jun 2010				
10.37/0.5		7.90/1.1	12.60	2.02	46.28	13.68/1.6	41.71	4.70	52.41	4:21.85
8729	1		NC	Eugene		24 Jun 2011				
10.33/0.6		7.80w/3.1	14.14	2.05	46.35	13.52/1.6	41.58	5.05	56.19	4:24.10
8505	2		World Champs	Daegu		28 Aug 2011				
10.46/-0.5		7.46/0.0	14.44	2.02	46.99	13.85/-0.8	46.17	4.60	55.17	4:18.94
9039 wr	1		NC/OT	Eugene		23 Jun 2012				
10.21/0.4		8.23/0.8	14.20	2.05	46.70	13.70/-0.8	42.81	5.30	58.87	4:14.48
8869	1		Olympics	London (OS)		9 Aug 2012				
10.35/0.4		8.03/0.8	14.66	2.05	46.90	13.56/0.1	42.53	5.20	61.96	4:33.59
8291	1		NC	Des Moines		22 Jun 2013				
10.48/1.2		7.59/0.3	15.00	1.90	46.89	14.68/0.0	43.99	4.60	60.36	4:34.15
8809	1		World Champs	Moskva		11 Aug 2013				
10.35/-0.5		7.73/0.3	14.39	1.93	46.02	13.72/0.4	45.00	5.20	64.83	4:29.80
–	dnf		Décastars	Talence		15 Sep 2013				
10.60/-0.3		7.50/-0.3	13.94							
9045 wr	1		World Champs	Beijing		29 Aug 2015				
10.23/-0.4		7.88/0.0	14.52	2.01	45.00	13.69/-0.2	43.34	5.20	63.63	4:17.52
8750	1		NC/OT	Eugene		3 Jul 2016				
10.34/1.8		7.84/1.4	14.04	2.00	46.30	13.60w/2.1	41.39	5.25	57.84	4:25.15
8893	1		Olympics	Rio de Janeiro		18 Aug 2016				
10.46/-0.1		7.94/1.7	14.73	2.01	46.07	13.80/0.7	45.49	5.20	59.77	4:23.33

Heptathlons

Mark	Pos	Meet	Venue	Date				
5370 o/s	2			Seattle		27 Jan 2007		
6.93		7.39	12.28	1.89	8.51	3.85	2:47.35	
5859 o/s	1			Seattle		2 Feb 2008		
6.83		7.22	12.03	2.05	7.97	4.55	2:44.23	
5676	6		NCAA	Fayetteville		15 Mar 2008		
6.93		7.28	10.87	1.84	7.96	4.75	2:40.90	
6174 o/s	1			Seattle		31 Jan 2009		
6.84		7.59	12.06	2.09	7.91	4.97	2:39.92	
5988	1		NCAA	College Station		14 Mar 2009		
6.86		7.39	11.68	2.02	7.90	5.10	2:47.68	
6256	1			College Station		30 Jan 2010		
6.78		7.66	12.56	2.07	7.86	4.96	2:38.02	
6499 wr	1		NCAA	Fayetteville		13 Mar 2010		
6.71		7.73	13.12	2.11	7.77	5.10	2:32.67	
6568 wr	1			Tallinn		6 Feb 2011		
6.66		7.77	14.45	2.01	7.60	5.20	2:34.74	
6645 wr	1		World Indoors	Istanbul		10 Mar 2012		
6.79		8.16	14.56	2.03	7.68	5.20	2:32.77	
6632	1		World Indoors	Sopot		8 Mar 2014		
6.66		7.78	14.88	2.06	7.64	5.20	2:34.72	
6470	1		World Indoors	Portland		19 Mar 2016		
6.81		8.08	14.16	1.99	7.78	5.10	2:35.22	

Where does Eaton rate among all-time decathletes? I think Daley Thompson still takes pride of place, but then it is Eaton vying with Dan O'Brien for next best. My colleague Mel Watman did a nice comparison in *Athletics International*:

THE ULTIMATE DECATHLON CONTEST
Who has the better set of individual personal bests: Ashton Eaton or Dan O'Brien? It's very, very close! This is how a contest between them would unfold if both matched their pbs. 100: Eaton 10.21 (1044 points) takes an early lead over O'Brien 10.32 (1018). LJ: Eaton goes further ahead (2164-2099) with 8.23 to 8.08. SP: O'Brien edges in front (2993-2978) thanks to 16.69 against 15.40. HJ: O'Brien greatly extends his lead (3985-3884) after clearing 2.20 to his opponent's 2.11. 400: Eaton claws back valuable points with 45.00 to 46.53, leaving O'Brien the overnight leader with 4967 to 4944. 110H: Both men are brilliant hurdlers, Eaton having the edge with 13.35 to 13.47, and now there are only 7 points between them: O'Brien 6011, Eaton 6004. DT: It's all over, surely, as O'Brien is in a different class: 55.07 against 47.36 and the scores are now 6988-6820. PV: Eaton narrows the deficit a little with 5.40 to 5.25 but O'Brien is still comfortably clear: 7976-7855. JT: Nothing in it here with O'Brien (66.90) scoring 4 more points than Eaton (66.64), so going into the final event O'Brien leads by a whopping 125 points (8818-8693). 1500: Would you believe it? Eaton (4:14.48) is so superior to his rival here (4:33.19) that he picks up 126 more points to win the contest by a single point: 9543 to 9542!

Yelena Gadzhievna ISINBAYEVA b. 3 Jan 1982 Volgograd.

Isinbayeva became the first woman to clear five metres in the pole vault at Crystal Palace, London on 22 July 2005. Four weeks later she won the World title with another world record of 5.01 and her margin of superiority over the rest of the world was emphasised with the runner-up clearing 4.60. Technically she was well-nigh perfect and thrilled athletics crowds with her supreme athleticism and consistency, often clearing heights at which her rivals peak by huge amounts.

Growing too tall (to 1.74m) to continue as a gymnast, she first cleared 4m at the age of 16 in 1998 and in successive years took gold medals at World Youths 1999, World Juniors 2000 and European Juniors 2001, with world junior indoor records at 4.45 in 2000 and 4.47 in 2001. She took the European silver medal in 2002, when her best was 4.60, and came to the top in 2003, with her first world record, 4.82 at Gateshead in July. She won the European U23 title but had to settle for silver indoors and bronze outdoors at the World Championships, both won by her great rival Svetlana Feofanova.

Isinbayeva set world indoor records with 4.81 and 4.83 at Donetsk in February 2004, and after Feofanova had regained the record with 4.85 in Athens, Isinbayeva was supreme at the World Indoors in Budapest, where she took the gold medal by soaring well clear with a new record at 4.86. Then came a brilliant outdoor season, at the end of which she was named as IAAF Woman Athlete of the Year. She set three world records in Britain, winning $50,000 each time: 4.87 at Gateshead, 4.89 at Birmingham (after Feofanova had taken the mark at 4.88 three weeks earlier) and 4.90 at Crystal Palace, London. At the Olympic Games she faced elimination and no medal when she failed at both 4.70 and 4.75 and, after Feofanova had cleared both those heights, gambled by passing to take her final attempt with the bar at 4.80. She succeeded and went on to first-time clearances at 4.85 and 4.91, her seventh world record of the year. Another came two weeks later in Brussels at 4.92, after which her celebrations went on deep into the night, including disco dancing to the delight of the fans while being driven slowly around the track in an open car.

She was again the IAAF Woman Athlete of the Year in 2005, in which she set world indoor records in each of her four indoor competitions (4.87, 4.88, 4.89 and finally 4.90 to win the European Indoor title) and her progress continued outdoors with world records at 4.93 in Lausanne and 4.95 at Crystal Palace before moving straight up to 5.00 in the same competition.

Although short of her 5.01 outdoors, she set a world indoor record of 4.91 in 2006, when she also won the World Indoor title in Moscow with 4.86. Having changed her coach, she had an outdoor best of 4.91 in the summer of 2006, but remained clearly the world's best, winning 4/4 indoors and 10/11 outdoors, including gold at Europeans, World Athletics Final and World Cup.

Apart from not getting back to 5m form, she had a perfect season in 2007, sharing the Golden League jackpot and winning all her 18 competitions – five indoors, including a world record 4.93, and 13 outdoors, including retaining her World title and winning for the fourth successive year at the World Athletics Final. She won her third World Indoor title in 2008 and outdoors set three more world records – 5.03 in Rome, 5.04 in Monaco and 5.05 in Beijing to retain her Olympic title.

In 2009 she set two more world indoor records – at 4.97 and 5.00 – and she shared the Golden League jackpot again. In all she won 13 of her 15 competitions in the year, but suffered set-backs when she lost at the London Grand Prix on count-back to Anna Rogowska at 4.68 (she first outdoor loss after 30 successive wins dating back to 2006) and when she failed to clear her opening height at the Worlds. However, she bounced back from this immediately with a world record 5.06 at Zürich. This took her total of world records to 28 (15 outdoors and 13 indoors) as she progressed towards her declared ambition of surpassing the 35 world records set at the men's event by Sergey Bubka.

After a disappointing fourth at the 2010 World Indoors, she took a rest from competition. She returned in 2011 and had indoor wins at 4.81 and 4.85, but disappointed outdoors with just 4.65 for 6th at the World Champs and a season's best of 4.76. However, she set her 13th world indoor record with 5.01 and then won her fourth World Indoor title in 2012, but by her standards a bronze medal at 4.70 at the Olympic Games was a disappointment in a summer of limited competition. In 2013 she competed just four times (outdoors) but won them all and was thrilled to take World gold with a season's best of 4.89 in Moscow.

She did not compete in 2014 or 2015 but made a magnificent return in 2016, clearing 4.90 to win the Russian title in what proved to be her one competition of the year. She was then bitterly disappointed to be denied the chance to win another Olympic title in Rio due to the overall ban on the Russian athletics team of which she was an outspoken critic. She was, however, elected as a member of the International Olympic Committee. At the end of the year she was appointed as head of the Russian Anti-Doping Agency.

She married Nikita Petinov (b. 29 Aug 1990, javelin best of 74.88 in 2013) in 2014; their daughter Eva was born on 28 Jun 2014.

Progression with positions on the World List and World Rankings (by Peter Matthews)

1997	3.30		
1998	4.00	64	
1999	4.20	37	
2000	4.45i, 4.40	13	
2001	4.47i, 4.46	16	9
2002	4.60, 4.65ex	8	6
2003	4.82	1	2
2004	4.92	1	1
2005	5.01	1	1
2006	4.91	1	1
2007	4.93i, 4.91	1	1
2008	5.05	1	1
2009	5.06	1	1
2010	4.85i	2	9
2011	4.85i, 4.76	2	5
2012	5.01i, 4.75	1	2
2013	4.89	3	1
2016	4.90	3=	nr

HALL OF FAME 2017

ASHTON EATON JOINS our Hall of Fame (Isinbayeva is already there), for which each year we add five new athletes.
Further new entrants:

Marjorie JACKSON (Australia) (b. 13 Sep 1931 Coffs Harbour, New South Wales). The 'Lithgow Flash' was undefeated in major competition with the 100m/200m double at the 1952 Olympics and the 100y/220y double at the 1950 and 1954 Commonwealth Games, with three relay golds as well. She set 18 world records: six at 100 yards to 10.4 in 1952 three at 100m to 11.4 in 1952; four at 200m or 220y to 23.4 (23.59 auto) in 1952; and five in relays

Hannes KOLEHMAINEN (Finland) (b. 9 Dec 1889 Kuopio. d. 11 Jan 1966 Helsinki). He was the first in a long line of great Finnish distance runners and the man who 'ran Finland onto the world map'. He won gold medals at 5000m, 10,000m and cross-country plus CC team silver at the 1912 Olympics and after WWI he won the Olympic marathon in 1920. His 8 world records include the first sub-15 minute – 14:36.6 at the the 1912 Games.

Wilma RUDOLPH (USA) (b. 23 Jun 1940 St Bethlehem, Tennessee. Later Ward, Eldridge. d. 12 Nov 1994 Brentwood, Tennessee) . Rudolph was triple sprint gold medallist at the 1960 Olympics after winning a relay bronze in 1956. Her first world record was 22.9 for 200m to win the 1960 AAU title and she added world records for 100m with 11.3 (11.41 auto) in the 1960 Olympic semi-final (running a wind-aided 11.0 (11.18) in the final), and 11.3 and 11.2 in 1961; she also ran on two US 4x100m ER teams.

Miruts YIFTER (Ethiopia) – See Obituary on page 100

NATIONAL CHAMPIONS 2016
and BIOGRAPHIES OF LEADING ATHLETES
By Peter Matthews

THIS SECTION incorporates biographical profiles of 809 of the world's top athletes this year – 429 men and 380 women, listed by nation. Also listed are national champions at standard events in 2016 for the leading countries prominent in athletics (for which I have such details).

The athletes profiled have, as usual, changed quite considerably from the previous year. All entries have been updated, but also many newcomers have been included to replace those who have retired or faded a little from the spotlight. The choice of who to include is always invidious, but I have concentrated on those who are currently in the world's top 10-15 per event, those who have the best championship records and some up-and-coming athletes who I consider may make notable impact during the coming year.

Since this section was introduced in the 1985 Annual, biographies have been given for a total of 4821 different athletes (2716 men and 2105 women).

The ever continuing high turnover in our sport is reflected in the fact that there are many newcomers to this section (127 in all, 66 men, 60 women), as well as 26 athletes (16 men, 10 women) reinstated from previous Annuals. The athlete who now has the longest continuous stretch herein is Bernard Lagat at 18 years, followed by Fabrzio Donato and Veronica Campbell-Brown on 17 and there are 11 athletes at 15 years or more. Athletes who have retired or who have been given drugs bans have generally been omitted.

No doubt some of those dropped from this compilation will also again make their presence felt; the keen reader can look up their credentials in previous Annuals, and, of course, basic details may be in the athletes' index at the end of this book.

Athletes included in these biographies are identified in the index at the end of this Annual by * for those profiled in this section and by ^ for those who were included in previous Annuals.

The biographical information includes:
a) Name, date and place of birth, height (in metres), weight (in kilograms).
b) Previous name(s) for married women; club or university; occupation.
c) Major championships record – all placings in such events as the Olympic Games, World Championships, European Championships, Commonwealth Games, World Cup and Continental Cup; leading placings in finals of the World Indoor Championships, European or World Junior Championships, European Under-23 Championships and other Continental Championships; and first three to six in European Indoors or World University Games. European Cup/Team Champs and IAAF Grand Prix first three at each event or overall. World Athletics Final (WAF) and Diamond League series (DL) winners
d) National (outdoor) titles won or successes in other major events.
e) Records set: world, continental and national; indoor world records/bests (WIR/WIB).
f) Progression of best marks over the years at each athlete's main event(s).
g) Personal best performances at other events.
h) Other comments.
See Introduction to this Annual for lists of abbreviations used for events and championships.

Information given is as known at 5 April 2017 (to include performances at the European Indoor Championships and World Cross-Country Championships as well as some other early indoor and outdoor events of 2017).

I am most grateful to various ATFS members who have helped check these details. Additional information or corrections would be welcomed for next year's Annual.

Peter Matthews

ALBANIA

Governing body: Federata Shqiptare e Atletikes, Rruga Dervish Hima n 31, Tirana.
National Championships first held in 1945 (women 1946).
Luiza GEGA b. 5 Nov 1988 Dibër 1.66m 56kg.
At 800m: WCh: '11- h. At 1500m: WCh: '13- sf, '15- h; EC: '12- sf, '14- h; WI: '14- 6; EI: '17-5;WUG: '13- 2. At 3000mSt: OG: '16- h; EC: '16- 2. Won Balkan 1500m 2011, 2015.
Albanian records: 800m (3) 2011-14, 1500m (4) 2013-15, 3000m (2) 2012-16, 5000m 2014, 3000mSt (4) 2011-16.
Progress at 1500m, 3000mSt: 2006- 4:38.0, 2010- 4:23.20, 2011- 4:14.22, 9:54.72; 2012- 4:08.65mx/4:09.76. 2013- 4:05.11, 2014- 4:03.12, 2015- 4:02.63, 2016- 4:06.89i, 9:28.52; 2017- 4:06.66i. pbs: 800m 2:01.31 '14, 3000m 8:52.53i '17, 8:53.78 '16; 5000m 15:46.89 '14.

ALGERIA

Governing body: Fédération Algerienne d'Athlétisme, BP n°61, Dely-Ibrahim 160410, Alger. Founded 1963.
National Champions 2016: Men: 100m: Djamil Skandar Athmani 10.63, 200m/400m: Soufiane Bouhada 20.53/46.43, 800m: Mohamed Belbachir 1:50.80, 1500m: Chenseddine Kiboua 3:57.46, 5000m: Lyès Belkhier 14:30.87, 3000mSt: Ali Messaoudi 8:51.94, 110mh: Lyès Mokdal 13.74, 400mh: Abdelmalik Lahoulou 49.89, HJ: Mohamed Temani 2.12, PV: Larbi Bouraada 4.90, LJ: Sid Ali Madani 7.30w, TJ: Louhab Kafia 16.33, SP: Mohamed Benzaaza 14.76, DT: Abdelmoumne Bourakba 48.97, HT: Abdelwahab Maamar 59.63, JT: Lardi Bouradaa 60.30, 20kW: Mohamed Ameur 1:31:04; **Women**. 100m/200m: Souheir Bouali 11.75w/23.84w, 400m/400mh: Dihia Haddar 54.50/57.56, 800m: Zahra Bouras 2:14.82, 1500m: Amina Betiche 4:32.43, 5000m: Kenza Dahmani 16:25.73, 3000mSt: Rima Chenah 10:28.13, 100mh/HJ: Yousra Arar 14.60/1.69, PV: Sonia Halliche 3.30, LJ: Romaissa Belbiod 6.52, TJ: Baha Rahouli 12.86w, SP/HT: Zouina Bouzebra 12.65/58.95, DT: Nabila Bounab 42.37, JT: Warda Benamrane 43.13, 20kW: Bariza Ghezelani 1:50:00.

Larbi BOURAADA b. 10 May 1988 Souk Ahras 1.87m 84kg.
At Dec (/PV): OG: '16- 5; WCh: '09- 13, '11- 10, '15- 5; AfG: '07- 3, '11- dnf/1; AfCh: '08- 1/2, '10-1/2, '14- 1. Won ALG PV 2016, JT 2015-16.
Four African decathlon records 2009-16, ALG record 2014.
Progress at Dec: 2007- 7349, 2008- 7697, 2009- 8171, 2010- 8148A, 2011- 8302, 2012- 8332dq, 2014- 8311, 2015- 8461, 2016- 8521. pbs: 60m 6.89i '10, 100m 10.67 '10, 10.61w '11, 10.58dq '12; 400m 46.69 '09, 1000m 2:39.86i '10, 1500m 4:12.15 '09, 60mh 8.05i '10, 110mh 14.00 '15, HJ 2.10 '09, PV 5.00 '11, LJ 7.69 '09, 7.94w '11; SP 14.00i '10, 13.78 '16; DT 42.39 '16, JT 66.49 '16, 67.68dq '12; Hep 5911i '10. Two-years drugs ban from positive test 15 Jun 2012.

Taoufik MAKHLOUFI b. 29 Apr 1988 Souk Ahras 1.81m 66kg.
At (800m)/1500m: OG: '12- h/1, '16- 2/2; WCh: '09/11- sf, '15- 4; AfG: '11- 1/3, '15- (2); AfCh: '10- h, '12- (1), '14- (3).
Algerian records 800m 2016, 1000m 2015.
Progress at 800m, 1500m: 2008- 3:43.4, 2009- 1:49.40, 3:34.34; 2010- 1:48.39, 3:32.94; 2011- 1:46.32, 3:34.4; 2012- 1:43.71, 3:30.80; 2013- 3:36.30, 2014- 1:43.53, 3:30.40; 2015- 1:44.24, 3:28.75; 2016- 1:42.61, 3:31.35. pbs: 600m 1:16.5+ '16, 1000m 2:13.08 '15, 1M 3:52.16 '14.

ANTIGUA & BARBUDA

Governing body: Athletic Association of Antigua & Barbuda, P.O.Box 979, St John's, Antigua. Founded 1960.

Miguel FRANCIS b. 28 Feb 1995 Montserrat 1.86m 75kg. Team Force 2000.
At 200m: WCh: '15- sf; WJ: '14- sf; CG: '14- 7R; PAm: '15- 6.
Three Antiguan 200m records 2015-16.
Progress at 100m: 2013- 20.60/20.58w, 2014- 20.71, 2015- 20.05/19.76dt, 2016- 19.67. pbs: 100m 10.28 '15, 400m 46.85 '16.

ARGENTINA

Governing body: Confederación Argentina de Atletismo (CADA), 21 de Noviembre No. 207. 3260 Concepción del Uruguay, Entre Ríos. Founded 1954 (original governing body founded 1919). **National Championships** first held in 1920 (men), 1939 (women). **2016 Champions: Men**: 100m: Matías Robledo 10.73, 200m: Daniel Londero 21.77, 400m: Martín Rojas 49.36, 800m: Leandro Paris 1:48.68, 1500m/5000m/3000mSt: Joaquín Arbe 3:51.56/14:30.65/8:53.18, 10000m: Luis Ariel Molina 30:35.03, Mar: Darío Ríos 2:24:06, 110mh: Agustín Carrera 14.72, 400mh: Jaime Rodríguez 52.65, HJ: Carlos Layoy 2.00, PV: Germán Chiaraviglio 5.50, LJ: Julián Cherit 7.45, TJ: Maximiliano Díaz 16.15, SP: Germán Lauro 19.20, DT: Juan Solito 49.14, HT: Joaquín Gómez 69.98, JT: Facundo Baudano 70.20, Dec: Jorge Jara 5798, 10,000mW: Leandro Orellano 45:11.46. **Women**: 100m: María Victoria Woodward 11.91, 200m: Juliana Menéndez 24.65, 400m: María Ayalén Diogo 56.12, 800m/1500m: Mariana Borelli 2:08.95/4:31.50, 5000m/10000m: Florencia Borelli 16:07.50/34:09.29, Mar: Luján Urrutia 2:48:34, 3000mSt: Carolina Lozano 10:04.24, 100mh: Martina Corrá 14.25, 400mh: Valeria Barón 63.06, HJ: Macarena Esparza 1.70, PV: Valeria Chiaraviglio 4.10, LJ: Florella Chiappe 5.98, TJ: Gloria Espinoza 12.14w, SP/DT: Rocío Comba

13.93/56.59, HT: Jennifer Dahlgren 65.04, JT: Yohana Arias 48.86, Hep: Evelin Ortiz 3231, 10000mW: Yenni Ortiz 55:02.85.

AUSTRALIA

Governing body: Athletics Australia, Suite 22, Fawkner Towers, 431 St.Kilda Rd, Melbourne, Victoria 3004. Founded 1897.
National Championships first held in 1893 (men) (Australasian until 1927), 1930 (women).
2016 Champions: **Men**: 100m/200m: Alex Hartmann 10.35/20.46, 400m: Steven Solomon 45.50, 800m: Luke Mathews 1:46.20, 1500m: Ryan Gregson 3:37.76, 3000m:, 5000m: Sam McEntee 13:37.95, 10000m: Patrick Tiernan 27:59.74, Mar: Thomas Do Canto 2:20:53, 3000mSt: James Nipperess 8:42.41, 110mh: Justino Merlino 13.81, 400mh: Leigh Bennett 50.67, HJ: Tom Brennan 2.17, PV: Kurtis Marschall 5.55, LJ: Fabrice Lapierre 8.27, TJ: Alwyn Jones 16.38, SP: Matt Cowie 16.98, DT/HT: Matthew Denny 60.47 68.44, JT: Hamish Peacock 82.84, Dec: Cedric Dubler 8114, 10000mW: Dane Bird-Smith 38:44.61, 20kW: Adam Garganis 1:34:23, 50kW: Matthew Griggs 4:36:14. **Women**: 100m: Melissa Breen 11.53, 200m: Ella Nelson 22.59, 400m: Morgan Mitchell 51.84, 800m: Brittany McGowan 2:04.13, 1500m: Heidi See 4:14.17, 3000m:, 5000m: Genevieve LaCaze 15:43.83, 10000m: Bridey Delaney 33:04.72, Mar: Virginia Moloney 2:34:27, 3000mSt: Madeline Hills 9:38.63, 100mh: Michelle Jenneke 12.93, 400mh: Lauren Wells 56.89, HJ: Eleanor Patterson 1.90, PV: Elizabeth Parnov 4.30, LJ: Brooke Stratton 6.68, TJ: Meggan O'Riley 13.42, SP: Chelsea Lenarduzzi 15.41, DT: Dani Samuels 63.44, HT: Lara Nielsen 65.33, JT: Tianah List 51.56, Hep: Sophie Stanwell 55.72, 10000mW: Bekki Smith 43:48.08, 20kW: .

Dane BIRD-SMITH b. 15 Jul 1992 Brisbane 1.78m 66kg. Racewalking Queensland.
At 20kW: OG: '16- 3; WCh: '13- 11, '15- 8; WCp: '14- 14, '16- 4; WUG: '15- 1; OCE Champion 2016-17; At 10000mW: WJ: '10- 5; WY: '09- 8. AUS 5000mW 2013, 10000mW 2014-17, 20kW 2013-14. Oceania 5000m walk record 2016.
Progress at 20kW: 2011- 1:26:38, 2012- 1:23:15, 2013- 1:22:03, 2014- 1:20:27, 2015- 1:20:05, 2016- 1:19:37, 2017- 1:19:37. pbs: 3000mW 10:56.23 '14, 5000mW 18:38.97 '16, 10000mW 38:34.23 '17.

Ryan GREGSON b. 26 Apr 1990 Bulli, NSW 1.84m 68kg. Kembla Joggers.
At 1500m: OG: '12- sf, '16- 9; WCh: '09-11-15: h/sf/h; CG: '14- h; WJ: '08- 5 (12 5000m); WY: '07- 5. AUS champion 2010, 2016-17.
Oceania 1500m record 2010.
Progress at 1500m: 2003- 4:26.00, 2004- 4:20,00, 2005- 4:06.00, 2006- 3:57.00, 2007- 3:43.84, 2008- 3:41.14, 2009- 3:37.24, 2010- 3:31.06, 2011- 3:36.64, 2012- 3:33.92, 2013- 3:35.25, 2014- 3:36.17, 2015- 3:36.51, 2016- 3:32.13. pbs: 800m 1:46.04 '10, 1000m 2:17.69 '10, 1M 3:52.24 '10, 3000m 7:44.90 '16, 5000m 13:56.83 '09, 10km Rd 29:09 '08.

Fabrice LAPIERRE b. 17 Oct 1983 Réduit, Mauritius 1.79m 66kg. Westfields. Science graduate of Texas A&M University, USA.
At LJ: OG: '08- dnq 15, '16- 10; WCh: '09-11-13-15: 4/dnq 21/dnq/2; CG: '06- 3, '10- 1, '14- 4; WJ: '02- 2 (qf 100m); WI: '10- 1, '16- 2; WCp: '06- 8, '10- 7. Won WAF 2008-09, DL 2016, NCAA 2005, AUS 2006, 2009-10, 2013, 2016.
Oceania indoor long jump records 2010 & 2016.
Progress at LJ: 2000- 7.39, 2001- 7.31, 2002- 7.74, 2003- 7.66i/7.57/7.85w, 2004- 7.61i/7.52/7.94Aw, 2005- 7.90i/7.83/8.15w, 2006- 8.19, 2007- 7.98, 2008- 8.15, 2009- 8.35/8.57w, 2010- 8.40/8.78w, 2011- 8.02, 2012- 8.10/8.14w, 2013- 8.25, 2014- 8.00, 2015- 8.29, 2016- 8.31/8.36w. pbs: 60m 6.89i '06, 100m 10.56/10.48w '02, 200m 21.40 '00, TJ 15.24 '04.
Former football player.

Jared TALLENT b. 17 Oct 1984 Ballarat 1.78m 60kg. Ballarat YCW. Graduate of University of Canberra.
At 20kW(/50kW): OG: '08- 3/2, '12- 7/1, '16- (2); WCh: '05- 18, '07- dq, '09- 5/6, '11- 23/2, '13- (3), '15- 26/2; CG: '06- 3, '10- 1; WCp: '06-08-10-12-14-16: 14/10/(3)/(1)/(3)/(1). At 10000mW: WJ: '02- 19; WY: '01- 7. Won AUS 5000mW 2012, 20kW 2008-13; 30kW 2004, 50kW 2007, 2009, 2011.
Commonwealth 5000m walk record 2009.
Progress at 20kW, 50kW: 2002- 1:40/21, 2003- 1:31:24, 2004- 1:27:02, 2005- 1:22:53, 2006- 1:21:36, 3:55:08; 2007- 1:21:25, 3:44:45, 2008- 1:19:41, 3:39:27; 2009- 1:19:42, 3:38:56; 2010- 1:19:15, 3:54:55; 2011- 1:19:57, 3:43:36; 2012- 1:20:02, 3:36:53; 2013- 1:20:41, 3:40:03; 2014- 1:20:55, 3:42:48; 2015- 1:24:05, 3:42.17; 2016- 1:21:50, 3:41:16. pbs: 3000mW 11:15.07 '09, 5000mW 18:41.83 '09, 10000mW 40:41.5 '06, 10kW 38:29 '10, 30kW 2:10:52 '13, 35kW 2:32:37 '12.
Won IAAF Walks Challenge 2008 and 2013.
Married Claire Woods on 30 Aug 2008, she has 20kW pb 1:28:53 '12, 2 CG '10. Younger sister Rachel Tallent (b. 20 Feb 1993) has 20kW pb 1:31:33 to win OCE 2016, 34 WCh '15, 40 OG '16.

Women

Madeline HILLS b. 15 May 1987 Shellharbour, New South Wales 1.74m 53kg. Kembla Joggers – Wollongong. Was at Sydney University.
At (5000m)/3000mSt OG: '16- 10/7; WCh: '15: h/h; CG: '14- 4. AUS champion 5000m 2015, 3000mSt 2016.
Progress at 5000m, 3000mSt: 2006- 9:56.54, 2014- 15:27.75, 9:34.01; 2015- 15:11.17, 9:21.56; 2016- 15:04.05, 9:20.38. pbs: 800m 2:06.13 '16, 1500m 4:06.47 '16, 1M 4:41.89 '06, 3000m 8:44.20 '15, 10000m 32:44.71 '14.
Had an eight-year break from athletics, during which she established a career as a pharmacist. Married to Chris Hills.

122 AUSTRALIA – AUSTRIA

Genevieve LaCAZE b. 4 Aug 1989 Benowa, Queensland 1.68m 54kg. Glenhuntly. Was at University of Florida, USA.
At 3000mSt OG: '12- h, '16- 9 (12 5000m); WCh: '15: h; CG: '14- 5. At 1500m: WJ: '04- h. AUS champion 5000m 2016, 3000mSt 2013, 2015.
Oceania records 2000mSt 2015, 3000mSt 2016.
Progress at 3000mSt: 2009- 10:26.92, 2010- 10:30.12, 2011- 9:59.44, 2012- 9:37.90, 2013- 9:37.62, 2014- 9:33.19, 2015- 9:35.17, 2016- 9:14.28. pbs: 800m 2:04.05 '16, 1500m 4:10.20 '16, 1M 4:32.19 '12, 3000m 8:45.81i '17, 8:52.28 '16; 2M 9:52.21 '14, 5000m 15:06.67 '16, 10k Rd 34:51 '15, 2000mSt 6:16.86 '15.

Kimberley MICKLE b. 28 Dec 1984 Perth 1.68m 70kg. Mandurah/Rockingham.
At JT: OG: '12/16- dnq 17/22; WCh: '09-11-13-15: dnq 15/6/2/dnq 22; CG: '06-10-14: 4/2/1; WJ: '02- 9; WY: '01- 1; WCp: '06-10-14: 5/3/4. AUS champion 2005-07, 2009-15.
Oceania javelin record 2014.
Progress at JT: 1999- 45.13, 2000- 45.76, 2001- 51.83, 2002- 52.77, 2003- 48.03, 2004- 50.38, 2005- 58.16, 2006- 58.56, 2007- 59.36, 2008- 57.64, 2009- 63.49, 2010- 61.36, 2011- 63.82, 2012- 64.12, 2013- 66.60, 2014- 66.83, 2015- 66.57, 2016- 57.20.

Kathryn MITCHELL b. 10 Jul 1982 Hamilton, Victoria 1.68m 72kg. Eureka AC.
At JT: OG: '12- 9, '16- 6; WCh: '13- 5, '15- dnq 17; CG: '06-10-14: 6/5/4; AUS champion 2008.
Progress at JT: 1999- 43.17, 2000- 51.44, 2001- 54.98, 2002- 54.72, 2003- 57.11, 2004- 48.10, 2005- 54.87, 2006- 58.81, 2007- 58.61, 2008- 58.77, 2010- 59.68, 2011- 59.47, 2012- 64.34, 2013- 63.77, 2014- 66.10, 2015- 63.70, 2016- 64.37.

Eleanor PATTERSON b. 22 May 1996 Leongatha, Victoria 1.82m 62kg. South Coast Athletics.
At HJ: OG: '16- dnq 22=; WCh: '15- 8; CG: '14: 1; WY: '13- 1. Won AUS 2014-15.
World youth and Oceania junior high jump record 2013.
Progress at HJ: 2010- 1.73, 2011- 1.82, 2012- 1.87, 2013- 1.96, 2014- 1.94, 2015- 1.96, 2016- 1.93.

Sally PEARSON b. 19 Sep 1986 Sydney 1.66m 60kg. née McLellan. Gold Coast Victory. Griffith University.
At (100m)/100mh: OG: '08- 2, '12- 1; WCh: '03- hR, '07- sf/sf, '09-11-13: 5/1/2; CG: '06- 7/fell/3R, '10- dq/1, '14- 1; WJ: '04- 3/4; WY: '03- 1; WCp: '06- 8/4, '10- 1. At 60mh: WI: '12- 1, '14- 2. At 200m: WY: '03- 5; AUS champion 100m & 100mh 2005-7, 2009, 2011, 2014-15; 100mh 2017. 200m 2011.
Records: Oceania 100mh (8) 2007-11, 60m 2009 & 60mh indoors (3) 2009-12; Commonwealth 100mh (2) 2011.
Progress at 100mh: 2003- 14.01, 2004- 13.30, 2005- 13.01, 2006- 12.95, 2007- 12.71, 2008- 12.53, 2009- 12.50, 2010- 12.57, 2011- 12.28, 2012- 12.35, 2013- 12.50, 2014- 12.5, 2015- 12.59, 2016- 13.14/12.92w, 2017- 12.53w. pbs: 60m 7.16 '11, 100m 11.14 '07, 150m 16.86 '10, 200m 23.02/22.66w '09, 300m 38.34 '09, 400m 53.86mx '11, 200mh 27.54 '06, 60mh 7.73i '12, 200mh 26.96 '09, 400mh 62.98 '07.
Married Kieran Pearson on 3 April 2010. IAAF female Athlete of the Year 2011.

Dani STEVENS b. 26 May 1988 Fairfield, Sydney 1.82m 82kg. née Samuels. Westfields, University of Western Sydney.
At DT/(SP): OG: '08- 8, '12- 11, '16- 4; WCh: '07-09-11-13-15: dnq 13/1/10/10/6; CG: '06- 3/12, '14- 1; WJ: '06- 1/7; WY: '05- 1/3; WCp: '06- 6; WUG: '07- 2, '09- 1; CCp: '10- 4, '14- 2. AUS champion SP 2006-07, 2009, 2012; DT 2005-12, 2014-15, 2017.
Progress at DT: 2001- 39.17, 2002- 45.52, 2003- 47.29, 2004- 52.21, 2005- 58.52, 2006- 60.63, 2007- 60.47, 2008- 62.95, 2009- 65.44, 2010- 65.84, 2011- 62.33, 2012- 63.97, 2013- 64.46, 2014- 67.99, 2015- 66.21, 2016- 67.77. pbs: SP 17.05 '14, HT 45.39 '05.
Sisters Jamie and Casey played basketball for Australia. Married Joe Stevens (SP: pb 17.34 '88; 11 WJ '06).

Brooke STRATTON b. 12 Jul 1993 Box Hill, Melbourne 1.68m 58kg. Nunawading. Was at Deakin University, Melbourne.
At LJ: OG: '16- 7; WCh: '15- dnq 14; WJ: '10- 6, '12- 7; WY: '09- 10; WI: '16- 5. Won AUS 2014.
Oceania long jump record 2016.
Progress at LJ: 2004- 5.38, 2005- 5.40, 2006- 5.52, 2007- 5.90, 2008- 6.06, 2009- 6.13, 2010- 6.30, 2011- 6.60, 2012- 6.56, 2013- 6.53, 2014- 6.70, 2015- 6.73, 2016- 7.05. Pbs: 100m 11.98 '13, 200m 24.79 '16, 100mh 14.18 '10, TJ 13.34 '12.

AUSTRIA

Governing body: Österreichischer Leichtathletik Verband OLV), 1040 Vienna, Prinz Eugenstrasse 12. Founded 1902.
National Championships first held in 1911 (men), 1918 (women). **2016 Champions**: **Men**: 100m/200m: Markus Fuchs 10.47/22.17, 400m: Mario Gebhardt 47.47, 800m: Günther Matzinger 1:55.00, 1500m: Andreas Vojta 3:48.46, 5000m: Brenton Rowe 14:50.34, 10000m/HMar: Valentin Pfeil 30:22.96/66:54 , Mar: Robert Gruber 2:25:17, 3000mSt: Christian Steinhammer 9:10.87, 110mh: Florian Domenig 14.85, 400mh: Dominik Hufnagl 51.38, HJ: Josip Kopic 2.06, PV/LJ: Dominik Distelberger 4.95/7.61, TJ: Philipp Kronsteiner 15.93w, SP: Georg Stamminger 15.60, DT: Lukas Weisshaidinger 64.42, HT: Matthias Hayek 57.20, JT: Matthias Kaserer 67.35, Dec: Felix Schmid-Schutti 6877, 20kW/50kW: Dietmar Hirschmugl 1:56:02/5:37:10. **Women**: 100m: Alexandra Toth 11.73, 200m: Carina Pölzi 24.79, 400m: Carina Schrempf 55.86, 800m/1500m: Cornelia Wohlfahrt 2:12.83/4:35.66, 5000m: Jennifer Werth 16:39.38, 10000m/HMar: Sandrina Illes 35:42.67/77:11, Mar: Anita

Baierl 2:42:35, 3000mSt Battina Bachl 11:33.46, 100mh: Stephanie Bendrat 13.65, 400mh/Hep: Verena Preiner 60.31/5609; HJ: Ekaterina Kuntsevich 1.77, PV: Brigitta Hesch 4.00, LJ/TJ: Michaela Egger 5.89/12.96, SP: Christina Scheffauer 13.88, DT: Veronika Watzek 56.18, HT: Tatjana Meklau 54.42, JT: Victoria Hudson 51.49, 20kW: Andrea Kovac HUN 2:02:24.

Lukas WEISSHAIDINGER b. 20 Feb 1992 Schärding 1.96m 136kg. ÖTB OÖ Leichtathletik.
At DT (SP): OG: '16- 6; WCh: '15: dnq 20; WJ: '10- dnq 16 (6); WY: '09- dnq 36 (4); EU23: '11- 7; EJ '11- 1 (5 SP). Won AUT SP 2012-15, DT 2015-16. Austrian discus record 2015.
Progress at DT: 2008- 43.47, 2009- 45.98, 2010- 54.21, 2011- 54.85, 2012- 58.00, 2013- 59.13, 2014- 60.68, 2015- 67.24, 2016- 66.00. pb SP 18.90 '13.

Women

Ivona DADIC b. 29 Dec 1993 Weis 1.79m 65kg. PSV Hornbach Weiss
At Hep: OG: '12- 23, '16- 21; EC: '16: 3; WJ: '12- dnf; WY: '09- 10; EU23: '13- 5, '15- 3; EJ: 11- 10 At Pen: EI: '17- 2. Won AUT Hep 2012.
5 Austrian heptathlon records 2012-16.
Progress at Hep: 2011- 5455, 2012- 5959, 2013- 5874, 2015- 6151, 2016- 6408. pbs: 200m 23.96 '12, 400m 56.27 '11, 800m 2:10.67 '12, 60mh 8.45i '17, 100mh 13.80 '16, HJ 1.87i '17, 1.80 '12; LJ 6.49 '16, SP 14.10 '16, JT 52.48 '15, Pen 4723i '17.
Improved heptathlon pb by 212 points for 3rd EC '16 and pentathlon best by 247 for 2nd EI '17.

AZERBAIJAN

Women

Hanna SKYDAN b. 14 May 1992 Krasnyi Luch, UKR 1.83m 114kg.
At HT: OG: '12/16- dnq 16/13; WCh: '15- dnq 23; EC: '16- 3; WJ: '10- dnq 27; WY: '09- 12; EJ: 11- dnq; WUG: '15- 1.
Seven AZE hammer records 2015-16.
Progress at HT: 2009- 56.90, 2010- 56.76, 2011- 67.56, 2012- 74.21, 2013- 68.44, 2014- 71.14, 2015- 72.31, 2016- 73.87. pbs: SP 13.76 '15, DT 49.50 '15.
Competed for Ukraine to 2012, AZE citizenship 15 Jan 2015 and cleared to compete for them from 1 Jun 2015.

BAHAMAS

Governing body: Bahamas Association of Athletics Associations, P.O.Box SS 5517, Nassau. Founded 1952.
National Champions 2016: **Men**: 100m: Shavez Hart 10.37, 200m: Ian Kerr 20.72, 400m: Steven Gardiner 44.46, 800m: Rocky Jean-Louis 1:52.09, 1500m: O'Neil Williams 3:56.37, 400mh: Jeffrey Gibson 50.24, HJ: Donald Thomas 2.27, LJ: Raymond Higgs 7.54, TJ: Leevan Sands 16.60, DT: Gerrard Burrows 48.72. **Women**: 100m/200m: Tynia Gaither 11.33/23.00, 400m: Shaunae Miller 52.17, 800m: Te'shon Adderley 2:08.81, 100mh: Ivanique Kemp 13.58, HJ: Celine Thompson 1.65. LJ: Bianca Stuart 6.66w, TJ: Tamara Myers 13.60, JT: Carlene Johnson 44.54.

Christopher BROWN b. 15 Oct 1978 Nassau 1.78m 68kg. Was at Norfolk State University.
At 400m/4x400mR: OG: '00- qf/3R, '04- sf, '08- 4/2R, '12- 4/1R, '16- h/3R; WCh: '01-03-05-07-09-11-13-15: h&1R/sf&3R/4&2R/4&2R/5/sf/sf/sf; CG: '02- 7/3R, '06- 4, '14- dns/2R; PAm: '07- 1/1R. '11- 7; PAm-J: '97- 2R; CAG: '98- 3R, '99- 1R, '03- 2/1R; CCp: '14- 3R; WI: '06-08-10-12-14: 3/3/1/3/2, '16- 2R; BAH champion 2002, 2004, 2007-09. At 800m: CG: '98- h.
Bahamas records 300m 2015, 400m 2007 & 2008, 800m 1998. CAC & Commonwealth 4x400m record 2012. World M35 records 400m 2014 & 2015, 300m 2015.
Progress at 400m: 1997- 47.46, 1998- 46.44, 1999- 45.96, 2000- 45.08, 2001- 45.45, 2002- 45.11, 2003- 44.94A/45.16, 2004- 45.09, 2005- 44.48, 2006- 44.80, 2007- 44.45, 2008- 44.40, 2009- 44.81, 2010- 45.05, 2011- 44.79, 2012- 44.67, 2013- 45.18, 2014- 44.59, 2015- 44.54, 2016- 45.56. pbs: 100m 10.26+ '14, 150mSt 15.10 '14, 200m 20.58 '15, 20.56w '06; 300m 31.99 '15, 800m 1:49.54 '98.
Fourth at four global championships outdoors. His 16-year span of winning Olympic medals is a men's record. Had fastest split (43.42 anchor leg) in 2005 World 4x400m. Men's record six WI medals.

Steven GARDINER b. 12 Sep 1995 Moore's Island 1.88m 75kg.
At 400m: OG: '16- sf/3R; WCh: '15- sf; WJ: '14- 6R (sf 200m); BAH champion 2015-16.
Bahamas 400m record 2015.
Progress at 400m: 2013- 47.78, 2015- 44.27, 2016- 44.46. pbs: 200m 20.64 '16, 20.51w '15; 300m 32.64 '16.

Jeffery GIBSON b. 15 Aug 1990 Freeport 1.86m 79kg. Was at Oral Roberts University, USA.
At 400mh: OG: '16- h; WCh: '13- sf. '15- 3; CG: '14- 3; PAm: '15- 1/3R. BAH champion 2011, 2013-16; NACAC 2012.
Seven BAH 400mh records 2013-5.
At 400mh: 2008- 52.45, 2010- 51.80, 2011- 50.82, 2012- 50.27A/50.69, 2013- 49,39, 2014- 48.78, 2015- 48.17, 2016- 48.96. pbs: 100m 10.56w '12, 200m 21.39w '12, 400m 46.30A '12, 46.62 '11.

Donald THOMAS b. 1 Jul 1984 Freeport 1.90m 75kg. Lindenwood University, USA.
At HJ: OG: '08/12- dnq 21=/30=, '16- 7= WCh: '07-09-11-13-15: 1/dnq 15/11/6/6; CG: '06-10-14: 4/1/9=; PAm: '07-11-15; 2/1/3; CAG: '06- 4=, '10- 1; CCp: '10- 2. Won WAF & NCAA indoors 2007, BAH 2007, 2010-11.
Progress at HJ: 2006- 2.24, 2007- 2.35, 2008- 2.28i/2.26, 2009- 2.30, 2010- 2.32, 2011- 2.32, 2012- 2.27, 2013- 2.32, 2014- 2.33i/2.25, 2015- 2.34, 2016- 2.37.
A basketball player, he made a sensational start

by clearing 2.22 indoors in January 2006 with no high jump training since he had jumped at school five years earlier. 19 months later he was world champion.

Women

Shaunae MILLER-UIBO b. 15 Apr 1994 Nassau 1.85m 69kg. University of Georgia, USA.
At (200m)/400m: OG: '12- ht, '16- 1; WCh: '13- (4), '15- 2; CG: '14- 6; WJ: '10- 1, '12- 4; WY: '11- 1; WI: '14- 3. Won BAH 400m 2010-11, 2014-16; NCAA indoor 400m 2013.
BAH 200m records 2015 & 2016. CAC junior records 200m 2013, 400m 2013.
Progress at 200m, 400m: 2009- 55.52, 2010- 24.09, 52.45; 2011- 23.70, 51.84; 2012- 22.70, 51.25; 2013- 22.45/22.41w, 50.70; 2014- 22.87, 51.63i/51.86; 2015- 22.14, 49.67; 2016- 22.05, 49.44. Pbs: 60m 7.59i '13, 100m 11.19 '16, 300m 35.71i '17.
Married Estonian decathlete Maicel Uibo (qv) on 4 Feb 2017. Great-uncle Leslie Miller set BAH 400m record of 46.99 at 1968 Olympics.

Pedrya SEYMOUR b. 29 May 1995 Nassau 1.68m 57kg. University of Illinois.
At 100mh: OG: '16- 6. At 400mh: WJ: '12- h. Won BAH 400mh 2012.
Five Bahamas 100mh records 2016.
Progress at 100mh: 2016- 12.64. pbs: 60m 7.66i '16, 200m 23.59 '16, 60mh 7.97i '17, 400mh 60.18 '16.
Having been a 300m/400m hurdler in 2010-13, she made an amazing breakthrough at 100mh in 2016 from her first race in 13.50 on April 9 to 6th in the Olympic final in 12.64.

Anthonique STRACHAN b. 22 Aug 1993 Nassau 1.68m 57kg. Auburn University, USA.
At (100m)/200m: OG: '12- sf, '16- h (6 4x400m); WCh: '11/13- sf; WJ: '10- sf, '12- 1/1; PAm: '15- dnf; CCp: '14- 4; PAm-J: '11- 1. Won BAH 100m 2014, 200m 2013, 2015.
Two CAC junior 200m records 2011-12.
Progress at 200m: 2009- 23.95, 2010- 23.66, 2011- 22.70, 2012- 22.53, 2013- 22.32, 2014- 22.50, 2015- 22.69, 2016- 22.96. Pbs: 100m 11.20 '12, 400m 52.42 '16.
Won IAAF Female Rising Star Award 2012.

BAHRAIN

Governing body: Bahrain Athletics Association, PO Box 29269, Isa Twon-Manama. Founded 1974.

Ali Khamis ABBAS b. 30 Jun 1995 1.82m 70kg.
At 400m: OG: '16- 6; AsiC: '13- 2; At 400mh: WJ: '12- h, '14- 2; WY: '11- h; AsiG: '14- 1. Won Arab 400mh 2015.
Three Bahrain 400m records 2016,
Progress at 400m: 2013- 45.65, 2014- 46.13, 2015- 45.88, 2016- 44.36. Pbs: 100m 10.69 '15, 200m 20.81 '15, 300m 32.0+ '16, 400mh 49.55 '14.

Abraham Naibei **CHEROBEN** b. 10 Nov 1992 1.76m 60kg.
At 10000m: OG: '16- 10.

BRN half marathon record (61:00) 2016.
Progress at 10000m, HMar: 2012- 63:53, 2013- 60:38, 2014- 58:48, 2015- 59:10, 2016- 27:31.86, 60:35. Road pbs: 15k 41:55 '14, 20k 55:50 '14, 25k 1:11:47 '14.
Transferred from Kenya to Bahrain on 19 Aug 2015, with eligibility from 1 Aug 2016.

Albert Kibichii **ROP** b. 17 Jul 1992 Kapsabet, Kenya 1.76m 55kg.
At 5000m: OG: '16- 7; WCh: '15- 11; AsiG: '14- 3; AsiC: '15- 2; CCp: '14- 4; Arab champion 2013, WMilG & Gulf 2015. World CC: '15- 11. Asian CC champion 2016.
Records: 1 Asian, 2 Bahrain 5000m and Bahrain 3000m 2013; Asian indoor 3000m (2) 2014 (if eligible), 5000m 2017.
Progress at 5000m: 2010- 14:15.81A, 2011- 13:03.70, 2012- 13:01.91, 2013- 12:51.96, 2014- 13:06.12, 2015- 13:06.74, 2016- 13:04.87, 2017- 13:09.43i. Pbs: 1500m 3:45.7A '13, 2000m 5:01.4+ '16, 3000m 7:32.02 '16.
Bahrain citizen from 2 Apr 2013, international eligibility 1 Apr 2014.

Women

Oluwakemi ADEKOYA b. 16 Jan 1993 Nigeria 1.68m 57kg. Accountancy graduate of University of Lagos.
At 400mh: WCh: '15- h (dq); AsiG: '14- 1 (1 400m); AsiC: '15- 1; CCp: '14- 3. At 400m: OG: '16- sf; WI: '16- 1; Won Arab 400m & W.MilG 400mh 2015, Asi Ind 400m 2016.
Records: Asian indoor 400m (4) to 51.45 in 2016. Bahrain 400m (4) 2015-16, 400mh (3) 2014-15.
Progress at 400m, 400mh: 2012- 57.16H, 2013- 52.57, 55.30; 2014- 51.11, 54.59; 2015- 50.86, 54.12; 2016- 50.72, 54.87. pbs: 100m 11.55 '14, 400m 50.86 '15.
Switched nationality from Nigeria to Bahrain from 11 Sep 2013, with international eligibility from 10 Sep 2014.

Rose CHELIMO b. 12 Jul 1989 Kenya 1.62m 45kg.
At Mar: OG: '16- 8. World CC: '17- 9.
Progress at HMar, Mar: 2010- 72:48, 2011- 69:45, 2012- 70:50, 2014- 68:40, 2015-68:22 , 2016- 68:08, 2:24:14. Road pbs: 10k 32:04 '11, 15k 50:33 '13, 20k 64:47 '15.
Transferred from Kenya to Bahrain on 19 Aug 2015; eligible to compete for them from 1 Aug 2016. Won in Seoul on marathon debut in 2016.

Ruth JEBET b. 17 Nov 1996 Kenya 1.65m 49kg.
At 3000mSt: OG: '16- 1; WCh: '15- 11; WJ: '14- 1; AsiG: '14- 1; AsiC: '13- 1 but ineligible; CCp: '14- 3. Won DL 2016, WMilG 2015, Arab 2015, Arab-J 3000m 2014 World CC: '15- 9J, '17- 7.
World 3000m steeplechase record 2016, four Asian 2014-16.
Progress at 3000mSt: 2013- 9:40.84, 2014- 9:20.55, 2015- 9:21.40, 2016- 8:52.78. pbs: 1500m 4:13.4A '16, 3000m 8:47.24i '16, 9:09.8A '13; 5000m 16:16.1A '13, road 10k 32:18 '14, 2000mSt 6:17.33

'13 (5:54.16 in 3000mSt WR).
Switched nationality from Kenya to Bahrain from 19 Aug 2015, with international eligibility from 19 May 2014 and won Bahrain's first Olympic medal. Formerly known as Chebet.
Eunice JEPKIRUI Kirwa b. 20 May 1984 Kenya 1.65m 52kg.
At Mar: OG: '16- 2; WCh: '15- 3; AsiG: '14- 1. At 1500m: WY: '99/01- h.
Bahrain records: marathon (3) 2014-17, half marathon 2016.
Progress at Mar: 2012- 2:21:41, 2013- 2:23:34, 2014- 2:25:37, 2015- 2:22:08, 2016- 2:22:40, 2017- 2:21:17. Pbs: 1500m 4:27.62 '99, 2000mSt 6:33.0A '03, 3000mSt 10:18.3A '05, Road: 10k 31:57 '12, 15k 48:37 '16, HMar 68:06 '16.
Won marathons in Asunción 2012, Lanzhou and Danzhou 2014, Nagoya 2015-17. Transferred from Kenya 11 Dec 2013 with eligibility to compete for Bahrain from 15 Jul 2014. Married to Joshua Kiprugut Kemei (pb HMar 62:53 '11) with one son.

BARBADOS
Governing body: Amateur Athletic Association of Barbados, P.O.Box 46, Bridgetown. Founded 1947.
National Champions 2016: **Men**: 100m/200m: Ramon Gittens 10.09/20.42, 400m: Wade Garner 47.40, 800m: Anthonio Mascoll 1:47.00, 1500m: Jonathan Jones 3:58.09, 110mh: Shane Brathwaite 13.62, 400mh: Kion Joseph 50.39, LJ: Shamar Rock 7.40, TJ: Barry Batson 15.26, DT: Dequan Lovell 49.75, JT: Janeil Craigg 69.11. **Women**: 100m: Ashley Marshall 11.55, 200m/400m: Sada Williams 22.88/52.90, 800m: Sadé Sealy 2:06.79, 1500m: Elizabeth Williams 4:42.64, 100mh: Kierre Beckles 12.93, HJ: Ashantia Phillips 1.70, LJ/TJ: Jamilah James 5.70/12.21, SP/DT: Ashley Williams 14.28/45.01, JT: Janita Austin 25.81.

Women
Akela JONES b. 21 Apr 1995 Saint Michael 1.86m 77kg. Student at Kansas State University.
At Hep: OG: '16- 20 (dnq 31 HJ). At LJ: WJ: '12- dnq 18; '14- 1; WY: '11- 6; PAm: '15- 6 (3 HJ, h 100mh).
BAR records: 100mh 2016, HJ (2) 2015-16, LJ (2) 2015-16, Hep (3) 2015, CAC Indoor pentathlon record 2016.
Progress at HJ, LJ, Hep: 2008- 1.71, 2009- 1.81, 5.85w; 2010- 1.85, 2011- 1.75, 6.16; 2012- 1.81, 6.36; 2013- 1.85i/1.80, 6.26i/6.35w; 2014- 1.87i/1.85, 6.55; 2015- 1.91, 6.64i/6.60, 6371(w); 2016- 1.98i/1.95, 6.80i/6.75, 6307. pbs: 60m 7.47i '15, 100m 11.64 '15, 11.59w '13; 200m 23.28 '16, 800m 2:21.62 '15, 60mh 8.00i '16, 100mh 12.94 '16, SP 14.85 '15, JT 38.97 '16, Pen 4643i '16.

BELARUS
Governing body: Belarus Athletic Federation, Kalinovskogo Street 111A, Minsk 220119. Founded 1991.
National Champions 2016: **Men**: 100m: Denis Konanov 10.63, 200m: Igor Popov 21.68, 400m: Aleksandr Krasovskiy 47.57, 800m: Yan Sloma 1:52.37, 1500m: Maksim Yushenko 3:52.55, 5000m: Sergey Platonov 14:23.45, 10000m: Vladislav Promov 29:39.09, 3000mSt: Sergey Litovchik 8:42.51, 110mh: Maksim Lynsha 14.02, 400mh: Mikhail Romanov 51.15, HJ: Andrey Skobeyko 2.23, PV: Stanislav Tivonchik 4.80, LJ: Konstantin Borichevskiy 7.91, TJ: Artyom Bondarenko 16.90, SP: Pavel Lyzhin 19.91, DT: Sergey Roganov 57.80, HT: Ivan Tikhon 80.04, JT: Vladimir Kozlov 77.85, Dec: Vitaliy Zhuk 7400, 20000mW: Ivan Trotskiy 1:24:46.1. **Women**: 100m/ 200m: Kristina Timanovskaya 11.62/23.87, 400m: Ilona Usovich 52.48, 800m: Dariya Borisevich 2:03.82, 1500m: Olga Rulevich 4:16.69, 5000m: Nina Savina 16:15.83, 10000m: Irina Somova 34:02.41, 3000mSt: Anastasiya Puzakova 9:53.23, 100mh: Alina Talay 12.71, 400mh: Yekaterina Belanovich 57.29, HJ: Yana Maksimova 1.90, PV: Irina Yakoltsevich 4.50, LJ: Veronika Shutkova 6.49w, TJ: Irina Vaskovskaya 14.19, SP: Yuliya Leontyuk 18.48,, DT: Svetlana Serova 52.89, HT: Anna Malyshik 72.31, JT: Tatyana Kholodovich 61.49, Hep: Yekaterina Netsvetayeva 6006, 20000mW: Viktoriya Roshchuplina 1:35:09.2

Ivan TIKHON b. 24 Jul 1976 Slonim 1.86m 110kg. Dynamo.
At HT: OG: '00- 4, '04- dq (2), '08- 3, '16- 2; WCh: '97- nt (12), '01- dnq 22, '03- 1, '05- dq (1), '07- 1, '15- dnq 21; EC: '98- dnq 30, '02- 9, '06- dq(1), 16- 2; EU23: '97- 1; EJ: '95- 9; WUG: '03- 1; WCp: '06- 2. Won WAF 2005(dq), 2007; BLR 2001-04, 2008, 2016.
Progress at HT: 1994- 62.66, 1995- 66.84, 1996- 75.32, 1997- 77.46, 1998- 78.03, 1999- 70.37, 2000- 79.85, 2001- 78.73, 2002- 79.04, 2003- 84.32, 2004- 84.46, 2005- dq86.73, 2006- 81.12, 2007- 83.63, 2008- 84.51, 2012- 82.81, 2015- 77.46, 2016- 80.04.
Missed Yuriy Sedykh's 19 year-old world record by just 1cm at Brest on 3 Jul 2005. Positive drugs test at 2008 Olympics, so originally lost medal, but was reinstated in 2010. Reappeared for one competition in 2012, but withdrawn from Olympic team, apparently after re-testing of 2004/05 samples. This led to his results from 22 Aug 2004 to 21 Aug 2006 being annulled (including two BLR records in 2005). He was also suspended in 2012-14.

Women
Marina ARZAMASOVA b. 17 Dec 1987 Minsk 1.73m 57kg. née Kotovich. Minsk.
At 800m: OG: '12- h, '16- 7; WCh: '11/13- sf, '15- 1; EC: '12- 2, '14- 1; WJ: '06- h; CCp: '14- 3; ET: '11-3, '13- 3; WI: '14- 3; EI: '13- 3. Won W.MilG 2011, BLR 800m 2008, 2013, 2015; 1500m 2013.
Progress at 800m: 2004- 2:09.37, 2005- 2:07.24, 2006- 2:06.39, 2007- 2:04.33, 2008- 2:02.67, 2009-

2:05.53i, 2011- 1:59.30, 2012- 1:59.63, 2013- 1:59.60, 2014- 1:58.15, 2015- 1:57.54, 2016- 1:58.36. pbs: 400m 52.81 '12, 600m 1:27.1+ '16, 1000m 2:37.93 '11, 1500m 4:15.99 '12.
Married to Ilya, with daughter Sashenka born 2010. Parents were Aleksandr Kotovich UKR (HJ 2.35i '85, 2.33 '84; 2 EI 85) and Ravilya Agletdinova BLR (800m 1:56.1 '82, 1500m 3:58.40 '85, 1 EC 86, 4 WCh 83).

Alyona DUBITSKAYA b. 25 Jan 1990 Grodno 1.82m 77k. née Hryshko. Grodnenskaya.
At SP: OG: '16- 8; WCh: '13- dnq 27, '15- 6; EC: '14- 7, '16- 6; WJ: '08- 4; WY: '07- 1; EJ: '09- 1; WI: '16- 9; EI: '17- 7; ET: '15- 3. BLR champion 2009, 2014-15.
Progress at SP: 2007- 15.91, 2008- 16.55, 2009- 17.95, 2010- 18.12i/17.75, 2012- 16.63, 2013- 17.88, 2014- 19.03, 2015- 18.88, 2016- 18.78. pb DT 46.30 '14. 6-month drugs ban 2014-15.

Tatyana KHOLODOVICH b. 21 Jun 1991 Brest 1.81m 83kg.
At JT: OG: '16- 5; WCh: '15- dnq 21; EC: '14- 5, '16- 1; WJ: '08/10- dnq 16/21; EU23: 13- dnq; WUG: '15- 1; ET: '15- 2. BLR champion 2012-16. Three Belarus javelin records 2014-16.
Progress at JT: 2007- 46.12, 2008- 53.51, 2009- 46.80, 2010- 51.17, 2011- 55.94, 2012- 59.15, 2013- 59.37, 2014- 63.61, 2015- 62.00, 2016- 66.34.

Yuliya LEONTYUK b. 31 Jan 1984 Pinsk 1.85m 80kg. Brest.
At SP: OG: '16- dnq 17; WCh: '13- dnq 16, '15- 7; EC: '14- 4, '16- 4; WJ: '02- 7; WY: '01- 3; EU23: '05- 4; EJ: '03- 2; WUG: '07- 2; ECp: '08- dq (1); WI: '14- 7; EI: '07-15-17: 4/2/3. BLR champion 2016.
Progress at SP: 2001- 15.16, 2002- 16.47, 2003- 17.44, 2004- 16.37, 2005- 17.91, 2006- 18.86, 2007- 18.86, 2008- 19.79, 2013- 18.47, 2014 18.87, 2015- 19.00i/18.86, 2016- 18.92. pb DT 48.72 '14.
Two-year drugs ban 2008-10.

Hanna MALYSHIK b. 4 Feb 1994 1.75m 90kg. née Zinchuk.
At HT: OG: '16- 7; EC: '16- dnq 26; WJ: '12- dnq; WY: '11- dnq 15, EJ: '13- 1. Won EY Oly 2011, BLR 2016.
Progress at HT: 2009- 50.70, 2010- 57.38, 2011- 60.11, 2012- 63.41, 2013- 66.36, 2014- 67.53, 2015- 66.50, 2016- 72.78.

Olga MAZURONAK b. 14 Apr 1989 1.76m 56kg. Minsk.
At Mar: OG: '16- 5. At 10000m: EC: '14- 7. At 10000mW: WJ: '06- 5; EJ: '07- dq. At 5000mW: WY: '05- 4. Won BLR 5000m 2013, 10000m 2013-14.
Progress at Mar: 2012- 2:33:56, 2013- 2:33:33, 2014- 2:27:33, 2015- 2:25:36, 2016- 2:23:54. pbs: 3000m 9:28.60i '15, 5000m 15:35.21 '15, 10000m 32:31.15, HMar 71:44 '16; 5000mW 22:36.55 '05, 10kW 44:30 '06..
Marathon wins: Debno & Siberia 2012, Sacramento 2014.

Yelena SOBOLEVA b. 11 May 1993 Grodno 1.80m 96kg. née Novogrodskaya. Grodnenskaya.
At HT: OG: '16- dnq 20; WCh: '15- 10; EC: '15- dnq 15; WJ: '12- 3; WY: '09- 11, EU23: '13- 6, '15- 2; EJ: '11- 4, Yth OG: '10- 2. BLR champion 2014-15.
Progress at HT: 2008- 53.49, 2009- 56.90, 2010- 60.42, 2011- 62.24, 2012- 67.13, 2013- 66.10, 2014- 68.96, 2015- 72.86, 2016- 70.43.

Alina TALAY b. 14 May 1989 Orsha, Vitebsk 1.64m 54kg.
At 100mh: OG: '12/16- sf; WCh: '13- sf, '15- 3; EC: '10-12-14-16: sf/1/5/2; WJ: '08- 4; EU23: '09- 3, '11- 1; WUG: '13- 2; ET: '11- 2, '15- 1; won W. MilG 2011, BLR 2009-10, 2013-16 (200m 2015). At 60mh: WI: '12- 3, '16- 6; EI: '11-13-15-17: 5/1/1/2. Two BLR 100m hurdles records 2015-16.
Progress at 100mh: 2007- 14.38/14.01w, 2008- 13.31, 2009- 13.07, 2010- 12.87, 2011- 12.91, 2012- 12.71, 2013- 12.78, 2014- 12.89, 2015- 12.66, 2016- 12.63. pbs: 60m 7.31i '15, 100m 11.48 '11, 200m 23.59 '11, 50mh 6.89i '11, 60mh 7.85i '15.

BELGIUM

Governing bodies: Ligue Royale Belge d'Athlétisme, Stade Roi Baudouin, avenue du Marathon 199B, 1020 Bruxelles (KBAB/LRBA). Vlaamse Atletiekliga (VAL); Ligue Belge Francophone d'Athlétisme (LBFA). Original governing body founded 1889.
National Championships first held in 1889 (women 1921). **2016**: **Men**: 100m: Andreas Vranken 10.63, 200m: Arnout Matthys 21.24, 400m: Julien Watrin 45.73, 800m: Aaron Botterman 1:50.68, 1500m: Pieter Claus 3:53.41, 5000m: Koen Naert 14:05.27, 10000m: Abdelhadi El Hachimi 29:11.51, Mar: Stijn De Vulder 2:19:53, 3000mSt: Abdellah Dacha MAR 8:59.15, 110mh: Damien Broothaerts 13.68w, 400mh: Eric Heggen 51.29, HJ: Bram Ghuys 2.13, PV: Jorg Vanlierde 4.81, LJ: Cedric Nolf 7.82, TJ: Leopold Kapata 15.21, SP/DT: Philip Milanov 16.69/62.03, HT: Walter De Wyngaert 60.11, JT: Timothy Herman 72.10, Dec: Benjamin Hougardy 7066, 20000mW: Dirk Bogaert 2:11:01, 50kW: Jacques Till 5:55:37. **Women**: 100m/200m: Olivia Borlée 11.54/23.02; 400m: Justien Grillet 54.03, 800m: Sofie Lauwers 2:11.49, 1500m: Sofie Van Accom 4:13.14, 5000m: Barbara Maveau 16:26.68, 10000m: Els Rens 35:53.79, Mar: Ann-Sofie Claeys 2:49:23, 3000mSt: Jolanda Verstraten 10:56.90, 100mh: Anne Zagré 13.01, 400mh: Axelle Dauwens 55.68, HJ: Hanne Van Hessche 1.85, PV: Fanny Smets 4.25, LJ: Jolien Leemans 6.32w, TJ: Elsa Loureiro 12.70, SP/HT: Jolien Boumkwo 16.54/ 67.30, DT: Anouska Hellebuyck 49.67, JT: Melissa Dupré 53.13, Hep: Ellen Hooyberghs 4940, 10000mW/20kW: Annelies Sarrazin 58:53.71/1:55:56

Jonathan BORLÉE b. 22 Feb 1988 Woluwe-Saint Lambert 1.80m 70kg. Racing Club of

Brussels. Was at Florida State University.
At 400m: OG: '08- sf/5R, '12- 6, '16- h (h 200m);
WCh: '11- 5, '13- 4, '15- sf; EC: '10- 7/3R, '12- 1R,
'14- dns, '16- h/1R; WJ: '06- 4; WY: '05- 5; EJ: '07-
h; WI: '10- 2R; EI: '11- 3R, '15- 1R. Won NCAA
2009. At 200m: EC: '12- 4. Won BEL 200m 2012-
13, 400m 2006, 2011, 2015.
Four Belgian 400m records 2009-12, 300m 2012.
Progress at 400m: 2005- 47.50, 2006- 46.06, 2007-
47.85, 2008- 45.11, 2009- 44.78, 2010- 44.71, 2011-
44.78, 2012- 44.43, 2013- 44.54, 2014- 45.37, 2015-
44.67, 2016- 45.34. pbs: 60m 6.81i '07, 100m 10.78
'07, 200m 20.31 '12, 300m 31.87 '12, 500m 1:00.76i
'15, 600m 1:18.60i '11.
Twin brother of Kevin Borlée, their sister
Olivia (b. 10 Apr 1986) has pbs 100m 11.39 '07,
200m 22.98 '06, 3 WCh '07, 2 OG '08 at 4x100mR.
Younger brother **Dylan** (b. 20 Sep 1992) pb
45.57 '15 and 2 EI '15 (the three brothers ran on
BEL 4x400m team 5th WCh 2013, 1st EI 2015 &
EC 2016, 4thn OG 2016). Their father Jacques
was an international 400m runner (45.4 '79),
mother Edith Demartelaere had pbs 200m 23.89
and 400m 54.09 in 1984.

Kévin BORLÉE b. 22 Feb 1988 Woluwe-Saint
Lambert 1.80m 71kg. Racing Club of Brussels.
Was at Florida State University.
At 400m: OG: '08- sf/5R, '12- 5, '16- h; WCh: '09-
sf/4R, '11- 3, '13-15: sf; EC: '10- 1/3R, '12- 1R,
'14- sf, '16- 4/1R; WJ: '06- sf; WI: '10- 2R; EI: '11-
15-17: 3R/1R/2R; CCp: '10- 4/2R. At 200m: WY:
'05- sf. Won DL 2012, BEL 200m 2009, 2011;
400m 2007, 2013.
Belgian 400m records 2008 and 2012.
Progress at 400m: 2005- 47.86, 2006- 46.63, 2007-
46.38, 2008- 44.88, 2009- 45.28, 2010- 45.01, 2011-
44.74, 2012- 44.56, 2013- 44.73, 2014- 45.28, 2015-
44.74, 2016- 45.17. pbs: 60m 6.85i '13, 100m 10.62
'07, 200m 20.72 '11, 300m 32.72i '13, 32.76 '08;
600m 1:15.65i '11.

Philip MILANOV b. 6 Jul 1991 Bruges 1.91m
118kg. Vilvoorde AC, Lille Metropole, FRA.
At DT: OG: '16- 9; WCh: '15- 2; EC: '14- dnq 20,
'16- 2; EU23: '13- 5; WUG: '15- 1. Won BEL DT
2011-16, SP 2016.
Six Belgian discus records 2014-16.
Progress at DT: 2011- 56.00, 2012- 57.66, 2013-
61.81, 2014- 66.02, 2015- 66.90, 2016- 67.26. pb SP
17.91 '15.
His father Emil Milanov had DT pb 58.28 '82,
moved from Bulgaria to Belgium in 1989.

Thomas VAN DER PLAETSEN b. 24 Dec 1990
Gent 1.85m 86kg. AC Deinze.
At Dec: OG: '16- 8; WCh: '11-13-15: 13/15/14; EC:
'14- 10, '16- 1; EU23: '11- 1; EJ: '09- 1; WUG: '13- 1,
'15- 1; Won BEL PV 2011, 2013; Dec 2010. At Hep:
WI: '14- 3; EI: '11- 6.
Belgian decathlon record 2011.
Progress at Dec: 2010- 7564, 2011- 8157, 2013-
8255, 2014- 8184, 2015- 8035, 2016- 8332. pbs:
60m 7.13i '14, 100m 11.04 '14, 200m 22.34 '10,
400m 48.64 '11, 1000m 2:40.50i '14, 1500m 4:32.52
'11, 60mh 8.06i '14, 110mh 14.39 '16, HJ 2.17 '11,
PV 5.41 '16, LJ 7.80 '13, SP 14.32i/14.12 '14, DT
44.48 '14, JT 65.31 '13, Hep 6259i '14.

Women

Nafissatou THIAM b. 19 Aug 1994 Namur
1.84m 69kg. RFCL. Student of geographical
science at University of Liège.
At Hep: OG: '16- 1; WCh: '13- 14, '15- 11; EC: '14-
3; WJ: '12- 14; WY: '11- 4; EJ: '13- 1. At Pen: EI:
'13-15-17: 6/2/1. At HJ: EC: '16- 4; EU23: '15- 2;
WI: '14- 8=. Won BEL Hep 2012, LJ 2015.
Two Belgian heptathlon records 2013-14. World
junior heptathlon best 2013.
Progress at HJ, Hep: 2010- 1.74, 2011- 1.81, 2012-
1.88, 5916; 2013- 1.92, 6298, 2014- 1.97, 6508; 2015-
1.92, 6412; 2016- 1.98, 6810. pbs: 60m 7.81i '13,
200m 24.78 '14, 800m 2:16.54 '16, 60mh 8.23i '17,
100mh 13.56 '16, LJ 6.58 '16, TJ 12.82 '14, SP
15.35i '17, 15.24 '15; JT 53.13 '15, Pen 4870i '17.
Tied world best in a heptathlon with 1.97 high
jump at EC 2014 and improved that to 1.98 at
the Olymoic Games, when she set five events
pbs en route to the gold medal and adding 319
points to her pb. IAAF female Rising Star
award 2016

BOSNIA & HERZEGOVINA

Amel TUKA b. 9 Jan 1991 Kakanj 1.87m 77kg.
AK Zenica. Mechanical engineering graduate.
At 800m: OG: '16- sf; WCh: '15- 3; EC: '12-14-16:
sf/6/4; EU23: '13- 3.
BIH records: 400m (4) 2012-16, 800m (5) 2013-15.
Progress at 800m: 2010- 1:51.04, 2011- 1:51.09,
2012- 1:48.31, 2013- 1:46.29, 2014- 1:46.12, 2015-
1:42.51, 2016- 1:44.54. pbs: 300m 34.46 '16, 400m
46.63 '16, 600m 1:15.21 '16.

BOTSWANA

Governing body: Botswana Athletics
Association, PO Box 2399, Gaborone. Fd 1972.

Nijel AMOS b. 15 Mar 1994 Marobela 1.79m
60kg.
At 800m: OG: '12- 2, '16- h; WCh: '15- sf; CG:
'14- 1; WJ: '12- 1, WY: '11- 5; AfG: '15- 1/2R;
AfCh: 14- 1/1R, '16- 1; CCp: '14- 1; WUG: '13- 1.
Won DL 2014-15.
World junior 800m and two Botswana 800m
records 2012.
Progress at 800m: 2011- 1:47.28, 2012- 1:41.73,
2013- 1:44.71, 2014- 1:42.45, 2015- 1:42.66, 2016-
1:44.66. pbs: 200m 21.34 '15, 400m 45.56 '14,
600m 1:15.0+ 12.

Isaac MAKWALA b. 29 Sep 1986 Tutume 1.83m
79kg.
At (200m)/400m: OG: '12- h, '16- sf; WCh: '09- h,
'13- (h), '15- 5; CG: '10- sf, '14- sf; AfG: '07- sf/1R,
'11- 7, '15- 1/2R; AfCh: '08-10-12-14-16: 2/sf/1/1
& (2),1R/4; CCp: '14- 6/2/1R.
Records: Commonwealth 400m 2015, African

400m (2) 2014-15, Botswana 100m (2) 2013-14, 200m 2013-14, 400m (4) 2014-15.
Progress at 200m, 400m: 2007- 46.48, 2008- 21.20, 45.64A; 2009- 20.73, 45.56; 2010- 21.33, 46.07; 2011- 21.17, 46.27; 2012- 20.87, 45.25; 2013- 20.21, 45.86; 2014- 19.96/19.7A, 44.01; 2015- 20.44A/20.77, 43.72; 2016- 20.42A, 44.85. Pbs: 100m 10.20A/10.14wA '14; 300m 31.5+ '15, 31.91 '16.

Karabo SIBANDA b. 2 Jul 1998 Shashe-Mooke 1.92m 79kg.
At 400m: OG: '16- 5; WJ: '14- sf, 16- 3/2R; WY: '15- 5; AfCh: '16- 2/1R; Af-J: '15- 1/1R; Yth OG: '14- 2; Comm-Y: '15- 1 (1 4x100m).
Progress at 400m: 2014- 46.76, 2015- 45.83, 2016- 44.25. Pb 200m 21.28A '16.

Baboloki THEBE b. 18 Mar 1997 Ramonake 1.86m 77kg.
At (200m)/400m: OG: '16- sf; WJ: '14- (sf), '16- dq sf/2R; AfCh: '16- 1/1R; Yth OG: '14- (2). Won BOT 200m & 400m 2016.
African junior 400m record 2016.
Progress at 200m, 400m: 2014- 20.85A, 2015- 20.56A, 2016- 20.21A, 44.22A/44.69. Pb: 100m 10.29A '15.

Women

Amantle MONTSHO b. 4 Jul 1983 Mabudutsa 1.73m 64kg.
At 400m: OG: '04- h, '08- 6, '12- 4; WCh: '05-07-09-11-13: h/sf/8/1/2; CG: '06-10-14: sf/1/4dq; AfG: '03-07-11: h/1/1; AfCh: '04-06-08-10-12: h/2/1/1/1; WI: '10- 4; CCp: '10- 1/3R. Won DL 2011-13.
Botswana records 100m 2011, 200m 2001-12, 400m 2003-13; African 300m 2010.
Progress at 400m: 2003- 55.03, 2004- 53.77, 2005- 52.59, 2006- 52.14, 2007- 50.90, 2008- 49.83A/50.54, 2009- 49.89, 2010- 49.89, 2011- 49.56, 2012- 49.54, 2013- 49.33, 2014- 50.37. pbs: 100m 11.60 '11, 200m 22.89 '12, 22.88w '11, 300m 36.33i '10.
First Botswana woman to win a major title.
Positive test at 2014 Commonwealth Games, for which she has received a two-year ban.

BRAZIL

Governing body: Confederação Brasileira de Atletismo (CBAt), Rua Jorge Chammas, 310, Vila Mariana, São Paulo, SP- CEP: 04.106-07. Founded 1914 (Confederação 1977).
National Championships first held in 1925.
2016: **Men**: 100m: Vitor Hugo dos Santos 10.21, 200m: Jorge Vides 20.40, 400m: Pedro de Oliveira 45.87, 800m: Cleiton Abrão 1:48.28, 1500m: Carlos de Oliveira Santos 3:45.94, 5000m/3000mSt: Altobelli da Silva 13:56.24/8:29.08, 10000m: Eder da Silva 29:19.36, 110mh: Gabriel Constantino 13.50, 400mh: Marco Teles 49.63, HJ: Guilherme Cobbo 2.18, PV: Thiago Braz da Silva 5.70, LJ: Higor Alves 8.19, TJ: Jean Rodsa 16.38, SP: Darlan Romani 20.21, DT: Mário David Júnior 56.87, HT: Wágner Domingos 74.49, JT: Júlio César de Oliveira 75.99, Dec: Luiz Alberto de Araújo 8070, 20kW: Caio Bonfim 1:23:26, 50kW: Jonathan Rieckmann 4:18:56.
Women: 100m: Rosângela Santos 11.34, 200m: Kauiza Venâncio 22.93, 400m: Geisa Coutinho 51.54, 800m: July da Silva 2:03.94, 1500m/3000mSt: Tatiane da Silva 4:19.05/9:49.22, 5000m: Jenifer Silva 16:32.01, 10000m: Tatiele de Carvalho 34:25.86, 100mh: Maila Machado 13.00, 400mh: Geisa dos Santos 57.43, HJ: Valdiléia Martins 1.85, PV: Fabiana Murer 4.87, LJ: Eliane Martins 6.72w, TJ: Nubia Soares 14.17, SP: Geisa Arcanjo 17.79, DT: Lidiane Cansian 55.35, HT: Mariana Marcelino 64.90, JT: Laila Ferrer e Silva Domingos 59.78, Hep: Vanessa Spínola 6188, 20000mW: Érica de Sena 1:37:38.

Caio BONFIM b. 19 Mar 1991 Brasilia 1.70m 58kg. CASO.
At 20kW: OG: '12- 39, '16- 4 (50kW 9); WCh: '11-18, '13- dq, '15- 6; WCp: '12-14-16: 15/16/8; PAm: 15- 3, SACh: '13- 1; BRA champion 2012-16, IbAm 2016. At 10000mW: WJ: '08- 6, '10- 4; WY: '07- 12.
Brazil 20kW & 50kW records 2016.
Progress at 20kW, 50kW: 2009- 1:30:17.9t, 2010- 1:27:21.3t, 2011- 1:20:58.5t, 2012- 1:21:26, 2013- 1:22:14, 2014- 1:20:28, 2015- 1:20:44, 4:02:20; 2016- 1:19:42, 3:47:02. Pbs: 5000mW 19:47.99 '11, 10000mW 40:23R '16, 40:40.0 '09.
National records at 20k and 50k walks at 2016 Olympics in Rio. His mother, Gianetti de Sena Bonfim (b. 13.3.65), won the 1996 Ibero-American 10,000m walk, and had pbs 5000m: 23:28.9 '96, 10000m: 47:42.0 '96, 20k: 1:41:07 '04.

Augusto Dutra de OLIVEIRA b. 16 Jul 1990 Marília, São Paulo 1.80m 70kg. BM&F Bovespa.
At PV: OG: '16- dnq 22=; WCh: '13- 11, '15- 9=; WI: '14- 7; SAG: '14- 1; SACh: '11- 4; CCp: '14- 4; won SAm-J '2009.
Two South American pole vault records and two indoors 2013.
Progress at PV: 2008- 4.60, 2009- 5.00, 2010- 5.40, 2011- 5.32, 2012- 5.45, 2013- 5.82, 2014- 5.70, 2015- 5.81, 2016- 5.70.

Darlan ROMANI b. 9 Apr 1991 Concórdia 1.88m 140kg.
At SP: OG: '16- 5; WCh: '15: dnq 15; WJ: '10- 7; PAm: '15- 6; SACh: '13- 2, won IbAm 2016, BRA 2012-16.
Nine Brazilian shot records 2012-16.
Progress at SP: 2009- 4.60, 2010- 17.66, 2011- 18.46, 2012- 20.48, 2013- 20.08, 2014- 20.84, 2015- 20.90, 2016- 21.02.

Thiago Braz da SILVA b. 16 Dec 1993 Marília 1.93m 84kg. Orcampi/Unimed.
At PV: OG: '16- 1; WCh: '13-15: dnq 14=/19; WJ: '12- 1; WI: '14- 4; PAm: '15- nh; SACh: '13- 1; Yth Oly: '10- 2, won BRA 2015-16, PAm-J 2011.
Six South American pole vault records 2013-16, indoors (5) 2014-16.

Progress at PV: 2009- 4.60, 2010- 5.10, 2011- 5.31, 2012- 5.55, 2013- 5.83, 2014- 5.76i/5.73, 2015- 5.92, 2016- 6.03.
Married Ana Paula de Oliveira (HJ 1.86 '15) on 13 Dec 2014.

Women
Érica Rocha de SENA b. 3 May 1985 Camaragibe, Pernambuco 1.68m 55kg. Orcampi Unimed.
At 20kW: OG: '16- 7; WCh: '15- 6; WCp: '16- 3; PAm: 15- 2; BRA champion 2011-16. Won IbAm 10000mW 2016.
S.American walk records 20k (5) 2014-16; BRA records: 10000mW 2014, 20kW (5) 2012-16.
Progress at 20kW: 2006- 1:51:45.5t, 2007- 1:44:52.96t, 2008- 1:44:14.6t, 2009- 1:44:27, 2010- 1:38:59, 2011- 1:35:29.6t, 2012- 1:31:53, 2013- 1:32:59, 2014- 1:30:43, 2015- 1:29:37, 2016- 1:27:18.
Pbs: 5000mW 23:10.59 '11, 10000mW 43:31.30 '14.
Married to and coached by Ecuadorian Andrés Chocho (qv). Lives in Cuenca, Ecuador.

BULGARIA
Governing body: Bulgarian Athletics Federation, 75 bl. Vassil Levski, Sofia 1000. Founded 1924.
National Championships first held in 1926 (men), 1938 (women). **2016 Champions: Men**: 100m/200m: Petar Kremenski 10.65/20.95, 400m: Krasimir Braykov 48.61, 800m: Velin Kovalenko 1:55.91, 1500m/5000m: Mitko Tsenov 3:50.98/14:19.82, 10000m/HMar/3000mSt: Yolo Nikolov 30:31.28/69:29/9:40.02, Mar:Ilia Kutsarov 2:28:25, 110mh: Alexander Alexandrov 14.78, 400mh: Nikolai Nikolov 53.88, HJ: Tikhomir Ivanov 2.29, PV: Plamen Piskov & Atanas Petrov 4.80, LJ: Denis Eradiri 7.64, TJ: Momchil Karailiev 16.79, SP: Georgi Ivanov 20.13, DT: Rosen Karamfilov 54.33, HT: Aykhan Apti 65.67, JT: Mark Slavov 65.31, Dec, 20kW: Nikolai Minkov 1:53:25. **Women**: 100m: Inna Eftimova 11.41, 200m: Nadezhda Racheva 23.90, 400m/800m: Katia Khristova 53.66/2:03.32, 1500m/: Dilyana Inkina 4:30.60, 5000m/1000m/HMar: Militsa Mircheva 17:06.63/39:15.33/1:21:23, Mar: Radosveta Simeonova 2:56:29, 3000mSt: Silvia Danekova 9:53.09, 100mh: Elena Miteva 14.09, 400mh: Kristina Borukova 61.26, HJ: Elena Petrova 1.70, PV: Polina Mitova 3.50, LJ: Milena Mitkova 6.03, TJ: Gabriela Petrova 13.65, SP/DT: Renata Petkova 14.20/49.41, HT: Ekaterina Dimova 48.92, JT: Elena Siminkovich 3973, Hep:, 20kW: Radosveta Simeonova 1:56:22.

Women
Mirela DEMIREVA b. 28 Sep 1989 Sofia 1.80m 58kg. Atletik Sf.
At HJ: OG: '16- 2; WCh: '13- dnq 26, '15- 9=; EC: '12- 8, 14- dnq 17, '16- 2=; WJ: '06- dnq 16, '08- 2; EU23: '09- 7, '11- dnq 17; EJ: '07- 3; EI: '13- 7. BUL champion 2007=08, 2011, 2013-14; Balkan 2015-16.

Progress at HJ: 2005- 1.76, 2006- 1.86, 2007- 1.88, 2008- 1.86, 2009- 1.86, 2011- 1.85i/1.84, 2012- 1.95, 2013- 1.92, 2014- 1.94, 2015- 1.94, 2016- 1.97.

Ivet LALOVA-COLLIO b. 18 May 1984 Sofia 1.68m 56kg. née Lalova. IL Sprint Academy.
At 100m/(200m): OG: '04- 4/5, '08- sf/qf, '12- sf/sf, '16- sf/8; WCh: '07- qf, '09- qf/h, '11- 7/sf, '13- sf/sf, '15- sf/7; EC: '10- h, '12- 1/sf, '14- 5/sf, '16- 2/2; WJ: '02- sf; WY: '01- h/sf; EJ: '03- 1/1; EI: '05- (1). At 60m: WI: '12- 8; EI: '13- 3. Won BUL 100m 2004-05, 200m 2004; Balkan 100m 2011, 2013, 2016.
Bulgarian 100m record 2004.
Progress at 100m, 200m: 1998- 13.0, 27.2; 1999- 12.71, 2000- 12.14, 25.24; 2001- 11.72, 24.03; 2002- 11.59, 24.4; 2003- 11.14, 22.87; 2004- 10.77, 22.51/22.36w; 2005- 11.03, 22.76; 2007- 11.26/11.15w, 23.00; 2008- 11.31/11.28w, 23.13; 2009- 11.48/11.24w, 23.60; 2010- 11.43, 23.71; 2011- 10.96, 22.66; 2012- 11.06/11.01w, 22.98; 2013- 11.04, 22.78; 2014- 11.10, 23.17/22.92w; 2015- 11.09, 22.32; 2016- 11.11, 22.42. pbs: 50m 6.23i+ '12, 60m 7.12i '13.
Broke her leg in a warm-up collision with two athletes on 14 Jun 2005. Married Simone Collio (Italy, 60m 6.55 ITA record 2008, 100m 10.06 in 2009) on 20 Sep 2013. Her father Miroslav Lalov had 100m best of 10.4 and won BUL 200m in 1966, mother Liliya was a pentathlete.

Gabriela PETROVA b. 29 Jun 1992 Haskovo 1.67m 61kg. Lokomtiv Plovdiv.
At SP: OG: '16- dnq 22; WCh: '15- 4; EC: '14- 5, '16- dnq 20; WJ: '10- dnq 17; WY: '09- dnq 18; EU23: '13- 1; EJ: '11- 5; EI: '15- 2; BUL champion 2010, 2013, 2016.
Progress at LJ: 2007- 12.43, 2008- 12.72i, 2009- 12.64, 2010- 13.35, 2011- 13.27/13.44w, 2012- 13.45, 2013- 14.14i/13.92/13.96w, 2014- 14.13, 2015- 14.66/14.85w, 2016- 14.32i/13.92. pb LJ 6.46 '15.

BURUNDI
Francine NIYONSABA b. 5 May 1993 Nkanda Bweru, Ruyiqi 1.61m 56kg.
At 800m: OG: '12- 5, '16- 2; AfCh: '12- 1; WI: '16- 1. Six Burundi 800m records 2012-16.
Progress at 800m: 2012- 1:56.59, 2013- 1:56.72, 2015- 1:57.62, 2016- 1:56.24. pbs: 400m 54.3 '13, 600m 1:26.8+ '16.
Won World title on her indoor debut in 2016 and first Olympic medal for a woman from Burundi.

CANADA
Governing body: Athletics Canada, Suite B1-110, 2445 S-Laurent Drive, Ottawa, Ontario K1G 6C3. Formed as Canadian AAU in 1884.
National Championships first held in 1884 (men), 1925 (women). **2016 Champions: Men**: 100m: Andre De Grasse 9.99, 200m: Brendon Rodney 19.96, 400m: Nathan George 45.94, 800m: Brandon McBride 1:45.25, 1500m: Charles

Philibert-Thiboutot 3:55.75, 5000m: Mohammed Ahmed 14:00.93, 10000m/Mar: Eric Gillis 29:00.93/2:13:44, HMar: Thomas Toth 67:27, 3000mSt: Taylor Milne 8:36.50; 110mh: Johnathan Cabral 13.63, 400mh: Jhalil Parris 51.49, HJ: Derek Drouin 2.30, PV: Aaron Unterberger 5.20, LJ: Jharyl Bowry 7.58, TJ: Aaron Hernandez 16.26, SP: Tim Nedow 20.28, DT: Marc-Antoine Dugas 53.65, HT: Charles Nguyen 59.70, JT: Evan Karakolis 71.77, 10,000mW: Mathieu Bilodeau 43:11.22. **Women**: 100m/200m: Crystal Emmanuel 11.26/22.83w, 400m: Carline Muir 51.79, 800m: Melisa Bishop 1:59.32, 1500m: Gabriella Stafford 4:18.51, 5000m: Andrea Seccafien 16:00.42, 10000m: Rachel Hannah 33:05.49, HMar: Emily Setlack 75:45, Mar: Krista Duchene 2:34:02, 3000mSt: Erin Teschuk 9:50.99, 100mh: Phylicia George 12.88, 400mh: Noelle Montcalm 55.83, HJ: Alyx Treasure 1.88, PV: Alysha Newman 4.40, LJ: Christabel Nettey 6.62w, TJ: Caroline Ehrhardt 12.97, SP: Brittany Crew 18.06, DT: Agnes Esser 50.32, HT: Heather Steacy 69.71, JT: Liz Gleadle 59.36, 10,000mW: Katelynn Ramage 50:26.65.

Mohammed AHMED b. 5 Jan 1991 Mogadishu, Somalia 1.82m 56kg. Niagara Olympic Club.
At (5000m)/10000m: OG: '12- 18, '16- 4/32; WCh: '13- 9, '15- (12); CG: '14- 5/6; PAm: '15- 1; WJ: '08- 9, '10- 4; PAm-J: '09- (1). At 3000m: WI: '16- 9. Won CAN 5000m 2016, 10000m 2012.
Canadian 10000m records 2015 & 2016.
Progress at 5000m, 10000m: 2008- 14:26.71, 30:03.53; 2009- 14:11.84, 2010- 14:02.04, 28:57.44; 2011- 13:34.23, 29:08.29; 2012- 13:41.06, 27:34.64, 2013- 13:40.43i, 27:35.76; 2014- 13:18.88, 28:02.96; 2015- 13:10.00, 27:46.90; 2016- 13:01.74, 29:32.84; 2017- 13:04.60i. pbs: 1500m 3:40.18 '15, 3000m 7:40.11i '16, 2M 8:13.16i '17.
Moved to Canada at age 11. Younger twin brother Ibrahim 25 WJ 10000m 2012.

Shawnacy BARBER b. 27 May 1994 Las Cruces, New Mexico, USA 1.90m 82kg. Student at Akron University, USA.
At PV: OG: '16- 10; WCh: '13- dnq 27, '15- 1; CG: '14- 3; WJ: '12- 3; PAm: '15- 1; PAm-J: 13- 1; WI: '16- 4=; Won CAN 2013-14, 2016; NCAA 2015.
Pole vault records: four Canadian 2013-15, indoors (7) 2014-16, N.American indoor 2016.
Progress at PV: 2010- 4.42, 2011- 5.03, 2012- 5.57, 2013- 5.71, 2014- 5.75Ai/5.65, 2015- 5.93, 2016- 6.00Ai/5.91.
He lost his Canadian title in 2016 following a positive test for cocaine (getting a Public Warning from the IAAF), but was cleared to compete at the Olympic Games. His father George vaulted 5.29 in 1985 and in 1993 competed for Canada at the Worlds (nh) and was Canadian champion.

Andre DE GRASSE b. 10 Nov 1994 Scarborough, Ontario 1.80m 73kg.University of Southern California (sociology).
At (100m)/200m: OG: '16- 3/2/3R; WCh: '15- (3=)/3R; CG: '14- sf; PAm: '15- 1/1; PAm-J: '13- 2/3. Won NCAA 100m & 200m 2015, CAN 100m 2015-16.
Four Canadian 200m records 2015-16.
Progress at 100m, 200m: 2012- 10.59, 2013- 10.25/9.96w, 20.74A/20.57w; 2014- 10.15/10.03w, 20.38; 2015- 9.92/9.75w, 19.88/19.58w; 2016- 9.91, 19.80. pbs: 55m 6.21i '13, 60m 6.60i '15, 400m 47.93 '14.
Father came from Barbados and mother from Trinidad. IAAF male Rising Star award 2016.

Derek DROUIN b. 6 Mar 1990 Sarnia, Ontario 1.95m 80kg. Student of exercise science at Indiana University.
At HJ: OG: '12- 3=, '16- 1; WCh: '13- 3, '15- 1; CG: '14- 1; WY: '07- 10; PAm: '15- 1; CCp: '14- 4. Won PAmJ 2009, CAN 2012-16, NCAA 2013, Franc G 2013.
Commonwealth high jump record 2014, four Canadian high jump records 2013-14.
Progress at HJ: 2007- 2.07, 2008- 2.11, 2009- 2.27, 2010- 2.28i/2.26, 2011- 2.33i/2.23, 2012- 2.31, 2013- 2.38, 2014- 2.40, 2015- 2.37, 2016- 2.38, 2017- 2.33i. pbs: 60mh 7.98i '12, 1000m 2:45.06i '13, 110mh 14.04 '13, PV 4.15i '13. 3.65 '11; LJ 7.20i '13, 6.85 '11; Hep 5817i '13.
Sister Jillian (b. 30 Sep 1986) heptathlon pb 5972w to win Pan-Am Cup 2014; 6th CG 2010.

Evan DUNFEE b. 28 Sep 1990 Richmond, BC 1.86m 68kg. Was at University of British Columbia.
At (20kW)/50kW: OG: '16- 10/4; WCh: '13- 36, '15- 12/12; CG: '10- (6); PAm: '15- (1), WCp: '14- (11); won NACAC 2012. At 10000mW: WJ: '08- 10; WY: '07- 23. CAN champion 10000mW 2012, 2015, 20kW 2010-11, 2014.
N.American records: 20k & 20,000m 2014, 50kW (2) 2015-16.
Progress at 50kW: 2013- 3:59:28, 2014- 3:58:34, 2015- 3:43:45, 2016- 3:41:38. pbs: 5000mW 18:53.06 '14, 10000mW 39:21.30 '16, 20kW 1:20:13 '14, 30kW 2:11:54 '14; HMar 70:44 '16.

Iñaki GÓMEZ Gorostieta b. 16 Jan 1988 Mexico City 1.72m 58kg. University of British Columbia.
At 20kW: OG: '12- 13, '16- 12; WCh: '13- 8, '15-14; CG: '10- 5; PAm: '15- 2; WCp: '12- 14-16: 12/12/7; WUG: '11/13- 5. At 10000mW: PAM-J: 07- 7. Won CAN 10000mW 2013
North American 20k walk records 2012 & 2016.
Progress at 20kW: 2008- 1:31:53, 2009- 1:29:55, 2010- 1:27:09, 2011- 1:22:06, 2012- 1:20:58, 2013- 1:22:21, 2014- 1:20:18, 2015- 1:21:55, 2016- 1:19:20. Pbs: 1MW 5:46.40 '12, 5000mW 18:45.64 '14, 10,000mW 40:01.0 '13, 50kW 4:04:12 '15.
Has lived in Vancouver from the age of 11.

Matthew **HUGHES** b. 3 Aug 1989 Oshawa, Ontario 1.80m 64kg. Was at University of Louisville, USA.

At 3000mSt: OG: '16- 10, WCh: '11- h, '13- 6, '15- 8; CG: '14- 4; WJ: '08- h; PAm: '15- 1; CCp: '14- 7; CAN champion 2013-15.
Canadian 3000m steeplechase record 2013.
Progress at 3000mSt: 2007- 9:20.61, 2008- 8:59.83, 2009- 8:47.36, 2010- 8:34.18, 2011- 8:24.87, 2012- 8:31.77, 2013- 8:11.64, 2014- 8:12.81, 2015- 8:18.63, 2016- 8:20.63. pbs: 1500m 3:41.49 '15, 1M 4:01.98 '16, 3000m 7:51.87i '15, 8:11.64 '13; 5000m 13:19.56 '15.

Tim NEDOW b. 16 Oct 1990 Brockville 1.98m 125kg. Ottawa Lions. Was at University of Tulsa and DePaul University, USA.
At SP: OG: '16- dnq 16; WCh: '13/15- dnq 24/20; CG: '14- 3; WI: '16- 7; PAm: '15- 2 (6 DT); PAm-J: '09- 3. Won CAN SP 2013-16, DT 2012-15
Progress at SP: 2010- 17.90, 2011- 19.18i/18.84, 2012- 20.51i/20.21, 2013- 20.74, 2014- 20.98, 2015- 20.78, 2016- 21.33i/20.88. pb DT 61.49 '15.

Benjamin THORNE b. 19 Mar 1993 Kitimat 1.80m 57kg. Racewalk West. University of British Columbia.
At 20kW: OG: '16- 27; WCh: '13- 20, '15- 5; WCp: '14- 13, '16- 5; WUG: 15- 2; At 10000mW: WJ: '12- dq. Won CAN 10kW 2011, 20kW 2012
North American 20k walk record 2015.
Progress at 20kW: 2012- 1:31:26, 2013- 1:24:26, 2014- 1:20:19, 2015- 1:19:57, 2016- 1:19:55. Pbs 5000mW 19:00.92 '14, 10000mW 40:26.0A '12.

Damian WARNER b. 4 Nov 1989 London, Ontario 1.85m 83kg. LWTF.
At Dec: OG: '12- 5, '16- 3; WCh: '11- 18, '13- 3, '15- 2; CG: '14- 1; PAm: '15- 1. Won Canadian 110mh 2014-15, Dec 2011-13. At Hep: WI: '14- 7.
Two Canadian decathlon records 2015.
Progress at Dec: 2010- 7449, 2011- 8102A/7832, 2012- 8442, 2013- 8512, 2014- 8282, 2015- 8695, 2016- 8666. pbs: 60m 6.74i '10, 100m 10.15/10.09w '16, 200m 20.96 '13, 400m 46.36i '15, 46.54 '16, 1000m 2:37.98i '14, 1500m 4:24.73 '15, 60mh 7.63i '16, 110mh 13.27 '15, HJ 2.09 '13, PV 4.90 '16, LJ 8.04 '16, TJ 14.75w '08, SP 14.44 '15, DT 50.26 '16, JT 64.67 '13, Hep: 6129 14.
Made 340 points improvement on pb when 5th at 2012 Olympics, setting six pbs, and 70 more at 2013 Worlds, with three pbs. Won Götzis & Talence 2013. Ran fastest ever in decathlons: 110mh 13.44 '15 and 100m 10.15 '16.

Women

Melissa BISHOP b. 5 Aug 1988 Eganville, Ontario 1.73m 57kg. Was at University of Windsor.
At 800m: OG: '12- h, '16- 4; WCh: '13- h, '15- 2; CG: '14- 8; PAm: '15- 1; CAN champion 2013-14, 2016. At 400m: WY: '05- h.
Two Canadian 800m records 2015-16.
Progress at 800m: 2007- 2:10.51 2008- 2:10.12, 2009- 2:06.77, 2010- 2:04.12, 2011- 2:02.69, 2012- 1:59.82, 2013- 1:59.76, 2014- 1:59.70, 2015- 1:57.52, 2016- 1:57.02. pbs: 400m 56.27 '10, 600m 1:27.2+ '16, 1000m 2:38.75 '14, 1500m 4:09.58 '16.

Sultana FRIZELL b. 24 Oct 1984 Perth, Ontario 1.83m 110kg. Was at University of Georgia.
At HT: OG: '08/12- dnq 31/23; WCh: '09- 10, '13/15- dnq 16/13; CG: '10- 1, '14- 1; PAm: '07-11- 15: 7/2/3; PAm-J: '03- 4; CCp: '14- 5; Canadian champion 2007-08, 2010, 2013-15.
Five Commonwealth hammer records 2009-14, North American 2012 & 2014, eight Canadian 2008-14 & 5 Wt 2017.
Progress at HT: 2002- 54.75, 2003- 57.95, 2004- 63.36, 2005- 66.42, 2006- 63.39, 2007- 67.92, 2008- 70.94, 2009- 72.07, 2010- 72.24, 2011- 71.46, 2012- 75.04, 2013- 71.57, 2014- 75.73, 2015- 73.66, 2016- 69.14. pbs: SP 15.82 '06, Wt 23.61i '17, JT 46.58 '04.

Phylicia GEORGE b. 16 Nov 1987 Toronto 1.78m 65kg. Was at University of Connecticut, USA.
At 100mh: OG: '12- 5, '16- 8; WCh: '11- 6, '15- sf; PAm: '15- 5; Canadian champion 2014. At 200m: WJ: 06- h.
Progress at 100mh: 2006- 14.53w, 2007- 14.44w, 2008- 13.71/13.62w, 2009- 13.74, 2010- 13.39, 2011- 12.73, 2012- 12.65, 2013- 13.75, 2014- 13.08, 2015- 12.94, 2016- 12.74/12.67w. pbs: 60m 7.35i '12, 100m 11.25 '12, 200m 23.10 '11, 50mh 6.90i '12, 55mh 7.69i '10, 60mh 8.03i '12.

Liz GLEADLE b. 5 Dec 1988 Vancouver 1.83m 95kg. Chinooks.
At JT: OG: '12- 12, '16- dnq 16; WCh: '15- 11; CG: '14- 5; PAm: '15- 1; WJ: '06- 12; WY: '05- 5; CCp: '14- 3. Canadian champion 2008-09, 2012, 2014- 16.
Five Canadian javelin records 2009-15.
Progress at JT: 2005- 50.53, 2006- 50.86, 2007- 52.36, 2008- 54.13, 2009- 58.21, 2010- 57.84, 2011- 58.40, 2012- 61.15, 2013- 54.13, 2014- 64.50, 2015- 64.83, 2016- 62.59.

Christabel NETTEY b. 2 Jun 1991 Brampton, Ontario 1.62m 59kg. Was at Arizona State University (justice studies).
At LJ: OG: '16- dnq 20; WCh: '13- dnq 19, '15- 4; CG: '14- 3; WY: '07- dnq 14 (8 100mh); PAm: '15- 1; PAm-J: '09- 2; CCp: '14- 4. At 100mh: WY: '07- 8 (3 MedR). Won CAN LJ 2013-16, NACAC 2012
Three Canadian long jump records 2015, four indoor 2014-15.
Progress at LJ: 2006- 6.12, 2007- 6.14, 2008- 6.21, 2009- 6.05/6.10w, 2010- 6.42i/6.28, 2011- 6.49/ 6.55i, 2012- 6.58, 2013- 6.75, 2014- 6.73, 2015- 6.99, 2016- 6.75/6.88w. pbs: 100m 12.14 '06, 60mh 8.25i '13, 100mh 13.42 '13, HJ 1.66 '11, TJ 12.80 '12, 12.90w '07; SP 12.16 '11, Hep 5068 '11.
Older sister Sabrina has LJ pbs 6.32i '14, 6.26 '12.

CHILE

Governing body: Federación Atlética de Chile, Calle Santo Toribio No 660, Ñuñoa, Santiago de Chile. Founded 1914.

2016 Champions: Men: 100m: Rodrigo Anguita 10.83, 200m: Sergio Germain 21.64, 400m: Sergio Aldea 46.49, 800m: Patrick Bravo 1:50.76, 1500m: Iván López 3:52.3, 5000m: Ariel Méndez 14:35.45, 10000m: Patrick Uribe 30:41.5, Mar: Víctor Aravena 2:16:10, 3000mSt: Roberto Tello 8:56.9, 110mh: Patricio Colarte 14.44, 400mh: Alfredo Sepúlveda 51.46, HJ: Rodolfo Arriagada 1.95, LJ: Daniel Pineda 7.50, TJ: Randy Hood 14.78, SP: Matías López 18.26, DT: Rodrigo Cárdenas 49.87, HT: Roberto Sáez 65.50, JT: Santiago de la Fuente 67.69, 10000mW: Yerko Araya 42:06.38. Women: 100m: Viviana Olivares 11.95, 200m: Paula Goñi 24.77, 400m: María Fernanda Mackenna 54.94, 800m: Carmen Mansilla 2:09.89, 1500m: Javiera Faletto 4:30.8, 5000m/10000m: Jennifer González 17:26.58/36:29.5, Mar: Clara Morales 2:46:32, 3000mSt: Margareta Masías 11:17.6, 100mh: María Ignacia Eguiguren 14.54, 400mh: María Echeverría 63.76, HJ: Marta Herrera 1.65, PV: Victoria Fernández 3.85, LJ: Macarena Reyes 6.07, TJ: Giscelia Aravena 11.28, SP: Ivanna Gallardo 16.35, DT: Karen Gallardo 56.97, HT: Constanza Avila 47.36, JT: Valentina Paz Salazar 50.80, Hep: Javiera Brahm 4852, 10000mW: Anita Rico 54:20.83

CHINA

Governing body: Athletic Association of the People's Republic of China, 2 Tiyuguan Road, Beijing 100763.
National Championships first held in 1910 (men), 1959 (women). **2016 Champions: Men**: 100m: Xu Zhouzheng 10.29, 200m: Liang Jinsheng 20.73, 400m: Guo Zhongze 46.16, 800m: Ma Junyi 1:49.38, 1500m: Gao Tongyou 3:44.38, 5000m: Sun Zhenlei 13:54.20, 10000m: Sun Jiahui 29:01.81, HMar: Jiang Junjie 67:53, Mar: Xu Wang 2:19:01, 3000mSt: Wang Qinglin 8:59.39, 110mh: Xie Wenjun 13.59, 400mh: Shang Shuo 49.97, HJ: Pai Long 2.28, PV: Yao Jie 5.65, LJ: Li Jinzhe 8.04, TJ: Zhu Yaming 16.97, SP: Liu Yang 19.68, DT: Wu Jian 59.14, HT: Wang Shizhu 72.25, JT: Zhao Qinggang 80.42, Dec: Hu Yufei 7616. **Women**: 100m/200m: Wei Yongli 11.44/23.55, 400m: Yang Huizhen 52.57, 800m/1500m: Zheng Xiaoqian 2:07.22/4:24.28, 5000m: Ding Changqin 15:40.33, 10000m: Wang Xueqin 33:11.55, HMar: Zhang Deshun 72:17, Mar: Cao Mojie 2:32:33, 3000mSt: Zhong Xiaoqian 10:05.72, 100mh: Kang Ya 13.32, 400mh: Huang Yan 56.48, HJ: Zheng Xingjuan 1.88, PV: Li Ling 4.40, LJ: Lu Minjia 6.45, TJ: Wang Wupin 13.73, SP: Gong Lijiao 18.94, DT: Yang Fei 58.43, HT: Wang Zheng 69.17, JT: Li Lingwei 61.56, Hep: Wang Qingling 5604.

CAI Zelin b. 11 Apr 1991 Dali, Yunnan 1.72m 55kg.
At 20kW: OG: '12- 4, '16- 2; WCh: '13- 26, '15- 5; AsiC: '14- 4; WCp: '14- 2, '16- 2. At 10000mW: WJ: '10- 2; WCp: '10- 2J. CHN 20kW champion 2012.

Progress at 20kW: 2010- 1:22:28, 2011- 1:21:07, 2012- 1:18:47, 2013- 1:18:55, 2014- 1:18:52, 2015- 1:19:45, 2016- 1:19:48, 2016- 1:19:26. Pbs: 5000mW 19:35.00 '14, 10,000mW 38:59.98 '12, 30kW 2:45:13 '09.

CAO SHUO b. 8 Oct 1991 Baoding, Hebei 1.80m 77kg.
At TJ: OG: '12- dnq 20, '16- 4; WCh: '15- dnq 15; AsiG: '10- 3, '14- 1; AsiC: '13- 1; CCp: '14- 5; WI: '14- 7. Won AsoJ 2010, CHN 2009, 2012-13, NG 2013. World youth triple jump record 2009.
Progress at TJ: 2007- 15.82, 2008- 16.42, 2009- 17.13, 2010- 16.85, 2011- 16.86, 2012- 17.35, 2013- 17.26, 2014- 17.30, 2015- 16.77/16.95w, 2016- 17.13.

CHEN Ding b. 5 Aug 1992 Dali, Yunnan 1.80m 62kg. Guangdong.
At 20kW: OG: '12- 1, '16- 39; WCh: '13- 2, '15- 9; WCp: '10- 5, '12- 7. At 10000mW: WJ: '08- 2; WCp: '08- 2J.
World youth 10,000m walk record 2008.
Progress at 20kW: 2008- 1:20:16, 2009- 1:21:21, 2010- 1:21:59, 2011- 1:18:52, 2012- 1:17:40, 2013- 1:21:09, 2014- 1:20:48, 2015- 1:18:44, 2016- 1:19:32. Pbs: 10kW 38:23 '10, 39:47.20t '08; 30kW 2:12:16 '10.

DONG Bin b. 22 Nov 1988 Changshan. 1.79m 67kg.
At TJ: OG: '12- 10, '16- 3; WCh: '13- 9, '15- dnq 18; WJ: '06- dnq 14; AsiG: '14- 2; AsiC: '11- 5, '15- 4; WI: '12- 8, '16- 1. Won Asian indoors 2010, 2012 Asian indoor triple jump record 2016.
Progress at TJ: 2006- 16.22, 2007- 16.25, 2008- 16.54, 2009- 16.89i/16.65, 2010- 16.86, 2011- 17.01i/16.86, 2012- 17.38, 2013- 17.16i/16.98, 2014- 16.95, 2015- 17.12/17.21w, 2016- 17.58. pb LJ 7.09 '07, 7.32w '06.

GAO Xinglong b. 12 Mar 1994 Heilongjiang Prov 1.81m 65kg.
At LJ: OG: '16- dnq nj; WCh: '15- 4; AsiG: '14- 3; AsiC: '15- 1. Won CHN 2014-15.
Progress at LJ: 2012- 7.27, 2013- 8.02i/7.98, 2014- 8.18/8.21w, 2015- 8.34, 2016- 8.23.

HAN Yucheng b. 16 Dec 1978 Fuxin 1.77m 59kg. Liaoning.
At 20kW (50kW): OG: '04- 40 (dnf), '16- (47); WCh: '05- (dnf), '07- 29; WCp: '04- 4, '06- 2; AsiG: '06- 1; AsiC: '03- 1. Won CHN 20kW 2004, 50kW 2004-05.
Asian 50km records 2004 & 2005.
Progress at 20kW, 50kW: 2003- 1:20:00, 3:54:45; 2004- 1:19:30, 3:39:10; 2005- 1:18:31, 3:36:20; 2006- 1:18:35, 2007- 1:19:15, 4:03:53; 2008- 1:21:46, 2009- 1:22:37, 4:01:33; 2010- 1:24:51, 2011- 1:29:47, 2012- 1:24:51, 2015- 3:55:44, 2016- 3:42:43. pbs: 10000mW 39:39.12 '06, 30kW 2:12:39 '05.

HUANG Changzhou b. 20 Aug 1994 Sichuan Prov 1.83m 64kg.
At LJ: OG: '16- 11; AsiC: '15- dnq; WI: '16- 3
Progress at LJ: 2012- 7.79, 2013- 7.97, 2014- 8.12, 2015- 8.17, 2016- 8.21i/8.12.

LI Jinzhe b. 1 Sep 1989 Beijing 1.88m 64kg.
At LJ: OG: '12- dnq 20; WCh: '09- dnq 13, '13- 12, '15- 5; WI: '14- 2; AsiG: '14- 1; AsiC: '07-09-11: 8/1/5; CCp: '10- 4, '14- 4; won E.Asian 2009, Asian indoors 2012, CHN 2009, 2016; CHN NG 2013.
Chinese long jump record 2014.
Progress at LJ: 2006- 7.19i, 2007- 7.85, 2008- 7.79, 2009- 8.18, 2010- 8.12/8.29w, 2011- 8.02, 2012- 8.25, 2013- 8.34, 2014- 8.47, 2015- 8.26, 2016- 8.04.

SU Bingtian b. 29 Aug 1989 Zhongshan, Guangdong Prov. 1.85m 65kg. Guandong.
At 100m: OG: '12- sf, '16- sf/4R; WCh: '13- sf, '15- 9/2R; AsiG: '14- 2/1R; AsiC: '13- 1; WUG: '11- 3. Won Chinese 100m 2009, 2011-13, E.Asian G 2013. At 60m: WI: '14- 4, '16- 5.
Records: Asian 4x100m 2016, indoor 60m 2016, Chinese 100m (3) 2011-15 and 200m 2013.
Progress at 100m: 2006- 10.59, 2007- 10.45, 2008- 10.41, 2009- 10.28, 2010- 10.32, 2011- 10.16, 2012- 10.19/10.04w, 2013- 10.06, 2014- 10.10, 2015- 9.99, 2016- 10.08/10.04w. pbs: 60m 6.50i '16, 200m 21.23 '08.

WANG Jianan b. 27 Aug 1996 Shenyang, Liaoning prov. 1.78m 61kg.
At LJ: OG: '16- 5; WCh: '13- dnq 23, '15- 3; WJ: '14- 1; AsiC: '13- 1; WI '16- 8.
Asian junior long jump record 2015.
Progress at LJ: 2012- 8.04, 2013- 7.95, 2014- 8.10, 2015- 8.25, 2016- 8.24. pbs: 60m 6.89i '12, 100m 10.88 '12, 60mh 8.46i '12, HJ 1.94 '12, PV 5.00 '12, Dec 7063 '12.
At 18 in 2015 he became the youngest ever male World Champs medallist at a field event.

WANG Zhen b. 24 Aug 1991 Changzhou 1.80m 62kg. Heilongjiang.
At 20kW: OG: '12- 3, '16- 1; WCh: 11- 2, '13- dq, '15- 2; AsiG: '14- 1; WCp: '12-14-16: 1/6/1; CHN champion 2011, 2015; NG 2013. Won World Race Walking Challenge 2016 & Final 10k 2010-12.
Walks records: World junior 10k 2010, Asian 20k 2012, 10,000m track 2012 & 2015.
Progress at 20kW: 2008- 1:28:01, 2009- 1:22:10, 2010- 1:20:42, 2011- 1:18:30, 2012- 1:17:36, 2013- 1:19:08, 2014- 1:19:40. 2015- 1:18:00, 2016- 1:19:12. Pbs: 3000mW 11:23.2 14, 5000mW 18:49.10 '14, 10kW 37:44 '10, 38:23.73 '15; 30kW 2:08:46 '08, 50kW 3:53:00 '09.
Won IAAF Race Walking Challenge 2016.

WANG Zhendong b. 11 Jan 1991 1.80m 65kg.
At 50kW: OG: '16- 11; AsiC: '14- 3.
Progress at 50kW: 2011- 4:16:44, 2012- 3:57:47, 2013- 4:09:17, 2014- 3:47:18, 2016- 3:41:02. Pbs: 5000mW 20:06.65 '14, 20kW 1:21:55 '13, 30kW 2:12:36 '10.

XIE Wenjun b. 11 Jul 1990 Shanghai 1.88m 77kg, Shanghai
At 110mh: OG: '12- sf, '16- h; WCh: '13- h, '15- sf AsiG: '14- 1; AsiC: '15- 1; CCp: '14- 4; Won CHN 2012, 2015-16; NG 2013.

Progress at 110mh: 2007- 14.09, 2008- 13.47, 2009- 13.53, 2010- 13.47, 2011- 13.45, 2012- 13.34, 2013- 13.28, 2014- 13.23, 2015- 13.36, 2016- 13.34. pbs: 100m 11.04 '06, 60mh 7.60i '13.

XUE Changrui b. 31 May 1991 Shandong prov. 1.83m 60kg
At PV: OG: '16- 6; WCh: '13- 12; WI: '14- 5, AsiG: '14- 1; AsiC: '13- 1; CCp: '14- 2; Won CHN NG 2013. Chinese pole vault record 2014.
Progress at PV: 2011- 5.30, 2012- 5.60, 2013- 5.75i/5.65, 2014- 5.80, 2015- 5.40, 2016- 5.81i/5.75. pb LJ 7.15 '08

YU Wei b. 11 Sep 1987 1.80m 60kg. Shandong.
At 50kW: OG: '16- 5; WCh: '15- 7. At 20kW: AsiC: '09- 2.
Progress at 50kW: 2008- 4:03:54, 2009- 3:58:00, 2010- 3:58:23, 2011- 3:51:46, 2014- 4:00:57, 2015- 3:45:21, 2016- 3:42:54. Pbs: 10,000mW 40:30.50 '12, 20kW 1:19:07 '13.

ZHANG Guowei b. 4 Jun 1991 Binzhon, Shandong prov. 2.00m 77kg.
At HJ: OG: '12/16- dnq 21=/25=; WCh: '11- 10, '13- 9, '15- 2=; WI: '12-14-16: 4=/7/6, AsiG: '14- 2; AsiC: '11- 8; CCp: '14- 6. CHN champion 2011.
Progress at HJ: 2010- 2.23, 2011- 2.31, 2012- 2.31, 2013- 2.32i/2.29, 2014- 2.34, 2015- 2.38, 2016- 2.33.

ZHANG Lin b. 11 Nov 1993 1.75m 55kg.
At 50kW: WCh: '15- 6; AsiC: '14- 6; WCp: '14- 7.
Progress at 50kW: 2013- 4:07:28, 2014- 3:48:49, 2015- 3:44:39, 2016- 3:48:23. Pbs: 10,000mW 40:36.84 '15, 20kW 1:28:39 '12, 30kW 2:14:24 '15, 35kW 2:36:18 '15.

Women

CHEN Yang b. 10 Jul 1991 1.80m 97kg. Hebei.
At DT: OG: '16- 7.
Progress at DT: 51.05- 53.79, 2011- 51.10, 2012- 53.10, 2013- 52.10, 2014- 58.53, 2015- 61.16, 2016- 63.61.

FENG Bin b. 3 Apr 1994 1.84m 95kg. Shandong.
At DT: OG: '16- 8; WY: '11- 4. W.MilG 2015.
Progress at DT: 2010- 53.77, 2011- 55.94, 2012- 55.62, 2013- 58.14, 2014- 59.73, 2015- 62.07, 2016- 65.14.

GAO Yang b. 1 Mar 1993. 1.78m 110kg. Army.
At SP: OG: '16- dnq 33; WCh: '15- 5; WJ: '12- 2; AsiC: '13- 3, '15- 2; WI: '16- 8. Won W.MilG 2015.
Progress at SP: 2012- 17.07, 2013- 17.76, 2014- 17.52, 2015- 19.04, 2016- 19.20.

GONG Lijiao b. 24 Jan 1989 Luquan, Hebei Prov. 1.74m 110kg. Hebei.
At SP: OG: '08- 3, '12- 2, '16- 4; WCh: '07-09-11-13-15: 7/3/4/3/2; WI: '10- 8, '14- 3; AsiG: '10- 2, '14- 1; AsiC: '09- 1; CCp: '10- 3, '14- 3. Chinese champion 2007-12, 2014, 2016; NG 2009, 2013; Asian indoor 2008.
Progress at SP: 2005- 15.41i, 2006- 17.92, 2007- 19.13, 2008- 19.46, 2009- 20.35, 2010- 20.13, 2011- 20.11, 2012- 20.22, 2013- 20.12, 2014- 19.65, 2015-

CHINA – COLOMBIA

20.34, 2016- 20.43. pb JT 53.94 '07.
LI Ling b. 6 Jul 1989 Zhubo, Henan Province 1.80m 65kg. Zhejiang
At PV: OG: '08/12/16- dnq 27=/30/16; WCh: '09-11-13-15: dnq 18/dnq 29/11/9; WJ: '06- nh; AsiG: '10- 2, '14- 1; AsiC: '11-13-15: 2/1/1; CCp: '14- 1; WUG: '15- 1. Won CHN 2008-09, 2011-13, 2015-16; NG 2013, Asian Indoors 2009, 2012, 2016.
Asian PV records: 2013 & 2015, indoor (4) 2015-16, junior 2008.
Progress at PV: 2005- 3.90i/3.70, 2006- 4.15, 2007- 4.30, 2008- 4.45, 2009- 4.40, 2010- 4.45i/4.40, 2011- 4.40, 2012- 4.50i/4.40, 2013- 4.65, 2014- 4.61, 2015- 4.66, 2016- 4.70.

LI Lingwei b. 26 Jan 1989 Yantai 1.72m 75kg.
At JT: OG: '12/16- dnq 30/15; WCh: '13- 8, '15- 5; WJ: '06- 8, '08- 2; AsiG: '10- 3, '14- 2; AsiC: '09- 2, '13- 1; won Asi-J 2008, CHN 2013, 2015-16; NG 2013.
Asian javelin record 2012.
Progress at JT: 2002- 49.60, 2003- 55.38, 2004- 51.19, 2005- 58.87, 2006- 58.87, 2007- 57.88, 2008- 59.25, 2009- 57.82, 2010- 60.60, 2011- 57.39, 2012- 65.11, 2013- 63.06, 2014- 62.56, 2015- 65.07, 2016- 62.89.

LIU Hong b. 12 May 1987 Anfu, Jiangxi Prov. 1.61m 48kg. Guangdong.
At 20kW: OG: '08- 4, '12- 3, '16- 1; WCh: '07-09-11-13-15: 19/2/1/3/1; WCp: '06-14-16: 6/2/dq1; AsiG: '06- 1, '10- 1; won CHN 2010-11, NG 2009.
At 10000mW: WJ: '06- 1; won IAAF Race Walking Challenge 10k 2012, 2014 (2nd 2011).
Walk records: World 20k 2015, Asian 5000m & 20k 2012.
Progress at 20kW: 2004- 1:35:04, 2005- 1:29:39, 2006- 1:28:26, 2007- 1:29:41, 2008- 1:27:17, 2009- 1:28:11, 2010- 1:30:06, 2011- 1:27:17, 2012- 1:25:46, 2013- 1:27:06, 2014- 1:26:58, 2015- 1:24:38, 2016- 1:25:56. pbs: 3000mW 12:18.18 '05, 5000mW 20:34.76 '12, 10kW 42:30R '10, 43:16.68t '12.
Running: Mar 2:51:23 '15.
Won IAAF Race Walking Challenge 2011-12 and 2015. Failed drugs test ahen 'winning; the World Cup 20k race in 2016 and received a three-months ban.

LU Huihui b. 26 Jun 1989 Huwan, Henan 1.71m 68kg.
At JT: OG: '12- 5, '16- 7; WCh: '15- 2.
Asian javelin records 2012 & 2015.
Progress at JT: 2005- 49.62, 2006- 49.96, 2010- 55.35, 2011- 58.72, 2012- 64.95, 2013- 64.48/65.62dq, 2015- 66.13, 2016- 64.03.
One-year drugs ban for positive test 27 Apr 2013.

LU Xiuzhi b. 26 Oct 1993 Chuzhou 1.67m 52kg.
At 20kW: OG: '12- 5, '16- 3; WCh: '15- 2; AsiG: '14- 1; WCp: '12-14-16: 4/6/5, won CHN 2014, NG 2013.
Asian 20k walk record 2015, junior 2012.
Progress at 20kW: 2011- 1:29:50, 2012- 1:27:01, 2013- 1:27:53, 2014- 1:27:15, 2015- 1:25:12, 2016- 1:28:07. pb 10kW 43:16 '12.

QIEYANG Shenjie b. 11 Nov 1990 Haiyan, Qinghai Prov. 1.60m 50kg.
At 20kW: OG: '12- 2, '16- 5; WCh: '11-4, '13- 15; WCp: '12- 14, '16- 2. CHN champion 2015. Tied first for IAAF Race Walking Challenge 2016.
Asian 20k walk record 2012.
Progress at 20kW: 2009- 1:35:54, 2010- 1:30:33, 2011- 1:28:04, 2012- 1:25:16, 2013- 1:28:05, 2015- 1:27:44, 2016- 1:26:49. pbs: 5000mW 20:42.67 '12, 10kW 43:16 '12.
First athlete from Tibet to win an Olympic medal.

SU Xinyue b. 8 Nov 1991 1.79m 70kg. Hebei
At DT: OG: '16- 5; WCh: '13- dnq 19, '15- 8; AsiC: '13- 1, '15- 1; WJ: '10- dnq 13.
Progress at DT: 2007- 48.29, 2009- 52.51, 2010- 56.11, 2011- 57.57, 2012- 60.32, 2013- 61.67, 2014- 61.31, 2015- 64.27, 2016- 65.59.

WANG Zheng b. 14 Dec 1987 Xian, Shanxi Province 1.74m 108kg.
At HT: OG: '08- dnq 30, '16- nt; WCh: '13- 4, '15- 5; WJ: '06- 9; AsiG: '10- 2, '14- 2; AsiC: '13- 1; CCp: '14- 4; won Asi-J 2006, E.Asian 2009, CHN 2014, 2016.
Asian hammer record 2014.
Progress at HT: 2000- 60.30, 2001- 66.30, 2002- 67.13, 2003- 70.60, 2004- 72.42, 2005- 73.24, 2006- 74.15, 2007- 74.86, 2008- 74.32, 2009- 74.25, 2010- 73.83, 2011- 75.65, 2012- 75.72, 2012- 76.99, 2013- 75.58, 2014- 77.68, 2015- 73.83, 2016- 74.50.

ZHANG Wenxiu b. 22 Mar 1986 Dalian 1.82m 108kg. Army.
At HT: OG: '04- 7, '08- 2, '12- 2, '16- 2; WCh: '01-03-05-07-09-11-13-15: 11/dnq 14/4/3/5/3/3/2; WJ: '02- dnq 20; AsiG: '06-10-14: 1/1/1; AsiC: '05- 1, '09- 1; WCp: '06- 4, '10- 2. Won Asi-J 2002, W.Mil 2003, 2007, 2011, 2015; CHN 2004, 2006-10, 2012, 2015; NG 2003, 2009, 2013.
Nine Asian hammer records 2001-12, world youth 2003, two world junior 2004-05.
Progress at HT: 2000- 60.30, 2001- 66.30, 2002- 67.13, 2003- 70.60, 2004- 72.42, 2005- 73.24, 2006- 74.15, 2007- 74.86, 2008- 74.32, 2009- 74.25, 2010- 73.83, 2011- 75.65, 2012- 76.99, 2013- 75.58, 2014- 77.33, 2015- 76.33, 2016- 76.75.
World age bests at 15-16-18. Originally lost third Asian Games title with a positive drugs test in 2014, but she was reinstated in May 2015 when it was ruled that her positive test was due to contaminated food.

COLOMBIA

Governing body: Federación Colombiana de Atletismo, Calle 27° No. 25-18, Apartado Aéreo 6024, Santafé de Bogotá. Founded 1937.
National Games Champions 2016: Men: 100m/200m: Diego Palomeque 10.26/20.66, 400m: Jhon Alejandro Perlaza 45.81, 800m:

Rafith Rodríguez 1:48.79, 1500m: Carlos San Martín 3:49.33, 5000m: Iván Darío González 14:25.00, 10000m: Javier Peña 29:59.74, Mar, 3000mSt: Mauricio Franco 9:05.13, 110mh: Yeison Rivas 13.63, 400mh: Ricardo Zapata 51.58, HJ: Daniel Cortez 2.15, PV: Hebert Gómez 4.90, LJ: Edwin Murillo 7.32, TJ: Jhon Fredy Murillo 16.74, SP: Eder Moreno 18.43, DT: Mauricio Ortega 52.67, HT: Jacoibo de León 59.34, JT: Arley Ibargüen 81.23, Dec: José Gregorio Lemus 6978, 20000mW: Freddy Hernández 1:27:20.3.
Women: 100m: Eliecit Palacios 11.53, 200m/400m: Yenifer Padilla 23.73/52.75, 800m: Rosibel García 2:05.22, 1500m/5000m: Muriel Coneo 4:23.87/16:39.72, 10000m: Gina Paola García 36:38.25, 100mh: Briggit Merlano 12.94, 400mh: Karen Palomeque 59.06, HJ: María Fernanda Murillo 1.79, PV: Luisa Martínez 3.60, LJ/ Hep: Evelis Aguilar 5.81/5917, TJ: Giselly Landázuri 13.42, SP: Sandra Lemus 16.85, DT: Johana Martínez 54.53, HT: Eli Johana Moreno 63.44, JT: Flor Dennis Ruiz 58.42, 20000mW: Lorena Arenas 1:36:48.6.

Eider ARÉVALO b. 9 Mar 1993 Bogotá 1.65m 58kg.
At 20kW: OG: '12- 20, '16- 15; WCh: '13- dnf, '15- 7; PAm: 15- 5, SACh: '13- 2; COL champion 2012- 13. At 10000mW: WJ: '12- 1; SAmJ: '11- 1; WCp: '10- 1J.
Colombian 20k walk record 2013.
Progress at 20kW: 2012- 1:21:49, 2013- 1:19:45, 2014- 1:21:28, 2015- 1:20:41, 2016- 1:20:47. Pb 10000mW 39:56.01A '11.

Jhon Fredy **MURILLO** b. 13 Jul 1984 Apartadó, Antioquia1.86m 85kg.
At HJ: OG: '16- 5; PAm: '15- 10; SACh: '06-07-13- 15: 3/4/2/1. Won COL LJ 2008, 2011, 2014, TJ 2007-16.
Colombia TJ record 2016.
Progress at TJ: 2006- 15.67A/16.33Aw, 2007- 15.93A, 2008- 16.02A, 2009- 16.20A, 2010- 15.61A, 2011- 16.18A, 2012- 16.37A, 2013- 16.58/16.82Aw, 2014- 16.47A, 2015- 16.55, 2016- 17.09. pbs: 100m 10.42A '08. LJ 7.74A '11, 7.78w A '08.
Women
Caterine IBARGÜEN b. 12 Feb 1984 Apartadó, Antioquia 1.81m 65kg. Studying nursing.
At TJ/(LJ): OG: '12- 2, '16- 1; WCh: '11- 3, '13- 1, '15- 1; WJ: '02: dnq 17; PAm: '11- 1/3; '15- 1; SACh: '03- 3/2, '05- 3/3, '06- 2/2, '07- (3), '09- 1, '11- 1/3; CAG: '02-06-10-14: 2/(2)/2/1; CCp: '14- 1. At HJ: OG: '04- dnq 28=; WCh: '09- dnq 28=; PAm: '07- 4; SACh: '99-05-06-07-09: 3/1/1/1/1; CAG: '02- 2, '06- 2. Won DL 2013-16, COL HJ 1999, 2001-03, 2005-12, 2015; LJ 2003-04, 2006-08, 2011-12, 2015; TJ 2002-05, 2007-12, 2014.
Records: South American triple jump (7) 2011- 14, junior HJ 2003. Colombia HJ (7) 2002-05, LJ (7) 2004-11, TJ (15) 2004-14.
Progress at TJ: 2001- 12.90, 2002- 13.38A, 2003- 13.23A, 2004- 13.64A, 2005- 13.66A, 2006- 13.91A/13.98Aw, 2007- 12.66A, 2008- 13.79A, 2009- 13.96A/13.93, 2010- 14.29, 2011- 14.99A/ 14.84, 2012- 14.95A/14.85, 2013- 14.85/14.93w, 2014- 15.31, 2015- 14.90/15.18w, 2016- 15.17. pbs: 200m 25.34 '08, 100mh 14.09 '11, HJ 1.93A '05, LJ 6.73A/6.87Aw/6.63/6.66w '12, SP 13.79 '10, JT 44.81 '09, Hep 5742 '09.
Formely a high jumper, concentrating fully on TJ from 2010. First Colombian woman to win a medal in world champs. Unbeaten in 9 competitions in 2013, 11 in 2014 and 9 in 2015 plus her first 4 in 2016, taking her to 34 in succession 2012-16. She lives in Puerto Rico.

Yosiri URRUTIA b. 26 Jun 1986 Chigorodó, Antioquia 1.75m 61kg. Graduated from nursing school at Universidad Metropolitana, Puerto Rico.
At (LJ/)TJ: OG: '16- dnq 20; WCh: '15- 10; PAm: '15- 3; SACh: '13- 5/2; CAG: '14- 3. Won Ib Am 2014, BolG 2013, COL LJ 2010, 2013.
Progress at TJ: 2005- 12.00, 2007- 12.43A, 2010- 12.94, 2013- 14.08, 2014- 14.58, 2015- 14.22/14.36w. 2016- 14.08A/13.95. pbs: 100mh 14.40 '10, LJ 6.53A/6.42 '10.
Previously a long jumper, she focused fully on the triple jump from 2013,

DEMOCRATIC REPUBLIC OF CONGO

Frank Dannique **ELEMBA** Owaka b. 21 Jul 1990 Brazzaville 1.98m 130kg.
At SP: OG: '16- 4; WCh: '15- dnq 21; AfG: '11- 5, '15- 1 (3 DT); AfCh: '10-12-14-16: 4/5/3/2; CCp: '10- 7, '14- 7.
Congo shot records 2010-16, DT 2016.
Progress at SP: 2009- 15.09, 2010- 15.90, 2011- 16.44, 2012- 17.58, 2013- 19.02, 2014- 19.72, 2015- 20.25, 2016- 21.20. pb DT 54.30 '16.
Lives in Paris. His 2016 4th was the best Olympic place for an athlete from Congo.

COSTA RICA

Governing body: Federación Costarricense de Atletismo, 1032-1007 San José. Founded 1960.

Nery BRENES b. 25 Sep 1985 Limón 1.74m 62kg. Student of political science.
At 400m: OG: '08- sf, '12- h, '16- sf (sf 200m); WCh: '05- h, '07/11/13/15- sf; PAm: '11- 1, '15- 4; CAG: '10- 1, '14- 8; WI: '08-10-12-14: 4/4/1/6; CCp: '10- 1R. Won IbAm 2010, C.American 2015. Seven CRC 400m records 2005-16, 200m (4) 2009-16.
Progress at 400m: 2004- 47.90A, 2005- 46.42, 2006- 47.57, 2007- 45.01, 2008- 44.94, 2009- 45.73A/45.92, 2010- 44.84, 2011- 44.65A/45.29, 2012- 45.11i/45.20, 2013- 46.16, 2014- 45.47, 2015- 44.80A/44.85, 2016- 44.60. pb 200m 20.20 '16.
Improved pb by 0.99 to win his heat at 2007 World Champs. Won Costa Rica's first ever

athletics gold medals at Pan-American Games in 2011 and World Indoors in 2012.

CROATIA

Governing body: Hrvatski Atletski Savez, Trg kralja Petra Svacica 17, 10000 Zagreb. Fd 1912.

National Champions 2016 Men: 100m/200m: Zvonimir Ivaskovic 10.88/21.81, 400m: Mateo Ruzic 46.62, 800m: Marino Bloudek 1:52.59, 1500m/5000m: Dino Bosnjak 3:50.55/14:48.67, 3000m: Goren Grdenic 8:54.53, Mar: Robert Radojkovic 2:31:16, 3000mSt: Filip Svalina 9:47.53, 110mh: Marin Jurjevic 14.88, 400mh: Hrvoje Ckman 51.36, HJ: Alen Melon 2.10, PV: Ivan Horvat 5.30, LJ: Dino Pervan 7.78, TJ: Ivan Djukic 15.13, SP: Stipe Zunic 20.53, DT: Filip Mihaljevic 61.151, HT: Mirko Micuda 67.03, JT: Sasa Milosevic 69.88. **Women**: 100m/200m/400m: Anita Banovic 12.16/24.69/53.98, 800m/1500m: Katarina Smiljanec 2:09.78/4:33.92, 3000m/5000m: Matea Parlov 10:10.83/16:47.72, Mar: Bojana Bjeljac 2:50:51, 3000mSt: Lora Ontl 10:48.28, 100mh: Andrea Ivancevic 13.11, 400mh: Valentina Juric 61.62, HJ: Ana Simic 1.85, PV: Petra Malkoc 3.80, LJ/TJ: Paola Borvoic 6.04/13.10, SP/DT: Marija Tolj 14.63/44.35, HT: Anamari Kozul 59.16, JT: Sara Kolak 62.90.

Filip MIHALJEVIC b. 31 Jul 1994 Livno, Bosnia & Herzegovina 2.01m 113kg. University of Virginia, USA.
At SP/(DT): OG: '16- dnq 21; EC: '16- dnq 22; EU23: '15- 1/4; EJ: '13- 2/11; WI: '16- 3. Won CRO SP 2013, DT 2015-16, NCAA SP 2016..
Progress at SP: 2012- 16.52, 2013- 17.54, 2014- 19.65, 2015- 20.16, 2016- 20.87i/20.71. pb DT 63.11 '15. Father Mirko was Yugoslav CC champion in 1987-8.

Stipe ZUNIC b. 13 Dec 1990 Zadar 1.88m 115kg. ASK Split. Sociology student at University of Florida, USA.
At SP: OG: '16- 11; EC: '14- 4, '16- 9; WY: '07- dnq 29; EI: '15- 7, '17- 5; NCAA indoor champion 2015. At JT: WJ: '08- dnq 18; WY: '07- 7; EJ: '09- 9 (11 DT); EU23: '11- 11; Croatian champion SP 2015-16, JT 2009-10.
Progress at SP: 2007- 15.36, 2008- 15.87, 2009- 16.83, 2011- 17.39i/16.60, 2012- 17.30i, 2014- 20.68, 2015- 21.11i/20.38, 2016- 20.61i/20.60, 2017- 21.04i. pbs: DT 59.09 '15, JT 77.89 '12
Huge improvement at shot in 2014-15 after switching from javelin. Formerly world junior champion at kick-boxing.

Women

Sara KOLAK b. 22 Jun 1995 Koprivnica 1.70m 74kg. AK Kvarner Rijeka.
At JT: OG: '16- 1; EC: '14- dnq 21, 16- 3; WJ: '12- dnq 23, '14- 3; EJ: '13- 3; Croatian champion 2012-14, 2016.
9 Croatian JT records 2013-16.
Progress at JT: 2008- 31.78, 2009- 43.13, 2010- 55.69, 2011- 45.94, 2012- 53.98, 2013- 57.79, 2014- 57.79, 2016- 66.18, 2017- 6523.
National javelin records 63.50 for 3rd EC, and at OG 64.30 qualifying and 66.18 for gold in final.

Sandra PERKOVIC b. 21 Jun 1990 Zagreb 1.83m 80kg. Zagreb.
At DT(/SP): OG: '12- 1, '16- 1; WCh: '09- 9, '13- 1, '15- 2; EC: '10-12-14-16: 1/1/1/1; WJ: '06- dnq 21, '08- 3/dnq 13; WY: '07- 2/dnq 13; EJ: '07- 2, '09- 1/5; CCp: '10- 2, '14- 3. Won DL 2012-16, Med G 2013; CRO SP 2008-10, DT 2010, 2012.
9 Croatian DT records 2009-14, 2 SP 2010-11.
Progress at DT: 2004- 30.37, 2005- 36.21, 2006- 50.11, 2007- 55.42, 2008- 55.89, 2009- 62.79, 2010- 66.93, 2011- 67.96/69.99dq, 2012- 69.11, 2013- 68.96, 2014- 71.08, 2015- 70.08, 2016- 70.88, 2017- 70.23. pb SP 16.99i/16.40 '11.
First woman to win European and Olympic gold for Croatia. Won 53 of 59 competitions 2012-16. Five successive wins for Diamond Race, and won all seven competitions in 2016. Her 70.51 and 71.08 to win her third European title in 2014 were the women's world's best discus throws since 1992. Six months drugs ban 2011.

Ana SIMIC b. 5 May 1990 Gradacac, Bosnia 1.77m 58kg. Zagreb.
At HJ: OG: '12/16- dnq 29=/22=; WCh: '13- dnq 19, '15- 9=; EC: '10-12-16: dnq 22=/20/14, '14- 3; WJ: '08- dnq 14=; WY: '07- dnq 21=; EU23: '11- 7; EJ: '09- dnq 18; CCp: '14- 3; EI: '17- 7; Croatian champion 2006-09, 2011, 2015.
Progress at HJ: 2003- 1.66, 2004- 1.73, 2005- 1.69, 2006- 1.78, 2007- 1.73, 2008- 1.82, 2009- 1.87, 2010- 1.92, 2011- 1.92, 2012- 1.91i/1.88, 2013- 1.96, 2014- 1.99, 2015- 1.95i/1.94, 2016- 1.96.

Blanka VLASIC b. 8 Nov 1983 Split 1.92m 75kg. ASK Split.
At HJ: OG: '00- dnq 17, '04- 11, '08- 2, '16- 3; WCh: '01-03-05-07-09-11-15: 6/7/dnq 19=/1/1/2/2; EC: '02- 5=, '06- 4, 10- 1; WJ: '00- 1, '02- 1; WY: '99- 8; EU23: '03- 1; EJ: '01- 7; WI: '03-04-06-08- 10-14: 4/3/2/1/1/6; EI: '07- 4, '09- 5=; CCp: '10- 1. Won WAF 2007-09, DL 2010-11, MedG 2001, CRO 2001-02, 2005.
Ten Croatian high jump records 2003-09.
Progress at HJ: 1998- 1.68, 1999- 1.80, 2000- 1.93, 2001- 1.95, 2002- 1.96, 2003- 2.01, 2004- 2.03, 2005- 1.95, 2006- 2.05i/2.03, 2007- 2.07, 2008- 2.06, 2009- 2.08, 2010- 2.06i/2.05, 2011- 2.03, 2013- 2.00, 2014- 2.00, 2015- 2.01, 2016- 1.97.
IAAF Woman Athlete of the Year 2010. Won 5/6 Golden League HJs in both 2007 and 2008. She has had 106 competitions at 2m or higher to the end of 2015 (and 174 jumps over 2m), including 42 successive Jul 2007- Feb 2009, but in 2008 lost on count-back both at Olympic Games (when she won first ever athletics medal for Croatia) and in the final Golden League meeting, thus losing her share of the Jackpot. She had 60 attempts at the world record 2007-10. Her father

Josko set the Croatian decathlon record with 7659 (1983) and named Blanka after Casablanca, where he won a Mediterranean Games title.

CUBA

Governing body: Federación Cubana de Atletismo, Calle 13 y C, Vedado 601, Zona Postal 4, La Habana 10400. Founded 1922.
National Champions 2016: Men: 100m: Reynier Mena 10.23, 200m: Roberto Skyers 20.42, 400m: Yoandys Lescay 46.56, 800m: Andy González 1:46.35, 1500m/5000m: José Alberto Sánchez 3:55.14/14:42.84, 10000m/HMar: Richer Pérez 30:42.86/66:19. Mar: Henrry Jaén 2:34:29, 110mh: Roger Iribarne 13.69, 400mh: Leandro Zamora 51.36, HJ: Luis Zayas 2.16, PV: Lázaro Borges 5.40, LJ: Juan Echeverría 7.93, TJ: Lázaro Martínez 16.61, SP: Lázaro Acosta 17.38, DT: Jorge Fernández 57.72, HT: Roberto Janet 75.29, JT: Guillermo Martínez 77.40, Dec: Leonel Suárez 8347, 10kW/20kW: Joel Vargas 44:20/1:38:49. **Women**: 100m/200m: Dulaimi Odelín 11.73/23.88, 400m: Roxana Gómez 53.06, 800m/1500m: Arletis Thaureaux 2:05.60/4:26.02, 5000m/10000m/HMar: Yudileyvis Castillo 16:51.79/34:29.05/1:17:58, 100mh: Belkis Milanés 13.46, 400mh: Nairobis Vicet 59.63, HJ: Isis Guerra 1.73, PV: Lisa Salomón 3.90, LJ: Paula Álvarez 6.36, TJ: Liadagmis Povea 14.56, SP: Yaniuvis López 18.62, DT: Yaimé Pérez 66.24, HT: Yirisleydi Ford 70.73, JT: Marisleisys Duarthe 51.57, Hep: Yorgelis Rodríguez 6307, 10kW/20kW: Misleidys Vargas 52:08/1:53:19.

Alexis COPELLO b. 12 Aug 1985 Santiago de Cuba 1.85m 80kg.
At TJ: OG: '08- dnq 13, '12- 8; WCh: '09- 3, '11- 4; WI: '12- 7; PAmG: '11- 1; CAG: '06- 2; CCp: '10- 2. Won IbAm 2010, CAC 2009, Cuban 2009, 2011.
Progress at TJ: 2002- 15.38, 2003- 16.34, 2004- 16.90, 2005- 16.95/17.09w, 2006- 17.38, 2007- 16.87/17.15w, 2008- 17.50, 2009- 17.65/17.69w, 2010- 17.55, 2011- 17.68A/17.47, 2012- 17.17, 2014- 17.05, 2015- 17.15/17.24w, 2016- 16.99i/16.98. pb LJ 7.35 '04.
Competes outside the authorization of the Cuban Federation. Elder brother Alexander (b. 19 Feb 1978) decathlon pb 7359 '02.

Jorge FERNÁNDEZ b. 2 Dec 1987 Matanzas 1.90m 100kg.
At DT: OG: '08- dnq 27, '12- 11, '16- dnq 22; WCh: '11- 8, '13- 10; WJ: '06- 5; PAmG: '11- 1, '15- 5; CAG: '14- 1; WJ: '06- 5; CCp: '14- 2; PAm-J: '05- 2. Won CAC 2008-09, Cuban 2009-16 (& SP 2014).
Progress at DT: 2005- 53.69, 2006- 54.77, 2007- 57.57, 2008- 63.31, 2009- 63.92, 2010- 66.00, 2011- 65.89, 2012- 66.05, 2013- 65.09, 2014- 66.50, 2015- 62.35, 2016- 65.30. pb SP 16.94 '14.

Roberto JANET b. 29 Aug 1986 Santiago de Cuba 1.87m 106kg.
At DT: OG: '12/16- dnq 19/14; WCh: '13- dnq 22, '15- 12; PAm: '11- 5, '15- 2; CAG: '14- 1, CCp: '10- 5, '14- 6. Won NACAC 2015, CAC 2009, 2011, Cuban 2009-12, 2014-16; IbAm 2010, 2012, PAm-J 2005. CAC hammer record 2015.
Progress at HT: 2005- 61.30, 2006- 68.43, 2007- 70.89, 2008- 71.92, 2009- 74.95, 2010- 76.50, 2011- 76.40, 2012- 77.08, 2013- 76.75, 2014- 75.99, 2015- 78.02, 2016- 76.52.

Lázaro MARTÍNEZ b. 3 Nov 1997 Guantánamo 1.92m 83kg.
At TJ: OG: '16- 8; WJ: '14- 1, '16- 1; WY: '13- 1; CAG: '14- 2; PAm-J: '13- 1. Won CUB 2016.
World youth triple jump record 2014.
Progress at TJ: 2011- 14.62, 2012- 15.38, 2013- 16.63, 2014- 17.24, 2015- 17.02, 2016- 17.06.

Yordan O'FARRILL b. 9 Feb 1993 Santa Cruz del Sur 1.85m 77kg.
At 110mh: OG: '16- sf; WCh: '15- h; WJ: '12- 1; PAm: '15- 6; CAG: '14- 1; CCp: '14- 7; Yth Oly: '10- 5. Won CAC-J 2012, CUB 2014, 2017.
Progress at 110mh: 2012- 13.91, 2013- 13.44, 2014- 13.19/12.9, 2015- 13.23, 2016- 13.51/13.46w, 2017- 13.33. Pbs: 100m 10.44 '14, 60mh 7.65i '13.

Pedro Pablo PICHARDO b. 30 Jun 1993 Santiago de Cuba 1.85m 71kg.
At TJ: WCh: '13- 2, '15- 2; WJ: '12- 1; PAm: '15- 1; WI: '14- 3. Won CAC-J 2012, CUB 2014-15.
Three CAC triple jump records 2015.
Progress at TJ: 2009- 14.55, 2010- 15.35/15.45w, 2011- 16.09, 2012- 16.79, 2013- 17.69, 2014- 17.76, 2015- 18.08. pb LJ 7.81 '15.
Injured in 2016. Father Jorge was a 2.10 high jumper.

Ernesto REVÉ b. 26 Feb 1992 Guantánamo 1.81m 70kg.
At TJ: OG: '16- dnq 14; WJ: '10- 2; PAm: '15- 3; CAG: '14- 1; WI: '14- 2. Won CUB 2012-13.
CAC junior triple jump record (=) 2011.
Progress at TJ: 2006- 14.97, 2007- 15.22, 2008- 16.32, 2009- 16.56, 2010- 16.73, 2011- 17.40, 2012- 17.13, 2013- 17.46, 2014- 17.58, 2015- 17.02, 2016- 16.91. pb LJ 7.00 '13.

Dayron ROBLES b. 19 Nov 1986 Guantánamo 1.91m 91kg.
At 110mh: OG: '08- 1, '12- dq; WCh: '05-07-09-11: sf/4/sf/dq(1); WJ: '04- 2, WY: '03- 6; CAG: '06- 1; PAm: '07- 1, '11- 1; WCp: '06- 3; won PAm-J 2005, WAF 2007, CAC 2009, Cuban 2006-07, DL 2011. At 60mh: WI: '06- 2, '10- 1.
World 110mh record 2008, three Cuban & CAC 2006-08, CAC junior record 2005. Two CAC 60mh indoor records 2008.
Progress at 110mh: 2002- 15.01, 2003- 14.30, 2004- 13.75, 2005- 13.46/13.2/13.41w, 2006- 13.00, 2007- 12.92, 2008- 12.87, 2009- 13.04, 2010- 13.01, 2011- 13.00, 2012- 13.10, 2013- 13.18, 2014- 13.29, 2015- 13.32. pbs: 100m 10.70 '06, 200m 21.85 '06, 50mh 6.39i '08, 60mh 7.33i '08.
Season's record 7 sub-13 second times in 2008.

Disqualified for obstructing Liu Xiang after finishing first at 2011 Worlds. Pulled muscle in 2012 Olympic final. Left Cuba in 2013 in agreement with Cuban authorities; competed in Europe representing AS Monaco. Returned in 2015 and rejoined the national team.

Leonel SUÁREZ b. 1 Sep 1987 Holguín 1.81m 76kg.
At Dec: OG: '08- 3, '12- 3, '16- 6; WCh: '09- 2, '11- 3, '13- 10; PAm: '07-11-15: 4/1/dnf. CAC champion 2009, Cuban 2009, 2015-16. At Hep: WI: '10- 7.
Decathlon records: 4 CUB 2008-09, CAC 2009.
Progress at Dec: 2005- 7267, 2006- 7357, 2007- 8156, 2008- 8527, 2009- 8654, 2010- 8328, 2011- 8501, 2012- 8523, 2013- 8317, 2015- 8027, 2016- 8460. pbs: 60m 7.11i '09, 100m 10.90 '08, 10.6w '06; 400m 47.65 '09, 1000m 2:36.12i '10, 1500m 4:16.70 '08, 60mh 7.90i '10, 110mh 14.12 '08, HJ 2.17 '08, PV 5.00 '09, LJ 7.52 '11, SP 15.20 '09, DT 47.32 '11, JT 78.29 '16, Hep 5964i '10.
Won at Talence 2010. Won IAAF Combined Events Challenge 2011.

Women

Rose Mary ALMANZA b. 13 Jul 1992 Camagüey 1.66m 53kg.
At 800m: OG: '12- sf, '16- h; WCh: '13/15- sf; WJ: '10- 4; WY: '09- 4; PAm: '11- 4, '15- 4; CAG: '14- 1. Won Cuban 800m 2010-11, 2014-15, 2017; 1500m 2013, 2015, 2017.
Two CAC junior 800m records 2010-11.
Progress at 800m: 2008- 2:11.1, 2009- 2:03.61, 2010- 2:02.04, 2011- 2:00.56, 2012- 1:59.55, 2013- 1:59.4, 2014- 1:59.48, 2015- 1:57.70, 2016- 1:58.49. pbs: 400m 54.48A '16, 54.64 '12; 600m 1:26.33mx '14, 1:26.9 '13; 1000m 2:38.1 '14, 1500m 4:14.53 '14.

Denia CABALLERO b. 13 Jan 1990 Caibarién, Villa Clara 1.75m 73kg. VCL.
At DT: OG: '12- dnq 25, '16- 3; WCh: '11-9, '13- 8, '15- 1; PAm: '11- 3, '15- 1; CAG: '14- 1. Won CAC 2011, Cuban 2015.
Progress at DT: 2006- 43.77, 2007- 46.08, 2008- 52.10, 2009- 57.21, 2010- 59.92, 2011- 62.94, 2012- 65.60, 2013- 63.47, 2014- 64.89, 2015- 70.65, 2016- 67.62.

Yaimé PÉREZ b. 29 May 1991 Santiago de Cuba 1.74m 78kg.
At DT: OG: '12- dnq 28, '16- nt; WCh: '13- 11, '15- 4; WJ: '10- 1; PAm: '15- 2; CAG: '14- 2; CCp: '14- 5. Cuban champion 2013-14, 2016-17.
Progress at DT: 2007- 46.29, 2008- 51.80, 2009- 55.23, 2010- 59.30, 2011- 59.26, 2012- 62.50, 2013- 66.01, 2014- 66.03, 2015- 67.13, 2016- 68.86. pbs SP 13.88 '08.

Yorgelis RODRÍGUEZ b. 25 Jan 1995 Guantánamo 1.73m 66kg.
At Hep: OG: '16- 7; WCh: '13- 12, '15- 21; WJ: '12- 1; '14- 2 (dnq 16= HJ); WY: '11- 2; PAm: '15- 1; won PAmCp 2013, 2015; CAG 2014, Cuban HJ 2017, Hep 2013, 2016.

Cuban heptathlon record 2016, three CAC junior records 2012-14..
Progress at Hep: 2012- 5994, 2013- 6186, 2014- 6231, 2015- 6332, 2016- 6481. pbs: 200m 24.06 '16, 800m 2:14.65 '16, 100mh 13.52 '16, HJ 1.87 '16, LJ 6.41 '17, SP 14.64 '16, JT 48.89 '16.

Yarisley SILVA b. 1 Jun 1987 Pinar del Rio 1.69m 68kg.
At PV: OG: '08- dnq 27=, '12- 2, '16- 7=; WCh: '11- 5, '13- 3, '15- 1; WI: '12- 7, '14- 1; WJ: '06- dnq; PAm: '07-11-15: 3/1/1; CAG: '14- 1; Won CAC 2009, Cuban 2004, 2006-07, 2009, 2012-13, 2015, 2017.
Pole vault records: 19 Cuban & CAC 2007-15 (9 in 2011), 8 CAC indoor 2012 & 2013 (to 4.82).
Progress at PV: 2001- 2.50, 2002- 3.10, 2003- 3.70, 2004- 4.00, 2005- 4.10, 2006- 4.20, 2007- 4.30, 2008- 4.50, 2009- 4.50, 2010- 4.40, 2011- 4.75A/4.70, 2012- 4.75, 2013- 4.90, 2014- 4.70, 2015- 4.91, 2016- 4.84.

CYPRUS

Governing body: Amateur Athletic Association of Cyprus, Olympic House, 2025 Strovolos, Nicosia. Founded 1983. **National Championships** first held in 1896, 1952 (women). **2016 Champions: Men**: 100m/200m: Paisios Dimitriades 10.62/21.53, 400m: Georgios Avraam 48.49, 800m: Christos Demetriou 1:48.36, 1500m: Amine Khadiri 3:43.84, 5000m: Marios Apostolides 15:10.05, 3000mSt: Nikolas Fraggou 9:23.94, 110mh: Milan Trajkovic 13.42w, 400mh: Michalis Andreou 53.63, HJ: Dimitrios Hondrokoukis 2.23, PV: Nikandros Stylianou 4.90, LJ: Mattheos Volou 7.41, TJ: Panayiotis Volou 15.97, SP: Michalis Lambrou 17.81, DT: Apostolos Parellis 63.74, HT: Constantinos Stathelakos 73.61, JT: Michail Kakotas 64.96. **Women**: 100m/200m: Ramona Papaioannou 11.25/23.24, 400m: Christiana Katsari 54.99, 800m/1500m: Natalia Evangelidou 2:11.47/4:22.62, 5000m: Meropi Panayiotou 17:44.31, 3000mSt: Zarina Mentayeva 11:03.74, 100mh: Natalia Christofi 13.92, 400mh: Kalypso Stavrou 63.34, HJ: Leontia Kallenou 1.75, PV: Maria Aristotelous 3.70, LJ: Nektaria Panayi 6.59, TJ: Eleftheria Christofi 12.63, SP: Gabriella Fella 16.26, DT: Androniki Lada 53.77, HT: Catherine Beatty 58.70, JT: Mariele Rousi 45.36,.

Kyriakos IOANNOU b. 26 Jul 1984 Limassol 1.93m 66kg. GS Olympia Limassol. Student of PE at University of Athens.
At HJ: OG: '04/08- dnq 18=/18, '12- 13, '16- 7=; WCh: '05- 10, '07- 3, '09- 2; EC: '12- dnq 21, '16- nh; CG: '06- 3, '14- 2; WJ: '02- dnq; WY: '01- dnq; EJ: '03- 6=; EU23: '05- 4; WI: '08- 3=, '10- 4; EI: '09- 2=, '15- nh; WUG: '07- 2. Won Med G 2005, 2009; Greek 2005, 2007, CYP 2004-05, 2009-12, 2014; EUR States 2005, 2009.
Nine Cyprus high jump records 2004-07.
Progress at HJ: 2001- 2.00, 2002- 2.15, 2003- 2.17,

2004- 2.28, 2005- 2.27, 2006- 2.30i/2.23, 2007- 2.35, 2008- 2.32i/2.27, 2009- 2.32, 2010- 2.30, 2011- 2.33, 2012- 2.30, 2014- 2.28, 2015- 2.29, 2016- 2.32i/2.29.
First athlete from Cyprus to win a medal at Olympics or World Championships.
Apostolos PARELLIS b. 24 Jul 1985 Limassol 1.86m 110kg.
At DT: OG: '12- dnq 13, '16- 8; WCh: '13- dnq 19, '15- 6; CG: '10- 4, '14- 2; EC: '10-12-14-16: dnq 17/13/16/18; EU23: '07- 3. Won CYP 2007-16.
17 CYP discus records 2007-16.
Progress at DT: 2004- 48.40, 2005- 50.88, 2006- 53.77, 2007- 58.16, 2008- 56.41, 2009- 61.07, 2010- 61.92, 201161.44, 2012- 65.36, 2013- 62.48, 2014- 63.89, 2015- 65.04, 2016- 65.69.

CZECH REPUBLIC

Governing body: Cesky atleticky svaz, Diskarská 100, 16900 Praha 6 -Strahov, PO Box 40. AAU of Bohemia founded in 1897.
National Championships first held in 1907 (Bohemia), 1919 (Czechoslovakia), 1993 CZE.
2016 Champions: **Men**: 100m: Jan Veleba 10.28, 200m: Jan Jirka 21.13, 400m: Patrik Sorm 46.60, 800m: Martin Sadil 1:54.61, 1500m: Jan Fris 3:50.92, 5000m: David Kucera 14:46.01, 10000m/3000mSt: Lukás Olejnícek 31:13.57/8:59.30, HMar: Vit Pavlista 66:19, Mar: Petr Pechek 2:22:14, 110mh: Petr Penáz 14.00, 400mh: Michal Broz 50.88, HJ: Jaroslav Bába 2.12, PV: Jan Kudlicka 5.55, LJ: Adam Zelinka 7.70, TJ: Lukás Kunc 15.68, SP: Tomás Stanek 20.39, DT: Marek Bárta 59.89, HT: Lukás Melich 74.88, JT: Vitezslav Vesely 77.92, Dec: Marek Lukás 7877, 20kW/50kW: Lukás Gdula 1:25:50/3:54:29. **Women**: 100m/200m: Barbora Procházková 11.51/23.71, 400m: Denisa Rosolová 54.11, 800m: Vendula Hluchá 2:09.79, 1500m/5000m: Simona Vrzalová 4:14.45/16:41.00, 10000m: Valerie Soukupová 35:15.96, HMar: Petra Kaminková 77:31, Mar: Eva Vrabcová Nyvltová 2:30:10 3000mSt: Lucie Sekanová 9:59.56, 100mh/Hep: Katerina Cachová 13.08/6285, 400mh: Tereza Vokálová 57.22, HJ: Michaela Hrubá 1.93, PV: Rebeka Silhanová 4.40, LJ: Jana Koresová 6.47, TJ: Lucie Májková 13.93, SP: Markéta Cervenková 16.69, DT: Eliska Stanková 55.43, HT: Katerina Safránková 71.06, JT: Barbora Spotáková 66.87, 20kW: Tereza Korvasová 1:50:55.

Jakub HOLUSA b. 20 Feb 1988 Opava 1.83m 72kg. Dukla Praha.
At 800m: OG: '08/12- h; EC: '10-12-16: 5/5; EU23: '09- h; WI: '10- 5, '12- 2. At 1500m: OG: , '16- sf; WCh: '15- h EC: '14- dns, '16- dq h; EU23: '09- 3; WI: '14- 5, '16- 2; EI: '11- 5, '15- 1; ET: '14- 1 (2 3000m). At 2000mSt: WY: '05- 7. At 3000mSt: EJ: '07- 1, Won CZE 800m 2008, 5000m 2014.
Czech 1500m records 2015 & 2016.
Progress at 1500m: 2003- 4:21.89, 2004- 4:04.47, 2005- 3:58.06, 2006- 3:56.23, 2007- 3:46.93, 2008- 3:41.88i/3:43.02, 2009- 3:42.15, 2010- 3:38.47, 2011- 3:38.10, 2012- 3:42.44i/3:42.79, 2013- 3:38.71, 2014- 3:35.26, 2015- 3:34.26, 2016- 3:33.36. pbs: 400m 47.29 '10, 800m 1:45.12 '12, 1000m 2:16.79 '14, 1M 3:53.46 '14, 3000m 7:51.43 '14, 5000m 14:06.32 '14, 2000mSt 5:43.39 '05, 3000mSt 8:50.30 '07, 400mh 54.46 '07.
Has used devastating sprint finish to good effect in major championships.

Jan KUDLICKA b. 29 Apr 1988 Opava 1.84m 76kg. Dukla Praha.
At PV: OG: '08- 9, '12- 7, '16- 4=; WCh: '09-11-13-15: dnq 23=/9/7/13=; EC: '10-12-14-16: 10/6/3=/2; WJ: '06- 5=; WY: '05- 6; EU23: '09- 8=; WI: '14- 3, '16- 4=; EI: '13-15-17: 5/7=/4; ET: '14- 2=; Won CZE 2008, 2010-16.
Czech pole vault record 2016.
Progress at PV: 2002- 3.65, 2003- 4.21, 2004- 4.80, 2005- 5.09, 2006- 5.30, 2007- 5.61/5.62ex, 2008- 5.70, 2009- 5.62, 2010- 5.65, 2011- 5.81ex/5.65, 2012- 5.73, 2013- 5.83ex/5.77i/5.76, 2014- 5.80i/5.72/5.76ex, 2015- 5.75, 2016- 5.83., 2017- 5.80i pbs: 60m 7.11i '07, HJ 2.05i/2.03 '07, LJ 7.55 '07, TJ 14.41 '07.

Pavel MASLÁK b. 21 Feb 1991 Havírov 1.76m 67kg. Dukla Praha.
At 400m: OG: '12- sf (h 200m), '16- sf; WCh: '13- 5, '15- h; EC: '12- 1, '16- 2; WY: '07- h; WI: '12-14-16: 5/1/1; EI: '13- 1/3R, '15&17- 1/3R. At 200m: WCh: '11- sf; WJ: '10- 7; EU23: '11- 3, '13- 3; EJ: '09- 5/2R. At 100m: WJ: '08- h. Won CZE 200m 2012-13, 2015; 400m 2011.
European indoor 300m & 500m bests 2014. CZE records: 200m (4) 2012-13, 400m (5) 2012-14.
Progress at 400m: 2006- 50.41, 2007- 48.30, 2008- 47.60, 2009- 47.44, 2010- 46.89, 2011- 47.05i/47.43, 2012- 44.91, 2013- 44.84, 2014- 44.79, 2015- 45.09, 2016- 45.06. pbs: 60m 6.65i '14, 100m 10.35 '16, 200m 20.49 '13, 300m 32.15i '14, 32.34 '13; 500m 1:00.35 '13.
European Athletics Rising Star Award 2012. Master of indoor running.

Tomás STANEK b. 13 Jun 1991 Prague 1.90m 127kg. Dukla Praha.
At SP: OG: '16- dnq 20; WCh: '15- dnq 19; EC: '14- dnq 14; EU23: '13- 5; EI: 17- 2. CZE champion 2016.
Progress at SP: 2011- 17.16, 2012- 18.52, 2013- 19.50, 2014- 20.93, 2015- 20.94i/20.64, 2016- 21.30i 21.26, 2017- 21.43i.

Jakub VADLEJCH b. 10 Oct 1990 Praha 1.90m 93kg. Dukla Praha.
At JT: OG: '12- dnq 24, '16- 8; WCh: '11/15- dnq 16/20; EC: '10/14- dnq 16/20, '16- 9; WJ: '08- 10; WY: '07- 12; EJ: '09- 8. Won DL 2016, Czech champion 2014-15.
Progress at JT: 2006- 55.24, 2007- 66.12, 2008- 76.59, 2009- 81.95, 2010- 84.47, 2011- 84.08, 2012- 80.40A, 2013- 75.85, 2014- 82.97, 2015- 86.21, 2016- 88.02.

Vitezslav VESELY b. 27 Feb 1983 Hodonin 1.86m 94kg. Dukla Praha.
At JT: OG: '08- 12, '12- 3, '16- 7; WCh: '09-11-13-15: dnq 28/4/1/8; EC: '10-12-14-16: 9/1/2/2; WJ: '02- 9; CCp: '14- 2. Won DL 2012-13, CZE 2008, 2010-12, 20-16.
Progress at JT: 2001- 66.18, 2002- 73.22, 2003- 66.95, 2004- 72.32, 2006- 75.98, 2007- 79.45, 2008- 81.20, 2009- 80.35, 2010- 86.45, 2011- 84.11, 2012- 88.34, 2013- 87.68, 2014- 87.38, 2015- 88.18, 2016- 84.82.

Women

Zuzana HEJNOVÁ b. 19 Dec 1986 Liberec 1.70m 54kg. Dukla Praha.
At 400mh/4x400mR: OG: '08- 7, '12- 3, '16- 4; WCh: '05-07-09- sf, '11- 7, '13- 1, '15- 1; EC: '06- sf, '10- 4, 12- 4/3R; EU23: '07- 3; WJ: '02- 5, '04- 2; EJ: '03- 3; '05- 1; WY: '03- 1; WI: '10- 3R; ET: '09- 3, '11- 1. Won DL 2013, 2015. At 400m: EI: '13- 4/3R, '17- 2. At Pen: EI: '11- 7. Won CZE 400m 2006, 2009.
12 Czech 400mh records 2005-13. 3 world bests 300mh 2011 (38.91) and 2013 (38.75 & 38.16).
Progress at 400mh: 2002- 58.42, 2003- 57.54, 2004- 57.44, 2005- 55.89, 2006- 55.83, 2007- 55.04, 2008- 54.96, 2009- 54.90, 2010- 54.13, 2011- 53.29, 2012- 53.38, 2013- 52.83, 2014- 55.86, 2015- 53.50, 2016- 53.92. pbs: 60m 7.66i '17, 150m 17.66 '13, 200m 23.65 '13, 300m 37.49A/37.80 '13, 400m 51.90/51.27i '13, 600m 1:28.04i '15, 800m 2:03.40i '16, 60mh 8.24i '17, 100mh 13.36 '11, 13.18w '10; 300mh 38.16 '13, HJ 1.80i '11, 1.74 '04; LJ 5.96i '11, 5.76 '07, SP 12.11i '11, JT 36.11 '10, Pen 4453i '11.
Unbeaten season at hurdles in 2013. Sister of Michaela Hejnová (b. 10 Apr 1980) pb Hep 6174w/6065 '04; OG: '04- 26; EC '02- 7; EU23: '01- 5; WJ: '98- 5; EJ: '97- 6/'99- 6 (100mh); WUG: '01- 5, '03- 3.

Jirina PTÁCNÍKOVÁ b. 20 May 1986 Plzen 1.75m 69kg. Was Svobodová. USK Praha.
At PV: OG: '12- 6=, '16- dnq 19=; WCh: '09-11-13-15: dnq 16=/7/8=/dnq; EC: '06-10-12-14-16: dnq 27/5/1/6/dnq 17=; WJ: '02/04- nh; EJ: '03- 6, '05- 4; WY: '03- 5; WUG: '09- 1; WI: '10-12-14: 5/6/2=; EI: '11- 4=, '13- 4; ET: '09-11-14: 5/3/2. CZE champion 2009-11, 2013, 2015.
Czech pole vault record 2013.
Progress at PV: 2001- 3.20, 2002- 4.00, 2003- 4.02, 2004- 4.11i/3.90, 2005- 4.15, 2006- 4.27, 2007- 4.22i/4.00, 2008- 4.28, 2009- 4.55, 2010- 4.66, 2011- 4.65, 2012- 4.72, 2013- 4.76, 2014- 4.71i/4.60, 2015- 4.72, 2016- 4.66i/4.65. pb LJ 5.85 '10, 5.95i '11.
Father Frantisek Ptacník was Czech indoor record holder at 60m (6.59 '87, 3= EI 1987), pb 100m 10.25 '85. She married Petr Svoboda (1 EI 60mh 2011, CZE 110mh record 13.27 '10) on 19 Sep 2012, but marriage ended two years later.

Barbora SPOTÁKOVÁ b. 30 Jun 1981 Jablonec nad Nisou 1.82m 80kg. Dukla Praha.
At JT: OG: '04- dnq 23, '08- 1, '12- 1, '16- 3; WCh: '05-07-09-11-15: dnq 13/1/2/2/9; EC: '02-06-10-14-16: dnq 17/2/3/1/5; EU23: '03- 6; WUG: '03- 4, '05- 1; CCp: '14- 1; ET: '09-11-14: 2/3/1; won DL 2010, 2012, 2014-15; WAF 2006-08, Czech 2003, 2005-12, 2015-16. At Hep: WJ: '00- 4.
World javelin record 2008, two European records 2008, 11 Czech records 2006-08. World heptathlon javelin best (60.90) in 2012.
Progress at JT: 1996- 31.32, 1997- 37.28, 1998- 44.56, new: 1999- 41.69, 2000- 54.15, 2001- 51.97, 2002- 56.76, 2003- 56.65, 2004- 60.95, 2005- 65.74, 2006- 66.21, 2007- 67.12, 2008- 72.28, 2009- 68.23, 2010- 68.66, 2011- 71.58, 2012- 69.55, 2013- 62.33, 2014- 67.99, 2015- 65.66, 2016- 66.87. pbs: 200m 25.33/25.11w '00, 800m 2:18.29 '00, 60mh 8.68i '07, 100mh 13.99 '00, 400mh 62.68 '98, HJ 1.78 '00, LJ 5.65 '00, SP 14.53 '07, DT 36.80 '02, Hep 5880 '12, Dec 6749 '04.
Son Janek born 24 May 2013.

DENMARK

Governing body: Dansk Athletik Forbund, Idraettens Hus, Brøndby Stadion 20, DK-2605 Brøndby. Founded 1907.
National Championships first held in 1894.
2016 Champions: **Men**: 100m: Festus Asante 10.56, 200m: Simon Hansen 21.12, 400m: Benjamin Lobo Vedel 47.00, 800m: Andreas Bube 1:50.26, 1500m/5000m: Thijs Nijhuis 3:44.59/14:29.93. 10000m: Abdi Hakin Ulad 29:41.17, HMar: Thijs Nijhuis 65:57, Mar: Jesper Faurschou 2:19:59, 3000mSt: Ole Hesselbjerg 8:59.16, 110mh: Andreas Martinsen 14.12, 400mh: Nicolai Hartling 50.82, HJ: Janick Klausen 2.22, PV: Rasmus W. Jørgensen 5.20, LJ: Morten Jensen 7.39, TJ: Peder P. Nielsen 15.36, SP: Kenneth Mertz 16.49, DT: Andreas Ellegaard 53.37, HT: Brian Nielsen 61.17, JT: Mikkel Bach Garbrecht 62.33, Dec: Christian Laugesen 6920, 5000mW: Andreas Nielsen 24:23.26, 50kW: Peer Jensen 5:49:17
Women: 100m/LJ: Martha Traoré 12.26/6.17, 200m: Sara Slott Petersen 23.64, 400m/400mh: Anne Sofie Kirkegaard 54.39/59.55, 800m/1500m: Anna Emilie Møller 2:05.91/4:37.24, 5000m/10000m: Simone Glad 16:26.55/35:14.48, HMar: Louise Langelund Batting 75:18, Mar: Marna Egholm 2:46:37, 100mh: Mette Graversgaard 13.57, HJ: Sandra B. Christensen 1.72, PV: Caroline Bonde Holm 4.05, TJ: Janne Nielsen 12.88, SP: Trine Mulbjerg 15.96, DT: Kathrine Bebe 54.02, HT: Celina Julin 60.17, JT: Marie Vestergaard 52.00, Hep: Sandra Böll 5275.

Sara SLOTT PETERSEN b. 9 Apr 1987 Nykøbing Falster, Sjælland 1.71m 57kg. Århus 1900 AM.
At 400mh: OG: 12- sf, '16- 2; WCh: 09/11- sf, '15- 4; EC: '10-12-14-16: h/sf/h/1; WJ: '04- h; WY: '03- 4; EU23: '07- 6, 09- 6; EJ: '05- 4; WUG: '09- 3, '11- 4. Won Danish 400mh 2002-09, 2011-12, 2014-15, 100m 2007, 2009, 200m 2009, 2012, 2016; 400m 2008-09.

12 Danish 400m records 2007-16.
Progress at 400mh: 2002- 60.67, 2003- 59.42, 2004- 60.60, 2005- 58.21, 2006- 57.65, 2007- 57.01, 2008- 57.06, 2009- 56.40, 2010- 57.28, 2011- 55.97, 2012- 55.68, 2014- 56.44, 2015- 53.99, 2016- 53.55. pbs: 60m 7.62i '15, 100m 12.07 '07, 11.93w '09; 200m 23.59 '16. 400m 52.59i/53.55 '16; 60mh 18.58i '07, 1500m 4:27.96 '11.
Her silver was the best ever for a Danish woman at the Olympics. Partner of Thomas Cortebeeck, their son Tobias born 8 Oct 2013.

DJIBOUTI

Hassan **Ayanleh SOULEIMAN** b. 3 Dec 1992 Djibouti City 1.72m 60kg.
At (800m)/1500m: OG: '16- sf/4; WCh: '13- 3/sf, '15- h; WI: '12- 5; AfG: '11- 6; AfCh: '12- 2, '14- 1; CCp: '14- 1; WI: '14- 1, '16- 9; won DL 2013, Arab G 2011, Franc G 2013. At 3000m: WY: '09- h. Won Arab 5000m 2015.
World indoor 1000m record 2016. DJI records: 800m (5) 2012-15, 1000m (2) 2013-16, 1500m (3) 2011-14, 1M (3) 2012-14, 3000m 2012.
Progress at 800m, 1500m: 2011- 1:51.78A, 3:34.32; 2012- 1:47.45, 3:30.31; 2013- 1:43.63, 3:31.64; 2014- 1:43.69, 3:29.58; 2015- 1:42.97, 3:30.17; 2016- 1:43.52, 3:31.68. pbs: 1000m 2:13.49 '16, 1M 3:47.32 '14, 3000m 7:39.81i '13, 7:42.22 '12, 5000m 13:17.97 '15.
Djibouti's first ever world champion 2013 and first to set an official world record.

DOMINICAN REPUBLIC

Governing body: Federación Dominicana de Asociaciones de Atletismo. Avenida J.F. Kennedy, Centro Olímpico "Juan Pablo Duarte". Santo Domingo. Founded 1953.
Luguelín SANTOS b. 12 Nov 1992 Bayaguana 1.73m 61kg. Universidad Interamericana de San Germán, Puerto Rico.
At 400m: OG: '12- 2, '16- sf; WCh: '13- 3 (h 200m), '15- 4; WJ: '10- 6, '12- 1; PAm: '11- 2/2R, '15- 1; CCp: '14- 5; YthOG: '10- 1; WUG: '15- 1.
DOM records 200m 2013, 400m (5) 2011-15. CAC indoor 600m best 2015.
Progress at 400m: 2009- 47.88, 2010- 46.19, 2011- 44.71A, 2012- 44.45, 2013- 44.52, 2014- 44.53, 2015- 44.11, 2016- 44.71. pbs: 200m 20.55A '13, 20.70 '16; 300m 32.0+, '15, 32.56 '12, 500m 59.75 '15, 600m 1:15.58 '16, 800m 1:49.18 '14.
Was over-age at the 2012 World Juniors. Younger brother Juander (b. 7 May 1995) has pbs 400m 45.93A '14, 400mh 50.27 '15.

ECUADOR

Governing body: Federación Ecuatoriana de Atletismo, Casilla 01-01-736, Cuenca. F'd 1925.
Andrés CHOCHO b. 4 Nov 1983 Cuenca 1.67m 67kg.
At 20kW: OG: '08- 38, '16- dq; WCh: '07-09-15: dq/38/dq; WCp: '16- 6; SACh: '11- 1, '13- 3; WUG: '11- 3. At 50kW: OG: '16- dq; WCh: '11-13-15: 10/dq/8; PAm: '15- 1; won BolG 2013. Won S.Am 20kW 2016, SAm-J 10,000W 2001.
Four S.American 50k records 2011-16.
Progress at 50kW: 2010- 3:54:42, 2011- 3:49:32, 2012- 3:49:26, 2013- 3:58:50, 2014- 3:57:00, 2015- 3:46:00, 2016- 3:42:57A. pbs: 10kW 40:28 '16, 41:55.50tA '15, 20kW 1:20:07 '16, 30kW 2:16:46 '14, 35kW 2:36:56 '15.
Married to Érica de Sena (Brazil) (qv).

EGYPT

Governing body: Egyptian Amateur Athletic Federation, Sport Federation Building, El Estad El Bahary, Nasr City – Cairo. Founded 1910.
Ihab ABDELRAHMAN El-Sayed b. 1 May 1989 Al-Sharqiyah 1.94m 96kg.
At JT: OG: '12- dnq 28; WCh: '11- dnq 35, '13- 7, '15- 2; AfG: '11- 5, '15- 1; AfCh: '10-12-14: 1/5/2; WJ: '08- 2; Af-J: '07- 3; CCp: '14- 1; Arab champion 2009, 2011, 2013, 2015.
African JT record 2014, six Egyptian 2010-14.
Progress at JT: 2007- 71.15, 2008- 76.20, 2009- 78.44, 2010- 81.84, 2011- 78.83, 2012- 82.25, 2013- 83.62, 2014- 89.21, 2015- 88.99, 2016- 87.37dq/81.51.
Egypt's first ever World Champs medal 2015. Reeived a 2-year ban following a positive test (that he is appealing) for testosterone on 21 Apr 2016
Mostafa Hicham AL-GAMAL b. 1 Oct 1988 Giza 1.91m 105kg.
At HT: OG: '12- dnq 27; WCh: '11- dnq 30, '15- 7; AfG: '11- 1, '15- 1; AfCh: '08-10-12-14: 2/3/3/1; CCp: '14- 2; Won Med G 2013, Arab Ch 2015.
African hammer record 2014.
Progress at HT: 2006- 61.44, 2007- 66.26, 2008- 71.15, 2009- 71.88, 2010- 73.27, 2011- 74.76, 2012- 77.14, 2013- 77.73, 2014- 81.27, 2015- 79.90.

ERITREA

Governing body: Eritrean National Athletics Federation, PO Box 1117, Asmara. F'd 1992.
Ghirmay GHEBRESLASSIE b. 14 Nov 1995 Kisadeka.
At Mar: OG: '16- 4; WCh: '15- 1. World HMar: '14- 7; CC: '13- 7J; AfCC: 12- 9J.
Progress at Mar: 2014- 2:09:08, 2015- 2:07:47. 2016- 2:07:46. pbs: 5000m 13:40.17 '12, 10000m 28:33.37 '12; Road: 10M 46:29 '12, HMar 60:09 '13, 25k 1:12:43 '16, 30k 1:28:13 '16.
Youngest ever world marathon champion at 19 in 2015 after 2nd in Hamburg Marathon. Won New York Marathon 2016.
Abrar OSMAN Adem b. 1 Jan 1994? Adi Shumakele, Debub 1.73m 55kg.
At 10000m: WCh: '15- 6 (h 5000m). At 5000m: OG: '12- h, '16- 10; WJ: '12- 6; AfG: '11- 5; AfCh: '14- 3. At 3000m: WY: '11- 3; CCp: '14- 6; Yth Oly: '10- 1. World CC: '13- 18, '15- 13; HMar: '16- 7.
Progress at 5000m, 10000m: 2011- 13:43.02, 2012-

ERITREA – ESTONIA

13:17.32, 2013- 13:20.79, 2014- 13:16.45, 2015- 13:14.00, 27:41.69; 2016- 13:04.12. pbs: 3000m 7:39.70 '13, 15k 42:19 '16, HMar 60:39 '15.
Zersenay TADESE b. 8 Feb 1982 Adi Bana 1.60m 56kg. C.A. Adidas. Madrid, Spain.
At (5000m)/10000m: OG: '04- 7/3, '08- 5, '12- 6, '16- 8; WCh: '03- (8), '05- 14/6, '07- 4, '09- 2, '11- 4; AfCh: '02- 6, AfG: '07- 1, '15 (1 HMar). World CC: 2002-03-04-05-06-07-08-09: 30/9/6/2/4/1/3/3; 20k: '06- 1; HMar: '02-03-07-08-09-10-12-14: 21/7/1/1/1/2/1/4.
Records: World 20km and half marathon 2010.
Eritrean 3000m (2), 2M, 5000m (4), 10000m (5) HMar (3) 2003-10.
Progress at 5000m, 10000m, HMar: 2002- 13:48.79, 28:47.29, 63:05; 2003- 13:05.57, 28:42.79, 61:26; 2004- 13:13.74, 27:22.57; 2005- 13:12.23, 27:04.70, 59:05; 2006- 12:59.27, 26:37.25, 59:16; 2007- 27:00.30, 58:59; 2008- 27:05.11, 59:56; 2009- 13:07.02, 26:50.12, 59:35; 2010- 58:23, 2011- 12:59.32, 26:51.09, 58:30; 2012- 27:33.51, 59:34; 2013- 60:10, 2014- 59.38, 2015- 28:05.34, 59:24; 2016- 13:26.23, 27:00.00. pbs: 3000m 7:39.93 '05, 2M 8:19.34 '07, Road: 15k 41:27 '05, 10M 45:52 '07, 20k 55:21+ '10, Mar 2:10:41 '12.
Won Eritrea's first medal at Olympics in 2004 and World CC in 2005 and first gold in 2006 World 20k before four more at half marathon. 15 wins in 18 half marathons 2002-13; ran 59:05 for the fastest ever to win the Great North Run (slightly downhill overall) in 2005 and won Lisbon 2010-11 in two fastest ever times. Won a national road cycling title in 2001 before taking up athletics. His younger brother **Kidane** (b. 31 Aug 1987) had pbs 5000m 13:11.85 '10, 10,000m 27:06.16 '08; at 5000m/(10000m): OG: '08- 10/12, WCh: '09- h/9; AfrCC: '12- 6.

ESTONIA

Governing body: Eesti Kergejôustikuliit, Maakri 23, Tallinn 10145. Founded 1920.
National Championships first held in 1917.
2016: Men: 100m/200m: Timo Tiisma 10.57/21.51, 400m: Rasmus Mägi 46.50, 800m: Raimond Valler 1:50.44, 1500m: Andi Noot 5:51.24, 5000m: Keio Kits 14:54.23, 10000m: Keio Kits 31:36.08., HMar: Tildrek Nurme 66:59, Mar: Heinar Vaine 2:23:18, 3000mSt: Kaur Kivistik 9:19.01, 110mh: Gert Valdsalu 14.56, 400mh: Jaak-Heinrich Jagor 50.76, HJ: Karl Lumi 2.13, PV: Anri Mulin 4.90, LJ: Henrik Kutberg 7.63, TJ: Igor Syunin 15.78, SP: Kristo Galeta 18.52, DT: Martin Kupper 64.76, HT: Mart Olman 63.14, JT: Tanel Laanmäe 84.06, Dec: Kristjan Rosenberg 7738, 10000mW/20kW: Lauri Lelumees 47:56.55/1:35:25. **Women**: 100m/LJ: Ksenija Balta 11.36/6.51, 200m: Maris Mägi 24.04, 400m/400mh: Annika Sakkarias 55.26/60.08, 800m/1500m: Liina Tsernov 2:06.79/4:22.31, 5000m: Egle-Helene Ervin 17:32.36, 10000m: Lily Luik 36:24.05, HMar: Kaisa Kukk 78:21, Mar: Moonika Pilli 2:52:17, 3000mSt: Olga Andrejeva 11:32.03, 100mh: Diana Suumann 13.91, HJ: Anna Iljustsenko 1.85, PV: Getter Marie Lemberg 3.50, LJ: Ksenija Balta 6.66, TJ: Merilyn Uudmäe 13.51, SP: Anu Teesaar 15.63, DT: Kätlin Töllasson 48.82, HT: Kati Ojaloo 65.14, JT: Marcella Liiv 51.11, Hep: Mari Klaup 5667, 10000mW: Anna Tipukina 55:57.86, 20kW: Angela Mandel 2:01:37.
Gerd KANTER b. 6 May 1979 Tallinn 1.96m 125kg. Tallinna SS Kalev. Business management graduate.
At DT: OG: '04- dnq 19, '08- 1, '12- 3, '16- 5; WCh: '03-05-07-09-11-13-15: dnq 25/2/1/3/2/3/4; EC: '02-06-10-12-14-16: 12/2/4/2/2/3; EU23: '01- 5; CCp: '14- 1; WUG: '05- 1. Won WAF 2007-08, DL 2012-13, Estonian 2004-09, 2011-15.
Five Estonian discus records 2004-06.
Progress at DT: 1998- 47.37, 1999- 49.65, 2000- 57.68, 2001- 60.47, 2002- 66.31, 2003- 67.13, 2004- 68.50, 2005- 70.10, 2006- 73.38, 2007- 72.02, 2008- 71.88, 2009- 71.64, 2010- 71.45, 2011- 67.99, 2012- 68.03, 2013- 67.59, 2014- 66.28, 2015- 66.02, 2016- 65.27. pb SP 17.31i '04, 16.11 '00.
Threw over 70m in four rounds at Helsingborg on 4 Sep 2006; a feat matched only by Virgilijus Alekna. Six successive seasons over 70m.
Martin KUPPER b. 31 May 1989 Tallinn 1.98m 119kg. Audentese SK.
At DT: OG: '16- 4; WCh: '15: dnq 16; EC: '14- 9, '16- 7; EU23: '11- dnq 15; Won EST 2016.
Five Estonian discus records 2004-06.
Progress at DT: 2010- 55.19, 2011- 60.18, 2012- 62.12, 2013- 65.03, 2014- 64.98, 2015- 66.67, 2016- 66.61. pb SP 17.84 '11.
Rasmus MÄGI b. 4 May 1992 Tartu 1.88m 74kg. Tartu University ASK.
At 400mh: OG: '12- h, '16- 6; WCh: '13 & 15- sf; EC: '12-14-16: 5/2/sf; WJ: '10- h; EU23: '13- 3; EJ: '11- 4; CCp: '14- 4. Won EST 400m 2012, 2016; 400mh 2009, 2014-15.
S3v3n Estonian 400mh records 2012-16
Progress at 400mh: 2010- 52.79, 2011- 50.14, 2012- 49.54, 2013- 49.19, 2014- 48.54, 2015- 48.65, 2016- 48.40. pbs: 200m 21.90 '11, 400m 46.40 '13, 200mh 24.01 '11, LJ 7.73 '12.
His sister Maris has won 22 Estonian titles in sprints and hurdles, pbs: 400m 52.21 '11, 400mh 56.56 '13 (EST record).
Maicel UIBO b. 27 Dec 1992 Pölva 1.88m 86kg. Pölva.
At Dec: OG: '16- 24; WCh: '13- 19, '15- 10; NCAA champion 2014-15. At HJ: EU23: '13- dnq 21. At HJ: WY: '09- dnq 19.
Progress at Dec: 2012- 7548, 2013- 8223, 2014- 8182, 2015- 8356, 2016- 8315. pbs: 60m 7.16Ai '14, 7.18 '15; 100m 10.99 '13, 400m 50.24 '15, 1000m 2:39.72i '13, 1500m 4:25.53 '15, 60mh 8.25Ai '14, 8.28i '13; 110mh 14.61 '16, HJ 2.18 '15; PV 5.25i/5.20 '15, LJ 7.82 '13, SP 14.98 '16; DT 49.14

'15, JT 64.51 '15, Hep 6044Ai '14.
Married Shaunae Miller (qv) on 4 Feb 2017..

Women

Ksenija BALTA b. 1 Nov 1986 Minsk, Belarus 1.68m 53kg. Tallinna SS Kalev.
At LJ: OG: '08- dnq 27, '16- 6; WCh: '09- 8; EC: '06- dnq 26 (h 100m), '10- dnq 16 (h 200m), '16- 4; WI: '10- 4, '16- 7; EI: '09- 1, '17- 5. At Hep: EJ: '05- 3; ECp: '06- 3. Won EST 100m 2006-08, 2013, 2016; 200m 2008, 2013; LJ 2008, 2010, 2015-16; Hep 2005.
EST records: 100m (3) 2006-14, 200m 2006, LJ (4) 2006-10.
Progress at LJ: 2003- 5.79, 2004- 6.01, 2005- 6.46i/6.32, 2006- 6.80, 2007- 6.55i, 2008- 6.65/6.76w, 2009- 6.87i/6.79/6.85w, 2010- 6.87, 2011- 6.73i, 2015- 6.66, 2016- 6.79, 2017- 6.79i. pbs: 50m 6.35i '08, 60m 7.29i '16, 100m 11.35 '14, 200m 23.05 '06, 400m 54.79i '05, 54.98 '13; 800m 2:09.80 '05, 60mh 8.16i '10, 100mh 13.89 '05, 13.70w '06; HJ 1.74 '06, SP 11.94 '05, JT 37.60 '05, Pen 4105i '05, Hep 6180 '06.

ETHIOPIA

Governing body: Ethiopian Athletic Federation, Addis Ababa Stadium, PO Box 3241, Addis Ababa. Founded 1961. **2016 National Champions**: **Men**: 800m: Bacha Morka 1:48.0, 1500m: Aman Wote 3:40.4, 5000m: Getaneh Tamire 13:47.6, 10000m: Abadi Hadis 28:43.2, HMar: Guye Adola 63:22, 3000mSt: Tafese Seboka 8:38.6. **Women**: 800m: Tigset Ketema 2:04.7, 1500m: Besu Sado 4:08.2, 5000m: Dera Dida 16:09.1, 10000m: Shure Demise 33:24.5, HMar: Netsanet Gudeta 73:45, 3000mSt: Weynshet Ansa 10:05.1.

Yenew ALAMIREW b. 27 May 1990 Tilili l.75m 57kg.
At 5000m: OG: '12- 12; WCh: '13- 9; AfG: '11- 2; AfCh: '14- 5; won DL 2013. At 3000m: WI: '12- 9, '16- 12.
Progress at 5000m: 2010- 13:16.53, 2011- 13:00.46, 2012- 12:48.77, 2013- 12:54.95, 2014- 13:00.21, 2015- 13:05.53, 2016- 13:04.29. pbs: 1500m 3:35.09+ '11, 1M 3:50.43 '11, 3000m 7:27.26 '11, Road: 10k 28:22 '15, 15k 42:30 '14, 10M 46:04 '15.

Mohamed AMAN Geleto b. 10 Jan 1994 Asella 1.69m 55kg.
At 800m: OG: '12- 6, '16- sf; WCh: '11- 8, '13- 1, '15- dq sf; WY: '11- 2; WI: '12-14-16: 1/1/4; AfCh: '14- 2; CCp: '14- 2; won DL 2012-13, Afr-J 2011, Yth OG 1000m 2010.
Records: Ethiopian 800m (6) 2011-13, 1000m 2014, world youth 800m indoors and out 2011, world junior 600m indoor 2013 (1:15.60), African indoor 800m 2014.
Progress at 800m: 2008- 1:50.29, 2009- 1:46.34, 2010- 1:48.5A, 2011- 1:43.37, 2012- 1:42.53, 2013- 1:42.37, 2014- 1:42.83, 2015- 1:43.56, 2016- 1:44.70. pbs: 600m 1:15.0+ '12, 1000m 2:15.75 '14, 1500m 3:43.52 '11, 1M 3:57.14 '11.
Was disqualified from taking the African Junior 800m gold in 2009 for being under-age (at 15). Youngest ever World Indoor champion at 18 years 60 days in 2012. Beat David Rudishsa in the latter's last races in both 2011 and 2012.

Kenenisa BEKELE b. 13 Jun 1982 near Bekoji, Arsi Province 1.62m 54kg.
At 5000m(/10000m): OG: '04- 2/1, '08- 1/1, '12- (4); WCh: '03- 3/1, '05- (1), '07- (1), '09- 1/1, '11- (dnf); WJ: '00- 2; AfG: '03- 1; AfCh: '06- 1, '08- 1. At 3000m: WY: '99- 2; WI: '06- 1; WCp: '06- 2. World CC: '99- 9J, 4k: '01- 1J/2 4k, '02-03-04-05-06: all 1/1, '08- 1. Won WAF 3000m 2003, 2009; 5000m 2006.
World records: 5000m 2004, 10000m 2004 & 2005, indoor 5000m (12:49.60) 2004, 2000m 2007, 2M 2008; World junior record 3000m 2001. ETH marathon record 2016.
Progress at 5000m, 10000m, Mar: 2000- 13:20.57, 2001- 13:13.33, 2002- 13:26.58, 2003- 12:52.26, 26:49.57; 2004- 12:37.35, 26:20.31; 2005- 12:40.18, 26:17.53; 2006- 12:48.09, 2007- 12:49.53, 26:46.19; 2008- 12:50.18, 26:25.97; 2009- 12:52.32, 26:46.31; 2011- 13:27e+, 26:43.16; 2012- 12:55.79, 27:02.59; 2013- 13:07.88, 27:12.08; 2014- 2:05:04, 2016- 2:03:03. pbs: 1000m 2:21.9+ '07, 1500m 3:32.35 '07, 1M 3:56.2+ '07, 2000m 4:49.99i '07, 4:58.40 '09, 3000m 7:25.79 '07, 2M 8:04.35i '08, 8:13.51 '07; Road: 15k 42:42 '01, 10M 46:06 '13, 20k 57:19 '13, HMar 60:09 '13, 25k 1:12:47 '16, 30k 1:27:25 '16.
At cross-country has a record 16 (12 individual, 4 team) world gold medals. Unbeaten in 27 races from Dec 2001 to March 2007 when he did not finish in the Worlds. After winning all his 12 10,000m track races including five major gold medals from 2003 until he dropped out of World 10,000 in 2011. 17 successive wins at 5000m 2006-09. Shared Golden League jackpot in 2009. Won Great North Run on half marathon debut 2013. Won in Paris on marathon debut 2014, then 4th Chicago; 3rd London and 1st Berlin 2016. IAAF Athlete of the Year 2004-05. He married film actress Danawit Gebregziabher on 18 Nov 2007.

Yigrem DEMELASH b. 28 Jan 1994 1.67m 52kg.
At 10000m: OG: '16- 4; WJ: '12- 1.
Progress at 5000m, 10000m: 2012- 13:03.30, 26:57.56; 2013- 13:13.18, 27:15.51; 2014- 13:11.80, 2015- 28:18.03, 2016- 13:05.64, 26:51.11. Pbs: 15k Rd 42:26 '14, HMar 59:19 '17.

Lelisa DESISA Benti b. 14 Jan 1990 Shewa 1.70m 52kg.
At 10000m: Af-J: '09- 1. At: HMar: WCh: '10- 7, AfG: '11- 1. At Mar: WCh: '13- 2, '15- 7.
Progress at 10000m, HMar, Mar: 2009- 28:46.74, 2010- 59:39; 2011- 59:30, 2012- 27:11.98, 62:50; 2013- 2:04:45, 2014- 59:36, 2:11:06; 2015- 2:05:52. pbs: 5000m 13:22.91 '12, Road: 15k 42:25 '10, 10M 45:36 '11., 2016- 60:37
Brilliant marathon debut to win Dubai 2013

and then won Boston and 2nd Worlds. 2nd New York 2014 (3rd 2015), Dubai 2015. Won Boston again in 2015 (2nd 2016).

Muktar EDRIS Awel b. 14 Jan 1994 Adio 1.72m 57kg.
At 5000m: OG: '16- dq; WCh: '13- 7; WJ: '12- 1. At 10000m: WCh: '15- 10; Af-J: '11- 4. World CC: '11-13-15-17: 7J/3J/3/6; AfCC: 12- 1J.
Progress at 5000m, 10000m: 2011- 28:44.95A, 2012- 13:04.34, 2013- 13:03.69, 2014- 12:54.83, 2015- 13:00.30, 27:17.18; 2016- 12:59.43. pbs: 3000m 7:33.28 '16.

Dejen GEBREMESKEL b. 24 Nov 1989 Adiqrat, Tigray region 1.78m 53kg.
At 5000m: OG: '12- 2, '16- 12; WCh: '11- 3; WJ: '08- 3; Af-J: '07- 2. At 10000m: WCh: '13- 16. At 3000m: WI: '10- 12-14: 10/5/3. World CC: '08-18J.
Progress at 5000m, 10000m: 2007- 13:21.05, 2008- 13:08.96, 2009- 13:03.13, 2010- 12:53.56, 2011- 12:55.89, 2012- 12:46.81, 2013- 13:31.02, 26:51.02; 2014- 13:09.73, 2015- 13:00.49, 2016- 12:59.89. pbs: 3000m 7:34.14i '12, 7:45.9+ '10, HMar 62:36 '14.
Fastest ever debut 10,000m at Sollentuna 2013.

Hagos GEBRHIWET Berhe b. 11 May 1994 Tsaedaenba, Tigray region 1.67m 55kg. Mesfen Engineering
At 5000m: OG: '12- 11, '16- 3; WCh: '13- 2, '15- 3; AfCh: '14- dnf; won DL 2016. At 3000m: WY: '11- 5; WI: '14- 5. World CC: '13- 1J, '15- 4, AfCC: '12- 4J.
World junior records 5000m 2012, indoor 3000m 2013.
Progress at 5000m: 2011- 14:10.0A, 2012- 12:47.53, 2013- 12:55.73, 2014- 13:06.88, 2015- 12:54.70, 2016- 13:00.20. pbs: 3000m 7:30.36 '13, 10k Rd 27:57dh '11.

Abadi HADIS Embaye b. 6 Nov 1997 1.70m 63kg.
At 10000m: OG: '16- 15; won ETH 2016. World CC: '17- 3.
Progress at 5000m, 10000m: 2015- 13:13.17, 2016- 13:02.49, 26:57.88. pbs: 3000m 7:33.28 '16.

Ibrahim JEYLAN Gashu b. 12 Jun 1989 Bale Province 1.68m 57kg. Muger Cement.
At 10000m: WCh: '11- 1, '13- 2; WJ: '06- 1, '08- 3; AfG: '11- 1; AfCh: '08- 2. At 3000m: WY: '05- 2. World CC: '06-08-17: 5J/1J/8. Won ETH 5000m 2014, 10000m 2006.
Two world youth 10,000m records 2006.
Progress at 5000m, 10000m: 2006- 13:09.38, 27:02.81; 2007- 13:17.99, 27:50.53; 2008- 13:15.12, 27:13.85; 2009- 13:19.70, 27:22.19; 2010- 13:21.29, 27:12.43; 2011- 13:09.95, 27:09.02; 2013- 13:09.16, 27:22.23; 2014- 13:09.67, 2015- 13:20.21, 2016- 13:03.22, 26:58.75. pbs: 3000m 8:04.21 '05, 15k 43:38 '08, HMar 61:47 '14.

Yomif KEJELCHA Atomsa b. 1 Aug 1997 1.86m 58kg.

At 5000m: WCh: '15- 4; WJ: '14- 1; Af-J: '15- 1; won DL 2015. At 3000m: WY: '13- 1; Yth OG: '14- 1; WI: '16- 1. World CC: '17- 2 MxR.
World junior 3000m record 2016.
Progress at 5000m: 2014- 13:25.19, 2015- 12:53.98, 2016- 13:03.29. pbs: 2000m 4:57.74i '14, 3000m 7:28.19 '16, 10k Rd 28:13 '13.

Abera KUMA Lema b. 31 Aug 1990 Ambo 1.60m 50kg.
At 5000m: WCh: '11- 5; Af-J: '09- 1. At 10000m: WCh: '13- 5. At 3000m: WY: '07- 5.
Tied world 30km record 2014.
Progress at 5000m, 10000m, Mar: 2009- 13:29.40, 2010- 13:07.83, 2011- 13:00.15, 27:22.54; 2012- 13:09.32, 27:18.39; 2013- 26:52.85, 2014- 2:05:56, 2015- 2:06:47, 2016- 2:07:48. pbs: 1500m 3:48.73 '09, 3000m 7:39.09i/7:40.85 '12, Road: 15k 42:01 '10, 10M 45:28 '11, HMar 60:19 '12, 25k 1:13:08 '14, 30k 1:27:38 '14.
3rd Berlin Marathon 2014, won Rotterdam 2015.

Hayle LEMI Berhanu b. 13 Sep 1994 Hasasa, 1.72m 56kg.
At Mar: OG: '16- 13; WCh: '15- 15.
Progress at Mar: 2014- 2:10:40, 2015- 2:05:28, 2016- 2:04:33. pbs: HMar 61:37 '15, 30k 1:27:21 '16.
Marathon wins: Zürich & Taiyuan 2014, Dubai 2015 (2nd 2016), Warsaw 2015, Boston 2016, Xiamen 2017.

Sisay LEMMA Kasaye b. 12 Dec 1990.
Progress at Mar: 2012- 2:11:58, 2013- 2:09:02, 2015- 2:06:26, 2016- 2:05:16, 2017- 2:08:04. pb HMar 61:11 '16, 25k 1:12:49 '16, 30k 1:27:20 '16.
Marathon wins: Carpi 2012 (debut), Warsaw 2013, Vienna & Frankfurt 2015; 3rd Dubai 2017.

Feyisa LILESA Gemechu b. 1 Feb 1990 Tullu Bultuma 1.58m 50kg.
At Mar: OG: '16- 2; WCh: '11- 3, '13- dnf, World CC: 2008-09-10-11-13: 14J/12/25/17/9. Won ETH CC 2013.
Progress at Mar: 2009- 2:09:12, 2010- 2:05:23, 2011- 2:10:32, 2012- 2:04:52, 2013- 2:07:46, 2014- 2:08:26, 2015- 2:06:35, 2016- 2:06:56. pbs: 5000m 13:34.80 '08, 10000m 27:46.97 '08; Road: 15k 42:15+ '13, 20k 56:19+ '12, HMar 59:22 '12, 25k 1:13:22 '13, 30k 1:28:05 '13.
Marathons won: Dublin 2009, Xiamen 2010, Tokyo 2016. 3rd/2nd Chicago 2010/2012, 4th Rotterdam 2010 in then fastest ever by 20 year-old, 4th London 2013. Now living in the USA.

Tsegaye MEKONNEN Asefa b. 15 Jun 1995 1.74m 56kg.
At 5000m: WJ: '12- 5.
World junior marathon record 2014.
Progress at Mar: 2014- 2:04:32, 2015- dnf, 2016- 2:04:46. pbs: 5000m 13:44.43 '14; Road: 10k 28:36 '12, HMar 61:05 '15.
Marathons: 1st Dubai 2014 (3rd 2016), 5th London 2014.

Imane MERGA Jida b. 15 Oct 1988 Tulu Bolo, Oromia region 1.74m 61kg. Defence.

At 5000m/(10000m): WCh: '09- (4), '11- dq/3, '13- (12), '15- 13/dnf; AfCh: '10- 5, '14- (5); Af-J: '07- (3); CCp: '10- 5; won DL 2010-11, WAF 2009. World CC: '07-11-13: 7J/1/2.
Progress at 5000m, 10000m: 2007- 13:33.52, 30:12.03; 2008- 13:08.20, 27:33.53, 2009- 12:55.66, 27:15.94; 2010- 12:53.58; 2011- 12:54.21, 26:48.35; 2012- 12:59.77, 27:14.02; 2013- 13:09.17, 26:57.33; 2014- 13:11.94, 28:17.75; 2015- 12:59.04, 27:17.63; 2016- 13:06.25, 27:27.33. pbs: 3000m 7:39.96 '15, HMar 59:56 '12.
Disqualified for running inside the kerb after finishing 3rd in World 5000m 2011.

Adugna TEKELE Bikila b. 26 Feb 1989 1.70m 55kg.
At 10000m: AfG: '15- 3; AfCh: '14- 4. At HMar: WCh: '14- 9.
Progress at 10000m: 2013- 29:13.1A, 2014- 28:12.28, 2015- 27:19.34, 2016- 27:20.65. pbs: HMar 60:15 '14, Mar 2:08:31 '14.

Adera Tamirat TOLA b. 11 Aug 1991 1.81m 59kg.
At 10000m: OG: '16- 3. At HMar: WCh: '16- 5; World CC: '15- 6.
Progress at 10000m, Mar: 2014- 2:06:17, 2015- 27:22.64, 2016- 26:57.33, dnf; 2017- 2:04:11. pbs: 15k 42:26 '127, 20k 56:36 '17, HMar 59:37 '17.
Won Dubai Marathon 2017.

Yemane TSEGAY Adhane b. 8 Apr 1985.
At Mar: WCh: '09- 4, '13- 8, '15- 2.
Progress at Mar: 2008- 2:13:29, 2009- 2:06:30, 2010- 2:07:11, 2011- 2:10:24, 2012- 2:04:48, 2013- 2:09:11, 2014- 2:06:51, 2015- 2:09:48dh, 2016- 2:08:48. pbs: HMar 61:37 '10, 30k 1:27:40 '12.
Marathon wins: Macau 2008, Gongju 2009, Lake Biwa 2010, Taipei 2011, Rotterdam 2012, Eindhoven 2013, Daegu & Ottawa 2014, Fukuoka 2016; 2nd/3rd Boston 2015/16.
Married Abeba Aregawi (qv) in January 2017.

Aman WOTE Fete b. 18 Apr 1984 Kabete 1.81m 64kg.
At 1500m: OG: '12- ht; WCh: 13- sf, '15- dnf; AfG: '11- 5; AfCh: '10- 7; WI: '12-14-16: 4/2/6. Won ETH 1500m 2014, 2016.
Ethiopian records 1500m (2) & 1M 2014.
Progress at 1500m: 2010- 3:38.89A 2011- 3:35.61, 2012- 3:35:38, 2013- 3:32.65, 2014- 3:29.91, 2015- 3:30.29, 2016- 3:34.58. pbs: 800m 1:44.99 '13, 1M 3:48.60 '14, 3000m 7:43.99i '13.

Tebalu ZAWEDE b. 2 Nov 1987 1.84m 65kg.
At 10000m: AfG: '15- 1; AfCh: '12- 4.
Progress at 10000m, Mar: 2012- 28:03.16, 2014- 2:07:10, 2015- 27:20.54, 2:08:46; 2016- 27:25.10. pb HMar 60:33 '13.
Won Joongang marathon in Seoul 2015.

Women

Sofia ASSEFA Abebe b. 14 Nov 1987 Tenta District, south Wello 1.71m 58kg. Ethiopian Bank.

At 3000mSt: OG: '08- h, '12- 2, '16- 5; WCh: '09-11-13-15: 12/5/3/4; AfG: '15- 1; AfCh: '08-10-14: 4/2/2; CCp: '10- 3.
Ethiopian 3000mSt records 2011 and 2012.
Progress at 3000mSt: 2006- 10:17.48, 2007- 9:48.46, 2008- 9:31.58, 2009- 9:19.91, 2010- 9:20.72, 2011- 9:15.04, 2012- 9:09.00, 2013- 9:12.84, 2014- 9:11.39, 2015- 9:12.63, 2016- 9:13.09. pbs: 1000m 2:49.79 '07, 5000m 15:59.74 '07, 2000mSt 6:33.49 '07.

Hiwot AYALEW Yemer b. 6 Mar 1990 Gojam, Amhara 1.73m 51kg. Commercial Bank.
At 3000mSt: OG: '12- 4, '16- h; WCh: '13- 4, '15- 6; AfG: '11- 2, 15- 2; AfCh: '14- 1; CCp: '14- 2; won DL 2014. At 3000m: WI: '14-11. World CC: '11- 11, '13- 2.
Progress at 3000mSt: 2011- 9:23.88, 2012- 9:09.61, 2013- 9:15.25, 2014- 9:10.64, 2015- 9:14.73, 2016- 9:35.09. pbs: 3000m 8:43.29i '14, 2M: 9:21.59i '14, 5000m 14:49.36 '12, 10k Rd 31:47 '14.
Younger sister of Wude Ayalew (qv).

Wude AYALEW Yimer b. 4 Jul 1987 Sekela, Amhara region 1.50m 44kg.
At 10000m: WCh: '09- 3; AfG: '11- 2, '15- 4; AfCh: '08- 3, '10- 4. At 5000m: WJ: '06- 5. World CC: '06-07-09-11: 5/10/5/6. Won ETH CC 2009.
Progress at 5000m, 10000m: 2006- 14:57.23, 33:57.0; 2008- 15:07.65, 31:06.84; 2009- 14:38.44, 30:11.87; 2010- 15:02.47, 32:29.92A; 2011- 14:59.71, 31:24.09; 2013- 31:16.68, 2015- 30:58.03. pbs: 1500m 4:14.85 '07, 3000m 8:30.93 '09; Road: 15k 48:15 '14, 20k 65:28 '14, HMar 67:58 '09, Mar 2:27:08 '16.
Won Great Ethiopian Run 2008. Older sister of Hiyot Ayalew.

Almaz AYANA Eba b. 21 Nov 1991 Benshangul 1.65m 50kg.
At 5000m/(10000m): OG: '16- 3/1; WCh: '13- 3, '15- 1; AfCh: '14- 1; CCp: '14- 1. At 3000mSt: WJ: '10- 5; won DL 5000m 2016, ETH 5000m 2014, 3000mSt 2013.
World record 10000m 2016, junior 3000m steeplechase 2010.
Progress at 5000m, 10000m, 3000mSt: 2009- 10:03.75, 2010- 9:22.51, 2011- 15:12.24, 9:30.23; 2012- 14:57.97, 9:38.62; 2013- 14:25.84, 9:27.49; 2014- 14:29.19, 2015- 14:14.32; 2016- 14:12.59, 29:17.45. pbs: 2000m 5:35.10+ '15, 3000m 8:22.22 '15, 10k rd 32:19 '10.
Ran 30:07.00 on 10000m track debut to win ETH trial race at Hengelo, then smashed WR in Rio.
Married to Soresa Fida (1500m 3:34.72 '11, 3 AfCh '11). IAAF female Athlete of the Year 2016.

Gelete BURKA Bati b. 15 Feb 1986 Kofele 1.65m 45kg.
At 1500m: OG: '08- h; WCh: '05- 8, '09- 10 (fell), '11- sf, '13- h; WI: '08- 1, '10- 3; AfG: '07- 1; AfCh: '08- 1, '10- 2; CCp: '10- 6. At 3000m: WI: '12- 3. At 5000m: OG: '12- 5; WCh: '07- 9. At 10000m: OG:

'16- 8; WCh: '15- 2; AfG: '15- 3. World CC: '03-05-06-07-08-09: 3J/1J/1 4k/4/6/8. Won ETH 800m 2011, 1500m 2004-05, 2007; 5000m 2005, 4k CC 2006.
African records: 1M 2008, 200m 2009, indoor 1500m 2008, junior 1500m 2005. World youth 1M best (4:30.81) 2003.
Progress at 1500m, 5000m, 10000m, Mar: 2003- 4:10.82, 16:23.8A, 2004- 4:06.10, 2005- 3:59.60, 14:51.47; 2006- 4:02.68, 14:40.92; 2007- 4:00.48, 14:31.20; 2008- 3:59.75i/4:00.44, 14:45.84; 2009- 3:58.79, 2010- 3:59.28, 2011- 4:03.28, 2012- 14:41.43, 2013- 4:04.36, 14:42.07, 2:30:40; 2014- 2:26:03, 2015- 14:40.50, 30:49.68; 2016- 14:52.4, 30:26.66. pbs: 800m 2:02.89 '10, 1M 4:18.23 '08, 2000m 5:30.19 '09, 3000m 8:25.92 '06; Rd: 15k 49:26 '12, HMar 69:32 '16, 25k 1:25:39 '14, 30k 1:43:03 '14. Married Taddele Gebrmehden in 2007.

Mamitu DASKA Molisa b. 16 Oct 1983 Liteshoa 1.64m 45kg.
At HMar: AfG: '11- 2, '15- 1. World CC: '09-10-15: 12/8/8. ETH half marathon record 2015.
Progress at 10,000m, Mar: 20008- 32:45.46, 2009- 31:36.88, 2:26:38; 2010- 2:24:19, 2011- 2:21:59, 2012- 32:54.9A, 2:23:52; 2013- 2:23:23, 2014- 2:29:35, 2015- 30:55.56, 2016- 2:25:27. pbs: Road: 5k 14:52 '15, 10M 51:54 '14, HMar 66:28 '15, 30k 1:39:46 '11. Marathon wins: Dubai 2010, Houston 2011, Frankfurt 2011 & 2016.

Buzunesh DEBA Dejene b. 8 Sep 1987 Arsi 1.62m 45kg.
Progress at Mar: 2009- 2:32:17, 2010- 2:27:24, 2011- 2:23:19, 2013- 2:24:26, 2014- 2:19:59dh/ 2:31:40, 2015- 2:25:09dh. pbs: 5000m 15:52.33 '04, Rd 10k 32:10 '10, 15k 49:05 '14, HMar 68:59 '14. Married Worku Bayi in 2005, lives in Bronx, New York. Marathon wins: Sacramento 2009, Jacksonville, Duluth, St.Paul & Sacramento 2010, Los Angeles & San Diego 2011, Boston 2014 (3rd 2015). 2nd New York 2011 & 2013, Houston 2013.

Meseret DEFAR b. 19 Nov 1983 Addis Ababa 1.55m 42kg.
At 5000m(/10000m): OG: '04- 1, '08- 2, '12- 1; WCh: '03- h, '05- 2, '07- 1, '09- 3/5, '11- 3/dnf, '13- 1; WJ: '00- 2, '02- 1; AfG: '03- 1, '07- 1; AfCh: '00-06-08-10: 2/1/2/2; WCp: '06- 1. At 3000m: WJ: '02- 1; WY: '99- 2; WI: '03-04-06-08-10-12-16: 3/1/1/1/1/2/2; CCp: '10- 1. Won WAF 3000m 2004-09, 5000m 2005, 2008-09; DL 5000m 2013. World CC: '02- 13J.
Records: World 5000m 2006 & 2007, 2M 2007 (2); indoor 3000m 2007, 2M 2008 (9:10.50) & 2009 (9:06.26), 5000m 2009; African 5000m 2005, Ethiopian 3000m (2) 2006-07. World 5k road best 14:46 Carlsbad 2006.
Progress at 3000m, 5000m, 10000m: 1999- 9:02.08, 33:54.9A; 2000- 8:59.90, 15:08.36; 2001- 8:52.47, 15:08.65; 2002- 8:40.28, 15:26.45; 2003- 8:38.31, 14:40.34; 2004- 8:33.44i/8:36.46, 14:44.81; 2005- 8:30.05i/8:33.57, 14:28.98; 2006- 8:24.66, 14:24.53; 2007- 8:23.72i/8:24.51, 14:16.63; 2008- 8:27.93i/8:34.53, 14:12.88; 2009- 8:26.99i/8:30.15, 14:24.37i/14:36.38, 29:59.20; 2010- 8:24.46i/8:36.09, 14:24.79i/14:38.87; 2011- 8:36.91i/8:50.36+, 14:29.52, 31:05.05; 2012- 8:31.56i/8:46.49, 14:35.85; 2013- 8:30.29, 14:26.90, 30:08.06; 2016- 8:30.83i. pbs: 1500m 4:02.00 '10, 1M: 4:28.5ei '06, 4:33.07+ '07; 2000m 5:34.74i/5:38.0 '06, 2M 8:58.58 '07, road 15k 47:30 '13, HMar 66:09 '13.
Married to Teodros Hailu. IAAF woman athlete of the year 2007. Record nine WAF wins. Reclrd 45 times under 15 mins for 5000m. Daughter Gabriella born on 23 June 2014. In first race since 2013 won at 3000m indoors in 8:30.83 at Boston on 14 Feb 2016.

Worknesh DEGEFA b. 28 Oct 1990.
At HMar: AfG: '15- 2.
Progress at HMar, Mar: 2012- 76:48, 2013- 67:49, 2014- 68:46, 2015- 67:14, 2016- 66:14. pbs: 10k 31:53 '12.
Won at Dubai 2017 on marathon debut.

Shure DEMISE Ware b. 21 Jan 1996 Bore 1.59m 45kg.
At 10000m: AfCh: '16- 5. Won ETH 2016.
World junior marathon record 2015 (4th on debut at Dubai).
Progress at Mar: 2015- 2:20:59, 2016- 2:25:04, 2017- 2:22:57. pbs: 10000m: 32:14.25 '16, 15k 49:22 '14, HMar 68:53 '14.
Won Toronto marathon 2015-1, 2nd Dubai 2017.

Birhane DIBABA b. 11 Sep 1993 Moyagajo 1.59m 44kg.
Progress at Mar: 2012- 2:29:22, 2013- 2:23:01, 2014- 2:22:30, 2015- 2:23:15, 2016- 2:23:16. pbs: HMar 67:47 '16.
Won Valencia marathon 2012, Tokyo 2015; 2nd São Paulo 2012, Nagoya 2013, Tokyo 2014 & 2017; 3rd Frankfurt 2013, Chicago 2014-15.

Genzebe DIBABA b. 8 Feb 1991 Bekoji. Muger Cement. 1.68m 52kg.
At 1500m: OG: '12- h, '16- 2; WCh: '13- 7, '15- 1; WI: '12- 1. At 3000m: CCp: '14- 1; WI: '14- 1, '16- 1. At 5000m: WCh: '09 -8, '11- 8, '15- 3; AfCh: '14- 2; WJ: '08- 2, '10- 1; Af-J: '09- 1. World CC: '07-08-09-10-11-17: 5J/1J/1J/11J/9/2 MxR. Won DL 5000m 2015, ETH 1500m 2010.
Records: World 1500m 2015, indoor 1500m, 3000m & 2M 2014, 5000m 2015, 1M 2016, 2000m 2017. Two African 1500m 2015. Ethiopian 1500m (3) 2012-15, 2000m 2014.
Progress at 1500m, 5000m: 2007- 15:53.46, 2008- 15:02.41, 2009- 14:55.52, 2010- 4:04.80i/4:06.10, 15:08.06; 2011- 4:05.90, 14:37.56; 2012- 3:57.77, 2013- 3:57.54, 14:37.68; 2014- 3:55.17i/4:01.00, 14:28.88; 2015- 3:50.07, 14:15.41; 2016- 3:56.46i+/3 :57.31, 2017- 3:58.80i. pbs: 1000m 2:33.06i '17, 2:35.6+ '15; 1M 4:13.31i/4:14.30 '16, 2000m 5:23.75i '17, 5:27.50 '14; 3000m 8:16.60i/8:26.21 '14, 2M 9:00.48i/9:14.28 '14.
Laureus World Sportswomen of the Year 2014,

IAAF Woman Athlete of the Year 2015. Younger sister of Ejegayehu (2 OG 10000m 2004, 3 WCh 5000 & 10000m 2005) and Tirunesh Dibaba.

Mare DIBABA Hurssa b. 20 Oct 1989 Sululta, Oromia 1.52m 40kg.
At Mar: OG: '12- 22, '16- 3; WCh: '15- 1. At HMar: AfG: '11- 1. Won AZE 3000m and 5000m 2009.
AZE records (as Mare Ibrahimova) at 3000m and 5000m 2009.
Progress at HMar, Mar: 2008- 70:28, 2009- 68:45, 2010- 67:13, 2:25:27, 2011- 68:39, 2:23:25; 2012- 67:44, 2:19:52; 2014- 68:56, 2:21:36/2:20:35dh; 2015- 2:19:52, 2016- 67:55, 2:24:09. pbs: 3000m 9:16.94 '09, 5000m 15:42.83 '09, Road: 10k 31:55+ '10, 15k 48:04+ '10, 10M 51:29+ '10, 20k 63:47+ '10, 30k 1:39:19 '14.
She switched to Azerbaijan in December 2008 but back to Ethiopia as of 1 Feb 2010. Major marathons: won at Xiamen 2014 and 2015, Chicago 2014; 2nd Boston 2014, 3rd Dubai 2012.

Tirunesh DIBABA Kenene b. 1 Oct 1985 Chefa near Bekoji, Arsi region 1.60m 47kg.
At 5000m(/10000m): OG: '04- 3, '08- 1/1, '12- 3/1, '16- (3); WCh: '03- 1, '05- 1/1, '07- (1), '13- (1); WJ: '02- 2; AfG: '03- 4; AfCh: '06- 2, '08- (1), '10- (1). At 3000m: WCp: '06- 1. World CC: '01-02-03-05-06-07-08-10: 5J/2J/1J/1/1/2/1/4; 4k: '03-04-05: 7/2/1. Won WAF 5000m 2006, ETH 4k CC & 5000m 2003. 8k CC 2005.
World records: 5000m 2008, indoor 5000m 2005 (14:32.93) & 2007, junior 5000m 2003-04, indoor 3000m & 5000m 2004, world road 5k best 14:51 2005, 15k 2009. African 10000m record 2008.
Progress at 5000m, 10000m, Mar: 2002- 14:49.90, 2003- 14:39.94, 2004- 14:30.88, 2005- 14:32.42, 30:15.67; 2006- 14:30.40, 2007- 14:27.42i/14:35.67, 31:55.41; 2008- 14:11.15, 29:54.66; 2009- 14:33.65, 2010- 14:34.07, 31:51.39A; 2012- 14:50.80, 30:20.75; 2013- 14:23.68, 30:26.67; 2014- 2:20:35, 2016- 14:41.73, 29:42.56. pbs: 2000m 5:42.7 '05, 3000m 8:29.55 '06, 2M 9:12.23i '10, road 15k 46:28 '09, 10M 51:49 '16, HMar 66:50 '17, 30k 1:39:14 '14.
In 2003 she became, at 17 years 333 days, the youngest ever world champion at an individual event and in 2005 the first woman to win the 5000m/10000m double (with last laps of 58.19 and 58.4) at a global event after earlier in the year winning both World CC titles. Now has women's record 21 World CC medals. Married Sileshi Sihine on 26 Oct 2008; son Natan Seleshi born 26 Mar 2015. Retained the Olympic 10,000m title and won the Great North Run on half marathon debut in 2012. Third in London on marathon debut 2014. She ran eleven 10,000m track races – and won them all – before her 3rd in the 2016 Ethiopian Trial.

Buze DIRIBA Kejela b. 9 Feb 1994 Arsi 1.60m 43kg.
At 5000m: WCh: '13- 5; WJ: '12- 1. World CC: '11- 10J, '13- 9J

Progress at 5000m, 10000m: 2012- 14:53.06, 2013- 14:50.02, 2014- 15:16.83, 2015- 31:33.27, 2016- 31:38.61. pbs: 1500m 4:10.96 '12, 3000m 8:39.65 '12, 2M 9:29.03i '15, 9:40.01 '14; 10M Rd 51:38 '16, HMar 71:49 '16.

Etenesh DIRO Neda b. 10 May 1991 Jeidu, Oromiya 1.69m 47kg.
At 3000mSt: OG: '12- 5, '16- 15; WCh: '13- 5, '15- h; AfG: '15- 6; AfCh: '14- 4.
Progress at 5000m, 3000mSt: 2011- 15:21.51, 9:49.18, 2012- 15:19.77, 9:14.07, 2013- 9:16.97, 2014- 9:19.71, 2015- 9:29.10, 2016- 14:33.30, 9:16.87. pbs: 3000m 8:38.32 '16, Road: 10k 33:32A '11, 15k 51:21 '09, HMar 71:35 '10.

Axumawit EMBAYE Abraya b. 18 Oct 1994 1.60m 50kg.
At 1500m: WJ: '12- 7; AfCh: '14- 4; WI: '14- 2, '16- 4.
Progress at 1500m: 2012- 4:12.92, 2013- 4:05.16, 2014- 4:02.35, 2015- 4:02.92i/4:03.00, 2016- 4:03.05 pbs: 800m 2:03.27i '15, 1000m 2:37.43 '15, 1M 4:23.50i/4:26.84 '15, 3000m 8:49.52i '17, 8:51.82 '15.

Letesenbet GIDEY b. 20 Mar 1998 Endameskel, Tigray region 1.63m 48kg.
At 3000m: WY: '15- 4. World CC: '15- 1J, '17- 1J. African junior 5000m record 2016.
Progress at 5000m: 2014- 16:19.3A, 2015- 15:39.83, 2016- 14:45.63. pbs: 3000m 8:53.3 '16.

Amane GOBENA Gemeda b. 1 Sep 1982. 1.63m 48kg.
World 4k CC: '02- 8, '04- 11.
Progress at Mar: 2009- 2:26:53, 2010- 2:24:13, 2011- 2:31:49, 2012- 2:28:38, 2013- 2:23:50, 2014- 2:27:05, 2015- 2:23:30, 2016- 2:21:51 pbs: 1500m 4:11.04 '04, 1M 4:41.57 '03, 3000m 9:01.46 '02, 5000m 15:19.50 '04, Road: 10km 31:44 '14, 15km 47:55 '10, HMar 68:16 '09, 30k 1:43:24 '09.
Marathon wins: Toronto 2009, Osaka and Seoul 2010, Xiamen 2011, Santa Monica 2014, Istanbul 2014-15; 2nd Paris 2015, Tokyo 2016.

Netsanet GUDETA b. 12 Feb 1991 1.62m 45kg.
At HMar: WCh: '14- 6, '16- 4. World CC: '15- 3. At 10000m: AfCh: '15- dnf..
Progress at 10000m: 2015- 31:06.53, 2016- 30:36.75. pbs: HMar 67:31 '15.

Meseret HAILU b. 12 Sep 1990 Oromia region 1.68m 54kg.
At Mar: WCh: '13- dnf. World HMar: '12- 1.
Progress at Mar: 2009- 2:43:29, 2010- 2:30:42, 2011- 2:34:38, 2012- 2:21:09, 2013- 2:26:58, 2014- 2:26:20, 2015- 2:24:33, 2016- 2:26:26. pbs: 10k 31:18 '13, HMar 66:56 '13, 30k 1:41:06 '12.
Won Amsterdam Marathon 2012, Hamburg 2015; 2nd Boston 2013, 3rd Berlin 2015.

Alemitu HAROYE Banata b. 9 May 1995 1.60m 44kg.
At 10000m: WCh: '15- 7; At 5000m: WJ: '14- 1; AfCh: '12- 4, Af-J: '13- 3. At 3000m: WY: '11- 5. World CC: '13- 3J, '15- 4; Af CC: '12- 5J, '14- 2J.

Progress at 5000m, 10000m: 2011- 16:14.3A, 2012- 15:55.36, 2013- 15:05.08, 2014- 14:52.67, 2015- 14:43.28, 30:50.83; 2016- 14:43.58. pbs: 3000m 8:36.87 '14, 2M 9:20.81 '14.

Aberu KEBEDE Shewaye b. 12 Sep 1989 Shewa 1.63m 50kg.
At Mar: WCh: '11- 12, '13- 13. World HMar: '09- 3; CC: '07- 16J. Won ETH 10000m 2009.
Progress at 10000m, Mar: 2009- 30:48.26, 2010- 32:17.74, 2:23:58; 2011- 2:24:34, 2012- 31:09.28, 2:20:30; 2013- 2:23:28, 2014- 2:22:21, 2015- 2:20:48, 2016- 2:20:45. pbs: 5km Rd 15:13 '09, HMar 67:39 '09, 30k 1:39:50 '14.
Won Rotterdam and Berlin marathons 2010 after 2nd Dubai on debut, won Berlin again in 2012 and 2016 (2nd 2015), and Tokyo and Shanghai 2013, Frankfurt 2014. Five sub-2:22 marathons ties record of five.

Yebrqual MELESE b. 18 Apr 1990 1.64m 55kg. Won ETH 10000m 2015.
Progress at Mar: 2014- 2:26:21, 2015- 2:23:23, 2016- 2:24:49, 2017- 2:23:13 pbs: 10000m: 32:40.3A '15, 10k 31:40 '13, HMar 68:21 '15.
Marathon wins: Hangzhou 2014, Houston & Prague 2015, 2nd Paris 2014, Chicago 2015.; 3rd Dubai 2017

Meselech MELKAMU b. 27 Apr 1985 Debre Markos, Amhara region 1.58m 47kg.
At 5000m(/10000m): OG: '08- 7; WCh: '05- 4, '07- 5, '09- 5/2, '11- (5); AfG: '07- 2, '11- (dnf); AfCh: '06- 6, '08- 1, '10- (2); WJ: '04- 1. At Mar: WCh: '13- dnf. At 3000m: WI: '08- 2. World CC: '03-04-05-06-07-08-09-10-11: 4J/1J/4 & 6/3 & 3/3/9/3/3/4 (17 medals). Won ETH 5000m 2004, 4k CC 2005, CC 2006-07.
African 10000m record 2009.
Progress at 5000m, 10000m, Mar: 2003- 15:27.93, 2004- 15:00.02, 2005- 14:38.97, 2006- 14:37.44, 2007- 14:33.83, 2008- 14:38.78, 31:04.93; 2009- 14:34.17, 29:53.80; 2010- 14:31.91, 31:04.52; 2011- 14:39.44, 30:56.55; 2012- 2:21:01, 2013- 2:25:46, 2014- 2:25:23, 2:21:28dh; 2015- 2:26:45, 2016- 2:21:54. pbs: 1500m 4:07.52 '07, 1M 4:33.94 '03, 2000m 5:39.2i+, 5:46.3+ '07; 3000m 8:23.74i '07, 8:34.73 '05, Road: 10M 53:12 '16, HMar 68:05 '13, 25k 1:23:23 '12, 1:22:27dh '14; 30k 1:39:58 '12, 1:39:21dh '14.
Third fastest ever marathon debut to win at Frankfurt 2012. 2nd Dubai 2014 (3rd 2016), won Daegu 2015, Hamburg & Amsterdam 2016.

Aselefech MERGIA b. 23 Jan 1985 Woliso 1.68m 51kg.
At Mar: OG: '12- 41; WCh: '09- 3, '11- dnf. HMar: WCh: '08- 2. World CC: '08- 16.
Ethiopian marathon record 2012.
Progress at HMar, Mar: 2006- 74:13, 2007- 74:50, 2008- 68:17, 2009- 67:48, 2:25:02; 2010- 67:22, 2:22:38; 2011- 67:21, 2:22:45; 2012- 69:42+, 2:19:31; 2014- 73:49, 2015- 71:42, 2:20:02; 2016- 2:23:57. pbs: 1500m 4:14.85 '07, 3000m 8:54.42 '08; Road: 10k 31:25+ '08, 15k 47:53 '09, 20k 63:41 '09, 30k 1:41:52 '09.
2nd Paris Marathon 2009 on debut, won London 2010 and Dubai 2011-12 and 2015; 2nd New York 2015. Daughter Sena born July 2013.

Belaynesh OLJIRA Jemane b. 26 Jun 1990 Welek'a, Amhara 1.65m 49kg.
At 10000m: OG: '12- 5; WCh: '13- 3, '15- 9; AfCh: '14- 3. World CC: '11-13-15-17: 10/3/9/8; AfCC: '12- 5. Won ETH 10000m 2011.
Ethiopian 1500m record 2012.
Progress at 10000m, Mar: 2011- 31:17.80, 2012- 30:26.70, 2013- 30:31.44, 2:25:01; 2014- 32:49.39, 2:24:21dh; 2015- 30:53.69, 2016- 30:50.25. pbs: 1500m 4:33.14 '12, 3000m 8:38.55 '16, 2M 9:23.32 '14, 5000m 14:42.57 '16, Road: 15k 49:08 '14, 10M 52:40 '14, HMar 67:27 '11, 30k 1:39:33dh '14.

Besu SADO Beko b. 12 Jun 1996 1.72m 56kg.
At 1500m: OG: '16- 9; WCh: '15- sf; AfG: '15- 2; AfCh: '14- 7; Af-J: '15- 2; won ETH 2014.
Progress at 1500m: 2014- 4:07.59, 2015- 4:00.65, 2016- 3:59.47. pbs: 800m 2:02.6A '14, 1000m 2:37.73 '15.

Mulu SEBOKA Seyfu b. 13 Jan 1984 1.58m 45kg. World 20k: '06- 25.
Progress at Mar: 2003- 2:43:30, 2004- 2:37:29, 2005- 2:30:54, 2006- 2:30:41, 2007- 2:33:27, 2008- 2:29:06, 2009- 2:29:38, 2010- 2:30:47, 2011- 2:35:14, 2012- 2:25:45, 2013- 2:23:43, 2014- 2:23:15, 2015- 2:21:56, 2016- 2:24:24. pbs: 15k 48:38 '12, HMar 69:11 '15, 30k 1:41:13 '14.
Marathon wins: Mumabi 2005-06, 2008; Toronto 2008, Melbourne 2010, Guangzhou 2012, Jakarta 2013, Dubai, Daegu & Toronto 2014.

Dawit SEYAUM Biratu b. 27 Jul 1996 Tumano 1.61m 49kg.
At 1500m: OG: '16- 8; WCh: '15- 4; WJ: '14- 1; WY: '13- 2; AfG: '15- 1; AfCh: '14- 2; Af-J: '13/15- 1; CCp: '14- 3; WI: '16- 2.
Progress at 1500m: 2013- 4:09.00, 2014- 3:59.53, 2015- 3:59.76, 2016- 3:58.09. pbs: 1M 4:32.13i '15, 2000m 5:35.46i '15, 3000m 8:37.65i "17.

Feysa TADESE Boru b. 19 Nov 1988 Shirka 1.67m 53kg.
At Mar: WCh: '13- dnf. World HMar: '10- 4, '12- 2; CC: '10- 7.
Progress at Mar: 2009- 2:36:57, 2011- 2:25:20, 2012- 2:23:07, 2013- 2:21:06, 2014- 2:20:27, 2016- 2:25:03. pbs: 10000m 32:29.07 '10, Road: 10k 32:21 '13, 15k 48:51 '12, 20k 65:41 '12, HMar 68:35 '13, 30k 1:39:18 '14.
Three wins in nine marathons: Seoul and Shanghai 2012, Paris 2013; 2nd Berlin 2014.

Senbere TEFERI Sora b. 3 May 1995 1.59m 45kg. Oromiya.
At 1500m: WCh: '13- h; WJ: '12- 3; WY: '11- 2; At 5000m: OG: '16- 5; WCh: '15- 2; World CC: '15- 2, '17- 10.
Progress at 1500m, 5000m, 10000m: 2011-

16:09.0A, 2012- 15:36.74, 2013- 4:04.55, 16:21.0A, 2014- 4:08.49, 2015- 4:01.86, 14:36:44; 2016- 14:29.82, 30:40.59. pbs: 2000m 5:34.27 '14, 3000m 8:34.32 '15, 10M Rd 52:51 '16.
Gudaf TSEGAY Desta b. 23 Jan 1997 1.59m 45kg.
At 1500m: WJ: '14- 2; WI: '16- 3. At 800m: OG: '16- h.
World junior indoor 1500m record 2016.
Progress at 1500m: 2013- 4:07.27, 2014- 4:02.83, 2015- 4:03.09, 2016- 4:00.18. pbs: 800m 1:59.77 '16, 1000m 2:38.05i '17, 1M 4:24.98i '16, 15k Rd 15:37 '15.
Tirfi TSEGAYE Beyene b. 25 Nov 1984 Bokoji 1.65m 54kg.
At Mar: OG: '16- 4; WCh: '15- 8. World HMar: '09- 6.
Progress at Mar: 2008- 2:35:32, 2009- 2:28:16, 2010- 2:22:44, 2011- 2:24:12, 2012- 2:21:19, 2013- 2:23:23, 2014- 2:20:18, 2015- 2:23:41, 2016- 2:19:41. pbs: 15k 49:48 '14, HMar 67:42 '12, 30k 1:39:17 '14.
Marathon wins: Porto 2008, Shanghai 2010, Paris 2012, Dubai 2013 & 2016, Tokyo & Berlin 2014. 3rd London 2015, 2nd Boston 2016.
Tigist TUFA Demisse b. 26 Jan 1987 1.55m 40kg.
At Mar: OG: '16- dnf; WCh: '15- 6.
Progress at Mar: 2011- 2:41:50, 2013- 2:29:24, 2014- 2:21:52, 2015- 2:23:22, 2016- 2:23:03. pbs: 15k 51:05 '14, HMar 70:03 '08, 25k 1:24:13 '16, 30k 1:41:39 '16.
Marathon wins: Ottawa & Shanghai 2014, London 2015 (2nd 2016); 3rd New York 2015.
Genet YALEW b. 31 Dec 1992 1.46m 46kg. Defense.
At HMar: WCh: '14- 10, '16- 5. World CC: '10-11-13-15: 5J/2J/15/10; AfCC: '12- 8. At 3000m: WJ: '10- 6' WY: '09- 3. At 5000m: Af-J: '11- 3; AfG: '15- 5. At 10000m: AfCh: '14- 4.
Progress at 5000m, 10000m: 2009- 16:25.6A, 2010- 15:03.52, 2011- 15:10.45, 32:05.90; 2012- 14:48.43, 2013- 15:04.38, 2014- 32:45.1A, 2015- 15:43.77, 31:08.82; 2016- 14:51.04, 30:37.38. pbs: 8:49.6 '16, HMar 66:26 '16.

FINLAND
Governing body: Suomen Urheiluliitto, Radiokatu 20, SF-00240 Helsinki. Founded 1906.
National Championships first held in 1907 (men), 1913 (women). **2016 Champions: Men**: 100m:Ville Myllymäki 10.38, 200m: Samuli Samuelsson 21.10, 400m/800m: Ville Lampinen 47.51/1:49.60, 1500m: Marco Bertolotti 3:45.33, 5000m: Ossi Kekki 14:27.71, 10000m: Arttu Vattulainen 29:33.70, HMar: Jussi Utriainen 66:00; Mar: Aki Nummela 2:24:18, 3000mSt: Hanu Granberg 8:58.60, 110mh: Elmo Lakka 13.81, 400mh: Petteri Monni 51.50, HJ: Jussi Viita 2.21, PV: Tomas Wecksten 5.42, LJ: Roni Ollikainen 7.80, TJ: Tuomas Kaukolahti 16.24,

SP: Arttu Kangas 19.38, DT: Pyry Niskala 59.97, HT: David Söderberg 76.64, JT: Tero Pitkämäki 82.05, Dec: Juuso Hassi 7734, 20kW: Aleksi Ojala 1:25:37, 30kW: Jarkko Kinnunen 2:12:29. **Women**: 100m/200m: Anna Hämäläinen 11.69/23.70, 400m: Katri Mustola 54.02, 800m: Sara Kuivisto 2:10.59, 1500m/5000m: Kristiina Mäki 4:30.32/16:12.88, 10000m: Camilla Richardsson 33:43.53, HMar: Hanna Jantunen 77:38, Mar: Laura Manninen 2:41:21, 3000mSt: Sandra Eriksson 9:40.70, 100mh: Nooralotta Neziri 13.05, 400mh: Hilla Uusimäki 57.40, HJ: Linda Sandblom 1.84, PV: Minna Nikkanen 4.40, LJ: Kristiina Vuorvirta 6.22, TJ: Kristiina Mäkelä 13.86, SP: Katri Hirvonen 15.35, DT: Salla Sipponen 56.75, HT: Inga Linna 67.15, JT: Heidi Nokelainen 60.98, Hep: Jutta Heikkinen 5603, 10kW/20kW: Elisa Neuvonen 47:47/1:40:19.

Ari MANNIO b. 23 Jul 1987 Lehtimäki 1.85m 104kg. Lehtimäen Jyske.
At JT: OG: '12- 10, '16- dnq 27; WCh: '11/15- dnq 14/dnq 14; EC: '12- 3, '16- dnq 19; WJ: '04- 6, '06- 2; EU23: '07- 4, '09- 1; EJ: '05- 3; ET: '10- 3. Finnish champion 2011, W.Military 2011, 2015.
Progress at JT: 2004- 70.83, 2005- 76.40, 2006- 79.68, 2007- 80.31, 2008- 81.54, 2009- 85.70, 2010- 85.12, 2011- 85.12, 2012- 84.62, 2013- 84.65, 2014- 83.70, 2015- 86.82, 2016- 81.38.

Tero PITKÄMÄKI b. 19 Dec 1982 Ilmajoki 1.95m 92kg. Nurmon Urheilijat. Electrical engineer.
At JT: OG: '04- 8, '08- 3, '12- 4, '16- dnq 21; WCh: '05-07-09-11-13-15: 4/1/5/dnq 17/2/3; EC: '06-10-12-14-16: 2/3/11/3/dnq 14; EU23: '03- 3; EJ: '01- 6; ECp: '06- 1, '15- 1. Won WAF 2005, 2007; DL 2015, Finnish 2004-07, 2013, 2016.
Progress at JT: 1999- 66.83, 2000- 73.75, 2001- 74.89, 2002- 77.24, 2003- 80.45, 2004- 84.64, 2005- 91.53, 2006- 91.11, 2007- 91.23, 2008- 87.70, 2009- 87.79, 2010- 86.92, 2011- 85.33, 2012- 86.98, 2013- 89.03, 2014- 86.63, 2015- 89.09, 2016- 86.13.
Partner is Niina Kelo (b. 26 Mar 1980) pb Hep 5956 (15 EC 2006).

Antti RUUSKANEN b. 21 Feb 1984 Kokkola 1.89m 86kg. Pielaveden Sampo.
At JT: OG: '12- 2, '16- 6; WCh: '09-11-13-15: 6/9/5/5; EC: '14- 1, '16- 3; EU23: '05- 2; EJ: '03- 3; CCp: '14- 8. Finnish champion 2012, 2014-15.
Progress at JT: 2002- 66.08, 2003- 72.87, 2004- 75.84, 2005- 79.75, 2006- 84.10, 2007- 82.71/87.88dh, 2008- 87.33, 2009- 85.39, 2010- 83.45, 2011- 82.29, 2012- 87.79, 2013- 85.70, 2014- 88.01, 2015- 88.98, 2016- 88.23.

David SÖDERBERG b. 11 Aug 1979 Vörå 1.85m 100kg. IF VOM Vöyri.
At HT: OG: '04-12: dnq 21/25, '16- 8; WCh: '07-09- dnq 20/18, '15- 6; EC: '06-10-12: dnq 18/16/13/dnq nt, '14-16: 8/7; EU23: '01- nt; WUG: '03- 3. Finnish champion 2013-16.
Progress at HT: 1997- 58.20, 1998- 61.02, 1999-

64.23, 2000- 68.53, 2001- 72.25, 2002- 76.51, 2003- 78.83, 2004- 75.56, 2005- 76.89, 2006- 75.58, 2007- 77.18, 2008- 75.82, 2009- 75.44, 2010- 76.05, 2011- 77.34, 2012- 77.53, 2013- 75.67, 2014- 77.57, 2015- 76.92, 2016- 77.60.

FRANCE

Governing body: Fédération Française d'Athlétisme, 33 avenue Pierre de Coubertin, 75640 Paris cedex 13. Founded 1920.
National Championships first held in 1888 (men), 1918 (women). **2016 Champions: Men**: 100m/200m: Jimmy Vicaut 9.88/20.62, 400m: Thomas Jordier 45.72, 800m: Aymeric Lusine 1:50.16, 1500m: Florian Carvalho 3:44.70, 5000m: Mourad Amdouni 14:12.33, 10000m: Freddy Guimard 29:03.54, HMar: Thierry Guibault 65:29, Mar: Paul Lalire 2:21:23, 3000mSt: Mahiedine Mekhissi Benabbad 8:29.01, 110mh: Dimitri Bascou 13.05w, 400mh: Mamadou Kasse Hann 50.26, HJ: Mickaël Hanany 2.21, PV: Renaud Lavillenie 5.95, LJ: Jean-Pierre Bertrand 8.01, TJ: Teddy Tamgho 17.15, SP: Fréderíc Dagée 19.21, DT: Lolassonn Djouhan 60.81, HT: Jérôme Bortoluzzi 72.81, JT: Killian Durechou 75.35, Dec: Bastien Auzeil 8191, 5000mW: Kevin Campion 18:59.46, 20kW: Jean Blancheteau 1:26:50, 50kW: Yohann Diniz 3:37:48.
Women: 100m: Stella Akakpo 11.17, 200m: Jennifer Galais 23.36, 400m: Floria Guei 51.21, 800m: Renelle Lamote 2:04.23, 1500m: Élodie Normand 4:13.39, 5000m: Alice Rocquain 16:20.28, 10000m: Christelle Daunay 32:43.38, HMar: Fanny Provost 75:55, Mar: Anais Quemener 2:55:26, 3000mSt: Aïssé Sow 9:54.18, 100mh: Cindy Billaud 12.83, 400mh: Phara Anacharsis 57.01, HJ: Marine Vallet 1.88, PV: Ninon Guillon-Romarin 4.40, LJ: Haoua Kessely 6.41, TJ: Jeanine Assani Issouf 14.40, SP: Jessica Cérival 17.47, DT: Mélina Robert-Michon 63.40, HT: Alexandra Tavernier 66.73, JT: Mathilde Andraud 54.05, Hep: Annaëlle Nyabeu Djapa 5768, 5000mW/20kW: Émilie Menuet 21:51.91/1:33:27.

Dimitri BASCOU b. 20 Jul 1987 Schoelcher, Martinique 1.82m 79kg. Racing Club de France.
At 110mh: OG: '12- sf, '16- 3; WCh: '09/11- sf, '15- 5; EC: '10- 4, 14- dq, '16- 1; EU23: '07- h, '09- 4; EJ: '05- h; won FRA 2009-11, 2016. At 60mh: WI: '16- 3; EI: '11- 6, '15- 2.
Progress at 110mh: 2004- 14.61w, 2005- 14.35, 2006- 14.24, 2007- 13.76, 2008- 13.61/13.39w, 2009- 13.49, 2010- 13.41, 2011- 13.37/13.26w, 2012- 13.34, 2013- 13.51, 2014- 13.25, 2015- 13.16, 2016- 13.12/13/05w. pbs: 60m 6.88i '14, 100m 10.72 '07, 200m 21.62 '09, 50mh 6.57i '12, 60mh 7.41i '16.
Disqualified for obstruction after finishing 3rd at the 2014 Europeans.

Wilhem BÉLOCIAN b. 22 Jun 1995 les Abymes, Guadeloupe 1.78m 78kg. Stade Lamertin.
At 110mh: OG: '16- h; EC: '16- 3; WJ: '12- 3, '14- 1;

WY: '11- 3 (3 Med R); EJ: '13- 1; At 60mh: EI: '15- 3. World junior record 99cm 110mh 12.99 in 2014, three European JR 2014-14.
Progress at 110mh: 2014- 13.54, 2015- 13.28, 2016- 13.25/13.15w. pbs: 60m 6.82i '12, 100m 10.61 '16, 60mh 7.52i '15.

Pierre-Ambroise BOSSE b. 11 May 1992 Nantes 1.85m 68kg. UA Gujan Mestras.
At 800m: OG: '12- sf, '16- 4; WCh: '13- 7, '15- 5; EC: '12-14-16: 3/8/5; WJ: '10- 8; EU23: '13- 1; EJ: '11- 1; ET: 15- 2; French champion 2012, 2014-15.
French 800m and European U23 1000m records 2014; European 600m record 2016.
Progress at 800m: 2007- 2:02.81, 2008- 1:56.05, 2010- 1:48.38, 2011- 1:46.18, 2012- 1:44.97, 2013- 1:43.76, 2014- 1:42.53, 2015- 1:43.88, 2016- 1:43.41. pbs: 400m 48.54 '11, 600m 1:13.21 '16, 1000m 2:15.31 '14, 1500m 3:54.81 '09.

Benjamin COMPAORÉ b. 5 Aug 1987 Bar-le-Duc 1.89m 86kg. Strasbourg AA.
At TJ: OG: '12- 6, '16- 10; WCh: '11- 8, '15- 12; EC: '10-14-16: 5/1/12; WJ: '06- 1; EJ: '05- 5; CCp: '14- 1; WI: '12- 6, '16- 3. FRA champion 2014.
Progress at TJ: 2003- 14.50, 2004- 15.48, 2005- 16.00/16.12w, 2006- 16.61, 2007- 16.62, 2008- 17.05, 2009- 16.98, 2010- 17.21/17.28w, 2011- 17.31, 2012- 17.17, 2013- 17.07, 2014- 17.48, 2015- 17.01, 2016- 17.09i/16.76. pbs: 60m 7.13i '08, 100m 10.76 '13, 400m 48.69 '12, 1500m 4:44.43 '12, 110mh 15.72 '12, HJ 1.98 '12, LJ 8.02 '16, Dec 6704 '12.
Father came from Burkina Faso.

Garfield DARIEN b. 22 Dec 1987 Lyon 1.87m 76kg. EA Chambéry.
At 110mh: OG: '12- sf; WCh: '09- sf, '15- 8; EC: '10- 2, '12- 2; WJ: '04- 7; EJ: '05- 1; CCp: '10- 4; ET: '11- 2; French champion 2012, 2015. At 60mh: WI: '14- 3; EI: '09-11-17: 6/2/4.
Progress at 110mh: 2004- 14.03/13.98w, 2005- 13.73, 2006- 13.94/13.92w, 2008- 13.50/13.43w, 2009- 13.36, 2010- 13.34, 2011- 13.37, 2012- 13.15, 2013- 14.47, 2014- 14.01, 2015- 13.17. pbs: 200m 22.05 '06, 60mh 7.47i '14, HJ 1.83 '04.
Father Daniel Darien had 110mh pb 13.76 '87.

Yohann DINIZ b. 1 Jan 1978 Epernay 1.85m 69kg. EFS Reims Athlétisme.
At 20kW: ECp: '07- 1, '15- 3; At 50kW: OG: '08- dnf, '12- dq, '16- 8; WCh: '05-07-09-11-13: dq/2/11/dq/10; EC: '06-10-14: 1/1/1; ECp: '05- 13: 4/1. Won French 10000mW 2010, 2012, 2014; 20kW 2007-09, 2015; 50kW 2005, 2016.
World walks records: track 50,000m 2011, road 50k 2014, 20k 2015. French records 5000mW (3) 2006-08, 10000mW 2014, 20000mW 2014, 20kW (4) 2005-15, 50kW 2006 & 2009, 1 Hr 2010.
Progress at 20kW, 50kW: 2001- 1:35:05.0t, 2002- 1:30:40, 2003- 1:26:54.99t, 2004- 1:24:25, 3:52:11.0t; 2005- 1:20:20, 3:45:17; 2006- 1:23:19, 3:41:39; 2007- 1:18:58, 3:44:22; 2008- 1:22:31, 2009- 1:22:50, 3:38:45; 2010- 1:20:23, 3:40:37; 2011- 3:35:27.2t, 2012- 1:17:43, 2013- 1:23:17, 3:41:07; 2014- 1:19:42.1t,

3:32:33; 2015- 1:17:02, 2016- 3:37:48. pbs: 3000mW 10:52.44 '08, 5000mW 18:16.76i '14, 18:18.01 '08; 10000mW 38:08.13 '14, 20000mW 1:19:42.1 '14, 1HrW 15,395m '10, 35kW 2:32:24 '12.

Kafétien GOMIS b. 23 Mar 1980 Saint Quentin 1.83m 67kg. Lille Metropole Athlétisme.
At LJ: OG: '04- dnq 14, '16- 8; WCh: '09- dnq 21, '15- 7; EC: '06-10-12-14-16: 5/2/9/3/7; WI: '16- 9; EI: '07-09-11: 4/4/2; CCp: '10- 2, '14- 8; ET: '10- 2, '15- 2. French champion 2007, 2015.
Progress at LJ: 2000- 7.35w, 2001- 7.56i/7.53, 2002- 7.77, 2003- 7.85, 2004- 8.21, 2005- 7.98, 2006- 8.03, 2007- 8.09i/7.91, 2008- 8.08, 2009- 8.15, 2010- 8.24, 2011- 8.12/8.22w, 2012- 8.05/8.13w, 2013- 8.02, 2014- 8.19, 2015- 8.26, 2016- 8.23i/8.05. pbs: 60m 6.91i '06, 100m 10.76 '03, HJ 2.07 '00.

Yoann KOWAL b. 28 May 1987 Nogent-le-Rotrou 1.72m 58kg. E. Périgueux Sarlat Trélissac.
At 1500m: OG: '12- sf; WCh: '09- h, '11- sf; EC: '10- 5; EU23: '09- 6; ET: '09- 3; EI: '09- 3. At 3000m: EI: '13- 4. At 3000mSt: OG: '16- 5; WCh: '13- 8, '15- h; EC: '14- 1, '16- 3; WJ: '06- h; EU23: '07- 11; ET: '13- 3, '14- 1. Won FRA 1500m 2008, 2010; 3000mSt 2014-15.
Progress at 3000mSt: 2006- 8:56.54, 2007- 8:36.11, 2008- 8:34.66, 2009- 9:02.38, 2011- 8:41.07, 2012- 8:21.66, 2013- 8:12.53, 2014- 8:25.50, 2015- 8:18.38, 2016- 8:16.21. pbs: 800m 1:47.95 '10, 1000m 2:20.43 '10, 1500m 3:33.75 '11, 2000m 5:04.18 '13, 3000m 7:44.26i '12, 7:45.11 '16; 5000m 14:40.02 '06, 10k Rd 29:01 '11.

Renaud LAVILLENIE b. 18 Sep 1986 Barbezieux-Saint-Hilaire 1.77m 69kg. Clermont Athl. Auvergne.
At PV: OG: '12- 1, '16- 2; WCh: '09-11-13-15: 3/3/2/3=; WI: '12- 1, '16- 1; EC: '10-12-14-16: 1/1/1/nh; EU23: '07- 10; EI: '09-11-13-15: 1/1/1/1; CCp: '10- 2, '14- 1; ET: '09-10-13-14-15: 1/1/1/1/1. Won DL 2010-16, French 2010, 2012-15.
World indoor pole vault record 2014. French record (indoors) 2011 and outdoors 2013.
Progress at PV: 2002- 3.40, 2003- 4.30, 2004- 4.60, 2005- 4.81i/4.70, 2006- 5.25i/5.22, 2007- 5.58i/5.45, 2008- 5.81i/5.65, 2009- 6.01, 2010- 5.94, 2011- 6.03i/5.90, 2012- 5.97, 2013- 6.02, 2014- 6.16i/5.93, 2015- 6.05, 2016- 6.03i/5.98. pbs: 60m 7.23i '08, 100m 11.04 '11, 60mh 8.41i '08, 100m 11.04 '11, 110mh 14.51 '10, HJ 1.89i '08, 1.87 '07; LJ 7.31 '10, Hep 5363i '08.
Broke Sergey Bubka's 21 year-old absolute world pole vault record indoors in 2014. 23 successive wins 31 Aug 2013 to EC 2014, only man to win all seven Diamond League titles from 2010. IAAF Male Athlete of the Year 2014.
His brother **Valentin** (b. 16 Jul 1991) has PV pb 5.80i '15, 5.65 '13; 3rd EU23 and nh WCh in 2013; 6 EI '15.

Christophe LEMAITRE b. 11 Jun 1990 Annecy 1.89m 74kg. AS Aix-les-Bains.
At 100m/(200m): OG: '12- (6)/3R, '16- sf/3; WCh: '09- qf, '11- 4/3/2R, '13- 7, '15- sf/sf; EC: '10- 1/1/1R, '12- 1/3R, '14- 2/2/3R; WJ: '08- (1); WY: '07- 4/5; EJ: '09- 1; CCp: '10- 1, '14- 5/4/2R; ET: '10- 2, '11- 1/1, '13- (1), '15- 1/2R. At 60m: EI: '11- 3. Won French 100m 2010-12, 2014; 200m 2010-15.
Records: European 4x200m 2014; French 100m (7) 2010-11, 200m (2) 2010-11, European junior 100m 2009. U23 100m 2010-11, 200m 2011.
Progress at 100m, 200m: 2005- 11.46, 2006- 10.96, 2007- 10.53, 21.08; 2008- 10.26, 20.83; 2009- 10.04/10.03w, 20.68; 2010- 9.97, 20.16; 2011- 9.92, 19.80; 2012- 10.04/9.94w, 19.91; 2013- 10.00/9.98w, 20.07; 2014- 10.10, 20.08; 2015- 10.07, 20.21; 2016- 10.07, 20.01. pbs: 60m 6.55i '10, 150m St 14.90 '13.
First Caucasian sub-10.00 100m runner and first to win sprint treble at European Champs; now has men's record eight EC medals.

Pascal MARTINOT-LAGARDE b. 22 Sep 1991 St Maur-des-Fossés 1.90m 80kg. Neuilly Plaisance Sport.
At 110mh: OG: '16- 4; WCh: '13- h, '15- 4; EC: '14- 3; WJ: '10- 1; EU23: '11- h; EJ: '09- 4; ET: '13-14-15: 2/3/2; won DL 2014, FRA 2014. At 60mh: WI: '12-14-16: 3/2/2; EI: '13-15-17: 3/1/2.
French 110m hurdles record 2014.
Progress at 110mh: 2008- 15.03, 2009- 14.13, 2010- 13.74, 2011- 13.94, 2012- 13.41/13.30w, 2013- 13.12, 2014- 12.95, 2015- 13.06, 2016- 13.12. pbs: 60m 7.07i '10, 100m 10.94 '13, 60mh 7.45i '14.
His brother **Thomas** (b. 7 Feb 1988) has 110mh pb 13.26, 7 WCh and French champion in 2013.

Kevin MAYER b. 10 Feb 1992 Argenteuil 1.86m 77kg. EA Tain-Tournon.
At Dec: OG: '16- 2; WCh: '13- 4; EC: '12- dnf, '14- 2; WJ: '10- 1; EJ: '11- 1; ECp: '13- 1. At Oct: WY: '09- 1. At Hep: EI: '13- 2, '17- 1.
Records: European indoor heptathlon 2017, French decathlon 2016.
Progress at Dec: 2011- 7992, 2012- 8447w/8415, 2013- 8446, 2014- 8521, 2015- 8469, 2016- 8834. pbs: 60m 6.95i '17, 100m 10.81 '16, 400m 48.28 '16, 1000m 2:37.30i '13, 1500m 4:18.04 '12, 60mh 7.88i '17, 110mh 14.01 '16, HJ 2.10i '10, 2.09 '12; PV 5.40 '16, LJ 7.65 '14, SP 15.97i/15.76 '16, DT 48.99 '16, JT 66.09 '13, Hep 6479i '17.
Four individual event pbs when adding 313 points to his decathlon best for 2016 OG silver.

Mahiédine MEKHISSI-BENABBAD b. 15 Mar 1985 Reims 1.90m 75kg. EFS Reims.
At 3000mSt: OG: '08- 2, '12- 2, '16- 3; WCh: '07/09-h, '11- 3, '13- 3; EC: '10-12-14-16: 1/1,dq (1 1500m)/1; WJ: '04- h; EU23: '05- h, '07- 1; CCp: '10- 3; ECp: '07- 2, '08- 1. At 1500m: WI: '10- 8; EI: '13- 1; WCp: '06- 7, '14- 3. Won FRA 1500m 2014, 3000mSt 2008, 2012-13, 2016.
Records: World best 2000m steeplechase 2010. European 3000mSt 2013, French 1M 2014.
Progress at 3000mSt: 2003- 9:52.07, 2004- 9:01.01, 2005- 8:34.45, 2006- 8:28.25, 2007- 8:14.22, 2008- 8:08.95, 2009- 8:06.98, 2010- 8:02.52, 2011- 8:02.09, 2012- 8:10.90, 2013- 8:00.09, 2014- 8:03.23, 2016-

8:08.15. pbs: 800m 1:53.61 '04, 1000m 2:17.14 '09, 1500m 3:33.12 '13, 1M 3:51.55 '14, 2000m 4:56.85 '13, 3000m 7:43.72i '13, 7:44.98 '10; 5000m 14:32.9 '05, 2000mSt 5:10.68 '10.
Disqualified after he took his vest off in the finishing straight when finishing well clear in 2014 EC steeplechase.

Kévin MENALDO b. 12 Jul 1992 Bordeaux 1.76m 66kg. E. Franconville Cesame Val d'Oise.
At PV: OG: '16- dnq 16=; WCh: '15- 6; EC: '14- 3=, '16- nh; WY: '09- 7; EU23: '13- dnq 15; EJ: '11- 2.
Progress at PV: 2007- 4.15i/4.00, 2008- 4.71, 2009- 5.05, 2010- 5.10i/5.05, 2011- 5.50, 2012- 5.43i/5.40, 2013- 5.65i/5.60, 2014- 5.75i/5.72, 2015- 5.81, 2016- 5.80.

Teddy TAMGHO b. 15 Jun 1989 Paris 1.87m 82kg. Bordeaux
At TJ: WCh: '09- 11, '13- 1; EC: '10- 3; WI: '10- 1; WJ: '08- 1; EJ: '07- 4; EI: '11- 1 (4 LJ); ET: '10- 3, '13- 2. Won DL 2010, French 2009-10, 2013, 2016.
Four World indoor triple jump records 2010 (17.90) & 2011, four absolute French records 2009-13; three Eur U23 records 2010.
Progress at TJ: 2004- 12.56, 2005- 14.89, 2006- 15.58, 2007- 16.53i/16.35/16.42w, 2008- 17.19/17.33w, 2009- 17.58i/17.11, 2010- 17.98, 2011- 17.92i/17.91, 2013- 18.04, 2015- 17.24, 2016- 17.15. pbs: 60m 6.92i '06, 100m 10.60 '09, LJ 8.01i '11, 7.81 '13.
2011 season ended when broke ankle in warm-up for European U23s and also missed all of 2012. His 18.04 to win 2013 World title was third best ever and world's best for 17 years. Fractured his shin in November 2013 and missed all the 2014 season.

Jimmy VICAUT b. 27 Feb 1992 Bondy 1.88m 83kg. SCO Sainte-Marguerite de Marseille.
At 100m/(200m)/4x100mR: OG: '12- sf/3R, '16- 7; WCh: '11- 6/2R, '13- sf/sf, '15- 8; EC: '10- 1R, '12- 2/3R (res), '14- sf, '16- 3/2R; WJ: '10- 3; WY: '09- 7; EJ: '11- 1/1R; ET: '13- 1, '14- 1. At 60m: EI: '13- 1. Won FRA 100m 2013, 2015-16; 200m 2016.
Equalled European 100m record 2015.
Progress at 100m: 2005- 13.0, 2006- 12.50, 2007- 11.0, 2008- 10.75/10.69w, 2009- 10.56, 2010- 10.16, 2011- 10.07, 2012- 10.02, 2013- 9.95, 2014- 9.95/9.89w, 2015- 9.86, 2016- 9.86. pbs: 60m 6.48i '13, 200m 20.30 '13.
His brother Willi was French U17 shot champion in 2012 and has senior pb of 17.33 '14.

Women

Cindy BILLAUD b. 11 Mar 1986 Coulommiers 1.65m 59kg. Athlé Sud 77.
At 100mh: OG: '16- sf; WCh: '09-11-13-15: sf/h/7/h; EC: '14- 2, '16- 7; WJ: '04- sf; EU23: '07- sf; EJ: '05- 3; ET: '14- 1; FRA champion 2013-16.
At 60mh: WI: '14- 4; EI: '09- 7.
French 100mh record 2014.
Progress at 100mh: 2004- 13.48, 2005- 13.57, 2006- 13.49/13.46w, 2007- 13.25, 2008- 12.99/12.97w,

2009- 12.97, 2010- 13.11, 2011- 12.93, 2012- 12.97, 2013- 12.59, 2014- 12.56, 2015- 12.83, 2016- 12.83. pbs: 60m 7.64i '08, 100m 12.00 '05, 200m 24.68 '08, 50mh 7.14+i '12, 60mh 7.87i '14.
Expecting a baby in 2017.

Floria GUEI b. 2 May 1990 Nantes 1.68m 53kg. E.Sud Lyonnais.
At 400m: OG: '16- sf; WCh: '11- hR, 13- sf, '15- sf; EC: '12- 2R, '14- sf/1R, '16- 2/2R; WJ: '08- h; EU23: '11- h/3R; EI: '11- 3R, '15- 1R, '17- 1; ET: '15- 1. French champion 2013, 2015-16.
Progress at 400m: 2008- 54.08, 2009- 52.90, 2010- 53.00, 2011- 52.77, 2012- 51.96, 2013- 51.42, 2014- 51.30, 2015- 50.89, 2016- 50.84. Pbs: 50m 6.62i '09, 60m 7.56i '17, 100m 11.82 '09, 200m 23.00 '16, 300m 36.46i '16.
Brilliant anchor 400m legs including 49.71 at '14 EC, 49.95 at '15 WCh and 49.92 '16 EC.

Rénelle LAMOTE b. 26 Dec 1993 Annecy 1.68m 57kg. Annecy Haute Savoie.
At 800m: OG: '16- h; WCh: '15- 8; EC: '14- sf, '16- 2; WJ: '12- sf; EU23: '13- h, 15- 1; ET: '14- 2, '15- 1. French champion 2014, 2016.
Progress at 800m: 2009- 2:18.24, 2010- 2:14.53, 2011- 2:08.39, 2012- 2:05.23, 2013- 2:02.40, 2014- 2:00.06, 2015- 1:58.86, 2016- 1:58.01. Pbs: 400m 53.92 '16, 1500m 4:35.93 '13, 10kRd 37:13 '14.

Antoinette NANA DJIMOU Ida b. 2 Aug 1985 Douala, Cameroon 1.74m 69kg. CA Montreuil.
At Hep: OG: '08- 18, '12- 4, '16- 11; WCh: '07-09-11-13: dnf/7/6/8; EC: '06-10-12-14-16: 21/dnf/1/1/2; WJ: '04- 4; EU23: '05- 5, '07- 7; ECp: '08- 2, '14- 2. At Pen: WI: '10- 4; EI: '09-11-13-15: 3/1/1/5. Won French LJ 2008, Hep 2006-07.
CMR heptathlon record 2003, French indoor pentathlon record 2011.
Progress at Hep: 2003- 5360, 2004- 5649, 2005- 6089w/5792, 2006- 5981, 2007- 5982, 2008- 6204, 2009- 6323, 2010- 5994, 2011- 6409, 2012- 6576, 2013- 6326, 2014- 6551, 2016- 6458. pbs: 60m 7.51i '11, 100m 11.78 '08, 200m 24.36 '11, 800m 2:15.22 '14, 60mh 8.11i '10, 100mh 12.96 '12, HJ 1.84i '10, 1.83 '11; LJ 6.44i '09, 6.43 '16, 6.61w '08; SP 16.17 '16, JT 57.27 '12, Pen 4723i '11.
Came to France at age 14, naturalised French citizen in 2004. Three pbs when winning European gold in 2012.

Mélina ROBERT-MICHON b. 18 Jul 1979 Voiron 1.80m 85kg. Lyon Athlétisme
At DT: OG: '00/04- dnq 29/30, '08- 7, '12- 5, '16- 2; WCh: '01-03-07-09-13-15: dnq 20/11/11/8/2/10; EC: '98-02-06-12-14-16: dnq 29/12/dnq 16/6/2/5; WJ: '98- 2; EU23: '99-12, '01- 1; WUG: '01- 3; CCp: '14- 4; ECp: '00-01-02-03-04-06-07-08-09-13-14- 15: 5/6/8/2/4/7/5/4/2/1/1/1. French champion 2000-09, 2011-16; MedG 2009.
Six French discus records 2000-16.
Progress at DT: 1997- 49.10, 1998- 59.27, 1999- 60.17, 2000- 63.19/63.61dh, 2001- 63.87, 2002- 65.78, 2003- 64.27, 2004- 64.54, 2005- 58.01, 2006-

59.89, 2007- 63.48, 2008- 62.21, 2009- 63.04, 2010- 56.52, 2011- 61.07, 2012- 63.98, 2013- 66.28, 2014- 65.51, 2015- 65.04, 2016- 66.73. pbs: SP 15.23 '07, HT 47.92 '02.
Daughter Elyssa born in 2010. Broke her 11 year-old French record in winning 2013 World silver.
Alexandra TAVERNIER b. 13 Dec 1993 Annecy 1.70m 82kg. Annecy Haute Savoie.
At HT: OG: '16- 11; WCh: '15- 3; EC: '14- 6, '16- dnq; WJ: '12- 1; EU23: '15- 1; EJ: '11- 6; ET: '15- 3. French champion 2014, 2016.
Progress at HT: 2009- 44.96, 2010- 58.44, 2011- 62.13, 2012- 70.62, 2013- 70.79, 2014- 71.17, 2015- 74.39, 2016- 72.16. Pbs: SP 11.81 '14, DT 41.58 '10.

GERMANY

Governing body: Deutscher Leichtathletik Verband (DLV), Alsfelder Str. 27, 64289 Darmstadt. Founded 1898.
National Championships first held in 1891.
2016 Champions: **Men**: 100m: Julian Reus 10.30, Robin Erewa 20.59, 400m: Johannes Trefz 46.59, 800m: Benedikt Huber 1:47.17, 1500m: Timo Benitz 3:40.28, 5000m: Richard Ringer 13:51.88, 10000m: Mitku Seboka 29:23.57, HMar:, Mar: Marcus Schönfisch 2:20:12, 3000mSt: Hannes Liebach 8:45.50, 110mh: Matthias Bühler 13.44, 400mh: Felix Franz 50.42, HJ: Eike Onne 2.20, PV: Tobias Scherbarth 5.70, LJ: Alyn Camara 2.20, TJ: Max Hess 17.06, SP: David Storl 20.75, DT: Robert Harting 69.04, HT: Alexander Ziegler 72.50, JT: Thomas Röhler 86.81, Dec: Felix Hepperle 7441, 10,000mW/20kW: Christopher Linke 38:40.25/1:21:14, 50kW: Carl Dohmann 3:47:57. **Women**: 100m: Tatjana Pinto 11.22, 200m: Gina Lückenkemper 22.84, 400m: Ruth Sophia Spelmeyer 52.17, 800m: Christina Hering 2:02.19, 1500m: Konstanze Klosterhalfen 4:07.92, 5000m: Geleto Tola 15:30.35, 10000m: Sabrina Mockenhaupt 32:40.80, HMar:, Mar: Fate Tola 2:25:42, 3000mSt: Gesa-Felicitas Krause 9:31.00, 100mh: Cindy Roleder 12.86, 400mh: Jackie Baumann 56.87, HJ: Marie-Laurence Jungfleisch 1.90, PV: Martina Strutz 4.70, LJ: Malaika Mihambo 6.72w, TJ: Jenny Elbe 14.28w, SP: Christina Schwanitz 19.49, DT: Nadine Müller 65.79, HT: Betty Heidler 75.32, JT: Christin Hussong 66.41, Hep: Mareike Arndt 5765, 5000mW: Teresa Zurek 22:14.94.

Arthur ABELE b. 30 Jul 1986 Mutlangen, Baden-Württemberg 1.84m 80kg. SSV Ulm 1846.
At Dec: OG: '08- dnf, '16- 15; WCh: '07- 9; EC: '14- 5; WJ: '04- 7; EJ: '05- 2; ECp: '04- 4. German champion 2013. At Hep: '15- 2.
Progress at Dec: 2006- 8012, 2007- 8269, 2008- 8372, 2013- 8251, 2014- 8477, 2016- 8605. pbs: 60m 6.93i '15, 100m 10.67 '14, 200m 22.41 '14, 400m 47.98 '05, 1000m 2:35.64i '15, 1500m 4:15.35 '08, 60mh 7.67i '15, 110mh 13.55 '14, 400mh 51.71 '04,

HJ 2.04 '07, PV 5.01 '14, LJ 7.57 '16. SP 15.79 '16, DT 46.20 '16, JT 71.89 '16, Hep 6279i '15.
Five individual event absolute bests in 2015 European Indoor heptathlon, but Achilles injury cost him the summer season.
Rico FREIMUTH b. 14 Mar 1988 Potsdam 1.96m 92kg. SV Halle.
At Dec: OG: '12- 6, '16- dnf; WCh: '11- dnf, '13- 7, '15- 3; EC: '14- 7; EU23: 09- 10; EJ: '07- 3.
Progress at Dec: 2009- 7689, 2010- 7826, 2011- 8287, 2012- 8322, 2013- 8488w/8382, 2014- 8356, 2015- 8561. pbs: 60m 6.98i '12, 100m 10.40 '14, 10.36w '13; 200m 21.39 '12, 400m 47.51 '12, 1000m 2:48.22i '12, 1500m 4:34.60 '13, 60mh 7.83i '14, 110mh 13.63 '14, HJ 1.99 '13, PV 4.90 '12, LJ 7.55 '13, SP 15.62 '15, DT 50.37 '14, JT 65.04 '11, Hep 5715i '12.
Won IAAF Combined Events Challenge 2014. His father Uwe had decathlon best of 8794 (1984), and was 4th at 1983 Worlds and 1986 Europeans and twice winner at Götzis. Uwe and Rico are the highest scoring father-son combination. His uncle Jörg won the high jump bronze medal at the 1980 Olympic Games in a pb of 2.31.
Christoph HARTING b. 4 Oct 1990 Cottbus 2.07m 120kg. SCC Berlin. Police officer.
At DT: OG: '16- 1; WCh: '13- dnq 13, '15- 8; EC: '16- 4; EU23: '11- 5. German champion 2015.
Progress at DT: 2008- 52.00, 2009- 50.19, 2010- 61.19, 2011- 62.12, 2012- 61.22, 2013- 64.99, 2014- 63.78, 2015- 67.93, 2016- 68.37. pb SP 17.75 '12.
The Hartings are the first siblings to win the same individual event in the history of the Summer Olympics.
Robert HARTING b. 18 Oct 1984 Cottbus 2.01m 127kg. SCC Berlin.
At DT: OG: 08- 4, '12- 1, '16- dnq 15; WCh: '07- 09-11-13: 2/1/1/1; EC: '06-10-12-14: dnq 13/2/1/1; CCp: '10- 1; ECp: '07-08-09-10-11-13-14: 2/2/2/1/1/1/1; WJ: '02- dnq 13; WY: '01- 2; EU23: '05- 1. German champion 2007-14, 2016.
Progress at DT: 2002- 54.25, 2003- 59.54, 2004- 64.05, 2005- 66.02, 2006- 65.22, 2007- 66.93, 2008- 68.65, 2009- 69.43, 2010- 69.69, 2011- 68.99, 2012- 70.66, 2013- 69.91, 2014- 68.47, 2016- 68.04. pb SP 18.63 '07.
35 successive wins 2011-13. Brother of Christoph (qv). His father Gert had pbs SP 16.05, DT 42.80 '88, and mother Bettina SP 15.04 and DT 43.06 '80. Married Julia Fischer (qv) on 17 Sep 2016.
Max HESS b. 13 Jul 1996 Chemnitz 1.85m 77kg. LAC Erdgas Chemnitz.
At TJ: OG: '16- dnq 15; EC: '16- 1; WJ: '14- 2; WY: '13- 8; WI: '16- 2; EI: '17- 3. GER champion 2016.
Progress at TJ: 2012- 14.58, 2013- 15.52, 2014- 16.55, 2015- 16.34i/16.07, 2016- 17.20, 2017- 17.52i. pbs: 60m 6.98i '16, LJ 8.03i '16.
Andreas HOFMANN b. 16 Dec 1991 Heidelberg 1.95m 108kg. MTG Mannheim. Sports student.

GERMANY

At JT: WCh: '15- 6; EC: '14- 9; EJ: '09- 1; ET: '14- 1. Progress at JT: 2008- 65.03, 2009- 77.84, 2010- 66.75, 2011- 73.98, 2012- 80.81, 2013- 75.56, 2014- 86.13, 2015- 86.14, 2016- 85.42. pb SP 18.59i '17.

Raphael HOLZDEPPE b. 28 Sep 1989 Kaiserslautern 1.81m 78kg. LAZ Zweibrücken.
At PV: OG: 08- 7, '12- 3, '16- dnq 26; WCh: '11- dnq 20, '13- 1, '15- 2; EC '10- 9, '12- 3; WJ: '06- 5, '08- 1; EU23: '09- 1; EJ: '07- dnq; ET: '15- 2; EI: '13- 8, '17- 5. GER champion 2015.
World junior pole vault record (=) 2008 (and indoors 5.68).
Progress at PV: 2002- 3.45, 2003- 4.25, 2004- 4.50, 2005- 5.00, 2006- 5.42, 2007- 5.50, 2008- 5.80, 2009- 5.65, 2010- 5.80, 2011- 5.72, 2012- 5.91, 2013- 5.91, 2014- 5.53, 2015- 5.94, 2016- 5.84i/5.70, 2017- 5.80i.

Daniel JASINSKI b. 5 Aug 1989 Bochum 2.07m 125kg. TV Wattenscheid.
At DT: OG: '16- 3; WCh: '15- dnq 15; EC: '14- 7; WJ: '08- dnq 24; EU23: '11- 6.
Progress at DT: 2008- 49.15, 2009- 55.01, 2010- 59.02, 2011- 61.28, 2012- 64.37, 2013- 64.69, 2014- 65.98, 2015- 65.93, 2016- 67.16.

Kai KAZMIREK b. 28 Jan 1991 Torgau 1.89m 91kg. LG Rhein-Wied.
At Dec: OG: '16- 4; WCh: '15- 6; EC: '14- 6; WJ: '10- 6; EU23: '11- 6, '13- 1; EJ: '09- 3. German champion 2012. At Hep: WJ: '14- 6.
Progress at Dec: 2011- 7802, 2012- 8130, 2013- 8366, 2014- 8471, 2015- 8462, 2016- 8580. pbs: 60m 7.01i '15, 100m 10.62 '16, 10.61w '13; 200m 21.40 '12, 400m 46.75 '11, 1000m 2:39.51i '14, 1500m 4:31.25 '16, 60mh 8.00i '14, 110mh 14.05 '14, HJ 2.15 '14, PV 5.20 '13, LJ 7.69 '16, SP 14.78 '16, DT 45.83 '15, JT 64.60 '16, Hep 6173i '13.
Won Götzis decathlon 2015, IAAF Combined Events Challenge 2016.

Christopher LINKE b. 24 Oct 1988 Potsdam 1.91m 66kg. SC Potsdam
At 20kW/(50kW): OG: '12- (21), '16- 5; WCh: '11- 17, '13- 9, '15- 38; EC: '10- (dnf), '14- 5; EU23: '09- 4; WCp: '12- (3), '16- 10; ECp: '11- (3), '13- 10, '15- 7. At 10000mW: EJ: '07- 6. Won GER 10000W 2011, 2014-16, 20kW 2012, 2014, 2016; 50kW 2008.
Progress at 20kW, 50kW: 2008- 1:25:25, 4:03:59; 2009- 1:24:29, 2010- 1:27:25, 3:53:24; 2011- 1:20:51, 3:52:56; 2012- 1:20:41, 3:47:33; 2013- 1:22:36, 2014- 1:21:00, 2015- 1:20:37, 2016- 1:19:19. pbs: 3000mW 11:49.10A '10, 5000mW 18:44.32i '16, 20:37.47 '08; 10000W 38:40.25 '16.

Thomas RÖHLER b. 30 Sep 1991 Jena 1.95m 86kg. LC Jena. Sports student.
At JT: OG: '16- 1; WCh: '13- dnq 29, '15- 4; EC: '12-14-16: dnq 13/12/5; WJ: '10- 9; EU23: '11- 7, '13- 3; ET: '13- 2. Won DL 2014, German champion 2012-16.
Progress at JT: 2009- 61.26, 2010- 76.37, 2011- 78.20, 2012- 80.79, 2013- 83.95, 2014- 87.63, 2015- 89.27, 2016- 91.28.

David STORL b. 21 Jul 1990 Rochlitz 1.99m 122kg. Leipzig SC DHfK. Federal police officer.
At SP: OG: '12- 2, '16- 7; ; WCh: '09- dnq 27, '11- 1, '13- 1, '15- 2; EC: '10-12-14-16: 4/1/1/1; WJ: '08- 1; WY: '07- 1; EU23: '11- 1; EJ: '09- 1; WI: '10-12-14: 6/2/2; EI: '11-15-17: 2/1/3; WCp: '14- 1; ET: '11-13-14-15: 1/1/1/1. GER champion 2011-12, 2014-16.
World junior shot record and three with 6kg (to 22.73) 2009.
Progress at SP: 2008- 18.46, 2009- 20.43, 2010- 20.77, 2011- 21.78, 2012- 21.88i/21.86, 2013- 21.73, 2014- 21.97, 2015- 22.20, 2016- 21.31.
9 major international titles & four second places.

Homiyu TESFAYE Heyi b. 23 Jun 1993 Debre Zeyit, Ethiopia 1.83m 66kg. LG Eintracht Frankfurt.
At 1500m: OG: '16- sf; WCh: '13- 5; EC: '14- 5, '16- 10; WI: '14- 7; EI: '15- 4; ET: '14- 2.
European U23 1500m record 2014.
Progress at 1500m: 2011- 3:46.02, 2012- 3:38.56, 2013- 3:34.18, 2014- 3:31.98, 2015- 3:34.13i, 2016- 3:35.05. pbs: 800m 1:46.40 '13, 1000m 2:17.56 '14, 1M 3:49.86 '14, 3000m 7:58.09i '14, 8:03.95 '12; 5000m 13:58.73 '13, 10000m 29:08.44 '13, Rd 10k 27:54 '15.
Claimed asylum in Germany in 2010, and German citizen from 27 Jun 2013.

Johannes VETTER b. 26 Mar 1993 Dresden 1.88m 105kg. LG Offenburg.
At JT: OG: '16- 4; WCh: '15- 7; EC: '16- dnq 16; EU23: '15- 4; EJ: '11- 12; ET: '15- 2.
Progress at JT: 2010- 63.60, 2011- 71.60, 2012- 60.19, 2013- 76.58, 2014- 79.75, 2015- 85.40, 2016- 89.57.

Julian WEBER b. 29 Aug 1994 Mainz 1.90m 94kg. USC Mainz.
At JT: OG: '16- 9; EU23: '15- 5; EJ: '13- 1.
Progress at JT: 2012- 71.12, 2013- 79.68, 2014- 80.72, 2015- 81.15, 2016- 88.29.

Martin WIERIG b. 10 Jun 1987 Neindorf 2.02m 127kg. SC Magdeburg. Federal police officer.
At DT: OG: '12- 6; WCh: '11- dnq 18, '13- 4, '15- dnq 19; EC: '10-12-14-16: 7/dnq 14/11/dnq 14; WJ: '04- 8, '06- 3; EU23: '07- 1, '09- 3; EJ: '05- 3 (dnq SP); ET: '15- 2.
Progress at DT: 2005- 57.44, 2006- 57.37, 2007- 61.10, 2008- 63.09, 2009- 63.90, 2010- 64.93, 2011- 67.21, 2012- 68.33, 2013- 67.46, 2014- 66.59, 2015- 65.94, 2016- 67.16. pb SP 17.30 '11.

Women

Shanice CRAFT b. 15 May 1993 Mannheim 1.85m 89kg. MTG Mannheim. Police officer.
At (SP)/DT: OG: '16- 11; WCh: '15- 7; EC: '14- 3, '16- 3; WJ: '12- 1/2; WY: '09- 3; EU23: '13- 2/2, '15- 2/1; EJ: '11- 1; ET: '14- 2. Won GER 2014, Yth Oly 2010.
Progress at DT: 2007- 44.86, 2008- 48.14, 2009- 50.57, 2010- 55.49, 2011- 58.65, 2012- 62.92, 2013- 60.77, 2014- 65.88, 2015- 64.79, 2016- 64.82. Pb SP 17.75 '14. US father.

Kristin GIERISCH b. 20 Aug 1990 Zwickau 1.78m 59kg. LAC Erdgas Chemnitz. Police.
At TJ: OG: '16- 11; WCh: '15- 8; EC: '14- 9, '16- 8; WY: '07- 6; EU23: '11- dns; EJ: '09- 5; EI: '15- 4, '17- 1; ET: '15- 2; WI: '16- 2. German champion 2014-15.
Progress at TJ: 2006- 12.09, 2007- 13.00, 2008- 12.22, 2009- 14.02, 2010- 13.84, 2011- 14.10i/13.47, 2012- 14.19i/13.94, 2013- 13.91i/13.67, 2014- 14.31/14.34w, 2015- 14.46i/14.38/14.46w, 2016- 14.31, 2017- 14.37i. pbs: 60m 7.59i '12, LJ 6.46i '15, 6.21 '14.

Julia HARTING b. 1 Apr 1990 Berlin 1.92m 95kg. née Fischer. SCC Berlin. Police officer.
At DT: OG: '12- dnq 20, '16- 9; WCh: '13- dnq 13, '15- 5; EC: '12-14-16: 5/5/2; WJ: '08- 2; WY: '07- 1; EU23: '11- 1; EJ: '09- 2; ET: '13- 2. GER champion 2015.
Progress at DT: 2005- 45.69, 2006- 50.23, 2007- 51.39, 2008- 55.92, 2009- 56.74, 2010- 57.49, 2011- 59.60, 2012- 64.22, 2013- 66.04, 2014- 66.46, 2015- 65.98, 2016- 68.49.
Married Robert Harting (qv) on 17 Sep 2016.

Betty HEIDLER b. 14 Oct 1983 Berlin 1.75m 80kg. LG Eintracht Frankfurt. Federal police officer.
At HT: OG: '04- 4, '08- 7, '12- 2, '16- 4; WCh: '03- 05-07-09-11-13-15: 11/dnq 29/1/2/2/dnq 18/7; EC: '06-10-12-14-16: 5/1/dnq 16/5/2; EU23: '03- 4, '05- 2; WJ: '00/02- dnq 19/17; EJ: '01- 9, WUG: '09- 1; CCp: '10- 4; ECp: '04-07-09-10-11-13-14-15: 3/1/2/1/1/1/1/2. Won WAF 2006, 2009; IAAF HT challenge 2010-12, German 2005-13, 2015-16. Hammer records: World 2011, 7 German 2004-11.
Progress at HT: 1999- 42.07, 2000- 56.02, 2001- 60.54, 2002- 63.38, 2003- 70.42, 2004- 72.73, 2005- 72.19, 2006- 76.55, 2007- 75.77, 2008- 74.11, 2009- 77.12, 2010- 76.38, 2011- 79.42, 2012- 78.07, 2013- 76.48, 2014- 78.00, 2015- 75.73, 2016- 75.77.

Christin HUSSONG b. 17 Apr 1994 Zweibrücken 1.87m 82kg. LAZ Zweibrücken. Sports student.
At JT: OG: '16- 12; WCh: '16- 6; EC: '14- 7, '16- dnq 17; WJ: '12- 7; WY: '11- 1; EU23: '13- 2, '15- 1; EJ: '13- 2, YthOG: '10- 4. GER champion 2016.
Progress at JT: 2009- 49.93, 2010- 55.35, 2011- 59.74, 2012- 55.74, 2013- 58.55, 2014- 63.34, 2015- 65.92, 2016- 66.41. Pbs: SP 15.02i '14, 14.02 '11.

Marie-Laurence JUNGFLEISCH b. 7 Oct 1990 Paris, France 1.81m 68kg. VfB Stuttgart. Soldier.
At HJ: OG: '16- 7=; WCh: '13- nh, '15- 6; EC: '12- 14-16: dnq 13=/5/5; EU23: '11- 8; EJ: '09- 6. Won GER 2013-16.
Progress at HJ: 2006- 1.70, 2007- 1.75, 2008- 1.78, 2009- 1.86, 2010- 1.90, 2011- 1.93, 2012- 1.95, 2013- 1.95, 2014- 1.97, 2015- 1.99, 2016- 2.00.
Father from Martinique, mother German.

Kathrin KLAAS b. 6 Feb 1984 Haiger 1.68m 72kg. LG Eintracht Frankfurt. Police inspector.
At HT: OG: '08- dnq 22, '12- 4, '16- dnq 18; WCh: '05-07-13: dnq -/27/20, '09-11-15: 4/7/6; EC: '06- 10-12-14-16: 6/dnq 15/4/4/dnq 25; EJ: '03-8, EU23: '05- 4; WUG: '09- 3. GER champion 2014.
Progress at HT: 2000- 44.24, 2001- 50.10, 2002- 57.74, 2003- 63.72, 2004- 68.01, 2005- 70.91, 2006- 71.67, 2007- 73.45, 2008- 70.39, 2009- 74.23, 2010- 74.53, 2011- 75.48, 2012- 76.05, 2013- 72.57, 2014- 74.62, 2015- 73.18, 2016- 71.78.

Konstanze KLOSTERHALFEN b. 18 Feb 1997 Königswinter 1.69m 52kg. TSV Bayer 04 Leverkusen.
At 1500m: OG: '16- sf; EJ: '15- 3, EI: '17- 2; YthOG: '14- 4. German champion 2016. At 3000m: WJ: '16- 3. Eur CC: 14-15-16: 28J/1J/1J.
Progress at 1500m: 2012- 55.74, 2013- 4:26.58, 2014- 4:19.97, 2015- 4:09.58, 2016- 4:06.91, 2017- 4:04.45i. Pbs: 800m 2:01.55 '16, 3000m 8:46.74 '16, 5000m 15:16.98 '16, 10kRd 32:24 '16.

Gesa Felicitas KRAUSE b. 3 Aug 1992 Ehringshausen 1.67m 55kg. LG Eintracht Frankfurt. Student.
At 3000mSt: OG: '12- 7, '16- 6; WCh: '11- 6, '13- 9, '15- 3; EC: '12-14-16: 3/5/1; WJ: '10- 4; EU23: '13- 1; EJ: '11- 1; ET: '15- 1; GER champion 2015-16. At 2000mSt: WY: '09- 7. At 1500m: EI: '15- 5.
European junior 3000mSt record 2011, two German 2000m Steeple 2015.
Progress at 3000mSt: 2010- 9:47.78, 2011- 9:32.74, 2012- 9:23.52, 2013- 9:37.11, 2014- 9:35.46, 2015- 9:19.25, 2016- 9:18.41. pbs: 800m 2:05.25 '11, 1000m 2:44.68 '10, 1500m 4:06.99 '16, 1M 4:29.58 '16, 3000m 8:49.43i '16, 9:02.04 '15; 5k Rd 16:15 '11, 10k Rd 33:26 '15, 2000mSt 6:04.20 '15.

Malaika MIHAMBO b. 3 Feb 1994 Heidelberg 1.70m 52kg. LG Kurpfalz. Political science student at Mannheim University.
At LJ: OG: '16- 4; WCh: '13- dnq 13, '15- 6; EC: '14- 4, '16- 3; WJ: '12- dnq 14; WY: '11- 9; EU23: '15- 1; EJ: '13- 1; ET: '14- 1. GER champion 2016
Progress at LJ: 2008- 5.55, 2009- 5.81, 2010- 5.96, 2011- 6.40, 2012- 6.45i/6.32/6.50w, 2013- 6.70/6.80w, 2014- 6.90, 2015- 6.84, 2016- 6.95. pbs: 200m 23.96 '15, HJ 1.78i/1.75 '10.
Tanzanian father, German mother.

Sosthene Taroum **MOGUENARA** b. 17 Oct 1989 Sarh, Moyen-Chari, Chad 1.82m 68kg. LG LAZ Saar 05 Saarbrücken.
At LJ: OG: '12- dnq 20, '16- 10; WCh: '11- dnq 31, '13- 11, '15- dnq 27; EC: '12- 4, '14- 9; EU23: '09- 4, '11- 3; ET: '15- 3; EI: '15- 2. GER champion 2013.
Progress at LJ: 2007- 6.22, 2008- 6.37, 2009- 6.61/6.69w, 2010- 6.65, 2011- 6.83, 2012- 6.88, 2013- 7.04, 2014- 6.82, 2015- 6.94, 2016- 7.16. pbs: 60m 7.66i '08, 100m 11.94 '10, 200m 24.85 '07.
Has lived in Germany from the age of nine.

Katharina MOLITOR b. 8 Nov 1983 Bedurg, Erft 1.82m 76kg. TSV Bayer 04 Leverkusen.
At JT: OG: '08- 7, 12- 6; WCh: '11- 5, '13- dnq 13, '15- 1; EC: '10-12-14-16: 4/5/9/4; EU23: '05- 2; WUG: '07- 6, '09- 4. German champion 2010, 2015.

Progress at JT: 2000- 42.94, 2001- 48.53, 2002- 49.01, 2003- 48.03, 2004- 50.04, 2005- 57.01, 2006- 57.58, 2007- 58.87, 2008- 61.74, 2009- 62.69, 2010- 64.53, 2011- 64.67, 2012- 63.20, 2013- 63.55, 2014- 63.40, 2015- 67.69, 2016- 63.20.
Played volleyball in the Bundesliga.

Nadine MÜLLER b. 21 Nov 1985 Leipzig 1.93m 90kg. Hallesche LA-Freunde. Federal police officer.
At DT: OG: '12- 4, '16- 6; WCh: '07-09-11-13-15: dnq 23/6/2/4/3; EC: '10-12-16: 8/2/4; WJ: '04- 3; EU23: '05- 10, '07- 8; EJ: '03- 2; ET: '10- 1. German champion 2010-13, 2016.
Progress at DT: 2000- 36.10, 2001- 46.27, 2002- 48.90, 2003- 53.44, 2004- 57.85, 2005- 59.35, 2006- 58.46, 2007- 62.93, 2008- 61.36, 2009- 63.46, 2010- 67.78, 2011- 66.99, 2012- 68.89, 2013- 66.89, 2014- 67.30, 2015- 65.72, 2016- 66.84.

Jennifer OESER b. 29 Nov 1983 Brunsbüttel 1.76m 65kg. TSV Bayer 04 Leverkusen. Federal police officer.
At Hep: OG: '08- 11, '12- 28 (dnf 800m), '16- 9; WCh: '07-09-11-15: 7/2/2/10; EC: '06- 4, '10- 3; WJ: '02- 8; EU23: '03- 1. German champion 2006.
Progress at Hep: 2000- 5167, 2001- 5531, 2002- 5595, 2003- 5901, 2004- 5936, 2005- 5637, 2006- 6376, 2007- 6378, 2008- 6436, 2009- 6493, 2010- 6683, 2011- 6663, 2012- 6345, 2015- 6308, 2016- 6401. pbs: 200m 23.95 '11, 800m 2:10.39 '11, 60mh 8.56i '09, 100mh 13.14 '11, HJ 1.86 '06, LJ 6.68 '10, 6.70w '11; SP 14.29 '09, JT 51.30 '11, Pen 4423i '09. Four pbs in EC Heptathlon bronze 2010. Won IAAF Challenge 2010-11. Son Jakob born on 6 Oct 2014.

Cindy ROLEDER b. 21 Aug 1989 Chemnitz 1.78m 68kg. LAZ Leipzig. Police officer.
At 100mh: OG: '12- sf, '16- 5, WCh: '11- sf, '15- 2; EC: '10-12-14-16: h/6/3/1; WJ: '08- sf; EU23: '09- sf, '11- 3; EJ: '07- 4; CCp: '14- 3; ET: '15- 3; GER champion 2011, 2015-16. At 60mh: WI: '14- 6; EI: '15- 4, '17- 1.
Progress at 100mh: 2007- 13.49, 2008- 13.72, 2009- 13.38, 2010- 12.97, 2011- 12.91, 2012- 12.91, 2013- 13.03/12.93w, 2014- 12.80, 2015- 12.59, 2016- 12.62. pbs: 60m 7.34i '15, 100m 11.72 '13, 150m 17.40 '15, 200m 23.35 '15, 800m 2:15.49 '15, 50mh 7.14+i '10, 60mh 7.84i '17, HJ 1.66 '15, LJ 6.32i '14, 6.17 '13, 6.18w '15; SP 13.59i '16, 13.25 '15; JT 36.33 '15, Pen 4187i '14, Hep 6055 '15.

Anna RÜH b. 17 Jun 1993 Greifswald 1.86m 78kg. SC Neubrandenburg.
At DT: '12- 9; EC: '12- 4, '14- 4; WJ: '10- dnq 21, '12- 1; EU23: '13- 1, '15- 2; EJ: '11- 2 (3 app).
Progress at DT: 2009- 44.43, 2010- 51.67, 2011- 59.97, 2012- 63.38, 2013- 64.33, 2014- 64.17, 2015- 66.14, 2016- 64.08. pb SP 17.68i/17.20 '16.

Elisaveta 'Lisa' RYZIH b. 27 Sep 1988 Omsk, Russia 1.79m 59kg. Formerly Ryshich. ABC Ludwigshafen. Psychology student.
At PV: OG: '12- 6=, '16- 10; WCh: '13- 8=, '15- 12;

EC: '10-12-14-16: 3/7/4/2; WJ: '04- 1, '06- nh; WY: '03- 1; EU23: '09- 1; EJ: '07- 4; EI: '11- 7, '17- 2; CCp: '10- 2, '14- 3. German champion 2014-15.
Progress at PV: 2002- 3.92, 2003- 4.10, 2004- 4.30, 2005- 4.15, 2006- 4.35, 2007- 4.35, 2008- 4.52i/4.50, 2009- 4.50, 2010- 4.65, 2011- 4.65i, 2012- 4.65, 2013- 4.55, 2014- 4.71, 2015- 4.72i/4.70, 2016- 4.73, 2017- 4.75i. pb HJ pb 1.91i '85 and 1.89 '81, and father Vladimir PV 5.30 '79.

Claudia SALMAN-RATH b. 25 Apr 1986 Hadamar, Hessen 1.75m 65kg. née Rath. LG Eintracht Frankfurt.
At Hep: OG: '16- 14; WCh: '11- 4, '15- 5; EC: '10-12-14: 10/6/8. German champion 2010-11. At WI Pen: '14- 5. At LJ: EI: '17- 3.
Progress at LJ, Hep: 2003- 5.64, 5231; 2004- 5.99, 5353; 2005- 6.09, 5323; 2006- 6.13, 5274; 2007- 6.22, 5274; 2008- 6.29, 5697; 2009- 6.44, 5941; 2010- 6.50, 6107; 2011- 6.28. 6098; 2012- 6.44, 6210; 2013- 6.67, 6462; 2014- 6.46, 6314, 2015- 6.73/6.84w, 6458; 2016- 6.62, 6310; 2017- 6.94i. pbs: 200m 23.77 '14, 800m 2:06.43 '13, 60mh 8.43i '14, 100mh 13.44 '15, HJ 1.83 '13, SP 13.78 '14, JT 43.65 '16, Pen 4681i '14.

Carolin SCHÄFER b. 5 Dec 1991 Bad Wildungen 1.78m 64kg. TV Friedrichstein.
At Hep: OG: '16- 5; WCh: '15- dnf; EC: '12- 10, '14- 4; WJ: '08- 1; EU23: '11- 5, '13- 6; EJ: '09- 1. German champion 2013.
Progress at Hep: 2007- 5545, 2008- 5833, 2009- 5697, 2010- 5333, 2011- 5941, 2012- 6072, 2013- 5972, 2014- 6395, 2015- 6547, 2016- 6557. pbs: 60m 7.86i '07, 200m 23.37 '16, 800m 2:14.10 '15, 60mh 8.45i '16, 100mh 13.12 '16, HJ 1.84 '14, LJ 6.31 '16, SP 14.57 '16, JT 50.76 '12, Pen 4098i '09.
Won IAAF Combined Events Challenge 2016. Her elder brother Sebastian had 400m best 47.10 '08 and ran at 4x100m in EJ 2005 & 2007.

Christina SCHWANITZ b. 24 Dec 1985 Dresden 1.80m 103kg. LV 90 Erzebirge. Soldier.
At SP: OG: '08- 9, '12- 9, '16- 6; WCh: '05-09-11-13-15: 7/12/12/2/1; EC: '12-14-16: 5/1/1; WJ: '04- 3; EU23: '05- 2; WI: '08- 6, '14- 2; EI: '11- 2, '13- 1; CCp: '14- 1; ET: '08-13-14-15: 1/1/1/1. Won DL 2015, German 2011, 2013-16.
Progress at SP: 2001- 13.57, 2002- 14.26, 2003- 15.25, 2004- 16.98, 2005- 18.84, 2007- 17.06, 2008- 19.68i/19.31, 2009- 19.06, 2010- 18.28, 2011- 19.20, 2012- 19.15i/19.05, 2013- 20.41, 2014- 20.22, 2015- 20.77, 2016- 20.17. pb DT 47.27 '03.

Silke SPIEGELBURG b. 17 Mar 1986 Georgsmarienhütte 1.73m 64kg. TSV Bayer 04 Leverkusen. Economics student.
At PV: OG: '04- 13, '08- 7, '12- 4; WCh: '07-09-11-13-15: nh/4/9/4/dnq 17=; EC: '06-10-12: 6/2/4=; WJ: '02- 8; WY: '01- 1; EU23: '07- 4; EJ: '03- 1, '05- 1; WI: '06-12-14: 8/4/7; EI: '07-09-11: 5/2/2; ECp: '08-09-10-11-13-15: 3/3/2/2/1/1; Won WAF 2008, DL 2011-13, German 2005-10, 2012.
PV records: World junior 2005, German 2012.
Progress at PV: 1998- 2.75, 1999- 3.30, 2000- 3.75, 2001- 4.00, 2002- 4.20, 2003- 4.20i/4.15, 2004- 4.40, 2005- 4.48i/4.42, 2006- 4.56, 2007- 4.60, 2008- 4.70, 2009- 4.75i/4.70, 2010- 4.71, 2011- 4.76i/4.75, 2012- 4.82, 2013- 4.79, 2014- 4.72i/4.50, 2015- 4.75, 2016- 4.56i/4.50.
Brothers: Henrik PV pb 4.80, Christian (b. 15 Apr 1976) 5.51 '98; **Richard** (b. 12 Aug 1977) 5.85 '01; 6= WCh 01, 1 WUG 99.

Linda STAHL b. 2 Oct 1985 Steinheim 1.74m 72kg. TSV Bayer 04 Leverkusen. Doctor.
At JT: OG: '12- 3, '16- 11; WCh: '07-09-11-13-15: 8/6/dns/4/10; EC: '10-12-14-16: 1/3/3/2; EU23: '07- 1; CCp: '10- 4, '14- 5; ET: '14- 3. Won GER 2013-14.
Progress at JT: 2000- 42.94, 2001- 43.96, 2002- 47.23, 2003- 47.32, 2004- 50.11, 2005- 53.94, 2006- 57.17, 2007- 62.80, 2008- 66.06, 2009- 63.86, 2010- 66.81, 2011- 60.78, 2012- 64.91, 2013- 65.76, 2014- 67.32, 2015- 64.65, 2015- 65.25, 2016- 65.25. pb SP 13.91i '06.

Martina STRUTZ b. 4 Nov 1981 Schwerin 1.60m 57kg. SC Neubrandenburg. Police officer.
At PV: OG: '12- 5, '16- 9; WCh: '11- 2, '15- 8; EC: '06-12-16: 5/2/10; WJ: '00- 5; EU23: '01- 4, '03- 9=; WCp: '06- 4. German champion 2011, 2013, 2016.
Two German pole vault records 2011.
Progress at PV: 1996- 3.30, 1997- 3.60i/3.50, 1998- 3.80, 1999- 4.10, 2000- 4.20, 2001- 4.42, 2002- 4.30, 2003- 4.20, 2004- 4.31, 2005- 4.40i/4.35, 2006- 4.50, 2007- 4.45, 2008- 4.52, 2009- 4.40, 2010- 4.30, 2011- 4.80, 2012- 4.60, 2013- 4.65, 2014- 4.46i/4.41, 2015- 4.65, 2016- 4.70.

Alexandra WESTER b. 21 Mar 1994 Bakau, The Gambia 1.73m 59kg. ASV Köln.
At LJ: OG: '16- dnq 34; EC: '16- 7; WI: '16- 6; EI: '17- 8.
Progress at LJ: 2009- 6.19, 2010- 5.97i/5.86, 2011- 5.83, 2012- 5.82, 2013- 6.29, 2014- 6.13, 2015- 6.59, 2016- 6.95i/6.79/7.00w. pbs: 60m 7.53i '15, 100m 12.00 '09, 200m 25.27i '10, 60mh 8.47i '15, HJ 1.68 '09, SP 11.51i '14, 11.42 '11; Hep 5523 '14.
German father, Ghanian mother. Has lived in Germany from the age of 3.

GREECE

Governing body: Hellenic Amateur Athletic Association (SEGAS), 137 Siggroú Avenue, 171 21 Nea Smirni, Athens. Founded 1897.
National Championships first held in 1896 (men), 1930 (women). **2016 Champions**: 100m/200m: Likoúrgos-Stéfanos Tsákonas 10.40/20.75, 400m: Pétros Kiriakídis 47.32, 800m/1500m: Andréas Dimitrákis 1:49.87/ 3:43.06, 5000m: Márkos Goúlias 14:40.28, 10000m: Hrístos Kallías 30:39.64, HMar: Konstadínos Gelaoúzos 68:35, Mar: Hristóforos Meroúsis 2:24:58, 3000mSt: Douíkis Dimosthénis 9:13.46, 110mh: Konstadínos Douvalídis 13.42, 400mh: Konstadínos Nákos 51.65, HJ: Konstadínos Baniótis 2.13, PV: Konstadínos Filippídis 5.55, LJ: Yeóryios Tsákonas 7.95, TJ: Dimítrios Baltadoúros 16.64, SP: Frántsi Latiflári 17.72, DT: Yeóryios Trémos 59.89, HT: Mihaíl Anastasákis 74.98, JT: Paraskevás Batzávalis 81.45, Dec: Panayiótis Mántis 6937, 20kW: Aléxandros Papamihaíl 1:26:05; 50kW: Konstadínos-Aléxandros Dedópoulos 4:09:33. **Women**: 100m/400mh: Ekateríni Daláka 11.70/ 58.43, 200m: María Belibasáki 23.21, 400m: Iríni Vasilíou 52.49, 800m: Konstadína Yiannopoúlou 2:03.91, 1500m: Anastasía-Panayióta Marinákou 4:24.11, 5000m: Alexi-Maria Pappas 15:47.56, 10000m/HMar/Mar: Ouranía Reboúli 34:06.80/76:57/2:49:24, 3000mSt: María Pardaloú 10:09.02, 100mh: Elisávet Pesirídou 12.93, HJ: Ioánna Zákka 1.82, PV: Ekateríni Stefanídi 4.80, LJ/TJ: Paraskevi Papahrístou 6.56/14.07, SP: Evaggelía Sofáni 15.64, DT: Hrisoúla Anagnostopoúlou 58.56, HT: Iliána Korosídou 65.87, JT/Hep: Sofía Ifantídou 56.02/5957, 20kW: Déspina Zapounídou 1:29:35.

Konstadínos FILIPÍDDIS b. 26 Nov 1986 Athens 1.88m 73kg. Panellínios YS Athens. Postgraduate student at Athens University of Economics and Business.
At PV: OG: '12- 6, '16- 7=; WCh: '05-09-11-13-15: dnq 14=/dnq 17/6/10/dnq 25=; EC: '06-10: dnq 26/21=, '12-14-16: 5/7/7=; WJ: '04- 4; WY: '03- 4; EJ: '05- 2; WI: '10-12-14-16: 4=/7/1/7; EI: '11-13-15-17: 5/4/5/2; WUG: '05- 2; ET: '09/10- 4; Won MedG 2005; Greek champion 2005, 2009-16.
Ten Greek pole vault records 2005-15.
Progress at PV: 2001- 3.70, 2002- 4.80, 2003- 5.22, 2004- 5.50, 2005- 5.75, 2006- 5.55, 2007- 5.35i/ 5.30/5.40dq, 2009- 5.65, 2010- 5.70i/5.55, 2011- 5.75, 2012- 5.80, 2013- 5.83i/5.82, 2014- 5.80i/5.70, 2015- 5.91, 2016- 5.84i/5.72, 2017- 5.85i.
Two-year drugs ban (reduced to 18 months) from positive test on 16 June 2007.

Women

Nikoléta KIRIAKOPOÚLOU b. 21 Mar 1986 Athens 1.67m 56kg. AYES Kámiros Rhodes.
At PV: OG: '08/12- dnq 27=/19=; WCh: '09-11-13-15: dnq 19/8/dnq 13=/3; EC: '10-12-14-16: dnq 13/3/7=/4; WJ: '04- 6; EJ: '05- 7; WI: '16- 6=; EI: '11- 9, '15- 5=. Won DL 2015, Balkan 2008, Med G 2009, Greek 2009, 2011-14.
Nine Greek pole vault records 2010-15.
Progress at PV: 2001- 2.90, 2002- 3.10, 2003- 3.70, 2004- 4.00, 2005- 4.10, 2006- 3.60, 2007- 4.00i/3.90,

2008- 4.45, 2009- 4.50, 2010- 4.55, 2011- 4.71, 2012- 4.60, 2013- 4.65, 2014- 4.72i/4.67, 2015- 4.83, 2016- 4.81i/4.75. Expecing a baby in 2017.

Paraskeví 'Voula' PAPAHRÍSTOU b. 17 Apr 1989 Athens 1.70m 53kg. AEK (Athens).
At TJ: OG: '16- 8; WCh: '09/11- dnq 29/16; EC: '12- 11, '16- 3; WJ: '08- 3; EU23: '09/11- 1/1; WI: '16- 3; EI: '17- 3. Won Greek LJ 2011-12, 2016; TJ 2009, 2011, 2015.
Progress at TJ: 2005- 12.75, 2006- 12.81/13.13w, 2007- 12.98i/12.92, 2008- 13.86i/13.79/13.94w, 2009- 14.47i/14.35, 2010- 13.94i/13.85, 2011- 14.72, 2012- 14.58/14.77w, 2013- 14.21, 2015- 13.99/14.20w, 2016- 14.73. pb LJ 6.40 '12.

Ekateríni STEFANÍDI b. 4 Feb 1990 Athens 1.72m 63kg. Was at Stanford University, USA and then as a graduate student in cognitive psychology at Arizona State University.
At PV: OG: '12- dnq 24, '16- 1; WCh: '15- dnq 15; EC: '12-14-16: nh/2/1; WJ: '08- 3; WY: '05- 1, '07- 2; EU23: '11- 2; WI: '16- 3; EI: '15- 2, '17- 1; WUG: '11- 3. Greek champion 2015-16, NCAA 2012. World youth pole vault best 2005. Greek PV record indoors and out 2016
Progress at PV: 2002- 3.40, 2003- 3.90, 2004- 4.14, 2005- 4.37i/4.30, 2006- 4.10, 2007- 4.25, 2008- 4.25, 2009- 4.13, 2010- 4.30, 2011- 4.45, 2012- 4.51, 2013- 4.45Ai/4.40, 2014- 4.71, 2015- 4.77Ai/4.71, 2016- 4.90i/4.86, 2017- 4.85i.
Married to Mitchell Krier.

GRENADA

Governing body: Grenada Athletic Assocation, PO Box 419, St George's. Founded 1924.

Kurt FELIX b. 4 Jul 1988 St. George's 1.90m 88kg. Was at Boise State University.
At Dec: OG: '12- dnf, '16- 9; WCh: '13- dnf, '15- 8; CG: '14- 3; PAm: '15- 2. At Hep: WI: '16- 6.
GRN records: decathlon (7) 2012-16, PV 2010-15.
Progress at Dec: 2008- 6946, 2009- 7091, 2010- 7412, 2012- 8062, 2013- dnf, 2014- 8070, 2015- 8302, 2016- 8323. pbs: 60m 7.00i '16, 100m 10.91 '15, 10.90w '12; 400m 48.63 '15, 1000m 2:42.91i '11, 1500m 4:30.53 '16, 60mh 8.31i '16, 110mh 14.58 '15, HJ 2.17i '11, 2.15 '09; PV 4.61i '16, 4.60 '12; LJ 7.74 '12, TJ 16.06 '09, SP 15.23 '15, DT 45.95 '15, JT 69.92 '16, Hep: 5986i '16.
Half brother of Lindon Victor (qv).

Kiraní JAMES b. 1 Sep 1992 St George's 1.85m 74kg. Student at University of Alabama, USA
At (200m)/400m: OG: '12- 1, '16- 2; WCh: '11- 1, '13- 7, '15- 3; CG: '14- 1; WJ: '08- 2, '10- 1; WY: '07- 2, '09- 1/1; WI: '12- 6. Won DL 2011, 2015; PAm-J 400m 2009, 200m 2011; NCAA 2010-11.
Records: CAC & Commonwealth 400m 2012 & 2014, GRN 200m 2011, 400m (2) 2011-12; Indoor 400m: CAC & Commonwealth 2010 (45.24) &. 2011, World Junior (44.80) 2011.
Progress at 400m: 2007- 46.96, 2008- 45.70, 2009- 45.24, 2010- 45.01, 2011- 44.36, 2012- 43.94, 2013- 43.96, 2014- 43.74, 2015- 43.78, 2016- 43.76. pbs: 200m 20.41A/20.53w '11, 20.76 '10; 300m 31.3+ '16.
He set world age bests at 14 and 15. In 2011 he became the youngest ever World or Olympic champion at 400m and in 2012 the first Olympic medallist for Grenada at any sport. In January 2012 the 'Kirani James Boulevard' was opened in the Grenadan capital St. George. IAAF Rising Star award 2011.

Bralon TAPLIN b. 8 May 1992 St George's 1.80m 73kg. Was at Texas A&M University, USA
At 400m: OG: '16- 7; WCh: '15- h; CG: '14- sf; PAm: '15- h; WI: '16- 4.
Progress at 400m: 2008- 49.21, 2009- 47.25, 2010- 47.03, 2011- 46.79, 2012- 45.36, 2013- 46.85i/47.50, 2014- 45.18, 2015- 44.89, 2016- 44.38. pbs: 100m 10.53A '12, 200m 20.80i '15, 20.83 '12; 300m 31.8+ '16, 31.97i '17; 600y 1:10.14i '11.

Lindon VICTOR b. 28 Feb 1993 St. George's 1.91m 89kg. Texas A&M University, USA.
At Dec: OG: '16- 16; CG: '14- 9; PAm: '15- 7.
Grenada decathlon records 2016 & 2017.
Progress at Dec: 2014- 7429, 2015- 7453, 2016- 8446, 2017- 8472. pbs: 60m 6.94i '17, 100m 10.60 '16, 400m 48.24 '17, 1000m 2:51.14i '17, 1500m 4:43.81 '16, 60mh 8.24i '16, 110mh 14.68 '16, HJ 2.09 '17, PV 4.76i '17, 4.55 '16; LJ 7.37 '17, SP 16.55i/16.52 '17, DT 54.56 '16, JT 71.23 '14, Hep: 5976i '17. Half brother of Kurt Felix (qv).

HUNGARY

Governing body: Magyar Atlétikai Szövetség, 1146 Budapest, Istvánmezei út 1-3. Fd 1897.
National Championships first held in 1896 (men), 1932 (women). **2016 Champions. Men**: 100m/200m: János Sipos 10.39/21.74, 400m: Marcell Deák Nagy 46.77, 800m/1500m: Tamás Kazi 1:51.35/3:40.93, 5000m: , 10000m: Benjamin Kovács 29:47.36, HMar/Mar: Gábor Józsa 67:45/2:22:39, 3000mSt: Balázs Juhász 8:52.07, 110mh: Balázs Baji 13.39w, 400mh: Tibor Koroknai 50.85, HJ: Péter Bakosi 2.12, PV: Tamás Kéri 5.00, LJ: István Virovecz 7.81, TJ: Dávid László 16.46w, SP: Lajos Kürthy 17.11, DT: Zoltán Kövágó 59.54, HT: Krisztián Pars 73.38, JT: Norbert Rivasz-Tóth 75.11, Dec: Botond Kriszt 6477, 20kW: Máté Helebrandt 1:22:38. **Women**: 100m/200m: Éva Kaptur 11.61/24.72, 400m/800m: Bianka Kéri 53.94/2:08.60, 1500m: Kriszta Kószás 4:28.70, 5000m/3000mSt: Viktória Gyürkés 16:40.64/10:15.99, 10000m/HMar: Zita Kácser 34:44.53/79:25, Mar: Simona Staicu 2:50:30, 100mh: Gréta Kerekes 13.28, 400mh: Noémi Szücs 60.34. HJ: Barbara Szabó 1.90, PV: Eniko Eros 4.25, LJ: Fanni Schmelcz 6.36w, TJ: Krisztina 13.02, SP/DT: Anita Márton 18.36/54.56, HT: Réka Gyurátz 69.66, JT: Réka Szilágyi 65.39, Hep: Luca Renner 5086, 20kW: Viktória Madarász 1:30:47.

HUNGARY – ICELAND – INDIA

Balázs BAJI b. 9 Jun 1989 Békéscsaba 1.92m 83kg. Békéscsabai AC.
At 110mh: OG: '12- h, '16- sf; WCh: '11-13-15: h/sf/sf; WJ: '08- 7; EC: '10-12-14-16: h/sf/4/2; EU23: '09- h,'11- 2; WUG: '11- 6; won HUN 200m 2009, 110mh 2007, 2011-16. At 60mh: WI: '16- 6; EI: '13- 4, '15- 7.
Four Hungarian 110mh records 2014-16.
Progress at 110mh: 2007- 14.48, 2008- 14.44/14.43w, 2009- 13.96/13.88w, 2010- 13.79, 2011- 13.58, 2012- 13.50, 2013- 13.36, 2014- 13.29, 2015- 13.45, 2016- 13.28. pbs: 60m 6.85i '13, 100m 10.60 '09, 200m 21.35 '13, 400m 49.6 '07, 60mh 7.55i '16, 400mh 56.38 '06.

Zoltán KÖVÁGÓ b. 10 Apr 1979 Szolnok 2.04m 127kg. Szolnoki Honvéd SE. Army lieutenant.
At DT: OG: '00- dnq, '04- 2, '08- dnq 21, '12- 7; WCh: '01-03-05-07-09-11-15: dnq 20/dnq 19/10/9/6/dnq 15/dnq 18; EC: '02-10-12-14-16: 7/dnq 21/dq (3)/dnq 14/6; WJ: '96- 4, '98- 1; EJ: '97- 3; EU23: '99- 6, '01- 1. HUN champion 2001, 2004-05, 2008-11, 2014-16; W.MilG 2015.
Progress at DT: 1995- 49.78, 1996- 59.70, 1997- 62.16, 1998- 60.27, 1999- 63.23, 2000- 66.76, 2001- 66.93, 2002- 65.98, 2003- 66.03, 2004- 68.93, 2005- 66.00, 2006- 69.95, 2007- 66.42, 2008- 68.17, 2009- 67.64, 2010- 69.69, 2011- 69.50, 2012- 68.21dq, 2014- 65.82, 2015- 67.39, 2016- 67.13. pb SP 15.93 '01.
2-year drugs ban 2011-13.

Krisztián PARS b. 18 Feb 1982 Körmend 1.88m 113kg. Dobó SE.
At HT: OG: '04- 4, '08- 4, '12- 1, '16- 7; WCh: '05-07-09-11-13-15: 6/5/4/2/2/4; EC: '06-10-12-14: 5/3/1/1; WY: '99- 1; EJ: '01- 1; EU23: '03- 1; CCp: '14- 1. Won HUN 2005-16; World HT challenge 2011-12, 2014.
World junior records with 6kg hammer: 80.64 & 81.34 in 2001.
Progress at HT: 1998- 54.00, 1999- 61.92, 2000- 66.80, 2001- 73.09, 2002- 74.18, 2003- 78.81, 2004- 80.90, 2005- 80.03, 2006- 82.45, 2007- 81.40, 2008- 81.96, 2009- 81.43, 2010- 79.64, 2011- 81.89, 2012- 82.28, 2013- 82.40, 2014- 82.69, 2015- 79.91, 2016- 77.38. pbs: SP 15.60 '05, DT 53.80 '03.

Women

Anita MÁRTON b. 15 Jan 1989 Szeged 1.71m 84kg. Békéscsabai AC.
At SP: OG: '12- dnq 22, '16- 3; WCh: '09-11-13: dnq 24/22/20, '15- 4; EC: '10-12-14-16: 11/7/3/2; WJ: '06- dnq 15, '08- 7; WY: '05- 11; EU23: '09- 5, '11- 5; EJ: '07- 7; WUG: '13- 4; WI: '14- 6, '16- 2; EI: '11-15-17: 5/1/1; won HUN SP 2006-16, DT 2008-16. Three Hungarian shot records 2014-16.
Progress at SP: 2004- 13.88, 2005- 14.12i/13.90, 2006- 15.57, 2007- 15.68, 2008- 16.90, 2009- 17.27, 2010- 18.20, 2011- 18.15, 2012- 18.48, 2013- 18.18, 2014- 19.04, 2015- 19.48, 2016- 19.87. pbs: DT 60.94 '16, HT 48.87 '08.
Improved pb from 18.48/18.63i to 19.04 to take EC bronze 2014, indoor best to 19.23i for EI gold and outdoor pb to 19.48 for World 4th 2015 and to 19.87 for Olympic silver 2016; HUN indoor record 19.33 for 2nd WI 2016.

Györgyi ZSIVOCZKY-FARKAS b. 13 Feb 1985 Budapest 1.70m 58kg. Honved SE.
At Hep: OG: '08- 28, '12- 20, '16- 8; WCh: '11- 22, '13- 15, '15- 6; EC: '12-14-16: 13/10/5; WJ: '02- 10, '04- 7; EU23: '05- 16.; WUG: 13- 2 At Pen: WI: '16- 5; EI: '15- 6, '17- 3. Won HUN LJ 2010, Hep 2008, 2010-11.
Progress at Hep: 2002- 5339, 2004- 5550, 2005- 5342, 2006- 5033, 2008- 5842, 2009- dnf, 2010- 5874, 2011- 6068, 2012- 6030, 2013- 6269, 2014- 6180, 2015- 6389, 2016- 6442. pbs: 200m 25.21 '15, 800m 2:11.76 '16, 60mh 8.44i '15, 100mh 13.79 '16, HJ 1.87 '16, LJ 6.38i '17, 6.32 '13; SP 14.95i '17, 14.62 '15; DT 42.06 '07, JT 50.73 '14, Pen 4723i '17.
Married to Attila Zsivoczky (Dec 8554 '00, 4/3 WCh 01/05, 8/6 OG 00/04. 2 EC 06).

ICELAND

Governing body: Frjálsíthróttasamband Islands, Engjavegur 6, IS-104 Reykjavik. Founded 1947.
National Championships first held in 1927.
2016 Champions: Men: 100m/200m: Kolbeinn Hödur Gunnarsson 10.61/21.48, 400m: Kormákur Ari Haflidason 50.30, 800m: Kristin Thór Kristinsson 1:54.91, 1500m/ 5000m: Hylnur Andrésson 4:01.77/15:26.39, 3000mSt:, 110mh: Gudmundur Gudmundsson 15.16, 400mh: Ivar Kristinn Jasonarson 52.70, HJ/JT: Örn Davidsson 1.93/63.22, PV: Krister Blær Jónsson 4.62, LJ/TJ: Thorsteinn Ingvarsson 6.98/13.54, SP: Ódinn Björn Thorsteinsson 17.28, DT: Gudni Valur Gudnason 56.83, HT: Hilmar Örn Jónsson 68.33. **Women**: 100m: Hrafnhild Eir Hermódsdóttir 11.83, 200m/400m/100mh: Arna Stefanía Gudmundsdóttir 24.21/53.91/13.68, 800m/1500m: Andrea Kolbeinsdóttir 4:59.82/10:43.17, 400mh: Gudbjörg Jóna Bjarnadóttir 62.90, HJ: María Rún Gunnlaugsdóttir 1.66, PV: Hilda Steinum Egilsdóttir 3.32, LJ: Irma Hunnarsdóttir 5.44, TJ: Vilborg María Loftsdóttir 11.36, SP/DT/JT: Ásdis Hjálmsdóttir 16.07/48.96/55.60, HT: Vigdis Jónsdóttir 57.11.

INDIA

Governing body: Athletics Federation of India, WZ-72, Todapur Main Road, Dev Prakash Shastri Marg, New Delhi – 110012. Fd 1946.
National Championships first held as Indian Games in 1924. **2016 Champions: Men**: 100m: Sanjeet Singh 10.55, 200m: Vidya Sagar 21.08, 400m: Arokia Rajiv 46.70, 800m/1500m: Ajay Kumar Saroj 1:56.25/3:51.82, 5000m/10000m: Govindan Lakshmanan 14:16.07/30:05.03, 3000mSt: Naveen Kumar 8:43.18, 110mh: Akhil Johnson 14.10, 400m: Jithin Paul 50.38, HJ: Tejaswin Shankar 2.22, PV: Jayaraj Preeth 4.95,

LJ: Muhammed Anees 7.65, TJ: Malkit Singh 16.57, SP: Om Prakash Singh 18.55, DT: Arjun Kumar Singh 56.67, HT: Neeraj Kumar 66.91, JT: Ravinder Singh 79.04, Dec: Abhishek Shetty 6991, 20kW: Devender Singh 1:29:48, 50kW: Basant Bahadur Rana 4:07:25. **Women**: 100m/200m: Hiriyur Manjunath Jyothi 11.57/23.73, 400m: Ashwini Chidananda Akkunji 53.25, 800m: Tintu Luka 2:03.21, 1500m: Sugandha Kumari 4:24.45, 5000m/10000m: Suriya Loganathan 16:05.90/33:33.74, 3000mSt: Preeti Lamba 10:31.88, 100mh: Purnima Hembram 13.96, 400mh: Santhosh Kumari 58.98, HJ: Jinu Maria Manuel 1.82, PV: Vakaharia Khyati 3.90, LJ: Narayanan V. Neena 6.43, TJ: Nellickal Varkey Sheena 13.54, SP: Manpreet Kaur 16.22, DT: Kamalpreet Kaur 54., HT: Sarita Prakash Singh 60.35, JT: Annu Rani 60.01, Hep: Liksy Joseph 5026, 20kW: Baby Soumya 1:44:32.

Women

Lalita Shivaji **BABAR** b. 2 Jun 1989 Mohi, Satara district 1.60m 58kg.
At 3000mSt: OG: '16- 10; WCh: '15- 8; AsiG: '14- 3; AsiC: '15- 1. At 10000m: CG: '10- 8. Won Indian 5000m 2010, 3000mSt 2015.
Indian records: HMar 2015, 3000mSt (5) 2014-16.
Progress at 3000mSt: 2013- 10:33.40, 2014- 9:35.37, 2015- 9:27.86, 2016- 9:19.76. pbs: 5000m 15:46.73 '15, 10000m 34:54.37 '10, road: 10k 34::10 '10, HMar 70:52 '15, Mar 2:38:21 '15.

IRAN

Governing body: Amateur Athletic Federation of Islamic Republic of Iran, Shahid Keshvari Sports Complex, Razaneh Junibi St Mirdamad Ave, Tehran. Founded 1936.

Ehsan HADADI b. 21 Jan 1985 Ahvaz 1.93m 125kg.
At DT: OG: '08- dnq 17, '12- 2, '16- dnq 24; WCh: '07- 7, '11- 3, '15- dnq 24; WJ: '04- 1; AsiG: '06-10-14: 1/1/1; AsiC: '03-05-07-09-11: 8/1/1/1/1; AsiJ: '04- 1; WCp: '06- 2, '10- 3. Won W.Asian 2005.
Eight Asian discus records 2005-08.
Progress at DT: 2002- 53.66, 2003- 54.40, 2004- 54.96, 2005- 65.25, 2006- 63.79, 2007- 67.95, 2008- 69.32, 2009- 66.19, 2010- 68.45, 2011- 66.08, 2012- 68.20, 2013- 66.98, 2014- 65.24, 2015- 65.22, 2016- 63.61. pb SP 17.82i '08, 16.00 '06.
First Iranian athlete to win an Olympic medal.

IRELAND

Governing Body: The Athletic Association of Ireland (AAI), Unit 19, Northwood Court, Northwood Business Campus, Santry, Dublin 9. Founded in 1999. Original Irish federation (Irish Champions AC) founded in 1873.
National Championships first held in 1873.
2016 Champions: Men: 100m: Jason Smyth 10.71, 200m: Eanna Madden 21.37, 400m: Brian Gregan 46.28, 800m: Mark English 1:51.48, 1500m: John Travers 4:01.19, 5000: Conor Duffy 14:32.85, 10000m: Brandon Hargreaves 29:45.01, HMar: Paul Pollock 65:10, Mar: Sergiu Ciobanu 2:17:40, 3000mSt: Rory Chesser 9:07.83, 110mh: Ben Reynolds 13.89, 400mh: Thomas Barr 50.28, HJ: Jaime Murtagh 2.10, PV: Thomas Houlihan 4.40, LJ: Adam McMullen 7.52, TJ: Denis Finnegan 14.80, SP: Sean Breathnach 17.34, DT: Marco Pons 53.22, HT: Padraig White 61.19, JT: Rory Gunning 61.15, Dec: Shane Aston 6398, 10000mW/20kW: Alex Wright 41:11.17/1:27:28.
Women: 100m: Amy Foster 11.83, 200m: Niamh Whelan 23.94, 400m: Sinead Denny 53.64, 800m: Siofra Cleirigh-Buttner 2:04.72, 1500m: Ciara Mageean 4:24.33, 5000m: Deirdre Byrne 16:07.56, HMar: Lizzie Lee 73:28, Mar: Laura Graham 2:41:54, 3000mSt: Michele Finn 9:46.81, 100mh: Lily Ann O'Hora 14.36, 400mh: Kelly McGrory 61.23, HJ: Summer Lecky 1.71, PV: Tori Pena 4.15, LJ: Imelda Morrisson 5.88w, TJ: Sarah Buggy 13.96, SP/DT: Clare Fitzgerald 15.07/53.38, HT: Cara Kennedy 58.36, JT: Anita Fitzgibbon 47.89, Hep: Naomi Morgan 4409, 5000mW: Emma Prendiville 25:15.57. 20kW: Maeve Curley 1:49:52.

Thomas BARR b. 24 Jul 1992 Waterford 1.83m 73kg. Ferrybank, Was at University of Limerick.
At 400mh: OG: '16- 4; WCh: '15- sf; EC: '12/14/16- sf, EU23: '13- 8; EJ: '11- 6; WUG: '15- 1. Irish champion 2014-16.
Five Irish 400mh records 2014-16.
Progress at 400mh: 2009- 56.53, 2010- 56.47. 2011- 50.06, 2012- 50.22, 2013- 49.78, 2014- 48.90, 2015- 48.65, 2016- 47.97. pbs: 200m 21.47i '16, 400m 46.87i '17, HJ 1.83 '09.
Sister Jessie Barr (b. 24 Jul 1989) pb 400mh 55.93 '12, 8 EC '12.

Robert HEFFERNAN b. 20 Feb 1978 Cork City 1.73m 55kg. Togher AC.
At 20kW/(50kW): OG: '00- 28, '04- dq, '08- 8, '12- 9/3, '16- (6); WCh: '01-05-07-09-13-15: 14/dq/6/14/(1)/(5); EC: '02- 8, '10- 3/4, '14- (dnf); WCp: '08- 9, '12- 9; ECp: '07-09-11-13: 5/4/8/9. At 10000mW: EJ: '97- 14; EU23: '99- 13. Won Irish 10000mW 2001-02, 2004-5, 2007-11; 20kW 2000- 02, 2004, 2009; 30kW 2008.
Irish records: 3000mW 2013, 20kW (4) 2001-08, 50kW (3) 2010-12. World M35 3000mW 2013.
Progress at 20kW, 50kW: 1999- 1:26:45, 2000- 1:22:43, 2001- 1:21:11, 2002- 1:20:25, 2003- 1:23:03, 2004- 1:20:55, 2005- 1:24:20, 2006- 1:22:24, 2007- 1:20:15, 2008- 1:19:22, 2009- 1:22:09, 2010- 1:20:45, 3:45:30; 2011- 1:20:54, 3:49:28; 2012- 1:20:18, 3:37:54; 2013- 1:21:59, 3:37:56; 2014- 1:20:57, 2015- 3:44:17, 2016- 1:22:41, 3:43:55. pbs: 1MW 5:39.75i '14, 3000mW 11:09.08 14, 5000mW 18:51.46i '08, 18:59.37 '07; 10000mW 38:27.57 '08, 30kW 2:07:48 '11, 35kW 2:31:19 '00.
Married to Marian Andrews (b. 16 Apr 1982, Irish 400m champion 2008-09, pb 53.10 '11).

ISRAEL

Governing body: Israeli Athletic Association, PO Box 24190, Tel Aviv 61241. Founded as Federation for Amateur Sport in Palestine 1931.
National Championships first held in 1935.
2016 Champions: Men: 100m: Imri Pressiado 10.66, 200m/110mh/400mh: Maor Szeged 21.69/14.38/52.02, 400m: Donald Blair-Sanford 45.26, 800m: Necho Taichaw 1:51.52, 1500m: Yimer Getahun 3:45.83, 5000m/10000m: Aimeru Almeya 13:57.47/28:48.21, HMar: Maru Teferri 66:16, Mar: Melkam Jamber 2:24:02, 3000mSt: Noam Neeman 9:10.69, HJ: Dmitriy Kroyter 2.19, PV: Itamar Basteker 5.20, LJ: Gilron Tzkevitz 7.31, TJ: Tom Yaacobov 16.23, SP/DT: Itamar Levi 18.27/54.75, HT: (Aleksndr Drygol 72.00) Viktor Zaginaiko 62.86, JT: Alan Ferber 65.03, Dec: Konstantin Krinitzkiy 6370. **Women**: 100m/200m: Olga Lenskiy 11.64/23.61, 400m: Gal Kadmon 56.05, 800m: Shanie Landen 2:09.84, 1500m: Rachel Gebretsadik 4:38.16, 5000m/100000m: Chemtai Korlima 16:41.03/35:01.33, HMar: Yelena Dolinin 1:20:08, Mar: Svetlana Bakhmula 2:56:23, 3000mSt: Advah Cohen 11:04.04, 100m: Noah Levi 14.73, 400m: Alexandra Lukshin 61.50, HJ: Maayan Shahaf 1.86, PV: Olga Bronstein 3.65 (31st title overall), LJ: Yiff'at Zelikovitz 5.99, TJ: Hanna Minenko 13.83, SP/DT: Anastasia Muchkaev 14.11/46.37, HT: Margarita Belov 56.76, JT: Dirit Naor 41.23 (19th title), Hep: Jouman Joubran 4766.

Women

Hanna MINENKO b. 25 Sep 1989 Periaslav-Khmelnytskyi 1.78m 61kg. née Knyazyeva. Maccabi Tel Aviv.
At TJ: OG: '12- 4, '16- 5; WCh: '13- 6, '15- 2; EC: '16- 2; WJ: '08- 4; EJ: '07- 2; EU23: '11- 5; WUG: '11- 4; EI: '14- 3. Won UKR TJ 2012, ISR LJ 2013-14; TJ 2014-15.
Eight Israeli triple jump records 2013-15 and one long jump 2014.
Progress at TJ: 2005- 12.87, 2006- 13.28, 2007- 13.85, 2009- 13.61, 2010- 13.65, 2011- 14.20, 2012- 14.71, 2013- 14.58, 2014- 14.29, 2015- 14.78, 2016- 14.68. pb LJ 6.52 '14.
Married Anatoliy Minenko (Dec 7046 '10) in November 2012 and switched from Ukraine to Israel on 12 May 2013.

ITALY

Governing Body: Federazione Italiana di Atletica Leggera (FIDAL), Via Flaminia Nuova 830, 00191 Roma. Constituted 1926. First governing body formed 1896.
National Championships first held in 1897 (one event)/1906 (men), 1927 (women). **2016 Champions: Men**: 100m: Filippo Tortu 10.32, 200m: Eseosa Desalu 20.31, 400m: Matteo Galvan 45.12, 800m: Giordano Benedetti 1:48.15, 1500m: Yemaneberhan Crippa 3:45.25, 5000m: Yassine Rachik 14:11.24, 10000m: Ahmed El Mazoury 28:43.18, HMar: Daniele D'Onofrio 63:29, 3000mSt: Yuri Floriani 8:30.03, 110mh: Hassane Fofana 13.62, 400mh: José Reynaldo Bencosme 49.76, HJ: Gianmarco Tamberi 2.36, PV: Giorgiorgio Piantella 5.35, LJ: Lamont Marcell Jacobs 7.89, TJ: Daniele Cavazzani 16.46, SP: Sebastiano Bianchetti 18.78, DT: Hannes Kirchler 62.34, HT: Marco Lingua 74.88, JT: Norbert Bonvecchio 78.85, Dec: Simone Cairoli 7463, 10kW: Francesco Fortunato 40:31, 20kW: Federico Tontodonati 1:21:56, 50kW: Michele Antonelli 3:56:57. **Women**: 100m/200m: Gloria Hooper 11.38/22.89, 400m: Libania Grenot 51.33, 800m: Yusneysi Santiusti 2:04.99, 1500m: Margherita Magnani 4:18.43, 5000m: Veronica Inglese 15:22.45, 10000m/HMar: Rosaria Console 33:22.66/73:01, 3000mSt: Francesca Bertoni 10:04.58, 100mh: Giulia Pennella 13.52, 400mh: Ayomide Folorunso 55.54, HJ: Alessia Trost 1.94, PV: Sonia Malavisi 4.45, LJ: Laura Strati 6.49, TJ: Dariya Derkach 14.15, SP: Chiara Rosa 17.52, DT: Stefania Strumillo 56.95, HT: Francesca Massobrio 62.31, JT: Eleonora Bacciotti 56.24, Hep: Federica Palumbo 5252, 10kW: Valentina Trapletti 44:41, 20kW: Sibilla Di Vincenzo 1:33:30.

Marco DE LUCA b. 12 May 1981 Rome 1.88m 69kg. Fiamme Gialle.
At 50kW: OG: '08- 19, '12- 14, '16- 21; WCh: 05-07-09-11-13-15: 13/dnf/7/11/15/16; EC: '06-10-14: 7/6/7; WCp: 06-08-10-12-16: 9/8/14/6/3; ECp: '07-09-11-15: 8/8/2/3. Won Italian 20kW 2011, 50kW 2006, 2009.
Progress at 50kW: 2002- 4:07:06, 2003- 4:13:24, 2004- 4:05:01, 2005- 3:55:30, 2006- 3:48:08, 2007- 3:47:04, 2008- 3:49:21, 2009- 3:46:31, 2010- 3:48:36, 2011- 3:49:40, 2012- 3:47:19, 2013- 3:48:05, 2014- 3:45:25, 2015- 3:46:21, 2016- 3:44:47. pbs: 3000mW 12:03.79 '09, 5000mW 19:29.54i '15, 20:03.6 '05, 10000mW 40:48.0 '09, 20kW 1:22:38 '10, 30kW 2:09:37 '04, 35kW 2:28:53 '10.

Fabrizio DONATO b. 14 Aug 1976 Latina 1.89m 82kg. Fiamme Gialle.
At TJ: OG: '00/04/08/16: dnq 25/21/21/17, '12- 3; WCh: '03/07/09-13: dnq 13/32/41/15, '11- 10; EC: '02-06-10-12-14: 4/dnq 16/9/1/7; EJ: '95- 5; WI: '01-08-10-12: 6/4/5/4; EI: '00-02-09-11-17: 6/4/1/2/2; ECp: '00-02-03-04-06-14-15: 2/2/1/6/1/2/1. Won MedG 2001, Italian 2000, 2004, 2006-08, 2010-11, 2015.
Italian triple jump record 2000, world M40 records 16.60 & 17.13 at EI '17.
Progress at TJ: 1992- 12.88, 1993- 14.36, 1994- 15.27, 1995- 15.81, 1996- 16.35, 1997- 16.40A, 1998- 16.73, 1999- 16.66i/16.53w, 2000- 17.60, 2001- 17.05, 2002- 17.17, 2003- 17.16, 2004- 16.90, 2005- 16.65/16.68w, 2006- 17.33i/17.24, 2007- 16.97/17.06w, 2008- 17.27i/16.91/17.29w, 2009- 17.59i/15.81, 2010- 17.39i/17.08, 2011- 17.73i/17.17, 2012- 17.53/17.63w, 2013- 16.86, 2014- 16.89/17.24w, 2015- 16.91/17.11w,

ITALY – IVORY COAST

2016- 16.93, 2017- 17.13i. pb LJ 8.03i '11, 8.00 '06. Italian indoor record to win 2009 European Indoor title. Married Patrizia Spuri (400m 51.74 '98, 8 EC 98, 800m 1:59.96 '98) on 27 Sep 2003.

Marco FASSINOTTI b. 29 Apr 1989 Turin 1.90m 71kg. Aeronautica Militare.
At HJ: EC: '10- 9, '14- 7; WJ: '08- 7; EU23: '09- 6, '11- 5; WI: '14- 6; EI: '11- 6; WUG: '09- 4; ET: '15- 2; Italian champion 2013, 2015.
ITA high jump record 2015, indoors (3) 2014-16.
Progress at HJ: 2005- 1.70, 2006- 1.90, 2007- 2.08, 2008- 2.17, 2009- 2.22, 2010- 2.28, 2011- 2.29i/2.25, 2012- 2.26i/2.24, 2013- 2.27, 2014- 2.34i/2.30, 2015- 2.34i/2.33, 2016- 2.35i/2.29.

Giorgio RUBINO b. 15 Apr 1986 Roma 1.74m 56kg. Fiamme Gialle.
At 20kW: OG: '08- 18, '12- 42; WCh: '07-09-11-13-15: 5/3/dq/28/20; EC: '06-10-14: 8/4/8/20; EU23: '07- dq; ECp: '09- 1, '11- 4. At 10000mW: WJ: '04- 10; WY: '03- 4; EJ: '05- 3; ECp: '05- 2J. Won Italian 10kW 2012, 2014; 20kW 2005, 2014.
Progress at 20kW: 2005- 1:23:58, 2006- 1:22:05, 2007- 1:21:17, 2008- 1:22:11, 2009- 1:19:37, 2010- 1:22:12, 2011- 1:20:44, 2012- 1:20:10, 2013- 1:21:07, 2014- 1:20:44, 2015- 1:21:38, 2016- 1:24:04. pbs: 5000mW 19:14.33i '08, 19:38.5 '06; 10000mW 39:43.20 '11, 38:00R '10; 35kW 2:36:50 '09.

Gianmarco TAMBERI b. 1 Jun 1992 Civitanove Marche 1.89m 71kg. Fiamme Gialle.
At HJ: OG: '12- dnq 21=; WCh: '15- 8=; EC: '12-14-16: 5/7=/1; WY: '09- dnq 18; EU23: '13- dnq 13=; EJ: '11- 3; WI: '16- 1; EI: '13- 5, '15- 7; Italian champion 2012, 2014, 2016.
Four Italian high jump records 2015-16 & three indoor 2016.
Progress at HJ: 2005- 1.52, 2006- 1.62i, 2007- 1.80, 2008- 2.01, 2009- 2.07, 2010- 2.14, 2011-2.25, 2012- 2.31, 2013- 2.30i/2.25, 2014- 2.29, 2015- 2.37, 2016- 2.39.
Suffered serious injury, costing him Olympic chance, just after setting Italian records at 2.37 and 2.39 in Monaco 2016. His father Marco had pb 2.28i (Italian indoor record)/2.27 '83, elder brother Gianluca 4th EJ JT 2009, pb 78.61 '10.

Women

Eleonora GIORGI b. 14 Sep 1989 Cuneo 1.63m 52kg. Fiamme Azzurre. Social-economic law graduate of University "Bocconi" of Milan.
At 20kW: OG: '12- 13, '16- dq; WCh: '13- 10, '15- dq; EC: '14- 5; EU23: '09- 11, '11- 3; WCp: '12- 13, '14- 5; ECp: '13- 6, '15- 2; won MedG 2013. At 10000mW: WJ: '08- 18.
Walk records: World best 5000m 2014, 25k & 30k 2016; Italian 20k (3) 2014-15.
Progress at 20kW: 2009- 1:34:27, 2010- 1:34:00, 2011- 1:33:46, 2012- 1:29:48, 2013- 1:30:01, 2014- 1:27:05, 2015- 1:26:17, 2016- 1:28:05. pbs: 3000mW 11:50.08i/12:05.83 '13, 5000mW 20:01.80 '14, 10kW 44:33.56t '13, 43:51R '11; 25kW 1:56:12 '16, 30kW 2:19:43 '16.

Libania GRENOT b. 12 Jul 1983 Santiago de Cuba 1.75m 61kg. Fiamme Galle.
At 400m: OG: '08/12- sf, '16- 8; WCh: '01- hR, '05- h, '09/13/15- sf; EC: '10-12-14-16: 4/6/1/1&3R; WY: '99- 5; PAm: '03- 4; CCp: '10- 6/2R, '14- 3/2R; ET: '09- 1, 15- 3. Won MedG 2009, CUB 2003-05, ITA 400m 2009-10, 2014-16; 200m 2012.
Four Italian 400m records 2008-09.
Progress at 400m: 1997- 56.2, 1998- 54.9, 1999- 53.87, 2000- 53.79, 2001- 52.91, 2002- 53.34A, 2003- 52.20, 2004- 51.68, 2005- 51.51, 2007- 54.21, 2008- 50.83, 2009- 50.30, 2010- 50.43, 2011- 52.17, 2012- 50.55, 2013- 50.47, 2014- 50.55, 2015- 51.07, 2016- 50.43. pbs: 200m 22.56 '16, 22.45w '12, 300m 36.82 '14. 500m 1:08.26 '09.
Switched from Cuba to Italy after she married Silvio Scaffetti in 2006 and gained Italian citizenship on 18 Mar 2008.

Antonella PALMISANO b. 6 Aug 1991 Mottola, Taranto 1.66m 49kg. Fiamme Galle.
At 20kW: OG: '16- 4; WCh: '13- 13, '15- 5; EC: '14- 7; EU23: '11- 2, '13- 3; WCp: '14- 9. At 10000mW: WJ: '08- 9, '10- 4; EJ: '09- 2; WCp: '10- 1J; ECp: '09- 3J. At 5000mW: WY: '07- 5.
Progress at 20kW: 2009- 1:38:47, 2010- 1:36:21, 2011- 1:34:31, 2012- 1:34:27, 2013- 1:30:50, 2014- 1:27:51, 2015- 1:28:40, 2016- 1:29:03. pbs: 3000mW 12:05.68i '15, 10kW 44:45.78t '13, 42:50R '14.

Alessia TROST b. 8 Mar 1993 Pordenone 1.88m 68kg. Fiamme Gialle.
At HJ: OG: '16- 5; WCh: '13- 7=; EC: '14- 9=, '16- 6=; WJ: '12- 1; WY: '09- 1; EU23: '13- 1, '15- 1; EJ: '11- 4; WI: '16- 7; EI: '13- 4=, '15- 2; ET: '13- 2; YthOly: '10- 2. Italian champion 2013-14, 2016.
Progress at HJ: 2003- 1.37, 2004- 1.55, 2005- 1.62, 2006- 1.68, 2008- 1.81, 2009- 1.89, 2010- 1.90, 2011- 1.87, 2012- 1.92, 2013- 2.00i/1.98, 2014- 1.96i/1.91, 2015- 1.97i/1.94, 2016- 1.95i/1.94. pbs: 100mh 15.5 '11, LJ 6.01 '14, SP 10.76i '14, Pen 4035i '14.

IVORY COAST

Governing Body: Fédération Ivoirienne d'Athlétisme, Abidjan. Founded 1960.

Ben Youssef MEITÉ b. 11 Nov 1986 Séguéla 1.79m 70kg.
At 100m/(200m): OG: '12- sf, '16- 6; WCh: '09- h/qf, '11- h/h, '15- sf; AfG: '07- sf/sf, '11- 2/2, '15- 1; AfCh: '06- sf, '10- 1/2, '12- h/1, '16- 1; CCp: '10- 5/3.
CIV records 100m (7) 2012-16, 200m 2009.
Progress at 100m: 2005- 10.40, 2006- 11.07, 2007- 10.49/10.46w, 2008- 10.49, 2009- 10.21/10.15w, 2010- 10.08A/10.25/10.19w, 2011- 10.21/10.14w, 2012- 10.06, 2015- 10.04, 2016- 9.96/9.95w. pbs: 60m 6.61i '11, 200m 20.37 '09, 300m 33.68i '07.
His brother Ibrahim (b. 18 Nov 1976) had pbs of 60m 6.58i '02 (CIV rec), 100m 10.24 '00, 200m 20.64 '94 and competed at Olympic Games of 1996 and 2000. Their father Amadou had 100m pb 10.32 '80 and competed at the Olympic

Games in 1972 and 1976 and won 1978 African Games 100m.

Women

Murielle AHOURÉ b. 23 Aug 1987 Abidjan 1.67m 57kg. Graduated in criminal law from the University of Miami, USA.
At 100m/200m: OG: '12- 7/6, '16- sf/sf; WCh: '13- 2/2, '15- sf/-; AfCh: '14- 2/1, '16- 1. At 60m: WI: '12- 2, 14- 2. Won NCAA Indoor 200m 2009. Two African 60m indoor records 2013. CIV records 100m (8) 2009-16, 200m (3) 2012-13.
Progress at 100m, 200m: 2005- 11.96, 2006- 11.42, 23.33; 2007- 11.41/11.28w, 23.34; 2008- 11.45, 23.50; 2009- 11.09, 22.78; 2010- 11.41, 2011- 11.06/10.86w, 2012- 10.99, 22.42; 2013- 10.91, 22.24; 2014- 10.97, 22.36; 2015- 10.81, 22.29; 2016- 10.78, 22.52. pbs: 60m 6.99i '13, 300m 38.09i '07, 400m 54.77 '08.
Lived in Paris from age 2, then USA from age 12. Won first medals for Ivory Coast at World Champs.

Marie Josée TA LOU Gonerie b. 18 Nov 1988 1.59m 57kg.
At 100m/200m: OG: '16- 4/4; WCh: '15- sf/sf; AfG: '11- 7/6, 15- 1/1/3R; AfCh: '10- sf/-, '12- 4/3/3R, '14- 3/2/2R, '16- 3/1; CCp: '14- 4/5. At 60m: WI: '16- 7
CIV 200m record 2016..
Progress at 100m: 2010- 12.10/11.6, 24.3; 2011- 11.56, 24.12; 2012- 11.53, 23.26; 2013- 11.58, 23.63; 2014- 11.20, 22.78; 2015- 11.02/10.95w, 22.56; 2016- 10.86, 22.21. pb 60m 7.06i '16.

JAMAICA

Governing body: Jamaica Athletics Administrative Association, PO Box 472, Kingston 5. Founded 1932.
2016 Champions: Men 100m/200m: Yohan Blake 9.95/20.29, 400m: Javon Francis 44.95, 800m: Jo-Wayne Hibbert 1:47.50, 1500m: Giovani Mowatt 3:55.97, 5000m: Kemoy Campbell 13:43.21, 110mh: Omar McLeod 13.01, 400mh: Annsert Whyte 48.66, HJ: Christofle Bryan 2.25, PV: Xavier Boland 4.60, LJ: Damar Forbes 8.16, TJ: Clive Pullen 16.90, SP: O'Dayne Richards 20.82, DT: Fredrick Dacres 62.27, HT: Caniggia Raynor 70.91, JT: Orlando Thomas 69.98. **Women**: 100m: Elaine Thompson 10.70, 200m: Simone Facey 22.65, 400m: Stephanie-Ann McPherson 50.04, 800m: Natolya Goule 2:00.23, 100mh: Megan Simmonds 12.79, 400mh: Ristananna Tracey 54.75, HJ: Kimberly Williamson 1.86, LJ: Chanice Porter 6.59, TJ: Kimberly Williams 14.66w, SP: Danniel Thomas 16.84, DT: Gleneve Grange 59.03, HT: Daina Levy 64.18, JT: Kateema Riettie 49.89.

Nickel ASHMEADE b. 7 Apr 1990 Ocho Rios, Saint-Ann 1.84m 87kg.
At 200m/4x100mR (100m): OG: '16- sf/sf/1R; WCh: '11- 5, '13- 4/1R (5), '15- 8/1R (sf); CG: 14- (3)/1R; WJ: '08- 2/2R (2 4x400m); WY: '07- 3 (2, 3 MedR); PAm-J: '09- 1; won DL 2012, JAM 2015, CAC 2009.
World 4x200m record 2014.
Progress at 100m, 200m: 2006- 10.60, 21.30; 2007- 10.39, 20.76; 2008- 10.34, 20.80/20.16w; 2009- 10.37/10.21w, 20.40; 2010- 10.39, 20.63; 2011- 9.96, 19.91; 2012- 9.93, 19.85; 2013- 9.90, 19.93; 2014- 9.97/9.95w, 19.95; 2015- 9.91, 20.18; 2016- 9.94, 20.07. pbs: 60m 6.62i '14, 400m 47.19 '12.

Kemar BAILEY-COLE b. 10 Jan 1992 St. Catherine 1.95m 83kg. Racers TC.
At 100m/4x100mR (200m): OG: '12- res (1)R, '16- res 1R; WCh: '13- 4/1R; CG: '14- 1/1R; WY: '09- sf/sf.
Progress at 100m: 2008- 10.85, 2009- 10.41/10.38w, 2010- 10.53, 2011- 10.28, 2012- 9.97, 2013- 9.93, 2014- 9.96/9.95w, 2015- 9.92, 2016- 10.00. pbs: 150mSt 15.00 '14, 200m 20.66 '15, 400m 47.36 '14.

Yohan BLAKE b. 26 Dec 1989 St. James 1.81m 79kg. Racers TC.
At 100m/4x100mR: OG: '12- 2/2/1R, '16- 4/sf/1R; WCh: '11- 1/1R; WJ: '06- 3/1R, '08- 4/2R; WY: '05- 7; PAm-J: '07- 2 (3 4x400m); won CAC-J 100m & 200m 2006; JAM 100m & 200m 2012 & 2016.
World record 4x100m 2012, 4x200m 2014.
Progress at 100m, 200m: 2005- 10.56, 22.10; 2006- 10.33, 20.92; 2007- 10.11, 20.62; 2008- 10.27/10.20w, 21.06; 2009- 10.07/9.93dq, 20.60; 2010- 9.89, 19.78; 2011- 9.82/9.80w, 19.26; 2012- 9.69, 19.44; 2013- 20.72, 2014- 10.02, 20.48; 2015- 10.12, 21.57; 2016- 9.93, 20.13. pbs: 60m 6.75i '08, 150mSt 14.71 '14, 400m 46.32 '13.
3-month drugs ban from positive test at Jamaican Champs 25 Jun 2009. Cut 200m pb from 20.60 to 19.78 in Monaco 2010 and then to 19.26 in Brussels 2011. Youngest ever World 100m champion at 21 in 2011.

Usain BOLT b. 21 Aug 1986 Sherwood Content, Trelawny 1.96m 88kg. Racers TC.
At (100m)/200m/4x100mR: OG: '04- h, '08- 1/1/dq1R, '12 & '16- 1/1/1R; WCh: '05- 8, '07- 2/2R, '09- 1/1/1R, '11- dq/1/1R, '13- 1/1/1R, '15- 1/1/1R; CG: '14- 1R; WJ: 02- 1/2R/2R; WY: '01- sf, '03- 1; PAm-J: '03- 1/2R; WCp: '06- 2; won WAF 200m 2009, DL 100m 2012, CAC 200m 2005, JAM 100m 2008-09, 2013; 200m 2005, 2007-09.
World records: 100m (3), 200m (2), 4x100m (4) 2008-12, best low altitude 300m 2010, CAC records 100m (4) 2008-09, 200m (3) 2007-09, WJR 200m 2003 & 2004, World U18 200m record 2003.
Progress at 100m, 200m, 400m: 2000- 51.7; 2001- 21.73, 48.28; 2002- 20.58, 47.12; 2003- 20.13, 45.35; 2004- 19.93, 2005- 19.99, 2006- 19.88, 2007- 10.03, 19.75, 45.28; 2008- 9.69, 19.30, 46.94; 2009- 9.58, 19.19, 45.54; 2010- 9.82, 19.56, 45.87; 2011- 9.76, 19.40; 2012- 9.63, 19.32; 2013- 9.77, 19.66, 46.44; 2014- 9.98, 2015- 9.79, 19.55, 46.38; 2016- 9.81,

19.78. pbs: 60m 6.31+ '09, 100y 9.14+ '11, 150m 14.35 straight & 14.44+ turn '09 (world bests), 300m 30.97 '10 (world low altitude best).
Bolt was the sensational superstar of the 2008 Olympics when he won triple gold – all in world records (but lost that for 4x100m when Nesta Carter tested positive for drugs). In 2009 he smashed both the 100m and 200m WRs at the World Champs and after two more golds at the 2011 Worlds (dq for false start at 100m) he repeated his Olympic treble in 2012 and again in 2016 and won further World trebles in 2013 and 2015, so that his 13 World Champs medals and 11 golds are records. In 2002, after running 20.61 to win the CAC U17 200m title, he became the youngest ever male world junior champion at 15y 332d and set a world age best with 20.58, with further age records for 16 and 17 in 2003-04. Won IAAF 'Rising Star' award for men in 2002 and 2003 and male Athlete of the Year award 2008-09, 2011-13 and 2016. He has won 46 of his 50 100m finals 2007-16. He was appointed an Ambassador-at-Large for Jamaica.

Roxroy CATO b. 1 May 1988 Saint Mary 1.83m 76kg.Was at Lincoln University, Missouri, USA.
At 400mh: OG: '12-h, '16- sf; WCh: '15- h; PAm: '15- 3; CG: '14- dq h.
Progress at 100m, 200m: 2007- 54.24; 2008- 52.75, 2009- 50.74, 2010- 49.45, 2011- 49.66, 2012- 49.03, 2013- 49.15, 2014- 48.48, 2015- 48.72, 2016- 48.56. pbs: 100m 11.01 '08, 200m 21.36Ai '11, 21.38 '13, 400m 46.97 '14.

Fedrick DACRES b. 28 Feb 1994 Kingston 1.91m 97kg.
At DT: OG: '16- dnq 34; WCh: '15- 7; PAm: '15- 1; WJ: '12- 1; WY '11- 1; won CAC-J 2012; JAM 2015-16. Two Jamaican discus records 2017.
Progress at DT: 2011- 53.05, 2012- 55.45, 2013- 59.30, 2014- 66.75, 2015- 66.40, 2016- 68.02, 2017- 68.88. pb SP 18.99 '14.

Rasheed DWYER b. 29 Jan 1989 St. Mary 1.88m 80kg. G.C.Foster College.
At 200m/4x100mR: WCh: '15- res 1R; CG : '10- sf/2R, '14- 1; WJ: '08- res2R; PAm: '15- 2; WUG: '11- 1, '13- 2; CCp: '14- 2. Won NACAC 2015. CAC 4x200m record 2014.
Progress at 200m: 2006- 21.67, 2007- 21.81, 2008- 21.84, 2009- 21.12/20.82w, 2010- 20.49, 2011- 20.20, 2012- 20.59, 2013- 20.15, 2014- 19.98, 2015- 19.80, 2016- 20.46. pbs: 100m 10.16 '15, 400m 46.76 '16.

Damar FORBES b. 18 Sep 1990 Saint Ann 1.85m 77kg. Sports administration degree from Louisiana State University.
At LJ: OG: '12- dnq 19, '16- 12; WCh: '11/15- dnq 20/26, '13- 8; CG: '14- 9. Jamaican champion 2012-16, NCAA 2013.
Progress at LJ: 2009- 7.51i/7.48, 2010- 9.93, 2011- 8.23, 2012- 8.13, 2013- 8.25/8.35w, 2014- 8.10, 2015- 8.17, 2016- 8.23. Pbs: 60m 6.73i '13, 100m 10.51 '13, 55mh 7.48i '09, 60mh 8.12i '09, TJ 16.11i '12, 15.85 '10.

Julian FORTE b. 1 Jul 1993 Saint Andrew 1.86m 73kg. University of Technology.
At 200m: WCh: '15: sf; CG: '14- res 1R; WJ: '12- 8.
Progress at 100m, 200m: 2009- 10.75, 21.93; 2010- 10.49, 21.04; 2011- 10.70, 21.18; 2012- 10.19m 20.38; 2013- 10.12/9.98w, 20.79/20.22w; 2014- 10.03, 20.49; 2015- 10.06, 20.04; 2016- 10.05/9.97w, 19.97. pbs: 60m 6.55 '17, 400m 47.18 '14, LJ 7.25 '09, TJ 14.77.

Javon FRANCIS b. 14 Dec 1994 Bull Bay 1.83m 73kg. Akan TC.
At 400m/4x400mR: OG: '16- sf/2R; WCh: '13- sf/2R, '15- sf; WJ: '12- 9. JAM champion 2015-16.
Progress at 400m: 2012- 46.06, 2013- 45.24, 2014- 45.00, 2015- 44.50, 2016- 44.77. Pb 200m 20.54 '16. Brilliant anchor relay legs at Worlds: 2013- 44.05 to move JAM from 5th to 2nd, and 43.52 in 2015, when pipped for 3rd place.

Jaheel HYDE b. 2 Feb 1997 1.80m 74kg.
At 400mh: OG: '16- sf; WJ: '14- 1/3R, '16- 1. At 110mh: WY: '13- 1; Yth OG: '14- 1.
Progress at 400mh: 2014- 49.29, 2015- 49.01, 2016- 48.81. Pbs: 200m 20.78 '17, 400m 46.66 '16. Scored a hat-trick for the Jamaican U17 football team against Bermuda in 2012. His father Lenworth played football for Jamaica.

Jason LIVERMORE b. 25 Apr 1988 Kingston 1.78m 77kg. Akan TC.
At (100m)/200m/4x100mR: WCh: '13- sf; CG: '14- 6/3/1R; PAm: '07-(h), '11- sf, '15- 7/h. CAC 4x200m record 2014.
Progress at 100m, 200m: 2007- 10.64, 22.02; 2008- 10.61, 2009- 10.66, 2010- 10.43, 21.61; 2011- 10.31, 20.73A; 2012- 10.31, 21.00; 2013- 10.07, 20.13; 2014- 10.05, 20.25; 2015- 10.06/10.10w, 20.54; 2016- 10.03. pbs: 200m 20.83 '12, 400m 47.36 '14.

Rusheen McDONALD b. 17 Aug 1992 Mandeville, Manchester 1.75m 73kg. Utech.
At 400m/4x400mR: OG: '12- h, '16- sf/res 2R; WCh: '13- 2R, '15- sf; CG: '14- sf. Jamaican 400m record 2015.
Progress at 400m: 2011- 47.32, 2012- 45.10, 2013- 45.28, 2014- 45.25, 2015- 43.93, 2016- 45.22. Pbs: 200m 20.57 '15, 300m 31.94 '15.

Omar McLEOD b. 25 Apr 1994 Kingston 1.80m 73kg. Studied business management at University of Arkansas, USA.
At 110mh: OG: '16- 1; WCh: '15- 6; WY: '11- 4 (8 400mh). At 60mh: WI: '16- 1.At 4x400m: WJ: '12-1. Won JAM 2015-16, NCAA 110mh 2015 (& 60mh indoors 2014-15).
Progress at 110mh: 2014- 13.44, 2015- 12.97, 2016- 12.98. Pbs: 60m 6.61i '17, 100m 9.99 '16, 200m 20.48i '17, 400m 47.41i '15, 60mh 7.41i '16, 400mh 49.98 '13.
First man ever to run under 10 secs for 100m and 13 secs for 110m hurdles,

Hansle PARCHMENT b. 17 Jun 1990 Saint

Thomas 1.96m 90kg. Student of psychology at University of the West Indies.
At 110mh: OG: '12- 3; WCh: '13- sf, '15- 2; CG: '10- 5; WY: '07- sf; WUG: '11- 1. Won JAM 2012.
Three Jamaican 110mh records 2012-13.
Progress at 110mh: 2010- 13.71, 2011- 13.24, 2012- 13.12, 2013- 13.05, 2014- 12.94, 2015- 13.03, 2016- 13.10. Pb 400mh 53.74 '08.

Asafa POWELL b. 23 Nov 1982 St Catherine 1.90m 88kg. MVP. Studied sports medicine at Kingston University of Technology.
At 100m/4x100mR: OG: '04- 5 (dns 200), '08- 5/dq1R, '12- 8, '16- 1R; WCh: '05- qf, '07- 3/2R, '09- 3/1R, '15- 7/1R; CG: '02- sf/2R, '06- 1/1R; PAm-J: '01- 2R. At 60m: WI: '16- 2. Won JAM 100m 2003-05, 2007, 2011, 2015; 200m 2006, 2010; WAF 100m 2004, 2006-08; 200m 2004; DL 100m 2011, 2016; GL 2006.
Four world 100m records, five CAC & Commonwealth 2005-07, seven JAM 2004-7; WR 4x100m 2008. Two world bests 100y 2010. Two CAC 60m indoor records 2016.
Progress at 100m, 200m: 2001- 10.50, 2002- 10.12, 20.48; 2003- 10.02/9.9, 2004- 9.87, 20.06; 2005- 9.77, 2006- 9.77, 19.90; 2007- 9.74, 20.00; 2008- 9.72, 2009- 9.82, 2010- 9.82/9.72w, 19.97; 2011- 9.78, 20.55; 2012- 9.85, 2013- 9.88, 2014- 9.87, 2015- 9.81, 2016- 9.92. pbs: 50m 5.64i '12, 60m 6.42+ '09, 6.44i '16; 100y 9.07+ '10, 400m 45.94 '09.
Disqualified for false start in World quarters 2003 after fastest time (10.05) in heats. In 2004 he tied the record of nine sub-10 second times in a season and in 2005 he took the world record for 100m at Athens, tying that at Gateshead and Zürich in 2006, when he ran a record 12 sub-10 times and was world athlete of the year. Took record to 9.74 in Rieti 2007 and ran 15 sub-10 times in 2008, including seven sub-9.90 in succession after 5th place at Olympics. Now has record 97 sub-10 times (plus 8w and 1 while banned). Withdrew from 2011 Worlds through injury. IAAF Athlete of the Year 2006. He tested positive for a banned stimulant on 21 Jun 2013; an original 18-month ban was reduced to 6 months by the CAS. Elder brother Donovan (b. 31 Oct 1971): at 60m: 6.51i '96 (won US indoors '96, 6 WI '99); 100m 10.07/9.7 '95.

O'Dayne RICHARDS b. 14 Dec 1988 St. Andrew 1.77m 120kg. Data communications graduate. MVP TC.
At SP: OG: '16- 8; WCh: '13- dnq 20, '15- 3; CG: '14- 1; PAm: '15- 1; WUG: '11- 1; CCp: '14- 2; won CAC 2011, 2013; JAM 2013-16.
Three CAC shot records 2014-15.
Progress at SP: 2008- 16.76, 2009- 18.05, 2010- 18.74, 2011- 19.93, 2012- 20.31, 2013- 20.97, 2014- 21.61, 2015- 21.69, 2016- 20.82. pb DT 58.31 '12.

Andrew RILEY b. 6 Sep 1988 Saint Thomas 1.88m 80kg. Economics graduate of University of Illinois.
At 110mh: OG: '12- h, '16- sf; WCh: '11- sf, '13- 8, '15- sf; CG: 14- 1. Jamaican champion 2011, 2013-14; won NCAA 100m 2012, 110mh 2010 & 2012. At 60mh: WI: '14 dns final.
Progress at 110mh: 2009- 13.74/13.61w, 2010- 13.45, 2011- 13.32, 2012- 13.19, 2013- 13.14, 2014- 13.19, 2015- 13.28, 2016- 13.35. Pbs: 60m 6.57i '12, 100m 10.02 '12, 200m 21.25w '12, 60mh 7.53i '12, HJ 2.10 '08.
First to win NCAA 100m and 110mh double 2012.

Warren WEIR b. 31 Oct 1989 Trelawny 1.78m 75kg. Racers TC.
At 200m/4x100mR: OG: '12- 3; WCh: '13- 2/res 1R, '15- sf; CG: '14- 2; won DL 2013, JAM 2013. At 110mh: WJ: '08- sf.
World 4x200m record 2014.
Progress at 200m: 2008- 22.26, 2009- 21.46w, 2010- 21.52, 2011- 20.43, 2012- 19.84, 2013- 19.79, 2014- 19.82, 2015- 20.24, 2016- 20.32. pbs: 100m 10.02 '13, 400m 46.23 '13, 110mh 13.65 '07, 13.45w '08; 400mh 53.28 '09.

Annsert WHYTE b. 4 Oct 1987 Kingston 1.88m 86kg. Racers TC.
At 400mh: OG: '16- 5; WCh: 13/15: sf. Jamaican champion 2015-16. At 400m: PAm: '11- h.
Progress at 400mh: 2013- 49.17, 2014- 48.58, 2015- 48.90, 2016- 48.07. pbs: 200m 21.03 '09, 400m 46.19 '09.

Women

Veronica CAMPBELL-BROWN b. 15 May 1982 Clarks Town, Trelawny 1.63m 61kg. Adidas. Was at University of Arkansas, USA.
At (100m)/200m/4x100mR: OG: '00- 2R, '04- 3/1/1R, '08- 1, '12- 3/4/2R, '16- h/2R; WCh: '05- 2/4/2R, '07- 1/2/2R, '09- 4/2, '11- 2/1/2R, '15- 4/3/1R; CG: '02- (2)/2R, '06- 2, 14- (2)/1R; WJ: '98- (qf), '00- 1/1/2R; WY: '99- (1)/1R; PAm-J: '99- 2R; CCp: '14- (1)/1R. At 60m: WI: '10-12-14: 1/1/5. Won WAF 100m 2004-05, 200m 2004; DL 100m 2014; CAC-J 100m 2000, JAM 100m 2002, 2004-05, 2007, 2011, 2014; 200m 2004-05, 2007-09, 2011.
Four CAC & Commonwealth 4x100m records 2004-15. CAC junior 100m record 2000.
Progress at 100m, 200m: 1999- 11.49, 23.73; 2000- 11.12/11.1, 22.87; 2001- 11.13/22.92; 2002- 11.00, 22.39; 2004- 10.91, 22.05; 2005- 10.85, 22.35/22.29w; 2006- 10.99, 22.51; 2007- 10.89, 22.34; 2008- 10.87/10.85w, 21.74; 2009- 10.89/10.81w, 22.29; 2010- 10.78, 21.98; 2011- 10.76, 22.22; 2012- 10.81, 22.32; 2013- 11.01/10.78w, 22.53/22.18w; 2014- 10.86, 22.94/22.30w, 2015- 10.89, 21.97; 2016- 10.83, 22.29. pbs: 50m 6.08i '12, 60m 7.00i '10, 100y 9.91+ '11 (world best), 400m 52.24i '05, 52.25 '11.
Has matched Merelene Ottey by winning medals at five Olympic Games. In 2000 became the first woman to become World Junior champion at both 100m and 200m. Unbeaten at 200m in 28 finals (42 races in all) from 11 March 2000 to 22 July 2005 (lost to Allyson Felix). Married Omar Brown (1 CG 200m 2006) on 3

166   JAMAICA

Nov 2007. She received a public warning for a positive test for a banned diuretic on 4 May 2013 and was suspended for the season, but the Court of Arbitration for Sport upheld her appeal in February 2014. Her brother Sean Bailey (b. 15 Jul 1997) has 400m pb 46.51 '16 and was 3rd at 4x400m at 2016 WJ.

Christine DAY b. 23 Aug 1986 St. Mary 1.68m 51kg. Cameron Blazers TC.
At 400m/4x400mR: OG: '12- sf/2R, '16- sf/res 2R; WCh: '09- sf, '15- 4/1R; CG: 14- 3/1R; CCp: '14- 1R. JAM champion 2015.
Progress at 400m: 2006- 55.33, 2007- 53.91, 2008- 53.10, 2009- 51.54, 2010- 52.43, 2011- 52.08, 2012- 50.85, 2013- 50.91, 2014- 50.16, 2015- 50.14, 2016- 50.29. pb 200m 23.73 '13.

Simone FACEY b. 7 May 1985 Manchester 1.62m 53kg. Was at Texas A&M University.
At 200m/4x100mR: OG: '16- sf/res 2R; WCh: '07- 2R, '09- 6/1R; PAm: '11- 2, '15- 3/2R; PAm-J: '03- 2R. At 100m: WJ: '02- 2; WY: '01- 4. Won JAM 200m 2016, NCAA 200m 2008, CAC-J 100m & 200m 2002.
CAC junior 200m record 2004.
Progress at 200m: 2000- 24.13, 2001- 23.67. 2002- 23.22, 2004- 22.71, 2005- 23.43i, 2006- 23.36, 2007- 22.49, 2008- 22.25, 2009- 22.58, 2010- 22.90, 2011- 22.86A/23.07, 2012- 23.12, 2013- 22.95, 2014- 22.67, 2015- 22.55, 2016- 22.50. pbs: 60m 7.14i '16, 100m 10.95A '08, 11.09 '14, 11.0 '04.

Shelly-Ann FRASER-PRYCE b. 27 Dec 1986 Kingston 1.60m 52kg. MVP. Graduate of the University of Technology. née Fraser. Married Jason Pryce on 7 Jan 2011.
At 100m/(200m)/4x100mR: OG: '08- 1, '12- 1/2/2R, '16- 3/2R; WCh: '07- res (2)R, '09- 1/1R, '11- 4/2R, '13- 1/1/1R, '15- 1/1R; CG: '14- 1R. At 60m: WI: '14- 1. Won WAF 2008, DL 100m 2012-13, 2015; 200m 2013; JAM 100m 2009, 2012, 2015; 200m 2012-13.
CAC and Commonwealth records 100m 2009 & 2012, 4x100m (4) 2011-15; CAC 4x100m 4x200m 2014.
Progress at 100m, 200m: 2002- 11.8, 2003- 11.57, 2004- 11.72, 24.08; 2005- 11.72; 2006- 11.74, 24.8; 2007- 11.31/11.21w, 23.5; 2008- 10.78, 22.15; 2009- 10.73, 22.58; 2010- 10.82dq, 22.47dq; 2011- 10.95, 22.59/22.10w; 2012- 10.70, 22.09; 2013- 10.71, 22.13; 2014- 11.01, 22.53; 2015- 10.74, 22.37; 2016- 10.86, 23.15. pb 60m 6.98i '14, 400m 55.67 '15.
Double World and Olympic champion with eight global gold medals (and four silver). Huge improvement in 2008 and moved to joint third on world all-time list for 100m when winning 2009 world 100m title. 6-month ban for positive test for a non-performance enhancing drug on 23 May 2010. IAAF Athlete of the Year 2013. Expecting a baby in 2017.

Shericka JACKSON b. 15 Jul 1994 1.74m 59kg. UTech.
At 400m/4x400mR: OG: '16- 3/2R; WCh: '15- 3/1R. At 200m: WJ: '12- 8/2R; WY: '11- 3/1 MedR; Yth OG: '10- 4.
Progress at 400m: 2008- 54.27, 2009- 53.13, 2010- 53.71, 2011- 52.94, 2012- 53.34, 2013- 51.60, 2014- 51.32, 2015- 49.99. 2016- 49.83. pbs: 100m 11.32 '17, 200m 22.84 '13.

Stephenie Ann McPHERSON b. 25 Nov 1988 Westmoreland 1.68m 55kg. MVP. Was at Kingston University of Technology.
At 400m/4x400mR: OG: '16- 6/2R; WCh: '13- 4, '15- 5/1R; CG: 14- 1/1R; CCp: '14- 1R; WI: 14- 2R, '16- 4. Won DL 2016, JAM 2016.
Progress at 400m: 2006- 56.42, 2007- 55.77, 2008- 52.80, 2009- 51.95, 2010- 51.64, 2012- 52.98, 2013- 49.92, 2014- 50.12, 2015- 50.32, 2016- 50.04. pbs: 100m 11.44 '10, 200m 22.93 '14, 800m 2:15.24 '12, 400mh 57.46 '12.

Natasha MORRISON b. 17 Nov 1992 1.70m 57kg. GGOF.
At 100m/4x100mR: WCh: '15- 7/1R.
CAC and Commonwealth 4x100m record 2015.
Progress at 100m: 2007- 12.06, 2008- 12.00, 2010- 11.98/11.47w, 2011- 11.42, 2013- 11.17/11.12w, 2014- 11.06, 2015- 10.96, 2016- 11.27. pbs: 60m 7.15i '16, 200m 23.08 '13.

Leah NUGENT b. 23 Nov 1992 Abington, Pennsylvania, USA 1.73m 66kg. Was at University of Kentucky.
At 400mh: OG: '16- 6.
Progress at 400mh: 2009- 60.72, 2010- 59.15, 2011- 57.72, 2012- 59.68, 2013- 58.47, 2014- 56.97, 2015- 55.63, 2016- 54.45. pbs: 60m 7.39i '16, 200m 24.03 '16, 400m 53.09i '16, 60mh 7.96i '17, 100mh 13.11 '16, 12.83w '17.
She competed in the 2016 US Champs but then got clearance to compete for Jamaica from 22 July (her father came from Jamaica) and reduced her pb from 55.44 to 54.98 and 54.45 at the Olympic Games,

Janeive RUSSELL b. 14 Nov 1993 Manchester 1.75m 63kg. UTech.
At 400mh/4x400mR: OG: '16- 7; WCh: '15- 5; CG: '14- 3; WJ: '12- 1/2R. At 400m: WJ: '10- sf/3R. At LJ: WY: '09- 9. Won JAM Hep 2011, 400mh 2015.
Progress at 400mh: 2011- 57.71, 2012- 56.62, 2013- 56.30, 2014- 54.75, 2015- 54.64, 2016- 53.96. pbs: 200m 24.10 '11, 400m 51.17 '16, 800m 2:11.5 '15, 100mh 13.80 '12, HJ 1.80 '09, LJ 6.20 '10, 6.26w '11; SP 10.86 '11, JT 26.53 '11, Hep 5361 '11.

Kaliese SPENCER b. 6 May 1987 Westmoreland 1.75m 63kg. Cameron Blazers TC. Was at University of Texas.
At 400mh/4x400mR: OG: '12- 4; WCh: '07-09-11-13-15: sf/4&res 2R/4/dq h/8; CG: 14- 1; WJ: '06-1/3R; CCp: '14- 1; Won DL 2010-12, 2014; JAM 2011, 2014. At 400m: WI: '14- 2/2R.
Progress at 400mh: 2006- 55.11, 2007- 55.62, 2009- 53.56, 2010- 53.33, 2011- 52.79, 2012- 53.49,

2013- 54.22, 2014- 53.41, 2015- 54.15, 2016- 55.02. pbs: 200m 23.11 '13, 400m 50.19 '13, 800m 2:03.01 '11.
Kerron STEWART b. 16 Apr 1984 Kingston 1.75m 61kg. Adult education student at Auburn University, USA.
At 100m/(200m)/4x100mR: OG: '08- 2=/3, '12- sf/2R; WCh: '07- 7/2R, '09- 2/1R, '11- 6/5/2R, '13- 5/1R, '15- res 1R; CG: '14- 3/1R; PAm: '15-(5)/2R; WJ: '02- 4/1R; WY: '01- 2/2R. Won NCAA 200m 2007, indoor 60m & 200m 2007; JAM 100m 2008, 2013.
Three CAC & Commonwealth 4x100m records 2011-13.
Progress at 100m, 200m: 2000- 11.89, 24.09w; 2001- 11.70, 23.90; 2002- 11.46, 24.21; 2003- 11.34, 23.50; 2004- 11.40, 23.63i/23.66; 2005- 11.63, 23.77i/24.22/23.46w; 2006- 11.03, 22.65; 2007- 11.03, 22.41; 2008- 10.80, 21.99; 2009- 10.75, 22.42; 2010- 10.96, 22.57/22.34w; 2011- 10.87, 22.63; 2012- 10.92, 22.70; 2013- 10.96, 22.71; 2014- 11.02, 23.64; 2015- 11.17, 22.72; 2016- 11.19, 22.99/22.69w. pbs: 55m 6.71i '06, 60m 7.14i '07, 400m 51.83 '13.
Shanieka THOMAS/RICKETTS b. 2 Feb 1992 Saint Andrew 1.82m 66kg. Was at San Diego State University, USA.
At TJ: OG: '16- dnq 14; WCh: '15- 11; CG: '14- 4; PAm: '15- 9; WI: '16- 8; Won NACAC 2015.
Progress at TJ: 2008- 11.83, 2011- 12.98i/12.90, 2012- 13.64, 2013- 14.15, 2014- 14.00, 2015- 14.23A/14.08, 2016- 14.57. pbs: 400m 55.38 '13, HJ 1.75 '10, LJ 6.63 '15.
Married coach Kerry-Lee Ricketts in 2016.
Elaine THOMPSON b. 28 Jun 1992 Manchester 1.69m 57kg. MVP. Kingston University of Technology.
At 200m/4x100mR: OG: '16- 1/1/2R; WCh: '15- 2/1R; CG: '14- res 1R. Won DL 100m 2016, JAM 100m 2016, 200m 2015. At 60m: WI: '16- 3.
CAC and Commonwealth records 4x100m 2015, 100m 2016.
Progress at 100m, 200m: 2008- 12.16, 25.56; 2009- 12.01, 24.35; 2010- 11.94w, 2012- 23.89, 2013- 11.41, 23.73; 2014- 11.17, 23.23; 2015- 10.84, 21.66, 2016- 10.70, 21.78. pbs: 60m 6.98i '17, 7.02 '17; 150mSt 15.00 '14, 400m 55.98 '17.
Ristananna TRACEY b. 9 May 1992 Kingston 1.73m 68kg. Racers TC.
At 400mh: OG: '16- 5; WCh: '11/13- sf, '15- h; PAm: '15- h; ; WJ: '10- 5; WY: '09- 8. Won CAC-J 2010, JAM 2013, 2016.
Progress at 400mh: 2009- 58.49, 2010- 57.77, 2011- 54.58, 2012- 55.64, 2013- 54.52, 2014- 55.12, 2015- 55.45, 2016- 54.15. pbs: 200m 23.63 '11, 400m 51.95 '11, 800m 2:03.97 '11.
Sister Nikita (b. 18 Sep 1990) 400mh pb 55.18 '14, 8 WJ '08.
Christania WILLIAMS b. 17 Oct 1994 Saint Mary 1.65m 63kg. U.Tech.
At 100m/4x100mR: OG: '16- 8/2R; WJ: '12- dnf hR; WY: '11- 3 (1 MedR).
Progress at 100m: 2009- 12.01, 2011- 11.39, 2012- 11.54, 2014- 11.19, 2015- 11.11, 2016- 10.96. pbs: 60m 7.05 '17, 200m 23.48 '15.
Danielle WILLIAMS b. 14 Sep 1992 St.Andrew 1.68m 59kg. Johnson C.Smith University, USA.
At 100mh: WCh: '13- sf, '15- 1; CG: '14- 4; WJ: '10- 4; WUG: '13- 3, '15- 1; PAm-J: '11- 2. JAM champion 2013, 2015.
CAC and Commonwealth 4x100m record 2015.
Progress at 100mh: 2010- 13.46/13.41w, 2011- 13.32/13.13w, 2012- 14.02, 2013- 12.69, 2014- 12.99, 2015- 12.57, 2016- 12.77/12.55w. pbs: 60m 7.32i '14, 100m 11.24A/11.41/11.34w '13, 200m 22.62A/23.43i '13, 23.48 '14; 60mh 8.02i '15.
Sister **Shermaine** (b. 4 Feb 1990) at 100mh: OG: '12/16- sf; WCh: '13- sf, '15- 7; WJ: '08- 2; WY: '05- 6, '07- 2; PAm-J: '09- 1; pb 12.78/12.65w '12.
Kimberly WILLIAMS b. 3 Nov 1988 Saint Thomas 1.69m 66kg. Florida State University, USA.
At TJ: OG: '12- 6, '16- 7; WCh: '09/11 dnq 15/14, '13- 4, '15- 5; CG: '14- 1; WJ: '06- dnq 15; WY: '05- dnq; CAG: '10- 1; PAm-J: '07- 2; CCp: '14- 4; WI: '12- 5, '14- 3. Won NCAA LJ & TJ 2009, JAM TJ 2010, 2012-16.
Progress at TJ: 2004- 12.53/12.65w, 2005- 12.63/13.09w, 2006- 13.18, 2007- 13.52, 2008- 13.82i/13.69/13.83w, 2009- 14.08/14.38w, 2010- 14.23, 2011- 14.25, 2012- 14.53, 2013- 14.62/14.78w, 2014- 14.59, 2015- 14.45, 2016- 14.56/14.66w. pbs: 100m 11.76 '12, 200m 24.55 '11, LJ 6.55i 11, 6.42/6.66w '09.
Novlene WILLIAMS-MILLS b. 26 Apr 1982 Saint Ann 1.70m 57kg. Studied recreation at University of Florida, USA.
At 400m/4x400mR: OG: '04- sf/3R, '08- sf/2R, '12- 5/2R, 16- 2R; WCh: '05- 2R, '07- 3/2R, '09- 4/2R, '11- 8/2R, '13- 8, '15- 6/1R; CG: '06- 3, '14- 2/1R; PAm: '03- 6/2R; WI: '06- 5; WCp: '06- 3/1R, '14- 2/1R. Won DL 2014, JAM 400m 2006-07, 2009-14.
Progress at 400m: 1999- 55.62, 2000- 53.90, 2001- 54.99, 2002- 52.05, 2003- 51.93, 2004- 50.59, 2005- 51.09, 2006- 49.63, 2007- 49.66, 2008- 50.11, 2009- 49.77, 2010- 50.04, 2011- 50.05, 2012- 49.78, 2013- 50.01, 2014- 50.05, 2015- 50.47, 2016- 50.64. pbs: 200m 23.25 '10, 500m 1:11.83i '03.
Married 2007. Younger sister Clora Williams (b. 26.11.83) joined her on JAM's 3rd place 4x400m team at 2010 WI; she has 400m pb 51.06 and won NCAA 2006.

JAPAN

Governing body: Nippon Rikujo-Kyogi Renmei, 1-1-1 Jinnan, Shibuya-Ku, Tokyo 150-8050. Founded 1911.
National Championships first held in 1914 (men), 1925 (women). **2016 Champions**: **Men**: 100m: Aska Cambridge 10.16, 200m: Shota

Iizuka 20.11, 400m: Julian Walsh 45.35, 800m: Sho Kawamoto 1:46.22, 1500m: Masaki Toda 3:46.66, 5000m/10000m: Suguru Osaka 13:37.13/28:07.44, Mar: Hisanori Kitajima 2:09:16, 3000mSt: Hironori Tsuetaki 8:36.39, 110mh: Wataru Yazawa 13.48w, 400mh: Keisuke Nozawa 49.14, HJ: Takashi Eto 2.29, PV: Daichi Sawano 5.60, LJ: Kota Minemura 7.93, TJ: Ryoma Yamamoto 16.52, SP: Satoshi Hatase 18.53, DT: Yuji Tsutsumi 60.00, HT: Ryota Kashimura 70.81, JT: Ryohei Arai 84.54, Dec: Akihiko Nakamura 8180, 20kW: Eiki Takahashi 1:18:26, 50kW: Takayuki Tanii 3:44:12. **Women**: 100m/200m: Chisato Fukushima 11.45/22.88, 400m: Seika Aoyama 53.04, 800m: Shoko Fukuda 2:05.92, 1500m: Tomoka Kimura 4:14.67, 5000m: Misaki Onishi 15:19.37, 10000m: Ayuko Suzuki 31:18.73, Mar: Tomoni Tanaka 2:23:19, 3000mSt: Anju Takamizawa 9:44.22, 100mh: Ayako Kimura 13.23w, 400mh: Satomi Kubokura 56.62, HJ: Moeko Kyoya 1.78, PV: Ayako Aoshima 4.10, LJ: Konomi Kai 6.36, TJ: Kaede Miyasaka 13.44, SP: Aya Ota 15.88, DT: Ayumi Sakaguchi 53.89, HT: Akane Watanabe 65.33, JT: Risa Miyashita 58.35, Hep: Meg Hemphill 5882, 20kW: Kumiko Okada 1:29:40.

Hirooki ARAI b. 18 May 1988 Obuse, Nagano Pref. 1.80m 62kg. Japan Self-Defense Forces Physical Training School, was at Fukui University of Technology.
At 50kW: OG: '16- 3; WCh: '11- 9, '13- 11, '15- 4; JPN champion 2015.
Progress at 50kW: 2009- 4:04:01, 2010- 3:55:56, 2011- 3:48:40, 2012- 3:47:08, 2013- 3:45:56, 2014- 3:40:34, 2015- 3:40:20, 2016- 3:41:24. Pbs: 3000mW 12:12.73 '09, 5000mW 19:05.46 '16, 10000m 39:17.66 '14, 20kW 1:19:54 '16.

Ryohei ARAI b. 23 Jun 1991 Nagatoro, Saitama pref. 1.83m 96kg. Suzuki Hamamatsu AC, was at Kokushikan University.
At JT: OG: '16- 11; WCh: '15- 9; AsiG: '14- 2. JPN champion 2014-16.
Progress at JT: 2011- 78.21, 2012- 78.00, 2013- 78.19, 2014- 86.83, 2015- 84.66, 2016- 84.54.

Daisuke MATSUNAGA b. 24 Mar 1995 Kanagawa pref. 1.74m 60kg. Fujitsu, was at Iwate University.
At 20kW: OG: '16- 7; WUG: '15- 3. At 10000mW: WJ: '14- 1; As-J 12- 2; WCp: '14-2J.
Asian junior 10000m walk records 2013.
Progress at 20kW: 2013- 1:23:56, 2014- 1:21:17, 2015- 1:19:08, 2016- 1:18:53, 2017- 1:19:40. pbs: 5000mW 19:28.91 '14, 10000mW 38:16.76 '16.

Yusuke SUZUKI b. 1 Feb 1988 Nomi, Iskikawa pref. 1.71m 58kg. Fujitsu. Was at Juntendo University.
At 20kW: OG: '12- 36; WCh: '09-11-13-15: 41/5/12/dnf WCp: '14- 4; AsiG: '10- 5, '14- 2; WUG: '07- 4; Asian champion 2013, 2015; JPN 2011, 2013-14. At 10000mW: WJ: 04- 17, '06- 3; WY: '05- 3.
Walk records: World 20k 2015, Asian 5000m 2015, 10000m (2) 2014-15, Japanese 10k (4) 2010-15, 20k (4) 2013-15.
Progress at 20kW: 2007- 1:24:40, 2008- 1:22:34, 2009- 1:22:05, 2010- 1:20:06, 2011- 1:21:13, 2012- 1:22:30, 2013- 1:18:34, 2014- 1:18:17, 2015- 1:16:36. pbs: 3000mW 18:37.60 '15, 5000mW 18:37.22 '15, 10kW 38:05 '15, track 38:10.23 '15.

Eiki TAKAHASHI b. 19 Nov 1992 Hanamaki, Iwate pref. 1.75m 56kg. Fujitsu, was at Iwate University.
At 20kW: OG: '16- 42; WCh: '15- 47; WCp: '14- 9, '16- 12; AsiG: '14- 7. JPN champion 2015-16.
Walk records: Asian 5000m & 10000m 2015, Japanese 20k 2015, 2017.
Progress at 20kW: 2011- 1:26:16, 2012- 1:22:33, 2013- 1:20:25, 2014- 1:18:41, 2015- 1:18:03, 2016- 1:18:26, 2017- 1:18:18. pbs: 5000mW 18:51.93 '15, 10000mW 38:01.49 '15.

Takayuki TANII b. 14 Feb 1983 Namerikawa, Toyama pref. 1.67m 57kg. Japan Self-Defense Forces Physical Training School, was at Nihon University.
At (20kW)/50kW: OG: '04- (15), '08- 29, '12- dnf, '16- 14; WCh: '05-07-09-11-13-15: (23)/(21)/dq/8/9/3; AsiG: '14- 1; WUG: '03- (6); At 10000mW: WJ: '02- 7; WY: '99- 3. Won Asian 20kW 2007, JPN 20kW 2004-05, 50kW 2013-14, 2016. Japanese 50k walk record 2003.
Progress at 50kW: 2003- 3:47:54, 2006- 3:47:23, 2007- 3:50:08, 2008- 3:49:33, 2009- 3:52:22, 2010- 3:53:27, 2011- 3:48:03, 2012- 3:43:56, 2013- 3:44:25, 2014- 3:40:19, 2015- 3:42:01, 2016- 3:44:12. pbs: 5000mW 19:07.58 '16, 10000mW 40:03.42 '03, 20kW 1:20:39 '04, 30kW 2:11:34 '14, 35kW 2:33:37 '14.

Women

Kayoko FUKUSHI b. 25 Mar 1982 Itayanagi, Aomori pref. 1.60m 47kg. Wacoal.
At Mar: OG: '16- 14; WCh: '13- 3. At 5000m/(10000m): OG: '04- (26), '08- h/9, '12- h/10; WCh: '03- h/11, '05- 12/11, '07- 13/9, '09- (9); WJ: '00- 4; AsiG: '02- 2/2, '06- (1), '10- 5/4; WCp: '06- 3 (5 3000m). World 20km: '06- 6; CC: '02- 15, '06- 6. Won JPN 5000m 2002, 2004-07, 2010; 10000m 2002-07, 2010.
World 15km record & Asian 20km & HMar records 2006, Japanese records: 3000m 2002, 5000m (4) 2002-05, 10k 2006
Progress at 5000m, 10,000m, Mar: 1998- 16:56.35, 1999- 16:38.69, 35:37.54; 2000- 15:29.70, 2001- 15:10.23, 31:42.05; 2002- 14:55.19, 30:51.81; 2003- 15:09.02, 31:10.57; 2004- 14:57.73, 31:05.68; 2005- 14:53.22, 31:03.75; 2006- 15:03.17, 30:57.90; 2007- 15:05.73, 32:13.58; 2008- 15:12.7, 31:01.14, 2:40:54; 2009- 15:23.44mx, 31:23.49; 2010- 15:17.86, 31:29.03; 2011- 15:50.66, 30:54.29, 2:24:38; 2012- 15:09.31, 31:10.35, 2:37:35; 2013- 15:49.64, 32:42.56, 2:24:21; 2014- 32:48.87, 2:26:25; 2015- 2:24:25,

2016- 16:17.73, 2:22:17. pbs: 1500m 4:21.61 '07, 3000m 8:44.40 '02, 15k 46:55 '06, 20k 63:41 '06, HMar 67:26 '06, 30k 1:40:13 '16.
Set Japanese junior records at 3000m, 5000m and 10000m in 2001. Won Osaka marathon 2013 & 2016; 2nd Chicago 2011.

KAZAKHSTAN

Governing body: Athletic Federation of the Republic of Kazakhstan, Abai Street 48, 480072 Almaty. Founded 1959.

2016 National Champions: Men: 100m: Vitaliy Zems 10.77, 200m: Vladislav Grigoryev 21.09, 400m/800m: Sergey Zaykov 47.53/1:50.14, 1500m: Artem Kosinov 4:05.74, 5000m: Konstantin Shibickiy 3:55.89, 10000m: Mikhail Krasilov 31:16.85, 3000mSt: Dmitriy Ivanchukov 9:27.53, 110mh: Denis Semenov 14.32, 400mh: Dmitriy Koblov 49.93, HJ: Yuriy Dergachev 2.20, PV: Sergey Grigoryev 5.30, LJ: Alexandr Kiselyev 7.57, TJ: Roman Valiyev 16.42, SP: Ivan Ivanov 19.12, DT: Yevgeniy Labutov 58.21, HT: Alexey Vladimirov 42.80, JT: Artur Gagner 59.01, Dec: Yevgeniy Marchenkov 6042. Women: 100m: Svetlana Golendova 11.84, 200m: Elina Mikhina 23.35, 400m: Yekaterin Yermak 54.61, 800m: Margarita Mukasheva 2:00.46, 1500m: Viktoriya Sergeyeva 4:51.63, 5000m: Tatyana Neroznak 17:40.15, 10000m: Zhanna Mamazhanova 37:39.88, 3000mSt: Tatyana Palkina 11:52.62, 100mh: Anastasiya Pipipenko 12.90, 400mh: Alexandra Romanova 56.17, HJ: Regina Kaysarova 1.75, PV: Yaroslava Vislobokova 3.50, LJ: Oksana Dzolba 5.75, TJ: Irina Ektova 13.19, SP/DT: Mariya Telushkina 13.71/60.30, HT: Diana Nusupbekova 58.12, JT: Asiya Rabayeva 46.80, Hep: Nadezhda Kimos 5349, 20kW: Florida Miniyanova 1:35:54.

Women

Olga RYPAKOVA b. 30 Nov 1984 Kamenogorsk 1.83m 62kg. née Alekseyeva.
At TJ/(LJ): OG: '08- 2 (dnq 29), '12- 1, '16- 3; WCh: '07-09-11-15: 10/10/2/3; WJ: '00- (dnq 23); AsiG: '06- (3), '10- 1/2, '14- 1; AsiC: '07- 1/1, '09- 1; WI: '08-10-12: 3/1/2; WUG: '07- (1); WCp: '06- (8), '10- 1/3; won DL TJ 2012, Asian Indoor LJ 2008-09, TJ 2009, 2016; Pen 2005-06. At Hep: WJ: '02- 2; WY: '01- 4; AsiG: '06- 1; won C.Asian 2003. Won KAZ LJ 2005, 2008, 2011, 2015; TJ 2008, 2011, 2015; Hep 2006.
Four Asian TJ records 2008-10, five indoors 2008-10, seven KAZ records 2007-10.
Progress at LJ, TJ: 2000- 6.23, 2001- 6.00, 2002- 6.26, 2003- 6.34i/6.14, 2004- 6.53i, 2005- 6.60, 2006- 6.63, 2007- 6.85, 14.69; 2008- 6.52/6.58w, 15.11; 2009- 6.58i/6.42, 14.53/14.69w; 2010- 6.60, 15.25; 2011- 6.56, 14.96; 2012- 14.98, 2014- 14.37, 2015- 14.77, 2016- 14.74. pbs: 200m 24.83 '02, 800m 2:20.12 '02, 60mh 8.67i '06, 100mh 14.02 '06, HJ 1.92 '06, SP 13.04 '06, JT 41.60 '03, Hep 6122 '06, Pen 4582i '06 (Asian rec).

Former heptathlete, concentrated on long jump after birth of daughter. Four KAZ and three Asian TJ records with successive jumps in Olympic final 2008, three Asian indoor records when won World Indoor gold in 2010. Son born June 2013.

KENYA

Governing body: Kenya Amateur Athletic Association, PO Box 46722, 00100 Nairobi. Founded 1951.

2016 National Champions: Men: 100m/200m: Mike Mokamba Nyangau 10.35/20.38, 400m: Alphas Kishoyan 45.71, 800m: Nicholas Kipkoech 1:43.91, 1500m: Vincent Letting 3:37.03, 5000m: Mang'ata Ndiwa 13:34.20, 10000m: Kenneth Kipkemoi 27:52.1, 3000mSt: Abraham Kibiwot 8:20.6, 110mh: William Mbevi 14.39, 400mh: Haron Koech 48.99, HJ: Matthew Sawe 2.12, TJ: Kennedy Magut 4.20, LJ: Bethwel Kibet 7.75, TJ: Elijah Kimetei 16.32, SP: Manasse Onyango 15.97, DT: David Limo 47.62, HT: Dominic Abuda 57.63, JT: Nelson Yego 71.34, 20kW: Samuel Kireri 1:20:2?. Women: 100m/200m: Eunice Kadogo 11.87/23.76, 400m: Margaret Wambui 51.39, 800m: Emily Cherotich 2:00.30, 1500m: Judy Kiyeng 4:05.45, 5000m: Sheila Chepkirui 15:30.8, 10000m: Alice Aprot Nawowuna 31:40.99, 3000mSt: Lydia Rotich 9:27.1; 400mh: Maureen Maiyo 57.39, HJ/LJ: Pricilah Tambunda 1.70/6.10, PV: Caroline Jerotich 3.10, TJ: Ivyn Chepkemoi 12.65, SP: Priscila Isiao 12.74, HT: Rebecca Kerubo 47.93, JT: Jane Jepleting 46.10, Hep: Jennifer Cheptoo 3690, 20kW: Grace Wanjiru 1:34:09.

Leonard Kiplimo **BARSOTON** b. 21 Oct 1994 1.66m 56kg.
At 10000m: AfG: '15- 2. World CC: '13-15-17: 2J/5/2; AfCC: '14- 1. Won KEN CC 2017.
Progress at 10000m: 2013- 27:33.13, 2014- 27:20.74, 2015- 27:27.55, 2016- 27:31.86. pbs: 1500m 3:47.95 '16, 5000m 13:16.25 '15.

Emmanuel Kipkemei **BETT** b. 30 Mar 1983 1.70m 55kg.
Progress at 10000m: 2011- 26:51.95, 2012- 26:51.16, 2013- 27:28.71, 2014- 27:21.61, 2015- 27:22.34, 2016- 27:53.05. pbs: 3000m 7:48.8 '14, 2M 8:25.55 '14, 5000m 13:08.35 '12, 15k 43:00+ '11, HMar 60:08 '15.

Kipyegon BETT b. 2 Jan 1998 1.82m 70kg.
At 800m: WJ: '16- 1; WY: '15- 2. Won Afr-Y 2015.
Progress at 800m: 2014- 1:52.45A, 2015- 1:44.55A, 2016- 1:43.76, 2017- 1:44.2A.

Nicholas BETT b. 20 Dec 1996 1.72m 52kg.
At 3000mSt: WY: '13- 2.
Progress at 3000mSt: 2013- 8:52.1A, 2014- 8:28.83, 2015- 8:19.26, 2016- 8:10.07. pbs: 5000m 14:33.6A '16, 2000mSt 5:20.92 '13.

Nicholas Kiptanui **BETT** b. 27 Jan 1990 1.86m 77kg. Kenya Police.

KENYA

At 400mh/4x400mR: OG: '16- h; WCh: '15- 1; AfCh: '14- 3/3R.
Kenyan 400mh record 2015.
Progress at 400mh: 2010- 53.11A, 2011- 50.35A, 2012- 53.2A, 2013- 49.70A, 2014- 49.03, 2015- 47.79, 2016- 48.01. pb 800m 1:49.34 '15.

Jairus Kipchoge **BIRECH** b. 14 Dec 1992 Uasin Gishu 1.70m 56kg.
At 3000mSt: WCh: '15- 4; CG: '14- 2; AfG: '11- 4; AfCh: '14- 1; Af-J: '11- 2; CCp: '14- 1. Won DL 2014-15, Kenyan 2014.
Progress at 3000mSt: 2010- 8:50.0A, 2011- 8:11.31, 2012- 8:03.43, 2013- 8:08.72, 2014- 7:58.41, 2015- 7:58.83, 2016- 8:03.90. pbs: 2000m 4:58.76 '11, 3000m 7:41.83 '13, 5000m 13:38.4A '15, 10000m 28:35.7A '16.

Bethwel Kiprotich **BIRGEN** b. 6 Aug 1988 Eldoret 1.78m 64kg.
At 1500m: WCh: '13- sf; WI: '14- 8.
Progress at 1500m: 2010- 3:35.60, 2011- 3:34.59, 2012- 3:31.00, 2013- 3:30.77, 2014- 3:31.22, 2015- 3:34.62i, 2016- 3:33.94. pbs: 800m 1:48.32 '11, 1M 3:50.42 '13, 3000m 7:32.48 '16, 5000m 14:01.0A '12.

Robert Kiptoo **BIWOTT** b. 28 Jan 1996 1.80m 68kg.
At 1500m: WY: '13- 1; Af-Y: '13-1 (1 800m).
Progress at 800m, 1500m: 2013- 1:46.98, 3:36.77; 2014- 1:44.69, 3:43.91A; 2015- 1:43.56, 3:30.10; 2016- 3:33.05. pbs: 600m 1:15.91 '15, 1000m 2:13.89 '16, 1M 3:55.62 '16.

Stanley Kipleting **BIWOTT** b. 21 Apr 1986 1.76m 60kg.
At Mar: OG: '16- dnf.
World record 30k road 2016.
Progress HMar, Mar: 2006- 2:14:25, 2007- 61:20, 2010- 2:09:41, 2011- 60:23, 2:07:03; 2012- 59:44, 2:05:12; 2013- 58:56, 2014- 59:18, 2:04:55; 2015- 59:20, 2:06:41; 2016- 60:40, 2:03:51. Road pbs: 10k 28:00 '12, 15k 42:13 '13, 20k 56:02 '13, 25k 1:12:40 '16, 30k 1:27:13 '16.
Marathon wins: São Paulo 2010, Chunchon 2011, Paris 2012, New York 2015; 2nd London 2014, 2016. His brother Norris Biwott had a marathon best of 2:11:29 in 2013.

Evans Kiplagat **CHEBET** b. 10 Nov 1988.
Progress at Mar: 2013- 2:11:26, 2014- 2:07:46, 2015- 2:08:50, 2016- 2:05:31. pb HMar 61:11+ '16.
Marathons: 2nd Prague 2014-15, Seoul Nov 2014 & Mar 2016, 3rd Berlin 2016.

Collins CHEBOI Kiprotich b. 25 Sep 1987 1.75m 64kg.
At 1500m: AfG: '11- 2.
World 4x1500m record 2014.
Progress at 1500m: 2007- 3:49.0A, 2009- 3:36.24, 2010- 3:34.17, 2011- 3:32.45, 2012- 3:32.08, 2013- 3:31.53, 2014- 3:32.00, 2015- 3:30.34, 2016- 3:35.74. pbs: 1M 3:49.56 '14, 2000m 4:59.5e+ '12, 3000m 7:45.32 '16, 5000m 13:51.3A '13.

Ferguson Rotich CHERUIYOT b. 30 Nov 1989 1.83m 73kg.
At 800m: OG: '16- 5; WCh: '13- sf, '15- 4; CG: '14- 4; AfCh: '14- 4. Won DL 2016, Kenyan 2014.
Progress at 800m: 2013- 1:43.22, 2014- 1:42.84, 2015- 1:43.60A, 2016- 1:43.43. pb 1000m 2:16.88 '14, 1500m 3:49.0A '14
Changed first name from Simon to Ferguson in honour of Manchester United manager Alex Ferguson.

Timothy CHERUIYOT b. 20 Nov 1995 1.78m 64kg.
At 1500m: WCh: '15- 7; AfCh: '16- 2.
Progress at 1500m: 2015- 3:34.86A, 2016- 3:31.34. pbs: 800m 1:45.92A '14, 1M 3:53.17 '16.

Augustine Kiprono **CHOGE** b. 21 Jan 1987 Kipsigat, Nandi 1.62m 53kg.
At 5000m: CG: '06- 1; WJ: '04- 1. At 3000m: WY: '03- 1; WI: '10-12-14-16: 11/2/9/3. At 1500m: OG: '08- 9; WCh: '05- h, '09- 5. World CC: '03-05-06-08: 4J/1J/7 (4k)/12. Won KEN 1500m 2013, E.African Youth 800m/1500m/3000m 2003, Junior 1500m 2004.
Records: World 4x1500m 2009, world youth 5000m 2004, world junior 3000m 2005.
Progress at 1500m, 5000m: 2003- 3:37.48, 13:20.08; 2004- 3:36.64, 12:57.01; 2005- 3:33.99, 12:53.66; 2006- 3:32.48, 12:56.41; 2007- 3:31.73, 2008- 3:31.57, 13:09.75; 2009- 3:29.47, 2010- 3:30.22, 13:04.64; 2011- 3:31.14, 13:21.24; 2012- 3:37.47, 13:15.50; 2013- 3:33.21, 13:05.31; 2014- 3:35.5A, 13:06.12. At HMar: 2016- 60:01, 2017- 59:26. pbs: 800m 1:44.86 '09, 1000m 2:17.79i '09, 1M 3:50.01 '13, 2000m 4:56.30i '07, 3000m 7:28.00i/7:28.76 '11, 10000m 28:22.8A '16.
At 17 in 2004 he become youngest to break 13 minutes for 5000m.

Dickson Kiptolo **CHUMBA** b. 27 Oct 1986 1.67m 50kg. Nandi.
Progress at Mar: 2010- 2:09:20dh, 2011- 2:07:23, 2012- 2:05:46, 2013- 2:10:15, 2014- 2:04:32, 2015- 2:06:34, 2016- 2:07:34. pbs: 1500m 3:44.33 '10, 5000m 13:41.34 '10, road: 10k 28:09 '13, HMar 61:34 '12, 60:39dh '14; 30k 1:28:36 '12.
Marathon wins: Rome 2011, Eindhoven 2012, Tokyo 2014 (3rd 2015-17), Chicago 2015 (2nd 2016, 3rd 2014).

Geoffrey Kipsang KAMWOROR b. 28 Nov 1992 Chepkorio, Keiyo district1.68m 54kg.
At 10000m: OG: '16- 11; WCh: '15- 2. World CC: '11-15-17: 1J/1/1; HMar: '14- 1, '16- 1. Won KEN 5000m 2015, CC 2016.
Tied world 30km record 2014.
Progress at 5000m, 10000m, HMar, Mar: 2010- 13:32.01, 2011- 13:12.23, 27:06.35, 59:31; 2012- 13:28.8A, 59:26, 2:06:12; 2013- 28:17.0A, 58:54, 2:06:26; 2014- 59:08, 2:06:39; 2015- 13:13.28A, 26:52.65, 2:10:48; 2016- 12:59.98, 27:31.94, 59:10. pbs: 1500m 3:40.7A '15, 3000m 7:54.15 '10; Road: 15k 41:41 '16, 20k 56:02 '13, 30k 1:27:37 '14.

3rd in Berlin Marathon 2012 (on debut) and 2013 (4th 2014), 2nd New York 2015. Won RAK half marathon 2013.

Bidan KAROKI Muchiri b. 21 Aug 1990 Nyandarua 1.69m 53kg. S&B Foods, Japan.
At 10000m: OG: '12- 5, '16- 7; WCh: '13- 6, '15- 4; AfG: '11- 2. World CC: '15- 2; HMar: '16- 2. Won Kenyan CC 2012.
Progress at 10000m, HMar: 2010- 27:23.62, 2011- 27:13.67, 2012- 27:05.50; 2013- 27:13.12, 2014- 26:52.36, 59:23; 2015- 27:04.77, 59:14; 2016- 27:07.30, 59:32; 2017- 59:10. pbs: 1500m 3:50.91 '08, 3000m 7:37.68 '13, 5000m 13:15.25 '14, 15k 41:41 '16, 10M 45:02 '14. Went to Japan in 2007.

Clement KEMBOI b. 1 Feb 1992 1.80m 65kg.
At 3000mSt: AfG: '15- 1.
Progress at 3000mSt: 2010- 9:03.4A, 2011- 8:28.13, 2012- 8:25.67, 2013- 8:17.18, 2014- 8:16.96, 2015- 8:12.68, 2016- 8:10.65. pbs: 1M 4:02.19 '14, 3000m 7:51.65 '16, 10kRd 28:44 '14.

Ezekiel KEMBOI Cheboi b. 25 May 1982 Matira, near Kapsowar, Marakwet District 1.75m 62kg.
At 3000mSt: OG: '04- 1, '08- 7, '12- 1, '16- dq; WCh: '03-05-07-09-11-13-15: 2/2/2/1/1/1/1; CG: '02-06-10-14: 2/1/2/3; AfG: '03- 1, '07- 2; AfCh: '02-06-10-14: 4/dq/2/3; Af-J: '01- 1. Won WAF 2009, Kenyan 2003, 2006-07.
Progress at 3000mSt: 2001- 8:23.66, 2002- 8:06.65, 2003- 8:02.49, 2004- 8:02.98, 2005- 8:09.04, 2006- 8:09.29, 2007- 8:05.50, 2008- 8:09.25, 2009- 7:58.85, 2010- 8:01.74, 2011- 7:55.76, 2012- 8:10.55, 2013- 7:59.03, 2014- 8:04.12, 2015- 8:01.71., 2016- 8:14.19 pbs: 1500m 3:40.8A '04, 3000m 7:44.24 '12, 5000m 13:50.61 '11, 10k Rd 28:38 '11.
Five gold and three silver medals from global 3000m steeplechase races. Disqualified after finishing third at 2016 Olympic Games for stepping inside lane one early in the race.

Stephen Kipkosgei **KIBET** b. 9 Nov 1986 1.72m 55kg.
At HMar: WCh: '12- 5.
Progress at HMar: 2009- 60:34, 2010- 60:09, 2011- 60:20, 2012- 58:54, 2013- 59:59, 2014- 59:21, 2015- 59:58, 2016- 59:27. pbs: 5000m 13:38.47 '15; road: 10k 27:44 '14, 15k 42:01+ '12, 20k 55:55+ '12, Mar 2:08:05 '12.
Six successive half marathon wins 2009-12.

Vincent KIBET b. 6 May 1991 Uasin Gishu 1.70m 57kg.
At 1500m: WI: '16- 7.
Progress at 1500m: 2010- 3:46.7A, 2011- 3:42.7A, 2012- 3:40.51A, 2013- 3:35.62, 2014- 3:31.96, 2015- 3:34.91i/3:36.80, 2016- 3:33.56. pbs: 800m 1:46.71 '14, 1000m 2:19.93i '15, 1M 3:52.15 '14, 3000m 7:44.87i '16, 7:58.9 '14.

Abraham KIBIWOT b. 4 Jun 1996 1.75m 55kg.
At 3000mSt: AfCh: '16- 3; won Af-J 2015, Kenyan 2016.
Progress at 3000mSt: 2014- 8:52.36A, 2015-

8:22.10, 2016- 8:09.25. pbs: 3000m 8:02.95 '16, 5000m 14:10.8A '15.

Dennis Kipruto **KIMETTO** b. 22 Jan 1984 near Kapngetuny 1.72m 57kg.
At Mar: WCh: '15- dnf.
World records 25km road 2012, marathon 2014.
Progress at Mar: 2012- 2:04:16, 2013- 2:03:45, 2014- 2:02:57, 2015- 2:05:50. Road pbs: 10k 28:21 '12, 15k 42:46 '11, HMar 59:14 '12, 25k 1:11:18 '12, 30k 1:27:38 '14.
Second Berlin 2012 in fastest ever marathon debut after major road wins at half marathon and 25k in Berlin in 2012. Won Tokyo and Chicago marathons 2013. Dnf Boston before WR in Berlin marathon 2014. 3rd London 2015.

Eliud KIPCHOGE b. 5 Nov 1984 Kapsisiywa, Nandi 1.67m 52kg.
At Mar: OG: '16- 1; At 5000m: OG: '04- 3, '08- 2; WCh: '03-05-07-09-11: 1/4/2/5/7; CG: '10- 2. At 3000m: WI: '06- 3. World CC: '02-03-04-05: 5J/1J/4/5; HMar: '12- 6. Won WAF 5000m 2003, 3000m 2004, Kenyan CC 2005.
World junior 5000m record 2003. World road best 4M 17:10 '05 and WR 30k 2016.
Progress at 1500m, 5000m, 10000m: 2002- 13:13.03, 2003- 3:36.17, 12:52.61; 2004- 3:33.20, 12:46.53; 2005- 3:33.80, 12:50.22; 2006- 3:36.25i, 12:54.94; 2007- 3:39.98, 12:50.38, 26:49.02; 2008- 13:02.06, 26:54.32; 2009- 12:56.46, 2010- 3:38.36, 12:51.21; 2011- 12:55.72i/12:59.01, 26:53.27; 2012- 12:55.34, 27:11.93. At HMar, Mar: 2012- 59:25, 2013- 60:04, 2:04:05, 2014- 60:52, 2:04:11; 2015- 60:50, 2:04:00; 2016- 59:44, 2:03:05. pbs: 1M 3:50.40 '04, 2000m 4:59.?+ '04, 3000m 7:27.66 '11, 2M 8:07.39i '12, 8:07.68 '05; Road: 10k 26:55dh '06, 27:34 '05; 25k 1:12:39 '16, 30k 1:27:13 '16.
Kenyan Junior CC champion 2002-03, followed World Junior CC win by winning the World 5000m title, becoming at 18 years 298 days the second youngest world champion. Age 19 bests for 3000m & 5000m 2004. Ran 26:49.02 in 10,000m debut at Hengelo in 2007. All his seven marathons were in 2:05:30 or better until his Olympic win in 2:08:44; he won at Hamburg on debut then 2nd Berlin in 2013, 1st Rotterdam & Chicago 2014, London & Berlin 2015, London 2016 (in second fastest of all-time). Won World Marathon Majors 2015/16.

Kenneth Kiprop **KIPKEMOI** b. 2 Aug 1984 1.65m 52kg.
At 10000m: WCh: '13- 7; AfCh: '12- 1. Kenyan champion 2012, 2016. World HMar: '14- 10.
Progress at 10000m, HMar: 2009- 62:59A, 2011- 27:48.5A, 59:47; 2012- 26:52.65, 59:11; 2013- 27:28.50, 60:45; 2014- 27:30.94, 59:01; 2015- 60:17, 2016- 27:52.1A, 60:05. pbs: 3000m 7:49.28+ '11, 5000m 13:03.37 '12, 15k 43:22 '12, 25k 1:22:32 '14.

Alfred KIPKETER b. 26 Dec 1996 1.69m 61kg.
At 800m: OG: '16- 7; WCh: '15- 8; WJ: '14- 1; WY: '13- 1.

Progress at 800m: 2013- 1:46.2A, 2014- 1:43.95, 2015- 1:44.07A, 2016- 1:42.87. pb 600m 1:15.60 '15.

Nicholas KIPKOECH b. 22 Oct 1992 1.68m 57kg.
At 800m: WY: '09- 3.
Progress at 800m: 2009- 1:47.4A, 2010- 1:47.0A, 2011- 1:45.47, 2012- 1:45.02, 2013- 1:47.14, 2014- 1:45.7A, 2015- 1:44.9A, 2016- 1:43.37A. pbs: 600m 1:15.87 '15, 1000m 2:165;68 '16, 1500m 3:44.07 '11.

Silas KIPLAGAT b. 20 Aug 1989 Siboh village, Marakwet 1.70m 57kg.
At 1500m: OG: '12- 7; WCh: '11-13-15: 2/6/5; CG: '10- 1; AfCh: '10- 4; WI: '12- 6. Won DL 2012, 2014; Kenyan 2011.
World 4x1500m record 2014.
Progress at 1500m: 2009- 3:39.1A, 2010- 3:29.27, 2011- 3:30.47, 2012- 3:29.63, 2013- 3:30.13, 2014- 3:27.64, 2015- 3:30.12, 2016- 3:33.68. pbs: 800m 1:44.8A '12, 1000m 2:19.80 '16, 1M 3:47.88 '14, 3000m 7:39.94 '10, 5000m 13:55.0A '13, 10k Rd 28:00 '09.

Asbel Kipruto **KIPROP** b. 30 Jun 1989 Uasin Gishu, Eldoret. North Rift 1.86m 70kg.
At (800m)/1500m: OG: '08- 1, '12- 12, '16- 6; WCh: '07- 4, '09- sf/4, '11-13-15: 1/1/1; AfG: '07- 1; AfCh: '10- 1, '14- 2; CCp: '10- 6, '14- 2; Won DL 2010, 2015-16. At 800m: AfCh: '08- 3. World CC: '07- 1J, '17- 1 MxR. Won Kenyan 800m 2015, 1500m 2007, 2010.
World 4x1500m record 2014.
Progress at 800m, 1500m: 2007- 3:35.24, 2008- 1:44.71, 3:31.64; 2009- 1:43.17, 3:31.20; 2010- 1:43.45, 3:31.78; 2011- 1:43.15, 3:30.46; 2012- 1:45.91, 3:28.88; 2013- 1:44.8A, 3:27.72; 2014- 1:43.34, 3:28.45; 2015- 1:44.4A, 3:26.69; 2016- 1:44.6A, 3:29.33. pbs: 1000m 2:14.23 '16, 1M 3:48.50 '09, 3000m 7:42.32 '07, 5000m 13:48.43A '10.
Father David Kebenei had 1M pb 3:59.35 (1982).

Brimin KIPRUTO b. 31 Jul 1985 Korkitony, Marakwet District 1.76m 54kg.
At 3000mSt: OG: '04- 2, '08- 1, '12- 5, '16- 6; WCh: '05-07-09-11-15: 3/1/7/2/3; CG: '10- 3; Af-J: '03- 2; KEN champion 2011. At 1500m: WJ: '04- 3. At 2000St: WY: '01- 2. World 4k CC: '06- 18.
Commonwealth & African 3000mSt record 2011.
Progress at 3000mSt: 2002- 8:33.0A, 2003- 8:34.5A, 2004- 8:05.52, 2005- 8:04.22, 2006- 8:08.32, 2007- 8:02.89, 2008- 8:10.26, 2009- 8:03.17, 2010- 8:00.90, 2011- 7:53.64, 2012- 8:01.73, 2013- 8:06.86, 2014- 8:04.64, 2015- 8:10:09, 2016- 8:18.79. pbs: 1500m 3:35.23 '06, 2000m 4:58.76i '07, 3000m 7:39.07i '12, 7:47.33 '06; 5000m 13:58.82 '04, 2000mSt 5:36.81 '01.
First name is actually Firmin, but he stayed with the clerical error of Brimin, written when he applied for a birth certificate in 2001.

Conseslus KIPRUTO b. 8 Dec 1994 Eldoret 1.71m 55kg.
At 3000mSt: OG: '16- 1; WCh: '13- 2, '15- 2; WJ: '12- 1; won DL 2013, 2016. At 2000St: WY: '11- 1.

World CC: 2013- 5J.
Progress at 3000mSt: 2011- 8:27.30, 2012- 8:03.49, 2013- 8:01.16, 2014- 8:09.81, 2015- 8:05.20, 2016- 8:00.12. pbs: 800m 1:49.0A '15, 1000m 2:19.85 '12, 1500m 3:39.57 '13, 3000m 7:44.09 '12, 5000m 13:47.5A 16, 2000mSt 5:28.65 '11.

Wilson KIPSANG Kiprotich b. 15 Mar 1982 Keiyo district 1.78m 59kg.
At Mar: OG: '12- 3; WCh: '15- dnf; HMar: WCh: '09- 4.
World marathon record 2013.
Progress at HMar, Mar: 2008- 59:16, 2009- 58:59, 2010- 60:04, 2:04:57; 2011- 60:49, 2:03:42; 2012- 59:06, 2:04:44; 2013- 61:02, 2:03:23; 2014- 60:25, 2:04:29; 2015- 61:23, 2:04:47; 2016- 61:11, 2:03:13. pbs: 5000m 13:55.7A '09, 10000m 28:37.0A '07; Road: 10k 27:42 '09, 15k 41:51+ '11, 10M 44:59+ '11, 20k 56:10+ '12, 25k 1:12:47 '16, 30k 1:27:26 '16.
Eight wins from 14 marathons: third in Paris in 2:07:13 on debut, won Frankfurt in 2010 and 2011, Lake Biwa 2011, London 2012 and 2014 (2nd 2015), Honolulu 2012, Berlin 2013 (2nd 2016) and New York 2014. Won World Marathon Majors 2013/14. Has record six marathons inside 2:05. Won Great North Run 2012. His brother Noah Kigen HMar pb 60:25 '17.

Eliud KIPTANUI b. 6 Jun 1989 Kaplelach, Uasin Gishu 1.69m 55kg.
At Mar: WCh: '11- 5.
Progress at Mar: 2009- 2:12:17, 2010- 2:05:39, 2011- 2:09:08, 2012- 2:06:44, 2013- 2:15:10, 2014- 2:07:24, 2015- 2:05:21, 2016- 2:07:47. pbs: 3000m 8:04.57 '09, Road: 25k 1:13:38 '14, 30k 1:29:18 '14; HMar 61:13 '16.
Won Safaricom Marathon in Kisimu in December 2009, then made a stunning improvement to win Prague Marathon in 2010; 3rd Seoul & 2nd Beijing 2012, 2nd Berlin 2015.

Bernard KIPYEGO Kiprop b. 16 Jul 1986 Kapkitony, Keiyo district 1.60m 50kg.
At 10000m: WCh: '09- 5; Af-J: '03- 3. At Mar: WCh: '13- 12. World CC: '05-07-08: 2J/3/10; HMar: '09- 2.
Progress at 10000m, Mar: 2003- 29:29.09, 2004- 28:18.94, 2005- 27:04.45, 2006- 27:19.45, 2007- 26:59.51, 2008- 27:08.06, 2009- 27:18.47, 2010- 2:07:01, 2011- 2:06:29, 2012- 2:06:40, 2013- 28:36.5A, 2:07:19, 2014- 2:06:22, 2015- 2:06:19, 2016- 2:06:45. pbs: 3000m 7:54.91 '05, 5000m 13:09.96 '05, Road: 15k 42:34 '11, 10M 45:44 '11, HMar 59:10 '09, 30k 1:29:51 '14.
Won in Berlin on half marathon debut in 59:34 in 2009, 5th Rotterdam on marathon debut 2010, won Amsterdam 2014-15, 2nd Paris 2011, Beijing 2013, Tokyo 2016; 3rd Chicago 2011, Boston 2012, Tokyo 2013 and Rotterdam 2014.

Abel KIRUI b. 4 Jun 1982 Bornet, Rift Valley 1.77m 62kg. Police.
At Mar: OG: '12- 2; WCh: '09- 1, '11- 1.
Progress at Mar: 2006- 2:15:22, 2007- 2:06:51,

2008- 2:07:38, 2009- 2:05:04, 2010- 2:08:04, 2011- 2:07:38, 2012- 2:07:56, 2014- 2:09:04, 2015- 2:10:55, 2016- 2:08:06. pbs: 1500m 3:46.10 '05, 3000m 7:55.90 '06, 5000m 13:52.71 '05, 10000m 28:16.86A '08; Road: 10k 27:59 '09, 15k 42:22 '07, 10M 46:40 '11, HMar 60:11 '07, 25k: 1:13:41 '08, 30k 1:28:25 '08.
Brilliantly retained World marathon title with halves of 65:07 and 62:31 and a fastest 5k split of 14:18. Won Vienna Marathon 2008, Chicago 2016, 2nd Berlin 2007, 3rd Rotterdam 2009. Uncle Mike Rotich had marathon pb 2:06:33 '03.

Jonathan KITILIT b. 24 Apr 1994 1.71m 61kg.
At 1500m: Af-J: '13- 2.
Progress at 800m: 2012- 1:47.8A, 2013- 1:48.03, 2015- 1:45.0A, 2016- 1:43.05. pbs: 2:13.95 '16, 1500m 3:39.81 '15.

Timothy KITUM b. 20 Nov 1994 Marakwet 1.72m 60kg.
At 800m: OG: '12- 3; WJ: '12- 2; WY: '11- 3; AfG: '15- 4.
Progress at 800m: 2011- 1:44.98, 2012- 1:42.53, 2013- 1:44.45, 2014- 1:43.65, 2015- 1:45.0A, 2016- 1:44.51A. pbs: 600m 1:14.4A '12, 1000m 2:17.62 '15.

Sammy Kiprop **KITWARA** b. 26 Nov 1986 Sagat village, Marakwet district 1.77m 54kg.
At 10000m: Kenyan champion 2009. World HMar: '09- 10, '10- 3.
Progress at 10,000m, HMar, Mar: 2007- 28:11.6A, 2008- 28:12.26A, 60:54; 2009- 27:44.46A, 58:58; 2010- 28:32.77A, 59:34; 2011- 58:47, 2012- 2:05:54, 2013- 61:53, 2:05:16; 2014- 60:24, 2:04:28; 2015- 60:25, 2:07:43; 2016- 59:47, 2:05:45. pbs: 5000m 13:34.0A '08, Road: 10k 27:11 '10, 15k 41:54 '09, 10M 45:17 '08, 20k 57:42 '08, 25k 1:13:42 '14, 30k 1:28:46 '14.
Won Taipei marathon 2016, 2nd marathon 2014-15 (3rd 2013, 4th 2012), 3rd Rotterdam 2013, Tokyo 2014

Haron KOECH b. 27 Jan 1990 1.88m 79kg. Central.
At 400mh/4x400mR: OG: '16- 7; WCh: '15- sf; AfCh: '16- 3/2R. Kenyan champion 2016.
Progress at 400mh: 2014- 51.14A, 2015- 49.38, 2016- 48.49.
Older brother of 400m hurdler Nicholas Bett.

Isiah Kiplangat **KOECH** b. 19 Dec 1993 Kericho 1.78m 60kg.
At 5000m: OG: '12- 5, '16- h; WCh: '11- 4, '13- 3, '15- 8; CG: '14- 2; AfCh: '14- 2; CCp: '14- 1; won DL 5000m 2012, Kenyan 2011, 2013. At 3000m: WY: '09- 1; WI: '16- 8. World CC: '10- 4J, '11- 10J. World junior records indoors: 5000m 2011, 3000m 2011 & 2012.
Progress at 5000m, 10000m: 2010- 13:07.70, 2011- 12:53.29i/12:54.18, 2012- 12:48.64, 27:17.03; 2013- 12:56.08, 2014- 13:07.55, 2015- 13:07.33, 2016- 13:08.34. pbs: 1500m 3:38.7A '12, 3000m 7:30.43 '12, 2M 8:14.16 '11.

Paul Kipsiele **KOECH** b. 10 Nov 1981 Cheplanget, Buret District 1.68m 57kg.
At 3000mSt: OG: '04- 3; WCh: '05- 7, '09- 4, '13- 4; AfG: '03- 2; AfCh: '06- 1; WCp: '06- 2; won DL 2010-12, WAF 2005-08. At 3000m: WI: 08- 2.
Progress at 3000mSt: 2001- 8:15.92, 2002- 8:05.44, 2003- 7:57.42, 2004- 7:59.65, 2005- 7:56.37, 2006- 7:59.94, 2007- 7:58.80, 2008- 8:00.57, 2009- 8:01.26, 2010- 8:02.07, 2011- 7:57.32, 2012- 7:54.31, 2013- 8:02.63, 2014- 8:05.47, 2015- 8:10.24, 2016- 8:08.32. pbs: 1500m 3:37.92 '07, 2000m 5:00.9+i '08, 5:01.84 '14; 3000m 7:32.78i '10, 7:33.93 '05; 2M 8:06.48i/8:13.31 '08, 5000m 13:02.69i 12, 13:05.18 '10.
Younger brother John Koech (b. 23 Aug 1995) transferred to Bahrain in 2013; 3000mSt: 8:14.75 '15; OG: '16- h; WCh: '15- 5, AsiC: '15- 1, CCP: '14- 5.

Ronald KWEMOI b. 19 Sep 1995 Mt. Elgon 1.80m 68kg.
At 1500m: OG: '16- 13; CG: '14- 2; AfG: '15- 4; AfCh: '14- 3; Kenyan champion 2014. World CC: '13- 9J.
World junior 1500m record 2014.
Progress at 1500m: 2013- 3:45.39, 2014- 3:28.81, 2015- 3:30.43, 2016- 3:30.49. pbs: 1M 3:52.57 '15, 3000m 7:53.85 '16, 5000m 13:16.14 '15, 10000m 27:33.94 '16.

Thomas Pkemei **LONGOSIWA** b. 14 Jan 1982 West Pokot 1.75m 57kg. North Rift.
At 5000m: OG: '08- 12, '12- 3; WCh: '11- 6, '13- 4; AfG: '07- 6, '15- 3; . World CC: '06- 13J (but dq after birthdate found to be 1982). Won Kenyan 5000m 2007.
Progress at 5000m: 2006- 13:35.3A, 2007- 12:51.95, 2008- 13:14.36, 2009- 13:03.43, 2010- 13:05.60, 2011- 12:56.08, 2012- 12:49.04, 2013- 12:59.81, 2014- 12:56.16, 2015- 12:59.72, 2016- 13:01.69. pbs: 1500m 3:41.92 '13, 2000m 5:01.6+ '10, 3000m 7:30.09 '09, 10000m 28:11.3A '06.

Wilson Erupe **LOYANAE** b. 20 Nov 1988 Lodwar, Turkana.
Progress at Mar: 2010- ?. 2011- 2:09:23, 2012- 2:05:37, 2015- 2:06:11, 2016- 2:05:13, 2017- 2:06:27. pb HMar 61:46 '12.
Marathon wins: Mombasa 2011-12, Gyongju 2011-12, 2015; Seoul 2012, 2015-16. Two-year drugs ban for EPO 2013-15.

James Kiplagat **MAGUT** b. 20 Jul 1990 Nandi 1.80m 64kg.
At 1500m: CG: '10- 2, '14- 1; WJ: '08- 2, AfCh: '12- 3, '14- 5; Af-J: '09- 1.
World 4x1500m record 2014.
Progress at 1500m: 2008- 3:42.3A, 2009- 3:36.8A, 2010- 3:40.47, 2012- 3:33.31, 2013- 3:35.2A, 2014- 3:30.61, 2015- 3:31.76, 2016- 3:35.18. pbs: 800m 1:48.0A '15, 1000m 2:19.72 '13, 1M 3:49.43 '14.

Elijah Motonei **MANANGOI** b. 5 Jan 1993 Narok 1.81m 65kg.
At 1500m: OG: '16- sf; WCh: '15- 2; CG: '14- 12. Kenyan champion 2015

KENYA

Progress at 1500m: 2014- 3:35.0A, 2015- 3:29.67, 2016- 3:31.19. pbs: 400m 47.0A '15, 47.33A '13; 800m 1:47.40 '15, 1000m 2:17.09i '16, 1M 3:52.04 '16.

Boniface MUCHERU Tumuti b. 2 May 1992 Laikipia District 1.85m 75kg. Central.
At 400mh/4x400mR (400m): OG: '12- h, '16- 2; WCh: '15- 5; CG: '14- 6; AfCh: '10- h, '12- 3/3R, 14- (3)/3R, '16- 1; WJ: '10- 8 (h). Kenyan champion 2012, 2015.
Kenyan 400mh records 2015 & 2016.
Progress at 400mh: 2008- 52.79A, 2010- 51.04A, 2011- 50.35A, 2012- 49.45, 2013- 49.59A, 2014- 49.25A/49.67, 2015- 48.29, 2016- 47.78. pbs: 200m 22.23 '15, 400m 45.07 '14, 800m 1:49.34 '15, 110mh 14.51A '15.

Abel Kiprop **MUTAI** b. 2 Oct 1988 Nandi 1.72m 73kg.
At 3000mSt: OG: '12- 3; WCh: '13- 7; AfCh: '12- 1; Af-J: '07- 1; Kenyan champion 2012. At 2000mSt: WY: '05- 1.
Progress at 3000mSt: 2006- 8:35.38, 2007- 8:29.76, 2009- 8:11.40, 2011- 8:21.02, 2012- 8:01.67, 2013- 8:08.83, 2014- 8:15.83, 2015- 8:20.38, 2016- 8:16.84. pbs: 3000m 8:05.16 '06, 5000m 14:07.80 '06, 2000mSt 5:24.69 '05.

Caleb Mwangangi **NDIKU** b. 9 Oct 1992 Machakos 1.83m 68kg.
At 1500m: WJ: '10- 1; WY: '09- 2; AfG: '11- 1; AfCh: '12- 1; Kenyan champion 2012. At 3000m: CCp: '14- 1; WI: '14- 1, '16- 5. At 5000m: OG: '16- h; WCh: '15- 2; CG: '14- 1; AfCh: '14- 1; won DL 2014 World CC: '10- 1J.
Progress at 1500m, 5000m: 2009- 3:38.2A, 2010- 3:37.30, 2011- 3:32.02, 2012- 3:32.39, 2013- 3:29.50, 13:03.80; 2014- 3:35.8A, 12:59.17; 2015- 3:38.13, 13:05.30; 2016- 13:12.25. pbs: 800m 1:52.6A '07, 1M 3:49.77 '11, 3000m 7:30.99 '12, 10000m 28:28.4A '14.
His father David was a javelin thrower.

Jonathan Muia **NDIKU** b. 18 Sep 1991 Machakos 1.73m 60kg. Team Hitachi Cable, Japan.
At 3000mSt: CG: '14- 1; AfCh: '14- 2; WJ: '08- 1, '10- 1; Af-J: '09- 1. At 2000mSt: WY: '07- 4.
Progress at 10,000m, 3000mSt: 2008- 28:08.28, 8:17.28; 2009- 27:37.72, 8:28.1A; 2010- 8:19.25A. 2011- 8:07.75, 2012- 8:17.88, 2013- 8:18.78, 2014- 8:10.44, 2015- 27:40.64, 8:11.64; 2016- 27:11.23. pbs: 1500m 3:39.27 '10, 3000m 7:39.63 '14, 5000m 13:11.99 '09, HMar 62:07 '17, 2000mSt 5:37.30 '07.

David Lekuta **RUDISHA** b. 17 Dec 1988 Kilgoris 1.89m 73kg. Masai.
At 800m: OG: '12- 1, '16- 1; WCh: '09- sf, '11- 1, '15- 1; CG: '14- 2; WJ: '06- 1/4R; AfCh: '08- 1, '10- 1; Af-J: '07- 1; CCp: '10- 1. Won DL 2010-11, WAF 2009, Kenyan 2009-11.
Three world 800m records 2010-12, four African records 2009-10., Commonwealth & African 600m record 2016.

Progress at 800m: 2006- 1:46.3A, 2007- 1:44.15, 2008- 1:43.72, 2009- 1:42.01, 2010- 1:41.01, 2011- 1:41.33, 2012- 1:40.91, 2013- 1:43.87, 2014- 1:42.98, 2015- 1:43.58, 2016- 1:42.15. pbs: 400m 45.50 '10, 45.2A '13; 600m 1:13.10 '16.
IAAF Male Athlete of the Year 2010, won 26 successive 800m finals 2009-11. His father Daniel won 4x400m silver medal at 1968 Olympics with 440y pb 45.5A '67.

Stephen Kiptoo **SAMBU** b. 3 Jul 1988 Eldoret 1.69m 55kg. Was at University of Arizona.
Progress at 10000m: 2009- 28:37.96, 2010- 29:01.34, 2011- 27:28.64, 2012- 28:06.16, 2014- 26:54.61, 2016- 26:58.25. pbs: 1500m 3:43.56 '12, 3000m 7:51.59i/8:13.69 '12, 5000m 13:13.74i '12, 13:21.14 '16; 10M Rd 43:20 '15, HMar 60:41 '13, Mar 2:13:35 '16.

William Malel **SITONIK** b. 1 Mar 1994 1.65m 52kg. Honda, Japan.
At 3000m: WY: '11- 1. At 5000m: WJ: '12- 3.
Progress at 10000m: 2012- 29:29.3A, 2013- 27:48.55, 2014- 27:25.56, 2015- 27:22.12, 2016- 26:54.66. pbs: 2000m 5:07.51 '11, 3000m 7:40.10 '11 '10, 5000m 13:19.83 '13.

Edwin Cheruiyot **SOI** b. 3 Mar 1986 Kericho 1.72m 55kg.
At 5000m: OG: '08- 3, '12- h; WCh: '13- 5, '15- 10; AfCh: '10- 1; CCp: '10- 4. At 3000m: WI: '08- 4, '12- 3; won WAF 3000m 2007, 5000m 2007-08. World CC: '06- 8 4k, '07- 9.
Progress at 5000m, 10000m: 2002- 29:06.5A, 2004- 13:22.57, 2005- 13:10.78, 2006- 12:52.40, 27:14.83; 2007- 13:10.21, 2008- 13:06.22, 2009- 12:55.03, 2010- 12:58.91, 2011- 12:59.15, 2012- 12:55.99, 2013- 12:51.34, 26:49.41; 2014- 12:59.82, 2015- 13:11.97, 2016- 13:03.26. pbs: 1500m 3:40.52 '13, 2000m 5:01.4+ '10, 3000m 7:27.55 '11, 2M 8:14.10 '11, 10k Rd 28:13 '08.

Paul Kipngetich **TANUI** b. 22 Dec 1990 Chesubeno village, Moio district 1.72m 54kg. Kyudenko Corporation, Japan.
At 10000m: OG: '16- 2; WCh: '11- 9, '13- 3, '15- 3. World CC: '09-10-11: 4J/8/2. Won Kenyan CC 2010.
Progress at 5000m, 10000m: 2008- 13:59.2A, 2009- 13:37.15, 27:25.24; 2010- 13:14.87, 27:17.61; 2011- 13:04.65, 26:50.63; 2012- 13:19.18, 27:27.56; 2013- 13:16.57, 27:21.50; 2014- 13:00.53, 26:49.41; 2015- 12:58.69, 26:51.86; 2016- 13:15.22, 27:05.64. pbs: 1500m 3:43.97 '10, 3000m 7:46.61 '16, HMar 62:48 '14.

Hillary Kipsang **YEGO** b. 2 Apr 1992 1.78m 60kg.
At 2000mSt: WY: '09- 1.
Progress at 3000mSt: 2009- 8:46.8A, 2010- 8:19.50, 2011- 8:07.71, 2012- 8:11.83, 2013- 8:03:57, 2014- 8:09.07, 2015- 8:13.10, 2016- 8:15.10. pbs: 1500m 3:43.3 '10, 3000m 7:53.18 '10, 5000m 13:53.82 '16, 2000mSt 5:25.33 '09.

Julius Kiplangat **YEGO** b. 4 Jan 1989 Cheptonon, Nandi district 1.75m 90kg.

KENYA   175

At JT: OG: '12- 11, '16- 2; WCh: '13- 4, '15- 1; CG: '10- 7, '14- 1; AfG: '11- 1; AfCh: '10-12-14: 3/1/1; CCp: '14- 4. Kenyan champion 2008-14.
Javelin records: Commonwealth & two African 2015, nine Kenyan 2011-15.
Progress at JT: 2008- 72.18A, 2009- 74.00A, 2010- 75.44, 2011- 78.34A, 2012- 81.81; 2013- 85.40, 2014- 84.72, 2015- 92.72, 2016- 88.24.
His winning throw at the 2015 Worlds was the world's best javelin throw since 2001.

Solomon Kirwa **YEGO** b. 10 May 1987 1.75m 58kg.
Af CC: 14- 4.
Progress at HMar: 2011- 64:40, 2012- 61:34, 2013- 61:56, 2014- 61:59, 2015- 60:04, 2016- 58:44, 2017- 59:50. pbs: 5000m 14:14.54 '12, 10000m 28:23.0A '15, Mar 2:08:31 '16.

Women

Alice APROT Nawowuna b. 2 Jan 1994 1.74m 55kg. Turkana.
At (5000m)/10000m: OG: '16- 4; WJ: '10- (3); AfG: '15- 3/1; AfCh: '16- 1. World CC: '10- 9J, '17- 2; AfCC: 14- 3. Won African & Kenyan CC 2016.
Progress at 5000m, 10000m: 2010- 15:16.74, 2011- 16:36.8A, 2014- 16:22.8A, 2015- 15:31.82, 31:24.18; 2016- 14:39.56, 29:53.51. pbs: 1500m 4:23.92 '14, 3000m 8:44.7 '16. 10M 51:59 '16.
Elder brother Joseph Ebuya won World CC in 2010, pb 5000m 12:51.00 '07.

Joyce CHEPKIRUI b. 20 Aug 1988 Bureti 1.52m 48kg.
At 10000m: OG: '12- dnf; CG: '14- 1; AfCh: '14- 1. At 5000m: CCp: '14- 2. At 1500m: AfG: '11- 2; Af-J: '07- 5. At HMar: WCh: '10- 5. AfCC: '12- 1. Won Kenyan CC 2012, 10000m 2015.
Progress at 10000m, HMar, Mar: 2007- 75:11, 2009- 71:47, 2010- 69:25, 2011- 31:26.10, 69:04; 2012- 32:34.71A, 67:03; 2013- 68:15, 2:35:54; 2014- 32:09.35, 66:19, 2:30:23; 2015- 32:08.00A, 68:42, 2:24:11; 2016- 67:41, 2:29:08. pbs: 1500m 4:08.80A '11, 5000m 15:58.31 '14, 3000mSt 10:26.7A '08; Road: 10k 30:37 '11, 15k 46:49 '14, 10M 51:30 '15, 20k 62:55 '14.
Won Honolulu Marathon 2014-15, Amsterdam 2015; 3rd Boston 2016. Married Erick Kibet, pb HMar 61:10 '10, in 2009.

Beatrice CHEPKOECH b. 6 Jul 1991 1.71m 57kg.
At 3000mSt: OG: '16- 4. At 1500m: AfG: '15- 3. World CC: '17- 1 MxR.
Progress at 1500m, 3000mSt: 2011- 10:41.3A, 2013- 4:16.6A, 2014- 4:12.37A, 2015- 4:03.28, 2016- 4:18.0A, 9:10.86. pbs: 800m 2:05.73 '15, 1500m 4:03.28 '15, 2000mSt 6:02.47 '15.

Lydia Tum **CHEPKURUI** b. 23 Aug 1984 1.70m 52kg.
At 3000mSt: WCh: '13- 2; AfG: '11- 4, Kenyan champion 2013.
Progress at 3000mSt: 2011- 9:30.73, 2012- 9:14.98,

2013- 9:12.55, 2014- 9:24.07, 2015- 9:20.44, 2016- 9:22.81. pbs: 1500m 4:14.97 '12, 3000m 8:55.21i '14, 2M 9:45.97i '14.

Irene Chebet **CHEPTAI** b. 4 Feb 1992 1.60m 45kg.
At 5000m: WCh: '15- 7. At 3000m: WY: '07- 7. World CC: '08-13-15-17: 2J/10/7/1. Won KEN CC 2017.
Progress at 5000m: 2012- 16:02.0A, 2013- 14:50.99, 2014- 15:17.76, 2015- 14:53.32, 2016- 14:43.42. pbs: 1500m 4:13.75 '14, 3000m 8:48.03 '15, 10k rd 31:45A '14.

Gladys Kiprono **CHERONO** b. 12 May 1983 Kericho 1.66m 50kg.
At 10000m: WCh: '13- 2; AfCh: '12- 1 (1 5000m). World HMar: '14- 1. Won Kenyan 5000m 2012.
Progress at 5000m, 10000m, Mar: 2005- 16:16.8A, 2007- 16:03.8A, 2008- 15:56.0A, 2012- 15:39.5A, 32:41.40; 2013- 14:47.12, 30:29.23; 2014- 16:49.8A, 34:13.0A; 2015- 15:50.3A, 32:24.10A, 2:19:25. pbs: 1500m 4:25.13 '04, 3000m 8:34.05 '13, Road: 15k 47:43 '13, 20k 63:26 '13, HMar 66:07 '16.
Second Dubai Marathon (2:20:03, third fastest ever debut) and won Berlin in 2015. Married to Joseph Bwambok (62:25 HMar 2010).

Mercy CHERONO b. 7 May 1991 Kericho 1.68m 54kg.
At (3000m)/5000m: OG: '16- 4; WCh: '11- 5, '13- 2, '15- 5; CG: '14- 1; AfCh: '14- 5; WJ: '08- (1), '10- 1/2; WY: '07- (1); Af-J: '09- 1/2; won DL 2014, KEN 5000m 2014. World CC: '07-09-10: 23J/2J/1J. Won Afr CC 2011.
Two world 4x1500m records 2014. Commonwealth 2M best 2014.
Progress at 1500m, 5000m: 2007- 16:49.13A, 2009- 4:13.70, 15:46.74A; 2010- 14:47.13, 2011- 4:02.31, 14:35.13; 2012- 4:06.42, 14:47.18; 2013- 4:05.82, 14:40.33; 2014- 4:08.57, 14:43.11; 2015- 4:01.26, 14:34.10; 2016- 14:33.95. pbs: 800m 2:05.7A '13, 1M 4:22.67 '15, 2000m 5:35.65 '10, 3000m 8:21.14 '14, 2M 9:11.49 '14, 10000m 34:33.4A '06, 3000mSt 10:41.4A '13.

Vivian Jepkemoi **CHERUIYOT** b. 11 Sep 1983 Keiyo 1.55m 38kg.
At 5000m (/10000m): OG: '04- 14, '08- 4, '12- 2/3, '16- 1/2; WCh: '07- 2, '09- 1, '11- 1/1, '15- (1); CG: '10- 1; WJ: '02- 3; AfG '99- 3; AfCh: '10- 1; Af-J: '01- 1; CCp: '10- 1; won DL 2010-12. At 3000m: WY: '99- 3; WI: '10- 2. World CC: '98-9-00-01-02-04-06-07-11: 5J/2J/1J/4J/3J/8 4k/8 4k/8/1. Won KEN 1500m 2009, 5000m 2010-11, 10000m 2011-12.
African 2000m record 2009, Commonwealth 5000m 2009 & 2011, 10000m 2016, indoor 3000m (8:30.53) 2009; Kenyan 5000m 2007 & 2011, 10000m 2016.
Progress at 5000m, 10000m: 1999- 15:42.79A, 2000- 15:11.11, 2001- 15:59.4A, 2002- 15:49.7A, 2003- 15:44.8A, 2004- 15:13.26, 2006- 14:47.43, 2007- 14:22.51, 2008- 14:25.43, 2009- 14:37.01,

176 KENYA

2010- 14:27.41, 2011- 14:20.87, 30:48.98; 2012- 14:35.62, 30:30.44; 2015- 14:46.69, 31:13.29; 2016- 14:26.17, 29:32.53. pbs: 1500m 4:06.6A '12, 4:06.65 '07; 2000m 5:31.52 '09, 3000m 8:28.66 '07, 2M 9:12.35i '10, 10M Rd 51:17 '15, HMar 67:54 '16.
Laureus Sportswomen of the Year for 2011. Married Moses Kirui on 14 Apr 2012; son Allan born 19 Oct 2013. Won Great North Run on half marathon debut 2016.

Flomena Daniel **CHEYECH** b. 5 Jul 1982 West Pokot 1.68m 49kg.
At Mar: CG: '14- 1. World HMar: 09- 8; CC: 99- 10J.
Progress at Mar: 2006- 2:42:15A, 2012- 2:34:13, 2013- 2:24:34, 2014- 2:22:44, 2015- 2:24:38, 2016- 2:23:18. pbs: 3000m 9:16.21 '07, 5000m 15:19.47 '09, 10000m 31:58.50 '08, road: 15k 48:26 '13, HMar 67:39 '13, 30k 1:40:33 '14.
Marathon wins: Porto Alegre 2012, Vienna & Toronto 2013, Paris 2014, Saitama 2016; 2nd Amsterdam 2015.

Irene JELAGAT b. 10 Dec 1988 Samutet, Nyanza 1.62m 45kg.
At 1500m: OG: '08- h; WCh: '09- h; CG: '10- 6; AfG: '11- 1; AfCh: '08- 5, '10- 4; WJ: '06- 1; WY: '05- dns; WI: '10- 5. At 3000m: WI: 14- 4.
Two world 4x1500m records 2014.
Progress at 1500m: 2005- 4:21.3A, 2006- 4:08.88, 2007- 4:10.27, 2008- 4:04.59, 2009- 4:03.62, 2010- 4:03.76, 2011- 4:02.59, 2014- 4:04.07, 2015- 4:07.75. pb 800m 2:02.99 '06, 2000m 5:46.4 '14, 3000m 8:28.51 '14, 2M 9:12.90 '14, 5000m 14:55.49 '15.

Peres JEPCHIRCHIR b. 27 Sep 1993 Usain Gishu 1.53m 40kg.
World HMar: '16- 1.
World records 20k and half marathon 2017.
Progress at HMar: 2014- 69:12, 2015- 67:17, 2016- 66:39, 2017- 65:06. pbs: Road: 10k 30:55 '15, 15k 46:32 '17, 20k 61:40 '17, Mar 2:47:33A '13.
7 wins in 8 half marathons 2014-17, inc. RAK 2017.

Violah JEPCHUMBA b. 23 Oct 1990 1.72m 52kg.
Progress at HMar: 2014- 73:20, 2015- 69:30, 2016- 65:51, 2017- 65:22. pbs: Road: 10k 30:05 '17, 15k 45:40 '17, 20k 61:50 '17.

Hyvin Kiyeng **JEPKEMOI** b. 13 Jan 1992 1.56m 45kg.
At 3000mSt: OG: '16- 2; WCh: '13- 6, '15- 1; AfG: '11- 1 (4 5000m); AfCh: '12- 3. Kenyan champion 2015. World CC: '17- 4.
African and Commonwealth 3000m steeplechase record 2016.
Progress at 3000mSt: 2011- 10:00.50, 2012- 9:23.53, 2013- 9:22.05, 2014- 9:22.58, 2015- 9:10.15, 2016- 9:00.01. pbs: 1500m 4:19.44 '11, 3000m 9:07.51 '11, 5000m 15:42.64 '11, 10000m 35:14.0A '14.

Joyciline JEPKOSGEI b. 8 Dec 1993 Nandi 1.56m 52kg.
World road records in Prague Half Marathon

2017: 10k 30:04, 15k 45:37, 20k 1:01:25, HMar 1:04.52.
Progress at HMar: 2015- 74:06A, 2016- 69:07, 2017- 64:52. pbs: 5000m 15:40.0A '16, 10000m 31:28.38 '16, Road: 10k 30:05 '17, 15k 45:40 '17, 20k 61:50 '17.
Married to Nicholas Koech (10k Rd 28:39 '07), son Brandon born 2011.

Priscah JEPTOO Chepsisor b. 26 Jun 1984 Chemnoet Village, Nandi 1.65m 49kg.
At Mar: OG: '12- 2; WCh: '11- 2. At 10000m: AfG: '99- 5. At 5000m: WJ: '00- 3. Won KEN CC 2014.
Progress at Mar: 2009- 2:30:40, 2010- 2:27:02, 2011- 2:22:55, 2012- 2:20:14, 2013- 2:20:15, 2015- 2:25:01, 2016- 2:25:57. pbs: 3000m 9:05.7 '13, road: 10k 31:18 '13, 15k 46:59 '14, 10M 50:38 '13, 20k 62:32 '13, HMar 65:45 '13.
Marathon wins: Porto 2009, Turin 2010, Paris 2011, London 2013 (3rd 2012), New York 2013. World Marathon Majors winner 2012/13. Won Great North Run 2013. Married to Douglas Chepsiro, son born 20 Feb 2009.

Lucy Wangui KABUU b. 24 Mar 1984 Ichamara, Nyeri region 1.55m 41kg. Suzuki, Japan.
At (5000m)/10000m: OG: '04- 9, '08- 6; CG: '06- 3/1; AfCh: '08- 4. At Mar: WCh: '13- 24. World 4k CC: '05- 5; HMar: '14- 4. Won KEN 10000m 2013.
Progress at 5000m, 10000m, HMar, Mar: 2001- 15:45.04, 2002- 15:33.03, 32:54.70; 2003- 15:10.23, 31:06.20; 2004- 14:47.09, 31:05.90, 69:47; 2005- 15:00.20, 31:22.37; 2006- 14:56.09, 31:29.66; 2007- 14:57.55, 31:32.52; 2008- 14:33.49, 30:39.96; 2009- 16:50.3A, 2011- 67:04, 2012- 2:19:34, 2013- 32:44.1A, 66:09, 2:24:06; 2014- 32:50.37A, 68:37, 2:24:16; 2015- 68:51, 2:20:21. pbs: 1500m 4:08.6A '12, 3000m 8:46.15 '08. Road 15k 47:13+ 13, 20k 62:48 '13, 25k 1:21:37 '13.
At the marathon set the pace in Osaka 2007, but at her first proper try was 2nd in 2:19:34 at Dubai 2012. 3rd Chicago 2012, Tokyo 2014, Dubai 2015. Won Great North Run 2011, RAK half marathon 2013.

Mary Jepkosgei **KEITANY** b. 18 Jan 1982 Kisok, Kabarnet 1.58m 45kg.
At Mar: OG: '12- 4. World HMar: '07- 2, '09- 1.
Records: World 25km 2010, 10M, 20km, half marathon 2011. African and two Kenyan half marathon 2009. Kenyan marathon 2012.
Progress at HMar, Mar: 2000- 72:53, 2002- 73:01, 2003- 73:25, 2004- 71:32, 2005- 70:18, 2006- 69:06, 2007- 66:48, 2009- 66:36, 2010- 67:14, 2:29:01; 2011- 65:50, 2:19:19; 2012- 66:49, 2:18:37; 2014- 65:39, 2:25:07; 2015- 66:02, 2:23:40; 2016- 68:53, 2:24:26; 2017- 65:13. pbs: 1500m 4:24.33 '99, 10000m 32:18.07 '07; Road: 5k 15:25 '11, 10k 30:45 '11, 15k 46:40 '11, 10M 50:05 '11, 20k 62:36 '11, 25k 1:19:53 '10.
15 wins in 17 half marathons 2006-17 (13 successive wins 2009-16) inc. Great North Run 2014-15, RAK 2011-12, 2015. Marathons: won

London 2011-12 (2nd 2015), New York 2014-16 (3rd 2010-11). Won World Marathon Majors 2011/12 & 2015/16. Married to Charles Koech (pbs 10k 27:56 & HMar 61:27 '07), son Jared born in June 2008 and daughter Samantha on 5 Apr 2013.

Viola Jelagat **KIBIWOT** b. 22 Dec 1983 Keiyo 1.67m 50kg.
At 1500m: OG: '08- h; WCh: '07- 5, '09/11- sf; CG: '06- 7, '10- 7; WJ: '02- 1. At 5000m: OG: '12- 6; WCh: '13- 4, '15- 4. World CC: '00-01-02-13: 3J/1J/1J/7; AfCC: '11-2.
Progress at 1500m, 5000m: 2003- 15:32.87, 2004- 4:06.64, 2006- 4:08.74, 2007- 4:02.10, 2008- 4:04.17, 14:51.59; 2009- 4:02.70, 2010- 4:03.39, 14:48.57; 2011- 4:05.51, 14:34.86; 2012- 3:59.25, 14:39.53; 2013- 4:00.76, 14:33.48; 2014- 4:00.46, 14:33.73; 2015- 4:01.41, 14:34.22. pbs: 800m 2:04.7A '12, 1M 4:24.31 '15, 2000m 5:38.2+ '14, 3000m 8:24.41 '14, 2M 9:12.59 '14, 10k Rd 31:14 '16, HMar 72:18 '14.

Valentine KIPKETER Jepkorir b. 5 Jan 1993 1.50m 40kg.
At Mar: WCh: '13- dnf.
Progress at Mar: 2012- 2:28:02, 2013- 2:23:02, 2016- 2:23:41. Pbs: 3000m 9:17.12 '10, 5000m 16:22.83 '10, Road: 10k 33:07 '11, HMar 68:21 '11.
Won Mumbai and Amsterdam marathons 2013, 3rd Chicago 2016.

Edna Ngeringwony **KIPLAGAT** b. 15 Nov 1979 Eldoret 1.71m 54kg. Corporal in Kenyan Police.
At Mar: OG: '12- 19; WCh: '11- 1, '13- 1, '15- 5. At 3000m: WJ: '96- 2, '98- 3. World CC: '96-97-06: 5J/4J/13.
African record 30km 2008.
Progress at Mar: 2005- 2:50:20, 2010- 2:25:38, 2011- 2:20:46, 2012- 2:19:50, 2013- 2:21:32, 2014- 2:20:21, 2015- 2:27:16, 2016- 2:22:36. pbs: 3000m 8:53.06 '96, 5000m 15:57.3A '06, 10000m 33:27.0A '07; Road: 5k 15:20 '10, 10k 31:06 '16, 15k 47:57 '10, 10M 54:56 '09, HMar 67:41 '12, 30k 1:39:11 '14.
Won Los Angeles and New York Marathons 2010, London 2014 (2nd 2011-13); 2nd Chicago & 3rd Tokyo 2016. Won World Marathon Majors 2010/11 & 2013/14. Married to Gilbert Koech (10000m 27:55.30 '01, 10k 27:32 '01, Mar 2:13:45 dh '05, 2:14:39 '09); two children.

Florence Jebet **KIPLAGAT** b. 27 Feb 1987 Kapkitony, Keiyo district 1.55m 42kg.
At 5000m: WJ: '06- 2. At 10000m: WCh: '09- 11; CG: '14- 2. World CC: '07- 5, '09- 1; HMar: '10- 1.
Won Kenyan 1500m 2007, 10000m 2014, CC 2007 & 2009.
World records 20k and half marathon 2014 & 2015, 15k 2015.. Kenyan 10000m record 2009.
Progress at 5000m, 10000m, HMar, Mar: 2006- 15:32.34, 2007- 14:40.74, 31:06.20; 2009- 14:40.14, 30:11.53; 2010- 14:52.64, 32:46.99A, 67:40; 2011- 2:19:44; 2012- 30:24.85, 66:38, 2:20:57; 2013- 67:13, 2:21:13; 2014- 31:48.6A, 65:12, 2:20:24; 2015- 65:09, 2:23:33; 2016- 69:19, 2:21:32. pbs: 1500m

4:09.0A '07, 3000m 8:40.72 '10, Road: 15k 46:14 '15, 20k 61:54 '15, 30k 1:39:11 '14.
Won half marathon debut in Lille in 2010, followed a month later by World title. Did not finish in Boston on marathon debut in 2011; won Berlin 2011 and 2013; Chicago 2015-16 (2nd 2014), 2nd London 2014 (3rd 2016). Formerly married to Moses Mosop, daughters Faith and Aisha Chelagat (born April 2008). Niece of William Kiplagat (Mar 2:06:50 '99, 8 WCh '07).

Helah KIPROP Jelagat b. 7 Apr 1985 Keiyo district 1.64m 48kg.
At Mar: OG: '16- dnf; WCh: '15- 2.
Progress at Mar: 2013- 2:28:02, 2014- 2:27:14, 2015- 2:24:03, 2016- 2:21:27. Pbs: 1500m 4:19.14 '07, 3000m 9:21.02 '06, 5000m 15:33.90 '07, 10000m 33:03.8A '09, 3000mSt 10:25.6A '09, Road: 10k 31:44 '12, 15k 47:32 '13, 20k 64:10 '13, HMar 67:39 '13.
Won Seoul marathon 2014, Tokyo 2016 (2nd 2015). Baby born 2008.

Faith Chepngetich **KIPYEGON** b. 10 Jan 1994 Bornet 1.57m 42kg.
At 1500m: OG: '12- h, '16- 1; WCh: '13- 5, '15- 2; CG: '14- 1; AfCh: '14- 5; WJ: '12- 1; WY: '11- 1. World CC: '10-11-13-17: 4J/1J/1J/6; AfCC: '12- 1J, '14- 1.
Records: World 4x1500m 2014, African junior 1500m 2013, African & Commonwealth 1M 2015, Kenyan & Commonwealth 1500m (3) 2013-16.
Progress at 1500m, 5000m: 2010- 4:17.1A, 2011- 4:09.48, 2012- 4:03.82, 2013- 3:56.98, 2014- 3:58.01, 2015- 3:59.32, 14:31.95; 2016- 3:56.41. pbs: 800m 1:58.02 '15, 1M 4:16.71 '15, 2000m 5:37.8+ '14, 3000m 8:23.55 '14.
Older sister Beatrice Mutai (b. 19 Apr 1987) 11 World CC 2013, HMar 69:30 '14.

Purity Cherotich **KIRUI** b. 13 Aug 1991 Kericho 1.62m 47kg.
At 3000mSt: CG: '14- 1; AfG: '15- 3; AfCh: '14- 6; WJ: '10- 1; Kenyan champion 2014-15.
Progress at 3000mSt: 2008- 10:27.19A, 2009- 10:05.1A, 2010- 9:36.34, 2011- 9:37.85, 2012- 9:35.61, 2013- 9:19.42, 2014- 9:23.43, 2015- 9:17.74, 2016- 9:22.47. pbs: 800m 2:07.6A '14, 1500m 4:31.83 '08, 5000m 16:13.42 '11.

Janet KISA b. 5 Mar 1992 near Mount Elgon 1.60m 48kg.
At 3000m: CCp: '14- 4. At 5000m: WCh: '15- 6; CG: '14- 2; AfCh: '14- 3; Af-J: '11- 2. World CC: '11-13-15: 5J/6/12; AfCC: '14- 2.
Progress at 5000m: 2010- 16:02.2A, 2011- 15:24.75, 2012- 14:57.68, 2013- 15:05.89, 2014- 14:52.59, 2015- 15:02.68, 2016- 14:38.70. pbs: 1500m 4:14.77 '11, 2000m 5:41.4+ '16, 3000m 8:28.33 '16, 10k Rd 33:55 '13, HMar 71:01 '14.

Cynthia Jerotich **LIMO** b. 18 Dec 1989 1.67m 52kg.
World HMar: '16- 2.
Progress at HMar: 2010- 73:19, 2011- 70:39, 2012-

70:06, 2013- 69:59, 2014- 68:24, 2015- 67:02, 2016- 66:04. pbs: Road: 1000m 32:25.18A '16, 10k 31:07 '15, 15k 47:11 '15, 20k 62:48 '16.
Won RAK Half marathon 2016.

Virginia NYAMBURA b. 20 Jul 1993 1.65m 48kg.
At 3000mSt: WCh: '15- 7; won DL 2015. 2000mSt: Yth OG: '10- 1.
World best 2000m steeplechase 2015.
Progress at 3000mSt: 2008- 10:27.46A, 2009- 10:13.6A, 2010- 10:28.19A, 2013- 9:58.08, 2014- 10:02.18, 2015- 9:13.85, 2016- 9:18.95. pbs: 1500m 4:10.0A '15, 2000m 6:05.45 '13, 5000m 16:38.6A '13, 2000mSt 6:02.16 '15.
Took 36.57 secs off pb at Doha 2015 after being the pacemaker and continuing to win.

Hellen Onsando **OBIRI** b. 13 Dec 1989 Nyangusu, Kisii 1.55m 45kg.
At 1500m: OG: '12- 8; WCh: '11- 10 (fell), '13- 3; CG: '14- 6; AfCh: '14- 1; CCp: '14- 4. At 3000m: WI: '12- 1, '14- 2. At 5000m: OG: '16- 2. Won Kenyan 1500m 2011-14.
Two world 4x1500m records 2014. African & Commonwealth 3000m record 2014.
Progress at 1500m, 5000m: 2011- 4:02.42, 2012- 3:59.68, 16:15.1A, 2013- 3:58.58, 15:49.7A; 2014- 3:57.05, 2016- 3:59.34, 14:25.78. pbs: 800m 2:00.54 '11, 1000m 2:46.00i '12, 2000m 5:37.7+ '14, 3000m 8:20.68 '14.
Daughter born in May 2015.

Betsy SAINA b. 30 Jun 1988 Sokosik, Nandi 1.63m 48kg. Bowerman TC, USA. Graduate of Iowa State University, USA
At 10000m: OG: '16- 5; WCh: '15- 8; AfCh: '12- 3. At 3000m: WI: '16- 7. Won NCAA indoor 5000m & CC 2012, 10000m 2013.
Progress at 5000m, 10000m: 2009- 16:15.74, 36:34.94; 2010- 16:10.69, 33:13.13; 2011- 15:50.74i/16:06.05, 33:13.87; 2012- 15:36.09i, 31:15.97; 2013- 15:12.05, 31:37.22; 2014- 14:39.49, 30:57.30; 2015- 15:00.48, 31:51.35; 2016- 14:44.67, 30:07.78. pbs: 1M 4:40.98i '13, 2000m 5:45.7 '14, 3000m 8:38.01 '14, 2M 9:16.95 '14, Rd 10k 30:46 '14, 10M 51:55 '14, HMar 69:27 '14.

Eunice Jepkoech **SUM** b. 2 Sep 1988 Burnt Forest, Uasin Gishu 1.72m 53kg. Police.
At 800m: OG: '16- sf; WCh: '11- sf, '13- 1, '15- 3; CG: '14- 1; AfCh: '10- h,'12- 2, '14- 1; CCp: '14- 1; won DL 2013-15. At 1500m: OG: '12- h, Won Kenyan 800m 2012, 2014.
World 4x1500m record 2014, Commonwealth & African 4x800m 2014..
Progress at 800m, 1500m: 2009- 2:07.4A, 2010- 2:00.28, 2011- 1:59.66A, 4:12.41; 2012- 1:59.13, 4:04.26; 2013- 1:57.38, 4:02.05; 2014- 1:57.92, 4:01.54; 2015- 1:56.99, 4:09.7A; 2016- 1:57.47. pb 3000m 8:53.12 '12.
Daughter Diana Cheruto born in 2008.

Jemima SUMGONG Jelagat b. 21 Dec 1984 Eldoret 1.61m 47kg.
At Mar: OG: '16- 1; WCh: '15- 4.
Progress at Mar: 2006- 2:35:22, 2007- 2:29:41, 2008- 2:30:18, 2010- 2:32:34, 2011- 2:28:32, 2012- 2:31:52, 2013- 2:20:48, 2014- 2:20:41dh/2:25:10, 2015- 2:24:23, 2016- 2:22:58. pbs: 1500m 4:26.95 '15, 5000m 16:51.0A '13, 10000m 33:08.0A '13, Road: 10k 31:15 '06, 15k 47:14 '13, 10M 50:38 '13, 20k 62:32 '13, HMar 66:43 '17, 30k 1:39:20dh '14.
Marathon wins: Las Vegas 2006, Castellón 2011, Rotterdam 2013. London 2016; 2nd Boston 2012, Chicago 2013 & New York 2014, 3rd Boston 2014. Married Noah Talam (Mar pb 2:14:54 '09) in 2009, daughter born in 2011. Originally given a 2-year ban in 2012, but later cleared by the IAAF.

Agnes Jebet **TIROP** b. 23 Oct 1995 Nandi, Chesumei 1.59m 44kg.
At 5000m: WJ: '12- 3, '14- 3; World CC: '13-15-17: 2J/1/5; AfCC: '12- 2J, '14- 1J.
Progress at 5000m: 2011- 16:09.0A, 2012- 15:36.74, 2013- 14:50.36, 2014- 15:00.19, 2016- 15:02.67. pbs: 1500m 4:12.68 '13, 2000m 5:48.65 '13, 3000m 8:39.13 '13, 10000m 32:55.41 '15, 3000mSt 10:27.4A '12.

Mercy WACERA Ngugi b. 17 Dec 1988 1.55m.
World HMar: '14- 2, '16- 3. At 5000m: WJ: '06- 3; Af-J: 07- 1.
Progress at HMar: 2012- 70:54, 2013- 70:32, 2014- 67:44, 2015- 70:21, 2016- 66:29. pbs: 1500m 4:24.4A '08, 3000m 8:55.89 '09, 5000m 15:20.30 '09, Road: 10k 31:28 '12, 15k 48:49 '15.
Widow of Samuel Wanjiru (2008 Olympic marathon champion). Daughter born 2010.

Margaret WAMBUI Nyairera b. 15 Sep 1995 Endarasha 1.75m 66kg.
At 800m: OG: '16- 3; WCh: '15- h; WJ: '14- 1; WI: '16- 3. At 400m: AfCh: '16- 2/3R.
Progress at 800m: 2014- 2:00.49, 2015- 2:01.32, 2016- 1:56.89 pbs: 400m 51.39A/51.97 '16, 6000m 1:27.1 '16.

KOREA

Governing body: Korea Athletics Federation, 10 Chamshil Dong, Songpa-Gu, Seoul. Founded 1945. **National Champions 2016**: **Men**: 100m: Kim Kuk-young 10.36, 200m: Park Bong-ko 20.65, 400m: Kim Kwang-yeol 47.58, 800m: Lee Moo-young 1:52.28, 1500m: Lee Jung-kuk 3:51.70, 5000m/10000m: Baek Seung-Ho 14:22.51/30:34.26, Mar:, 3000mSt: Choi Dong-il 9:12.51, 110mh: Lee Jung-joon 13.86, 400mh: Han Se-hyun 51.30, HJ: Woo Sang-hyuk 2.23, PV: Han Do-hyun 5.50, LJ: Kim Duk-hyung 7.84, TJ: Kim Dong-hyun 16.46, SP: Jung Il-woo 18.29, DT: Lee Hyun-jae 55.10, HT: Lee Yun-chul 72.21, JT: Jung Sang-jin 72.21, Dec: Kang Ki-won 7054, 20kW: Kim Hyun-sub 1:24:01. **Women**: 100m/200m: Kang Da-seul 11.85/24.31, 400m: Kim Kyong-hwa 55.73, 800m/1500m: Shin So-mang 2:09.47/4:34.12, 5000m: Kim Do-youn

16:49.97, 10000m: Kim Sung-eun 34:51.10Mar:, 3000mSt: Jo Ha-rim 10:49.98, 100mh: Jung Hyelim 13.28, 400mh: Kim Kyong-hwa 59.90, HJ: Han Da-rye 1.79, PV: Lim Eun-ji 4.30, LJ: Kim Min-ji 5.98, TJ: Bae Chan-mi 13.23, SP: Lee Su-kyung 15.73, DT: Cho Hye-rim 51.29, HT: Park Syeo-jin 56.85, JT: Kim Kyong-ae 57.50, Hep: Jung Su-hye 5108, 20kW: Jeon Young-eun 1:35:10.
KIM Hyun-sub b. 31 May 1985 Sokcho 1.75m 53kg.
At 20kW: OG: '08- 23, '12- 17, '16- 17 (dnf 50kW); WCh: '07-09-11-13-15: 20/33/3/10/10; AsiG: '06-10-14: 2/3/3; WUG: '05-07-09: 2/6/5. Asian champion 2011, 2014, 2017 (2nd 2015); KOR 2005-06, 2008-13, 2016. At 10000m/10kW: WJ: '04- 3; WCp: '04- 8.
Five Korean 20km road walk records 2008-15. Progress at 20kW: 2004- 1:24:58, 2005- 1:22:15, 2006- 1:21:45, 2007- 1:20:54, 2008- 1:19:41, 2009- 1:22:00, 2010- 1:19:36, 2011- 1:19:31, 2012- 1:21:36, 2013- 1:21:22, 2014- 1:19:24, 2015- 1:19:13, 2016- 1:21:44. Pb 10000mW 39:30.56 '09, 38:13R '10; 50kW 4:01:06 '16.

LATVIA

Governing body: Latvian Athletic Association, 1 Augsiela Str, Riga LV-1009. Founded 1921.
National Championships first held in 1920 (men), 1922 (women). **2016 Champions: Men:** 100m/200m: Janis Mezitis 10.67/21.43, 400m: Valerijs Valinscikovs 48.45, 800m/1500m: Pauls Arents 1:53.08/3:52.59, 3000m/5000m: Reimis Hartmanis 8:25.91/14:31.56, HMar: Dmitrijs Serjogins 68:02, Mar: Anatolijs Macuks 2:28:31, 3000mSt: Kaspars Gulbis 9:43.24, 110mh: Kristaps Sietins 14.08, 400mh: Janis Baltuss 50.78, HJ: Janis Mucenieks 1.99, PV: Mareks Arents 5.55, LJ/TJ: Elvijs Misans 7.68/16.13, SP: Maris Urtans 16.09, DT: Oskars Vaisjuns 53.68, HT: Igors Sokolovs 75.44, JT: Zigismunds Sirmais 82.49, Dec: Ingus Zarins 6294, 10000mW: Arturs Makars 42:12.8. **Women**: 100m/200m: Sindija Buksa 11.85/24.27, 400m: Anna Paula Auzina 57.15, 800m: Elena Miezava 2:16.67. 1500m: Liga Jansone 4:58.31, 3000m/5000m/HMar: Jolanta Leipina 10:33.28/18:12.03/1:23:32, 10000m: Leide Neimana 38:49.2, Mar: Kristina Kuznecova 3:09:06, 3000mSt: Lina Sulgina 11:32.29, 100mh/Hep: Ilona Dramaconoka 14.49/4938, 400mh: Liga Velvere 57.47, HJ: Madara Onuzane 1.74, PV: Ildze Bortascenoka 3.75, LJ: Mara Griva 6.07, TJ: Madara Apine 13.12, SP: Linda Ozola 14.29, DT: Dace Steinerte 49.76, HT: Liene Rozina 39.90, JT: Gundega Griva 52.20, 10000mW: Agnese Pastare 48:06.8.
Zigismunds SIRMAIS b. 6 May 1992 Riga 1.90m 96kg. Riga Arkadija.
At JT: OG: '12- dnq, '16- dnq 14; WCh: '11: dnq 32; EC: '12- dnq 23, '16- 1; WJ: '10- 7; EU23: '13- 1; EJ: '11- 1; WUG: '15- 3. Latvian champion 2016.
Two world junior javelin records 2011.
Progress at JT: 2009- 65.03, 2010- 82.27, 2011- 84.69, 2012- 84.06, 2013- 82.77, 2014- 86.61, 2015- 79.37, 2016- 86.66.
Sister Katrina Sirma (b. 31 Mar 1994) JT 55.87 '14.

Women

Laura IKAUNIECE-ADMIDINA b. 31 May 1992 Jürmala 1.79m 60kg. Jürmalas SS.
At Hep: OG: '12- 7, '16- 4; WCh: '13- 11, '15- 3; EC: '12- 2, '14- 6; WJ: '10- 6; WY: '09- 2; EJ: '11- 3; WUG: '13- 1. At 100mh: EC: '16- h. Won LAT 100m 2012-13, 200m 2009, 2013; 100mh & HJ 2010.
Five Latvian heptathlon records 2012-16.
Progress at Hep: 2010- 5618, 2011- 6063, 2012- 6414, 2013- 6321, 2014- 6320, 2015- 6516, 2016- 6622. Pbs: 60m 7.58i '16, 100m 11.78 '16, 200m 23.64 '16, 800m 2:09.43 '16, 60mh 8.38i '14, 100mh 13.07 '16, HJ 1.85i '12, 1.84 '14; LJ 6.49i '16, 6.32 '15; SP 13.78 '16, JT 55.93 '16, Pen 4496i '14.
Won IAAF Challenge 2015. Her mother Vineta Ikauniece set Latvian records at 100m 11.34A '87, 200m 22.49A '87 and 400m 50.71 '88, and her father Aivars Ikaunieks had 110mh bests of 13.71A '87 and 13.4 '84. Married Rolands Admidins in 2014.
Madara PALAMEIKA b. 18 Jun 1987 Valdemarpils 1.85m 76kg. Ventspils.
At JT: OG: '12- 8, '16- 10; WCh: '09-13-15: dnq 27/27/13, '11- 11; EC: '10-12-14-16: 8/8/4/7; WJ: '06- dnq 16; EU23: '07- 3, '09- 1; EJ: '05- dnq 17. Won DL 2016, LAT 2009-11, 2014-15.
Three Latvian javelin records 2009-16.
Progress at JT: 2002- 42.31, 2003- 49.11, 2004- 51.50, 2005- 51.75, 2006- 54.19, 2007- 57.98, 2008- 53.45, 2009- 64.51, 2010- 62.02, 2011- 63.46, 2012- 62.74, 2013- 62.72, 2014- 66.15, 2015- 65.01, 2016- 66.18.

LITHUANIA

Governing body: Athletic Federation of Lithuania, Kareiviu 6, LT-09117 Vilnius. Founded 1921.
National Championships first held in 1921 (women 1922). **2016 Champions: Men:** 100m: Rytis Sakalauskas 10.29, 200m: Ugnius Savickas 21.52, 400m: Rokas Pacevicius 47.77, 800m: Benediktas Mickus 1:52.38, 1500m/5000m: Simas Bertasius 3:52.36/14:58.17, 10000m:, HMar:, Mar: Serhiy Marchuk 2:22:20, 3000mSt:, 110mh: Rapolas Saulius 14.13, 400mh: Rapolas Saulius 53.72, HJ: Adrijus Glebauskas 2.15, PV: , LJ: Marius Vadeikis 7.60, TJ: Paulius Svarauskas 15.25w, SP: Sarunas Banevicius 18.35, DT: Domantas Poska 62.47, HT: Lukas Simonavicius 61.28, JT: Edis Matusevicius 79.62, Dec: Alvydas Misius 7144, 20kW: Marius Ziukas 1:24:31 **Women**: 100m: Karolina Deliautaite 11.50w, 200m/400m: Eva Misiunaite 23.79/54.24, 800m:

LITHUANIA – LUXEMBOURG – MEXICO – MOLDOVA

Monika Elenska 2:06.50, 1500m/5000m: Milda Vilcinskaite 4:30.57/16:50.86, 10000m:, HMar:, Mar: Viktoriya Khapilina 2:37:44, 3000mSt:, 100mh: Sonata Tamosaityte 13.99, 400mh: Rūta Okulic-Kazarinaite 61.65, HJ: Airine Palsyte 1.90, PV:, LJ: Austra Skujyte 6.08w, TJ: Jolanta Versevkaite 13.47, SP: Giedre Kupstyte 16.03, DT: Zinaida Sendriute 60.00, HT: Aiste Ziginskaite 51.51, JT: Liveta Jasiunaite 57.06, Hep: Diana Prankute 5313, 20kW: Brigita Virbalyte-Dimsiene 1:31:34.

Women

Airine PALSYTE b. 13 Jul 1992 Vilnius 1.86m 62kg. COSMA. Vilnius University.
At HJ: OG: '12- 11, '16- 13=; WCh: '13- 12, '15- dnq 14=; WJ: '08- dnq 23, '10- 2; WY: '09- 4; EC: '10-12-14-16: dnq 18/9/13/2; EJ: '11- 2; EU23: '13- 2; WUG: '11- 2, '15- 1; WI: '16- 4; EI: '15- 4, '17- 1; Lithuanian champion 2010, 2012-16.
Three LTU high jump records 2011-14 and absolute records 2.00 & 2.01i 17.
Progress at HJ: 2003- 1.45, 2004- 1.40i, 2005- 1.60, 2006- 1.71, 2007- 1.70i/1.55, 2008- 1.80, 2009- 1.86i/1.83, 2010- 1.92, 2011- 1.96, 2012- 1.95, 2013- 1.95, 2014- 1.98, 2015- 1.98i/1.95, 2016- 1.97i/1.96, 2017- 2.01i. pb 200m 24.78 '12, TJ 12.70i '12.

Zinaida SENDRIUTE b. 20 Dec 1984 Klaisiai, Skuodas 1.88m 89kg. COSMA.
At DT: OG: '08- dnq 32, '12- 8, '16- 10; WCh: '09-11-13-15: dnq 31/12/9/dnq 13; EC: '06-10-12-14-16: dnq 17/5/dnq 17/6/13; EJ: '03- 7; EU23: '05- 6; WUG: '11- 2; Lithuanian champion 2003, 2005-08, 2010-16.
Progress at DT: 2000- 33.37, 2001- 40.55, 2002- 48.66, 2003- 50.62, 2004- 51.38, 2005- 55.25, 2006- 57.26, 2007- 56.74, 2008- 59.42, 2009- 60.21, 2010- 60.70, 2011- 62.49, 2012- 64.03, 2013- 65.97, 2014- 65.83, 2015- 61.37, 2016- 61.89. pbs: SP 14.15 '10, HT 33.19 '04.

LUXEMBOURG

Governing body: Fédération Luxembourgeoise d'Athlétisme, 3 Route d'Arlon, L-8009 Strassen, Luxembourg. Founded 1928.
2016 National Champions: Men: 100m: Olivier Boussong 11.14, 200m: Pol Bidaine 22.10, 400m: Vincent Karger 48.33, 800m: Christophe Bestgen 1:58.23, 1500m: Charles Grethen 3:53.16, 5000m: Bob Bertemes 14:57.16, Mar: Christian Molitor 2:37:00, 3000mSt: Luc Scheller 9:51.61, 110mh: Christopher Weber 16.52, HJ: Kevin Rutare 2.02, PV: Sebastien Hoffelt 4.80, LJ: Nils Liefgen 7.11, TJ: Ben Kiffer 13.07, SP/JT: Tom Reuter 12.78/66.48, DT: Sven Forster 52.47, HT: Gilles Lorang 48.07, Dec: Kevin Steffen 4647. Women: 100m/200m: Anais Bauer 12.22/25.08, 400m: Carole Hill 60.02. 800m/1500m: Vera Hoffmann 2:07.23/4:36.06, 3000m: Pascale Schmoetten-Steffen 10:29.84, Mar: Fabienne Gehlen 3:05:56, 3000mSt: Liz Weiler 11:34.92, 100m: Lara Merx 14.48, HJ: Cathy Zimmer 1.74, PV: Edna Semedo Monteiro 3.75, LJ: Laurence Jones 5.50, TJ: Nita Bokomba 11.37, SP: Isabeau Pleimling 11.08, DT: Noémie Pleimling 36.35.

MEXICO

Governing body: Federación Mexicana de Atletismo, Anillo Periférico y Av. del Conscripto, 11200 México D.F. Founded 1933.
National Champions 2016: Men: 100m/200m: José Carlos Herrera 10.22/20.46, 400m: Ivan Nuñez 46.79, 800m: Jesús López 1:46.57, 1500m: Fernando Martínez 3:44.94, 5000m: Fabián Guerrero 14:10.62, 10000m: Juan Carlos Romero 29:50.44, 3000mSt: Quetzalcóatl Delgado 8:58.77, 110mh: Genaro Rodríguez 13.84, 400mh: Alejandro Orozco 51.41, HJ: Edgar Rivera 2.29, PV: Victor Manuel Castillero 5.15, LJ: Luis Rivera 7.98w, TJ: Alberto Álvarez 16.83w, SP: Stephen Sáenz 18.73, DT: Mario Cota 61.16, HT: Diego del Real 72.99, JT: David Carreón 77.00, Dec: Felipe Ruiz 6923. **Women**: 100m: Iza Daniela Flores 11.63, 200m: Evelin Rivera 23.83, 400m: Paola Morán 52.78, 800m: Gabriela Medina 2:06.97, 1500m/3000mSt: Ana Narvaez 4:20.77/10:12.22, 5000m: Brenda Flores 16:24.75, 10000m: Marisol Romero 33:49.30, 100mh: Elizabeth López 13.40, 400mh: Zudikey Rodríguez 57.31, HJ: Ximena Esquivel 1.80, PV: Carmelita Correa 4.20, LJ: Ivonne Treviño 6.70, TJ: Ivonne Rangel 13.39, SP: María Fernanda Orozco 16.02, DT: Alma Pollorena 51.75, HT: Miranda Vázquez 54.76, JT: Abigail Gómez 55.66, Hep: Jessamyn Sauceda 5563/

Jorge **Horacio NAVA** b. 20 Jan 1982 Chihuahua 1.75m 62kg.
At 50kW: OG: '08- 6, '12- 13, '16- 13; WCh: '05-07-09-13: 9/9/18/32; PAm: '07-11-15: 2/1/3; CAG: '10- 1; WCp: '06-08-10-12: 7/5/2/9. At 20kW: WCh: '11- 16, '15- 28; CAG: '14- 1. At 10000mW: WY: '99- 5; PAm-J: '01- 1. Won MEX 20000mW 2013, 20kW 2014; PAmCp 50k 2015.
Progress at 50kW: 2005- 3:53:57, 2006- 3:48:22, 2007- 3:52:35, 2008- 3:45:21, 2009- 3:56:26, 2010- 3:54:16, 2011- 3:45:29, 2012- 3:46:59, 2013- 3:58:00, 2014- 3:42:51, 2015- 3:45:41, 2016- 3:47:44. pbs: 5000m 18:40.11 '09, 10000mW 40:33.52 '04, 20kW 1:22:04 '12.

Women

María Guadalupe 'Lupita' GONZÁLEZ Romero b. 9 Jan 1989 Mexico City 1.62m 48kg.
At 20kW: OG: '16- 2; PAm: '15- 1; WCp: '14- 16, '16- 1. Won CAC 10kW 2013, PAmCp 20k 2015. Tied first IAAF Race Walking Challenge 2016.
20k walk records 2014 & 2016, CAC 2016.
Progress at 20kW: 2013- 1:37:02, 2014- 1:28:48, 2015- 1:29:21, 2016- 1:26:17. pbs: 10kW 43:49 '15.

MOLDOVA

Governing Body: Federatia de Atletism din Republica Moldova. Founded 1991.

Zalina PETRIVSKAYA b. 5 Feb 1988 Vladikavkaz, North Osetia, Russia 1.74m 90kg. née Marghieva. AS-CSPLN.
At HT: OG: '08- dnq 35, '12- dq8, '16- 5; WCh: '09- dq dnq 26, '11- dq8, '15- 8; EC: '10- dq5, '12-dq8, '16- 5; WJ: '06- 4; WY: '05- 7; EU23: '09- 1; EJ: '07- 5; WUG: '11- dq1, '13- dq3. Won Balkan 2015-16, MDA 2016.
Nine Moldovan hammer records 2005-16 (and 3 disqualified).
Progress at HT: 2005- 61.80, 2006- 65.50, 2007-65.40, 2008- 70.22, 2009- 71.56, 2015- 73.97, 2016-74.21; DQ: 2010- 71.50, 2011- 72.93, 2012- 74.47, 2013- 74.28.
Drugs ban announced in 2013 with all results annulled from 2009 Worlds to 2013. Sister **Marina** (now **Nikisenko**) (b. 28 Jun 1986) HT: 72.53 '09, seven MDA records 2007-09, OG: '08-16: dnq/41/24; WCh: '09/11/15- dnq 32/17/25; EC: '10- 5, '12/16- dnq 14/14; received a 3-year drugs ban from 24 July 2012. Brother **Serghei** (b. 6 Nov 1992) four MDA HT recs to 78.72 '15, 2 EJ '11, 8 EC 16, 10 OG 16.

MOROCCO
Governing Body: Fédération Royale Marocaine d'Athlétisme, Complex Sportif Prince Moulay Abdellah, PO Box 1778 R/P, Rabat. Fd. 1957.
2016 National Champions: Men: 100m: Aziz Ouhadi 10.50, 200m: Brahim Raggui 21.71, 400m: Mohammed Laalou 47.28, 800m: Badr El Jalaoui 1:47.14, 1500m: Youness Essalhi 3:39.27, 5000m: El Mahjoub Dazza 13:45.26, 10000m: Mohamed Ziani 28:30.74, 3000mSt: Hamid Ezzine 8:23.34, 110mh: Mohamed Soughi 14.73, 400mh: Mohamed-Reda El Bilaoui 53.01, HJ: Zakaria Mejhour 2.00, PV: Issam Madani 4.40, LJ: Abderrahim Zahouani 7.30 TJ: Adil Gandou 15.87, SP: Frank Elemba 20.58, DT: El Bachir Mbarki 53.62, HT: Dreiss Barid 59.90, JT: Abdullah Charii 63.69, 20kW: Ali Daghiri 1:32:58. **Women**: 100m: Hajar Edaou 12.21, 200m: Khadija Ouardi 25.48, 400m/400mh: Hasna Grioui 56.09/60.03, 800m: Siham Hilali 2:05.57, 1500m: Fadwa Sidi Madane 4:25.41, 5000m: Amina Tahiri 16:23.90, 10000m: Kaltoum Bouaasayriya 34:20.77, 3000mSt: Sanae El Mansouri 10:35.97, 100mh: Houria Kabouchi 14.76, HJ: Hanane Sadik1.65, PV: Dinar Nasrine 3.60, LJ/TJ: Jihad Bakhchi 5.76/12.81, SP: Rachid Lakhal 12.25, DT: Amina Moudden 46.91, HT/JT: Soukana Zakkour 61.30/38.56.

Soufiane EL BAKKALI b. 7 Jan 1996 1.88m 70kg.
At 3000mSt: OG: '16- 4; WJ: '14- 4; AfCh: '14- 10. Progress at 3000mSt: 2013- 8:52.00, 2014- 8:32.66, 2015- 8:27.79, 2016- 8:14.35. pbs: 1500m 3:45.36 '15, 3000m 7:49.68 '16, 5000m 13:10.80i '17, 13:47.76 '14.

Abdelaati IGUIDER b. 25 Mar 1987 Errachidia 1.70m 52kg.
At 1500m(/5000m): OG: '08- 5, '12- 3/6, '16- 5; WCh: '07-09-11-13-15: h/11/5/sf/3; WJ: '04- 1, '06- 2; WI: '10-12-14: 2/1/3. At 3000m: WI: '16- 4.
Progress at 1500m, 5000m: 2004- 3:35.53, 2005-3:35.63, 2006- 3:32.68, 2007- 3:32.75, 2008- 3:31.88, 2009- 3:31.47, 2010- 3:34:25, 2011- 3:31.60, 2012-3:33.99, 13:09.17; 2013- 3:33.29, 2014- 3:29.83, 2015-3:28.79, 12:59.25; 2016- 3:31.40, 13:08.61. pbs: 800m 1:46.67 '15, 1000m 2:19.14 '07, 1M 3:49.09 '14, 2000m 4:59.20 '16, 3000m 7:30.09 '16.

Women
Malika AKKAOUI b. 25 Dec 1987 Zaida, Meknès-Tafilalet 1.60m 46kg.
At 800m/(1500m): OG: '12- sf, '16- h/sf; WCh: '11- (h), '13- sf, '15- sf/12; AfCh: '10-12-14-16: 3/3/6/2; WJ: '06- h. Won MAR 400m 2014, 800m 2007-08, MedG 800m 2013, Arab 800m 2015.
Progress at 800m: 2004- 2:09.2, 2005- 2:08.1, 2006- 2:06.29, 2007- 2:05.04, 2008- 2:04.25, 2009-2:02.10, 2010- 2:00.6, 2011- 1:59.75, 2012- 1:59.01i/ 1:59.54, 2013- 1:57.64, 2014- 2:00.58, 2015- 1:59.03, 2016- 1:59.93. pbs: 400m 53.19 '13, 1000m 2:39.86 '13, 1500m 4:04.49 '15.

Rabab ARRAFI b. 12 Jan 1991 1.67m 54kg. ASOAK.
At (800m)/1500m: OG: '16- h/12; WCh: '13- sf, '15- 4/9; AfCh: 12- 1, '14- 3, '16- 5/2; WI: '14- dq after finishing 3rd. At 3000m: WY: '07- 12. Won FrancG 2013.
Progress at 800m, 1500m: 2006- 24:21.59, 2011-2:09.24, 2012- 2:04.60, 4:05.80; 2013- 2:00.58, 4:05.22; 2014- 2:03.18i, 4:02.71; 2015- 1:58.55, 4:02.94; 2016- 2:01.49, 4:03.95. pbs: 1M 4:23.50 '15, 3000m 8:58.32i '13, 9:34.78 '07.

NETHERLANDS
Governing body: Koninklijke Nederlandse Atletiek Unie (KNAU), Postbus 60100, NL-6800 JC Arnhem. Founded 1901.
National Championships first held in 1910 (men), 1921 (women). **2016 Champions: Men**: 100m/200m: Churandy Martina 10.11/20.11, 400m: Leemarvin Bonevacia 46.29, 800m: Thijmen Kupers 1:45.25, 1500m: Mike Foppen 3:54.10, 5000m: Dennis Licht 14:08.13, 10000m/Mar: Khalid Choukoud 28:37.13/2:11:23, HMar: Abdi Nageeye 62:08, 3000mSt: Simon Grannetia 9:08.29, 110mh: Koen Smet 13.71, 400mh: Jesper Arts 51.18, HJ: Jan Peter Larsen 2.17, PV: Menno Vloon 5.05, LJ: Ignisious Gaiseh 7.63, TJ: Fabian Florant 16.28, SP: Patrick Cronie 18.60, DT: Erik Cadée 61.47, HT: Sander Styok 56.88, JT: Mart Ten Berge 75.46, Dec: Bas Markies 7794, 20kW: Rob Tersteeg 1:39:10. **Women**: 100m: Naomi Sedney 11.44, 200m: Tessa van Schagen 22.86, 400m: Lisanne de Witte 53.12, 800m: Sanne Verstegen 2:01.28, 1500m: Manon Kruiver 4:28.26, 5000m: Susan Kuijken 15:37.26, 10000m: , HMar: Inge de Jong 75:24, Mar: Ruth van der Meijden 2:33:44, 3000mSt: Veerle Bakker 10:33.49, 100mh: Eefje Boons 13.08w, 400mh: Bianca Baak 58.14,

HJ: Narlies van Haaren 1.76, PV: Femke Pluim 4.17, LJ: Astrid Ekelmans 6.02, TJ: Nora Ritzen 13.38, SP: Melissa Boekelman 18.09, DT: Corinne Nugter 54.04, HT: Wendy Koolhaas 62.65, JT: Emma Oosterwegel 52.45, Hep: Sophie Klumper 5338.

Churandy MARTINA b. 3 Jul 1984 Willemstad, Curaçao 1.78m 75kg. Rotterdam Atletiek. Studied civil engineering at University of Texas at El Paso, USA.
At 100m/(200m): OG: '04- qf, '08- 4/dq, '12- 5/5, '16- h/5; WCh: '03- h, '05- qf, '07- 5/5, '09- qf, '11/15- sf/sf, '13- sf/7; EC: '12- (1)/1R, '14- sf/4, '16- 1/dq(1); WJ: '00- h/h, '02- qf; WY: '99- sf; PAm: '03- sf, '07- 1; CAG: '06- 1/1R, '10- 1/1/3R; CCp: '10- (2)/1R. Won PAm-J 2003; NED 100m 2011-16; 200m 2011, 2014, 2016.
Records: AHO 100m (8) 2004-08, 200m (6) 2005-10, 400m 2007; NED 100m (2) 2011-12, 200m (3) 2012-16.
Progress at 100m, 200m: 2000- 10.73, 21.73; 2001- 10.64A, 21.55; 2002- 10.30, 20.81; 2003- 10.29/10.26w, 20.71; 2004- 10.13, 20.75; 2005- 10.13/9.93Aw,20.32/20.31w;2006- 10.04A/10.06/9.76Aw/ 9.99w, 20.27A; 2007- 10.06, 20.20; 2008- 9.93, 20.11; 2009- 9.97, 20.76; 2010- 10.03A/10.07/9.92w, 20.08; 2011- 10.10, 20.38; 2012- 9.91, 19.85; 2013- 10.03, 20.01; 2014- 10.13, 20.25; 2015- 10.06, 20.20; 2016- 10.01, 19.81. pbs: 60m 6.58i '10, 400m 46.13A '07.
At 2008 Olympics set three national records at 100m and one at 200m before crossing line in second place in final in 19.82 only to be disqualified for running out of his lane. Competed for Netherlands Antilles until 2010.

Eelco SINTNICOLAAS b. 7 Apr 1987 Dordrecht 1.86m 81kg. AV '34 (Apeldoorn). Economics student.
At Dec: OG: '12- 11, '16- dnf; WCh: '09-11-13-15: dnf/5/5.dnf; EC: '10-14-16: 2/4/16; WJ: '06- 8; EU23: '09- 1; EJ: '05- 14; ECp: '14- 1. At Hep: WI: '14- 4; EI: '11-13-15: 4/1/3.
Dutch decathlon record 2012.
Progress at Dec: 2007- 7466, 2008- 7507w, 2009- 8112, 2010- 8436, 2011- 8304, 2012- 8506, 2013- 8391, 2014- 8478, 2015- 8298. pbs: 60m 6.88i '13, 100m 10.62 '15, 200m 21.62 '10, 400m 47.88 '10, 1000m 2:37.42i '06, 1500m 4:22.29 '11, 60mh 7.88i '13, 110mh 13.92/13.89w '13, 400mh 51.59 '10, HJ 2.08i/2.02 '13, PV 5.52i '11, 5.45 '10; LJ 7.65i, 7.76w '09, 7.65 '12; SP 14.67 '15, DT 43.38 '14, JT 63.59 '12, Hep 6372i '13.
Set six pbs in improving pb by 277 points for European silver 2010.

Women

Nadine BROERSEN b. 29 Apr 1990 Hoorn 1.71m 62kg. AV Sprint Breda.
At Hep: OG: '12- 11, '16- 13; WCh: '13- 10, '15- 4; EC: '14- 2, '16- dnf; EU23: '11- 9; EJ: '09- 5; ECp: '14- 1. At Pen: WI: '14- 1; EI: '15- 5. Won NED HJ 2010-11, 2014; LJ 2015; JT 2013.

Four Dutch high jump records 2013-14 and indoors 2014.
Progress at Hep: 2009- 5507, 2010- 5967, 2011- 5932(w)/5854, 2012- 6319, 2013- 6345, 2014- 6539, 2015- 6531, 2016- 6377. pbs: 200m 24.57 '14, 800m 2:11.11 '14, 60mh 8.32i '13, 100mh 13.39 '14, HJ 1.94 '14, LJ 6.39 '14, 6.40w '16; SP 14.93i '14, 14.82 '15; JT 54.97 '12, Pen 4830i '14.
Lost c.200 points in stumbling at last hurdle in first event of 2013 World heptathlon. Won IAAF Combined Events Challenge 2014.

Sifan HASSAN b. '1 Jan' 1993 Adama, Ethiopia 1.70m 49kg. Eindhoven Atletiek.
At 1500m/(5000m): OG: '16- 5 (h 800m); WCh: '15- 3 (sf 800m); EC: '14- 1/2, '16- 2; CCp: '14- 1; WI: '16- 1; EI: 15- 1; won DL 2015. At 3000m: WI: '14- 5; ET: '14- 1. Eur CC: '13- 1 U23, '15- 1.
Records: European U23 1500m (3) 2014-15, Dutch 1500m (4), 1M, 3000m & 5000m 2014-15.
Progress at 800m, 1500m, 5000m: 2011- 4:20.13, 2012- 4:08.74, 2013- 2:00.86, 4:03.73. 2014- 1:59.95, 3:57.00, 14:59.23; 2015- 1:58.50, 3:56.05; 2016- 2:00.27, 3:57.13. pbs: 1000m 2:34.68 '15, 1M 4:18.20 '15, 2000m 5:46.1 '14, 3000m 8:29.38 '14, 10kRd 34:28 '12, HMar 77:10 '11.
Came to the Netherlands as a refugee at age 15. Dutch eligibility from 29 Nov 2013.

Maureen KOSTER b. 3 Jul 1992 Gouda 1.75m 56kg. Phanos.
At 1500m: OG: '16- h; WCh: '13/15- sf; EC: '14- h; WJ: '10- h. At 3000m: WI: '16- 4; EI: '15- 3, '17- 4. At 5000m: WCh: '15- h. Eur CC: '14- 5 U23, '15- 9. Won NED 1500m 2012-13, 2015.
Progress at 1500m: 2007- 4:37.38, 2008- 4:28.11, 2009- 4:24.32, 2010- 4:19.28, 2011- 4:17.64, 2012- 4:13.48; 2013- 4:06.50, 2014- 4:04.92, 2015- 3:59.79, 2016- 4:03.84. pbs: 800m 2:02.15 '14, 1000m 2:40.09 '14, 3000m 8:44.63i '17, 8:48.46mx; 5000m 15:07.20 '16, 10kRd: 34:27 '14.

Susan KRUMINS b. 8 Jul 1986 Nijmegen 1.72m 54kg. née Kuijken. Zevenheuvelen. Was at Florida State University, USA.
At 1500m: WCh: '09- h; EC: '10- h; E23: '07- 4. At 3000m: WJ: '04- dnf; EJ: '05- 2; CCp: '14- 3. At 5000m/(10000m): OG: '16- 8/14; WCh: '13- 8, '15- 8/10; EC: '14- 3, '16- 4. Eur CC: '05- 3J, '08- 1 U23. Won NED 1500m 2014, 5000m 2016; NCAA 1500m 2009..
Progress at 5000m, 10000m: 2003- 16:41.31, 2006- 16:20.30, 2009- 16:31.68, 2013- 15:04.36, 2014- 15:32.82, 2015- 15:07.38, 31:31.97; 2016- 15:00.69, 31:32.43. pbs: 800m 2:02.24 '09, 1000m 2:38.01 '14, 1500m 4:05.38 '13, 1M 4:34.11i '09, 2000m 5:38.37 '13, 3000m 8:36.08 '14, HMar 70:32 '17, 3000mSt 10:42.93 '05.
In September 2016 married Andrew Krumins, who competed for Australia at the 2001 World Youth Champs, pb 800m 1:47.16 '06.

Dafne SCHIPPERS b. 15 Jun 1992 Utrecht 1.79m 68kg. Hellas.

At Hep: OG: '12- 10; WCh: '13- 3; WJ: '10- 1; EJ: '09- 4, '11- 1. At (100m)/200m/4x100mR: OG: '16- 5/2; WCh: '11- sf, '15- 2/1; EC: 12- 5/2R, '14- 1/1, '16- 1/-/1R; WJ: '10- 3R; EU23: '13- (1) (3 LJ); CCp: '14- 3/1; ET: '14- 1. At 60m: WI: '16- 2; EI: '13- 4, 15- 1. Won DL 200m 2016, NED 100m 2011-12, 2014-15; LJ 2012, 2014.
European 200m record 2015, Dutch records: 100m (5) 2014-15, 200m (5) 2011-15, LJ 2014, Hep 2013 & 2014.
Progress at 100m, 200m, Hep: 2007- 12.09/ 12.08w, 2008- 12.26/12.01w, 2009- 11.79, 24.21, 5507; 2010- 11.56, 23.70/23.41w, 5967; 2011- 11.19/ 11.13w, 22.69, 6172; 2012- 11.36, 22.70, 6360; 2013- 11.09, 22.84, 6477; 2014- 11.03, 22.03, 6545; 2015- 10.81, 21.63; 2016- 10.83, 21.88. pbs: 60m 7.00i '16, 150m 16.93 '13, 800m 2:08.59 '14, 60mh 8.18i '12, 100mh 13.13 '14, HJ 1.80 '12, LJ 6.78 '14, SP 14.66 '15, JT 42.22 '15.
Added 117 points to pb and reduced 800m best from 2:15.52 to 2:08.62 in taking 2013 World heptathlon bronze. First Dutch woman to win a medal in World Championships and emulated Fanny Blankers-Koen (1950) by winning EC sprint double 2014. European Athlete of the Year 2014-15.

Anouk VETTER b. 4 Feb 1993 Amsterdam 1.77m 62kg. Sprint.
At Hep: OG: '16- 10; WCh: '15- 12; EC: '14- 7, '16- 1; WJ: '12- dnf; EJ: '11- dnf. At Pen: EI: '15- 8.
Dutch heptathlon record 2016.
Progress at Hep: 2011- 5549, 2012- 5764, 2013- 5872, 2014- 6316, 2015- 6458, 2016- 6626. pbs: 60m 7.46i '16, 100m 11.61 '16, 200m 23.70 '16, 800m 2:17.71 '16, 60mh 8.25i '16, 100mh 13.29 '16, HJ 1.81 '13, LJ 6.34 '15, 6.38w '16, SP 15.69 '16, JT 55.76 '16, Pen 4548i '15.
Mother Gerda Blokziel was NED javlin champion 1987-8. pb 58.22 '86.

Nadine VISSER b. 9 Feb 1995 Hoorn 1.75m 63kg. SAV.
At Hep (100mh): OG: '16- 19 (h); WCh: '15- 8; EC: '14 (h), '16- (sf); WJ: '12- 11, 14- 3 (3); EU23: '15- (3, 11 LJ); EJ: '13- 4. At 60mh: EI: '17- 7. Won NED 100mh 2015.
Progress at Hep: 2011- 5171, 2012- 5475, 2013- 5774, 2014- 6110, 2015- 6467, 2016- 6190. pbs: 100m 11.60 '14, 150m 17.69 '15, 200m 23.62 '15, 800m 2:13.08 '15, 60mh 7.92i '17, 100mh 12.81 '15, HJ 1.80 '14, LJ 6.48 '15, SP 13.89i '17, 13.24 '15; JT 44.01 '15, Pen 4428i '17.

NEW ZEALAND

Governing body: Athletics New Zealand, PO Box 305 504, Triton Plaza, Auckland.
National Championships first held in 1887 (men), 1926 (women). **2016 Champions: Men**: 100m/LJ: Matthew Wyatt 10.68/7.58, 200m: Alex Jordan 22.00, 400m: Andrew Whyte 46.70, 800m: Brad Mathas 1:50.47, 1500m: Hamish Carson 3:44.42, 3000m: Nick Willis 8:00.09, 5000m: Hayden McLaren 14:37.26, 10000m: Aaron Pulford 30:09.02, HMar: Oska Inkster-Bayne 66:34, Mar: Nick Horspool 2:27:39, 3000mSt: Mike Banks 9:35.12, 110mh: Joshua Hawkins 14.25, 400mh: Phil Simms 51.85, HJ: Sam Pinson 1.96, PV: Nick Southgate 5.10, TJ: Ebuka Okpala 15.85w, SP: Tom Walsh 21.11, DT: Marshall Hall 56.77, HT: Matt Bloxham 61.63, JT: Stuart Farquhar 77.77, Dec: Brent Newdick 7115, 3000mW/20kW: Jonathon Lord 13:01.48/ 1:45:32. **Women**: 100m: Rochelle Coster 11.64, 200m/400m: Louise Jones 24.39/54.05, 800m/ 1500m: Angie Petty 2:02.08/4:12.02, 3000m: Rosa Flanagan 9:09.33, 5000m: Camille Buscomb 16:03.75, 10000m: Lydia O'Donnell 34:32.80, HMar: Olivia Burne 75:29, Mar: Lisa Hunter-Galvan 2:55:25, 100mh: Fiona Morrison 13.21, 400mh: Anna Percy 61.58, HJ: Elizabeth Lamb 1.86, PV: Eliza McCartney 4.80, LJ: Kelsey Berryman 5.93w, TJ: Anna Thomson 19.43, SP: Valerie Adams 19.43, DT: Siositina Hakeai 56.11, HT: Julia Ratcliffe 65.93, JT: Laura Overton 47.80, Hep: Veronica Torr 5774, 3000mW: Roseanne Robinson 14:31.35, 20kW: Kate Newitt 1:54:18.

Jacko GILL b. 20 Dec 1994 Auckland 1.90m 118kg. Takapuna.
At SP: OG: '16- 9; WCh: '15- 8; CG: '14- 11; WJ: '10- 1, '12- 1; WY: '11- 1, YthOG: '10- 2. Oceania champion 2014.
Five World youth shot records 5kg 23.86 '10, 24.35 and 24.45 '11; 6kg (4) 21.34 to 22.31, 7.26kg (3) in 2011. World junior 6kg record 23.00 '13. Three NZL records 2011.
Progress at SP: 2010- 18.57, 2011- 20.38, 2012- 20.05, 2014- 20.70, 2015- 20.75, 2016- 20.83, 2017- 21.01.
First name actually Jackson. World age 15 and 16 bests for 5kg, 6kg and 7.26kg shot. His father Walter was NZ champion at SP 1987 & 1989, DT 1975, pbs 16.57 '86 & 53.78 (1975); his mother Nerida (née Morris) had discus best of 51.32 and was NZ champion in 1990. His sister Ayla was 6th in WJ hammer 2010.

Zane ROBERTSON b. 14 Nov 1989 Hamilton 1.80m 65kg. Hamilton City Hawks.
At 5000m: WCh: '13- 14; CG: 14- 3 (h 1500m); CCp: '14- 2. At 10000m: OG: '16- 12.
Oceania 15k, 20k and half marathon records 2015, 10k 2016; NZ 10000m record 2016.
Progress at 5000m, 10000m: 2011- 13:58.37, 2013- 13:13.83, 2014- 13:14.69, 2015- 13:25.41, 27:46.82; 2016- 13:25.41, 27:33.67. pbs: 1500m 3:34.19 '14, 1M 3:53.72 '14, 3000m 7:41.37 '14, 2M 8:22.82 '14, road: 10k 27:28 '16, 15k 42:17 '15, 20k 56:40 '15, HMar 59:47 '15.
Twin brother **Jake** pbs 5000m 13:15.54 '13, 10000m 27:45.46 '13, HMar 60:01 '17. CG '14: 7 10000m, 9 5000m; WC 5000m: '11- h, '11- 14

Tomas WALSH b. 1 Mar 1992 Timaru 1.86m 123kg. South Canterbury.
At SP: OG: '16- 3; WCh: '15- 4; CG: '14- 2; WJ:

NEW ZEALAND – NIGERIA

'10- dnq 16; WY: '09- 6 (dnq 31 DT), CCp: '14- 4; WI: '14- 3. '16- 1. Won DL 2016, NZ SP 2010-16, DT 2013.
Shot records: 7 Oceania 2016, 8 NZL 2013-16 & 6 Oceania indoor 2014-16, = Comm rec 2016.
Progress at SP: 2010- 17.57, 2011- 18.83, 2012- 19.33, 2013- 20.61, 2014- 21.26i/21.16, 2015- 21.62, 2016- 22.21. pb DT 53.58 '14.
At World Indoors: set four NZ indoor records in 2014 and three Oceania records in 2016.

Nick WILLIS b. 25 Apr 1983 Lower Hutt 1.83m 68kg. Economics graduate of University of Michigan, USA.
At 1500m: OG: '04- sf, '08- 2, '12- 9, '16- 3; WCh: '05- 07-11-13-15: sf/10/12/sf/6; CG: '06-1, '10- 3, '14-3 (10 5000m); WJ: '02- 4; WI: '08/14- dq, '16- 3; WCp: '06- 3, '14- 6 (4 3000m). Won NCAA indoor 2005, NZ 1500m 2006, 2015; 3000m 2013, 2016; 5000m 2011-12.
Records: NZ 1500m (6) 2005-15, 3000m 2014. Oceania 1500m (3) 2012-15 and indoors 1500m (3:35.80) 2010, 1M 2015 & 2016 (3:50.63).
Progress at 1500m: 2001- 3:43.54, 2002- 3:42.69, 2003- 3:36.58, 2004- 3:32.64, 2005- 3:32.38, 2006- 3:32.17, 2007- 3:35.85, 2008- 3:33.51, 2009- 3:38.85i, 2010- 3:35.17, 2011- 3:31.79, 2012- 3:30.35, 2013- 3:32.57, 2014- 3:29.91, 2015- 3:29.66, 2016- 3:34.29. pbs: 800m 1:45.54 '04, 1000m 2:16.58 '12, 1M 3:49.83 '14, 3000m 7:36.91 '14, 5000m 13:20.33 '14, HMar 67:06 '14.
His brother Steve (b. 25 Apr 1975) had pbs: 1500m 3:40.29 '99, 1M 3:59.04 '00.

Women

Valerie ADAMS b. 6 Oct 1984 Rotorua 1.93m 123kg. Auckland City.
At SP: OG: '04- 7, '08- 1, '12- 1, '16- 2; WCh: '03- 05-07-09-11-13: 5/2/1/1/1/1; CG: '02-06-10-14: 2/1/1/1; WJ: '02- 1; WY: '99- 10, '01- 1; WI: '04- 08-10-12-14-16: dnq 10/1/2/1/1/3; WCp: '02- 6, '06- 1, '10- 1. Won WAF 2005, 2008-09, DL 2011-14, 2016; NZL SP 2001-11, 2013-14, 2016; DT 2004, HT 2003.
Nine Oceania & Commonwealth shot records 2005-11, 22 NZ 2002-11, 10 OCE indoor 2004-13.
Progress at SP: 1999- 14.83, 2000- 15.72, 2001- 17.08, 2002- 18.40, 2003- 18.93, 2004- 19.29, 2005- 19.87, 2006- 20.20, 2007- 20.54, 2008- 20.56, 2009- 21.07, 2010- 20.86, 2011- 21.24, 2012- 21.11, 2013- 20.98i/20.90, 2014- 20.67i/20.59, 2015- 18.73, 2016- 20.42. pbs: DT 58.12 '04, HT 58.75 '02.
Nine senior global shot titles. IAAF Female Athlete of the Year 2014. Matched her age with metres at the shot from 14 to 18 and missed that at 19 by only two months. 28 successive shot wins from September 2007 to World Indoor silver in March 2010, and another 56 from August 2010 to July 2015. Her father came from England and her mother from Tonga. Married New Caledonia thrower Bertrand Vili (SP 17.81 '02, DT 63.66 '09, 4 ECp '07 for France) in November 2004 (divorced in 2010), and married Gabriel Price on 2 April 2016. She was made a Dame Companion of the New Zealand Order of Merit for services to athletics in the 2017 New Year's Honours.

Eliza McCARTNEY b. 11 Dec 1996 Auckland 1.79m 65kg. North Harbour Bays.
At PV: OG: '16- 3; WJ: '14- 3; WY: '13- 4; WUG: '15- 2; WI: '16- 5. NZ champion 2016.
Pole vault records: World junior 2015, Oceania & Commonwealth 2016, seven NZ 2014-16.
Progress at PV: 2012- 3.85, 2013- 4.11, 2014- 4.45, 2015- 4.64, 2016- 4.80, 2017- 4.70i.

NIGERIA

Governing body: The Athletic Federation of Nigeria, P.O.Box 18793, Garki, Abuja. F'd 1944.
2016 National Champions: Men: 100m: Seye Ogunlewe 10.12, 200m: Divine Oduduru 20.51, 400m: Kunle Fasasi 46.22, 800m/1500m: Soudi Hamadjan 1:49.80/3:49.0, 5000m/10000m: Emmanuel Gyang 14:52.75/31:31.58, 110mh: Antwon Hicks 13.27, 400mh: Henry Okorie 50.12, HJ: Tadius Okpara 2.10, PV: Melody Bassey 4.00, LJ: Blessing Oluwayemi 7.54, TJ: Olu Olamigoke 16.70, SP: Chukwuewuka Enekwechi 19.60, DT: Augustine Nwoye 54.11, HT: Ganiyu Monsuru 45.57, JT: Samuel Adams 66.89, 20kW: Fatoyinbo Gbenga 1:45:59. **Women**: 100m/200m: Blessing Okagbare 11.02/22.77, 400m: Patience Okon George 51.67, 800m: Philomena Ikehandu 2:06.94, 1500m: Comfort James 4:37, 5000m/10000m: Deborah Pam 17:23.50/36:53.73, 100mh: Lindsay Lindley 13.16, 400mh: Amaka Ogoegbunam 57.61, HJ: Grace Anigbata 1.70, LJ: Ese Brume 6.45, TJ: Blessing Ibrahim 13.12, SP/DT: Nwanneka Okwelogu 16.17/52.93, HT: Daramola Feyisayo 49.06, JT: Kelechi Nwangaa 53.52, 20kW: Joy Davies 2:04:17.

Tosin OKE b. 1 Oct 1980 London, UK 1.78m 77kg. Woodford Green, UK. Chemistry graduate of Manchester University.
At TJ: OG: '12- 7, '16- dnq 23; WCh: '09/11- dnq 16/16, '15- 8; EC: '02- nj; CG: '02-10-14: 5/1/2; AfG: '11- 1, '15- 1; AfCh: '10-12-14-16: 1/1/2/1; EJ: '99- 1; CCp: '10- 6; '14- 4; ECp: '03- 4; WI: '16- 6. Won UK 2007, NGR 2009-10, 2012-13, 2015.
Progress at TJ: 1997- 14.07, 1998- 15.16/15.62w, 1999- 16.57, 2000- 16.04/16.37w, 2001- 16.08i/15.72, 2002- 16.65, 2003- 16.61i/16.59, 2004- 16.49/16.75w, 2005- 16.12/16.30w, 2006- 16.33/16.50w, 2007- 16.86, 2008- 16.47/16.63w, 2009- 16.87, 2010- 17.22A/17.16, 2011- 17.21, 2012- 17.23, 2013- 16.87i/16.64, 2014- 16.97/17.21w, 2015- 17.00, 2016- 17.13. pb LJ 7.31 '05.
Switched allegiance from Britain to Nigeria (grandfather) from 10 Feb 2009.

Women

Ese BRUME b. 20 Jan 1996 Ugheli, Delta State 1.67m 58kg. Student at University of Benin.
At LJ: OG: '16- 5; CG: '14- 1; WJ: '14- dnq 33; AfG:

'15- 4; Af Ch: '14- 1, '16- 1; CCp: '14- 5. Won Af-J LJ & 4x100m 2013 & 2015, TJ 2015.
Progress at LJ: 2012- 6.02, 2013- 6.53, 2014- 6.68, 2015- 6.61, 2016- 6.83. pbs: 100m 11.84 '14, 400m 55.53 '16, TJ 13.16A '15.

Blessing OKAGBARE b. 9 Oct 1988 Sapele 1.80m 68kg. Married name Ighoteguonor. Was at University of Texas at El Paso, USA.
At LJ/(100m): OG: '08- 2, '12- dnq 16/8; '16- (sf, sf 100m), WCh: '11- dnq 18/5, '13- 2/6 (3 200m), '15- (8); CG: '14- 1 100m & 200m/2R; AfG: '07- 2 (4 TJ), '11- 1/2; AfCh: '10- 1/1/1R, '12- 1/2, '14- (1)/1R; WJ: '06- 16 (dnq 17 TJ); CCp: '10- 6/3/3R; Won Nigerian 100m 2009-14, 2016; 200m 2013-14, 2016; LJ 2008-09, 2011-13; TJ 2008; NCAA 100m & LJ 2010.
Two African 100m records 2013, 4x200m 2015, Nigerian & African junior TJ record 2007.
Progress at 100m, 200m, LJ: 2004- 5.85 irreg, 2006- 6.16, 2007- 6.51, 2008- 23.76A, 6.91; 2009- 11.16, 6.73/6.90w; 2010- 11.00/10.98w/10.7Aw, 22.71, 6.88; 2011- 11.08/11.01w, 22.94, 6.78/6.84w; 2012- 10.92, 22.63, 6.97; 2013- 10.79/10.75w, 22.31, 7.00/7.14w; 2014- 10.85, 22.23, 6.86; 2015- 10.80, 22.67, 6.66; 2016- 11.02/10.92w, 22.58, 6.73. pbs: 60m 7.18i '10, 300m 37.04 '13, 400m 53.34 '15, TJ 14.13 '07.
Majestic winner of Commonwealth Games sprint double in 2014. Married football international Jude Igho Otegheri on 7 Nov 2014.

NORWAY

Governing body: Norges Friidrettsforbund, Serviceboks 1, Ullevaal Stadium, 0840 Oslo. Founded 1896.
National Championships first held in 1896 (men), 1947 (women, walks 1937). **2016 Champions: Men**: 100m/200m: Jaysuma Saidy Ndure 10.59/21.01, 400m/400mh: Karsten Warholm 45.8/50.72, 800m: Filip Ingebrigtsen 1:52.09, 1500m: Snorre Holtan Løken 4:01.00, 5000m: Marius Vedvik 14:19.63. 10000m: Okubamichael Mesfun 29:10.10, HMar/Mar: Marius Vedvik 65:14sh/2:21:50, 3000mSt: Tom Erling Kårbo 8:57.88, 110mh: Vladimir Vukicevic 13.89, HJ: Brede Raa Ellingsen 2.07, PV: Eirik Dolve 5.50, LJ: Ingar Kiplesund 7.64w, TJ: Sindre Almsengen 15.51, SP/DT: Sven Martin Skagestad 18.18/61.58, HT: Eivind Henriksen 69.35, JT: Paul Redford 66.45, Dec: *not held*, 5000mW: Erik Tysse 19:15.33; 10000mW: Fredrik Vaeng Røtnes 42:01.1, 20kW: Håvard Haukenes 1:25:44. **Women**: 100m: Ezinne Okparaebo 11.58, 200m: Helene Rønningen 23.98, 400m: Line Kloster 53.02, 800m: Yngvild Elvemo 2:07.43, 1500m: Ida Fillingsnes 4:25.22, 5000m: Aurora Dybedokken 16:35.53, 10000m: Live Solheimdal 34:47.70, HMar: Anne Kristine Nevin 77:52sh, Mar: Marthe Katrine Myhre 2:43:31, 3000mSt: Ingeborg Løvnes 10:00.13, 100mh: Isabelle Pedersen 13.37, 400mh: Amalie Hammild Iuel 57.06, HJ: Tonje Angelsen 1.80,

PV: Lene Retzius 4.10, LJ: Nadia Akpana Assa 6.49, TJ: Oda Utsi Onstad 13.03, SP: Kristin Sundsteigen 13.63, DT: Grete Etholm 50.69, HT: Beatrice Nedberge Llano 65.48, JT: Sigrid Borge 56.36, Hep: Caroline Fleischer 5063, 3000mW: Merete Heigheim 13:39.80, 5000mW/10kW: Josefin Greiff 27:16.3/57:09.

Håvard HAUKENES b. 22 Apr 1990 Bergen 1.80m 68kg. IL Gular
At 50kW: OG: '16- 7; WCh: '13- dq, '15- 24; At 20kW: EC: '14- dq. Won NOR 20kW 2014, 2016; 50kW 2012.
Progress at 50kW: 2011- 4:04:48, 2012- 3:56:38, 2015- 3:56:50, 2016- 3:46:33, 2017- 3:43:40. pbs: 3000mW 11:44.17 '15, 5000mW 19:19.79 '16, 10000mW 42:39.5 '16, 20kW 1:23:15 '16.

Henrik INGEBRIGTSEN b. 24 Feb 1991 Stavanger 1.80m 69kg. Sandnes IL
At 1500m (3000m): OG: '12- 5, '16- sf; WCh: '13- 8, '15- h; EC: '10-12-14-16: h/1/2/3; WJ: '10- h; EU23: '11- h; EJ: '09- h; CCp: '14- 4; EI: '15- 6 (3), '17- (2). At 5000m: EC: '16-4; EU23: '13- 1. Won NOR 800m 2013, 1500m 2010, 2012, 2014; 5000m 2015. Eur U23 CC: '12- 1.
Norwegian records: 1500m (4) 2012-14, 1M (3) 2012-14.
Progress at 1500m: 2004- 4:30.63, 2005- 4:22.48, 2006- 4:04.15, 2007- 3:54.08, 2008- 3:50.63, 2009- 3:44.53, 2010- 3:38.61, 2011- 3:39.50, 2012- 3:35.43, 2013- 3:33.95, 2014- 3:31.46, 2015- 3:32.85, 2016- 3:34.57. pbs: 800m 1:48.09 '14, 1M 3:50.72 '14, 3000m 7:42.19 '13, 5000m 13:27.10 '15, 2000mSt 5:41.03 '09, 3000mSt 8:52.56 '09.
Younger brothers: **Filip** (b. 20 Apr 1993) 1500m pb 3:32.43 '16 (EC: '14- h, '16- 1; 10 WJ '12, 6 EU23 '13), 1000m 2:16.95 '16, 1M 3:55.02 '16, 3000m 7:49.70 '16; **Jakob** (b. 19 Sep 00) European age 14 1500m bests to 3:48.37 '15, pb 3:42.44 '16 and won Eur-U20 CC 2016.

Karsten WARHOLM b. 28 Feb1992 Volda 1.87m 78kg. Dimna IL.
At 400mh: OG: '16- sf; EC: '16- 6; At 400m: EC: '14- h; EJ: '15- 2; At Oct: WY: '13- 1; At Dec: WJ: '14- 10; EJ: '15- 2. Won NOR 400m & 400mh 2015-16, 110mh 2013-14.
Norwegian records; 400m, 400mh (4) 2016.
Progress at 400mh: 2014- 52.20, 2015- 51.09, 2016- 48.49. pbs: 60m 6.75i '17, 100m 10.49i '17, 10.52 '16; 200m 20.92i/21.09 '16, 21.00w '15; 400m 45.96i '17, 45.8/46.10 '16; 1000m 2:45.80i '13, 1500m 4:44.73 '15, 60mh 8.10i '15, 110mh 14.30 '15, HJ 2.05 '14, PV 4.30 '15, LJ 7.66 '15, TJ 14.48i/14.33 '12, SP 9.18 '14, DT 29.40 '14, JT 45.82 '15.
Won multiple NOR age group titles at a wide range of events. EJ silver medals at 400m & Dec in 2015 even though 400m was in the middle of the decathlon first day.

Women

Karoline Bjerkeli GRØVDAL b. 14 Jun 1990 Alesund1.67m 52kg. Sportsklubben Vidar.

At 5000m/(10000m): OG: '12- h, '16- 7/9; WCh: 13- 13, '15- h; EC: '10- 9/dnf, '14- 12, '16- (3); EJ: '09- 1; ET: '10- 3. At 3000mSt: WCh: '09- h; EU23: '11- h; EJ: '07- 1, '09- 1. At 2000mSt: WY: '07- 3. Eur CC: '06-09-13-15-16: 2J/1J/5/3/3. Won NOR 1500m 2013, 2015; 5000m 2008, 2010, 2012, 2014; 3000mSt 2006, 2009-10.
NOR records 1M 2016, 3000mSt 2007.
Progress at 5000m, 10000m: 2007- 15:55.62, 2008- 16:08.22; 2009- 15:29.82, 2010- 15:25.40, 2011- 15:44.92, 2012- 15:24.86, 2013- 15:16.27mx, 2014- 15:47.63, 2015- 15:15.18, 2016- 14:57.53, 31:14.07. pbs: 800m 2:04.23 '16, 1500m 4:09.03 '16, 1M 4:26.23 '16, 3000m 8:39.47 '16, HMar 69:41 '12, 2000mSt 6:21.39 '08, 3000mSt 9:33.19 '07.

PANAMA

Governing body: Federación Panameña de Atletismo, Apartado 0860-00684, Villa Lucre, Ciudad de Panamá. Founded 1945.

Alonso EDWARD b. 8 Dec 1989 Ciudad de Panamá 1.83m 73kg. Was at Barton County CC.
At (100m)/200m: OG: '12- h, '16- 7; WCh: '09-11-13-15: 2/dnf/sf/4; WJ: '08- (h); PAm: '15- 3; SAG: '14- (1); SACh: '09- 1/1, SAm-J: '07- (1), SAm-Y: '06- 1/1; CCp: '14- 1. Won DL 2014-16, C. American 2012, C.AmG 100m 2010, 200m 2013; SAmG 100m 2014.
Records: S.American 200m 2009, Panama 100m (2) 2009-14, 200m (5) 2007-09; South American Junior 100m 2007.
Progress at 100m, 200m: 2006- 10.60, 21.18; 2007- 10.28/10.25w, 20.62; 2008- 10.63, 20.96; 2009- 10.09/9.97w, 19.81; 2010- 10.24/10.08w, 2011- 20.28, 2012- 21.23A, 2013- 10.13, 20.37/20.32w; 2014- 10.02, 19.84; 2015- 10.29, 19.87; 2016- 19.92. pbs: 300m 34.17 '17, 400m 47.40i '10.
World age-19 best 19.81 in World final 2009. Suffered a 10cm career-threatening hamstring tear in the 2011 World 200m final. Younger brother Mateo (b. 1 May 1993): 60m 6.73i PAN record, 100m 10.29, and 200m 21.48 in 2014.

POLAND

Governing body: Polski Zwiazek Lekkiej Atletyki (PZLA), ul. Myslowicka 4, 01-612 Warszawa. Founded 1919.
National Championships first held in 1920 (men), 1922 (women). **2016 Champions: Men**: 100m/200m: Karol Zalewski 10.30/20.61, 400m: Rafal Omelko 45.57, 800m/1500m: Marcin Lewandowski 1:48.31/3:39.45, 5000m/3000mSt: Krystian Zalewski 14:16.49/8:53.94, 10000m: Tomasz Grycko 29:19.56, HMar: Szymon Kulka 64:28; Mar: Artur Kozlowski 2:11:54, 110mh: Damian Czykier 13.35, 400mh: Patryk Dobek 50.06, HJ: Sylwester Bednarek 2.25, PV: Pawel Wojciechowski 5.40, LJ: Tomasz Jaszczuk 7.82, TJ: Karol Hoffmann 16.67, SP: Konrad Bukowiecki 20.80, DT: Piotr Malachowski 68.10, HT: Pawel Fajdek 81.87, JT: Marcin Krukowski 83.63, Dec: Pawel Wiesiolek 8095, 20kW: Lukasz Nowak1:26:31, 50kW: Rafal Augustyn 3:43:22. **Women**: 100m: Ewa Swoboda 11.34, 200m: Anna Kielbasinska 23.27, 400m: Justyna Swiety 51.66, 800m/1500m: Angelika Cichocka 2:10.62/4:08.48, 5000m/3000mSt: Katarzyna Kowalska 16:18.05/10:06.09, 10000m: Katarzyna Rutkowska 34:25.71, HMar: Izabela Trzaskalska 72:44; Mar: Agnieszka Mierzejewska 2:32:04, 100mh: Karolina Koleczek 13.03, 400mh: Joanna Linkiewicz 55.55, HJ: Kamila Licwinko 1.93, PV: Justyna Smietanka 4.20, LJ/TJ: Anna Jagaciak-Michalska 6.55/14.00, SP: Klaudia Kardasz 16.79, DT: Joanna Wisniewska 58.89, HT: Anita Wlodarczyk 78.69, JT: Maria Andrejczyk 60.70, Hep: Izabela Mikolajczyk 5720, 20kW: Paulina Buziak 1:36:52.

Rafal AUGUSTYN b. 14 May 1984 Chyki-Debiaki, near Mielec 1.78m 71kg. LKS Stal Mielec.
At 50kW: OG: '16- 22; WCh: '09- 21, '15- 28; EC: '14- 9; WCp: '12- 7; ECp: '11- 6. At 20kW: OG: '08- 29, '12- 29; WCh: '07-11-13: 26/20/19; EC: '10- 9; EU23: '05- 4; ECp: '09- 7, '13- 8. Won POL 20kW 2007, 50kW 2010-11, 2014-17.
Progress at 50kW: 2009- 3:52:16, 2010- 3:49:54, 2011- 3:46:56, 2012- 3:49:53, 2013- 3:51:33, 2014- 3:45:32, 2015- 3:43:55, 2016- 3:43:22, 2017- 3:44:42. pbs: 3000mW 11:17.82 '11, 5000mW 19:16.51i '14, 19:26.55 '11; 10kW 39:47 '10, 40:37.73t '06; 20kW 1:20:53 '12.

Sylwester BEDNAREK b. 28 Apr 1989 Glówno 1.98m 75kg. RKS Lódz.
At HJ: OG: '16- dnq 30=; WCh: '09- 3, '15- dnq 33=; EC: '10- 10=; WJ: '06- 4, '08- 2; WY: '05- 4; E23: '09- 1; EJ: '07- 6; EI: '17- 1. Polish champion 2014-15.
Progress at HJ: 2003- 1.76, 2004- 2.06, 2005- 2.22, 2006- 2.26, 2007- 2.22, 2008- 2.24, 2009- 2.32, 2010- 2.26, 2012- 2.20, 2013- 2.22, 2014- 2.25, 2015- 2.30, 2016- 2.30, 2017- 2.33i.

Konrad BUKOWIECKI b. 17 Mar 1997 Olsztyn 1.91m 129kg. PKS Gwardia Szczytno.
At SP: OG: '16- nt; WCh: '15- dnq; EC: '16- 4; WJ: '14- 1, '16- 1; WY: '13- 5; EJ: '15- 1 (dnq 13 DT); Yth OG: '10- 1; WI: '16- 4; EI: '15- 6. Polish champion 2016.
Shot records: Four world junior 7.26kg 2015-16, 6kg 23.34 '16, indoor 6kg (4) 22.38 '15 to 22.96 '16, World youth 5kg 2 out to 22.24 & 5 indoor to 24.24 in 2014; European junior (5) 2015, indoor (3) 2016., U23 indoor 2017.
Progress at SP: 2014- 17.29i, 2015- 20.78, 2016- 21.14, 2017- 21.97i/21.17. Pb DT 55.47 '16.

Patryk DOBEK b. 13 Feb 1994 Koscierzyna 1.83m 75kg. SKLA Sopot.
At 400mh: OG: '16- h; WCh: '15- 7; EC: '14- sf; EU23: '15- 1/2R; ET: '15- 2; Polish champion 2014-16. At 400m: WJ: '12- sf/2R; WY: '11- 3; EJ: '13- 2/2R.

Progress at 400mh: 2012- 52.00, 2013- 50.67, 2014- 49.13, 2015- 48.40, 2016- 49.01. pbs: 200m 21.38 '15, 300m 33.34 '13, 400m 46.15 '13, 600m 1:15.78 '14.

Pawel FAJDEK b. 4 Jun 1989 Swiebodzice 1.86m 118kg. KS Agros Zamosc.
At HT: OG: '12- dnq, '16- dnq 17; WCh: '11- 11, '13- 1, '15- 1; EC: 14- 2, '16- 1; WJ: '08- 4; EU23: '09- 8, '11- 1; WUG: '11-13-15: 1/1/1; CCp: '14- 3; ET: '11-13-14-15: 2/1/2/1. Won POL 2012, 2014-16; Franc G 2013, World HT challenge 2013, 2015-16.
Two Polish hammer records 2014-15.
Progress at HT: 2008- 64.58, 2009- 72.36, 2010- 76.07, 2011- 78.54, 2012- 81.39, 2013- 82.27, 2014- 83.48, 2015- 83.93, 2016- 82.47. pb Wt 23.22i '14.
Won 16 of 17 competitions in 2015 and 13/14 in 2016, with the top 12 performances of the year at hammer each year. The clear favourite, he failed to qualify with only 72.00 for Olympic final 2016 after 27 successive wins, all over 78m.

Michal HARATYK b. 10 Apr 1992 Cieszyn 1.94m 136kg. KS AZS AWF Kraków.
At SP: OG: '16- dnq 18; EC: '16- 2.
Progress at SP: 2012- 17.72, 2013- 17.24, 2014- 19.95, 2015- 20.10i/19.95, 2016- 21.35i/21.23. pb DT 53.53 '13.
Elder brother Lukasz SP 18.82 '10.

Karol HOFFMANN b. 1 Jun 1989 Warsaw 1.97m 80kg. MKS Aleksandrów Lódzki.
At TJ: OG: '16- 12; EC: '12- 6, '16- 2; WJ: '08- 10; EU23: '11- 10; EJ: '07- dnq 22; WI: '14- 5. Polish champion 2011-12, 2014, 2016.
Progress at TJ: 2006- 15.00/15.23w, 2007- 15.74/15.88w, 2008- 15.94, 2009- 16.00, 2010- 15.92, 2011- 16.50/16.87w, 2012- 17.09, 2013- 16.66, 2014- 16.89i/16.64, 2015- 16.29, 2016- 17.16. pb LJ 7.76 '11.
His father Zdzislaw was TJ world champion in 1983, Polish record 17.53 '85.

Adam KSZCZOT b. 2 Sep 1989 Opoczno 1.78m 64kg. RKS Lódz. Studied organisation and management.
At 800m: OG: '12/16- sf; WCh: '09/13- sf, '11- 6, '15- 2; EC: '10-14-16: 3/1/1; WJ: '08- 4; EU23: '09/11- 1; EJ: '07- 3; WI: '10-12-14: 3/4/2; EI: '09-11-13-17: 4/1/1/1; CCp: '14- 3; ET: '11-13-14-15: 1/1/2/3. Polish champion 2009-10, 2012, 2014-15.
Polish 1000m record 2011 and 2014.
Progress at 800m: 2005- 1:59.57, 2006- 1:51.09, 2007- 1:48.10, 2008- 1:47.16, 2009- 1:45.72, 2010- 1:45.07, 2011- 1:43.30, 2012- 1:43.83, 2013- 1:44.76, 2014- 1:44.02, 2015- 1:43.45, 2016- 1:43.76. pbs: 400m 46.51 '11, 600m 1:14.55 '10, 1000m 2:15.72 '14, 1500m 3:46.53 '10.

Marcin LEWANDOWSKI b. 13 Jun 1987 Szczecin 1.80m 64kg. SL WKS Zawisza Bydgoszcz. PE student.
At 800m: OG: '08/12- sf, '16- 6; WCh: '09-11-13-15: 8/4/4/sf; EC: '10-14-16: 1/52; WJ: '06- 4; EU23: '07- 1, '09- 2; WI: '14- dq; EI: '09-11-15: 6/2/1; CCp: '10- 2; ECp: '08- 2, '10- 3; won W.MilG 2011.
At 1500m: EJ: '05- 7; EI: '13- 4, "17- 1; ET: '13-14-15: 3/3/2. Won Polish 800m 2011, 2016; 1500m 2008, 2010, 2014, 2016.
Polish 1000m record 2011 & 2016.
Progress at 800m: 2002- 1:57.86, 2003- 1:53.31, 2004- 1:51.73, 2005- 1:48.86, 2006- 1:46.69, 2007- 1:45.52, 2008- 1:45.84, 2009- 1:43.84, 2010- 1:44.10, 2011- 1:44.53, 2012- 1:44.34, 2013- 1:43.79, 2014- 1:44.03, 2015- 1:43.72, 2016- 1:43.73. pbs: 400m 47.76 '09, 600m 1:15.17 '14, 1000m 2:14.30 '16, 1500m 3:37.37i '14, 3:37.69 '16.
Coached by brother Tomasz (1:51.00 '03).

Piotr LISEK b. 16 Aug 1992 Duszniki, Poznan 1.88m 85kg. OSOT Szczecin.
At PV: OG: '16- 4=; WCh: '15- 3=; EC: '14- 6, '16- 4=; EU23: '13- dnq 17; ET: '15- 3; WI: 16- 3; EI: '15- 3, '17- 1.
Three Polish indoor pole vault records 2015-17.
Progress at PV: 2006- 3.20, 2007- 3.30, 2008- 4.10, 2009- 4.42, 2010- 4.70, 2011- 5.10i/5.00, 2012- 5.20, 2013- 5.60, 2014- 5.82, 2015- 5.90i/5.82, 2016- 5.77i/5.75, 2017- 6.00i.
6-months drugs ban in 2012.

Piotr MALACHOWSKI b. 7 Jun 1983 Zuromin 1.94m 135kg. WKS Slask Wroclaw. Army corporal.
At DT: OG: '08- 2, '12- 5, '16- 2; WCh: '07-09-11-13-15: 12/2/9/2/1; EC: '06-10-14-16: 6/1/4/1; WJ: '02- 6; EU23: '03- 9, '05- 2; EJ: '01- 5; CCp: '10- 4; ECp: '06-07-08-09-10-11-14: 1/1/3/1/2/3/2. Won DL 2010, 2014-16; POL 2005-10, 2012-15.
Nine Polish discus records 2006-13.
Progress at DT: 1999- 39.48, 2000- 52.04, 2001- 54.19, 2002- 56.84, 2003- 57.83, 2004- 62.04, 2005- 64.74, 2006- 66.21, 2007- 66.61, 2008- 68.65, 2009- 69.15, 2010- 69.83, 2011- 68.49, 2012- 68.94, 2013- 71.84, 2014- 69.28, 2015- 68.29, 2016- 68.15.

Wojciech NOWICKI b. 22 Feb 1989 Bialystok 1.96m 112kg. KS Podlasie Bialystok.
At HT: OG: '16- 3; WCh: '15- 3; EC: '16- 3; EU23: '11- 5.
Progress at HT: 2008- 55.71, 2009- 64.41, 2010- 69.59, 2011- 72.72, 2012- 73.52, 2013- 75.87, 2014- 76.14, 2015- 78.71, 2016- 78.36. pb Wt 22.72i '14.

Robert SOBERA b. 19 Jan 1991 Wroclaw 1.90m 77kg. KS AZS AWF Wroclaw.
At PV: OG: '16- dnq 13; WCh: '13- dnq, '15- 15; EC: '14- nh, '16- 1; WJ: '10- 4; EU23: '11- 11, '13- 2; EJ: '09- nh; WUG: '15- 3; WI: '14- 6, '16- 6; EI: '13- 6=, '15- 4. Polish champion 2014.
Progress at PV: 2005- 2.80, 2006- 4.12, 2007- 4.60, 2008- 5.00, 2009- 5.30, 2010- 5.30, 2011- 5.40, 2012- 5.42, 2013- 5.71i/5.61, 2014- 5.75i/5.70/5.80exh, 2015- 5.81i/5.70, 2016- 5.77i/5.70.

Robert URBANEK b. 29 Apr 1987 Leczyca 2.00m 120kg. MKS Aleksandrów Lódzki.
At DT: OG: '12/16- dnq 32/17; WCh: '13- 6, '15-

3; EC: '12-14-16: 6/3/9; EU23: '09- 7; CCp: '14- 6; ET: '15- 1.
Progress at PV: 2004- 47.09, 2005- 47.83, 2006- 50.84, 2007- 56.18, 2008- 62.22, 2009- 60.54, 2010- 60.74, 2011- 64.37, 2012- 66.93, 2013- 65.30, 2014- 65.75, 2015- 66.31, 2016- 65.56. pb SP 16.21 '07.

Pawel WOJCIECHOWSKI b. 6 Jun 1989 Bydgoszcz 1.90m 81kg. CWKS Zawisza Bydgoszcz. PE student.
At PV: OG: '12- dnq, '16- dnq 16=; WCh: '11- 1, '15- 3=; EC: '14- 2, '16- 7=; WJ: '08- 2; EU23: '11- 1; EJ: '07- dnq 16; EI: '11- 4, '17- 3; CCp: '14- 5. Won W.MilG 2011, POL 2015-16.
Polish pole vault record 2011.
Progress at PV: 2001- 2.50, 2002- 2.70, 2003- 3.10, 2004- 3.50, 2005- 4.10, 2006- 4.70, 2007- 5.00, 2008- 5.51, 2009- 5.40i/5.22, 2010- 5.60, 2011- 5.91, 2012- 5.62, 2014- 5.80, 2015- 5.84, 2016- 5.84i/5.71, 2017- 5.85i.

Women

Maria ANDREJCZYK b. 9 Mar 1996 Sejny 1.74m 77kg. LUKS Hancza Suwalki.
At JT: OG: '16- 4; WCh: '15- dnq 28; EC: '16- dnq 13; WJ: '14- 5; WY: '13- dnq 26; EJ: '15- 1. Polish champion 2016. Polish javelin record 2016.
Progress at JT: 2010- 28.51, 2011- 41.21, 2012- 44.58, 2014- 56.53, 2015- 62.11, 2016- 67.11.

Angelika CICHOCKA b. 15 Mar 1988 Kartuzy 1.69m 54kg. SKLA Sopot.
At 800m: OG: '16- sf; EC: '10/14- h; EJ: '07- h; WI: '14- 2. At 1500m: WCh: '15- 8; EC: '12- h, '16- 1; E23: '09- 8; WI: '12- 5; EI: '15- 2. Polish champion 800m 2011-13, 2016; 1500m 2011, 2014, 2016.
Progress at 800m, 1500m: 2005- 2:12.50, 2006- 2:06.50, 4:32.04; 2007- 2:06.51, 4:26.85; 2008- 2:04.24, 4:21.47; 2009- 2:03.24, 4:12.31; 2010- 2:00.86i/2:01.17, 4:10.54i/4:12.80; 2011- 2:00.20, 4:06.50; 2012- 2:01.32, 4:06.79; 2013- 2:00.60, 4:11.33; 2014- 2:00.30, 4:07.55; 2015- 1:59.55, 4:03.06; 2016- 1:58.97, 4:03.25. pbs: 400m 54.44 '10, 600m 1:28.38 '11, 1000m 2:34.84 '16, 1M 4:25.39 '16, 3000m 9:10.65 '12.

Sofia ENNAOUI b. 30 Aug 1995 Ben Guerir Morocco 1.58m 45kg. MKL Szczecin.
At 1500m: OG: '16- 10; WCh: '15- sf; EC: '16- 7; WJ: '12- 10, '14- 5; EU23: '15- 2; EJ: '13- 2; EI: '17- 3. At 800m: WCh: '15- sf; WY: '11- h, At 3000m: WJ: '14- dnf; ET: '15- 1; EI: '15- 6; Eur CC: '13- 2J, '16- 1 U23. Won POL 1500m 2015.
Progress at 1500m: 2012- 4:13.68, 2013- 4:12.05, 2014- 4:07.34, 2015- 4:04.26. 2016- 4:01.00. pbs: 400m 56.07 '15, 800m 2:00.11 '15, 1000m 2:35.15 '16, 1M 4:25.34 '16, 3000m 8:45.29i '17, 8:59.44 '14. Moved to Poland with her Polish mother at the age of 2.

Joanna FIODOROW b. 4 Mar 1989 Augustów 1.69m 89kg. OS AZS Poznan.
At HT: OG: '12- 7, '16- 9; WCh: '11-15: dnq 21/17; EC: '14- 3, '16- 10; WJ: '08- dnq 19; EU23: '09- 4, '11- 2; ET: '14- 2; WUG: '15- 2.

Progress at HT: 2005- 40.96, 2006- 50.18, 2007- 55.93, 2008- 61.22, 2009- 62.80, 2010- 64.66, 2011- 70.06, 2012- 74.18, 2013- 68.92, 2014- 74.39, 2015- 72.67, 2016- 72.98. pbs: SP 12.87 '10, JT 35.56 '09.

Anna JAGACIAK-MICHALSKA (née Jagaciak) b. 10 Feb 1990 Zielona Góra 1.76m 68kg. OS AZS Poznan.
At (LJ)/TJ: OG: '16- 10; WCh: '11- dnq 28, '13- 10; EC: '10- 10/dnq 15, '12- (dnq 22), '14- dnq 15, '16- 4; WJ: '08- 7/dnq 14; WY: '07- (dnq 13); EU23: '11- 4/3; EJ: '09- 3/4; EI: '17- 4; WUG: '13- 2, 15-2/3. Won POL LJ 2010, 2016; TJ 2013-14, 2016; FrancG LJ & TJ 2013.
Progress at TJ: 2007- 12.62, 2008- 13.43, 2009- 13.55, 2010- 13.93/14.16w, 2011- 14.25, 2012- 13.87/14.06w, 2013- 14.21, 2014- 14.20, 2015- 14.17, 2016- 14.33/14.40w. pb LJ 6.74 '10.
Married Lukasz Michalski (PV 5.85 '11, 4 WCh & 1 WUG 2011) in July 2014.

Joanna JÓZWIK b. 30 Jan 1991 Walbrzych 1.68m 53kg. AZS-AWF Warszawa.
At 800m: OG: '16- 5; WCh: '15- 7; EC: '14- 3, '16- 6; WJ: '10- sf; EU23: '11- h, '13- 8; ET: '15- 2; EI: '15- 4. Polish champion 2014-15.
Progress at 800m: 2007- 2:12.90, 2008- 2:11.55, 2009- 2:07.31, 2010- 2:05.09, 2011- 2:03.15, 2012- 2:05.87, 2013- 2:02.39, 2014- 1:59.63, 2015- 1:58.35, 2016- 1:57.37. pbs: 200m 24.16 '14, 300m 39.83 '11, 400m 53.08 '14, 600m 1:25.04 '15, 1000m 2:34.93 '16.

Kamila LICWINKO b. 22 Mar 1986 Bielsk Podlaski 1.83m 66kg. née Stepaniuk. KS Podlasie Bialystok.
At HJ: OG: '16- 9; WCh: '09- dnq 16, '13- 7=, '15- 4; EC: '14- 9=; EU23: '07- 4; EJ: '05- 7; WI: '14- 1=,'16- 3; EI: '09- 8, '15- 3; ET: '13-14-15: 2/3=/3; WUG: '13- 1. Won POL 2007-09, 2015-16.
Polish high jump records 2013 & 2014, three indoor 2015.
Progress at HJ: 1999- 1.46, 2000- 1.61, 2001- 1.66, 2002- 1.75, 2003- 1.75, 2004- 1.84, 2005- 1.86, 2006- 1.85i/1.84, 2007- 1.90, 2008- 1.91, 2009- 1.93, 2010- 1.92i/1.89, 2011- 1.88i, 2012- 1.89, 2013- 1.99, 2014- 2.00i/1.97, 2015- 2.02i/1.99, 2016- 1.99.
Married her trainer Michal Licwinko in 2013.

Anita WLODARCCZYK b. 8 Aug 1985 Rawicz 1.78m 95kg. RKS Skra Warszawa. PE student.
At HT: OG: '08- 4, '12- 1, '16- 1; WCh: '09-11-13-15: 1/5/2/1; EC: '10-12-14-16: 3/1/1/1; EU23: '07- 9; CCp: '14- 1; ET: '09-13-15: 1/2/1. Won POL 2009, 2011-12, 2014-16; Franc G 2013, IAAF HT challenge 2013-16.
Six world hammer records 2009-16, six Polish records 2009-14.
Progress at HT: 2002- 33.83, 2003- 43.24, 2004- 54.74, 2005- 60.51, 2006- 65.53, 2007- 69.07, 2008- 72.80, 2009- 77.96, 2010- 78.30, 2011- 75.33, 2012- 77.60, 2013- 78.46, 2014- 79.58, 2015- 81.08, 2016- 82.98. pbs: SP 13.25 '06, DT 52.26 '08, Wt 20.09i '14.

Won all 11 hammer competitions in 2015 and had the eight best throws of the year, including when she became first woman to throw hammer over 80m with 81.08 at Cetniewo on 1 Aug 2015, and two 80m throws (80.27 and 80.85) later that month at the World Champs. In 2016 she won all her 12 competitions to take her win streak to 30 from a last loss on 16 June 2014.

PORTUGAL

Governing body: Federação Portuguesa de Atletismo, Largo da Lagoa, 1799-538 Linda-a-Velha. Founded in 1921.
National Championships first held in 1910 (men), 1937 (women). **2016 Champions: Men**: 100m: Diego Antunes 10.29, 200m: David Lima 20.88w, 400m: Vitor Ricardo Santos 48.05, 800m: Sandy Martins 1:52.07, 1500m: Hélio Gomes 3:54.95, 5000m: Eduardo Mbengani 14:13.74, 10000m: Bruno Albuquerque 29:07.10, Mar: Paulo Machado 2:35:26, 3000mSt: André Pereira 8:58.24, 110mh: João Fontela 14.25w, 400mh: Ricardo Lima 51.68, HJ: Paulo Conceição 2.17, PV: Diogo Ferreira 5.25, LJ/TJ: Nelson Évora 7.77w/16.60, SP: Tsanko Arnaudov 19.93, DT: Filipe Vital e Silva 56.40, HT: António Vital e Silva 67.78, JT: Tiago Aperta 61.98, Dec: Pedro Ferreira 6139w, 10,000mW: João Vieira 41:24.07, 20kW: Pedro Isidro 1:25:08, 35kW: João Vieira 2:35:59. **Women**: 100m/200m: Lorène Bazolo 11.40/23.86w, 400m: Cátia Azevedo 52.96, 800m: Salomé Afonso 2:10.81, 1500m: Marta Pen Freitas 4:16.12, 5000m/10000m: Carla Salomé Rocha 16:29.95/32:23.68, Mar: Rosa Madureira 2:55:20, 3000mSt: Joana Soares 10:24.29, 100mh: Olimpia Barbosa 13.46w, 400mh: Vera Barbosa 57.70, HJ: Anabela Neto 1.74, PV: Marta Onofre 4.38, LJ: Evelise Veiga 6.51w, TJ: Patricia Mamona 14.53w, SP: Ophélie Oliveira 12.58, DT: Irina Rodrigues 61.03, HT: Vânia Silva 57.35, JT: Claudia Ferreira 47.80, Hep: Lecabela Quaresma 5802, 10000mW: Ana Cabecinha 43:29.57, 20kW: Inês Henriques 1:30:52.

Nelson ÉVORA b. 20 Apr 1984 Abidjan, Côte d'Ivoire 1.81m 70kg. Sport Lisboa e Benfica.
At (LJ/)TJ: OG: '04- dnq 40, '08- 1, '16- 6; WCh: '05-07-09-11-15: dnq 14/1/2/5/3; EC: '06- 6/4, '14- 6, '16- dnq 17; WJ: '02- dnq 18/6; EU23: '05- 3; EJ: '03- 1/1; WUG: '09- 1, '11- 1; WI: '06-08-16: 6/3/4; EI: '07-15-17: 5/1/1; ECp: '09- 2/1; Won WAF TJ 2008, POR LJ 2006-07, 2016; TJ 2003-04, 2006-07, 2009-11, 2013-16.
Six Portuguese triple jump records 2006-07, Cape Verde LJ & TJ records 2001-02.
Progress at TJ: 1999- 14.35, 2000- 14.93i, 2001- 16.15, 2002- 15.87, 2003- 16.43, 2004- 16.85i/16.04, 2005- 16.89, 2006- 17.23, 2007- 17.74, 2008- 17.67, 2009- 17.66/17.82w, 2010- 16.36, 2011- 17.35, 2013- 16.68, 2014- 16.97, 2015- 17.52, 2016- 17.03, 2017- 17.20i. pbs: HJ 2.07i '05, 1.98 '99; LJ 8.10 '07.
Portugal's first male world champion in 2007.

He suffered a serious injury in right tibia (in same place where he had an operation in February 2010) in January 2012 and missed season. Father from Cape Verde, mother from Côte d'Ivoire, relocating to Portugal when he was five. Switched nationality in 2002. Sister Dorothé (b. 28 May 1991) 400m pb 54.43 '14.

Women

Jéssica AUGUSTO b. 8 Nov 1981 Paris, France 1.65m 46kg. Sporting CP.
At Mar: OG: '12- 6, '16- dnf; EC: '14- 3. At HMar: EC: '16- 3; At 3000mSt: OG: '08- h (h 5000); WCh: '09- 9. At 5000m/(10000m): WCh: '05- h, '07- 14, '11- (10); EC: '10- 3/2; EU23: '03- dnf; WUG: '07- 1; CCp: '10- 7; ECp: '14- (2). At 3000m (1500m): WJ: '00- 8; EU23: '01- (10); EJ: '99- 6 (12); WI: '08- 8, '10- 7; EI: '09- 9. World CC: '07- 12, '10- 21; Eur CC: '98-99-00-02-04-05-06-07-08-09-10: 12J/8J/1J/16/18/30/9/11/2/4/1. Won POR 1500m 2007, 2011; 5000m 2006, 10000m 2014; IbAm 3000m 2004, 2006, 2010.
Two Portuguese 3000m steeplechase records 2008-10, European indoor 2M best 2010.
Progress at 5000m, 10000m, Mar, 3000mSt: 2003- 15:51.63, 2004- 15:15.76, 2005- 15:20.45, 2006- 15:37.55, 2007- 14:56.39, 2008- 15:19.67, 9:22.50; 2009- 9:25.25, 2010- 14:37.07, 31:19.15, 9:18.54; 2011- 15:19.60, 32:06.68, 2:24:33; 2012- 2:24:59, 2013- 15:38.73, 2:29:11; 2014- 31:55.56, 2:24:25; 2016- 15:52.53, 32:30.71, 2:28:53. pbs: 800m 2:07.97i '02, 1500m 4:07.89i/4:08.32 '10, 1M 4:32.58i '09, 4:42.15 '99, 2000m 5:45.6i '09, 3000m 8:41.53 '07, 2M 9:19.39i '10, 9:22.89 '07; road 15k 48:40 '08, 10M 53:15 '08, HMar 69:08 '09, 30k 1:41:37 '11.
Won Great North Run 2009. Daughter Leonor born 15 Jun 2015 (father is football goalkeeper Eduardo Carvalho).

Ana CABECINHA b. 29 Apr 1984 Beja 1.68m 52kg. CO Pechão.
At 20kW: OG: '08- 8, '12- 8, '16- 6; WCh: '11-13-15: 6/8/4; EC: '10- 7, '14- 6; EU23: '05- 4; WCp '08-10-12-14-16: 11/8/8/8/6; ECp: '13- 5, '15- 9. At 5000mW: WY: '01- 10. At 10000mW: WJ: '02- 12; EJ: '03- 3; won IbAm 2006, 2010; 2nd RWC 2012; POR 10000mW 2005, 2008, 2010, 2012, 2014-16; 20kW 2012-15.
POR records 10,000m and 20km walk 2008.
Progress at 20kW: 2004- 1:37:39, 2005- 1:34:13, 2006- 1:31:02, 2007- 1:32:46, 2008- 1:27:46, 2009- 1:33:05, 2010- 1:31:14, 2011- 1:31:08, 2012- 1:28:03, 2013- 1:29:17, 2014- 1:27:49, 2015- 1:28:28, 2016- 1:28:40. pbs: 3000mW 12:17.50 '14, 5000mW 21:22.23 '15, 21:21R '12; 10000mW 43:08.17 '08; running 1500m 4:31.73 '07, 3000m 9:46.08 '13, 5000m 17:57.34 '12.

Inês HENRIQUES b 1 May 1980 Santarém 1.56m 48kg. CN Rio Maior.
At 20kW: OG: '04- 25, '12- 14, '16- 12; WCh: '01-05-07-09-11-13-15: dq/27/7/10/9/11/23; EC: '02-

06-10-14: 15/12/8/13; EU23: '01- 10; WCp: '06-10-12-16: 13/3/9/8; ECp: '07- 7, '13- 8; Won POR 10000mW 2006, 2009, 2011, 2013; 20kmW 2009, 2011, 2016. At 5000mW: EJ: '99- 12.
World record 50k walk 2017.
Progress at 20kW: 2000- 1:41:09, 2001- 1:34:49, 2002- 1:34:46.5t, 2003- 1:36:03, 2004- 1:31:23.7t, 2005- 1:33:24, 2006- 1:30:28, 2007- 1:30:24, 2008- 1:31:06, 2009- 1:30:34, 2010- 1:29:36, 2011- 1:30:29, 2012- 1:29:54, 2013- 1:29:30, 2014- 1:29:33, 2015- 1:29:52, 2016- 1:29:00. pbs: 3000mW 12:25.36i '13, 12:38.75 '07; 5000mW 21:32.08 '14, 10000mW 43:22.05 '08, 43:09R '10; 50kW: 4:08:25 '17.

Patrícia MAMONA b. 21 Nov 1988 Lisbon 1.68m 53kg. Sporting CP. Was at Clemson University, USA.
At TJ: OG: '12- dnq 13, '16- 6; WCh: '11-15: dnq 27/16; EC: '10-12-14-16: 8/2/dnq 13;/1 WJ: '06- 4; WY: '05- 7; EU23: '09- 5; EJ: '07- dnq 15; WI: '14- 4; EI: '13-15-17: 8/5/2; WUG: '11- 2. POR champion 2008-16, NCAA 2010-11.
Nine Portuguese triple jump records 2009-16.
Progress at TJ: 2004- 12.71, 2005- 12.87, 2006- 13.37/13.38w, 2007- 13.24, 2008- 13.51, 2009- 13.83, 2010- 14.12, 2011- 14.42, 2012- 14.52, 2013- 14.02/14.07w, 2014- 14.36/14.49w, 2015- 14.32i/14.19, 2016- 14.65. pbs: 200m 24.42 '10, 800m 2:19.70i '09, 60mh 8.41i '09, 100mh 13.53/13.49w '10, HJ 1.69 '04; LJ 6.28i '17, 6.16 '05; Pen 4081i '09, Hep 5293 '11.

Sara MOREIRA b. 17 Oct 1985 Santo Tirso 1.68m 51kg. Sporting CP.
At (5000m)/3000mSt: OG: '08- h; WCh: '07- 13, '09- 10/h, '11- dq; EC: '10- (2), '12- (3), '14- (6); EU23: '07- 3; WUG: '07- 4, '09- 1/1, '11- (2); ET: '11- 2. At 3000m: WI: '10- 5; EI: '09- 2, '13- 1; CCp: '10- 6. At 1500m: EI: '11- 7. At 10000m: OG: '12- 14; WCh: '15- 12; EC: '10/16- dnf, '14- 5; ECp: '10-11-12-14: 3/1/1/3. At HMar: EC: '16- 1. At Mar: OG: 16- dnf. Eur CC: '09-10-12: 10/9/12. Won IbAm 5000m 2016, POR 1500m 2010, 2012; 5000m 2014-15, 10000m 2015, 3000mSt 2007-09, 2011.
POR 3000mSt record 2008.
Progress at 5000m, 10000m, Mar, 3000mSt: 2005- 10:27.72, 2007- 9:42.47, 2008- 9:34.30; 2009- 14:58.11, 9:28.64; 2010- 14:54.71, 31:26.55; 2011- 15:11.97, 31:39.11, 9:35.11; 2012- 15:08.33, 31:16.44; 2014- 15:20.01, 32:01.42, 2:26:00; 2015- 15:50.09, 31:12.93, 2:24:49; 2016- 15:34.93, 2:25:53. pbs: 1500m 4:07.11 '10, 3000m 8:42.69 '10, 2M 9:47.99i '10, 15kRd 48:48 '13, HMar 69:18 '15.
Third in New York on marathon debut 2014, 2nd Prague 2015. 6-months drugs ban 2011-12. Married to Pedro Ribeiro (POR 3000mSt champion 2010, pb 8:32.20 '06). Son Guillermo born 1 Nov 2013.

PUERTO RICO
Governing body: Federación de Atletismo Amateur de Puerto Rico, 90, Ave. Río Hondo, Bayamón, PR 00961-3113. Founded 1947.
National Champions 2016: Men: 100m/200m: Pedro Cruz 10.54/21.24, 400m: Eric Gomez 47.18, 800m: Félix Soto 1:52.50, 1500m: Víctor Ortiz 3:59.80, 3000mSt: Richard Estremera 9:17.56, 110mh: Ricardo Torres 14.14, 400mh: Eric Alejandro 49.79, HJ: Abiam Salas 2.05, PV: Emanuel Rivera 5.00, LJ: Abdel Merced 7.38, TJ: Alexis Caraballo 13.80w, SP/DT: Alfredo Romero 14.81/49.60, HT: Jerome Vega 63.68, Dec: Tristán Faure 6999. **Women**: 100m: Beatriz Cruz 11.67, 200m: Génesis Lozada 24.94, 400m: Janice Machuca 58.03, 800m: Emily Rosa 2:16.19, 1500m: Angelín Figueroa 4:35.41, 100mh: Alma Vega 14.97, 400mh: Kathyenid Rivera 61.33, HJ: Reina Hernández 1.60, PV: Diamara Planell 4.30, LJ: María Hodge 5.92, TJ: Noelys Morales 12.30w, SP: Lysbeth Vega 12.33, DT: Sylvia Galarza 54.04, HT: Gianna Castro 52.97, JT: Odalis Romero 48.71.

Javier CULSON b. 25 Jul 1984 Ponce 1.98m 79kg.
At 400mh: OG: '08- sf, '12- 3, '16- dq; WCh: '07-09-11-13-15: sf/2/2/6/sf; PAm: '07- 6, '15- 2; CAG: '06- 5, '10- 2; PAm-J: '03- 3; WUG: '07- 3; CCp: '10- 2, '14- 3/3R; won DL 2012-13, IbAm 2006, CAC 2009, NACAC 2015.
Seven Puerto Rican 400mh records 2007-10.
Progress at 400mh: 2002- 54.47, 2003- 51.10, 2004- 50.77, 2005- 50.62, 2006- 49.48, 2007- 49.07, 2008- 48.87, 2009- 48.09, 2010- 47.72. 2011- 48.32, 2012- 47.78, 2013- 48.14, 2014- 48.03, 2015- 48.48, 2016- 48.46. pbs: 200m 21.64w '07, 400m 45.99 '12, 800m 1:49.83 '14, 110mh 13.84 '07.

QATAR
Governing body: Qatar Association of Athletics Federation, PO Box 8139, Doha. Founded 1963.

Mutaz Essa BARSHIM b. 24 Jun 1991 Doha 1.92m 70kg. Team Aspire.
At HJ: OG: '12- 3=, '16- 2; WCh: '11- 7, '13- 2, '15- 4; WJ: '10- 1; AsiG: '10- 1, '14- 1; AsiC: '11- 1; WI: '12-14-16: 9=/1/4; CCp: '14- 3; won DL 2014-15, Asian indoors 2010, 2012, 2014, 2016; Asi-J 2010, W.Mil G 2011, Arab 2011, 2013, 2015; Gulf 2013.
Five Asian high jump records 2012-14 and indoors (3) 2013-15, 14 Qatar records 2010-13.
Progress at HJ: 2008- 2.07, 2009- 2.14, 2010- 2.31, 2011- 2.35, 2012- 2.39, 2013- 2.40, 2014- 2.43, 2015- 2.41, 2016- 2.40.
His 2.43 at Brussels in 2014 was the world's best since 1993, second only to Javier Sotomayor. Qatari father (who was a race walker), Sudanese mother. Younger brother Muamer Aissa Barshim (b. 3 Jan 1994) has HJ pb 2.28 '14 and was 3rd 2014 Asian Games.

Ashraf Amjad EL-SEIFY (Al-Saifi) b. 20 Feb 1995 Egypt 1.83m 93kg.
At HT: OG: '16- 6; WCh: '13- dnq 25, '15- 9; WJ: '12- 1, '14- 1. Won Asi=J 2014,

Records: world youth 5kg 85.26 '11, world junior 6kg 85.57 '12, Asian junior 7.36k 2013, three Qatar 2013-16.
Progress at HT: 2013- 76.37, 2014- 71.81, 2015- 78.04, 2016- 78.19. Former Egyptian.
Abdelilah HAROUN b. 1 Jan 1997 Sudan 1.78m 73kg.
At 400m: OG: '16- sf; AsiC: '15- 1/1R; WJ: '16- 1; WI: '16- 2. Won Asian indoor 2016, Arab 2015. Asian 400m records indoors and out 2015. World best 500m indoors 2016.
Progress at 400m: 2014- 45.74, 2015- 44.27, 2016- 44.81. Pb 500m 59.83i '16.
Qatar citizen from 2 Feb 2015, having lived there from 2013.
Femi Seun **OGUNODE** b. 15 May 1991 Nigeria 1.83m 79kg.
At (100m)/200m: OG: '16- h/h; WCh: '11- sf (8 400m), '15- sf/7; AsiG: '10- 1 (1 400m), 14- 1/1; AsiC: '11- 1, '15- 1/1; CCp: '14- 3/3; Won Arab 100m 2011, 100m/200m 2015; W.Asian 100m/200m 2010, W.MilG 100m/200m 2011. At 60m: WI: '14- 3.
Asian records 100m (3) 2014-16, 200m 2015, four Qatar 200m 2011-15.
Progress at 100m, 200m: 2010- 10.25, 20.43; 2011- 10.07, 20.30; 2014- 9.93, 20.06; 2015- 9.91, 19.97; 2016- 9.91, 20.10. pbs: 60m 6.51Ai/6.52i '14, 400m 45.12 '10.
Two-year drugs ban 2012-14. Switched allegiance from Nigeria to Qatar from 31 Oct 2009. Younger brother Tosin suddenly emerged with 6.50i for 60m in 2014 and has pb 100m 10.18 '16.

ROMANIA
Governing body: Federatia Romana de Atletism, 2 Primo Nebiolo Str, 011349 Bucuresti. Founded 1912.
National Championships first held in 1914 (men), 1925 (women). **2016 Champions: Men**: 100m: Ioan Melnicescu 10.43, 200m: Alexandru Terpezan, 400m: Adrian Dragan, 800m: Valentin Voicu 1:49.73, 1500m: Ioan Zaizan 3:47.03, 5000m: Ilie Corneschi 14:30.02, 10000m: Nicolae Soare 29:58.78, HMar: Nicolae Soare 66:25, Mar: Sorin Mineran 2:30:22, 3000mSt: Catalin Atanasoaei 8:55.62, 110mh: Cosmin Dumitrache 14.07, 400mh: Attila Nagy, HJ: Mihai Donisan 2.20, PV: Andrei Deliu 5.00, LJ: Christian Staicu 7.72, TJ: Marius Anghel 15.77, SP: Andrei Gag 21.06, DT: Alin Firfirica 61.29, HT: Ion Sorescu 63.46, JT: George Zaharia 73.73, Dec: Ionel Cojan 7121; 20kW: Marius Cocioran 1:26:21, 50kW: Narcis Mihaila 4:28:20. **Women**: 100m: Andreea Ograzeanu 11.64, 200m: 400m: Sanda Belgyan 57.96, 800m: Mihaela Nunu 2:06.21, 1500m: Florina Pierdevara 4:17.90, 5000m/3000mSt: Ancuta Bobocel 16:04.81/ 9:42.02, 10000m: Monica Florea 34:03.19, HMar: Andreea Piscu 76:26, Mar/10kW/20kW: Ana Rodean 2:51:05/49:25.2/1:34:07, 100mh: Anamaria Nesteriuc 13.45, 400mh: Sanda Belgyan 57.96, HJ/Hep: Beatrice Puiu 1.75/5674, PV: Lavinia Bulov 3.70, LJ: Alina Rotaru 6.48, TJ: Elena Panturoiu 14.07, SP: Lenuta Burueana 15.36, DT: Ileana Sorescu 47.11, HT: Bianca Ghelber-Perie 64.23, JT: Nicoleta Anghelescu 51.23.
Andrei GAG b. 27 Apr 1991 Bocsig 1.95m 118kg. CSM Arad, University of Suceava.
At SP: OG: '16- dnq 13; WCh: '15- dnq 17; EC: '14-16: dnq 20/16, WUG: '15- 2; WI: '16- 2; At DT: WJ: '08- dnq 30, '10- 2; EU23: '11/13- dnq 19/11; EJ: '09- 10. Won ROU SP 2014-16, DT 2014; Balkan SP 2015.
Romanian shot records 2015 & 2016.
Progress at SP: 2008- 14.71i, 2009- 15.91, 2010- 16.00i/15.92, 2011- 16.95, 2012- 17.73, 2013- 18.41, 2014- 20.17i/19.64, 2015- 20.96, 2016- 21.06. pb DT 61.27 '14.

Women
Alina ROTARU b. 5 Jun 1993 Bucharest 1.75m 54kg. CSA Steaua Bucharest.
At LJ: OG: '16- dnq 18; WCh: '15- dnq 15; EC: '12- dnq 20, '14- 7; WJ: '10- dnq 19, '12- 5; WY: '09- 2 (4 HJ); Yth OG: '10- 2; EU23: '13- 5, '15- 3; EJ: '11- 2; EI: '15- 4. ROU champion 2014-16.
Progress at LJ: 2008- 6.08i/5.99, 2009- 6.26, 2010- 6.40, 2011- 6.46, 2012- 6.57/6.58w, 2013- 6.63, 2014- 6.74, 2015- 6.75, 2016- 6.67. pbs: 60m 7.63i '15, 60mh 8.86i '14, HJ 1.85i '12, 1.82 '09; TJ 13.24i/13.21 '12, Pen 4111i '12.

RUSSIA
Governing body: All-Russia Athletic Federation, Luzhnetskaya Nab. 8, Moscow 119992. Founded 1911.
National Championships first held 1908, USSR women from 1922. **2016 Champions: Men**: 100m/200m: Denis Ogarkov 10.31/21.13, 400m: Pavel Ivashko 45.71, 800m: Konstantin Kholmogorov 1:48.54, 1500m: Aleksey Kharitonov 3:40.26, 5000m: Vladimir Nikitin 13:31.81, 10000m: Anatoliy Rybakov 28:23.04, HMar/Mar: Fyodor Shutov 73:27/2:11:26, 3000mSt: Viktor Bakharev 8:25.34, 110mh: Sergey Shubenkov 13.20, 400mh: Tomofey Chalyy 48.96, HJ: Ivan Ukhov 2.30, PV: Georgiy Gorokhov 5.65, LJ: Vasiliy Kopeykin 8.06, TJ: Lyukman Adams 16.89, SP: Maksim Afonin 20.98, DT: Viktor Butenko 62.97, HT: Sergey Litvinov 77.67, JT: Dmitriy Tarabin 84.70, Dec: Ilya Shkurenyov 8292, 20kW: Sergey Shirobokov 1:22:31, 50kW: Denis Nizhegorodov 3:44:47. **Women**: 100m: Kristina Sivkova 11.22, 200m: Anastasiya Kocherzhova 23.76, 400m: Antonina Krivoshapka 50.70, 800m: Aleksandra Gulyayeva 2:01.22, 1500m: Anastasiya Kalina 4:07.76, 5000m: Yelena Korobkina 15:44.64, 10000m: Alla Kulyatina 32:12.70, HMar: Gulnara Vygovskaya 74:41, Mar: Tatyana

Arkhipova 2:28:34, 3000mSt: Yekaterina Ivonina 9:24.66, 100mh: Yekaterina Galitskaya 13.18, 400mh: Vera Rudakova 55.29, HJ: Anna Chicherova 1.98, PV: Yelena Isinbayeva 4.90, LJ: Darya Klishina 6.84, TJ: Viktoriya Prokopenko 14.28, SP: Yevgeniya Solovyova 18.03, DT: Yekaterina Strokova 61.83, HT: Oksana Kondratyeva 68.81, JT: Vera Rebrik 63.92, Hep: Mariya Gromysheva 5970, 20kW: Yelena Lashmanova 1:24:58.

Lyukman ADAMS b. 24 Sep 1988 St. Petersburg 1.94m 87kg.
At TJ: OG: '12- 9; WCh: '15- 5; EC: '10- 6, '14- 2; EJ: '07- 1; CCp: '14- 6; WI: '12- 3, '14- 1. Russian champion 2012, 2015-16.
Progress at TJ: 2005- 15.97, 2006- 15.16, 2007- 16.75, 2008- 16.86i/16.78, 2009- 16.22i/16.20, 2010- 17.17/17.21w, 2011- 17.32i/15.60, 2012- 17.53, 2013- 16.82, 2014- 17.37i/17.29, 2015- 17.34, 2016- 17.15. pb LJ 8.01 '15.
Married Yevgeniya Polyakova (60m 7.09 '08, 1 EI '09; 100m 11.09 '07; 4x100m 1 OG '08) on 5 Apr 2014.

Sergey BAKULIN b. 13 Nov 1986 Insar, Mordoviya. 1.69m 58kg. Mordoviya VS.
At 20kW: EC: '06- 5; EU23: '07- 3; WCp: '06- 6, '10- 7; WUG: '09- 1. At 50kW: OG: '12- dq6; WCh: '11- dq1; EC: '10- 3; WCp: '12-dq 4; ECp: '09- 4; Russian champion 2011.
Progress at 20kW, 50kW: 2006- 1:19:54, 2007- 1:19:14, 2008- 1:18:18, 3:52:38; 2010- 1:24:05, 3:43:26; dq: 2011- 3:38:46dq, 2012- 3:38:55dq, 2017- 1:18:51. pbs: 5000mW 18:26.82i '12, 10kW: 39:03 '06, 30kW: 2:05:19dq '13, 35kW 2:24:25 '09.
3 year 2 month ban announced in January 2015 for biological passport anomaly and with results annulled 25 Feb 2011 to 24 Dec 2012 lost 2011 World title and 2012 Olympic 5th place. Back competing in 2017.

Viktor BUTENKO b. 10 Mar 1993 Stavropol 1.96m 116kg. Stavropolskiy.
At DT: WCh: '13- 8; EC: '14- 5; WJ: '12- 4; EU23: '13- 2; EJ: '11- 6; ET: '14- 3. RUS champion 2016.
Progress at DT: 2011- 51.89, 2012- 57.32, 2013- 65.97, 2014- 65.89, 2015- 65.44, 2016- 65.17.

Dmitriy CHIZHIKOV b. 6 Dec 1993 Sankt-Peterburg 1.94m 85kg.
At TJ: EU23: '15- 1; EJ: '11- 4.
Progress at TJ: 2011- 15.75/15.95w, 2012- 15.82i/15.72/15.80w, 2013- 16.16, 2014- 16.51, 2015- 17.20, 2016- 16.85i/16.78. pb LJ 7.67 '16.

Aleksey DMITRIK b. 12 Apr 1984 Slantsy. Leningrad reg, 1.91m 69kg. St Petersburg YR.
At HJ: WCh: '11- 2, '13- dnq 25=; EC: '10- 7, '14- dnq 23; WJ: '02- 14; WY: '01- 1; EJ: '03- 2; EU23: '05- 6; EI: '09- 2=, '13- 2; ECp: '05- 1, '11- 2. Russian champion 2011.
Progress at HJ: 2000- 2.08, 2001- 2.23, 2002- 2.26, 2003- 2.28, 2004- 2.30, 2005- 2.34i/2.30, 2006- 2.28, 2007- 2.30, 2008- 2.33i/2.27, 2009- 2.33, 2010- 2.32i/2.31, 2011- 2.36, 2012- 2.35i/2.33, 2013- 2.36i/2.30, 2014- 2.40i/2.30, 2015- 2.32, 2016- 2.28i/2.26.
Mother Yelana was a 1.75m high jumper.

Aleksey FYODOROV b. 25 May 1991 Smolensk 1.84m 73kg. Mosoovskaya Smolenskaya.
At TJ: WCh: '11- dnq 18, 13- 5; EC: '12- 4, '14- 3; WJ: '10- 1; WY: '07- 2; EU23: '11-2, '13- 1; EJ: '09- 1; EI: '13- 3, '15- 4; WUG: '13- 2; ET: '13-14-15: 1/1/2. Russian champion 2011, 2013-14.
Progress at TJ: 2007- 15.59, 2008- 16.08, 2009- 16.62, 2010- 17.12/17.18w, 2011- 17.05i/17.01, 2012- 17.19, 2013- 17.13, 2014- 17.07/17.12w, 2015- 17.42, 2016- 17.02.
Parents Leonid and Tatyana were triple jumpers.

Aleksandr IVANOV b. 25 Apr 1993 Nizhny Tagiul, Sverdlovsk reg. 1.82m 68kg. Mordoviya VS.
At 20kW: WCh: '13- 1; EC: '14- 2; EU23: '13- 2; ECp: '13- 4. At 10000mW: WJ: '12- 2; WCp: 'EJ: '11- 6; 12- 2J.
Progress at 20kW: 2013- 1:20:58, 2014- 1:19:45, 2015- 1:20:06, 2016- 1:22:25. pbs: 5000mW 19:35.0 '12, 10000mW: 40:12.90 '12, 39:29R '13.
At 20 in 2013 he became the youngest ever World walking champion. Married Elmira Alembekova in August 2015.

Denis KUDRYAVTSEV b. 13 Apr 1992 Chelyabinsk 1.87m 77kg. Tyumenskaya Chelyabinsk.
At 400mh: WCh: '13- h, '15- 2; EC: '14- 3; EU23: '13- sf; EJ: '11- sf; ET: '14- 1, '15- 1. RUS champion 2013, 2015.
Russian 400mh record 2015.
Progress at 400mh: 2010- 53.18, 2011- 51.45, 2012- 52.68, 2013- 49.40, 2014- 48.95, 2015- 48.05, 2016- 49.43. pbs: 200m 21.44 '14, 400m 45.86 '15.

Aleksandr LESNOY b. 28 Jul 1988 Krasnodar 1.94m 116kg.
At SP: WCh: '13-15: dnq 21/16; EC: '14- 10; WUG: '13- 1; WI: '14- 8; ET: '13-14: 3/3. RUS champion 2014.
Progress at SP: 2008- 16.46, 2009- 16.80, 2010- 19.09, 2011- 19.60, 2012- 20.05, 2013- 20.60, 2014- 21.40, 2015- 20.70i/20.55, 2016- 21.03. pb DT 58.80 '12.

Sergey LITVINOV b. 27 Jan 1986 Rostov-on-Don 1.85m 110kg.
At HT: WCh: '09-11-13-15: 5/dnq 15/11/5; EC: '14- 3; WJ: '04- 9; EU23: '07- 11; EJ: '05- 9; WUG: '13- 3; ET: '14- 1. German champion 2009, Russian 2013, 2015-16.
Progress at HT: 2004- 60.00, 2005- 73.98, 2006- 66.46, 2007- 74.80, 2008- 75.35, 2009- 77.88, 2010- 78.98, 2011- 78.90, 2012- 80.98, 2013- 80.89, 2014- 79.35, 2015- 77.24, 2016- 75.74.
Switched from Belarus to Germany 15 Jul 2008 and from 1 Jan 2011 to Russia. His father Sergey Litvinov (USSR) set three world records at hammer 1980-3 with a pb of 86.04 '86; he was

Olympic champion 1988 (2nd 1980) and World champion 1983 and 1987. His mother was born in Germany.

Aleksandr MENKOV b. 7 Dec 1990 Minusinsk, Krasnoyarsk reg. 1.78m 74kg. Krasnoyarsk VS. Krasnoyarsk State University.
At LJ: OG: '12- 11; WCh: '09-11-13-15: dnq 32/6/1/6; EC: '14- dnq 13; WI: '12- 3, '14- 5; EU23: '11- 1; EJ: '09- 1; EI: '13- 1; WUG: '13- 2; ET: '11-13-15: 1/1/1. Won DL 2012-13, Russian 2012.
Two Russian records 2013.
Progress at LJ: 2008- 6.98, 2009- 8.16, 2010- 8.10, 2011- 8.28, 2012- 8.29, 2013- 8.56, 2014- 8.30i/8.02, 2015- 8.27, 2016- 7.91. pbs: HJ 2.15 '10, TJ 15.20 '09.

Denis NIZHEGORODOV b. 26 Jul 1980 Saransk 1.80m 61kg. Saransk VS.
At 50kW: OG: '04- 2, '08- 3; WCh: '03-07-09-11: 5/4/dnf/1; EC: '06- dq; WCp: '06- 1, '08- 1; ECp: '09- 1, '11- 1; Russian champion 2003-04, 2007, 2016. At 20kW: EU23: '01- 5; WUG: '01- 4; ECp: '00- 17, '01- 7.
World record 50km walk 2008, best (no drugs test) 2004.
Progress at 20kW, 50kW: 2000- 1:21:47, 2001- 1:18:20; 2003- 1:23:23, 3:38:23; 2004- 3:35:29, 2005- dnf, 2006- 1:22:45, 3:38:02; 2007- 3:40:53, 2008- 3:34:14, 2009- 3:42:47, 2011- 3:42:45, 2016- 3:44:47. pbs: 5000mW 18:58.81i '12, 30kW 2:05:08 '06, 35kW 2:24:50 '06.

Ilya SHKURENYOV b. 11 Jan 1991 Linevo, Volgograd reg. 1.91m 82kg. Volgograd Dyn.
At Dec: OG: '12- 16; WCh: '13- 8, '15- 4; EC: '12- 3, '14- 3; WJ: '10- 2; EU23: '11- 5, '13- 2; ECp: '15- 1. Russian champion 2013, 2016. At Hep: WI: '12- 4; EI: '13- 5, '15- 1.
Progress at Dec: 2011- 7894, 2012- 8219, 2013- 8370, 2014- 8498, 2015- 8538, 2016- 8292. pbs: 60m 6.98i '15, 100m 10.91 '13, 400m 47.88 '15, 1000m 2:41.65i '13, 1500m 4:24.98 '15, 60mh 7.86i '15, 110mh 14.02 '15, HJ 2.11i '15, 2.10 '14; PV 5.40 '13, LJ 7.78 '16, SP 14.84i '11, 14.24 '15; DT 46.04 '14, JT 63.58 '14, Hep 6353i '15.
Won IAAF Challenge 2015.

Sergey SHUBENKOV b. 4 Oct 1990 Barnaul, Altay Kray 1.90m 75kg. Tyumen State University.
At 110mh: OG: '12- sf; WCh: '11- h, '13- 3, '15- 1; EC: '12- 1, '14- 1; EU23: '11- 1; EJ: '09- 2, WUG: '13- 3; CCp: '14- 1; ET: '13-14-15: 1/1. Won WMilG 2015, Russian 2013, 20-16. At 60mh: EI: '13- 1.
Six Russian 110mh records 2012-15.
Progress at 110mh: 2010- 13.54, 2011- 13.46, 2012- 13.09, 2013- 13.16/13.10w, 2014- 13.13, 2015- 12.98, 2016- 13.20. pb 60mh 7.49i '13.
Mother Natalya Shubenkova had heptathlon pb 6859 '04; 4th 1988 OG and 3rd 1986 EC.

Andrey SILNOV b. 9 Sep 1984 Shakhty, Rostov region 1.98m 83kg. Moskva Reg. VS.
At HJ: OG: '08- 1, '12- 12; WCh: '07- 11=; EC: '06- 1; EU23: '05- 9; WI: '12- 2; WCp: '06- 2; ECp: '06-08-14: 1/1/2. Won WAF 2008, Russian 2006.
Progress at HJ: 2002- 2.10, 2003- 2.10, 2004- 2.15, 2005- 2.28, 2006- 2.37, 2007- 2.36i/2.30, 2008- 2.38, 2009- 2.21, 2010- 2.33, 2011- 2.36, 2012- 2.37, 2013- 2.32i/2.18, 2014- 2.29i/2.28, 2016- 2.34.
Elected vice-president of the Russian Athletics Federation in December 2016.

Aleksiy SOKIRSKIY b. 16 Mar 1985 Gorlivka, Ukraine 1.85m 108kg. Krim Sakhi.
At HT: OG: '12- 4; WCh: '09-11: dnq 22/17; EC: '10- 6, '12- nt; WJ: '04- 8, EU23: '07- 6; WUG: '09- 3; ET: '11- 3. UKR champion 2010-11.
Progress at HT: 2005- 70.23, 2006- 71.95, 2007- 73.44, 2008- 75.54, 2009- 76.50, 2010- 76.62, 2011- 78.33, 2012- 78.91, 2013- 77.38, 2014- 77.86, 2015- 75.29, 2016- 77.78.
Switched from Ukraine to Russia 2015.

Dmitriy SOROKIN b. 27 Sep 1992 Khabarovsk 1.76m 73kg. Siberian Sate University of Physical Culture. Omsk.
At TJ: WCh: '15- 7; WY: 09- dnq 13; WUG: '15- 1; EI: '15- 6. Won WMilG 2015.
Progress at TJ: 2009- 15.62, 2010- 16.28/16.41w, 2011- 16.38dq, 2013- 15.30, 2014- 16.96, 2015- 17.29, 2016- 17.05i/16.49. pb LJ 7.94i '16, 7.55 '10.
2-year drugs ban 2011-13.

Dmitriy TARABIN b. 29 Oct 1991 Berlin, Germany 1.76m 85kg. Student at Russian State University of Physical Education, Moscow
At JT: WCh: '11- 10, '13- 3, '15- dnq 25; EC: '14- 5; WJ: '10- 3; WY: '07- dnq 23; EU23: '11- 3; EJ: '09- dnq 13; WUG: '13- 1; ET: '13- 1, '14- 2. Won RUS 2013, 2015-16.
Progress at JT: 2007- 55.18, 2008- 67.39, 2009- 69.63, 2010- 77.65, 2011- 85.10, 2012- 82.75, 2013- 88.84, 2014- 85.92, 2015- 84.70, 2016- 81.56.
Switched from Moldova to Russia 9 June 2010.
Married Mariya Abakumova on 12 Oct 2012.

Daniyil TSYPLAKOV b. 29 Jul 1992 Khabarovsk reg. 1.78m 70kg. Khabarovskiy.
At HJ: WCh: '15- 5; EC: '14- 5; WY: '09- 3; EU23: '13- 2; EJ: '11- 4; ET: '15- 1; WUG: '15- 1; WI: '14- 5; EI: '15- 1. RUS champion 2014-15.
Progress at HJ: 2008- 2.11, 2009- 2.21, 2010- 2.21, 2011- 2.26, 2012- 2.31, 2013- 2.30, 2014- 2.34i/2.33, 2015- 2.33, 2016- 2.30i/2.28.

Ivan UKHOV b. 29 Mar 1986 Chelyabinsk 1.92m 83kg. Sverdlovsk TU.
At HJ: OG: '12- 1; WCh: '09-11-13-15: 10/5=/4/dnq 24; EC: '06-10-14: 12=/2/3; WJ: '04- dnq 13; EJ: '05- 1; CCp: '14- 2; WUG: '05- 4; WI: '10-12-14: 1/3/2; EI: '09- 1, '11- 1. Won DL 2010, Russian 2009, 2012-13, 2016.
Russian high jump record 2014 (& 2 indoors, inc. one European).
Progress at HJ: 2004- 2.15, 2005- 2.30, 2006- 2.37i/2.33, 2007- 2.39i/2.20, 2008- 2.36i/2.30, 2009- 2.40i/2.35, 2010- 2.38i/2.36, 2011- 2.38i/

2.34, 2012- 2.39, 2013- 2.35, 2014- 2.42i/2.41, 2015- 2.32, 2016- 2.35.
Former discus thrower.
Stanislav YEMELYANOV b. 23 Oct 1990 Pavlovo, Nizhni Novgorod Reg. 1.75m 62kg. Mordoviya VS. Law student.
At 20kmW: WCh: '11- dq5; EC: '10- dq1; ECp: '11- 1dq; RUS champion 2010. At 10000mW: WJ: '08- 1; WY: '07- 1; EJ: '09- 1; ECp: '09- 1J.
World junior 10k walk record 2009.
Progress at 20kW: 2010- 1:19:43, (DQ: 2011- 1:19:33, 2012- 1:18:29), 2015- 1:20:10, 2016- 1:21:57, 2017- 1:19:48. pbs: 10kW 38:28 '09, 39:35.01t '08; 30kW 2:24:25 '09.
Two-year drugs ban announced in 2014 and all results annulled from 26 Jul 2010.

Women

Mariya ABAKUMOVA b. 15 Jan 1986 Stavropol 1.78m 85kg. Krasnodar VS.
At JT: OG: '08- dq2, '12- 10; WCh: '07- 09-11-13-15: 7/3/1/3/dnq 30; EC: '10- 5; WJ: '04- dnq 25; WY: '03- 4; EU23: '07- 6; EJ: '05- 1; WUG: '13- 1; CCp: '10- 1; ECp: '08-09-10: 2/3/3. Won WAF 2009, Russian 2008, 2011-13.
European javelin record 2008, four Russian 2008-11.
Progress at JT: 2002- 51.81, 2003- 51.41, 2004- 58.26, 2005- 59.53, 2006- 60.12, 2007- 64.28, 2008- 70.78, 2009- 68.92, 2010- 68.89, 2011- 71.99, 2012- 66.86, 2013- 70.53, 2015- 61.27, 2016- 59.55.
Tested positive for turinabol on re-testing of samples from the 2008 Olympic Games, so lost her silver medal. Married Dmitriy Tarabin on 12 Oct 2012, twin daughters Kira and Milana born 17 Jun 2014.

Anna BULGAKOVA b. 17 Jan 1988 Stavropol 1.73m 90kg. Stavropol VS.
At HT: OG: '08- dnq 20; WCh: '13- 5; EC: '12- 3, '14- nt; WJ: '04- 4, '06- 2; WY: '05- 2; EJ: '07- 4; ET: '14- 3. RUS champion 2014.
Progress at HT: 2003- 57.24, 2004- 63.83, 2005- 64.43, 2006- 67.79, 2007- 68.49, 2008- 73.79, 2010- 66.29, 2011- 69.10, 2012- 74.02, 2013- 76.17, 2014- 74.16, 2015- 72.15, 2016- 72.07. pb DT 44.19 '06.

Irina GORDEYEVA b. 9 Oct 1986 Leningrad 1.85m 55kg. Yunost Rossii.
At HJ: OG: '12- 10; WCh: '13- 9=; EC: '10- dnq 13=, '12- 3=; WJ: '04- 9; WY: '03- 7=; EJ: '05- 4; EI: '09- 5=.
Progress at HJ: 2001- 1.75, 2002- 1.82, 2003- 1.84, 2004- 1.88, 2005- 1.88, 2006- 1.88, 2007- 1.87i/1.83, 2008- 1.95, 2009- 2.02, 2010- 1.97, 2011- 1.94, 2012- 2.04, 2013- 1.99, 2014- 1.95, 2015- 1.96i/1.94, 2016- 1.94.

Olga KANISKINA b. 19 Jan 1985 Napolnaya Tavla, Mordoviya 1.61m 45kg. Saransk VS. Mathematics student at University of Mordovia.
At 20kW: OG: '08- 1, '12- dq2; WCh: '07-09-11: 1/dq1/dq1; EC: '06- 2, '10- dq1; WCp: '06-08-12: 5/1/dq2; EU23: '05- 2; ECp: '07- 2.

Progress at 20kW: 2005- 1:29:25, 2006- 1:26:02, 2007- 1:26:47, 2008- 1:25:11, 2009- 1:24:56, 2016- 1:25:54; DQ: 2010- 1:27:44, 2011- 1:28:35, 2012- 1:25:09. pbs: 3000mW 11:57.86i '13, 12:23.5 '05; 5000mW 20:38.2 '05, 10kW 41:42R '09.
Eight successive 20km walk wins 2007-09 and 11 wins in 12 races 2008-11. 3 year 2 month ban announced in January 2015 for biological passport anomaly and results from 15 Aug 2009 to 15 Oct 2012 annulled, so she therefore loses 2009 and 2011 World titles and 2011 IAAF Challenge.

Anisya KIRDYAPKINA b. 23 Oct 1989 Saransk, Mordoviya 1.65m 51kg. née Kornikova. Mordovia TU.
At 20kW: OG: '12- 4; WCh: '09- 3, '11- 2, '13- 2; EC: '10- 1; WCp: '10-12-14: 6/5/1; ECp: '09-11-13: 2/2/1; WUG: '13- 1, '15- 1; RUS champion 2010, 2012. At 10000mW: EJ: '07- 1; ECp: '07- 1J.
World junior 20km walk best 2008.
Progress at 20kW: 2007- 1:28:00, 2008- 1:25:30, 2009- 1:25:26, 2010- 1:25:11, 2011- 1:25:09, 2012- 1:26:26. 2013- 1:25:59, 2014- 1:26:31, 2015- 1:26:44. pbs: 3000mW 11:44.10i '12, 5000mW 21:06.3 '06, 10000mW 43:27.30 '07, 42:04R '11.
Married to Sergey Kirdyapkin (50kW: dq1 OG 12, 1/1dq WCh 05/09, 1dq WCp 12, pb 3:38:08 '05, 3:35:59dq '12).

Darya KLISHINA b. 15 Jan 1991 Tver 1.80m 57kg. Moskva. Model.
At LJ: OG: '16- 9; WCh: '11- 6, '13- 6, '15- 10; EC: '14- 3; WY: '07- 1; EU23: '11- 1; EJ: '09- 1; WI: '10-12-14: 5/4/7; EI: '11-13-17: 1/1/4, WUG: '13- 1; ET: '11-13-15: 1/2/1. RUS champion 2014.
Progress at LJ: 2005- 5.83, 2006- 6.33/6.47w, 2007- 6.49, 2008- 6.52i/6.20, 2009- 6.80, 2010- 7.03, 2011- 7.05, 2012- 6.93, 2013- 7.01i/6.90/6.98w, 2014- 6.90, 2015- 6.95, 2016- 6.84, 2017- 6.84i.
The one Russian athlete permitted to compete (as a neutral) at OG '16 and EI 17.

Oksana KONDRATYEVA b. 22 Nov 1985 Moskva 1.80m 80kg. Moscow State University of PE.
At HT: WCh: '13- 7; WUG: '13- 2. Won RUS 2015-16.
Progress at HT: 2004- 57.36, 2005- 62.24, 2006- 61.81, 2007- 64.09, 2008- 66.08, 2009- 67.84, 2010- 71.90, 2011- 69.87, 2012- 73.31, 2013- 77.13, 2014- 72.17, 2015- 72.01, 2016- 70.75.
Mother Lydmila Kondratyeva (1980 Olympic 100m champion) and father Yuriy Sedykh (hammer world record holder).

Yekaterina KONEVA b. 25 Sep 1988 Khabarovsk 1.69m 55kg. Khabarovskiy.
At TJ: WCh: '13- 2, '15- 7; EC: '14- 2; WI: '14- 1; WUG: '11-13-15: 1/1/1; CCp: '14- 2; EI: '15- 1; ET: '13-14-15: 2/1/1. RUS champion 2014-15, WMilG LJ & TJ 2015.
Progress at TJ: 2010- 13.93/14.00w, 2011- 14.46, 2012- 14.60i/14.36, 2013- 14.82, 2014- 14.89, 2015-

15.04, 2016- 14.42. pbs: 60m 7.39i '07, 100m 11.76 '09, 200m 23.89 '09, LJ 6.82i '15, 6.70/6.80w '11. Married Sergey Polyanskiy (LJ 8.20 '15, 8 WCh '15) in October 2016. Two-year drugs ban 2007-09.

Angelina KRASNOVA b. 7 Feb 1991 Moskva 1.68m 55kg. née Zhuk. Irkutskaya.
At PV: WCh: '13- 7; EC: '14- 3; EU23: '13- 1; CCp: '14- 2; EI: '13- 5, '15- 4.
Progress at PV: 2007- 3.60i, 2008- 3.80, 2010- 4.10, 2011- 4.30i/4.25, 2012- 4.40, 2013- 4.70, 2014- 4.65, 2015- 4.67i/4.60, 2016- 4.66i/4.50.

Mariya KUCHINA/LASITSKENE b. 14 Jan 1993 Prokhladny, Kabardino-Balkar 1.82m 60kg. Moskovskaya.
At HJ: WCh: '15- 1; EC: '14- 2; WJ: '12- 3; WY: '09- 2=; EU23: '15- 12; EJ: '11- 1; WI: '14- 1=; EI: '15- 1; WUG: '13- 2; CCp: '14- 1; ET: '13-14-15: 1/1/1. Won DL 2014, Yth Oly 2010, RUS champion 2014, W.MilG 2015.
World junior indoor high jump record 2011.
Progress at HJ: 2009- 1.87, 2010- 1.91, 2011- 1.97i/1.95, 2012- 1.96i/1.89, 2013- 1.98i/1.96, 2014- 2.01i/2.00, 2015- 2.01, 2016- 2.00, 2017- 2.03i.
Married journalist Vladas Lasitskas on 17 Mar 2017.

Yelena LASHMANOVA b. 9 Apr 1992 Saransk 1.70m 48kg. Biology student at Mordoviya State University.
At 20kmW: OG: '12- 1; WCh: '13- 1; WCp: '12- 1; won RUS 2016. At 10000mW: WJ: '10- 1; EJ: '11- 1; ECp: '11- 1J. At 5000mW: WY: '09- 1.
Official world 20km walk record 2012, world junior 10,000m walk record 2011.
Progress at 20kW: 2012- 1:25:02, 2013- 1:25:49, 2016- 1:24:58, 2017- 1:25:18. pbs: 5000mW 20:15.6 '16, 10000mW 42:59.48 '11.
Best ever debut at 20k walk (1:26:30 in 2012) and has won all seven of her career 20k walks 2012-3. Won IAAF Walks Challenge 2013. Received two-year drugs ban from test on 4 Jan 2014.

Yekaterina MEDVEDYEVA b. 29 Mar 1994. Mordoviya.
At 10000mW: WJ: '12- 1; WCp: '12- 4J.
Progress at 20kW: 2015- 1:29:32, 2016- 1:26:40, 2017- 1:25:22. pbs: 10000mW 43:50.0 '13.

Marina PANDAKOVA 1 Mar 1989. Churvashkaya Reg.
At 20kW: WCp: '14- 10. ECp: '13- 3, '15- 5; WUG: '15- 2.
Progress at 20kW: 2008- 1:38:19, 2011- 1:33:00, 2012- 1:28:29, 2013- 1:27:39, 2014- 1:27:54, 2015- 1:25:03, 2016- 1:27:18. pbs: 3000mW: 11:50.30 '16, 5000mW 21:40.41i '13, 10kW 43:29 '12.

Vira REBRIK b. 25 Feb 1989 Yalta 1.76m 65kg.
At JT: OG: '08/12- dnq 15/19; WCh: '09- 11-13-15: 9/dnq 16/11.dnq 24; EC: '10- dnq 17, '12- 1; WJ: '06- 2, '08- 1; WY: '05- 2; EU23: '09- 2, '11- 2; EJ: '07- 1; WUG: '09- 2, '11- 4; ET: '13- 3. Won UKR 2010-12, RUS 2015-16.
World junior javelin record 2008; three UKR records 2012.
Progress at JT: 2003- 44.94, 2004- 52.47, 2005- 57.48, 2006- 59.64, 2007- 58.48, 2008- 63.01, 2009- 62.26, 2010- 63.36, 2011- 61.60, 2012- 66.86, 2013- 64.30, 2014- 61.57, 2015- 64.93, 2016- 67.30.
Crimean athlete, transferred to Russia in 2015.

Anastasiya SAVCHENKO b. 15 Nov 1989 Omsk 1.75m 65kg. Luch Moskva.
At PV: OG: '12- dnq 26-; WCh: '13- 5=; EC: '12- 4; EU23: '09- 8, '11- 6; WUG: '13- 1; WI: '12/14-10/11; EI: '13- 5=.
Progress at PV: 2005- 3.80, 2006- 3.80i/3.70, 2007- 3.90, 2008- 4.20i/4.10, 2009- 4.30i/4.20, 2010- 4.30, 2011- 4.40, 2012- 4.60, 2013- 4.73, 2014- 4.50, 2015- 4.60i/4.20, 2016- 4.40.

Anzhelika SIDOROVA b. 28 Jun 1991 Moskva 1.70m 52kg. Moskva Youth.
At PV: WCh: '15- nh; EC: '14- 1; WJ: '10- 4; EU23: '13- 2; WI: '14- 2=; EI: '13- 3, '15- 1; ET: '13-14-15:- 2/1/2. RUS champion 2014-15.
Progress at PV: 2007- 3.80, 2008- 4.00, 2009- 4.10i/4.00, 2010- 4.30, 2011- 4.40i/4.30, 2012- 4.50, 2013- 4.62i/4.60, 2014- 4.72i/4.70, 2015- 4.80i/4.79, 2016- 4.85.

Irina TARASOVA b. 15 Apr 1987 Kovrov 1.83m 110kg. Army.
At SP: OG: '12- 7; WCh: '13- 7; ECh: '12- 2, '14- 6; WI: '12- 8; WJ: '04- 5, '06- 3; WY: '03- 5; EU23: '07- 1, '09- 2; EJ: '05- 2; EI: '11- 8, '13- 5; WUG: '07-11-13: 1/1/1; ET: '14- 2, '15- 2. RUS champion 2015.
Progress at SP: 2002- 14.01, 2003- 15.04, 2004- 16.16, 2005- 16.79i/16.53, 2006- 17.11, 2007- 18.27, 2008- 18.45, 2009- 18.21, 2010- 18.18, 2011- 18.72, 2012- 19.35, 2013- 19.20, 2014- 18.38, 2015- 18.53, 2016- 18.78.

Svetlana VASILYEVA b. 24 Jul 1992. Mordovia VS.
At 20kW: EU23: '13- 1; ECp: '15- 3. At 10000mW: EJ: '11- 2; WCp: '10- 5J; ECp: '11- 2J. At 5000mW: WY: '09- 3.
Progress at 20kW: 2012- 1:28:30. 2013- 1:29:56, 2014- 1:28:49, 2015- 1:25:04, 2016- 1:27:58. pbs: 3000m 11:57.71i '14, 10kW 42:43.0t '11.

SAINT KITTS & NEVIS

Governing body: Saint Kitts Amateur Athletic Association, PO Box 932, Basseterre, St Kitts. Founded 1961.

Kim COLLINS b. 5 Apr 1976 Ogees, Saint-Peter 1.75m 64kg. Studied sociology at Texas Christian University, USA.
At 100m (/200m): OG: '96- qf, 00- 7/sf, '04- 6, '08- sf/6, '16- sf; WCh: '95- hR, '97- h, 99- h/h, '01- 5/3=, '03- 1, '05- 3, '07- sf, '09- qf/qf, '11- 3/sf/3R, '15- h; CG: '02- 1; PAm: '07- 5, '11- 2; PAm-J: '95- 2; CAC: '99- 2, '01- 1/1, '03- 1; WCp: '02- 2/2R, '14- 1R/3 4x400mR. At 60m: WI: '03-08-16: 2/2=/8. Won NCAA indoor 60m & 200m 2001.

SKN records: 100m from 1996 to 2016, 200m from 1998, 400m 2000. CAC indoor 60m 2015. M35 world records: 100m (3) 2013-16, indoor 60m (4) 2014-15; M40 100m 2016, 60m indoor (6) 2017.
Progress at 100m, 200m: 1995- 10.63, 21.85; 1996- 10.27, 21.06; 1998- 10.18/10.16w, 20.88/20.78w; 1999- 10.21, 20.43, 2000- 10.13A/10.15/10.02w, 20.31A/20.18w; 2001- 10.04A/10.00?/9.99w, 20.20/ 20.08w; 2002- 9.98, 20.49; 2003- 9.99/9.92w, 20.40w; 2004- 10.00, 20.98; 2005- 10.00, 2006- 10.33, 21.53; 2007- 10.14, 2008- 10.05, 20.25; 2009- 10.15/10.08w, 20.45; 2010- 10.20, 21.35/20.76w; 2011- 10.00A/10.01, 20.52; 2012- 10.01/9.96w, 2013- 9.97, 21.37i, 2014- 9.96, 2015- 9.98/9.94w, 2016- 9.93. pbs: 60m 6.47i '15, 400m 46.93 '00.
The first athlete from his country to make Olympic and World finals and in 2003 the first to win a World Indoor medal and a World title; won a further medal in 2011 and has now competed in ten World Champs. Oldest man to have broken 10 secs for 100m. There is a 'Kim Collins Highway' in St Kitts.

ST LUCIA
Governing body: Saint Lucia Athletics Association, Olympic House, Barnard Hill P.O.GM 697 Gable Woods Mall, Castries.
Levern SPENCER b. 23 Jun 1984 Cacao Babonneau 1.80m 54kg. Was at University of Georgia.
At HJ: OG: '08/12- dnq 26/19, '16- 6; WCh: '05- 07-09-11-13-15: dnq 22/15=/dnq 24=/dnq 13/11/12=; CG: '02-06-10-14: 12=/5/3/3; WJ: '02- 8; WY: '01- 3; PAm: '03-07-11-15: 5/3/6/1; CAG: '06-10-14: 3/1/1; WI: '14- 7, '16- 5=; CCp: '10- 3=, '14- 5. CAC champion 2001, 2005, 2008-09, 2011, 2013; NACAC 2007, 2015.
Nine St. Lucia high jump records 2004-10.
Progress at HJ: 2000- 1.80, 2001- 1.81, 2002- 1.83, 2003- 1.86, 2004- 1.88, 2005- 1.94, 2006- 1.90, 2007- 1.94, 2008- 1.93, 2009- 1.95, 2010- 1.98, 2011- 1.94, 2012- 1.91, 2013- 1.95A, 2014- 1.96, 2015- 1.94, 2016- 1.96. pbs: 200m 24.22 '05, LJ 6.08 '14.

SERBIA
Governing body: Athletic Federation of Serbia, Strahinjica Bana 73a, 11000 Beograd. Founded in 1921 (as Yugoslav Athletic Federation).
National Championships (Yugoslav) first held in 1920 (men) and 1923 (women). **2016 Champions**: **Men**: 100m: Aleksa Kijanovic 10.77, 200m: Goran Podunavac 21.91, 400m: Milos Ravic 47.73, 800m: Marko Vozab 1:51.86, 1500m: Elzan Bibic 3:52.65, 3000m: Milos Pendic 8:43.26, 5000m: Nemanja Stojanovic 15:02.10, 10000m: Sasa Stolic 31:37.9, HMar: Ognjen Stojanovic 71:48, Mar: Sinisa Radivojevic 2:38:59, 3000mSt: Milos Krstic 9:14.93, 110mh: Milan Ristic 14.03, 400mh: Milos Markovic 53.46, HJ: Milos Todosijevic 2.16, PV: Djordje Mijailovic 4.90, LJ: Lazar Anic 7.98, TJ: Nemanja Koviljac 14.59, SP: Armin Sinancevic 17.28, DT: Marko Peric 48.25, HT: Laslo Eperjesi 56.56, JT: Vedran Samac 74.19, Dec: Mihail Dudas 8174, 10kW: Vladimir Savanovic 43:25. **Women**: 100m: Zorana Barjaktarovic 11.88, 200m: Tamara Salaski 24.26, 400m: Katarina Ilic 55.54, 800m/1500m: Amela Terzic 2:06.97/4:18.51, 3000m: Teodora Simovic 9:47.64, 5000m: Olivera Jevtic 16:21.14, 10000m: Teodora Simovic 33:56.37, HMar: Nevena Jovanovic 1:24:02, Mar: Marijana Cegar-Lukic 3:01:06, 3000mSt: Biljana Cvijanovic 10:18.88, 100mh: Ivana Petkovic 13.79, 400mh: Iva Saviv 66.78, HJ: Dunja Spajic 1.60, PV: Milica Emini 3.10, LJ: Milica Kovacevic 5.82, TJ/Hep: Ivana Ognjanovic 13.04/4467, SP: Dijana Sefcic 13.71, DT: Dragana Tomasevic 60.10, HT: Sara Savatovic 59.85, JT: Marija Vucenovic 50.87, 5000mW/5kW: Dusica Topic 23:33.49/25:22.

Asmir KOLASINAC b. 15 Oct 1984 Skopje, Macedonia 1.86m 137kg. AC Partizan, Belgrade.
At SP: OG: '08- dnq 30, '12- 7, '16- dnq 15; WCh: '09-11-13-15: dnq 21/10/10/7; EC: '10-12-14-16: 8/3/5/5; EU23: '05- dnq; EI: '13- 1, '15- 2; Won Balkan 2011; SRB 2008, 2010-15.
Progress at SP: 2004- 15.50, 2005- 17.88, 2006- 17.85, 2007- 19.30, 2008- 19.99, 2009- 20.41, 2010- 20.52i/20.38, 2011- 20.50, 2012- 20.85, 2013- 20.80, 2014- 20.79, 2015- 21.58, 2016- 20.96.
Older brother Almir BIH had JT best 68.32 '09.

Women
Ivana SPANOVIC b. 10 May 1990 Zrenjanin 1.76m 65kg. AC Vojvodina, Novi Sad.
At LJ: OG: '08- dnq 30, '12- 10, '16- 3; WCh: '13- 3, '15- 3; EC: '10-12-14-16: 8/dnq 14/2/1; WJ: '06- 7, '08- 1; WY: '05- dnq, '07- 2; EU23: '11- 2; EJ: '07- 5, '09- 2; WUG: '09- 1; CCp: '14- 2; WI: '14- 3, '16- 2; EI: '13-15-17: 5/1/1. Won DL 2016, Serbian 2006, 2008, 2011-13, Balkan 2011, 2013.
11 Serbian long jump records 2009-16 (f9 indoor 2007-16), indoor records 60m & Pen.
Progress at LJ: 2003- 5.36, 2004- 5.91, 2005- 6.43, 2006- 6.48i/6.38, 2007- 6.53i/6.41, 2008- 6.65, 2009- 6.71, 2010- 6.78, 2011- 6.71/6.74w, 2012- 6.64, 2013- 6.82, 2014- 6.92i/6.88, 2015- 7.02, 2016- 7.10, 2017- 7.24i. pbs: 60m 7.31i '15, 100m 11.90 '13, 60mh 8.49i '13, HJ 1.78i '13, 1.65 '05; TJ 13.78 '14, SP 12.40i '13, Pen 4240i '13.
Won first medal for Serbia at World Champs and at the Olympic Games. Her 7.24 at EI '17 was the world's longest indoor women's LJ for 28 years.

SLOVAKIA
Governing body: Slovak Athletic Federation, Junácka 6, 832 80 Bratislava. Founded 1939.
National Championships first held in 1939. **2016 Champions**: **Men**: : 100m/200m: Ján Volko 10.47/20.96, 400m: Denis Danac 48.18,

800m: Matús Talán 1:54.62, 1500m/5000m: Peter Durec 3:55.44/14:41.64, 10000m: Branislav Sarkan 31:30.88, HMar: Jozef Urban 67:49, Mar: Gabriel Svajda 2:37:13, 3000mSt: Jakub Valachovic 9:26.45, 110mh: Marco Adrien Drozda 15.08, 400mh: Martin Kucera 51.07, HJ: Matús Bubeník 2.23, PV: Ján Zmoray 4.80, LJ: Jan Suba 7.12, TJ: Tomas Veszelka 16.20, SP: Matus Olej 17.82, DT: Michal Holica 54.63, HT: Marcel Lomnicky 76.87, JT: Patrik Zenúch 67.73, 20kW: Anton Kucmín 1:20:43, 50kW: Dusan Majdan 3:58:41. **Women**: 100m: Lenka Krsáková 11.74, 200m: Alexandra Bezeková 23.41w, 400m: Iveta Putalová 53.63, 800m: Pavla Habovstiaková 2:13.49, 1500m: Kristina Hegedüsová 4:40.47, 5000m: Sona Vnencáková 17:44.62, 10000m Zuzana Durcová 36:31.04, HMar: Petra Fasungová 79:48, Mar: Monika Pisová 3:26:28, 3000mSt: Zuzana Gejdosová 11:51.89, 100mh: Stanislava Lajcáková 13.82, 400mh: Lucia Slanícková 57.76, HJ: Katarína Kustárová 1.77, PV: Anna Mária Hrvolová 3.60, LJ: Jana Veldáková 6.75, TJ: Dana Veldáková 13.79, SP: Patrícia Slosárová 13.83, DT: Ivana Kristofícová 44.50, HT: Martina Hrasnová 72.34, JT: Miroslava Vargová 45.22, 20kW: Maria Czaková 1:30:53.

Marcel LOMNICKY b. 6 Jul 1987 Nitra 1.77m 106kg. TJ Stavbár Nitra. Was at Virginia Tech University, USA.
At HT: OG: '12- dnq 14, '16- 5; WCh: '11- dnq 21, '13- 8, '15- 8; WJ: '04- dnq 17, '06- 3; EC: '10-12-14-16: dnq 24/11/7/5; EU23: '07- 3, '09- 6; EJ: '05- 8; WUG: '11- 2, '13- 2. SVK champion 2012-16, won NCAA HT 2009, indoor Wt 2012.
Progress at HT: 2005- 64.27, 2006- 69.53, 2007- 72.17, 2008- 72.66, 2009- 71.78, 2010- 74.83, 2011- 75.84, 2012- 77.43, 2013- 78.73, 2014- 79.16, 2015- 77.63, 2016- 77.48. pbs: SP 15.73 '07, DT 43.82 '08, Wt 23.05i '12.
Sister Nikola Lomnická (b. 16 Sep 1988) has hammer best 71.58 '14, won NCAA 2010 and was 8th EC 2014.

Matej TÓTH b. 10 Feb 1983 Nitra 1.85m 73kg. Dukla Banská Bystrica.
At 20kW/(50kW): OG: '04- 32, '08- 26, '12- (5), '16- (1); WCh: '05- 21, 07- 14, '09- 8/9, '11- 10/dnf, '13- (5), '15- (1); EC: '06- 6, '10- 6, '14- (2); EU23: '03- 6; WCp: '10- (1); ECp: '09-11-13-15: 9/1/3/2.
At 10000mW: WJ: '02- 16, WY: '99- 8; EJ: '01- 6. Won SVK 20kW 2005-08, 2010-12, 2015; 50kW 2011.
Four SVK 50k walk records 2009-15.
Progress at 20kW, 50kW: 1999- 1:34:29, 2000- 1:30:28, 2001- 1:29:33, 2003- 1:13:17, 2004- 1:23:18, 2005- 1:21:38, 2006- 1:21:39, 2007- 1:25:10, 2008- 1:21:24, 2009- 1:20:53, 3:41:32; 2010- 1:22:04, 3:53:30; 2011- 1:20:16, 3:39:46; 2012- 1:20:25, 3:41:24; 2013- 1:20:14, 3:41:07; 2014- 1:19:48, 3:36:21; 2015- 1:20:21, 3:34:38; 2016- 1:29:04, 3:40:58. pbs: 3000mW 10:57.32i '11, 11:05.95 '12; 5000mW 18:34.56i '12, 18:54.39 '11; 10000W 39:45.03 '06, 39:07R '10; 30kW 2:12:44 '13, 35kW 2:34:23 '13.
First ever World and Olympic gold medallist for Slovakia. Won IAAF Race Walking Challenge 2015.

Women

Martina HRASNOVÁ b. 21 Mar 1983 Bratislava 1.77m 88kg. née Danisová. Dukla Banská Bystrica.
At HT: OG: '08- 6, '12/16- dnq 17/19; WCh: '01-07-13-15: dnq 23/12/21/16, '09- 3; EC: '02 & '06- dnq 26, '12—14-16: 2/2.7; WJ: '00- 5, '02- 2; EJ: '99- 4, '01- 2; CCp: '14- 3; WUG: '07- 5, '09- 2.
Won SVK SP 2003, 2006; HT 2000-01, 2006, 2008-09, 2011-15.
14 Slovakian hammer records 2001-09.
Progress at HT: 1999- 58.61, 2000- 61.62, 2001- 68.50, 2002- 68.22, 2003- 66.36, 2005- 69.24, 2006- 73.84, 2007- 69.22, 2008- 76.82, 2009- 76.90, 2011- 72.47, 2012- 73.34, 2013- 72.41, 2014- 75.27, 2015- 74.27, 2016- 72.34. pbs: 60m 7.96i '12, SP 15.60i '15, 15.02 '06; DT 43.15 '06, Wt 21.74i '11.
Two-year drugs ban (nandrolone) from July 2003. Daughter Rebeka born on 4 July 2010. Brother of Branislav Danis (HT 69.20 '06).

Dana VELDÁKOVÁ b. 3 Jun 1981 Roznava 1.79m 60kg. Dukla Banská Bystrica.
At (LJ/)TJ: OG: '08- dnq, '12- 10, '16- dnq 17; WCh: '05-07-09-11-13-15: dnq 17/11/8/11/11.dnq 15; EC: '02/06- dnq 15/24, '10-12-14-16: 7/5/6/11; WJ: '98- 6, '00- 4/3; EU23: '01- 5, '03- 4; EJ: '99- 8; WI: '06-10-12-14: 8/6/8/8; EI: '07-09-11: 6/3/3; WUG: '03- 5, '07- 2. Won SVK 100mh 2003, TJ 2002-05, 2007-16 (& 15 indoors), Hep 2001, 2004.
Two SVK triple jump records 2007-08.
Progress at TJ: 1998- 13.12, 1999- 13.13/13.19w, 2000- 13.92, 2001- 13.73, 2002- 13.99, 2003- 14.02, 2004- 13.96A, 2005- 14.16, 2006- 14.19, 2007- 14.41, 2008- 14.51, 2009- 14.43, 2010- 14.32/14.59w, 2011- 14.48, 2012- 14.36, 2013- 14.31, 2014- 14.10i/13.91, 2015- 14.27, 2016- 14.11. pbs: 60m 7.73i '06, 100m 11.99 '14, 60mh 8.82i '03, 100mh 14.38 '01, HJ 1.75 '01, LJ 6.56 '08, SP 11.56i '04, Hep 5191 '01, Pen 3746i '03.
Twin **Jana** LJ 6.75 '16, 6.88w '10; TJ 13.40 '04; 20 Slovak LJ titles.

SLOVENIA

Governing body: Atletska Zveza Slovenije, Letaliska cesta 33c, 1122 Ljubljana. Current organisation founded 1948.
2016 National Champions: Men: 100m: Enej Leban 10.79, 200m/400m: Luka Janezic 20.96/45.94, 800m: Jan Petrac 1:49.15, 1500m: Jan Breznik 3:55.92, 3000m: Jan Kokalj 8:30.05, 5000m: Primoz Kobe 14:50.91, 10000m: Domen Hafner 31:43.38, HMar: Peter Lamovec 67:51, Mar: Janez Mulej 2:34:57, 3000mSt: Blaz Grad 9:30.08, 110mh: Gregor Kokalovic 15.16, 400mh: Mitja Lindic 51.69, HJ: Axel Luxa 2.00, PV:

Robert Renner 5.60, LJ: Nino Celec 7.28, TJ: Jan Luxa 15.63, SP: Marko Spiler 18.61, DT: Tadej Hribar 55.00, HT: Nejc Plesko 73.51, JT: Matija Kranjc 78.20, Dec: Simon Blatnik 4852. **Women:** 100m/200m: Maja Mihalinec 11.64/23.17, 400m: Anita Horvat 53.47, 800m: Jerneja Smonkar 2:10.60, 1500m/3000m: Marusa Mismas 4:30.91/9:19.55, 5000m: Neja Krsinar 18:19.13, 10000m: Sara Jaklic 37:49.92, HMar: Sonja Roman 77:50, Mar: Helena Javornik 3:01:32, 3000mSt: Urska Arzensek 11:54.07, 100mh: Marina Tomic 13.66, 400mh: Agata Zupin 60.46, HJ: Marusa Cernjul 1.93, PV: Tina Sutej 4.55i, LJ: Maja Bedrac 6.21, TJ: Petra Koren 13.82, SP: Tina Vaupot 10.63, DT: Veronika Domjan 59.36, HT: Barbara Spiler 65.96, JT: Martina Ratej 59.76, Hep: Brina Mljac 4168.

Women

Martina RATEJ b. 2 Nov 1981 Celje 1.78m 69kg. AD Kladivar Celje.
At JT: OG: '08- dnq 36, '12- 7, '16- dnq 18; WCh: '09-11-13-15: 11/7/dnq 20/dnq 23; EC: '06-10-12-14-16: dnq 21/7/dnq 21/6/6; WJ: '00- dnq 15.
SLO champion 2005-14, 2016; MedG 2013, Balkan 2015.
Five SLO javelin records 2008-10.
Progress at JT: 1999- 48.74, 2000- 46.83, 2005- 50.86, 2006- 57.49, 2007- 58.49, 2008- 63.44, 2009- 63.42, 2010- 67.16, 2011- 65.89, 2012- 65.24, 2013- 62.60, 2014- 66.13, 2015- 65.75, 2016- 61.03.

SOUTH AFRICA

Governing body: Athletics South Africa, PO Box 2712, Houghton 2041. Original body founded 1894.
National Championships first held in 1894 (men), 1929 (women). **2016 Champions: Men:** 100m: Henricho Bruintjies 10.17, 200m: Clarence Munyai 20.73, 400m: Wade van Niekerk 44.98, 800m: Jacob Rozani 1:46.26, 1500m: Flávio Seholhe MOZ 3:42.41, 5000m/10000m/HMar: Stephen Mokoka 13:40.81/27:57.50/61:26, Mar: Lucas Jani 2:21:32, 3000mSt: Rantso Mokopane 8:35.09, 110mh: Antonio Alkana 13.37, 400mh: L.J.van Zyl 49.34, HJ: Keegan Fourie 2.15, PV: Eben Beukes 5.50, LJ: Rushwal Samaai 8.34, TJ: Menzi Mthembu 16.10, SP: Orazio Cremona 19.85, DT: Victor Hogan 67.62, HT: Chris Harmse 73.32 (21st successive title), JT: Phil-Mar Janse van Rensburg 78.88, Dec: Friedrich Pretorius 7482, 20kW: Lebogang Shange 1:20:42. **Women:** 100m/200m: Alyssa Conley 11.36/23.01, 400m/800m/1500m: Caster Semenya 50.74/1:58.45/4:10.91. 5000m/HMar: Irvette van Zyl 16:02.63/71:00, 10000m: Glenrose Xaba 34:23.56, Mar: Patience Khumalo 2:47:21, 3000mSt: Nolene Conrad 10:38.35, 100mh: Claudia Heunis 13.42, 400mh: Wenda Nel 54.84, HJ: Julia du Plessis 1.80, PV: Christy Nel 3.50, LJ: Lynique Prinsloo 6.59, TJ: Patience Ntshingila 13.57, SP/DT: Ischke Senekal 15.28/56.86, HT:
Stefanie Greyling 54.61, JT: Sunette Viljoen 59.39, Hep: Bianca Erwee 5395, 20kW: Anél Oosthuizen 1:37:21.

Luvo MANYONGA b. 18 Nov 1991 Mbekweni 1.85m 65kg. Tuks, University of Pretoria.
At LJ: OG: '16- 2; WCh: '11- 5; WJ: '10- 1; AfG: '11- 1, AfCh; '16- 2; Af-J: '09- 3.
African jlong jump record 2017, junior 2010.
Progress at LJ: 2009- 7.65, 2010- 8.19, 2011- 8.26, 2012- 8.00, 2016- 8.48, 2017- 8.62A. pb TJ 15.71A '10.
18 months drugs ban from positive test 20 Mar 2012.

Godfrey Khotso MOKOENA b. 6 Mar 1985 Heidelberg, Gauteng 1.90m 73kg. University of Johannesburg.
At LJ/(TJ): OG: '04- (dnq 29), '08- 2, '12- 8, '16- (dnq 21); WCh: '05-07-09-11-13-15: 7/5/2/dnq 15=/7/dnq 13 & 9; CG: '06- 4/2, '14- (1); WJ: '02- 12, '04- 2/1; AfG: '03- 3/2, '07- 3; AfCh: '06- 2/2, '10- 1, '14- 2/1, '16- (3); CCp: '14- (2); WI: '06-08-10: 5/1/2. At HJ: WY: '01- 5. Won DL LJ 2014, RSA LJ 2005-07, 2009-11; TJ 2004-06, 2014--15.
Records: African LJ (3) 2009, RSA LJ (5) 2005-09, TJ (3) 2004-14, African junior TJ 2004.
Progress at LJ, TJ: 2001- 7.17A, 2002- 7.82A, 16.03A; 2003- 7.84A/7.83, 16.28; 2004- 8.09, 16.96A/16.77; 2005- 8.37A/8.22, 17.25; 2006- 8.39/8.45w, 16.95; 2007- 8.34A/8.28/8.32w, 16.75; 2008- 8.25/8.35w, 2009- 8.50, 2010- 8.23A/8.15/8.22w, 2011- 8.25/8.31w, 2012- 8.29A/8.24, 2013- 8.30, 15.68i; 2014- 8.19, 17.35; 2015- 8.16, 16.85; 2016- 16.77. pbs: 100m 10.7A '09, HJ 2.10 '01.
Returned to triple jumping in 2014.

Rushwal SAMAAI b. 25 Sep 1991 Paarl 1.78m 73kg. Was at University of Johannesburg.
At LJ: OG: '16- 9; WCh: '15- dnq 20; CG: '14- 3; AfCh: '14- 3, '16- 1; WI: '16- 5; RSA champion 2015.
Progress at LJ: 2009- 6.93A, 2010- 7.41, 2011- 7.75/7.80w, 2012- 7.94A/7.61w, 2013- 7.96A/7.74, 2014- 8.13A/8.08, 2015- 8.38, 2016- 8.38/8.40w. pb TJ 16.10A '14.

Akani SIMBINE b. 21 Sep 1993 Kempton Park 1.74m 67kg. Tuks, University of Pretoria.
At 100m/(200m): OG: '16- 5; WCh: '13- h, '15- sf/sf; CG: 14- sf/5; AfCh: '14- 8, 16- 3; WUG: '15- 1. Won RSA 100m 2015.
Three South African 100m records 2015-16.
Progress at 100m, 200m: 2010- 10.61A, 2011- 10.57A, 21.27A; 2012- 10.19A, 20.68A; 2013- 10.36, 20.79A/20.78w; 2015- 9.97, 20.23; 2016- 9.89, 20.16. pb 60m 6.60Ai '15, 6.66i '13.

Wayde van NIEKERK b. 15 Jul 1992 Cape Town 1.83m 73kg. University of the Free State, Bloemfontein.
At (200m)/400m: OG: '16- 1; WCh: '13- h, '15- 1; CG: '14- sf/2; AfCh: '14- 2, '16- (1); WJ: '10- (4); CCp: '14- 4/1R. Won RSA 200m 2011, 400m 2013-15

Records: World 400m 2016, Commonwealth 400m 2015, African 300m (2) 2016-16. 400m (2) 2015, RSA 200m & 400m (2) 2015.
Progress at 200m, 400m: 2010- 21.02, 2011- 20.57, 2012- 20.91, 46.43; 2013- 20.84A, 45.09; 2014- 20.19, 44.38; 2015- 19.94, 43.48; 2016- 20.02, 43.03. pbs: 100m 9.98A '16, 10.51 '10; 300m 31.03 '16.
The only man to run under 10,0, 20.0 and 44.0, he ranks as the fourth best ever combination 100-200-400 man.

Louis J. van ZYL b. 20 Jul 1985 Bloemfontein 1.86m 75kg. Tuks, University of Pretoria.
At 400mh/4x400mR: OG: '08- 5, '12- h, '16- sf; WCh: '05-07-09-11-13-15: 6/h/sf/3&2R/h/sf; CG: '06- 1/2R, '10- 2, '14- h; AfG: '07- 1; AfCh: '06-08-10-14-16: 1/1&1R/1/4&3R; WJ: '02- 1, '04- 4/2R; WY: '01- 3; WCp: '06- 2, '10- 5; RSA champion 2003, 2005-06, 2008, 2011, 2015.
Two RSA 400m hurdles records 2011. Tied world best for 200m hurdles straight 2015.
Progress at 400mh: 2001- 51.14A, 2002- 48.89, 2003- 49.22, 2004- 49.06, 2005- 48.11, 2006- 48.05, 2007- 48.24, 2008- 48.22, 2009- 47.94, 2010- 48.51A/48.63, 2011- 47.66, 2012- 49,42A, 2013- 49.11, 2014- 48.96A/48.97, 2015- 48.78, 2016- 48.67. pbs: 100m 10.62 '07, 10.3Aw '03, 10.5A '01; 200m 20.71A '15, 300m 32.32 '09, 400m 44.86A '11, 46.02 '08; 200mhSt 22.10 '15, 300mh 35.76 '04.
Ran world U18 record of 48.89 to win World Junior title in 2002 after world age record at 15 in 2001. Commonwealth Games record to win 400mh gold and ran brilliant final leg in 4x400m to take RSA from fifth to second in 2006. Married Irvette van Blerk (pbs HMar 70:56 '11, Mar 2:31:26 '13) on 29 Sep 2012.

Zarck VISSER b. 15 Sep 1989 Welkom 1.78m 70kg. University of Johannesburg.
At LJ: WCh: '13/15- dnq 13/19; CG: '14- 2; AfCh: '12- 2, '14- 1; CCp: '14- 3; RSA champion 2012-14.
Progress at LJ: 2007- 7.21A, 2008- 7.62A, 2009- 7.77, 2010- 7.76A/7.79Aw, 2011- 7.85, 2012- 8.15A/8.07/8.21w, 2013- 8.32, 2014- 8.31A/8.18, 2015- 8.41, 2016- 7.93A/7.81. pb TJ 15.66A '08.

Women

Wenda NEL b. 27 May 1988 Worcester, Western Cape 1.69m 52kg. née Theron. Tuks, University of Pretoria.
At 400mh: OG: '16- sf; WCh: '11- sf, '15- 7; CG: '14- h; AfG: '11- 2; AfCh: '10-12-14-16: 7/5/1/1&1R; CCp: '14- 5. RSA champion 2011-2, 2014- 16. At 100m/200m: WJ: '06- h/h; WY: '05: h/-.
Progress at 400mh: 2008- 60.23A, 2009- 56.45, 2010- 56.97, 2011- 56.13, 2012- 55.36A/55.79, 2013- 55.80, 2014- 54.82, 2015- 54.37, 2016- 54.47. pbs: 100m 11.57Aw/11.80A '15, 200m 23.55A '15, 300m 37.59A '17, 400m 52.09A '15, 600 1:28.05A '15, 100mh 14.23 '07.

Caster SEMENYA b. 7 Jan 1991 Polokwane, Limpopo Province 1.70m 64kg. NWU Pukke. Student of sports science at North West University, Potchefstroom.
At 800m (/1500m): OG: '12- 1, '16- 1; WCh: ' 09- 1, '11- 1, '15- sf; AfG: '15- 1/8; AfCh: '16- 1/1/1R; WJ: '08- h; Afr-J: '09- 1 (1), won DL 2016. RSA 400m 2016, 800m 2011-12, 2014-16; 1500m 2011, 2016.
Four RSA 800m records 2009-16, 600m 2012.
Progress at 800m: 2007- 2:09.35, 2008- 2:04.23, 2009- 1:55.45, 2010- 1:58.16, 2011- 1:56.35, 2012- 1:57.23, 2013- 1:58.92, 2014- 2:02.66, 2015- 1:59.59, 2016- 1:55.28. pbs: 300m 37.22A '17, 400m 50.40 '16, 600m 1:25.56 '12, 1500m 4:01.99 '16, 3000m 9:36.29A '17.
Questions over her gender arose at the African Junior and World Champs in 2009, and she was barred from competing by Athletics South Africa until the IAAF determined whether she was free to compete again. They did so in July 2010 but saying that the medical details of her case remained confidential.

Sunette VILJOEN b. 6 Oct 1983 Johannesburg 1.70m 73kg. North West University, Potchefstroom.
At JT: OG: '04/08- dnq 35/32, '12- 4, '16- 2; WCh: '03/09- dnq 16/18, '11-13-15: 3/6/3; CG: '06-10-14: 1/1/2; AfG: '03- 3, '07- 3; AfCh: '04-06-08-10-14- 16: 1/2/1/1/1/1; WUG: '07- 5, '09- 1, '11- 1; CCp: '10- 2, '14- 2. Won Afro-Asian Games 2003, RSA 2003-04, 2006, 2009-16.
Four African javelin records 2009-12, two Commonwealth 2011-12.
Progress at JT: 1999- 43.89A, 2000- 45.50A, 2001- 50.70A, 2002- 58.33A, 2003- 61.59, 2004- 61.15A, 2005- 57.31, 2006- 60.72, 2007- 58.39, 2008- 62.24A, 2009- 65.43, 2010- 66.38, 2011- 68.38, 2012- 69.35, 2013- 64.51, 2014- 65.32, 2015- 66.62, 2016- 65.14.
She played one Test and 17 ODIs for South Africa as an all-rounder at cricket 2000-02. Son Henré born in 2005.

SPAIN

Governing body: Real Federación Española de Atletismo (RFEA), Avda. Valladolid, 81 – 1°, 28008 Madrid, Spain. Founded 1918.
National Championships first held in 1917 (men), 1931 (women). **2016 Champions: Men**: 100m: Ángel David Rodríguez 10.39, 200m: Oscar Husillos 20.83, 400m: Lucas Bua 46.36, 800m: Álvaro de Arriba 1:50.18, 1500m: Marc Alcalá 3:51.04, 5000m: Ilias Fifa 13:38.22, 10000m: Antonio Abadia 28:07.14, HMar: Javier Guerra 62:22, Mar: Carles Castillejo 2:11:29, 3000mSt: Sebastián Martos 8:37.63, 110mh: Orlando Ortega 13.09, 400mh: Sergio Fernández 50.21, HJ: Miguel Ángel Sancho 2.23, PV: Igor Bychkov 5.51, LJ: Jean Marie Okutu 7.65, TJ: José Alfonso Palomares 15.96, SP: Borja Vivas 20.59, DT: Frank Casañas 61.25, HT: Javier Cienfuegos 72.92, JT: Nicolás Quijera 75.86, Dec: Jorge Ureña 7900, 10000mW: Miguel Ángel López

SPAIN – SRI LANKA

38:06.28, 20kW: Alvaro Martín 1:21:23. **Women**: 100m: Estela García 11.41, 200m: Christina Lara 23.60, 400m: Aauri Lorena Bokesa 53.44, 800m: Esther Guerrero 2:01.72, 1500m: Marta Pérez 4:12.74, 5000m/10000m: Trihas Gebre 16:02.12/ 32:14.25, HMar/Mar: Paula González 71:04/ 2:31:18, 3000mSt: María José Pérez 9:50.45, 100mh: Caridad Jerez 13.15, 400mh: Maryia Roshchyn 59.88, HJ: Ruth Beitia 1.90, PV: Naroa Agirre 4.32m LJ: Juliet Itoya 6.51, TJ: Patricia Sarrapio 13.66, SP: Úrsula Ruiz 17.24, DT: Sabina Asenjo 58.20, HT: Berta Castells 69.41, JT: Lidia Parada 57.18, Hep: Andrea Medina 5641, 10000mW: Raquel González 42:14.12, 20kW: Ainhoa Pinedo 1:32:52.

Miguel Ángel LÓPEZ b. 3 Jul 1988 Murcia 1.81m 70kg. CA Llano de Brujas-Murcia.
At 20kW: OG: '12- 5, '16- 11 (dnf 50kW); WCh: '11- 13, '13- 3, '15- 1; EC: '10- 13, '14- 1; EU23: '09- 1; WCp: '10- 12, '14- 5; ECp: '11- 5, '13- 2, '15- 1. At 10kW: WJ: '06- 14; WY: '05- 6; EJ: '05- 9, '07- 8; WCp: '06- 2J; ECp: '07- 2J. Won Spanish 10000mW 2010, 2012-16; 20kW 2010, 2012, 2015; 50kW 2016.
Progress at 20kW: 2008- 1:23:44, 2009- 1:22:23, 2010- 1:23:08, 2011- 1:21:41, 2012- 1:19:49, 2013- 1:21:21, 2014- 1:19:21, 2015- 1:19:14, 2016- 1:20:34. pbs: 3000mW 11:39.92 '13, 5000mW 18:46.95 '16, 10000mW 38:06.28 '16, 35kW 2:32:56 '15, 50kW 3:53:52 '16.

Alvaro MARTÍN b. 18 Jun 1994 Llerena 1.81m 62kg. Playas de Castellón.
At 20kW: OG: '16- 22; WCh: '13- 24, '15- 16; EC: '14- 6; EU23: '15- 2; WCp: '16- 3. At 10kW: WJ: '12- 5; WY: '11- 8; EJ: '13- 3; ECp: '11- 6J. Won Spanish 20kW 2016-17.
Progress at 20kW: 2012- 1:22:12, 2013- 1:22:25, 2014- 1:20:39, 2015- 1:20:19, 2016- 1:19:36. pbs: 5000mW 18:39.65 '15, 10000mW 39:23.51 '16, 35kW 2:37:17 '14.

Orlando ORTEGA b. 29 Jul 1991 La Habana 1.85m 70kg. Club d'Atletisme de la Vall d'Albaida.
At 110mh: OG: '12- 6, '16- 2; WCh: '13- h; WJ: '10- h; PAm: '11- 3. Won DL 2016, Cuban 2011, Spanish 2016. At 60mh: EI: '17- 7.
Two Spanish 110mh records 2016.
Progress at 110mh: 2009- 14.11, 2010- 13.99, 2011- 13.29/13.1w, 2012- 13.09, 2013- 13.08, 2014- 13.01, 2015- 12.94, 2016- 13.04. pbs: 60m 6.71i '16, 100m 10.62 '11, 400m 47.84 '09, 50mh 6.66+i '12, 60mh 7.45i '15, 7.48i '17 ESP record.
Left Cuba in 2013 and given Spanish citizenship on 9 Sep 2015 with eligibility to compete for them if agreed by the Cuban federation. Eligibility confirmed just before 2016 Olympic Games.

Women

Ruth BEITIA b. 1 Apr 1979 Santander 1.92m 71kg. Piélagos Inelecma. Graduate of physical therapy at University of Santander.
At HJ: OG: '04- dnq 16=, '08- 6=, '12- 4, '16- 1; WCh: '03-05-07-09-11-13-15: 11=/dnq 19=/6/5/ dnq 16/3=/5; EC: '02-06-10-12-14-16: 11/9/6=/ 1/1/1; WJ: '96- dnq, '98- 8, EU23: '01- 1; EJ: '97- 9; WI: '01-03-06-08-10-12-14-16: 7/5=/3/4/2/6/3/2; EI: '05-07-09-11-13-15-17: 2/3/2/2/1/5/2; WCp: '02- 6=; ECp: '03-06-07-09-11-14-15: 2/2/2/2/3/ 3/2; Won DL 2015-16, IbAm 2010, Med G 2005, Spanish 2003, 2006-16 (and 16 indoors 2002-17). Nine Spanish HJ records 1998-2007 (and eight indoors 2001-07). Equal world W35 record 2014.
Progress at HJ: 1989- 1.29, 1990- 1.39, 1991- 1.50, 1992- 1.55, 1993- 1.66, 1994- 1.74, 1995- 1.80, 1996- 1.85, 1997- 1.87i/1.86, 1998- 1.89, 1999- 1.83, 2000- 1.86i/1.85, 2001- 1.94i/1.91, 2002- 1.94, 2003- 2.00, 2004- 2.00i/1.96, 2005- 1.99i/1.97, 2006- 1.98i/1.97; 2007- 2.02, 2008- 2.01, 2009- 2.01, 2010- 2.00, 2011- 1.96i/1.95, 2012- 2.00, 2013- 1.99i/1.97, 2014- 2.01, 2015- 2.00, 2016- 1.98. pbs: 200m 25.26 '02, 100mh 14.95 '97, 14.93w '00; LJ 6.04 '03, TJ 12.43/12.73w '11.
Became the oldest Olympic champion at any jumps event and Spain's first female Olympic champion in 2016. Has competed at a record nine World Indoor Champs. She is a deputy of the Parliament of Cantabria, her autonomous community. Her sister Inmaculada (b. 8 Sep 1975) had TJ pb 13.43 '00.

Beatriz PASCUAL b. 9 May 1982 Barcelona 1.63m 64kg. Valencia Terra i Mar.
At 20kW: OG: '08- 6, '12- 7, '16- 8; WCh: '07-09- 11-13: 13/5/8/6; EC: '02-06-10-14: 12/20/4/8; EU23: '03- 4; WCp: '10- 11, '12- 4; ECp: '07-09-13: 9/6/9. At 10kW: WJ: '00- 6; EJ: '01- 3. Won Spanish 10000mW 2008, 2010, 2012; 20kW 2006, 2008-09, 2011, 2016.
Spanish walk records 5000m (3) 2008-12, 10000m 2010.
Progress at 20kW: 2002- 1:32:38, 2003- 1:31:31, 2004- 1:30:22, 2005- 1:32:49, 2006- 1:33:55, 2007- 1:30:37, 2008- 1:27:44, 2009- 1:29:54, 2010- 1:28:05, 2011- 1:28:51, 2012- 1:27:56, 2013- 1:29:00, 2014- 1:29:02, 2015- 1:31:51, 2016- 1:29:27. pbs: 3000mW 13:06.48 '04, 5000mW 20:45:11 '12, 10000mW 42:35.69 '16; HMar (run) 82:43 '08.

SRI LANKA

Governing body: Athletic Association of Sri Lanka, n°33 Torrington Avenue, Colombo 7. Founded 1922.
National Champions 2016: Men: 100m: W.K. Himasha Eashan 10.5, 200m: Vinod Suranjaya De Silva 21.2, 400m: A.D.P.Ruwan Kumara 47.2, 800m: Indunil Herath 1:50.4, 1500m: R.A.D. Hemantha Kumara 3:51.9, 5000m: D.M.D.S. Dissanayake 15:02.9, 10000m: B.U.Vijitha Kumara 31:17.9, 3000mSt: R.M.S.Pushpakumara 9:15.0, 110mh: Salinda Randeewa 14.6, 400mh: S.M.Aravinda Chathuranga 52.3, HJ: Manjula Kumara Wijesekara 2.24, PV: M.H.Ishara

Sandaruwan 5.00, LJ: W.P.Amila Jayasiri 7.69, TJ: Atheetha N.Karunasinghe 16.21, SP: Joy Danuskha Perera 14.94, DT: Z.T.M.Aasik 43.77, HT: K.Nilantha 45.99, JT: Waruna Lakshan Dayarathne 75.98, Dec: Ajith Kumara Karunathilake 6724. Women: 100m: Shashika L.Vidanadurage 12.1, 200m: A.P.G. Nirmali Madushika 25.0, 400m/800m: W.K.L.A. Nimali 54.6/2:04.8, 1500m: K.K.Jayasundara 4:37.3, 5000m/3000mSt: U.K.Nilani Rathnayake 16:39.9/10:10.3, 10000m: Nilanthi L.Ariyadasa 36:02.9, 100mh: Ireshani Rajasinghe 14.9, 400mh: Kaushalya Madushani 61.0, HJ: Dulanjali Ranasinghe 1.76; PV: Aniththa Jegatheshwaran 3.30, LJ: Lakshika Sarangi Silva 6.04, TJ: Harshani Pramoda Balasooriya 12.79, SP: Tharika Kumudumali Fernando 14.47, DT/HT: Ayesha Maduwanthi 40.10/44.14, JT: Dilhani Lekamge 56.06, Hep: W.V.L. Sugandhi 4547.

SWEDEN

Governing body: Svenska Friidrottsförbundet, Heliosgatan 3, 120 30 Stockholm. Founded 1895.
National Championships first held in 1896 (men), 1928 (women). **2016: Men:** 100m/200m: Tom Kling-Baptiste 10.27w/21.09, 400m: Benjamin Mullen USA (later SWE) 47.12, 800m: Johan Rogestedt 1:49.92, 1500m: Kalle Berglund 3:50.24, 5000m: Jonas Leanderson 14:30.04, 10000m/Mar: Mustafa Mohamed 29:22.07/2:20:01, HMar: Abraham Adhanom ERI 64:50, 3000mSt: Vidar Johansson 8:57.22, 110mh: Alexander Brorsson 14.27, 400mh: Isak Andersson 52.04, HJ: Andreas Carlsson 2.11, PV: Oscar Janson 5.09, LJ/TJ: Michel Tornéus 7.74/16.10, SP/DT: Daniel Ståhl 19.38/68.72, HT: Oscar Vestlund 70.32, JT: Kim Amb 83.46, Dec: Fredrik Samuelsson 7788, 10000mW/20kW/50kW: Perseus Karlström 44:38.4/1:22:25/4:06:33. **Women**: 100m/LJ: Khaddi Sagnia 11.48/6.69w, 200m: Gladys Bamane 24.19, 400m: Matilda Hellqvist 54.04, 800m: Lovisa Lindh 2:01.25, 1500m: Anna Silvander 4:25.27, 5000m: Sarah Lahti 15:32.46, 10000m: Malin Liljestedt 34:54.59, HMar/Mar: Isabellah Andersson 76:21/2:35:47, 3000mSt: Maria Larsson 10:04.23, 100mh: Elin Westerlund 13.42, 400mh: Hanna Palmqvist 59.07, HJ: Sofie Skoog 1.90, PV: Angelica Bengtsson 4.35, TJ: Malin Marmbrandt 13.11, SP: Fanny Roos 16.80, DT: Sofia Larsson 50.42, HT: Marinda Petersson 69.22, JT: Anna Wessman 57.76, Hep: Bianca Salming 5565, 5000mW/10kW: Monica Svensson 23:57.2/51:00, 20kW: Lizbeth Silvia Miranda 2:00:00.

Kim AMB b. 31 Jul 1990 Solna 1.80m 85kg. F Bålsta IK.
At JT: OG: '12/16- dnq 17/17; WCh: '13- 10, '15- 11; EC: '12-14-16: 7/dnq/7; WJ: '08- dnq 13; EU23: '11- 4. Swedish champion 2011-13, 2015-16.
Progress at JT: 2007- 55.01, 2008- 69.34, 2009- 66.06, 2010- 77.81, 2011- 80.09, 2012- 81.84, 2013- 84.61, 2014- 84.14, 2015- 82.40, 2016- 84.50. Pb PV 3.45 '06.
His father Björn had a best with the old javelin of 62.60 '79 and sister Emilia JT best of 49.34 '12.

Armand 'Mondo' DUPLANTIS b. 10 Nov 1999 1.68m 61kg.
At PV: WJ: '16- 3; WY: '15- 1.
Four world junior pole vault records 2017.
Progress at PV: 2009- 2.89i, 2010- 3.86, 2012- 3.97i, 2013- 4.15, 2014- 4.60, 2015- 5.30, 2016- 5.51, 2017- 5.90i. Pb LJ 6.95w '17.
Has dual citizenship Sweden/USA. Has been setting world age records from the age of 7 in 2007. His father Greg (USA) had pb 5.80 '93, his mother Helena was a Swedish heptathlete, and his brother Andreas (b. 2 May 1993) had PV pb 5.43i/5.36 '13, WJ: '12- 10, EJ: '11- 9.

Daniel STÅHL b. 27 Aug 1992 2.00m 145kg. Spårvägens FK.
At (SP)/DT: OG: '16- dnq 14; WCh: '15- 5; EC: '14- dnq 24, '16- 5; EU23: '13- 4; WJ: '10- (dnq 27); WY: '09- dnq 16/dnq 16; EJ: '11- (dnq 20). Won SWE SP 2015-16, DT 2014, 2016.
Progress at DT: 2008- 40.36, 2009- 44.34, 2010- 50.32, 2011- 55.60, 2012- 62.16, 2013- 61.29, 2014- 66.89, 2015- 64.73, 2016- 68.72. pbs: SP 19.60i '17, 19.38 '16; HT 45.50 '14, JT 43.78 '13.
Father Jan had pbs SP 16.80 & HT 59.14 '80, mother Gaina DT 51.90 '88, sister Annell HT 59.74 '13.

Michel TORNÉUS b. 26 May 1986 Botkyrka 1.84m 70kg. Hammarby IF.
At LJ: OG: '12- 4, '16- dnq 26; WCh: '09-11-13-15: dnq 28/27/19.dnq; EC: '10-12-14-16: 9/3/5/2; EU23: '07- 10; EJ: '05- 4; WI: '14- 3; EI: '11-13-15- 17: 7/2/1/2; ET: '11- 2. Won Swedish LJ 2005, 2007-10, 2012-16 (indoor 2008, 2010-17); TJ 2012, 2016. Swedish long jump records 2012 & 2016.
Progress at LJ: 2001- 6.48, 2002- 6.74/6.86w, 2003- 7.07, 2004- 7.41, 2005- 7.94, 2006- 7.68, 2007- 7.85, 2008- 7.86, 2009- 8.11, 2010- 8.12/8.21w, 2011- 8.19, 2012- 8.22, 2013- 8.29i/8.00/8.12w, 2014- 8.21i/8.09/8.10w, 2015- 8.30i/7.83/8.07w, 2016- 8.44A/8.07/8.21w. pbs: 60m 6.93i '12, 100m 10.71/10.63w '11, 400mh 55.48 '04, HJ 1.99i '05, 1.92 '04; TJ 16.10 '16, Dec 6115 '04.
Father came from DR of Congo.

Women

Abeba AREGAWI Gebretsadik b. 5 Jul 1990 Adigrat, Tigray, Ethiopia 1.69m 48kg. Hammarby IF.
At 1500m: OG: '12- 3; WCh: '13- 1, '15- 6; EC: '14- 2; WI: 14- 1; EI: '13- 1; ET: '14- 1; won DL 2012-13. At 800m: Af-J: '09- 3. Won ETH 800m 2009.
Records: Swedish 800m 2013, 1M 2015; 1500m: ETH 2012, SWE 2013, European indoor 2014.
Progress at 1500m: 2010- 4:01.96, 2011- 4:01.47i/4:10.30, 2012- 3:56.54, 2013- 3:56.60,

2014- 3:57.57, 2015- 4:01.97. pbs: 800m 1:59.20 '13, 1M 4:23.07 '15.
Lived in Stockholm from 2009; granted Swedish citizenship on 28 Jun 2012 and accepted by the IAAF to compete for Sweden from 10 Dec 2012 but from then has lived in Ethiopia and divorced from her husband and coach Henok Weldegebriel. Unbeaten at 1500m in 2013. Married in January 2017 to Yemane Tsegay (qv). Expecting a baby in 2017.

Meraf BAHTA Ogbagaber b. 24 Jun 1989 Dekishahay, Eritrea 1.77m 51kg. Hälle IF.
At 5000m: EC: '14- 1, '16- 6; ET: '14- 1. At 3000m: CCp: '14- 2. At 1500m: OG: '16- 6; WJ: '06- 5; EI: '17- 4. World CC: '06- 12J, '07- 6J; Eur CC: '14- 3. Won SWE 5000m 2011, 4k & 8k CC 2013-14.
SWE records 3000m 2016, 5000m 2014 & 2016.
Progress at 1500m, 5000m: 2006- 4:16.01, 2007- 4:15.12, 15:56.30; 2008- 4:12.52, 15:58.31; 2009- 4:28.93, 2010- 4:22.86, 16:28.77; 2011- 4:19.82, 16:29.08; 2012- 4:14.09, 2013- 4:05.11, 2014- 4:01.34, 14:59.49; 2015- 4:06.42i, 15:46.97; 2016- 4:02.62, 14:49.95. pbs: 800m 2:07.19 '08, 1M 4:25.26 '16, 3000m 8:43.00i '17, 8:43.08 '16; 10000m 33:11.45 '16, 10k road 32:40 '14.
Came from Eritrea to Sweden as a refugee in 2009; Swedish citizenship on 23 Dec 2013.

Angelica BENGTSSON b. 8 July 1993 Väckelsång 1.64m 51kg. Hässelby SK.
At PV: OG: '12/16- dnq 19=/14=, WCh: '13- dnq 16, '15- 4=; EC: '12-14-16: 10/5/3; WJ: '10- 1, '12- 1; WY: '09- 1; EU23: '13- 3, '15- 1; EJ: '11- 1; YthOG: '10- 1; EI: '15- 3, '17- 3=; ET: '15- 3. SWE champion 2012, 2014-16.
Pole vault records: Two world youth 2010; four world junior indoors 2011, two world junior outdoor bests, six Swedish 2011-15.
Progress at PV: 2005- 3.10, 2006- 3.40, 2007- 3.90, 2008- 4.12, 2009- 4.37, 2010- 4.47, 2011- 4.63i/4.57, 2012- 4.58, 2013- 4.55, 2014- 4.62i/4.50, 2015- 4.70, 2016- 4.66i/4.65. pbs: LJ 5.22i '13, JT 34.67 '14.
Rising Star Awards: IAAF 2010, European Athletics 2012. Her father Glenn had JT pb 67.08 '82, sisters Victoria (b. 1990) PV 4.00 '09 and Maria (b. 1988) DT 43.95 '07.

Khaddijatou 'Khaddi' SAGNIA b. 20 Apr 1994 Helsingborg 1.73cm 63kg. Ullevi FK.
At LJ: OG: '16- dnq 27; WCh: '15- 7; EC: '16- 6; WY: '11- 11; EU23: '15- 4. At TJ: WY: '11- 9; YthOG: '10- 1. Won SWE TJ 2011, LJ 2015-16, 100m 2016.
Progress at LJ: 2007- 5.18i, 2008- 5.56, 2009- 6.03i/5.89/6.00w, 2010- 6.26, 2011- 6.32, 2014- 6.55, 2015- 6.78, 2016- 6.74. Pbs: 60m 7.40i '15, 100m 11.48 '16, 200m 25.14 '14, 100mh 13.93 '15, 13.62w '14; HJ 1.78 '11, TJ 13.65/13.86w '11, JT 41.47 '14, Hep 5287 '11.

SWITZERLAND
Governing body: Schweizerischer Leichtathletikverband (SLV), Haus des Sports, Postfach 606, 3000 Bern 22. Formed 1905 as Athletischer Ausschuss des Schweizerischen Fussball-Verbandes.
National Championships first held in 1906 (men), 1934 (women). **2016**: **Men**: 100m/200m: Alex Wilson 10.31/20.64, 400m: Joel Burgunder 46.88, 800m: Hugo Santacruz 1:53.03, 1500m: Jan Hochstrasser 3:57.78, 5000m: Julien Wanders 14:12.22, 10000m: Adrian Lehmann 29:37.86, HMar: Fabian Kuert 67:40, Mar: Stefan Trummer 2:30:24, 3000mSt: Jari Piller 9:21.78, 110mh: Tobias Furrer 13.99, 400mh: Alain-Hervé Mfomkpa 50.42, HJ: Loïc Gasch 2.18, PV: Dominik Alberto 5.45, LJ: Christopher Ullmann 7.73, TJ: Nils Wicki 15.42, SP: Lukas Jost 15.87, DT: Lukas Jost 52.59, HT: Martin Bingisser 59.75, JT: Bruno Schürch 69.59, Dec: Jonas Fringelli 7777, 1000mW: Nathan Bozon 50:08.3, 20kW: Patrick Gavillet 1:56:16. **Women**: 100m: Mujinga Kambundji 11.38, 200m: Léa Sprunger 22.38, 400m: Selina Büchel 53.99, 800m: Pamela Märzendorfer 2:13.41, 1500m/5000m: Fabienne Schlumpf 4:31.73/16:27.38, 10000m: Martina Tresch 34:27.32, HMar: Laura Hrebec 75:49, Mar: Susanne Rüegger 2:40:24, 100mh/LJ: Clélia Rard-Reuse 12.98/6.07, 400mh: Robine Schürmann 57.94, HJ: Giovanna Demo 1.82, PV: Olivia Fischer 4.00, TJ: Barbara Leuthard 12.92, SP: Michelle Zeltner 13.72, DT/JT: Nadia-Marie Pasternack 44.48/52.22, HT: Nicole Zihlmann 64.63, Hep: Caroline Agnou 5822, 10000mW: Marie Polli 50:46.4, 20kW: Corinne Henchoz 2:01:22.

Tadesse ABRAHAM b. 12 Aug 1982 Asmara, Eritrea 1.78m 61kg. LC Uster.
At HMar: EC: '16- 1; at Mar: OG: '16- 7; WCh: '15- 19; EC: '14- 9. Won Swiss 10000m 2014, HMar 2015.
Swiss records: half marathon 2015, marathon 2016.
Progress at Mar: 2009- 2:10:09, 2010- 2:09:24, 2011- 2:12:48, 2012- 2:10:26, 2013- 2:07:45, 2014- 2:15:05, 2015- 2:11:37, 2016- 2:06:40. pbs: 10000m 28:41.37 '15, Road: 10k 28:28 '13, 10 47:12 '12, HMar 60:42 '15.
Competed for Eritrea in World Junior CC in 2003 & 2004, but later disqualified when it was found that he was over-age. Lived in Switzerland from 30 Mar 2004, Swiss citizenship 10 Jun 2014. Won Zürich marathon 2009, 2013.

Kariem HUSSEIN b. 1 Apr 1989 Münsterlingen 1.90m 77kg. TV Amriswil
At 400mh: OG: '16- h; WCh: '15- sf; EC: '12- sf; '14- 1, '16- 3; EU23: '11- sf; CCh: '14- 2; Swiss champion 2011-15.
Swiss 300mh record 2014.
Progress at 400mh: 2009- 52.33, 2010- 51.64, 2011- 51.09, 2012- 49.61, 2013- 49.78, 2014- 48.47, 2015- 48.45, 2016- 48.87. pbs: 60mh 8.14i '11, 110mh 14.51 '11, 300mh 35.54 '15.

Successive pbs at end of 2014 from 49.08 to 48.96 EC, 48.70 WK, 48.47 CCp. Father Ehab came from Egypt to Switzerland in the early 1980s.

Women

Selina BÜCHEL b. 26 Jul 1991 Mosnang 1.68m 58kg. KTV Bütschwil
At 800m: OG: '16- sf; WCh: '15- sf; EC: '14- sf, '16- 4; WJ: '10- sf; EU23: '11- 5, 13- 3; EJ: '09- 7; WI: '14- 4; EI: '15- 1, '17- 1. Won Swiss 400m 2016, 800m 2011, 2013.
Swiss 800m record 2015.
Progress at 800m: 2008- 2:11.68, 2009- 2:06.20, 2010- 2:05.95, 2011- 2:04.25, 2012- 2:04.02, 2013- 2:01.64i/2:01.66, 2014- 2:00.93i/2:01.42, 2015- 1:57.95, 2016- 1:58.77. pbs: 400m 53.99 '16, 600m 1:25.45 '15, 1500m 4:08.95i '16, 4:18.57 '15.

Nicole BÜCHLER b. 17 Dec 1983 Biel 1.62m 56kg. LC Zürich.
At PV: OG: '08/12- dnq 22/25, '16- 6; WCh: '09/11/13/15- dnq 14/16/15/17=; EC: '14- dnq 17; EU23: '05- 12; WUG: '07- 3, '09- 2; WI: '12- 8, '16- 4. Won Swiss 400m 2016, 800m 2009, 2012-13, 2015.
12 Swiss pole vault records (and 14 indoors).
Progress at PV: 2004- 3.80, 2005- 4.15, 2006- 4.10, 2007- 4.35, 2008- 4.40, 2009- 4.50, 2010- 4.47i/4.00, 2011- 4.50, 2012- 4.60, 2013- 4.61, 2014- 4.67, 2015- 4.71, 2016- 4.80i/4.78. pbs: 60mh 8.65i '09, 100mh 14.01 '09, LJ 5.65 '07.
She competed for Switzerland at two World and four European championships at rhythmic gymnastics, taking up pole vaulting at the age of 20. Married US pole vaulter Mitch Greeley (5.56sq '08, 5.55i '09) in 2010.

SYRIA

Majed El Dein GHAZAL b. 21 Apr 1987 Damascus 1.93m 72kg.
At HJ: OG: '08/12- dnq 24/=/28=, 16- 7=; WCh: '09/11/13/15– dnq 28/=/23=/21/15; AsiG: '10- dnq 13=, '14- 6; AsiC: '11- 2. Won WMilG 2015.
13 Syrian records 2007-16.
Progress at HJ: 2006- 2.09, 2007- 2.17, 2008- 2.21i/2.20, 2009- 2.16, 2010- 2.22, 2011- 2.28, 2012- 2.326, 2013- 2.23, 2014- 2.26, 2015- 2.31, 2016- 2.36.

TADJIKISTAN

Governing body: Athletics Federation of Tadjikistan, Rudski Avenue 62, Dushanbe 734025. Founded 1932.

Dilshod NAZAROV b. 6 May 1982 Dushanbe 1.87m 115kg.
At HT: OG: '08- 11, '12- 9, '16- 1; WCh: '05-07-09-11-13-15: dnq 15/dnq 21/11/10/5/2; WJ: '98- dnq 15, '00- 5, AsiG: '98-02-06-10-14: 7/9/1/1/1; AsiC: '03-05-07-09-13-15: 3/2/2/1/1/1; CCp: '10- 2, '14- 4. Won Asi-J 1999, 2001, C.Asian 2003.
Progress at HT: 1998- 63.91, 1999- 63,56, 2000- 66.50, 2001- 68.08, 2002- 69.86, 2003- 75.56, 2004- 76.58, 2005- 77.63, 2006- 74.43, 2007- 78.89, 2008- 79.05, 2009- 79.28, 2010- 80.11, 2011- 80.30, 2012- 77.70, 2013- 80.71, 2014- 80.62, 2015- 79.36, 2016- 78.87.
President of national federation. In 2016 he won the first Olympic gold medal at any sport for Tadjikistan.

TRINIDAD & TOBAGO

Governing body: National Association of Athletics Administrations of Trinidad & Tobago, PO Box 605, Port of Spain, Trinidad. Founded 1945, reformed 1971.
National Championships first held in 1946 (men) and 1947 (women). **2016 Champions**: Men: 100m: Richard Thompson 9.97, 200m: Rondell Sorrillo 20.24, 400m: Machel Cedonio 44.45, 800m: Nicholas Landeau 1:49.55, 1500m: Antoneil Prince 4:08.83, 5000m: Jules La Rode 16:27.19, 110mh: Mikel Thomas 13.67, 400mh: Jehue Gordon 50.44, HJ: Kareem Roberts 2.05, LJ: Che Richards 7.53, TJ: Lyron Blaise 15.47w, SP: Hezekiel Romeo 17.72, DT: Quincy Wilson 58.65, HT: Emmanuel Stewart 53.05, JT: Keshorn Walcott 80.45, Dec: Shevon Smith 4091. Women: 100m/200m: Michelle-Lee Ahye 11.00/22.33, 400m: Domonique Williams 52.83, 800m: Alena Brooks 2:10.32, 1500m: April Francis 5:19.89, 100mh: Deborah John 13.36, 400mh: Janeil Bellille 56.11, HJ: Deandra Daniel 1.75, LJ: Safiya John 5.51, TJ: Ayanna Alexander 13.69, SP: Cleopatra Borel 17.88, DT: Chelsea James 45.91, HT: Latoya Gilding 27.47, JT: Chuntal Mohan 41.82, Hep: Kechelle Douglas 5025.

Keston BLEDMAN b. 8 Mar 1988 San Fernando 1.83m 75kg. Simplex.
At 100m/4x100mR: OG: '08- 1R, '12- sf/2R, '16- h; WCh: '07- qf, '09- res(2)R, '11/13- sf, '15- h; CG: '14- sf/3R; WJ: '06- 7 (h 200m); WY: '05- 3; PAm: '07- sf, '15- 4/3R; CAG: '10- 7/1R. Won PAm-J 2007, CAC 2011, TTO 2012-13, 2015.
Progress at 100m: 2005- 10.48, 2006- 10.32, 2007- 10.14/10.05w, 2008- 10.18, 2009- 10.10/10.0, 2010- 10.01/9.93w, 2011- 9.93, 2012- 9.86/9.85w, 2013- 10.02/9.86w, 2014- 10.00, 2015- 9.86, 2016- 10.07. pbs: 60m 6.62i '12, 200m 20.73 '08.

Machel CEDENIO b. 6 Sep 1995 San Fernando 1.83m 70kg. Simplex.
At 400m/4x400mR: OG: '16- 4; WCh: '15- 7/2R; WJ: '12- 5/3R, '14- 1; WY: '11- 4; PAm: '15- 2/1R; WI: '16- res 3R. Won CAC-J 2014, TTO 2016.
TTO 400m record 2016.
Progress at 400m: 2010- 48.12, 2011- 46.89, 2012- 46.02, 2013- 45.93, 2014- 45.13, 2015- 44.36, 2016- 44.01. Pbs: 200m 21.15 '13, 300m 31.7+ '16.

Lalonde GORDON b. 25 Nov 1988 Lowlands, Tobago 1.88m 83kg. Tigers. Studied at Mohawk Valley CC.
At 400m/4x400mR: OG: '12- 3/3R, '16- sf; WCh: '15- sf/2R; CG: '10- sf, '14- 3/3R; CAG: '10- 3R;

WI: '12- 3R, '14- 5, '16- 6/3R. At 200m: WCh: '13- sf. Won NACAC 2015, TTO 200m 2013-14, 400m 2012.
Progress at 400m: 2009- 49.47, 2010- 46.33, 2011- 45.51, 2012- 44.52, 2013- 45.67, 2014- 44.78, 2015- 44.64A/44.70, 2016- 44.69. pbs: 100m 10.45 '12, 200m 20.26 '13, 300m 32.47i '14 (CAC record), 32.5+ '12.
Moved with his family to New York at the age of seven, and still lives there.

Deon LENDORE b. 28 Oct 1992 Arima 1.79m 75kg. Abilene. Was at Texas A&M University, USA.
At 400m/4x400mR: OG: '12- h/3R, '16- h; WCh: '13- sf, '15- 2R; WJ: '10- sf; WY: '09- sf; WI: '16- 3/3R. TTO champion 2013, NCAA 2014.
Progress at 400m: 2009- 47.61, 2010- 46.59, 2011- 46.50, 2012- 45.13, 2013- 44.94, 2014- 44.36, 2015- 44.41, 2016- 45.31. pb 200m 20.68i '14, 21.20 '11.

Richard THOMPSON b. 7 Jun 1985 Cascade 1.87m 79kg. Rebirth. Was at Louisiana State University.
At 100m: OG: '08- 2/1R, '12- 6/2R, '16- h; WCh: '07- qf, '09- 5/2R, '11/13- sf; CG: '14- sf/3R; PAm: '07- h; CCp: '14- 8/1R. Won TTO 100m 2009-11, 2014, 2016; 200m 2010; NACAC 100m 2007, NCAA 100m & 60m indoor 2008.
Progress at 100m, 200m: 2004- 10.65, 2005- 10.47, 21.73; 2006- 10.27/10.26w, 21.24; 2007- 10.09/9.95w, 20.90; 2008- 9.89, 20.18; 2009- 9.93, 20.65; 2010- 10.01/9.89w, 20.37; 2011- 9.85, 20.85; 2012- 9.96, 20.80; 2013- 10.14/9.91w, 21.06; 2014- 9.82/9.74w, 20.81/20.63w; 2015- 10.04, 20.81w; 2016- 9.97/20.54w. pbs: 60m 6.45+ '09, 6.51i '08.

Keshorn WALCOTT b. 2 Apr 1993 Toco 1.88m 90kg. Rebirth.
At JT: OG: '12- 1, '16- 3; WCh: '13/15- dnq 19/26; CG: '14- 2; WJ: '10- dnq, '12- 1; WY: '09- dnq 13; PAm: '11- 7, '15- 1; CCp: '14- 3. Won CAC-J 2010, 2012; TTO 2012, 2015-16.
Javelin records: CAC 2015, nine TTO 2012-15, eight CAC junior 2011-12.
Progress at JT: 2009- 60.02, 2010- 67.01, 2011- 75.77A, 2012- 84.58, 2013- 84.39, 2014- 85.77, 2015- 90.16, 2016- 88.68. pb TJ 14.28 '10.
First Caribbean Olympic champion and youngest ever Olympic champion in throwing events. Won IAAF Rising Star Award 2012. Elder brother Elton TJ pb 16.43/16.51w '11 & 4 WY '09, aunt Anna Lee Walcott Hep pb 5224 '00.

Women

Michelle-Lee AHYE b. 10 Apr 1992 Port of Spain 1.68m 59kg. Rebirth.
At 100m/(200m): OG: '12- sf, '16- 6/6; WCh: '11- sf, '13- sf, '15- 5/3R; CG: '14- sf; WY: '07- qf; CCp: '14- 2/1R; PAm-J: '11- 1. At 60m: WI: '14- 6, '16- 4. TTO champion 100m & 200m 2014, 2016.
Two TTO 200m records 2016.
Progress at 100m, 200m: 2006- 11.94, 24.60; 2007- 11.76/11.63w, 24.30/24.23w; 2008- 11.48, 23.80; 2009- 11.69, 2010- 11.32, 24.14/13.71w; 2011- 11.20/11.15w, 22.92w; 2012- 11.19, 23.13; 2013- 11.06, 22.98; 2014- 10.85, 22.77; 2015- 10.97/10.87w, 23.19i, 22.01w; 2016- 10.90, 22.25. pbs: 50m 6.33i '13, 60m 7.09i '16.

Kelly-Ann BAPTISTE b. 14 Oct 1986 Plymouth, Tobago 1.68m 58kg. Zenith. Studied psychology at Louisiana State University.
At 100m/(200m): OG: '08- qf, '12- 6, '16- h; WCh: '05- qf, '09: sf/sf, '11- 3, '15- 6/3R; WJ: '02- sf, '04- (4); WY: '03- 3; PAm: '03- h, '15- 5; CCp: '10- 1/1R. Won NCAA 100m & indoor 60m 2008, TTO 100m 2005-06, 2008-10, 2012-13, 2015; 200m 2005, 2013.
TTO records: 100m (6) 2005-14, 200m (5) 2005-13.
Progress at 100m, 200m: 2002- 11.71, 24.03; 2003- 11.48, 23.22; 2004- 11.40, 23.41/22.99w; 2005- 11.17/11.04w, 22.93; 2006- 11.08, 22.73; 2007- 11.22, 22.90i/22.95; 2008- 11.06/10.97w, 22.67; 2009- 10.94/10.91w, 22.60; 2010- 10.84, 22.78/22.58w; 2011- 10.90, 2012- 10.86, 22.33w; 2013- 10.83, 22.36; 2015- 10.84, 22.91w; 2016- 11.04, 22.73. pbs: 55m 6.73i '06, 60m 7.13i '08.
She was withdrawn from 2013 World Champs team after failing a drugs test and was given a 2-year ban by the IAAF, but that was withdrawn by her governing body in August 2014 and after the IAAF appealed this to the CAS the suspension was lifted.

Cleopatra BOREL b. 3 Oct 1979 Port of Spain 1.68m 93kg. Rebirth. Was at University of Maryland; assistant coach at Virginia Tech University.
At SP: OG: '04- 9, '08- dnq 15, '12- dnq 1111, '16- 7; WCh: '05-07-09-13: dnq 17/18/13/14, '11/15-13/12; CG: '02-06-10-14: 4/3/2/2; PAm: '03-07-11-15: 6/3/2/1; CAG: '06-10-14: 3/1/1; CCp: '14- 5; WI: '04-06-08-16: dnq 11/7/7/4. Won NACAC 2007, CAC 2008, 2011, 2013; TTO 2002, 2004, 2006-10, 2012, 2014-16.
Eight TTO records at shot 2004-11.
Progress at SP: 2000- 14.64i, 2001- 16.44, 2002- 17.50i/16.90, 2003- 17.95i/17.79, 2004- 19.48i/18.90, 2005- 18.44, 2006- 18.81, 2007- 18.91, 2008- 18.87, 2009- 18.52, 2010- 19.30, 2011- 19.42, 2012- 18.82, 2013- 17.84, 2014- 19.13, 2015- 19.26, 2016- 18.78. pb HT 51.28 '01.
Formerly competed under married name Borel-Brown.

TUNISIA

Governing body: Fédération Tunisienne d'Athlétisme, B.P. 264, Cité Mahrajane 1082, Tunis. Founded 1957.

Women

Habiba GHRIBI b. 9 Apr 1984 Kairouan 1.70m 57kg. Entente Franconville Cesame Va, FRA.
At 3000mSt: OG: '08- 12, '12- 1, '16- 12; WCh: '05-09-11-15: h/4/1/2; AfCh: '06- 2, '14- 5 (6

1500m). At 5000m: AfCh: '02- 11. Won FRA 1500m 2014
African 3000mSt record 2015, Tunisian: 1500m 2014, 3000m (3) 2008-13, 3000mSt (10) 2005-15.
Progress at 3000mSt: 2005- 9:51.49, 2006- 10:14.36, 2007- 9:50.04, 2008- 9:25.50, 2009- 9:12.52, 2011- 9:11.97, 2012- 9:08.37, 2014- 9:15.23, 2015- 9:05.36, 2016- 9:18.71. pbs: 1500m 4:06.38 '14, 3000m 8:46.61i '15, 8:49.5+ '13; 5000m 16:12.9 '03, 10000m 35:03.83 '05, 10kRd 33:30 '04.
Missed 2010 season after toe surgery. Won first Olympic medal for a woman from Tunisia.

TURKEY

Governing body: Türkiye Atletizm Federasyonu, 19 Mayis Spor Kompleksi, Ulus-Ankara. Founded 1922.

National Champions 2016: Men: 100m: Jak Ali Harvey 9.92, 200m: Ramil Guliyev 20.44, 400m: Furkan Can 49.25 ?, 800m: Ramazan Barbaros 1:49.07, 1500m: Ramazan Özdemir 3:41.24, 5000m: Hakan Çoban 14:30.69, 10000m: Polat Kemboi Arikan 27:59.59, HMar: Fatih Bilgiç 64:53, 3000mSt: Hakan Duvar 8:34.43, 110mh: Mustafa Günes 14.05, 400mh: Enis Ünsal 52.88, HJ: Ümit Tan 2.06, PV: Hasan Birinci 5.05; LJ: Alper Kulaksiz 7.78, TJ: Askin Karaca 15.78, SP: Murat Gündüz 17.60, DT: Tuna Ceylan 49.70, HT: Özkan Baltaci 72.88, JT: Emin Önce;l 74.56. Dec: Yusuf Pehlevan 6200. **Women**. 100m: Berfe Sancak 11.94, Mizgin Ay 24.29, 400m: Maryam Kasap 55.82, 800m: Hatice Ünzir 2:11.35, 1500m: Asli Arik 4:18.71, 5000m: Pinar Demirtas 16:49.77. 10000m: Yasemin Can 31:30.58, HMar: Alemitu Bekele 75:07, 3000mSt: Sebahat Akpinar 10:08.95, 100mh: Özge Solu 14.27, 400mh/LJ: Emel Senli 58.72/6.07, HJ: Burcu Yüksel 1.85, PV: Demet Parlak 4.10; TJ: Tugba Aydin 13.18w, SP: Sinem Yildirim 13.41, DT: Elçin Kaya 50.70, HT: Zeliha Uzunbilek 61.61, JT: Eda Tugsuz 52.96.

Polat Kemboi ARIKAN (ex Paul KEMBOI) b. 12 Dec 1990 Cheptirte, Kenya 1.73m 62kg.
At (5000m)/10000m: OG: '12- h/9, '16- 13; WCh: '13- dnf; EC: '12- 3/1, '14- 4, '16- 1; ECp: '12-14-15: 1/1/1; won Med G 2013. At 3000m: EI: '13- 10. Eur CC: '12-13-14-16: 7/2/1/2. World HMar: 14- 16, CC: '15- 22.
Turkish records 3000m 2012, 5000m 2011, HMar 2014.
Progress at 5000m, 10000m: 2006- 14:23.4A, 2009- 13:24.25, 2010- 13:18.12, 2011- 13:05.98, 2012- 13:12.55i/13:27.21, 27:38.81; 2013- 28:17.26, 2014- 28:11.11, 2015- 13:30.76, 28:05.64; 2016- 27:35.50. pbs: 1500m 3:47.05 '12, 3000m 7:42.31 '12, HMar 61:22 '14.
Became a Turkish citizen 9 Jun 2011, originally with 2-year wait for international eligibility, but waiting period ended in February 2012.

Yasmani COPELLO Escobar. b. 15 Apr 1987 La Habana, Cuba 1.96m 86kg. Fenerbahçe.

At 400mh: OG: '16- 3; WCh: '15- 6; EC: '16- 1; Ibero-American champion 2008, Balkan 2015, Cuban NG 2010.
Six Turkish 400mh records 2015-16.
Progress at 400mh: 2006- 52.30, 2007- 49.99, 2008- 50.08, 2009- 49.56, 2010- 51.23, 2011- 49.76, 2012- 50.28, 2013- 49.89, 2014- 50.62, 2015- 48.46, 2016- 47.92. pbs: 200m 21.44 '09, 400m 46.77 '09, 110mh 14.35A '08.
Former Cuban, has lived in Turkey from 2012, acquired citizenship 21 Oct 2013, cleared to compete for them from 30 Apr 2014.

Ramil GULIYEV b. 29 May 1990 Baku, Azerbaijan 1.87m 73kg. Fenerbahçe. Student teacher
At (100m)/200m: OG: '08- qf, '16- 8; WCh: '09- 7, '15- 6; EC: '14- h/6, '16- 6/2; WJ: '06- (h), '08- 5; WY: '07- 2; EJ: '09- 2/1; WUG: '09- 1, '15- 3/3; ET: '14- 3/2. At 60m: EI: '09- 7. Won Balkan 100m 2014, 2016; 200m 2014-16, TUR 100m 2012, 200m 2016.
Records: European Junior 200m 2009; AZE 100m (2) 2009, 200m (4) 2007-09; TUR 100m (2) & 200m (4) 2011-15.
Progress at 200m: 2006- 21.74, 2007- 20.72, 2008- 20.66, 2009- 20.04, 2010- 20.73, 2011- 20.32, 2012- 20.53, 2013- 20.46, 2014- 20.38, 2015- 19.88, 2016- 20.09. pbs: 60m 6.58i '12, 100m 10.07 '16, 300m 32.61 '16.
Switched from Azerbaijan to Turkey on 26 Apr 2011, and cleared to compete for Turkey from 4 Apr 2013.

Jak Ali HARVEY b. 5 Apr 1989 Hanover Parish, Jamaica 1.82m 73kg. ENKA.
At 100m/(200m): OG: '16- sf/h; WCh: '15- sf; EC: '16- 2; WUG: '11- 1; Balkan champion 2015, TUR 2016.
Four Turkish 100m records 2015-16.
Progress at 400mh: 2007- 10.90, 2008- 10.53, 2009- 10.57/10.46w, 2010- 10.26, 2011- 10.09/10.03w, 2012- 10.08, 2013- 10.04, 2014- 10.17, 2015- 10.01, 2016- 9.92A/10.03. pb 200m 20.38 '15.
Born Jacques Montgomery Harvey. Turkey citizen from 25 Jul 2014, cleared to compete for them from 24 Jul 2015.

Ali KAYA b. 20 Apr 1994 Eldoret, Kenya 1.71m 55kg. Ex Stanley Kiprotich KEN. Fenerbahçe.
At 5000m/(10000m): OG: '16- h/dnf; WCh: '15- 9/7; EC: '14- 9/3. '16- (2); EU23: '15- 1/1; ECp: '14- 3/2; EJ: '13- 1/1; CCp: '14- 5. At 3000m: EI: '15- 1, '17- 9. World CC: '17- 3 MxR; Eur CC: '13- 1J, '14- 2, '15- 1.
Records: European U23 & Turkish 5000m & 10,000m 2015, HMar 2016; TUR 3000m & half marathon 2015.
Progress at 5000m, 10000m: 2013- 13:31.39, 28:31.16; 2014- 13:34.83, 28:08.72; 2015- 13:00.31, 27:24.09; 2016- 28:21.42. pbs: 1500m 3:44.62 '16, 3000m 7:38.42i/7:38.65 '15, HMar 60:16 '16.
Moved to Turkey in 2010 and became a Turkish citizen on 6 Jun 2013.

TURKEY – UGANDA – UKRAINE

Kaan Kigen ÖZBILEN (Mike Kipruto **KIGEN)** b. 15 Jan 1986 Keiyo district, Kenya 1.70m 54kg.
At 5000m/(10000m): AfCh: '06- 2/2; WCp: '06- 2. At HMar: EC: '16- 2. At Mar: OG: '16- 17. World CC: '06- 5. Won Kenyan 5000m 2006.
Progress at 5000m, 10000m, Mar: 2005- 13:22.48, 2006- 12:58.58, 28:03.70; 2008- 13:09.84, 2009- 13:04.38, 2011- 13:11.65, 27:30.53; 2012- 13:21.55A, 27:03.49; 2013- 13:36.51, 2:08:24; 2014- 13:26.6, 2:06:59; 2015- 2:07:42, 2016- 2:06:10. pbs: 3000m 7:35.87 '06, 2M 8:20.09 '05, Road: 10M 45:34 '14, HMar 59:58 '11, 25k 1:14:17 '14, 30k 1:29:15 '14.
2nd Frankfurt marathon 2014, 3rd Amsterdam 2015. Acquired Turkish citizenship as Kaan Kigen Özbilen on 24 Jun 2015. 3rd Seoul Marathon 2016, but his 2:06:10 may not be eligible for European record.

Women

Yasemin CAN (formerly **Vivian Jemutai** KEN) b. 11 Dec 1996 Kenya. 1.66m 49kg. ENKA.
At 5000m/10000m: OG: 16- 6/7, EC: '16- 1/1; At 3000m: EI: '17- 2. World CC: '17- 3 MxR; Eur CC: '16- 1. Won TUR 10000m 2016.
European U23 records 10000m (3), 15k Rd 2016
Progress at 5000m, 10000m: 2015- 15:39.90, 32:42.31; 2016- 14:37.61, 30:26.41. pbs: 1500m 4:11.54i '17, 3000m 8:43.46i '17, 8:48.8 '16, 15k Rd 48:40 '16.
Became a Turkish citizen on 25 May 2015, cleared to compete for Turkey from 13 Mar 2016.

UGANDA

Governing body: Uganda Athletics Federation, PO Box 22726, Kampala. Founded 1925.
National Champions 2016: Men: 100m: Musa Isabirye 10.54, 200m: Pius Adome 20.96, 400m: Leonard Opiny 45.66, 800m/1500m: Abu Mayanja 1:46.82/3:44.1, 5000m: Joshua Cheptegei 13:17.80, 10000m: Thomas Ayeko 27:57.3, 3000mSt: Benjamin Kiplagat 8:33.72, HJ: Francis Isaano 1.90, PV: Peter Kizito 2.70, LJ: Francis Oketayot 7.09, TJ: Felix Watmon 15.31, SP/DT: Jacob Wokorach 13.25/40.05, JT: Robert Okello 60.04. **Women**: 100m: Mildred Gamba 12.02, 200m: Maureen Banura 23.84, 400m: Leni Shida 52.57, 800m: Halima Nakaayi 2:01.44, 1500m: Dorcus Ajok 4:20.5, 5000m: Janet Achola 16:06.23, 10000m: Rebecca Cheptegei 35:05.3, 3000mSt: Annet Chebet 10:56.3, HJ: Joyce Ajok 1.53, LJ: Mary Zawadi Unyuthfua 5.50, TJ: Sarah Nambawa 12.39, SP: Janneth Acan 11.93, DT: Josephine Lalam 36.81, JT: Lucy Aber 49.08.

Joshua Kiprui **CHEPTEGEI** b. 12 Sep 1996 1.79m 61kg.
At (5000m)/10000m: OG: '16- 8/6; WCh: '15- 9; WJ: '14- 4/1; won Afr-J 2015. UGA champion 5000m 2014-16.
Progress at 10000m: 2013- 28:53.52A, 2014- 13:32.84, 27:56.26; 2015- 13:28.50A, 27:27.57; 2016- 13:00.60, 27:10.06. pbs: 1500m 3:37.82 '16, 15k Rd 42:08 '16, 3000mSt 8:43.21A '13.
Had big lead at 3/4 distance in World Cross 2017, but faded badly to 30th.

Stephen KIPROTICH b. 27 Feb 1989 Kapchorwa 1.72m 56kg.
At Mar: OG: '12- 1, '16- 14; WCh: '11- 8, '13- 1, '15- 6. At 5000m: WCh: '07- h. At 10000m: WJ: '08- 5, AfCh: '10- 6, World CC: '08-11-17: 12J/6/17; AfChC: '11- 2.
Ugandan marathon records 2011 & 2015.
Progress at Mar: 2011- 2:07:20, 2012- 2:07:50, 2013- 2:08:05, 2014- 2:11:37, 2015- 2:06:33, 2016- 2:07:46. Pbs: 3000m 7:48.06 '07, 5000m 13:23.70 '08, 10000m 27:58.03 '10, HMar 61:15 '13, 3000mSt 8:26.66 '10.
Won Enschede marathon on debut 2011. Became the second man ever to win Olympic and World titles at marathon. 2nd Tokyo 2015.

UKRAINE

Governing body: Ukrainian Athletic Federation, P.O. Box 607, Kiev 01019. Founded 1991. **National Champions 2016: Men**: 100m: Igor Bodrov 10.55, 200m: Serhiy Smelyk 20.40, 400m: Vitaliy Butrym 45.85, 800m: Roman Yarko 1:46.80, 1500m: Volodymyr Kyts 3:52.19, 5000m: Artem Kazban 13:57.45, 10000m: Dmytro Lashyn 28:59.60, HMar: Yuriy Rusyuk 64:12, Mar: Serhiy Marchuk 2:22:20, 3000mSt: Vadym Slobodenyuk 8:36.68, 110mh: Serhiy Kopaneyko 13.87, 400mh: Anatoliy Synyanskyy 50.34, HJ: Dmytro Yakovenko 2.26, PV: Ivan Yeryomin 5.30, LJ: Serhiy Nykyforov 8.18w, TJ: Andriy Stanchev 16.60, SP: Viktor Samolyuk 18.48, DT: Mykyta Nesterenko 59.88, HT: Andriy Martynyuk 74.90, JT: Dmytro Kosynskyy 81.10, Dec: Serhiy Yarokhovych 7108, 20kW: Ivan Losev 1:23:29, 50kW: Andrit Hrechkovskyy 3:53:04. **Women**: 100m/200m: Nataliya Pohrebnyak 11.11/22.76, 400m: Olha Bibik 51.69, 800m/1500m: Nataliya Pryshchepa 1:59.08/4:10.51, 5000m: Viktoriya Pohoryelska 15:50.67, 10000m: Olha Kotovska 33:54.98, HMar: Kateryna Karmanenko 78:47, Mar: Viktoriya Khapilina 2:37:44, 3000mSt: Mariya Shatalova 9:44.25, 100mh: Anna Plotitsyna 13.06, 400mh: Hanna Titimets 55.00, HJ: Oksana Okuneva 1.97, PV: Maryna Kylypko 4.30, LJ: Maryna Bekh 6.93, TJ: Ruslana Tsyhotska 14.41, SP: Halyna Obleshchuk 17.84, DT: Nataliya Semenova 62.41, HT: Iryna Novozhylova 71.00, JT: Hanna Hatsko-Fedyusova 60.12, Hep: Daryna Sloboda 5644, 20kW: Olena Shevchuk 1:39:07, 50kW: Ksenitya Radko 4:39:09.

Bohdan BONDARENKO b. 30 Aug 1989 Kharkiv 1.97m 80kg.
At HJ: OG: '12- 7, '16- 3; WCh: '11- dnq 15=, '13- 1, '15- 2=; EC: '12- 11, '14- 1; WJ: '06- 3, '08- 1; EU23: '11- 1; EJ: '07- 9; WUG: '11- 1, CCp: '14- 1; ET: '13- 1. Won DL 2013.

Two UKR high jump records 2013-14.
Progress at HJ: 2005- 2.15, 2006- 2.26, 2007-
2.25i/2.19, 2008- 2.26, 2009- 2.27/2.15, 2010- 2.10,
2011- 2.30, 2012- 2.31, 2013- 2.41, 2014- 2.42, 2015-
2.37, 2016- 2.37.
His father Viktor had decathlon pb of 7480 '87.
Ruslan DMYTRENKO b. 22 Mar 1986 Kirove,
Kyiv region 1.80m 62kg. Donetsk.
At 20kW: OG: '12- 30, '16- 16; WCh: '09-11-13-15:
32/4/7/21; EC: '10- 11, '14- 4; WCp: '12-14-16:
3/1/9; EU23: '07- 6; ECp: '13- 5; WUG: '13- 2;
Won IAAF Race Walking Challenge 2014; UKR
champion 2009, 2011. At 10000m/10kW: EJ: '05-
11; ECp: '05- 6J.
UKR 20k walk record 2014 (and unofficial
10,000mW).
Progress at 20kW: 2006- 1:27:16, 2007- 1:23:31, 2008-
1:25:26, 2009- 1:21:21, 2010- 1:21:54, 2011- 1:21:31,
2012- 1:20:17, 2013- 1:20:38, 2014- 1:18:37, 2015-
1:21:25, 2016- 1:20:33. pbs: 5000mW 18:21.76i '14,
10000mW 39:26.90i '12, 39:33.91 '10, 38:50R '14.
Igor HLAVAN b. 25 Sep 1990 Nazarivka,
Kirovohrad 1.72m 62kg.
At (20kW)/50kW: OG: '12- 16, '16- 35/dnf; WCh:
'13- 4, '15- 4/dq; EC: '14- 6; WCp: '12- 10, '14- (7),
'16- 2; ECp: '13- 4, '15- (5). Won UKR 35kW 2013.
UKR 50km walk record 2013.
Progress at 20kW, 50kW: 2010- 1:30:31, 4:08:08;
2011- 1:25:58, 4:03:18; 2012- 3:48:07, 3- 1:22:32,
3:40:39; 2014- 1:19:59, 3:45:08; 2015- 1:20:29, 2016-
1:21:55, 3:44:02. pbs: 5000mW 19:11.87 '14,
10000mW 39:15.1 '14, 35k 2:31:15 '13.
Oleksiy KASYANOV b. 26 Aug 1985
Stakhanov, Lugansk 1.91m 87kg. Spartak
Zaporozhye.
At Dec: OG: '08- 6, '12- 7, '16- dnf; WCh: '09-11-
13-15: 4/12/dnf/9; EC: '10-12-14-16: dnf/2/8/4;
EU23: '07- 4; WUG: '07- 4; ECp: '09- 3, '15- 2.
UKR champion 2008. At Hep: WI: '10-12-14-16:
6/2/5/2; EI: '09- 2.
Progress at Dec: 2006- 7599, 2007- 7964, 2008-
8238, 2009- 8479, 2010- 8381, 2011- 8251, 2012-
8312, 2014- 8231, 2015- 8262, 2016- 8077. pbs: 60m
6.83i '09, 100m 10.50 '11, 200m 21.54 '15, 400m
47.46 '08, 1000m 2:39.44i '14, 1500m 4:22.27 '08,
60mh 7.85i '13, 110mh 13.92 '15, HJ 2.08i 14, 2.05
'09; PV 4.82 '09, LJ 8.04i/7.97 '10, SP 15.72 '09, DT
51.95 '10, JT 55.84 '07, Hep 6254i '10.
Won Talence decathlon 2009 & 2016. Married
Hanna Melnychenko (qv) on 18 Oct 2014.
Dmytro KOSYNSKYY b. 31 Mar 1989 Malyn
2.00m 105kg. Kyivska.
At JT: OG: '16- 5; EC: '10- 12, '14/16- dnq 14/18;
WJ: '08- 7; EU23: '11- dq (8); ET: '11- dq (1). UKR
champion 2010, 2014-16.
Progress at JT: 2008- 72.61, 2009- 75.18, 2010-
79.53, 2011- 83.39, 2014- 82.28, 2015- 79.00, 2016-
84.08.
Two-year drugs ban after failing a test when 1st
at 2011 European Team Champs.

Andriy PROTSENKO b. 20 May 1988 Kherson
1.94m 80kg. Khersonskaya. Biotechnology
graduate.
At HJ: OG: '12- 9, '16- 4=; WCh: '09-11-13-15: dnq
25/27/23=/17; EC: '10-12: dnq 17/13=, '14- 2, '16=
9=; EU23: '09- 3; EJ: '07- 2; WI: '14- 3, '16- 7; EI:
'15- 6; WUG: '13- 2; ET: '10- 3, '14- 1. UKR
champion 2012.
Progress at HJ: 2005- 2.10, 2006- 2.18i/2.10, 2007-
2.21, 2008- 2.30, 2009- 2.25, 2010- 2.25, 2011- 2.31,
2012- 2.31, 2013- 2.32, 2014- 2.40, 2015- 2.33i/2.32,
2016- 2.33.
Women
Anastasiya MOKHNYUK b. 1 Jan 1991 Kiev
1.75m 67kg. Kyivskiya.
At Hep: WCh: '15- 7; EC: '14- 14; EU23: '13- 3;
WJ: '10- 11. At Pen: WI: '16- 2. At LJ: EI: '13- 7.
Won UKR LJ 2013.
Progress at Hep: 2009- 4970, 2010- 5496, 2011-
5497, 2012- 5830, 2013- 5941, 2014- 6220, 2015-
6359. pbs: 200m 24.30 '15, 800m 2:15.52 '14, 60mh
8.11i '16, 100mh 13.00 '15, HJ 1.85i '16, 1.83 '15; LJ
6.66i '16, 6.57 '13; SP 15.01i '16, 14.96 '15; JT 39.76
'15, Pen 4847i '16.
Oksana OKUNEVA b. 14 Mar 1990 Mykolaiv
1.75m 61kg. Mykolaivska.
At HJ: OG: '16- dnq 22=; WCh: '11-13-15: dnq
19/15/14=; EC: '14- 6, '16- 6=; WY: '07- 6; EU23:
'11- 2; EJ: '09- 6; EI: '11- 7, '17- 4; ET: '14- 2. UKR
champion 2011, 2013-14, 2016.
Progress at HJ: 2005- 1.60, 2006- 1.75, 2007- 1.78,
2008- 1.80, 2009- 1.90, 2010- 1.92, 2011- 1.94, 2012-
1.93i/1.87, 2013- 1.92, 2014- 1.98, 2015- 1.92, 2016-
1.97.
Olesya POVH b. 18 Oct 1987 Dnipropetrovsk
1.69m 63kg. Zaporizhye.
At 100m/4x100mR: OG: '12- sf/3R, '16- sf; WCh:
'11- sf/3R, '13- sf, '15- hR; EC: '10- sf/1R, '12- 2,
'14/16- sf; WUG: '13- 1R; ET: '13- 2/1R. At 60m:
EI: '11-15-17: 1/6/2. Won UKR 100m 2010, 2012.
Progress at 100m: 2005- 12.19, 2006- 11.81, 2007-
11.85, 2008- 11.76, 2009- 11.70, 2010- 11.29, 2011-
11.24, 2012- 11.08, 2013- 11.14, 2014- 11.42/11.0h/
11.40w, 2015- 11.32, 2016- 11.21. pbs: 50m 6.21i
'12, 60m 7.11i '15, 200m 22.58 '11.
Nataliya PRYSHCHEPA b. 11 Sep 1994 Kiev
1.63m 50kg. Rivnenska.
At 800m: OG: '16- sf; EC: '16- 1; WY: '11- sf. At
1500m: EC: '14- 10, '16- h; WJ: '12- h; E23: '15- 3;
EJ: '13- 1; ET: '14- 3. Won UKR 800m 2016, 1500m
2013 & 2016.
Progress at 800m. 1500m: 2011- 2:08.02, 2012-
2:04.47, 4:22.63; 2013- 2:05.52, 4:13.81; 2014-
4:08.89, 2015- 2:05.22, 4:06.29; 2016- 1:58.60,
4:10.51.
Olga SALADUKHA b. 4 Jun 1983 Donetsk
1.75m 55kg.
At TJ: OG: '08- 7, '12- 3, '16- dnq 18; WCh: '07-11-
13-15: 6/1/3/6; EC: '06-10-12-14-16: 4/1/1/1/6;
WJ: '02- 5; EU23: '05- 4; EJ: '01- 9; WI: '08- 5, '14-

2; EI: '13- 1; WUG: '05- 2, '07- 1; WCp: '06-10-14: 6/2/3; ECp: '06-08-10-11-13-14: 1/1/1/1/1/2. Won DL 2011, UKR 2007-08.
Progress at TJ: 1998- 13.32, 1999- 12.86, 2000- 13.26, 2001- 13.48, 2002- 13.66i/13.63, 2003- 13.26i/13.03, 2004- 13.22, 2005- 14.04, 2006- 14.41/14.50w, 2007- 14.79, 2008- 14.84, 2010- 14.81, 2011- 14.98/15.06w, 2012- 14.99, 2013- 14.88i/14.85, 2014- 14.73, 2015- 14.62, 2016- 14.40. pb LJ 6.37 '06.
Married to professional road cyclist Denys Kostyuk with a daughter Diana born 2009.

Anna TITIMETS b. 5 Mar 1989 Pavlograd, Dnipropetrovsk 1.73m 63kg. Dnipropetrovsk.
At 400mh: OG: '12- sf, '16- sf; WCh: '09- h, '11- sf, '13- 4; EC: '10/12/16- sf, '14- 2; WJ: '08- 4; EU23: '09- 4, '11- 2; EJ: '07- 8 (2 4x100m); CCp: '14- 4; ET: '15- 2; WUG: '11- 1 4x100m, '13- 1. UKR champion 2010, 2012-14, 2016.
Progress at 400mh: 2006- 59.79, 2007- 58.35, 2008- 57.22, 2009- 55.95, 2010- 55.58, 2011- 54.69, 2012- 54.98, 2013- 54.63, 2014- 54.56, 2015- 54.75, 2016- 55.00. pbs: 60m 7.46i '11, 200m 23.60 '09, 400m 52.73 '11, 60mh 8.50i '13.

Olha ZEMLYAK b. 16 Jan 1990 Rivne 1.65m 56kg. Rivnenska.
At 400m: OG: '12- 3R, 16- 7; WCh: '13- hR, '15- h; EC: '12- 4/1R, '14- 2/2R, '16- sf; WJ: '08- sf/2R; WY: '07- 4/2R; EJ: '09- dq1R; CCp: '14- 5/2R; ET: '14- 3/1R.
Progress at 400mh: 2006- 55.95, 2007- 54.05, 2008- 53.69, 2009- 53.40, 2012- 51.82, 2013- 51.95, 2014- 51.00, 2015- 51.61, 2016- 50.75. pbs: 60m 7.72i '09, 100m 11.68 '14, 200m 23.49 '14.
Two-year drugs ban from positive test on 26 Jul 2009 after running 4x400m first leg at European Juniors.

UNITED KINGDOM

Governing body: British Athletics, Alexander Stadium, Walsall, Perry Barr, Birmingham B42 2BE. Founded 1999 (replacing British Athletics, founded 1991, which succeeded BAAB, founded 1932). The Amateur Athletic Association was founded in 1880 and the Women's Amateur Athletic Association in 1922.
National Championships (first were English Championships 1866-79, then AAA 1880-2006, WAAA from 1922). **2016 UK Champions**:
Men: 100m: James Dasaolu 9.93w, 200m: Adam Gemili 20.44, 400m: Matthew Hudson-Smith 44.88, 800m: Elliot Giles 1:48.00, 1500m: Charlie Grice 3:43.41, 5000m: Andrew Butchart 13:44.00, 10000m: Ross Millington 28:28.20, HMar: Mo Farah 60:04, Mar: Callum Hawkins 2:10:52, 3000mSt: Rob Mullett 8:41.67, 110mh: Andrew Pozzi 13.31, 400mh: Sebastian Rodger 49.45, HJ: Robbie Grabarz 2.26, PV: Luke Cutts 5.40, LJ: Daniel Gardiner 7.67, TJ: Nathan Douglas 16.58, SP: Scott Lincoln 19.03, DT: Nick Percy 60.43, HT: Chris Bennett 75.67, JT: Matti Mortimore 74.40, Dec: Aiden Davies 6914, 5000mW/20kW: Tom Bosworth 19:13.56/1:30:29, 50kW: Matthew Haddock 5:32:33. **Women**: 100m: Asha Philip 11.17, 200m: Dina Asher-Smith 23.11, 400m: Emily Diamond 51.94, 800m: Shelayna Oskan-Clarke 2:01.99, 1500m: Laura Muir 4:10.14, 5000m: Stephanie Twell 15:53.35, 10000m: Jessica Andrews 31:58.00, HMar: Charlotte Purdue 72:13, Mar: Alyson Dixon 2:31:52, 3000mSt: Rosie Clarke 9:52.20, 100mh: Tiffany Porter 12.91, 400mh: Eilidh Doyle 54.93, HJ: Morgan Lake 1.90, PV: Holly Bradshaw 4.60, LJ: Jazmin Sawyers 6.75, TJ: Laura Samuel 14.09, SP: Rachel Wallader 16.67, DT: Jade Lally 59.15, HT: Sophie Hitchon 69.99, JT: Jo Blair 57.44, Hep: Jessica Taylor 5913(w), 5000mW: Bethan Davies 22:03.82, 20k: Hannah Hunter 1:55:39.

Tom BOSWORTH b. 17 Jan 1990 Pembury, Kent 1.84m 64kg. Tonbridge, was at Leeds Metropolitan University.
At 20kW: OG: '16-6, WCh: '15- 24; EC: '14- 12; CG: '10- 11; won RWA 2010-11, 2016' UK 56000mWb 2011, 2014-16; 10kW 2011.
UK walk records: 5000m (3) 2011-15, 10k road 2015, 20k (2) 2016.
Progress at 20kW: 2010- 1:28:24, 2011- 1:27:18, 2012- 1:24:49, 2013- 1:24:44, 2014- 1:22:20, 2015- 1:22:33, 2016- 1:20:13 pbs: 3000mW 10:58.21i/11:29.54 '16, 5000mW 18:39.47i '17, 19:00.73 '15, 10kW 39:36 '15, 41:34.19t '15.

Andrew BUTCHART b. 14 Oct 1991 Dunblane 1.75m 64kg. Central.
At 5000m: OG: '16- 6; won UK 2016. At 3000m: ET: '15- 3. Eur CC: '16- 4.
Progress at 5000m: 2009- 14:49.93, 2010- 15:18.33, 2013- 15:14.18, 2014- 13:58.05, 2015- 13:29.49, 2016- 13:08.61 pbs: 800m 1:51.39 '14, 1500m 3:44.57 '15, 1M 3:45.23i '17,4:05.40 '13; 3000m 7:41.05i '17, 7:45.00 '13; 2M 8:12.63i '17, 10000m 29:32.43 '15, 10k Rd 28:28 '16.

(Sir) **Mohamed FARAH** b. 23 March 1983 Mogadishu, Somalia 1.71m 65kg. Newham & Essex Beagles.
At 5000m (/10000m): OG: '08- h, '12- 1/1, '16- 1/1; WCh: '07- 6, '09- 7, '11- 1/2, '13- 1/1, '15- 1/1; EC: '06- 2, '10- 1/1, '12- 1, '14- 1/1; CG: '06- 9; WJ: '00- 10; EJ: '01- 1; EU23: '03 & '05- 2; ECp: '08-09-10-13: 1/1/1 &(1)/1. At 3000m: WY: '99- 6; WI: '08- 6, '12- 4; EI: '05-07-09-11: 6/5/1/1; ECp: '05- 06: 2/2. World CC: '07- 11, '10- 20; HMar: '16- 3; Eur CC: '99-00-01-04-05-06-08-09: 5J/7J/2J/15/21/1/2/2. Won UK 5000m 2007, 2011; Mar 2014, HMar 2016.
Records: World indoor 2M 2015, European 10000m 2011, indoor 5000m 2011 (u) & 2017, 1500m 2013; indoor 2M 2012, 20k and half marathon 2015, 15k 2016; UK 3000m 2016, 2M 2014, 5000m 2010 & 2011, half marathon (3) 2011-15.
Progress at 1500m, 5000m, 10000m: 1996- 4:43.9, 1997- 4:06.41, 1998- 3:57.67, 1999- 3:55.78, 2000-

3:49.60, 14:05.72; 2001- 3:46.1, 13:56.31; 2002- 3:47.78, 14:00.5; 2003-3:43.17, 13:38.41; 2004- 3:43.4, c.14:25; 2005- 3:38.62, 13:30.53; 2006- 3:38.02, 13:09.40; 2007- 3:45.2i+, 3:46.50, 13:07.00; 2008- 3:39.66, 13:08.11, 27:44.54; 2009- 3:33.98, 13:09.14; 2010- 12:57.94, 27:28.86; 2011- 12:53.11, 26:46.57; 2012- 3:34.66, 12:56.98, 27:30.42; 2013- 3:28.81, 13:05.88, 27:21.71; 2014- 13:23.42, 28:08.11; 2015- 3:28.93, 13:11.77, 26:50.97; 2016- 3:31.74, 12:59.29, 26:53.71; 2017- 13:09.16i. pbs: 800m 1:48.69 '03, 1M 3:56.49 '05, 2000m 5:02.1+ '16, 3000m 7:32.62 '16, 2M 8:03.40i '15, 8:07.85 '14, 2000mSt 5:55.72 '00; road 15k 42:03+ '16, 10M 45:32+ '15, 20k 56:27 '15, HMar 59:22dh/59:32 '15, Mar 2:08:21 '14.
Joined his father in England in 1993. Sixth man ever to win Olympic 5000m/10,000m double at same Games and uniquely repeated that in 2016; first British athlete to win either title and to win three/four Olympic golds. In 2013 became third man to win World 5000m/ 10000m double and he repeated that in 2015; now has record eight global distance running titles. Won in New York on his debut in 2011 and has six wins, including Great North Run 2014-16, and three 2nds in his nine half marathons. He was knighted in the 2017 New Year's Honours

Adam GEMILI b. 6 Oct 1993 London 1.78m 73kg. Blackheath & Bromley.
At 100m/(200m)/4x100mR: OG: '12- sf, '16- (4); WCh: '13- (5); EC: '14- (1)/1R, '16- 1R; CG: '14- 2/1R; WJ: '12- 1; EU23: '13- 1/4/1R; EJ: '11- 2/2R; ET: '13/14- 1R. Won UK 200m 2016.
Progress at 100m, 200m: 2009- 11.2, 2010- 10.80/ 10.72w, 21.87w; 2011- 10.35/10.23w, 20.98; 2012- 10.05, 20.38; 2013- 10.06, 19.98; 2014- 10.04, 19.98; 2015- 9.97; 2016- 10.11, 19.97. Pb 60m 6.59i '16.
Sixth equal all-time junior list 10.05 to win World Junior 100m in 2012, improved 200m best from 20.30 to 20.17 and 19.98 at 2013 Worlds before 5th in final in 20.08. As a footballer he was a member of the youth academy at Chelsea before playing for Dagenham & Redbridge and then making a huge impact as a sprinter. Won European Athletics Rising Star award 2014.

Robbie GRABARZ b. 3 Oct 1987 Enfield 1.92m 87kg. Newham & Essex Beagles.
At HJ: OG: '12- 3=, '16- 4=; WCh: '13- 8, '15- dnq 18=; EC: '12- 1, '16- 2; WJ: '06- 12; EU23: '09- 11; EJ: '05- dnq 18; WI: '12- 6=, '16- 2; EI: '13- 6, '17- 2; won DL 2012, UK 2012-13, 2015-16.
UK high jump record 2012.
Progress at HJ: 2002- 1.75, 2004- 2.00, 2005- 2.22, 2006- 2.20i/2.14, 2007- 2.21, 2008- 2.27, 2009- 2.23i/2.22, 2010- 2.28, 2011- 2.28, 2012- 2.37, 2013- 2.31, 2014- 2.27i, 2015- 2.28, 2016- 2.33. pb TJ 14.40 '09.

Matthew HUDSON-SMITH b. 26 Oct 1994 Wolverhampton 1.96m. Birchfield H.
At 400m/4x400mR: OG: '16- 8; EC: '14- 2/1R, '16- 3R; CG: '14- 1R. At 200m: EJ: '13- 3/3R. Won UK 2016.
Progress at 400m: 2009- 52.09, 2011- 50.61, 2013- 48.76i, 2014- 44.75, 2015- 45.09, 2016- 44.48. pbs: 60m 6.96i '12, 100m 10.9 '13, 10.8w '12; 200m 20.88 '13, 300m 32.3+ '16.

Zharnell HUGHES b. 13 Jul 1995 Sandy Ground, Anguilla 1.90m 79kg. Racers TC, Jamaica.
At (100m)/200m: WCh: '15- 5; EC: '16- h; WJ: '12- sf/h, '14- 5. Won CAC-J 2014, UK 2015, PAm-J 100m 2013.
Records: Anguilla: 100m (4), 200m (6) 2012-14.
Progress at 200m: 2012- 20.90, 2013- 20.79/20.77w, 2014- 20.32, 2015- 20.02, 2016- 20.62. pbs: 100m 10.10 '16, 400m 46.95 '16.
Switched from Anguilla and cleared to compete for Britain from 19 June 2015.

Richard KILTY b. 2 Sep 1989 Middlesbrough 1.84m 80kg. Gateshead H.
At 200m/4x100mR: CG: '14- sf/2R; EU23: '09- 7, '11- 2R; WJ: '08- sf. At 100m: WCh: '13- hR, '15- sf; EC: '14- 1R, '16- dq; CCp: '14- 2R; ET: '14- 1R, '15- 2/1R. At 60m: WI: '14- 1; EI: 15- 1, '17- 1.
Progress at 100m, 200m: 2004- 11.43/11.3w, 2005- 10.96/10.90w, 22.60; 2006- 10.76/10.75w, 21.96; 2007- 10.61, 21.37; 2008- 10.60/10.5/10.51w, 21.19; 2009- 10.43, 20.80; 2010- 10.44, 21.41i; 2011- 10.32, 20.53; 2012- 10.23/10.15w, 20.50; 2013- 10.10, 20.34; 2014- 10.12, 20.73; 2015- 10.05, 20.54; 2016- 10.01/9.92w, 20.60. pbs: 60m 6.49i '14, 150mSt 15.32 '14, 14.64w '15; 400m 48.58 '13.
His partner is Dovile Dzindzaletaite, the Lithuanian who won the European U23 triple jump in 2015 after the World Junior silver in 2012; LTU record 14.23 '15.

Nick MILLER b. 1 May 1993 Carlisle 1.88m 112kg. Border H, Oklahoma State University, USA.
At HT: OG: '16- dnq 22/ WCh: '15- 11; EC: '16- dnq 25; CG: '14- 2; WJ: '12- dnq 25; EU23: '13- 9, '15- 1; ET: '15- 2. UK champion 2014-15, NCAA 2016. UK hammer record 2015.
Progress at HT: 2010- 49.86, 2011- 57.74, 2012- 67.56, 2013- 71.60, 2014- 74.38, 2015- 77.55, 2016- 76.93 '16. Pbs: DT 45.37 '13, Wt 22.46i '15.

Andrew POZZI b. 15 May 1992 Leamington Spa 1.86m 79kg. Stratford-upon-Avon. Bristol University.
At 110mh: OG: '12- h, '16- sf; EC: '16- dns; EJ: '11- 2. UK champion 2012, 2016. At 60mh: WI: '12- 4, '14- 4; EI: '17- 1.
Progress at 110mh: 2009- 14.8, 2011- 13.73/13.66w, 2012- 13.34, 2015- 13.62, 2016- 13.19. pbs: 100m 10.9 '11, 60mh 7.43i '17, LJ 6.73 '09.

Martyn ROONEY b. 3 Apr 1987 Croydon 1.98m 78kg. Croydon H. Was at Loughborough University.
At 400m/4x400mR: OG: '08- 6/3R, '12- sf, '16- h; WCh: '07- h, '09- sf/2R, '11- sf, '13- 4R, '15- sf/3R;

EC: '10- 3/2R, '14- 1/1R, '16- 1; CG: '06- 5, '14- 4; WJ: '06- 3/3R; EJ: '05- 2/1R; CCp: '10- 2R, '14-7/2R; ECp: '07-08-10: 3R/1&2R/1. Won UK 2008, 2010-12, 2014.
Progress at 400m: 2003- 49.4, 2004- 47.46, 2005- 46.44, 2006- 45.35, 2007- 45.47, 2008- 44.60, 2009- 45.35, 2010- 44.99, 2011- 45.30, 2012- 44.92, 2013- 45.05, 2014- 44.71, 2015- 44.45, 2016- 45.04. pbs: 60m 7.12i '09, 200m 21.08 '13, 20.87w '11; 300m 32.72 '16, 600m 1:16.9 '05, 800m 1:50.55 '05.
Ran anchor leg in 43.73 on 4x400m at 2008 Olympics. Married Kate Dennison (six UK PV records to 4.60 '09, 3= CG 2010) on 19 Sep 2014.

Greg RUTHERFORD b. 17 Nov 1986 Milton Keynes 1.88m 84kg. Marshall Milton Keynes.
At LJ: OG: '08- 9, '12- 1, '16- 3; WCh: '09- 5, '15- 1, '07-11-13- dnq 21/15=/14; EC: '06-14-16: 2/1/1; CG: '06-10-14: 8/2/1; EJ: '05- 1; EI: '09- 6; ET: '13- 3, '14- 2. Won DL 2015, AAA 2005-06, UK 2008, 2012, 2015.
Three UK Long jump records 2009-14.
Progress at LJ: 1999- 5.04, 2001- 6.16, 2003- 7.04, 2004- 7.28, 2005- 8.14, 2006- 8.26, 2007- 7.96, 2008- 8.20, 2009- 8.30, 2010- 8.22, 2011- 8.27/8.32w, 2012- 8.35, 2013- 8.22, 2014- 8.51, 2015- 8.41, 2016- 8.31/8.36w. pbs: 60m 6.68i '09, 100m 10.26 '10.
European Athlete of the Year 2015. Great-grandfather Jock Rutherford played 11 internationals for England at football 1904-08.

Chijindu UJAH b. 5 Mar 1994 Enfield 1.80m 75kg. Enfield & Haringey.
At 100m: OG: '16- sf; WCh: '15- sf; EC: '16- 1R; WJ: '12- 6; WY: '11- 8; EJ: '13- 1; Won UK 2015.
Progress at 2009- 11.61, 2010- 10.83, 2011- 10.58/10.49w, 2012- 10.26, 2013- 10.32, 2014- 9.96, 2015- 9.96, 2016- 10.01/9.97w. pbs: 60m 6.53i '15, 200m 20.47 '15.

Rabah YOUSIF Bkheit b. 11 Dec 1986 Khartoum, Sudan 1.83m 73kg. Newham & Essex Beagles.
At 400m/4x400mR: OG: '12- sf; WCh: '09- sf, '11- sf, '15- 6/3R; EC: '14- res 1R, '16- 3R; AfG: '11- 1; AfCh: '08- sf/2R, '10- 2/4R; CCp: '10- 5/3R; Won UK 2015, Arab 2009, 2011.
Progress at 400m: 2004- 46.36, 2005- 46.33, 2006- 46.89, 2007- 45.72, 2008- 47,13, 2009- 45.15, 2010- 45.18A/45.38, 2011- 45.13, 2012- 45.13, 2013- 46.06, 2014- 45.41, 2015- 44.54, 2016- 45.45. pbs: 60m 6.88i '07, 100m 10.79 '07, 200m 21.06 '12, 20.85w '07; 300m 32.31 '14, HJ 2.05i '04, LJ 7.61 '07.
Came to Britain in 2002, granted British nationality 23 Jan 2013, eligible to compete from 13 Jun 2013, previously Sudan.

Women

Dina ASHER-SMITH b. 4 Dec 1995 Farnborough 1.65m 55kg. Blackheath & Bromley. Student at King's College, London.
At 200m/4x100mR (100m): OG: '16- 5/3R; WCh: '13- 3R, '15- 5; EC: '14- dnf, '16- 1/2R; WJ: '12- 7, '14- (1); EJ: '13- 1/1R. At 60m: WI: '16- dns; EI: '15- 2. Won UK 100m 2015.
UK records 100m (2) & 200m 2015, 4x100m (2) 2016.
Progress at 100m, 200m: 2009- 12.10, 24.83; 2010- 12.00/24.50; 2011- 11.96, 24.16/24.11w; 2012- 11.54, 23.49; 2013- 11.38/11.30w, 23.14; 2014- 11.14/11.93w, 22.61; 2015- 10.99, 22.07; 2016- 11.08, 22.31. pbs: 60m 7.08i '15, 150mSt 16.82 '15, 400m 53.49 '14.

Holly BRADSHAW b. 2 Nov 1991 Preston 1.75m 68kg. née Bleasdale. Blackburn Harriers.
At PV: OG: '12- 6=, '16- 5; WCh: '11- dnq, '15- 7; WI: '12- 3, '14- 9; WJ: '10- 3; EU23: '11- 1; EI: '13- 1. UK champion 2011-12, 2015-16.
Three UK pole vault records 2011-12, five indoors 2011-12.
Progress at PV: 2007- 2.30, 2008- 3.10i, 2009- 4.05, 2010- 4.35, 2011- 4.71i/4.70, 2012- 4.87i/4.71, 2013- 4.77i/4.60, 2014- 4.73i, 2015- 4.70, 2016- 4.76i/4.70. pbs: SP 11.32 '11, JT 37.60 '11.
World age-19 best 2011, age-20 best 2012.
Married 800m runner Paul Bradshaw (1:47.37 '09) on 25 Oct 2014.

Eilidh CHILD/DOYLE b. 20 Feb 1987 Perth 1.72m 59kg. Pitreavie. PE degree from Edinburgh University.
At 400mh/4x400mR: OG: '12- sf, '16- 8/3R; WCh: '09/11- sf, '13- 5/3R, '15- 6/3R; EC: '10- 8, '12- 4R, '14- 1/3R, '16- 1R; CG: '10- 2, '14- 2; EU23: '07- 5, '09- 2; CCp: '14- 2; ET: '09-10-13-14-15: 3R/2/1&1R/2/1; UK champion 2014-16. At 400m: WI: '14- 3R; EI: '13- 2/1R, '17- 2R.
Progress at 400mh: 2003- 59.8mx, 2004- 59.53, 2005- 59.78, 2006- 59.7/60.05, 2007- 57.11, 2008- 56.84, 2009- 55.32, 2010- 55.16, 2011- 55.67, 2012- 54.96, 2013- 54.22, 2014- 54.39, 2015- 54.46, 2016- 54.09. pbs: 200m 24.51i '13, 24.56 '08; 300m 37.1i '13, 400m 51.45i/51.83 '13, 800m 2:24.2 '04, 60mh 8.89i '06, 100mh 14.51 '04, 14.38w '07, 200mhSt 25.84 '14.
Married Brian Doyle (400m 47.12 '06) Oct 2015.

Desiree HENRY b. 26 Aug 1995 Enfield, London 1.72m 60kg. Enfield & Haringey.
At 100m/(200m): OG: '16- sf/3R; WCh: '15- 4R; EC: '14- 7/1R, '16- dnf; WJ: '12- (4), '14- 4; WY: '11- (1); EJ: '13- (2)/1R; WCp: '14- 2R.
Progress at 100m, 200m: 2007- 27.05i, 2008- 12.58/12.4w, 25.37/25.01w; 2009- 12.04/12.01w/12.0,24.18;2010-12.11/11.93w,23.93i/24.06/23.66w; 2011- 11.92/11.51w, 23.25; 2012- 11.84/11.48w, 23.28; 2013- 11.50/11.43w, 23.32; 2014- 11.13/11.04w, 23.29/23.16w; 2015- 11.11, 22.94; 2016- 11.06, 22.46. pbs: 60m 7.22i '14, 150mSt 16.57 '16 (UK best), 400m 52.27 '16.
One of the seven torchbearers who lit the cauldron at the Opening Ceremony of the 2012 Olympic Games.

Sophie HITCHON b. 11 Jul 1991 Burnley 1.70m 74kg. Blackburn H.

At HT: OG: '12- 8, '16- 3; WCh: '11- dnq 25, '13- dnq 19, '15- 4; EC: '12- 10, '14- dnq 19, '16- 4; CG: '14- 3; WJ: '08- 7, '10- 1; WY: '07- dnq 17; EU23: '11- 3, '13- 1; EJ: '09- 3; ET: '13- 3; won Comm-Y 2008, UK 2011-12, 2014-16.
13 UK hammer records 2011-16.
Progress at HT: 2006- 40.98, 2007- 54.56, 2008- 60.73, 2009- 63.18, 2010- 66.01, 2011- 69.59, 2012- 71.98, 2013- 72.97, 2014- 71.53, 2015- 73.86, 2016- 74.54. pbs: 100m 12.2/12.40 '09, 200m 25.2 '08, 25.51 '09; SP 10.75 '08.

Katarina JOHNSON-THOMPSON b. 9 Jan 1993 Liverpool 1.83m 70kg. Liverpool H.
At Hep: OG: '12- 13, '16- 6; WCh: '13- 5, '15- 28 (11); WY: '09- 1; EU23: '13- 1; EJ: '09- 8, '11- 6. At LJ: WJ: '12- 1 (sf 100mh); WI: '14- 2. At Pen: EI: '15- 1. Won UK LJ 2014.
UK indoor records: high jump (2) 2014-15, long jump & pentathlon 2015.
Progress at LJ, Hep: 2006- 5.11, 2007- 5.77i/5.65, 2008- 6.11i/5.90/6.07w, 5343; 2009- 6.31, 5481; 2010- 6.25i/5.58, 2011- 6.44, 5787; 2012- 6.51/6.81w, 6267; 2013- 6449, 6.56; 2014- 6.92, 6682; 2015- 6.93i/6.79, 5039; 2016- 6.84, 6523. pbs: 60m 7.50i '14, 100m 12.35 '08, 12.2 '09, 11.30w '14; 200m 22.79 '16, 300m 38.56i '08, 400m 53.7 '14, 800m 2:07.64 '13, 60mh 8.18i '15, 100mh 13.37 '15, 200mHS 25.31 '15, 400mh 58.3 '14, HJ 1.98 '16, TJ 12.83, 13.35w '14; SP 12.49i '14, 12.47 '15; JT 42.01 '15, Pen 5000i '12.
Set pbs in the each of the last four events when adding 182 points to her pb for 5th at the 2013 Worlds and 474 points to pentathlon best to win 2015 European Indoors, including a 6.89 long jump, the best ever in a pentathlon. Three no-jumps (last by 1 cm) in 2015 WCh Hep LJ. World heptathlon best HJ 1.98 at 2016 Olympic Games. Has all all-time record 27 English age-group titles U15 to U23.

Morgan LAKE b. 12 May 1997 Milton Keynes 1.78m 64kg. Windsor, Slough, Eton & Honslow.
At Hep/(HJ): OG: '16- (10=); WCh: '15- (dnq 14=); EC: '14- (dnq 17=), '16- dnf; WJ: '14- 1/1; WY: '13- dnf; EJ: '15- (1). At Pen: WI: '16- 7; EI: '15- 9, '17- (8). Won UK HJ 2016.
World youth indoor pentathlon record 2014.
Progress at HJ, Hep: 2007- 1.28, 2008- 1.50, 2009- 1.57, 2010- 1.70, 2011- 1.76, 2012- 1.80, 2013- 1.90, 2014- 1.94, 6148; 2015- 1.94, 5082; 2016- 1.94, 5951. pbs: 60m 7.98i '13, 200m 24.59 '14, 800m 2:18.53i '16, 2:21.06 '14; 60mh 8.63i '16, 100mh 14.25 '14, LJ 6.32 '14, TJ 12.35, 12.45w '13; SP 14.85 '14, JT 41.66 '14, Pen 4527i '15.
27 English age-group titles 2010-15 (12 indoors, 15 out). Father Eldon had a TJ pb of 15.43 (1989).

Eilish McCOLGAN b. 25 Nov 1990 Dundee 1.76m 59kg. Dundee Hawkhill, was at Dundee University.
At 5000m: OG: '16- 13; EC: '16- 6. At 3000m: EI: '17- 3; At 3000mSt: OG: '12- h; WCh: '13- 10, CG: '14- 6; EU23: '11- 6; UK 2012-14.

Progress at 1500m, 5000m: 2002- 5:22.8, 2003- 4:58.14, 2004- 4:36.70, 2005- 4:37.78, 2006- 4:38.00, 2007- 4:35.56, 2008- 4:27.11, 2010- 4:21.38, 2011- 4:14.44, 15:52.69; 2012- 4:11.78mx/4:13.19, 15:44.62; 2013- 4:09.67, 2014- 4:15.23mx, 2016- 4:03.74, 15:05.00. pbs: 800m 2:12.22 '08, 3000m 8:43.27 '16, 10000m 32:10.59 '17, 2000mSt 6:42.24 '11, 3000mSt 9:35.82 '13.
Her mother Liz (10,000m OG: '88- 2, WCh: '91- 1, 30:57.07 '91), father Peter (3000mSt 8:27.93 '91).

Laura MUIR b. 9 May 1993 Milnathort, Kinross 1.62m 54kg. Dundee Hawkhill H. Was at Glasgow University.
At 1500m /(3000m): OG: '16- 7; WCh: '15- 5; EC: '14- h; CG: '14- 11; WJ: '12- (16); EU23: '13- 3; EI: '13- 7, '15- (4), '17- 1/1, won DL 2016. At 800m: WCh: '13- sf. Won UK 2015-16. Eur CC: '15- 4 U23.
Two UK 1500m records 2016, Indoor records: Commonwealth 30000m & European 1000m & 3000m 2017.
Progress at 1500m: 2005- 5:33.16, 2006- 5:12.39, 2007- 4:48.97, 2008- 4:47.92, 2009- 4:58.77, 2010- 4:50.91. 2011- 4:38.90, 2012- 4:14.52mx/4:17.81, 2013- 4:07.76, 2014- 4:00.07, 2015- 3:58.66. 2016- 3:55.22, 2017- 4:02.39i. pbs: 400m 55.36i mx '16, 55.71i '14, 56.78 '12; 800m 2:00.42 '15, 1000m 2:31.93i '17, 2:40.5 '16, 1M 4:19.12 '16, 3000m 8:26.41i '17, 8:38.47 '15; 5000m: 14:49.12i '17, 10k Rd 38:23 '11.

Cindy OFILI b. 5 Aug 1994 Ypsilanti, USA 1.78m 68kg. University of Michigan.
At 100mh: OG: '16- 4; WCh: '15- sf. Won NCAA indoor 60mh 2016.
Progress at 100mh: 2012- 13.61, 2013- 13.34/13.30w, 2014- 12.93, 2015- 12.60, 2016- 12.63. pbs: 60m 7.37i '14, 100m 11.39 '15, 200m 23.46/23.43w '16, 60mh 7.89i '16.
Sister of Tiffany Porter. Has dual British/US nationality.

Christine OHURUOGU b. 17 May 1984 Forest Gate, London 1.75m 70kg. Newham & Essex Beagles. Studied linguistics at University College, London.
At 400m/4x400mR: OG: '04- sf/4R, '08- 1, '12- 2, '16- sf/3R; WCh: '05- sf/3R, '07- 1/3R, '09- 5, '11- h, '13- 1/3R, '15- 8/3R; EC: '14- 4, '16- 4; CG: '06- 1, '14- 3R; EU23: '05- 2/2R; EJ: '03- 3/3R; WI: '12- 1R, '14- 3R; EI: '13- 1R; ET: '13- 1R. At 200m: ECp: '08- 2, '09- 3. Won AAA 400m 2004, UK 2009, 2012-13.
UK 400m record 2013.
Progress at 400m: 2000- 59.0, 2001- 55.29, 2003- 54.21, 2004- 50.50, 2005- 50.73, 2006- 50.28, 2007- 49.61, 2008- 49.62, 2009- 50.21, 2010- 50.88, 2011- 50.85, 2012- 49.70, 2013- 49.41, 2014- 51.38, 2015- 50.16, 2016- 51.05. pbs: 60m 7.39i '06, 100m 11.35 '08, 150mStr 16.94 '09, 200m 22.85 '09, 300m 36.76+ '09.
Played for England U17 and U19 at netball. Withdrawn from GB European Champs team in 2006 after missing three drugs tests, receiving a

one-year ban. Younger sister Victoria (b. 28 Feb 1993) 400m pb 52.62 '13; res 3R WI '14.

Asha PHILIP b. 25 Oct 1990 Leytonstone, London 1.63m 54kg. Newham & Essex Beagles, was at Kingston University.
At 100m/4x100mR: OG: '16- sf/3R; WCh: '13- sf, '15- sf/4R; EC: '14- sf/1R, '16- 4/2R; CG: '14-4/3R; WJ: 06- 4/6R; WY: 07- 1; E23: 13- 4 200m; EJ: '07- 1R; ET: '15- 1. At 60m: WI: '14- 4, '16- 5; EI: '13- 5. '17- 1. Won UK 100m 2013-14, 16.
Progress at 100m: 2004- 12.14/12.04w, 2005- 11.83, 2006- 11.45, 2007- 11.37, 2010- 12.0, 2011- 11.47, 2012- 11.53, 2013- 11.20, 2014- 11.18/11.11w, 2015- 11.10, 2016- 11.16. pbs: 60m 7.06i '17, 150mSt 16.69 '14, 200m 23.45, 23.07w '13.
World U17 double-mini trampoline champion in 2006, but ruptured her knee in 2007 and unable to compete until 2010.

Tiffany PORTER b. 13 Nov 1987 Ypsilanti, USA 1.72m 62kg. née Ofili. Doctorate in pharmacy from University of Michigan.
At 100mh: OG: '12- sf, '16- 7; WCh: '11- 4, '13- 3, '15- 5; EC: '14- 1, '16- 3; CG: '14- 2; WJ: '06- 3 (for USA); CCp: '14- 2; ET: '13- 1. At 60mh: WI: '12-14-16: 2/3/3; EI: '11- 2. Won UK 100mh 2011, 2013-16; NCAA 100mh & 60mh indoors 2009.
Records: British 100mh (4) 2011-14, 50mh/55mh/ 60mh indoors; world best 4x100mh 2014 & 2015
Progress at 100mh: 2005- 14.19, 2006- 13.37/13.15w, 2007- 12.80, 2008- 12.73, 2009- 12.77/12.57w, 2010- 12.85, 2011- 12.56, 2012- 12.65/12.47w, 2013- 12.55, 2014- 12.51, 2015- 12.56, 2016- 12.70. pbs: 60m 7.41i '11, 100m 11.70 '09, 11.63w '08; 200m 23.90 '08, 50mh 6.83i '12, 55mh 7.38i '12, 60mh 7.80i '11, 400mh 61.96 '06, LJ 6.48 '09.
Opted for British nationality in September 2010; her mother being born in London (father born in Nigeria). Married US hurdler Jeff Porter (qv) in May 2011. Sister of Cindy Ofili (qv).

Shara PROCTOR b. 16 Sep 1988 The Valley, Anguilla 1.74m 56kg. Birchfield H. Was at University of Florida, USA.
At LJ: OG: '12- 8, '16- dnq 21; WCh: '07-09-11-13-15: dnq 29/6/dnq 20/5/2; WI: '12-14-16: 3/4/8; CG: '06- dnq 13, '14- nj; WJ: '06- dnq 16; WY: '05- 6; EI: '13- 4; ET: '13- 3. Won DL 2013, CAC 2009, UK 2011-13.
Records: Anguilla: LJ 2005-09, TJ 2007-09; UK LJ (4) 2012-15.
Progress at LJ: 2003- 5.64, 2004- 5.99A, 2005- 6.24, 2006- 6.17, 2007- 6.17, 2008- 6.54A/6.52/6.61w, 2009- 6.71, 2010- 6.69, 2011- 6.81, 2012- 6.95, 2013- 6.92, 2014- 6.82, 2015- 7.07, 2016- 6.91i/6.80. pbs: 60m 7.36i '16, 100m 12.27 '08, 12.10w '10; TJ 13.88i '10, 13.74 '09.
Switched from Anguilla (a British Dependent Territory without a National Olympic Committee) to Britain from 16 Nov 2010. Younger sister Shinelle (b. 27 Jun 91) set Anguillan high jump records at 1.70 in 2009 and 2010 and 1.72i in 2014.

JAZMIN SAWYERS b. 21 May 1994 Stoke-on-Trent 1.67m 52kg. City of Stoke. Studying law at Bristol University.
At LJ: OG: '16- 8; EC: '16- 2; CG: '14- 2; WJ: '12- 3; EU23: '15- 2; EJ: '13- 2; EI: '17- 6. UK champion 2016. At Hep: WY: '11- 9.
Progress at LJ: 2005- 4.21/4.64w, 2006- 5.05, 2007- 5.65, 2008- 5.72, 2009- 5.96, 2010- 5.60i, 2011- 6.23/6.27w, 2012- 6.67, 2013- 6.63, 2014- 6.54, 2015- 6.71, 2016- 6.75/6.86w. pbs: 200m 25.24 '11, 800m 2:28.71 '11, 100mh 14.29 '13, HJ 1.77i '08, 1.75 '11; SP 10.42 '11, JT 28.02 '11, Hep 5077 '11.
Silver medal for Britain at bobsleigh at 2012 Youth Olympics.

Lynsey SHARP b. 11 Jul 1990 Dumfries 1.75m 60kg. Edinburgh AC. Law graduate of Edinburgh Napier University.
At 800m: OG: '12- sf, '16- 6; WCh: '15- sf; EC: '12- 1, '14- 2; CG: '14- 2; WJ: '08- sf; WY: '07- sf; EU23: '11- 2; CCp: '14- 5. Won UK 2012, 2014-15.
Progress at 800m: 2000- 2:38.2, 2002- 2:25.97, 2003- 2:16.57, 2004- 2:09.98, 2005- 2:10.44, 2006- 2:10.91i, 2007- 2:06.92, 2008- 2:04.44, 2011- 2:00.65, 2012- 2:00.52, 2013- 2:02.63, 2014- 1:58.80, 2015- 1:57.71, 2016- 1:57.69. pbs: 400m 54.43 '16, 600m 1:27.51 '14, 1500m 4:36.27 '11.
Father Cameron (1982: 4th 100m, 2nd 200m EC; 3rd 100m, 200m, 4x100m CG; pbs: 100m 10.20 '83, 200m 20.47 '82); mother Carol Lightfoot (800m 2:02.91 '82).

Lorraine UGEN b. 22 Aug 1991 London 1.78m 64kg. Blackheath & Bromley. Was at Texas Christian University, USA.
At LJ: OG: '16- 11; WCh: '13- dnq, '15- 5; EC: '16- dnq 18; CG: '14- 5; WJ: '10- dnq 17; EU23: '13- dns F; EJ: '09- dnq 21; WI: '16- 3; EI: 17- 2; won NCAA 2013.
UK indoor LJ record 2017.
Progress at LJ: 2007- 5.55, 2008- 5.79, 2009- 6.29, 2010- 6.35/6.42w, 2011- 6.54, 2012- 6.74/6.83w, 2013- 6.77, 2014- 6.73Ai/6.59i/6.39/6.40w, 2015- 6.92/6.96w, 2016- 6.93i/6.80/6.82w, 2017- 6.97i. pbs: 60m 7.50Ai '12, 7.51i '14; 100m 11.42 '15, 11.34w '12; 200m 23.81/23.71w '15, 100mh 15.2/15.42 '08, HJ 1.56 '08, Hep 4307 '08.

Laura WEIGHTMAN b. 1 Jul 1991 Alnwick 1.72m 58kg. Morpeth H. Leeds Met University.
At 1500m: OG: '12- 7, '16- 11; WCh: '13- h, '15- sf; EC: '14- 3; CG: '14- 2; WJ: '10- 6. Won UK 2012, 2014. At 3000m: ET: '13- 2. Eur U23 CC: '13- 8.
Progress at 1500m: 2004- 4:50.5, 2005- 4:44.0, 2006- 4:37.20, 2007- 4:26.02, 2008- 4:22.20, 2009- 4:14.9mx/4:19.9, 2010- 4:09.60mx/4:12.82, 2011- 4:07.94mx/4:15.51, 2012- 4:02.99, 2013- 4:05.36, 2014- 4:00.17, 2015- 4:04.70, 2016- 4:02.66. pbs: 400m 58.43 '09, 800m 2:02.52 '12, 1000m 2:38.49 '13, 1M 4:52.7 '09, 2000m 5:44.22 '13, 3000m 8:43.46mx '13, 9:02.62 '12; 5k Rd 16:43 '12.

USA

Governing body: USA Track and Field, One RCA Dome, Suite #140, Indianapolis, IN 46225. Founded 1979 as The Athletics Congress, when it replaced the AAU (founded 1888) as the governing body.

National Championships first held in 1876 (men), 1923 (women). **2016 Champions: Men**: 100m/200m: Juston Gatlin 9.80/19.75, 400m: LaShawn Merritt 43.97, 800m: Clayton Murphy 1:44.76, 1500m: Matthew Centrowitz 3:34.09, 5000m: Bernard Lagat 13:35.50, 10000m: Galen Rupp 27:55.04, HMar: Christo Landry 62:52, 3000mSt: Evan Jager 8:22.48, 110mh: Devon Allen 13.03, 400mh: Kerron Clement 48.50, HJ: Erik Kynard 2.29, PV: Sam Kendricks 5.91, LJ: Jeff Henderson 8.59w, TJ: Will Claye 17.65, SP: Ryan Crouser 22.11, DT: Mason Finley 63.42. HT: Rudy Winkler 76.76, JT: Cyrus Hostetler 83.24, Dec: Ashton Eaton 8750, 20kW/50kW: John Nunn 1:25:36/4:03:21. **Women**: 100m: English Gardner 10.74, 200m: Tori Bowie 22.25, 400m: Allyson Felix 49.68, 800m: Kate Grace 1:59.10, 1500m: Jenny Simpson 4:04.74, 5000m/10000m: Molly Huddle 15:05.01/31:41.62, HMar: Tara Welling 70:25, 3000mSt: Emma Coburn 9:17.48, 100mh: Brianna Rollins 12.34, 400mh: Dalilah Muhammad 52.88, HJ: Chaunté Lowe 2.01, PV: Jenn Suhr 4.80, LJ: Brittney Reese 7.31, TJ: Keturah Orji 14.32, SP: Michelle Carter 19.39, DT: Whitney Ashley 62.25, HT: Amber Campbell 74.03; JT: Maggie Malone 60.84, Hep: Barbara Nwaba 6494, 20kW: Maria Michta-Coffey 1:33:40, 50kW: Taylor-Talcott 4:44:26.

NCAA Championships first held in 1921 (men), 1982 (women). **2016 Champions: Men**: 100m/200m/LJ: Jarrion Lawson 10.22/20.19/8.15, 400m: Arman Hall 44.82, 800m: Donavan Brazier 1:43.55, 1500m: Clayton Murphy 3:36.38, 5000m/10000m: Edward Chesarek 13:25.59/29:09.57, 3000mSt: Mason Ferlic 8:27.16. 110mh: Devon Allen 13.50, 400mh: Eric Futch 48.91, HJ: Randall Cunningham 2.25, PV: Jake Blankenship 5.60, TJ: Latario Collie-Minns BAH 16.97, SP: Filip Mihaljevic CRO 20.71, DT: Nicholas Percy GBR 61.27, HT: Nick Miller GBR 73.98, JT: Curtis Thompson 77.64, Dec: Lindon Victor GRN 8379. **Women**: 100m/200m: Ariana Washington 10.95w/22.21, 400m: Courtney Okolo 50.36, 800m: Raevyn Rogers 2:00.75, 1500m: Marta Pen POR 4:09.53, 5000m/10000m: Dominique Scott RSA 15:57.07/32:35.69, 3000mSt: Courtney Frerichs 9:24.41, 100mh: Jasmine Camacho-Quinn PUR 12.54w, 400mh: Shamier Little 53.51, HJ: Kimberly Williamson JAM 1.88, PV: Lexi Weeks 4.50, LJ: Chanice Porter JAM 6.67, TJ: Keturah Orji 14.53, SP: Raven Saunders 19.33, DT: Kelsey Card 63.52, HT: DeAnna Price 71.53, JT: Maggie Malone 62.19, Hep: Kendell Williams 6225.

Devon ALLEN b. 12 Dec 1994 Phoenix, Arizona 1.83m 84kg. Student at University of Oregon.
At 110mh: OG: '16- 5; Won US 2014, 2016; NCAA 2014, 2016.
Progress at 110mh: 2014- 13.16, 2016- 13.03. pbs: 60m 6.85Ai '14, 100m 10.36 '16, 200m 20.68 '16, 60mh 7.56i '16, 400mh 51.19 '14.
On a football scholarship, wide receiver. Suffered a knee injury on the opening kickoff of the Rose Bowl at the end of 2014 and missed 2015 track season.

Robby ANDREWS b. 29 Mar 1991 Mamalapan Township, New Jersey 1.77m 68kg. adidas. Was at University of Virginia.
At 800m: WJ: '10- 3. At 1500m: OG: '16- sf; WCh: '15- 11; WI: '16- 4. Won US 1500m (& indoor 1000m) 2015; NCAA 800m 2011.
Progress at 800m, 1500m: 2008- 4:12.48Mi/4:12.82M, 2009- 1:48.66, 4:03.49M; 2010- 1:45.54, 3:14.09; 2011- 1:44.71, 3:40.77; 2012- 1:45.06, 3:34.78; 2013- 1:47.13Ai/1:48.18, 3:43.52; 2014- 1:46.28, 3:42.54; 2015- 1:45.98, 3:35.52; 2016- 1:46.06, 3:34.88. pbs: 1000m 2:17.90i '13, 1M 3:53.16i '16, 3:57.15 '15.

Ronnie ASH b. 2 Jul 1988 Raleigh NC 1.88m 86kg. Nike. Was at University of Oklahoma.
At 110mh: OG: '16- dq; WCh: '15- h; CCp: '14- 2; won NACAC 2010, NCAA 2009.
Progress at 110mh: 2008- 13.44, 2009- 13.27, 2010- 13.19/12.98w, 2011- 13.25/13.24w, 2012- 13.20/13.10w, 2014- 12.99, 2015- 13.13, 2016- 13.21. pbs: 200m 22.08 '08, 60mh 7.55i '10.

Ronnie BAKER b. 15 Oct 1993 Louisville, Kentucky 1.78m 73kg. Texas Christian University.
At 100m: WUG: '15- 4. Won NCAA indoor 60m 2015-16, US 2017.
Progress at 100m: 2011- 10.57, 2012- 10.59/10.55w, 2013- 10.58/10.33w, 2014- 10.21/10.14w, 2015- 10.05/9.94w, 2016- 10.09/9.95w. pbs: 60m 6.45Ai/6.46i '17, 200m 20.60Ai, 20.64 '16; 400m 46.18 '13. Fastest in the world indoor 60m in 2016 & 2017.

Boris BERIAN b. 19 Dec 1992 Colorado Springs 1.83m 71kg. Adams State University.
At 800m: OG: '16- 8; WI: '16- 1.
Progress at 800m: 2011- 1:52.18A, 2012- 1:48.93, 2013- 1:48.89, 2015- 1:43.34, 2016- 1:44.20. pbs: 400m 46.93A '11, 600m 1:15.51i '16, 1:16.14 '15.

Hillary BOR b. 22 Nov 1989 Eldoret, Kenya 1.68m 57kg. Was at Iowa State University.
At 3000mSt: OG: '16- 7.
Progress at 3000mSt: 2008- 8:36.84, 2009- 8:35.12, 2010- 8:38.05, 2011- 8:40.83, 2012- 8:36.44, 2013- 8:32.41, 2014- 8:38.42, 2015- 8:45.94, 2016- 8:13.68. pbs: 1500m 3:44.30 '07, 1M 4:03.43i '08, 3000m 8:10.77i '10, 5000m 14:03.45 '08, 10M Rd 48:31 '15.

Marvin BRACY b. 15 Dec 1993 Orlando, Florida 1.75m 74kg. adidas. Was at Florida State University.

At 100m/4x100mR: OG: '16- sf; WJ: '10- res 1R; PAm-J: 11- 1. At 60m: WI: '14- 2, '16- 7; won US indoor 2014-16.
Progress at 100m: 2010- 10.42/10.19w, 2011- 10.28/10.05w, 2012- 10.25/10.06w, 2013- 10.09, 2014- 10.08, 2015- 9.93, 2016- 9.94. pbs: 55m 6.08i '12, 60m 6.48Ai/6.51i '14, 200m 20.55 '14.
Wide receiver at American Football at University.

Trayvon BROMELL b 10 Jul 1995 St. Petersburg, Florida 1.75m 71kg. New Balance. Baylor University.
At 100m/4x100mR: OG: '16- 8; WCh: '15- 3=; WJ: '14- 2/1R; PAm-J: 13- 3/1R. At 60m: WI: '16- 1.
Two world junior 100m records 2014.
Progress at 100m, 200m: 2012- 10.40, 21.01; 2013- 10.27/9.99Aw, 20.91/20.86w; 2014- 9.97/9.77w, 20.59/20.23w; 2015- 9.84/9.76w, 20.03/19.86w; 2016- 9.84, 20.30. pb 60m 6.47i '16.
Fastest ever teenager with 9.84 for 100m in 2015.

Christian CANTWELL b. 30 Sep 1980 Jefferson City, Missouri 1.93m 154kg. Nike. Studied hotel and restaurant management at University of Missouri.
At SP: OG: '08- 2, '12- 4; WCh: '05-09-11-15: 4/1/3/dns; WI: '04-08-10: 1/1/1; CCp: '10- 1; won DL 2010, WAF 2003, 2009; US 2005, 2009-10. At DT: PAm-J: '99- 2.
Progress at SP: 1999- 15.85, 2000- 19.67, 2001- 19.71, 2002- 21.45, 2003- 21.62, 2004- 22.54, 2005- 21.67, 2006- 22.45, 2007- 21.96, 2008- 22.18i/21.76, 2009- 22.16, 2010- 22.41, 2011- 22.07, 2012- 22.31, 2013- 20.13i/19.86, 2014- 21.85, 2015- 21.64, 2016- 19.72. pbs: DT 59.32 '01, HT 57.18 '01, Wt 22.04i '03.
Three competitions over 22m in 2004, then 4th in US Olympic Trials. Married Teri Steer (b. 3 Oct 1975, SP pb 19.21 '01, 3 WI 1999) 29 Oct 2005.

Chris CARTER b. 11 Mar 1989 Austin 1.86m 80kg. Was at University of Houston.
At TJ: PAm: '11- 6; WI: '14- 6. Won US indoor 2014.
Progress at TJ: 2005- 14.43, 2006- 13.78/14.69w, 2007- 15.88, 2008- 15.41i/15.31/15.69Aw, 2009- 16.34, 2010- 15.98, 2011- 16.86, 2012- 16.61, 2013- 16.69, 2014- 17.15Ai/17.09, 2015- 16.71i/16.70, 2016- 17.18. pbs: 400mh 53.90 '07, LJ 7.67 '13.

Matthew CENTROWITZ b. 18 Nov 1989 Beltsville, Maryland 1.76m 61kg. Nike Oregon Project. Studied sociology at the University of Oregon.
At 1500m: OG: '12- 4, '16- 1; WCh: '11-13-15: 3/2/8; WI: '12- 7, '16- 1. At 5000m WJ: '08- 11. Won US 2011, 2013, 2015-16; NCAA 2011, PAm-J 2007.
Progress at 1500m: 2007- 3:49.54, 2008- 3:44.98, 2009- 3:36.92, 2010- 3:40.14, 2011- 3:34.46, 2012- 3:31.96, 2013- 3:33.58, 2014- 3:31.09, 2015- 3:30.40, 2016- 3:34.09. pbs: 800m 1:44.62 '15, 1000m 2:16.67 '16, 1M 3:50.53 '14, 3000m 7:40.74i '16, 2M 8:21.07i '17, 8:40.55 '07; 5000m 13:20.06 '14.
Father Matt pbs: 1500m 3:36.60 '76, 3:54.94 '82, 5000m US record 13:12.91 '82, 10000m 28:32.7 '83; h OG 1500m 1976; 1 PAm 5000m 1979. Sister Lauren (b. 25 Sep 1986) 1500m pb 4:10.23 '09.

Paul Kipkemoi CHELIMO b. 27 Oct 1990 Iten, Kenya 1.71m 57kg. US Army. Went to the University of North Carolina.
At 5000m: OG: '16- 2; WUG: '13- 2 (1500m 6). At 3000m: WI: '16- 7.
Progress at 5000m: 2011- 13:53.02, 2012- 13:21.89, 2013- 13:36.27, 2015- 13:37.02, 2016- 13:03.90. pbs: 1500m 3:39.33 '16, 1M 4:02.80i '12, 3000m 7:37.98 '16, 2M 8:28.53Ai '17, 10000m 29:44.42 '11, 10M Rd 48:19 '15.
Came to the USA in 2010, granted US citizenship on 23 Jul 2014 and cleared to compete for the US from 15 Jun 2015. Reduced his 5000m best from 13:19.54 to 13:03.90 at the 2016 Olympic Games.

Jordan CLARKE b. 10 Jul 1990 Anchorage, Alaska 1.93m 125kg. Was at Arizona State University.
At SP: WCh: '15- dnq 13; PAm-J: '09- 2. Won NCAA 2011-12.
Progress at SP: 2009- 19.49, 2010- 19.21, 2011- 19.75, 2012- 20.86i/20.40, 2013- 20.59i/20.28, 2014- 21.37, 2015- 21.49, 2016- 21.11. pbs: DT 61.16 '09, HT 66.18 '13, Wt 19.96i '13.

Will CLAYE b. 13 Jun 1991 Phoenix 1.80m 68kg. Nike. Was at University of Oklahoma, then Florida.
At (LJ)/TJ: OG: '12- 3/2, '16- 2; WCh: '11- 9/3, '13- 3, '15- dnq 19; WI: '12- 4/1; CCp: '14- 2/3; won US 2014, 2016; PAm-J and NCAA 2009.
Progress at LJ, TJ: 2007- 14.91/15.19w, 2008- 7.39/7.48w, 15.97; 2009- 7.89/8.00w, 17.19/17.24w; 2010- 7.30w, 16.30; 2011- 8.29, 17.50/17.62w; 2012- 8.25, 17.70i/17.62; 2013- 8.10, 17.52; 2014- 8.19/8.29w, 17.75; 2015- 8.07/8.11w, 17.48/17.50w; 2016- 8.14/8.42w, 17.76. pb 100m 10.64/10.53w '12.
Possibly youngest ever NCAA champion – he won 2009 title on his 18th birthday with 17.24w (and US junior record 17.19). First athlete to win Olympic medals at both LJ and TJ since 1936.

Kerron CLEMENT b. 31 Oct 1985 Port of Spain, Trinidad 1.88m 84kg. Was at University of Florida.
At 400mh/4x400mR: OG: '08- 2/res1R, '12- 8, '16- 1; WCh: '05- 4, '07- 1/res 1R, '09- 1/1R, '11- 13-15: sf/8/4; WJ: '04- 1/1R; PAm: '15- 4/2R; WI: '10- res 1R; WCp: '06- 1. Won WAF 2008-09, DL 2016, US 2005-06, 2016; NCAA 2004-05.
World junior 4x400m record 2004, world indoor records: 400m 2005, 4x400m 2006.
Progress at 400mh: 2002- 49.77, 2003- 50.13, 2004- 48.51; 2005- 47.24; 2006- 47.39; 2007- 47.61; 2008- 47.79; 2009- 47.91; 2010- 47.86; 2011- 48.74; 2012- 48.12; 2013- 48.06; 2015- 48.18, 2016- 47.73. pbs: 60m 6.89i '10, 100m 10.23 '07, 200m 20.40i '05, 20.49 '07; 300m 31.94i '06, 400m 44.48 '07,

55mh 7.28i '05, 60mh 7.80i '04, 110mh 13.78 '04. Born in Trinidad, moved to Texas in 1998, US citizenship confirmed in 2005. Ran 47.24, the world's fastest time since 1998, to win 2005 US 400mh title.

Christian COLEMAN b. 6 Mar 1996 Atlanta 1.75m 73kg. University of Tennessee.
At 100m: OG: 16- resR; PAm-J: '15- 3. Won NCAA indoor 60m & 200m 2017.
Progress at 100m, 200m: 2013- 22.43, 2014- 10.30/10.29w, 20.94; 2015- 10.18/10.16w, 20.61; 2016- 9.95, 20.26; 2017- 20.11i. pbs: 60m 6.45i '17, LJ: 7.21 '14.

Omar CRADDOCK b. 26 Apr 1991 Killeen, Texas 1.78m 79kg. Jump Corps. Was at University of Florida.
At TJ: WCh: '13- dnq 13, '15- 4; WJ: '10- 3; WI: '16- 5. Won US 2015, NCAA 2012-13.
Progress at TJ: 2006- 14.67, 2007- 15.16A, 2008- 15.53, 2009- 14.87i, 2010- 16.56, 2011- 16.57i/16.46, 2012- 16.75i/16.71/16.92w, 2013- 16.92/17.15w, 2014- 16.98/17.26w, 2015- 17.53, 2016- 17.16/17.42w. pb LJ 7.63i '13, 7.60 '15, 7.70w '12.

Ryan CROUSER b. 18 Dec 1992 Portland 2.01m 127kg. University of Texas.
At SP(/DT): OG: '16- 1; WY: '09- 1/2. Won US SP 2016, NCAA SP 2013-14, indoors 2014.
Progress at SP: 2011- 19.48i, 2012- 20.29i/19.32, 2013- 21.09, 2014- 21.39, 2015- 21.14i/21.11, 2016- 22.52. pbs: DT 63.90 '14, JT 61.16 '09.
Set High School 1.62kg DT record 72.40 '11. His father Mitch SP 20.04i '83, 19.94 '82, DT 67.22 '85; uncle Dean SP 21.07 '82, DT 65.88 '83, won NCAA SP 1982 & DT 1982-3; uncle Brian JT 83.00 '87, old JT 95.10 '85, won NCAA 1982 & 1985, dnq OG 1988 & 1992; Dean's children: Sam SP 17.62 '13, JT 83.30 '15 (dnq 34 OG 16), US junior & HS record '10, won NCAA 2014-15; Haley US junior JT record 55.22 '12, 4 WY '11.

Marquis DENDY b. 17 Nov 1992 Middleton, Delaware 1.92m 75kg. Nike. Was at University of Florida.
At LJ/(TJ): WCh: '13- dnq 27, '15- dnq 21/dnq 13; WI: '16- 1. At TJ: WJ: '10- 8; won US LJ 2015; NACAC LJ 2012, NCAA LJ 2015, TJ 2014-15, indoor LJ 2013, 2015-16; TJ 2015.
Progress at LJ, TJ: 2009- 7.20, 15.40; 2010- 7.45, 16.03; 2011- 7.47/7.56w, 15.62; 2012- 8.06i/7.81, 15.55; 2013- 8.28i/8.10/8.29w, 16.25i/16.03; 2014- 8.00, 16.52/17.05w; 2015- 8.39/8.68w, 17.50/17.71w; 2016- 8.42, 16.36. pbs: 60m 6.88i '14, 100m 10.31 '15.

Dedric DUKES b. 4 Feb 1992 Miami 1.80m 70kg. Was at University of Florida.
At 200m: WY: '09- 4/1 MedR. Won NCAA 2014.
Progress at 200m: 2007- 21.88/21.79w, 2008- 21.19/21.12w, 2009- 20.94, 2011- 20.88w, 2012- 20.47, 2013- 20.45/20.34w, 2014- 19.97/19.91w, 2015- 19.99/19.86w, 2016- 20.41/20.14w. pbs: 60m 6.77i '14, 100m 10.13 '16, 400m 45.66 '14.
Football wide receiver in high school.

Johnny DUTCH b. 20 Jan 1989 Clayton NC 1.80m 82kg. Studied media arts at University of South Carolina.
At 400mh: WCh: '09/15- sf; WJ: '08- 2; PAm-J: '07- 1/2R. Won US 2014, NCAA 2010.
Progress at 400mh: 2005- 52.06, 2006- 51.72, 2007- 50.07, 2008- 48.52, 2009- 48.18, 2010- 47.63, 2011- 48.47, 2012- 48.90, 2013- 48.02, 2014- 48.93, 2015- 48.13, 2016- 48.10. pbs: 400m 46.75 '13, 500m 1:03.25i '15, 55mh 7.31i '10, 60mh 7.71i '09, 110mh 13.50/13.30w '10.

Justin GATLIN b. 10 Feb 1982 Brooklyn, NY 1.85m 79kg. XTEP. Was at University of Tennessee.
At 100m/(200m)/4x100mR: OG: '04- 1/3/2R, '12- 3/dq2R, '16- 2/sf; WCh: '05- 1/1, '11- sf, '13- 2/2R, '15- 2/2. At 60m: WI: '03- 1, '12- 1. Won DL 100m 2013-15, US 100m 2005-06, 2012, 2016; 200m 2005, 2015-16; (indoor 60m 2003), NCAA 100m & 200m 2001-02 (& indoor 60m/200m 2002). N.American 4x100m record 2015.
Progress at 100m, 200m: 2000- 10.36, 2001- 10.08, 20.29/19.86w; 2002: under international suspension 10.05/10.00w, 19.86; 2003- 9.97, 20.04; 2004- 9.85, 20.01; 2005- 9.88/9.84w, 20.00; 2006- 9.77dq, 2010- 10.09, 20.63; 2011- 9.95, 20.20; 2012- 9.79, 20.11; 2013- 9.85, 20.21; 2014- 9.77/9.76w, 19.68; 2015- 9.74, 19.57, 2016- 9.80, 19.75. pbs: 60m 6.45i '03, 100y 9.10 '14, 55mh 7.39i '02, 60mh 7.86i '01, 110mh 13.41dq '02, 13.78/13.74w '01; LJ 7.34i '01, 7.21 '00.
Top hurdler in high school (110mh 13.66 and 300mh 36.74 on junior hurdles). Retained NCAA sprint titles while ineligible for international competition in 2002 after failing a drugs test in 2001 (when he won 100m, 200m and 110mh at the US Juniors) for a prescribed medication to treat Attention Deficit Disorder. Reinstated by IAAF in July 2002. Won 2005 World 100m title by biggest ever winning margin of 0.17. Won all five 100m competitions in 2006, including tying the world record with 9.77 in Doha and taking the US title, but had tested positive for testosterone before these performances. He received a four-year drugs ban but returned to competition in August 2010. In 2014 he was unbeaten at 100m and 200m and in Brussels on 5 September recorded the best-ever one-day sprint double with 9.77 and 19.71. His run of successive wins (26 finals and 7 prelims) in 2014-15 ended by Usain Bolt in World 100m in 2015.

Tyson GAY b. 9 Aug 1982 Lexington 1.83m 73kg. adidas. Studied marketing at University of Arkansas.
At 100m/(200m)/4x100mR: OG: '08- sf, '12- dq(4/2R), '16- dq hR; WCh: '05- (4), '07- 1/1/1R, '09- 2, 15- 6; WCp: '06- 1/1R, '10- 1R. Won DL 2010, WAF 100m 2009, 200m 2005-06, US 100m 2007-08, 2013, 2015; 200m 2007, 2013; NCAA 100m 2004.

Five N.American 100m records 2008-12, 4x100m 2015.
Progress at 100m, 200m: 1999- 10.81, 22.29i; 2000- 10.56, 21.27; 2001- 10.46/10.28w, 21.23; 2002- 10.27/10.08w, 20.88/20.21w; 2003- 10.01Aw/10.14w, 21.15/20.31w; 2004- 10.06/10.10w, 20.07; 2005- 10.08, 19.93; 2006- 9.84, 19.68; 2007- 9.84/9.76w, 19.62; 2008- 9.77/9.68w, 20.00; 2009- 9.69, 19.58; 2010- 9.78, 19.76; 2011- 9.79, 2012- 9.86/9.80dq, 20.21dq; 2013- 9.75dq, 19.74dq; 2014- 9.93, 20.22; 2015- 9.87/9.79w, 2016- 9.97, 20.16. pbs: 60m 6.39+ '09, 6.55i '05; 150mSt 14.51 '11, 200m/220ySt 19.41/19.54 '10, 400m 44.89 '10.
Ran four 200m races in under 19.85 in 2006. Then greatest ever sprint double (9.84 and 19.62) at 2007 US Champs and ran fastest ever 100m 9.68w/+4.1 (after US record in qf) to win US Olympic Trials in 2008 but pulled hamstring in 200m qf and unable to compete again until Olympics. IAAF Athlete of the Year 2007. He tested positive for a banned substance (later reported as a steroid) in May 2013 and withdrew from the World Championships; case resolved with a 1-year ban and annulment of results from 15 Jul 2012, thus including his Olympic 2012 results.

Marquise GOODWIN b. 19 Nov 1990 Austin, Texas 1.78m 82kg. Studied kinesiology at University of Texas.
At LJ: OG: '12- 10; WCh: '11- dnq 13; WJ: '10-1/1R; PAm: '15- 2; WUG: '11- 2; won NCAA 2010, 2012; US 2011-12.
Progress at LJ: 2007- 7.62, 2008- 7.74/7.96w, 2009- 8.18, 2010- 8.15, 2011- 8.17/8.33w, 2012- 8.33, 2015- 8.13/8.37w, 2016- 8.45. pbs: 60m 6.68i '16, 100m 10.35 '12, 10.24w '09; 200m 21.57/21.24w '09, TJ 15.20/15.38w '09.
A wide receiver at American football. Returned to athletics in 2015.

Arman HALL b. 12 Feb 1994 Pembroke Pines, Florida 1.88m 77kg. Student at University of Florida.
At 400m/4x400mR: OG: '16- 1R; WCh: '13-sf/1R; WJ: '12- 2/1R; WY: '11- 1/1 medley R. Won NCAA 2016.
Progress at 400m: 2009- 48.27, 2010- 47.43, 2011- 46.01, 2012- 45.39, 2013- 44.82, 2014- 45.19, 2015- 45.94, 2016- 44.82. pbs: 6.63i '16, 200m 20.34/20.33w '16.

James Edward 'Trey' HARDEE b. 7 Feb 1984 Birmingham, Alabama 1.96m 95kg. Nike. Was at Mississippi State University and University of Texas.
At Dec: OG: '08- dnf, '12- 2; WCh: '09-11-13-15: 1/1/dnf/dnf; won NCAA 2005, US 2009, 2014-15. At Hep: WI: '10- 2.
Progress at Dec: 2003- 7544, 2004- 8041(w), 2005- 7881, 2006- 8465, 2008- 8534, 2009- 8790, 2011- 8689, 2012- 8671, 2013- dnf, 2014- 8599w/8518, 2015- 8725. pbs: 55m 6.30i '06, 60m 6.71i '06, 100m 10.39 '10, 10.28w '06; 200m 20.98

'06, 300m 33.69 '14, 400m 47.51 '06, 1000m 2:45.67i '12, 1500m 4:40.94 '12, 60mh 7.70i '10, 110mh 13.54 '12; HJ 2.06i '10, 2.05 '08; PV 5.35 '15, LJ 7.88 '11, SP 15.94i '09, 15.72 '12; DT 52.68 '08, JT 68.99 '11, Hep 6208Ai '06.
Won IAAF Combined Events Challenge 2009 and in Götzis 2014. Married Chelsea Johnson (PV 4.73 '08, 2= WCh 2009) in 2014; her father Jan Johnson set a world indoor PV best 5.36 '70, won at the 1971 Pan-Ams and was the 1972 Olympic bronze medallist.

Aleec HARRIS b. 31 Oct 1990 Lawrenceville, Georgia 1.85m 77kg. adidas. Studied sociology at University of Southern California.
At 110mh: WCh: '15- sf. Won US indoor 60mh 2015. World 4x110mh best 2015.
Progress at 110mh: 2010- 14.15/13.88w, 2011- 13.65/13.55w, 2013- 13.69/13.55w, 2014- 13.14, 2015- 13.11, 2016- 13.43/13.32w. pbs: 55mh 7.18i '11, 60mh 7.50i '15.

Mike HARTFIELD b. 29 Mar 1990 Manchester, Connecticut 1.90m 77kg. adidas. Was at Ohio State University.
At LJ: OG: '16- dnq 25; WCh: '15- nj.
Progress at LJ: 2007- 7.19w, 2008- 7.42/7.52w, 2009- 7.57, 2010- 7.61i, 2011- 7.91/7.95w, 2012- 7.96, 2013- 8.15, 2014- 8.15/8.17w, 2015- 8.27/8.42w, 2016- 8.34/8.39w. pb TJ 15.84 '13.
Broke 77 year-old Ohio State University record set by Jesse Owens.

Jeffery HENDERSON b. 16 Feb 1989 Sherwood, Arkansas 1.78m 82kg. Was at Florida Memorial University and Stillman College.
At LJ: OG: '16- 1; WCh: '15- 9; PAm: '15- 1; WI: '16- 4; US champion 2014, 2016; indoors 2012.
Progress at LJ: 2006- 7.14i, 2007- 7.51i/7.41, 2008- 7.74/7.77w, 2009- 8.15u/7.88/8.19w, 2010- 7.94Ai/7.90i, 2011- 7.78, 2012- 7.91w, 2013- 8.22, 2014- 8.43/8.52w, 2015- 8.52/8.54w, 2016- 8.38/8.59w. pbs: 55m 6.31i '09, 60m 6.58i '16, 100m 10.18A '13, 10.25 '11, 10.19w '15; 200m 20.65A '13, TJ 14.90i '08.

Dsrrell HILL b. 17 Aug 1993 Darby, Pennsylvania 1.93m 135kg. Was at Penn State University.
At SP: OG: '16- dnq 23; PAm: '15- 4. Won NCAA 2011-12.
Progress at SP: 2012- 17.62i/17.53, 2013- 19.13, 2014- 20.57, 2015- 20.86, 2016- 21.63. pbs: DT 50.20 '15, Wt 19.12i '15.

Ryan HILL b. 31 Jan 1990 Hickory, North Carolina 1.76m 60kg. Bowerman TC. Was at North Carolina State University.
At 5000m: WCh: '13- 10, '15- 7. At 3000m: WI: '16- 2. Won US 5000m 2015.
Progress at 5000m: 2009- 14:09.63, 2010- 13:44.36, 2011- 13:31.67, 2012- 13:26.34, 2013- 13:14.22, 2014- 13:14.31, 2015- 13:05.69, 2016- 13:15.59, 2017- 13:07.61. pbs: 800m 1:50.22iA '14, 1000m 2:20.26 '13, 1500m 3:35.59 '16, 1M 3:54.89i '14, 3:56.78 '12;

3000m 7:30.93 '16, 2M 8:11.56i '17, 10000m 29:32.28 '10.

Daniel HULING b. 16 Jul 1983 Denver 1.85m 70kg. Nike. Was at Miami University (Ohio).
At 3000mSt: WCh: '09/11/13- h, '15- 5; CCp: '10- 8; US champion 2010.
Progress at 3000mSt: 2004- 8:58.88, 2005- 8:43.59, 2006- 8:27.41, 2008- 8:20.84, 2009- 8:14.69, 2010- 8:13.29, 2011- 8:25.95, 2012- 8:20.81, 2013- 8:21.92, 2014- 8:15.61, 2015- 8:14.11, 2016- 8:18.58. pbs: 1500m 3:37.53 '12, 1M 3:58.24i '12, 2000m 5:02.41i '14, 3000m 7:44.42 '13, 5000m 13:18.42 '13, 10000m 30:37.25 '06.

Bershawn JACKSON b. 8 May 1983 Miami 1.73m 69kg. Nike. Studied accountancy at St Augustine's University, Florida.
At 400mh/4x400mR: OG: '08- 3; WCh: '03- h (dq), '05- 1, '07- sf/res 1R, '09- 3/res 1R, '11- 6/1R, '13- sf, '15- h; WJ: '02- 3/1R; CCp: '10- 3/1R; won DL 2010, 2015; WAF 2004-05, US 2003, 2008-10, 2015. At 400m: WI: '10- 5/1R; won US indoor 2005, 2010.
Progress at 400mh: 1999- 54.53, 2000- 52.17, 2001- 50.86, 2002- 50.00, 2003- 48.23, 2004- 47.86, 2005- 47.30, 2006- 47.48, 2007- 48.13, 2008- 48.02, 2009- 47.98, 2010- 47.32, 2011- 47.93, 2012- 48.20, 2013- 48.09, 2014- 48.76, 2015- 48.09, 2016- 49.04. pbs: 200m 21.03/20.46w '04, 400m 45.06 '07, 500m 1:00.70i '15, 600m 1:17.85i '16, 800m 1:53.40 '11, 200mhSt 22.26 '11.

Evan JAGER b. 8 Mar 1989 Algonquin, Illinois 1.86m 66kg. Bowerman TC. Was at University of Wisconsin.
At 3000mSt: OG: '12- 6, '16- 2; WCh: '13- 5, '15- 6; CCp: '14- 2; US champion 2012-16. At 1500m: WJ: '08- 8. At 5000m: WCh: '09- h.
Three N.American 3000m steeplechase records 2012-15.
Progress at 5000m, 3000mSt: 2009- 13:22.18, 2012- 8:06.81, 2013- 13:02.40, 8:08.60; 2014- 13:08.63, 8:04.71; 2015- 8:00.45, 2016- 13:16.86, 8:04.01. pbs: 800m 1:50.10i '10, 1:51.04 '08; 1000m 2:20.29i '15, 1500m 3:32.97 '15, 1M 3:53.33 '14, 2000m 4:57.56 '14, 3000m 7:35.16 '12, 2M 8:14.95i '13.
Set US record in only his fifth steeplechase race, improving pb by 10.59 secs. In 2009 he had come 3rd in the US Champs in only his second race at 5000m.

Sam KENDRICKS b. 7 Sep 1992 Oxford, Mississippi 1.89m 79kg. Nike. Army reservist (2nd Lt.). Was at University of Mississippi.
At PV: OG: '16- 3; WCh: '15- 9=; WUG: '13- 1; WI: '16- 2; US champion 2014-16, NCAA 2013-4.
Progress at PV: 2010- 4.68, 2011- 5.18, 2012- 5.50, 2013- 5.81, 2014- 5.75, 2015- 5.86Ai/5.82, 2016- 5.92.

Joe KOVACS b. 28 Jun 1989 Bethlehem, Pennsylvania 1.81m 132kg. Nike. Was at Penn State University.
At SP: OG: '16- 2; WCh: '15- 1; CCp: '14- 3; Won DL 2015, US 2014-15.
Progress at SP: 2007- 16.49, 2008- 16.86i, 2009- 18.53, 2010- 19.36i/18.73, 2011- 19.84i/19.15, 2012- 21.08, 2013- 20.82, 2014- 22.03. 2015- 22.56, 2016- 22.13. pbs: DT 56.08 '11, HT 61.50 '11, Wt 19.07i '11.

Erik KYNARD b. 3 Feb 1991 Toledo, Ohio 1.93m 86kg. Nike Jordan. Was at Kansas State University.
At HJ: OG: '12- 2, '16- 6; WCh: '11- dnq 14, '13- 5, '15- 8=; WJ: '08- dnq 19=; CCp: '14- 5; WI: '14- 4, '16- 3; Won DL 2016, US 2013-14, 2016; NCAA 2011-12.
Progress at HJ: 2007- 2.13i/2.05, 2008- 2.23i/2.15, 2009- 2.24i/2.22, 2010- 2.25, 2011- 2.33i/2.31, 2012- 2.34, 2013- 2.37, 2014- 2.37, 2015- 2.37, 2016- 2.35. pb LJ 7.15i '09.

Bernard LAGAT b. 12 Dec 1974 Kapsabet, Kenya 1.75m 61kg. Nike. Studied business management at Washington State University, USA.
At 1500m (/5000m): OG: '00- 3, '04- 2, '08- sf/9, '12- (4), '16- (5); WCh: '01- 2, '05- sf, '07- 1/1, '09- 3/2, '11- (2), '13- (6); WI: '03- 2; AfCh: '02- 1; WUG: '99- 1; WCp: '02- 1; 2nd GP 1999-2000-02, WAF 2005-06. At 3000m: WI: '01-04-10-12-14: 6/1/1/1/2; CCp: '10- 1/(1), '14- 3. Won WAF 3000m 2005, 2008; KEN 1500m 2002, US 1500m 2006, 2008; 5000m 2006-08, 2010-11, 2013-14, 2016; NCAA 5000m 1999 (and indoor 1M/3000m).
Records: Commonwealth and KEN 1500m 2001, N.American 1500m 2005, 3000m 2010, 5000m 2010 & 2011, indoor 2000m 2014, 3000m 2007, 2M 2011 & 2013, 5000m 2010, 2012. World M35 3000m & 5000m 2010, 1M and 5000m 2011, 2000m 2014; M40 1500m, 1M, 3000m (2), 5000m, 10k Rd; indoor 1500m, 1M, 3000m (3), 2M 2015; 5000m (2) & 10,000m 2016.
Progress at 1500m, 5000m: 1996- 3:37.7A, 1997- 3:41.19, 13:50.33; 1998- 3:34.48, 13:42.73; 1999- 3:30.56, 13:36.12; 2000- 3:28.51, 13:23.46; 2001- 3:26.34, 13:30.54; 2002- 3:27.91, 13:19.14; 2003- 3:30.55, 2004- 3:27.40, 2005- 3:29.30, 12:59.29; 2006- 3:29.68, 12:59.22; 2007- 3:33.85, 13:30.73; 2008- 3:32.75, 13:16.29; 2009- 3:32.56, 13:03.06; 2010- 3:32.51, 12:54.12; 2011- 3:33.11, 12:53.60; 2012- 3:34.63, 12:59.92; 2013- 3:36.36, 12:58.99; 2014- 13:06.68, 2015- 3:40.20i/3:41.87, 13:14.97; 2016- 13:06.78. pbs: 800m 1:46.00 '03, 1000m 2:16.18 '08, 1M 3:47.28 '01, 2000m 4:54.74i '14, 4:55.49 '99; 3000m 7:29.00 '10, 2M 8:09.49i '13, 8:12.45 '08, 10000m 27:49.35 '16, 10k 27:48 '15, HMar 62:33 '13.
Gave up his final year of scholastic eligibility (as under NCAA rules no payments can be received) at his university in order to compete (for money) in the 1999 GP Final, in which he was 2nd. He was 2nd to Hicham El Guerrouj six times in 2001, including his 3:26.34 at Brussels for 2nd on the world all-time list, and

six times in 2002. Withdrew from 2003 Worlds after testing positive for EPO, but this was later repudiated. Lives in Tucson, Arizona, gained US citizenship 2005. First man ever to win 1500m/5000m double at the US Champs in 2006 and at World Champs in 2007. Oldest ever male World Indoor champion at 37y 89d in 2012 and medallist at 39y 87d in 2014.
A sister **Mary Chepkemboi** competed at the 1982 Commonwealth Games and won African 3000m in 1984, and another **Evelyne Jerotich Langat** has 71:35 half marathon pb. Of his brothers **William Cheseret** has a marathon pb of 2:12:09 '04 and **Robert Cheseret** won NCAA 5000m in 2004 and 10000m in 2005, pbs 5000m 13:13.23 & 10000m 28:20.11 '05.

Jarrion LAWSON b. 6 May 1994 Texarcana, Texas 1.88m 75kg. University of Arkansas.
At LJ: OG: '16- 4 (res dqR); WJ: '12- 3 (dnq 22 TJ). Won NCAA 100m, 200m & LJ 2016.
Progress at LJ: 2011- 7.26/7.46w, 2012- 7.82/7.89w, 2013- 7.93, 2014- 8.39Ai/7.92/8.13w, 2015- 8.34/8.36w, 2016- 8.58. pbs: 60m 6.60i '16, 100m 10.04/9.9/9.90w '15, 200m 20.17 '16, TJ 15.80 '12.

Noah LYLES b. 18 Jul 1997 Gainesville, Florida 1.82m 73kg.
At 100m: WJ: '16- 1/1R; PAM-J '15- 2 (1 200m); at 200m: WY: 13- sf/2Med R; Yth OG: '14- 1.
World indoor 300m record 2017.
Progress at 100m, 200m: 2013- 21.23; 2014- 10.45, 20.71; 2015- 10.14/10.07w, 20.18; 2016- 10.16/10.08w, 20.09/20.04w. pbs: 60m 6.63i '17, 300m 31.87i/32.67i '17, 400m 47.04 '16, HJ: 2.03i '16.
His younger brother **Josephus** (b. 22 Jul 1998) 1 4x400m WJ '14, 3 200m & 2 400m WY '15; pbs 200m 20.74 '15, 20.73w '16; 400m 45.46 '15. Their father Kevin had a 400m pb 45.01 '95 and mother Keisha Caine 52.48 '94.

Tony McQUAY b. 16 Apr 1990 West Palm Beach, Florida 1.80m 70kg. adidas. Was at University of Florida.
At 400m: OG: '12- sf/2R, '16- 1R; WCh: '11- h, '13- 2/1R, '15- 1R; Won US 2011, NCAA 2012.
Progress at 400m: 2008- 48.09, 2009- 46.84, 2010- 45.37, 2011- 44.68, 2012- 44.49, 2013- 44.40, 2014- 44.92, 2015- 44.81, 2016- 44.24. pbs: 100m 10.22 '13, 10.13w '14; 200m 20.60 '12, 300m 31.64 '16.

Aries MERRITT b. 24 Jul 1985 Marietta, Georgia 1.83m 74kg. Nike. Studied sports management at University of Tennessee.
At 110mh: OG: '12- 1; WCh: '09-11-13-15: h/5=/6/3; WJ: '04- 1. At 60mh: WI: '12-1, Won DL 110mh 2012, NCAA 60mh indoors & 110mh 2006, US indoor 60mh & 110mh 2012.
World 110mh record 2012.
Progress at 110mh: 2004- 13.47, 2005- 13.38/13.34w, 2006- 13.12, 2007- 13.09, 2008- 13.24, 2009- 13.15, 2010- 13.61, 2011- 13.12, 2012- 12.80, 2013- 13.09, 2014- 13.27, 2015- 13.04, 2016- 13.22. pbs: 55m 6.43i '05, 60m 6.90i '10, 200m 21.31 '05, 50mh 6.54i '12, 55mh 7.02+i '12, 60mh 7.43Ai/7.44i '12, 400mh 51.94 '04.
Record 8 (and 2w) sub-13 second times in 2012. Revealed in 2015 that he had been suffering for two years from a kidney disorder and remarkably won World bronze medal just before undergoing a kidney transplant.

LaShawn MERRITT b. 27 Jun 1986 Portsmouth, Virginia 1.88m 82kg. Nike. Studied sports management at Old Dominion University, Norfolk, Virginia.
At 400m/4x400mR: OG: '08- 1/1R, '12- dnf ht, '16- 3/1R (6 200m); WCh: '05- res(1)R, '07- 2/1R, '09- 1/1R, '11- 2/1R, '13- 1/1R, '15- 2/1R; WJ: '04- 1/1R (1 at 4x100); WI: '06- 1R; WCp: '06- 1/1R, '14- 1/3R; won WAF 2007-09, DL 2013-14, 2016; US 2008-09, 2012-13, 2016.
World junior records 4x100m and 4x400m 2004, World indoor 400m junior best (44.93) 2005. World 4x110mh best 2015,
Progress at 200m, 400m: 2002- 21.46, 2003- 21.33, 47.69, 2004- 20.72/20.69w, 45.25; 2005- 20.38, 44.66; 2006- 20.10, 44.14; 2007- 19.98, 43.96; 2008- 20.08/19.80w, 43.75; 2009- 20.07, 44.06; 2011- 20.13, 44.63; 2012- 20.16, 44.12; 2013- 20.26, 43.74; 2014- 20.42, 43.92; 2015- 43.65, 2016- 19.74, 43.85. pbs: 55m 6.33i '04, 60m 6.68i '06, 100m 10.47/10.38w '04, 300m 31.23 '16, 500m 1:01.39i '12.
World age-18 400m record with 44.66 in 2005 and world low-altitude 300m best 2006 and 2009. Spent a year at East Carolina University before signing for Nike and returning home to Portsmouth. Two-year drugs ban for three positive tests from October 2009, reduced by three months after US arbitration panel declared that he had taken the steroid accidentally in buying a product intended for sexual enhancement; successfully challenged IOC rule preventing anyone serving 6 months or more from a drugs offence from competing in the next Games. Has won six successive World 4x400m gold medals.

Clayton MURPHY b. 26 Feb 1995 New Madison, Ohio 1.82m 68kg. Nike. University of Akron.
At 800m: OG: '16- 3; WCh: '15- sf; PAm: '15- 1. Won US 800m 2016, NCAA 1500m 2016.
Progress at 800m, 1500m: 2013- 1600m 4:11.72, 2014- 1:50.03, 3:44.53; 2015- 1:45.59, 3:40.69; 2016- 1:42.93, 3:36.23. pbs: 600m 1:165.9+ '16, 1000m 2:18.60Ai '17, 2:20.12 '16; 1M 3:54.31i '17, 3000m 8:18.44i '16, 5000m 14:15.61 '15.

Michael NORMAN b. 3 Dec 1997 San Diego 1.83m 73kg. University of Southern California.
At 200m: WJ: '16- 1/1R.
Progress at 200m: 2014- 20.82, 2015- 20.24, 2016- 20.14/20.06w. pbs: 100m 10.27 '16, 400m 45.19 '15.

Vernon NORWOOD b. 10 Apr 1992 New Orleans 1.87m 77kg. New Balance. Was at Louisiana State University.

At 400m/4x400mR: WCh: '15- sf/res1R; WI: '16- 1R. Won NCAA indoors and out 2015.
Progress at 400m: 2011- 47.47, 2012- 45.72A/45.98, 2013- 45.56A/45.67, 2014- 45.02, 2015- 44.44, 2016- 45.00 pbs: 200m 20.77 '15, 300m 32.07 '15, 500m 1:00.11i '17, 600y 1:08.80i '13, 600m 1:18.57Ai '15.

David OLIVER b. 24 Apr 1982 Orlando 1.88m 93kg. Nike. Marketing graduate of Howard University.
At 110mh: OG: '08- 3; WCh: '07-11-13-15: sf/4/1/7; PAm: '15- 1; CCp: '10- 1. Won DL 2010, 2013, 2015; WAF 2008, US 2008, 2010-11, 2015. At 60mh: WI: '10- 3.
Two North American 110mh records 2010, world 4x110mh best 2015.
Progress at 110mh: 2001- 14.04, 2002- 13.92/13.88w, 2003- 13.60, 2004- 13.55, 2005- 13.29/13.23w, 2006- 13.20, 2007- 13.14, 2008- 12.95/12.89w, 2009- 13.09, 2010- 12.89, 2011- 12.94, 2012- 13.07, 2013- 13.00, 2014- 13.21, 2015- 12.98. pbs: 60m 6.88i '04, 50mh 6.50i '12, 55mh 7.01+i '12, 60mh 7.37i '11.
Mother, Brenda Chambers, 400mh pb 58.54 '80.

Jeff PORTER b. 27 Nov 1985 Summit, New Jersey 1.83m 84kg. Sports management degree from University of Michigan.
At 110mh: OG: '12/16- sf; PAm: '11- 4. Won NCAA indoor 60mh 2007.
Progress at 110mh: 2004- 14.08, 2005- 14.12, 2006- 13.93/13.92w, 2007- 13.57, 2008- 13.47, 2009- 13.37, 2010- 13.45, 2011- 13.26, 2012- 13.08, 2013- 13.35, 2014- 13.27/13.12w, 2015- 13.25, 2016- 13.21. pbs: 60m 6.77i '14, 100m 10.56 '11, 50mh 6.50i '12, 60mh 7.46i '14.
Married to Tiffany Porter (see UK). His twin brother Joe played in the NFL.

Jason RICHARDSON b. 4 Apr 1986 Houston 1.86m 73kg. Nike. Was at University of South Carolina.
At 110mh: OG: '12- 2; WCh: '11- 1, '13- 4; WY: '03- 1 (1 400mh); won NCAA 2008.
World 4x110mh best 2015.
Progress at 110mh: 2004- 13.76, 2005- 13.50, 2006- 13.43/13.36w, 2008- 13.21, 2009- 13.29, 2010- 13.34, 2011- 13.04, 2012- 12.98, 2013- 13.20/13.17w, 2014- 13.29/13.27w, 2015- 13.12, 2016- 13.28. pbs: 100m 10.90 '03, 200m 21.13 '03, 400m 46.96 '12, 60mh 7.53i '08, 400mh 49.79 '04.

Gil ROBERTS b. 15 Mar 1989 Oklahoma City 1.88m 81kg. Nike. Was at Texas Tech University.
At 400m/4x400mR: OG: '16- sf/1R; WCh: '09- h; WI: '12- 1R; US champion 2014, indoors 2012.
Progress at 400m: 2005- 47.47, 2006- 47.72A, 2007- 46.16, 2008- 46.14, 2009- 44.86, 2011- 45.22, 2012- 44.84, 2013- 45.73, 2014- 44.53, 2015- 45.29, 2016- 44.65. pbs: 55m 6.26i '12, 100m 10.12/9.92w '14, 200m 20.22 '14, 300m 31.81 '16.

Kurt ROBERTS b. 20 Feb 1988 Lancaster, Ohio 1.91m 127kg. Nike, Was at Ashland University.

Won NACAC 2010, US indoor SP 2016.
Progress at SP: 2007- 16.39, 2008- 17.81, 2009- 18.78, 2010- 19.80i/18.76, 2011- 19.55, 2012- 21.14, 2013- 20.98, 2014- 21.50i/21.47, 2015- 20.45, 2016- 21.57i/21.40.

Michael RODGERS b. 24 Apr 1985 Brenham, Texas 1.78m 73kg. Nike. Studied kinesiology at Oklahoma Baptist University.
At 100m/4x100mR: OG: '16- dqR; WCh: '09- sf, '13- 6/2R, '15- 5; CCp: '14- 2/1R. At 60m: WI: '08-10-16: 4/2/6. Won US 100m 2009, 2014; indoor 60m 2008.
N.American 4x100m record 2015.
Progress at 100m: 2004- 10.55/10.31w, 2005- 10.30/10.25w, 2006- 10.29/10.18w, 2007- 10.10, 10.07w, 2008- 10.06/10.01w, 2009- 9.94/9.9/9.85w, 2010- 10.00/9.99w, 2011- 9.85, 2012- 9.94, 2013- 9.90, 2014- 9.91/9.80w, 2015- 9.86, 2016- 9.97. pbs: 60m 6.48Ai/6.50i '11, 150mSt 15.33 '14, 200m 20.24 '09.
Dropped out of US World Champs team after positive test for stimulant on 19 July 2011, for which he subsequently received a 9-month suspension. Younger sister Alishea Usery won US junior 400m 2009, pb 53.27 '09.

Galen RUPP b. 8 May 1986 Portland 1.80m 62kg. Nike Oregon Project. Studied business at University of Oregon.
At (5000/)10000m: OG: '08- 13, '12- 7/2, '16- 5 (3 Mar); WCh: '07- 11, '09- 8, '11- 9/7, '13- 8/4, '15- 5/5. At 5000m: WJ: '04- 9; PAm-J: '03- 1. At 3000m: WI: '10- 5, '14- 4; WY: '03- 7. Won US 5000m 2012, 10000m 2009-16, NCAA 5000m & 10000m (& indoor 3000m & 5000m) 2009, CC 2008.
N.American records: 10000m 2011 & 2014, junior 5000m 2004, 10000m 2005; indoor 5000m (13:11.44) 2011 & 2014, 3000m 2013, 2M 2012, 2014.
Progress at 5000m, 10000m: 2002- 14:34.05, 2003- 14:20.29, 2004- 13:37.91, 29:09.56; 2005- 13:44.72. 28:15.52; 2006- 13:47.04, 30:42.10; 2007- 13:30.49, 27:33.48; 2008- 13:49.8+, 27:36.99; 2009- 13:18.12i/13:42.59+, 27:37.99; 2010- 13:07.35, 27:10.74; 2011- 13:06.86, 26:48.00; 2012- 12:58.90, 27:25.33; 2013- 13:01.37, 27:24.39; 2014- 13:00.99, 26:44.36; 2015- 13:08.38, 27:08.91; 2016- 13:20.69, 27:08.92. pbs: 800m 1:49.87i/1:50.00 '09, 1500m 3:34.15 '14, 1M 3:50.92i/3:52.11 '13, 3000m 7:30.16i '13, 7:43.24 '10, 2M 8:07.41i '14, HMar 60:30 '11, Mar 2:10:05 '16. Won US Olympic Trials on marathon debut 2016.

Duane SOLOMON b. 28 Dec 1984 Lompoc, California 1.91m 77kg. Saucony. Sociology graduate of University of Southern California.
At 800m: OG: '12- 4; WCh: '07- h, '13- 6; PAm: '07- h; CCp: '14- 6. Won US 2013-14, US indoor 2011.
World indoor 4x800m record 2014.
Progress at 800m: 2002- 1:51.76, 2003- 1:49.79, 2005- 1:47.84, 2006- 1:47.45, 2007- 1:45.69, 2008- 1:45.71, 2009- 1:46.82, 2010- 1:45.23, 2011- 1:45.86,

2012- 1:42.82, 2013- 1:43.27, 2014- 1:43.88, 2015- 1:45.56, 2016- 1:45.47. pbs: 400m 45.98 '12, 600m 1:13.28 '13, 1000m 2:17.84 '10, 1500m 3:48.29 '08, 1M 4:03.26 '10.

Wallace SPEARMAN b. 24 Dec 1984 Chicago 1.90m 80kg. Was at University of Arkansas.
At 200m/4x100mR: OG: '08- dq, '12- 4; WCh: '05-07-09-13: 2/3&1R/3/sf; PAm: '15- 5/1R; WCp: '06- 1/1R, '10- 1/1R. Won DL 2010, US 2006, 2010, 2012; NCAA 2004-05. At 4x400m: WI: '06- 1R.
WIR 4x400m and world indoor best 300m 2006. Two US indoor 200m records 2005.
Progress at 100m, 200m: 2003- 21.05, 2004- 10.38, 20.25/20.12w; 2005- 10.35/10.21w, 19.89; 2006- 10.11, 19.65; 2007- 9.96, 19.82; 2008- 10.07, 19.90; 2009- 10.18, 19.85; 2010- 10.15, 19.79/19.77w; 2011- 20.18; 2012- 10.26/10.06w, 19.90/19.82w; 2013- 10.29/9.92w, 20.10; 2014- 20.19, 20.03, 2016- 20.31. pbs: 60m 6.66i '12, 100m 9.96 '07, 150mSt 14.87 '12, 300m 31.88i '06, 32.14 '09; 400m 45.22 '06.
Disqualified for running out of his lane after crossing the line in 3rd place at the 2008 Olympics. 3-month doping ban for use of a stimulant on 6 Jul 2014. His father (also Wallace, b. 3 Sep 1962) had pbs: of 100m 10.19 '87, 10.05w '86, 10.0w '81; 200m 20.27/20.20w '87; 1 WUG 200/4x100m, 3 PAm 200m 1987.

Jeremy TAIWO b. 15 Jan 1990 Ballard, Washington 1.96m 85kg. Brooks Beats TC. Graduate of University of Washington.
At Dec:OG: '16- 11; WCh: '13/15- dnf.
Progress at Dec: 2009- 7299, 2010- 7521, 2011- 7742, 2013- 8239, 2015- 8303, 2016- 8425. pbs: 60m 6.97i '13, 100m 10.84 '13, 400m 47.83 '15, 1000m 2:30.85i '15, 1500m 4:16.34 '13, 60mh 7.87i '15, 110mh 14.22 '10, 14.16w '13; HJ 2.25i '13, 2.21 '16; PV 5.00 '13, LJ 7.57 '15, SP 14.93 '15, DT 44.27 '15, JT 53.71 '09, Hep 6344i '15.
His father Joseph Taiwo was 9th at triple jump for Nigeria at both 1984 & 1988 Olympics, 6th WCh & WI '87, African chamnpion 1984, pb 17.22 88, 17.47w '92; mother Colombian.

Christian TAYLOR b. 18 Jun 1990 Fayetteville 1.90m 75kg. Li Ning. Studied at the University of Florida.
At (LJ/)TJ: OG: '12- 1, '16- 1; WCh: '11- 1, '13- 4, '15- 1; WI: '12- 2; WJ: '08- 7/8 (res 1 4x400m); WY: '07- 3/1. Won DL 2012-16, NACAC 2010-11, US 2011-12, NCAA indoor 2009-10.
North American triple jump record 2015.
Progress at LJ, TJ: 2007- 7.29, 15.98; 2008- 7.79i/7.68/7.77w, 16.05; 2009- 8.02i/7.72, 16.98i/16.65/16.91w; 2010- 8.19, 17.18i/ 17.02/17.09w; 2011- 8.00/8.07w/17.96; 2012- 8.12, 17.81; 2013- 8.01/8.07w, 17.66; 2014- 8.09, 17.51; 2015- 8.18, 18.21; 2016- 7.96, 17.86. pbs: 60m 6.79i '11, 200m 20.70 '13, 400m 45.17 '14.
His 18.21 in the final round of the 2015 World Champs was the second longest ever legal TJ mark; it was 18.32 from take-off to landing. Both parents came from Barbados.

Michael TINSLEY b. 21 Apr 1984 Little Rock, Arkansas 1.85m 74kg. adidas. Studied criminal justice at Jackson State University.
At 400mh: OG: '12- 2, '16- h; WCh: '13- 2, '15- 8; CCp: '14- 7; won DL 2014, NCAA 2008, US 2012-13.
Progress at 400mh: 2002- 52.5, 2004- 50.87, 2005- 48.55, 2006- 48.25, 2007- 48.02, 2008- 48.84, 2009- 48.53, 2010- 48.46, 2011- 48.45, 2012- 47.91, 2013- 47.70, 2014- 48.25, 2015- 48.34, 2016- 48.74. pbs: 60m 6.92i '05, 200m 20.66 '09, 20.34w '13; 400m 46.02i '06, 46.05 '07; 55mh 7.39i '04, 60mh 7.84i '06, 110mh 13.86 '04.

Ben TRUE b. 29 Dec 1985 North Yarmouth, Maine 1.83m 70kg. Saucony. Studied art history and architecture at Dartmouth College.
At 5000m: WCh: '15- 6. World CC: '13- 6.
Progress at 5000m: 2006- 14:18.61, 2007- 13:14.85, 2010- 13:43.98, 2011- 13:24.11, 2012- 13:20.53, 2013- 13:11.59, 2014- 13:02.74, 2015- 13:05.54, 2016- 13:12.67, 2017- 13:06.74i. pbs: 800m 1:50.07 '07, 1500m 3:36.05 '16, 1M 3:57.31i '17, 4:02.61 '07; 3000m 7:36.59 '13, 2M 8:11.33i '17, 10000m 27:41.17 '12, road: 10M 46:48 '11, 15k 43:04 '14.
Married to Sarah Groff, 4th at 2012 Olympics in triathlon.

David VERBURG b. 14 May 1991 Oklahoma 1.68m 64kg. adidas. Was at George Mason University.
At 400m/4x400mR: OG: '16- sf/res 1R; WCh: '13- 1R, '15- sf/1R; WJ: 10- 1R; WI: '14- 4/1R. US champion 2015.
Progress at 400m: 2009- 47.15, 2010- 46.27, 2011- 46.09, 2012- 45.06, 2013- 44.75, 2014- 45.03, 2015- 44.41, 2016- 44.82. pbs: 200m 20.63 '15, 300m 32.17 '15, 500m 1:01.29i '13, 600m 1:18.06i '12.
Engaged to Cassandra Tate (qv).

Ameer WEBB b. 19 Mar 1991 Carson, California 1.75m 75kg. Nike. Was at Texas A & M University.
At 200m: OG: '16- sf; won NCAA 2014 (indoor 2013-13).
Progress at 100m, 200m: 2008- 10.70w, 21.81w; 2009- 10.67, 21.25/21.24w; 2010- 10.37, 20.70; 2011- 10.37, 20.49; 2012- 10.17/10.05w, 20.46/20.20w; 2013- 10.14/10.07w, 20.20/20.05w; 2014- 10.37, 20.38; 2015- 10.04, 20.02; 2016- 9.94/9.90w, 19.85. pb 60m 6.60Ai/6.65i '16.

Ryan WHITING b. 24 Nov 1986 Harrisburg, Pennsylvania 1.91m 134kg. Nike. Studied civil engineering at Arizona State University.
At SP: OG: '12- 9; WCh: '11- 6, '13- 2; WI: '12- 1, '14- 1; PAm-J: '05- 1 (1 DT); Won DL 2013, US 2013, NACAC 2009, NCAA 2009-10, indoor 2008-10, DT 2010.
Progress at SP: 2006- 19.75, 2007- 20.35, 2008- 21.73i/20.60, 2009- 20.99, 2010- 21.97, 2011- 21.76, 2012- 22.00i/21.66, 2013- 22.28, 2014- 22.23i/21.31, 2015- 21.80i/21.37, 2016- 21.06. pb DT 61.11 '08, Wt 18.94i '10.

Jesse WILLIAMS b. 27 Dec 1983 Modesto 1.84m 75kg. Oregon TC Elite. Graduate of University of Southern California, formerly at North Carolina State.
At HJ: OG: '08- dnq 19=, '12- 9=; WCh: '05/07- dnq 15/26, '11- 1, '13/15- dnq 23=/22=; WJ: '02- 4=; PAm: '15- 4=; WI: '08-10-12: 6=/5/6=; Won US 2008, 2010-11; NCAA indoors and out 2005-06; DL 2011.
Progress at HJ: 2001- 2.16, 2002- 2.21, 2003- 2.24, 2004- 2.24, 2005- 2.30, 2006- 2.32, 2007- 2.33, 2008- 2.32i/2.30, 2009- 2.36i/2.34, 2010- 2.34Ai/2.30, 2011- 2.37, 2012- 2.36, 2013- 2.31, 2014- 2.29, 2015- 2.31, 2016- 2.23. pb LJ 7.53 '06. Also a wrestler in high school.

Isiah YOUNG b. 5 Jan 1990 Manhattan, Kansas 1.83m 75kg. Was at University of Mississippi.
At 200m: OG: '12- sf; WCh: '13- sf, '15- h.
Progress at 100m, 200m: 2008- 10.96; 2009- 10.44, 21.22; 2010- 10.32, 20.98; 2011- 10.31, 20.81; 2012- 10.09/10.08w, 20.33/20.16w; 2013- 9.99/9.93w, 19.86; 2014- 10.23, 20.58/20.55w; 2015- 10.00/ 9.82w, 19.93/19.75w; 2016- 10.03, 20.24. pb 60m 6.61i '12.

Zachery ZIEMEK b. 23 Feb 1993 Itaska, Illinois 1.94m 88 kg. University of Wisconsin.
At Dec: OG: '16- 7; WCh: '15- 15.
Progress at Dec: 2012- 7042, 2013- 7640, 2014- 7981, 2015- 8107, 2016- 8413. pbs: 60m 6.75i '16, 100m 10.57 '15, 400m 49.04 '16, 1000m 2:48.25i '13, 1500m 4:42.52 '16, 60mh 8.10i '16, 110mh 14.71 '16, HJ 2.10 '14, PV 5.45 '15, LJ 7.73 '14, SP 14.77 '15, DT 49.42 '16, JT 60.92 '16, Hep 6173i '16.

Women

Morolake AKINOSUN b. 17 May 1994 Lagos, Nigeria 1.63m 61kg. University of Texas.
At 100m/200m: OG: '16- res 1R; PAm: '15- sf/1R. Won US Indoor 60m 2017.
Progress at 100m, 200m: 2010- 11.94, 24.58/24.07w; 2011- 11.42, 23.49/23.44w; 2012- 11.41, 24.34; 2013- 11.45/11.29w, 23.26/23.18w; 2014- 11.04/10.96w, 22.68/22.17w; 2015- 11.29/ 10.94w, 22.52; 2016- 10.95, 22.54. pbs: 60m 7.08Ai/7.17i '17.

Nia ALI b. 23 Oct 1988 Philadelphia 1.70m 64kg. Nike. Was at University of Southern California.
At 100mh: OG: '16- 2; WCh: '13- sf; WUG: '11- 1. Won NCAA 2011. At 60mh: WI: '14- 1, '16- 1; won US indoor 2013-14.
Progress at 100mh: 2005- 14.20, 2006- 13.63/13.55w, 2007- 13.25, 2008- 13.14, 2009- 13.17, 2011- 12.73/12.63w, 2012- 12.78, 2013- 12.48, 2014- 12.75, 2016- 12.55. pbs: 60m 7.43i '14, 200m 23.90 '09, 800m 2:24.55 '07, 60mh 7.80i '14, HJ 1.86 '11, LJ 5.89 '09, SP 13.61 '09, JT 39.24 '09, Hep 5870 '16.
Son Titus born to her and Michael Tinsley in May 2015.

Joanna ATKINS b. 31 Jan 1989 Stone Mountain, Georgia 1.80m 64kg. LifeSpeed. Was at Auburn University.
At 200m: CCp: '14- 2. At 400m: WCh: '13- res2R; WI: '14- 6/1R; Won NCAA 400m 2009.
Progress at 200m, 400m: 2004- 24.25w, 56.12; 2005- 24.02, 54.32; 2006- 23.82, 55.42; 2007- 24.35i/23.69w, 53.93; 2008- 23.30, 52.94; 2009- 22.89, 50.39; 2010- 23.32, 51.52; 2011- 22.68, 51.50; 2012- 23.10/22.83w, 51.12; 2013- 23.27, 50.77; 2014- 22.27/22.19w, 50.74; 2015- 23.82i, 2016- 22.40, 52.39. pbs: 55m 6.91i '09, 600m 7.28i '09, 100m 11.02 '14, 10.99w '16; 300m 36.18Ai '17.

Tianna BARTOLETTA b. 30 Aug 1985 Elyria, Ohio 1.68m 60kg. née Madison. Nike. Studied biology at University of Central Florida, formerly at University of Tennessee.
At 100m/4x100mR: OG: '12- 4/1R, '16- sf/1R; won US 2014. At LJ: OG: '16- 1; WCh: '05- 1, '07- 10, '15- 1; CCp: '14- 3/1R; WI: '06- 1; PAm-J: '03- 4, won DL 2014-15, US 2015, NCAA indoors and out 2005. At 60m: WI: '12- 3, '14- 3; won US indoor 2012.
Progress at 100m, LJ: 2000- 5.73, 2001- 6.07, 2002- 11.98/11.91w, 6.20; 2003- 11.68, 6.28; 2004- 11.50/11.35w, 6.60; 2005- 11.41, 6.89/6.92w; 2006- 11.52/11.50w, 6.80i/6.60; 2007- 6.60/6.61w; 2008- 11.54, 6.53/6.58w; 2009- 11.05, 6.48; 2010- 11.20, 6.44; 2011- 11.29, 6.21/6.58w; 2012- 10.85, 6.48; 2013- 11.41; 2014- 10.92, 7.02; 2015- 10.94/10.90w, 7.14; 2016- 10.78, 7.17. pbs: 55m 6.69i '09, 60m 7.02i '12, 200m 22.37/22.33w '12.
Set long jump pbs in qualifying and final of 2005 Worlds. Competed on the US bobsled team in 2012/13. Married John Bartoletta in 2012.

Gewn BERRY b. 29 Jun 1989 St. Louis, Missouri. 1.76m 80kg. New York AC. Was at University of Southern Illinois.
At HT: OG: '16- dnq 14; US champion indoor weight 2013-14, 2017.
World 20lb weight indoor record record 2017.
Progress at HT: 2008- 53.70, 2009- 59.58, 2010- 62.55, 2011- 70.52, 2012- 71.95, 2013- 73.81, 2014- 72.04, 2015- 72.326, 2016- 73.09/76.12dq. Pbs: SP 16.99 '11, Wt 25.60i '17.
3-month ban from 29 Mar 2016 for use of a stimulant that cost her a North American 'record' of 76.31 and US indoor wight title.

Amanda BINGSON b. 20 Feb 1990 Victorville, California 1.70m 89kg. New York AC. Sports psychology graduate of University of Nevada, Las Vegas.
At HT: OG: '12- dnq 25; WCh: '13- 10, '15- 9; CCp: '14- 2; US champion 2013-14, NACAC 2012. North American hammer record 2013.
Progress at HT: 2009- 55.19, 2010- 64.07, 2011- 69.79, 2012- 71.78, 2013- 75.73, 2014- 75.12, 2015- 72.35, 2016- 71.90. Pbs: DT 46.08A '11, Wt 22.42i '14.
Former gymnast.

Tori BOWIE b. 27 Aug 1990 Sandhill, Mississippi 1.75m 61kg. adidas. Studied psychology at University of Southern Mississippi.
At 100m/(200m): OG: '16- 2/3/1R; WCh: '15- 3. At 60m: WI: '16- 6. Won US 100m 2015, 200m 2016. At LJ: won NCAA 2011.
Progress at 100m, 200m, LJ: 2008- 12.21w, 6.03w; 2009- 11.82, 23.99, 6.30/6.60w; 2010- 11.76/11.72w, 24.55/23.98w, 6.43/6.50w; 2011- 6.64, 2012- 11.28, 24.06, 6.78; 2013- 11.14/11.04w, 6.91, 2014- 10.80, 22.18, 6.95i/6.82; 2015- 10.81/10.72w, 22.23; 2016- 10.78/10.74w, 21.99. pbs: 60m 7.11i '16, TJ 13.09i/12.65 '14. First name actually Frentorish.

Tia BROOKS b. 2 Aug 1990 Saginaw, Michigan 1.83m 109kg. Nike. Was at University of Oklahoma.
At SP: OG: '12- dnq 19, WCh: '13- 8, '15- dnq 13. NCAA champion indoors and out 2012-13.
Progress at SP: 2008- 14.64, 2009- 14.13i/14.09, 2010- 17.37, 2011- 18.00, 2012- 19.00i/18.47, 2013- 19.22i/18.96, 2014- 18.83, 2015- 19.00, 2016- 19.73. pb DT 46.64 '08.

Dezerea BRYANT b. 27 Apr 1993 Milwaukee 1.57m 50kg. University of Kentucky.
At 100m/200m: WJ: '10- 1R, '12-sf/3/1R; Won NCAA 200m 2015.
Progress at 100m, 200m: 2007- 25.33, 2009- 11.86/11.76w, 24.02; 2010- 11.59, 23.51; 2012- 11.29, 22.97; 2013- 11.20, 22.87/22.54w; 2014- 11.24/10.96w, 22.68; 2015- 11.00/10.99w, 22.18; 2016- 11.23w, 23.07. pbs: 60m 7.11Ai/7.12i '17; 300m 36.70i '15, 400m 54.46 '13.

Quanesha BURKS b. 15 Mar 1995 Ozark, Alabama 1.60m 55kg. University.of Alabama
At LJ: WJ: '14- 5; PAm: '15- 8; Won NCAA 2015, NACAC 2015-16.
Progress at LJ: 2012- 6.13, 2013- 5.84w, 2014- 6.38, 2015- 6.93A/6.84/6.91w, 2016- 6.80i/6.77. pbs: 60m 7.27i '17, 100m 11.52 '14.

Mary CAIN b. 3 May 1996 New York 1.70m 50kg. Nike Elite. Student at Fordham University (formerly Portland).
At 1500m: WCh: '13- 9; WJ: '12- 6. At 3000m: WJ: '14- 1.
Two world junior indoor 1000m records 2014; North American junior records: 800m, 1500m, indoor 1500m 2013-14, 1M 2014.
Progress at 1500m: 2011- 4:23.59, 2012- 4:11.01, 2013- 4:04.62, 2014- 4:06.34, 2015- 4:09.08, 2016- 4:10.84. pbs: 500m 1:21.43i '14, 800m 1:59.51 '13, 1000m 2:35.80i '14, 2:38.57 '15; 1M 4:24.11i '14, 4:39.28 '12; 3000m 8:58.48 '14, 2M 9:38.68i '13, 5000m 15:45.46 '13.

Amber CAMPBELL b. 5 Jun 1981 Indianapolis 1.70m 91kg. Mjolnar. Was at Coastal Carolina University.
At HT: OG: '08/12- dnq 19/10, '16- 6; WCh: '05-11-13: dnq 18/13/13, '09- 11, '15- nt; PAm: '11- 3, '15- 2. Won NACAC 2015, US 2012, 2015-16; indoor Wt 2007-11.
Progress at HT: 2000- 49.16, 2001- 62.08, 2002- 63.76, 2003- 64.58, 2004- 67.23, 2005- 69.52, 2006- 67.52, 2007- 70.33, 2008- 70.19, 2009- 70.61, 2010- 71.94, 2011- 72.59, 2012- 71.80, 2013- 73.03, 2014- 73.61, 2015- 72.81, 2016- 74.03. pbs: SP 14.81i '02, 14.42 '04; 20lb Wt 24.78i '12.

Kori CARTER b. 6 Mar 1992 Pasadena, California 1.65m 57kg. Nike. Human biology student at Stanford University.
At 400mh: WCh: '15- sf; WJ: '08- h; CCp: '14- 7; Won US 2014, NCAA 2013. At 100mh: WY: '09- 2.
Progress at 400mh: 2007- 62.21, 2008- 60.22, 2009- 59.89, 2010- 60.47, 2011- 57.10, 2012- 57.60, 2013- 53.21, 2014- 53.84, 2015- 54.41, 2016- 54.47. pbs: 100m 11.57 '11, 200m 23.07 '17, 60mh 8.11i '17, 100mh 12.76 '13.

Michelle CARTER b. 12 Oct 1985 San Jose 1.75m 110kg. Nike. Liberal arts graduate from University of Texas.
At SP: OG: '08- 13, '12- 4, '16- 1; WCh: '09-11-13-15: 6/9/4/3; WI: '12-14-16: 3/5/1; WJ: '04- 1; WY: '01- 2; PAm: '11- 3; PAm-J: '03- 1; CCp: '14- 2. Won US 2008-09, 2011, 2013-16; NCAA indoor 2006.
North American shot records 2013 and 2016 and indoors (20.21) 2016.
Progress at SP: 2000- 14.76, 2001- 15.23, 2002- 16.25, 2003- 16.73, 2004- 17.55, 2005- 18.26, 2006- 17.98, 2007- 17.57, 2008- 18.85, 2009- 19.13, 2010- 18.80, 2011- 19.86, 2012- 19.60, 2013- 20.24, 2014- 19.84, 2015- 20.02, 2016- 20.63. pbs: DT 54.06 '07.
First US woman to win Olympic shot. Her father Mike set a world junior shot record in 1979 and won the Olympic silver in 1984, seven NCAA titles (4 in, 3 out) (for a unique father-daughter double) and WUG gold in 1981 and 1983, pb 21.76 '84. Her younger sister D'Andra (b. 17 Jun 1987) won the NCAA discus in 2009, pb 57.73 '08.

Kristi CASTLIN b. 7 Jul 1988 Douglasville, Georgia 1.70m 75kg. adidas. Political science graduate of Virginia Tech University.
At 100mh: OG: '16- 3; won PAm-J 2007. At 60mh: won US indoors 2012.
World best 4x100mh 2014 & 2015.
Progress at 100mh: 2005- 13.85, 2006- 13.73, 2007- 12.91/12.82w, 2008- 12.81, 2009- 12.89, 2010- 12.83/12.59w, 2011- 12.83/12.68w, 2012- 12.56 12.48w, 2013- 12.61, 2014- 12.58, 2015- 12.71, 2016- 12.50. pbs: 55m 7.04i '08, 60m 7.47i '08, 100m 11.60 '12, 11.49w '11; 200m 23.46 '12, 50mh 6.81+i '12, 55mh 7.37i '12, 60mh 7.84Ai/7.91i '12, 400mh 60.44 '07.
Married to Alonzo Nelson.

Emma COBURN b. 19 Oct 1990 Boulder 1.73m 55kg. New Balance. Marketing graduate of University of Colorado.
At 3000mSt: OG: '12- 8, '16- 3; WCh: '11- 9, '15- 5; CCp: '14- 1; US champion 2011-12, 2014-16; NCAA 2011, 2013.

Three North American 3000m steeple records 2014 (unratified as no doping test) & 2016 (2). Progress at 3000mSt: 2009- 10:06.21, 2010- 9:51.86, 2011- 9:37.16, 2012- 9:23.54, 2013- 9:28.26, 2014- 9:11.42, 2015- 9:15.59, 2016- 9:07.63. pbs: 800m 2:09.81 '10, 1500m 4:05.10 '15, 1M 4:29.86i '13, 4:33.24 '12; 2000m 5:41.11i '15, 3000m 8:59.76 '15.

Vashti CUNNINGHAM b. 18 Jan 1998 Las Vegas 1.85m 66kg. Nike. High school in Las Vegas, Nevada.
At HJ: OG: '16- 13=; WI: '16- 1; PAm-J: 15- 1; won US indoor 2016.
High jump records: World youth (=) 2015, World junior indoor 2016.
Progress at HJ: 2012- 1.76, 2013- 1.83, 2014- 1.90, 2015- 1.96, 2016- 1.99i/1.97. Pb LJ 5.85w '15.
Father Randall Cunningham was a quarterback in the NFL. Her brother Randall (b. 4 Jan 1996) has HJ pbs 2.27i '17, 2.25 '16and won PAm-J 2015 and NCAA 2016.

Sharon DAY-MONROE b. 9 Jun 1985 Brooklyn, New York 1.75m 70kg. née Day. Asics. Was at Cal Poly San Luis Obispo.
At Hep: OG: '12- 14; WCh: '09-11-13-15: 9/16/6/14. US champion 2011, 2013-14. At Hep: WI: '14- 4. At HJ: OG: '08- dnq 23=; WCh: '09- dnq 17=; WJ: '04- 3; PAm: '07- 6; won PAm-J 2003, USA 2014, NCAA 2005.
US indoor heptathlon record 2014.
Progress at Hep: 2007- 5244, 2008- 5642, 2009- 6177, 2010- 6006(w), 2011- 6058, 2012- 6343, 2013- 6550, 2014- 6470, 2015- 6458, 2016- 6385. pbs: 200m 24.02 '13, 400m 56.54 '07, 800m 2:08.94 '13, 55mh 7.98i '12, 60mh 8.43i '14, 100mh 13.31 '15, HJ 1.95 '08, LJ 6.15 '12, 6.16w '13; SP 15.62 '15, JT 47.38 '12, Pen 4805Ai '14.
Married Dan Monroe on 1 Sep 2014.

Taylor ELLIS-WATSON b. 6 May 1993 Philadelphia 1.83m 64kg. Was at University of Pittsburgh, then Arkansas.
At 400m/4x400mR: OG: '16- res1R.
Progress at 400m: 2008- 55.65, 2011- 55.26i, 2012- 52.75i, 2014- 50.51.78, 2015- 51.18, 2016- 50.25. pbs: 60m 7.57i '12, 100m 11.33 '16, 200m 22.40 '16.

Allyson FELIX b. 18 Nov 1985 Los Angeles 1.68m 57kg. Nike. Elementary education graduate of University of Southern California.
At 400m: OG: '16- 2/1R/1R; At 200m/4x400mR: OG: '04- 2, '08- 2/1R, '12- 1/1R (1 4x100mR); WCh: '03- qf, '05- 1, '07- 1/1 4x100mR/1R, '09- 1/1R, '11- 3/1R (2 400m, 1 4x100m), '13- dnf, '15- 1 400m (2 4x100m & 4x400m); WJ: '02- 5; PAm: '03- 3; WI: '10- 1R. At 100m: OG: '12- 5; WY: '01- 1 (1 Medley R). Won DL 200m 2010, 2014-15; 400m 2010, WAF 200m 2005-06, 2009; US 100m 2010, 200m 2004-05, 2007-09, 2012; 400m 2011, 2015-16.
World junior record 200m 2004 after unratified mark (no doping test) at age 17 in 2003.

Progress at 100m, 200m, 400m: 2000- 12.19/11.99w, 23.90; 2001- 11.53, 23.31/23.27w; 2002- 11.40, 22.83/22.69w, 55.01; 2003- 11.29/11.12w, 22.11A/22.51, 52.26; 2004- 11.16, 22.18, 51.83A; 2005- 11.05, 22.13, 51.12; 2006- 11.04, 22.11; 2007- 11.01, 21.81, 49.70; 2008- 10.93, 21.93/21.82w, 49.83; 2009- 11.08, 21.88, 49.83; 2010- 11.27, 22.03, 50.15; 2011- 11.26+, 22.32, 49.59; 2012- 10.89, 21.69; 2013- 11.06+, 22.30, 50.19; 2014- 11.01, 22.02, 50.81; 2015- 11.09, 21.98, 49.26; 2016- 22.02, 49.51. pbs: 50m 6.43i '02, 60m 7.10i '12, 150mSt 16.36 '13 (world best), 300m 36.33i '07.
Women's record 6 Olympic gold medals from 9 medals to equal record. First teenager to won a World sprint title. Unbeaten in ten 200m competitions 2005 and in five 2007. Has women's record nine World gold medals including three in 2007 when she had a record 0.53 winning margin at 200m and ran a 48.0 400m relay leg, and four Olympic gold medals. Ran 47.72 relay leg at the 2015 Worlds. IAAF female Athlete of the Year 2012. Older brother Wes Felix won World Junior bronze at 200m and gold in WJR at 4x100m in 2002, pbs: 100m 10.23 '05, 200m 20.43 '04.

Shalane FLANAGAN b. 8 Jul 1981 Boulder 1.65m 50kg. Bowerman TC. Was at University of North Carolina.
At 5000m/(10000m): OG: '04- h, '08- 9/2; WCh: '05- h, '07- 8, '09- (13), '11- (7), '13- (8), '15- (6). At Mar: OG: '12- 9, '16- 6. World CC: '10- 12, '11-3; 4k: '04- 14, 05- 20. Won US 5000m 2005, 10000m 2008, 2011, 2013; HMar 2010, Mar 2012, CC 2008, 2010-11, 2013; 4km CC 2004-05, indoor 3000m 2007, NCAA CC 2002-03, indoor 3000m 2003.
North American records: 5000m and indoor 3000m 2007, 10000m (2) 2008, 15km & 25km road 2014.
Progress at 5000m, 10000m, Mar: 2001- 16:29.68, 2003- 15:20.54, 2004- 15:05.08, 2005- 15:10.96, 2007- 14:44.80, 2008- 14:59.69, 30:22.22; 2009- 14:47.62i/15:10.86, 31:23.43; 2010- 14:49.08, 2:28:40; 2011- 14:45.20, 30:39.57; 2012- 31:59.69, 2:25:38; 2013- 31:04.85, 2:27:08; 2014- 2:21:14, 2015- 15:10.02, 31:09.02, 2:27:47dh; 2016- 2:25:26. pbs: 800m 2:09.28 '02, 1500m 4:05.86 '07, 1M 4:33.81i '11, 4:48.47 '00; 3000m 8:33.25i/8:35.34 '07, Road: 15k 47:03 '14, 10M 51:45 '10, HMar 67:51dh '16, 68:31 '13, 25k 1:22:36 '14, 30k 1:39:15 '14.
2nd New York 2010 on marathon debut and won Olympic Trials 2012; 3rd Berlin 2014. Married to Steve Edwards. Mother, Cheryl Bridges, set marathon world best with 2:49:40 in 1971 and was 4th in 1969 International CC, father Steve ran in World Cross 1976-7, 1979.

Phyllis FRANCIS b. 4 May 1992 New York 1.78m 61kg. Nike. Was at University of Oregon.
At 400m/4x400mR: OG: '16- 5/1R; WCh: '15- 7/res2R; PAm-J: '11- 3/1R. Won NCAA indoors 2014.

Progress at 400m: 2010- 55.82i, 2011- 52.93, 2012- 51.22, 2013- 50.86, 2014- 50.46Ai/50.59, 2015- 50.50, 2016- 49.94. pbs: 60m 7.30i '17, 100m 11.34w '16, 200m 22.50 '16, 300m 36.15Ai '17, 600m 1:27.38i '11, 800m 2:04.83 '08.
Younger sister Claudia pbs 400m 52.51 '15, 800m 2:02.92 '15

Stephanie GARCIA b. 3 May 1988 Austin, Texas 1.68m 52kg. New Balance. Was at University of Virginia.
At 3000mSt: WCh: '11- h, '15- 9.
North American 3000m steeple record 2014 (unratified as no doping test).
Progress at 3000mSt: 2007- 10:15.83, 2008- 10:17.38, 2009- 10:08.48, 2010- 10:05.05, 2011- 9:41.12, 2012- 9:47.76, 2013- 9:45.78, 2014- 9:24.28, 2015- 9:23.48, 2016- 9:19.48. pbs: 800m 2:05.65i '17, 1500m 4:05.39 '15, 1M 4:28.84 '15, 2000m 5:48.25i '14, 3000m 8:53.20i '16, 8:58.09 '14, 2M 10:04.14i '15, 5000m 15:16.56 '16.

English GARDNER b. 22 Apr 1992 Philadelphia 1.62m 50kg. Nike. Was at University of Oregon.
At 100m/4x100mR: OG: '16- 7/1R; WCh: '13- 4/2R, '15- sf/2R; Won US 100m 2016, NCAA 100m 2013, indoor 60m 2012.
Progress at 100m, 200m: 2005- 11.99, 24.53; 2007- 11.61, 24.01; 2008- 11.82/11.49w, 24.27/24.19w; 2011- 11.03, 23.02; 2012- 11.10/11.00w, 22.82; 2013- 10.85, 22.62; 2014- 11.01, 22.81; 2015- 10.79/10.76w, 22.74; 2016- 10.74. pbs: 60m 7.12i '12, 400m 53.73 '12.

Kate GRACE b. 24 Oct 1988 Sacramento 1.73m 55kg. Oiselle. Was at Yale University.
At 800m: OG: '16- 8. US champion 2016.
Progress at 800m: 2007- 2:10.18, 2008- 2:06.12, 2009- 2:04.72i/2:05.82, 2010- 2:04.22, 2011- 2:03.41, 2012- 2:01.63, 2013- 1:59.47, 2014- 2:01.22, 2016- 1:58.28. pbs: 400m 55.96 '06, 600m 1:27.8 '16, 1000m 2:36.97i '17, 1500m 4:05.65 '16, 1M 4:22.93 '17, 3000m 8:47.26i '17, 5k Rd 16:03 '16.

Dawn HARPER NELSON b. 13 May 1984 Norman, Oklahoma 1.68m 61kg. Nike. Studied psychology at UCLA.
At 100mh: OG: '08- 1, '12- 2; WCh: '09-11-13-15: 7/3/4/sf; CCp: '14- 1; won DL 2012-15, PAm-J 2003, US 2009, 2014-15.
World best 4x100mh 2015.
Progress at 100mh: 2002- 13.63, 2003- 13.33/13.21w, 2004- 13.16/12.91w, 2005- 12.91, 2006- 12.80A/12.86, 2007- 12.67, 2008- 12.54, 2009- 12.48/12.36w, 2010- 12.77w, 2011- 12.47, 2012- 12.37, 2013- 12.48, 2014- 12.44, 2015- 12.48, 2016- 12.65. pbs: 60m 7.70i '05, 100m 11.66 '07, 200m 23.97 '06, 50mh 6.96i '12, 60mh 7.98i '06.
Married Craig Everhart (b. 13 Sep 1983, 400m 44.89 '04) in October 2007, and then Alonzo Nelson on 27 March 2013. Given 3-months drugs suspension from 1 Dec 2016 for inadvertent use of a masking agent.

Kendra 'Keni' HARRISON b. 18 Sep 1992 Clayton, North Carolina 1.63m 52kg. University of Kentucky.
At 100mh: WC: '15- sf. At 60mh: WI: '16- 8. Won DL 100mh 2016, NCAA 100mh & 60mh indoors 2015.
World and two N.American 100m hurdles records 2016.
Progress at 100mh, 400mh: 2010- 13.79, 59.19; 2011- 13.49, 59.13; 2012- 13.03/13.02w, 56.72; 2013- 12.88/12.87w, 55.75; 2014- 12.71/12.68w, 54.76; 2015- 12.50/12.46w, 54.09; 2016- 12.20. pbs: 60m 7.31i '14, 100m 11.35 '16, 200m 23.00 '16, 300m 37.84i '15, 400m 53.82i '13, 60mh 7.74Ai/7.75i '17.

Queen HARRISON b. 10 Sep 1988 Loch Sheldrake, New York 1.70m 60kg. Studied of business marketing at Virginia Tech.
At 100mh: OG: '08- sf; WCh: '11- sf; PAm-J: '07- 1 (2 100mh); won NCAA 100mh, 400mh & 60mh indoors 2010. World best 4x100mh 2014 & 2015.
Progress at 100mh, 400mh: 2007- 12.98, 55.81; 2008- 12.70, 54.60; 2009- 13.14/12.98w, 56.03; 2010- 12.61/12.44w, 54.55; 2011- 12.88, 54.78; 2012- 12.62, 55.32; 2013- 12.43, 2014- 12.46, 2015- 12.52/12.50w, 2016- 12.57/12.54w. pbs: 400m 52.88 '08, 60mh 7.74Ai/7.75i 17, LJ 5.82i '06.

Natasha HASTINGS b. 23 Jul 1986 Brooklyn, New York 1.73m 63kg. Under Armour. Studied exercise science at University of South Carolina.
At 400m/4x400m: OG: '08- res 1R, '16- 4/1R; WCh: '07- sf/res 1R, '09/11- res 1R, '13- 5/2R, '15- sf/2R; WJ: '04- 1/1R; WY: '03- 1; WI: '10/14/16- 1R, '12- 3/2R; PAm-J: '03- 1R, '05- 1/1R. Won US 2013, NCAA indoors and out 2007. World junior 500m indoor best 2005, North American indoor 4x400m record 2014.
Progress at 400m: 2000- 54.21, 2001- 55.06, 2002- 53.42, 2003- 52.09, 2004- 52.04, 2005- 51.34, 2006- 51.45, 2007- 49.84, 2008- 50.80, 2009- 50.89, 2010- 50.53, 2011- 50.83Ai/50.97, 2012- 50.72, 2013- 49.94, 2014- 50.53, 2015- 50.24, 2016- 49.90. pbs: 55m 7.08i '02, 60m 7.26i '13, 100m 11.24 '13, 11.08w '14; 200m 22.57 '16, 22.55w '14; 300m 35.9+ '07, 36.25i '16; 500m 1:10.05i '05.
Father from Jamaica, mother Joanne Gardner was British (ran 11.89 to win WAAA U15 100m at 14 in 1977).

Quanera HAYES b. 7 Mar 1992. Hope Mills, North Carolina 1.72m 59kg. Wsa at Livingstone College.
At 400m/4x400mR: WI: '16- 3/1R.
North American indoor 300m record 2017.
Progress at 400m: 2012- 54.18A, 2013- 51.54A, 2014- 51.91, 2015- 50.84, 2016- 49.91. pbs: 60m 7.34i '17, 100m 11.27 '16, 200m 22.89 '16, 22.81w '15; 300m 35.71i '17.

Candace HILL b. 11 Feb 1999 Conyers, Georgia. 1.75m 59kg.
At 100/(200m): WJ: '16- 1/1R; WY: '15- 1/1.

World youth records 100m & 200m 2015, world indoor 300m record 2017.
Progress at 100m, 200m: 2013- 11.81, 23.85; 2014- 11.44/11.34w, 23.14; 2015- 10.98, 22.43A/23.05; 2016- 11.07, 22.76/22.38w. Pbs: 60m 7.30i '17, 300m 36.56Ai/36.86i '17, 400m 52.94 '17.

Molly HUDDLE b. 31 Aug 1984 Elmira, New York 1.63m 48kg. Saucony. Was at University of Notre Dame.
At 5000m: OG: '12- 11; WCh: '11- h, '13- 6; CCp: '10- 3. At 10000m: OG: '16- 5; WCh: '15- 4. Won US 5000m 2011, 2014, 2016; 10000m 2015-16. World CC: '10- 19, '11- 17.
North American 5000m (2) records 2010-14, 10000m 2016.
Progress at 5000m, 10000m: 2003- 15:36.95, 2004- 15:32.55, 2005- 16:12.17i, 2006- 15:40.41, 32:37.87; 2007- 15:17.13, 33:09.27; 2008- 15:25.47, 31:27.12; 2009- 15:53.91, 32:42.11; 2010- 14:44.76, 31:27.12; 2011- 15:10.01, 31:28.66; 2012- 15:01.32, 2013- 14:58.15, 2014- 14:42.64, 30:47.59; 2015- 14:57.23, 31:39.20; 2016- 14:48.14, 30:13:17. pbs: 1500m 4:08.09 '13, 1M 4:26.84 '14, 3000m 8:42.99 '13, Rd: 15k 48:52 '14, 10M 51:44 '15, 20k 64:06 '16, HMar 67:41 '16, Mar 2:28:13 '16.
Married Kurt Benninger CAN (pbs 1500m 3:38.03 '08, 1M 3:56.99 '08, 5000m 13:30.27 '09) in 2009. Won US road running titles in 2014 at a women's record four distances. 3rd New York 2016 on marathon debut.

Emily INFELD b. 21 Mar 1990 University Heights, Ohio 1.63m 48kg. Saucony. Was at Georgetown University.
At 10000m: OG: '16- 11; WCh: '15- 3. World CC: '13-21. Won NCAA indoor 3000m 2012.
Progress at 10000m: 2015- 31:38.71, 2016- 31:26.94. pbs: 800m 2:06.05 '09, 1000m 2:44.56i '09, 1500m 4:07.77 '12, 1M 4:31.50i '13, 4:38.01 '10; 3000m 8:41.43 '13, 5000m 15:00.91i '16, 15:07.18 '15.
Older sister Maggie (b.10 Apr 1986) has pb 1500m 4:08.31 '12.

Oluwafunmilayo 'Funmi' JIMOH b. 29 May 1984 Seattle 1.73m 64kg. Nike. Was at Rice University.
At LJ: OG: '08- 11; WCh: '09/11/13- dnq 21/nj/dnq 12; won US 2008-09, NCAA 2008.
Progress at LJ: 2004- 6.14, 2005- 6.31, 2006- 6.44, 2007- 6.46/6.62w, 2008- 6.91, 2009- 6.96, 2010- 6.81/6.87w, 2011- 6.88, 2012- 6.82, 2013- 6.92, 2014- 6.81, 2015- 6.74i/6.72, 2016- 6.76. pbs: 60m 7.67i '04, 100m 12.03 '08, 11.65w '11; 200m 23.91A '11, 24.28 '08, 23.65w '06; 400m 59.57i '09, 60mh 8.32i '07, 100mh 13.51 '05, 13.39w '07; HJ 1.75i '05, 1.66 '07; SP 10.68i '06, Pen 3937i '06, Hep 5335 '07.

Sally Jepkosgei **KIPYEGO** b. 19 Dec 1985 Kapsowar, Marakwet district, Kenya 1.68m 52kg. Was at Texas Tech University, USA.
At (5000m)/10000m: OG: '12- 4/2; WCh: '11- 2, '15- 5. World CC: '01- 8J. Won record equalling nine NCAA titles 5000m 2008, 10000m 2007, CC 2006-08, indoor 3000m 2007, 5000m 2007-09.
Progress at 5000m, 10000m: 2005- 16:34.90, 2006- 16:13.39, 2007- 15:19.72, 31:56.72; 2008- 15:11.88, 31:25.48; 2009- 15:09.03, 33:44.7A; 2010- 14:38.64, 2011- 14:30.42, 30:38.35; 2012- 14:43.11, 30:26.37; 2014- 14:37.18, 30:42.26; 2015- 14:47.75, 31:44.42; 2016- 14:43.98, 32:37.11A. pbs: 800m 2:08.26 '08, 1500m 4:06.23 '11, 1M 4:27.19i/4:29.64 '09, 2000m 5:35.20 '09, 3000m 8:34.18 '14, 2M 9:21.04i, 9:22.10 '14, Road: 15k 48:51 '14, 20k 64:54 '14, HMar 68:31 '14, Mar 2:28:01 '16.
2nd New York Marathon 2016. Married to Kevin Chelimo (5000m 13:14.57 '12) and expecting a baby in 2017. One of her eight brothers is Mike Kipyego (3000mSt 8:08.48). She received US citizenship in January 2017.

Shamier LITTLE b. 20 Mar 1995 Louisville, Kentucky 1.63m 52kg. Texas A&M University.
At 400mh: WCh: '15- 2; WJ: '12- dnf, '14- 1/1R; PAm: '15- 1/1R; won US 2015, NCAA 2014-16.
Progress at 400mh: 2011- 57.83, 2012- 57.44, 2013- 58.80, 2014- 55.07, 2015- 53.74, 2016- 53.51. pbs: 200m 23.17 '16, 400m 51.06 '14, 60mh 8.43i '14, 100mh 13.77 '14.
Mother Tiffany Mayfield had HJ pb 1.73.

Chaunté LOWE b. 12 Jan 1984 Templeton, California 1.75m 59kg. née Howard. Nike. Economics graduate of Georgia Tech University.
At HJ: OG: '04- dnq 26=, '08- 6, '12- 5, '16- 4; WCh: '05- 2, '09- 7=, '15- dnq; PAm-J: '03- 3; CCp: '14- 2; WI: '06-10-12: 8/3/1; Won DL 2012, US 2006, 2008-10, 2012, 2014-16; NCAA 2004, indoors 2004-05.
North American HJ records (3) 2010, indoors 2012.
Progress at HJ: 2000- 1.75, 2001- 1.84, 2002- 1.87, 2003- 1.89, 2004- 1.98A, 2005- 2.00, 2006- 2.01, 2008- 2.00, 2009- 1.98, 2010- 2.05, 2011- 1.78, 2012- 2.02Ai/2.01, 2014- 1.97, 2015- 1.91, 2016- 2.01. pbs: 100m 11.83 '05, 200m 24.47 '16, 100mh 13.78 '04, LJ 6.90 '10, TJ 12.93 '04, 12.98w '05; Hep 5133 '16.
Married Mario Lowe (b. 20 Apr 1980, TJ pb 16.15 '02) in 2005, daughters Jasmine born 30 Jul 2007 and Aurora in 4 Apr 2011 and son Mario Josiah in August 2013.

Molly LUDLOW b. 4 Aug 1987 Worthington, Ohio 1.73m 59kg. née Beckwith. Saucony. Was at University of Indiana.
At 800m: WCh: '15- sf.
North American 4x800m record 2015.
Progress at 800m: 2007- 2:13.99i/2:14.17, 2008- 2:06.46, 2009- 2:02.51, 2010- 1:59.83, 2011- 1:59.12, 2012- 1:59.18, 2014- 1:59.30, 2015- 1:58.68, 2016- 1:57.68. pbs: 400m 54.13 '09, 600m 1:27.22i '10, 1000m 2:37.19i '14, 1500m 4:07.88 '14, 1M 4:34.44i '14. Went to university on a soccer scholarship. Married Reed Ludlow in 2013.

Francena McCORORY b. 20 Oct 1988 Hampton, Virginia 1.70m 60kg. adidas. Psychology graduate of Hampton University.

At 400m/4x400mR: OG: '12- 7/1R, '16- res 1R; WCh: '11- 4/1R, '13- 6/2R, '15- 2R; CCp: '14- 1/1R; WI: '14- 1/1R; won DL 2015, US 2014, NCAA indoors 2009-10, out 2010.
World junior indoor 300m best 2007, North American indoor 4x400m record 2014.
Progress at 400m: 2004- 54.54, 2005- 55.26i, 2006- 51.93i, 2008- 51.54, 2009- 50.58, 2010- 50.52, 2011- 50.24, 2012- 50.06, 2013- 49.86, 2014- 49.48, 2015- 49.83, 2016- 50.23. pbs: 55m 6.86i '06, 60m 7.43i '07, 100m 11.55 '16, 200m 22.92 '10, 300m 35.7+ '13, 500m 1:09.01i '12, 600m 1:29.07i '13, 800m 2:20.25i '07.

Candyce McGRONE b. 29 Mar 1989 Indianapolis 1.68m 59kg. adidas. Was at Florida State University, then Oklahoma.
At 200m: WCh: '15- 4; won NCAA 100m 2011.
Progress at 100m, 200m: 2007- 11.54/11.29w, 23.82/23.24w; 2008- 11.50/11.37w, 23.47; 2009- 11.44, 23.30/23.17w; 2010- 22.84; 2011- 11.08/11.07w, 22.81; 2012- 11.38, 23.49; 2013- 11.19, 22.85; 2014- 11.26/11.20w, 23.43; 2015- 11.00/10.91w, 22.01; 2016- 11.13/11.06w, 22.98. pbs: 60m 7.21Ai/7.27i '12, 400m 55.34 '11.

Sydney McLAUGHLIN b. 7 Aug 1999 New Brunswick, New Jersey. 1.74m 61kg. Going to University of Kentucky.
At 400mh: OG: '16- sf; WY: '15- 1.
World junior 400mh record 2016, world youth records 400mh (2) and 400m indoors 2016.
Progress at 400mh: 2013- 11.81, 23.85; 2014- 11.44/11.34w, 23.14; 2015- 10.98, 22.43A/23.05; 2016- 54.15. pbs: 200m 23.97 '16, 300m 36.82i '17, 400m 51.61i '17, 51.87 '16; 55mh 7.66i '15, 60mh 8.17i '15, 100mh 13.34 '14. LJ 5.89i '15. 5.81w '14.
Her brother Taylor (b. 3 Aug 1997) was 2nd at the 2016 World Juniors.

Inika McPHERSON b. 29 Sep 1986 Galveston, Texas 1.63m 55kg. Was at University of California.
At HJ: OG: '16- 10=; WCh: '11/13- dnq 26/18; WJ: '04- 11; PAm: '07- 11.
Progress at HJ: 2002- 1.83, 2004- 1.83, 2005- 1.88, 2006- 1.80i/1.78, 2007- 1.84, 2008- 1.78, 2009- 1.83, 2011- 1.86, 2012- 1.95, 2013- 1.92, 2014- 2.00dq/1.96, 2016- 1.94. pb LJ 5.69 '04.
Before the mark was annulled her 2.00 US women's high jump in 2014 was a world record height differential for a woman of 37cm. She tested positive for a banned substance at this meeting and received 21-month ban.

Christina MANNING b. 29 May 1990 Waldorf, Maryland 1.63m 54kg. adidas. Was at Ohio State University.
At 100mh: WUG: '11- 3/2R.
Progress at 100mh: 2008- 13.86, 2009- 13.08, 2010- 13.10, 2011 12.86/12.72w, 2012- 12.68/12.57w, 2014- 13.61, 2015- 13.04, 2016- 12.87/12.67w. pbs: 60m 7.23i '12, 100m 11.29 '11, 200m 23.27 '12, 60mh 7.82i '17; LJ 5.75 '08.

Brenda MARTINEZ b. 8 Sep 1987 Upland, California 1.63m 52kg. New Balance. Studied sociology and law at University of California – Riverside.
At 800m: WCh: '13- 2, '15- sf. At 1500m: OG: '16- sf; WI: '16- 5.
N.American 4x800m & 4x1500m records 2014.
Progress at 800m, 1500m: 2007- 2:04.22, 4:21.18; 2008- 2:02.34, 4:17.09; 2009- 2:00.85, 4;09.52; 2010- 2:04.76, 4:18.17; 2011- 2:01.07, 4:10.77; 2012- 1:59.14, 4:06.96; 2013- 1:57.91, 4:00.94; 2014- 1:58.84, 4:01.36; 2015- 1:59.06; 2016- 1:59.64, 4:03.57. pbs: 1000m 2:38.48 '12, 1M 4:26.76 '12, 3000m 9:07.99+i '13, 2M 9:51.91i '13, 5000m 15:30.89mx '13, 15:41.50 '14; 5km Rd 15:24 '14.
Married coach Carlos Handler in October 2012.

Georganne MOLINE b. 6 Mar 1990 Phoenix, Arizona 1.78m 59kg. Nike Psychology and communications student at University of Arizona.
At 400mh: OG: '12- 5; WCh: '13- h.
Progress at 400mh: 2010- 57.88, 2011- 57.41, 2012- 53.92, 2013- 53.72, 2014- 54.00, 2015- 54.24, 2016- 53.97. pbs: 200m 23.37 '13, 400m 52.08 '15, 500m 1:08.84i '15, 600m 1:26.70Ai '16, 1:27.15 '15; 800m 2:08.67i '13. 2:09.58 '14.
53.92 in Olympic final was seventh 400mh pb of her 2012 season.

Alysia MONTAÑO b. 26 Apr 1986 Queens, New York 1.70m 61kg. née Johnson. Nike. Was at University of California.
At 800m: OG: '12- 4; WCh: '07-11-13-15: h/3/3/h; PAm: '07- 6, '15- 2/res 1R; WI: '10- 3; CCp: '10- 7; won US 2007, 2010-13, 2015; NCAA 2007.
North American records: 4x800m 2015, indoor 600m 2013.
Progress at 800m: 2004- 2:08.97, 2005- 2:05.49, 2006- 2:01.80, 2007- 1:59.29, 2008- 2:00.57, 2009- 2:01.09, 2010- 1:57.34, 2011- 1:57.48, 2012- 1:57.37, 2013- 1:57.75, 2015- 1:59.15, 2016- 2:00.20. pbs: 200m 24.41iA '13, 400m 52.09 '10, 500m 1:09.55i '17, 600m 1:23.59i '13, 1:26.7+ '12; 1500m 4:28.43 '09.
Always runs with a flower in her hair. Married Louis Montaño on 19 Mar 2011, daughter Linnea Dori born 15 Aug 2014.

Sandi MORRIS b. 8 Jul 1992 Downers Grove, Illinois 1.74m 65kg. Student at University of Arkansas, formerly North Carolina.
At PV: OG: '16- 2; WCh: '15- 4=; WI: '16- 2; PAm-J: 11- 2. Won NACAC 2014.
Three North American outdoor pole vault records 2016.
Progress at PV: 2009- 3.81, 2010- 4.05, 2011- 4.30, 2012- 4.23i/4.15, 2013- 4.43i/4.02, 2014- 4.55, 2015- 4.76, 2016- 5.00.

Dalilah MUHAMMAD b. 7 Feb 1990 Jamaica, Queens, New York 1.70m 62kg. Nike. Business graduate of University of Southern California.
At 400mh: OG: '16- 1; WCh: '13- 2; WY: '07- 1;

PAm-J: '09- 2; US champion 2013, 2016.
Progress at 400mh: 2005- 61.25, 2006- 59.82, 2007- 57.09, 2008- 57.81, 2009- 56.49, 2010- 57.14, 2011- 56.04, 2012- 56.19, 2013- 53.83, 2014- 58.02, 2015- 55.76, 2016- 52.88. pbs: 60m 7.64i '10, 100m 11.42 '13, 200m 23.61 '16, 400m 52.64 '16, 600m 1:09.66i '17, 60mh 8.23i '12, 100mh 13.33 '12, 200mhSt 25.90 '14, HJ 1.75 '10.

Sharika NELVIS b. 10 May 1990 Memphis 1.78m 64kg. adidas. Sociology student at Arkansas State University.
At 100mh: WCh: '15- 8. Won NCAA 100mh & indoor 60mh 2014. World best 4x100mh 2015.
Progress at 100mh: 2008- 14.23, 2009- 14.03, 2011- 13.45, 2012- 13.22/12.99w, 2013- 12.84, 2014- 12.71/12.52w, 2015- 12.34. 2016- 12.60. pbs: 60m 7.28i '14, 100m 11.27/11.17w '14, 200m 23.19 '15, 22.70w '14; 400m 54.62 '13, 60mh 7.83i '15, LJ 6.32i '13, 6.27 '14.

Barbara NWABA b. 18 Jan 1989 Los Angeles 1.75m 64kg. Santa Barbara TC .Was at UC Santa Barbara.
At Hep: OG: '16- 12; WCh: '15- 27 (dnf 100mh). US champion 2016. At Pen: WI: '16- 4;
Progress at Hep: 2009- 5039, 2010- 5552, 2011- 5733, 2012- 5986, 2014- 6307, 2015- 6500, 2016- 6494. pbs: 200m 23.76 '15, 800m 2:07.13 '15, 60mh 8.40i '15, 100mh 13.38 '15, 400mh 60.51 '10, HJ 1.90 '16, LJ 6.23 '15, SP 15.00i /14.81 '16, JT 49.19 '16, Pen 4661i '16.

Courtney OKOLO b. 15 Mar 1994 Carrolltown, Texas 1.68m 54kg. Student at University of Texas.
At 400m/4x400mR: OG: '16- 1R; WI: '16- 1R; PAm-J: '13- 1/1R. Won NACAC 2015, NCAA 2014, 2016.
Progress at 400m: 2009- 56.50, 2010- 54.34, 2011- 53.03, 2012- 52.40, 2013- 51.04, 2014- 50.03, 2015- 50.82A/50.99, 2016- 49.71. pbs: 60m 7.52i '14, 100m 11.53 '16, 200m 22.93 '15, 22.79i '16; 300m 35.74 '16, 500m 1:07.34i '17, 600y 1:18.24i '15, 600m 1:24.00Ai/1:25.21 '17.

Keturah ORJI b. 5 May 1996 Mount Olive, New Jersey 1.65m 52kg. University of Georgia.
At TJ: OG: '16- 4; WJ: '14- 9; WY: '13- 3 (2 LJ); WI: '16- 4; won US 2016, NCAA 2015-16. North American and 3 US triple jump records 2016.,N.Am indoors 2017.
Progress at TJ: 2012- 12.46/12.51w, 2013- 13.69, 2014- 13.46, 2015- 14.15, 2016- 14.71, 2017- 14.32i. pbs: 60m 7.58i '16, LJ 6.72i '17, 6.63 '15.

Demi PAYNE b. 30 Sep 1991 New Braunfels, Texas 1.82m 65kg. Student at Stephen F.Austin University, formerly University of Kansas.
At PV: WCh: '15- dnq 19; PAm: '15- 4; Won NCAA 2015.
Progress at PV: 2008- 3.81, 2009- 3.94, 2010- 3.92i/3.86, 2011- 4.06, 2012- 4.22i/4.20, 2013- 4.25i, 2014- 4.29irr/4.21, 2015- 4.75i/4.71, 2016- 4.90i/4.85.
Big improvement to three US collegiate records

indoors in January 2015. Daughter Carlee born October 2013. Her father Bill Payne (b. 21 Dec 1967) in 1991 had pb best of 5.86 (US collegiate best) and was 2nd WUG.

Barbara PIERRE b. 28 Apr 1987 Port-au-Prince, Haiti 1.75m 60kg. Nike. Was at St. Augustine's College.
At 100m/4x100mR: OG: '08- qf; PAm: '11- 2/2R, '15- 3/1R. Won NACAC 2015. At 60m: WI: '12- 4, '16- 1.
Haiti records at 100m 2009, 200m 2008-09.
Progress at 100m: 2003- 11.98, 2005- 11.78, 2006- 11.66, 2007- 11.30, 2008- 11.40A, 2009- 11.18, 2010- 11.35, 2011- 11.14, 2012- 11.34, 2013- 10.85, 2014- 11.05, 2015- 10.92, 2016- 11.07/11.01w. pbs: 50m 6.22+i '12, 55m 6.89i '07, 60m 7.00i '16, 100y 10.38y '11, 200m 23.23 '10, 400m 57.04 '08.
With dual citizenship, she switched from US to Haiti 31 Dec 2007, and back to US 24 Mar 2010.

Jenna PRANDINI b. 20 Nov 1992 Clovis, California 1.72m 59kg. Student of psychology at University of Oregon.
At 200/4x100mR: OG: '16- sf; WCh: '15- sf/2R. Won NCAA 100m 2015, LJ 2014; US 200m 2015.
Progress at 100m, 200m, LJ: 2008- 12.18/11.74w, 5.86; 2009- 11.81, 24.48/24.02w; 2010- 11.34, 24.61, 6.15/6.29w; 2011- 11.51/11.44w, 23.75/23.51w, 6.20; 2012- 24.07, 2013- 11.31/11.14w, 23.15, 6.15; 2014- 11.11, 22.60, 6.55; 2015- 10.92, 22.20/22.18w, 6.80; 2016- 10.95/10.81w, 22.39. pbs: 60m 7.15i '15, TJ 12.73/12.98w '10.

DeAnna PRICE b. 8 Jun 1993 Moscow Mills, Missouri 1.73m 99kg. Was at Southern Illinois University.
At HT: OG: '16- 8; WCh: '15- dnq 18; WJ: '12- dnq 11; PAm: '15- 4. NCAA champion 2015-16. North American hammer record 2013.
Progress at HT: 2011- 55.20, 2012- 62.62, 2013- 65.18, 2015- 72.30, 2016- 73.09. Pbs: SP 16.30 '15, DT 53.46 '15, Wt 23.46i '17.

Brittney REESE b. 9 Sep 1986 Gulfport, Mississippi 1.73m 64kg. Nike. English graduate of University of Mississippi.
At LJ: OG: '08- 5, '12- 1, '16- 2; WCh: '07-09-11-13-15: 8/1/1/1/dnq 24; WI: '10-12-16: 1/1/1; won DL 2010-11, WAF 2009, US 2008-12, 2014, 2016 (& 3 indoors); NCAA 2007-08.
North American indoor long jump record 2012.
Progress at LJ: 2004- 6.31, 2006- 5.94, 2007- 6.83, 2008- 6.95, 2009- 7.10, 2010- 6.94/7.05w, 2011- 7.19, 2012- 7.23i/7.15, 2013- 7.25, 2014- 6.92, 2015- 6.97, 2016- 7.31. pbs: 50m 6.23i '12, 60m 7.24i '11, 100m 11.63 '09, 11.20w '11; HJ 1.88i/1.84 '08, TJ 13.16 '08.
Concentrated on basketball at Gulf Coast Community College in 2005-06. Has won six successive global titles

Brianna ROLLINS b. 18 Aug 1991 Miami 1.64m 55kg. Nike. Was at Clemson University.
At 100mh: OG: '16- 1; WCh: '13- 1, '15- 4; Won

US 2013, 2016; NACAC 2012. At 60mh: WI: '16- 2; won US indoor 60mh 2016, NCAA 100mh 2013, indoor 60mh 2011 & 2013.
North American 100m hurdles record 2013, world best 4x100mh 2014 & 2015.
Progress at 100mh: 2007- 14.48, 2008- 13.93, 2009- 13.83, 2011- 12.99/12.88w, 2012- 12.70/12.60Aw, 2013- 12.26, 2014- 12.53, 2015- 12.56, 2016- 12.34. pbs: 60m 7.29Ai '16, 200m 23.04/23.02w '13, 300m 37.90i '10, 400m 53.93 '13, 60mh 7.76i '16, 400mh 60.58 '09.
Undefeated in 2013: inc. heats 200m- 7, 400m- 1, 60mh- 8, 100mh- 18.

Shannon ROWBURY b. 19 Sep 1984 San Francisco 1.65m 52kg. Nike Oregon Project. Was at Duke University.
At 1500m: OG: '08- 7, '12- 4, '16- 4; WCh: '09- 3, '11- sf, '15- 7; CCp: '14- 2; Won US 2008-09, NCAA indoor mile 2007. At 3000m: WI: '14- 8, '16- 3; CCp: '10- 2. At 5000m: WCh: '13- 7.
WR distance medley 2015, North American records: 2M 2014, 1500m 2015, 5000m 2016.
Progress at 1500m, 5000m: 2004- 4:17.41, 2005- 4:14.81, 2006- 4:12.31, 15:38.42; 2007- 16:59.97i, 2008- 4:00.33, 2009- 4:00.81, 15:12.95; 2010- 4:01.30, 15:00.51; 2011- 4:05.73, 2012- 4:03.15, 2013- 4:01.28, 15:06.10, 2014- 3:59.49, 14:48.68; 2015- 3:56.29, 2016- 3:57.78, 14:38.92. pbs: 800m 1:59.97 '16, 1000m 2:40.25i '15, 1M 4:20.34 '08, 2000m 5:46.2 '14, 3000m 8:29.93 '14, 2M 9:20.25 '14, 3000mSt 9:59.4 '06.
Former ballet and Irish dancer. Married Pablo Solares (Mexican 1500m record 3:36.67 '09) on 11 April 2015.

Raven SAUNDERS b. 15 May 1996 Charleston, SC 1.65m 89kg. Student at Southern Illinois University.
At SP: OG: '16- 5; WJ: 14- 2. Won PAm-J 2015, NCAA 2016.
Progress at SP: 2014- 17.82, 2015- 18.62i/18.35, 2016- 19.35, 2017- 19.56i. pbs: DT 56.85 '16, HT 56.91 '16, Wt 21.67i '17.
4 indoor and 4 outdoor US junior records 2015.

Mary SAXER SIBEARS b. 21 Jun 1987 Buffalo, NY 1.69m 57kg. Nike. Marketing graduate of University of Notre Dame.
At PV: WI: '12- 4, 14- 8.
Progress at PV: 2004- 4.09i/3.81, 2005- 4.32i/4.19, 2006- 4.05i/3.90, 2007- 3.86i/3.80, 2008- 4.06, 2009- 4.30, 2010- 4.50, 2011- 4.60, 2012- 4.62Ai/4.53, 2013- 4.70, 2014- 4.71Ai/4.58, 2015- 4.62, 2016- 4.71Ai/4.43.
Married Justin Sibears on 9 Nov 2013.

Jennifer SIMPSON b. 23 Aug 1986 Webster City, Iowa 1.65m 50kg. née Barringer. New Balance. Studied political science at University of Colorado.
At 1500m: OG: '12- sf, '16- 3; WCh: '11- 1, '13- 2, '15- 11; won DL 2014. At 3000mSt: OG: '08- 8; WCh: '07- h, '09- 3; won NCAA 2006, 2008-09. Won US 1500m 2014-16, 5000m 2013, 3000mSt 2009.
North American records: 3000m steeplechase (3) 2008-09, indoor 2 miles 2015.
Progress at 1500m, 5000m, 3000mSt: 2006- 16:15.23, 9:53.04, 2007- 4:21.53, 15:48.24, 9:33.95; 2008- 4:11.36, 9:22.26; 2009- 3:59.90, 15:01.70i/15:05.25, 9:12.50; 2010- 4:03.63, 15:33.33; 2011- 4:03.54, 15:11.49; 2012- 4:04.07, 2013- 4:00.48, 14:56.26; 2014- 3:57.22, 2015- 3:57.30, 2016- 3:58.19. pbs: 800m 2:00.45 '13, 1M 4:22.18 '15, 2000m 5:45.7 '14, 3000m 8:29.58 '14, 2M 9:18.35i '15.
Married Jason Simpson on 8 Oct 2010. Won 5th Avenue Mile 2011.

Brittany SMITH b. 25 Mar 1991 Oak Park, Illinois 1.78m 89kg. Was at Illinois State University.
At SP: WJ: 10- 6. Won NACAC 2012.
Progress at SP: 2008- 13.52, 2009- 13.88, 2010- 15.98, 2011- 17.19i/15.83, 2012- 17.92, 2013- 17.85, 2014- 18.57, 2015- 19.01i/18.96, 2016- 18.94. pbs: DT 55.15 '15, HT 70.27 '14, Wt 21.51i '13.

Shalonda SOLOMON b. 19 Dec 1985 Inglewood, California 1.69m 56kg. Reebok. Was at University of South Carolina.
At (100m)/200m/4x100m: WCh: '11- 4/res (1)R; WJ: '04- 1/1R; PAm-J: '03- 1/1/1R; CCp: '10- (2)/1R. Won NCAA 200m 2006, NCAAC 100m & 200m 2006.
Progress at 100m, 200m: 2001- 11.57/11.37w, 23.65/23.22w; 2002- 11.51/11.46w, 23.31; 2003- 11.35/11.25w, 22.93; 2004- 11.41/11.32w, 22.82; 2005- 11.29, 22.74/22.72w; 2006- 11.09/11.07w, 22.36/22.30w; 2007- 11.33, 22.77; 2008- 11.16, 22.48/22.36w; 2009- 11.04/11.00w, 22.41; 2010- 10.90, 22.47; 2011- 11.08/10.90w, 22.15; 2012- 11.26, 22.82; 2013- 11.04/10.97w, 22.41/22.33w; 2014- 11.12, 22.64/22.54w; 2015- 11.06/10.97w, 22.56; 2016- 11.16/11.05w, 22.63/22.58w. pbs: 55m 6.72i '09, 60m 7.15Ai '11, 7.21i '06; 300m 36.45i '09, 400m 52.83 '16.

Cynthia 'Janay' SOUKUP b. 12 Oct 1985 Panama City, Florida 1.65m 59kg. née DeLoach. Nike. Psychology graduate of Colorado State University.
At LJ: OG: '12- 3, '16- dnq 13; WCh: '11- 5, '13- 10, '15- 8; WI: '12- 2, '16- 4; PAm: '07- 10. Won US 2013, US indoor 2011-13. At 60mh: WI: '14- 5.
Progress at LJ: 2004- 6.14Ai/6.05/6.14w, 2005- 6.27A/6.43w, 2006- 6.21Ai, 2007- 6.42Ai/6.41/6.45w, 2008- 6.48/6.51w, 2009- 6.33i/6.04, 2010- 6.61, 2011- 6.99Ai/6.97, 2012- 7.03/7.15w, 2013- 6.99/7.08w, 2014- 6.53Ai/6.41, 2015- 6.95, 2016- 6.93. pb 55m 6.85Ai '05, 60m 7.31Ai '06, 100m 11.45 '08, 200m 24.60 '07, 24.26Aw '08; 60mh 7.82Ai '14, 7.85i '16; 100mh 12.84 '15, HJ 1.73i '11, SP 13.44i '14, Pen 4289i '11.
Married Patrick Soukup in September 2012.

Ashley SPENCER b. 8 Jun 1993 Indianapolis 1.68m 54kg. Student at University of Texas,

formerly Illinois.
At 400mh: OG: '16- 3. At 400m/4x400mR: WCh: '13- sf/2R; WJ: '12- 1/1R; WI: '16- 2/1R. Won NCAA 2012-13.
Progress at 400m, 400mh: 2012- 50.50, 59.43; 2013- 50.28, 56.32; 2014- 51.38, 59.78; 2015- 51.72, 2016- 51.09, 53.72. pbs: 60m 7.42i '13, 100m 11.34/11.27w '14, 200m 22.92/22.69w '14, 300m 36.27i '17, 100mh 14.40/14.28w '11.

Deajah STEVENS b. 19 May 1995 Tarrytown, New York 1.72m 60kg. University of Oregon.
At 200m: OG: '16- 7.
Progress at 200m: 2008- 25.54, 2009- 24.48, 2011- 24.20, 2012- 24.38, 2013- 24.15, 2015- 23.18, 2016- 22.25. Pbs: 60m 7.17i '17, 100m 11.18/11.04w '16, 300m 37.90i '13, 400m 53.63 '15. LJ 5.95 '15.

Jeneva STEVENS b. 28 Oct 1989 Dolton, Illinois 1.78m 102kg. née McCall. Was at Southern Illinois University.
At HT: WCh: '11- dnq 14, '13- 9; WUG: '13- 1. At SP: WCh: '15- 10; PAm: '15- 6; WI: '14- 8. Won NCAA DT 2010, HT 2012.
Progress at SP, HT: 2009- 15.22, 55.83; 2010- 17.25i/16.54, 64.17; 2011- 17.22i/16.96, 69.55; 2012- 17.97i/17.89, 69.38; 2013- 19.10i/18.47, 74.77; 2014- 18.45i/17.86, 70.78; 2015- 18.84, 72.69; 2016- 19.11, 71.10. Pbs: DT 59.45 '12, Wt 23.94i '13.
Daughter of 1994-5 WBC world heavyweight boxing champion Oliver McCall.

Jasmin STOWERS b. 23 Sep 1991 Pendleton, SC 1.75m 64kg. Degree in nutrition from Louisiana State University.
At 100mh: WY: '07- 4; won NCAA indoor 60mh 2013, US 2015. World best 4x100mh 2015.
Progress at 100mh: 2005- 14.27w, 2006- 14.05/13.82Aw, 2007- 13.69/13.68w, 2008- 13.66/13.46w, 2009- 13.59/13.32Aw, 2010- 14.47, 2011- 12.88/12.86w, 2012- 12.92, 2013- 13.00/12.88w, 2014- 12.71 12.54w, 2015- 12.35, 2016- 12.55. pbs: 60m 7.51i '12, 100m 11.82 '11, 60mh 7.82Ai '17, 7.84i '15; 400mh 61.17 '08.

Jennifer SUHR b. 6 Feb 1982 Fredonia, New York 1.80m 64kg. adidas. née Stuczynski. Graduate of Roberts Wesleyan University, now studying child psychology.
At PV: OG: '08- 2, '12- 1, '16- 7=; WCh: '07-11-13-15: 10/4/2/4=; PAm: '15- 3; WI: '08-14-16: 2/5=/1; WCp: '06- nh; US champion 2006-10, 2012-16; indoors 2005, 2007-09, 2011-13.
Records: world indoors 2013 & 2016, four North American pole vault records 2007-08, four indoors 2009-13.
Progress at PV: 2002- 2.75, 2004- 3.49, 2005- 4.57i/4.26, 2006- 4.68i/4.66, 2007- 4.88, 2008- 4.92, 2009- 4.83i/4.81, 2010- 4.89, 2011- 4.91, 2012- 4.88i/4.81, 2013- 5.02Ai/4.91, 2014- 4.73i/4.71, 2015- 4.82, 2016- 5.03i/4.82. pbs: 55m 8.07i '05, JT 46.82 '05.
All-time top scorer at basketball at her university, then very rapid progress at vaulting.

Cassandra TATE b. 11 Sep 1990 Hammond, Louisiana 1.74m 64kg. Management graduate of Louisiana State University.
At 400m/4x400m: WI: '14- 1R. At 400mh: WCh: '15- 3; won DL 2016, NCAA & NACAC 2012.
Progress at 400mh: 2010- 56.87, 2011- 55.99, 2012- 55.22, 2013- 55.45, 2014- 54.70, 2015- 54.01, 2016- 54.47. pbs: 60m 7.49i '11, 100m 11.79 '08, 11.47w '10; 200m 23.37i '10, 23.68 '09; 400m 52.40Ai '14, 52.51 '15; 60mh 8.61i '09, 100mh 14.21 '08, 14.08w '07. Engaged to David Verburg (qv).

Ariana WASHINGTON b. 4 Sep 1996 Signal Hill, California 1.75m 59kg. Student at University of Oregon.
At 100/(200m): WJ: '14- 7/1R; WY: '13- 2/3. Won NCAA 100m & 200m 2016.
Progress at 100m, 200m: 2010- 12.78/12.55w, 25.176; 2011- 12.07, 24.01; 2012- 11.47, 23.41; 2013- 11.39/11.18Aw, 23.18/23.05Aw; 2014- 11.22, 22.96; 2015- 23.07i; 2016- 11.01/10.95w, 22.21; 2017- 22.42i. pbs: 60m 7.20i '17, HJ 1.57 '11, LJ 5.79 '11.

Kaylin WHITNEY b. 9 Mar 1998 Kissimmee, Florida 1.67m 57kg. Nike.
At (100m)/200m: WJ: '14- 3/1/1R; PAm: '15- 1/1R. World youth records 100m 2014, 200m (3) 2014-15
Progress at 100m, 200m: 2012- 11.91, 2013- 11.54/11.47Aw, 23.40/23.28Aw; 2014- 11.10, 22.49; 2015- 11.37/11.01w, 22.47; 2016- 11.17/11.15w, 22.84.

Charonda WILLIAMS b. 27 Mar 1987 Richmond, California 1.67m 55kg. adidas. Was at Arizona State University.
At 200m: WCh: '09- sf, '13- 6. Won DL 2012.
Progress at 200m: 2006- 24.19/24.08w, 2007- 23.53, 2008- 23.09, 2009- 22.55/22.39w, 2010- 22.97, 2011- 22.85/22.78w, 2012- 22.52, 2013- 22.71, 2014- 23.41, 2015- 22.32, 2016- 23.44/23.08w. pbs: 55m 6.99Ai '08, 60m 7.29Ai '09, 7.36i '11; 100m 11.07 '13, 10.95w '12; 300m 37.04i '11, 400m 52.71 '11, LJ 5.91 '07, 6.03w '00.

Kendell WILLIAMS b. 14 Jun 1995 Marietta 1.73m 64kg. Student at University of Georgia.
At Hep: OG: '16- 17; WJ: '12- 8; WY: '11- 11; won NCAA 2016. At Pen: WI: '16- 6. At 100mh: WJ: '14- 1; WY: '11- 3.
Progress at Hep: 2011- 5169, 2012- 5578, 2014- 5572A, 2014- 6018, 2015- 6223, 2016- 6402. pbs: 200m 23.67 '16, 800m 2:15.31 '16, 60mh 8.34i '17, 100mh 12.83 '16, 400mh 58.63 '10, HJ 1.88Ai '14, 1.84 '16; LJ 6.54i/6.46 '15, SP 13.55i/12.95 '16, JT 42.21 '16, Pen 4703i '16.
Her brother Devon (b. 17 Dec 1994) had decathlon pb 8116 '16.

Tiffany WILLIAMS b. 5 Feb 1983 Miami 1.58m 57kg. née Ross. Reebok. Retail management graduate of University of Southern Carolina.
At 400mh: OG: '08- 8; WCh: '07- 7, '09- 5; WJ: '02- 4/1R; WI: '06- 2R. Won NACAC 2015, US 2007-08.

Progress at 400mh: 2000- 58.50, 2001- 57.91, 2002- 55.22, 2003- 55.89, 2005- 54.56, 2006- 53.79, 2007- 53.28, 2008- 53.54, 2009- 53.83, 2011- 55.77, 2012- 55.01, 2013- 55.04, 2014- 54.74, 2015- 54.27, 2016- 56.06. pbs: 200m 24.40 '08, 24.35i '06; 300m 37.36 '12, 400m 52.43i '05, 52.45 '06; 55mh 7.63i '03, 60mh 8.29i '05, 100mh 12.99 '05, 12.8 '08; TJ 12.49.
Married to Steven Williams, they have a daughter, Samya, born in 2004.

Ajee' WILSON b. 8 May 1994 Neptune, New Jersey 1.69m 55kg. adidas. Student of kinesiology at Temple University, Philadelphia.
At 800m: OG: '16- sf; WCh: '13- 5; WJ: '10- 5, '12- 1; WY: 11- 1; CCp: '14- 2; WI: '16- 2; won US 2014, indoor 2013-14, 2016.
Records: WR distance medley 2015, North American 4x800m 2014, world junior 600m & North American junior 800m 2013.
Progress at 800m: 2008- 2:11.43, 2009- 2:07.08, 2010- 2:04.18, 2011- 2:02.64, 2012- 2:00.91, 2013- 1:58.21, 2014- 1:57.67, 2015- 1:57.87, 2016- 1:59.44, 2017- 1:58.27i. pbs: 400m 53.63 '14, 500m 1:10.27i '15, 600m 1:23.84Ai/1:25.23 '17, 1000m 2:42.71i '16, 1500m 4:12.10 '14, 1M 4:33.57 '16, 3000m 10:13.41 '07.
Elder sister Jade has 400mh pb 59.90 '12.

Kara WINGER b. 10 Apr 1986 Seattle 1.83m 84kg. née Patterson. Studied interior design at Purdue University.
At JT: OG: '08/12/16- dnq 40/31/13; WCh: '09/11/15- dnq 29/21/8; PAm: '15- 2; PAm-J: '05- 2; CCp: '10- 6, '14- 7. Won NACAC 2015, US 2008-11, 2014-15.
North American javelin record 2010.
Progress at JT: 2003- 44.75, 2004- 48.51. 2005- 52.09, 2006- 56.19, 2008- 61.56, 2009- 63.95, 2010- 66.67, 2011- 62.76, 2012- 60.49, 2013- 57.12, 2014- 62.90, 2015- 66.47, 2016- 61.86. Pb DT 35.17 '11.
Married Russ Winger (SP 21.29i '08, 21.25 '10; DT 66.04 '11, dnq 26 WCh 15) on 28 Sep 2014.

UZBEKISTAN

Governing body: Athletic Federation of Uzbekistan, Navoi str. 30, 100129 Tashkent.

Svetlana RADZIVIL b. 17 Jan 1987 Tashkent 1.84m 61kg
At HJ: OG: '08- dnq 17, '12- 7, '16- 13=; WCh: '09- dnq 21=, '11- 8=, '15- 9=; AsiG: '06-10-14: 7/1/1; AsiC: '09-11-13-15: 3/2/2/1; WJ: '02- dnq, '04- 13, '06- 1; WY: '03- dnq; CCp: '14- 4; WI: '12- 8. Won Asi-J 2006, Asian indoor 2014, 2016.
Progress at HJ: 2002- 1.84, 2003- 1.78, 2004- 1.88, 2005- 1.85, 2006- 1.91, 2007- 1.91, 2008- 1.93, 2009- 1.91, 2010- 1.95, 2011- 1.95, 2012- 1.97, 2013- 1.94, 2014- 1.96, 2015- 1.94, 2016- 1.95.

VENEZUELA

Governing body: Federación Venezolana de Atletismo, Apartado Postal 29059, Caracas. Founded 1948.

National Champions 2016: Men 100m: Yeiker Mendoza 10.55, 200m: Rafael Vásquez 21.22, 400m: Freddy Mezones 45.55, 800m: Sixto León 1:51.57, 1500m: *not held*, 3000m: Whinton Palma 8:25.82, 3000mSt: Jordan Camejo 9:12.58, 110mh: Geormis Jaramillo 14.34, 400mh: Wilson Bello 51.17, HJ: Eure Yáñez 2.20, PV: José Milanesse 4.20, LJ: Héctor Germaya 7.01, TJ: Leodan Torrealba 15.60, SP: Yosner Ortiz 17.80, DT: Carlos Herrera 45.30, HT: Prinston Quailey 56.70, JT: Billy Julio 62.25, Dec: Gerson Izaguirre 7071, 20000mW: Yerenman Salazar 1:29:29.1.
Women: 100m: Nelsibeth Villalobos 11.4h, 200m: Emilet Pirela 24.91, 400m: Maryury Valdez 55.03, 800m: Ydanis Navas 2:13.53, 1500m *not held*, 3000m: Nubia Arteaga 10:27.46, 3000mSt: Wilyeska Suárez 11:42.24, 100mh: Nelsibeth Villalobos 14.21, 400mh: Magdalena Mendoza 61.09, HJ: Thaylor Vergara 1.70, PV: Carmen Villanueva 3.70 LJ: Aries Sánchez 6.08, TJ: Keidy Morles 12.33w, SP: Yohana Vargas 14.04, DT: Elizabeth Álvarez 45.84, HT: Adriana Pérez 50.70, JT: Estefany Chacón 53.20, Hep: Luisaris Toledo 5291, 20000mW: Milánggela Rosales 1:47:57.5.

Women

Rosa RODRÍGUEZ b. 2 Jul 1986 Acarigua, Portuguesa 1.80m 85kg. Zheus.
At HT: OG: '12- dnq 24, '16- 10; WCh: '07-09-13: dnq 34/29/15, '15- 11; WJ: '04- dnq; WY: '03- 13; PAm: '11- 8, '15- 1; SACh: '05-09-11-13-15: 3/4/3/1/1; Won IbAm 2012, SAm-U23 2008; VEN 2005, 2007-08, 2010-11.
Six Venezuelan hammer records 2006-13.
Progress at HT: 2002- 53.75, 2003- 56.23, 2004- 59.24, 2005- 62.85, 2006- 64.22, 2007- 66.96, 2008- 65.96, 2009- 69.46, 2010- 69.10, 2011- 67.90, 2012- 72.83, 2013- 73.64, 2014- 72.20, 2015- 73.06, 2016- 72.41. pb SP 15.07 '11.

Yulimar ROJAS b. 21 Oct 1995 Caracas 1.89m 75kg. FC Barcelona, Spain.
At TJ (LJ): OG: '16- 2; WJ: '14- dnq 17 (11); PAm: '15- 4 (11); SACh: '15- 1; WI: '16- 1. Won SAu23 LJ & TJ 2014, SAmJ HJ 2011.
Venezuelan records: LJ 2015, TJ (5) 2015-16. Four South American indoor TJ records 2016-17.
Progress at TJ: 2014- 13.65, 2015- 14.20, 2016- 15.02, 2017- 14.79i. Pbs: 100m 11.94 '13, HJ 1.87 '13, LJ 6.57 '15.
Lives in Guadalajara, Spain and coached by Iván Pedroso. First woman to win an Olympic medal for Venezuela.

INTRODUCTION TO WORLD LISTS AND INDEX

Records
World, World U20 and U18, Olympic, Area and Continental records are listed for standard events. In running events up to and including 400 metres, only fully automatic times are shown. Marks listed are those which are considered statistically acceptable by the ATFS, and thus may differ from official records. These are followed by 'odd events', road bests and bests by over 35/40 masters.

World All-time and Year Lists
Lists are presented in the following format: Mark, Wind reading (where appropriate), Name, Nationality (abbreviated), Date of birth, Position in competition, Meeting name (if significant), Venue, Date of performance.

In standard events the best 30 or so performances are listed followed by the best marks for other athletes. Position, meet and venue details have been omitted beyond 100th in year lists.

In the all-time lists performances which have been world records (or world bests, thus including some unratified marks) are shown with WR against them (or WIR for world indoor records).

Juniors (U20) are shown with-J after date of birth, and Youths (U18) with -Y.

Indexes
These contain the names of all athletes ranked with full details in the world year lists for standard events (and others such as half marathon). The format of the index is as follows:

Family name, First name, Nationality, Birthdate, Height (cm) and Weight (kg), 2016 best mark, Lifetime best (with year) as at the end of 2016.

* indicates an athlete who is profiled in the Biographies section, and ^ one who has been profiled in previous editions.

General Notes
Altitude aid
Marks set at an altitude of 1000m or higher have been suffixed by the letter "A" in events where altitude may be of significance.

Although there are no separate world records for altitude assisted events, it is understood by experts that in all events up to 400m in length (with the possible exclusion of the 110m hurdles), and in the horizontal jumps, altitude gives a material benefit to performances. For events beyond 800m, however, the thinner air of high altitude has a detrimental effect.

Supplementary lists are included in relevant events for athletes with seasonal bests at altitude who have low altitude marks qualifying for the main list.

Some leading venues over 1000m
Addis Ababa ETH	2365m
Air Force Academy USA	2194
Albuquerque USA	1555
Antananarivo MAD	1350
Ávila ESP	1128
Bloemfontein RSA	1392
Bogotá COL	2644
Boulder USA	1655
Bozeman USA	1467
Calgary CAN	1045
Cali COL	1046
Ciudad de Guatemala GUA	1402
Ciudad de México MEX	2247
Cochabamba BOL	2558
Colorado Springs USA	1823
Cuenca ECU	2561
Denver USA	1609
El Paso USA	1187
Flagstaff USA	2107
Fort Collins USA	1521
Gabarone BOT	1006
Germiston RSA	1661
Guadalajara MEX	1567
Harare ZIM	1473
Johannesburg RSA	1748
Kampala UGA	1189
Krugersdorp RSA	1740
La Paz BOL	3630
Levelland USA	1069
Logan USA	1372
Medellín COL	1541
Monachil ESP	2302
Nairobi KEN	1675
Orem USA	1455
Pietersburg RSA	1230
Pocatello USA	1361
Potchefstroom RSA	1351
Pretoria RSA	1400
Provo USA	1380
Pueblo USA	1487
Reno USA	1369
Roodepoort RSA	1623
Rustenburg RSA	1215
Salt Lake City USA	1321
San José CRC	1200
Sasolberg RSA	1488
Secunda RSA	1628
Sestriere ITA	2050
Soría ESP	1056
South Lake Tahoe USA	1909
Sucre BOL	2750
Toluca MEX	2680
Windhoek NAM	1725
Xalapa MEX	1356

Some others over 500m
Albertville FRA	550
Almaty KZK	847
Ankara TUR	902
Bangalore, IND	949
Bern SUI	555
Blacksburg USA	634
Boise USA	818
Canberra AUS	581

La Chaux de Fonds SUI	997
Caracas VEN	922
Edmonton CAN	652
Jablonec CZE	598
Las Vegas USA	619
Lausanne SUI	597
Lubbock USA	981
Madrid ESP	640
Magglingen SUI	751
Malles ITA	980
Moscow, Idaho USA	787
München GER	520
Nampa, Idaho USA	760
Salamanca ESP	806
Santiago de Chile CHI	520
São Paulo BRA	725
Sofia BUL	564
Spokane USA	576
Trípoli GRE	655
Tucson USA	728
Uberlândia BRA	852
350m–500m	
Banská Bystrica SVK	362
Fayetteville USA	407
Genève SUI	385
Götzis AUT	448
Johnson City USA	499
Rieti ITA	402
Sindelfingen GER	440
Stuttgart GER	415
Tashkent UZB	477
Zürich SUI	410

Automatic timing
In the main lists for sprints and hurdles, only times recorded by fully automatic timing devices are included.

Hand timing
In the sprints and hurdles supplementary lists are included for races which are hand timed. Athletes with a hand timed best 0.01 seconds or more better than his or her automatically timed best has been included, but hand timed lists have been terminated close to the differential levels considered by the IAAF to be equivalent to automatic times, i.e. 0.24 sec. for 100m, 200m, 100mh, 110mh, and 0.14 sec. for 400m and 400mh. It should be noted that this effectively recognises bad hand timekeeping, for there should be no material difference between hand and auto times, but badly trained timekeepers anticipate the finish, having reacted to the flash at the start.

In events beyond 400m, auto times are integrated with hand timed marks, the latter identifiable by times being shown to tenths. All-time lists also include some auto times in tenths of a second, identified with '.

Indoor marks
Indoor marks are included in the main lists for field events and straightway track events, but not for other track events as track sizes vary in circumference (200m is the international standard) and banking, while outdoor tracks are standardised at 400m. Outdoor marks for athletes with indoor bests are shown in a supplemental list.

Mixed races
For record purposes athletes may not, except in road races, compete in mixed sex races. Statistically there would not appear to be any particular logic in this, and women's marks set in such races are shown in our lists – annotated with mx. In such cases the athlete's best mark in single sex competition is appended.

Field event series
Field event series are given (where known) for marks in the top 30 performances lists.

Tracks and Courses
As well as climatic conditions, the type and composition of tracks and runways will affect standards of performance, as will the variations in road race courses.

Wind assistance
Anemometer readings have been shown for sprints and horizontal jumps in metres per second to one decimal place. If the figure was given to two decimal places, it has been rounded to the next tenth upwards, e.g. a wind reading of +2.01m/s, beyond the IAAF legal limit of 2.0, is rounded to +2.1; or -1.22m/s is rounded up to -1.2.

Drugs bans
The IAAF Council may decertify an athlete's records, titles and results if he or she is found to have used a banned substance before those performances. Performances at or after such a positive finding are shown in footnotes. Such athletes are shown with ¶ after their name in year lists, and in all-time lists if at any stage of their career they have served a drugs suspension of a year or more (thus not including athletes receiving public warnings or 3 month bans for stimulants etc., which for that year only are indicated with a #). This should not be taken as implying that the athlete was using drugs at that time. Nor have those athletes who have subsequently unofficially admitted to using banned substances been indicated; the ¶ is used only for those who have been caught.

Venues
Place names occasionally change. Our policy is to use names in force at the time that the performance was set. Thus Leningrad prior to 1991, Sankt-Peterburg from its re-naming.

Amendments
Keen observers may spot errors in the lists. They are invited to send corrections as well as news and results for 2017.

Peter Matthews
Email p.matthews121@btinternet.com

WORLD & CONTINENTAL RECORDS

As at 1 April 2015. **Key**: W = World, Afr = Africa, Asi = Asia, CAC = Central America & Caribbean, Eur = Europe, NAm = North America, Oce = Oceania, SAm = South America, Com = Commonwealth, W20 = World Junior (U20), W18 = World Youth (U18, not officially ratified by IAAF). h hand timed.
Successive columns show: World or Continent, performance, name, nationality, venue, date.
A altitude over 1000m, + timing by photo-electric-cell, # awaiting ratification, § not officially ratified

100 METRES

W,CAC,Com	9.58	Usain BOLT	JAM	Berlin	16 Aug 2009
NAm	9.69	Tyson GAY	USA	Shanghai	20 Sep 2009
Afr	9.85	Olusoji FASUBA	NGR	Doha	12 May 2006
Eur	9.86	Francis OBIKWELU	POR	Athína	22 Aug 2004
	9.86	Jimmy VICAUT	FRA	Saint-Denis	4 Jul 2015
	9.86	Jimmy VICAUT	FRA	Montreuil-sous-Bois	7 Jun 2016
Asi	9.91	Femi Seun OGUNODE	QAT	Wuhan 4 Jun 15 & Gainesville	22 Apr 2016
Oce	9.93	Patrick JOHNSON	AUS	Mito	5 May 2003
SAm	10.00A	Róbson da SILVA	BRA	Ciudad de México	22 Jul 1988
W20	9.97	Trayvon BROMELL	USA	Eugene	13 Jun 2014
W18	10.19	Yoshihide KIRYU	JPN	Fukuroi	3 Nov 2012

200 METRES

W,CAC,Com	19.19	Usain BOLT	JAM	Berlin	20 Aug 2009
NAm	19.32	Michael JOHNSON	USA	Atlanta	1 Aug 1996
Afr	19.68	Frank FREDERICKS	NAM	Atlanta	1 Aug 1996
Eur	19.72A	Pietro MENNEA	ITA	Ciudad de México	12 Sep 1979
SAm	19.81	Alonso EDWARD	PAN	Berlin	20 Aug 2009
Asi	19.97	Femi Seun OGUNODE	QAT	Bruxelles	11 Sep 2015
Oce	20.06A	Peter NORMAN	AUS	Ciudad de México	16 Oct 1968
W20	19.93	Usain BOLT	JAM	Hamilton, BER	11 Apr 2004
W18	20.13	Usain BOLT	JAM	Bridgetown	20 Jul 2003

400 METRES

W, Afr, Com	43.03	Wayde van NIEKERK	RSA	Rio de Janeiro	14 Aug 16
NAm	43.18	Michael JOHNSON	USA	Sevilla	26 Aug 1999
CAC	43.74	Kirani JAMES	GRN	Lausanne	3 Jul 2014
Asi	43.93	Yousef Ahmed AL-MASRAHI	KSA	Beijing	23 Aug 2015
SAm	44.29	Sanderlei PARRELA	BRA	Sevilla	26 Aug 1999
Eur	44.33	Thomas SCHÖNLEBE	GER	Roma	3 Sep 1987
Oce	44.38	Darren CLARK	AUS	Seoul	26 Sep 1988
W20	43.87	Steve LEWIS	USA	Seoul	28 Sep 1988
W18	45.14	Obea MOORE	USA	Santiago de Chile	2 Sep 1995

800 METRES

W, Afr, Com	1:40.91	David RUDISHA	KEN	London (OS)	9 Aug 2012
Eur	1:41.11	Wilson KIPKETER	DEN	Köln	24 Aug 1997
SAm	1:41.77	Joaquim CRUZ	BRA	Köln	26 Aug 1984
NAm	1:42.60	Johnny GRAY	USA	Koblenz	28 Aug 1985
Asi	1:42.79	Youssef Saad KAMEL	BRN	Monaco	29 Jul 2008
CAC	1:42.85	Norberto TELLEZ	CUB	Atlanta	31 Jul 1996
Oce	1:44.3+ h	Peter SNELL	NZL	Christchurch	3 Feb 1962
W20	1:41.73	Nijel AMOS	BOT	London (OS)	9 Aug 2012
W18	1:43.37	Mohamed AMAN	ETH	Rieti	10 Sep 2011

1000 METRES

W, Afr, Com	2:11.96	Noah NGENY	KEN	Rieti	5 Sep 1999
Eur	2:12.18	Sebastian COE	GBR	Oslo	11 Jul 1981
NAm	2:13.9	Rick WOHLHUTER	USA	Oslo	30 Jul 1974
SAm	2:14.09	Joaquim CRUZ	BRA	Nice	20 Aug 1984
Asi	2:14.72	Youssef Saad KAMEL	BRN	Stockholm	22 Jul 2008
Oce	2:16.09	Jeff RISELEY	AUS	Ostrava	17 Jun 2014
CAC	2:17.0	Byron DYCE	JAM	København	15 Aug 1973
W20	2:13.93 §	Abubaker KAKI	SUD	Stockholm	22 Jul 2008
W18	2:17.44	Hamza DRIOUCH	QAT	Sollentuna	9 Aug 2011

1500 METRES

W, Afr	3:26.00	Hicham EL GUERROUJ	MAR	Roma	14 Jul 1998
Com	3:26.34	Bernard LAGAT	KEN	Bruxelles	24 Aug 2001
Eur	3:28.81	Mo FARAH	GBR	Monaco	19 Jul 2013
Asi	3:29.14	Rashid RAMZI	BRN	Roma	14 Jul 2006

NAm	3:29.30	Bernard LAGAT	USA	Rieti	28 Aug 2005
Oce	3:29.26	Nick WILLIS	NZL	Monaco	17 Jul 2015
SAm	3:33.25	Hudson Santos de SOUZA	BRA	Rieti	28 Aug 2005
CAC	3:35.03	Maurys CASTILLO	CUB	Huelva	7 Jun 2012
W20	3:28.81	Ronald KWEMOI	KEN	Monaco	18 Jul 2014
W18	3:33.72	Nicholas KEMBOI	KEN	Zürich	18 Aug 2006

1 MILE

W, Afr	3:43.13	Hicham El GUERROUJ	MAR	Roma	7 Jul 1999
Com	3:43.40	Noah NGENY	KEN	Roma	7 Jul 1999
Eur	3:46.32	Steve CRAM	GBR	Oslo	27 Jul 1985
NAm	3:46.91	Alan WEBB	USA	Brasschaat	21 Jul 2007
Asi	3:47.97	Daham Najim BASHIR	QAT	Oslo	29 Jul 2005
Oce	3:48.98	Craig MOTTRAM	AUS	Oslo	29 Jul 2005
SAm	3:51.05	Hudson de SOUZA	BRA	Oslo	29 Jul 2005
CAC	3:57.34	Byron DYCE	JAM	Stockholm	1 Jul 1974
	3:57.34	Juan Luis BARRIOS	MEX	Dublin	17 Jul 2013
W20	3:49.29	William Biwott TANUI (now ÖZBILEN)	KEN	Oslo	3 Jul 2009
W18	3:54.56	Isaac SONGOK	KEN	Linz	20 Aug 2001

2000 METRES

W, Afr	4:44.79	Hicham EL GUERROUJ	MAR	Berlin	7 Sep 1999
Com	4:48.74	John KIBOWEN	KEN	Hechtel	1 Aug 1998
Oce	4:50.76	Craig MOTTRAM	AUS	Melbourne	9 Mar 2006
Eur	4:51.39	Steve CRAM	GBR	Budapest	4 Aug 1985
NAm	4:52.44	Jim SPIVEY	USA	Lausanne	15 Sep 1987
Asi	4:55.57	Mohammed SULEIMAN	QAT	Roma	8 Jun 1995
SAm	5:03.34	Hudson Santos de SOUZA	BRA	Manaus	6 Apr 2002
CAC	5:03.4	Arturo BARRIOS	MEX	Nice	10 Jul 1989
W20	4:56.25	Tesfaye CHERU	ETH	Reims	5 Jul 2011
W18	4:56.86	Isaac SONGOK	KEN	Berlin	31 Aug 2001

3000 METRES

W, Afr, Com	7:20.67	Daniel KOMEN	KEN	Rieti	1 Sep 1996
Eur	7:26.62	Mohammed MOURHIT	BEL	Monaco	18 Aug 2000
NAm	7:29.00	Bernard LAGAT	USA	Rieti	29 Aug 2010
Asi	7:30.76	Jamal Bilal SALEM	QAT	Doha	13 May 2005
Oce	7:32.19	Craig MOTTRAM	AUS	Athína	17 Sep 2006
CAC	7:35.71	Arturo BARRIOS	MEX	Nice	10 Jul 1989
SAm	7:39.70	Hudson Santos de SOUZA	BRA	Lausanne	2 Jul 2002
W20	7:28.19	Yomif KEJELCHA	ETH	Saint-Denis	27 Aug 2016
W18	7:32.37	Abreham CHERKOS Feleke	ETH	Lausanne	11 Jul 2006

5000 METRES

W, Afr	12:37.35	Kenenisa BEKELE	ETH	Hengelo	31 May 2004
Com	12:39.74	Daniel KOMEN	KEN	Bruxelles	22 Aug 1997
Eur	12:49.71	Mohammed MOURHIT	BEL	Bruxelles	25 Aug 2000
Asi	12:51.96	Albert ROP	BRN	Monaco	19 Jul 2013
NAm	12:53.60	Bernard LAGAT	USA	Monaco	22 Jul 2011
Oce	12:55.76	Craig MOTTRAM	AUS	London	30 Jul 2004
CAC	13:07.79	Arturo BARRIOS	MEX	London (CP)	14 Jul 1989
SAm	13:19.43	Marilson dos SANTOS	BRA	Kassel	8 Jun 2006
W20	12:47.53	Hagos GEBRHIWET	ETH	Saint-Denis	6 Jul 2012
W18	12:54.19	Abreham CHERKOS Feleke	ETH	Roma	14 Jul 2006

10,000 METRES

W, Afr	26:17.53	Kenenisa BEKELE	ETH	Bruxelles	26 Aug 2005
Com	26:27.85	Paul TERGAT	KEN	Bruxelles	22 Aug 1997
Asi	26:38.76	Abdullah Ahmad HASSAN	QAT	Bruxelles	5 Sep 2003
NAm	26:44.36	Galen RUPP	USA	Eugene	30 May 2014
Eur	26:46.57	Mohamed FARAH	GBR	Eugene	3 Jun 2011
CAC	27:08.23	Arturo BARRIOS	MEX	Berlin	18 Aug 1989
Oce	27:24.95	Ben ST LAWRENCE	AUS	Stanford	1 May 2011
SAm	27:28.12	Marilson dos SANTOS	BRA	Neerpelt	2 Jun 2007
W20	26:41.75	Samuel WANJIRU	KEN	Bruxelles	26 Aug 2005
W18	27:02.81	Ibrahim JAYLAN Gashu	ETH	Bruxelles	25 Aug 2006

HALF MARATHON

W, Afr	58:23	Zersenay TADESE	ERI	Lisboa	21 Mar 2010
Com	58:33	Samuel WANJIRU	KEN	Den Haag	17 Mar 2007
Eur	59:32	Mohamed FARAH	GBR	Lisboa	21 Mar 2015

WORLD AND CONTINENTAL RECORDS 235

SAm	59:33	Marilson dos SANTOS	BRA	Udine	14 Oct 2007
NAm	59:43	Ryan HALL	USA	Houston	14 Jan 2007
Oce	59:47	Zane ROBERTSON	NZL	Marugame	1 Feb 2015
CAC	60:14	Armando QUINTANILLA	MEX	Tokyo	21 Jan 1996
Asi	60:25	Atsushi SATO	JPN	Udine	14 Oct 2007
W20	59:16	Samuel WANJIRU	KEN	Rotterdam	11 Sep 2005
W18	60:38	Faustin BAHA Sulle	TAN	Lille	4 Sep 1999

MARATHON

W, Afr, Com	2:02:57	Dennis KIMETTO	KEN	Berlin	28 Sep 2014
NAm	2:05:38	Khalid KHANNOUCHI (ex MAR)	USA	London	14 Apr 2002
SAm	2:06:05	Ronaldo da COSTA	BRA	Berlin	20 Sep 1998
Asi	2:06:16	Toshinari TAKAOKA	JPN	Chicago	13 Oct 2002
Eur	2:06:36 §	António PINTO	POR	London	16 Apr 2000
	2:06:36	Benoît ZWIERZCHIEWSKI	FRA	Paris	6 Apr 2003
	2:06:10 §	Kaan Kigen ÖZBILEN	TUR	Seoul	20 Mar 2016
Oce	2:08:16	Steve MONEGHETTI	AUS	Berlin	30 Sep 1990
CAC	2:08:30	Dionicio CERÓN	MEX	London	2 Apr 1995
W20	2:04:32	Tsegaye MEKONNEN	ETH	Dubai	24 Jan 2014
W18	2:11:43	LI He	CHN	Beijing	14 Oct 2001

3000 METRES STEEPLECHASE

W, Asi	7:53.63	Saïf Saaeed SHAHEEN	QAT	Bruxelles	3 Sep 2004
Afr, Com	7:53.64	Brimin KIPRUTO	KEN	Monaco	22 Jul 2011
Eur	8:00.09	Mahiedine MEKHISSI-BENABBAD	FRA	Saint-Denis	6 Jul 2013
NAm	8:00.45	Evan JAGER	USA	Saimt-Denis	4 Jul 2015
Oce	8:14.05	Peter RENNER	NZL	Koblenz	29 Aug 1984
SAm	8:14.41	Wander MOURA	BRA	Mar del Plata	22 Mar 1995
CAC	8:25.69	Salvador MIRANDA	MEX	Barakaldo	9 Jul 2000
W20	7:58.66	Stephen CHERONO (now Shaheen)	KEN	Bruxelles	24 Aug 2001
W18	8:17.28 §	Jonathan NDIKU	KEN	Bydgoszcz	13 Jul 2008

110 METRES HURDLES

W, NAm	12.80	Aries MERRITT	USA	Bruxelles	7 Sep 2012
CAC	12.87	Dayron ROBLES	CUB	Ostrava	12 Jun 2008
Asi	12.88	LIU Xiang	CHN	Lausanne	11 Jul 2006
Eur, Com	12.91	Colin JACKSON	GBR/Wal	Stuttgart	20 Aug 1993
Afr	13.24	Lehann FOURIE	RSA	Bruxelles	7 Sep 2012
SAm	13.27A	Paulo César VILLAR	COL	Guadalajara	28 Oct 2011
Oce	13.29	Kyle VANDER-KUYP	AUS	Göteborg	11 Aug 1995
W20	13.12	LIU Xiang (with 3'6" hurdles)	CHN	Lausanne	2 Jul 2002
W20 99cm h	12.99	Wilhem BELOCIAN	FRA	Eugene	24 Jul 2014
W18	13.43	SHI Dongpeng	CHN	Shanghai	6 May 2001
W18 91cm h	12.96	Jaheel HYDE	JAM	Nanjing	23 Aug 2014

400 METRES HURDLES

W, NAm	46.78	Kevin YOUNG	USA	Barcelona	6 Aug 1992
Afr, Com	47.10	Samuel MATETE	ZAM	Zürich	7 Aug 1991
CAC	47.25	Felix SÁNCHEZ	DOM	Saint-Denis	29 Aug 2003
Eur	47.37	Stéphane DIAGANA	FRA	Lausanne	5 Jul 1995
Asi	47.53	Hadi Soua'an AL-SOMAILY	KSA	Sydney	27 Sep 2000
SAm	47.84	Bayano KAMANI	PAN	Helsinki	7 Aug 2005
Oce	48.28	Rohan ROBINSON	AUS	Atlanta	31 Jul 1996
W20	48.02	Danny HARRIS	USA	Los Angeles	17 Jun 1984
W18	48.89	L.J. VAN ZYL	RSA	Kingston	19 Jul 2002

HIGH JUMP

W, CAC	2.45	Javier SOTOMAYOR	CUB	Salamanca	27 Jul 1993
Asi	2.43	Mutaz Essa BARSHIM	QAT	Bruxelles	5 Sep 2014
Eur	2.42	Patrik SJÖBERG	SWE	Stockholm	30 Jun 1987
	2.42 i§	Carlo THRÄNHARDT	FRG	Berlin	26 Feb 1988
	2.42i	Ivan UKHOV	RUS	Praha	25 Feb 2014
	2.42	Bohdan BONDARENKO	UKR	New York	14 Jun 2014
NAm	2.40 i§	Holis CONWAY	USA	Sevilla	10 Mar 1991
	2.40	Charles AUSTIN	USA	Zürich	7 Aug 1991
NAm=, Com	2.40	Derek DROUIN	CAN	Des Moines	25 Apr 2014
Afr	2.38	Jacques FREITAG	RSA	Oudtshoorn	5 Mar 2005
Oce	2.36	Tim FORSYTH	AUS	Melbourne	2 Mar 1997
SAm	2.33	Gilmar MAYO	COL	Pereira	17 Oct 1994
W20	2.37	Dragutin TOPIC	YUG	Plovdiv	12 Aug 1990
		Steve SMITH	GBR	Seoul	20 Sep 1992
W18	2.33	Javier SOTOMAYOR	CUB	La Habana	19 May 1984

WORLD AND CONTINENTAL RECORDS

POLE VAULT

W, Eur	6.16 i	Renaud LAVILLENIE	FRA	Donetsk	15 Feb 2014
	6.14 A	Sergey BUBKA (best outdoor mark)	UKR	Sestriere	31 Jul 1994
Oce, Com	6.06i	Steve HOOKER	AUS	Boston (R)	7 Feb 2009
	6.05	Dmitriy MARKOV	AUS	Edmonton	9 Aug 2001
NAm	6.04	Brad WALKER	USA	Eugene	8 Jun 2008
Afr	6.03	Okkert BRITS	RSA	Köln	18 Aug 1995
Asi	5.92i	Igor POTAPOVICH	KAZ	Stockholm	19 Feb 1998
	5.90	Grigoriy YEGOROV	KAZ	Stuttgart	19 Aug 1993
	5.90	Grigoriy YEGOROV	KAZ	London (CP)	10 Sep 1993
	5.90	Igor POTAPOVICH	KAZ	Nice	10 Jul 1996
SAm	6.03	Thiago BRAZ da SILVA	BRA	Rio de Janeiro	15 Aug 2016
CAC	5.90	Lázaro BORGES	CUB	Daegu	29 Aug 2011
W20	5.82i	Armand DUPLANTIS	SWE	New York (Armory)	11 Mar 2017
	5.80	Maksim TARASOV	RUS	Bryansk	14 Jul 1989
	5.80	Raphael HOLZDEPPE	GER	Biberach	28 Jun 2008
W18	5.55	Emmanouil KARÁLIS	GRE	Ostrava	20 May 1206

LONG JUMP

W, NAm	8.95	Mike POWELL	USA	Tokyo	30 Aug 1991
Eur	8.86 A	Robert EMMIYAN	ARM	Tsakhkadzor	22 May 1987
SAm	8.73	Irving SALADINO	PAN	Hengelo	24 May 2008
CAC	8.71	Iván PEDROSO	CUB	Salamanca	18 Jul 1995
Com	8.62	James BECKFORD	JAM	Orlando	5 Apr 1997
Afr, Com	8.62A	Luva MANYONGA	RSA	Pretoria	17 Mar 2017
Oce	8.54	Mitchell WATT	AUS	Stockholm	29 Jul 2011
Asi	8.48	Mohamed Salim AL-KHUWALIDI	KSA	Sotteville	2 Jul 2006
W20	8.35	Sergey MORGUNOV	RUS	Cheboksary	20 Jun 2012
W18	8.28	Maykel D MASSÓ	CUB	La Habana	28 May 2016

TRIPLE JUMP

W, Eur, Com	18.29	Jonathan EDWARDS	GBR/Eng	Göteborg	7 Aug 1995
NAm	18.21	Christian TAYLOR	USA	Beijing	27 Aug 2015
CAC	18.08	Pedro Pablo PICHARDO	CUB	La Habana	28 May 2015
SAm	17.90	Jadel GREGÓRIO	BRA	Belém	20 May 2007
Asi	17.59	LI Yanxi	CHN	Jinan	26 Oct 2009
Oce	17.46	Ken LORRAWAY	AUS	London (CP)	7 Aug 1982
Afr	17.37	Tareq BOUGTAÏB	MAR	Khémisset	14 Jul 2007
W20	17.50	Volker MAI	GDR	Erfurt	23 Jun 1985
W18	17.24	Lazaro MARTÍNEZ	CUB	La Habana	1 Feb 2014

SHOT

W, NAm	23.12	Randy BARNES	USA	Los Angeles (Westwood)	20 May 1990
Eur	23.06	Ulf TIMMERMANN	GER	Haniá	22 May 1988
Com	22.21	Dylan ARMSTRONG	CAN	Calgary	25 Jun 2011
Oce, com =	22.21	Tom WALSH	NZL	Zagreb	5 Jun 2016
AfC	21.97	Janus ROBBERTS	RSA	Eugene	2 Jun 2001
CAC	21.69	O'Dayne RICHARDS	JAM	Beijing	23 Aug 2015
SAm	21.26	Germán LAURO	ARG	Doha	10 May 2013
Asi	21.13	Sultan Abdulmajeed AL-HEBSHI	KSA	Doha	8 May 2009
W20	21.14	Konrad BUKOWIECKI	POL	Oslo	9 Jun 2016
W18	20.38	Jacko GILL	NZL	Auckland (North Shore)	5 Dec 2011
W20 6kg	23.34	Konrad BUKOWIECKI	POL	Bydgoszcz	19 Jul 2016
W18 5kg	24.45	Jacko GILL	NZL	Auckland (North Shore)	19 Dec 2011

DISCUS

W, Eur	74.08	Jürgen SCHULT	GDR	Neubrandenburg	6 Jun 1986
NAm	72.34 ¶	Ben PLUCKNETT	USA	Stockholm	7 Jul 1981
	71.32 §	Ben PLUCKNETT	USA	Eugene	4 Jun 1983
CAC	71.06	Luis DELIS	CUB	La Habana	21 May 1983
Afr, Com	70.32	Frantz KRUGER	RSA	Salon-de-Provence	26 May 2002
Asi	69.32	Ehsan HADADI	IRI	Tallinn	3 Jun 2008
Oce	68.20	Benn HARRADINE	AUS	Townsville	10 May 2013
SAm	66.32	Jorge BALLIENGO	ARG	Rosario	15 Apr 2006
W20	65.62 §	Werner REITERER	AUS	Melbourne	15 Dec 1987
W18/20	65.31	Mykyta NESTERENKO	UKR	Tallinn	3 Jun 2008
W20 1.75kg	70.13	Mykyta NESTERENKO	UKR	Halle	24 May 2008
W18 1.5kg	77.50	Mykyta NESTERENKO	UKR	Koncha Zaspa	19 May 2008

¶ Disallowed by the IAAF following retrospective disqualification for drug abuse, but ratified by the AAU/TAC

WORLD AND CONTINENTAL RECORDS 237

HAMMER

W, Eur	86.74	Yuriy SEDYKH	UKR/RUS	Stuttgart	30 Aug 1986
Asi	84.86	Koji MUROFUSHI	JPN	Praha	29 Jun 2003
NAm	82.52	Lance DEAL	USA	Milano	7 Sep 1996
Afr	81.27	Mostafa Hicham AL-GAMAL	EGY	Al-Qáhira	21 Mar 2014
Com	80.63	Chris HARMSE	RSA	Durban	15 Apr 2005
Oce	79.29	Stuart RENDELL	AUS	Varazdin	6 Jul 2002
SAm	78.63	Wagner DOMINGOS	BRA	Celje	19 Jun 2016
CAC	78.02	Roberto JANET	CUB	La Habana	28 May 2015
W20	78.33	Olli-Pekka KARJALAINEN	FIN	Seinäjoki	5 Aug 1999
W18	73.66	Vladislav PISKUNOV	UKR	Kyiv	11 Jun 1994
W20 6kg	85.57	Ashraf Amgad EL-SEIFY	QAT	Barcelona	14 Jul 2012
W18 5kg	87.16	Bence HALÁSZ	HUN	Baku	31 May 2014

JAVELIN

W, Eur	98.48	Jan ZELEZNY	CZE	Jena	25 May 1996
Afr, Com	92.72	Julius YEGO	KEN	Beijing	26 Aug 2015
NAm	91.29	Breaux GREER	USA	Indianapolis	21 Jun 2007
CAC	90.16	Keshorn WALCOTT	TTO	Lausanne	9 Jul 2015
Asi	89.15	ZHAO Qinggang	CHN	Incheon	2 Oct 2014
Oce	89.02	Jarrod BANNISTER	AUS	Brisbane	29 Feb 2008
SAm	84.70	Edgar BAUMANN	PAR	San Marcos	17 Oct 1999
W20	86.48	Neeraj CHOPRA	IND	Bydgoszcz	23 Jul 2016
W18 700g	89.34	Braian Ezequiel TOLEDO	ARG	Mar del Plata	6 Mar 2010

DECATHLON

W, NAm	9045	Ashton EATON	USA	Beijing	29 Aug 2015
Eur	9026	Roman SEBRLE	CZE	Götzis	27 May 2001
Com	8847	Daley THOMPSON	GBR/Eng	Los Angeles	9 Aug 1984
Asi	8725	Dmitriy KARPOV	KAZ	Athína	24 Aug 2004
CAC	8654	Leonel SUÁREZ	CUB	La Habana	4 Jul 2009
Afr	8521	Larbi BOURAADA	ALG	Rio de Janeiro	18 Aug 2016
Oce	8490	Jagan HAMES	AUS	Kuala Lumpur	18 Sep 1998
SAm	8393	Carlos Eduardo CHININ	BRA	São Paulo	8 Jun 2013
W20	8397	Torsten VOSS (with 3'6" hurdles)	GDR	Erfurt	7 Jul 1982
W18	8104h	Valter KÜLVET	EST	Viimsi	23 Aug 1981
	7829	Valter KÜLVET	EST	Stockholm	13 Sep 1981

4 X 100 METRES RELAY

W, CAC, Com	36.84	JAM (Carter, M Frater, Blake, Bolt)		London (OS)	11 Aug 2012
NAm	37.38	USA (Demps, Patton, Kimmons, Gatlin)		London (OS)	10 Aug 2012
	37.38	USA (Rodgers, Gatlin, Gay, Bailey)		Nassau	2 May 2015
Asi	37.60	JPN (Yamagata, Iizuka, Kiryu, Cambridge)		Rio de Janeiro	19 Aug 2016
Eur	37.73	GBR (Gardener, Campbell, Devonish, Chambers)		Sevilla	29 Aug 1999
SAm	37.90	BRA (V Lima, Ribeiro, A da Silva, Cl da Silva)		Sydney	30 Sep 2000
Afr	37.94	NGR (O Ezinwa, Adeniken, Obikwelu, D Ezinwa)		Athína	9 Aug 1997
Oce	38.17	AUS (Henderson, Jackson, Brimacombe, Marsh)		Göteborg	12 Aug 1995
	38.17	AUS (Alozie, Ntiamoah, McCabe, Ross)		Ldon (OS)	10 Aug 2012
W20	38.66	USA (Kimmons, Omole, Williams, Merritt)		Grosseto	18 Jul 2004
W18	40.03	JAM (W Smith, M Frater, Spence, O Brown)		Bydgoszcz	18 Jul 1999

4 X 400 METRES RELAY

W, NAm	2:54.29	USA (Valmon, Watts, Reynolds, Johnson)		Stuttgart	22 Aug1993
Eur	2:56.60	GBR (Thomas, Baulch, Richardson, Black)		Atlanta	3 Aug 1996
CAC, Com	2:56.72	BAH (Brown, Pinder, Mathieu, Miller)		London (OS)	10 Aug 2012
SAm	2:58.56	BRA (C da Silva, A J dosSantos, de Araújo, Parrela)		Winnipeg	30 Jul 1999
Afr	2:58.68	NGR (Chukwu, Monye, Bada, Udo-Obong)		Sydney	30 Sep 2000
Oce	2:59.70	AUS (Frayne, Clark, Minihan, Mitchell)		Los Angeles	11 Aug 1984
Asi	3:00.76	JPN (Karube, K Ito, Osakada, Omori)		Atlanta	3 Aug 1996
W20	3:01.09	USA (Johnson, Merritt, Craig, Clement)		Grosseto	18 Jul 2004
W18	3:11.66A	TTO (Guevara, Cedenio, Walters, Lewis)		Morelia	1 Jul 2012

20 KILOMETRES WALK

W, Asi	1:16:36	Yusuke SUZUKI	JPN	Nomi	15 Mar 2015
Eur	1:17:02	Yohann DINIZ	FRA	Arles	8 Mar 2015
	1:16:43 §	Sergey MOROZOV	RUS	Saransk	8 Jun 2008
SAm	1:17:21	Jefferson PÉREZ	ECU	Saint-Denis	23 Aug 2003
CAC	1:17:25.6 t	Bernardo SEGURA	MEX	Bergen (Fana)	7 May 1994
Oce, Com	1:17:33	Nathan DEAKES	AUS	Cixi	23 Apr 2005
Afr	1:19:02	Hatem GHOULA	TUN	Eisenhüttenstadt	10 May 1997
NAm	1:19:20	Inaki GÓMEZ	CAN	Nomi	20 Mar 2016

238 WORLD AND CONTINENTAL RECORDS

W20	1:18:06 §	Viktor BURAYEV	RUS	Adler	4 Mar 2001
W18	1:18:07	LI Gaobo	CHN	Cixi	23 Apr 2005

20,000 METRES TRACK WALK

W, CAC	1:17:25.6	Bernardo SEGURA	MEX	Bergen (Fana)	7 May 1994
Asi	1:18:03.3	BU Lingtang	CHN	Beijing	7 Apr 1994
Eur	1:18:35.2	Stefan JOHANSSON	SWE	Bergen (Fana)	15 May 1992
Oce, Com	1:19:48.1	Nathan DEAKES	AUS	Brisbane	4 Sep 2001
SAm	1:20:23.8	Andrés CHOCHO	ECU	Buenos Aires	5 Jun 2011
NAm	1:21:57.0	Evan DUNFEE	CAN	Moncton	27 Jun 2014
Afr	1:22:51.84	Hatem GHOULA	TUN	Leutkirch	8 Sep 1994
W20	1:20:11.72	LI Gaobo	CHN	Wuhan	2 Nov 2007
W18	1:24:28.3	ZHU Hongjun	CHN	Xian	15 Sep 1999

50 KILOMETRES WALK

W, Eur	3:32:33	Yohann DINIZ	FRA	Zürich	15 Aug 2014
Oce, Com	3:35:47	Nathan DEAKES	AUS	Geelong	2 Dec 2006
Asi	3:36:06	YU Chaohong	CHN	Nanjing	22 Oct 2005
CAC	3:41:09	Erick BARRONDO	GUA	Dudince	23 Mar 2013
NAm	3:41:38	Evan DUNFEE	CAN	Rio de Janeiro	19 Aug 2016
SAm	3:42:57	Andrés CHOCHO	ECU	Ciudad Juárez	6 Mar 2016
Afr	3:54:12	Marc MUNDELL	RSA	Melbourne	13 Dec 2015
W20	3:41:10	ZHAO Jianguo	CHN	Wajima	16 Apr 2006
W18	3:45:46	YU Guoping	CHN	Guangzhou	23 Nov 2001

50,000 METRES TRACK WALK

W, Eur	3:35:27.2	Yoahnn DINIZ	FRA	Reims	12 Mar 2011
CAC	3:41:38.4	Raúl GONZÁLEZ	MEX	Bergen (Fana)	25 May 1979
Oce, Com	3:43:50.0	Simon BAKER	AUS	Melbourne	9 Sep 1990
Asi	3:48:13.7	ZHAO Yongshen	CHN	Bergen (Fana)	7 May 1994
NAm	3:52:21.0	Tim BERRETT	CAN	Victoria	29 Oct 2000
SAm	3:57:58.0	Claudio dos SANTOS	BRA	Blumenau	20 Sep 2008
Afr	4:21:44.5	Abdelwahab FERGUÈNE	ALG	Toulouse	25 Mar 1984

World Records at other men's events recognised by the IAAF

20,000m	56:25.98+	Haile GEBRSELASSIE	ETH	Ostrava	27 Jun 2007
1 Hour	21,285 m	Haile GEBRSELASSIE	ETH	Ostrava	27 Jun 2007
25,000m	1:12:25.4	Moses MOSOP	KEN	Eugene	3 Jun 2011
30,000m	1:26:47.4	Moses MOSOP	KEN	Eugene	3 Jun 2011
U18 Octathlon	6491	Jake STEIN	AUS	Villeneuve d'Ascq	7 Jul 2011
4 x 200m	1:18.63	National team	JAM	Nassau	24 May 2014
		(Nickel Ashmeade, Warren Weir, Jermaine Brown, Yohan Blake)			
4 x 800m	7:02.43	National Team	KEN	Bruxelles	25 Aug 2006
		(Joseph Mutua, William Yiampoy, Ismael Kombich, Wilfred Bungei)			
4 x 1500m	14:22.22	C Cheboi, A Kiplagat, Magut, A Kiprop	KEN	Nassau	25 May 2014
Distance Medley	9:15.50	Merber,Spratting,Johnson,Blankenship	USA	Nassau	3 May 2015
Walking					
2 Hours track	29,572m+	Maurizio DAMILANO	ITA	Cuneo	3 Oct 1992
30km track	2:01:44.1	Maurizio DAMILANO	ITA	Cuneo	3 Oct 1992
U20 10,000m track	38:46.4	Viktor BURAYEV	RUS	Moskva	20 May 2000
U20 10km road	37:44	WANG Zhen	CHN	Beijing	18 Sep 2010
W18 10km road	38:57	LI Tianlei	CHN	Beijing	18 Sep 2010

WOMEN

100 METRES

W, NAm	10.49	Florence GRIFFITH JOYNER	USA	Indianapolis	16 Jul 1988
CAC, Com	10.70	Shelly-Ann FRASER	JAM	Kingstobn	29 Jun 2012
	10.70	Elaine THOMPSON	JAM	Kingston	1 Jul 2016
Eur	10.73	Christine ARRON	FRA	Budapest	19 Aug 1998
Afr	10.79	Blessing OKAGBARE	NGR	London (OS)	27 Jul 2013
Asi	10.78	Murielle AHOURÉ	CIV	Montverde	11 Jun 2016
SAm	10.99	Angela TENORIO	ECU	Toronto	22 Jul 2015
Oce	11.11	Melissa BREEN	AUS	Canberra	9 Feb 2014
W20	10.88	Marlies OELSNER/GÖHR	GDR	Dresden	1 Jul 1977
W18	10.98	Candace HILL	USA	Shoreline	20 Jun 2015

200 METRES

W, NAm	21.34	Florence GRIFFITH JOYNER	USA	Seoul	29 Sep 1988
CAC, Com	21.64	Merlene OTTEY	JAM	Bruxelles	13 Sep 1991
Eur	21.63	Dafne SCHIPPERS	NED	Beijing	28 Aug 2015
Asi	22.01	LI Xuemei	CHN	Shanghai	22 Oct 1997

WORLD AND CONTINENTAL RECORDS

Afr	22.06 A§	Evette DE KLERK	RSA	Pietersburg	8 Apr 1989
	22.07	Mary ONYALI	NGR	Zürich	14 Aug 1996
Oce	22.23	Melinda GAINSFORD-TAYLOR	AUS	Stuttgart	13 Jul 1997
SAm	22.48	Ana Cláudia da SILVA	BRA	São Paulo	6 Aug 2011
W20	22.18	Allyson FELIX	USA	Athína	25 Aug 2004
	22.11A §	Allyson FELIX (no doping control)	USA	Ciudad de México	3 May 2003
W18	22.43A	Candace HILL	USA	Cali	19 Jul 2015

400 METRES

W, Eur	47.60	Marita KOCH	GDR	Canberra	6 Oct 1985
Oce, Com	48.63	Cathy FREEMAN	AUS	Atlanta	29 Jul 1996
NAm	48.70	Sanya RICHARDS	USA	Athína	16 Sep 2006
CAC	48.89	Ana GUEVARA	MEX	Saint-Denis	27 Aug 2003
Afr	49.10	Falilat OGUNKOYA	NGR	Atlanta	29 Jul 1996
SAm	49.64	Ximena RESTREPO	COL	Barcelona	5 Aug 1992
Asi	49.81	MA Yuqin	CHN	Beijing	11 Sep 1993
W20	49.42	Grit BREUER	GER	Tokyo	27 Aug 1991
W18	50.01	LI Jing	CHN	Shanghai	18 Oct 1997

800 METRES

W, Eur	1:53.28	Jarmila KRATOCHVÍLOVÁ	CZE	München	26 Jul 1983
Afr,W20,Com	1:54.01	Pamela JELIMO	KEN	Zürich	29 Aug 2008
CAC	1:54.44	Ana Fidelia QUIROT	CUB	Barcelona	9 Sep 1989
Asi	1:55.54	LIU Dong	CHN	Beijing	9 Sep 1993
NAm	1:56.40	Jearl MILES CLARK	USA	Zürich	11 Aug 1999
SAm	1:56.68	Letitia VRIESDE	SUR	Göteborg	13 Aug 1995
Oce	1:58.25	Toni HODGKINSON	NZL	Atlanta	27 Jul 1996
W18	1:57.18	WANG Yuan	CHN	Beijing	8 Sep 1993

1000 METRES

W, Eur	2:28.98	Svetlana MASTERKOVA	RUS	Bruxelles	23 Aug 1996
Afr	2:29.34	Maria Lurdes MUTOLA	MOZ	Bruxelles	25 Aug 1995
Com	2:29.66	Maria Lurdes MUTOLA	MOZ	Bruxelles	23 Aug 1996
NAm	2:31.80	Regina JACOBS	USA	Brunswick	3 Jul 1999
SAm	2:32.25	Letitia VRIESDE	SUR	Berlin	10 Sep 1991
CAC	2:33.21	Ana Fidelia QUIROT	CUB	Jerez de la Frontera	13 Sep 1989
Asi	2:33.6 §	Svetlana ULMASOVA	UZB	Podolsk	5 Aug 1979
	2:40.53	ZHAO Jing	CHN	Changbaishan	2 Sep 2014
Oce	2:37.28	Angie PETTY	NZL	Chiba	15 Aug 2015
W20	2:35.4a	Irina NIKITINA	RUS	Podolsk	5 Aug 1979
	2:35.4	Katrin WÜHN	GDR	Potsdam	12 Jul 1984
W18	2:38.58	Jo WHITE	GBR	London (CP)	9 Sep 1977

1500 METRES

W, Afr	3:50.07	Genzebe DIBABA	ETH	Monaco	17 Jul 15
As i	3:50.46	QU Yunxia	CHN	Beijing	11 Sep 1993
Eur	3:52.47	Tatyana KAZANKINA	RUS	Zürich	13 Aug 1980
Com	3:55.22	Laura MUIR	Sco/GBR	Saint-Denis	27 Aug 2016
NAm	3:56.29	Shannon ROWBURY	USA	Monaco	17 Jul 2015
Oce	4:00.93	Sarah JAMIESON	AUS	Stockholm	25 Jul 2006
CAC	4:01.84	Yvonne GRAHAM	JAM	Monaco	25 Jul 1995
SAm	4:05.67	Letitia VRIESDE	SUR	Tokyo	31 Aug 1991
W20	3:51.34	LANG Yinglai	CHN	Shanghai	18 Oct 1997
W18	3:54.52	ZHANG Ling	CHN	Shanghai	18 Oct 1997

1 MILE

W, Eur	4:12.56	Svetlana MASTERKOVA	RUS	Zürich	14 Aug 1996
Afr	4:14.30	Genzebe DIBABA	ETH	Rovereto	6 Sep 2016
NAm	4:16.71	Mary SLANEY	USA	Zürich	21 Aug 1985
Com	4:16.71	Faith KIPYEGON	KEN	Bruxelles	11 Sep 2015
Asi	4:17.75	Maryam Yusuf JAMAL	BRN	Bruxelles	14 Sep 2007
Oce	4:22.66	Lisa CORRIGAN	AUS	Melbourne	2 Mar 2007
CAC	4:24.64	Yvonne GRAHAM	JAM	Zürich	17 Aug 1994
SAm	4:30.05	Soraya TELLES	BRA	Praha	9 Jun 1988
W20	4:17.57	Zola BUDD	GBR	Zürich	21 Aug 1985
W18	4:30.81	Gelete BURKA	ETH	Heusden	2 Aug 2003

2000 METRES

W, Eur	5:25.36	Sonia O'SULLIVAN	IRL	Edinburgh	8 Jul 1994
Com	5:26.93	Yvonne MURRAY	GBR/Sco	Edinburgh	8 Jul 1994
Afr	5:27.50	Genzebe DIBABA	ETH	Ostrava	17 Jun 2014

240 WORLD AND CONTINENTAL RECORDS

Asi	5:29.43+§	WANG Junxia	CHN	Beijing	12 Sep 1993
	5:31.88	Maryam Yusuf JAMAL	BRN	Eugene	7 Jun 2009
NAm	5:32.7	Mary SLANEY	USA	Eugene	3 Aug 1984
Oce	5:37.71	Benita JOHNSON	AUS	Ostrava	12 Jun 2003
W20	5:33.15	Zola BUDD	GBR	London (CP)	13 Jul 1984
W18	5:46.5+	Sally BARSOSIO	KEN	Zürich	16 Aug 1995

3000 METRES

W, Asi	8:06.11	WANG Junxia	CHN	Beijing	13 Sep 1993
Afr, Com	8:20.68	Hellen OBIRI	KEN	Doha	9 May 2014
Eur	8:21.42	Gabriela SZABO	ROU	Monaco	19 Jul 2002
NAm	8:25.83	Mary SLANEY	USA	Roma	7 Sep 1985
Oce	8:35.31	Kimberley SMITH	NZL	Monaco	25 Jul 2007
CAC	8:37.07	Yvonne GRAHAM	JAM	Zürich	16 Aug 1995
SAm	9:02.37	Delirde BERNARDI	BRA	Linz	4 Jul 1994
W20	8:28.83	Zola BUDD	GBR	Roma	7 Sep 1985
W18	8:36.45	MA Ningning	CHN	Jinan	6 Jun 1993

5000 METRES

W, Afr	14:11.15	Tirunesh DIBABA	ETH	Oslo	6 Jun 2008
Com	14:20.87	Vivian CHERUIYOT	KEN	Stockho;lm	29 Jul 2011
Eur	14:23.75	Liliya SHOBUKHOVA	RUS	Kazan	19 Jul 2008
Asi	14:28.09	JIANG Bo	CHN	Shanghai	23 Oct 1997
NAm	14:38.92	Shannon ROWBURY	USA	Bruxelles	9 Sep 1206
Oce	14:45.93	Kimberley SMITH	NZL	Roma	11 Jul 2008
CAC	15:04.32	Adriana FERNÁNDEZ	MEX	Gresham	17 May 2003
SAm	15:18.85	Simone Alves da SILVA	BRA	São Paulo	20 May 2011
W20	14:30.88	Tirunesh DIBABA	ETH	Bergen (Fana)	11 Jun 2004
W18	14:45.71	SONG Liqing	CHN	Shanghai	21 Oct 1997

10,000 METRES

W, Afr	29:17.45	Almaz AYANA	ETH	Rio de Janeiro	12 Aug 2016
Asi	29:31.78	WANG Junxia	CHN	Beijing	8 Sep 1993
Com	29:32.53	Vivian CHERUIYOT	KEN	Rio de Janeiro	12 Aug 2016
Eur	29:56.34	Elvan ABEYLEGESSE	TUR	Beijing	15 Aug 2008
NAm	30:13.17	Molly HUDDLE	USA	Rio de Janeiro	12 Aug 2016
Oce	30:35.54	Kimberley SMITH	NZL	Stanford	4 May 2008
CAC	31:10.12	Adriana FERNANDEZ	MEX	Brunswick	1 Jul 2000
SAm	31:47.76	Carmen de OLIVEIRA	BRA	Stuttgart	21 Aug 1993
W20	30:26.50	Linet MASAI	KEN	Beijing	15 Aug 2008
W18	31:11.26	SONG Liqing	CHN	Shanghai	19 Oct 1997

HALF MARATHON

W, Afr, Com	65:06	Peres JEPCHIRCHIR	KEN	Ra's Al-Khaymah	10 Feb 2017
Eur	66:25	Lornah KIPLAGAT	NED	Udine	14 Oct 2007
Oce	67:11	Kimberley SMITH	NZL	Philadelphia	18 Sep 2011
Asi	67:26	Kayoko FUKUSHI	JPN	Marugame	5 Feb 2006
NAm	67:34	Deena KASTOR	USA	Berlin	2 Apr 2006
CAC	68:34 dh	Olga APPELL	MEX	Tokyo	24 Jan 1993
	69:28	Adrian FERNÁNDEZ	MEX	Kyoto	9 Mar 2003
SAm	70:14	Gladys TEJEDA	PER	Cardiff	26 Mar 2016
W20	67:57	Abebu GELAN	ETH	Ra's Al Khaymah	20 Feb 2009
W18	72:31	LIU Zhuang	CHN	Yangzhou	24 Apr 2011

MARATHON

W, Eur, Com	2:15:25	Paula RADCLIFFE	GBR/Eng	London	13 Apr 2003
Afr	2:18:37	Mary KEITANY	KEN	London	22 Apr 2012
Asi	2:19:12	Mizuki NOGUCHI	JPN	Berlin	25 Sep 2005
NAm	2:19:36	Deena KASTOR	USA	London	23 Apr 2006
Oce	2:22:36	Benita JOHNSON	AUS	Chicago	22 Oct 2006
CAC	2:22:59	Madai PÉREZ	MEX	Chicago	22 Oct 2006
SAm	2:26:48	Inés MELCHOR	PER	Berlin	28 Sep 2014
W20	2:20:59	Shure DEMISE	ETH	Dubai	23 Jan 2015

3000 METRES STEEPLECHASE

W, Asi	8:52.78	Ruth JEBET	BRN	Sant-Denis	27 Aug 2016
Eur	8:58.81	Gulnara GALKINA	RUS	Beijing	17 Aug 2008
Afr	9:00.01	Hyvin JEPKEMOI	KEN	Eugene	28 May 2016
Com	9:07.14	Milcah CHEMOS Cheywa	KEN	Oslo	7 Jun 2012
NAm	9:07.63	Emma COBURN	USA	Rio de Janeiro	15 Aug 2016
Oce	9:14.28	Genevieve LaCAZE	AUS	Saint-Denis	27 Aug 2016

WORLD AND CONTINENTAL RECORDS 241

CAC	9:27.21	Mardrea HYMAN	JAM	Monaco	9 Sep 2005
SAm	9:38.63	Juliana dos SANTOS	BRA	Praha	6 Jun 2016
W20	9:20.37	Birtukan ADAMU	ETH	Roma	26 May 2011
W18	9:24.73	Celphine CHESPOL	KEN	Shanghai	14 May 2016

100 METRES HURDLES

W, NAm	12.20	Kendra HARRISON	USA	London (OS)	22 Jul 2016
Eur	12.21	Yordanka DONKOVA	BUL	Stara Zagora	20 Aug 1988
Oce, Com	12.28	Sally PEARSON	AUS	Daegu	3 Sep 2011
Asi	12.44	Olga SHISHIGINA	KAZ	Luzern	27 Jun 1995
Afr	12.44	Glory ALOZIE	NGR	Monaco	8 Aug 1998
	12.44	Glory ALOZIE	NGR	Bruxelles	28 Aug 1998
	12.44	Glory ALOZIE	NGR	Sevilla	28 Aug 1999
CAC	12.45	Brigitte FOSTER	JAM	Eugene	24 May 2003
SAm	12.67	Yvette LEWIS	PAN	Lahti	17 Jul 2013
W20	12.74	Dior HALL	USA	Eugene	13 Jun 2015
W18	12.84	Tia JONES	USA	Clovis	25 Jun 2016

400 METRES HURDLES

Eur, W	52.34	Yuliya PECHONKINA	RUS	Tula	8 Aug 2003
CAC, Com	52.42	Melaine WALKER	JAM	Berlin	20 Aug 2009
NAm	52.47	Lashinda DEMUS	USA	Daegu	1 Sep 2011
Afr	52.90	Nezha BIDOUANE	MAR	Sevilla	25 Aug 1999
Oce	53.17	Debbie FLINTOFF-KING	AUS	Seoul	28 Sep 1988
Asi	53.96	HAN Qing	CHN	Beijing	9 Sep 1993
	53.96	SONG Yinglan	CHN	Guangzhou	22 Nov 2001
SAm	55.84	Lucimar TEODORO	BRA	Belém	24 May 2009
W20, W18	54.15	Sydney McLAUGHLIN	USA	Eugene	10 Jul 2016

HIGH JUMP

W, Eur	2.09	Stefka KOSTADINOVA	BUL	Roma	30 Aug 1987
Afr, Com	2.06	Hestrie CLOETE	RSA	Saint-Denis	31 Aug 2003
NAm	2.05	Chaunté HOWARD-LOWE	USA	Des Moines	26 Jun 2010
CAC	2.04	Silvia COSTA	CUB	Barcelona	9 Sep 1989
Asi	1.99	Marina AITOVA	KAZ	Athína	13 Jul 2009
Oce	1 98	Vanessa WARD	AUS	Perth	12 Feb 1989
	1.98	Alison INVERARITY	AUS	Ingolstadt	17 Jul 1994
SAm	1.96	Solange WITTEVEEN	ARG	Oristano	8 Sep 1997
W20	2.01	Olga TURCHAK	KAZ	Moskva	7 Jul 1986
	2.01	Heike BALCK	GDR	Chemnitz	18 Jun 1989
W18	1.96A	Charmaine GALE	RSA	Bloemfontein	4 Apr 1981
	1.96	Olga TURCHAK	UKR	Donetsk	7 Sep 1984
	1.96	Eleanor PATTERSON	AUS	Townsville	7 Dec 2013
	1.96	Vashti CUNNINGHAM	USA	Edmonton	1 Aug 2015

POLE VAULT

W, Eur	5.06	Yelena ISINBAYEVA	RUS	Zürich	28 Aug 2009
NAm	5.03i	Jennifer SUHR	USA	Brockport	30 Jan 2016
	4.92	Jennifer STUCZYNSKI/SUHR	USA	Eugene	6 Jul 2008
CAC	4.91	Yarisley SILVA	CUB	Beckum	2 Aug 2015
SAm	4.87	Fabiana MURER	BRA	ßão Bernardo do Campo	3 Jul 2016
Com	4.87i	Holly BLEASDALE	GBR	Villeurbanne	21 Jan 2012
Com, Oce	4.82	Eliza McCARTNEY	NZL	Auckland	26 Feb 2017
Asi	4.70i	LI Ling	CHN	Doha	19 Feb 2016
	4.66	LI Ling	CHN	Wuhan	6 Jun 2015
Afr	4.42	Elmarie GERRYTS	RSA	Wesel	12 Jun 2000
W20	4.64	Eliza McCARTNEY	NZL	Auckland	19 Dec 2015
W18	4.47	Angelica BENGTSSON	SWE	Moskva	22 May 2010

LONG JUMP

W, Eur	7.52	Galina CHISTYAKOVA	RUS	Sankt-Peterburg	11 Jun 1988
NAm	7.49	Jackie JOYNER-KERSEE	USA	New York	22 May 1994
	7.49A §	Jackie JOYNER-KERSEE	USA	Sestriere	31 Jul 1994
SAm	7.26A	Maurren MAGGI	BRA	Bogotá	26 Jun 1999
CAC, Com	7.16A	Elva GOULBOURNE	JAM	Ciudad de México	22 May 2004
Afr	7.12	Chioma AJUNWA	NGR	Atlanta	1 Aug 1996
Asi	7.01	YAO Weili	CHN	Jinan	5 Jun 1993
Oce	7.05	Brooke STRATTON	AUS	Perth	12 Mar 2016
W20	7.14	Heike DAUTE/Drechsler	GDR	Bratislava	4 Jun 1983
W18	6.91	Heike DAUTE/Drechsler	GDR	Jena	9 Aug 1981

WORLD AND CONTINENTAL RECORDS

TRIPLE JUMP
W, Eur	15.50	Inessa KRAVETS	UKR	Göteborg		10 Aug 1995
Afr, Com	15.39	Françoise MBANGO Etone	CMR	Beijing		17 Aug 2008
SAm	15.31	Caterine IBARGÜEN	COL	Monaco		18 Jul 2014
CAC	15.29	Yamilé ALDAMA	CUB	Roma		11 Jul 2003
Asi	15.25	Olga RYPAKOVA	KAZ	Split		4 Sep 2010
NAm	14.71	Keturah ORJI	USA	Rio de Janeiro		14 Aug 2016
Oce	14.04	Nicole MLADENIS	AUS	Hobart		9 Mar 2002
	14.04	Nicole MLADENIS	AUS	Perth		7 Dec 2003
W20	14.62	Tereza MARINOVA	BUL	Sydney		25 Aug 1996
W18	14.57	HUANG Qiuyan	CHN	Shanghai		19 Oct 1997

SHOT
W, Eur	22.63	Natalya LISOVSKAYA	RUS	Moskva	7 Jun 1987
Asi	21.76	LI Meisu	CHN	Shijiazhuang	23 Apr 1988
Oce, Com	21.24	Valerie ADAMS	NZL	Daegu	29 Aug 2011
CAC	20.96	Belsy LAZA	CUB	Ciudad de México	2 May 1992
NAm	20.63	Michelle CARTER	USA	Rio de Janeiro	12 Aug 2016
SAm	19.30	Elisângela ADRIANO	BRA	Tunja	14 Jul 2001
Afr	18.43	Vivian CHUKWUEMEKA	NGR	Walnut	19 Apr 2003
W20	20.54	Astrid KUMBERNUSS	GDR	Orimattila	1 Jul 1989
W18	19.08	Ilke WYLUDDA	GDR	Karl-Marx-Stadt	9 Aug 1986

DISCUS
W, Eur	76.80	Gabriele REINSCH	GDR	Neubrandenburg	9 Jul 1988
Asi	71.68	XIAO Yanling	CHN	Beijing	14 Mar 1992
CAC	70.88	Hilda RAMOS	CUB	La Habana	8 May 1992
NAm	69.17	Gia LEWIS-SMALWOOD	USA	Angers	30 Aug 2014
Oce, Com	68.72	Daniela COSTIAN	AUS	Auckland	22 Jan 1994
Afr	64.87	Elizna NAUDE	RSA	Stellenbosch	2 Mar 2007
SAm	64.21	Andressa de MORAIS	BRA	Barquisimeto	10 Jun 2012
W20	74.40	Ilke WYLUDDA	GDR	Berlin	13 Sep 1988
W18	65.86	Ilke WYLUDDA	GDR	Neubrandenburg	1 Aug 1986

HAMMER
W, Eur	82.98	Anita WLODARCZYK	POL	Warszawa	28 Aug 2016
øπAsi	77.68	WANG Zheng	CHN	Chengdu	29 Mar 2014
CAC	76.62	Yipsi MORENO	CUB	Zagreb	9 Sep 2008
NAm	75.73	Amanda BINGSON	USA	Des Moines	22 Jun 2013
NAm, Com	75.73	Sultana FRIZELL	CAN	Tucson	22 May 2014
SAm	73.74	Jennifer DAHLGREN	ARG	Buenos Aires	10 Apr 2010
Oce	71.12	Bronwyn EAGLES	AUS	Adelaide	6 Feb 2003
Afr	69.70	Amy SÈNE	SEN	Forbach	25 May 2014
W20	73.24	ZHANG Wenxiu	CHN	Changsha	24 Jun 2005
W18	70.60	ZHANG Wenxiu	CHN	Nanning	5 Apr 2003
W18 3kg	76.04	Réka GYURÁTZ	HUN	Zalaegerszeg	23 Jun 2013

JAVELIN
W, Eur	72.28	Barbora SPOTÁKOVÁ	CZE	Stuttgart	13 Sep 2008
CAC	71.70	Osleidys MENÉNDEZ	CUB	Helsinki	14 Aug 2005
Afr, Com	69.35	Sunette VILJOEN	RSA	New York	9 Jun 2012
Oce	66.83	Kimberley MICKLE	AUS	Melbourne	22 Mar 2014
NAm	66.67	Kara PATTERSON	USA	Des Moines	25 Jun 2010
Asi	66.13	LU Huihui	CHN	Beijing	30 Aug 2015
SAm	63.80A	Flor Dennis RUIZ	COL	Xalapa	27 Nov 2014
W20	63.86	Yulenmis AGUILAR	CUB	Edmonton	2 Aug 2015
W18	62.93	XUE Juan	CHN	Changsha	27 Oct 2003

HEPTATHLON
W, NAm	7291	Jackie JOYNER-KERSEE	USA	Seoul	24 Sep 1988
Eur	7032	Carolina KLÜFT	SWE	Osaka	26 Aug 2007
Com	6955	Jessica ENNIS	GBR/Eng	London (OS)	4 Aug 2012
Asi	6942	Ghada SHOUAA	SYR	Götzis	26 May 1996
Oce	6695	Jane FLEMMING	AUS	Auckland	28 Jan 1990
CAC	6527	Diane GUTHRIE-GRESHAM	JAM	Knoxville	3 Jun 1995
Afr	6423	Margaret SIMPSON	GHA	Götzis	29 May 2005
SAm	6160	Lucimara DA SILVA	BRA	Barquisimeto	10 Jun 2012
W20	6542	Carolina KLÜFT	SWE	München	10 Aug 2002
W18	6185	SHEN Shengfei	CHN	Shanghai	18 Oct 1997
U18 spec	6186	Alina SHUKH	UKR	Tbilisi	15 Jul 2016

DECATHLON

W, Eur	8358		Austra SKUJYTE	LTU	Columbia, MO	15 Apr 2005
Asi	7798	§	Irina NAUMENKO	KAZ	Talence	26 Sep 2004
NAm	7577	§	Tiffany LOTT-HOGAN	USA	Lage	10 Sep 2000
CAC	7245	§	Magalys GARCÍA	CUB	Wien	29 Jun 2002
Afr, Com	6915		Margaret SIMPSON	GHA	Réduit	19 Apr 2007
SAm	6570		Andrea BORDALEJO	ARG	Rosario	28 Nov 2004
Oce	6428		Simone CARRÉ	AUS	Melbourne	11 Mar 2012

4 X 100 METRES RELAY

W, NAm	40.82	USA (Madison, Felix, Knight, Jeter)		London (OS)	10 Aug 2012
CAC, Com	41.07	JAM (Campbell-Brown, Morrison, Thompson, Fraser-Pryce)		Beijing	29 Aug 2015
Eur	41.37	GDR (Gladisch, Rieger, Auerswald, Göhr)		Canberra	6 Oct 1985
Asi	42.23	Sichuan CHN (Xiao Lin, Li Yali, Liu Xiaomei, Li Xuemei)		Shanghai	23 Oct 1997
SAm	42.29	BRA (E dos Santos, Silva, Krasucki, R Santos)		Moskva	18 Aug 2013
Afr	42.39	NGR (Utondu, Idehen, Opara-Thompson, Onyali)		Barcelona	7 Aug 1992
Oce	42.99A	AUS (Massey, Broadrick, Lambert, Gainsford-Taylor)		Pietersburg	18 Mar 2000
W20	43.29	USA (Knight, Tarmoh, Olear, Mayo)		Eugene	8 Aug 2006
W18	44.05	GDR (Koppetsch, Oelsner, Sinzel, Brehmer)		Athína	24 Aug 1975

4 X 400 METRES RELAY

W, Eur	3:15.17	URS (Ledovskaya, Nazarova, Pinigina, Bryzgina)		Seoul	1 Oct 1988
NAm	3:15.51	USA (D.Howard, Dixon, Brisco, Griffith Joyner)		Seoul	1 Oct 1988
CAC, Com	3:18.71	JAM (Whyte, Prendergast, N Williams-Mills, S Williams)		Daegu	3 Sep 2011
Afr	3:21.04	NGR (Bisi Afolabi, Yusuf, Opara, Ogunkoya)		Atlanta	3 Aug 1996
Oce	3:23.81	AUS (Peris, Lewis, Gainsford-Taylor, Freeman)		Sydney	30 Sep 2000
Asi	3:24.28	Hebei CHN (An X, Bai X, Cao C, Ma Y)		Beijing	13 Sep 1993
SAm	3:26.68	BRA (Coutinho, de Oliveira, Souza, de Lima)		São Paulo	7 Aug 2011
W20	3:27.60	USA (Anderson, Kidd, Smith, Hastings)		Grosseto	18 Jul 2004
W18	3:36.98	GBR (Ravenscroft, E McMeekin, Kennedy, Pettett)		Duisburg	26 Aug 1973

10 KILOMETRES WALK

W, Eur	41:04		Yelena NIKOLAYEVA	RUS	Sochi	20 Apr 1996
Asi	41:16		WANG Yan	CHN	Eisenhüttenstadt	8 May 1999
Oce, Com	41:30		Kerry SAXBY-JUNNA	AUS	Canberra	27 Aug 1988
CAC	42:42		Graciela MENDOZA	MEX	Naumburg	25 May 1997
SAm	43:56+		Erica de SEÑA	BRA	Roma	7 May 2016
NAm	44:09+		Maria MICHTA-COFFEY	USA	St. Louis	3 Apr 2016
Afr	45:02		Chahinez NASRI	TUN	La Coruña	28 May 2016
W20	41:52	§	Tatyana MINEYEVA	RUS	Penza	5 Sep 2009
	41:57	§	GAO Hongmiao	CHN	Beijing	8 Sep 1993
W18	43:28		Aleksandra KUDRYASHOVA	RUS	Adler	19 Feb 2006

10,000 METRES TRACK WALK

W, Asi	41:37.9 §	GAO Hongmiao	CHN	Beijing		7 Apr 1994
W, Eur	41:56.23	Nadyezhda RYASHKINA	RUS	Seattle		24 Jul 1990
Oce, Com	41:57.22	Kerry SAXBY-JUNNA	AUS	Seattle		24 Jul 1990
SAm	43:41.30	Erica de SEÑA	BRA	São Paulo		1 Aug 2014
NAm	44:30.1 m	Alison BAKER	CAN	Bergen (Fana)		15 May 1992
	44:06 no kerb	Michelle ROHL	USA	Kenosha		2 Jun 1996
CAC	44:16.21	Cristina LÓPEZ	ESA	San Salvador		13 Jul 2007
Afr	44:41.8A	Grace Njue WANJIRU	KEN	Thika		5 Mar 1206
W20	42:47.25	Anezka DRAHOTOVÁ	CZE	Eugene		23 Jul 2014
W18	42:56.09	GAO Hongmiao	CHN	Tangshan		27 Sep 1991

20,000 METRES TRACK WALK

W, Eur	1:26:52.3	Olimpiada IVANOVA	RUS	Brisbane		6 Sep 2001
Asi, W20	1:29:32.4 §	SONG Hongjuan	CHN	Changsha		24 Oct 2003
SAm	1:31:02.25	Sandra Lorena ARENAS	COL	Lima		13 Jun 2015
CAC	1:31:53.8A	Mirna ORTIZ	GUA	Ciudad de Guatemala		9 Aug 2014
NAm, Com	1:32:54.0	Rachel SEAMAN	CAN	Moncton		27 Jun 2014
Oce	1:33:40.2	Kerry SAXBY-JUNNA	AUS	Brisbane		6 Sep 2001
Afr	1:36:18.22	Nicolene CRONJE	RSA	Durban		17 Apr 2004
W18	1:34:21.56	WANG Xue	CHN	Wuhan		1 Nov 2007

20 KILOMETRES WALK

W,Asi	1:24:38	LIU Hong	CHN	La Coruna		6 Jun 2015
Eur	1:24:47 §	Elmira ALEMBEKOVA	RUS	Sochi		27 Feb 2015
	1:25:02	Yeoena LASHMANOVA	RUS	London		11 Aug 2012
SAm	1:27:18	Erica de SEÑA	BRA	Roma		7 May 2016

Oce, Com	1:27:44	Jane SAVILLE	AUS	Naumburg		2 May 2004
CAC	1:28:31	Mima ORTIZ	GUA	Rio Maior		6 Apr 2013
NAm	1:29:54	Rachel SEAMAN	CAN	Nomi		15 Mar 2015
Afr	1:30:43	Grace Njue WANJIRU	KEN	Durban		26 Jun 2016
W20	1:25:30	Anisya KIRDYAPKINA	RUS	Adler		23 Feb 2008
W18	1:30:28	ZHOU Tongmei	CHN	Cixi		23 Apr 2005

World Records at other track & field events recognised by the IAAF

1 Hour	18,517 m	Dire TUNE	ETH	Ostrava	12 Jun 2008
20,000m	1:05:26.6	Tegla LOROUPE	KEN	Borgholzhausen	3 Sep 2000
25,000m	1:27:05.84	Tegla LOROUPE	KEN	Mengerskirchen	21 Sep 2002
30,000m	1:45:50.0	Tegla LOROUPE	KEN	Warstein	6 Jun 2003
4x200m	1:27.46	L Jenkins, L Colander, N Perry, M Jones	USA	Philadelphia	29 Apr 2000
4x800m	7:50.17	Olizarenko, Gurina, Borisova, Podyalovskaya	USSR	Moskva	5 Aug 1984
4x1500m	16:33.58	M Cherono, Kipyegon, I Jelagat, Obiri	KEN	Nassau	24 May 2014

WORLD BESTS AT NON-STANDARD EVENTS

Men

50m	5.47+e	Usain Bolt	JAM	Berlin (in 100m)	16 Aug 2009
60m	6.31+	Usain Bolt	JAM	Berlin (in 100m)	16 Aug 2009
100 yards	9.07	Asafa Powell	JAM	Ostrava	27 May 2010
150m turn	14.44+	Usain Bolt	JAM	Berlin (in 200m)	20 Aug 2009
150m straight	14.35	Usain Bolt	JAM	Manchester	17 May 2009
300m	30.85A	Michael Johnson	USA	Pretoria	24 Mar 2000
	30.97	Usain Bolt	JAM	Ostrava	27 May 2010
500m	59.32	Orestes Rodríguez	CUB	La Habana	15 Feb 2013
600m	1:12.81	Johnny Gray	USA	Santa Monica	24 May 1986
2 miles	7:58.61	Daniel Komen	KEN	Hechtel	19 Jul 1997
2000m Steeple	5:10.68	Mahiedine Mekhissi	FRA	Reims	30 Jun 2010
200mh	22.55	Laurent Ottoz	ITA	Milano	31 May 1995
(hand time)	22.5	Martin Lauer	FRG	Zürich	7 Jul 1959
200mh straight	22.10	Andrew Turner	GBR	Manchester	15 May 2011
	22.10	L.J. van Zyl	RSA	Manchester	9 May 2015
220yh straight	21.9	Don Styron	USA	Baton Rouge	2 Apr 1960
300mh	34.48	Chris Rawlinson	GBR	Sheffield	30 Jun 2002
35lb weight	25.41	Lance Deal	USA	Azusa	20 Feb 1993
Pentathlon	4282 points	Bill Toomey	USA	London (CP)	16 Aug 1969
(1985 tables)		(7.58, 66.18, 21.3, 44.52, 4:20.3)			
Double decathlon	14,571	Joe Detmer	USA	Lynchburg	24/25 Sep 2010
		10.93w, 7.30, 200mh 24.25w, 12.27, 5k 18:25.32, 2:02.23, 1.98, 400m 50.43, HT 31.82, 3kSt 11:22.47			
		15.01, DT 40.73, 200m 22.58, 4.85, 3k 10:25.99, 400mh 53.83, 51.95, 4:26.66, TJ 13.67, 10k 40:27.26			
4x110mh	52.94	USA Richardson, Harris, Merritt, Oliver		Des Moines	25 Apr 2015
3000m track walk	10:47.11	Giovanni De Benedictis	ITA	San Giovanni Valdarno	19 May 1990
5000m track walk	18:05.49	Hatem Ghoula	TUN	Tunis	1 May 1997
10,000m track walk	37:53.09	Francisco Javier Fernández	ESP	Santa Cruz de Tenerife	27 Jul 2008
10 km road walk	37:11	Roman Rasskazov	RUS	Saransk	28 May 2000
30 km road walk	2:01:13+	Vladimir Kanaykin	RUS	Adler	19 Feb 2006
35 km road walk	2:21:31	Vladimir Kanaykin	RUS	Adler	19 Feb 2006
100 km road walk	8:38:07	Viktor Ginko	BLR	Scanzorosciate	27 Oct 2002

Women

50m	5.93+	Marion Jones	USA	Sevilla (in 100m)	22 Aug 1999
60m	6.85+	Marion Jones	USA	Sevilla (in 100m)	22 Aug 1999
100 yards	9.91	Veronica-Campbell-Brown	JAM	Ostrava	31 May 2011
150m	16.10+	Florence Griffith-Joyner	USA	Seoul (in 200m)	29 Sep 1988
300m	34.1+	Marita Koch	GDR	Canberra (in 400m)	6 Oct 1985
500m	1:05.9	Tatána Kocembová	CZE	Ostrava	2 Aug 1984
600m	1:22.63	Ana Fidelia Quirot	CUB	Guadalajara, ESP	25 Jul 1997
2 miles	8:58.58	Meseret Defar	ETH	Bruxelles	14 Sep 2007
2000m Steeple	6:02.16	Virginia Nyambura	KEN	Berlin	6 Sep 2015
200mh	24.8	Yadisleidis Pedroso	ITA	Caserta	6 Apr 2013
	25.79	Noemi Zbären	SUI	Basel	17 May 2014
300mh	38.16	Zuzana Hejnová	CZE	Cheb	2 Aug 2013
Double heptathlon	10,798	Milla Kelo	FIN	Turku	7/8 Sep 2002
		100mh 14.89, HJ 1.51, 1500m 5:03.74, 400m 62.21, SP 12.73, 200m 25.16, 100m 12.59			
		LJ 5.73w, 400m 56.10, JT 32.69, 800m 2:23.94, 200mh 28.72, DT 47.86, 3000m 11:48.68			
4x100mh	50.50	USA Castlin, Q Harrison, Harper-Nelson, Rollins		Des Moines	24 Apr 2015
3000m track walk	11:35.34i	Gillian O'SAullivan	IRL	Belfast	15 Feb 2003
	11:48.24	Ileana Salvador	ITA	Padova	29 Aug 1993
5000m track walk	20:01.80	Eleonora Giorgi	ITA	Misterbianco	17 May 2014
25km road walk	1:56:12+	Eleonora GIORGI	ITA	Catania	31 Jan 2016
30 km road walk	2:19:43	Eleonora Giorgi	ITA	Catania	31 Jul 2016

WORLD AND CONTINENTAL RECORDS

50 km road walk	4:08:26	Inês Henriques	POR	Porto de Mos	15 Jan 2017
100 km road walk	10:04:50	Jolanta Dukure	LAT	Scanzorosciate	21 Oct 2007

LONG DISTANCE WORLD BESTS – MEN TRACK

	hr:min:sec	Name	Nat	Venue	Date
15,000m	0:42:18.7+	Haile Gebrselassie	ETH	Ostrava	27 Jun 2007
10 miles	0:45:23.8+	Haile Gebrselassie	ETH	Ostrava	27 Jun 2007
15 miles	1:11:43.1	Bill Rodgers	USA	Saratoga, Cal.	21 Feb 1979
20 miles	1:39:14.4	Jack Foster	NZL	Hamilton, NZ	15 Aug 1971
30 miles	2:42:00+	Jeff Norman	GBR	Timperley, Cheshire	7 Jun 1980
50 km	2:48:06	Jeff Norman	GBR	Timperley, Cheshire	7 Jun 1980
40 miles	3:48:35	Don Ritchie	GBR	London (Hendon)	16 Oct 1982
50 miles	4:51:49	Don Ritchie	GBR	London (Hendon)	12 Mar 1983
100 km	6:10:20	Don Ritchie	GBR	London (CP)	28 Oct 1978
150 km	10:34:30	Denis Zhalybin	RUS	London (CP)	20 Oct 2002
100 miles	11:28:03	Oleg Kharitonov	RUS	London (CP)	20 Oct 2002
200 km	15:10:27+	Yiannis Kouros	AUS	Adelaide	4-5 Oct 1997
200 miles	27:48:35	Yiannis Kouros	GRE	Montauban	15-16 Mar 1985
500 km	60:23.00+ ??	Yiannis Kouros	GRE	Colac, Aus	26-29 Nov 1984
500 miles	105:42:09+	Yiannis Kouros	GRE	Colac, Aus	26-30 Nov 1984
1000 km	136:17:00	Yiannis Kouros	GRE	Colac, Aus	26-31 Nov 1984
1500 km	10d 17:28:26	Petrus Silkinas	LTU	Nanango, Qld	11-21 Mar 1998
1000 mile	11d 13:54:58+	Petrus Silkinas	LTU	Nanango, Qld	11-22 Mar 1998
2 hrs	37.994 km	Jim Alder	GBR	Walton-on-Thames	17 Oct 1964
12 hrs	162.400 km +	Yiannis Kouros	GRE	Montauban	15 Mar 1985
24 hrs	303.506 km	Yiannis Kouros	AUS	Adelaide	4-5 Oct 1997
48 hrs	473.797 km	Yiannis Kouros	AUS	Surgères	3-5 May 1996
6 days	1036.8 km	Yiannis Kouros	GRE	Colac, Aus	20-26 Nov 2005

LONG DISTANCE ROAD RECORDS & BESTS – MEN

Where superior to track bests (over 10km) and run on properly measured road courses. (I) IAAF recognition.

10 km (I)	0:26:44	Leonard Patrick Komon	KEN	Utrecht	26 Sep 2010
15 km (I)	0:41:13	Leonard Patrick Komon	KEN	Nijmegen	21 Nov 2010
10 miles	0:44:24 §	Haile Gebrselassie	ETH	Tilburg	4 Sep 2005
	0:44:45	Paul Koech	KEN	Amsterdam-Zaandam	21 Sep 1997
20 km (I)	0:55:21+	Zersenay Tadese	ERI	Lisboa	21 Mar 2010
25 km (I)	1:11:18	Dennis Kimetto	KEN	Berlin	6 May 2012
30 km (I)	1:27:13+	Eliud Kipchoge	KEN	London	24 Apr 2016
	1:27:13+	Stanley Biwott	KEN	London	24 Apr 2016
20 miles	1:35:22+	Steve Jones	GBR	Chicago	10 Oct 1985
30 miles	2:37:31+	Thompson Magawana	RSA	Claremont-Kirstenbosch	2 Apr 1988
50km	2:43:38+	Thompson Magawana	RSA	Claremont-Kirstenbosch	2 Apr 1988
40 miles	3:45:39	Andy Jones	CAN	Houston	23 Feb 1991
50 miles	4:50:21	Bruce Fordyce	RSA	London-Brighton	25 Sep 1983
100 km (I)	6:13:33	Takahiro Sunada	JPN	Yubetsu	21 Jun 1998
1000 miles	10d:10:30:35	Yiannis Kouros	GRE	New York	21-30 May 1988
12 hrs	162.543 km	Yiannis Kouros	GRE	Queen's, New York	7 Nov 1984

LONG DISTANCE WORLD BESTS – WOMEN TRACK

15 km	0:48:54.91+	Dire Tune	ETH	Ostrava	12 Jun 2008
10 miles	0:54:21.8	Lorraine Moller	NZL	Auckland	9 Jan 1993
20 miles	1:59:09 !	Chantal Langlacé	FRA	Amiens	3 Sep 1983
30 miles	3:12:25+	Carolyn Hunter-Rowe	GBR	Barry, Wales	3 Mar 1996
50 km	3:18:52+	Carolyn Hunter-Rowe	GBR	Barry, Wales	3 Mar 1996
40 miles	4:26:43	Carolyn Hunter-Rowe	GBR	Barry, Wales	7 Mar 1993
50 miles	5:48:12.0+	Norimi Sakurai	JPN	San Giovanni Lupatoto	27 Sep 2003
100 km	7:14:05.8	Norimi Sakurai	JPN	San Giovanni Lupatoto	27 Sep 2003
150 km	13:45:54	Hilary Walker	GBR	Blackpool	5-6 Nov 1988
100 miles	13:52.02+	Mami Kudo	JPN	Soochow	10-11 Dec 2011
200 km	17:52.18+	Mami Kudo	JPN	Soochow	10-11 Dec 2011
200 miles	39:09:03	Hilary Walker	GBR	Blackpool	5-7 Nov 1988
500 km	77:53:46	Eleanor Adams	GBR	Colac, Aus.	13-16 Nov 1989
500 miles	130:59:58+	Sandra Barwick	NZL	Campbelltown, AUS	18-23 Nov 1990
1000 km	8d 00:27:06+	Eleanor Robinson	GBR	Nanango, Qld	11-19 Mar 1998
1500 km	12d 06:52:12+	Eleanor Robinson	GBR	Nanango, Qld	11-23 Mar 1998
1000 miles	13d 02:16:49	Eleanor Robinson	GBR	Nanango, Qld	11-24 Mar 1998
2 hrs	32.652 km	Chantal Langlacé	FRA	Amiens	3 Sep 1983
12 hrs	147.600 km	Ann Trason	USA	Hayward, Cal	3-4 Aug 1991
24 hours	255.303 km	Mami Kudo	JPN	Soochow	10-11 Dec 2011
48 hrs	385.130 km	Mami Kudo	JPN	Surgères	22-24 May 2010

WORLD AND CONTINENTAL RECORDS

6 days	883.631 km	Sandra Barwick	NZL	Campbelltown, AUS	18-24 Nov 1990

! Timed on one running watch only

LONG DISTANCE ROAD RECORDS & BESTS – WOMEN

	hr:min:sec	Name	Nat	Venue	Date
10 km (l)	0:30:21	Paula Radcliffe	GBR	San Juan	23 Feb 2003
15 km (l)	46:14+	Florence Kiplaget	KEN	Barcelona	15 Feb 2015
10 miles	0:50:05+	Mary Keitany	KEN	Ra's Al-Khaymah	18 Feb 2011
	0:50:01+ dh	Paula Radcliffe	GBR	Newcastle	21 Sep 2003
20 km (l)	1:01:54+	Florence Kiplaget	KEN	Barcelona	15 Feb 2015
25 km (l)	1:19:53	Mary Keitany	KEN	Berlin	9 May 2010
30 km (l)	1:38:23+ §	Liliya Shobukhova	RUS	Chicago	9 Oct 2011
	1:36:36+ dh	Paula Radcliffe	GBR	London	13 Apr 2003
20 miles	1:43:33+	Paula Radcliffe	GBR	London	13 Apr 2003
30 miles	3:01:16+	Frith van der Merwe	RSA	Claremont-Kirstenbosch	25 Mar 1989
50 km	3:08:39	Frith van der Merwe	RSA	Claremont-Kirstenbosch	25 Mar 1989
40 miles	4:26:13+	Ann Trason	USA	Houston	23 Feb 1991
50 miles	5:40:18	Ann Trason	USA	Houston	23 Feb 1991
100 km (l)	6:33:11	Tomoe Abe	JPN	Yubetsu	25 Jun 2000
100 miles	13:47:41	Ann Trason	USA	Queen's, New York	4 May 1991
200 km	18:45:51	Mami Kudo	JPN	Steenbergen	11-12 May 2013
1000 km	7d 01:11:00+	Sandra Barwick	NZL	New York	16-23 Sep 1991
1000 miles	12d 14:38:40	Sandra Barwick	NZL	New York	16-29 Sep 1991
12 hours	144.840 km	Ann Trason	USA	Queen's, New York	4 May 1991
24 hours	252.205 km	Mami Kudo	JPN	Steenbergen	12 May 2013

100 KILOMETRES CONTINENTAL RECORDS

Men

W, Asi	6:13:33	Takahiro SUNADA	JPN	Yubetsu	21 Jun 1998
Eur	6:16:41	Jean-Paul PRAET	BEL	Torhout	24 Jun 1989
SAm	6:18:09	Valmir NUNES	BRA	Winschoten	16 Sep 1995
Afr	6:24:05	Bongmusa MTHEMBU	RSA	Los Alcazares	27 Nov 2016
NAm	6:27:43	Maxwell KING	USA	Doha	21 Nov 2014
Oce	6:29:23	Tim SLOAN	AUS	Ross-Richmond	23 Apr 1995

Women

W, Asi	6:33:11	Tomoe ABE	JPN	Yubetsu	25 Jun 2000
NAm	7:00:48	Ann TRASON	USA	Winschoten	16 Sep 1995
Eur	7:10:32	Tatyana ZHYRKOVA	RUS	Winschoten	11 Sep 2004
SAm	7:20:22	Maria VENÂNCIO	BRA	Cubatão	8 Aug 1998
Afr	7:31:47	Helena JOUBERT	RSA	Winschoten	16 Sep 1995
Oce	7:34:35	Kirstin BULL	AUS	Los Alcazares	27 Nov 2016

WORLD INDOOR RECORDS

Men
to March 2015

50 metres	5.56A	Donovan Bailey	CAN	Reno	9 Feb 1996
60 metres	6.39	Maurice Greene	USA	Madrid	3 Feb 1998
	6.39	Maurice Greene	USA	Atlanta	3 Mar 2001
100 metres	9.98	Usain Bolt	JAM	Warszawa	23 Aug 2014
200 metres	19.92	Frank Fredericks	NAM	Liévin	18 Feb 1996
400 metres	44.57	Kerron Clement	USA	Fayetteville	12 Mar 2005
800 metres	1:42.67	Wilson Kipketer	KEN	Paris (Bercy)	9 Mar 1997
1000 metres	2:14.20	Ayanleh Souleiman	DJI	Stockholm	17 Feb 2016
1500 metres	3:31.18	Hicham El Guerrouj	MAR	Stuttgart	2 Feb 1997
1 mile	3:48.45	Hicham El Guerrouj	MAR	Gent	12 Feb 1997
2000 metres #	4:49.99	Kenenisa Bekele	ETH	Birmingham	17 Feb 2007
3000 metres	7:24.90	Daniel Komen	KEN	Budapest	6 Feb 1998
2 miles #	8:04.35	Kenenisa Bekele	ETH	Birmingham	16 Feb 2008
5000 metres	12:49.60	Kenenisa Bekele	ETH	Birmingham	20 Feb 2004
10000 metres #	27:50.29	Mark Bett	KEN	Gent	10 Feb 2002
50 m hurdles	6.25	Mark McKoy	CAN	Kobe	5 Mar 1986
60 m hurdles	7.30	Colin Jackson	GBR	Sindelfingen	6 Mar 1994
110 m hurdles	13.03	Orlando Ortega	CUB	Warszawa	23 Aug 2014
High jump	2.43	Javier Sotomayor	CUB	Budapest	4 Mar 1989
Pole vault	6.16	Renaud Lavillenie	FRA	Donetsk	15 Feb 2014
Long jump	8.79	Carl Lewis	USA	New York	27 Jan 1984
Triple jump	17.92	Teddy Tamgho	FRA	Paris (Bercy)	6 Mar 2011
Shot	22.66	Randy Barnes	USA	Los Angeles	20 Jan 1989
Javelin #	85.78	Matti Närhi	FIN	Kajaani	3 Mar 1996
35 lb weight #	25.86	Lance Deal	USA	Atlanta	4 Mar 1995

WORLD AND CONTINENTAL RECORDS

3000m walk #	10:31.42	Andreas Erm	GER	Halle	4 Feb 2001
5000m walk	18:07.08	Mikhail Shchennikov	RUS	Moskva	14 Feb 1995
10000m walk #	38:31.4	Werner Heyer	GDR	Berlin	12 Jan 1980
4 x 200m	1:22.11	United Kingdom		Glasgow	3 Mar 1991
		(Linford Christie, Darren Braithwaite, Ade Mafe, John Regis)			
4 x 400m	3:02.13	USA		Sopot	9 Mar 2014
		(Kyle Clemons, David Verburg, Kind Butler, Calvin Smith)			
	3:01.96 §	USA (not ratified – no EPO analysis)		Fayetteville	11 Feb 2006
		(Kerron Clement, Wallace Spearmon, Darold Williamson, Jeremy Wariner)			
4 x 800m	7:13.11	USA All-Stars		Boston (Roxbury)	8 Feb 2014
		(Richard Jones, David Torrence, Duane Solomon, Erik Sowinski)			
Distance Med	9:19.93	USA		New York (Armory)	31 Jan 2015
		(Matthew Centrowitz, Mike Berry, Erik Sowinski, Pat Casey)			
Heptathlon	6645 points	Ashton Eaton	USA	Istanbul	9/10 Mar 2012
		(6.79 60m, 8.16 LJ, 14.56 SP, 2.03 HJ, 7.68 60mh, 5.20 PV, 2:32.77 1000m)			

Women

50 metres	5.96+	Irina Privalova	RUS	Madrid	9 Feb 1995
60 metres	6.92	Irina Privalova	RUS	Madrid	11 Feb 1993 & 9 Feb 1995
200 metres	21.87	Merlene Ottey	JAM	Liévin	13 Feb 1993
400 metres	49.59	Jarmila Kratochvílová	CZE	Milano	7 Mar 1982
800 metres	1:55.82	Jolanda Ceplak	SLO	Wien	3 Mar 2002
1000 metres	2:30.94	Maria Lurdes Mutola	MOZ	Stockholm	25 Feb 1999
1500 metres	3:55.17	Genzebe Dibaba	ETH	Karlsruhe	1 Feb 2014
1 mile	4:13.31	Genzebe Dibaba	ETH	Stockholm	17 Feb 2016
2000 metres #	5:23.75	Genzebe Dibaba	ETH	Sabadell	7 Feb 2017
3000 metres	8:16.60	Genzebe Dibaba	ETH	Stockholm	6 Feb 2014
2 miles #	9:00.48	Genzebe Dibaba	ETH	Birmingham	15 Feb 2014
5000 metres	14:18.86	Genzebe Dibaba	ETH	Stockholm	19 Feb 2015
50 m hurdles	6.58	Cornelia Oschkenat	GDR	Berlin	20 Feb 1988
60 m hurdles	7.68	Susanna Kallur	SWE	Karlsruhe	10 Feb 2008
100 m hurdles	12.64	Ludmila Engquist	SWE	Tampere	10 Feb 1997
High jump	2.08	Kajsa Bergqvist	SWE	Arnstadt	4 Feb 2006
Pole vault	5.03	Jenn Suhr	USA	Brockport	30 Jan 2016
Long jump	7.37	Heike Drechsler	GDR	Wien	13 Feb 1988
Triple jump	15.36	Tatyana Lebedeva	RUS	Budapest	5 Mar 2004
Shot	22.50	Helena Fibingerová	CZE	Jablonec	19 Feb 1977
Javelin #	61.29	Taina Uppa/Kolkkala	FIN	Mustasaari	28 Feb 1999
20 lb weight #	25.60	Gwen Berry	USA	Albuquerque	4 Mar 2017
3000m walk	11:35.34 un	Gillian O'Sullivan	IRL	Belfast	15 Feb 2003
	11:40.33	Claudia Iovan/Stef	ROU	Bucuresti	30 Jan 1999
5000m walk #	20:37.77	Margarita Turova	BLR	Minsk	13 Feb 2005
10000m walk	43:54.63	Yelena Ginko	BLR	Mogilyov	22 Feb 2008
4 x 200m	1:32.41	Russia		Glasgow	29 Jan 2005
		(Yekaterina Kondratyeva, Irina Khabarova, Yuliya Pechonkina, Yuliya Gushchina)			
4 x 400m	3:23.37	Russia		Glasgow	28 Jan 2006
		(Yuliya Gushchina, Olga Kotlyarova, Olga Zaytseva, Olesya Krasnomovets)			
4 x 800m	8:06.24	Moskva	RUS	Moskva	18 Feb 2011
		(Aleksandra Bulanova, Yekaterina Martynova, Yelena Kofanova , Anna Balakshina)			
Distance Med	10:42.57	Newa Balance TC	USA	Boston (Roxbury)	7 Feb 2015
		(Sarah Brown, Mahogany Jones, Megan Krumpoch, Brenda Martinez)			
Pentathlon	5013 points	Nataliya Dobrynska	UKR	Istanbul	9 Mar 2012
		(8.38 60mh, 1.84 HJ, 16.51 SP, 6.57 LJ, 2:11.15 800m)			

events not officially recognised by the IAAF

WORLD INDOOR JUNIOR (U20) RECORDS

First approved by IAAF Council in 2011. **Men**

60 metres	6.51	Mark Lewis-Francis	GBR	Lisboa	11 Mar 2001
200 metres	20.37	Walter Dix	USA	Fayetteville	11 Mar 2005
400 metres	44.80	Kirani James	GRN	Fayetteville	27 Feb 2011
800 metres	1:44.35	Yuriy Borzakovskiy	RUS	Dortmund	30 Jan 2000
1000 metres	2:15.77	Abubaker Kaki	SUD	Stockholm	21 Feb 2008
1500 metres	3:36.28	Belal Mansoor Ali (overage!)	BRN	Stockholm	20 Feb 2007
One mile	3:55.02	German Fernandez	USA	College Station	28 Feb 2009
3000 metres	7:32.87	Hagos Gebrhiwet	ETH	Boston (Roxbury)	2 Feb 2013
5000 metres	12:53.29	Isiah Koech	KEN	Düsseldorf	11 Feb 2011
60mh (99cm)	7.49	Trey Cunningham	USA	New York (Armory)	12 Mar 2017
High jump	2.35	Volodymyr Yashchenko	URS	Milano	12 Mar 1978
Pole vault	5.82	Armand Duplantis	SWE	New York (Armory)	11 Mar 2017
Long jump	8.22	Viktor Kuznetsov	UKR	Brovary	22 Jan 2005
Triple jump	17.14	Volker Mai	GDR	Piréas	2 Mar 1985

248 WORLD AND CONTINENTAL RECORDS

Shot (6kg)	22.48	Konrad Bukowiecki	POL	Torun	8 Jan 2016
Heptathlon	6022	Gunnar Nixon	USA	Fayetteville	27/28 Jan 2012
(jnr imps)		(7.10, 7.53, 13.97, 2.15, 8.21, 4.50, 2:40.15)			

Women

60 metres	7.07	Ewa Swoboda	POL	Torun	12 Feb 2016
200 metres	22.40	Bianca Knight	USA	Fayetteville	14 Mar 2008
400 metres	50.82	Sanya Richards	USA	Fayetteville	13 Mar 2004
800 metres	2:01.03	Meskerem Legesse	ETH	Fayetteville	14 Feb 2004
1000 metres	2:35.80	Mary Cain	USA	Boston (Roxbury)	8 Feb 2014
1500 metres	4:01.81	Gudaf Tsegay	ETH	Glasgow	20 Feb 2016
One mile	4:24.10	Kalkidan Gezahegne	ETH	Birmingham	20 Feb 2010
3000 metres	8:33.56	Tirunesh Dibaba	ETH	Birmingham	20 Feb 2004
5000 metres	14:53.99	Tirunesh Dibaba	ETH	Boston	31 Jan 2004
60m hurdles	8.00	Klaudia Siciarz	POL	Torun	18 Feb 2017
High jump	1.99	Vashti Cunningham	USA	Portland	12 Mar 2016
Pole vault	4.71	Wilma Murto	FIN	Zweibrücken	31 Jan 2016
Long jump	6.88	Heike Daute	GDR	Berlin	1 Feb 1983
Triple jump	14.37	Ren Ruiping	CHN	Barcelona	11 Mar 1995
Shot	20.51	Heidi Krieger	GDR	Budapest	8 Feb 1984
Pentathlon	4635A	Kendell Williams	USA	Albuquerque	15 Mar 2014
		(8.21, 1.88, 12.05, 6.32, 2:17.31)			
	4550	Alina Shukh	UKR	Zaporizhzhya	27 Jan 2017
		(8.85, 1.88, 14.27, 6.04, 2:17.69)			

WORLD VETERANS/MASTERS RECORDS

MEN – aged 35-39

100 metres	9.93	Kim Collins (5.4.76)	SKN	Bottrop	29 May 2016
200 metres	20.11	Linford Christie (2.4.60)	GBR	Villeneuve d'Ascq	25 Jun 1995
400 metres	44.54	Chris Brown (15.10.78)	BAH	Eugene	30 May 2015
800 metres	1:43.36	Johnny Gray (19.6.60)	USA	Zürich	16 Aug 1995
1000 metres	2:18.8+	William Tanui (22.2.64)	KEN	Rome	7 Jul 1999
1500 metres	3:32.45	William Tanui (22.2.64)	KEN	Athína	16 Jun 1999
1 mile	3:51.38	Bernard Lagat (12.12.74)	USA	London (CP)	6 Aug 2011
2000 metres	4:58.3+ e	William Tanui (22.2.64	KEN	Monaco	4 Aug 1999
	4:54.74i	Bernard Lagat (12.12.74)	USA	New York	15 Feb 2014
3000 metres	7:29.00	Bernard Lagat (12.12.74)	USA	Rieti	29 Aug 2010
5000 metres	12:53.60	Bernard Lagat (12.12.74)	USA	Monaco	22 Jul 2011
10000 metres	26:51.20	Haile Gebrselassie (18.4.73)	ETH	Hengelo	24 May 2008
20000 metres	57:44.4+	Gaston Roelants (5.2.37)	BEL	Bruxelles	20 Sep 1972
1 Hour	20,822m	Haile Gebrselassie (18.4.73)	ETH	Hengelo	1 Jun 2009
Half Marathon	59:10 dh	Paul Tergat (17.6.69)	KEN	Lisboa	13 Mar 2005
	59:31	Gilbert Masai (20.5.81)	KEN	København	18 Sep 2016
Marathon	2:03:59	Haile Gebrselassie (18.4.73)	ETH	Berlin	28 Sep 2008
3000m steeple	8:04.95	Simon Vroemen (11.5.69)	NED	Bruxelles	26 Aug 2005
110m hurdles	12.96	Allen Johnson (1.3.71)	USA	Athína	17 Sep 2006
400m hurdles	48.10	Felix Sánchez (30.8.77)	DOM	Moskva	13 Aug 2013
High jump	2.31	Dragutin Topic (12.3.71)	SRB	Kragujevac	28 Jul 2009
	2.31	Jamie Nieto (2.11.76)	USA	New York	9 Jun 2012
Pole vault	5.90i	Björn Otto (16.10.77)	GER	Cottbus	30 Jan 2013
	5.90i	Björn Otto		Düsseldorf	8 Feb 2013
	5.90	Björn Otto		Eugene	1 Jun 2013
Long jump	8.50	Larry Myricks (10.3.56)	USA	New York	15 Jun 1991
	8.50	Carl Lewis (1.7.61)	USA	Atlanta	29 Jul 1996
Triple jump	17.92	Jonathan Edwards (10.5.66)	GBR	Edmonton	6 Aug 2001
Shot	22.67	Kevin Toth ¶ (29.12.67)	USA	Lawrence	19 Apr 2003
Discus	71.56	Virgilijus Alekna (13.2.72)	LTU	Kaunas	25 Jul 2007
Hammer	83.62	Igor Astapkovich (4.1.63)	BLR	Staiki	20 Jun 1998
Javelin	92.80	Jan Zelezny (16.6.66)	CZE	Edmonton	12 Aug 2001
Decathlon	8241	Kip Janvrin (8.7.65)	USA	Eugene	22 Jun 2001
		(10.98, 7.01, 14.21, 1.89, 48.41, 14.72, 45.59, 5.20, 60.41, 4:14.96)			
20 km walk	1:17:02	Yohann Diniz (1.1.78)	FRA	Arles	8 Mar 2015
20000m t walk	1:19:42.1	Yohann Diniz (1.1.78)	FRA	Bogny-sur-Meuse	25 May 2014
50 km walk	3:32:33	Yohann Diniz (1.1.78)	FRA	Zürich	15 Aug 2014
50000m t walk	3:49:29.7	Alain Lemercier (11.1.57)	FRA	Franconville	3 Apr 1994

MEN – aged 40 or over

100 metres	9.93	Kim Collins (5.4.76)	SKN	Bottrop	29 May 2016
200 metres	20.64	Troy Douglas (30.11.62)	NED	Utrecht	9 Aug 2003
400 metres	47.82	Enrico Saraceni (19.5.64)	ITA	Århus	25 Jul 2004
	47.5u	Lee Evans (25.2.47)	USA		Apr 1989
800 metres	1:48.05	Anthony Whiteman (13.11.71)	GBR	Manchester (Stretford)	12 Jul 2014

WORLD AND CONTINENTAL RECORDS 249

Event	Mark	Athlete	Nat	Venue	Date
1000 metres	2:24.93i	Vyacheslav Shabunin (27.9.69)	RUS	Moskva	10 Jan 2010
1500 metres	3:40.20i+	Bernard Lagat (12.12.74)	USA	New York (Armory)	14 Feb 2015
	3:41.87	Bernard Lagat		Birmingham	7 Jun 2015
1 mile	3:54.91i+	Bernard Lagat		New York (Armory)	14 Feb 2015
	3:57.91	Bernard Lagat		London (OS)	25 Jul 2015
3000 metres	7:37.92i+	Bernard Lagat (12.12.74)	USA	Metz	25 Feb 2015
	7:42.75	Bernard Lagat		Luzern	14 Jul 2015
5000 metres	13:06.78	Bernard Lagat		Rio de Janeiro	20 Aug 2016
10000 metres	27:49.35	Bernard Lagat		Stanford	1 May 2016
10 km road	27:48	Bernard Lagat (12.12.74)	USA	Manchester	10 May 2015
1 Hour	19.710k	Steve Moneghetti (26.9.62)	AUS	Geelong	17 Dec 2005
Half marathon	60:41 dh	Haile Gebrselassie (18.4.73)	ETH	South Shields	15 Sep 2013
	61:09	Haile Gebrselassie		Glasgow	6 Oct 2013
Marathon	2:08:38	Kenneth Mungara KEN (7.9.73)	KEN	Milano	3 Apr 2016
3000m steeple	8:38.40	Angelo Carosi (20.1.64)	ITA	Firenze	11 Jul 2004
110m hurdles	13.97	David Ashford (24.1.63)	USA	Indianapolis	3 Jul 2004
	13.79 ?	Roger Kingdom (26.8.62)	USA	Slippery Rock	23 Jun 2004
400m hurdles	49.69	Danny McFarlane (14.2.72)	JAM	Kingston	29 Jun 2012
High jump	2.28	Dragutin Topic (12.3.71)	SRB	Beograd	20 May 2012
Pole vault	5.71i	Jeff Hartwig (25.9.67)	USA	Jonesboro	31 May 2008
	5.70	Jeff Hartwig		Eugene	29 Jun 2008
Long jump	7.68A	Aaron Sampson (20.9.61)	USA	Cedar City, UT	21 Jun 2002
	7.59i	Mattias Sunneborn (27.9.70)	SWE	Sätra	3 Feb 2013
	7.57	Hans Schicker (3.10.47)	FRG	Kitzingen	16 Jul 1989
Triple jump	17.13i	Fabrizio Donato (14.8.76	ITA	Beograd	3 Mar 2017
	16.93	Fabrizio Donato (14.8.76	ITA	Rovereto	6 Sep 2016
Shot	21.41	Brian Oldfield USA (1.6.45)	USA	Innsbruck	22 Aug 1985
Discus	70.28	Virgilijus Alekna (13.2.72)	LTU	Klaipeda	23 Jun 2012
Hammer	82.23	Igor Astapkovich (4.1.63)	BLR	Minsk	10 Jul 2004
Javelin	85.92	Jan Zelezny (16.6.66)	CZE	Göteborg	9 Aug 2006
Pentathlon	3510	Werner Schallau (8.9.38)	FRG	Gelsenkirchen	24 Sep 1978
	6.74, 59.20, 23.0, 43.76, 5:05.7				
Decathlon	7525	Kip Janvrin (8.7.65)	USA	San Sebastián	24 Aug 2005
	11.56, 6.78, 14.01, 1.80, 49.46, 15.40, 42.70, 4.70, 58.43, 4:25.87				
20 km walk	1:20:20	Andriy Kovenko (25.11.73)	UKR	Alushta	28 Feb 2014
20000m t walk	1:24:46.1	Ivan Trotskiy (27.5.76)	BLR	Grodno	23 Jun 2016
50 km walk	3:40:46	Yuriy Andronov (6.11.71)	RUS	Moskva	11 Jun 2012
50000m t walk	3:51:54.5	José Marín (21.1.50)	ESP	Manresa	7 Apr 1990
4x100m	42.20	SpeedWest TC	USA	Irvine	2 May 2004
	(Frank Strong, Cornell Stephenson, Kettrell Berry, Willie Gault)				
4x400m	3:20.83	S Allah, K Morning, E Gonera, R Blackwell USA		Philadelphia	27 Apr 2001

WOMEN – aged 35-39

Event	Mark	Athlete	Nat	Venue	Date
100 metres	10.74	Merlene Ottey (10.5.60)	JAM	Milano	7 Sep 1996
200 metres	21.93	Merlene Ottey (10.5.60)	JAM	Bruxelles	25 Aug 1995
400 metres	50.27	Jearl Miles Clark (4.9.66)	USA	Madrid	20 Sep 2002
800 metres	1:56.53	Lyubov Gurina (6.8.57)	RUS	Hechtel	30 Jul 1994
1000 metres	2:31.5	Maricica Puica (29.7.50)	ROU	Poiana Brasov	1 Jun 1986
1500 metres	3:57.73	Maricica Puica (29.7.50)	ROU	Bruxelles	30 Aug 1985
1 mile	4:17.33	Maricica Puica (29.7.50)	ROU	Zürich	21 Aug 1985
2000 metres	5:28.69	Maricica Puica (29.7.50)	ROU	London (CP)	11 Jul 1986
3000 metres	8:23.23	Edith Masai (4.4.67)	KEN	Monaco	19 Jul 2002
5000 metres	14:33.84	Edith Masai (4.4.67)	KEN	Oslo	2 Jun 2006
10000 metres	30:30.26	Edith Masai (4.4.67)	KEN	Helsinki	6 Aug 2005
Half Marathon	67:16	Edith Masai (4.4.67)	KEN	Berlin	2 Apr 2006
Marathon	2:19:19	Irina Mikitenko (23.8.72)	GER	Berlin	28 Sep 2008
3000m steeple	9:24.26	Marta Domínguez (3.11.75)	ESP	Huelva	7 Jun 2012
100m hurdles	12.40	Gail Devers (19.11.66)	USA	Lausanne	2 Jul 2002
400m hurdles	52.94	Marina Styepanova (1.5.50)	RUS	Tashkent	17 Sep 1986
High jump	2.01	Inga Babakova (27.6.67)	UKR	Oslo	27 Jun 2003
	2.01	Ruth Beitia (1.4.79)	ESP	Zürich	17 Aug 2014
Pole vault	4.87	Fabiana Murer (16,3,81)	BRA	São Bernardo do Campo	3 Jul 2016
Long jump	6.99	Heike Drechsler (16.12.64)	GER	Sydney	29 Sep 2000
Triple jump	14.68	Tatyana Lebedeva (21.7.76)	RUS	Cheboksary	3 Jul 2012
	14.82i	Yamilé Aldama (14.8.72)	GBR	Istanbul	10 Mar 2012
Shot	21.46	Larisa Peleshenko (29.2.64)	RUS	Moskva	26 Aug 2000
	21.47i	Helena Fibingerová (13.7.49)	CZE	Jablonec	9 Feb 1985
Discus	69.60	Faina Melnik (9.7.45)	RUS	Donetsk	9 Sep 1980
Hammer	74.03	Amber Campbell (5.6.81)	USA	Eugene	6 Jul 2016
Javelin	68.34	Steffi Nerius (1.7.72)	GER	Berlin (Elstal)	31 Aug 2008
Heptathlon	6533	Jane Frederick (7.4.52)	USA	Talence	27 Sep 1987
	13.60, 1.82, 15.50, 24.73; 6.29, 49.70, 2:14.88				

WORLD AND CONTINENTAL RECORDS

Event	Mark	Athlete	Nat	Venue	Date
5000m walk	20:12.41	Elisabetta Perrone (9.7.68)	ITA	Rieti	2 Aug 2003
10km walk	41:41	Kjersti Tysse Plätzer (18.1.72)	NOR	Kraków	30 May 2009
10000m t walk	43:26.5	Elisabetta Perrone (9.7.68)	ITA	Saluzzo	4 Aug 2004
20km walk	1:25:59	Tamara Kovalenko (5.6.64)	RUS	Moskva	19 May 2000
20000m t walk	1:27:49.3	Yelena Nikolayeva (1.2.66)	RUS	Brisbane	6 Sep 2001
4x100m	48.63	Desmier, Sulter, Andreas, Apavou	FRA	Eugene	8 Jun 1989
4x400m	3:50.80	Mitchell, Mathews, Beadnall, Gabriel	GBR	Gateshead	8 Aug 1999

WOMEN – aged 40 or over

Event	Mark	Athlete	Nat	Venue	Date
100 metres	10.99	Merlene Ottey (10.5.60)	JAM	Thessaloniki	30 Aug 2000
200 metres	22.72	Merlene Ottey (10.5.60)	SLO	Athína	23 Aug 2004
400 metres	53.05A	María Figueirêdo (11.11.63)	BRA	Bogotá	10 Jul 2004
	53.14	María Figueirêdo (11.11.63)	BRA	San Carlos, VEN	19 Jun 2004
800 metres	1:59.25	Yekaterina Podkopayeva (11.6.52)	RUS	Luxembourg	30 Jun 1994
1000 metres	2:36.16	Yekaterina Podkopayeva (11.6.52)	RUS	Nancy	14 Sep 1994
	2:36.08i	Yekaterina Podkopayeva	RUS	Liévin	13 Feb 1993
1500 metres	3:59.78	Yekaterina Podkopayeva (11.6.52)	RUS	Nice	18 Jul 1994
1 mile	4:23.78	Yekaterina Podkopayeva (11.6.52)	RUS	Roma	9 Jun 1993
3000 metres	9:01.1+	Jo Pavey (20.9.73)	GBR	Roma	5 Jun 2014
	8:58.20i	Nuria Fernández (16.8.76)	ESP	Beograd	3 May 2017
5000 metres	15:04.87	Jo Pavey (20.9.73)	GBR	Roma	5 Jun 2014
10000 metres	31:31.18	Edith Masai (4.4.67)	KEN	Alger	21 Jul 2007
1 hour	16.056k	Jackie Fairweather (10.11.67)	AUS	Canberra	24 Jan 2008
Half Marathon	69:37	Deena Kastor (14.2.73)	USA	Philadelphia	21 Sep 2014
Marathon	2:24:54	Irina Mikitenko (23.8.72)	GER	Berlin	21 Sep 2013
3000m steeple	10:00.75	Minori Hayakari (29.11.72)	JPN	Kumagaya	22 Sep 2013
100 m hurdles	13.20	Patricia Girard (8.4.68)	FRA	Paris	14 Jul 2008
400 m hurdles	58.35	Barbara Gähling (20.3.65)	GER	Erfurt	21 Jul 2007
	58.3 h	Gowry Retchakan (21.6.60)	GBR	Hoo	3 Sep 2000
High jump	1.94i	Venelina Veneva-Mateeva (13.6.74)	BUL	Dobrich 15 Feb & Praha	6 Mar 2015
	1.90	Venelina Veneva-Mateeva	BUL	Plovdiv 12 Jul & Pitesti	27 Jul 2014
Pole vault	4.10	Doris Auer (10.5.71)	AUT	Innsbruck	6 Aug 2011
	4.11 §	Doris Auer	AUT	Wien	5 Jul 2011
Long jump	6.64	Tatyana Ter-Mesrobian (12.5.68)	RUS	Sankt-Peterburg	31 May 2008
	6.64i	Tatyana Ter-Mesrobian	RUS	Sankt-Peterburg	5 Jan 2010
Triple jump	14.06	Yamilé Aldama (14.8.72)	GBR	Eugene	1 Jun 2013
Shot	19.05	Antonina Ivanova (25.12.32)	RUS	Oryol	28 Aug 1973
	19.16i	Antonina Ivanova	RUS	Moskva	24 Feb 1974
Discus	67.89	Iryna Yatchenko (31.10.65)	BLR	Staiki	29 Jun 2008
Hammer	59.29	Oneithea Lewis (11.6.60)	USA	Princeton	10 May 2003
Javelin	61.96	Laverne Eve (16.6.65)	BAH	Monaco	9 Sep 2005
Heptathlon	5449	Tatyana Alisevich (22.1.69)	BLR	Staiki	3 Jun 2010
	14.80, 1.62, 13.92, 26.18, 5.55, 45.44, 2:24.39				
5000m walk	21:46.68	Kelly Ruddick (19.4.73)	AUS	Brisbane	29 Mar 2014
10000m t walk	44:50.19	Susana Feitor (28.1.75)	POR	Leiria	25 Jul 2015
20km walk	1:31:58	Susana Feitor		Rio Maior	18 Apr 2015
	1:31:58	Susana Feitor		Murcia	17 May 2015
20000m t walk	1:33:28.15t	Teresa Vaill (20.11.62)	USA	Carson	25 Jun 2005
4x100m	48.22	Cadinot, Barilly, Valouvin, Lapierre	FRA	Le Touquet	24 Jun 2006
4x400m	3:57.28	Loizou, Kay, Smithe, Cearns	AUS	Brisbane	14 Jul 2001

WORLD AND CONTINENTAL RECORDS SET IN 2016

OUTDOORS – MEN   § Not ratified

Event	Cat	Mark	Athlete	Nat	Venue	Date
100	Asi =	9.91	Femi Seun OGUNODE	QAT	Gainesville	22 Apr 16
	W40	10.09	Kim COLLINS	SKN	Kingston	7 May 16
	W35, 40	9.93	Kim COLLINS	SKN	Bottrop	29 May 16
	Eur =	9.86	Jimmy VICAUT	FRA	Montreuil-sous-Bois	7 Jun 16
300	Afr	31.03	Wayde van NIEKERK	RSA	Kingston	11 Jun 16
400	W, Afr	43.03	Wayde van NIEKERK	RSA	Rio de Janeiro	14 Aug 16
600	Afr, Com	1:13.10	David RUDISHA	KEN	Birmingham	5 Jun 16
3000	W20	7:28.19	Yomif KEJELCHA	ETH	Saint-Denis	27 Aug 16
5000	W40	13:14.96	Bernard LAGAT	USA	London (OS)	23 Jul 16
	W40	13:06.78	Bernard LAGAT	USA	Rio de Janeiro	20 Aug 16
10000	W40	27:49.35	Bernard LAGAT	USA	Stanford	1 May 16
10k	Oce	27:28	Zane ROBERTSON	NZL	Berlin	9 Oct 16
15k	Eur	42:03+	Mo FARAH	GBR	Cardiff	26 Mar 16
HMar	W35	59:31	Gilbert MASAI	KEN	København	18 Sep 16
30k	W, Afr	1:27:20+	Sisay LEMMA	ETH	Dubai	22 Jan 16
	W,Afr,Com	1:27:13+	Eliud KIPCHOGE	KEN	London	24 Apr 16
	W,Afr,Com	1:27:13+	Stanley BIWOTT	KEN	London	24 Apr 16
Mar	Eur	2:06:10 §	Kaan Kigen ÖZBILEN	TUR	Seoul	20 Mar 16

WORLD AND CONTINENTAL RECORDS 251

	W40	2:08:38	Kenneth MUNGARA	KEN	Milano	3 Apr 16
100k	Afr	6:24:05	Bongmusa MTHEMBU	RSA	Los Alcazares	27 Nov 16
PV	W18	5.55	Emmanouil KARÁLIS	GRE	Ostrava	20 May 16
	SAm	5.93 & 6.03	Thiago BRAZ da SILVA	BRA	Rio de Janeiro	15 Aug 16
LJ	W18	8.28	Maykel D MASSÓ	CUB	La Habana	28 May 16
TJ	W40	16.93	Fabrizio DONATO	ITA	Rovereto	6 Sep 16
SP/6	W20	23.34	Konrad BUKOWIECKI	POL	Bydgoszcz	19 Jul 16
SP	W20	20.69 & 21.01	Konrad BUKOWIECKI	POL	Ostrava	20 May 16
	W20	21.14	Konrad BUKOWIECKI	POL	Oslo	9 Jun 16
	Oce	21.81 & 22.00	Tom WALSH	NZL	Saint-Denis	27 Aug 16
	Oce	22.20	Tom WALSH	NZL	Zürich	1 Sep 16
	Oce,Com =	22.21	Tom WALSH	NZL	Zagreb	5 Sep 16
HT	SAm	76.81 & 78.63	Wagner DOMINGOS	BRA	Celje	19 Jun 16
JT	W20	86.48	Neeraj CHOPRA	IND	Bydgoszcz	23 Jul 16
Dec	Afr	8521	Larbi BOURAADA	ALG	Rio de Janeiro	18 Aug 16
		(10.75, 7.52, 13.78, 2.10, 47.98 / 14.15, 42.39, 4.60, 66.49, 4:14.60)				
4x100 R	Asi	37.82	Tang Xingqiang, Xie Zhenye, Su Bingtian, Zhang Peimeng			
				CHN	Rio de Janeiro	18 Aug 16
	Asi	37.68	Yamagata, Iizuka, Kiryu, Cambridge	JPN	Rio de Janeiro	18 Aug 16
	Asi	37.60	Yamagata, Iizuka, Kiryu, Cambridge	JPN	Rio de Janeiro	19 Aug 16
4x800 R	W35	7:51.47	Sotomayor, Pérez, Pouz, Gil	ESP	Madrid	14 May 16
5000W	Oce	18:38.97	Dane BIRD-SMITH	AUS	Melbourne	5 Mar 16
20000W	W40	1:24:46.1t	Ivan TROTSKIY	BLR	Grodno	23 Jun 16
20kW	NAm	1:19:20	Iñaki GÓMEZ	CAN	Nomi	20 Mar 16
50kW	SAm	3:42:57	Andres CHOCHO	ECU	Ciudad Juárez	6 Mar 16
	NAm	3:41:38	Evan DUNFEE	CAN	Rio de Janeiro	19 Aug 16

OUTDOORS – WOMEN

100	Afr	10.78	Murielle AHOURÉ	CIV	Montverde	11 Jun 16
	CAC=,Com=	10.70	Elaine THOMPSON	JAM	Kingston	1 Jul 16
1500	Com	3:56.82	Faith KIPYEGON	KEN	Shanghai	14 May 16
	Com	3:56.41	Faith KIPYEGON	KEN	Eugene	28 May 16
	Com	3:55.22	Laura MUIR	Sco/GBR	Saint-Denis	27 Aug 16
1M	Afr	4:14.30	Genzebe DIBABA	ETH	Rovereto	6 Sep 16
5000	NAm	14:38.92	Shannon ROWBURY	USA	Bruxelles	9 Sep 16
10000	W, Afr	29:17.45	Almaz AYANA	ETH	Rio de Janeiro	12 Aug 16
	Com	29:32.53	Vivian CHERUIYOT	KEN	Rio de Janeiro	12 Aug 16
	NAm	30:13.17	Molly HUDDLE	USA	Rio de Janeiro	12 Aug 16
HMar	SAm	70:14	Gladys TEJEDA	PER	Cardiff	26 Mar 16
100k	Oce	7:34:35	Kirstin BULL	AUS	Los Alcazares	27 Nov 16
24Hr	Eur	250.647k	Maria JANSSON	SWE	Albi	23 Oct 16
3000SC	Asi	9:15.98	Ruth JEBET	BRN	Shanghai	14 May 16
	W18	9:24.73	Celphine CHESPOL	KEN	Shanghai	14 May 16
	SAm	9:39.33	Juliana dos SANTOS	BRA	Oordegem	28 May 16
	Asi	8:59.97	Ruth JEBET	BRN	Eugene	28 May 16
	Afr, Com	9:00.01	Hyvin JEPKEMOI	KEN	Eugene	28 May 16
	NAm	9:10.76	Emma COBURN	USA	Eugene	28 May 16
	SAm	9:38.63	Juliana dos SANTOS	BRA	Praha	6 Jun 16
	Asi	8:59.75	Ruth JEBET	BRN	Rio de Janeiro	15 Aug 16
	NAm	9:07.63	Emma COBURN	USA	Rio de Janeiro	15 Aug 16
	W,Asi	8:52.78	Ruth JEBET	BRN	Saint-Denis	27 Aug 16
	Oce	9:14.28	Genevieve LaCAZE	AUS	Saint-Denis	27 Aug 16
100H	NAm	12.24	Keni HARRISON	USA	Eugene	28 May 16
	W18	12.84	Tia JONES	USA	Clovis	25 Jun 16
	W, NAm	12.20	Keni HARRISON	USA	London	22 Jul 16
400H	W18	54.46	Sydney McLAUGHLIN	USA	Greensboro	19 Jun 16
	W18, W20	54.15	Sydney McLAUGHLIN	USA	Eugene	10 Jul 16
HJ	WB/Hep	1.98	Nafissatou THIAM	BEL	Rio de Janeiro	12 Aug 16
	WB/Hep	1.98	Katarina JOHNSON-THOMPSON	GBR	Rio de Janeiro	12 Aug 16
PV	Oce	4.77	Alana BOYD	AUS	Sippy Downs	28 Jan 16
	Oce	4.80	Eliza McCARTNEY	NZL	Dunedin	5 Mar 16
	W18	4.50	Lisa GUNNARSSON	SWE	Pézenas	28 May 16
	W18=	4.50	Lisa GUNNARSSON	SWE	Angers	25 Jun 16
	Oce, Com	4.81	Alana BOYD	AUS	Sippy Downs	2 Jul 16
	W35, SAm	4.87	Fabiana de Almeida MURER	BRA	São Bernardo do Campo	3 Jul 16
LJ	Oce	7.05	Brooke STRATTON	AUS	Perth	12 Mar 16
TJ	NAm	14.53	Keturah ORJI	USA	Eugene	11 Jun 16
	NAm	14.71	Keturah ORJI	USA	Rio de Janeiro	14 Aug 16
SP	NAm	20.63	Michelle CARTER	USA	Rio de Janeiro	12 Aug 16
HT	W35	74.03	Amber CAMPBELL	USA	Eugene	6 Jul 16
	W,Eur	82.29	Anita WLODARCZYK	POL	Rio de Janeiro	15 Aug 16

252 WORLD AND CONTINENTAL RECORDS

	W,Eur	82.98	Anita WLODARCZYK	POL	Warszawa	28 Aug 16
JT	SAm	63.84A	Flor RUIZ	COL	Cali	25 Jun 16
Hep/U18	W18	6186	Alina SHUKH	UKR	Tbilisi	15 Jul 16
		(14.43, 1.88, 14.85, 26.68 / 5.98, 50.04, 2:14.89)				
Hep	SAm	6270A	Evelis AGUILAR	COL	Cali	26 Jun 16
		(13.56w, 1.71, 13.25, 23.76w / 6.06, 45.98, 2:10.06)				
5000W	Afr	21:49.27t	Chahinez NASRI	TUN	Blois	8 Jun 16
10000W	Afr	44:41.8At	Grace Njue WANJIRU	KEN	Thika	5 Mar 16
10kW	NAm	44:09+	Maria MICHTA-COFFEY	USA	St. Louis	3 Apr 16
	SAm	43:56+	Erica de SENA	BRA	Roma	7 May 16
	Afr	45:02	Chahinez NASRI	TUN	La Coruña	28 May 16
20kW	Afr	1:34:35	Chahinez NASRI	TUN	St-Sebastien-sur-Loire	13 Mar 16
	SAm	1:28:22	Erica de SENA	BRA	Dudince	19 Mar 16
	CAC	1:26:17	Maria Guadelupe GONZÁLEZ	MEX	Roma	7 May 16
	SAm	1:27:18	Erica de SENA	BRA	Roma	7 May 16
	Afr	1:34:09A	Grace Njue WANJIRU	KEN	Nairobi	27 May 16
	Afr	1:30:43	Grace Njue WANJIRU	KEN	Durban	26 Jun 16
25kW	W,Eur	1:56:12+	Eleonora GIORGI	ITA	Catania	31 Jan 16
30kW	W,Eur	2:19:43	Eleonora GIORGI	ITA	Catania	31 Jan 16
50kW	Asi	4:34:01	ZHOU Kang	CHN	Huangshan	6 Mar 16

See ATHLETICS 2016 for Indoor Records set in January - March 2016 – and add

INDOORS – MEN
4x400 R	W35,40	4:03.72A	Friend-Uhl, Gentile, Walles, McGowan	USA	Albuquerque	6 Mar 16

WORLD AND CONTINENTAL RECORDS SET IN JAN–MAR 2017

INDOORS – MEN   # on oversized track

60	W40	6.71 & 6.64	Kim COLLINS	SKN	Jablonec	28 Jan 17
	W40	6.58 & 6.56	Kim COLLINS	SKN	Düsseldorf	1 Feb 17
	W40	6.54 & 6.52	Kim COLLINS	SKN	Mondeville	4 Feb 17
200	W18	21.05	Tyrese COOPER	USA	New York (Armory)	12 Mar 17
300	W20, W18	32.87	Tyrese COOPER	USA	New York (Armory)	4 Feb 17
	W, NAm	31.87A	Noah LYLES	USA	Albuquerque	5 Mar 17
400	W18	46.01	Tyrese COOPER	USA	Fayetteville	10 Feb 17
	SAm	46.26#	Stephan JAMES	GUY	Nashville	24 Feb 17
	SAm	46.15#	Jermaine GRIFFITH	GUY	Geneva,OH	25 Feb 17
600	W, Afr	1:14.97A	Emmanuel KORIR	KEN	Albuquerque	20 Jan 17
	W, NAm	1:14.91	Casimir LOXSOM	USA	State College	28 Jan 17
5000	W40	14:19.59	Kevin CASTILLE	USA	Boston (Allston)	28 Jan 17
	Eur	13:09.16	Mohamed FARAH	GBR	Birmingham	18 Feb 17
	Asi	13:09.43	Albert ROP	BRN	Birmingham	18 Feb 17
	CAC	13:14.45	Kemoy CAMPBELL	JAM	Boston (Allston)	26 Feb 17
Mar	W	2:21:47	Chris ZABLOCKI	USA	New York (Armory)	25 Mar 17
60H/99	W20	7.49	Trey CUNNINGHAM	USA	Birmingham,AL	27 Jan 17
	W20	7.45	Trey CUNNINGHAM	USA	New York (Armory)	11 Mar 17
	W20	7.40	Trey CUNNINGHAM	USA	New York (Armory)	12 Mar 17
PV	W20	5.72	Armand DUPLANTIS	SWE	Baton Rouge	4 Feb 17
	W20	5.75	Armand DUPLANTIS	SWE	New York (Armory)	11 Feb 17
	W20	5.82	Armand DUPLANTIS	SWE	New York (Armory)	11 Mar 17
TJ	W20	17.20	Melvin RAFFIN	FRA	Beograd	3 Mar 17
	W40	16.70	Fabrizio DONATO	ITA	Beograd	3 Mar 17
	W40	17.13	Fabrizio DONATO	ITA	Beograd	5 Mar 17
SP/6kg	W20	22.72 & 22.96 §	Konrad BUKOWIECKI	POL	Spala	29 Dec 16
Hep	Eur	6479	Kevin MAYER	FRA	Beograd	5 Mar 17
		(6.95, 7.54, 15.66, 2.10 / 7.88, 5.40, 2:41.08)				
4x800 R	W35	7:54.51	Ramón, Gil, Pérez, Sotomayor	ESP	Madrid	2 Feb 17
4x1M R	W, NAm	16:12.81	Cabral, Palmer, Crawford, Merber	USA	New York (Armory)	17 Feb 17
5000W	Com	18:39.47	Tom BOSWORTH	GBR	Sheffield	12 Feb 17
	W40	19:32.08	João VIEIRA	POR	Pombal	18 Feb 17

INDOORS – WOMEN

200	SAm	23.36	Brenessa THOMPSON	GUY	Clemson	11 Feb 17
300	NAm	35.71	Quanera HAYES	USA	Clemson	7 Jan 17
	W20	36.56A	Candace HILL	USA	Albuquerque	4 Mar 17
500	NAm	1:08.40	Sage WATSON	CAN	New York	4 Feb 17
	NAm	1:07.34	Courtney OKOLO	USA	New York	11 Feb 17
600	CAC, Com	1:25.76	Natoya GOULE	JAM	Clemson	28 Jan 17
	CAC, Com	1:25.35	Natoya GOULE	JAM	Clemson	17 Feb 17
800	NAm	1:58.27	Ajee' WILSON	USA	New York (Armory)	11 Feb 17
1000	Eur	2:31.93	Laura MUIR	GBR	Birmingham	18 Feb 17
1500	Com	4:02.39	Laura MUIR	GBR	Beograd	4 Mar 17

WORLD AND CONTINENTAL RECORDS

1M	SAm	4:38.86	Rolanda BELL	PAN	New York (Armory)	21 Jan 17	
2000	W, Afr	5:23.75	Genzebe DIBABA	ETH	Sabadell	7 Feb 17	
3000	Eur, Com	8:26.41	Laura MUIR	GBR	Karlsruhe	4 Feb 17	
	W40	9:01.42	Nuria FERNÁNDEZ	ESP	Karlsruhe	4 Feb 17	
	W40	8:58.20	Nuria FERNÁNDEZ	ESP	Beograd	3 Mar 17	
Mar	W	2:42:30	Laura MANNINEN	FIN	New York (Armory)	25 Mar 17	
60H 76cm	W18	8.10	Cyrena SAMBA-MAYELA	FRA	Nantes	11 Feb 17	
60H	W20	8.00	Klaudia SICIARZ	POL	Torun	18 Feb 17	
HJ	W35=	1.98	Ruth BEITIA	ESP	Madrid	24 Feb 17	
TJ	SAm	14.79	Yulimar ROJAS	VEN	Madrid	28 Jan 17	
	NAm	14.32 (twice)	Keturah ORJI	USA	Nashville	25 Feb 17	
Wt	Eur	23.73	Ida STORM	SWE	Malmö	15 Feb 17	
	W, NAm	25.60A	Gwen BERRY	USA	Albuquerque	4 Mar 17	
Pen	W20	4550	Alina SHUKH	UKR	Zaporizhzhya	27 Jan 17	
		(8.85, 1.88, 14.27, 6.04, 2:17.69)					
4x200 R	Asi	1:36.40	Tulapina, Rakhmanova, Shynazbekova, Zyabkina				
				KAZ	Ust-Kamenogorsk	11 Feb 17	
Dist MedR	W,NAm	10:40.31	Coburn, McLaughlin, Martinez, Simpson	USA	Boston (Allston)	28 Jan 17	
3000W	CAC	12:59.45	Mirna ORTIZ	GUA	Bordeaux	19 Feb 17	

OUTDOORS – MEN

400H 84cm	W18	48.84A	Sokwakhana ZAZINI	RSA	Pretoria	17 Mar 17
LJ	Afr, Com	8.62A	Luvo MANYONGA	RSA	Pretoria	17 Mar 17

OUTDOORS – WOMEN

20k	W,Afr,Com	61:40	Peres JEPCHIRCHIR	KEN	Ra's Al-Khaymah	10 Feb 17
HMar	W,Afr,Com	65:06	Peres JEPCHIRCHIR	KEN	Ra's Al-Khaymah	10 Feb 17
PV	Oce, Com	4.82	Eliza McCARTNEY	NZL	Auckland	26 Feb 17
50kW	W, Eur	4:08:26	Inés HENRIQUES	POR	Porto de Mos	15 Jan 17
	NAm	4:26:37	Katie BURNETT	USA	Santee	28 Jan 17
	Asi	4:22:22	Yin Hang	CHN	Huangshan	5 Mar 17

Most World Records: Sergey Bubka USR/UKR set a total of 35 at pole vault: 17 outdoors from 5.85 (1984) to 6.14 (1994) and 18 indoors (9 ratified by IAAF) from 5.81 (1844) to 6.15 (1993). Paavi Nurmi FIN set 22 official and 13 unofficial world records at distances from 1500m to 20,000m between 1921 and 1931.
The most world records by a woman at one event is 28 at pole vault (15 outdoors, 13 indoors) by Yelena Isinbayeva RUS 2003-09.

Oldest: 41y 238d Yekaterina Podkopayeva RUS women's 4x800m indoor 8:18.71 Moskva 4 Feb 1994.

Youngest: 14y 334d Wang Yan CHN 5000m walk 21:33.8 Jian 9 Mar 1986 (unratified).

Youngest male: 17y 198d Thomas Ray PV 3.42m Ulverston 19 Sep 1879 (prior to IAAF jurisdiction (from 1913).

Most world records set in one day: 6 Jesse Owens USA at Ann Arbor 25 May 1935: 100y 9.4, LJ 8.13m, 220y straight (& 200m) 20.3, 220y hurdles straight (& 220yh) 22.6.

Record span of setting world records: Men: 15 years Haile Gebrselassie ETH 1994-2009

SPLIT TIMES IN WORLD RECORDS

Men

			400m	800m	1200m	1600m	2000m	2400m	2800m
800m	1:40.91	Rudisha 2010	49.28	1:40.91					
1000m	2:11.96	Ngeny 1999	49.66	1:44.62		(200m 24.12, 600m 1:17.14)			
1500m	3:26.00	El Guerrouj 1998	54.3	1:50.7	2:46.4	(1000m 2:18.8)			
1M	3:43.13	El Guerrouj 1999	55.2	1:51.2	2:47.0	(1000m 2:19.2)			
2000m	4:44.79	El Guerrouj 1999	57.1	1:55.4	2:52.4	3:49.60			
3000m	7:20.67	Komen 1996	57.6	1:57.0	2:54.9	3:53.6	4:53.4	5:51.3	6:51.2 (1500m 3:38.6)
2M	7:58.61	Komen 1997	58.6	2:00.4		3:58.4	4:58.2	5:56.7	6:57.5 (1M 3:59.2)
5000m	12:37.35	Bekele 2004	kms:	2:33.24, 5:05.47, 7:37.34, 10:07.93, last 400m 57.9					
10,000m	26:17.53	Bekele 2005	kms:	2:40.6, 5:16.4, 7:53.3, 10:30.4, 13:09.4, 15:44.66, 18:23.98,					
				21:04.63, 23:45.09, 26:17.53, last 400m 57.1					
3kmSt	7:53.63	Shaheen 2004	1000m 2:36.13, 2000m 5:18.09						

Women

800m	1:53.28	Kratochvílová 1983	56.1	1:53.28	(600m 1:25.0)		
1000m	2:28.98	Masterkova 1996	58.3	1:59.8	(200m 28.4, 600m 1:29.7)		
1500m	3:50.46	Qu Yunxia 1993	57.2	2:00.8	3:05.2		
1M	4:12.56	Masterkova 1996	62.0	2:06.7	3:12.2	(1000m 2:39.5, 1500m 3:56.77)	
2000m	5:25.36	O'Sullivan 1994	64.9	2:07.8	3:14.8	4:23.5	5:25.36
			1km	2km	3km	4km	5km
3000m	8:06.11	Wang J 1993	2:42.0	5:29.7	(last 400m 62.7)		
2M	8:58.58	Defar 2007	2:48.4	5:37.5	8:24.1 (1M 4:33.07, last 400m 62.6)		
5000m	14:11.15	Dibaba 2008	2:48.3	5:43.8	8:39.0	11:28.44	14:11.15
10000m	29:17.45	Ayana 2016	3:01.53	5:55.79	8:52.70	11:49.79	14:46.81
			6k: 17:3674. 7k: 20:29.98, 8k: 23:25.37, 9k: 26:22.8				
3kmSt	8:52.78	Jebet 2016	1000m 2:56.36, 2000m 5:54.21				

WORLD MEN'S ALL-TIME LISTS
100 METRES

Mark	Wind	Name		Nat	Born	Pos	Meet	Venue	Date
9.58 WR	0.9	Usain	Bolt	JAM	21.8.86	1	WCh	Berlin	16 Aug 09
9.63	1.5		Bolt			1	OG	London (OS)	5 Aug 12
9.69 WR	0.0		Bolt			1	OG	Beijing	16 Aug 08
9.69	2.0	Tyson	Gay ¶	USA	9.8.82	1		Shanghai	20 Sep 09
9.69	-0.1	Yohan	Blake	JAM	26.12.89	1	Athl	Lausanne	23 Aug 12
9.71	0.9		Gay			2	WCh	Berlin	16 Aug 09
9.72 WR	1.7		Bolt			1	Reebok	New York (RI)	31 May 08
9.72	0.2	Asafa	Powell	JAM	23.11.82	1rA	Athl	Lausanne	2 Sep 08
9.74 WR	1.7		Powell			1h2	GP	Rieti	9 Sep 07
9.74	0.9	Justin	Gatlin ¶	USA	10.2.82	1	DL	Doha	15 May 15
9.75	1.1		Blake			1	NC	Kingston	29 Jun 15
9.75	1.5		Blake			2	OG	London (OS)	5 Aug 12
9.75	0.9		Gatlin			1	GGala	Roma	4 Jun 15
9.75	1.4		Gatlin			1	Athl	Lausanne	9 Jul 15
9.76	1.8		Bolt			1		Kingston	3 May 08
9.76	1.3		Bolt			1	VD	Bruxelles	16 Sep 11
9.76	-0.1		Bolt			1	GGala	Roma	31 May 12
9.76	1.4		Blake			1	WK	Zürich	30 Aug 12
9.77 WR	1.6		Powell			1	Tsik	Athína	14 Jun 05
9.77 WR	1.5		Powell			1	BrGP	Gateshead	11 Jun 06
9.77 WR	1.0		Powell			1rA	WK	Zürich	18 Aug 06
9.77	1.6		Gay			1q1	NC/OT	Eugene	28 Jun 08
9.77	-1.3		Bolt			1	VD	Bruxelles	5 Sep 08
9.77	0.9		Powell			1h1	GP	Rieti	7 Sep 08
9.77	0.4		Gay			1	GGala	Roma	10 Jul 09
9.77	-0.3		Bolt			1	WCh	Moskva	11 Aug 13
9.77	0.6		Gatlin			1	VD	Bruxelles	5 Sep 14
9.77	0.9		Gatlin			1s2	WCh	Beijing	23 Aug 15
9.78	0.0		Powell			1	GP	Rieti	9 Sep 07
9.78	-0.4		Gay			1	LGP	London (CP)	13 Aug 10
9.78	0.9	Nesta	Carter ¶?	JAM	10.11.85	1		Rieti	29 Aug 10
9.78	1.0		Powell			1	Athl	Lausanne	30 Jun 11
9.78	-0.3		Gatlin			1	Herc	Monaco	17 Jul 15
		(34 performances by 6 athletes)							
9.79 WR	0.1	Maurice	Greene	USA	23.7.74	1rA	Tsik	Athína	16 Jun 99
9.80	0.4	Steve	Mullings ¶	JAM	29.11.82	1	Pre	Eugene	4 Jun 11
9.82	1.7	Richard	Thompson	TTO	7.6.85	1	NC	Port of Spain	21 Jun 14
9.84 WR	0.7	Donovan	Bailey	CAN	16.12.67	1	OG	Atlanta	27 Jul 96
		(10)							
9.84	0.2	Bruny	Surin	CAN	12.7.67	2	WCh	Sevilla	22 Aug 99
9.84	1.3	Trayvon	Bromell	USA	10.7.95	1h4	NC	Eugene	25 Jun 15
9.85 WR	1.2	Leroy	Burrell	USA	21.2.67	1rA	Athl	Lausanne	6 Jul 94
9.85	1.7	Olusoji	Fasuba	NGR	9.7.84	2	SGP	Doha	12 May 06
9.85	1.3	Michael	Rodgers	USA	24.4.85	2	Pre	Eugene	4 Jun 11
9.86 WR	1.2	Carl	Lewis	USA	1.7.61	1	WCh	Tokyo	25 Aug 91
9.86	-0.4	Frank	Fredericks	NAM	2.10.67	1rA	Athl	Lausanne	3 Jul 96
9.86	1.8	Ato	Boldon	TTO	30.12.73	1rA	MSR	Walnut	19 Apr 98
9.86	0.6	Francis	Obikwelu	NGR/POR	22.11.78	2	OG	Athína	22 Aug 04
9.86	1.4	Keston	Bledman	TTO	8.3.88	1	NC	Port of Spain	23 Jun 12
		(20)							
9.86	1.3	Jimmy	Vicaut	FRA	27.2.92	2	DL	Saint-Denis	4 Jul 15
9.87	0.3	Linford	Christie ¶	GBR	2.4.60	1	WCh	Stuttgart	15 Aug 93
9.87A	-0.2	Obadele	Thompson	BAR	30.3.76	1	WCp	Johannesburg	11 Sep 98
9.88	1.8	Shawn	Crawford ¶	USA	14.1.78	1	Pre	Eugene	19 Jun 04
9.88	0.6	Walter	Dix	USA	31.1.86	2		Nottwil	8 Aug 10
9.88	0.9	Ryan	Bailey	USA	13.4.89	2		Rieti	29 Aug 10
9.88	1.0	Michael	Frater	JAM	6.10.82	2	Athl	Lausanne	30 Jun 11
9.89	1.6	Travis	Padgett	USA	13.12.86	1q2	NC/OT	Eugene	28 Jun 08
9.89	1.6	Darvis	Patton	USA	4.12.77	1q3	NC/OT	Eugene	28 Jun 08
9.89	1.3	Ngonidzashe	Makusha	ZIM	11.3.87	1	NCAA	Des Moines	10 Jun 11
		(30)							
9.89	1.9	Akani	Simbine	RSA	21.9.93	1	Gyulai	Székesfehérvár	18 Jul 16
9.90	0.4	Nickel	Ashmeade	JAM	7.4.90	1s2	WCh	Moskva	11 Aug 13
9.91	1.2	Dennis	Mitchell ¶	USA	20.2.66	3	WCh	Tokyo	25 Aug 91
9.91	0.9	Leonard	Scott	USA	19.1.80	2	WAF	Stuttgart	9 Sep 06
9.91	-0.5	Derrick	Atkins	BAH	5.1.84	2	WCh	Osaka	26 Aug 07
9.91	-0.2	Daniel	Bailey	ANT	9.9.86	2	GL	Saint-Denis	17 Jul 09

100 METRES A-T

Mark	Wind	Name		Nat	Born	Pos	Meet	Venue	Date
9.91	0.7	Churandy	Martina	NED	3.7.84	2s1	OG	London (OS)	5 Aug 12
9.91	1.1	James	Dasaolu	GBR	5.9.87	1s2	NC	Birmingham	13 Jul 13
9.91	1.8	Femi Seun	Ogunode ¶	QAT	15.5.91	1	AsiC	Wuhan	4 Jun 15
9.91	0.2	Andre	De Grasse	CAN	10.11.94	3	OG	Rio de Janeiro	14 Aug 16
		(40)							
9.92	0.3	Andre	Cason	USA	20.1.69	2	WCh	Stuttgart	15 Aug 93
9.92	0.8	Jon	Drummond	USA	9.9.68	1h3	NC	Indianapolis	12 Jun 97
9.92	0.2	Tim	Montgomery ¶	USA	28.1.75	2	NC	Indianapolis	13 Jun 97
9.92A	-0.2	Seun	Ogunkoya	NGR	28.12.77	2	WCp	Johannesburg	11 Sep 98
9.92	1.0	Tim	Harden	USA	27.1.74	1	Spitzen	Luzern	5 Jul 99
9.92	2.0	Christophe	Lemaitre	FRA	11.6.90	1	NC	Albi	29 Jul 11
9.92	-0.8	Kemar	Bailey-Cole	JAM	10.1.92	3	DL	London (OS)	24 Jul 15
9.92A	0.9	Jak Ali	Harvey	JAM/TUR	5.4.89	1		Erzurum	12 Jun 16
9.93A	wR1.4	Calvin	Smith	USA	8.1.61	1	USOF	USAF Academy	3 Jul 83

9.93 Michael Marsh USA 4.8.67 Walnut 18 Apr 92. Patrick Johnson AUS 26.9.72 Mito 5 May 03, Ivory Williams # USA 2.5.85 Réthimno 20 Jul 09, Kemarley Brown JAM 20.7.92 Walbut 17 May 14, Clayton Vaughn USA 15.5.92 Mobile 10 May 15, Marvin Bracy USA 15.12.93 Birmingham 7 Jun 15

(55)   100th man 9.99, 200th 10.06, 300th 10.10, 400th 10.13, 500th 10.16

Doubtful wind reading

| 9.91 | -2.3 | Davidson | Ezinwa ¶ | NGR | 22.11.71 | 1 | | Azusa | 11 Apr 92 |

Wind-assisted – performances to 9.76, performers listed to 9.89

Mark	Wind	Name		Nat	Born	Pos	Meet	Venue	Date
9.68	4.1	Tyson	Gay ¶	USA	9.8.82	1	NC/OT	Eugene	29 Jun 08
9.69A	5+	Obadele	Thompson	BAR	30.3.76	1		El Paso	13 Apr 96
9.72	2.1		Powell			1	Bisl	Oslo	4 Jun 10
9.74	w	Richard	Thompson	TTO	7.6.85	1		Clermont	31 May 14
9.75	3.4		Gay			1h1	NC	Eugene	25 Jun 09
9.75	2.6		Powell			1h2	DL	Doha	14 May 10
9.75	4.3	Darvis	Patton	USA	4.12.77	1rA	TexR	Austin	30 Mar 13
9.75	2.7	Andre	De Grasse	CAN	10.11.94	1	NCAA	Eugene	12 Jun 15
9.76A	6.1	Churandy	Martina	AHO	3.7.84	1		El Paso	13 May 06
9.76	2.2		Gay			1	GP	New York	2 Jun 07
9.76	2.7		Gatlin			1	Pre	Eugene	31 May 14
9.76	3.7	Trayvon	Bromell	USA	10.7.95	1s1	NC	Eugene	26 Jun 15
9.78	5.2	Carl	Lewis	USA	1.7.61	1	NC/OT	Indianapolis	16 Jul 88
9.78	3.7	Maurice	Greene	USA	23.7.74	1	GP II	Stanford	31 May 04
9.79	5.3	Andre	Cason	USA	20.1.69	1h4	NC	Eugene	16 Jun 93
9.80	4.1	Walter	Dix	USA	31.1.86	2	NC/OT	Eugene	29 Jun 08
9.80	2.7	Michael	Rodgers	USA	24.4.85	2	Pre	Eugene	31 May 14
9.82	3.0	Isiah	Young	USA	5.1.90	1		Clermont	16 May 15
9.82	4.9	Remontay	McClain	USA	21.9.92	1h3	NC	Eugene	25 Jun 15
9.83	7.1	Leonard	Scott	USA	19.1.80	1r1	Sea Ray	Knoxville	9 Apr 99
9.83	2.2	Derrick	Atkins	BAH	5.1.84	2	GP	New York	2 Jun 07
9.84	5.4	Francis	Obikwelu	NGR/POR	22.11.78	1		Zaragoza	3 Jun 06
9.85	4.8	Dennis	Mitchell ¶	USA	20.2.66	2	NC	Eugene	17 Jun 93
9.85A	3.0	Frank	Fredericks	NAM	2.10.67	1		Nairobi	18 May 02
9.85	4.1	Travis	Padgett	USA	13.12.86	4	NC/OT	Eugene	29 Jun 08
9.85	3.6	Keston	Bledman	TTO	8.3.88	1rA		Clermont	2 Jun 12
9.85	3.2	Charles	Silmon	USA	4.7.91	1s1	NC	Des Moines	21 Jun 13
9.85A	3.0	Kemar	Hyman	CAY	11.10.89	1s2	NACAC	San José, CRC	7 Aug 15
9.86	2.6	Shawn	Crawford ¶	USA	14.1.78	1	GP	Doha	14 May 04
9.86	3.6	Michael	Frater	JAM	6.10.82	2h4	NC	Kingston	23 Jun 11
9.86	3.2	Rakieem "Mookie"	Salaam	USA	5.4.90	2s1	NC	Des Moines	21 Jun 13
9.86	3.7	Diondre	Batson	USA	13.7.92	2s1	NC	Eugene	26 Jun 15
9.87	11.2	William	Snoddy	USA	6.12.57	1		Dallas	1 Apr 78
9.87	4.9	Calvin	Smith	USA	8.1.61	1s2	NC/OT	Indianapolis	16 Jul 88
9.87	2.4	Michael	Marsh	USA	4.8.67	1rA	MSR	Walnut	20 Apr 97
9.87	3.3	Yoshihide	Kiryu	JPN	15.12.95	1r1	TexR	Austin	28 Mar 15
9.87	2.1	Tevin	Hester	USA	10.1.94	1	ACC	Tallahassee	16 May 15
9.88	2.3	James	Sanford	USA	27.12.57	1		Los Angeles (Ww)	3 May 80
9.88	5.2	Albert	Robinson	USA	28.11.64	4	NC/OT	Indianapolis	16 Jul 88
9.88	4.9	Tim	Harden	USA	27.1.74	1	NC	New Orleans	20 Jun 98
9.88	4.5	Coby	Miller	USA	19.10.76	1		Auburn	1 Apr 00
9.88	3.6	Patrick	Johnson	AUS	26.9.72	1		Perth	8 Feb 03
9.88	3.0	Darrel	Brown	TTO	11.10.84	1	NC	Port of Spain	23 Jun 07
9.88	3.7	Ivory	Williams #	USA	2.5.85	1	TexR	Austin	3 Apr 10
9.89	4.2	Ray	Stewart	JAM	18.3.65	1s1	PAm	Indianapolis	9 Aug 87
9.89	4.4	Henricho	Bruintjies	RSA	16.7.93	1		Gavardo	29 May 16

Hand timing and three men at 9.7w

| 9.7 | 1.9 | Donovan | Powell ¶ | JAM | 31.10.71 | 1rA | | Houston | 19 May 95 |
| 9.7 | 1.9 | Carl | Lewis | USA | 1.7.61 | 2rA | | Houston | 19 May 95 |

256   100 – 200 METRES A-T

Mark	Wind	Name		Nat	Born	Pos	Meet	Venue	Date
9.7	1.9	Olapade	Adeniken	NGR	19.8.69	3rA		Houston	19 May 95
Drugs disqualification									
9.75	1.1		Gay ¶			(1)	NC	Des Moines	21 Jun 13
9.77	1.7		Gatlin ¶	USA	10.2.82	(1)	SGP	Doha	12 May 06
9.78	2.0	Tim	Montgomery ¶	USA	28.1.75	(1)	GPF	Paris (C)	14 Sep 02
9.79	1.1	Ben	Johnson ¶	CAN	30.12.61	(1)	OG	Seoul	24 Sep 88
9.87	2.0	Dwain	Chambers ¶	GBR	5.4.78	(2)	GPF	Paris (C)	14 Sep 02
9.7w ht	3.5		Johnson	CAN	30.12.61	(1)		Perth	24 Jan 87
9.75w	2.4		Gay			(1s2)	NC	Des Moines	21 Jun 13

200 METRES

Mark	Wind	Name		Nat	Born	Pos	Meet	Venue	Date
19.19	WR -0.3	Usain	Bolt	JAM	21.8.86	1	WCh	Berlin	20 Aug 09
19.26	0.7	Yohan	Blake	JAM	26.12.89	1	VD	Bruxelles	16 Sep 11
19.30	WR -0.9		Bolt			1	OG	Beijing	20 Aug 08
19.32	WR 0.4	Michael	Johnson	USA	13.9.67	1	OG	Atlanta	1 Aug 96
19.32	0.4		Bolt			1	OG	London (OS)	9 Aug 12
19.40	0.8		Bolt			1	WCh	Daegu	3 Sep 11
19.44	0.4		Blake			2	OG	London (OS)	9 Aug 12
19.53	0.7	Walter	Dix	USA	31.1.86	2	VD	Bruxelles	16 Sep 11
19.54	0.0		Blake			1	VD	Bruxelles	7 Sep 12
19.55	-0.1		Bolt			1	WCh	Beijing	27 Aug 15
19.56	-0.8		Bolt			1		Kingston	1 May 10
19.57	0.0		Bolt			1	VD	Bruxelles	4 Sep 09
19.57	0.4	Justin	Gatlin ¶	USA	10.2.82	1	NC	Eugene	28 Jun 15
19.58	1.3	Tyson	Gay ¶	USA	9.8.82	1	Reebok	New York	30 May 09
19.58	1.4		Bolt			1	Athl	Lausanne	23 Aug 12
19.59	-0.9		Bolt			1	Athl	Lausanne	7 Jul 09
19.62	-0.3		Gay			1	NC	Indianapolis	24 Jun 07
19.63	0.4	Xavier	Carter	USA	8.12.85	1	Athl	Lausanne	11 Jul 06
19.63	-0.9		Bolt			1	Athl	Lausanne	2 Sep 08
19.65	0.0	Wallace	Spearmon	USA	24.12.84	1		Daegu	28 Sep 06
19.66	WR 1.7		M Johnson			1	NC	Atlanta	23 Jun 96
19.66	0.0		Bolt			1	WK	Zürich	30 Aug 12
19.66	0.0		Bolt			1	WCh	Moskva	17 Aug 13
19.67	-0.5		Bolt			1	GP	Athína	13 Jul 08
19.68	0.4	Frank	Fredericks	NAM	2.10.67	2	OG	Atlanta	1 Aug 96
19.68	-0.1		Gay			1	WAF	Stuttgart	10 Sep 06
19.68	-0.1		Bolt			1	WAF	Thessaloníki	13 Sep 09
19.68	-0.5		Gatlin			1	Herc	Monaco	18 Jul 14
19.68	0.9		Gatlin			1	Pre	Eugene	30 May 15
19.69	0.9		Dix			1	NCAA-r	Gainesville	26 May 07
		(30/9)							
19.72A	WR 1.8	Pietro	Mennea (10)	ITA	28.6.52	1	WUG	Ciudad de México	12 Sep 79
19.73	-0.2	Michael	Marsh	USA	4.8.67	1s1	OG	Barcelona	5 Aug 92
19.75	1.5	Carl	Lewis	USA	1.7.61	1	NC	Indianapolis	19 Jun 83
19.74	1.4	LaShawn	Merritt ¶	USA	27.6.86	1s3	NC/OT	Eugene	8 Jul 16
19.75	1.7	Joe	DeLoach	USA	5.6.67	1	OG	Seoul	28 Sep 88
19.77	0.7	Ato	Boldon	TTO	30.12.73	1rA		Stuttgart	13 Jul 97
19.79	1.2	Shawn	Crawford ¶	USA	14.1.78	1	OG	Athína	26 Aug 04
19.79	0.9	Warren	Weir	JAM	31.10.89	1	NC	Kingston	23 Jun 13
19.80	0.8	Christophe	Lemaitre	FRA	11.6.90	3	WCh	Daegu	3 Sep 11
19.80	2.0	Rasheed	Dwyer	JAM	29.1.89	1s1	PAm	Toronto	23 Jul 15
19.80	-0.3	Andre	De Grasse	CAN	10.11.94	2s2	OG	Rio de Janeiro	17 Aug 16
		(20)							
19.81	-0.3	Alonso	Edward	PAN	8.12.89	2	WCh	Berlin	20 Aug 09
19.81	0.4	Churandy	Martina	NED	3.7.84	1	Athl	Lausanne	25 Aug 16
19.83A	WR 0.9	Tommie	Smith	USA	6.6.44	1	OG	Ciudad de México	16 Oct 68
19.84	1.7	Francis	Obikwelu	NGR/POR	22.11.78	1s2	WCh	Sevilla	25 Aug 99
19.85	-0.3	John	Capel ¶	USA	27.10.78	1	NC	Sacramento	23 Jul 00
19.85	-0.5	Konstadínos	Kedéris ¶	GRE	11.7.73	1	EC	München	9 Aug 02
19.85	0.0	Nickel	Ashmeade	JAM	4.7.90	2	WK	Zürich	30 Aug 12
19.85	1.9	Ameer	Webb	USA	19.3.91	1	DL	Doha	6 May 16
19.86A	1.0	Don	Quarrie	JAM	25.2.51	1	PAm	Cali	3 Aug 71
		(30)							
19.86	1.6	Maurice	Greene	USA	23.7.74	2rA	DNG	Stockholm	7 Jul 97
19.86	1.5	Jason	Young	JAM	21.3.91	1	Spitzen	Luzern	17 Jul 13
19.86	1.6	Isiah	Young	USA	5.1.90	1	NC	Des Moines	23 Jun 13
19.87	0.8	Lorenzo	Daniel	USA	23.3.66	1	NCAA	Eugene	3 Jun 88
19.87A	1.8	John	Regis	GBR	13.10.66	1		Sestriere	31 Jul 94
19.87	1.2	Jeff	Williams	USA	31.12.65	1		Fresno	13 Apr 96

200 – 300 – 400 METRES A-T

Mark	Wind	Name		Nat	Born	Pos	Meet	Venue	Date
19.87	-0.1	Anaso	Jobodwana	RSA	30.7.92	3	WCh	Beijing	27 Aug 15
19.88	-0.3	Floyd	Heard	USA	24.3.66	2	NC	Sacramento	23 Jul 00
19.88	0.1	Joshua 'J.J'	Johnson	USA	10.5.76	1	VD	Bruxelles	24 Aug 01
19.88	-0.4	Ramil	Guliyev	AZE/TUR	29.5.90	1		Zagreb	8 Sep 15
		(40)							
19.88	1.2	Miguel	Francis	ANT	28.2.95	1		Kingston	11 Jun 16
19.89	-0.8	Claudinei	da Silva	BRA	19.11.70	1	GPF	München	11 Sep 99
19.89	1.3	Jaysuma	Saidy Ndure	NOR	1.1.84	1	WAF	Stuttgart	23 Sep 07
19.90	1.3	Asafa	Powell	JAM	23.11.82	1	NC	Kingston	25 Jun 06
19.92A WR	1.9	John	Carlos	USA	5.6.45	1	FOT	Echo Summit	12 Sep 68
19.94	0.6	Wayde	van Niekerk	RSA	15.7.92	1rB		Luzern	14 Jul 15
19.95	0.4	Nethaneel	Mitchell-Blake	GBR	2.4.94	1	SEC	Tuscaloosa	14 May 16
19.96	-0.9	Kirk	Baptiste	USA	20.6.63	2	OG	Los Angeles	8 Aug 84
19.96	0.4	Robson	da Silva	BRA	4.9.64	1	VD	Bruxelles	25 Aug 89
19.96	-0.3	Coby	Miller	USA	19.10.76	3	NC	Sacramento	23 Jul 00
19.96	-0.4	Isaac	Makwala	BOT	29.9.86	1		La Chaux-de-Fonds	6 Jul 14
19.96	1.1	Brendon	Rodney	CAN	9.4.92	1	NC	Edmonton	10 Jul 16
		(52)							

100th man 20.10, 200th 20.22, 300th 20.31, 400th 20.37, 500th 20.41

Wind-assisted 2 performances to 19.69, performers listed to 19.92

19.58	2.4	Andre	De Grasse	CAN	10.11.94	1	NCAA	Eugene	12 Jun 15
19.61	>4.0	Leroy	Burrell	USA	21.2.67	1	SWC	College Station	19 May 90
19.73	3.3	Shawn	Crawford ¶	USA	14.1.78	1	NC	Eugene	28 Jun 09
19.75	4.1	Isiah	Young	USA	5.1.90	1rA		Clermont	16 May 15
19.83	9.2	Bobby	Cruse	USA	20.3.78	1r2	Sea Ray	Knoxville	9 Apr 99
19.86	4.6	Roy	Martin	USA	25.12.66	1	SWC	Houston	18 May 86
19.86	2.4	Dedric	Dukes	USA	2.4.92	2	NCAA	Eugene	12 Jun 15
19.86	2.4	Trayvon	Bromell	USA	10.7.95	3	NCAA	Eugene	12 Jun 15
19.90	3.8	Steve	Mullings ¶	JAM	29.11.82	1		Fort Worth	17 Apr 04
19.91		James	Jett	USA	28.12.70	1		Morgantown	18 Apr 92

Low altitude mark for athletes with lifetime bests at high altitude
19.94 0.3 Regis   2 WCh Stuttgart 20 Aug 93   19.96 0.0 Mennea   1 Barletta   17 Aug 80

Hand timing
19.7A James Sanford USA 27.12.57 1 El Paso 19 Apr 80, 19.7A 0.2 Robson C. da Silva BRA 4.9.64 1 AmCp Bogotá 13 Aug 89, 19.7A 1.4 Isaac Makwala BOT 29.9.86 1 Germiston 15 Mar 14

300 METRES

In 300m races only, not including intermediate times in 400m races

30.85A		Michael	Johnson	USA	13.9.67	1		Pretoria	24 Mar 00
30.97		Usain	Bolt	JAM	21.8.86	1	GS	Ostrava	27 May 10
31.03		Wayde	van Niekerk	RSA	15.7.92	1		Kingston	11 Jun 16
31.23		LaShawn	Merritt ¶	USA	27.6.86	2		Kingston	11 Jun 16
31.48		Danny	Everett	USA	1.11.66	1		Jerez de la Frontera	3 Sep 90
31.48		Roberto	Hernández	CUB	6.3.67	2		Jerez de la Frontera	3 Sep 90
31.56		Doug	Walker ¶	GBR	28.7.73	1		Gateshead	19 Jul 98
31.61		Anthuan	Maybank	USA	30.12.69	1		Durham	13 Jul 96
31.64		Tony	McQuay	USA	16.4.90	3		Kingston	11 Jun 16
31.67		John	Regis (10)	GBR	13.10.66	1	Vaux	Gateshead	17 Jul 92
31.70		Kirk	Baptiste	USA	20.6.63	1	Nike	London (CP)	18 Aug 84
31.72		Jeremy	Wariner	USA	31.1.84	1	GS	Ostrava	12 Jun 08
31.73		Thomas	Jefferson	USA	8.6.62	1	DCG	London (CP)	22 Aug 87

400 METRES

43.03 WR		Wayde	van Niekerk	RSA	15.7.92	1	OG	Rio de Janeiro	14 Aug 16
43.18 WR		Michael	Johnson	USA	13.9.67	1	WCh	Sevilla	26 Aug 99
43.29 WR		Butch	Reynolds ¶	USA	8.6.64	1	WK	Zürich	17 Aug 88
43.39			Johnson			1	WCh	Göteborg	9 Aug 95
43.44			Johnson			1	NC	Atlanta	19 Jun 96
43.45		Jeremy	Wariner	USA	31.1.84	1	WCh	Osaka	31 Aug 07
43.48			van Niekerk			1	WCh	Beijing	26 Aug 15
43.49			Johnson			1	OG	Atlanta	29 Jul 96
43.50		Quincy	Watts	USA	19.6.70	1	OG	Barcelona	5 Aug 92
43.50			Wariner			1	DNG	Stockholm	7 Aug 07
43.62			Wariner			1rA	GGala	Roma	14 Jul 06
43.65			Johnson			1	WCh	Stuttgart	17 Aug 93
43.65		LaShawn	Merritt ¶	USA	27.6.86	2	WCh	Beijing	26 Aug 15
43.66			Johnson			1	NC	Sacramento	16 Jun 95
43.66			Johnson			1rA	Athl	Lausanne	3 Jul 96
43.68			Johnson			1	WK	Zürich	12 Aug 98
43.68			Johnson			1	NC	Sacramento	16 Jul 00
43.71			Watts			1s2	OG	Barcelona	3 Aug 92
43.72		Isaac	Makwala	BOT	29.9.86	1		La Chaux-de-Fonds	5 Jul 15
43.74			Johnson			1	NC	Eugene	19 Jun 93

400 – 600 METRES A-T

Mark	Wind	Name		Nat	Born	Pos	Meet	Venue	Date
43.74			Merritt			1	WCh	Moskva	13 Aug 13
43.74		Kirani	James	GRN	1.9.92	1	Athl	Lausanne	3 Jul 14
43.75			Johnson			1		Waco	19 Apr 97
43.75			Merritt			1	OG	Beijing	21 Aug 08
43.76			Johnson			1	GWG	Uniondale, NY	22 Jul 98
43.76			James			2	OG	Rio de Janeiro	14 Aug 16
43.78			James			3	WCh	Beijing	26 Aug 15
43.81		Danny	Everett	USA	1.11.66	1	NC/OT	New Orleans	26 Jun 92
43.82			Wariner			1	WK	Zürich	29 Aug 08
43.83			Watts			1	WK	Zürich	19 Aug 92
		(30/10)							
43.86A WR		Lee	Evans	USA	25.2.47	1	OG	Ciudad de México	18 Oct 68
43.87		Steve	Lewis	USA	16.5.69	1	OG	Seoul	28 Sep 88
43.93		Youssef	Al-Masrahi	KSA	31.12.87	1h2	WCh	Beijing	23 Aug 15
43.93		Rusheen	McDonald	JAM	17.8.92	2h2	WCh	Beijing	23 Aug 15
43.97A		Larry	James	USA	6.11.47	2	OG	Ciudad de México	18 Oct 68
44.01		Machel	Cedenio	TTO	6.9.95	4	OG	Rio de Janeiro	14 Aug 16
44.05		Angelo	Taylor	USA	29.12.78	1	NC	Indianapolis	23 Jun 07
44.09		Alvin	Harrison ¶	USA/DOM	20.1.74	3	NC	Atlanta	19 Jun 96
44.09		Jerome	Young ¶	USA	14.8.76	1	NC	New Orleans	21 Jun 98
44.10		Gary	Kikaya	COD	4.2.78	2	WAF	Stuttgart	9 Sep 06
44.11		Luguelín	Santos	DOM	12.11.92	4	WCh	Beijing	26 Aug 15
		(20)							
44.13		Derek	Mills	USA	9.7.72	1	Pre	Eugene	4 Jun 95
44.14		Roberto	Hernández	CUB	6.3.67	2		Sevilla	30 May 90
44.15		Anthuan	Maybank	USA	30.12.69	1rB	Athl	Lausanne	3 Jul 96
44.16		Otis	Harris	USA	30.6.82	2	OG	Athína	23 Aug 04
44.17		Innocent	Egbunike	NGR	30.11.61	1rA	WK	Zürich	19 Aug 87
44.18		Samson	Kitur	KEN	25.2.66	2s2	OG	Barcelona	3 Aug 92
44.20A		Charles	Gitonga	KEN	5.10.71	1	NC	Nairobi	29 Jun 96
44.21		Ian	Morris	TTO	30.11.61	3s2	OG	Barcelona	3 Aug 92
44.22A		Baboloki	Thebe	BOT	18.3.97	1	NC	Gaborone	21 May 16
44.24		Tony	McQuay	USA	16.4.90	1s1	NC/OT	Eugene	2 Jul 16
		(30)							
44.25		Karabo	Sibanda	BOT	2.7.98	5	OG	Rio de Janeiro	14 Aug 16
44.26		Alberto	Juantorena	CUB	21.11.50	1	OG	Montreal	29 Jul 76
44.27		Alonzo	Babers	USA	31.10.61	1	OG	Los Angeles	8 Aug 84
44.27		Antonio	Pettigrew ¶	USA	3.11.67	1	NC	Houston	17 Jun 89
44.27		Darold	Williamson	USA	19.2.83	1s1	NCAA	Sacramento	10 Jun 05
44.27		Steven	Gardiner	BAH	12.9.95	1	NC	Nassau	27 Jun 15
44.27		Abdelilah	Haroun	QAT	1.1.97	2		La Chaux-de-Fonds	5 Jul 15
44.28		Andrew	Valmon	USA	1.1.65	4	NC	Eugene	19 Jun 93
44.28		Tyree	Washington	USA	28.8.76	1		Los Angeles (ER)	12 May 01
44.29		Derrick	Brew	USA	28.12.77	1	SEC	Athens, GA	16 May 99
		(40)							
44.29		Sanderlei	Parrela	BRA	7.10.74	2	WCh	Sevilla	26 Aug 99
44.30		Gabriel	Tiacoh	CIV	10.9.63	1	NCAA	Indianapolis	7 Jun 86
44.30		Lamont	Smith	USA	11.12.72	4	NC	Atlanta	19 Jun 96
44.31		Alejandro	Cárdenas	MEX	4.10.74	3	WCh	Sevilla	26 Aug 99
44.33		Thomas	Schönlebe	GDR	6.8.65	1	WCh	Roma	3 Sep 87
44.34		Darnell	Hall	USA	26.9.71	1	Athl	Lausanne	5 Jul 95
44.35		Andrew	Rock	USA	23.1.82	2	WCh	Helsinki	12 Aug 05
44.36		Iwan	Thomas	GBR	5.1.74	1	NC	Birmingham	13 Jul 97
44.36		Deon	Lendore	TTO	28.10.92	1	SEC	Lexington	18 May 14
44.36		Ali Khamis	Abbas	BRN	30.6.95	6	OG	Rio de Janeiro	14 Aug 16
		(50)							

100th man 44.59, 200th 44.84, 300th 45.04, 400th 45.21, 500th 45.33

Drugs disqualification

| 44.21 | | Antonio | Pettigrew ¶ | USA | 3.11.67 | 1 | | Nassau | 26 May 99 |

Hand timing *440 yards time less 0.3 secs*

44.1		Wayne	Collett	USA	20.10.49	1	OT	Eugene	9 Jul 72
44.2*		John	Smith	USA	5.8.50	1	AAU	Eugene	26 Jun 71
44.2		Fred	Newhouse	USA	8.11.48	1s1	OT	Eugene	7 Jul 72

600 METRES

1:12.81		Johnny	Gray	USA	19.6.60	1		Santa Monica	24 May 86
1:13.10		David	Rudisha	KEN	17.12.88	1	DL	Birmingham	5 Jun 16
1:13.2 + ?		John	Kipkurgat	KEN	16.3.44	1		Pointe-à-Pierre	23 Mar 74
1:13.21		Pierre-Ambroise	Bosse	FRA	11.5.92	2	DL	Birmingham	5 Jun 16
1:13.28		Duane	Solomon	USA	28.12.84	1		Burnaby	1 Jul 13
1:13.49		Joseph	Mutua	KEN	10.12.78	1		Liège (NX)	27 Aug 02
1:13.80		Earl	Jones	USA	17.7.64	2		Santa Monica	24 May 86

800 METRES

Mark	Wind	Name		Nat	Born	Pos	Meet	Venue	Date
1:40.91 WR		David	Rudisha	KEN	17.12.88	1	OG	London (OS)	9 Aug 12
1:41.01 WR			Rudisha			1rA		Rieti	29 Aug 10
1:41.09 WR			Rudisha			1	ISTAF	Berlin	22 Aug 10
1:41.11 WR		Wilson	Kipketer	DEN	12.12.70	1	ASV	Köln	24 Aug 97
1:41.24 WR			Kipketer			1rA	WK	Zürich	13 Aug 97
1:41.33			Rudisha			1		Rieti	10 Sep 11
1:41.51			Rudisha			1	NA	Heusden-Zolder	10 Jul 10
1:41.54			Rudisha			1	DL	Saint-Denis	6 Jul 12
1:41.73!WR		Sebastian	Coe	GBR	29.9.56	1		Firenze	10 Jun 81
1:41.73 WR			Kipketer			1rA	DNG	Stockholm	7 Jul 97
1:41.73		Nijel	Amos	BOT	15.3.94	2	OG	London (OS)	9 Aug 12
1:41.74			Rudisha			1	adidas	New York	9 Jun 12
1:41.77		Joaquim	Cruz	BRA	12.3.63	1	ASV	Köln	26 Aug 84
1:41.83			Kipketer			1	GP II	Rieti	1 Sep 96
1:42.01			Rudisha			1	GP	Rieti	6 Sep 09
1:42.04			Rudisha			1	Bisl	Oslo	4 Jun 10
1:42.12A			Rudisha			1	OT	Nairobi	23 Jun 12
1:42.15			Rudisha			1	OG	Rio de Janeiro	15 Aug 16
1:42.17			Kipketer			1	TOTO	Tokyo	16 Sep 96
1:42.20			Kipketer			1	VD	Bruxelles	22 Aug 97
1:42.23		Abubaker	Kaki	SUD	21.6.89	2	Bisl	Oslo	4 Jun 10
1:42.27			Kipketer			1	VD	Bruxelles	3 Sep 99
1:42.28		Sammy	Koskei	KEN	14.5.61	2	ASV	Köln	26 Aug 84
1:42.32			Kipketer			1	GP II	Rieti	8 Sep 02
1:42.33 WR			Coe			1	Bisl	Oslo	5 Jul 79
1:42.34			Cruz			1r1	WK	Zürich	22 Aug 84
1:42.34		Wilfred	Bungei	KEN	24.7.80	2	GP II	Rieti	8 Sep 02
1:42.37		Mohammed	Aman	ETH	10.1.94	1	VD	Bruxelles	6 Sep 13
1:42.41			Cruz			1	VD	Bruxelles	24 Aug 84
1:42.45			Amos			1	Herc	Monaco	18 Jul 14
1:42.47		Yuriy	Borzakovskiy	RUS	12.4.81	1	VD	Bruxelles	24 Aug 01
(31/10)					! photo-electric cell time				
1:42.51		Amel	Tuka	BIH	9.1.91	1	Herc	Monaco	17 Jul 15
1:42.53		Timothy	Kitum	KEN	20.11.94	3	OG	London (OS)	9 Aug 12
1:42.53		Pierre-Ambroise	Bosse	FRA	11.5.92	2	Herc	Monaco	18 Jul 14
1:42.55		André	Bucher	SUI	19.10.76	1rA	WK	Zürich	17 Aug 01
1:42.58		Vebjørn	Rodal	NOR	16.9.72	1	OG	Atlanta	31 Jul 96
1:42.60		Johnny	Gray	USA	19.6.60	2r1		Koblenz	28 Aug 85
1:42.61		Taoufik	Makhloufi	ALG	29.4.88	2	OG	Rio de Janeiro	15 Aug 16
1:42.62		Patrick	Ndururi	KEN	12.1.69	2rA	WK	Zürich	13 Aug 97
1:42.67		Alfred	Kirwa Yego	KEN	28.11.86	2	GP	Rieti	6 Sep 09
1:42.69		Hezekiél	Sepeng ¶	RSA	30.6.74	2	VD	Bruxelles	3 Sep 99
(20)									
1:42.69		Japheth	Kimutai	KEN	20.12.78	3	VD	Bruxelles	3 Sep 99
1:42.79		Fred	Onyancha	KEN	25.12.69	3	OG	Atlanta	31 Jul 96
1:42.79		Youssef Saad	Kamel	KEN/BRN	29.3.83	2	Herc	Monaco	29 Jul 08
1:42.81		Jean-Patrick	Nduwimana	BDI	9.5.78	2rA	WK	Zürich	17 Aug 01
1:42.82		Duane	Solomon	USA	28.12.84	4	OG	London (OS)	9 Aug 12
1:42.84		Ferguson	Cheruiyot	KEN	30.11.89	4	Herc	Monaco	18 Jul 14
1:42.85		Norberto	Téllez	CUB	22.1.72	4	OG	Atlanta	31 Jul 96
1:42.86		Mbulaeni	Mulaudzi	RSA	8.9.80	3	GP	Rieti	6 Sep 09
1:42.87		Alfred	Kipketer	KEN	26.12.96	1	DL	Saint-Denis	27 Aug 16
1:42.88		Steve	Cram	GBR	14.10.60	1rA	WK	Zürich	21 Aug 85
(30)									
1:42.91		William	Yiampoy	KEN	17.5.74	3	GP II	Rieti	8 Sep 02
1:42.93		Clayton	Murphy	USA	26.2.95	3	OG	Rio de Janeiro	15 Aug 16
1:42.95		Boaz	Lalang	KEN	8.2.89	2rA		Rieti	29 Aug 10
1:42.95		Nick	Symmonds	USA	30.12.83	5	OG	London (OS)	9 Aug 12
1:42.97		Peter	Elliott	GBR	9.10.62	1		Sevilla	30 May 90
1:42.97		Ayanleh	Souleiman	DJI	3.12.92	3	Herc	Monaco	17 Jul 15
1:42.98		Patrick	Konchellah	KEN	20.4.68	2	ASV	Köln	24 Aug 97
1:43.03		Kennedy/Kenneth	Kimwetich	KEN	1.1.73	2		Stuttgart	19 Jul 98
1:43.05		Jonathan	Kitilit	KEN	24.4.94	3	DL	Saint-Denis	27 Aug 16
1:43.06		Billy	Konchellah	KEN	20.10.62	1	WCh	Roma	1 Sep 87
(40)									
1:43.07		Yeimer	López	CUB	20.8.82	1		Jerez de la Frontera	24 Jun 08
1:43.08		José Luiz	Barbosa	BRA	27.5.61	1		Rieti	6 Sep 91
1:43.09		Djabir	Saïd-Guerni	ALG	29.3.77	5	VD	Bruxelles	3 Sep 99
1:43.13		Abraham Kipchirchir	Rotich	KEN	26.6.93	1	Herc	Monaco	20 Jul 12

800 – 1000 – 1500 METRES A-T

Mark	Wind	Name		Nat	Born	Pos	Meet	Venue	Date
1:43.15		Mehdi	Baala	FRA	17.8.78	5	GP II	Rieti	8 Sep 02
1:43.15		Asbel	Kiprop	KEN	30.6.89	2	Herc	Monaco	22 Jul 11
1:43.16		Paul	Ereng	KEN	22.8.67	1	WK	Zürich	16 Aug 89
1:43.17		Benson	Koech	KEN	10.11.74	1		Rieti	28 Aug 94
1:43.20		Mark	Everett	USA	2.9.68	1rA	Gugl	Linz	9 Jul 97
1:43.22		Pawel	Czapiewski	POL	30.3.78	5rA	WK	Zürich	17 Aug 01
		(50)		100th man 1:43.82, 200th 1:44.57, 300th 1:45.00, 400th 1:45.33, 500th 1:45.6					

1000 METRES

Mark		Name		Nat	Born	Pos	Meet	Venue	Date
2:11.96 WR		Noah	Ngeny	KEN	2.11.78	1	GP II	Rieti	5 Sep 99
2:12.18 WR		Sebastian	Coe	GBR	29.9.56	1	OsloG	Oslo	11 Jul 81
2:12.66			Ngeny			1	Nik	Nice	17 Jul 99
2:12.88		Steve	Cram	GBR	14.10.60	1		Gateshead	9 Aug 85
2:13.08		Taoufik	Makhloufi	ALG	29.4.88	1		Tomblaine	1 Jul 15
2:13.40 WR			Coe			1	Bisl	Oslo	1 Jul 80
2:13.49		Ayanleh	Souleiman	DJI	3.12.92	1	Athl	Lausanne	25 Aug 16
2:13.56		Kennedy/Kenneth	Kimwetich	KEN	1.1.73	2	Nik	Nice	17 Jul 99
2:13.62		Abubaker	Kaki	SUD	21.6.89	1	Pre	Eugene	3 Jul 10
2:13.73		Noureddine	Morceli	ALG	28.2.70	1	BNP	Villeneuve d'Ascq	2 Jul 93
2:13.89		Robert	Biwott	KEN	28.1.96	2	Athl	Lausanne	25 Aug 16
2:13.9 WR		Rick	Wohlhuter	USA	23.12.48	1	King	Oslo	30 Jul 74
2:13.95		Jonathan	Kitilit	KEN	24.4.94	3	Athl	Lausanne	25 Aug 16
2:13.96		Mehdi	Baala	FRA	17.8.78	1		Strasbourg	26 Jun 03
2:14.09		Joaquim	Cruz	BRA	12.3.63	1	Nik	Nice	20 Aug 84
		(13)		50th man 2:15.81, 100th 2:16.58, 200th 2:17.51					

1500 METRES

Mark		Name		Nat	Born	Pos	Meet	Venue	Date
3:26.00 WR		Hicham	El Guerrouj	MAR	14.9.74	1	GGala	Roma	14 Jul 98
3:26.12			El Guerrouj			1	VD	Bruxelles	24 Aug 01
3:26.34		Bernard	Lagat	KEN/USA	12.12.74	2	VD	Bruxelles	24 Aug 01
3:26.45			El Guerrouj			1 rA	WK	Zürich	12 Aug 98
3:26.69		Asbel	Kiprop	KEN	30.6.89	1	Herc	Monaco	17 Jul 15
3:26.89			El Guerrouj			1	WK	Zürich	16 Aug 02
3:26.96			El Guerrouj			1	GP II	Rieti	8 Sep 02
3:27.21			El Guerrouj			1	WK	Zürich	11 Aug 00
3:27.34			El Guerrouj			1	Herc	Monaco	19 Jul 02
3:27.37 WR		Noureddine	Morceli	ALG	28.2.70	1	Nik	Nice	12 Jul 95
3:27.40			Lagat			1rA	WK	Zürich	6 Aug 04
3:27.52			Morceli			1	Herc	Monaco	25 Jul 95
3:27.64			El Guerrouj			2rA	WK	Zürich	6 Aug 04
3:27.64		Silas	Kiplagat	KEN	20.8.89	1	Herc	Monaco	18 Jul 14
3:27.65			El Guerrouj			1	WCh	Sevilla	24 Aug 99
3:27.72			Kiprop			1	Herc	Monaco	19 Jul 13
3:27.91			Lagat			2	Herc	Monaco	19 Jul 02
3:28.12		Noah	Ngeny	KEN	2.11.78	2	WK	Zürich	11 Aug 00
3:28.21+			El Guerrouj			1	in 1M	Roma	7 Jul 99
3.28.37			Morceli			1	GPF	Monaco	9 Sep 95
3:28.37			El Guerrouj			1	Herc	Monaco	8 Aug 98
3:28.38			El Guerrouj			1	GP	Saint-Denis	6 Jul 01
3:28.40			El Guerrouj			1	VD	Bruxelles	5 Sep 03
3:28.45			Kiprop			2	Herc	Monaco	18 Jul 14
3:28.51			Lagat			3	WK	Zürich	11 Aug 00
3:28.57			El Guerrouj			1rA	WK	Zürich	11 Aug 99
3:28.6+			Ngeny			2	in 1M	Roma	7 Jul 99
3:28.73			Ngeny			2	WCh	Sevilla	24 Aug 99
3:28.75		Taoufik	Makhloufi	ALG	29.4.88	2	Herc	Monaco	17 Jul 15
3:28.79		Abdelaati	Iguider	MAR	25.3.87	3	Herc	Monaco	17 Jul 15
		(30/8)							
3:28.81		Mohamed	Farah	GBR	23.3.83	2	Herc	Monaco	19 Jul 13
3:28.81		Ronald	Kwemoi (10)	KEN	19.9.95	3	Herc	Monaco	18 Jul 14
3:28.95		Fermín	Cacho	ESP	16.2.69	2rA	WK	Zürich	13 Aug 97
3:28.98		Mehdi	Baala	FRA	17.8.78	2	VD	Bruxelles	5 Sep 03
3:29.02		Daniel Kipchirchir	Komen	KEN	27.11.84	1	GGala	Roma	14 Jul 06
3:29.14		Rashid	Ramzi ¶	MAR/BRN	17.7.80	2	GGala	Roma	14 Jul 06
3:29.18		Vénuste	Niyongabo	BDI	9.12.73	2	VD	Bruxelles	22 Aug 97
3:29.29		William	Chirchir	KEN	6.2.79	3	VD	Bruxelles	24 Aug 01
3:29.46 WR		Saïd	Aouita	MAR	2.11.59	1	ISTAF	Berlin	23 Aug 85
3:29.46		Daniel	Komen	KEN	17.5.76	1	Herc	Monaco	16 Aug 97
3:29.47		Augustine	Choge	KEN	21.1.87	1	ISTAF	Berlin	14 Jun 09
3:29.50		Caleb	Ndiku (20)	KEN	9.10.92	3	Herc	Monaco	19 Jul 13

1500 METRES – 1 MILE A-T

Mark	Wind	Name		Nat	Born	Pos	Meet	Venue	Date
3:29.51		Ali	Saïdi-Sief ¶	ALG	15.3.78	1	Athl	Lausanne	4 Jul 01
3:29.53		Amine	Laâlou ¶	MAR	13.5.82	2	Herc	Monaco	22 Jul 10
3:29.58		Ayanleh	Souleiman	DJI	3.12.92	4	Herc	Monaco	18 Jul 14
3:29.66		Nick	Willis	NZL	25.4.83	5	Herc	Monaco	17 Jul 15
3:29.67	WR	Steve	Cram	GBR	14.10.60	1	Nik	Nice	16 Jul 85
3:29.67		Elijah	Manangoi	KEN	5.1.93	6	Herc	Monaco	17 Jul 15
3:29.77		Sydney	Maree	USA	9.9.56	1	ASV	Köln	25 Aug 85
3:29.77		Sebastian	Coe	GBR	29.9.56	1		Rieti	7 Sep 86
3:29.77		Nixon	Chepseba	KEN	12.12.90	2	Herc	Monaco	20 Jul 12
3:29.91		Laban	Rotich	KEN	20.1.69	2rA	WK	Zürich	12 Aug 98
		(30)							
3:29.91		Aman	Wote	ETH	18.4.84	6	Herc	Monaco	14 Jul 14
3:30.04		Timothy	Kiptanui	KEN	5.1.80	2	GP	Saint-Denis	23 Jul 04
3:30.07		Rui	Silva	POR	3.8.77	3	Herc	Monaco	19 Jul 02
3:30.10		Robert	Biwott	KEN	28.1.96	7	Herc	Monaco	17 Jul 15
3:30.18		John	Kibowen	KEN	21.4.69	3rA	WK	Zürich	12 Aug 98
3:30.20		Haron	Keitany	KEN	17.12.83	2	ISTAF	Berlin	14 Jun 09
3:30.24		Cornelius	Chirchir	KEN	5.6.83	4	Herc	Monaco	19 Jul 02
3:30.33		Ivan	Heshko	UKR	19.8.79	2	VD	Bruxelles	3 Sep 04
3:30.34		Collins	Cheboi	KEN	25.9.87	9	Herc	Monaco	17 Jul 15
3:30.40		Matthew	Centrowitz	USA	18.10.89	10	Herc	Monaco	17 Jul 15
		(40)							
3:30.46		Alex	Kipchirchir	KEN	26.11.84	3	VD	Bruxelles	3 Sep 04
3:30.54		Alan	Webb	USA	13.1.83	1	Gaz	Saint-Denis	6 Jul 07
3:30.55		Abdi	Bile	SOM	28.12.62	1		Rieti	3 Sep 89
3:30.57		Reyes	Estévez	ESP	2.8.76	3	WCh	Sevilla	24 Aug 99
3:30.58		William	Tanui	KEN	22.2.64	3	Herc	Monaco	16 Aug 97
3:30.61		James	Magut	KEN	20.7.90	5	DL	Doha	9 May 14
3:30.67		Benjamin	Kipkurui	KEN	28.12.80	2	Herc	Monaco	20 Jul 01
3:30.72		Paul	Korir	KEN	15.7.77	3	VD	Bruxelles	5 Sep 03
3:30.77	WR	Steve	Ovett	GBR	9.10.55	1		Rieti	4 Sep 83
3:30.77		Bethwel	Birgen	KEN	6.8.88	4	Herc	Monaco	19 Jul 13
		(50)							

100th man 3:31.96, 200th 3:33.79, 300th 3:34.77, 400th 3:35.65, 500th 3:36.19

Drugs disqualification: 3:30.77 Adil Kaouch ¶ MAR 1.1.79 1 GGala Roma 13 Jul 07

1 MILE

Mark		Name		Nat	Born	Pos	Meet	Venue	Date
3:43.13	WR	Hicham	El Guerrouj	MAR	14.9.74	1	GGala	Roma	7 Jul 99
3:43.40		Noah	Ngeny	KEN	2.11.78	2	GGala	Roma	7 Jul 99
3:44.39	WR	Noureddine	Morceli	ALG	28.2.70	1		Rieti	5 Sep 93
3:44.60			El Guerrouj			1	Nik	Nice	16 Jul 98
3:44.90			El Guerrouj			1	Bisl	Oslo	4 Jul 97
3:44.95			El Guerrouj			1	GGala	Roma	29 Jun 01
3:45.19			Morceli			1	WK	Zürich	16 Aug 95
3:45.64			El Guerrouj			1	ISTAF	Berlin	26 Aug 97
3:45.96			El Guerrouj			1	BrGP	London (CP)	5 Aug 00
3:46.24			El Guerrouj			1	Bisl	Oslo	28 Jul 00
3:46.32	WR	Steve	Cram	GBR	14.10.60	1	Bisl	Oslo	27 Jul 85
3:46.38		Daniel	Komen	KEN	17.5.76	2	ISTAF	Berlin	26 Aug 97
3:46.70		Vénuste	Niyongabo	BDI	9.12.73	3	ISTAF	Berlin	26 Aug 97
3:46.76		Saïd	Aouita	MAR	2.11.59	1	WG	Helsinki	2 Jul 87
3:46.78			Morceli			1	ISTAF	Berlin	27 Aug 93
3:46.91		Alan	Webb	USA	13.1.83	1		Brasschaat	21 Jul 07
3:46.92			Aouita			1	WK	Zürich	21 Aug 85
3:47.10			El Guerrouj			1	BrGP	London (CP)	7 Aug 99
3:47.28		Bernard	Lagat	KEN/USA	12.12.74	2	GGala	Roma	29 Jun 01
3:47.30			Morceli			1	VD	Bruxelles	3 Sep 93
3:47.32		Ayanleh	Souleiman (10)	DJI	3.12.92	1	Pre	Eugene	31 May 14
3:47.33	WR	Sebastian	Coe	GBR	29.9.56	1	VD	Bruxelles	28 Aug 81
		(22/11)							
3:47.65		Laban	Rotich	KEN	20.1.69	2	Bisl	Oslo	4 Jul 97
3:47.69		Steve	Scott	USA	5.5.56	1	OsloG	Oslo	7 Jul 82
3:47.79		José Luis	González	ESP	8.12.57	2	Bisl	Oslo	27 Jul 85
3:47.88		John	Kibowen	KEN	21.4.69	3	Bisl	Oslo	4 Jul 97
3:47.88		Silas	Kiplagat	KEN	20.8.89	2	Pre	Eugene	31 May 14
3:47.94		William	Chirchir	KEN	6.2.79	2	Bisl	Oslo	28 Jul 00
3:47.97		Daham Najim	Bashir	KEN/QAT	8.11.78	1	Bisl	Oslo	29 Jul 05
3:48.17		Paul	Korir	KEN	15.7.77	1	GP	London (CP)	8 Aug 03
3:48.23		Ali	Saïdi-Sief ¶	ALG	15.3.78	1	Bisl	Oslo	13 Jul 01
		(20)							
3:48.28		Daniel Kipchirchir	Komen	KEN	27.11.84	1	Pre	Eugene	10 Jun 07

1 MILE – 2000 – 3000 METRES A-T

Mark	Wind	Name		Nat	Born	Pos	Meet	Venue	Date
3:48.38		Andrés Manuel	Díaz	ESP	12.7.69	3	GGala	Roma	29 Jun 01
3:48.40	WR	Steve	Ovett	GBR	9.10.55	1	R-W	Koblenz	26 Aug 81
3:48.50		Asbel	Kiprop	KEN	30.6.89	1	Pre	Eugene	7 Jun 09
3:48.60		Aman	Wote	ETH	18.4.84	3	Pre	Eugene	31 May 14
3:48.78		Haron	Keitany	KEN	17.12.83	2	Pre	Eugene	7 Jun 09
3:48.80		William	Kemei	KEN	22.2.69	1	ISTAF	Berlin	21 Aug 92
3:48.83		Sydney	Maree	USA	9.9.56	1		Rieti	9 Sep 81
3:48.95		Deresse	Mekonnen	ETH	20.10.87	1	Bisl	Oslo	3 Jul 09
3:48.98		Craig	Mottram	AUS	18.6.80	5	Bisl	Oslo	29 Jul 05
(30)									
3:49.08		John	Walker	NZL	12.1.52	2	OsloG	Oslo	7 Jul 82
3:49.09		Abdelaati	Iguider	MAR	25.3.87	4	Pre	Eugene	31 May 14
3:49.20		Peter	Elliott	GBR	9.10.62	2	Bisl	Oslo	2 Jul 88
3:49.22		Jens-Peter	Herold	GDR	2.6.65	3	Bisl	Oslo	2 Jul 88
3:49.29		William	Biwott/Özbilen	KEN/TUR	5.3.90	2	Bisl	Oslo	3 Jul 09
3:49.31		Joe	Falcon	USA	23.6.66	1	Bisl	Oslo	14 Jul 90
3:49.34		David	Moorcroft	GBR	10.4.53	3	Bisl	Oslo	26 Jun 82
3:49.34		Benjamin	Kipkurui	KEN	28.12.80	3	VD	Bruxelles	25 Aug 00
3:49.38		Andrew	Baddeley	GBR	20.6.82	1	Bisl	Oslo	6 Jun 08
3:49.40		Abdi	Bile	SOM	28.12.62	4	Bisl	Oslo	2 Jul 88
(40)									
3:49.43		James	Magut	KEN	20.7.90	5	Pre	Eugene	31 May 14
3:49.45		Mike	Boit	KEN	6.1.49	2	VD	Bruxelles	28 Aug 81
3:49.50		Rui	Silva	POR	3.8.77	3	GGala	Roma	12 Jul 02
3:49.56		Fermín	Cacho	ESP	16.2.69	2	Bisl	Oslo	5 Jul 96
3:49.56		Collins	Cheboi	KEN	25.9.87	6	Pre	Eugene	31 May 14
3:49.60		José Antonio	Redolat	ESP	17.2.76	4	GGala	Roma	29 Jun 01
3:49.70		Mekonnen	Gebremedhin	ETH	11.10.88	4	Pre	Eugene	4 Jun 11
3:49.75		Leonard	Mucheru	KEN/BRN	13.6.78	5	GGala	Roma	29 Jun 01
3:49.77		Ray	Flynn	IRL	22.1.57	3	OsloG	Oslo	7 Jul 82
3:49.77		Wilfred	Kirochi	KEN	12.12.69	2	Bisl	Oslo	6 Jul 91
3:49.77		Caleb	Ndiku	KEN	9.10.92	5	Pre	Eugene	4 Jun 11
(51)									

100th 3:51.05, 200th 3:53.17, 300th 3:54.78

2000 METRES

Mark	Wind	Name		Nat	Born	Pos	Meet	Venue	Date
4:44.79	WR	Hicham	El Guerrouj	MAR	14.9.74	1	ISTAF	Berlin	7 Sep 99
4:46.88		Ali	Saïdi-Sief ¶	ALG	15.3.78	1		Strasbourg	19 Jun 01
4:47.88	WR	Noureddine	Morceli	ALG	28.2.70	1		Paris (JB)	3 Jul 95
4:48.36			El Guerrouj			1		Gateshead	19 Jul 98
4:48.69		Vénuste	Niyongabo	BDI	9.12.73	1	Nik	Nice	12 Jul 95
4:48.74		John	Kibowen	KEN	21.4.69	1		Hechtel	1 Aug 98
4:49.00			Niyongabo			1		Rieti	3 Sep 97
4:49.55			Morceli			1	Nik	Nice	10 Jul 96
4:50.08		Noah	Ngeny	KEN	2.11.78	1	DNG	Stockholm	30 Jul 99
4:50.76		Craig	Mottram	AUS	18.6.80	1		Melbourne (OP)	9 Mar 06
4:50.81	WR	Saïd	Aouita	MAR	2.11.59	1	BNP	Paris (JB)	16 Jul 87
4:51.30		Daniel	Komen	KEN	17.5.76	1		Milano	5 Jun 98
4:51.39	WR	Steve	Cram (10)	GBR	14.10.60	1	BGP	Budapest	4 Aug 85

Indoors

| 4:49.99 | | Kenenisa | Bekele | ETH | 13.6.82 | 1 | | Birmingham | 17 Feb 07 |

3000 METRES

Mark	Wind	Name		Nat	Born	Pos	Meet	Venue	Date
7:20.67	WR	Daniel	Komen	KEN	17.5.76	1		Rieti	1 Sep 96
7:23.09		Hicham	El Guerrouj	MAR	14.9.74	1	VD	Bruxelles	3 Sep 99
7:25.02		Ali	Saïdi-Sief ¶	ALG	15.3.78	1	Herc	Monaco	18 Aug 00
7:25.09		Haile	Gebrselassie	ETH	18.4.73	1	VD	Bruxelles	28 Aug 98
7:25.11	WR	Noureddine	Morceli	ALG	28.2.70	1	Herc	Monaco	2 Aug 94
7:25.16			Komen			1	Herc	Monaco	10 Aug 96
7:25.54			Gebrselassie			1	Herc	Monaco	8 Aug 98
7:25.79		Kenenisa	Bekele	ETH	13.6.82	1	DNG	Stockholm	7 Aug 07
7:25.87			Komen			1	VD	Bruxelles	23 Aug 96
7:26.02			Gebrselassie			1	VD	Bruxelles	22 Aug 97
7:26.03			Gebrselassie			1	GP II	Helsinki	10 Jun 99
7:26.5 e			Komen			1	in 2M	Sydney	28 Feb 98
7:26.62		Mohammed	Mourhit ¶	BEL	10.10.70	2	Herc	Monaco	18 Aug 00
7:26.69			K Bekele			1	BrGP	Sheffield	15 Jul 07
7:27.18		Moses	Kiptanui	KEN	1.10.70	1	Herc	Monaco	25 Jul 95
7:27.26		Yenew	Alamirew	ETH	27.5.90	1	DL	Doha	6 May 11
7:27.3+			Komen			1	in 2M	Hechtel	19 Jul 97
7:27.42			Gebrselassie			1	Bisl	Oslo	9 Jul 98

3000 METRES A-T

Mark	Wind	Name		Nat	Born	Pos	Meet	Venue	Date
7:27.50			Morceli			1	VD	Bruxelles	25 Aug 95
7:27.55		Edwin	Soi (10)	KEN	3.3.86	2	DL	Doha	6 May 11
7:27.59		Luke	Kipkosgei	KEN	27.11.75	2	Herc	Monaco	8 Aug 98
7:27.66		Eliud	Kipchoge	KEN	5.11.84	3	DL	Doha	6 May 11
7:27.67			Saïdi-Sief			1	Gaz	Saint-Denis	23 Jun 00
7:27.72			Kipchoge			1	VD	Bruxelles	3 Sep 04
7:27.75		Thomas	Nyariki	KEN	27.9.71	2	Herc	Monaco	10 Aug 96
7:28.04			Kiptanui			1	ASV	Köln	18 Aug 95
7:28.19		Yomif	Kejelcha	ETH	1.8.97	1	DL	Saint-Denis	27 Aug 16
7:28.28			Kipkosgei			2	Bisl	Oslo	9 Jul 98
7:28.28		James	Kwalia	KEN/QAT	12.6.84	2	VD	Bruxelles	3 Sep 04
7:28.37			Kipchoge			1	SGP	Doha	8 May 09
		(30/15)							
7:28.41		Paul	Bitok	KEN	26.6.70	3	Herc	Monaco	10 Aug 96
7:28.45		Assefa	Mezegebu	ETH	19.6.78	3	Herc	Monaco	8 Aug 98
7:28.67		Benjamin	Limo	KEN	23.8.74	1	Herc	Monaco	4 Aug 99
7:28.70		Paul	Tergat	KEN	17.6.69	4	Herc	Monaco	10 Aug 96
7:28.70		Tariku	Bekele	ETH	21.1.87	1		Rieti	29 Aug 10
		(20)							
7:28.72		Isaac K.	Songok	KEN	25.4.84	1	GP	Rieti	27 Aug 06
7:28.76		Augustine	Choge	KEN	21.1.87	4	DL	Doha	6 May 11
7:28.93		Salah	Hissou	MAR	16.1.72	2	Herc	Monaco	4 Aug 99
7:28.94		Brahim	Lahlafi	FRA/MAR	15.4.68	3	Herc	Monaco	4 Aug 99
7:29.00		Bernard	Lagat	USA	12.12.74	2		Rieti	29 Aug 10
7:29.09		John	Kibowen	KEN	21.4.69	3	Bisl	Oslo	9 Jul 98
7:29.34		Isaac	Viciosa	ESP	26.12.69	4	Bisl	Oslo	9 Jul 98
7:29.45	WR	Saïd	Aouita	MAR	2.11.59	1	ASV	Köln	20 Aug 89
7:29.92		Sileshi	Sihine	ETH	29.1.83	1	GP	Rieti	28 Aug 05
7:30.09		Ismaïl	Sghyr	MAR/FRA	16.3.72	2	Herc	Monaco	25 Jul 95
		(30)							
7:30.09		Thomas	Longosiwa	KEN	14.1.82	2	SGP	Doha	8 May 09
7:30.09		Abdelaati	Iguider	MAR	25.3.87	2	DL	Saint-Denis	27 Aug 16
7:30.15		Vincent	Chepkok	KEN	5.7.88	5	DL	Doha	6 May 11
7:30.36		Mark	Carroll	IRL	15.1.72	5	Herc	Monaco	4 Aug 99
7:30.36		Hagos	Gebrhiwet	ETH	11.5.94	1	DL	Doha	10 May 13
7:30.43		Isiah	Koech	KEN	19.12.93	1	DNG	Stockholm	17 Aug 12
7:30.50		Dieter	Baumann ¶	GER	9.2.65	6	Herc	Monaco	8 Aug 98
7:30.53		El Hassan	Lahssini	MAR/FRA	1.1.75	6	Herc	Monaco	10 Aug 96
7:30.53		Hailu	Mekonnen	ETH	4.4.80	1	VD	Bruxelles	24 Aug 01
7:30.62		Boniface	Songok	KEN	25.12.80	3	VD	Bruxelles	3 Sep 04
		(40)							
7:30.76		Jamal Bilal	Salem	KEN/QAT	12.9.78	4	SGP	Doha	13 May 05
7:30.78		Mustapha	Essaïd	FRA	20.1.70	7	Herc	Monaco	8 Aug 98
7:30.84		Bob	Kennedy	USA	18.8.70	8	Herc	Monaco	8 Aug 98
7:30.93		Ryan	Hill	USA	31.1.90	4	DL	Saint-Denis	27 Aug 16
7:30.95		Moses	Kipsiro	UGA	2.9.86	1	Herc	Monaco	28 Jul 09
7:30.99		Khalid	Boulami	MAR	7.8.69	1	Nik	Nice	16 Jul 97
7:30.99		Caleb	Ndiku	KEN	9.10.92	2	DNG	Stockholm	17 Aug 12
7:31.13		Julius	Gitahi	KEN	29.4.78	6	Bisl	Oslo	9 Jul 98
7:31.14		William	Kalya	KEN	4.8.74	3	Herc	Monaco	16 Aug 97
7:31.20		Joseph	Kiplimo	KEN	20.7.88	1	GP	Rieti	6 Sep 09
		(50)							

100th man 7:34.77, 200th man 7:39.24, 300th 7:41.74, 400th 7:43.59, 500th 7:45.2

Indoors

Mark	Wind	Name		Nat	Born	Pos	Meet	Venue	Date
7:24.90	WIR		Komen			1		Budapest	6 Feb 98
7:26.15	WIR		Gebrselassie			1		Karlsruhe	25 Jan 98
7:26.80			Gebrselassie			1		Karlsruhe	24 Jan 99
7:27.80			Alamirew			1	Spark	Stuttgart	5 Feb 11
7:27.93			Komen			1	Spark	Stuttgart	1 Feb 98
7:28.00		Augustine	Choge	KEN	21.1.87	2	Spark	Stuttgart	5 Feb 11
7:30.16		Galen	Rupp	USA	8.5.86	1		Stockholm	21 Feb 13

2 MILES

Mark	Wind	Name		Nat	Born	Pos	Meet	Venue	Date
7:58.61	WR	Daniel	Komen	KEN	17.5.76	1		Hechtel	19 Jul 97
7:58.91			Komen			1		Sydney	28 Feb 98
8:01.08	WR	Haile	Gebrselassie	ETH	18.4.73	1	APM	Hengelo	31 May 97
8:01.72			Gebrselassie			1	BrGP	London (CP)	7 Aug 99
8:01.86			Gebrselassie			1	APM	Hengelo	30 May 99
8:03.50		Craig	Mottram	AUS	18.6.80	1	Pre	Eugene	10 Jun 07
8:03.54	WR		Komen			1		Lappeenranta	14 Jul 96

A – mark made at an altitude of 1000m or higher, i – indoors, Q – in qualifying competition, WR – world record

264 2 MILES – 5000 METRES A-T

Mark	Wind	Name		Nat	Born	Pos	Meet	Venue	Date
Indoors									
8:03.40		Mohamed	Farah	GBR	23.3.83	1	GP	Birmingham	21 Feb 15
8:04.35		Kenenisa	Bekele	ETH	13.6.82	1	GP	Birmingham	16 Feb 08
5000 METRES									
12:37.35 WR		Kenenisa	Bekele	ETH	13.6.82	1	FBK	Hengelo	31 May 04
12:39.36 WR		Haile	Gebrselassie	ETH	18.4.73	1	GP II	Helsinki	13 Jun 98
12:39.74 WR		Daniel	Komen	KEN	17.5.76	1	VD	Bruxelles	22 Aug 97
12:40.18			K Bekele			1	Gaz	Saint-Denis	1 Jul 05
12:41.86 WR			Gebrselassie			1	WK	Zürich	13 Aug 97
12:44.39 WR			Gebrselassie			1	WK	Zürich	16 Aug 95
12:44.90			Komen			2	WK	Zürich	13 Aug 97
12:45.09			Komen			1	WK	Zürich	14 Aug 96
12:46.53		Eliud	Kipchoge	KEN	5.11.84	1	GGala	Roma	2 Jul 04
12:46.81		Dejen	Gebremeskel	ETH	24.11.89	1	DL	Saint-Denis	6 Jul 12
12:47.04		Sileshi	Sihine	ETH	29.9.83	2	GGala	Roma	2 Jul 04
12:47.53		Hagos	Gebrhiwet	ETH	11.5.94	2	DL	Saint-Denis	6 Jul 12
12:48.09			K Bekele			1	VD	Bruxelles	25 Aug 06
12:48.25			K Bekele			1	WK	Zürich	18 Aug 06
12:48.64		Isiah	Koech	KEN	19.12.93	3	DL	Saint-Denis	6 Jul 12
12:48.66		Isaac K.	Songok	KEN	25.4.84	2	WK	Zürich	18 Aug 06
12:48.77		Yenew	Alamirew (10)	ETH	27.5.90	4	DL	Saint-Denis	6 Jul 12
12:48.81		Stephen	Cherono/Shaheen	KEN/QAT	15.10.82	1	GS	Ostrava	12 Jun 03
12:48.98			Komen			1	GGala	Roma	5 Jun 97
12:49.04		Thomas	Longosiwa	KEN	14.1.82	5	DL	Saint-Denis	6 Jul 12
12:49.28		Brahim	Lahlafi	MAR	15.4.68	1	VD	Bruxelles	25 Aug 00
12:49.50		John	Kipkoech	KEN	29.12.91	6	DL	Saint-Denis	6 Jul 12
12:49.53			K Bekele			1	Aragón	Zaragoza	28 Jul 07
12:49.64			Gebrselassie			1	WK	Zürich	11 Aug 99
12:49.71		Mohammed	Mourhit ¶	BEL	10.10.70	2	VD	Bruxelles	25 Aug 00
12:49.87		Paul	Tergat	KEN	17.6.69	3	WK	Zürich	13 Aug 97
12:50.16			Sihine			1	VD	Bruxelles	14 Sep 07
12:50.18			K Bekele			1	WK	Zürich	29 Aug 08
12:50.22			Kipchoge			1	VD	Bruxelles	26 Aug 05
12:50.24		Hicham (30/17)	El Guerrouj	MAR	14.9.74	2	GS	Ostrava	12 Jun 03
12:50.25		Abderrahim	Goumri ¶	MAR	21.5.76	2	VD	Bruxelles	26 Aug 05
12:50.55		Moses	Masai	KEN	1.6.86	1	ISTAF	Berlin	1 Jun 08
12:50.72		Moses (20)	Kipsiro	UGA	2.9.86	3	VD	Bruxelles	14 Sep 07
12:50.80		Salah	Hissou	MAR	16.1.72	1	GGala	Roma	5 Jun 96
12:50.86		Ali	Saïdi-Sief ¶	ALG	15.3.78	1	GGala	Roma	30 Jun 00
12:51.00		Joseph	Ebuya	KEN	20.6.87	4	VD	Bruxelles	14 Sep 07
12:51.34		Edwin	Soi	KEN	3.3.86	1	Herc	Monaco	19 Jul 13
12:51.45		Vincent	Chepkok	KEN	5.7.88	2	DL	Doha	14 May 10
12:51.96		Albert	Rop	KEN/BRN	17.7.92	2	Herc	Monaco	19 Jul 13
12:52.33		Sammy	Kipketer	KEN	29.9.81	2	Bisl	Oslo	27 Jun 03
12:52.45		Tariku	Bekele	ETH	21.1.87	2	ISTAF	Berlin	1 Jun 08
12:52.80		Gebre-egziabher	Gebremariam	ETH	10.9.84	3	GGala	Roma	8 Jul 05
12:52.99		Abraham (30)	Chebii	KEN	23.12.79	4	Bisl	Oslo	27 Jun 03
12:53.11		Mohamed	Farah	GBR	23.3.83	1	Herc	Monaco	22 Jul 11
12:53.41		Khalid	Boulami	MAR	7.8.69	4	WK	Zürich	13 Aug 97
12:53.46		Mark	Kiptoo	KEN	21.6.76	1	DNG	Stockholm	6 Aug 10
12:53.58		Imane	Merga	ETH	15.10.88	3	DNG	Stockholm	6 Aug 10
12:53.60		Bernard	Lagat	USA	12.12.74	2	Herc	Monaco	22 Jul 11
12:53.66		Augustine	Choge	KEN	21.1.87	4	GGala	Roma	8 Jul 05
12:53.72		Philip	Mosima	KEN	2.1.77	2	GGala	Roma	5 Jun 96
12:53.84		Assefa	Mezegebu	ETH	19.6.78	1	VD	Bruxelles	28 Aug 98
12:53.98		Yomif	Kejelcha	ETH	1.8.97	1	VD	Bruxelles	11 Sep 15
12:54.07		John (40)	Kibowen	KEN	21.4.69	4	WCh	Saint-Denis	31 Aug 03
12:54.15		Dejene	Berhanu	ETH	12.12.80	3	GGala	Roma	2 Jul 04
12:54.19		Abreham	Cherkos	ETH	23.9.89	5	GGala	Roma	14 Jul 06
12:54.46		Moses	Mosop	KEN	17.7.85	3	Gaz	Saint-Denis	8 Jul 05
12:54.58		James	Kwalia	KEN/QAT	12.6.84	5	Bisl	Oslo	27 Jun 03
12:54.70		Dieter	Baumann ¶	GER	9.2.65	5	WK	Zürich	13 Aug 97
12:54.83		Muktar	Edris	ETH	14.1.94	1	DNG	Stockholm	21 Aug 14
12:54.85		Moses	Kiptanui	KEN	1.10.70	3	GGala	Roma	5 Jun 96
12:54.99		Benjamin	Limo	KEN	23.8.74	3	Gaz	Saint-Denis	4 Jul 03

5000 – 10,000 METRES A-T   265

Mark	Wind	Name		Nat	Born	Pos	Meet	Venue	Date
12:55.06		Lucas	Rotich	KEN	16.4.90	4	Bisl	Oslo	4 Jun 10
12:55.52		Hicham	Bellani	MAR	15.9.79	7	GGala	Roma	14 Jul 06
		(50)	100th man 13:00.60, 200th 13:08.03, 300th 13:12.14, 400th 13:15.62, 500th 13:18.21						
Indoors: 12:49.60			K Bekele			1		Birmingham	20 Feb 04

10,000 METRES

MEN All-time

Mark		Name		Nat	Born	Pos	Meet	Venue	Date
26:17.53	WR	Kenenisa	Bekele	ETH	13.6.82	1	VD	Bruxelles	26 Aug 05
26:20.31	WR		K Bekele			1	GS	Ostrava	8 Jun 04
26:22.75	WR	Haile	Gebrselassie	ETH	18.4.73	1	APM	Hengelo	1 Jun 98
26:25.97			K Bekele			1	Pre	Eugene	8 Jun 08
26:27.85	WR	Paul	Tergat	KEN	17.6.69	1	VD	Bruxelles	22 Aug 97
26:28.72			K Bekele			1	FBK	Hengelo	29 May 05
26:29.22			Gebrselassie			1	VD	Bruxelles	5 Sep 03
26:30.03		Nicholas	Kemboi	KEN/QAT	25.11.83	2	VD	Bruxelles	5 Sep 03
26:30.74		Abebe	Dinkesa	ETH	6.3.84	2	FBK	Hengelo	29 May 05
26:31.32	WR		Gebrselassie			1	Bisl	Oslo	4 Jul 97
26:35.63		Micah	Kogo	KEN	3.6.86	1	VD	Bruxelles	25 Aug 06
26:36.26		Paul	Koech	KEN	25.6.69	2	VD	Bruxelles	22 Aug 97
26:37.25		Zersenay	Tadese	ERI	8.2.82	2	VD	Bruxelles	25 Aug 06
26:38.08	WR	Salah	Hissou	MAR	16.1.72	1	VD	Bruxelles	23 Aug 96
26:38.76		Abdullah Ahmad	Hassan (10)	QAT	4.4.81	3	VD	Bruxelles	5 Sep 03
		(Formerly Albert Chepkurui KEN)							
26:39.69		Sileshi	Sihine	ETH	29.9.83	1	FBK	Hengelo	31 May 04
26:39.77		Boniface	Kiprop	UGA	12.10.85	2	VD	Bruxelles	26 Aug 05
26:41.58			Gebrselassie			2	FBK	Hengelo	31 May 04
26:41.75		Samuel	Wanjiru	KEN	10.11.86	3	VD	Bruxelles	26 Aug 05
26:41.95			Kiprop			3	VD	Bruxelles	25 Aug 06
26:43.16			K Bekele			1	VD	Bruxelles	16 Sep 11
26:43.53	WR		Gebrselassie			1	APM	Hengelo	5 Jun 95
26:43.98		Lucas	Rotich	KEN	16.4.90	2	VD	Bruxelles	16 Sep 11
26:44.36		Galen	Rupp	USA	8.5.86	1	Pre	Eugene	30 May 14
26:46.19			K Bekele			1	VD	Bruxelles	14 Sep 07
26:46.31			K Bekele			1	WCh	Berlin	17 Aug 09
26:46.44			Tergat			1	VD	Bruxelles	28 Aug 98
26:46.57		Mohamed	Farah	GBR	23.3.83	1	Pre	Eugene	3 Jun 11
26:47.89			Koech			2	VD	Bruxelles	28 Aug 98
26:48.00			Rupp			3	VD	Bruxelles	16 Sep 11
		(30/16)							
26:48.35		Imane	Merga	ETH	15.10.88	2	Pre	Eugene	3 Jun 11
26:48.99		Josphat	Bett	KEN	12.6.90	3	Pre	Eugene	3 Jun 11
26:49.02		Eliud	Kipchoge	KEN	5.11.84	2	FBK	Hengelo	26 May 07
26:49.20		Moses	Masai	KEN	1.6.86	2	VD	Bruxelles	14 Sep 07
		(20)							
26:49.38		Sammy	Kipketer	KEN	29.9.81	1	VD	Bruxelles	30 Aug 02
26:49.41		Paul	Tanui	KEN	22.12.90	2	Pre	Eugene	30 May 14
26:49.55		Moses	Mosop	KEN	17.7.85	3	FBK	Hengelo	26 May 07
26:49.90		Assefa	Mezegebu	ETH	19.6.78	2	VD	Bruxelles	30 Aug 02
26:50.20		Richard	Limo	KEN	18.11.80	3	VD	Bruxelles	30 Aug 02
26:51.02		Dejen	Gebremeskel	ETH	24.11.89	1		Sollentuna	27 Jun 13
26:51.11		Yigrem	Demelash	ETH	28.1.94	1	OT	Hengelo	29 Jun 16
26:51.16		Emmanuel	Bett	KEN	30.3.83	1	VD	Bruxelles	7 Sep 12
26:51.49		Charles	Kamathi	KEN	18.5.78	1	VD	Bruxelles	3 Sep 99
26:51.68		Vincent	Chepkok	KEN	5.7.88	2	VD	Bruxelles	7 Sep 12
		(30)							
26:52.23	WR	William	Sigei	KEN	14.10.69	1	Bisl	Oslo	22 Jul 94
26:52.30		Mohammed	Mourhit ¶	BEL	10.10.70	2	VD	Bruxelles	3 Sep 99
26:52.33		Gebre-egziabher	Gebremariam	ETH	10.9.84	4	FBK	Hengelo	26 May 07
26:52.36		Bidan	Karoki	KEN	21.8.90	3	Pre	Eugene	30 May 14
26:52.65		Kenneth	Kipkemoi	KEN	2.8.84	3	VD	Bruxelles	7 Sep 12
26:52.65		Geoffrey	Kamworor	KEN	28.11.92	3	Pre	Eugene	29 May 15
26:52.85		Abera	Kuma	ETH	31.8.90	2		Sollentuna	27 Jun 13
26:52.87		John Cheruiyot	Korir	KEN	13.12.81	5	VD	Bruxelles	30 Aug 02
26:52.93		Mark	Bett	KEN	22.12.76	6	VD	Bruxelles	26 Aug 05
26:54.25		Mathew	Kisorio ¶	KEN	16.5.89	7	Pre	Eugene	3 Jun 11
		(40)							
26:54.61		Stephen	Sambu	KEN	3.7.88	4	Pre	Eugene	30 May 14
26:54.64		Mark	Kiptoo	KEN	21.6.76	8	Pre	Eugene	3 Jun 11
26:54.66		William Malel	Sitonik	KEN	1.3.94	2	Pre	Eugene	27 May 16
26:55.29		Leonard Patrick	Komon	KEN	10.1.88	9	Pre	Eugene	3 Jun 11
26:55.73		Geoffrey	Kirui	KEN	16.2.93	6	VD	Bruxelles	16 Sep 11

266 10,000 METRES – HALF MARATHON A-T

Mark	Wind	Name		Nat	Born	Pos	Meet	Venue	Date
26:56.74		Josphat	Menjo	KEN	20.8.79	1		Turku	29 Aug 10
26:57.33		Tamirat	Tola	ETH	11.8.91	3	Pre	Eugene	27 May 16
26:57.36		Josphat	Muchiri Ndambiri	KEN	12.2.85	1		Fukuroi	3 May 09
26:57.88		Abadi	Embaye	ETH	6.11.97	3	OT	Hengelo	29 Jun 16
26:58.38	wr	Yobes	Ondieki	KEN	21.2.61	1	Bisl	Oslo	10 Jul 93
		(50)							

100th man 27:13.94, 200th 27:28.67, 300th 27:36.90, 400th 27:43.29, 500th 27:48.7

20,000 METRES & 1 HOUR

Mark			Name		Nat	Born	Pos	Meet	Venue	Date
56:25.98+	21 285m		Haile	Gebrselassie	ETH	18.4.73	1	GS	Ostrava	27 Jun 07
56:55.6+	21 101		Arturo	Barrios	MEX	12.12.63	1		La Flèche	30 Mar 91
57:24.19+	20 944		Jos	Hermens	NED	8.1.50	1		Papendal	1 May 76
57:18.4+	20 943		Dionísio	Castro	POR	22.11.63	1		La Flèche	31 Mar 90

HALF MARATHON

Included are the slightly downhill courses: Newcastle to South Shields 30.5m, Tokyo 33m, Lisboa (Spring to 2008) 69m

Mark		Name		Nat	Born	Pos	Meet	Venue	Date
58:23	wr	Zersenay	Tadese	ERI	8.2.82	1		Lisboa	21 Mar 10
58:30			Z Tadese			1		Lisboa	20 Mar 11
58:33	wr	Samuel	Wanjiru	KEN	10.11.86	1		Den Haag	17 Mar 07
58:44		Solomon	Yego	KEN	10.5.87	1		Ostia	13 Mar 16
58:46		Mathew	Kisorio ¶	KEN	16.5.89	1		Philadelphia	18 Sep 11
58:47		Atsedu	Tsegay	ETH	17.12.91	1		Praha	31 Mar 12
58:48		Sammy	Kitwara	KEN	26.11.86	2		Philadelphia	18 Sep 11
58:48		Abreham	Cheroben	KEN/BRN	11.10.92	1		Valencia	19 Oct 14
58:52		Patrick	Makau	KEN	2.3.85	1		Ra's Al Khaymah	20 Feb 09
58:53	wr		Wanjiru			1		Ra's Al Khaymah	9 Feb 07
58:54		Stephen	Kibet	KEN	9.11.86	1		Den Haag	11 Mar 12
58:54		Geoffrey	Kamworor (10)	KEN	28.11.92	1		Ra's Al-Khaymah	15 Feb 13
58:55	wr	Haile	Gebrselassie	ETH	18.4.73	1		Tempe	15 Jan 06
58:56			Makau			1		Berlin	1 Apr 07
58:56	dh	Martin	Mathathi	KEN	25.12.85	1	GNR	South Shields	18 Sep 11
58:56		Stanley	Biwott	KEN	21.4.86	2		Ra's Al-Khaymah	15 Feb 13
58:58			Kitwara			1		Rotterdam	13 Sep 09
58:58		Geoffrey	Mutai	KEN	7.10.81	3		Ra's Al-Khaymah	15 Feb 13
58:59			Z Tadese			1	WCh	Udine	14 Oct 07
58:59		Wilson	Kipsang	KEN	15.3.82	2		Ra's Al Khaymah	20 Feb 09
59:01		Kenneth	Kipkemoi	KEN	2.8.84	2		Valencia	19 Oct 14
59:02			Makau			2	WCh	Udine	14 Oct 07
59:02		Jonathan	Maiyo	KEN	5.5.88	2		Den Haag	11 Mar 12
59:05	dh		Tadese			1	GNR	South Shields	18 Sep 05
59:05		Evans	Cheruiyot	KEN	10.5.82	3	WCh	Udine	14 Oct 07
59:05		Ezekiel	Chebii	KEN	3.1.91	1		Lille	1 Sep 12
59:06	dh	Paul	Tergat (20)	KEN	17.6.69	1		Lisboa	26 Mar 00
59:06	dh		Kipsang			1	GNR	South Shields	16 Sep 12
59:06			G Mutai			1		Udine	22 Sep 13
59:06		Guye	Adola	ETH	20.10.90	1		New Delhi	23 Nov 14
		(30/21)							
59:07		Paul	Kosgei	KEN	22.4.78	1		Berlin	2 Apr 06
59:07	dh	Micah	Kogo	KEN	3.6.86	2	GNR	South Shields	16 Sep 12
59:07		James	Wangari	KEN	23.3.94	1		København	18 Sep 16
59:09		James Kipsang	Kwambai	KEN	28.2.83	3		Rotterdam	13 Sep 09
59:10		Bernard	Kipyego	KEN	16.7.86	4		Rotterdam	13 Sep 09
59:10		Bernard	Koech	KEN	31.1.88	2		Lille	1 Sep 12
59:11		Mosinet	Geremew	ETH	12.2.92	3		New Delhi	23 Nov 14
59:12		Cyprian	Kotut	KEN	.92	4		New Delhi	23 Nov 14
59:14		Dennis	Kimetto	KEN	22.1.84	1		Berlin	1 Apr 12
		(30)							
59:14		Leonard Patrick	Komon	KEN	10.1.88	1		Berlin	30 Mar 14
59:14		Bidan	Karoki	KEN	21.8.90	1		København	13 Sep 15
59:15		Deriba	Merga	ETH	26.10.80	1		New Delhi	9 Nov 08
59:15		Wilson	Chebet	KEN	12.7.85	5		Rotterdam	13 Sep 09
59:15		Wilson	Kiprop	KEN	14.4.87	2		Berlin	1 Apr 12
59:18		Leonard	Langat	KEN	7.8.90	2		Ostia	13 Mar 16
59:19		Tilahun	Regassa	ETH	18.1.90	1		Abu Dhabi	7 Jan 10
59:19		Robert	Chemosin	KEN	1.2.89	2		Ostia	3 Mar 13
59:20	dh	Hendrick	Ramaala	RSA	2.2.72	2		Lisboa	26 Mar 00
59:20		Moses	Mosop	KEN	17.7.85	1	Stra	Milano	21 Mar 10
		(40)							
59:20		Simon	Cheprot	KEN	2.7.93	3		Ostia	3 Mar 13
59:20		Berhanu	Legesse	ETH	11.9.94	1		New Delhi	29 Nov 15
59:20		Daniel	Wanjiru	KEN	25.5.92	1		Praha	2 Apr 16

HALF MARATHON – MARATHON A-T

Mark	Wind	Name		Nat	Born	Pos	Meet	Venue	Date
59:21	dh	Robert Kipkoech	Cheruiyot	KEN	26.9.78	2		Lisboa	13 Mar 05
59:21		Samuel	Tsegay	ERI	24.2.88	2	WCh	København	29 Mar 14
59:22		Feyisa	Lilesa	ETH	1.2.90	1		Houston	15 Jan 12
59:22		Peter Cheruiyot	Kirui	KEN	2.1.88	1		Praha	5 Apr 14
59:22	dh	Mohamed	Farah	GBR	23.3.83	1	GNR	South Shields	13 Sep 15
59:23		John Kiprotich	Chemisto	KEN	5.6.83	6		Rotterdam	13 Sep 09
59:25		Pius	Kirop	KEN	8.1.90	4		Berlin	1 Apr 12
59:25		Eliud	Kipchoge	KEN	5.11.84	3		Lille	1 Sep 12
59:25		Aziz	Lahbabi	MAR	3.2.91	1		Ostia	2 Mar 14
(52)			100th man 59:44, 200th man 60:14, 300th 60:35, 400th 60:53, 500th 61:05						
Short course:		58:51	Paul Tergat	KEN	17.6.69	1	Stra	Milano 49m sh	30 Mar 96
Excessively downhill:		58:42	Bernard Koech	KEN	31.1.88	1		San Diego (dh 86m)	2 Jun 13

MARATHON

Mark		Name		Nat	Born	Pos		Venue	Date
2:02:57	WR	Dennis	Kimetto	KEN	22.1.84	1		Berlin	28 Sep 14
2:03:03		Kenenisa	Bekele	ETH	13.6.82	1		Berlin	25 Sep 16
2:03:05		Eliud	Kipchoge	KEN	5.11.84	1		London	24 Apr 16
2:03:13		Emmanuel	Mutai	KEN	12.10.84	2		Berlin	28 Sep 14
2:03:13		Wilson	Kipsang	KEN	15.3.82	2		Berlin	25 Sep 16
2:03:23	WR		W Kipsang			1		Berlin	29 Sep 13
2:03:38	WR	Patrick	Makau	KEN	2.3.85	1		Berlin	25 Sep 11
2:03:42			W Kipsang			1		Frankfurt	30 Oct 11
2:03:45			Kimetto			1		Chicago	13 Oct 13
2:03:51		Stanley	Biwott	KEN	21.4.86	2		London	24 Apr 16
2:03:52			Mutai			2		Chicago	13 Oct 13
2:03:59	WR	Haile	Gebrselassie	ETH	18.4.73	1		Berlin	28 Sep 08
2:04:00			Kipchoge			1		Berlin	27 Sep 15
2:04:05			Kipchoge			2		Berlin	29 Sep 13
2:04:11			Kipchoge			1		Chicago	12 Oct 14
2:04:15		Geoffrey	Mutai	KEN	7.10.81	1		Berlin	30 Sep 12
2:04:16			Kimetto			2		Berlin	30 Sep 12
2:04:23		Ayele	Abshero (10)	ETH	28.12.90	1		Dubai	27 Jan 12
2:04:24		Tesfaye	Abera	ETH	31.3.92	1		Dubai	22 Jan 16
2:04:26	WR		Gebrselassie			1		Berlin	30 Sep 07
2:04:27		Duncan	Kibet	KEN	25.4.78	1		Rotterdam	5 Apr 09
2:04:27		James Kipsang	Kwambai	KEN	28.2.83	2		Rotterdam	5 Apr 09
2:04:28		Sammy	Kitwara	KEN	26.11.86	2		Chicago	12 Oct 14
2:04:29			W Kipsang			1		London	13 Apr 14
2:04:32		Tsegaye	Mekonnen	ETH	15.6.95	1		Dubai	24 Jan 14
2:04:32		Dickson	Chumba	KEN	27.10.86	3		Chicago	12 Oct 14
2:04:33		Hayle	Lemi Berhanu	ETH	13.9.94	2		Dubai	22 Jan 16
2:04:38		Tsegaye	Kebede	ETH	15.1.87	1		Chicago	7 Oct 12
2:04:40			E Mutai			1		London	17 Apr 11
2:04:42			Kipchoge			1		London	26 Apr 15
(30/18)									
2:04:45		Lelisa	Desisa	ETH	14.1.90	1		Dubai	25 Jan 13
2:04:48		Yemane	Tsegay Adhane	ETH	8.4.85	1		Rotterdam	15 Apr 12
(20)									
2:04:48		Berhanu	Shiferaw	ETH	31.5.93	2		Dubai	25 Jan 13
2:04:49		Tadesse	Tola	ETH	31.10.87	3		Dubai	25 Jan 13
2:04:50		Dino	Sefir	ETH	28.5.88	2		Dubai	27 Jan 12
2:04:50		Getu	Feleke	ETH	28.11.86	2		Rotterdam	15 Apr 12
2:04:52		Feyisa	Lilesa	ETH	1.2.90	2		Chicago	7 Oct 12
2:04:52		Endeshaw	Negesse	ETH	13.3.88	4		Dubai	25 Jan 13
2:04:53		Bernard	Koech	KEN	31.1.88	5		Dubai	25 Jan 13
2:04:54		Markos	Geneti	ETH	30.5.84	3		Dubai	27 Jan 12
2:04:55	WR	Paul	Tergat	KEN	17.6.69	1		Berlin	28 Sep 03
2:04:56		Sammy	Korir	KEN	12.12.71	2		Berlin	28 Sep 03
(30)									
2:04:56		Jonathan	Maiyo	KEN	5.5.88	4		Dubai	27 Jan 12
2:05:03		Moses	Mosop	KEN	17.7.85	3		Rotterdam	15 Apr 12
2:05:04		Abel	Kirui	KEN	4.6.82	3		Rotterdam	5 Apr 09
2:05:10		Samuel	Wanjiru	KEN	10.11.86	1		London	26 Apr 09
2:05:13		Vincent	Kipruto	KEN	13.9.87	3		Rotterdam	11 Apr 10
2:05:13		Wilson	Loyanae ¶	KEN	20.11.88	1		Seoul	20 Mar 16
2:05:15		Martin	Lel	KEN	29.10.78	1		London	13 Apr 08
2:05:16		Levi	Matebo Omari	KEN	3.11.89	2		Frankfurt	30 Oct 11
2:05:16		Sisay	Lemma	ETH	12.12.90	4		Dubai	22 Jan 16
2:05:21		Eliud	Kiptanui	KEN	6.6.89	2		Berlin	27 Sep 15
(40)									

MEN All-time

MARATHON – 2000m – 3000m STEEPLECHASE A-T

Mark	Wind	Name		Nat	Born	Pos	Meet	Venue	Date
2:05:25		Bazu	Worku	ETH	15.9.90	3		Berlin	26 Sep 10
2:05:25		Albert	Matebor	KEN	20.12.80	3		Frankfurt	30 Oct 11
2:05:27		Jaouad	Gharib	MAR	22.5.72	3		London	26 Apr 09
2:05:27		Wilson	Chebet	KEN	12.7.85	1		Rotterdam	10 Apr 11
2:05:27		Tilahun	Regassa	ETH	18.1.90	3		Chicago	7 Oct 12
2:05:30		Abderrahim	Goumri ¶	MAR	21.5.76	3		London	13 Apr 08
2:05:31		Evans Kiplagat	Chebet	KEN	10.11.88	3		Berlin	25 Sep 16
2:05:38 WR		Khalid	Khannouchi	MAR/USA	22.12.71	1		London	14 Apr 02
2:05:38		Peter	Some	KEN	5.6.90	1		Paris	7 Apr 13
2:05:41		Yami	Dadi	ETH	.82	6		Dubai	27 Jan 12
		(50)	100th man 2:06:27, 200th 2:07:18, 300th 2:07:58, 400th 2:08:29, 500th 2:08:52						

Downhill point-to-point course – Boston marathon is downhill overall (139m) and sometimes strongly wind-aided.

Mark	Wind	Name		Nat	Born	Pos	Meet	Venue	Date
2:03:02		Geoffrey	Mutai	KEN	7.10.81	1		Boston	18 Apr 11
2:03:06		Moses	Mosop	KEN	17.7.85	2		Boston	18 Apr 11
2:04:53		Gebre-egziabher	Gebremariam	ETH	10.9.84	3		Boston	18 Apr 11
2:04:58		Ryan	Hall	USA	14.10.82	4		Boston	18 Apr 11

2000 METRES STEEPLECHASE

Mark	Wind	Name		Nat	Born	Pos	Meet	Venue	Date
5:10.68		Mahiedine	Mekhissi-Benabbad	FRA	15.3.85	1		Reims	30 Jun 10
5:13.47		Bouabdellah	Tahri	FRA	20.12.78	1		Tomblaine	25 Jun 10
5:14.43		Julius	Kariuki	KEN	12.6.61	1		Rovereto	21 Aug 90
5:14.53		Saïf Saaeed	Shaheen	QAT	15.10.82	1	SGP	Doha	13 May 05
5:16.22		Phillip	Barkutwo	KEN	6.10.66	2		Rovereto	21 Aug 90
5:16.46		Wesley	Kiprotich	KEN	31.7.79	2	SGP	Doha	13 May 05
5:16.85		Eliud	Barngetuny	KEN	20.5.73	1		Parma	13 Jun 95

3000 METRES STEEPLECHASE

Mark	Wind	Name		Nat	Born	Pos	Meet	Venue	Date
7:53.63 WR		Saïf Saaeed	Shaheen	KEN/QAT	15.10.82	1	VD	Bruxelles	3 Sep 04
7:53.64		Brimin	Kipruto	KEN	31.7.85	1	Herc	Monaco	22 Jul 11
7:54.31		Paul Kipsiele	Koech	KEN	10.11.81	1	GGala	Roma	31 May 12
7:55.28 WR		Brahim	Boulami ¶	MAR	20.4.72	1	VD	Bruxelles	24 Aug 01
7:55.51			Shaheen			1	VD	Bruxelles	26 Aug 05
7:55.72 WR		Bernard	Barmasai	KEN	6.5.74	1	ASV	Köln	24 Aug 97
7:55.76		Ezekiel	Kemboi	KEN	25.5.82	2	Herc	Monaco	22 Jul 11
7:56.16		Moses	Kiptanui	KEN	1.10.70	2	ASV	Köln	24 Aug 97
7:56.32			Shaheen			1	Tsik	Athína	3 Jul 06
7:56.34			Shaheen			1	GGala	Roma	8 Jul 05
7:56.37			P K Koech			2	GGala	Roma	8 Jul 05
7:56.54			Shaheen			1	WK	Zürich	18 Aug 06
7:56.58			P K Koech			1	DL	Doha	11 May 12
7:56.81		Richard	Mateelong	KEN	14.10.83	2	DL	Doha	11 May 12
7:56.94			Shaheen			1	WAF	Monaco	19 Sep 04
7:57.28			Shaheen			1	Tsik	Athína	14 Jun 05
7:57.29		Reuben	Kosgei	KEN	2.8.79	2	VD	Bruxelles	24 Aug 01
7:57.32			P K Koech			3	Herc	Monaco	22 Jul 11
7:57.38			Shaheen			1	WAF	Monaco	14 Sep 03
7:57.42			P K Koech			2	WAF	Monaco	14 Sep 03
7:58.09			Boulami			1	Herc	Monaco	19 Jul 02
7:58.10			S Cherono			2	Herc	Monaco	19 Jul 02
7:58.41		Jairus	Birech (10)	KEN	14.12.92	1	VD	Bruxelles	5 Sep 14
7:58.50			Boulami			1	WK	Zürich	17 Aug 01
7:58.66			S Cherono			3	VD	Bruxelles	24 Aug 01
7:58.80			P K Koech			1	VD	Bruxelles	14 Sep 07
7:58.83			Birech			1	DL	Saint-Denis	4 Jul 15
7:58.85			Kemboi			1	SGP	Doha	8 May 09
7:58.98			Barmasai			1	Herc	Monaco	4 Aug 99
7:59.03			Kemboi			1	DL	Saint-Denis	6 Jul 13
		(30/10)							
7:59.08 WR		Wilson	Boit Kipketer	KEN	6.10.73	1	WK	Zürich	13 Aug 97
8:00.09		Mahiedine	Mekhissi-Benabbad	FRA	15.3.85	2	DL	Saint-Denis	6 Jul 13
8:00.12		Conseslus	Kipruto	KEN	8.12.94	1	DL	Birmingham	5 Jun 16
8:00.45		Evan	Jager	USA	8.3.89	2	DL	Saint-Denis	4 Jul 15
8:01.18		Bouabdellah	Tahri	FRA	20.12.78	3	WCh	Berlin	18 Aug 09
8:01.67		Abel	Mutai	KEN	2.10.88	2	GGala	Roma	31 May 12
8:01.69		Kipkirui	Misoi	KEN	23.12.78	4	VD	Bruxelles	24 Aug 01
8:03.41		Patrick	Sang	KEN	11.4.64	3	ASV	Köln	24 Aug 97
8:03.57		Ali	Ezzine	MAR	3.9.78	1	Gaz	Saint-Denis	23 Jun 00
8:03.57		Hillary	Yego	KEN	2.4.92	3	DL	Shanghai	18 May 13
		(20)							
8:03.74		Raymond	Yator	KEN	7.4.81	3	Herc	Monaco	18 Aug 00

3000m STEEPLECHASE

Mark	Wind	Name		Nat	Born	Pos	Meet	Venue	Date
8:03.81		Benjamin	Kiplagat	UGA	4.3.89	2	Athl	Lausanne	8 Jul 10
8:03.89		John	Kosgei	KEN	13.7.73	3	Herc	Monaco	16 Aug 97
8:04.95		Simon	Vroemen ¶	NED	11.5.69	2	VD	Bruxelles	26 Aug 05
8:05.01		Eliud	Barngetuny	KEN	20.5.73	1	Herc	Monaco	25 Jul 95
8:05.35 WR		Peter	Koech	KEN	18.2.58	1	DNG	Stockholm	3 Jul 89
8:05.37		Philip	Barkutwo	KEN	6.10.66	2		Rieti	6 Sep 92
8:05.4 WR		Henry	Rono	KEN	12.2.52	1		Seattle	13 May 78
8:05.43		Christopher	Kosgei	KEN	14.8.74	2	WK	Zürich	11 Aug 99
8:05.51		Julius	Kariuki	KEN	12.6.61	1	OG	Seoul	30 Sep 88
(30)									
8:05.68		Wesley	Kiprotich	KEN	1.8.79	4	VD	Bruxelles	3 Sep 04
8:05.75		Mustafa	Mohamed	SWE	1.3.79	1	NA	Heusden-Zolder	28 Jul 07
8:05.88		Bernard	Mbugua Nganga	KEN	17.1.85	2	ISTAF	Berlin	11 Sep 11
8:05.99		Joseph	Keter	KEN	13.6.69	1	Herc	Monaco	10 Aug 96
8:06.13		Tareq Mubarak	Taher	BRN	24.3.84	3	Tsik	Athína	13 Jul 09
8:06.16		Roba	Gari	ETH	12.4.82	3	DL	Doha	11 May 12
8:06.77		Gideon	Chirchir	KEN	24.2.66	2	WK	Zürich	16 Aug 95
8:06.88		Richard	Kosgei	KEN	29.12.70	2	GPF	Monaco	9 Sep 95
8:06.96		Gilbert	Kirui	KEN	22.1.94	2	DL	London (OS)	27 Jul 13
8:07.02		Brahim	Taleb	MAR	16.2.85	2	NA	Heusden-Zolder	28 Jul 07
(40)									
8:07.13		Paul	Kosgei	KEN	22.4.78	2	GP II	Saint-Denis	3 Jul 99
8:07.18		Obaid Moussa	Amer ¶	KEN/QAT	18.4.85	4	OG	Athína	24 Aug 04
8:07.44		Luis Miguel	Martín	ESP	11.1.72	2	VD	Bruxelles	30 Aug 02
8:07.59		Julius	Nyamu	KEN	1.12.77	5	VD	Bruxelles	24 Aug 01
8:07.62		Joseph	Mahmoud	FRA	13.12.55	1	VD	Bruxelles	24 Aug 84
8:07.75		Jonathan	Ndiku Muia	KEN	18.9.91	6	Herc	Monaco	22 Jul 11
8:07.96		Mark	Rowland	GBR	7.3.63	3	OG	Seoul	30 Sep 88
8:08.02 WR		Anders	Gärderud	SWE	28.8.46	1	OG	Montreal	28 Jul 76
8:08.12		Matthew	Birir	KEN	5.7.72	3	GGala	Roma	8 Jun 95
8:08.14		Sa'ad Shaddad	Al-Asmari	KSA	24.9.68	4	DNG	Stockholm	16 Jul 02
(50)		100th man 8:12.25, 200th 8:17.49, 300th 8:20.98, 400th 8:23.4, 500th 8:25.6							

7:53.63 Shaheen formerly Stephen Cherono KE0
Drugs disqualification: 7:53.17 Brahim Boulami ¶ MAR 20.4.72 1 WK Zürich 16 Aug 02

110 METRES HURDLES

Mark	Wind	Name		Nat	Born	Pos	Meet	Venue	Date
12.80 WR	0.3	Aries	Merritt	USA	24.7.85	1	VD	Bruxelles	7 Sep 12
12.87 WR	0.9	Dayron	Robles	CUB	19.11.86	1	GS	Ostrava	12 Jun 08
12.88 WR	1.1		Liu Xiang	CHN	13.7.83	1rA	Athl	Lausanne	11 Jul 06
12.88	0.5		Robles			1	Gaz	Saint-Denis	18 Jul 08
12.89	0.5	David	Oliver	USA	24.4.82	1	DL	Saint-Denis	16 Jul 10
12.90	1.1	Dominique	Arnold	USA	14.9.73	2rA	Athl	Lausanne	11 Jul 06
12.90	1.6		Oliver			1	Pre	Eugene	3 Jul 10
12.91 WR	0.5	Colin	Jackson	GBR	18.2.67	1	WCh	Stuttgart	20 Aug 93
12.91 WR	0.3		Liu Xiang			1	OG	Athína	27 Aug 04
12.91	0.2		Robles			1	DNG	Stockholm	22 Jul 08
12.92 WR	-0.1	Roger	Kingdom	USA	26.8.62	1	WK	Zürich	16 Aug 89
12.92	0.9	Allen	Johnson	USA	1.3.71	1	NC	Atlanta	23 Jun 96
12.92	0.2		Johnson			1	VD	Bruxelles	23 Aug 96
12.92	1.5		Liu Xiang			1	GP	New York	2 Jun 07
12.92	0.0		Robles			1	WAF	Stuttgart	23 Sep 07
12.92	-0.3		Merritt			1	OG	London (OS)	8 Aug 12
12.93 WR	-0.2	Renaldo	Nehemiah	USA	24.3.59	1	WK	Zürich	19 Aug 81
12.93	0.0		Johnson			1	WCh	Athína	7 Aug 97
12.93	-0.6		Liu Xiang			1	WAF	Stuttgart	9 Sep 06
12.93	0.1		Robles			1	OG	Beijing	21 Aug 08
12.93	1.7		Oliver			1	NC	Des Moines	27 Jun 10
12.93	-0.3		Oliver			1	WK	Zürich	19 Aug 10
12.93	1.2		Merritt			1	NC/OT	Eugene	30 Jun 12
12.93	0.6		Merritt			1	LGP	London (CP)	13 Jul 12
12.93	0.0		Merritt			1	Herc	Monaco	20 Jul 12
12.94	1.6	Jack	Pierce (10)	USA	23.9.62	1s2	NC	Atlanta	22 Jun 96
12.94	1.8		Oliver			1	Pre	Eugene	4 Jun 11
12.94	0.1		Merritt			1s2	OG	London (OS)	8 Aug 12
12.94	0.8	Hansle	Parchment	JAM	17.6.90	1	DL	Saint-Denis	5 Jul 14
12.94	0.5	Orlando	Ortega	CUB/ESP	29.7.91	1	DL	Saint-Denis	4 Jul 15
(30/12)									
12.95	1.5	Terrence	Trammell	USA	23.11.78	2	GP	New York	2 Jun 07
12.95	0.2	Pascal	Martinot-Lagarde	FRA	22.9.91	1	Herc	Monaco	18 Jul 14
12.97	1.0	Ladji	Doucouré	FRA	28.3.83	1	NC	Angers	15 Jul 05

270   110m HURDLES A-T

Mark	Wind	Name		Nat	Born	Pos	Meet	Venue	Date
12.97	1.0	Omar	McLeod	JAM	25.4.94	1	NC	Kingston	27 Jun 15
12.98	0.6	Mark	Crear	USA	2.10.68	1		Zagreb	5 Jul 99
12.98	1.5	Jason	Richardson	USA	4.4.86	1s3	NC/OT	Eugene	30 Jun 12
12.98	0.2	Sergey	Shubenkov	RUS	4.10.90	1	WCh	Beijing	28 Aug 15
12.99	1.2	Ronnie (20)	Ash	USA	2.7.88	1s1	NC	Sacramento	29 Jun 14
13.00	0.5	Anthony	Jarrett	GBR	13.8.68	2	WCh	Stuttgart	20 Aug 93
13.00	0.6	Anier	García	CUB	9.3.76	1	OG	Sydney	25 Sep 00
13.01	0.3	Larry	Wade ¶	USA	22.11.74	1rA	Athl	Lausanne	2 Jul 99
13.02	1.5	Ryan	Wilson	USA	19.12.80	3	GP	New York	2 Jun 07
13.02	1.7	David	Payne	USA	24.7.82	3	WCh	Osaka	31 Aug 07
13.03	-0.2	Greg	Foster	USA	4.8.58	2	WK	Zürich	19 Aug 81
13.03	1.0	Reggie	Torian	USA	22.4.75	1	NC	New Orleans	21 Jun 98
13.03	1.0	Devon	Allen	USA	12.12.94	1	NC/OT	Eugene	9 Jul 16
13.05	1.4	Tony	Dees ¶	USA	6.8.63	1		Vigo	23 Jul 91
13.05	-0.8	Florian (30)	Schwarthoff	GER	7.5.68	1	NC	Bremen	2 Jul 95
13.08	1.2	Mark	McKoy	CAN	10.12.61	1	BNP	Villeneuve-d'Ascq	2 Jul 93
13.08	0.0	Stanislav	Olijar	LAT	22.3.79	2	Athl	Lausanne	1 Jul 03
13.08	1.2	Jeff	Porter	USA	27.11.85	3	NC/OT	Eugene	30 Jun 12
13.09	2.0	Antwon	Hicks	USA	12.3.83	2s2	NC/OT	Eugene	6 Jul 08
13.11	0.5	Aleec	Harris	USA	31.10.90	4	DL	Saint-Denis	4 Jul 15
13.12	1.5	Falk	Balzer ¶	GER	14.12.73	2	EC	Budapest	22 Aug 98
13.12	1.0	Duane	Ross ¶	USA	5.12.72	3	WCh	Sevilla	25 Aug 99
13.12	1.9	Anwar	Moore	USA	5.3.79	1	ModR	Modesto	5 May 07
13.12	0.0	Dimitri	Bascou	FRA	20.7.87	2	Herc	Monaco	15 Jul 16
13.13	1.6	Igor (40)	Kovác	SVK	12.5.69	1	DNG	Stockholm	7 Jul 97
13.13	2.0	Dexter	Faulk	USA	14.4.84	2	GS	Ostrava	17 Jun 09
13.14	0.1	Ryan	Brathwaite	BAR	6.6.88	1	WCh	Berlin	20 Aug 09
13.14	0.0	Andrew	Riley	JAM	6.9.88	4	DL	Saint-Denis	6 Jul 13
13.15	0.3	Robin	Korving	NED	29.7.74	5rA	Athl	Lausanne	2 Jul 99
13.15	0.1	Dwight	Thomas	JAM	23.9.80	2	Bisl	Oslo	9 Jun 11
13.15	-0.3	Garfield	Darien	FRA	22.12.87	1s3	EC	Helsinki	1 Jul 12
13.16	0.4	William	Sharman	GBR	12.9.84	1s1	EC	Zürich	14 Aug 14
13.17	-0.4	Sam	Turner	USA	17.6.57	2	Pepsi	Los Angeles (Ww)	15 May 83
13.17	0.0	Tonie	Campbell	USA	14.6.60	3	WK	Zürich	17 Aug 88
13.17	0.5	Courtney	Hawkins	USA	11.7.67	1		Ingolstadt	26 Jul 98
13.17	0.4	Mike	Fenner	GER	24.4.71	1		Leverkusen	9 Aug 98
13.17	-0.1	Maurice	Wignall	JAM	17.4.76	1s1	OG	Athína	26 Aug 04
13.17	0.8	Mikel (53)	Thomas	TTO	23.11.87	2	PAm	Toronto	24 Jul 15

100th man 13.26, 200th 13.40, 300th 13.48, 400th 13.54, 500th 13.59

Rolling start but accepted by race officials

| 13.10A | 2.0 | Falk | Balzer ¶ | GER | 14.12.73 | 1 | WCp | Johannesburg | 13 Sep 98 |

Doubtful timing: Scheessel 4 Jun 95 +1.3 1. Mike Fenner GER 24.4.71 13.06, 2. Eric Kaiser ¶ GER 7.3.71 13.08

Wind-assisted marks   Performances to 12.94, performers to 13.17

12.87	2.6	Roger	Kingdom	USA	26.8.62	1	WCp	Barcelona	10 Sep 89
12.87	2.4	Liu	Xiang	CHN	13.7.83	1	Pre	Eugene	2 Jun 12
12.89	3.2	David	Oliver	USA	24.4.82	1s1	NC/OT	Eugene	6 Jul 08
12.91	3.5	Renaldo	Nehemiah	USA	24.3.59	1	NCAA	Champaign	1 Jun 79
12.94A	2.8		Jackson			1rA		Sestriere	31 Jul 94
12.98	3.1	Ronnie	Ash	USA	2.7.88	1	NACAC	Miramar	9 Jul 10
13.00	2.6	Anwar	Moore	USA	5.3.79	1	DrakeR	Des Moines	28 Apr 07
13.05	3.6	Ryan	Brathwaite	BAR	6.6.88	1		Austin	2 May 09
13.05	2.1	Dimitri	Bascou	FRA	20.7.87	1	NC	Angers	26 Jun 16
13.06	2.1	Mark	McKoy	CAN	10.12.61	1	Gugl	Linz	13 Aug 92
13.12	2.4	Dexter	Faulk	USA	14.4.84	1	Pre	Eugene	2 Jun 12
13.14	2.9	Igor	Kazanov	LAT	24.9.63	1r1	Znam	Leningrad	8 Jun 86
13.14	4.7	Lawrence	Clarke	GBR	12.3.90	1h1		Madrid	7 Jul 12
13.14	3.8	Wayne	Davis	TTO	22.8.91	1	NCAA	Eugene	8 Jun 13
13.15	2.1	Courtney	Hawkins	USA	11.7.67	1		Salamanca	10 Jul 98
13.15	2.1	Wilhem	Bélocian	FRA	22.6.95	2	NC	Angers	26 Jun 16

Hand timing

12.7		Sergey	Shubenkov	RUS	4.10.90	1		Barnaul	2 Jul 16
12.8	1.0	Renaldo	Nehemiah	USA	24.3.59	1		Kingston	11 May 79
12.9	0.0	Yordan	O'Farrill	CUB	9.2.93	1	Barr	La Habana	23 May 14

Wind-assisted

12.8	2.4	Colin	Jackson	GBR	18.2.67	1		Sydney	10 Jan 90
12.9	4.1	Mark	Crear	USA	2.10.68	1rA	S&W	Modesto	8 May 93
12.9	3.1	William	Sharman	GBR	12.9.84	1r2		Madrid	2 Jul 10

400 METRES HURDLES

Mark	Wind	Name		Nat	Born	Pos	Meet	Venue	Date
46.78 WR		Kevin	Young	USA	16.9.66	1	OG	Barcelona	6 Aug 92
47.02 WR		Edwin	Moses	USA	31.8.55	1		Koblenz	31 Aug 83
47.03		Bryan	Bronson ¶	USA	9.9.72	1	NC	New Orleans	21 Jun 98
47.10		Samuel	Matete	ZAM	27.7.68	1rA	WK	Zürich	7 Aug 91
47.13 WR			Moses			1		Milano	3 Jul 80
47.14			Moses			1	Athl	Lausanne	14 Jul 81
47.17			Moses			1	ISTAF	Berlin	8 Aug 80
47.18			Young			1	WCh	Stuttgart	19 Aug 93
47.19		Andre	Phillips	USA	5.9.59	1	OG	Seoul	25 Sep 88
47.23		Amadou	Dia Bâ	SEN	22.9.58	2	OG	Seoul	25 Sep 88
47.24		Kerron	Clement	USA	31.10.85	1	NC	Carson	26 Jun 05
47.25		Félix	Sánchez	DOM	30.8.77	1	WCh	Saint-Denis	29 Aug 03
47.25		Angelo	Taylor	USA	29.12.78	1	OG	Beijing	18 Aug 08
47.27			Moses			1	ISTAF	Berlin	21 Aug 81
47.30		Bershawn	Jackson (10)	USA	8.5.83	1	WCh	Helsinki	9 Aug 05
47.32			Moses			1		Koblenz	29 Aug 84
47.32			Jackson			1	NC	Des Moines	26 Jun 10
47.35			Sánchez			1rA	WK	Zürich	16 Aug 02
47.37			Moses			1	WCp	Roma	4 Sep 81
47.37			Moses			1	WK	Zürich	24 Aug 83
47.37			Moses			1	NC/OT	Indianapolis	17 Jul 88
47.37			Young			1	Athl	Lausanne	7 Jul 93
47.37		Stéphane	Diagana	FRA	23.7.69	1	Athl	Lausanne	5 Jul 95
47.38			Moses			1	Athl	Lausanne	2 Sep 86
47.38		Danny	Harris ¶	USA	7.9.65	1	Athl	Lausanne	10 Jul 91
47.38			Sánchez			1rA	WK	Zürich	17 Aug 01
47.39			Clement			1	NC	Indianapolis	24 Jun 06
47.40			Young			1	WK	Zürich	19 Aug 92
47.42			Young			1	ASV	Köln	16 Aug 92
47.43			Moses			1	ASV	Köln	28 Aug 83
47.43		James (31/13)	Carter	USA	7.5.78	2	WCh	Helsinki	9 Aug 05
47.48		Harald	Schmid	FRG	29.9.57	1	EC	Athína	8 Sep 82
47.53		Hadi Soua'an	Al-Somaily	KSA	21.8.76	2	OG	Sydney	27 Sep 00
47.54		Derrick	Adkins	USA	2.7.70	2	Athl	Lausanne	5 Jul 95
47.54		Fabrizio	Mori	ITA	28.6.69	2	WCh	Edmonton	10 Aug 01
47.60		Winthrop	Graham	JAM	17.11.65	1	WK	Zürich	4 Aug 93
47.63		Johnny	Dutch	USA	20.1.89	2	NC	Des Moines	26 Jun 10
47.66A		L.J. 'Louis' (20)	van Zyl	RSA	20.7.85	1		Pretoria	25 Feb 11
47.67		Bennie	Brazell	USA	2.6.82	2	NCAA	Sacramento	11 Jun 05
47.69		Jehue	Gordon	TTO	15.12.91	1	WCh	Moskva	15 Aug 13
47.70		Michael	Tinsley	USA	21.4.84	2	WCh	Moskva	15 Aug 13
47.72		Javier	Culson	PUR	25.7.84	1		Ponce	8 May 10
47.75		David	Patrick	USA	12.6.60	4	NC/OT	Indianapolis	17 Jul 88
47.78		Boniface Mucheru	Tumuti	KEN	2.5.92	2	OG	Rio de Janeiro	18 Aug 16
47.79		Nicholas	Bett	KEN	14.6.92	1	WCh	Beijing	25 Aug 15
47.81		Llewellyn	Herbert	RSA	21.7.77	3	OG	Sydney	27 Sep 00
47.82 WR		John	Akii-Bua	UGA	3.12.49	1	OG	München	2 Sep 72
47.82		Kriss (30)	Akabusi	GBR	28.11.58	3	OG	Barcelona	6 Aug 92
47.82		Periklis	Iakovákis	GRE	24.3.79	2	GP	Osaka	6 May 06
47.84		Bayano	Kamani	PAN	17.4.80	2s1	WCh	Helsinki	7 Aug 05
47.84		David	Greene	GBR	11.4.86	2	DL	Saint-Denis	6 Jul 12
47.89		Dai	Tamesue	JPN	3.5.78	3	WCh	Edmonton	10 Aug 01
47.91		Calvin	Davis	USA	2.4.72	1s2	OG	Atlanta	31 Jul 96
47.92		Aleksandr	Vasilyev	BLR	26.7.61	2	ECp	Moskva	17 Aug 85
47.92		Yasmani	Copello	CUB/TUR	15.4.87	3	OG	Rio de Janeiro	18 Aug 16
47.93		Kenji	Narisako	JPN	25.7.84	3	GP	Osaka	6 May 06
47.93		Jeshua	Anderson	USA	22.6.89	1	NC	Eugene	26 Jun 11
47.93		Omar (40)	Cisneros	CUB	19.11.89	1s3	WCh	Moskva	13 Aug 13
47.94		Eric	Thomas	USA	1.12.73	1	GGala	Roma	30 Jun 00
47.97		Maurice	Mitchell	USA	14.5.71	2rA	WK	Zürich	14 Aug 96
47.97		Joey	Woody	USA	22.5.73	3	NC	New Orleans	21 Jun 98
47.97		Thomas	Barr	IRL	24.7.92	4	OG	Rio de Janeiro	18 Aug 16
47.98		Sven	Nylander	SWE	1.1.62	4	OG	Atlanta	1 Aug 96
48.00		Danny	McFarlane	JAM	14.2.72	1s2	OG	Athína	24 Aug 04

400 METRES HURDLES – HIGH JUMP A-T

Mark	Wind	Name	Name	Nat	Born	Pos	Meet	Venue	Date
48.02A		Ockert	Cilliers	RSA	21.4.81	1		Pretoria	20 Feb 04
48.04		Eronilde	de Araújo	BRA	31.12.70	2	Nik	Nice	12 Jul 95
48.05		Ken	Harnden	ZIM	31.3.73	1	GP	Paris (C)	29 Jul 98
48.05		Kemel	Thompson	JAM	25.9.74	1	GP	London (CP)	8 Aug 03
48.05		Isa	Phillips	JAM	22.4.84	1	NC	Kingston	27 Jun 09
48.05		Emir	Bekric	SRB	14.3.91	3	WCh	Moskva	15 Aug 13
48.05		Denis	Kudryavtsev	RUS	13.4.92	2	WCh	Beijing	25 Aug 15
(53)			100th man 48.46, 200th man 48.95, 300th man 49.19, 400th 49.39, 500th 49.56						
Best at low altitude:		47.66	van Zyl	1	GS		Ostrava		31 May 11
Drugs disqualification		47.15	Bronson ¶	1	GWG		Uniondale, NY		19 Jul 98

HIGH JUMP

Mark		Name	Name	Nat	Born	Pos	Meet	Venue	Date
2.45 WR		Javier	Sotomayor ¶	CUB	13.10.67	1		Salamanca	27 Jul 93
2.44 WR			Sotomayor			1	CAC	San Juan	29 Jul 89
2.43 WR			Sotomayor			1		Salamanca	8 Sep 88
2.43i			Sotomayor			1	WI	Budapest	4 Mar 89
2.43		Mutaz Essa	Barshim	QAT	24.6.91	1	VD	Bruxelles	5 Sep 14
2.42 WR		Patrik	Sjöberg	SWE	5.1.65	1	DNG	Stockholm	30 Jun 87
2.42i WR		Carlo	Thränhardt	FRG	5.7.57	1		Berlin	26 Feb 88
2.42			Sotomayor			1		Sevilla	5 Jun 94
2.42i		Ivan	Ukhov	RUS	29.3.86	1		Praha	25 Feb 14
2.42		Bohdan	Bondarenko	UKR	30.8.89	1	adidas	New York	14 Jun 14
2.42			Barshim			2	adidas	New York	14 Jun 14
2.41 WR		Igor	Paklin	KGZ	15.6.63	1	WUG	Kobe	4 Sep 85
2.41i			Sjöberg			1		Pireás	1 Feb 87
2.41i			Sotomayor			1	WI	Toronto	14 Mar 93
2.41			Sotomayor			1	NC	La Habana	25 Jun 94
2.41			Sotomayor			1	TSB	London (CP)	15 Jul 94
2.41			Bondarenko			1	Athl	Lausanne	4 Jul 13
2.41			Bondarenko			1	WCh	Moskva	15 Aug 13
2.41i			Ukhov			1		Chelyabinsk	16 Jan 14
2.41			Ukhov			1	DL	Doha	9 May 14
2.41			Barshim			1	GGala	Roma	5 Jun 14
2.41			Barshim			1		Eberstadt	22 Aug 14
2.41i			Barshim			1		Athlone	18 Feb 15
2.41		(24/7)	Barshim			1	Pre	Eugene	30 May 15
2.40 WR		Rudolf	Povarnitsyn	UKR	13.6.62	1		Donetsk	11 Aug 85
2.40		Sorin	Matei	ROU	6.7.63	1	PTS	Bratislava	20 Jun 90
2.40i		Hollis	Conway (10)	USA	8.1.67	1	WI	Sevilla	10 Mar 91
2.40		Charles	Austin	USA	19.12.67	1	WK	Zürich	7 Aug 91
2.40		Vyacheslav	Voronin	RUS	5.4.74	1	BrGP	London (CP)	5 Aug 00
2.40i		Stefan	Holm	SWE	25.5.76	1	El	Madrid	6 Mar 05
2.40i		Aleksey	Dmitrik	RUS	12.4.84	1		Arnstadt	8 Feb 14
2.40		Derek	Drouin	CAN	6.3.90	1	DrakeR	Des Moines	25 Apr 14
2.40		Andriy	Protsenko	UKR	20.5.88	2	Athl	Lausanne	3 Jul 14
2.40	25 more performances: Sotomayor 13, Bondarenko 4, Barshom 3, Sjöberg, Ukhov 2, Thränhardt1 for (58/16)								
2.39 WR			Zhu Jianhua	CHN	29.5.63	1		Eberstadt	10 Jun 84
2.39i		Dietmar	Mögenburg	FRG	15.8.61	1		Köln	24 Feb 85
2.39i		Ralf	Sonn	GER	17.1.67	1		Berlin	1 Mar 91
2.39		Gianmarco	Tamberi	ITA	1.6.92	1	Herc	Monaco	15 Jul 16
		(20)							
2.38i		Gennadiy	Avdeyenko	UKR	4.11.63	2	WI	Indianapolis	7 Mar 87
2.38		Sergey	Malchenko	RUS	2.11.63	1		Banská Bystrica	4 Sep 88
2.38		Dragutin	Topic ¶	YUG	12.3.71	1		Beograd	1 Aug 93
2.38i		Steve	Smith	GBR	29.3.73	2		Wuppertal	4 Feb 94
2.38i		Wolf-Hendrik	Beyer	GER	14.2.72	1		Weinheim	18 Mar 94
2.38		Troy	Kemp	BAH	18.6.66	1	Nik	Nice	12 Jul 95
2.38		Artur	Partyka	POL	25.7.69	1		Eberstadt	18 Aug 96
2.38i		Matt	Hemingway	USA	24.10.72	1	NC	Atlanta	4 Mar 00
2.38i		Yaroslav	Rybakov	RUS	22.11.80	1		Stockholm	15 Feb 05
2.38		Jacques	Freitag	RSA	11.6.82	1		Oudtshoorn	5 Mar 05
		(30)							
2.38		Andriy	Sokolovskyy	UKR	16.7.78	1	GGala	Roma	8 Jul 05
2.38i		Linus	Thörnblad	SWE	6.3.85	2	NC	Göteborg	25 Feb 07
2.38		Andrey	Silnov	RUS	9.9.84	1	LGP	London (CP)	25 Jul 08
2.38			Zhang Guowei	CHN	4.6.91	2	Pre	Eugene	30 May 15
2.37		Valeriy	Sereda	RUS	30.6.59	1		Rieti	2 Sep 84
2.37		Tom	McCants	USA	27.11.62	1	Owens	Columbus	8 May 88
2.37		Jerome	Carter	USA	25.3.63	2	Owens	Columbus	8 May 88
2.37		Sergey	Dymchenko	UKR	23.8.67	1		Kyiv	16 Sep 90

HIGH JUMP – POLE VAULT A-T

MEN All-time

Mark	Wind	Name		Nat	Born	Pos	Meet	Venue	Date
2.37i		Dalton	Grant	GBR	8.4.66	1	EI	Paris	13 Mar 94
2.37i		Jaroslav	Bába	CZE	2.9.84	2		Arnstadt	5 Feb 05
		(40)							
2.37		Jesse	Williams	USA	27.12.83	1	NC	Eugene	26 Jun 11
2.37		Robbie	Grabarz	GBR	3.10.87	3	Athl	Lausanne	23 Aug 12
2.37		Eric	Kynard	USA	3.2.91	2	Athl	Lausanne	4 Jul 13
2.37		Donald	Thomas	BAH	1.7.84	1	Gyulai	Székesfehérvár	18 Jul 16
2.36 WR		Gerd	Wessig	GDR	16.7.59	1	OG	Moskva	1 Aug 80
2.36		Sergey	Zasimovich	KZK	6.9.62	1		Tashkent	5 May 84
2.36		Eddy	Annys	BEL	15.12.58	1		Gent	26 May 85
2.36i		Jim	Howard	USA	11.9.59	1		Albuquerque	25 Jan 86
2.36i		Jan	Zvara	CZE	12.2.63	1	vGDR	Jablonec	14 Feb 87
2.36i		Gerd	Nagel	FRG	22.10.57	1		Sulingen	17 Mar 89
		(50)							

Mark	Name		Nat	Date	Mark	Name		Nat	Date
2.36	Nick	Saunders	BER	1 Feb 90	2.36	Martin	Buss	GER	8 Aug 01
2.36	Doug	Nordquist	USA	15 Jun 90	2.36	Aleksander	Walerianczyk	POL	20 Jul 03
2.36	Georgi	Dakov	BUL	10 Aug 90	2.36	Michal	Bieniek	POL	28 May 05
2.36	Lábros	Papakóstas	GRE	21 Jun 92	2.36i	Andrey	Tereshin	RUS	17 Feb 06
2.36i	Steinar	Hoen	NOR	12 Feb 94	2.36A	Dusty	Jonas	USA	18 May 08
2.36	Tim	Forsyth	AUS	2 Mar 97	2.36	Aleksandr	Shustov	RUS	23 Jul 11
2.36	Sergey	Klyugin	RUS	12 Aug 98	2.36i	Chris	Baker	GBR	13 Feb 16
2.36	Konstantin	Matusevich	ISR	5 Feb 00	2.36	Majed El Dein	Ghazal	SYR	18 May 16
	(66)								

100th man 2.34, 200th 2.31, 300th 2.30, 400th 2.28, 500th 2.27

Best outdoor marks for athletes with indoor bests

Mark	Name	Pos	Meet	Venue	Date	Mark	Name	Pos	Meet	Venue	Date
2.41	Ukhov	1	DL	Doha	9 May 14	2.36	Mögenburg	3		Eberstadt	10 Jun 87
2.39	Conway	1	USOF	Norman	30 Jul 89	2.36	Howard	1		Rehlingen	8 Jun 87
2.38	Avdeyenko	2=	WCh	Roma	6 Sep 87	2.36	Zvara	1		Praha	23 Aug 87
2.37	Thränhardt	2		Rieti	2 Sep 84	2.36	Grant	4	WCh	Tokyo	1 Sep 91
2.37	Smith	1	WJ	Seoul	20 Sep 92	2.36	Hoen	1		Oslo	1 Jul 97
2.37	Holm	1		Athína	13 Jul 08	2.36	Bába	2=	GGala	Roma	8 Jul 05
						2.36	Dmitrik	1	NC	Chelyabinsk	23 Jul 11

Ancillary jumps – en route to final marks

Mark	Name	Date		Mark	Name	Date
2.40	Sotomayor	8 Sep 88	2.40	Sotomayor	5 Jun 94	2.40	Barshim	14 Jun 14
2.40	Sotomayor	29 Jul 89	2.40	Bondarenko	14 Jun 14	2.40	Barshim	5 Sep 14

POLE VAULT

Mark	Wind	Name		Nat	Born	Pos	Meet	Venue	Date
6.16i WR		Renaud	Lavillenie	FRA	18.9.86	1		Donetsk	15 Feb 14
6.15i WR		Sergey	Bubka	UKR	4.12.63	1		Donetsk	21 Feb 93
6.14i WIR			Bubka			1		Liévin	13 Feb 93
6.14A WIR			Bubka			1		Sestriere	31 Jul 94
6.13i WIR			Bubka			1		Berlin	21 Feb 92
6.13 WR			Bubka			1	TOTO	Tokyo	19 Sep 92
6.12i WIR			Bubka			1	Mast	Grenoble	23 Mar 91
6.12 WR			Bubka			1		Padova	30 Aug 92
6.11i WIR			Bubka			1		Donetsk	19 Mar 91
6.11 WR			Bubka			1		Dijon	13 Jun 92
6.10i WIR			Bubka			1		San Sebastián	15 Mar 91
6.10 WR			Bubka			1	MAI	Malmö	5 Aug 91
6.09 WR			Bubka			1		Formia	8 Jul 91
6.08i WIR			Bubka			1	NC	Volgograd	9 Feb 91
6.08 WR			Bubka			1	Znam	Moskva	9 Jun 91
6.08i			Lavillenie			1		Bydgoszcz	31 Jan 14
6.07 WR			Bubka			1	Super	Shizuoka	6 May 91
6.06 WR			Bubka			1	Nik	Nice	10 Jul 88
6.06i		Steve	Hooker	AUS	16.7.82	1		Boston (R)	7 Feb 09
6.05 WR			Bubka			1	PTS	Bratislava	9 Jun 88
6.05i			Bubka			1		Donetsk	17 Mar 90
6.05i			Bubka			1		Berlin	5 Mar 93
6.05			Bubka			1	GPF	London (CP)	10 Sep 93
6.05i			Bubka			1	Mast	Grenoble	6 Feb 94
6.05			Bubka			1	ISTAF	Berlin	30 Aug 94
6.05			Bubka			1	GPF	Fukuoka	13 Sep 97
6.05		Maksim	Tarasov	RUS	2.12.70	1	GP II	Athína	16 Jun 99
6.05		Dmitriy	Markov	BLR/AUS	14.3.75	1	WCh	Edmonton	9 Aug 01
6.05			Lavillenie			1	Pre	Eugene	30 May 15
6.04		Brad	Walker	USA	21.6.81	1	Pre	Eugene	8 Jun 08
6.04i			Lavillenie			1		Rouen	25 Jan 14
6.04i			Lavillenie			1	EI	Praha (O2)	7 Mar 15
		(32/6)							
6.03		Okkert	Brits	RSA	22.8.73	1	ASV	Köln	18 Aug 95
6.03		Jeff	Hartwig	USA	25.9.67	1		Jonesboro	14 Jun 00

274 POLE VAULT – LONG JUMP A-T

Mark	Wind	Name		Nat	Born	Pos	Meet	Venue	Date
6.03		Thiago	Braz da Silva	BRA	16.12.93	1	OG	Rio de Janeiro	15 Aug 16
6.02i		Rodion	Gataullin	RUS	23.11.65	1	NC	Gomel	4 Feb 89
		(10)							
6.01		Igor	Trandenkov	RUS	17.8.66	1	NC	Sankt Peterburg	4 Jul 96
		Hit bar hard, but kept it on with his hand illegally. Next best 5.95 1						Dijon	26 May 96
6.01		Tim	Mack	USA	15.9.72	1	WAF	Monaco	18 Sep 04
6.01		Yevgeniy	Lukyanenko	RUS	23.1.85	1	EAF	Bydgoszcz	1 Jul 08
6.01	sq	Björn	Otto	GER	16.10.77	1		Aachen	5 Sep 12
6.00		Tim	Lobinger	GER	3.9.72	1	ASV	Köln	24 Aug 97
6.00i		Jean	Galfione	FRA	9.6.71	1	WI	Maebashi	6 Mar 99
6.00i		Danny	Ecker	GER	21.7.77	1		Dortmund	11 Feb 01
6.00		Toby	Stevenson	USA	19.11.76	1eA	CalR	Modesto	8 May 04
6.00		Paul	Burgess	AUS	14.8.79	1		Perth	25 Feb 05
6.00Ai		Shawnacy	Barber	CAN	27.5.94	1		Reno	15 Jan 16
		(20)							
5.98		Lawrence	Johnson	USA	7.5.74	1		Knoxville	25 May 96
5.97		Scott	Huffman	USA	30.11.64	1	NC	Knoxville	18 Jun 94
5.96		Joe	Dial	USA	26.10.62	1		Norman	18 Jun 87
5.95		Andrei	Tivontchik	GER	13.7.70	1	ASV	Köln	16 Aug 96
5.95		Michael	Stolle	GER	17.12.74	1	Herc	Monaco	18 Aug 00
5.95		Romain	Mesnil	FRA	13.6.77	1		Castres	6 Aug 03
5.94i		Philippe	Collet	FRA	13.12.63	1	Mast	Grenoble	10 Mar 90
5.94		Raphael	Holzdeppe	GER	28.9.89	1	NC	Nürnberg	26 Jul 15
5.93i	WIR	Billy	Olson	USA	19.7.58	1		East Rutherford	8 Feb 86
5.93i		Tye	Harvey	USA	25.9.74	2	NC	Atlanta	3 Mar 01
		(30)							
5.93		Alex	Averbukh	ISR	1.10.74	1	GP	Madrid (C)	19 Jul 03
5.92		István	Bagyula	HUN	2.1.69	1	Gugl	Linz	5 Jul 91
5.92		Igor	Potapovich	KAZ	6.9.67	2		Dijon	13 Jun 92
5.92		Dean	Starkey	USA	27.3.67	1	Banes	São Paulo	21 May 94
5.92		Sam	Kendricks	USA	7.9.92	1		Beijing	18 May 16
5.91	WR	Thierry	Vigneron	FRA	9.3.60	2	GGala	Roma	31 Aug 84
5.91i		Viktor	Ryzhenkov	UZB	25.8.66	2		San Sebastián	15 Mar 91
5.91A		Riaan	Botha	RSA	8.11.70	1		Pretoria	2 Apr 97
5.91		Pawel	Wojciechowski	POL	6.6.89	1		Szczecin	15 Aug 11
5.91		Malte	Mohr	GER	24.7.86	1		Ingolstadt	22 Jun 12
		(40)							
5.91		Konstadinos	Filippídis ¶	GRE	26.11.86	1	DL	Saint-Denis	4 Jul 15
5.90		Pierre	Quinon	FRA	20.2.62	2	Nik	Nice	16 Jul 85
5.90i		Ferenc	Salbert	HUN/FRA	5.8.60	1	Mast	Grenoble	14 Mar 87
5.90		Miroslaw	Chmara	POL	9.5.64	1	BNP	Villeneuve d'Ascq	27 Jun 88
5.90i		Grigoriy	Yegorov	KAZ	12.1.67	1		Yokohama	11 Mar 90
5.90		Denis	Petushinskiy ¶	RUS	28.6.67	1	Znam	Moskva	13 Jun 93
5.90i		Pyotr	Bochkaryov	RUS	3.11.67	1	EI	Paris (B)	12 Mar 94
5.90		Jacob	Davis	USA	29.4.78	1	TexR	Austin	4 Apr 98
5.90		Viktor	Chistyakov	RUS/AUS	9.2.75	1		Salamanca	15 Jul 99
5.90		Pavel	Gerasimov	RUS	29.5.79	1		Rüdlingen	12 Aug 00
		(50)							
5.90		Nick	Hysong	USA	9.12.71	1	OG	Sydney	29 Sep 00
5.90		Giuseppe	Gibilisco	ITA	5.1.79	1	WCh	Saint-Denis	28 Aug 03
5.90i		Igor	Pavlov	RUS	18.7.79	1	EI	Madrid	5 Mar 05
5.90		Lázaro	Borges	CUB	19.6.86	2	WCh	Daegu	29 Aug 11
5.90i		Dmitriy	Starodubtsev	RUS	3.1.86	1		Chelyabinsk	18 Dec 11
5.90i		Piotr	Lisek	POL	16.8.92	1		Bad Oeynhausen	28 Feb 15
		(56)		100th man 5.81, 200th 5.72, 300th 5.66, 400th 5.61, 500th 5.59					

Best outdoor marks for athletes with lifetime bests indoors

6.00		Gataullin	1	Tokyo	16 Sep 89	5.93	Ecker	1	Ingolstadt	26 Jul 98
6.00		Hooker	1	Perth	27 Jan 08	5.93	Barber	2	DL London (OS)	25 Jul 15
5.98		Galfione	1	Amiens	23 Jul 99	5.90	Yegorov	2	WCh Stuttgart	19 Aug 93

Exhibition or Market Square competitions   Ancillary jump: 6.05i Bubka   13 Feb 93

6.00		Jean	Galfione	FRA	9.6.71	1		Besançon	23 May 97
5.95		Viktor	Chistiakov	RUS/AUS	9.2.75	1		Chiari	8 Sep 99
5.90		Pyotr	Bochkaryov	RUS	3.11.67	1		Karlskrona	28 Jun 96

LONG JUMP

Mark	Wind	Name		Nat	Born	Pos	Meet	Venue	Date
8.95	WR 0.3	Mike	Powell	USA	10.11.63	1	WCh	Tokyo	30 Aug 91
8.90A	WR 2.0	Bob	Beamon	USA	29.8.46	1	OG	Ciudad de México	18 Oct 68
8.87	-0.2	Carl	Lewis	USA	1.7.61	*	WCh	Tokyo	30 Aug 91
8.86A	1.9	Robert	Emmiyan	ARM	16.2.65	1		Tsakhkadzor	22 May 87
8.79	1.9		Lewis			1	TAC	Indianapolis	19 Jun 83
8.79i	-		Lewis			1		New York	27 Jan 84

LONG JUMP A-T

Mark	Wind	Name		Nat	Born	Pos	Meet	Venue	Date
8.76	1.0		Lewis			1	USOF	Indianapolis	24 Jul 82
8.76	0.8		Lewis			1	NC/OT	Indianapolis	18 Jul 88
8.75	1.7		Lewis			1	PAm	Indianapolis	16 Aug 87
8.74	1.4	Larry	Myricks ¶	USA	10.3.56	2	NC/OT	Indianapolis	18 Jul 88
8.74A	2.0	Erick	Walder	USA	5.11.71	1		El Paso	2 Apr 94
8.74	1.2	Dwight	Phillips	USA	1.10.77	1	Pre	Eugene	7 Jun 09
8.73	1.2	Irving	Saladino	PAN	23.1.83	1	FBK	Hengelo	24 May 08
8.72	-0.2		Lewis			1	OG	Seoul	26 Sep 88
8.71	-0.4		Lewis			1	Pepsi	Los Angeles (Ww)	13 May 84
8.71	0.1		Lewis			1	OT	Los Angeles	19 Jun 84
8.71	1.9	Iván	Pedroso	CUB	17.12.72	1		Salamanca	18 Jul 95
8.71i		Sebastian	Bayer (10)	GER	11.6.86	1	EI	Torino	8 Mar 09
8.70	0.8		Myricks			1	NC	Houston	17 Jun 89
8.70	0.7		Powell			1		Salamanca	27 Jul 93
8.70	1.6		Pedroso			1	WCh	Göteborg	12 Aug 95
8.68	1.0		Lewis			Q	OG	Barcelona	5 Aug 92
8.68	1.6		Pedroso			1		Lisboa	17 Jun 95
8.67	0.4		Lewis			1	WCh	Roma	5 Sep 87
8.67	-0.7		Lewis			1	OG	Barcelona	6 Aug 92
8.66	0.8		Lewis			*	MSR	Walnut	26 Apr 87
8.66	1.0		Myricks			1		Tokyo	23 Sep 87
8.66	0.9		Powell			1	BNP	Villeneuve d'Ascq	29 Jun 90
8.66A	1.4		Lewis			*		Sestriere	31 Jul 94
8.66	0.3		Pedroso			1		Linz	22 Aug 95
8.66	1.6	Loúis	Tsátoumas (31/11)	GRE	12.2.82	1		Kalamáta	2 Jun 07
8.63	0.5	Kareem	Streete-Thompson	CAY/USA	30.3.73	1	GP II	Linz	4 Jul 94
8.62	0.7	James	Beckford	JAM	9.1.75	1		Orlando	5 Apr 97
8.59i		Miguel	Pate	USA	13.6.79	1	NC	New York	1 Mar 02
8.58	1.8	Jarrion	Lawson	USA	6.5.94	2	NC/OT	Eugene	3 Jul 16
8.56i	-	Yago	Lamela	ESP	24.7.77	2	WI	Maebashi	7 Mar 99
8.56	0.2	Aleksandr	Menkov	RUS	7.12.90	1	WCh	Moskva	16 Aug 13
8.54	0.9	Lutz	Dombrowski	GDR	25.6.59	1	OG	Moskva	28 Jul 80
8.54	1.7	Mitchell	Watt	AUS	25.3.88	1	DNG	Stockholm	29 Jul 11
8.53	1.2	Jaime	Jefferson (20)	CUB	17.1.62	1	Barr	La Habana	12 May 90
8.52	0.7	Savanté	Stringfellow	USA	6.11.78	1	NC	Stanford	21 Jun 02
8.52	1.8	Jeff	Henderson	USA	19.2.89	*	PAm	Toronto	22 Jul 15
8.51	1.7	Roland	McGhee	USA	15.10.71	2		São Paulo	14 May 95
8.51	1.7	Greg	Rutherford	GBR	17.11.86	1		Chula Vista	24 Apr 14
8.50	0.2	Llewellyn	Starks	USA	10.2.67	2		Rhede	7 Jul 91
8.50	1.3	Godfrey Khotso	Mokoena	RSA	6.3.85	2	GP	Madrid	4 Jul 09
8.49	2.0	Melvin	Lister	USA	29.8.77	1	SEC	Baton Rouge	13 May 00
8.49	0.6	Jai	Taurima	AUS	26.6.72	2	OG	Sydney	28 Sep 00
8.49	0.7	Christian	Reif	GER	24.10.84	1		Weinheim	31 May 14
8.48	0.8	Joe	Greene (30)	USA	17.2.67	3		São Paulo	14 May 95
8.48	0.6	Mohamed Salim	Al-Khuwalidi	KSA	19.6.81	1		Sotteville-lès-Rouen	2 Jul 06
8.48	0.1	Luvo	Manyonga ¶	RSA	18.11.91	1	VD	Bruxelles	9 Sep 16
8.47	1.9	Kevin	Dilworth	USA	14.2.74	1		Abilene	9 May 96
8.47	0.9	John	Moffitt	USA	12.12.80	2	OG	Athína	26 Aug 04
8.47	-0.2	Andrew	Howe	ITA	12.5.85	2	WCh	Osaka	30 Aug 07
8.47	0.0		Li Jinzhe	CHN	1.9.89	1		Bad Langensalza	28 Jun 14
8.46	1.2	Leonid	Voloshin	RUS	30.3.66	1	NC	Tallinn	5 Jul 88
8.46	1.6	Mike	Conley	USA	5.10.62	2		Springfield	4 May 96
8.46	1.8	Cheikh Tidiane	Touré	SEN/FRA	25.1.70	1		Bad Langensalza	15 Jun 97
8.46	0.3	Ibrahim	Camejo (40)	CUB	28.6.82	1		Bilbao	21 Jun 08
8.46	1.3	Luis	Rivera	MEX	21.6.87	1	WUG	Kazan	12 Jul 13
8.45	2.0	Nenad	Stekic	YUG	7.3.51	1	PO	Montreal	25 Jul 75
8.45	0.8	Marquise	Goodwin	USA	19.11.90	1		Baie Mahault	14 May 16
8.44	1.7	Eric	Metcalf	USA	23.1.68	1	NC	Tampa	17 Jun 88
8.44A	1.8	Michel	Tornéus	SWE	26.5.86	1		Monachil	10 Jul 16
8.43	0.8	Jason	Grimes	USA	10.9.59	*	NC	Indianapolis	16 Jun 85
8.43	1.8	Giovanni	Evangelisti	ITA	11.9.61	1		San Giovanni Valdarno	16 May 87
8.43i	-	Stanislav	Tarasenko	RUS	23.7.66	1		Moskva	26 Jan 94
8.43	0.1	Luis Felipe	Méliz	CUB/ESP	11.8.79	2	OD	Jena	3 Jun 00
8.43	-0.2	Ignisious	Gaisah (50)	GHA/NED	20.6.83	2	GGala	Roma	14 Jul 06

100th man 8.34, 200th 8.23, 300th 8.18, 400th 8.13, 500th 8.10

Best at low altitude: 8.61 1.3 Emmiyan 1 GWG Moskva 6 Jul 86   8.58 1.8 Walder 1 Springfield 4 May 86

276 LONG JUMP – TRIPLE JUMP A-T

Mark	Wind	Name		Nat	Born	Pos	Meet	Venue	Date
Wind-assisted marks performances to 8.70, performers to 8.43									
8.99A	4.4	Mike	Powell	USA	10.11.63	1		Sestriere	21 Jul 92
8.96A	1.2+	Iván	Pedroso	CUB	17.12.72	1		Sestriere	29 Jul 95
8.95A	3.9		Powell			1		Sestriere	31 Jul 94
8.91	2.9	Carl	Lewis	USA	1.7.61	2	WCh	Tokyo	30 Aug 91
8.90	3.7		Powell			1	S&W	Modesto	16 May 92
8.79	3.0		Pedroso			1	Barr	La Habana	21 May 92
8.78	3.1	Fabrice	Lapierre	AUS	17.10.83	1	NC	Perth	18 Apr 10
8.77	3.9		Lewis			1	Pepsi	Los Angeles (Ww)	18 May 85
8.77	3.4		Lewis			1	MSR	Walnut	26 Apr 87
8.73	4.6		Lewis			Q	NC	Sacramento	19 Jun 81
8.73	3.2		Lewis			Q	NC	Indianapolis	17 Jun 83
8.73A	2.6		Powell			1		Sestriere	31 Jul 91
8.73	4.8		Pedroso			1		Madrid	20 Jun 95
8.72	2.2		Lewis			1	NYG	New York	24 May 92
8.72A	3.9		Lewis			2		Sestriere	31 Jul 94
8.70	2.5		Pedroso			1		Padova	16 Jul 95
8.68	4.9	James	Beckford	JAM	9.1.75	1	JUCO	Odessa, Tx	19 May 95
8.68	3.7	Marquis	Dendy	USA	17.11.92	1	NC	Eugene	25 Jun 15
8.66A	4.0	Joe	Greene	USA	17.2.67	2		Sestriere	21 Jul 92
8.64	3.5	Kareem	Streete-Thompson	CAY/USA	30.3.73	2	NC	Knoxville	18 Jun 94
8.63	3.9	Mike	Conley	USA	5.10.62	2	NC	Eugene	20 Jun 86
8.59	2.9	Jeff	Henderson	USA	19.2.89	1	NC/OT	Eugene	3 Jul 16
8.57	5.2	Jason	Grimes	USA	10.9.59	1	vFRG,AFR	Durham	27 Jun 82
8.53	4.9	Kevin	Dilworth	USA	14.2.74	1		Fort-de-France	27 Apr 02
8.51	3.7	Ignisious	Gaisah	GHA	20.6.83	1	AfCh	Bambous	9 Aug 06
8.49	2.6	Ralph	Boston	USA	9.5.39	1	OT	Los Angeles	12 Sep 64
8.49	4.5	Stanislav	Tarasenko	RUS	23.7.66	2		Madrid	20 Jun 95
8.48	2.8	Kirill	Sosunov	RUS	1.11.75	1		Oristano	18 Sep 95
8.48	3.4	Peter	Burge	AUS	3.7.74	1		Gold Coast (RB)	10 Sep 00
8.48	2.1	Brian	Johnson	USA	25.3.80	1	Conseil	Fort-de-France	8 May 08
8.48	2.8	Lamont Marcell	Jacobs	ITA	26.9.94	1	NC-23	Bressanone	10 Jun 16
8.46	3.4	Randy	Williams	USA	23.8.53	1		Eugene	18 May 73
8.46		Vernon	George	USA	6.10.64	1		Houston	21 May 89
8.44		Keith	Talley	USA	28.1.64	Q		Odessa, Tx	16 May 85
Exhibition: 8.46 Yuriy			Naumkin	RUS	4.11.68	1		Iglesias	6 Sep 96
Best outdoors									
8.56 1.3 Lamela 1 Torino 24 Jun 99 8.49 1.6 Bayer 1 NC Ulm 4 Jul 09									
8.46A 0.0 Pate 1 Cd. de México 3 May 03 and 8.45 1.5 2 NC Stanford 21 Jun 02, 8.48w 5.6 1 Fort Worth 21 Apr 01									
Ancillary marks – other marks during series (to 8.67/8.70w)									
8.84	1.7	Lewis		30 Aug 91	8.89Aw 2.4	Pedroso	29 Jul 95	8.75w 2.1 Lewis	16 Aug 87
8.71	0.6	Lewis		19 Jun 83	8.84Aw 3.8	Powell	21 Jul 92	8.75Aw 3.4 Powell	21 Jul 92
8.68	0.3	Lewis		18 Jul 88	8.83w 2.3	Lewis	30 Aug 91	8.73w 2.4 Lewis	18 May 85
8.68	0.0	Lewis		30 Aug 91	8.80Aw 4.0	Powell	21 Jul 92	8.73w Powell	16 May 92
8.67	-0.2	Lewis		5 Sep 87	8.78Aw	Powell	21 Jul 92	8.71Aw Powell	31 Jul 91

TRIPLE JUMP

Mark	Wind	Name		Nat	Born	Pos	Meet	Venue	Date
18.29 WR	1.3	Jonathan	Edwards	GBR	10.5.66	1	WCh	Göteborg	7 Aug 95
18.21	0.2	Christian	Taylor	USA	18.6.90	1	WCh	Beijing	27 Aug 15
18.09	-0.4	Kenny	Harrison	USA	13.2.65	1	OG	Atlanta	27 Jul 96
18.08	0.0	Pedro Pablo	Pichardo	CUB	30.6.93	1	Barr	La Habana	28 May 15
18.06	0.8		Pichardo			1	DL	Doha	15 May 15
18.06	1.1		Taylor			1	Athl	Lausanne	9 Jul 15
18.04	0.3	Teddy	Tamgho	FRA	15.6.89	1	WCh	Moskva	18 Aug 13
18.04	0.8		Taylor			2	DL	Doha	15 May 15
18.01	0.4		Edwards			1	Bisl	Oslo	9 Jul 98
18.00	1.3		Edwards			1	McD	London (CP)	27 Aug 95
17.99	0.5		Edwards			1	EC	Budapest	23 Aug 98
17.99	1.8		Pichardo			2	Athl	Lausanne	9 Jul 15
17.98 WR	1.8		Edwards			1		Salamanca	18 Jul 95
17.98	1.2		Tamgho			1	DL	New York	12 Jun 10
17.97 WR	1.5	Willie	Banks	USA	11.3.56	1	TAC	Indianapolis	16 Jun 85
17.96	0.1		Taylor			1	WCh	Daegu	4 Sep 11
17.96	-0.4		Pichardo			1	GGala	Roma	4 Jun 15
17.94	0.0		Pichardo			1		La Habana	8 May 15
17.93	1.6		Harrison			1	DNG	Stockholm	2 Jul 90
17.92	1.6	Khristo	Markov	BUL	27.1.65	1	WCh	Roma	31 Aug 87
17.92	1.9	James	Beckford	JAM	9.1.75	1	JUCO	Odessa, TX	20 May 95
17.92i WIR	-		Tamgho			1	EI	Paris (Bercy)	6 Mar 11

TRIPLE JUMP A-T

MEN All-time

Mark	Wind	Name		Nat	Born	Pos	Meet	Venue	Date
17.92	0.7		Edwards			1	WCh	Edmonton	6 Aug 01
17.91i	wr -		Tamgho			1	NC	Aubière	20 Feb 11
17.91	1.4		Tamgho			1	Athl	Lausanne	30 Jun 11
17.90	1.0	Vladimir	Inozemtsev	UKR	25.5.64	1	PTS	Bratislava	20 Jun 90
17.90	0.4	Jadel	Gregório (10)	BRA	16.9.80	1	GP	Belém	20 May 07
17.90i			Tamgho			1	WI	Doha	14 Mar 10
17.89A	wr 0.0	João Carlos	de Oliveira	BRA	28.5.54	1	PAm	Ciudad de México	15 Oct 75
17.88	0.9		Edwards			2	OG	Atlanta	27 Jul 96
		(30/11)							
17.87	1.7	Mike	Conley	USA	5.10.62	1	NC	San José	27 Jun 87
17.86	1.3	Charles	Simpkins	USA	19.10.63	1	WUG	Kobe	2 Sep 85
17.85	0.9	Yoelbi	Quesada	CUB	4.8.73	1	WCh	Athína	8 Aug 97
17.83i	wr -	Aliecer	Urrutia	CUB	22.9.74	1		Sindelfingen	1 Mar 97
17.83i	wr -	Christian	Olsson	SWE	25.1.80	1	WI	Budapest	7 Mar 04
17.81	1.0	Marian	Oprea	ROU	6.6.82	1	Athl	Lausanne	5 Jul 05
17.81	0.1	Phillips	Idowu	GBR	30.12.78	1	EC	Barcelona	29 Jul 10
17.78	1.0	Nikolay	Musiyenko	UKR	16.12.59	1	Znam	Leningrad	7 Jun 86
17.78	0.6	Lázaro	Betancourt ¶	CUB	18.3.63	1	Barr	La Habana	15 Jun 86
		(20)							
17.78	0.8	Melvin	Lister	USA	29.8.77	1	NC/OT	Sacramento	17 Jul 04
17.77	1.0	Aleksandr	Kovalenko	RUS	8.5.63	1	NC	Bryansk	18 Jul 87
17.77i	-	Leonid	Voloshin	RUS	30.3.66	1		Grenoble	6 Feb 94
17.76	0.4	Will	Claye	USA	13.6.91	2	OG	Rio de Janeiro	16 Aug 16
17.75	0.3	Oleg	Protsenko	RUS	11.8.63	1	Znam	Moskva	10 Jun 90
17.74	1.4	Nelson	Évora	POR	20.4.84	1	WCh	Osaka	27 Aug 07
17.73i		Walter	Davis	USA	2.7.79	1	WI	Moskva	12 Mar 06
17.73i	-	Fabrizio	Donato	ITA	14.8.76	2	EI	Paris (Bercy)	6 Mar 11
17.72i		Brian	Wellman	BER	8.9.67	1	WI	Barcelona	12 Mar 95
17.72	1.3	Sheryf	El-Sheryf	UKR	2.1.89	1	EU23	Ostrava	17 Jul 11
		(30)	El-Sheryf now Seref Osmanoglou TUR						
17.70i		Daniele	Greco	ITA	1.3.89	1	EI	Göteborg	2 Mar 13
17.69	1.5	Igor	Lapshin	BLR	8.8.63	1		Stayki	31 Jul 88
17.69i		Yoandri	Betanzos	CUB	15.2.82	2	WI	Doha	14 Mar 10
17.68	0.4	Danil	Burkenya	RUS	20.7.78	1	NC	Tula	31 Jul 04
17.68A	1.6	Alexis	Copello	CUB	12.8.85	1		Ávila	17 Jul 11
17.66	1.7	Ralf	Jaros	GER	13.12.65	1	ECp	Frankfurt-am-Main	30 Jun 91
17.65	1.0	Aleksandr	Yakovlev	UKR	8.9.57	1	Znam	Moskva	6 Jun 87
17.65	0.8	Denis	Kapustin	RUS	5.10.70	2	Bisl	Oslo	9 Jul 98
17.64	1.4	Nathan	Douglas	GBR	4.12.82	1	NC	Manchester (SC)	10 Jul 05
17.63	0.9	Kenta	Bell	USA	16.3.77	1c2	MSR	Walnut	21 Apr 02
		(40)							
17.62i	-	Yoel	García	CUB	25.11.73	2		Sindelfingen	1 Mar 97
17.62	-0.2	Arne David	Girat	CUB	26.8.84	3	ALBA	La Habana	25 Apr 09
17.60	0.6	Vladimir	Plekhanov	RUS	11.4.58	2	NC	Leningrad	4 Aug 85
17.59i	-	Pierre	Camara	FRA	10.9.65	1	WI	Toronto	13 Mar 93
17.59	0.3	Vasiliy	Sokov	RUS	7.4.68	1	NC	Moskva	19 Jun 93
17.59	0.8	Charles	Friedek	GER	26.8.71	1		Hamburg	23 Jul 97
17.59	0.9	Leevan	Sands	BAH	16.8.81	3	OG	Beijing	21 Aug 08
17.59	0.0		Li Yanxi	CHN	26.6.84	1	NG	Jinan	26 Oct 09
17.58	1.5	Oleg	Sakirkin	KZK	23.1.66	2	NC	Gorkiy	23 Jul 89
17.58	1.6	Aarik	Wilson	USA	25.10.82	1	LGP	London (CP)	3 Aug 07
17.58	-1.7	Ernesto	Revé	CUB	26.2.92	2		La Habana	7 Feb 14
		(51)	100th man 17.39, 200th 17.19, 300th 17.02, 400th 16.90, 500th 16.81						

Wind-assisted marks – performances to 17.91, performers to 17.59

18.43	2.4	Jonathan	Edwards	GBR	10.5.66	1	ECp	Villeneuve d'Ascq	25 Jun 95
18.20	5.2	Willie	Banks	USA	11.3.56	1	NC/OT	Indianapolis	16 Jul 88
18.17	2.1	Mike	Conley	USA	5.10.62	1	OG	Barcelona	3 Aug 92
18.08	2.5		Edwards			1	BrGP	Sheffield	23 Jul 95
18.03	2.9		Edwards			1	GhG	Gateshead	2 Jul 95
18.01	3.7		Harrison			1	NC	Atlanta	15 Jun 96
17.97	7.5	Yoelbi	Quesada	CUB	4.8.73	1		Madrid	20 Jun 95
17.93	5.2	Charles	Simpkins	USA	19.10.63	2	NC/OT	Indianapolis	16 Jul 88
17.92	3.4	Christian	Olsson	SWE	25.1.80	1	GP	Gateshead	13 Jul 03
17.91	3.2		Simpkins			1	NC	Eugene	21 Jun 86
17.82	2.5	Nelson	Évora	POR	20.4.84	1	NC	Seixal	26 Jul 09
17.81	4.6	Keith	Connor	GBR	16.9.57	1	CG	Brisbane	9 Oct 82
17.76A	2.2	Kenta	Bell	USA	16.3.77	1		El Paso	10 Apr 04
17.75		Gennadiy	Valyukevich	BLR	1.6.58	1		Uzhgorod	27 Apr 86
17.75	7.1	Brian	Wellman	BER	8.9.67	2		Madrid	20 Jun 95
17.73	4.1	Vasiliy	Sokov	RUS	7.4.68	1		Riga	3 Jun 89
17.71	2.4	Marquis	Dendy	USA	17.11.92	1	NCAA	Eugene	12 Jun 15

278 TRIPLE JUMP – SHOT A-T

Mark	Wind	Name		Nat	Born	Pos	Meet	Venue	Date
17.69	3.9	Alexis	Copello	CUB	12.8.85	1	ALBA	La Habana	25 Apr 09
17.63	4.3	Robert	Cannon	USA	9.7.58	3	NC/OT	Indianapolis	16 Jul 88
17.59	2.1	Jerome	Romain	DMA/FRA	12.6.71	3	WCh	Göteborg	7 Aug 95

Best outdoor marks for athletes with indoor bests

Mark	Wind	Name				Nat	Born		Pos	Meet	Venue	Date
17.79	1.4	Olsson	1	OG	Athína		22 Aug 04	17.65	1.4	Betanzos 2 ALBA	La Habana	25 Apr 09
17.75	1.0	Voloshin	2	WCh	Tokyo		26 Aug 91			17.67w 5.4 1	Bilbao	1 Jul 06
17.71		Davis	1	NC	Indianapolis		25 Jun 06	17.62A	0.1	Wellman 1	El Paso	15 Apr 95
17.70	1.7	Urrutia	1	GP II	Sevilla		6 Jun 96	17.60	1.9	Donato 1	Milano	7 Jun 00
17.67w	3.4	Greco	1	NC	Bressanone		8 Jul 12			17.63w 2.8 1 EC	Helsinki	30 Jun 12

Low altitude best: 17.65 0.1 Copello 1 Barr La Habana 30 May 09

Ancillary marks – other marks during series (to 17.90)

18.16 WR	1.3	Edwards	7 Aug 95	17.93	0.2	Pichardo	28 May 15	18.06w	4.9	Banks	16 Jul 88
18.02	0.8	Taylor	9 Jul 15	17.92i		Tamgho	6 Mar 11	17.90w	2.5	Edwards	25 Jun 95
17.99	0.1	Harrison	27 Jul 96	18.39w	3.7	Edwards	25 Jun 95				

SHOT

Mark		Name		Nat	Born	Pos	Meet	Venue	Date
23.12 WR	Randy	Barnes ¶		USA	16.6.66	1		Los Angeles (Ww)	20 May 90
23.10		Barnes				1	Jenner	San José	26 May 90
23.06 WR	Ulf	Timmermann		GDR	1.11.62	1	Veniz	Haniá	22 May 88
22.91 WR	Alessandro	Andrei		ITA	3.1.59	1		Viareggio	12 Aug 87
22.86	Brian	Oldfield		USA	1.6.45	1	ITA	El Paso	10 May 75
22.75	Werner	Günthör		SUI	1.6.61	1		Bern	23 Aug 88
22.67	Kevin	Toth ¶		USA	29.12.67	1	KansR	Lawrence	19 Apr 03
22.66i		Barnes				1	Sunkist	Los Angeles	20 Jan 89
22.64 WR	Udo	Beyer		GDR	9.8.55	1		Berlin	20 Aug 86
22.62 WR		Timmermann				1		Berlin	22 Sep 85
22.61		Timmermann				1		Potsdam	8 Sep 88
22.60		Timmermann				1	vURS	Tallinn	21 Jun 86
22.56		Timmermann				1		Berlin	13 Sep 88
22.56	Joe	Kovacs		USA	28.6.89	1	Herc	Monaco	17 Jul 15
22.55i		Timmermann				1	NC	Senftenberg	11 Feb 89
22.54	Christian	Cantwell		USA	30.9.80	1	GP II	Gresham	5 Jun 04
22.52	John	Brenner (10)		USA	4.1.61	1	MSR	Walnut	26 Apr 87
22.52	Ryan	Crouser		USA	18.12.92	1	OG	Rio de Janeiro	18 Aug 16
22.51		Timmermann				1		Erfurt	1 Jun 86
22.51	Adam	Nelson		USA	7.7.75	1		Gresham	18 May 02
22.47		Timmermann				1		Dresden	17 Aug 86
22.47		Günthör				1	WG	Helsinki	2 Jul 87
22.47		Timmermann				1	OG	Seoul	23 Sep 88
22.45		Oldfield				1	ITA	El Paso	22 May 76
22.45		Cantwell				1	GP	Gateshead	11 Jun 06
22.43		Günthör				1	v3-N	Lüdenscheid	18 Jun 87
22.43	Reese	Hoffa		USA	8.10.77	1	LGP	London (CP)	3 Aug 07
22.42		Barnes				1	WK	Zürich	17 Aug 88
22.41		Cantwell				1	Pre	Eugene	3 Jul 10
22.40		Barnes				1		Rüdlingen	13 Jul 96
22.40i		Nelson				1		Fayetteville	15 Feb 08
	(31/12)								
22.28	Ryan	Whiting		USA	24.11.86	1	DL	Doha	10 May 13
22.24	Sergey	Smirnov		RUS	17.9.60	2	vGDR	Tallinn	21 Jun 86
22.21	Dylan	Armstrong		CAN	15.1.81	1	NC	Calgary	25 Jun 11
22.21	Tom	Walsh		NZL	1.3.92	2	Hanz	Zagreb	5 Sep 16
22.20	John	Godina		USA	31.5.72	1		Carson	22 May 05
22.20	David	Storl		GER	27.7.90	1	Athl	Lausanne	9 Jul 15
22.10	Sergey	Gavryushin		RUS	27.6.59	1		Tbilisi	31 Aug 86
22.10	Cory	Martin		USA	22.5.85	1		Tucson	22 May 10
	(20)								
22.09	Sergey	Kasnauskas		BLR	20.4.61	1		Stayki	23 Aug 84
22.09i	Mika	Halvari		FIN	13.2.70	1		Tampere	7 Feb 00
22.02i	George	Woods		USA	11.2.43	1	LAT	Inglewood	8 Feb 74
22.02	Dave	Laut		USA	21.12.56	1		Koblenz	25 Aug 82
22.00 WR	Aleksandr	Baryshnikov		RUS	11.11.48	1	vFRA	Colombes	10 Jul 76
21.98	Gregg	Tafralis ¶		USA	9.4.58	1		Los Gatos	13 Jun 92
21.97	Janus	Robberts		RSA	10.3.79	1	NCAA	Eugene	2 Jun 01
21.96	Mikhail	Kostin		RUS	10.5.59	1		Vitebsk	20 Jul 86
21.95	Tomasz	Majewski		POL	30.8.81	1	DNG	Stockholm	30 Jul 09
21.93	Remigius	Machura ¶		CZE	3.7.60	1		Praha	23 Aug 87
	(30)								
21.92	Carl	Myerscough ¶		GBR	21.10.79	1	NCAA	Sacramento	13 Jun 03
21.87	C.J.	Hunter ¶		USA	14.12.68	2	NC	Sacramento	15 Jul 00

SHOT – DISCUS A-T 279

Mark	Wind	Name		Nat	Born	Pos	Meet	Venue	Date
21.85	WR	Terry	Albritton	USA	14.1.55	1		Honolulu	21 Feb 76
21.83i		Aleksandr	Bagach ¶	UKR	21.11.66	1		Brovary	21 Feb 99
21.82	WR	Al	Feuerbach	USA	14.1.48	1		San José	5 May 73
21.82		Andy	Bloom	USA	11.8.73	1	GPF	Doha	5 Oct 00
21.81		Yuriy	Bilonog ¶	UKR	9.3.74	1	NC	Kiev	3 Jul 03
21.78	WR	Randy	Matson	USA	5.3.45	1		College Station	22 Apr 67
21.78		Dan	Taylor	USA	12.5.82	1		Tucson	23 May 09
21.77i		Mike (40)	Stulce ¶	USA	21.7.69	1	v GBR	Birmingham	13 Feb 93
21.77		Dragan	Peric	YUG	8.5.64	1		Bar	25 Apr 98
21.76		Michael	Carter	USA	29.10.60	2	NCAA	Eugene	2 Jun 84
21.76		Stephen	Mozia	NGR	16.8.93	1		Ustí nad Labem	19 Jul 16
21.74		Janis	Bojars	LAT	12.5.56	1		Riga	14 Jul 84
21.73		Augie	Wolf ¶	USA	3.9.61	1		Leverkusen	12 Apr 84
21.69		Reijo	Ståhlberg	FIN	21.9.52	1	WCR	Fresno	5 May 79
21.69		Andrey	Mikhnevich ¶	BLR	12.7.76	1	WCh	Saint-Denis	23 Aug 03
21.69		O'Dayne	Richards	JAM	14.2.88	1	PAm	Toronto	21 Jul 15
21.68		Geoff	Capes	GBR	23.8.49	1	4-N	Cwmbrân	18 May 80
21.68		Edward (50)	Sarul	POL	16.11.58	1		Sopot	31 Jul 83

100th man 21.21, 200th 20.78, 300th 20.45, 400th 20.15, 500th 19.96
Not recognised by GDR authorities: 22.11 Rolf Oesterreich GDR 24.8.49 1 Zschopau 12 Sep 76
Drugs disqualification
22.84			Barnes					Malmö	7 Aug 90
22.10		Andrey	Mikhnevich ¶	BLR	12.7.76	1		Minsk	11 Aug 11
21.82		Mike	Stulce ¶	USA	21.7.69	1		Brenham	9 May 90

Best outdoor marks for athletes with indoor bests
21.70   Stulce ¶   1   OG   Barcelona   31 Jul 92 | 21.63   Woods   2   CalR   Modesto   22 May 76

Ancillary marks – other marks during series (to 22.45)
22.84 WR	Andrei	12 Aug 87	22.72 WR	Andrei	12 Aug 87	22.55	Barnes	20 May 90
22.76	Barnes	20 May 90	22.70	Günthör	23 Aug 88	22.49	Nelson	18 May 02
22.74	Andrei	12 Aug 87	22.58	Beyer	20 Aug 86	22.45	Timmermann	22 May 88

DISCUS

Mark		Name		Nat	Born	Pos	Meet	Venue	Date
74.08	WR	Jürgen	Schult	GDR	11.5.60	1		Neubrandenburg	6 Jun 86
73.88		Virgilijus	Alekna	LTU	13.2.72	1	NC	Kaunas	3 Aug 00
73.38		Gerd	Kanter	EST	6.5.79	1		Helsingborg	4 Sep 06
72.02			Kanter			1eA		Salinas	3 May 07
71.88			Kanter			1eA		Salinas	8 May 08
71.86	WR	Yuriy	Dumchev	RUS	5.8.58	1		Moskva	29 May 83
71.84		Piotr	Malachowski	POL	7.6.83	1	FBK	Hengelo	8 Jun 13
71.70		Róbert	Fazekas ¶	HUN	18.8.75	1		Szombathely	14 Jul 02
71.64			Kanter			1		Kohila	25 Jun 09
71.56			Alekna			1		Kaunas	25 Jul 07
71.50		Lars	Riedel	GER	28.6.67	1		Wiesbaden	3 May 97
71.45			Kanter			1		Chula Vista	29 Apr 10
71.32		Ben	Plucknett ¶	USA	13.4.54	1	Pre	Eugene	4 Jun 83
71.26		John	Powell	USA	25.6.47	1	NC	San José	9 Jun 84
71.26		Rickard	Bruch	SWE	2.7.46	1		Malmö	15 Nov 84
71.26		Imrich	Bugár (10)	CZE	14.4.55	1	Jenner	San José	25 May 85
71.25			Fazekas			1	WCp	Madrid (C)	21 Sep 02
71.25			Alekna			1	Danek	Turnov	20 May 08
71.18		Art	Burns	USA	19.7.54	1		San José	19 Jul 83
71.16	WR	Wolfgang	Schmidt	GDR	16.1.54	1		Berlin	9 Aug 78
71.14			Plucknett			1		Berkeley	12 Jun 83
71.14		Anthony	Washington	USA	16.1.66	1eA		Salinas	22 May 96
71.12			Alekna			1	WK	Zürich	11 Aug 00
71.08			Alekna			1		Réthimno	21 Jul 06
71.06		Luis Mariano	Delís ¶	CUB	12.12.57	1	Barr	La Habana	21 May 83
71.06			Riedel			1	WK	Zürich	14 Aug 96
71.00			Bruch			1		Malmö	14 Oct 84
70.99			Alekna			1		Stellenbosch	30 Mar 01
70.98		Mac	Wilkins	USA	15.11.50	1	WG	Helsinki	9 Jul 80
70.98			Burns (30/16)			1	Pre	Eugene	21 Jul 84
70.82		Aleksander	Tammert	EST	2.2.73	1		Denton	15 Apr 06
70.66		Robert	Harting	GER	18.10.84	1	Danek	Turnov	22 May 12
70.54		Dmitriy	Shevchenko ¶	RUS	13.5.68	1		Krasnodar	7 May 02
70.38	WRu	Jay (20)	Silvester	USA	27.8.37	1		Lancaster	16 May 71

DISCUS – HAMMER A-T

Mark	Wind	Name		Nat	Born	Pos	Meet	Venue	Date
70.32		Frantz	Kruger	RSA/FIN	22.5.75	1		Salon-de-Provence	26 May 02
70.06		Romas	Ubartas ¶	LTU	26.5.60	1		Smalininkay	8 May 88
70.00		Juan	Martínez ¶	CUB	17.5.58	2	Barr	La Habana	21 May 83
69.95		Zoltán	Kövágó ¶	HUN	10.4.79	1		Salon-de-Provence	25 May 06
69.91		John	Godina	USA	31.5.72	1		Salinas	19 May 98
69.90		Jason	Young	USA	27.5.81	1		Lubbock	26 Mar 10
69.70		Géjza	Valent	CZE	3.10.53	2		Nitra	26 Aug 84
69.62		Knut	Hjeltnes ¶	NOR	8.12.51	2	Jen	San José	25 May 85
69.62		Timo	Tompuri	FIN	9.6.69	1		Helsingborg	8 Jul 01
69.50		Mario (30)	Pestano	ESP	8.4.78	1	NC	Santa Cruz de Tenerife	27 Jul 08
69.46		Al	Oerter	USA	19.9.36	1	TFA	Wichita	31 May 80
69.44		Georgiy	Kolnootchenko	BLR	7.5.59	1	vUSA	Indianapolis	3 Jul 82
69.40		Art	Swarts ¶	USA	14.2.45	1		Scotch Plains	8 Dec 79
69.36		Mike	Buncic	USA	25.7.62	1		Fresno	6 Apr 91
69.32		Ehsan	Hadadi	IRI	21.1.85	1		Tallinn	3 Jun 08
69.28		Vladimir	Dubrovshchik	BLR	7.1.72	1	NC	Staiki	3 Jun 00
69.26		Ken	Stadel	USA	19.2.52	2	AAU	Walnut	16 Jun 79
68.94		Adam	Setliff	USA	15.12.69	1		Atascadero	25 Jul 01
68.91		Ian	Waltz	USA	15.4.77	1		Salinas	24 May 06
68.90		Jean-Claude (40)	Retel	FRA	11.2.68	1		Salon-de-Provence	17 Jul 02
68.88		Vladimir	Zinchenko	UKR	25.7.59	1		Dnepropetrovsk	16 Jul 88
68.76		Jarred	Rome	USA	21.12.76	2cA		Chula Vista	6 Aug 11
68.72		Daniel	Ståhl	SWE	27.8.92	1	NC	Sollentuna	28 Aug 16
68.64		Dmitriy	Kovtsun ¶	UKR	29.9.55	1		Riga	6 Jul 84
68.58		Attila	Horváth	HUN	28.7.67	1		Budapest	24 Jun 94
68.52		Igor	Duginyets	UKR	20.5.56	1	NC	Kyiv	21 Aug 82
68.50		Armin	Lemme	GDR	28.10.55	1	vUSA	Karl-Marx-Stadt	10 Jul 82
68.49A		Casey	Malone	USA	6.4.77	1		Fort Collins	20 Jun 09
68.48 WR		John	van Reenen	RSA	26.3.47	1		Stellenbosch	14 Mar 75
68.44		Vaclovas (50)	Kidykas	LTU	17.10.61	1		Sochi	1 Jun 88

100th man 67.20, 200th 65.46, 300th 64.43, 400th 63.28, 500th 62.41

Subsequent to or at drugs disqualification ! recognised as US record

72.34!		Ben	Plucknett ¶	USA	13.4.54	(1)	DNG	Stockholm	7 Jul 81
71.20			Plucknett			(1)	CalR	Modesto	16 May 81
70.84		Kamy	Keshmiri ¶	USA	23.1.69	(1)		Salinas	27 May 92

Sloping ground

72.08		John	Powell	USA	25.6.47	1		Klagshamn	11 Sep 87
69.80		Stefan	Fernholm	SWE	2.7.59	1		Klagshamn	13 Aug 87
69.44		Adam	Setliff	USA	15.12.69	1		La Jolla	21 Jul 01
68.46		Andy	Bloom	USA	11.8.73	2cA		La Jolla	25 Mar 00

Ancillary marks – other marks during series (to 70.98)
72.35 Alekna 3 Aug 00   72.30 Kanter 4 Sep 06   71.08 Plucknett 4 Jun 83

HAMMER

Mark	Wind	Name		Nat	Born	Pos	Meet	Venue	Date
86.74 WR		Yuriy	Sedykh	RUS	11.6.55	1	EC	Stuttgart	30 Aug 86
86.66 WR			Sedykh			1	vGDR	Tallinn	22 Jun 86
86.34 WR			Sedykh			1		Cork	3 Jul 84
86.04		Sergey	Litvinov	RUS	23.1.58	1	OD	Dresden	3 Jul 86
85.74			Litvinov			2	EC	Stuttgart	30 Aug 86
85.68			Sedykh			1	BGP	Budapest	11 Aug 86
85.60			Sedykh			1	PTG	London (CP)	13 Jul 84
85.60			Sedykh			1	Drz	Moskva	17 Aug 84
85.20			Litvinov			2		Cork	3 Jul 84
85.14			Litvinov			1	PTG	London	11 Jul 86
85.14			Sedykh			1	Kuts	Moskva	4 Sep 88
85.02			Sedykh			1	BGP	Budapest	20 Aug 86
84.92			Sedykh			2	OD	Dresden	3 Jul 86
84.90		Vadim	Devyatovskiy ¶	BLR	20.3.77	1		Staiki	21 Jul 05
84.88			Litvinov			1	GP-GG	Roma	10 Sep 86
84.86		Koji	Murofushi	JPN	8.10.74	1	Odlozil	Praha	29 Jun 03
84.80			Litvinov			1	OG	Seoul	26 Sep 88
84.72			Sedykh			1	GWG	Moskva	9 Jul 86
84.64			Litvinov			2	GWG	Moskva	9 Jul 86
84.62		Igor	Astapkovich	BLR	4.1.63	1	Expo	Sevilla	6 Jun 92
84.60			Sedykh			1	8-N	Tokyo	14 Sep 84
84.58			Sedykh			1	Znam	Leningrad	8 Jun 86
84.51		Ivan	Tikhon ¶	BLR	24.7.76	1	NC	Grodno	9 Jul 08
84.48		Igor	Nikulin	RUS	14.8.60	1	Athl	Lausanne	12 Jul 90

HAMMER – JAVELIN A-T   281

Mark	Wind	Name		Nat	Born	Pos	Meet	Venue	Date
84.46			Sedykh			1		Vladivostok	14 Sep 88
84.46			Tikhon			1		Minsk	7 May 04
84.40		Jüri	Tamm	EST	5.2.57	1		Banská Bystrica	9 Sep 84
84.36			Litvinov			2	vGDR	Tallinn	22 Jun 86
84.32			Tikhon			1		Staiki	8 Aug 03
84.26			Sedykh			1	Nik	Nice	15 Jul 86
(30/8)									
84.19		Adrián	Annus ¶	HUN	28.6.73	1		Szombathely	10 Aug 03
83.93		Pawel	Fajdek	POL	4.6.89	1	Kuso	Szczecin	9 Aug 15
(10)									
83.68		Tibor	Gécsek ¶	HUN	22.9.64	1		Zalaegerszeg	19 Sep 98
83.46		Andrey	Abduvaliyev	TJK/UZB	30.6.66	1		Adler	26 May 90
83.43		Aleksey	Zagornyi	RUS	31.5.78	1		Adler	10 Feb 02
83.40 @		Ralf	Haber	GDR	18.8.62	1		Athína	16 May 88
82.54						1		Potsdam	9 Sep 88
83.38		Szymon	Ziólkowski	POL	1.7.76	1	WCh	Edmonton	5 Aug 01
83.30		Olli-Pekka	Karjalainen	FIN	7.3.80	1		Lahti	14 Jul 04
83.04		Heinz	Weis	GER	14.7.63	1	NC	Frankfurt	29 Jun 97
83.00		Balázs	Kiss	HUN	21.3.72	1	GP II	Saint-Denis	4 Jun 98
82.78		Karsten	Kobs	GER	16.9.71	1		Dortmund	26 Jun 99
82.69		Krisztián	Pars	HUN	18.2.82	1	EC	Zürich	16 Aug 14
(20)									
				@ competitive meeting but unsanctioned by GDR federation					
82.64		Günther	Rodehau	GDR	6.7.59	1		Dresden	3 Aug 85
82.62		Sergey	Kirmasov ¶	RUS	25.3.70	1		Bryansk	30 May 98
82.62		Andrey	Skvaruk	UKR	9.3.67	1		Koncha-Zaspa	27 Apr 02
82.58		Primoz	Kozmus	SLO	30.9.79	1		Celje	2 Sep 09
82.54		Vasiliy	Sidorenko	RUS	1.5.61	1		Krasnodar	13 May 92
82.52		Lance	Deal	USA	21.8.61	1	GPF	Milano	7 Sep 96
82.40		Plamen	Minev	BUL	28.4.65	1	NM	Plovdiv	1 Jun 91
82.38		Gilles	Dupray	FRA	2.1.70	1		Chelles	21 Jun 00
82.28		Ilya	Konovalov ¶	RUS	4.3.71	1	NC	Tula	10 Aug 03
82.24		Benjaminas	Viluckis	LIT	20.3.61	1		Klaipeda	24 Aug 86
(30)									
82.24		Vyacheslav	Korovin	RUS	8.9.62	1		Chelyabinsk	20 Jun 87
82.23		Vladislav	Piskunov ¶	UKR	7.6.78	2		Koncha-Zaspa	27 Apr 02
82.22		Holger	Klose	GER	5.12.72	1		Dortmund	2 May 98
82.16		Vitaliy	Alisevich	BLR	15.6.67	1		Parnu	13 Jul 88
82.08		Ivan	Tanev	BUL	1.5.57	1	NC	Sofia	3 Sep 88
82.00		Sergey	Alay ¶	BLR	11.6.65	1		Stayki	12 May 92
81.88		Jud	Logan ¶	USA	19.7.59	1		State College	22 Apr 88
81.81		Libor	Charfreitag	SVK	11.9.77	3	Odlozil	Praha	29 Jun 03
81.79		Christophe	Épalle	FRA	23.1.69	1		Clermont-Ferrand	30 Jun 00
81.78		Christoph	Sahner	FRG	23.9.63	1		Wemmetsweiler	11 Sep 88
(40)									
81.70		Aleksandr	Seleznyov	RUS	25.1.63	2		Sochi	22 May 93
81.66		Aleksandr	Krykun	UKR	1.3.68	1		Kiev	29 May 04
81.64		Enrico	Sgrulletti	ITA	24.4.65	1		Ostia	9 Mar 97
81.56		Sergey	Gavrilov	RUS	22.5.70	1	Army	Rostov	16 Jun 96
81.56		Zsolt	Németh	HUN	9.11.71	1		Veszprém	14 Aug 99
81.52		Juha	Tiainen	FIN	5.12.55	1		Tampere	11 Jun 84
81.49		Valeriy	Svyatokho	BLR	20.7.81	1	NCp	Brest	27 May 06
81.45		Esref	Apak ¶	TUR	3.1.82	1	Cezmi	Istanbul	4 Jun 05
81.44		Yuriy	Tarasyuk	BLR	11.4.57	1		Minsk	10 Aug 84
81.35		Wojciech	Kondratowicz	POL	18.4.80	1		Bydgoszczcz	13 Jul 03
(50)		100th man 80.08, 200th 77.68, 300th 75.90, 400th 74.56, 500th 73.60							

Drugs disqualification

| 86.73 | | Ivan | Tikhon ¶ | BLR | 24.7.76 | 1 | NC | Brest | 3 Jul 05 |

Ancillary marks – other marks during series (to 84.85)

86.68	Sedykh	30 Aug 86	85.82	Sedykh	22 Jun 86	85.42	Sedykh	11 Aug 86	85.20	Sedykh	3 Jul 84
86.62	Sedykh	30 Aug 86	85.52	Sedykh	13 Jul 84	85.28	Sedykh	30 Aug 86	85.04	Sedykh	13 Jul 84
86.00	Sedykh	3 Jul 84	85.46	Sedykh	30 Aug 86	85.26	Sedykh	11 Aug 86	84.98	Sedykh	4 Sep 88
86.00	Sedykh	22 Jun 86	85.42	Litvinov	3 Jul 84	85.24	Sedykh	11 Aug 86	84.92	Litvinov	3 Jul 86

JAVELIN

98.48 WR		Jan	Zelezny	CZE	16.6.66	1		Jena	25 May 96
95.66 WR			Zelezny			1	McD	Sheffield	29 Aug 93
95.54A WR			Zelezny			1		Pietersburg	6 Apr 93
94.64			Zelezny			1	GS	Ostrava	31 May 96
94.02			Zelezny			1		Stellenbosch	26 Mar 97
93.09		Aki	Parviainen	FIN	26.10.74	1		Kuortane	26 Jun 99
92.80			Zelezny			1	WCh	Edmonton	12 Aug 01

JAVELIN A-T

Mark	Wind	Name		Nat	Born	Pos	Meet	Venue	Date
92.72		Julius	Yego	KEN	4.1.89	1	WCh	Beijing	26 Aug 15
92.61		Sergey	Makarov	RUS	19.3.73	1		Sheffield	30 Jun 02
92.60		Raymond	Hecht	GER	11.11.68	1	Bisl	Oslo	21 Jul 95
92.42			Zelezny			1	GS	Ostrava	28 May 97
92.41			Parviainen			1	ECp-1A	Vaasa	24 Jun 01
92.28			Zelezny			1	GPF	Monaco	9 Sep 95
92.28			Hecht			1	WK	Zürich	14 Aug 96
92.12			Zelezny			1	McD	London (CP)	27 Aug 95
92.12			Zelezny			1	TOTO	Tokyo	15 Sep 95
91.82			Zelezny			1	McD	Sheffield	4 Sep 94
91.69		Kostadínos	Gatsioúdis	GRE	17.12.73	1		Kuortane	24 Jun 00
91.68			Zelezny			1	GP	Gateshead	1 Jul 94
91.59		Andreas	Thorkildsen	NOR	1.4.82	1	Bisl	Oslo	2 Jun 06
91.53		Tero	Pitkämäki	FIN	19.12.82	1		Kuortane	26 Jun 05
91.50			Zelezny			1	Kuso	Lublin	4 Jun 94
91.50A			Zelezny			1		Pretoria	8 Apr 96
91.50			Hecht			1		Gengenbach	1 Sep 96
91.46 WR		Steve	Backley	GBR	12.2.69	1		Auckland (NS)	25 Jan 92
91.40			Zelezny			1	BNP	Villeneuve d'Ascq	2 Jul 93
91.39			Yego			1	DL	Birmingham	7 Jun 15
91.34			Zelezny			1		Cape Town	8 Apr 97
91.33			Pitkämäki			1	WAF	Monaco	10 Sep 05
91.31			Parviainen			2	WCh	Edmonton	12 Aug 01
91.30			Zelezny			1	ISTAF	Berlin	1 Sep 95
91.29		Breaux	Greer	USA	19.10.76	1	NC	Indianapolis	21 Jun 07
(32/10) 84 over 90m (most: Zelezny 34, Parviainen 8, Thorkildsen 8, Hecht & Pitkämäki 6, Makarov 5)									
91.28		Thomas	Röhler	GER	30.9.91	1	PNG	Turku	29 Jun 16
90.73		Vadims	Vasilevskis	LAT	5.1.82	1		Tallinn	22 Jul 07
90.60		Seppo	Räty	FIN	27.4.62	1		Nurmijärvi	20 Jul 92
90.44		Boris	Henry	GER	14.12.73	1	Gugl	Linz	9 Jul 97
90.16		Keshorn	Walcott	TTO	2.4.93	1	Athl	Lausanne	9 Jul 15
89.57		Johannes	Vetter	GER	26.3.93	1	ISTAF	Berlin	3 Sep 16
89.21		Ihab	Abdelrahman ¶	EGY	1.5.89	1	DL	Shanghai	18 May 14
89.16A		Tom	Petranoff	USA	8.4.58	1		Potchefstroom	1 Mar 91
89.15			Zhao Qinggang	CHN	24.7.85	1	AsiG	Incheon	2 Oct 14
89.10 WR		Patrik	Bodén	SWE	30.6.67	1		Austin	24 Mar 90
(20)									
89.02		Jarrod	Bannister ¶	AUS	3.10.84	1	NC	Brisbane	29 Feb 08
88.98		Antti	Ruuskanen	FIN	21.2.84	1	NC	Pori	2 Aug 15
88.90		Aleksandr	Ivanov	RUS	25.5.82	1	Znam	Tula	7 Jun 03
88.84		Dmitriy	Tarabin	RUS	29.10.91	1	NC	Moskva	24 Jul 13
88.75		Marius	Corbett	RSA	26.9.75	1	CG	Kuala Lumpur	21 Sep 98
88.70		Peter	Blank	GER	10.4.62	1	NC	Stuttgart	30 Jun 01
88.36		Matthias	de Zordo	GER	21.2.88	1	VD	Bruxelles	16 Sep 11
88.34		Vitezslav	Vesely	CZE	27.2.83	Q	OG	London (OS)	8 Aug 12
88.29		Julian	Weber	GER	29.8.94	2	ISTAF	Berlin	3 Sep 16
88.24		Matti	Närhi	FIN	17.8.75	1		Soini	27 Jul 97
(30)									
88.23		Petr	Frydrych	CZE	13.1.88	1	GS	Ostrava	27 May 10
88.22		Juha	Laukkanen	FIN	6.1.69	1		Kuortane	20 Jun 92
88.20		Gavin	Lovegrove	NZL	21.10.67	1	Bisl	Oslo	5 Jul 96
88.02		Jakub	Vadlejch	CZE	10.10.90	1	DL	Saint-Denis	27 Aug 16
88.00		Vladimir	Ovchinnikov	RUS	2.8.70	1		Tolyatti	14 May 95
87.83		Andrus	Värnik	EST	27.9.77	1		Valga	19 Aug 03
87.82		Harri	Hakkarainen	FIN	16.10.69	1		Kuortane	24 Jun 95
87.60		Kazuhiro	Mizoguchi	JPN	18.3.62	1	Jenner	San José	27 May 89
87.40		Vladimir	Sasimovich ¶	BLR	14.9.68	2		Kuortane	24 Jun 95
87.34		Andrey	Moruyev	RUS	6.5.70	1	ECp	Birmingham	25 Jun 94
(40)									
87.23		Teemu	Wirkkala	FIN	14.1.84	1		Joensuu	22 Jul 09
87.20		Viktor	Zaytsev	UZB	6.6.66	1	OT	Moskva	23 Jun 92
87.20		Peter	Esenwein	GER	7.12.67	1		Rehlingen	31 May 04
87.20A		Guillermo	Martínez	CUB	28.6.81	1	PAm	Guadalajara	28 Oct 11
87.17		Dariusz	Trafas	POL	16.5.72	1		Gold Coast (RB)	17 Sep 00
87.14		Ioánnis	Kiriazis	GRE	19.1.96	1	NC-23	Lárisa	31 Jul 16
87.12		Tom	Pukstys	USA	28.5.68	2	OD	Jena	25 May 97
87.12		Emeterio	González	CUB	11.4.73	1	OD	Jena	3 Jun 00
86.98		Yuriy	Rybin	RUS	5.3.63	1		Nitra	26 Aug 95
86.94		Mick	Hill	GBR	22.10.64	1	NC	London (CP)	13 Jun 93
(50) 100th man 84.81, 200th 82.38, 300th 80.50, 400th 79.48 new javelin introduced in 1986									

JAVELIN – DECATHLON AT 283

Mark	Wind	Name	Nat	Born	Pos	Meet	Venue	Date

Ancillary marks – other marks during series (to 91.40)
95.34		Zelezny	29 Aug 93	92.26		Zelezny	26 Mar 97	91.44	Zelezny	25 May 96
92.88		Zelezny	25 May 96	91.88		Zelezny	27 Aug 95	91.44	Zelezny	26 Mar 97
92.30		Zelezny	26 Mar 97	91.48		Zelezny	15 Sep 95			

Javelins with roughened tails, now banned by the IAAF
96.96 WR	Seppo	Räty	FIN	27.4.62	1		Punkalaidun	2 Jun 91
94.74 Irreg		Zelezny			1	Bisl	Oslo	4 Jul 92
91.98 WR		Räty			1	Super	Shizuoka	6 May 91
90.82	Kimmo	Kinnunen	FIN	31.3.68	1	WCh	Tokyo	26 Aug 91
87.00	Peter	Borglund	SWE	29.1.64	1	vFIN	Stockholm	13 Aug 91

DECATHLON

9045 WR	Ashton	Eaton	USA	21.1.88	1	WCh	Beijing	29 Aug 15
	10.23/-0.4	7.88/0.0	14.52	2.01	45.00		13.69/-0.2	43.34	5.20	63.63	4:17.52
9039 WR		Eaton			1	NC/OT	Eugene	23 Jun 12
	10.21/0.4	8.23/0.8	14.20	2.05	46.70		13.70/-0.8	42.81	5.30	58.87	4:14.48
9026 WR	Roman	Sebrle	CZE	26.11.74	1		Götzis	27 May 01
	10.64/0.0	8.11/1.9	15.33	2.12	47.79		13.92/-0.2	47.92	4.80	70.16	4:21.98
8994 WR	Tomás	Dvořák	CZE	11.5.72	1	ECp	Praha	4 Jul 99
	10.54/-0.1	7.90/1.1	16.78	2.04	48.08		13.73/0.0	48.33	4.90	72.32	4:37.20
8902		Dvořák			1	WCh	Edmonton	7 Aug 01
	10.62/1.5	8.07/0.9	16.57	2.00	47.74		13.80/-0.4	45.51	5.00	68.53	4:35.13
8900		Dvořák			1		Götzis	4 Jun 00
	10.54/1.3	8.03/0.0	16.68	2.09	48.36		13.89/-1.0	47.89	4.85	67.21	4:42.33
8893		Sebrle			1	OG	Athína	24 Aug 04
	10.85/1.5	7.84/0.3	16.36	2.12	48.36		14.05/1.5	48.72	5.00	70.52	4:40.01
8893		Eaton			1	OG	Rio de Janeiro	18 Aug 16
	10.46/-0.1	7.94/1.7	14.73	2.01	46.07		13.80/0.7	45.49	5.20	59.77	4:23.33
8891 WR	Dan	O'Brien	USA	18.7.66	1		Talence	5 Sep 92
	10.43w/2.1	8.08/1.8	16.69	2.07	48.51		13.98/-0.5	48.56	5.00	62.58	4:42.10
8869		Eaton			1	OG	London (OS)	9 Aug 12
	10.35/0.4	8.03/0.8	14.66	2.05	46.90		13.56/0.1	42.53	5.20	61.96	4:33.59
8847 WR	Daley	Thompson	GBR	30.7.58	1	OG	Los Angeles	9 Aug 84
	10.44/-1.0	8.01/0.4	15.72	2.03	46.97		14.33/-1.1	46.56	5.00	65.24	4:35.00
8844w		O'Brien			1	TAC	New York	13 Jun 91
	10.23	7.96	16.06	2.08	47.70		13.95W/4.2	48.08	5.10	57.40	4:45.54
8842		Sebrle			1		Götzis	30 May 04
	10.92/0.5	7.86w/3.3	16.22	2.09	48.59		14.15/0.3	47.44	5.00	71.10	4:34.09
8837		Dvořák			1	WCh	Athína	6 Aug 97
	10.60/0.8	7.64/-0.7	16.32	2.00	47.56		13.61/0.8	45.16	5.00	70.34	4:35.40
8834	Kevin	Mayer	FRA	10.2.92	2	OG	Rio de Janeiro	18 Aug 16
	10.81/-0.4	7.60/0.1	15.76	2.04	48.28		14.02/0.7	46.78	5.40	65.04	4:25.49
8832 WR	Jürgen	Hingsen	FRG	25.1.58	1	OT	Mannheim	9 Jun 84
	10.70w/2.9	7.76/-1.6	16.42	2.07	48.05		14.07/0.2	49.36	4.90	59.86	4:19.75
8832	Bryan	Clay	USA	3.1.80	1	NC/OT	Eugene	30 Jun 08
	10.39/-0.4	7.39/-1.6	15.17	2.08	48.41		13.75/1.9	52.74	5.00	70.55	4:50.97
8825 WR		Hingsen			1		Bernhausen	5 Jun 83
	10.92/0.0	7.74	15.94	2.15	47.89		14.10	46.80	4.70	67.26	4:19.74
8824		O'Brien			1	OG	Atlanta	1 Aug 96
	10.50/0.7	7.57/1.4	15.66	2.07	46.82		13.87/0.3	48.78	5.00	66.90	4:45.89
8820		Clay			2	OG	Athína	24 Aug 04
	10.44w/2.2	7.96/0.2	15.23	2.06	49.19		14.13/1.5	50.11	4.90	69.71	4:41.65
8817		O'Brien			1	WCh	Stuttgart	20 Aug 93
	10.57/0.9	7.99/0.4	15.41	2.03	47.46		14.08/0.0	47.92	5.20	62.56	4:40.08
8815	Erki	Nool	EST	25.6.70	2	WCh	Edmonton	7 Aug 01
	10.60/1.5	7.63/2.0	14.90	2.03	46.23		14.40/0.0	43.40	5.40	67.01	4:29.58
8812		O'Brien			1	WCh	Tokyo	30 Aug 91
	10.41/-1.6	7.90/0.8	16.24	1.91	46.53		13.94/-1.2	47.20	5.20	60.66	4:37.50
8811		Thompson			1	EC	Stuttgart	28 Aug 86
	10.26/2.0	7.72/1.0	15.73	2.00	47.02		14.04/-0.3	43.38	5.10	62.78	4:26.16
8809		Eaton			1	WCh	Moskva	11 Aug 13
	10.35/-0.5	7.73/0.3	14.39	1.93	46.02		13.72/0.4	45.00	5.20	64.83	4:29.80
8807		Sebrle			1		Götzis	1 Jun 03
	10.78/-0.2	7.86/1.2	15.41	2.12	47.83		13.96/0.0	43.42	4.90	69.22	4:28.63
8800		Sebrle			1		Götzis	2 Jun 02
	10.95/0.5	7.79/1.8	15.50	2.12	48.35		13.89/1.6	48.02	5.00	68.97	4:38.16
8800		Sebrle			1	EC	München	8 Aug 02
	10.83/1.3	7.92/0.8	15.41	2.12	48.48		14.04/0.0	46.88	5.10	68.51	4:42.94
8792	Uwe	Freimuth (10)	GDR	10.9.61	1	OD	Potsdam	21 Jul 84
	11.06/0.4	7.79/1.2	16.30	2.03	48.43		14.66/1.9	46.58	5.15	72.42	4:25.19

284　DECATHLON A-T

Mark	Wind	Name		Nat	Born	Pos	Meet	Venue		Date
8791		Clay				1	OG	Beijing		22 Aug 08
	10.44/0.3	7.78/0.0	16.27	1.99	48.92		13.93/-0.5	53.79	5.00　70.97	5:06.59
	(30/10)									
8790		Trey	Hardee	USA	7.2.84	1	WCh	Berlin		20 Aug 09
	10.45/0.2	7.83/1.9	15.33	1.99	48.13		13.86/0.3	48.08	5.20　68.00	4:48.91
8784		Tom	Pappas	USA	6.9.76	1	NC	Stanford		22 Jun 03
	10.78/0.2	7.96/1.4	16.28	2.17	48.22		14.13/1.7	45.84	5.20　60.77	4:48.12
8762		Siegfried	Wentz	FRG	7.3.60	2		Bernhausen		5 Jun 83
	10.89	7.49/	15.35	2.09	47.38		14.00	46.90	4.80　70.68	4:24.90
8735		Eduard	Hämäläinen	FIN/BLR	21.1.69	1		Götzis		29 May 94
	10.50w/2.1	7.26/1.0	16.05	2.11	47.63		13.82/-3.0	49.70	4.90　60.32	4:35.09
8727		Dave	Johnson	USA	7.4.63	1		Azusa		24 Apr 92
	10.96/0.4	7.52w/4.5	14.61	2.04	48.19		14.17/0.3	49.88	5.28　66.96	4:29.38
8725		Dmitriy	Karpov	KAZ	23.7.81	3	OG	Athína		24 Aug 04
	10.50w/2.2	7.81/-0.9	15.93	2.09	46.81		13.97/1.5	51.65	4.60　55.54	4:38.11
8709		Aleksandr	Apaychev	UKR	6.5.61	1	vGDR	Neubrandenburg		3 Jun 84
	10.96/	7.57/	16.00	1.97	48.72		13.93/	48.00	4.90　72.24	4:26.51
8706		Frank	Busemann	GER	26.2.75	2	OG	Atlanta		1 Aug 96
	10.60/0.7	8.07/0.8	13.60	2.04	48.34		13.47/0.3	45.04	4.80　66.86	4:31.41
8698		Grigoriy	Degtyaryov	RUS	16.8.58	1	NC	Kiyev		22 Jun 84
	10.87/0.7	7.42/0.1	16.03	2.10	49.75		14.53/0.3	51.20	4.90　67.08	4:23.09
8695		Damian	Warner	CAN	4.11.89	2	WCh	Beijing		29 Aug 15
	10.31/-0.4	7.65/0.2	14.44	2.04	47.30		13.63/-0.2	44.99	4.80　63.50	4:31.51
	(20)									
8694		Chris	Huffins	USA	15.4.70	1	NC	New Orleans		20 Jun 98
	10.31w/3.5	7.76w/2.5	15.43	2.18	49.02		14.02/1.0	53.22	4.60　61.59	4:59.43
8680		Torsten	Voss	GDR	24.3.63	1	WCh	Roma		4 Sep 87
	10.69/-0.3	7.88/1.2	14.98	2.10	47.96		14.13/0.1	43.96	5.10　58.02	4:25.93
8670		Michael	Schrader	GER	1.7.87	2	WCh	Moskva		11 Aug 13
	10.73/-0.5	7.85/0.2	14.56	1.99	47.66		14.29/0.4	46.44	5.00　65.67	4:25.38
8667 WR		Guido	Kratschmer	FRG	10.1.53	1		Bernhausen		14 Jun 80
	10.58w/2.4	7.80/	15.47	2.00	48.04		13.92/	45.52	4.60　66.50	4:24.15
8654		Leonel	Suárez	CUB	1.9.87	1	CAC	La Habana		4 Jul 09
	11.07/0.7	7.42/0.8	14.39	2.09	47.65		14.15/-0.6	46.07	4.70　77.47	4:27.29
8644		Steve	Fritz	USA	1.11.67	4	OG	Atlanta		1 Aug 96
	10.90/0.8	7.77/0.9	15.31	2.04	50.13		13.97/0.3	49.84	5.10　65.70	4:38.26
8644		Maurice	Smith	JAM	28.9.80	2	WCh	Osaka		1 Sep 07
	10.62/0.7	7.50/0.0	17.32	1.97	47.48		13.91/-0.2	52.36	4.80　53.61	4:33.52
8634 WR		Bruce	Jenner	USA	28.10.49	1	OG	Montreal		30 Jul 76
	10.94/0.0	7.22/0.0	15.35	2.03	47.51		14.84/0.0	50.04	4.80　68.52	4:12.61
8627		Robert	Zmelík	CZE	18.4.69	1		Götzis		31 May 92
	10.62w/2.1	8.02/0.2	13.93	2.05	48.73		13.84/1.2	44.44	4.90　61.26	4:24.83
8626		Michael	Smith	CAN	16.9.67	1		Götzis		26 May 96
	11.23/-0.6	7.72/0.6	16.94	1.97	48.69		14.77/-2.4	52.90	4.90　71.22	4:41.95
	(30)									
8617		Andrey	Kravchenko	BLR	4.1.86	1		Götzis		27 May 07
	10.86/0.2	7.90/0.9	13.89	2.15	47.46		14.05/-0.1	39.63	5.00　64.35	4:29.10
8605		Arthur	Abele	GER	30.7.86	1		Ratingen		26 Jun 16
	10.95/-0.6	748/0.4　1579		198	49.43		14.07/-0.94620	490	7189	4:24.12
8603		Dean	Macey	GBR	12.12.77	3	WCh	Edmonton		7 Aug 01
	10.72/-0.7	7.59/0.4	15.41	2.15	46.21		14.34/0.0	46.96	4.70　54.61	4:29.05
8583w		Jón Arnar	Magnússon	ISL	28.7.69	1	ECp-2	Reykjavik		5 Jul 98
	10.68/2.0	7.63/2.0	15.57	2.07	47.78		14.33W/5.2	44.53	5.00　64.16	4:41.60
8573						3		Götzis		31 May 98
	10.74/0.5	7.60/-0.2	16.03	2.03	47.66		14.24/0.7	47.82	5.10　59.77	4:46.43
8580		Kai	Kazmirek	GER	28.1.91	4	OG	Rio de Janeiro		18 Aug 16
	10.78/-0.1	7.69/-1.0　14.20		2.10	46.75		14.62/0.7	43.25	5.00　64.60	4:31.25
8574		Christian	Plaziat	FRA	28.10.63	1	EC	Split		29 Aug 90
	10.72/-0.6	7.77/1.1	14.19	2.10	47.10		13.98/0.7	44.36	5.00　54.72	4:27.83
8574		Aleksandr	Yurkov	UKR	21.7.75	4		Götzis		4 Jun 00
	10.69/0.9	7.93/1.8	15.26	2.03	49.74		14.56/-0.9	47.85	5.15　58.92	4:32.49
8571		Lev	Lobodin	RUS	1.4.69	3	EC	Budapest		20 Aug 98
	10.66w/2.2	7.42/0.2	15.67	2.03	48.65		13.97/0.9	46.55	5.20　56.55	4:30.27
8566		Sebastian	Chmara	POL	21.11.71	1		Alhama de Murcia		17 May 98
	10.97w/2.9	7.56/1.2	16.03	2.10	48.27		14.32/1.8	44.39	5.20　57.25	4:29.66
8561		Rico	Freimuth	GER	14.3.88	3	WCh	Beijing		29 Aug 15
	10.51/-0.4	7.51/0.5	15.50	1.95	47.82		13.91/-0.2	50.17	4.80　60.61	4:37.05
	(40)									
8558		Pascal	Behrenbruch	GER	19.1.85	1	EC	Helsinki		28 Jun 12
	10.93/0.8	7.15/-0.8	16.89	1.97	48.54		14.16/0.2	48.24	5.00　67.45	4:34.02

DECATHLON – 4x100m A-T

Mark	Wind	Name	Nat	Born	Pos	Meet	Venue	Date
8554		Attila Zsivoczky	HUN	29.4.77	5		Götzis	4 Jun 00
	10.64w/2.1 7.24/-1.0 15.72			2.18 48.13		14.87/-0.9 45.64 4.65 63.57		4:23.13
8548		Paul Meier	GER	27.7.71	3	WCh	Stuttgart	20 Aug 93
	10.57/0.9 7.57/1.1 15.45			2.15 47.73		14.63/0.0 45.72 4.60 61.22		4:32.05
8547		Igor Sobolevskiy	UKR	4.5.62	2	NC	Kiyev	22 Jun 84
	10.64/0.7 7.71/0.2 15.93			2.01 48.24		14.82/0.3 50.54 4.40 67.40		4:32.84
8538		Ilya Shkurenyov	RUS	11.1.91	4	WCh	Beijing	29 Sep 15
	11.01/-0.7 7.50/0.5 14.09			2.10 47.88		14.27/-0.2 44.53 5.20 60.99		4:24.98
8534		Siegfried Stark	GDR	12.6.55	1	OT	Halle	4 May 80
	11.10w 7.64 15.81			2.03 49.53		14.86w 47.20 5.00 68.70		4:27.7
8534w/8478		Antonio Peñalver	ESP	1.12.68	1		Alhama de Murcia	24 May 92
(7.19w/4.0)		10.76w/3.9 7.42W/6.2 16.50		2.12 49.50		14.32/0.8 47.38 5.00 59.32		4:39.94
8528		Aleksandr Pogorelov ¶	RUS	10.1.80	3	WCh	Berlin	20 Aug 09
	10.95/-0.3 7.49/-0.4 16.65			2.08 50.27		14.19/0.3 48.46 5.10 63.95		4:48.70
8526		Francisco Javier Benet	ESP	25.3.68	2		Alhama de Murcia	17 May 98
	10.72w/2.9 7.45/-1.2 14.57			1.92 48.10		13.83/1.8 46.12 5.00 65.37		4:26.81
8526		Kristjan Rahnu	EST	29.8.79	1		Arles	5 Jun 05
	10.52w/2.2 7.58/1.6 15.51			1.99 48.60		14.04w/3.1 50.81 4.95 60.71		4:52.18
(50)		100th man 8356, 200th 8187, 300th 8082, 400th 7990, 500th 7912						

MEN All-time

4 x 100 METRES RELAY

Mark		Nat	Team	Pos	Meet	Venue	Date
36.84 WR		JAM	N Carter 10.1, Frater 8.9, Blake 9.0, Bolt 8.8	1	OG	London (OS)	11 Aug 12
37.04 WR		JAM	N Carter, Frater, Blake, Bolt	1	WCh	Daegu	4 Sep 11
37.10 WR		JAM	N Carter, Frater, Bolt, Powell	1	OG	Beijing	22 Aug 08
37.27		JAM	Powell, Blake, Ashmeade, Bolt	1	OG	Rio de Janeiro	19 Aug 16
37.31		JAM	Mullings, Frater, Bolt, Powell	1	WCh	Berlin	22 Aug 09
37.36		JAM	Carter, Bailey Cole, Ashmeade, Bolt	1	WCh	Moskva	18 Aug 13
37.36		JAM	Carter, Powell, Ashmeade, Bolt	1	WCh	Beijing	29 Aug 15
37.38		USA	Demps, Patton, Kimmons, Gatlin	1h2	OG	London (OS)	10 Aug 12
37.38		USA	Rodgers, Gatlin, Gay, R.Bailey	1	W.Rly	Nassau	2 May 15
37.39		JAM	Carter, Frater, Blake, Bailey-Cole	1h1	OG	London (OS)	10 Aug 12
37.40 WR		USA	Marsh, Burrell, Mitchell, C Lewis	1	OG	Barcelona	8 Aug 92
37.40 WR		USA	Drummond, Cason, D Mitchell, L Burrell	1s1	WCh	Stuttgart	21 Aug 93
37.41		JAM	Carter, Powell, Dwyer, Ashmeade	1h2	WCh	Beijing	29 Aug 15
37.45		USA	Kimmons, Spearmon, Gay, Rodgers	1	WK	Zürich	19 Aug 10
37.48		USA	Drummond, Cason, D Mitchell, L Burrell	1	WCh	Stuttgart	22 Aug 93
37.50 WR		USA	Cason, Burrell, Mitchell, C Lewis	1	WCh	Tokyo	1 Sep 91
37.58		USA	'Red' Silmon, Rodgers, Salaam, Gatlin	1	Herc	Monaco	19 Jul 13
37.58		JAM	Livermore, Bailey-Cole, Ashmeade, Bolt	1	CG	Glasgow	2 Aug 14
37.59		USA	Drummond, Montgomery, B Lewis, Greene	1	WCh	Sevilla	29 Aug 99
37.59		USA	Conwright, Spearmon, Gay, Smoots	1	WCp	Athína	16 Sep 06
37.60		JPN	Yamagata, Iizuka, Kiryu, Cambridge	2	OG	Rio de Janeiro	19 Aug 16
37.61		USA	Drummond, Williams, B Lewis, Greene	1	OG	Sydney	30 Sep 00
37.61		USA	Kimmons, Gatlin, Gay, Bailey	1	Herc	Monaco	20 Jul 12
37.62		TTO	Brown, Burns, Callander, Thompson	2	WCh	Berlin	22 Aug 09
37.64		CAN	Haynes, A.Brown, Rodney, DeGrasse	3	OG	Rio de Janeiro	19 Aug 16
37.65		USA	Drummond, Williams, C Johnson, Greene	1	ISTAF	Berlin	1 Sep 00
37.65		USA	Rodgers, Coleman, Gay, Lawson	1h1	OG	Rio de Janeiro	18 Aug 16
37.66		USA	Silmon, Rodgers, Salaam, Gatlin	2	WCh	Moskva	18 Aug 13
37.67 WR		USA	Marsh, Burrell, Mitchell, C Lewis	1	WK	Zürich	7 Aug 91
37.68		JAM	Carter, Bailey Cole, Ashmeade, Bolt	2	W.Rly	Nassau	2 May 15
37.68		JPN	Yamagata, Iizuka, Kiryu, Cambridge	1h2	OG	Rio de Janeiro	18 Aug 16
		(31 performances by teams from 5 nations) Further bests by nations:					
37.73		GBR	Gardener, Campbell, Devonish, Chambers	2	WCh	Sevilla	29 Aug 99
37.79 WR	FRA	Morinière, Sangouma 8.90, Trouabal, Marie-Rose	1	EC	Split	1 Sep 90
37.82		CHN	Tang, Xie, Su, Zhang	2h1	OG	Rio de Janeiro	18 Aug 16
37.90		BRA	de Lima, Ribeiro, A da Silva, Cl da Silva	2	OG	Sydney	30 Sep 00
37.94		NGR	O Ezinwa, Adeniken, Obikwelu, D Ezinwa	1s2	WCh	Athína	9 Aug 97
(10)							
38.00		CUB	Simón, Lamela, Isasi, Aguilera	3	OG	Barcelona	8 Aug 92
38.01		ANT	Walsh, D.Bailey, Jarvis, Francis	4h2	WCh	Beijing	29 Aug 15
38.02		URS	Yevgenyev, Bryzgin, Muravyov, Krylov	2	WCh	Roma	6 Sep 87
38.02		GER	Reus, Unger, Kosenkow, Jakubczyk	1		Weinheim	27 Jul 12
38.12		GHA	Duah, Nkansah, Zakari, Tuffour	1s1	WCh	Athína	9 Aug 97
38.17		AUS	Henderson, Jackson, Brimacombe, Marsh	1s2	WCh	Göteborg	12 Aug 95
38.17		ITA	Donati, Collio, Di Gregorio, Checcucci	2	EC	Barcelona	1 Aug 10
38.29		NED	Mariano, Martina, Codrington, van Luijk	3h1	OG	London (OS)	10 Aug 12
38.30		TUR	Safer, Harvey, Barnes, Guliyev	4h1	OG	Rio de Janeiro	18 Aug 16
38.31		POL	Masztak, Kuc, Kubaczyk, Krynski	6h2	OG	London (OS)	10 Aug 12
(20)							

286 4x100m – 4x200m – 4x400m RELAY A-T

Mark	Wind	Name	Nat	Born	Pos	Meet	Venue	Date
38.35		RSA Bruintjies, Magakwe, Titi, Simbine			4	CG	Glasgow	2 Aug 14
38.41		SKN Lestrod, Rogers, Adams, Lawrence			6h1	OG	London (OS)	10 Aug 12
38.45		AHO Goeloe, Raffaela, Duzant, Martina			6	WCh	Helsinki	13 Aug 05
38.46		URS/RUS Zharov, Krylov, Fatun, Goremykin			4	EC	Split	1 Sep 90
38.46		ESP Viles, Ruiz, Hortelano, Rodríguez			4h1	WCh	Moskva	18 Aug 13
38.47		HKG Tang Yik Chun, Lai Chun Ho, Ng Ka Fung, Tsui Chi Ho					Taipei	26 May 12
38.52		BAH Griffith, Fraser, Hart, T.Smith			3h1	CG	Glasgow	1 Aug 14
38.52		DOM De Oloe, Andujar, Del Carmen, Martinez			1	IbAm	Rio de Janeiro	16 May 16
38.53		UKR Rurak, Osovich, Kramarenko, Dologodin			1	ECp	Madrid	1 Jun 96
38.54		SUI Mancini, Schenkel, Somasundaran, Wilson			2h1	EC	Zürich	18 Aug 14
38.55A		BAR Cadogan, Gittens, Deshong, Ellis			3	NACAC	San José, CRC	9 Aug 15
38.60		CIV Meité, Douhou, Sonan, N'Dri (30)			3s1	WCh	Edmonton	12 Aug 01

Multi-nation team

| 37.46 | | Racers TC Bailey/ANT, Blake JAM, Forsythe JAM, Bolt JAM | | | 1 | LGP | London (CP) | 25 Jul 09 |

One man disqualified for drugs

| 37.04 | | USA Kimmons 10.1, Gatlin 8.9, Gay ¶ 9.0, Bailey 9.0 | | | (2) | OG | London (OS) | 11 Aug 12 |
| 37.91 | | NGR Asonze ¶, Obikwelu, Effiong, Aliu | | | (3) | WCh | Sevilla | 29 Aug 99 |

4 x 200 METRES RELAY

1:18.63	WR	JAM Ashmeade 20.5, Weir 19.2, J Brown 19.6, Y Blake 19.4	1	WRly	Nassau	24 May 14
1:18.68	WR	USA - Santa Monica Track Cluc				
		Marsh 20.0, Burrell 19.6, Heard 19.7, C Lewis 19.4	1	MSR	Walnut	17 Apr 94
1:19.10		World All-Stars	2	MSR	Walnut	17 Apr 94
		Drummond USA 20.4, Mitchell USA 19.3, Bridgewater USA 20.3, Regis GBR 19.1				
1:19.11	WR	Santa Monica TC/USA M.Marsh, L Burrell, Heard, C Lewis	1	Penn	Philadelphia	25 Apr 92
1:19.16		USA Red Team Crawford, Clay, Patton, Gatlin	1	PennR	Philadelphia	26 Apr 03
1:19.20		CAN Smellie, Rodney, DeGrasse, A.Brown	1	FlaR	Gainesville	2 Apr 16
1:19.38	WR	Santa Monica TC/USA Everett, Burrell, Heard, C Lewis	1	R-W	Koblenz	23 Aug 89
1:19.39		USA Blue Drummond, Crawford, B Williams, Greene	1	PennR	Philadelphia	28 Apr 01
1:19.45		Santa Monica TC/USA DeLoach, Burrell, C.Lewis, Heard	1	Penn	Philadelphia	27 Apr 91
1:19.47		Nike Int./USA Brokenburr, A Harrison, Greene, M Johnson	1	Penn	Philadelphia	24 Apr 99

Best non-US nations

1:20.51		SKN A Adams, L Roland, BJ Lawrence, A Clarke	2	WRly	Nassau	24 May 14
1:20.66		FRA Lemaitre, Fonsat, Bassaw, Romain	3	WRly	Nassau	25 May 14
1:21.10		ITA Tilli, Simionato, Bongiorno, Mennea	1		Cagliari	29 Sep 83
1:21.22		POL Tulin, Balcerzak, Pilarczyk, Urbas	2		Gdansk	14 Jul 01
1:21.29		GBR Adam, Mafe, Christie, Regis	1	vURS	Birmingham	23 Jun 89

4 x 400 METRES RELAY

2:54.29	WR	USA Valmon 44.5, Watts 43.6, Reynolds 43.23, Johnson 42.94	1	WCh	Stuttgart	22 Aug 93
2:55.39		USA Merritt 44.4, Taylor 43.7, Neville 44.16, Wariner 43.18	1	OG	Beijing	23 Aug 08
2:55.56		USA Merritt 44.4, Taylor 43.7, Williamson 44.32, Wariner 44.10	1	WCh	Osaka	2 Sep 07
2:55.74	WR	USA Valmon 44.6, Watts 43.00, M Johnson 44.73, S Lewis 43.41	1	OG	Barcelona	8 Aug 92
2:55.91		USA O Harris 44.5, Brew 43.6, Wariner 43.98, Williamson 43.83	1	OG	Athína	28 Aug 04
2:55.99		USA L Smith 44.62, A Harrison 43.84, Mills 43.66, Maybank 43.87	1	OG	Atlanta	3 Aug 96
2:56.16A	WR	USA Matthews 45.0, Freeman 43.2, James 43.9, Evans 44.1	1	OG	Ciud. México	20 Oct 68
2:56.16	WR	USA Everett 43.79, S Lewis 43.69, Robinzine 44.74, Reynolds 43.94	1	OG	Seoul	1 Oct 88
2:56.60		GBR I Thomas 44.92, Baulch 44.19, Richardson 43.62, Black 43.87	2	OG	Atlanta	3 Aug 96
2:56.65		GBR Thomas 44.8, Black 44.2, Baulch 44.08, Richardson 43.57	2	WCh	Athína	10 Aug 97
2:56.72		BAH Brown 44.9, Pinder 43.5, Mathieu 44.25, Miller 44.01	1	OG	London (OS)	10 Aug 12
2:56.75		JAM McDonald 44.5, Haughton 44.4, McFarlane 44.37, Clarke 43.51	3	WCh	Athína	10 Aug 97
2:56.91		USA Rock 44.7, Brew 44.3, Williamson 44.40, Wariner 43.49	1	WCh	Helsinki	14 Aug 05
2:57.05		USA Nellum 45.2, Mance 43.5, McQuay 43.41, Taylor 44.85	2	OG	London (OS)	10 Aug 12
2:57.25		USA Verburg 44.8, McQuay 44.1, C Taylor 44.4, L Merritt 43.8	1	WRly	Nassau	25 May 14
2:57.29		USA Everett 45.1, Haley 44.0, McKay 44.20, Reynolds 44.00	1	WCh	Roma	6 Sep 87
2:57.30		USA Hall 45.3, McQuay 43.2, Roberts 44.79, Merritt 43.97	1	OG	Rio de Janeiro	20 Aug 16
2:57.32		USA Ramsey 44.9, Mills 44.6, Reynolds 43.74, Johnson 44.11	1	WCh	Göteborg	13 Aug 95
2:57.32		BAH McKinney 44.9, Moncur 44.6, A Williams 44.43, Brown 43.42	2	WCh	Helsinki	14 Aug 05
2:57.53		GBR Black 44.7, Redmond 44.0, Regis 44.22, Akabusi 44.59	1	WCh	Tokyo	1 Sep 91
2:57.57		USA Valmon 44.9, Watts 43.4, D.Everett 44.31, Pettigrew 44.93	2	WCh	Tokyo	1 Sep 91
2:57.59		BAH Williams 45.0, Pinder 43.8, C Brown 44.2, Mathieu 44.6	2	WRly	Nassau	25 May 14
2:57.82		USA Verburg 45.0, McQuay 45.4, Nellum 44.38, Merritt 44.18	1	WCh	Beijing	30 Aug 15
2:57.86		USA Taylor 45.4, Wariner 43.6, Clement 44.72, Merritt 44.16	1	WCh	Berlin	23 Aug 09
2:57.87		USA L Smith 44.59, Rouser 44.33, Mills 44.32, Maybank 44.63	1s2	OG	Atlanta	2 Aug 96
2:57.91		USA Nix 45.59, Armstead 43.97, Babers 43.75, McKay 44.60	1	OG	Los Angeles	11 Aug 84
2:57.97		JAM McDonald, Haughton McFarlane, D Clarke	1	PAm	Winnipeg	30 Jul 99
2:58.00		POL Rysiukiewicz 45.6, Czubak 44.2, Haczek 44.0, Mackowiak 44.2	2	GWG	Uniondale, NY	22 Jul 98
2:58.03		BAH Bain 45.0, Mathieu 44.1, A Williams 44.02, Brown 44.05	2	OG	Beijing	23 Aug 08
2:58.07		JAM Ayre 44.9, Simpson 44.4, Spence 44.48, Clarke 43.81	3	WCh	Helsinki	14 Aug 05

(30/5 plus 7 times for teams that contained an athlete who was subsequently banned for drugs abuse

4 x 400m – 4 x 800m – 4x1500m RELAY A-T

Mark	Wind	Nat	Name	Born Pos	Meet	Venue	Date
2:58.20		TTO	Quow 44.8, L Gordon 44.1, Lendore 44.85, Cedenio 44.47	2	WCh	Beijing	30 Aug 15
2:58.52		BEL	Watrin 46.0, J.Borlée 44.1, D.Borlée 44.71, K.Borlée 43.67	4	OG	Rio de Janeiro	20 Aug 16
2:58.56		BRA	Cl. da Silva 44.6, A dos Santos 45.1, de Araújo 45.0, Parrela 43.9	2	PAm	Winnipeg	30 Jul 99
2:58.68		NGR	Chukwu 45.18, Monye 44.49, Bada 44.70, Udo-Obong 44.31	1	OG	Sydney	30 Sep 00
2:58.96		FRA	Djhone 45.4, Keita 44.7, Diagana 44.69, Raquil 44.15	2	WCh	Saint-Denis	31 Aug 03
(10)							
2:59.06		BOT	Makwala 44.9, Sibanda 43.9, Nkobolo 44.94, Maotoanong 45.28	5 OG		Rio de Janeiro	20 Aug 16
2:59.13		CUB	Martínez 45.6, Herrera 44.38, Tellez 44.81, Hernández 44.34	1h2 OG		Barcelona	7 Aug 92
2:59.21		RSA	Pistorius 45.58, Mogawane 43.97, de Beer 44.46, Victor 45.20	3h1 WCh		Daegu	1 Sep 11
2:59.38		RUS	Dyldin 45.1, Ivashko 44.1, Uglov 45.28, Krasnov 44.83	2	EC	Zürich	17 Aug 14
2:59.63		KEN	D Kitur 45.4, S Kitur 45.13, Kipkemboi 44.76, Kemboi 44.34	3h2 OG		Barcelona	7 Aug 92
2:59.70		AUS	Frayne 45.38, Clark 43.86, Minihan 45.07, Mitchell 45.39	4	OG	Los Angeles	11 Aug 84
2:59.86		GDR	Möller 45.8, Schersing 44.8, Carlowitz 45.3, Schönlebe 44.1	1	vURS	Erfurt	23 Jun 85
2:59.95		YUG	Jovkovic, Djurovic, Macev, Brankovic 44.3	2h3 WCh		Tokyo	31 Aug 91
2:59.96		FRG	Dobeleit 45.7, Henrich 44.3, Itt 45.12, Schmid 44.93	4	WCh	Roma	6 Sep 87
3:00.15		DOM	Cuesta 45.4, Soriano 43.8, J.Santos 46.58, L.Santos 44.36	6h2 WCh		Beijing	29 Aug 15
(20)							
3:00.64		SEN	Diarra 46.53, Dia 44.94, Ndiaye 44.70, Faye 44.47	4	OG	Atlanta	3 Aug 96
3:00.76		JPN	Karube 45.88, Ito 44.86, Osakada 45.08, Omori 44.94	5	OG	Atlanta	3 Aug 96
3:00.79		ZIM	Chiwira 46.2, Mukomana 44.6, Ngidhi 45.79, Harnden 44.20	2h3 WCh		Athína	9 Aug 97
3:00.82A		VEN	A Ramírez 45.7, Aguilar 45.3, Acevedo 44.7, Longart 45.2	3	PAm	Guadalajara	28 Oct 11
3:00.91		IND	Kunhu, Anas, Dharun, Rajiv	1		Bengaluru	10 Jun 16
3:01.12		FIN	Lönnqvist 46.7, Salin 45.1, Karttunen 44.8, Kukkoaho 44.5	6	OG	München	10 Sep 72
3:01.16 A		COL	Zambrano, Lemos, Palomeque, Perlaza	1		Medellín	10 Jul 16
3:01.26		IRL	Gregan 46.1, Murphy 45.2, Barr 45.05, English 44.96	8h2 WCh		Beijing	29 Aug 15
3:01.37		ITA	Bongiorni 46.2, Zuliani 45.0, Petrella 45.3, Ribaud 44.9	4	EC	Stuttgart	31 Aug 86
3:01.42		ESP	I Rodríguez 46.0, Canal 44.1, Andrés 45.88, Reina 45.48	4h1 WCh		Edmonton	11 Aug 01
(30)							

Including subsequently banned athlete

Mark	Nat	Name	Pos	Meet	Venue	Date
2:54.20(WR)	USA	Young 44.3, Pettigrew ¶ 43.2, Washington 43.5, Johnson 43.2 (1)		GWG	Uniondale, NY	22 Jul 98
2:56.35	USA	A Harrison 44.36, Pettigrew 44.17, C Harrison 43.53, Johnson 44.29 (1)		OG	Sydney	30 Sep 00
2:56.45	USA	J Davis 45.2, Pettigrew 43.9, Taylor 43.92, M Johnson 43.49 (1)		WCh	Sevilla	29 Aug 99
2:56.47	USA	Young 44.6, Pettigrew 43.1, Jones 44.80, Washington 44.80 (1)		WCh	Athína	10 Aug 97
2:56.60	USA Red	Taylor 45.0, Pettigrew 44.2, Washington 43.7, Johnson 43.7 (1)		PennR	Philadelphia	29 Apr 00
2:57.54	USA	Byrd 45.9, Pettigrew 43.9, Brew 44.03, Taylor 43.71	1	WCh	Edmonton	12 Aug 01
2:58.06	RUS	Dyldin 45.5, Frolov 44.6, Kokorin 44.34, Alekseyev 43.56	3	OG	Beijing	23 Aug 08

4 x 800 METRES RELAY

Mark	Nat	Name	Pos	Meet	Venue	Date
7:02.43	KEN	Mutua 1:46.73, Yiampoy 1:44.38, Kombich 1:45.92, Bungei 1:45.40	1	VD	Bruxelles	25 Aug 06
7:02.82	USA		2	VD	Bruxelles	25 Aug 06
		J Harris 1:47.05, Robinson 1:44.03, Burley 1:46.05, Krummenacker 1:45.69				
7:03.89 WR	GBR	Elliott 1:49.14, Cook 1:46.20, Cram 1:44.54, Coe 1:44.01	1		London (CP)	30 Aug 82
7:04.70	RSA	van Oudtshoorn 1:46.9, Sepeng 1:45.2, Kotze 1:48.3, J Botha 1:44.3	1		Stuttgart	6 Jun 99
7:06.66	QAT	Sultan 1:45.81, Al-Badri 1:46.71, Suleiman 1:45.89, Ali Kamal 1:48.25	4	VD	Bruxelles	25 Aug 06
7:07.40	URS	Masunov, Kostetskiy, Matvetev, Kalinkin	1		Moskva	5 Aug 84
7:08.5 WR	FRG	Kinder 1:46.9, Adams 1:47.5, Bogatzki 1:47.9, Kemper 1:46.2	1		Wiesbaden	13 Aug 66
7:08.89	POL	Konieczny 1:48.9, Krawczyk 1:49.1, Lewandowski 1:45.9, Kszczot 1:44.8	2 WRly		Nassau	24 May 14

4 x 1500 METRES RELAY

Mark	Nat	Name	Pos	Meet	Venue	Date
14:22.22 WR	KEN	C Cheboi 3:38.5, S Kiplagat 3:32.4, Magut 3:39.0, A Kiprop 3:32.3	1 WRly		Nassau	25 May 14
14:36.23 WR	KEN	W Biwott 3:38.5, Gathimba 3:39.5, G Rono 3:41.4, Choge 3:36.9	1	VD	Bruxelles	4 Sep 09
14:38.8 WR	FRG	Wessinghage 3:38.8, Hudak 3:39.1, Lederer 3:44.6, Fleschen 3:36.3	1		Köln	16 Aug 77
14:40.4 WR	NZL	Polhill 3:42.9, Walker 3:40.4, Dixon 3:41.2, Quax 3:35.9	1		Oslo	22 Aug 73
14:40.80	USA	Casey 3:38.2, Torrence 3:36.6, Leer 3:39.3, Manzano 3:46.7	2 WRly		Nassau	25 May 14
14:41.22	ETH	Gebremedhin 3:39.9, Fida 3:37.5, Z Alemayehu 3:46.5, Wote 3:37.3	3 WRly		Nassau	25 May 14
14:45.63	URS	Kalutskiy, Yakovlev, Legeda, Lotarev	1		Leningrad	4 Aug 85
14:46.04	AUS	Gregson 3:39.1, McEntee 3:44.9, Birmingham 3:38.3, Williamsz 3:43.7	4 WRly		Nassau	25 May 14
14:46.16		Larios, GER Jiménez 3:40.9, Pancorbo 3:41.2, A García 3:43.9, Viciosa 3:40.2	1		Madrid	5 Sep 97
14:48.2	FRA	Bégouin 3:44.5, Lequement 44.3, Philippe 3:42.2, Dien 3:37.2	2		Bourges	23 Jun 79
Mixed Team:		14:44.31 Ali BRN, Birgen KEN, N Kemboi KEN, Campbell IRL	2 VD		Bruxelles	4 Sep 09

4 x 1 MILE RELAY

Mark	Nat	Name	Pos	Venue	Date
15:49.08	IRL	Coghlan 4:00.2, O'Sullivan 3:55.3, O'Mara 3:56.6, Flynn 3:56.98	1	Dublin	17 Aug 85
15:59.57	NZL	Rogers 3:57.2, Bowden 4:02.5, Gilchrist 4:02.8, Walker 3:57.07	1	Auckland	2 Mar 83

4 x 110m/120y HURDLES

Mark	Nat	Name	Pos	Meet	Venue	Date
52.94	USA Blue	Richardson, Harris, Merritt, Oliver	1	DrakeR	Des Moines	25 Apr 15
53.08	All Stars	Riley JAM, R Brathwaite BAR, Parchment JAM, Swift BAR	2	DrakeR	Des Moines	25 Apr 15
53.31y	USA Red	Oliver, Herring, Brown, Merritt	1	PennR	Philadelphia	25 Apr 08
53.36	USA	Bramlett, Moore, Payne, Merritt	1	DNG	Stockholm	7 Aug 07
53.62	USA (ACC All-Stars)	A Johnson, Reese, Brown, Ross	1		Clemson	16 May 98

3000m, 5000m, 10,000m WALK A-T

Mark	Wind	Name		Nat	Born	Pos	Meet	Venue	Date

3000 METRES TRACK WALK

Mark		Name		Nat	Born	Pos	Meet	Venue	Date
10:47.11		Giovanni	De Benedictis	ITA	8.1.68	1		S.Giovanni Valdarno	19 May 90
10:52.44+		Yohann	Diniz	FRA	1.1.78	1	in 5k	Villeneuve d'Ascq	27 Jun 08
10:56.22		Andrew	Jachno	AUS	13.4.62	1		Melbourne	7 Feb 91
10:56.23		Dane	Bird-Smith	AUS	15.7.92	1		Cork	8 Jul 14
10:56.34+		Roman	Mrázek	SVK	21.1.62	1	in 5k	Bratislava	14 Jun 89
10:58.16		Kevin	Campion	FRA	23.5.88	2		Cork	8 Jul 14
10:58.47		Alex	Wright	IRL	19.12.90	3		Cork	8 Jul 14
10:59.04		Luke	Adams	AUS	22.10.76	1		Cork	3 Jul 10
11:00.2+		Jozef	Pribilinec	SVK	6.7.60	1	in 10k	Banská Bystrica	30 Aug 85
11:00.50+		Francisco Javier	Fernández ¶	ESP	6.3.77	1	in 5k	Villeneuve d'Ascq	8 Jun 07

Indoors

10:31.42		Andreas	Erm	GER	12.3.76	1		Halle	4 Feb 01
10:50.0		Denis	Nizhegorodov	RUS	26.7.80	1		Saransk	4 Dec 06
10:53+		Mikhail	Shchennikov	RUS	24.12.67	1	in 5k	Moskva	14 Feb 95
10:53.3		Igor	Yerokhin	RUS	4.9.85	2		Saransk	4 Dec 06
10:54.61		Carlo	Mattioli	ITA	23.10.54	1		Milano	6 Feb 80
10:56.77+		Ivano	Brugnetti	ITA	1.9.76	1	in 5k	Torino	21 Feb 09
10:56.88		Reima	Salonen	FIN	19.11.55	1		Turku	5 Feb 84
10:57.32		Matej	Tóth	SVK	10.2.83	1		Wien	12 Feb 11

5000 METRES TRACK WALK

Mark		Name		Nat	Born	Pos	Meet	Venue	Date
18:05.49		Hatem	Ghoula	TUN	7.6.73	1		Tunis	1 May 97
18:17.22		Robert	Korzeniowski	POL	30.7.68	1		Reims	3 Jul 92
18:18.01		Yohann	Diniz	FRA	1.1.78	1		Villeneuve d'Ascq	27 Jun 08
18:27.34		Francisco Javier	Fernández ¶	ESP	6.3.77	1		Villeneuve d'Ascq	8 Jun 07
18:28.80		Roman	Mrázek	SVK	21.1.62	1	PTS	Bratislava	14 Jun 89
18:30.43		Maurizio	Damilano	ITA	6.4.57	1		Caserta	11 Jun 92

Indoors

18:07.08		Mikhail	Shchennikov	RUS	24.12.67	1		Moskva	14 Feb 95
18:08.86		Ivano	Brugnetti	ITA	1.9.76	1	NC	Ancona	17 Feb 07
18:11.41		Ronald	Weigel	GDR	8.8.59	1mx		Wien	13 Feb 88
18:11.8		Valeriy	Borchin ¶	RUS	11.9.86	1		Saransk	30 Dec 10
18:15.25		Grigoriy	Kornev	RUS	14.3.61	1		Moskva	7 Feb 92
18:15.54		Andrey	Ruzavin	RUS	28.3.86	1		Samara	30 Jan 14
18:16.54 ?		Frants	Kostyukevich	BLR	4.4.63	2	NC	Gomel	4 Feb 89
18:16.76		Yohann	Diniz	FRA	1.1.78	1		Reims	7 Dec 14
18:19.97		Giovanni	De Benedictis	ITA	8.1.68	1	EI	Genova	28 Feb 92
18:21.76		Ruslan	Dmytrenko	UKR	22.3.86	2		Samara	30 Jan 14
18:22.25		Andreas	Erm	GER	12.3.76	1	NC	Dortmund	25 Feb 01
18:23.18		Rishat	Shafikov	RUS	23.1.70	1		Samara	1 Mar 97
18:24.13		Francisco Javier	Fernández ¶	ESP	6.3.77	1		Belfast	17 Feb 07
18:27.15		Alessandro	Gandellini	ITA	30.4.73	1	NC	Genova	12 Feb 00
18:27.80		Jozef	Pribilinec	SVK	6.7.60	2	WI	Indianapolis	7 Mar 87
18:27.95		Stefan	Johansson	SWE	11.4.67	3	EI	Genova	28 Feb 92
18:28.54		Igor	Yerokhin	RUS	4.9.85	1		Samara	31 Jan 13
Drugs dq: 18:17.13	Vladimir	Kanaykin ¶		RUS	21.3.85	(2)	Winter	Moskva	5 Feb 12
18:26.82		Sergey	Bakulin ¶	RUS	13.11.86	(3)	Winter	Moskva	5 Feb 12

10,000 METRES TRACK WALK

Mark		Name		Nat	Born	Pos	Meet	Venue	Date
37:53.09		Francisco Javier	Fernández ¶	ESP	6.3.77	1	NC	Santa Cruz de Tenerife	27 Jul 08
37:58.6		Ivano	Brugnetti	ITA	1.9.76	1		Sesto San Gioavnni	23 Jul 05
38:01.49		Eiki	Takahashi	JPN	19.11.92	1		Isahaya	13 Dec 15
38:02.60		Jozef	Pribilinec	SVK	6.7.60	1		Banská Bystrica	30 Aug 85
38:06.6		David	Smith	AUS	24.7.55	1		Sydney	25 Sep 86
38:06.28		Miguel Ángel	López	ESP	3.7.88	1	NC	Gijón	24 Jul 16
38:08.13		Yohann	Diniz	FRA	1.1.78	1	NC	Reims	12 Jul 14
38:10.23		Yusuke	Suzuki	JPN	2.1.88	1		Abashiri	16 Jul 15
38:12.13		Ronald	Weigel	GDR	8.8.59	1		Potsdam	10 May 86
38:16.76		Daisuke	Matsunaga (10)	JPN	24.3.95	1		Yokohama	21 May 16
38:18.0+		Valdas	Kazlauskas	LTU	23.2.58	1		Moskva	18 Sep 83
38:20.0		Moacir	Zimmermann	BRA	30.12.83	1		Blumenau	7 Jun 08
38:23.73			Wang Zhen	CHN	24.8.91	1		Genova	8 Feb 15
38:24 0+		Bernardo	Segura	MEX	11.2.70	1	SGP	Fana	7 May 94
38:24.31		Hatem	Ghoula	TUN	7.6.73	1		Tunis	30 May 98
38:26.4		Daniel	García	MEX	28.10.71	1		Sdr Omme	17 May 97
38:26.53		Robert	Korzeniowski	POL	30.7.68	1		Riga	31 May 02
38:27.57		Robert	Heffernan	IRL	20.2.78	1	NC	Dublin	20 Jul 08
38:32.0		Erik	Tysse	NOR	4.12.80	1	NC	Bergen (Fana)	13 Jun 08
38:37.02		Kevin	Campion	FRA	23.5.88	1	NC	Paris (C)	13 Jul 13
Indoors: 38:31.4	Werner	Heyer		GDR	14.11.56	1		Berlin	12 Jan 80

20 KILOMETRES WALK

Mark	Wind	Name		Nat	Born	Pos	Meet	Venue	Date
1:16:36wr		Yusuke	Suzuki	JPN	2.1.88	1	AsiC	Nomi	15 Mar 15
1:16:43		Sergey	Morozov ¶	RUS	21.3.88	1	NC	Saransk	8 Jun 08
1:17:02		Yohann	Diniz	FRA	1.1.78	1	NC	Arles	8 Mar 15
1:17:16wr		Vladimir	Kanaykin ¶	RUS	21.3.85	1	RWC	Saransk	29 Sep 07
1:17:21wr		Jefferson	Pérez	ECU	1.7.74	1	WCh	Saint-Denis	23 Aug 03
1:17:22wr		Francisco Javier	Fernández ¶	ESP	6.3.77	1		Turku	28 Apr 02
1:17:23		Vladimir	Stankin	RUS	2.1.74	1	NC-w	Adler	8 Feb 04
1:17:24			Diniz			1		Lugano	15 Mar 15
1:17:25.6t		Bernardo	Segura	MEX	11.2.70	1	SGP	Bergen (Fana)	7 May 94
1:17:30		Alex	Schwazer ¶	ITA	26.12.84	1		Lugano	18 Mar 12
1:17:33		Nathan	Deakes (10)	AUS	17.8.77	1		Cixi	23 Apr 05
1:17:36			Kanaykin			1	NC	Cheboksary	17 Jun 07
1:17:36			Wang Zhen	CHN	24.8.91	1		Taicang	30 Mar 12
1:17:38		Valeriy	Borchin ¶	RUS	11.9.86	1	NC-w	Adler	28 Feb 09
1:17:40			Chen Ding	CHN	5.8.92	2		Taicang	30 Mar 12
1:17:41			Zhu Hongjun	CHN	18.8.83	2		Cixi	23 Apr 05
1:17:43			Diniz			2		Lugano	18 Mar 12
1:17:46		Julio	Martínez	GUA	27.9.73	1		Eisenhüttenstadt	8 May 99
1:17:46		Roman	Rasskazov	RUS	28.4.79	1	NC	Moskva	19 May 00
1:17:52			Fernández			1		La Coruña	4 Jun 05
1:17:53			Cui Zhide	CHN	11.1.83	3		Cixi	23 Apr 05
1:17:55			Borchin			1	NC-w	Adler	23 Feb 08
1:17:56		Alejandro	López	MEX	9.2.75	2		Eisenhüttenstadt	8 May 99
1:18:00			Fernández			2	WCh	Saint-Denis	23 Aug 03
1:18:00			Wang Zhen			1		La Coruña	6 Jun 15
1:18:03		Eiki	Takahashi	JPN	19.11.92	1	NC	Kobe	15 Feb 15
1:18:03.3twr			Bo Lingtang (20)	CHN	12.8.70	1	NC	Beijing	7 Apr 94
1:18:05		Dmitriy	Yesipchuk	RUS	17.11.74	1	NC-w	Adler	4 Mar 01
1:18:06		Viktor	Burayev ¶	RUS	23.8.82	2	NC-w	Adler	4 Mar 01
1:18:06		Vladimir (30/23)	Parvatkin	RUS	10.10.84	1	NC-w	Adler	12 Mar 05
1:18:07			Li Gaobo	CHN	4.5.89	4		Cixi	23 Apr 05
1:18:12		Artur	Meleshkevich	BLR	11.4.75	1		Brest	10 Mar 01
1:18:13wr		Pavol	Blazek	SVK	9.7.58	1		Hildesheim	16 Sep 90
1:18:13			Wang Hao	CHN	16.8.89	1	NG	Jinan	22 Oct 09
1:18:14		Mikhail	Khmelnitskiy	BLR	24.7.69	1	NC	Soligorsk	13 May 00
1:18:14		Noé	Hernández	MEX	15.3.78	4	WCh	Saint-Denis	23 Aug 03
1:18:16		Vladimir (30)	Andreyev	RUS	7.9.66	2	NC	Moskva	19 May 00
1:18:17		Ilya	Markov	RUS	19.6.72	2	NC-w	Adler	12 Mar 05
1:18:18		Yevgeniy	Misyulya	BLR	13.3.64	1		Eisenhüttenstadt	11 May 96
1:18:18		Sergey	Bakulin ¶	RUS	13.11.86	2	NC-w	Adler	23 Feb 08
1:18:20wr		Andrey	Perlov	RUS	12.12.61	1	NC	Moskva	26 May 90
1:18:20		Denis	Nizhegorodov	RUS	26.7.80	3	NC-w	Adler	4 Mar 01
1:18:22		Robert	Korzeniowski	POL	30.7.68	1		Hildesheim	9 Jul 00
1:18:23		Andrey	Makarov	BLR	2.1.71	2	NC	Soligorsk	13 May 00
1:18:25		Andrey	Krivov	RUS	14.11.85	3	NC-w	Sochi	18 Feb 12
1:18:25		Erick	Barrondo	GUA	14.6.91	3		Lugano	18 Mar 12
1:18:27		Daniel (40)	García	MEX	28.10.71	2	WCp	Podebrady	19 Apr 97
1:18:27			Xing Shucai	CHN	4.8.84	5		Cixi	23 Apr 05
1:18:28		Pyotr	Trofimov	RUS	28.11.83	1	NC-w	Sochi	23 Feb 13
1:18:30			Yu Chaohong	CHN	12.12.76	6		Cixi	23 Apr 05
1:18:31			Han Yucheng	CHN	16.12.78	7		Cixi	23 Apr 05
1:18:32			Li Zewen	CHN	5.12.73	4	WCp	Podebrady	19 Apr 97
1:18:33			Liu Yunfeng ¶	CHN	3.8.79	8		Cixi	23 Apr 05
1:18:34		Eder	Sánchez	MEX	21.5.86	3	WCp	Cheboksary	10 May 08
1:18:35.2t		Stefan	Johansson	SWE	11.4.67	1	SGP	Bergen (Fana)	15 May 92
1:18:36		Mikhail	Shchennikov	RUS	24.12.67	1	NC	Sochi	20 Apr 96
1:18:37		Aleksandr	Pershin	RUS	4.9.68	2	NC	Moskva	26 May 90
1:18:37		Ruslan	Shafikov	RUS	27.6.75	1	NC-w23	Adler	11 Feb 95
1:18:37		Ruslan (52)	Dmytrenko	UKR	22.3.86	1	WCp	Taicang	4 May 14

100th man 1:19:22, 200th 1:20:19, 300th 1:21:02.5, 400th 1:21:43, 500th 1:22:09

Probable short course

| 1:18:33 | | Mikhail | Shchennikov | RUS | 24.12.67 | 1 | 4-N | Livorno | 10 Jul 93 |

Drugs disqualification

1:16:53		Vladimir	Kanaykin ¶	RUS	21.3.85	(2)	NC	Saransk	8 Jun 08
1:17:47		Andrey	Ruzavin ¶	RUS	28.3.86	(1)	NC-w	Sochi	18 Feb 12
1:17:52			Morozov ¶			(2)	NC-w	Sochi	18 Feb 12

30 – 35 – 50 KILOMETRES WALK A-T

Mark	Wind	Name		Nat	Born	Pos	Meet	Venue	Date
1:18:29		Stanislav	Yemelyanov ¶	RUS	23.10.90	(4)	NC-w	Sochi	18 Feb 12

30 KILOMETRES WALK

Mark	Name		Nat	Born	Pos	Meet	Venue	Date
2:01:13+	Vladimir	Kanaykin ¶	RUS	21.3.85	1	in 35k	Adler	19 Feb 06
2:01:44.1t	Maurizio	Damilano	ITA	6.4.57	1		Cuneo	3 Oct 92
2:01:47+		Kanaykin			1	in 35k	Adler	13 Mar 05
2:02:27+		Kanaykin			1	in 35k	Adler	8 Feb 04
2:02:41	Andrey	Perlov	RUS	12.12.61	1	NC-w	Sochi	19 Feb 89
2:02:45	Yevgeniy	Misyulya	BLR	13.3.64	1		Mogilyov	28 Apr 91
2:03:06	Daniel	Bautista	MEX	4.8.52	1		Cherkassy	27 Apr 80
2:03:50+	Vladimir	Parvatkin	RUS	10.10.84	2	in 35k	Adler	19 Feb 06
2:03:56.5t	Thierry	Toutain	FRA	14.2.62	1		Héricourt	24 Mar 91
2:04:00	Aleksandr	Potashov	BLR	12.3.62	1		Adler	14 Feb 93
2:04:24	Valeriy	Spitsyn	RUS	5.12.65	1	NC-w	Sochi	22 Feb 92
2:04:30	Vitaliy	Matsko (10)	RUS	8.6.60	2	NC-w	Sochi	19 Feb 89
2:04:49+	Semyon	Lovkin	RUS	14.7.77	1=	in 35k	Adler	1 Mar 03
2:04:49+	Stepan	Yudin	RUS	3.4.80	1=	in 35k	Adler	1 Mar 03
2:04:50+	Sergey	Kirdyapkin ¶	RUS	16.1.80	2	in 35k	Adler	13 Mar 05
2:04:55.5t	Guillaume	Leblanc	CAN	14.4.62	1		Sept-Iles	16 Jun 90
2:05:01	Sergey	Katureyev	RUS	29.9.67	2	NC-w	Sochi	22 Feb 92
2:05:05	Pyotr	Pochenchuk	UKR	26.7.54	2		Cherkassy	27 Apr 80
2:05:06	Nathan	Deakes	AUS	17.8.77	1	NC	Hobart	27 Aug 06
2:05:08+	Denis	Nizhegorodov	RUS	26.7.80	3	in 35k	Adler	19 Feb 06
2:05:09	Mikhail	Shchennikov	RUS	24.12.67	1	NC-w	Adler	11 Feb 96
2:05:12	Valeriy	Suntsov (20)	RUS	10.7.55	3		Cherkassy	27 Apr 80

35 KILOMETRES WALK

Mark	Name		Nat	Born	Pos	Meet	Venue	Date
2:21:31	Vladimir	Kanaykin ¶	RUS	21.3.85	1	NC-w	Adler	19 Feb 06
2:23:17		Kanaykin			1	NC-w	Adler	8 Feb 04
2:23:17		Kanaykin			1	NC-w	Adler	13 Mar 05
2:24:25	Semyon	Lovkin	RUS	14.7.77	1	NC-w	Adler	1 Mar 03
2:24:25	Sergey	Bakulin ¶	RUS	13.11.86	1	NC-w	Adler	1 Mar 09
2:24:50	Denis	Nizhegorodov	RUS	26.7.80	2	NC-w	Adler	19 Feb 06
2:24:56		Nizhegorodov			2	NC-w	Adler	1 Mar 09
2:25:19	Andrey	Ruzavin ¶	RUS	28.3.86	3	NC-w	Adler	1 Mar 09
2:25:38	Stepan	Yudin	RUS	3.4.80	2	NC-w	Adler	1 Mar 03
2:25:54	Mikhail	Ryzhov	RUS	17.12.91	1	NC-w	Sochi	27 Feb 15
2:25:57		Kirdyapkin			2	NC-w	Adler	13 Mar 05
2:25:58	German	Skurygin ¶	RUS	15.9.63	1	NC-w	Adler	20 Feb 98
2:25:59		Kanaykin ¶			1	NC-w	Adler	23 Feb 08
2:25:59		Ryzhov			1	NC-w	Sochi	18 Feb 12
2:26:16	(15/9) Alex	Schwazer ¶ (10)	ITA	26.12.84	1		Montalto Di Castro	24 Jan 10
2:26:25	Aleksey	Voyevodin ¶	RUS	9.8.70	2	NC-w	Adler	8 Feb 04
2:26:29	Yuriy	Andronov	RUS	6.11.71	4	NC-w	Adler	1 Mar 09
2:26:33	Ivan	Noskov	RUS	16.7.88	2	NC-w	Sochi	18 Feb 12
2:26:36	Igor	Yerokhin ¶	RUS	4.9.85	1	NC-w	Sochi	26 Feb 11
2:26:46	Oleg	Ishutkin	RUS	22.7.75	2	NC-w	Adler	9 Feb 97
2:27:02	Yevgeniy	Shmalyuk	RUS	14.1.76	1	NC-w	Adler	20 Feb 00
2:27:07	Dmitriy	Dolnikov	RUS	19.11.72	2	NC-w	Adler	20 Feb 98
2:27:21	Pavel	Nikolayev	RUS	18.12.77	3	NC-w	Adler	20 Feb 98
2:27:29	Nikolay	Matyukhin	RUS	13.12.68	2	NC-w	Adler	9 Feb 97
2:27:42	Aleksey	Bartsaykin (20)	RUS	22.3.89	2	NC-w	Sochi	23 Feb 13
DQ: 2:25:42	Sergey	Kirdyapkin ¶	RUS	18.6.80	(1)	NC-w	Sochi	18 Feb 12

50 KILOMETRES WALK

Mark	Name		Nat	Born	Pos	Meet	Venue	Date
3:32:33 WR	Yohann	Diniz	FRA	1.1.78	1	EC	Zürich	15 Aug 14
3:34:14 WR	Denis	Nizhegorodov	RUS	26.7.80	1	WCp	Cheboksary	11 May 08
3:34:38	Matej	Tóth	SVK	10.2.83	1		Dudince	21 Mar 15
3:35:27.2t WR		Diniz			1		Reims	12 Mar 11
3:35:29		Nizhegorodov			1	NC	Cheboksary	13 Jun 04
3:35:47	Nathan	Deakes	AUS	17.8.77	1	NC	Geelong	2 Dec 06
3:36:03 WR	Robert	Korzeniowski	POL	30.7.68	1	WCh	Saint-Denis	27 Aug 03
3:36:04	Alex	Schwazer ¶	ITA	26.12.84	1	NC	Rosignano Solvay	11 Feb 07
3:36:06		Yu Chaohong	CHN	12.12.76	1	NG	Nanjing	22 Oct 05
3:36:13		Zhao Chengliang	CHN	1.6.84	2	NG	Nanjing	22 Oct 05
3:36:20		Han Yucheng	CHN	16.12.78	1	NC	Nanning	27 Feb 05
3:36:21		Tóth			2	EC	Zürich	15 Aug 14
3:36:39 WR		Korzeniowski			1	EC	München	8 Aug 02
3:36:42	German	Skurygin ¶ (10)	RUS	15.9.63	2	WCh	Saint-Denis	27 Aug 03

50 – 100 KILOMETRES WALK A-T

Mark	Wind	Name		Nat	Born	Pos	Meet	Venue	Date
3:36:53		Jared	Tallent	AUS	17.10.84	1	OG	London	11 Aug 12
3:37:04			Schwazer			2	WCp	Cheboksary	11 May 08
3:37:09			Schwazer			1	OG	Beijing	22 Aug 08
3:37:16		Si Tianfeng		CHN	17.6.84	2	OG	London	11 Aug 12
3:37:26	WR	Valeriy	Spitsyn	RUS	5.12.65	1	NC	Moskva	21 May 00
3:37:41	WR	Andrey	Perlov	RUS	12.12.61	1	NC	Leningrad	5 Aug 89
3:37:41		Ivan	Noskov ¶	RUS	16.7.88	3	EC	Zürich	15 Aug 14
3:37:46		Andreas	Erm	GER	12.3.76	3	WCh	Saint-Denis	27 Aug 03
3:37:48			Diniz			1	NC	St.Sebastien-sur-Loire	13 Mar 16
3:37:54		Robert	Heffernan	IRL	20.2.78	3	OG	London	11 Aug 12
3:37:56			Heffernan			1	WCh	Moskva	14 Aug 13
3:37:58		Xing Shucai		CHN	4.8.84	2	NC	Nanning	27 Feb 05
3:38:01		Aleksey	Voyevodin ¶	RUS	9.8.70	4	WCh	Saint-Denis	27 Aug 03
3:38:02			Nizhegorodov			1	WCp	La Coruña	14 May 06
3:38:08		Sergey	Kirdyapkin ¶ (20)	RUS	16.1.80	1	WCh	Helsinki	12 Aug 05
3:38:08		Igor	Yerokhin ¶	RUS	4.9.85	1	NC	Saransk	8 Jun 08
3:38:08			Kirdyapkin			1	WCp	Saransk	13 May 12
		(31/21)							
3:38:17	WR	Ronald	Weigel	GDR	8.8.59	1	IM	Potsdam	25 May 86
3:38:29		Vyacheslav	Ivanenko	RUS	3.3.61	1	OG	Seoul	30 Sep 88
3:38:43		Valentí	Massana	ESP	5.7.70	1	NC	Orense	20 Mar 94
3:38:58		Mikhail	Ryzhov ¶	RUS	17.12.91	2	WCh	Moskva	14 Aug 13
3:39:01			Li Jianbo	CHN	14.11.86	4	OG	London	11 Aug 12
3:39:17			Dong Jimin	CHN	10.10.83	4	NC	Nanning	27 Feb 05
3:39:21		Vladimir	Potemin	RUS	15.1.80	2	NC	Moskva	21 May 00
3:39:22		Sergey	Korepanov	KAZ	9.5.64	1	WCp	Mézidon-Canon	2 May 99
3:39:34		Valentin	Kononen	FIN	7.3.69	1		Dudince	25 Mar 00
		(30)							
3:39:45		Hartwig	Gauder	GDR	10.11.54	3	OG	Seoul	30 Sep 88
3:39:54		Jesús Angel	García	ESP	17.10.69	1	WCp	Podebrady	20 Apr 97
3:40:02		Aleksandr	Potashov	BLR	12.3.62	1	NC	Moskva	27 May 90
3:40:07		Andrey	Plotnikov	RUS	12.8.67	2	NC	Moskva	27 May 90
3:40:08		Tomasz	Lipiec ¶	POL	10.5.71	2	WCp	Mézidon-Canon	2 May 99
3:40:12		Oleg	Ishutkin	RUS	22.7.75	2	WCp	Podebrady	20 Apr 97
3:40:12		Yuki	Yamazaki	JPN	16.1.84	1		Wajima	12 Apr 09
3:40:13		Nikolay	Matyukhin	RUS	13.12.68	3	WCp	Mézidon-Canon	2 May 99
3:40:19		Takayuki	Tanii	JPN	14.2.83	2	AsiG	Incheon	1 Oct 14
3:40:20		Hirooki	Arai	JPN	18.5.88	1	NC	Wajima	19 Apr 15
		(40)							
3:40:23			Gadasu Alatan	CHN	27.1.84	3	NG	Nanjing	22 Oct 05
3:40:39		Igor	Hlavan	UKR	25.9.90	4	WCh	Moskva	14 Aug 13
3:40:40		Vladimir	Kanaykin ¶	RUS	21.3.85	1	NC	Saransk	12 Jun 05
3:40:46	WR	José	Marin	ESP	21.1.50	1	NC	Valencia	13 Mar 83
3:40:46		Yuriy	Andronov ¶	RUS	6.11.71	1		Moskva	11 Jun 12
3:40:57.9t		Thierry	Toutain	FRA	14.2.62	1		Héricourt	29 Sep 96
3:41:02		Francisco Javier	Fernández ¶	ESP	6.3.77	1	NC	San Pedro del Pinatar	1 Mar 09
3:41:02			Wang Zhendong	CHN	11.1.91	1		Huangshan	6 Mar 16
3:41:09		Érick	Barrondo	GUA	14.6.91	1		Dudince	23 Mar 13
3:41:10			Zhao Jianguo	CHN	19.1.88	1	AsiC	Wajima	16 Apr 06
		(50)	100th man 3:44:36, 200th 3:49:11, 300th 3:51:47, 400th 3:54:20, 500th 3:56:53						

Drugs disqualification Russians – Noskov, Ryzhov, Strelkov and Yargunkin suspended pending investigation

3:35:59		Sergey	Kirdyapkin ¶	RUS	16.1.80	(1)	OG	London	11 Aug 12
3:36:55		Vladimir	Kanaykin ¶	RUS	21.3.85	(2)	WCp	Cheboksary	11 May 08
3:37:54		Igor	Yerokhin ¶	RUS	4.9.85	(5)	OG	London	11 Aug 12
3:38:46		Sergey	Bakulin ¶	RUS	13.11.86	(1)	NC	Saransk	12 Jun 11

100 KILOMETRES WALK

Mark		Name		Nat	Born	Pos	Meet	Venue	Date
8:38.07		Viktor	Ginko	BLR	7.12.65	1		Scanzorosciate	27 Oct 02
8:43:30			Ginko			1		Scanzorosciate	29 Oct 00
8:44:28			Ginko			1		Scanzorosciate	19 Oct 03
8:48:28		Modris	Liepins	LAT	30.8.66	1		Scanzorosciate	28 Oct 01
8:54:35		Aleksey	Rodionov	RUS	5.3.57	1		Scanzorosciate	15 Nov 98
8:55:12		Pascal	Kieffer	FRA	6.5.61	1		Besançon	18 Oct 92
8:55:40		Vitaliy	Popovich	UKR	22.10.62	1		Scanzorosciate	31 Oct 99
8:58:12		Gérard	Lelièvre	FRA	13.11.49	1		Laval	7 Oct 84
8:58:47		Zóltan	Czukor	HUN	18.12.62	2		Scanzorosciate	27 Oct 02

Oldest mark in top 50 World Lists: Men: in wind assisted section: LJ 8.49w Ralph Boston USA 2 Sep 1964,; in main lists: SP: 38= 21.78 Randy Matson USA 22 Apr 1967
Women: by an individual – just outside: 100mh 52= 12.59 Anneliese Ehrhardt GDR 8 Sep 1972.

WOMEN'S ALL-TIME WORLD LISTS

100 METRES

Mark	Wind	Name		Nat	Born	Pos	Meet	Venue	Date
10.49WR	0.0	Florence	Griffith Joyner	USA	21.12.59	1q1	NC/OT	Indianapolis	16 Jul 88
		@ Probably strongly wind-assisted, but recognised as a US and world record							
10.61	1.2		Griffith Joyner			1	NC/OT	Indianapolis	17 Jul 88
10.62	1.0		Griffith Joyner			1q3	OG	Seoul	24 Sep 88
10.64	1.2	Carmelita	Jeter	USA	24.11.79	1		Shanghai	20 Sep 09
10.65A	1.1	Marion	Jones ¶	USA	12.10.75	1	WCp	Johannesburg	12 Sep 98
10.67	-0.1		Jeter			1	WAF	Thessaloníki	13 Sep 09
10.70 (WR)	1.6		Griffith Joyner			1s1	NC/OT	Indianapolis	17 Jul 88
10.70	-0.1		Jones			1	WCh	Sevilla	22 Aug 99
10.70	2.0		Jeter			1	Pre	Eugene	4 Jun 11
10.70	0.6	Shelly-Ann	Fraser-Pryce	JAM	27.12.86	1	NC	Kingston	29 Jun 12
10.70	0.3	Elaine	Thompson	JAM	28.6.92	1	NC	Kingston	1 Jul 16
10.71	0.1		Jones			1		Chengdu	12 May 98
10.71	2.0		Jones			1s2	NC	New Orleans	19 Jun 98
10.71	-0.3		Fraser-Pryce			1	WCh	Moskva	12 Aug 13
10.71	0.5		Thompson			1	OG	Rio de Janeiro	13 Aug 16
10.72	2.0		Jones			1	NC	New Orleans	20 Jun 98
10.72	0.0		Jones			1	Herc	Monaco	8 Aug 98
10.72	0.0		Jones			1	Athl	Lausanne	25 Aug 98
10.72	-0.3		Fraser-Pryce			1	VD	Bruxelles	6 Sep 13
10.73	2.0	Christine	Arron	FRA	13.9.73	1	EC	Budapest	19 Aug 98
10.73	0.1		Fraser-Pryce			1	WCh	Berlin	17 Aug 09
10.74	1.3	Merlene	Ottey	JAM/SLO	10.5.60	1	GPF	Milano	7 Sep 96
10.74	0.2		Fraser-Pryce			1	DL	Saint-Denis	4 Jul 15
10.74	1.0	English	Gardner	USA	22.4.92	1	NC	Eugene	3 Jul 16
10.75	0.6		Jones			1	GGala	Roma	14 Jul 98
10.75	0.4	Kerron	Stewart	JAM	16.4.84	1	GGala	Roma	10 Jul 09
10.75	0.1		Stewart			2	WCh	Berlin	17 Aug 09
10.75	1.5		Fraser-Pryce			1	OG	London (OS)	4 Aug 12
10.76 WR	1.7	Evelyn	Ashford (10)	USA	15.4.57	1	WK	Zürich	22 Aug 84
10.76	0.9		Jones			1	VD	Bruxelles	22 Aug 97
10.76	0.3		Jones			1q4	WCh	Sevilla	21 Aug 99
10.76	1.1	Veronica	Campbell-Brown	JAM	15.5.82	1	GS	Ostrava	31 May 11
10.76	-0.3		Fraser-Pryce			1	WCh	Beijing	24 Aug 15
		(32 performances by 11 athletes)							
10.77	0.9	Irina	Privalova	RUS	22.11.68	1rA	Athl	Lausanne	6 Jul 94
10.77	0.7	Ivet	Lalova-Collio	BUL	18.5.84	1	ECp-1A	Plovdiv	19 Jun 04
10.78A	1.0	Dawn	Sowell	USA	27.3.66	1	NCAA	Provo	3 Jun 89
10.78	1.8	Torri	Edwards ¶	USA	31.1.77	1s2	OT	Eugene	28 Jun 08
10.78	1.6	Murielle	Ahouré	CIV	23.8.87	1		Montverde	11 Jun 16
10.78	1.0	Tianna	Bartoletta '	USA	30.8.85	2	NC	Eugene	3 Jul 16
10.78	1.0	Tori	Bowie	USA	27.8.90	3	NC	Eugene	3 Jul 16
10.79	0.0		Li Xuemei	CHN	5.1.77	1	NG	Shanghai	18 Oct 97
10.79	-0.1	Inger	Miller	USA	12.6.72	2	WCh	Sevilla	22 Aug 99
		(20)							
10.79	1.1	Blessing	Okagbare	NGR	9.10.88	1	DL	London (OS)	27 Jul 13
10.81 WR	1.7	Marlies	Göhr'	GDR	21.3.58	1	OD	Berlin	8 Jun 83
10.81	-0.3	Dafne	Schippers	NED	15.6.92	2	WCh	Beijing	24 Aug 15
10.82	-1.0	Gail	Devers	USA	19.11.66	1	OG	Barcelona	1 Aug 92
10.82	0.4	Gwen	Torrence	USA	12.6.65	2	GPF	Paris	3 Sep 94
10.82	-0.3	Zhanna	Pintusevich-Block ¶	UKR	6.7.72	1	WCh	Edmonton	6 Aug 01
10.82	-0.7	Sherone	Simpson	JAM	12.8.84	1	NC	Kingston	24 Jun 06
10.83	1.7	Marita	Koch	GDR	18.2.57	2	OD	Berlin	8 Jun 83
10.83	-1.0	Juliet	Cuthbert	JAM	9.4.64	2	OG	Barcelona	1 Aug 92
10.83	0.1	Ekateríni	Thánou ¶	GRE	1.2.75	2s1	WCh	Sevilla	22 Aug 99
		(30)							
10.83	1.6	Kelly-Ann	Baptiste	TTO	14.10.86	1	NC	Port of Spain	22 Jun 13
10.84	1.3	Chioma	Ajunwa ¶	NGR	25.12.70	1		Lagos	11 Apr 92
10.84	1.9	Chandra	Sturrup	BAH	12.9.71	1	Athl	Lausanne	5 Jul 05
10.85	2.0	Anelia	Nuneva	BUL	30.6.62	1h1	NC	Sofia	2 Sep 88
10.85	1.0	Muna	Lee	USA	30.10.81	1	OT	Eugene	28 Jun 08
10.85	2.0	Barbara	Pierre	HAI/USA	28.4.87	1s1	NC	Des Moines	21 Jun 13
10.85	1.6	Michelle-Lee	Ahye	TTO	10.4.92	1	NC	Port of Spain	21 Jun 14
10.86	0.6	Silke	Gladisch'	GDR	20.6.64	1	NC	Potsdam	20 Aug 87
10.86	1.2	Chryste	Gaines ¶	USA	14.9.70	1	WAF	Monaco	14 Sep 03
10.86	2.0	Marshevet	Hooker/Myers	USA	25.9.84	2	Pre	Eugene	4 Jun 11
		(40)							

100 – 200 METRES A-T

Mark	Wind	Name		Nat	Born	Pos	Meet	Venue	Date
10.86	0.5	Marie Josée	Ta Lou	CIV	18.11.88	4	OG	Rio de Janeiro	13 Aug 16
10.87	1.8	Octavious	Freeman	USA	20.4.92	2	NC	Des Moines	21 Jun 13
10.88	0.4	Lauryn	Williams	USA	11.9.83	2	WK	Zürich	19 Aug 05
10.89	1.8	Katrin	Krabbe ¶	GDR	22.11.69	1		Berlin	20 Jul 88
10.89	0.0		Liu Xiaomei	CHN	11.1.72	2	NG	Shanghai	18 Oct 97
10.89	1.5	Allyson	Felix	USA	18.11.85	5	OG	London (OS)	4 Aug 12
10.90	1.4	Glory	Alozie	NGR/ESP	30.12.77	1		La Laguna	5 Jun 99
10.90	1.8	Shalonda	Solomon	USA	19.12.85	2		Clermont	5 Jun 10
10.91	0.2	Heike	Drechsler'	GDR/GER	16.12.64	2	GWG	Moskva	6 Jul 86
10.91	1.1	Savatheda	Fynes	BAH	17.10.74	2	Athl	Lausanne	2 Jul 99
10.91	1.5	Debbie	Ferguson McKenzie	BAH	16.1.76	1	CG	Manchester	27 Jul 02
10.91	1.7	Alexandria	Anderson	USA	28.1.87	3s2	NC	Des Moines	21 Jun 13
(53)			100th women 11.01, 200th 11.11, 300th 11.17, 400th 11.22, 500th 11.26						

Doubtful wind reading

10.83	0.0	Sheila	Echols	USA	2.10.64	1q2	NC/OT	Indianapolis	16 Jul 88
10.88	0.0	Diane	Williams	USA	14.12.60	2q1	NC/OT	Indianapolis	16 Jul 88

Probably semi-automatic timing

10.87	1.9	Lyudmila	Kondratyeva	RUS	11.4.58	1		Leningrad	3 Jun 80

Low altitude best: 10.91 1.6 Sowell 1 NC Houston 16 Jun 89

Wind-assisted performances to 10.75 and performers to 10.88

Mark	Wind	Name		Nat	Born	Pos	Meet	Venue	Date
10.54	3.0		Griffith Joyner			1	OG	Seoul	25 Sep 88
10.60	3.2		Griffith Joyner			1h1	NC/OT	Indianapolis	16 Jul 88
10.68	2.2		Jones			1	DNG	Stockholm	1 Aug 00
10.70	2.6		Griffith Joyner			1s2	OG	Seoul	25 Sep 88
10.71	2.2		Fraser-Pryce			1	Pre	Eugene	1 Jun 13
10.71	2.4		Thompson			1		Kingston	7 May 16
10.72	3.0		Jeter			1s1	NC	Eugene	26 Jun 09
10.72	3.2	Tori	Bowie	USA	27.8.90	1s2	NC	Eugene	26 Jun 15
10.74	2.7		Jeter			1	NC	Eugene	24 Jun 11
10.74	3.1		Bowie			1s1	NC	Eugene	3 Jul 16
10.74	2.5		Gardner			1s3	NC	Eugene	3 Jul 16
10.75	2.2	Blessing	Okagbare	NGR	9.10.88	2	Pre	Eugene	1 Jun 13
10.76	3.4	Marshevet	Hooker/Myers	USA	25.9.84	1q1	NC/OT	Eugene	27 Jun 08
10.77	2.3	Gail	Devers	USA	19.11.66	1	Jen	San José	28 May 94
10.77	2.3	Ekateríni	Thánou ¶	GRE	1.2.75	1		Rethymno	28 May 99
10.78	5.0	Gwen	Torrence	USA	12.6.65	1q3	NC/OT	Indianapolis	16 Jul 88
10.78	3.3	Muna	Lee	USA	30.10.81	2	NC	Eugene	26 Jun 09
10.79	3.3	Marlies	Göhr'	GDR	21.3.58	1	NC	Cottbus	16 Jul 80
10.80	2.9	Pam	Marshall	USA	16.8.60	1	NC	Eugene	20 Jun 86
10.80	2.8	Heike	Drechsler'	GDR	16.12.64	1	Bisl	Oslo	5 Jul 86
10.81	3.6	Jenna	Prandini	USA	20.11.92	1h4	NC	Eugene	2 Jul 16
10.82	2.2	Silke	Gladisch/Möller	GDR	20.6.64	1s1	WCh	Roma	30 Aug 87
10.83	3.9	Sheila	Echols	USA	2.10.64	1h2	NC/OT	Indianapolis	16 Jul 88
10.84	2.9	Alice	Brown	USA	20.9.60	2	NC	Eugene	20 Jun 86
10.86	3.4	Lauryn	Williams	USA	11.9.83	2q1	NC/OT	Eugene	27 Jun 08
10.86	3.2	Jasmine	Todd	USA	23.12.93	3s2	NC	Eugene	26 Jun 15
10.87	3.0	Me'Lisa	Barber	USA	4.10.80	1s1	NC	Carson	25 Jun 05
10.88	5.9	Alexandria	Anderson	USA	28.1.87	1		Austin	14 Apr 12

Hand timing: 10.6 0.1 Zhanna Pintusevich ¶ UKR 6.7.72 1 Kiev 12 Jun 97

Drugs disqualification

10.75	-0.4		Jones			(1)	OG	Sydney	23 Sep 00
10.78	0.1		Jones			(1)	ISTAF	Berlin	1 Sep 00
10.85	0.9	Kelli	White ¶	USA	1.4.77	(1)	WCh	Saint-Denis	24 Aug 03
10.79w	2.3	Kelli	White ¶	USA	1.4.77	(1)		Carson	1 Jun 03
10.89w	4.6	Tahesia	Harrigan-Scott	IVB	15.2.82	(1h1)		Clermont	4 Jun 11

200 METRES

Mark	Wind	Name		Nat	Born	Pos	Meet	Venue	Date
21.34WR	1.3	Florence	Griffith Joyner	USA	21.12.59	1	OG	Seoul	29 Sep 88
21.56WR	1.7		Griffith Joyner			1s1	OG	Seoul	29 Sep 88
21.62A	-0.6	Marion	Jones ¶	USA	12.10.75	1	WCp	Johannesburg	11 Sep 98
21.63	0.2	Dafne	Schippers	NED	15.6.92	1	WCh	Beijing	28 Aug 15
21.64	0.8	Merlene	Ottey	JAM	10.5.60	1	VD	Bruxelles	13 Sep 91
21.66	-1.0		Ottey			1	WK	Zürich	15 Aug 90
21.66	0.2	Elaine	Thompson	JAM	28.6.92	2	WCh	Beijing	28 Aug 15
21.69	1.0	Allyson	Felix	USA	18.11.85	1	NC/OT	Eugene	30 Jun 12
21.71WR	0.7	Marita	Koch	GDR	18.2.57	1	v CAN	Karl-Marx-Stadt	10 Jun 79
21.71WR	0.3		Koch			1	OD	Potsdam	21 Jul 84
21.71WR	1.2	Heike	Drechsler'	GDR	16.12.64	1	NC	Jena	29 Jun 86
21.71WR	-0.8		Drechsler			1	EC	Stuttgart	29 Aug 86
21.72	1.3	Grace	Jackson	JAM	14.6.61	2	OG	Seoul	29 Sep 88
21.72	-0.1	Gwen	Torrence (10)	USA	12.6.65	1s2	OG	Barcelona	5 Aug 92

294 200 METRES A-T

Mark	Wind	Name		Nat	Born	Pos	Meet	Venue	Date
21.74	0.4	Marlies	Göhr'	GDR	21.3.58	1	NC	Erfurt	3 Jun 84
21.74	1.2	Silke	Gladisch'	GDR	20.6.64	1	WCh	Roma	3 Sep 87
21.74	0.6	Veronica	Campbell-Brown	JAM	15.5.82	1	OG	Beijing	21 Aug 08
21.75	-0.1	Juliet	Cuthbert	JAM	9.4.64	2s2	OG	Barcelona	5 Aug 92
21.76	0.3		Koch			1	NC	Dresden	3 Jul 82
21.76	0.7		Griffith Joyner			1q1	OG	Seoul	28 Sep 88
21.76	-0.8		Jones			1	WK	Zürich	13 Aug 97
21.77	-0.1		Griffith Joyner			1q2	NC/OT	Indianapolis	22 Jul 88
21.77	1.0		Ottey			1	Herc	Monaco	7 Aug 93
21.77	-0.3		Torrence			1	ASV	Köln	18 Aug 95
21.77	0.6	Inger	Miller	USA	12.6.72	1	WCh	Sevilla	27 Aug 99
21.78	-1.3		Koch			1	NC	Leipzig	11 Aug 85
21.78	-0.1		Thompson			1	OG	Rio de Janeiro	17 Aug 16
21.79	1.7		Gladisch			1	NC	Potsdam	22 Aug 87
21.80	-1.1		Ottey			1	Nik	Nice	10 Jul 90
21.80	0.4		Jones			1	GWG	Uniondale, NY	20 Jul 98
		(30/15)							
21.81	-0.1	Valerie	Brisco-Hooks	USA	6.7.60	1	OG	Los Angeles	9 Aug 84
21.83	-0.2	Evelyn	Ashford	USA	15.4.57	1	WCp	Montreal	24 Aug 79
21.85	0.3	Bärbel	Wöckel'	GDR	21.3.55	2	OD	Potsdam	21 Jul 84
21.87	0.0	Irina	Privalova	RUS	22.11.68	2	Herc	Monaco	25 Jul 95
21.93	1.3	Pam	Marshall	USA	16.8.60	2	NC/OT	Indianapolis	23 Jul 88
		(20)							
21.95	0.3	Katrin	Krabbe ¶	GDR	22.11.69	1	EC	Split	30 Aug 90
21.97	1.9	Jarmila	Kratochvílová	CZE	26.1.51	1	PTS	Bratislava	6 Jun 81
21.99	0.9	Chandra	Cheeseborough	USA	10.1.59	2	NC	Indianapolis	19 Jun 83
21.99	1.1	Marie-José	Pérec	FRA	9.5.68	1	BNP	Villeneuve d'Ascq	2 Jul 93
21.99	1.1	Kerron	Stewart	JAM	16.4.84	2	NC	Kingston	29 Jun 08
21.99	1.9	Tori	Bowie	USA	27.8.90	1	Pre	Eugene	28 May 16
22.00	1.3	Sherone	Simpson	JAM	12.8.84	1	NC	Kingston	25 Jun 06
22.01	-0.5	Anelia	Nuneva'	BUL	30.6.62	1	NC	Sofia	16 Aug 87
22.01	0.0		Li Xuemei	CHN	5.1.77	1	NG	Shanghai	22 Oct 97
22.01	0.6	Muna	Lee	USA	30.10.81	4	OG	Beijing	21 Aug 08
		(30)							
22.01	0.2	Candyce	McGrone	USA	24.3.89	4	WCh	Beijing	28 Aug 15
22.04A	0.7	Dawn	Sowell	USA	27.3.66	1	NCAA	Provo	2 Jun 89
22.05	0.8	Shaunae	Miller	BAH	15.4.94	1		Kingston	11 Jun 16
22.06A	0.7	Evette	de Klerk'	RSA	21.8.65	1		Pietersburg	8 Apr 89
22.07	-0.1	Mary	Onyali	NGR	3.2.68	1	WK	Zürich	14 Aug 96
22.07	0.2	Dina	Asher-Smith	GBR	4.12.95	5	WCh	Beijing	28 Aug 15
22.09	-0.3	Sanya	Richards-Ross	USA	26.2.85	1	DL	New York	9 Jun 12
22.09	-0.2	Shelly-Ann	Fraser-Pryce	JAM	27.12.86	2	OG	London (OS)	8 Aug 12
22.10	-0.1	Kathy	Cook'	GBR	3.5.60	4	OG	Los Angeles	9 Aug 84
22.11	1.0	Carmelita	Jeter	USA	24.11.79	2	NC/OT	Eugene	30 Jun 12
		(40)							
22.11	0.1	Myriam	Soumaré	FRA	29.10.86	2	VD	Bruxelles	5 Sep 14
22.13	1.2	Ewa	Kasprzyk	POL	7.9.57	2	GWG	Moskva	8 Jul 86
22.14	-0.6	Carlette	Guidry	USA	4.9.68	1	NC	Atlanta	23 Jun 96
22.15	1.0	Shalonda	Solomon	USA	19.12.85	1	NC	Eugene	26 Jun 11
22.17A	-2.3	Zhanna	Pintusevich-Block ¶	UKR	6.7.72	1		Monachil	9 Jul 97
22.18	-0.6	Dannette	Young-Stone	USA	6.10.64	2	NC	Atlanta	23 Jun 96
22.18	0.9	Galina	Malchugina	RUS	17.12.62	1s2	NC	Sankt Peterburg	4 Jul 96
22.18	0.5	Merlene	Frazer	JAM	27.12.73	1s2	WCh	Sevilla	25 Aug 99
22.18	1.9	Dezerea	Bryant	USA	27.4.93	1	NCAA	Eugene	13 Jun 15
22.19	1.5	Natalya	Bochina	RUS	4.1.62	2	OG	Moskva	30 Jul 80
22.19	0.0	Debbie	Ferguson McKenzie	BAH	16.1.76	1	GP II	Saint-Denis	3 Jul 99
22.19	1.9	Kimberlyn	Duncan	USA	2.8.91	1s2	NCAA	Des Moines	7 Jun 12
22.19	1.0	Aleksandra	Fedoriva	RUS	13.9.88	1	NC	Cheboksary	6 Jul 12
		(53)	100th woman 22.32, 200th 22.57, 300th 22.71, 400th 22.81, 500th 22.89						
Wind-assisted			*Performers listed to 22.16*						
21.80	3.2	Kimberlyn	Duncan	USA	2.8.91	1	NC	Des Moines	23 Jun 13
21.82	3.1	Irina	Privalova	RUS	22.11.68	1	Athl	Lausanne	6 Jul 94
21.91	2.8	Muna	Lee	USA	30.10.81	1		Fort-de-France	10 May 08
22.01	2.9	Michelle-Lee	Ahye	TTO	10.4.92	1		San Marcos	25 Apr 15
22.06	3.8	Jeneba	Tarmoh	USA	27.9.89	1	NC	Sacramento	29 Jun 14
22.16	3.1	Dannette	Young-Stone	USA	6.10.64	2	Athl	Lausanne	6 Jul 94
22.16	3.2	Nanceen	Perry	USA	19.4.77	1		Austin	6 May 00
22.16	3.2	Kamaria	Brown	USA	21.12.92	4	NC	Des Moines	23 Jun 13
Hand timing									
21.9	-0.1	Svetlana	Goncharenko	RUS	28.5.71	1		Rostov-na-Donu	31 May 98

200 – 300 – 400 METRES A-T

Mark	Wind	Name		Nat	Born	Pos	Meet	Venue	Date
21.6w	2.5	Pam	Marshall	USA	16.8.60	1	NC	San José	26 Jun 87
Drugs disqualification									
22.05	-0.3	Kelli	White ¶	USA	1.4.77	1	WCh	Saint-Denis	28 Aug 03
22.18i		Michelle	Collins ¶	USA	12.2.71	1	WI	Birmingham	15 Mar 03

Times in 300m races only

300 METRES

35.30A		Ana Gabriela	Guevara	MEX	4.3.77	1		Ciudad de México	3 May 03
35.46		Kathy	Cook'	GBR	3.5.60	1	Nike	London (CP)	18 Aug 84
35.46		Chandra	Cheeseborough	USA	10.1.59	2	Nike	London (CP)	18 Aug 84
Indoors									
35.45		Irina	Privalova	RUS	22.11.68	1		Moskva	17 Jan 93
35.48	#	Svetlana	Goncharenko	RUS	28.5.71	1		Tampere	4 Feb 98

400 METRES

47.60 WR	Marita	Koch	GDR	18.2.57	1	WCp	Canberra	6 Oct 85
47.99 WR	Jarmila	Kratochvílová	CZE	26.1.51	1	WCh	Helsinki	10 Aug 83
48.16 WR		Koch			1	EC	Athína	8 Sep 82
48.16		Koch			1	Drz	Praha	16 Aug 84
48.22		Koch			1	EC	Stuttgart	28 Aug 86
48.25	Marie-José	Pérec	FRA	9.5.68	1	OG	Atlanta	29 Jul 96
48.26		Koch			1	GO	Dresden	27 Jul 84
48.27	Olga	Vladykina'	UKR	30.6.63	2	WCp	Canberra	6 Oct 85
48.45		Kratochvílová			1	NC	Praha	23 Jul 83
48.59	Tatána	Kocembová'	CZE	2.5.62	2	WCh	Helsinki	10 Aug 83
48.60 WR		Koch			1	ECp	Torino	4 Aug 79
48.60		Vladykina			1	ECp	Moskva	17 Aug 85
48.61		Kratochvílová			1	WCp	Roma	6 Sep 81
48.63	Cathy	Freeman	AUS	16.2.73	2	OG	Atlanta	29 Jul 96
48.65		Bryzgina'			1	OG	Seoul	26 Sep 88
48.70	Sanya	Richards	USA	26.2.85	1	WCp	Athína	16 Sep 06
48.73		Kocembová			2	Drz	Praha	16 Aug 84
48.77		Koch			1	v USA	Karl-Marx-Stadt	9 Jul 82
48.82		Kratochvílová			1	Ros	Praha	23 Jun 83
48.83	Valerie	Brisco	USA	6.7.60	1	OG	Los Angeles	6 Aug 84
48.83		Pérec			1	OG	Barcelona	5 Aug 92
48.83		Richards			1	VD	Bruxelles	4 Sep 09
48.85		Kratochvílová			2	EC	Athína	8 Sep 82
48.86		Kratochvílová			1	WK	Zürich	18 Aug 82
48.86		Koch			1	NC	Erfurt	2 Jun 84
48.87		Koch			1	VD	Bruxelles	27 Aug 82
48.88		Koch			1	OG	Moskva	28 Jul 80
48.89 WR		Koch			1		Potsdam	29 Jul 79
48.89		Koch			1		Berlin	15 Jul 84
48.89	Ana Gabriela	Guevara	MEX	4.3.77	1	WCh	Saint-Denis	27 Aug 03
(30/9)								
49.05	Chandra (10)	Cheeseborough	USA	10.1.59	2	OG	Los Angeles	6 Aug 84
49.07	Tonique	Williams-Darling	BAH	17.1.76	1	ISTAF	Berlin	12 Sep 04
49.10	Falilat	Ogunkoya	NGR	12.5.68	3	OG	Atlanta	29 Jul 96
49.11	Olga	Nazarova ¶	RUS	1.6.65	1s1	OG	Seoul	25 Sep 88
49.16	Antonina	Krivoshapka ¶	RUS	21.7.87	1	NC	Cheboksary	5 Jul 12
49.19	Mariya	Pinigina'	UKR	9.2.58	3	WCh	Helsinki	10 Aug 83
49.24	Sabine	Busch	GDR	21.11.62	2	NC	Erfurt	2 Jun 84
49.26	Allyson	Felix	USA	18.11.85	1	WCh	Beijing	27 Aug 15
49.28 WR	Irena	Szewinska'	POL	24.5.46	1	OG	Montreal	29 Jul 76
49.28	Pauline	Davis-Thompson	BAH	9.7.66	4	OG	Atlanta	29 Jul 96
49.28	Yuliya	Gushchina	RUS	4.3.83	2	NC	Cheboksary	5 Jul 12
(20)								
49.29	Charity	Opara ¶	NGR	20.5.72	1	GGala	Roma	14 Jul 98
49.30	Petra	Müller'	GDR	18.7.65	1		Jena	3 Jun 88
49.30	Lorraine	Fenton'	JAM	8.9.73	2	Herc	Monaco	19 Jul 02
49.32	Shericka	Williams	JAM	17.9.85	2	WCh	Berlin	18 Aug 09
49.33	Amantle	Montsho ¶	BOT	4.7.83	1	Herc	Monaco	19 Jul 13
49.35	Anastasiya	Kapachinskaya ¶	RUS	21.11.79	1	NC	Cheboksary	22 Jul 11
49.40	Jearl	Miles-Clark	USA	4.9.66	1	NC	Indianapolis	14 Jun 97
49.41	Christine	Ohuruogu	GBR	17.5.84	1	WCh	Moskva	12 Aug 13
49.42	Grit	Breuer ¶	GER	16.2.72	2	WCh	Tokyo	27 Aug 91
49.43	Kathy	Cook'	GBR	3.5.60	3	OG	Los Angeles	6 Aug 84
(30)								
49.43A	Fatima	Yusuf	NGR	2.5.71	1	AfG	Harare	15 Sep 95
49.44	Shaunae	Miller	BAH	15.4.94	1	OG	Rio de Janeiro	15 Aug 16

WOMEN All-time

400 – 600 – 800 METRES A-T

Mark	Wind	Name		Nat	Born	Pos	Meet	Venue	Date
49.47		Aelita	Yurchenko	UKR	1.1.65	2	Kuts	Moskva	4 Sep 88
49.48		Francena	McCorory	USA	20.10.88	1	NC	Sacramento	28 Jun 14
49.49		Olga	Zaytseva	RUS	10.11.84	1	NCp	Tula	16 Jul 06
49.53		Vanya	Stambolova ¶	BUL	28.11.83	1	GP	Rieti	27 Aug 06
49.56		Bärbel	Wöckel'	GDR	21.3.55	1		Erfurt	30 May 82
49.56		Monique	Hennagan	USA	26.5.76	1	NC/OT	Sacramento	17 Jul 04
49.57		Grace	Jackson	JAM	14.6.61	1	Nik	Nice	10 Jul 88
49.58		Dagmar	Rübsam'	GDR	3.6.62	3	NC	Erfurt	2 Jun 84
(40)									
49.59		Marion	Jones ¶	USA	12.10.75	1r6	MSR	Walnut	16 Apr 00
49.59		Katharine	Merry	GBR	21.9.74	1	GP	Athína	11 Jun 01
49.61		Ana Fidelia	Quirot	CUB	23.3.63	1	PAm	La Habana	5 Aug 91
49.63		Novlene	Williams-Mills	JAM	26.4.82	1		Shanghai	23 Sep 06
49.64		Gwen	Torrence	USA	12.6.65	2	Nik	Nice	15 Jul 93
49.64		Ximena	Restrepo	COL	10.3.69	3	OG	Barcelona	5 Aug 92
49.64		Deedee	Trotter	USA	8.12.82	1	NC	Indianapolis	23 Jun 07
49.64		Debbie	Dunn ¶	USA	26.3.78	1	NC	Des Moines	26 Jun 10
49.65		Natalya	Nazarova	RUS	26.5.79	1	NC	Tula	31 Jul 04
49.65		Nicola	Sanders	GBR	23.6.82	2	WCh	Osaka	29 Aug 07
(50)				100th woman 50.17, 200th 50.79, 300th 51.14, 400th 51.38, 500th 51.59					
Hand timing									
48.9		Olga	Nazarova ¶	RUS	1.6.65	1	NP	Vladivostok	13 Sep 88
49.2A		Ana Fidelia	Quirot	CUB	23.3.63	1	AmCp	Bogotá	13 Aug 89

600 METRES

Mark		Name		Nat	Born	Pos	Meet	Venue	Date
1:22.63		Ana Fidelia	Quirot	CUB	23.3.63	1		Guadalajara, ESP	25 Jul 97
1:22.87		Maria Lurdes	Mutola	MOZ	27.10.72	1		Liège (NX)	27 Aug 02
1:23.35		Pamela	Jelimo	KEN	5.12.89	1		Liège (NX)	5 Jul 12
1:23.5A		Doina	Melinte	ROU	27.12.56	1		Poiana Brasov	27 Jul 86

800 METRES

Mark		Name		Nat	Born	Pos	Meet	Venue	Date
1:53.28 WR		Jarmila	Kratochvílová	CZE	26.1.51	1		München	26 Jul 83
1:53.43 WR		Nadezhda	Olizarenko'	UKR	28.11.53	1	OG	Moskva	27 Jul 80
1:54.01		Pamela	Jelimo	KEN	5.12.89	1	WK	Zürich	29 Aug 08
1:54.44		Ana Fidelia	Quirot	CUB	23.3.63	1	WCp	Barcelona	9 Sep 89
1:54.68			Kratochvílová			1	WCh	Helsinki	9 Aug 83
1:54.81		Olga	Mineyeva	RUS	1.9.52	2	OG	Moskva	27 Jul 80
1:54.82			Quirot			1	ASV	Köln	24 Aug 97
1:54.85 WR			Olizarenko			1	Prav	Moskva	12 Jun 80
1:54.87			Jelimo			1	OG	Beijing	18 Aug 08
1:54.94 WR		Tatyana	Kazankina ¶	RUS	17.12.51	1	OG	Montreal	26 Jul 76
1:54.97			Jelimo			1	Gaz	Saint-Denis	18 Jul 08
1:54.99			Jelimo			1	ISTAF	Berlin	1 Jun 08
1:55.04			Kratochvílová			1	OsloG	Oslo	23 Aug 83
1:55.05		Doina	Melinte	ROU	27.12.56	1	NC	Bucuresti	1 Aug 82
1:55.1 '			Mineyeva			1	Znam	Moskva	6 Jul 80
1:55.16			Jelimo			1	VD	Bruxelles	5 Sep 08
1:55.19		Maria Lurdes	Mutola	MOZ	27.10.72	1	WK	Zürich	17 Aug 94
1:55.19		Jolanda	Ceplak ¶	SLO	12.9.76	1rA	NA	Heusden	20 Jul 02
1:55.26		Sigrun	Wodars/Grau (10)	GDR	7.11.65	1	WCh	Roma	31 Aug 87
1:55.28		Caster	Semenya	RSA	7.1.91	1	OG	Rio de Janeiro	20 Aug 16
1:55.29			Mutola			2	ASV	Köln	24 Aug 97
1:55.32		Christine	Wachtel	GDR	6.1.65	2	WCh	Roma	31 Aug 87
1:55.33			Semenya			1	Herc	Monaco	15 Jul 16
1:55.41			Mineyeva			1	EC	Athína	8 Sep 82
1:55.41			Jelimo			1	Bisl	Oslo	6 Jun 08
1:55.42		Nikolina	Shtereva	BUL	25.1.55	2	OG	Montreal	26 Jul 76
1:55.43			Mutola			1	WCh	Stuttgart	17 Aug 93
1:55.45			Semenya			1	WCh	Berlin	19 Aug 09
1:55.46		Tatyana	Providokhina	RUS	26.3.53	3	OG	Moskva	27 Jul 80
1:55.5			Mineyeva			1	Kuts	Podolsk	21 Aug 82
		(30/14)							
1:55.54		Ellen	van Langen	NED	9.2.66	1	OG	Barcelona	3 Aug 92
1:55.54			Liu Dong	CHN	24.12.73	1	NG	Beijing	9 Sep 93
1:55.56		Lyubov	Gurina	RUS	6.8.57	3	WCh	Roma	31 Aug 87
1:55.60		Elfi	Zinn	GDR	24.8.53	3	OG	Montreal	26 Jul 76
1:55.68		Ella	Kovacs	ROU	11.12.64	1	RomIC	Bucuresti	2 Jun 85
1:55.69		Irina	Podyalovskaya	RUS	19.10.59	1	Izv	Kyiv	22 Jun 84
		(20)							
1:55.74		Anita	Weiss'	GDR	16.7.55	4	OG	Montreal	26 Jul 76

800 – 1000 – 1500 METRES A-T   297

Mark	Wind	Name		Nat	Born	Pos	Meet	Venue	Date
1:55.87		Svetlana	Masterkova	RUS	17.1.68	1	Kuts	Moskva	18 Jun 99
1:55.96		Lyudmila	Veselkova	RUS	25.10.50	2	EC	Athína	8 Sep 82
1:55.96		Yekaterina	Podkopayeva'	RUS	11.6.52	1		Leningrad	27 Jul 83
1:55.99		Liliya	Nurutdinova ¶	RUS	15.12.63	2	OG	Barcelona	3 Aug 92
1:56.00		Tatyana	Andrianova	RUS	10.12.79	1	NC	Kazan	18 Jul 08
1:56.0 WR		Valentina	Gerasimova	KAZ	15.5.48	1	NC	Kyiv	12 Jun 76
1:56.0		Inna	Yevseyeva	UKR	14.8.64	1		Kyiv	25 Jun 88
1:56.04		Janeth	Jepkosgei	KEN	13.12.83	1	WCh	Osaka	28 Aug 07
1:56.09		Zulia	Calatayud	CUB	9.11.79	1	Herc	Monaco	19 Jul 02
(30)									
1:56.1		Ravilya	Agletdinova'	BLR	10.2.60	2	Kuts	Podolsk	21 Aug 82
1:56.2 '		Totka	Petrova ¶	BUL	17.12.56	1		Paris (C)	6 Jul 79
1:56.2		Tatyana	Mishkel	UKR	10.6.52	3	Kuts	Podolsk	21 Aug 82
1:56.21		Martina	Kämpfert'	GDR	11.11.59	4	OG	Moskva	27 Jul 80
1:56.21		Zamira	Zaytseva	UZB	16.2.53	2		Leningrad	27 Jul 83
1:56.21		Kelly	Holmes	GBR	19.4.70	2	GPF	Monaco	9 Sep 95
1:56.24			Qu Yunxia	CHN	8.12.72	2	NG	Beijing	9 Sep 93
1:56.24		Francine	Niyonsaba	BDI	5.5.93	2	Herc	Monaco	15 Jul 16
1:56.40		Jearl	Miles-Clark	USA	4.9.66	3	WK	Zürich	11 Aug 99
1:56.42		Paula	Ivan	ROU	20.7.63	1	Balk	Ankara	16 Jul 88
(40)									
1:56.43		Hasna	Benhassi	MAR	1.6.78	2	OG	Athína	23 Aug 04
1:56.44		Svetlana	Styrkina	RUS	1.1.49	5	OG	Montreal	26 Jul 76
1:56.51		Slobodanka	Colovic	YUG	10.1.65	1		Beograd	17 Jun 87
1:56.53		Patricia	Djaté	FRA	3.1.71	3	GPF	Monaco	9 Sep 95
1:56.56		Ludmila	Formanová	CZE	2.1.74	4	WK	Zürich	11 Aug 99
1:56.57		Zoya	Rigel	RUS	15.10.52	3	EC	Praha	31 Aug 78
1:56.59		Natalya	Khrushchelyova	RUS	30.5.73	2	NC	Tula	31 Jul 04
1:56.60		Natalya	Tsyganova	RUS	7.2.71	1	NC	Tula	25 Jul 00
1:56.6		Tamara	Sorokina'	RUS	15.8.50	5	Kuts	Podolsk	21 Aug 82
1:56.61		Yelena	Afanasyeva	RUS	1.3.67	3	WK	Zürich	13 Aug 97
(50)		100th woman 1:57.48, 200th 1:58.5, 300th 1:59.24, 400th 1:59.68, 500th 2:00.13							
Indoors: 1:55.85		Stephanie	Graf	AUT	26.4.73	2	EI	Wien	3 Mar 02
Drugs disqualification									
1:54.85		Yelena	Soboleva ¶	RUS	3.10.82	(1)	NC	Kazan	18 Jul 08
1:55.87		Mariya	Savinova ¶	RUS	13.8.85	1	WCh	Daegu	4 Sep 11

1000 METRES

Mark	Wind	Name		Nat	Born	Pos	Meet	Venue	Date
2:28.98 WR		Svetlana	Masterkova	RUS	17.1.68	1	VD	Bruxelles	23 Aug 96
2:29.34 WR		Maria Lurdes	Mutola	MOZ	27.10.72	1	VD	Bruxelles	25 Aug 95
2:30.6 WR		Tatyana	Providokhina	RUS	26.3.53	1		Podolsk	20 Aug 78
2:30.67 WR		Christine	Wachtel	GDR	6.1.65	1	ISTAF	Berlin	17 Aug 90
2:30.85		Martina	Kämpfert'	GDR	11.11.59	1		Berlin	9 Jul 80
2:31.50		Natalya	Artyomova ¶	RUS	5.1.63	1	ISTAF	Berlin	10 Sep 91
2:31.5 A		Maricica	Puica	ROU	29.7.50	1		Poiana Brasov	1 Jun 86
2:31.51		Sandra	Gasser ¶	SUI	27.7.62	1		Jerez de la Frontera	13 Sep 89

1500 METRES

Mark	Wind	Name		Nat	Born	Pos	Meet	Venue	Date
3:50.07 WR		Genzebe	Dibaba	ETH	8.2.91	1	Herc	Monaco	17 Jul 15
3:50.46 WR			Qu Yunxia	CHN	8.12.72	1	NG	Beijing	11 Sep 93
3:50.98			Jiang Bo	CHN	13.3.77	1	NG	Shanghai	18 Oct 97
3:51.34			Lang Yinglai	CHN	22.8.79	2	NG	Shanghai	18 Oct 97
3:51.92			Wang Junxia	CHN	9.1.73	2	NG	Beijing	11 Sep 93
3:52.47 WR		Tatyana	Kazankina ¶	RUS	17.12.51	1	WK	Zürich	13 Aug 80
3:53.91			Yin Lili ¶	CHN	11.11.79	3	NG	Shanghai	18 Oct 97
3:53.96		Paula	Ivan'	ROU	20.7.63	1	OG	Seoul	1 Oct 88
3:53.97			Lan Lixin	CHN	14.2.79	4	NG	Shanghai	18 Oct 97
3:54.11			Dibaba			1		Barcelona	8 Jul 15
3:54.23		Olga	Dvirna (10)	RUS	11.2.53	1	NC	Kyiv	27 Jul 82
3:54.52			Zhang Ling	CHN	13.4.80	5	NG	Shanghai	18 Oct 97
3:55.0 ' WR			Kazankina ¶			1	Znam	Moskva	6 Jul 80
3:55.01			Lan Lixin			1h2	NG	Shanghai	17 Oct 97
3:55.07			Dong Yanmei	CHN	16.2.77	6	NG	Shanghai	18 Oct 97
3:55.22		Laura	Muir	GBR	9.5.93	1	DL	Saint-Denis	27 Aug 16
3:55.30		Hassiba	Boulmerka	ALG	10.7.68	1	OG	Barcelona	8 Aug 92
3:55.33		Süreyya	Ayhan ¶	TUR	6.9.78	1	VD	Bruxelles	5 Sep 03
3:55.38			Qu Yunxia			2h2	NG	Shanghai	17 Oct 97
3:55.47			Zhang Ling			3h2	NG	Shanghai	17 Oct 97
3:55.60			Ayhan			1	WK	Zürich	15 Aug 03
3:55.68		Yuliya	Chizhenko ¶	RUS	30.8.79	1	Gaz	Saint-Denis	8 Jul 06
3:55.82			Dong Yanmei			4h2	NG	Shanghai	17 Oct 97

1500 METRES – 1 MILE – 2000 METRES A-T

Mark	Wind	Name		Nat	Born	Pos	Meet	Venue	Date
3:56.0 WR			Kazankina ¶			1		Podolsk	28 Jun 76
3:56.05		Sifan	Hassan	ETH/NED	.93	2	Herc	Monaco	17 Jul 15
3:56.14		Zamira	Zaytseva	UZB	16.2.53	2	NC	Kyiv	27 Jul 82
3:56.18		Maryam	Jamal	BRN	16.9.84	1	GP	Rieti	27 Aug 06
3:56.22			Ivan			1	WK	Zürich	17 Aug 88
3:56.29		Shannon	Rowbury	USA	19.9.84	3	Herc	Monaco	17 Jul 15
3:56.31			Liu Dong	CHN	24.12.73	5h2	NG	Shanghai	17 Oct 97
(30/20)									
3:56.41		Faith	Kipyegon	KEN	10.1.94	1	Pre	Eugene	28 May 16
3:56.43		Yelena	Soboleva ¶	RUS	3.10.82	2	Gaz	Saint-Denis	8 Jul 06
3:56.50		Tatyana	Pozdnyakova	RUS	4.3.56	3	NC	Kyiv	27 Jul 82
3:56.54		Abeba	Aregawi	ETH/SWE	5.7.90	1	GGala	Roma	31 May 12
3:56.63		Nadezhda	Ralldugina	UKR	15.11.57	1	Drz	Praha	18 Aug 84
3:56.65		Yekaterina	Podkopayeva'	RUS	11.6.52	1		Rieti	2 Sep 84
3:56.7 '		Lyubov	Smolka	UKR	29.11.52	2	Znam	Moskva	6 Jul 80
3:56.7		Doina	Melinte	ROU	27.12.56	1		Bucuresti	12 Jul 86
3:56.77+		Svetlana	Masterkova	RUS	17.1.68	1	WK	Zürich	14 Aug 96
3:56.8 '		Nadezhda	Olizarenko'	UKR	28.11.53	3	Znam	Moskva	6 Jul 80
(30)									
3:56.91		Lyudmila	Rogachova	RUS	30.10.66	2	OG	Barcelona	8 Aug 92
3:56.91		Tatyana	Tomashova ¶	RUS	1.7.75	1	EC	Göteborg	13 Aug 06
3:56.97		Gabriela	Szabo	ROU	14.11.75	1	Herc	Monaco	8 Aug 98
3:57.03			Liu Jing	CHN	3.2.71	6h2	NG	Shanghai	17 Oct 97
3:57.05		Svetlana	Guskova	MDA	19.8.59	4	NC	Kyiv	27 Jul 82
3:57.05		Hellen	Obiri	KEN	13.12.89	1	Pre	Eugene	31 May 14
3:57.12		Mary	Decker/Slaney	USA	4.8.58	1	vNord	Stockholm	26 Jul 83
3:57.22		Maricica	Puica	ROU	29.7.50	1		Bucuresti	1 Jul 84
3:57.22		Jennifer	Simpson	USA	23.8.86	2	DL	Saint-Denis	5 Jul 14
3:57.40		Suzy	Favor Hamilton	USA	8.8.68	1	Bisl	Oslo	28 Jul 00
(40)									
3:57.4 '		Totka	Petrova ¶	BUL	17.12.56	1	Balk	Athína	11 Aug 79
3:57.41		Jackline	Maranga	KEN	16.12.77	3	Herc	Monaco	8 Aug 98
3:57.46			Zhang Linli	CHN	6.3.73	3	NG	Beijing	11 Sep 93
3:57.71		Christiane	Wartenberg'	GDR	27.10.56	2	OG	Moskva	1 Aug 80
3:57.71		Carla	Sacramento	POR	10.12.71	4	Herc	Monaco	8 Aug 98
3:57.72		Galina	Zakharova	RUS	7.9.56	1	NP	Baku	14 Sep 84
3:57.73		Natalya	Yevdokimova	RUS	17.3.78	2	GP	Rieti	28 Aug 05
3:57.90		Kelly	Holmes	GBR	19.4.70	1	OG	Athína	28 Aug 04
3:57.92		Tatyana	Samolenko/Dorovskikh ¶	UKR	12.8.61	4	OG	Barcelona	8 Aug 92
3:58.12		Naomi	Mugo	KEN	2.1.77	5	Herc	Monaco	8 Aug 98
(50)		100th woman 3:59.95, 200th 4:02.26, 300th 4:04.10, 400th 4:05.5, 500th 4:06.45							
Indoors: 3:55.17 WIR			G Dibaba			1		Karlsruhe	1 Feb 14
Drugs disqualification: 3:56.15			Mariem Alaoui Selsouli ¶	MAR	8.4.84	(1)	DL	Saint-Denis	6 Jul 12
3:56.62		Asli	Çakir Alptekin ¶	TUR	20.8.85	(2)	DL	Saint-Denis	6 Jul 12
3:57.65		Anna	Alminova ¶	RUS	17.1.85	(1)	DL	Saint-Denis	16 Jul 10

1 MILE

Mark		Name		Nat	Born	Pos	Meet	Venue	Date
4:12.56 WR		Svetlana	Masterkova	RUS	17.1.68	1	WK	Zürich	14 Aug 96
4:14.30		Genzebe	Dibaba	ETH	8.2.91	1		Rovereto	6 Sep 16
4:15.61 WR		Paula	Ivan'	ROU	20.7.63	1	Nik	Nice	10 Jul 89
4:15.8		Natalya	Artyomova ¶	RUS	5.1.63	1		Leningrad	5 Aug 84
4:16.71 WR		Mary	Slaney (Decker)	USA	4.8.58	1	WK	Zürich	21 Aug 85
4:16.71		Faith	Kipyegon	KEN	10.1.94	1	VD	Bruxelles	11 Sep 15
4:17.25		Sonia	O'Sullivan	IRL	28.11.69	1	Bisl	Oslo	22 Jul 94
Indoors									
4:13.31 WIR		Genzebe	Dibaba	ETH	8.2.91	1	Globen	Stockholm	17 Feb 16
4:17.14 WIR		Doina	Melinte	ROU	27.12.56	1		East Rutherford	9 Feb 90
Drugs dq: 4:15.63		Yelena	Soboleva ¶	RUS	3.10.82	1		Moskva	29 Jun 07

2000 METRES

Mark		Name		Nat	Born	Pos	Meet	Venue	Date
5:25.36 WR		Sonia	O'Sullivan	IRL	28.11.69	1	TSB	Edinburgh	8 Jul 94
5:26.93		Yvonne	Murray	GBR	4.10.64	2	TSB	Edinburgh	8 Jul 94
5:27.50		Genzebe	Dibaba	ETH	8.2.91	1	GS	Ostrava	17 Jun 14
5:28.69 WR		Maricica	Puica	ROU	29.7.50	1	PTG	London (CP)	11 Jul 86
5:28.72 WR		Tatyana	Kazankina ¶	RUS	17.12.51	1		Moskva	4 Aug 84
5:29.43+			Wang Junxia	CHN	9.1.73	1h2	NG	Beijing	12 Sep 93
5:29.64		Tatyana	Pozdnyakova	UKR	4.3.56	2		Moskva	4 Aug 84
5:30.19		Zola	Budd'	GBR	26.5.66	3	PTG	London (CP)	11 Jul 86
5:30.19		Gelete	Burka	ETH	15.2.86	1	VD	Bruxelles	4 Sep 09
5:30.92		Galina	Zakharova	RUS	7.9.56	3		Moskva	4 Aug 84
Indoors: 5:30.53		Gabriela	Szabo	ROU	14.11.75	1		Sindelfingen	8 Mar 98

3000 METRES A-T 299

Mark	Wind	Name		Nat	Born	Pos	Meet	Venue	Date
3000 METRES									
8:06.11 WR			Wang Junxia	CHN	9.1.73	1	NG	Beijing	13 Sep 93
8:12.18			Qu Yunxia	CHN	8.12.72	2	NG	Beijing	13 Sep 93
8:12.19 WR			Wang Junxia			1h2	NG	Beijing	12 Sep 93
8:12.27			Qu Yunxia			2h2	NG	Beijing	12 Sep 93
8:16.50			Zhang Linli	CHN	6.3.73	3	NG	Beijing	13 Sep 93
8:19.78			Ma Liyan	CHN	6.9.68	3h2	NG	Beijing	12 Sep 93
8:20.68		Hellen	Obiri	KEN	13.12.89	1	DL	Doha	9 May 14
8:21.14		Mercy	Cherono	KEN	7.5.91	2	DL	Doha	9 May 14
8:21.26			Ma Liyan			4	NG	Beijing	13 Sep 93
8:21.42		Gabriela	Szabo	ROU	14.11.75	1	Herc	Monaco	19 Jul 02
8:21.64		Sonia	O'Sullivan	IRL	28.11.69	1	TSB	London (CP)	15 Jul 94
8:21.84			Zhang Lirong	CHN	3.3.73	5	NG	Beijing	13 Sep 93
8:22.06 WR			Zhang Linli			1h1	NG	Beijing	12 Sep 93
8:22.20		Paula	Radcliffe (10)	GBR	17.12.73	2	Herc	Monaco	19 Jul 02
8:22.22		Almaz	Ayana	ETH	21.11.91	1		Rabat	14 Jun 15
8:22.34			Ayana			1	WK	Zürich	3 Sep 15
8:22.44			Zhang Lirong			2h1	NG	Beijing	12 Sep 93
8:22.62 WR		Tatyana	Kazankina ¶	RUS	17.12.51	1		Leningrad	26 Aug 84
8:23.11			Ayana			1	DL	Doha	6 May 16
8:23.23		Edith	Masai	KEN	4.4.67	3	Herc	Monaco	19 Jul 02
8:23.26		Olga	Yegorova ¶	RUS	28.3.72	1	WK	Zürich	17 Aug 01
8:23.55		Faith	Kipyegon	KEN	10.1.94	3	DL	Doha	9 May 14
8:23.75			Yegorova			1	GP	Saint-Denis	6 Jul 01
8:23.96			Yegorova			1	GGala	Roma	29 Jun 01
8:24.19			Szabo			2	WK	Zürich	17 Aug 01
8:24.27			Obiri			1	Herc	Monaco	15 Jul 16
8:24.31			Szabo			1	GP	Paris (C)	29 Jul 98
8:24.41		Viola	Kibiwot	KEN	22.12.83	4	DL	Doha	9 May 14
8:24.51+		Meseret	Defar	ETH	19.11.83	1	in 2M	Bruxelles	14 Sep 07
8:24.58			Ayana			5	DL	Doha	9 May 14
		(30/17)							
8:25.40		Yelena	Zadorozhnaya	RUS	3.12.77	2	GGala	Roma	29 Jun 01
8:25.56		Tatyana	Tomashova ¶	RUS	1.7.75	3	GGala	Roma	29 Jun 01
8:25.62		Berhane	Adere (20)	ETH	21.7.73	3	WK	Zürich	17 Aug 01
8:25.83		Mary	Slaney	USA	4.8.58	1	GGala	Roma	7 Sep 85
8:25.92		Gelete	Burka	ETH	15.2.86	2	DNG	Stockholm	25 Jul 08
8:26.21		Genzebe	Dibaba	ETH	8.2.91	6	DL	Doha	9 May 14
8:26.48		Zahra	Ouaziz	MAR	20.12.69	2	WK	Zürich	11 Aug 99
8:26.53		Tatyana	Samolenko' ¶	UKR	12.8.61	1	OG	Seoul	25 Sep 88
8:26.78 WR		Svetlana	Ulmasova	UZB	4.2.53	1	NC	Kyiv	25 Jul 82
8:27.10 WR		Lyudmila	Bragina	RUS	24.7.43	1	v USA	College Park	7 Aug 76
8:27.15		Paula	Ivan'	ROU	20.7.63	2	OG	Seoul	25 Sep 88
8:27.62		Getenesh	Wami	ETH	11.12.74	4	WK	Zürich	17 Aug 01
8:27.83		Maricica	Puica	ROU	29.7.50	2	GGala	Roma	7 Sep 85
		(30)							
8:28.33		Janet	Kisa	KEN	5.3.92	3	Herc	Monaco	15 Jul 16
8:28.41		Sentayehu	Ejigu	ETH	21.6.85	1	Herc	Monaco	22 Jul 10
8:28.51		Irene	Jelagat	KEN	10.12.88	7	DL	Doha	9 May 14
8:28.66		Vivian	Cheruiyot	KEN	11.9.83	1	WAF	Stuttgart	23 Sep 07
8:28.80		Marta	Domínguez	ESP	3.11.75	3	WK	Zürich	11 Aug 00
8:28.83		Zola	Budd'	GBR	26.5.66	3	GGala	Roma	7 Sep 85
8:28.87		Maryam	Jamal	BRN	16.9.84	1	Bisl	Oslo	29 Jul 05
8:29.02		Yvonne	Murray	GBR	4.10.64	3	OG	Seoul	25 Sep 88
8:29.06		Priscah	Cherono	KEN	27.6.80	3	WAF	Stuttgart	23 Sep 07
8:29.14		Lydia	Cheromei ¶	KEN	11.5.77	5	WK	Zürich	11 Aug 00
		(40)							
8:29.36		Svetlana	Guskova	MDA	19.8.59	2	NC	Kyiv	25 Jul 82
8:29.38		Sifan	Hassan	NED	.93	2	VD	Bruxelles	5 Sep 14
8:29.52		Mariem Alaoui	Selsouli ¶	MAR	8.4.84	1	Herc	Monaco	25 Jul 07
8:29.55		Tirunesh	Dibaba	ETH	1.10.85	1	LGP	London (CP)	28 Jul 06
8:29.58		Jennifer	Simpson'	USA	23.8.86	4	VD	Bruxelles	5 Sep 14
8:29.93		Shannon	Rowbury	USA	19.9.84	5	VD	Bruxelles	5 Sep 14
8:30.00		Mimi	Belete	BRN	9.6.88	8	DL	Doha	9 May 14
8:30.18		Mariya	Pantyukhova	RUS	14.8.74	4	WK	Zürich	11 Aug 99
8:30.22		Carla	Sacramento	POR	10.12.71	2	Herc	Monaco	4 Aug 99
8:30.39		Irina	Mikitenko	GER	23.8.72	6	WK	Zürich	11 Aug 00
		(50)		100th woman 8:35.89, 200th 8:42.68, 300th 8:46.71					
Indoors:									
8:16.60 WIR		Genzebe	Dibaba	ETH	8.2.91	1		Stockholm	6 Feb 14

WOMEN All-time

Mark	Wind	Name		Nat	Born	Pos	Meet	Venue	Date
8:23.72	WIR	Meseret	Defar	ETH	19.11.83	1	Spark	Stuttgart	3 Feb 07
8:23.74		Meselech	Melkamu	ETH	27.4.85	2	Spark	Stuttgart	3 Feb 07
8:25.27		Sentayehu	Ejigu	ETH	21.6.85	2	Spark	Stuttgart	6 Feb 10
8:27.86	WIR	Liliya	Shobukhova ¶	RUS	13.11.77	1	NC	Moskva	17 Feb 06
8:28.49		Anna	Alminova ¶	RUS	17.1.85	2	Spark	Stuttgart	7 Feb 09
8:29.00		Olesya	Syreva ¶	RUS	25.11.83	2	NC	Moskva	17 Feb 06

5000 METRES

Mark		Name		Nat	Born	Pos	Meet	Venue	Date
14:11.15	WR	Tirunesh	Dibaba	ETH	1.10.85	1	Bisl	Oslo	6 Jun 08
14:12.59		Almaz	Ayana	ETH	21.11.91	1	GGala	Roma	2 Jun 16
14:12.88		Meseret	Defar	ETH	19.11.83	1	DNG	Stockholm	22 Jul 08
14:14.32			Ayana			1	DL	Shanghai	17 May 15
14:15.41		Genzebe	Dibaba	ETH	8.2.91	1	DL	Saint-Denis	4 Jul 15
14:16.31			Ayana			1		Rabat	22 May 16
14:16.63	WR		Defar			1	Bisl	Oslo	15 Jun 07
14:18.89			Ayana			1	VD	Bruxelles	9 Sep 16
14:19.76			G Dibaba			1	Pre	Eugene	30 May 15
14:20.87		Vivian	Cheruiyot	KEN	11.9.83	1	DNG	Stockholm	29 Jul 11
14:21.29			G Dibaba			1	Bisl	Oslo	11 Jun 15
14:21.97			Ayana			2	DL	Saint-Denis	4 Jul 15
14:22.51			Cheruiyot			2	Bisl	Oslo	15 Jun 07
14:23.46			T Dibaba			1	GP	Rieti	7 Sep 08
14:23.68			T Dibaba			1	DL	Saint-Denis	6 Jul 13
14:23.75		Liliya	Shobukhova ¶	RUS	13.11.77	1	NC	Kazan	19 Jul 08
14:24.53	WR		Defar			1		New York (RI)	3 Jun 06
14:24.68	WR	Elvan	Abeylegesse ¶	TUR	11.9.82	1	Bisl	Bergen (Fana)	11 Jun 04
14:25.43			Cheruiyot			1	VD	Bruxelles	5 Sep 08
14:25.52			Defar			2	VD	Bruxelles	5 Sep 08
14:25.78		Hellen	Obiri	KEN	13.12.89	2	VD	Bruxelles	9 Sep 16
14:25.84			Ayana			2	DL	Saint-Denis	6 Jul 13
14:26.17			Cheruiyot			1	OG	Rio de Janeiro	19 Aug 16
14:26.83			Ayana			1	WCh	Beijing	30 Aug 15
14:26.90			Defar			1	Bisl	Oslo	13 Jun 13
14:27.41			Cheruiyot			1	DL	Saint-Denis	16 Jul 10
14:28.09	WR		Jiang Bo	CHN	13.3.77	1	NG	Shanghai	23 Oct 97
14:28.39		Sentayehu	Ejigu (10)	ETH	21.6.85	2	DL	Saint-Denis	16 Jul 10
14:28.88			G Dibaba			1	Herc	Monaco	18 Jul 14
14:28.98			Defar			1	VD	Bruxelles	26 Aug 05
		(30/10)							
14:29.11		Paula	Radcliffe	GBR	17.12.73	1	ECpS	Bydgoszcz	20 Jun 04
14:29.32		Olga	Yegorova ¶	RUS	28.3.72	1	ISTAF	Berlin	31 Aug 01
14:29.32		Berhane	Adere	ETH	21.7.73	1	Bisl	Oslo	27 Jun 03
14:29.50		Viola	Kibiwot	KEN	22.12.83	2		Rabat	22 May 16
14:29.82			Dong Yanmei	CHN	16.2.77	2	NG	Shanghai	23 Oct 97
14:29.82		Senbere	Teferi	ETH	3.5.95	3	VD	Bruxelles	9 Sep 16
14:30.42		Sally	Kipyego	KEN	19.12.85	2	WK	Zürich	8 Sep 11
14:30.88		Getenesh	Wami	ETH	11.12.74	1	NA	Heusden-Zolder	5 Aug 00
14:31.14		Linet	Masai	KEN	5.12.89	2	DL	Shanghai	23 May 10
14:31.20		Gelete	Burka	ETH	15.2.86	2	GS	Ostrava	27 Jun 07
		(20)							
14:31.48		Gabriela	Szabo	ROU	14.11.75	1	ISTAF	Berlin	1 Sep 98
14:31.91		Meselech	Melkamu	ETH	27.4.85	3	DL	Shanghai	23 May 10
14:31.91		Sylvia	Kibet	KEN	28.3.84	4	DL	Shanghai	23 May 10
14:31.95		Faith	Kipyegon	KEN	10.1.94	2	Pre	Eugene	30 May 15
14:32.08		Zahra	Ouaziz	MAR	20.12.69	2	ISTAF	Berlin	1 Sep 98
14:32.33			Liu Shixiang ¶	CHN	13.1.71	3h1	NG	Shanghai	21 Oct 97
14:32.74		Ejagayehu	Dibaba	ETH	25.6.82	3	Bisl	Bergen (Fana)	11 Jun 04
14:33.04		Werknesh	Kidane	ETH	21.11.81	2	Bisl	Oslo	27 Jun 03
14:33.13		Gulnara	Galkina'	RUS	9.7.78	2	NC	Kazan	19 Jul 08
14:33.30		Etenesh	Diro	ETH	10.5.91	4	VD	Bruxelles	9 Sep 16
		(30)							
14:33.49		Lucy Wangui	Kabuu	KEN	24.3.84	2	Bisl	Oslo	6 Jun 08
14:33.84		Edith	Masai	KEN	4.4.67	3	Bisl	Oslo	2 Jun 06
14:34.10		Mercy	Cherono	KEN	7.5.91	3	DL	Saint-Denis	4 Jul 15
14:35.30		Priscah	Jepleting/Cherono	KEN	27.6.80	4	Bisl	Oslo	2 Jun 06
14:36.45	WR	Fernanda	Ribeiro	POR	23.6.69	1		Hechtel	22 Jul 95
14:36.52		Mariem Alaoui	Selsouli ¶	MAR	8.4.84	1	G Gala	Roma	13 Jul 07
14:37.07		Jéssica	Augusto	POR	8.11.81	5	DL	Saint-Denis	16 Jul 10
14:37.33	WR	Ingrid	Kristiansen'	NOR	21.3.56	1		Stockholm	5 Aug 86
14:37.61		Yasemin	Can	TUR	11.12.96	6	GGala	Roma	2 Jun 16

5000 – 10,000 METRES A-T

Mark	Wind	Name		Nat	Born	Pos	Meet	Venue	Date
14:38.09		Mariya	Konovalova ¶ (40) RUS		14.8.74	3	NC	Kazan	19 Jul 08
14:38.21		Isabella	Ochichi	KEN	28.10.79	4	VD	Bruxelles	26 Aug 05
14:38.44		Wude	Ayalew	ETH	4.7.87	5	Bisl	Oslo	3 Jul 09
14:38.70		Janet	Kisa	KEN	5.3.92	4		Rabat	22 May 16
14:39.19		Ines	Chenonge	KEN	1.2.82	6	DL	Saint-Denis	16 Jul 10
14:39.22		Tatyana	Tomashova ¶	RUS	1.7.75	4	ISTAF	Berlin	31 Aug 01
14:39.49		Betsy	Saina	KEN	30.6.88	5	Herc	Monaco	18 Jul 14
14:39.56		Alice Aprot	Nawowuna	KEN	2.1.94	6	VD	Bruxelles	9 Sep 16
14:39.83		Leah	Malot	KEN	7.6.72	1	ISTAF	Berlin	1 Sep 00
14:39.96		Yin Lili ¶		CHN	11.11.79	4	NG	Shanghai	23 Oct 97
14:39.96		Jo (50)	Pavey	GBR	20.9.73	3	VD	Bruxelles	25 Aug 06

100th woman 14:48.07, 200th 15:04.07, 300th 15:09.84, 400th 15:16.04, 500th 15:20.13

Indoors: 14:18.86

			G Dibaba			1	XL-G	Stockholm	19 Feb 15
14:24.37	WIR		Defar			1		Stockholm	18 Feb 09
14:24.79			Defar			1	GE Galan	Stockholm	10 Feb 10
14:27.42	WIR		T Dibaba			1	BIG	Boston (R)	27 Jan 07
14:39.89		Kimberley	Smith	NZL	19.11.73	1		New York (Armory)	27 Feb 09

Drugs disqualification: 14:36.79 Alemitu Bekele ¶ TUR 17.9.77 4 VD Bruxelles 27 Aug 10

10,000 METRES

Mark	Wind	Name		Nat	Born	Pos	Meet	Venue	Date
29:17.45	WR	Almaz	Ayana	ETH	21.11.91	1	OG	Rio de Janeiro	12 Aug 16
29:31.78	WR		Wang Junxia	CHN	9.1.73	1	NG	Beijing	8 Sep 93
29:32.53		Vivian	Cheruiyot	KEN	11.9.83	2	OG	Rio de Janeiro	12 Aug 16
29:42.56		Tirunesh	Dibaba	ETH	1.10.85	3	OG	Rio de Janeiro	12 Aug 16
29:53.51		Alice Aprot	Nawowuna	KEN	2.1.94	4	OG	Rio de Janeiro	12 Aug 16
29:53.80		Meselech	Melkamu	ETH	27.4.85	1		Utrecht	14 Jun 09
29:54.66			T Dibaba			1	OG	Beijing	15 Aug 08
29:59.20		Meseret	Defar	ETH	19.11.83	1	NC	Birmingham	11 Jul 09
30:01.09		Paula	Radcliffe	GBR	17.12.73	1	EC	München	6 Aug 02
30:04.18		Berhane	Adere (10)	ETH	21.7.73	1	WCh	Saint-Denis	23 Aug 03
30:07.00			Ayana			1	OT	Hengelo	29 Jun 16
30:07.15		Werknesh	Kidane	ETH	21.11.81	2	WCh	Saint-Denis	23 Aug 03
30:07.20			Sun Yingjie ¶	CHN	3.10.77	3	WCh	Saint-Denis	23 Aug 03
30:07.78		Betsy	Saina	KEN	30.6.88	5	OG	Rio de Janeiro	12 Aug 16
30:08.06			Defar			1		Sollentuna	27 Jun 13
30:11.53		Florence	Kiplagat	KEN	27.2.87	2		Utrecht	14 Jun 09
30:11.87		Wude	Ayalew	ETH	4.7.87	3		Utrecht	14 Jun 09
30:12.53		Lornah	Kiplagat (KEN)	NED	1.5.74	4	WCh	Saint-Denis	23 Aug 03
30:13.17		Molly	Huddle	USA	31.8.84	6	OG	Rio de Janeiro	12 Aug 16
30:13.37			Zhong Huandi	CHN	28.6.67	2	NG	Beijing	8 Sep 93
30:13.74	WR	Ingrid	Kristiansen'	NOR	21.3.56	1	Bisl	Oslo	5 Jul 86
30:15.67			T Dibaba			1		Sollentuna	28 Jun 05
30:17.15			Radcliffe			1	GP	Gateshead	27 Jun 04
30:17.49		Derartu	Tulu	ETH	21.3.72	1	OG	Sydney	30 Sep 00
30:18.39		Ejegayehu	Dibaba (20)	ETH	25.6.82	2		Sollentuna	28 Jun 05
30:19.39			Kidane			1	GP II	Stanford	29 May 05
30:20.75			T Dibaba			1	OG	London (OS)	3 Aug 12
30:21.67		Elvan	Abeylegesse ¶	TUR	11.9.82	1	ECp	Antalya	15 Apr 06
30:22.22		Shalane	Flanagan	USA	8.7.81	3	OG	Beijing	15 Aug 08
30:22.48		Getenesh	Wami	ETH	11.12.74	2	OG	Sydney	30 Sep 00
30:22.88		Fernanda (30/23)	Ribeiro	POR	23.6.69	3	OG	Sydney	30 Sep 00
30:23.07		Alla	Zhilyayeva	RUS	5.2.69	5	WCh	Saint-Denis	23 Aug 03
30:24.36			Xing Huina	CHN	25.2.84	1	OG	Athína	27 Aug 04
30:26.20		Galina	Bogomolova	RUS	15.10.77	6	WCh	Saint-Denis	23 Aug 03
30:26.37		Sally	Kipyego	KEN	19.12.85	2	OG	London (OS)	3 Aug 12
30:26.41		Yasemin	Can	TUR	11.12.96	7	OG	Rio de Janeiro	12 Aug 16
30:26.50		Linet (30)	Masai	KEN	5.12.89	1	OG	Beijing	15 Aug 08
30:26.66		Gelete	Burka	ETH	23.1.86	8	OG	Rio de Janeiro	12 Aug 16
30:26.70		Belaynesh	Oljira	ETH	26.6.90	3	Pre	Eugene	1 Jun 12
30:29.21mx		Philes	Ongori	KEN	19.7.86	1mx		Yokohama	23 Nov 08
30:29.23		Gladys	Cherono	KEN	12.5.83	2	GS	Ostrava	27 Jun 13
30:29.36		Liliya	Shobukhova ¶	RUS	13.11.77	1	NC	Cheboksary	23 Jul 09
30:30.26		Edith	Masai	KEN	4.4.67	5	WCh	Helsinki	6 Aug 05
30:31.03		Mariya	Konovalova ¶	RUS	14.8.74	2	NC	Cheboksary	23 Jul 09
30:31.42		Inga	Abitova ¶	RUS	6.3.82	1	EC	Göteborg	7 Aug 06
30:32.03		Tegla	Loroupe	KEN	9.5.73	3	WCh	Sevilla	26 Aug 99
30:32.36		Susanne (40)	Wigene	NOR	12.2.78	2	EC	Göteborg	7 Aug 06
30:32.72		Lidiya	Grigoryeva ¶	RUS	21.1.74	3	EC	Göteborg	7 Aug 06

WOMEN All-time

HALF MARATHON A-T

Mark	Wind	Name		Nat	Born	Pos	Meet	Venue	Date
30:35.54		Kimberley	Smith	NZL	19.11.81	2		Stanford	4 May 08
30:35.91		Birhane	Ababel	ETH	10.6.90	4	GS	Ostrava	27 Jun 13
30:36.75		Netsanet	Gudeta	ETH	12.2.91	4	OT	Hengelo	29 Jun 16
30:37.38		Genet	Yalew	ETH	31.12.92	5	OT	Hengelo	29 Jun 16
30:37.68		Benita	Johnson	AUS	6.5.79	8	WCh	Saint-Denis	23 Aug 03
30:38.09			Dong Yanmei	CHN	16.2.77	1	NG	Shanghai	19 Oct 97
30:38.33		Mestawat	Tufa	ETH	14.9.83	1		Nijmegen	25 Jun 08
30:38.78		Jelena	Prokopcuka	LAT	21.9.76	6	EC	Göteborg	7 Aug 06
30:39.41			Lan Lixin	CHN	14.2.79	2		Shanghai	19 Oct 97

(50) 100th woman 31:08.89, 200th 31:29.22, 300th 31:43.55, 400th 31:55.51, 500th 32:04.27

Drugs dq: 29:56.34 Elvan Abeylegesse ¶ TUR 11.9.82 (2) OG Beijing 15 Aug 08

HALF MARATHON
Slightly downhill courses included: Newcastle-South Shields 30.5m, Tokyo 33m (to 1998), Lisboa (Spring to 2008) 69m

Mark	Wind	Name		Nat	Born	Pos	Meet	Venue	Date
65:09	WR	Florence	Kiplagat	KEN	27.2.87	1		Barcelona	15 Feb 15
65:12	WR		F Kiplagat			1		Barcelona	16 Feb 14
65:39	dh	Mary	Keitany	KEN	18.1.82	1	GNR	South Shields	7 Sep 14
65:40	dh	Paula	Radcliffe	GBR	17.12.73	1	GNR	South Shields	21 Sep 03
65:44	dh	Susan	Chepkemei	KEN	25.6.75	1		Lisboa	1 Apr 01
65:45	dh	Priscah	Jeptoo	KEN	26.6.84	1	GNR	South Shields	15 Sep 13
65:50	WR		Keitany			1		Ra's Al Khaymah	18 Feb 11
65:51		Violah	Jepchumba	KEN	23.10.90	1		Praha	2 Apr 16
66:02			Keitany			1		Ra's Al-Khaymah	13 Feb 15
66:04		Cynthia	Limo	KEN	18.12.89	1		Ra's Al-Khaymah	12 Feb 16
66:07		Gladys	Cherono	KEN	12.5.83	2		Ra's Al-Khaymah	12 Feb 16
66:09		Lucy Wangui	Kabuu	KEN	24.3.84	1		Ra's Al-Khaymah	15 Feb 13
66:09	dh	Meseret	Defar (10)	ETH	19.11.83	2	GNR	South Shields	15 Sep 13
66:11			P Jeptoo			2		Ra's Al-Khaymah	15 Feb 13
66:14		Worknesh	Degefa	ETH	28.10.90	2		Praha	2 Apr 16
66:19		Joyce	Chepkirui	KEN	20.8.88	1		Praha	5 Apr 14
66:25		Lornah	Kiplagat	NED	1.5.74	1	WCh	Udine	14 Oct 07
66:26		Genet	Yalew	ETH	31.12.92	3		Ra's Al-Khaymah	12 Feb 16
66:27		Rita	Jeptoo ¶	KEN	15.2.81	3		Ra's Al-Khaymah	15 Feb 13
66:28		Mamitu	Daska	ETH	16.10.83	2		Ra's Al-Khaymah	13 Feb 15
66:29		Mercy Wacera	Ngugi	KEN	17.12.88	1		Houston	17 Jan 16
66:34	dh		Kiplagat			2		Lisboa	1 Apr 01
66:36			Keitany			1	WCh	Birmingham	11 Oct 09
66:38			F Kiplagat			1		Ostia	26 Feb 12
66:38			G Cherono			1		Istanbul	26 Apr 15
66:38			Keitany			1		Olomouc	20 Jun 15
66:39		Peres	Jepchirchir	KEN	27.9.93	4		Ra's Al-Khaymah	12 Feb 16
66:40*		Ingrid	Kristiansen	NOR	21.3.56	1	NC	Sandnes	5 Apr 87
66:41			C Limo			2		Houston	17 Jan 16
66:43	dh	Masako	Chiba	JPN	18.7.76	1		Tokyo	19 Jan 97

(30/20) * uncertain course measurement

Mark	Wind	Name		Nat	Born	Pos	Meet	Venue	Date
66:44		Elana	Meyer	RSA	10.10.66	1		Tokyo	15 Jan 99
66:49		Esther	Wanjiru	KEN	27.3.77	2		Tokyo	15 Jan 99
66:56		Meseret	Hailu	ETH	12.9.90	4		Ra's Al-Khaymah	15 Feb 13
66:56	dh	Tirunesh	Dibaba	ETH	1.10.85	3	GNR	South Shields	15 Sep 13
66:57	dh	Kara	Goucher	USA	9.7.78	1	GNR	South Shields	30 Sep 07
66:57		Gladys	Chesire	KEN	20.2.93	5		Ra's Al-Khaymah	12 Feb 16
66:58		Jemima Jelagat	Sumgong	KEN	21.12.84	6		Ra's Al-Khaymah	12 Feb 16
67:03	dh	Derartu	Tulu	ETH	21.3.72	3		Lisboa	1 Apr 01
67:07		Elvan	Abeylegesse	TUR	11.9.82	1		Ra's Al Khaymah	19 Feb 10
67:08		Sharon	Cherop	KEN	16.3.84	2		New Delhi	21 Nov 11

(30)

Mark	Wind	Name		Nat	Born	Pos	Meet	Venue	Date
67:11	dh	Liz	McColgan	GBR	24.5.64	1		Tokyo	26 Jan 92
67:11		Kimberley	Smith	NZL	19.11.81	1		Philadelphia	18 Sep 11
67:12	dh	Tegla	Loroupe	KEN	9.5.73	1		Lisboa	10 Mar 96
67:13		Mare	Dibaba	ETH	20.10.89	2		Ra's Al Khaymah	19 Feb 10
67:16		Edith	Masai	KEN	4.4.67	1		Berlin	2 Apr 06
67:16		Angela	Tanui	KEN	27.7.92	2		Ostia	13 Mar 16
67:17		Pasalia	Kipkoech	KEN	22.12.88	1		Rio de Janeiro	19 Aug 12
67:18		Dire	Tune	ETH	19.6.85	1		R'as Al Khaymah	20 Feb 09
67:19	dh	Sonia	O'Sullivan	IRL	28.11.69	1	GNR	South Shields	6 Oct 02
67:21		Aselefech	Mergia	ETH	23.1.85	3		New Delhi	21 Nov 11

(40)

Mark	Wind	Name		Nat	Born	Pos	Meet	Venue	Date
67:22		Agnes	Kiprop	KEN	12.12.79	2		Ostia	26 Feb 12
67:23		Margaret	Okayo	KEN	30.5.76	1		Udine	28 Sep 03
67:26		Kayoko	Fukushi	JPN	25.3.82	1		Marugame	5 Feb 06

HALF MARATHON – MARATHON A-T   303

Mark	Wind	Name		Nat	Born	Pos	Meet	Venue	Date
67:26		Lydia	Cheromei ¶	KEN	11.5.77	2		Praha	31 Mar 12
67:27		Belaynesh	Oljira	ETH	26.6.90	4		New Delhi	27 Nov 11
67:28		Worknesh	Kidane	ETH	21.11.81	2		Philadelphia	18 Sep 11
67:31		Netsanet	Gudeta	ETH	12.2.91	1		Valencia	18 Oct 15
67:31		Magdalene	Masai	KEN	4.4.93	3		Ostia	13 Mar 16
67:32	dh	Berhane	Adere	ETH	21.7.73	2	GNR	South Shields	21 Sep 03
67:34		Deena	Kastor	USA	14.2.73	2		Berlin	2 Apr 06
67:34		Atsede	Baysa	ETH	16.4.87	1		Barcelona	17 Feb 13
(51)									

100th woman 68:11, 200th 69:06, 300th 69:36, 400th 70:01, 500th 70:21

MARATHON

P = point-to-point or start and finish more than 30% apart, 2nd column

WOMEN All-time

Mark	Wind	Name		Nat	Born	Pos	Meet	Venue	Date
2:15:25	WR	Paula	Radcliffe	GBR	17.12.73	1		London	13 Apr 03
2:17:18	WR		Radcliffe			1		Chicago	13 Oct 02
2:17:42			Radcliffe			1		London	17 Apr 05
2:18:37		Mary	Keitany	KEN	18.1.82	1		London	22 Apr 12
2:18:47	WR	Catherine	Ndereba	KEN	21.7.72	1		Chicago	7 Oct 01
2:18:56			Radcliffe			1		London	14 Apr 02
2:18:58		Tiki	Gelana	ETH	22.10.87	1		Rotterdam	15 Apr 12
2:19:12		Mizuki	Noguchi	JPN	3.7.78	1		Berlin	25 Sep 05
2:19:19		Irina	Mikitenko	GER	23.8.72	1		Berlin	28 Sep 08
2:19:19			Keitany			1		London	17 Apr 11
2:19:25		Gladys	Cherono	KEN	12.5.83	1		Berlin	27 Sep 15
2:19:26			Ndereba			2		Chicago	13 Oct 02
2:19:31		Aselefech	Mergia	ETH	23.1.85	1		Dubai	27 Jan 12
2:19:34		Lucy Wangui	Kabuu	KEN	24.3.84	2		Dubai	27 Jan 12
2:19:36		Deena	Kastor (10)	USA	14.2.73	1		London	23 Apr 06
2:19:39			Sun Yingjie ¶	CHN	3.10.77	1		Beijing	19 Oct 03
2:19:41		Yoko	Shibui	JPN	14.3.79	1		Berlin	26 Sep 04
2:19:41		Tirfi	Tsegaye	ETH	25.11.84	1		Dubai	22 Jan 16
2:19:44		Florence	Kiplagat	KEN	27.2.87	1		Berlin	25 Sep 11
2:19:46	WR	Naoko	Takahashi	JPN	6.5.72	1		Berlin	30 Sep 01
2:19:50		Edna	Kiplagat	KEN	15.11.79	2		London	22 Apr 12
2:19:51	P		Zhou Chunxiu	CHN	15.11.78	1	Dong-A	Seoul	12 Mar 06
2:19:52		Mare	Dibaba	ETH	20.10.89	3		Dubai	27 Jan 12
2:19:52			M Dibaba			1		Xiamen	3 Jan 15
2:19:55			Ndereba			2		London	13 Apr 03
2:19:57		Rita	Jeptoo ¶	KEN	15.2.81	1		Chicago	13 Oct 13
2:20:02			Mergia			1		Dubai	23 Jan 15
2:20:03			Cherono			2		Dubai	23 Jan 15
2:20:14		Priscah	Jeptoo	KEN	26.6.84	3		London	22 Apr 12
2:20:15			P Jeptoo			1		London	21 Apr 13
		(30/20)							
2:20:27		Feyse	Tadesse	ETH	19.11.88	2		Berlin	28 Sep 14
2:20:30		Bezunesh	Bekele	ETH	29.1.83	4		Dubai	27 Jan 12
2:20:30		Aberu	Kebede	ETH	12.9.89	1		Berlin	30 Sep 12
2:20:35		Tirunesh	Dibaba	ETH	1.10.85	3		London	13 Apr 14
2:20:42		Berhane	Adere	ETH	21.7.73	1		Chicago	22 Oct 06
2:20:43	WR	Tegla	Loroupe	KEN	9.5.73	1		Berlin	26 Sep 99
2:20:47		Galina	Bogomolova	RUS	15.10.77	2		Chicago	22 Oct 06
2:20:48		Jemima Jelagat	Sumgong	KEN	21.12.84	2		Chicago	13 Oct 13
2:20:48		Amane	Beriso	ETH	13.10.91	2		Dubai	22 Jan 16
2:20:59		Shure	Demise	ETH	21.1.96	4		Dubai	23 Jan 15
		(30)							
2:21:01		Meselech	Melkamu	ETH	27.4.85	1		Frankfurt	28 Oct 12
2:21:06	WR	Ingrid	Kristiansen	NOR	21.3.56	1		London	21 Apr 85
2:21:09		Meseret	Hailu	ETH	12.9.90	1		Amsterdam	21 Oct 12
2:21:14		Shalane	Flanagan	USA	8.7.81	3		Berlin	28 Sep 14
2:21:21		Joan	Benoit'	USA	16.5.57	1		Chicago	20 Oct 85
2:21:27		Helah	Kiprop	KEN	7.4.85	1		Tokyo	28 Feb 16
2:21:29		Lyudmila	Petrova	RUS	7.10.68	2		London	23 Apr 06
2:21:30		Constantina	Dita	ROU	23.1.70	2		Chicago	9 Oct 05
2:21:30		Lydia	Cheromei ¶	KEN	11.5.77	6		Dubai	27 Jan 12
2:21:31		Svetlana	Zakharova	RUS	15.9.70	4		Chicago	13 Oct 02
		(40)							
2:21:31		Askale	Tafa	ETH	27.9.84	2		Berlin	28 Sep 08
2:21:34		Getenesh	Wami	ETH	11.12.74	1		Berlin	25 Sep 06
2:21:39		Georgina	Rono	KEN	19.5.84	2		Frankfurt	28 Oct 12
2:21:41		Eunice	Jepkirui Kirwa	KEN	20.5.84	2		Amsterdam	21 Oct 12
2:21:45		Masako	Chiba	JPN	18.7.76	2		Osaka	26 Jan 03

MARATHON – 2000m, 3000m STEEPLECHASE A-T

Mark	Wind	Name		Nat	Born	Pos	Meet	Venue	Date
2:21:46		Susan	Chepkemei ¶	KEN	25.6.75	3		London	23 Apr 06
2:21:51		Naoko	Sakamoto	JPN	14.11.80	3		Osaka	26 Jan 03
2:21:51		Amane	Gobena	ETH	1.9.82	2		Tokyo	28 Feb 16
2:21:52		Tigist	Tufa	ETH	26.1.87	1		Shanghai	2 Nov 14
2:21:56		Mulu	Seboka	ETH	24.9.84	6		Dubai	23 Jan 15
		(50)	100th woman 2:23:30, 200th 2:25:15, 300th 2:26:26, 400th 2:27:26, 500th 2:28:16						

Downhill point-to-point course – Boston marathon is downhill overall (139m) and sometimes strongly wind-aided.

Mark	Wind	Name		Nat	Born	Pos	Meet	Venue	Date
2:19:59	D	Buzunesh	Deba	ETH	8.9.87	2		Boston	21 Apr 14
2:20:41	D	Jemima Jelagat	Sumgong	KEN	21.12.84	4		Boston	21 Apr 14
2:20:43	D	Margaret	Okayo	KEN	30.5.76	1		Boston	15 Apr 02
2:21:45	D	Uta	Pippig ¶	GER	7.9.65	1		Boston	18 Apr 94

Drugs disqualification

Mark	Wind	Name		Nat	Born	Pos	Meet	Venue	Date
2:18:20		Liliya	Shobukhova	RUS	13.11.77	1		Chicago	9 Oct 11
2:20:15			Shobukhova			2		London	17 Apr 11
2:20:23			Wei Yanan ¶	CHN	6.12.81	1		Beijing	20 Oct 02
2:18:57	D	Rita	Jeptoo ¶	KEN	15.2.81	1		Boston	21 Apr 14
2:21:29	D	Aleksandra	Duliba ¶	BLR	9.1.88	6		Boston	21 Apr 14

2000 METRES STEEPLECHASE

Mark	Name		Nat	Born	Pos	Meet	Venue	Date
6:02.16	Virginia	Nyambura	KEN	20.7.93	1	ISTAF	Berlin	6 Sep 15
6:02.47	Beatrice	Chepkoech	KEN	6.7.91	2	ISTAF	Berlin	6 Sep 15
6:03.38	Wioletta	Janowska	POL	9.6.77	1		Gdansk	15 Jul 06
6:04.20	Gesa-Felicitas	Krause	GER	3.8.92	3	ISTAF	Berlin	6 Sep 15
6:04.46	Dorcus	Inzikuru	UGA	2.2.82	1	GP II	Milano	1 Jun 05
6:10.82	Magdalene	Masai	KEN	4.4.93	4	ISTAF	Berlin	6 Sep 15

3000 METRES STEEPLECHASE

Mark		Name		Nat	Born	Pos	Meet	Venue	Date
8:52.78	WR	Ruth	Jebet	KEN/BRN	17.11.96	1	DL	Saint-Denis	27 Aug 16
8:58.81	WR	Gulnara	Samitova/Galkina	RUS	9.7.78	1	OG	Beijing	17 Aug 08
8:59.75			Jebet			1	OG	Rio de Janeiro	15 Aug 16
8:59.97			Jebet			2	DL	Shanghai	14 May 16
9:00.01		Hyvin	Jepkemoi	KEN	13.1.92	2	Pre	Eugene	28 May 16
9:01.59	WR		Samitova/Galkina			1		Iráklio	4 Jul 04
9:01.96			Jepkemoi			2	DL	Saint-Denis	27 Aug 16
9:05.36		Habiba	Ghribi	TUN	9.4.84	1	VD	Bruxelles	11 Sep 15
9:06.57		Yekaterina	Volkova	RUS	16.2.78	1	WCh	Osaka	27 Aug 07
9:07.00			Jebet			1	WK	Zürich	1 Sep 16
9:07.12			Jepkemoi			2	OG	Rio de Janeiro	15 Aug 16
9:07.14		Milcah	Chemos Cheywa	KEN	24.2.86	1	Bisl	Oslo	7 Jun 12
9:07.41		Eunice	Jepkorir	KEN	17.2.82	2	OG	Beijing	17 Aug 08
9:07.42			Jepkemoi			1	DL	Shanghai	14 May 16
9:07.63		Emma	Coburn	USA	19.10.90	3	OG	Rio de Janeiro	15 Aug 16
9:07.64			Volkova			3	OG	Beijing	17 Aug 08
9:08.21			Galkina			1	NC	Kazan	18 Jul 08
9:08.33	WR		Samitova			1	NC	Tula	10 Aug 03
9:08.37			Ghribi			2	OG	London (OS)	6 Aug 12
9:08.37			Jebet			1	DL	Stockholm	16 Jun 16
9:08.39		Yuliya	Zaripova' ¶	RUS	26.4.86	2	WCh	Berlin	17 Aug 09
9:08.57			Chemos			3	WCh	Berlin	17 Aug 09
9:09.00		Sofia	Assefa (10)	ETH	14.11.87	2	Bisl	Oslo	7 Jun 12
9:09.19		Tatyana	Petrova	RUS	8.4.83	2	WCh	Osaka	27 Aug 07
9:09.39		Marta	Dominguez ¶	ESP	3.11.75	1		Barcelona	25 Jul 09
9:09.57			Jepkemoi			1	Bisl	Oslo	9 Jun 16
9:09.61		Hiwot	Ayalew	ETH	6.3.90	3	Bisl	Oslo	7 Jun 12
9:09.84			Samitova			1		Réthimno	23 Jun 04
9:09.84			Assefa			3	OG	London (OS)	6 Aug 12
9:09.88			Chemos			4	OG	London (OS)	6 Aug 12
		(30/13)							
9:10.86		Beatrice	Chepkoech	KEN	6.7.91	4	DL	Saint-Denis	27 Aug 16
9:12.50		Jennifer	Simpson'	USA	23.8.86	5	WCh	Berlin	17 Aug 09
9:12.55		Lydia	Chepkurui	KEN	23.8.84	2	WCh	Moskva	13 Aug 13
9:13.16		Ruth	Bisibori	KEN	2.1.88	7	WCh	Berlin	17 Aug 09
9:13.22		Gladys	Kipkemboi	KEN	15.10.86	2	GGala	Roma	10 Jun 10
9:13.53		Gülcan	Mingir	TUR	21.5.89	1	Pavlov	Sofia	9 Jun 12
9:13.85		Virginia	Nyambura	KEN	20.7.93	3	Herc	Monaco	17 Jul 15
		(20)							
9:14.07		Etenesh	Diro	ETH	10.5.91	3	DNG	Stockholm	17 Aug 12
9:14.28		Genevieve	LaCaze	AUS	4.8.89	6	DL	Saint-Denis	27 Aug 16
9:15.04		Dorcus	Inzikuru	UGA	2.2.82	1	SGP	Athína	14 Jun 05
9:16.51	WR	Alesya	Turova	BLR	6.12.79	1		Gdansk	27 Jul 02

3000m STEEPLE – 100m HURDLES A-T

Mark	Wind	Name		Nat	Born	Pos	Meet	Venue	Date
9:16.85		Cristina	Casandra	ROU	21.10.77	5	OG	Beijing	17 Aug 08
9:16.94		Mercy	Njoroge	KEN	10.6.86	2	DL	Doha	6 May 11
9:17.15		Wioletta	Frankiewicz/Janowska	POL	9.6.77	1	SGP	Athína	3 Jul 06
9:17.74		Purity	Kirui	KEN	13.8.91	5	VD	Bruxelles	11 Sep 15
9:17.85		Zemzem	Ahmed	ETH	27.12.84	7	OG	Beijing	17 Aug 08
9:18.03		Lydia (30)	Rotich	KEN	8.8.88	3	Bisl	Oslo	4 Jun 10
9:18.35		Donna	MacFarlane	AUS	18.6.77	3	Bisl	Oslo	6 Jun 08
9:18.41		Gesa Felicitas	Krause	GER	3.8.92	6	OG	Rio de Janeiro	15 Aug 16
9:18.54		Antje	Möldner-Schmidt	GER	13.6.84	9	WCh	Berlin	17 Aug 09
9:18.54		Jéssica	Augusto	POR	8.11.81	4		Huelva	9 Jun 10
9:18.85		Leah	O'Connor	USA	30.8.92	6	Pre	Eugene	28 May 16
9:19.48		Stephanie	Garcia	USA	3.5.88	8	DL	Saint-Denis	27 Aug 16
9:19.76		Lalita	Babar	IND	2.6.89	4h2	OG	Rio de Janeiro	13 Aug 16
9:20.00		Colleen	Quigley	USA	20.11.92	9	DL	Saint-Denis	27 Aug 16
9:20.38		Madeline	Heiner/Hills	AUS	15.5.87	7	OG	Rio de Janeiro	15 Aug 16
9:20.92		Courtney (40)	Frerichs	USA	18.1.93	2	NC	Eugene	7 Jul 16
9:20.23		Mekdes	Bekele	ETH	20.1.87	2		Huelva	13 Jun 08
9:20.37		Birtukan	Adamu	ETH	29.4.92	4	GGala	Roma	26 May 11
9:20.64		Salima	El Ouali	MAR	29.12.83	7	Herc	Monaco	17 Jul 15
9:20.65		Tigist	Mekonen	BRN	7.7.97	8	Herc	Monaco	17 Jul 15
9:21.94		Lyubov	Ivanova' ¶	RUS	2.3.81	2	Tsik	Athína	3 Jul 06
9:22.12		Hanane	Ouhaddou	MAR	.82	1	NA	Heusden-Zolder	18 Jul 09
9:22.15		Yelena	Sidorchenkova	RUS	30.5.80	2	NC	Cheboksary	23 Jul 09
9:22.29 WR		Justyna	Bak	POL	18.7.74	1		Milano	5 Jun 02
9:22.51		Almaz	Ayana	ETH	21.11.91	3	VD	Bruxelles	27 Aug 10
9:22.76		Anna (50)	Willard/Pierce	USA	31.3.84	2	NA	Heusden-Zolder	20 Jul 08

100th woman 9:31.06, 200th 9:41.26, 300th 9:49.05, 400th 9:54.86

Drugs disqualification

Mark	Wind	Name		Nat	Born	Pos	Meet	Venue	Date
9:05.02		Yuliya	Zaripova	RUS	26.4.86	(1)	DNG	Stockholm	17 Aug 12
9:06.72			Zaripova			(1)	OG	London (OS)	6 Aug 12
9:07.03			Zaripova	RUS	26.4.86	(1)	WCh	Daegu	30 Aug 11
9:07.32		Marta	Dominguez ¶	ESP	3.11.75	(1)	WCh	Berlin	17 Aug 09

WOMEN All-time

100 METRES HURDLES

Mark	Wind	Name		Nat	Born	Pos	Meet	Venue	Date
12.20 WR	0.3	Kendra	Harrison	USA	18.9.92	1	DL	London (OS)	22 Jul 16
12.21 WR	0.7	Yordanka	Donkova	BUL	28.9.61	1		Stara Zagora	20 Aug 88
12.24	0.9		Donkova			1h		Stara Zagora	28 Aug 88
12.24	0.5		K Harrison			1	Pre	Eugene	28 May 16
12.25 WR	1.4	Ginka	Zagorcheva	BUL	12.4.58	1	v TCH,GRE	Drama	8 Aug 87
12.26 WR	1.5		Donkova			1	Balk	Ljubljana	7 Sep 86
12.26	1.7	Lyudmila (later Ludmila Engquist SWE)	Narozhilenko ¶	RUS	21.4.64	1rB		Sevilla	6 Jun 92
12.26	1.2	Brianna	Rollins	USA	18.8.91	1	NC	Des Moines	22 Jun 13
12.27	-1.2		Donkova			1		Stara Zagora	28 Aug 88
12.28	1.8		Narozhilenko			1	NC	Kyiv	11 Jul 91
12.28	0.9		Narozhilenko			1rA		Sevilla	6 Jun 92
12.28	1.1	Sally	Pearson'	AUS	19.9.86	1	WCh	Daegu	3 Sep 11
12.29 WR	-0.4		Donkova			1	ASV	Köln	17 Aug 86
12.32	1.6		Narozhilenko			1		Saint-Denis	4 Jun 92
12.33	1.4		Donkova			1		Fürth	14 Jun 87
12.33	-0.3	Gail	Devers	USA	19.11.66	1	NC	Sacramento	23 Jul 00
12.34	-0.5		Zagorcheva			1	WCh	Roma	4 Sep 87
12.34	1.9	Sharika	Nelvis	USA	10.5.90	1h3	NC	Eugene	26 Jun 15
12.34	1.2		Rollins			1	NC	Eugene	8 Jul 16
12.35 WR	0.1		Donkova			1h2	ASV	Köln	17 Aug 86
12.35	-0.2		Pearson			1	OG	London (OS)	7 Aug 12
12.35	0.9	Jasmin	Stowers	USA	23.9.91	1	DL	Doha	15 May 15
12.36 WR	1.9	Grazyna	Rabsztyn (10)	POL	20.9.52	1	Kuso	Warszawa	13 Jun 80
12.36 WR	-0.6		Donkova			1	NC	Sofia	13 Aug 86
12.36	1.1		Donkova			1		Schwechat	15 Jun 88
12.36	0.3		Pearson			1s2	WCh	Daegu	3 Sep 11
12.36	1.4		K Harrison			1	Towns	Athens GA	8 Apr 16
12.37	1.4		Donkova			1	ISTAF	Berlin	15 Aug 86
12.37	0.7		Devers			1	WCh	Sevilla	28 Aug 99
12.37	1.5	Joanna	Hayes	USA	23.12.76	1	OG	Athína	24 Aug 04
12.37	-0.2	Dawn	Harper Nelson	USA	13.5.84	2	OG	London (OS)	7 Aug 12
12.37	2.0	(32/11)	Nelvis			1s1	NC	Eugene	27 Jun 15

100 – 400 METRES HURDLES A-T

Mark	Wind	Name		Nat	Born	Pos	Meet	Venue	Date
12.39	1.5	Vera	Komisova'	RUS	11.6.53	1	GGala	Roma	5 Aug 80
12.39	1.8	Natalya	Grigoryeva ¶	UKR	3.12.62	2	NC	Kyiv	11 Jul 91
12.42	1.8	Bettine	Jahn	GDR	3.8.58	1	OD	Berlin	8 Jun 83
12.42	2.0	Anjanette	Kirkland	USA	24.2.74	1	WCh	Edmonton	11 Aug 01
12.43	-0.9	Lucyna	Kalek (Langer)	POL	9.1.56	1		Hannover	19 Aug 84
12.43	-0.3	Michelle	Perry	USA	1.5.79	1s1	NC	Carson	26 Jun 05
12.43	0.2	Lolo	Jones	USA	5.8.82	1s1	OG	Beijing	18 Aug 08
12.43	1.2	Queen	Harrison	USA	10.9.88	2	NC	Des Moines	22 Jun 13
		(20)							
12.44	-0.5	Gloria	Uibel (-Siebert)	GDR	13.1.64	2	WCh	Roma	4 Sep 87
12.44	-0.8	Olga	Shishigina ¶	KAZ	23.12.68	1	Spitzen	Luzern	27 Jun 95
12.44	0.4	Glory	Alozie	NGR/ESP	30.12.77	1	Herc	Monaco	8 Aug 98
12.44	0.6	Damu	Cherry ¶	USA	29.11.77	2rA	Athl	Lausanne	11 Jul 06
12.45	1.3	Cornelia	Oschkenat'	GDR	29.10.61	1		Neubrandenburg	11 Jun 87
12.45	1.4	Brigitte	Foster-Hylton	JAM	7.11.74	1	Pre	Eugene	24 May 03
12.45	1.5	Olena	Krasovska	UKR	17.8.76	2	OG	Athína	24 Aug 04
12.45	1.4	Virginia	Powell/Crawford	USA	7.9.83	1	GP	New York	2 Jun 07
12.46	0.7	Perdita	Felicien	CAN	29.8.80	1	Pre	Eugene	19 Jun 04
12.47	1.1	Marina	Azyabina	RUS	15.6.63	1s2	NC	Moskva	19 Jun 93
		(30)							
12.47	1.1	Danielle	Carruthers	USA	22.12.79	2	WCh	Daegu	3 Sep 11
12.48	-0.2	Kellie	Wells	USA	16.7.82	3	OG	London (OS)	7 Aug 12
12.48	1.2	Nia	Ali	USA	23.10.88	3	NC	Des Moines	22 Jun 13
12.49	0.9	Susanna	Kallur	SWE	16.2.81	1	ISTAF	Berlin	16 Sep 07
12.49	1.0	Priscilla	Lopes-Schliep	CAN	26.8.82	2	VD	Bruxelles	4 Sep 09
12.50	0.0	Vera	Akimova'	RUS	5.6.59	1		Sochi	19 May 84
12.50	-0.1	Delloreen	Ennis-London	JAM	5.3.75	3	WCh	Osaka	29 Aug 07
12.50	0.8	Josephine	Onyia ¶	NGR/ESP	15.7.86	1	ISTAF	Berlin	1 Jun 08
12.50	1.8	Kendra	Harrison	USA	18.9.92	1	SEC	Starkville	16 May 15
12.50	1.2	Kristi	Castlin	USA	7.7.88	2	NC	Eugene	8 Jul 16
12.51	1.4	Miesha	McKelvy	USA	26.7.76	2	Pre	Eugene	24 May 03
		(40)							
12.51	0.7	Tiffany	Porter'	USA/GBR	13.11.87	2	C.Cup	Marrakech	14 Sep 14
12.52	-0.4	Michelle	Freeman	JAM	5.5.69	1s1	WCh	Athína	10 Aug 97
12.53	0.2	Tatyana	Reshetnikova	RUS	14.10.66	1rA	GP II	Linz	4 Jul 94
12.53	-0.4	Svetla	Dimitrova ¶	BUL	27.1.70	1	Herc	Stara Zagora	16 Jul 94
12.53	1.0	Melissa	Morrison	USA	9.7.71	1	DNG	Stockholm	5 Aug 98
12.54	0.4	Kerstin	Knabe	GDR	7.7.59	3	EC	Athína	9 Sep 82
12.54	0.9	Sabine	Paetz/John'	GDR	16.10.57	1		Berlin	15 Jul 84
12.54	1.7	Nichole	Denby	USA	10.10.82	2s2	OT	Eugene	6 Jul 08
12.54	1.3	Jessica	Ennis	GBR	28.1.86	1H5	OG	London (OS)	3 Aug 12
12.56	1.2	Johanna	Klier'	GDR	13.9.52	1r2		Cottbus	17 Jul 80
12.56	1.2	Monique	Ewanjé-Epée	FRA	11.7.67	1	BNP	Villeneuve d'Ascq	29 Jun 90
12.56	1.2	Cindy	Billaud	FRA	11.3.86	1h1	NC	Reims	12 Jul 14
		(52)							

100th woman 12.67, 200th 12.82, 300th 12.91, 400th 13.00, 500th 13.08

Wind assisted performances to 12.36, performers to 12.53

12.28	2.7	Cornelia	Oschkenat'	GDR	29.10.61	1		Berlin	25 Aug 87
12.29	3.5		Donkova			1	Athl	Lausanne	24 Jun 88
12.29	2.7	Gail	Devers	USA	19.11.66	1	Pre	Eugene	26 May 02
12.29	3.8	Lolo	Jones	USA	5.8.82	1	NC/OT	Eugene	6 Jul 08
12.30	2.8		Rollins			1s1	NC	Des Moines	22 Jun 13
12.33	2.3		Rollins			1h3	NC	Des Moines	21 Jun 13
12.35	2.4	Bettine	Jahn	GDR	3.8.58	1	WCh	Helsinki	13 Aug 83
12.35	3.7	Kellie	Wells	USA	16.7.82	1		Gainesville	16 Apr 11
12.36	2.2	Dawn	Harper Nelson	USA	13.5.84	1	NC	Eugene	28 Jun 09
12.37	2.7	Gloria	Uibel/Siebert'	GDR	13.1.64	2		Berlin	25 Aug 87
12.37	3.4	Danielle	Carruthers	USA	22.12.79	1s1	NC	Eugene	26 Jun 11
12.40	2.1	Michelle	Freeman	JAM	5.5.69	1	GPF	Fukuoka	13 Sep 97
12.41	2.2	Olga	Shishigina ¶	KAZ	23.12.68	1rA	Athl	Lausanne	5 Jul 95
12.42	2.4	Kerstin	Knabe	GDR	7.7.59	2	WCh	Helsinki	13 Aug 83
12.43	2.7	Yvette	Lewis	USA/PAN	16.3.85	1	MSR	Walnut	20 Apr 13
12.44	2.6	Melissa	Morrison	USA	9.7.71	1		Carson	22 May 04
12.45	2.1	Perdita	Felicien	CAN	29.8.80	1	NC	Victoria	10 Jul 04
12.47	3.0	Tiffany	Porter	USA/GBR	13.11.87	1		Gainesville	21 Apr 12
12.48	3.8	Kristi	Castlin	USA	7.7.88	1		Clermont	2 Jun 12
12.50	2.7	Svetla	Dimitrova ¶	BUL	27.1.70	1		Saint-Denis	10 Jun 94
12.51	3.2	Johanna	Klier'	GDR	13.9.52	1	NC	Cottbus	17 Jul 80
12.51	3.6	Sabine	Paetz/John'	GDR	16.10.57	1		Dresden	27 Jul 84
12.51A	3.3	Yuliya	Graudyn	RUS	13.11.70	1		Sestriere	31 Jul 94
12.52	3.1	Angela	Whyte	CAN	22.5.80	2		Edmonton	29 Jun 13
12.53	2.2	Mihaela	Pogacian	ROU	27.1.58	1	IAC	Edinburgh	6 Jul 90

100 – 400 METRES HURDLES A-T

Mark	Wind	Name		Nat	Born	Pos	Meet	Venue	Date
Probably hand timed		Officially 12.36, but subsequent investigations showed this unlikely to have been auto-timed							
12.4	0.7	Svetla	Dimitrova ¶	BUL	27.1.70	1		Stara Zagora	9 Jul 97
Hand timed									
12.3 WR	1.5	Anneliese	Ehrhardt	GDR	18.6.50	1	NC	Dresden	22 Jul 73
12.3		Marina	Azyabina	RUS	15.6.63	1		Yekaterinburg	30 May 93
12.0w	2.1	Yordanka	Donkova	BUL	28.9.61	1		Sofia	3 Aug 86
12.1w	2.1	Ginka	Zagorcheva	BUL	12.4.58	2		Sofia	3 Aug 86

400 METRES HURDLES

Mark	Name		Nat	Born	Pos	Meet	Venue	Date
52.34 WR	Yuliya	Nosova-Pechonkina'	RUS	21.4.78	1	NC	Tula	8 Aug 03
52.42	Melaine	Walker	JAM	1.1.83	1	WCh	Berlin	20 Aug 09
52.47	Lashinda	Demus	USA	10.3.83	1	WCh	Daegu	1 Sep 11
52.61 WR	Kim	Batten	USA	29.3.69	1	WCh	Göteborg	11 Aug 95
52.62	Tonja	Buford-Bailey	USA	13.12.70	2	WCh	Göteborg	11 Aug 95
52.63		Demus			1	Herc	Monaco	28 Jul 09
52.64		Walker			1	OG	Beijing	20 Aug 08
52.70	Natalya	Antyukh	RUS	26.6.81	1	OG	London (OS)	8 Aug 12
52.73		Walker			2	WCh	Daegu	1 Sep 11
52.74 WR	Sally	Gunnell	GBR	29.7.66	1	WCh	Stuttgart	19 Aug 93
52.74		Batten			1	Herc	Monaco	8 Aug 98
52.77	Faní	Halkiá	GRE	2.2.79	1s2	OG	Athína	22 Aug 04
52.77		Demus			2	OG	London (OS)	8 Aug 12
52.79	Sandra	Farmer-Patrick	USA	18.8.62	2	WCh	Stuttgart	19 Aug 93
52.79	Kaliese	Spencer (10)	JAM	6.5.87	1	LGP	London (CP)	5 Aug 11
52.82	Deon	Hemmings	JAM	9.10.68	1	OG	Atlanta	31 Jul 96
52.82		Halkiá			1	OG	Athína	25 Aug 04
52.82		Demus			1	GGala	Roma	10 Jun 10
52.83	Zuzana	Hejnová	CZE	19.12.86	1	WCh	Moskva	15 Aug 13
52.84		Batten			1	WK	Zürich	12 Aug 98
52.88	Dalilah	Muhammad	USA	7.2.90	1	NC	Eugene	10 Jul 16
52.89	Daimí	Pernía	CUB	27.12.76	1	WCh	Sevilla	25 Aug 99
52.90		Buford			1	WK	Zürich	16 Aug 95
52.90	Nezha	Bidouane	MAR	18.9.69	2	WCh	Sevilla	25 Aug 99
52.90		Pechonkina			1	WCh	Helsinki	13 Aug 05
52.92		Antyukh			1	EC	Barcelona	30 Jul 10
52.94 WR	Marina	Styepanova'	RUS	1.5.50	1s	Spart	Tashkent	17 Sep 86
52.95	Sheena	Johnson/Tosta	USA	1.10.82	1	NC/OT	Sacramento	11 Jul 04
52.96A		Bidouane			1	WCp	Johannesburg	11 Sep 98
52.96		Demus			2	WCh	Berlin	20 Aug 09
	(30/17)							
53.02	Irina	Privalova	RUS	22.11.68	1	OG	Sydney	27 Sep 00
53.11	Tatyana	Ledovskaya	BLR	21.5.66	1	WCh	Tokyo	29 Aug 91
53.17	Debbie	Flintoff-King	AUS	20.4.60	1	OG	Seoul	28 Sep 88
	(20)							
53.20	Josanne	Lucas	TTO	14.5.84	3	WCh	Berlin	20 Aug 09
53.21	Marie-José	Pérec	FRA	9.5.68	2	WK	Zürich	16 Aug 95
53.21	Kori	Carter	USA	6.3.92	1	NCAA	Eugene	7 Jun 13
53.22	Jana	Pittman/Rawlinson	AUS	9.11.82	1	WCh	Saint-Denis	28 Aug 03
53.24	Sabine	Busch	GDR	21.11.62	1	NC	Potsdam	21 Aug 87
53.25	Ionela	Târlea-Manolache	ROU	9.2.76	2	GGala	Roma	7 Jul 99
53.28	Tiffany	Ross-Williams	USA	5.2.83	1	NC	Indianapolis	24 Jun 07
53.32	Sandra	Glover	USA	30.12.68	3	WCh	Helsinki	13 Aug 05
53.36	Andrea	Blackett	BAR	24.1.76	4	WCh	Sevilla	25 Aug 99
53.36	Brenda	Taylor	USA	9.2.79	2	NC/OT	Sacramento	11 Jul 04
	(30)							
53.37	Tetyana	Tereshchuk	UKR	11.10.69	3s2	OG	Athína	22 Aug 04
53.47	Janeene	Vickers	USA	3.10.68	3	WCh	Tokyo	29 Aug 91
53.48	Margarita	Ponomaryova'	RUS	19.6.63	3	WCh	Stuttgart	19 Aug 93
53.51	Shamier	Little	USA	20.3.95	1	NCAA	Eugene	11 Jun 16
53.55	Sara Slott	Petersen	DEN	9.4.87	3	OG	Rio de Janeiro	18 Aug 16
53.58	Cornelia	Ullrich'	GDR	26.4.63	2	NC	Potsdam	21 Aug 87
53.63	Ellen	Fiedler'	GDR	26.11.58	3	OG	Seoul	28 Sep 88
53.65A mx	Myrtle	Bothma'	RSA	18.2.64	mx		Pretoria	12 Mar 90
	53.74A				1		Johannesburg	18 Apr 86
53.67	Perri	Shakes-Drayton	GBR	21.12.88	2	DL	London (OS)	26 Jul 13
53.68	Vania	Stambolova ¶	BUL	28.11.83	1		Rabat	5 Jun 11
	(40)							
53.72	Yekaterina	Bikert	RUS	13.5.80	2	NC	Tula	30 Jul 04
53.72	Georgeanne	Moline	USA	6.3.90	2	NCAA	Eugene	7 Jun 13
53.72	Ashley	Spencer	USA	8.6.93	3	OG	Rio de Janeiro	18 Aug 16

WOMEN All-time

400m HURDLES – HIGH JUMP A-T

Mark	Wind	Name		Nat	Born	Pos	Meet	Venue	Date
53.77		Irina	Davydova	RUS	27.5.88	1	EC	Helsinki	29 Jun 12
53.84		Natasha	Danvers	GBR	19.9.77	3	OG	Beijing	20 Aug 08
53.85		Angela	Morosanu	ROU	26.7.86	2	DL	Shanghai	18 May 13
53.86		Anna	Jesien	POL	10.12.78	1s3	WCh	Osaka	28 Aug 07
53.88		Debbie-Ann	Parris	JAM	24.3.73	3s1	WCh	Edmonton	6 Aug 01
53.93		Yevgeniya	Isakova	RUS	27.11.78	1	EC	Göteborg	9 Aug 06
53.96			Han Qing ¶	CHN	4.3.70	1	NG	Beijing	9 Sep 93
53.96			Song Yinglan	CHN	14.9.75	1	NG	Guangzhou	22 Nov 01
53.96		Anastasiya	Rabchenyuk	UKR	14.9.83	4	OG	Beijing	20 Aug 08
53.96		Janeive	Russell	JAM	14.11.93	1	GGala	Roma	2 Jun 16

(52) 100th woman 54.54, 200th 55.35, 300th 55.78, 400th 56.14, 500th 56.44

Drugs disqualification: 53.38 Jiang Limei ¶ CHN .3.70 (1) 89 Shanghai 22 Oct 97

HIGH JUMP

Mark	Wind	Name		Nat	Born	Pos	Meet	Venue	Date
2.09 WR		Stefka	Kostadinova	BUL	25.3.65	1	WCh	Roma	30 Aug 87
2.08 WR			Kostadinova			1	NM	Sofia	31 May 86
2.08i		Kajsa	Bergqvist	SWE	12.10.76	1		Arnstadt	4 Feb 06
2.08		Blanka	Vlasic	CRO	8.11.83	1	Hanz	Zagreb	31 Aug 09
2.07 WR		Lyudmila	Andonova ¶	BUL	6.5.60	1	OD	Berlin	20 Jul 84
2.07 WR			Kostadinova			1		Sofia	25 May 86
2.07			Kostadinova			1		Cagliari	16 Sep 87
2.07			Kostadinova			1	NC	Sofia	3 Sep 88
2.07i		Heike	Henkel'	GER	5.5.64	1	NC	Karlsruhe	8 Feb 92
2.07			Vlasic			1	DNG	Stockholm	7 Aug 07
2.07		Anna	Chicherova ¶	RUS	22.7.82	1	NC	Cheboksary	22 Jul 11
2.06			Kostadinova			1	ECp	Moskva	18 Aug 85
2.06			Kostadinova			1		Fürth	15 Jun 86
2.06			Kostadinova			1		Cagliari	14 Sep 86
2.06			Kostadinova			1		Wörrstadt	6 Jun 87
2.06			Kostadinova			1		Rieti	8 Sep 87
2.06i			Kostadinova			1		Pireás	20 Feb 88
2.06			Bergqvist			1		Eberstadt	26 Jul 03
2.06		Hestrie	Cloete	RSA	26.8.78	1	WCh	Saint-Denis	31 Aug 03
2.06		Yelena	Slesarenko	RUS	28.2.82	1	OG	Athína	28 Aug 04
2.06			Vlasic			1		Thessaloníki	30 Jul 07
2.06			Vlasic			1	ECp-1B	Istanbul	22 Jun 08
2.06			Vlasic			1	GP	Madrid	5 Jul 08
2.06		Ariane	Friedrich	GER	10.1.84	1	ISTAF	Berlin	14 Jun 09
2.06i			Vlasic			1		Arnstadt	6 Feb 10
2.06i			Chicherova			1		Arnstadt	4 Feb 12
2.05 WR		Tamara	Bykova (10)	RUS	21.12.58	1	Izv	Kyiv	22 Jun 84
2.05		Inga	Babakova	UKR	27.6.67	1		Tokyo	15 Sep 95
2.05i		Tia	Hellebaut	BEL	16.2.78	1	EI	Birmingham	3 Mar 07
2.05		Chaunté	Lowe'	USA	12.1.84	1	NC	Des Moines	26 Jun 10

Further 2.05 performances: Kostadinova 10, Vlasic 10, Bergqvist, Chicherova 2, Hellebaut, Henkel, Cloete, Friedrich 1 (58/13)

Mark	Wind	Name		Nat	Born	Pos	Meet	Venue	Date
2.04		Silvia	Costa	CUB	4.5.64	1	WCp	Barcelona	9 Sep 89
2.04i		Alina	Astafei	GER	7.6.69	1		Berlin	3 Mar 95
2.04		Venelina	Veneva ¶	BUL	13.6.74	1		Kalamáta	2 Jun 01
2.04i		Antonietta	Di Martino	ITA	1.6.78	1		Banská Bystrica	9 Feb 11
2.04		Irina	Gordeyeva	RUS	9.10.86	1		Eberstadt	19 Aug 12
2.04		Brigetta	Barrett	USA	24.12.90	1	NC	Des Moines	22 Jun 13
2.03 WR		Ulrike	Meyfarth (20)	FRG	4.5.56	1	ECp	London (CP)	21 Aug 83
2.03		Louise	Ritter	USA	18.2.58	1		Austin	8 Jul 88
2.03		Tatyana	Motkova	RUS	23.11.68	2		Bratislava	30 May 95
2.03		Níki	Bakoyiánni	GRE	9.6.68	2	OG	Atlanta	3 Aug 96
2.03i		Monica	Iagar/Dinescu	ROU	2.4.73	1		Bucuresti	23 Jan 99
2.03i		Marina	Kuptsova	RUS	22.12.81	1	EI	Wien	2 Mar 02
2.03		Svetlana	Shkolina	RUS	9.3.86	3	OG	London (OS)	11 Aug 12
2.02i		Susanne	Beyer'	GDR	24.6.61	2	WI	Indianapolis	8 Mar 87
2.02		Yelena	Yelesina	RUS	4.4.70	1	GWG	Seattle	23 Jul 90
2.02		Viktoriya	Styopina	UKR	21.2.76	3	OG	Athína	28 Aug 04
2.02		Ruth	Beitia (30)	ESP	1.4.79	1	NC	San Sebastián	4 Aug 07
2.02i		Kamila	Licwinko'	POL	22.3.86	1	NC	Torun	21 Feb 15
2.01 WR		Sara	Simeoni	ITA	19.4.53	1	v Pol	Brescia	4 Aug 78
2.01		Olga	Turchak	UKR	5.3.67	2	GWG	Moskva	7 Jul 86
2.01A		Desiré	du Plessis	RSA	20.5.65	1		Johannesburg	16 Sep 86
2.01i		Gabriele	Günz	GDR	8.9.61	2		Stuttgart	31 Jan 88

HIGH JUMP – POLE VAULT A-T

Mark	Wind	Name		Nat	Born	Pos	Meet	Venue	Date
2.01		Heike	Balck	GDR	19.8.70	1	vUSSR-j	Karl-Marx-Stadt	18 Jun 89
2.01i		Ioamnet	Quintero	CUB	8.9.72	1		Berlin	5 Mar 93
2.01		Hanne	Haugland	NOR	14.12.67	1	WK	Zürich	13 Aug 97
2.01i		Tisha	Waller	USA	1.12.70	1	NC	Atlanta	28 Feb 98
2.01		Yelena	Gulyayeva	RUS	14.8.67	2		Kalamáta	23 May 98
		(40)							
2.01		Vita	Palamar	UKR	12.10.77	2=	WK	Zürich	15 Aug 03
2.01		Amy	Acuff	USA	14.7.75	4	WK	Zürich	15 Aug 03
2.01		Iryna	Myhalchenko	UKR	20.1.72	1		Eberstadt	18 Jul 04
2.01		Emma	Green Tregaro	SWE	8.12.84	2	EC	Barcelona	1 Aug 10
2.01i		Mariya	Kuchina	RUS	14.1.93	1		Stockholm	6 Feb 14
2.00 WR		Rosemarie	Ackermann'	GDR	4.4.52	1	ISTAF	Berlin	26 Aug 77

2.00 by 22 others (68)   100th woman 1.98, 200th 1.95, 300th 1.93, 400th 1.92, 500th 1.90

Best outdoor marks

2.05	Henkel	1	WCh Tokyo	31 Aug 91	2.02	Kuptsova	1	FBK Hengelo	1 Jun 03
2.05	Hellebaut	1	OG Beijing	23 Aug 08	2.01	Astafei	2	Wörrstadt	27 May 95
2.03	Di Martino	1	ECp-1B Milano	24 Jun 07	2.01	Kuchina	1	WCh Beijing	29 Aug 15
2.02	Iagar/Dinescu	1	Budapest	6 Jun 98	2.00	four women			

Ancillary jumps: 2.06 Kostadinova 30 Aug 87, 2.05i Henkel 8 Feb 92, 2.05i Bergqvist 4 Feb 06, 2.05 Vlasic 31 Aug 09

POLE VAULT

Mark		Name		Nat	Born	Pos	Meet	Venue	Date
5.06 WR		Yelena	Isinbayeva	RUS	3.6.82	1	WK	Zürich	28 Aug 09
5.05 WR			Isinbayeva			1	OG	Beijing	18 Aug 08
5.04 WR			Isinbayeva			1	Herc	Monaco	29 Jul 08
5.03 WR			Isinbayeva			1	GGala	Roma	11 Jul 08
5.03i WIR		Jennifer	Suhr	USA	5.2.82	1		Brockport	30 Jan 16
5.02Ai WIR			Suhr			1	NC	Albuquerque	2 Mar 13
5.01 WR			Isinbayeva			1	WCh	Helsinki	12 Aug 05
5.01i WIR			Isinbayeva			1	XL Galan	Stockholm	23 Feb 12
5.01i			Suhr			1		Fredonia	1 Oct 16
5.00 WR			Isinbayeva			1	LGP	London (CP)	22 Jul 05
5.00i			Isinbayeva			1		Donetsk	15 Feb 09
5.00		Sandi	Morris	USA	8.7.92	1	VD	Bruxelles	9 Sep 16
4.95 WR			Isinbayeva			1	GP	Madrid	16 Jul 05
4.95i			Isinbayeva			1		Donetsk	16 Feb 08
4.95i			Morris			1	NC	Portland	12 Mar 16
4.93 WR			Isinbayeva			1	Athl	Lausanne	5 Jul 05
4.93			Isinbayeva			1	VD	Bruxelles	26 Aug 05
4.93i			Isinbayeva			1		Donetsk	10 Feb 07
4.93			Isinbayeva			1	LGP	London (CP)	25 Jul 08
4.93			Morris			1		Houston	23 Jul 16
4.92 WR			Isinbayeva			1	VD	Bruxelles	3 Sep 04
4.92			Stuczynski/Suhr			1	NC/OT	Eugene	6 Jul 08
4.91 WR			Isinbayeva (this jump on 25 Aug)			1	OG	Athína	25 Aug 04
4.91i			Isinbayeva			1		Donetsk	12 Feb 06
4.91			Isinbayeva			1	LGP	London (CP)	28 Jul 06
4.91			Isinbayeva			1	Gaz	Saint-Denis	6 Jul 07
4.91			Suhr			1		Rochester, NY	26 Jul 11
4.91			Suhr			1		Lyndonville	14 Jun 13
4.91		Yarisley	Silva	CUB	1.6.87	1		Beckum	2 Aug 15
4.91i			Suhr			1		Kent	16 Jan 16
		(30/4)							
4.90i		Ekateríni	Stefanídi	GRE	4.2.90	1	Mill	New York (A)	20 Feb 16
4.90i		Demi	Payne	USA	30.9.91	2	Mill	New York (A)	20 Feb 16
4.88 WR		Svetlana	Feofanova	RUS	16.7.80	1		Iráklio	4 Jul 04
4.87i		Holly	Bleasdale/Bradshaw	GBR	2.11.91	1		Villeurbanne	20 Jan 12
4.87		Fabiana	Murer	BRA	16.3.81	1	NC	São Bernardo do Campo	3 Jul 16
4.85i		Anna	Rogowska	POL	21.5.81	1	EI	Paris (Bercy)	6 Mar 11
		(10)							
4.85		Anzhelika	Sidorova	RUS	28.6.91	2	NC	Cheboksary	21 Jun 16
4.83		Stacy	Dragila	USA	25.3.71	1	GS	Ostrava	8 Jun 04
4.83		Nikoléta	Kiriakopoúlou	GRE	21.3.86	1	DL	Saint-Denis	4 Jul 15
4.82		Monika	Pyrek	POL	11.8.80	2	WAF	Stuttgart	22 Sep 07
4.82		Silke	Spiegelburg	GER	17.3.86	1	Herc	Monaco	20 Jul 12
4.81		Alana	Boyd	AUS	10.5.84	1		Sippy Downs	2 Jul 16
4.80		Martina	Strutz	GER	4.11.81	2	WCh	Daegu	30 Aug 11
4.80		Eliza	McCartney	NZL	11.12.96	1	NC	Dunedin	5 Mar 16
4.80i		Nicole	Büchler	SUI	17.12.83	4	WI	Portland	17 Mar 16
4.78		Tatyana	Polnova	RUS	20.4.79	2	WAF	Monaco	19 Sep 04
		(20)							

POLE VAULT – LONG JUMP A-T

Mark	Wind	Name		Nat	Born	Pos	Meet	Venue	Date
4.77		Annika	Becker	GER	12.11.81	1	NC	Wattenscheid	7 Jul 02
4.76		Jirina	Ptácníková'	CZE	20.5.86	1		Plzen	4 Sep 13
4.75		Katerina	Badurová	CZE	18.12.82	2	WCh	Osaka	28 Aug 07
4.75i		Yuliya	Golubchikova	RUS	27.3.83	1		Athína (P)	13 Feb 08
4.75Ai		Kylie	Hutson	USA	27.11.87	2	NC	Albuquerque	2 Mar 13
4.73		Chelsea	Johnson	USA	20.12.83	1		Los Gatos	26 Jun 08
4.73		Anastasiya	Savchenko	RUS	15.11.89	1	NCp	Yerino	15 Jun 13
4.73		Lisa	Ryzih	GER	27.9.88	1		Jockgrim	19 Jul 16
4.72i		Kym	Howe	AUS	12.6.80	2		Donetsk	10 Feb 07
4.72i		Jillian	Schwartz	USA/ISR	19.9.79	1		Jonesboro	15 Jun 08
		(30)							
4.72		Carolin	Hingst	GER	18.9.80	1		Biberach	9 Jul 10
4.71i		Tina	Sutej	SLO	7.11.88	1		Moskva	2 Feb 14
4.71Ai		Mary	Saxer Sibears	USA	21.6.87	1	NC	Albuquerque	23 Feb 14
4.71i		Marion	Fiack	FRA	13.10.92	1		Aubière	10 Jan 15
4.71i		Wilma	Murto	FIN	11.6.98	1		Zweibrücken	31 Jan 16
4.70		Yvonne	Buschbaum	GER	14.7.80	1	NC	Ulm	29 Jun 03
4.70		Vanessa	Boslak	FRA	11.6.82	2	ECp-S	Málaga	28 Jun 06
4.70		Angelina	Zhuk/Krasnova	RUS	7.2.91	1	EU23	Tampere	13 Jul 13
4.70i		Angelica	Bengtsson	SWE	8.7.93	3	EI	Praha (O2)	8 Mar 15
4.70i			Li Ling	CHN	6.7.89	1	AsC	Doha	19 Feb 16
		(40)							
4.70		Kristen	Brown	USA	26.5.92	1		Chula Vista	26 Jun 16
4.70		Lexi	Weeks	USA	20.11.96	3	NC	Eugene	10 Jul 16
4.68		Anna	Battke	GER	3.1.85	5	ISTAF	Berlin	14 Jun 09
4.67i		Kellie	Suttle	USA	9.5.73	1		Jonesboro	16 Jun 04
4.66i		Christine	Adams	GER	28.2.74	1	IHS	Sindelfingen	10 Mar 02
4.66i		Lacy	Janson	USA	20.2.83	1		Fayetteville	12 Feb 10
4.66i		Kristina	Gadschiew	GER	3.7.84	1		Potsdam	18 Feb 11
4.66			Li Ling	CHN	6.7.89	1	AsiC	Wuhan	6 Jun 15
4.65		Mary	Sauer/Vincent	USA	31.10.75	2		Madrid (C)	3 Jul 02
4.65		Anastasiya	Ivanova/Shvedova	RUS/BLR	3.5.79	1	Odlozil	Praha	13 Jun 07
4.65		Aleksandra	Kiryashova	RUS	21.8.85	1	NCp	Tula	1 Aug 09
		(50)							
4.65i		Becky	Holliday	USA	12.3.80	1		Jonesboro	16 Apr 15
4.65		Katharina	Bauer	GER	12.6.90	3		Beckum	2 Aug 15
4.65i		Kristen	Hixson	USA	1.7.92	4	NC	Portland	12 Mar 16
4.65		Olga	Mullina	RUS	1.8.92	3	NC	Cheboksary	21 Jun 16
4.65		Marina	Kylypko	UKR	10.11.95	1		Trani	3 Sep 16
		(55)							

100th woman 4.55, 200th 4.40, 300th 4.32, 400th 4.26, 500th 4.21

Outdoor bests

4.86		Stefanidi	1		Athínai (F)	8 Jun 16	4.70	Saxer	1	Chula Vista	6 Jun 13
4.75		Golubchikova	4	OG	Beijing	18 Aug 08	4.70	Bengtsson	4= WCh	Beijing	26 Aug 15
4.71		Bleasdale	1	NC	Birmingham	24 Jun 12	4.66	Li Ling	1 AsiC	Wuhan	6 Jun 15
4.71		Payne	1		Hammond	8 May 15	4.65	Howe	1	Saulheim	30 Jun 07
4.70		Hutson	1		Terre Haute	15 Jun 13	4.65	Hixson	1	Chula Vista	18 Jun 16

Ancillary jumps: Isinbayeva: 4.97 15 Feb 09, 4.96 WR 22 Jul 05, 4.95 18 Aug 08, 4.93 29 Jul 08, 4.92i 23 Feb 12
Exhibition: 4.72 Anastasiya Shvedova RUS 3.5.79 1 Aosta 5 Jul 08

LONG JUMP

Mark	Wind	Name		Nat	Born	Pos	Meet	Venue	Date
7.52 WR	1.4	Galina	Chistyakova	RUS	26.7.62	1	Znam	Leningrad	11 Jun 88
7.49	1.3	Jackie	Joyner-Kersee	USA	3.3.62	1	NYG	New York	22 May 94
7.49A	1.7		Joyner-Kersee			1		Sestriere	31 Jul 94
7.48	1.2	Heike	Drechsler	GER	16.12.64	1	v ITA	Neubrandenburg	9 Jul 88
7.48	0.4		Drechsler			1	Athl	Lausanne	8 Jul 92
7.45 WR	0.9		Drechsler'			1	v USSR	Tallinn	21 Jun 86
7.45 WR	1.1		Drechsler			1	OD	Dresden	3 Jul 86
7.45 WR	0.6		Joyner-Kersee			1	PAm	Indianapolis	13 Aug 87
7.45	1.6		Chistyakova			1	BGP	Budapest	12 Aug 88
7.44 WR	2.0		Drechsler			1		Berlin	22 Sep 85
7.43 WR	1.4	Anisoara	Cusmir/Stanciu	ROU	28.6.62	1	RomIC	Bucuresti	4 Jun 83
7.42	2.0	Tatyana	Kotova ¶	RUS	11.12.76	1	ECp-S	Annecy	23 Jun 02
7.40	1.8		Daute' (Drechsler)			1		Dresden	26 Jul 84
7.40	0.7		Drechsler			1	NC	Potsdam	21 Aug 87
7.40	0.9		Joyner-Kersee			1	OG	Seoul	29 Sep 88
7.39	0.3		Drechsler			1	WK	Zürich	21 Aug 85
7.39	0.5	Yelena	Byelevskaya'	BLR	11.10.63	1	NC	Bryansk	18 Jul 87
7.39			Joyner-Kersee			1		San Diego	25 Jun 88
7.37i	-		Drechsler			1	v2N	Wien ·	13 Feb 88
7.37A	1.8		Drechsler			1		Sestriere	31 Jul 91
7.37		Inessa	Kravets ¶	UKR	5.10.66	1		Kyiv	13 Jun 92

LONG JUMP A-T

Mark	Wind	Name		Nat	Born	Pos	Meet	Venue	Date
7.36	0.4		Joyner			1	WCh	Roma	4 Sep 87
7.36	1.8		Byelevskaya			2	Znam	Leningrad	11 Jun 88
7.36	1.8		Drechsler			1		Jena	28 May 92
7.35	1.9		Chistyakova			1	GPB	Bratislava	20 Jun 90
7.34	1.6		Daute'			1		Dresden	19 May 84
7.34	1.4		Chistyakova			2	v GDR	Tallinn	21 Jun 86
7.34			Byelevskaya			1		Sukhumi	17 May 87
7.34	0.7		Drechsler			1	v USSR	Karl-Marx-Stadt	20 Jun 87
7.33	0.4		Drechsler			1	v USSR	Erfurt	22 Jun 85
7.33	2.0		Drechsler			1		Dresden	2 Aug 85
7.33	-0.3		Drechsler			1	Herc	Monaco	11 Aug 92
7.33	0.4	Tatyana	Lebedeva	RUS	21.7.76	1	NC	Tula	31 Jul 04
		(33/8)							
7.31	1.5	Yelena	Kokonova'	UKR	4.8.63	1	NP	Alma-Ata	12 Sep 85
7.31	1.9	Marion	Jones ¶	USA	12.10.75	1	Pre	Eugene	31 May 98
		(10)							
7.31	1.7	Brittney	Reese	USA	9.9.86	1	NC	Eugene	2 Jul 16
7.27	-0.4	Irina	Simagina/Meleshina	RUS	25.5.82	2	NC	Tula	31 Jul 04
7.26A	1.8	Maurren	Maggi ¶	BRA	25.6.76	1	SACh	Bogotá	26 Jun 99
7.24	1.0	Larisa	Berezhnaya	UKR	28.2.61	1		Granada	25 May 91
7.21	1.6	Helga	Radtke	GDR	16.5.62	2		Dresden	26 Jul 84
7.21	1.9	Lyudmila	Kolchanova	RUS	1.10.79	1		Sochi	27 May 07
7.20 WR	-0.5	Valy	Ionescu	ROU	31.8.60	1	NC	Bucuresti	1 Aug 82
7.20	2.0	Irena	Ozhenko'	LTU	13.11.62	1		Budapest	12 Sep 86
7.20	0.8	Yelena	Sinchukova'	RUS	23.1.61	1	BGP	Budapest	20 Jun 91
7.20	0.7	Irina	Mushayilova	RUS	6.1.67	1	NC	Sankt-Peterburg	14 Jul 94
		(20)							
7.17	1.8	Irina	Valyukevich	BLR	19.11.59	2	NC	Bryansk	18 Jul 87
7.17	0.6	Tianna	Bartoletta'	USA	30.8.85	1	OG	Rio de Janeiro	17 Aug 16
7.16		Iolanda	Chen	RUS	26.7.61	1		Moskva	30 Jul 88
7.16A	-0.1	Elva	Goulbourne	JAM	21.1.80	1		Ciudad de México	22 May 04
7.16	1.6	Sosthene	Moguenara	GER	17.10.89	1		Weinheim	28 May 16
7.14	1.8	Nijole	Medvedeva ¶	LTU	20.10.60	1		Riga	4 Jun 88
7.14	1.2	Mirela	Dulgheru	ROU	5.10.66	1	Balk G	Sofia	5 Jul 92
7.13	2.0	Olga	Kucherenko ¶	RUS	5.11.85	1		Sochi	27 May 10
7.12	1.6	Sabine	Paetz/John'	GDR	16.10.57	2		Dresden	19 May 84
7.12	0.9	Chioma	Ajunwa ¶	NGR	25.12.70	1	OG	Atlanta	2 Aug 96
		(30)							
7.12	1.3	Naide	Gomes	CPV/POR	10.11.79	1	Herc	Monaco	29 Jul 08
7.11	0.8	Fiona	May	GBR/ITA	12.12.69	2	EC	Budapest	22 Aug 98
7.11	1.3	Anna	Nazarova	RUS	3.2.86	1	Mosc Ch	Moskva	20 Jun 12
7.10	1.6	Chelsea	Hayes	USA	9.2.88	2	NC/OT	Eugene	1 Jul 12
7.10	0.3	Ivana	Spanovic	SRB	10.5.90	1		Beograd	11 Sep 16
7.09 WR	0.0	Vilhelmina	Bardauskiené	LTU	15.6.53	Q	EC	Praha	29 Aug 78
7.09	1.5	Ljudmila	Ninova	AUT	25.6.60	1	GP II	Sevilla	5 Jun 94
7.08	0.5	Marieta	Ilcu ¶	ROU	16.10.62	1	RumIC	Pitesti	25 Jun 89
7.08	1.9	Anastasiya	Mironchik-Ivanova	BLR	13.4.89	1		Minsk	12 Jun 12
7.07	0.0	Svetlana	Zorina	RUS	2.2.60	1		Krasnodar	15 Aug 87
		(40)							
7.07	0.5	Yelena	Sokolova	RUS	23.7.86	2	OG	London (OS)	8 Aug 12
7.07	0.4	Shara	Proctor	AIA/GBR	16.9.88	2	WCh	Beijing	28 Aug 15
7.06	0.4	Tatyana	Kolpakova	KGZ	18.10.59	1	OG	Moskva	31 Jul 80
7.06	-0.1	Niurka	Montalvo	CUB/ESP	4.6.68	1	WCh	Sevilla	23 Aug 99
7.06		Tatyana	Ter-Mesrobyan	RUS	12.5.68	1		Sankt Peterburg	22 May 02
7.05	0.6	Lyudmila	Galkina	RUS	20.1.72	1	WCh	Athína	9 Aug 97
7.05	-0.4	Eunice	Barber	FRA	17.11.74	1	WAF	Monaco	14 Sep 03
7.05	1.1	Darya	Klishina	RUS	15.1.91	1	EU23	Ostrava	17 Jul 11
7.05	2.0	Brooke	Stratton	AUS	12.7.93	1		Perth	12 Mar 16
7.04	0.5	Brigitte	Wujak' (50)	GDR	6.3.55	2	OG	Moskva	31 Jul 80
7.04	0.9	Tatyana	Proskuryakova'	RUS	13.1.56	1		Kyiv	25 Aug 83
7.04	2.0	Yelena	Yatsuk	UKR	16.3.61	1	Znam	Moskva	8 Jun 85
7.04	0.3	Carol	Lewis	USA	8.8.63	5	WK	Zürich	21 Aug 85
		(53)							

100th woman 6.93, 200th 6.82, 300th 6.70, 400th 6.70, 500th 6.65

Wind assisted *Performances to 7.35, performers to 7.05*

7.63A	2.1	Heike	Drechsler	GER	16.12.64	1		Sestriere	21 Jul 92
7.45	2.6		Joyner-Kersee			1	NC/OT	Indianapolis	23 Jul 88
7.39	2.6		Drechsler			1		Padova	15 Sep 91
7.39	2.9		Drechsler			1	Expo	Sevilla	6 Jun 92
7.39A	3.3		Drechsler			2		Sestriere	31 Jul 94
7.36	2.2		Chistyakova			1	Znam	Volgograd	11 Jun 89
7.35	3.4		Drechsler			1	NC	Jena	29 Jun 86

312 LONG JUMP – TRIPLE JUMP A-T

Mark	Wind	Name		Nat	Born	Pos	Meet	Venue	Date
7.23A	4.3	Fiona	May	ITA	12.12.69	1		Sestriere	29 Jul 95
7.22	4.3	Anastasiya	Mironchik-Ivanova	BLR	13.4.89	1	NC	Grodno	6 Jul 12
7.19A	3.7	Susen	Tiedtke ¶	GER	23.1.69	1		Sestriere	28 Jul 93
7.17	3.6	Eva	Murková	SVK	29.5.62	1		Nitra	26 Aug 84
7.15	2.8	Janay	DeLoach-Soukup	USA	12.10.85	Q	NC/OT	Eugene	29 Jun 12
7.14A	4.5	Marieke	Veltman	USA	18.9.71	2		Sestriere	29 Jul 95
7.14	2.2	Blessing	Okagbare	NGR	9.10.88	2	DL	Doha	10 May 13
7.12A	5.8	Níki	Xánthou	GRE	11.10.73	3		Sestriere	29 Jul 95
7.12A	4.3	Nicole	Boegman	AUS	5.3.67	4		Sestriere	29 Jul 95
7.09	2.9	Renata	Nielsen	DEN	18.5.66	2		Sevilla	5 Jun 94
7.08	2.2	Lyudmila	Galkina	RUS	20.1.72	1		Thessaloniki	23 Jun 99
7.07A	5.6	Valentina	Uccheddu	ITA	26.10.66	5		Sestriere	29 Jul 95
7.07A	2.7	Sharon	Couch	USA	13.9.67	1		El Paso	12 Apr 97
7.07A	w	Erica	Johansson	SWE	5.2.74	1		Vygieskraal	15 Jan 00
7.06	3.4		Ma Miaolan	CHN	18.1.70	1	NG	Beijing	10 Sep 93

Best at low altitude:

7.06	0.8	Maggi ¶	1	Milano	3 Jun 03	7.12w	3.4	May	1 NC Bologna 25 May 96
		7.17w	2.6	1	São Paulo	13 Apr 02			

Ancillary marks – other marks during series (to 7.34/7.36w):

7.45	1.0	Chistyakova	11 Jun 88	7.47Aw	3.1 Drechsler	21 Jul 92	7.38w	2.2	Chistyakova 11 Jun 88
7.37		Drechsler	9 Jul 88	7.39Aw	3.1 Drechsler	21 Jul 92	7.36w		Joyner-Kersee 31 Jul 94

TRIPLE JUMP

Mark	Wind	Name		Nat	Born	Pos	Meet	Venue	Date
15.50 WR	0.9	Inessa	Kravets ¶	UKR	5.10.66	1	WCh	Göteborg	10 Aug 95
15.39	0.5	Françoise	Mbango	CMR	14.4.76	1	OG	Beijing	17 Aug 08
15.36i		Tatyana	Lebedeva ¶	RUS	21.7.76	1	WI	Budapest	6 Mar 04
15.34	-0.5		Lebedeva			1		Iráklio	4 Jul 04
15.33	-0.1		Kravets			1	OG	Atlanta	31 Jul 96
15.33	1.2		Lebedeva			1	Athl	Lausanne	6 Jul 04
15.32	0.5		Lebedeva			1	Super	Yokohama	9 Sep 00
15.32	0.9	Hrisopiyi	Devetzí ¶	GRE	2.1.76	Q	OG	Athína	21 Aug 04
15.32	0.5		Lebedeva			2	OG	Beijing	17 Aug 08
15.31	0.0	Caterine	Ibargüen	COL	12.2.84	1	Herc	Monaco	18 Jul 14
15.30	0.6		Mbango			1	OG	Athína	23 Aug 04
15.29	0.3	Yamilé	Aldama	CUB/SUD/GBR	14.8.72	1	GGala	Roma	11 Jul 03
15.28	0.3		Aldama			1	GP	Linz	2 Aug 04
15.28	0.9	Yargelis	Savigne	CUB	13.11.84	1	WCh	Osaka	31 Aug 07
15.27	1.3		Aldama			1	GP	London (CP)	8 Aug 03
15.25	-0.8		Lebedeva			1	WCh	Edmonton	10 Aug 01
15.25	-0.1		Devetzí			2	OG	Athína	23 Aug 04
15.25	1.7	Olga	Rypakova	KAZ	30.11.84	1	C.Cup	Split	4 Sep 10
15.23	0.8		Lebedeva			1		Réthimno	23 Jun 04
15.23	0.6		Lebedeva			1	Tsik	Athína	3 Jul 06
15.21	1.2		Aldama			2		Réthimno	23 Jun 04
15.20	0.0	Sarka	Kaspárková	CZE	20.5.71	1	WCh	Athína	4 Aug 97
15.20	-0.3	Tereza	Marinova (10)	BUL	5.9.77	1	OG	Sydney	24 Sep 00
15.20	1.3		Savigne			1	Vard	Réthimno	14 Jul 08
15.19	0.5		Lebedeva			1	Athl	Lausanne	11 Jul 06
15.18	0.3	Iva	Prandzheva ¶	BUL	15.2.72	2	WCh	Göteborg	10 Aug 95
15.18	-0.2		Lebedeva			1	WCh	Saint-Denis	26 Aug 03
15.17	0.4		Ibargüen			1	OG	Rio de Janeiro	14 Aug 16
15.16	0.1	Rodica	Mateescu ¶	ROU	13.3.71	2	WCh	Athína	4 Aug 97
15.16i WIR	-	Ashia	Hansen	GBR	5.12.71	1	EI	Valencia	28 Feb 98
15.16	0.7	Trecia (31/14)	Smith	JAM	5.11.75	2	GP	Linz	2 Aug 04
15.14	1.9	Nadezhda	Alekhina	RUS	22.9.78	1	NC	Cheboksary	26 Jul 09
15.09 WR	0.5	Anna	Biryukova	RUS	27.9.67	1	WCh	Stuttgart	21 Aug 93
15.09	-0.5	Inna	Lasovskaya	RUS	17.12.69	1	ECCp-A	Valencia	31 May 97
15.08i		Marija	Sestak	SLO	17.4.79	1		Athína (P)	13 Feb 08
15.07	-0.6	Paraskeví	Tsiamíta	GRE	10.3.72	Q	WCh	Sevilla	22 Aug 99
15.04	1.7	Yekaterina (20)	Koneva	RUS	25.9.88	2	Pre	Eugene	30 May 15
15.03i		Iolanda	Chen	RUS	26.7.61	1	WI	Barcelona	11 Mar 95
15.03	1.9	Magdelin	Martinez	ITA	10.2.76	1		Roma	26 Jun 04
15.02	0.9	Anna	Pyatykh	RUS	4.4.81	3	EC	Göteborg	8 Sep 06
15.02	-0.4	Yulimar	Rojas	VEN	21.10.95	1		Madrid	23 Jun 16
15.00	1.2	Kène	Ndoye	SEN	20.11.78	2		Iráklio	4 Jul 04
14.99	0.2	Olha	Saladukha	UKR	4.6.83	1	EC	Helsinki	29 Jun 12
14.98	1.8	Sofia	Bozhanova ¶	BUL	4.10.67	1		Stara Zagora	16 Jul 94
14.98	0.2	Baya	Rahouli	ALG	27.7.79	1	MedG	Almeria	1 Jul 05

TRIPLE JUMP – SHOT A-T   313

Mark	Wind	Name		Nat	Born	Pos	Meet	Venue	Date
14.96	0.7	Yelena	Hovorova	UKR	18.9.73	4	OG	Sydney	24 Sep 00
14.94i	–	Cristina	Nicolau	ROU	9.8.77	1	NC	Bucuresti	5 Feb 00
		(30)							
14.94i		Oksana	Udmurtova	RUS	1.2.82	1		Tartu	20 Feb 08
14.90	1.0		Xie Limei	CHN	27.6.86	1		Urumqi	20 Sep 07
14.85	1.2	Viktoriya	Gurova	RUS	22.5.82	3	NC	Kazan	19 Jul 08
14.83i	–	Yelena	Lebedenko	RUS	16.1.71	1		Samara	1 Feb 01
14.83	0.5	Yelena	Oleynikova	RUS	9.12.76	1	Odlozil	Praha	17 Jun 02
14.79	1.7	Irina	Mushayilova	RUS	6.1.67	1	DNG	Stockholm	5 Jul 93
14.78i		Adelina	Gavrila	ROU	26.11.78	1		Bucuresti	3 Feb 08
14.78	-0.1	Hanna	Minenko	UKR/ISR	25.9.89	2	WCh	Beijing	24 Aug 15
14.76	0.9	Galina	Chistyakova	RUS	26.7.62	1	Spitzen	Luzern	27 Jun 95
14.76	1.1	Gundega	Sproge ¶	LAT	12.12.72	3		Sheffield	29 Jun 97
		(40)							
14.76	0.4	Kseniya	Detsuk	BLR	23.4.86	*	NCp	Brest	26 May 12
14.73	-1.3	Paraskeví	Papahrístou	GRE	17.4.89	1		Athína (F)	8 Jun 16
14.72	1.8		Huang Qiuyan	CHN	25.1.80	1	NG	Guangzhou	22 Nov 01
14.71	1.4	Athanasía	Pérra	GRE	2.2.83	1	NC	Athína	16 Jun 12
14.71	0.0	Keturah	Orji	USA	5.3.96	4	OG	Rio de Janeiro	14 Aug 16
14.70i		Oksana	Rogova	RUS	7.10.78	1		Volgograd	6 Feb 02
14.69	1.2	Anja	Valant	SLO	8.9.77	3		Kalamáta	4 Jun 00
14.69	1.2	Simona	La Mantia	ITA	14.4.83	1		Palermo	22 May 05
14.69	2.0	Teresa	N'zola Meso	ANG/FRA	30.11.83	1	ECp-S	München	23 Jun 07
14.68i		Anastasiya	Taranova-Potapova	RUS	6.9.85	1	EI	Torino	8 Mar 09
		(50)	100th woman 14.45, 200th 14.16, 300th 13.99, 400th 13.83, 500th 13.70						

Wind assisted   *Performances to 15.14, performers to 14.75*

Mark	Wind	Name		Nat	Born	Pos	Meet	Venue	Date
15.24A	4.2	Magdelin	Martinez	ITA	10.2.76	1		Sestriere	1 Aug 04
15.18	2.1	Caterine	Ibargüen	COL	12.2.84	1	Pre	Eugene	30 May 15
15.17	2.4	Anna	Pyatykh	RUS	4.4.81	2	SGP	Athína	3 Jul 06
15.10	2.7	Keila	Costa	BRA	6.2.83	1		Uberlandia	6 May 07
15.06	2.6	Olga	Saladukha	UKR	4.6.83	1	DNG	Stockholm	29 Jul 11
14.99	6.8	Yelena	Hovorova	UKR	18.9.73	1	WUG	Palma de Mallorca	11 Jul 99
14.85	2.5	Gabriela	Petrova	BUL	29.6.92	1	ET-2	Stara Zagora	20 Jun 15
14.84	4.1	Galina	Chistyakova	RUS	26.7.62	1		Innsbruck	28 Jun 95
14.83	8.3		Ren Ruiping	CHN	1.2.76	1	NC	Taiyuan	21 May 95
14.83	2.2	Heli	Koivula-Kruger	FIN	27.6.75	2	EC	München	10 Aug 02
14.81	2.4	Kseniya	Detsuk	BLR	23.4.86	1	NCp	Brest	26 May 12
14.78	2.7	Kimberly	Williams	JAM	3.11.88	3	Pre	Eugene	1 Jun 13
14.77	2.3	Paraskeví	Papahrístou	GRE	17.4.89	1		Ankara	5 Jun 12
14.75	4.2	Jelena	Blazevic	LAT	11.5.70	1	v2N	Kaunas	23 Aug 97

Best outdoor mark for athlete with all-time best indoors

15.15	1.7	Hansen	1 GPF	Fukuoka	13 Sep 97	14.85	1.4 Udmurtova	1	Padova	31 Aug 08
15.03	1.1	Sestak	6 OG	Beijing	17 Aug 08	14.75	1.1 Gavrila	3 GP II	Rieti	7 Sep 03
14.97WR	0.9	Chen	1 NC	Moskva	18 Jun 93	14.70	1.3 Nicolau	1 EU23	Göteborg	1 Aug 99

Ancillary marks – other marks during series (to 15.19)

15.30	0.5	Mbango	23 Aug 04	15.28	-0.3	Ledebeva	4 Jul 04	15.25i	Ledebeva	6 Mar 04
15.21	-0.2	Mbango	23 Aug 04	15.19	1.0	Lebedeva	3 Jul 06	15.19	1.3 Mbango	17 Aug 08

Drugs disqualification

15.23	1.6		Devetzí ¶			3	OG	Beijing	17 Aug 08
15.22	1.5		Devetzí ¶			1		Thessaloníki	9 Jul 08

SHOT

Mark		Name		Nat	Born	Pos	Meet	Venue	Date
22.63 WR		Natalya	Lisovskaya	RUS	16.7.62	1	Znam	Moskva	7 Jun 87
22.55			Lisovskaya			1	NC	Tallinn	5 Jul 88
22.53 WR			Lisovskaya			1		Sochi	27 May 84
22.53			Lisovskaya			1		Kyiv	14 Aug 88
22.50i		Helena	Fibingerová	CZE	13.7.49	1		Jablonec	19 Feb 77
22.45 WR		Ilona	Slupianek' ¶	GDR	24.9.56	1		Potsdam	11 May 80
22.41			Slupianek			1	OG	Moskva	24 Jul 80
22.40			Slupianek			1		Berlin	3 Jun 83
22.38			Slupianek			1		Karl-Marx-Stadt	25 May 80
22.36 WR			Slupianek			1		Celje	2 May 80
22.34			Slupianek			1		Berlin	7 May 80
22.34			Slupianek			1	NC	Cottbus	18 Jul 80
22.32 WR			Fibingerová			1		Nitra	20 Aug 77
22.24			Lisovskaya			1	OG	Seoul	1 Oct 88
22.22			Slupianek			1		Potsdam	13 Jul 80
22.19		Claudia	Losch	FRG	10.1.60	1		Hainfeld	23 Aug 87
22.14i			Lisovskaya			1	NC	Penza	7 Feb 87
22.13			Slupianek			1		Split	29 Apr 80

314   SHOT A-T

Mark	Wind	Name		Nat	Born	Pos	Meet	Venue	Date
22.06			Slupianek			1		Berlin	15 Aug 78
22.06			Lisovskaya			1		Moskva	6 Aug 88
22.05			Slupianek			1	OD	Berlin	28 May 80
22.05			Slupianek			1		Potsdam	31 May 80
22.04			Slupianek			1		Potsdam	4 Jul 79
22.04			Slupianek			1		Potsdam	29 Jul 79
21.99 WR			Fibingerová			1		Opava	26 Sep 76
21.98			Slupianek			1		Berlin	17 Jul 79
21.96			Fibingerová			1	GS	Ostrava	8 Jun 77
21.96			Lisovskaya			1	Drz	Praha	16 Aug 84
21.96			Lisovskaya			1		Vilnius	28 Aug 88
21.95			Lisovskaya			1	IAC	Edinburgh	29 Jul 88
		(30/4)							
21.89 WR		Ivanka	Khristova	BUL	19.11.41	1		Belmeken	4 Jul 76
21.86		Marianne	Adam	GDR	19.9.51	1	v URS	Leipzig	23 Jun 79
21.76			Li Meisu	CHN	17.4.59	1		Shijiazhuang	23 Apr 88
21.73		Natalya	Akhrimenko	RUS	12.5.55	1		Leselidze	21 May 88
21.70i		Nadezhda	Ostapchuk ¶	BLR	12.10.80	1	NC	Mogilyov	12 Feb 10
21.69		Viktoriya	Pavlysh ¶	UKR	15.1.69	1	EC	Budapest	20 Aug 98
		(10)							
21.66			Sui Xinmei ¶	CHN	29.1.65	1		Beijing	9 Jun 90
21.61		Verzhinia	Veselinova	BUL	18.11.57	1		Sofia	21 Aug 82
21.60i		Valentina	Fedyushina	UKR	18.2.65	1		Simferopol	28 Dec 91
21.58		Margitta	Droese/Pufe	GDR	10.9.52	1		Erfurt	28 May 78
21.57 @		Ines	Müller'	GDR	2.1.59	1		Athína	16 May 88
21.45						1		Schwerin	4 Jun 86
21.53		Nunu	Abashidze ¶	UKR	27.3.55	2	Izv	Kyiv	20 Jun 84
21.52			Huang Zhihong	CHN	7.5.65	1	NC	Beijing	27 Jun 90
21.46		Larisa	Peleshenko ¶	RUS	29.2.64	1	Kuts	Moskva	26 Aug 00
21.45 WR		Nadezhda	Chizhova	RUS	29.9.45	1		Varna	29 Sep 73
21.43		Eva	Wilms	FRG	28.7.52	2	HB	München	17 Jun 77
		(20)	@ competitive meeting, but unsanctioned by GDR federation						
21.42		Svetlana	Krachevskaya'	RUS	23.11.44	2	OG	Moskva	24 Jul 80
21.31 @		Heike	Hartwig'	GDR	30.12.62	2		Athína	16 May 88
21.27						1		Haniá	22 May 88
21.27		Liane	Schmuhl	GDR	29.6.61	1		Cottbus	26 Jun 82
21.24		Valerie	Adams	NZL	6.10.84	1	WCh	Daegu	29 Aug 11
21.22		Astrid	Kumbernuss	GDR/GER	5.2.70	1	WCh	Göteborg	5 Aug 95
21.21		Kathrin	Neimke	GDR	18.7.66	2	WCh	Roma	5 Sep 87
21.19		Helma	Knorscheidt	GDR	31.12.56	1		Berlin	24 May 84
21.15i		Irina	Korzhanenko ¶	RUS	16.5.74	1		Moskva	18 Feb 99
21.10		Heidi	Krieger	GDR	20.7.65	1	EC	Stuttgart	26 Aug 86
21.06		Svetlana	Krivelyova ¶	RUS	13.6.69	1	OG	Barcelona	7 Aug 92
		(30)							
21.05		Zdenka	Silhavá' ¶	CZE	15.6.54	2	NC	Praha	23 Jul 83
21.01		Ivanka	Petrova-Stoycheva	BUL	3.2.51	1	NC	Sofia	28 Jul 79
21.00		Mihaela	Loghin	ROU	1.6.52	1		Formia	30 Jun 84
21.00		Cordula	Schulze	GDR	11.9.59	4	OD	Potsdam	21 Jul 84
20.96		Belsy	Laza	CUB	5.6.67	1		Ciudad de México	2 May 92
20.95		Elena	Stoyanova ¶	BUL	23.1.52	2	Balk	Sofia	14 Jun 80
20.91		Svetla	Mitkova	BUL	17.6.64	1		Sofia	24 May 87
20.80		Sona	Vasícková	CZE	14.3.62	1		Praha	2 Jun 88
20.77		Christina	Schwanitz	GER	24.12.85	1		Beijing	20 May 15
20.72		Grit	Haupt/Hammer	GDR	4.6.66	3		Neubrandenburg	11 Jun 87
		(40)							
20.70		Natalya	Mikhnevich' ¶	BLR	25.5.82	2	NC	Grodno	8 Jul 08
20.63		Michelle	Carter	USA	12.10.85	1	OG	Rio de Janeiro	12 Aug 16
20.61		María Elena	Sarría	CUB	14.9.54	1		La Habana	22 Jul 82
20.61		Yanina	Korolchik' ¶	BLR	26.12.76	1	WCh	Edmonton	5 Aug 01
20.60		Marina	Antonyuk	RUS	12.5.62	1		Chelyabinsk	10 Aug 86
20.54			Zhang Liuhong	CHN	16.1.69	1	NC	Beijing	5 Jun 94
20.53		Iris	Plotzitzka	FRG	7.1.66	1	ASV	Köln	21 Aug 88
20.50i		Christa	Wiese	GDR	25.12.67	2	NC	Senftenberg	12 Feb 89
20.47		Nina	Isayeva	RUS	6.7.50	1		Bryansk	28 Aug 82
20.47			Cong Yuzhen	CHN	22.1.63	2	IntC	Tianjin	3 Sep 88
		(50)	100th woman 19.73, 200th 18.87, 300th 18.2, 400th 17.84, 500th 17.53						

Best outdoor marks
21.58	Ostapchuk ¶	1	Minsk	18 Jul 12		20.82	Korzhanenko ¶	1	Rostov na Donu	30 May 98
21.08	Fedyushina	1	Leselidze	15 May 88		21.06 drugs dq	(1) OG		Athína	18 Aug 04

SHOT – DISCUS A-T 315

Mark	Wind	Name		Nat	Born	Pos	Meet	Venue	Date
Ancillary marks – other marks			22.33	Slupianek		2 May 80	22.12	Slupianek	13 Jul 80
during series (to 22.09)			22.20	Slupianek		13 Jul 80	22.11	Slupianek	7 May 80
22.60	Lisovskaya (WR)	7 Jun 87	22.19	Lisovskaya		5 Jul 88	22.10	Slupianek	25 May 80
22.40	Lisovskaya	14 Aug 88	22.14	Reinsch		25 May 80	22.09	Slupianek	7 May 80
22.34	Slupianek	11 May 80	22.14	Slupianek		13 Jul 80			

DISCUS

Mark	Wind		Name		Nat	Born	Pos	Meet	Venue	Date
76.80	WR	Gabriele	Reinsch		GDR	23.9.63	1	v ITA	Neubrandenburg	9 Jul 88
74.56	WR	Zdenka	Silhavá' ¶		CZE	15.6.54	1		Nitra	26 Aug 84
74.56		Ilke	Wyludda		GDR	28.3.69	1	NC	Neubrandenburg	23 Jul 89
74.44			Reinsch				1		Berlin	13 Sep 88
74.40			Wyludda				2		Berlin	13 Sep 88
74.08		Diana	Gansky'		GDR	14.12.63	1	v USSR	Karl-Marx-Stadt	20 Jun 87
73.90			Gansky				1	ECp	Praha	27 Jun 87
73.84		Daniela	Costian ¶		ROU	30.4.65	1		Bucuresti	30 Apr 88
73.78			Costian				1		Bucuresti	24 Apr 88
73.42			Reinsch				1		Karl-Marx-Stadt	12 Jun 88
73.36	WR	Irina	Meszynski		GDR	24.3.62	1	Drz	Praha	17 Aug 84
73.32			Gansky				1		Neubrandenburg	11 Jun 87
73.28		Galina	Savinkova'		RUS	15.7.53	1	NC	Donetsk	8 Sep 84
73.26	WR		Savinkova				1		Leselidze	21 May 83
73.26			Sachse/Gansky				1		Neubrandenburg	6 Jun 86
73.24			Gansky				1		Leipzig	29 May 87
73.22		Tsvetanka	Khristova ¶		BUL	14.3.62	1		Kazanlak	19 Apr 87
73.10		Gisela	Beyer		GDR	16.7.60	1	OD	Berlin	20 Jul 84
73.04			Gansky				1		Potsdam	6 Jun 87
73.04			Wyludda				1	ECp	Gateshead	5 Aug 89
72.96			Savinkova				1	v GDR	Erfurt	23 Jun 85
72.94			Gansky				2	v ITA	Neubrandenburg	9 Jul 88
72.92		Martina	Opitz/Hellmann		GDR	12.12.60	1	NC	Potsdam	20 Aug 87
72.90			Costian				1		Bucuresti	14 May 88
72.78			Hellmann				2		Neubrandenburg	11 Jun 87
72.78			Reinsch				1	OD	Berlin	29 Jun 88
72.72			Wyludda				1		Neubrandenburg	23 Jun 89
72.70			Wyludda				1	NC-j	Karl-Marx-Stadt	15 Jul 88
72.54			Gansky				1	NC	Rostock	25 Jun 88
72.52			Hellmann				1		Frohburg	15 Jun 86
72.52		(31/10)	Khristova				1	BGP	Budapest	11 Aug 86
72.14		Galina	Murashova		LTU	22.12.55	2	Drz	Praha	17 Aug 84
71.80	WR	Maria	Vergova/Petkova		BUL	3.11.50	1	NC	Sofia	13 Jul 80
71.68			Xiao Yanling ¶		CHN	27.3.68	1		Beijing	14 Mar 92
71.58		Ellina	Zvereva'		BLR	16.11.60	1	Znam	Leningrad	12 Jun 88
71.50	WR	Evelin	Schlaak/Jahl		GDR	28.3.56	1		Potsdam	10 May 80
71.30		Larisa	Korotkevich		RUS	3.1.67	1	RusCp	Sochi	29 May 92
71.22		Ria	Stalman		NED	11.12.51	1		Walnut	15 Jul 84
		Disallowed as Dutch record in 2016 after Stalman admitted drugs use								
71.08		Sandra	Perkovic		CRO	21.6.90	1	EC	Zürich	16 Aug 14
70.88		Hilda Elia	Ramos ¶		CUB	1.9.64	1		La Habana	8 May 92
70.80		Larisa (20)	Mikhalchenko		UKR	16.5.63	1		Kharkov	18 Jun 88
70.68		Maritza	Martén		CUB	16.8.63	1	Ib Am	Sevilla	18 Jul 92
70.65		Denia	Caballero		CUB	13.1.90	1		Bilbao	20 Jun 15
70.50	WR	Faina	Melnik		RUS	9.6.45	1	Znam	Sochi	24 Apr 76
70.34	@	Silvia	Madetzky		GDR	24.6.62	3		Athína	16 May 88
69.34							1		Halle	26 Jun 87
70.02		Natalya	Sadova ¶		RUS	15.7.72	1		Thessaloniki	23 Jun 99
69.86		Valentina	Kharchenko		RUS	.49	1		Feodosiya	16 May 81
69.72		Svetla	Mitkova		BUL	17.6.64	2	NC	Sofia	15 Aug 87
69.68		Mette	Bergmann		NOR	9.11.62	1		Florø	27 May 95
69.51		Franka	Dietzsch		GER	22.1.68	1		Wiesbaden	8 May 99
69.50		Florenta (30)	Craciunescu'		ROU	7.5.55	1	Balk	Stara Zagora	2 Aug 85
69.17		Gia	Lewis-Smallwood		USA	1.4.79	1	Déca	Angers	30 Aug 14
69.14		Irina	Yatchenko ¶		BLR	31.10.65	1		Staiki	31 Jul 04
69.08		Carmen	Romero		CUB	6.10.50	1	NC	La Habana	17 Apr 76
69.08		Mariana	Ionescu/Lengyel		ROU	14.4.53	1		Constanta	19 Apr 86
68.92		Sabine	Engel		GDR	21.4.54	1	v URS,POL	Karl-Marx-Stadt	25 Jun 77
68.89		Nadine	Müller		GER	21.11.85	1	ECp-w	Bar	18 Mar 12
68.86		Yaimí	Pérez		CUB	29.5.91	1		La Habana	13 Feb 16
68.80	A	Nicoleta	Grasu		ROU	11.9.71	1		Poiana Brasov	7 Aug 99
68.64		Margitta	Pufe'		GDR	10.9.52	1	ISTAF	Berlin	17 Aug 79

WOMEN All-time

316   DISCUS – HAMMER A-T

Mark	Wind	Name		Nat	Born	Pos	Meet	Venue	Date
68.62	(40)	Yu	Hourun	CHN	9.7.64	1		Beijing	6 May 88
68.62		Hou	Xuemei	CHN	27.2.62	1	IntC	Tianjin	4 Sep 88
68.60		Nadezhda	Kugayevskikh	RUS	19.4.60	1		Oryol	30 Aug 83
68.58		Lyubov	Zverkova	RUS	14.6.55	1	Izv	Kyiv	22 Jun 84
68.52		Beatrice	Faumuiná	NZL	23.10.74	1	Bisl	Oslo	4 Jul 97
68.49		Julia	Fischer	GER	1.4.90	1	Werfer	Halle	21 May 16
68.38		Olga	Burova'	RUS	17.9.63	2	RusCp	Sochi	29 May 92
68.18		Tatyana	Lesovaya	KAZ	24.4.56	1		Alma-Ata	23 Sep 82
68.18		Irina	Khval	RUS	17.5.62	1		Moskva	8 Jul 88
68.18		Barbara	Hechevarría	CUB	6.8.66	2		La Habana	17 Feb 89
68.03		Yarelis	Barrios ¶	CUB	12.7.83	1	NC	La Habana	22 Mar 12
	(50)		100th woman 65.96, 200th 63.86, 300th 61.98, 400th 60.36, 500th 59.16						

Unofficial meeting: Berlin 6 Sep 88: 1. Martina Hellmann 78.14, 2. Ilke Wyludda 75.36
Downhill: 69.44 Suzy   Powell   USA   3.9.76 1   La Jolla   27 Apr 02
Drugs disqualification:
70.69   Darya   Pishchalnikova ¶   RUS   19.7.85   (1)   NC   Cheboksary   5 Jul 12
Ancillary marks – other marks during series (to 72.92)
73.32   Reinsch   13 Sep 88   73.28   Gansky   27 Jun 87   73.10   Reinsch   9 Jul 88
73.28   Gansky   11 Jun 87   73.16   Wyludda   13 Sep 88   73.06   Gansky   27 Jun 87
                                                                                        72.92   Hellmann   20 Aug 87

HAMMER

Mark	Wind	Name		Nat	Born	Pos	Meet	Venue	Date
82.98 WR		Anita	Wlodarczyk	POL	8.8.85	1	Skol	Warszawa	28 Aug 16
82.29 WR			Wlodarczyk			1	OG	Rio de Janeiro	14 Aug 16
81.08			Wlodarczyk			1	Skol	Cetniewo	1 Aug 15
80.85			Wlodarczyk			1	WCh	Beijing	27 Aug 15
80.26			Wlodarczyk			1		Cetniewo	12 Jul 16
79.61			Wlodarczyk			1	Kuso	Szczecin	18 Jun 16
79.58 WR			Wlodarczyk			1	ISTAF	Berlin	31 Aug 14
79.48			Wlodarczyk			1	Werfer	Halle	21 May 16
79.45			Wlodarczyk			1		Forbach	29 May 16
79.42 WR		Betty	Heidler	GER	14.10.83	1		Halle	21 May 11
78.80		Tatyana	Lysenko ¶	RUS	9.10.83	1	WCh	Moskva	16 Aug 13
78.76			Wlodarczyk			1	EC	Zürich	15 Aug 14
78.69		Oksana	Menkova	BLR	28.3.82	1		Minsk	18 Jul 12
78.69			Wlodarczyk			1	NC	Bydgoszcz	26 Jun 16
78.54			Wlodarczyk			1	GS	Ostrava	19 May 16
78.51			Lysenko			1	NC	Cheboksary	5 Jul 12
78.46			Wlodarczyk			2	WCh	Moskva	16 Aug 13
78.30 WR			Wlodarczyk			1	EAF	Bydgoszcz	6 Jun 10
78.28			Wlodarczyk			1	ET	Cheboksary	21 Jun 15
78.24			Wlodarczyk			1	NC	Kraków	21 Jul 15
78.22			Wlodarczyk			1		Dubnica nad Vahom	21 Aug 13
78.19			Menkova			1		Brest	28 Apr 12
78.19			Menkova			1		Minsk	12 Jun 12
78.18			Lysenko			1	OG	London (OS)	10 Aug 12
78.17			Wlodarczyk			1		Cetniewo	26 Jul 14
78.16			Wlodarczyk			1	Skol	Warszawa	13 Sep 15
78.15			Lysenko			1	NC	Moskva	24 Jul 13
78.14			Wlodarczyk			1	EC	Amsterdam	8 Jul 16
78.10			Wlodarczyk			1	Gyulai	Székesfehérvár	18 Jul 16
78.07			Heidler			1	GS	Ostrava	24 May 12
	(30/4)								
77.68		Wang	Zheng	CHN	14.12.87	1		Chengdu	29 Mar 14
77.33		Zhang	Wenxiu ¶	CHN	22.3.86	(1)	AsiG	Incheon	28 Sep 14
77.26 WR		Gulfiya	Khanafeyeva ¶	RUS	4.6.82	1	NC	Tula	12 Jun 06
77.13		Oksana	Kondratyeva	RUS	22.11.85	1	Znam	Zhukovskiy	30 Jun 13
76.90		Martina	Hrasnová' ¶	SVK	21.3.83	1		Trnava	16 May 09
76.83		Kamila	Skolimowska	POL	4.11.82	1	SGP	Doha	11 May 07
	(10)								
76.72		Mariya	Bespalova ¶	RUS	21.5.86	2		Zhukovskiy	23 Jun 12
76.66		Olga	Tsander	BLR	18.5.76	1		Staiki	21 Jul 05
76.63		Yekaterina	Khoroshikh ¶	RUS	21.1.83	2	Znam	Moskva	24 Jun 06
76.62		Yipsi	Moreno	CUB	19.11.80	1	GP	Zagreb	9 Sep 08
76.56		Alena	Matoshko	BLR	23.6.82	2		Minsk	12 Jun 12
76.33		Darya	Pchelnik	BLR	20.12.81	2		Staiki	29 Jun 08
76.21		Yelena	Konevtsova	RUS	11.3.81	3		Sochi	26 May 07
76.17		Anna	Bulgakova ¶	RUS	17.1.88	2	NC	Moskva	24 Jul 13
76.07 WR		Mihaela	Melinte ¶	ROU	27.3.75	1		Rüdlingen	29 Aug 99
76.05		Kathrin	Klaas	GER	6.2.84	5	OG	London (OS)	10 Aug 12
	(20)								

HAMMER – JAVELIN A-T

Mark	Wind	Name		Nat	Born	Pos	Meet	Venue	Date
75.73		Amanda	Bingson	USA	20.2.90	1	NC	Des Moines	22 Jun 13
75.73		Sultana	Frizell	CAN	24.10.84	1		Tucson	22 May 14
75.68		Olga	Kuzenkova ¶	RUS	4.10.70	1	NCp	Tula	4 Jun 00
75.09		Yelena	Rigert'	RUS	2.12.83	1	Kuts	Moskva	15 Jul 13
75.08		Ivana	Brkljacic	CRO	25.1.83	2	Kuso	Waszawa	17 Jun 07
74.77		Jeneva	McCall/Stevens	USA	28.10.89	2		Dubnica nad Vahom	21 Aug 13
74.66		Manuèla	Montebrun	FRA	13.11.79	1	GP II	Zagreb	11 Jul 05
74.65		Mariya	Smolyachkova	BLR	10.2.85	2		Staiki	19 Jul 08
74.54		Sophie	Hitchon	GBR	11.7.91	3	OG	Rio de Janeiro	15 Aug 16
74.52		Iryna	Sekachyova	UKR	21.7.76	1	NC	Kyiv	2 Jul 08
		(30)							
74.39		Joanna	Fiodorow	POL	4.3.89	2	Werfer	Halle	17 May 14
74.39		Alexandra	Tavernier	FRA	13.12.93	Q	WCh	Beijing	26 Aug 15
74.21		Hanna	Skydan	UKR/AZE	14.5.92	1	NC	Yalta	14 Jun 12
74.21		Zalina	Marghieva ¶	MDA	5.2.88	1	NC-w	Chisinau	6 Feb 16
74.20		Jessica	Cosby Toruga	USA	31.5.82	3		Tucson	22 May 14
74.17		Tugçe	Sahutoglu ¶	TUR	1.5.88	1		Izmir	19 May 12
74.10		Iryna	Novozhylova	UKR	7.1.86	1		Kyiv	19 May 12
74.03		Amber	Campbell	USA	5.6.81	1	NC	Eugene	6 Jul 16
73.97		Zalina	Marghieva ¶	MDA	5.2.88	1	BalkC	Pitesti	2 Aug 15
73.90		Arasay	Thondike	CUB	28.5.86	1		La Habana	18 Jun 09
73.87		Erin	Gilreath	USA	11.10.80	1	NC	Carson	25 Jun 05
		(40)							
73.81		Gwen	Berry	USA	29.6.89	1		Lisle	8 Jun 13
73.74		Jennifer	Dahlgren	ARG	21.4.84	1		Buenos Aires	10 Apr 10
73.64		Rosa	Rodríguez	VEN	2.7.86	1		Barquisimeto	16 May 13
73.59		Ester	Balassini	ITA	20.10.77	1	NC	Bressanone	25 Jun 05
73.52		Bianca	Ghelber-Perie	ROU	1.6.90	1	NC	Bucuresti	16 Jul 10
73.44		Éva	Orbán	HUN	29.11.84	2	Werfer	Halle	25 May 13
73.40		Stéphanie	Falzon	FRA	7.1.83	1	NC	Albi	26 Jul 08
73.21		Eileen	O'Keeffe	IRL	31.5.81	1	NC	Dublin	21 Jul 07
73.16		Yunaika	Crawford	CUB	2.11.82	3	OG	Athína	25 Aug 04
73.09		DeAnna	Price	USA	8.6.93	3	NC	Eugene	6 Jul 16
		(50)							

100th woman 70.48, 200th 67.33, 300th 65.21, 400th 63.50, 500th 62.52

Downhill: 75.20 Manuéla Montebrun FRA 13.11.79 1 Vineuil 18 May 03

Ancillary marks – other marks during series to 78.80 – all by Wlodarczyk

81.77	28 Aug 16	80.40	14 Aug 16	79.68	28 Aug 16	79.58	12 Jul 16	79.04	31 Aug 14
81.74	14 Aug 16	80.31	28 Aug 16	79.67	12 Jul 16	79.39	12 Jul 16	79.04	18 Jun 16
81.27	28 Aug 16	80.27	27 Aug 15	79.62	12 Jul 16	79.31	27 Aug 15	78.90	18 Jun 16

Drugs disqualification   79.60 14 Aug 16   79.07   1 Aug 15   78.80   18 Jun 16

78.61			Lysenko			(1)		Sochi	26 May 07
77.36		Gulfiya	Khanafeyeva ¶	RUS	4.6.82	(2)		Sochi	26 May 07
76.31		Gwen	Berry #	USA	29.6.89	(1)		San Diego	21 May 16
74.47		Zalina	Marghieva ¶	MDA	5.2.88	1	Univ Ch	Chisinau	7 May 12

JAVELIN

Mark		Name		Nat	Born	Pos	Meet	Venue	Date
72.28 WR		Barbora	Spotáková	CZE	30.6.81	1	WAF	Stuttgart	13 Sep 08
71.99		Mariya	Abakumova ¶	RUS	15.1.86	1	WCh	Daegu	2 Sep 11
71.70 WR		Osleidys	Menéndez	CUB	14.11.79	1	WCh	Helsinki	14 Aug 05
71.58			Spotáková			2	WCh	Daegu	2 Sep 11
71.54 WR			Menéndez			1		Réthimno	1 Jul 01
71.53			Menéndez			1	OG	Athína	27 Aug 04
71.42			Spotáková			1	OG	Beijing	21 Aug 08
70.78			Abakumova			2	OG	Beijing	21 Aug 08
70.53			Abakumova			1	ISTAF	Berlin	1 Sep 13
70.20		Christina	Obergföll	GER	22.8.81	1	ECp-S	München	23 Jun 07
70.03			Obergföll			2	WCh	Helsinki	14 Aug 05
69.82			Menéndez			1	WUG	Beijing	29 Aug 01
69.81			Obergföll			1		Berlin (Elstal)	31 Aug 08
69.75			Abakumova			1		Berlin (Elstal)	25 Aug 13
69.57			Obergföll			1	WK	Zürich	8 Sep 11
69.55			Spotáková			1	OG	London (OS)	9 Aug 12
69.53			Menéndez			1	WCh	Edmonton	7 Aug 01
69.48 WR		Trine	Hattestad	NOR	18.4.66	1	Bisl	Oslo	28 Jul 00
69.45			Spotáková			1	Herc	Monaco	22 Jul 11
69.35		Sunette	Viljoen	RSA	6.1.83	1	DL	New York	9 Jun 12
69.34			Abakumova			1	ECp-w	Castellón	16 Mar 13
69.15			Spotáková			1		Zaragoza	31 May 08
69.09			Abakumova			Q	WCh	Moskva	16 Aug 13
69.05			Obergföll			1	WCh	Moskva	18 Aug 13

JAVELIN – HEPTATHLON A-T

Mark	Wind	Name		Nat	Born	Pos	Meet	Venue	Date
68.94			Abakumova			1	WK	Zürich	29 Aug 13
68.92			Abakumova			Q	WCh	Berlin	16 Aug 09
68.91			Hattestad			1	OG	Sydney	30 Sep 00
68.89			Abakumova			1	DL	Doha	14 May 10
68.86			Obergföll			1	NC	Kassel	24 Jul 11
68.81	(30/6)		Spotáková			1	Odlozil	Praha	16 Jun 08
68.34		Steffi	Nerius	GER	1.7.72	2		Berlin (Elstal)	31 Aug 08
67.69		Katharina	Molitor	GER	8.11.83	1	WCh	Beijing	30 Aug 15
67.67		Sonia	Bisset	CUB	1.4.71	1		Salamanca	6 Jul 05
67.51		Miréla	Manjani/Tzelíli	GRE	21.12.76	2	OG	Sydney	30 Sep 00
	(10)								
67.32		Linda	Stahl	GER	2.10.85	1	adidas	New York	14 Jun 14
67.30		Vera	Rebrik	RUS	25.2.89	1	NC-w	Adler	19 Feb 16
67.29		Hanna	Hatsko-Fedusova	UKR	3.10.90	1	NC	Kirovohrad	26 Jul 14
67.20		Tatyana	Shikolenko	RUS	10.5.68	1	Herc	Monaco	18 Aug 00
67.16		Martina	Ratej	SLO	2.11.81	3	DL	Doha	14 May 10
67.11		Maria	Andrejczyk	POL	9.3.96	Q	OG	Rio de Janeiro	16 Aug 16
66.91		Tanja	Damaske	GER	16.11.71	1	NC	Erfurt	4 Jul 99
66.83		Kimberley	Mickle	AUS	28.12.84	1		Melbourne	22 Mar 14
66.80		Louise	McPaul/Currey	AUS	24.1.69	1		Gold Coast (RB)	5 Aug 00
66.67		Kara	Patterson/Winger	USA	10.4.86	1	NC	Des Moines	25 Jun 10
	(20)								
66.41		Christin	Hussong	GER	17.4.94	1	NC	Kassel	19 Jun 16
66.34		Tatyana	Kholodovich	BLR	21.6.91	1	EC	Amsterdam	9 Jul 16
66.18		Sara	Kolak	CRO	22.6.95	1	OG	Rio de Janeiro	18 Aug 16
66.17		Goldie	Sayers	GBR	16.7.82	1	LGP	London (CP)	14 Jul 12
66.15		Madara	Palameika	LAT	18.6.87	1		Jelgava	26 Jun 14
66.13			Lu Huihui ¶	CHN	26.6.89	2	WCh	Beijing	30 Aug 15
66.10		Kathryn	Mitchell	AUS	10.7.82	2		Adelaide	15 Feb 14
65.91		Nikola	Brejchová'	CZE	25.6.74	1	GP	Linz	2 Aug 04
65.64			Liu Shiying	CHN	24.9.93	1	NGP	Shaoxing	16 Apr 16
65.47			Zhang Li	CHN	17.1.89	1	AsiG	Incheon	1 Oct 14
	(30)								
65.30		Claudia	Coslovich	ITA	26.4.72	1		Ljubljana	10 Jun 00
65.29		Xiomara	Rivero	CUB	22.11.68	1		Santiago de Cuba	17 Mar 01
65.17		Karen	Forkel	GER	24.9.70	2	NC	Erfurt	4 Jul 99
65.11			Li Lingwei	CHN	26.1.89	1		Fuzhou	23 Jun 12
65.08		Ana Mirela	Termure ¶	ROU	13.1.75	1	NC	Bucuresti	10 Jun 01
64.90		Paula	Huhtaniemi'	FIN	17.2.73	1	NC	Helsinki	10 Aug 03
64.89		Yekaterina	Ivakina	RUS	4.12.64	4	Bisl	Oslo	28 Jul 00
64.87		Kelly	Morgan	GBR	17.6.80	1	NC	Birmingham	14 Jul 02
64.83		Christina	Scherwin	DEN	11.7.76	3	WAF	Stuttgart	9 Sep 06
64.83		Liz	Gleadle	CAN	5.12.88	1		Kawasaki	10 May 15
	(40)								
64.75		Brittany	Borman	USA	1.7.89	2		Kawasaki	10 May 15
64.62		Joanna	Stone	AUS	4.10.72	2		Gold Coast (RB)	5 Aug 00
64.62		Nikolett	Szabó	HUN	3.3.80	1		Pátra	22 Jul 01
64.61		Oksana	Makarova	RUS	21.7.71	2	ECp	Paris (C)	19 Jun 99
64.56		Margaryta	Dorozhon	UKR/ISR	4.9.87	1	Bisl	Oslo	11 Jun 15
64.51		Monica	Stoian	ROU	25.8.82	4	WCh	Berlin	18 Aug 09
64.49		Valeriya	Zabruskova	RUS	29.7.75	1	Znam	Tula	7 Jun 03
64.46		Dörthe	Friedrich	GER	21.6.73	1	NC	Wattenscheid	7 Jul 02
64.38		Sinta	Ozolina/Sprudzane	LAT	26.2.88	1		Riga	30 May 13
64.21		Tatjana	Jelaca	SRB	10.8.90	2	EC	Zürich	14 Aug 14
	(50)		100th woman 62.06, 200th 59.12, 300th 57.19						

Ancillary marks – other marks during series (to 68.90)

71.25	Abakumova	2 Sep 11	69.32	Abakumova	21 Aug 08	68.95	Obergföll	8 Sep 11
69.42	Menéndez	7 Aug 01	69.22	Spotáková	21 Aug 08	Spec. changed from 1 May 1999.		
69.35	Abakumova	25 Aug 13	69.08	Abakumova	21 Aug 08			

HEPTATHLON

7291 WR	Jackie	Joyner-Kersee	USA	3.3.62	1	OG	Seoul	24 Sep 88
		12.69/0.5	1.86	15.80	22.56/1.6	7.27/0.7	45.66	2:08.51
7215 WR		Joyner-Kersee			1	NC/OT	Indianapolis	16 Jul 88
		12.71/-0.9	1.93	15.65	22.30/ 0.0	7.00/-1.3	50.08	2:20.70
7158 WR		Joyner-Kersee			1	USOF	Houston	2 Aug 86
		13.18/-0.5	1.88	15.20	22.85/1.2	7.03w/2.9	50.12	2:09.69
7148 WR		Joyner-Kersee			1	GWG	Moskva	7 Jul 86
		12.85/0.2	1.88	14.76	23.00/0.3	7.01/-0.5	49.86	2:10.02
7128		Joyner-Kersee			1	WCh	Roma	1 Sep 87
		12.91/0.2	1.90	16.00	22.95/1.2	7.14/0.9	45.68	2:16.29

HEPTATHLON A-T

Mark	Wind	Name			Nat	Born	Pos	Meet	Venue		Date
7044		Joyner-Kersee					1	OG	Barcelona		2 Aug 92
		12.85/-0.9	1.91	14.13		23.12/0.7	7.10/1.3		44.98	2:11.78	
7032		Carolina	Klüft		SWE	2.2.83	1	WCh	Osaka		26 Aug 07
		13.15/0.1	1.95	14.81		23.38/0.3	6.85/1.0		47.98	2:12.56	
7007		Larisa	Nikitina ¶		RUS	29.4.65	1	NC	Bryansk		11 Jun 89
		13.40/1.4	1.89	16.45		23.97/1.1	6.73w/4.0		53.94	2:15.31	
7001			Klüft				1	WCh	Saint-Denis		24 Aug 03
		13.18/-0.4	1.94	14.19		22.98/1.1	6.68/1.0		49.90	2:12.12	
6985		Sabine	Braun		GER	19.6.65	1		Götzis		31 May 92
		13.11/-0.4	1.93	14.84		23.65/2.0	6.63w/2.9		51.62	2:12.67	
6979			Joyner-Kersee				1	NC	San José		24 Jun 87
		12.90/2.0	1.85	15.17		23.02/0.4	7.25/2.3		40.24	2:13.07	
6955		Jessica	Ennis-Hill		GBR	28.1.86	1	OG	London (OS)		4 Aug 12
		12.54/1.3	1.86	14.28		22.83/-0.3	6.48/-0.6		47.49	2:08.65	
6952			Klüft				1	OG	Athína		21 Aug 04
		13.21/0.2	1.91	14.77		23.27/-0.1	6.78/0.4		48.89	2:14.15	
6946 WR		Sabine	Paetz'		GDR	16.10.57	1	NC	Potsdam		6 May 84
		12.64/0.3	1.80	15.37		23.37/0.7	6.86/-0.2		44.62	2:08.93	
6942		Ghada	Shouaa		SYR	10.9.72	1		Götzis		26 May 96
		13.78/0.3	1.87	15.64		23.78/0.6	6.77/0.6		54.74	2:13.61	
6935 WR		Ramona	Neubert		GDR	26.7.58	1	v USSR	Moskva		19 Jun 83
		13.42/1.7	1.82	15.25		23.49/0.5	6.79/0.7		49.94	2:07.51	
6910			Joyner				1	MSR	Walnut		25 Apr 86
		12.9/0.0	1.86	14.75		23.24w/2.8	6.85/2.1		48.30	2:14.11	
6906			Ennis				1		Götzis		27 May 12
		12.81/0.0	1.85	14.51		22.88/1.9	6.51/0.8		47.11	2:09.00	
6897			John'				2	wOG	Seoul		24 Sep 88
		12.85/0.5	1.80	16.23		23.65/1.6	6.71/0.0		42.56	2:06.14	
6889		Eunice	Barber		FRA	17.11.74	1		Arles		5 Jun 05
		12.62w/2.9	1.91	12.61		24.12/1.2	6.78w/3.4		53.07	2:14.66	
6887			Klüft				1	WCh	Helsinki		7 Aug 05
		13.19/-0.4	1.82	15.02		23.70/-2.5	6.87/0.2		47.20	2:08.89	
6878			Joyner-Kersee				1	NC	New York		13 Jun 91
		12.77	1.89	15.62		23.42	6.97/0.4		43.28	2:22.12	
6875			Nikitina				1	ECp-A	Helmond		16 Jul 89
		13.55/-2.1	1.84	15.99		24.29/-2.1	6.75/-2.5		56.78	2:18.67	
6861			Barber				1	WCh	Sevilla		22 Aug 99
		12.89/-0.5	1.93	12.37		23.57/0.5	6.86/-0.3		49.88	2:15.65	
6859		Natalya	Shubenkova (10)		RUS	25.9.57	1		Kyiv		21 Jun 84
		12.93/1.0	1.83	13.66		23.57/-0.3	6.73/0.4		46.26	2:04.60	
6858		Anke	Vater/Behmer		GDR	5.6.61	3	OG	Seoul		24 Sep 88
		13.20/0.5	1.83	14.20		23.10/1.6	6.68/0.1		44.54	2:04.20	
6847			Nikitina				1	WUG	Duisburg		29 Aug 89
		13.47	1.81	16.12		24.12	6.66		59.28	2:22.07	
6845 WR			Neubert				1	v URS	Halle		20 Jun 82
		13.58/1.8	1.83	15.10		23.14/1.4	6.84w/2.3		42.54	2:06.16	
6845		Irina	Belova ¶		RUS	27.3.68	2	OG	Barcelona		2 Aug 92
		13.25/-0.1	1.88	13.77		23.34/0.2	6.82/0.0		41.90	2:05.08	
6842			Barber				1		Götzis		4 Jun 00
	12.97/0.2 (30/12)		1.88			12.23 23.84/0.5	6.85/-0.1		51.91	2:11.55	
6832		Lyudmila	Blonska ¶		UKR	9.11.77	2	WCh	Osaka		26 Aug 07
		13.25/0.1	1.92	14.44		24.09/0.3	6.88/1.0		47.77	2:16.68	
6831		Denise	Lewis		GBR	27.8.72	1		Talence		30 Jul 00
		13.13/1.0	1.84	15.07		24.01w/3.6	6.69/-0.4		49.42	2:12.20	
6810		Nafissatou	Thiam		BEL	19.8.94	1	OG	Rio de Janeiro		13 Aug 16
		13.56/0.3	1.98	14.91		25.10/-0.7	6.58/-0.5		53.13	2:16.54	
6808		Brianne	Theisen-Eaton		CAN	18.12.88	1	Hypo	Götzis		31 May 15
		13.05/-0.2	1.84	13.73		23.34/1.4	6.72/0.9		42.96	2:09.37	
6803		Jane	Frederick		USA	7.4.52	1		Talence		16 Sep 84
		13.27/1.2	1.87	15.49		24.15/1.6	6.43/0.2		51.74	2:13.55	
6778		Nataliya	Dobrynska		UKR	29.5.82	2	EC	Barcelona		31 Jul 10
		13.59/-1.6	1.86	15.88		24.23/-0.2	6.56/0.3		49.25	2:12.06	
6768w		Tatyana	Chernova ¶		RUS	29.1.88	1		Arles		3 Jun 07
		13.04w/6.1	1.83	13.57		23.59w/5.2	6.61/1.2		53.43	2:15.05	
6765		Yelena	Prokhorova (20)		RUS	16.4.78	1	NC	Tula		23 Jul 00
		13.54/-2.8	1.82	14.30		23.37/-0.2	6.72/1.0		43.40	2:04.27	
6750			Ma Miaolan		CHN	18.1.70	1	NG	Beijing		12 Sep 93
		13.28/1.5	1.89	14.98		23.86/	6.64/		45.82	2:15.33	

WOMEN All-time

HEPTATHLON – DECATHLON

Mark	Wind	Name	Nat	Born	Pos	Meet	Venue	Date
6741		Heike Drechsler	GER	16.12.64	1		Talence	11 Sep 94
	13.34/-0.3	1.84 13.58		22.84/-1.1	6.95/1.0		40.64 2:11.53	
6735(w)		Hyleas Fountain	USA	14.1.81	1	NC	Des Moines	26 Jun 10
	12.93w/2.6	1.90 13.73		23.28w/3.3	6.79w/2.7		42.26 2:17.80	
6703		Tatyana Blokhina	RUS	12.3.70	1		Talence	11 Sep 93
	13.69/-0.6	1.91 14.94		23.95/-0.4	5.99/-0.3		52.16 2:09.65	
6702		Chantal Beaugeant ¶	FRA	16.2.61	2		Götzis	19 Jun 88
	13.10/1.6	1.78 13.74		23.96w/3.5	6.45/0.2		50.96 2:07.09	
6695		Jane Flemming	AUS	14.4.65	1	CG	Auckland	28 Jan 90
	13.21/1.4	1.82 13.76		23.62w/2.4	6.57/1.6		49.28 2:12.53	
6683		Jennifer Oeser	GER	29.11.83	3	EC	Barcelona	31 Jul 10
	13.37/-1.0	1.83 13.82		24.07/-0.3	6.68/-0.3		49.17 2:12.28	
6682		Katarina Johnson-Thompson	GBR	9.1.93	1		Götzis	1 Jun 14
	13.47/-1.2	1.90 12.17		22.89/1.5	6.70/-0.1		41.44 2:08.16	
6681		Kristina Savitskaya	RUS	10.6.91	1	NC	Cheboksary	3 Jun 12
	13.52/0.0	1.88 15.27		24.61/0.0	6.65/0.0		46.83 2:14.73	
6660		Ines Schulz	GDR	10.7.65	3		Götzis	19 Jun 88
	13.56/0.4	1.84 13.95		23.93w/2.8	6.70/0.7		42.82 2:06.31	
	(30)							
6658		Svetla Dimitrova ¶	BUL	27.1.70	2		Götzis	31 May 92
	13.41/-0.7	1.75 14.72		23.06w/2.4	6.64/1.9		43.84 2:09.60	
6649		Lilli Schwarzkopf	GER	28.8.83	2	OG	London (OS)	4 Aug 12
	13.26/0.9	1.83 14.77		24.77/0.9	6.30/-0.7		51.73 2:10.50	
6646		Natalya Grachova	UKR	21.2.52	1	NC	Moskva	2 Aug 82
	13.80	1.80 16.18		23.86	6.65w/3.5		39.42 2:06.59	
66635		Sibylle Thiele	GDR	6.3.65	2	GWG	Moskva	7 Jul 86
	13.14/0.6	1.76 16.00		24.18	6.62/1.0		45.74 2:15.30	
6635		Svetlana Buraga	BLR	4.9.65	3	WCh	Stuttgart	17 Aug 93
	12.95/0.1	1.84 14.55		23.69/0.0	6.58/-0.2		41.04 2:13.65	
6633		Natalya Roshchupkina	RUS	13.1.78	2	NC	Tula	23 Jul 00
	14.05/-2.8	1.88 14.28		23.47/-0.2	6.45/0.4		44.34 2:07.93	
6626		Anouk Vetter	NED	4.2.93	1	EC	Amsterdam	9 Jul 16
	13.29/-0.7	1.74 15.69		23.89	6.38w/2.9		55.76 2:21.50	
6623		Judy Simpson'	GBR	14.11.60	3	EC	Stuttgart	30 Aug 86
	13.05/0.8	1.92 14.73		25.09/0.0	6.56w/2.5		40.92 2:11.70	
6622		Laura Ikauniece-Admidina	LAT	31.5.92	2	Hypo	Götzis	29 May 16
	13.07/0.5	1.83 13.00		23.64/1.3	6.16/-0.1		54.83 2:14.77	
6619		Liliana Nastase	ROU	1.8.62	4	OG	Barcelona	2 Aug 92
	12.86/-0.9	1.82 14.34		23.70/0.2	6.49/-0.3		41.30 2:11.22	
	(40)							
6616		Malgorzata Nowak'	POL	9.2.59	1	WUG	Kobe	31 Aug 85
	13.27w/4.0	1.95 15.35		24.20/0.0	6.37w/3.9		43.36 2:20.39	
6604		Remigija Nazaroviene'	LTU	2.6.67	2	URSCh	Bryansk	11 Jun 89
	13.26/1.4	1.86 14.27		24.12/0.7	6.58/0.9		40.94 2:09.98	
6604		Irina Tyukhay	RUS	14.1.67	3		Götzis	28 May 95
	13.20/-0.7	1.84 14.97		24.33/1.7	6.71/0.5		43.84 2:17.64	
6599A		Jessica Zelinka	CAN	3.9.81	1	NC	Calgary	28 Jun 12
	12.76/-0.6	1.77 14.74		23.42w/2.1	5.98w/2.9		46.60 2:08.95	
6599		Austra Skujyté	LTU	12.8.79	33	OG	London (OS)	4 Aug 12
	14.00/0.7	1.92 17.31		25.43/0.9	6.25/-0.6		51.13 2:20.59	
6598		Svetlana Moskalets	RUS	22.1.69	1	NC	Vladimir	17 Jun 94
	13.20/0.8	1.82 13.78		23.56/0.1	6.74/0.8		42.48 2:14.54	
6591		Svetlana Sokolova	RUS	9.1.81	1	NC	Tula	23 Jun 04
	13.56/1.1	1.82 15.09		24.02/0.6	6.26/0.3		45.07 2:07.23	
6586		Anna Melnychenko	UKR	24.4.83	1	WCh	Moskva	13 Aug 13
	13.29/-0.6	1.86 13.85		23.87/0.0	6.49/0.2		41.87 2:09.85	
6577		DeDee Nathan	USA	20.4.68	1		Götzis	30 May 99
	13.28/-0.1	1.76 14.74		24.23/0.2	6.59/1.6		50.08 2:16.92	
6576		Antoinette Nana Djimou	FRA	2.8.85	4	OG	London (OS)	4 Aug 12
	12.96/1.3	1.80 14.26		24.72/0.3	6.13/-0.2		55.87 2:15.94	
	(50)	100th woman 6423, 200th 6213, 300th 6102, 400th 6010, 500th 5928						

Drugs disqualification

Mark	Wind	Name	Nat	Born	Pos	Meet	Venue	Date
6880		Tatyana Chernova ¶	RUS	29.1.88	(1)	WCh	Daegu	30 Aug 11
	13.32/0.9	1.83 14.17		23.50/-1.5	6.61/-0.7		52.95 2:08.04	
6618		Lyudmyla Yosypenko ¶	UKR	24.9.84	4	OG	London (OS)	4 Aug 12
	13.25/0.9	1.83 13.90		23.68/0.6	6.31/-0.6		49.63 2:13.28	

DECATHLON

Mark		Name		Nat	Born	Pos		Venue	Date
8358 WR		Austra Skujyte		LTU	12.8.79	1		Columbia, MO	15 Apr 05
	12.49/1.6	46.19 3.10	48.78		57.19	14.22w/2.4	6.12/1.6	16.42 1.78	5:15.86
8150		Marie Collonvillé		FRA	23.11.73	1		Talence	26 Sep 04
	12.48/0.4	34.69 3.50	47.19		56.15	13.96/0.4	6.18/1.0	11.90 1.80	5:06.09

4 x 100m – 4 x 200m RELAY A-T   321

Mark	Wind	Nat	Name	Born	Pos	Meet	Venue	Date

4 x 100 METRES RELAY

Mark	Wind	Nat	Name	Pos	Meet	Venue	Date
40.82	WR	USA	Madison (-Bartoletta), Felix, Knight, Jeter	1	OG	London (OS)	10 Aug 12
41.01		USA	Bartoletta, Felix, Gardner, Bowie	1	OG	Rio de Janeiro	19 Aug 16
41.07		JAM	Campbell-Brown, Morrison, Thompson, Fraser-Pryce	1	WCh	Beijing	29 Aug 15
41.29		JAM	Russell, Stewart, Calvert, Fraser-Pryce	1	WCh	Moskva	18 Aug 13
41.36		JAM	C.Williams, Thompson, Campbell-Brown, Fraser-Pryce	2	OG	Rio de Janeiro	19 Aug 16
41.37	WR	GDR	Gladisch, Rieger, Auerswald, Göhr	1	WCp	Canberra	6 Oct 85
41.41		JAM	Fraser-Pryce, Simpson, Campbell-Brown, Stewart	2	OG	London (OS)	10 Aug 12
41.47		USA	Gaines, Jones, Miller, Devers	1	WCh	Athína	9 Aug 97
41.49		RUS	Bogoslovskaya, Malchugina, Voronova, Privalova	1	WCh	Stuttgart	22 Aug 93
41.49		USA	Finn, Torrence, Vereen, Devers	2	WCh	Stuttgart	22 Aug 93
41.52		USA	Gaines, Jones, Miller, Devers	1h1	WCh	Athína	8 Aug 97
41.53	WR	GDR	Gladisch, Koch, Auerswald, Göhr			Berlin	31 Jul 83
41.55		USA	Brown, Williams, Griffith, Marshall	1	ISTAF	Berlin	21 Aug 87
41.56		USA	B Knight, Felix, Myers, Jeter	1	WCh	Daegu	4 Sep 11
41.58		USA	Brown, Williams, Griffith, Marshall	1	WCh	Roma	6 Sep 87
41.58		USA	L.Williams, Felix, Lee, Jeter	1		Cottbus	8 Aug 09
41.60	WR	GDR	Müller, Wöckel, Auerswald, Göhr	1	OG	Moskva	1 Aug 80
41.60		JAM	Simpson, Morrison, Thompson, Fraser-Pryce	1	WK	Zürich	3 Sep 15
41.61A		USA	Brown, Williams, Cheeseborough, Ashford	1	USOF	USAF Academy	3 Jul 83
41.62		GER	Pinto, Mayer, Lückenkemper, Haase	1		Mannheim	29 Jul 16
41.63		USA	Brown, Williams, Cheeseborough, Ashford	1	v GDR	Los Angeles	25 Jun 83
41.64		USA	Madison, Tarmoh, Knight, L Williams	1h1	OG	London (OS)	9 Aug 12

(22 performances by 4 nations) from here just best by nation

Mark		Nat	Name	Pos	Meet	Venue	Date
41.77		GBR	Philip, Henry, Asher-Smith, Neita	3	OG	Rio de Janeiro	19 Aug 16
41.78		FRA	Girard, Hurtis, Félix, Arron	1	WCh	Saint-Denis	30 Aug 03
41.92		BAH	Fynes, Sturrup, Davis-Thompson, Ferguson	1	WCh	Sevilla	29 Aug 99
42.03		TTO	Baptiste, Ahye, Thomas, Hackett	3	WCh	Beijing	29 Aug 15
42.04		UKR	Povh, Stuy, Ryemyen, Bryzgina	3	OG	London (OS)	10 Aug 12
42.04		NED	Samuel, Schippers, van Schagen, Sedney (10)	1	EC	Amsterdam	10 Jul 16
42.08mx		BUL	Pavlova, Nuneva, Georgieva, Ivanova	mx		Sofia	8 Aug 84
42.29			Penchova, Nuneva, Georgieva, Donkova	1		Sofia	26 Jun 88
42.23		CHN	(Sichuan) Xiao Lin, Li Yali, Liu Xiaomei, Li Xuemei	1	NG	Shanghai	23 Oct 97
42.29		BRA	E dos Santos, Silva, Krasucki, R Santos	2h3	WCh	Moskva	18 Aug 13
42.39		NGR	Utondu, Idehen, Opara-Thompson, Onyali	2h2	OG	Barcelona	7 Aug 92
42.54		BEL	Borlée, Mariën, Ouédraogo, Gevaert	2	OG	Beijing	22 Aug 08
42.56		BLR	Nesterenko, Sologub, Nevmerzhitskaya, Dragun	3	WCh	Helsinki	13 Aug 05
42.59		FRG	Possekel, Helten, Richter, Kroniger	2	OG	Montreal	31 Jul 76
42.60		CAN	Emmanuel, Hyacinthe, Fofanah, Bingham	3h1	WCh	Beijing	29 Aug 15
42.67		GHA	Owusu-Agyapong, Acheampong, Gyaman, Amponsah	1		Cape Coast	8 Jul 16
42.68		POL	Popowicz, Korczynska, Jeschke, Wedler (20)	3	EC	Barcelona	1 Aug 10
42.87		SUI	Del Ponte, Atcho, E.Sprunger, Kora	2h1	EC	Amsterdam	9 Jul 16
42.89		CUB	Ferrer, López, Duporty, Allen	6	WCh	Stuttgart	22 Aug 93
42.92		KAZ	Kashafutdinova, Zyabkina, Rakhmanova, Safronova	1		Almaty	4 Jul 16
42.98		CZE/TCH	Sokolová, Soborová, Kocembová, Kratochvílová	1	WK	Zürich	18 Aug 82
42.99A		AUS	Massey, Broadrick, Lambert, Gainsford-Taylor	1		Pietersburg	18 Mar 00
43.03A		COL	M.Murillo, Palacios, Obregón, D Murillo	2	SAm-r	Bogotá	10 Jul 04
43.04		ITA	Pistone, Calí, Arcioni, Alloh	3	ECp-S	Annecy	21 Jun 08
43.07		GRE	Tsóni, Kóffa, Vasarmídou, Thánou	2	MedG	Bari	18 Jun 97
43.25A		RSA	Hartman, Moropane, Holtshausen, Seyerling	2		Pietersburg	18 Mar 00
43.28		DOM	M Sánchez, Chala, Mejía, Manzueta (30)	5h1	WCh	Moskva	18 Aug 13

Best at low altitude

| 43.03 | | COL | M.Murillo, Palacios, Obregón, N.González | 3h2 | WCh | Helsinki | 12 Aug 05 |
| 43.18 | | AUS | Wilson, Wells, Robertson, Boyle | 5 | OG | Montreal | 31 Jul 76 |

One or more athlete subsequently drugs dq

| 41.67 | | USA | A Williams, Jones ¶, L Williams, Colander | (1) | 3-N | München | 8 Aug 04 |
| 41.67 | | USA | A Williams, Jones ¶, L Williams, Colander | (1h1) | OG | Athína | 26 Aug 04 |

4 x 200 METRES RELAY

Mark		Nat	Name	Pos	Meet	Venue	Date
1:27.46	WR	USA	Blue Jenkins, Colander-Richardson, Perry, M Jones	1	PennR	Philadelphia	29 Apr 00
1:28.15	WR	GDR	Göhr, R.Müller, Wöckel, Koch			Jena	9 Aug 80
1:29.42			Texas A & M (USA) Tarmoh, Mayo, Beard, Lucas	1	Penn R	Philadelphia	24 Apr 10
1:29.45		USA	Solomon, Meadows, Knight, K Duncan	1	WRly	Nassau	25 May 14
1:29.61		GBR	Henry, A Onuora, B Williams, A Philip	2	WRly	Nassau	25 May 14

Drugs dq: 1:29.40 USA Red Colander, Gaines, Miller, M Jones ¶ | 1 | Penn | Philadelphia | 24 Apr 04

4 x 400 METRES RELAY

| 3:15.17 | WR | URS | | 1 | OG | Seoul | 1 Oct 88 |

Ledovskaya 50.12, O.Nazarova 47.82, Pinigina 49.43, Bryzgina 47.80

WOMEN All-time

322   4 x 400m, 4 x 800m, 4x 1500m RELAY

Mark	Wind	Name	Nat	Born	Pos	Meet	Venue	Date
3:15.51		USA			2	OG	Seoul	1 Oct 88
		D.Howard 49.82, Dixon 49.17, Brisco 48.44, Griffith Joyner 48.08						
3:15.92 WR		GDR G.Walther 49.8, Busch 48.9, Rübsam 49.4, Koch 47.8			1	NC	Erfurt	3 Jun 84
3:16.71		USA Torrence 49.0, Malone 49.4, Kaiser-Brown 49.48, Miles 48.78			1	WCh	Stuttgart	22 Aug 93
3:16.87		GDR Emmelmann 50.9, Busch 48.8, Müller 48.9, Koch 48.21			1	EC	Stuttgart	31 Aug 86
3:16.87		USA Trotter 50.3, Felix 48.1, McCorory 49.39, Richards-Ross 49.10			1	OG	London (OS)	11 Aug 12
3:17.83		USA Dunn 50.5, Felix 48.8, Demus 50.14, Richards 48.44			1	WCh	Berlin	23 Aug 09
3:18.09		USA Richards-Ross 49.3, Felix 49.4, Beard 49.84, McCorory 49.52			1	WCh	Daegu	3 Sep 11
3:18.29		USA				1	OG	Los Angeles	11 Aug 84
		Leatherwood 50.50, S.Howard 48.83, Brisco-Hooks 49.23, Cheeseborough 49.73						
3:18.29		GDR Neubauer 50.58, Emmelmann 49.89, Busch 48.81, Müller 48.99			3	OG	Seoul	1 Oct 88
3:18.38		RUS			2	WCh	Stuttgart	22 Aug 93
		Ruzina 50.8, Alekseyeva 49.3, Ponomaryova 49.78, Privalova 48.47						
3:18.43		URS Ledovskaya 51.7, Dzhigalova 49.2, Nazarova 48.87, Bryzgina 48.67			1	WCh	Tokyo	1 Sep 91
3:18.54		USA Wineberg 51.0, Felix 48.6, Henderson 50.06, Richards 48.93			1	OG	Beijing	23 Aug 08
3:18.55		USA Trotter 51.2, Felix 48.0, Wineberg 50.24, Richards 49.07			1	WCh	Osaka	2 Sep 07
3:18.58		URS I.Nazarova, Olizarenko, Pinigina, Vladykina				ECp	Moskva	18 Aug 85
3:18.63		GDR Neubauer 51.4, Emmelmann 49.1, Müller 48.64, Busch 49.48			1	WCh	Roma	6 Sep 87
3:18.71		JAM Whyte 50.0, Prendergast 49.6, Williams-Mills 49.84, Williams 49.22			2	WCh	Daegu	3 Sep 11
3:19.01		USA Trotter 49.8, Henderson 49.7, Richards 49.81, Hennagan 49.73			(1)	OG	Athína	28 Aug 04
		Note team was disqualified as Crystal Cox (subject of retrospective drugs ban) ran for them in the heat						
3:19.04 WR		GDR Siemon' 51.0, Busch 50.0, Rübsam 50.2, Koch 47.9			1	EC	Athína	11 Sep 82
3:19.06		USA Okolo 50.3, Hastings 49.2, Francis 49.82, Felix 49.66			1	OG	Rio de Janeiro	20 Aug 16
3:19.12		URS Baskakova, I.Nazarova, Pinigina, Vladykina			1	Drz	Praha	18 Aug 84
3:19.23 WR		GDR Maletzki 50.05, Rohde 49.00, Streidt 49.51, Brehmer 49.79			1	OG	Montreal	31 Jul 76
3:19.36		RUS			3	WCh	Daegu	3 Sep 11
		Krivoshapka 50.3, Antyukh 50.0, Litvinova 49.96, Kapachinskaya 49.22						
3:19.49		GDR Emmelmann, Busch, Neubauer, Koch 47.5			1	WCp	Canberra	4 Oct 85
		(24/5 with USSR and Russia counted separately)						
3:20.04		GBR Ohuruogu 50.6, Okoro 50.9, McConnell 49.79, Sanders 48.76			3	WCh	Osaka	2 Sep 07
3:20.32		CZE/TCH			2	WCh	Helsinki	14 Aug 83
		Kocembová 48.93, Matejkovicová 52.13, Moravcíková 51.51, Kratochvílová 47.75						
3:21.04		NGR Afolabi 51.13, Yusuf 49.72, Opara 51.29, Ogunkoya 48.90			2	OG	Atlanta	3 Aug 96
3:21.21		CAN Crooks 50.30, Richardson 50.22, Killingbeck ¶ 50.62, Payne 50.07			2	OG	Los Angeles	11 Aug 84
3:21.88		BLR Yushchenko 51.40, Khlyustova 50.7, I Usovich 49.97, S Usovich 49.78			5	WCh	Osaka	2 Sep 07
		(10)						
3:21.94		UKR Dzhigalova, Olizarenko, Pinigina, Vladykina			1	URS Ch	Kyiv	17 Jul 86
3:22.34		FRA Landre 51.3, Dorsile 51.1, Elien 50.54, Pérec 49.36			1	EC	Helsinki	14 Aug 94
3:22.49		FRG Thimm 50.81, Arendt 49.95, Thomas 51.40, Abt 50.23			4	OG	Seoul	1 Oct 88
3:23.21		CUB Díaz 51.1, Calatayud 51.2, Clement 50.47, Terrero 50.46			6	OG	Beijing	23 Aug 08
3:23.81		AUS Peris-K 51.71, Lewis 51.69, Gainsford-T 51.06, Freeman 49.35			4	OG	Sydney	30 Sep 00
3:24.28		CHN (Hebei) An X, Bai X, Cao C, Ma Y			1	NG	Beijing	13 Sep 93
3:24.49		POL Guzowska 52.2, Bejnar 50.2, Prokopek 50.47, Jesien 51.59			4	WCh	Helsinki	14 Aug 05
3:25.16		ITA Chigbolu 52.1, Spacca 51.3, Folorunso 51.44, Grenot 50.18			4h2	OG	Rio de Janeiro	19 Aug 16
3:25.68		ROU Ruicu 52.69, Rîpanu 51.09, Barbu 52.64, Tîrlea 49.26			2	ECp	Paris (C)	20 Jun 99
3:25.7a		FIN Eklund 53.6, Pursiainen 50.6, Wilmi 51.6, Salin 49.9			2	EC	Roma	8 Sep 74
		(20)						
3:25.81		BUL Ilieva, Stamenova, Penkova, Damyanova			1	v Hun,Pol	Sofia	24 Jul 83
3:26.33		GRE Kaidantzi 53.2, Goudenoúdi 51.6, Boudá 51.76, Halkiá 49.75			3	ECpS	Bydgoszcz	20 Jun 04
3:26.36		BAH L Clarke 52.4, Strachan 51.9, Cox 50.91, Amertil 51.07			6h2	OG	Rio de Janeiro	19 Aug 16
3:26.68		BRA (Bovespa) Coutinho, de Oliveira, Sousa, de Lima			1	NC	São Paulo	7 Aug 11
3:26.89		IND R Kaur 53.1, Beenamol 51.4, Soman 52.51, M Kaur 49.85			3h2	OG	Athína	27 Aug 04
3:26.98		NED			6h1	OG	Rio de Janeiro	19 Aug 16
		Ghafoor 52.4, Lisanne de Witte 51.0, van Leuveren 50.99, Laura de Witte 52.49						
3:27.08		CMR Nguimgo 51.7, Kaboud 52.1, Atangana 51.98, Béwouda 51.35			7	WCh	Saint-Denis	31 Aug 03
3:27.14		MEX Rodríguez 53.3, Medina 51.2, Vela 52.94, Guevara 49.70			4h2	WCh	Osaka	1 Sep 07
3:27.48		IRL Andrews 53.4, Cuddihy 49.9, Bergin 52.60, Carey 51.54			4h3	WCh	Daegu	2 Sep 11
3:27.54		LTU Navickaite, Valiuliene, Mendzoryte, Ambraziene (30)			3	SPART	Moskva	22 Jun 83
Drugs dq:		3:18.82 RUS Gushchina 50.6, Litvinova 49.2, Firova 49.20, Kapachinskaya 49.82			(2)	OG	Beijing	23 Aug 08
3:21.85		BLR Kozak 52.0, Khlyustova 50.7, I Usovich 49.85, S Usovich 49.69			(4)	OG	Beijing	23 Aug 08

4 x 800 METRES RELAY

7:50.17 WR		USSR Olizarenko, Gurina, Borisova, Podyalovskaya			1		Moskva	5 Aug 84
7:54.10 WR		GDR Zinn, Hoffmeister, Weiss, Klapezynski			1	NC	Karl-Marx-Stadt	6 Aug 76
8:00.62		USA Price 2:01.30, Vessey 2:00.92, Ludlow 1:59.50, Montaño 1:58.70			1	WRly	Nassau	3 May 15

4 x 1500 METRES RELAY

16:33.58 WR		KEN M Cherono 4:07.5, Kipyegon 4:08.5, Jelagat 4:10.5, Obiri 4:07.1			1	WRly	Nassau	24 May 14
16:55.33		USA Kampf 4:09.2, Mackey, Grace, Martinez 4:10.2			2	WRly	Nassau	24 May 14
17:08.65		AUS Buckman 4:08.1, Delaney 4:15.5, McGowan, Duncan 4:16.0			3	WRly	Nassau	25 May 14

5000m – 10 – 20 KILOMETRES WALK A-T   323

Mark	Wind	Name		Nat	Born	Pos	Meet	Venue	Date

5000 METRES WALK (TRACK)

Mark	Wind	Name		Nat	Born	Pos	Meet	Venue	Date
20:01.80	WR	Eleonora	Giorgi	ITA	14.9.89	1		Misterbianco	18 May 14
20:02.60	WR	Gillian	O'Sullivan	IRL	21.8.76	1	NC	Dublin (S)	13 Jul 02
20:03.0	WR	Kerry	Saxby-Junna	AUS	2.6.61	1		Sydney	11 Feb 96
20:07.52	WR	Beate	Anders/Gummelt	GDR	4.2.68	1	vURS	Rostock	23 Jun 90
20:11.45		Sabine	Zimmer/Krantz	GER	6.2.81	1	NC	Wattenscheid	2 Jul 05
20:12.41		Elisabetta	Perrone	ITA	9.7.68	1	NC	Rieti	2 Aug 03
20:15.71		Lyudmyla	Olyanovska ¶	UKR	20.2.93	1		Kyiv	4 Jun 14
20:18.87		Melanie	Seeger	GER	8.1.77	1	NC	Braunschweig	10 Jul 04
20:21.69		Annarita	Sidoti	ITA	25.7.69	1	NC	Cesenatico	1 Jul 95
20:27.59	WR	Ileana	Salvador	ITA	16.1.62	1		Trento	3 Jun 89

10 KILOMETRES WALK

Mark	Wind	Name		Nat	Born	Pos	Meet	Venue	Date
41:04	WR	Yelena	Nikolayeva	RUS	1.2.66	1	NC	Sochi	20 Apr 96
41:16			Wang Yan	CHN	3.5.71	1		Eisenhüttenstadt	8 May 99
41:16		Kjersti	Plätzer (Tysse)	NOR	18.1.72	1	NC	Os	11 May 02
41:17		Irina	Stankina	RUS	25.3.77	1	NC-w	Adler	9 Feb 97
41:24		Olimpiada	Ivanova ¶	RUS	26.8.70	2	NC-w	Adler	9 Feb 97
41:29	WR	Larisa	Ramazanova	RUS	23.9.71	1	NC	Izhevsk	4 Jun 95
41:30	WR	Kerry	Saxby-Junna	AUS	2.6.61	1	NC	Canberra	27 Aug 88
41:30			O Ivanova			2	NC	Izhevsk	4 Jun 95
41:31		Yelena	Gruzinova	RUS	24.12.67	2	NC	Sochi	20 Apr 96
41:37.9t			Gao Hongmiao	CHN	17.3.74	1	NC	Beijing	7 Apr 94
41:38		Rossella	Giordano (10)	ITA	1.12.72	1		Naumburg	25 May 97
41:41			Nikolayeva			2		Naumburg	25 May 97
41:41			Tysse Plätzer			1		Kraków	30 May 09
41:42		Olga	Kaniskina ¶	RUS	19.1.85	2		Kraków	30 May 09
41:42.5t		Lyudmyla	Olyanovska ¶	UKR	20.2.93	1		Mukachevo	1 Nov 14
41:45			Liu Hongyu	CHN	11.1.75	2		Eisenhüttenstadt	8 May 99
41:46		Annarita	Sidoti	ITA	25.7.69	1		Livorno	12 Jun 94
41:46			O Ivanova			1	NC/w	Adler	11 Feb 96
41:47			Saxby-Junna			1		Eisenhüttenstadt	11 May 96
41:48		(20/15)	Li Chunxiu	CHN	13.8.69	1	NG	Beijing	8 Sep 93
41:50		Yelena	Arshintseva	RUS	5.4.71	1	NC-w	Adler	11 Feb 95
41:51		Beate	Anders/Gummelt	GER	4.2.68	2		Eisenhüttenstadt	11 May 96
41:52		Tatyana	Mineyeva ¶	RUS	10.8.90	1	NCp-j	Penza	5 Sep 09
41:52		Tatyana	Korotkova	RUS	24.4.80	1		Buy	19 Sep 10
41:53		Tatyana	Sibileva	RUS	17.5.80	1	RWC-F	Beijing	18 Sep 10
41:56		(20) Yelena	Sayko	RUS	24.12.67	2	NC/w	Adler	11 Feb 96
41:56.23t		Nadezhda	Ryashkina	RUS	22.1.67	1	GWG	Seattle	24 Jul 90
41:59		Marina	Pandakova	RUS	1.3.89	1		Podolsk	8 May 16
42:01		Tamara	Kovalenko	RUS	5.6.64	3	NC-w	Adler	11 Feb 95
42:01		Olga	Panfyorova	RUS	21.8.77	1	NC-23	Izhevsk	16 May 98
42:03		Lina	Bikulova	RUS	1.10.88	1		Bui	13 Sep 14
42:04+		Vera	Sokolova ¶	RUS	8.6.87	1=	in 20k	Sochi	26 Feb 11
42:04+		Anisya	Kirdyapkina	RUS	23.10.89	1=	in 20k	Sochi	26 Feb 11
42:04+		Tatyana	Shemyakina	RUS	3.9.87	1=	in 20k	Sochi	26 Feb 11
42:05+		Margarita	Turova	BLR	28.12.80	1+	in 20k	Adler	12 Mar 05
42:06		(30) Valentina	Tsybulskaya	BLR	19.2.68	4		Eisenhüttenstadt	8 May 99
42:07		Ileana	Salvador	ITA	16.1.62	1		Sesto San Giovanni	1 May 92
42:09		Elisabetta	Perrone	ITA	9.7.68	4		Eisenhüttenstadt	11 May 96
42:11		Nina	Alyushenko	RUS	29.5.68	3	NC	Izhevsk	4 Jun 95
42:12+		Elmira	Alembekova ¶	RUS	30.6.90	1	in 20k	Sochi	27 Feb 15
42:12+		Svetlana	Vasilyeva	RUS	24.7.92	3	in 20k	Sochi	27 Feb 15
		(36)	50th woman 42:29.06, 100th 43:08.17, 200th 43:56, 300th 44:31, 400th 44:55						

Best track times

Mark	Wind	Name		Nat	Born	Pos	Meet	Venue	Date
41:57.22		Kerry	Saxby-Junna	AUS	2.6.61	2	GWG	Seattle	24 Jul 90
42:11.5		Beate	Anders/Gummelt	GER	4.2.68	1	SGP	Fana	15 May 92

20 KILOMETRES WALK

Mark	Wind	Name		Nat	Born	Pos	Meet	Venue	Date
1:24:38	WR		Liu Hong	CHN	12.5.87	1		La Coruña	6 Jun 15
1:24:47		Elmira	Alembekova ¶	RUS	30.6.90	1	NC-w	Sochi	27 Feb 15
1:24:50		Olimpiada	Ivanova ¶	RUS	26.8.70	1	NC-w	Adler	4 Mar 01
1:24:56		Olga	Kaniskina ¶	RUS	19.1.85	1	NC-w	Adler	28 Feb 09
1:24:58		Yelena	Lashmanova ¶	RUS	9.4.92	1	NC	Cheboksary	25 Jun 16
1:25:02	WR		Lashmanova			1	OG	London	11 Aug 12
1:25:03		Marina	Pandakova	RUS	1.3.89	2	NC-w	Sochi	27 Feb 15
1:25:04		Svetlana	Vasilyeva	RUS	24.7.92	3	NC-w	Sochi	27 Feb 15

WOMEN All-time

20 – 50 KILOMETRES WALK A-T

Mark	Wind	Name		Nat	Born	Pos	Meet	Venue	Date
1:25:08	WR	Vera	Sokolova	RUS	8.6.87	1	NC-w	Sochi	26 Feb 11
1:25:09		Anisya	Kirdyapkina ¶	RUS	23.10.89	2	NC-w	Sochi	26 Feb 11
1:25:11			Kaniskina			1	NC-w	Adler	23 Feb 08
1:25:11			Kirdyapkina			1	NC-w	Sochi	20 Feb 10
1:25:12			Lu Xiuzhi (10)	CHN	26.10.93	1	WCT	Beijing	20 Mar 15
1:25:16			Qieyang Shenjie	CHN	11.11.90	2	OG	London	11 Aug 12
1:25:18		Tatyana	Gudkova	RUS	23.1.78	1	NC	Moskva	19 May 00
1:25:20		Olga	Polyakova	RUS	23.9.80	2	NC	Moskva	19 May 00
1:25:26			Sokolova			2	NC-w	Adler	28 Feb 09
1:25:26			Kirdyapkina			3	NC-w	Adler	28 Feb 09
1:25:27			Alembekova			1	NC-w	Sochi	18 Feb 12
1:25:29		Irina	Stankina	RUS	25.3.77	3	NC	Moskva	19 May 00
1:25:30			Kirdyapkina			2	NC-w	Adler	23 Feb 08
1:25:32		Yelena	Shumkina	RUS	24.1.88	4	NC-w	Adler	28 Feb 09
1:25:35			Sokolova			2	NC-w	Sochi	20 Feb 10
1:25:38			Sokolova			4	NC-w	Sochi	27 Feb 15
1:25:41	WR		Ivanova			1	WCh	Helsinki	7 Aug 05
1:25:42			Kaniskina			1	WCp	Cheboksary	11 May 08
1:25:46		Tatyana	Shemyakina	RUS	3.9.87	3	NC-w	Adler	23 Feb 08
1:25:46			Liu Hong			1		Taicang	30 Mar 12
1:25:49			Lashmanova			1	NC-w	Sochi	23 Feb 13
1:25:52		Larisa	Yemelyanova	RUS	6.1.80	5	NC-w	Adler	28 Feb 09
1:25:52		Tatyana (31/18)	Sibileva	RUS	17.5.80	3	NC-w	Sochi	20 Feb 10
1:25:59		Tamara	Kovalenko	RUS	5.6.64	4	NC	Moskva	19 May 00
1:26:11		Margarita	Turova (20)	BLR	28.12.80	1	NC	Nesvizh	15 Apr 06
1:26:14		Irina	Petrova	RUS	26.5.85	2	NC-w	Adler	19 Feb 06
1:26:16		Lyudmila	Arkhipova	RUS	25.11.78	5	NC-w	Adler	23 Feb 08
1:26:17		Eleonora	Giorgi	ITA	14.9.89	2	ECp	Murcia	17 May 15
1:26:17		María Guadalupe	González	MEX	9.1.89	1	WCp	Roma	7 May 16
1:26:22	WR		Wang Yan	CHN	3.5.71	1	NG	Guangzhou	19 Nov 01
1:26:22	WR	Yelena	Nikolayeva	RUS	1.2.66	1	ECp	Cheboksary	18 May 03
1:26:23			Wang Liping	CHN	8.7.76	2	NG	Guangzhou	19 Nov 01
1:26:28		Iraida	Pudovkina	RUS	2.11.80	1	NC-w	Adler	12 Mar 05
1:26:34		Tatyana	Kalmykova	RUS	10.1.90	1	NC	Saransk	8 Jun 08
1:26:35		(30)	Liu Hongyu	CHN	11.1.75	3	NG	Guangzhou	19 Nov 01
1:26:40		Yekaterina	Medvedyeva	RUS	29.3.94	2	NC-w	Sochi	27 Feb 16
1:26:46			Song Hongjuan	CHN	4.7.84	1	NC	Guangzhou	20 Mar 04
1:26:46		Mariya	Ponomaryova	RUS	18.6.95	3	NC	Cheboksary	25 Jun 16
1:26:47		Irina	Yumanova ¶	RUS	6.11.90	3	NC-w	Sochi	18 Feb 12
1:26:47		Klavdiya	Afanasyeva	RUS	15.1.96	4	NC	Cheboksary	25 Jun 16
1:26:50		Natalya	Fedoskina	RUS	25.6.80	2	ECp	Dudince	19 May 01
1:26:53		Anezka	Drahotová	CZE	22.7.95	4	ECp	Murcia	17 May 15
1:26:57		Lyudmila	Yefimkina	RUS	22.8.81	3	NC-w	Adler	19 Feb 06
1:27:07		Kjersti	Tysse Plätzer	NOR	18.1.72	2	OG	Beijing	21 Aug 08
1:27:09		Elisabetta (40)	Perrone	ITA	9.7.68	3	ECp	Dudince	19 May 01
1:27:09		Lyudmyla	Olyanovska ¶	UKR	20.2.93	7	ECp	Murcia	17 May 15
1:27:12		Elisa	Rigaudo	ITA	17.6.80	3	OG	Beijing	21 Aug 08
1:27:14		Antonina	Petrova	RUS	1.5.77	1	NC-w	Adler	1 Mar 03
1:27:18		Alena	Nartova	RUS	1.1.82	6	NC-w	Adler	23 Feb 08
1:27:18		Érica	de Sena	BRA	3.5.85	3	WCp	Roma	7 May 16
1:27:19			Jiang Jing	CHN	23.10.85	1	NC	Nanning	25 Feb 05
1:27:22		Gillian	O'Sullivan	IRL	21.8.76	1		Sesto San Giovanni	1 May 03
1:27:25		María	Vasco	ESP	26.12.75	5	OG	Beijing	21 Aug 08
1:27:27		Vira	Zozulya	UKR	31.8.70	1	NC	Sumy	7 Jun 08
1:27:29		Erica (50)	Alfridi	ITA	22.2.68	4	ECp	Dudince	19 May 01
			100th best woman 1:28:44, 200th 1:30:40, 300th 1:32:05, 400th 1:33:36						
Drugs dq: 1:25:09			Kaniskina			(2)	OG	London	11 Aug 12
1:27:08		Anna	Lukyanova ¶	RUS	23.4.91	(5)	NC-w	Sochi	18 Feb 12

50 KILOMETRES WALK

Mark		Name		Nat	Born	Pos	Meet	Venue	Date
4:10:59		Monica	Svensson	SWE	26.12.78	1		Scanzorosciate	21 Oct 07
4:12:16		Yelena	Ginko	BLR	30.7.76	1		Scanzorosciate	17 Oct 04
4:16:27		Jolanta	Dukure	LAT	20.9.79	1		Paralepa	9 Sep 06
4:25:22		Brigita	Virbalyte-Dimsiene	LTU	1.2.85	1		Villa di Serio	17 Oct 10
4:28:13		Evaggelía	Xinoú	GRE	22.11.81	2		Scanzorosciate	17 Oct 04
4:28:53		Neringa	Aidietyté	LTU	5.6.83	1		Ivano-Frankivsk	1 Oct 06
4:28:59		Kora	Boufflért	FRA	23.4.66	1		Charly-sur-Marne	18 Feb 07

JUNIOR MEN'S ALL-TIME LISTS

Mark	Wind	Name		Nat	Born	Pos	Meet	Venue	Date

100 METRES

Mark	Wind	Name		Nat	Born	Pos	Meet	Venue	Date
9.97	1.8	Trayvon	Bromell	USA	10.7.95	1	NCAA	Eugene	13 Jun 14
10.00	1.6	Trentavis	Friday	USA	5.6.95	1h1	NC-j	Eugene	5 Jul 14
10.01	0.0	Darrel	Brown	TTO	11.10.84	1	WCh	Saint-Denis	24 Aug 03
10.01	1.6	Jeffery	Demps	USA	8.1.90	2q1	NC/OT	Eugene	28 Jun 08
10.01	0.9	Yoshihide	Kiryu	JPN	15.12.95	1h3	Oda	Hiroshima	29 Apr 13
10.03	0.7	Marcus	Rowland	USA	11.3.90	1	PAm-J	Port of Spain	31 Jul 09
10.04	1.7	DeAngelo	Cherry	USA	1.8.90	1h4	NCAA	Fayetteville	10 Jun 09
10.04	0.2	Christoph	Lemaitre	FRA	11.6.90	1	EJ	Novi Sad	24 Jul 09
10.04	1.9	Abdullah Abkar	Mohammed	KSA	.97	1	MSR	Norwalk	15 Apr 16
10.05		Davidson	Ezinwa	NGR	22.11.71	1		Bauchi	4 Jan 90
10.05	0.1	Adam	Gemili	GBR	6.10.93	1	WJ	Barcelona	11 Jul 12
Wind assisted to 10.02									
9.77	4.2	Trayvon	Bromell	USA	10.7.95	1	Big 12	Lubbock	18 May 14
9.83	7.1	Leonard	Scott	USA	19.1.80	1		Knoxville	9 Apr 99
9.96	4.5	Walter	Dix	USA	31.1.86	1rA	TexR	Austin	9 Apr 05
9.96	5.0	André	De Grasse	CAN	10.11.94	1	JUCO	Hutchinson, KS	18 May 13
9.97	??	Mark	Lewis-Francis	GBR	4.9.82	1q3	WCh	Edmonton	4 Aug 01
9.98	5.0	Tyreek	Hill	USA	1.3.94	2	JUCO	Hutchinson, KS	18 May 13
10.02	2.8	DeAngelo	Cherry	USA	1.8.90	1h2	NC-j	Eugene	26 Jun 09
10.02	2.4	Marcus	Rowland	USA	11.3.90	1	NC-j	Eugene	26 Jun 09

200 METRES

Mark	Wind	Name		Nat	Born	Pos	Meet	Venue	Date
19.93	1.4	Usain	Bolt	JAM	21.8.86	1		Hamilton, BER	11 Apr 04
20.04	0.1	Ramil	Guliyev	AZE	29.5.90	1	WUG	Beograd	10 Jul 09
20.07	1.5	Lorenzo	Daniel	USA	23.3.66	1	SEC	Starkville	18 May 85
20.09	1.6	Noah	Lyles	USA	18.7.97	4	NC/OT	Eugene	9 Jul 16
20.13	1.7	Roy	Martin	USA	25.12.66	1		Austin	11 May 85
20.14	1.8	Tyreek	Hill	USA	1.3.94	1		Orlando	26 May 12
20.14	1.6	Michael	Norman	USA	3.12.97	5	NC/OT	Eugene	9 Jul 16
20.16A	-0.2	Riaan	Dempers	RSA	4.3.77	1	NC-j	Germiston	7 Apr 95
20.18	1.0	Walter	Dix	USA	31.1.86	1s2	NCAA	Sacramento	9 Jun 05
20.21A	1.4	Baboloki	Thebe	BOT	18.3.97	1	NC-j	Gaborone	22 May 16
Wind assisted to 20.16									
19.86	4.0	Justin	Gatlin	USA	10.2.82	1h2	NCAA	Eugene	30 May 01
20.01	2.5	Derald	Harris	USA	5.4.58	1		San José	9 Apr 77
20.03	2.9	Trentavis	Friday	USA	5.6.95	1	NC-j	Eugene	6 Jul 14
20.04	3.3	Noah	Lyles	USA	18.7.97	1h1	NC/OT	Eugene	7 Jul 16
20.06	2.8	Michael	Norman	USA	3.12.97	1h4	NC/OT	Eugene	7 Jul 16
20.08	9.2	Leonard	Scott	USA	19.1.80	2r2		Knoxville	9 Apr 99
20.10	4.6	Stanley	Kerr	USA	19.6.67	2r2	SWC	Houston	18 May 86
20.16	5.2	Nickel	Ashmeade	JAM	4.7.90	1	Carifta	Basseterre	24 Mar 08

400 METRES

Mark	Wind	Name		Nat	Born	Pos	Meet	Venue	Date
43.87		Steve	Lewis	USA	16.5.69	1	OG	Seoul	28 Sep 88
44.22A		Baboloki	Thebe	BOT	18.3.97	1	NC-j	Gaborone	21 May 16
44.25		Karabo	Sibanda	BOT	2.7.98	5	OG	Rio de Janeiro	14 Aug 16
44.27		Abdelilah	Haroun	QAT	1.1.97	2		La Chaux-de-Fonds	5 Jul 15
44.36		Kirani	James	GRN	1.9.92	1	WK	Zürich	8 Sep 11
44.66		Hamdam Odha	Al-Bishi	KSA	5.5.81	1	WJ	Santiago de Chile	20 Oct 00
44.66		LaShawn	Merritt	USA	27.6.86	1		Kingston	7 May 05
44.69		Darrell	Robinson	USA	23.12.63	2	USOF	Indianapolis	24 Jul 82
44.71A		Luguelín	Santos	DOM	12.11.93	2	PAm	Guadalajara	26 Oct 11
44.73A		James	Rolle	USA	2.2.64	1	USOF	USAF Academy	2 Jul 83
44.75		Darren	Clark	AUS	6.9.65	4	OG	Los Angeles	8 Aug 84
44.75		Deon	Minor	USA	22.1.73	1s1	NCAA	Austin	5 Jun 92

800 METRES

Mark	Name		Nat	Born	Pos	Meet	Venue	Date
1:41.73	Nijel	Amos	BOT	15.3.94	2	OG	London (OS)	9 Aug 12
1:42.37	Mohammed	Aman	ETH	10.1.94	1	VD	Bruxelles	6 Sep 13
1:42.53	Timothy	Kitum	KEN	20.11.94	3	OG	London (OS)	9 Aug 12
1:42.69	Abubaker	Kaki	SUD	21.6.89	1	Bisl	Oslo	6 Jun 08
1:43.13	Abraham Kipchirchir	Rotich	KEN	26.6.93	1	Herc	Monaco	20 Jul 12
1:43.40	Leonard	Kosencha	KEN	21.8.94	2	Herc	Monaco	20 Jul 12
1:43.55	Donavan	Brazier	USA	15.4.97	1	NCAA	Eugene	10 Jun 16
1:43.56	Robert	Biwott	KEN	28.1.96	2		Barcelona	8 Jul 15
1:43.64	Japheth	Kimutai	KEN	20.12.78	3rB	WK	Zürich	13 Aug 97
1:43.76	Kipyegon	Bett	KEN	2.1.98	2	ISTAF	Berlin	3 Sep 16
1:43.81	Edwin	Melly	KEN	24.3.94	2		Rieti	9 Sep 12

JUNIOR MEN ALL-TIME

Mark	Wind	Name		Nat	Born	Pos	Meet	Venue	Date
1000 METRES									
2:13.93		Abubaker	Kaki	SUD	21.6.89	1	DNG	Stockholm	22 Jul 08
2:15.00		Benjamin	Kipkurui	KEN	28.12.80	5	Nik	Nice	17 Jul 99
1500 METRES									
3:28.81		Ronald	Kwemoi	KEN	19.9.95	3	Herc	Monaco	18 Jul 14
3:30.10		Robert	Biwott	KEN	28.1.96	7	Herc	Monaco	17 JUl 15
3:30.24		Cornelius	Chirchir	KEN	5.6.83	4	Herc	Monaco	19 Jul 02
3:31.13		Mulugueta	Wondimu	ETH	28.2.85	2rA	NA	Heusden	31 Jul 04
3:31.42		Alex	Kipchirchir	KEN	26.11.84	5	VD	Bruxelles	5 Sep 03
3:31.54		Isaac	Songok	KEN	25.4.84	1	NA	Heusden	2 Aug 03
3:31.64		Asbel	Kiprop	KEN	30.6.89	1	GGala	Roma	11 Jul 08
3:31.70		William	Biwott	KEN	5.3.90	3	GGala	Roma	10 Jul 09
3:32.02		Caleb	Ndiku	KEN	9.10.92	4	FBK	Hengelo	29 May 11
3:32.48		Augustine	Choge	KEN	21.1.87	1	ISTAF	Berlin	3 Sep 06
3:32.68		Abdelaati	Iguider	MAR	25.3.87	5	VD	Bruxelles	25 Aug 06
1 MILE									
3:49.29		William	Biwott	KEN	5.3.90	2	Bisl	Oslo	3 Jul 09
3:49.77		Caleb	Ndiku	KEN	9.10.92	5	Pre	Eugene	4 Jun 11
3:50.25		Alex	Kipchirchir	KEN	26.11.84	2	GP II	Rieti	7 Sep 03
3:50.39		James	Kwalia	KEN	12.6.84	1	FBK	Hengelo	1 Jun 03
3:50.41		Noah	Ngeny	KEN	2.11.78	2	Nik	Nice	16 Jul 97
3:50.69		Cornelius	Chirchir	KEN	5.6.83	5	GGala	Roma	12 Jul 02
3:50.83		Nicholas	Kemboi	KEN	18.12.89	6	Bisl	Oslo	6 Jun 08
2000 METRES									
4:56.25		Tesfaye	Cheru	ETH	2.3.93	1		Reims	5 Jul 11
4:56.86		Isaac	Songok	KEN	25.4.84	6	ISTAF	Berlin	31 Aug 01
4:58.18		Soresa	Fida	ETH	27.5.93	4		Reims	5 Jul 11
4:58.76		Jairus	Kipchoge	KEN	15.12.92	7		Reims	5 Jul 11
3000 METRES									
7:28.19		Yomlf	Kejelcha	ETH	1.8.97	1	DL	Saint-Denis	27 Aug 16
7:28.78		Augustine	Choge	KEN	21.1.87	2	SGP	Doha	13 May 05
7:29.11		Tariku	Bekele	ETH	21.1.87	2	GP	Rieti	27 Aug 06
7:30.36		Hagos	Gebrhiwet	ETH	11.5.94	1	DL	Doha	10 May 13
7:30.43		Isiah	Koech	KEN	19.12.93	1	DNG	Stockholm	17 Aug 12
7:30.67		Kenenisa	Bekele	ETH	13.6.82	2	VD	Bruxelles	24 Aug 01
7:30.91		Eliud	Kipchoge	KEN	5.11.84	2	VD	Bruxelles	5 Sep 03
7:32.37		Abreham	Cherkos	ETH	23.9.89	2	Athl	Lausanne	11 Jul 06
7:32.72		John	Kipkoech	KEN	29.12.91	4		Rieti	29 Aug 10
7:33.00		Hailu	Mekonnen	ETH	4.4.80	2		Stuttgart	6 Jun 99
7:33.01		Levy	Matebo	KEN	3.11.89	2	GP	Rieti	7 Sep 08
5000 METRES									
12:47.53		Hagos	Gebrhiwet	ETH	11.5.94	2	DL	Saint-Denis	6 Jul 12
12:48.64		Isiah	Koech	KEN	19.12.93	3	DL	Saint-Denis	6 Jul 12
12:52.61		Eliud	Kipchoge	KEN	5.11.84	3	Bisl	Oslo	27 Jun 03
12:53.66		Augustine	Choge	KEN	21.1.87	4	GGala	Roma	8 Jul 05
12:53.72		Philip	Mosima	KEN	2.1.77	2	GGala	Roma	5 Jun 96
12:53.81		Tariku	Bekele	ETH	21.1.87	4	GGala	Roma	14 Jul 06
12:53.98		Yomif	Kejelcha	ETH	1.8.97	1	VD	Bruxelles	11 Sep 15
12:54.07		Sammy	Kipketer	KEN	29.9.81	2	GGala	Roma	30 Jun 00
12:54.19		Abreham	Cherkos	ETH	23.9.89	5	GGala	Roma	14 Jul 06
12:54.58		James	Kwalia	KEN	12.6.84	5	Bisl	Oslo	27 Jun 03
12:56.15		Daniel	Komen	KEN	17.5.76	2	GG	Roma	8 Jun 95
10,000 METRES									
26:41.75		Samuel	Wanjiru	KEN	10.11.86	3	VD	Bruxelles	26 Aug 05
26:55.73		Geoffrey	Kirui	KEN	16.2.93	6	VD	Bruxelles	16 Sep 11
26:57.56		Yigrem	Demelash	ETH	28.1.94	4	VD	Bruxelles	7 Sep 12
27:02.81		Ibrahim	Jeylan	ETH	12.6.89	4	VD	Bruxelles	25 Aug 06
27:04.00		Boniface	Kiprop	UGA	12.10.85	5	VD	Bruxelles	3 Sep 04
27:04.45		Bernard	Kipyego	KEN	16.7.86	4	FBK	Hengelo	29 May 05
27:06.35		Geoffrey	Kipsang	KEN	28.11.92	10	Pre	Eugene	3 Jun 11
27:06.47		Habtanu	Fikadu	ETH	13.3.88	8	FBK	Hengelo	26 May 07
27:07.29		Moses	Masai	KEN	1.6.86	7	VD	Bruxelles	3 Sep 04
27:11.18		Richard	Chelimo	KEN	21.4.72	1	APM	Hengelo	25 Jun 91
27:12.42		Sammy Alex	Mutahi	KEN	1.6.89	1		Tokamchi	29 Sep 07

JUNIOR MEN ALL-TIME 327

Mark	Wind	Name		Nat	Born	Pos	Meet	Venue	Date
3000 METRES STEEPLECHASE									
7:58.66		Stephen	Cherono	KEN	15.10.82	3	VD	Bruxelles	24 Aug 01
8:01.16		Conseslus	Kipruto	KEN	8.12.94	1	DL	Shanghai	18 May 13
8:03.74		Raymond	Yator	KEN	7.4.81	3	Herc	Monaco	18 Aug 00
8:05.52		Brimin	Kipruto	KEN	31.7.85	1	FBK	Hengelo	31 May 04
8:06.96		Gilbert	Kirui	KEN	22.1.94	2	DL	London (OS)	27 Jul 13
8:07.18		Moussa	Omar Obaid	QAT	18.4.85	4	OG	Athína	24 Aug 04
8:07.69		Paul	Kosgei	KEN	22.4.78	5	DNG	Stockholm	7 Jul 97
8:07.71		Hillary	Yego	KEN	2.4.92	3	DL	Shanghai	15 May 11
8:09.37		Abel	Cheruiyot/Yugut	KEN	26.12.84	2	NA	Heusden	2 Aug 03
8:11.31		Jairus	Birech	KEN	15.12.92	5	DL	Saint Denis	8 Jul 11
8:12.91		Thomas	Kiplitan	KEN	15.6.83	7	GP	Doha	15 May 02
110 METRES HURDLES (106cm)									
13.12	1.6		Liu Xiang	CHN	13.7.83	1rB	Athl	Lausanne	2 Jul 02
13.23	0.0	Renaldo	Nehemiah	USA	24.3.59	1r2	WK	Zürich	16 Aug 78
13.40	-1.0		Shi Dongpeng	CHN	6.1.84	1	NC	Shanghai	14 Sep 03
13.44	-0.8	Colin	Jackson	GBR	18.2.67	1	WJ	Athína	19 Jul 86
13.46	1.8	Jon	Ridgeon	GBR	14.2.67	1	EJ	Cottbus	23 Aug 85
13.46	-1.6	Dayron	Robles	CUB	19.11.86	1	PAm-J	Windsor	29 Jul 05
13.47	1.9	Holger	Pohland	GDR	5.4.63	2	vUSA	Karl-Marx-Stadt	10 Jul 82
13.47	1.2	Aries	Merritt	USA	24.7.85	4	NCAA	Austin	12 Jun 04
13.47	0.2		Xie Wenjun	CHN	11.7.90	2	GP	Shanghai	20 Sep 08
13.49	0.6	Stanislav	Olijar	LAT	22.3.79	1		Valmiera	11 Jul 98
13.49	1.2	Booker	Nunley	USA	2.7.90	2	SEC	Gainesville	17 May 09
Wind assisted									
13.41	2.6	Dayron	Robles	CUB	19.11.86	2	CAC	Nassau	10 Jul 05
13.42	4.5	Colin	Jackson	GBR	18.2.67	2	CG	Edinburgh	27 Jul 86
13.42	2.6	Antwon	Hicks	USA	12.3.83	1	WJ	Kingston	21 Jul 02
13.47	2.1	Frank	Busemann	GER	26.2.75	1	WJ	Lisboa	22 Jul 94
99 cm Hurdles									
12.99	0.5	Wilhem	Belocian	FRA	22.6.95	1	WJ	Eugene	24 Jul 14
13.06	0.5	Tyler	Mason	JAM	15.1.95	2	WJ	Eugene	24 Jul 14
13.08	2.0	Wayne	Davis	USA	2.7.90	1	PAm-J	Port of Spain	31 Jul 09
13.14	1.6	Eddie	Lovett	USA	25.6.92	1	PAm-J	Miramar	23 Jul 11
13.17	-0.7	David	Omoregie	GBR	1.11.95	1	NC-j	Bedford	22 Jun 14
13.18	1.0	Yordan	O'Farrill	CUB	9.2.93	1	WJ	Barcelona	12 Jul 12
13.20	0.6	Dejour	Russell	JAM	1.4.00	1s3	WJ	Bydgoszcz	20 Jul 16
13.21	1.5	Misana	Viltz	USA	21.2.96	1	NC-j	Eugene	25 Jun 15
Wind assisted to 13.20									
13.03	2.9	Eddie	Lovett	USA	25.6.92	1h1	PAm-J	Miramar	23 Jul 11
13.15	2.7	Brendan	Ames	USA	6.10.88	1	NC-j	Indianapolis	21 Jun 07
13.18		Arthur	Blake	USA	19.8.66	1	GWest	Sacramento	9 Jun 84
13.19	3.8	Chad	Zallow	USA	25.4.97	1		Greensboro	20 Jun 15
Hand timed: 12.9y Renaldo			Nehemiah	USA	24.3.59	1		Jamaica, NY	30 May 77
400 METRES HURDLES									
48.02		Danny	Harris	USA	7.9.65	2s1	OT	Los Angeles	17 Jun 84
48.26		Jehue	Gordon	TTO	15.12.91	4	WCh	Berlin	18 Aug 09
48.51		Kerron	Clement	USA	31.10.85	1	WJ	Grosseto	16 Jul 04
48.52		Johnny	Dutch	USA	20.1.89	5	NC/OT	Eugene	29 Jun 08
48.62		Brandon	Johnson	USA	6.3.85	2	WJ	Grosseto	16 Jul 04
48.68		Bayano	Kamani	USA	17.4.80	1	NCAA	Boise	4 Jun 99
48.68		Jeshua	Anderson	USA	22.6.89	1	WJ	Bydgoszcz	11 Jul 08
48.72		Angelo	Taylor	USA	29.12.78	2	NCAA	Bloomington	6 Jun 97
48.74		Vladimir	Budko	BLR	4.2.65	2	DRZ	Moskva	18 Aug 84
48.76A		Llewellyn	Herbert	RSA	21.7.77	1		Pretoria	7 Apr 96
48.79		Kenneth	Ferguson	USA	22.3.84	1	SEC	Knoxville	18 May 03
HIGH JUMP									
2.37		Dragutin	Topic	YUG	12.3.71	1	WJ	Plovdiv	12 Aug 90
2.37		Steve	Smith	GBR	29.3.73	1	WJ	Seoul	20 Sep 92
2.36		Javier	Sotomayor	CUB	13.10.67	1		Santiago de Cuba	23 Feb 86
2.35i		Vladimir	Yashchenko	UKR	12.1.59	1	EI	Milano	12 Mar 78
	2.34					1	Prv	Tbilisi	16 Jun 78
2.35		Dietmar	Mögenburg	FRG	15.8.61	1		Rehlingen	26 May 80
2.34		Tim	Forsyth	AUS	17.8.73	1	Bisl	Oslo	4 Jul 92
2.33			Zhu Jianhua	CHN	29.5.63	1	AsiG	New Delhi	1 Dec 82
2.33		Patrik	Sjöberg	SWE	5.1.65	1	OsloG	Oslo	9 Jul 83
2.32i		Jaroslav	Bába	CZE	2.9.84	3		Arnstadt	8 Feb 03
2.32			Huang Haiqiang	CHN	8.2.88	1	WJ	Beijing	17 Aug 06

328   JUNIOR MEN ALL-TIME

Mark	Wind	Name		Nat	Born	Pos	Meet	Venue	Date
POLE VAULT									
5.80		Maksim	Tarasov	RUS	2.12.70	1	vGDR-j	Bryansk	14 Jul 89
5.80		Raphael	Holzdeppe	GER	28.9.89	2		Biberach	28 Jun 08
5.75		Konstadínos	Filippídis	GRE	26.11.86	2	WUG	Izmir	18 Aug 05
5.72		Andrew	Irwin	USA	23.1.93	1	SEC	Baton Rouge	13 May 12
5.71		Lawrence	Johnson	USA	7.5.74	1		Knoxville	12 Jun 93
5.71		Germán	Chiaraviglio	ARG	16.4.87	1	WJ	Beijing	19 Aug 06
5.71		Shawnacy	Barber	CAN	27.5.94	2	TexR	Austin	29 Mar 13
5.70		Viktor	Chistyakov	RUS	9.2.75	1		Leppävirta	7 Jun 94
5.70		Artyom	Kuptsov	RUS	22.4.84	1	Znam	Tula	7 Jun 03
5.70		Kurtis	Marschall	AUS	25.4.97	1		Mannheim	26 Jun 16
LONG JUMP									
8.35	1.1	Sergey	Morgunov	RUS	9.2.93	1	NC-j	Cheboksary	19 Jun 12
8.34	0.0	Randy	Williams	USA	23.8.53	Q	OG	München	8 Sep 72
8.30	1.3		Shi Yuhao	CHN	26.9.98	1	NC-j	Ordos	27 Jun 16
8.28	0.8	Luis Alberto	Bueno	CUB	22.5.69	1		La Habana	16 Jul 88
8.28	1.8	Maykel	Massó	CUB	8.5.99	1	Barr	La Habana	28 May 16
8.27	1.7	Eusebio	Cáceres	ESP	10.9.91	Q	EC	Barcelona	30 Jul 10
8.25	0.9		Wang Jianan	CHN	27.8.96	3	DL	Shanghai	17 May 15
8.24	0.2	Eric	Metcalf	USA	23.1.68	1	NCAA	Indianapolis	6 Jun 86
8.24	1.8	Vladimir	Ochkan	UKR	13.1.68	1	vGDR-j	Leningrad	21 Jun 87
8.22		Larry	Doubley	USA	15.3.58	1	NCAA	Champaign	3 Jun 77
8.22		Iván	Pedroso	CUB	17.12.72	1		Santiago de Cuba	3 May 91
8.22i		Viktor	Kuznetsov	UKR	14.7.86	1		Brovary	22 Jan 05
Wind assisted to 8.24									
8.40	3.2	Kareem	Streete-Thompson	CAY	30.3.73	1		Houston	5 May 91
8.35	2.2	Carl	Lewis	USA	1.7.61	1	NCAA	Austin	6 Jun 80
8.29	2.3	James	Beckford	JAM	9.1.75	1		Tempe	2 Apr 94
TRIPLE JUMP									
17.50	0.4	Volker	Mai	GDR	3.5.66	1	vURS	Erfurt	23 Jun 85
17.42	1.3	Khristo	Markov	BUL	27.1.65	1	Nar	Sofiya	19 May 84
17.40A		Pedro	Pérez	CUB	23.2.52	1	PAm	Cali	5 Aug 71
17.40	0.8	Ernesto	Revé	CUB	26.2.92	1		La Habana	10 Jun 11
17.31	-0.2	David	Girat Jr.	CUB	26.8.84	Q	WCh	Saint-Denis	23 Aug 03
17.29	1.3	James	Beckford	JAM	9.1.75	1		Tempe	2 Apr 94
17.27		Aliecer	Urrutia	CUB	22.9.74	1		Artemisa	23 Apr 93
17.24	0.7	Lázaro	Martínez	CUB	3.11.97	2		La Habana	1 Feb 14
17.23	0.2	Yoelbi	Quesada	CUB	4.8.73	1	NC	La Habana	13 May 92
17.19	-0.4	Teddy	Tamgho	FRA	15.6.89	4	Herc	Monaco	29 Jul 08
17.19	2.0	Will	Claye	USA	13.6.91	*	NCAA	Fayetteville	13 Jun 09
Wind assisted									
17.33	2.1	Teddy	Tamgho	FRA	15.6.89	1	WJ	Bydgoszcz	11 Jul 08
17.24	2.5	Will	Claye	USA	13.6.91	1	NCAA	Fayetteville	13 Jun 09
SHOT									
21.14		Konrad	Bukowiecki	POL	17.3.97	2	Bisl	Oslo	9 Jun 16
21.05i		Terry	Albritton	USA	14.1.55	1	AAU	New York	22 Feb 74
		20.38				2	MSR	Walnut	27 Apr 74
20.82i		Jordan	Geist	USA	21.7.98	1		Greensburg	22 Dec 76
20.65		Mike	Carter	USA	29.10.60	1	vSU-j	Boston	4 Jul 79
20.54	?	Andrei	Toader	ROU	26.5.97	1	ROU IC	Pitesti	4 Jun 16
20.43		David	Storl	GER	27.7.90	2		Gerlingen	6 Jul 09
20.39		Janus	Robberts	RSA	10.3.79	1	NC	Germiston	7 Mar 98
20.38		Jacko	Gill	NZL	10.12.94	1		Auckland (NS)	5 Dec 11
20.20		Randy	Matson	USA	5.3.45	2	OG	Tokyo	17 Oct 64
20.20		Udo	Beyer	GDR	9.8.55	2	NC	Leipzig	6 Jul 74
6 kg Shot									
23.34		Konrad	Bukowiecki	POL	17.3.97	1	WJ	Bydgoszcz	19 Jul 16
23.00		Jacko	Gill	NZL	10.12.94	1		Auckland	18 Aug 13
22.73		David	Storl	GER	27.7.90	1		Osterode	14 Jul 09
22.30 dq?		Andrei	Toader	ROU	26.5.97	2	WJ	Bydgoszcz	19 Jul 16
21.96		Edis	Elkasevic	CRO	18.2.83	1	NC-j	Zagreb	29 Jun 02
21.90		John	Maurins	USA	3.8.96	1	NC-j	Eugene	25 Jun 15
21.79		Mustafa Amer	Ahmed	EGY	16.12.95	1	Arab	Cairo	23 Feb 14
21.78		Krzysztof	Brzozowski	POL	15.7.93	2	WJ	Barcelona	11 Jul 12
DISCUS									
65.62		Werner	Reiterer	AUS	27.1.68	1		Melbourne	15 Dec 87
65.31		Mykyta	Nesterenko	UKR	15.4.91	3		Tallinn	3 Jun 08

JUNIOR MEN ALL-TIME

Mark	Wind	Name		Nat	Born	Pos	Meet	Venue	Date
63.64		Werner	Hartmann	FRG	20.4.59	1	vFRA	Strasbourg	25 Jun 78
63.26		Sergey	Pachin	UKR	24.5.68	2		Moskva	25 Jul 87
63.22		Brian	Milne	USA	7.1.73	1		State College	28 Mar 92
62.58		Matthew	Denny	AUS	2.6.96	2	WUG	Gwangju	11 Jul 15
62.52		John	Nichols	USA	23.8.69	1		Baton Rouge	23 Apr 88
62.43		Martin	Markovic	CRO	13.1.96	1	NC-w	Split	8 Mar 15
62.36		Tulake	Nuermaimaiti	CHN	8.3.82	2	NG	Guangzhou	21 Nov 01
62.16		Zoltán	Kövágó	HUN	10.4.79	1		Budapest	9 May 97
1.75kg Discus									
70.13		Mykyta	Nesterenko	UKR	15.4.91	1		Halle	24 May 08
68.48		Martin	Markovic	CRO	13.1.96	1	NC-j	Varazdin	28 Jun 15
68.02		Bartlomiej	Stój	POL	15.5.96	1	EJ	Eskilstuna	19 Jul 15
67.32		Margus	Hunt	EST	14.7.87	1	WJ	Beijing	16 Aug 06
66.88		Traves	Smikle	JAM	7.5.92	1		Kingston	31 Mar 11
66.81		Matthew	Denny	AUS	2.6.96	1		Brisbane	23 Nov 14
66.45		Gordon	Wolf	GER	17.1.90	1		Halle	23 May 09
66.27		Clemens	Prüfer	GER	13.8.97	1		Wiesbaden	15 May 16
65.88		Omar	El-Ghazaly	EGY	9.2.84	1		Cairo	7 Nov 03
65.71		Marin	Premeru	CRO	29.8.90	1		Split	31 May 09
HAMMER									
78.33		Olli-Pekka	Karjalainen	FIN	7.3.80	1	NC	Seinäjoki	5 Aug 99
78.14		Roland	Steuk	GDR	5.3.59	1	NC	Leipzig	30 Jun 78
78.00		Sergey	Dorozhon	UKR	17.2.64	1		Moskva	7 Aug 83
76.54		Valeriy	Gubkin	BLR	3.9.67	2		Minsk	27 Jun 86
76.42		Ruslan	Dikiy	TJK	18.1.72	1		Togliatti	7 Sep 91
76.37		Ashraf Amjad	El-Seify	QAT	20.2.95	1		Doha	10 Apr 13
75.52		Sergey	Kirmasov	RUS	25.3.70	1		Kharkov	4 Jun 89
75.42		Szymon	Ziolkowski	POL	1.7.76	1	EJ	Nyíregyhazá	30 Jul 95
75.24		Christoph	Sahner	FRG	23.9.63	1	vPOL-j	Göttingen	26 Jun 82
6kg Hammer									
85.57		Ashraf Amjad	El-Seify	QAT-Y	20.2.95	1	WJ	Barcelona	14 Jul 12
82.97		Javier	Cienfuegos	ESP	15.7.90	1		Madrid	17 Jun 09
82.84		Quentin	Bigot	FRA	1.12.92	1		Bondoufle	16 Oct 11
82.64		Bence	Halász	HUN	4.8.97	1	NC-j	Szombathely	25 Jun 16
82.62		Yevgeniy	Aydamirov	RUS	11.5.87	1	NC-j	Tula	22 Jul 06
81.34		Krisztián	Pars	HUN	18.2.82	1		Szombathely	2 Sep 01
81.16		Özkan	Baltaci	TUR	13.2.94	1		Ankara	31 Jul 13
81.15		Ákos	Hudi	HUN	10.8.91	1		Veszprém	7 Jul 10
JAVELIN									
86.48		Neeraj	Chopra	IND	24.12.97	1	WJ	Bydgoszcz	23 Jul 16
84.69		Zigismunds	Sirmais	LAT	6.5.92	2		Bauska	22 Jun 11
84.58		Keshorn	Walcott	TTO	2.4.93	1	OG	London (OS)	11 Aug 12
83.87		Andreas	Thorkildsen	NOR	1.4.82	1		Fana	7 Jun 01
83.55		Aleksandr	Ivanov	RUS	25.5.82	2	NC	Tula	14 Jul 01
83.07		Robert	Oosthuizen	RSA	23.1.87	1	WJ	Beijing	19 Aug 06
82.52		Harri	Haatainen	FIN	5.1.78	4		Leppävirta	25 May 96
82.52		Till	Wöschler	GER	9.6.91	1	WJ	Moncton	23 Jul 10
81.95		Jakub	Vadlejch	CZE	10.10.90	1		Domazlice	26 Sep 09
81.80		Sergey	Voynov	UZB	26.2.77	1		Tashkent	6 Jun 96

DECATHLON

8397	Torsten		Voss		GDR	24.3.63	1	NC	Erfurt			7 Jul 82
	10.76	7.66		14.41	2.09	48.37		14.37	41.76	4.80	62.90	4:34.04
8257	Yordani		García		CUB	21.11.88	8	WCh	Osaka			1 Sep 07
	10.73/0.7	7.15/0.2		14.94	2.09	49.25		14.08/-0.2	42.91	4.70	68.74	4:55.42
8114	Michael		Kohnle		FRG	3.5.70	1	EJ	Varazdin			26 Aug 89
	10.95	7.09/0.1		15.27	2.02	49.91		14.40	45.82	4.90	60.82	4:49.43
8104	Valter		Külvet		EST	19.2.64	1		Viimsi			23 Aug 81
	10.7	7.26		13.86	2.09	48.5		14.8	47.92	4.50	60.34	4:37.8
8082	Daley		Thompson		GBR	30.7.58	1	ECp/s	Sittard			31 Jul 77
	10.70/0.8	7.54/0.7		13.84	2.01	47.31		15.26/2.0	41.70	4.70	54.48	4:30.4
8041	Qi Haifeng				CHN	7.8.83	1	AsiG	Busan			10 Oct 02
	11.09/0.2	7.22/0.0		13.05	2.06	49.09		14.54/0.0	43.16	4.80	61.04	4:35.17
8036	Christian		Schenk		GDR	9.2.65	5		Potsdam			21 Jul 84
	11.54	7.18		14.26	2.16	49.23		15.06	44.74	4.20	65.98	4:24.11
7992	Kevin		Mayer		FRA	10.2.92	8		Kladno			16 Jun 11
	11.23/0.1	7.34/0.2		12.44	2.01	48.66		14.74/-2.0	38.64	4.90	60.96	4:19.79
7938	Frank		Busemann		GER	26.2.75	1		Zeven			2 Oct 94
	10.68/1.6	7.37/1.1		13.08	2.03	50.41		14.34/-1.1	39.84	4.40	63.00	4:37.31

JUNIOR MEN ALL-TIME

Mark	Wind	Name		Nat	Born	Pos	Meet	Venue			Date
IAAF Junior specification with 99cm 110mh, 6kg shot, 1.75kg Discus											
8162		Miklas	Kaul	GER	11.2.98	1	WJ	Bydgoszcz			20 Jul 16
	11.52/0.8	6.79/-1.9	14.80	2.10	49.69		14.72/0.9	41.80	4.80	71.59	4:21.70
8135		Jiri	Sykora	CZE	20.1.95	1	WJ	Eugene			23 Jul 14
	10.92/0.5	7.35/2.0	15.50	1.94	49.00		14.23/-0.1	48.55	4.40	60.56	4:42.10
8131		Arkadiy	Vasilyev	RUS	19.1.87	1		Sochi			27 May 06
	11.28/-0.8	7.70/2.0	14.59	2.00	49.17		14.67/0.6	46.30	4.70	56.96	4:32.10
8126		Andrey	Kravchenko	BLR	4.1.86	1	WJ	Grosseto			15 Jul 04
	11.09/-0.5	7.46-0.2	14.51	2.16	48.98		14.55*/0.4	43.41	4.50	52.84	4:28.46
8124		Kévin	Mayer	FRA	10.2.92	1	EJ	Tallin			24 Jul 11
	11.40/-1.7	7.52/1.5	14.65	2.04	49.41		14.09/0.7	41.00	4.80	56.60	4:25.23

10,000 METRES WALK

Mark	Name		Nat	Born	Pos	Meet	Venue	Date
38:46.4	Viktor	Burayev	RUS	23.8.82	1	NC-j	Moskva	20 May 00
38:54.75	Ralf	Kowalsky	GDR	22.3.62	1		Cottbus	24 Jun 81
38:58.21	Vasiliy	Mizinov	RUS	29.12.97	1	NC-j	Cheboksary	25 Jun 16
39:08.23	Daisuke	Matsunaga	JPN	24.3.95	1		Tama	14 Dec 13
39:28.63	Toshizuka	Yamanishi	JPN	15.2.96	2		Osaka	13 Sep 15
39:28.45	Andrey	Ruzavin	RUS	28.3.86	1	EJ	Kaunas	23 Jul 05
39:30.15	Yuga	Yamashita	JPN	6.2.96	1		Tama	12 Dec 15
39:35.01	Stanislav	Yemelyanov	RUS	23.10.90	1	WJ	Bydgoszcz	11 Jul 08

20 KILOMETRES WALK

Mark	Name		Nat	Born	Pos	Meet	Venue	Date
1:18:06	Viktor	Burayev	RUS	23.8.82	2	NC-w	Adler	4 Mar 01
1:18:07		Li Gaobo	CHN	23.7.89	4		Cixi	23 Apr 05
1:18:44		Chu Yafei	CHN	5.9.88	5		Yangzhou	22 Apr 06
1:18:52		Chen Ding	CHN	5.8.92	3		Taicang	22 Apr 11
1:18:57		Bai Xuejin	CHN	6.6.87	7		Yangzhou	22 Apr 06
1:19:02	Éder	Sánchez	MEX	21.5.86	11		Cixi	23 Apr 05
1:19:14		Xu Xingde	CHN	12.6.84	3	NC	Yangzhou	12 Apr 03
1:19:34		Li Jianbo	CHN	14.11.86	16		Cixi	23 Apr 05

4 x 100 METRES RELAY

Mark	Nat	Names	Pos	Meet	Venue	Date
38.66	USA	Kimmons, Omole, I Williams, L Merritt	1	WJ	Grosseto	18 Jun 04
38.97	JAM	Tracey, Skeen, Minzie, Murphy	2	WJ	Barcelona	14 Jul 12
39.01	JPN	Oseto, Hashimoto, Cambridge, Kanamori	1h1	WJ	Barcelona	13 Jul 12
39.05	GBR	Edgar, Grant, Benjamin, Lewis-Francis	1	WJ	Santiago de Chile	22 Oct 00
39.13	GER	Gurski, Vartel, Giese, Eitel	3	WJ	Bydgoszcz	23 Jul 16
39.17	TTO	Simpson, Burns, Holder, Brown	3	WJ	Kingston	21 Jul 02
39.29	BRA	de Araújo, Monteiro, R dos Santos Jnr, Rocha	2h1	WJ	Barcelona	13 Jul 12
39.31	POL	Bijowski, Slowikowski, Zalewski, Jabłonski	3h1	WJ	Barcelona	13 Jul 12

4 x 400 METRES RELAY

Mark	Nat	Names	Pos	Meet	Venue	Date
3:01.09	USA	B Johnson, L Merritt, Craig, Clement	1	WJ	Grosseto	18 Jul 04
3:02.81	BOT	Poo, Thebe, Sibanda, Talane	2	WJ	Bydgoszcz	24 Jul 16
3:03.80	GBR	Grindley, Patrick, Winrow, Richardson	2	WJ	Plovdiv	12 Aug 90
3:04.06	JAM	S Clarke, Bolt, Myers, Gonzales	2	WJ	Kingston	21 Jul 02
3:04.11	JPN	Walsh, Yui, Kitagawa, Kato	2	WJ	Eugene	27 Jul 14
3:04.22	CUB	Cadogan, Mordoche, González, Hernández	2	WJ	Athína	20 Jul 86
3:04.50	RSA	le Roux, Gebhardt, Julius, van Zyl	2	WJ	Grosseto	18 Jul 04
3:04.58	GDR	Preusche, Löper, Trylus, Carlowitz	1	EJ	Utrecht	23 Aug 81

JUNIOR WOMEN'S ALL-TIME LISTS

100 METRES

Mark	Wind	Name		Nat	Born	Pos	Meet	Venue	Date
10.88	2.0	Marlies	Oelsner	GDR	21.3.58	1	NC	Dresden	1 Jul 77
10.89	1.8	Katrin	Krabbe	GDR	22.11.69	1rB		Berlin	20 Jul 88
10.98	2.0	Candace	Hill	USA	11.2.99	1		Shoreline	20 Jun 15
10.99	0.9	Angela	Tenorio	ECU	27.1.96	2	PAm	Toronto	22 Jul 15
11.03	1.7	Silke	Gladisch	GDR	20.6.64	3	OD	Berlin	8 Jun 83
11.03	0.6	English	Gardner	USA	22.4.92	1	Pac10	Tucson	14 May 11
11.04	1.4	Angela	Williams	USA	30.1.80	1	NCAA	Boise	5 Jun 99
11.07	0.7	Bianca	Knight	USA	2.1.89	4q2	NC/OT	Eugene	27 Jun 08
11.08	2.0	Brenda	Morehead	USA	5.10.57	1	OT	Eugene	21 Jun 76
11.10	0.9	Kaylin	Whitney	USA	9.3.98	1	NC-j	Eugene	5 Jul 14

Uncertain timing: 10.99 1.9 Natalya Bochina RUS 4.1.62 2   Leningrad 3 Jun 80
Wind assisted to 11.08

10.96	3.7	Angela	Williams	USA	30.1.80	1		Las Vegas	3 Apr 99
10.97	3.3	Gesine	Walther	GDR	6.10.62	4	NC	Cottbus	16 Jul 80
11.01	5.4	Kaylin	Whitney	USA	9.3.98	3	Athl	Lausanne	9 Jul 15
11.02	2.1	Nikole	Mitchell	JAM	5.6.74	1	Mutual	Kingston	1 May 93

JUNIOR WOMEN ALL-TIME

Mark	Wind	Name		Nat	Born	Pos	Meet	Venue	Date
11.03	2.2	Dina	Asher-Smith	GBR	4.12.95	1		Mannheim	5 Jul 14
11.04	5.6	Kelly-Ann	Baptiste	TTO	14.10.86	1rB	TexR	Austin	9 Apr 05
11.04	3.1	Desiree	Henry	GBR	26.8.95	1		Clermont	26 Apr 14
11.06	2.2	Brenda	Morehead	USA	5.10.57	1s2	OT	Eugene	21 Jun 76

200 METRES

Mark	Wind	Name		Nat	Born	Pos	Meet	Venue	Date
22.11A	-0.5	Allyson	Felix	USA	18.11.85	1		Ciudad de México	3 May 03
22.18	0.8					2	OG	Athína	25 Aug 04
22.19	1.5	Natalya	Bochina	RUS	4.1.62	2	OG	Moskva	30 Jul 80
22.37	1.3	Sabine	Rieger	GDR	6.11.63	2	vURS	Cottbus	26 Jun 82
22.42	0.4	Gesine	Walther	GDR	6.10.62	1		Potsdam	29 Aug 81
22.43	0.8	Bianca	Knight	USA	2.1.89	1	Reebok	New York (RI)	31 May 08
22.43A	-0.7	Candace	Hill	USA	11.2.99	1		Calí	19 Jul 15
22.45	0.5	Grit	Breuer	GER	16.2.72	2	ASV	Köln	8 Sep 91
22.45	0.9	Shaunae	Miller	BAH	15.4.94	2	NC	Freeport	22 Jun 13
22.47	0.4	Kaylin	Whitney	USA	9.3.98	4	NC	Eugene	28 Jun 15
22.51	2.0	Katrin	Krabbe	GDR	22.11.69	3		Berlin	13 Sep 88
22.52	1.2	Mary	Onyali	NGR	3.2.68	6	WCh	Roma	3 Sep 87
Indoors									
22.40		Bianca	Knight	USA	2.1.89	1r2	NCAA	Fayetteville	15 Mar 08
22.49		Sanya	Richards	USA	26.2.85	2rA	NCAA	Fayetteville	12 Mar 04
Wind assisted									
22.25	5.6	Bianca	Knight	USA	2.1.89	5	NC/OT	Eugene	6 Jul 08
22.34	2.3	Katrin	Krabbe	GDR	22.11.69	1	WJ	Sudbury	30 Jul 88
22.38	2.1	Candace	Hill	USA	11.2.99	1		Montverde	11 Jun 16
22.41	3.1	Shaunae	Miller	BAH	15.4.94	1		Athens, GA	13 Apr 13
22.41	2.6	Gina	Lückenkemper	GER	21.11.96	1	EJ	Eskilstuna	18 Jul 15
22.44	2.5	Lauren Rain	Williams	USA	25.7.99	1		Norwalk	21 May 16

400 METRES

Mark	Wind	Name		Nat	Born	Pos	Meet	Venue	Date
49.42		Grit	Breuer	GER	16.2.72	2	WCh	Tokyo	27 Aug 91
49.77		Christina	Brehmer	GDR	28.2.58	1		Dresden	9 May 76
49.89		Sanya	Richards	USA	26.2.85	2	NC/OT	Sacramento	17 Jul 04
50.01		Li Jing		CHN	14.2.80	1	NG	Shanghai	18 Oct 97
50.19		Marita	Koch	GDR	18.2.57	3	OD	Berlin	10 Jul 76
50.46		Kendall	Baisden	USA	5.3.95	2	Big 12	Lubbock	18 May 14
50.50		Ashley	Spencer	USA	8.6.93	1	WJ	Barcelona	13 Jul 12
50.59		Fatima	Yusuf	NGR	2.5.71	1	HGP	Budapest	5 Aug 90
50.70		Shaunae	Miller	BAH	15.4.94	2	NCAA	Eugene	7 Jun 13
50.74		Monique	Henderson	USA	18.2.83	1		Norwalk	3 Jun 00
50.78		Danijela	Grgic	CRO	28.9.88	1	WJ	Beijing	17 Aug 06

800 METRES

Mark	Wind	Name		Nat	Born	Pos	Meet	Venue	Date
1:54.01		Pamela	Jelimo	KEN	5.12.89	1	WK	Zürich	29 Aug 08
1:55.45		Caster	Semenya	RSA	7.1.91	1	WCh	Berlin	19 Aug 09
1:56.59		Francine	Niyonsaba	BDI	5.5.93	1	VD	Bruxelles	7 Sep 12
1:57.18		Wang Yuan		CHN	8.4.76	2h2	NG	Beijing	8 Sep 93
1:57.45		Hildegard	Ullrich	GDR	20.12.59	5	EC	Praha	31 Aug 78
1:57.62		Lang Yinglai		CHN	22.8.79	1	NG	Shanghai	22 Oct 97
1:57.63		Maria	Mutola	MOZ	27.10.72	4	WCh	Tokyo	26 Aug 91
1:57.74		Sahily	Diago	CUB	26.8.95	1	Barr	La Habana	25 Jul 14
1:57.77		Lu Yi		CHN	10.4.74	4	NG	Beijing	9 Sep 93
1:57.86		Katrin	Wühn	GDR	19.11.65	1		Celje	5 May 84
1:58.16		Lin Na		CHN	18.1.80	3	NG	Shanghai	22 Oct 97

1000 METRES

Mark	Wind	Name		Nat	Born	Pos	Meet	Venue	Date
2:35.4		Irina	Nikitina	RUS	16.6.61	5	Kuts	Podolsk	5 Aug 79
2:35.4		Katrin	Wühn	GDR	19.11.65	3		Potsdam	12 Jul 84

1500 METRES

Mark	Wind	Name		Nat	Born	Pos	Meet	Venue	Date
3:51.34		Lang Yinglai		CHN	22.8.79	2	NG	Shanghai	18 Oct 97
3:53.91		Yin Lili		CHN	11.11.79	3	NG	Shanghai	18 Oct 97
3:53.97		Lan Lixin		CHN	14.2.79	4	NG	Shanghai	18 Oct 97
3:54.52		Zhang Ling		CHN	13.4.80	5	NG	Shanghai	18 Oct 97
3:56.98		Faith	Kipyegon	KEN	10.1.94	2	DL	Doha	10 May 13
3:59.53		Dawit	Seyaum	ETH	27.7.96	1		Marrakech	8 Jun 14
3:59.60		Gelete	Burka	ETH	15.2.86	5	GP	Rieti	28 Aug 05
3:59.81		Wang Yuan		CHN	8.4.76	7	NG	Beijing	11 Sep 93
3:59.96		Zola	Budd	GBR	26.5.66	3	VD	Bruxelles	30 Aug 85
4:00.05		Lu Yi		CHN	10.4.74	8	NG	Beijing	11 Sep 93
4:00.18		Gudaf	Tsegay	ETH	23.1.97	3	Pre	Eugene	28 May 16

JUNIOR WOMEN ALL-TIME

Mark	Wind	Name		Nat	Born	Pos	Meet	Venue	Date
3000 METRES									
8:28.83		Zola	Budd	GBR	26.5.66	3	GG	Roma	7 Sep 85
8:35.89		Sally	Barsosio	KEN	21.3.78	2	Herc	Monaco	16 Aug 97
8:36.45			Ma Ningning	CHN	1.6.76	4	NC	Jinan	6 Jun 93
8:36.87		Alemitu	Haroye	ETH	9.5.95	14	VD	Bruxelles	5 Sep 14
8:38.61		Kalkedan	Gezahegn	ETH	8.5.91	5	WAF	Thessaloníki	13 Sep 09
8:38.97		Linet	Masai	KEN	5.12.89	5	GP	Rieti	9 Sep 07
8:39.13		Agnes	Tirop	KEN	23.10.95	3		Rieti	8 Sep 13
8:39.65		Buze	Diriba	ETH	9.2.94	3	Herc	Monaco	20 Jul 12
8:39.90		Gelete	Burka	ETH	15.2.86	3	SGP	Doha	13 May 05
8:40.08		Gabriela	Szabo	ROU	14.11.75	3	EC	Helsinki	10 Aug 94
8:40.28		Meseret	Defar	ETH	19.11.83	10	VD	Bruxelles	30 Aug 02
5000 METRES									
14:30.88		Tirunesh	Dibaba	ETH	1.10.85	2	Bisl	Bergen (Fana)	11 Jun 04
14:35.18		Sentayehu	Ejigu	ETH	21.6.85	4	Bisl	Bergen (Fana)	11 Jun 04
14:39.96			Yin Lili	CHN	11.11.79	4	NG	Shanghai	23 Oct 97
14:43.29		Emebet	Anteneh	ETH	13.1.92	5	Bisl	Oslo	9 Jun 11
14:45.33			Lan Lixin	CHN	14.2.79	2h2	NG	Shanghai	21 Oct 97
14:45.63		Letesenbet	Gidey	ETH	20.3.98	1		Barcelona (S)	30 Jun 16
14:45.71			Song Liqing	CHN	20.1.80	3h2	NG	Shanghai	21 Oct 97
14:45.90			Jiang Bo	CHN	13.3.77	1		Nanjing	24 Oct 95
14:45.98		Pauline	Korikwiang	KEN	1.3.88	7	Bisl	Oslo	2 Jun 06
14:46.71		Sally	Barsosio	KEN	21.3.78	3	VD	Bruxelles	22 Aug 97
14:47.13		Mercy	Cherono	KEN	7.5.91	7	DL	Shanghai	23 May 10
10,000 METRES									
30:26.50		Linet	Masai	KEN	5.12.89	4	OG	Beijing	15 Aug 08
30:31.55			Xing Huina	CHN	25.2.84	7	WCh	Saint-Denis	23 Aug 03
30:39.41			Lan Lixin	CHN	14.2.79	2	NG	Shanghai	19 Oct 97
30:39.98			Yin Lili	CHN	11.11.79	3	NG	Shanghai	19 Oct 97
30:59.92		Merima	Hashim	ETH	.81	3	NA	Heusden-Zolder	5 Aug 00
31:06.20		Lucy	Wangui	KEN	24.3.84	1rA		Okayama	27 Sep 03
31:11.26			Song Liqing	CHN	20.1.80	7	NG	Shanghai	19 Oct 97
31:15.38		Sally	Barsosio	KEN	21.3.78	3	WCh	Stuttgart	21 Aug 93
31:16.50		Evelyne	Kimwei	KEN	25.8.87	1		Kobe	21 Oct 06
31:17.30			Zhang Yingying	CHN	4.1.90	1		Wuhan	2 Nov 07
31:20.38		Tigist	Kiros	ETH	8.6.92	4	GS	Ostrava	31 May 11
MARATHON									
2:20:59		Shure	Demise	ETH	21.1.96	4		Dubai	23 Jan 15
2:22:38			Zhang Yingying	CHN	4.1.90	1	NC	Xiamen	5 Jan 08
2:23:06		Merima	Mohamed	ETH	10.6.92	3		Toronto	26 Sep 10
2:23:37			Liu Min	CHN	29.11.83	1		Beijing	14 Oct 01
2:23:57			Zhu Xiaolin	CHN	20.4.84	4		Beijing	20 Oct 02
2:25:48			Jin Li	CHN	29.5.83	6		Beijing	14 Oct 01
2:26:34			Wei Yanan	CHN	6.12.81	1		Beijing	15 Oct 00
2:27:05			Chen Rong	CHN	18.5.88	1		Beijing	21 Oct 07
3000 METRES STEEPLECHASE									
9:20.37		Birtukan	Adamu	ETH	29.4.92	4	GGala	Roma	26 May 11
9:20.55		Ruth	Chebet	KEN/BRN	17.11.96	4	WK	Zürich	28 Aug 14
9:20.65		Tigist	Mekonen	BRN	7.7.97	8	Herc	Monaco	17 Jul 15
9:22.51		Almaz	Ayana	ETH	21.11.91	3	VD	Bruxelles	27 Aug 10
9:24.51		Ruth	Bisibori	KEN	2.1.88	1		Daegu	3 Oct 07
9:24.73		Celphine	Chespol	KEN	23.3.99	7	DL	Shanghai	14 May 16
9:25.91		Rosefline	Chepngetich	KEN	17.6.97	3h2	WCh	Beijing	24 Aug 15
9:26.25			Liu Nian	CHN	26.4.88	1		Wuhan	2 Nov 07
9:29.52		Korahubish	Itaa	ETH	28.2.92	1		Huelva	10 Jun 09
9:30.70		Melissa	Rollison	AUS	13.4.83	1	GWG	Brisbane	4 Sep 01
100 METRES HURDLES									
12.74	1.7	Dior	Hall	USA	2.1.96	3	NCAA	Eugene	13 Jun 15
12.83A	0.4	Tobi	Amusan	NGR	23.4.97	1		El Paso	30 Apr 16
12.84	1.5	Aliuska	López	CUB	29.8.69	2	WUG	Zagreb	16 Jul 87
12.84	1.2	Tia	Jones	USA	8.9.00	1h1	NC-j	Clovis	25 Jun 16
12.85	2.0	Elvira	German	BLR	19.6.97	1	WJ	Bydgoszcz	24 Jul 16
12.87	2.0	Kendell	Williams	USA	14.6.95	1	NC-j	Eugene	6 Jul 14
12.87	2.0	Rushelle	Burton	JAM	4.12.97	2	WJ	Bydgoszcz	24 Jul 16
12.88	1.5	Yelena	Ovcharova	UKR	17.6.76	2	ECp	Villeneuve d'Ascq	25 Jun 95
12.89	1.3	Anay	Tejeda	CUB	3.4.83	1		Padova	1 Sep 02

JUNIOR WOMEN ALL-TIME 333

Mark	Wind	Name		Nat	Born	Pos	Meet	Venue	Date
12.91	1.8	Kristina	Castlin	USA	7.7.88	1	NCAA-r	Gainesville	26 May 07
12.92	0.0	Sun Hongwei		CHN	24.11.79	6	NG	Shanghai	18 Oct 97
Wind assisted									
12.79	3.8	Tobi	Amusan	NGR	23.4.97	2	NCAA	Eugene	11 Jun 16
12.81	3.4	Anay	Tejeda	CUB	3.4.83	1	WJ	Kingston	21 Jul 02
12.82	2.1	Kristina	Castlin	USA	7.7.88	1		College Park	21 Apr 07
12.90	3.0	Adrianna	Lamalle	FRA	27.9.82	1		Fort-de-France	28 Apr 01

400 METRES HURDLES

Mark		Name		Nat	Born	Pos	Meet	Venue	Date
54.15		Sydney	McLaughlin	USA	7.8.99	3	NC	Eugene	10 Jul 16
54.40		Wang Xing		CHN	30.11.86	2	NG	Nanjing	21 Oct 05
54.58		Ristananna	Tracey	JAM	5.9.92	2	NC	Kingston	24 Jun 11
54.70		Lashinda	Demus	USA	10.3.83	1	WJ	Kingston	19 Jul 02
54.93		Li Rui		CHN	22.11.79	1	NG	Shanghai	22 Oct 97
55.07		Shamier	Little	USA	20.3.95	1	NCAA	Eugene	13 Jun 14
55.11		Kaliese	Spencer	JAM	6.4.87	1	WJ	Beijing	17 Aug 06
55.15		Huang Xiaoxiao		CHN	3.3.83	2	NG	Guangzhou	22 Nov 01
55.20		Lesley	Maxie	USA	4.1.67	2	TAC	San Jose	9 Jun 84
55.20A		Jana	Pittman	AUS	9.11.82	1		Pietersburg	18 Mar 00
55.20		Anna	Cockrell	USA	28.8.97	1	WJ	Bydgoszcz	22 Jul 16 **Drugs**
disqualification: 54.54		Peng Yinghua ¶		CHN	21.2.79	(2)	NG	Shanghai	22 Oct 97

HIGH JUMP

Mark		Name		Nat	Born	Pos	Meet	Venue	Date
2.01		Olga	Turchak	UKR	5.3.67	2	GWG	Moskva	7 Jul 86
2.01		Heike	Balck	GDR	19.8.70	1	vURS-j	Karl-Marx-Stadt	18 Jun 89
2.00		Stefka	Kostadinova	BUL	25.3.65	1		Sofia	25 Aug 84
2.00		Alina	Astafei	ROU	7.6.69	1	WJ	Sudbury	29 Jul 88
1.99i		Vashti	Cunningham	USA	18.1.98	1	NC	Portland	12 Mar 16
	1.97					2	NC	Eugene	3 Jul 16
1.98		Silvia	Costa	CUB	4.5.64	2	WUG	Edmonton	11 Jul 83
1.98		Yelena	Yelesina	RUS	5.4.70	1	Druzh	Nyiregyháza	13 Aug 88
1.97		Svetlana	Isaeva	BUL	18.3.67	2		Sofia	25 May 86
1.97i		Mariya	Kuchina	RUS	14.1.93	1		Trinec	26 Jan 11
1.96A		Charmaine	Gale	RSA	27.2.64	1	NC-j	Bloemfontein	4 Apr 81
1.96i		Desislava	Aleksandrova	BUL	27.10.75	2	EI	Paris (B)	12 Mar 94
1.96		Marina	Kuptsova	RUS	22.12.81	1	NC	Tula	26 Jul 00
1.96		Blanka	Vlasic	CRO	8.11.83	1	WJ	Kingston	20 Jul 02
1.96		Airine	Palsyte	LTU	13.7.92	2	WUG	Shenzhen	21 Aug 11
1.96		Eleanor	Patterson	AUS	22.5.96	1	N.Sch	Townsville	7 Dec 13

POLE VAULT

Mark		Name		Nat	Born	Pos	Meet	Venue	Date
4.71i		Wilma	Murto	FIN	11.6.98	1		Zweibrücken	31 Jan 16
	4.52					2	PNG	Turku	29 Jun 16
4.64		Eliza	McCartney	NZL	11.12.96	1		Auckland	19 Dec 15
4.63i		Angelica	Bengtsson	SWE	8.7.93	2		Stockholm	22 Feb 11
	4.58					1		Sollentuna	5 Jul 12
4.61		Alyona	Lutkovskaya	RUS	15.3.96	1		Irkutsk	21 May 15
4.60i		Hanna	Shelekh	UKR	14.7.93	3		Donetsk	11 Feb 12
4.60i		Roberta	Bruni	ITA	8.3.94	1	NC	Ancona	17 Feb 13
4.60		Robeilys	Peinado	VEN	26.11.97	1		Barquisimeto	20 May 15
4.59		Nina	Kennedy	AUS	5.4.97	1		Perth	14 Feb 15
4.57		Angelica	Moser	SUI	9.10.97	1		Frauenkappelen	1 Aug 16
4.52i		Katie	Byres	GBR	11.9.93	2		Nevers	18 Feb 12

LONG JUMP

Mark	Wind	Name		Nat	Born	Pos	Meet	Venue	Date
7.14	1.1	Heike	Daute	GDR	16.12.64	1	PTS	Bratislava	4 Jun 83
7.03	1.3	Darya	Klishina	RUS	15.1.91	1	Znam	Zhukovskiy	26 Jun 10
7.00	-0.2	Birgit	Grosshennig	GDR	21.2.65	2		Berlin	9 Jun 84
6.94	-0.5	Magdalena	Khristova	BUL	25.2.77	2		Kalamáta	22 Jun 96
6.91	0.0	Anisoara	Cusmir	ROU	28.6.62	1		Bucuresti	23 May 81
6.90	1.4	Beverly	Kinch	GBR	14.1.64	*	WCh	Helsinki	14 Aug 83
6.88	0.6	Natalya	Shevchenko	RUS	28.12.66	2		Sochi	26 May 84
6.84		Larisa	Baluta	UKR	13.8.65	2		Krasnodar	6 Aug 83
6.83	1.7	Kate	Hall	USA	12.1.97	1		Greensboro NC	21 Jun 15
6.82	1.8	Fiona	May	GBR	12.12.69	*	WJ	Sudbury	30 Jul 88
6.81	1.6	Carol	Lewis	USA	8.8.63	1	TAC	Knoxville	20 Jun 82
6.81	1.4	Yelena	Davydova	KZK	16.11.67	1	NC-j	Krasnodar	17 Jul 85
Wind assisted to 6.82									
7.27	2.2	Heike	Daute	GDR	16.12.64	1	WCh	Helsinki	14 Aug 83
6.93	4.6	Beverly	Kinch	GBR	14.1.64	5	WCh	Helsinki	14 Aug 83
6.88	2.1	Fiona	May	GBR	12.12.69	1	WJ	Sudbury	30 Jul 88

JUNIOR WOMEN ALL-TIME

Mark	Wind	Name		Nat	Born	Pos	Meet	Venue	Date
6.84	2.8	Anu	Kaljurand	EST	16.4.69	2		Riga	4 Jun 88

TRIPLE JUMP
Mark	Wind		Name	Nat	Born	Pos	Meet	Venue	Date
14.62	1.0	Tereza	Marinova	BUL	5.9.77	1	WC	Sydney	25 Aug 96
14.57	0.2		Huang Qiuyan	CHN	25.1.80	1	NG	Shanghai	19 Oct 97
14.52	0.6	Anastasiya	Ilyina	RUS	16.1.82	q	WJ	Santiago de Chile	20 Oct 00
14.46	1.0		Peng Fengmei	CHN	2.7.79	1		Chengdu	18 Apr 98
14.43	0.6	Kaire	Leibak	EST	21.5.88	1	WJ	Beijing	17 Aug 06
14.38	-0.7		Xie Limei	CHN	27.6.86	1	AsiC	Inchon	1 Sep 05
14.37i	-		Ren Ruiping	CHN	1.2.76	3	WI	Barcelona	11 Mar 95
			14.36			0.0			1	NC	Beijing	1 Jun 94
14.36	0.0	Dailenys	Alcántara	CUB	10.8.91	3	Barr/NC	La Habana	29 May 09
14.35		Yana	Borodina	RUS	21.4.92	1J	Mosc Ch	Moskva	15 Jun 11
14.32	-0.1	Yelena	Lysak ¶	RUS	19.10.75	1		Voronezh	18 Jun 94
Wind assisted									
14.83	8.3		Ren Ruiping	CHN	1.2.76	1	NC	Taiyuan	21 May 95
14.55	3.7	Dailenis	Alcántara	CUB	10.8.91	1	Barr/NC	La Habana	21 Mar 10
14.43	2.7	Yelena	Lysak ¶	RUS	19.10.75	1	WJ	Lisboa	21 Jul 94

SHOT
Mark		Name		Nat	Born	Pos	Meet	Venue	Date
20.54		Astrid	Kumbernuss	GDR	5.2.70	1	vFIN-j	Orimattila	1 Jul 89
20.51i		Heidi	Krieger	GDR	20.7.65	2		Budapest	8 Feb 84
			20.24			5		Split	30 Apr 84
20.23		Ilke	Wyludda	GDR	28.3.69	1	NC-j	Karl-Marx-Stadt	16 Jul 88
20.12		Ilona	Schoknecht	GDR	24.9.56	2	NC	Erfurt	23 Aug 75
20.02			Cheng Xiaoyan	CHN	30.11.75	3	NC	Beijing	5 Jun 94
19.90		Stephanie	Storp	FRG	28.11.68	1		Hamburg	16 Aug 87
19.63			Wang Yawen	CHN	23.8.73	1		Shijiazhuang	25 Apr 92
19.57		Grit	Haupt	GDR	4.6.66	1		Gera	7 Jul 84
19.48		Ines	Wittich	GDR	14.11.69	5		Leipzig	29 Jul 87
19.46			Gong Lijiao	CHN	24.1.89	Q	OG	Beijing	16 Aug 08
19.42		Simone	Michel	GDR	18.12.60	3	vSU	Leipzig	23 Jun 79

DISCUS
Mark		Name		Nat	Born	Pos	Meet	Venue	Date
74.40		Ilke	Wyludda	GDR	28.3.69	2		Berlin	13 Sep 88
			75.36 unofficial meeting			2		Berlin	6 Sep 88
67.38		Irina	Meszynski	GDR	24.3.62	1		Berlin	14 Aug 81
67.00		Jana	Günther	GDR	7.1.68	6	NC	Potsdam	20 Aug 87
66.80		Svetla	Mitkova	BUL	17.6.64	1		Sofia	2 Aug 83
66.60		Astrid	Kumbernuss	GDR	5.2.70	1		Berlin	20 Jul 88
66.34		Franka	Dietzsch	GDR	22.1.68	2		Saint-Denis	11 Jun 87
66.30		Jana	Lauren	GDR	28.6.70	1	vURS-j	Karl-Marx-Stadt	18 Jun 89
66.08			Cao Qi	CHN	15.1.74	1	NG	Beijing	12 Sep 93
65.96		Grit	Haupt	GDR	4.6.66	3		Leipzig	13 Jul 84
65.22		Daniela	Costian	ROU	30.4.65	3		Nitra	26 Aug 84

HAMMER
Mark		Name		Nat	Born	Pos	Meet	Venue	Date
73.24			Zhang Wenxiu	CHN	22.3.86	1	NC	Changsha	24 Jun 05
71.71		Kamila	Skolimowska	POL	4.11.82	1	GPF	Melbourne	9 Sep 01
70.62		Alexandra	Tavernier	FRA	13.12.93	1	WJ	Barcelona	14 Jul 12
70.39		Mariya	Smolyachkova	BLR	10.2.85	1		Staiki	26 Jun 04
70.39		Réka	Gyurátz	HUN	31.5.96	1		Budapest	23 May 15
69.73		Natalya	Zolotukhina	UKR	4.1.85	1		Kyiv	24 Jul 04
69.63		Bianca	Perie	ROU	1.6.90	1	NC-j	Bucuresti	14 Aug 09
69.25		Audrey	Ciofani	FRA	13.3.96	1		Gagny	10 May 15
68.98		Ayamey	Medina	CUB	21.2.98	2	Barr	La Habana	27 May 16
68.74		Arasay	Thondike	CUB	28.5.86	2	Barr	La Habana	2 May 05
68.50		Martina	Danisová	SVK	21.3.83	1		Kladno	16 Jun 01

JAVELIN
Mark		Name		Nat	Born	Pos	Meet	Venue	Date
63.86		Yulenmis	Aguilar	CUB	3.8.96	1	PAm-J	Edmonton	2 Aug 15
63.01		Vira	Rebryk (now RUS)	UKR	25.2.89	1	WJ	Bydgoszcz	10 Jul 08
62.93			Xue Juan	CHN	10.2.86	1	NG	Changsha	27 Oct 03
62.11		Maria	Andrejczyk	POL	9.3.96	1	Skol	Cetniewo	1 Aug 15
62.09			Zhang Li	CHN	17.1.89	1		Beijing	25 May 08
61.99			Wang Yaning	CHN	4.1.80	1	NC	Huizhou	14 Oct 99
61.96		Sofi	Flink	SWE	8.7.95	Q	WCh	Moskva	16 Aug 13
61.79		Nikolett	Szabó	HUN	3.3.80	1		Schwechat	23 May 99
61.61			Chang Chunfeng	CHN	4.5.88	1	NC-j	Chengdu	4 Jun 07
61.49			Liang Lili	CHN	16.11.83	1	NC	Benxi	1 Jun 02
61.38		Annika	Suthe	GER	15.10.85	1-j		Halle	23 May 04

JUNIOR WOMEN ALL-TIME 335

Mark	Wind	Name		Nat	Born	Pos	Meet	Venue	Date
61.38		Haruka	Kitaguchi	JPN	16.3.98	3		Kawasaki	8 May 16

HEPTATHLON

Mark	Wind	Name		Nat	Born	Pos	Meet	Venue	Date
6768w		Tatyana	Chernova	RUS	29.1.88	1		Arles	3 Jun 07
	13.04w/6.1	1.82	13.57	23.59w/5.2	6.61/1.2	53.43	2:15.05		
6227						1	WJ	Beijing	19 Aug 06
	13.70/1.6	1.80	12.18	24.05/0.3	6.35/-0.4	50.51	2:25.49		
6542		Carolina	Klüft	SWE	2.2.83	1	EC	München	10 Aug 02
	13.33/-0.3	1.89	13.16	23.71/-0.3	6.36/1.1	47.61	2:17.99		
6465		Sibylle	Thiele	GDR	6.3.65	1	EJ	Schwechat	28 Aug 83
	13.49	1.90	14.63	24.07	6.65	36.22	2:18.36		
6436		Sabine	Braun	FRG	19.6.65	1	vBUL	Mannheim	9 Jun 84
	13.68	1.78	13.09	23.88	6.03	52.14	2:09.41		
6428		Svetla	Dimitrova ¶	BUL	27.1.70	1	NC	Sofia	18 Jun 89
	13.49/-0.7	1.77	13.98	23.59/-0.2	6.49/0.7	40.10	2:11.10		
6403		Emilia	Dimitrova	BUL	13.11.67	6	GWG	Moskva	7 Jul 86
	13.73	1.76	13.46	23.17	6.29	43.30	2:09.85		
6298		Nafissatou	Thiam	BEL	19.8.94	1	EJ	Rieti	19 Jul 13
	13.87/1.2	1.89	14.26	25.15/-0.6	6.37/0.1	46.94	2:24.89		
6276		Larisa	Nikitina	RUS	29.4.65	8	URS Ch	Kiyev	21 Jun 84
	13.87/1.6	1.86	14.04	25.26/-0.7	6.31/0.1	48.62	2:22.76		
6267		Katarina	Johnson-Thompson	GBR	9.1.93	15	OG	London (OS)	4 Aug 12
	13.48/0.9	1.89	11.32	23.73/-0.3	6.19/-0.4	38.37	2:10.76		
6231		Yorgelis	Rodríguez	CUB	25.1.95	1		La Habana	22 Feb 14
	14.01/0.0	1.84	14.21	24.93/0.0	6.03/0.0	47.58	2:17.93		
6218		Jana	Sobotka	GDR	3.10.65	6	OD	Potsdam	21 Jul 84
	14.40	1.74	13.28	24.19	6.27	43.64	2:06.83		

Drugs disqualification: 6534 Svetla Dimitrova BUL 27.1.70 (3) ECp Helmond 16 Jul 89
13.30/1.0 1.84 14.35 23.33/-2.2 6.47/-1.4 39.20 2:13.56

10 KILOMETRES WALK

Mark		Name		Nat	Born	Pos	Meet	Venue	Date
41:52		Tatyana	Mineyeva	RUS	10.8.90	1	NCp-j	Penza	5 Sep 09
41:55		Irina	Stankina	RUS	25.3.77	1	NC-wj	Adler	11 Feb 95
41:57			Gao Hongmiao	CHN	17.3.74	2	NG	Beijing	8 Sep 93
42:15+		Anisya	Kirdyapkina	RUS	23.10.89	1=	in 20k	Adler	23 Feb 08
42:29		Tatyana	Kalmykova	RUS	10.1.90	1	NC-wj	Adler	23 Feb 08
42:31		Irina	Yumanova	RUS	17.6.90	2	NC-wj	Adler	23 Feb 08
42:43.0	t	Svetlana	Vasilyeva	RUS	24.7.92	1	NC-wj	Sochi	27 Feb 11
42:44			Long Yuwen	CHN	1.8.75	3	NC	Shenzen	18 Feb 93

20 KILOMETRES WALK

Mark	Name		Nat	Born	Pos	Meet	Venue	Date
1:25:30	Anisya	Kirdyapkina	RUS	23.10.89	2	NC-w	Adler	23 Feb 08
1:26:36	Tatyana	Kalmykova	RUS	10.1.90	1	NC	Saransk	8 Jun 08
1:27:01		Lu Xiuzhi	CHN	26.10.93	2		Taicang	30 Mar 12
1:27:16		Song Hongjuan	CHN	4.7.84	1	NC	Yangzhou	14 Apr 03
1:27:34		Jiang Jing	CHN	23.10.85	2	WCp	Naumburg	2 May 04
1:27:35	Natalya	Fedoskina	RUS	25.6.80	2	WCp	Mézidon-Canon	2 May 99
1:28:08	Anezka	Drahotová	CZE	22.7.95	3	EC	Zürich	14 Aug 14
1:28:23		Song Xiaoling	CHN	21.12.87	2		Yangzhou	22 Apr 06

4 X 100 METRES RELAY

Mark	Nat	Names	Pos	Meet	Venue	Date
43.29	USA (Blue)	Knight, Tarmoh, Olear, Mayo	1		Eugene	8 Aug 06
43.40	JAM	Simpson, Stewart, McLaughlin, Facey	1	WJ	Kingston	20 Jul 02
43.42	GER	Burghardt, Grompe, Pinto, Frese	1	EJ	Tallinn	24 Jul 11
43.44A	NGR	Utondu, Iheagwam, Onyali, Ogunkoya	1	AfrG	Nairobi	9 Aug 87
43.68	FRA	Vouaux, Jacques-Sebastien, Kamga, Banco	3	WJ	Grosseto	18 Jul 04
43.81	GBR	Miller, Asher-Smith, S Wilson, Henry	1	EJ	Rieti	21 Jul 13
43.87	URS	Lapshina, Doronina, Bulatova, Kovalyova	1	vGDR-j	Leningrad	20 Jun 87
43.98	BRA	Silva, Leoncio, Krasucki, Santos	2	PAm-J	São Paulo	7 Jul 07
44.04	CUB	Riquelme, Allen, López, Valdivia	2	WJ	Sudbury	31 Jul 88

4 X 400 METRES RELAY

Mark	Nat	Names	Pos	Meet	Venue	Date
3:27.60	USA	Anderson, Kidd, Smith, Hastings	1	WJ	Grosseto	18 Jul 04
3:28.39	GDR	Derr, Fabert, Wöhlk, Breuer	1	WJ	Sudbury	31 Jul 88
3:29.66	JAM	Stewart, Morgan, Walker, Hall	1	PennR	Philadelphia	28 Apr 01
3:30.03	RUS	Talko, Shapayeva, Soldatova, Kostetskaya	2	WJ	Grosseto	18 Jul 04
3:30.38	AUS	Scamps, R Poetschka, Hanigan, Andrews	1	WJ	Plovdiv	12 Aug 90
3:30.46	GBR	Wall, Spencer, James, Miller	2	WJ	Kingston	21 Jul 02
3:30.72	BUL	Kireva, Angelova, Rashova, Dimitrova	3	v2N	Sofia	24 Jul 83
3:30.84	NGR	Abugan, Odumosu, Eze, Adesanya	2	WJ	Beijing	20 Aug 06
3:31.57	ROU	Petrea, Florea, Tîrlea, Nedelcu	1	WJ	Seoul	20 Sep 92

MEN'S WORLD LISTS 2016

60 METRES INDOORS

Mark	Name		Nat	Born	Pos	Meet	Venue	Date	
6.44	Asafa	Powell	JAM	23.11.82	1h5	WI	Portland	18	Mar
6.44		Powell			1s3	WI	Portland	18	Mar
6.47	Ronnie	Baker	USA	15.10.93	1	NCAA	Birmingham	12	Mar
6.47	Trayvon	Bromell	USA	10.7.95	1	WI	Portland	18	Mar
6.48	Cameron	Burrell	USA	11.9.94	2	NCAA	Birmingham	12	Mar
6.49		Powell			1s2		Houston	12	Feb
6.49	Kim	Collins	SKN	5.4.76	1s2	WI	Portland	18	Mar
6.50		Powell			1h1		Houston	12	Feb
6.50	Richard	Kilty	GBR	2.9.89	1		Jablonec nad Nisou	5	Mar
6.50		Burrell			1h2	NCAA	Birmingham	11	Mar
6.50		Su Bingtian	CHN	29.8.89	2s3	WI	Portland	18	Mar
6.50		Powell			2	WI	Portland	18	Mar
	(12/7)								
6.51	Marvin	Bracy	USA	15.12.93	1	NC	Portland	12	Mar
6.51	Mike	Rodgers	USA	24.4.85	2s2	WI	Portland	18	Mar
6.51	Ramon	Gittens	BAR	20.7.87	3	WI	Portland	18	Mar
	(10)								
6.52	Julian	Reus	GER	29.4.88	1	NC	Leipzig	27	Feb
6.52	Christian	Coleman	USA	6.3.96	3	NCAA	Birmingham	12	Mar
6.53	Yunier	Pérez	CUB	16.2.85	1	Pedros	Lódz	5	Feb
6.53	James	Dasaolu	GBR	5.9.87	1	NC	Sheffield	27	Feb
6.53	John	Teeters	USA	19.5.93	4	NCAA	Birmingham	12	Mar
6.53		Xie Zhenye	CHN	17.8.93	4	WI	Portland	18	Mar
6.54	Andrew	Robertson	GBR	17.12.90	2	NC	Sheffield	27	Feb
6.55	Sean	Safo-Antwi	GBR/GHA	31.10.90	1		Mondeville	6	Mar
6.55		Yang Yang	CHN	26.6.91	1	NGP	Nanjing	3	Mar
6.56	Joe	Morris	USA	4.10.89	1		Torun	12	Feb
	(20)								
6.56	Hassan	Taftian	IRI	4.5.93	1	AsiC	Doha	19	Feb
6.56		Tang Xingqiang	CHN	11.8.95	2	NGP	Nanjing	3	Mar
6.56	Theo	Etienne	GBR	3.9.96	2		Jablonec nad Nisou	5	Mar
6.56	Kenzo	Cotton	USA	13.5.96	2h1	NCAA	Birmingham	11	Mar
6.56	Yoshihide	Kiryu	JPN	15.12.95	3s1	WI	Portland	18	Mar
6.57	Eric	Cray	PHI	6.11.88	1s1	AsiC	Doha	19	Feb
6.57	Mobolade	Ajomale	CAN	31.8.95	1	NCAA-II	Pittsburg	12	Mar
6.57	D'Angelo	Cherry	USA	1.8.90	4	NC	Portland	12	Mar
6.58	Emmanuel	Matadi	LBR	15.4.91	1		Mankato	22	Jan
6.58	Antoine	Adams	SKN	31.8.88	1		Houston	12	Feb
	(30)								
6.58	Jeffrey	Henderson	USA	19.2.89	2h1	NC	Portland	11	Mar
6.59	Warren	Fraser	BAH	8.7.91	1		Clemson	29	Jan
6.59	Chevaughn	Walsh	ANT	29.12.87	1		Houston	30	Jan
6.59	Adam	Gemili	GBR	6.10.93	1	Welsh	Cardiff	31	Jan
6.59	Keitavious	Walter	USA	16.4.96	1		Birmingham AL	31	Jan
6.59	Christophe	Lemaitre	FRA	11.6.90	1h3		Mondeville	6	Feb
6.59	Markesh	Woodson	USA	6.9.93	1s1		Fayetteville	12	Feb
6.60	Adrian	Griffith	BAH	11.11.84	1		Birmingham AL	31	Jan
6.60	Kevaughn	Rattray	JAM	16.4.96	1h2		New York (Arm)	5	Feb
6.60	Churandy	Martina	NED	3.7.84	2h1		Karlsruhe	6	Feb
	(40)								
6.60A	Ameer	Webb	USA	19.3.91	1h7		Flagstaff	13	Feb
6.60	Daveon	Collins	USA	3.10.92	1		Seattle	13	Feb
6.60	Christian	Blum	GER	10.3.87	2	NC	Leipzig	27	Feb
6.60	Bryce	Robinson	USA	13.11.93	3h2	NCAA	Birmingham	11	Mar
6.60	Jarrion	Lawson	USA	6.5.94	5	NCAA	Birmingham	12	Mar
6.61	Rondell	Sorrillo	TTO	21.1.86	3		Lexington	23	Jan
6.61	Quentin	Butler	USA	18.9.92	1h3		Houston	30	Jan
6.61	Diondre	Batson	USA	13.7.92	1		Nashville	30	Jan
6.61	Andre	De Grasse	CAN	10.11.94	1	Mill	New York (Arm)	20	Feb
6.61	Tevin	Hester	USA	10.1.94	1	ACC	Boston	27	Feb
	(50)								
6.61	Kyle	de Escofet	GBR	4.10.96	5	NC	Sheffield	27	Feb
6.61	Sean	McLean	USA	23.3.92	2h3	NC	Portland	11	Mar
6.61	Albert	Huntley	USA	3.1.90	5s1	NC	Portland	12	Mar
6.61	Kemar	Hyman	CAY	11.10.89	4s2	WI	Portland	18	Mar
6.62	Keenan	Brock	USA	1.6.92	2h1		Birmingham AL	15	Jan
6.62	Odean	Skeen	JAM	28.8.94	2		Birmingham AL	16	Jan

60 – 100 METRES

Mark	Wind	Name		Nat	Born	Pos	Meet	Venue	Date	
6.62A		Wilfried	Koffi	CIV	12.10.87	2		Flagstaff	30	Jan
6.62		Levi	Cadogan	BAR	8.11.95	7		Karlsruhe	6	Feb
6.62		Likoúrgos-Stéfanos Tsákonas		GRE	8.3.90	1	NC	Pireás	13	Feb
6.62		Henricho	Bruintjies	RSA	16.7.93	2	ISTAF	Berlin	13	Feb
		(60)								
6.62		Odain	Rose	SWE	19.7.92	4	Globen	Stockholm	17	Feb
6.62		Darrell	Wesh	HAI	21.1.92	1		Blacksburg	19	Feb
6.62		Lamar	Hargrove	USA	21.4.94	1		Tiffin	28	Feb
6.62		Remigiusz	Olszewski	POL	20.9.92	1	NC	Torun	5	Mar
6.62		Ryota	Yamagata	JPN	10.6.92	1rB		Osaka	13	Mar
Drugs disqualification: 6.55 Trell Kimmons ¶				USA	13.7.85	2s1	NC	Portland	12	Mar

100 METRES

Mark	Wind	Name		Nat	Born	Pos	Meet	Venue	Date	
9.80	1.6	Justin	Gatlin	USA	10.2.82	1	NC/OT	Eugene	3	Jul
9.81	0.2	Usain	Bolt	JAM	21.8.86	1	OG	Rio de Janeiro	14	Aug
9.83	1.7		Gatlin			1s1	NC/OT	Eugene	3	Jul
9.84	1.6	Trayvon	Bromell	USA	10.7.95	2	NC/OT	Eugene	3	Jul
9.86	1.8	Jimmy	Vicaut	FRA	27.2.92	1		Montreuil-sous-Bois	7	Jun
9.86	2.0		Bromell			1s2	NC/OT	Eugene	3	Jul
9.86	0.2		Bolt			1s2	OG	Rio de Janeiro	14	Aug
9.88	1.0		Bolt			1		Kingston	11	Jun
9.88	1.9		Vicaut			1	NC	Angers	25	Jun
9.89	1.9	Akani	Simbine	RSA	21.9.93	1	Gyulai	Székesfehérvár	18	Jul
9.89	0.2		Gatlin			2	OG	Rio de Janeiro	14	Aug
9.91	0.6	Femi Seun	Ogunode	QAT	15.5.91	1		Gainesville	22	Apr
9.91	0.2	Andre	De Grasse	CAN	10.11.94	3	OG	Rio de Janeiro	14	Aug
9.92A	0.9	Jak Ali	Harvey	TUR	5.4.89	1		Erzurum	12	Jun
9.92	1.9	Asafa	Powell	JAM	23.11.82	2	Gyulai	Székesfehérvár	18	Jul
9.92	0.2		De Grasse			2s2	OG	Rio de Janeiro	14	Aug
9.93	1.9	Kim	Collins (10)	SKN	5.4.76	1		Bottrop	29	May
9.93	1.0		Gatlin			1	GGala	Roma	2	Jun
9.93	0.2	Yohan	Blake	JAM	26.12.89	4	OG	Rio de Janeiro	14	Aug
9.94	0.0		Gatlin			1	DL	Shanghai	14	May
9.94	-0.1		Gatlin			1		Beijing	18	May
9.94	1.0	Ameer	Webb	USA	19.3.91	2	GGala	Roma	2	Jun
9.94	1.8	Marvin	Bracy	USA	15.12.93	1		Montverde, FL	11	Jun
9.94	1.0	Nickel	Ashmeade	JAM	7.4.90	2		Kingston	11	Jun
9.94	1.0		Blake			3		Kingston	11	Jun
9.94	1.7		Vicaut			1h1	NC	Angers	25	Jun
9.94	1.2		Bromell			1h3	NC/OT	Eugene	2	Jul
9.94	0.2		Simbine			5	OG	Rio de Janeiro	14	Aug
9.94	0.0		Gatlin			1s3	OG	Rio de Janeiro	14	Aug
9.94	0.4		Powell			1	WK	Zürich	1	Sep
		[30 performances by 14 athletes]								
9.95	1.7	Christian	Coleman	USA	6.3.96	2s1	NC/OT	Eugene	3	Jul
9.96	1.6	Senoj-Jay	Givans	JAM	30.12.93	1s3	NCAA	Eugene	8	Jun
9.96	2.0	Aaron	Brown	CAN	27.5.92	1h1		Montverde, FL	11	Jun
9.96	2.0	Joel	Fearon	GBR	11.10.88	1		Bedford	30	Jul
9.96	0.2	Ben Youssef	Meité	CIV	11.11.86	6	OG	Rio de Janeiro	14	Aug
9.97	-0.1	Michael	Rodgers	USA	24.4.85	2		Beijing	18	May
		(20)								
9.97	2.0	Tyson	Gay	USA	9.8.82	2h1		Montverde, FL	11	Jun
9.97	1.7	Richard	Thompson	TTO	7.6.85	1	NC	Port of Spain	25	Jun
9.98A	1.5	Wayde	van Niekerk	RSA	15.7.92	1		Bloemfontein	12	Mar
9.99	2.0	Omar	McLeod	JAM	25.4.94	1		Fayetteville	23	Apr
9.99	1.7	Rondell	Sorrillo	TTO	21.1.86	2	NC	Port of Spain	25	Jun
10.00	1.0	Kemar	Bailey-Cole	JAM	10.1.92	5		Kingston	11	Jun
10.00	1.9	John	Teeters	USA	19.5.93	1h5	NC/OT	Eugene	2	Jul
10.01	1.1	Hua Wilfried	Koffi	CIV	24.9.89	1		Tempe	9	Apr
10.01	0.0	Cejhae	Greene	ANT	6.10.95	1		Athens, GA	30	Apr
10.01	1.8	Yoshihide	Kiryu	JPN	15.12.95	1s4		Hiratsuka	11	Jun
		(30)								
10.01	1.9	Richard	Kilty	GBR	2.9.89	1		Hexham	16	Jul
10.01	1.8	Julian	Reus	GER	29.4.88	1		Mannheim	29	Jul
10.01	0.2	Chijindu	Ujah	GBR	5.3.94	4s2	OG	Rio de Janeiro	14	Aug
10.01	-0.1	Churandy	Martina	NED	3.7.84	3	DL	Saint-Denis	27	Aug
10.02	1.8	Clayton	Vaughn	USA	15.5.92	3		Montverde, FL	11	Jun
10.02	0.7	Jevaughn	Minzie	JAM	20.7.95	3	NC	Kingston	1	Jul
10.03	0.6	Isiah	Young	USA	5.1.90	2		Gainesville	22	Apr

100 METRES

Mark	Wind	Name		Nat	Born	Pos	Meet	Venue	Date	
10.03	0.9	Kemarley	Brown	JAM/BRN	20.7.92	1rB		Kingston	7	May
10.03	2.0	Walter	Dix	USA	31.1.86	1		Tampa	27	May
10.03	1.0	Ramon	Gittens	BAR	20.7.87	7		Kingston	11	Jun
(40)										
10.03	1.6	Jason	Livermore	JAM	25.4.88	1rB		Kingston	11	Jun
10.03	0.5	Ryota	Yamagata	JPN	10.6.92	1		Osaka	25	Sep
10.04	1.9	Abdullah Abkar	Mohammed	KSA-J	.97	1	MSR	Norwalk	15	Apr
10.04	1.0	Michael	Frater	JAM	6.10.82	8		Kingston	11	Jun
10.04	1.0	Hassan	Taftian	IRI	4.5.93	1		Madrid	23	Jun
10.04	1.5	James	Ellington	GBR	6.9.85	2s1	EC	Amsterdam	7	Jul
10.04	1.5	Reece	Prescod	GBR	29.2.96	1h1		Bedford	30	Jul
10.05	1.6	Markesh	Woodson	USA	6.9.93	3s3	NCAA	Eugene	8	Jun
10.05	1.1	Barakat	Al-Harthi	OMA	15.6.88	1		Stara Zagora	9	Jun
10.05	2.0	Justin	Walker	USA	30.11.90	3h1		Montverde, FL	11	Jun
[50]										
10.05	0.3	Julian	Forte	JAM	1.7.93	2h2	DL	London (OS)	22	Jul
10.06	0.0	Kendal	Williams	USA	23.9.95	2		Athens, GA	30	Apr
10.06	1.7	Jeff	Demps	USA	8.1.90	1h2		Clermont	30	Apr
10.06	1.0	Bruno	Hortelano	ESP	18.9.91	2		Madrid	23	Jun
10.06	2.0	Quentin	Butler	USA	18.9.92	1		Eugene	29	Jul
10.07	1.6	Warren	Weir	JAM	31.10.89	1rB		Kingston	16	Apr
10.07	1.9	Chris	Belcher	USA	29.1.94	1		Greensboro, NC	7	May
10.07	1.0	Andrew	Fisher	JAM/BRN	15.12.91	4rA		Kingston	7	May
10.07	1.6	Kenzo	Cotton	USA	13.5.96	4s3	NCAA	Eugene	8	Jun
10.07	2.0	Keston	Bledman	TTO	8.3.88	1rB		Montverde, FL	11	Jun
(60)										
10.07	1.6	Jarrion	Lawson	USA	6.5.94	7	NC/OT	Eugene	3	Jul
10.07	1.5	Ramil	Guliyev	TUR	29.5.90	3s1	EC	Amsterdam	7	Jul
10.07	0.0	Christophe	Lemaitre	FRA	11.6.90	3s3	OG	Rio de Janeiro	14	Aug
10.08	1.8	Gerald	Phiri	ZAM	6.10.88	4		Montverde, FL	11	Jun
10.08	1.8	Desmond	Lawrence	USA	19.12.91	5		Montverde, FL	11	Jun
10.08	0.4	Everton	Clarke	JAM	24.12.92	6s2	NC	Kingston	1	Jul
10.08	1.7	Sean	McLean	USA	23.3.92	4s1	NC/OT	Eugene	3	Jul
10.08	1.7	Harry	Aikines-Aryeetey	GBR	29.8.88	2		Loughborough	16	Jul
10.08	-0.1		Xie Zhenye	CHN	17.8.93	1h3	OG	Rio de Janeiro	13	Aug
10.08	0.0		Su Bingtian	CHN	29.8.89	4s3	OG	Rio de Janeiro	14	Aug
(70)										
10.09	1.0	Nethaneel	Mitchell-Blake	GBR	2.4.94	1		Austin	16	Apr
10.09	0.7	BeeJay	Lee	USA	5.3.93	1		Phoenix, AZ	21	May
10.09	1.6	Ronnie	Baker	USA	15.10.93	5s3	NCAA	Eugene	8	Jun
10.09	1.6	Daniel	Bailey	ANT	9.9.86	2rB		Kingston	11	Jun
10.10	1.4	Rasheed	Dwyer	JAM	29.1.89	2rA		Kingston	16	Apr
10.10	1.4	Zharnel	Hughes	GBR	13.7.95	3rA		Kingston	16	Apr
10.10	0.7	Aska	Cambridge	JPN	31.5.93	1h8		Kumagaya	21	May
10.10A	0.9	Sergiy	Smelyk	UKR	19.4.87	2		Erzurum	12	Jun
10.10	1.5	James	Dasaolu	GBR	5.9.87	3	Hanz	Zagreb	6	Sep
10.11	0.0	Roberto	Skyers	CUB	12.11.91	1s1	Barr	La Habana	27	May
(80)										
10.11	1.1	Henricho	Bruintjies	RSA	16.7.93	2	Odlozil	Praha	6	Jun
10.11	2.0	Adrian	Griffith	BAH	11.11.84	2rB		Montverde, FL	11	Jun
10.11	1.7	Vitor Hugo	dos Santos	BRA	1.2.96	1s1	NC	São Bernardo do Campo	30	Jun
10.11	0.4	Adam	Gemili	GBR	6.10.93	5	WK	Zürich	1	Sep
10.12	1.2	Emre Zafer	Barnes	TUR	7.11.88	1		San Antonio	26	Mar
10.12	0.0	Dentarius	Locke	USA	12.12.89	3		Athens, GA	30	Apr
10.12	1.1	Mosito	Lehata	LES	8.4.89	3	Odlozil	Praha	6	Jun
10.12	1.6	Chadic	Hinds	JAM	11.8.92	3rB		Kingston	11	Jun
10.12	1.5	Kemar	Hyman	CAY	11.10.89	1h2		Madrid	23	Jun
10.12	1.9	Stuart	Dutamby	FRA	24.4.94	2	NC	Angers	25	Jun
(90)										
10.12	0.0	Seye	Ogunlewe	NGR	30.8.91	1	NC/	Sapele	8	Jul
10.13	1.0	Oshane	Bailey	JAM	9.8.89	7rA		Kingston	7	May
10.13	1.4	Dedric	Dukes	USA	2.4.92	1rC		Clermont	14	May
10.13	1.6	Jurgen	Themen	SUR	26.10.85	1	NCAA-2	Bradenton, FL	28	May
10.13	1.8	Trentavis	Friday	USA	5.6.95	6		Montverde, FL	11	Jun
10.13	0.8	Calesio	Newman	USA	20.8.86	1h2		Chula Vista	18	Jun
10.13	1.5	Solomon	Bockarie	NED	18.5.87	4s1	EC	Amsterdam	7	Jul
10.14	1.1	Emmanuel	Matadi	LBR	15.4.91	1		Redlands, CA	18	Mar
10.14	1.2	Gabriel	Mvumuvre	ZIM	23.4.88	1		Baton Rouge	9	Apr
10.14	-0.9	Dexter	Lee	JAM	18.1.91	4s1	NC	Kingston	1	Jul
[100]										
10.14	1.7	Remontay	McClain	USA	21.9.92	6s1	NC/OT	Eugene	3	Jul

100 METRES

Mark	Wind	Name		Nat	Born	Pos	Meet	Venue	Date
10.15	0.8	Joshua	Clarke	AUS	19.5.95	6		Feb	
10.15	0.7	Elijah	Hall-Thompson	USA	22.8.94	30		Apr	
10.15	1.1	Yancarlos	Martinez	DOM	8.7.92	30		Apr	
10.15	1.1	Danny	Talbot	GBR	1.5.91	30		Apr	
10.15	0.3	Diondre	Batson	USA	13.7.92	14		May	
10.15	-1.4	LeShon	Collins	USA	11.12.93	15		May	
10.15	1.3	Egweru	Ogho-Oghene	NGR	26.11.88	21		May	
10.15	1.1	Damian	Warner	CAN	4.11.89	28		May	
10.15	1.9	Joe	Morris	USA	4.10.89	29		May	
10.15	0.8	Carlin	Isles	USA	21.11.89	18		Jun	
10.15	0.3	Mobolade	Ajomale	CAN	31.8.95	9		Jul	
10.15	1.8	Aleixo Platini	Menga	GER	29.9.87	29		Jul	
10.15	2.0	Andrew	Robertson	GBR	17.12.90	30		Jul	
10.16	1.4	Nigel	Ellis	JAM-J	8.8.97	26		Mar	
10.16	1.9	Jahvid	Best	USA/LCA	30.1.89	2		Apr	
10.16	1.9	Cameron	Burrell	USA	11.9.94	6		May	
10.16A		Karabo	Mothibi	BOT	15.10.96	7		May	
10.16	1.4	Jamial	Rolle	BAH	16.4.80	14		May	
10.16	1.9	Rae	Edwards	NGR	7.5.81	12		Jun	
10.16	1.8	Noah	Lyles	USA-J	18.7.97	2		Jul	
10.16	1.5	Lucas	Jakubczyk	GER	28.4.85	7		Jul	
10.16	2.0	Akeem	Haynes	CAN	3.11.92	9		Jul	
10.17	1.7	Lamar	Hargrove	USA	21.4.94	16		Apr	
10.17	1.7	Kirk	Wilson	USA	27.5.91	16		Apr	
10.17	1.6	Burkheart	Ellis	BAR	18.9.92	28		May	
10.17	1.4	D'Angelo	Cherry	USA	1.8.90	29		May	
10.17	1.3	Tatenda	Tsumba	ZIM	12.11.91	26		Jun	
10.18	0.0	Antoine	Adams	SKN	31.8.88	2		Apr	
10.18	2.0	Wallace	Spearmon	USA	24.12.84	23		Apr	
10.18	0.7	Alonso	Edward	PAN	8.12.89	30		Apr	
10.18A	0.8	Emeilo	Ferguson	JAM	16.4.93	19		May	
10.18A	0.8	Xavier	Atkins	USA	24.6.96	19		May	
10.18	1.2	Sean	Safo-Antwi	GHA	31.10.90	22		May	
10.18	0.8	Denis	Dimitrov	BUL	10.2.94	29		May	
10.18	0.8	Tosin	Ogunode	QAT	2.3.94	11		Jun	
10.18	1.1	Khairul Hafiz	Jantan	MAS-J	22.7.98	27		Jul	
10.19	2.0	Marqueze	Washington	USA	29.9.93	23		Apr	
10.19	1.9	Darrell	Wesh	HAI	21.1.92	30		Apr	
10.19	1.7	Kazuma	Oseto	JPN	5.8.94	11		Jun	
10.19	1.5	Carl	Horsley	USA	17.6.92	18		Jun	
10.19	1.7	Emmanuel	Callender	TTO	10.5.84	25		Jun	
10.19	0.2	Ojie	Edoburun	GBR	2.6.96	25		Jun	
10.19	0.9	Filippo	Tortu	ITA-J	15.6.98	7		Jul	
10.20A	0.1	Brian	Kasinda	ZAM-J	31.12.97	20		Feb	
10.20	1.6	Jermaine	Hamilton	JAM	22.10.84	16		Apr	
10.20	1.8	Malcolm	White	USA	16.9.95	7		May	
10.20	1.8	Arthur	Delaney	USA	23.6.93	26		May	
10.20	1.2	Banuve	Tabakaucoro	FIJ	4.9.92	8		Jul	
10.20	0.7	Tlotliso Gift	Leotlela	RSA-J	12.5.98	20		Jul	
10.21	0.2	Kavean	Smith	JAM	12.5.91	1		Apr	
10.21	1.4	Jason	Rogers	SKN	31.8.91	16		Apr	
10.21	1.4	Keenan	Brock	USA	1.6.92	23		Apr	

Mark	Wind	Name		Nat	Born	Pos	Meet	Venue	Date
10.21A	1.1	Emile	Erasmus	RSA	3.4.92	29		Apr	
10.21A	2.0	Lebokeng	Sesele	RSA	10.12.90	6		May	
10.21A	0.8	Keitavious	Walter	USA	16.4.96	19		May	
10.21	1.5	Cravon	Gillespie	USA	31.7.96	21		May	
10.21	0.7	Jeremy	Dodson	SAM	30.8.87	21		May	
10.21	1.8	Remigiusz	Olszewski	POL	20.9.92	5		Jun	
10.21	2.0	Phil	DeRosier	USA	11.4.84	11		Jun	
10.21	0.0	Gavin	Smellie	CAN	26.6.86	18		Jun	
10.21	1.7	Ricardo Mário	de Souza	BRA	21.9.94	19		Jun	
10.21	1.9	Mickaël-Meba	Zézé	FRA	19.5.94	25		Jun	
10.21	1.6	Jack	Hale	AUS-J	22.5.98	25		Jun	
10.21	0.7	Adam	Harris	GUY	21.7.87	29		Jul	
10.21	-1.4	Rodrigo	do Nascimento	BRA	26.9.94	24		Sep	
10.22	1.8	Cordero	Gray	USA	9.5.89	26		Mar	
10.22	1.1	Devin	Jenkins	USA	16.2.94	9		Apr	
10.22	1.0	Abdul Hakim Sani	Brown	JPN-Y	6.3.99	14		May	
10.22	-0.6	Tevin	Hester	USA	10.1.94	26		May	
10.22	1.2	José Carlos	Herrera	MEX	5.2.86	3		Jun	
10.22	0.1	Levi	Cadogan	BAR	8.11.95	26		Jun	
10.22	1.8	Alexander	Kosenkow	GER	14.3.77	29		Jul	
10.23	0.8	Aaron	Stubbs	AUS	13.7.90	20		Feb	
10.23	0.1	Reynier	Mena	CUB	21.11.96	18		Mar	
10.23	0.4	Hensley	Paulina	NED	26.6.93	22		Apr	
10.23	1.9	Josh	Swaray	SEN	2.2.86	14		May	
10.23	1.2	Lamont Marcell	Jacobs	ITA	26.9.94	25		May	
10.23	0.7	Likoúrgos-Stéfanos	Tsákonas	GRE	8.3.90	4		Jun	
10.23A	0.2	Diego	Palomeque	COL	5.12.93	10		Jul	
10.23A	0.2	Isidro	Montoya	COL	3.11.90	10		Jul	
10.23	0.6	Theo	Etienne	GBR	3.9.96	20		Jul	
10.24	0.1	Yaniel	Carrero	CUB	17.8.95	18		Mar	
10.24	0.3	Aziz	Ouhadi	MAR	24.7.84	23		Apr	
10.24	1.0	John	Lundy	USA	15.3.92	15		May	
10.24	-0.1	Zhang	Peimeng	CHN	13.3.87	15		May	
10.24	2.0	Kenji	Fujimitsu	JPN	1.5.86	21		May	
10.24	1.4	Segun	Makinde	CAN	6.7.91	11		Jun	
10.24	1.5	Ángel David	Rodríguez	ESP	25.4.80	23		Jun	
10.24	1.8	Sven	Knipphals	GER	20.9.85	25		Jun	
10.25	0.9	Jhevaughn	Matherson	JAM-Y	27.2.99	5		Mar	
10.25	0.0	Raheem	Chambers	JAM-J	6.10.97	18		Mar	
10.25	1.5	Jaylen	Bacon	USA	5.8.96	15		May	
10.25	0.9	Adama	Jammeh	GAM	10.6.93	15		May	
10.25	-0.3	Andre	Ewers	USA	7.6.95	4		Jun	
10.25	-0.5	Kei	Takase	JPN	25.11.88	5		Jun	
10.25	1.3	Ryan	Clark	USA	14.9.96	8		Jun	
10.25	1.0	Takuya	Nagata	JPN	14.6.94	11		Jun	
10.25	1.7	Marcus	Duncan	TTO	4.12.86	25		Jun	
10.25	0.1	Mario	Burke [200]	BAR-J	18.3.97	26		Jun	
10.25	-0.2	José Carlos	Moreira	BRA	28.9.83	30		Jun	
10.25	0.0	Divine	Oduduru	NGR	7.10.96	8		Jul	
10.25	-0.1	Shuhei	Tada	JPN	24.6.96	4		Aug	
Irregular									
10.24	1.3	Michael	Pohl	GER	18.11.89	22		May	

Wind assisted

Mark	Wind	Name		Nat	Born	Pos	Meet	Venue	Date
9.88	2.6		Gatlin			1	Pre	Eugene	28 May
9.89	4.4	Henricho	Bruintjies	RSA	16.7.93	1		Gavardo	29 May
9.90	2.3		Gatlin			1		Nassau	16 Apr
9.90	2.4	Ameer	Webb	USA	19.3.91	1rA	MSR	Norwalk	16 Apr
9.92	4.4	Richard	Kilty	GBR	2.9.89	2		Gavardo	29 May
9.93	3.0	James	Dasaolu	GBR	5.9.87	1	NC	Birmingham	25 Jun
9.94	2.6	Julian	Forte	JAM	1.7.93	1		Spanish Town	12 Mar
9.95	2.7	Ronnie	Baker	USA	15.10.93	1		Fort Worth	18 Mar
9.95	3.1	Aaron	Brown	CAN	27.5.92	1		Baton Rouge	30 Apr
9.95	2.4	Ben Youssef	Meité	CIV	11.11.86	1	AfCh	Durban	23 Jun
9.96	3.0	James	Ellington	GBR	6.9.85	2	NC	Birmingham	25 Jun
9.97	4.5	Emmanuel	Matadi	LBR	15.4.91	1		Las Vegas	23 Mar
9.97	3.0	Chijindu	Ujah	GBR	5.3.94	3	NC	Birmingham	25 Jun
9.99	3.0	Tevin	Hester	USA	10.1.94	1	TexR	Austin	2 Apr
10.01	2.7	Jarrion	Lawson	USA	6.5.94	3s3	NC/OT	Eugene	3 Jul
10.01	2.7	Dentarius	Locke	USA	12.12.89	4s3	NC/OT	Eugene	3 Jul
10.02	2.3	Adrian	Griffith	BAH	11.11.84	3		Nassau	16 Apr
10.02	3.0	Ojie	Edoburun	GBR	2.6.96	4	NC	Birmingham	25 Jun
10.02	3.0	Harry	Aikines-Aryeetey	GBR	29.8.88	5	NC	Birmingham	25 Jun
10.03	5.5	Kieran	Showler-Davis	GBR	14.11.91	1A2		London (LV)	3 Aug
10.04	3.1	Cravon	Gillespie	USA	31.7.96	1		Lancaster, CA	14 May
10.04	2.6		Su Bingtian	CHN	29.8.89	7	Pre	Eugene	28 May
10.04	2.4	Mosito	Lehata	LES	8.4.89	2	AfCh	Durban	23 Jun

100 METRES

Mark	Wind	Name		Nat	Born	Pos	Meet	Venue		Date	
10.04	2.4	Remontay	McClain	USA	21.9.92	3h4	NC/OT	Eugene		2	Jul
10.04	2.7	Kendal	Williams	USA	23.9.95	5s3	NC/OT	Eugene		3	Jul
10.05	2.5	Kemar	Hyman	CAY	11.10.89	1		Athens, GA		9	Apr
10.06	4.9	Brandon	Carnes	USA	6.3.95	1		Terre Haute		15	May
10.07A	2.9	Diego	Palomeque	COL	5.12.93	1		Cali		25	Jun
10.08	2.6	Rasheed	Dwyer	JAM	29.1.89	2		Spanish Town		12	Mar
10.08	2.3	Antoine	Adams	SKN	31.8.88	4rA		Nassau		16	Apr
10.08	2.4	BeeJay	Lee	USA	5.3.93	4rA	MSR	Norwalk		16	Apr
10.08	7.5	Ralph	Quinlee	TTO	2.3.91	1		Lubbock		6	May
10.08A	3.0	Shivnarine	Smalling	JAM	28.9.96	1		Albuquerque		4	Jun
10.08	2.2	Noah	Lyles	USA-J	18.7.97	1	NC-j	Clovis		24	Jun
10.09	5.3	Damian	Warner	CAN	4.11.89	1		London, ONT		14	May
10.09	2.4	Moriba	Morain	TTO	8.10.92	1	NAIA	Gulf Shores, AL		28	May
10.09A	3.0	Jace	Comick	USA-J	10.7.98	2		Albuquerque		4	Jun
10.09	3.8	Joe	Morris	USA	4.10.89	3h1	NC/OT	Eugene		2	Jul
10.10	2.6	Ronald	Levy	JAM	30.10.92	3		Spanish Town		12	Mar
10.11	2.8	Yancarlos	Martinez	DOM	8.7.92	1		San Germán		23	Apr
10.11	3.4	Arthur	Delaney	USA	23.6.93	1		Corvallis		30	Apr
10.11	3.0	Dwain	Chambers	GBR	5.4.78	7	NC	Birmingham		25	Jun
10.12	3.5	Bruno	de Barros	BRA	7.1.87	1		Maringá		27	Feb
10.12	7.5	Ian	Kerr	BAH	1.5.96	3		Lubbock		6	May
10.14	2.1	Alex	Wilson	SUI	19.9.90	22 May		10.21	3.9 Kyran Stewart USA 1.3.91	3	Apr
10.14	2.9	Sean	Safo-Antwi	GHA	31.10.90	26 Jun		10.21	3.2 Nic Bowens USA 28.6.93	13	May
10.14	3.2	Theo	Etienne	GBR	3.9.96	20 Jul		10.21	3.4 Bismark Boateng CAN 15.3.92	14	May
10.15	3.3	Ernie	Wiggins	USA	18.6.82	1 Apr		10.21	2.1 Kevin Snead USA .94	15	May
10.15	2.3	Shavez	Hart	BAH	6.9.92	16 Apr		10.21	5.5 Tommy Ramdhan GBR 28.11.96	3	Aug
10.15	2.4	Akeem	Haynes	CAN	3.11.92	16 Apr		10.22	2.2 Reynier Mena CUB 21.11.96	26	Feb
10.15	2.2	Keitavious	Walter	USA	16.4.96	23 Apr		10.22	3.5 Jorge Henrique Vides BRA 24.11.92	27	Feb
10.15	4.0	Darrell	Wesh	HAI	21.1.92	4 May		10.22	3.5 Brijesh "BJ" Lawrence SKN 27.12.89	9	Apr
10.15	4.8	Micah	Larkins	USA	8.12.94	8 May		10.22	3.0 Riak Reese USA 23.11.94	23	Apr
10.15	2.6	Thando	Roto	RSA	26.9.95	4 Jun		10.22	2.6 Daveon Collins USA 3.10.92	6	May
10.16	4.6	Nick	Taylor	USA	8.4.93	13 May		10.22	2.6 Kameron Cowan USA 17.1.91	6	May
10.17	3.5	Karabo	Mothibi	BOT	15.10.96	9 Jul		10.22	2.2 Blake Bartlett BAH 3.2.93	14	May
10.17	2.5	Segun	Makinde	CAN	6.7.91	9 Jul		10.22	2.3 Josh Swaray SEN 2.2.86	20	Jul
10.18	6.8	Jeffrey	Josephs	JAM	15.4.91	6 May		10.23	3.5 Roland Lestrod SKN 5.9.92	31	Jan
10.18	3.0	Eli	Minor	USA	.96	8 May		10.23	2.2 Yanlel Carrero CUB 17.8.95	26	Feb
10.18A	3.8	Seyi	Smith	CAN	21.2.87	5 Jun		10.23	2.8 Yoandry Andujar DOM 5.7.90	23	Apr
10.18A	2.9	Eric	de Jesus	BRA	29.1.90	25 Jun		10.23	2.2 Shermund Allsop TTO 21.3.91	23	Apr
10.18	6.3	Stanly	del Carmen	DOM	20.9.95	2 Jul		10.23	2.2 Jermey Hicks USA 1.8.94	23	Apr
10.18	3.7	Salum	Kashafali	NOR	25.11.93	12 Aug		10.23	2.3 Aaron Ernest USA 8.11.93	23	Apr
10.19	7.5	Andrew	Hudson	USA	14.12.96	6 May		10.23	2.1 Blake Smith USA 28.5.93	14	May
10.19	4.8	Aaron	Piper	USA	.95	8 May		10.23	2.3 Chris Royster USA 26.1.92	15	May
10.19	4.8	Amir	James	USA	7.12.95	8 May		10.23	2.4 Rechmial Miller GBR-J 27.6.98	25	Jun
10.19	3.3	Bentrell	McGee	USA	15.12.93	8 May		10.23	2.4 Divine Oduduru NGR 7.10.96	7	Jul
10.19	3.1	James	Alaka	GBR	8.9.89	5 Jun		10.23	2.5 Justyn Warner CAN 28.6.87	9	Jul
10.19	3.0	Tom	Kling-Baptiste	SWE	29.8.90	19 Jun		10.24	2.1 Jeffrey Vanan SUR 21.12.92	16	Apr
10.19A	2.9	Isidro	Montoya	COL	3.11.90	25 Jun		10.24	2.1 Reggie Thomas USA .96	6	May
10.20	2.3	Levi	Cadogan	BAR	8.11.95	16 Apr		10.24	3.1 Greg Cackett GBR 14.11.89	5	Jun
10.20	2.1	Parker	Bluth	USA	2.2.92	14 May		10.24	2.1 Kristoffer Hari DEN-J 23.12.97	11	Jun
10.20	3.4	Moulaye	Sonko	SEN	1.3.88	25 May		10.24	2.9 Patrick Chinedu NGR 26.4.84	23	Jun
10.20	5.4	David	Lima	POR	6.9.90	25 Jun		10.24	3.6 Hikaru Kurosawa JPN .94	30	Jul
10.20	5.5	Reuben	Arthur	GBR	12.10.96	3 Aug		10.24	5.9 Antonio Infantino GBR/ITA 22.3.91	3	Aug
10.21A	2.4	Samkelo	Sabela	RSA	4.4.95	1 Apr		10.24	2.5 Kotaro Iwasaki JPN .96	17	Sep
								10.24?w?	Winston George GUY 19.5.87	4	Nov
Low altitude bests											
10.03	0.2	Harvey		4s1 OG	Rio de Janeiro 14 Aug			10.23	0.1 Erasmus 1s2 NC Stellenbosch	15	Apr
Hand timing											
9.9	0.9	Noah	Lyles	USA-J	18.7.97	1		Fairfax		27	May
10.0		Divine	Oduduru	NGR	7.10.96	4 May		10.0	Antoine Adams SKN 31.8.88	18	Jun
								10.0	Jason Rogers SKN 31.8.91	18	Jun
Hand timing - Wind assisted											
9.9A	4.8	Karabo	Mothibi	BOT	15.10.96	1		Windhoek		28	May

JUNIORS

Mark	Wind	Name		Nat	Born	Pos	Meet	Venue		Date	
10.04	1.9	Abdullah Abkar	Mohammed	KSA	.97	1	MSR	Norwalk		15	Apr
10.16	1.4	Nigel	Ellis	JAM	8.8.97	1	Carifta	St. Georges		26	Mar
		10.18	0.0 1	N.Sch Kingston	18 Mar	10.20	1.9 1		Montego Bay	4	Feb
10.16	1.8	Noah	Lyles	USA	18.7.97	4h2	NC/OT	Eugene		2	Jul
		10.17	1.2 1	Arcadia	9 Apr	10.17	0.2 1	WJ	Bydgoszcz	20	Jul
10.18	1.1	Khairul Hafiz	Jantan	MAS	22.7.98	1		Kuching		27	Jul
10.19	0.6	Filippo	Tortu	ITA	15.6.98	3s2	EC	Amsterdam		7	Jul
10.20A	0.1	Brian	Kasinda	ZAM	31.12.97	1	NC	Lusaka		20	Feb
10.20	0.7	Tlotliso Gift	Leotlela	RSA	12.5.98	1s3	WJ	Bydgoszcz		20	Jul
(11 performances by 7 men to 10.20)											
10.21	1.6	Jack	Hale	AUS	22.5.98	1h2		Mannheim		25	Jun
10.22	1.0	Abdul Hakim	Sani Brown	JPN-Y	6.3.99	2	DL	Shanghai		14	May

100 – 200 METRES

Mark	Wind	Name		Nat	Born	Pos	Meet	Venue	Date	
10.25	0.9	Jhevaughn	Matherson (10)	JAM-Y	27.2.99	1		Kingston	5	Mar
10.25	0.0	Raheem	Chambers	JAM	6.10.97	2		Kingston	18	Mar
10.25	0.1	Mario	Burke	BAR	18.3.97	3	NC	Waterford	26	Jun
10.26	0.1	Paulo André	de Oliveira	BRA	20.8.98	2h5	NC	São Bernardo do Campo	30	Jun
10.27	1.2	Trae	Williams	AUS	5.5.97	1		Perth	12	Mar
10.27	-1.2	Michael	Norman	USA	3.12.97	1-HSMSR		Norwalk	16	Apr
10.27	1.0	Ippei	Takeda	JPN-	13.3.97	1		Mito	5	May
10.28A	0.7	Clarence	Munyai	RSA	20.2.98	2		Sasolburg	8	Apr
10.28	1.8	Sydney	Siame	ZAM	7.10.97	3h1		Regensburg	5	Jun
10.30	1.5	Hakim	Montgomery	USA	23.6.97	2		Lafayette	15	May
10.31	1.6	Manuel	Eitel (20)	GER	28.1.97	2h2		Mannheim	25	Jun
10.31	1.4	Daisuke	Miyamoto	JPN-Y	17.4.99	1s3		Kitakami	7	Oct
Wind assisted										
10.08	2.2	Noah	Lyles	USA	18.7.97	1	NC-j	Clovis	24	Jun
10.09A	3.0	Jace	Comick	USA	10.7.98	2		Albuquerque	4	Jun
10.23	2.4	Rechmial	Miller	GBR	27.6.98	1h4		Mannheim	25	Jun
10.24	2.1	Kristoffer	Hari	DEN	23.12.97	1		Hvidovre	11	Jun
10.26	3.2	Derick	Slva	BRA	23.4.98	1s1		São Bernardo do Campo	15	Apr
10.26	w	Brandon	Taylor	USA	24.6.98	1		Lufkin	22	Apr
10.26	2.4	Anthony	Schwartz	USA-Y	5.9.00	1		Fort Lauderdale	28	Apr
10.27	5.2	Tarrick	Brock	USA	3.2.98	1h		Costa Mesa	14	May
10.27	2.6	Rohan	Browning	AUS	31.12.97	1		Canberra	19	Nov
10.28	2.5	Nick	Gray	USA	2.6.97	2h2	NC-j	Clovis	24	Jun

150 METRES: 14.95 Miguel Francis ANT 28.2.95 1 Somerville 18 Jun

200 METRES

Mark	Wind	Name		Nat	Born	Pos	Meet	Venue	Date	
19.74	1.4	LaShawn	Merritt	USA	27.6.86	1s3	NC/OT	Eugene	8	Jul
19.75	1.6	Justin	Gatlin	USA	10.2.82	1	NC/OT	Eugene	9	Jul
19.78	0.9		Merritt			1		Nassau	16	Apr
19.78	-0.3	Usain	Bolt	JAM	21.8.86	1s2	OG	Rio de Janeiro	17	Aug
19.78	-0.5		Bolt			1	OG	Rio de Janeiro	18	Aug
19.79	1.6		Merritt			2	NC/OT	Eugene	9	Jul
19.80	-0.3	Andre	De Grasse	CAN	10.11.94	2s2	OG	Rio de Janeiro	17	Aug
19.81	0.4	Churandy	Martina	NED	3.7.84	1	Athl	Lausanne	25	Aug
19.85	1.9	Ameer	Webb	USA	19.3.91	1	DL	Doha	6	May
19.88	1.2	Miguel	Francis	ANT	28.2.95	1		Kingston	11	Jun
19.89	-0.3		Bolt			1	DL	London	22	Jul
19.91	1.0		Webb			1	MSR	Norwalk	16	Apr
19.92	0.4	Alonso	Edward	PAN	8.12.89	2	Athl	Lausanne	25	Aug
19.94	-0.4		Merritt			1s1	OG	Rio de Janeiro	17	Aug
19.95	0.4	Nethaneel	Mitchell-Blake	GBR	2.4.94	1	SEC	Tuscaloosa	14	May
19.96	1.1	Brendon	Rodney (10)	CAN	9.4.92	1	NC	Edmonton	10	Jul
19.97	1.4		Webb			2s3	NC/OT	Eugene	8	Jul
19.97	0.8	Julian	Forte	JAM	1.7.93	1	VD	Bruxelles	9	Sep
19.97	0.8	Adam	Gemili	GBR	6.10.93	2	VD	Bruxelles	9	Sep
19.98	0.8		Martina			3	VD	Bruxelles	9	Sep
20.00	1.1	Aaron	Brown	CAN	27.5.92	1		Baton Rouge	30	Apr
20.00	1.6		Webb			3	NC/OT	Eugene	9	Jul
20.01	-0.4	Christophe	Lemaitre	FRA	11.6.90	2s1	OG	Rio de Janeiro	17	Aug
20.02	1.8	Wayde	van Niekerk	RSA	15.7.92	1	AfCh	Durban	26	Jun
20.02	-0.5		De Grasse			2	OG	Rio de Janeiro	18	Aug
20.03	1.2		van Niekerk			1s1	AfCh	Durban	25	Jun
20.04	0.6		Webb			1	GGala	Roma	2	Jun
20.04	-0.3		Edward			2	DL	London (OS)	22	Jul
20.06	1.9		Edward			2	DL	Doha	6	May
20.07	0.2	Nickel	Ashmeade	JAM	7.4.90	1rA		Clermont	30	Apr
20.07	-0.3		Gemili			3	DL	London (OS)	22	Jul
20.07	-0.2		Edward			1s3	OG	Rio de Janeiro	17	Aug
		[32/16]								
20.09	1.6	Noah	Lyles	USA-J	18.7.97	4	NC/OT	Eugene	9	Jul
20.09	-0.3	Ramil	Guliyev	TUR	29.5.90	4s2	OG	Rio de Janeiro	17	Aug
20.10	1.9	Femi Seun	Ogunode	QAT	15.5.91	3	DL	Doha	6	May
20.11	1.8	Shota	Iizuka (20)	JPN	25.6.91	1	NC	Nagoya	26	Jun
20.12	1.5	Jamiel	Trimble	USA	25.6.95	1h1	NCAA-W	Lawrence	28	May
20.12	-0.2	Bruno	Hortelano	ESP	18.9.91	1h2	OG	Rio de Janeiro	16	Aug
20.13	0.9	Tevin	Hester	USA	10.1.94	1	ACC	Tallahassee	15	May
20.13	-0.2	Yohan	Blake	JAM	26.12.89	2h2	OG	Rio de Janeiro	16	Aug
20.14	1.9	Walter	Dix	USA	31.1.86	4	DL	Doha	6	May

200 METRES

Mark	Wind	Name		Nat	Born	Pos	Meet	Venue	Date	
20.14	1.6	Michael	Norman	USA-J	3.12.97	5	NC/OT	Eugene	9	Jul
20.15	0.4	Renard	Howell	USA/JAM	3.3.95	2	SEC	Tuscaloosa	14	May
20.16	2.0	Ahmed	Ali	SUD	15.11.93	1	FlaR	Gainesville	1	Apr
20.16	1.4	Tyson	Gay	USA	9.8.82	3s3	NC/OT	Eugene	8	Jul
20.16	0.7	Akani	Simbine	RSA	21.9.93	1	Gyulai	Székesfehérvár	18	Jul
		(30)								
20.17	0.9	José Carlos	Herrera	MEX	2.5.86	1rB	MSR	Norwalk	16	Apr
20.17	1.5	Jarrion	Lawson	USA	6.5.94	2h1	NCAA-W	Lawrence	28	May
20.19	0.3	Yancarlos	Martinez	DOM	8.7.92	1	IbAm	Rio de Janeiro	16	May
20.19	0.3	Mohamed	Yacoub Salem	BRN	1.3.96	1h3	OG	Rio de Janeiro	16	Aug
20.20	1.5	Cravon	Gillespie	USA	31.7.96	1		Lancaster	14	May
20.20	0.2	Nery	Brenes	CRC	25.9.85	1h7	OG	Rio de Janeiro	16	Aug
20.21A	1.4	Baboloki	Thebe	BOT-J	18.3.97	1	NC-j	Gaborone	22	May
20.21	0.4	Likoúrgos-Stéfanos	Tsákonas	GRE	8.3.90	4	Athl	Lausanne	25	Aug
20.23	1.0	BeeJay	Lee	USA	5.3.93	2rA	MSR	Norwalk	16	Apr
20.24	-1.5	Sean	McLean	USA	23.3.92	3	DL	Birmingham	5	Jun
		(40)								
20.24	0.7	Isiah	Young	USA	5.1.90	2	Gyulai	Székesfehérvár	18	Jul
20.25	-0.4	Danny	Talbot	GBR	1.5.91	3s1	OG	Rio de Janeiro	17	Aug
20.26	-0.2	Christian	Coleman	USA	6.3.96	2	NCAA	Eugene	10	Jun
20.26	1.6	Justin	Walker	USA	30.11.90	2		Montverde, FL	11	Jun
20.26	-0.3	Karol	Zalewski	POL	7.8.93	1	Sidlo	Sopot	28	Jul
20.27	0.0	Aleixo Platini	Menga	GER	29.9.87	1		Clermont	14	May
20.27	1.0	Rondell	Sorrillo	TTO	21.1.86	3h10	OG	Rio de Janeiro	16	Aug
20.29A	1.0	Correion	Mosby	USA	31.1.96	1	JUCO	Levelland, TX	19	May
20.30	-0.3	Trayvon	Bromell	USA	10.7.95	1		Waco	9	Apr
20.31	1.2	James	Ellington	GBR	6.9.85	2rB		Clermont	30	Apr
		[50]								
20.31	1.2	Eseosa	Desalu	ITA	19.2.94	1	NC	Rieti	26	Jun
20.31	1.8	Kei	Takase	JPN	25.11.88	2	NC	Nagoya	26	Jun
20.31	0.4	Kendal	Williams	USA	23.9.95	2s2	NC/OT	Eugene	8	Jul
20.31	0.3	Wallace	Spearmon	USA	24.12.84	1		Houston	23	Jul
20.32	0.9	Aldemir	Gomes da Silva	BRA	8.6.92	2rB	MSR	Norwalk	16	Apr
20.32	1.2	Warren	Weir	JAM	31.10.89	3		Kingston	11	Jun
20.33	1.8	Shota	Hara	JPN	18.7.92	3	NC	Nagoya	26	Jun
20.34	0.4	Arman	Hall	USA	12.2.94	3	SEC	Tuscaloosa	14	May
20.34	0.6	Divine	Oduduru	NGR	7.10.96	2h9	OG	Rio de Janeiro	16	Aug
20.35	0.8	Kenzo	Cotton	USA	13.5.96	1h6	NCAA-W	Lawrence	28	May
		(60)								
20.36A	1.5	Clarence	Munyai	RSA-J	20.2.98	1	NC-j	Germiston	2	Apr
20.36	1.2	Burkheart	Ellis	BAR	18.9.92	1		Charlotte, NC	23	Apr
20.37	1.0	Curtis	Mitchell	USA	11.3.89	3rA	MSR	Norwalk	16	Apr
20.37A	1.0	Elijah	Hall-Thompson	USA	22.8.94	2	JUCO	Levelland, TX	19	May
20.37	0.4	Solomon	Bockarie	NED	18.5.87	1		Velenje	31	Aug
20.38A	1.3	Mike Mokamba	Nyangau	KEN	28.8.94	1	NC	Nairobi	28	May
20.38	1.3	Antoine	Adams	SKN	31.8.88	1		Road Town	3	Jul
20.38	0.4	Reece	Prescod	GBR	29.2.96	5	Athl	Lausanne	25	Aug
20.39	0.5	Devin	Jenkins	USA	16.2.94	2		Tempe	9	Apr
20.39	1.2	Chris	Belcher	USA	29.1.94	1		Greensboro, NC	7	May
		[70]								
20.39	0.4	Julian	Reus	GER	29.4.88	3h8	OG	Rio de Janeiro	16	Aug
20.40	1.9	Nigel	Ellis	JAM-J	8.8.97	1		Montego Bay	4	Feb
20.40	0.5	Sergiy	Smelyk	UKR	19.4.87	1	NC	Lutsk	19	Jun
20.40	0.3	Jorge Henrique	Vides	BRA	24.11.92	1	NC	São Bernardo do Campo	3	Jul
20.40	0.9	Robin	Erewa	GER	24.6.91	1		Mannheim	29	Jul
20.41	0.0	Dedric	Dukes	USA	2.4.92	1		Clermont	14	May
20.41	0.8	Reynier	Mena	CUB	21.11.96	1	NACAC	San Salvador	17	Jul
20.42A	1.0	Isaac	Makwala	BOT	29.9.86	1		Potchefstroom	15	Mar
20.42	1.0	Roberto	Skyers	CUB	12.11.91	1	NC	La Habana	20	Mar
20.42	0.6	Oshane	Bailey	JAM	9.8.89	2		Kingston	16	Apr
		[80]								
20.42	0.9	Michael	Rodgers	USA	24.4.85	3		Nassau	16	Apr
20.42A	0.2	Bernardo	Baloyes	COL	6.1.94	1		Medellín	30	Apr
20.42	0.0	Ramon	Gittens	BAR	20.7.87	1	NC	Waterford	26	Jun
20.43	1.6	Gavin	Smellie	CAN	26.6.86	1rB	FlaR	Gainesville	31	Mar
20.43	0.4	Khalil	Henderson	USA	18.11.94	4	SEC	Tuscaloosa	14	May
20.43	0.1	LeShon	Collins	USA	11.12.93	1		Orlando	15	May
20.43	-0.3	Jaysuma	Saidy Ndure	NOR	1.7.84	2		Bruxelles	19	Jun
20.44	0.3	Aldrich	Bailey	USA	6.2.94	1		Austin	16	Apr
20.44	0.9	Emmanuel	Matadi	LBR	15.4.91	3rB	MSR	Norwalk	16	Apr
20.44A	0.1	Jeremy	Dodson	SAM	30.8.87	1		Longmont, CO	13	May
		[90]								

200 METRES

Mark	Wind	Name		Nat	Born	Pos	Meet	Venue	Date	
20.44	1.3	Tatenda	Tsumba	ZIM	12.11.91	1		Chula Vista	26	Jun
20.44	1.2	Davide	Manenti	ITA	16.4.89	2	NC	Rieti	26	Jun
20.45	-0.5	Alex	Hartmann	AUS	7.3.93	1		Canberra	7	Feb
20.45	0.3	Demetrius	Pinder	BAH	13.2.89	2		Austin	16	Apr
20.45	0.9	Asafa	Powell	JAM	23.11.82	1		Kingston	7	May
20.45	1.0	Nick	Gray	USA-J	2.6.97	1h2	NCAA-E	Jacksonville	27	May
20.45	1.2	Terrel	Cotton	USA	19.7.88	5		Kingston	11	Jun
20.45	1.3	Aaron	Ernest	USA	8.11.93	1rB		Montverde, FL	11	Jun
20.45	1.8	Adama	Jammeh	GAM	10.6.93	2	AfCh	Durban	26	Jun
20.45	0.0	Levi	Cadogan	BAR	8.11.95	2	NC	Waterford	26	Jun
		[100]								
20.45	1.0	Everton	Clarke	JAM	24.12.92	2h3	NC	Kingston	2	Jul
20.46	1.6	Carvin	Nkanata	KEN	6.5.91	11	Jun	20.58	0.9	James	Alaka	GBR	8.9.89	5	Jun
20.46	0.0	Trentavis	Friday	USA	5.6.95	22	Jun	20.58	1.4	Trey	Hadnot	USA	7.3.92	10	Jun
20.46	1.9	Stanly	del Carmen	DOM	20.9.95	26	Jun	20.58	0.0	Nicholas	Deshong	BAR	24.4.92	12	Jun
20.46	1.0	Rasheed	Dwyer	JAM	29.1.89	2	Jul	20.58	0.7	Jak Ali	Harvey	TUR	5.4.89	16	Aug
20.47	0.5	Calesio	Newman	USA	20.8.86	9	Apr	20.59	2.0	Ryan	Clark	USA	14.9.96	1	Apr
20.47	0.1	Mookie	Salaam	USA	5.4.90	30	Apr	20.59	1.7	Manteo	Mitchell	USA	6.7.87	29	Apr
20.47A	0.5	Tlotliso Gift	Leotlela	RSA-J	12.5.98	18	Jun	20.59A	1.0	Akeem	Sirleaf	USA/LBR-J	10.3.97	19	May
20.48	1.0	Bryshon	Nellum	USA	1.5.89	16	Apr	20.59	0.9	Mobolade	Ajomale	CAN	31.8.95	28	May
20.48	0.3	Chijindu	Ujah	GBR	5.3.94	8	May	20.60	1.7	Gábor	Pásztor ¶	HUN	25.11.82	19	Mar
20.48	1.0	Wilfried	Koffi Hua	CIV	24.8.89	16	Aug	20.60	-0.1	Harris	Edwards	USA	.95	16	Apr
20.49	0.7	Stirley	Jones	USA	13.12.84	23	Apr	20.60	-0.4	Richard	Kilty	GBR	2.9.89	22	Apr
20.49	0.3	Arthur	Delaney	USA	23.6.93	20	May	20.60	1.2	Malcolm	White	USA	16.9.95	14	May
20.49	0.1	Mickaël-Meba	Zézé	FRA	19.5.94	5	Jun	20.60	1.4	Reggie	Lewis	USA	18.8.93	28	May
20.49	-0.9	Igor	Bodrov	UKR	9.7.87	24	Jun	20.60	0.9	Roscoe	Engel	RSA	6.3.89	24	Jun
20.49	-0.1	Kenji	Fujimitsu	JPN	1.5.86	24	Jun	20.60	1.3	Mitchel	Davis	DMA	17.8.91	3	Jul
20.49	0.7	Emmanuel	Dasor	GHA	14.9.95	8	Jul	20.60	-0.1	Yoshihide	Kiryu	JPN	15.12.95	4	Sep
20.50	0.7	Bruno	de Barros	BRA	7.1.87	31	Mar	20.61	1.3	Fred	Kerley	USA	7.5.95	19	Mar
20.50A	0.0	César	Ramirez	MEX	21.11.94	11	May	20.61	0.1	Joe	Morris	USA	4.10.89	23	Apr
20.50	1.2	Matteo	Galvan	ITA	24.8.88	26	Jun	20.61	1.3	Elijah	Morrow	USA	95	12	May
20.50	0.3	Vitor Hugo	dos Santos	BRA	1.2.96	3	Jul	20.61	0.6	Kyle	Greaux	TTO	26.4.88	16	Aug
20.51A	1.4	Hendrik	Maartens	RSA	24.5.96	2	Apr	20.62	-1.3	Zharnel	Hughes	GBR	13.7.95	7	May
20.52	0.5	Tinashe Samuel	Mutanga	ZIM	27.1.93	25	Mar	20.62	0.8	Devon	Allen	USA	12.12.94	28	May
20.52A	-1.1	Parker	Bluth	USA	2.2.92	4	May	20.62	0.0	David	Lima	POR	6.9.90	4	Jun
20.52	1.5	Tubotein	Taylor	NGR	1.11.91	8	May	20.62	0.3	Julius	Morris	MNT	14.4.94	8	Jun
20.52	1.3	Adrian	Griffith	BAH	11.11.84	11	Jun	20.62	0.9	Hensley	Paulina	NED	26.6.93	24	Jun
20.53	0.3	Senoj-Jay	Givans	JAM	30.12.93	16	Apr	20.62	1.3	Joel	Redhead	GRN	3.7.86	3	Jul
20.53	-1.2	Jimmy	Vicaut	FRA	27.2.92	8	May	20.62	0.4	Aska	Cambridge	JPN	31.5.93	16	Jul
20.53	2.0	Winston	George	GUY	19.5.87	14	May	20.62	0.4	Tyrese	Cooper	USA-Y	21.3.00	2	Aug
20.53	0.0	Paul	Dedewo	NGR/USA	5.6.91	8	Jun	20.63	0.3	Teray	Smith	BAH	28.9.94	16	Apr
20.53	0.7	Michael	Mathieu	BAH	24.6.83	10	Jul	20.63A	1.7	Bruno	Rojas da Silva	BOL	27.5.93	24	Apr
20.53	1.9	Soufiane	Bouhada	ALG	8.6.90	16	Jul	20.63	1.0	Kyree	King	USA	9.7.94	27	May
20.53	1.9	Antonio	Infantino	GBR/ITA	22.3.91	20	Jul	20.63	0.8	Terrell	Smith	USA	10.10.94	28	May
20.53	-0.2	Anaso	Jobodwana	RSA	30.7.92	16	Aug	20.63	0.3	Sibusiso	Matsenjwa	SWZ	2.5.88	16	Aug
20.54	0.6	Javon	Francis	JAM	14.12.94	16	Apr	20.63A	1.5	Thando	Dlodlo	RSA-Y	22.4.99	28	Oct
20.54	1.0	Abdul Hakim	Sani Brown	JPN-Y	6.3.99	3	May	20.64	0.2	Ronnie	Baker	USA	15.10.93	22	Apr
20.54	0.0	Marqueze	Washington	USA	29.9.93	28	May	20.64	1.6	Steven	Gardiner	BAH	12.9.95	30	Apr
20.55	0.9	Daveon	Collins	USA	3.10.92	16	Apr	20.64	-1.0	Cejhae	Greene	ANT	6.10.95	14	May
20.55	0.1	Diondre	Batson	USA	13.7.92	23	Apr	20.64	0.0	Alexander	Gladitz	GER	19.12.94	21	May
20.55	0.0	Robert	Hering	GER	14.6.90	14	May	20.64	1.5	Roger	Gurski	GER-J	11.7.97	21	Jul
20.55	0.6	Kazuma	Oseto	JPN	5.8.94	22	May	20.64	0.6	Jonathan	Borlée	BEL	22.2.88	16	Aug
20.55	1.2	Jason	Young	JAM	21.3.91	11	Jun	20.65A	-0.2	Pavel	Maslák	CZE	21.2.91	26	Jan
20.55A	0.0	Sydney	Siame	ZAM-J	7.10.97	18	Jun	20.65	1.4	Sam	Watts	GBR	14.2.92	28	May
20.56	0.2	Cameron	Williams	USA	11.9.95	7	May	20.65	0.1	Yuichi	Kobayashi	JPN	25.8.89	29	May
20.56A	0.3	Shamon	Ehiemua	USA-J	30.9.98	4	Jun	20.65	1.1		Park Bong-ko	KOR	8.5.91	3	Jun
20.57	0.8	James	Harrington	USA	3.7.93	16	Apr	20.65	1.5	Samuel	Garcia	ESP	4.12.91	8	Jun
20.57	0.8	Dentarius	Locke	USA	12.12.89	16	Apr	20.65	1.8	Takanori	Kawase	JPN	9.9.94	26	Jun
20.57	1.4	Keitavious	Walter	USA	16.4.96	30	Apr	20.65	0.7	Mosito	Lehata	LES	8.4.89	16	Aug
20.57	-0.6	Bentrell	McGee	USA	15.7.93	8	May			[201]	224 to 20.69				
20.57	1.5	Alex	Wilson	SUI	19.9.90	22	May	**Indoors**							
20.57	0.3	Shavez	Hart	BAH	6.9.92	23	Jul	20.60A		Ronnie	Baker	USA	15.10.93	30	Jan
20.58	0.0	Brijesh "BJ"	Lawrence	SKN	27.12.89	23	Apr	20.60		Sam	Watts	GBR	14.2.92	13	Feb
20.58A	1.7	Andy	Martínez	PER	28.9.93	24	Apr	20.61		David	Winters	USA	19.2.94	26	Feb
20.58A	1.0	Emeilo	Ferguson	JAM	16.4.93	19	May	20.63		Bryce	Robinson	USA	13.11.93	5	Feb

Uncertified track

19.67	0.4	Miguel	Francis	ANT	28.2.95	1	NC	St.John's	10	Jul

Wind assisted

19.96	3.6		Mitchell-Blake			1q2	NCAA-E	Jacksonville	28	May
19.97	4.3		Rodney			1q1	NCAA-E	Jacksonville	28	May
20.04	3.3	Noah	Lyles	USA-J	18.7.97	1h1	NC/OT	Eugene	7	Jul
20.06	2.8	Michael	Norman	USA-J	3.12.97	1h4	NC/OT	Eugene	7	Jul
20.11	3.3	Kendal	Williams	USA	23.9.95	2h1	NC/OT	Eugene	7	Jul
20.14	3.3	Dedric	Dukes	USA	2.4.92	3h1	NC/OT	Eugene	7	Jul
20.20	4.6	Jeremy	Dodson	SAM	30.8.87	1		Paradise Valley, Phoenix	21	May
20.20	2.9	Khalil	Henderson	USA	18.11.94	1q3	NCAA-E	Jacksonville	28	May

200 – 300 METRES

Mark	Wind	Name		Nat	Born	Pos	Meet	Venue	Date	
20.23	3.1	Arthur	Delaney	USA	23.6.93	1		Eugene	6	May
20.23	2.3	Julian	Reus	GER	29.4.88	1		Zeulenroda	24	Jun
20.24	2.1	Rondell	Sorrillo	TTO	21.1.86	1	NC	Port of Spain	26	Jun
20.26	4.3	Stanly	del Carmen	DOM	20.9.95	1		Mouscron	2	Jul
20.29	2.7	Abdullah Abkar	Mohammed	KSA-J	.97	1	MSR	Norwalk	15	Apr
20.31	3.3	Calesio	Newman	USA	20.8.86	2		Norwalk	4	Jun
20.33A	2.7	Clarence	Munyai	RSA-J	20.2.98	1s1	NC-j	Germiston	2	Apr
20.33	3.4	Arman	Hall	USA	12.2.94	1h4	SEC	Tuscaloosa	12	May
20.33	3.3	Trentavis	Friday	USA	5.6.95	5h1	NC/OT	Eugene	7	Jul
20.34	3.3	John	Lundy	USA	15.3.92	3		Norwalk	4	Jun
20.35	3.8	Wilfried	Koffi Hua	CIV	24.9.89	2	DL	Rabat	22	May
20.37	4.3	Kyree	King	USA	9.7.94	2q1	NCAA-E	Jacksonville	28	May
20.38	3.1	Bruno	de Barros	BRA	7.1.87	1		Azusa	15	Apr
20.39	3.1	Joe	Morris	USA	4.10.89	2		Eugene	6	May
20.39	3.3	Lalonde	Gordon	TTO	25.11.88	4		Norwalk	4	Jun
20.40	4.6	Tremaine	Harris	CAN	10.2.92	2		Paradise Valley, Arizona	21	May
20.42	3.3	Winston	George	GUY	19.5.87	5		Norwalk	4	Jun
20.44	2.8	Terrell	Smith	USA	10.10.94	23 Apr	20.53	2.3 Steven Gardiner	BAH	12.9.95 14 May
20.44	2.6	Julius	Morris	MNT	14.4.94	28 May	20.54	2.8 Brandon Carnes	USA	-.3.95 15 May
20.45	3.9	Mookie	Salaam	USA	5.4.90	7 May	20.54	2.1 Richard Thompson	TTO	7.6.85 26 Jun
20.45	3.3	Daveon	Collins	USA	3.10.92	4 Jun	20.55	2.8 Remontay McClain	USA	21.9.92 7 Jul
20.46	2.2	Tyrese	Cooper	USA-Y	21.3.00	16 Apr	20.56	LaMarion Arnold	USA	.96 9 Apr
20.47	3.5	Ben Youssef Meité		CIV	11.11.86	25 May	20.57	2.6 Ncincihli Titi	RSA	15.12.93 28 May
20.48	2.9	Blake	Bartlett	BAH	3.2.93	14 May	20.59	2.4 Vernon Norwood	USA	10.4.92 16 Apr
20.49	2.8	Marquese	Washington	USA	29.9.93	23 Apr	20.59	2.6 Mustaqeem Williams	USA	24.8.95 28 May
20.49	3.9	Diondre	Batson	USA	13.7.92	7 May	20.60	2.6 David Lima	POR	6.9.90 22 May
20.49	2.5	Aska	Cambridge	JPN	31.5.93	22 May	20.60	2.2 Shermund Allsop	TTO	21.3.91 4 Jun
20.50	2.4	Tinashe Samuel Mutanga		ZIM	27.1.93	16 Apr	20.60	2.8 Tom Gamble	AUS	25.11.91 19 Nov
20.50	2.5	Tremayne	Acy	USA	21.1.95	23 May	20.63	2.8 Josh Washington	USA	28.8.95 23 Apr
20.50	4.0	Ojie	Edoburun	GBR	2.6.96	22 May	20.63	2.9 Quashawn Cunningham	USA	3.4.96 28 May
20.51	4.3	Yoandry	Andujar	DOM	5.7.90	2 Jul	20.64	2.4 Maurice Freeman	USA	22.11.93 1 Apr
20.53	3.6	Jaron	Flournoy	USA	24.11.96	23 Apr	20.64	3.6 Jordan Landburg	USA	17.4.92 2 Apr

Hand timing - Wind assisted

| 20.0A | | Hendrik | Maartens | RSA | 24.5.96 | 1 | | Bulawayo | 5 | Aug |

Low altitude bests

| 20.40 | -1.2 | Munyai | | 1h4 WJ | Bydgoszcz | 21 Jul | 20.47 | | Dodson | 23 Jul | 20.58 2.0 Leotlela | 21 Jul |
| | | | | | | | | | | 20.60 0.3 Baloyes | 16 May |

Drugs disqualification

| 20.45dq | 1.0 | Dharambir | Singh ¶ | IND | 10.12.90 | (1) | | Bengaluru | 11 | Jul |

JUNIORS

See main list for top 6 juniors. 14 performances by 4 men to 20.40. Additional marks and further juniors:

Lyles		20.23	0.2 1		Fairfax	27 May	20.33	2.0 1		Alexandria VA	7	May
		20.26	0.4 1s2 NC		Eugene	8 Jul						
Norman		20.15	1.2 1	NC-j	Clovis	26 Jun	20.21	-1.1 1s1 NC		Eugene	8	Jul
		20.17	1.2 1	WJ	Bydgoszcz	22 Jul	20.23	-1.0 1		Norwalk	27	May
Munyai		20.39A	1.4 1		Johannesburg	18 Mar	20.40	-1.2 1h4 WJ		Bydgoszcz	21	Jul
20.47A	0.5	Tlotliso Gift		Leotlela	RSA	12.5.98	1			Lusaka	18	Jun
		20.58		2.0			2s3 WJ			Bydgoszcz	21	Jul
20.54	1.0	Abdul Hakim		Sani Brown	JPN-Y	6.3.99	2			Fukuroi	3	May
20.55A	0.0	Sydney		Siame	ZAM	7.10.97	2			Lusaka	18	Jun
20.56A	0.3	Shamon		Ehiemua (10)	USA	30.9.98	1			Albuquerque	4	Jun
20.59A	1.0	Akeem		Sirleaf	USA/LBR	10.3.97	4	JUCO		Levelland, TX	19	May
20.62	0.4	Tyrese		Cooper	USA-Y	21.3.00	1h14	Jnr Oly		Humble, TX	2	Aug
20.63A	1.5	Thando		Dlodlo	RSA-Y	22.4.99	1			Pretoria	28	Oct
20.64	1.5	Roger		Gurski	GER	11.7.97	2s1	WJ		Bydgoszcz	21	Jul
20.66	0.4	Akeem		Bloomfield	JAM	10.11.97	1h11			Kingston	21	May
20.67	1.5	Jun		Yamashita	JPN	23.8.97	3s1	WJ		Bydgoszcz	21	Jul
20.71A	0.3	Maxwell		Willis	USA	2.9.98	2			Albuquerque	4	Jun
20.71	1.1	Champion		Allison	USA	5.11.98	1			Greensboro, NC	19	Jun
20.71	1.5	Cameron		Tindle	GBR	5.6.98	4s1	WJ		Bydgoszcz	21	Jul
20.73	0.5	(20)		Yang Chun-Han	TPE	1.1.97	1	Asi-J		Ho Chi Minh	6	Jun

Wind assisted. See main list for top 4 juniors. 4 performances by 4 men to 20.40. Further juniors:

20.46	2.2	Tyrese	Cooper	USA-Y	21.3.00	1		Tallahassee	16	Apr
20.66A	2.7	Kyle	Appel	RSA	10.5.98	3s1	NC-j	Germiston	2	Apr
20.67A	2.5	Phemelo	Matlhabe	RSA	31.5.97	1		Potchefstroom	12	Mar

300 METRES

31.03		Wayde	van Niekerk	RSA	15.7.92	1		Kingston	11	Jun
31.23		LaShawn	Merritt	USA	27.6.86	2		Kingston	11	Jun
31.64		Tony	McQuay	USA	16.4.90	3		Kingston	11	Jun
31.81		Gil	Roberts	USA	15.3.89	4		Kingston	11	Jun
31.91		Isaac	Makwala	BOT	29.9.86	5		Kingston	11	Jun

300 – 400 METRES   345

Mark	Wind	Name		Nat	Born	Pos	Meet	Venue	Date	
32.35		Javere	Bell	JAM	20.9.92	6		Kingston	11	Jun
32.48		Bastien	Mouthon	SUI	25.7.94	5 May	32.61	Demetrius Pinder BAH	13.2.89	17 Jun
32.51		Pavel	Maslák	CZE	21.2.91	2 Aug	32.61	Ramil Guliyev TUR	29.5.90	27 Jul
32.61		Luka	Janezic	SLO	14.11.95	28 May	32.64	Steven Gardiner BAH	12.9.95	9 Jan

Estimated intermediate times in Olympic final, Rio de Janeiro 14 Aug
Wayde van Niekerk 31.0, LaShawn Merritt 31.2, Kirani James 31.3, Machel Cedenio 31.7, Braion Taplin 31.8, Ali Khamis Abbas 32.0, Matthew Hudson-Smith 32.3, Karabo Sibanda 32.5

400 METRES

Mark	Wind	Name		Nat	Born	Pos	Meet	Venue	Date	
43.03		Wayde	van Niekerk	RSA	15.7.92	1	OG	Rio de Janeiro	14	Aug
43.76		Kirani	James	GRN	1.9.92	2	OG	Rio de Janeiro	14	Aug
43.85		LaShawn	Merritt	USA	27.6.86	3	OG	Rio de Janeiro	14	Aug
43.97			Merritt			1	NC/OT	Eugene	3	Jul
44.01		Machel	Cedenio	TTO	6.9.95	4	OG	Rio de Janeiro	14	Aug
44.02			James			1s1	OG	Rio de Janeiro	13	Aug
44.08			James			1	DrakeR	Des Moines	29	Apr
44.11A			van Niekerk			1h2		Bloemfontein	6	May
44.12			van Niekerk			1	Herc	Monaco	15	Jul
44.15			James			1		Baie Mahault	14	May
44.19			van Niekerk			1	GGala	Roma	2	Jun
44.21			Merritt			2s1	OG	Rio de Janeiro	13	Aug
44.22			Merritt			2	DrakeR	Des Moines	29	Apr
44.22A		Baboloki	Thebe	BOT-J	18.3.97	1	NC-j	Gaborone	21	May
44.22			James			1	Pre	Eugene	28	May
44.23			James			1	DL	Birmingham	5	Jun
44.24		Tony	McQuay	USA	16.4.90	1s1	NC/OT	Eugene	2	Jul
44.25		Karabo	Sibanda	BOT-J	2.7.98	5	OG	Rio de Janeiro	14	Aug
44.28			van Niekerk			1		Somerville, MA	17	Jun
44.34			Cedenio			2	Herc	Monaco	15	Jul
44.36			James			1		Nassau	16	Apr
44.36		Ali Khamis	Abbas	BRN	30.6.95	6	OG	Rio de Janeiro	14	Aug
44.37			Cedenio			1		Kingston	11	Jun
44.38		Bralon	Taplin	GRN	8.5.92	3	Herc	Monaco	15	Jul
44.39			Merritt			2	Pre	Eugene	28	May
44.39			Cedenio			1s2	OG	Rio de Janeiro	13	Aug
44.41			Taplin			1		Tempe	9	Apr
44.41			Merritt			1	DL	Doha	6	May
44.43			Taplin			2	GGala	Roma	2	Jun
44.44			Taplin			1s3	OG	Rio de Janeiro	13	Aug
		[30/9]								
44.46		Steven	Gardiner (10)	BAH	12.9.95	1	NC	Nassau	25	Jun
44.48		Matthew	Hudson-Smith	GBR	26.10.94	2s3	OG	Rio de Janeiro	13	Aug
44.60		Nery	Brenes	CRC	25.9.85	1		Madrid	23	Jun
44.65		Gil	Roberts	USA	15.3.89	4s3	OG	Rio de Janeiro	13	Aug
44.69		Lalonde	Gordon	TTO	25.11.88	2	NC	Port of Spain	26	Jun
44.71		Luguelín	Santos	DOM	12.11.92	4s1	OG	Rio de Janeiro	13	Aug
44.77		Javon	Francis	JAM	14.12.94	3		Baie Mahault	14	May
44.79		Najee	Glass	USA	12.6.94	3s1	NC/OT	Eugene	2	Jul
44.79		Kyle	Clemons	USA	27.8.90	4s1	NC/OT	Eugene	2	Jul
44.81		Abdelilah	Haroun	QAT-J	.97	3	DL	Doha	6	May
44.81		Michael	Cherry	USA	23.3.95	5s1	NC/OT	Eugene	2	Jul
		(20)								
44.82		Arman	Hall	USA	12.2.94	1	NCAA	Eugene	10	Jun
44.82		David	Verburg	USA	14.5.91	3	NC/OT	Eugene	3	Jul
44.85		Isaac	Makwala	BOT	29.9.86	3	GGala	Roma	2	Jun
44.96A		Alphas	Kishoyan	KEN	12.10.94	1	OT	Eldoret	1	Jul
45.00		Vernon	Norwood	USA	10.4.92	2		Kingston	7	May
45.00		Yoandys	Lescay	CUB	5.1.94	6s3	OG	Rio de Janeiro	13	Aug
45.03		Liemarvin	Bonevacia	NED	5.4.89	7s1	OG	Rio de Janeiro	13	Aug
45.04		Martyn	Rooney	GBR	3.4.87	1s2	EC	Amsterdam	7	Jul
45.06		Fitzroy	Dunkley	JAM	20.5.93	2	NCAA	Eugene	10	Jun
45.06		Pavel	Maslák	CZE	21.2.91	3s2	OG	Rio de Janeiro	13	Aug
		(30)								
45.07		Nathan	Strother	USA	6.9.95	1s3	NCAA	Eugene	8	Jun
45.07		Luka	Janezic	SLO	14.11.95	4s2	OG	Rio de Janeiro	13	Aug
45.10		Fred	Kerley	USA	7.5.95	2		Tempe	9	Apr
45.12		Dontavius	Wright	USA	3.1.94	1		Rock Hill, SC	16	May
45.12		Matteo	Galvan	ITA	24.8.88	1	NC	Rieti	25	Jun
45.13		Kahmari	Montgomery	USA-J	16.8.97	1	SEC	Tuscaloosa	14	May

MEN 2016

400 METRES

Mark	Name		Nat	Born	Pos	Meet	Venue	Date	
45.14	Rafal	Omelko	POL	16.1.89	3s2	EC	Amsterdam	7	Jul
45.17	Kévin	Borlée	BEL	22.2.88	3		Kingston	7	May
45.18	Michael	Berry	USA	10.12.91	2		Atlanta	4	Jun
45.22	Rusheen	McDonald	JAM	17.8.92	2h6	OG	Rio de Janeiro	12	Aug
	(40)								
45.23	Tyrese	Cooper	USA-Y	21.3.00	1	Jnr Sel	Humble, TX	6	Aug
45.25A	Diego	Palomeque	COL	5.12.93	1		Medellín	30	Apr
45.25	Alonzo	Russell	BAH	8.2.92	2	NC	Nassau	25	Jun
45.26	Donald	Blair-Sanford	ISR	5.2.87	1	NC	Tel Aviv	22	Jun
45.27	Izaiah	Brown	USA-J	1.1.97	1	Big 10	Lincoln	15	May
45.27	Marcus	Chambers	USA	3.11.94	4	NCAA	Eugene	10	Jun
45.27	Wilbert	London	USA-J	17.8.97	2	WJ	Bydgoszcz	22	Jul
45.30	Demish	Gaye	JAM	20.1.93	2		George Town	14	May
45.31	Deon	Lendore	TTO	28.10.92	4		Baie Mahault	14	May
45.33	Kyle	Collins	USA	9.9.94	2		Waco	23	Apr
	[50]								
45.34	Jonathan	Borlée	BEL	22.2.88	1	NA	Heusden-Zolder	16	Jul
45.35	Julian Jrummi	Walsh	JPN	18.9.96	1	NC	Nagoya	25	Jun
45.36	Peter	Matthews	JAM	13.11.89	2s3	NC	Kingston	2	Jul
45.38	Geoffrey	Kiprotich	KEN-J	23.11.97	1s3	WJ	Bydgoszcz	21	Jul
45.39	Mame-Ibra	Anne	FRA	7.11.89	4s2	EC	Amsterdam	7	Jul
45.39	Nathon	Allen	JAM	28.10.95	1	NACAC	San Salvador	16	Jul
45.40	Anas	Beshr	EGY	19.7.93	1		Montverde, FL	11	Jun
45.40	Mohammed	Anas	IND	17.9.94	1rB	POL Ch	Bydgoszcz	25	Jun
45.42	Michael	Mathieu	BAH	24.6.83	2		Montverde, FL	11	Jun
45.42	Aldrich	Bailey	USA	6.2.94	6s1	NC/OT	Eugene	2	Jul
	(60)								
45.42	Jarrin	Solomon	TTO	11.8.86	4	Gyulai	Székesfehérvár	18	Jul
45.43	Kunle	Fasasi	NGR	23.6.96	1	FlaR	Gainesville	1	Apr
45.44A	Takeshi	Fujiwara	JPN	5.8.85	1	CRC Ch	San José, CRC	7	May
45.44	Steven	Solomon	AUS	16.5.93	1		Townsville	4	Jun
45.45A	Jhon	Perlaza	COL	26.8.94	1		Cali	25	Jun
45.45	Rabah	Yousif	GBR	11.12.86	3	DL	London (OS)	23	Jul
45.47	Arokia	Rajiv	IND	22.5.91	1	Fed Cup	New Delhi	29	Apr
45.50	Delano	Williams	GBR	23.12.93	1rB		Kingston	11	Jun
45.50	Bryshon	Nellum	USA	1.5.89	3		Houston	23	Jul
45.51	Michael	Norman	USA-J	3.12.97	1		Arcadia, CA	9	Apr
	(70)								
45.51	Javere	Bell	JAM	20.9.92	3s2	NC	Kingston	2	Jul
45.51	Yavuz	Can	TUR	23.2.87	5s2	EC	Amsterdam	7	Jul
45.51	Jeremy	Wariner	USA	31.1.84	3		Edmonton	15	Jul
45.52	Cody	Rush	USA	11.11.93	2	Big 10	Lincoln	15	May
45.53	Alberth	Bravo	VEN	29.8.87	5		Madrid	23	Jun
45.54	Ricky	Morgan	USA	7.1.96	1		Los Angeles	26	Mar
45.54	Renny	Quow	TTO	25.8.87	1		Lignano	13	Jul
45.55	Freddy	Mezones	VEN	24.9.87	1	NC	Barinas	8	Apr
45.56	Chris	Brown	BAH	15.10.78	4h4	OG	Rio de Janeiro	12	Aug
45.59A	Mohammad Nasser	Abbas	QAT	.96	2		Monachil	10	Jul
	(80)								
45.60A	Raymond	Kibet	KEN	4.2.96	2	OT	Eldoret	1	Jul
45.61	Calvin	Smith	USA	10.12.87	4		Atlanta	4	Jun
45.61	Jonia	McDonald	JAM	16.12.89	2s1	NC	Kingston	2	Jul
45.61	Dylan	Borlée	BEL	20.9.92	3	VD	Bruxelles	9	Sep
45.63	Brunson	Miller	USA	10.2.91	2rB		Montverde, FL	11	Jun
45.63	Ashton	Eaton	USA	21.1.88	5		Houstonernan	23	Jul
45.64A	Thapelo	Phora	RSA	21.11.91	1		Pretoria	8	Mar
45.64	Pedro	de Oliveira	BRA	17.2.92	3	IbAm	Rio de Janeiro	15	May
45.65	Samuel	Garcia	ESP	4.12.91	6		Madrid	23	Jun
45.66	Joel	Roberson	USA	15.12.93	1		Greensboro, NC	7	May
	(90)								
45.66	Christopher	Taylor	JAM-Y	29.9.99	2rB		Kingston	11	Jun
45.66A	Leonard	Opiny	UGA		1	NC	Kampala	7	Jul
45.67	Paul	Dedewo	NGR/USA	5.6.91	1		New York	8	Jun
45.67	Sadam	Koumi	SUD	6.4.94	1		København	18	Jun
45.69	Chris	Giesting	USA	10.12.92	1		Allendale, MI	13	May
45.69	Hugo	Souza	BRA	5.3.87	4	IbAm	Rio de Janeiro	15	May
45.69	Luis	Pérez	PUR	6.1.95	2	NCAA-2	Bradenton, FL	28	May
45.70A	Shaun	de Jager	RSA	28.6.91	1		Pretoria	11	Jun
45.70	Je'Von	Hutchison	USA	4.5.92	1		Charlotte, NC	17	Jun
45.71	Artyom	Denmukhametov	RUS	15.5.93	1		Sochi	26	May
	[100]								

400 METRES

Mark	Name		Nat	Born	Pos	Meet	Venue	Date	
45.71	Nicholas	Parks	USA	19.11.93	3q2	NCAA-E	Jacksonville	27	May
45.71	Pavel	Ivashko	RUS	16.11.94	1	NC	Cheboksary	21	Jun
45.71	Nobuya	Kato	JPN	16.4.95	2	NC	Nagoya	25	Jun
45.72	Brycen	Spratling	USA	10.3.92	11	Jun			
45.72	Thomas	Jordier	FRA	12.8.94	26	Jun			
45.72	Julien	Watrin	BEL	27.6.92	9	Sep			
45.73	Nijel	Amos	BOT	15.3.94	19	Apr			
45.74	Khallifah	Rosser	USA	13.7.95	9	Apr			
45.74	Champ	Page	USA	1.6.94	15	May			
45.75	Alfred	Larry	USA	9.4.93	13	May			
45.75	Aleksandr	Linnik	BLR	28.1.91	22	Jun			
45.76	Jermaine	Griffith	GUY	28.5.95	23	Apr			
45.76	Mar'yea	Harris	USA-J	24.11.97	15	May			
45.76	Chidi	Okezie	NGR	8.8.93	24	Jun			
45.76	Winston	George	GUY	19.5.87	22	Jul			
45.77	Maurice	Freeman	USA	22.11.93	26	Mar			
45.78A	Ranti	Dikgale	RSA	12.7.87	11	Jun			
45.79	Josh	Mance	USA	21.3.92	15	May			
45.80	Stephen	Newbold	BAH	5.8.94	25	Jun			
45.81	Elbert	Rogers	USA	11.7.94	15	May			
45.81	Warren	Hazel	STK	10.1.96	16	Jul			
45.81	Anthony	Zambrano	COL-J	17.1.98	21	Jul			
45.82	Emmanuel	Dasor	GHA	14.9.95	15	May			
45.82		Guo Zhongze	CHN	7.8.96	3	Jul			
45.83	Elija	Godwin	USA-Y	.99	16	Jul			
45.84	Carlos Andrés	Lemos	COL	3.6.88	15	May			
45.84	Karol	Zalewski	POL	7.8.93	30	Jul			
45.85	Vitaliy	Butrym	UKR	10.1.91	17	Jun			
45.86A	Pieter	Conradie	RSA	20.10.94	29	Apr			
45.86	Ceolamar	Ways	USA	22.11.94	15	May			
45.86	Timofey	Chalyy	RUS	7.4.94	26	May			
45.86	Lukasz	Krawczuk	POL	15.6.89	7	Jul			
45.86	Philip	Osei	CAN	30.10.90	15	Jul			
45.86	Nigel	Levine	GBR	30.4.89	23	Jul			
45.87	Manteo	Mitchell	USA	6.7.87	17	Jun			
45.88	LaToy	Williams	BAH	28.5.88	30	Apr			
45.90	Ricardo	Chambers	JAM	7.10.84	2	Jul			
45.91	Cyril	Grayson	USA	5.12.93	30	Apr			
45.92	Jesse	White	USA	24.10.93	9	Apr			
45.92	Williams	Collazo	CUB	31.8.86	15	May			
45.93	Takamasa	Kitagawa	JPN	5.9.96	25	Jun			
45.94	Gaone	Maotoanong	BOT	7.5.91	15	Mar			
45.94	Josephus	Lyles	USA-J	22.7.98	9	Apr			
45.94	Alexander	Gladitz	GER	19.12.94	4	Jun			
45.94	Nathan	George	CAN	7.1.94	9	Jul			
45.95A	Stanley	Kieti	KEN	30.12.96	28	May			
45.96	Brendon	Rodney	CAN	9.4.92	1	Apr			
45.96	Vladimir	Krasnov	RUS	19.8.90	21	Jun			
45.96	Michal	Pietrzak	POL	3.4.89	24	Jun			
45.96	Patrick	Feeney	USA	29.12.91	1	Jul			
45.98A	Zacharia	Kamberuka	BOT	28.12.87	15	Mar			
45.98	Lucas	Carvalho	BRA	16.7.93	4	Jun			
45.98	My'Lik	Kerley	USA	6.6.96	8	Jun			
45.98	Pavel	Trenikhin	RUS	24.3.86	21	Jun			
45.98	Robin	Vanderbemden	BEL	10.2.94	26	Jun			
45.99	Chris	Tate	USA	5.12.93	15	May			
45.99	Lamar	Bruton	USA	26.5.95	27	May			
46.00	William	Shell	USA	12.6.91	23	Apr			
46.00	Hederson	Estefani	BRA	11.9.91	30	Apr			
46.00	Troy	Pollard	USA	12.6.91	7	May			
46.00	Lucas	Búa	ESP	12.1.94	3	Jun			
46.00	Onkabetse	Nkobolo	BOT	22.7.93	3	Jun			
46.00A	Collins	Omae	KEN	9.4.89	1	Jul			
46.00	Jarryd	Dunn	GBR	30.1.92	7	Jul			
46.01	Akeem	Bloomfield	JAM-J	10.11.97	26	Mar			
46.02	Joshua	Cunningham	CAN	2.2.95	23	Apr			
46.02	Johannes	Trefz	GER	7.6.92	4	Jun			
46.02	Dwayne	Cowan	GBR	1.1.85	4	Jun			
46.02	Conrad	Williams	GBR	20.3.82	18	Jun			
46.02	Theo	Campbell	GBR	14.7.91	18	Jun			
46.02	Jereem	Richards	TTO	13.1.94	26	Jun			
46.03	Soufiane	Bouhada	ALG	8.6.90	29	May			
46.03	Joey	Hughes	USA	26.10.90	18	Jun			
46.03		Quach Cong Lich	VIE	27.8.93	23	Nov			
46.04	Naoki	Kobayashi	JPN	20.12.90	3	Apr			
46.04	Jimmy	Brooks	USA	19.2.95	15	May			
46.04	Chinedu	Amonu	USA	7.5.95	15	May			
46.04	Myles	Pringle	USA-J	5.9.97	28	May			
46.04	Demetrius	Pinder	BAH	13.2.89	24	Jun			
46.04A	Abderrahmane	Samba	QAT	5.9.95	10	Jul			
46.05	Luke	Stevens	AUS	8.6.94	2	Apr			
46.05	Zack	Bilderback	USA	27.8.93	23	Apr			
46.05	James	Harris	USA	19.3.91	14	May			
46.05	Abbas	Abubakar	BRN	17.5.96	9	Jun			
46.05A	Joseph	Loshangar	KEN	2.7.90	1	Jul			
46.07	Dane	Hyatt	JAM	22.1.84	4	May			
46.07	Patrick	Schneider	GER	30.11.92	16	Jul			
46.08	P.P.Kunhu	Muhammed	IND	5.3.87	29	Apr			
46.08	Steven	Coles	USA	19.8.93	7	May			
46.08	Youssef	Al-Masrahi ¶	KSA	31.12.87	28	May			
46.08	Ilya	Krasnov	RUS	17.5.96	21	Jun			
46.08	Jakub	Krzewina	POL	10.10.89	25	Jun			
46.08	Jamal	Walton	CAY-J	25.11.98	15	Jul			
46.09	Daniel	Gyasi	GHA	25.9.94	26	May			
46.09	Peterson [195]	dos Santos	BRA	17.6.91	1	Jul			

Hand timing
| 45.8 | Karsten | Warholm | NOR | 28.2.96 | 31 | Jul | | | |

Low altitude bests
44.69	Thebe		1	AfCh	Durban	24	Jun	45.81 Perlaza 15 May
								45.86 Palomeque 19 Jun
								45.90 de Jager 16 Apr

Drugs disqualification
| 45.51 | Youssef | Al-Masrahi ¶ | KSA | 31.12.87 | 3 | | Madrid | 23 Jun |

Indoors
| 45.27 | Zack | Bilderback | USA | 27.8.93 | 1 | Big 12 | Ames | 27 Feb |
| 45.72 | Marqueze | Washington | USA | 29.9.93 | 19 Feb | 45.91 Neil Braddy | USA | 18.10.91 19 Feb |

JUNIORS
See main list for top 10 juniors. 12 performances by 7 men to 45.27. Additional marks and further juniors:

Thebe	44.69	1	AfCh	Durban	24 Jun				
Sibanda	44.47	3s1	OG	Rio de Janeiro	13 Aug	45.15	1s1	WJ Budgoszcz	21 Jul
Haroun	44.81	1	WJ	Budgoszcz	22 Jul	45.05	4	GGala Roma	2 Jun
45.76	Mar'yea	Harris	USA	24.11.97	4	Big 10	Lincoln	15 May
45.81	Anthony	Zambrano	COL	17.1.98	3s1	WJ	Bydgoszcz	21 Jul
45.83	Elija	Godwin	USA-Y	.99	1		Orlando	16 Jul
45.94	Josephus	Lyles	USA	22.7.98	2		Arcadia	9 Apr
46.01	Akeem	Bloomfield	JAM	10.11.97	1		St.Georges	26 Mar
46.04	Myles	Pringle	USA	5.9.97	3	NCAA-2	Bradenton, FL	28 May
46.08	Jamal	Walton	CAY	25.11.98	2		Orlando	15 Jul
46.11	Keshun	Reed	USA	17.3.98	1		Waco	21 May
46.16	Nick	Gray	USA	2.6.97	3		Los Angeles	26 May
46.17	Sean	Hiooper (20)	USA	28.10.98	1	Jnr Oly	Humble	6 Aug

+ intermediate time in longer race, A made at an altitude of 1000m or higher, D made in a decathlon, h made in a heat, qf quarter-final, sf semi-final, i indoors, Q qualifying round, r race number, -J juniors, -Y youths (b. 1999 or later)

600 – 800 METRES

Mark	Name		Nat	Born	Pos	Meet	Venue		Date

600 METRES

Mark	Name		Nat	Born	Pos	Meet	Venue		Date
1:13.10	David	Rudisha	KEN	17.12.88	1	DL	Birmingham		5 Jun
1:13.21	Pierre-Ambroise	Bosse	FRA	11.5.92	2	DL	Birmingham		5 Jun
1:14.92	Charles	Jock	USA	23.11.89	1		Murfreesboro		4 Jun
1:14.96	Casimir	Loxsom	USA	17.3.91	2		Murfreesboro		4 Jun
1:15.06	Erik	Sowinski	USA	21.12.89	3	DL	Birmingham		5 Jun
1:15.21	Amel	Tuka	BIH	9.1.91	1		Pliezhausen		8 May
1:15.40	Eliud	Rutto	KEN	13.3.94	3		Murfreesboro		4 Jun
1:15.49	Zan	Rudolf	SLO	9.5.93	2		Pliezhausen		8 May
1:15.50	Joshua	Ralph	AUS	27.10.91	4	DL	Birmingham		5 Ju
1:15.57	Wesley Vázquez	PUR 27.3.94 19 Mar		1:15.74A	Pieter		Conradie	RSA 20.10.94	9 Feb
1:15.58	Luguelín Santos	DOM 12.11.92 19 Mar		1:15.87	Michael		Rimmer	GBR 3.2.86	5 Jun
1:15.64	Carter Lilly	USA 19.10.95 23 Apr		1:16.06A	Patryk		Dobek	POL 13.2.94	9 Feb

Indoors

1:15.51	Boris	Berian	USA	19.12.92	1		Boston (R)		14 Feb
1:16.02	Daniel Kuhn	USA 11.8.95 27 Feb		1:16.21	Mitch		Hechsel	USA .94	27 Feb
1:16.12	Jermaine Griffith	USA 28.5.95 27 Feb		1:16.29	Nate		Roese	USA 19.9.94	27 Feb

800 METRES

Mark	Name		Nat	Born	Pos	Meet	Venue	Date
1:42.15	David	Rudisha	KEN	17.12.88	1	OG	Rio de Janeiro	15 Aug
1:42.61	Taoufik	Makhloufi	ALG	29.4.88	2	OG	Rio de Janeiro	15 Aug
1:42.87	Alfred	Kipketer	KEN	26.12.96	1	DL	Saint-Denis	27 Aug
1:42.93	Clayton	Murphy	USA	26.2.95	3	OG	Rio de Janeiro	15 Aug
1:42.98		Makhloufi			2	DL	Saint-Denis	27 Aug
1:43.05	Jonathan	Kitilit	KEN	24.4.94	3	DL	Saint-Denis	27 Aug
1:43.31		Rudisha			1	ISTAF	Berlin	3 Sep
1:43.35		Rudisha			1	Gyulai	Székesfehérvár	18 Jul
1:43.37A	Nicholas	Kipkoech	KEN	22.10.92	1		Nairobi	29 May
1:43.4A		Rudisha			1h3	OT	Eldoret	30 Jun
1:43.41	Pierre-Ambroise	Bosse	FRA	11.5.92	4	OG	Rio de Janeiro	15 Aug
1:43.43	Ferguson	Cheruiyot	KEN	30.11.89	4	DL	Saint-Denis	27 Aug
1:43.48A		Kitilit			2		Nairobi	29 Apr
1:43.52	Ayanleh	Souleiman	DJI	3.12.92	5	DL	Saint-Denis	27 Aug
1:43.55	Donavan	Brazier (10)	USA-J	15.4.97	1	NCAA	Eugene	10 Jun
1:43.55		Cheruiyot			5	OG	Rio de Janeiro	15 Aug
1:43.58		Bosse			6	DL	Saint-Denis	27 Aug
1:43.73A		Kipketer			1	OT	Eldoret	1 Jul
1:43.73	Marcin	Lewandowski	POL	13.6.87	7	DL	Saint-Denis	27 Aug
1:43.76	Adam	Kszczot	POL	2.9.89	8	DL	Saint-Denis	27 Aug
1:43.76	Kipyegon	Bett	KEN-J	2.1.98	2	ISTAF	Berlin	3 Sep
1:43.85		Kipkoech			1		Montreuil-sous-Bois	7 Jun
1:43.85		Bosse			1s1	OG	Rio de Janeiro	13 Aug
1:43.85		Makhloufi			2s1	OG	Rio de Janeiro	13 Aug
1:43.88		Bosse			1	DL	London (OS)	22 Jul
1:43.88		Rudisha			1s3	OG	Rio de Janeiro	13 Aug
1:43.89		Kitilit			2		Montreuil-sous-Bois	7 Jun
1:43.91A		Kipkoech			1	NC	Nairobi	28 May
1:43.92		Makhloufi			1		Saint Maur	5 Jul
1:43.95	Brandon McBride [30/14]		CAN	15.6.94	2	DL	London (OS)	22 Jul
1:44.0A	Jackson	Kivuva	KEN	11.8.88	2h3	OT	Eldoret	30 Jun
1:44.07	Samir	Dahmani	FRA	3.4.91	9	DL	Saint-Denis	27 Aug
1:44.20	Boris	Berian	USA	19.12.92	1	Pre	Eugene	28 May
1:44.51A	Timothy	Kitum	KEN	20.11.94	3		Nairobi	29 Apr
1:44.54	Amel	Tuka	BIH	9.1.91	3	VD	Bruxelles	9 Sep
1:44.6A	Asbel Kiprop (20)		KEN	30.6.89	1s1		Eldoret	15 Apr
1:44.64A	Boaz	Kiprugut	KEN-J	18.5.98	3	NC	Nairobi	28 May
1:44.66	Nijel	Amos	BOT	15.3.94	4	DL	London (OS)	22 Jul
1:44.70	Mohamed	Aman	ETH	10.1.94	3	Pre	Eugene	28 May
1:44.75	Wesley	Vázquez	PUR	27.3.94	1	FlaR	Gainesville	1 Apr
1:44.81	Yassine	Hathat	ALG	30.7.91	3s2	OG	Rio de Janeiro	13 Aug
1:44.84	Willy	Tarbei	KEN-J	30.5.98	1		Herzogenaurach	14 May
1:44.93	Michael	Rimmer	GBR	3.2.86	1		Barcelona (S)	30 Jun
1:44.99	Shaquille	Walker	USA	24.6.93	1		Tempe	9 Apr
1:45.01	Mohamed Amine	Belferrar	ALG	6.2.91	3		Barcelona (S)	30 Jun
1:45.04A	Peter Kiplangat (30)		KEN	6.9.93	4	NC	Nairobi	28 May
1:45.05	Mostafa	Smaïli	MAR-J	9.1.97	2	PTS	Samorín	4 Jun

Mark	Name		Nat	Born	Pos	Meet	Venue	Date	
1:45.1A	Elijah	Manangoi	KEN	5.1.93	1		Nairobi	23	Apr
1:45.13	Jeff	Riseley	AUS	11.11.86	5	DL	London (OS)	22	Jul
1:45.16	Luke	Mathews	AUS	21.6.95	2		Melbourne	5	Mar
1:45.20	Edwin	Melly	KEN	23.4.94	1		Montbéliard	1	Jun
1:45.23	Thijmen	Kupers	NED	4.10.91	6	DL	London (OS)	22	Jul
1:45.24	Antoine	Gakémé	BDI	24.12.91	2		Madrid	23	Jun
1:45.25	Jeremiah	Mutai	KEN	27.12.92	4		Montreuil-sous-Bois	7	Jun
1:45.25	Mohamed Ahmed	Hamada	EGY	22.10.92	2		Barcelona	9	Jul
1:45.28	Abubaker Haydar (40)	Abdallah	QAT	28.8.96	1		Doha	6	May
1:45.33	Rynhardt	van Rensburg	RSA	23.3.92	5s2	OG	Rio de Janeiro	13	Aug
1:45.35	Erik	Sowinski	USA	21.12.89	7	DL	London (OS)	22	Jul
1:45.36	Mark	English	IRL	18.3.93	8	DL	London (OS)	22	Jul
1:45.38	Jacob	Rozani	RSA	24.1.88	2	AfCh	Durban	24	Jun
1:45.4A	Leonard	Kosencha	KEN	21.8.94	2h1	OT	Eldoret	30	Jun
1:45.41	Peter	Bol	AUS	22.2.94	1		Ninove	23	Jul
1:45.42	Lutimar	Paes	BRA	14.12.88	1	IbAm	Rio de Janeiro	15	May
1:45.47	Duane	Solomon	USA	28.12.84	1	MSR	Norwalk	16	Apr
1:45.48A	Timothy Olodaru	Sein	KEN	1.2.88	5	NC	Nairobi	28	May
1:45.48	Charles [50]	Jock	USA	23.11.89	3	NC/OT	Eugene	4	Jul
1:45.53	Charlie	Grice	GBR	7.11.93	9	DL	London (OS)	22	Jul
1:45.54	Elliot	Giles	GBR	26.5.94	3	EC	Amsterdam	10	Jul
1:45.59	Eliud	Rutto	KEN	4.6.88	2	MSR	Norwalk	16	Apr
1:45.60	Anthony	Romaniw	CAN	15.9.91	2		Edmonton	15	Jul
1:45.6A	Sammy	Kirongo	KEN	4.2.94	2		Nakuru	19	Mar
1:45.61	Kevin	López	ESP	12.6.90	2		Huelva	3	Jun
1:45.61	Daniel	Andújar	ESP	14.5.94	3		Huelva	3	Jun
1:45.65	Drew	Windle	USA	22.7.92	1r1		Portland	12	Jun
1:45.75	Yeimer	López	CUB	20.8.82	1	Bisl	Oslo	9	Jun
1:45.76	Isaiah (60)	Harris	USA	18.10.96	4	NCAA	Eugene	10	Jun
1:45.77	Harun	Abda	USA	1.1.90	3		Eugene	29	Jul
1:45.78	Andrés	Arroyo	PUR	7.6.95	2	FlaR	Gainesville	1	Apr
1:45.79	Kléberson	Davide	BRA	20.7.85	2	IbAm	Rio de Janeiro	15	May
1:45.83	Abraham	Rotich	BRN	26.6.93	2	NA	Heusden-Zolder	16	Jul
1:45.84	Robert	Biwott	KEN	28.1.96	2	DL	Shanghai	14	May
1:45.87	Abdellatif	El Guesse	MAR	27.2.93	4	PTS	Samorín	4	Jun
1:45.87	Boitumelo	Masilo	BOT	5.8.95	1r4		Kortrijk	9	Jul
1:45.87	Andreas	Bube	DEN	13.7.87	7s2	OG	Rio de Janeiro	13	Aug
1:45.88A	Mathew	Rono	KEN		6	NC	Nairobi	28	May
1:45.93	Álvaro (70)	de Arriba	ESP	2.6.94	5		Madrid	23	Jun
1:45.93	Casimir	Loxsom	USA	17.3.91	3s1	NC/OT	Eugene	2	Jul
1:45.96	James	Bowness	GBR	26.11.91	2		Ninove	23	Jul
1:45.97	Sho	Kawamoto	JPN	1.3.93	1		Yokohama	2	Jul
1:45.98	Jinson	Johnson	IND	15.3.91	1		Bengaluru	11	Jul
1:45.98	Abdessalem	Ayouni	TUN	16.5.94	1r2	DL	Saint-Denis	27	Aug
1:46.03	Craig	Engels	USA	1.5.94	4	NC/OT	Eugene	4	Jul
1:46.04	Andy	González	CUB	17.10.87	1h1	Barr	La Habana	28	May
1:46.06	Robby	Andrews	USA	29.3.91	1		Philadelphia	25	Jun
1:46.09	James	Gurr	AUS	20.12.83	3		Melbourne	5	Mar
1:46.1A	Job (80)	Kinyor	KEN	2.9.90	3		Nairobi	23	Apr
1:46.12	Brandon	Johnson	USA	6.3.85	3	IbAm	Rio de Janeiro	15	May
1:46.15	Hector	Hernandez	PUR	25.9.94	2	SEC	Tuscaloosa	14	May
1:46.19	Marc	Reuther	GER	23.6.96	2		Wiesbaden	29	Jun
1:46.21	Khalid	Benmahdi	ALG	22.10.88	3		Ninove	23	Jul
1:46.22	Brannon	Kidder	USA	18.11.93	3h2	NC/OT	Eugene	1	Jul
1:46.22	Jamal	Al-Hayrani	QAT	26.5.93	2r4		Kortrijk	9	Jul
1:46.24	Edward	Kemboi	KEN	12.12.91	2r1		Portland	12	Jun
1:46.25	Saïd Aden	Saïd	QAT	.93	7		Barcelona (S)	30	Jul
1:46.27	Alex	Rowe	AUS	8.7.92	2		Pfungstadt	6	Jul
1:46.3A	Thomas (90)	Lemiso	KEN	95	3		Nakuru	19	Mar
1:46.31	Edose	Ibadin	USA	27.2.93	4h2	NC/OT	Eugene	1	Jul
1:46.32	Alberto	Mamba	MOZ	9.10.94	2	Bisl	Oslo	9	Jun
1:46.35	Ronald	Musagala	UGA	16.12.92	1		Oordegem	4	Jun
1:46.37	Manuel	Olmedo	ESP	17.5.83	1		Carmona	8	Jun
1:46.39	Sofiane	Selmouni	FRA	22.9.89	6		Tomblaine	14	Jun
1:46.41	Giordano	Benedetti	ITA	22.5.89	6s3	OG	Rio de Janeiro	13	Aug

350 800 METRES

Mark	Name		Nat	Born	Pos	Meet	Venue	Date	
1:46.42	Filip	Sasinek	CZE	8.1.96	1	WK	Zürich	1	Sep
1:46.43	Sören	Ludolph	GER	25.2.88	1		Regensburg	5	Jun
1:46.44	Charel	Grethen	LUX	22.6.92	2		Oordegem	4	Jun
1:46.44	Sampson	Laari	GHA	3.3.93	3s2	NCAA	Eugene	8	Jun
[100]									
1:46.45A	Kabelo	Mohlosi	RSA	20.1.93	22 Apr				
1:46.45	Maurys Surel	Castillo	ESP	19.10.84	23 Jun				
1:46.47	Brice	Leroy	FRA	26.6.89	4 Jun				
1:46.49	Nasredine	Khatir	FRA	30.1.95	1 Jun				
1:46.52	Chris	Sanders	USA	29.4.94	8 Jun				
1:46.53	Jonah	Koech	KEN	12.12.96	8 Jun				
1:46.57	Jesús	López	MEX-J	2.8.97	5 Jun				
1:46.57	Benedikt	Huber	GER	13.10.89	5 Jun				
1:46.59	Jamie	Webb	GBR	1.6.94	28 May				
1:46.60	David	Palacio	ESP	8.6.88	8 Jun				
1:46.60A	Cornelius	Kiplangat	KEN	21.12.92	1 Jul				
1:46.61	Konstantin	Kholmogorov	RUS	7.2.96	5 Jun				
1:46.62	Alex	Amankwah	USA/GHA	2.3.92	30 Apr				
1:46.63	Alejandro	Estévez	ESP	21.1.92	3 Jun				
1:46.65	Robert	Farken	GER-J	20.9.97	6 Jul				
1:46.65	Rafith	Rodríguez	COL	1.6.89	12 Aug				
1:46.66	Joseph	White	USA	16.11.95	8 Jun				
1:46.69	Daniel	Kuhn	USA	11.8.95	26 Mar				
1:46.69	Christian	Harrison	USA	27.9.93	14 May				
1:46.69	Homiyu	Tesfaye	GER	23.6.93	27 May				
1:46.69	Joshua	Ralph	AUS	27.10.91	6 Jul				
1:46.70	James	Gilreath	USA	7.8.89	12 Jun				
1:46.70	Paul	Renaudie	FRA	2.4.90	14 Jun				
1:46.70A	Duncan	Oloirusha	KEN	.96	7 May				
1:46.71	William	Mothosola	RSA	31.3.90	16 Apr				
1:46.72	Lucirio Antonio	Garrido	VEN	8.4.92	15 May				
1:46.73	Nick	Hartle	USA	14.1.94	16 Apr				
1:46.73	Kyle	Langford	GBR	2.2.96	22 Jul				
1:46.78	Robert	Heppenstall	CAN-J	28.2.97	10 Jul				
1:46.78	Zak	Curran	IRL	17.12.93	22 Jul				
1:46.8A	Edwin	Kemboi	KEN	22.8.86	28 Apr				
1:46.80	Roman	Yarko	UKR	6.11.89	19 Jun				
1:46.8A	Wycliffe	Kinyamal	KEN-J	2.7.97	22 Jun				
1:46.81	Goaner	Deng	USA	30.6.93	9 Apr				
1:46.82A	Abu	Mayanja	UGA	.90	7 Jul				
1:46.83	Dennis	Krüger	GER	24.4.93	9 Jul				
1:46.84	Mamush	Lencho	ETH	24.3.96	16 Jun				
1:46.85A	Moses	Kibet	KEN	20.11.94	29 Apr				
1:46.85	Michal	Rozmys	POL	13.3.95	9 Sep				
1:46.90	Collins	Kibet	KEN	.88	26 Mar				
1:46.90	Patrick	Zwicker	GER	13.7.94	5 Jun				
1:46.90	Abraham	Alvarado	USA	4.8.95	12 Jun				
1:46.93	Isaac	Kimeli	BEL	9.3.94	4 Jun				
1:46.93	Zan	Rudolf	SLO	9.5.93	12 Aug				
1:46.94	Emmanuel	Korir	KEN	15.6.95	28 May				
1:46.96	Carlton	Orange	USA-J	11.3.97	23 Apr				
1:46.97	Vincent	Crisp	USA-J	17.8.97	25 Jun				
1:46.99	Ryan	Sánchez	PUR-J	22.6.98	15 Apr				
1:47.00	Anthonio	Mascoll	BAR	17.1.93	26 Jun				
1:47.02	Ahmed	Bile	USA	21.9.93	9 Jul				
1:47.02	Christoph	Kessler	GER	28.4.95	1 Sep				
1:47.08	Guy	Learmonth	GBR	24.4.92	1 May				
1:47.10	Youssef Saad	Kamel	BRN	29.3.83	13 Jul				
1:47.11	Jesse	Garn	USA	4.6.93	22 Apr				
1:47.11	Riadh	El Chenini	TUN-J	25.3.97	23 Jul				
1:47.12	Stijn	Baeten	BEL	3.6.94	16 Jul				
1:47.13	Holland	Sherrer	USA	17.8.93	27 May				
1:47.13	Jake	Wightman	GBR	11.7.94	28 May				
1:47.14	Badr	El Jalaoui	MAR	28.1.93	5 Jun				
1:47.14	Chris	Low	USA	29.8.92	23 Jun				
1:47.15	Brad	Mathas	NZL	24.6.93	6 Jul				
1:47.16	Amine	El Manaoui	MAR	20.11.91	23 Apr				
1:47.16	Kalle	Berglund	SWE	11.3.96	25 May				
1:47.17	Baptiste	Mischler	FRA-J	23.11.97	26 Jun				
1:47.17	Matthew	Centrowitz	USA	18.10.89	29 Jul				
1:47.18	Dusty	Solis	USA	28.6.90	9 Apr				
1:47.18	Leandro	Paris	ARG	16.2.95	14 May				
1:47.18	Brian	Bell	USA-J	6.2.97	25 Jun				
1:47.19	David	Bustos	ESP	25.8.90	25 Jun				
1:47.2A	Bernard	Kipyegon	KEN	94	16 Apr				
1:47.20	Michael	Rutt	USA	28.10.87	7 May				
1:47.20	Alberto	Guerrero	ESP	4.4.95	8 Jun				
1:47.20	Timo	Benitz	GER	24.12.91	24 Jul				
1:47.21	Antonio Manuel	Reina	ESP	13.6.81	22 May				
1:47.21	Jan	Riedel	GER	14.10.89	5 Jun				
1:47.24	Eugene	Hamilton	USA	13.2.95	26 Mar				
1:47.24A	Geoffrey	Rutto	UGA		7 Jul				
1:47.24	Aurèle	Vandeputte	BEL	14.5.95	16 Jul				
1:47.24	Andreas	Kramer	SWE-J	13.4.97	27 Jul				
1:47.25	Jena	Umar	ETH	24.12.95	4 Jun				
1:47.26	Jordan	Williamsz	AUS	21.8.92	29 Jun				
1:47.27	Patrick	Joseph	USA	7.9.95	12 Jun				
1:47.27	Jacopo	Lahbi	ITA	1.6.93	7 Jul				
1:47.27	Leonel	Manzano	USA	12.9.84	27 Jul				
1:47.28	Tayron	Reyes	DOM	4.1.90	15 May				
1:47.30	Blair	Henderson	USA	4.10.94	30 Apr				
1:47.3A	Julius	Kipchirchir	KEN-J	.97	7 May				
1:47.32	Carter	Lilly	USA	19.10.95	16 Apr				
1:47.33	Andrew	Wheating	USA	21.11.87	2 Jun				
1:47.34	Charles	Jones	USA	1.11.95	23 Apr				
1:47.35	Bryan Antonio	Martínez	MEX	1.8.94	5 Mar				
1:47.37	Richard	Jones	USA	15.7.88	19 Jun				
1:47.39	Ayoub	Labser	MAR	7.4.93	5 Jun				
1:47.39	Saquille	Dill	BER	4.9.93	18 Jun				
1:47.4A	Silas	Kiplagat	KEN	20.8.89	14 Apr				
1:47.41	Mason	Cohen	AUS	19.9.96	2 Apr				
1:47.41	Balázs	Vindics	HUN	28.3.94	18 Jul				
1:47.42	Fabiano	Peçanha	BRA	5.6.82	22 May				
1:47.44	Aaron	Botterman	BEL	1.5.94	25 Jun				
1:47.45	Nabil	Oussama	MAR	18.2.96	16 Apr				
[200]									
1:47.45	George	Kusche	RSA-J	6.8.98	16 Jul				
1:47.45	Masato	Yokota	JPN	19.11.87	25 Jun				
1:47.45	Brian	Gagnon	USA	8.5.87	25 Jun				

Indoors

| 1:45.93 | Abdulrahman Musaeb | Balla | QAT | 19.3.89 | 2 | | Stockholm | 17 | Feb |
| 1:47.28 | Drew | Piazza | USA | 28.1.95 | 30 Jan | 1:47.37 | Ryan | Manahan | USA | 14.7.94 | 30 Jan |

JUNIORS

See main list for top 5 juniors. 11 performances by 5 men to 1:45.2. Additional marks and further juniors:

Brazier	1:45.07	s2	NCAA	Eugene		8 Jun				
Bett	1:44.4A	1	NC-j	Nairobi		22 Jun	1:44.95	1	WJ	Bydgoszcz	24 Jul
	1:44.44	2	VD	Bruxelles		9 Sep					
Tarbei	1:45.11	1B	VD	Bruxelles		9 Sep	1:45.2A	2	NC-j	Nairobi	22 Jun
1:46.65	Robert	Farken		GER	20.9.97	1J		Pfungstadt		6 Jul
1:46.57	Jesús	López		MEX	2.8.97	1	NC	Monterrey		5 Jun
1:46.78	Robert	Heppenstall		CAN	28.2.97	3	NC	Edmonton		10 Jul
1:46.8A	Wycliffe	Kinyamal		KEN	2.7.97	3	NC-j	Nairobi		22 Jun
1:46.96	Carlton	Orange (10)		USA	11.3.97	1		Fayetteville		23 Apr
1:46.97	Vincent	Crisp		USA	17.8.97	1	NC-j	Clovis		25 Jun
1:46.99	Ryan	Sánchez		PUR	22.6.98	1	MSR	Norwalk		15 Apr
1:47.11	Riadh	El Chenini		TUN	25.3.97	2s1	WJ	Bydgoszcz		23 Jul
1:47.17	Baptiste	Mischler		FRA	23.11.97	1		Mannheim		26 Jun

800 – 1000 – 1500 METRES   351

Mark	Name		Nat	Born	Pos	Meet	Venue	Date
1:47.18	Brian	Bell	USA	6.2.97	2	NC-j	Clovis	25 Jun
1:47.24	Andreas	Kramer	SWE	13.4.97	5		Karlstad	27 Jul
1:47.3A	Julius	Kipchirchir	KEN	.97	3		Nairobi	7 May
1:47.45	George	Kusche	RSA	6.8.98	4	NC	Stellenbosch	16 Apr
1:47.5A	Peter	Kiptum	KEN	22.12.98	4	NC-j	Nairobi	22 Jun
1:47.53	Teddese	Lemi (20)	ETH-Y	20.1.99	4s3	WJ	Bydgoszcz	23 Jul

1000 METRES

Mark	Name		Nat	Born	Pos	Meet	Venue	Date
2:13.49	Ayanleh	Souleiman	DJI	3.12.92	1	Athl	Lausanne	25 Aug
2:13.89	Robert	Biwott	KEN	28.1.96	2	Athl	Lausanne	25 Aug
2:13.95	Jonathan	Kitilit	KEN	24.4.94	3	Athl	Lausanne	25 Aug
2:14.23	Asbel	Kiprop	KEN	30.6.89	4	Athl	Lausanne	25 Aug
2:14.30	Marcin	Lewandowski	POL	13.6.87	5	Athl	Lausanne	25 Aug
2:16.67	Matthew	Centrowitz	USA	18.10.89	6	Athl	Lausanne	25 Aug
2:16.68	Nicholas	Kipkoech	KEN	22.10.92	7	Athl	Lausanne	25 Aug
2:16.95	Filip	Ingebrigtsen	NOR	20.4.93	8	Athl	Lausanne	25 Aug
2:17.66	Mohamed Ahmed Hamada		EGY	22.10.92	15 Jul	2:18.56 Michal	Rozmys	POL	13.3.95	27 Aug
2:17.67	Johan	Rogestedt	SWE	27.1.93	15 Jul	2:18.63 Gilbert	Kwemboi	KEN-J	3.10.97	25 Aug
2:18.5	Ismael	Debjani	BEL	25.9.90	20 Jul	2:18.66 Jan	Hochstrasser	SUI	23.10.88	25 Aug
2:18.54	Timo	Benitz	GER	24.12.91	8 May	2:18.94 Charel	Grethen	LUX	22.6.92	8 May

Indoors

Mark	Name		Nat	Born	Pos	Meet	Venue	Date
2:14.20		Souleiman			1		Stockholm	17 Feb
2:17.02	Thijmen	Kupers	NED	4.10.91	2		Stockholm	17 Feb
2:17.09	Elijah	Manangoi	KEN	5.1.93	3		Stockholm	17 Feb
2:18.24	Manuel	Olmedo	ESP	17.5.83	16 Jan	2:18.27 Jakub	Holusa	CZE	20.2.88	17 Feb
2:18.26	Brannon	Kidder	USA	18.11.93	16 Jan	2:18.68 Andrew	Wheating	USA	21.11.87	14 Feb

1500 METRES

Mark	Name		Nat	Born	Pos	Meet	Venue	Date
3:29.33	Asbel	Kiprop	KEN	30.6.89	1	DL	Birmingham	5 Jun
3:30.49	Ronald	Kwemoi	KEN	19.9.95	1	Herc	Monaco	15 Jul
3:31.19	Elijah	Manangoi	KEN	5.1.93	2	Herc	Monaco	15 Jul
3:31.34	Timothy	Cheruiyot	KEN	20.11.95	1	VD	Bruxelles	9 Sep
3:31.35	Taoufik	Makhloufi	ALG	29.4.88	3	Herc	Monaco	15 Jul
3:31.40	Abdelaati	Iguider	MAR	25.3.87	2	VD	Bruxelles	9 Sep
3:31.54		Iguider			4	Herc	Monaco	15 Jul
3:31.68	Ayanleh	Souleiman	DJI	3.12.92	1	NA	Heusden-Zolder	16 Jul
3:31.74	Mohamed	Farah	GBR	23.3.83	5	Herc	Monaco	15 Jul
3:31.87		Kiprop			3	VD	Bruxelles	9 Sep
3:32.03		Kiprop			6	Herc	Monaco	15 Jul
3:32.13	Ryan	Gregson	AUS	26.4.90	7	Herc	Monaco	15 Jul
3:32.15		Kiprop			1	DL	Doha	6 May
3:32.21		Makhloufi			4	VD	Bruxelles	9 Sep
3:32.30	Sadik	Mikhou (10)	BRN	25.7.90	1		Huelva	3 Jun
3:32.43	Filip	Ingebrigtsen	NOR	20.4.93	5	VD	Bruxelles	9 Sep
3:32.85		Mikhou			1	Odlozil	Praha	6 Jun
3:32.97	Hillary	Ngetich	KEN	15.9.95	2	NA	Heusden-Zolder	16 Jul
3:33.05	Robert	Biwott	KEN	28.1.96	6	VD	Bruxelles	9 Sep
3:33.10		Iguider			2	DL	Birmingham	5 Jun
3:33.36	Jakub	Holusa	CZE	20.2.88	8	Herc	Monaco	15 Jul
3:33.56	Vincent	Kibet	KEN	6.5.91	7	VD	Bruxelles	9 Sep
3:33.60	Charlie	Grice	GBR	7.11.93	9	Herc	Monaco	15 Jul
3:33.61		Cheruiyot			1	DL	Rabat	22 May
3:33.67		Manangoi			2	DL	Doha	6 May
3:33.68	Silas	Kiplagat	KEN	20.8.89	2	DL	Rabat	22 May
3:33.71	Gilbert	Kwemboi	KEN-J	3.10.97	3	NA	Heusden-Zolder	16 Jul
3:33.72		Ingebrigtsen			10	Herc	Monaco	15 Jul
3:33.86		Kiplagat			3	DL	Doha	6 May
3:33.94	Bethwel	Birgen	KEN	6.8.88	4	DL	Doha	6 May
3:33.96		Manangoi			1	GGala	Roma	2 Jun
3:33.98	Dawit (32/20)	Wolde	ETH	19.5.91	4	NA	Heusden-Zolder	16 Jul
3:34.09	Matthew	Centrowitz	USA	18.10.89	1	NC/OT	Eugene	10 Jul
3:34.24	Charles	Philibert-Thiboutot	CAN	31.12.90	11	Herc	Monaco	15 Jul
3:34.26	Ben	Blankenship	USA	15.12.89	9	VD	Bruxelles	9 Sep
3:34.29	Nick	Willis	NZL	25.4.83	3	DL	Birmingham	5 Jun
3:34.55	Abdi Waiss	Mouhyadin	DJI	3.7.96	5	DL	Doha	6 May
3:34.57	Henrik	Ingebrigtsen	NOR	24.2.91	12	Herc	Monaco	15 Jul
3:34.58	Aman	Wote	ETH	18.4.84	6	DL	Doha	6 May
3:34.88	Robby	Andrews	USA	29.3.91	2	NC/OT	Eugene	10 Jul

MEN 2016

1500 METRES

Mark	Name		Nat	Born	Pos	Meet	Venue	Date	
3:34.88	Colby	Alexander	USA	13.6.91	1		Eugene	29	Jul
3:34.95	David	Torrence	USA/PER	26.11.85	2		Eugene	29	Jul
(30)									
3:34.96	Fouad	El Kaam	MAR	27.5.88	4	DL	Rabat	22	May
3:35.05	Homiyu	Tesfaye	GER	23.6.93	5	DL	Rabat	22	May
3:35.12	Vincent	Letting	KEN	16.6.93	5	NA	Heusden-Zolder	16	Jul
3:35.18	James	Magut	KEN	20.7.90	5	DL	Birmingham	5	Jun
3:35.24	Adel	Mechaal	ESP	5.12.90	1		Barcelona (S)	30	Jun
3:35.28	Benson	Seurei	BRN	27.3.84	2		Barcelona (S)	30	Jun
3:35.29	Florian	Carvalho	FRA	9.3.89	14	Herc	Monaco	15	Jul
3:35.37	Chris	O'Hare	GBR	23.11.90	7	GGala	Roma	2	Jun
3:35.38	Pieter Jan	Hannes	BEL	30.10.92	6	NA	Heusden-Zolder	16	Jul
3:35.50	Mekonnen	Gebremedhin	ETH	11.10.88	3		Barcelona (S)	30	Jun
(40)									
3:35.58	Mourad	Amdouni	FRA	21.1.88	10	GGala	Roma	2	Jun
3:35.59	Ryan	Hill	USA	31.1.90	7	NA	Heusden-Zolder	16	Jul
3:35.62	Ismael	Debjani	BEL	25.9.90	8	NA	Heusden-Zolder	16	Jul
3:35.74	Collins	Cheboi	KEN	25.9.87	13	VD	Bruxelles	9	Sep
3:35.76	Brahim	Kaazouzi	MAR	15.6.90	1		Amiens	11	Jun
3:35.77	Richard	Douma	NED	17.4.93	9	NA	Heusden-Zolder	16	Jul
3:35.83	Kyle	Merber	USA	19.11.90	4		Eugene	29	Jul
3:35.94	Eric	Jenkins	USA	24.11.91	5		Eugene	29	Jul
3:35.99	Luke	Mathews	AUS	21.6.95	2		Nijmegen	18	May
3:36.04	John	Gregorek	USA	7.12.91	6		Eugene	29	Jul
[50]									
3:36.05	Ben	True	USA	29.12.85	3		Somerville, MA	17	Jun
3:36.14	Julian	Matthews	NZL	21.7.88	2		Swarthmore	16	May
3:36.14	David	Bustos	ESP	25.8.90	2		Huelva	3	Jun
3:36.19	Younès	Essalhi	MAR	20.2.93	2		Amiens	11	Jun
3:36.23	Ronald	Musagala	UGA	16.12.94	1		Montreuil-sous-Bois	7	Jun
3:36.23	Clayton	Murphy	USA	26.2.95	1r1		Portland	12	Jun
3:36.25	Hamish	Carson	NZL	1.11.88	3		Swarthmore	16	May
3:36.29	Lee	Emanuel	GBR	24.1.85	4		Swarthmore	16	May
3:36.32	Filip	Sasinek	CZE	8.1.96	1	GS	Ostrava	20	May
3:36.37	Eric	Avila	USA	3.10.89	1		Padova	17	Jul
(60)									
3:36.40	Timo	Benitz	GER	24.12.91	2	GS	Ostrava	20	May
3:36.41	Maurys Surel	Castillo	ESP	19.10.84	5		Barcelona (S)	30	Jun
3:36.58	Johan	Rogestedt	SWE	27.1.93	2		Sollentuna	28	Jun
3:36.62	Leonel	Manzano	USA	12.9.84	4	NC/OT	Eugene	10	Jul
3:36.64	Jake	Wightman	GBR	11.7.94	5		Somerville, MA	17	Jun
3:36.65	Dumisani	Hlaselo	RSA	8.6.89	9	DL	Doha	6	May
3:36.67	Adam Ali	Musaab	QAT	17.4.95	10	DL	Doha	6	May
3:36.84	Nathan	Brannen	CAN	8.9.82	2		Windsor	21	May
3:36.92	Jonas	Leandersson	SWE	26.1.91	3		Sollentuna	28	Jun
3:36.93	Marc	Alcalá	ESP	7.11.94	6		Barcelona (S)	30	Jun
(70)									
3:37.03	Bryan	Cantero	FRA	28.4.91	4	GS	Ostrava	20	May
3:37.08	Graham	Crawford	USA	29.12.92	2		Princeton	18	Jun
3:37.18	Martin	Sperlich	GER	28.8.91	11	NA	Heusden-Zolder	16	Jul
3:37.24	Valentin	Smirnov	RUS	13.2.86	1		Sochi	26	May
3:37.24	Antonio	Abadía	ESP	2.7.90	1rB		Huelva	3	Jun
3:37.44	Eric	Speakman	NZL	29.8.90	5		Windsor, CAN	21	May
3:37.47	Tom	Lancashire	GBR	2.7.85	7		Barcelona (S)	30	Jun
3:37.49	Johan	Cronje	RSA	13.4.82	3		Tomblaine	14	Jun
3:37.62	Sebastian	Keiner	GER	22.8.89	5		Sollentuna	28	Jun
3:37.63	Aman	Kedi	ETH	16.9.94	5		Huelva	3	Jun
(80)									
3:37.65	Hassan	Mead	USA	28.8.89	1rA		Los Angeles (ER)	20	May
3:37.66	Craig	Engels	USA	1.5.94	5	NC/OT	Eugene	10	Jul
3:37.69	Marcin	Lewandowski	POL	13.6.87	3	Hanz	Zagreb	6	Sep
3:37.73A	Erick	Kiptanui	KEN	.90	3	NC	Nairobi	28	May
3:37.73	Ahmed	Bile	USA	21.9.93	1		Princeton	3	Jun
3:37.74	Izaic	Yorks	USA	17.4.94	1	Jordan	Stanford	1	May
3:37.74	Hélio	Gomes	POR	27.12.84	6		Huelva	3	Jun
3:37.75	Thomas	Awad	USA	27.5.94	5		Swarthmore	16	May
3:37.79	Isaac	Kimeli	BEL	9.3.94	12	NA	Heusden-Zolder	16	Jul
3:37.82	Joshua	Cheptegei	UGA	12.9.96	3		Nijmegen	18	May
(90)									
3:37.82A	Abednego	Chesebe	KEN	20.6.82	4	NC	Nairobi	28	May
3:37.82	Carlos Martín	Díaz	CHI	9.7.93	8		Huelva	3	Jun

1500 METRES

Mark	Name		Nat	Born	Pos	Meet	Venue	Date	
3:37.87	Peter	Callahan	USA/BEL	1.6.91	7		Swarthmore	16	May
3:37.90	João	Bussotti (Neves)	ITA	10.5.93	5		Padova	17	Jul
3:38.05	Henry	Wynne	USA	18.4.95	1		Charlottesville	23	Apr
3:38.05	Stijn	Baeten	BEL	3.6.94	2		Ninove	23	Jul
3:38.07	Jordan	McNamara	USA	7.3.87	2r1		Portland	12	Jun
3:38.11	Abderrahmane	Anou	ALG	29.1.91	3		Amiens	11	Jun
3:38.19	Rabie	Doukkana	MAR	6.12.87	2		Kortrijk	9	Jul
3:38.20	Brandon [100]	Hudgins	USA	14.1.87	4		Greenville, SC	4	Jun
3:38.23	Will	Leer	USA	15.4.85	21 May	3:39.44	Carlos	Alonso	ESP	15.9.89	3 Jun
3:38.28	Duncan	Phillips	USA	7.6.89	4 Jun	3:39.46	Amin	Cheniti	ALG	22.5.93	23 Jul
3:38.29	Mathew	Kiptanui	KEN	20.10.94	18 Jul	3:39.49	Benjamin	Kovács	HUN	24.1.95	6 Jun
3:38.3A	Edwin	Kiptoo	KEN-J	20.7.98	16 Apr	3:39.49	Adam	Palamar	CAN	12.3.94	17 Jun
3:38.34	Dorian	Ulrey	USA	11.7.87	12 Jun	3:39.5	Boaz	Kiprugut	KEN-J	18.5.98	30 Apr
3:38.35	Ford	Palmer	USA	6.10.90	4 Jun	3:39.50	Amine	Khadiri	CYP	20.11.88	3 Jun
3:38.35	Michal	Rozmys	POL	13.3.95	17 Jul	3:39.5A	Anthony	Kiptoo	KEN-J	19.8.97	22 Jun
3:38.37	Yemaneberhan	Crippa	ITA	15.10.96	17 Jul	3:39.52	Samir	Dahmani	FRA	3.4.91	7 Jun
3:38.40	Ben	Saarel	USA	8.3.95	12 Jun	3:39.58	Baptiste	Mischler	FRA-J	23.11.97	11 Jun
3:38.43	Sam	Prakel	USA	29.10.94	26 Jun	3:39.60	Víctor José	Corrales	ESP	12.3.89	16 May
3:38.44	Aleksey	Kharitonov	RUS	4.7.91	26 May	3:39.60	Quentin	Tison	FRA	16.4.96	4 Jun
3:38.44	Salim	Keddar	ALG	23.11.93	30 Jun	3:39.60	Marius	Probst	GER	20.8.95	16 Jul
3:38.55	Lyès	Belkhier	ALG	5.10.87	17 Jun	3:39.61	Joshua	Thompson	USA	9.5.93	18 Jun
3:38.58	Jordan	Gusman	AUS	30.1.94	20 May	3:39.64	Sam	Penzenstadler	USA	11.9.92	20 May
3:38.60	Andrew	Wheating	USA	21.11.87	20 May	3:39.67	Masaki	Toda	JPN	21.6.93	24 Apr
3:38.61	Volodymyr	Kyts	UKR	15.1.87	20 May	3:39.71	Jan	Hochstrasser	SUI	23.10.88	23 Jul
3:38.62	Yassine	Hathat	ALG	30.7.91	31 Mar	3:39.76	Abubaker	Kaki	SUD	21.6.89	31 Mar
3:38.62	Matthew	Maton	USA	28.3.96	12 Jun	3:39.76	Nikita	Vysotskiy	RUS	16.10.93	26 May
3:38.63	Snorre Holtan	Løken	NOR	25.10.94	9 Jun	3:39.79	Llorenç	Sales	ESP	14.7.88	22 Jun
3:38.64	Iván	López	CHI	10.3.90	16 May	3:39.82	Ben	Malone	USA	13.11.94	18 Jun
3:38.64	Jonathan	Cook	GBR	31.7.87	23 Jul	3:39.84	Mohamed Ismail	Ibrahim	DJI-J	,97	8 Jun
3:38.67	Evan	Jager	USA	8.3.89	1 May	3:39.85	Petr	Vitner	CZE	27.1.90	4 Jun
3:38.74	Mohad	Abdikadar	ITA	12.6.93	2 Jun	3:39.85	Marco	Pettenazzo	ITA	28.10.92	1 Jun
3:38.77	Lex	Williams	USA	21.3.87	21 May	3:39.85	Andreas	Bueno	DEN	7.7.88	9 Jun
3:38.77	Riley	Masters	USA	5.4.90	17 Jul	3:39.89	Weston	Strum	USA	17.1.92	12 Jun
3:38.8A	Kumari	Taki	KEN-Y	6.5.99	22 Jun	3:39.9	Belete	Mekonnen	ETH-J	97?	30 May
3:38.81	Daniel	Winn	USA	30.7.91	4 Jun	3:39.92	Neil	Gourley	GBR	7.2.95	3 Jul
3:38.83	Richard	Ringer	GER	27.2.89	1 Jun	3:39.96	Guillaume	Adam	FRA	15.1.90	1 Jun
3:38.84	Hillary	Maiyo	KEN	2.10.93	18 Jul	3:39.98	Andreas	Vojta	AUT	9.6.89	20 May
3:38.86	Tarik	Moukrime	BEL	3.3.92	22 May	3:39.99	Thomas	Riva	CAN	31.1.92	20 May
3:38.86	Alexandre	Saddédine	FRA	29.9.94	1 Jun	3:40.0	James	West	GBR	30.1.96	15 Jun
3:38.95	Tamás	Kazi	HUN	16.5.85	4 Jun	3:40.03	Robert	Denault	CAN	27.4.93	25 Jun
3:39.0A	Job	Kinyor	KEN	2.9.90	16 Apr	3:40.05	Patrick	Casey	USA	23.5.90	20 May
3:39.03	Cornelius	Kiplangat	KEN	21.12.92	28 May	3:40.11	Brannon	Kidder	USA	18.11.93	22 Apr
3:39.03	Robbie	Fitzgibbon	GBR	23.3.96	23 Jul	3:40.13	Staffan	Ek	SWE	13.11.91	23 Jul
3:39.11	Pieter	Claus	BEL	1.3.93	23 Jul	3:40.13	John	Maina	KEN	3.8.94	24 Sep
3:39.15	Chad	Noelle	USA	12.4.93	4 Jun	3:40.15	James	Randon	USA	16.6.94	23 Apr
3:39.18	Nixon	Chepseba	KEN	12.12.90	14 May	3:40.16	Collis	Birmingham	AUS	27.12.84	5 Mar
3:39.23	Justyn	Knight	CAN	19.7.96	23 Apr	3:40.16	Dan	Castle	USA	20.2.87	21 May
3:39.24	Andy	Bayer	USA	3.2.90	18 Jul	3:40.17	Josh	Wright	AUS	3.5.91	17 Jun
3:39.24	Elijah	Kiptoo	KEN	9.6.86	18 Jul	3:40.20	Mac	Fleet	USA	17.10.90	20 May
3:39.27	Martin	Casse	FRA	23.6.90	17 Jun	3:40.24	Linus	Kiplagat	BRN	23.12.94	29 May
3:39.30	Ismael	Kombich	KEN	16.10.85	1 Jun	3:40.26	Kota	Murayama	JPN	23.2.93	24 Sep
3:39.32	Dusty	Solis	USA	28.6.90	16 May	3:40.28	Florian	Orth	GER	24.7.89	28 Jun
3:39.33	Cristian	Soratos	USA	26.9.92	17 Jun	3:40.31	Justin	Brinkley	USA	16.1.94	15 May
3:39.33	Paul	Chelimo	USA	27.10.90	6 Sep	3:40.33	Sergey	Dubrovskiy	RUS	20.1.95	26 May
3:39.34	Garrett	O'Toole	USA	22.3.96	16 May	3:40.34	Emanuel	Rolim	POR	30.1.93	12 Jun
3:39.38	Jerry	Motsau	RSA	12.3.90	17 Jul	3:40.36	Antoine	Gakémé	BDI	24.12.91	28 May
3:39.4	Thomas	Farrell	GBR	23.3.91	15 Jun	3:40.36	Christopher	Sandoval	MEX	29.10.91	12 Jun
3:39.41	Tom	Marshall	GBR	12.6.89	4 Jun	3:40.42	Reda [200]	Jaafar	MAR	18.10.90	17 Jun

Indoors

3:36.35	Mohamed	Al-Garni ¶		QAT	2.7.92	1	AsiC	Doha	20	Feb
3:37.29	Saïd Aden	Saïd		QAT	.93	3	AsiC	Doha	20	Feb
3:37.67+	Cory	Leslie		USA	24.10.89	3	Mill	New York	20	Feb
3:38.25	Manuel	Olmedo		ESP	17.5.83	7 Feb	3:39.89i	Yassine	Bensghir	MAR	3.1.83	19 Feb
3:38.48+	Garrett	Heath		USA	3.11.85	20 Feb	3:40.09+	Blake	Haney	USA	29.3.96	20 Feb

JUNIORS

3:33.71	Gilbert	Kwemboi	KEN	3.10.97	3	NA	Heusden-Zolder	16	Jul
	3:37.76	3	Sotteville-les-Rouen	18	Jul				
3:38.3A	Edwin	Kiptoo	KEN	20.7.98	2		Eldoret	16	Apr
	3:39.0A	2	NC-j Nairobi	22	Jun				
3:38.8A	Kumari	Taki	KEN-Y	6.5.99	1		Nairobi	22	Jun
	3:39.15A	6	NC Nairobi	28	May	11 performances by 8 men to 3:39.9			
3:39.5	Boaz	Kiprugut	KEN	18.5.98	1		Dar-es-Salaam	30	Apr
3:39.5A	Anthony	Kiptoo	KEN	19.8.97	3	NC-j	Nairobi	22	Jun
3:39.58	Baptiste	Mischler	FRA	23.11.97	4		Amiens	11	Jun
3:39.84	Mohamed Ismail	Ibrahim	DJI	.97	1		Barcelona	8	Jun

1500 METRES – 1 MILE

Mark	Name		Nat	Born	Pos	Meet	Venue	Date	
3:39.9	Belete	Mekonnen	ETH	97?	2		Dar-es-Salaam	30	Apr
3:40.87	Ayoub	Sniba	MAR	5.4.97	3	NC	Rabat	5	Jun
3:40.88	Idriss Mousa	Youssouf (10)	QAT	1.1.97?	6		Lokeren	3	Jul
3:40.9A	Terese	Tolosa	ETH	15.6.98	2	NC	Addis Ababa	24	Apr
3:40.92	Jordi	Torrents	ESP	25.9.97	13		Barcelona	30	Jun
3:41.08	Josh	Kerr	GBR	8.10.97	5s2	NCAA	Eugene	8	Jun
3:41.5A	Aron	Kirui	KEN	5.5.98	4	NC-j	Nairobi	22	Jun
3:41.78	Ramazan	Barbaros	TUR	5.1.98	3	NC	Mersin	12	Jun
3:41.8A	Kelvin	Kipkosgei	KEN	18.8.98	5	NC-j	Nairobi	22	Jun
3:41.85+	Drew	Hunter	USA	5.9.97	11	in 1M	Eugene	28	May
3:42.0A	Evans	Keitany	KEN	.98	5		Eldoret	16	Apr
3:42.2A	Aaron	Kibet	KEN	12.11.98	3		Nairobi	4	Apr
3:42.3A	Justus	Kiplagat (20)	KEN-Y	.99	6	NC-j	Nairobi	22	Jun

1 MILE

Mark	Name		Nat	Born	Pos	Meet	Venue	Date	
3:51.48	Asbel	Kiprop	KEN	30.6.89	1	Bisl	Oslo	9	Jun
3:51.54		Kiprop			1	Pre	Eugene	28	May
3:51.96	Abdelaati	Iguider	MAR	25.3.87	2	Pre	Eugene	28	May
3:52.04	Elijah	Manangoi	KEN	5.1.93	2	Bisl	Oslo	9	Jun
3:52.24	Taoufik	Makhloufi	ALG	29.4.88	3	Bisl	Oslo	9	Jun
3:52.26	Nick	Willis	NZL	25.4.83	4	Bisl	Oslo	9	Jun
3:52.39		Manangoi			3	Pre	Eugene	28	May
3:52.59	Ryan	Gregson	AUS	26.4.90	5	Bisl	Oslo	9	Jun
3:52.64	Charlie	Grice	GBR	7.11.93	1rB	Pre	Eugene	28	May
3:52.71	Vincent	Kibet	KEN	6.5.91	4	Pre	Eugene	28	May
	[10/8]								
3:53.04	Silas	Kiplagat	KEN	20.8.89	1	DL	London (OS)	22	Jul
3:53.17	Timothy	Cheruiyot	KEN	20.11.95	2	DL	London (OS)	22	Jul
	10)								
3:53.19	Henrik	Ingebrigtsen	NOR	24.2.91	7	Bisl	Oslo	9	Jun
3:53.23	Aman	Wote	ETH	18.4.84	6	Pre	Eugene	28	May
3:53.83	Ben	Blankenship	USA	15.12.89	7	Pre	Eugene	28	May
3:54.20	Jake	Wightman	GBR	11.7.94	4	DL	London (OS)	22	Jul
3:54.21	Evan	Jager	USA	8.3.89	8	Pre	Eugene	28	May
3:54.57	Kyle	Merber	USA	19.11.90	1		Raleigh	5	Aug
3:54.94	Colby	Alexander	USA	13.6.91	2		Raleigh	5	Aug
3:54.99	David	Torrence	USA/PER	26.11.85	1		Huntington, NY	31	Aug
3:55.25	Charles	Philibert-Thiboutot	CAN	31.12.90	2		Huntington, NY	31	Aug
3:55.27	John	Gregorek	USA	7.12.91	3		Raleigh	5	Aug
	(20)								
3:55.31	Nathan	Brannen	CAN	8.9.82	6	DL	London (OS)	22	Jul
3:55.43	Lee	Emanuel	GBR	24.1.85	7	DL	London (OS)	22	Jul
3:55.46	Andy	Bayer	USA	3.2.90	8	DL	London (OS)	22	Jul
3:55.60	Ford	Palmer	USA	6.10.90	31 Aug	3:56.72	Hamish	Carson	NZL	1.11.88	19 Jan
3:55.62	Robert	Biwott	KEN	28.1.96	9 Jun	3:56.73	Daniel	Winn	USA	30.7.91	22 Jul
3:55.80	Dawit	Wolde	ETH	19.5.91	28 May	3:56.89	James	Magut	KEN	20.7.90	28 May
3:56.05	Graham	Crawford	USA	29.12.92	5 Aug	3:57.15	Drew	Hunter	USA-J	5.9.97	5 Aug
3:56.14	Peter	Callahan	BEL	1.6.91	22 Jul	3:57.24	Frezer	Legesse	USA	4.6.90	2 Jun
3:56.39	Jordan	McNamara	USA	7.3.87	2 Jun	3:57.30	Eric	Speakman	NZL	29.8.90	19 Jan
3:56.44	Tom	Lancashire	GBR	2.7.85	22 Jul	3:57.39	Cristian	Soratos	USA	26.9.92	2 Jun
3:56.50	Eric	Avila	USA	3.10.89	31 Aug	3:57.58	Mikey	Brannigan	USA	12.11.96	5 Aug
3:56.62	Jerry	Motsau	RSA	12.3.90	22 Jul	3:57.60	Richard	Douma	NED	17.4.93	22 Jul
3:56.7	Luke	Mathews	AUS	21.6.95	23 Feb	3:57.80	Sam	Penzenstadler	USA	11.9.92	2 Jun
							[43]				

Indoors

Mark	Name		Nat	Born	Pos	Meet	Venue	Date	
3:50.63	Matthew	Centrowitz	USA	18.10.89	1	Mill	New York (A) (A)	20	Feb
3:51.06	Nick	Willis	NZL	25.4.83	2	Mill	New York (A)	20	Feb
3:52.91	Chris	O'Hare	GBR	23.11.90	3	Mill	New York (A)	20	Feb
3:53.16	Robby	Andrews	USA	29.3.91	4	Mill	New York (A)	20	Feb
3:53.87	Cory	Leslie	USA	24.10.89	5	Mill	New York (A)	20	Feb
3:53.89	Izaic	Yorks	USA	17.4.94	1		Seattle	27	Feb
3:53.95	Sean	McGorty	USA	8.3.95	2		Seattle	27	Feb
3:54.02	Dawit	Wolde	ETH	19.5.91	1		Athlone	17	Feb
3:55.10	Garrett	Heath	USA	3.11.85	6	Mill	New York (A)	20	Feb
3:55.41	Bethwel	Birgen	KEN	6.8.88	2		Boston (R)	14	Feb
3:56.05	Cristian	Soratos	USA	26.9.92	20 Feb	3:57.38	Edward	Cheserek	KEN	2.2.94	30 Jan
3:56.36	Blake	Haney	USA	29.3.96	20 Feb	3:57.38	David	Elliott	USA	21.7.93	13 Feb
3:56.87	Justyn	Knight	CAN	19.7.96	30 Jan	3:57.46	Jacob	Burcham	USA	13.2.95	13 Feb
3:56.91	Julian	Matthews	NZL	21.7.88	20 Feb	3:57.83i	Morgan	McDonald	AUS	23.4.96	6 Feb
3:57.03	Thomas	Awad	USA	27.5.94	20 Feb	3:57.84i	Ahmed	Bile	USA	21.9.93	6 Feb
3:57.11	Clayton	Murphy	USA	26.2.95	6 Feb	3:57.88i	Cole	Williams	USA	19.2.93	6 Feb
3:57.29	Sam	Penzenstadler	USA	11.9.92	6 Feb	3:57.95i	Sam	Prakel	USA	29.10.94	13 Feb

1 MILE – 2000 – 3000 METRES

Mark	Name		Nat	Born	Pos	Meet	Venue	Date
			JUNIORS					
3:57.15	Drew		Hunter	USA	5.9.97	6		Raleigh	5 Aug
	3:57.81i	4B	Mill	New York (Arm)	6 Feb		3:58.25i	7		New York (Arm)	6 Feb
3:59.53	Michael		Slagowski	USA	16.6.97	1		Portland	29 Apr

2000 METRES

4:59.20+	Abdelaati		Iguider	MAR	25.3.87	1	DL	Saint-Denis	27 Aug
4:59.5+e	Collins		Cheboi	KEN	25.9.87	2	DL	Saint-Denis	27 Aug
5:01.4+	Albert	Rop		BRN	17.7.92	27 Aug	5:01.9+	Mohamed Farah	GBR	23.3.83	5 Jun
5:01.75+	Vincent	Rono		KEN	22.12.90	5 Jun				

3000 METRES

Mark	Name		Nat	Born	Pos	Meet	Venue	Date
7:28.19	Yomif	Kejelcha	ETH-J	1.8.97	1	DL	Saint-Denis	27 Aug
7:30.09	Abdelaati	Iguider	MAR	25.3.87	2	DL	Saint-Denis	27 Aug
7:30.45	Hagos	Gebrhiwet	ETH	11.5.94	3	DL	Saint-Denis	27 Aug
7:30.93	Ryan	Hill	USA	31.1.90	4	DL	Saint-Denis	27 Aug
7:32.02	Albert	Rop	BRN	17.7.92	5	DL	Saint-Denis	27 Aug
7:32.48	Bethwel	Birgen	KEN	6.8.88	6	DL	Saint-Denis	27 Aug
7:32.62	Mohamed	Farah	GBR	23.3.83	1	DL	Birmingham	5 Jun
7:33.28	Muktar	Edris	ETH	14.1.94	7	DL	Saint-Denis	27 Aug
7:36.85		Iguider			1	DL	Rabat	22 May
7:37.76	Hayle	Ibrahimov	AZE	18.1.90	2	DL	Rabat	22 May
7:37.98	Paul	Chelimo	USA	27.10.90	8	DL	Saint-Denis	27 Aug
(11/10)								
7:39.02	Sadik	Mikhou	BRN	25.7.90	9	DL	Saint-Denis	27 Aug
7:39.51	Adel	Mechaal	ESP	5.12.90	3	DL	Rabat	22 May
7:41.31	Thomas	Longosiwa	KEN	14.1.82	10	DL	Saint-Denis	27 Aug
7:42.69	John	Kipkoech	KEN	29.12.91	4	DL	Rabat	22 May
7:43.00	Augustine	Choge	KEN	21.1.87	1	ISTAF	Berlin	3 Sep
7:43.30	Edwin	Soi	KEN	3.3.86	11	DL	Saint-Denis	27 Aug
7:43.63	Bernard	Lagat	USA	12.12.74	2	ISTAF	Berlin	3 Sep
7:44.16	Mathew	Kiptanui	KEN	20.10.94	2	DL	Birmingham	5 Jun
7:44.29	Birhanu	Yemataw	BRN	27.2.96	3	ISTAF	Berlin	3 Sep
7:44.90	Ryan	Gregson	AUS	26.4.90	12	DL	Saint-Denis	27 Aug
(30)								
7:44.96	Dejene	Debela	ETH	.94	5	DL	Rabat	22 May
7:44.99	Hillary	Maiyo	KEN	2.10.93	3	DL	Birmingham	5 Jun
7:45.00	Andrew	Butchart	GBR	14.10.91	4	DL	Birmingham	5 Jun
7:45.11	Yoann	Kowal	FRA	28.5.87	13	DL	Saint-Denis	27 Aug
7:45.22	Hillary	Ngetich	KEN	15.9.95	4	ISTAF	Berlin	3 Sep
7:45.24	Andy	Bayer	USA	3.2.90	5	ISTAF	Berlin	3 Sep
7:45.32	Collins	Cheboi	KEN	25.9.87	1		Göteborg	15 Jul
7:45.80	Zouhair	Aouad	BRN	7.4.89	1		Fès	30 Apr
7:46.24	Younès	Essalhi	MAR	20.2.93	1		Montgeron	15 May
7:46.37	Soufiyan	Bouqantar	MAR	30.8.93	1		Dessau	27 May
(40)								
7:46.58	Brahim	Kaazouzi	MAR	15.6.90	2		Montgeron	15 May
7:46.59	Richard	Ringer	GER	27.2.89	2		Dessau	27 May
7:46.61	Paul	Tanui	KEN	22.12.90	14	DL	Saint-Denis	27 Aug
7:48.04	Davis	Kiplangat	KEN-J	10.7.98	27 May	7:50.67	Biyazen	Alehegn	ETH-Y	16.9.99	3 Sep
7:48.27	Nelson	Kipkosgei	BRN	9.3.93	27 May	7:50.98+	Dejen	Gebremeskel	ETH	24.11.89	17 Jun
7:48.35	Sam	McEntee	AUS	3.2.92	30 Jan	7:50.98	Olivier	Irabaruta	BDI	25.8.90	23 Jun
7:49.24	Abayneh	Ayele	ETH	4.11.87	22 May	7:51.11	David	McNeill	AUS	6.10.86	3 Sep
7:49.42	Mohamed	Moustaoui	MAR	2.4.85	15 May	7:51.31	Illias	Fifa	MAR/ESP	16.5.89	11 Jun
7:49.56	Emmanuel	Kipsang	KEN	13.6.91	22 May	7:51.36	Zak	Patterson	AUS	29.5.95	30 Jan
7:49.68	Soufiane	El Bakkali	MAR	7.1.96	15 May	7:51.36	Ben	St. Lawrence	AUS	7.11.81	22 May
7:49.70	Filip	Ingebrigtsen	NOR	20.4.93	31 Aug	7:51.64	Joseph Macharia Ndirangu		KEN	9.9.94	17 Sep
7:50.65	Benson	Seurei	BRN	27.3.84	23 Jun	7:51.65	Clement	Kemboi	KEN	1.2.92	15 Jul
7:50.66	Ali	Kaya	TUR	20.4.94	29 May	(52)				

Indoors

7:38.03	Dejen	Gebremeskel	ETH	24.11.89	1		Boston	28 Feb
7:38.85	Hassan	Mead	USA	28.8.89	2	Mill	New York	20 Feb
7:39.23	Mohamed	Al-Garni ¶	QAT	2.7.92	1	AsiC	Doha	21 Feb
7:39.23	Augustine	Choge	KEN	21.1.87	1		Düsseldorf	3 Feb
7:39.43	Eric	Jenkins	USA	24.11.91	3	Mill	New York	20 Feb
7:39.82	Caleb	Ndiku	KEN	9.10.92	2		Düsseldorf	3 Feb
7:40.10	Evan	Jager	USA	8.3.89	4	Mill	New York	20 Feb
7:40.11	Mohammed	Ahmed	CAN	5.1.91	5	Mill	New York	20 Feb
7:40.24	Yenew	Alamirew	ETH	27.5.90	3		Düsseldorf	3 Feb
7:40.51	Edward	Cheserek	KEN	2.2.94	6	Mill	New York	20 Feb
7:40.74	Matthew	Centrowitz	USA	18.10.89	1		Portland	5 Feb

3000 METRES – 5000 METRES

Mark	Name		Nat	Born	Pos	Meet	Venue	Date	
7:40.79	Kemoy	Campbell	JAM	14.1.91	7	Mill	New York	20	Feb
7:41.25	Bernard	Lagat	USA	12.12.74	4	NC	Portland	11	Mar
7:41.26	Garrett	Heath	USA	3.11.85	5	NC	Portland	11	Mar
7:41.69	Dawit	Wolde	ETH	19.5.91	3		Glasgow	20	Feb
7:42.18	Yasin	Haji	ETH	22.1.96	5		Düsseldorf	3	Feb
7:42.33	Andy	Bayer	USA	3.2.90	8	Mill	New York	20	Feb
7:42.47	Thomas	Farrell	GBR	23.3.91	3		Portland	5	Feb
7:42.53	Isiah	Koech	KEN	19.12.93	6		Düsseldorf	3	Feb
7:43.01	Lopez	Lomong	USA	1.1.85	9	Mill	New York	20	Feb
7:43.04	Vincent	Rono	KEN	22.12.90	7		Düsseldorf	3	Feb
7:43.33	Trevor	Dunbar	USA	29.4.91	4		Portland	5	Feb
7:43.44	Youssouf Hiss	Bachir	DJI	87	4		Stockholm	17	Feb
7:44.29	Brett	Robinson	AUS	8.5.91	2		Boston (R)	14	Feb
7:44.50	Leul	Gebrselassie	ETH	20.9.93	1		Sabadell	19	Feb
7:44.69	Saïd Aden	Saïd	QAT	.93	3	AsiC	Doha	21	Feb
7:44.87	Vincent	Kibet	KEN	6.5.91	5		Karlsruhe	6	Feb
7:44.96	Ben	Blankenship	USA	15.12.89	4		Glasgow	20	Feb
7:45.07	Lawi	Lalang	KEN	15.6.91	3		Boston (R)	14	Feb
7:45.09	Paul Kipsiele	Koech	KEN	10.11.81	8		Düsseldorf	3	Feb
7:45.15	Soufiyan	Bouqantar	MAR	30.8.93	2		Sabadell	19	Feb
7:45.44	Cameron	Levins	CAN	28.3.89	10	Mill	New York	20	Feb
7:46.72	Jeff	See	USA	6.6.86	1		Nashville	13	Feb
7:47.18	Donn	Cabral	USA	12.12.89	11	Mill	New York	20	Feb
7:47.70	Mourad	Amdouni	FRA	21.1.88	3		Metz	21	Feb

7:48.34	Galen	Rupp	USA	8.5.86	11 Mar		7:50.70	Saïd	El Otmani	ITA	14.10.91	19 Feb
7:48.55	Patrick	Tiernan	AUS	11.9.94	12 Feb		7:50.74	Othmane	El Goumri ¶	MAR	28.5.92	20 Feb
7:48.71	Justyn	Knight	CAN	19.7.96	12 Feb		7:50.96	Colby	Gilbert	USA	17.3.95	13 Feb
7:48.79	Sean	McGorty	USA	8.3.95	12 Feb		7:51.04	Florian	Orth	GER	24.7.89	6 Feb
7:48.89	William	Kincaid	USA	21.9.92	22 Jan		7:51.21	Vladimir	Nikitin	RUS	5.8.92	14 Feb
7:49.53	Antonio	Abadía	ESP	2.7.90	6 Feb		7:51.29	Victor	García	ESP	13.3.85	19 Feb
7:50.06	Grant	Fisher	USA-J	22.4.97	13 Feb		7:51.38	Jefferson	Abbey	USA	93	13 Feb
7:50.20	Izaic	Yorks	USA	17.4.94	13 Feb		7:51.51	Pierce	Murphy	USA	92	27 Feb
7:50.41	Kyle	Merber	USA	19.11.90	27 Feb		7:51.56	Lucas	Bruchet	CAN	23.2.91	13 Feb
7:50.58	Aman	Kedi	ETH	16.9.94	19 Feb		7:51.73	Stephen	Sambu	KEN	3.7.88	5 Feb
7:50.60	Patrick	Corona	USA	17.3.94	13 Feb		7:51.77	Ahmed	Bile	USA	21.9.93	13 Feb
							7:51.85	Connor	Winter	USA	18.2.93	27 Feb

JUNIORS
See main list for top 2 juniors. 5 performances by 5 men to 7:55.0, Further juniors:

7:50.67	Biyazen	Alehegn	ETH-Y	16.9.99	6	ISTAF	Berlin	3	Sep
7:52.94	Jacob	Kiplimo	UGA-Y	14.11.00	3		Lignano	13	Jul
7:54.15	Yemane	Hailesilassie	ERI	21.2.98	19	DL	Saint-Denis	27	Aug
7:59.18	Hyuga	Endo	JPN	5.8.98	1		Itami	16	Aug
8:00.70	Tesfu	Tewelde	ERI	21.7.97	6		Madrid	23	Jun
8:01.63	Alex	Yee	GBR	18.2.98	1	LI	Loughborough	22	May
8:01.90	Elzan	Bibic	SRB-Y	8.1.99	1		Zenica	1	Jun

Indoors 5 performances by 2 men to 7:55.0

Kejelcha	7:39.11	2		Stockholm	17 Feb	7:43.77	1		Metz	21 Feb
	7:43.45	2		Karlsruhe	6 Feb	7:51.01	1h1 WI		Portland	18 Mar
7:50.06	Grant	Fisher	USA	22.4.97	1		Seattle	13	Feb
7:55.20	Morgan	McDonald	AUS	23.4.96	1		Ames	14	Feb

5000 METRES

12:59.29	Mohamed	Farah	GBR	23.3.83	1	DL	London (OS)	23	Jul
12:59.43	Muktar	Edris	ETH	14.1.94	1	Pre	Eugene	28	May
12:59.89	Dejen	Gebremeskel	ETH	24.11.89	1		Somerville, MA	17	Jun
12:59.96		Edris			1	DL	Shanghai	14	May
12:59.98	Geoffrey	Kamworor	KEN	28.11.92	2	Pre	Eugene	28	May
13:00.20	Hagos	Gebrhiwet	ETH	11.5.94	2		Somerville, MA	17	Jun
13:00.60	Joshua	Cheptegei	UGA	12.9.96	2	DL	Shanghai	14	May
13:00.99		Gebremeskel			1	FBK	Hengelo	22	May
13:01.69	Thomas	Longosiwa	KEN	14.1.82	3	DL	Shanghai	14	May
13:01.74	Mohammed	Ahmed	CAN	5.1.91	3	Pre	Eugene	28	May
13:02.49	Abadi	Hadis	ETH-J	6.11.97	4	DL	Shanghai	14	May
13:02.91		Longosiwa			4	Pre	Eugene	28	May
13:03.22	Ibrahim	Jeylan (10)	ETH	12.6.89	1	DL	Stockholm	16	Jun
13:03.26	Edwin	Soi	KEN	3.3.86	5	Pre	Eugene	28	May
13:03.29	Yomif	Kejelcha	ETH-J	1.8.97	5	DL	Shanghai	14	May
13:03.30		Farah			1	OG	Rio de Janeiro	20	Aug
13:03.66		Kejelcha			2	DL	Stockholm	16	Jun
13:03.90	Paul	Chelimo	USA	27.10.90	2	OG	Rio de Janeiro	20	Aug

5000 METRES

Mark	Name		Nat	Born	Pos	Meet	Venue	Date	
13:04.12		Gebrhiwet			6	DL	Shanghai	14	May
13:04.12	Abrar	Osman	ERI	1.1.94	2	FBK	Hengelo	22	May
13:04.17	Hassan	Mead	USA	28.8.89	6	Pre	Eugene	28	May
13:04.29	Yenew	Alamirew	ETH	27.5.90	7	Pre	Eugene	28	May
13:04.35		Gebrhiwet			3	OG	Rio de Janeiro	20	Aug
13:04.66	Bethwel	Birgen	KEN	6.8.88	3	FBK	Hengelo	22	May
13:04.87	Albert	Rop	BRN	17.7.92	7	DL	Shanghai	14	May
13:04.88	Elroy	Gelant	RSA	25.8.86	4	FBK	Hengelo	22	May
13:04.95		Hadis			5	FBK	Hengelo	22	May
13:05.54		Edris			3	DL	Stockholm	16	Jun
13:05.59	Getaneh	Tamire (20)	ETH	.94	6	FBK	Hengelo	22	May
13:05.64	Yigrem	Demelash	ETH	28.1.94	2	DL	Stockholm	16	Jun
13:05.94		Ahmed			4	OG	Rio de Janeiro	20	Aug
	[31/21]								
13:06.25	Imane	Merga	ETH	15.10.88	8	DL	Shanghai	14	May
13:06.78	Bernard	Lagat	USA	12.12.74	5	OG	Rio de Janeiro	20	Aug
13:08.34	Isiah	Koech	KEN	19.12.93	9	Pre	Eugene	28	May
13:08.61	Abdelaati	Iguider	MAR	25.3.87	4	Bisl	Oslo	9	Jun
13:08.61	Andrew	Butchart	GBR	14.10.91	6	OG	Rio de Janeiro	20	Aug
13:09.26	Birhanu	Yemataw	BRN	27.2.96	9	OG	Rio de Janeiro	20	Aug
13:10.80	Cornelius	Kangogo	KEN	31.12.93	1		Huelva	3	Jun
13:11.83	Illias	Fifa	ESP	16.5.89	2		Huelva	3	Jun
13:12.25	Caleb	Ndiku	KEN	9.10.92	10	Pre	Eugene	28	May
	(30)								
13:12.67	Ben	True	USA	29.12.85	11	Pre	Eugene	28	May
13:12.67	Solomon	Berihu	ETH-J	22.10.99?	6	DL	Stockholm	16	Jun
13:12.68	Antonio	Abadía	ESP	2.7.90	8	FBK	Hengelo	22	May
13:13.07	Victor	Chumo	KEN	1.1.87	2		Bellinzona	6	Jun
13:13.35	Douglas	Kipserem	KEN	87	1	AfCh	Durban	26	Jun
13:13.39	Aron	Kifle	ERI-J	20.2.98	3		Huelva	3	Jun
13:13.88	Leul	Gebrselassie	ETH	20.9.93	4		Huelva	3	Jun
13:13.92	Hayle	Ibrahimov	AZE	18.1.90	8	Bisl	Oslo	9	Jun
13:13.93	James Mwangi	Wangari	KEN	23.3.94	1		Kumamoto	2	Apr
13:14.06	Mathew	Kiptanui	KEN	20.10.94	2		Barcelona	9	Jul
	(40)								
13:14.16	Zouhaïr	Aouad	BRN	7.4.89	3		Barcelona (S)	30	Jun
13:14.92	Bashir	Abdi	BEL	10.2.89	10	FBK	Hengelo	22	May
13:15.22	Paul	Tanui	KEN	22.12.90	12	Pre	Eugene	28	May
13:15.32	Jonathan	Ndiku	KEN	18.9.91	1		Yokohama	23	Oct
13:15.40	Adel	Mechaal	ESP	5.12.90	5		Huelva	3	Jun
13:15.59	Fredrick	Kipkosgei	KEN	13.11.96	11	FBK	Hengelo	22	May
13:15.59	Ryan	Hill	USA	31.1.90	5	DL	London (OS)	23	Jul
13:15.94	Remmy	Limo	KEN	3.2.88	3		Bellinzona	6	Jun
13:16.12	Jaouad	Tougane	MAR	10.1.89	6		Huelva	3	Jun
13:16.35	Davis	Kiplangat	KEN-J	10.7.98	2	NA	Heusden-Zolder	16	Jul
	[50]								
13:16.82	John	Maina	KEN	14.7.93	2		Yokohama	23	Oct
13:16.85	Mang'ata	Ndiwa	KEN	12.12.87	3	AfCh	Durban	26	Jun
13:16.86	Evan	Jager	USA	8.3.89	3	WK	Zürich	1	Sep
13:17.08	Nicholas	Kosimbei	KEN	1.10.96	3	NA	Heusden-Zolder	16	Jul
13:17.24	Hizkel	Tewelde	ERI	15.9.86	3		Carquefou	3	Jun
13:17.32	Younès	Essalhi	MAR	20.2.93	7		Huelva	3	Jun
13:17.50	Paul	Kamais	KEN	24.10.96	1		Nobeoka	7	May
13:17.98	Olivier	Irabaruta	BDI	25.8.90	1		Ponzano Veneto	10	Jun
13:18.15	Aweke	Ayalew	BRN	23.2.93	11	DL	Shanghai	14	May
13:18.17	John	Kipkoech	KEN	29.12.91	4		Bellinzona	6	Jun
	(60)								
13:18.52	Shadrack	Kipchirchir	USA	22.2.89	1	Jordan	Stanford	1	May
13:18.78	Peter	Lagat	KEN	26.5.92	5	AfCh	Durban	26	Jun
13:18.98	Rodgers Kemoi	Chumo	KEN-J	3.3.97	2		Kumamoto	2	Apr
13:19.09	Emmanuel	Kipsang	KEN	13.6.91	5		Bellinzona	6	Jun
13:19.29	Brett	Robinson	AUS	8.5.91	12	FBK	Hengelo	22	May
13:19.36	El Hassan	El Abbassi	BRN	13.4.84	5		Barcelona	9	Jul
13:19.38	Alfred	Ngeno	KEN-J	2.5.97	3		Yokohama	23	Oct
13:19.42	David	Torrence	USA/PER	26.11.85	3	Jordan	Stanford	1	May
13:19.50	Yasin	Haji	ETH	22.1.96	12	DL	Shanghai	14	May
13:19.54	Jacob	Kiplimo	KEN-Y	14.11.00	2		Ponzano Veneto	10	Jun
	(70)								
13:19.89	William Malel	Sitonik	KEN	1.3.94	3		Kumamoto	2	Apr
13:20.32	Cyrus	Rutto	KEN	21.4.92	1		Nijmegen	18	May

MEN 2016

5000 METRES

Mark	Name		Nat	Born	Pos	Meet	Venue	Date	
13:20.39	Ambrose	Bore	KEN	8.8.95	2		Nijmegen	18	May
13:20.51	Josephat	Menjo	KEN	20.8.79	1	PNG	Turku	29	Jun
13:20.69	Galen	Rupp	USA	8.5.86	1		Portland	12	Jun
13:20.72	Sam	McEntee	AUS	3.2.92	4	Jordan	Stanford	1	May
13:20.88	Patrick	Tiernan	AUS	11.9.94	2	PNG	Turku	29	Jun
13:21.14	Stephen	Sambu	KEN	3.7.88	5	Jordan	Stanford	1	May
13:21.21	Selemon	Birega	ETH-Y	20.1.00	1	WJ	Bydgoszcz	23	Jul
13:21.50	Djamal Abdi	Dirieh	DJI-J	.97	2	WJ	Bydgoszcz	23	Jul
(80)									
13:21.68	Namakoe	Nkhasa	LES	10.1.94	6	AfCh	Durban	26	Jun
13:21.70	Soufiyan	Bouqantar	MAR	30.8.93	1		Kortrijk	9	Jul
13:21.90	Alexander	Mutiso	KEN	10.9.96	5		Kumamoto	2	Apr
13:22.53	Jamal	Chatbi ¶	ITA	30.4.84	3		Nijmegen	18	May
13:22.64	Mourad	Amdouni	FRA	21.1.88	9	DL	Stockholm	16	Jun
13:22.90	Awet Niftalem	Kibrab	ERI	9.5.95	1		Oordegem	28	May
13:23.03	Dawit	Fikadu	ETH	95	4		Barcelona (S)	30	Jun
13:23.04	Tsegay	Tuemay	ERI	20.12.95	2		Portland	12	Jun
13:23.06	Garrett	Heath	USA	3.11.85	6	Jordan	Stanford	1	May
13:23.10	Paul Kipsiele	Koech	KEN	10.11.81	8	DL	London (OS)	23	Jul
(90)									
13:23.34	Wesley	Ledama	KEN-Y	2.7.99	3	WJ	Bydgoszcz	23	Jul
13:23.43	Joseph Macharia	Ndirangu	KEN	9.9.94	1r1		Osaka	25	Sep
13:23.66	Teressa	Nyakora	ETH	26.2.95	3		Nobeoka	7	May
13:23.66	Stephen	Mokoka	RSA	31.1.85	9	DL	London (OS)	23	Jul
13:23.67	Florian	Orth	GER	24.7.89	2		Oordegem	28	May
13:23.79	Charles	Muneria	KEN	10.2.96	2		Yokohama	24	May
13:23.87	David	McNeill	AUS	6.10.86	3	PNG	Turku	29	Jun
13:23.94	Jonathan	Davies	GBR	28.10.94	3		Oordegem	28	May
13:24.10	Lucas	Bruchet	CAN	23.2.91	3		Portland	12	Jun
13:24.13	Teklit	Tewaldebrhan	ERI	1.10.93	1		Yokohama	15	May
[100]									
13:24.25	Sean	McGorty	USA	7.3.95	1	May	13:30.27	Reed	Connor	USA	25.9.90	12	Jun
13:24.33	Eric	Jenkins	USA	24.11.91	23	Jul	13:30.3A	Elijah	Kiptoo	KEN	9.6.86	26	May
13:24.40	Awet	Habte	ERI-J	29.9.97	15	May	13:30.35	George	Alex	USA	20.1.90	23	Jun
13:24.46	Leonard	Barsoton	KEN	21.10.94	7	May	13:30.47	Charles	Ndirangu	KEN	8.2.93	29	Apr
13:24.54	El Mahjoub	Dazza	MAR	3.3.91	9	Jul	13:30.61A	Thomas	Ayeko	UGA	10.2.92	7	Jul
13:24.66	Phillip	Kipyeko	UGA	10.1.95	17	Aug	13:30.97	Jonathan	Taylor	GBR	10.10.87	28	May
13:24.74	David	Njuguna	KEN	6.9.89	25	Sep	13:31.0A	Geoffrey	Rono	KEN	21.4.87	26	May
13:24.93	Mamiyo	Nuguse	ETH	13.2.82	2	Apr	13:31.08	Kassa	Mekashaw	ETH	19.3.84	13	Nov
13:24.97	Mohamed	Al-Outaibi ¶	KSA	20.6.76	9	Jul	13:31.09	Hiko	Tonosa	ETH	9.10.95	13	Nov
13:25.16	Hillary	Maiyo	KEN	2.10.93	6	Sep	13:31.21	Jeff	See	USA	6.6.86	20	May
13:25.32	Charles	Ndungu	KEN	20.2.96	2	Apr	13:31.30	Ryan	Walling	USA	10.12.92	10	Jun
13:25.35	Leonard	Korir	KEN/USA	10.12.86	1	May	13:31.45	Suguru	Osako	JPN	23.5.91	17	Aug
13:25.59	Edward	Cheserek	KEN	2.2.94	10	Jun	13:31.56	Shuho	Dairokuno	JPN	23.12.92	29	Apr
13:25.64	Bidan	Karoki	KEN	21.8.90	13	Nov	13:31.57	Samuel	Mwangi	KEN-J	19.9.97	24	Apr
13:25.66	Gabriel	Geay	TAN	10.9.96	12	Jun	13:31.66	Patrick	Corona	USA	17.3.94	10	Jun
13:25.91	Amos	Kirui	KEN-J	9.2.98	2	Apr	13:31.67	Berhanu	Legesse	ETH	11.9.94	14	May
13:26.16	Andrew	Vernon	GBR	7.1.86	29	Jun	13:31.76	John	Koech	BRN	23.8.95	29	Jun
13:26.23	Zersenay	Tadese	ERI	8.2.82	16	Jun	13:31.89	Marouan	Razine	ITA	9.4.91	6	Sep
13:26.24	Thierry	Ndikumwenayo	BDI-J	26.3.97	26	Jun	13:31.91	Jean-Marie Vianney	Niyomukiza	RWA-J	.97	26	Jun
13:26.36	Justyn	Knight	CAN	19.7.96	23	Jun	13:32.00	Yevgeniy	Rybakov	RUS	27.2.85	27	May
13:26.79	Cameron	Levins	CAN	28.3.89	28	May	13:32.12	Anatoliy	Rybakov	RUS	27.2.85	27	May
13:27.32	William	Kincaid	USA	21.9.92	23	Jun	13:32.3A	Franklin	Ngelel	KEN	.86	26	May
13:27.44	Dejene	Debela	ETH	.95	9	Jun	13:33.03	Debele	Gezmu	ETH	14.4.96	17	Jun
13:27.53	Samuel	Chelanga	USA	23.2.85	20	May	13:33.16	Hiram	Ngatia	KEN	1.1.96	2	Apr
13:27.63	Patrick	Wambui	KEN	2.11.96	24	Apr	13:33.25	Charles Philibert-Thiboutot		CAN	31.12.90	1	May
13:27.64	Thomas	Curtin	USA	8.8.93	10	Jun	13:33.82	Lawi	Lalang	KEN	15.6.91	3	Jun
13:27.70	Daniel	Kipkemoi	KEN	5.7.96	24	Apr	13:33.84	Martin	Sperlich	GER	28.8.91	6	Jun
13:27.71	James	Rungaru	KEN	14.1.93	17	Sep	13:33.94	Dennis	Licht	NED	30.5.84	22	May
13:27.77	Thomas	Farrell	GBR	23.3.91	20	May	13:34.04	Daniel	Kitonyi	KEN	12.1.94	7	May
13:27.77	Ronald	Kwemoi	KEN	19.9.95	13	Nov	13:34.29	Yoann	Kowal	FRA	28.5.87	16	Jun
13:28.25	Vincent	Rono	KEN	22.12.90	16	Jul	13:34.31	Ross	Proudfoot	CAN	4.7.92	3	Jun
13:28.41	Biyazen	Alehegn	ETH-Y	16.9.99	23	Jul	13:34.52	Yuichiro	Ueno	JPN	29.7.85	29	Apr
13:28.45	Tariq	Al-Amri	KSA	23.12.90	9	Jul	13:34.52	Abdallah	Mande	UGA	10.5.95	26	Jun
13:28.53	Zelalem	Bacha	BRN	10.1.88	16	Jun	13:34.54	Onésphore	Nkunzimana	BDI	23.7.85	26	Jun
13:28.91	Takanori	Ichikawa	JPN	3.11.90	2	Apr	13:34.64	Hazuma	Hattori	JPN	7.2.95	7	May
13:29.13	Brian	Shrader	USA	22.7.91	23	Jun	13:34.95	Carlos	Mayo	ESP	18.9.95	3	Jun
13:29.20	Moses	Kurong	UGA	7.7.94	16	Jun	13:34.98	Cameron	Marantz	USA	29.8.87	23	Jun
13:29.51	Abbabiya	Simbassa	USA	30.6.93	12	Jun	13:34.99	Isaac	Korir	BRN	26.8.90	27	Apr
13:29.79	Morgan	McDonald	AUS	23.4.96	10	Jun	13:35.06	Kota	Murayama	JPN	23.2.93	5	Jun
13:29.87	Donn	Cabral	USA	12.12.89	1	May	13:35.10	Moses	Koech	KEN-J	5.4.97	23	Jul
13:30.05	Tariq	Haddadi	MAR	7.6.90	16	Jul	13:35.19	Takashi	Ichida	JPN	16.6.92	29	Apr
13:30.06	Vladimir	Nikitin	RUS	5.8.92	27	May	13:35.20	Colby	Gilbert	USA	17.3.95	15	May
13:30.09	Kemoy	Campbell	JAM	14.1.91	20	May	13:35.28	Elijah	Kipchirchir	KEN	.96	5	Mar
13:30.13	Grant	Fisher	USA-J	22.4.97	10	Jun	13:36.08	Hideyuki	Tanaka	JPN	23.2.84	29	Apr
13:30.18	Kirubel	Erassa	USA	17.6.93	23	Jun	13:36.14	Fabiano	Sulle	TAN	1.10.94	7	May

5000 – 10,000 METRES

Mark	Name		Nat	Born	Pos	Meet	Venue		Date
13:36.33	Cyrus	Kingori	KEN-J	5.1.97	7	May			
13:36.65	Yemaneberhan	Crippa	ITA	15.10.96	6	Jun			
13:36.79	Morgan	Pearson	USA	22.9.93	15	May			
13:36.83	Sydney	Gidabuday	USA	21.8.96	15	Apr			
13:36.88	Frezer	Legesse	USA	4.6.90	20	May			
13:37.34A	Peter	Langat	KEN-J	20.10.98					28 May
13:37.41		Bekele					Shiferaw	ETH	14.10.95 11 Jul
13:37.52	Mitch	Brown						AUS	30.1.88 20 May
13:37.54	Ben						St. Lawrence	AUS	7.11.81 5 Mar
13:37.56	Mason (200)						Ferlic	USA	5.8.93 15 Apr

Disqualified for obstruction
13:04.79 Edris (4) OG Rio de Janeiro 20 Aug

JUNIORS
See main list for top 11 juniors. 16 performances by 8 men to 13:20.0. Additional marks and further juniors:

Hadis 2+	13:11.45	7	Bisl	Oslo		9 Jun			
Kejelcha 2+	13:06.24	1		Barcelona		30 Jun	13:11.97	1	Barcelona (S) 9 Jul
	13:08.34	3	Bisl	Oslo		9 Jun	13:19.90	7 WK	Zürich 1 Sep
Kiplangat	13:16.46	2		Carquefou		3 Jun			
13:24.40	Awet		Habte	ERI	29.9.97	2		Yokohama	15 May
13:25.91	Amos		Kirui	KEN	9.2.98	3rB		Kumamoto	2 Apr
13:26.24	Thierry		Ndikumwenayo	BDI-	26.3.97	7	AfCh	Durban	26 Jun
13:28.41	Biyazen		Alehegn	ETH	16.9.99	4	WJ	Bydgoszcz	23 Jul
13:30.13	Grant		Fisher	USA	22.4.97	6	NCAA	Eugene	10 Jun
13:31.57	Samuel		Mwangi	KEN	19.9.97	6		Yokohama	24 Apr
13:31.91	Jean-Marie		Vianney Niyomukiza	RWA	.97	8	AfCh	Durban	26 Jun
13:35.10	Moses		Koech	KEN	5.4.97	6	WJ	Bydgoszcz	23 Jul
13:36.33	Cyrus		Kingori (20)	KEN	5.1.97	13		Nobeoka	7 May
13:37.34A	Peter		Langat	KEN	20.10.98	3	NC	Nairobi	28 May

Best European: 13:51.40 Elzan Bibic SRB-Y 8.1.99 8 WJ Bydgoszcz 23 Jul

10,000 METRES

Mark	Name		Nat	Born	Pos	Meet	Venue	Date
26:51.11	Yigrem	Demelash	ETH	28.1.94	1	OT	Hengelo	29 Jun
26:53.71	Mohamed	Farah	GBR	23.3.83	1	Pre	Eugene	27 May
26:54.66	William Malel	Sitonik	KEN	1.3.94	2	Pre	Eugene	27 May
26:57.33	Tamirat	Tola	ETH	11.8.91	3	Pre	Eugene	27 May
26:57.45		Tola			2	OT	Hengelo	29 Jun
26:57.88	Abadi	Hadis	ETH-J	6.11.97	3	OT	Hengelo	29 Jun
26:58.25	Stephen	Sambu	KEN	3.7.88	4	Pre	Eugene	27 May
26:58.75	Ibrahim	Jeylan	ETH	12.6.89	5	Pre	Eugene	27 May
27:00.66	Zersenay	Tadese	ERI	8.2.82	6	Pre	Eugene	27 May
27:02.59	Nicholas	Kosimbei	KEN	1.10.96	7	Pre	Eugene	27 May
27:05.17		Farah			1	OG	Rio de Janeiro	13 Aug
27:05.64	Paul	Tanui (10)	KEN	22.12.90	2	OG	Rio de Janeiro	13 Aug
27:06.26		Tola			3	OG	Rio de Janeiro	13 Aug
27:06.27		Demelash			4	OG	Rio de Janeiro	13 Aug
27:07.30	Bidan	Karoki	KEN	21.8.90	1		Yokohama	13 Nov
27:08.92	Galen	Rupp	USA	8.5.86	5	OG	Rio de Janeiro	13 Aug
27:09.78	Guye	Adola	ETH	20.10.90	8	Pre	Eugene	27 May
27:10.06	Joshua	Cheptegei	UGA	12.9.96	6	OG	Rio de Janeiro	13 Aug
27:11.23	Jonathan	Ndiku	KEN	18.9.91	2		Yokohama	13 Nov
27:11.83	Belay	Tilahun	ETH	.95	4	OT	Hengelo	29 Jun
27:19.71	Leul	Gebrselassie	ETH	20.9.93	1		Herzogenaurach	13 May
27:20.65	Adugna	Tekele	ETH	26.2.89	5	OT	Hengelo	29 Jun
27:21.97	John	Maina	KEN	3.8.94	3		Yokohama	13 Nov
27:22.28		Tanui			1		Kobe	24 Apr
27:22.93		Karoki			7	OG	Rio de Janeiro	13 Aug
27:22.99	Emmanuel	Kipsang (20)	KEN	13.6.91	2		Herzogenaurach	13 May
27:23.04	James Mwangi	Wangari	KEN	23.3.94	1		Kobe	23 Apr
27:23.86		Tadese			8	OG	Rio de Janeiro	13 Aug
27:24.85	Mamiyo	Nuguse	ETH	13.2.82	2		Kobe	24 Apr
27:25.10	Tebalu [30/23]	Zawude	ETH	2.11.87	3		Herzogenaurach	13 May
27:25.23	Rodgers Chumo	Kwemoi	KEN-J	3.3.97	1	WJ	Bydgoszcz	19 Jul
27:25.94	Vincent	Yator	KEN	11.7.89	9	Pre	Eugene	27 May
27:26.20	Aron	Kifle	ERI-J	20.2.98	2	WJ	Bydgoszcz	19 Jul
27:26.68	Jacob	Kiplimo	KEN-Y	14.11.00	3	WJ	Bydgoszcz	19 Jul
27:27.30	Birhan	Nebebew	ETH	14.8.94	10	Pre	Eugene	27 May
27:27.33	Imane	Merga	ETH	15.10.88	11	Pre	Eugene	27 May
27:27.43	Moses	Kurong (30)	UGA	7.7.94	2		Leiden	11 Jun
27:30.17	James	Rungaru	KEN	14.1.93	1		Tajimi	15 Oct
27:30.50	Hizkel	Tewelde	ERI	15.9.86	3		Leiden	11 Jun
27:30.75	Hiram	Ngatia	KEN	1.1.96	2		Tajimi	15 Oct
27:30.79	Nguse	Tesfaldet	ERI	10.11.86	9	OG	Rio de Janeiro	13 Aug

10,000 METRES

Mark	Name		Nat	Born	Pos	Meet	Venue	Date
27:31.86	Leonard	Barsoton	KEN	21.10.94	12	Pre	Eugene	27 May
27:31.86	Abreham	Cheroben	BRN	11.10.92	10	OG	Rio de Janeiro	13 Aug
27:31.94	Geoffrey	Kamworor	KEN	28.11.92	11	OG	Rio de Janeiro	13 Aug
27:33.67	Zane	Robertson	NZL	14.11.89	12	OG	Rio de Janeiro	13 Aug
27:33.94	Ronald	Kwemoi	KEN	19.9.95	1rA		Machida	26 Nov
27:35.50	Polat Kemboi	Arikan	TUR	12.12.90	13	OG	Rio de Janeiro	13 Aug
(40)								
27:35.65	Leonard	Korir	KEN/USA	10.12.86	14	OG	Rio de Janeiro	13 Aug
27:35.83	Abayneh	Ayele	ETH	4.11.87	7	OT	Hengelo	29 Jun
27:37.65	Goitom	Kifle	ERI	3.12.93	5		Leiden	11 Jun
27:38.69	Chris	Derrick	USA	17.10.90	3rA		Machida	26 Nov
27:39.25	Alexander	Mutiso	KEN	10.9.96	4rA		Machida	26 Nov
27:40.23	Edward	Waweru	KEN	3.10.90	3		Tajimi	15 Oct
27:40.76	Azmeraw	Mengistu	ETH	15.9.92	9	OT	Hengelo	29 Jun
27:41.28	Patrick	Mwaka	KEN	2.11.92	5rA		Machida	26 Nov
27:42.34	Teklemariam	Medhin	ERI	24.6.89	14	Pre	Eugene	27 May
27:42.75	Teressa	Nyakora	ETH	26.2.95	6rA		Machida	26 Nov
[50]								
27:43.55	Kassa	Mekashaw	ETH	19.3.84	7rA		Machida	26 Nov
27:44.39	Kota	Murayama	JPN	23.2.93	8rA		Machida	26 Nov
27:45.04	Abiyot	Abinet	ETH	10.5.89	1		Abashiri	11 Jul
27:45.27	Samuel	Mwangi	KEN-J	19.9.97	9rA		Machida	26 Nov
27:47.29	El Hassan	El Abbassi	BRN	13.4.84	15	Pre	Eugene	27 May
27:48.02	Eric	Jenkins	USA	24.11.91	16	Pre	Eugene	27 May
27:48.35	Yuta	Shitara	JPN	18.12.91	2		Abashiri	11 Jul
27:48.56	Minato	Oishi	JPN	19.5.88	10rA		Machida	26 Nov
27:48.84	Stephen	Mokoka	RSA	31.1.85	17	Pre	Eugene	27 May
27:49.35	Bernard	Lagat	USA	12.12.74	1	Jordan	Stanford	1 May
(60)								
27:49.57	David	Njuguna	KEN	6.9.89	1rB		Machida	26 Nov
27:49.89	Daniel	Kitonyi	KEN	12.1.94	2rB		Machida	26 Nov
27:50.27	Suguru	Osako	JPN	23.5.91	2	Jordan	Stanford	1 May
27:50.81	Bernard	Kimani	KEN	10.9.93	4		Kobe	24 Apr
27:51.71	David	McNeill	AUS	6.10.86	16	OG	Rio de Janeiro	13 Aug
27:52.1A	Kenneth	Kipkemoi	KEN	2.8.84	1	NC	Nairobi	28 May
27:52.70	Futsum	Zienasellassie	USA	16.12.92	3	Jordan	Stanford	1 May
27:53.05	Emmanuel	Bett	KEN	30.3.83	18	Pre	Eugene	27 May
27:53.30	Cleophas	Ngetich	KEN	12.11.95	2	ISR Ch	Tel Aviv	21 Apr
27:53.38	Abraham	Habte	ERI	14.7.96	4	Jordan	Stanford	1 May
(70)								
27:53.50	Simon	Kariuki	KEN	13.2.92	14rA		Machida	26 Nov
27:53.59	Takashi	Ichida	JPN	16.6.92	3		Abashiri	11 Jul
27:54.2A	Wilfred	Kimitei	KEN	11.3.85	2	NC	Nairobi	28 May
27:54.57	Samuel	Chelanga	USA	23.2.85	5	Jordan	Stanford	1 May
27:54.75	Shuho	Dairokuno	JPN	23.12.92	15rA		Machida	26 Nov
27:54.80	Luis	Ostos	PER	9.12.92	6	Jordan	Stanford	1 May
27:54.99	Vincent	Chepkok	KEN	5.7.88	4		Herzogenaurach	13 May
27:55.06	Ross	Millington	GBR	19.9.89	6		Leiden	11 Jun
27:55.92	Olivier	Irabaruta	BDI	25.8.90	1		Fucecchio	9 Apr
27:56.47	Dominic	Nyairo	KEN-J	22.8.97	3		Kobe	23 Apr
(80)								
27:56.48	Hassan	Chani	BRN	5.5.88	5		Herzogenaurach	13 May
27:56.98	Mogos	Shumay	ERI-J	1.1.97	8	Jordan	Stanford	1 May
27:57.07A	Charles	Muneria	KEN	10.2.96	2	OT	Eldoret	1 Jul
27:57.3A	Thomas	Ayeko	UGA	10.2.92	1	NC	Kampala	7 Jul
27:57.36	Charles	Ndungu	KEN	20.2.96	5		Kobe	23 Apr
27:57.57	Joseph	Ndirangu	KEN	9.9.94	6		Kobe	23 Apr
27:58.22	Yetwale	Kende	ETH	10.1.91	11	OT	Hengelo	29 Jun
27:58.32	Shadrack	Kipchirchir	USA	22.2.89	19	OG	Rio de Janeiro	13 Aug
27:58.32	Daniel	Kipkemoi	KEN	5.7.96	16rA		Machida	26 Nov
27:59.0A	Stephen	Arita	KEN	26.6.88	3	NC	Nairobi	28 May
(90)								
27:59.72	Mitsunori	Asaoka	JPN	11.1.93	4		Abashiri	11 Jul
27:59.74	Patrick	Tiernan	AUS	11.9.94	1	Zátopek	Melbourne	8 Dec
28:00.14	Amedework	Walelegn	ETH-Y	11.3.99	4	WJ	Bydgoszcz	19 Jul
28:00.43	Scott	Fauble	USA	5.11.91	3		Stanford	1 May
28:01.49	Bashir	Abdi	BEL	10.2.89	20	OG	Rio de Janeiro	13 Aug
28:01.53	Fabiano	Sulle	TAN	1.10.94	7		Kobe	23 Apr
28:01.76	Cyrus	Kingori	KEN-J	5.1.97	8		Kobe	23 Apr
28:04.84	Timothy	Toroitich	UGA	10.10.91	23	OG	Rio de Janeiro	13 Aug
28:04.98	Gabriel	Geay	TAN	10.9.96	1		Portland	11 Jun

10,000 METRES

Mark	Name		Nat	Born	Pos	Meet	Venue		Date
28:06.33	Namakoe [100]	Nkhasi	10.1.94?	LES	10.1.93	3	AfCh	Durban	22 Jun
28:06.64	German	Fernandez	USA	2.11.90	1 Apr		28:21.69	Patrick	Wambui	KEN	2.11.96	19 May
28:06.92	Joseph	Kamathi	KEN	23.11.96	11 Jul		28:21.92	Abdallah	Mande	UGA	10.5.95	22 Jun
28:07.14	Antonio	Abadía	ESP	2.7.90	9 Apr		28:22.17	Masaki	Toda	JPN	21.6.93	26 Nov
28:07.53	Hiroyuki	Yamamoto	JPN	30.4.86	11 Jul		28:22.32	Aron	Rono	USA	1.11.82	1 Apr
28:07.55	Alex	Cherop	UGA	15.1.93	11 Jun		28:22.62	Noah	Droddy	USA	22.9.90	11 Jun
28:08.56	Akinobu	Murasawa	JPN	28.3.91	11 Jul		28:22.63	Karemi Jeremiah	Thuku	KEN	7.7.94	7 Jul
28:08.92	Yimer	Mekonnen	ETH		22 Jun		28:22.8A	Augustine	Choge	KEN	21.1.87	23 Apr
28:08.98	Amos	Kirui	KEN-J	9.2.98	7 May		28:22.97	Shun	Sakuraoka	JPN	1.9.94	11 Jul
28:09.21	Fikadu	Haftu	ETH	21.2.94	22 Jun		28:23.04	Anatoliy	Rybakov	RUS	27.2.85	22 Jun
28:09.35	Andrew	Bumbalough	USA	14.3.87	26 Nov		28:24.27	Scott	Smith	USA	13.7.86	11 Jun
28:09.57	Gizachew	Hailu	ETH-J	18.4.98	19 Jul		28:24.50	Gladwin	Mzazi	RSA	28.8.88	22 Jun
28:09.74	Yuma	Hattori	JPN	13.11.93	15 Oct		28:24.71	Daniele	Meucci	ITA	7.10.85	5 Jun
28:10.07	Josephat	Onsarigo	KEN	.93	3 Dec		28:25.09	Naoki	Kudo	JPN	5.9.95	11 Jul
28:10.54	Bekele	Shiferaw	ETH	14.10.95	26 Nov		28:25.29	Okbay	Tsegay	ERI	86	11 Jun
28:10.62	Shun	Inoura	JPN	26.7.92	26 Nov		28:25.32	Ben	Bruce	USA	10.9.82	1 May
28:10.77	Yuichiro	Ueno	JPN	29.7.85	3 Dec		28:25.52	Keijiro	Mogi	JPN	21.10.95	24 Jun
28:11.04	Soufiane	Bouchikhi	BEL	22.3.90	11 Jun		28:25.85	Hiroki	Nagayama	JPN	20.7.96	26 Nov
28:11.52	Aimeru	Almeya	ISR	8.6.90	11 Jun		28:25.9A	Peter	Emase	KEN	12.12.93	28 May
28:11.64	Martin	Musau	UGA-J	5.10.98	11 Jun		28:26.11	Alex	Mwangi	KEN	14.6.90	23 Apr
28:12.70	Sota	Hoshi	JPN	6.1.88	26 Nov		28:26.12	Akihiko	Tsumurai	JPN	10.7.84	24 Apr
28:13.43	Ronald	Kiprotich	KEN-J	6.12.98	19 Jul		28:26.70	Takaya	Sato	JPN	5.5.94	24 Sep
28:13.46	Ismail	Juma Gallet	TAN	3.8.91	22 Jun		28:27.10	Xolisa	Tyali	RSA	2.12.89	11 Jun
28:13.84	Bonsa	Dida	ETH	21.1.95	29 Jun		28:27.50	Shogo	Nakamura	JPN	16.9.92	7 May
28:13.97	Tsubasa	Hayakawa	JPN	2.7.90	15 Oct		28:27.54	Keigo	Yano	JPN	3.12.91	26 Nov
28:14.01	Mohamed	Ziani	MAR	.93	29 Jun		28:27.75	Yevgeniy	Rybakov	RUS	27.2.85	22 Jun
28:14.10	Alfred	Ngeno	KEN-J	2.5.97	26 Nov		28:27.90	Dmytro	Lashyn	UKR	17.2.88	8 Jul
28:15.18	Enoch	Omwamba	KEN	4.4.93	24 Sep		28:28.40	Titus	Mogusu	KEN	.96	24 Sep
28:15.42	Ryo	Matsumoto	JPN	19.10.90	15 Oct		28:28.50	Tatsuya	Oike	JPN	18.5.90	26 Nov
28:15.56	Masato	Terauchi	JPN	18.10.93	15 Oct		28:28.55	Dewi	Griffiths	GBR	9.8.91	8 Jul
28:16.49	Hironori	Tsuetaki	JPN	8.5.93	26 Nov		28:28.56	Benjamin	Gandu	KEN	21.5.91	21 May
28:16.91	Tsegay	Tadese	ETH	30.11.96	16 Jan		28:28.92	Kazuma	Ito	JPN	17.6.88	26 Nov
28:17.03	Alex	Monroe	USA	30.3.92	1 Apr		28:28.93	Juan Antonio	Pérez	ESP	6.11.88	5 Jun
28:17.4A	John	Langat	KEN	31.12.96	28 May		28:29.01	Hiroki	Matsueda	JPN	20.5.93	24 Sep
28:17.5A	Joseph	Kiptum	KEN	25.9.87	23 Apr		28:29.43	Atsushi	Yamato	JPN-J	13.3.97	26 Nov
28:17.54	Daichi	Kamino	JPN	13.9.93	11 Jul		28:29.61	Hideyuki	Tanaka	JPN	9.10.90	26 Nov
28:18.31	Kazuki	Tamura	JPN	16.7.95	26 Nov		28:29.65	Stewart	McSweyn	AUS	1.6.95	8 Dec
28:18.45	Johana	Maina	KEN	24.12.90	23 Apr		28:29.94	Melaku	Abera	ETH	20.4.94	24 Sep
28:18.48	Yusuke	Ogura	JPN	16.4.93	11 Jul		28:30.09	Chihiro	Miyawaki	JPN	28.8.91	26 Nov
28:18.5A	Boniface	Nduwa	KEN	1.6.84	28 May		28:30.16	Kengo	Suzuki	JPN	11.6.95	14 Jul
28:19.16	Workneh	Derese	ETH	23.7.95	26 Nov		28:30.85	Willy	Kwemoi	KEN-J	8.10.97	24 Sep
28:19.36	Andrew	Vernon	GBR	7.1.86	13 Aug		28:30.89	Vyacheslav	Shalamov	RUS	8.7.89	22 Jun
28:19.4A	Mathew	Kipkorir	KEN-J	1.4.98	28 May		28:31.66	Takato	Suzuki	JPN-J	23.7.97	26 Nov
28:19.45	Jason	Witt	USA	9.12.89	1 May		28:31.91	Robert	Cheseret	USA	8.10.83	1 May
28:21.42	Ali	Kaya	TUR	20.4.94	8 Jul		28:31.91	Mustapha (188)	Houdadi	MAR	5.8.86	5 Jun

200th 28:34.58

JUNIORS
See main list for top 9 juniors. 14 performances by 8 men to 28:01.0.0. Additional marks and further juniors:

Hadis		27:36.34	15	OG	Rio de Janeiro	13 Aug			
Chumo		27:43.85	3		Kobe	24 Apr	27:53.82	1	Gifu	7 May
		27:53.49	13rA		Machida	26 Nov	28:00.13	5	Tajimi	15 Oct
Kifle		27:27.04	1		Leiden	11 Jun			
28:08.98	Amos	Kirui (10)		KEN	9.2.98	2		Gifu	7 May
28:09.57	Gizachew	Hailu		ETH	18.4.98	5	WJ	Bydgoszcz	19 Jul
28:11.64	Martin	Musau		UGA	5.10.98	10		Leiden	11 Jun
28:13.43	Ronald	Kiprotich		KEN	6.12.98	6	WJ	Bydgoszcz	19 Jul
28:14.10	Alfred	Ngeno		KEN	2.5.97	18rA		Machida	26 Nov
28:19.4A	Mathew	Kipkorir		KEN	1.4.98	7	NC	Nairobi	28 May
28:29.43	Atsushi	Yamato		JPN-	13.3.97	3rD		Machida	26 Nov
28:30.85	Willy	Kwemoi		KEN	8.10.97	8		Yokohama	24 Sep
28:31.66	Takato	Suzuki		JPN-	23.7.97	3		Kanagawa	26 Nov
28:36.32	Titus	Wambua		KEN		10		Yokohama	24 Sep
28:40.21	Julius	Tanki (20)		KEN	15.7.97	1		Isahaya	8 Oct

Best European: 29:25.09 Pietro Riva ITA 1.5.97 10 WJ Bydgoszcz 19 Jul

10 KILOMETRES ROAD

27:15 +	James Ndirangu	Mwangi	KEN	29.3.94		København	18 Sep
27:28 +	Bedan Karoki	Muchiri	KEN	21.8.90		København	18 Sep
27:28 +	Abraham	Kiptum	KEN	.89		København	18 Sep
27:28 +	Stephen	Kibet	KEN	9.11.86		København	18 Sep
27:28 +	Edwin	Rotich	KEN	.88		København	18 Sep
27:28	Zane	Robertson	NZL	14.11.89	1	Berlin	9 Oct
27:29 +	Mathew	Kisorio	KEN	16.5.89		København	18 Sep
27:29 +	Albert	Kangogo	KEN	16.8.87		København	18 Sep

10 - 15 KILOMETRES ROAD

Mark	Name		Nat	Born	Pos Meet	Venue	Date
27:29 +	Gilbert	Masai	KEN	20.5.81		København	18 Sep
27:31 +	Geoffrey	Yegon	KEN	28.8.88		København	18 Sep
27:33	Mustapha	El Aziz	MAR	24.12.85	1	Marrakech	16 Oct
27:37 +	Alex	Oleitiptip	KEN	20.12.90		København	18 Sep
27:40	Abraham	Kipyatich	KEN	10.5.93	1	Praha	10 Sep
27:43	Daniel	Wanjiru	KEN	26.5.92	2	Praha	10 Sep
27:45 +	Thomas	Ayeko	UGA	10.2.92		København	18 Sep
27:46 +	Fikadu	Haftu	ETH	21.2.94		København	18 Sep
27:50	Kenneth	Keter	KEN	4.8.96	4	Praha	10 Sep
27:53	Mathew	Kimeli	KEN	4.1.98	5	Praha	10 Sep
27:55	Daniel	Chebii	KEN	28.5.85	1	Boston	26 Jun
27:56	Dawit	Fikadu	ETH	.95	1	Casablanca	29 May
27:57	Rhonzas	Kilimo	KEN	5.5.96	2	Casablanca	29 May
27:58	John	Langat	KEN	31.12.96	1	Appingedam	25 Jun
27:58 +	Japhet	Korir	KEN	30.6.93		København	18 Sep
27:59	Wilson	Kipsang	KEN	15.3.82	2	Appingedam	25 Jun
27:59 +	Birhanu	Legese	ETH	11.5.94		København	18 Sep
27:59 +	Mosinet	Geremew	ETH	12.2.92		København	18 Sep
28:00	Philip	Kiprono	KEN	23.4.90	4	San Juan, PUR	28 Feb
28:00	John	Mwangangi	KEN	1.11.90	5	San Juan, PUR	28 Feb
28:00 +	Simon	Cheprot	KEN	2.7.93		Cardiff	26 Mar
28:01	Bernard	Korir	KEN	.92	1	Abu Dhabi	19 Mar
28:01 +	Edwin Kiprop	Kiptoo	KEN	14.8.93		Zaandam	18 Sep
28:02	Antonio	Abadía	ESP	2.7.90	2	Laredo	19 Mar
28:02	John	Muritu	KEN	.96	1	New Orleans	26 Mar
28:02 +	Mourad	Marofit	MAR	26.1.82		Valencia	23 Oct
28:02 +	Solomon Kirwa	Yego	KEN	10.5.87		Valencia	23 Oct
28:04 +	Barselius	Kipyego	KEN	23.7.93		Ústí nad Labem	17 Sep
28:05 +	Richard	Mengich	KEN	3.4.89		Göteborg	21 May
28:06 +	Cosmas	Birech	KEN	21.3.86		Ostia	13 Mar
28:06 +	Leonard	Langat	KEN	7.8.90		Ostia	13 Mar
28:06 +	Peter	Ndorobo	KEN	11.8.93		Ostia	13 Mar
28:06 +	Mule	Wasihun	ETH	20.10.93		Cardiff	26 Mar
28:07	Silas	Kipruto	KEN	26.9.84	26 Mar		
28:08 +	Emmanuel	Gniki Gisamoda	TAN	18.5.88	24 Apr		
28:08	Kenenisa	Bekele	ETH	13.6.82	22 May		
28:08	Daniel	Salel	KEN	11.12.90	26 Jun		
28:09 +	Abrar	Osman	ERI	.94	26 Mar		
28:10	Aziz	Lahbabi	MAR	3.2.91	19 Mar		
28:10	Amos	Kurgat	KEN	7.3.92	10 Sep		
28:11 +	Nicholas	Korir	KEN	18.11.90	2 Oct		
28:12	Dathan	Ritzenhein	USA	30.12.82	26 Jun		
28:12 +	Sammy	Kitwara	KEN	26.11.86	18 Sep		
28:12 +	Peter	Kirui	KEN	2.1.88	2 Oct		
28:13 +	Nguse	Amlosom	ERI	10.11.86	26 Mar		
28:13 +	Teshome	Mekonen	ETH	5.8.95	26 Mar		
28:13	Dominic	Ondoro	KEN	.88	26 Mar		
28:13 +	Adugna	Takele	ETH	26.2.89	17 Sep		
28:14 +	Norbert	Kigen	KEN	24.1.93	2 Apr		
28:14 +	Yohannes	Ghebregergish	ERI	11.1.94	2 Apr		
28:14 +	Geoffrey	Koech	KEN	28.8.93	2 Apr		
28:14 +	Felix	Kandie	KEN	10.4.87	2 Apr		
28:15 +	Bernard	Bett	KEN	4.1.93	2 Apr		
28:15 +	Morris Munene Gachaga		KEN	7.4.95	24 Apr		
28:15 +	Dickson	Chumba	KEN	27.10.86	24 Apr		
28:15	Robert	Kaptingei	KEN	8.12.86	18 Jun		
28:15	Kalipus	Lomwai	KEN	.95	11 Sep		
28:15 +	Geoffrey	Kipyego	KEN	17.7.87	17 Sep		
28:16	Jacob	Kendagor	KEN	19.9.84	25 Jun		
28:16	Zelalem	Mengistu	ETH	.93	11 Sep		
28:17	Ben	True	USA	29.12.85	6 Aug		
28:18 +	Leonard Patrick Komon		KEN	10.1.88	18 Sep		
28:18 +	Nicholas	Kamakya	KEN	2.3.85	18 Sep		
28:18	Fathi	Abdenasir	MAR	25.1.87	16 Oct		
28:19	Muktar	Edris	ETH	14.1.94	28 Feb		
28:19	Erick	Koskei	KEN	93	11 Sep		
28:19	Bernard	Matheka	KEN	7.8.88	30 Oct		
28:19	Cornelius	Kangogo	KEN	15.12.93	18 Dec		
28:19	Jemal	Yimer	ETH	11.5.96	18 Dec		
28:19	El Mahjoub	Dazza	MAR	3.3.91	18 Dec		
28:19	Thiery	Ndikumwenayo	BDI	26.3.97	18 Dec		
28:20 +	Victor	Chumo	KEN	.87	20 Mar		
28:20 +	Paul	Mwangi	KEN	2.1.93	20 Mar		
28:20	Philemon	Maritim	KEN	.88	11 Sep		
28:21 +	Edwin	Kipyego	KEN	16.11.90	26 Mar		
28:22 +	Remmy Limo Ndiwa		KEN	3.2.88	13 Mar		
28:22	Samir	Jouahri	MAR	29.4.85	19 Mar		
28:22 +	Henry	Kiplagat	KEN	16.12.82	20 Mar		
28:22	Julien	Wanders	SUI	18.3.96	18 Dec		
28:23	Joel	Mmone	RSA	29.3.91	29 May		
28:23	David	Manja	RSA	80691	29 May		
28:23	Youssef	Nasir	MAR	15.2.90	16 Oct		
28:25	Khalil	Lemciyeh	MAR	10.12.86	29 May		
28:26 +	Jameson	Wangechi	KEN		6 Mar		
28:26 +	Eliud	Tarus	KEN	3.3.93	6 Mar		
28:26 +	Abel	Kirui	KEN	4.6.82	20 Mar		
28:26 +	Hillary	Maiyo	KEN	.94	20 Mar		
28:26 +	Wycliffe	Biwott	KEN	.88	20 Mar		
28:27	Salah	Bounasr	MAR	27.5.90	19 Mar		
28:27	Simon	Tesfay	ERI	15.3.85	28 Mar		
28:27 +	Festus	Talam	KEN	20.10.94	21 May		
28:27	Brett	Robinson	AUS	8.5.91	23 Oct		
28:28	Andrew	Butchart	GBR	14.10.91	30 May		
28:28	Awit	Habte	ERI	29.5.97	9 Oct		
28:29	Henry	Kipsang	KEN	.92	19 Mar		
28:29	Lucas	Rotich	KEN	16.4.90	14 May		
28:29	Zakaria	Boudad	MAR	2.10.93	29 May		
28:29	Sondre Nordstad Moen		NOR	12.1.91	25 Jun		
28:30	Elhassan	Elabbassi	BRN	13.4.84	28 Feb		
28:30	Patrick	Ereng	KEN	.87	11 Sep		
28:30	Thomen	Bellani	MAR	15.9.79	16 Oct		

Probable short course: Mar 6, Casablanca: 1. El Hassan El Abbassi BRN 27:26, 2. Morris Munene KEN 27:27, 3. Mohamed Ziani MAR 27:28, 4, Amos Kaptich KEN 27:28, 5. Abdennacer Fathi MAR 27:35, 6. Ahmed Tamri MAR 27:54; 7, Zakaria Boudad MAR 28:03, 8, Hassan Toriss MAR 28:18.

15/20 KILOMETRES ROAD

See also in 10M and Half Marathon lists

| 42:08+ | Geoffrey | Yegon | KEN | 28.8.88 | in HMar | Göteborg | 21 May |

15 – 20 KILOMETRES – 10M ROAD – HALF MARATHON

Mark			Name		Nat	Born	Pos	Meet	Venue	Date
		42:08	Joshua	Cheptegei	UGA	12.9.96	1		Nijmegen	20 Nov
		42:31+	Cosmas Jairus	Kipchoge	KEN	21.3.86		in HMar	Ostia	13 Mar
		42:32+	Evans Kigen	Kurui	KEN	.1.93		in HMar	Istanbul	24 Apr
		42:33+	Kenneth	Kipkemoi	KEN	2.8.84		in HMar	Istanbul	24 Apr
		42:33+	Titus	Mbishei	KEN	28.10.90		in HMar	Istanbul	24 Apr
		42:34+	Emmanuel	Bor	KEN	14.4.88		in HMar	Istanbul	24 Apr
		42:44+	Stephen	Mokoka	RSA	31.1.85		in HMar	Cardiff	26 Mar
		42:48+	Geoffrey	Koech	KEN	28.8.93		in HMar	Praha	2 Apr
		42:49+	Edwin	Kipyego	KEN	16.11.90		in HMar	Cardiff	26 Mar
		42:56+	Abreham	Cheroben	BRN	11.10.92		in HMar	København	18 Sep
		42:57+	Nguse	Tesfaldet	ERI	10.11.86		in HMar	Cardiff	26 Mar
		43:02	Herpasa	Negasa	ETH	.93	1		s'Heerenberg	4 Dec
57:43		43:04+	Morris Munene	Gachaga	KEN	7.4.95		in HMar	Yangzhou	24 Apr
		43:06	Hiskel	Tewelde	ERI	15.9.86	3		Nijmegen	20 Nov
		43:06	Fredrik	Kiptoo	KEN	13.11.96	2		s'Heerenberg	4 Dec
		43:07+	Amos	Kurgat	KEN	7.3.92		in HMar	Milano	20 Mar
56:56+			Solomon Kirwa	Yego	KEN	10.5.87		in HMar	Valencia	23 Oct
57:19+			Leonard	Langat 2.8.96?	KEN	7.8.90		in HMar	Istanbul	24 Apr
57:38+			Mosinet	Geremew	ETH	12.2.92		in HMar	Houston	17 Jan

15k

45:25	42:14		Elijah	Kiptoo	KEN	9.6.86	1		Zaandam	18 Sep
45:38	42:21		Joshua	Cheptegei	UGA	12.9.96	2		Zaandam	18 Sep
46:04	43:04		Rodgers Chumo	Kwemoi	KEN-J	3.3.97	1		Tilburg	4 Sep
46:04	43:04		John	Langat	KEN	31.12.96	2		Tilburg	4 Sep
46:05	43:04		Moses	Kurong	UGA	7.7.94	3		Tilburg	4 Sep
46:12	42:53		Abrar	Osman	ERI	1.1.94	3		Zaandam	18 Sep
46:19			Jeremiah	Thuku	KEN	7.7.94	1		Kosa	27 Nov

20k   15k   Slightly downhill race: 30.5m South Shields

10 MILES ROAD

HALF MARATHON

58:44		41:54	Solomon Kirwa	Yego	KEN	10.5.87	1		Ostia	13 Mar
59:07	56:01	41:32	James	Wangari	KEN	23.3.94	1		København	18 Sep
59:10	56:05	41:41	Geoffrey	Kamworor	KEN	28.11.92	1	WCh	Cardiff	26 Mar
59:12				Wangari			1		Milano	20 Mar
59:15		41:59	Barselius	Kipyego	KEN	23.7.93	1		Usti nad Labem	17 Sep
59:18		41:55	Leonard	Langat	KEN	7.8.90	2		Ostia	13 Mar
59:20	56:19	42:26	Daniel	Wanjiru	KEN	26.5.92	1		Praha	2 Apr
59:27	56:25		Stephen	Kibet	KEN	9.11.86	1		Valencia	23 Oct
59:28	56:26	42:01		Kibet			2		København	18 Sep
59:29	56:27	42:02	Albert	Kangogo	KEN	16.8.87	3		København	18 Sep
59:29	56:27	42:21	Mustapha	El Aziz	MAR	24.12.85	2		Valencia	23 Oct
59:30	56:26	42:26?		Kipyego			2		Praha	2 Apr
59:31	56:27	42:02	Gilbert	Masai (10)	KEN	20.5.81	4		København	18 Sep
59:32	56:23	41:41	Bidan	Karoki	KEN	21.8.90	5		København	18 Sep
59:32			Edwin	Rotich	KEN	88	3		Valencia	23 Oct
59:33	56:27	42:20	Mourad	Marofit	MAR	26.1.82	4		Valencia	23 Oct
59:35	56:28	42:08	Richard	Mengich	KEN	3.4.89	1		Göteborg	21 May
59:36	56:13	41:41		Karoki			2	WCh	Cardiff	26 Mar
59:36	56:27	42:02	Abraham	Kiptum	KEN	.89	6		København	18 Sep
59:40	56:36	42:26	Adugna	Takele	ETH	26.2.89	3		Praha	2 Apr
59:42	56:36	42:26	Nobert	Kigen	KEN	24.1.93	4		Praha	2 Apr
59:44	56:46	42:37	Geoffrey	Yegon	KEN	28.8.88	1		Venlo	20 Mar
59:44			Eliud	Kipchoge	KEN	5.11.84	1		New Delhi	20 Nov
59:46	56:36			Yegon			5		Valencia	23 Oct
59:47	56:41		Sammy	Kitwara (20)	KEN	26.11.86	1		Lisboa	20 Mar
59:48	56:46	42:36	Kenneth	Keter	KEN	4.8.96	2		Venlo	20 Mar
59:48			Yigrem	Demelash	ETH	28.1.94	2		New Delhi	20 Nov
59:49	56:46	42:36		Demelash			3		Venlo	20 Mar
59:50	56:42	42:26	Peter	Kirui	KEN	2.1.88	5		Praha	2 Apr
59:50		42:30	Nicholas	Korir	KEN	18.11.90	1		Breda	2 Oct
59:53				P Kirui			1		Krems	18 Sep
59:54	56:40	42:02		Rotich			7		Købehavn	18 Sep
59:58				Mengich			1		Berlin	3 Apr
59:59	56:55	42:03	Mohamed	Farah	GBR	23.3.83	3	WCh	Cardiff	26 Mar
59:59	56:54	42:00	Abayneh	Ayele	ETH	4.11.87	4	WCh	Cardiff	26 Mar
			(35/26)							
60:01			Augustine	Choge	KEN	21.1.87	3		New Delhi	20 Nov

MEN 2016

364 HALF MARATHON

Mark			Name		Nat	Born	Pos	Meet	Venue	Date	
60:04	56:56	42:26	Felix	Kandie	KEN	10.4.87	6		Praha	2	Apr
60:05	56:51		Kenneth	Kipkemoi	KEN	2.8.84	2		Lisboa	20	Mar
60:06		42:36	Remmy	Limo	KEN	3.2.88	3		Ostia	13	Mar
			(30)								
60:06	56:55	41:56	Tamirat	Tola	ETH	11.8.91	5	WCh	Cardiff	26	Mar
60:11	56:59		Paul	Lonyangata	KEN	12.12.92	3		Lisboa	20	Mar
60:12	56:55	41:51	Simon	Cheprot	KEN	2.7.93	6	WCh	Cardiff	26	Mar
60:12dh			Dathan	Ritzenhein	USA	30.12.82	2	GNR	South Shields	11	Sep
60:13		42:31	Peter	Ndorobo	KEN	11.8.93	4		Ostia	13	Mar
60:14	56:59		Emmanuel	Kipsang	KEN	13.6.91	4		Lisboa	20	Mar
60:16	57:00	42:27	Abraham	Kipyatich	KEN	10.5.93	7		Praha	2	Apr
60:16	57:09	42:32	Ali	Kaya	TUR	20.4.94	1		Istanbul	24	Apr
60:21	57:04	42:26	Yohannes	Ghebregergish	ERI	11.1.94	8		Praha	2	Apr
60:24			Joshua	Kipkorir	KEN	.94	1		Haicang	10	Dec
			(40)								
60:26	57:19	42:28	Thomas	Ayeko	UGA	10.2.92	8		København	18	Sep
60:27	57:29		Edwin	Kipyego	KEN	16.11.90	1		Den Haag	6	Mar
60:31		42:32	Zersenay	Tadese	ERI	8.2.82	2		Istanbul	24	Apr
60:33	57:23	42:28	Alex	Oleitiptip	KEN	22.9.82	10		København	18	Sep
60:35	57:31		Abreham	Cheroben	BRN	11.10.92	3		Den Haag	6	Mar
60:35			Morris Munene	Gachaga	KEN	7.4.95	2		Krems	18	Sep
60:36	57:25	42:27	Bernard	Bett	KEN	4.1.93	9		Praha	2	Apr
60:37	57:38	43:06	Lelisa	Desisa	ETH	14.1.90	1		Houston	17	Jan
60:40	57:51		Berhanu	Legesse	ETH	11.9.94	1		Ra's Al-Khaymah	12	Feb
60:40	57:51		Stanley	Biwott	KEN	21.4.86	2		Ra's Al-Khaymah	12	Feb
			[50]								
60:41	57:51		Nguse	Tesfaldet	ERI	10.11.86	3		Ra's Al-Khaymah	12	Feb
60:41	57:32	43:02	Bernard	Kimani	KEN	10.9.93	4		Den Haag	6	Mar
60:43		43:04	Mosinet	Geremew	ETH	12.2.92	1		Yangzhou	24	Apr
60:45	57:43	43:04	Feyisa	Lilesa	ETH	1.2.90	3		Yangzhou	24	Apr
60:47	57:44	42:50	Emanuel	Gniki Gisamoda	TAN	18.5.88	5		Yangzhou	24	Apr
60:48	57:32	42:31	Leonard Patrick	Komon	KEN	10.1.88	4		Istanbul	24	Apr
60:49	57:36	43:05	Goitom	Kifle	ERI	3.12.93	1		Marugame	7	Feb
60:50	57:41	43:05	Dominic	Nyairo	KEN-J	22.8.97	2		Marugame	7	Feb
60:52			Henry	Kiplagat	KEN	16.12.82	2		Ceske Budejovice	4	Jun
60:53	57:58		Shadrack	Korir Kimining	KEN	10.2.96	1		Cardiff	2	Oct
			(60)								
60:54	57:40	43:05	Keijiro	Mogi	JPN	21.10.95	3		Marugame	7	Feb
60:56			Thomas	Lokomwa	KEN	26.12.87	1		Piacenza	8	May
60:57			Paul	Kipkorir	KEN	.82	2		Adana	3	Jan
60:58	57:37	42:19	Abrar	Osman	ERI	1.1.94	7	WCh	Cardiff	26	Mar
60:59			Alexander	Mutiso	KEN	10.9.96	1		Ichinoseki	18	Sep
60:59			Daniel	Rotich	UGA	10.10.92	1		Porto	18	Sep
61:00	57:52		Edwin Kiprop	Kiptoo	KEN	14.8.93	7		Ra's Al-Khaymah	12	Feb
61:00	57:42		Charles	Ndirangu	KEN	8.2.93	1		Yamaguchi	14	Feb
61:00		43:01	Simon	Tesfay	ERI	15.3.85	2		Berlin	3	Apr
61:00	57:50	42:56	Japhet	Korir	KEN	30.6.93	12		København	18	Sep
			(70)								
61:02			Cosmas Jairus	Kipchoge	KEN	21.3.86	1		Lugano	22	May
61:02	57:50	42:546	Fikadu	Haftu	ETH	21.2.94	13		København	18	Sep
61:03			Nicholas	Makau	KEN	15.10.90	2		Lugano	22	May
61:04			Emmanuel	Bor	KEN	14.4.88	2		Granollers	7	Feb
61:04			Cyprian	Kotut	KEN	.92	1		Paris	6	Mar
61:11			Amos	Kipruto	KEN	.92	2		Paris	6	Mar
61:11	57:57	43:02	Eliud	Tarus	KEN	3.3.93	5		Den Haag	6	Mar
61:11			Kebede	Tulu	ETH	.96	5		Ostia	13	Mar
61:11	57:42	42:24	Mule	Wasihun	ETH	20.10.93	8	WCh	Cardiff	26	Mar
61:11+			Kenenisa	Bekele	ETH	13.6.82	1=	in Mar	Berlin	25	Sep
			(80)								
61:11+			Wilson	Kipsang	KEN	15.3.82	1=	in Mar	Berlin	25	Sep
61:11+			Evans Kiplagat	Chebet	KEN	10.11.88	1=	in Mar	Berlin	25	Sep
61:11+			Sisay	Lemma	ETH	12.12.90	1=	in Mar	Berlin	25	Sep
61:11+			Geoffrey	Ronoh	KEN	29.11.82	1=	in Mar	Berlin	25	Sep
61:11+			Alfers	Lagat	KEN	7.8.86	1=	in Mar	Berlin	25	Sep
61:11+			Jacob	Kendagor	KEN	24.8.84	1=	in Mar	Berlin	25	Sep
61:13+			Eliud	Kiptanui	KEN	6.6.89	8	in Mar	Berlin	25	Sep
61:15			Stephen	Arita	KEN	26.6.88	3		Adana	3	Jan
61:15+			Emmanuel	Mutai	KEN	12.10.84	9	in Mar	Berlin	25	Sep
61:16	57:57		Stephen	Sambu	KEN	3.7.88	1		New York	20	Mar
			(90)								
61:16			Edwin	Koech	KEN	15.5.83	1		Port Elizabeth	30	Jul

HALF MARATHON

Mark			Name		Nat	Born	Pos	Meet	Venue	Date
61:17			Azmeraw	Mengistu	ETH	15.9.92	3		Paris	6 Mar
61:19	57:56	43:05	Fabiano	Sulle	TAN	1.10.94	4		Marugame	7 Feb
61:19			Johana	Maina	KEN	24.12.90	2		Yamaguchi	14 Feb
61:19			Simon	Muthoni	KEN	27.2.95	2		Piacenza	8 May
61:19+			Vincent	Kipruto	KEN	13.9.87	10	in Mar	Berlin	25 Sep
61:21		43:18	Keisuke	Nakatani	JPN	12.1.95	5		Marugame	7 Feb
61:21			Kennedy	Kipyeko	KEN	12.12.90	6		Ostia	13 Mar
61:21			Mohamed	Ziani	MAR	.93	1		Rabat	13 Mar
61:21			Fentahun	Hunegnaw	ETH		6		Yangzhou	24 Apr
61:21			[100] William	Kibor	KEN	10.1.85	1		Las Vegas	13 Nov
61:22 dh	Emmanuel		Bett		KEN	30.3.83	11 Sep	61:42	Ezekiel	Chebotibin	KEN	10.7.92	14 Feb
61:23	42:32 Vincent		Rono		KEN	22.12.90	24 Apr	61:42	Joseph	Ndirangu	KEN	9.9.94	14 Feb
61:24+	Gideon		Kipketer		KEN	10.11.92	24 Apr	61:43	Abayneh	Degu	ETH	1.12.88	6 Mar
61:24+	Tilahun		Regassa		ETH	18.1.90	24 Apr	61:43	Samuel	Chelanga	USA	23.2.85	20 Mar
61:25	43:18 Naoki		Kudo		JPN-J	5.9.95	7 Feb	61:43	Ronald	Kirui	KEN-J	6.12.98	20 Nov
61:25+	Ghirmay		Ghebrselassie		ERI	14.11.95	24 Apr	61:44	Sibusiso	Nzima	RSA	23.11.86	20 Nov
61:25	Paul		Mwangi		KEN	2.1.93	9 Oct	61:45	Robert	Mbithi	KEN	26.6.89	13 Mar
61:26	Stephen		Mokoka		RSA	31.1.85	30 Jul	61:46	Ezekiel	Chepkorim	UGA	.92	20 Nov
61:28	Samson		Gebreyohanes		ERI	7.2.92	17 Jan	61:47	Anas	Selmouni	MAR	15.3.79	13 Mar
61:28	Stephen		Chebogut		KEN	9.1.85	6 Mar	61:48	Festus	Talam	KEN	20.10.94	21 May
61:28+	Abera		Kuma		ETH	31.8.90	24 Apr	61:48+	Geoffrey	Koech	KEN	28.8.93	25 Sep
61:29	Luke		Puskedra		USA	8.2.90	17 Jan	61:49	Jameson	Wangechi	KEN	.96	6 Mar
61:29	Evans		Korir		KEN	.87	6 Mar	61:49	Elijah	Tirop	KEN	1.1.92	24 Apr
61:29	Tadesse		Abraham		SUI	12.8.82	22 May	61:51	Takuya	Fujimoto	JPN	11.9.89	7 Feb
61:30	Vincent		Chepkok		KEN	5.7.88	13 Mar	61:51	Mohamed Réda El Araaby		MAR	12.11.89	13 Mar
61:30+	Dennis		Kimetto		KEN	22.1.84	24 Apr	61:51	Patrick	Mwaka	KEN	2.11.92	15 May
61:32	43:13 Shuho		Dairokuno		JPN	23.12.92	7 Feb	61:51	Belay	Tilahun	ETH	.95	23 Oct
61:33	Mathew		Kisorio		KEN	16.5.89	7 Feb	61:52	Benjamin	Somikwo	UGA	4.10.96	24 Jan
61:35	Joseph		Kamathi		KEN	23.11.96	14 Feb	61:53	Shogo	Nakamura	JPN	16.9.92	14 Feb
61:35	Wilson Kwambai Chebet				KEN	12.7.85	20 Mar	61:54	Ouais	Zitane	MAR	17.1.86	24 Jan
61:35	Charles		Muneria		KEN	10.2.96	2 Oct	61:54	Keita	Shitara	JPN	18.12.91	7 Feb
61:36	Asefa		Mengistu		ETH	18.1.85	30 Jul	61:54	Paul	Kuira	KEN	25.1.90	15 May
61:37+	Ernest		Ngeno		KEN	20.5.95	22 Jan	61:54	Pius	Kirop	KEN	8.1.90	18 Sep
61:37+	Asbel		Kipsang		KEN	10.9.93	22 Jan	61:55	Terefa	Deleba	ETH-J	.98	17 Jan
61:37+	Tebalu		Zawude		ETH	2.11.87	22 Jan	61:55	Joel	Muaura	KEN-Y	20.1.99	28 Feb
61:37	Ahmed		Tamri		MAR	8.2.85	13 Mar	61:55	Joseph	Tophil	TAN	26.6.95	24 Apr
61:37	Moses		Kibet		UGA	23.3.91	20 Mar	61:55	Wilson	Cheruiyot	KEN	15.11.87	17 Sep
61:38+	Tsegaye		Mekonnen		ETH	15.6.95	22 Jan	61:55	Sammy	Kurui	KEN	20.12.87	18 Sep
61:38+	Alemu		Bekele		BRN	23.3.90	22 Jan	61:55	Shadrack	Biwott	KEN	19.2.85	2 Oct
61:38+	Tesfaye		Abera		ETH	31.3.92	22 Jan	61:56	Amos	Kurgat	KEN	7.3.92	20 Mar
61:38+	Hayle		Lemi		ETH	13.9.94	22 Jan	61:56	Titus	Mbishei	KEN	28.10.90	24 Apr
61:39+	Samuel Kiplimo Kosgei				KEN	20.1.86	22 Jan	61:56	Benjamin	Siwa	UGA	27.5.89	2 Oct
61:39+	Mesfin		Teshome		ETH		22 Jan	61:56A	Nicodemus	Kipkurui	KEN	4.4.94	13 Nov
61:39+	Tadesse		Tola		ETH	31.10.87	22 Jan	61:57	Philimon	Maritim	KEN	88	18 Sep
61:39	42:44 Teshome		Mekonen		ETH	5.8.95	26 Mar	61:58	Kaoru	Hirosue	JPN	8.11.93	7 Feb
61:39+	Meshak		Koech		KEN	.88	25 Sep	61:58	Richard	Sigei	KEN	11.5.85	24 Apr
61:40	Vincent		Yator		KEN	11.7.89	7 Feb	61:59	Moses	Bowen	KEN	.91	16 Apr
61:40	Fethi		Abdenacer		MAR		13 Mar	61:59	Rintaro	Takeda	JPN	5.4.94	20 Nov
61:40	Moussaab		Hadout		MAR	11.03.88	11 Dec	61:59	Alphonce (178)	Felix	TAN	14.2.92	20 Nov

149.7m short: Glasgow 2 Oct:1. 60:24 Callum Hawkins GBR 22.6.92. 2. 60:54 Moses Kipsiro UGA 2.9.86, 3. 61:34 Joel Kipkoech Kimutai KEN 5.10.88, 4. 61:58 Chris Thompson GBR 17.4.81
400m short: Nairobi 6 Mar 1. 60:38A Wilfred Kimitei KEN 11.3.85 1 Nairobi 6 Mar, 2. 60:40A Hillary Kipchumba KEN 25.11.92, 3. 60:42A Philemon Rono KEN 8.2.91, 5. 61:02 Sammy Kirui 20.12.87, 6. 61:16 Vincent Kipchumba KEN, 7. 61:17 Edwin Soi KEN 3.3.86; 8. 61:25 Stephen Chemlany KEN 9.8.82, 9. 61:28 Francis Kiplagat .90, 10. 61:29 Alpha Maringa

JUNIORS

Mark	Name		Nat	Born	Pos	Venue	Date
62:03	Shota	Onitsuka	JPN	13.9.97	3	Ageo	20 Nov
62:05	Akira	Aizawa	JPN	18.7.97	5	Ageo	20 Nov
62:17	Junnosuke	Matsuo	JPN	15.6.97	9	Ageo	20 Nov
62:21	Justus	Kanda	KEN	29.6.97	2	Warszawa	3 Apr
62:48	Tomoki	Ota	JPN	17.10.97	12	Ageo	20 Nov
62:55	Robert	Chemonges	UGA	15.10.97	1	Pordenone	9 Oct
62:55	Takato	Suzuki	JPN	23.7.97	2	Tokyo	13 Nov
63:01	Kiyoshi	Nagato	JPN	13.1.97	13	Ageo	20 Nov
63:03	Rintaro	Takata	JPN	22.7.97	16	Ageo	20 Nov
63:04	Shota	Nakagawa	JPN	17.8.97	19	Ageo	20 Nov
63:05	Takumi	Yokokama	JPN	20.1.98	23	Ageo	20 Nov
63:07	Moses	Wamaitha	KEN	.98	1	Genova	24 Apr
63:08	Kedir	Besher	ETH	.97	1	Dronten	17 Dec
63:12	Mogos	Shumay	ERI	.97	9	Nanning	4 Dec

25-30 KILOMETRES ROAD

25k	30k						
		In addition to those shown in Marathon listing					
1:12:48	1:27:26+	Alfers	Lagat	KEN	7.8.86	Berlin	25 Sep

25 – 30 KILOMETRES – MARATHON

Mark			Name		Nat	Born	Pos	Meet	Venue	Date	
1:12:47	1:28:00+		Geoffrey	Ronoh	KEN	29.11.82	6		Berlin	25	Sep
1:14:39+			Laban	Korir	KEN	30.12.85	1	in Mar	Paris	3	Apr
	1:29:32+		Dejene	Debela	ETH	.94		in Mar	Eindhoven	9	Oct
	1:29:33+		Jacob Kibet	Kendagor	KEN	24.8.84		in Mar	Seoul	20	Mar
	1:29:33+		Paul	Kipkorir	KEN	.82		in Mar	Seoul	20	Mar
	1:29:33+		Norbert	Kigen	KEN	24.1.93		in Mar	Eindhoven	9	Oct
	1:29:33+		Richard	Mengich	KEN	3.4.89		in Mar	Einhoven	9	Oct

MARATHON

	25k	30k									
2:03:03	1:12:47	1:27:30	Kenenisa	Bekele	ETH	13.6.82	1		Berlin	25	Sep
2:03:05	1:12:39	1:27:13	Eliud	Kipchoge	KEN	5.11.84	1		London	24	Apr
2:03:13	1:12:47	1:27:26	Wilson	Kipsang	KEN	15.3.82	2		Berlin	25	Sep
2:03:51	1:12:40	1:27:13	Stanley	Biwott	KEN	21.4.86	2		London	24	Apr
2:04:24	1:12:50	1:27:25	Tesfaye	Abera	ETH	31.3.92	1		Dubai	22	Jan
2:04:33	1:12:49	1:27:21	Hayle	Lemi Berhanu	ETH	13.9.94	2		Dubai	22	Jan
2:04:46	1:12:49	1:27:21	Tsegaye	Mekonnen	ETH	15.6.95	3		Dubai	22	Jan
2:05:13		1:29:33	Wilson	Loyanae	KEN	20.11.88	1		Seoul	20	Mar
2:05:16	1:12:49	1:27:20	Sisay	Lemma	ETH	12.12.90	4		Dubai	22	Jan
2:05:21	1:14:43	1:29:46	Daniel	Wanjiru (10)	KEN	26.5.92	1		Amsterdam	16	Oct
2:05:31	1:12:49	1:27:29	Evans Kiplagat	Chebet	KEN	10.11.88	3		Berlin	25	Sep
2:05:33		1:29:33		Chebet			2		Seoul	20	Mar
2:05:44	1:12:50	1:27:21	Mule	Wasihun	ETH	20.10.93	5		Dubai	22	Jan
2:05:45	1:14:43	1:29:44	Sammy	Kitwara	KEN	26.11.86	2		Amsterdam	16	Oct
2:05:47	1:14:44	1:29:46	Marius	Kimutai	KEN	.89	3		Amsterdam	16	Oct
2:05:54	1:14:45	1:29:46	Laban	Korir	KEN	30.12.85	4		Amsterdam	16	Oct
2:06:07	1:14:43	1:29:45	Ezekiel	Chebii	KEN	3.1.91	5		Amsterdam	16	Oct
2:06:10		1:29:33	Kaan Kigen	Özbilen	TUR	15.1.86	3		Seoul	20	Mar
2:06:11	1:14:05	1:29:04	Marius	Kipserem	KEN	17.5.88	1		Rotterdam	10	Apr
2:06:22	1:14:06	1:29:04	Solomon	Deksisa	ETH	11.3.94	2		Rotterdam	10	Apr
2:06:25	1:14:45	1:29:46	Felix	Kandie (20)	KEN	10.4.87	6		Amsterdam	16	Oct
2:06:26		1:29:32	Festus	Talam	KEN	20.10.94	1		Eindhoven	9	Oct
2:06:27	1:14:42	1:29:44	Geoffrey	Kirui	KEN	16.2.93	7		Amsterdam	16	Oct
2:06:36	1:12:42	1:27:25		Bekele			3		London	24	Apr
2:06:40		1:29:33	Tadesse	Abraham	SUI	12.8.82	4		Seoul	20	Mar
2:06:45	1:12:49	1:27:27	Abayneh	Ayele	ETH	4.11.87	6		Dubai	22	Jan
2:06:45	1:14:44	1:29:46	Bernard	Kipyego	KEN	16.7.86	8		Amsterdam	16	Oct
2:06:48			Mark	Korir	KEN	10.1.85	1		Frankfurt	30	Oct
2:06:51			Frankline	Chepkwony	KEN	15.6.84	5		Seoul	20	Mar
2:06:53	1:12:57		Samuel Kiplimo	Kosgei	KEN	20.1.86	7		Dubai	22	Jan
2:06:56		1:29:51	Feyisa	Lilesa	ETH	1.2.90	1		Tokyo	28	Feb
2:06:56	1:12:47	1:27:34		Lemma			4		Berlin	25	Sep
2:06:58	1:14:31	1:29:29		Abera			1		Hamburg	17	Apr
2:06:58			Felix (34/30)	Kiprotich	KEN	.88	1		Gyeongju	16	Oct
2:07:11	1:14:42	1:30:02	Cyprian	Kotut	KEN	.92	1		Paris	3	Apr
2:07:20			Philemon	Rono	KEN	8.2.91	2		Hamburg	17	Apr
2:07:21			Luka	Kanda	KEN	.87	1		Chuncheon	23	Oct
2:07:22			Martin	Kosgei	KEN	.89	2		Frankfurt	30	Oct
2:07:24			Lawrence	Cherono	KEN	7.8.88	1		Praha	8	May
2:07:30		1:29:33	Asbel	Kipsang	KEN	10.9.93	6		Seoul	20	Mar
2:07:34		1:29:50	Dickson	Chumba	KEN	27.10.86	3		Tokyo	28	Feb
2:07:37	1:14:41	1:30:03	Stephen	Chemlany	KEN	9.8.82	3		Paris	3	Apr
2:07:39			Victor	Kipchirchir	KEN	5.12.87	1		Valencia	20	Nov
2:07:46		1:29:52	Stephen (40)	Kiprotich	UGA	27.2.89	4		Tokyo	28	Feb
2:07:46	1:12:53	1:28:13	Ghirmay	Ghebreslassie	ERI	14.11.95	4		London	24	Apr
2:07:47	1:12:50	1:28:07	Eliud	Kiptanui	KEN	6.6.89	5		Berlin	25	Sep
2:07:48		1:29:46	Abera	Kuma	ETH	31.8.90	10		Amsterdam	16	Oct
2:07:49			Ernest	Ngeno	KEN	20.5.95	2		Gyeongju	16	Oct
2:08:03			Micah	Kogo	KEN	3.6.86	3		Paris	3	Apr
2:08:03			Robert Kipkorir	Kwambai	KEN	22.11.85	3		Gyeongju	16	Oct
2:08:04	1:14:15		Gilbert Yegon	Koech	KEN	6.8.88	2		Valencia	20	Nov
2:08:06		1:29:50	Abel	Kirui	KEN	4.6.82	5		Tokyo	28	Feb
2:08:07			Joel	Kimurer	KEN	21.1.88	1		Seoul	6	Nov
2:08:11	1:12:50		Tilahun [50]	Regassa	ETH	18.1.90	8		Dubai	22	Jan

MARATHON

Mark			Name		Nat	Born	Pos	Meet	Venue	Date	
2:08:12			Amos	Kipruto	KEN	.92	1		Roma	10	Apr
2:08:12	1:14:15		Peter	Kirui	KEN	2.1.88	3		Valencia	20	Nov
2:08:14			Cosmas	Lagat	KEN	.95	1		Sevilla	21	Feb
2:08:14			Dino	Sefir	ETH	28.5.88	1		Ottawa	29	May
2:08:17			Gebretsadik	Adhana	ETH	16.7.92	5		Paris	3	Apr
2:08:19	1:29:45		Sammy	Korir	KEN	29.9.85	11		Amsterdam	16	Oct
2:08:19	1:29:46		Wilson	Chebet	KEN	12.7.85	12		Amsterdam	16	Oct
2:08:20			Ishmael	Busendich	KEN	7.7.91	2		Milano	3	Apr
2:08:23			Hillary	Kipchumba	KEN	25.11.92	4		Gyeongju	16	Oct
2:08:28			Alfers	Lagat	KEN	7.8.86	6		Paris	3	Apr
			(60)								
2:08:31			Solomon Kirwa	Yego	KEN	10.5.87	3		Praha	8	May
2:08:31			John	Mwangangi	KEN	1.11.90	4		Valencia	20	Nov
2:08:34			Thomas	Kiplagat	KEN		9		Dubai	22	Jan
2:08:35			Gideon	Kipketer	KEN	10.11.92	1		Mumbai	17	Jan
2:08:38			Kenneth	Mungara	KEN	7.9.73	3		Milano	3	Apr
2:08:39			Raymond	Choge	KEN	.88	1		Köln	2	Oct
2:08:41			Asefa	Mengistu	ETH	18.1.85	1		Cape Town	18	Sep
2:08:47			Emmanuel	Keter	KEN	.80	2		Cape Town	18	Sep
2:08:48	1:14:06	1:29:03	Limenih	Getachew	ETH	30.4.90	4		Rotterdam	10	Apr
2:08:48			Yemane	Tsegay	ETH	8.4.85	1		Fukuoka	4	Dec
			(70)								
2:08:51			Dominic	Ondoro	KEN	.88	1		St Paul	9	Oct
2:08:53			Yitayal	Atnafu	ETH	20.1.93	7		Paris	3	Apr
2:08:53			Lucas	Rotich	KEN	16.4.90	2		New York	6	Nov
2:08:55			Ezequiel	Omullo	KEN		1		Warszawa	25	Sep
2:08:56			Jacob Kibet	Kendagor	KEN	24.8.84	7		Seoul	20	Mar
2:08:56			Kelkile	Gezahegn	ETH	.91	1		Hefei	12	Nov
2:08:57			Patrick	Makau	KEN	2.3.85	2		Fukuoka	4	Dec
2:08:58			David	Kiyeng	KEN	22.4.83	1		Kosice	2	Oct
2:09:01			Yuki	Kawauchi	JPN	5.3.87	2		Gold Coast	3	Jul
2:09:01			Ronald	Korir	KEN	.91	2		Seoul	6	Nov
			(80)								
2:09:05			Reuben	Kerio	KEN	.94	1		Brescia	13	Mar
2:09:05			Birhanu	Teshome	ETH		2		Hefei	12	Nov
2:09:07			Edwin (1:27:20)	Koech	KEN	15.5.83	1		Linz	3	Apr
2:09:16			Hisanori	Kitajima	JPN	16.10.84	2		Otsu	6	Mar
2:09:16			Laban	Mutai	KEN	.85	1		Ljubljana	30	Oct
2:09:19			Alphonce	Felix	TAN	14.2.92	3		Otsu	6	Mar
2:09:19			Norbert	Kigen	KEN	24.1.93	3		Eindhoven	9	Oct
2:09:19			Philip	Kimutai	KEN	10.9.83	2		Ljubljana	30	Oct
2:09:19			Chala	Dechase	ETH	13.6.84	3		Seoul	6	Nov
2:09:20			Seboka	Tola	ETH	10.11.87	2		Mumbai	17	Jan
			(90)								
2:09:21			Barnabas	Kiptum	KEN	8.10.86	3		Cape Town	18	Sep
2:09:24			Mesfin	Teshome	ETH		10		Dubai	22	Jan
2:09:24			Elijah	Kemboi	KEN	10.9.84	2		Kosice	2	Oct
2:09:25			Suehiro	Ishikawa	JPN	27.9.79	4		Otsu	6	Mar
2:09:25			Duncan	Maiyo	KEN	5.8.90	4		Eindhoven	9	Oct
2:09:27			Melaku	Abera	ETH	20.4.94	1		Oita	7	Feb
2:09:27			Birhanu	Addisie	ETH	13.9.95	2		Roma	10	Apr
2:09:27			Dickson	Tuwei	KEN	31.10.92	1		Dongying	8	May
2:09:28			Dominic	Ruto	KEN	.90	3		Roma	10	Apr
2:09:28			Tujuba	Megersa	ETH	15.10.87	4		Roma	10	Apr
			(100)								
2:09:29			Geoffrey	Ronoh	KEN	29.11.82	6		Berlin	25	Sep
2:09:29 dh			Justus	Kimutai	KEN		1		Rennes (dh 65m)	23	Oct
2:09:31	Takuya	Fukatsu	JPN	10.11.87	6 Mar		2:10:04	Tola	Shura	ETH	9.6.96	29 May
2:09:33	Moses	Mosop	KEN	17.7.85	8 May		2:10:05	Afewerk	Mesfin	ETH	12.10.92	22 May
2:09:37	Levi	Omari	KEN	3.11.89	30 Oct		2:10:05	Galen	Rupp	USA	8.5.86	21 Aug
2:09:39	Fumihiro	Maruyama	JPN	1.7.90	6 Mar		2:10:05	Jamin	Ngaukon	KEN		23 Oct
2:09:42	Feyera	Gemeda	ETH	.82	8 May		2:10:06	Siboke	Nigusse	ETH	.84	8 May
2:09:44 dh	Mutai	Kipkemei	KEN	25.7.86	23 Oct		2:10:08	Albert	Korir	KEN	.94	13 Mar
2:09:45	Samuel	Mwaniki	KEN	.84	3 Apr		2:10:09	Charles	Cheruiyot	KEN	4.8.88	10 Apr
2:09:47	Abraraw	Misganaw	ETH	.88	30 Oct		2:10:13	Dejene	Debela	ETH	.94	9 Oct
2:09:48	Yihunilign	Adane	ETH	29.2.96	22 Jan		2:10:15	Emmanuel	Kichwen	KEN	.95	13 Mar
2:09:48	Robert	Chemosin	KEN	1.2.89	10 Apr		2:10:15	Suleiman	Simotwo	KEN	21.4.80	10 Apr
2:09:48	Yohanes	Gebregergish	ERI	11.1.94	25 Sep		2:10:16	Silah	Limo	KEN	1.2.92	10 Apr
2:09:49	Belachew	Alemayehu	ETH	.85	22 Jan		2:10:17	Herpasa	Negassa	ETH	.93	17 Jan
2:09:49 dh	Alfonce	Kigen	KEN	.93	23 Oct		2:10:17	Tadesse	Mamo	ETH	.91	2 Oct
2:10:01	Peter	Some	KEN	5.6.90	20 Mar		2:10:18	Vincent	Kipruto	KEN	13.9.87	2 Jan
2:10:04	Evans	Korir	KEN	.87	3 Apr		2:10:18	Stephen	Mokoka	RSA	31.1.85	30 Oct

MEN 2016

MARATHON – 100 KILOMETRES – 24 HOURS

Mark	Name		Nat		Born	Pos	Meet	Venue		Date
2:10:18	Japhet	Kosgei	KEN	.88	30 Oct					
2:10:21	Elisha	Barno	KEN	.85	9 Oct					
2:10:21	Joseph Kyengo Munywoki		KEN	.92	23 Oct					
2:10:22	Nicholas	Kamakya	KEN	2.3.85	2 Oct					
2:10:22	Julius	Rotich	KEN	.88	23 Oct					
2:10:23	Emmanuel	Mutai	KEN	12.10.84	28 Feb					
2:10:23	Jared	Kipchumba	KEN	8.8.83	13 Mar					
2:10:24	Mark Kosgei	Kiptoo	KEN	21.06.76	25 Sep					
2:10:27	Alfred	Kering	KEN	.80	2 Oct					
2:10:28	Evans	Sambu	KEN		18 Dec					
2:10:31	Daniel Kiprop	Limo	KEN	10.12.83	2 Oct					
2:10:32	Vincent	Torotich	KEN		23 Oct					
2:10:35	Abdelhadi	El Hachimi	BEL	15.12.74	3 Jul					
2:10:38	Kibrom	Ghebrezgiabhier	ERI	1.2.87	20 Nov					
2:10:39	Richard	Mengich	KEN	3.4.89	9 Oct					
2:10:40	Henry	Chirchir	KEN	14.5.85	2 Oct					
2:10:40	Hayato	Sonoda	JPN	5.4.89	7 Dec					
2:10:41	Allan	Kiprono	KEN	15.2.90	2 Oct					
2:10:43	Chiharu	Takada	JPN	9.7.81	3 Jul					
2:10:44	Josphat	Letting	KEN	1.1.88	17 Apr					
2:10:45	Elisha	Kipchirchir	KEN	.90	13 Nov					
2:10:46	James	Kwambai	KEN	28.2.83	3 Apr					
2:10:46	Emmanuel	Ngatuny	KEN	10.10.92	27 Nov					
2:10:48	Amenuel	Mesel	ERI	29.12.90	7 Dec					
2:10:49	John	Langat	KEN	31.12.96	3 Apr					
2:10:49	Alex	Saekwo	KEN	.90	2 Oct					
2:10:51	William Kiprono Yegon		KEN	10.1.83	26 Feb					
2:10:52	Callum	Hawkins	GBR	22.6.92	24 Apr					
2:10:53	Henrik	Szost	POL	20.1.82	7 Dec					
2:10:55	Raymond	Kemboi	KEN	8.2.86	17 Apr					
2:10:55dh	Kipkemoi	Kipsang	KEN	.90	23 Oct					
2:10:55	Reid	Coolsaet	CAN	29.7.79	7 Dec					
2:10:56	Tsegaye	Kebede	ETH	15.1.87	10 Apr					
2:10:57	Yuki	Takamiya	JPN	2.12.87	28 Feb					
2:10:57	Lani	Kiplagat	KEN		6 Nov					
2:10:58	Stanley	Koech	KEN		4 Jun					
2:10:59	Stephen	Chebogut	KEN	9.1.85	9 Oct					
2:11:00	Deribe	Robi (170)	ETH	26.9.90	9 Oct					
2:11:01	Javier	Guerra	ESP	10.11.83	28 Feb					
2:11:02	Abebe	Negewo	ETH	20.5.84	10 Apr					
2:11:02	Motlokoa	Nkhabutlane	LES	15.11.84	18 Sp					
2:11:02	Hassane	Ahouchar	MAR	.75	20 Nov					
2:11:04	Robert	Chemonges	UGA	15.10.97	30 Oct					
2:11:05	Sergiy	Lebid	UKR	15.7.75	30 Oct					

Drugs disqualification

Mark	Name		Nat	Born	Pos	Meet	Venue	Date
2:10:54	Gebo	Burka ¶	ETH	27.9.87				17 Jan

JUNIORS

Mark	Name	Nat	Born	Pos	Venue	Date
2:11:04	Robert Chemonges	UGA	15.10.97	7	Ljubljana	30 Oct
2:11:45	1 Trieste		8 May			
2:16:25	Mogos Shumay	ERI	.97	5	Sydney	18 Sep

100 KILOMETRES

Mark	Name		Nat	Born	Pos	Meet	Venue	Date
6:18:22	Hideaki	Yamauchi	JPN	16.12.85	1	WCh	Los Alcazares	27 Nov
6:24:06	Bongmusa	Mthembu	RSA	27.6.83	2	WCh	Los Alcazares	27 Nov
6:30:37	Geoffrey	Burns	USA	5.3.90	1		Madison	9 Apr
6:33:52	Wouter	De Cock	BEL	23.9.83	1		Steenwerck	5 May
6:35:42	Patrick	Reagan	USA	7.12.86	3	WCh	Los Alcazares	27 Nov
6:35:56		Reagan			1		Madison	9 Apr
6:37:05	Tatsuya	Itagaki	JPN	4.1.88	1		Yubetsu	26 Jun
6:37:23	Tomasz	Walerowicz	POL	16.1.81	4	WCh	Los Alcazares	27 Nov
6:38:34		Burns			5	WCh	Los Alcazares	27 Nov
6:39:24		Yamauchi			2		Yubetsu	26 Jun
	(10/7)							
6:40:37	Yoshiki	Takada	JPN	18.7.83	3		Yubetsu	26 Jun
6:40:50	Kaitaro	Sotoike	JPN	2.9.86	4		Yubetsu	26 Jun
6:41:08	José Antonio	Requejo	ESP	12.12.82	6	WCh	Los Alcazares	27 Nov
6:41:17	Giorgio	Calcaterra	ITA	11.2.72	7	WCh	Los Alcazares	27 Nov
6:43:00	Gift	Kelehe	RSA	9.11.81	9	WCh	Los Alcazares	27 Nov
6:44:20	Brendan	Davies	AUS	3.1.77	10	WCh	Los Alcazares	27 Nov
6:44:24	Elov	Olsson	WE	26.7.89	11	WCh	Los Alcazares	27 Nov
6:44:34	David	Gatebe	RSA	13.8.81	12	WCh	Los Alcazares	27 Nov
6:44:54	André	Collet	GER	21.9.71	13	WCh	Los Alcazares	27 Nov
6:45:00	Tetsuo	Toyonaga	JPN	26.1.86	5		Yubetsu	26 Jun
6:45:21	Hiromi	Kamada	JPN	5.6.95	6		Yubetsu	26 Jun
6:45:28	Fritjof	Fagerlund	SWE	27.6.74	14	WCh	Los Alcazares	27 Nov
6:45:29	Yoshikazu	Hara	JPN	13.8.72	7		Yubetsu	26 Jun
6:45:43	Didrik	Hermansen	NOR	24.3.80	15	WCh	Los Alcazares	27 Nov
6:46:16	Henri	Ansio	FIN	27.5.85	16	WCh	Los Alcazares	27 Nov
6:47:40	Ranno	Erala	EST	28.3.73	17	WCh	Los Alcazares	27 Nov
6:48:48	Shin-ya	Tsuchihashi	JPN	.91	8		Yubetsu	26 Jun
6:48:48	Chikara	Omine	USA	24.11.82	18	WCh	Los Alcazares	27 Nov
6:49:30	Takeshi	Ozaki	JPN	.78	9		Yubetsu	26 Jun
6:50:51	Yoshifumi	Kiyomoto	JPN	27.11.78	26 Jun			
6:52:43	Rufus	Photo	RSA	17.3.80	27 Nov			
6:52:50	Zach	Bitter	USA	21.1.86	27 Nov			
6:53:15	Hideo	Nojo	JPN	24.12.76	26 Jun			
6:53:52	Jérôme	Andrieu	FRA	3.10.73	7 May			
6:54:35	Jarle	Risa	NOR	20.5.76	27 Nov			
6:54:52	Karsten	Fischer	GER	17.9.84	27 Nov			
6:54:54	Yoshiki	Takada	JPN	18.7.83	27 Nov			
6:55:13	Pascal	van Norden	NED	5.9.72	27 Nov			
6:55:48	Suke	Obayashi	JPN	30.1.85	16 Oct			

Indoor

| 6:40:35 | Vasiliy | Larkin | RUS | 19.8.91 | 1 | | Moskva | 13 Feb |

24 HOURS

Mark	Name	Nat	Born	Pos	Meet	Venue	Date
263.127	Yoshihiko Ishikawa	JPN	25.4.88	1		Tokyo	18 Dec
261.843	Dan Lawson	GBR	13.2.73	1	EC	Albi	22 Oct
260.491	Aleksandr Sorokin	LTU	30.9.81	1		Athínai	19 Mar
258.661	Ondrej Velicka	CZE	27.4.83	2	EC	Albi	22 Oct

24 HOURS – STEEPLECHASE

Mark	Name		Nat		Born	Pos	Meet	Venue	Date	
258.110t	James	Stewart	GBR		2.4.76	1		London (TB)	18	Sep
257.953t	Barry	Loveday	AUS		5.10.77	1		Bruce	20	Mar
257.296	Stéphane	Ruel	FRA		21.1.66	3	EC	Albi	22	Oct
255.250	Tamás	Rudolf	HUN		12.12.79	1	NC	Sárvár	24	Apr
253.631	Piero	Lattarico	FRA		8.2.69	4	EC	Albi	22	Oct
252.364	Patrick	Ruiz	FRA		28.12.69	5	EC	Albi	22	Oct
251.611	Aleksandr	Sorokin	LTU		30.9.81	6	EC	Albi	22	Oct
251.599	Stefan Stu	Thoms	GER		18.10.66	7	EC	Albi	22	Oct
250.263	Marco	Consani	GBR		15.11.74	8	EC	Albi	22	Oct
250.240	Guillaume	Laroche	FRA		25.5.76	9	EC	Albi	22	Oct
249.804	Nobuyuki	Takahashi	JPN	1.2.83	18 Dec	247.058	Bjørn Tore Kronen Taranger	NOR	23.4.79	22 Oct
248.404	Shuhei	Kotani	JPN	25.8.88	18 Dec	247.040	Bela Mazur	HUN	13.4.78	24 Apr
247.994	Toshiro	Naraki	JPN	10.8.76	18 Dec	245.245t	Yuriy Galkin	RUS	6.3.58	15 May

3000 METRES STEEPLECHASE

Mark	Name		Nat		Born	Pos	Meet	Venue	Date	
8:00.12	Conseslus	Kipruto	KEN		8.12.94	1	DL	Birmingham	5	Jun
8:01.41		C Kipruto				1	GGala	Roma	2	Jun
8:02.77		C Kipruto				1	DL	Rabat	22	May
8:03.28		C Kipruto				1	OG	Rio de Janeiro	17	Aug
8:03.74		C Kipruto				1	VD	Bruxelles	9	Sep
8:03.90	Jairus	Birech	KEN		14.12.92	2	DL	Rabat	22	May
8:04.01	Evan	Jager	USA		8.3.89	2	VD	Bruxelles	9	Sep
8:04.28		Jager				2	OG	Rio de Janeiro	17	Aug
8:05.13		C Kipruto				1	DL	Doha	6	May
8:08.11		C Kipruto				1	Herc	Monaco	15	Jul
8:08.15	Mahiedine	Mekhissi-Benabbad	FRA		15.3.85	3	VD	Bruxelles	9	Sep
8:08.28		Birech				2	DL	Doha	6	May
8:08.32	Paul Kipsiele	Koech	KEN		10.11.81	2	Herc	Monaco	15	Jul
8:09.13	Barnabas	Kipyego	KEN		12.6.95	3	Herc	Monaco	15	Jul
8:09.25	Abraham	Kibiwot	KEN		4.6.96	3	DL	Doha	6	May
8:09.58		Kibiwot				1	Athl	Lausanne	25	Aug
8:09.62	John	Koech	BRN		23.8.95	4	DL	Doha	6	May
8:10.07	Nicholas	Bett	KEN		20.12.96	2	Athl	Lausanne	25	Aug
8:10.11		Kipyego				5	DL	Doha	6	May
8:10.19		P K Koech				2	DL	Birmingham	5	Jun
8:10.65	Clement	Kemboi (10)	KEN		1.2.92	6	DL	Doha	6	May
8:11.20		Bett				4	VD	Bruxelles	9	Sep
8:11.39		Birech				2	GGala	Roma	2	Jun
8:11.52		Mekhissi-Benabbad				3	OG	Rio de Janeiro	17	Aug
8:12.33		P K Koech				3		Rabat	22	May
8:12.81		Kibiwot				5	VD	Bruxelles	9	Sep
8:13.68	Hillary	Bor	USA		22.11.89	6	VD	Bruxelles	9	Sep
8:14.04		Bett				1	NA	Heusden-Zolder	16	Jul
8:14.19	Ezekiel	Kemboi	KEN		25.5.82	1		Beijing	18	May
8:14.35	Soufiane	El Bakkali	MAR		7.1.96	4	OG	Rio de Janeiro	17	Aug
	[30/13]									
8:15.10	Hillary	Yego	KEN		2.4.92	2	NA	Heusden-Zolder	16	Jul
8:16.11	Andrew	Bayer	USA		3.2.90	7	VD	Bruxelles	9	Sep
8:16.14	Tesfaye	Girma	ETH		.95	3	NA	Heusden-Zolder	16	Jul
8:16.21	Yoann	Kowal	FRA		28.5.87	8	VD	Bruxelles	9	Sep
8:16.84	Abel	Mutai	KEN		2.10.88	8	DL	Doha	6	May
8:17.75	Tafese	Soboka	ETH		29.9.93	2		Huelva	3	Jun
8:17.79	Lawrence	Kemboi	KEN		15.6.93	9	DL	Doha	6	May
	(20)									
8:17.84	Chala	Beyo	ETH		18.1.96	3		Huelva	3	Jun
8:18.28	Alex	Kibet	KEN		20.10.90	4	NA	Heusden-Zolder	16	Jul
8:18.52	Stanley	Kebenei	USA		6.11.89	5	GGala	Roma	2	Jun
8:18.58	Dan	Huling	USA		16.7.83	2		Los Angeles (ER)	20	May
8:18.79	Brimin	Kipruto	KEN		31.7.85	6	OG	Rio de Janeiro	17	Aug
8:19.12	Cory	Leslie	USA		24.10.89	3		Los Angeles (ER)	20	May
8:19.31	Hamid	Ezzine	MAR		5.10.83	6	DL	Rabat	22	May
8:19.33	Sebastián	Martos	ESP		20.6.89	8	Herc	Monaco	15	Jul
8:19.91	Krystian	Zalewski	POL		11.4.89	7	GGala	Roma	2	Jun
8:20.26	Bilal	Tabti	ALG		7.6.93	8	GGala	Roma	2	Jun
	(30)									
8:20.35	Benjamin	Kiplagat	UGA		4.3.89	10	Herc	Monaco	15	Jul
8:20.43	Amos	Kirui	KEN-J		9.2.98	1	WJ	Bydgoszcz	24	Jul
8:20.53	Hicham	Sigueni	MAR		30.1.93	5	NA	Heusden-Zolder	16	Jul
8:20.63	Matt	Hughes	CAN		3.8.89	4		Los Angeles (ER)	20	May
8:20.72	Amor	Benyahia	TUN		1.7.85	2		Sotteville-les-Rouen	18	Jul

3000m STEEPLECHASE

Mark	Name		Nat	Born	Pos	Meet	Venue	Date	
8:20.72	Donn	Cabral	USA	12.12.89	1		Eugene	29	Jul
8:21.10	Hailemariyam	Amare	ETH-J	22.2.97	5		Beijing	18	May
8:21.23	Phenus	Kipleting	KEN	.89	4		Huelva	3	Jun
8:21.30	Birhan	Getahun	ETH	5.9.91	2		Montbéliard	1	Jun
8:21.33	Jigisa	Tolosa	ETH	29.3.90	10	GGala	Roma	2	Jun
(40)									
8:21.34	Mitko	Tsenov	BUL	13.6.93	10	DL	Doha	6	May
8:21.53	Jacob	Araptany	UGA	11.2.92	2h3	OG	Rio de Janeiro	15	Aug
8:21.57	Mason	Ferlic	USA	5.8.93	2		Eugene	29	Jul
8:21.92	Jamal	Chatbi ¶	ITA	30.4.84	9	DL	Rabat	22	May
8:22.42	Rob	Mullett	GBR	31.7.87	5		Los Angeles (ER)	20	May
8:22.5A	Justus	Lagat	KEN	20.5.96	3	NC	Nairobi	28	May
8:22.52	Yemane	Haileselassie	ERI-J	21.2.98	6		Huelva	3	Jun
8:22.7A	Vincent	Kipyegon	KEN-J	31.12.98	1	NC-j	Nairobi	22	Jun
8:22.83	Getnet	Wale	ETH-Y	20.7.99	3	WJ	Bydgoszcz	24	Jul
8:23.38	Donnie	Cowart	USA	24.10.85	6		Los Angeles (ER)	20	May
[50]									
8:23.51	Hichem	Bouchicha	ALG	19.5.89	4		Montbéliard	1	Jun
8:23.77	Mohamed Ismail	Ibrahim	DJI-J	.97	11	DL	Doha	6	May
8:25.34	Viktor	Bakharev	RUS	5.5.94	1	NC	Cheboksary	21	Jun
8:25.44	Travis	Mahoney	USA	25.7.90	8		Los Angeles (ER)	20	May
8:25.81	Ilgizar	Safiulin	RUS	9.12.92	2	NC	Cheboksary	21	Jun
8:26.15	Abdelaziz	Merzougui	ESP	30.8.91	7		Huelva	3	Jun
8:26.21	Maksim	Yakushev	RUS	15.3.92	3	NC	Cheboksary	21	Jun
8:26.23	Nelson	Kipkosgei	BRN	9.3.93	7	NA	Heusden-Zolder	16	Jul
8:26.30	Altobeli	da Silva	BRA	3.12.90	10	OG	Rio de Janeiro	17	Aug
8:26.36	Andrey	Farnosov	RUS	9.7.80	4	NC	Cheboksary	21	Jun
(60)									
8:26.36	José Gregorio	Peña	VEN	12.1.87	8	NA	Heusden-Zolder	16	Jul
8:26.97	Taylor	Milne	CAN	14.6.81	1		Guelph	25	Jun
8:27.18	Chris	Winter	CAN	22.7.86	9		Los Angeles (ER)	20	May
8:27.19	Craig	Forys	USA	13.7.89	10		Los Angeles (ER)	20	May
8:27.62	Anthony	Rotich	KEN	.93	4	Jordan	Stanford	1	May
8:27.99	Ali	Messaoudi	Al G	13.10.95	1		Alger	28	Jun
8:28.01	Belayneh	Shimelis	ETH	.96	2		Sollentuna	28	Jun
8:28.14	Abdelhamid	Zerrifi	ALG	20.6.86	11	Herc	Monaco	15	Jul
8:28.34	Djilali	Bédrani	FRA	1.10.93	5		Montbéliard	1	Jun
8:28.45	Patrick	Churkor	KEN	17.2.91	6		Montbéliard	1	Jun
(70)									
8:29.0A	Hillary	Kemboi	KEN	.86	5	NC	Nairobi	28	May
8:29.78	Hironori	Tsuetaki	JPN	8.5.93	1		Osaka	24	Sep
8:29.91	Aras	Kaya	TUR	4.4.94	2	EC	Amsterdam	8	Jul
8:30.03	Yuri	Floriani	ITA	25.12.81	1	NC	Rieti	26	Jun
8:30.14A	Joash	Kiplimo	KEN	.91	1h1	NC	Nairobi	26	May
8:30.23	Mohammed	Tindouft	MAR	12.3.93	2	NC	Rabat	5	Jun
8:30.25	Alexandre	Genest	CAN	30.6.86	9	Jordan	Stanford	1	May
8:30.28	Valentin	Pépiot	FRA	6.7.91	12	Herc	Monaco	15	Jul
8:30.38	Ivan	Lukyanov	RUS	31.1.81	5	NC	Cheboksary	21	Jun
8:30.51	Ole	Hesselbjerg	DEN	23.4.90	1rB	Jordan	Stanford	1	May
(80)									
8:30.67	Franklin	Tonui	KEN	2.8.93	2	NCAA	Eugene	10	Jun
8:30.71	Edwin	Kibichy	KEN	2.4.92	3	NCAA	Eugene	10	Jun
8:30.85	Younès	Kniya	MAR	15.8.95	3	NC	Rabat	5	Jun
8:30.87	Bernard Nganga	Mbugua	KEN	17.1.85	8		Beijing	18	May
8:31.02	Chris	Dulhanty	CAN	6.4.92	11		Los Angeles (ER)	20	May
8:31.05	Mohammed	Boulama	MAR	31.12.93	1		Oordegem	28	May
8:31.20	Yousif Abdalla	Targan	SUD	28.9.96	8		Montbéliard	1	Jun
8:31.42	Isaac	Updike	USA	21.3.92	1rB		Los Angeles (ER)	20	May
8:31.48	Issam	Zeghdane	ALG	9.3.93	1		Alger	2	Jul
8:31.54	Jeroen	D'Hoedt	BEL	10.1.90	9	NA	Heusden-Zolder	16	Jul
(90)									
8:31.72	Rantso	Makopane	RSA	8.8.94	2		Oordegem	28	May
8:31.87	Jaouad	Chemlal	MAR	11.4.94	13	DL	Rabat	22	May
8:31.89	Kazuya	Shiojiri	JPN	8.11.96	1		Inba	7	Jul
8:32.10	Collins	Chebii	KEN-J	.97	2		Doha	26	Apr
8:32.20	Amos	Kibitok	KEN	4.4.94	1		Mersin	1	May
8:32.20	Osama	Zoghlami	ITA	19.6.94	1		Castiglione d.Pescaia	17	May
8:32.54	Abdoullah	Bamoussa	ITA	2.6.86	6h1	EC	Amsterdam	6	Jul
8:32.55	Mike	Hardy	USA	13.1.90	2rB		Los Angeles (ER)	20	May
8:32.59	James	Nipperess	AUS	21.5.90	12		Los Angeles (ER)	20	May
8:32.63	Silas	Kitum	KEN	25.5.90	10		Huelva	3	Jun
[100]									

3000m STEEPLECHASE – 60 METRES HURDLES

Mark	Name		Nat	Born		Mark	Name		Nat	Born	
8:32.66	Yohannes	Chiappinelli	ITA-J	18.8.97	24 Jul	8:36.24	Darren	Fahy	USA	14.5.94	8 Jun
8:32.74	Dylan	Lafond	USA	18.3.93	18 Jun	8:36.30	Kosei	Yamaguchi	JPN	19.8.91	7 Jul
8:32.79	Dikotsi	Lekopa	RSA	7.7.88	28 May	8:36.37	Hashim Salah	Abbas	QAT	15.4.94	30 Jun
8:32.86	Tabor	Stevens	USA	21.6.91	4 Jun	8:36.4A	Geoffrey	Rotich	KEN-J	28.10.98	28 May
8:32.94	Aric	Van Halen	USA	6.10.89	20 May	8:36.42	Antoine	Thibeault	CAN	24.3.94	1 May
8:33.09	Zak	Seddon	GBR	28.6.94	1 Apr	8:36.47	Bjørnar Ustad	Kristensen	NOR	26.1.82	28 May
8:33.09	Nikolay	Chavkin	RUS	24.4.84	21 Jun	8:36.51	Troy	Reeder	USA	8.8.94	8 Jun
8:33.12	Halil	Akkas	TUR	1.7.83	15 Aug	8:36.58	Austin	Bussing	USA	17.4.90	12 Jun
8:33.13	Hakan	Duvar	TUR	21.8.90	6 Jul	8:36.60	Austin	O'Neil	USA	7.11.93	20 May
8:33.23	Malek	Ben Amor	TUN	4.5.94	1 Jun	8:36.65	Bailey	Roth	USA	17.1.96	12 Jun
8:33.35	Ibrahim	Chakir	ESP	4.9.94	30 Jun	8:36.68	Edwin	Melly	KEN	10.8.96	17 May
8:33.61	Tumisang	Monnatlala	RSA	31.1.95	28 May	8:36.68	Vadym	Slobodenyuk	UKR	17.3.81	18 Jun
8:33.69	Fernando	Carro	ESP	1.4.92	6 Jul	8:36.78	Mohammed	Merbouhi	ALG	2.7.91	2 Jul
8:33.75	Benard	Keter	KEN	.94	8 Jun	8:36.81	Aaron	Fletcher	USA	89	8 Jun
8:33.75	Kaur	Kivistik	EST	29.4.91	8 Jul	8:36.85	Haron	Lagat	KEN	15.8.83	7 May
8:33.77	Caleb	Hoover	USA	22.7.92	8 Jun	8:36.9A	James	Bunuka	KEN-J	1.11.97	22 Jun
8:33.82	Andrés Camilo	Camargo	COL	30.6.86	15 Apr	8:37.05	Fabian	Clarkson	GER	13.12.90	25 Jun
8:33.92	Wogene	Sebisibe	ETH-J	23.6.98	28 Jun	8:37.1A	Willy	Komen	KEN	22.12.87	27 Feb
8:34.04	Jakob	Abrahamsen	DEN	29.7.94	27 May	8:37.12	Tomas	Cotter	IRL	28.12.90	20 May
8:34.07A	Kennedy	Njiru	KEN	.87	29 Apr	8:37.43	Jonathan	Hopkins	GBR	3.6.92	5 Jun
8:34.09	Ryan	Brockerville	CAN	29.7.89	20 May	8:37.44	Elmar	Engholm	SWE	2.10.92	8 Jun
8:34.13	MJ	Erb	USA	2.2.94	8 Jun	8:37.62	Matt	Cleaver	USA	7.11.89	1 May
8:34.28	Abdelkarim	Ben Zahra	MAR-J	27.10.98	24 Jul	8:37.76	Albert	Chemutai	KEN-Y	25.11.99	24 Jul
8:34.32	Bryce	Miller	USA	1.5.95	8 Jun	8:37.80	Tom	Wade	GBR	14.1.89	18 Jun
8:34.45	Stewart	McSweyn	AUS	1.6.95	28 Jun	8:37.89	Sisay	Korme	ETH	9.1.85	31 Mar
8:34.64	Tarik Langat	Akdag	TUR	16.6.88	29 May	8:37.9A	Daniel	Kipchumba	KEN-J	12.12.97	22 Jun
8:34.66	Mouname	Sassaoui	MAR	20.3.95	5 Jun	8:37.92	Ricardo	Estremera	PUR	11.3.86	1 May
8:34.69	Dylan	Blankenbaker	USA	6.1.94	10 Jun	8:38.08	Boris	Zakharov	RUS	1.4.84	21 Jun
8:34.81	Jun	Shinoto	JPN	2.4.85	1 May	8:38.28	Sibusiso	Madikizela	RSA	.91	22 Mar
8:34.81	Emil	Blomberg	SWE	9.4.92	6 Jul	8:38.28	Jordan	Mann	USA	.94	27 May
8:35.29A	Hillary	Maiyo	KEN	2.10.93	26 May	8:38.80	Andrea	Sanguinetti	ITA	25.1.92	4 Jun
8:35.30	Michael	Jordan	USA	21.5.91	18 Jun	8:38.85	Yevgeniy	Bykov	RUS	15.5.90	26 May
8:35.5A	Philemon	Ruto	KEN-Y	20.9.01	22 Jun	8:38.93	Ibrahim	Ezzaydouny	MAR	28.4.91	24 Jul
8:35.56	Mark	Parrish	USA	2.12.91	20 May	8:39.05	Kidanemariam	Dessie	ETH-Y	12.9.99	21 Jul
8:35.56A	Isaac	Yego	KEN	89	26 May	8:39.15	Hannes	Liebach	GER	23.5.87	28 May
8:35.59	Carl	Stones	USA	1.11.89	12 Jun	8:39.24	Eric	Peñalver	ESP	23.9.93	24 Jul
8:35.63	Yuriy	Kloptsov	RUS	22.12.89	26 May	8:39.26	Meron	Simon	USA	14.1.93	14 May
8:35.71	Luke	Gunn	GBR	22.3.85	28 May	8:39.27	Henry	Sterling	USA	19.7.91	18 Jun
8:35.84	Tom Erling	Kårbø	NOR	4.2.89	28 May	8:39.58	Aaron	Nelson	USA	16.7.92	14 May
8:35.93	Patrick	Karl	GER	3.5.96	16 May	8:39.82	Tumelo	Motlagale	RSA	26.11.86	16 Apr
8:36.03	Evans	Chematot	BRN	19.3.96	18 May	8:39.97	Tim	Stegemann	GER	4.8.92	4 Jun
8:36.06A	Vincent	Ruto	KEN	17.9.95	26 May		[183]				

Disqualified – stepping off inside of track
8:08.47 Ezekiel Kemboi KEN 25.5.82 [3] OG Rio de Janeiro 17 Aug

Drugs disqualification
8:25.84 Ildar Minshin ¶ RUS 5.2.85 (3) NC Cheboksary 21 Jun
8:39.80 Abdellah Dacha ¶ MAR 26.1.92 (11) NA Heusden-Zolder 16 Jul

JUNIORS

See main list for top 7 juniors. 11 performances by 6 men to 8:28.0. Additional marks and further juniors:

Mark	Name		Nat	Born	Pos	Meet	Venue	Date
Kurui	8:22.59	7	Athl	Lausanne		25 Aug	8:27.4A	2 NC-j Nairobi 22 Jun
Haileselassie	8:22.67	2	WJ	Bydgoszcz		24 Jul	8:26.72	4h2 OG Rio de Janeiro 15 Aug
Kipyegon	8:22.84	4	WJ	Bydgoszcz		24 Jul		
8:32.66	Yohannes	Chiappinelli	ITA	18.8.97	5	WJ	Bydgoszcz	24 Jul
8:33.92	Wogene	Sebisibe	ETH	23.6.98	3		Sollentuna	28 Jun
8:34.28	Abdelkarim	Ben Zahra (10)	MAR	27.10.98	6	WJ	Bydgoszcz	24 Jul
8:35.5A	Philemon	Ruto	KEN-Y	20.9.01	3	NC-j	Nairobi	22 Jun
8:36.4A	Geoffrey	Rotich	KEN	28.10.98	8	NC	Nairobi	28 May
8:36.9A	James	Bunuka	KEN	1.11.97	4	NC-j	Nairobi	22 Jun
8:37.76	Albert	Chemutai	KEN-Y	25.11.99	7	WJ	Bydgoszcz	24 Jul
8:37.9A	Daniel	Kipchumba	KEN	12.12.97	5	NC-j	Nairobi	22 Jun
8:39.05	Kidanemariam	Dessie	ETH-Y	12.9.99	2h2	WJ	Bydgoszcz	21 Jul
8:40.98	Daniel	Kipchumba	KEN	.97	7h1	NC	Nairobi	26 May
8:41.79	Mohamed Amine	Jihnaoui	TUN	2.4.97	9	WJ	Bydgoszcz	24 Jul
8:42.56	Soufien	Cherni	TUN	8.1.97	11	WJ	Bydgoszcz	24 Jul
8:43.53	Louis	Gilavert (20)	FRA	1.1.98	2rB		Oordegem	28 May

60 METRES HURDLES INDOORS

Mark	Name		Nat	Born	Pos	Meet	Venue	Date
7.41	Dimitri	Bascou	FRA	20.7.87	1	ISTAF	Berlin	13 Feb
7.41	Omar	McLeod	JAM	25.4.94	1	WI	Portland	20 Mar
7.46		McLeod			1	Mill	New York	20 Feb
7.46	Pascal	Martinot-Lagarde	FRA	22.9.91	2	WI	Portland	20 Mar
7.48		Martinot-Lagarde			1h4	WI	Portland	19 Mar
7.48		Bascou			3	WI	Portland	20 Mar
7.49	Orlando	Ortega	ESP	29.7.91	1		Düsseldorf	3 Feb

372 60 METRES HURDLES

Mark	Name		Nat	Born	Pos	Meet	Venue	Date	
7.49		Martinot-Lagarde			1		Metz	21	Feb
7.50	Jarret	Eaton	USA	24.6.89	4	WI	Portland	20	Mar
7.51		Ortega			2	ISTAF	Berlin	13	Feb
(10/5)									
7.53	Ashton	Eaton	USA	21.1.88	2	Mill	New York (Arm)	20	Feb
7.53	Myles	Hunter	USA	16.8.95	1	NCAA-II	Pittsburg KS	12	Mar
7.55	Balázs	Baji	HUN	9.6.89	1h1	NC	Budapest	21	Feb
7.56	Devon	Allen	USA	12.12.94	1	NCAA	Birmingham	12	Mar
7.57	Jeff	Porter	USA	27.11.85	3		Jablonec nad Nisou	5	Mar
(10)									
7.58	Greggmar	Swift	BAR	16.2.91	2	Pedros	Lódz	5	Feb
7.58A	Aries	Merritt	USA	24.7.85	1h3		Flagstaff	13	Feb
7.58	Jordan	Moore	USA	13.12.93	1h1	NCAA	Birmingham	11	Mar
7.58	Spencer	Adams	USA	10.9.89	2	NC	Portland	12	Mar
7.59	Terence	Somerville	USA	5.11.89	1		Bloomington, IN	30	Jan
7.60	Abdulaziz	Al-Mandeel	KUW	22.5.89	1	AsiC	Doha	21	Feb
7.61	Andy	Pozzi	GBR	15.5.92	1h1	South	London (LV)	17	Jan
7.61	Yordan	O'Farrill	CUB	9.2.93	2		Mondeville	6	Feb
7.61	Erik	Balnuweit	GER	21.9.88	1	NC	Leipzig	27	Feb
7.62	Garfield	Darien	FRA	22.12.87	3		Düsseldorf	3	Feb
(20)									
7.63	Damian	Warner	CAN	4.11.89	1h1		Toronto	30	Jan
7.63		Xie Wenjun	CHN	11.7.90	1	GP	Glasgow	20	Feb
7.63	Eddie	Lovett	ISV	25.6.92	1h1	WI	Portland	19	Mar
7.64	Yidiel	Contreras	ESP	27.11.91	3	Pedros	Lódz	5	Feb
7.64	Alexander	John	GER	3.5.86	2	NC	Leipzig	27	Feb
7.64	Freddie	Crittenden	USA	3.8.94	2	NCAA	Birmingham	12	Mar
7.64	Shane	Brathwaite	BAR	8.2.90	3s1	WI	Portland	20	Mar
7.65	Aleec	Harris	USA	31.10.90	1		Winston-Salem	30	Jan
7.65	Lawrence	Clarke	GBR	12.3.90	3	ISTAF	Berlin	13	Feb
7.65	Yaqoub	Al-Yoha	KUW	31.1.93	2	AsiC	Doha	21	Feb
(30)									
7.65	Ronald	Forbes	CAY	5.4.85	1		New York (Arm)	4	Mar
7.65	Artur	Noga	POL	2.5.88	1	NC	Torun	6	Mar
7.66	David	King	GBR	13.6.94	1h1		Gent	13	Feb
7.66		Zhang Honglin	CHN	12.1.94	2		Reims	17	Feb
7.67	Koen	Smet	NED	9.8.92	1r1		Amsterdam	6	Feb
7.67	Will	Barnes	USA	17.3.94	1		Kent	20	Feb
7.67	Konstantin	Shabanov	RUS	17.11.89	1	NC	Moskva	24	Feb
7.67	Martin	Vogel	GER	16.3.92	3	NC	Leipzig	27	Feb
7.67	Mikel	Thomas	TTO	23.11.87	2		New York (Arm)	4	Mar
7.68	Simon	Krauss	FRA	12.2.92	1h2		Reims	16	Jan
(40)									
7.68	Kevin	Craddock	USA	25.6.87	4		Düsseldorf	3	Feb
7.68	David	Omoregie	GBR	1.11.95	3		Mondeville	6	Feb
7.68	Dominik	Bochenek	POL	14.5.87	1		Spala	20	Feb
7.68	Fábio	dos Santos	BRA	11.10.83	1		São Caetano do Sul	27	Feb
7.69	Israel	Nelson	USA	.96	1		Pittsburg	29	Jan
7.69	Konstadínos	Douvalídis	GRE	10.3.87	3h1		Düsseldorf	3	Feb
7.69	Dondre	Echols	USA	6.7.93	1		Fayetteville	12	Feb
7.69	Chad	Zallow	USA-J	25.4.97	1		Akron	19	Feb
7.69	Damien	Broothaerts	BEL	13.3.83	1	NC	Gent	20	Feb
7.69	Andreas	Martinsen	DEN	17.7.90	1r1		Rud	21	Feb
(50)									
7.69	Aaron	Mallett	USA	26.9.94	1	Big 10	Geneva	27	Feb
7.69	Francisco Javier	López	ESP	8.4.89	2	NCAA-II	Pittsburg	12	Mar
7.70	Trey	Holloway	USA	7.7.94	1		Newport News	23	Jan
7.70	Serhiy	Kopanayko	UKR	5.11.88	1		Kyiv	4	Feb
7.70	Artem	Shamatryn	UKR	15.6.91	2		Kyiv	4	Feb
7.70	Jhoanis	Portilla	CUB	24.7.90	3		Metz	21	Feb
7.70	Brahian	Peña	SUI	3.4.94	1	NC	St. Gallen	28	Feb
7.71	Benjamin	Sedecias	FRA	18.1.95	1		Gent	13	Feb
7.71	Maksim	Lynsha	BLR	6.4.85	1	NC	Mogilyov	21	Feb
7.71	Dapo	Akinmoladun	USA	28.2.94	2	Big 10	Geneva	27	Feb
(60)									
7.71	Yanick	Hart	JAM	1.10.93	2	SEC	Fayetteville	27	Feb
7.71	Marcus	McWilliams	USA-J	20.2.97	4	NCAA	Birmingham	12	Mar
7.72	Chris	Williams	USA	5.3.94	1h5		Seattle	26	Feb
7.73	Kirk	Thornton	USA	13.7.86	2		Houston	30	Jan
7.73	Jason	Richardson	USA	4.4.86	7	Mill	New York (Arm)	20	Feb
7.73	Jonathas Felipe	Brito	BRA	30.11.92	2		São Caetano do Sul	27	Feb

60 – 110 METRES HURDLES

Mark	Wind	Name		Nat	Born	Pos	Meet	Venue	Date	
7.73		Ben	Reynolds	IRL	26.9.90	1	NC	Athlone	28	Feb
7.74		Khai	Riley-La Borde	GBR	8.11.95	1A1		London (LV)	3	Jan
7.74		Michael	Dickson	USA-J	25.1.97	2s2		New York (Arm)	5	Feb
7.74		Chris	Caldwell	USA	6.4.94	1	Big 12	Ames	27	Feb
		(70)								
7.74		Jonathan	Mendes	BRA	14.4.90	3		São Caetano do Sul	27	Feb
7.74		Tobias	Furer	SUI	13.8.87	2	NC	St. Gallen	28	Feb
7.74		Thomas	Delmestre	FRA	31.3.91	3	NC	Aubière	28	Feb
7.74		Martin	Mazáč	CZE	6.5.90	4		Jablonec nad Nisou	5	Mar
7.75		Kemar	Clarke	USA	20.5.88	1		New York (Arm)	5	Feb
7.75		Damian	Czykier	POL	10.8.92	3		Torun	12	Feb
7.75		Alexander	Brorsson	SWE	29.5.90	1	v3N	Växjö	13	Feb
7.75		Johnathan	Cabral	CAN	31.12.92	2	NC	Montréal	20	Feb
7.75		Cam	Viney	USA	6.9.93	1h1	Big 10	Geneva	26	Feb
7.75		Nicolas	Borome	FRA	7.10.93	5	NC	Aubière	28	Feb
		(80)								
7.75		Ramón	Sosa	DOM	11.1.86	3		New York (Arm)	4	Mar
7.75		Vladimir	Vukicevic	NOR	6.5.91	2	NC	Rud	6	Mar

110 METRES HURDLES

Mark	Wind	Name		Nat	Born	Pos	Meet	Venue	Date	
12.98	1.2	Omar	McLeod	JAM	25.4.94	1	DL	Shanghai	14	May
13.01	1.4		McLeod			1	NC	Kingston	2	Jul
13.03	1.0	Devon	Allen	USA	12.12.94	1	NC/OT	Eugene	9	Jul
13.04	0.0	Orlando	Ortega	ESP	29.7.91	1	Herc	Monaco	15	Jul
13.05	1.4		McLeod			1	DL	Dha	6	May
13.05	0.2		McLeod			1	OG	Rio de Janeiro	16	Aug
13.06	0.7		McLeod			1	Pre	Eugene	28	May
13.08	-0.1		McLeod			1r1	DrakeR	Des Moines	30	Apr
13.08	0.2		Ortega			1	VD	Bruxelles	9	Sep
13.09	0.2	David	Oliver	USA	24.4.82	1		Kingston	11	Jun
13.09	1.0		Ortega			1	NC	Gijón	24	Jul
13.10	1.4	Hansle	Parchment	JAM	17.6.90	2	DL	Doha	6	May
13.11	0.5		Ortega			1	Athl	Lausanne	25	Aug
13.12	1.4		Ortega			3	DL	Doha	6	May
13.12	1.2		Parchment			2	DL	Shanghai	14	May
13.12	1.4		Oliver			1	DL	Rabat	22	May
13.12	0.0	Dimitri	Bascou	FRA	20.7.87	2	Herc	Monaco	15	Jul
13.12	0.5		McLeod			2	Athl	Lausanne	25	Aug
13.12	0.2	Pascal	Martinot Lagarde	FRA	22.9.91	2	VD	Bruxelles	9	Sep
13.13	1.4		Ortega			2		Rabat	22	May
13.15	-0.1		McLeod			1s2	OG	Rio de Janeiro	16	Aug
13.16	1.4		Oliver			4	DL	Doha	6	May
13.17	0.9		Ortega			1		Madrid	23	Jun
13.17	0.0		Martinot Lagarde			3	Herc	Monaco	15	Jul
13.17	0.2		Ortega			2	OG	Rio de Janeiro	16	Aug
13.18	1.4	Ronnie	Ash	USA	2.7.88	1h1		Montverde, FL	11	Jun
13.19	-0.8	Andrew	Pozzi	GBR	15.5.92	1h1	DL	London (OS)	23	Jul
13.20	0.2	Deuce	Carter (10)	JAM	28.9.90	2		Kingston	11	Jun
13.20	-0.2	Sergey	Shubenkov	RUS	4.10.90	1	NC	Cheboksary	21	Jun
13.20	-0.5		Bascou			1s3	EC	Amsterdam	9	Jul
13.20	-1.0		Bascou			1		London (OS)	23	Jul
		[31/11]								
13.21	1.0	Jeff	Porter	USA	27.11.85	3	NC/OT	Eugene	9	Jul
13.21	1.8	Gregor	Traber	GER	2.12.92	1		Mannheim	29	Jul
13.22	1.0	Aries	Merritt	USA	24.7.85	4	NC/OT	Eugene	9	Jul
13.24	0.6	David	Omoregie	GBR	1.11.95	1	ISTAF	Berlin	3	Sep
13.25	0.0	Jarret	Eaton	USA	24.6.89	1	GS	Ostrava	20	May
13.25	0.5	Wilhem	Bélocian	FRA	22.6.95	4	Athl	Lausanne	25	Aug
13.27	0.6	Antwon	Hicks	NGR	12.3.83	1	NC/	Sapele	7	Jul
13.28	1.4	Antonio	Alkana	RSA	12.4.90	3	DL	Rabat	22	May
13.28	0.0	Balázs	Baji	HUN	9.6.89	2	EC	Amsterdam	9	Jul
		(20)								
13.28	1.0	Jason	Richardson	USA	4.4.86	5	NC/OT	Eugene	9	Jul
13.31	0.3	Milan	Trajkovic	CYP	17.3.92	2s3	OG	Rio de Janeiro	16	Aug
13.32	-1.8	Damian	Czykier	POL	10.8.92	3s2	EC	Amsterdam	9	Jul
13.33	1.7	Aurel	Manga	FRA	24.7.92	3h1	NC	Angers	26	Jun
13.34	1.2		Xie Wenjun	CHN	11.7.90	3	DL	Shanghai	14	May
13.35	1.9	Johnathan	Cabral	CAN	31.12.92	1	MSR	Norwalk	16	Apr
13.35	1.8	Andrew	Riley	JAM	6.9.88	1		Eugene	29	Jul

110 METRES HURDLES

Mark	Wind	Name		Nat	Born	Pos	Meet	Venue	Date	
13.36	0.4	Ronald	Forbes	CAY	5.4.85	2		Clermont	30	Apr
13.36A	0.3	Yeison	Rivas	COL	24.9.87	1		Medellín	10	Jul
13.38	0.6	Alexander (30)	John	GER	3.5.86	1h2		Clermont	14	May
13.38	1.4	Konstadínos	Douvalídis	GRE	10.3.87	4	DL	Rabat	22	May
13.39	1.9	Eddie	Lovett	ISV	25.6.92	1	FlaR	Gainesville	1	Apr
13.39	2.0	Milan	Ristic	SRB	8.8.91	1		Clermont	14	May
13.40	1.9	Mikel	Thomas	TTO	23.11.87	2	MSR	Norwalk	16	Apr
13.40	1.1	Adarius	Washington	USA	19.10.92	1r2	DrakeR	Des Moines	30	Apr
13.41	1.1	Will	Barnes	PUR	17.3.94	2r2	DrakeR	Des Moines	30	Apr
13.42	1.3	Damian	Warner	CAN	4.11.89	1		Lexington	7	May
13.42	-0.7	Lawrence	Clarke	GBR	12.3.90	1		Luzern	14	Jun
13.43	1.9	Isaac	Williams	USA	30.11.93	3	MSR	Norwalk	16	Apr
13.43	0.1	Aleec (40)	Harris	USA	31.10.90	2		Baie Mahault	14	May
13.43	1.9	Maximilian	Bayer	GER	5.12.90	2		Mannheim	29	Jul
13.44	1.4	Spencer	Adams	USA	10.9.89	7	DL	Doha	6	May
13.44	1.0	Devon	Hill	USA	26.10.89	1		Coral Gables	4	Jun
13.44	0.3	Matthias	Bühler	GER	2.9.86	1	NC	Kassel	18	Jun
13.45	1.9	Benjamin	Sédécias	FRA	18.1.95	1		La Roche sur Yon	13	Jul
13.45	1.0	Yidiel	Contreras	ESP	27.11.92	2	NC	Gijón	24	Jul
13.46	0.2	Tyler	Mason	JAM	15.1.95	5		Kingston	11	Jun
13.47	2.0	Jeffrey	Julmis	HAI	6.1.87	2		Clermont	14	May
13.47	1.4	Wataru	Yazawa	JPN	2.7.91	1		Tottori	5	Jun
13.48	1.9	Ashton [50]	Eaton	USA	21.1.88	4	MSR	Norwalk	16	Apr
13.48	0.8	Freddie	Crittenden	USA	3.8.94	1		Auburn	23	Apr
13.48	0.5	Ryan	Fontenot	USA	4.5.86	1		Houston	6	May
13.48	2.0	Logan	Taylor	USA	3.4.86	3		Clermont	14	May
13.48	0.3	Aaron	Mallett	USA	26.9.94	1	Big 10	Lincoln	15	May
13.48	0.0	Gregory	Sedoc	NED	16.10.81	3		Weinheim	28	May
13.49	1.8	Ronald	Brookins	USA	5.7.89	1		Irvine	30	Apr
13.50	0.3	Ronald	Levy	JAM	30.10.92	1		Kingston	12	Jun
13.50	0.1	Gabriel	Constantino	BRA	9.2.95	1	NC	São Bernardo do Campo	3	Jul
13.51	1.6	Abdulaziz	Al-Mandeel	KUW	22.5.89	1		Al-Kuwait	14	May
13.51	0.0	Yordan (60)	O'Farrill	CUB	9.2.93	1h1	Barr	La Habana	26	May
13.51	1.0	Jhoanis	Portilla	CUB	24.7.90	1	Barr	La Habana	26	May
13.51	1.1	Shane	Brathwaite	BAR	8.2.90	3	Odlozil	Praha	6	Jun
13.52	0.0	William	Sharman	GBR	12.9.84	2r2		Bellinzona	6	Jun
13.52A	0.0	Javier	McFarlane	PER	21.10.91	1		Cali	26	Jun
13.52	-0.5	Hassane	Fofana	ITA	28.4.92	5s3	EC	Amsterdam	9	Jul
13.52	0.5	Hideki	Omuro	JPN	25.7.90	1		Hiratsuka	23	Jul
13.53	1.2	Jordan	Moore	USA	13.12.93	1	SEC	Tuscaloosa	14	May
13.53	1.0	Roger	Iribarne	CUB	2.1.96	2	Barr	La Habana	26	May
13.53	-0.6	Simon	Krauss	FRA	12.2.92	1		Forbach	29	May
13.53A	0.3	Jorge (70)	McFarlane	PER	20.2.88	2		Medellín	10	Jul
13.54	1.2	Dondre	Echols	USA	6.7.93	2	SEC	Tuscaloosa	14	May
13.54	2.0	Ryan	Wilson	USA	19.12.80	4		Clermont	14	May
13.54	1.5	David	King	GBR	13.6.94	2		Loughborough	22	May
13.54	0.4	Thingalaya	Siddhanth	IND	1.3.91	1		Tempe	11	Jun
13.54	-1.8	Emanuele	Abate	ITA	8.7.85	4s2	EC	Amsterdam	9	Jul
13.54	-1.8	Vladimir	Vukicevic	NOR	6.5.91	5s2	EC	Amsterdam	9	Jul
13.54	-0.1	Petr	Svoboda	CZE	10.10.84	1		Usti nad Orlicí	4	Sep
13.55	1.6	Yacoub	Al-Yoha	KUW	31.1.93	2		Al-Kuwait	14	May
13.55	1.4	Tyrone	Akins	NGR	6.1.86	1		Nassau	10	Jul
13.56	0.7	Eduardo (80)	de Deus	BRA	8.10.95	2	IbAm	Rio de Janeiro	16	May
13.56	0.0	Erik	Balnuweit	GER	21.9.88	4		Weinheim	28	May
13.56	0.9	Nick	Hough	AUS	20.10.93	2		Barcelona (S)	30	Jun
13.58	1.9	Yanick	Hart	JAM	10.1.93	2q1	NCAA-E	Jacksonville	28	May
13.58	1.4	Javier	Colomo	ESP	26.3.94	1		Castellón	11	Jun
13.58	1.4	Shun-ya	Takayama	JPN	3.9.94	1		Okayama	20	Aug
13.59	1.5	Chris	Caldwell	USA	6.4.94	1		Lubbock	6	May
13.59	-0.6		Zhang Honglin	CHN	12.1.94	2		Kawasaki	8	May
13.59	1.8	Amere	Lattin	USA-J	17.2.97	1		Orlando	15	May
13.59	1.4	Genta	Masuno	JPN	24.5.93	2		Tottori	5	Jun
13.60	1.2	Nick (90)	Anderson	USA	28.4.95	2rC	FlaR	Gainesville	1	Apr
13.60	1.5	Ruebin	Walters	TTO	2.4.95	1		Tempe	9	Apr

110 METRES HURDLES

Mark	Wind	Name		Nat	Born	Pos	Meet	Venue	Date	
13.60	1.9	Joshua	Thompson	USA	16.1.93	1		Baton Rouge	23	Apr
13.60	0.2	Lu	Yang	CHN	9.1.96	1		Taiyuan	22	May
13.60	1.9	Vincent	Wyatt	USA	18.10.92	3q1	NCAA-E	Jacksonville	28	May
13.60	1.7	Khai	Riley-La Borde	GBR	8.11.95	1		Castres	20	Jul
13.61	0.2	Jiang	Fan	CHN	16.9.89	2		Taiyuan	22	May
13.61	1.1	Lloyd	Sicard	USA	31.5.95	1h1	NCAA-W	Lawrence	8	May
13.61	1.7	Yang	Wei-Ting	TPE	22.9.94	1s5		Hiratsuka	10	Jun
13.61	0.7	Thomas	Martinot Lagarde	FRA	7.2.88	2h2	NC	Angers	26	Jun
13.61	-0.2	Éder Antônio	de Souza	BRA	15.10.86	4h5	OG	Rio de Janeiro	15	Aug
(100)										
13.62	0.8	Jamiel	Trimble	USA	25.6.95	26 May		13.77A	0.7	Pedro Bustamante MEX 5.3.90 18 Mar
13.63A	1.2	Ruan	de Vries	RSA	1.2.86	13 Feb		13.77	2.0	Ingvar Moseley CAN 24.11.91 21 May
13.63	1.5	Omo	Osaghae	USA	18.5.88	6 May		13.77	0.8	Konstantin Shabanov RUS 17.11.89 21 Jun
13.63	1.4	Ryan	Brathwaite	BAR	6.6.88	11 Jun		13.77	0.9	Dominik Bochenek POL 14.5.87 26 Jun
13.63	1.7		Kim Byung-jun	KOR	15.8.91	3 Jul		13.77	0.1	Jonathas Brito BRA 30.11.92 3 Jul
13.63	1.4	João Vitor	de Oliveira	BRA	15.5.92	15 Aug		13.78	0.2	Terence Somerville USA 5.11.89 2 Apr
13.64	1.5	Gabriel	Odujobi	GBR	15.7.87	14 May		13.78	-0.1	Tiaan Smit RSA 14.3.95 16 Apr
13.64	0.8	Sekou	Kaba	CAN	25.8.90	10 Jul		13.78	1.7	Loic Desbonnes FRA 26.7.91 26 Jun
13.65	-0.1	Tshepo	Lefete	RSA	2.2.92	16 Apr		13.79A	-0.1	Ricardo Torres PUR 13.2.96 30 Apr
13.65	1.9	Desmond	Wallace	USA	4.7.93	28 May		13.79	-0.4	Yuta Notoya JPN 8.7.89 8 May
13.65	0.3	Andreas	Martinsen	DEN	17.7.90	8 Jul		13.79	1.8	Maksim Lynsha BLR 6.4.85 20 May
13.66	1.0	Nate	Pozolinski	USA	8.8.95	23 Apr		13.79	0.1	René Mählmann GER 24.10.93 9 Jun
13.66	1.0	David	Payne	USA	24.7.82	23 Apr		13.80	1.3	Trey Holloway USA 7.7.94 25 Mar
13.67	0.9	Michael	Dickson	USA-J	25.1.97	23 Apr		13.80	1.1	Matheus Rocha BRA 19.12.94 9 Apr
13.67	1.1	Fábio	dos Santos	BRA	11.10.83	4 Jun		13.80	1.9	Tramaine Maloney BAR 1.6.94 23 Apr
13.67	1.2	Lorenzo	Perini	ITA	22.7.94	11 Jun		13.80	-0.8	Fred Townsend USA 19.2.82 29 May
13.67	-1.0	Cameron	Hall	USA	12.5.93	22 Jun		13.80	1.0	Jermaine Collier USA 5.7.93 8 Jun
13.67	0.4	Rohan	Cole	JAM-J	28.10.97	2 Jul		13.80	0.8	Robert Semien USA 15.4.93 12 Jun
13.68	-0.6	Teivaskie	Lewin	JAM	27.12.91	28 May		13.80	-0.1	Damien Broothaerts BEL 12.11.84 13 Jul
13.68	0.3	Isaiah	Moore	USA	12.6.96	27 May		13.80	0.3	Masanori Nishizawa JPN 16.7.87 10 Oct
13.69	0.3	Antoine	Lloyd	USA	10.6.96	15 May		13.81	0.6	Justin Merlino AUS 10.12.86 3 Apr
13.69	0.3	Mohamed	Koussi	MAR	15.3.94	22 May		13.81	-0.2	Hiroki Fudaba JPN 4.2.94 8 May
13.69	1.7	Ludovic	Payen	FRA	18.2.95	20 Jul		13.81	0.9	Loïc Herkenrath FRA 11.7.94 5 Jun
13.70A	0.7	Salvador	García	MEX	8.3.96	18 Mar		13.81	-0.3	Aleksey Dryomin RUS 10.5.89 20 Jul
13.70	-0.4	Myles	Hunter	USA	16.8.95	19 Mar		13.82A	1.9	Jordan Charles USA 29.4.95 6 May
13.70	1.9	Francisco Javier	López	ESP	29.12.89	23 Apr		13.82	1.2	Davon Anderson USA 24.8.96 14 May
13.70	2.0	Alex	Al-Ameen	NGR	2.3.89	14 May		13.82	0.3	Matheus Inocêncio BRA 17.5.81 2 Jul
13.70	1.6	Dario	De Borger	BEL	20.3.92	21 May		13.82	-0.6	Ogierakhi Martins NGR 30.6.91 7 Jul
13.71	-0.8	Tony	Brown	USA	13.7.95	8 Jun		13.82	0.2	Ma Lei CHN 29.6.89 15 Sep
13.71	0.1	Koen	Smet	NED	9.8.92	18 Jun		13.82	0.2	Yutaro Furukawa JPN 3.6.85 25 Sep
13.71	1.9	Valdó	Szücs	HUN	29.6.95	26 Jun		13.83	1.3	Marcus Neely USA 10.2.94 25 Mar
13.71	1.8	Julian	Marquart	GER	2.4.91	29 Jul		13.83	1.6	Desmond Palmer USA 30.7.95 15 May
13.71	1.8	Arnau	Erta	ESP	5.4.92	29 Jul		13.83	-0.5	Filipp Shabanov RUS 29.1.91 26 May
13.72	-0.3	Kevin	Craddock	USA	25.6.87	19 Mar		13.83	0.9	Artur Noga POL 2.5.88 26 Jun
13.72	0.5	Masahiro	Kagimoto	JPN	29.9.95	13 May		13.83	0.8	Artem Shamatryn UKR 15.6.91 16 Jul
13.72	1.7	Nicolas	Borome	FRA	7.10.93	16 Jun		13.83	0.2	Ji Wei CHN 5.2.84 15 Sep
13.72	0.3	Elmo	Lakka	FIN	10.4.93	8 Jul		13.83	0.7	Yoichi Iwafune JPN 12.6.85 25 Sep
13.73	1.8	Bentrell	McGee	USA	15.7.93	19 Mar		13.84	2.0	Genaro Rodríguez MEX 10.10.90 5 Jun
13.73	0.9	Denis	Hanjoul	BEL	17.1.91	21 May		13.84	1.4	Anthony Tyrell Kuriki JPN .96 10 Jun
13.73	1.0	Ashtyn	Davis	USA	10.10.96	8 Jun		13.84	1.3	Elie Agot FRA 9.4.91 23 Jun
13.73	0.4	Takumu	Furuya	JPN-J	12.3.97	25 Jun		13.85	0.5	Ni Mingchao CHN 20.4.94 14 May
13.74	0.8	Don	Pollitt	USA	1.10.91	23 Apr		13.85	1.4	Moussa Dembélé SEN 30.10.88 25 Jun
13.74	0.3	Cameron	Viney	USA	6.9.93	15 May		13.86	0.6	Joshua Hawkins NZL 9.2.94 3 Apr
13.74	0.3	Serhiy	Kopanayko	UKR	5.11.88	8 Jul		13.86	1.7	Kemar Jones BAR 5.2.93 6 May
13.74	-1.0	Lyès	Mokdel	ALG	20.6.90	15 Jul		13.86	0.0	Max Hairston USA 8.5.94 7 May
13.74	0.3	Taio	Kanai	JPN	28.9.95	10 Oct		13.86	1.8	Vitaliy Parakhonko BLR 18.8.93 20 May
13.75	1.0	Wellington	Zaza	LBR	20.1.95	8 Jun		13.86	0.0	Brahian Peña SUI 3.4.94 28 May
13.75	0.2	Hiroyuki	Sato	JPN	6.8.90	25 Jun		13.86	0.6	Lee Jung-joon KOR 26.3.84 2 Jun
13.76	-0.2	Malcolm	Anderson	USA	18.9.89	19 May		13.86	1.4	Job Beintema NED 24.5.95 11 Jul
13.76	0.0	Tobias	Furer	SUI	13.8.87	28 May		(199)		21 men 13.87 to 13.89

Wind assisted

13.05	2.1	Dimitri	Bascou	FRA	20.7.87	1	NC	Angers	26	Jun
13.15	2.1	Wilhem	Bélocian	FRA	22.6.95	2	NC	Angers	26	Jun
13.15	2.4		Allen			1		Eugene	29	Jun
13.25	2.6	Aurel	Manga	FRA	24.7.92	2		Montreuil-sous-Bois	7	Jun
13.31	4.2	Damian	Czykier	POL	10.8.92	1		København	18	Jun
13.31A	2.6	Javier	McFarlane	PER	21.10.91	1		Cali	25	Jun
13.32	2.7	Aleec	Harris	USA	31.10.90	2		Nassau	16	Apr
13.33	2.2	Devon	Hill	USA	26.10.89	1		Montverde, FL	11	Jun
13.35	2.1	Dondre	Echols	USA	6.7.93	1q2	NCAA-E	Jacksonville	28	May
13.35	2.4	Ronald	Brookins	USA	5.7.89	1		Chula Vista	18	Jun
13.37	2.1	Konstadínos	Douvalídis	GRE	10.3.87	2h1		Madrid	23	Jun
13.40	4.1	Ryan	Fontenot	USA	4.5.86	1		Austin	7	May
13.43	2.1	Freddie	Crittenden	USA	3.8.94	2q2	NCAA-E	Jacksonville	28	May
13.45	2.6	Simon	Krauss	FRA	12.2.92	4		Montreuil-sous-Bois	7	Jun
13.46	2.6	Yordan	O'Farrill	CUB	9.2.93	5		Montreuil-sous-Bois	7	Jun

110 METRES HURDLES

Mark	Wind	Name		Nat	Born	Pos	Meet	Venue	Date
13.47	2.1	Thingalaya	Siddhanth	IND	1.3.91	1		Redlands, CA	19 May
13.47	3.2	Hideki	Omuro	JPN	25.7.90	1		Yokohama	18 Jun
13.47	2.4	Logan	Taylor	USA	3.4.86	2		Chula Vista	18 Jun
13.48A	2.6	Jorge	McFarlane	PER	20.2.88	2		Cali	25 Jun
13.51	2.4	Genta	Masuno	JPN	24.5.93	2	NC	Nagoya	26 Jun
13.52	3.0	Tony	Brown	USA	13.7.95	2q3	NCAA-E	Jacksonville	28 May
13.54	2.3	Isaiah	Moore	USA	12.6.96	1rB	FlaR	Gainesville	1 Apr
13.55	2.6	Thomas	Martinot Lagarde	FRA	7.2.88	6		Montreuil-sous-Bois	7 Jun
13.56	3.7	Francisco Javier	López	ESP	29.12.89	1		Arlington, TX	26 Mar
13.56	2.1	Javier	Colomo	ESP	26.3.94	4h1		Madrid	23 Jun
13.57	3.7	Gabriel	Odujobi	GBR	15.7.87	1rB		Clermont	30 Apr
13.58	2.3	Joshua	Thompson	USA	16.1.93	2		Leonora/GUY	18 Jun
13.59	3.7	Teivaskie	Lewin	JAM	27.12.91	1		Long Beach	16 May
13.59	2.1	Wellington	Zaza	LBR	20.1.95	3q2	NCAA-E	Jacksonville	28 May
13.59	3.0	Nick	Anderson	USA	28.4.95	3q3	NCAA-E	Jacksonville	28 May
13.59	2.9	Andreas	Martinsen	DEN	17.7.90	1h1		København	18 Jun
13.60	3.7	Myles	Hunter	USA	16.8.95	2		Long Beach	16 Apr
13.61	3.0	Jermaine	Collier	USA	5.7.93	28 May	13.71	2.4 Takumu Furuya JPN-J 12.3.97	26 Jun
13.61	2.4	Taio	Kanai	JPN	28.9.95	26 Jun	13.72	4.1 Rhys Phillips USA/BAR 28.4.93	7 May
13.62	3.0	Max	Hairston	USA	8.5.94	28 May	13.72	2.5 Moussa Dembélé SEN 30.10.88	11 Jun
13.63	4.1	Robert	Semien	USA	15.4.93	7 May	13.75	2.1 Kemar Mowatt JAM 12.3.95	23 Jun
13.63	2.1	Trey	Holloway	USA	7.7.94	28 May	13.78	2.6 Jonathas Brito BRA 30.11.92	4 Mar
13.63	3.4	Petr	Penáz	CZE	27.8.91	6 Jun	13.78	2.7 Marcus McWilliams USA-J 20.2.97	2 Apr
13.67	4.1	Damien	Broothaerts	BEL	12.11.84	2 Jul	13.78	3.7 René Mählmann GER 24.10.93	30 Apr
13.70	3.7	Malcolm	Anderson	USA	18.9.89	30 Apr	13.78	3.7 Jonathan Santiago PUR 7.4.92	30 Apr
13.70	3.4	Marcus	Neely	USA	10.2.94	15 May	13.79	2.7 Yoichi Iwafune JPN 12.6.85	10 Jul

Low altitude bests

13.55	0.7	Javier McFarlane							
		1	IbAm	Rio de Janeiro	16 May	13.65	0.7 de Vries 1	Pretoria	12 Mar
13.57	2.0	Jorge McFarlane				13.83	1.0 Torres	16 Apr	
		1	MEX Ch	Monterrey	4 Jun	13.79w	2.4 Bustamante	16 Apr	

Hand timing

12.7		Sergey	Shubenkov	RUS	4.10.90	1		Barnaul	2 Jul
	13.0					1		Barnaul	20 May

Bellinzona 6 Jun (0.1) 2. Milan Ristic SRB 8.8.91 13.4, 4. Lawrence Clarke GBR 12.3.90 13.4, 5. David King GBR 13.6.94 13.4, 6. William Sharman GBR 12.9.84 3.5

JUNIORS

13.59	1.8	Amere	Lattin	USA	17.2.97	1		Orlando	15 May
	13.64	1.0 1s3	NCAA Eugene		8 Jun				
13.67	0.9	Michael	Dickson	USA	25.1.97	1		Atlanta	23 Apr
13.67	0.4	Rohan	Cole	JAM	28.10.97	5	NC	Kingston	2 Jul
	13.75	-0.3 6	NACAC San Salvador		16 Jul	6 performances by 4 men to 13.75.			
13.73	0.4	Takumu	Furuya	JPN	12.3.97	2h1	NC	Nagoya	25 Jun
13.90	0.1	Marcus	McWilliams	USA	20.2.97	3	PennR	Philadelphia	30 Apr
13.91	0.2	John	Burt	USA	10.2.97	2h5	NCAA-W	Lawrence	28 May
13.92	1.2	Chad	Zallow	USA	25.4.97	5rC	FlaR	Gainesville	1 Apr
13.94	1.2	Papdemba	Hiramatsu	JPN	15.12.97	3		Hiratsuka	10 Jun
13.95	1.9	Michael	Nicholls	BAR	6.4.97	6		Baton Rouge	23 Apr
13.95	1.1	Akeem	Chumney	SKN	2.11.97	1	NC	Basseterre	18 Jun
13.98	1.2	Takuma	Kato	JPN	25.9.98	1		Okayama	2 Aug
13.99	0.3	Orlando	Smith	JAM	23.9.97	2		Kingston	12 Jun

Wind assisted

13.71	2.4	Takumu	Furuya	JPN-J	12.3.97	5	NC	Nagoya	26 Jun
13.78	2.7	Marcus	McWilliams	USA-J	20.2.97	3	TexR	Austin	2 Apr
13.90	3.2	Papdemba	Hiramatsu	JPN	15.12.97	2		Sagamihara	17 Sep
13.91	2.7	Michael	Nicholls	BAR	6.4.97	1		Corpus Christi	8 May
13.95	3.2	Shun	Taue	JPN	30.5.97	3		Sagamihara	17 Sep

110 Metres Hurdles – 99 cm hurdles

13.20	0.6	Dejour	Russell	JAM-Y	1.4.00	1s3	WJ	Bydgoszcz	20 Jul
13.25	1.6	Markus	Krah	USA	30.10.97	1	NC-j	Clovis	24 Jun
	13.25	0.2 1	WJ Bydgoszcz		21 Jul	13.36	-0.1 1s2 WJ	Bydgoszcz	20 Jul
	13.32	1.1 1	Greensboro		21 May				
13.30	0.2	Amere	Lattin	USA	17.2.97	2	WJ	Bydgoszcz	21 Jul
	13.32	1.6 2	NC-j Clovis		24 Jun	12 performances by 8 men to 13.37			
13.31	0.2	Takumu	Furuya	JPN	12.3.97	3	WJ	Bydgoszcz	21 Jul
13.33	1.2	James	Weaver	GBR	25.7.97	1		Mannheim	25 Jun
13.33	1.6	Nicholas	Andrews	AUS	2.2.97	1h4		Mannheim	25 Jun
13.37	1.6	Grant	Holloway	USA	19.11.97	3	NC-j	Clovis	24 Jun
13.37	1.6	Trey	Cunningham	USA	26.8.98	4	NC-j	Clovis	24 Jun
13.42	-0.2	Damion	Thomas	JAM-Y	29.6.99	1		Pompano Beach	28 Apr
13.42	0.6	Michael	Nicholls (10)	BAR	6.4.97	3s3	WJ	Bydgoszcz	20 Jul

110m – 200m – 400 METRES HURDLES   377

Mark	Wind	Name		Nat	Born	Pos	Meet	Venue	Date	
13.45	1.8	Matt	Moore	USA	23.3.98	1h1		Jefferson GA	14	May
13.45	0.2	David	Zebrowski	POL	8.8.97	5	WJ	Bydgoszcz	21	Jul
13.46	1.7	John	Burt	USA	10.2.97	1h3	NC-j	Clovis	24	Jun
13.46		Mikdat	Sevier	TUR	21.1.98	1		Ankara	24	Aug
13.48	-0.7	Rohan	Cole	JAM	28.10.97	1		Kingston	6	Mar
13.48	1.9	Matthew	Treston	GBR	20.7.98	1	NC-j	Bedford	19	Jun
13.49A	1.3	Mpho	Tladi	RSA	1.2.98	1		Bloemfontein	16	Mar
13.51	1.7	Chad	Zallow	USA	25.4.97	2h3	NC-j	Clovis	24	Jun
13.51	1.2	Roje Jackson	Chin	JAM	5.1.97	4	PAm-J	Edmonton	1	Aug
13.55A	1.5	Thabo	Maganyele (20)	RSA	10.1.98	1	NC-j	Germiston	2	Apr
Wind assisted										
13.33		Matt	Moore	USA		1		Marietta	21	May
13.35		Trey	Cunningham	USA	26.8.98	1		Winfield	29	Apr

200 METRES HURDLES

Inba 13 Aug: (-2.2) 1. Hideki Omuro JPN 25.7.90 22.80, 2. Hiroyuki Sato JPN 6.8.80 22.90
Straight Track
Manchester 20 May: (4.1) 1, Sebastian Rodger GBR 22.66w, 2. Jacob Paul GBR 22.84w
Brussels 4 Sep: L.J. van Zyl RSA 22.77

300 METRES HURDLES

Mark	Name		Nat	Born	Pos	Venue	Date	
35.34	José	Bencosme de Leon	ITA	16.5.92	1	Cuneo	11	Sep
35.59	Mark	Ujakpor	ESP	18.1.87	1	Fuenlabrada	26	May
35.70	Sergio	Fernández	ESP	1.4.93	2	Fuenlabrada	26	May
35.70	Naoto	Noguchi	JPN	.91	1	Inda	13	Aug

400 METRES HURDLES

Mark	Name		Nat	Born	Pos	Meet	Venue	Date	
47.73	Kerron	Clement	USA	31.10.85	1	OG	Rio de Janeiro	18	Aug
47.78	Boniface Mucheru	Tumuti	KEN	2.5.92	2	OG	Rio de Janeiro	18	Aug
47.92	Yasmani	Copello	TUR	15.4.87	3	OG	Rio de Janeiro	18	Aug
47.97	Thomas	Barr	IRL	24.7.92	4	OG	Rio de Janeiro	18	Aug
48.01	Nicholas	Bett	KEN	14.6.92	1	DL	Saint-Denis	27	Aug
48.07	Annsert	Whyte	JAM	10.4.87	5	OG	Rio de Janeiro	18	Aug
48.10	Johnny	Dutch	USA	20.1.89	1		Kingston	11	Jun
48.19		Clement			2	DL	Saint-Denis	27	Aug
48.24		Copello			3	DL	Saint-Denis	27	Aug
48.26		Clement			1s1	OG	Rio de Janeiro	16	Aug
48.32		Whyte			1s2	OG	Rio de Janeiro	16	Aug
48.36		Dutch			1		Nassau	16	Apr
48.37		Whyte			1h5	OG	Rio de Janeiro	15	Aug
48.39		Barr			1s3	OG	Rio de Janeiro	16	Aug
48.40		Clement			1	DL	London (OS)	23	Jul
48.40	Rasmus	Mägi	EST	4.5.92	6	OG	Rio de Janeiro	18	Aug
48.42		Copello			1s2	EC	Amsterdam	7	Jul
48.46	Javier	Culson	PUR	25.7.84	2s2	OG	Rio de Janeiro	16	Aug
48.49	Karsten	Warholm (10)	NOR	28.2.96	1h3	OG	Rio de Janeiro	15	Aug
48.49	Haron	Koech	KEN	27.1.90	2s3	OG	Rio de Janeiro	16	Aug
48.50		Clement			1	NC/OT	Eugene	10	Jul
48.53		Culson			2h3	OG	Rio de Janeiro	15	Aug
48.55		Mägi			3h3	OG	Rio de Janeiro	15	Aug
48.55		Culson			4	DL	Saint-Denis	27	Aug
48.56	Roxroy	Cato	JAM	1.5.88	4h3	OG	Rio de Janeiro	15	Aug
48.57	Timofey	Chalyy	RUS	7.4.94	1		Moskva	28	Jul
48.59		Mägi			1	Athl	Lausanne	25	Aug
48.61		Copello			3s2	OG	Rio de Janeiro	16	Aug
48.62	Abdelmalik	Lahoulou	ALG	7.5.92	1h1	OG	Rio de Janeiro	15	Aug
48.62	Keisuke	Nozawa	JPN	7.6.91	1h4	OG	Rio de Janeiro	15	Aug
48.63		Culson			2	DL	London (OS)	23	Jul
	[31/15]								
48.65	Byron	Robinson	USA	16.2.95	3s3	OG	Rio de Janeiro	16	Aug
48.67	Louis 'L.J'	van Zyl	RSA	20.7.85	1	GS	Ostrava	20	May
48.74	Michael	Tinsley	USA	21.4.84	1	Pre	Eugene	28	May
48.81	Jaheel	Hyde	JAM-J	2.2.97	2	NC	Kingston	1	Jul
48.87	Kariem	Hussein	SUI	1.4.89	2s1	EC	Amsterdam	7	Jul
	(20)								
48.87	Sergio	Fernández	ESP	1.4.93	3s1	OG	Rio de Janeiro	16	Aug
48.88	Jeshua	Anderson	USA	22.6.89	1		Atlanta	4	Jun
48.88	Ricky	Babineaux	USA	14.12.90	4	NC/OT	Eugene	10	Jul

MEN 2016

400 METRES HURDLES

Mark	Name		Nat	Born	Pos	Meet	Venue	Date	
48.91	Eric	Futch	USA	25.4.93	1	NCAA	Eugene	10	Jun
48.96	Jeffery	Gibson	BAH	15.8.90	1		Kingston	7	May
48.96	Mahau	Suguimati	BRA	13.11.84	2		Kumagaya	22	May
48.96	Jack	Green	GBR	6.10.91	2h5	OG	Rio de Janeiro	15	Aug
48.98	Eric	Cray	PHI	6.11.88	2		Madrid	23	Jun
49.01	Patryk	Dobek	POL	13.2.94	2	DL	Shanghai	14	May
49.03A	Lindsay	Hanekom	RSA	15.5.93	1h2		Bloemfontein	6	May
(30)									
49.04	Khallifah	Rosser	USA	13.7.95	1	NCAA-2	Bradenton, FL	28	May
49.04	Bershawn	Jackson	USA	8.5.83	3	Pre	Eugene	28	May
49.04	Oskari	Mörö	FIN	31.1.93	4h5	OG	Rio de Janeiro	15	Aug
49.08	Martin	Kucera	SVK	10.5.90	4s1	EC	Amsterdam	7	Jul
49.09	Márcio	Teles	BRA	27.1.94	2		Genève	11	Jun
49.10	Yuki	Matsushita	JPN	9.9.91	3		Kawasaki	8	May
49.15	Mamadou Kassé	Hann	FRA	10.10.86	3		Genève	11	Jun
49.16	Eric	Alejandro	PUR	15.4.86	1		Road Town	3	Jul
49.17	José Luis	Gaspar	CUB	25.8.95	1		La Habana	11	Jun
49.21	Andrés	Silva	URU	27.3.86	3h6	OG	Rio de Janeiro	15	Aug
(40)									
49.22	Rhys	Williams	GBR	27.2.84	1		Oordegem	28	May
49.22A	Kiprono	Kosgei	KEN	85	1	OT	Eldoret	1	Jul
49.24A	Le Roux	Hamman	RSA	6.1.92	1		Pretoria	11	Jun
49.26	Jordin	Andrade	CPV	5.5.92	4		Kingston	11	Jun
49.27	Michaël	Bultheel	BEL	30.6.86	5h5	OG	Rio de Janeiro	15	Aug
49.29	Sebastian	Rodger	GBR	29.6.91	1		Oordegem	11	Jul
49.31	Kenny	Selmon	USA	27.8.96	2s1	NCAA	Eugene	8	Jun
49.31	Timothy "TJ"	Holmes	USA	2.7.95	2	NCAA	Eugene	10	Jun
49.31	Isa	Phillips	JAM	22.4.84	1h2	NC	Kingston	30	Jun
49.32	Quincy	Downing	USA	16.1.93	2		Atlanta	4	Jun
[50]									
49.32	Romel	Lewis	JAM	28.1.88	5q2	NC	Kingston	1	Jul
49.32	Ivan	Shablyuyev	RUS	17.4.88	2		Moskva	28	Jul
49.33	Aleksandr	Skorobogatko	RUS	7.8.94	1	NC-23	Saransk	16	Jul
49.35	Mario	Lambrughi	ITA	5.2.92	1		Lignano	13	Jul
49.36	Omar	Cisneros	CUB	19.11.89	1		Salamanca	4	Jun
49.36	Robert	Grant	USA	31.1.96	1s3	NCAA	Eugene	8	Jun
49.39	Dmitriy	Koblov	KAZ	30.11.92	1		Bishkek	19	Jun
49.41	Amadou	Ndiaye	SEN	6.12.92	2	AfCh	Durban	24	Jun
49.43	Juander	Santos	DOM	7.5.95	1		Aarhus	25	Jun
49.43	Denis	Kudryavtsev	RUS	13.4.92	3		Moskva	28	Jul
[60]									
49.44	Yuta	Konishi	JPN	31.7.90	2		Osaka	24	Sep
49.45	Taylor	McLaughlin	USA-J	2.8.97	2	WJ	Bydgoszcz	23	Jul
49.48	Tobias	Giehl	GER	25.7.91	1		Mönchengladbach	10	Jul
49.51	Naoya	Nakano	JPN	3.7.94	1h2	NC	Nagoya	24	Jun
49.56	Kyron	McMaster	IVB-J	3.1.97	3	WJ	Bydgoszcz	23	Jul
49.60	Miles	Ukaoma	NGR	21.7.92	4		Nassau	16	Apr
49.62	Mikael Antonio	de Jesús	BRA-J	19.8.97	2	IbAm	Rio de Janeiro	15	May
49.62	Tom	Burton	GBR	29.10.88	4		Genève	11	Jun
49.64	Shotaro	Tanabe	JPN	23.4.94	1		Osaka	8	May
49.64	Andre	Clarke	JAM	6.6.92	1		Kingston	12	Jul
[70]									
49.65	Mark	Ujakpor	ESP	18.1.87	3	IbAm	Rio de Janeiro	15	May
49.65	Jaak-Heinrich	Jagor	EST	11.5.90	5s2	EC	Amsterdam	7	Jul
49.65	Miloud	Rahmouni	ALG	13.12.83	1r2		Tarare	9	Jul
49.66	Desmond	Palmer	USA	30.7.95	1	ACC	Tallahassee	15	May
49.66	Ricardo	Cunningham	JAM	3.10.80	2		Kingston	12	Jun
49.67	Kotaro	Miyao	JPN	12.7.91	2h2	NC	Nagoya	24	Jun
49.68	Michael	Stigler	USA	5.4.92	4		Atlanta	4	Jun
49.69	Kohei	Ueno	JPN	13.7.94	1		Kumagaya	4	Sep
49.72	Patryk	Adamczyk	POL	5.1.94	1	NC-23	Jelenia Gora	31	Jul
49.73	Nikita	Andriyanov	RUS	7.2.90	3	NCp	Zhukovskiy	21	Jul
[80]									
49.74A	William	Mutunga	KEN	17.9.93	1		Nairobi	29	Apr
49.74	Kurt	Couto	MOZ	14.5.85	6h5	OG	Rio de Janeiro	15	Aug
49.75	Cornel	Fredericks	RSA	3.3.90	2	NC	Stellenbosch	15	Apr
49.76	José	Bencosme de Leon	ITA	16.5.92	1	NC	Rieti	26	Jun
49.76	Ian	Dewhurst	AUS	13.11.90	2		Oordegem	11	Jul
49.77	Amaechi	Morton	NGR	30.10.89	6		Nassau	16	Apr
49.77	Naoto	Noguchi	JPN	27.5.94	2		Osaka	8	May
49.78	Kazuaki	Yoshida	JPN	31.8.87	1		Chiba	4	Jun

400 METRES HURDLES

Mark	Name		Nat	Born	Pos	Meet	Venue	Date	
49.78	Viktor	Leptikov	KAZ	2.7.87	2		Bishkek	19	Jun
49.79	Jithin	Paul	IND	13.3.90	2	PTS	Samorín	4	Jun
[90]									
49.82	LaRon	Bennett	USA	25.11.82	5		Atlanta	4	Jun
49.82	Rai	Benjamin	ANT-J	27.7.97	6	NCAA	Eugene	10	Jun
49.86	Michael	Cochrane	NZL	13.8.91	1		Canberra	20	Feb
49.86	Alfredo	Sepúlveda	CHI	3.8.93	6	IbAm	Rio de Janeiro	15	May
49.86	Artur Langowski	Terezan	BRA	8.5.91	1h3	NC	Santiago de Chile	2	Jul
49.87	Jussi	Kanervo	FIN	1.2.93	1q1	NCAA-E	Jacksonville	27	May
49.87	Cameron	French	NZL	17.5.92	1rA		Bruxelles	19	Jun
49.87	Curtis	Beach	USA	22.7.90	3		Houston	23	Jul
49.88	Robert	Brylinski	POL	2.4.91	1		Kraków	12	Jun
49.89	Takayuki	Kishimoto	JPN	6.5.90	3		Osaka	24	Sep
[100]									
49.90	Leford	Green	JAM	14.11.86	16 Apr				
49.93	Shawn	Rowe	JAM	7.12.92	28 May				
49.94	Mattia	Contini	ITA	27.10.94	26 Jun				
49.96	Yoshihiro	Watanabe	JPN-J	7.1.97	22 May				
49.97	Shang Shuo		CHN	1.6.95	16 Sep				
49.98	Jehue	Gordon	TTO	15.12.91	15 Aug				
49.98	Tomoharu	Kino	JPN	4.8.89	22 Oct				
50.00	Constant	Pretorius	RSA	26.1.94	15 Apr				
50.01	Saber	Boukmouche	ALG	20.4.92	22 May				
50.01	Atsushi	Yamada	JPN	3.7.91	24 Jun				
50.02A	Okeem	Williams	JAM	1.1.96	19 May				
50.02	David 'Dai'	Greene	GBR	11.4.86	14 Jun				
50.03	Niall	Flannery	GBR	26.4.91	6 Jun				
50.05	Javan	Gallimore	JAM	7.8.93	30 Jun				
50.05	Emanuel	Mayers	TTO	9.3.89	10 Jul				
50.07	Ikpefan	Obokhare	NGR	6.7.95	15 May				
50.07	Marvin	Williams	JAM	13.6.96	1 Jul				
50.08	Carlos Eduardo Maciel		BRA	28.5.93	25 May				
50.09	Takahiro	Matsumoto	JPN	19.9.94	22 May				
50.09	Henry	Okorie	NGR	11.4.87	9 Jul				
50.09	Mohamed	Sghaier	TUN	18.7.88	15 Aug				
50.11	Jakub	Smolinski	POL	21.7.92	12 Jun				
50.12	Neil	Braddy	USA	18.10.91	6 May				
50.15	Masayuki	Obayashi	JPN	6.2.96	14 May				
50.15A	Hardus	Maritz	NAM	10.5.90	11 Jun				
50.16	Craig "CJ"	Allen	USA	14.2.95	9 Apr				
50.16	Ryosuke	Hamai	JPN	17.8.94	13 Aug				
50.17	Jacob	Paul	GBR	6.2.95	25 Jun				
50.18	Yoan	Décimus	FRA	30.11.87	22 May				
50.21	Jurmarcus	Shelvin	USA	4.4.94	26 Mar				
50.21	Kenneth	Medwood	BIZ	14.12.87	19 May				
50.21	Wang Yang		CHN	20.9.96	16 Sep				
50.22	Chen Chieh		TPE	8.5.92	4 May				
50.26	Pavel	Agafonov	RUS	28.8.95	16 Jul				
50.27	Javier	Delgado	ESP	9.6.96	26 Jun				
50.28	Arnaud	Ghislain	BEL	2.12.88	28 May				
50.29	Josef	Robertson	JAM	14.5.87	21 May				
50.30	Davide	Piccolo	ITA	18.5.91	25 Jun				
50.32	Xun Zhizhun		CHN	22.4.92	22 Apr				
50.32	Abdullah	Al-Mehili	KSA	10.7.94?	28 May				
50.32	Ludvy	Vaillant	FRA	15.3.95	18 Jun				
50.33	Yusuke	Ishida	JPN	25.5.95	12 Jun				
50.34	Mickaël	François	FRA	12.3.88	8 May				
50.34	Anatoliy	Synyanskiy	UKR	4.2.91	19 Jun				
50.36	M.P.	Jabir	IND	8.6.96	1 Sep				
50.36	Tatsuhiro	Yamamoto	JPN-J	23.4.97	3 Sep				
50.37	Durgesh	Kumar Pal	IND	20.4.94	30 Apr				
50.38	Leigh	Bennett	AUS	20.4.86	9 Jul				
50.39	Keyunta	Hayes	USA	15.2.92	16 Apr				
50.39	Øyvind	Kjerpeset	NOR	12.12.91	28 May				
50.39	Kion	Joseph	BAR	27.4.94	26 Jun				
50.40	Richard	Yates	GBR	26.1.86	19 Jun				
50.40	Georg	Fleischhauer	GER	21.10.88	6 Aug				
50.40	Lee Seung-yun		KOR	28.2.89	26 Aug				
50.41	Kei	Maeno	JPN	10.5.91	29 May				
50.42	Takatoshi	Abe	JPN	12.11.91	22 May				
50.42	Felix	Franz	GER	6.5.93	19 Jun				
50.42	Alain-Hervé	Mfomkpa	SUI	4.6.96	17 Jul				
50.43	Michal	Broz	CZE	16.6.92	26 Jun				
50.43	Mitsuru	Sugai	JPN	7.1.94	23 Jul				
50.45	Tim	Rummens	BEL	16.12.87	4 Jun				
50.45	Vit	Müller	CZE	31.8.96	18 Jun				
50.46	Richard	Lowe	USA	24.2.89	21 May				
50.46	Rilwan	Alowonle	USA	12.12.93	8 Jul				
50.46	Stéphane	Yato	FRA	11.9.92	10 Jul				
50.47	Victor	Coroller	FRA-J	21.9.97	10 Jun				
50.48	Jermel	Kindred	USA	22.1.91	6 May				
50.48	William	Wynne	USA	30.1.90	15 May				
50.49	Tristan	Thomas	AUS	23.5.86	20 Feb				
50.49	J.W.	Smith	USA	1.1.95	24 Mar				
50.49	Michael	Williams	USA	2.3.93	27 May				
50.49	Janis	Baltuss	LAT	26.6.91	4 Jun				
50.49	Mica-Jonathan Petit-Homme		HAI	9.4.94	8 Jun				
50.49	Florian	Handt	GER	9.8.91	17 Jul				
50.50	Norman	Grimes	USA-J	6.1.98	24 Mar				
50.50	Javonte	Lipsey	USA	17.10.92	27 May				
50.51	Chris	Davis	USA	13.7.89	4 Jun				
50.51	Nicolai	Hartling	DEN	17.1.94	25 Jun				
50.51	Ayyasamy	Dharun	IND	31.12.96	11 Jul				
50.52	Máximo	Mercedes	DOM	14.9.88	7 Apr				
50.52	Luke	Campbell	USA	22.11.94	28 May				
50.52	YUtaro	Mano	JPN	.96	16 Jul				
50.53	David	Aristil	USA	12.12.88	12 Jun				
50.53	Kefiloe	Mogawane	RSA-J	11.10.97	21 Jul				
50.54	Seiya	Kato	JPN	22.11.92	22 May				
50.54	Armando	Creve Machava	MOZ	8.2.96	25 May				
50.56	Randy	Bermea	USA	2.9.93	31 Mar				
50.57	Stanislav	Melnykov	UKR	26.2.87	6 Jul				
50.58	Leonardo	Capotosti	ITA	24.7.88	1 Jun				
50.59	Yumi	Takahashi	JPN	.95	15 May				
50.61	Antonio	Blanks	USA	17.10.92	27 May				
50.62	Feng Zhiqiang		CHN-J	14.4.98	13 May				
50.63	Václav	Barák	CZE	22.10.90	12 Jun				
50.63	Yu Chia-Hsuan		TPE	22.5.95	22 Oct				
50.65	Lorenzo	Vergani	ITA	4.9.93	13 Jul				
50.66	Kemar	Mowatt	JAM	12.3.95	31 Mar				
50.66	Ran Hong		CHN	16.12.95	22 Apr				
50.66	Cam	Viney	USA	6.9.93	23 Apr				
50.67	Stanley	Broaden	USA	26.9.93	15 May				
50.67	Yusuke	Sakanashi	JPN	26.4.95	1 Apr				
50.67	Isshu	Takada	JPN-J	27.11.97	3 Sep				
[201]									

Hand timed
| 50.5A | Emerson | Chalá | ECU | 2.8.91 | 26 Mar | | | | |

Low altitude bests
| 49.60 | Hamman | | 2 | Aarhus | 25 Jun | 49.81 | Hanekom | 2 | Cape Town | 22 Mar |

JUNIORS
See main list for top 5 juniors. 12 performances by 4 men to 49.80. Additional marks and further juniors:

Hyde	49.03	1	WJ	Bydgoszcz	23 Jul	49.24	4h4	OG	Rio de Janeiro	15 Aug
	49.16	2		Kingston	7 May	49.31	2h2	NC	Kingston	30 Jun
	49.17	5s1	OG	Rio de Janeiro	16 Aug	49.77	1s3	WJ	Bydgoszcz	22 Jul
McLaughlin	49.73	3s3	NCAA	Eugene	8 Jun	49.74	5	NCAA	Eugene	10 Jun
49.96	Yoshihiro	Watanabe	JPN	7.1.97	2		Yokohama	22 May
50.47	Victor	Coroller	FRA	21.9.97	3		Colmar	10 Jun

400m HURDLES – HIGH JUMP

Mark	Name			Nat	Born	Pos	Meet	Venue	Date	
50.36	Tatsuhiro		Yamamoto	JPN	23.4.97	2h3		Kumagaya	3	Sep
50.50	Norman		Grimes	USA	6.1.98	2		Lubbock	24	Mar
50.53	Kefiloe		Mogawane (10)	RSA	11.10.97	1h2	WJ	Bydgoszcz	21	Jul
50.62			Feng Zhiqiang	CHN	14.4.98	2		Zhengzhou	13	May
50.67	Isshu		Takada	JPN	27.11.97	2h4		Kumagaya	3	Sep
50.70	Infinite		Tucker	USA	22.5.98	1		Greensboro, NC	19	Jun
50.71	Amere		Lattin	USA	17.2.97	1		Orlando	15	May
50.74	Ned		Azemia	SEY	21.8.97	8h3	OG	Rio de Janeiro	15	Aug
50.82	Mohammed Fares		Jelassi	TUN	29.7.97	1s1	WJ	Bydgoszcz	22	Jul
50.97			Wang Yijie	CHN	23.3.97	3		Taiyuan	21	May
50.98	Ivan		Loginov	RUS	19.6.97	3	NC-23	Saransk	16	Jul
50.99			Gong Debin	CHN	9.9.97	1h5		Zhengzhou	12	May
51.01	Kazuki		Hamamura (20)	JPN	.97	2		Osaka	10	Jul

HIGH JUMP

Mark				Name		Venue			Date	
2.40			Mutaz Essa		Barshim	QAT	24.6.91	1	Opole	11	Jun
						2.23/1 2.27/1 2.30/1 2.35/1 2.38/3 2.40/1 2.45/xxx					
	2.37	1	DL		Birmingham	5 Jun	2.20/1 2.23/1 2.26/1 2.29/2 2.35/2 2.37/2 2.40/xx 2.44/x				
	2.36i	1			Malmö	13 Feb	2.17/1 2.20/1 2.25/1 2.30/2 2.36/1 2.38/xxx				
	2.36	2	OG		Rio de Janeiro	16 Aug	2.20/1 2.25/1 2.29/1 2.33/1 2.36/1 2.38/xxx				
	2.35i	1	AsiC		Doha	19 Feb	2.24/1 2.28/1 2.31/2 2.35/2 2.40/xxx				
	2.35	1	Athl		Lausanne	25 Aug	2.20/1 2.25/1 2.29/1 2.32/1 2.35/3				
	2.35	1	Skol		Warszawa	28 Aug	2.20/1 2.25/1 2.30/1 2.35/1 2.41/xxx				
	2.34i	1			Malmö	31 Jan	2.14/1 2.20/1 2.25/2 2.30/1 2.34/2 2.38/xxx				
	2.34	2			Eberstadt	17 Jul	2.20/1 2.27/1 2.32/3 2.34/1 2.36/x 2.38/x 2.40/x				
2.39			Gianmarco		Tamberi	ITA	1.6.92	1	Herc	Monaco	15 Jul
						2.22/1 2.27/1 2.31/2 2.34/2 2.37/1 2.39/3 2.41/xxx					
	2.38i	1			Hustopece	13 Feb	2.20/1 2.25/1 2.30/1 2.34/1 2.38/1 2.40/xxx				
	2.36i	1	NC		Ancona	6 Mar	2.22/2 2.28/1 2.33/2 2.36/1 2.40/xxx				
	2.36i	1	WI		Portland	19 Mar	2.20/2 2.25/1 2.29/3 2.33/3 2.36/1 2.40/xxx				
	2.36	1	NC		Rieti	26 Jun	2.20/1 2.29/1 2.33/1 2.36/2 2.41/xxx				
	2.35i	1			Banská Bystrica	4 Feb	2.20/1 2.24/1 2.27/2 2.30/1 2.33/3 2.35/1 2.37/xx 2.40/x				
2.38			Derek		Drouin	CAN	6.3.90	1		Eberstadt	17 Jul
						2.15/1 2.20/1 2.24/1 2.27/1 2.30/1 2.32/1 2.34/1 2.36/1 2.38/1					
	2.38	1	OG		Rio de Janeiro	16 Aug	2.20/1 2.25/1 2.29/1 2.33/1 2.36/1 2.38/1 2.40/x				
2.37			Bogdan		Bondarenko	UKR	30.8.89	2	Herc	Monaco	15 Jul
						2.22/1 2.31/2 2.34/1 2.37/2 2.39/xxx					
	2.35	2	Gyulai		Székesfehérvár	18 Jul	2.23/1 2.29/1 2.33/xx 2.35/1 2.39/x				
2.37			Donald		Thomas	BAH	1.7.84	1	Gyulai	Székesfehérvár	18 Jul
						2.10/1 2.20/1 2.26/2 2.29/1 2.33/2 2.37/3 2.39/x 2.41/xx					
2.36i			Chris		Baker	GBR	2.2.91	2		Hustopece	13 Feb
						2.15/1 2.20/1 2.25/1 2.28/1 2.30/1 2.34/1 2.36/2 2.40/xxx					
2.36			Majed El Dein		Ghazal	SYR	21.4.87	1		Beijing	18 May
						2.20/1 2.25/1 2.29/1 2.32/1 2.3.4/22.36/2					
	2.34	3	Herc		Monaco	15 Jul	2.22/1 2.27/1 2.31/2 2.34/1 2.37/xxx				
2.35i			Marco		Fassinotti	ITA	29.4.89	2		Banská Bystrica	4 Feb
						2.24/1 2.27/3 2.30/2 2.33/2 2.35/2 2.37/xxx					
2.35			Eric		Kynard	USA	3.2.91	2	DL	Birmingham	5 Jun
						2.20/1 2.23/1 2.26/1 2.29/1 2.32/xx 2.35/1 2.37/xx 2.40/x					
2.35			Ivan		Ukhov (10)	RUS	29.3.86	1		Moskva	28 Jul
						2.15/1 2.25/1 2.30/2 2.35/3 2.41/xxx					
	2.35i	1			Yekaterinburg	29 Dec					
	2.34	1	NCp		Zhukovskiy	21 Jul	2.15/1 2.23/1 2.30/1 2.34/1 2.36/xxx				
2.34			Andrey		Silnov	RUS	9.9.84	2	NCp	Zhukovskiy	21 Jul
						2.15/1 2.19/1 2.23/1 2.28/2 2.30/1 2.34/1 2.36/xxx					
	(29/11)				16 perfromances at 2.33 by 11 men						
2.33i			Robbie		Grabarz	GBR	3.10.87	4		Banská Bystrica	4 Feb
						2.20/2 2.24/1 2.27/2 2.30/2 2.33/3 2.35/xxx					
2.33i			Konstadínos		Baniótis	GRE	6.11.86	1	NC	Pireás	13 Feb
						2.14/2 2.20/1 2.24/2 2.30/2 2.33/2 2.35/x 2.37/xx					
2.33					Zhang Guowei	CHN	4.6.91	1		Kawasaki	8 May
						2.20/1 2.23/1 2.26/2 2.29/2 2.33/1 2.35/xxx					
2.33					Wang Yu	CHN	18.8.91	2		Kawasaki	8 May
						2.10/1 2.15/1 2.20/1 2.23/1 2.26/2 2.29/1 2.31/1 2.33/3 2.35/xxx					
2.33			Andriy		Protsenko	UKR	20.5.88	4=	OG	Rio de Janeiro	16 Aug
						2.20/1 2.25/1 2.29/2 2.33/1 2.36/xxx					
2.32i			Kyriakos		Ioannou	CYP	26.7.84	3		Hustopece	13 Feb
2.32			Eike		Onnen	GER	3.8.82	3		Eberstadt	17 Jul
2.31i			Danyil		Lysenko	RUS-J	19.5.97	1		Moskva	29 Jan
2.31i			Jamal (20)		Wilson	BAH	1.9.88	1		Linz	12 Feb

HIGH JUMP

Mark	Name		Nat	Born	Pos	Meet	Venue	Date	
2.31	Avion	Jones	USA	31.1.94	1		Orlando	14	May
2.31A	Arturo	Chávez	PER	12.1.90	1		Ciudad de México	11	Jun
2.30i	Daniyil	Tsyplakov	RUS	29.7.92	1		Volgograd	19	Jan
2.30i	Matús	Bubeník	SVK	14.11.89	5		Banská Bystrica	4	Feb
2.30i	Andrey	Churylo	BLR	19.5.93	1		Minsk	7	Feb
2.30i	Edgar	Rivera	MEX	13.2.91	1		Brno	9	Feb
2.30i	Silvano	Chesani	ITA	17.7.88	4		Hustopece	13	Feb
2.30	Pavel	Seliverstov	BLR	2.9.96	1		Andujar	16	Jul
2.30	Sylwester	Bednarek	POL	28.4.89	1	Sidlo	Sopot	28	Jul
2.29i	Mateusz (30)	Przybylko	GER	9.3.92	1		Leverkusen	16	Jan
2.29i	Bradley	Adkins	USA	30.12.93	1		Fayetteville	13	Feb
2.29i	Dmitriy	Nabokov	BLR	20.1.96	1	NC	Mogilev	20	Feb
2.29Ai	Jeron	Robinson	USA	30.4.91	1		Alamosa, CO	20	Feb
2.29	Talles	Silva	BRA	20.8.91	1		Campinas	27	Mar
2.29	David	Smith	PUR	2.5.92	1		Auburn	23	Apr
2.29	Nauraj Singh	Randhawa	MAS	27.1.92	1		Singapore	28	Apr
2.29	Luis Joel	Castro	PUR	28.1.91	1		Sinn	28	May
2.29	Tihomir	Ivanov	BUL	11.7.94	1	NC	Sofia	16	Jun
2.29	Ricky	Robertson	USA	19.9.90	1		Chula Vista	19	Jun
2.29	Takashi (40)	Eto	JPN	5.2.91	1	NC	Nagoya	26	Jun
2.29	Joel	Baden	AUS	1.2.96	1		Cairns	26	Jun
2.29	Wojciech	Theiner	POL	25.6.86	1		Opole	2	Jul
2.29	Michael	Mason	CAN	30.9.86	1		Surrey, BC	3	Jul
2.29		Woo Sang-hyuk	KOR	23.4.96	1		Osaka	10	Jul
2.29	Trevor	Barry	BAH	14.6.83	Q	OG	Rio de Janeiro	14	Aug
2.29	Brandon	Starc	AUS	24.11.93	Q	OG	Rio de Janeiro	14	Aug
2.28i	Dmitriy	Semyonov	RUS	2.8.92	2		Chelyabinsk	9	Jan
2.28i	Aleksey	Dmitrik	RUS	12.4.84	1		Volgograd	6	Feb
2.28i	Jaroslav	Bába	CZE	2.9.84	6=		Hustopece	13	Feb
2.28i	Vasilios [50]	Konstantinou	CYP	13.9.92	8		Hustopece	13	Feb
2.28	Mikhail	Akimenko	RUS	6.12.95	1	NC-23	Saransk	17	Jul
2.28		Pai Long	CHN	8.10.89	1	NC	Tianjin	14	Sep
2.27i	Sergey	Mudrov	RUS	8.9.90	3		Yekaterinburg	7	Jan
2.27Ai	Deante	Kemper	USA	27.3.93	2		Flagstaff	19	Feb
2.27i		Sun Zhao	CHN	8.2.90	1		Xi'an	8	Mar
2.27	Yuriy	Krymarenko	UKR	11.8.83	1		Berdychev	25	Jun
2.27	Luis	Zayas	CUB-J	7.6.97	1	WJ	Bydgoszcz	22	Jul
2.26i	Barry	Pender	IRL	2.4.90	2		Cardiff	10	Jan
2.26i	Randall	Cunningham	USA	4.1.96	1		Birmingham, AL	22	Jan
2.26i	Allan (60)	Smith	GBR	6.11.92	1		Hirson	23	Jan
2.26i	Marius	Dumitrache	ROU	15.6.89	1		Bucuresti	30	Jan
2.26i	Yuriy	Dergachev	KAZ	8.11.94	1	NC	Ust-Kamenogorsk	31	Jan
2.26Ai	Bryan	McBride	USA	10.12.91	1		Albuquerque	5	Feb
2.26i	Hiromi	Takahari	JPN	13.11.87	1		Praha	7	Feb
2.26	Trey	Culver	USA	18.7.96	2	TexR	Austin	2	Apr
2.26	Jah-Nhai	Perinchief	BER-J	31.12.97	1		Wichita	16	Apr
2.26	Eure	Yáñez	VEN	20.5.93	1	IbAm	Rio de Janeiro	16	May
2.26	Miguel Ángel	Sancho	ESP	24.4.90	1		Lloret de Mar	5	Jun
2.26	Dmytro	Yakovenko	UKR	17.9.92	1	NC	Lutsk	19	Jun
2.26	Simón (70)	Siverio	ESP	2.8.88	1		Barcelona (S)	22	Jun
2.26	Oleksandr	Barannikov	UKR-J	23.1.97	2=		Berdychev	25	Jun
2.26	Eugenio	Rossi	SMR	6.3.92	2	NC	Rieti	26	Jun
2.26	Péter	Bakosi	HUN	23.6.93	1		Miskolc	1	Jul
2.26	Kyle	Landon	USA	16.10.94	2	NC/OT	Eugene	10	Jul
2.26	Dimitrios	Hondrokoukis	CYP	26.1.88	4	Gyulai	Székesfehérvár	18	Jul
2.26	Tejaswin	Shankar	IND-J	21.12.98	1	NC-j	Coimbatore	10	Nov
2.25i	Ali Mohamed	Younes Idris	SUD	15.9.89	2		Leverkusen	16	Jan
2.25i		Yoon Seung-hyun	KOR	1.6.94	1=		Manhattan, KS	23	Jan
2.25i	Christoffe	Bryan	JAM	26.4.96	2		Fayetteville	13	Feb
2.25i	Ilya (80)	Ivanyuk	RUS	9.3.93	2		Moskva	14	Feb
2.25i	Ivan	Ilyichev	RUS	14.10.86	4	NC	Moskva	24	Feb
2.25	Guilherme	Cobbo	BRA	1.10.87	1		São Bernardo do Campo	27	Feb
2.25	Trey	McRae	USA	12.7.93	1		Raleigh	25	Mar
2.25A	Kabelo Mmono	Kgosiemang	BOT	7.1.86	1		Pietersburg	30	Apr
2.25	Vernon	Turner	USA-J	21.8.98	1		Moore, OK	14	May

MEN 2016

382   HIGH JUMP – POLE VAULT

Mark	Name		Nat	Born	Pos	Meet	Venue	Date	
2.25	Hoova	Taylor	USA	11.6.87	1		Greensboro	15	May
2.25		Guo Jinqi	CHN	21.9.92	4		Beijing	18	May
2.25	Dakarai	Hightower	USA	15.7.94	1		Gresham	24	May
2.25	Andrei	Miticov	MDA	15.11.86	1		Tiraspol	28	May
2.25	Ryo	Sato	JPN	21.7.94	2	NC	Nagoya	26	Jun
(90)									
2.25	Nikita	Anishchenkov	RUS	25.7.92	1		Chelyabinsk	9	Jul
2.25	Bram	Ghuys	BEL	14.2.93	1		Oordegem	11	Jul
2.25	Darius	Carbin	USA-J	4.3.98	2	WJ	Bydgoszcz	22	Jul
2.25	Naoto	Tobe	JPN	31.3.92	1		Tokyo	25	Sep
2.24i	Mohammad Reza Vazifehdoost		IRI	13.10.93	1	NC	Tehran	22	Jan
2.24i	Anton	Bodnar	KAZ	12.4.92	2		Ust-Kamenogorsk	23	Jan
2.24i	Mikhail	Veryovkin	RUS	28.6.91	4		Moskva	29	Jan
2.24i	Manjula Kumara	Wijesekara	SRI	30.1.84	3	AsiC	Doha	19	Feb
2.24i	Andrea	Lemmi	ITA	12.5.84	1		Lucca	27	Feb
2.24i		Yu Shisuo	CHN	20.2.90	1		Nanjing	28	Feb
(100)									
2.24i		Bi Xiaoliang	CHN	26.12.92	2		Nanjing	3	Mar
2.24i	Paulo	Conceição	POR	29.12.93	1		Pombal	6	Mar
2.24	Mickaël	Hanany	FRA	25.3.83	1		Palafrugell	28	May
2.24	Andrey	Rybakov	BLR	14.12.96	1		Minsk	1	Jun
2.24	Zurab	Gogochuri	GEO	22.3.90	1		Baku	3	Jun
2.24	Matthew	Roberts	GBR	22.12.84	1		Genève	11	Jun
2.24	Chris	Kandu	GBR	10.9.95	1	NC-23	Bedford	18	Jun
2.24	Shuichi	Matsumoto	JPN	14.11.96	1		Kyoto	3	Jul
2.24		Park Yeon-su	KOR	24.4.94	1		Asan	11	Oct

Mark	Name		Nat	Born	Pos		Mark	Name		Nat	Born	Pos
2.235 7'4"	Darryl	Sullivan	USA-J	28.12.97	13 May		2.20i	Landon	Cuskelly	USA-J	4.6.97	19 Feb
2.23i	Alen	Melon	CRO	25.10.91	30 Jan		2.20i	Jacorian	Duffield	USA	2.9.92	20 Feb
2.23i	Batyrkhan Baymukhambetov		KAZ	7.9.92	13 Jan		2.20i	Taylor	Smith	USA	10.5.95	26 Feb
2.23i	Andrey	Skobeyko	BLR	11.6.95	20 Feb		2.20i	Jaron	Brooks	USA-J	26.7.98	26 Feb
2.23i	Mihai	Anastasiu	ROU	11.3.93	20 Feb		2.20i	Lysvanys	Pérez	ESP	24.1.82	27 Feb
2.23i	Viktor	Lonskyy	UKR	27.10.95	27 Feb		2.20i	Emil	Svensson	SWE	2.5.89	27 Feb
2.23	Jesse	Williams	USA	27.12.83	16 Apr		2.20i	Ümit	Tan	TUR	16.7.90	27 Feb
2.23	Django	Lovett	CAN	6.7.92	16 Apr		2.20i	Milos	Todosijevic	SRB	8.3.86	27 Feb
2.23	Fernando	Ferreira	BRA	13.12.94	8 May		2.20i	Robert	Atwater	USA	30.9.96	28 Feb
2.23	Loïc	Gasch	SUI	13.8.94	28 May		2.20i		Zhu Gezhen	CHN	14.4.93	28 Feb
2.23	Kris	Kornegay-Gober	USA	6.10.91	29 May		2.20i		Chen Ji	CHN	27.1.90	28 Feb
2.23	Raivydas	Stanys	LTU	3.2.87	3 Jun		2.20i		Huang Longkang	CHN	5.7.95	28 Feb
2.23	Mike	Edwards	GBR	11.7.90	15 Jun		2.20i	Riley	Northrup	USA	25.3.87	5 Mar
2.23	Geoff	Davis	USA	8.8.90	16 Jun		2.20i	David	Bolado	ESP	10.9.92	12 Mar
2.23A	Chris	Moleya	RSA-J	27.1.97	18 Jun		2.20	Keegan	Fourie	RSA	7.9.91	12 Mar
2.23	Dmitriy	Kroyter	ISR	18.2.93	9 Jul		2.20	Carlos	Layoy	ARG	26.2.91	12 Mar
2.23	Hamdi Mahamat Alamine		QAT-J	15.4.97	22 Jul		2.20	Javen	Reeves	USA	4.12.95	17 Mar
2.22i	Lev	Missirov	RUS	4.8.90	9 Jan		2.20	Wally	Ellenson	USA	4.5.94	9 Apr
2.22i	Lukás	Beer	SVK	23.8.89	15 Jan		2.20	Arturo Joaquin Abascal		MEX	19.6.95	10 Apr
2.22i	David	Nopper	GER	25.1.95	24 Jan		2.20	Bobby	Harris	USA	8.12.95	15 Apr
2.22i	Mihai	Donisan ¶	ROU	24.7.88	7 Feb		2.20	Keenon	Laine	USA-J	.97	16 Apr
2.22i	Norbert	Kobielski	POL-J	28.1.97	14 Feb		2.20		Ding Shuo	CHN-J	8.4.98	22 Apr
2.22i	Matthew	Sawe	KEN	2.7.88	16 Feb		2.20	Ryan	Lockard	USA	30.8.95	23 Apr
2.22i	Stefano	Sottile	ITA-J	26.1.98	27 Feb		2.20	Justice	Summerset	USA-J	20.1.98	23 Apr
2.22i	David	Smith	GBR	14.7.91	28 Feb		2.20	Tanner	Anderson	USA	4.5.92	30 Apr
2.22		Lee Hup-Wei	MAS	5.5.87	9 Apr		2.20	Enrique	Esquer	MEX	2.12.91	30 Apr
2.22	Garrett	Huyler	USA	15.1.87	12 May		2.20	Tiago	Pereira	POR	19.9.93	1 May
2.22	Yuji	Hiramatsu	JPN-J	11.1.97	21 May		2.20		Hsiang Chun-Hsien	TPE	4.9.93	4 May
2.22	Piotr	Sleboda	POL	22.1.87	28 May		2.20	Tom	Parsons	GBR	5.5.84	7 May
2.22	Janick	Klausen	DEN	3.4.93	28 Aug		2.20	Pavel	Kipra	BLR	3.7.94	12 May
2.21i	Keyvan	Ghanbarzadeh	IRI	26.5.90	22 Jan		2.20	Demar	Robinson	JAM	13.8.93	14 May
2.21i	Abdoulaye	Diarra	MLI	27.5.88	13 Feb		2.20	Nik	Bojic	AUS	18.1.92	18 May
2.21	Ed	Wright	USA	3.3.86	1 Apr		2.20	Ryan	Ingraham	BAH	2.11.93	21 May
2.21	Ed'Ricus	Williams	USA	6.7.94	1 Apr		2.20	d'Chaz	Moss	BAH-J	.97	21 May
2.21	Tiago	Portela	BRA	31.7.91	10 Apr		2.20		Wang Chen	CHN	27.2.90	21 May
2.21	Zack	Blackham	USA	10.8.92	23 Apr		2.20		Qiao Yuefeng	CHN	26.12.92	21 May
2.21	Noah	Martin	USA	19.9.96	23 Apr		2.20		Sun Bin	CHN	10.12.94	21 May
2.21	Thane	Pierson	USA	1.8.94	30 Apr		2.20	Tim	Schenker	GER	27.8.95	22 May
2.21	Yevgeniy	Korshunov	RUS	11.4.86	5 Jun		2.20	Martin	Günther	GER	8.10.86	26 May
2.21	Fernand	Djoumessi	CMR	5.9.89	26 Jun		2.20	Martyn	Bernard	GBR	15.12.84	28 May
2.21	Semyen	Pozdnyakov	RUS	28.11.92	2 Jul		2.20	Eugenio	Meloni	ITA	28.8.94	18 Jun
2.21	Jeremy	Taiwo	USA	15.1.90	2 Jul		2.20	Sebastien	Deschamps	FRA	12.4.87	19 Jun
2.21	Tomohiro	Shinno	JPN	17.8.96	3 Jul		2.20	Maksim	Nedasekov	BLR-J	21.1.98	21 Jun
2.21	John	Dodds	AUS-Y	24.2.99	22 Jul		2.20	Dmytro	Demyanyuk	UKR	30.6.83	19 Jun
2.21	Jussi	Viita	FIN	26.9.85	23 Jul		2.20	Artur	Kolesnyk	UKR	6.7.95	25 Jun
2.21	Daisuke	Nakajima	JPN	18.4.95	7 Aug		2.20	Ryoichi	Akamatsu	JPN	2.5.95	26 Jun
2.20i	Viktor	Shapoval	UKR	17.10.79	16 Jan		2.20	Naoto	Hasegawa	JPN	.96	26 Jun
2.20i	Roland	Sales	USA	94	6 Feb		2.20	Usman	Usmanov	RUS	26.10.95	12 Mar
2.20i	Josué	da Costa	BRA	15.3.93	13 Feb		2.20	Jakob	Thorvaldsson	SWE	6.2.88	31 Jul
2.20i	Eric	Moore	USA	14.8.96	15 Feb		2.20	Balasubramiam Chethan		IND	18.8.92	29 Sep

HIGH JUMP – POLE VAULT

Mark	Name		Nat	Born	Pos	Meet	Venue	Date
2.20	Sreenith	Mohan	IND	24.3.95			Nassau	29 Sep
2.20	Rai	Mizutani	JPN-J	12.1.97				23 Oct

Best outdoor marks

2.30	Wilson	1		Nassau	9 Jan
2.30	Lysenko	1		Sochi	27 May
2.29	Fassinotti	3	DL	Doha	6 May
2.29	Rivera	1	NC	Monterrey	5 Jun
2.29	Przybylko	1		Leverkusen	8 Jul
2.29	Baker	3=	EC	Amsterdam	10 Jul
2.29	Ioannou	7=	OG	Rio de Janeiro	16 Aug
2.28	Tsyplakov	3		Sochi	27 May
2.27	Sun Zhao	2		Shaoxing	15 Apr
2.26	Robinson	1	TexR	Austin	2 Apr
2.26	Dmitrik	4		Sochi	27 May
2.26	Bába	5=	DL	Birmingham	5 Jun
2.23	Lemmi		22 May	2.22	D Smith	22 Jul
2.23	Dergachev		24 May	2.22	Churylo	14 Aug
2.23	Conceição	4	Jun	2.22	Chesani	14 Aug
2.23	Skobeyko	25	Jun	2.22	Sottile	6 Sep
2.23	Vazifehdoost	5	Jul	2.21	Ghanbarzadeh	3 May
2.22A	Sawe		29 Apr	2.21	Ivanyuk	5 Jun

2.26	A Smith	1=		Köln	29 Jun
2.26	Takahari	2		Osaka	10 Jul
2.26	Adkins	21Q	OG	Rio de Janeiro	14 Aug
2.25	Bryan	1		Manhattan, KS	7 May
2.25	Baniótis	3=	DL	Rabat	22 May
2.25	Cunningham	1	NCAA	Eugene	10 Jun
2.25	Konstantinou	Q	EC	Amsterdam	9 Jul
2.24	McBride	2	DrakeR	Des Moines	29 Apr
2.24	Yoon Seung-hyun	1		Munggyeong	2 May
2.24	Bi Xiaoliang	1		Taiyuan	21 May
2.24	Bubeník	1		Samorin	11 Jun
2.24	Nabokov	2		Hérouville	16 Jun
2.24	Wijesekara	1	NC	Diyagama	8 Jul
2.21	Kemper		26 Jun	2.20	Zhu Gezhen	15 Apr
2.21	Roberts		15 Jul	2.20	da Costa	21 Apr
2.21	Beer		10 Sep	2.20	Melon	7 May
2.20	Huang Longkang	15 Apr		2.20	Pender	7 May
2.20	Chen Ji	15 Apr		2.20	Diarra	8 May
2.20	Yu Shisuo	15 Apr		2.20	Dumitrache	21 May
				2.20	Todosijevic	25 Jun

Drugs disqualification

2.26i	Mihai		Donisan ¶	ROU	24.7.88	1	NC	Bucuresti	20 Feb
	2.23					2		Zoetemeer	22 Jun

JUNIORS

See main list for top 7 juniors. 12 performances (inc. 6 indoors) by 5 men to 2.26. Additional marks and further juniors:

Lysenko 2+	2.30i	1	NC-j	Novocheboksarsk	9 Feb	2.28	2	NC	Cheboksary	22 Jun
	2.28i	1		Chelyabinsk	9 Jan	2.28i	3	NC	Moskva	24 Feb
	2.28i	1		Sankt-Peterburg	7 Feb	2.27i	2		Yekaterinburg	7 Jan
2.235 7'4"	Darryl		Sullivan	USA	28.12.97	1		Marion, IL	13 May
2.23A	Chris		Moleya	RSA	27.1.97	1		Lusaka	18 Jun
2.23	Hamdi Mahamat		Alamine (10)	QAT	15.4.97	3	WJ	Bydgoszcz	22 Jul
2.22i	Norbert		Kobielski	POL	28.1.97	1	NC-j	Spala	14 Feb
2.22i	Stefano		Sottile	ITA	26.1.98	1		Padova	27 Feb
	2.22					1		Livorno	6 Sep
2.22	Yuji		Hiramatsu	JPN	11.1.97	1		Yokohama	21 May
2.21	John		Dodds	AUS-Y	24.2.99	5	WJ	Bydgoszcz	22 Jul
2.20i	Landon		Cuskelly	USA	4.6.97	1		Pittsburg, KS	19 Feb
2.20i	Jaron		Brooks	USA	26.7.98	1		Huntington, WV	26 Feb
2.20	Keenon		Laine	USA	.97	1		Clarksville, TN	16 Apr
2.20			Ding Shuo	CHN	8.4.98	4		Huaian	22 Apr
2.20	Justice		Summerset	USA	20.1.98	1		Tucson	23 Apr
2.20	d'Chaz		Moss (20)	BAH	.97	2		Nassau	21 May
2.20	Maksim		Nedasekov	BLR	21.1.98	1	NC-j	Brest	21 Jun
2.20	Rai		Mizutani	JPN	12.1.97	1	NC-j	Nagoya	23 Oct
2.20i	Metin		Dogu	TUR	19.1.97	1		Istanbul	24 Dec

POLE VAULT

6.03i	Renaud		Lavillenie	FRA	18.9.86	1		Jablonec	5 Mar
				5.74/1	5.90/1	6.03/2	6.10/xxx		
	6.02i	1		Clermont-Ferrand	21 Feb	5.70/1	5.84/1	5.91/1	6.02/1 6.17/xxx
	6.02i	1	WI	Portland	17 Mar	5.75/1	5.90/1	6.02/1	6.17/xxx
	5.98	2	OG	Rio de Janeiro	15 Aug	5.75/1	5.85/1	5.98/1	6.03/xx 6.08/x
	5.96	1		Sotteville-les-Rouen	18 Jul	5.70/1	5.84/2	5.96/1	6.01/xxx
	5.95	1	NC	Angers	26 Jun	5.75/1	5.85/1	5.95/2	6.01/xx
	5.93i	1	NC	Aubière	27 Feb	5.77/1	5.93/1	6.03/xxx	
	5.93	1	DL	Saint-Denis	27 Aug	5.61/1	5.71/1	5.81/3	5.87/2 5.93/1 6.00/xxx
	5.91i	1		Karlsruhe	6 Feb	5.70/3	5.84/1	5.91/3	6.01/xxx
	5.90	1	DL	London (OS)	22 Jul	5.65/1	5.75/1	5.83/1	5.90/1 5.97/xxx
	5.90	1=	WK	Zürich	1 Sep	5.62/2	5.72/1	5.78/1	5.84/2 5.90/2 6.01/xxx
	5.85i	2	ISTAF	Berlin	13 Feb	5.69/3	5.85/1	5.93/xxx	
6.03	Thiago		Braz da Silva	BRA	16.12.93	1	OG	Rio de Janeiro	15 Aug
				5.65/1	5.75/2	5.93/2	6.03/2		
	5.93i	1	ISTAF	Berlin	13 Feb	5.45/1	5.60/1	5.69/xx	5.77/1 5.85/1 5.93/2 6.01/xxx
	5.90	1sq		Schlanders	22 Jul	...	5.90/2	6.00/xxx	
	5.85	2		Leverkusen	24 Jun	5.55/x	5.61/1	5.75/1	5.85/1 6.00/xxx
	5.84	3	WK	Zürich	1 Sep	5.52/3	5.72/2	5.84/2	
6.00Ai	Shawnacy		Barber	CAN	27.5.94	1		Reno	15 Jan
				5.30/1	5.45/1	5.65/1	5.77/1	5.83/1 5.94/3 6.00/1
	5.91i	2		Clermont-Ferrand	21 Feb	5.42/3	5.57/1	5.70/2	5.84/1 5.91/2 6.02/xxx

384 POLE VAULT

Mark		Name		Nat	Born	Pos	Meet	Venue	Date
	5.91	1	TexR Austin 2 Apr		5.35/1 5.50/3 5.60/2 5.70/1 5.80/1 5.91/1 6.01/xxx				
	5.90	1	Leverkusen 24 Jun		5.40/2 5.55/1 5.65/1 5.75/x 5.80/1 5.85/x 5.90/2 6.00/xxx				
	5.89i	1	Glasgow 20 Feb		5.40/1 5.60/2 5.77/1 5.89/1 6.01/xxx				
	5.88i	1	Belton, TX 2 Jan						
5.92		Sam	Kendricks	USA	7.9.92	1		Beijing	18 May
					5.20/1 5.40/1 5.50/1 5.60/2 5.70/1 5.76/2 5.82/1 5.92/2 6.00/xxx				
	5.92	1	Athl Lausanne 25 Aug		5.32/1 5.47/1 5.62/1 5.72/1 5.80/1 5.92/2				
	5.91	1	NC/OT Eugene 4 Jul		5.40/1 5.50/1 5.60/1 5.65/1 5.70/1 5.80/1 5				
	5.90i	1	NC Portland 11 Mar		5.35/1 5.50/1 5.55/1 5.60/1 5.65/1 5.80/1 5.90/3				
	5.90	1=	WK Zürich 1 Sep		5.42/1 5.62/1 5.72/1 5.78/3 5.84/1 5.90/2 6.01/xxx				
	5.88	1	DL Shanghai 14 May		5.40/1 5.52/1 5.62/1 5.70/1 5.78/2 5.83/3 5.88/3 5.93/xxx				
	5.85	3	OG Rio de Janeiro 15 Aug		5.50/1 5.65/2 5.75/x 5.85/1 5.93/xxx				
	5.84i	3=	Clermont-Ferrand 21 Feb		5.42/1 5.57/1 5.70/1 5.77/x 5.84/1 5.91/xxx				
5.84i		Raphael	Holzdeppe	GER	28.9.89	1		Rouen	23 Jan
					5.70/2 5.84/3 5.91/xxx				
5.84i		Konstadinos	Filippídis	GRE	26.11.86	3=		Clermont-Ferrand	21 Feb
					5.42/1 5.57/1 5.70/2 5.84/1 5.91/xxx				
5.84i		Pawel	Wojciechowski	POL	6.6.89	5		Clermont-Ferrand	21 Feb
		(34/7)			5.57/1 5.70/1 5.77/x 5.84/1 5.91/xxx				
5.81i			Xue Changrui	CHN	31.5.91	1		Orléans	16 Jan
5.80i		Timur	Morgunov (10)	RUS	12.10.96	1	NC-23	Volgograd	2 Mar
5.80		Kévin	Menaldo	FRA	12.7.92	2	NC	Angers	26 Jun
5.80		Ilya	Mudrov	RUS	17.11.91	1		Moskva	28 Jul
5.77Ai		Seito	Yamamoto	JPN	11.3.92	2		Reno	15 Jan
5.77i		Carlo	Paech	GER	18.12.92	1		Potsdam	6 Feb
5.77i		Jérôme	Clavier	FRA	3.5.83	2		Potsdam	6 Feb
5.77i		Robert	Sobera	POL	19.1.91	1		Torun	12 Feb
5.77i		Piotr	Lisek	POL	16.8.92	2		Torun	12 Feb
5.77Ai		Mike	Arnold	USA	13.8.90	1		Flagstaff	13 Feb
5.77		Florian	Gaul	GER	21.9.91	2		Rottach-Egern	16 Jul
5.75i			Huang Bokai	CHN	26.9.96	1	AsiC	Doha	20 Feb
		(20)							
5.75		Tobias	Scherbarth	GER	17.8.85	3		Leverkusen	24 Jun
5.75		Stanley	Joseph	FRA	24.10.91	3	NC	Angers	26 Jun
5.75		Daichi	Sawano	JPN	16.9.80	1		Tokyo	3 Jul
5.72i		Jake	Blankenship	USA	15.3.94	1		Blacksburg	6 Feb
5.72A		Cale	Simmons	USA	5.2.91	1		Highlands Ranch, CO	26 Jun
5.72		Joseph	Uhle	USA	14.11.92	1		Chula Vista	26 Jun
5.71		Valentin	Lavillenie	FRA	16.7.91	1		St.Denis, Réunion	23 Apr
5.71		Logan	Cunningham	USA	30.5.91	1		Phoenix	21 May
5.71A		Mark	Hollis	USA	1.12.84	1		Ciudad de México	29 May
5.70i		Michal	Balner	CZE	12.9.82	3		Cottbus	27 Jan
		(30)							
5.70i		Luke	Cutts	GBR	13.2.88	1		Cardiff	7 Feb
5.70i		Georgiy	Gorokhov	RUS	20.4.93	1		Moskva	10 Feb
5.70i		Pauls	Pujats	LAT	6.8.91	1		Black Springs, AR	28 Feb
5.70		Devin	King	USA	12.3.96	1	TexR	Austin	2 Apr
5.70		Melker	Svärd Jacobsson	SWE	8.1.94	2	TexR	Austin	2 Apr
5.70		Hiroki	Ogita	JPN	30.12.87	3	TexR	Austin	2 Apr
5.70			Yao Jie	CHN	21.9.90	4		Beijing	18 May
5.70		Mareks	Arents	LAT	6.8.86	1		Jablonec	8 Jun
5.70		Augusto	Dutra de Oliveira	BRA	16.7.90	1		São Bernardo do Campo	19 Jun
5.70A		Dylan	Bell	USA	21.7.93	1		Pueblo	19 Jun
		(40)							
5.70		Kurtis	Marschall	AUS-J	25.4.97	1		Mannheim	26 Jun
5.70		Karsten	Dilla	GER	17.7.89	2		Landau	28 Jun
5.70		Germán	Chiaraviglio	ARG	16.4.87	Q	OG	Rio de Janeiro	13 Aug
5.70		Ivan	Horvat	CRO	17.8.93	1	Hanz	Zagreb	6 Sep
5.67i		Jason	Colwick	USA	25.1.88	1		Houston	12 Feb
5.66		Eirik Greibrokk	Dolve	NOR	5.5.95	2		Praha	22 Jun
5.65i		Yevgeniy	Lukyanenko	RUS	23.1.85	1		Slavyansk	31 Jan
5.65i		Adam	Bragg	USA	18.4.93	1		New York (SI)	12 Feb
5.65		Audie	Wyatt	USA	30.4.96	2	TexR	Austin	2 Apr
5.65		John	Prader	USA	10.2.91	1		Chula Vista	21 Apr
		[50]							
5.65		Scott	Houston	USA	11.6.90	1		Durham	23 Apr
5.65		Chase	Wolfle	USA	9.10.92	1		Waco	23 Apr
5.65		Axel	Chapelle	FRA	24.4.95	1		Pierre-Bénite	10 Jun
5.65		Mike	Woepse	USA	29.5.91	1		Phoenix	11 Jun
5.65		Tray	Oates	USA	14.3.95	1		Rock Hill	25 Jun
5.65		Robert	Renner	SLO	8.3.94	5	DL	London (OS)	22 Jul

Mark	Name		Nat	Born	Pos	Meet	Venue	Date	
5.65	Deakin	Volz	USA-J	12.1.97	1	WJ	Bydgoszcz	23	Jul
5.64i	Max	Eaves	GBR	31.5.88	4		Jablonecvnad Nisou	5	Mar
5.62i	Torben	Laidig	GER	13.3.94	2		Blacksburg	6	Feb
5.62i	Drew	Volz	USA	20.11.92	1		Blacksburg	20	Feb
	(60)								
5.62i	Jeff	Coover	USA	1.12.87	1		Jonesboro	9	Jun
5.62	Jordan	Scott	USA	22.2.88	1		Lawrence	25	Jun
5.62A	Sam	Pierson	USA	7.4.88	2		Highlands Ranch, CO.	26	Jun
5.62	Rasmus	Jørgensen	DEN	23.1.89	4		Jockgrim	19	Jul
5.61	Hendrik	Gruber	GER	28.9.86	1		Leverkusen	7	May
5.61	Ben	Broeders	BEL	21.6.95	1		Oordegem	21	May
5.61	Levi	Keller	USA	30.1.86	1		Seattle	15	Jun
5.61i	Arnaud	Art	BEL	28.1.93	1		Rennes	17	Dec
5.60i	Dimítrios	Patsoukákis	GRE	18.3.87	1		Pireás	30	Jan
5.60A	Eben	Beukes	RSA	9.3.90	1		Pretoria	13	Feb
	(70)								
5.60i	Baptiste	Boirie	FRA	26.12.92	1		Clermont-Ferrand	20	Feb
5.60	Steve	Lewis	GBR	20.5.86	1		Phoenix	26	Mar
5.60		Jin Min-sub	KOR	2.9.92	2	MSR	Norwalk	16	Apr
5.60	Chris	Nilsen	USA-J	13.1.98	1		Kansas City (72mm pegs)	21	May
5.60	Ivan	Gertleyn	RUS	25.9.87	1	Znam	Zhukovskiy	5	Jun
5.60	Dmitry	Zhelyabin	RUS	20.5.90	1		Moskva	10	Jun
5.60	Alioune	Sène	FRA	3.2.96	2		Pierre-Bénite	10	Jun
5.60	Zach	Siegmeier	USA	8.1.91	1		Ames	19	Jun
5.60i	Peter	Geraghty	USA	11.6.91	1		Champaign	26	Jun
5.58	Menno	Vloon	NED	11.5.94	1		Kessel-Lo	30	Jul
	(80)								
5.55Ai	Victor	Weirich	USA	25.10.87	5		Reno	15	Jan
5.55i	Anton	Ivakin	RUS	3.2.91	2		Slavyansk	31	Jan
5.55	Ernest John	Obiena	PHI	17.11.95	1		Singapore	29	Apr
5.55	João Gabriel	Sousa	BRA	6.11.84	1		Belo Horizonte	30	Apr
5.55	Diogo	Ferreira	POR	30.7.90	1		Fátima	19	May
5.55	Emmanouil	Karális	GRE-Y	20.10.99	7	GS	Ostrava	20	May
5.55	Dominik	Alberto	SUI	28.4.92	1		Gräfeling	29	May
5.55	Tyler	Wallace	USA	31.7.90	1		Norwalk	4	Jun
5.55	Lukás	Posekany	CZE	30.12.92	4=		Praha	22	Jun
5.55	Kyrylo	Kiru	UKR	6.5.96	1		Kyiv	24	Jun
	(90)								
5.55	Vladyslav	Malykhin	UKR-J	15.1.98	1	NC-j	Kirovohrad	2	Jul
5.53i	Adam	Hague	GBR-J	29.8.97	2		Cardiff	7	Feb
5.53i	Igor	Bychkov	ESP	7.3.87	1		Madrid	26	Feb
5.53i	Pau Gaspar	Tonnesen	ESP	24.10.92	1		Seattle	27	Feb
5.53	Rutger	Koppelaar	NED	1.5.93	2		Kessel-Lo	30	Jul
5.52i	Luke	Winder	USA	2.8.95	1	NCAA-3	Grinnell, IA	11	Mar
5.52i	Jeremy	Scott	USA	1.5.81	1		Jonesboro	13	Jun
5.52	Alex	Bishop	USA	17.5.91	2		Chula Vista	26	Jun
5.51i	Daniel	Clemens	GER	28.4.92	5		Zweibrücken	31	Jan
5.51i	Tom	Konrad	GER	30.3.91	5		Bad Oeynhausen	5	Mar
	[100]								
5.51	Sean	Collins	USA-J	29.8.97	1		Lafayette, LA	15	May
5.51	Chase	Brannon	USA	8.2.91	1		Knoxville	21	May
5.51	Nikandros	Stylianou	CYP	22.8.89	1		Oordegem	28	May
5.51	Mathieu	Collet	FRA	15.3.95	1	Med U23	Radès	5	Jun
5.51	Armand	Duplantis	SWE-Y	10.11.99	1		Norrköping	13	Jul
5.51	Kota	Suzuki	JPN	18.12.95	1		Gifu	10	Oct

Mark	Name		Nat	Born	Date		Mark	Name		Nat	Born	Date	
5.50i	Anatoliy	Bednyuk	RUS	30.1.89	22 Jan		5.50	Reese	Watson	USA	8.10.93	2	Jul
5.50i	Mikhail	Gelmanov	RUS	18.3.90	9 Jan		5.50	Tomas	Wecksten	FIN	2.11.96	9	Jul
5.50i	Leonid	Kivalov	RUS	1.4.88	22 Jan		5.48i	Noël	Ost	FRA	15.11.89	23	Jan
5.50i	Sergey	Grigoryev	KAZ	24.6.92	23 Jan		5.48i	Mehdi Amar	Rouana	FRA	30.3.94	23	Jan
5.50i	Aleksandr	Gripich	RUS	21.9.86	7 Feb		5.47	Nicholas	Southgate	NZL	9.4.94	3	Apr
5.50i	Edi	Maia	POR	10.11.87	20 Feb		5.47	Chris	Uhle	USA	14.11.92	5	May
5.50i	Leonid	Kobelev	RUS	24.6.95	24 Feb		5.46i	Jacob	Wooten	USA-J	22.4.97	6	Feb
5.50i	Artem	Burya	RUS	11.4.86	24 Feb		5.46i	Nate	Richartz	USA	2.11.94	27	Feb
5.50i	Jax	Thoirs	GBR	7.4.93	11 Mar		5.46	Matthew	Ludwig	USA	5.7.96	30	Apr
5.50i	Darren	Niedermeyer	USA	2.4.82	11 Mar		5.46	Icaro	Miranda	POR	13.12.94	23	Jun
5.50	Nick	Meyer	USA	5.2.95	7 May		5.46	Masaki	Ejima	JPN-Y	6.3.99	8	Oct
5.50	Jake	Albright	USA	22.12.93	13 May		5.45Ai	Andrew	Irwin	USA	23.1.93	15	Jan
5.50		Han Do-hyun	KOR	28.7.94	2 Jun		5.45i	Alessandro	Sinno	ITA	17.7.94	7	Feb
5.50	Alexandre	Feger	FRA	22.1.90	10 Jun		5.45i	Matti	Mononen	FIN	25.11.83	28	Feb
5.50	Hiroki	Sasase	JPN	17.8.89	24 Jun		5.45i	Andrew	Sutcliffe	GBR	10.7.91	28	Feb
5.50	Adrián	Vallés	ESP	16.3.95	25 Jun		5.45	Marvin	Caspari	GER	9.8.91	16	May
5.50	Dídac	Salas	ESP	19.5.93	30 Jun		5.45	Nikita	Filippov	KAZ	7.10.91	29	May
5.50	Danyil	Kotov	RUS	14.11.95	1 Jul		5.45	Craig	Hunter	USA	18.11.94	8	Jun

POLE VAULT

Mark	Name		Nat	Born	Pos	Meet	Venue	Date	
5.45	Damiel	Dossévi	FRA	3.2.83	15			Jun	10 Mar
5.45	Lázaro	Borges	CUB	19.6.86	2			Jul	12 Mar
5.43i	Casey	Bowen	USA	11.1.93	6			Feb	12 Mar
5.43i	Max	Babits	USA	30.5.92	19			Feb	21 Apr
5.42i	Kyle	Wait	USA	20.2.92	29			Jan	23 Apr
5.42i	Sean	Young	USA	27.12.85	6			Feb	18 May
5.42i	Marquis	Richards	SUI	29.7.91	6			Feb	21 May
5.42i	Justin	Estala	USA	94	19			Feb	21 May
5.42i	Kyle	Thompson	USA	11.2.93	19			Feb	22 May
5.42i	Austin	Crenshaw	USA	22.1.92	20			Feb	25 May
5.42i	Derek	O'Connell	USA	94	28			May	26 May
5.42i	Mike	Vani	USA	20.6.91	9			Jun	11 Jun
5.42	Derick	Hinch	USA	2.2.91	26			Jun	18 Jun
5.41i	Per Magne	Florvaag	NOR	21.2.93	17			Feb	24 Jun
5.41i	Kyle	Pater	USA	24.12.94	27			Feb	24 Jun
5.41i	Mitch	Greeley	USA	5.5.86	5			Mar	24 Jun
5.41i	Niko	Koskinen	FIN	14.7.96	6			Mar	3 Jul
5.41i	Jordan	Yamoah	GHA	30.9.93	12			Mar	14 Jul
5.41	Cole	Walsh	USA	14.6.95	16			Apr	21 Jul
5.41	Lev	Skorish	ISR	12.4.96	21			May	24 Jul
5.41	Thomas	Van Der Plaetsen	BEL	24.12.90	28			May	13 Aug
5.41	Pascal	Koehl	GER	1.9.91	29			Jun	18 Aug
5.41	Nikólaos	Nerántzis	GRE-J	13.3.98	9			Jul	2 Sep
5.40i	Stanislav	Tivonchik	BLR	3.3.85	7			Feb	
5.40i	Ashton	Eaton	USA	21.1.88	14			Feb	
5.40i	Sergey	Safonov	RUS	18.2.95	2			Mar	
5.40A	Michael	Cilliers	RSA	25.4.93	5			Mar	

Mark	Name		Nat	Born	Pos	Meet	Venue	Date
5.40	Angus	Armstrong	AUS-J	17.3.97				10 Mar
5.40	Declan	Carruthers	AUS-J	7.9.97				12 Mar
5.40i	Zachary	Ziemek	USA	23.2.93				12 Mar
5.40	Jack	Whitt	USA	12.4.90				21 Apr
5.40	Peter	Roach	USA	18.8.90				23 Apr
5.40		Xia Xiang	CHN	28.3.91				18 May
5.40	Koki	Kuruma	JPN	25.3.96				21 May
5.40	Karol	Pawlik	POL	17.3.94				21 May
5.40	Tomoki	Yamamoto	JPN	25.8.92				22 May
5.40	Danil	Polyanskiy	KAZ	17.12.91				25 May
5.40	Francesco	Lama	ITA-J	8.4.97				26 May
5.40	Przemyslaw	Czerwinski	POL	28.7.83				11 Jun
5.40	Dylan	Duvio	USA	6.4.95				18 Jun
5.40	Yusaku	Kogiso	JPN	19.12.94				24 Jun
5.40	Nariharu	Matsuzawa	JPN	6.1.92				24 Jun
5.40	Ivan	Yeryomin	UKR	30.5.89				24 Jun
5.40	Shingo	Sawa	JPN	28.9.96				3 Jul
5.40	Eemeli	Salomäki	FIN	11.10.87				14 Jul
5.40	Ilya	Prosvirin	RUS	28.2.95				21 Jul
5.40	Lamin	Krubally	GER	13.2.95				24 Jul
5.40	Paul	Malquist	USA	10.9.91				13 Aug
5.40	Kevin	Mayer	FRA	10.2.92				18 Aug
5.40	Ryohei	Yamakata [192]	JPN	26.10.92				2 Sep

Doubtful mark

| 5.45 | Leonid | Andreyev | UZB | 6.10.83 | | | | 10 Jun |

Drugs disqualification

| 5.47Ai | Nick | Mossberg ¶ | USA | 5.4.86 | | | | 13 Feb |

Best outdoor marks

Mark	Name		Pos	Meet	Venue	Date
5.75	Xue	Changrui	1		Tomblaine	14 Jun
5.75	Lisek		4=	OG	Rio de Janeiro	15 Aug
5.72	Filippídis		1	ISTAF	Berlin	3 Sep
5.71	Wojciechowski		3=	Pre	Eugene	28 May
5.70	Sobera		5		Beijing	18 May
5.70	Holzdeppe		1		Mannheim	29 Jul
5.66	Balner		1		Linz	29 Jun
5.65	Blankenship		1	SEC	Tuscaloosa	14 May
5.65	Gorokhov		1	NC	Cheboksary	22 Jun
5.63	S Yamamoto		5	GS	Ostrava	20 May
5.61	Cutts		2		Linz	29 Jun
5.60	Laidig		3	TexR	Austin	2 Apr
5.60	Art		1		St-André-de-Cubzac	29 May
5.50	Weirich	31 Mar	5.50	Kivalov	1 Jul
5.50	Volz	2 Apr	5.50	Hague	21 Sep
5.50	Clemens	21 May	5.45	Geraghty	30 Apr
5.50	Grigoryev	25 May	5.45	Patsoukákis	10 May
5.50	Maia	4 Jun	5.45	Clavier	25 May

5.60	Morgunov	1		Chelyabinsk	9 Jul
5.60	Huang Bokai	2		La Roche-sur-Yon	13 Jul
5.60	Boirie	3		La Roche-sur-Yon	13 Jul
5.60	Pujats	Q	OG	Rio de Janeiro	13 Aug
5.57	Eaves	1		Eton	7 May
5.57	Coover	1		Dublin (S)	22 Jul
5.56	Arnold	3		Chula Vista	28 May
5.55	Colwick	1		Waco	23 Apr
5.55	Lukyanenko	1		Sochi	26 May
5.53	Bragg	1		Princeton	7 May
5.51	Winder	1		Rock Island, IL	7 May
5.51	Bychkov	1	NC	Gijón	23 Jul
5.45	Konrad	29 May	5.40	Pater	14 May
5.45	Thoirs	8 Jun	5.40	Florvaag	3 Jun
5.41	Ost	14 Jun	5.40	Rouana	10 Jun
5.41	Young	25 Jun	5.40	Kobelev	16 Jul
5.40	Yamoah	9 Apr			

Irregular: Street/beach vaults downhill

5.80	Logan	Cunningham	USA	30.5.91	1		Port Aransas, TX	18 Jun
5.70	Scott	Houston	USA	11.6.90	1		Louisville	4 Jun
5.70	Audie	Wyatt	USA	30.4.96	2		Port Aransas, TX	18 Jun
5.56	Peter	Geraghty	USA	11.6.91	2		Louisville	4 Jun
5.50	Garrett	Larson	USA	27.4.95	3		Port Aransas, TX	18 Jun

JUNIORS

See main list for top 8 juniors. 13 performances (inc. 3 indoors) by 6 men to 5.53. Additional marks and further juniors:

Mark	Name		Nat	Born	Pos	Meet	Venue	Date
Marschall	5.60				15q	OG	Ro de Janeiro	13 Aug
	5.55				1	NC	Sydney	3 Apr
Nilsen	5.56A				1		Albuquerque	4 Jun
Karális	5.54i				5		Jablonec	5 Mar
	5.53i				3	NC	Pireás	13 Feb
5.46i	Jacob	Wooten	USA	22.4.97	1		College Station	6 Feb
5.46	Masaki	Ejima (10)	JPN-Y	6.3.99	1		Kitakami	8 Oct
5.41	Nikólaos	Nerántzis	GRE-J	13.3.98	1	NC-j	Sérres	9 Jul
5.40	Angus	Armstrong	AUS-J	17.3.97	2	NC-j	Perth	10 Mar
5.40	Declan	Carruthers	AUS-J	7.9.97	2		Perth	12 Mar
5.40	Francesco	Lama	ITA-J	8.4.97	1		Orvieto	26 May
5.38	Brandon	Bray	USA	24.4.97	5q	NCAA-W	Lawrence	27 May
5.38	Paulo	Benavides	USA	27.7.97	2		Lawrence	11 Jun
5.36	Blake	Scott	USA	2.7.97	1		Auston	7 May
5.35	Muntaher Faleh	Abdelwahid	IRQ	1.2.98	1	NC	Al Najaf	2 Mar
5.35	Koen	van der Wijst	NED	7.8.97	1		Lisse	7 May
5.35	Pierre	Cottin (20)	FRA	26.1.98	4		Moulins	18 Jun
Best out: 5.50 Adam			Hague		3c2		Paris	21 Sep

Symbols/Abbreviations

+ intermediate time in longer race, A made at an altitude of 1000m or higher, D made in a decathlon, h made in a heat, qf quarter-final, sf semi-final, i indoors, Q qualifying round, r race number, -J juniors, -Y youths (b. 1999 or later)

LONG JUMP

Mark	Wind	Name		Nat	Born	Pos	Meet	Venue			Date
8.58	1.8	Jarrion	Lawson	USA	6.5.94	2	NC/OT	Eugene			3 Jul
					8.20w	8.32w/2.5	x	8.58	p	p	
	8.25 -0.5 4 OG		Rio de Janeiro	13 Aug	8.19	8.15	8.25	x	x	7.78	
8.48	0.1	Luvo	Manyonga	RSA	18.11.91	1	VD	Bruxelles			9 Sep
					8.24/-0.5	8.26/0.2	x	8.28/0.1	8.48	x	
	8.37 -0.3 2 OG		Rio de Janeiro	13 Aug	8.16	x	x	8.28/-0.2	8.37	x	
	8.30A 0.2 1		Pretoria	11 Mar							
8.45	0.8	Marquise	Goodwin	USA	19.11.90	1		Baie Mahault			14 May
					7.90	8.43/0.6	8.21	x	8.44/0.6	8.45	
	8.42 1.0 1 DL		Birmingham	5 Jun	x	8.42	7.92	p	p	x	
8.44A	1.8	Michel	Tornéus	SWE	26.5.86	1		Monachil			10 Jul
					8.44	p	p	p	p	p	
8.42	1.6	Marquis	Dendy	USA	17.11.92	4	NC/OT	Eugene			3 Jul
					7.75w	x	8.42	x	p	p	
	8.41i 1 NC		Portland	11 Mar	7.90	7.78	8.10	7.83	8.41	p	
	8.38i 1		Fayetteville	12 Feb	8.35	8.19	x	8.38	8.04	x	
	8.26i Dendy			1	WI	Portland	20	Mar			
					8.05	8.26	x	8.06	x	x	
8.38	0.8	Rushwal	Samaai	RSA	25.9.91	1	DL	Rabat			22 May
					8.03	8.09	8.12	8.38	7.96	p	
	8.34 0.6 1 NC		Stellenbosch	16 Apr	8.34	8.21	x	x	p	7.94	
	8.38 0.2	Jeff	Henderson	USA 19.2.89	1	OG	Rio de Janeiro	13	Aug		
					8.20	7.94	8.10	7.96	8.22	8.38	
8.34	0.3	Mike	Hartfield	USA	29.3.90	2		Baie Mahault			14 May
					8.20	x	x	8.34	x	8.32/0.6	
	8.29 -1.3 2 DL		Birmingham	5 Jun	8.17	8.29	x	8.03	p	8.22	
8.31	-0.4	Fabrice	Lapierre	AUS	17.10.83	*	DL	Rabat			22 May
					7.86	7.84	8.31	p	8.36w/5.2	7.97	
	8.27 2.0 1 NC		Sydney	3 Apr	x	8.27	8.09	8.20	8.10	x	
	8.25i 2 WI		Portland	20 Mar	7.29	7.78	8.25	x	7.79	x	
8.31	-0.3	Greg	Rutherford (10)	GBR	17.11.86	1	GGala	Roma			2 Jun
					8.03	8.31	x	p	p	8.19	
	8.30 0.4 1		Long Beach	16 Apr	8.30	8.18	8.19	p	p	p	
	8.29 0.3 3 OG		Rio de Janeiro	13 Aug	8.18	8.11	8.22	8.26/-0.2	8.09	8.29	
	8.26iA 1		Albuquerque	5 Feb	7.96	8.26	p	p	p	p	
	8.25 0.5 1 EC		Amsterdam	7 Jul	8.12	x	x	8.13	8.25	8.12	
	8.24 0.9 *		Phoenix	14 May	x	x	8.36w/2.8	x	8.24	p	
8.30	1.3		Shi Yuhao	CHN-J	26.9.98	1	NC-j	Ordos			27 Jun
					7.84	8.18w	8.02	8.15	8.13	8.30	
8.28	1.8	Maykel	Massó	CUB-Y	8.5.99	1	Barr	La Habana			28 May
					8.28	p	7.75	p	x	p	
8.25i		Bachana	Khorava	GEO	15.3.93	1	NC	Tbilisi			7 Feb
					8.10	x	x	8.25	8.01	x	
8.24	1.7	Jarvis	Gotch	USA	25.3.92	1	TexR	Austin			2 Apr
					8.14	7.96	p	x	8.24	p	
8.24	0.3		Wang Jianan	CHN	27.8.96	Q	OG	Rio de Janeiro			12 Aug
	(31/15)				8.24	p		p			
8.23i		Kafétien	Gomis	FRA	23.3.80	1	NC	Aubière			28 Feb
8.23	0.5		Gao Xinglong	CHN	12.3.94	1		Beijing			18 May
8.23	1.5	Damar	Forbes	JAM	18.9.90	1	Herc	Monaco			15 Jul
8.22	1.3	Stefan	Brits	RSA	19.1.92	1	ACC	Tallahassee			14 May
8.22	0.4		Kim Duk-hyung	KOR	8.12.85	1		Ried			10 Jun
	(20)										
8.22	1.2	Vasiliy	Kopeykin	RUS	9.3.88	Q	NC	Cheboksary			20 Jun
8.21i			Huang Changzhou	CHN	20.8.94	3	WI	Portland			20 Mar
8.21	0.2	Alyn	Camara	GER	31.3.89	1		Oberteuringen			10 Jul
8.19	2.0	Miltiádis	Tentóglou	GRE-J	18.3.98	1		Kalamáta			28 May
8.19	0.1	Ankit	Sharma	IND	20.7.92	1		Almaty			26 Jun
8.19	1.0	Higor	Alves	BRA	23.2.94	1	NC	São Bernardo do Campo			1 Jul
8.18	1.0	Tyrone	Smith	BER	7.8.86	4	DL	Birmingham			5 Jun
8.17i		Jonathan	Addison	USA	27.2.95	1		Blacksburg			5 Feb
8.17A	0.0	Jean Marie	Okutu	ESP	4.8.88	2		Monachil			10 Jul
8.16A	0.2	Dylan	Cotter	RSA	23.8.91	1		Johannesburg			13 Feb
	(30)										
8.16	-0.5	Emiliano	Lasa	URU	25.1.90	1		São Bernardo do Campo			6 Mar
8.16	1.4	Henry	Frayne	AUS	14.4.90	2	NC	Sydney			3 Apr
8.16	0.0	Mohammad	Arzandeh	IRI	30.10.87	2		Almaty			26 Jun
8.15	?	W.P. Amila	Jayasiri	SRI	24.1.94	1		Diyagama			16 Aug
8.14	0.2	Mauro Vinícius	da Silva	BRA	26.12.86	2		Rio de Janeiro			28 Feb

388 LONG JUMP

Mark	Wind	Name		Nat	Born	Pos	Meet	Venue	Date	
8.14i		Daniel	Bramble	GBR	14.10.90	6	WI	Portland	20	Mar
8.14	1.9	Luis	Rivera	MEX	21.6.87	2		Phoenix	14	May
8.14	1.0	Will	Claye	USA	13.6.91	Q	NC/OT	Eugene	2	Jul
8.13	1.0	Benjamin	Gföhler	SUI	27.1.94	1		Oberteuringen	5	Jun
8.12i		Andreas	Otterling	SWE	25.5.86	1		Stockholm	17	Feb
		(50)								
8.12	0.4		Chan Ming Tai	HKG	30.1.95	1	NC	Hong Kong	7	May
8.12	2.0	Damarcus	Simpson	USA	14.7.93	8	NC/OT	Eugene	3	Jul
8.11	1.8	Sergiy	Nykyforov	UKR	6.2.94	*	NC	Lutsk	17	Jun
8.11	-0.9		Zhong Peifeng	CHN-J	3.3.97	2	NC-j	Ordos	27	Jun
8.11	1.0	KeAndre	Bates	USA	24.5.96	Q	NC/OT	Eugene	2	Jul
8.11	1.6	Radek	Juska	CZE	8.3.93	Q	EC	Amsterdam	6	Jul
8.10	1.1	Braxton	Drummond	USA	1.7.94	1		Coral Gables	9	Apr
8.09i			Zhang Yaoguang	CHN	21.6.93	3		Nanjing	3	Mar
8.08	0.2	Danylo	Martins	BRA	21.11.92	2		São Bernardo do Campo	6	Mar
8.08i		Ashton	Eaton	USA	21.1.88	1H	WI	Portland	18	Mar
		[50]								
8.08	1.0	Elvijs	Misans	LAT	8.4.89	1		Saldus	12	Jul
8.07i		Kirill	Sukharev	RUS	24.5.92	1		Moskva	10	Jan
8.07A	1.2	Henri	Väyrynen	FIN	16.10.91	1		Potchefstroom	26	Jan
8.07	0.0	Taras	Neledva	UKR	7.6.92	1		Kyiv	24	Jun
8.05	2.0	Lavon	Allen	USA	26.11.90	1		Mount Pleasant, SC	23	Apr
8.05	1.5	Ted	Hooper (Hou Yubo)	TPE	31.1.91	*		Norwalk	4	Jun
8.05	1.7	Viktor	Kuznetsov	UKR	17.7.86	3	NC	Lutsk	17	Jun
8.04	1.3	Damian	Warner	CAN	4.11.89	1		Athens, GA	30	Apr
8.04	0.5		Lin Hung-Min	TPE	7.9.90	1		Taitung	3	May
8.04	2.0	Norris	Frederick	USA	17.2.86	9	NC/OT	Eugene	3	Jul
		(60)								
8.04	0.5		Li Jinzhe	CHN	1.9.89	1	NC	Tianjin	15	Sep
8.03i		Julian	Howard	GER	3.4.89	1		Karlsruhe	6	Feb
8.03	0.7		Tang Gongchen	CHN	24.4.89	3		Beijing	18	May
8.03	0.6	Izmir	Smajlaj	ALB	29.3.93	1		Elbasan	21	May
8.03	1.4	Jean-Pierre	Bertrand	FRA	5.11.92	4		Montreuil-sous-Bois	7	Jun
8.02i		Raihau	Maiau	PYF	1.8.92	1		Nantes	4	Feb
8.02	0.6	Benjamin	Compaoré	FRA	5.8.87	1		Longueville-les-Metz	8	May
8.02A	0.0	Eusebio	Cáceres	ESP	10.9.91	3		Monachil	10	Jul
8.01	1.2	Konstantin	Borichevskiy	BLR	29.5.90	1		Minsk	1	Jun
8.01	1.8	Fabian	Heinle	GER	14.5.94	1		Madrid	23	Jun
		(70)								
8.01	1.2	Shotaro	Shiroyama	JPN	6.3.95	1		Hiratsuka	23	Jul
8.00	1.7	Nikólaos	Kapsís	GRE	5.12.91	2		Kalamáta	28	May
8.00	1.8	Tomasz	Jaszczuk	POL	9.3.92	1		Biala Podlaska	18	Jun
8.00	1.8	Ignisious	Gaisah	NED	20.6.83	2		Madrid	23	Jun
8.00	1.5	Natsuki	Yamakawa	JPN	24.7.95	1		Tokyo	3	Jul
7.99i			Li Chengbin	CHN	22.2.90	4		Nanjing	28	Feb
7.98i		Bilal	Abdullah	USA	6.10.93	1		Birmingham	16	Jan
7.98	2.0	Yeóryios	Tsákonas	GRE	22.1.88	3		Kalamáta	28	May
7.98	1.0	Lazar	Anic	SRB	14.12.91	1		Novi Sad	18	Jun
7.97i		Sadeekie	Edie	JAM	28.10.93	1	NCAA-2	Pittsburg, KS	11	Mar
		(80)								
7.97	0.1	Fyodor	Kiselkov	RUS	3.6.95	2	NC	Cheboksary	21	Jun
7.96i		Pavel	Shalin	RUS	15.3.87	2		Moskva	10	Jan
7.96i		Sergey	Polyanskiy	RUS	29.10.89	1		Slavyansk	31	Jan
7.96	0.8	Juan Miguel	Echevarría	CUB-J	11.8.98	*		La Habana	12	Feb
7.96	0.8	Christian	Taylor	USA	18.6.90	7	DL	Birmingham	5	Jun
7.96	1.0	Vladyslav	Mazur	UKR	21.11.96	2		Kyiv	24	Jun
7.96	0.4	Ja'Mari	Ward	USA-J	21.7.98	Q	WJ	Bydgoszcz	19	Jul
7.96	1.6	Daniel	Gardiner	GBR	25.6.90	1		Bedford	31	Jul
7.95A	0.6	Eero	Haapala	FIN	10.7.89	2		Potchefstroom	26	Jan
7.95	0.6	Kota	Minemura	JPN	22.12.92	1		Redlands, CA	18	Mar
		(90)								
7.95	1.9	Terrell	McClain	USA	10.11.95	1		Akron	16	Apr
7.95	1.4	Kristian	Bäck	FIN	18.7.96	1		Formia	15	May
7.95	1.9	Miháil	Mertzanídis-Despotéris	GRE	21.8.87	4		Kalamáta	28	May
7.95	1.0	Lamont Marcell	Jacobs	ITA	26.9.94	1	Med U23	Radès	4	Jun
7.95	2.0	Adrian	Strzalkowski	POL	28.3.90	1		Opole	2	Jul
7.94i		Stefano	Tremigliozzi	ITA	7.5.85	1		Ancona	24	Jan
7.94i		Dmitriy	Sorokin	RUS	27.9.92	2		Slavyansk	31	Jan
7.94	1.9	Corentin	Campener	BEL	5.10.90	*		Nivelles	21	May
7.94		Ronald	Taylor	USA	13.8.90	1		San Diego	11	Jun
7.94	2.0	Mikese	Morse	USA	30.10.87	Q	NC/OT	Eugene	3	Jul
		[100]								

LONG JUMP

Mark	Wind	Name		Nat	Born	Pos	Meet	Venue		Date	
7.94A	0.4	Daniel	Solis	ESP	5.11.96	4		Monachil		10	Jul
7.94		Dhanuka Liyana	Pathirana	SRI	25.6.93	2		Diyagama		16	Aug
7.93i		Pavel	Karavayev	RUS	27.8.88	9 Feb	7.87	1.7 Cristian Staicu	ROU	30.7.73	25 Jun
7.93i	0.4	Rogério	Bispo	BRA	16.11.85	12 Mar	7.86i	Mitchell Watt	AUS	25.3.88	20 Feb
7.93i		Rayvon	Grey	USA-J	2.12.97	12 Mar	7.86i	Jared Belardo	USA	29.12.96	27 Feb
7.93	1.6	Shin-ichiro	Shimono	JPN	10.10.90	19 Mar	7.86	1.4 Tomoya Nomura	JPN-J	18.3.97	4 May
7.93	-0.3	Stephan	Hartmann	GER	13.1.94	5 Jun	7.86	Li Zhipeng	CHN	1.5.95	15 May
7.93	0.4	Roelf	Pienaar	RSA	23.12.93	8 Jun	7.86	-0.3 Mohcine Khoua	MAR-J	26.7.98	4 Jun
7.93A	-0.8	Zarck	Visser	RSA	15.9.89	1 Jul	7.86	Lyndon Wyse	USA	2.4.86	11 Jun
7.93	0.0	Daiki	Oda	JPN	15.1.96	16 Oct	7.86	1.9 Alper Kulaksiz	TUR	6.4.92	15 Jun
7.92i		Steven	Barze	USA	1.3.96	8 Jan	7.86	1.6 Jakub Andrzejczak	POL-J	13.6.98	1 Jul
7.92A	0.6	Kristian	Pulli	FIN	2.9.94	26 Jan	7.86	0.7 Tiago da Silva	BRA	23.10.93	1 Jul
7.92i		Kumaravel	Premkumar	IND	6.2.93	21 Feb	7.85i	Eric Sloan	USA	20.6.94	23 Jan
7.92	2.0	Aleksandr	Melo	BRA	26.9.95	27 Feb	7.85i	Will Williams	USA	31.1.95	23 Jan
7.92	0.0	Ankit	Sharma	IND	20.7.92	6 May	7.85	1.4 Shem James	AUS-J	12.7.97	14 Feb
7.92	0.2	Corey	Crawford	USA	12.12.91	25 Jun	7.85	0.6 Marcos Chuva	POR	8.8.89	19 Jun
7.92	0.9	Strahinja	Jovancevic	SRB	28.2.93	25 Jun	7.85	1.3 Kendall Spencer	USA	24.7.91	19 Jun
7.92	1.6	Melvin	Echard	USA	29.8.89	10 Jul	7.85	0.6 Takahiri Nakajima	JPN	31.1.90	16 Oct
7.92	0.9	Chris	Mitrevski	AUS	12.7.96	20 Nov	7.84i	Valentin Toboc	ROU	17.3.92	31 Jan
7.91i		Aleksandr	Petrov	RUS	9.8.86	10 Jan	7.84	1.7 Masamine Momiyama	JPN	6.6.93	4 May
7.91i		Grant	Holloway	USA-J	19.11.97	30 Jan	7.84	0.0 Adam McMullen	IRL	5.7.90	14 May
7.91i		Lutalo	Boyce	CAY	11.8.91	13 Feb	7.84	-0.7 Marcel Kirstges	GER	29.5.91	5 Jun
7.91i		Maksim	Kolesnikov	RUS	28.2.91	25 Feb	7.84	-0.7 Roni Ollikainen	FIN	27.8.90	9 Jul
7.91	0.8	Luca	Wieland	GER	7.12.94	23 Apr	7.84	0.1 Ryoma Yamamoto	JPN	14.7.95	3 Sep
7.91A	1.6	Fabian	Edoki	NGR-J	30.3.98	18 May	7.83i	Aleksey Chyharevskiy	BLR	15.4.93	21 Feb
7.91	0.0	Aleksandr	Menkov	RUS	7.12.90	21 Jun	7.83	-0.4 Alberto Álvarez	MEX	8.3.91	4 Mar
7.90	1.2	Angus	Gould	AUS	8.1.94	11 Feb	7.83	1.6 Charles Brown	USA-J	28.5.97	24 Mar
7.90i		Maksim	Yunyakin	RUS	13.2.96	2 Mar	7.83A	Kiplagat Ruto	KEN	1.11.94	23 Apr
7.90A		Tera	Langat	KEN	26.12.85	15 Apr	7.83	1.3 Emmanuel Williams	USA	27.2.93	6 May
7.90	-0.2	Paulo Sérgio	Oliveira	BRA	1.6.93	7 May	7.83	0.2 Sergey Morgunov	RUS	9.2.93	4 Jun
7.90	0.3	Sobhan	Taherkhani	IRI	21.9.92	26 Jun	7.83	-1.0 Cedric Nolf	BEL	18.6.89	19 Jun
7.90	2.0	Ndiss Kaba	Badji	SEN	21.9.83	13 Jul	7.83	1.9 Ronald Brookins	USA	5.7.89	26 Jun
7.89i		Loúis	Tsátoumas	GRE	12.2.82	31 Jan	7.83	1.3 Adoreé Jackson	USA	18.9.95	3 Jul
7.89i		Julian	Harvey	USA	17.6.95	26 Feb	7.82i	Louis Rollins	USA	30.9.96	11 Mar
7.89	1.2	Salim	Sdiri	FRA	26.10.78	26 Jun	7.82	0.0 Trey McRae	USA	12.7.93	18 Mar
7.88i		Adrian	Vasile	ROU	9.4.86	21 Feb	7.82	0.4 Jiang Zhaodan	CHN	19.2.89	16 Apr
7.88	1.8	Allan	Hamilton	GBR	14.7.92	15 Apr	7.82	0.8 Joseph Oduho	USA	10.3.93	13 May
7.88	1.6	Kim Sang-su		KOR	5.6.84	1 May	7.82	Jemal Parham	USA	5.4.93	14 May
7.88		Willie	Alexander	USA	94	13 May	7.82	0.4 Serhiy Kruk	UKR	7.10.93	23 Jul
7.88	2.0	Marquise	Corbett	USA	93	26 May	7.82i	Yann Randrianasolo	FRA	3.2.94	18 Dec
7.88	-0.7	Vincent	Vogel	GER	14.1.94	5 Jun	7.81i	Cedric Dufag	FRA	22.8.96	20 Feb
7.88	1.4	Vladislav	Syaglo	RUS	27.10.95	20 Jun	7.81	Tyler Askew	USA	1.3.92	7 May
7.88	0.0	Kevin	Ojiaku	ITA	20.4.89	7 Jul	7.81	1.1 Maximilian Entholzner	GER	18.8.94	7 May
7.88	0.6	Leon	Hunt	ISV	17.5.87	10 Jul	7.81	-0.2 José Luis Despaigne	CUB	1.2.95	28 May
7.88	0.6	Ifeanyi	Otuonye	TKS	27.6.94	15 Jul	7.81	1.1 Thierno Amadou Barry	ESP-J	3.6.97	23 Jun
7.88	-1.0	Darcy	Roper	AUS-J	31.3.98	20 Jul	7.81		Hamza Lahoual	MAR	2.93	9 Jul
7.88	0.6	Shunsuke	Narisada	JPN	11.7.93	11 Aug	7.81	0.8 Jan Uder	GER	21.11.88	10 Jul
7.88	0.6	Shun-ya	Fujiwara	JPN	3.12.94	3 Sep	7.81	-1.5 Yasser Triki	ALG-J	24.3.97	20 Jul
7.87i		Andreas	Trajkovski	DEN	18.3.93	27 Feb	7.81	2.0 István Virovecz	HUN	1.12.89	30 Jul
7.87	0.0	Robert	Martey	GHA	27.12.84	5 Jun		(197) 7.80 ten men			

Wind assisted

Mark	Wind	Name		Nat	Born	Pos	Meet	Venue		Date	
8.59	2.9	Jeff	Henderson	USA	19.2.89	1	NC/OT	Eugene		3	Jul
					8.41w/2.3	8.04w	8.59w	8.34w/3.1	p	8.19	
8.48	2.8	Lamont Marcell	Jacobs	ITA	26.9.94	1	NC-23	Bressanone		10	Jun
					8.09w	x	7.04w	8.15w	x	8.48w	
8.42	5.0	Will	Claye	USA	13.6.91	3	NC/OT	Eugene		3	Jul
					x	8.09w	8.05w	8.38w/3.3	8.42w	7.93w	
8.40	2.9	Rushwal	Samaai	RSA	25.9.91	1	AfCh	Durban		23	Jun
					8.20w	8.19w	8.40w	x	p	p	
8.39	3.2		Hartfield			5	NC/OT	Eugene		3	Jul
					x	8.23w	8.34w/3.4	8.39w	8.34w/4.1	8.22w	
8.36	2.8	Greg	Rutherford	GBR	17.11.86	1		Phoenix		14	May
						see 8.24ok					
8.36	5.2	Fabrice	Lapierre	AUS	17.10.83	2	DL	Rabat		22	May
						see 8.31ok					
8.35	2.7	Jarvis	Gotch	USA	25.3.92	1		Baton Rouge		23	Apr
					x	8.35w	8.23w	p	p	p	
	8.31	4.0 1		Dakar	25 May	7.26	7.82w	8.01	x	8.17	8.31w
8.32	3.6	KeAndre	Bates	USA	24.5.96	2	NC/OT	Eugene		3	Jul
					7.95w	7.84w	8.32w	8.00	8.29w/2.6	8.19w	
8.25	2.7		Goodwin			7	NC/OT	Eugene		3	Jul
		[11 performances by 9 athletes]				7.92w	x		8.25w	x	8.17w	8.17w
8.23	2.9		Kim Duk-hyung	KOR	8.12.85	1		Mungyeong		1	May
8.18	2.2	Sergiy	Nykyforov	UKR	6.2.94	1	NC	Lutsk		17	Jun
8.15	2.9	Juan Miguel	Echevarría	CUB-J	11.8.98	1		La Habana		12	Feb

LONG JUMP

Mark	Wind	Name		Nat	Born	Pos	Meet	Venue	Date	
8.15	2.7	Ted	Hooper (Hou Yubo)	TPE	31.1.91	1		Norwalk	4	Jun
8.13	3.4	Ndiss	Kaba	SEN	21.9.83	1		La Chaux de Fonds	26	Jun
8.11	3.0	Taras	Neledva	UKR	7.6.92	2	NC	Lutsk	17	Jun
8.11	3.0	Fabian	Heinle	GER	14.5.94	Q	EC	Amsterdam	6	Jul
8.09	2.2	Ashton	Eaton	USA	21.1.88	1	MSR	Norwalk	16	Apr
8.09	2.3	Adrian	Strzalkowski	POL	28.3.90	2		Montreuil-sous-Bois	7	Jun
8.08	8.1	Roelf	Pienaar	RSA	23.12.93	1		Memphis	30	Apr
8.08	3.9	Konstantin	Borichevskiy	BLR	29.5.90	Q	EC	Amsterdam	6	Jul
8.06	3.0	Aleksandro	Melo	BRA	26.9.95	1		Maringá	27	Feb
8.05	2.6	Corentin	Campener	BEL	5.10.90	1		Nivelles	21	May
8.04	2.5	Elbert	Maxwell	USA	20.10.92	3		Phoenix	14	May
8.04	2.1	Ronald	Taylor	USA	13.8.90	1		Chula Vista	18	Jun
8.02A	2.3	Fabian	Edoki	NGR-J	30.3.98	1		El Paso	26	Mar
8.02	2.1	Shunsuke	Narisada	JPN	11.7.93	1		Osaka	11	Aug
8.00	2.3	Hiroshi	Tebira	JPN	6.8.92	1		Kitakami	7	Oct
7.99A	2.3	Eero	Haapala	FIN	10.7.89	1		Potchefstroom	15	Jan
7.99	2.7	Aaron	George	USA	2.8.95	1		San Marcos	30	Apr
7.98	4.0	Jonathan	Drack	MRI	6.11.88	1		St.Denis, Reunion	23	Apr
7.98	2.4	Kemonie	Briggs	USA	21.5.96	1		Long Beach	13	May
7.97	3.5	Marquise	Corbett	USA	93	2	NCAA-2	Bradenton, FL	26	May
7.97	4.8	Mohcine	Khoua	MAR-J	26.7.98	1		Safi	29	May
7.97	4.0	Kevin	Ojiaku	ITA	20.4.89	1		Latina	7	Jul
7.97	2.9	Stephan	Zenker	GER	18.11.91	1		Mannheim	29	Jul
7.96	2.5	Yasuhiro	Moro	JPN	21.12.94	1		Yokohama	20	May
7.96	2.6	Kristian	Bäck	FIN	18.7.96	Q	EC	Amsterdam	6	Jul

Mark	Wind	Name		Nat	Born	Date		Mark	Wind	Name		Nat	Born	Date	
7.95	4.2	Jerome	Wilson	JAM	10.9.91	6 May		7.89	4.1	Adoreé	Jackson	USA	18.9.95	26 May
7.95	2.7	Lutalo	Boyce	USA	11.8.91	7 May		7.88	2.3	Trey	McRae	USA	12.7.93	2 Apr
7.93	3.4	Corey	Crawford	USA	12.12.91	14 May		7.88	2.9	George	Fields	USA	29.12.86	16 Apr
7.92	3.7	Christopher	Ullmann	SUI	21.8.93	26 Jun		7.87	2.5	Andre	Dorsey	USA	11.3.93	8 Apr
7.91	2.1	Julian	Harvey	USA	17.6.95	26 Mar		7.86	2.9	Hibiki	Tsuha	JPN-J	21.1.98	11 Jun
7.91	3.2	Isaiah	Holmes	USA-J	18.10.98	27 May		7.86	2.3	Naoya	Yoshizawa	JPN	.95	6 Aug
7.90	5.5	Ruri	Rammokolodi	BOT	17.11.89	23 Jun		7.85	2.6	Will	Williams	USA	31.1.95	19 Mar
7.90	5.0	Yasumichi	Konishi	JPN	13.4.90	14 Aug		7.85	3.9	Basil	Fares	USA	94	7 May
								7.84	7.1	Taishi	Endo	JPN-J	3.9.97	21 Mar

Best outdoor marks

Mark	Wind	Name		Nat	Meet	Venue	Date		Mark	Wind	Name		Meet	Venue	Date
8.12	0.4	Huang Changzhou	2			Beijing	18 May		8.01	0.8	Zhang Yaoguang	2	NC Tianjin		15 Sep
8.05	0.0	Gomis	8		OG	Rio de Janeiro	13 Aug		8.00	1.4	Bramble	4	DL	Rabat	22 May
8.02	1.0	Khorava	1			Marsa/MLT	11 Jun		7.95	2.0	Shalin	2		Sochi	26 May
8.01	1.6	Eaton	*		MSR	Norwalk	16 Apr								
7.93	0.1	Polyanskiy	26				7.90 May		Kolesnikov	8	Jul		7.80	1.3 Sloan	9 Apr
7.92	0.2	Addison	26	May		7.88	0.0	Premkumar 29	Jun			7.91w 2.3 Maiau		23 Apr
7.91	0.7	Tremigliozzi	26	May		7.80	0.7	Petrov	21	Jul				

Low altitude bests

Mark	Wind	Name			Nat	Venue	Date		Mark	Wind	Name		Venue	Date
8.07	0.3	Tornéus	*	EC		Amsterdam	7 Jul		7.94	1.8	Cáceres	1	Murcia	26 Jun
	8.21w	2.1	2	EC		Amsterdam	7 Jul		7.94	0.5	Haapala	1	Jyväskylä	22 Jun
7.95	2.0	Okutu	3			Madrid	23 Jun		7.90	0.8	Visser	1 NA	Hengelo	18 Jul

Doubtful marks

Mark	Wind	Name		Nat	Born	Pos	Venue	Date
8.20	2.0	Aubrey	Smith	CAN	30.6.88	1	Miami	7 May
8.12	-1.0	Mikese	Morse	USA	30.10.87	1	Miramar, FL	15 Jun
8.06	2.0	Bavon	Sylvain	DMA	16.11.86	2	Miami	7 May
8.02	-0.7	Aubrey	Smith	JAM	30.6.88	2	Miramar, FL	15 Jun
7.88	-1.3	Innocent	Jacob	USA	11.5.92	3	Miramar, FL	15 Jun

Prosthetic Limbs: 8.24 Markus Rehm GER 22.8.88 1 Rio de Janeiro 28 Feb

JUNIORS

See main list for top 16 juniors. 11 performances (inc. 2 indoors) by 7 men to 7.92. Additional marks and further juniors:

Mark	Wind	Name		Nat	Born	Pos	Meet	Venue	Date
Shi Yuhao		8.02	1					Suzhou	1 May
Massó		8.00 -1.8	1	WJ				Bydgoszcz	20 Jul
Zhong Peifeng		8.01i	4					Nanjing	3 Mar
						7.92	1.0 1	Zhengzhou	13 May
Echeverría		7.93 1.3	1	NC				La Habana	19 Mar
7.93i		Rayvon	Grey	USA	2.12.97	1		New York	12 Mar
7.91i		Grant	Holloway	USA	19.11.97	1		Blacksburg	30 Jan
7.91A	1.6	Fabian	Edoki	NGR	30.3.98	1	JUCO	Levelland	18 May
7.88	-1.0	Darcy	Roper (10)	AUS	31.3.98	3	WJ	Bydgoszcz	20 Jul
7.86	1.4	Tomoya	Nomura	JPN	18.3.97	1		Hiratsuka	4 May
7.86	-0.3	Mohcine	Khoua	MAR	26.7.98	2	Med U23	Radès	4 Jun
7.86	1.6	Jakub	Andrzejczak	POL	13.6.98	1	NC-j	Suwalki	1 Jul
7.85	1.4	Shem	James	AUS	12.7.97	1		Brisbane	14 Feb
7.83	1.6	Charles	Brown	USA	28.5.97	1		Lubbock	24 Mar
7.81	1.1	Thierno Amadou	Barry	ESP	3.6.97	4		Madrid	23 Jun
7.81	-1.5	Yasser	Triki	ALG	24.3.97	4	WJ	Bydgoszcz	20 Jul
7.80	1.2	Yugant	Shekhar Singh	IND-	2.10.97	2		Bengaluru	10 Jul

LONG JUMP – TRIPLE JUMP

Mark	Wind		Name	Nat	Born	Pos	Meet	Venue	Date
7.78i		Gabriele	Chilà	ITA	17.9.97	1	v2N	Padova	27 Feb
7.76	2.0	Kazuma	Adachi (20)	JPN	16.10.97	1		Wakayama	31 Jul
7.76	1.4	Taishi	Endo	JPN	3.9.97	1		Kyoto	3 Jul
7.76	-2.2	Grant	Holloway (best out)	USA	19.11.97	1		Newport News	4 Jun

Wind assisted see main lists for top 3 juniors

Tentoglou	7.98	2.4 1	Grevená		25 May				
7.91	3.2	Isaiah	Holmes	USA	18.10.98	1		Elk Grove	27 May
7.86	2.9	Hibiki	Tsuha	JPN	21.1.98	2		Hiratsuka	11 Jun
7.84	7.1	Taishi	Endo	JPN	3.9.97	1		Nara	21 Mar
7.79	3.3	Shown-D	Thompson	JAM	20.1.97	1	NC-j	Kingston	19 Jun
7.78	2.4	Héctor	Santos	ESP	6.1.98	5		Madrid	23 Jun

Mark	Wind			Name	Nat	Born	Pos	Meet	Venue				Date
17.86	-0.6		Christian	Taylor	USA	18.6.90	1	OG	Rio de Janeiro				16 Aug
						17.86	17.77/-0.8 x	17.77/0.5 x	x				
17.80	0.1	1	WK	Zürich	1 Sep	16.69	17.34/-0.4 x	17.17/0.0	17.80	17.26/0.0			
17.78	0.6	1	DL	London (OS)	22 Jul	17.18	x	x	17.43/0.3 x	17.78			
17.76	0.8	1	Pre	Eugene	28 May	17.09	16.96	17.46/1.2 p	17.38/1.3	17.76			
17.59	-0.6	1	DL	Stockholm	16 Jun	16.70	17.24/-0.3	17.06	p	17.27/-0.4	17.59		
17.39	-0.8	2	NC/OT	Eugene	9 Jul	16.72	16.90	17.37/1.0	17.02	x	17.39		
17.24	0.2	Q	OG	Rio de Janeiro	15 Aug	17.24							
17.23	0.3	1	DL	Doha	6 May	16.63	17.08	17.19/1.4 x	17.23	p			
17.76	0.4		Will	Claye	USA	13.6.91	2	OG	Rio de Janeiro				16 Aug
						17.76	x	x	17.61/0.4 x	17.55/0.4			
	17.65	2.0 1	NC/OT	Eugene	9 Jul	17.06	17.26w/2.1	17.31w/3.3	17.09	17.65	p		
	17.56	0.8 2	Pre	Eugene	28 May	16.93w	x	17.26w/2.1	17.40/0.3	17.24/1.9	17.56		
	17.40	1.5 *		Eugene	29 Jul	16.83	17.40	17.33w/2.3	17.52w	17.10	p		
17.58	-0.2			Dong Bin	CHN	22.11.88	3	OG	Rio de Janeiro				16 Aug
						17.58	x	x	p	p	p		
	17.41i	1		Nanjing	29 Feb	16.61	17.41	p	p	p	p		
	17.33i	1	WI	Portland	19 Mar	17.18	16.20	17.29	16.98	17.33	p		
	17.25i	1		Nanjing	4 Mar	17.25	p	p	p	p	p		
	17.24	0.5 1		Beijing	18 May	x	17.24	p	p	p	p		
17.30	0.8		Renjith	Maheswary	IND	30.1.86	1		Bengaluru				11 Jul
						16.55	16.75	16.93	17.30	x	p		
17.21	-0.9		Chris	Benard	USA	4.4.90	3	NC/OT	Eugene				9 Jul
						16.93w	17.12/-1.8	17.18/0.4	16.26	17.21	17.12/-1.4		
	17.19	1.6 1		Chula Vista	28 May	x	x	16.72w	17.12/1.6	17.19	17.09		
17.20	0.5		Max	Hess	GER	13.7.96	1	EC	Amsterdam				9 Jul
						x	17.20	p	p	x	x		
	17.14i	2	WI	Portland	19 Mar	16.25	16.37	x	17.14	x	17.14		
17.18	1.7		Troy	Doris	GUY	12.4.89	1		Clermont				14 May
						x	x	15.86	17.18	p	p		
17.18	0.7		Chris	Carter	USA	11.3.89	3		Eugene				29 Jul
						16.39	17.18	16.75w	16.48	16.87w	16.96w		
17.16	0.1		Karol	Hoffmann	POL	1.6.89	2	EC	Amsterdam				9 Jul
						16.59w	16.96	17.16	x	16.93	16.92		
17.16	1.8		Omar	Craddock (10)	USA	26.4.91	4	NC/OT	Eugene				9 Jul
						16.97w	16.93	16.73	16.73	17.16	16.31		
	17.15	1.2 3	Pre	Eugene	28 May	17.13/1.4	16.93	16.73	17.00	p	17.15		
17.15			Lyukman	Adams	RUS	24.9.88	1		Yerino				12 Jun
						17.15	x	16.78	x	x	x		
17.15	1.8		Teddy	Tamgho	FRA	15.6.89	1	NC	Angers				25 Jun
						14.89	x	16.75	16.46	17.15	p		
	1.0		Tosin	Oke	NGR	1.10.80	1	AfCh	Durban				25 Jun
						16.64	17.13	p	p	15.11	15.67		
17.13	-0.2			Cao Shuo	CHN	8.10.91	4	OG	Rio de Janeiro				16 Aug
	(31/14)					16.78	x	16.89	x	17.13	15.27		
17.09i			Benjamin	Compaoré	FRA	5.8.87	3	WI	Portland				19 Mar
17.09	0.0		Jhon Fredy	Murillo	COL	13.7.84	5	OG	Rio de Janeiro				16 Aug
17.08	1.2		Harold	Corréa	FRA	26.6.88	1		Villeneuve d'Ascq				22 May
17.06	-1.1		Lázaro	Martínez	CUB-J	3.11.97	1	WJ	Bydgoszcz				21 Jul
17.05i			Dmitriy	Sorokin	RUS	27.9.92	1		Sankt Peterburg				7 Feb
17.03i			Eric	Sloan	USA	20.6.94	1		Fayetteville				13 Feb
	(20)												
17.03	0.1		Nelson	Évora	POR	20.4.84	6	OG	Rio de Janeiro				16 Aug
17.02	1.1		Aleksey	Fyodorov	RUS	25.5.91	1		Smolensk				3 Jun
17.02	1.6		Donald	Scott	USA	23.2.92	1		Leonora, GUY				18 Jun
16.99i			Alexis	Copello	ex-CUB	12.8.85	1		Karlsruhe				6 Feb
16.99	1.9		Alberto	Álvarez	MEX	8.3.91	1	MSR	Norwalk				16 Apr

TRIPLE JUMP

Mark	Wind	Name		Nat	Born	Pos	Meet	Venue	Date	
16.99	0.4	Muhammad	Halim	ISV	26.10.86	1		Baltimore	23	Apr
16.97	1.4	Latario	Collie-Minns	BAH	10.3.94	1	NCAA	Eugene	10	Jun
16.97	0.2		Zhu Yaming	CHN	4.5.94	1	NC	Tianjin	17	Sep
16.93	-0.3	Fabrizio	Donato	ITA	14.8.76	2		Rovereto	6	Sep
16.92	2.0	Fabian	Florant	NED	1.2.83	1		Clermont	30	Apr
(30)										
16.92	0.3	Cristian Atanay	Nápoles	CUB-J	27.11.98	1		La Habana	17	Jun
16.92	1.5	Matthew	O'Neal	USA	10.6.94	*	NC/OT	Eugene	9	Jul
16.91	0.0	Ernesto	Revé	CUB	26.2.92	2		La Habana	17	Jun
16.90	2.0	Artyom	Bondarenko	BLR	19.6.91	1	NC	Grodno	25	Jun
16.90	1.9	Dmitriy	Plotnitskiy	BLR	26.8.88	2	NC	Grodno	25	Jun
16.90	1.9	Clive	Pullen	JAM	18.10.94	1	NC	Kingston	30	Jun
16.89A	-0.3	Pablo	Torrijos	ESP	12.5.92	1		Monachil	2	Jul
16.88	0.2	Daigo	Hasegawa	JPN	27.2.90	1	Oda	Hiroshima	29	Apr
16.87i		Roman	Valiyev	KAZ	27.3.84	1	NC	Ust-Kamenogorsk	31	Jan
16.87A ?0.9		Lasha	Torgvaidze	GEO	26.5.93	1		Almaty	24	May
16.62i			Torgvaidze			1		Tbilisi	24	Jan
(40)										
16.86	0.1	Vladimir	Letnicov	MDA	7.10.81	1		Brest	10	Jun
16.85i		Dmitriy	Chizhikov	RUS	6.12.93	2		Sankt Peterburg	7	Feb
16.85	-1.1	Kohei	Yamashita	JPN	6.9.94	1		Yokohama	22	May
16.85	0.3	Seref	Osmanoglu	TUR	2.1.89	1		Mersin	24	May
16.85A	0.9	Levon	Aghasyan	ARM	19.1.95	1	NC	Artashat	29	May
16.85	1.9	Maksim	Nesterenko	BLR	1.9.92	3	NC	Grodno	25	Jun
16.83	1.0	Nazim	Babayev	AZE-J	8.10.97	1	NC	Baku	4	Jun
16.82i		Marian	Oprea	ROU	6.6.82	1	NC	Bucuresti	20	Feb
16.82i		Fabrizio	Schembri	ITA	27.1.81	1	NC	Ancona	5	Mar
16.81	1.4	Momchil	Karailiev	BUL	21.5.82	1	Veniz	Haniá	4	Jun
[50]										
16.81	1.2	Fabrice	Zango	BUR	25.6.93	2	AfCh	Durban	25	Jun
16.80	0.7	Andy	Díaz	CUB	25.12.95	4		La Habana	13	Feb
16.78A	0.8	Roger	Haitengi	NAM	12.9.83	1		Johannesburg	13	Feb
16.78	0.7	Josh	Honeycutt	USA	7.3.89	1		Phoenix, AZ	11	Jun
16.77	1.4	Kazuyoshi	Ishikawa	JPN	6.11.82	2	Oda	Hiroshima	29	Apr
16.77	1.7	Dimítrios	Tsiámis	GRE	12.1.82	1		Kalamáta	28	May
16.77	1.6	Elvijs	Misans	LAT	8.4.89	1		Riga	3	Jun
16.77	1.7	Khotso	Mokoena	RSA	6.3.85	3	AfCh	Durban	25	Jun
16.76	0.5	Julian	Reid	GBR	23.9.88	3	EC	Amsterdam	9	Jul
16.75	-0.3	Jean Marc	Pontvianne	FRA	6.8.94	1		Pierre-Bénite	10	Jun
[60]										
16.74	0.0	Louhab	Kafia	ALG	24.2.87	1		Alger	24	Jun
16.73		Sergey	Laptev	RUS	7.2.91	3		Yerino	12	Jun
16.71i		Liu	Ruihai	CHN	23.12.96	2		Nanjing	29	Feb
16.71	2.0	Zlatozar	Atanasov	BUL	12.12.89	3		Sofia	15	Jun
16.70	1.2	Louis-Grégory	Occin	FRA	2.6.89	1		Blois	8	Jun
16.70	0.2	Olu	Olamigoke	NGR	19.9.90	5	NC	Sapele	8	Jul
16.69	0.5	Fu	Haitao	CHN	1.11.93	2	NC	Tianjin	17	Sep
16.68i		Jeremiah	Green	USA	9.2.94	2		Fayetteville	13	Feb
16.68	1.1	Ryoma	Yamamoto	JPN	14.7.95	2		Yokohama	22	May
16.68	0.7	Adrian	Swiderski	POL	26.9.86	1		Biala Podlaska	28	May
[70]										
16.67i		Jonathan	Drack	MRI	6.11.88	2		Karlsruhe	6	Feb
16.67	-0.4	Jean	Rosa	BRA	1.2.90	1		São Bernardo do Campo	6	Mar
16.67	1.6	Georgi	Tsonov	BUL	2.5.93	*	NC	Sofia	15	Jun
16.65	0.0		Xu Xiaolong	CHN	20.12.92	Q	OG	Rio de Janeiro	15	Aug
16.64	0.6	Samyr	Laine	HAI	17.7.84	6	DL	Doha	6 May-13
16.64	0.0	Dimítrios	Baltadoúros	GRE	1.10.89	1	NC	Pátra	18	Jun
16.63	1.7	Leevan	Sands	BAH	16.8.81	3		Nassau	16	Apr
16.63		Mateus Daniel	de Sá	BRA	21.11.95	1		São Bernardo do Campo	23	Apr
16.63	1.6	Askin	Karaca	TUR	20.10.90	1		Antalya	11	May
16.63	1.0	KeAndre	Bates	USA	24.5.96	Q	NC/OT	Eugene	7	Jul
[80]										
16.62i		Simone	Forte	ITA	20.1.96	3	NC	Ancona	5	Mar
16.60	0.1	Andriy	Stanchev	UKR	10.7.93	1		Lutsk	19	Jun
16.60	0.0		Wu Ruiting	CHN	29.11.95	2		Marseille	13	Sep
16.59i		Rumen	Dimitrov	BUL	19.9.86	1		Bratislava	31	Jan
16.59	1.8	Alwyn	Jones	AUS	28.2.85	1		Perth	12	Mar
16.58	0.2	Nathan	Douglas	GBR	4.12.82	1	NC	Birmingham	25	Jun
16.58	0.5	Shawn	Johnson	USA	11.1.94	8	NC/OT	Eugene	9	Jul
16.58	1.8	Fyodor	Kiselkov	RUS	3.6.95	1	NC-23	Saransk	17	Jul

TRIPLE JUMP

Mark	Wind	Name		Nat	Born	Pos	Meet	Venue	Date
16.57	-0.6	Tim	White-Edwards	USA	15.7.94	4	NCAA	Eugene	10 Jun
16.57	1.8	Malkit	Singh	IND	5.10.88	1	NC	Lucknow	30 Sep
[90]									
16.55i		Yevgeniy	Ektov	KAZ	1.9.86	2	NC	Ust-Kamenogorsk	31 Jan
16.55A		Betwell	Langat	KEN	20.11.96	1		Nairobi	7 May
16.55	0.8	Martin	Jasper	GER	6.1.89	2		Kassel	18 Jun
16.55	-0.2	Pavlo	Beznits	UKR-J	17.6.97	2	NC	Lutsk	19 Jun
16.54	-0.3	Leslie	Caesa	CUB-J	14.1.97	*		La Habana	13 Feb
16.54		Aleksandr	Yurchenko	RUS	30.7.92	2		Smolensk	2 Jul
16.53	1.0	Aleksandro	Melo	BRA	26.9.95	1		São Bernardo do Campo	5 Jun
16.53	1.7	Kevin	Luron	FRA	8.11.91	2		Blois	8 Jun
16.53	0.5	Jonathan	Gardner	USA	10.12.91	1		Miramar, FL	12 Jun
16.52	-1.2	Paulo Sérgio	Oliveira	BRA	1.6.93	2		São Bernardo do Campo	23 Apr
(100)									
16.50	0.0	Osviel	Hernández	CUB	31.5.89	13 Feb			
16.48	-0.6	José Emilio	Bellido	ESP	25.5.87	4 Jun			
16.48	?	Mikhail	Lopin	RUS	8.5.91	11 Jun			
16.47	-0.8	Álvaro	Cortéz	CHI	27.10.95	10 Apr			
16.47	0.0	Melvin	Raffin	FRA-J	9.8.98	5 Jun			
16.47	2.0	Marcel	Kornhardt	GER	3.8.93	18 Jun			
16.47	-0.9	Ronald	Woodley	USA	31.5.90	25 Jun			
16.46	0.9	Kim Dong-hyun		KOR	5.6.89	4 Jun			
16.46	-0.7	Ilya	Potaptsev	RUS	19.4.93	22 Jun			
16.46	-0.3	Daniele	Cavazzani	ITA	4.12.92	26 Jun			
16.46	0.3	Lu Zhiwei		CHN	4.4.96	17 Sep			
16.45A	0.2	Yoann	Rapinier	FRA	29.9.89	30 Apr			
16.45	0.4	Mamadou Cherif Dia		MLI	13.3.85	15 Aug			
16.45	0.1	Kim Duk-hyung		KOR	8.12.85	12 Oct			
16.44i		Alexandru	Baciu	ROU	25.2.91	13 Feb			
16.44	1.7	Nathan	Fox	GBR	21.10.90	30 Apr			
16.44	0.8	Tom	Ya'acobov	ISR	30.6.92	26 Jun			
16.44	1.1	Daniele	Greco	ITA	1.3.89	5 Jul			
16.44	1.1	Felix	Obi	USA	16.5.94	8 Jul			
16.43A	1.9	Menzi	Mthembu	RSA	7.2.95	2 Apr			
16.42	0.0	Damon	McLean	JAM	21.11.90	18 Jun			
16.41	1.4	Preston	Woodard	USA	27.9.91	2 Apr			
16.41	1.3	Brandon	Roulhac	USA	13.12.83	16 Apr			
16.41	1.7	Ben	Williams	GBR	25.1.92	15 May			
16.40	0.0	José Ernesto Martínez		CUB	1.1.91	17 Jun			
16.40	0.9	Ruslan	Kurbanov	UZB	10.2.93	19 Jun			
16.40	-0.4	Hiroshi	Abe	JPN	20.6.92	25 Sep			
16.39	-1.9	O'Brien	Wasome	JAM-J	24.1.97	18 Mar			
16.38	2.0	Liu Mingxuan		CHN-J	16.5.97	28 Jun			
16.38	1.8	Denis	Obertsyhev	RUS-J	16.2.97	28 Jun			
16.37i		Yuriy	Kovalyov	RUS	18.6.91	7 Feb			
16.37	-0.2	Raúl	Spank	GER	13.7.88	18 Jun			
16.36i		Fang Yaoqing		CHN	20.4.96	29 Feb			

16.36	1.7	Marquis	Dendy	USA	17.11.92	22 Apr
16.36	1.6	Jadel	Gregório	BRA	16.9.80	23 Apr
16.35A	1.1	Maximiliano	Díaz	ARG	15.11.88	13 Feb
16.35	-0.5	Michal	Lewandowski	POL	28.8.88	24 Jun
16.35	0.8	Charles	Brown	USA-J	28.5.97	25 Jun
16.35	-1.0	Jefferson	Sabino	BRA	4.11.82	3 Jul
16.34i		Martin	Lamou	FRA-Y	13.5.99	27 Feb
16.34i		Ilya	Glazunov	RUS	20.4.94	3 Mar
16.34	1.9	Ja'Mari	Ward	USA-J	21.3.98	28 Apr
16.33	0.0	Tetteh	Anang	AUS	5.4.93	2 Apr
16.33	0.0	Jonathan	Reid	JAM	9.5.92	16 Apr
16.33	0.2	Julio César	Carbonell	CUB-Y	16.5.99	17 Jun
16.33	-0.1	Tomás	Veszelka	SVK	9.7.95	10 Sep
16.32A		Elijah	Kimitei	KEN	25.12.86	27 May
16.31i		Nate	Moore	USA	28.5.96	12 Mar
16.31	0.2		Liu Yan	CHN	18.1.94	17 Apr
16.31	0.1	Mamadou	Guèye	SEN	1.4.86	16 Jul
16.30i		Sergio	Solanas	ESP	28.4.87	16 Jan
16.30	-0.2	Izmir	Smajlaj	ALB	29.3.93	7 Jun
16.30	1.2	Yevgeniy	Chettykbayev	KAZ	29.3.85	25 Jun
16.30	-0.7	I.D.S. Sanjaya	Jayasinghe	SRI	20.4.82	24 Sep
16.29i		Viktor	Yastrebov	UKR	13.1.82	9 Jan
16.29		Muhammad Hakimilsmail		MAS	8.4.91	28 May
16.29	0.3	Mark Harry	Diones	PHI	3.1.93	5 Nov
16.28i		Alphonso	Jordan	USA	1.11.87	29 Jan
16.28	0.6	Miguel	van Assen	SUR-J	30.7.97	18 Mar
16.27	2.0	Brian	Leap	USA	17.8.92	16 Apr
16.27	0.5	John	Warren	USA	2.3.96	28 May
16.26	1.2	Tony	Carodine	USA	18.6.94	7 Jul
16.26	1.9	K.V.Rakesh	Babu	IND	20.3.90	11 Jul
16.26		Marouane	Aissaoui	MAR	12.8.96	16 Jul
16.25	0.9	Yordanys	Durañona	DMA	16.6.88	5 Jun
16.25	-0.3	Philipp	Kronsteiner	AUT-J	25.4.97	21 Jul
(166)						

Wind assisted

Mark	Wind	Name		Nat	Born	Pos	Meet	Venue	Date
17.52	2.2		Claye			1		Eugene	29 Jul
		see 17.40 ok							
17.42	3.1	Omar	Craddock	USA	26.4.91	2		Eugene	29 Jul
		16.73 17.42w 17.11/1.7 16.78 17.29w/2.3 16.58							
17.15	3.8	Leslie	Caesa	CUB-J	14.1.97	1		La Habana	13 Feb
		15.70w x 16.54 17.15w x x							
17.11	2.2	Harold	Corréa	FRA	26.6.88	1		Montgeron	15 May
17.01	3.0	Matthew	O'Neal	USA	10.6.94	1Q	NCAA-E	Jacksonville	28 May
16.96	3.1	Julian	Reid	GBR	23.9.88	1		Bedford	28 May
16.93	2.8	Melvin	Raffin	FRA-J	9.8.98	1	NC-j	Châteauroux	2 Jul
16.89	2.2	Kevin	Luron	FRA	8.11.91	3	NC	Angers	25 Jun
16.88	2.9	Osviel	Hernández	CUB	31.5.89	2		La Habana	13 Feb
16.85	3.9	Shawn	Johnson	USA	11.1.94	Q	NC/OT	Eugene	7 Jul
16.84	2.3	Hugues	Zango	BUR	25.6.93	2		Forbach	29 May
16.81	2.1	Josh	Honeycutt	USA	7.3.89	1		Phoenix	14 May
16.73	3.2	KeAndre	Bates	USA	24.5.96	2	NCAA	Eugene	10 Jun
16.73	2.2	Georgi	Tsonov	BUL	2.5.93	2	NC	Sofia	15 Jun
16.61	4.0	Jordan	Scott	JAM-J	29.6.97	1	NC-j	Kingston	19 Jun
16.57	2.3	Kim Duk-hyung		KOR	8.12.85	1		Asan	12 Oct
16.55	2.2	José Ernesto	Martínez	CUB	1.1.91	5		La Habana	13 Feb
16.54	2.3	Brandon	Roulhac	USA	13.12.83	2		Clermont	14 May
16.46	3.1	Damon	McLean	JAM	21.11.90	30 Jun			
16.46	4.1	Martin	Lamou	FRA-Y	13.5.99	2 Jul			
16.46	4.3	Dávid	László	HUN	25.2.92	31 Jul			
16.42	2.5	Jadel	Gregório	BRA	16.9.80	19 Jun			
16.42	3.1	Wilbert	Walker	JAM	7.1.85	30 Jun			
16.39	3.2	Liu Mingxuan		CHN-J	16.5.97	28 Jun			

16.37	4.4	Brian	Leap	USA	17.8.92	28 May
16.36	4.5	Eric	England	USA	15.6.94	29 Apr
16.31w	2.8	Maksim	Lustin	RUS	19.9.94	17 Jul
16.31w	2.4	Igor	Syunin	EST	4.12.90	2 Aug
16.28w	3.1	Nonso	Okolo	NGR	7.12.90	28 May
16.28w	2.4	Phillip	Young	USA	9.10.92	11 Jun

TRIPLE JUMP – SHOT

Mark	Wind	Name		Nat	Born	Pos	Meet	Venue	Date
Best outdoor marks									
16.98	0.5	Copello	3 DL Doha		6 May	1.5	Compaoré 1	Sidi Sopot	28 Jul
16.80	1.1	Valiyev	1 Almaty		25 Jun	1.8	Drack 1	Réduit	2 Apr
16.78	-0.1	Chizhikov	2 Sochi		27 May				
16.49	-0.1	Sorokin	27 May 16.37	0.5	Liu Ruihai	14 May	16.25	1.0 Green	14 May
16.46	1.0	Dimitrov	29 May 16.27	1.9	Glazunov	17 Jul			
Low altitude bests						16.49	0.2	Aghasyan 1 Balk C Pitesti	26 Jun
16.71	1.6	Torrijos	1 Salamanca		4 Jun	16.48	1.9	Haitengi 2 Réduit	2 Apr
Beach event – downhill: 16.63 Nguyen Van Hung VIE 4.3.89 1 Danang 28 Sep									
Doubtful marks									
16.87	1.2	Ruslan	Kurbanov	UZB	10.2.93	1	NC	Andijan	8 Jul
16.54	1.8	Rex	Parker	USA	8.3.90	1		Lisle	25 Jun

JUNIORS

See main list for top 5 juniors (and 3 wa). 14 performances by 3 men to 16.60. Additional marks and further juniors:

	Mark	Wind		Name	Venue						
Martínez	16.90	0.7	3		La Habana	17 Jun	16.61	0.0	1	NC	La Habana	20 May
	16.71		1		La Habana	14 May	16.61	-0.7	1		Remire Montjoly	4 Jun
	16.68	-0.5	8	OG	Rio de Janeiro	16 Aug	16.61	0.0	Q	OG	Rio de Janeiro	16 Aug
	16.64	0.1	1		Barr	La Habana	29 May	16.60		1	La Habana	24 Dec
Nápoles	16.62	-0.6	2	WJ	Bydgoszcz	21 Jul	16.60	0.0	2	Barr	La Habana	29 May
Babayev	16.79A	0.4	1	NC	Erzurum	12 Jun						
16.47	0.0	Melvin		Raffin	FRA	9.8.98	1	Med U23	Radès		5 Jun
16.39	-1.9	O'Brien		Wasome	JAM	24.1.97	1		Kingston		18 Mar
16.38	2.0			Liu Mingxuan	CHN	16.5.97	*	NC-j	Ordos		28 Jun
16.38	1.8	Denis		Obertsyhev	RUS	16.2.97	1	NC-j	Kazan		28 Jun
16.35	0.8	Charles		Brown (10)	USA	28.5.97	1	NC-j	Clovis		25 Jun
16.34i		Martin		Lamou	FRA-Y	13.5.99	2	3-N	Padova		27 Feb
16.34	1.9	Ja'Mari		Ward	USA	21.3.98	1		Belleville, IL		28 Apr
16.33	0.2	Julio César		Carbonell	CUB-Y	16.5.99	6		La Habana		17 Jun
16.28	0.6	Miguel		van Assen	SUR	30.7.97	1		Tampa		18 Mar
16.25	-0.3	Philipp		Kronsteiner	AUT	25.4.97	4	WJ	Bydgoszcz		21 Jul
16.22	0.7	Christoph		Garritsen	GER	15.4.97	5	NC	Kassel		18 Jun
16.19	-0.2			Sung Jin-syuk	KOR	2.1.97	1	AsiJ	Ho Chi Minh		6 Jun
16.16	1.2	Musuki		Harada	JPN	4.2.97	2		Hiratsuka		10 Jun
16.14	0.0	Oleksandr		Malosilov	UKR	6.6.97	3	NC	Lutsk		19 Jun
16.12	1.8	Armani		Wallace (20)	USA	11.2.97	2	ACC	Tallahassee		15 May
16.15	1.3	Martin		Lamou (best out)	FRA-Y	13.5.99	*		Chateauroux		2 Jul
Wind assisted											
Nápoles	16.82	4.1	3		La Habana	13 Feb	16.65	w	1	La Habana	27 Feb
16.46	4.1	Martin		Lamou	FRA-Y	13.5.99			Chateauroux		2 Jul
16.39	3.2			Liu Mingxuan	CHN	16.5.97	1	NC-j	Ordos		28 Jun

SHOT

Mark				Name			Nat	Born	Pos	Meet	Venue	Date
22.52			Ryan		Crouser		USA	18.12.92	1	OG	Rio de Janeiro	18 Aug
				21.15	22.22	22.26	21.93	22.52	21.74			
	22.28	1		Hanz	Zagreb	5 Sep	19.91	20.70	20.73	21.95	22.28	21.67
	22.11	1	NC/OT	Eugene		1 Jul	20.42	22.11	21.43	21.47	X	21.07
	22.00	2	WK	Zürich		1 Sep	21.45	20.70	21.92	22.00	x	21.66
	21.99	2	DL	Saint-Denis		27 Aug	21.28	21.33	21.99	X	X	21.14
	21.85	1		Chula Vista		18 Jun	21.76	21.52	21.62	x	21.01	21.85
	21.73i	1	Big 12	Ames		27 Feb	19.62	20.72	21.00	21.29	21.13	21.73
	21.59	Q	OG	Rio de Janeiro		18 Aug	21.59					
	21.34	1		Austin		16 Apr	x	19.98	p	20.60	21.34	x
22.21			Tom		Walsh		NZL	1.3.92	2		Hanz Zagreb	5 Sep
				20.85	x		21.56	21.87	22.21	21.11		
	22.20	1	WK	Zürich		1 Sep	21.45	20.70	21.92	22.20	x	21.66
	22.00	1	DL	Saint-Denis		27 Aug	21.14	21.81	x	21.12	20.93	22.00
	21.78i	1	WI	Portland		18 Mar	20.38	21.60	21.40	21.64	21.49	21.78
	21.54	2	DL	London (OS)		23 Jul	20.64	21.54	20.89	21.38	21.01	20.83
	21.53	1		Athens, GA		6 Aug	21.40	21.53	x	20.45	21.26	21.09
	21.48	1	Skol	Warszawa		28 Aug	20.92	x	x	x	x	21.48
	21.36	3	OG	Rio de Janeiro		18 Aug	20.54	21.20	x	20.75	21.36	21.25
22.13			Joe		Kovacs		USA	28.6.89	1	Pre	Eugene	27 May
				20.41	20.49	21.26	21.57	21.66	22.13			
	22.04	1	DL	London (OS)		23 Jul	19.65	21.31	20.93	21.17	22.04	x
	22.01	1	Bisl	Oslo		9 Jun	20.18	20.73	20.69	20.45	21.51	22.01
	21.95	2	NC/OT	Eugene		1 Jul	20.69	21.03	20.88	21.09	20.93	21.95
	21.78	2	OG	Rio de Janeiro		18 Aug	21.78	x		21.52	x	21.35
	21.47	1		La Jolla		23 Apr	20.74	20.21	21.11	21.47	21.06	p
21.76			Stephen		Mozia		NGR	16.8.93	1		Ustí nad Labem	19 Jul
				19.15	21.27	x	21.76	x	x			

SHOT

Mark	Wind	Name		Nat	Born	Pos	Meet	Venue	Date	
21.63		Darrell	Hill	USA	17.8.93	3	NC/OT	Eugene	1	Jul
		20.93	21.63		19.46	20.47	20.08	x		
	21.44	3 Hanz	Zagreb	5 Sep	19.86	21.44	20.60	20.65	x	0.69
21.57i		Kurt	Roberts	USA	20.2.88	1		Boston (R)	14	Feb
		21.15	20.28		21.30	20.90	x	21.57		
	21.40	1 DL	Shanghai	14 May	20.53	20.12	19.95	x	20.31	21.40
21.39		David	Storl	GER	27.7.90	3	DL	London (OS)	23	Jul
		20.56	21.02		21.00	21.39	21.19	21.04		
21.35i		Michael	Haratyk	POL	10.4.92	1		Lodz	5	Feb
		(30/8)			20.80	x	20.75	20.81	21.10	21.35
21.33i		Tim	Nedow	CAN	16.10.90	1		Stockholm	17	Feb
21.30i		Tomás	Stanek (10)	CZE	13.6.91	1		Jablonec	5	Mar
21.21		Damien	Birkinhead	AUS	8.4.93	1		Hobart	13	Feb
21.20		Franck	Elemba	CGO	21.7.90	4	OG	Rio de Janeiro	18	Aug
21.14		Konrad	Bukowiecki	POL-J	17.3.97	2	Bisl	Oslo	9	Jun
21.11		Jordan	Clarke	USA	10.7.90	1		Tucson	21	May
21.08		Tomasz	Majewski	POL	30.8.81	2	Skol	Warszawa	28	Aug
21.06		Ryan	Whiting	USA	24.11.86	3		Chula Vista	18	Jun
21.06		Andrei	Gag	ROU	7.4.91	1	NC	Cluj Napoca	17	Jul
21.03		Aleksandr	Lesnoy	RUS	28.7.88	1		Sochi	27	May
21.02i		Reese	Hoffa	USA	8.10.77	2		Boston (R)	14	Feb
21.02		Darlan	Romani	BRA	9.4.91	5	OG	Rio de Janeiro	18	Aug
		(20)								
20.96		Asmir	Kolasinac	SRB	15.10.84	1		Senta	7	May
20.96		Maksim	Afonin	RUS	6.1.92	1	NC	Cheboksary	21	Jun
20.88i		Konstantin	Lyadusov	RUS	2.3.88	1	NC	Moskva	24	Feb
20.87i		Filip	Mihaljevic	CRO	31.7.94	3	WI	Portland	18	Mar
20.83		Jacko	Gill	NZL	20.12.94	1		Christchurch	8	Feb
20.82i		Jonathan	Jones	USA	23.4.91	1		State College	30	Jan
20.82i		Jordan	Geist	USA-J	21.7.98	1		Greensburg	22	Dec
20.82		O'Dayne	Richards	JAM	14.12.88	1	NC	Kingston	3	Jul
20.80		Ivan	Emilianov	MDA	19.2.77	1		Onesti	14	May
20.79		Garrett	Appier	USA	15.10.92	1		Joplin, MO	29	Apr
		(30)								
20.74		Kemal	Mesic	BIH	4.8.85	1		Radford, VA	30	Apr
20.72		Borja	Vivas	ESP	26.5.84	1		Málaga	22	Jan
20.70i		Pavel	Lyzhin	BLR	24.3.81	1		Mogilev	22	Jan
20.70		Stipe	Zunic	CRO	13.12.90	1		Split	1	Jul
20.67		Soslan	Tsirikhov	RUS	24.11.84	2		Sochi	27	May
20.62		Georgi	Ivanov	BUL	13.3.85	1	Balk C	Pitesti	25	Jun
20.61		Nicholas	Skarvélis	GRE	2.2.93	2		La Jolla	23	Apr
20.59		Tsanko	Arnaudov	POR	14.3.92	3	EC	Amsterdam	10	Jul
20.58		Mesud	Pezer	BIH	27.8.94	2		Irvine	30	Apr
20.57		Hamza	Alic	BIH	20.1.79	1		Zenica	1	Jun
		(40)								
20.56i		Tobias	Dahm	GER	23.5.87	1		Sassnitz	14	Feb
20.54		Andrei	Toader	ROU-J	26.5.97	1	ROU IC	Pitesti	4	Jun
20.53i		Maksim	Sidorov	RUS	13.5.86	1		Moskva	14	Feb
20.51		Jacob	Thormaehlen	USA	13.2.90	1		San Marcos	30	Apr
20.50i		Carlos	Tobalina	ESP	2.8.85	1	NC	Madrid	5	Mar
20.48		Adam	Nelson	USA	7.7.75	2		Athens, GA	30	Apr
20.40		Cory	Martin	USA	22.5.85	1		Carbondale	22	Jun
20.37i		Rafal	Kownatke	POL	24.3.85	1	NC	Torun	6	Mar
20.37		Chukwuebuka	Enekwechi	USA	28.1.93	1		Bloomington	23	Apr
20.37		David	Pless	USA	19.11.90	Q	NC/OT	Eugene	1	Jul
		[50]								
20.33		Darien	Moore	USA	10.6.91	1		Rathdrum, ID	4	Jun
20.32		Mohamed	Hamza	EGY	30.8.96	1	NC	El Maadi	13	Apr
20.30		Arttu	Kangas	FIN	13.7.93	1		Raasepori	12	Jun
20.29i		Germán	Lauro	ARG	2.4.84	4		Madrid	26	Feb
20.28		Mitchell	Pope	USA	21.1.84	1		Boone, NC	7	May
20.21		Braheme	Days	USA	18.1.95	3		La Jolla	23	Apr
20.21		JC	Murasky	USA	6.2.93	1	Big 10	Lincoln	15	May
20.19		Mustafa Amr	Ahmed Hassan	EGY	16.12.95	3	NCAA	Eugene	8	Jun
20.19		Ladislav	Prásil	CZE	17.5.90	2	NC	Tábor	17	Jun
20.18i		Mikhail	Abramchuk	BLR	15.11.92	1		Minsk	28	Jan
		(60)								
20.18		Bobby	Grace	USA	10.10.90	1		Berea, OH	23	Apr
20.18		Mateusz	Mikos	POL	10.4.87	2	PNG	Turku	29	Jun
20.14		Bob	Bertemes	LUX	24.5.93	1		Zweibrücken	5	Jun
20.11		Curtis	Jensen	USA	1.11.90	1		Naperville	5	Jun

MEN 2016

SHOT

Mark	Name		Nat	Born	Pos	Meet	Venue	Date	
20.11	Josh	Awotunde	NGR	12.6.95	1		Princeton	18	Jun
20.06i	Ashinia	Miller	JAM	6.6.93	1	SEC	Fayetteville	27	Feb
20.06	Richard	Garrett	USA	21.12.90	5		Rathdrum	4	Jun
20.06i	Josh	Freeman	USA	22.8.94	1		Carbondale	10	Dec
20.05	Orazio	Cremona	RSA	1.7.89	1		Pretoria	8	Mar
20.01	Nedzad	Mulabegovic	CRO	4.2.81	3		Slovenska Bistrica	28	May
(70)									
20.00i	Leif	Arrhenius	SWE	15.7.86	1		Ogden	29	Jan
20.00	Jaco	Engelbrecht	RSA	8.3.87	1	AfCh	Durban	22	Jun
19.97	Roger	Steen	USA	17.5.92	1		Rock Island	19	May
19.96i	Rob	Golabek	USA	27.4.89	1		Boone, NC	19	Feb
19.94	Aleksey	Kulayev	RUS	7.5.94	5		Sochi	27	May
19.93	Tejinder Pal	Singh	IND	13.11.94	1	Fed Cup	New Delhi	28	Apr
19.93	Marco	Fortes	POR	26.9.82	3		Lisboa (I)	12	Jun
19.90	Paul	Davis	USA	11.9.90	1		Abilene	4	Jun
19.87i	Nick	Vena	USA	16.4.93	1		Princeton	11	Dec
19.86	Miháíl	Stamatóyiannis ¶	GRE	20.5.82	1		Pátra	13	Jul
(80)									
19.85	Martin	Stasek	CZE	8.4.89	1		Olomouc	8	May
19.85	Inderjeet	Singh	IND	19.4.88	1		Bengaluru	10	Jul
19.82	Raigo	Toompuu	EST	17.7.81	1		Clarksville	16	Apr
19.81	Sultan	Al-Hebshi	KSA	23.2.83	5		La Jolla	23	Apr
19.78	Sebastiano	Bianchetti	ITA	20.1.96	3	ECp-w	Arad	13	Mar
19.78	Kristo	Galeta	EST	9.4.83	1		Tallinn	30	May
19.75	Aleksey	Nichipor	BLR	10.4.93	3	NC	Grodno	24	Jun
19.74	Jan	Marcell	CZE	4.6.85	1		Kladno	23	Jul
19.72	Christian	Cantwell	USA	30.9.80	8	KansR	Lawrence	22	Apr
19.68		Liu Yang	CHN	29.10.86	1	NC	Tianjin	14	Sep
(90)									
19.67	Michal	Rozporski	POL	20.12.88	1		Lillestrøm	28	May
19.65	Derrick	Vicars	USA	8.5.89	1		Bedford	25	Jun
19.63	Ivan	Ivanov	KAZ	3.1.92	2		Almaty	24	May
19.59	Scott	Lincoln	GBR	7.5.93	1		Oordegem	28	May
19.59	Martin	Novák	CZE	5.10.92	6	Odlozil	Praha	6	Jun
19.59	Om Prakash	Singh	IND	11.1.87	2		Bengaluru	11	Jul
19.58	Francisco	Belo	POR	27.3.91	2		Lisboa (AL)	15	May
19.57	Oghenakpobo	Efekoro	NGR	15.7.96	4	AfCh	Durban	22	Jun
19.56i	Aleksandr	Bulanov	RUS	26.12.89	4		Moskva	14	Feb
19.56	Matt	DeChant	USA	31.5.89	2		Ashland, OH	30	Apr
(100)									
19.55	Patrick	Cronie	NED	5.11.89	28 May	19.23	Kevin	Farley	USA	18.7.93	22 Jun
19.55	Tomas	Djurovic	MNE	14.2.94	1 Oct	19.19i	Robert	Dippl	GER	21.10.83	24 Jan
19.54	Luke	Johnson	USA	10.7.92	15 May	19.19	Ayomidotun	Ogundeji	USA	24.2.96	28 May
19.54	Meshari	Suroor Saad	KUW	2.7.87	30 Sep	19.18	Dillon	Simon	DMA	5.3.92	28 May
19.53	Denzel	Comenentia	NED	25.11.95	13 May	19.17	Grant	Cartwright	USA	19.11.94	15 May
19.52	Luke	Pinkelman	USA	5.5.88	23 Apr	19.16	Brett	Neelly	USA	22.11.96	8 Jun
19.52	Gaëtan	Bucki	FRA	9.5.80	14 May	19.15	Niklas	Arrhenius	SWE	10.9.82	27 Aug
19.48	Frédéric	Dagée	FRA	11.12.92	29 May	19.13	Stephen	Sáenz	MEX	23.8.90	30 Apr
19.47	Dennis	Lewke	GER	23.7.93	31 May	19.11	Isaiah	Simmons	USA	3.12.92	30 Apr
19.47	Kole	Weldon	USA	25.3.92	11 Jun	19.11	Aldo	González	BOL	5.9.84	11 Jun
19.47i	Willie	Morrison	USA	23.11.96	9 Dec	19.10	Timothy	Hendry-Gallagher	CAN	3.2.90	29 May
19.44	Coy	Blair	USA	10.6.94	11 Jun	19.10i	Maksim	Zakharenko	BLR	15.10.91	29 Dec
19.43i	Nick	Ponzio	USA	5.1.95	16 Jan	19.09i	Ali	Samari	IRI	7.1.93	22 Jan
19.42i	Sergey	Dementyev	UZB	1.6.90	11 Feb	19.09	Christian	Jagusch	GER	13.7.92	21 May
19.42	Jonathan	Kalnas	USA	18.4.80	3 Jun	19.08i		Wu Jiaxing	CHN	29.3.90	3 Mar
19.40	Anton	Tikhomirov	RUS	29.4.88	27 May	19.08		Chang Ming-Huang	TPE	7.8.82	30 Apr
19.40	Jacek	Wisniewski	POL	29.1.91	28 May	19.07i	Nick	Baatz	USA	4.1.90	20 Feb
19.39	Eldred	Henry	IVB	9.5.94	28 May	19.06		Han Zibin	CHN	5.4.87	7 Apr
19.38	Daniel	Ståhl	SWE	27.8.92	27 Aug	19.05	Kord	Ferguson	USA	19.6.95	13 May
19.36	Justin	Baker	USA	7.7.89	6 May	19.04	Amin Atia	Al-Aradi	KSA	13.5.86	25 Jun
19.36	Hayden	Baillio	USA	22.7.91	17 Jun	19.03i	Devon	Patterson	USA	27.4.96	13 May
19.35i	Daniele	Secci	ITA	9.3.92	6 Mar	19.03	Joshua	Uikilifi	TGA/USA	11.9.90	27 Feb
19.35	Colt	Feltes	USA	8.4.93	9 Apr	19.03		Jung Il-woo	KOR	28.3.86	21 Apr
19.32	Mario	Cota	MEX	11.9.90	18 Jun	19.02	Riley	Budde	USA	31.5.95	6 May
19.31	Andrzej	Regin	POL	21.2.94	28 May	19.01	Alex	Renner	USA	.94	16 Apr
19.31	Artyom	Podolskiy	RUS	21.7.93	21 Jun	19.01	Willian	Dourado	BRA	6.1.94	5 Jun
19.30	Péter	Simon	HUN	18.9.94	1 May	19.00	Dawid	Krzyzan	POL	20.4.94	28 May
19.30	Jakub	Szyszkowski	POL	21.8.91	21 May	18.97i	Bodo	Göder	GER	27.6.93	23 Jan
19.29i		Tian Zhizhong	CHN	15.12.92	28 Jan	18.97	Fedrick	Dacres	JAM	28.2.94	20 Feb
19.29	Odinn Björn	Thorsteinsson	ISL	3.12.81	21 May	18.96	Osman Can	Özdevici	TUR	23.8.95	14 Feb
19.28i	Jan Josef	Jeuschede	GER	23.4.93	27 Feb	18.94	Aaron	Castle	USA	7.10.93	28 May
19.25i	Nicolai	Ceban	MDA	4.2.95	13 Feb	18.94		Guo Yanxiang	CHN	29.1.87	20 Jun
19.25	Patrick	Müller	GER	4.2.96	4 Jun	18.94i	Richard	Chavez	USA	30.7.92	3 Dec
19.23	Hüseyin	Atici	TUR	3.5.86	30 Apr	18.92	Jasdeep	Singh	IND	6.10.90	25 Aug

SHOT

Mark	Name		Nat	Born		Pos	Meet	Venue		Date
18.90	Tom	Anderson	USA	26.7.93				15 Apr		
18.89	Gian Piero	Ragonesi	ITA	19.4.95				14 May		
18.88		Ding Weiye	CHN	13.4.90				20 Jun		
18.84	Simon	Bayer	GER	23.11.95				23 Jul		
18.84	Timo	Kööpikkä	FIN	10.5.94				20 Aug		
18.82	Ryan	Cribbin	USA	5.5.95				18 Mar		
18.81		Wang Guangfu	CHN	15.11.87				17 Apr		
18.80i	Nick	Demaline	USA	1.3.96				6 Feb		
18.80	Maris	Urtans	LAT	9.2.81				3 Jun		
18.80	Viktor	Samolyuk	UKR	5.9.86				4 Jun		
18.79i	David	Noguera	ESP	11.3.93				19 Feb		
18.79	Matt	Katnik	USA	10.10.96				19 Mar		
18.79	Kyle	Felpel	USA	26.7.93				28 May		
18.78	Jagroop	Singh	IND	7.1.85				7 Sep		
18.77i	Chase	Sammons	USA	9.12.92				30 Jan		
18.77i	Yegor	Klimanov	RUS	2.11.89				24 Feb		
18.77	Armin	Sinancevic	SRB	14.8.96				24 Sep		
18.76i	Mohamed	Eskandari	IRI					22 Jan		
18.76	Sarunas				Banevicius	LTU		20.11.91		13 May
18.76	Frank				Catelli	USA		93		15 May
18.75	Valeriy				Kokuyev	RUS		22.7.88		20 Jun
18.73i	Marko				Spiler	SLO		8.1.90		27 Feb
18.73	Ahmed				Hassan	EGY		28.7.94		21 May
18.72	Benik				Abramyan	GEO		31.7.85		18 Aug
18.71	Valdivino				Nunes	BRA		9.1.95		19 Jun
18.70	Michael				King	USA		93		23 Apr
18.70	Hendrik				Müller	GER		28.8.90		7 May
18.70	Valentin				Döbler	GER		21.11.96		27 Jul
18.68	Pavel				Derkach	RUS		2.11.93		13 May
18.67i	Derek				Sievers	USA		18.10.92		26 Feb
18.67	Rashad				Williams	PUR		13.3.90		8 Apr
18.66i	Zack				Stetler	USA		28.11.91		13 Feb
	(200									

Drugs disqualification

| 18.97i | Rimantas | | | | Martisauskas | LTU | | 18.9.86 | | 6 Feb |

Best outdoor marks

21.26	Stanek	1		Thum			2 Sep
21.23	Haratyk	1		Kielce			8 May
20.88	Nedow	1		Irvine			29 Apr
20.83	Hoffa	3		Tucson			21 May
20.71	Mihaljevic	1	NCAA	Eugene			8 Jun
20.62	Lyadusov	2	NC	Cheboksary			21 Jun
20.42	Dahm	Q	EC	Amsterdam			9 Jul
20.36	Jones	Q	NC/OT	Eugene			1 Jul
20.16	Tobalina	Q	EC	Amsterdam			9 Jul
19.42	Ponzio	23 Apr	19.24	Bulanov	28 Jul	18.87	Tian Zhizhong	20 Jun
19.33	Secci	17 May	19.08	Samari	1 Aug	18.80	Wu Jiaxing	14 May
19.27	Morrison	28 May	19.01	Baatz	30 Apr	18.68	Eskandari	10 Jul

20.13	Abramchuk	1		Brest		20 May
20.10	Lauro	2	Sidlo	Sopot		28 Jul
20.02	Miller	3Q	NCAA-E	Jacksonville		28 May
20.00	Arrhenius	1		Bottnaryd		18 Jun
19.95	Sidorov	3	NCp	Zhukovskiy		21 Jul
19.92	Freeman	1		Columbia, MO		16 May
19.91	Lyzhin	1	NC	Grodno		24 Jun
19.72	Kownatke	2		Warszawa		28 May
19.71	Vena	4		Athens, GA		30 Apr
18.97	Göder	11 Jul				
18.90	Chavez	2 Apr				
18.89	Dementyev	9 Jul				

Doubtful marks

| 20.54dm | Benik | | Abramyan | GEO | 31.7.85 | 1 | | Almaty | 24 May |
| 20.51i | Ivan | | Ivanov | KAZ | 3.1.92 | 1 | NC | Ust-Kamenogorsk | 30 Jan |

JUNIORS

21.14	Konrad			Bukowiecki	POL	17.3.97	2	Bisl	Oslo		9 Jun
	21.02	1	Kuso	Szzcecin		18 Jun	20.62	1		Werfer Halle	21 May
	21.01	1	GS	Ostrava		20 May	20.61i	2		Madrid	26 Feb
	20.83	1	EAF	Bydgoszcz		5 Jun	20.58i	2		Pedros Lódz	5 Feb
	20.82	3	Skol	Warszawa		28 Aug	20.58	4	EC	Amsterdam	9 Jul
	20.71	Q	OG	Rio de Janeiro		18 Aug	20.53i	4	WI	Portland	18 Mar
	20.65	1	EC	Amsterdam		9 Jul	20.51	2	ISTAF	Berlin	3 Sep
	16 performances by 3 men over 20.50										
20.82i	Jordan			Geist	USA	21.7.98	1		Greensburg		22 Dec
20.54 dq?	Andrei			Toader	ROU-J	26.5.97	1	ROU IC	Pitesti		4 Jun
18.43	Vashon			McCarthy	JAM	4.6.97	1		Mona		2 Apr
18.30	Andrew			Liskowitz	USA	22.5.97	1		Adrian		16 Apr
18.27	Nathan			Bultman	USA	6.4.97	4		Eugene		9 Apr
18.26	Marcus			Thomsen	NOR	7.1.98	1		København		10 Sep
18.18	Wictor			Petersson	SWE	1.5.98	4	NC	Sollentuna		27 Aug
18.01i	Sterling			Mungro	USA	4.6.97	1	JUCO	Winston-Salem		4 Mar
17.90i	Merten			Howe	GER	7.1.97	5		Sassnitz		14 Feb

6 KG SHOT

23.34	Konrad			Bukowiecki	POL	17.3.97	1	WJ	Bydgoszcz		19 Jul
	22.94	1		Bojanowo		1 May	22.29	1	NC-j	Suwalki	3 Jul
	22.61	1		Bialystok		1 Jun	21.73	Q	WJ	Bydgoszcz	19 Jul
	22.61	1		Cetniewo		12 Jul	21.59	1	NC-j	Suwalki	3 Jul
	22.48i	1		Torun		8 Jan	21.21i	1	NC-j	Spala	14 Feb
22.30 dq?	Andrei			Toader	ROU	26.5.97	2	WJ	Bydgoszcz		19 Jul
	21.67i	1		Bucuresti		9 Jan	21.47	1		Nicosia	23 May
21.27	Bronson			Osborn	USA	5.7.98	3	WJ	Bydgoszcz		19 Jul
	13 performances by 2 men to 21.20										
20.65	Wictor			Petersson	SWE	1.5.98	4	WJ	Bydgoszcz		19 Jul
20.62	Adrian			Piperi	USA	20.1.99	5	WJ	Bydgoszcz		19 Jul
20.40	Szymon			Mazur	POL	2.9.98	6	WJ	Bydgoszcz		19 Jul
20.30i	Marcus			Thomsen	NOR	7.1.98	1	NC-j	Steinkjer		28 Feb
	20.23						1		Göteborg		2 Jul
20.17i	Merten			Howe	GER	7.1.97	1	NC-j	Wattenscheid		20 Feb
	19.90						2	Werfer	Halle		21 May
19.97	Warren			Barrett	JAM	9.9.97	1		St. George;s		28 Mar
19.88	Cedric			Trinemeier (10)	GER	21.11.97	1		Rochlitz		31 Jan
	19.81						1		Neubrandenburg		28 May

MEN 2016

SHOT

Mark	Name		Nat	Born	Pos	Meet	Venue	Date
19.77	Burger	Lambrechts	RSA	6.8.98	1	NC-j	Germiston	2 Apr
19.76	Tobias	Köhler	GER	23.8.98	7	WJ	Bydgoszcz	19 Jul
19.61	Isaiah	Rogers	USA	28.4.98	1		Marietta	8 May
19.61	Demyan	Seskin	RUS	4.8.97	1	NC-j	Kazan	26 Jun
19.59	Jordan	Geist	USA	21.7.98	3	NC-j	Clovis	25 Jun
19.58	Andrew	Liskowitz	USA	22.5.97	4	NC-j	Clovis	25 Jun
19.53	Clemens	Prüfer	GER	13.8.97	2		Osterode	31 May
19.50	Jason	van Rooyen	RSA	4.2.97	1		Lusaka	17 Jun
19.48	Nathan	Bultman	USA	6.4.97	5	NC-j	Clovis	25 Jun
19.46i	Marius	Musteata (20)	ROU	11.1.97			Bacau	5 Feb

12 lb (5.44kg) Shot

Mark	Name		Nat	Born	Pos	Meet	Venue	Date
22.67	Jordan	Geist	USA	21.7.98	1		Rathdrum	4 Jun
22.38	Adrian	Piperi	USA-Y	20.1.99	1	N.Sch	Greensboro	19 Jun

DISCUS

Mark			Name		Nat	Born	Pos	Meet	Venue		Date
68.72			Daniel	Ståhl	SWE	27.8.92	1	NC	Sollentuna		28 Aug
						x	65.09	x	63.83	x	68.72
	66.92	2	Gyulai	Székesfehérvár	18 Jul	63.13	66.28	65.27	x	66.92	66.34
	66.74	1		Salinas	17 Apr	64.50e-	63e		66.74	x	65e	66e
68.37			Christoph	Harting	GER	4.10.90	1	OG	Rio de Janeiro		13 Aug
						62.38	66.34	x	x	64.77	68.37
	68.06	1		Dessau	27 May	65.08	66.55	x	65.14	65.51	68.06
68.15			Piotr	Malachowski	POL	7.6.83	1		Warszawa		28 May
						x	63.88	68.15	65.51		
	68.10	1	NC	Bydgoszcz	26 Jun	64.89	64.94-	63.24	x	68.10	65.67
	68.03	1	DL	Doha	6 May	61.31	64.40	62.90	65.81	65.33	68.03
	67.55	2	OG	Rio de Janeiro	13 Aug	67.32	67.06	67.55	x	65.51-	65.38
	67.50	1	DL	Birmingham	5 Jun	62.33	62.83	65.08	66.91	x	67.50
	67.45	1		Rabat	22 May	63.24	63.72	65.91	66.88	x	67.45
	67.16	1		Cetniewo	12 Jul	65.08	65.24	63.83	x	67.16	66.81
	67.06	1	EC	Amsterdam	9 Jul	62.73	65.96	66.15	67.06	65.68	64.97
	66.93	1		Stalowa Wola	8 May	66.93	x	x	64.41	x	64.45
68.04			Robert	Harting	GER	18.10.84	1	NC	Kassel		19 Jun
						63.53	x	62.26	65.15	65.60	68.04
	66.95	1		Schönebeck	29 Jul	66.87	x	x	x	x	66.95
68.02			Fedrick	Dacres	JAM	28.2.94	1		La Jolla		23 Apr
						64.85	65.77	63.42	67.87	65.86	68.02
67.60			Martin	Wierig	GER	10.6.87	1		Wiesbaden		15 May
						67.60	65.50	63.46	x	65.11	x
67.45			Sam	Mattis	USA	19.3.94	1		Philadelphia		19 Mar
						67.45	63.28	x	x	66.51	67.21
67.26			Philip	Milanov	BEL	6.7.91	2	DL	Doha		6 May
						63.73	61.61	65.47	62.37	67.26	x
	67.07	1		Lokoren	3 Jul	58.55	63.99	67.07	64.28	x	62.52
	66.88	1		Herentals	1 May	x	65.99	66.88	x	65.33	x
67.16			Daniel	Jasinski	GER	5.8.89	2		Wiesbaden		15 May
						65.08	61.78	62.46	67.16	64.20	62.61
	67.05	3	OG	Rio de Janeiro	13 Aug	65.77	x	66.08	64.83	63.31	67.05
67.13			Zoltán	Kövágó (10)	HUN	10.4.79	1	Gyulai	Székesfehérvár		18 Jul
						64.23	67.13	x	x- x	x	
66.96			Lois Maikel	Martínez	ESP	3.6.81	1		Castellón		30 Jun
						58.75	66.96	x	x	x	58.81
	66.89	1		Málaga	2 Jun	61.67	63.54	66.89	x	p	64.50
66.78			Markus	Münch	GER	13.6.86	1		Schönebeck		3 Jun
						64.14	63.36	66.78	x	x	62.17
66.72			Mason	Finley	USA	7.10.90	Q	NC/OT	Eugene		7 Jul
						54.75	66.72	p			
66.61			Martin	Kupper	EST	31.5.89	1		Tallinn		18 Jun
		(30/14)				62.38	62.63	63.05	66.61		
66.23			Mykyta	Nesterenko	UKR	15.4.91	1		Kyiv		25 Jun
66.03			Axel	Härstedt	SWE	28.2.87	1		Helsingborg		11 Jul
66.02A			Niklas	Arrhenius	SWE	10.9.82	1		Provo		19 Jul
66.00			Rodney	Brown	USA	21.5.93	1	MSR	Norwalk		16 May
66.00			Lukas	Weißhaidinger	AUT	20.2.92	1	ISTAF	Berlin		3 Sep
65.84			Mauricio	Ortega	COL	4.8.94	1		Jablonec		1 Jun
		(20)									
65.82			Tavis	Bailey	USA	6.1.92	1		Salinas		29 May
65.74			Alex	Rose	SAM	7.11.91	1		Claremont		15 May
65.69			Apostolos	Parellis	CYP	24.7.85	1		Iráklio		28 May
65.67			Jason	Young	USA	27.5.81	1		Lubbock		6 May

DISCUS

Mark	Name		Nat	Born	Pos	Meet	Venue	Date	
65.56	Robert	Urbanek	POL	29.4.87	2	Kuso	Szczecin	18	Jun
65.52	Sultan Mubarak	Al-Dawoodi	KSA	16.6.77	1		Biala Podlaska	18	Jun
65.41	Andrew	Evans	USA	25.1.91	2		Chula Vista	21	Apr
65.37	Matthew	Denny	AUS	2.6.96	1		Salinas	28	May
65.34	Oleksiy	Semenov	UKR	27.6.82	1	NC	Tiraspol	28	May
65.32	Frank	Casañas	ESP	18.10.78	2		Castellón	30	Jun
	(30)								
65.30	Jorge	Fernández	CUB	2.10.87	1		Las Tunas	20	Feb
65.27	Gerd	Kanter	EST	6.5.79	3	EC	Amsterdam	9	Jul
65.20	Sven Martin	Skagestad	NOR	13.1.95	1-u23		Wiesbaden	15	May
65.18	Andrius	Gudzius	LTU	14.2.91	Q	OG	Rio de Janeiro	12	Aug
65.17	Viktor	Butenko	RUS	10.3.93	1		Yerino	12	Jun
65.03	Alin Alexandru	Firfirica	ROU	3.11.95	1		Leiria	23	Jul
65.00	Mahmoud	Samimi	IRI	18.9.88	1		Szombathely	16	Apr
64.97	Hannes	Kirchler	ITA	22.12.78	1		Tarquinia	15	Jun
64.89	János	Huszák	HUN	5.2.92	1		Szentes	16	Apr
64.64	Bartlomiej	Stój	POL	15.5.96	2	NC	Bydgoszcz	26	Jun
	(40)								
64.49	Nathaniel	Moses	USA	1.4.90	2		Salinas	28	May
64.46	Nikolay	Sedyuk	RUS	29.4.88	1	NC-w	Adler	20	Feb
64.45	Chad	Wright	JAM	25.3.91	3		Salinas	28	May
64.24A	Russel	Tucker	RSA	4.11.90	1		Pretoria	29	Feb
64.24	Erik	Cadée	NED	15.2.84	1		Heerhugowaard	1	Jul
64.15	Péter	Savanyú	HUN	26.6.87	1		Szekszárd	22	Jun
64.04	Victor	Hogan #	RSA	25.7.89	1		Cape Town	22	Mar
63.92	Jared	Schuurmans	USA	20.8.87	2		Claremont	15	May
63.85	Danijel	Furtula	MNE	31.7.92	1		Split	6	Mar
63.85	Rutger	Smith	NED	9.7.81	Q	EC	Amsterdam	7	Jul
	[50]								
63.81	Mohammed	Samimi	IRI	29.3.87	1		Zalaegerszeg	23	Apr
63.63	Lance	Brooks	USA	1.1.84	2		Lubbock	7	May
63.61	Ehsan	Hadadi	IRI	21.1.85	4		Cetniewo	12	Jul
63.51	David	Wrobel	GER	13.2.91	5	NC	Kassel	19	Jun
63.47	Russ	Winger	USA	2.8.84	2		Salinas	29	May
63.42	Traves	Smikle	JAM	7.5.92	2	PennR	Philadelphia	30	Apr
63.38	Nick	Percy	GBR	5.12.94	1		Helsingborg	22	Jul
63.35	Mario	Cota	MEX	11.9.90	1		Chula Vista	18	Jun
63.23	Brian	Williams	USA	18.12.94	1		Mt. Vernon, IA	9	Apr
63.18	Tomás	Vonavka	CZE	4.6.90	1		Kolin	12	Jun
	(60)								
63.15	Roman	Ryzhyy	UKR	17.1.85	2		Kyiv	25	Jun
63.14	Róbert	Szikszai	HUN	30.9.94	1		Veszprém	12	Jun
63.11	Jason	Morgan	JAM	6.10.82	1		Ruston	19	Mar
63.10	Simon	Pettersson	SWE	3.1.94	1	NC-23	Hässleholm	7	Aug
63.08	Brett	Morse	GBR	11.2.89	4		Chula Vista	21	Apr
62.87	Ronald	Julião	BRA	16.6.85	2		Chula Vista	7	May
62.71	Phillip	Jagers	USA	12.8.95	1Q	NCAA-E	Jacksonville	27	May
62.64	Roland	Varga	CRO	22.10.77	1		Abbeville	14	May
62.59	Aleksas	Abromavicius	LTU	6.12.84	1	NC-w	Palanga	30	Apr
62.56	Mitch	Cooper	AUS	2.6.95	1	KansR	Lawrence	23	Apr
	(70)								
62.55	Sergiu	Ursu ¶	ROU	26.4.80	2		Nicosia	14	May
62.50	Macklin	Tudor	USA	13.6.94	3		La Jolla	22	Apr
62.50A	Leif	Arrhenius	SWE	15.7.86	1		Orem, UT	11	Jun
62.48	Kole	Weldon	USA	25.3.92	4		Salinas	29	May
62.47	Domantas	Poska	LTU	10.1.96	1	NC	Palanga	18	Jun
62.43	Filip	Mihaljevic	CRO	31.7.94	1	ACC	Tallahassee	15	May
62.28	Zane	Duquemin	GBR	23.9.91	2		Helsingborg	11	Jul
62.23	Aleksey	Khudyakov	RUS	31.3.95	2		Adler	12	Feb
62.20	Stephen	Mozia	NGR	16.8.93	1	TexR	Austin	1	Apr
62.20	Benn	Harradine	AUS	14.10.82	3	SWE Ch	Sollentuna	28	Aug
	(80)								
62.12	Jason	Harrell	USA	10.1.91	2		Chula Vista	26	Jun
62.11	Jan-Louw	Kotze	RSA	18.3.94	1	FlaR	Gainesville	2	Apr
62.01	Martin	Markovic	CRO	13.1.96	1		Varazdin	11	Jun
61.97	Gerhard	de Beer	RSA	5.7.94	3		Tucson	21	May
61.95	Lolassonn	Djouhan	FRA	18.5.91	1		Salon-de-Provence	8	Jun
61.92	Mike	Torie	USA	12.3.86	1		Claremont	27	Feb
61.91	Matthew	Kosecki	USA	1.7.91	2		Lubbock	25	Jun
61.85	Gudni Valur	Gudnason	ISL	11.10.95	3		Heerhugowaard	1	Jul
61.68	Jan	Marcell	CZE	4.6.85	1		Brno	13	Jul

400 DISCUS

Mark	Name		Nat	Born	Pos Meet	Venue	Date
61.64	Reggie (90)	Jagers	USA	13.8.94	1	Ashland	16 Jun
61.62	Clemens	Prüfer	GER-J	13.8.97	2-u23	Wiesbaden	15 May
61.58	Pyry	Niskala	FIN	6.11.90	1	Laihia	7 Sep
61.57	Bryan	Powlen	USA	3.12.87	4	Tucson	21 May
61.53	Eligijus	Ruskys	LTU	1.12.90	1	Vilnius	9 May
61.53	Märt	Israel	EST	23.9.83	6	Halle	21 May
61.52	Jeff	Milliron	USA	18.1.92	1	Philadelphia	25 Jun
61.51	Mario	Pestano	ESP	8.4.78	2	Leiria	22 Jun
61.49	Ahmed Mohamed	Dheeb	QAT	29.9.85	1	Heilbronn	26 Jun
61.38	Marek	Bárta	CZE	8.12.92	2	Charlottesville, VA	22 Apr
61.36	Ola Stunes [100]	Isene	NOR	29.1.95	3	Helsingborg	11 Jun
61.33	James	Plummer	USA	19.8.90	30 Apr
61.21	Gleb	Sidorchenko	RUS	15.5.86	12 May
61.19	Nazzareno	Di Marco	ITA	30.4.85	15 Jun
61.18	Sebastian	Scheffel	GER	17.11.93	3 Jun
61.09	Luke	Bryant	USA	5.12.88	12 Jun
61.02	Aleksandr	Kirya	RUS	23.3.92	23 Jun
60.96	Federico	Apolloni	ITA	14.3.87	15 Jun
60.90	Chase	Madison	USA	13.9.85	19 Mar
60.89	Henning	Prüfer	GER	7.3.96	19 Jun
60.83	Hayden	Reed	USA	4.4.94	2 Apr
60.81	Aleksandr	Dobrenshkiy	RUS	11.3.94	23 Jun
60.80	Ercüment	Olgundeniz	TUR	7.7.76	27 Feb
60.75	David	Lucas	USA	6.6.96	18 Jun
60.71	Reno	Tuufuli	USA	15.2.96	2 Apr
60.69	Brian	Trainor	USA	14.3.80	6 May
60.67	Carl	Myerscough	GBR	21.10.79	15 May
60.58	Giovanni	Faloci	ITA	13.10.85	30 Apr
60.56	Josh	Syrotchen	USA	19.4.94	2 Apr
60.53	Sergey	Roganov	BLR	17.4.86	12 Mar
60.48	Behnam	Shiri	IRI	21.3.93	11 Jun
60.47	András	Seres	HUN	31.1.89	14 May
60.40	Joe	Williams	USA	21.8.94	2 Apr
60.37	Carter	Comito	USA	26.10.90	10 May
60.35	Ivan	Panasyuk	UKR	8.10.91	25 May
60.32	Pedro José	Cuesta	ESP	22.8.83	27 Feb
60.32	Benedikt	Stienen	GER	12.1.92	24 Jul
60.27	Julian	Wruck	AUS	6.7.91	19 Nov
60.26	Michael	Salzer	GER	25.10.91	15 May
60.23	Yevgeniy	Labutov	KAZ	17.11.84	25 May
60.18	Vladimir	Tocari	MDA	16.1.84	7 Feb
60.13	Kord	Ferguson	USA	19.6.95	2 Apr
60.12	Wojciech	Praczyk	POL	10.1.93	8 May
60.00	Yuji	Tsutsumi	JPN	22.12.89	26 Jun
59.89	Yeóryios	Trémos	GRE	21.3.89	19 Jun
59.80	Jacob	Armbrust	USA	22.2.94	18 Jun
59.76	Kirpal	Singh Bath	IND	16.5.92	11 Jul
59.75	Dewald	van Heerden	RSA	4.4.91	15 Apr
59.74	Magomed	Magomedov	RUS	26.7.91	20 Feb
59.71	Damian	Kaminski	POL	15.12.93	8 May
59.69	Stéphane	Marthély	FRA	9.9.79	15 May
59.65	Quincy	Wilson	TTO	3.4.91	9 Jul
59.61	Przemyslaw	Czajkowski	POL	26.10.88	1 Jun
59.53	Virgilijus	Alekna	LTU	13.2.72	21 Apr
59.53	Daniel	Haugh	USA	3.5.95	14 May
59.47	Michael	Ohakwe	USA	0.92	21 May

Mark	Name		Nat	Date
59.45	Cody	Snyder	USA	27.4.92 22 Mar
59.43	Gerhard	Mayer	AUT	20.5.80 5 Jul
59.32	Ryan	Crouser	USA	18.12.92 1 Apr
59.29	Muhd Irfan	Shamsuddin	MAS	16.8.95 11 Jun
59.29	János	Káplar	HUN	8.2.94 21 Jun
59.27	Jaromír	Mazgal	CZE	20.1.93 17 Sep
59.26	Petr	Vuklisevic	CZE	25.2.82 30 Jun
59.25	Frantz	Kruger	FIN	22.5.75 3 Sep
59.24	Marshall	Hall	NZL	7.10.88 17 Apr
59.22	Gregory	Thompson	GBR	5.5.94 10 Jul
59.16	Andreas	Christou	CYP	14.4.93 18 Jun
59.15	Maksim	Gigashvili	RUS	22.4.92 30 May
59.14	Arjun Kumar	Singh	IND	1.7.93 26 Aug
59.14		Wu Jian	CHN	25.5.86 14 Sep
59.08	Colin	Quirke	IRL	17.6.90 15 May
59.03	Justin	Ramirez	USA	3.11.93 12 Jun
59.01	Casey	Malone	USA	6.4.77 18 Jun
59.00	Cole	Walderzak	USA	93 2 Apr
58.99	Mike	Guidry	USA	29.10.79 6 May
58.99	Vikas	Gowda	IND	5.7.83 12 Aug
58.97	Jayson	Kovar	USA	30.4.94 16 Apr
58.96	Sam	Elsner	USA	95 14 Apr
58.88	Yevgeniy	Bratko	RUS	26.2.88 1 Jul
58.82	Maarten	Persoon	NED	15.3.87 28 Mar
58.81	Alan	Toward	GBR	31.10.92 22 May
58.79	Nikólaos	Skarvélis	GRE	2.2.93 2 Apr
58.79	Pawel	Pasinski	POL	6.3.93 8 May
58.77	Nicolai	Ceban	MDA	4.2.95 28 May
58.71	Courtland	Clavette	USA	4.7.93 2 Apr
58.62	Mihai	Grasu	ROU	21.4.87 1 Mar
58.55	Filipe	Silva	POR	27.1.83 23 Jul
58.50	Stanislav	Nesterovskiy	UKR	31.7.80 19 Jun
58.36	Go	Chinen	JPN	7.2.92 26 Jun
58.34	Kevin	Farley	USA	18.7.93 28 May
58.34	Igor	Gondor	CZE	10.3.79 18 Jun
58.23	Kino	Dunkley	JAM	27.12.96 2 Apr
58.19	Jordan	Williams	USA	22.5.90 19 May
58.16	Jeff	Bartlett	USA	94 28 May
58.12	Basil	Bingham	JAM	1.9.94 2 Apr
58.10	Tulake	Nuermaimaiti	CHN	8.3.82 6 May
58.08	Aleksander	Tammert	EST	2.2.73 9 Sep
58.05	Caniggia	Raynor	JAM	3.11.90 29 Apr
58.02	JT	Van Veen	USA	3.5.93 14 May
58.01	Ihor	Musiyenko [189]	UKR	22.8.93 25 Jun

Very doubtful mark
| 65.94 | Yevgeniy | Labutov | KAZ | 17.11.84 | 1 | NC | Dushanbe | 13 Jun |

Drugs disqualification
67.62	Victor	Hogan #	RSA	25.7.89	(1) NC	Stellenbosch	15 Apr
				x	59.65 x	67.62 x	x
61,00	Martin	Maric ¶	CRO	19.4.84	(1)	Poughkeepsie, NY	6 May

Sloping Ground – beach
At Oostende 22 Jul: 1. Philip Milanov BEL 68.44, 2. Andrius Gudzius LTU 67.96, 3. Mauricio Ortega COL 67.45, 4. Erik Cadée NED 65.48, 5. David Wrobel GER 64.93. 6. Igor Gondor CZE 60.37, 7. Stephan Dekker NED 17.2.87 59.87

JUNIORS

Mark	Name		Nat	Born	Pos	Venue	Date
61.62	Clemens	Prüfer	GER	13.8.97	2	Wiesbaden	15 May
	57.99 5	Halle		22 May			
57.01	Ruslan	Valitov	UKR	24.2.97	4	Kyiv	25 Jun
56.97	Wout	Zijlstra	NED	25.11.97	1	Hilversum	4 Sep
56.83	Merten	Howe	GER	7.1.97	4	Wiesbaden	15 May
55.84	Kevin	Benson	USA	5.1.97	3	Princeton	7 May
56.63	Cleveson	Oliviera	BRA	7.5.97	1	São Bernardo do Campo	22 May

DISCUS – HAMMER

Mark	Name		Nat	Born	Pos	Meet	Venue	Date
55.47	Konrad	Bukowiecki	POL	17.3.97	1	WJ	Bydgoszcz	19 Jul
55.25	Nathan	Bultman	USA	6.4.97	18		La Jolla	22 Apr
55.22	Sun	Shichen	CHN	23.7.97	4		Shaoxing	17 Apr
55.19	Vadim	Rybkin	RUS	9.1.97	3	NC-23	Saransk	17 Jul
54.92	Yume	Ando	JPN	3.2.97	2		Hiratsuka	4 May

1.75 KG DISCUS

Mark	Name			Nat	Born	Pos	Meet	Venue	Date
66.27	Clemens		Prüfer	GER	13.8.97	1		Wiesbaden	15 May
	64.63	1		Osterode	31 May	63.64	1	Neubrandenburg	28 May
	64.35	1		Halle	21 May	63.00	1	Potsdam	7 Jul
63.63	Mouad Mohamed		Ibrahim	QAT-Y	8.2.99	1	WJ	Bydgoszcz	24 Jul
63.44	Merten		Howe	GER	7.1.97	2		Wiesbaden	15 May
	63.29	1	NC-j	Mönchengladbach	30 Jul	63.18	2	Neubrandenburg	28 May
	62.94	2		Halle	21 May	10 performances by 3 men to 62.94			
62.83	Oskar		Stachnik	POL	1.3.98	2	WJ	Bydgoszcz	24 Jul
62.78	Henrik		Janssen	GER	19.5.98	3	NC-j	Mönchengladbach	30 Jul
62.58	Jakob		Gardenkrans	SWE	15.8.97	1		Bottnaryd	18 Jun
62.20	Konrad		Bukowiecki	POL	17.3.97	1		Bialystok	1 Jun
62.18	Vadim		Rybkin	RUS	9.1.97	1	NC-j	Kazan	28 Jun
61.83	Srefan		Mura	MDA	2.7.97	1	NC-w	Chisinau	7 Feb
61.75	Connor		Bandel (10)	USA	21.10.97	1	NC-j	Clovis	26 Jun
61.72	Wictor		Petersson	SWE	1.5.98	1		Malmö	22 Jun
61.70	Gleb		Zhuk	BLR	24.3.98	3	WJ	Bydgoszcz	24 Jul
60.76	Wout		Zijlstra	NED	25.11.97	1		Leiden	11 Jun
59.72	Ryan		Camp	USA	25.11.97	1		Marietta	8 May
59.35	Bence		Halász	HUN	4.8.97	1		Szombathely	1 May
59.24			Cheng Yulong	CHN	1.2.97	Q	WJ	Bydgoszcz	24 Jul
59.05	George		Evans	GBR	21.1.98	1		Bedford	4 Sep
58.96	Georgios		Koniarakis	CYP-Y	7.2.99	1		Nicosia	23 May
58.94	Jordan		Guehaseim	FRA	16.6.97	3		Mannheim	25 Jun

1.62 kg Discus

Mark	Name		Nat	Born	Pos	Meet	Venue	Date
65.16	Terrell	Adams	USA	19.3.98	1		Apex	14 May
62.92	A.J.	Epenesa	USA		1		Edwardsville	23 Apr
62.28	Bronson	Osborn	USA	5.7.98	1	MSR	Norwalk	15 Apr
62.26	Adrian	Piperi	USA	20.1.99	1	TexR	Austin	2 Apr
62.25	Connor	Bandel	USA	21.10.97	1		Oxford, MI	23 Apr
62.20	Ryan	Camp	USA	25.11.97	1		Marietta	24 Apr

HAMMER

Mark	Name				Nat	Born	Pos	Meet	Venue			Date	
82.47	Pawel			Fajdek	POL	4.6.89	1	Skol	Warszawa			28 Aug	
						78.52		80.03	79.71	79.57	82.47	80.89	
	81.87	1	NC		Bydgoszcz	25 Jun	81.87	x	x	78.11	x	x	
	81.71	1	EAF		Bydgoszcz	5 Jun	77.70	76.18	x	77.28	79.80	81.71	
	81.59	1			Cetniewo	12 Jul	x		76.24	x	81.59	x	
	81.12	1	PNG		Turku	29 Jun	77.87	78.75	x	81.12	80.95	80.79	
	81.11	1	Gyulai		Székesfehérvár	18 Jul	72.70	78.10	76.55	78.50	81.11	79.95	
	81.08	1			Czestochowa	3 Sep	x	81.08	x	x			
	80.93	1	EC		Amsterdam	10 Jul	80.46	78.85	79.09	80.37	80.93	79.69	
	80.66	1	GS		Ostrava	19 May	78.71	x	78.46	x	80.66	78.09	
	80.39	1			Halle	21 Jan	73.70	79.02	x	79.51	78.03	80.39	
	80.28	1	Pre		Eugene	27 May	x	80.28	79.66	79.48	78.82	x	
	80.10	1	Kuso		Szczecin	18 Jun	x	x	79.99	x	x	80.10	
	79.12	1			Kielce	8 May	x	x	78.64	x	x	79.12	
	78.82	Q	EC		Amsterdam	8 Jul	x	x	78.82				
80.04	Ivan			Tikhon	BLR	24.7.76	1	NC	Grodno			24 Jun	
						76.06	77.87	80.04	78.54	x	77.71		
	78.84	2	EC		Amsterdam	10 Jul	76.60	75.16	76.42	76.18	75.84	78.84	
	77.79	2	OG		Rio de Janeiro	19 Aug	76.13	77.43	73.48	x	77.79	76.34	
78.87	Dilshod			Nazarov	TJK	6.5.82	2	PNG	Turku			29 Jun	
						76.53	77.79	77.71	78.87	78.56	78.02		
	78.82	2	GS		Ostrava	19 May	73.71	78.82	75.73	76.85	75.85	78.63	
	78.68	1	OG		Rio de Janeiro	19 Aug	76.16	77.27	78.07	77.17	78.68	77.68	
	78.34	2			Halle	21 May	74.88	76.90	76.80	77.47	78.59	78.34	
	78.12	2	Pre		Eugene	27 May	75.11	78.12	76.12	77.02	x	77.96	
78.63	Wágner			Domingos	BRA	23.6.83	1	CRO Ch	Celje			19 Jun	
						75.09	73.95	76.81	78.63	76.06	74.72		
78.60	Pavel			Boreysha	BLR	16.2.91	1		Brest			21 May	
						74.80	78.60	p	p	p	p		
78.48	Serghei			Marghiev	MDA	6.11.92	1	NC-w	Chisinau			6 Feb	
						x	x	x	78.48	x	x		

MEN 2016

HAMMER

Mark	Name		Nat	Born	Pos	Meet	Venue	Date
78.39	Hassan Mohamed	Mahmoud	EGY	10.2.84	1		Potchefstroom	1 Mar
				x	72.27	74.90	73.76 74.93	78.39
78.36	Wojciech	Nowicki	POL	22.2.89	1		Bialystok	1 Jun
				x	76.85	78.05	77.00 78.36	x
78.04	3	PNG Turku	29 Jun	74.75	78.04	x	x 73.57	75.64
78.19	Ashraf Amjad	El-Seify	QAT	20.2.95	1		Doha	27 Mar
				77.61	x	78.19	76.04 74.48	x
77.78	Aleksey	Sokirskiy	RUS	16.3.85	1		Moskva	28 Jul
	(30/10)			75.88	77.78	77.13	x	
77.70	Oleksandr	Dryhol ¶	ISR	25.4.66	1		Jablonec nad Nisou	1 Jun
77.67	Sergey	Litvinov	RUS	27.1.86	1	NC	Cheboksary	22 Jun
77.60	David	Söderberg	FIN	11.8.79	4	PNG	Turku	29 Jun
77.49	Diego	del Real	MEX	6.3.94	1		Querátaro	24 Apr
77.48	Marcel	Lomnicky	SVK	6.7.87	3	GS	Ostrava	19 May
77.41	Zakhar	Makhrosenko	BLR	10.10.91	1		Zhirovichi	8 Jul
77.40	Kaveh	Mousavi	IRI	27.5.85	2		Zhirovichi	8 Jul
77.38	Krisztián	Pars	HUN	18.2.82	1	NC-w	Szombathely	27 Feb
77.18	Peyman	Ghalenouei	IRI	29.1.92	3		Zhirovichi	8 Jul
77.15	Yevhen	Vynohradov	UKR	30.4.84	1		Kyiv	4 Jun
	(20)							
77.15	Roberto	Sawyers	CRC	17.10.86	1		Liberec	12 Jun
77.08	Mihaíl	Anastasákis	GRE	3.12.94	1	Med U23	Radès	4 Jun
76.93	Nick	Miller	GBR	1.5.93	1Q	NCAA-W	Lawrence	26 May
76.76	Rudy	Winkler	USA	6.12.94	1	NC/OT	Eugene	6 Jul
	77.76?				1		New York	22 Jun
76.52	Roberto	Janet	CUB	29.8.86	1	Barr	La Habana	28 May
76.45	Chris	Bennett	GBR	17.12.89	1		Budapest	18 Jun
76.45	Esref	Apak	TUR	3.1.82	1	Balk C	Pitesti	25 Jun
76.37	Javier	Cienfuegos	ESP	15.7.90	1		Montijo	4 Jul
76.26	Kirill	Ikonnikov ¶	RUS	5.3.84	2	NC-w	Adler	21 Feb
76.26	Mark	Dry	GBR	11.10.87	1		Loughborough	17 Apr
	(30)							
76.20	Tuomas	Seppänen	FIN	16.5.86	3		Halle	21 May
76.10	Quentin	Bigot ¶	FRA	1.12.92	1		Sarreguemines	20 Jul
76.03	Marco	Lingua	ITA	4.6.78	1		Boissano	28 Sep
76.00	Sergey	Kolomoyets	BLR	11.8.89	2		Brest	21 May
75.97	Lukás	Melich	CZE	16.9.80	4	GS	Ostrava	19 May
75.92	Denis	Lukyanov	RUS	11.7.89	2	NC	Cheboksary	22 Jun
75.77	Özkan	Baltaci	TUR	13.2.94	1		Ankara	1 Jul
75.74	Yuriy	Shayunov	BLR	22.10.87	3		Brest	21 May
75.74	Oleg	Dubitskiy	BLR	14.10.90	4		Brest	21 May
75.44	Igors	Sokolovs	LAT	17.8.74	1	NC	Salaspils	30 Jul
	(40)							
75.39	Valeriy	Pronkin	RUS	15.6.94	3	NC-w	Adler	21 Feb
75.32	A.G.	Kruger	USA	18.2.79	1		Ashland, OH	17 Jun
75.13	Jérôme	Bortoluzzi	FRA	20.5.82	1		Luxembourg	17 Jul
75.11	Kibwé	Johnson	USA	17.7.81	2	NC/OT	Eugene	6 Jul
75.10	Konstadínos-Ioánnis	Kostoglídis	GRE	10.8.90	1		Athina (E)	7 May
74.97	Eivind	Henriksen	NOR	14.9.90	2		Fränkisch-Crumbach	15 May
74.90	Andriy	Martynyuk	UKR	25.9.90	1	NC	Lutsk	16 Jun
74.79	Conor	McCullough	USA	31.1.91	1		Chula Vista	18 Jun
74.60	Andrey	Romanov	RUS	19.9.94	1	NC-w23	Adler	19 Feb
74.47	Libor	Charfreitag	SVK	11.9.77	1		El Paso	30 Apr
	[50]							
74.46	Yevgeniy	Korotovskiy	RUS	21.6.92	4	NC	Cheboksary	22 Jun
74.35	Sean	Donnelly	USA	1.4.93	1		Tempe	18 Mar
74.33	Valeriy	Svyatokho	BLR	20.7.81	2		Brest	29 Apr
73.97	Bence	Halász	HUN-J	4.8.97	1		Szombathely	29 Jun
73.83	Aleksey	Korolyov	RUS	5.4.82	4	NC-w	Adler	21 Feb
73.78	Simone	Falloni	ITA	26.9.91	1		Chiari	7 Feb
73.77	Igor	Vinichenko ¶	RUS	11.4.84	5	NC	Cheboksary	22 Jun
73.77	Aleksi	Jaakkola	FIN-J	17.11.97	1		Kaustinen	2 Jul
73.70	Michael	Lihrman	USA	6.12.91	1		Madison	6 May
73.61	Konstantinos	Stathelakos	CYP	30.12.87	1	NC	Nicosia	19 Jun
	(60)							
73.58	Serhiy	Reheda	UKR	6.2.94	1		Kyiv	4 May
73.51	Nejc	Plesko	SLO	9.10.92	2	NC	Celje	19 Jun
73.45	Bence	Pásztor	HUN	5.2.95	1		Veszprém	12 Jun
73.33	Andy	Fryman	USA	3.2.85	1		Edmonton	15 Jul

HAMMER

Mark	Name		Nat	Born	Pos	Meet	Venue	Date	
73.32	Chris	Harmse	RSA	31.5.73	1	NC	Stellenbosch	16	Apr
73.26	Darien	Thornton	USA	14.7.94	2		Ashland, OH	17	Jun
73.22	Alexander	Ziegler	GER	7.7.87	4		Fränkisch-Crumbach	15	May
73.11	Anatoliy	Pozdnyakov	RUS	1.2.87	4		Adler	26	May
73.09	Ákos	Hudi	HUN	10.8.91	1		Szombathely	25	Jun
73.09	Jesse	Lehto	FIN	12.2.93	3	NC	Oulu	23	Jul
(70)									
72.86	Gleb	Dudarov	BLR	17.10.96	5		Brest	21	May
72.74	Nicola	Vizzoni	ITA	4.11.73	1		Firenze	5	Jun
72.70	Taylor	Campbell	GBR	30.6.96	1		Leiria	24	Jul
72.67	Humberto	Mansilla	CHI	22.5.96	1	SACh-23	Lima	24	Sep
72.61	Simon	Lang	GER	16.8.95	1-u23		Fränkisch-Crumbach	15	May
72.61	Nikolay	Bashan	RUS	18.11.92	7	NC	Cheboksary	22	Jul
72.59	Colin	Dunbar	USA	27.6.88	1		Tucson	19	May
72.56	Reinier	Mejias	CUB	22.9.90	2	Barr	La Habana	28	May
72.55	Tommi	Remes	FIN	20.1.94	1	Tiainen	Parikkala	21	May
72.55		Lee Yun-chul	KOR	28.3.82	1		Goseong	15	Jun
(80)									
72.52	Matthias	Tayala	USA	27.4.93	6	NC/OT	Eugene	6	Jul
72.47	Alex	Young	USA	1.9.94	1		Hammond, LA	15	Apr
72.41	Islam Ahmed	Taha	EGY	23.7.94	2	NC	El Maadi	15	Apr
72.25		Wang Shizhu	CHN	20.2.89	1	NC	Tianjin	14	Sep
72.24	Matija	Greguric	CRO	17.9.96	2	NC-w	Split	6	Mar
72.17	Marco	Bortolato	ITA	11.2.94	1		Udine	25	Apr
72.12	Henri	Liipola	FIN	24.4.94	1		Forssa	30	Apr
72.12	Hilmar Örn	Jonsson	ISL	6.5.96	2		Budapest	18	Jun
72.02	Nikólaos	Gavriilidis	GRE	15.3.95	4		Nikítii	12	Jun
71.94	James "JC"	Lambert	USA	12.4.90	1		Carbondale	22	Jun
(90)									
71.84	Maksim	Mitskov	BLR	1.12.95	2	Klim	Minsk	9	Jun
71.82	Ilya	Terentyev	RUS	25.1.95	2	NC-w23	Adler	19	Feb
71.77	Garland	Porter	USA	10.2.82	6		Fränkisch-Crumbach	15	May
71.69	Allan	Wolski	BRA	18.1.90	3	IbAm	Rio de Janeiro	14	May
71.53	Hlib	Piskunov	UKR-J	25.11.98	2		Kirovohrad	21	Apr
71.50	Sukhrob	Khodjayev	UZB	21.5.93	1		Tashkent	9	Jun
71.50		Wan Yong	CHN	22.7.87	2	NC	Tianjin	14	Sep
71.50	Joaquín	Gómez	ARG	14.10.96	2	SACh-23	Lima	24	Sep
71.39	Greg	Skipper	USA	26.3.93	3	NCAA	Eugene	8	Jun
71.33	Gabriel	Kehr	CHI	3.9.96	1		Temuco	1	Oct
[100]									
71.28	Andreas	Sahner	GER	27.1.85	3 Sep	69.83	Markus	Kokkonen	FIN	17.5.95	21 May
71.20	Miguel Alberto Blanco		ESP	22.2.96	7 Feb	69.80	Frédéric	Pouzy	FRA	18.2.83	15 Jun
71.14	Anders	Eriksson	SWE	22.3.94	22 Apr	69.79	Craig	Murch	GBR	27.6.93	22 May
71.02	Johannes	Bichler	GER	3.7.90	21 May	69.71	Igor	Buryi	RUS	8.4.93	12 May
71.00	Yuiy	Kuziv	RUS	29.5.96	26 May	69.71	Naoki	Uematsu	JPN	13.11.94	18 Jun
70.96	Connor	Neu	USA	5.11.92	2 Apr	69.66	Matt	Denny	AUS	2.6.96	20 Feb
70.95	Oscar	Vestlund	SWE	27.4.93	28 May	69.62	Ryan	Loughney	USA	21.8.89	14 May
70.91	Caniggia	Raynor	JAM	3.11.90	2 Jul	69.62	Dorian	Collaku	ALB	2.6.77	15 May
70.87	Arkadiusz	Rogowski	POL	30.3.93	25 Jun	69.50	Noleisis	Vicet	CUB	6.2.81	11 Mar
70.81	Ryota	Kashimura	JPN	13.8.91	24 Jun	69.50	Yevgeniy	Ivanov	BLR	11.6.92	25 Nov
70.79	Tom	Postema	USA	17.7.89	16 Apr	69.49	Eric	Flores	USA	30.12.86	25 Mar
70.77	Ahmed Tariq	Ismail	EGY-J	18.10.97	24 Jun	69.49	Iván	Menglebéi	GRE	25.1.95	12 Jun
70.73	Neeraj	Kumar	IND	17.9.90	29 Jun	69.42	Denzel	Comenentia	NED	25.11.95	1 Apr
70.58	Alexej	Mikhailov	GER	12.4.96	24 Jul	69.34	Elias	Håkansson	SWE	29.2.92	16 Oct
70.56	Paul	Hützen	GER	7.3.91	19 Jun	69.33	Collin	Post	USA	13.2.82	11 Jun
70.26	Tshepang	Makhethe	RSA	9.2.96	5 Mar	69.28	Kevin	Arreaga	ESP	23.10.95	16 Jul
70.26	Yasmani	Fernández	CUB	7.4.95	27 May	69.23	Joachim	Koivu	FIN	5.9.88	16 May
70.23	Ainars	Vaiculens	LAT	21.1.83	4 Jun	69.19	Mattias	Lindberg	SWE	2.1.90	19 Jun
70.19	Aykhan	Apti	BUL	25.4.93	27 Feb	69.15	Ivan	Aksyonov	RUS	16.8.95	6 Jul
70.17	Yushiro	Hosaka	JPN	16.10.91	22 May	69.13	Justin	Welch	USA	29.9.91	17 Jun
70.16	Ali Mohamed Al-Zankawi		KUW	27.2.84	28 Apr	69.09	Ahmed Amgad El-Seify		QAT	1.10.96	27 May
70.16	Mohsen	Anani	EGY	25.5.85	12 Jun	68.98		Qi Dakai	CHN	23.5.87	10 Apr
70.14	Adam	Keenan	CAN	26.3.93	14 May	68.98	Mirko	Micuda	CRO	22.12.89	7 May
70.13	Tristan	Schwandke	GER	23.5.92	23 Jul	68.80	Igor	Yevseyev	RUS	27.3.96	11 Feb
70.08	Alexandros	Poursanides	CYP	23.1.93	1 Apr	68.79	Artem	Poleshko	UKR	13.2.95	12 Feb
70.08	Reza	Moghaddam	IRI	17.11.88	9 Jun	68.71	Oleksandr	Myahkyh	UKR	7.5.86	6 Feb
70.06	António	Silva	POR	23.1.88	17 Jul	68.70	Aleksandr	Shimanovich	BLR-J	9.2.98	21 May
70.05	Juho	Saarikoski	FIN	19.5.93	9 May	68.66	Chris	Shorthouse	GBR	23.6.88	28 May
70.04	Chukwuebuka Enekwechi		USA	28.1.93	6 May	68.62	Volodymyr	Myslyvchuk	UKR	25.4.96	21 Apr
69.94	Tomás	Kruzliak	SVK	9.2.92	22 May	68.57	Joe	Frye	USA	20.7.88	17 Mar
69.94	Carel	Haasbroek	RSA-J	22.2.98	8 Apr	68.57	Dániel	Rába	HUN-J	24.4.98	29 Jun
69.90	Dempsey	McGuigan	IRL	30.8.93	29 Apr	68.51	Dário	Manso	POR	1.7.82	2 Jul
69.85	Andrey	Yeshbekov	RUS	31.5.90	11 Feb	68.45	Colin	Cashner	USA	9.12.92	17 Jun
69.85	Pedro José	Martin	ESP	12.8.92	23 Jul	68.36	Michal	Fiala	CZE	22.6.85	10 May

HAMMER – JAVELIN

Mark	Name		Nat	Born	Pos	Meet	Venue	Date
68.25	Joseph	Ellis	GBR	10.4.96	26 May		68.01 Sebastian Janusz POL 21.12.95	8 May
68.23	Ken-ichi	Hirose	JPN	5.9.89	4 Jun		[171]	

JUNIORS

See main list for top 3 juniors. 10 performances by 3 men over 59.00. Additional marks and further juniors:

Mark	Name			Venue	Date			Venue	Date
Halász	73.70	2		Budapest	4 Sep	72.27	2	Tapolca	6 Aug
	72.97	1		Szombathely	11 Jul	72.22	2 NC	Székesfehérvár	30 Jul
	72.47	1		Szombathely	8 Jun	71.80	1	Szombathely	2 Apr
Jaakkola	73.42	2		Kuortane	25 Jun	71.90	1	Espoo	6 Jun
	72.07	1		Nokia	21 Jun	11 performances by 2 men to 71.80			
70.77	Ahmed Tariq		Ismail	EGY	18.10.97	1		Kapfenberg	24 Jun
69.94	Carel		Haasbroek	RSA	27.2.98	2		Sasolburg	8 Apr
68.70	Aleksandr		Shimanovich	BLR	9.2.98	8		Brest	21 May
68.57	Dániel		Rába	HUN	24.4.98	3		Szombathely	29 Jun
67.60			Ding Yuanbo	CHN	26.1.97	2		Taiyuan	20 May
67.50	Adam		Kelly	USA	6.7.97	2		Princeton	7 May
67.32	Myhaylo		Havrylyuk (10)	UKR-Y	19.10.99	3	NC-w	Mukachevo	12 Feb
66.58	Danyil		Danilov	RUS	5.1.98	6	Kuts	Moskva	1 Jul
64.60	Owen		Russell	IRL	21.8.97	3		Princeton	7 May

6KG HAMMER

Mark	Name			Venue	Date			Venue	Date
82.64	Bence		Halász	HUN	4.8.97	1	NC-j	Szombathely	25 Jun
	81.76	1		Szombathely	1 May	80.93	1 WJ	Bydgoszcz	22 Jul
	81.74	1		Szombathely	8 Jun	80.89	1	Halle	21 May
	81.21	1		Potchefstroom	22 Apr	80.77	1	Tapolca	6 Aug
	81.16	1		Veszprém	12 Jun				
80.54	Aleksi		Jaakkola	FIN	17.11.97	1		Nokia	28 Apr
	80.48	1	NC-j	Lappeenranta	6 Aug	79.93	1	Nordic Hafnarfjördur	14 Aug
	80.12	1		Tampere	20 Aug	14 performances by 4 men over 79.50			
79.84	Ahmed Tariq		Ismail	EGY	18.10.97	1		Kapfenberg	24 Jun
79.58	Hlib		Piskunov	UKR	25.11.98	2	WJ	Bydgoszcz	22 Jul
78.10	Aaron		Kangas	FIN	3.7.97	1		Nkoia	28 Apr
77.76	Dániel		Rába	HUN	24.4.98	2	NC-j	Szombathely	25 Jun
76.10	Aleksadr		Shimanovich	BLR	9.2.98	1		Minsk	9 Apr
75.73	Danyil		Danilov	RUS	5.1.98	1		Adler	11 Feb
75.52	Alberto		González	ESP	1.1.98	5	WJ	Bydgoszcz	22 Jul
74.40	Tomas		Vasilauskas (10)	LTU	28.11.97	1		Alytus	12 May
74.12	Bobby		Colantonio	USA	18.5.98	1	NC-j	Clovis	24 Jun
73.75	Ned		Weatherly	AUS	12.1.98	7	WJ	Bydgoszcz	22 Jul
73.63	Ilya		Yevgenyev	RUS	31.7.98	2		Adler	11 Feb
73.22	Balázs		Varga	HUN	30.1.98	3	NC-w	Szombathely	5 Mar
73.17	Adam		Kelly	USA	6.7.97	8	WJ	Bydgoszcz	22 Jul
73.07	Myhaylo		Havrylyuk	UKR-Y	19.10.99	1		Nicosia	7 May
72.60			Ding Yuanbo	CHN	26.1.97	1	NC-j	Ordos	28 Jun
71.84	Pyotr		Neikiporets	RUS	6.5.97	2		Adler	12 May
71.70	Adam		King	IRL	2.2.97	11	WJ	Bydgoszcz	22 Jul
71.55	Jake		Norris (20)	GBR	30.6.99	1		Woodford	25 Sep

JAVELIN

Mark	Name				Nat	Born	Pos	Meet	Venue			Date
91.28	Thomas		Röhler		GER	30.9.91	1	PNG	Turku			29 Jun
						85.81	89.34	91.28	86.25	91.04	86.56	
	90.30	1	OG	Rio de Janeiro		20 Aug	87.40	85.61- 87.07	84.84	90.30	x	
	89.30	1	Bisl	Oslo		9 Jun	84.71	89.30	85.35	84.12	81.59	x
	87.91	1		Jena		4 Jun	82.41	84.90	81.07	87.91	x	83.44
	87.37	1	GS	Ostrava		20 May	81.58	83.11	84.28	84.50	x	87.37
	86.81	1	NC	Kassel		18 Jun	83.71	86.81	x	78.43	82.60	84.45
	86.56	2	WK	Zürich		1 Sep	86.56	x	x	80.70	85.10	84.34
	86.30	3		Kuortane		25 Jun	77.73	71.40	81.55	85.10	86.26	86.30
	86.25	1		Thum		2 Sep	86.25	85.83	p	83.58	85.55	x
89.57	Johannes		Vetter		GER	26.3.93	1	ISTAF	Berlin			3 Sep
						89.57	85.20	84.38	81.19	x	84.00	
	88.23	1		Kuortane		25 Jun	79.16	88.23	79.57	83.88	81.93	x
	87.11	2	Bisl	Oslo		9 Jun	87.11	83.67	84.03	x	83.76	82.83
88.68	Keshorn		Walcott		TTO	2.4.93	Q	OG	Rio de Janeiro			17 Aug
						88.68	p	p				
	86.35	3	Bisl	Oslo		9 Jun	82.91	84.78	83.85	86.35	79.68	x
88.29	Julian		Weber		GER	29.8.94	2	ISTAF	Berlin			3 Sep
						83.99	88.29	83.80	83.33	p	82.98	
	88.04	1		Offenburg		10 Jul	x	77.62	74.85	80.87	83.64	88.04
	87.39	2	DL	Saint-Denis		27 Aug	79.15	83.87	87.39	82.40	78.16	80.39
	86.83	2	PNG	Turku		29 Jun	80.63	81.19	84.45	83.44	86.83	83.39

JAVELIN

Mark		Name		Nat	Born	Pos	Meet	Venue		Date	
88.24		Julius	Yego	KEN	4.1.89	2	OG	Rio de Janeiro		20 Aug	
					88.24	x	p	x	p	p	
88.23		Antti	Ruuskanen	FIN	21.2.84	Q	EC	Amsterdam		6 Jul	
					88.23						
	86.90	2	Kuortane	25 Jun	83.57	79.15	84.52	79.35	83.58	86.90	
88.02		Jakub	Vadlejch	CZE	10.10.90	1	DL	Saint-Denis		27 Aug	
					x	76.08	88.02	x	84.22	85.50	
	87.28	1 WK	Zürich	1 Sep	82.12	84.93	x	87.28	85.67	x	
	87.20	1	Kolin	4 Aug							
	86.76	1	Kawasaki	8 May	85.07	79.84	82.97	x	86.76	x	
	86.37	1	Usti nad Orlicii	4 Sep	82.27	x	x	81.24	86.37	p	
87.14		Ioánnis	Kiriazis	GRE	19.1.96	1	NC-23	Lárisa		31 Jul	
					87.14	p		p	p	p	
86.66		Zigismunds	Sirmais	LAT	6.5.92	1	EC	Amsterdam		7 Jul	
					81.86	81.36	80.88	78.36	86.66	75.57	
86.48		Neeraj	Chopra (10)	IND-J	24.12.97	1	WJ	Bydgoszcz		23 Jul	
					79.66	86.48	78.36	x			
86.13		Tero	Pitkämaki	FIN	19.12.82	1		Lappeenranta		27 Aug	
		(30/11)			x	x	82.78	80.94	86.13	78.85	
85.95		Paraskevás	Batzávalis	GRE	25.11.94	1		Thiva		20 Jul	
85.79		Lars	Hamann	GER	4.4.89	2		Thum		2 Sep	
85.42		Andreas	Hofmann	GER	16.12.91	3	ISTAF	Berlin		3 Sep	
85.11		Joshua	Robinson	AUS	4.10.85	1		Perth		14 May	
85.04		Tanel	Laanmäe	EST	29.9.89	1	Sule	Tartu		13 Jun	
84.82		Vitezslav	Vesely	CZE	27.2.83	Q	EC	Amsterdam		6 Jul	
84.74		Marcin	Krukowski	POL	14.6.92	3	GS	Ostrava		20 May	
84.74		Ahmed Bader	Magour	QAT	3.3.96	1		Riihimäki		6 Jul	
84.54		Ryohei	Arai	JPN	23.6.91	1	NC	Nagoya		25 Jun	
		(20)									
84.50		Kim	Amb	SWE	31.7.90	1	vFIN	Tampere		4 Sep	
84.47		Magnus	Kirt	EST	10.4.90	2	Sule	Tartu		13 Jun	
84.39		Hamish	Peacock	AUS	15.10.90	1		Hobart		22 May	
84.10		Petr	Frydrych	CZE	13.1.88	1		Letterkenny		2 Jul	
84.08		Dmytro	Kosynskyy	UKR	31.3.89	4	DL	Saint-Denis		27 Aug	
83.93		Stuart	Farquhar	NZL	15.3.82	1	AUS Ch	Sydney		3 Apr	
83.83		Cyrus	Hostetler	USA	8.8.86	1		Tucson		21 May	
83.82			Huang Shih-Feng	TPE	2.3.92	3		Kawasaki		8 May	
83.60		Lukasz	Grzeszczuk	POL	3.3.90	1		Warszawa		21 May	
83.28		Oleksandr	Pyatnytsya	UKR	14.7.85	1		Kyiv		5 May	
		(30)									
83.19		Jaroslav	Jílek	CZE	22.10.89	5		Kawasaki		8 May	
83.09		John	Ampomah	GHA	11.7.90	1		Cape Coast		8 Jul	
83.09		Risto	Mätas	EST	30.4.84	1		Tallinn		10 Jul	
83.03		Ivan	Zaytsev	UZB	7.11.88	1	TJK Ch	Dushanbe		13 Jun	
82.88		Curtis	Thompson	USA	8.2.96	2	NC/OT	Eugene		4 Jul	
82.81		Gabriel	Wallin	SWE	14.10.81	1		Saarijärvi		26 Jun	
82.39A		Dayron	Márquez	COL	11.6.83	1		Medellín		10 Jul	
81.96		Braian	Toledo	ARG	8.9.93	Q	OG	Rio de Janeiro		17 Aug	
81.89		Jiannis	Smaliós	SWE	17.2.87	3	vFIN	Tampere		4 Sep	
81.88		Sampo	Lehtola	FIN	10.5.89	1		Aanekoski		11 Aug	
		(40)									
81.81		Yukifumi	Murakami	JPN	23.12.79	2	Nambu	Sapporo		10 Jul	
81.76		Leslie	Copeland	FIJ	23.4.88	3	AUS Ch	Sydney		3 Apr	
81.76		Rolands	Strobinders	LAT	14.4.92	1		Jelgava		19 Jun	
81.63		Dejan	Mileusnic	BIH	16.11.91	1	NC	Zenica		18 Jun	
81.56		Júlio César	de Oliveira	BRA	4.2.86	1		Chula Vista		7 May	
81.56		Dmitriy	Tarabin	RUS	29.10.91	1	Znam	Zhukovskiy		5 Jun	
81.55		Kohei	Hasegawa	JPN	1.1.90	1		Kumatori		21 May	
81.51		Ihab	Abdelrahman ¶	EGY	1.5.89	1	NC	El Maadi		13 Apr	
81.49		Guillermo	Martínez	CUB	28.6.81	1		La Habana		27 Feb	
81.38		Ari	Mannio	FIN	23.7.87	2	NC	Oulu		24 Jul	
		[50]									
81.28		Edis	Matusevicius	LTU	30.6.96	1	ECCp	Mersin		29 May	
81.23A		Arley	Ibargüen	COL	4.12.82	1	NC	Medellín		23 Apr	
81.16		Teemu	Wirkkala	FIN	14.1.84	4	vSWE	Tampere		4 Sep	
81.13		Matija	Kranjc	SLO	12.6.84	1		Brezice		23 Jun	
81.05		Roberto	Bertolini	ITA	9.10.85	1		Nembro		18 Jun	
80.97		Kacper	Oleszczuk	POL	15.5.94	Q	EC	Amsterdam		6 Jul	
80.86		Ben	Woodruff	USA	9.5.89	2		Tucson		21 May	
80.59		Johannes	Grobler	RSA-J	6.8.97	2	WJ	Bydgoszcz		23 Jul	

406 JAVELIN

Mark	Name		Nat	Born	Pos	Meet	Venue	Date	
80.42	Hubert	Chmielak	POL	19.6.89	1		Slupsk	14	May
80.42	Riley	Dolezal	USA	16.11.85	1	Jerome	Burnaby	17	Jun
(60)									
80.42		Zhao Qinggang	CHN	24.7.85	1	NC	Tianjin	15	Sep
80.38	Bartosz	Osewski	POL	20.3.91	1		Gdansk	11	Jun
80.32	Harri	Haatainen	FIN	5.1.78	1		Urjala	31	Jul
80.27	Luke	Cann	AUS	17.7.94	1		Townsville	5	Jun
80.25	R.M.Sumedha	Ranasinghe	SRI	10.2.91	2		Guwahati	10	Feb
80.21	Devender	Singh	IND	18.12.88	1		Bengaluru	11	Jul
80.04	Joni	Karvinen	FIN	7.2.94	2		Raasepori	12	Jun
79.88	Oleksandr	Nychyporchuk	UKR	14.4.92	1		Kyiv	24	Jun
79.84	David	Ocampo	MEX	14.2.92	1		Tucson	21	May
79.80	Benjamin	Langton-Burnell	NZL	10.7.92	1		Hamilton	10	Dec
(70)									
79.77	Shivpal	Singh	IND	6.7.95	1		Patiala	6	May
79.71	Matthew	Outzen	AUS	12.10.87	2		Newcastle	30	Jan
79.65	Anderson	Peters	GRN-J	21.10.97	3	WJ	Bydgoszcz	23	Jul
79.62	Tim	van Liew	USA	25.5.90	3		Tucson	21	May
79.59	Genki	Dean	JPN	30.12.91	2	Oda	Hiroshima	29	Apr
79.53	Shakiel	Waithe	TTO	10.6.95	2	NC	Port of Spain	26	Jun
79.47	Norbert	Rivasz-Tóth	HUN	6.5.96	1		Miskolc	28	May
79.42	Emin	Öncel	TUR-J	1.5.97	1	NC-j	Bolu	29	Jun
79.36	Janis Svens	Griva	LAT	23.4.93	2		Ventspils	12	Jun
79.34	Vladimir	Kozlov	BLR	20.4.85	1	ECp-w	Arad	13	Mar
(80)									
79.34	Bernhard	Seifert	GER	15.2.93	2		Dessau	27	May
79.30	Evan	Karakolis	CAN	30.3.94	1	KansR	Lawrence	23	Apr
79.21	Norbert	Bonvecchio	ITA	14.8.85	1		Conegliano	15	Jun
79.14	Amit	Kumar	IND	18.9.92	1		Hyderabad	2	Jul
79.04	Ravinder	Singh Khaira	IND	19.3.86	1	NC	Lucknow	28	Sep
79.02	Ainars	Kovals	LAT	21.11.81	1		Tallinn	25	Jun
79.02	Sami	Peltomäki	FIN	11.1.91	2		Vantaa	28	May
78.88	Phil-Mar	van Rensburg	RSA	23.6.89	1	NC	Stellenbosch	15	Apr
78.82		Ma Qun	CHN	8.2.94	1		Kimchun	3	Jul
78.77	Sam	Humphreys	USA	12.9.90	4		Tucson	21	May
(90)									
78.66	Alexandru	Novac	ROU-J	24.3.97	1	NC-w	Arad	1	Mar
78.56	Piotr	Lebioda	POL	28.5.92	3		Slupsk	14	May
78.52	Waruna Lakshan	Dayarathne	SRI	14.5.88	1		Jaffna	2	Oct
78.48	Adrian	Mardare	MDA	20.6.95	1	ROU Ch	Cluj Napoca	16	Jul
78.48	Rocco	van Rooyen	RSA	23.12.92	24q	OG	Rio de Janeiro	17	Aug
78.45	Gatis	Cakss	LAT	13.6.95	3		Tallinn	21	May
78.41	Jani	Kiiskilä	FIN	28.12.89	1		Rovaniemi	12	Jun
78.33	Arshad	Nadeem	PAK-J	2.1.97	3		Guwahati	10	Feb
78.29	Jarrod	Bannister ¶	AUS	3.10.84	6		Halle	21	May
78.29	Leonel	Suárez	CUB	1.9.87	1D	NC	La Habana	18	Mar
[100]									

Mark	First	Last	Nat	Born	Pos		Mark	First	Last	Nat	Born
78.26	Yegor	Yermoshin	RUS	6.7.93	5 Jun		77.16	Dmytro	Sheremet	UKR	19.11.92 19 Jun
78.25	Ansis	Bruns	LAT	30.3.89	12 Jun		77.15	Jérémy	Nicollin	FRA	8.4.91 27 May
78.24	Daan	Meijer	NED	17.2.83	18 Sep		77.07	Patrik	Zenúch	SVK	30.12.90 21 May
78.17	Marcin	Plener	POL	22.8.90	4 Jun		77.00	David	Carreón	MEX	23.3.94 4 Jun
78.12	Jami	Kinnunen	FIN	31.3.95	27 Aug		76.98	Peerachet	Janthra	THA	9.9.90 3 Sep
78.07	Pawel	Rakoczy	POL	15.5.87	22 May		76.92	Mykola	Shama	UKR	5.4.91 12 Feb
78.06	Sam	Crouser	USA	31.12.91	4 Jul		76.91	D.G.Sampath	Ranasinghe	SRI	1.9.88 16 Aug
78.03	Tim	Glover	USA	1.11.90	21 May		76.89	Matthias	de Zordo	GER	21.2.88 4 Jun
77.97	Jun-ya	Sado	JPN-J	17.1.97	6 Jun		76.86	Tyler	Renton	CAN	8.6.94 19 Mar
77.97	Mart	ten Berge	NED	27.4.91	25 Sep		76.81	Chad	Herman	RSA	25.5.92 15 Apr
77.94	Antonio	Fent	ITA	31.3.88	20 Feb		76.77		Sun Jianjun	CHN	9.6.91 15 Apr
77.94	Vipin	Kasana	IND	4.8.89	2 Jul		76.74	Cody	Danielson	USA	1.12.93 18 Mar
77.91		Liu Qizhen	CHN	17.9.95	20 Jun		76.74	Ranno	Koorep	EST	24.1.90 27 Aug
77.89	Osmani	Laffita	CUB	14.8.94	28 May		76.68		Jung Sang-jin	KOR	16.4.84 4 Jun
77.89	Katsuya	Nakamura	JPN	14.12.95	15 Oct		76.65	Rajender	Singh Dalvir	IND	5.4.89 3 Jul
77.84	Aleksandr	Ashomko	BLR	18.2.84	1 Jun		76.64	Mateusz	Kwasniewski	POL	16.7.95 24 Jun
77.79	George	Zaharia	ROU	3.8.95	30 Jul		76.58	Shu	Mori	JPN	14.11.96 2 Jul
77.77	Eetu	Vanhamäki	FIN	3.3.89	16 Jul		76.50		Jiang Xingyu	CHN	16.3.87 11 Apr
77.76	Yegor	Nikolayev	RUS	5.6.96	21 Feb		76.38		Park Won-kil	KOR	24.2.90 3 Sep
77.64	Takuma	Nakanishi	JPN	8.4.94	16 Apr		76.36	Josué	Menéndez	MEX	4.5.90 21 May
77.61	Killian	Duréchou	FRA	15.8.92	16 May		76.35	Abhishek	Singh	IND	29.4.94 2 Jul
77.50	Chris	Carper	USA	19.4.92	21 May		76.26	Sean	Furey	USA	31.8.82 2 Jul
77.34	Rhys	Stein	AUS	15.5.96	20 Feb		76.12	Omid	Taji	IRI	18.8.91 12 Jun
77.25	Yutaka	Kakishima	JPN	12.4.94	3 Sep		76.11	Ryan	Young	USA	3.1.87 21 May
77.23	Albert	Reynolds	LCA	28.3.88	3 Jul		76.07	Caleb	Nieves	PUR	28 May
77.17	Valeriy	Iordan	RUS	14.2.92	22 Jun		76.01	Oleksandr	Chehlatyy	UKR	27.9.89 22 Apr

JAVELIN – DECATHLON

Mark	Name		Nat	Born	Pos	Meet	Venue		Date
76.00	Majid Mohsen	Ali Al-Badri	EGY-J	27.6.97	5	Oct	Wöschler	GER	9.6.91 10 Jun
75.99	Yuya	Koriki	JPN	19.10.89	24	Jul			
75.95	Juan José	Méndez	MEX	27.4.88	19	May			
75.91	Reinhardt	van Zyl	RSA	7.2.94	13	May			
75.91	Werner	Bouwer	RSA-J	21.9.98	15	Oct			
75.86	Nicolás	Quijera	ESP	24.6.96	23	Jul			
75.85	Takuto	Kominami	JPN	26.7.95	10	Oct			
75.79	Matti	Mortimore	GBR	16.5.93	9	Apr			
75.77	Kenji	Ogura	JPN	8.6.95	25	Jun			
75.74	Devin	Bogert	USA	27.5.93	1	May			
75.72	Emron	Gibbs	GRN	18.5.92	23	Apr			
75.70	Vladislav	Panasenkov	RUS	22.5.96	2	Jul			
75.62	Janeil	Craigg	BAR	29.3.94	16	Jul			
75.60	Matija	Muhar	SLO	22.7.96	15	May			
75.56	Amrendra	Singh	IND	15.8.91	24	Apr			
75.51	Jonas	Bonewit	GER	30.7.95	4	Jun			
75.50		Deng Sheng	CHN	14.11.92	22	May			
75.48	Robert	Robbins	USA	16.11.92	31	Jul			
75.46	Harry	Hughes	GBR-J	26.9.97	21	May			
75.44	Serhiy	Dyachok	UKR	12.6.90	4	Jun			
75.40	Zakhar	Mishchenko	UKR-J	4.1.98	19	Jun			
75.39	Samarjeet	Singh	IND	7.11.88	10	Feb			
75.37	Gyanesh	Pathak	IND	11.7.95	1	Jan			
75.36	Andrés	Valencia	COL	9.1.95	23	Jul			

75.35	Till			Wöschler		GER	9.6.91	10 Jun
75.27	Mykola			Kalyush		UKR	12.8.87	26 May
75.24	Yoshihiro			Nakajima		JPN	12.3.93	29 Oct
75.21A	Tobie			Holtzhausen		RSA	25.5.87	5 Mar
75.20	Víctor			Fatecha		PAR	10.3.88	30 Jan
75.20	Ioánnis			Houlákis		GRE	10.6.88	20 Jul
75.15	Cruz			Hogan		AUS	22.2.94	5 Feb
75.10	Gudmundur			Sverrisson		ISL	24.5.90	21 May
75.03	Skirmantas			Simoliunas		LTU	13.3.94	3 Jun
75.01	Orrin			Powell		JAM	2.2.92	20 Feb
74.99				Li Yingchang		CHN	22.6.91	15 Sep
74.96	Bobur			Shokirjanov		UZB	5.12.90	25 Jun
74.92	Vedran			Samac		SRB	22.1.90	22 May
74.90	Raul			Rusu		ROU	20.7.95	1 Mar
74.90	Cyprian			Mrzygłód		POL-J	2.2.98	12 Jun
74.80	Adriaan			Beukes		BOT	14.7.94	15 Apr
74.80	Márk			Schmölcz		HUN-J	14.10.97	22 Jul
74.76	Marian			Spannowsky		GER	20.9.96	5 May
74.72	Wojciech			Cwik		POL	20.5.94	8 May
74.71	Toma			Pop		ROU	11.3.92	1 Mar
74.71	Kennosuke			Sogawa		JPN	12.7.94	4 Sep
74.70	Pavel			Meleshko		BLR	24.11.92	14 Feb
74.63	Teo			Takala		FIN	6.6.94	22 Jun
74.61	Yuya			Mizuno		JPN-J	.97	4 Sep
[200]				215 over 74.00				

Unconfirmed – probably too light implement and not accepted as new NR
77.06   Ayoub   Arokhi   IRI   23.5.82   28 May
Not accepted as record as illegally taped: 76.20 Arokhi   2 Aug

Drugs disqualification
87.37   Ihab   Abdelrahman ¶   EGY   1.5.89   (1) Pre   Eugene   28 May
          76.42   84.06   79.94   84.45   87.37   x
86.00   Abdelrahman   (1) DL   Stockholm   16 Jun
          x   x   86.00   79.38   82.05   81.96

JUNIORS
See main list for top 6 juniors. 10 performances by 4 men over 79.00. Additional marks and further juniors:

Chopra	82.23	1	S.Asian	Guwahati	10 Feb	79.54	1		New Delhi	24 Apr
	79.95	1		Patiala	1 Jan	79.51	5		Rehlingen	16 May
	79.73	2		Warszawa	21 May	79.23	3		Offenburg	10 Jul
77.97	Jun-ya		Sado		JPN-	17.1.97	1	Asi-J	Ho Chi Minh	6 Jun
76.00	Majid Mohsen Ali		Al-Badri		EGY	27.6.97	1		El Maadi	5 Oct
75.91	Werner		Bouwer		RSA	21.9.98	1		Pretoria	15 Oct
75.46	Harry		Hughes (10)		GBR	26.9.97	1J		Halle	21 May
75.40	Zakhar		Mishchenko		UKR	4.1.98	5	NC	Lutsk	19 Jun
74.90	Cyprian		Mrzygłód		POL	2.2.98	1		Gdansk	12 Jun
74.80	Márk		Schmölcz		HUN	14.10.97	Q	WJ	Bydgoszcz	22 Jul
74.61	Yuya		Mizuno		JPN	.97	4		Kuamagaya	4 Sep
74.02	Patriks		Gailums		LAT	10.5.98	Q-7	WJ	Bydgoszcz	22 Jul
73.47	Valeriy		Izotov		BLR	12.4.97	1	NC-j	Brest	21 Jun
73.20	Rikinari		Ishizaka		JPN	.97	1	NC-j	Nagoya	21 Oct
73.18	Lukas		Moutarde		FRA	1.4.98	Q	WJ	Bydgoszcz	22 Jul
73.11	Atsushi		Kawano		JPN	6.1.97	1		Kitakyushu	26 Mar
73.08	Hudson		Keffer (20)		USA	13.7.97	1		Tucson	30 Apr

DECATHLON

8893	Ashton	Eaton	USA	21.1.88	1	OG	Rio de Janeiro	18 Aug
	10.46/-0.1	7.94/1.7	14.73	2.01	46.07	13.80/0.7	45.49 5.20 59.77	4:23.33
8834	Kevin	Mayer	FRA	10.2.92	2	OG	Rio de Janeiro	18 Aug
	10.81/-0.4	7.60/0.1	15.76	2.04	48.28	14.02/0.7	46.78 5.40 65.04	4:25.49
8750		Eaton			1	NC/OT	Eugene	3 Jul
	10.34/1.8	7.84/1.4	14.04	2.00	46.30	13.60w/2.1	41.39 5.25 57.84	4:25.15
8666	Damian	Warner	CAN	4.11.89	3	OG	Rio de Janeiro	18 Aug
	10.30/-0.1	7.67/0.5	13.66	2.04	47.35	13.58/0.7	44.93 4.70 63.19	4:24.90
8605	Arthur	Abele	GER	30.7.86	1		Ratingen	26 Jun
	10.95/-0.6	7.48/0.4	15.79	1.98	49.43	14.07/-0.9	46.20 4.90 71.89	4:24.12
8580	Kai	Kazmirek	GER	28.1.91	4	OG	Rio de Janeiro	18 Aug
	10.78/-0.1	7.69/-1.0	14.20	2.10	46.75	14.62/0.7	43.25 5.00 64.60	4:31.25
8523		Warner			1	Hypo	Götzis	29 May
	10.15/1.1	7.12/-0.2	14.64	2.00	47.13	13.72/-1.1	47.79 4.70 58.72	4:32.83
8521	Larbi	Bouraada	ALG	10.5.88	5	OG	Rio de Janeiro	18 Aug
	10.75/-0.4	7.52/0.5	13.78	2.10	47.98	14.15/0.4	42.39 4.60 66.49	4:14.60
8460	Leonel	Suárez	CUB	1.9.87	6	OG	Rio de Janeiro	18 Aug
	11.21/0.5	7.14/0.1	14.27	2.07	48.15	14.48/0.1	47.07 4.90 72.32	4:28.32

408 DECATHLON

Mark	Name		Nat	Born	Pos	Meet	Venue			Date
8446	Lindon	Victor	GRN	28.2.93	1	SEC	Tuscaloosa			13 May
	10.72/0.6	7.09/1.4 15.73	2.02	48.33		14.70/0.7	54.56	4.55	68.96	4:47.12
8446		Mayer			2	Hypo	Götzis			29 May
	10.92/0.3	7.32/-0.2 15.22	2.00	50.07		14.06/-0.6	48.99	5.00	65.77	4:35.45
8425	Jeremy	Taiwo	USA	15.1.90	2	NC/OT	Eugene			3 Jul
	10.94/1.6	7.55/1.1 14.88	2.21	48.76		14.22/1.0	42.10	4.75	52.82	4:17.35
8413	Zach	Ziemek (10)	USA	23.2.93	3	NC/OT	Eugene			3 Jul
	10.60/1.8	7.72/0.7 14.11	2.09	49.30		14.94/1.0	48.17	5.25	57.24	4:48.21
8392		Ziemek			7	OG	Rio de Janeiro			18 Aug
	10.71/-0.1	7.49/0.2 13.44	2.10	49.83		14.77/0.4	49.42	5.20	60.92	4:42.97
8379		Victor			1	NCAA	Eugene			9 Jun
	10.60/0.9	7.34/1.6 15.62	1.95	48.73		14.68/0.4	53.46	4.50	65.63	4:43.81
8347		Suárez			1	NC	La Habana			18 Mar
	11.30/0.0	7.40/-1.4 13.74	2.06	49.72		14.65/0.5	43.48	4.80	78.29	4:29.20
8332	Thomas	Van Der Plaetsen	BEL	24.12.90	8	OG	Rio de Janeiro			18 Aug
	11.24/0.5	7.66/0.7 12.84	2.16	49.63		15.01/0.7	43.58	5.40	62.09	4:34.21
8323		Kazmirek			2		Ratingen			26 Jun
	10.79/-0.6	759/-0.6 1478	207	48.46		14.40/-0.94059	500		5954	4:38.52
8323	Kurt	Felix	GRN	4.7.88	9	OG	Rio de Janeiro			18 Aug
	10.93/0.5	7.42/-0.6 14.77	2.07	49.14		14.79/0.4	45.10	4.50	69.92	4:30.53
8318		Kazmirek			3	Hypo	Götzis			29 May
	10.62/1.1	7.45/-0.6 14.05	2.06	47.01		14.25/-1.1	39.56	5.00	57.63	4:38.32
8315	Maicel	Uibo	EST	27.12.92	2	SEC	Tuscaloosa			13 May
	11.13/0.6	7.36w/2.3 14.98	2.11	50.97		14.84/-0.8	44.92	5.05	64.20	4:27.91
8315	Luiz Alberto	de Araújo	BRA	27.9.87	10	OG	Rio de Janeiro			18 Aug
	10.77/-0.4	7.48/-0.2 15.26	1.92	48.14		14.17/0.1	45.10	4.90	57.28	4:31.46
8300		Ziemek			2	NCAA	Eugene			9 Jun
	10.63/0.9	7.72w/2.5 14.05	2.01	49.04		14.85/0.3	46.91	5.00	58.32	4:42.52
8300		Taiwo			11	OG	Rio de Janeiro			18 Aug
	11.01/-0.4	7.45/0.2 14.92	2.19	48.78		14.57/0.7	39.91	5.00	51.29	4:21.96
8294		Uibo			3	NCAA	Eugene			9 Jun
	11.16/1.0	7.39w/2.3 14.36	2.07	50.85		15.06/1.1	44.76	5.30	63.96	4:27.53
8292	Ilya	Shkurenyov	RUS	11.1.91	1		Cheboksary			21 Jun
	11.02w/2.2	7.78/1.6 13.81	2.05	49.44		14.47/0.8	45.20	5.20	58.86	4:46.73
8291	Adam Sebastian	Helcelet	CZE	27.10.91	12	OG	Rio de Janeiro			18 Aug
	11.06/-0.4	7.35/0.0 15.11	2.04	49.51		14.37/0.1	44.13	4.70	68.20	4:34.41
8228	Garrett	Scantling	USA	19.5.93	4	NC/OT	Eugene			3 Jul
	10.86/1.2	7.24w/3.0 15.97	2.06	51.04		14.13/1.2	43.76	4.85	69.37	5:02.32
8218		Van Der Plaetsen			1	EC	Amsterdam			7 Jul
	11.23/0.8	7.64w/2.1 13.17	2.10	50.50		14.64/-1.0	44.32	5.40	57.23	4:37.84
8203		Taiwo			4	Hypo	Götzis			29 May
	10.89/1.1	7.30/1.0 14.84	2.18	49.25		14.69/-0.5	42.14	4.90	52.20	4:31.62
	(30/17)									
8191	Bastien	Auzeil	FRA	22.10.89	1	NC	Angers			25 Jun
	11.18/-0.3	7.14/1.8 15.06	2.04	49.97		14.57/1.0	47.02	5.00	61.80	4:38.79
8180	Akihiko	Nakamura	JPN	23.10.90	1	NC	Nagano			12 Jun
	10.69/1.8	7.65/0.8 12.47	2.02	47.82		14.12w/2.1	35.58	4.90	54.18	4:16.30
8175	Dominik	Distelberger	AUT	16.3.90	5	Hypo	Götzis			29 May
	10.71/1.1	7.25/0.3 13.76	1.94	48.47		14.45/-0.6	43.93	5.00	59.97	4:34.21
	(20)									
8174	Mihail	Dudas	SRB	1.11.89	1	NC	Novi Sad			13 May
	10.75/-0.2	7.47/-0.1 13.78	1.92	48.96		14.52/-1.9	46.70	4.80	59.55	4:32.11
8160	Keisuke	Ushiro	JPN	24.7.86	1		Wakayama			1 May
	11.32/-1.3	7.18/-0.8 15.13	2.02	50.36		15.00/-0.6	48.12	4.90	66.71	4:37.77
8121	Jirí	Sykora	CZE	20.1.95	6	Hypo	Götzis			29 May
	10.86/1.1	7.41/1.6 14.19	2.00	48.97		14.36/0.0	45.21	4.60	58.64	4:36.47
8116	Devon	Williams	USA	17.1.94	3	SEC	Tuscaloosa			13 May
	10.70/0.9	7.39/1.2 13.95	1.93	48.51		14.03/-0.8	42.40	4.65	58.59	4:33.15
8114	Cedric	Dubler	AUS	13.1.95	1	NC	Sydney			1 Apr
	10.71/1.3	7.72/0.7 11.93	2.15	48.47		14.25/0.7	42.81	4.90	53.29	4:55.71
8114	Gaël	Quérin	FRA	26.6.87	1		Hexham			10 Jul
	11.10/1.9	7.40w/3.3 13.30	1.96	49.45		14.18/0.8	40.79	5.05	54.34	4:12.71
8108	Karl Robert	Saluri	EST	6.8.93	1		Athens, GA			7 Apr
	10.66/1.3	7.42/1.2 14.29	1.85	48.34		15.09/1.5	43.80	4.95	57.99	4:27.43
8103	Pau Gaspar	Tonnesen	ESP	24.10.92	4	NCAA	Eugene			9 Jun
	11.35/1.0	7.37/0.7 14.10	1.95	50.91		14.39/1.1	45.93	5.30	60.44	4:38.20
8095	Pawel	Wiesiolek	POL	13.8.91	1	NC	Warszawa			5 Jun
	10.74/1.0	7.20/1.6 14.15	2.11	49.78		14.62/0.6	41.50	4.60	59.75	4:32.28
8087	Basile	Rolnin	FRA	21.1.94	1		Caorle			7 Aug
	11.28/-0.7	7.25/-0.3 14.718	2.04	50.17		14.45/1.4	48.22	5.00	48.22	4:41.91
	(30)									

DECATHLON

Mark	Name		Nat	Born	Pos	Meet	Venue			Date
8077	Oleksiy	Kasyanov	UKR	26.8.85	1		Talence			18 Sep
	10.65w/2.7	7.42/1.1 14.82	1.99	49.19		14.08/0.5	45.26	4.46	47.94	4:28.49
8073	Florian	Geffrouais	FRA	5.12.88	2	NC	Angers			25 Jun
	11.28/-0.3	7.10/1.5 15.14	1.89	49.41		14.88/1.4	45.86	5.00	58.61	4:19.50
8068	Yordani	García	CUB	21.11.88	2	NC	La Habana			18 Mar
	10.86/0.0	6.66/-1.5 14.48	2.00	49.19		14.32/0.5	39.90	4.90	65.38	4:31.84
8065	Sergey	Sviridov	RUS	20.10.90	1	NCp	Adler			22 May
	10.93/1.5	7.46/1.7 14.31	1.91	49.59		15.07	45.17	4.50	67.88	4:31.91
8058	Pieter	Braun	NED	21.1.93	8	Hypo	Götzis			29 May
	11.11/0.0	7.40/0.0 14.75	2.00	49.28		14.59/-0.6	44.65	4.60	55.70	4:27.06
8056	Ashley	Bryant	GBR	17.5.91	9	Hypo	Götzis			29 May
	11.08/0.3	7.58/0.8 13.28	2.00	49.54		14.70/-0.5	43.48	4.40	66.47	4:29.75
8055	Artem	Lukyanenko	RUS	30.1.90	2	NC	Cheboksary			21 Jun
	11.16w/2.2	7.15/0.4 15.02	1.93	49.68		14.55/1.3	45.71	5.20	53.97	4:34.66
8051	Niels	Pittomvils	BEL	18.7.92	10	Hypo	Götzis			29 May
	11.15/0.3	7.24w/3.0 13.40	2.00	50.14		14.77/-0.7	44.43	5.20	57.89	4:30.85
8032	Harrison	Williams	USA	7.3.96	5	NCAA	Eugene			9 Jun
	10.69/0.9	6.86/1.1 13.52	1.92	47.06		14.07/2.0	41.66	5.00	50.94	4:27.88
8027	Pierce	Lepage	CAN	22.1.96	3		Talence			18 Sep
	10.46w/2.7 (40)	7.75/1.3 14.18	2.02	48.01		14.69/0.2	40.79	4.86	48.88	4.58.77
8017	Yevgeniy	Sarantsev	RUS	5.8.88	3	NC	Cheboksary			21 Jun
	11.20w/2.2	7.13/0.0 15.04	1.99	50.99		15.17/1.3	45.97	4.90	63.47	4:34.94
8007	Romain	Barras	FRA	1.8.80	1		Perpignan			5 Jun
	11.12/1.9	7.16/0.7 15.36	1.96	49.02		14.47/1.8	44.00	4.80	59.20	4:45.54
7985	Jorge	Ureña	ESP	8.10.93	12	Hypo	Götzis			29 May
	10.93/1.1	7.47/1.6 12.71	2.03	49.42		14.24/-1.1	37.51	4.80	55.61	4:24.60
7958u	Jefferson	Carvalho	BRA	13.9.90	1		São Bernardo do Campo			23 Sep
	11.02	7.50 14.53	2.01	49.76		14.70	43.81	4.90	50.09	4:41.78
7942	Marcus	Nilsson	SWE	3.5.91	8	EC	Amsterdam			7 Jul
	11.29/0.8	7.02/0.9 14.15	1.98	50.93		14.97/-2.3	45.31	4.60	64.01	4:19.12
7940	Roman	Kondratyev	RUS	15.5.95	4	NC	Cheboksary			21 Jun
	10.76w/2.2	6.93 14.00	2.11	49.25		14.30	41.94	4.50	50.82	4:30.02
7936	Solomon	Simmons	USA	26.9.93	6	NCAA	Eugene			9 Jun
	10.88/0.9	7.03/0.7 15.15	1.8949.37	14.21/2.0		42.00		4.70	59.45	4:40.46
7925	Lars Vikan	Rise	NOR	23.11.88	1		Kladno			11 Jun
	11.32/-1.6	702/1.7 1602	201	50.71		15.56/1.1 4440	460		6682	4:36.84
7917	Steve	Bastien	USA	4.3.94	8	NCAA	Eugene			9 Jun
	10.68/1.3	7.48w/2.6 12.68	1.98	48.89		14.86/0.9	38.80	4.80	54.36	4:29.82
7907	Kristjan	Rosenberg	EST	16.5.94	1		Arona			5 Jun
	11.19/-0.4 [50]	7.42/0.0 13.73	2.11	50.07		15.27/0.0	39.44	4.82	58.19	4:35.72
7903	Marek	Lukás	CZE	16.7.91	2		Kladno			11 Jun
	11.00/-0.5	685/-0.1 1458	192	50.00		14.27/+0.94018	450		6896	4:35.05
7886	Mathias	Brugger	GER	6.8.92	9	EC	Amsterdam			7 Jul
	11.16/-1.0	7.22w/2.5 14.39	1.98	49.76		14.99/-1.3	42.79	4.70	57.35	4:30.24
7882	Ben	Gregory	GBR	21.11.90	1	MSR	Azusa			14 Apr
	11.14/1.8	7.34w/2.7 13.51	1.90	50.23		14.60/0.9	40.77	5.00	54.78	4:23.09
7879	Willem	Coertzen	RSA	30.12.82	6		Talence			18 Sep
	10.90w/2.7	7.25/2.0 13.18	1.90	49.50		14.62/0.5	41.57	4.46	65.25	4:31.56
7876	Scott	Filip	USA	28.1.95	1	vGER	Fayetteville			30 Jul
	10.63/1.1	7.57/1.2 13.88	2.02	49.07		14.92/1.3	39.47	4.75	48.33	4:42.18
7875	Fredrik	Samuelsson	SWE	16.2.95	10	EC	Amsterdam			7 Jul
	11.13/-1.0	7.30/0.5 13.99	2.07	51.02		14.65/-1.3	39.50	4.70	58.44	4:34.78
7862	Jonas	Fringeli	SUI	12.1.88	13	Hypo	Götzis			29 May
	11.17/0.7	7.05/1.3 13.30	2.00	48.87		14.54/-0.7	41.41	4.80	53.03	4:25.41
7860	Romain	Martin	FRA	12.7.88	2		Arona			5 Jun
	11.21/-0.4	7.11/0.0 13.59	2.02	49.49		14.94/-0.4	39.09	4.92	62.53	4:40.30
7859	Felipe Vinícius	dos Santos	BRA	30.7.94	2	NC	São Bernardo do Campo			2 Jul
	10.50/-0.2	7.49/0.2 12.63	1.97	48.24		14.34/-1.0	35.96	4.70	59.28	4:57.68
7856	Yevgeniy	Likhanov	RUS	10.1.95	3	NCp	Adler			22 May
	11.08/1.5 (60)	7.56/1.8 13.79	2.03	50.28		14.69	44.43	4.70	49.20	4:40.48
7855	Martin	Roe	NOR	1.4.92	2		Firenze			30 Apr
	10.82/1.8	7.15/-1.0 15.36	1.92	49.90		15.52/1.4	46.25	4.35	59.31	4:34.10
7838	Tim	Nowak	GER	13.8.95	14	Hypo	Götzis			29 May
	11.09/0.7	6.89/-1.9 14.07	1.94	50.29		14.82/0.0	45.15	4.60	60.32	4:28.84
7835	Feliks	Shestopalov	RUS	11.3.96	5	NC	Cheboksary			21 Jun
	11.21w/2.3	7.32 12.41	1.90	47.79		15.16	42.02	4.70	58.88	4:23.16
7830	Kale	Wolken	USA	13.9.93	1	NAIA	Gulf Shores, AL			27 May
	10.94/1.0	7.16/1.7 13.15	1.97	49.77		14.88w/3.3	43.79	4.85	57.16	4:43.01

MEN 2016

410 DECATHLON

Mark	Name			Nat	Born	Pos	Meet	Venue			Date
7827	Darko	Pesic		MNE	30.11.92	1	Balk C	Pitesti			26 Jun
	11.38/-0.6	7.33/0.4	14.67	1.99	51.04		14.59/-0.6	44.01	4.40	59.27	4:33.50
7822	Miller	Moss		USA	14.3.88	1		Chula Vista			29 May
	11.01/1.1	7.19/0.0	14.32	1.91	49.11		14.24/1.8	42.19	4.80	49.83	4:38.53
7814	Mikk	Pahapill		EST	18.7.83	3		Kladno			11 Jun
	11.37/-0.2	704/-0.1	1514	195	52.15		14.89/0.9	4708	480	6118	4:43.45
7812	René	Stauß		GER	17.9.87	1		Marburg			22 May
	11.42/-1.9	7.08/0.5	14.30	2.09	50.95		15.47/-1.0	44.21	5.00	55.22	4:39.45
7812	Sergey	Timshin		RUS	25.11.92	6	NC	Cheboksary			21 Jun
	11.01w/2.2	6.91	13.28	2.02	48.80		14.66	42.49	4.90	53.62	4:43.70
7807	Jérémy	Lelièvre		FRA	8.2.91	3	NC	Angers			25 Jun
	10.84/0.3	7.12/1.6	14.67	1.86	49.31		14.55/1.0	43.12	4.40	51.86	4:22.78
	(70)										
7800	Atsu	Nyamadi		GHA	1.6.94	4		Athens, GA			7 Apr
	11.15/1.8	7.51/-0.5	13.76	2.00	50.06		14.63/1.5	45.35	3.75	64.07	4:38.48
7795	Kurtis	Brondyke		USA	24.1.89	1		Dallas			5 Jun
	11.11+1.6	735+2.2	1517	193	50.46		14.88+1.34	680	441	5678	4:47.27
7794	Bas	Markies		NED	24.7.84	1	NC	Amsterdam			18 Jun
	10.81w/2.5	7.33/0.1	14.36	1.92	50.59		14.35/0.2	37.96	4.90	52.01	4:40.39
7785	Mitch	Modin		USA	12.4.95	7	NC/OT	Eugene			3 Jul
	10.87/1.2	7.42w/2.3	13.92	1.97	49.67		14.55/1.0	38.10	4.75	57.87	4:56.49
7784w	Luca	Wieland		GER	7.12.94	1	Big 10	Lincoln			14 May
	10.83w/2.6	7.71w/5.3	14.43	2.06	50.67		14.90w/2.6	44.53	4.31	50.50	4:56.56
7780	Friedrich	Pretorius		RSA	4.8.95	1	AfCh	Durban			23 Jun
	11.10	7.26	13.30	1.97	49.89		14.44	38.60	4.70	53.11	4:25.28
7776	James	Turner		CAN	4.8.93	2	MSR	Azusa			14 Apr
	11.04/0.4	7.42/1.2	13.48	1.87	49.60		15.03/0.9	43.34	4.80	57.74	4:43.27
7776	Austin	Bahner		USA	7.7.91	8	NC/OT	Eugene			3 Jul
	10.84/1.2	7.38/0.9	13.86	1.88	49.87		15.52/1.4	45.49	4.85	54.59	4:44.93
7762	Janek	Oiglane		EST	25.4.94	12	EC	Amsterdam			7 Jul
	11.21/0.8	7.10w/2.2	14.68	1.98	51.48		16.47/-1.3	44.62	4.80	67.41	4:42.01
7740	Aleksandr	Tabala		RUS	23.5.86	7	NC	Cheboksary			21 Jun
	11.60w/2.3	7.07	14.82	1.99	51.99		15.07	42.28	4.90	60.27	4:36.0
	(80)										
7734	Juuso	Hassi		FIN	4.4.93	1	NC	Oulu			24 Jul
	10.96/0.3	7.19/1.3	14.09	1.93	49.72		15.10/1.0	40.77	4.50	58.69	4:35.58
7730	Jan	Dolezal		CZE	6.6.96	4		Kladno			11 Jun
	11.09/-0.2	703/-1.8	1338	198	49.76		14.72/0.6	4852	460	5307	4:49.94
7728	Curtis	Beach		USA	22.7.90	9	NC/OT	Eugene			3 Jul
	10.75/1.8	7.33/1.7	12.61	1.88	48.23		14.95/1.2	36.85	4.65	47.65	4:12.13
7720	Ruben	Gado		FRA	13.12.93	4	NC	Angers			25 Jun
	10.83/0.3	7.20/1.2	11.80	1.92	49.98		15.12/1.4	39.44	5.00	51.79	4:21.01
7711	Gonzalo	Barroilhet		CHI	19.8.86	5		Athens, GA			7 Apr
	11.36/1.8	6.93/0.0	14.41	2.00	51.79		14.03/1.6	43.63	4.95	53.92	4:54.8
7709	Briander	Rivero		CUB	23.4.91	3	NC	La Habana			18 Mar
	11.02/0.0	6.77/-0.3	14.32	2.06	50.59		14.62/0.5	44.05	4.00	63.63	4:45.66
7709	Tim	Duckworth		GBR	18.6.96	4	SEC	Tuscaloosa			13 May
	10.85/0.6	7.44/1.3	11.17	2.11	51.21		14.84/-0.3	39.79	5.05	55.01	5:00.84
7704	Elmo	Savola		FIN	10.3.95	2	NC	Oulu			24 Jul
	11.01/0.3	6.95/1.2	13.57	1.96	50.17		14.66/1.0	39.64	4.70	63.28	4:50.83
7703	Kyle	Cranston		AUS	3.9.92	1		Sydney			10 Jan
	11.18/0.0	6.96/-0.8	13.31	1.97	49.53		14.74/0.2	42.43	4.40	59.31	4:32.66
7695	Román	Gastaldi		ARG	25.9.89	7		Kladno			11 Jun
	11.06/-0.5	6.98/-1.0	14.19	2.01	49.79		14.93/0.6	43.48	4.50	54.08	4:43.33
	(90)										
7683	Vasyl	Ivanytskyy		UKR	29.1.91	1	NC	Lutsk			17 Jun
	11.19/0.0	7.18/0.4	12.59	1.96	50.46		14.68/-0.7	40.16	4.70	60.88	4:40.55
7680	José Ángel	Mendieta		CUB	16.10.91	1	Barr	La Habana			27 May
	11.09/0.0	6.82w/2.9	15.26	1.94	50.22		13.80/0.0	42.46	4.30	61.88	5:00.47
7667	Patrick	Scherfose		GER	28.11.91	2		Marburg			22 May
	11.10/-1.9	7.34w/2.2	14.56	1.91	50.74		14.64/-1.3	42.98	4.80	48.82	4:48.62
7665	Kazuya	Kawasaki		JPN	2.9.92	1		Kumagaya			3 Sep
	10.88/0.9	7.46/1.2	11.56	2.02	49.23		15.61/2.0	38.16	4.60	57.74	4:36.55
7659	Pelle	Rietveld		NED	4.2.85	3		Ratingen			26 Jun
	11.19/-1.0	6.67/0.1	12.68	1.80	49.45		14.89/-0.9	40.72	4.80	71.66	4:49.46
7659	Alex	Soares		BRA	2.2.95	3	NC	São Bernardo do Campo			2 Jul
	11.19/-0.2	7.47/-0.1	14.76	1.97	50.22		14.77/-1.0	43.43	4.40	64.10	5:27.08
7643	Jake	Stein		AUS	17.1.94	2	NC	Sydney			1 Apr
	11.41/1.9	7.21/0.4	15.01	1.97	52.02		14.87/0.7	48.16	4.20	62.81	xxx
7643	Edgars	Erins		LAT	18.6.86	9		Kladno			11 Jun
	11.10/-0.2	6.65/0.3	13.85	1.80	49.39		14.94/0.6	46.60	4.40	53.86	4:14.49

DECATHLON

Mark	Name		Nat	Born	Pos	Meet	Venue			Date
7639	Jonay	Jordán	ESP	12.5.91	1	POR Ch	Maia			26 Jun
	11.07/1.8	7.18w/2.8 14.24	1.93	50.59		14.72/0.5	44.43	4.60	54.72	4:56.93
7620w	Cody	Walton	USA	14.6.95	3	Big 10	Lincoln			14 May
	10.98w/3.5	6.79w/2.1 12.74	1.91	49.55		14.45w/2.6	38.97	4.81	63.51	4:56.92
	[100]									
7616	Simone	Cairoli ITA	12.9.90	15 May	7481	Guillaume	Thierry	MRI	15.9.86	3 Apr
7616		Hu Yufei CHN	9.11.93	17 Sep	7480		Chen Xiaohong	CHN-J	9.2.97	22 Apr
7601	Rostam	Turner CAN	95	17 Jul	7478		Xiong Shanhu	CHN	24.3.93	21 May
7594	Yaroslav	Novitskiy RUS	4.4.88	21 Jun	7474	Brent	Newdick	NZL	31.1.85	11 Jun
7593	Johannes	Erm EST-J	26.3.98	7 Aug	7471	Taylor	Sanderson	USA	2.10.92	8 Apr
7590	Nils	Merten GER	20.2.91	22 May	7469w	Kimihito	Morimoto	JPN	21.4.93	12 Jun
7590	Cody	Thomas NZL	5.10.91	27 May	7446	Román	Garibay	MEX	30.10.88	31 Mar
7588	Ibn	Short USA	16.3.95	13 May	7446	Japheth	Cato	USA	25.12.90	25 Jun
7587	Manuel	González CUB	23.3.93	27 May	7444	Sybren	Blok	NED	25.6.96	10 Jul
7576	Thomas	FitzSimons USA	8.3.89	2 Apr	7441	Felix	Hepperle	GER	23.11.89	14 Aug
7570	Yevgeniy	Chernov RUS	9.11.91	22 May	7439	Ippei	Nimaida	JPN	21.7.90	12 Jun
7543	Michael	Morrison USA	18.3.88	7 Apr	7439	Taavi	Tsernjavski	EST	4.3.95	7 Aug
7541	Torben	Blech GER	12.2.95	14 Aug	7438	Brad	Culp	USA	5.5.93	26 Mar
7535	Tsuyoshi	Shimizu JPN	21.12.93	12 Jun	7433	Michele	Calvi	ITA	7.6.90	30 Apr
7521	Liam	Ramsay GBR	18.11.92	29 May	7432	Joe	Delgado	USA	8.1.95	9 Jun
7520	Axel	McCune USA	7.4.93	13 May	7424	Mat	Clark	USA	31.5.87	5 Jun
7519	Yevgeniy	Teptin RUS	16.3.90	22 May	7422	Suguru	Shiozaki	JPN	21.11.96	3 Sep
7517	David	Brock AUS	8.6.94	1 Apr	7417	Ánderson	Venâncio	BRA	6.1.87	22 Apr
7513	Dennis	Hutterer GER	4.5.96	26 Jun	7411	Maxime	Maugein	FRA	27.9.92	17 Jul
7511	Axel	Martin FRA	13.4.94	18 Sep	7403A	Jackson	Walker	USA	18.1.92	22 Apr
7488	Sergey	Whitaker USA	4.6.93	13 May	7400	Vitaliy	Zhuk	BLR	10.9.96	25 Jun
7488	Maksim	Korolyov RUS	6.1.88	21 Jun	7400	Asuka	Kashiwagura	JPN	17.12.94	3 Sep
7485	Thomas	Hopkins USA	28.5.91	25 Jun	(145)					

Doubtful Mark

8250	Leonid	Andreyev	UZB	6.10.83	1		Tashkent			10 Jun
	11.01	7.30 16.27	2.09	50.13		14.57	46.20	5.45	61.02	5:21.21

JUNIORS

7593	Johannes	Erm	EST	26.3.98	2	NC	Rakvere			7 Aug
	10.78/0.6	7.25/0.6 12.36	1.92	49.19		15.51/-0.8	40.02	4.50	55.14	4:33.89
7480		Chen Xiaohong	CHN	9.2.97	1		Huaian			22 Apr
	10.86/-0.4	7.28/2.0 12.74	1.83	49.53		15.30/0.5	43.23	4.60	64.77	5:25.22
7338	2	Taiyuan		21 May						
7318	Artyom	Makarenko	RUS	23.4.97	2	NC-j	Saransk			17 Jul
	11.09/1.3	6.91 12.97	1.94	49.39		14.88/-1.1	35.03	4.60	45.55	4:38.87
7211	Sebastian	Ruthström	SWE	4.8.97	2	NC	Falun			11 Sep
	11.69/0.7	7.12/1.0 13.12	1.99	51.63		15.63/1.5	38.16	4.45	58.99	4:57.43
7260	Jan	Dolezal	CZE	6.6.96	25	ECp	Aubagne			5 Jul
	10.94/0.3	7.08/-0.1 12.55	2.01	49.47		15.79/-0.9	43.04	4.30	48.90	5:10.04
7179A	Andy	Preciado	ECU	12.10.97	1	NC-j	Ambato			21 Aug
	11.00	6.82 14.28	2.05	52.10		14.70	42.96	3.80	59.02	5:26.20
7093		Yue Xuesong	CHN	31.10.97	8	NC	Tianjin			17 Sep
	11.06/-0.3	7.05/0.3 11.35	1.86	50.75		15.12/-0.7	30.46	4.70	58.03	5:00.05
7057w	Cale	Wagner	USA	25.7.97	8	Big10	Lincoln			14 May
	10.79w/2.6	7.25/1.8 12.15	1.97	50.64		15.89/1.4	31.76	4.11	46.57	4:41.95

IAAF JUNIOR SPECIFICATION – WITH 99CM 110MH, 6KG SP, 1.75KG DT

8162	Miklas	Kaul	GER	11.2.98	1	WJ	Bydgoszcz			20 Jul
	11.52/0.8	6.79/-1.9 14.80	2.10	49.69		14.72/0.9	41.80	4.80	71.59	4:21.70
7910	1	Kreutzal		12 Jun						
	11.51/0.2	6.69/-1.8 15.30	2.08	49.85		14.71/-0.2	43.57	4.70	58.82	4:29.245
8046	Maksim	Andraloits	BLR	17.6.97	2	WJ	Bydgoszcz			20 Jul
	10.97/0.7	7.20/-1.1 15.00	2.04	49.33		13.95/0.4	48.62	4.60	48.79	4:43.65
7972	Jan	Ruhrmann	GER	14.7.97	1		Marburg			22 May
	11.37/-1.3	7.05/0.3 17.15	1.93	49.77		15.56/-0.8	49.17	4.40	63.01	4:32.33
7795	6	WJ Bydgoszcz		20 Jul						
	11.29/0.0	6.78/-0.7 15.83	1.98	49.61		15.11/1.1	45.95	4.30	56.72	4:27.10
7943h	Santiago	Ford	CUB	25.8.97	1		La Habana			4 May
	10.9h/1.6	7.00/1.7 15.78	2.01	49.9h		13.9h/-2.4	49.76	4.00	64.85	4:55.7h
7819	4	WJ Bydgoszcz		20 Jul		10 performances by 7 men over 7700				
	11.40/0.7	7.05/-0.9 13.09	1.95	50.09		14.20/0.4	51.67	4.00	63.57	4:34.54
7879	Johannes	Erm	EST	26.3.98	3	WJ	Bydgoszcz			20 Jul
	11.06/0.7	7.42/-0.3 13.44	1.92	48.17		14.66/0.9	43.61	4.50	54.19	4:28.96
7815	Toraiv	Opsal	NOR	9.3.98	5	WJ	Bydgoszcz			20 Jul
	11.30/0.8	7.11/-0.1 13.73	1.98	49.17		14.66/1.1	43.08	4.70	50.23	4:21.61
7701	Rik	Taam	NED	17.1.97	1	NC-j	Alphen aan den Rijn			15 May
	10.95/-0.1	6.90/1.7 14.98	1.80	48.92		14.10w/2.8	45.08	4.30	54.15	4:40.49
7693	Dmitriy	Solomatin	RUS	15.4.98	1	NCp	Adler			22 May
	11.26/0.0	7.12/0.0 15.49	1.91	49.18		15.21/1.2	40.67	4.60	50.76	4:27.80

DECATHLON – 4 x 100 METRES

Mark	Name	Nat	Born	Pos	Meet	Venue	Date
7663h	Rafael Noguera 10.7h/1.6 6.81/1.7 14.22	CUB 1.89	28.2.97 48.5h	2 13.8h/-2.4	37.64 4.10 53.64	La Habana	4 May 4:18.6h
7650	Artem Makarenko (10) 11.25/-1.4 7.26w/2.3 14.71	RUS 1.99	23.4.97 49.87	1 14.41/-0.5	NC-j 38.07 4.60 49.51	Kazan	27 Jun 4:42.76
7592	Hans-Christian Hausenberg 10.91/1.2 7.52w/2.3 14.83	EST 1.94	18.9.98 52.34	1 14.31/1.0	v2N 43.35 5.00 52.31	Jekabpils	23 May 5:44.21
7592	Nathaniel Mechler 11.05/0.0 7.17/-0.3 12.02	CAN 2.02	31.3.97 48.66	1 14.84/0.9	38.73 4.50 48.53	Ottawa	19 Jun 4:29.78
7539	Lennard Biere 11.61/-1.0 7.12/-0.1 16.81	GER 1.93	3.2.97 50.61	2 14.70/-0.4	46.27 4.50 49.13	Kreutzal	12 Jun 5:06.35
7532	Cale Wagner 10.67/1.7 7.43w/2.6 13.56	USA 2.00	25.7.97 50.67	1 14.75/1.2	NC-j 37.29 4.20 52.02	Clovis	25 Jun 4:51.54
7468	Tristan Freyr Jónsson 10.91/0.7 6.89/-0.8 12.56	ISL 1.95	20.9.97 49.06	9 14.19/0.4	WJ 41.41 4.30 51.51	Bydgoszcz	20 Jul 4:55.32
7452	Rody de Wolff 11.40/0.8 6.69/-1.1 15.57	NED 1.89	9.4.97 51.82	10 14.93/0.9	WJ 51.44 4.10 56.75	Bydgoszcz	20 Jul 4:56.23
7376	Risto Lillemets 11.54/0.1 6.85/0.4 13.62	EST 1.89	20.11.97 51.57	1 14.80/-0.8	43.22 4.30 57.68	Rakvere	7 Aug 4:38.36
7330	Maximilian Vollmer 11.22/-1.0 6.87/0.0 14.62	GER 1.78	12.3.98 49.53	3 14.97/-0.2	38.13 4.20 56.60	Kreutzal	12 Jun 4:39.53
7330	Ludovic Besson 11.11/1.9 6.79/0.7 15.39	FRA 1.87	27.1.98 51.58	1 15.13/1.3	44.92 4.30 49.79	Guéret	19 Jun 4:53.04

4 X 100 METRES RELAY

Mark	Nat	Names	Pos	Meet	Venue	Date
37.27	JAM	Powell, Blake, Ashmeade, Bolt	1	OG	Rio de Janeiro	19 Aug
37.60	JPN	Yamagata, Iizuka, Kiryu, Cambridge	2	OG	Rio de Janeiro	19 Aug
37.64	CAN	Haynes, A.Brown, Rodney, DeGrasse	3	OG	Rio de Janeiro	19 Aug
37.65	USA	Rodgers, Coleman, Gay, Lawson	1h1	OG	Rio de Janeiro	18 Aug
37.68	JPN	Yamagata, Iizuka, Kiryu, Cambridge	1h2	OG	Rio de Janeiro	18 Aug
37.78	GBR A	Dasaolu, Gemili, Ellington, Ujah	1	DL	London (OS)	23 Jul
37.81	GBR B	Kilty, Aikines-Aryeetey, Talbot, Edoburun	2	DL	London (OS)	23 Jul
37.82	CHN	Tang, Xie, Su, Zhang	2h1	OG	Rio de Janeiro	18 Aug
37.89	CAN	Haynes, A.Brown, Rodney, Ajomale	3h1	OG	Rio de Janeiro	18 Aug
37.90	CHN	Tang, Xie, Su, Zhang	4	OG	Rio de Janeiro	19 Aug
37.94	JAM	Minzie, Powell, Ashmeade, Bailey-Cole	2h2	OG	Rio de Janeiro	18 Aug
37.96	TTO	Bledman, Sorrillo, Callender, Thompson	3h2	OG	Rio de Janeiro	18 Aug
37.98	GBR	Kilty, Aikines-Aryeetey, Ellington, Gemili	5	OG	Rio de Janeiro	19 Aug
38.06	GBR	Kilty, Aikines-Aryeetey, Ellington, Ujah	4h2	OG	Rio de Janeiro	18 Aug
38.11	CAN	Haynes, A.Brown, Rodney, DeGrasse	1	FlaR	Gainesville	2 Apr
38.12	GBR	Dasaolu, Gemili, Ellington, Ujah	1h1	EC	Amsterdam	9 Jul
38.17	GBR	Dasaolu, Gemili, Ellington, Ujah	1	EC	Amsterdam	10 Jul
38.17	CAN	Haynes, Ajomale, Rodney, A.Brown	3	DL	London (OS)	23 Jul
38.19	BRA	R de Souza, V dos Santos, de Barros, Vides	5h2	OG	Rio de Janeiro	18 Aug
38.21	CHN	Yang, Xie, Su, Zhang	1		Beijing	18 May
38.22	GER	Reus, Knipphals, Hering, Jakubczyk	1		Mannheim	29 Jul
		(21 perfromances by teams from 9 nations)				
38.30	TUR	Safer, Harvey, Barnes, Guliyev	4h1	OG	Rio de Janeiro	18 Aug
38.35	FRA	René, Dutamby, Zézé, Vicaut	5h1	OG	Rio de Janeiro	18 Aug
38.44	CUB	Ruíz, Skyers, Mena, Carrero	1h1	IbAm	Rio de Janeiro	15 May
38.44	NED	Bockarie, Martina, van Luijk, Paulina	1	GGala	Roma	2 Jun
38.44	ANT	C.Walsh, Greene, Jarvis, T.Walsh	6h1	OG	Rio de Janeiro	18 Aug
38.52	DOM	De Oloe, Andujar, Del Carmen, Martinez	1	IbAm	Rio de Janeiro	16 May
38.58	ITA	Ferraro, Cattaneo, Manenti, Tortu	3h1	EC	Amsterdam	9 Jul
38.64	POL	Zimniewicz, Slowikowski, Pawlowski, Zalewski	1h2	EC	Amsterdam	9 Jul
38.84	RSA	Erasmus, van Niekerk, Leotlela, Simbine	1	AfCh	Durban	24 Jul
38.88	SUI	Mancini, Schenkel, Somasundaram, Wilson	4h1	EC	Amsterdam	9 Jul
38.95	POR	Antunes, Lima, Abrantes, Nascimento	2		Lisboa (U)	19 Jun
	(20)					
38.98	CIV	Cissé, Koffi, Tchan, Meité	2	AfCh	Durban	24 Jun
39.11	BAR	Cadogan, Ellis, Deshong, Burke	3		Road Town	3 Jul
39.12	UKR	Kravtsov, Suprun, Bodrov, Korzh	5h1	EC	Amsterdam	9 Jul
39.15	ESP	Triana, Husillos, Gavaldá, A.Rodriguez	6h1	EC	Amsterdam	9 Jul
39.23	HKG	So Chun Hong, Ng Ka Fung, Tang Yik Chun, Lai Chun Ho	2		Beijing	18 May
39.25	FIN	Hamalainen, Ahlfors, Samuelsson, Myllymäki	1	vSWE	Tampere	4 Sep
39.26	AUS	T.Williams, Jung, Hartmann, Jaworski	1		Canberra	19 Feb
39.26	BAH		1		Nassau	10 Jul
39.28	INA	Iswandi, Bobi, Fadlin, Nugroho	1		Singapore	29 Apr
39.35	NOR	Halonen, Quarcoo, Morken, Saidy Ndure	4h2	EC	Amsterdam	9 Jul
	(30)					

4 x 100m – 4 x 200m – 4 x 400 METRES

Mark		Name		Nat		Born		Pos	Meet	Venue		Date	
39.37	SWE	9	Jul	39.51	TPE	19	May	39.55	CZE	18 Jun	39.57A	KEN	26 May	39.68	GHA	7 Aug
39.39	SKN	3	Jul	39.52	IRL	9	Jul	39.55	KOR	3 Jul	39.60 A	ROU	12 Jun	39.69	THA	8 May

JUNIORS

Mark	Nat	Name	Pos	Meet	Venue	Date
38.93	USA	Norman, Montgomery, B Taylor, N Lyles	1	WJ	Bydgoszcz	23 Jul
39.01	JPN	Takeda, Yamashita, Inuzuka, Oshima	2	WJ	Bydgoszcz	23 Jul
39.13	GER	Gurski, Vartel, Giese, Eitel	3	WJ	Bydgoszcz	23 Jul
39.13	JAM	Chanbers, Ellis, Matherson, Russell	4	WJ	Bydgoszcz	23 Jul
39.51	TPE	Yeh S-P, Yang C-H, Liu ChH, Shen Y-S	1h1		Taoyuan	19 May
39.57	AUS	Williams, Hale, Searle, Andrews	5	WJ	Bydgoszcz	23 Jul
39.57	GBR	Plummer, Bromby, Gorman, Matthew	6	WJ	Bydgoszcz	23 Jul
39.88A	RSA	(Tuks Sports School)	1		Johannesburg	18 Mar
39.91	MAS		2	Asi-J	Ho Chih Moinh	5 Jun
39.98	POL	Galandziej, Wesela, Sztekkowski, Hampel	3h2	WJ	Bydgoszcz	22 Jul

4 X 200 METRES RELAY

Mark	Nat	Name	Pos	Meet	Venue	Date
1:19.20	CAN	Smellie, Rodney, DeGrasse, A.Brown	1	FlaR	Gainesville	2 Apr
1:20.79		Star Athletucs	2	FlaR	Gainesville	2 Apr
1:20.94	USA	Young, Gatlin, Spearmon, Rodgers	1	PennR	Philadelphia	30 Apr
1:21.11		Texas A&M Un. Grant, Kerley, Morrow, Jenkins	1	TexR	Austin	2 Apr
1:21.14		Louisiana State Un (USA/JAM/ZIM.GBR)	2	TexR	Austin	2 Apr

4 X 400 METRES RELAY

Mark	Nat	Name	Pos	Meet	Venue	Date
2:57.30	USA	Hall 45.3, McQuay 43.2, Roberts 44.79, Merritt 43.97	1	OG	Rio de Janeiro	20 Aug
2:58.16	JAM	Matthews 45.5, Allen 44.0, Dunkley 44.82, Francis 43.78	2	OG	Rio de Janeiro	20 Aug
2:58.29	JAM	MacDonald 45.8, Matthews 44.4, Allen 43.52, Francis 44.55	1h1	OG	Rio de Janeiro	19 Aug
2:58.38	USA	Hall 45.3, McQuay 43.4, Clemons 44.98, Verburg 44.59	2h1	OG	Rio de Janeiro	19 Aug
2:58.49	BAH	Russell 45.3, Mathieu 45.2, Gardiner 43.79, Brown 44.20	3	OG	Rio de Janeiro	20 Aug
2:58.52	BEL	Watrin 46.0, J.Borlée 44.1, D.Borlée 44.71, K.Borlée 43.67	4	OG	Rio de Janeiro	20 Aug
2:59.06	BOT	Makwala 44.9, Sibanda 43.9, Nkobolo 44.94, Maotaonong 45.28	5	OG	Rio de Janeiro	20 Aug
2:59.25	BEL	Watrin 45.8, J.Borlée 44.1, D.Borlée 45.20, K.Borlée 44.15	1h2	OG	Rio de Janeiro	19 Aug
2:59.35	BOT	Makwala 45.0, Sibanda 44.0, Nkobolo 45.23, Maotaonong 45.15	3h1	OG	Rio de Janeiro	19 Aug
2:59.53	CUB	Collazo 45.7, Chacón 44.7, Pellicier 45.33, Lescay 43.60	6	OG	Rio de Janeiro	20 Aug
2:59.58	POL	Krawczuk 45.7, Pietrzak 44.7, Krzewina 44.72, Omelko 44.42	4h1	OG	Rio de Janeiro	19 Aug
2:59.64	BAH	Russell 45.2, Brown 44.7, Gardiner 44.90, Newbold 44.83	2h2	OG	Rio de Janeiro	19 Aug
3:00.16	CUB	Collazo 46.0, Chacón 44.5, Pellicier 45.40, Lescay 44.21	3h2	OG	Rio de Janeiro	19 Aug
3:00.43	BRA	de Oliveira 45.3, Russo 45.0, P.dos Santos 45.02, H So.usa 44.96	4h2	OG	Rio de Janeiro	19 Aug
3:00.50	POL	Krawczuk 46.0, Pietrzak 45.0, Krzewina 44.94, Omelko 44.59	7	OG	Rio de Janeiro	20 Aug
3:00.82	FRA	Anne 45.5, Venel 45.0, Hann 45.04, Jordier 45.23	5h1	OG	Rio de Janeiro	19 Aug
3:00.89	USA	Wright, Grant, Rosser, Cherry	1	NACAC	San Salvador	17 Jul
3:00.91	IND	Kunhu, Anas, Dharun, Rajiv	1		Bengaluru	10 Jun
	(18/10)					
3:01.16A	COL	Zambrano, Lemos, Palomeque, Perlaza	1		Medellín	10 Jul
3:01.44	GBR	Yousif 45.6, D.Williams 44.8, J.Green 45.64, Hudson-Smith 45.32	3	EC	Amsterdam	10 Jul
3:01.67A	VEN	A.Ramírez, Longart, Meléndez, Mezones	2		Medellín	10 Jul
3:01.76	DOM	Soriano 46.4, Santos 44.4, Charles 45.92, Cuesta 46.01	5h2	OG	Rio de Janeiro	19 Aug
3:02.11	JPN	Walsh, Tamura, Kitagawa, Kato	1		Osaka	10 Jul
3:02.22A	TUR	Kiliç, Copello, Altintas, Can	2		Erzurum	12 Jul
3:02.66	CZE	Tesar 46.4, Maslák 44.2, Desensky 46.54, Sorm 45.49	3h1	EC	Amsterdam	9 Jul
3:03.10A	UKR	Butrym, Burakov, Danylenko, Hutsol	3		Erzurum	12 Jun
3:03.91	QAT	Samba, Balla, Abdallah, Haroun	3	DL	Doha	6 May
3:03.97	GER	C.Schmidt 47.2, Schneider 45.2, Gaba 45.61, Trefz 45.95	3h2	EC	Amsterdam	9 Jul
	(20)					
3:04.04	NED	Bonevacia 46.7, Agard 45.6, Blauwhof 45.87, Stuivenberg 45.81	4h2	EC	Amsterdam	9 Jul
3:04.25	KEN	Mucheru, Kishoyan, Mweresa, H.Koech	2	AfCh	Durban	26 Jun
3:04.32	IRL	Gregan 45.9, Lynch 46.3, Gillick 46.13, Barr 45.98	5	EC	Amsterdam	10 Jul
3:04.73	RSA	Seeliger, de Jager, Mogawane, van Zyl	3	AfCh	Durban	26 Jun
3:04.77	ESP	García 46.4, Bua 45.3, Fernández 46.03, Vallejo 47.05	5h2	EC	Amsterdam	9 Jul
3:04.95	SWE	Bergrahm 47.2, Martinsson 45.6, Francois 45.91, Danielsson 46.25	6h2	EC	Amsterdam	9 Jul
3:05.20	KSA	Al-Yassin, Al-Nasser, Souleiman, Al-Masrahi	1	TexR	Austin	2 Apr
3:05.93	CAN	Cunningham, Parris, Bellemore, George	4	NACAC	San Salvador	17 Jul
3:06.07	ITA	Valentini 47.1, Tricca 47.2, Lambrughi 45.85, Galvan 45.88	6h1	EC	Amsterdam	9 Jul
3:06.38	CHN-Shandong	Wang, Zhang, Zhai, Zhu	1		Tianjin	17 Sep
	(30)					
3:06.52 SUI	9 Jul	3:07.22 PUR	4 Jun	3:07.56 CHI	16 May	3:08.28 TTO	24 Jul						
3:06.81 NGR	30 Apr	3:07.32 ALG	26 Jun	3:07.59 SRI	11 Feb	3:08.54 CRO	26 Jun						

Mixed nationalities

Mark	Nat	Name	Pos	Meet	Venue	Date
3:00.38	LSU - USA/JAM	Bruton, Cherry, Grayson, Dunkley JAM	1		Baton Rouge	23 Apr
3:00.48	LSU - USA/JAM	Bruton 45.9, Cherry 44.3, Grayson 45.16, Dunkley 45.16	1	SEC	Tuscaloosa	14 May
3:00.69	LSU - USA/JAM	Bruton 46.4, Cherry 44.2, Grayson 45.80, Dunkley 44.29	1	NCAA	Eugene	10 Jun

4 x 400m - 3000 METRES WALK - 5000 METRES WALK

Mark		Name		Nat	Born	Pos Meet	Venue	Date

Low altitude best
3:02.69 VEN A.Ramírez 46.1, Longart 45.2, Bravo 44.70, Mezones 46.55   6h2 OG   Rio de Janeiro 19 Aug

Disqualified- Relay zone infringement
2:58.82 GBR Levine 45.7, D.Williams 44.0, Hudson-Smith 45.32, Rooney 43.75 [1h2] OG   Rio de Janeiro 19 Aug
2:58.84 TTO J.Solomon 45.0, L.Gordon 44.5, Lendore 44.78, Cedenio 44.57   [3h1] OG   Rio de Janeiro 19 Aug

JUNIORS

3:02.39 USA Allison 46.8, Cogdell 45.5, Montgomery 45.27, London 44.82 1   WJ Bydgoszcz 24 Jul
3:02.81 BOT Poo 47.5, Thebe 43.5, Sibanda 45.38, Talane 46.44 2 WJ Bydgoszcz 24 Jul
         3:03.75 Poo 47.8, Thebe 44.2, Sibanda 45.28, Talane 46.47 1h1 WJ Bydgoszcz 24 Jul
3:04.83 JAM Carpenter 47.1, S Bailey 46.3, Thomas 46.31, C Taylor 45.12 3 WJ Bydgoszcz 24 Jul
3:07.02 JPN Obuchi 47.4, Kitakami 46.4, Watanabe 47.08, Matsukiyo 46.14 4 WJ Bydgoszcz 24 Jul
3:08.13 GER Sanders 47.7, Wagner 47.0, Dammermann 47.02, Schlegel 46.41 5 WJ Bydgoszcz 24 Jul
3:08.28 TTO St. Clair 47.3, St. Hillare 46.9, Taylor, 47.4, King 46.67 6 WJ Bydgoszcz 24 Jul
3:08.89 IND Luran 47.5, Kumar, 47.1 Malik 47.89, Jacob 46.65 7 WJ Bydgoszcz 24 Jul
3:09.42 ITA Mezzaluna 47.7, Aceti 47.1, Lopez, Sibilio 47.88 3h2 WJ Bydgoszcz 23 Jul
3:09.42 POL Rzeznuiczak, Miroslaw, Mroczek, 46.74Zimny 6h1 WJ Bydgoszcz 23 Jul
3:10.08 THA Kongkraphan, Thumcha, Sunthonthuam, Phosri 7h1 WJ Bydgoszcz 23 Jul

3000 METRES WALK

Mark	Name		Nat	Born	Pos	Meet	Venue	Date
11:13.94	Alex	Wright	IRL	19.12.90	1		Cork	28 Jun
11:14.95+	Miguel Ángel	López	ESP	3.7.88	1	in 10k	Gijón	24 Jul
11:18.65	Robert	Heffernan	IRL	20.2.78	2		Cork	28 Jun
11:22.36	Antón	Kucmín	SVK	7.6.84	1	PTS	Samorín	4 Jun
11:29.15	Grzegorz	Sudoł	POL	28.8.78	3		Cork	28 Jun
11:31.69	Matej	Tóth	SVK	10.2.83	2	PTS	Samorín	4 Jun
11:32.53	Miroslav	Úradník	SVK	24.3.96	3	PTS	Samorín	4 Jun
11:34.06	Brendan	Boyce	IRL	15.10.86	4		Cork	28 Jun
11:34.6	Quentin	Rew	NZL	16.7.84	1		Melbourne	30 Jan

Indoors
10:58.21	Tom	Bosworth	GBR	17.1.90	1	NC	Sheffield	28 Feb
11:25.57+	Grzegorz	Sudol	POL	28.8.78	3	in 5k	Bratislava	31 Jan
11:36.46	Erik	Tysse	NOR	4.12.80	1		Bergen	23 Jan

JUNIORS

11:35.49	Dominik	Cerny	SVK	1.11.97	4	PTS	Samorín	4 Jun
11:36.2	Callum	Wilkinson	GBR	14.3.97	1		Bury St Edmonds	15 May
11:40.32	Declan	Tingay	AUS	6.2.99	1		Geelong	17 Dec

Indoors
| 11:47.12 | Cameron | Corbishley | GBR | 31.3.97 | 1 | | Cardiff | 13 Dec |

5000 METRES WALK

Mark	Name		Nat	Born	Pos	Meet	Venue	Date
18:38.97	Dane	Bird-Smith	AUS	15.7.92	1		Melbourne	5 Mar
18:42.96	Yohann	Diniz	FRA	1.1.78	1		Tomblaine	14 Jun
18:46.47		Bird-Smith			1		Brisbane	6 Feb
18:46.95	Miguel Ángel	López	ESP	3.7.88	1		Murcia	26 Jun
18:53.91	Francesco	Fortunato	ITA	13.12.94	1		Borgo Valsugana	18 Jun
18:55.0+		López			1	in 10k	Gijón	24 Jul
18:59.46	Kevin	Campion	FRA	23.5.88	1	NC	Angers	26 Jun
19:02.91	Eiki	Takahashi	JPN	19.11.92	1		Kumagaya	21 May
19:04.93	Álvaro	Martín	ESP	18.6.94	1		Cáceres	29 Jun
19:05.46	Hirooki	Arai	JPN	18.5.88	2		Kumagaya	21 May
	(10/8)							
19:05.91	Luís Alberto	Amezcua	ESP	1.5.92	1		Torremolinos	9 Jul
19:07.03	Iván	Pajuelo (10)	ESP	27.8.93	2		Cáceres	29 Jun
19:07.58	Takayuki	Tanii	JPN	14.2.83	3		Kumagaya	21 May
19:10.25	Takumi	Saito	JPN	23.3.93	1		Tajimi	15 Oct
19:11.94	Kai	Kobayashi	JPN	28.2.93	1		Abashiri	11 Jul
19:13.56	Tom	Bosworth	GBR	17.1.90	2	NC	Birmingham	26 Jun
19:15.33	Erik	Tysse	NOR	4.12.80	1	NC	Askøy	29 Jul
19:15.94	Kirill	Frolov	RUS	29.9.93	1		Moskva	28 Jul
19:18.33	Matteo	Giupponi	ITA	8.10.88	1		Milano	22 Apr
19:19.63	Roman	Yevstifeyev	RUS	19.9.92	2		Moskva	28 Jul
19:19.79	Håvard	Haukenes	NOR	22.4.90	2	NC	Askøy	29 Jul
19:22.64	Leonardo	Dei Tos	ITA	27.4.92	2		Milano	22 Apr
19:26.76	Rhydian	Cowley	AUS	4.1.91	5 Mar	19:35.4	Callum Wilkinson GBR-J 14.3.97	2 Jul
19:28.75	Sergey	Sharipov	RUS	14.4.92	28 Jul	19:35.82	Máté Helebrandt HUN 12.1.89	22 Jul
19:31.24	Michael	Hosking	AUS	16.10.85	5 Mar	19:36.39	Marc Tur ESP 30.11.94	18 Jun
19:31.55	Evan	Dunfee	CAN	28.9.90	17 Jun	19:37.93	Hassanine Sbaï TUN 21.1.84	22 May
						19:37.96	Robert Heffernan IRL 20.2.78	26 Jun

Indoors
| 18:44.32 | Christopher | Linke | GER | 24.10.88 | 1 | NC | Erfurt | 14 Feb |

5000 – 10,000 METRES WALK

Mark	Name		Nat	Born	Pos	Meet	Venue		Date	
18:46.77	Nils	Brembach	GER	23.2.93	2	NC	Erfurt		14	Feb
18:47.55	Ruslan	Dmytrenko	UKR	22.3.86	1		Kyiv		8	Jan
18:51.9	Vasiliy	Mizinov	RUS-J	29.12.97	1		Chelyabinsk		6	Jan
18:54.18	Tom	Bosworth	GBR	17.1.90	1		Bratislava		31	Jan
18:54.32	Hagen	Pohle	GER	5.3.92	3	NC	Erfurt		14	Feb
18:56.87	Perseus	Karlström	SWE	2.5.90	1	NC	Eskilstuna		17	Apr
19:00.4	Sergey	Shirobokov	RUS-Y	16.2.99	1		Saransk		30	Dec
(8/8)										
19:08.74	Aléxandros	Papamihaíl	GRE	18.9.88	1	NC	Pireás		13	Feb
19:09.62	Grzegorz	Sudol	POL	28.8.78	2		Bratislava		31	Jan
19:12.00	Francesco	Fortunato	ITA	13.12.94	1	NC	Ancona		5	Mar
19:13.25	Ihor	Hlavan	UKR	25.9.90	2		Kyiv		8	Jan
19:19.83	Robert	Heffernan	IRL	20.2.78	3		Bratislava		31	Jan
19:23.07	Leonardo	Dei Tos	ITA	27.4.92	1		Padova		20	Feb
19:25.42	Matej	Tóth	SVK	10.2.83	31 Jan	19:36.82	Dawid	Tomala	POL	27.8.89	5 Mar
19:32.62	Alex	Wright	IRL	19.12.90	31 Jan	19:37.10	Ato	Ibanez	SWE	14.11.85	17 Apr
19:33.72	Marius	Ziukas	LTU	29.6.85	30 Jan	19:37.99	Marius	Savelskis	LTU	30.7.94	30 Jan
19:35.81	Yevgeniy	Zaleski	BLR	18.7.93	29 Jan	19:38.75	Rafal	Augustyn	POL	14.5.84	5 Mar

JUNIORS

Mark	Name		Nat	Born	Pos	Meet	Venue	Date	
19:35.4	Callum	Wilkinson	GBR-J	14.3.97	1		Tamworth	2	Jul
19:39.69i 6			Bratislava	31 Jan	19:54.47	3	NC	Birmingham	26 Jun
19:40.04	Manuel	Bernúdez	ESP	12.12.97	4		Murcia	26	Jun
19:56.66	Ryutaro	Yamamoto	JPN	17.9.98	1		Kitakami	10	Oct

10,000 METRES WALK

Mark	Name		Nat	Born	Pos	Meet	Venue	Date	
38:06.28	Miguel Ángel	López	ESP	3.7.88	1	NC	Gijón	24	Jul
38:16.76	Daisuke	Matsunaga	JPN	24.3.95	1		Yokohama	21	May
38:21.88	Eiki	Takahashi	JPN	19.11.92	1		Kitakami	9	Oct
38:40.22		Matsunaga			2		Kitakami	9	Oct
38:40.25	Christopher	Linke	GER	24.10.88	1	NC	Bühlertal	11	Jun
38:44.61	Dane	Bird-Smith	AUS	15.7.92	1	NC	Sydney	1	Apr
38:53.11		Wang Zhen	CHN	24.8.91	1		Asti	21	May
38:58.21	Vasiliy	Mizinov	RUS-J	29.12.97	1	NC-j	Cheboksary	25	Jun
39:16.06		Takahashi			1		Isahaya	12	Nov
39:18.09		Cai Zelin	CHN	11.4.91	2		Asti	21	May
(10/8)									
39:21.30	Evan	Dunfee	CAN	28.9.90	1		Coquitlam	12	Jun
39:23.51	Álvaro	Martín (10)	ESP	18.6.94	2	NC	Gijón	24	Jul
39:29.00	Luís Alberto	Amezcua	ESP	1.5.92	3	NC	Gijón	24	Jul
39:31.09A	Ricardo	Ortíz	MEX	7.2.95	1		Tlaxcala	18	Dec
39:32.03	Kai	Kobayashi	JPN	28.2.93	2		Kitami	14	Jul
39:41.81A	Jorge	Martínez	MEX	25.10.90	2		Tlaxcala	18	Dec
39:46.25	Francesco	Fortunato	ITA	13.12.94	1	Med-23	Radès	4	Jun
39:49.26		Yu Wei	CHN	11.9.87	3		Asti	21	May
39:50.32	Ivan	Kakayev	RUS-J	13.8.97	2	NC-j	Cheboksary	25	Jun
39:55.80	Toshikazu	Yamanishi	JPN	15.2.96	4		Kitakami	9	Oct
39:56.02	Máté	Helebrandt	HUN	12.1.89	1		Budapest	19	Jun
39:57.41	Kota	Yamada	JPN	27.4.94	1		Koshigaya	19	Nov
(20)									
39:59.02	Fumitaka	Oikawa	JPN	5.4.95	1		Konosu	9	Apr
40:06.44	Carl	Dohmann	GER	18.5.90	2	NC	Bühlertal	11	Jun
40:08.32	Takumi	Saito	JPN	23.3.93	3		Osaka	24	Sep
40:15.38	Satoshi	Maruo	JPN	28.11.91	24 Sep	40:22.86	Tomohiro	Noda	JPN	24.1.96	21 May
40:16.98	Iván	Pajuelo	ESP	27.8.93	24 Jul	40:23.25	Jean	Blancheteau	FRA	7.1.96	4 Jun
40:19.72A	Noel Ali	Chama	MEX-J	15.9.97	18 Dec	40:24.57	Federico	Tontodonati	ITA	30.10.89	21 May
40:22.00	Leonardo	Dei Tos	ITA	27.4.92	3 Apr	40:29.71A	Andrés	Chocho	ECU	4.11.83	27 Mar

Indoors

| 40:12.56 | Aleksandr | Lyakhovich | BLR | 4.7.89 | 1 | NC | Mogilyov | 20 | Feb |
| 40:25.58 | Dmitriy | Dyubin | BLR | 12.7.90 | 2 | NC | Mogilyov | 20 | Feb |

JUNIORS

See main list for top 2 juniors. 8 performances by 7 men to 40:50.0. Additional marks and further juniors:

Mizinov	40:05.0	1	NC-w	Sochi		28 Feb				
40:32.69	Timofey	Parkayev	RUS	19.10.97	3	NC-j	Cheboksary	25	Jun
40:41.62	Callum	Wilkinson	GBR	14.3.97	1	WJ	Bydgoszcz	23	Jul
40:43.0	Vladislav	Saraykin	RUS	3.3.97	2	NC-w	Sochi	28	Feb
40:43.33	Jonathan Javier	Amores	ESP	29.8.89	2	WJ	Bydgoszcz	23	Jul
40:45.53	Salih	Korkmaz	TUR	14.4.97	3	WJ	Bydgoszcz	23	Jul
40:55.96	Yohanis	Algaw	ETH-Y	14.8.99	4	WJ	Bydgoszcz	23	Jul
40:58.0	Sergey	Shirobokov	RUS-Y	16.2.99	1	NC-wy	Sochi	28	Feb
41:01.33		Zhu Guowen (10)	CHN	20.8.97	5	WJ	Bydgoszcz	23	Jul

416 10,000m – 10 KILOMETRES – 20 KILOMETRES WALK

Mark	Name		Nat	Born	Pos	Meet	Venue	Date
41:04.37	Aleksey	Shevchuk	RUS	10.8.97	5	NC-j	Cheboksary	25 Jun
41:06.14		Bai Liga	CHN	21.1.98	6	WJ	Bydgoszcz	23 Jul
41:08.87	Federico	González	MEX	17.11.98	1		Monterrey	14 May
41:23.3	Manuel	Bermúdez	ESP	12.12.97	1		Palafrugell	10 Apr
41:32.80	Andrey	Tryapkin	RUS	1.12.97	6	NC-j	Cheboksary	25 Jun
41:33.10	Leo	Köpp	GER	23.5.98	8	WJ	Bydgoszcz	23 Jul
41:34.01	Shunta	Saito	JPN	.97	2		Koshigaya	19 Nov
41:38.97	Zakhar	Silva	RUS	1.3.98	7	NC-j	Cheboksary	25 Jun

10 KILOMETRES ROAD WALK

Where better than track times above or as intermediate times in 20k lists below.

Mark	Name		Nat	Born	Pos	Meet	Venue	Date
38:03	Eiki	Takahashi	JPN	19.11.92	1		Wajima	16 Apr
39:17+	Takumi	Saito	JPN	23.3.93		in 20k	Kobe	21 Feb
39:25+	Satoshi	Maruo	JPN	28.11.91		in 20k	Kobe	21 Feb
39:53	Eider	Arévalo	COL	9.3.93	1		Suzhou	26 Sep
39:58+	Tom	Bosworth	GBR	17.1.90	1	in 20k	Dudince	19 Mar
40:03	Ersin	Tacir	TUR	1.4.85	1		Ayvalik	28 Feb
40:10	Zhang Jun		CHN-J	20.7.98	1	NGP-j	Huangshan	5 Mar
40:19+	Krishnan	Ganapathi	IND	29.6.89	20 Mar	40:27+	Hagen Pohle	GER 5.3.92	22 May
40:19+	Manuel	Soto	COL	28.1.94	9 Apr	40:28	Mert Atli	TUR 23.7.93	28 Feb
40:22+	Richard	Vargas	VEN	28.12.94	12 Aug	40:28+	Moacir Zimmerman	BRA 30.12.83	7 May
40:22+	Benjamin	Thorne	CAN	19.3.93	12 Aug	40:29+	Hamid Reza Zouravand	IRI	7 May
40:23+	Ever	Palma	MEX	18.3.92	12 Aug	40:29+	Lebogang Shange	RSA 1.8.90	7 May
40:23+	Luis Fernando	López	COL	3.6.79	12 Aug	40:30	Callum Wilkinson	GBR-J 14.3.97	7 May
40:23+	Ruslan	Dmytrenko	UKR	22.3.86	12 Aug	40:30+	Chen Ding	CHN 5.8.92	7 May
40:23+	Hassanine	Sbaï	TUN	21.1.84	12 Aug	40:30+	Diego Flores	MEX 23.3.87	22 May
40:27	Manuel	Bermúdez	ESP-J	12.12.97	7 May				

JUNIORS
3 Sep

Mark	Name		Nat	Born	Pos	Meet	Venue	Date
Mizinov	39:59	1		Kostroma				
40:10		Zhang Jun	CHN	20.7.98	1	NGP-j	Huangshan	5 Mar
40:27	Manuel	Bermúdez	ESP	12.12.97	2	WCp-J	Roma	7 May
40:30	Callum	Wilkinson	GBR	14.3.97	4	WCp-J	Roma	7 May
40:31		Wang Libo	CHN	9.2.97	1		Huhehaote	8 Sep
40:43		Jin Xiangqian	CHN	18.3.97	1y		Taicang	23 Apr
40:43	Andrés	Olivas	MEX	27.5.98	5	WCp-J	Roma	7 May
40:44		Hu Linfeng	CHN	1.2.98	2		Huangshan	5 Mar
40:45		Zhu Guowen	CHN	20.8.97	3		Huangshan	5 Mar
40:46		Niu Wenchao	CHN	20.4.98	3		Huhehaote	8 Sep
40:47		Bai Liga	CHN	21.1.98	2y		Taicang	23 Apr
40:53		Zhang Yao	CHN-Y	11.1.00	1		Taicang	23 Apr
40:56		Wei Ximeng	CHN	5.6.97	4		Huangshan	5 Mar
40:56		Zhang Hongliang	CHN-Y	1.1.99	2		Taicang	23 Apr
41:00		Zhou Xiaojun	CHN-Y	9.9.99	1y		Huhehaote	8 Sep
41:01	Masaya	Ishikawa	JPN	.97	1	NC-j	Kobe	21 Feb
41:04	Masatora	Kawano	JPN	23.10.98	1		Wajima	16 Apr
41:08	César Augusto	Rodríguez	PER	26.6.97	6	WCp-J	Roma	7 May

20 KILOMETRES WALK

20k	10k	Name		Nat	Born	Pos	Meet	Venue	Date
1:18:26	38:51	Eiki	Takahashi	JPN	19.11.92	1	NC	Kobe	21 Feb
1:18:45	38:51	Isamu	Fujisawa	JPN	12.10.87	2	NC	Kobe	21 Feb
1:18:53	39:07	Daisuke	Matsunaga	JPN	24.3.95	1		Nomi	20 Mar
1:19:11	39:40	Perseus	Karlström	SWE	2.5.90	1		Podébrady	9 Apr
1:19:12			Wang Zhen	CHN	24.8.91	1		Huangshan	5 Mar
1:19:14	40:22		Wang Zhen			1	OG	Rio de Janeiro	12 Aug
1:19:19	40:02	Christopher	Linke	GER	24.10.88	2		Podébrady	9 Apr
1:19:20	39:21	Iñaki	Gómez	CAN	16.1.88	2		Nomi	20 Mar
1:19:20	40:06	Omar	Pineda	MEX	2.12.94	3		Podébrady	9 Apr
1:19:20	40:10	Jesús Tadeo	Vega	MEX	23.5.94	4		Podébrady	9 Apr
1:19:22	40:29		Wang Zhen			1		Roma	7 May
1:19:24		Samuel	Gathimba (10)	KEN	26.10.87	1	AfCh	Durban	26 Jun
1:19:26	40:22		Cai Zelin	CHN	11.4.91	2	OG	Rio de Janeiro	12 Aug
1:19:32			Chen Ding	CHN	5.8.92	2		Huangshan	5 Mar
1:19:34	40:27		Cai Zelin			2	WCp	Roma	7 May
1:19:36	40:29	Álvaro	Martín	ESP	18.6.94	3	WCp	Roma	7 May
1:19:37	40:22	Dane	Bird-Smith	AUS	15.7.92	3	OG	Rio de Janeiro	12 Aug
1:19:38		Ever	Palma	MEX	18.3.92	5		Podébrady	9 Apr
1:19:38	40:28		Bird-Smith			4	WCp	Roma	7 May
1:19:42		Caio	Bonfim	BRA	19.3.91	4	OG	Rio de Janeiro	12 Aug

20 KILOMETRES WALK

Mark		Name		Nat	Born	Pos	Meet	Venue	Date	
1:19:44	39:21	Takumi	Saito	JPN	23.3.93	3		Nomi	20 Mar	
1:19:48			Cai Zelin			3		Huangshan	5 Mar	
1:19:51			Wang Kaihua	CHN	16.2.94	4		Huangshan	5 Mar	
1:19:54	39:44	Hirooki	Arai	JPN	18.5.88	3	NC	Kobe	21 Feb	
1:19:55	40:29	Benjamin	Thorne (20)	CAN	19.3.93	5	WCp	Roma	7 May	
1:19:57	39:13	Kai	Kobayashi	JPN	28.2.93	4		Nomi	20 Mar	
1:19:58	40:38	Hagen	Pohle	GER	5.3.92	6		Podébrady	9 Apr	
1:20:00			Linke			5	OG	Rio de Janeiro	12 Aug	
1:20:04			Bird-Smith			1		Adelaide	21 Feb	
1:20:05		Pedro	Gómez	MEX	31.12.90	7		Podébrady	9 Apr	
		(30/23)								
1:20:06		Lebogang	Shange	RSA	1.8.90	2		Adelaide	21 Feb	
1:20:07	40:28	Andrés	Chocho	ECU	4.11.83	6	WCp	Roma	7 May	
1:20:13	40:10	Tom	Bosworth	GBR	17.1.90	6	OG	Rio de Janeiro	12 Aug	
1:20:14	39:36	Satoshi	Maruo	JPN	28.11.91	5	NC	Kobe	21 Feb	
1:20:21	40:19	Devender	Singh	IND	5.12.83	5		Nomi	20 Mar	
1:20:24	40:34	Julio César	Salazar	MEX	8.7.93	8		Podébrady	9 Apr	
1:20:26	40:19	Manish	Singh Rawat	IND	5.5.91	7		Nomi	20 Mar	
		(30)								
1:20:27	40:23	Matteo	Giupponi	ITA	8.10.88	8	OG	Rio de Janeiro	12 Aug	
1:20:29	40:18	Gurmeet	Singh	IND	1.7.85	8	1 AsiC	Nomi	20 Mar	
1:20:33	40:28	Ruslan	Dmytrenko	UKR	22.3.86	9	WCp	Roma	7 May	
1:20:34		Evan	Dunfee	CAN	28.9.90	5		Adelaide	21 Feb	
1:20:34		Miguel Ángel	López	ESP	3.7.88	2		La Coruña	28 May	
1:20:36	40:23	Manuel	Soto	COL	28.1.94	9	OG	Rio de Janeiro	12 Aug	
1:20:43	40:38	Antón	Kucmín	SVK	7.6.84	10		Podébrady	9 Apr	
1:20:44	40:19	Sandeep	Kumar Sangwan	IND	16.12.86	9		Nomi	20 Mar	
1:20:45	40:06	Kevin	Campion	FRA	23.5.88	11		Podébrady	9 Apr	
1:20:46		Wayne	Snyman	RSA	8.3.85	2	NC	Stellenbosch	16 Apr	
		(40)								
1:20:47		Eider	Arévalo	COL	9.3.93	4		La Coruña	28 May	
1:20:49		Hassanine	Sbaï	TUN	21.1.84	6		La Coruña	28 May	
1:20:50	40:38	Toshikazu	Yamanishi	JPN	15.2.96	7		La Coruña	28 May	
1:20:51	40:06	Jorge Alejandro	Martínez	MEX	25.10.90	12		Podébrady	9 Apr	
1:20:54	40:10	Anatole	Ibáñez	SWE	14.11.85	3		Dudince	19 Mar	
1:20:54	40:12	Isaac	Palma	MEX	26.10.90	13		Podébrady	9 Apr	
1:20:55	40:18	Fumitaka	Oikawa	JPN	5.4.95	11		Nomi	20 Mar	
1:20:56	40:27	Horacio	Nava	MEX	20.1.82	1		Naumburg	22 May	
1:20:58	40:13	Nils	Brembach	GER	23.2.93	14		Podébrady	9 Apr	
1:21:08		Mauricio	Arteaga	ECU	8.8.88	11	WCp	Roma	7 May	
		[50]								
1:21:14		Aleksandr	Lyakhovich	BLR	4.7.89	1		Brest	2 Apr	
1:21:21	40:29	Nazar	Kovalenko	UKR	9.2.89	14	WCp	Roma	7 May	
1:21:21		Francisco	Arcilla	ESP	14.1.84	8		La Coruña	28 May	
1:21:23	39:44	Takayuki	Tanii	JPN	14.2.83	6	NC	Kobe	21 Feb	
1:21:23			Wang Rui	CHN	6.1.96	4		Taicang	23 Apr	
1:21:26		Yerko	Araya	CHI	14.2.86	7		Adelaide	21 Feb	
1:21:26		Carl	Dohmann	GER	18.5.90	15	WCp	Roma	7 May	
1:21:31	40:17	Eder	Sánchez	MEX	21.5.86	3		Naumburg	22 May	
1:21:32		Luis Fernando	López	COL	3.6.79	17		Podébrady	9 Apr	
1:21:33	40:38	Aléxandros	Papamihaíl	GRE	18.9.88	17	WCp	Roma	7 May	
		(60)								
1:21:35		James	Rendón	COL	7.7.85	18		Podébrady	9 Apr	
1:21:35		Iván	Garrido	COL	25.1.94	18	WCp	Roma	7 May	
1:21:36		Diego	García	ESP	19.1.96	19	WCp	Roma	7 May	
1:21:38	40:13	Jakub	Jelonek	POL	7.7.85	19		Podébrady	9 Apr	
1:21:39			Li Tianlei	CHN	13.1.95	5		Huangshan	5 Mar	
1:21:39	40:20	Luis Alberto	Amezcua	ESP	1.5.92	2	NC	Cáceres	20 Mar	
1:21:41	40:29	Krishnan	Ganapathi	IND	29.6.89	22	WCp	Roma	7 May	
1:21:44	40:23		Kim Hyun-sub	KOR	31.5.85	17	OG	Rio de Janeiro	12 Aug	
1:21:45		Ricardo	Ortíz	MEX	7.2.95	5		Taicang	23 Apr	
1:21:46			Wei Xubao	CHN	1.2.93	1r2		Taicang	23 Apr	
		(70)								
1:21:47	40:13	Rafal	Fedaczynski	POL	3.12.80	20		Podébrady	9 Apr	
1:21:48	40:30	Denis	Simanovich	BLR	20.4.87	23	WCp	Roma	7 May	
1:21:49		Brian	Pintado	ECU	29.7.95	24	WCp	Roma	7 May	
1:21:49		Paolo César	Yaurivilca	PER	23.4.96	25	WCp	Roma	7 May	
1:21:50		Jared	Tallent	AUS	17.10.84	6		Taicang	23 Apr	
1:21:50		Dawid	Tomala	POL	27.8.89	1		Alytus	10 Jun	
1:21:50		Pyotr	Bogatyrev	RUS	11.3.91	1		Kostroma	3 Sep	

20 KILOMETRES WALK

Mark		Name		Nat	Born	Pos	Meet	Venue	Date	
1:21:51			Sun Song	CHN	15.12.96	2r2		Taicang	23	Apr
1:21:52	40:19	Georgiy	Sheyko	KAZ	24.8.89	12	3 AsiC	Nomi	20	Mar
1:21:54		Erwin	González	MEX	7.2.94	7		Dudince	19	Mar
(80)										
1:21:54		Quentin	Rew	NZL	16.7.84	26	WCp	Roma	7	May
1:21:55		Igor	Hlavan	UKR	25.9.90	12		La Coruña	28	May
1:21:56		Federico	Tontodonati	ITA	30.10.89	1	NC	Cassino	20	Mar
1:21:56		Alex	Wright	IRL	19.12.90	13		La Coruña	28	May
1:21:57		Stanislav	Yemelyanov ¶	RUS	23.10.90	2		Kostroma	3	Sep
1:22:01		Marco	De Luca	ITA	12.5.81	4		Rio Maior	9	Apr
1:22:06		Pyotr	Trofimov	RUS	28.11.83	1	NC-w	Sochi	27	Feb
1:22:07		Rhydian	Cowley	AUS	4.1.91	9		Adelaide	21	Feb
1:22:08			Wang Qin #	CHN	8.5.94	13		Nomi	20	Mar
1:22:10	40:30	Richard	Vargas	VEN	28.12.94	28	WCp	Roma	7	May
(90)										
1:22:11		Artur	Brzozowski	POL	18.12.88	2		Alytus	10	Jun
1:22:12		Erik	Tysse	NOR	4.12.80	1		Vallensbaek	1	May
1:22:15		Kolothum Thodi	Irfan	IND	8.2.90	4	NC	Jaipur	27	Feb
1:22:15		José Alessandro	Bagio	BRA	16.4.81	5		Rio Maior	9	Apr
1:22:18		Yevgeniy	Zaleski	BLR	18.7.93	3		Brest	2	Apr
1:22:19		Ersin	Tacir	TUR	1.4.85	21		Poděbrady	9	Apr
1:22:19			Jiang Jie	CHN	25.10.94	3r2		Taicang	23	Apr
1:22:19			Zeng Qingcun	CHN	3.4.95	4r2		Taicang	23	Apr
1:22:19		Omar	Segura	MEX	24.3.81	9		Taicang	23	Apr
1:22:25		Aleksandr	Ivanov	RUS	25.4.93	2	NC-w	Sochi	27	Feb
(100)										
1:22:25		Ivan	Trotskiy	BLR	27.5.76	4		Brest	2	Apr
1:22:27		Jarkko	Kinnunen	FIN	19.1.84	23	Apr				
1:22:27		Marius	Ziukas	LTU	29.6.85	12	Aug				
1:22:29		Tomohiro	Noda	JPN	24.1.96	20	Mar				
1:22:31		Sergey	Shiroborokov	RUS-Y	16.2.99	25	Jun				
1:22:31		Máté	Helebrandt	HUN	12.1.89	12	Aug				
1:22:34		João	Vieira	POR	20.2.76	29	May				
1:22:41		Robert	Heffernan	IRL	20.2.78	19	Mar				
1:22:43		Moacir	Zimmerman	BRA	30.12.83	19	Mar				
1:22:43		Dmitriy	Dyubin	BLR	12.7.90	2	Apr				
1:22:43		Ivan	Losev	UKR	26.1.86	7	May				
1:22:46		Tsuyoshi	Tasaka	JPN	30.7.93	20	Mar				
1:22:47		Aleksey	Golovin	RUS	24.12.88	27	Feb				
1:22:49			Choi Byung-kwang	KOR	7.4.91	20	Mar				
1:22:52		Hamid Reza	Zouravand	IRI	13.1.90	20	Mar				
1:22:54		Dementiy	Cheparev	RUS	28.10.92	25	Jun				
1:22:55		Andriy	Hrechkovskyy	UKR	30.8.93	19	Mar				
1:22:57		Francesco	Fortunato	ITA	13.12.94	20	Mar				
1:23:02		Kota	Yamada	JPN	27.4.94	23	Oct				
1:23:05			Yin Jiaxing	CHN	16.3.94	5	Mar				
1:23:07			Sun Chenggang	CHN	11.3.91	23	Apr				
1:23:07			Chen Rui	CHN	11.8.96	8	Sep				
1:23:09		Rafal	Augustyn	POL	14.5.84	7	May				
1:23:10		Leonardo	Dei Tos	ITA	27.4.92	9	Apr				
1:23:13			Li Jichao	CHN	10.5.96	8	Sep				
1:23:14		Marius	Savelskis	LTU	30.7.94	9	Apr				
1:23:14		Mohamed	Ameur	ALG	1.11.84	30	Apr				
1:23:15		Håvard	Haukenes	NOR	22.4.90	7	May				
1:23:18			Bian Tongda	CHN	1.4.91	23	Apr				
1:23:21		Kazuki	Takahashi	JPN	.96	23	Oct				
1:23:22		Antonin	Boyez	FRA	9.11.84	9	Apr				
1:23:25		Seiya	Watanabe	JPN	23.5.88	21	Feb				
1:23:26		Igor	Saharuk	UKR	3.6.88	2	Apr				
1:23:26		Omar	Zepeda	MEX	8.7.77	23	Apr				
1:23:26		Simon	Wachira	KEN	6.5.84	26	Jun				
1:23:26			Gao Wenkui	CHN	28.7.95	8	Sep				
1:23:29		Kirill	Frolov	RUS	29.9.93	27	Feb				
1:23:29		José Luis	Doctor	MEX	14.6.96	19	Mar				
1:23:29			Nguyen Thanh Ngung	VIE	8.4.92	20	Mar				
1:23:30			Byun Young-jun	KOR	20.3.84	20	Mar				
1:23:30			Zhao Qi	CHN	14.1.93	8	Sep				
1:23:31		Nikolay	Markov	RUS	1.2.95	25	Jun				
1:23:32			Zhang Rongjin	CHN	24.4.96	5	Mar				
1:23:32			Han Jijiang	CHN	20.7.93	23	Apr				
1:23:33		Kostyantyn	Puzanov	UKR	19.5.91	11	Jun				
1:23:35		Neeraj	Rathi Singh	IND	15.8.94	27	Feb				
1:23:35		Marc	Tur	ESP	30.11.94	9	Apr				
1:23:37		Jonathan	Hilbert	GER	24.1.95	9	Apr				
1:23:40		Takeshi	Okuma	JPN	14.12.83	21	Feb				
1:23:40		Lukasz	Nowak	POL	18.12.88	10	Jun				
1:23:41		Teodorico	Caporaso	ITA	14.9.87	9	Apr				
1:23:44		Yuki	Yamazaki	JPN	16.1.84	21	Feb				
1:23:45		Andriy	Kovenko	UKR	25.11.73	5	Mar				
1:23:45			Zhao Fujie	CHN	11.11.93	8	Sep				
1:23:46			Li Shuai	CHN	6.1.95	8	Sep				
1:23:48			Kim Dae-ho	KOR	30.4.88	20	Mar				
1:23:50		Mert	Atli	TUR	23.7.93	19	Mar				
1:23:53		Karl	Junghannß	GER	6.4.96	9	Apr				
1:23:55		Michele	Antonelli	ITA	23.5.94	20	Mar				
1:24:00		Juan Manuel	Cano	ARG	12.12.87	9	Apr				
1:24:04		Giorgio	Rubino	ITA	15.4.86	9	Apr				
1:24:05		Aurelien	Quinion	FRA	27.1.93	28	May				
1:24:05		Genadij	Kozlovskij	LTU	7.1.91	8	Oct				
1:24:12		Yuga	Yamashita	JPN	6.2.96	21	Feb				
1:24:18		Koichiro	Morioka	JPN	2.4.85	21	Feb				
1:24:20			Yan Dexiang	CHN	18.693	23	Apr				
1:24:21			Xie Sichao	CHN	28.2.93	8	Apr				
1:24:25			Wang Gang	CHN	2.4.91	8	Sep				
1:24:33		Andrea	Agrusti	ITA	30.8.95	20	Mar				
1:24:34		Oleksiy	Kazanin	UKR	22.5.82	11	Jun				
1:24:34			Liu Xu	CHN	11.12.94	8	Sep				
1:24:35		Kohei	Kowaki	JPN	.96	20	Mar				
1:24:36			Ceng Qingsheng	CHN	3.4.95	23	Apr				
1:24:37		Recep	Çelik	TUR	10.6.83	30	Jan				
1:24:37			Dong Guozhu	CHN	2.8.92	8	Apr				
1:24:39		Ryota	Shiojima	JPN	1.7.94	1	Jan				
1:24:41		Diego	Flores	MEX	23.3.87	22	May				
1:24:42		Michael	Hosking	AUS	16.10.85	21	Feb				
1:24:42		Vito	Minei	ITA	16.6.94	7	May				
1:24:43		Hichem	Medjber	ALG	10.2.82	30	Apr				
1:24:46		Brandon	Segura	MEX	30.4.96	23	Apr				
1:24:49		Yuki	Kurumisawa	JPN	11.12.95	1	Jan				
1:24:50			Luo Yadong	CHN	15.1.92	8	Sep				
1:24:50			Liu Jianmin	CHN	9.3.88	23	Apr				
1:24:50		Benjamin	Sánchez	ESP	10.3.85	7	May				
1:24:54		Hatem	Ghoula	TUN	7.6.73	28	May				
1:24:54		José Alejandro	Barrondo	GUA	16.9.96	28	May				
1:24:57			Ma Haijun	CHN	24.11.92	8	Apr				
1:24:57			Cao Wenlong	CHN-J	4.3.98	23	Apr				
1:24:59		Vladimir	Kolesnik	BLR	7.2.92	2	Apr				
1:24:59		Aleksi	Ojala	FIN	9.12.92	7	May				
1:25:00A		José Marie	Raymundo	GUA	1.9.93	28	Feb				
[192]										

Best track times
1:24:41.3t	Iván	Garrido	COL	25.1.94	24	Sep
1:24:46.1t	Ivan	Trotskiy	BLR	27.5.76	23	Jun

20 – 30 – 35 KILOMETRES WALK

Mark		Name		Nat	Born	Pos	Meet	Venue	Date	
Drugs disqualification										
1:20:23dq		Alex	Schwazer ¶	ITA	26.12.84	(2)		La Coruña	29	May
			JUNIORS							
1:22:31		Sergey	Shiroborokov	RUS	16.2.99	1	NC	Cheboksary	25	Jun
1:24:57			Cao Wenlong	CHN	4.3.98	11		Taicang	23	Apr
1:25:06			Xin Zhaoyang	CHN	30.6.98	12		Taicang	23	Apr
1:25:13		Aleksey	Shevchuk	RUS	10.8.97	2		Kostroma	3	Sep
1:25:15			Zheng Ke	CHN	10.1.98	13		Taicang	23	Apr
1:25:23			Niu Wenchao	CHN	20.4.98	15		Taicang	23	Apr
1:25:37		Masatora	Kawano	JPN	23.10.98	29		Nomo	20	Mar
1:26.07		Hiroki	Makitani	JPN	.97	30		Nomo	20	Mar
1:26:22			Zhu Guowen	CHN	20.8.97	13		Rio Maior	9	Apr
1:26:29			Cha Jinhong (10)	CHN	27.5.97	22		Huangshan	5	Mar
1:26:31		Hayato	Takata	JPN	.97	33		Nomo	20	Mar
1:26:50		Shunta	Saito	JPN	.97	9		Takahata	23	Oct

30-35 KILOMETRES WALK

Mark		Name	Nat	Born	Pos	Meet	Venue	Date	
	2:28:29	Sergey	Bakulin	RUS	13.11.86	1	NC-w	Sochi	27 Feb
	2:28:49	Dementiy	Cheparev	RUS	28.10.92	1		Kostroma	3 Sep
	2:29:56	Sergey	Sharipov	RUS	14.4.92	2		Kostroma	3 Sep
	2:30:40	Sergey	Kirdyapkin	RUS	18.6.80	2	NC-w	Sochi	27 Feb
	2:31:49	Roman	Yevstifeyev	RUS	13.11.86	3	NC-w	Sochi	27 Feb
2:09:21A?		José Maria	Raymundo	GUA	1.9.93	1		Ciudad de Guatemala	28 Feb
2:10:21		Chris	Erickson	AUS	1.12.81	1	in 20M	Canberra (2:19:51)	10 Jun
2:10:26	2:32:49	Ihor	Hlavan	UKR	25.9.90	1	NC-w	Ivano-Frankivsk	6 Mar
2:10:25	2:33:13	Ivan	Banzeruk	UKR	9.2.90	2	NC-w	Ivano-Frankivsk	6 Mar
2:12:23	2:34:32	Serhiy	Budza	UKR	6.12.84	3	NC-w	Ivano-Frankivsk	6 Mar
2:11:29	2:34:47+	Yohann	Diniz	FRA	1.1.78		in 50k	Rio de Janeiro	19 Aug
2:11:41		Quentin	Rew	NZL	16.7.84	2	in 20M	Canberra (2:21:26)	10 Jun
2:12:05			Jin Xiangqian	CHN-J	18.3.97	1		Huangshan	6 Mar
2:12:29		Jarkko	Kinnunen	FIN	19.1.84	1	NC	Turku	12 Jun
2:12:57	2:34:39	Evan	Dunfee	CAN	28.9.90		in 50k	Rio de Janeiro	19 Aug
2:12:57	2:34:45+	Jared	Tallent	AUS	17.10.84		in 50k	Roma	8 May
2:12:57	2:34:45+		Han Yucheng	CHN	16.12.78		in 50k	Roma	8 May
2:13:04	2:34:48	Maryan	Zakolnytskyy	UKR	19.8.94	4	NC-w	Ivano-Frankivsk	6 Mar
2:12:59	2:34:53+	Matej	Tóth	SVK	10.2.83		in 50k	Rio de Janeiro	19 Aug
2:13:02	2:34:53+	Hirooki	Arai	JPN	18.5.88		in 50k	Rio de Janeiro	19 Aug
2:13:02	2:34:53+		Yu Wei	CHN	11.9.87		in 50k	Rio de Janeiro	19 Aug
2:13:02	2:34:55+	Robert	Heffernan	IRL	20.2.78		in 50k	Rio de Janeiro	19 Aug
2:12:51	2:35:03+	Takayuki	Tanii	JPN	14.2.83	1		Wajima	17 Apr
2:12:57	2:35:06	Matteo	Giupponi	ITA	8.10.88		in 50k	Roma	8 May
2:13:02+		Andrés	Chocho	ECU	4.11.83		in 50k	Rio de Janeiro	19 Aug
2:13:02A		Luis Ángel	Sánchez	GUA	15.12.93	2		Ciudad de Guatemala	28 Feb
2:13:38	2:35:25	Ihor	Saharuk	UKR	3.6.88	5	NC-w	Ivano-Frankivsk	6 Mar
2:13:16	2:36:01+	Horacio	Nava	MEX	20.1.82		in 50k	Rio de Janeiro	19 Aug
2:13:50	2:35:51+	Kai	Kobayashi	JPN	28.2.93	1	in 50k	Takahata	22 Oct
2:14:03	2:36:31+	Marco	De Luca	ITA	12.5.81		in 50k	Roma	8 May
2:14:33	2:36:43+	Perseus	Karlström	SWE	2.5.90		in 50k	Roma	8 May
	2:36:43+	Anatole	Ibáñez	SWE	14.11.85		in 50k	Roma	8 May
	2:36:51+	Rafal	Augustyn	POL	14.5.84	1	in 50k	Dudince	19 Mar
2:14:35	2:36:59	Denis	Nizhegorodov	RUS	26.7.80	1	in 50k	Cheboksary	26 Jun
Drugs disqualification									
2:12:29	2:33:57+	Alex	Schwazer ¶	ITA	26.12.84		in 50k	Roma	8 May

50 KILOMETRES WALK

Mark		Name	Nat	Born	Pos	Meet	Venue	Date	
3:37:48		Yohann	Diniz	FRA	1.1.78	1	NC	St.Sebastien sur Loire	13 Mar
3:40:58		Matej	Tóth	SVK	10.2.83	1	OG	Rio de Janeiro	19 Aug
3:41:02			Wang Zhendong	CHN	11.1.91	1		Huangshan	6 Mar
3:41:16		Jared	Tallent	AUS	17.10.84	2	OG	Rio de Janeiro	19 Aug
3:41:24		Hirooki	Arai	JPN	18.5.88	3	OG	Rio de Janeiro	19 Aug
3:41:38		Evan	Dunfee	CAN	28.9.90	4	OG	Rio de Janeiro	19 Aug
3:42:08		Kai	Kobayashi	JPN	28.2.93	1		Takahata	23 Oct
3:42:36			Tallent			1	WCp	Roma	8 May
3:42:43			Han Yucheng	CHN	16.12.78	2		Huangshan	6 Mar
3:42:54			Yu Wei	CHN	11.9.87	3		Huangshan	6 Mar
3:42:57A		Andrés	Chocho (10)	ECU	4.11.83	1		Ciudad Juárez	6 Mar
3:43:00			Yu Wei			5	OG	Rio de Janeiro	19 Aug
3:43:22		Rafal	Augustyn	POL	14.5.84	1		Dudince	19 Mar
3:43:31			Zhang Hang	CHN	28.10.91	4		Huangshan	6 Mar

420 50 KILOMETRES WALK

Mark	Name		Nat	Born	Pos	Meet	Venue	Date	
3:43:55	Robert	Heffernan	IRL	20.2.78	6	OG	Rio de Janeiro	19	Aug
3:44:02	Igor	Hlavan	UKR	25.9.90	2	WCp	Roma	8	May
3:44:12	Takayuki	Tanii	JPN	14.2.83	1	NC	Wajima	17	Apr
3:44:47		Arai			2	NC	Wajima	17	Apr
3:44:47	Marco	De Luca	ITA	12.5.81	3	WCp	Roma	8	May
3:44:47	Denis	Nizhegorodov	RUS	26.7.80	1	NC	Cheboksary	26	Jun
3:45:28A	Omar	Zepeda	MEX	8.7.77	2		Ciudad Juárez	6	Mar
3:46:25	Aleksi	Ojala	FIN	9.12.92	2		Dudince	19	Mar
3:46:33	Håvard	Haukenes (20)	NOR	22.4.90	7	OG	Rio de Janeiro	19	Aug
3:46:43		Diniz			8	OG	Rio de Janeiro	19	Aug
3:46:51	Sergey	Sharipov	RUS	14.4.92	2	NC	Cheboksary	26	Jun
3:47:02	Caio	Bonfim	BRA	19.3.91	9	OG	Rio de Janeiro	19	Aug
3:47:16	Adrian	Blocki	POL	11.4.90	3		Dudince	19	Mar
3:47:42		Haukenes			4		Dudince	19	Mar
3:47:44	Horacio	Nava	MEX	20.1.82	5		Dudince	19	Mar
3:47:51		Liu Jian	CHN	19.5.95	5		Huangshan	6	Mar
3:47:57	Carl (31/26)	Dohmann	GER	18.5.90	1	NC	Andernach	8	Oct
3:48:07		Xu Faguang	CHN	17.5.87	6		Huangshan	6	Mar
3:48:23		Zhang Lin	CHN	11.11.93	7		Huangshan	6	Mar
3:48:29	Teodorico	Caporaso	ITA	14.9.87	4	WCp	Roma	8	May
3:48:31	Alex (30)	Wright	IRL	19.12.90	6		Dudince	19	Mar
3:48:32		Niu Wenbin	CHN	20.1.91	8		Huangshan	6	Mar
3:48:40	Chris	Erickson	AUS	1.12.81	10	OG	Rio de Janeiro	19	Aug
3:48:42	Rafal	Fedaczynski	POL	3.12.80	7		Dudince	19	Mar
3:49:05	João	Vieira	POR	20.2.76	8		Dudince	19	Mar
3:49:32	Quentin	Rew	NZL	16.7.84	12	OG	Rio de Janeiro	19	Aug
3:50:16		Wang Qin #	CHN	8.5.94	9		Huangshan	6	Mar
3:50:40	José	Leyver Ojeda	MEX	12.11.85	9		Dudince	19	Mar
3:50:40	Jarkko	Kinnunen	FIN	19.1.84	10		Dudince	19	Mar
3:51:10	José Ignacio	Díaz	ESP	22.11.79	5	WCp	Roma	8	May
3:51:11A	Jorge Alejandro (40)	Martínez	MEX	25.10.90	3		Ciudad Juárez	6	Mar
3:51:18	Rafal	Sikora	POL	17.2.87	11		Dudince	19	Mar
3:51:42	Jorge	Ruiz	COL	17.5.89	17	OG	Rio de Janeiro	19	Aug
3:51:57	Ivan	Banzeruk	UKR	9.2.90	6	WCp	Roma	8	May
3:52:07	Hayato	Katsuki	JPN	28.11.90	3	NC	Wajima	17	Apr
3:52:26		Park Chil-sung	KOR	8.7.82	12		Dudince	19	Mar
3:52:27	Matteo	Giupponi	ITA	8.10.88	7	WCp	Roma	8	May
3:52:46	Karl	Junghannß	GER	6.4.96	2	NC	Andernach	8	Oct
3:52:48A	José Leonardo	Montaña	COL	21.3.92	4		Ciudad Juárez	6	Mar
3:53:01	Jaime	Quiyuch	GUA	24.4.88	13		Dudince	19	Mar
3:53:04	Andrey [50]	Hrechkovskyy	UKR	30.8.93	1	NC	Ivano-Frankivsk	16	Oct
3:53:08	Michele	Antonelli	ITA	23.5.94	3	GER Ch	Andernach	8	Oct
3:53:12	Ivan	Trotskiy	BLR	27.5.76	14		Dudince	19	Mar
3:53:22	Sergiy	Budza	UKR	6.12.84	18	OG	Rio de Janeiro	19	Aug
3:53:23	Pedro	Gómez	MEX	31.12.90	15		Dudince	19	Mar
3:53:52	Miguel Ángel	López	ESP	3.7.88	1	NC	Motril	28	Feb
3:53:54	Máté	Helebrandt	HUN	12.1.89	16		Dudince	19	Mar
3:53:56	Mathieu	Bilodeau	CAN	27.11.83	2	FRA Ch	St.Sebastien sur Loire	13	Mar
3:53:59	Brendan	Boyce	IRL	15.10.86	19	OG	Rio de Janeiro	19	Aug
3:54:02	Veli-Matti	Partanen	FIN	28.10.91	17		Dudince	19	Mar
3:54:21	Mikel (60)	Odriozola	ESP	25.5.73	2	NC	Motril	28	Feb
3:54:26	Damian	Blocki	POL	28.4.89	9	WCp	Roma	8	May
3:54:29	Lukás	Gdula	CZE	6.12.91	18		Dudince	19	Mar
3:54:29	Jesús Ángel	García	ESP	17.10.69	20	OG	Rio de Janeiro	19	Aug
3:54:32	Rolando	Saquipay	ECU	21.7.79	10	WCp	Roma	8	May
3:55:06	Francisco	Arcilla	ESP	14.1.84	11	WCp	Roma	8	May
3:55:17	Federico	Tontodonati	ITA	30.10.89	12	WCp	Roma	8	May
3:55:26	Jonathan	Riekmann	BRA	20.8.87	19		Dudince	19	Mar
3:55:48	Dominic	King	GBR	30.5.83	4	GER Ch	Andernach	8	Oct
3:56:12	Marc	Mundell	RSA	7.7.83	20		Dudince	19	Mar
3:56:17	Andrea (70)	Agrusti	ITA	30.8.95	5	GER Ch	Andernach	8	Oct
3:56:30	Maryan	Zakalnytskyy	UKR	19.8.94	2	NC	Ivano-Frankivsk	16	Oct
3:57:02		Wu Qianlong	CHN	30.1.90	10		Huangshan	6	Mar
3:57:06	Miklós	Srp	HUN	6.3.93	21		Dudince	19	Mar

50 KILOMETRES WALK

Mark	Name		Nat	Born	Pos	Meet	Venue	Date	
3:58:03	Nathaniel	Seiler	GER	6.4.96	6	NC	Andernach	8	Oct
3:58:25	Dusan	Majdán	SVK	8.9.87	26	OG	Rio de Janeiro	19	Aug
3:58:32	Pavel	Chihuán	PER	19.1.86	22		Dudince	19	Mar
3:58:33	Valeriy	Litanyuk	UKR	2.4.94	3	NC	Ivano-Frankivsk	16	Oct
3:58:38	Cheng Min		CHN	6.7.91	11		Huangshan	6	Mar
3:58:49	Dmytro	Sobchuk	UKR	7.11.95	4	NC	Ivano-Frankivsk	16	Oct
3:58:54A	Edward (80)	Araya	CHI	14.2.86	5		Ciudad Juárez	6	Mar
3:58:56	Claudio	Villanueva	ECU	3.8.88	13	WCp	Roma	8	May
3:58:59	Koichiro	Morioka	JPN	2.4.85	27	OG	Rio de Janeiro	19	Aug
3:59:10	Luo Dongpo		CHN	23.6.95	4		Huhehaote	10	Sep
3:59:21	Aléxandros	Papamihaíl	GRE	18.9.88	28	OG	Rio de Janeiro	19	Aug
3:59:30	Takeshi	Okuma	JPN	14.12.83	3		Takahata	23	Oct
3:59:35	Darien	Molmy	FRA	2.10.88	7		Andernach	8	Oct
4:00:11	Zhang Kuo		CHN	12.12.89	4		Huhehaote	10	Sep
4:00:21A	Omar	Sierra	COL	10.9.88	6		Ciudad Juárez	6	Mar
4:00:31	Pablo	Oliva	ESP	15.10.96	4	NC	Motril	28	Feb
4:00:31	James (90)	Rendón	COL	7.7.85	15	WCp	Roma	8	May
4:00:43	Martin	Tistan	SVK	12.11.92	24		Dudince	19	Mar
4:00:50	Geng Yudong		CHN	13.6.94	12		Huangshan	6	Mar
4:01:06	Kim Hyun-sub		KOR	31.5.85	25		Dudince	19	Mar
4:01:23A	Anders	Hansson	SWE	10.3.92	7		Ciudad Juárez	6	Mar
4:01:59A	Luis	López Menjivar	ESA	18.1.94	8		Ciudad Juárez	6	Mar
4:02:00	Ronald	Quispe	BOL	5.3.89	30	OG	Rio de Janeiro	19	Aug
4:02:01	Fang Hongzhen		CHN	6.3.96	13		Huangshan	6	Mar
4:02:35	Bence	Venyercsán	HUN	8.1.96	26		Dudince	19	Mar
4:02:36	Satoshi	Maruo	JPN	28.11.91	4		Takahata	23	Oct
4:02:37	Alex [100]	Florez-Studer	SUI	11.5.71	27		Dudince	19	Mar

4:02:46	Narcis	Mihaila	ROU	4.8.87	19 Aug	4:05:50	Shuto	Goto	JPN	26.2.94	23 Oct
4:02:48	Yerenman	Salazar	VEN	24.10.78	8 May	4:06:26	Yuki	Ito	JPN	12.4.92	23 Oct
4:03:01		Li Tengliang	CHN	23.5.94	6 Mar	4:06:33	Perseus	Karlström	SWE	2.5.90	1 Oct
4:03:14		Bian Tongda	CHN	1.4.91	10 Sep	4:06:48		Li Peng	CHN	10.11.94	10 Sep
4:03:21	John	Nunn	USA	3.2.78	21 Feb	4:07:25	Basant Bahadur Rana		IND	18.1.84	28 Feb
4:03:23	Luis Manuel	Corchete	ESP	14.5.84	28 Feb	4:07:51		Wang Chao	CHN	2.5.96	10 Sep
4:03:39	Igor	Saharuk	UKR	3.6.88	16 Oct	4:07:53	Grzegorz	Sudol	POL	28.8.78	8 May
4:03:42	Pedro	Isidro	POR	17.7.85	19 Aug	4:07:55	Sandeep Kumar Sangwan		IND	16.12.86	19 Aug
4:03:47		Wang Hao	CHN	16.8.89	6 Mar	4:08:01		Zhao Qingwei	CHN	16.4.95	6 Mar
4:04:10	Tadas	Suskevicius	LTU	22.5.85	19 Aug	4:08:16	Miguel	Carvalho	POR	2.9.94	19 Aug
4:04:19		Jiang Shu	CHN	8.4.95	6 Mar	4:08:22		Luo Yadong	CHN	15.1.92	10 Sep
4:04:29	Jonathan	Cáceres	ECU	20.1.90	8 May	4:08:36	Jitender	Singh Rathore	IND	20.3.84	8 May
4:04:42	Vladimir	Saksin	RUS	28.4.95	26 Jun	4:08:40	Gregorio	Angelini	ITA	24.6.96	31 Jan
4:04:48	Volodymyr	Hontsovskyy	UKR	23.8.91	16 Oct	4:08:52	Ondrej	Motl	CZE	25.7.94	19 Mar
4:04:49	Artur	Mastianica	LTU	30.7.92	19 Mar	4:08:56	Dávid	Tokodi	HUN	3.5.91	8 Oct
4:05:09	Pavel	Schrom	CZE	17.3.91	19 Mar	4:09:15	Hugo	Andrieu	FRA	16.10.92	13 Mar
4:05:20	Arnis	Rumbenieks	LAT	4.4.88	19 Mar	4:09:25		Shan Rongjiang	CHN	26.10.96	10 Sep
4:05:31	Pavel	Yerokhov	BLR	21.7.82	19 Mar	4:09:33	Konstadinos	Dedópoulos	GRE	1.5.94	10 Jan
4:05:37A	Mario Alfonso	Bran	GUA	17.10.89	6 Mar	4:09:40	Dionisio	Ventura	POR	13.12.79	19 Mar
4:05:43	Yuki	Yamazaki	JPN	16.1.84	23 Oct	4:09:51	Chandan	Singh	IND	8.6.87	28 Feb
4:05:47	Luis	Campos	PER	10.11.95	8 May	4:09:55A	Cristian [142]	Berdeja	MEX	21.6.81	6 Mar

Drugs disqualification

3:39:00	Alex	Schwazer ¶	ITA	26.12.84	(1)	WCp	Roma	8 May

60 METRES

7.17	1.6	Elaine	Thompson	JAM	28.6.92	1		Kingston	30 Jan
7.18	1.7	Audrea	Segree	JAM	5.10.90	1rB		Kingston	30 Jan

WOMEN'S WORLD LISTS 2016

60 METRES

Mark		Name		Nat	Born	Pos	Meet	Venue	Date	
7.17	1.6	Elaine	Thompson	JAM	28.6.92	1		Kingston	30	Jan
7.18	1.7	Audrea	Segree	JAM	5.10.90	1rB		Kingston	30	Jan
7.19	1.1	Gayon	Evans	JAM	15.1.90	1		Spanish Town	23	Jan
7.21	1.7	Shimayra	Williams	JAM	2.12.95	2rB		Kingston	30	Jan
7.24	1.0	Sheniqua	Ferguson	BAH	24.11.89	1rC		Kingston	30	Jan
Indoors										
7.00		Dafne	Schippers	NED	15.6.92	1	ISTAF	Berlin	13	Feb
7.00		Barbara	Pierre	USA	28.4.87	1	NC	Portland	12	Mar
7.02			Pierre			1	WI	Portland	19	Mar
7.03			Schippers			1	NC	Apeldoorn	27	Feb
7.04			Schippers			1h1	ISTAF	Berlin	13	Feb
7.04		Elaine	Thompson	JAM	28.6.92	1s3	WI	Portland	19	Mar
7.04			Schippers			2	WI	Portland	19	Mar
7.06		Marie Josée	Ta Lou	CIV	18.11.88	2	ISTAF	Berlin	13	Feb
7.06			Pierre			1s1	WI	Portland	19	Mar
7.06			Thompson			3	WI	Portland	19	Mar
7.07			Schippers			1h1		Karlsruhe	6	Feb
7.07		Ewa	Swoboda (10)	POL-J	26.7.97	1		Torun	12	Feb
7.07		Tatjana	Pinto	GER	2.7.92	1	NC	Leipzig	27	Feb
7.09		Michelle-Lee	Ahye	TTO	10.4.92	1h4	WI	Portland	19	Mar
7.10		Asha	Philip	GBR	25.10.90	1	NC	Sheffield	27	Feb
7.11		Dina	Asher-Smith	GBR	4.12.95	3		Karlsruhe	6	Feb
7.11		Teahna	Daniels	USA-J	27.3.97	1	NCAA	Birmingham, AL	12	Mar
7.11		Tori	Bowie	USA	27.8.90	2s2	WI	Portland	19	Mar
7.12		Stella	Akakpo	FRA	28.2.94	2		Metz	21	Feb
7.12		Hannah	Cunliffe	USA	9.1.96	1h2	NCAA	Birmingham, AL	11	Mar
7.14		Simone	Facey	JAM	7.5.85	1		Eaubonne	9	Feb
7.14		Jamile (20)	Samuel	NED	24.4.92	2h2	ISTAF	Berlin	13	Feb
7.15		Natasha	Morrison	JAM	17.11.92	1s1		Houston	12	Feb
7.15		English	Gardner	USA	22.4.92	1		Boston (R)	14	Feb
7.15		Allyson	Felix	USA	18.11.85	1	Mill	New York (A)	20	Feb
7.16		Rebekka	Haase	GER	2.1.93	1		Leipzig	13	Feb
7.16		Kelly-Ann	Baptiste	TTO	14.10.86	4s1	WI	Portland	19	Mar
7.17		Shayla	Sanders	USA	6.1.94	1		Fayetteville	30	Jan
7.17		Rosângela	Santos	BRA	20.12.90	4	ISTAF	Berlin	13	Feb
7.17			Wei Yongli	CHN	11.10.91	1	NGP	Nanjing	28	Feb
7.17		Ezinne	Okparaebo	NOR	3.3.88	1	NC	Rud	5	Mar
7.17		Tianna (30)	Bartoletta	USA	30.8.85	3	NC	Portland	12	Mar
7.17		Mikiah	Brisco	USA	14.7.96	3	NCAA	Birmingham, AL	12	Mar
7.18		Nataliya	Pohrebnyak	UKR	19.2.88	1		Zaporizhzhya	27	Feb
7.18		Carole	Zahi	FRA	12.6.94	2	NC	Aubière	27	Feb
7.18		Jenna	Prandini	USA	20.11.92	4	NC	Portland	12	Mar
7.19		Carina	Horn	RSA	9.3.89	5	ISTAF	Berlin	13	Feb
7.19		Morolake	Akinosun	USA	17.5.94	4h2	NCAA	Birmingham, AL	11	Mar
7.19		Jasmine	Todd	USA	23.12.93	4	NCAA	Birmingham, AL	12	Mar
7.19		Mikele	Barber	USA	4.10.80	5	NC	Portland	12	Mar
7.20		Kristina	Sivkova	RUS-J	28.2.97	1		Yekaterinburg	7	Jan
7.20		Olesya (40)	Povh	UKR	18.10.87	1		Zaporizhzhya	16	Jan
7.20		Viktoriya	Zyabkina	KAZ	4.9.92	1	NC	Ust-Kamenogorsk	29	Jan
7.20		Kerron	Stewart	JAM	16.4.84	1		Boston	28	Feb
7.20		Tahesia	Harrigan	IVB	15.2.82	1		New York	4	Mar
7.20		Marika	Popowicz-Drapala	POL	28.4.88	1	NC	Torun	5	Mar
7.20		Javianne	Oliver	USA	26.12.94	5h2	NCAA	Birmingham, AL	11	Mar
7.21		Mujinga	Kambundji	SUI	17.6.92	1	NC	St.Gallen	27	Feb
7.21		Ángela	Tenorio	ECU	27.1.96	5s3	WI	Portland	19	Mar
7.22		Alex	Anderson	USA	28.1.87	1		Nashville	30	Jan
7.22		Dezerea	Bryant	USA	27.4.93	3s2	NC	Portland	12	Mar
7.23		Tawanna (50)	Meadows	USA	4.8.86	3		Eaubonne	9	Feb
7.23		Crystal	Emmanuel	CAN	27.11.91	1		New York (SI)	12	Feb
7.23		Flings	Owusu-Agyapong	GHA	16.10.88	5	Mill	New York (A)	20	Feb
7.23		Felicia	Brown	USA	27.10.93	1h3	SEC	Fayetteville	26	Feb

60 – 100 METRES

Mark	Wind	Name		Nat	Born	Pos	Meet	Venue		Date	
7.23			Liang Xiaojing	CHN-J	7.4.97	1	NGP	Nanjing		3	Mar
7.24		Myasia	Jacobs	USA	8.1.94	1		Boston (R)		27	Feb
7.24		Maja	Mihalinec	SLO	17.12.89	2		Jablonec nad Nisou		5	Mar
7.25		Khamica	Bingham	CAN	15.6.94	6	Mill	New York (A)		20	Feb
7.26		Adeline	Gouenon	CIV	20.10.94	2r5		London (LV)		31	Jan
7.26		Anna	Kukushkina	RUS	13.12.92	1		Sankt Peterburg		7	Feb
7.26		Laverne	Jones-Ferrette	ISV	16.9.81	2s3		Houston		12	Feb
		(60)									
7.26		Desiree	Henry	GBR	26.8.95	4h2	GP	Glasgow		20	Feb
7.26		Jennifer	Madu	USA	23.9.94	1h1	SEC	Fayetteville		26	Feb
7.27		Octavious	Freeman	USA	20.4.92	16 Jan	7.29A	Brianna	Rollins	USA	18.8.91	22 Jan
7.27A		Muna	Lee	USA	30.10.81	30 Jan	7.29	Daryll	Neita	GBR	29.8.96	31 Jan
7.27		Samantha	Henry-Robinson	JAM	25.9.88	13 Feb	7.29	Ashley	Marshall	BAR	10.9.93	13 Feb
7.27		Chantal	Butzek	GER-J	25.2.97	21 Feb	7.29A	LeKeisha	Lawson	USA	3.6.87	13 Feb
7.27		Jennifer	Galais	FRA	7.3.92	27 Feb	7.29	Yevgeniya	Polyakova	RUS	29.5.83	14 Feb
7.27		Kennadi	Bouyer	USA	16.9.95	11 Mar	7.29	Sherone	Simpson	JAM	12.8.84	19 Feb
7.28		Kali	Davis-White	JAM	24.10.94	15 Jan	7.29	Ksenija	Balta	EST	1.11.86	27 Feb
7.28		Erica	Alexander	USA	24.6.90	30 Jan	7.29	Shaina	Harrison	CAN	11.3.94	27 Feb
7.28		Kristina	Knott	USA	.95	7 Feb	7.29	Andrea	Ivancevic	CRO	21.8.84	1 Mar
7.28		Dutee	Chand	IND	3.2.96	19 Feb	7.29	Gloria	Hooper	ITA	3.3.92	19 Mar
7.28		Nadine	Gonska	GER	23.1.90	27 Feb		(83)				

100 METRES

Mark	Wind	Name		Nat	Born	Pos	Meet	Venue	Date	
10.70	0.3	Elaine	Thompson	JAM	28.6.92	1	NC	Kingston	1	Jul
10.71	0.5		Thompson			1	OG	Rio de Janeiro	13	Aug
10.72	0.6		Thompson			1	VD	Bruxelles	9	Sep
10.74	1.0	English	Gardner	USA	22.4.92	1	NC	Eugene	3	Jul
10.78	1.6	Murielle	Ahouré	CIV	23.8.87	1		Montverde	11	Jun
10.78	1.0	Tianna	Bartoletta	USA	30.8.85	2	NC	Eugene	3	Jul
10.78	1.0	Tori	Bowie	USA	27.8.90	3	NC	Eugene	3	Jul
10.78	0.8		Thompson			1	Athl	Lausanne	25	Aug
10.80	0.7		Bowie			1	DL	Doha	6	May
10.81	1.5		Gardner			1	Pre	Eugene	28	May
10.83	0.7	Dafne	Schippers	NED	15.6.92	2	DL	Doha	6	May
10.83	1.6	Veronica	Campbell-Brown	JAM	15.5.82	2		Montverde	11	Jun
10.83	0.5		Bowie			2	OG	Rio de Janeiro	13	Aug
10.85	0.2		Thompson			1s1	NC	Kingston	1	Jul
10.86	0.5	Shelly-Ann	Fraser-Pryce	JAM	27.12.86	3	OG	Rio de Janeiro	13	Aug
10.86	0.5	Marie Josée	Ta Lou	CIV	18.11.88	4	OG	Rio de Janeiro	13	Aug
10.87	0.8		Thompson			1	GGala	Roma	2	Jun
10.88	0.3		Fraser-Pryce			1s2	OG	Rio de Janeiro	13	Aug
10.88	0.6		Thompson			1s3	OG	Rio de Janeiro	13	Aug
10.90	1.8		Gardner			1h1	NC	Eugene	2	Jul
10.90	-0.2		Schippers			1	EC	Amsterdam	8	Jul
10.90	1.0		Bowie			1s1	OG	Rio de Janeiro	13	Aug
10.90	1.0	Michelle-Lee	Ahye	TTO	10.4.92	2s1	OG	Rio de Janeiro	13	Aug
10.90	0.3		Schippers			2s2	OG	Rio de Janeiro	13	Aug
10.90	0.6		Gardner			2s3	OG	Rio de Janeiro	13	Aug
10.90	0.6		Schippers			5	OG	Rio de Janeiro	13	Aug
10.91	0.7		Campbell-Brown			3	DL	Doha	6	May
10.91	1.2		Bowie			1		Herzogenaurach	14	May
10.91	1.8		Bowie			1h5	NC	Eugene	2	Jul
10.92	0.8		Gardner			2	GGala	Roma	2	Jun
10.92	0.6		Ahye			6	OG	Rio de Janeiro	13	Aug
		(31/10)								
10.95	1.7	Jenna	Prandini	USA	20.11.92	1	MSR	Norwalk	16	Apr
10.95	1.0	Morolake	Akinosun	USA	17.5.94	4	NC	Eugene	3	Jul
10.96	1.0	Christania	Williams	JAM	17.10.94	3s1	OG	Rio de Janeiro	13	Aug
10.99	1.7	Hannah	Cunliffe	USA	9.1.96	2	MSR	Norwalk	16	Apr
11.00	0.4	Simone	Facey	JAM	7.5.85	1		Gainesville	22	Apr
11.00	1.2	Tatjana	Pinto	GER	2.7.92	1r1		Mannheim	29	Jul
11.01	2.0	Ariana	Washington	USA	4.9.96	2h3	NC	Eugene	2	Jul
11.02	0.3	Blessing	Okagbare	NGR	9.10.88	1	NC	Sapele	8	Jul
11.04	1.5	Kelly-Ann	Baptiste	TTO	14.10.86	2s2	NC	Port of Spain	25	Jun
11.04	1.2	Gina	Lückenkemper	GER	21.11.96	2r1		Mannheim	29	Jul
		(20)								
11.06	1.5	Desiree	Henry	GBR	26.8.95	1		Azusa	15	Apr
11.07	1.5	LeKeisha	Lawson	USA	3.6.87	1		Chula Vista	18	Jun
11.07	2.0	Carina	Horn	RSA	9.3.89	2	AfCh	Durban	23	Jun
11.07	1.0	Semoy	Hackett	TTO	27.11.88	2	NC	Port of Spain	25	Jun
11.07	1.8	Barbara	Pierre	USA	28.4.87	2h5	NC	Eugene	2	Jul

100 METRES

Mark	Wind	Name		Nat	Born	Pos	Meet	Venue	Date	
11.07	0.9	Candace	Hill	USA-Y	11.2.99	1	WJ	Bydgoszcz	21	Jul
11.07	-1.3	Dina	Asher-Smith	GBR	4.12.95	3h2	DL	London (OS)	23	Jul
11.09	0.8	Olga	Safronova	KAZ	5.11.91	1	NCp	Almaty	24	May
11.09	1.6	Joanna	Atkins	USA	31.1.89	3		Montverde	11	Jun
11.10	1.7	Mikele	Barber	USA	4.10.80	3	MSR	Norwalk	16	Apr
		(30)								
11.11	1.7	Kimberlyn	Duncan	USA	2.8.91	4	MSR	Norwalk	16	Apr
11.11	-0.1	Ivet	Lalova-Collio	BUL	18.5.84	2		Beijing	18	May
11.11	-2.2	Nataliya	Pohrebnyak	UKR	19.2.88	1	NC	Lutsk	17	Jun
11.11	1.0	Tiffany	Townsend	USA	14.6.89	8	NC	Eugene	3	Jul
11.12	0.9	Ewa	Swoboda	POL-J	26.7.97	2	WJ	Bydgoszcz	21	Jul
11.13	1.2	Shayla	Sanders	USA	6.1.94	1		Los Angeles	26	Mar
11.13	0.4	Candyce	McGrone	USA	24.3.89	3		Gainesville	22	Apr
11.13	1.0	Ángela	Tenorio	ECU	27.1.96	2		Madrid	23	Jun
11.13	1.8	Tawanna	Meadows	USA	4.8.86	2h1	NC	Eugene	2	Jul
11.14	0.1	Mujinga	Kambundji	SUI	17.6.92	1h1		Weinheim	28	May
		(40)								
11.14	1.8	Brenessa	Thompson	GUY	22.7.96	1		Leonora	18	Jun
11.14	1.4	Octavious	Freeman	USA	20.4.92	1rB	NC	Port of Spain	25	Jun
11.14A	0.7	Ana Cláudia	Silva #	BRA	6.11.88	1		Medellín	10	Jul
11.16	1.5	Carmelita	Jeter	USA	24.11.79	7	Pre	Eugene	28	May
11.16	1.0	Khalifa	St.Fort	TTO-J	13.2.98	4	NC	Port of Spain	25	Jun
11.16	1.8	Shalonda	Solomon	USA	19.12.85	3h1	NC	Eugene	2	Jul
11.16	-1.3	Asha	Philip	GBR	25.10.90	5h2	DL	London (OS)	23	Jul
11.17	0.2	Kyra	Jefferson	USA	23.9.94	1rC		Gainesville	22	Apr
11.17	1.6	Kaylin	Whitney	USA-J	9.3.98	4		Montverde	11	Jun
11.17	-0.4	Stella	Akakpo	FRA	28.2.94	1	NC	Angers	25	Jun
		(50)								
11.17	0.7	Sashalee	Forbes	JAM	10.5.96	3s2	NC	Kingston	1	Jul
11.17	1.7	Imani	Lansiquot	GBR-J	17.12.97	1h3	WJ	Bydgoszcz	20	Jul
11.18	0.8	Deajah	Stevens	USA	19.5.95	2h2	NC	Eugene	2	Jul
11.19	0.8	Alex	Anderson	USA	28.1.87	1		Austin	16	Apr
11.19	0.0	Shaunae	Miller	BAH	15.4.94	2		Clermont	30	Apr
11.19	1.8	Shillonie	Calvert	JAM	27.7.88	1		Phoenix	21	May
11.19	-1.3	Kerron	Stewart	JAM	16.4.84	3		Rabat	22	May
11.19	1.8	Ashleigh	Nelson	GBR	20.2.91	2		Weinheim	28	May
11.19	1.1	Tynia	Gaither	BAH	16.3.93	2s2	NCAA	Eugene	9	Jun
11.19	0.9	Floriane	Gnafoua	FRA	30.1.96	2h2	NC	Angers	25	Jun
		(60)								
11.20	1.7	Jasmine	Todd	USA	23.12.93	5	MSR	Norwalk	16	Apr
11.20	1.3	Kianna	Gray	USA	30.12.96	1s3	NCAA	Eugene	9	Jun
11.20A	0.7	Evelin	Rivera	COL-J	8.12.97	2		Medellín	10	Jul
11.21	1.2	Teahna	Daniels	USA-J	27.3.97	2		Los Angeles	26	Mar
11.21	1.1	Olesya	Povh	UKR	18.10.87	1	NCp	Kirovohrad	25	May
11.21	1.9	Lorène	Bazolo	POR	4.5.83	1		Salamanca	4	Jun
11.21	1.5	Ashley	Henderson	USA	4.12.95	1s1	NCAA	Eugene	9	Jun
11.21	1.3	Deanna	Hill	USA	13.4.96	2s3	NCAA	Eugene	9	Jun
11.21	1.6	Shelbi	White	USA	3.7.96	6		Montverde	11	Jun
11.21A	0.7	Eliecit	Palacios	COL	15.8.87	3		Medellín	10	Jul
		(70)								
11.22	0.3	Rebekka	Haase	GER	2.1.93	3		Clermont	14	May
11.22	1.8	Reyare	Thomas	TTO	23.11.87	2		Leonora	18	Jun
11.22	1.0	Kristina	Sivkova	RUS-J	28.2.97	1	NC	Cheboksary	20	Jun
11.23	0.6	Alyssa	Conley	RSA	27.4.91	2		Gavardo	29	May
11.23	0.3	Rosângela	Santos	BRA	20.12.90	1		Rio de Janeiro	5	Jun
11.23	1.2	Daryll	Neita	GBR	29.8.96	1s1	NC	Birmingham	25	Jun
11.24	-0.1	Wei Yongli		CHN	11.10.91	4		Beijing	18	May
11.24	1.8	Gloria	Asumnu	NGR	22.5.85	2		Phoenix	21	May
11.24	0.0	Hrystyna	Stuy	UKR	3.2.88	1h1	NCp	Kirovohrad	25	May
11.24	1.5	Mikiah	Brisco	USA	14.7.96	2s1	NCAA	Eugene	9	Jun
		(80)								
11.24	0.6	Gayon	Evans	JAM	15.1.90	4		Kingston	11	Jun
11.24	0.6	Remona	Burchell	JAM	15.9.91	5		Kingston	11	Jun
11.25	1.1	Jura	Levy	JAM	4.11.90	1		Kingston	16	Apr
11.25	1.1	Lisa	Mayer	GER	2.5.96	2		Wetzlar	7	May
11.25	0.5	Felicia	Brown	USA	27.10.93	1h3	SEC	Tuscaloosa	13	May
11.25	1.6	Jennifer	Galais	FRA	7.3.92	1h1		Vénissieux	4	Jun
11.25	1.9	Me'Lisa	Barber	USA	4.10.80	2	Bush	Norwalk	4	Jun
11.25	1.3	Ramona	Papaioannou	CYP	15.6.89	1	NC	Nicosia	18	Jun
11.25	-0.6	Tahesia	Harrigan	IVB	15.2.82	1		Road Town	3	Jul
11.26A	0.5	Narcisa	Landázuri	ECU	25.11.92	1		Cuenca	26	Mar
		(90)								

100 METRES

Mark	Wind	Name		Nat	Born	Pos	Meet	Venue		Date	
11.26	0.3	Flings	Owusu-Agyapong	GHA	16.10.88	4		Clermont		14	May
11.26A	1.9	Katia	Seymour	USA-J	3.10.97	1		Albuquerque		4	Jun
11.26	-0.9	Kali	Davis-White	JAM	24.10.94	2s3	NC	Kingston		1	Jul
11.26	1.1	Phylicia	George	CAN	16.11.87	1h3	NC	Edmonton		9	Jul
11.26	0.6	Crystal	Emmanuel	CAN	27.11.91	1	NC	Edmonton		9	Jul
11.27	0.4	Quanera	Hayes	USA	7.3.92	2rB		Gainesville		22	Apr
11.27	1.6	Kortnei	Johnson	USA-J	11.8.97	1q2	NCAA-E	Jacksonville		27	May
11.27	0.1	Viktoriya	Zyabkina	KAZ	4.9.92	2		Riga		31	May
11.27	0.8	Ezinne	Okparaebo	NOR	3.3.88	6h2	DL	Birmingham		5	Jun
11.27	1.5	Jennifer	Madu	USA	23.9.94	3s1	NCAA	Eugene		9	Jun
11.27 (100)	0.7	Natasha	Morrison	JAM	17.11.92	4s2	NC	Kingston		1	Jul
11.27	1.6	Sophie	Papps	GBR	6.10.94	1s1	Eng Ch	Bedford		30	Jul
11.28	1.1	Carole	Zahi	FRA	12.6.94					4	Jun
11.28	1.9	Mandy	White	USA	23.10.88					4	Jun
11.28	1.6	Hajar Saad	Al-Khaldi	BRN	17.3.95					18	Jun
11.28+	0.0	Natasha	Hastings	USA	23.7.86					10	Sep
11.29	-0.1		Yuan Qiqi	CHN	26.10.95					18	May
11.29	0.0	Alexis	Love	USA	24.4.91					27	May
11.29	1.6	Javianne	Oliver	USA	26.12.94					27	May
11.29	0.8	Jeneba	Tarmoh	USA	27.9.89					2	Jul
11.29	1.9	Toea	Wisil	PNG	1.1.88					9	Jul
11.30	2.0	Gabrielle	Thomas	USA	7.12.96					1	Apr
11.30	0.4	Arialis	Gandulla	CUB	22.6.95					27	May
11.30	-0.9	Audrea	Segree	JAM	5.10.94					1	Jul
11.31	1.8	Franciela	Krasucki	BRA	26.4.88					14	May
11.31	0.8	Nigina	Sharipova	UZB	10.8.95					24	May
11.31	0.8	Melissa	Breen	AUS	17.9.90					5	Jun
11.31	1.2	Anastasiya	Grigoryeva	RUS	7.11.93					20	Jun
11.31	1.4	Céline	Distel-Bonnet	FRA	25.7.87					25	Jun
11.32	1.6	Gabrielle	Farquharson	USA	12.12.92					14	May
11.32	1.5	Jessica	Davis	USA	31.10.92					18	Jun
11.32	1.9	Alexis	Faulknor	USA	22.9.94					26	Jun
11.33	1.4	Rushell	Harvey	USA	9.9.95					9	Apr
11.33	1.2	Cambrya	Jones	USA	20.9.90					9	Apr
11.33	1.5	Taylor	Ellis-Watson	USA	6.5.93					23	Apr
11.33	-0.3	Taylor	Bennett	USA-J	15.1.97					23	Apr
11.33	0.3	Dutee	Chand	IND	3.2.96					28	Apr
11.33	1.5	Samantha	Henry-Robinson	JAM	25.9.88					14	May
11.33	2.0	Tameka	Williams	SKN	31.8.89					11	Jun
11.33	0.2	Josefina	Elsler	GER	7.6.91					23	Jul
11.34A	-0.2	Isidora	Jiménez	CHI	10.8.93					23	Apr
11.34	1.6	Gloria	Hooper	ITA	3.3.92					30	Apr
11.34	0.6	Marissa	Kurtimah	CAN	25.5.94					15	May
11.34	1.2	Aniekeme	Alphonsus	NGR-J	25.12.98					25	May
11.34	0.7	Aleia	Hobbs	USA	24.2.96					26	May
11.34	0.0	Kamaria	Brown	USA	21.12.92					27	May
11.34A	1.9	Sha'carri	Richardson	USA-Y	25.3.00					4	Jun
11.34	1.0	Kaylor	Harris	USA-Y	10.7.00					18	Jun
11.34	0.6	Kimberly	Hyacinthe	CAN	28.3.89					9	Jul
11.34	1.2	Alexandra	Burghardt	GER	28.4.94					29	Jul
11.34	1.5	Maja	Mihalinec	SLO	17.12.89					10	Sep
11.35	1.0	Savannah	Carson	USA	30.3.95					23	Apr
11.35	0.7	Keni	Harrison	USA	18.9.92					7	May
11.35	1.1	Destiny	Carter	USA	.93					27	May
11.35	0.2	Phumlile	Ndzinisa	SWZ	21.8.92					29	May
11.35		Agnes	Osazuwa	NGR	21.6.90					8	Jul
11.35	1.2	Inna	Weit	GER	5.8.88					29	Jul
11.36	1.7	Moesha	Davidson	USA	.95					23	Apr
11.36	-0.2	Krystal	Sparling	USA-J	15.9.97					14	May
11.36	1.6	Yasmin	Kwadwo	GER	9.11.90					28	May
11.36	-0.5	Naomi	Sedney	NED	17.12.94					7	Jul
11.36	1.7	Ksenija	Balta	EST	1.11.86					16	Jul
11.37	0.0	Laura	Müller	GER	11.12.95					28	May
11.37	1.2	Bianca	Knight	USA	2.1.89					4	Jun
11.37	1.3	Aaliyah	Brown		USA				6.1.95		9	Jun
11.37	2.0	Kai	Selvon		TTO				13.4.92		11	Jun
11.37	2.0	Ornella	Livingston		JAM				19.5.91		11	Jun
11.37	0.3	Peace	Uko		NGR				26.12.95		8	Jul
11.37	-1.3	Khamica	Bingham		CAN				15.6.94		23	Jul
11.38	1.3	Jodie	Williams		GBR				28.9.93		16	Apr
11.38	0.1	Kylie	Price		USA				1.10.93		1	May
11.38A	1.2	Eboni	Coby		USA				23.12.94		19	May
11.38	0.8	Svetlana	Golendova		KAZ				25.7.93		24	May
11.38	1.4	Chisato	Fukushima		JPN				27.6.88		5	Jun
11.38	0.3	Jamile	Samuel		NED				24.4.92		5	Jun
11.38	1.1	Inna	Eftimova		BUL				19.6.88		15	Jun
11.39	0.9	Khadija	Suleman		NGR				16.8.93		26	Mar
11.39	1.5	Kiara	Parker		USA				28.10.96		23	Apr
11.39	1.4	Shimayra	Williams		JAM				2.12.95		7	May
11.39	1.4	Lauren Rain	Williams		USA-Y				25.7.99		4	Jun
11.39	-0.1	Cassandra	Hall		USA-J				23.7.97		18	Jun
11.39	1.4	Véronique	Mang		FRA				15.12.84		25	Jun
11.39	2.0	Hannah	Brier		GBR-J				3.2.98		21	Jul
11.40A	0.8	Tebogo	Mamathu		RSA				27.5.95		8	Mar
11.40	0.8	Kimone	Shaw		JAM-Y				28.9.99		18	Mar
11.40	-0.2	Jada	Martin		USA				8.6.95		14	May
11.40	0.8	Yuliya	Rakhmanova		KAZ				25.10.91		24	May
11.40	1.8	Laverne	Jones-Ferrette		ISV				16.9.81		18	Jun
11.40	1.9	Melanise	Chapman		USA				28.4.91		26	Jun
11.41	0.0	Anneisha	McLaughlin-Whilby		JAM				6.1.86		9	Apr
11.41	1.2	Celera	Barnes		USA-J				2.12.98		24	Jun
11.41	1.6	Tristie	Johnson		USA				20.11.93		27	May
11.41	1.0	Twanisha	Terry		USA-Y				24.1.99		18	Jun
11.41	1.2	Jayla	Kirkland		USA-Y				13.2.99		24	Jun
11.41	1.2	Celera	Barnes		USA-J				2.12.98		24	Jun
11.41	1.4	Estela	García		ESP				20.3.89		23	Jul
11.42	1.7	Ella	Nelson		AUS				10.5.94		20	Feb
11.42	1.5	Shenel	Crooke		SKN				12.10.93		18	Mar
11.42	2.0	Ashley	Marshall		BAR				10.9.93		8	Apr
11.42	-1.4	Nikia	Squire		USA				5.12.93		9	Apr
11.42	1.0	Nediam	Vargas		VEN				2.9.94		30	Apr
11.42	0.6	Amy	Foster		IRL				2.10.88		14	May
11.42	1.1	Yelizaveta	Bryzgina		UKR				28.11.89		25	May
11.42	-0.5	Anna	Kukushkina		RUS				13.12.92		20	Jul
11.43	1.3	Shai-Anne	Davis		CAN				4.12.93		6	Apr
11.43	0.9	Carmiesha	Cox		BAH				16.5.95		4	May
11.43	0.9	Cindy	Ofili		GBR				5.8.94		4	May
11.43	2.0	Anglerne	Annelus		USA-J				10.1.97		4	May
11.43	1.4	Gina	Bass		GAM				3.5.95		5	May
11.43	0.7	Precious	Hitchcock		USA				.95		6	May
11.43	0.5	Nadine	Gonska		GER				23.1.90		8	May
11.43	1.0	Katrin	Fehm		GER-J				16.4.98		5	Jun
11.43	-0.4	Ayodelé	Ikuesan		FRA				15.5.85		5	Jun
11.43	0.2	Gemma	Acheampong		GHA				13.2.93		8	Jul

Running with guide runner

| 11.40 | 0.2 | Omara | Durand | CUB | 26.11.91 | 1 | | Kingston | | 9 | Sep |

Wind assisted

10.71	2.4		Thompson			1		Kingston		7	May
10.74	3.1	Tori	Bowie	USA	27.8.90	1s1	NC	Eugene		3	Jul
10.74	2.5		Gardner			1s3	NC	Eugene		3	Jul
10.79	2.5		Bartoletta			2s3	NC	Eugene		3	Jul
10.80	2.1		Ahouré			1h1		Montverde		11	Jun
10.81	3.6	Jenna	Prandini	USA	20.11.92	1h4	NC	Eugene		2	Jul
10.85	2.4		Gardner			2		Kingston		7	May
10.86	4.5		Prandini			1s2	NC	Eugene		3	Jul
10.92	2.6	Blessing	Okagbare	NGR	9.10.88	1	Gyulai	Székesfehérvár		18	Jul
10.95	2.6	Ariana	Washington	USA	4.9.96	1	NCAA	Eugene		11	Jun

100 METRES

Mark	Wind	Name		Nat	Born	Pos	Meet	Venue	Date	
10.96	2.6	Ashley	Henderson	USA	4.12.95	2	NCAA	Eugene	11	Jun
10.97	5.3	Alex	Anderson	USA	28.1.87	1		Austin	7	May
10.98	3.4	Rebekka	Haase	GER	2.1.93	1r3		Mannheim	29	Jul
10.99	3.6	Joanna	Atkins	USA	31.1.89	2h4	NC	Eugene	2	Jul
11.01	2.5	Barbara	Pierre	USA	28.4.87	3s3	NC	Eugene	3	Jul
11.03	4.5	Tiffany	Townsend	USA	14.6.89	3s2	NC	Eugene	3	Jul
11.04	3.1	Deajah	Stevens	USA	19.5.95	3s1	NC	Eugene	3	Jul
11.04	3.4	Lisa	Mayer	GER	2.5.96	2r3		Mannheim	29	Jul
11.05	3.6	Octavious	Freeman	USA	20.4.92	4h4	NC	Eugene	2	Jul
11.05	4.5	Shalonda	Solomon	USA	19.12.85	5s2	NC	Eugene	3	Jul
11.06	4.5	Candyce	McGrone	USA	24.3.89	6s2	NC	Eugene	3	Jul
11.08	2.6	Tynia	Gaither	BAH	16.3.93	4	NCAA	Eugene	11	Jun
11.10	2.7	Ewa	Swoboda	POL-J	26.7.97	1h4	WJ	Bydgoszcz	20	Jul
11.11	3.8	Destiny	Carter	USA	.93	1		Baton Rouge	30	Apr
11.11	2.4	Jura	Levy	JAM	4.11.90	5		Kingston	7	May
11.11	3.6	Mandy	White	USA	23.10.88	5h4	NC	Eugene	2	Jul
11.12	3.8	Kianna	Gray	USA	30.12.96	2		Baton Rouge	30	Apr
11.13	3.8	Kortnei	Johnson	USA-J	11.8.97	3		Baton Rouge	30	Apr
11.13	2.6	Mikiah	Brisco	USA	14.7.96	5	NCAA	Eugene	11	Jun
11.14	3.5	Phylicia	George	CAN	16.11.87	2		Baton Rouge	23	Apr
11.15	4.5	Kaylin	Whitney	USA-J	9.3.98	7s2	NC	Eugene	3	Jul
11.16	3.8	Javianne	Oliver	USA	26.12.94	4		Baton Rouge	30	Apr
11.16	5.3	Remona	Burchell	JAM	15.9.91	2		Austin	7	May
11.17	3.5	Lauren Rain	Williams	USA-Y	25.7.99	1		Norwalk	21	May
11.18	3.5	Kali	Davis-White	JAM	24.10.94	4		Baton Rouge	23	Apr
11.18	2.6	Crystal	Emmanuel	CAN	27.11.91	1h2	NC	Edmonton	9	Jul
11.18	3.4	Alexandra	Burghardt	GER	28.4.94	3r3		Mannheim	29	Jul
11.21	2.2	Audrea	Segree	JAM	5.10.90	1		Spanish Town	12	Mar
11.21	3.9	Khamica	Bingham	CAN	15.6.94	1		Toronto	11	Jun
11.21	3.4	Nadine	Gonska	GER	23.1.90	4r3		Mannheim	29	Jul
11.22A	4.2	Rochene	Smith	JAM	.95	1		Hobbs	23	Apr
11.22	2.2	María	Belibasáki	GRE	19.6.91	1		Kalamáta	28	Ma
11.23	3.5	Dezerea	Bryant	USA	27.4.93	5		Baton Rouge	23	Apr
11.24	3.5	Jada	Martin	USA	8.6.95	6		Baton Rouge	23	Apr
11.24	5.3	Cleo	VanBuren	USA	1.5.86	3		Austin	7	May
11.25	2.1	Alexis	Love	USA	24.4.91	5h1		Montverde	11	Jun
11.26	3.9	Jessica	Davis	USA	31.10.92	1r3	MSR	Norwalk	15	Apr
11.26	4.9	Aaliyah	Brown	USA	6.1.95	1rB		Baton Rouge	30	Apr
11.26	3.8	Rushell	Harvey	USA	9.9.95	5		Baton Rouge	30	Apr
11.26	2.1	Ezinne	Okparaebo	NOR	3.3.88	2h1		Madrid	23	Jun
11.26	2.8	Jeneba	Tarmoh	USA	27.9.89	3		Eugene	29	Jul
11.27	3.7	Mahagony	Jones	USA	20.12.90	15		Apr		
11.27	3.8	Krystal	Sparling	USA-J	15.9.97	30		Apr		
11.28	3.4	Inna	Weit	GER	5.8.88	29		Jul		
11.29	5.3	Chauntae	Bayne	USA	4.4.84	7		May		
11.30	3.8	Gina	Bass	GAM	3.5.95	19		Mar		
11.30	2.5	Anastasiya	Grigoryeva	RUS	7.11.93	30		Jun		
11.31	2.1	Kiana	Horton	USA-J	29.1.97	26		Mar		
11.31	3.8	Kiara	Parker	USA	28.10.96	30		Apr		
11.31	3.4	Yasmin	Kwadwo	GER	9.11.90	29		Jul		
11.32	3.7	Ashton	Purvis	USA	12.7.92	15		Apr		
11.32	2.6	Destiny	Smith-Barnett	USA	26.7.96	13		May		
11.32	2.9	Leslie	Cole	USA	16.2.87	19		May		
11.32	2.2	Kimberly	Hyacinthe	CAN	28.3.89	9		Apr		
11.34	3.3	Phyllis	Francis	USA	4.5.92	6		May		
11.34	2.6	Drea	Austin	USA	24.1.96	13		May		
11.35	4.2	Precious	Hitchcock	USA	.95	9		Apr		
11.35	2.9	Briana	Guillory	USA-J	21.11.97	23		Apr		
11.35	3.0	Lauren	Williams	USA	27.7.89	29		Apr		
11.35	4.9	Jellisa	Westney	CAN	6.10.93	30		Apr		
11.35	3.5	Celera	Barnes	USA-J	2.12.98	21		May		
11.35	3.1	Anna	Kukushkina	RUS	13.12.92	20		Jul		
11.36	3.5	Nikia	Squire	USA	5.12.93	19		Mar		
11.36	2.8	Zainab	Sanni	NGR	20.1.95	23		Apr		
11.36	4.0	Riley	Day	AUS-Y	30.3.00	3		Dec		
11.37	3.9	Dominique	Booker	USA	10.2.92	15		Apr		
11.37	3.9	Shai-Anne	Davis	CAN	4.12.93	15		Apr		
11.37	2.4	Cassondra	Hall	USA-J	23.9.97	30		Apr		
11.37A	3.0	Tamzin	Thomas	RSA-J	6.10.97	17		Jun		
11.37	3.3	Rachel	Johncock	GBR	4.10.93	30		Jul		
11.38	3.4	Jadzia	Beasley	USA-J	13.1.97	15		May		
11.38	3.6	Tristie	Johnson	USA	20.11.93	2		Jul		
11.39	4.2	Jasmine	Camacho-Quinn	PUR	21.8.96	9		Apr		
11.39	4.9	Diamond	Spaulding	USA	29.9.96	30		Apr		
11.39	4.1	Charonda	Williams	USA	27.3.87	7		May		
11.39	2.4	Agata	Forkasiewicz	POL	13.1.94	21		May		
11.40	2.4	Amy	Foster	IRL	2.10.88	14		May		
11.41	4.2	Rochelle	Coster	NZL	6.6.88	22		Jan		
11.41	3.7	LaTessa	Johnson	USA	13.4.97	15		Apr		
11.41	4.2	Debbie Ferguson McKenzie		BAH	16.1.76	6		May		

Best at low altitude

11.27	0.2	A C Silva #7h1 DL		London (OS)	23	Jul
11.27	0.3	Landázuri 6s2 OG		Rio de Janeiro	13	Aug
11.37	0.8	Jiménez		19	Mar	
11.42	1.5	Coby		26	Mar	

Hand timing

11.0A		Narcisa	Landázuri	ECU	25.11.92	1h1		Cuenca	26	Mar
11.0A	0.3	Nedian	Vargas	VEN	5.9.94	1h2		Cuenca	26	Mar
11.1A		Andrea	Purica	VEN	29.11.95	26		Mar		
11.1A		Eliecit	Palacios	COL	15.8.87	26		Mar		

Doubtful marks at Almaty 25 Jun:
1. Viktoriya Zyabkina KAZ 4.9.92 11.15, 2. Dutee Chand IND 3.2.96 11.24, 3. Iman Isa Jassim BRN-J 9.7.97 11.26,
4. Roma Kashafutdinova KAZ 22.10.93 11.31

JUNIORS

See main list for top 10 juniors (& 4 wa). 12 performances by 5 women to 11.18. Additional marks and further juniors:

100 – 150 – 200 METRES

Mark	Wind	Name		Nat	Born	Pos	Meet	Venue	Date
C Hill	11.09	1.9 1h2 NC-j	Clovis	24 Jun		11.12	2.0 1s2 WJ	Bydgoszcz	21 Jul
Swoboda	11.17	0.4 1s3 WJ	Bydgoszcz	21 Jul		11.18	1.0 7s1 OG	Rio de Janeiro	13 Aug
	11.18	1.2 2	St. Polten	26 May					
St. Fort	11.18	0.9 3 WJ	Bydgoszcz	21 Jul					
Whitney	11.18	2.0 3h3 NC	Eugene	2 Jul					
11.33	-0.3	Taylor	Bennett	USA	15.1.97	2	Johnson	Waco	23 Apr
11.34	1.2	Aniekeme	Alphonsus	NGR	25.12.98	1h4		Lagos	25 May
11.34A	1.9	Sha'carri	Richardson	USA-Y	25.3.00	2		Albuquerque	4 Jun
11.34	1.0	Kaylor	Harris	USA-Y	10.7.00	1	HS N.Bal	Grensboro	18 Jun
11.36	-0.2	Krystal	Sparling	USA	15.9.97	4	SEC	Tuscaloosa	14 May
11.39	1.4	Lauren Rain	Williams	USA-Y	25.7.99	1		Clovis	4 Jun
11.39	-0.1	Cassandra	Hall	USA	23.7.97	1		Renton	18 Jun
11.39	2.0	Hannah	Brier	GBR	3.2.98	3s2	WJ	Bydgoszcz	21 Jul
11.40	0.8	Kimone	Shaw	JAM-Y	28.9.99	1	N.Sch-y	Kingston	18 Mar
11.41	1.2	Celera	Barnes (20)	USA	2.12.98	3	NC-j	Clovis	24 Jun
11.41	1.0	Twanisha	Terry	USA-Y	24.1.99	2	HS N.Bal	Greensboro	18 Jun
11.41	1.2	Jayla	Kirkland	USA-Y	13.2.99	2	NC-j	Clovis	24 Jun
11.41	1.2	Celera	Barnes	USA	2.12.98	3	NC-j	Clovis	24 Jun
Wind assisted:			4 performances by 4 women to 11.17w.						
11.27	3.8	Krystal	Sparling	USA	15.9.97	6		Baton Rouge	30 Apr
11.31	2.1	Kiana	Horton	USA	29.1.97	1		San Antonio	26 Mar
11.35	2.9	Briana	Guillory	USA	21.11.97	1		Iowa City	23 Apr
11.35	3.5	Celera	Barnes	USA	2.12.98	2		Norwalk	21 May
11.36	4.0	Riley	Day	AUS-J	30.3.00	1		Canberra	3 Dec
11.37	2.4	Cassandra	Hall	USA-J	23.9.97	1h1		Conyers	30 Apr
11.37A	3.0	Tamzin	Thomas	RSA-J	6.10.97	1		Lusaka	17 Jun
11.38	3.4	Jadzia	Beasley	USA-J	13.1.97	1rC	MSR	Norwalk	15 Apr

150 METRES STRAIGHT

Mark	Wind	Name		Nat	Born	Pos	Meet	Venue	Date
16.57	1.1	Desiree	Henry	GBR	26.8.95	1		Gateshead	10 Sep
16.67	1.1	Natasha	Hastings	USA	23.7.86	2		Gateshead	10 Sep
16.80	1.1	Jodie	Williams	GBR	28.9.93	3		Gateshead	10 Sep
16.99	-0.1	Tiffany	Townsend	USA	14.6.89	1		Bston	18 Jun

200 METRES

Mark	Wind	Name		Nat	Born	Pos	Meet	Venue	Date
21.78	-0.1	Elaine	Thompson	JAM	28.6.92	1	OG	Rio de Janeiro	17 Aug
21.85	0.2		Thompson			1	WK	Zürich	1 Sep
21.86	0.2	Dafne	Schippers	NED	15.6.92	1	WK	Zürich	1 Sep
21.88	-0.1		Schippers			2	OG	Rio de Janeiro	17 Aug
21.93	0.7		Schippers			1	Bisl	Oslo	9 Jun
21.96	0.1		Schippers			1s1	OG	Rio de Janeiro	16 Aug
21.99	1.9	Tori	Bowie	USA	27.8.90	1	Pre	Eugene	28 May
22.02	-0.3		Schippers			1	FBK	Hengelo	22 May
22.02	0.2	Allyson	Felix	USA	18.11.85	3	WK	Zürich	1 Sep
22.05	0.8	Shaunae	Miller	BAH	15.4.94	1		Kingston	11 Jun
22.11	1.9		Schippers			2	Pre	Eugene	28 May
22.13	-0.8		Schippers			1	DL	Saint-Denis	27 Aug
22.13	0.8		Bowie			1s3	OG	Rio de Janeiro	16 Aug
22.13	0.1		Thompson			2s1	OG	Rio de Janeiro	16 Aug
22.13	0.1		Schippers			1	DL	London (OS)	23 Jul
22.15	-0.1		Bowie			3	OG	Rio de Janeiro	17 Aug
22.16	1.9		Thompson			3	Pre	Eugene	28 May
22.21	1.9	Ariana	Washington	USA	4.9.96	1	NCAA	Eugene	11 Jun
22.21	-0.1	Marie Josée	Ta Lou	CIV	18.11.88	4	OG	Rio de Janeiro	17 Aug
22.25	-0.2		Schippers			1		Gainesville	22 Apr
22.25	1.9	Deajah	Stevens	USA	19.5.95	2	NCAA	Eugene	11 Jun
22.25	-0.6		Bowie			1	NC	Eugene	9 Jul
22.25	0.8	Michelle-Lee	Ahye	TTO	10.4.92	2s3	OG	Rio de Janeiro	16 Aug
22.26	0.3		Bowie			1		Nassau	16 Apr
22.26	-1.3	Felicia	Brown (10)	USA	27.10.93	1	SEC	Tuscaloosa	14 May
22.27	0.4		Bowie			1s3	NC	Eugene	9 Jul
22.28	0.1		Ta Lou			1s2	OG	Rio de Janeiro	16 Aug
22.29	0.5	Veronica	Campbell-Brown	JAM	15.5.82	1		Clermont	30 Apr
22.29	0.2		Campbell-Brown			1		Beijing	18 May
22.30	-0.6		Stevens			2	NC	Eugene	9 Jul
		(30/11)							
22.31	-0.1	Dina	Asher-Smith	GBR	4.12.95	5	OG	Rio de Janeiro	17 Aug
22.38	0.4	Léa	Sprunger	SUI	5.3.90	1	NC	Genève	17 Jul
22.39	0.8	Jenna	Prandini	USA	20.11.92	2		Kingston	11 Jun

428   200 METRES

Mark	Wind	Name		Nat	Born	Pos	Meet	Venue	Date	
22.40	1.4	Joanna	Atkins	USA	31.1.89	1		Clermont	14	May
22.42	0.1	Ivet	Lalova-Collio	BUL	18.5.84	2s2	OG	Rio de Janeiro	16	Aug
22.46	0.1	Desiree	Henry	GBR	26.8.95	2	DL	Saint-Denis	27	Aug
22.47	1.9	Gabrielle	Thomas	USA	7.12.96	3	NCAA	Eugene	11	Jun
22.48	-1.3	Taylor	Ellis-Watson	USA	6.5.93	2	SEC	Tuscaloosa	14	May
22.49	-1.1	Hannah (20)	Cunliffe	USA	9.1.96	1	Pac 12	Seattle	15	May
22.50	0.1	Phyllis	Francis	USA	4.5.92	2	ATL	Houston	23	Jul
22.50	0.1	Ella	Nelson	AUS	10.5.94	3s2	OG	Rio de Janeiro	16	Aug
22.50	0.2	Simone	Facey	JAM	7.5.85	5	WK	Zürich	1	Sep
22.52	0.1	Murielle	Ahouré	CIV	23.8.87	2h8	OG	Rio de Janeiro	15	Aug
22.54	1.9	Morolake	Akinosun	USA	17.5.94	4	NCAA	Eugene	11	Jun
22.54	1.9	Tynia	Gaither	BAH	16.3.93	5	NCAA	Eugene	11	Jun
22.56	1.6	Kyra	Jefferson	USA	23.9.94	1h4	SEC	Tuscaloosa	12	May
22.56	0.9	Shakima	Wimbley	USA	23.4.95	1	ACC	Tallahassee	15	May
22.56	1.9	Libania	Grenot	ITA	12.7.83	1		Tampa	27	May
22.57	0.3	Natasha (30)	Hastings	USA	23.7.86	2		Nassau	16	Apr
22.58	1.8	Blessing	Okagbare	NGR	9.10.88	1		Sollentuna	28	Jun
22.60	-1.3	Jada	Martin	USA	8.6.95	3	SEC	Tuscaloosa	14	May
22.60	0.7	Deanna	Hill	USA	13.4.96	1h2	NCAA-W	Lawrence	28	May
22.61	1.6	Sada	Williams	BAR-J	1.12.97	1		Waterford	18	Mar
22.61	1.6	Semoy	Hackett	TTO	27.11.88	2	NC	Port of Spain	26	Jun
22.63	1.9	Alexis	Love	USA	24.4.91	2		Tampa	27	May
22.63	1.0	Shalonda	Solomon	USA	19.12.85	2	Gyulai	Székesfehérvár	18	Jul
22.63	1.0	Tiffany	Townsend	USA	14.6.89	3	Gyulai	Székesfehérvár	18	Jul
22.64	1.0	Ashley	Henderson	USA	4.12.95	1	Jordan	Stanford	1	May
22.64	0.5	Nataliya (40)	Pohrebnyak	UKR	19.2.88	2h1	OG	Rio de Janeiro	15	Aug
22.65	1.0	Daye Shon	Roberson	USA	3.7.95	2	Jordan	Stanford	1	May
22.66	0.7	Viktoriya	Zyabkina	KAZ	4.9.92	1	Kozanov	Almaty	26	Jun
22.67	0.0	Gina	Lückenkemper	GER	21.11.96	1		Regensburg	5	Jun
22.69	0.5	Jodie	Williams	GBR	28.9.93	3h7	OG	Rio de Janeiro	15	Aug
22.71	-1.0	Taylor	Bennett	USA-J	15.1.97	1		Waco	9	Apr
22.72	1.6	Reyare	Thomas	TTO	23.11.87	3	NC	Port of Spain	26	Jun
22.73	1.4	Kelly-Ann	Baptiste	TTO	14.10.86	2		Clermont	14	May
22.74	0.6	Edidiong Ofonime	Odiong	BRN-J	13.3.97	1h9	OG	Rio de Janeiro	15	Aug
22.75	1.3	Alex	Anderson	USA	28.1.87	1		Montreuil	7	Jun
22.76	1.7	Candace (50)	Hill	USA-Y	11.2.99	1h2	NC-j	Clovis	25	Jun
22.77	0.1	Shayla	Sanders	USA	6.1.94	1		Los Angeles	26	Mar
22.78	0.7	Anneisha	McLaughlin-Whilby	JAM	6.1.86	1		Kingston	16	Apr
22.78	1.9	Kortnei	Johnson	USA-J	11.8.97	1h3	SEC	Tuscaloosa	12	May
22.78	0.1	Mujinga	Kambundji	SUI	17.6.92	3h8	OG	Rio de Janeiro	15	Aug
22.79	1.0	Kianna	Gray	USA	30.12.96	1h2	NCAA-E	Jacksonville	27	May
22.79	1.3	Katarina	Johnson-Thompson	GBR	9.1.93	1H	Hypo	Götzis	28	May
22.79	1.0	Nadine	Gonska	GER	23.1.90	1r2		Mannheim	29	Jul
22.80	1.7	Cambrya	Jones	USA	20.9.90	1		Coral Gables	9	Apr
22.80	-0.1	Lauren Rain	Williams	USA-Y	25.7.99	1		Norwalk	27	May
22.80	1.2	LaTessa (60)	Johnson	USA-J	13.4.97	2h3	NCAA-W	Lawrence	28	May
22.80	0.5	Crystal	Emmanuel	CAN	27.11.91	3h1	OG	Rio de Janeiro	15	Aug
22.81	-0.8	Jeneba	Tarmoh	USA	27.9.89	4	DL	London (OS)	23	Jul
22.81	0.8	Laura	Müller	GER	11.12.95	1r1		Mannheim	29	Jul
22.83	-0.4	Jamile	Samuel	NED	24.4.92	4	EC	Amsterdam	7	Jul
22.84	0.3	Kaylin	Whitney	USA-J	9.3.98	4		Nassau	16	Apr
22.84	1.2	Alyssa	Conley	RSA	27.4.91	2	AfCh	Durban	26	Jun
22.85	0.7	Anastasia	Le-Roy	JAM	11.9.87	2		Kingston	16	Apr
22.85	1.9	Felecia	Majors	USA	2.12.95	2h2	SEC	Tuscaloosa	12	May
22.86	0.4	Kali	Davis-White	JAM	24.10.94	2		Tallahassee	16	Apr
22.86	0.4	Tessa (70)	van Schagen	NED	2.2.94	1	NC	Amsterdam	19	Jun
22.86	0.8	Lisa	Mayer	GER	2.5.96	2h2	OG	Rio de Janeiro	15	Aug
22.87	0.3	Jasmine	Camacho-Quinn	PUR	21.8.96	2h3	NCAA-E	Jacksonville	27	May
22.88	1.8	Chisato	Fukushima	JPN	27.6.88	1	NC	Nagoya	26	Jun
22.88	1.6	Kai	Selvon	TTO	13.4.92	5	NC	Port of Spain	26	Jun
22.88	0.8	Nercely	Soto	VEN	23.8.90	7s3	OG	Rio de Janeiro	16	Aug
22.89	-0.2	Quanera	Hayes	USA	7.3.92	2		Gainesville	22	Apr
22.89	0.8	Audrea	Segree	JAM	5.10.90	3		Kingston	11	Jun
22.89	1.4	Gloria	Hooper	ITA	3.3.92	1	NC	Rieti	26	Jun
22.89	0.4	Ellen	Sprunger	SUI	5.8.86	2	NC	Genève	17	Jul

200 METRES

Mark	Wind	Name		Nat	Born	Pos	Meet	Venue	Date	
22.92	1.2	Gina	Bass	GAM	3.5.95	3	AfCh	Durban	26	Jun
		(80)								
22.93	1.1	Kauiza	Venâncio	BRA	11.6.87	1	NC	São Bernardo do Campo	3	Jul
22.94	0.9	A'Keyla	Mitchell	USA	25.11.95	1		Baton Rouge	9	Apr
22.94	1.7	Jessica	Beard	USA	8.1.89	3		Coral Gables	9	Apr
22.94	0.8	Ángela	Tenorio	ECU	27.1.96	4h2	OG	Rio de Janeiro	15	Aug
22.95	0.3	Shericka	Jackson	JAM	15.7.94	2		Kingston	30	Jan
22.95	0.7	Briana	Guillory	USA-J	21.11.97	1	Big 10	Lincoln, NE	15	May
22.95	0.7	Olga	Safronova	KAZ	5.11.91	2	Kozanov	Almaty	26	Jun
22.95	0.5	Anna	Kielbasinska	POL	26.6.90	4h1	OG	Rio de Janeiro	15	Aug
22.96	-0.2	Ashleigh	Nelson	GBR	20.2.91	1rB	Johnson	Waco	23	Apr
22.96	-0.1	Anthonique	Strachan	BAH	22.8.93	3h5	OG	Rio de Janeiro	15	Aug
		(90)								
22.97	0.2	Destiny	Carter	USA	.93	1h6	NCAA-E	Jacksonville	27	May
22.97	2.0	Lauryn	Ghee	USA-J	30.10.98	1h3	HS N.Bal	Greensboro	19	Jun
22.98	1.9	Marie	Veale	USA	17.11.94	1	Bush	Norwalk	4	Jun
22.98	1.2	LeKeisha	Lawson	USA	3.6.87	1rB	Bush	Norwalk	4	Jun
22.99	2.0	Kerron	Stewart	JAM	16.4.84	4		Austin	16	Apr
22.99	1.2	Brenessa	Thompson	GUY	22.7.96	3h3	NCAA-W	Lawrence	28	May
22.99	0.9	Janet	Amponsah	GHA	12.4.93	1		Cape Coast	8	Jul
23.00	1.4	Kendra	Harrison	USA	18.9.92	1		Lexington	7	May
23.00	-0.4	Lilla	McMillan	USA	31.8.94	1		Orlando	15	May
23.00	-0.1	Floria	Guei	FRA	2.5.90	1		Genève	11	Jun
		(100)								
23.00	0.8	Celiangely	Morales	PUR	2.11.85	5h2	OG	Rio de Janeiro	15	Aug
23.01	1.9	Kimberlyn	Duncan	USA	2.8.91	16	Apr	23.19	1.1	Ashton	Purvis	USA	12.7.92	15	Apr
23.01	1.2	Courtney	Okolo	USA	15.3.94	14	May	23.19	0.4	Leslie	Cole	USA	16.2.87	19	May
23.01	0.7	Aisha	Cavin	USA	3.12.92	15	May	23.19	0.0	Eleni	Artymata	CYP	16.5.86	2	Jun
23.01	0.2	Maja	Mihalinec	SLO	17.12.89	6	Jul	23.20	0.1	Francena	McCorory	USA	20.10.88	16	Apr
23.01	0.4	Candyce	McGrone	USA	24.3.89	9	Jul	23.20	1.2	Amarachi	Pipi	GBR	26.11.95	28	May
23.01	0.5	Lorène	Bazolo	POR	4.5.83	15	Aug	23.20	2.0	Ornella	Livingston	JAM	19.5.91	11	Jun
23.02	0.2	Mahagony	Jones	USA	20.12.90	9	Apr	23.20	1.1	Rosângela	Santos	BRA	20.12.90	3	Jul
23.02	-0.1	Kiana	Horton	USA-J	29.1.97	23	Apr	23.21	0.3	Farah	Jacques	CAN	8.2.90	31	Mar
23.02	1.5	Krystal	Sparling	USA-J	15.9.97	12	May	23.21	0.9	Rushell	Harvey	USA	9.9.95	9	Apr
23.02	0.1	Kimberly	Hyacinthe	CAN	28.3.89	14	May	23.21	0.9	Bianca	Knight	USA	2.1.89	30	Apr
23.02	1.3	Olivia	Borlée	BEL	10.4.86	26	Jun	23.21	0.9	Trisana	Fairweather	USA		28	May
23.03	1.1	Elexis	Guster	USA	7.7.94	14	May	23.21	0.6	Evelin	Rivera	COL-J	8.12.97	23	Jul
23.03	0.5	Schillonie	Calvert	JAM	27.7.88	4	Jun	23.22	1.1	Ngozi	Onwumere	NGR	23.1.92	15	Apr
23.03	0.7	María	Belibasáki	GRE	19.6.91	6	Jul	23.22	0.9	Aiyanna	Stiverne	CAN	20.2.95	15	May
23.04	1.6	Yelizaveta	Bryzgina	UKR	28.11.89	26	May	23.22	0.9	Carly	Muscaro	USA	18.5.95	28	May
23.05	1.6	Shimayra	Williams	JAM	2.12.95	21	May	23.22	1.2	Anglerne	Annelus	USA-J	10.1.97	28	May
23.05	1.9	Kamaria	Brown	USA	21.12.92	27	May	23.22	2.0	Arialis	Gandulla	CUB	22.6.95	29	May
23.05	2.0	Tameka	Williams	SKN	31.8.89	11	Jun	23.22	1.2	Laniece	Clarke	BAH	4.11.87	11	Jun
23.06	-0.3	Samantha	Henry-Robinson	JAM	25.9.88	2	Jul	23.22	1.2	Justine	Palframan	RSA	4.11.93	26	Jun
23.07A	0.0	Isidora	Jiménez	CHI	10.8.93	27	Mar	23.23	-1.2	Jaide	Stepter	USA	25.4.94	19	Mar
23.07	0.4	Dezerea	Bryant	USA	27.4.93	16	Apr	23.23	1.6	Hrystyna	Stuy	UKR	3.2.88	26	May
23.07	0.7	Gabrielle	Farquharson	USA	12.12.92	15	May	23.23	0.7	Kristina	Knott	USA		28	May
23.07	1.1	Jennifer	Galais	FRA	7.3.92	5	Jun	23.23	0.9	Laura	de Witte	NED	7.8.95	6	Jul
23.07	0.7	Srabani	Nanda	IND	7.5.91	26	Jun	23.24A	0.4	Tobi	Amusan	NGR-J	23.4.97	30	Apr
23.08A	1.1	Mupopo	Kabange	ZAM	21.9.92	5	Mar	23.24	0.2	Tahesia	Harrigan	IVB	15.2.82	19	Jun
23.08	0.9	Deja	Parrish	USA	14.7.96	15	May	23.25A	0.1	Leungo	Mathlaku	BOT	24.3.95	22	May
23.09	-0.4	Kenya	Woodall	USA	17.7.94	15	May	23.25	0.3	Elina	Mikhina	KAZ	16.7.94	5	Jul
23.10	1.1	LaQuisha	Jackson	USA	7.1.94	1	Apr	23.26	-0.2	Jess	Thornton	AUS-J	12.8.98	20	Feb
23.10	2.0	Salwa	Eid Nasser	BRN-J	23.5.98	16	Apr	23.26	0.6	India	Brown	USA	29.1.96	1	Apr
23.10	0.0	Ramona	Papaioannou	CYP	5.6.86	15	Aug	23.26	1.1	Zainab	Sanni	USA	20.1.95	28	May
23.12	-2.8	Stephenie Ann	McPherson	JAM	25.11.88	9	Apr	23.26	-0.7	Katia	Seymour	USA-J	3.10.97	16	Jul
23.12	0.2	Laverne	Jones-Ferrette	ISV	16.9.81	30	Apr	23.27	2.0	Kiara	Porter	USA	22.10.93	1	Apr
23.12	-0.6	Aaliyah	Brown	USA	6.1.95	28	May	23.27	0.1	Olga	Lenskiy	ISR	24.12.92	26	May
23.13	-0.7	Mariely	Sánchez	DOM	30.12.88	26	Jun	23.27	-0.6	Diamond	Spaulding	USA	29.9.96	28	May
23.13	1.6	Kamaria	Durant	TTO	24.2.91	26	Jun	23.27	-0.1	Bianca	Williams	GBR	18.12.93	11	Jun
23.13	1.6	Brigitte	Ntiamoah	FRA	5.3.94	30	Jun	23.28	0.6	Kiersten	Duncan	USA	7.3.94	9	Apr
23.15	1.6	Jayla	Kirkland	USA-Y	13.2.99	19	Jun	23.28	1.7	Flings	Owusu-Agyapong	GHA	16.10.88	9	Apr
23.15	-1.1	Shelly-Ann	Fraser-Pryce	JAM	27.12.86	2	Jul	23.28	1.9	Akela	Jones	BAR	22.4.95	13	Apr
23.16	1.1	Carmiesha	Cox	BAH	16.5.95	14	May	23.28	1.1	Dominique	Booker	USA	10.2.92	15	May
23.16	1.4	Rebekka	Haase	GER	2.1.93	14	May	23.28	-1.3	Diamond	Gause	USA	4.4.94	14	May
23.16A	1.5	Kayelle	Clarke	TTO	28.2.96	19	May	23.28	0.5	Sashalee	Forbes	JAM	10.5.96	21	May
23.16	0.6	Inna	Weit	GER	5.8.88	24	Jun	23.29	-0.2	Patricia	Hall-Pritchett	JAM	16.10.82	23	Apr
23.16	-1.1	Cierra	White	USA	29.4.93	10	Jul	23.29	1.9	Danyel	White	USA	12.12.93	30	Apr
23.16	1.1	Josefina	Elsler	GER	7.6.91	23	Jul	23.29	0.7		Wei Yongli	CHN	11.10.91	14	May
23.17	0.3	Ashley	Kelly	IVB	25.3.91	31	Mar	23.29	0.9	Yekaterina	Vukolova	RUS	10.8.87	1	Jul
23.17	0.0	Lake	Kwaza	USA	7.11.93	9	Apr	23.30	1.9	Franciela	Krasucki	BRA	26.4.88	16	Apr
23.17	0.9	Rachel	Misher	USA-J	4.2.97	9	Apr	23.30	1.1	Jaílma	de Lima	BRA	31.12.86	3	Jul
23.17	-0.1	Shamier	Little	USA	20.3.95	23	Apr	23.30	0.4	Sarah	Atcho	SUI	1.6.95	17	Jul
23.17	-1.2	Mercy	Ntia-Obong	NGR-J	4.10.97	25	May			(201)					
23.17	0.0	Nigina	Sharipova	UZB	10.8.95	19	Jun	**Running with guide runner**							
23.17	-0.7	Estela	García	ESP	20.3.89	26	Jun	23.05	0.1	Omara	Durand	CUB	26.11.91	12	Sep
23.18	1.0	Precious	Hitchcock	USA	.95	27	May								

430   200 – 300 METRES

Mark	Wind	Name		Nat	Born	Pos	Meet	Venue		Date
Indoors										
22.79		Courtney	Okolo	USA	15.3.94	1	Big 12	Ames		27 Feb
23.10		Robin	Reynolds	USA	22.2.94	13 Feb	23.19	Ashley	Spencer	USA 8.6.93 6 Feb
23.10		Rebekka	Haase	GER	2.1.93	28 Feb	23.19	Diamond	Spaulding	USA 29.9.96 27 Feb
							23.27	Stella	Akakpo	FRA 28.2.94 28 Feb
Wind assisted										
22.14	2.2		Miller			1		Kingston		7 May
22.19	2.6	Felicia	Brown	USA	27.10.93	1h1	SEC	Tuscaloosa		12 May
22.27	4.1		Brown			1q2	NCAA-E	Jacksonville		28 May
22.37	3.4	Gabrielle	Thomas	USA	7.12.96	1q3	NCAA-E	Jacksonville		28 May
22.38	3.7	Tiffany	Townsend	USA	14.6.89	1	FlaR	Gainesville		31 Mar
22.38	2.1	Candace	Hill	USA-Y	11.2.99	1		Montverde		11 Jun
22.41	2.6	Destiny	Carter	USA	.93	2h1	SEC	Tuscaloosa		12 May
22.41	3.4	Jada	Martin	USA	8.6.95	2q3	NCAA-E	Jacksonville		28 May
22.44	2.3	Ashley	Henderson	USA	4.12.95	1	MWC	Clovis		14 May
22.44	2.5	Lauren Rain	Williams	USA-Y	25.7.99	1		Norwalk		21 May
22.53	4.7	Alex	Anderson	USA	28.1.87	1		Austin		7 May
22.58	3.7	Shalonda	Solomon	USA	19.12.85	3	FlaR	Gainesville		31 Mar
22.58	4.7	Kianna	Gray	USA	30.12.96	1q1	NCAA-E	Jacksonville		28 May
22.66	2.6	Kali	Davis-White	JAM	24.10.94	1-22	NACAC	San Salvador		17 Jul
22.67	4.7	Kortnei	Johnson	USA-J	11.8.97	2q1	NCAA-E	Jacksonville		28 May
22.69	2.1	Kerron	Stewart	JAM	16.4.84	3		Montverde		11 Jun
22.70	4.1	Jasmine	Camacho-Quinn	PUR	21.8.96	2q2	NCAA-E	Jacksonville		28 May
22.75	3.7	LaTessa	Johnson	USA	13.4.97	1		San Marcos		2 Apr
22.75	4.7	Carmiesha	Cox	BAH	16.5.95	3q1	NCAA-E	Jacksonville		28 May
22.76	3.7	Cambrya	Jones	USA	20.9.90	4	FlaR	Gainesville		31 Mar
22.84	4.7	Aisha	Cavin	USA	3.12.92	4q1	NCAA-E	Jacksonville		28 May
22.85	2.3	Jessica	Beard	USA	8.1.89	1rC		Clermont		30 Apr
22.86	2.2	Shericka	Jackson	JAM	15.7.94	4		Kingston		7 May
22.88	2.1	Kimberly	Hyacinthe	CAN	28.3.89	2	NC	Edmonton		10 Jul
22.91	3.4	Gabrielle	Farquharson	USA	12.12.92	4q3	NCAA-E	Jacksonville		28 May
22.92	4.1	Precious	Hitchcock	USA	.95	4q2	NCAA-E	Jacksonville		28 May
22.93	2.6	Diamond	Gause	USA	4.4.94	3h1	SEC	Tuscaloosa		12 May
22.94	4.1	Rachel	Misher	USA-J	4.2.97	5q2	NCAA-E	Jacksonville		28 May
22.98	4.7	Savannah	Roberson	USA	15.1.96	5q1	NCAA-E	Jacksonville		28 May
22.98	2.2	Candyce	McGrone	USA	24.3.89	2h5	NC	Eugene		8 Jul
23.01	4.7	Drea	Austin	USA	24.1.96	13 May	23.12	3.4 Rushell	Harvey	USA 9.9.95 28 May
23.01	2.1	Lexis	Lambert	USA	12.5.94	18 Jun	23.17	4.7 Simone	Glenn	USA 16.5.96 13 May
23.03	4.7	Jenae	Ambrose	BAH-J 29.12.97	28 May		23.23	Alex	Swanson	USA 8 Apr
23.04	3.7	Francena	McCorory	USA	20.10.88	31 Mar	23.23	2.4 Agata	Forkasiewicz	POL 13.1.94 12 Jun
23.07	4.7	Bianca	Knight	USA	2.1.89	7 May	23.25	2.9 Celera	Barnes	USA-J 2.12.98 4 Jun
23.08	4.7	Charonda	Williams	USA	27.3.87	7 May	23.26	Danyel	White	USA-J 10.2.98 13 Apr
23.08	4.7	India	Brown	USA	29.1.96	28 May	23.26	2.1 Lesline	Gilzene	JAM 29.4.86 14 Apr
23.12	2.7	Shavonne	Husbands	BAR	24.10.94	22 Apr	23.26	2.6 Khadija	Suleman	NGR 16.8.93 12 May
23.12	2.7	Marissa	Kurtimah	CAN	25.5.94	22 Apr	23.27	3.7 Franciela	Krasucki	BRA 26.4.88 31 Mar
							23.29	2.2 Sonikqua	Walker	JAM 24.9.94 14 May

Best at low altitude: 23.19 0.3 Jiménez 15 May

JUNIORS

See main list for top 10 juniors (& 4 wa). 11 performances by 7 women to 22.85. Additional marks and further juniors:

Mark	Wind	Name		Nat	Born	Pos	Meet	Venue	Date
Odiong		22.84	0.6 1	WJ	Bydgoszcz	23 Jul	22.84 0.8 6s3 OG	Rio de Janeiro	16 Aug
Johnson		22.82	-1.3 4	SEC	Tuscaloosa	14 May			
Whitney		22.85	1.0 4	Gyulai Székesfehérvár	18 Jul				
23.02	-0.1	Kiana	Horton	USA	29.1.97	1	Johnson	Waco	23 Apr
23.02	1.5	Krystal	Sparling	USA	15.9.97	3h5	SEC	Tuscaloosa	12 May
23.10	2.0	Salwa	Eid Nasser	BRN	23.5.98	1	WAs-J	Manama	16 Apr
23.15	1.6	Jayla	Kirkland	USA-Y	13.2.99	1	HS N.Bal	Greensboro	19 Jun
23.17	0.9	Rachel	Misher	USA	4.2.97	3		Baton Rouge	9 Apr
23.17	-1.2	Mercy	Ntia-Obong	NGR	4.10.97	1h1		Lagos	25 May
23.21	0.6	Evelin	Rivera	COL	8.12.97	2	WJ	Bydgoszcz	23 Jul
23.22	1.2	Anglerne	Annelus	USA	10.1.97	5h3	NCAA-W	Lawrence	28 May
23.24A	0.4	Tobi	Amusan	NGR	23.4.97	1		El Paso	30 Apr
23.26	-0.2	Jess	Thornton (20)	AUS	12.4.98	2		Canberra	20 Feb
23.26	-0.7	Katia	Seymour	USA	3.10.97	1		Kissimmee	16 Jul

Wind assisted: 3 performances to 22.80 by 3 women. See main list for top 4.

23.03	4.7	Jenae	Ambrose	BAH-J	29.12.97	6q1	NCAA-E	Jacksonville	28 May
23.23	2.4	Agata	Forkasiewicz	POL	13.1.94	1		Kraków	12 Jun
23.25	2.9	Celera	Barnes	USA-J	2.12.98	1		Clovis	4 Jun
23.26		Danyel	White	USA-J	10.2.98	1		Duncanville	13 Apr

300 METRES

35.74		Courtney	Okolo	USA	15.3.94	1	ATL	Houston	23 Jul
36.24		Nicky	van Leuveren	NED	25.5.90	1		Lisse	7 May

300 – 400 METRES

Mark	Wind	Name		Nat		Born	Pos	Meet	Venue		Date	
36.27		Léa	Sprunger	SUI		5.3.90	1		Langenthal		5	May
36.39		Kendall	Baisden	USA		5.3.95	2	ATL	Houston		23	Jul
36.71		Mariam	Kromah	LBR		1.1.94	3	ATL	Houston		23	Jul
36.88		Laura	de Witte	NED	7.8.95	7 May	37.06		Kanika	Beckles GRN	3.10.92	23 Jul
36.90		Kineke	Alexander	VIN	21.2.86	23 Jul	37.42		Patrycja	Wyciszkiewicz POL	8.1.94	10 Sep

Estimated intermediate times in 400m OG Rio de Janeiro 15 Aug
Shaunae Miller 35.3, Natasha Hastings 35.7, Allyson Felix 35.8, Shericka Jackson 35.9, Phyllis Francis & Stephanie Ann McPherson 36.3, Libania Grenot 36.6, Olha Zemlyak 37.4

Indoors

Mark	Wind	Name		Nat		Born	Pos	Meet	Venue		Date	
36.25		Natasha	Hastings	USA		23.7.86	1		Boston (R)		14	Feb
36.46		Floria	Guei	FRA		2.5.90	1		Metz		21	Feb
36.94		Jessica	Beard	USA	8.1.89	14 Feb	37.22		Felicia	Brown	USA 27.10.93	15 Jan

400 METRES

Mark	Wind	Name		Nat	Born	Pos	Meet	Venue	Date	
49.44		Shaunae	Miller	BAH	15.4.94	1	OG	Rio de Janeiro	15	Aug
49.51		Allyson	Felix	USA	18.11.85	2	OG	Rio de Janeiro	15	Aug
49.55			Miller			1	DL	London (OS)	22	Jul
49.67			Felix			1s3	OG	Rio de Janeiro	14	Aug
49.68			Felix			1	NC	Eugene	3	Jul
49.69			Miller			1		Nassau	16	Apr
49.71		Courtney	Okolo	USA	15.3.94	1		Baton Rouge	23	Apr
49.83		Shericka	Jackson	JAM	15.7.94	1s2	OG	Rio de Janeiro	14	Aug
49.85			Jackson			3	OG	Rio de Janeiro	54	Aug
49.90		Natasha	Hastings	USA	23.7.86	2s2	OG	Rio de Janeiro	14	Aug
49.91		Quanera	Hayes	USA	7.3.92	2		Nassau	16	Apr
49.91			Miller			2s3	OG	Rio de Janeiro	14	Aug
49.94		Phyllis	Francis	USA	4.5.92	2	NC	Eugene	3	Jul
50.04		Stephenie Ann	McPherson	JAM	25.11.88	1	NC	Kingston	3	Jul
50.06			Hastings			1	DL	Saint-Denis	27	Aug
50.15			Miller			1	Pre	Eugene	28	May
50.17			Hastings			3	NC	Eugene	3	Jul
50.23		Francena	McCorory	USA	20.10.88	2	Pre	Eugene	28	May
50.25		Taylor	Ellis-Watson (10)	USA	6.5.93	4	NC	Eugene	3	Jul
50.28			McCorory			1s1	NC	Eugene	2	Jul
50.29		Christine	Day	JAM	23.8.86	2	NC	Kingston	3	Jul
50.31			McPherson			1s2	NC	Kingston	2	Ju
50.31			Felix			2s1	NC	Eugene	2	Jul
50.31			Francis			1s1	OG	Rio de Janeiro	14	Aug
50.33			McPherson			2	DL	Saint-Denis	27	Aug
50.34			Hastings			4	OG	Rio de Janeiro	15	Aug
50.36			Okolo			1	NCAA	Eugene	11	Jun
50.37			Okolo			1s2	NC	Eugene	2	Jul
50.37			McCorory			5	NC	Eugene	3	Jul
50.39			Okolo			6	NC	Eugene	3	Jul
		(30/11)								
50.40		Caster	Semenya	RSA	7.1.91	1	VD	Bruxelles	9	Sep
50.43		Libania	Grenot	ITA	12.7.83	1s3	EC	Amsterdam	7	Jul
50.64		Novlene	Williams-Mills	JAM	26.4.82	4	NC	Kingston	3	Jul
50.70		Antonina	Krivoshapka	RUS	21.7.87	1	NC	Cheboksary	21	Jun
50.72		Kemi	Adekoya	BRN	16.1.93	2h3	OG	Rio de Janeiro	13	Aug
50.75		Olha	Zemlyak	UKR	16.1.90	3s1	OG	Rio de Janeiro	14	Aug
50.84		Floria	Guei	FRA	2.5.90	1	DL	Birmingham	5	Jun
50.88		Salwa	Eid Naser	BRN-J	23.5.98	3s2	OG	Rio de Janeiro	14	Aug
50.90		Shakima	Wimbley	USA	23.4.95	1	ACC	Tallahassee	15	May
		(20)								
50.91		Jaide	Stepter	USA	25.4.94	1		Los Angeles	26	Mar
51.02		Chris-Ann	Gordon	JAM	18.9.94	1	NACAC	San Salvador	16	Jul
51.03		Anneisha	McLaughlin-Whilby	JAM	6.1.86	5	NC	Kingston	3	Jul
51.04A		Mupopo	Kabange	ZAM	21.9.92	1		Ndola	5	Mar
51.05		Carline	Muir	CAN	1.10.87	1		Madrid	23	Jun
51.05		Christine	Ohuruogu	GBR	17.5.84	5	DL	London (OS)	22	Jul
51.06		Patience	George	NGR	25.11.91	1		Akure	6	Jun
51.09		Ashley	Spencer	USA	8.6.93	7	NC	Eugene	3	Jul
51.11		Margaret	Bamgbose	NGR	19.10.93	2	ACC	Tallahassee	15	May
51.17		Janeive	Russell	JAM	14.11.93	1		Kingston	2	Apr
		(30)								
51.17		Carly	Muscaro	USA	18.5.95	1		New Haven	14	May
51.23		Emily	Diamond	GBR	11.6.91	1		Regensburg	4	Jun
51.25		Morgan	Mitchell	AUS	3.10.94	3	DL	Birmingham	5	Jun
51.26		Seren	Bundy-Davies	GBR	30.12.94	1		Genève	11	Jun

400 METRES

Mark	Name		Nat	Born	Pos	Meet	Venue	Date	
51.29	Felecia	Majors	USA	2.12.95	2	SEC	Tuscaloosa	14	May
51.32	Tiffany	James	JAM-J	31.1.97	1	WJ	Bydgoszcz	21	Jul
51.38	Lilla	McMillan	USA	31.8.94	1		Orlando	15	May
51.39A	Margaret	Wambui	KEN	15.9.95	1	NC	Nairobi	28	May
51.39	Ebony	Eutsey	USA	3.5.92	3		Kingston	11	Jun
51.39	Lynna (40)	Irby	USA-J	6.12.98	2	WJ	Bydgoszcz	21	Jul
51.40	Kineke	Alexander	VIN	21.2.86	1		San Marcos	20	May
51.42	Daye Shon	Roberson	USA	3.7.95	1	Jordan	Stanford	1	May
51.43	Ruth Sophia	Spelmeyer	GER	19.9.90	3h5	OG	Rio de Janeiro	13	Aug
51.47	Anyika	Onuora	GBR	28.10.84	3	EC	Amsterdam	8	Jul
51.48	Nirmala	Sheoran	IND	15.7.95	1	I-S	Hyderabad	1	Jul
51.50A	Lydia	Jele	BOT	22.6.90	1		Gaborone	10	Apr
51.50	Alena	Mamina	RUS	30.5.90	1		Sochi	26	May
51.54	Geisa	Coutinho	BRA	1.6.80	1	NC	São Bernardo do Campo	1	Jul
51.55	Claudia	Francis	USA	14.11.93	2		Baton Rouge	30	Apr
51.58	Omolara (50)	Omotoso	NGR	25.5.93	2h1	NC	Sapele	7	Jul
51.62	Justyna	Swiety	POL	3.12.92	5s3	OG	Rio de Janeiro	14	Aug
51.63	Cátia	Azevedo	POR	9.3.94	2		Madrid	23	Jun
51.64	Patricia	Hall-Pritchett	JAM	16.10.82	2	Johnson	Waco	23	Apr
51.66	Jasmine	Blocker	USA	9.6.92	2		Orlando	15	May
51.67	Malgorzata	Holub	POL	30.10.92	2s3	EC	Amsterdam	7	Jul
51.69	Olha	Bibik	UKR	5.2.90	1	NC	Lutsk	17	Jun
51.69	Laura	Müller	GER	11.12.95	1		Mannheim	29	Jul
51.70	Yuliya	Olishevska	UKR	2.2.89	2	NC	Lutsk	17	Jun
51.72	Monica	Hargrove	USA	30.12.82	2	Bush	Norwalk	4	Jun
51.74	Junelle (60)	Bromfield	JAM-J	8.2.98	1	N.Sch	Kingston	19	Mar
51.74	Kseniya	Aksyonova	RUS	14.1.88	3	NC	Cheboksary	21	Jun
51.75	Deedee	Trotter	USA	8.12.82	2		Atlanta	4	Jun
51.75	Deborah	Sananès	FRA	26.10.95	1	NC-23	Aubagne	17	Jul
51.76	Jessica	Beard	USA	8.1.89	4		Nassau	16	Apr
51.82	Kendall	Ellis	USA	8.3.96	1	MSR	Norwalk	16	Apr
51.83	Kenya	Woodall	USA	17.7.94	2q1	NCAA-E	Jacksonville	27	May
51.84	Robin	Reynolds	USA	22.2.94	6	NCAA	Eugene	11	Jun
51.84	Alicia	Brown	CAN	21.1.90	2	NC	Edmonton	9	Jul
51.85	Elexis	Guster	USA	7.7.94	1		Tucson	9	Apr
51.87	Sydney (70)	McLaughlin	USA-Y	7.8.99	1		Bayville	8	Jun
51.89	Tamara	Salaski	SRB	16.10.88	2		Stara Zagora	9	Jun
51.92	Tetyana	Melnyk	UKR	2.4.95	4	NC	Lutsk	17	Jun
51.92	Anneliese	Rubie	AUS	22.4.92	3h1	OG	Rio de Janeiro	13	Aug
51.93	Sonikqua	Walker	JAM	24.9.94	1q2	NCAA-E	Jacksonville	27	May
51.96A	Tsholofelo	Thipe	RSA	9.12.86	1		Pretoria	5	Mar
51.97	Micha	Powell	CAN	12.1.95	2q2	NCAA-E	Jacksonville	27	May
51.99	Jaílma	de Lima	BRA	31.12.86	1	IbAm	Rio de Janeiro	15	May
52.00	Kala	Funderburk	USA	14.9.92	3		Atlanta	4	Jun
52.00	Anastasia	Le-Roy	JAM	11.9.87	4		Kingston	11	Jun
52.01	Sage (80)	Watson	CAN	20.6.94	1		Tucson	30	Apr
52.01	Ekundayo	Sogbesan	USA	29.3.92	1		Philadelphia	25	Jun
52.01	Maria Benedicta	Chigbolu	ITA	27.7.89	3		Padova	17	Jul
52.02	Nicky	van Leuveren	NED	25.5.90	3s1	EC	Amsterdam	7	Jul
52.02	Patrycja	Wyciszkiewicz	POL	8.1.94	4h3	OG	Rio de Janeiro	13	Aug
52.03	Tjipekapora	Herunga	NAM	1.1.88	2		Kingston	9	Apr
52.04	Aliyah	Abrams	GUY-J	3.4.97	4	SEC	Tuscaloosa	14	May
52.05	Jess	Thornton	AUS-J	12.4.98	4	WJ	Bydgoszcz	21	Jul
52.06	Lisneidy	Veitía	CUB	29.4.94	1		La Habana	16	Jun
52.07	Sada	Williams	BAR-J	1.12.97	1	Carifta	St. George	26	Mar
52.08	Jody Ann (90)	Muir	JAM	1.1.91	1		Kingston	7	May
52.08	Aiyanna	Stiverne	CAN	20.2.95	3	ACC	Tallahassee	15	May
52.09	Kendall	Baisden	USA	5.3.95	4		Atlanta	4	Jun
52.09	Elina	Mikhina	KAZ	16.7.94	1	Kazanov	Almaty	25	Jun
52.09	Maureen	Thomas	KEN-J	29.12.97	5	WJ	Bydgoszcz	21	Jul
52.10	Kiara	Porter	USA	22.10.93	4h1	NC	Eugene	1	Jul
52.11	Kyra	Jefferson	USA	23.9.94	2	FlaR	Gainesville	1	Apr
52.11	Alexandra	Gholston	USA	1.3.95	5	SEC	Tuscaloosa	14	May
52.11	Mariam	Kromah	LBR	1.1.94	1	Conf USA	Murfreesboro	15	May
52.12	Iríni	Vasilíou	GRE	18.3.90	1h1	NC	Pátra	18	Jun

400 METRES

Mark	Name		Nat	Born	Pos	Meet	Venue		Date
52.13	Chrishuna	Williams (100)	USA	31.3.93	1		Fayetteville		6 May
52.14	Maureen	Maiyo	KEN	28.5.85				20 May	
52.14	Lisanne	de Witte	NED	10.9.92				5 Jun	
52.15A	Christine	Botlogetswe	BOT	1.10.95				21 May	
52.16	Sanya	Richards-Ross	USA	26.2.85				28 May	
52.19	Kendra	Clarke	CAN	16.11.96				9 Jul	
52.21	Marie	Gayot	FRA	18.12.89				9 Jun	
52.23	Regina	George	NGR	17.2.91				8 Jul	
52.23	Elea Mariama	Diarra	FRA	8.3.90				23 Jul	
52.24	Djénébou	Danté	MLI	7.8.89				10 Jun	
52.24	Ewelina	Ptak	POL	20.3.87				24 Jun	
52.24	Roxana	Gómez	CUB-Y	7.1.99				21 Jul	
52.26	Sharrika	Barnett	USA-J	16.4.97				26 May	
52.26	Yuliya	Kuznetsova	RUS	20.2.90				4 Jun	
52.26	Kadecia	Baird	GUY	24.2.95				18 Jun	
52.27A	Wenda	Nel	RSA	30.7.88				12 Mar	
52.27	Desiree	Henry	GBR	26.8.95				31 Mar	
52.27	Yinka	Ajayi	NGR-J	11.8.97				6 Jun	
52.28	Laviai	Nielsen	GBR	13.3.96				14 May	
52.28	Kaelin	Roberts	USA-Y	6.1.99				4 Jun	
52.29	Ashley	Kelly	IVB	25.3.91				3 Jul	
52.30	Raevyn	Rogers	USA	7.9.96				19 Mar	
52.30	Gilda	Casanova	CUB	19.12.95				16 Jun	
52.31	Machettira Raju	Poovamma	IND	5.6.90				24 Jun	
52.31	Anastasiya	Kudinova	KAZ	27.2.88				25 Jun	
52.31	Brigitte	Ntiamoah	FRA	5.3.94				26 Jun	
52.33	Carol	Rodríguez	PUR	16.12.85				4 Jun	
52.34	A'Keyla	Mitchell	USA	25.11.95				23 Apr	
52.34	Yekaterina	Renzhina	RUS	18.10.94				28 Jul	
52.35	Dawnalee	Loney	JAM	15.5.96				11 Jun	
52.36	Daina	Harper	USA	26.6.95				30 Apr	
52.37A	Jacinta	Shikanda	KEN	14.7.86				1 Jul	
52.38	Jenna	Martin-Evans	CAN	31.3.88				11 Jun	
52.39	Joanna	Atkins	USA	31.1.89				22 Apr	
52.39	Georganne	Moline	USA	6.3.90				23 Apr	
52.39	Autumne	Franklin	USA	20.7.94				17 Jun	
52.39	Aauri Lorena	Bokesa	ESP	14.12.88				7 Jul	
52.40	Anilda	Thomas	IND	6.5.93				29 Apr	
52.41	Kanika	Beckles	GRN	3.10.91				13 Aug	
52.42	Tovea	Jenkins	JAM	27.10.92				28 May	
52.42	Anthonique	Strachan	BAH	22.8.93				11 Jun	
52.42	Bianca	Razor	ROU	8.8.94				13 Aug	
52.43	Perri	Shakes-Drayton	GBR	21.12.88				14 Jun	
52.43	Alina	Lohvynenko	UKR	18.7.90				17 Jun	
52.43	Agnès	Raharolahy	FRA	7.11.92				23 Jul	
52.44	Shapri	Romero	USA	13.11.91				4 Jun	
52.48	Brionna	Thomas	USA	21.3.96				26 May	
52.48	Ilona	Usovich	BLR	14.11.82				24 Jun	
52.50	Shaquania	Dorsett	BAH-J	16.9.97				26 Mar	
52.50A	Arria	Minor	USA-Y	9.2.01				21 May	
52.50	Tiffany	Harris	USA	28.9.91				11 Jun	
52.50	Ánna	Vasilíou	GRE	18.3.90				18 Jun	
52.51	Makenzie	Dunmore	USA-J	17.10.97				20 Apr	
52.52	Tatum	Waggoner	USA	6.9.95				9 Apr	
52.52	Jasmine	Mitchell	USA	25.3.95				26 May	
52.53	Diamond	Dixon	USA	29.6.92				23 Jun	
52.54A	Hellen	Syombua	KEN-J	8.8.97				28 May	
52.55	Verone	Chambers	JAM	16.12.88				2 Apr	
52.55	Paola	Morán	MEX-J	25.2.97				14 May	
52.55	Friederike	Möhlenkamp	GER	19.11.92				4 Jun	
52.57	Rita	Ossai	NGR	21.10.95				31 May	
52.57A	Leni	Shida	UGA	22.5.94				7 Jul	
52.57		Yang Huizhen	CHN	13.8.92				15 Sep	
52.58	Déborah	Rodríguez	URU	2.12.92				8 Apr	
52.58	Olha	Lyakhova	UKR	18.3.92				23 May	
52.58	Viktoriya	Tkachuk	UKR	8.11.94				25 May	
52.59	Ebonie	Floyd	USA	21.10.83				23 Jun	
52.59	Tabata	de Carvalho	BRA	23.4.96				1 Jul	
52.60	Anastasiya	Rabchenyuk	UKR	14.9.83				17 Jun	
52.61	Kaliese	Spencer	JAM	6.5.87				31 Aug	
52.63	Kiah	Seymour	USA	11.1.94				1 Apr	
52.63	Ristananna	Tracey	JAM	9.5.92				28 May	
52.64	D'Airrien	Jackson	USA-J	3.3.97				26 Mar	
52.64	Dalilah	Muhammad	USA	7.2.90				1 Apr	
52.64	Kai	Selvon	TTO	13.4.92				9 Apr	
52.64	Letícia	de Souza	BRA	6.5.96				1 Jul	
52.65	Domonique	Williams	TTO	8.8.94				24 Jun	
52.69	Briyahna	Desrosiers	USA	11.3.96				9 Apr	
52.69	Sterling	Lester	USA-Y	13.11.00				22 Apr	
52.69	Santina	Williams	USA	.92				27 Ma	
52.69	Rosangélica	Escobar	COL	13.11.93				5 Jun	
52.70	Ayiana	Gaines	USA	1.2.96				13 May	
52.70	Andrea	Miklos	ROU-Y	17.4.99				16 Jul	
52.70	Laura	de Witte	NED	7.8.95				29 Jul	
52.71	Iga	Baumgart	POL	11.4.89				25 Jun	
52.71	Pariis	Garcia	PUR	24.11.94				26 Jun	
52.72		Quach Thi Lan	VIE	18.10.95				23 Nov	
52.73	Laniece	Clarke	BAH	4.11.87				31 Mar	
52.73A	Yenifer	Padilla	COL	1.1.90				30 Apr	
52.73	Montené	Speight	GBR	5.11.92				6 May	
52.73	Yelena	Zuykevich	RUS	26.2.90				26 May	
52.74	Shayla	Luckett	USA	18.2.93				1 Apr	
52.74	Ciara	Short	USA	11.3.89				16 Apr	
52.75	Margaret	Adeoye	GBR	22.4.85				23 Jul	
52.75	Anastasiya	Bednova	RUS	18.10.96				28 Jul	
52.78	Vivian	Mills	GHA	10.5.91				29 May	
52.78	Marina	Konovalova	RUS	17.9.90				7 Jun	
52.79	Sparkle	McKnight	TTO	21.12.91				7 May	
52.79	Madiea	Ghafoor	NED	9.9.92				11 Jul	
52.79	Dzhoys	Koba	UKR-J	26.2.98				20 Jul	
52.80	Deja	Parrish	USA	14.7.96				15 May	
52.80	Hannah	Williams (200)	GBR-J	23.4.98				20 Jul	

Unknown irregularity

52.15	Anastasiya	Kudinova	KAZ	27.2.88				9 Jun	

Hand timed

52.1	Gilda	Casanova	CUB	19.12.95				3 May	
52.4A	Leni	Shida	UGA	22.4.94				2 Jul	

Indoors

51.74	Shamier	Little	USA	20.3.95	3	NCAA	Birmingham, AL		12 Mar
51.84	Sydney	McLaughlin	USA-Y	7.8.99	1	HS N.Bal	New York		13 Mar
52.34	Briana	Haith	USA	8.6.94				27 Feb	
52.34	Zuzana	Hejnová	CZE	19.12.86				28 Feb	
52.36	Léa	Sprunger	SUI	5.3.90				31 Jan	
52.48	Brionna	Thomas	USA	21.3.96				27 Feb	
52.52	Amalie Hammild	Iuel	NOR	17.4.94				12 Feb	
52.59	Sara Slott	Petersen	DEN	9.4.87				13 Feb	
52.77	Yana	Glotova	RUS	8.4.95				24 Feb	
52.78	Symone	Black	USA	26.10.95				27 Feb	

Best at low altitude

51.35	Kabange	1					Regensburg		4 Jun
51.97	Wambui	1s2 AfCh					Durban		23 Jun

52.14	Jele			14 Jun					
52.37	Botlogetswe			13 Aug					
52.80	Thipe			13 Aug					

Running with guide runner

51.77	Omara		Durand	26.11.91	1	ParaOG	Rio de Janeiro		17 Sep

JUNIORS

See main list for top 9 juniors. 11 performances (1 indoor) by 6 women to 52.04. Additional marks and further juniors:

Naser	51.06	1h6 OG		Rio de Janeiro	13 Aug		51.63	1	Stara Zagora	9 Jun
James	51.77	1s3 WJ		Bydgoszcz	20 Jul					
Irby	51.90	1s1 WJ		Bydgoszcz	20 Jul					
52.24	Roxana		Gómez (10)	CUB-Y	7.1.99	6	WJ	Bydgoszcz		21 Jul
52.26	Sharrika		Barnett	USA	16.4.97	2h4	NCAA-E	Jacksonville		26 May
52.27	Yinka		Ajayi	NGR	11.8.97	2		Akure		6 Jun
52.28	Kaelin		Roberts	USA-Y	6.1.99	1		Clovis		4 Jun

434   400 – 600 – 800 METRES

Mark	Name		Nat	Born	Pos	Meet	Venue	Date
52.50	Shaquania	Dorsett	BAH	16.9.97	2	Carifta	St. George	26 Mar
52.50A	Arria	Minor	USA-Y	9.2.01	1		Lakewood	21 May
52.51	Makenzie	Dunmore	USA	17.10.97	1		Marietta	20 Apr
52.54A	Hellen	Syombua	KEN	8.8.97	3	NC	Nairobi	28 May
52.55	Paola	Morán	MEX	25.2.97	1		Monterrey	14 May
52.64	D'Airrien	Jackson	USA	3.3.97	1		Nashville	26 Mar
52.69	Sterling	Lester (20)	USA-Y	13.11.00	2		Marietta	22 Apr

600 METRES

Mark	Name		Nat	Born	Pos	Meet	Venue		Date
1:26.76+	Caster	Semenya	RSA	7.1.91	1	in 800m	Zürich		1 Sep
1:26.8+	Francine	Niyonsaba	BDI	5.5.93	2	in 800m	Rio de Janeiro		20 Aug
1:27.1+	Margaret	Wambui	KEN	15.9.95	20 Aug	1:27.2+	Melissa	Bishop	CAN 5.8.88 20 Aug
1:27.1+	Marina	Arzamasova	BLR	17.12.87	20 Aug	1:27.8+	Kate	Grace	USA 24.10.88 20 Aug
1:27.11	Christina	Hering	GER	9.10.94	8 May	1:27.8+	Lynsey	Sharp	GBR 11.7.90 20 Aug
1:27.12	Selina	Büchel	SUI	26.7.91	8 May	1:27.79	Fabienne	Kohlmann	GER 6.11.89 8 May
						1:27.92	Alexandra	Stuková	SVK 2.7.90 2 Aug

Indoors

Mark	Name		Nat	Born	Pos	Meet	Venue	Date
1:26.34i	Raevyn	Rogers	USA	7.9.96	1		Seattle	16 Jan
1:26.70Ai	Georganne	Moline	USA	6.3.90	1		Albuquerque	12 Feb

800 METRES

Mark	Name		Nat	Born	Pos	Meet	Venue	Date
1:55.28	Caster	Semenya	RSA	7.1.91	1	OG	Rio de Janeiro	20 Aug
1:55.33		Semenya			1	Herc	Monaco	15 Jul
1:55.68		Semenya			1	ISTAF	Berlin	3 Sep
1:56.24	Francine	Niyonsaba	BDI	5.5.93	2	Herc	Monaco	15 Jul
1:56.44		Semenya			1	WK	Zürich	1 Sep
1:56.49		Niyonsaba			2	OG	Rio de Janeiro	20 Aug
1:56.64		Semenya			1		Rabat	22 May
1:56.64		Semenya			1	GGala	Roma	2 Jun
1:56.76		Niyonsaba			2	WK	Zürich	1 Sep
1:56.89	Margaret	Wambui	KEN	15.9.95	3	OG	Rio de Janeiro	20 Aug
1:56.92		Niyonsaba			1	DL	Birmingham	5 Jun
1:57.02	Melissa	Bishop	CAN	5.8.88	4	OG	Rio de Janeiro	20 Aug
1:57.04		Wambui			3	WK	Zürich	1 Sep
1:57.37	Joanna	Józwik	POL	30.1.91	5	OG	Rio de Janeiro	20 Aug
1:57.43		Bishop			1		Edmonton	15 Jul
1:57.47	Eunice	Sum	KEN	2.9.88	3	Herc	Monaco	15 Jul
1:57.52		Wambui			1		Montreuil-sous-Bois	7 Jun
1:57.58		Niyonsaba			2	ISTAF	Berlin	3 Sep
1:57.68	Molly	Ludlow	USA	4.8.87	4	Herc	Monaco	15 Jul
1:57.69	Lynsey	Sharp	GBR	11.7.90	6	OG	Rio de Janeiro	20 Aug
1:57.71		Niyonsaba			1	Athl	Lausanne	25 Aug
1:57.74		Niyonsaba			2		Rabat	22 May
1:57.75		Sharp			5	Herc	Monaco	15 Jul
1:57.95		Sum			3	ISTAF	Berlin	3 Sep
1:58.01	Renelle	Lamote	FRA	26.12.93	2	DL	Birmingham	5 Jun
1:58.15		Semenya			1s3	OG	Rio de Janeiro	18 Aug
1:58.20		Niyonsaba			2	GGala	Roma	2 Jun
1:58.20		Semenya			1	AfCh	Durban	26 Jun
1:58.20		Józwik			4	ISTAF	Berlin	3 Sep
1:58.21		Józwik			4	WK	Zürich	1 Sep
	(30/9)							
1:58.28	Kate	Grace	USA	24.10.88	5	WK	Zürich	1 Sep
1:58.36	Marina	Arzamasova	BLR	17.12.87	6	WK	Zürich	1 Sep
1:58.49	Rose Mary	Almanza	CUB	13.7.92	1		Barcelona (S)	30 Jun
1:58.60	Nataliya	Pryshchepa	UKR	11.9.94	7	WK	Zürich	1 Sep
1:58.77	Selina	Büchel	SUI	26.7.91	5	Athl	Lausanne	25 Aug
1:58.84A	Sahily	Diago	CUB	26.8.95	1		Puebla	17 Apr
1:58.93	Lisneidy	Veitía	CUB	29.4.94	2		Barcelona (S)	30 Jun
1:58.97	Angelika	Cichocka	POL	15.3.88	6	Herc	Monaco	15 Jul
1:58.99	Habitam	Alemu	ETH-J	9.7.97	3h4	OG	Rio de Janeiro	17 Aug
1:59.12	Noélie	Yarigo	BEN	26.12.85	4h4	OG	Rio de Janeiro	17 Aug
1:59.29mx	Sanne	Verstegen	NED	10.11.85	1		Hilversum	1 Sep
	2:00.74				1		Sollentuna	28 Jun
	(20)							
1:59.38	Natoya	Goule	JAM	30.3.91	1		Atlanta	4 Jun
1:59.41	Lovisa	Lindh	SWE	9.7.91	4s2	OG	Rio de Janeiro	18 Aug
1:59.44	Ajee'	Wilson	USA	8.5.94	2h2	OG	Rio de Janeiro	17 Aug
1:59.45	Shelayna	Oskan-Clarke	GBR	20.1.90	5s2	OG	Rio de Janeiro	18 Aug
1:59.59	Chrishuna	Williams	USA	31.3.93	3	NC	Eugene	4 Jul

800 METRES

Mark	Name		Nat	Born	Pos	Meet	Venue	Date	
1:59.64	Brenda	Martinez	USA	8.9.87	1s2	NC	Eugene	2	Jul
1:59.70	Nataliya	Lupu	UKR	4.11.87	2	NC	Lutsk	19	Jun
1:59.77	Gudaf	Tsegay	ETH-J	23.1.97	8	Herc	Monaco	15	Jul
1:59.78	Halimah	Nakaayi	UGA	16.10.94	5h4	OG	Rio de Janeiro	17	Aug
1:59.86	Justine	Fédronic	FRA	11.5.91	2		Atlanta	4	Jun
(30)									
1:59.88	Svetlana	Uloga	RUS	23.11.86	1	Kuts	Moskva	1	Jul
1:59.88	Winny	Chebet	KEN	20.12.90	4	DL	London (OS)	23	Jul
1:59.93	Malika	Akkaoui	MAR	25.12.87	4	DL	Doha	6	May
1:59.93		Wang Chunyu	CHN	17.1.95	4h2	OG	Rio de Janeiro	17	Aug
1:59.97	Shannon	Rowbury	USA	19.9.84	3		Eugene	29	Jul
2:00.00	Renée	Eykens	BEL	8.6.96	4h5	OG	Rio de Janeiro	17	Aug
2:00.0A	Emily	Jerotich	KEN	.86	1		Nairobi	23	Apr
2:00.04	Yusneysi	Santiusti	ITA	24.12.84	9	Herc	Monaco	15	Jul
2:00.04mx	Adelle	Tracey	GBR	27.5.93	1mx		Watford	7	Sep
2:01.16					1		London (Elt)	17	Aug
2:00.14	Aníta	Hinriksdóttir	ISL	13.1.96	6h4	OG	Rio de Janeiro	17	Aug
(40)									
2:00.15	Laura	Roesler	USA	19.12.91	1		Los Angeles (ER)	20	May
2:00.20	Alysia	Montaño	USA	23.4.86	3s2	NC	Eugene	2	Jul
2:00.21	Tigist	Assefa	ETH	28.3.94	5h5	OG	Rio de Janeiro	17	Aug
2:00.24	Aleksandra	Gulyayeva	RUS	30.4.94	1	NCp	Zhukovskiy	21	Jul
2:00.27	Sifan	Hassan	NED	1.1.93	5h3	OG	Rio de Janeiro	17	Aug
2:00.32	Olha	Lyakhova	UKR	18.3.92	2		Bellinzona	6	Jun
2:00.34	Sofia	Ennaoui	POL	30.8.95	3		Bellinzona	6	Jun
2:00.37	Christina	Hering	GER	9.10.94	1		Dessau	27	May
2:00.46	Margarita	Mukasheva	KAZ	4.1.86	1		Almaty	5	Jul
2:00.49	Fabienne	Kohlmann	GER	6.11.89	1h1	NC	Kassel	18	Jun
(50)									
2:00.52	Alison	Leonard	GBR	17.3.90	5	DL	London (OS)	23	Jul
2:00.53	Alexandra	Bell	GBR	4.11.92	1		Dublin (S)	22	Jul
2:00.55	Heather	Kampf	USA	19.1.87	3	BostonG	Somerville	17	Jun
2:00.57	Laura	Muir	GBR	9.5.93	1		Montbéliard	1	Jun
2:00.57	Winnie	Nanyondo	UGA	23.8.93	1	GS	Leiden	11	Jun
2:00.57	Lucia	Hrivnák Klocová	SVK	20.11.83	4h8	OG	Rio de Janeiro	17	Aug
2:00.58	Tintu	Luka	IND	26.4.89	6h3	OG	Rio de Janeiro	17	Aug
2:00.59	Raevyn	Rogers	USA	7.9.96	5	NC	Eugene	4	Jul
2:00.62	Angela	Petty	NZL	16.8.91	2		Liège	13	Jul
2:00.65	Charlene	Lipsey	USA	16.7.91	5		Atlanta	4	Jun
(60)									
2:00.7A	Nelly	Jepkosgei	KEN	14.7.91	2		Nairobi	23	Apr
2:00.74	Jennifer	Meadows	GBR	17.4.81	4		Bellinzona	6	Jun
2:00.76	Kendra	Chambers	USA	11.9.90	1		Lignano	13	Jul
2:00.79	Ciara	Mageean	IRL	12.3.92	2		Dublin (S)	22	Jul
2:00.80	Chanelle	Price	USA	22.8.90	6	DL	Birmingham	5	Jun
2:00.81	Kenia	Sinclair	JAM	14.7.80	6		Atlanta	4	Jun
2:00.82	Maggie	Vessey	USA	23.12.81	3	Jordan	Stanford	1	May
2:00.94	Hedda	Hynne	NOR	13.3.90	7	EC	Amsterdam	9	Jul
2:00.96A	Sylivia	Chesebe	KEN	17.5.87	4	OT	Eldoret	1	Jul
2:00.98A	Eglay	Nalyanya	KEN	28.5.96	5	OT	Eldoret	1	Jul
(70)									
2:00.99	Alexa	Efraimson	USA-J	20.2.97	2		Portland	15	May
2:00.99	Amela	Terzic	SRB	2.1.93	2h1	OG	Rio de Janeiro	17	Aug
2:01.02	Olivia	Baker	USA	12.6.96	4	Jordan	Stanford	1	May
2:01.03	Phoebe	Wright	USA	30.8.88	3		Los Angeles (ER)	20	May
2:01.09	Yuliya	Karol	BLR	26.6.91	5h8	OG	Rio de Janeiro	17	Aug
2:01.10	Sarah	McDonald	GBR	2.8.93	1		Oxford	23	Jul
2:01.12	Simoya	Campbell	JAM	1.3.94	2		Lignano	13	Jul
2:01.17	Yelena	Arzhakova	RUS	8.9.89	1	Mosc	Moskva	10	Jun
2:01.20	Esther	Guerrero	ESP	7.2.90	5		Madrid	23	Jul
2:01.21	Santa	Tkhakur	RUS	23.4.93	2	NCp	Zhukovskiy	21	Jul
(80)									
2:01.22	Anastasiya	Tkachuk	UKR	20.4.93	4	NA	Heusden	16	Jul
2:01.23	Florina	Pierdevara	ROU	29.3.90	1		Florø	4	Jun
2:01.27	Selma	Kajan	AUS	30.7.91	4		Barcelona (S)	30	Jun
2:01.29	McKayla	Fricker	USA	19.4.92	3	ATL	Houston	23	Jul
2:01.34	Hannah	England	GBR	6.3.87	3		Padova	17	Jul
2:01.47	Katie	Mackey	USA	12.11.87	5	Jordan	Stanford	1	May
2:01.49	Claudia	Bobocea	ROU	11.6.92	3	GS	Leiden	11	Jun
2:01.49	Rabab	Arrafi	MAR	12.1.91	5	AfCh	Durban	26	Jun
2:01.55	Konstanze	Klosterhalfen	GER-J	18.2.97	1		Leverkusen	8	Jul

800 METRES

Mark	Name		Nat	Born	Pos	Meet	Venue	Date	
2:01.56	Shelby	Houlihan	USA	8.2.93	3		Portland	15	May
	(90)								
2:01.59	Lauren	Johnson	USA	4.5.87	1rB		Portland	12	Jun
2:01.62	Anna	Shchagina	RUS	7.12.91	2	Mosc	Moskva	10	Jun
2:01.63	Brittany	McGowan	AUS	24.4.91	1		Nivelles	18	Jun
2:01.63	Tanja	Spill	GER	16.12.95	2		Leverkusen	8	Jul
2:01.65	Clarisse	Moh	FRA	6.12.86	2		Nivelles	18	Jun
2:01.67	Lora	Storey	AUS	19.10.89	1rB	Jordan	Stanford	1	May
2:01.73	Trine	Mjåland	NOR	30.6.90	6s2	EC	Amsterdam	7	Jul
2:01.75	Megan	Krumpoch	USA	31.8.92	4		Kessel-Lo	30	Jul
2:01.77	Yngvild	Elvemo	NOR	28.5.90	4	DL	Stockholm	16	Jun
2:01.80	Anastasiya	Kalina	RUS	16.2.94	4	NC	Cheboksary	21	Jun
	(100)								
2:01.81	Yelena	Kotulskaya	RUS	8.8.88	1	Jul			
2:01.84	Jessica	Smith	CAN	11.10.89	1	May			
2:01.86	Déborah	Rodríguez	URU	2.12.92	17	Aug			
2:01.91	Marta	Zenoni	ITA-Y	9.3.99	6	Jun			
2:01.93	Darya	Borisevich	BLR	6.4.90	16	Jul			
2:01.94	Cory	McGee	USA	29.5.92	11	Jun			
2:01.94	Treniere	Moser	USA	27.10.81	17	Jun			
2:01.97	Kaela	Edwards	USA	8.12.93	16	Apr			
2:01.97	Jenna	Westaway	CAN	19.6.94	23	Jun			
2:01.98	Katie	Snowden	GBR	9.3.94	28	May			
2:01.98	Siofra	Cleirigh-Buttner	IRL	21.7.95	9	Jul			
2:02.00	Abby	Farley	USA	15.10.92	11	Jun			
2:02.00	Morgan	Uceny	USA	10.3.85	17	Jun			
2:02.10	Natalia	Evangelidou	CYP	10.3.91	28	May			
2:02.11	Chaltu	Shume	ETH	.96	4	Jun			
2:02.14	Amanda	Eccleston	USA	18.6.90	25	Jun			
2:02.14	Claudia	Saunders	USA	19.5.94	28	Jun			
2:02.18	Natalya	Peryakova	RUS	4.3.83	27	May			
2:02.20	Dana	Mecke	USA	20.9.87	23	Apr			
2:02.22	Olicia	Williams	USA	26.2.94	1	Jul			
2:02.23	Helen	Crofts	CAN	28.5.90	30	Jul			
2:02.29	Morgan	Schuetz	USA	8.1.94	23	Apr			
2:02.3A	Selah	Busienei	KEN	27.12.91	29	Apr			
2:02.30	Annie	Leblanc	CAN	29.4.92	12	Jun			
2:02.32	Revee	Walcott-Nolan	GBR	6.3.95	15	Jun			
2:02.35	Rose-Anne	Galligan	IRL	9.12.87	1	May			
2:02.36	Nicole	Sifuentes	CAN	30.6.86	25	Jun			
2:02.37	Lidya	Melese	ETH	.96	16	Jul			
2:02.38	Violah	Lagat	KEN	13.3.89	7	May			
2:02.39	Carsyn	Koch	USA	5.1.96	7	May			
2:02.39	Dominique	Jackson	USA	10.6.89	20	May			
2:02.39	Anima	Banks	USA	30.3.94	1	Jul			
2:02.4mx	Tamsyn	Manou	AUS	20.7.78	15	Mar			
2:03.5					23	Feb			
2:02.40	Katia	Hristova	BUL	18.7.93	29	May			
2:02.43	Olga	Rulevich	BLR	27.5.89	21	May			
2:02.44	Bethany	Praska	USA	10.6.89	20	Jun			
2:02.44	Amina	Bakhit	SUD	14.11.90	1	Jun			
2:02.45	Hanna	Green	USA	16.10.94	15	May			
2:02.49	Dina	Aleksandrova	RUS	9.8.92	27	May			
2:02.49	Latavia	Thomas	USA	17.12.88	17	Jun			
2:02.52	Anneliese	Rubie	AUS	22.4.92	10	Jun			
2:02.57	Baylee	Mires	USA	10.12.92	1	Jul			
2:02.57	Anna	Silvander	SWE	22.6.93	28	Aug			
2:02.58	Stephanie	Twell	GBR	17.8.89	15	Jun			
2:02.62	Cecilia	Barowski	USA	7.12.92	2	Apr			
2:02.64	Alena	Shukhtuyeva	RUS	7.12.93	21	Jun			
2:02.67		Zhao Jing	CHN	9.7.88	7	May			
2:02.67	Lauren	Wallace	USA	4.5.90	4	Jun			
2:02.67	Lindsey	Butterworth	CAN	27.9.92	30	Jul			
2:02.70	Katherine	Marshall	NZL	6.2.92	22	Jul			
2:02.71	Liga	Velvere	LAT	10.2.90	12	Jul			
2:02.71	Paulina	Mikiewicz-Lapinska	POL	13.7.92	30	Jul			
2:02.74	Hilary	Stellingwerff	CAN	7.8.81	8	May			
2:02.76	Yelena	Murashova	RUS	5.10.87	20	Jun			

Mark	Name		Nat	Born	Pos	Meet	Venue	Date	
2:02.79	Irene	Baldessari	ITA	21.1.93	29	May			
2:02.82	Ce'aira	Brown	USA	4.11.93	1	Apr			
2:02.83	Shea	Collinsworth	USA	19.2.95	11	Jun			
2:02.84	Anna	Musina	RUS	3.11.84	21	Jul			
2:02.85	Linden	Hall	AUS	29.6.91	12	Jun			
2:02.85	Raquel	Lambdin	USA	23.7.93	16	Jun			
2:02.86	Inessa	Gusarova	RUS	29.10.95	21	Jul			
2:02.88	Marilyn	Okoro	GBR	23.9.84	27	May			
2:02.88	Tola	Kore	ETH-J	.97	4	Jun			
2:02.91	Gabriela	Stafford	CAN	13.9.95	19	Jun			
2:02.91	Alexandra	Stuková	SVK	2.7.90	22	Jun			
2:02.91	Samantha	Watson	USA-Y	10.11.99	25	Jun			
2:02.93	Erin	Donohue	USA	8.5.83	1	Jul			
2:02.94	Olena	Zhushman	UKR	30.12.85	28	Jun			
2:02.96	Aaliyah	Miller	USA-J	28.8.98	25	Jun			
2:02.98	Egle	Balciunaite	LTU	31.10.88	17	Aug			
2:03.00	Rachel	Aubry	CAN	18.5.90	25	Jun			
2:03.01	Bianka	Kéri	HUN	19.4.94	22	Jun			
2:03.03	Maureen	Koster	NED	3.7.92	28	May			
2:03.03	Grace	Annear	CAN	.92	25	Jun			
2:03.07	Anna	Kupayeva	RUS	24.11.90	21	Jul			
2:03.10	Yelena	Kobeleva	RUS	12.6.88	27	May			
2:03.1A	Esther	Chebet	UGA-J	10.9.97	2	Sep			
2:03.11	Fiona	Benson	CAN	25.5.92	16	Jun			
2:03.18	Rachel	François	CAN	14.11.92	12	Jun			
2:03.19	Shannon	Leinert	USA	30.6.87	2	Jun			
2:03.19	Ayvika	Malanova	RUS	28.11.92	10	Jun			
2:03.20	Megan	Malasarte	USA	1.8.92	23	Jun			
2:03.21	Devan	Wiebe	CAN	9.12.93	12	Jun			
2:03.22	Anastasiya	Nemykina	RUS	13.5.93	20	Jun			
2:03.23	Katy	Brown	GBR	18.11.93	4	Jun			
2:03.24	Ariah	Graham	USA	19.2.94	1	Apr			
2:03.25A	Dorcus	Ajok	UGA	12.7.94	9	Apr			
2:03.25	Jazmine	Fray	USA-J	6.6.97	23	Apr			
2:03.26	Alisha	Brown	USA	8.11.92	23	Jun			
2:03.27	Emily	Dudgeon	GBR	3.3.93	14	May			
2:03.29	Claire	Tarplee	IRL	22.9.88	28	May			
2:03.29	Hanna	Klein	GER	6.4.93	27	Jul			
2:03.32	Hanna	Hermansson	SWE	18.5.89	28	Jun			
2:03.32	Anastasiya	Komarova	AZE	23.3.93	7	Jul			
2:03.33	Emma	Keenan	USA	8.12.94	27	May			
2:03.33	Sasha	Gollish	CAN	27.12.81	30	Jul			
2:03.34	Geena	Gall	USA	18.1.87	12	Jun			
2:03.34	Siham	Hilali	MAR	2.5.86	18	Jul			
2:03.35	Samantha	Murphy	CAN	18.3.92	1	May			
2:03.36	Anna	Sabat	POL	9.11.93	11	Jun			
	(200)								

Indoors

2:02.81	Stina	Troest	DEN	17.1.94	30	Jan
2:02.88	Stephanie	Brown	USA	29.7.91	19	Feb
2:02.96	Natalija	Piliusina	LTU	22.10.90	28	Feb
2:02.97	Yekaterina	Kupina	RUS	2.2.86	31	Jan
2:03.00	Bianka	Kéri	HUN	19.4.94	30	Jan
2:03.10	Sabrina	Southerland	USA	18.12.95	6	Feb
2:03.18	Leah	Barrow	GBR	21.1.93	28	Feb

JUNIORS

See main list for top 4 juniors. 11 performances by 3 women to 2:01.0. Additional mark and further juniors:

Alemu	1:59.14	2	DL	Doha	6 May	2:00.07	6s2	OG	Rio de Janeiro	18 Aug
	1:59.68	7	Herc	Monaco	15 Jul	2:00.46	6	Athl	Lausanne	25 Aug
	1:59.70	6		Rabat	22 May					
Tsegay	1:59.90	3		Barcelona (S)	30 Jun	2:00.13	4h3	OG	Rio de Janeiro	17 Aug
	2:01.91		Marta	Zenoni	ITA-Y	9.3.99	10		Bellinzona	6 Jun
	2:02.88		Tola	Kore	ETH	.97	7	PTS	Samorín	4 Jun

800 – 1000 – 1500 METRES

Mark	Name		Nat	Born	Pos	Meet	Venue	Date	
2:02.91	Samantha	Watson	USA-Y	10.11.99	1	NC-j	Clovis	25	Jun
2:02.96	Aaliyah	Miller	USA	28.8.98	2	NC-j	Clovis	25	Jun
2:03.1A	Esther	Chebet	UGA	10.9.97	1		Eldoret	2	Sep
2:03.25	Jazmine	Fray (10)	USA-J	6.6.97	1	Johnson	Waco	23	Apr
2:03.43	Ruby	Stauber	USA-J	30.9.97	3	NC-j	Clovis	25	Jun
2:03.54A	Josphine	Chelangat	KEN-J	2.2..98	5	NC	Nairobi	28	May
2:03.57	Alina	Ammann	GER-J	16.2.98	3		Dessau	27	May
2:03.58	Victoria	Tachinski	CAN-Y	15.6.99	1		Murfreesboro	4	Jun
2:03.61A	Sigei	Chepkemoi	KEN	30.9.98	6	NC	Nairobi	28	May
2:03.72	Sage	Hurta	USA	23.6.98	1		Greensboro	19	Jun
2:04.0A	Lilian	Odira	KEN	18.4.99	3		Eldoret	2	Sep
2:04.1A	Agnes	Mule	KEN	7.7.98	4		Nairobi	29	Apr
2:04.13	Ersula	Farrow	USA	20.11.97	3	ACC	Tallahassee	15	May
2:04.29	Shoko	Fukuda (20)	JPN	20.8.98	1		Okayama	1	Aug

1000 METRES

Mark	Name		Nat	Born	Pos	Meet	Venue		Date	
2:34.84	Angelika	Cichocka	POL	15.3.88	1	Sidlo	Sopot		28	Jul
2:34.90	Anna	Shchagina	RUS	7.12.91	1		Moskva		28	Jul
2:34.93	Joanna	Józwik	POL	30.1.91	2	Sidlo	Sopot		28	Jul
2:35.15	Sofia	Ennaoui	POL	30.8.95	3	Sidlo	Sopot		28	Jul
2:36.04	Lovisa	Lindh	SWE	9.7.91	1		Göteborg		15	Jul
2:36.07	Dina	Aleksandrova	RUS	9.8.92	2		Moskva		28	Jul
2:36.67	Inessa	Gusarova	RUS	29.10.95	3		Moskva		28	Jul
2:36.89	Santa	Tkhakur	RUS	23.4.93	4		Moskva		28	Jul
2:37.09	Anastasiya	Kalina	RUS	16.2.94	5		Moskva		28	Jul
2:37.48	Anastasiya	Tkachuk	UKR	20.4.93	4	Sidlo	Sopot		28	Jul
2:37.53	Svetlana	Uloga	RUS	23.11.86	6		Moskva		28	Jul
2:37.78	Anna	Silvander	SWE	22.6.93	2		Göteborg		15	Jul
2:38.00	Danuta	Urbanik	POL	24.12.89	5	Sidlo	Sopot		28	Jul
2:38.05	Sanne	Verstegen	NED	10.11.85	15	Jul	c. 2:40	Jennifer	Meadows	GBR	17.4.81	9	Jun
2:38.28	Yekaterina	Sokolova	RUS	16.12.95	28	Jul	2:40.5+	Laura	Muir	GBR	9.5.93	22	Jul
2:38.63	Sarah	McDonald	GBR	2.8.93	15	Jul	Indoors						
2:39.19	Darya	Borisevich	BLR	6.4.90	28	Jul	2:39.22i	Renata	Plis	POL	5.2.85	6	Feb
2:39.3+	Genzebe	Dibaba	ETH	8.2.91	6	Sep	2:40.54i	Katarzyna	Broniatowska	POL	22.2.90	6	Feb
2:39.95	Monika	Halasa	POL	5.4.92	28	Jul							
Best junior: 2:42.52	Mareen	Kalis		GER	21.5.97	2		Pliezhausen		8	May

1500 METRES

Mark	Name		Nat	Born	Pos	Meet	Venue	Date	
3:55.22	Laura	Muir	GBR	9.5.93	1	DL	Saint-Denis	27	Aug
3:56.41	Faith	Kipyegon	KEN	10.1.94	1	Pre	Eugene	28	May
3:56.72		Kipyegon			2	DL	Saint-Denis	27	Aug
3:56.82		Kipyegon			1	DL	Shanghai	14	May
3:57.13	Sifan	Hassan	NED	1.1.93	3	DL	Saint-Denis	27	Aug
3:57.31+	Genzebe	Dibaba	ETH	8.2.91	1		Rovereto	6	Sep
3:57.49		Muir			1	DL	London (OS)	22	Jul
3:57.78	Shannon	Rowbury	USA	19.9.84	1	WK	Zürich	1	Sep
3:57.85		Muir			2	WK	Zürich	1	Sep
3:58.00		Rowbury			4	DL	Saint-Denis	27	Aug
3:58.09	Dawit	Seyaum	ETH	27.7.96	5	DL	Saint-Denis	27	Aug
3:58.10		Seyaum			2	Pre	Eugene	28	May
3:58.19	Jenny	Simpson	USA	23.8.86	6	DL	Saint-Denis	27	Aug
3:58.43		Hassan			3	WK	Zürich	1	Sep
3:58.54		Simpson			4	WK	Zürich	1	Sep
3:58.63		Seyaum			5	WK	Zürich	1	Sep
3:59.34	Hellen	Obiri	KEN	13.12.89	2	DL	Shanghai	14	May
3:59.47	Besu	Sado	ETH	12.1.96	6	WK	Zürich	1	Sep
3:59.71+		Kipyegon			1	in 1M	Oslo	9	Jun
3:59.83		G Dibaba			1		Barcelona (S)	9	Jul
3:59.87		Seyaum			3	DL	Shanghai	14	May
3:59.96		Sado			7	DL	Saint-Denis	27	Aug
4:00.08		Sado			4	DL	Shanghai	14	May
4:00.18	Gudaf	Tsegay (10)	ETH-J	23.1.97	3	Pre	Eugene	28	May
4:00.53+		Muir			2	in 1M	Oslo	9	Jun
4:00.87		Hassan			2	DL	London (OS)	22	Jul
4:01.00	Sofia	Ennaoui	POL	30.8.95	8	DL	Saint-Denis	27	Aug
4:01.46	Ciara	Mageean	IRL	12.3.92	9	DL	Saint-Denis	27	Aug
4:01.57		Simpson			4	Pre	Eugene	28	May
4:01.78	Linden (30/13)	Hall	AUS	29.6.91	5	Pre	Eugene	28	May
4:01.99	Caster	Semenya	RSA	7.1.91	1	AfCh	Durban	24	Jun

1500 METRES

Mark	Name		Nat	Born	Pos	Meet	Venue	Date	
4:02.62	Meraf	Bahta	SWE	24.6.89	3	DL	London (OS)	22	Jul
4:02.66	Laura	Weightman	GBR	1.7.91	4	DL	London (OS)	22	Jul
4:02.66	Winny	Chebet	KEN	20.12.90	10	DL	Saint-Denis	27	Aug
4:03.05	Axumawit	Embaye	ETH	18.10.94	5	DL	London (OS)	22	Jul
4:03.22	Zoe	Buckman	AUS	21.12.88	11	DL	Saint-Denis	27	Aug
4:03.25	Angelika	Cichocka	POL	15.3.88	1	DL	Stockholm	16	Jun
(20)									
4:03.25	Amanda	Eccleston	USA	18.6.90	6	DL	London (OS)	22	Jul
4:03.39	Shelby	Houlihan	USA	8.2.93	7	Pre	Eugene	28	May
4:03.57	Brenda	Martinez	USA	8.9.87	8	Pre	Eugene	28	May
4:03.70	Betlhem	Desalegn	UAE	13.11.91	2		Beijing	18	May
4:03.74	Eilish	McColgan	GBR	25.11.90	7	DL	London (OS)	22	Jul
4:03.84	Maureen	Koster	NED	3.7.92	9	DL	London (OS)	22	Jul
4:03.94	Morgan	Uceny	USA	10.3.85	1		Greenville SC	4	Jun
4:03.95	Rabab	Arrafi	MAR	12.1.91	2	AfCh	Durban	24	Jun
4:03.96	Sheila	Reid	CAN	2.8.89	9	Pre	Eugene	28	May
4:03.97	Nicole	Sifuentes	CAN	30.6.86	2		Greenville SC	4	Jun
(30)									
4:04.13	Mary	Kuria	KEN	29.11.87	1		Huelva	3	Jun
4:04.26	Nelly	Jepkosgei	KEN	14.7.91	3		Beijing	18	May
4:04.46	Heather	Kampf	USA	19.1.87	3		Greenville SC	4	Jun
4:04.62	Jenny	Blundell	AUS	9.5.94	4		Beijing	18	May
4:05.22	Nancy	Chepkwemoi	KEN	8.10.93	8	DL	Shanghai	14	May
4:05.22	Feyisa	Adanech	ETH-J	23.1.98	3	AfCh	Durban	24	Jun
4:05.29	Lauren	Johnson	USA	4.5.87	5		Beijing	18	May
4:05.35	Ingvill	Måkestad Bovim	NOR	7.8.81	11	DL	London (OS)	22	Jul
4:05.40	Renata	Plis	POL	5.2.85	12	DL	London (OS)	22	Jul
4:05.45A	Judy	Kiyeng	KEN	.94	1	NC	Nairobi	28	May
(40)									
4:05.53	Amela	Terzic	SRB	2.1.93	2		Huelva	3	Jun
4:05.61	Hilary	Stellingwerff	CAN	7.8.81	5		Greenville SC	4	Jun
4:05.65	Kate	Grace	USA	24.10.88	1		Los Angeles (ER)	20	May
4:05.67	Anastasiya	Kalina	RUS	16.2.94	1	Znam	Zhukovskiy	5	Jun
4:05.84	Taye	Fantu	ETH-Y	29.3.99	4	AfCh	Durban	24	Jun
4:05.98	Charlene	Thomas	GBR	6.5.82	2	NA	Heusden	16	Jul
4:06.00	Violah	Lagat	KEN	13.3.89	7		Beijing	18	May
4:06.20	Stephanie	Twell	GBR	17.8.89	13	DL	London (OS)	22	Jul
4:06.28A	Selah	Busienei	KEN	27.12.91	2	NC	Nairobi	28	May
4:06.33	Katie	Mackey	USA	12.11.87	3		Los Angeles (ER)	20	May
(50)									
4:06.38	Alexa	Efraimson	USA-J	20.2.97	6		Greenville SC	4	Jun
4:06.43	Sara	Sutherland	USA	31.1.92	7		Greenville SC	4	Jun
4:06.47	Madeline	Hills	AUS	15.5.87	4	NA	Heusden	16	Jul
4:06.53	Gabriela	Stafford	CAN	13.9.95	3		Portland	12	Jun
4:06.53	Tigist	Gashaw	BRN	25.12.96	3		Sollentuna	28	Jun
4:06.54	Marta	Pen Freitas	POR	31.7.93	2		Barcelona (S)	30	Jun
4:06.58	Danuta	Urbanik	POL	24.12.89	1	PNG	Turku	29	Jun
4:06.75	Yelena	Korobkina	RUS	25.11.90	2	Znam	Zhukovskiy	5	Jun
4:06.80	Stephanie	Garcia	USA	3.5.88	8		Greenville SC	4	Jun
4:06.91	Konstanze	Klosterhalfen	GER-J	18.2.97	1	GS	Ostrava	20	May
(60)									
4:06.92	Emma	Coburn	USA	19.10.90	5		Los Angeles (ER)	20	May
4:06.96	Yekaterina	Sokolova	RUS	16.12.95	1		Sochi	26	May
4:06.99	Muriel	Coneo	COL	15.3.87	3		Huelva	3	Jun
4:06.99	Gesa Felicitas	Krause	GER	3.8.92	9	DL	Stockholm	16	Jun
4:07.04	Treniere	Moser	USA	27.10.81	11	Pre	Eugene	28	May
4:07.18	Nikki	Hamblin	NZL	20.5.88	9		Greenville SC	4	Jun
4:07.18	Sarah	McDonald	GBR	2.8.93	1	DL	Birmingham	5	Jun
4:07.21	Kate	Murphy	USA-Y	15.8.99	1-j	BostonG	Somerville	17	Jun
4:07.30	Sofie	Van Accom	BEL	7.6.86	5	NA	Heusden	16	Jul
4:07.34	Cory	McGee	USA	29.5.92	6	NA	Heusden	16	Jul
(70)									
4:07.39	Siham	Hilali	MAR	2.5.86	5	AfCh	Durban	24	Jun
4:07.40	Diana	Sujew	GER	2.11.90	1		Kortrijk	9	Jul
4:07.42	Malika	Akkaoui	MAR	25.12.87	5h2	OG	Rio de Janeiro	12	Aug
4:07.55	Melissa	Courtney	GBR	30.8.93	2	DL	Birmingham	5	Jun
4:07.74	Anna	Shchagina	RUS	7.12.91	1	NCp	Zhukovskiy	20	Jul
4:07.78	Hannah	England	GBR	6.3.87	4		Kortrijk	9	Jul
4:07.83	Angela	Petty	NZL	16.8.91	2	PNG	Turku	29	Jun
4:07.84	Rachel	Schneider	USA	18.7.91	7	NA	Heusden	16	Jul
4:07.91	Margherita	Magnani	ITA	26.2.87	8	NA	Heusden	16	Jul

1500 METRES

Mark	Name		Nat	Born	Pos	Meet	Venue	Date
4:07.96	Lucia	Hrivnák Klocová	SVK	20.11.83	2	GS	Ostrava	20 May
(80)								
4:08.11	Janet	Achola	UGA	26.6.88	6	AfCh	Durban	24 Jun
4:08.13	Ashley	Higginson	USA	17.3.89	7		Los Angeles (ER)	20 May
4:08.14	Denise	Krebs	GER	27.6.87	3	PNG	Turku	29 Jun
4:08.29	Solange Andreia	Pereira	ESP	12.12.89	5		Barcelona (S)	30 Jun
4:08.36A	Sandra Felis	Chebet	KEN-J	20.1.98	3	NC	Nairobi	28 May
4:08.45	Heidi	See	AUS	9.7.89	9		Los Angeles (ER)	20 May
4:08.56	Hanna	Klein	GER	6.4.93	5		Kortrijk	9 Jul
4:08.64	Claudia	Bobocea	ROU	11.6.92	3	DL	Birmingham	5 Jun
4:08.68	Kristiina	Mäki	CZE	22.9.91	5	PNG	Turku	29 Jun
4:08.71	Christina	Aragon	USA-J	17.6.97	3	WJ	Bydgoszcz	24 Jul
(90)								
4:08.75	Beatha	Nishimwe	RWA-J	1.12.98	7	AfCh	Durban	24 Jun
4:08.91	Sarah	Lahti	SWE	18.2.95	2		Oordegem	28 May
4:08.94	Federica	Del Buono	ITA	12.12.94	1		Cles	25 Aug
4:08.95	Darya	Borisevich	BLR	6.4.90	4	Kuso	Szczecin	18 Jun
4:08.96mx	Alison	Leonard	GBR	17.3.90	1mx		Manchester (Str)	9 Aug
4:09.59					4	FBK	Hengelo	22 May
4:09.03	Karoline Bjerkeli	Grøvdal	NOR	14.6.90	3		Oordegem	28 May
4:09.08	Shannon	Osika	USA	15.6.93	1		Guelph	25 Jun
4:09.16	Stephanie	Brown	USA	29.7.91	4		Portland	12 Jun
4:09.25	Winfredah	Nzisa	KEN-J	30.5.97	4	WJ	Bydgoszcz	24 Jul
4:09.28		Zhao Jing	CHN	9.7.88	10	DL	Shanghai	14 May
(100)								
4:09.30	Aleksandra	Gulyayeva	RUS	30.4.94	23 Jun			
4:09.33	Maren	Kock	GER	22.6.90	27 May			
4:09.41	Stephanie	Schappert	USA	25.4.93	4 Jun			
4:09.54	Elise	Cranny	USA	8.5.96	11 Jun			
4:09.58	Melissa	Bishop	CAN	5.8.88	21 May			
4:09.58	Dalilah Abdelkadir	Gosa	BRN-J	27.6.98	18 Jun			
4:09.68	Sasha	Gollish	CAN	27.12.81	25 Jun			
4:09.70	Melissa	Duncan	AUS	30.1.90	30 Jan			
4:09.75	Rebecca	Tracy	USA	20.2.91	20 May			
4:09.88	Regan	Yee	CAN	4.7.95	25 Jun			
4:09.89	Kim	Conley	USA	14.3.86	20 May			
4:10.12	Renée	Eykens	BEL	8.6.96	30 Jul			
4:10.13	Nicole	Tully	USA	30.10.86	22 Apr			
4:10.15	Élodie	Normand	FRA	6.10.88	4 Jun			
4:10.19	Viktoriya	Kushnir	BLR	9.2.93	12 May			
4:10.19	Sara	Vaughn	USA	16.5.86	12 Jun			
4:10.20	Genevieve	LaCaze	AUS	4.8.89	30 Jan			
4:10.30	Mariah	Kelly	CAN	19.8.91	5 Jun			
4:10.32		Zheng Xiaoqian	CHN	15.8.96	14 May			
4:10.43	Marta	Pérez	ESP	19.4.93	26 Jun			
4:10.51	Nataliya	Pryshchepa	UKR	11.9.94	17 Jun			
4:10.59	Meryem	Akdag	TUR	5.8.92	24 May			
4:10.61	Bobby	Clay	GBR-J	19.5.97	5 Jun			
4:10.63	Anastasía-Panayióta	Marinákou	GRE	12.6.96	4 Jun			
4:10.65	Claire	Tarplee	IRL	22.9.88	20 May			
4:10.70	Andrea	Seccafien	CAN	27.8.90	19 Jun			
4:10.83	Dina	Aleksandrova	RUS	9.8.92	23 Jun			
4:10.84	Mary	Cain	USA	3.5.96	17 Jun			
4:11.05	Geneviève	Lalonde	CAN	5.9.91	25 Jun			
4:11.22	Erin	Donohue	USA	8.5.83	18 Jun			
4:11.23	Anastasiya	Tkachuk	UKR	20.4.93	13 Jul			
4:11.28	Natalia	Evangelidou	CYP	10.3.91	30 Jul			
4:11.3A	Janet	Kisa	KEN	5.3.92	23 Apr			
4:11.32	Jamie	Cheever	USA	28.2.87	12 Jun			
4:11.35	Yekaterina	Ishova	RUS	17.1.89	5 Jun			
4:11.40	Katarzyna	Broniatowska	POL	22.2.90	27 May			
4:11.44	Liina	Tsernov	EST	28.12.87	19 Jun			
4:11.45	Leah	O'Connor	USA	30.8.92	7 May			
4:11.53	Marina	Pospelova	RUS	23.7.90	23 Jun			
4:11.55	Florina	Pierdevara	ROU	29.3.90	12 Aug			
4:11.57	Aisha	Praught	JAM	14.12.89	16 Jul			
4:11.67	Shuru	Bulo	ETH-J	27.6.98	11 Jul			
4:11.67	Sammy	Silva	USA	24.1.95	30 Jul			
4:11.71	Carolina	Lozano	ARG	27.2.96	16 May			
4:11.72	Inessa	Gusarova	RUS	29.10.95	20 Jul			
4:11.75	Johanna	Geyer Carles	FRA	10.10.95	19 Jun			
4:11.8A	Margaret Chelimo	Kipkemboi	KEN	9.2.93	23 Apr			
4:11.8A	Adanech	Ansa	ETH		24 Apr			
4:11.82	Tereza	Capková	CZE	24.7.87	20 May			
4:11.82	Katelyn	Simpson	AUS	28.1.94	12 Jun			
4:11.86	Dana	Giordano	USA	30.12.93	11 Jun			
4:11.86	Gabe	Grunewald	USA	25.6.86	8 Jul			

4:11.87	Ann	Mwangi	KEN	8.12.88 24 Sep
4:11.91	Megan	Moye	USA	27.3.94 15 May
4:12.09	Laura	Carlyle	CAN	16.7.89 16 Jul
4:12.13	Brie	Felnagle	USA	9.12.86 12 Jun
4:12.21	Colleen	Quigley	USA	20.11.92 23 Jun
4:12.25	Dana	Mecke	USA	20.9.87 20 May
4:12.3A	Virginia	Nyambura	KEN	20.7.93 23 Apr
4:12.30	Hawi	Alemu	ETH-J	24.1.98 20 May
4:12.30	Louise	Carton	BEL	16.4.94 19 Jun
4:12.31	Emily	Lipari	USA	19.11.92 17 Jun
4:12.35	Lianne	Farber	USA	12.6.92 12 Jun
4:12.40	Sanne	Verstegen	NED	10.11.85 22 May
4:12.41	Rosie	Clarke	GBR	17.11.91 5 Jun
4:12.41	Maya	Iino	JPN	5.2.88 24 Sep
4:12.44	Manon	Kruiver	NED	3.1.88 30 Jul
4:12.45	Jessica	Judd	GBR	7.1.95 14 May
4:12.47+	Emily	Jerotich	KEN	.86 6 Sep
4:12.58	Sarah	Inglis	GBR	28.8.91 5 Jun
4:12.61	María Pía	Fernández	URU	1.4.95 16 May
4:12.62	Anna	Maxwell	USA	8.2.96 1 May
4:12.62	Phoebe	Wright	USA	30.8.88 1 May
4:12.62	Katie	Rainsberger	USA-Y	18.8.98 12 Jun
4:12.7A	Celphine	Chespol	KEN-Y	23.3.99 17 Jun
4:12.73	Tatyana	Tomashova	RUS	1.7.75 22 Jun
4:12.75	Chiaki	Morikawa	JPN	22.9.87 24 Sep
4:12.78	Sara	Kuivisto	FIN	18.8.91 29 Jun
4:12.84	Mimi	Belete	BRN	9.6.88 22 May
4:12.85	Alena	Shukhtuyeva	RUS	7.12.93 22 Jun
4:12.89	Lydia	Wafula	KEN	15.2.88 14 May
4:12.90	Helen	Ekarare	KEN-Y	3.3.99 9 Apr
4:13.03	Olena	Sidorska	UKR	30.7.94 17 Jun
4:13.06mx	Katie	Snowden	GBR	9.3.94 24 Aug
4:13.09+	Nuria	Fernández	ESP	16.8.76 9 Jun
4:13.18	Olena	Zhushman	UKR	30.12.85 24 Jun
4:13.18	Yolanda	Ngarambe	SWE	14.9.91 28 Jun
4:13.22	Greta	Feldman	USA	30.3.91 20 May
4:13.22	Caterina	Granz	GER	14.3.94 4 Jun
4:13.37	Anastasiya	Nemykina	RUS	13.5.93 20 Jul
4:13.39	Shalaya	Kipp	USA	19.8.90 12 Jun
4:13.4A	Ruth	Jebet	BRN	17.11.96 16 Apr
4:13.44	Dani	Jones	USA	21.8.96 9 Jun
4:13.45	Anzhela	Shevchenko	UKR	29.10.87 24 Jun
4:13.48	Sanaa	Koubaa	GER	6.1.85 30 Jul
4:13.54	Simona	Vrzalová	CZE	7.4.88 20 May
4:13.55	Georgia	Griffith	AUS	5.12.96 17 Dec
4:13.63	Kaela	Edwards	USA	8.12.93 9 Jun
4:13.67	Elina	Sujew	GER	2.11.90 20 May
4:13.74	Sophie	Connor	GBR	21.5.93 9 Jun
4:13.74	Sarah	MacPherson	CAN	8.5.91 12 Jun
4:13.74	Helen	Ekolor	KEN-J		9 Oct
(201)				

WOMEN 2016

1500 METRES – 1 MILE

Mark	Name		Nat	Born	Pos	Meet	Venue	Date	
Indoors									
3:56.46+	Genzebe	Dibaba	ETH	8.2.91	1	Globen	Stockholm	17	Feb
4:00.28		Seyaum			1		Bsoton (A)	28	Feb
4:06.89	Luiza	Gega	ALB	5.11.88	1	BalkC	Istanbul	27	Feb
4:06.93	Melissa	Duncan	AUS	30.1.90	4		Boston (R)	14	Feb
4:08.53+	Kerri	Gallagher	USA	31.5.89	2	Mill	New York (A)	20	Feb
4:08.95	Selina	Büchel	SUI	26.7.91	5		Karlsruhe	6	Feb
4:11.07	Rose-Anne	Galligan	IRL	9.12.87	17 Feb				
4:11.42+	Heather	Wilson	USA	13.6.90	20 Feb				
4:12.72i	Olga	Vovk	RUS	13.2.93	14 Feb				
4:13.04+	Sandra	Eriksson	FIN	4.6.89	17 Feb				
4:13.38+	Dominique	Scott	RSA	24.6.92	20 Feb				
4:13.48i	Kokebe	Tesfaye	ETH-J	5.5.97	19 Feb				
4:13.68i	Josephine	Moultrie	GBR	19.11.90	30 Jan				

JUNIORS

See main list for top 10 juniors. 10 performances by 5 women to 4:07.21. Additional marks and further juniors:

Mark	Name		Nat	Born	Pos	Meet	Venue	Date	
Tsegay	4:02.73	5	DL	Shanghai		14 May			
	4:04.37	3	DL	Stockholm		16 Jun			
	4:04.29	9	WK	Zürich		1 Sep			
	4:05.54	13	DL	Saint-Denis		27 Aug			
4:09.58	Dalilah Abdelkadir	Gosa	BRN	27.6.98	7	Kuso	Szczecin	18	Jun
4:10.61	Bobby	Clay	GBR	19.5.97	4	DL	Birmingham	5	Jun
4:11.67	Shuru	Bulo	ETH	27.6.98	1		Abashiri	11	Jul
4:12.30	Hawi	Alemu	ETH	24.1.98	10	GS	Ostrava	20	May
4:12.62	Katie	Rainsberger	USA-Y	18.8.98	3rB		Portland	12	Jun
4:12.7A	Celphine	Chespol	KEN-Y	23.3.99	1		Embu	17	Jun
4:12.90	Helen	Ekarare	KEN-Y	3.3.99	1		Rifu	9	Apr
4:13.74	Helen	Ekolor	KEN		1		Kitakami	9	Oct
4:14.11	Ella	Donaghu	USA	13.4.98	4rB		Portland	12	Jun
4:14.64	Alina	Reh (20)	GER	23.5.97	5		Regensburg	5	Jun
Indoors									
Tsegay	4:01.81	2		Glasgow		20 Feb	4:05.71	3	WI	Portland	19 Mar
4:13.48	Kokebe	Tesfaye	ETH	5.5.97	2		Sabadell	19	Feb

1 MILE

Mark	Name		Nat	Born	Pos	Meet	Venue	Date	
4:14.30	Genzebe	Dibaba	ETH	8.2.91	1		Rovereto	6	Sep
4:18.60	Faith	Kipyegon	KEN	10.1.94	1	Bisl	Oslo	9	Jun
4:19.12	Laura	Muir	GBR	9.5.93	2	Bisl	Oslo	9	Jun
4:25.04	Lauren	Johnson	USA	4.5.87	1		Raleigh	5	Aug
4:25.26	Meraf	Bahta	SWE	24.6.89	3	Bisl	Oslo	9	Jun
4:25.34	Sofia	Ennaoui	POL	30.8.95	4	Bisl	Oslo	9	Jun
4:25.39	Angelika	Cichocka	POL	15.3.88	5	Bisl	Oslo	9	Jun
4:25.48	Katie	Mackey	USA	12.11.87	1		Dublin (S)	22	Jul
4:25.50	Sifan	Hassan	NED	1.1.93	2		Rovereto	6	Sep
4:25.64	Amanda	Eccleston	USA	18.6.90	2		Raleigh	5	Aug
4:26.23	Karoline Bjerkeli	Grøvdal	NOR	14.6.90	6	Bisl	Oslo	9	Jun
4:27.23	Heather	Kampf	USA	19.1.87	3		Raleigh	5	Aug
4:27.39	Alexa	Efraimson	USA-J	20.2.97	3		Rovereto	6	Sep
4:28.13	Federica	Del Buono	ITA	12.12.94	4		Rovereto	6	Sep
4:28.45	Shannon	Osika	USA	15.6.93	3		South Huntington"	31	Aug
4:28.55	Cory	McGee	USA	29.5.92	3		Dublin (S)	22	Jul
4:28.82	Violah	Lagat	KEN	13.3.89	5		Rovereto	6	Sep
4:29.06	Stephanie	Brown	USA	29.7.91	5		Raleigh	5	Aug
4:29.29	Judy	Kiyeng	KEN	.94	6		Rovereto	6	Sep
4:29.55	Emily	Jerotich	KEN	.86	6 Sep	4:31.72	Rachel	Schneider	USA	18.7.91	31 Aug
4:29.58	Gesa Felicitas	Krause	GER	3.8.92	9 Jun	4:32.6	Genevieve	LaCaze	AUS	4.8.89	23 Feb
4:29.59	Axumawit	Embaye	ETH	18.10.94	9 Jun	4:32.72	Brie	Felnagle	USA	9.12.86	2 Jun
4:29.78	Nicole	Tully	USA	30.10.86	5 Aug	4:33.48	Hannah	England	GBR	6.3.87	22 Jul
4:30.07	Stephanie	Schappert	USA	25.4.93	22 Jul	4:33.50	Lianne	Farber	USA	12.6.92	5 Aug
4:30.67	Nancy	Chepkwemoi	KEN	8.10.93	9 Jun	4:33.57	Ajee'	Wilson	USA	8.5.94	31 Aug
4:30.86	Darya	Borisevich	BLR	6.4.90	6 Sep	4:33.72	Morgan	Uceny	USA	10.3.85	5 Aug
4:30.93	Zoe	Buckman	AUS	21.12.88	6 Sep	4:33.83	Emily	Lipari	USA	19.11.92	2 Jun
4:31.16	Nikki	Hamblin	NZL	20.5.88	22 Jul	4:33.88	Nuria	Fernández	ESP	16.8.76	9 Jun
4:31.23	Aisha	Praught	JAM	14.12.89	6 Sep	4:33.90	Ashley	Higginson	USA	17.3.89	30 Apr
4:31.57	Ingvill	Måkestad Bovim	NOR	7.8.81	9 Jun	4:34.01	Angela	Bizzarri	USA	15.2.88	2 Jun
Indoors											
4:13.31	Genzebe	Dibaba	ETH	8.2.91	1	Globen	Stockholm	17	Feb
4:24.39	Shannon	Rowbury	USA	19.9.84	1	Mill	New York (A)	20	Feb
4:24.98	Gudaf	Tsegay	ETH-J	23.1.97	2	Globen	Stockholm	17	Feb
4:26.18	Kerri	Gallagher	USA	31.5.89	2	Mill	New York (A)	20	Feb
4:27.57	Sheila	Reid	CAN	2.8.89	1		Boston	28	Feb
4:27.75	Axumawit	Embaye	ETH	18.10.94	3	Globen	Stockholm	17	Feb
4:27.88	Kim	Conley	USA	14.3.86	1		New York (A)	24	Jan
4:27.93	Nicole	Sifuentes	CAN	30.6.86	2		Boston (A)	12	Feb
4:27.99	Morgan	Uceny	USA	10.3.85	5	Mill	New York (A)	20	Feb
4:28.30	Kate	Grace	USA	24.10.88	2		New York (A)	24	Jan

1 MILE – 2000 – 3000 METRES

Mark	Name		Nat	Born	Pos	Meet	Venue		Date
4:28.40	Ciara	Mageean	IRL	12.3.92	6	Mill	New York (A)		20 Feb
4:28.47	Stephanie	Garcia	USA	3.5.88	2		Winston-Salem		30 Jan
4:28.50	Rachel	Schneider	USA	18.7.91	2		Boston		28 Feb
4:29.07	Gabriela	Stafford	CAN	13.9.95	1		New York (A)		6 Feb
4:29.07	Erin	Donohue	USA	8.5.83	3		Boston (A)		12 Feb
4:29.71	Elinor	Purrier	USA	20.2.95	12 Feb	4:31.57	Dominique	Scott	RSA 24.6.92	20 Feb
4:30.10	Rabab	Arrafi	MAR	12.1.91	17 Feb	4:31.68	Emily	Lipari	USA 19.11.92	12 Feb
4:30.16	Ashley	Higginson	USA	17.3.89	6 Feb	4:31.83	Leah	O'Connor	USA 30.8.92	20 Feb
4:30.42	Sarah	Lahti	SWE	18.2.95	17 Feb	4:32.05	Brenda	Martinez	USA 8.9.87	29 Jan
4:30.65	Heather	Wilson	USA	13.6.90	12 Feb	4:32.14	Kaela	Edwards	USA 8.12.93	30 Jan
4:30.91	Sandra	Eriksson	FIN	4.6.89	17 Feb	4:32.71	Rebecca	Tracy	USA 20.2.91	20 Feb
4:31.50	Abbey	D'Agostino	USA	25.5.92	29 Jan	4:33.07	Linn	Nilsson	SWE 15.10.90	17 Feb
4:31.53	Hannah	England	GBR	6.3.87	17 Feb	4:33.24	Andrea	Keklak	USA 1.10.93	12 Feb
						4:33.30	Heidi	See	AUS 8.9.89	30 Jan

2000 METRES

Mark	Name		Nat	Born	Pos	Meet	Venue	Date
5:36.80+	Almaz	Ayana	ETH	21.11.91	1	in 3000m	Doha	6 May
c.5:40.0+	Mercy	Cherono	KEN	7.5.91	2	in 3000m	Doha	6 May
5:40.89+	Hellen	Obiri	KEN	13.12.89	1	Herc	Monaco	15 Jul
5:41.4+	Janet	Kisa	KEN	5.3.92	3	in 3000m	Monaco	15 Jul
5:41.61+	Beatrice	Chepkoech	KEN	6.7.91	1	in 5000m	Roma	2 Jun
5:45.51	Aisha	Praught	JAM	14.12.89	1	Déca	Marseille	13 Sep
Indoors								
c.5:39+	Genzebe	Dibaba	ETH	8.2.91	1	in 3000m	Sabadell	19 Feb

3000 METRES

Mark	Name		Nat	Born	Pos	Meet	Venue	Date
8:23.11	Almaz	Ayana	ETH	21.11.91	1	DL	Doha	6 May
8:24.27	Hellen	Obiri	KEN	13.12.89	1	Herc	Monaco	15 Jul
8:26.36	Mercy	Cherono	KEN	7.5.91	2	DL	Doha	6 May
8:27.25		Cherono			2	Herc	Monaco	15 Jul
8:28.33	Janet	Kisa	KEN	5.3.92	3	Herc	Monaco	15 Jul
8:28.49	Gelete	Burka	ETH	23.1.86	3	DL	Doha	6 May
8:30.43+		Ayana			1	in 5000	Roma	2 Jun
8:31.84	Genzebe	Dibaba	ETH	8.2.91	1	Athl	Lausanne	25 Aug
8:31.86	Vivian	Cheruiyot	KEN	11.9.83	4	DL	Doha	6 May
8:32.13		Kisa			5	DL	Doha	6 May
8:32.33+		Ayana			1	in 5000	Rabat	22 May
8:33.96		Obiri			2	Athl	Lausanne	25 Aug
8:34.49		Cherono			3	Athl	Lausanne	25 Aug
8:34.50	Viola	Kibiwot	KEN	22.12.83	6	DL	Doha	6 May
(15/8)								
8:37.54	Margaret Chelimo	Kipkemboi	KEN	9.2.93	4	Athl	Lausanne	25 Aug
8:38.32	Etenesh	Diro (10)	ETH	10.5.91	7	DL	Doha	6 May
8:38.55	Belaynesh	Oljira	ETH	26.6.90	1	GS	Ostrava	20 May
8:39.47	Karoline Bjerkeli	Grøvdal	NOR	14.6.90	4	Herc	Monaco	15 Jul
8:40.80	Haftamnesh	Tesfay	ETH	28.4.94	2	GS	Ostrava	20 May
8:40.98	Stephanie	Twell	GBR	17.8.89	5	Herc	Monaco	15 Jul
8:41.76	Beyenu	Degefu	ETH-Y	12.7.99	1	WJ	Bydgoszcz	20 Jul
8:42.01	Selah	Busienei	KEN	27.12.91	8	DL	Doha	6 May
8:43.08	Meraf	Bahta	SWE	24.6.89	9	DL	Doha	6 May
8:43.27	Eilish	McColgan	GBR	25.11.90	10	DL	Doha	6 May
8:44.7+	Alice Aprot	Nawowuna	KEN	2.1.94	2	in 5000	Bruxelles	9 Sep
8:45.1+	Senbere	Teferi (20)	ETH	3.5.95	4	in 5000	Bruxelles	9 Sep
8:46.25	Nicole	Sifuentes	CAN	30.6.86	6	Herc	Monaco	15 Jul
8:46.38	Agnes	Tirop	KEN	23.10.95	2	Hanz	Zagreb	6 Sep
8:46.42	Dalilah Abdelkadir	Gosa	BRN-J	27.6.98	2	WJ	Bydgoszcz	20 Jul
8:46.58	Katie	Mackey	USA	12.11.87	7	Herc	Monaco	15 Jul
8:46.65	Dominique	Scott	RSA	24.6.92	8	Herc	Monaco	15 Jul
8:46.74	Konstanze	Klosterhalfen	GER-J	18.2.97	3	WJ	Bydgoszcz	20 Jul
8:46.88	Susan	Kuijken	NED	8.7.86	3	Hanz	Zagreb	6 Sep
8:47.46	Fotyen	Tesfay	ETH-J	17.2.98	4	WJ	Bydgoszcz	20 Jul
8:47.83	Anna Emilie	Møller	DEN-J	28.7.97	5	Hanz	Zagreb	6 Sep
8:48.31	Dera (30)	Dida	ETH	26.10.96	9	Herc	Monaco	15 Jul
8:48.46mx	Maureen	Koster	NED	3.7.92	1mx		Utrecht	24 Jun
8:48.60	Tigist	Gashaw	BRN	25.12.96	11	DL	Doha	6 May
8:48.8+	Yasemin	Can	TUR	11.12.96	2	in 5000	Roma	2 Jun
8:49.6+	Genet	Yalew	ETH	31.12.92	6	in 5000	Roma	2 Jun
8:50.8+	Goytatom	Gebreselassie	ETH	15.1.95	13	in 5000	Roma	2 Jun
8:50.97mx	Sarah	Lahti	SWE	18.2.95	1r2		Utrecht	24 Jun

3000 METRES

Mark	Name		Nat	Born	Pos	Meet	Venue	Date	
8:51.00	Mimi	Belete	BRN	9.6.88	12	DL	Doha	6	May
8:51.04	Shuru	Bulo	ETH-J	27.6.98	1		Isahaya	24	Sep
8:51.2+	Shannon	Rowbury	USA	19.9.84	8	in 5000	Bruxelles	9	Sep
8:51.48mx	Laura	Whittle	GBR	27.6.85	1		Manchester (Str)	7	Jun
	(40)								
8:52.08	Alemitu	Hawi	ETH	14.11.96	3		Göteborg	15	Jul
8:52.28	Genevieve	LaCaze	AUS	4.8.89	6	Hanz	Zagreb	6	Sep
8:53.3+	Letesenbet	Gidey	ETH-J	20.3.98	14	in 5000	Roma	2	Jun
8:53.78 ?	Luiza	Gega	ALB	5.11.88	1		Elbasan	21	May
8:53.94mx	Beth	Potter	GBR	27.12.91	1		Watford	27	Jul
8:54.51	Svetlana	Kudzelich	BLR	7.5.87	7	Hanz	Zagreb	6	Sep
8:55.06	Helen	Ekarare	KEN-Y	18.9.99	1		Okayama	2	Aug
8:55.77	Sandra Felis	Chebet	KEN-J	20.1.98	5	WJ	Bydgoszcz	20	Jul
8:57.31	Eloise	Wellings	AUS	9.11.82	8	Hanz	Zagreb	6	Sep
8:57.65	Gulshat	Fazlitdinova	RUS	28.8.92	1		Moskva	28	Jul
	(50)								
8:58.25	Louise	Carton	BEL	16.4.94	29	Jun			
8:58.35	Kamau	Njeri	KEN-J		2	Aug			
8:58.72	Miriam	Muthoni	KEN	18.6.95	25	Jun			
8:58.86	Misembi	Takamatsu	JPN-Y	23.2.00	2	Aug			
8:58.93	Monica	Margaret	KEN-J	.98	23	Apr			
8:59.34	Madeline	Hills	AUS	15.5.87	6	May			
8:59.72	Gabe	Grunewald	USA	25.6.86	15	Jul			
8:59.89	Sheila	Chelangat	KEN-J	11.4.98	20	Jul			
8:59.94	Yekaterina	Sokolenko	RUS	13.9.92	28	Jul			
8:59.96	Harumi	Okamoto	JPN-J	7.2.98	14	Jul			
9:00.06	Susan	Wairimu	KEN	11.10.92	23	Oct			
9:00.19	Ann	Mwangi	KEN	8.12.88	14	Jul			
9:00.42	Sasha	Gollish	CAN	27.12.81	15	Jul			
9:00.62	Katie	Rainsberger	USA-J	18.8.98	20	Jul			
9:00.81	Ririka	Hironaka	JPN-Y	24.11.00	16	Oct			
9:01.16	Nozomi	Tanaka	JPN-Y	4.9.99	20	Jul			
9:01.5+	Juliet		Chekwel		UGA	25.5.90	2	Jun	
9:01.58mx	Katrina		Wootton		GBR	2.9.85	9	Aug	
9:01.9+	Meryem		Akdag		TUR	5.8.92	2	Jun	
9:02.11mx	Elinor		Kirk		GBR	26.4.89	9	Aug	
9:02.59	Natalya		Vlasova		RUS	19.7.88	28	Jul	
9:02.84	Özlem		Kaya		TUR	20.4.90	23	May	
9:03.11	Juliana Paula		dos Santos		BRA	12.7.83	14	May	
9:03.62	Etagegne		Woldu		ETH	10.5.96	20	May	
9:03.63mx	Melissa		Courtney		GBR	30.8.93	24	Aug	
9:04.24	Rosemary		Wanjiru		KEN	9.12.94	2	Apr	
9:04.32mx	Victoria		Mitchell		AUS	25.4.82	19	Nov	
9:04.5	Suriya		Loganathan		IND	7.7.90	24	Apr	
9:04.54mx	Dominika		Napieraj		POL	12.12.91	7	May	
9:04.57mx	Lauren		Howarth		GBR	21.4.90	9	Aug	
9:04.7+	Jessica		O'Connell		CAN	10.2.89	9	Sep	
9:04.79	Muriel		Coneo		COL	15.3.87	14	May	
9:04.99	Annie		St.Geme Beck		USA	8.11.87	30	Jul	

Indoors

Mark	Name		Nat	Born	Pos	Meet	Venue	Date	
8:22.50	Genzebe	Dibaba	ETH	8.2.91	1		Sabadell	19	Feb
8:30.83	Meseret	Defar	ETH	19.11.83	1		Boston (R)	14	Feb
8:33.76		Burka			2		Sabadell	19	Feb
8:44.59	Betlhem	Desalegn	UAE	13.11.91	1	AsC	Doha	20	Feb
8:47.24	Ruth	Jebet	BRN	17.11.96	2	AsC	Doha	20	Feb
8:48.62	Alia Mohammed	Saeed	UAE	18.5.91	3	AsC	Doha	20	Feb
8:49.06	Nancy	Chepkwemoi	KEN	8.10.93	1	GP	Glasgow	20	Feb
8:49.07	Sofia	Ennaoui	POL	30.8.95	2	GP	Glasgow	20	Feb
8:49.43	Gesa Felicitas	Krause	GER	3.8.92	4	GP	Glasgow	20	Feb
8:50.75	Renata	Plis	POL	5.2.85	6	GP	Glasgow	20	Feb
8:51.88mx	Abbey	D'Agostino	USA	25.5.92	1		Boston	2	Jan
8:53.20	Stephanie	Garcia	USA	3.5.88	7	GP	Glasgow	20	Feb
8:54.27	Allie	Ostrander	USA	24.12.96	1		Seattle	13	Feb
8:54.70	Marielle	Hall	USA	28.1.92	1		New York (A)	6	Feb
8:54.87	Gabriela	Stafford	CAN	13.9.95	2		Seattle	13	Feb
8:56.50	Sheila	Reid	CAN	2.8.89	2		New York (A)	6	Feb
8:56.52	Kerri	Gallagher	USA	31.5.89	1		Winston-Salem	30	Jan
8:56.55	Gemeda	Feyne	ETH	28.6.92	2		Mondeville	6	Feb
8:56.58	Jessica	O'Connell	CAN	10.2.89	1		Boston (A)	12	Feb
8:57.11	Laura	Thweatt	USA	17.12.88	3		Boston (R)	14	Feb
8:57.13	Molly	Seidel	USA	12.7.94	1		Notre Dame	6	Feb
8:57.14mx	Josephine	Moultrie	GBR	19.11.90	1		Glasgow	3	Jan
8:57.66	Heidi	See	AUS	8.9.89	5		Boston (R)	14	Feb
8:57.78	Lauren	Paquette	USA	27.6.86	1		Nashville	13	Feb
8:57.87mx	Cory	McGee	USA	29.5.92	1		Boston (A)	31	Dec
8:58.34	Heather	Kampf	USA	19.1.87	6	Feb			
8:58.84	Rachel	Schneider	USA	18.7.91	30	Jan			
8:59.04	Sara	Moreira	POR	17.10.85	21	Feb			
8:59.06	Nicole	Tully	USA	30.10.86	4	Mar			
8:59.44	Leah	O'Connor	USA	30.8.92	22	Jan			
8:59.69	Amanda	Eccleston	USA	18.6.90	6	Feb			
8:59.77	Sandra	Eriksson	FIN	4.6.89	28	Feb			
8:59.85	Shalaya	Kipp	USA	19.8.90	11	Mar			
8:59.94	Svetlana	Aplachkina	RUS	28.11.92	23	Feb			
9:00.44mx	Liz	Costello	USA	23.2.88	31	Dec			
9:00.82+	Molly	Huddle	USA	31.8.84	20	Feb			
9:01.05+	Betsy	Saina	KEN	30.6.88	20	Feb			
9:01.11	Shelby	Houlihan	USA	8.2.93	11	Mar			
9:01.20	Yuliya	Zaripova	RUS	26.4.86	23	Feb			
9:01.25	Erin	Finn	USA	19.11.94	6	Feb			
9:01.25+	Emily		Infeld		USA	21.3.90	20	Feb	
9:01.26	Wesley		Frazier		USA	3.9.95	30	Jan	
9:01.31	Kim		Conley		USA	14.3.86	16	Jan	
9:01.74	Yekaterina		Ishova		RUS	17.1.89	23	Feb	
9:02.15	Diana		Sujew		GER	2.11.90	14	Feb	
9:02.76	Siham		Hilali		MAR	2.5.86	20	Feb	
9:02.77	Ashley		Higginson		USA	17.3.89	12	Feb	
9:03.06	Ancuta		Bobocel		ROU	3.10.87	1	Mar	
9:03.17	Jordan		Hasay		USA	21.9.91	6	Feb	
9:03.22	Mel		Lawrence		USA	29.8.89	13	Feb	
9:03.39	Amela		Terzic		SRB	2.1.93	1	Mar	
9:03.59	Calli		Thackery		GBR	9.1.93	13	Feb	
9:03.60mx	Kate		Hulls/Maltby		GBR	26.7.85	11	Dec	
9:03.85	Lyudmila		Lebedeva		RUS	23.5.90	16	Jan	
9:04.10	Rabab		Arrafi		MAR	12.1.91	6	Feb	

3000 – 5000 METRES

Mark	Name		Nat	Born	Pos	Meet	Venue		Date
9:04.13	Nicol	Traynor	USA	6.5.89	4 Mar		Chelsea Sodaro	USA	9.5.89 13 Feb
9:04.38	Sarah	Boyle	USA	27.5.86	6 Feb	9:04.87	Morgan Uceny	USA	10.3.85 29 Jan
Best in women's race: 8:49.18i Maureen Koster						20 Feb			

JUNIORS
See main list for top 9 juniors. 11 performances (1 indoors) by 8 women to 8:57.0 and further juniors:

Gosa	8:51.31	3	GS	Ostrava		20 May			
Klosterhalfen	8:55.66	1		Pliezhausen		8 May	8:56.36i	1 NC Leipzig	28 Feb
8:58.35	Kamau	Njeri (10)	KEN-J		2		Okayama		2 Aug
8:58.86	Misembi	Takamatsu	JPN-Y	23.2.00	3		Okayama		2 Aug
8:58.93	Monica	Margaret	KEN-J	.98	2		Yokohama		23 Apr
8:59.89	Sheila	Chelangat	KEN-J	11.4.98	6	WJ	Bydgoszcz		20 Jul
8:59.96	Harumi	Okamoto	JPN-J	7.2.98	1		Kitami		14 Jul
9:00.62	Katie	Rainsberger	USA-J	18.8.98	7	WJ	Bydgoszcz		20 Jul
9:00.81	Ririka	Hironaka	JPN-Y	24.11.00	1		Fukuoka		16 Oct
9:01.16	Nozomi	Tanaka	JPN-Y	4.9.99	8	WJ	Bydgoszcz		20 Jul
9:05.15	Akari	Ogasawara	JPN-Y	3.10.00	7		Okayama		2 Aug
9:05.64	Rika	Kaseda	JPN-Y	2.3.99	8		Okayama		2 Aug
9:06.16	Mai	Misaki (20)	JPN-Y	.99	3		Fukuoka		16 Oct
9:00.58i	Alina	Reh	GER-J	23.5.97	2	NC	Leipzig		28 Feb

5000 METRES

Mark	Name		Nat	Born	Pos	Meet	Venue	Date
14:12.59	Almaz	Ayana	ETH	21.11.91	1	GGala	Roma	2 Jun
14:16.31		Ayana			1		Rabat	22 May
14:18.89		Ayana			1	VD	Bruxelles	9 Sep
14:25.78	Hellen	Obiri	KEN	13.12.89	2	VD	Bruxelles	9 Sep
14:26.17	Vivian	Cheruiyot	KEN	11.9.83	1	OG	Rio de Janeiro	19 Aug
14:29.50	Viola	Kibiwot	KEN	22.12.83	2		Rabat	22 May
14:29.77		Obiri			2	OG	Rio de Janeiro	19 Aug
14:29.82	Senbere	Teferi	ETH	3.5.95	3	VD	Bruxelles	9 Sep
14:32.02		Obiri			1	Pre	Eugene	27 May
14:33.30	Etenesh	Diro	ETH	10.5.91	4	VD	Bruxelles	9 Sep
14:33.59		Ayana			3	OG	Rio de Janeiro	19 Aug
14:33.95	Mercy	Cherono	KEN	7.5.91	2	GGala	Roma	2 Jun
14:34.39		Kibiwot			3	GGala	Roma	2 Jun
14:35.09		Teferi			3		Rabat	22 May
14:35.13		Kibiwot			2	Pre	Eugene	27 May
14:35.69		Cheruiyot			3	Pre	Eugene	27 May
14:37.08		Cherono			4	Pre	Eugene	27 May
14:37.19		Teferi			4	GGala	Roma	2 Jun
14:37.51		Diro			5	GGala	Roma	2 Jun
14:37.61	Yasemin	Can	TUR	11.12.96	6	GGala	Roma	2 Jun
14:38.70	Janet	Kisa	KEN	5.3.92	4		Rabat	22 May
14:38.92	Shannon	Rowbury (10)	USA	19.9.84	5	VD	Bruxelles	9 Sep
14:39.56	Alice	Aprot Nawowuna	KEN	2.1.94	6	VD	Bruxelles	9 Sep
14:41.58	Yeshaneh	Ababel	ETH	10.6.90	5		Rabat	22 May
14:41.73	Tirunesh	Dibaba	ETH	1.10.85	1		Kortrijk	9 Jul
14:42.57	Belaynesh	Oljira	ETH	26.6.90	5	Pre	Eugene	27 May
14:42.61		Kisa			7	GGala	Roma	2 Jun
14:42.84	Dera	Dida	ETH	26.10.96	8	GGala	Roma	2 Jun
14:42.89		Cherono			4	OG	Rio de Janeiro	19 Aug
14:43.42	Irene	Cheptai (30/16)	KEN	4.2.92	6	Pre	Eugene	27 May
14:43.58	Alemitu	Haroye	ETH	9.5.95	6		Rabat	22 May
14:43.98	Sally	Kipyego	KEN	19.12.85	7	Pre	Eugene	27 May
14:44.67	Betsy	Saina	KEN	30.6.88	8	Pre	Eugene	27 May
14:45.63	Letesenbet	Gidey (20)	ETH-J	20.3.98	1		Barcelona (S)	30 Jun
14:47.24	Margaret Chelimo	Kipkemboi	KEN	9.2.93	8	VD	Bruxelles	9 Sep
14:48.14	Molly	Huddle	USA	31.8.84	11	Pre	Eugene	27 May
14:49.95	Meraf	Bahta	SWE	24.6.89	7		Rabat	22 May
14:51.04	Genet	Yalew	ETH	31.12.92	9	GGala	Roma	2 Jun
14:52.4+	Gelete	Burka	ETH	23.1.86	7	in 10k	Rio de Janeiro	12 Aug
14:57.53	Karoline Bjerkeli	Grøvdal	NOR	14.6.90	7	OG	Rio de Janeiro	19 Aug
14:59.00	Stephanie	Twell	GBR	17.8.89	11	GGala	Roma	2 Jun
15:00.21	Goytatom	Gebreselassie	ETH	15.1.95	13	GGala	Roma	2 Jun
15:00.69	Susan	Kuijken	NED	8.7.86	8	OG	Rio de Janeiro	19 Aug
15:01.59	Eloise	Wellings (30)	AUS	9.11.82	9	OG	Rio de Janeiro	19 Aug
15:02.67	Agnes	Tirop	KEN	23.10.95	9	VD	Bruxelles	9 Sep

5000 METRES

Mark	Name		Nat	Born	Pos	Meet	Venue	Date	
15:04.05	Madeline	Hills	AUS	15.5.87	10	OG	Rio de Janeiro	19	Aug
15:04.08	Nicole	Tully	USA	30.10.86	2	Jordan	Stanford	1	May
15:05.00	Eilish	McColgan	GBR	25.11.90	13	VD	Bruxelles	9	Sep
15:05.45	Sheila	Chepkirui	KEN	27.12.90	1	AfCh	Durban	23	Jun
15:06.14	Shelby	Houlihan	USA	8.2.93	2	NC	Eugene	10	Jul
15:06.49	Sintayehu	Lewetegn	ETH	9.5.96	8		Rabat	22	May
15:06.67	Genevieve	LaCaze	AUS	4.8.89	15	VD	Bruxelles	9	Sep
15:06.96	Meseret	Defar	ETH	19.11.83	1	BostonG	Somerville	17	Jun
15:07.20	Maureen (40)	Koster	NED	3.7.92	3	Jordan	Stanford	1	May
15:07.72	Jessica	O'Connell	CAN	10.2.89	16	VD	Bruxelles	9	Sep
15:08.58	Laura	Whittle	GBR	27.6.85	4	Jordan	Stanford	1	May
15:10.13	Alemitu	Hawi	ETH	14.11.96	1		Huelva	3	Jun
15:10.30	Stella	Chesang	UGA	1.12.96	3	FBK	Hengelo	22	May
15:10.62	Kim	Conley	USA	14.3.86	3	NC	Eugene	10	Jul
15:10.76	Sarah	Lahti	SWE	18.2.95	4	FBK	Hengelo	22	May
15:10.79	Dalilah Abdelkadir	Gosa	BRN-J	27.6.98	3		Barcelona (S)	30	Jun
15:10.85	Haftamnesh	Tesfay	ETH	28.4.94	5	FBK	Hengelo	22	May
15:12.89	Helen	Ekarare	KEN-Y	3.3.99	1		Yokohama	3	Dec
15:13.07	Shuru (50)	Bulo	ETH-J	27.6.98	1		Kitami	14	Jul
15:13.66	Marielle	Hall	USA	28.1.92	2	BostonG	Somerville	17	Jun
15:13.87	Emily	Infeld	USA	21.3.90	4	NC	Eugene	10	Jul
15:14.04	Abbey	D'Agostino	USA	25.5.92	5	NC	Eugene	10	Jul
15:14.45	Lauren	Paquette	USA	27.6.86	7	Jordan	Stanford	1	May
15:15.14	Rosemary	Wanjiru	KEN	9.12.94	1	Oda	Hiroshima	29	Apr
15:16.44	Grace	Kimanzi	KEN	1.3.92	2	Oda	Hiroshima	29	Apr
15:16.56	Stephanie	Garcia	USA	3.5.88	8	Jordan	Stanford	1	May
15:16.98	Bezunesh	Getachew	ETH-J	.97	2		Huelva	3	Jun
15:16.98	Konstanze	Klosterhalfen	GER-J	18.2.97	1		Bergisch Gladbach	25	Aug
15:17.43	Ann (60)	Mwangi	KEN	8.12.88	1		Osaka	25	Sep
15:17.81	Andrea	Seccafien	CAN	27.8.90	1		Los Angeles (ER)	20	May
15:18.06	Meskerem	Mamo	ETH		4	AfCh	Durban	23	Jun
15:18.08	Tomoko	Kimura	JPN	12.11.94	2		Yokohama	3	Dec
15:18.11	Risa	Yokoe	JPN	12.10.94	1		Abashiri	11	Jul
15:18.60	Katie	Mackey	USA	12.11.87	6	NC	Eugene	10	Jul
15:19.37	Misaki	Onishi	JPN	24.2.85	1	NC	Nagoya	26	Jun
15:19.47	Felista	Wanjugu	KEN	18.2.90	3	Oda	Hiroshima	29	Apr
15:19.50	Gabe	Grunewald	USA	25.6.86	2		Portland	12	Jun
15:20.13	Lucy	Oliver	NZL	18.11.88	3		Portland	12	Jun
15:20.15	Juliet (70)	Chekwel	UGA	25.5.90	15	GGala	Roma	2	Jun
15:20.94	Mariam	Waithera	KEN	23.12.96	3		Osaka	25	Sep
15:21.31	Kaori	Morita	JPN	19.9.95	3		Yokohama	3	Dec
15:21.88	Jessica	Tebo	USA	8.4.88	2		Los Angeles (ER)	20	May
15:22.10	Kellyn	Taylor	USA	22.7.86	3		Los Angeles (ER)	20	May
15:22.29	Yukari	Abe	JPN	21.8.89	4		Yokohama	3	Dec
15:22.34	Rina	Nabeshima	JPN	16.12.93	5		Yokohama	3	Dec
15:22.45	Veronica	Inglese	ITA	22.11.90	1	NC	Rieti	25	Jun
15:22.56	Enatnesg	Alamirew	ETH	.95	7	FBK	Hengelo	22	May
15:23.11	Alisha	Williams	USA	5.2.82	4		Portland	12	Jun
15:23.19	Renata (80)	Plis	POL	5.2.85	1	NA	Heusden	16	Jul
15:23.41	Miyuki	Uehara	JPN	22.11.95	7h1	OG	Rio de Janeiro	16	Aug
15:23.53	Yuka	Hori	JPN	13.6.96	6		Yokohama	3	Dec
15:23.94mx	Rachel	Cliff	CAN	1.4.88	1		Surrey, BC	28	Jun
15:28.60					3		Gresham	23	Jun
15:23.98	Misaki	Kato	JPN	15.6.91	4		Osaka	25	Sep
15:24.02	Jessica	Andrews	GBR	1.10.92	2	NA	Heusden	16	Jul
15:24.17	Nuria	Fernández	ESP	16.8.76	3		Huelva	3	Jun
15:24.27	Azmera	Gebru	ETH	5.5.92	4	BostonG	Somerville	17	Jun
15:24.47	Ayuko	Suzuki	JPN	8.10.91	2	NC	Nagoya	26	Jun
15:24.60	Meryem	Akdag	TUR	5.8.92	16	GGala	Roma	2	Jun
15:24.73	Maren (90)	Kock	GER	22.6.90	10	Jordan	Stanford	1	May
15:24.74	Jo	Pavey	GBR	20.9.73	5	BostonG	Somerville	17	Jun
15:24.74	Hanami	Sekine	JPN	26.2.96	3	NC	Nagoya	26	Jun
15:24.74	Allie	Ostrander	USA	24.12.96	8	NC	Eugene	10	Jul
15:24.83	Emily	Sisson	USA	12.10.91	6	BostonG	Somerville	17	Jun
15:25.10	Dominique	Scott	RSA	24.6.92	1		Stanford	1	Apr

5000 – 10,000 METRES 445

Mark	Name		Nat	Born	Pos	Meet	Venue	Date	
15:25.12	Bontu	Edao	BRN-J	12.12.97	1		Bilbao	25	Jun
15:25.37	Gulshat	Fazlitdinova	RUS	28.8.92	1		Sochi	27	May
15:25.87	Mikuni	Yada	JPN-Y	29.10.99	7		Yokohama	3	Dec
15:25.95	Susan	Wairimu	KEN	11.10.92	5		Osaka	25	Sep
15:26.28	Laura (100)	Thweatt	USA	17.12.88	6		Portland	12	Jun
15:26.51	Pauline	Kamulu	KEN	30.12.94	14	Jul			
15:26.53	Mary	Cullen	IRL	17.8.82	1	Apr			
15:26.79	Sarah	Pagano	USA	23.7.91	2	Jun			
15:26.82	Tara	Welling	USA	14.6.89	10	Jul			
15:27.09	Hanna	Klein	GER	6.4.93	16	Jul			
15:27.67	raelle	Kanuho	USA	4.7.90	1	May			
15:27.80	Riko	Matsuzaki	JPN	24.12.92	25	Sep			
15:27.83	Nahura	Sato	JPN	2.10.97	3	Dec			
15:28.16	Alla	Kulyatina	RUS	9.6.90	27	May			
15:28.25	Sara	Hall	USA	15.4.83	20	May			
15:28.32	Beth	Potter	GBR	27.12.91	1	May			
15:28.47	Kate	Spencer	AUS	23.6.95	12	Jul			
15:28.56	Natosha	Rogers	USA	7.5.91	20	May			
15:28.88	Liz	Costello	USA	23.2.88	17	Jun			
15:29.02	Kate	Avery	GBR	10.10.91	1	May			
15:29.12	Hisami	Ishii	JPN	10.8.95	26	Jun			
15:29.32	Shuri	Ogasawara	JPN-Y	3.10.00	3	Dec			
15:29.64	Kalkidan	Fenite	ETH-J	9.5.98	23	Jul			
15:29.72	Mimi	Belete	BRN	9.6.88	16	Aug			
15:29.77	Jordan	Hasay	USA	21.9.91	23	Jun			
15:29.85	Sammy	Silva	USA	24.1.95	16	Jul			
15:29.89	Kaitlin	Goodman	USA	31.1.87	17	Jun			
15:30.02	Aliphine	Bolton	KEN	5.4.89	15	Apr			
15:30.12	Yuliya	Shmatenko	UKR	10.10.91	23	Jul			
15:30.15	Yui	Fukuda	JPN	1.6.95	24	Dec			
15:30.34	Jessica	Tonn	USA	15.2.92	20	May			
15:30.35	Geleto	Tola	GER	22.10.87	19	Jun			
15:30.97	Miriam	Muthoni	KEN	18.6.95	3	Jul			
15:31.12	Imaculata	Chepkurui	KEN-Y	3.8.00	23	Jul			
15:31.15	Kristiina	Mäki	CZE	22.9.91	23	Jul			
15:31.53	Yekaterina	Ishova	RUS	17.1.89	27	May			
15:31.62	Miki	Moribayashi	JPN-Y	5.9.99	3	Dec			
15:31.95	Kelsey	Smith	USA	5.11.91	20	May			
15:32.10	Kimberley	Smith	NZL	19.11.81	2	Jun			
15:32.46	Viktoriya	Pohoryelska	UKR	4.8.90	24	Jun			
15:33.08	Harumi	Okamoto	JPN-J	7.2.98	11	Jul			
15:33.58	Louise	Carton	BEL	16.4.94	16	Jul			
15:33.78	Alexi	Pappas	GRE	28.3.90	15	Apr			
15:33.95	Natsuki	Sekiya	JPN-J	.97	11	Jul			
15:34.09	Mercyline	Chelangat	UGA-J	17.12.97	23	Jul			
15:34.37	Yitayish	Mekonene	ETH-Y	17.3.00	23	Jul			
15:34.50	Erin	Finn	USA	19.11.94	12	Jun			
15:34.93	Sara	Moreira	POR	17.10.85	17	Jul			
15:35.12	Aisling	Cuffe	USA	12.9.93	23	Jun			
15:35.16	Brenda	Flores	MEX	4.9.91	15	Apr			
15:35.16	Sasha	Gollish	CAN	27.12.81	1	May			
15:35.34	Alycia	Cridebring	USA	11.1.92	12	Jun			
15:35.46	Misaki	Tanabe	JPN	31.8.95	3	Dec			
15:35.56	Maki	Izumida	JPN	22.1.96	3	Dec			
15:35.72	Nozomi	Tanaka	JPN-Y	4.9.99	20	Nov			
15:36.02	Amy	Van Alstine	USA	11.11.87	23	Jun			
15:36.10	Natsuki	Omori	JPN	22.6.94	26	Jun			
15:36.27	Mina	Ueda	JPN-J	11.2.97	3	Dec			
15:37.08	Natalya	Leontyeva	RUS	5.7.87	27	May			
15:37.12	Dulce	Félix	POR	23.10.82	12	Jun			
15:37.16	Natsuko	Goto	JPN	4.8.87	10	Dec			
15:37.21	Yuka	Ando	JPN	16.3.94	29	Apr			
15:37.25	Kasumi	Nishihara	JPN	1.3.89	7	Oct			
15:37.39	Azusa	Sumi	JPN	12.8.96	3	Dec			
15:37.44	Calli	Thackery	GBR	9.1.93	1	May			
15:37.58	Nao	Yamamoto	JPN	20.10.96	11	Jul			
15:37.62	Margarita	Hernández	MEX	3.12.85	15	Apr			
15:37.65	Elinor	Kirk	GBR	26.4.89	16	Jul			
15:37.69	Meseret	Taye	ETH	.94	30	Jun			
15:37.70	Natasha	Wodak	CAN	17.12.81	20	May			
15:37.79	Catherine	Syokau	KEN-Y	20.8.99	23	Jul			
15:37.85	Moeno	Nakamura	JPN	21.3.90	26	Jun			
15:38.23	Jip	Vastenburg	NED	21.3.94	19	Jun			
15:38.33	Leah	O'Connor	USA	30.8.92	23	Apr			
15:39.04	Paulina	Kaczynska	POL	24.7.91	28	May			
15:39.27	Kidsan	Alema	ETH		95	23	Jun		
15:39.45	Deirdre	Byrne	IRL	21.9.82	28	May			
15:39.47	Rei	Ohara	JPN	10.8.90	19	Nov			
15:39.55	Birtukan	Fente	ETH	18.6.89	5	Jun			
15:39.59	Suriya	Loganathan	IND	7.7.90	28	Jun			
15:39.59	Natalya	Vlasova	RUS	19.7.88	21	Jul			
15:39.66	Rika	Kaseda	JPN-Y	2.3.99	3	Jul			
15:39.68	Meskerem	Amare	ETH-J	.97	30	Jun			
15:39.70	Sakiho	Tsutsui	JPN	19.1.96	11	Jul			
15:39.8A	Jackline	Chepngeno	KEN	16.1.93	16	May			
15:40.0A	Joyciline	Jepkosgei	KEN	8.12.93	27	Apr			
15:40.03	Sabrina	Mockenhaupt	GER	6.12.80	14	May			
15:40.15	Camille	Buscomb	NZL	11.7.90	22	May			
15:40.33		Ding Changqin	CHN	27.11.91	16	Sep			
15:40.57	Chiaki	Morikawa	JPN	22.9.87	3	Dec			
15:40.92	Simona	Vrzalová	CZE	7.4.88	3	Jun			
15:41.19		Li Zhixuan	CHN	23.3.94	6	May			
15:41.24mx	Jennifer	Wenth	AUT	24.7.91	1	Jun			
15:41.35	Erin	Teschuk	CAN	25.10.94	15	Apr			
15:41.47	Dominika	Napieraj	POL	12.12.91	5	Jun			
15:41.62	Alina	Reh	GER-J	23.5.97	23	Jul			
15:41.64	Vanessa	Fraser	USA	27.7.95	1	May			
15:41.94	Louise	Small	GBR	27.3.92	28	May			
15:42.0A	Sheila	Chelangat	KEN-J	11.4.98	28	May			
15:42.23		Xu Qiuzi	CHN	4.9.91	15	Apr			
15:42.23	Ririka	Hironaka	JPN-Y	24.11.00	22	Oct			
15:42.29	Sakie	Arai	JPN	3.6.94	7	May			
15:42.59	Katja	Goldring	USA	11.8.90	23	Jun			
15:43.49	Monica (200)	Margaret	KEN-J	.98	3	Dec			

Indoors

Mark	Name		Nat	Born	Pos	Meet	Venue	Date	
15:00.91	Emily	Infeld	USA	21.3.90	3	Mill	New York (A)	20	Feb
15:06.05	Marielle	Hall	USA	28.1.92	4	Mill	New York (A)	20	Feb
15:09.31	Kim	Conley	USA	14.3.86	1		Seattle	29	Jan
15:15.21	Molly	Seidel	USA	12.7.94	1	NCAA	Birmingham, AL	11	Mar
15:19.27	Meryem	Akdag	TUR	5.8.92	2	NC	Istanbul	20	Feb
15:21.85	Allie	Ostrander	USA	24.12.96	2		Seattle	29	Jan
15:23.16	Erin	Finn	USA	19.11.94	2	NCAA	Birmingham, AL	11	Mar
15:28.95	Yelena	Sedova	RUS	1.3.90	25	Feb			
15:32.03	Anna	Rohrer	USA-J	27.2.98	26	Feb			
15:36.73	Chelsea	Sodaro	USA	9.5.89	20	Feb			
15:37.40	Karissa	Schweizer	USA	4.5.96	3	Dec			
15:42.07	Chelsea	Blaase	USA	10.4.94	11	Mar			

JUNIORS

See main list for top 8 juniors. 11 performances by 6 women to 15:26.0. Additional marks and further juniors:

Gidey	14:58.44	1	FBK	Hengelo	22 May	15:20.84	3	Kortrijk	9 Jul
	15:09.45	14	GGala	Roma	2 Jun				
Bulo	15:18.54	1		Nobeoka	7 May	15:21.09	1	Yamaguchi	10 Dec
15:29.32	Shuri	Ogasawara	JPN-Y	3.10.00	9		Yokohama	3 Dec
15:29.64	Kalkidan	Fenite (10)	ETH	9.5.98	1	WJ	Bydgoszcz	23 Jul
15:31.12	Imaculata	Chepkurui	KEN-Y	3.8.00	2	WJ	Bydgoszcz	23 Jul
15:31.62	Miki	Moribayashi	JPN-Y	5.9.99	10		Yokohama	3 Dec
15:33.08	Harumi	Okamoto	JPN	7.2.98	2		Abashiri	11 Jul

WOMEN 2016

5000 – 10,000 METRES

Mark	Name		Nat	Born	Pos	Meet	Venue	Date	
15:33.95	Natsuki	Sekiya	JPN	.97	3		Abashiri	11	Jul
15:34.09	Mercyline	Chelangat	UGA	17.12.97	4	WJ	Bydgoszcz	23	Jul
15:34.37	Yitayish	Mekonene	ETH-Y	17.3.00	5	WJ	Bydgoszcz	23	Jul
15:35.72	Nozomi	Tanaka	JPN-Y	4.9.99	1		Fukuroi	20	Nov
15:36.27	Mina	Ueda	JPN	11.2.97	13		Yokohama	3	Dec
15:37.79	Catherine	Syokau	KEN-Y	20.8.99	6	WJ	Bydgoszcz	23	Jul
15:39.66	Rika	Kaseda (20)	JPN-Y	2.3.99	8	WJ	Bydgoszcz	23	Jul
15:39.68	Meskerem	Amare	ETH	.97	6		Barcelona (S)	30	Jun
15:32.03i	Anna	Rohrer	USA	27.2.98	2		Boston (R)	26	Feb

10,000 METRES

Mark	Name		Nat	Born	Pos	Meet	Venue	Date	
29:17.45	Almaz	Ayana	ETH	21.11.91	1	OG	Rio de Janeiro	12	Aug
29:32.53	Vivian	Cheruiyot	KEN	11.9.83	2	OG	Rio de Janeiro	12	Aug
29:42.56	Tirunesh	Dibaba	ETH	1.10.85	3	OG	Rio de Janeiro	12	Aug
29:53.51	Alice Aprot	Nawowuna	KEN	2.1.94	4	OG	Rio de Janeiro	12	Aug
30:07.00		Ayana			1	OT	Hengelo	29	Jun
30:07.78	Betsy	Saina	KEN	30.6.88	5	OG	Rio de Janeiro	12	Aug
30:13.17	Molly	Huddle	USA	31.8.84	6	OG	Rio de Janeiro	12	Aug
30:26.41	Yasemin	Can	TUR	11.12.96	7	OG	Rio de Janeiro	12	Aug
30:26.66	Gelete	Burka	ETH	23.1.86	8	OG	Rio de Janeiro	12	Aug
30:26.94		Nawowuna			1	AfCh	Durban	25	Jun
30:28.47		Burka			2	OT	Hengelo	29	Jun
30:28.53		T Dibaba			3	OT	Hengelo	29	Jun
30:36.75	Netsanet	Gudeta	ETH	12.2.91	4	OT	Hengelo	29	Jun
30:37.38	Genet	Yalew (10)	ETH	31.12.92	5	OT	Hengelo	29	Jun
30:40.59	Senbere	Teferi	ETH	3.5.95	6	OT	Hengelo	29	Jun
30:50.25	Belaynesh	Oljira	ETH	26.6.90	7	OT	Hengelo	29	Jun
30:54.12	Yeshaneh	Ababel	ETH	10.6.90	8	OT	Hengelo	29	Jun
30:54.61	Tadelech	Bekele	ETH	11.4.91	9	OT	Hengelo	29	Jun
30:56.26		Gudeta			1		Herzogenaurach	13	May
30:56.26		G Yalew			2		Herzogenaurach	13	May
31:04.59		Oljira			1		Dubai	23	Apr
31:10.25	Alia Mohammed	Saeed	UAE	18.5.91	2		Dubai	23	Apr
31:12.86		Can			1	EC	Amsterdam	6	Jul
31:14.07	Karoline Bjerkeli	Grøvdal	NOR	14.6.90	9	OG	Rio de Janeiro	12	Aug
31:14.52	Goytatom	Gebreselassie	ETH	15.1.95	10	OT	Hengelo	29	Jun
31:14.94	Eloise	Wellings	AUS	9.11.82	10	OG	Rio de Janeiro	12	Aug
31:15.38	Irene	Cheptai	KEN	4.2.92	1	Jordan	Stanford	1	May
31:16.38	Caroline	Kipkirui	KEN	26.5.94	2	Jordan	Stanford	1	May
31:18.16	Ayuko	Suzuki (20)	JPN	8.10.91	3	Jordan	Stanford	1	May
31:18.73		Suzuki			1	NC	Nagoya	24	Jun
	(30/21)								
31:19.03	Dulce	Félix	POR	23.10.82	2	EC	Amsterdam	6	Jul
31:22.92	Hanami	Sekine	JPN	26.2.96	2	NC	Nagoya	24	Jun
31:26.94	Emily	Infeld	USA	21.3.90	11	OG	Rio de Janeiro	12	Aug
31:27.73	Jackline	Chepngeno	KEN	16.1.93	2	AfCh	Durban	25	Jun
31:28.28	Joyciline	Jepkosgei	KEN	8.12.93	3	AfCh	Durban	25	Jun
31:28.43	Sarah	Lahti	SWE	18.2.95	12	OG	Rio de Janeiro	12	Aug
31:28.69	Diane	Nukuri	BDI	1.12.84	13	OG	Rio de Janeiro	12	Aug
31:30.74	Fionnuala	McCormack	IRL	24.9.84	4	EC	Amsterdam	6	Jul
31:32.43	Susan	Kuijken	NED	8.7.86	14	OG	Rio de Janeiro	12	Aug
	(30)								
31:33.44	Jo	Pavey	GBR	20.9.73	15	OG	Rio de Janeiro	12	Aug
31:35.76	Yuka	Takashima	JPN	12.5.88	3	NC	Nagoya	24	Jun
31:35.92	Jessica	Andrews	GBR	1.10.92	16	OG	Rio de Janeiro	12	Aug
31:36.16	Alexi	Páppas	GRE	28.3.90	17	OG	Rio de Janeiro	12	Aug
31:36.90	Darya	Maslova	KGZ	6.5.95	19	OG	Rio de Janeiro	12	Aug
31:37.43	Veronica	Inglese	ITA	22.11.90	6	EC	Amsterdam	6	Jul
31:37.45	Marielle	Hall	USA	28.1.92	4	Jordan	Stanford	1	May
31:37.99	Juliet	Chekwel	UGA	25.5.90	1		Rubiera	24	Apr
31:38.61	Buze	Diriba	ETH	9.2.94	6	Jordan	Stanford	1	May
31:38.80	Miyuki	Uehara	JPN	22.11.95	7	Jordan	Stanford	1	May
	(40)								
31:40.70	Kellyn	Taylor	USA	22.7.86	8	Jordan	Stanford	1	May
31:42.9mx	Johanna	Peiponen	FIN	18.12.90	1		Kempele	21	May
31:43.79	Liz	Costello	USA	23.2.88	10	Jordan	Stanford	1	May
31:45.82	Salomé	Nyirarukundo	RWA-J	20.12.97	4	AfCh	Durban	25	Jun
31:48.24	Hisami	Ishii	JPN	10.8.95	1		Abashiri	11	Jul
31:51.47	Dominique	Scott	RSA	24.6.92	21	OG	Rio de Janeiro	12	Aug

10,000 METRES

Mark	Name		Nat	Born	Pos	Meet	Venue	Date	
31:51.84	Erin	Finn	USA	19.11.94	13	Jordan	Stanford	1	May
31:52.94	Laura	Thweatt	USA	17.12.88	1		Stanford	1	Apr
31:53.14	Natasha	Wodak	CAN	17.12.81	22	OG	Rio de Janeiro	12	Aug
31:54.20	Aliphine	Bolton	KEN	5.4.89	2		Stanford	1	Apr
(50)									
31:55.26	Riko	Matsuzaki	JPN	24.12.92	14	Jordan	Stanford	1	May
31:56.70	Pauline	Kamulu	KEN	16.4.95	1		Fukagawa	7	Jul
31:57.77	Sitora	Khamidova	UZB	12.5.89	24	OG	Rio de Janeiro	12	Aug
31:57.92	Moeno	Nakamura	JPN	21.3.90	2		Abashiri	11	Jul
31:58.33	Jordan	Hasay	USA	21.9.91	17	Jordan	Stanford	1	May
31:58.46	Yuki	Munehisa	JPN-J	15.12.97	3		Abashiri	11	Jul
31:58.71	Yuka	Ando	JPN	16.3.94	4		Abashiri	11	Jul
31:59.12	Mizuki	Matsuda	JPN	31.5.95	1		Osaka	23	Sep
31:59.23	Alia	Gray	USA	12.11.88	18	Jordan	Stanford	1	May
31:59.72	Misaki	Kato	JPN	15.6.91	2		Osaka	23	Sep
(60)									
32:02.48	Linet	Masai	KEN	5.12.89	2		London (PH)	21	May
32:02.80	Tara	Welling	USA	14.6.89	3		Stanford	1	Apr
32:03.45	Beth	Potter	GBR	27.12.91	4		Stanford	1	Apr
32:04.00	Jip	Vastenburg	NED	21.3.94	8	EC	Amsterdam	6	Jul
32:04.11	Felista	Wanjugu	KEN	18.2.90	1		Kumagaya	21	May
32:04.21	Lanni	Marchant	CAN	11.4.84	25	OG	Rio de Janeiro	12	Aug
32:05.05	Mao	Kiyota	JPN	12.9.93	5		Abashiri	11	Jul
32:05.82	Carla Salomé	Rocha	POR	25.4.90	4		London (PH)	21	May
32:06.23	Clémence	Calvin	FRA	17.5.90	19	Jordan	Stanford	1	May
32:06.82	Natosha	Rogers	USA	7.5.91	1		Portland	11	Jun
(70)									
32:07.56	Ai	Inoue	JPN	13.1.90	6		Abashiri	11	Jul
32:07.77	Kasumi	Nishihara	JPN	1.3.89	20	Jordan	Stanford	1	May
32:08.02	Sule	Utura	ETH	8.2.90	11	OT	Hengelo	29	Jun
32:08.32	Courtney	Smith	USA	1.5.96	6		Stanford	1	Apr
32:08.39	Chelsea	Blaase	USA	10.4.94	7		Stanford	1	Apr
32:09.14	Tatiele	de Carvalho	BRA	22.11.89	2		Portland	11	Jun
32:09.67	Trihas	Gebre	ESP	29.4.90	29	OG	Rio de Janeiro	12	Aug
32:10.99	Inés	Melchor	PER	30.8.86	22	Jordan	Stanford	1	May
32:11.04	Margarita	Hernández	MEX	3.12.85	2rB	Jordan	Stanford	1	May
32:11.84	Kate	Avery	GBR	10.10.91	5	2 UK Ch	London (PH)	21	May
(80)									
32:12.70	Alla	Kulyatina	RUS	9.6.90	1	NC	Cheboksary	22	Jun
32:13.03	Sara	Slattery	USA	2.10.81	3rB	Jordan	Stanford	1	May
32:13.17	Marisol	Romero	MEX	26.11.83	23	Jordan	Stanford	1	May
32:13.44	Yelena	Sedova	RUS	1.3.90	2	NC	Cheboksary	22	Jun
32:14.25	Shure	Demise	ETH	21.1.96	5	AfCh	Durban	25	Jun
32:14.40	Kanayo	Miyata	JPN	12.10.90	1		Yamaguchi	10	Dec
32:14.42	Stephanie	Bruce	USA	14.1.84	8		Stanford	1	Apr
32:14.43	Yelena	Nagovitsyna	RUS	7.12.82	3	NC	Cheboksary	22	Jun
32:15.40		Liu Ruihuan	CHN	29.6.92	1	NGP	Zhengzhou	14	May
32:15.53	Elizeba	Cherono	NED	6.6.88	12	OT	Hengelo	29	Jun
(90)									
32:15.73	Mao	Ichiyama	JPN-J	29.5.97	2		Yamaguchi	10	Dec
32:16.03	Sarah	Pagano	USA	23.7.91	3		Portland	11	Jun
32:17.35A	Gladys	Chesire	KEN	20.2.93	3	OT	Eldoret	30	Jun
32:17.38	Yenenesh	Tilahun	ETH	.94	6	AfCh	Durban	25	Jun
32:17.66	Yuko	Kikuchi	JPN	8.6.92	3		Yamaguchi	10	Dec
32:18.14	Mizuki	Tanimoto	JPN	18.12.94	4		Yamaguchi	10	Dec
32:19.15	Krisztina	Papp	HUN	17.12.82	2		Maia	9	Apr
32:20.94	Shiho	Takechi	JPN	18.8.90	8	NC	Nagoya	24	Jun
32:21.20	Risa	Kikuchi	JPN	5.2.90	7		Abashiri	11	Jul
32:21.98	Rachel	Cliff	CAN	1.4.88	4		Portland	11	Jun
(100)									

32:22.94	Miho	Shimizu	JPN	13.5.90	10 Dec	32:27.51	Rei	Ohara	JPN	10.8.90	24 Apr
32:23.85	Natsuko	Goto	JPN	4.8.87	11 Jul	32:28.60	Reia	Iwade	JPN	8.12.94	11 Jul
32:24.07	Yuka	Miyazaki	JPN	21.8.92	1 May	32:28.77	Kaho	Tanaka	JPN	24.6.91	24 Apr
32:24.73	Carolina	Tabares	COL	18.7.86	1 May	32:28.78	Wakaba	Kawakami	JPN	28.4.96	23 Sep
32:24.87	Risa	Yokoe	JPN	12.10.94	24 Apr	32:30.71	Jéssica	Augusto	POR	8.11.81	22 Jun
32:25.18A	Cynthia	Limo	KEN	18.12.89	30 Jun	32:30.83	Gulshat	Fazlitdinova	RUS	28.8.92	22 Jun
32:25.33	Doricah	Obare	KEN	10.1.90	21 May	32:31.18	Catarina	Ribeiro	POR	31.5.90	22 Jun
32:26.84	Yukari	Abe	JPN	21.8.89	24 Apr	32:31.32	Mary	Davies	NZL	27.8.82	11 Jun
32:26.99	Ai	Hosoda	JPN	27.11.95	11 Jul	32:31.92	Grace	Kimanzi	KEN	1.3.92	23 Sep
32:27.01	Lindsey	Scherf	USA	18.9.86	11 Jun	32:32.05	Rochelle	Kanuho	USA	4.7.90	2 Jul
32:27.22	Yukari	Ishizawa	JPN	16.4.88	11 Jul	32:32.85	Becky	Wade	USA	9.2.89	1 May
32:27.28	Elaina	Balouris	USA	17.12.91	11 Jun	32:34.41	Camille	Buscomb	NZL	11.7.90	8 Dec

10,000 METRES – 10 KILOMETRES ROAD

Mark	Name		Nat	Born	Pos	Meet	Venue		Date
32:34.97	Lily	Partridge	GBR	9.3.91	9		Apr		
32:36.11	Alice	Wright	GBR	3.11.94	1		May		
32:36.66	Ai	Utsunomiya	JPN	19.9.95	11		Jul		
32:37.11A	Sally	Kipyego	KEN	19.12.85	30		Jun		
32:38.29	Saki	Fukui	JPN	25.3.96	26		Nov		
32:39.08	Brenda	Flores	MEX	4.9.91	12		Aug		
32:39.18	Maki	Izumida	JPN	22.1.96	26		Nov		
32:39.48A	Beatrice	Mutai	KEN	19.4.87	30		Jun		
32:39.86	Suriya	Loganathan	IND	7.7.90	11		Feb		
32:40.28	Kanna	Tamaki	JPN	7.10.96	26		Nov		
32:40.57	Yuri	Karasawa	JPN	25.11.95	26		Nov		
32:40.79	Kureha	Seki	JPN	15.9.96	26		Nov		
32:40.80	Sabrina	Mockenhaupt	GER	6.12.80	7		May		
32:43.38	Christelle	Daunay	FRA	5.12.74	27		Apr		
32:43.42	Honami	Maeda	JPN	17.7.96	11		Jul		
32:44.48	Sara	Hall	USA	15.4.83	11		Jun		
32:44.64	Misaki	Hayashida	JPN	31.1.96	23		Sep		
32:46.02	Hanae	Tanaka	JPN	12.2.90	24		Jun		
32:46.93	Hiroko	Miyauchi	JPN	19.6.83	10		Dec		
32:47.25	Hannah	Everson	USA	21.4.94	9		Jun		
32:47.30	Lauren	LaRocco	USA	.96	9		Jun		
32:47.74	Yukari	Wada	JPN	20.7.95	26		Nov		
32:49.18	Maho	Shimizu	JPN	.95	26		Nov		
32:49.19	Mariam	Waithera	KEN	23.12.96	21		May		
32:49.43	Sharon	Lokedi	KEN		9		Jun		
32:51.05	Lyudmila	Lebedeva	RUS	23.5.90	22		Jun		
32:52.13	Eri	Hayakawa	JPN	15.11.81	23		Sep		
32:52.23	Nami	Hashimoto	JPN	8.8.91	23		Sep		
32:52.75	Saori	Noda	JPN	30.3.93	24		Apr		
32:52.92	Tara	Jameson	IRL	19.9.91	4		Jun		
32:53.04mx	Virginia	Moloney	AUS	6.5.90	17		Dec		
32:53.41	Saori	Imamura	JPN	24.3.96	26		Nov		
32:53.73	Swati	Gadhave	IND	1.6.90	30		Apr		
32:53.91	Ayano	Ikemitsu	JPN	18.4.91	23		Sep		
32:54.07	Emily	Sisson	USA	12.10.91	2		Jul		
32:54.36	Yuki	Mitsunobu	JPN	9.11.92	10		Dec		
32:54.41	Anna	Matsuda	JPN	18.4.94	11		Jul		
32:55.21	Kaitlin	Goodman	USA	31.1.87	?		Jul		
32:55.97	Nanako	Kanno	JPN	30.12.94	24		Apr		
32:56.19	Risa	Taguchi	JPN	15.3.95	21		May		
32:56.43	Eri	Makikawa	JPN	22.4.93	24		Apr		
32:56.66				Zheng Zhiling	CHN	25.12.96	7		May
32:56.78	Kana	Furuya	JPN	.96	11		Jul		
32:57.76	Kikuyo	Tsuzaki	JPN	27.8.89	11		Jul		
32:57.87	Asami	Furuse	JPN	17.3.88	23		Sep		
32:57.99	Mari	Ozaki	JPN	16.7.75	11		Jul		
32:58.28	Nazret	Weldu	ERI	1.1.90	29		Jun		
32:58.70	Yoko	Miyauchi	JPN	19.6.83	10		Dec		
32:58.78	Brenna	Peloquin	USA	2.9.96	9		Jun		
32:59.30	Sakie	Arai	JPN	3.6.94	26		Nov		
32:59.52	Asami	Kato	JPN	12.10.90	10		Dec		
32:59.91	Moeno	Shimizu	JPN-J	20.3.97	26		Nov		
33:00.13	Elinor	Kirk	GBR	26.4.89	11		Jun		
33:00.14	Akane	Fujiwara	JPN	.96	26		Nov		
33:00.27	Sakura	Kawakami	JPN	28.4.96	10		Dec		
33:00.31	Erika	Ikeda	JPN	10.6.91	10		Dec		
33:00.44	Agnieszka	Mierzejewska	POL	22.10.85	11		Jun		
33:01.81	Rina	Yamazaki	JPN	6.5.88	24		Jun		
33:02.15	Reno	Okura	JPN	14.12.95	10		Dec		
33:02.65	Susan	Wairimu	KEN	11.10.92	7		Jul		
33:02.78	Katja	Goldring	USA	11.8.90	11		Jun		
33:02.90	Sarah	Pease	USA	9.11.87	1		Apr		
33:02.94	Mai	Ito	JPN	23.5.84	20		May		
33:03.18	Misato	Horie	JPN	10.3.87	23		Sep		
33:03.35	Kristen	Heckert	USA	11.11.86	12		May		
33:03.93	Suzuna	Seiyama	JPN	19.9.94	2		Sep		
33:04.10	Angela	Bizzarri	USA	15.2.88	1		May		
33:04.20	Yomogi	Akasaka	JPN	.95	10		Dec		
33:04.27	Mami	Onuki	JPN	9.10.91	11		Jul		
33:04.29	Meghan	Peyton	USA	6.1.86	11		Jun		
33:04.40	Miharu	Shimokado	JPN	24.4.90	7		Jul		
33:04.72	Bridey	Delaney	AUS	16.7.89	8		Dec		
33:05.31	Katy	Moen	USA	20.4.92	1		May		
33:05.49	Rachel	Hannah	CAN	2.10.86	25		Jun		
33:05.55	Lauren	Deadman	GBR	27.3.84	21		May		
(200)									

JUNIORS
See main list for top 3 juniors. 7 performances by 4 women to 33:08.0. Additional marks and further juniors:

Nyirarukundo	32:07.80	27	OG	Rio de Janeiro	12 Aug				
Munehisa	33:06.18	2		Kumagaya	2 Sep				
Shimizu	33:00.02	21		Abashiri	11 Jul				
32:59.91	Moeno	Shimizu	JPN	20.3.97	10		Yokohama	26	Nov
33:09.72	Natsuki	Sekiya	JPN	.97	12r2		Yokohama	26	Nov
33:24.37	Kasumi	Yamguchi	JPN	.97	14r2		Yokohama	26	Nov
33:28.22	Sachiho	Suzuki	JPN	.97	15r2		Yokohama	26	Nov

10 KILOMETRES ROAD

Mark		Name		Nat	Born	Pos		Venue		Date
30:24		Violah	Jepchumba	KEN	23.10.90	1		Praha	10	Sep
30:29+			Jepchumba			1	in HMar	Praha	2	Apr
30:34+		Worknesh	Degefa	ETH	28.10.90	2	in HMar	Praha	2	Apr
30:45		Mary	Keitany	KEN	18.1.82	1		Cape Elizabeth	6	Aug
30:52		Shalane	Flanagan	USA	8.7.81	1		Boston	26	Jun
30:55+			Jepchumba			1	in HMar	Valencia	23	Oct
31:01+		Peres	Jepchirchir	KEN	27.9.93	2	in HMar	Valencia	23	Oct
31:04+			Jepchumba			1	in HMar	Göteborg	21	May
31:06		Edna	Kiplagat	KEN	15.11.79	2		Boston	26	Jun
31:07		Edith	Chelimo	KEN	16.7.86	1		Brunssum	3	Apr
31:08		Joyciline	Jepkosgei	KEN	8.12.93	2		Praha	10	Sep
31:14		Viola	Kibiwot	KEN	22.12.83	1		Houilles	18	Dec
31:16		Tirunesh	Dibaba	ETH	1.10.85	1		Manchester	22	May
Where better than 10,000m track times										
31:26		Jemima	Sumgong	KEN	21.12.84	1		New York	11	Jun
31:26+		Angela	Tanui	KEN	27.7.92		in HMar	Göteborg	21	May
31:31		Amy	Cragg	USA	21.1.84	3		Boston	26	Jun
31:32 +		Gladys	Cherono	KEN	12.5.83		in HMar	Ra's Al-Khaymah	12	Feb
31:32+		Gladys	Chesire	KEN	20.2.93		in HMar	Ra's Al-Khaymah	12	Feb
31:32+		Cynthia	Limo	KEN	18.12.89		in HMar	Ra's Al-Khaymah	12	Feb
31:33+		Rose	Chelimo	BRN	12.7.89		in HMar	Ra's Al-Khaymah	12	Feb
31:34 +		Priscah	Jeptoo	KEN	26.6.84		in HMar	Ra's Al-Khaymah	12	Feb
31:37+		Lucy	Cheruiyot	KEN-J	4.1.97		in HMar	Ústí nad Labem	17	Sep
31:38+		Mercy Wacera	Ngugi	KEN	17.12.88		in HMar	Houston	17	Jan
31:38+		Mare	Dibaba	ETH	20.10.89		in HMar	Houston	17	Jan

10 KILOMETRES ROAD

Mark	Name		Nat	Born	Pos	Meet	Venue	Date	
31:38+	Afera	Godfay	ETH	25.9.91	3	in HMar	Ústí nad Labem	17	Sep
31:39+	Ruti	Aga	ETH	16.1.94		in HMar	Houston	17	Jan
31:40	Wude	Ayalew	ETH	4.7.87	2		Cape Elizabeth	6	Aug
31:41+	Gladys	Chesire	KEN	20.2.93		in HMar	København	18	Sep
31:41+	Eunice	Chumba	BRN	23.5.93		in HMar	København	18	Sep
31:41+	Veronica	Nyaruai	KEN	29.10.89		in HMar	København	18	Sep
31:42+	Hiwot	Gebrekidan	ETH	11.5.95		in HMar	København	18	Sep
31:44+	Birhane	Dibaba	ETH	11.9.93		in HMar	Yangzhou	24	Apr
31:46+	Gulume	Tollesa	ETH	11.9.92		in HMar	Ra's Al-Khaymah	12	Feb
31:46+	Pascalia	Kipkoech	KEN	22.12.88		in HMar	Yangzhou	24	Apr
31:47	Emily	Sisson	USA	12.10.91	1		Boston	10	Oct
31:47	Katrina	Wootton	GBR	2.9.85	2		Houilles	18	Dec
31:49	Mercy	Ngugi	KEN	17.12.88	1		San Juan	28	Feb
31:51+	Eunice	Jepkirui Kirwa	BRN	20.5.84			Marugame	7	Feb
31:52+	Gladys	Yator	KEN	8.8.92		in HMar	Praha	2	Apr
31:52	Antonina	Kwambai	KEN	.92	1		Hamburg	11	Sep
31:56	Linet	Masai	KEN	5.12.89	4		San Juan	28	Feb
31:57	Naomi	Rotich	KEN	.94	2		Hamburg	11	Sep
31:58	Monicah	Wanjuhi	KEN	7.11.93	5		San Juan	28	Feb
31:58	Gladys	Cherono	KEN	12.5.83	4		Praha	10	Sep
32:04	Rosemary	Wanjiru	KEN	9.12.94	1		Okayama	23	Dec
32:07	Elizeba	Cherono	NED	6.6.88	1		Utrecht	2	Oct
32:08	Mamitu	Daska	ETH	16.10.83	2		Ottawa	28	May
32:09+	Magdalene	Masai	KEN	4.4.93		in HMar	Ostia	13	Mar
32:10+	Lucy	Karimi	KEN	9.10.86		in HMar	Praha	2	Apr
32:10+	Isabella	Ochichi	KEN	28.10.79		in HMar	Praha	2	Apr
32:10	Carolyne	Jepkosgei	KEN	.91	2		Utrecht	2	Oct
32:11	Lineth	Chepkurui	KEN	23.2.88	6		San Juan	28	Feb
32:12	Veronicah	Maina	KEN	8.8.89	2		Edinburg, TX	6	Feb
32:12+	Peninah	Arusei	KEN	23.2.79		in HMar	Ostia	13	Mar
32:12+	Parendis	Lekapana	KEN	4.8.91		in HMar	Yangzhou	24	Apr
32:12	Nancy	Nzisa	KEN	29.12.95	5		Boston	26	Jun
32:13+	Rebecca	Kangogo Chesir	KEN	.92			Gifu	15	May
32:14	Risper	Gesabwa	KEN	10.2.89	3		Edinburg, TX	6	Feb
32:14+	Marta	Lema	ETH	30.12.90		in HMar	Ostia	13	Mar
32:14	Biruktayit	Degefa	ETH	29.9.90	3		Mobile	20	Mar
32:15	Maryanne	Wanjiru	KEN	86	2		Brunssum	3	Apr
32:16A	Sheila	Chepkurui	KEN	27.12.90	1		Kericho	17	Sep
32:18+	Filomena	Cheyech	KEN	5.7.82		in HMar	Cardiff	2	Oct
32:19	Pascalia	Kipkoech	KEN	22.12.88	2		Ziwa	10	Dec
32:20	Tejitu	Daba	BRN	20.8.91	1		Hem	28	Aug
32:21A	Fancy	Chemutai	KEN		2		Kericho	17	Sep
32:21	Grace	Kimanzi	KEN	1.3.92	2		Okayama	23	Dec
32:22	Dominika	Napieraj	POL	12.12.91	22 May	32:40+	Bizuneh Deba	ETH 8.9.87	17 Jan
32:23+	Emmaculate	Jebet	KEN	.92	13 Mar	32:40	Magdalina Crispin	TAN	16 Oct
32:23	Christelle	Daunay	FRA	5.12.74	22 May	32:41	Susan Jerotich	KEN .87	20 Mar
32:23	Mary	Wangari	KEN	4.10.86	11 Sep	32:41	Kimberley Smith	NZL 19.11.81	11 Jun
32:24	Konstanze	Klosterhalfen	GER-J	18.2.97	6 Mar	32:42	Viola Jelagat	KEN 20.4.92	11 Sep
32:27+	Risper	Chebet	KEN	6.6.92	2 Apr	32:43+	Dehininet Demsew	ETH 15.9.84	26 Mar
32:27	Florence	Kiplagat	KEN	27.2.87	4 Sep	32:43	Gemma Steel	GBR 12.11.85	22 May
32:28	Helah	Kiprop	KEN	7.4.85	15 May	32:44	Helaria Johannes	NAM 13.8.80	18 Sep
32:29+	Pauline Wanjiku	Njeru	KEN	.88	24 Jan	32:45	Susan Jeptoo	KEN 7.3.87	26 Mar
32:29	Sylvia	Kiberenge	KEN	.90	12 Mar	32:45	Joan Aiyabei	KEN 17.5.79	2 Oct
32:29+	Ashete	Bekele	ETH	17.4.88	21 May	32:47	Beata Naigambo	NAM 11.3.80	14 Feb
32:30	Dibabe	Kuma	ETH	14.9.96	25 Jun	32:47	Simone Glad	DEN 12.8.90	12 Mar
32:30	Chaltu	Bedo Dida	ETH	.94	14 Jul	32:47	Faith Chepkoech	KEN .93	19 Mar
32:31+	Gebeyanesh	Ayele	ETH	1.5.95	20 Nov	32:47	Yeshi Chekole	ERI	18 Jun
32:32+	Bornes	Kitur	KEN	.88	18 Sep	32:47A	Pamela Cherotich	KEN .86	17 Sep
32:32+	Desi	Jisa Mokonin	BRN-J	12.7.97	18 Sep	32:48	Failuna Abdi Matanga	TAN 28.10.92	15 May
32:32+	Helen	Bekele Tola	ETH	21.11.94	18 Sep	32:48+	Damaris Areba	KEN 95	20 Nov
32:32	Eilish	McColgan	GBR	25.11.90	4 Dec	32:50	Etalemahu Habtewold	ETH .90	19 Mar
32:33+	Visiline	Jepkesho	KEN	30.12.89	3 Jan	32:50+	Gladys Tejeda	PER 30.9.85	26 Mar
32:33	Olga	Kimaiyo	KEN	24.7.88	6 Feb	32:51+	Mizuki Matsuda	JPN 31.5.95	26 Mar
32:33	Aselefech	Mergia	ETH	23.1.85	26 Jun	32:51	Makda Harun	ETH 5.9.88	2 Jun
32:34+	Guteni	Shone	ETH	17.11.91	18 Sep	32:51	Mary Wangechi	KEN .93	11 Sep
32:35	Elinor	Kirk	GBR	26.4.89	11 Dec	32:51	Belaynesh Zemedkun	ETH 23.12.87	24 Nov
32:36	Laura	Whittle	GBR	27.6.85	20 Mar	32:52	Edinah Koech	KEN	19 Mar
32:36A	Sheila	Chelangat	KEN-J	11.4.98	17 Sep	32:52	Joyce Chepkirui	KEN 20.8.88	20 Mar
32:37	Chaltu	Begassa	ETH	13.12.96	20 Mar	32:52	Dorcas Nzembi	KEN-J 22.12.97	26 Mar
32:37+	Linah	Cheruto	KEN	18.3.95	24 Apr	32:52	Fate Tola Geleto	ETH/GER 12.10.87	11 Jun
32:38+	Sara	Hall	USA	15.4.83	17 Jan	32:52	Lauren Paquette	USA 27.6.86	10 Oct
32:38+	Rael	Kguriatukei (Kiyara)	KEN	4.4.84	20 Mar	32:53	Esther Kakuri	KEN 26.10.94	15 May
32:38+	Amane	Gobena	ETH	1.9.82	24 Apr	32:55	Sheila Cherotich	KEN 89	18 Jun
32:38	Monica	Ngige	KEN		15 Oct	32:55+	Ivy Kibet	KEN 4.2.90	2 Oct

WOMEN 2016

450   10 – 15 – 20 KILOMETRES & 10 MILES ROAD

Mark	Name	Nat	Born	Pos Meet	Venue	Date
32:56+	Nancy Arusei	KEN	.86 25 Sep	33:00 Lavinia	Haitope	NAM 3.3.90 14 Feb
32:57	Webalem Ayele	ETH	.89 22 Oct	33:00 Azmera	Gebru	ETH 5.5.92 26 Jun
32:59	Jane Jelagat	KEN	25.11.83 15 May	33:00 Sentayehu	Ejigu	ETH 21.6.85 26 Jun
32:59A	Rena Chesser	USA	17.5.83 25 Jul	33:00 Winfridah	Moseti	KEN 12.11.96 18 Sep
32:59	Tabitha Wambui	KEN	29.12.83 18 Sep	33:00+ Meselech	Melkamu	ETH 27.4.85 18 Sep

Downhill 55m: Dec 13, Madrid: 1. Brigid Kosgei KEN .80 32:07, 2. Karolina Jarzynska POL 6.9.81 32:13, 3. Liv Westphal FRA 22.12.93 32:42
Downhill 86m: Nov 6, Morlaix: 1.Mekdes Woldu ERI 20.10.92 32:59
Probable short course: Mar 6, Casablanca: 1. Pascalia Kipkoech KEN 31:14, 2. Bezunesh Getachew ETH-J 31:21, 3. Meraf Bahta SWE 31:26. 4, Hajiba El Hasnaoui MAR 31:27, 5. Souad Aït Salem MAR 31:53, 6. Kaltoum Bouaasayriya MAR 32:07, 7. Souad Kanbouchia MAR 32:14
Drugs disqualification: 32:17 Mailika Asahssah MAR (1) San Sebastián 10 Jan

JUNIORS

Mark	Name		Nat	Born	Pos Meet	Venue	Date
31:37+	Lucy	Cheruiyot	KEN-J	4.1.97	in HMar	Ústí nad Labem	17 Sep
32:24	Konstanze	Klosterhalfen	GER-J	18.2.97 1		Leverkusen	6 Mar
32:32+	Desi	Jisa Mokonin	BRN-J	12.7.97	in HMar	København	18 Sep
32:36A	Sheila	Chelangat	KEN-J	11.4.98 3		Kericho	17 Sep
32:52	Dorcas	Nzembi	KEN-J	22.12.97 3		Paderborn	26 Mar

15 KILOMETRES ROAD

Mark	Name			Nat	Born	Pos Meet	Venue	Date
47:20+			Jepchumba			1 in HMar	Valencia	23 Oct
47:22+			Jepchumba			1 in HMar	Göteborg	21 May
48:37		Eunice	Jepkirui	BRN	20.5.84 1		's-Heerenberg	4 Dec
48:40		Yasemin	Can	TUR	1.8.92 1		Istanbul	13 Nov
48:50		Cynthia	Limo	KEN	18.12.89 1		Utica	11 Jul
48:54		Edna	Kiplagat	KEN	15.11.79 2		's-Heerenberg	4 Dec
48:57+		Diane	Nukuri	BDI	1.12.84	in HMar	New York	20 Mar
49:00		Gebeyanesh	Ayele	ETH	1.5.95 2		Istanbul	13 Nov
49:21+		Perendis	Lekepana	KEN	4.8.91	in HMar	Yangzhou	24 Apr
49:25		Veronica	Nyaruai	KEN	29.10.89 2		Utica	11 Jul
49:30+	Rebecca	Kangogo	KEN	.92 15 May	49:41+ Mizuki	Matsuda	JPN 31.5.95 26 Mar
49:30	Susan	Krumins	NED	8.7.86 20 Nov	49:46 Dibabe	Kuma	ETH 14.9.96 1 May
49:31+	Martha	Akeno	KEN	15.12.93 13 Mar	49:46 Muliye	Dekebo	ETH-J .98 1 May
49:31+	Emmaculate	Jebet	KEN	.23 13 Mar	49:51+ Miho	Shimizu	JPN 13.5.90 26 Mar
49:36	Maryanne	Wanjiru	KEN	.86 19 Mar	49:54 Mercy	Ngugi	KEN 17.12.88 11 Jul
49:40+	Yuka	Ando	JPN	16.3.94 26 Mar	49:56 Lucy	Murigi	KEN 7.7.85 19 Mar

10 MILES ROAD

10M	15k	Name		Nat	Born	Pos	Venue	Date
51:38		Buze	Diriba	ETH	9.2.94	1	Pittsburgh	6 Nov
51:49	48:30	Tirunesh	Dibaba	ETH	1.10.85	1	Portsmouth	23 Oct
51:59	48:23	Alice Aprot	Nawowuna	KEN	2.1.94	1	Zaandam	18 Sep
52:03		Emily	Sisson	USA	12.10.91	2	Pittsburgh	6 Nov
52:34	49:04	Tejitu	Daba	BRN	20.8.91	2	Zaandam	18 Sep
52:49		Jordan	Hasay	USA	21.9.91	1	St.Paul	9 Oct
52:51		Senbere	Teferi	ETH	3.5.95	1	Portsmouth	23 Oct
53:01		Aliphine	Bolton	USA	5.4.89	2	St.Paul	9 Oct
53:03	49:31	Lucy	Karimi	KEN	9.10.86	3	Zaandam	18 Sep
53:12		Veronica	Nyaruai	KEN	29.10.89	1	Washington DC	3 Apr
53:12	49:32	Meselech	Melkamu	ETH	27.4.85	4	Zaandam	18 Sep
53:13		Gwen	Jorgensen	USA	25.4.86	3	St.Paul	9 Oct
53:21		Jane	Kibii	KEN	10.3.85	1	Sacramento	3 Apr
53:26		Elizeba	Cherono	NED	6.6.88	5	Zaandam	18 Sep
53:33		Sara	Hall	USA	15.4.83	4	St.Paul	9 Oct

20 KILOMETRES ROAD

20k	15k	Name		Nat	Born	Pos Meet	Venue	Date
64:37+48:07		Priscah	Jeptoo	KEN	26.6.84	in HMar	Ra's Al-Khaymah	12 Feb
65:47		Aliphine	Bolton	USA	5.4.89 1		New Haven	5 Sep
66:03		Emily	Sisson	USA	12.10.91 2		New Haven	5 Sep
66:24		Etagegne	Woldu	ETH	10.5.96 1		Paris	9 Oct
66:24		Dera	Dida	ETH	26.10.96 2		Paris	9 Oct
66:31		Susan	Jeptoo	KEN	7.3.87 3		Paris	9 Oct
66:35		Beatrice	Cherono	KEN	.93 4		Paris	9 Oct
66:40+49:33		Pauline Wanjiku	Njeru	KEN	.88	in HMar	Santa Pola	24 Jan
66:47+		Florence	Kiplagat	KEN	27.2.87	in Mar	Chicago	9 Oct
66:48+		Valentine	Kipketer	KEN	5.1.93	in Mar	Chicago	9 Oct
67:00+		Dibaba	Kuma	ETH	14.9.96	in HMar	København	18 Sep
67:02		Joyciline	Jepkosgei	KEN	8.12.93 1		Cassis	30 Oct
67:05		Chaltu	Bedo Dida	ETH	.94 5		Paris	9 Oct
67:39		Nancy	Arusei	KEN	.86 6		Paris	9 Oct

HALF MARATHON 451

HALF MARATHON

Mark	20k	15k	Name		Nat	Born	Pos	Meet	Venue	Date
			Slightly downhill course: South Shields 30.5m							
65:51	62:24	46:21	Violah	Jepchumba	KEN	23.10.90	1		Praha	2 Apr
66:04	62:48	47:21	Cynthia	Limo	KEN	18.12.89	1		Ra's Al-Khaymah	12 Feb
66:07	62:49	47:22	Gladys	Cherono	KEN	12.5.83	2		Ra's Al-Khaymah	12 Feb
66:14	62:47	46:34	Worknesh	Degefa	ETH	28.10.90	2		Praha	2 Apr
66:26	62:57	47:22	Genet	Yalew	ETH	31.12.92	3		Ra's Al-Khaymah	12 Feb
66:29	63:09	47:24	Mercy Wacera	Ngugi	KEN	17.12.88	1		Houston	17 Jan
66:39	63:13	47:21	Peres	Jepchirchir	KEN	27.9.93	4		Ra's Al-Khaymah	12 Feb
66:41	63:15	47:24		Limo			2		Houston	17 Jan
66:57	63:29	47:22	Gladys	Chesire	KEN	20.2.93	5		Ra's Al-Khaymah	12 Feb
66:58	63:29	47:23	Jemima Jelagat	Sumgong	KEN	21.12.84	6		Ra's Al-Khaymah	12 Feb
67:08		47:57		Degefa			1		Ostia	13 Mar
67:09		46:59		Jepchirchir			1		Valencia	23 Oct
67:16		47:58	Angela	Tanui (10)	KEN	27.7.92	2		Ostia	13 Mar
67:21	63:57	47:27		Jepchirchir			1		Yangzhou	24 Apr
67:24		47:38		Jepchirchir			1		Ústí nad Labem	17 Sep
67:31		47:58	Magdalene	Masai	KEN	4.4.93	3		Ostia	13 Mar
67:31	64:13	48:14		Jepchirchir			1	WCh	Cardiff	26 Mar
67:32	63:57	47:22		Degefa			7		Ra's Al-Khaymah	12 Feb
67:34	64:13	48:14		Limo			2	WCh	Cardiff	26 Mar
67:41	64:06	48:19	Molly	Huddle	USA	31.8.84	1		New York	20 Mar
67:41		48:19	Joyce	Chepkirui	KEN	20.8.88	2		New York	20 Mar
67:42				Degefa			1		New Delhi	20 Nov
67:47	64:21	47:55	Birhane	Dibaba	ETH	11.9.93	2		Yangzhou	24 Apr
67:52			Yeshaneh	Ababel	ETH	10.6.90	2		New Delhi	20 Nov
67:52			Sarah	Chepchirchir	KEN	27.7.84	1		Haicang	10 Dec
67:54	64:19	48:15		Ngugi			3	WCh	Cardiff	26 Mar
67:54dh			Vivian	Cheruiyot	KEN	11.9.83	1	GNR	South Shields	11 Sep
67:55	64:23	47:47	Mare	Dibaba	ETH	20.10.89	3		Houston	17 Jan
67:55dh			Priscah	Jeptoo	KEN	26.6.84	2	GNR	South Shields	11 Sep
67:58		48:23	Marta	Lema (20)	ETH	30.12.90	4		Ostia	13 Mar
67:58	64:28	47:55	Pascalia	Kipkoech	KEN	22.12.88	3		Yangzhou	24 Apr
			(31/21)							
68:00	64:39	48:21	Hiwot	Gebrekidan	ETH	11.5.95	1		København	18 Sep
68:01	64:25	48:14	Netsanet	Gudeta	ETH	12.2.91	4	WCh	Cardiff	26 Mar
68:04dh			Tirunesh	Dibaba	ETH	1.10.85	3	GNR	South Shields	11 Sep
68:04	64:42	48:20	Eunice	Chumba	BRN	23.5.93	2		København	18 Sep
68:06	64:33	48:09	Eunice	Jepkirui Kirwa	BRN	20.5.84	1		Marugame	7 Feb
68:06	64:44	48:22	Veronica	Nyaruai	KEN	29.10.89	3		København	18 Sep
68:07	64:36	47:44	Ruti	Aga	ETH	16.1.94	4		Houston	17 Jan
68:08	64:37	48:05	Rose	Chelimo	BRN	12.7.89	9		Ra's Al-Khaymah	12 Feb
68:11			Helah	Kiprop	KEN	7.4.85	3		New Delhi	20 Nov
			(30)							
68:17		47:44	Lucy	Cheruiyot	KEN-J	4.1.97	2		Ústí nad Labem	17 Sep
68:32		47:52	Afera	Godfay	ETH	25.9.91	3		Ústí nad Labem	17 Sep
68:38			Diana Chemtai	Kipyokei	KEN	.94	2		Haicang	10 Dec
68:39	65:06	48:37	Gladys	Yator	KEN	8.8.92	3		Praha	2 Apr
68:40	65:13	48:24	Gulume	Tollesa	ETH	11.9.92	10		Ra's Al-Khaymah	12 Feb
68:43	65:14	48:49	Lucy	Karimi	KEN	9.10.86	4		Praha	2 Apr
68:53			Mary	Keitany	KEN	18.1.82	1		Olomouc	25 Jun
69:03	65:28	48:47	Isabella	Ochichi	KEN	28.10.79	5		Praha	2 Apr
69:05A			Valentine	Kipketer Jepkorir	KEN	5.1.93	1		Nairobi	6 Mar
69:07			Joyciline	Jepkosgei	KEN	8.12.93	1		Karlovy Vary	21 May
			(40)							
69:08	65:32	48:27	Tadelech	Bekele	ETH	11.4.91	11		Ra's Al-Khaymah	12 Feb
69:08		48:45	Peninah	Arusei	KEN	23.2.79	5		Ostia	13 Mar
69:16			Tigist	Jabore	ETH	.93	3		Haicang	10 Dec
69:19			Florence	Kiplagat	KEN	27.2.87	1		Barcelona	14 Feb
69:21			Dibaba	Kuma	ETH	14.9.96	1		Paris	6 Mar
69:23	65:46	48:58	Diane	Nukuri	BDI	1.12.84	2		Marugame	7 Feb
69:23	65:52		Wude	Ayalew	ETH	4.7.87	2		Lisboa	20 Mar
69:24	65:51	49:20	Risper	Chebet	KEN	6.6.92	6		Praha	2 Apr
69:27+	65:52	49:40	Aberu	Kebede	ETH	12.9.86	1	in Mar	Berlin	25 Sep
69:29	65:45	48:58	Eloise	Wellings	AUS	9.11.82	3		Marugame	7 Feb
			(50)							
69:32			Gelete	Burka	ETH	23.1.86	7		New Delhi	20 Nov
69:33	65:52		Linet	Masai	KEN	5.12.89	3		Lisboa	20 Mar
69:33			Valary	Aiyabei	KEN	8.6.91	2		Zwolle	11 Jun
69:39	66:09	48:27	Meskerem	Assefa	ETH	20.9.85	2		Istanbul	24 Apr

WOMEN 2016

452 HALF MARATHON

Mark			Name		Nat	Born	Pos	Meet	Venue	Date
69:41	66:06	49:43	Miho	Shimizu	JPN	13.5.90	1		Yamaguchi	14 Feb
69:43			Visiline	Jepkesho	KEN	30.12.89	2		Adana	3 Jan
69:45A			Edith	Chelimo	KEN	16.7.86	1		Njabini	13 Nov
69:49			Perendis	Lekepana	KEN	4.8.91	1		Krems	18 Sep
69:51			Fate Tola	Geleto	ETH/GER	22.10.87	1		Paderborn	26 Mar
69:51	66:10	48:46	Amane (60)	Gobena	ETH	1.9.82	3		Istanbul	24 Apr
69:52			Pauline Wanjiku	Njeru	KEN	.88	2		Paris	6 Mar
69:52			Muliye	Dekebo	ETH-J	13.3.98	1		Lugano	22 May
69:53			Sally	Kipyego	KEN	19.12.85	1		San José	2 Oct
69:58			Christelle	Daunay	FRA	5.12.74	3		Paris	6 Mar
70:00	66:29	49:40	Bornes	Kitur	KEN	.88	5		København	18 Sep
70:02	66:18	49:53	Felista	Wanjugu	KEN	18.2.90	2		Yamaguchi	14 Feb
70:04	66:27	49:47	Rei	Ohara	JPN	10.8.90	1		Okayama	23 Dec
70:05		49:05	Filomena	Cheyech	KEN	5.7.82	2		Cardiff	2 Oct
70:06	66:30	49:51	Katarzyna	Kowalska	POL	7.4.85	7		Praha	2 Apr
70:07	66:31	49:23	Sara (70)	Hall	USA	15.4.83	5		Houston	17 Jan
70:09	66:06	49:53	Hisami	Ishii	JPN	10.8.95	3		Yamaguchi	14 Feb
70:10	66:35		Yuka	Ando	JPN	16.3.94	4		Marugame	7 Feb
70:13			Maryanne	Wanjiru	KEN	.86	2		Paderborn	26 Mar
70:13	66:35	49:19	Dihihinet	Demsew	ETH	15.9.84	8	WCh	Cardiff	26 Mar
70:14	66:35	49:19	Gladys	Tejeda	PER	30.9.85	9	WCh	Cardiff	26 Mar
70:17+	66:42		Sutume	Asefa	ETH			in Mar	Dubai	22 Jan
70:17+	66:42		Amane	Beriso	ETH	13.10.91	2=	in Mar	Dubai	22 Jan
70:17+	66:42		Tirfi	Tsegaye	ETH	25.11.84		in Mar	Dubai	22 Jan
70:17+	66:42		Mestawat	Tufa	ETH	14.9.83		in Mar	Dubai	22 Jan
70:17	66:36		Sara (80)	Moreira	POR	17.10.85	5		Lisboa	20 Mar
70:18+	66:42		Mamitu	Daska	ETH	16.10.83	1	in Mar	Dubai	22 Jan
70:18+	66:43		Yebrqual	Melese	ETH	18.4.90		in Mar	Dubai	22 Jan
70:18+	66:43		Meselech	Melkamu	ETH	27.4.85		in Mar	Dubai	22 Jan
70:18+	66:43		Mulu	Seboka	ETH	24.9.84		in Mar	Dubai	22 Jan
70:19		49:32	Rael	Kguriatukei (Kihara)	KEN	4.4.84	1	Stra	Milano	20 Mar
70:21+	66:43		Dinknesh	Mekasha	ETH	11.9.85		in Mar	Dubai	22 Jan
70:21			Gebeyanesh	Ayele	ETH	1.5.95	1		Boulogne-Billancourt	20 Nov
70:23	66:51	49:59	Guteni	Shone	ETH	17.11.91	6		København	18 Sep
70:24			Viola	Jelagat	KEN	20.4.92	2		Krems	18 Sep
70:25	66:42		Mizuki (90)	Matsuda	JPN	31.5.95	4		Yamaguchi	14 Feb
70:25			Tara	Welling	USA	14.6.89	1		Columbus	30 Apr
70:27	66:44		Mai	Ito	JPN	23.5.84	1		Osaka	31 Jan
70:27+	66:42		Risa	Takenaka	JPN	6.1.90		in Mar	Osaka	31 Jan
70:28+	66:42		Kayoko	Fukushi	JPN	25.3.82	1	in Mar	Osaka	31 Jan
70:28			Naomi	Rotich	KEN	.94	1		Otterndorf	18 Sep
70:28			Margaret	Agai	KEN	10.6.88	2		Lisboa	2 Oct
70:30	66:49		Asami	Kato	JPN	12.10.90	2		Osaka	31 Jan
70:30+	66:48		Purity	Rionoripo	KEN	10.6.93		in Mar	Chicago	9 Oct
70:31+	66:48		Edna	Kiplagat	KEN	15.11.79		in Mar	Chicago	9 Oct
70:35+	66:45		Etaferahu (100)	Wodaj	ETH	.89		in Mar	Dubai	22 Jan
70:35			Veronica	Inglese	ITA	22.11.90	2	EC	Amsterdam	10 Jul
70:36	66:53	49:31	Ashete	Bekele	ETH	17.4.88	4		Göteborg	21 May
70:39			Emmaculate	Chebet	KEN	.92	6		Ostia	13 Mar
70:42	67:00		Misaki	Kato	JPN	15.6.91	2		Okayama	23 Dec
70:43+			Shure	Demise	ETH	21.1.96		in Mar	Tokyo	28 Feb
70:43			Elizeba	Cherono	NED	6.6.88	1		Berlin	3 Apr
70:44			Fionnuala	McCormack	IRL	24.9.84	4		New York	20 Mar
70:45			Caroline	Rotich	KEN	13.5.84	5		New York	20 Mar
70:46		49:41	Janet	Bawcom	USA	22.8.78	11	WCh	Cardiff	26 Mar
70:48			Milly	Clark	AUS	1.3.89	13	WCh	Cardiff	26 Mar
70:49+	67:00		Risa	Shigemoto	JPN	29.8.87		in Mar	Osaka	31 Jan
70:49		49:56	Susan	Jeptoo	KEN	7.3.87	2		Berlin	3 Apr

Mark			Name		Nat	Born			Venue	Date
70:50	Isabellah		Andersson		SWE	12.11.80			14 Feb	
70:53	Reia		Iwade		JPN	8.12.94			14 Feb	
70:55	Jéssica		Augusto		POR	8.11.81			10 Jul	
70:58	Sheila		Chesang		KEN	17.7.80			30 Jul	
71:00	Ayantu		Gemechu		ETH	1.3.92			1 May	
71:00	Irvette		van Zyl		RSA	5.7.87			30 Jul	
71:02	Yukari		Abe		JPN	21.8.89			14 Feb	
71:03	49:58 Miho		Ihara		JPN	4.2.88			14 Feb	
71:04	Paula		González		ESP	2.5.85			24 Jan	
71:05	Sasha		Gollish		CAN	27.12.81			5 Nov	
71:06	Eva		Vrabcová-Nyvltová		CZE	6.2.86			2 Apr	
71:06	Desiree		Linden		USA	26.7.83			30 Apr	
71:07	Mao		Kiyota		JPN	12.9.93			23 Oct	
71:08	Ai		Utsunomiya		JPN	19.9.95			14 Feb	
71:09	Souad		Aït Salem		ALG	6.1.79			24 Jan	
71:09	67:36 Betelhem		Moges		ETH	3.5.91			15 May	
71:09	Rebecca		Kangogo Chesir		KEN	.92			15 May	
71:11+	Shitaye		Eshete		BRN	21.5.90			22 Jan	

HALF MARATHON – 25 – 30 KILOMETRES ROAD

Mark	Name		Nat	Born	Pos Meet	Venue	Date
71:11	Martha	Akeno	KEN	15.12.93	13 Mar		
71:11+	Meseret	Hailu	ETH	12.9.90	16 Oct		
71:12+	Fasika	Metaferiya	ETH	.96	22 Jan		
71:12+	Abebech	Afework	ETH	11.12.90	16 Oct		
71:13	Hannah	Gatheru	KEN	6.6.86	7 Feb		
71:13	Cassie	Fien	AUS	15.9.85	26 Mar		
71:14	Kotomi	Takayama	JPN	18.2.93	7 Feb		
71:14	Sylvia	Medugu	KEN	14.2.90	2 Apr		
71:17	Akane	Sekino	JPN	28.7.90	7 Feb		
71:17	Anja	Scherl	GER	12.4.86	14 Feb		
71:17	Clémence	Calvin	FRA	17.5.90	20 Mar		
71:17	Tsehay	Desalegn	ETH	28.10.91	18 Sep		
71:17	Tejitu	Daba	BRN	20.8.91	23 Oct		
71:18+	Winfridaj	Kebaso	KEN	16.4.95	17 Apr		
71:20	Ayaka	Fujimoto	JPN-J	8.7.97	23 Dec		
71:21	Kelly	Arias	COL	3.6.89	26 Mar		
71:22A	Alice	Kibor	KEN	.92	22 May		
71:22	Filomena	Costa	POR	22.2.85	2 Oct		
71:22A	Meseret	Mengistu	ETH	6.3.90	4 Dec		
71:23	Lenah	Cherotich	KEN	27.3.88	2 Oct		
71:24	Brianne	Nelson	USA	27.10.80	30 Apr		
71:24	Ivy	Kibet	KEN	4.2.90	2 Oct		
71:26	Lanni	Marchant	CAN	11.4.84	26 Mar		
71:26	Linah	Cheruto	KEN	18.3.95	24 Apr		
71:26A	Lydia	Orango	KEN		22 May		
71:27	Winnie	Jepkorir	KEN	10.6.90	20 Mar		
71:27+	Nancy	Kiprop	KEN	7.7.79	20 Nov		
71:28+	Sarah	Jebet	KEN	.88	30 Oct		
71:28	Rochelle	Kanuho	USA	4.7.90	5 Nov		
71:30	Nazret	Weldu	ERI	1.1.90	17 Jan		
71:30	Nancy	Kiprono	KEN		7 Feb		
71:33	Moeno	Nakamura	JPN	21.3.90	7 Feb		
71:33	Diana	Lobacevske	LTU	7.8.80	17 Apr		
71:33	Izabela	Trzaskalska	POL	9.1.88	16 Oct		
71:34	Saori	Noda	JPN	30.3.93	14 Feb		
71:34	Helen	Jepkurgat	KEN	21.2.89	20 Mar		
71:35	Mary	Wanjohi	KEN	4.10.86	20 Mar		
71:35	Dinahrose Lebogang Phalula		RSA	9.12.83	30 Jul		
71:35	Agnes	Barsosio	KEN	5.8.82	14 Aug		
71:35	Violet	Yator	KEN	30.7.93	13 Nov		
71:36	Ayano	Ikemitsu	JPN	18.4.91	23 Dec		
71:38+	Helen	Bekele Tola	ETH	21.11.94	30 Oct		
71:39	Lily	Partridge	GBR	9.3.91	2 Oct		
71:40	Desi	Jisa Mokonin	BRN-J	12.7.97			18 Sep
71:41	Yomogi	Akasaka	JPN	.95			7 Feb
71:41	Agnieszka	Mierzejewska	POL	22.10.85			3 Apr
71:42	Bekelech	Daba	ETH	29.12.91			21 May
71:42	Biruktayit	Degefa	ETH	29.9.90			20 Nov
71:43	Olga	Kimaiyo	KEN	24.7.88			7 May
71:44	Jelena	Prokopcuka	LAT	21.9.76			20 Mar
71:44	Olga	Mazuronak	BLR	14.4.89			4 Sep
71:45	Lucy	Macharia	KEN	.91			17 Dec
71:46+	Monica	Jepkoech	KEN	.85			13 Mar
71:46+	Shiho	Takechi	JPN	18.8.90			13 Mar
71:46+	Tomomi	Tanaka	JPN	25.1.88			13 Mar
71:46+	Sayaka	Kuwahara	JPN	8.3.93			13 Mar
71:46+	Ryoko	Kizaki	JPN	21.6.85			13 Mar
71:47	Rasa	Drazdauskaite	LTU	20.3.81			10 Jul
71:48	Miharu	Shimokado	JPN	24.4.90			20 Mar
71:49	Hillary	Montgomery	USA	11.2.93			17 Jan
71:49	Alisha	Williams	USA	5.2.82			20 Mar
71:49	Debele	Beyene	ETH				1 May
71:49	Esma	Aydemir	TUR	1.1.92			10 Jul
71:49	Buze	Diriba	ETH	9.2.94			18 Sep
71:50	Misaki	Ogata	JPN-J	.97			20 Mar
71:50	Martina	Strähl	SUI	7.5.87			17 Apr
71:50	Nina	Savina	BLR	21.7.93			4 Sep
71:51	Betty	Lempus	KEN				11 Jun
71:52	Keiko	Nogami	JPN	6.12.85			31 Jan
71:52	Vianney (200)	De La Rosa	MEX	4.8.86			26 Mar
71:52	Ouranía	Reboúli	GRE	16.5.89			10 Jul
71:53	Ayumi	Uehara	JPN	23.11.94			20 Mar
71:54+	Megertu	Ifa	ETH	.91			22 Mar
71:54	Susan	Partridge	GBR	4.1.80			2 Apr
71:54	Yukari	Ishizawa	JPN	16.4.88			23 Dec
71:56	Margarita	Hernández	MEX	3.12.85			26 Mar
71:56+	Aliphine	Bolton	USA	5.4.89			14 May
71:56	Monica	Florea	ROU	3.2.93			10 Jul
71:57	Kenza	Dahmani	ALG	18.11.80			4 Mar
71:58	Belaynesh	Tsegaye	ETH-J	.97			15 May
71:59+	Madaí	Pérez	MEX	2.2.80			17 Apr
71:59	Damaris	Kemunto	KEN	.95			20 Nov
Uncertain measurement							
71:55	? Luz Mery	Rojas	PER	20.6.93			28 Aug
71:59	Rocío Marisol Cántara		PER	4.1.87			28 Aug

149.7m short Glasgow 2 Oct: 1. Betsy Saina KEN 67:22, 3. Doris Changeiywo KEN 12.12.84 71:34; 4, L Partridge 9.3.91 71:39.

Short course: 71:21 Jacqueline Gandar FRA 17.6.94 St-Pierre-les-Elb 13 Mar

Exceessively downhill
67:51dh	Shalane	Flanagan	USA	8.7.81	1	San Diego	5 Jun
69:50dh	Amy	Cragg	USA	21.1.84	2	San Diego (86.5m dh)	5 Jun

JUNIORS
See main list for top 2 juniors. 8 performances by 6 women to 72:00. Additional marks and further juniors:

Cheruiyot	71:17	1	Casablanca	15 May	71:41	2 Baringo	5 Nov
71:20	Ayaka	Fujimoto	JPN-J	8.7.97	3	Okayama	23 Dec
71:40	Desi	Jisa Mokonin	BRN-J	12.7.97	10	København	18 Sep
71:50	Misaki	Ogata	JPN-J	.97	1	Matsue	20 Mar
71:58	Belaynesh	Tsegaye	ETH-J	.97	3	Casablanca	15 May
72:21	Honoka	Tanaike	JPN	.97	5	Matsue	20 Mar
72:44	Genet	Abdukadir	ETH	.97	2	Nanning	4 Dec
72:47	Dorcas	Nzembi	KEN	22.12.97	4	Berlin	3 Apr
73:41	Meskerem	Amare	ETH	.97	5	Luzhou	20 Nov

25 – 30 KILOMETRES ROAD

In addition to those shown in Marathon listing

25k	30k							
1:23:09+		Hiwot	Gebrekidan	ETH	11.5.95	in Mar	Dubai	22 Jan
1:23:25	1:40:12+	Filomena	Cheyech	KEN	5.7.82	in Mar	Osaka	31 Jan
1:23:34	1:41:10	Risa	Takenaka	JPN	6.1.90	in Mar	Osaka	31 Jan
1:23:29	1:41:18	Sally	Chepyego	KEN	3.10.85	in Mar	Osaka	31 Jan
1:23:41		Eunice	Chumba	BRN	23.5.93	in Mar	Dubai	22 Jan
1:24:01+		Angela	Tanui	KEN	27.7.92	in Mar	London	24 Apr
1:24:01+		Helah	Kiprop	KEN	7.4.85	in Mar	London	24 Apr
1:24:13	1:41:40+	Mary	Keitany	KEN	18.1.82	in Mar	London	24 Apr
1:24:16	1:41:06+	Meseret	Hailu	ETH	12.9.90	in Mar	Amsterdam	16 Oct
1:24:19+	1:42:18	Dinknesh	Mekasha	ETH	.85	in Mar	Dubai	22 Jan
1:24:19	1:42:06+	Risa	Shigemoto	JPN	29.8.87	in Mar	Osaka	31 Jan

25-30K – MARATHON

Mark			Name		Nat	Born	Pos	Meet	Venue	Date	
1:24:29	1:42:20+		Misaki	Kato	JPN	15.6.91		in Mar	Osaka	31	Jan
1:24:30+			Fasika	Metaferiya	ETH	.96		in Mar	Dubai	22	Jan
1:24:30+			Afera	Godfay	ETH	25.9.91		in Mar	Dubai	22	Jan
1:24:39+			Mamitu	Daska	ETH	16.10.83		in Mar	Dubai	22	Jan
1:24:57	1:42:32+		Sarah	Jebet	KEN	.88		in Mar	Frankfurt	30	Oct
1:25:06+	1:42:15		Visiline	Jepkesho	KEN	30.12.89		in Mar	Nagoya	13	Mar
1:25:06+	1:42:15		Sarah	Chepchirchir	KEN	27.7.84		in Mar	Nagoya	13	Mar
1:25:06+			Monica	Jepkoech	KEN	.85		in Mar	Nagoya	13	Mar
1:25:07+	1:42:16		Ryoko	Kizaki	JPN	21.6.85		in Mar	Nagoya	13	Mar
1:25:08+	1:42:17		Betelhem	Moges	ETH	3.5.91		in Mar	Nagoya	13	Mar
1:25:54	1:43:06		Janet	Rono	KEN	8.12.88		in Mar	Seoul	20	Mar
1:25:08+	1:43:09		Bekelech	Daba	ETH	29.12.91		in Mar	Nagoya	13	Mar
1:25:28+	1:43:09		Michi	Numata	JPN	6.5.89		in Mar	Nagoya	13	Mar
1:25:31+	1:43:06		Madaí	Pérez	MEX	2.2.80		in Mar	Hamburg	17	Apr
1:25:36			Aliphine	Bolton	USA	5.4.89	1	NC	Grand Rapids	14	May

MARATHON

	25k	30k									
2:19:41	1:23:09	1:39:28	Tirfi	Tsegaye	ETH	25.11.84	1		Dubai	22	Jan
2:20:45	1:22:17	1:38:42	Aberu	Kebede	ETH	12.9.86	1		Berlin	25	Sep
2:20:48	1:23:09	1:39:28	Amane	Beriso	ETH	13.10.91	2		Dubai	22	Jan
2:21:27	1:23:39	1:40:26	Helah	Kiprop	KEN	7.4.85	1		Tokyo	28	Feb
2:21:32	1:23:51	1:40:29	Florence	Kiplagat	KEN	27.2.87	1		Chicago	9	Oct
2:21:51	1:23:39	1:40:26	Amane	Gobena	ETH	1.9.82	2		Tokyo	28	Feb
2:21:54	1:23:56	1:40:38	Meselech	Melkamu	ETH	27.4.85	1		Hamburg	17	Apr
2:22:17	1:23:26	1:40:13	Kayoko	Fukushi	JPN	25.3.82	1		Osaka	31	Jan
2:22:29	1:23:10	1:39:44		Melkamu			3		Dubai	22	Jan
2:22:36	1:23:39	1:40:26	Edna	Kiplagat	KEN	15.11.79	3		Tokyo	28	Feb
2:22:40	1:25:06	1:42:15	Eunice	Jepkirui Kirwa (10)	BRN	20.5.84	1		Nagoya	13	Mar
2:22:58	1:24:13	1:41:40	Jemima	Sumgong	KEN	21.12.84	1		London	24	Apr
2:23:01	1:23:39	1:40:26		Kebede			4		Tokyo	28	Feb
2:23:03	1:24:13	1:41:39	Tigist	Tufa	ETH	26.1.87	2		London	24	Apr
2:23:16	1:23:39	1:40:26	Birhane	Dibaba	ETH	11.9.93	5		Tokyo	28	Feb
2:23:18	1:24:50	1:41:32	Filomena	Cheyech	KEN	5.7.82	1		Saitama	13	Nov
2:23:19	1:25:07	1:42:16	Tomomi	Tanaka	JPN	25.1.88	2		Nagoya	13	Mar
2:23:20	1:25:06	1:42:16	Rei	Ohara	JPN	10.8.90	3		Nagoya	13	Mar
2:23:21	1:24:16	1:40:59		Melkamu			1		Amsterdam	16	Oct
2:23:28				E Kiplagat			2		Chicago	9	Oct
2:23:39	1:24:13	1:41:39		F Kiplagat			3		London	24	Apr
2:23:41	1:23:52		Valentine	Kipketer	KEN	5.1.93	3		Chicago	9	Oct
2:23:54		1:43:13	Olga	Mazuronak	BLR	14.4.89	4		London	24	Apr
2:23:57	1:24:14	1:41:40	Aselefech	Mergia	ETH	23.1.85	5		London	24	Apr
2:23:58	1:22:23	1:39:06		B Dibaba			2		Berlin	25	Sep
2:24:00	1:23:09	1:40:11	Sutume	Asefa (20)	ETH	.94	4		Dubai	22	Jan
2:24:04			Worknesh	Edesa	ETH	11.9.92	1		Xiamen	2	Jan
2:24:04				Sumgong			1	OG	Rio de Janeiro	14	Aug
2:24:09	1:24:13	1:41:39	Mare	Dibaba	ETH	20.10.89	6		London	24	Apr
2:24:13				Jepkirui			2	OG	Rio de Janeiro	14	Aug
2:24:13			Sarah (31/23)	Chepchirchir	KEN	27.7.84	1		Lisboa	2	Oct
2:24:14	1:25:59	1:43:06	Rose	Chelimo	BRN	12.7.89	1		Seoul	20	Mar
2:24:24	1:23:10	1:40:11	Mulu	Seboka	ETH	24.9.84	5		Dubai	22	Jan
2:24:26			Mary	Keitany	KEN	18.1.82	1		New York	6	Nov
2:24:27	1:24:16	1:41:01	Abebech	Afework	ETH	11.12.90	2		Amsterdam	16	Oct
2:24:28	1:25:59	1:43:06	Melkaw	Gizaw	ETH	17.9.90	2		Seoul	20	Mar
2:24:31			Shuko	Genemo	ETH	.95	1		Wien	10	Apr
2:24:32			Marta (30)	Lema	ETH	30.12.90	2		Xiamen	2	Jan
2:24:32	1:25:07	1:42:16	Mao	Kiyota	JPN	12.9.93	4		Nagoya	13	Mar
2:24:38	1:25:06	1:42:16	Reia	Iwade	JPN	8.12.94	5		Nagoya	13	Mar
2:24:41	1:22:41	1:39:57	Ruti	Aga	ETH	16.1.94	3		Berlin	25	Sep
2:24:45		1:42:35	Brigid	Kosgei	KEN	.94	2		Lisboa	2	Oct
2:24:46	1:25:47		Lucy	Karimi	KEN	9.10.86	1		Praha	8	May
2:24:47	1:23:51		Purity	Rionoripo	KEN	10.6.93	4		Chicago	9	Oct
2:24:48	1:24:29	1:41:50	Valary	Aiyabei	KEN	8.6.91	1		Valencia	20	Nov
2:24:49	1:23:51		Yebrqual	Melese	ETH	18.4.90	5		Chicago	9	Oct
2:24:59	1:25:59	1:43:06	Agnes	Barsosio	KEN	5.8.82	3		Seoul	20	Mar
2:25:00	1:24:16	1:41:00	Eunice (40)	Chumba	BRN	23.5.93	3		Amsterdam	16	Oct

MARATHON 455

Mark			Name		Nat	Born	Pos	Meet	Venue	Date	
2:25:03	1:24:13	1:41:40	Feyse	Tadesse	ETH	19.11.88	7		London	24	Apr
2:25:04			Shure	Demise	ETH	21.1.96	6		Tokyo	28	Feb
2:25:09	1:25:06	1:42:16	Sayaka	Kuwahara	JPN	8.3.93	6		Nagoya	13	Mar
2:25:13	1:24:58	1:42:21	Nancy	Kiprop	KEN	.79	2		Valencia	20	Nov
2:25:26		1:43:22	Shalane	Flanagan	USA	8.7.81	6	OG	Rio de Janeiro	14	Aug
2:25:27	1:23:38	1:40:28	Mamitu	Daska	ETH	16.10.83	1		Frankfurt	30	Oct
2:25:29	1:25:06	1:42:16	Shiho	Takechi	JPN	18.8.90	7		Nagoya	13	Mar
2:25:36	1:24:30	1:41:38	Shitaye	Eshete	BRN	21.5.90	6		Dubai	22	Jan
2:25:42		1:43:18	Fate Tola	Geleto	GER	22.10.87	2		Frankfurt	30	Oct
2:25:50			Ashete (50)	Bekele	ETH	17.4.88	7		Tokyo	28	Feb
2:25:53	1:25:54	1:43:16	Visiline	Jepkesho	KEN	30.12.89	1		Paris	3	Apr
2:25:56			Meseret	Mengistu	ETH	6.3.90	1		Beijing	17	Sep
2:25:57	1:24:16	1:41:09	Priscah	Jeptoo	KEN	26.6.84	4		Amsterdam	16	Oct
2:26:07			Biruktayit	Degefa	ETH	29.9.90	1		Houston	17	Jan
2:26:08			Meseret	Legesse	ETH	28.8.87	1		Wuhan	10	Apr
2:26:08		1:43:34	Desiree	Linden	USA	26.7.83	7	OG	Rio de Janeiro	14	Aug
2:26:11			Betelhem	Moges	ETH	3.5.91	3		Valencia	20	Nov
2:26:13			Liu	Ruihuan	CHN	29.6.92	1		Chongqing	20	Mar
2:26:14	1:23:51	1:43:39	Gulume	Tollesa	ETH	11.9.92	2		Paris	3	Apr
2:26:15			Letebrhan (60)	Gebreslasea	ETH	29.10.90	1		Rotterdam	10	Apr
2:26:18			Roza	Dereje	ETH		1		Shanghai	30	Oct
2:26:20			Margaret	Agai	KEN	10.6.88	2		Shanghai	30	Oct
2:26:26	1:25:00	1:43:05	Meseret	Hailu	ETH	12.9.90	2		Hamburg	17	Apr
2:26:31			Tadelech	Bekele	ETH	11.4.91	2		Toronto	16	Oct
2:26:34	1:23:09	1:40:06	Mestawat	Tufa	ETH	14.9.83	7		Dubai	22	Jan
2:26:40			Misato	Horie	JPN	10.3.87	1		Gold Coast	3	Jul
2:26:53			Fantu	Jimma Eticha	ETH	11.9.87	3		Xiamen	2	Jan
2:27:06			Korene	Jelela	ETH	18.1.87	1		Ottawa	29	May
2:27:07			Sarah	Jebet	KEN	.88	3		Frankfurt	30	Oct
2:27:08			Wude (70)	Ayalew	ETH	4.7.87	3		Shanghai	30	Oct
2:27:23			Janet	Rono	KEN	8.12.88	4		Seoul	20	Mar
2:27:23			Risper	Chebet	KEN	6.6.92	3		Praha	8	May
2:27:27			Michi	Numata	JPN	6.5.89	9		Nagoya	13	Mar
2:27:35			Lisa	Weightman	AUS	16.1.79	2		Houston	17	Jan
2:27:36			Maja	Neuenschwander	SUI	13.2.80	8		Tokyo	28	Feb
2:27:39			Leah	Kiprono	KEN	15.4.80	1		Zhengzhou	27	Mar
2:27:39			Caroline	Kilel	KEN	21.3.81	1		Daegu	3	Apr
2:27:40			Inés	Melchor	PER	30.8.86	2		Daegu	3	Apr
2:27:41			Priscah	Cherono	KEN	27.6.80	1		Venezia	23	Oct
2:27:41			Aberu (80)	Mekuria	ETH	24.12.83	4		Valencia	20	Nov
2:27:50			Anja	Scherl	GER	12.4.86	3		Hamburg	17	Apr
2:27:53			Rael	Kguriatukei (Kiyara)	KEN	4.4.84	4		Shanghai	30	Oct
2:28:01			Sally	Kipyego	KEN	19.12.85	2		New York	6	Nov
2:28:06			Pamela	Rotich Chepkosgei	KEN	.84	1		Rabat	13	Mar
2:28:06				Kim Ji-hyang	PRK	26.9.95	1		Pyongyang	10	Apr
2:28:11			Dinknesh	Mekasha	ETH	11.9.85	3		Paris	3	Apr
2:28:13			Molly	Huddle	USA	31.8.84	3		New York	6	Nov
2:28:20			Amy	Cragg	USA	21.1.84	1	OT	Los Angeles	13	Feb
2:28:26			Monika	Stefanowicz	POL	15.5.80	4		Hamburg	17	Apr
2:28:28			Grace (90)	Momanyi	KEN	3.3.82	1		Hefei	12	Nov
2:28:34			Tatyana	Arkhipova	RUS	8.4.83	1	NC	Volgograd	1	May
2:28:34			Katharina	Heinig	GER	22.8.89	5		Berlin	25	Sep
2:28:36				Kim Hye-song	PRK	9.3.93	10	OG	Rio de Janeiro	14	Aug
2:28:36				Kim Hye-gyong	PRK	9.3.93	11	OG	Rio de Janeiro	14	Aug
2:28:37			Esther	Chemtai	KEN	4.6.88	2		Rabat	13	Mar
2:28:43			Sechale	Delasa	ETH	20.9.91	3		Houston	17	Jan
2:28:43			Kumeshi	Sichala	ETH	.95	1		Warszawa	24	Apr
2:28:46			Winnie	Jepkorir	KEN	10.6.90	1		Firenze	27	Nov
2:28:48				Sin Yong-sun	PRK	20.5.90	2		Pyongyang	10	Apr
2:28:49			Ryoko (100)	Kizaki	JPN	21.6.85	10		Nagoya	13	Mar
2:28:49			Rahma	Tusa	ETH	.93	1		Roma	10	Apr
2:28:53	Jéssica	Augusto	POR	8.11.81	24 Apr	2:28:57	Meselech	Tsegaye	ETH	.94	12 Nov
2:28:53	Atsede	Baysa	ETH	16.4.87	9 Oct	2:28:59	Alina	Prokopyeva	RUS	16.8.85	1 May
2:28:54	Rebecca Kangogo (Chesire)		KEN	.92	16 Oc	2:29:01	Askale	Alemaheyu	ETH	11.1.96	30 Oct
2:28:56	Monica	Jepkoech	KEN	1.1.83	13 Nov	2:29:08	Joyce	Chepkirui	KEN	20.8.88	6 Nov

WOMEN 2016

MARATHON – 100 KILOMETRES

Mark	Name		Nat	Born	Pos	Meet	Venue		Date
2:29:09	Rose	Chepchumba	KEN	14.3.79	17	Apr			
2:29:13	Loice	Kiptoo	KEN	.86	6	Nov			
2:29:14	Risa	Takenaka	JPN	6.1.90	31	Jan			
2:29:15		Hua Shaoqing	CHN	12.2.94	20	Mar			
2:29:16	Rebecca	Jepchirchir	KEN	.89	10	Apr			
2:29:21	Helen	Bekele Tola	ETH	21.11.94	17	Apr			
2:29:21	Peninah	Arusei	KEN	23.2.79	24	Apr			
2:29:27	Madaí	Pérez	MEX	2.2.80	17	Apr			
2:29:28	Lindsay	Flanagan	USA	24.1.91	30	Oct			
2:29:32	Jelena	Prokopcuka	LAT	21.9.76	14	Aug			
2:29:32	Purity	Changwony	KEN	.90	30	Oct			
2:29:33	Asami	Kato	JPN	12.10.90	13	Mar			
2:29:36	Kelly	Arias	COL	3.6.89	17	Apr			
2:29:44	Valeria	Straneo	ITA	5.4.76	14	Aug			
2:29:44	Atsede	Habtamu	ETH	26.10.87	13	Nov			
2:29:45	Megeretu	Geletu	ETH	20.9.91	22	Jan			
2:29:47	Katarzyna	Kowalska	POL	7.4.85	24	Apr			
2:29:50	Bekelech	Daba	ETH	29.12.91	13	Mar			
2:29:55		Zhang Yingying	CHN	4.1.90	20	Mar			
2:29:55	Gladys	Tejeda	PER	30.9.85	14	Aug			
2:29:57	Margarita	Hernández	MEX	3.12.85	17	Jan			
2:29:57		Jo Un-ok	PRK		10	Apr			
2:29:59	Mulu	Diro	ETH	.92	10	Apr			
2:30:01	Jane	Kibii	KEN	10.3.85	9	Oct			
2:30:02	Isabellah	Andersson	SWE	12.11.80	28	Feb			
2:30:04	Charlotte	Purdue	GBR	10.6.91	30	Oct			
2:30:05	Fasika	Metaferiya	ETH	.96	22	Jan			
2:30:06	Sara	Hall	USA	15.4.83	24	Apr			
2:30:09	Diana	Lobacevske	LTU	7.8.80	31	Jan			
2:30:10	Eva	Vrabcová-Nvltová	CZE	6.2.86	8	May			
2:30:10	Sara Catarine	Ribeiro	POR	31.5.90	6	Nov			
2:30:13	Meskerem	Assefa	ETH	20.9.85	30	Oct			
2:30:14	Naomi	Tuei	KEN	.93	13	Mar			
2:30:15	Iwona	Lewandowska	POL	19.2.85	13	Mar			
2:30:19	Catherine	Bertone	ITA	6.5.72	10	Apr			
2:30:24	Kara	Goucher	USA	9.7.78	13	Feb			
2:30:27		Yue Chao	CHN	5.1.91	20	Mar			
2:30:27	Filomena	Costa	POR	22.2.85	6	Nov			
2:30:30	Gladys	Chemweno	KEN	4.7.88	16	May			
2:30:32	Truphena	Chepchirchir	KEN		9	Oct			
2:30:35	Anna	Hahner	GER	20.11.89	10	Apr			
2:30:39	Dulce	Félix	POR	23.10.82	14	Aug			
2:30:40	Risa	Shigemoto	JPN	29.8.87	31	Jan			
2:30:40	Serena	Burla	USA	29.7.82	9	Oct			
2:30:47	Salome	Biwott	KEN	8.11.82	10	Apr			
2:30:47	Natalya	Starkova	RUS	8.11.87	1	May			
2:30:47	Marta	Esteban	ESP	6.11.82	20	Nov			
2:30:51	Aynalem	Kassahun	ETH		13	Mar			
2:30:51	Jane	Moraa	Onyangi	KEN	21.9.91	27	Nov		
2:30:52	Fatna		Maraoui	ITA	10.7.77	27	Nov		
2:30:53	Milly		Clark	AUS	1.3.89	14	Aug		
2:30:53	Shasho		Insermu	ETH	..93	30	Oct		
2:30:54	Kaoru		Nagao	JPN	26.9.89	13	Mar		
2:30:57	Emma		Quaglia	ITA	15.8.80	20	Nov		
2:30:58	Martina		Strähl	SUI	7.5.87	30	Oct		
2:31:04	Misaki		Kato	JPN	15.6.91	31	Jan		
2:31:05	Bechadu		Bekele	ETH	.91	30	Oct		
2:31:07dh	Helen		Jepkurgat	KEN	21.2.89	23	Oct		
2:31:13	Janet		Bawcom	USA	22.8.78	13	Feb		
2:31:16	Nancy		Koech	KEN	12.11.86	10	Apr		
2:31:17	Yukiko		Okuno	JPN	12.9.92	28	Feb		
2:31:17	Haruna		Takada	JPN	17.2.90	13	Mar		
2:31:18	Paula		González	ESP	2.5.85	21	Feb		
2:31:21	Anne		Cheptanui	KEN	4.11.82	9	Nov		
2:31:22	Miriam		Wangari	KEN	22.2.79	8	May		
2:31:22	Fionnuala		McCormack	IRL	24.9.84	14	Aug		
2:31:23	Adriana		da Silva	BRA	22.7.81	17	Apr		
2:31:26	Boulaid		Kaoutar	MAR	10.10.89	21	Feb		
2:31:28	Aya		Higashimoto	JPN	7.4.92	31	Jan		
2:31:30	Mona		Stockhecke	GER	11.10.83	30	Oct		
2:31:33	Jovana		de la Cruz	PER	12.7.92	17	Jan		
2:31:34	Wilma		Arizapana	PER	1.10.82	10	Apr		
2:31:34	Hirut		Tibebu	ETH	13.12.94	6	Nov		
2:31:41	Racheal		Mutgaa	KEN	.88	17	Apr		
2:31:41	Esther		Chemutai	KEN	6.6.87	2	Oct		
2:31:42	Abeba		Gebremeskel	ETH	.89	30	Oct		
2:31:44	Jessica		Trengove	AUS	15.8.87	14	Aug		
2:31:45			Ri Kwang-ok	PRK		10	Apr		
2:31:45	Azucena		Díaz	ESP	19.12.82	10	Apr		
2:31:45	Tizita		Terecha	ETH	.92	30	Oct		
2:31:47	Eri		Hayakawa	JPN	15.11.81	13	Mar		
2:31:48	Agnes		Kiprop	KEN	12.12.79	20	Mar		
2:31:50	Doris		Changeiywo	KEN	12.12.86	10	Apr		
2:31:52	Alyson		Dixon	GBR	24.9.78	24	Apr		
2:31:58dh	Eunice		Jeptoo	KEN	24.6.83	23	Oct		
2:32:00	Bornes		Kitur	KEN	.88	17	Jan		
2:32:00	Sonia		Samuels	GBR	16.5.79	24	Apr		
2:32:02	Ehite		Bizuayehu	ETH	.91	8	May		
2:32:04	Agnieszka		Mierzejewska	POL	22.10.85	17	Apr		
2:32:05	Tracy		Barlow	GBR	18.6.85	30	Oct		
2:32:07	Motu (200)		Megersa	ETH	22.10.94	13	Mar		

Excessively downhill

2:30:40	Nataliya	Lehonkova	UKR	27.2.82	14	Feb
2:31:20	Sarah	Kiptoo	KEN	.89	4	Dec

Drugs disqualification

2:29:17	Edinah	Kwambai ¶	KEN	22.3.86	10	Apr

100 KILOMETRES

Mark	Name		Nat	Born	Pos	Meet	Venue	Date	
7:29:04	Nele	Alder-Baerens	GER	1.4.78	1	NC	Leipzig	20	Aug
7:34:25	Kirstin	Bull	AUS	2.8.81	1	WCh	Los Alcazares	27	Nov
7:36:10	Nikolina	Sustic	CRO	24.7.87	2	WCh	Los Alcazares	27	Nov
7:39:51	Hisayo	Matsumoto	JPN	.78	1		Yubetsu	26	Jun
7:40:39		Sustic			1		Firenze	29	May
7:41:38	Joasia	Zakrzewski	GBR	19.1.76	3	WCh	Los Alcazares	27	Nov
7:42:48	Mai	Fujisawa	JPN	21.9.74	2		Yubetsu	26	Jun
7:45:58	Karin	Freitag	AUT	1.4.80	4	WCh	Los Alcazares	27	Nov
7:47:06	Aiko	Kanematsu	JPN	18.5.80	3		Yubetsu	26	Jun
7:47:38	Mikiko	Ota	JPN	28.4.75	5	WCh	Los Alcazares	27	Nov
7:47:41		Kanematsu			6	WCh	Los Alcazares	27	Nov
7:47:55	Chiyuki	Mochizuki	JPN	29.9.86	7	WCh	Los Alcazares	27	Nov
7:48:27		Fujisawa			8	WCh	Los Alcazares	27	Nov
7:51:19	Veronika	Jurisic	CRO	6.4.77	9	WCh	Los Alcazares	27	Nov
7:51:22	Frida (15/12)	Södermark	SWE	5.8.78	10	WCh	Los Alcazares	27	Nov
7:53:22	Riitta	Paasio	FIN	6.4.84	11	WCh	Los Alcazares	27	Nov
7:54:59	Sophia	Sundberg	SWE	5.9.84	1		Winschoten	10	Sep
7:56:48	Pam	Smith	USA	22.9.74	12	WCh	Los Alcazares	27	Nov
7:58:22	Meghan	Arbogast	USA	16.4.61	13	WCh	Los Alcazares	27	Nov
8:06:35	Julie	Hamulecki	CAN	21.11.80	27	Nov			
8:08:56	Chiyuki	Mochizuki	JPN	29.9.86	26	Jun			
8:09:39	Arielle	Fitzgerald	CAN	31.1.94	27	Nov			
8:09:52	Samantha	Amend	GBR	25.5.79	25	Jun			
8:10:18	Marita	Eisler	AUS	7.3.80	11	Jun			
8:10:23	Traci	Falbo	USA	12.11.71	27	Nov			
8:10:31	Sophia	Sundberg	SWE	5.9.84	27	Nov			
8:11:29	Kim	Mulder	NED	21.5.75	27	Nov			
8:11:40	Rejane	Lecamus	FRA	18.10.77	8	Oct			

Indoor

8:11:20	Natalya	Sotnikova	RUS	17.10.89	13	Feb

Mark	Name		Nat	Born	Pos	Meet	Venue	Date
							24 HOURS	
250.647	Maria	Jansson	SWE	10.7.85	1	EC	Albi	22 Oct
242.686		Jansson			1		Basel	1 May
241.633	Patrycja	Bereznowska	POL	17.10.75	2	EC	Albi	22 Oct
241.334t		Ying Shan	CHN	.82	1		Taipei	4 Dec
237.362t	Courtney	Dauwalter	USA	13.2.85	1		Phoenix	11 Dec
235.228t	Antje	Krause	GER	1.5.72	1		Barcelona	18 Dec
232.285	Agata	Matejczuk	POL	27.11.81	3	EC	Albi	22 Oct
231.200t	Pam	Smith	USA	22.9.74	1		Sharon Hill PA	15 May
230.609	Mizuki	Aotani	JPN	5.12.73	1		Tokyo	17 Dec
230.395t	Jessica	Baker	GBR	6.6.82	1		Bruce	20 Mar
228.809	Yuri	Matsumoto	JPN	27.2.78	2		Tokyo	17 Dec
228.639	Jennifer	Hoffman	USA	1.7.78	1		Cleveland	18 Sep
228.323	Therese	Falk	NOR	5.8.75	4	EC	Albi	22 Oct
227.511	Milena	Grabska-Grzegorczyk	POL	18.6.78	5	EC	Albi	22 Oct
225.727		Bereznowska			1		Krakow	4 Sep
225.724	Anne Marie Geisler Andersen		DEN	15.4.81	6	EC	Albi	22 Oct
225.600	Viktória	Makai	HUN	1.7.80	1	NC	Sárvár	24 Apr
225.190t	Tatyana	Maslova	RUS	23.6.75	1		Moskva	15 May
	(18/16)							
224.193	Monika	Biegasiewicz	POL	25.5.76	7	EC	Albi	22 Oct
224.176	Julia	Fatton	GER	24.4.72	8	EC	Albi	22 Oct
224.106	Szilvia	Lubics	HUN	27.5.74	9	EC	Albi	22 Oct
223.676	Veronika	Jurisic	CRO	6.4.77	10	EC	Albi	22 Oct
	(20)							
223.551t	Linda	Voets	NED	17.8.81	1		Driehuis	18 Dec
223.540	Boglárka	Vágó	HUN	5.1.85	2	NC	Sárvár	24 Apr
223.427	Anne-Marie	Vernet	FRA	15.12.67	11	EC	Albi	22 Oct
222.760	Sayuri	Oka	JPN	6.8.70	3		Tokyo	17 Dec
222.537	Annika	Nilrud	SWE	7.12.75	12	EC	Albi	22 Oct
221.719	Lorena	Brusamento	ITA	19.8.73	13	EC	Albi	22 Oct
221.367t	Noora	Honkala	FIN	1.7.92	2		Barcelona	18 Dec
220.613	Christine	Zanconato	FRA	23.10.62	14	EC	Albi	22 Oct
220.400t	Melanie	Rabb	USA	21.5.80	2		Sharon Hill PA	15 May
218.472	Sandra	Lundqvist	SWE	5.7.77	15	EC	Albi	22 Oct
	(30)							
218.387	Courtney	Dauwalter	USA	13.2.85	1		Minneapolis	5 Jun
217.811	Eva María Esnaola	ESP	23.11.60	18 Dec	217.266	Nicole Barker	AUS	16.7.71 10 Jul
217.787	Nathalie Derault-Hediou	FRA	15.10.73	22 Oct	215.310	Amy Masner	IRL	22.11.73 22 Oct
217.369	Anke Libuda	GER	3.4.79	22 Oct	215.253	Alison Young	GBR	26.11.73 22 Oct
Indoors								
226.194	Sandra	Lundqvist	SWE	5.7.77	1		Espoo	28 Feb
217.608	Amy Masner	IRL	22.11.73	28 Feb	216.284	Anna Grundahl	SWE	6.4.76 19 Nov
						2000 METRES STEEPLECHASE		
6:09.46	Gesa Felicitas	Krause	GER	3.8.92	1		Rehlingen	16 May
6:16.54	Viktoriya	Ivanova	RUS	21.11.91	1		Moskva	1 Jul
6:20.64	Jana	Sussmann	GER	12.10.90	1		Kiel	11 May
6:20.67	Fabienne	Schlumpf	SUI	17.11.90	1		Uster	27 May
6:21.05	Maya	Rehberg	GER	28.4.94	2		Kiel	11 May
6:21.98	Matylda	Kowal	POL	11.1.89	2		Rehlingen	16 May
6:25.12	Zita Kácser	HUN	2.10.88	22 May	6:27.38	Sara Treacy	IRL	22.6.89 14 May
6:26.08	Louise Webb	GBR	9.2.91	16 Apr	6:28.61	Natalya Leontyeva	RUS	5.7.87 1 Jul
6:26.45	Silvia Danekova	BUL	7.2.83	18 May	6:30.32	Kriszta Kószás	HUN	26.8.94 22 May
6:26.63	Viktória Gyürkés	HUN	15.10.92	22 May				
				JUNIORS				
6:31.32	Aneta	Konieczek	POL-J	8.6.97	1		Czestochowa	17 Sep
6:34.52	Anna Mark	Helwigh	DEN-Y	12.3.00	1	EY	Tbilisi	16 Jul
						3000 METRES STEEPLECHASE		
8:52.78	Ruth	Jebet	BRN	17.11.96	1	DL	Saint-Denis	27 Aug
8:59.75		Jebet			1	OG	Rio de Janeiro	15 Aug
8:59.97		Jebet			2	DL	Shanghai	14 May
9:00.01	Hyvin	Jepkemoi	KEN	13.1.92	1	Pre	Eugene	28 May
9:01.96		Jepkemoi			2	DL	Saint-Denis	27 Aug
9:07.00		Jebet			1	WK	Zürich	1 Sep
9:07.12		Jepkemoi			2	OG	Rio de Janeiro	15 Aug
9:07.42		Jepkemoi			1	DL	Shanghai	14 May
9:07.63	Emma	Coburn	USA	19.10.90	3	OG	Rio de Janeiro	15 Aug
9:08.37		Jebet			1	DL	Stockholm	16 Jun

3000m STEEPLECHASE

Mark	Name		Nat	Born	Pos	Meet	Venue	Date	
9:09.57		Jepkemoi			1	Bisl	Oslo	9	Jun
9:10.15		Jepkemoi			2	WK	Zürich	1	Sep
9:10.19		Coburn			3	DL	Saint-Denis	27	Aug
9:10.76		Coburn			3	Pre	Eugene	28	May
9:10.86	Beatrice	Chepkoech	KEN	6.7.91	4	DL	Saint-Denis	27	Aug
9:12.62		Jebet			1h1	OG	Rio de Janeiro	13	Aug
9:13.09	Sofia	Assefa	ETH	14.11.87	5	DL	Saint-Denis	27	Aug
9:14.28	Genevieve	LaCaze	AUS	4.8.89	6	DL	Saint-Denis	27	Aug
9:15.98		Jebet			2	DL	Shanghai	14	May
9:16.05		Chepkoech			4	OG	Rio de Janeiro	15	Aug
9:16.87	Etenesh	Diro	ETH	10.5.91	1		Rabat	22	May
9:17.15		Assefa			5	OG	Rio de Janeiro	15	Aug
9:17.41		Chepkoech			4	Pre	Eugene	28	May
9:17.42		Coburn			3	WK	Zürich	1	Sep
9:17.48		Coburn			1	NC	Eugene	7	Jul
9:17.55		Chepkoech			1h2	OG	Rio de Janeiro	13	Aug
9:18.12		Coburn			2h2	OG	Rio de Janeiro	13	Aug
9:18.16		Assefa			5	Pre	Eugene	28	May
9:18.41	Gesa Felicitas	Krause	GER	3.8.92	6	OG	Rio de Janeiro	15	Aug
9:18.53		Assefa			2	Bisl	Oslo	9	Jun
(30/8)									
9:18.71	Habiba	Ghribi	TUN	9.4.84	3h2	OG	Rio de Janeiro	13	Aug
9:18.85	Leah	O'Connor (10)	USA	30.8.92	6	Pre	Eugene	28	May
9:18.95	Virginia	Nyambura	KEN	20.7.93	7	DL	Saint-Denis	27	Aug
9:19.48	Stephanie	Garcia	USA	3.5.88	8	DL	Saint-Denis	27	Aug
9:19.76	Lalita	Babar	IND	2.6.89	4h2	OG	Rio de Janeiro	13	Aug
9:20.00	Colleen	Quigley	USA	20.11.92	9	DL	Saint-Denis	27	Aug
9:20.38	Madeline	Hills	AUS	15.5.87	7	OG	Rio de Janeiro	15	Aug
9:20.92	Courtney	Frerichs	USA	18.1.93	2	NC	Eugene	7	Jul
9:22.47	Purity	Kirui	KEN	13.8.91	5	DL	Shanghai	14	May
9:22.81	Lydia	Chepkurui	KEN	23.8.84	8	Pre	Eugene	28	May
9:23.49	Lydia	Rotich	KEN	8.8.88	6	DL	Shanghai	14	May
9:24.66	Yekaterina	Ivonina	RUS	14.6.94	1	NC	Cheboksary	21	Jun
(20)									
9:24.73	Celphine	Chespol	KEN-Y	23.3.99	7	DL	Shanghai	14	May
9:25.07	Norah	Tanui	KEN	2.10.95	1	AfCh	Durban	26	Jun
9:26.36	Gladys	Kipkemboi	KEN	15.10.86	2		Rabat	22	May
9:26.55	Sudha	Singh	IND	25.6.86	8	DL	Shanghai	14	May
9:27.22	Agnes	Chesang	KEN	1.4.86	2	AfCh	Durban	26	Jun
9:28.52	Luiza	Gega	ALB	5.11.88	2	EC	Amsterdam	10	Jul
9:28.54		Zhang Xinyan	CHN	9.2.94	1	NGP	Luoyang	6	May
9:28.72	Shalaya	Kipp	USA	19.8.90	4	NC	Eugene	7	Jul
9:28.81	Caroline	Chepkurui	KEN	12.3.90	3		Rabat	22	May
9:29.02	Yekaterina	Sokolenko	RUS	13.9.92	2	NC	Cheboksary	21	Jun
(30)									
9:29.77	Ashley	Higginson	USA	17.3.89	1		Princeton	18	Jun
9:30.11	Charlotta	Fougberg	SWE	19.6.85	5	Bisl	Oslo	9	Jun
9:30.24	Geneviève	Lalonde	CAN	5.9.91	4h3	OG	Rio de Janeiro	13	Aug
9:30.54	Fabienne	Schlumpf	SUI	17.11.90	6h2	OG	Rio de Janeiro	13	Aug
9:30.89	Mariya	Shatalova	UKR	3.3.89	6h1	OG	Rio de Janeiro	13	Aug
9:31.03	Peruth	Chemutai	UGA-Y	10.7.99	7h1	OG	Rio de Janeiro	13	Aug
9:31.75	Aisha	Praught	JAM	14.12.89	4	DL	London (OS)	23	Jul
9:31.84	Tigist	Mekonen	BRN-J	7.7.97	8	DL	Stockholm	16	Jun
9:31.88	Sandra	Eriksson	FIN	4.6.89	9	DL	Stockholm	16	Jun
9:31.95	Natalya	Vlasova	RUS	19.7.88	3	NC	Cheboksary	21	Jun
(40)									
9:32.03	Özlem	Kaya	TUR	20.4.90	9h1	OG	Rio de Janeiro	13	Aug
9:32.68	Anna Emilie	Møller	DEN-J	28.7.97	6h3	OG	Rio de Janeiro	13	Aug
9:32.93	Svetlana	Kudzelich	BLR	7.5.87	10h1	OG	Rio de Janeiro	13	Aug
9:32.94	Fadwa	Sidi Madane	MAR	20.11.94	11h1	OG	Rio de Janeiro	13	Aug
9:33.51	Bridget	Franek	USA	8.11.87	6	NC	Eugene	7	Jul
9:33.70	Olga	Vovk	RUS	13.2.93	4	NC	Cheboksary	21	Jun
9:34.96	Ophélie	Claude-Boxberger	FRA	18.10.88	1	PNG	Turku	29	Jun
9:35.09	Hiwot	Ayalew	ETH	6.3.90	7h2	OG	Rio de Janeiro	13	Aug
9:35.13	Matylda	Kowal	POL	11.1.89	8h2	OG	Rio de Janeiro	13	Aug
9:35.15	Sanaa	Koubaa	GER	6.1.85	9h2	OG	Rio de Janeiro	13	Aug
(50)									
9:35.22	Rosefline	Chepngetich	KEN-J	17.6.97	11	DL	Shanghai	14	May
9:35.31	Megan	Rolland	USA	30.8.88	7	NC	Eugene	7	Jul
9:35.91	Lennie	Waite	GBR	4.5.86	1		Portland	12	Jun

3000m STEEPLECHASE

Mark	Name		Nat	Born	Pos	Meet	Venue	Date
9:35.97	Birtukan	Adamu	ETH	29.4.92	5		Rabat	22 May
9:36.35	Mel	Lawrence	USA	29.8.89	8	NC	Eugene	7 Jul
9:36.54	Meryem	Akdag	TUR	5.8.92	1		Mersin	1 May
9:37.12	Jamie	Cheever	USA	28.2.87	1		Los Angeles (ER)	20 May
9:37.17	Agrie	Belachew	ETH-Y	20.1.99	3	WJ	Bydgoszcz	22 Jul
9:37.85	Woynshet	Ansa	ETH	9.4.96	3		Huelva	3 Jun
9:38.27	Betty	Kibet	KEN-Y	3.4.00	4	WJ	Bydgoszcz	22 Jul
(60)								
9:38.63	Juliana Paula	dos Santos	BRA	12.7.83	1		Odlozil Praha	6 Jun
9:39.18	Maya	Rehberg	GER	28.4.94	2		Odlozil Praha	6 Jun
9:39.40	Victoria	Mitchell	AUS	25.4.82	10h2	OG	Rio de Janeiro	13 Aug
9:39.41	Sara	Treacy	IRL	22.6.89	6	DL	London (OS)	23 Jul
9:39.84	Nicole	Bush	USA	4.4.86	4		Portland	12 Jun
9:40.19	Maeva	Danois	FRA	10.3.93	2		Oordegem	28 May
9:40.49	Rena	Chesser	USA	17.5.83	10	NC	Eugene	7 Jul
9:40.87	Ancuta	Bobocel	ROU	3.10.87	1	IntC	Pitesti	4 Jun
9:40.94	Sarah	Pease	USA	9.11.87	5		Portland	12 Jun
9:41.05	Jana	Sussmann	GER	12.10.90	5	ISTAF	Berlin	3 Sep
(70)								
9:41.22	Katie	Landwehr	USA	23.1.93	11	NC	Eugene	7 Jul
9:41.23	Diana	Martín	ESP	1.4.81	12	DL	Stockholm	16 Jun
9:41.26	Alycia	Butterworth	CAN	1.10.92	6		Portland	12 Jun
9:41.28	Jessica	Kamilos	USA	3.8.93	2	NCAA	Eugene	11 Jun
9:42.39	Elena	Panaet	ROU	5.6.93	2		Cluj-Napoca	16 Jul
9:42.49	Natalya	Aristarkhova	RUS	31.10.89	3		Sochi	26 May
9:42.64	Birtukan	Fente	ETH	18.6.89	1		Madrid	23 Jun
9:42.83	Viktoriya	Ivanova	RUS	21.11.91	1	Znam	Zhukovskiy	5 Jun
9:42.91	Anastasiya	Puzakova	BLR	12.12.93	6	EC	Amsterdam	10 Jul
9:42.93	Belén	Casetta	ARG	26.9.94	1	IbAm	Rio de Janeiro	14 May
(80)								
9:42.94	Marisa	Howard	USA	9.8.92	3		Los Angeles (ER)	20 May
9:43.16	Muriel	Coneo	COL	15.3.87	1	MSR	Norwalk	15 Apr
9:43.19	Michele	Finn	IRL	16.12.89	7	EC	Amsterdam	10 Jul
9:43.37	Megan	Patrignelli	USA	22.6.92	1		Portland	23 Jun
9:43.97	Ingeborg	Løvnes	NOR	5.9.92	4	PNG	Turku	29 Jun
9:44.22	Anju	Takamizawa	JPN	6.3.96	1	NC	Nagoya	25 Jun
9:44.5A	Ruth	Bisibori	KEN	2.1.88	1h1	NC	Nairobi	27 May
9:44.50	Eliane	Sahalinirina	MAD	20.3.82	4	AfCh	Durban	26 Jun
9:44.62	Charlotte	Prouse	CAN-J	9.2.97	6	WJ	Bydgoszcz	22 Jul
9:44.81	Maria	Bernard	CAN	6.4.93	7		Portland	12 Jun
(90)								
9:44.83	Salima	Alami	MAR	29.12.83	10h3	OG	Rio de Janeiro	13 Aug
9:44.93	Bezuayehu	Mohamed	ETH	4.1.96	4		Huelva	3 Jun
9:45.27	Chikako	Mori	JPN	25.11.92	2	NC	Nagoya	25 Jun
9:45.31	Fancy	Cherotich	KEN	10.8.90	3		Kawasaki	8 May
9:45.35	Kerry	O'Flaherty	IRL	15.7.81	14h1	OG	Rio de Janeiro	13 Aug
9:45.69	Marie	Bouchard	FRA	7.12.93	5		Oordegem	28 May
9:46.17	Elif	Karabulut	TUR	8.8.91	1		Mersin	23 May
9:46.49	Amina	Bettiche	ALG	14.12.87	2		Kortrijk	9 Jul
9:46.73	Lyudmila	Lebedeva	RUS	23.5.90	4		Sochi	26 May
9:46.86	Tatiane Raquel	da Silva	BRA	10.6.90	2	IbAm	Rio de Janeiro	14 May
(100)								

Mark	Name		Nat	Born	Pos	Date		Mark	Name		Nat	Born	Pos	Date
9:46.87	Rachel	Johnson	USA	30.4.93	4 Jun			9:50.54	Emily	Oren	USA	20.9.93	5 May	
9:47.17	Elinor	Purrier	USA	20.2.95	16 Apr			9:50.57	Sarah	Boyle	USA	27.5.86	18 Jun	
9:47.74	Maddie	Van Beek	USA	20.8.91	12 Jun			9:50.90	Brianna	Nerud	USA	16.9.94	23 Jun	
9:48.06	Zita	Kácser	HUN	2.10.88	19 Jun			9:50.9A	Gladys	Kemboi	KEN	.94	7 May	
9:48.29	Emily	Ritter	USA	28.12.92	20 May			9:51.48	Erica	Richardson	USA	23.5.89	17 Jun	
9:48.36	Silvia	Danekova	BUL	7.2.83	4 Jun			9:51.51	Nicol	Traynor	USA	6.5.89	20 May	
9:48.61	Joan	Chepkemoi	KEN	24.11.93	8 May			9:51.54	Camilla	Richardsson	FIN	14.9.93	3 Jun	
9:48.65	Erin	Teschuk	CAN	25.10.94	23 Jun			9:51.66	Cornelia	Griesche	GER	28.8.93	13 May	
9:48.72	Erin	Clark	USA	28.12.94	14 May			9:51.97	Rosie	Clarke	GBR	17.11.91	23 Jul	
9:48.81	Danielle	Winslow	USA	2.9.93	16 May			9:52.24	Aïssé	Sow	FRA	19.8.91	28 May	
9:48.97	María José	Pérez	ESP	12.6.92	9 Jul			9:52.61	Carmen	Graves	USA	27.1.91	18 Jun	
9:49.05	Rosa	Flanagan	NZL	28.2.96	30 Jan			9:52.62	Becky	Wade	USA	9.2.89	4 Jun	
9:49.16	Rosie	Donegan	AUS	1.7.93	7 May			9:52.88	Zulema	Arenas	PER	15.11.95	3 Jun	
9:49.25	Devin	Clark	USA-J	10.6.97	11 Jun			9:53.13	Anna	Petrova	RUS	15.7.94	21 Jun	
9:49.70	Viktória	Gyürkés	HUN	15.10.92	19 Jun			9:53.63	Nawal	Yahi	ALG	9.12.91	1 Jun	
9:49.93	Tugba	Güvenç	TUR	9.7.94	13 Aug			9:53.99	Regan	Yee	CAN	4.7.95	17 Jun	
9:50.07	Alex	Wilson	USA	.90	20 May			9:54.21	Misaki	Sango	JPN	21.4.89	25 Jun	
9:50.08	Betsy	Graney	USA	23.10.89	4 Jul			9:54.51	Eunice	Jepkorir	KEN	17.2.82	23 Jun	
9:50.16	Maria	Larsson	SWE	24.3.94	8 Jul			9:55.00	Emily	Myers	USA	23.5.94	12 Jun	
9:50.21	Paige	Kouba	USA	8.1.94	1 Apr			9:55.08	Lucie	Sekanová	CZE	5.8.89	22 May	
9:50.30	Marion	Kibor	KEN	27.9.94	1 May			9:55.14	Nega	Asmarech	ETH-Y	8.6.99	22 Jul	

460 3000m STEEPLE – 60 METRES HURDLES

Mark	Name		Nat	Born	Pos	Meet	Venue		Date
9:55.61	Amber	Schultz	USA	27.12.90	23	Jun			
9:55.62	Allix	Potratz-Lee	USA	3.5.86	20	May			
9:55.77	Claire	Perraux	FRA	6.10.87	9	Jun			
9:55.79	Madelin	Talbert	USA	23.4.94	15	Apr			
9:55.86	Ana Cristina	Narváez	MEX	12.8.91	15	Apr			
9:56.01	Katelyn	Steen	USA	9.7.96	20	May			
9:56.14	Irene Sánchez-Escribano		ESP	25.9.92	23	Jul			
9:56.42	Mara	Olson	USA	8.3.93	4	Jun			
9:56.79	Frida	Berge	NOR	13.3.94	14	May			
9:56.96	Marusa	Mismas	SLO	24.10.94	30	Jun			
9:57.17	Sofie	Gallein	BEL	7.8.92	23	Jun			
9:57.18	Louise	Webb	GBR	9.2.91	26	Jun			
9:57.45	Valeria	Roffino	ITA	9.4.90	1	May			
9:57.56	Nataliya	Strebkova	UKR	6.3.95	1	Jun			
9:57.68A	Magdalene	Masai	KEN	4.4.93	1	Jul			
9:58.10	Francesca	Bertoni	ITA	29.12.93	28	May			
9:58.52	Alicia	Nelson	USA	20.10.90	1	May			
9:58.81	Soyoka	Segawa	JPN	28.7.94	8	May			
9:59.17	Kako	Okada	JPN-J	.98	4	Sep			
9:59.18	Carolina	Robles	ESP	4.12.91	23	Jul			
9:59.32	Antonia	Hehr	GER	28.6.96	27	May			
9:59.35	Maki	Izumida	JPN	22.1.96	24	Jun			
9:59.54	Bri	Ilarda	AUS	19.2.96	14	May			
9:59.56	Svetlana	Shestakova	RUS	30.4.92	5	Jun			
9:59.64	Silvia	Oggioni	ITA	18.8.95	24	Sep			
9:59.73	Liz	Weiler	USA	22.2.93	27	May			
10:00.03	Eva	Krchová	CZE	10.9.89	2	Jul			
10:00.40	Chika	Mukai	JPN-J	26.2.98	1	May			
10:00.58	Aneta	Konieczek	POL-J	8.6.97	22	Jul			
10:00.65	Yui	Yabuta	JPN	.96	4	Sep			
10:00.95	Carolina	Lozano	ARG	27.2.96	14	May			
10:01.1A	Elizabeth	Mueni	KEN	28.12.91	28	May			
10:01.60	Emma	Oudiou	FRA	2.1.95	14	May			
10:01.60	Erika	Barr	USA	.94	9	Jun			
10:01.68		Xu Shuangshuang	CHN	6.4.96	23	Apr			
10:01.70	Natalya	Leontyeva	RUS	5.7.87	20	Jul			
10:01.73	Chantelle	Groenewoud	CAN	3.3.89	17	Jun			
10:01.80	Urszula	Necka	POL	28.6.84	6	Jun			
10:01.97	Justyna	Korytkowska	POL	12.3.86	3	Jun			
10:02.00	Isobel	Batt-Doyle	AUS	14.9.95	9	Apr			
10:02.02	Valentina	Costanza	ITA	27.2.87	28	May			
10:02.04A	Daisy	Jepkemei	KEN	13.2.96	1	Jul			
10:02.35	Jessica	Furlan	CAN	15.3.90	17	Jun			
10:02.47	Rachel	Sorna	USA	15.4.92	18	Jun			
10:02.84	Yekaterina	Doseykina	RUS	30.3.90	21	Jun			
10:03.52	Madeline	Strandemo	USA	12.7.95	22	Apr			
10:04.02	Natalya	Gorchakova	RUS	17.4.83	5	Jun			
10:04.17	Lili	Tóth	HUN-J	17.9.98	22	Jul			
10:04.28	Nana	Sato	JPN	24.9.89	25	Jun			
10:04.43	Bethany	Blomquist	USA	4.10.85	12	Jun			
10:04.69	Hannah	Waggoner	USA	6.2.95	13	May			
10:04.8A	Mercy	Njoroge	KEN	10.6.86	27	Apr			
10:04.89	Collier	Lawrence	USA	4.10.86	20	May			
10:05.03	Katelyn	Greenleaf	USA	9.3.94	1	Apr			
10:05.04	Caroline	Austin	USA	1.7.91	23	Jun			
10:05.25	Marwa	Bouzayani	TUN-J	26.3.97	22	Jul			
10:05.50	Molly	Renfer	SUI	22.8.93	28	May			
10:05.52	Moeno (200)	Shimizu	JPN-J	20.3.97	4	Sep			
10:05.65	Val	Constien	USA	21.3.96	14	May			

JUNIORS

See main list for top 8 juniors. 13 performances by 7 women to 9:40.0. Additional marks and further juniors:

Chespol	9:25.15	1	WJ	Bydgoszcz	22 Jul	9:32.30	8	WK Zürich	1 Sep
	9:25.49	1	ISTAF	Berlin	3 Sep				
Chemutai	9:31.34	10	DL	Shanghai	14 May				
Mekonen	9:34.08	2	WJ	Bydgoszcz	22 Jul				
Chepngetich	9:35.90	2		Kawasaki	8 May				
9:49.25	Devin		Clark	USA	10.6.97	5	NCAA	Eugene	11 Jun
9:55.14	Nega		Asmarech (10)	ETH-Y	8.6.99	8	WJ	Bydgoszcz	22 Jul
9:59.17	Kako		Okada	JPN	.98	2		Kumagaya	4 Sep
10:00.40	Chika		Mukai	JPN	26.2.98	1		Wakayama	1 May
10:00.58	Aneta		Konieczek	POL	8.6.97	9	WJ	Bydgoszcz	22 Jul
10:04.17	Lili		Tóth	HUN	17.9.98	10	WJ	Bydgoszcz	22 Jul
10:05.25	Marwa		Bouzayani	TUN	26.3.97	11	WJ	Bydgoszcz	22 Jul
10:05.52	Moeno		Shimizu	JPN	20.3.97	4		Kumagaya	4 Sep
10:05.72			Zhong Xiaoqian	CHN	24.10.97	1	NC	Tianjin	14 Sep
10:07.2A	Winfred		Mutile	KEN-Y	31.12.99	2		Embu	17 Jun
10:08.92	Yuki		Shibata	JPN-Y	19.1.99	2		Wakayama	1 May
10:10.6A	Emily		Kipchumba (20)	KEN	16.2.98	3	NC-j	Nairobi	22 Jun

60 METRES HURDLES INDOORS

7.76	Brianna		Rollins	USA	18.8.91	1	NC	Portland	12 Mar
7.77	Kendra		Harrison	USA	18.9.92	2	NC	Portland	12 Mar
7.81			K Harrison			1h3	WI	Portland	18 Mar
7.81	Nia		Ali	USA	23.10.88	1	WI	Portland	18 Mar
7.82			K Harrison			1h2		Karlsruhe	6 Feb
7.82			Rollins			1h1	WI	Portland	18 Mar
7.82			Rollins			2	WI	Portland	18 Mar
7.83			K Harrison			1		Lexington	23 Jan
7.83	Queen		Harrison	USA	10.9.88	3	NC	Portland	12 Mar
7.84			Rollins			1s2	WI	Portland	18 Mar
7.85	Janay		DeLoach	USA	12.10.85	1	Mill	New York (A)	20 Feb
7.85			Ali			1s1	NC	Portland	12 Mar
	(13/5)								
7.88	Cindy		Roleder	GER	21.8.89	1		Leipzig	27 Feb
7.89	Tiffany		Porter	GBR	13.11.87	1		Jablonec ned Nisou	5 Mar
7.89	Cindy		Ofili	GBR	5.8.94	1	NCAA	Birmingham, AL	12 Mar
7.90	Christina		Manning	USA	29.5.90	1		Montréal	20 Feb
7.90	Sharika (10)		Nelvis	USA	10.5.90	1h2	NC	Portland	11 Mar
7.91	Sasha		Wallace	USA	21.9.95	2	NCAA	Birmingham, AL	12 Mar
7.91	Andrea		Ivancevic	CRO	21.8.84	2h3	WI	Portland	18 Mar
7.92	Kristi		Castlin	USA	7.7.88	1		Athlone	17 Feb

60 METRES HURDLES

Mark	Name		Nat	Born	Pos	Meet	Venue	Date	
7.93	Jackie	Coward	USA	5.11.89	2		Montréal	20	Feb
7.93	Jasmin	Stowers	USA	23.9.91	3	Mill	New York (A)	20	Feb
7.95A	Lolo	Jones	USA	5.8.82	1		Albuquerque	6	Feb
7.96	Alina	Talay	BLR	14.5.89	2h1	WI	Portland	18	Mar
7.97	Devynne	Charlton	BAH	26.11.95	1	Big 10	Geneva	27	Feb
7.99	Angela	Whyte	CAN	22.5.80	5	WI	Portland	18	Mar
8.00	Akela	Jones	BAR	22.4.95	1	Big 12	Ames	27	Feb
	(20)								
8.01	Lucy	Hatton	GBR	8.11.94	2h1		Karlsruhe	6	Feb
8.01	Sandra	Gomis	FRA	21.11.83	1		Gent	13	Feb
8.01	Nadine	Hildebrand	GER	20.9.87	2	NC	Leipzig	27	Feb
8.02	Serita	Solomon	GBR	1.3.90	2h2		Jablonec ned Nisou	5	Mar
8.02	Tonea	Marshall	USA-J	17.12.98	1	HS N.Bal	New York	13	Mar
8.03	Bridgette	Owens	USA	14.3.92	2		Eaubonne	9	Feb
8.03	Dawn	Harper Nelson	USA	13.5.84	6		Boston (R)	14	Feb
8.04	Cindy	Billaud	FRA	11.3.86	1		Metz	21	Feb
8.04	Daeshon	Gordon	JAM	8.11.96	4	NCAA	Birmingham, AL	12	Mar
8.04	Mikiah	Brisco	USA	14.7.96	5	NCAA	Birmingham, AL	12	Mar
	(30)								
8.04	Brianne	Theisen-Eaton	CAN	18.12.88	1P	WI	Portland	18	Mar
8.05	Karolina	Koleczek	POL	15.1.93	2		Torun	12	Feb
8.05	Kaila	Barber	USA	4.4.93	3h2	NCAA	Birmingham, AL	11	Mar
8.06	Jade	Barber	USA	4.4.93	2		Notre Dame	6	Feb
8.06	Hanna	Plotitsyna	UKR	1.1.87	3		Jablonec	5	Mar
8.07	Danielle	Williams	JAM	14.9.92	1s1		State College	30	Jan
8.08	Pamela	Dutkiewicz	GER	28.9.91	4h1		Karlsruhe	6	Feb
8.08	Fabiana	Moraes	BRA	5.6.86	1		São Caetano do Sul	13	Feb
8.08	Mulern	Jean	USA	25.9.92	1h1		Boston (R)	26	Feb
8.08	Alaysha	Johnson	USA	20.7.96	3h1	NCAA	Birmingham, AL	11	Mar
	(40)								
8.09	Candice	Davis-Price	USA	26.10.85	4		Notre Dame	6	Feb
8.09	Ginnie	Crawford	USA	7.9.83	3		Torun	12	Feb
8.09	Nina	Morozova	RUS	15.9.89	1	NC	Moskva	24	Feb
8.09	Payton	Stumbaugh	USA	29.11.95	4h2	NCAA	Birmingham, AL	11	Mar
8.09	Kendell	Williams	USA	14.6.95	1P	NCAA	Birmingham, AL	11	Mar
8.10	Nikkita	Holder	CAN	7.5.87	1		Toronto	8	Jan
8.10A	Kaylon	Eppinger	USA	17.9.97	1		Albuquerque	23	Jan
8.10	Anastasiya	Pilipenko	KAZ	13.9.86	1	NC	Ust-Kamenogorsk	31	Jan
8.10	Aisseta	Diawara	FRA	29.6.89	2		Gent	13	Feb
8.10	Raven	Clay	USA	5.10.90	2		Baton Rouge	19	Feb
	(50)								
8.10	Ricarda	Lobe	GER	13.4.94	3	NC	Leipzig	27	Feb
8.10	Nooralotta	Neziri	FIN	9.11.92	1	NC	Tampere	28	Feb
8.10	LaTisha	Holden-Palmer	USA	29.8.89	5h1	NC	Portland	11	Mar
8.10	Michelle	Jenneke	AUS	23.6.93	4h1	WI	Portland	18	Mar
8.11	Giulia	Pennella	ITA	27.10.89	2	Pedro	Lódz	5	Feb
8.11	Tiffani	McReynolds	USA	4.12.91	1h2		Metz	21	Feb
8.11	Caridad	Jerez	ESP	23.1.91	1		Madrid	26	Feb
8.11	Monika	Zapalska	GER	24.5.94	4	NC	Leipzig	27	Feb
8.11	Candice	Price	USA	26.10.85	6h1	NC	Portland	11	Mar
8.11	Anastasiya	Mokhnyuk	UKR	1.1.91	2P	WI	Portland	18	Mar
	(60)								
8.12	Franziska	Hofmann	GER	27.3.94	3		Chemnitz	20	Feb
8.12	Ebony	Morrison	USA	28.12.94	6h2	NCAA	Birmingham, AL	11	Mar
8.12	Samantha	Scarlett	JAM	7.4.93	7h2	NCAA	Birmingham, AL	11	Mar
8.13	Phylicia	George	CAN	16.11.87	1s1		Houston	30	Jan
8.14	Brianna	McGhee	USA	8.11.93	1h2	Big 12	Ames	26	Feb
8.14	Katerina	Cachová	CZE	26.2.90	1	NC	Ostrava	27	Feb
8.14	Clélia	Rard-Reuse	SUI	1.8.88	1	NC	St.Gallen	28	Feb
8.14	Alexis	Duncan	USA-J	16.8.98	2	HS N.Bal	New York	13	Mar
8.15	Mariya	Aglitskaya	RUS	20.6.91	1		Sankt Peterburg	24	Jan
8.15A	Tiana	Davis	USA	12.8.89	2s2		Albuquerque	13	Feb
	(70)								
8.15	Matilda	Bogdanoff	FIN	8.10.90	1		Turku	14	Feb
8.15	Pedrya	Seymour	BAH	29.5.95	5h1	WI	Portland	18	Mar
8.16A	Danielle	Demas	USA	28.8.93	2		Albuquerque	23	Jan
8.16	Yasmin	Miller	GBR	24.5.95	2h1		Mondeville	6	Feb
8.16	Monique	Morgan	JAM	14.10.85	1h1		New York (SI)	12	Feb
8.16	Lindsay	Lindley	NGR	6.10.89	1h1		Birmingham	13	Feb
8.16	Yekaterina	Poplavskaya	BLR	7.5.87	2	NC	Mogilyov	21	Feb

100 METRES HURDLES

Mark		Name		Nat	Born	Pos	Meet	Venue	Date	
12.20	0.3	Kendra	Harrison	USA	18.9.92	1	DL	London (OS)	22	Jul
12.24	0.5		K Harrison			1	Pre	Eugene	28	May
12.34	1.2	Brianna	Rollins	USA	18.8.91	1	NC	Eugene	8	Jul
12.36	1.4		K Harrison			1	Towns	Athens GA	8	Apr
12.40	0.2		K Harrison			1h2	DL	London (OS)	22	Jul
12.42	0.1		K Harrison			1		George Town	14	May
12.42	0.7		K Harrison			1	Athl	Lausanne	25	Aug
12.44	0.2		K Harrison			1	DL	Saint-Denis	27	Aug
12.46	-0.3		K Harrison			1	DL	Birmingham	5	Jun
12.47	0.2		Rollins			1s1	OG	Rio de Janeiro	17	Aug
12.48	0.0		Rollins			1	OG	Rio de Janeiro	17	Aug
12.50	1.2	Kristi	Castlin	USA	7.7.88	2	NC	Eugene	8	Jul
12.53	0.7		Rollins			2	Pre	Eugene	28	May
12.54	0.4		Rollins			1h6	OG	Rio de Janeiro	16	Aug
12.55	0.7	Jasmin	Stowers	USA	23.9.91	3	Pre	Eugene	28	May
12.55	1.2	Nia	Ali	USA	23.10.88	3	NC	Eugene	8	Jul
12.56	1.5		K Harrison			1	DrakeR	Des Moines	30	Apr
12.56	-0.4		Rollins			1	Bisl	Oslo	9	Jun
12.56	0.7		Rollins			1h5	NC	Eugene	7	Jul
12.57	-0.3		Rollins			2	DL	Birmingham	5	Jun
12.57	0.2		K Harrison			1h1	NC	Eugene	7	Jul
12.57	1.2	Queen	Harrison	USA	10.9.88	4	NC	Eugene	8	Jul
12.57	0.3		Rollins			2	DL	London (OS)	22	Jul
12.58	0.2		Stowers			2h2	DL	London (OS)	22	Jul
12.59	0.3		Castlin			3	DL	London (OS)	22	Jul
12.59	0.0		Ali			2	OG	Rio de Janeiro	17	Aug
12.60	-1.0		Rollins			1s1	NC	Eugene	8	Jul
12.60	1.2	Sharika	Nelvis	USA	10.5.90	5	NC	Eugene	8	Jul
12.61	0.3		Nelvis			1		Kingston	11	Jun
12.61	0.0		Castlin			3	OG	Rio de Janeiro	17	Aug
		(30/7)								
12.62	-0.7	Cindy	Roleder	GER	21.8.89	1	EC	Amsterdam	7	Jul
12.63	0.0	Alina	Talay	BLR	14.5.89	1		Regensburg	5	Jun
12.63	0.0	Cindy	Ofili	GBR	5.8.94	4	OG	Rio de Janeiro	17	Aug
		(10)								
12.64	1.8	Nadine	Hildebrand	GER	20.9.87	1r4		Mannheim	29	Jul
12.64	0.2	Pedrya	Seymour	BAH	29.5.95	2s1	OG	Rio de Janeiro	17	Aug
12.65	0.2	Dawn	Harper Nelson	USA	13.5.84	2	DL	Saint-Denis	27	Aug
12.68	1.0	Jackie	Coward	USA	5.11.89	1		Eugene	29	Jul
12.69	0.7	Jasmine	Camacho-Quinn	USA/PUR	21.8.96	1	SEC	Tuscaloosa	14	May
12.70	0.3	Tiffany	Porter	GBR	13.11.87	6	DL	London (OS)	22	Jul
12.74	0.1	Phylicia	George	CAN	16.11.87	2		George Town	14	May
12.75	1.4	Candice	Price	USA	26.10.85	1		Montverde	11	Jun
12.76	1.3	Ebony	Morrison	USA	28.12.94	1q2	NCAA-E	Jacksonville	28	May
12.76	0.3	Jessica	Ennis-Hill	GBR	28.1.86	3h1	DL	London (OS)	22	Jul
		(20)								
12.77	0.3	Danielle	Williams	JAM	14.9.92	2		Kingston	11	Jun
12.78	1.2	Evonne	Britton	USA	10.10.91	1		Fairburn	29	May
12.78	0.3	Anne	Zagré	BEL	13.3.90	4h1	DL	London (OS)	22	Jul
12.79	1.6	Sandra	Gomis	FRA	21.11.83	1h2	NC	Angers	25	Jun
12.79	0.9	Megan	Simmonds	JAM	18.3.94	1	NC	Kingston	3	Jul
12.80	0.6	Monique	Morgan	JAM	14.10.85	1		Clermont	14	May
12.81	0.1	Ginnie	Crawford	USA	7.9.83	3		George Town	14	May
12.81	1.6	Nooralotta	Neziri	FIN	9.11.92	1		Kuortane	25	Jun
12.83	1.7	Payton	Stumbaugh	USA	29.11.95	1		Fayetteville	23	Apr
12.83A	0.4	Tobi	Amusan	NGR-J	23.4.97	1		El Paso	30	Apr
		(30)								
12.83	1.4	Kendell	Williams	USA	14.6.95	1H	NCAA	Eugene	10	Jun
12.83	0.1	Cindy	Billaud	FRA	11.3.86	1	NC	Angers	25	Jun
12.84	1.2	Tia	Jones	USA-Y	8.9.00	1h1	NC-j	Clovis	25	Jun
12.85	0.0	Pamela	Dutkiewicz	GER	28.9.91	3		Regensburg	5	Jun
12.85	2.0	Elvira	German	BLR-J	19.6.97	1	WJ	Bydgoszcz	24	Jul
12.85	1.5	Angela	Whyte	CAN	22.5.80	1		Edmonton	25	Jul
12.86	1.8	Morgan	Snow/Goodwin	USA	26.7.93	1rB		Nassau	16	Apr
12.86	1.2	Cassandra	Lloyd	USA	27.1.90	1		Halifax	22	Jun
12.86	0.9	Isabelle	Pedersen	NOR	27.1.92	3h3	OG	Rio de Janeiro	16	Aug
12.86	0.2	Shermaine	Williams	JAM	4.2.90	5s1	OG	Rio de Janeiro	17	Aug
		(40)								

100 METRES HURDLES

Mark	Wind	Name		Nat	Born	Pos	Meet	Venue	Date
12.87	0.8	Anastasiya	Pilipenko	KAZ	13.9.86	1h	NCp	Almaty	25 May
12.87	1.6	Clélia	Rard-Reuse	SUI	1.8.88	1		Thun	22 Jun
12.87	-0.7	Christina	Manning	USA	29.5.90	1		Sotteville-lès-Rouen	18 Jul
12.87	2.0	Rushelle	Burton	JAM-J	4.12.97	2	WJ	Bydgoszcz	24 Jul
12.88	0.2	Tiffani	McReynolds	USA	4.12.91	1	Johnson	Waco	23 Apr
12.88	1.7	Brianna	McGhee	USA	8.11.93	1h2	Big 12	Fort Worth	14 May
12.88	-0.5	Janay	DeLoach	USA	12.10.85	1r1		Bellinzona	6 Jun
12.88	-0.2	Yekaterina	Poplavskaya	BLR	7.5.87	2		Lapinlahti	19 Jun
12.89	1.8	Nadine	Visser	NED	9.2.95	2h1		Gainesville	22 Apr
12.89	-0.1	Nickiesha	Wilson	JAM	28.7.86	3h4	OG	Rio de Janeiro	16 Aug
		(50)							
12.90	1.3	Alexis	Perry	USA	8.8.94	2q2	NCAA-E	Jacksonville	28 May
12.90	1.9	Jacklyn	Howell	USA	3.10.96	2q3	NCAA-E	Jacksonville	28 May
12.90	0.9	Andrea	Ivancevic	CRO	21.8.84	4h3	OG	Rio de Janeiro	16 Aug
12.91	-0.2	Fabiana	Moraes	BRA	5.6.86	1	IbAm	Rio de Janeiro	16 May
12.91	2.0	Kaila	Barber	USA	4.4.93	1h6	NCAA-E	Jacksonville	27 May
12.91	1.6	Susanna	Kallur	SWE	16.2.81	2		Kuortane	25 Jun
12.92	1.0	Nikkita	Holder	CAN	7.5.87	4h5	OG	Rio de Janeiro	16 Aug
12.93	2.0	Michelle	Jenneke	AUS	23.6.93	1	NC	Sydney	3 Apr
12.93	2.0	Raven	Clay	USA	5.10.90	1		Coral Gables	9 Apr
12.93	0.5	Brianne	Theisen-Eaton	CAN	18.12.88	2H	Hypo	Götzis	28 May
		(60)							
12.93	0.5	Elisávet	Pesirídou	GRE	12.2.92	1	NC	Pátra	18 Jun
12.93	0.0	Kierre	Beckles	BAR	21.5.90	1	NC	Waterford	26 Jun
12.93	2.0	Alexis	Duncan	USA-J	16.8.98	4	WJ	Bydgoszcz	24 Jul
12.94A	-0.2	Briggitte	Merlano	COL	29.4.82	1	NC	Medellín	23 Apr
12.94	1.7	Akela	Jones	BAR	22.4.95	2		Fayetteville	23 Apr
12.94	0.1	Bridgette	Owens	USA	14.3.92	4		George Town	14 May
12.94	1.0	Chanice	Chase	CAN	6.8.93	1h2	NCAA-E	Jacksonville	27 May
12.95	1.1	Sasha	Wallace	USA	21.9.95	1s2	NCAA	Eugene	9 Jun
12.95	0.2	Chanel	Brissett	USA-Y	10.8.99	5h1	NC	Eugene	7 Jul
12.96	1.3	Nnenya	Hailey	USA	23.2.94	1		Tucson	9 Apr
		(70)							
12.96	1.6	Oksana	Shkurat	UKR	30.7.93	1		Minsk	5 Jul
12.96	0.3	Alaysha	Johnson	USA	20.7.96	4h2	NC	Eugene	7 Jul
12.97	1.7	Danielle	Demas	USA	28.8.93	2s1	NCAA	Eugene	9 Jun
12.98	1.7	Alex	Gochenour	USA	17.2.93	1H	SEC	Tuscaloosa	12 May
12.98	1.9	Nicole	Setterington	CAN	18.4.95	3q3	NCAA-E	Jacksonville	28 May
12.98	0.9	Aygerim	Shynyzbekova	KAZ	1.7.92	2		Almaty	5 Jul
12.99	0.1	Tenaya	Jones	USA	22.3.89	6		George Town	14 May
12.99	-0.2	Maíla Paula	Machado	BRA	22.1.81	2	IbAm	Rio de Janeiro	16 May
12.99	0.7	Caridad	Jerez	ESP	23.1.91	1		Barcelona (S)	1 Jun
13.00	2.0	Jade	Barber	USA	4.4.93	3	MSR	Norwalk	16 Apr
		(80)							
13.00	-0.2	Valentina	Kibalnikova	UZB	16.10.90	1h1	Kozanov	Almaty	25 Jun
13.00	1.3	Olena	Yanovska	UKR	15.2.90	1	Kozanov	Almaty	25 Jun
13.01	1.3	Mulern	Jean	USA	25.9.92	1h3	ACC	Tallahassee	14 May
13.01	1.6	Ricarda	Lobe	GER	13.4.94	3r3		Mannheim	29 Jul
13.02	0.8		Wu Shuijiao	CHN	19.6.91	1	NGP	Shaoxing	17 Apr
13.02	0.3	Franziska	Hofmann	GER	27.3.94	3		Weinheim	28 May
13.02	0.1	Hanna	Plotitsyna	UKR	1.1.87	6s1	EC	Amsterdam	7 Jul
13.03	2.0	Brianna	Beahan	AUS	1.11.91	2	NC	Sydney	3 Apr
13.03	1.2	Chastity	Stewart	USA	2.5.93	1		San Marcos	30 Apr
13.03	0.8	Karolina	Koleczek	POL	15.1.93	1	NC	Bydgoszcz	26 Jun
		(90)							
13.04	1.2	Tonea	Marshall	USA-J	17.12.98	1	TexR	Austin	2 Apr
13.04	1.9	Erica	Bougard	USA	26.7.93	4q3	NCAA-E	Jacksonville	28 May
13.04	1.9		Jung Hye-lim	KOR	1.7.87	1		Goseong	15 Jun
13.04	1.3	Giulia	Pennella	ITA	27.10.89	1h1	EC	Amsterdam	6 Jul
13.05	1.3	Katerina	Cachová	CZE	26.2.90	3	Odlozil	Praha	6 Jun
13.07	1.1	Breana	Norman	USA	14.9.92	1		Baltimore	23 Apr
13.07	0.5	Deborah	John	TTO	10.4.90	1	Jackson	Abilene	27 Apr
13.07	0.5	Laura	Ikauniece-Admidina	LAT	31.5.92	3H	Hypo	Götzis	28 May
13.07	0.9	Kimberley	Laing	JAM	8.1.89	5	NC	Kingston	3 Jul
13.07	0.1	Eefje	Boons	NED	18.7.94	1h3	EC	Amsterdam	6 Jul
		(100)							
13.08	0.7	Brandee'	Johnson	USA-J	3.4.98	18 Jun	13.10	1.0 Hitomi Shimura	JPN 8.11.90 25 Sep
13.09	2.0	Génesis	Romero	VEN	6.11.95	9 Apr	13.11	1.1 Tiana Davis	USA 12.8.89 23 Apr
13.09	0.6	Chelsea	Eades	USA	21.8.89	14 May	13.11	0.0 Stephanie Bendrat	AUT 5.3.91 26 May
13.09	-0.3	Ivana	Loncarek	CRO	8.4.91	26 Jun	13.11	0.0 Elin Westerlund	SWE 4.2.90 28 Jun
13.10	0.8	Rochelle	Coster	NZL	6.6.88	3 Apr	13.12	1.8 Melia Cox	USA 23.11.92 4 Jun
13.10	0.4	Mikiah	Brisco	USA	14.7.96	13 May	13.12	1.9 Lucie Koudelová	CZE 6.7.94 18 Jun

WOMEN 2016

100 METRES HURDLES

Mark	Wind	Name		Nat	Born	Pos	Meet	Venue		Date
13.12	1.8	Eva	Strogies	GER	21.3.91	29		Jul		
13.12	0.0	Carolin	Schäfer	GER	5.12.91	12		Aug		
13.13	0.7	Yvette	Lewis	PAN	16.3.85	25		Jun		
13.14	-0.4	Sally	Pearson	AUS	19.9.86	9		Jun		
13.15	1.0	Vanessa	Clerveaux	USA	17.6.94	27		May		
13.15	0.8	Olibía	Petsoúdi	GRE	6.12.86	29		May		
13.15	1.4	Marina	Tomic	SLO	30.4.83	10		Jun		
13.15	1.2	Gréta	Kerekes	HUN	9.10.92	18		Jun		
13.15	2.0	Alicia	Barrett	GBR-J	25.3.98	24		Jul		
13.16	2.0	Fiona	Morrison	NZL	24.10.88	3		Apr		
13.16	1.3	Reetta	Hurske	FIN	15.5.95	6		Jul		
13.16	0.5	Lindsay	Lindley	NGR	6.10.89	8		Jul		
13.17	1.7	Lina	Florez	COL	2.11.84	7		May		
13.17	0.9	Paige	Knodle	USA	15.8.93	15		May		
13.17	0.7	Lavonne	Idlette	DOM	31.10.85	11		Jun		
13.17	0.7	Anna	Cockrell	USA-J	28.8.97	18		Jun		
13.17	0.1	Aisseta	Diawara	FRA	29.6.89	25		Jun		
13.18	0.7	Valerie	Thames	USA	27.2.95	14		May		
13.18	1.2	Lucy	Hatton	GBR	8.11.94	22		May		
13.18	1.2	Rosina	Hodde	NED	10.2.83	22		May		
13.18	1.3	Alexia	Fortenberry	USA	19.9.93	28		May		
13.18	-0.1	Yekaterina	Galitskaya	RUS	24.2.87	21		Jun		
13.18	1.6	Sandra	Sogoyou	FRA	15.9.91	25		Jun		
13.19	1.6	Laura	Valette	FRA-J	16.2.97	25		Jun		
13.20	1.5	Jessica	Flax	USA	4.9.90	13		Apr		
13.20	1.2	Luca	Kozák	HUN	1.6.96	18		Jun		
13.20		Adanaca	Brown	BAH	23.10.93	25		Jun		
13.20	0.9	Micol	Cattaneo	ITA	14.5.82	16		Jul		
13.21	1.2	Monika	Zapalska	GER	24.5.94	28		May		
13.21	1.4	Taliyah	Brooks	USA	8.2.95	10		Jun		
13.21	1.2	Jasmyne	Graham	USA-J	6.5.97	25		Jun		
13.22	1.9	Ayako	Kimura	JPN	11.6.88	5		May		
13.22	-0.4	Kendra	Newton	USA	3.8.87	4		Jun		
13.22	0.3	Ashley	Miller	USA-J	17.2.98	25		Jun		
13.22	1.2	Chantae	McMillan	USA	1.5.88	29		Jul		
13.23	1.2	Taylor	Larch-Miller	USA	13.8.94	26		Mar		
13.23	0.8	Alice	Decaux	FRA	10.4.85	15		May		
13.24	0.9	Brittley	Humphrey	USA-J	6.3.98	16		Apr		
13.24	2.0	Sirena Alise	Williams	USA	26.12.87	16		Apr		
13.25	2.0	Kimberly	Golding	JAM	15.12.92	14		May		
13.24	2.0	Yekaterina	Bleskina	RUS	29.1.93	1		Jul		
13.25	1.7	Olivia	Haggerty	USA	22.6.95	14		May		
13.25	-1.2	Javette	Lee	USA	1.4.94	15		May		
13.25	1.9	Toyin	Augustus	NGR	24.12.79	21		May		

Mark	Wind	Name		Nat	Born	Pos	Meet	Venue		Date
13.25	1.9	Kaylon	Eppinger	USA	17.9.89	21		May		
13.26	1.5	Lorenda	Holston	USA	15.8.95	13		May		
13.26	1.3	Peta Gaye	Williams	JAM	13.9.95	14		May		
13.26	1.6	Clémence	Vifquin	FRA	9.6.86	25		Jun		
13.26	-0.7	Antoinette	Nana Djimou	FRA	2.8.85	8		Jul		
13.27	0.5	Adelly	Santos	BRA	8.7.87	22		Apr		
13.27	1.7	Eliecit	Palacios	COL	15.8.87	7		May		
13.27	1.3	Micha	Auzenne	USA	10.6.95	28		May		
13.27	1.4	Marthe	Koala	BUR	8.3.94	24		Jun		
13.28	1.6	Megan	George	USA	5.4.95	26		Mar		
13.28	-0.1	Jasmine	Edgerson	USA	6.6.91	22		Apr		
13.28	1.3	Skylar	Ross Ransom	USA	19.2.95	28		May		
13.28	1.0	Lutisha	Bowen	USA	9.7.90	11		Jun		
13.28	1.2	Anamaria	Nesteriuc	ROU	29.11.93	18		Jun		
13.28	-1.1	Sharona	Bakker	NED	12.4.90	25		Jun		
13.28	1.3	Mollie	Courtney	GBR-J	2.7.97	22		Jul		
13.29	2.0	Daniela	Roman	AUS	7.1.96	3		Apr		
13.29	0.8	Ariel	Jones	USA	18.7.95	28		May		
13.29	1.1	Rosvitha	Okou	CIV	5.9.86	12		Jun		
13.29	1.1	Mathilde	Raibaut	FRA	18.4.92	25		Jun		
13.29	0.6	Jayla	Stewart	USA-J	23.7.97	25		Jun		
13.29	-0.7	Anouk	Vetter	NED	4.2.93	8		Jul		
13.30	1.7	Abbie	Taddeo	AUS	8.2.94	20		Feb		
13.30	-0.7	Chari	Hawkins	USA	21.5.91	1		Apr		
13.30	0.1	Christie	Moerman	CAN	5.10.86	15		Apr		
13.30	0.3	Letícia	Gaspar	BRA	24.1.90	25		May		
13.30	0.6	Mobolaji	Adeokun	NGR	14.1.94	28		May		
13.30	1.7	Sarah	Koutouan	FRA-J	4.2.98	25		Jun		
13.30	1.1	Awa	Sène	FRA	24.7.94	25		Jun		
13.31	1.7	Kelsey	Herman	USA	15.6.96	12		May		
13.31	1.5	Samantha	Scarlett	JAM	7.4.93	13		May		
13.31	1.9	Stefani	Kerrison	USA	7.6.96	28		May		
13.32	0.1	Belkis	Milanés	CUB	16.1.90	26		May		
13.32	1.0	Kyra	Atkins	USA	1.9.92	27		May		
13.32	1.4	Uhunoma	Osazuwa	NGR	23.11.87	24		Jun		
13.32	1.6	Aurore	Isnard	FRA	14.2.84	25		Jun		
13.32	-0.5	Ashlea	Maddex	CAN	16.12.92	10		Jul		
13.32	0.3		Kang Ya	CHN	16.3.90	15		Sep		
13.32	1.0	Eriko	Soma	JPN	30.9.91	25		Sep		
13.33	0.0	Karelle	Edwards	CAN	30.3.90	30		Apr		
13.33	1.9	Chantel	Ray	USA	3.1.96	28		May		
13.33	1.9	Masumi	Aoki	JPN	16.4.94	10		Jun		
13.33	-0.3		Wang Dou	CHN	18.5.93	13		Sep		
		(199)			228 to 13.39					

Wind assisted

Mark	Wind	Name		Nat	Born	Pos	Meet	Venue		Date
12.52	2.9		Rollins			1		Kingston	7	May
12.54	2.9	Queen	Harrison	USA	10.9.88	2		Kingston	7	May
12.54	3.8	Jasmine	Camacho-Quinn	USA/PUR	21.8.96	1	NCAA	Eugene	11	Jun
12.55	2.9	Danielle	Williams	JAM	14.9.92	3		Kingston	7	May
12.61	3.3		Q Harrison			1		Montreuil-sous-Bois	7	Jun
12.67	2.7	Phylicia	George	CAN	16.11.87	1		Baton Rouge	23	Apr
12.67	2.9	Christina	Manning	USA	29.5.90	1		Austin	7	May
12.76	2.9	Tiffany	McReynolds	USA	4.12.91	2		Austin	7	May
12.79	3.8	Tobi	Amusan	NGR-J	23.4.97	2	NCAA	Eugene	11	Jun
12.81	2.9	Angela	Whyte	CAN	22.5.80	1rB	MSR	Norwalk	16	Apr
12.81	3.8	Sasha	Wallace	USA	21.9.95	3	NCAA	Eugene	11	Jun
12.85	2.6	Briggitte	Merlano	COL	29.4.82	4rA		Nassau	16	Apr
12.86	2.5	Nikkita	Holder	CAN	7.5.87	2		Clermont	30	Apr
12.86	3.1		Jung Hye-lim	KOR	1.7.87	1	Nambu	Sapporo	10	Jul
12.87	2.1	Jacklyn	Howell	USA	3.10.96	2		Baton Rouge	30	Apr
12.87	3.8	Alexis	Perry	USA	8.8.94	5	NCAA	Eugene	11	Jun
12.88	2.3	Andrea	Ivancevic	CRO	21.8.84	2	Hanz	Zagreb	6	Sep
12.90	3.8	Chanice	Chase	CAN	6.8.93	6	NCAA	Eugene	11	Jun
12.92	3.3	Sally	Pearson	AUS	19.9.86	6		Montreuil	7	Jun
12.96	2.9	Christie	Moerman	CAN	5.10.86	2rB	MSR	Norwalk	16	Apr
12.96	3.0	Tiana	Davis	USA	12.8.93	1r1		Fort Lauderdale	25	Jun
12.99	2.7	Daeshon	Gordon	JAM	8.11.96	4		Baton Rouge	23	Apr
13.00	2.4	Ricarda	Lobe	GER	13.4.94	2		Zeulenroda	24	Jun
13.00	2.4	Franziska	Hofmann	GER	27.3.94	2		Zeulenroda	24	Jun
13.01	2.4	Karolina	Koleczek	POL	15.1.93	2	EAF	Bydgoszcz	5	Jun
13.01	2.7	Melia	Cox	USA	23.11.92	1		Chula Vista	26	Jun
13.02	2.6	Yvette	Lewis	PAN	16.3.85	5rA		Nassau	16	Apr
13.02	2.6	Mikiah	Brisco	USA	14.7.96	3q1	NCAA-E	Jacksonville	28	May
13.02	3.1	Chelsea	Eades	USA	21.8.89	H		Ottawa	17	Jun
13.04	2.9	Ayako	Kimura	JPN	11.6.88	4rB	MSR	Norwalk	16	Apr

100 – 200 – 300 – 400 METRES HURDLES

Mark	Wind	Name		Nat	Born	Pos	Meet	Venue	Date
13.04	2.5	Stephanie	Bendrat	AUT	5.3.91	2h2		Clermont	30 Apr
13.05	3.1	Lucie	Koudelová	CZE	6.7.94	1		Plzeň	14 May
13.05	2.8	Lucy	Hatton	GBR	8.11.94	1h2	NC	Birmingham	25 Jun
13.06	2.9	Hitomi	Shimura	JPN	8.11.90	6rB	MSR	Norwalk	16 Apr
13.08	2.5	Rosina	Hodde	NED	10.2.83				30 Apr
13.11	3.0	Kimberly	Golding	JAM	15.12.92				30 Apr
13.11	2.4	Kendra	Newton	USA	3.8.87				15 May
13.12	2.6	Vanessa	Clerveaux	USA	17.6.94				28 May
13.12	2.5	Heather	Miller Koch	USA	30.3.87				18 Jun
13.14	2.3	Deborah	John	TTO	10.4.90				16 Apr
13.14	2.4	Ariel	Jones	USA	18.7.95				14 May
13.14	2.1	Toyin	Augustus	NGR	24.12.79				21 May
13.16	2.9	Taliyah	Brooks	USA	8.2.95				30 Mar
13.16	3.0	Adanaca	Brown	BAH	23.10.93				25 Jun
13.16	2.7	Kaylon	Eppinger	USA	17.9.89				26 Jun
13.18	2.1	Skylar	Ross Ransom	USA	19.2.95				1 Apr
13.18	2.6	Micha	Auzenne	USA	10.6.95				14 May
13.18	2.4	Ashley	Miller	USA-J	17.2.98				14 May
13.20	3.0	Emma	Spagnola	USA	18.3.96				30 Apr
13.21	2.1	Antoinette	Nana Djimou	FRA	2.8.85				17 Sep
13.22	2.1	Samantha	Scarlett	JAM	7.4.93				9 Apr
13.22	3.0	Yvana	Hepburn-Bailey	BAH/USA	9.11.87				25 Jun
13.23	2.6	Mofiyinfoluwa	Olusola	USA	23.8.96				14 May
13.23	2.5	Karelle	Edwards	CAN	30.3.90				19 May
13.25	3.5	Sharona	Bakker	NED	12.4.90				18 Jun
13.27	3.1	Holly	Pattie-Belleli	GBR	9.6.94				14 May
13.28	3.3	Kseniya	Medvedeva	BLR	24.10.91				1 Jun
13.28	4.7	Devyani	Biswal	CAN	.93				12 Jun
13.29	2.2	Melaine	Walker	JAM	1.1.83				2 Apr
13.29	2.6	Angelita	Broadbelt-Blake	GBR	12.9.85				30 Jul
13.31	2.9	Janice	Jackson	JAM	30.10.91				11 Jun
13.31	3.1	Jessica	Zelinka	CAN	3.9.81				17 Jun
13.31	2.7	Tale	Ørving	NOR	17.3.89				19 Jun

Best at low altitude
| 12.91 | -0.1 | Amusan (J) | | | | 3s2 | OG | Rio de Janeiro | 17 Aug |
| 12.94 | 1.3 | Merlano | | | | 1 | | Odlozil Praha | 6 Jun |

JUNIORS
See main list for top 7 juniors. 13 performances by 6 women to 13.00. Additional marks and further juniors:

Amusan	12.91	-0.1	3s2	OG	Rio de Janeiro	17 Aug	12.99	0.6 1s1 WJ	Bydgoszcz	23 Jul
	12.95	2.0	5	WJ	Bydgoszcz	24 Jul	12.99	1.0 5h5 OG	Rio de Janeiro	16 Aug
	12.98	0.9	4s3	NCAA	Eugene	9 Jun			
Jones	12.89	2.0	3	WJ	Bydgoszcz	24 Jul			
German	12.97	0.9	1s3	WJ	Bydgoszcz	23 Jul			

Mark	Wind	Name		Nat	Born	Pos	Meet	Venue	Date
13.08	0.7	Brandee'	Johnson	USA	3.4.98	2	HS N.Bal	Greensboro	18 Jun
13.15	2.0	Alicia	Barrett	GBR	25.3.98	6	WJ	Bydgoszcz	24 Jul
13.17	0.7	Anna	Cockrell (10)	USA	28.8.97	4	HS N.Bal	Greensboro	18 Jun
13.19	1.6	Laura	Valette	FRA	16.2.97	3h2	NC	Angers	25 Jun
13.21	1.2	Jasmyne	Graham	USA	6.5.97	3h1	NC-j	Clovis	25 Jun
13.22	0.3	Ashley	Miller	USA	17.2.98	4	NC-j	Clovis	25 Jun
13.24	0.9	Brittley	Humphrey	USA	6.3.98	1	MSR	Norwalk	16 Apr
13.28	1.3	Mollie	Courtney	GBR	2.7.97	2h3	WJ	Bydgoszcz	22 Jul
13.29	0.6	Jayla	Stewart	USA	23.7.97	4h2	NC-j	Clovis	25 Jun
13.30	1.7	Sarah	Koutouan	FRA	4.2.98	1-j		Mannheim	25 Jun
13.34	1.4	Pauline	Salies	FRA	18.9.97	1		Vineuil	28 May
13.35	0.9	Chanel	Freeman	GUY	27.3.97	1		Tempe	26 Mar
13.35	0.9	Taylon	Bieldt (20)	RSA	4.11.98	3s3	WJ	Bydgoszcz	23 Jul

Wind assisted see main list for 1 junior performance to 13.00
| 13.18 | 2.4 | Ashley | Miller | USA-J | 17.2.98 | 3h1 | Big 12 | Fort Worth | 14 May |
| 13.32 | 2.1 | Jasmine | Barge | USA-J | 2.1.97 | 1 | KansR | Lawrence | 23 Apr |

200 METRES HURDLES

| 26.93 | 1.4 | Robine | Schürmann | SUI | 31.1.89 | 1 | | Basel | 7 May |

Straight track
| 26.61 | | Axelle | Dauwens | BEL | 1.12.90 | 1 | | Bruxelles | 4 Sep |

300 METRES HURDLES

38.93		Léa	Sprunger	SUI	5.3.90	1		Langenthal	3 Aug
39.44		Zuzana	Hejnová	CZE	19.12.86	1		Cheb	2 Aug
39.69		Jackie	Baumann	GER	24.8.95	2		Langenthal	3 Aug
39.2h		Joanna	Linkiewicz	POL	2.5.90	1		Pliezhausen	8 May

400 METRES HURDLES

52.88		Dalilah	Muhammad	USA	7.2.90	1	NC	Eugene	10 Jul
53.13			Muhammad			1	OG	Rio de Janeiro	18 Aug
53.51		Shamier	Little	USA	20.3.95	1	NCAA	Eugene	11 Jun
53.55		Sara Slott	Petersen	DEN	9.4.87	2	OG	Rio de Janeiro	18 Aug
53.72		Ashley	Spencer	USA	8.6.93	3	OG	Rio de Janeiro	18 Aug
53.78			Muhammad			1	Athl	Lausanne	25 Aug
53.89			Muhammad			1s3	OG	Rio de Janeiro	16 Aug
53.90			Muhammad			1	DL	London (OS)	22 Jul
53.92		Zuzana	Hejnová	CZE	19.12.86	4	OG	Rio de Janeiro	18 Aug
53.96		Janeive	Russell	JAM	14.11.93	1	GGala	Roma	2 Jun
53.97		Georganne	Moline	USA	6.3.90	1		Tucson	21 May
53.97			Little			1	WK	Zürich	1 Sep
54.02			Spencer			2	NC	Eugene	10 Jul

400 METRES HURDLES

Mark	Name		Nat	Born	Pos	Meet	Venue	Date	
54.09	Eilidh	Doyle	GBR	20.2.87	1	Herc	Monaco	15	Jul
54.14		Muhammad			1s2	NC	Eugene	8	Jul
54.15	Sydney	McLaughlin	USA-Y	7.8.99	3	NC	Eugene	10	Jul
54.15	Ristananna	Tracey (10)	JAM	9.5.92	5	OG	Rio de Janeiro	18	Aug
54.16		Russell			1		Rabat	22	May
54.22		Petersen			2	WK	Zürich	1	Sep
54.33		Petersen			2	DL	London (OS)	22	Jul
54.37		Muhammad			1		Montreuil-sous-Bois	7	Jun
54.45	Leah	Nugent	JAM	23.11.92	6	OG	Rio de Janeiro	18	Aug
54.45		Doyle			2	Athl	Lausanne	25	Aug
54.46		McLaughlin			1	N.Bal HS	Greensboro	19	Jun
54.47	Kori	Carter	USA	3.6.92	4	NC	Eugene	10	Jul
54.47	Wenda	Nel	RSA	30.7.88	3	DL	London (OS)	22	Jul
54.47	Cassandra	Tate	USA	11.9.90	1	VD	Bruxelles	9	Sep
54.48	Vera	Rudakova	RUS	20.3.92	1	NCp	Zhukovskiy	21	Jul
54.51		Spencer			1		Atlanta	4	Jun
54.53		Doyle			1	DL	Doha	6	May
	(30/15)								
54.65	Autumne	Franklin	USA	20.7.94	6	NC	Eugene	10	Jul
54.67	Kiah	Seymour	USA	11.1.94	2	NCAA	Eugene	11	Jun
54.82	Sage	Watson	CAN	20.6.94	3		Tucson	21	May
54.87	Kemi	Adekoya	BRN	16.1.93	2	DL	Doha	6	May
54.92	Léa	Sprunger	SUI	5.3.90	1		Genève	11	Jun
	(20)								
54.94	Chanice	Chase	CAN	6.8.93	5	NCAA	Eugene	11	Jun
54.95	Jaide	Stepter	USA	25.4.94	7	NC	Eugene	10	Jul
54.98	Nnenya	Hailey	USA	23.2.94	2		Baton Rouge	23	Apr
55.00	Anna	Titimets	UKR	5.3.89	1	NC	Lutsk	19	Jun
55.02	Kaliese	Spencer	JAM	6.5.87	3	DL	Doha	6	May
55.20	Anna	Cockrell	USA-J	28.8.97	1	WJ	Bydgoszcz	22	Jul
55.22	Turquoise	Thompson	USA	31.7.91	1		San Diego	11	Jun
55.23	Lauren	Wells	AUS	3.8.88	1		Kawasaki	8	May
55.25	Joanna	Linkiewicz	POL	2.5.90	1		Warszawa	28	May
55.28	Alexis	Franklin	USA	9.10.93	2q2	NCAA-E	Jacksonville	27	May
	(30)								
55.30	T'erea	Brown	USA	24.10.89	2		Atlanta	4	Jun
55.32	Viktoriya	Tkachuk	UKR	8.11.94	1		Lutsk	4	Jun
55.43	Meghan	Beesley	GBR	15.11.89	1	DrakeR	Des Moines	30	Apr
55.48	Olena	Kolesnychenko	UKR	3.6.93	2	NC	Lutsk	19	Jun
55.50	Ayomide	Folorunso	ITA	17.10.96	4	EC	Amsterdam	10	Jul
55.53	Kaila	Barber	USA	4.4.93	3q2	NCAA-E	Jacksonville	27	May
55.55	Claudia	Francis	USA	14.11.93	4q2	NCAA-E	Jacksonville	27	May
55.58	Rhonda	Whyte	JAM	6.11.90	1		Kingston	16	Apr
55.59	Yekaterina	Belanovich	BLR	14.1.91	2		Warszawa	28	May
55.68	Axelle	Dauwens	BEL	1.12.90	1	NC	Bruxelles	26	Jun
	(40)								
55.69	Marzia	Caravelli	ITA	23.10.81	1		Orvieto	26	May
55.75	Jade	Miller	USA	13.1.95	5q2	NCAA-E	Jacksonville	27	May
55.78	Yadisleidy	Pedroso	ITA	28.1.87	5s2	OG	Rio de Janeiro	16	Aug
55.79	Amalie Hammild	Iuel	NOR	17.4.94	2s2	EC	Amsterdam	9	Jul
55.82	Tia Adana	Belle	BAR	16.6.96	1	CIAA	Charlotte	23	Apr
55.83	Noelle	Montcalm	CAN	3.4.88	1	NC	Edmonton	8	Jul
55.84	Phara	Anacharsis	FRA	17.12.83	4		Montreuil-sous-Bois	7	Jun
55.85	Grace	Claxton	PUR	19.8.93	5s3	OG	Rio de Janeiro	16	Aug
55.89	Emilia	Ankiewicz	POL	22.11.90	3h4	OG	Rio de Janeiro	15	Aug
55.95	Aleksandra	Romanova	KAZ	26.12.90	1	UZB Cp	Tashkent	9	Jun
	(50)								
56.00	Stina	Troest	DEN	17.1.94	4s1	OG	Rio de Janeiro	16	Aug
56.03	Symone	Black	USA	26.10.95	2	Big 10	Lincoln, NE	15	May
56.05	Maeva	Contion	FRA	31.5.92	2		Tarare	9	Jul
56.06	Tiffany	Williams	USA	5.2.83	2h4	NC	Eugene	7	Jul
56.06	Christine	McMahon	IRL	6.7.92	2	NA	Heusden	16	Jul
56.06	Janeil	Bellille	TTO	18.6.89	6s3	OG	Rio de Janeiro	16	Aug
56.08	Arna Stefania	Gudmundsdóttir	ISL	1.9.95	1	Nord-23	Espoo	20	Aug
56.12	Maureen	Maiyo	KEN	28.5.85	2	AfCh	Durban	26	Jun
56.14	Satomi	Kubokura	JPN	27.4.82	2		Kawasaki	8	May
56.16	Brandee'	Johnson	USA-J	3.4.98	3	NC-j	Clovis	25	Jun
	(60)								
56.17	Yanique	Haye-Smith	JAM	22.3.90	3		Atlanta	4	Jun
56.19	Jackie	Baumann	GER	24.8.95	1		Oordegem	28	May

400 METRES HURDLES

Mark	Name		Nat	Born	Pos	Meet	Venue	Date	
56.20	Vera	Barbosa	POR	13.1.89	1rB		Genève	11	Jun
56.21	Nikita	Tracey	JAM	18.9.90	2		Kingston	12	Jun
56.23	Sparkle	McKnight	TTO	21.12.91	1		Kingston	21	May
56.27	Nenah	De Coninck	BEL	2.9.96	2	NC	Bruxelles	26	Jun
56.29	Shannon	Kalawan	JAM-J	25.11.97	1	Carifta	St. George	27	Mar
56.33	Natalya	Asanova	UZB	29.11.89	2	NC	Tashkent	9	Jun
56.33	Hilla	Uusimäki	FIN	12.6.96	2	Nord-23	Espoo	20	Aug
56.34A	Zurian	Hechavarría	CUB	10.8.95	1		Ciudad de México	2	Jul
(70)									
56.34	Bianca	Baak	NED	25.1.92	4s2	EC	Amsterdam	9	Jul
56.36	Denisa	Rosolová	CZE	21.8.86	4h3	OG	Rio de Janeiro	15	Aug
56.38	Kymber	Payne	USA	4.6.96	2q3	NCAA-E	Jacksonville	27	May
56.42A	Zudikey	Rodríguez	MEX	14.3.87	1		Ciudad de México	25	Jun
56.42	Rushell	Clayton	JAM	18.10.92	4	NC	Kingston	1	Jul
56.44		Wang Huan	CHN	21.9.94	1	NGP	Taiyuan	21	May
56.44	Tameka	Jameson	NGR	11.8.89	4		Tucson	21	May
56.45	Landria	Buckley	USA	2.7.88	1		Los Angeles (ER)	7	May
56.45	Tyler	Brockington	USA	6.2.94	3q3	NCAA-E	Jacksonville	27	May
56.45	Sarah	Wells	CAN	10.11.89	4	NC	Edmonton	8	Jul
(80)									
56.46	Damajahnee	Birch	USA-J	29.1.97	1		Fayetteville	6	May
56.48	Taysia	Radoslav	CAN	17.9.96	3		Princeton	8	May
56.48	Petra	Fontanive	SUI	10.10.88	1	WK-23	Zürich	1	Sep
56.48		Huang Yan	CHN	12.1.96	1	NC	Tianjin	16	Sep
56.49	Jasmine	Hyder	USA	25.8.88	2		Austin	16	Apr
56.50	Erica	Twiss	USA	17.6.92	4		Atlanta	4	Jun
56.53	Aurélie	Chaboudez	FRA	9.5.93	3		Genève	11	Jun
56.55	Ariel	Jones	USA	18.7.95	1		Los Angeles	26	Mar
56.63	Ka'lynn	Jupiter	USA	12.1.95	3q1	NCAA-E	Jacksonville	27	May
56.65	Amaka	Ogoegbunam	NGR	3.3.90	1	NC	Maia	26	Jun
56.66	Tina	Matusinska	POL	12.7.88	1	EAF	Bydgoszcz	5	Jun
56.67		Quach Thi Lan	VIE	18.10.95	1	NC	Hanoi	25	Nov
56.70	Montayla	Holder	USA	7.2.94	3		Tucson	9	Apr
56.75	Haruko	Ishizuka	JPN-J	2.6.97	3		Kawasaki	8	May
56.75	Yelena	Zuykevich	RUS	26.2.90	2		Sochi	27	May
56.79	Déborah	Rodríguez	URU	2.12.92	1		Bruxelles	19	Jun
56.79	Satsuki	Umehara	JPN	22.5.94	1		Kumagaya	4	Sep
56.81	Kelsey	Balkwill	CAN	19.9.92	1		Guelph	25	Jun
56.84	Jen	Cotten	CAN	14.10.87	1r2		Ottawa	18	Jun
56.85	Liga	Velvere	LAT	10.2.90	1		Valmiera	1	Jul
(100)									
56.85	Sayaka	Aoki	JPN	15.12.86	2		Osaka	24	Sep
56.86	Katrina	Seymour	BAH	7.1.93	15 May		57.46	Shona	Richards	GBR	1.9.95	11 Jun
56.89	Ghofrane	Al-Mohamed	SYR	6.6.89	5 Jul		57.47	Lucie	Slaníčková	SVK	8.11.88	12 Jun
56.90	Latosha	Wallace	USA	25.3.85	18 Jun		57.48	Kiana	Hawn	USA	5.12.95	31 Mar
56.90	Xahria	Santiago	CAN-Y	9.10.99	22 Jul		57.49	Anaïs	Lufutucu	FRA	24.4.92	9 Jul
56.91	Danielle	Dowie	JAM	5.5.92	14 May		57.56	Brenna	Detra	USA	.95	14 May
56.91	Ellen	Wortham	USA	5.1.90	11 Jun		57.56	Dihia	Haddar	ALG	29.4.95	16 Jul
56.93	Nicole	Leach	USA	18.7.87	14 May		57.61	Jaclyn	Siefring	USA	.95	16 Apr
56.94	Aminat Yusuf	Odeyemi	BRN-J	27.6.97	20 Jul		57.62	Claire	Privat	FRA	5.7.89	25 Jun
56.94		Xiao Xia	CHN	6.6.91	16 Sep		57.64	Eva	Duinslaeger	BEL	21.9.88	26 Jun
56.98	Andrenette	Knight	JAM	19.11.96	18 Mar		57.65	Viivi	Lehikoinen	FIN-Y	27.8.99	24 Jul
56.98	Francesca	Doveri	ITA	21.12.82	11 Jun		57.68	Daje	Pugh	USA	22.8.94	26 May
56.99	Nicolee	Foster	JAM-J	11.1.98	18 Mar		57.69	Jauna	Murmu	IND	16.8.90	11 Feb
57.00	Jessica	Turner	GBR	8.8.95	5 Jun		57.69	Mariam	Abdul-Rashid	CAN-J	21.9.97	21 Jul
57.04	Jen	Esposito	USA	22.7.94	26 May		57.69	Aleksandra	Kurakina	RUS	15.8.87	28 Jul
57.04	Manami	Kira	JPN	23.10.91	24 Sep		57.70	Bethany	Close	GBR	30.12.95	26 Jun
57.05	Toria	Levy	USA	5.10.94	26 May		57.71	Chastity	Stewart	USA	2.5.93	27 May
57.05	Ugonna	Ndu	NGR	27.6.91	11 Jun		57.73	Klaudia	Zurek	POL	22.9.91	28 May
57.05	Irina	Takuntseva	RUS	14.11.90	22 Jun		57.73	Abigail	Lewis	JAM	7.5.93	10 Jun
57.06	Lamiae	Lhabze	MAR	1.5.93	10 Jul		57.74	Alena	Hrusoci	CRO	14.3.95	15 May
57.07	Valeriya	Khramova	RUS	13.8.92	21 Jul		57.74	Irina	Davydova	RUS	27.5.88	21 Jul
57.13	Eileen	Demes	GER-J	13.10.97	21 Jul		57.75	Gezelle	Magerman	RSA-J	21.4.97	20 Jul
57.16	Valerie	Thames	USA	27.2.95	12 May		57.75	Djamila	Böhm	GER	15.7.94	23 Jul
57.17	Darya	Korableva	RUS	23.5.88	21 Jun		57.76	Sashel	Brown	JAM	20.1.94	23 Apr
57.20	Sanique	Walker	JAM-Y	4.00.80	18 Mar		57.77	Daisy	Akpofa	NGR	26.9.96	21 May
57.22	Tereza	Vokálová	CZE-J	16.6.98	19 Jun		57.78	Shiann	Salmon	JAM-Y	31.3.99	18 Mar
57.31	Rita	Ossai	NGR	21.10.95	16 Jun		57.78	Kiani	Profit	USA	18.2.90	16 Apr
57.34	Gianna	Woodruff	PAN	15.5.93	15 May		57.78	Kimone	Green	JAM	23.5.95	8 May
57.39		Nguyen Thi Huyen	VIE	19.8.93	25 Nov		57.80	Ese	Okoro	GBR	4.7.90	16 May
57.40	Tetyana	Melnyk	UKR	2.4.95	25 May		57.80	Ranae	McKenzie	JAM	28.10.96	30 Jun
57.40	Kateryna	Slyusarenko	UKR	15.3.93	19 Jun		57.81	Méghane	Grandson	FRA	15.9.95	17 Jul
57.43	Elif	Yildirim	TUR	11.2.90	19 Jun		57.84	Aisha	Naibe-Wey	SLE	3.8.93	15 May
57.43	Geisa	dos Santos	BRA	13.10.92	3 Jul		57.85	Bryiana	Richardson	USA	26.1.95	12 May
57.44	Lora	Storey	AUS	19.10.89	28 Feb		57.85	Kyra	Johnson	USA	15.1.94	27 May

WOMEN 2016

400 METRES HURDLES – HIGH JUMP

Mark	Name		Nat	Born	Pos	Meet	Venue		Date
57.85	Jean-Marie	Senekal	RSA	11.12.92	26	Jun			
57.86	Laura	Gläsner	GER	20.1.96	28	May			
57.86	Glory	Nathaniel	NGR	23.1.96	8	Jul			
57.89	Farah	Clerc	FRA	31.7.90	5	Jun			
57.89	Moe	Oshiden	JPN	19.8.93	26	Jun			
57.90	Lisa	Meneau	USA	.95	15	May			
57.91	Nickiesha	Wilson	JAM	28.7.86	16	Apr			
57.91	Anastasiya	Lebid	UKR	30.10.93	4	Jun			
57.91	Anna	Berghii	MDA	19.2.93	5	Jun			
57.91	Nadezhda	Moseyeva	RUS	16.7.88	15	Jun			
57.91	Liliane Cristina	Fernandes	BRA	8.10.87	3	Jul			
57.91	Robine	Schürmann	SUI	31.1.89	8	Jul			
57.94	Keia	Pinnick	USA	23.1.91	26	Mar			
57.94	Jasmine	Barge	USA-J	2.1.97	14	May			
57.95	Melissa	Gonzalez	USA	24.6.94	23	Apr			
57.95	Karolina	Pahlitzsch	GER	5.4.94	14	May			
57.95	Christine	Salterberg	GER	9.6.94	19	Jun			
57.96	Sanda	Belgyan	ROU	17.12.92	17	Jul			
57.97	Anna	Raukuc	GER	7.1.90	5	Jun			
57.97	Natalya	Antyukh	RUS	26.6.81	21	Jun			
57.98	Alessandra	Silva	BRA	2.7.91	5	Jun			
57.98	Yelena	Kurakina	RUS	14.2.85	21	Jul			
57.99	Sara	Klein	AUS	19.5.94	3	Apr			
57.99	Daeshon	Gordon	JAM	8.11.96	23	Apr			
57.99	Ilaria	Vitale	ITA	25.5.90	26	Jun			
58.00	Emel	Sanli	TUR	7.7.93	19	Jun			
58.01	Joan	Medjid	FRA	29.9.95	11	Jun			
58.02	Maddie	Gipson	AUS	14.4.95	14	May			
58.02	Haruka	Shibata	JPN	13.1.91	26	Jun			
58.02	Eri	Utsunomiya	JPN	11.4.93	17	Jul			
58.03	Philippa	Lowe	GBR	7.4.92	22	May			
58.03	Kana	Koyama	JPN-J	.98	25	Jun			
58.04	Lyndsay (200)	Pekin	AUS	13.6.86	19	Mar			

Best at low altitude
56.89 Z Rodríguez 5 Jun, 57.17 Hechavarría 17 Jul
Very doubtful mark: 56.5A Lilit Harutyanyan ARM 4.4.93 1 NC Artashat 29 May

JUNIORS

See main list for top 6 juniors. 10 performances by 3 women to 56.22. Additional marks and further juniors:

Mark	Name		Nat	Born	Pos	Meet	Venue	Date	
McLaughlin	54.54	1	NC-j	Clovis	25 Jun	55.46	1h2 NC	Eugene	7 Jul
2+	55.23	1s1	NC	Eugene	8 Jul	56.22	5s1 OG	Rio de Janeiro	16 Aug
Cockrell	55.89	2	NC-j	Clovis	25 Jun	56.10	1s3 WJ	Bydgoszcz	21 Jul
56.90	Xahria		Santiago	CAN-Y	9.10.99	3	WJ	Bydgoszcz	22 Jul
56.94	Aminat Yusuf		Odeyemi	BRN	27.6.97	1h5	WJ	Bydgoszcz	20 Jul
56.99	Nicolee		Foster	JAM	11.1.98	3	N.Sch	Kingston	18 Mar
57.13	Eileen		Demes (10)	GER	13.10.97	1s1	WJ	Bydgoszcz	21 Jul
57.20	Sanique		Walker	JAM-Y	8.4.00	4	N.Sch	Kingston	18 Mar
57.22	Tereza		Vokálová	CZE	16.6.98	1	NC	Tábor	19 Jun
57.65	Viivi		Lehikoinen	FIN-Y	27.8.99	2	NC	Oulu	24 Jul
57.69	Mariam		Abdul-Rashid	CAN	21.9.97	2s2	WJ	Bydgoszcz	21 Jul
57.75	Gezelle		Magerman	RSA	21.4.97	2h2	WJ	Bydgoszcz	20 Jul
57.78	Shiann		Salmon	JAM-Y	31.3.99	5	N.Sch	Kingston	18 Mar
57.94	Jasmine		Barge	USA	2.1.97	3h1	Big 10	Lincoln, NE	14 May
58.03	Kana		Koyama	JPN	.98	3h1	NC	Nagoya	25 Jun
58.08	Michaela		Pesková	SVK	22.10.97	3s1	WJ	Bydgoszcz	21 Jul
58.14	Lakeisha		Warner (20)	IVB	15.9.97	2	Carifta	St. George	27 Mar

HIGH JUMP

2.01	Chaunté	Lowe	USA	12.1.84	1	NC	Eugene	3 Jul

1.79/1 1.84/1 1.89/1 1.91/1 1.93/1 1.95/1 1.97/1 1.99/2 2.01/2
    1.97 4 OG Rio de Janeiro 20 Aug 1.88/1 1.93/1 1.97/3 2.00/xxx

2.00	Marie-Laurence	Jungfleisch	GER	7.10.90	1		Eberstadt	16 Jul

1.80/1 1.84/1 1.87/1 1.90/1 1.93/1 1.96/3 2.00/2

2.00	Mariya	Kuchina	RUS	14.1.93	1	NCp	Zhukovskiy	21 Jul

1.80/1 1.84/1 1.88/1 1.91/1 1.95/1 2.00/2 2.03/xx
    1.98i 1 Moskva 14 Feb 1.80/1 1.85/1 1.89/1 1.93/1 1.98/2 2.02/xxx

1.99i	Vashti	Cunningham	USA-J	18.1.98	1	NC	Portland	12 Mar

1.75/1 1.81/1 1.85/1 1.90/1 1.93/1 1.96/1 1.99/2 2.01/x
    1.97 2 NC Eugene 3 Jul 1.79/1 1.84/1 1.89/1 1.91/1 1.95/3 1.97/1 1.99/xxx

1.99	Kamila	Licwinko	POL	22.3.86	1	Kuso	Szczecin	18 Jun

1.88/1 1.91/2 1.93/2 1.95/2 1.97/1 1.99/1 2.01/xxx
    1.97i 1 Pedro Lódz 5 Feb 1.88/1 1.91/1 1.94/1 1.97/2 2.00/xxx

1.98i	Ruth	Beitia	ESP	1.4.79	1	NC	Madrid	6 Mar

1.83/1 1.90/1 1.93/1 1.96/1 1.98/3 2.00/xxx
    1.98 1 EC Amsterdam 7 Jul 1.84/1 1.89/1 1.93/2 1.96/1 1.98/1 2.00/xxx
    1.98 1 DL London (OS) 22 Jul 1.85/1 1.92/1 1.95/1 1.98/3 2.00/xxx
    1.98 1 DL Saint-Denis 27 Aug 1.85/1 1.90/1 1.93/1 1.96/1 1.98/1 2.02/xxx
    1.97 1 OG Rio de Janeiro 20 Aug 1.88/1 1.93/1 1.97/1 2.00/xxx

1.98i	Akela	Jones	BAR	22.4.95	1P	NCAA	Birmingham, AL	11 Mar

1.74/1 1.77/1 1.80/1 1.83/1 1.86/1 1.89/1 1.91/1 1.95/1 1.98/1 2.01/xxx

1.98	Anna	Chicherova	RUS	22.7.82	1	NC	Cheboksary	23 Jun

1.80/1 1.84/2 1.91/1 1.94/2 1.98/2 2.00/xxx

1.98	Nafissatou	Thiam	BEL	19.8.94	1H	OG	Rio de Janeiro	12 Aug

1.83/1 1.86/1 1.89/1 1.92/1 1.95/3 1.98/1 2.01/XXX

1.98	Katarina	Johnson-Thompson	GBR	9.1.93	2H	OG	Rio de Janeiro	12 Aug

1.80/1 1.86/1 1.89/1 1.92/1 1.95/1 1.98/2 2.01/XXX

1.97i	Airine	Palsyte	LTU	13.7.92	1		Cottbus	27 Jan

1.80/1 1.84/1 1.88/1 1.91/1 1.94/1 1.97/1 2.00/xxx

HIGH JUMP

Mark	Name		Nat	Born	Pos	Meet	Venue	Date
1.97	Desirée	Rossit	ITA	19.3.94	1	NC-23	Bressanone	10 Jun
	1.75/1 1.79/1 1.8/1 1.89/2 1/94/1 1.97/1 2.00/xxx							
1.97	Oksana	Okuneva	UKR	14.3.90	1	NC	Lutsk	17 Jun4
	1.75/1 1.80/1 1.83/1 1.86/2 1.89/1 1.91/1 1.93/1 1.95/1 1.97/1 2.00/xx							
1.97	Mirela	Demireva	BUL	28.9.89	2	Kuso	Szczecin	18 Jun
	1.80/1 1.84/1 1.88/1 1.91/1 1.93/3 1.95/1 1.97/2 1.99/xxx							
1.97	2 OG Rio de Janeiro 20 Aug 1.88/2 1.93/1 1.97/1 2.00/xxx							
1.97	Blanka	Vlasic	CRO	8.11.83	3	OG	Rio de Janeiro	20 Aug
	(24/15)	1.88/2 1.93/2 1.97/2 2.00/xxx						
1.96	Ana	Simic	CRO	5.5.90	1		Bühl	24 Jun
1.96	Levern	Spencer	LCA	23.6.84	2	DL	Saint-Denis	27 Aug
1.95i	Michaela	Hrubá	CZE-J	21.2.98	1	NC-j	Praha	20 Feb
1.95i	Alessia	Trost	ITA	8.3.93	1		Madrid	26 Feb
1.95	Doreen	Amata	NGR	6.5.88	1		Fairburn	29 May
	(20)							
1.95	Svetlana	Radzivil	UZB	17.1.87	1		Filothei	8 Jun
1.95	Yuliya	Levchenko	UKR-J	28.11.97	2	NC	Lutsk	17 Jun
1.95	Marija	Vukovic	MNE	21.1.92	1		Berane	24 Jul
1.94i	Sofie	Skoog	SWE	7.6.90	1	v3N	Växjö	13 Feb
1.94i	Irina	Gordeyeva	RUS	9.10.86	1	NC	Moskva	25 Feb
1.94	Nadezhda	Dusanova	UZB	17.11.87	2	DL	Shanghai	14 May
1.94	Inika	McPherson	USA	29.9.86	Q	OG	Rio de Janeiro	18 Aug
1.94	Iryna	Herashchenko	UKR	10.3.95	Q	OG	Rio de Janeiro	18 Aug
1.94	Alyx	Treasure	CAN	15.5.92	Q	OG	Rio de Janeiro	18 Aug
1.94	Morgan	Lake	GBR-J	12.5.97	Q	OG	Rio de Janeiro	18 Aug
	(30)							
1.93i	Daniela	Stanciu	ROU	15.10.87	1		Bucuresti	31 Jan
1.93i	Isobel	Pooley	GBR	21.12.92	3	GP	Glasgow	20 Feb
1.93i	Yuliya	Chumachenko	UKR	2.10.94	1		Kherson	5 Mar
1.93	Eleanor	Patterson	AUS	22.5.96	1		Melbourne	5 Mar
1.93i	Urszula	Gardzielewska	POL	21.7.88	1P	NC	Torun	5 Mar
1.93i	Elizabeth	Patterson	USA	9.6.88	2	NC	Portland	12 Mar
1.93i	Erika	Kinsey	SWE	10.3.88	8	WI	Portland	20 Mar
1.93	Rachel	McCoy	USA	1.8.95	1	TexR	Austin	2 Apr
1.93	Marusa	Cernjul	SLO	30.6.92	1	NC	Celje	19 Jun
1.93	Linda	Sandblom	FIN	18.10.89	1		Kuortanei	25 Jun
	(40)							
1.93	Tonje	Angelsen	NOR	17.1.90	1		Oslo	6 Jul
1.92	Alina	Shukh	UKR-Y	12.2.99	1H	NC	Lutsk	18 Jun
1.92	Natalya	Aksyonova	RUS-J	6.6.97	1	NC-23	Saransk	16 Jul
1.91i	Kristina	Korolyova	RUS	6.11.90	2		Moskva	22 Jan
1.91i	Tatyana	Mnatsakanova	RUS	25.5.83	4	NC	Moskva	25 Feb
1.91	Erika	Furlani	ITA	2.1.96			Rietii	21 May
1.91	Jeannelle	Scheper	LCA	21.11.94	1	NC	Vieux-Fort	26 Jun
1.91	Amina	Smith	USA	10.1.92	4	NC	Eugene	3 Jul
1.90i	Ulyana	Aleksandrova	RUS	1.1.91	1P		Smolensik	19 Feb
1.90i	Priscilla	Frederick	ANT	14.2.89	1		New York (SI)	27 Feb
	(50)							
1.90i	Raquel	Álvarez	ESP	13.6.83	2	NC	Madrid	6 Mar
1.90i	Zibby	Boyer	USA	23.9.92	4	NC	Portland	12 Mar
1.90A	Ximena	Esquivel	MEX-J	22.8.97	1		Querétaro	24 Apr
1.90		Zheng Xingjuan	CHN	20.3.89	3		Kawasaki	8 May
1.90	Maya	Pressley	USA	1.2.91	2		Fairburn	29 May
1.90	Valentina	Liashenko	GEO	30.1.81	1	CSSE	Marsa	11 Jun
1.90	Yana	Maksimova	BLR	9.1.89	1	NC	Grodno	24 Jun
1.90	Anna	Iljustsenko	EST	12.10.85	3		Bühl	24 Jun
1.90	Lada	Pejchalová	CZE-J	15.11.98	1	v5N-j	Miskolc	1 Jul
1.90	Emma	Green	SWE	8.12.84	1		Torremolinos	9 Jul
	(60)							
1.90	Barbara	Nwaba	USA	18.1.89	1H	NC	Eugene	9 Jul
1.90		Liu Jingyi	CHN	27.10.94	1		Dalian	22 Jul
1.90	Jossie	Graumann	GER	18.3.94	1		Mannheim	29 Jul
1.90	Barbara	Szabó	HUN	17.2.90	1	NC	Székesfehérvár	31 Jul
1.89i	Abby	Ward	GBR-Y	19.4.99	1		Cardiff	7 Feb
1.89i	Lissa	Labiche	SEY	18.2.93	10	WI	Portland	20 Mar
1.89	Niamh	Emerson	GBR-Y	22.4.99	1	LI	Loughborough	22 May
1.89	Ty	Butts	USA	10.6.90	1		Chula Vista	28 May
1.89	Kaitlin	Whitehorn	USA	16.8.94	5	NC	Eugene	3 Jul
1.89	Jessica	Ennis-Hill	GBR	28.1.86	3H	OG	Rio de Janeiro	12 Aug
	(70)							
1.88i	Margarita	Mazina	RUS	7.7.95	3		Moskva	22 Jan

WOMEN 2016

HIGH JUMP

Mark	Name		Nat	Born	Pos	Meet	Venue	Date	
1.88i	Katarina	Mögenburg	NOR	16.6.91	7		Cottbus	27	Jan
1.88i	Ariane	Friedrich	GER	10.1.84	8		Cottbus	27	Jan
1.88i	Claudia	García	ESP	30.9.92	2		State College	30	Jan
1.88i	Svetlana	Nikolenko	RUS	26.9.91	5	NC	Moskva	25	Feb
1.88i		Wang Yang	CHN	14.2.89	1	NGP	Nanjing	4	Mar
1.88i	Michalina	Kwasniewska	POL	22.10.91	3	NC	Torun	6	Mar
1.88	Erica	Bougard	USA	26.7.93	1	FlaR	Gainesville	1	Apr
1.88	Valdiléia	Martins	BRA	19.9.89	1		São Bernardo do Campo	21	Apr
1.88	Hanna	Gorodskaya	BLR	31.1.93	1		Brest	12	May
(80)									
1.88	Regina	Kaysarova	KAZ	7.4.93	1	NCp	Almaty	25	May
1.88	Kimberly	Williamson	JAM	2.10.93	1	NCAA	Eugene	11	Jun
1.88	Marine	Vallet	FRA	9.9.93	1	NC	Angers	25	Jun
1.88	Nicola	McDermott	AUS	28.12.96	1-22		Eberstadt	15	Jul
1.88	Yekaterina	Stepanova	RUS	24.7.94	2	NC-23	Saransk	16	Jul
1.88i	Natalya	Baluyeva	RUS	.92	1		Sankt Peterburg	25	Dec
1.88i	Aleksandra	Yaryshkina	RUS	10.6.94	2		Sankt Peterburg	25	Dec
1.87i	Burcu	Yüksel	TUR	3.5.90	1		Istanbul	16	Jan
1.87i	Imke	Onnen	GER	17.8.94	1		Hannover	22	Jan
1.87i	Yevgeniya	Kononova	RUS	28.9.89	1	SP	Sankt Peterburg	24	Jan
(90)									
1.87i	Kendell	Williams	USA	14.6.95	1P		Fayetteville	29	Jan
1.87i	Lisa	Maihöfer	GER-J	28.10.98	1P	NC-j	Hamburg	31	Jan
1.87i	Chanice	Porter	JAM	25.5.94	1		Blacksburg	6	Feb
1.87i	Réka	Czuth	HUN	27.6.94	2		Lincoln NE	6	Feb
1.87i	Paulina	Borys	POL-J	14.5.98	1	NC-j	Spala	13	Feb
1.87i	Hanne	Van Hessche	BEL	5.7.91	3		Gent	13	Feb
1.87i	Oldriska	Maresová	CZE	14.10.86	5		Hustopece	13	Feb
1.87	Zoe	Timmers	AUS	25.5.89	2		Canberra	20	Feb
1.87i	Salome	Lang	SUI-J	18.11.97	1	NC	St.Gallen	28	Feb
1.87i	Cristina	Ferrando	ESP	12.1.92	3	NC	Madrid	6	Mar
(100)									
1.87	Yorgelis	Rodríguez	CUB	25.1.95	1H	NC	La Habana	18	Mar
1.87	Uhunoma	Osazuwa	NGR	23.11.87	1		Long Beach	16	Apr
1.87	Hannah	Joye	AUS	4.1.96	1		Townsville	5	Jun
1.87	Györgyi	Zsivoczky-Farkas	HUN	13.2.85	1H	Décastar	Talence	17	Sep
1.87i	Tatyana	Yermachenkova	RUS-J	9.9.98	1		Sankt-Peterburg	4	Dec
1.86i	Loretta	Blaut	USA	22.3.96	16	Jan		1.85	
1.86i	Tatiána	Goúsin	GRE	26.1.94	22	Jan		1.85	
1.86i	Mariya	Shulgina	BLR	14.8.89	28	Jan		1.85	
1.86Ai	Susan	Jackson	USA	26.7.89	6	Feb		1.85	
1.86i	Taisya	Roslova	BLR	7.2.92	7	Feb		1.85	
1.86i	Anna	Pau	ITA	30.1.94	7	Feb		1.85	
1.86i	Jailah	Mason	USA	12.9.96	12	Feb		1.85	
1.86i	Monika	Gollner	AUT	23.10.74	21	Feb		1.85	
1.86i	Nawal	Méniker	FRA-J	9.12.97	27	Feb		1.85	
1.86	Elizabeth	Lamb	NZL	12.5.91	5	Mar		1.85	
1.86	Liz	Evans	USA	1.12.90	9	Apr		1.85	
1.86	Madeline	Fagan	USA	4.6.96	9	Apr		1.84i	
1.86	Natasha	Jackson	CAN	10.6.89	13	Apr		1.84i	
1.86	Bethan	Partridge	GBR	11.7.90	22	May		1.84i	
1.86	Aneta	Rydz	POL	30.3.94	4	Jun		1.84i	
1.86	Darya	Kuchyna	UKR	14.6.93	4	Jun		1.84	
1.86	Maayan	Shahaf	ISR	9.11.86	23	Jun		1.84	
1.86	Yekaterina	Kuntsevich	AUT	13.7.84	23	Jun		1.84	
1.86	Anne	Klebsch	GER	20.2.96	15	Jul		1.84	
1.86	Brianne	Theisen-Eaton	CAN	18.12.88	12	Aug		1.84	
1.86	Jennifer	Oeser	GER	29.11.83	12	Aug		1.84	
1.86		Duong Thi Viet Anh	VIE	30.12.90	23	Nov		1.84	
1.85i	Hannelore	Desmet	BEL	25.2.89	10	Jan		1.84	
1.85i	Lisa	Engman	SWE	27.7.94	23	Jan		1.84	
1.85i	Yekaterina	Fedotova	RUS	3.7.92	14	Feb		1.84	
1.85A	Julia	du Plessis	RSA	27.5.96	23	Feb		1.84	
1.85i	Livia	Odermatt	SUI	18.8.95	28	Feb		1.84	
1.85i	Alina	Fyodorova	UKR	31.7.89	18	Mar		1.84	
1.85i	Anastasiya	Mokhnyuk	UKR	1.1.91	18	Mar		1.84	
1.85	Dakota	Dailey-Harris	USA	28.6.94	9	Apr		1.84	
1.85	Kaysee	Pilgrim	USA	11.7.95	16	Apr		1.84	
1.85	Saniel	Grier	JAM	2.7.91	16	Apr		1.84	
1.85	Solène	Gicquel	FRA	1.12.94	8	May			

1.85	Karla Yazmin	Teran	MEX-J	8.3.98	13	May			
1.85	Madara	Onuzane-Salina	LAT	7.6.89	20	May			
1.85	Eleonora	Omoregie	ITA	22.5.96	24	May			
1.85	Mareike	Max	GER-J	19.8.98	26	Jun			
1.85	Mona	Gottschämmer	GER-J	11.5.98	26	Jun			
1.85	Eleriin	Haas	EST	4.7.92	6	Jul			
1.85	Grete	Udras	EST	11.3.88	17	Jul			
1.85	Tyra	Gittens	TTO-J	6.6.98	30	Jul			
1.85	Yekaterina	Bolshova	RUS	4.2.88	8	Sep			
1.85	Brigetta	Barrett	USA	24.12.90	13	Sep			
1.85	María Fernanda	Murillo	COL-Y	21.1.99	13	Nov			
1.84i	Erika	Hurd	USA	8.4.94	29	Jan			
1.84i	Elina	Smolander	FIN	11.10.89	2	Feb			
1.84i	Nicole	Greene	USA-J	2.5.97	6	Feb			
1.84i	Sofia	Linde	SWE	12.1.95	6	Feb			
1.84		Wang Xueyi	CHN	3.8.91	17	Apr			
1.84	Amalie Hammild	Iuel	NOR	17.4.94	7	May			
1.84	Haleigh	Knapp	USA		13	May			
1.84	Claire	Orcel	BEL-J	21.12.97	14	May			
1.84	Lara	Omerzu	SLO-J	10.5.98	18	May			
1.84		Hu Linpeng	CHN	29.12.95	21	May			
1.84		Wang Lin	CHN	8.1.95	20	Jun			
1.84	Tatyana	Odineva	RUS	23.5.83	23	Jun			
1.84	Laura	Rautanen	FIN	13.2.88	24	Jun			
1.84	Olena	Zhmur	UKR-Y	30.1.01	25	Jun			
1.84	Teresa Maria	Rossi	ITA	12.4.92	5	Jul			
1.84	Margarita	Churikova	RUS-J	20.2.97	6	Jul			
1.84	Aleksandra	Yaryshkina	RUS	10.6.94	16	Jul			
1.84	Margarita	Korneychuk	RUS	21.2.95	16	Jul			
1.84	Lavinja	Jürgens	GER-Y	,00	30	Jul			
1.84		Zhang Yu	CHN-J	13.11.98	17	Sep			
1.84	Paige	Wilson	AUS	15.7.99	3	Dec			
(170)									

1.94	Trost		1	NC	Rieti			25	Jun
1.94	Skoog		Q	OG	Rio de Janeiro			18	Aug
1.93	Patterson		1		Kawasaki			8	May
1.93	Hrubá (J)		1		Praha			2	Jun

Best outdoors

1.97	Cunningham	2	NC	Eugene	3	Jul	
1.96	Palsyte	2	EC	Amsterdam	7	Jul	
1.95	A Jones	1H	MSR	Azusa	13	Apr	
1.94	Gordeyeva	2		Sochi	27	May	

HIGH JUMP – POLE VAULT

Mark	Name			Nat	Born	Pos	Meet	Venue	Date
1.90	Boyer	2	MSR	Norwalk	16 Apr	1.88	Nikolenko 2= NCp	Zhukovskiy	21 Jul
1.90	Kinsey	1		Clermont	14 May	1.88	Wang Yang 2 NC	Tianjin	17 Sep
1.89	Chumachenko	5	NC	Lutsk	17 Jun	1.87	García 1	Baton Rouge	23 Apr
1.89	Frederick	28q	OG	Rio de Janeiro	18 Aug	1.87	Labiche 1	Dillingen	5 May
1.88	Korolyova	4		Sochi	27 May	1.87	Mögenburg 1	Garbsen	22 May
1.88	Pooley	8	Pre	Eugene	28 May	1.87	Ferrando 5	Madrid	23 Jun
1.86	Roslova	20 May	1.86	Gardzielewska	11 Jun	1.85	Méniker 5 Jun	1.84 Friedrich	19 Jun
1.86	Ward	22 May	1.86	Shulgina	24 Jun	1.85	Van Hessche 26 Jun	1.84 Smolander	24 Jun
1.86	Kwasniewska	3 Jun	1.86	Lang	3 Jul	1.84	Czuth 9 Apr	1.84 KWilliams	9 Jul
1.86	Yüksel	5 Jun	1.85	Jackson	29 Apr	1.84	Álvarez 14 May		

JUNIORS

See main list for top 13 juniors. 18 performances (inc. 8 indoors) by 4 women to 1.93. Additional marks and further juniors:

Mark	Name			Venue	Date	Mark	Pos Meet	Venue	Date
Cunningham	1.96i	1	WI	Portland	20 Mar	1.94	Q OG	Rio de Janeiro	18 Aug
2+	1.95Ai	1		Albuquerque	5 Feb	1.93	1 MSR	Norwalk	16 Apr
	1.94	1		Las Vegas	20 Feb				
Hrubá 2+	1.94i	1		Trinec	7 Feb	1.93i	1 NC	Ostrava	28 Feb
	1.93i	2		Split	29 Jan	1.93	1 NC	Tábor	18 Jun
	1.93i	3		Hustopece	13 Feb				
Lake	1.93i	1P		Salamanca	20 Feb	1.93	10 OG	Rio de Janeiro	20 Aug
1.86i	Nawal			Méniker	FRA- 9.12.97	1	v2N-j	Padova	27 Feb
1.85	Karla Yazmin			Teran	MEX 8.3.98	2	NC-J	Monterrey	13 May
1.85	Mareike			Max	GER 19.8.98	1-j		Mannheim	26 Jun
1.85	Mona			Gottschämmer	GER 11.5.98	2-j		Mannheim	26 Jun
1.85	Tyra			Gittens	TTO- 6.6.98	1H	Jun Oly	Humble	30 Jul
1.85	María Fernanda			Murillo (20)	COL-Y 21.1.99	1	SACh-y	Concordia	13 Nov

Best out

1.86	Abby	Ward	GBR-Y 19.4.99	3	LI	Loughborough	22 May
1.86	Salome	Lang	SUI 18.11.97	1		Düdingen	3 Jul
1.85	Nawal	Méniker	FRA 9.12.97	3	Med-23	Radès	5 Jun

POLE VAULT

Mark	Name			Venue	Date			Venue	Date
5.03i	Jenn			Suhr	USA 5.2.82	1		Brockport	30 Jan
	4.60/2 4.82/1 5.03/3 5.07/xxx								
	5.01i	1		Fredonia	1 Oct	4.57/1 4.72/1 4.87/1 5.01/3			
	4.91i	1		Kent	16 Jan	4.61/1 4.81/2 4.91/3 5.03/xxx			
	4.90i	2	NC	Portland	12 Mar	4.65/1 4.75/2 4.85/1 4.90/1 4.95/x 5.00/xx			
	4.90i	1	WI	Portland	17 Mar	4.60/1 4.75/1 4.85/1 4.90/1			
	4.87i	1		Rochester	23 Sep	4.57/1 4.72/1 4.87/3 5.01/xx			
	4.85i	1		Boston (A)	28 Feb	4.65/1 4.75/1 4.85/2 5.07/xxx			
	4.82i	1		Boston (R)	14 Feb	4.62/1 4.72/1 4.82/2 5.07/xxx			
	4.82	1		San Marcos	30 Apr	4.62/3 4.82/1 4.94/xxx			
5.00	Sandi			Morris	USA 8.7.92	1	VD	Bruxelles	9 Sep
	4.52/2 4.58/1 4.64/1 4.70/2 4.76/x 4.82/1 4.88/1 4.94/1 5.00/2 5.07/xxx								
	4.95i	1	NC	Portland	12 Mar	4.50/1 4.65/2 4.75/3 4.85/x 4.90/2 4.95/1 5.00/xxx			
	4.93	1		Houston	23 Jul	4.35/1 4.50/1 4.60/1 4.70/1 4.80/2 4.93/1 5.07/xxx			
	4.85i	2	WI	Portland	17 Mar	4.50/1 4.60/1 4.70/1 4.75/2 4.80/1 4.85/1 4.90/xx 4.95/x			
	4.85	2	OG	Rio de Janeiro	19 Aug	4.50/1 4.60/1 4.70/2 4.80/2 4.85/2 4.90/xxx			
	4.83	1	DL	Doha	6 May	4.43/1 4.53/2 4.63/2 4.73/2 4.83/1 4.93/xxx			
	4.81	1		Fayetteville	23 Apr	4.52/2 4.64/1 4.74/2 4.81/1 4.93/xxx			
4.90i	Ekateríni			Stefanídi	GRE 4.2.90	1	Mill	New York (A)	20 Feb
	4.50/1 4.60/1 4.80/1 4.90/2 5.00/xxx								
	4.86	1		Athínai (F)	8 Jun	4.60/1 4.74/1 4.86/1			
	4.85	1	OG	Rio de Janeiro	19 Aug	4.60/1 4.70/1 4.80/2 4.85/2 4.90/xxx			
	4.81	1	EC	Amsterdam	9 Jul	4.55/1 4.65/1 4.70/1 4.81/3 4.94/xxx			
	4.81	1	Herc	Monaco	15 Jul	4.65/1 4.76/1 4.81/2 4.93/xxx			
4.90i	Demi			Payne	USA 30.9.91	2	Mill	New York (A)	20 Feb
	4.50/3 4.70/1 4.80/1 4.90/2 5.00/xxx								
	4.88Ai	1		Albuquerque	6 Feb	4.45/2 4.65/2 4.76/2 4.82/2 4.88/1			
	4.85i	3	NC	Portland	12 Mar	4.50/1 4.65/1 4.75/1 4.85/1 4.90/xx 4.95/x			
4.90	Yelena			Isinbayeva	RUS 3.6.82	1	NC	Cheboksary	21 Jun
	4.60/1 4.70/1 4.80/2 4.90/3 5.07/x								
4.87	Fabiana			Murer	BRA 16.3.81	1	NC	São Bernardo do Campo	3 Jul
	4.50/1 4.65/1 4.75/1 4.87/3 5.00/xx								
4.85	Anzhelika			Sidorova	RUS 28.6.91	2	NC	Cheboksary	21 Jun
	4.60/1 4.75/1 4.85/2 4.90/xxx								
4.84	Yarisley			Silva	CUB 1.6.87	1	DL	Birmingham	5 Jun
	4.50/1 4.60/1 4.70/2 4.77/2 4.84/3 4.92/xx								
4.81i	Nikoléta			Kiriakopoúlou	GRE 21.3.86	1	Globen	Stockholm	17 Feb
	4.49/1 4.59/1 4.71/2 4.81/1 4.91/xxx								

POLE VAULT

Mark	Name		Nat	Born	Pos	Meet	Venue	Date	
4.81	Alana	Boyd	AUS	10.5.84	1		Sippy Downs	2	Jul
	(30/10)			4.50/1 4.65/1	4.75/3	4.81/2	4.87/xxx		
4.80	Eliza	McCartney	NZL	11.12.96	1	NC	Dunedin	5	Mar
4.80i	Nicole	Büchler	SUI	17.12.83	4	WI	Portland	17	Mar
4.76i	Holly	Bradshaw	GBR	2.11.91	1	WK	Zürich	31	Aug
4.73	Lisa	Ryzih	GER	27.9.88	1		Jockgrim	19	Jul
4.71Ai	Mary	Saxer Sibears	USA	21.6.87	3		Reno	15	Jan
4.71i	Wilma	Murto	FIN-J	11.6.98	1		Zweibrücken	31	Jan
4.70i		Li Ling	CHN	6.7.89	1	AsC	Doha	19	Feb
4.70	Kylie	Hutson	USA	27.11.87	1		Phoenix	11	Jun
4.70	Martina	Strutz	GER	4.11.81	1	NC	Kassel	18	Jun
4.70	Kristen	Brown	USA	26.5.92	1		Chula Vista	26	Jun
	(20)								
4.70	Lexi	Weeks	USA	20.11.96	3	NC	Eugene	10	Jul
4.66i	Angelica	Bengtsson	SWE	8.7.93	1	v3N	Växjö	13	Feb
4.66i	Angelina	Krasnova	RUS	7.2.91	2		Moskva	14	Feb
4.66i	Jirina	Ptácníková	CZE	20.5.86	1		Praha	17	Feb
4.65i	Kristen	Hixson	USA	1.7.92	4	NC	Portland	12	Mar
4.65	Olga	Mullina	RUS	1.8.92	3	NC	Cheboksary	21	Jun
4.65	Marina	Kylypko	UKR	10.11.95	1		Trani	3	Sep
4.63i	Katie	Nageotte	USA	30.6.91	1	Starks	Columbus	4	Mar
4.63	Megan	Clark	USA	10.6.94	1		Durham	23	Apr
4.62i	Romana	Malácová	CZE	15.5.87	4		Clermont-Ferrand	21	Feb
	(30)								
4.62	Michaela	Meijer	SWE	30.7.93	1		Randers	4	Jun
4.61i	Minna	Nikkanen	FIN	9.4.88	2	v3N	Växjö	13	Feb
4.61	Alysha	Newman	CAN	29.6.94	1		London, CAN	28	Jul
4.60i	Vanessa	Boslak	FRA	11.6.82	1	NC	Aubière	28	Feb
4.60	Annika	Roloff	GER	10.3.91	1		Landau	28	Jun
4.60	Morgann	LeLeux	USA	14.11.92	4	NC	Eugene	10	Jul
4.57	Angelica	Moser	SUI-J	9.10.97	1		Frauenkappelen	1	Aug
4.56i	Silke	Spiegelburg	GER	17.3.86	1	NC	Leipzig	27	Feb
4.56	Robeilys	Peinado	VEN-J	26.11.97	1		Budapest	10	Jun
4.56 sq	Tina	Sutej	SLO	7.11.88	1		Linz	29	Jun
	(40)								
4.55Ai	Melinda	Withrow	USA	30.10.84	1		Air Force Academy	23	Jan
4.55	Anjuli	Knäsche	GER	18.10.93	1		Paderborn	26	May
4.55	April	Steiner Bennett	USA	22.4.80	2		Phoenix	11	Jun
4.55	Kelsie	Ahbe	CAN	6.7.91	8q	OG	Rio de Janeiro	16	Aug
4.52	Tori	Pena	IRL	30.7.87	1=		Long Beach	16	Apr
4.51i	Marta	Onofre	POR	28.1.91	1		Pombal	6	Mar
4.51i	Katy	Viuf	USA	23.5.87	1		Jonesboro	20	Jun
4.51	Sonia	Malavisi	ITA	31.10.94	2		Padova	17	Jul
4.51	Irina	Yakoltsevich	BLR	26.1.93	1		Rovereto	6	Sep
4.50i	Femke	Pluim	NED	10.5.94	1		Gent	16	Jan
	(50)								
4.50i	Emily	Grove	USA	22.5.93	1		Ames	13	Feb
4.50i	Leslie	Brost	USA	28.9.89	6	NC	Portland	12	Mar
4.50	Diamara	Planell	PUR	16.2.93	1	MSR	Norwalk	16	Apr
4.50	Anicka	Newell	CAN	5.8.93	1	Jackson	Abilene	27	Apr
4.50	Kaitlin	Petrillose	USA	10.12.92	2		Austin	7	May
4.50	Lisa	Gunnarsson	SWE-Y	20.8.99	1		Pézenas	28	May
4.50	Kat	Majester	USA	22.5.87	1		Rock Hill	28	May
4.50	Joana	Ribeiro Costa	BRA	15.8.81	2	NC	São Bernardo do Campo	3	Jul
4.50	Maria Eleonor	Tavares	POR	24.9.85	1		Franconville	6	Jul
4.46i	Kayla	Caldwell	USA	19.6.91	1		Jonesboro	23	Jun
	(60)								
4.46	Allie	Koressel	USA	2.3.91	2		Chula Vista	26	Jun
4.45	Annie	Rhodes	USA	13.5.95	1		San Antonio	26	Mar
4.44	Carolina	Carmichael	USA	28.4.94	1		Memphis	30	Apr
4.43	Jessie	Johnson	USA	21.11.93	1		Athens	30	Apr
4.43	Kortney	Ross	USA	26.7.92	2		Phoenix	21	May
4.42	Sydney	Clute	USA	15.11.93	1	Big 10	Lincoln, NE	13	May
4.41i	Sophie	Gutermuth	USA	2.11.92	1		Bloomington	12	Feb
4.41Ai	Carmelita	Correa	MEX	5.12.88	2		Flagstaff	12	Feb
4.41i	Melissa	Gergel	USA	24.4.89	1		Blacksburg	20	Feb
4.41	Mackenzie	Shell	USA-J	6.1.97	1		Norman	23	Apr
	(70)								
4.40i	Rianna	Galiart	NED	22.11.85	1		Gent	13	Feb
4.40i	Tori	Weeks	USA	20.11.96	1		Fayetteville	19	Feb
4.40i	Natalya	Demidenko	RUS	7.8.93	4	NC	Moskva	23	Feb

POLE VAULT — WOMEN 2016

Mark	Name		Nat	Born	Pos	Meet	Venue	Date	
4.40i	Yelizaveta	Bondarenko	RUS-Y	1.7.99	4	NC	Moskva	23	Feb
4.40	Liz	Parnov	AUS	9.5.94	1		Perth	12	Mar
4.40	Vicky	Parnov	AUS	24.10.90	1		Perth	20	Mar
4.40	Sally	Peake	GBR	8.2.86	4=		Chula Vista	21	Apr
4.40	Malin	Dahlström	SWE	26.8.89	4=		Chula Vista	21	Apr
4.40	Chloé	Henry	BEL	5.3.87	8		Chula Vista	21	Apr
4.40	Regine	Kramer	GER	5.4.93	1		Engen	8	May
(80)									
4.40	Carolin	Hingst	GER	18.9.80			Wipperfürth	22	May
4.40	Katharina	Bauer	GER	12.6.90	1		Bottrop	29	May
4.40	Fanny	Smets	BEL	21.4.86	2		Montreuil-sous-Bois	7	Jun
4.40	Rebeka	Silhanová	CZE	22.3.95	1	NC	Tábor	19	Jun
4.40	Justyna	Smietanka	POL	24.9.94	1		Warszawa	19	Jun
4.40	Anastasiya	Savchenko	RUS	15.11.89	5	NC	Cheboksary	21	Jun
4.40	Naroa	Agirre	ESP	15.5.79	1		Pamplona	22	Jun
4.40	Ninon	Guillon-Romarin	FRA	15.4.95	2	NC	Angers	25	Jun
4.39i	Becky	Holliday	USA	12.3.80	4		Akron	9	Jan
4.38i	Marion	Fiack	FRA	13.10.92	4		Rouen	23	Jan
(90)									
4.36i	Marion	Lotout	FRA	19.11.89	5		Zweibrücken	31	Jan
4.35	Karla	da Silva	BRA	12.11.84	1		São Bernardo do Campo	23	Jan
4.35i	Elienor	Werner	SWE-J	5.5.98	1		Norrköping	30	Jan
4.35i	Tatyana	Shvydkina	RUS	8.5.90	1		Sankt Peterburg	7	Feb
4.35i	Elizabeth	Quick	USA	14.11.94	2		Seattle	13	Feb
4.35i	Tatyana	Stetsyuk	RUS	27.8.92	6		Moskva	14	Feb
4.35	Lindsey	Mix	CAN	14.1.89	1		Tempe	9	Apr
4.35	Natasha	Kolbo	USA	5.4.92	1		Chula Vista	21	Apr
4.35	Mariya	Zakharutkina	RUS	14.8.96	1	NC-23	Saransk	15	Jul
4.35	Polina	Knoroz	RUS-Y	20.7.99	2	NC-23	Saransk	15	Jul
(100)									
4.34	Rachel	Baxter	USA-Y	5.4.99	23	Apr			
4.34	Lindsey	Murray	USA	22.7.96	30	Apr			
4.33i	Friedelinde	Petershofen	GER	19.8.95	30	Jan			
4.33	Tomomi	Abiko	JPN	17.3.88	2	Apr			
4.32i	Kristina	Owsinski	USA	16.2.93	16	Jan			
4.32	Hunter	Wilkes	USA	17.8.94	16	Apr			
4.32	Kally	Long	USA	28.8.95	30	Apr			
4.32	Alina	McDonald	USA-J	26.8.97	28	May			
4.32	Lene	Retzius	NOR	4.1.96	5	Aug			
4.31i	Janice	Keppler	USA	22.3.87	16	Jan			
4.31i	Reena	Koll	EST	15.11.96	9	Feb			
4.31i	Martina	Schultze	GER	12.9.90	27	Feb			
4.31i	Anna	Felzmann	GER	18.1.92	27	Feb			
4.31	Jax	Williams	USA	13.11.94	21	May			
4.31	Sara	Bercan	SLO	31.5.92	23	Jun			
4.30Ai	Jenny	Wartinbee	USA	1.3.87	15	Jan			
4.30i	Chanel	Krause	USA	31.10.94	12	Feb			
4.30i	Olga	Frackowiak	POL	14.2.90	14	Feb			
4.30i		Ren Mengqian	CHN	4.10.93	19	Feb			
4.30i	Patrícia	dos Santos	BRA	13.6.84	27	Feb			
4.30i		Song Tingting	CHN	8.10.93	29	Feb			
4.30i		Xu Huiqin	CHN	4.9.93	29	Feb			
4.30i	Anastasiya	Sadovnikova	RUS	22.6.95	1	Mar			
4.30i	Aino	Siitonen	FIN	29.9.94	5	Mar			
4.30i	Giorgia	Benecchi	ITA	9.7.89	6	Mar			
4.30i	Kamila	Przybyla	POL	3.5.96	6	Mar			
4.30i	Nina	Kennedy	AUS-J	5.4.97	12	Mar			
4.30i	Madison	Heath	USA	3.11.95	26	Mar			
4.30		Chen Qiaoling	CHN-Y	22.11.99	16	Apr			
4.30	Olivia	Gruver	USA-J	29.7.97	22	Apr			
4.30	Vera	Schmitz	USA	3.12.87	23	Apr			
4.30	Mariya	Temnikova	RUS	9.7.95	6	May			
4.30	Brysun	Stately	USA	22.11.86	7	May			
4.30	Lilli	Schnitzerling	GER	5.12.93	8	May			
4.30	Stélla-Iró	Ledáki	GRE	18.7.88	10	May			
4.30	Megan	Zimlich	USA	30.9.93	14	May			
4.30	Roberta	Bruni	ITA	8.3.94	22	May			
4.30	Fanni	Juhász	HUN	31.3.81	22	May			
4.30	Demet	Parlak	TUR	26.7.96	28	May			
4.30		Lim Eun-ji	KOR	2.4.89	2	Jun			
4.30	Caroline Bonde	Holm	DEN	19.7.90	24	Jun			
4.30	Carla	Franch	ESP	25.10.89	9	Jul			
4.30	Lyudmila	Yeryomina	RUS	8.8.91	13	Aug			

Mark	Name		Nat	Born	Pos	Meet	Venue	Date	
4.30	Kristina	Bondarenko	RUS	10.8.95	13	Aug			
4.30	Amálie	Svábíková	CZE-Y	22.11.99	11	Sep			
4.30	Olivia	McTaggart	NZL-Y	9.1.00	26	Nov			
4.29	Bonnie	Draxler	USA	13.10.95	1	May			
4.28	Desiree	Freier	USA	24.7.96	23	Apr			
4.27	Paula	Andrie	USA	26.1.93	7	May			
4.27	Aneta	Morysková	CZE	19.9.92	22	Jun			
4.26	Caroline	Hasse	GER	8.3.91	1	Apr			
4.26	Jessica	Harter	USA	26.10.94	13	May			
4.26	Malen	Ruiz de Azua	ESP	17.11.95	2	Jul			
4.26	Isabelle	Leroy	FRA	18.5.88	6	Jul			
4.25Ai	Madison	Mills	USA	18.1.94	5	Feb			
4.25i	Giulia	Cargnelli	ITA	18.3.88	20	Feb			
4.25i	Robin	Bone	CAN	13.2.94	11	Mar			
4.25A	Martha	Villalobos	MEX	20.3.90	26	Mar			
4.25	Leanna	Carrière	CAN	3.4.85	9	Apr			
4.25	Sydney	White	USA	22.6.94	5	May			
4.25	Mandissa	Marshall	USA	2.4.91	14	May			
4.25	Lauren	Chorny	USA	22.6.93	27	May			
4.25	Alyssa	McBride	USA	2.2.94	27	May			
4.25		Wu Zuocheng	CHN-Y	26.5.99	11	Jun			
4.25	Gil	Le Bris-Finot	FRA	29.11.95	29	Jun			
4.25sq	Elien	De Vocht	BEL	18.7.95	14	Jul			
4.25	Carson	Dingler	USA-Y	14.5.99	21	Jul			
4.25	Enikő	Erős	HUN	8.9.86	30	Jul			
4.25	Lucy	Bryan	GBR	22.5.95	6	Aug			
4.23	Erica	Hjerpe	FIN	20.8.93	23	Apr			
4.23	Bridget	Guy	USA	18.3.96	29	Apr			
4.22i	Sophie	Dangla	FRA	19.10.87	20	Feb			
4.22i	Sirine	Ebondo	TUN	31.10.83	20	Feb			
4.22i	Kristen	Denk	USA	15.2.97	27	Feb			
4.22i	Alyssa	Applebee	USA	12.1.94	27	Feb			
4.22i	Clara	Amat	ESP	31.7.94	28	Feb			
4.22	Nicole	Casper	USA	29.6.94	23	Apr			
4.22	Samantha	Tollerud	USA	6.2.96	7	May			
4.22	Jill	Marois	USA	8.6.94	11	May			
4.21i	Anais	Poumarat	FRA	25.2.89	6	Feb			
4.21i	Lexi	Masterson	USA	30.6.94	26	Feb			
4.21	Katherine	Pitman	USA	.95	26	May			
4.21sq	Nastja	Modic	SLO-Y	28.1.99	29	Jun			
4.21	Mallaury	Sautereau	FRA	1.8.96	20	Jul			
4.21	Karleigh	Parker	CAN	10.5.92	28	Jul			
(185)									
4.20 by 28 women									

Symbols/Abbreviations
+ intermediate time in longer race, A made at an altitude of 1000m or higher, D made in a decathlon, h made in a heat, qf quarter-final, sf semi-final, i indoors, Q qualifying round, r race number, -J juniors, -Y youths (b. 1999 or later)

POLE VAULT – LONG JUMP

Mark	Wind		Name		Nat	Born	Pos	Meet	Venue	Date
Best outdoors										
4.82			Suhr	1		San Marcos	30 Apr	4.50	Spiegelburg	2=		Zweibrücken	12 Jun
4.78			Büchler	2	DL	Doha	6 May	4.50	Krasnova	4	NC	Cheboksary	21 Jun
4.75			Kiriakopoúlou	2	GGala	Roma	2 Jun	4.50	Grove	10	NC	Eugene	10 Jul
4.70			Bradshaw	5	OG	Rio de Janeiro	19 Aug	4.45	Payne	1		San Antonio	19 Mar
4.65			Ptácníková	1		Praha	2 Jun	4.45	Pluim	2	FBK	Hengelo	22 May
4.65			Hixson	1		Chula Vista	18 Jun	4.43	Saxer Sibears	7	DL	Doha	6 May
4.65			Bengtsson	3	EC	Amsterdam	9 Jul	4.42	Brost	1		La Crosse	19 May
4.63			Li Ling	4	DL	Doha	6 May	4.40	T Weeks	3		Fayetteville	23 Apr
4.60			Nageotte	5	NC	Eugene	10 Jul	4.40	Viuf	1		Joplin	29 Apr
4.55			Malácová	2		Praha	2 Jun	4.38	Onofre	1	NC	Maia	26 Jun
4.55			Nikkanen	13q	OG	Rio de Janeiro	16 Aug	4.35A	Correa	1		Ciudad de México	18 Mar
4.52			Murto	2	PNG	Turku	29 Jun	4.35	Galiart	Q	EC	Amsterdam	7 Jul
4.50			Withrow	2		Chula Vista	7 May	4.35	Caldwell	15q	NC	Eugene	8 Jul
4.32			Holliday	16 Apr		4.30	Song Tingting	16 Apr	4.30	Boslak	18 Jun		4.25	Benecchi	26 Jun
4.32			Gutermuth	23 Apr		4.30	Lotout	8 May	4.30	Siitonen	24 Jun		4.25	Sadovnikova	15 Jul
4.31			Gergel	21 May		4.30	Xu Huiqin	22 May	4.30	Petershofen	23 Jul		4.22	Felzmann	26 May
4.30			Ren Mengqian	16 Apr		4.30	Y Bondarenko	30 May	4.25	Schultze	8 May		4.22	Applebee	27 May
												4.22	Quick	27 May

JUNIORS
See main list for top 8 juniors. 18 performances (inc. 7 indoors) by 4 women to 4.49. Additional marks and further juniors:

Mark		Name			Name	Nat	Born	Pos	Meet	Venue	Date
Murto 2+	4.55i	1		Turku			17 Jan	4.50	5	DL	Birmingham	5 Jun
	4.50i	1		Nastola			9 Jan	4.50	2	Spitz	Luzern	14 Jun
Moser	4.55	1	WJ	Bydgoszcz			21 Jul	4.50i	1		Dornbirn	14 Feb
Peinado	4.55	1		Montreuil			7 Jun	4.50	2		Athína	10 May
	4.52i	6		Clermont-Ferrand			21 Feb	4.50	3	GS	Ostrava	20 May
	4.50i	1		Spala			14 Feb					
Gunnarsson	4.50	1	NC	Angers			25 Jun	4.49i	4		Globen Stockholm	17 Feb
4.34		Rachel			Baxter	USA-Y	5.4.99	1		Mission Viejo (75mm pegs)	23 Apr
4.32		Alina			McDonald (10)	USA	26.8.97	2		Rock Hill	28 May
4.30		Nina			Kennedy	AUS	5.4.97	3		Perth	12 Mar
4.30					Chen Qiaoling	CHN-Y	22.11.99	2	NGP	Shaoxing	16 Apr
4.30		Olivia			Gruver	USA	29.7.97	1		Charlottesville	22 Apr
4.30		Amálie			Svábíková	CZE-Y	22.11.99	1		Kladno	11 Sep
4.30		Olivia			McTaggart	NZL-Y	9.1.00	1		Auckland	26 Nov
4.25					Wu Zuocheng	CHN-Y	26.5.99	1	NC-y	Jinan	11 Jun
4.25		Carson			Dingler	USA-Y	14.5.99	5	WJ	Bydgoszcz	21 Jul
4.21	sq	Nastja			Modic	SLO-Y	28.1.99	2		Linz	29 Jun
4.20i		Anna			Shpak	BLR	14.2.97	2	NC	Mogilyov	20 Feb
4.20		Aksana			Gataullina (20)	RUS-Y	17.7.00	2	NC-y	Chelyabinsk	22 Jun
4.20					Li Chaoqun	CHN	20.2.97	6	WJ	Bydgoszcz	21 Jul
4.20i		Thiziri			Daci	FRA	15.12.97	1		Eaubonne	12 Nov
Best out: 4.30		Yelizaveta			Bondarenko	RUS-Y	1.7.99	1j		Cheboksary	30 May

LONG JUMP

Mark	Wind		Name		Name	Nat	Born				Venue		Date
7.31	1.7		Brittney		Reese	USA	9.9.86	1	NC		Eugene		2 Jul
							6.99/1.9	x		5.42	7.31	x	
	7.22i		1	WI	Portland		18 Mar	6.97	x	x	6.88	7.00	7.22
	7.15	0.6	2	OG	Rio de Janeiro		17 Aug	x	x	6.79	x	7.09/0.6	7.15
	7.04	-1.2	1		Bellinzona		6 Jun	6.91/0.3	x	x	7.04/0.0	7.04/-0.2	x
	6.95	-0.2	1	WK	Zürich		1 Sep	6.76	x	x	6.95	p	6.83
	6.92	1.1	1	Pre	Eugene		27 May	6.92	6.53	x	6.80/0.8	x	x
	6.92	1.3	1		Eugene		29 Jul	6.91/1.4	6.84	x	x	6.69	6.92
	6.89i		1	NC	Portland		12 Mar	6.89	6.80	x	x	6.70	x
7.17	0.6		Tianna		Bartoletta	USA	30.8.85	1	OG		Rio de Janeiro		17 Aug
								x	6.94/0.4	6.95/0.0	6.74	7.17	7.13/0.8
7.16	1.6		Sosthene		Moguenara	GER	17.10.89	1			Weinheim		28 May
								6.79/0.6	x		6.96/1.8	7.07/0.0	7.16	p
7.10	0.3		Ivana		Spanovic	SRB	10.5.90	1			Beograd		11 Sep
								7.10	6.74	6.97/-0.3	7.03/0.9	6.80	6.83
	7.08	0.6	3	OG	Rio de Janeiro		17 Aug	6.95/-0.1	x	x	6.91/0.4	7.08	7.05/0.7
	7.07i		2	WI	Portland		18 Mar	7.00	6.88	x	x	7.07	6.76
	6.96	1.1	*	Hanz	Zagreb		6 Sep	6.88/1.0	6.96/1.1	6.81	x	p	7.03w
	6.95	0.7	1	DL	Shanghai		14 May	6.95	6.82	6.64	6.88/0.1	p	6.75
	-6.94	-0.5	1	Bisl	Oslo		9 Jun	6.63	6.79/0.3	x	x	6.94	p
	6.94	0.9	1	EC	Amsterdam		8 Jul	x	6.94	6.81/1.9	6.71/0.6	6.72/1.6	x
	6.93	0.0	2	WK	Zürich		1 Sep	6.93	x	6.74/-1.3	x	6.90/-0.1	x
	-6.90	-0.3	1	DL	Stockholm		16 Jun	6.73	6.90	6.52	p	6.57	p
	6.90	1.7	Q	EC	Amsterdam		6 Jul	6.90					
	6.90	0.0	1	DL	Saint-Denis		27 Aug	x	6.90		retired		

LONG JUMP

Mark	Wind	Name		Nat	Born	Pos	Meet	Venue			Date	
7.05	2.0	Brooke	Stratton	AUS	12.7.93	1		Perth			12	Mar
					6.71w	7.05	6.69w	6.82w	6.79w	6.84		
	6.94	0.0 1	Canberra	20 Feb	x	x	6.94	x	6.82/1.7	x		
6.95i		Alexandra	Wester	GER	21.3.94	1	ISTAF	Berlin			13	Feb
					6.44	6.82	6.95	x	x	6.76		
6.95	0.6	Malaika	Mihambo	GER	3.2.94	4	OG	Rio de Janeiro			17	Aug
					6.83/-0.8	x	x	6.58	6.95	6.79		
6.93i		Lorraine	Ugen	GBR	22.8.91	3	WI	Portland			18	Mar
					6.62	6.64	6.65	x	6.93	6.86		
6.93	2.0	Maryna	Bekh	UKR	18.7.95	1	NC	Lutsk			17	Jun
					6.63	6.93	x	6.80	6.88w	p		
6.93	1.7	Janay	DeLoach (10)	USA	12.10.85	3	NC	Eugene			2	Jul
					x	x	6.58	6.48	4.94	6.93		
	6.89i	4 WI	Portland	18 Mar	x	6.80	x	x	6.85	6.89		
6.91i		Shara	Proctor	GBR	16.9.88	2	ISTAF	Berlin			13	Feb
					6.65	6.91	5.18	6.87	6.59	6.86		
6.89	1.8	Sha'Keela	Saunders	USA	18.12.93	4	NC	Eugene			2	Jul
	(31/12)				6.89	6.68	x	6.79	6.83	x		
6.88A	1.9	Concepción	Montaner	ESP	14.1.81	1		Monachil			2	Jul
6.85A	0.3	Karin	Melis Mey	TUR	31.5.84	1		Johannesburg			13	Feb
6.84i		Anastasiya	Mironchik-Ivanova	BLR	13.4.89	1	NCp	Minsk			7	Feb
6.84	1.1	Darya	Klishina	RUS	15.1.91	1	NC	Cheboksary			21	Jun
6.84	0.9	Katarina	Johnson-Thompson	GBR	9.1.93	1	DL	London (OS)			23	Jul
6.83	1.2	Ese	Brume	NGR	20.1.96	1		Akure			6	Jun
6.81	1.2	Kenyattia	Hackworth	USA	15.9.93	1		Lexington			7	May
6.80i		Quanesha	Burks	USA	15.3.95	1	NCAA	Birmingham, AL			11	Mar
	(20)											
6.80i		Akela	Jones	BAR	22.4.95	1P	NCAA	Birmingham, AL			11	Mar
6.79	1.5	Juliet	Itoya	ESP	17.8.86	1		Salamanca			4	Jun
6.79	-0.2	Ksenija	Balta	EST	1.11.86	6	OG	Rio de Janeiro			17	Aug
6.78A		Lynique	Prinsloo	RSA	30.3.91	1		Polokwane			30	Apr
6.78	1.2	Háido	Alexoúli	GRE	29.3.91	1		Kalamáta			28	May
6.76i		Anna	Misochenko	RUS	15.4.92	1		Slavyansk-na-Kubani			31	Jan
6.76	0.3	Funmi	Jimoh	USA	29.5.84	5	NC	Eugene			2	Jul
6.75i		Yuliya	Pidluzhnaya	RUS	1.10.88	1	NC	Moskva			24	Feb
6.75	0.3	Christabel	Nettey	CAN	2.6.91	2	DL	Shanghai			14	May
6.75	0.2	Jazmin	Sawyers	GBR	21.5.94	1	NC	Birmingham			26	Jun
	(30)											
6.75	-0.5	Jana	Veldáková	SVK	3.6.81	1	NC	Banská Bystrica			26	Jun
6.74	1.5	Khaddi	Sagnia	SWE	20.4.94	1	vFIN	Tampere			4	Sep
6.73	1.6	Blessing	Okagbare	NGR	9.10.88	4	Pre	Eugene			27	May
6.73	0.8	Anna	Lunyova	UKR	1.10.91	1		Kyiv			24	Jun
6.72	1.9	Whitney	Gipson	USA	20.9.90	1	Bush	Norwalk			4	Jun
6.72	0.9	Eliane	Martins	BRA	26.5.86	1		São Bernardo do Campo			19	Jun
6.72	0.8	Marestella	Sunang	PHI	20.2.81	1		Almaty			4	Jul
6.71i		Veronika	Semashko	RUS	17.10.90	2	NC	Moskva			24	Feb
6.71	1.2	Svetlana	Biryukova	RUS	1.4.91	Q	NC	Cheboksary			20	Jun
6.71	0.0	Krystyna	Hryshutyna	UKR	21.3.92	2		Kyiv			24	Jun
	(40)											
6.70i		Yekaterina	Koneva	RUS	25.9.88	2		Slavyansk-na-Kubani			31	Jan
6.70	-0.1	Chelsea	Jaensch	AUS	6.1.85	2		Canberra			20	Feb
6.70	1.4	Ivonne	Treviño	MEX	8.3.89	1	NC	Monterrey			5	Jun
6.70	-0.3	Melanie	Bauschke	GER	14.7.88	2		Oberteuringen			5	Jun
6.70	2.0	Oksana	Zubkovska	UKR	15.7.81	2	NC	Lutsk			17	Jun
6.70	2.0	Anna	Kornuta	UKR	10.11.88	3	NC	Lutsk			17	Jun
6.69	0.5	Jéssica Carolina	dos Reis	BRA	17.3.93	2	NC	São Bernardo do Campo			1	Jul
6.68	0.9	Tori	Polk	USA	21.9.83	*		Phoenix			21	May
6.67	-0.5	Chanice	Porter	JAM	25.5.94	2	NCAA	Eugene			9	Jun
6.67	0.1	Alina	Rotaru	ROU	5.6.93	1		Oberteuringen			10	Jul
	(50)											
6.66i		Xu Xiaoling		CHN	13.5.92	1	NGP	Nanjing			28	Feb
6.66i		Anastasiya	Mokhnyuk	UKR	1.1.91	1P	WI	Portland			18	Mar
6.66	0.8	Chantel	Malone	IVB	2.12.91	1	FlaR	Gainesville			1	Apr
6.66	1.4	Efthimía	Kolokithá	GRE	9.7.87	2		Kalamáta			28	May
6.66	0.7	Narayanan V.	Neena	IND	2.5.91	1		Bengaluru			11	Jul
6.66	-1.0	Alexis	Perry	USA	8.8.94	3	NACAC	San Salvador			17	Jul
6.63i		Xenia	Stolz	GER	14.1.89	3	ISTAF	Berlin			13	Feb
6.63	1.8	Ja'nia	Sears	USA	15.4.93	1		Clovis			23	Apr
6.63	0.6	Nadja	Käther	GER	29.9.88	3		Oberteuringen			5	Jun
6.63	1.2	Jessica	Ennis-Hill	GBR	28.1.86	1H		Ratingen			26	Jun
	(60)											

LONG JUMP

Mark	Wind	Name		Nat	Born	Pos	Meet	Venue	Date	
6.62A	1.3	Abigail	Irozuru	GBR	3.1.90	1		El Paso	30	Apr
6.62	1.6	Claudia	Rath	GER	25.4.86	4		Bad Langensalza	21	May
6.62	-0.4	Keturah	Orji	USA	5.3.96	1q	NCAA-E	Jacksonville	26	May
6.62	1.6	Hafdís	Sigurdardóttir	ISL	12.2.87	1		Hilversum	9	Jul
6.61i			Jiang Yanfei	CHN	5.7.92	2	NGP	Nanjing	3	Mar
6.61A	1.0	Olatz	Arrieta	ESP	1.12.90	2		Monachil	2	Jul
6.60	1.7	Jessica	Penney	AUS	21.12.87	2	NC	Sydney	3	Apr
6.60A	0.6	Erica	Jarder	SWE	2.4.86	3		Monachil	2	Jul
6.59	0.0		Bul Thi Thu Thuo	VIE	29.4.92	1		Singapore	28	Apr
6.59	-0.3	Nektaria	Panagi	CYP	20.3.90	1		Árgos Orestikó	11	Jun
		(70)								
6.59	0.0	Yelena	Sokolova	RUS	23.7.86	4	NC	Cheboksary	21	Jun
6.59	1.6	Laura	Strati	ITA	3.10.90	1		Ljubljana	30	Jun
6.59	0.2	Maryse	Luzolo	GER	13.3.95	1-22		Oberteuringen	10	Jul
6.59	0.5	Marina	Buchelgnikova	RUS	8.2.94	2	NCp	Zhukovskiy	21	Jul
6.58	0.0	Rougui	Sow	FRA	7.6.95	1	Med-23	Radès	5	Jun
6.58	-0.4	Haoua	Kessely	FRA	2.2.88	1		Pierre-Bénite	10	Jun
6.58	-0.5	Nafissatou	Thiam	BEL	19.8.94	1H	OG	Rio de Janeiro	13	Aug
6.57i		Andrea	Geubelle	USA	21.6.91	3	NC	Portland	12	Mar
6.57	-0.2	Éloyse	Lesueur	FRA	15.7.88	1	Déca	Marseille	13	Sep
6.56A		Maryke	Brits	RSA	25.2.94	2		Polokwane	30	Apr
		(80)								
6.56	0.2	Brianne	Theisen-Eaton	CAN	18.12.88	1H	Hypo	Götzis	29	May
6.56	0.1	Romaissa	Belbiod	ALG	28.2.91	1	PTS	Samorín	4	Jun
6.56	0.0	Paraskeví	Papahrístou	GRE	17.4.89	1	NC	Pátra	18	Jun
6.56	1.5	María del Mar	Jover	ESP	21.4.88	1		Castellón	30	Jun
6.56	1.6	Keila	Costa	BRA	6.2.83	3	NC	São Bernardo do Campo	1	Jul
6.55	2.0	Veronika	Shutkova	BLR	26.5.86	1		Minsk	10	Jun
6.55	0.1	Heather	Miller Koch	USA	30.3.87	1		Chula Vista	18	Jun
6.55	1.4	Anna	Jagaciak Michalska	POL	10.2.90	1	NC	Bydgoszcz	26	Jun
6.54i		Kate	Hall	USA-J	12.1.97	2		Fayetteville	29	Jan
6.54	0.0	Gabrielle	Farquharson	USA	12.12.92	1		Tallahassee	15	Apr
		(90)								
6.54	-0.3	Der'Renae	Freeman	USA	15.4.94	1	ACC	Tallahassee	14	May
6.54	1.9	Kylie	Price	USA	1.10.93	8	NC	Eugene	2	Jul
6.53	1.4	Malaina	Payton	USA	16.10.91	1		Chula Vista	7	May
6.53	0.4	Nadia	Akpana Assa	NOR	22.12.95	1		København	18	Jun
6.52	1.3	Bianca	Stuart	BAH	17.5.88	2		Baie-Mahault	14	May
6.52	0.0	Bohdana	Melnyk	UKR	25.10.94	2		Kyiv	31	May
6.52	1.3	Yelena	Mashinistova	RUS	29.3.94	3q	NC	Cheboksary	20	Jun
6.52	0.0	Jessie	Gaines	USA	12.8.90	1		Philadelphia	25	Jun
6.51i		Darrielle	McQueen	USA	29.5.96	5	SEC	Fayetteville	26	Feb
6.51	1.7	Tânia	da Silva	BRA	17.12.86	1		São Bernardo do Campo	27	Feb
		(100)								
6.51	1.3	Destiny	Carter	USA	.93	3		Charlottesville	23	Apr
6.51	1.9	Neja	Filipic	SLO	22.4.95	1		Slovenska Bistrica	28	May
6.51	-0.3		Lu Minjia	CHN	29.12.92	1	NGPF	Chongqing	18	Jun
6.51	0.6	Jana	Koresová	CZE	8.4.81	1	Pán	Tábor	27	Jul

Mark	Wind	Name		Nat	Born	Date		Mark	Wind	Name		Nat	Date	
6.50	-0.8	Jogaile	Petrokaite	LTU	30.9.95	14 May		6.46	2.0	Stachia	Reuwsaat	USA	.94	26 May
6.50	2.0	Malin	Marmbrandt	SWE	29.4.85	25 May		6.46		Sabina	Allen	JAM	27.12.94	3 Jun
6.50	0.2	Tilde	Johansson	SWE-Y	5.1.01	1 Jul		6.45i		Kendell	Williams	USA	14.6.95	11 Mar
6.49i		Florentina	Marincu	ROU	8.4.96	31 Jan		6.45	-2.2	Paula Beatriz	Álvarez	CUB	11.9.95	29 May
6.49i		Laura	Ikauniece-Admidina	LAT	31.5.92	9 Mar		6.45	1.9	Naa	Anang	AUS	10.3.95	19 Jun
6.49	0.9	Elizabeth	López	MEX	12.11.91	21 May		6.45	1.1	Eszter	Bajnok	HUN-J	26.4.97	26 Jun
6.49	0.5	Ivona	Dadic	AUT	29.12.93	10 Jun		6.45	1.4	Filippa	Fotopoulou	CYP	20.12.96	26 Jun
6.49	1.1	Bria	Matthews	USA-J	22.7.97	25 Jun		6.44i		Julienne	McKee	USA	6.12.91	13 Feb
6.49	0.5	Martina	Lorenzetto	ITA	18.4.92	25 Jun		6.44i		Clairwin	Dameus	USA	12.6.94	26 Feb
6.49	0.0	Sophie	Weißenberg	GER-J	24.9.97	26 Jun		6.44	1.4	Savannah	Carson	USA	30.3.95	9 Apr
6.48i		Yekaterina	Levitskaya	RUS	2.1.87	20 Jan		6.44	-1.1	Tierra	Williams	USA	10.6.95	7 May
6.48i		Jasmine	Simmons	USA	28.2.89	5 Feb		6.44	1.0	Karolina	Zawila	POL	21.11.86	28 May
6.48i		Yekaterina	Khalyutina	RUS	16.1.91	9 Feb		6.44	1.9	Milena	Mitkova	BUL	26.1.90	29 May
6.48i		Samiyah	Samuels	USA-J	2.10.97	12 Mar		6.44	1.3	Polina	Yurchenko	RUS	20.8.93	1 Jul
6.48	0.0	Yanis	David	FRA-J	12.12.97	26 Mar		6.43	0.5	Mayookha	Johny	IND	9.4.88	9 Feb
6.48	1.7	Dominique	Bullock	USA	14.5.96	23 Apr		6.43		Irisdaymi	Herrera	CUB	18.4.92	13 May
6.48	0.8	Hanne	Maudens	BEL-J	12.3.97	21 May		6.43	-1.6	Antoinette	Nana Djimou	FRA	2.8.85	13 Aug
6.48	1.5	Konomi	Kai	JPN	10.7.93	19 Jun		6.42i		Mariya	Gromysheva	RUS	10.1.90	20 Jan
6.48	0.3	Aiga	Grabuste	LAT	24.3.88	21 Jun		6.42i		Darya	Reznichenko	UZB	3.4.91	27 Jan
6.48	2.0	Shana	Woods	USA	7.7.88	26 Jun		6.42		Crystal	Walker	USA	23.6.91	9 Apr
6.47i			Chen Liwen	CHN-J	3.1.98	28 Feb		6.42	1.8	Irène	Pusterla	SUI	21.6.88	11 Jun
6.47	-0.6	Anna	Bühler	GER-J	3.6.97	22 May		6.42	?	Joëlle	Mbumi	CMR	25.5.86	12 Jun
6.47	2.0	Jasmine	Todd	USA	23.12.93	29 Jul		6.42	-0.6	Margrethe	Renstrøm	NOR	21.3.85	2 Jul
6.47	0.0	Gesa Katharina	Kratzsch	GER	5.11.91	3 Aug		6.42i		Heather	Arneton	FRA-Y	27.7.02	10 Dec
6.46	1.7	Viktoriya	Rybalko	UKR	26.10.82	7 May		6.41i		Lisa	Maihöfer	GER-J	28.10.98	23 Jan

LONG JUMP

Mark	Wind	Name		Nat	Born	Pos	Meet	Venue	Date	
6.41Ai		Margaux	Jones	USA-J	11.2.97	5		Feb	6.37Ai	Tara Davis USA-Y 20.5.99 20 Feb
6.41	1.8	Teresa	Dobija	POL	9.10.82	21		May	6.37i	Jhoanmy Luque VEN 20.12.95 26 Feb
6.41	0.4	Yilian	Durruthy	CUB	30.1.90	29		May	6.37i	Li Ying CHN 29.3.94 28 Feb
6.41	0.0	Marharyta	Tverdohlib	UKR	2.6.91	31		May	6.37A 0.9	Alejandra Maldonado MEX 18.4.92 11 May
6.41	1.7	Kaede	Miyasaka	JPN	12.12.92	15		Oct	6.36i	Anastasiya Yeremina RUS 14.7.95 19 Jan
6.40		Yiff'at	Zelikovitz	ISR	19.12.92	24		May	6.36i	Li Li CHN 5.12.89 28 Feb
6.40	0.5	Tania	Vicenzino	ITA	1.4.86	29		May	6.36	1.0 Taylor DeLoach USA-J22.10.97 19 Jun
6.39i			Wang Wupin	CHN	18.1.91	28		Feb	6.36	1.2 Olga Sudareva BLR 22.2.84 23 Jun
6.39	-2.0	Taliyah	Brooks	USA	8.2.95	6		May	6.36	1.6 Paola Borovic CRO 26.6.95 26 Jun
6.39	1.8	Tayler	Fleming	USA		7		May	6.36	1.0 Maja Bedrac SLO-Y 10.9.99 2 Jul
6.39	1.6	Jessamyn	Sauceda	MEX	22.5.89	14		May	6.36	1.2 Yekaterina Bolshova RUS 4.2.88 21 Jul
6.39	1.0	Caroline	Klein	GER	4.3.96	23		Jul	6.35i	Nina Djordjevic SLO 15.5.88 20 Feb
6.38i		Elena	Panturoiu	ROU	24.2.95	21		Feb	6.35	1.8 Giulia Liboà ITA 3.6.93 1 May
6.38	1.6	Maria Natalia	Londa	INA	29.10.90	16		May	6.35	Yuliya Tarasova UZB 13.3.86 31 May
6.38	1.5	Emmi	Mäkinen	FIN	29.5.93	19		May	6.35	1.1 Zhou Xiaoxue CHN 19.6.92 18 Jun
6.38		Jovanna	Klaczynski	GER	8.4.94	22		May	6.35	1.9 Diana Ion ROU-Y27.11.00 19 Jun
6.38	1.7	Nadine	Broersen	NED	29.4.90	18		Sep	6.35	0.5 Nadine Visser NED 9.2.95 13 Aug
6.37i		Lyudmila	Yeryomina	RUS	8.8.91	19		Jan		(189)

Wind assisted

Mark	Wind		Name		Nat	Born	Pos	Meet	Venue		Date
7.03	2.5	(see 6.96)	Spanovic				1		Hanz Zagreb		6 Sep
7.02	2.3		Bartoletta				2	NC	Eugene		2 Jul
							7.02w p	p	6.82	p	p
7.01	2.7	(only jump)	Reese				Q	NC	Eugene		1 Jul
	6.90	2.8 1		Chula Vista 26		Jun	6.87/1.6	x	x	6.90w	p p
7.00	3.3		Alexandra Wester	GER		21.3.94	2		Weinheim		28 May
			x				7.00w	6.94w/2.2	6.61	6.78	x
6.90	2.8		Melanie Bauschke	GER		14.7.88	3		Weinheim		28 May
			6.63				6.68	6.90w. x	6.61w	6.65	
6.88	2.2		Christabel Nettey	CAN		2.6.91	1		Tempe		9 Apr
6.86	2.8		Jazmin Sawyers	GBR		21.5.94	2	EC	Amsterdam		8 Jul
6.84	4.2		Whitney Gipson	USA		20.9.90	1		Chula Vista		28 May
6.82	3.5		Lorraine Ugen	GBR		22.8.91	1	DrakeR	Des Moines		29 Apr
6.77	2.7		Tori Polk	USA		21.9.83	1		Phoenix		21 May
6.76	2.2		Bianca Stuart	BAH		17.5.88	1		Auburn		9 Apr
6.70	3.5		Der'Renae Freeman	USA		15.4.94	6	NC	Eugene		2 Jul
6.68	2.9		María del Mar Jover	ESP		21.4.88	1		Castellón		11 Jun
6.66	2.5		Kylie Price	USA		1.10.93	5q	NC	Eugene		1 Jul
6.64	2.3		Nadja Käther	GER		29.9.88	4		Weinheim		28 May
6.59	2.2		Kate Hall	USA-J		12.1.97	8q	NC	Eugene		1 Jul
6.58	2.1		Bohdana Melnyk	UKR		25.10.94	6	NC	Lutsk		17 Jun
6.57	3.3		Ottavia Cestonaro	ITA		12.1.95	1	NC-23	Bressanone		10 Jun
6.52	2.2		Jogaile Petrokaite	LTU		30.9.95	2	ACC	Tallahassee		14 May
6.52	3.7		Malin Marmbrandt	SWE		29.4.85	1		Torremolinos		25 May
6.51A	2.4		Patience Ntshingila	RSA		26.8.89	13 Feb	6.40	3.3 Nadine Broersen NED 29.4.90 9 Jul
6.51	3.5		Marharyta Tverdohlib	UKR		2.6.91	17 Jun	6.40	2.2 Martha Traoré DEN 8.1.95 10 Sep
6.51	2.4		Evelise Veiga	POR		3.3.96	26 Jun	6.39	2.6 Cidae'a Woods USA 26.6.96 13 May
6.50	4.2		Euphemia Edem	NGR		3.3.89	3 Mar	6.38	2.4 Chelsea Hayes USA 9.2.88 16 Apr
6.50	2.2		Tierra Williams	USA		10.6.95	14 May	6.38	5.0 Jhoanmy Luque VEN 20.12.95 23 Apr
6.48	2.7		Tissanna Hickling	JAM-J		7.1.98	19 Jun	6.38	2.9 Anouk Vetter NED 4.2.93 9 Jul
6.47	3.4		Margaux Jones	USA-J		11.2.97	16 Apr	6.37	3.8 Ayana Gales USA .94 13 May
6.47	2.1		Nikia Squire	USA		5.12.93	26 May	6.36	4.2 Fanni Schmelcz HUN 19.4.92 31 Jul
6.45	3.3		Heather Arneton	FRA-Y		27.7.02	8 Jul	6.36	2.8 Kaiza Karlén SWE-J 4.12.98 6 Aug
6.43	3.9		Jessamyn Sauceda	MEX		22.5.89	21 May	6.35	3.2 Stormm Phillips USA .94 22 Apr
6.43	2.7		Anastasiya Angioi	ITA		28.4.95	10 Jun	6.35	4.2 Bae Chan-mi KOR 24.3.91 1 May
6.40	2.6		Lisa Kurschilgen	GER		27.3.91	28 May	6.35	2.2 Judith Nagy ROU 14.9.89 22 May

Best outdoors

Mark	Wind		Name						Venue		Date
6.80	0.1		Proctor		2	DL		London (OS)		23	Jul	6.75	1.8 Jones 1 Big 12 Fort Worth 14 May
6.80	0.0		Ugen		2	DL		Saint-Denis		27	Aug	6.69	1.5 Misochenko 2 NC Cheboksary 21 Jun
6.79	0.5		Wester		1			Oberteuringen		5	Jun	6.65	0.2 Pidluzhnaya 1 Sochi 26 May
6.77	-0.4		Burks		1		SEC	Tuscaloosa		13	May	6.56	1.5 Stolz 6 Weinheim 28 May
												6.53	1.6 Hall Q NC Eugene 1 Jul
6.49	0.0		Koneva		4			Jun	6.44	1.8	Samuels 25 Jun	6.38 1.8 Dameus 13 May
6.45	0.3		Xu Xiaoling		15			Apr	6.41	0.0	Chen Liwen 27 Jun	6.37 1.2 M Jones 25 Jun
6.47w	2.7		Xu Xiaoling		8			May	6.40	0.1	Levitskaya 26 May	6.36 2.0 K Williams 30 Apr
									6.39	0.1	Jiang Yanfei 15 Apr	6.35 0.8 McQueen 26 Mar

Best at low altitude

6.62	1.1	Melis Mey	5	EC	Amsterdam	8 Jul	6.53i		Jarder	4	Globen Stockholm	17 Feb
6.59	0.3	Prinsloo	1	NC	Stellenbosch	16 Apr			6.53w 2.1	1	København	14 Aug
6.54	-0.7	Brits	2	NC	Stellenbosch	16 Apr			6.49 1.1	8	Bad Langensalza	21 May
6.46i		Montaner 13 Feb, 6.37 1.5 Arrieta 26 Jun										

JUNIORS

Mark	Wind		Name		Nat	Born	Pos	Meet	Venue	Date
6.54i		Kate	Hall		USA	12.1.97	2		Fayetteville	29 Jan
	6.53	1.6					Q	NC	Eugene	1 Jul
6.50	0.2	Tilde	Johansson		SWE-Y	5.1.01	1		Göteborg	1 Jul
6.49	1.1	Bria	Matthews		USA	22.7.97	1	NC-j	Clovis	25 Jun
	6.47	0.6 4		ACC	Tallahassee		14May	10 performances (inc. 3 indoors) by 9 women to 6.47		

WOMEN 2016

LONG JUMP – TRIPLE JUMP

Mark	Wind	Name		Nat	Born	Pos	Meet	Venue	Date	
6.49	0.0	Sophie	Weißenberg	GER	24.9.97	1-j		Mannheim	26	Jun
6.48i		Samiyah	Samuels	USA	2.10.97	1	HS N.Bal	New York	12	Mar
		6.44	1.8			2	NC-j	Clovis	25	Jun
6.48	0.0	Yanis	David	FRA	12.12.97	1	Carifta	St. George	26	Mar
6.48	0.8	Hanne	Maudens	BEL-	12.3.97	1		Oordegem	21	May
6.47i			Chen Liwen	CHN	3.1.98	2	NGP	Nanjing	28	Feb
		6.41	0.0			1	NC-j	Ordos	27	Jun
6.47	-0.6	Anna	Bühler	GER	3.6.97	1		Garbsen	22	May
6.45	1.1	Eszter	Bajnok (10)	HUN	26.4.97	1	NC-j	Szombathely	26	Jun
6.42i		Heather	Arneton	FRA-Y	27.7.02	1		Eaubonne	10	Dec
6.41i		Lisa	Maihöfer	GER	28.10.98	1		Karlsruhe	23	Jan
6.41Ai		Margaux	Jones	USA	11.2.97	3		Albuquerque	5	Feb
		6.37	1.2			3	NC-j	Clovis	25	Jun
6.37Ai		Tara	Davis	USA-Y	20.5.99	1		Pocatello	20	Feb
6.36	1.0	Taylor	DeLoach	USA-J	22.10.97	1	HS N.Bal	Greensboro	19	Jun
6.36	1.0	Maja	Bedrac	SLO-Y	10.9.99	1	Balk-y	Krusevac	2	Jul
6.35	1.9	Diana	Ion	ROU-Y	27.11.00	1	NC-y	Pitesti	19	Jun
6.34			Nguyen Thi Truc Mai	VIE	20.3.97	1	Asi-J	Ho Chi Minh	3	Jun
6.34	2.0	Polina	Lukyanenkova	RUS	15.7.98	1	NC-j	Kazan	27	Jun
6.33	0.7	Hilary	Kpatcha (20)	FRA	5.5.98	3	WJ	Bydgoszcz	22	Jul
Wind assisted			3 performances by 3 women to 6.47							
6.59	2.2	Kate	Hall	USA	12.1.97	8q	NC	Eugene	1	Jul
6.48	2.7	Tissanna	Hickling	JAM	7.1.98	1	NC-j	Kingston	19	Jun
6.47	3.4	Margaux	Jones	USA	11.2.97	2	MSR	Norwalk	16	Apr
6.45	3.3	Heather	Arneton	FRA-Y	27.7.02	1		Saint-Florentin	8	Jul
6.36	2.8	Kaiza	Karlén	SWE	4.12.98	1	NC-j	Hässleholm	6	Aug

TRIPLE JUMP

Mark	Wind	Name		Nat	Born	Pos	Meet	Venue	Date					
15.17	0.4	Caterine	Ibargüen	COL	12.2.84	1	OG	Rio de Janeiro	14 Aug					
						14.65/-0.1	15.03/0.0	14.38	15.17	14.76/0.2	14.80/0.0			
	15.04	1.5 1 DL	Doha		6 May	14.46	14.77/?	x	x	15.04	14.98/1.3			
	14.96	-0.2 1 Herc	Monaco		15 Jul	14.56/1.3	14.82/0.4	14.87/0.6	x	x	14.96			
	14.78	-0.1 1 GGala	Roma		2 Jun	14.28	x	14.64/-0.4	x	x	14.78			
	14.76	0.5 1 Athl	Lausanne		25 Aug	14.41	14.34	x	14.70/0.6	14.76	13.79			
	14.66	-0.4 1 VD	Bruxelles		9 Sep	13.94	14.54/0.4	14.52/0.0	14.18	14.56/0.4	14.66			
	14.56	0.8 2 DL	Birmingham		5 Jun	13.98	14.51/1.4	14.56	14.35	14.42	14.53/0.7			
	14.52	0.1 Q OG	Rio de Janeiro		13 Aug	14.52								
	14.51	-0.4 1	Rabat		22 May	14.38	14.41	13.87	x	14.20	14.51			
	14.51A	-1.4 1	Cali		25 Jun	14.36	14.26	x	x	14.51	14.48			
15.02	-0.4	Yulimar	Rojas	VEN	21.10.95	1		Madrid	23 Jun					
						x	14.53w/2.1	14.57/1.6	x	14.78/0.7	15.02			
	14.98	0.8 2 OG	Rio de Janeiro		14 Aug	14.32	x	14.87/0.7	14.98	14.66/0.0	14.95/0.1			
	14.79	1.3 * DL	Doha		6 May	13.91	14.61/0.9	14.79/1.3	x	14.92w	x			
	14.69i	1	Madrid		23 Jan	x	x	13.53	14.19	14.25	14.69			
	14.64	0.7 2 Herc	Monaco		15 Jul	14.23/0.3	13.97	14.55/0.2	x	14.64	x			
	14.63i	1	Madrid		26 Feb	x	14.32	14.56	x	14.63	x			
14.74	0.3	Olga	Rypakova	KAZ	30.11.84	3	OG	Rio de Janeiro	14 Aug					
						14.73/0.5	14.49	14.52/0.0	14.74	14.58/0.2				
	14.61	1.1 3 DL	Doha		6 May	14.23		14.31	13.88	14.61	x			
	14.61	1.5 1 DL	Birmingham		5 Jun	14.42	14.25	14.35	14.22	p	14.61			
	14.53	1.0 2 Athl	Lausanne		25 Aug	14.16	x	x	14.53	14.49/0.7	14.29			
	14.51	0.7 2 GGala	Roma		2 Jun	14.25	14.51	14.08	14.13	14.36	14.37			
14.73	-1.3	Paraskeví	Papahrístou	GRE	17.4.89	1		Athína (F)	8 Jun					
						14.73	p	x	p	p	p			
14.71	0.0	Keturah	Orji	USA	5.3.96	4	OG	Rio de Janeiro	14 Aug					
						14.71	x	x	14.50/0.4	14.40	14.39			
	14.53	1.2 1 NCAA	Eugene		11 Jun	x	13.93	13.98	13.96w	14.53	11.86			
14.68	0.5	Hanna	Minenko	ISR	25.9.89	5	OG	Rio de Janeiro	14 Aug					
						14.25	14.39	14.32	14.68	x	14.33			
14.65	0.1	Patrícia	Mamona	POR	21.11.88	6	OG	Rio de Janeiro	14 Aug					
					14.39	14.14	14.45	14.42	14.65		14.59/0.2			
	14.58	0.8 1 EC	Amsterdam		10 Jul	x	13.95	14.38w/2.6	x	x	14.58			
14.57	-1.1	Shanieka	Thomas	JAM	2.2.92	1		Mona	2 Apr					
14.56	1.8	Liadagmis	Povea	CUB	6.2.96	1	NC	La Habana	19 Mar					
						14.43	14.45	14.56	14.43	14.09w	p			
14.56	1.5	Kimberly	Williams (10)	JAM	3.11.88	*	NC	Kingston	3 Jul					
						14.56/1.5	14.16w	14.54/1.5	x	14.66w	14.27			
	14.53	0.4 7 OG	Rio de Janeiro		14 Aug	14.33	14.48	x	14.38	x	14.53			
14.51A	0.3	Liuba M.	Zaldívar	CUB	5.4.93	1		Medellín	10 Jul					
		(31/11)				14.18	13.86	14.26	x	13.78	14.51			

TRIPLE JUMP

Mark	Wind	Name		Nat	Born	Pos	Meet	Venue	Date	
14.42	1.5	Yekaterina	Koneva	RUS	25.9.88	1	Kuts	Moskva	1	Jul
14.41	1.4	Ruslana	Tsyhotska	UKR	23.3.86	1	NC	Lutsk	19	Jun
14.40	1.8	Olha	Saladukha	UKR	4.6.83	3	DL	Birmingham	5	Jun
14.40	1.1	Jeanine	Assani Issouf	FRA	17.8.92	1	NC	Angers	26	Jun
14.34	0.0	Susana	Costa	POR	22.9.84	5	EC	Amsterdam	10	Jul
14.33	1.0	Elena	Panturoiu	ROU	24.2.95	1	BalkC	Pitesti	25	Jun
14.33	0.6	Anna	Jagaciak Michalska	POL	10.2.90	Q	EC	Amsterdam	8	Jul
14.32i		Gabriela	Petrova	BUL	29.6.92	1	BalkC	Istanbul	27	Feb
14.31	0.2	Kristin	Gierisch	GER	20.8.90	1		Garbsen	22	May
		(20)								
14.28	1.4	Jenny	Elbe	GER	18.4.90	1		Dresden	14	May
14.28	0.6	Viktoriya	Prokopenko	RUS	17.4.91	1	NC	Cheboksary	23	Jun
14.24	-0.2	Kristiina	Mäkelä	FIN	20.11.92	Q	OG	Rio de Janeiro	13	Aug
14.23i		Irina	Vaskovskaya	BLR	2.4.91	1	NC	Mogilyov	20	Feb
14.22	1.2	Ana José	Tima	DOM	10.10.89	3		Madrid	23	Jun
14.22	2.0	Natalya	Vyatkina	BLR	10.2.87	Q	NC	Grodno	24	Jun
14.17	0.0	Núbia	Soares	BRA	26.3.96	1	NC	São Bernardo do Campo	3	Jul
14.17	0.6	Christina	Epps	USA	20.6.91	2	NC	Eugene	7	Jul
14.16i		Rouguy	Diallo	FRA	5.2.95	2	NC	Aubière	27	Feb
14.16	1.0	Yekaterina	Ektova	KAZ	30.8.92	1	NCp	Almaty	24	May
		(30)								
14.16A	-0.5	Patricia	Sarrapio	ESP	16.11.82	1		Monachil	10	Jul
14.15	0.1	Andrea	Geubelle	USA	21.6.91	1		Chula Vista	18	Jun
14.15	0.6	Dariya	Derkach	ITA	27.3.93	1	NC	Rieti	26	Jun
14.11	0.7	Dana	Veldáková	SVK	3.6.81	Q	EC	Amsterdam	8	Jul
14.10	0.8	Ayanna	Alexander	TTO	20.7.82	1		Lynchburg	23	Jul
14.09	0.0	Yargelis	Savigne	CUB	13.11.84	2		La Habana	13	Feb
14.09A	0.6	Mayookha	Johny	IND	9.4.88	1		Potchefstroom	22	Apr
14.09	0.6	Laura	Samuel	GBR	19.2.91	1	NC	Birmingham	25	Jun
14.08A	0.4	Yosiri	Urrutia	COL	26.6.86	2		Medellín	30	Apr
14.08	0.0	Davisleidis L.	Velazco	CUB-Y	4.9.99	1	Barr	La Habana	28	May
		(40)								
14.08	0.9	Svetlana	Biryukova	RUS	1.4.91	3	NC	Cheboksary	23	Jun
14.03	0.0	Nathalie	Marie-Nély	FRA	24.11.86	2		Forbach	29	May
14.02	1.5	Keila	Costa	BRA	6.2.83	2	NC	São Bernardo do Campo	3	Jul
14.02	1.6	Imani	Oliver	USA	7.3.93	Q	NC	Eugene	4	Jul
13.99	1.6	Ciarra	Brewer	USA	12.3.93	Q	NC	Eugene	4	Jul
13.96i		Natalya	Alekseyeva	RUS	27.5.86	1	Mosc	Moskva	10	Feb
13.96	-0.2	Tânia	da Silva	BRA	17.12.86	3	NC	São Bernardo do Campo	3	Jul
13.94i		Carmen	Toma	ROU	28.3.89	2	NGP	Bucuresti	30	Jan
13.94	1.7	Crystal	Manning	USA	15.4.86	1	Johnson	Waco	23	Apr
13.94	1.4	Cristina	Sandu	ROU	4.3.90	*		Pitesti	21	May
		(50)								
13.93	0.4	Neele	Eckhardt	GER	2.7.92	3		Garbsen	22	May
13.93	0.5	Anna	Krylova	RUS	3.10.85	4		Sochi	27	May
13.93	0.8	Lucie	Májková	CZE	9.7.88	1	NC	Tábor	19	Jun
13.91i		Ana	Peleteiro	ESP	2.12.95	2		Madrid	26	Feb
13.91i			Chen Mudan	CHN	4.10.93	1	NGP	Nanjing	29	Feb
13.91i			Wang Wupin	CHN	18.1.91	2	NGP	Nanjing	29	Feb
13.91	0.0	Nneka	Okpala	NZL	27.4.88	1	NC	Sydney	2	Apr
13.91	0.2	Olesya	Zabara	RUS	6.10.82	5		Sochi	27	May
13.91	0.8	Irina	Ektova	KAZ	8.1.87	31		Almaty	5	Jul
13.90i		Kseniya	Detsuk	BLR	23.4.86	2	NC	Mogilyov	20	Feb
		(60)								
13.90A		Patience	Ntshingila	RSA	26.8.89	1		Polokwane	29	Apr
13.89i		Olesya	Tikhonova	RUS	28.1.90	2	NC	Moskva	25	Feb
13.88		Amy	Zongo-Filet	FRA	4.10.80	1		Castres	20	Jul
13.86	1.7	Natalya	Yevdokimova	RUS	7.9.93	7	NC	Cheboksary	23	Jun
13.85	1.4	Andriana	Bânova	BUL	1.5.87	1		Sofia	18	May
13.85	1.4		Chen Ting	CHN-J	28.8.97	1	WJ	Bydgoszcz	23	Jul
13.83i		Petia	Dacheva	BUL	10.3.85	1		Bucuresti	27	Feb
13.83	2.0	April	Sinkler	USA	1.9.81	1		Chula Vista	26	Jun
13.82	1.4	Nadia	Eke	GHA	11.1.93	2		Chula Vista	18	Jun
13.82	1.7	Petra	Koren	SLO	30.7.93	1	NC	Celje	19	Jun
		(70)								
13.80	0.0	Malgorzata	Trybanska-Stronska	POL	21.6.81	1		Warszawa	19	Jun
13.78	2.0	Eva	Mustar	SLO	30.9.96	1		Ljubljana	30	Jun
13.78i		Irina	Gumenyuk	RUS	6.1.88	1		Sankt Peterburg	25	Dec
13.77	1.8	Simone	Charley	USA	4.2.95	2	NCAA	Eugene	11	Jun
13.75i		Anastasiya	Mironchik-Ivanova	BLR	13.4.89	2		Mogilyov	23	Jan
13.74	0.1	Yamilé	Aldama	GBR	14.8.72	1		Clermont	30	Apr

480 TRIPLE JUMP

Mark	Wind	Name		Nat	Born	Pos	Meet	Venue	Date	
13.74	1.2	Iryna	Pimenova	UKR	19.12.88	2	NC	Lutsk	19	Jun
13.74			Chen Yanzhen	CHN		1		Quanzhou	19	Jul
13.73	-1.7		Li Xiaohong	CHN	8.1.95	5		Kawasaki	8	May
13.73	1.2	Bria	Matthews	USA-J	22.7.97	1	ACC	Tallahassee	15	May
(80)										
13.72i		Darya	Nidbaykina	RUS	26.12.94	1	NC-23	Volgograd	3	Mar
13.71i		Veronika	Semashko	RUS	17.10.90	3		Moskva	14	Feb
13.71	-1.2	Claudine	de Jesus	BRA	9.9.94	2		São Bernardo do Campo	6	Mar
13.70i		Martyna	Bielawska	POL	15.11.90	1		Spala	20	Feb
13.70		Sineade	Gutzmore	GBR	9.10.86	2		Castres	20	Jul
13.69	1.9	Aleksandra	Nikitsina	BLR	12.9.93	3	NC	Grodno	25	Jun
13.68i		Tetyana	Ptashkina	UKR	10.1.93	1	NC	Sumy	26	Feb
13.67	1.0	Sasa	Babsek	SLO	27.3.92	*	NC	Celje	19	Jun
13.66i		Tori	Franklin	USA	7.10.92	2	NC	Portland	11	Mar
13.65	2.0	Olga	Velmyakina	RUS	3.8.92	8	NC	Cheboksary	23	Jun
(90)										
13.64	0.0		Deng Linuo	CHN	16.3.92	3	NGP	Shaoxing	16	Apr
13.64			Li Yanmei	CHN	6.2.90	3		Kawasaki	8	May
13.63i		Sanna	Nygård	FIN	22.3.88	2		Mustasaari	6	Feb
13.63	0.2		Tran Hue Hoa	VIE	8.8.91	2		Taoyuan	20	May
13.63	0.0	Iryna	Nikolayeva	UKR	20.1.84	3	NC	Lutsk	19	Jun
13.61i		Thea	LaFond	DMA	5.4.94	2		State College	20	Feb
13.61i		Darrielle	McQueen	USA	29.5.96	2	SEC	Fayetteville	27	Feb
13.61i			Rao Fan	CHN	1.1.96	3	NGP	Nanjing	4	Mar
13.61	1.9	Dilyara	Abuova	KAZ	6.1.94	4	Kozanov	Almaty	25	Jun
13.60A	0.3	Zinzi	Chanbangu	RSA	28.9.96	1		Johannesburg	13	Feb
(100)										
13.60	0.0	Simona	La Mantia	ITA	14.4.83	1		Palermo	8	May
13.60	1.0	Blessing	Ibrahim	NGR	4.4.90	1		Abuja	14	May
13.60	0.7	Jolanta	Verseckaite	LTU	9.2.88	1		Kaunas	21	May
13.60	0.9	Mariya	Ovchinnikova	KAZ-J	19.10.98	1		Almaty	24	May
13.60	1.0	Birte	Damerius	GER	13.12.91	1		Bremen	10	Jun
13.60	0.6	Toni	Smith	USA	13.10.84	5		Chula Vista	18	Jun
13.60	1.5	Tamara	Myers	BAH	27.7.93	1	NC	Nassau	25	Jun
13.59i		Katja	Demut	GER	21.12.83	20 Feb				
13.59	0.2		Bae Chan-mi	KOR	24.3.91	4 May				
13.59	1.8	Joëlle	Mbumi	CMR	25.5.86	9 Jul				
13.58i		Anastasiya	Potapova	RUS	6.9.85	14 Feb				
13.58i		Anna	Starzak	POL	15.5.88	6 Mar				
13.58	1.7	Giselly	Landázuri	COL	8.8.92	7 May				
13.58	1.4	Lynnika	Pitts	USA	19.5.92	18 Jun				
13.58	1.2	Nellickal Varkey	Sheena	IND	22.11.92	25 Jun				
13.57	2.0	Keri	Emanuel	USA	30.6.92	18 Jun				
13.57	1.8	Alsu	Murtazina	RUS	12.12.87	23 Jun				
13.57	1.9	Anastasiya	Leonova	BLR	6.4.94	25 Jun				
13.56	1.6	Tierra	Williams	USA	10.6.95	15 May				
13.55		Jihad	Bakhchi	MAR	22.8.91	16 Apr				
13.55	-0.6	Snezana	Vukmirovic	SLO	19.8.82	21 May				
13.55	0.7	Konstadína	Roméou	GRE-J	30.5.97	23 Jul				
13.54i			Jiang Yanfei	CHN	5.7.92	29 Feb				
13.54	1.0	Dannielle	Gibson	BAH	5.4.96	16 Jul				
13.53	1.8	Malaikah	Love	USA	2.5.90	25 Jun				
13.53	1.2	Yekaterina	Sariyeva	AZE	18.12.95	25 Jun				
13.52	0.8	Maria Natalia	Londa	INA	29.10.90	25 Sep				
13.52	0.7	Kaede	Miyasaka	JPN	12.12.92	15 Oct				
13.51	1.8	Merilyn	Uudmäe	EST	26.3.91	16 Jul				
13.50i		Yanis	David	FRA-J	12.12.97	13 Feb				
13.50	2.0	Kristína	Alvertsián	GRE	4.7.90	8 May				
13.49	1.0	Cristina	Bujin	ROU	12.4.88	2 Jul				
13.49	1.7	Georgiana	Anitei	ROU-Y	26.3.99	23 Jul				
13.48	1.4	Dailenis	Alcántara	CUB	10.8.91	17 Mar				
13.48	0.5		Hung Pei-Ning	TPE	10.2.94	2 May				
13.48	-1.8	Alitta	Boyd	USA	7.12.91	12 Jun				
13.48			Vu Thi Men	VIE	10.7.90	25 Nov				
13.47i			Wang Rong	CHN	1.7.96	29 Feb				
13.47	1.1	Sandisha	Antoine	LCA	5.11.91	26 Jun				
13.46	0.5	Amber	Hughes	USA	23.8.94	30 Apr				
13.46	0.2	Natasha	Dicks	USA	6.7.95	14 May				
13.46	1.7	Katarzyna	Plonka	POL	28.6.88	24 Jun				
13.45	1.0	Violetta	Skvortsova	BLR-J	5.4.98	12 May				
13.45	0.9	Krisztina	Hoffer	HUN	6.8.90	10 Sep				
13.44	0.8	Amanda	Smock	USA	27.7.82	4 Jul				
13.43i		Eleonora	D'Elicio	ITA	28.5.89	19 Feb				
13.43	0.5	Klaudia	Kaczmarek	GER	13.3.90	22 May				
13.43	1.5	Madara	Apine	LAT	2.3.89	31 May				
13.42	1.8	Meggan	O'Riley	AUS	18.3.89	2 Apr				
13.42	0.4		Xu Ting	CHN-J	23.2.97	16 Apr				
13.42	1.5	Blessing	Ufodiama	USA	28.11.81	18 Jun				
13.41i		Francesca	Lanciano	ITA	3.4.94	5 Mar				
13.41	0.6		Li Ying	CHN	29.3.94	21 May				
13.41	0.8	Shilpa	Chacko	IND	18.12.92	10 Jul				
13.41		H.D.Vidusha	Lakshani	SRI	28.12.96	23 Sep				
13.40i			Li Li	CHN	5.12.89	4 Mar				
13.40A	0.9	Ivonne	Rangel	MEX	24.8.93	18 Mar				
13,40		Iryna	Konstants	RUS	1.3.90	10 Jun				
13.40	1.8	Norka	Moretic	CHI-J	26.3.98	23 Jul				
13.39i		Andreea	Lefcenco	ROU	10.5.95	13 Feb				
13.39	-0.5	Anna	Kornuta	UKR	10.11.88	22 Jun				
13.39	1.6	Silvana	Segura	PER	6.11.90	4 Nov				
13.38i		Elina	Sterzing	GER	30.5.93	27 Feb				
13.38	0.3	Nora	Ritzen	NED	3.7.93	18 Jun				
13.38	1.9	Yelena	Mashinistova	RUS	29.3.94	1 Jul				
13.38	1.3	Marshay	Ryan	USA	4.2.95	4 Jul				
13.37i			Wei Mingchen	CHN	4.1.91	4 Mar				
13.37	-1.6	Valentina	Kosolapova	RUS-J	11.7.97	30 May				
13.37	1.1	Jhoanmy	Luque	VEN	20.12.95	11 Jun				
13.37	1.0	Ilionis	Guillaume	FRA-J	13.1.98	26 Jun				
13.37		Noor Shahidatun Nadia	Zuki	MAS	5.6.96	28 Jul				
13.36	0.4	Jannell	Hadnot	USA	17.10.95	28 May				
13.36	0.4	Liliana	Breto	CUB-J	4.2.97	28 May				
13.36	1.3		Chen Liwen	CHN-J	3.1.98	28 Jun				
13.36			Xiang Jia	CHN	1.8.96	16 Jul				
13.35i		Haoua	Kessely	FRA	2.2.88	9 Jan				
13.35	1.9	Jazzy	Black	USA	31.5.94	2 Apr				
13.34i		Violetta	Maksimchuk	RUS	1.12.90	10 Feb				
13.34i		Paola	Borovic	CRO	26.6.95	21 Feb				
13.34		Deborah	Acquah	GHA		16 Apr				
13.34	1.7	Chioma	Matthews	GBR	12.3.81	28 May				
13.34	0.6	Mara	Griva	LAT	4.8.89	3 Jul				
13.32	1.0	Valeriya	Zavyalova	RUS	16.1.88	2 Apr				
13.32	1.1	Anna	Gorodkova	KAZ-J	7.4.97	24 May				
13.32	0.9	Andrea	Calleja	ESP	3.10.92	30 May				
13.31i		Viershanie	Latham	USA	1.8.95	13 Feb				
13.31	-0.2	Isabella	Marten	GER	12.5.96	15 May				
13.31	0.0	Kateryna	Popova	UKR	7.8.96	1 Jun				
13.31		Kirthana	Ramasamy	MAS-J	20.1.97	28 Jul				
(189)										

TRIPLE JUMP

Mark	Wind	Name		Nat	Born	Pos	Meet	Venue	Date
Wind assisted									
14.92	2.6	(see 14.79)	Rojas			2	DL	Doha	6 May
14.66	2.6	Kimberly	Williams (see 14.56)	JAM	3.11.88	1	NC	Kingston	3 Jul
14.60	2.9		Orji			1	SEC	Tuscaloosa	14 May
					14.02	x		14.19 x	14.60w x
14.54	2.7		Povea			1		La Habana	13 Feb
					14.25	14.29w	14.08	14.33 14.23	14.54w
14.53	3.5		Mamona			1	NC	Maia	25 Jun
					x	13.91	x	x 14.53w	x
14.51	2.9		Minenko			2	EC	Amsterdam	10 Jul
					x	x	14.51w	x x	x
14.40	3.2	Anna	Jagaciak Michalska	POL	10.2.90	4	EC	Amsterdam	10 Jul
14.19	2.1	Yargelis	Savigne	CUB	13.11.84	2	NC	La Habana	19 Mar
14.10	2.1	Cristina	Sandu	ROU	4.3.90	1		Pitesti	21 May
14.05	2.5	Irina	Gumenyuk	RUS	6.1.88	4	NC	Cheboksary	23 Jun
13.92	2.3	Olesya	Tikhonova	RUS	28.1.90	5	NC	Cheboksary	23 Jun
13.81	2.1	Sasa	Babsek	SLO	27.3.92	2	NC	Celje	19 Jun
13.79	2.8	Madara	Apine	LAT	2.3.89	1		Rīga	20 May
13.77	4.1	Tamara	Myers	BAH	27.7.93	1		Nassau	30 Apr
13.74	4.3	Valentina	Kosolapova	RUS-J	11.7.97	1	NC-23	Saransk	17 Jul
13.73	3.0	Yosleivis	Ribalta	CUB	2.5.90	4	NC	La Habana	19 Mar
13.70	2.7	Thea	LaFond	DMA	5.4.94	2		Eugene	6 May
13.68	2.8	Marshay	Ryan	USA	4.2.95	2q	NCAA-E	Jacksonville	28 May
13.67	2.2	Mariya	Ovchinnikova	KAZ-J	19.10.98	3	Kozanov	Almaty	25 Jun
13.67	2.3	Toni	Smith	USA	13.10.84	7q	NC	Eugene	4 Jul
13.65	3.3	Yelena	Mashinistova	RUS	29.3.94	3		Saransk	17 Jul
13.64	5.3	Yanis	David	FRA-J	12.12.97	3	NCAA	Eugene	11 Jun
13.63	3.0	Dannielle	Gibson	BAH	5.4.94	3q	NCAA-E	Jacksonville	28 May
13.60	2.4	Rita	Rosado	MEX	17.8.90	16 Apr	13.41	2.6 Evelise Veiga POR 3.3.96	19 Jun
13.60	4.0	Viershanie	Latham	USA	1.8.95	6 May	13.40	3.3 Yekaterina Kropivko RUS-J 13.6.97	28 Jun
13.60	2.1	Natasha	Dicks	USA	6.7.95	28 May	13.40	2.2 Alexandra Russell GBR 27.3.90	31 Jul
13.52	2.2	Marjorie	Sánchez	CUB	3.10.85	21 May	13.38	2.1 Asa Garcia USA-J 15.5.97	23 Apr
13.50	2.9	Amber	Hughes	USA	23.8.94	28 May	13.38	3.0 Kaitlyn Beans USA 21.4.95	28 May
13.47	2.2	Irina	Konstants	RUS	1.3.90	22 Jun	13.35	4.4 Isabella Marten GER 12.5.96	11 Jun
13.46	3.4	Ilionis	Guillaume	FRA-J	13.1.98	2 Jul	13.34	3.7 Sha'Keela Saunders USA 18.12.93	28 May
Best outdoors									
14.19	1.9	Vaskovskaya	1	NC	Grodno	25 Jun	13.76	0.5 Gumenyuk 3 NCp Zhukovskiy	20 Jul
13.94	0.5	Diallo	3		Forbach	29 May	13.73	0.3 Wang Wupin 1 NC Tianjin	16 Sep
13.92	0.2	Petrova	22q	OG	Rio de Janeiro	13 Aug	13.64	1.0 Nidbaykina 9 NC Cheboksary	23 Jun
13.82	1.4	Detsuk	1		Minsk	1 Jun		13.67w 3.3 2 NC-23 Saransk	17 Jul
13.76	-0.1	Chen Mudan	1	NGP	Shaoxing	16 Apr	13.61	-0.1 Tikhonova 7 Sochi	27 May
13.56	0.2	Rao Fan	21 May	13.44	2.0 David	2 Jul	13.36	2.0 Alekseyeva	20 Jul
13.55	0.7	Peleteiro	12 Jun	13.42	0.7 D'Elicio	26 Jun		13.65w 3.4	20 Jul
13.54	1.7	Franklin	16 Apr	13.41	0.7 LaFond	15 May	13.35	1.6 Sterzing	12 Jun
13.53	0.6	Nygård	18 May	13.41	0.3 Wang Rong	16 Sep	13.33	-1.5 Ptashkina	22 May
13.48	1.1	Demut	9 Jul	13.37	0.1 Li Li	16 Apr		13.54w 2.4	26 May
		13.51w 2.6	3 Jul				13.31	1.8 Latham	23 Apr
Best at low altitude							13.30w	2.3 McQueen	30 Apr
14.00i		Johny	2	AsC	Doha	20 Feb			
13.92	0.3	Zaldívar	1		São Bernardo	19 Jun	13.84i	Sarrapio 2 Madrid	23 Jan
		14.03w 3.21			Cartagena	7 May	13.84	0.3 5 Madrid	23 Jun
13.85	0.0	Johny	1	SAsG	Guwahati	19 Feb	13.57	0.5 Ntshingila	15 Apr
13.95	-0.1	Urrutia	20q	OG	Rio de Janeiro	18 Aug	13.53	0.6 Chanbangu	15 Apr

JUNIORS

See main list for top 3 juniors (and 3 wa). 11 performances by 5 women to 13.54 (plus 3 by 3 wa). Additional marks and further juniors:

Mark	Wind	Name		Nat	Born	Pos	Meet	Venue	Date
		Velazco	13.67	0.0 *		La Habana	13 Feb	13.58 0.6 Q Barr La Habana	26 May
		Chen Ting	13.77	-0.3 Q	WJ	Bydgoszcz	22 Jul	13.54 1.5 1 NC-j Ordos	28 Jun
		Ovchinnikova	13.54	1.4 *		Almaty	25 Jun		
13.60	0.9	Mariya	Ovchinnikova	KAZ	19.10.98	1		Almaty	24 May
13.55	0.7	Konstadína	Roméou	GRE	30.5.97	2	WJ	Bydgoszcz	23 Jul
13.50i		Yanis	David	FRA	12.12.97	1		Fayetteville	13 Feb
		13.44	2.0				2	NC-j Châteauroux	2 Jul
13.49	1.7	Georgiana	Anitei	ROU-Y	26.3.99	3	WJ	Bydgoszcz	23 Jul
13.45	1.0	Violetta	Skvortsova	BLR	15.4.98	2		Brest	12 May
13.42	0.4		Xu Ting	CHN	23.2.97	4	NGP	Shaoxing	16 Apr
13.40	1.8	Norka	Moretic (10)	CHI	26.3.98	5	WJ	Bydgoszcz	23 Jul
13.37	-1.6	Valentina	Kosolapova	RUS	11.7.97	1J		Cheboksary	30 May
13.37	1.0	Ilionis	Guillaume	FRA	13.1.98	6	NC	Angers	26 Jun
13.36	0.4	Liliana	Breto	CUB	4.2.97	4	Barr	La Habana	28 May
13.36	1.3		Chen Liwen	CHN	3.1.98	2	NC-j	Ordos	28 Jun

WOMEN 2016

482 TRIPLE JUMP – SHOT

Mark			Name		Nat	Born	Pos	Meet	Venue	Date
13.32	1.1	Anna	Gorodkova		KAZ	7.4.97	2-j		Almaty	24 May
13.31		Kirthana	Ramasamy		MAS	20.1.97	2		Kuching	28 Jul
13.27		Anastasiya	Kolbasova		RUS	16.11.97	2		Cheboksary	30 May
13.23		Alexandra	Mihai		ROU	18.7.97	1	Balk-j	Bolu	2 Jul
13.21A		Nagyla	Renteria		COL	12.10.97	6		Medellín	30 Apr
13.20i		Diana	Zagainova (20)		LTU	20.6.97	1	v4N-j	Minsk	27 Feb
Wind assisted					see main list for three juniors					
13.46	3.4	Ilionis	Guillaume		FRA-	13.1.98	1	NC-j	Châteauroux	2 Jul
13.40	3.3	Yekaterina	Kropivko		RUS	13.6.97	1	NC-j	Kazan	28 Jun
13.38	2.1	Asa	Garcia		USA	15.5.97	1		Baton Rouge	23 Apr
13.25		Jasmine	Moore		USA-Y	1.5.01	1		Greensboro	18 Jun

SHOT

Mark				Name		Nat	Born	Pos	Meet	Venue	Date
20.63			Michelle	Carter		USA	12.10.85	1	OG	Rio de Janeiro	12 Aug
			19.12				19.82		19.44	19.87	19.84	20.63
	20.21i	1	WI	Portland	19 Mar	x	18.90	19.31	19.28	x	20.21
	19.98	1	VD	Bruxelles	8 Sep	x	19.98	19.61	18.69	x	19.69
	19.68	1	ISTAF	Berlin	3 Sep	19.31	x	19.68	18.64	19.08	x
	19.59	1	NC	Eugene	7 Jul	19.07	19.12	19.06	x	x	19.59
	19.58	3	Herc	Monaco	15 Jul	18.75	19.51	19.19	19.58	19.41	19.45
	19.56	3	Gyulai	Székesfehérvár	18 Jul	18.61	x	18.11	x	19.56	19.24
20.43				Gong Lijiao		CHN	24.1.89	1	Werfer	Halle	21 May
			19.90				20.43	p	p	p	p
	19.77	1		Husian	23 Apr						
	19.74	1		Osterode	31 May	19.25	19.64	19.63	19.24	19.74	19.73
	19.73	1		Schönebeck	29 Jul	x	19.35	19.04	x	19.30	19.73
20.42			Valerie	Adams		NZL	6.10.84	2	OG	Rio de Janeiro	12 Aug
			19.79				20.42	19.80	x	x	20.39
	20.19	1	Gyulai	Székesfehérvár	18 Jul	19.00	20.14	19.80	20.05	x	20.19
	20.05	1	Herc	Monaco	15 Jul	19.25	19.76	19.70	x	20.05	19.76);
	19.94	1	Athl	Lausanne	25 Aug	18.98	19.83	19.09	19.31	19.48	19.94
	19.75	1		Bad Köstritz	28 Aug	19.24	19.72	19.74	19.63	19.75	19.35
	19.74	Q	OG	Rio de Janeiro	12 Aug	19.74					
	19.69	1	GGala	Roma	2 Jun	19.46	18.95	19.69	19.63	19.52	19.56
	19.68	1		Rabat	22 May	18.93	19.30	19.20	19.48	19.68	19.64
	19.63	2	DL	Birmingham	5 Jun	19.32	19.31	19.54	19.44	19.63	19.44
	19.63	2	ISTAF	Berlin	3 Sep	19.15	19.63	19.61	19.42	x	19.52
	19.57	2	VD	Bruxelles	8 Sep	18.97	19.32	19.48	19.34	19.11	19.57
20.17			Christina	Schwanitz		GER	24.12.85	1	EC	Amsterdam	7 Jul
			20.17				19.28	19.55	x	x	19.46
	20.14	2	Gyulai	Székesfehérvár	18 Jul	19.13	20.14	19.71	20.13	19.86	x
	19.92	1		Gotha	31 Jul						
	19.81	2	Herc	Monaco	15 Jul	18.74	x	18.67	19.67	19.81	19.54
	19.71	2		Schönebeck	29 Jul	19.31	x	18.93	19.71	19.25	19.29
	19.53	1		Biberach	11 Jul	19.22	19.39	19.53	x	19.19	19.37
19.87			Anita	Márton		HUN	15.1.89	3	OG	Rio de Janeiro	12 Aug
			17.60				18.72	19.39	19.38	19.10	19.87
19.73			Tia	Brooks		USA	2.8.90	1	DL	Birmingham	5 Jun
		(30/6)	19.37				x	19.25	19.73	x	19.52
19.35			Raven	Saunders		USA	15.5.96	5	OG	Rio de Janeiro	12 Aug
19.26			Felisha	Johnson		USA	24.7.89	1		Naperville	5 Jun
19.20				Gao Yang		CHN	1.3.93	1		Neubrandenburg	20 Jul
19.11			Jeneva	Stevens		USA	28.10.89	1		Carbondale	22 Jun
		(10)									
18.99			Jill	Camarena-Williams		USA	2.3.82	1		Tucson	21 May
18.94			Brittany	Smith		USA	25.3.91	4	Athl	Lausanne	25 Aug
18.92			Yuliya	Leontyuk		BLR	31.1.84	1		Brest	10 Jun
18.87i			Dani	Bunch		USA	16.5.91	1		Notre Dame	20 Feb
18.78			Alyona	Dubitskaya		BLR	25.1.90	1		Mersin	24 May
18.78			Irina	Tarasova		RUS	15.4.87	1		Sochi	27 May
18.78			Cleopatra	Borel		TTO	10.3.79	3	DL	Birmingham	5 Jun
18.67			Yaniuvis	López		CUB	1.2.86	1	Barr	La Habana	27 May
18.63i			Paulina	Guba		POL	14.5.91	1	NC	Torun	5 Mar
18.57			Emel	Dereli		TUR	25.2.96	3	DL	Doha	6 May
		(20)									
18.56			Kelsey	Card		USA	20.8.92	1		Madison	6 May
18.52			Yanina	Provalinskaya-Korolchik		BLR	26.12.76	1		Minsk	10 Jun
18.50			Yevgeniya	Solovyova		RUS	28.6.86	3		Sochi	27 May
18.46			Chase	Ealey		USA	20.7.94	7	NC	Eugene	7 Jul
18.45			Olha	Holodnaya		UKR	14.11.91	1		Kyiv	4 May

Mark	Name		Nat	Born	Pos	Meet	Venue	Date	
18.36		Bian Ka	CHN	5.1.93	1	NGP	Chengdu	11	Apr
18.36	Melissa	Boekelman	NED	11.5.89	1		Burcht	9	Jul
18.35i	Irina	Kirichenko	RUS	18.5.87	1		Irkutsk	19	Jan
18.32i	Lena	Urbaniak	GER	31.10.92	1	NC	Leipzig	27	Feb
18.28i	Jessica	Ramsey	USA	26.7.91	3		Nashville	30	Jan
	(30)								
18.27	Radoslava	Mavrodieva	BUL	13.3.87	1		Ruse	13	May
18.27	Geisa	Arcanjo	BRA	19.9.91	Q	OG	Rio de Janeiro	12	Aug
18.24		Guo Tianqian	CHN	1.6.95	2	NGP	Huaian	23	Apr
18.19	Ahymará	Espinoza	VEN	28.5.85	1	IbAm	Rio de Janeiro	15	May
18.19	Natalia	Ducó	CHI	31.1.89	1		Leiria	23	Jul
18.13	Halyna	Obleshchuk	UKR	23.2.89	1	Ga	Kyiv	4	Jun
18.06i		Geng Shuang	CHN	9.7.93	1	AsC	Doha	19	Feb
18.06	Brittany	Crew	CAN	3.6.94	1	NC	Edmonton	9	Jul
18.02i	Alena	Abramchuk	BLR	14.2.88	1		Minsk	16	Jan
17.98		Liu Xiangrong	CHN	6.6.88	2	NGPF	Chongqing	20	Jun
	(40)								
17.97i	Dani	Winters	USA	18.2.93	1	NCAA	Birmingham, AL	12	Mar
17.95	Sara	Gambetta	GER	18.2.93	7	EC	Amsterdam	7	Jul
17.94	Manpreet	Kaur	IND	6.7.90	1	SAsG	Guwahati	9	Feb
17.94	Alyona	Bugakova	RUS-J	24.4.97	1		Moskva	15	Jun
17.94	Saily	Viart	CUB	10.9.95	1		Cali	25	Jun
17.93i	Christina	Hillman	USA	6.10.93	1	Big 12	Ames	27	Feb
17.92	Auriole	Dongmo	CMR	3.8.90	10q	OG	Rio de Janeiro	12	Aug
17.91	Nikki	Okwelogu	NGR	5.5.95	1q	NCAA-E	Jacksonville	28	May
17.90i	Chiara	Rosa	ITA	28.1.83	1		Padova	20	Feb
17.90	Claudine	Vita	GER	19.9.96	1-22		Neubrandenburg	6	Jul
	(50)								
17.89	Kearsten	Peoples	USA	20.12.91	3		Carbondale	22	Jun
17.88	Taryn	Suttie	CAN	7.12.90	1		Tempe	9	Apr
17.88	Jessica	Woodard	USA	4.2.95	3	NCAA	Eugene	9	Jun
17.87i	Olesya	Sviridova ¶	RUS	28.10.89	2	NC	Madrid	24	Feb
17.80		Meng Qianqian	CHN	6.1.91	3	NGP	Chengdu	7	Apr
17.80	Erin	Farmer	USA	11.8.95	1		Lafayette	14	May
17.74i	Anastasiya	Podolskaya	RUS	18.8.90	1		Moskva	10	Jan
17.73	Monique	Riddick	USA	8.11.89	3		Tucson	21	May
17.68i	Anna	Rüh	GER	17.6.93	2	NC	Leipzig	27	Feb
17.68i	Cassie	Wertman	USA	14.6.93	2	NCAA	Birmingham, AL	12	Mar
	(60)								
17.67	Nia	Henderson/Gailliard	USA	5.11.94	1		Ashland	17	Jun
17.67	Anna	Avdeyeva	RUS	6.4.85	4	NC	Cheboksary	23	Jun
17.67	Valeriya	Zyryanova	RUS	12.8.90	1		Moskva	5	Jul
17.63	Jill	Rushin	USA	18.7.91	1		Columbia	16	Apr
17.62i	Whitney	Ashley	USA	18.2.89	1		Portland	29	Jan
17.60	Danniel	Thomas	JAM	11.11.92	1		Akron	7	May
17.58	Alina	Kenzel	GER-J	10.8.97	1	WJ	Bydgoszcz	20	Jul
17.58	Fanny	Roos	SWE	2.1.95	1		Växjö	13	Aug
17.56		Song Jiayuan	CHN-J	15.9.97	2	NC	Tianjin	17	Sep
17.53	Rachel	Wallader	GBR	1.9.89	1		Swansea	4	Jun
	(70)								
17.50	Torie	Owers	NZL/USA	6.3.94	1		Los Angeles (Ww)	16	Apr
17.49	Brittany	Mann	USA	16.4.94	5	NCAA	Eugene	9	Jun
17.48	Becky	O'Brien	USA	30.4.90	1		Rathdrum	4	Jun
17.47	Jessica	Cérival	FRA	20.1.82	1	NC	Angers	25	Jun
17.41	Shanice	Craft	GER	15.5.93	7	Werfer	Halle	21	May
17.41	Josephine	Terlecki	GER	17.2.86	2		Frankenberg	28	May
17.39i	Cion	Hicks	USA	14.10.94	2		Fayetteville	13	Feb
17.37	Valentina	Muzaric	CRO	23.7.92	1		Atlanta	26	Mar
17.36	Keely	Medeiros	BRA	30.4.87	5		La Jolla	23	Apr
17.36	Breana	Jemison	USA	11.12/93	1		Long Beach	14	May
	(80)								
17.34	Leyla	Rajabi	IRI	18.4.83	1	Kozanov	Almaty	25	Jun
17.33	Viktoryia	Kolb	BLR	26.10.93	4	NC	Grodno	24	Jun
17.31i	Úrsula	Ruiz	ESP	11.8.83	1		Sabadell	19	Feb
17.29i	Alexis	Cooks	USA	11.9.93	1		Akron	19	Feb
17.29	Ányela	Rivas	COL	13.8.89	4	IbAm	Rio de Janeiro	15	May
17.27i	Rachel	Fatherly	USA	20.4.94	1		State College	6	Feb
17.26	McKenzie	Warren	USA	3.12.93	1		Portland	25	Jun
17.22i	Vera	Kunova	RUS	2.4.90	6	NC	Moskva	24	Feb
17.21	Megan	Smith	USA	31.3.93	1		Fort Worth	18	Mar

484 SHOT

Mark	Name		Nat	Born	Pos	Meet	Venue	Date	
17.14	Sophie (90)	McKinna	GBR	31.8.94	1		Norwich	9	Jul
17.09	Jolien	Boumkwo	BEL	27.8.93	1		Bruxelles	19	Jun
17.06	Lloydricia	Cameron	USA	8.4.96	4	FlaR	Gainesville	2	Apr
17.04	Sandra	Lemus	COL	1.1.89	1		Cartagena	6	May
17.02	Yekaterina	Burmistrova	RUS	18.8.90	1		Sankt Peterburg	9	Jun
17.00i	Alyssa	Wilson	USA-Y	20.2.99	1		New York (SI)	17	Dec
16.99	Jamie	Sindelar	USA	.93	1		Ashland	30	Apr
16.99	Yevgeniya	Smirnova	RUS	16.3.91	8	NC	Cheboksary	23	Jun
16.98	Madison	McLaughlin	USA	14.11.96	1	NCAA-II	Bradenton	28	May
16.96i		Dong Yangzi	CHN	22.10.92	3	NGP	Nanjing	4	Mar
16.96i	Cassie	Caswell	USA	3.7.94	1	NCAA-II	Pittsburg	12	Mar
16.96	Tanya (100)	Sapa	USA	13.6.95	1		Los Angeles (Ww)	1	May
16.95	Rachel	Dincoff	USA	24.12.93	30 Apr	16.38	Anna	Omarova	RUS	3.10.81	13 May
16.94i	Alena	Pasechnik	BLR	17.4.95	28 Jan	16.36	Rosario	Sánchez	MEX?	3.4.88	28 May
16.93	Emmonie	Henderson	USA	5.11.94	16 Apr	16.35	Alysiah	Whittaker	USA	17.3.95	14 May
16.92	María Fernanda	Orozco	MEX-J	25.1.98	20 Mar	16.34i	Emmaline	Berg	USA	27.9.91	10 Jan
16.91		Lee Mi-young	KOR	19.8.79	1 Jul	16.32		Wang Xiaoyun	CHN	7.12.93	7 Apr
16.90	Yiliena	Otamendi	CUB	12.4.96	18 Mar	16.32	Haley	Teel	USA	20.6.96	13 May
16.90	Claire	Uke	NGR	31.12.92	28 May	16.31	Janeah	Stewart	USA	21.7.96	30 Apr
16.87	Christine	Bohan	USA	14.7.95	8 Apr	16.30i	Julia	Ritter	GER-J	13.5.98	14 Feb
16.86i	Natalya	Troneva	RUS	24.3.93	24 Feb	16.30	Alyssa	Gary	USA	.93	28 May
16.86	Markéta	Cervenková	CZE	20.8.91	12 Mar	16.30	María Belén	Toimil	ESP	5.5.94	5 Jun
16.85i	Maggie	Ewen	USA	23.9.94	27 Feb	16.27	Jess	St.John	ANT	15.12.95	18 May
16.85	Chioma	Onyekwere	USA/NGR	28.6.94	14 May	16.26i	Noora	Salem Jassem	BRN	27.11.96	19 Feb
16.82i	Itohan	Aikhonbare	USA	29.3.94	16 Jan	16.26	Sydney	Giampietro	ITA-Y	27.1.99	29 May
16.80i	Sarah	Howard	CAN	11.10.93	21 Feb	16.26	Gavriella	Fella	CYP-J	21.1.98	13 Jun
16.79	Klaudia	Kardasz	POL	2.5.96	24 Jun	16.25		Rong Jun	CHN	7.4.89	7 Apr
16.78	Manpreet	Kaur II	IND	5.3.96	28 Jun	16.25	Lena	Giger	USA	7.6.96	23 Apr
16.78	Raisa	Blinova	RUS	22.11.94	28 Jul	16.25	Izabela	da Silva	BRA	2.8.95	24 Sep
16.77i	Kätlin	Piirimäe	EST	8.11.95	27 Feb	16.24	Heavin	Warner	USA	4.3.93	28 May
16.77	Tochi	Nlemchi	USA	.95	9 Jun	16.24	Adele	Nicoll	GBR	28.9.96	19 Jun
16.75	Stamatía	Skarvélis	GRE	17.8.95	9 Apr	16.24		Chen Xiarong	CHN-J	21.12.98	20 Jun
16.74	Sara	Wells	USA	11.8.92	19 Apr	16.24	Nanaka	Kori	JPN-J	2.5.97	23 Oct
16.72i	Dimitriana	Surdu	MDA	12.5.94	9 Jan	16.23i	Yelena	Bezruchenko	RUS	23.7.96	2 Mar
16.72	Giedre	Kupstyte	LTU	9.3.92	20 May	16.23	Julie	Labonté	CAN	12.1.90	9 Apr
16.70	Evaggelía	Sofáni	GRE	28.1.85	5 Jun	16.21	Svitlana	Marusenko	UKR	17.5.93	4 May
16.67	Amber	Monroe	USA	14.10.93	28 May	16.18	DeAnna	Price	USA	8.6.93	29 Apr
16.66i	Markéta	Cervenková	CZE	20.8.91	5 Mar	16.18	Norma	Cunigan	USA-J	25.6.97	14 May
16.66	Alessandra	Gamboa	PER	24.2.92	16 Apr	16.17	Aliyah	Gustafson	USA	3.5.95	28 May
16.65i	Austra	Skujyte	LTU	12.8.79	6 Feb	16.17	Antoinette	Nana Duimou	FRA	2.8.85	8 Jul
16.65i	Nickolette	Dunbar	USA-J	5.4.98	12 Mar	16.15	Tera	Novy	USA	10.2.94	1 May
16.65	Katharina	Maisch	GER-J	12.6.97	21 May	16.15i	Amelia	Strickler	GBR	24.1.94	9 Dec
16.64	Elena	Bruckner	USA-J	19.4.98	13 May	16.14	Toni	Tupper	USA	3.11.95	23 Apr
16.64	Julaika	Nicoletti	ITA	20.3.88	26 Jun	16.13i	Rose Sharon	Pierre-Louis	FRA	7.9.94	27 Feb
16.63	Talore	Kelly	USA	11.3.94	25 Mar	16.12i	Jamie	Lindstrom	USA	.93	19 Feb
16.59	Ischke	Senekal	RSA	8.1.93	29 Apr	16.12	Aya	Ota	JPN	13.4.95	23 Jul
16.55i	LaPorscha	Wells	USA	.95	23 Feb	16.10	Jana	Kárníková	CZE	14.2.81	22 Jun
16.53	Alex	Porlier-Langlois	CAN	16.7.93	14 May	16.09i	Obeng	Marfo	CAN	11.4.96	26 Feb
16.53	Ivana	Gallardo	CHI	20.3.93	29 Oct	16.09	Micah	Dennis	USA	21.9.92	30 Apr
16.52i	Anna	Wloka	POL	14.3.93	31 Jan	16.08	Kristine	Hanks	USA	.95	23 Apr
16.51	Alyssa	Robinson	USA	10.5.95	14 May	16.08	Ásdís	Hjálmsdóttir	ISL	28.10.85	7 May
16.50i	Courtney	Pasiowitz	USA	.95	30 Jan	16.08	Jorinde	van Klinken	NED-Y	2.2.00	19 May
16.50i	Trine	Mulbjerg	DEN	23.4.90	31 Jan	16.07	Jessica	Inchude	GBS	25.3.96	23 Jul
16.50i	Ashlie	Blake	USA	7.6.96	6 Feb	16.06	Katelyn	Daniels	USA	11.4.95	14 May
16.49i	Avione	Allgood	USA	14.12.93	30 Jan	16.05	Sireta	Roach	JAM	.94	15 Jun
16.48	Eden	Francis	GBR	19.10.88	22 May	16.04i	Sade	Olatoye	USA-J	25.1.97	16 Jan
16.47	Livia	Avancini	BRA	8.5.92	3 Jul	16.03i	Devene	Brown	JAM	16.3.93	6 Feb
16.47		Lee Su-kyung	KOR	15.2.93	9 Oct	16.03	Jakayla	Daniels	USA	11.11.94	9 Apr
16.45i	Sarah	Schmidt	GER-J	9.7.97	20 Feb	16.02i	Tiffany	Okieme	USA	8.1.94	16 Jan
16.43i	Alexus	Scott	USA	18.11.93	12 Feb	16.02i	Heavin	Warner	USA	4.3.93	12 Mar
16.43	Portious	Warren	TTO	2.3.96	27 Feb						
16.41	Agnieszka	Maluskiewicz	POL	18.3.89	24 Jun	16.00i	Viktoriya	Klochko	UKR	2.9.92	27 Jan
16.39	Aaliyah	Pete	USA	15.3.95	28 May	16.00i (200)	Megan	Tomei	USA	.94	19 Feb

Best outdoors

18.18	Bunch	3		Baie-Mahault	14 May	17.52	Rosa	1	NC	Rieti	26 Jun
18.02	Urbaniak	2	NC	Kassel	19 Jun	17.39	Winters	1	Big 12	Fort Worth	14 May
17.93	Kirichenko	3		Sochi	27 May	17.24	Ruiz	1	NC	Gijón	23 Jul
17.87	Geng Shuang	2	NGP	Chengdu	11 Apr	17.20	Wertman	2q	NCAA-E	Jacksonville	28 May
17.82	Abramchuk	1		Brest	12 May	17.20	Rüh	4		Schönebeck	3 Jun
17.74	Guba	4		Rabat	22 May	17.09	Hicks	5	Big 12	Fort Worth	14 May
17.74	Ramsey	3		Eugene	29 Jul	17.00	A Wilson (Y)	1	HS N.Bal	Greensboro	19 Jun
17.73	Sviridova ¶	2		Adler	13 May	16.96	Fatherly	1		Tempe	26 Mar
17.70	Podolskaya	3	NC	Cheboksary	23 Jun	16.82	Ewen	8q	NCAA-W	Lawrence	28 May
17.69	Hillman	10q	NC	Eugene	7 Jul	16.80	Dong Yangzi	4	NGP	Chengdu	11 Apr

Mark	Name	Nat	Born	Pos	Meet	Venue	Date

16.72	Pasechnik	3	Brest	12 May	16.64	Caswell	2	NCAA-II	Bradenton	28 May	
16.72	Troneva	5	Adler	13 May							

16.57	Aikhonbare	15 Apr	16.41	Dunbar	3 Jul	16.31	Skujyte	8 Jul	16.06	Allgood	14 May
16.47	Pasiowitz	6 May	16.34	S Howard	6 May	16.20	Wells	14 May	16.04	Pierre-Louis	16 Jul
16.42	Schmidt	21 May	16.33	Scott	29 Apr	16.09	Berg	23 Apr	16.01	Mulbjerg	16 Aug

Downhill/irregular

Stoke Rochford 8 May: 1. Sophie McKinna GBR 18.41, Rachel Wallader GBR 18.00

Drugs disqualification

18.66	Olesya	Sviridova ¶	RUS	28.10.89	(2)	Sochi	27 May

JUNIORS

See main list for top 4 juniors. 12 performances (3 indoors) by 3 women to 17.22. Additional marks and further juniors:

Bugakova	17.58i	1	NC-j	Novochebokarsk	9 Feb	17.29	1	NC-j	Kazan	26 Jun
	17.45i	1	NC-23	Volgograd	2 Mar	17.26	1		Moskva	30 May
	17.33i	3		Moskva	14 Feb	17.22	6	NC	Cheboksary	23 Jun
Kenzel	17.48	1		Mannheim	25 Jun	17.24	3		Biberach	11 Jul
	17.27	3		Gotha	31 Jul					

16.92	María Fernanda	Orozco	MEX	25.1.98	1		Ciudad de México	20 Mar
16.65i	Nickolette	Dunbar	USA	5.4.98	1	HS N.Bal	New York	12 Mar
	16.41				1		Millersville	3 Jul
16.65	Katharina	Maisch	GER	12.6.97	1-j	Werfer	Halle	21 May
16.64	Elena	Bruckner	USA	19.4.98	1		Mountain View	13 May
16.45i	Sarah	Schmidt	GER	9.7.97	2	NC-j	Wattenscheid	20 Feb
	16.42				2-j	Werfer	Halle	21 May
16.30i	Julia	Ritter (10)	GER	13.5.98	2-j		Sassnitz	14 Feb
16.26	Sydney	Giampietro	ITA-Y	27.1.99	2		Gavardo	29 May
16.26	Gavriella	Fella	CYP-J	21.1.98	1	NC	Nicosia	19 Jun
16.24		Chen Xiarong	CHN-J	21.12.98	6	NGPF	Chongqing	20 Jun
16.24	Nanaka	Kori	JPN-J	2.5.97	1	NC-j	Nagoya	23 Oct
16.18	Norma	Cunigan	USA-J	25.6.97	1		Amarillo	14 May
16.08	Jorinde	van Klinken	NED-Y	2.2.00	2	NC	Amsterdam	19 Jun
16.04i	Sade	Olatoye	USA-J	25.1.97	5		Lexington	16 Jan
15.84	Kathleen	Young	USA-Y	31.7.99	1		Moweaqua	28 Apr
15.75	Anna	Niedbala	POL	10.7.98	1	NC-j	Suwalki	1 Jul
15.75	Maja	Siepowronska	POL	2.12.98	6	WJ	Bydgoszcz	20 Jul

DISCUS

70.88				Sandra	Perkovic	CRO	21.6.90	1	DL	Shanghai		14 May
							x	65.37	67.73	70.88	x	x
	70.59	1	Nc-w	Split		6 Mar	**68.04**	**70.59**	**68.44**	**x**	**x**	**x**
	69.97	1	EC	Amsterdam		8 Jul	62.60	63.09	x	66.03	69.97	x
	69.94	1	DL	London (OS)		23 Jul	64.80	69.94	67.80	66.63	66.98	66.42
	69.21	1	OG	Rio de Janeiro		16 Aug	x	x	69.21	x	x	x
	68.57	1	Pre	Eugene		27 May	62.75	x	x	62.89	68.57	67.57
	68.44	1	WK	Zürich		1 Sep	64.23	66.57	x	67.98	x	68.44
	68.32	1	DL	Stockholm		16 Jun	66.11	65.44	x	x	68.32	67.26
	67.86	1	Hanz	Zagreb		6 Sep	66.41	67.62	67.86	x	x	64.32
	67.62	1	DL	Saint-Denis		27 Aug	61.75	64.03	x	66.80	65.65	67.62
	67.10	1	Bisl	Oslo		9 Jun	65.34	66.28	67.10	x	64.10	x
68.86				Yaimí	Pérez	CUB	29.5.91	1		La Habana		13 Feb
							x	62.71	65.72	62.69	65.90	68.86
	67.91	1		Montreuil-sous-Bois		7 Jun	59.40	65.68	62.88	63.09	67.91	66.14
	67.63	1		Las Tunas		20 Feb	x	64.33	67.63	66.15	62.35	65.68
	67.02	Q	Barr	La Habana		26 May	67.02					
	66.30	Q	NC	La Habana		17 Mar	66.30					
68.49				Julia	Fischer	GER	1.4.90	1	Werfer	Halle		21 May
							x	x	64.14. x	65.16	68.49	
	67.47	1	Sole	Schönebeck		29 Jul	61.08	66.01	x	60.91	67.47	x
	66.59	1	Werfer	Wiesbaden		15 May	65.24	x	x	63.28	66.59	66.14
	66.29	1		Schönebeck		3 Jun	59.51	65.22	66.29	x	x	65.92
67.77				Dani	Stevens	AUS	26.5.88	2	DL	Shanghai		14 May
							64.00	x	62.85	64.65	64.27	67.77
	67.02	2	Sole	Schönebeck		29 Jul	64.65	61.72	65.12	66.80	63.77	67.02
	66.41	1		Waitakare		25 Feb	63.14	61.04	64.02	x	65.99	66.41
67.62				Denia	Caballero	CUB	13.1.90	1		Leiria		29 Jun
	67.53	2		La Habana		13 Feb	65.61	65.49	67.53	x	x	x
	67.30	2		Las Tunas		20 Feb	x	x	67.30	63.24	66.78	x
	67.00	1		Leiria		22 Jun	x	x	45.74	64.87	x	67.00
	66.41	2	Werfer	Halle		21 May	60.79	63.89	x	61.70	66.41	x
66.84				Nadine	Müller	GER	21.11.85	3	Sole	Schönebeck		29 Jul
							60.85	59.28	63.40	63.92	66.84	61.47

WOMEN 2016

486 DISCUS

Mark		Name		Nat	Born	Pos	Meet	Venue	Date	
66.73		Mélina	Robert-Michon	FRA	18.7.79	2	OG	Rio de Janeiro	16 Aug	
					65.52	64.83	65.08	x	66.73	x
		(30/7)								
65.59			Su Xinyue	CHN	8.11.91	1		Neubrandenburg	28 May	
65.26		Yekaterina	Strokova	RUS	17.12.89	1		Adler	12 May	
65.14			Feng Bin	CHN	3.4.94	4	Werfer	Halle	21 May	
		(10)								
65.10		Jade	Lally	GBR	30.3.87	1		Sydney	27 Feb	
64.62		Whitney	Ashley	USA	18.2.89	1		Chula Vista	21 Apr	
64.62		Shanice	Craft	GER	15.5.93	3		Wiesbaden	15 May	
64.08		Anna	Rüh	GER	17.6.93	2		Schönebeck	3 Jun	
63.96		Irina	Rodrigues	POR	5.2.91	1		Leiria	5 Mar	
63.61			Chen Yang	CHN	10.7.91	1cB	Werfer	Halle	21 May	
63.52		Kelsey	Card	USA	20.8.92	1	NCAA	Eugene	11 Jun	
63.27		Yuliya	Maltseva	RUS	30.11.90	2		Adler	12 May	
63.09		Stephanie	Brown Trafton	USA	1.12.79	1		Salinas	29 May	
62.93		Nataliya	Semenova	UKR	7.7.82	2		Montreuil	7 Jun	
		(20)								
62.77		Claudine	Vita	GER	19.9.96	4		Schönebeck	3 Jun	
62.76			Lu Xiaoxin	CHN	22.2.89	1	NGP	Chengdu	11 Jun	
62.74		Fernanda Raquel	Borges	BRA	26.7.88	1		Chula Vista	7 May	
62.68		Pauline	Pousse	FRA	17.9.87	2	NC	Angers	25 Jun	
62.62		Seema	Punia-Antil	IND	27.7.83	1		Salinas	28 May	
62.60		Yelena	Panova	RUS	2.3.87	3		Adler	12 May	
62.50		Yarelis	Barrios	CUB	12.7.83	3		Las Tunas	20 Feb	
61.97		Hannah	Carson	USA	26.1.93	1		Lubbock	6 May	
61.89		Sabina	Asenjo	ESP	3.8.86	2		Bilbao	25 Jun	
61.89		Zinaida	Sendriute	LTU	20.12.84	10	OG	Rio de Janeiro	16 Aug	
		(30)								
61.86		Vera	Ganeyeva	RUS	6.11.88	4		Adler	12 May	
61.85	?	Natalia	Stratulat	MDA	24.7.87	1	NC-w	Chisinau	7 May	
61.67		Liz	Podominick	USA	5.12.84	4		La Jolla	22 Apr	
61.58		Chinwe	Okoro	NGR	20.6.89	1		Athens	2 Apr	
61.44		Kellion	Knibb	JAM	25.12.93	2	NCAA	Eugene	11 Jun	
61.42		Valarie	Allman	USA	23.2.95	3	NCAA	Eugene	11 Jun	
61.37			Yang Yanbo	CHN	9.3.90	1		Tucson	21 May	
61.28		Tara-Sue	Barnett	JAM	9.10.93	1		Irvine	30 Apr	
61.20		Mariya	Telushkina	KAZ	3.4.94	1	NC	Tashkent	10 Jun	
61.18		Shadae	Lawrence	JAM	31.12.95	4	NCAA	Eugene	11 Jun	
		(50)								
61.16		Paige	Blackburn	USA	5.3.90	1		Los Angeles	25 Mar	
61.12		Subenrat	Insaeng	THA	10.2.94	1	Kozanov	Almaty	26 Jun	
61.10		Tera	Novy	USA	10.2.94	2		Los Angeles	14 Apr	
61.01		Kristin	Pudenz	GER	9.2.93	6		Wiesbaden	15 May	
61.01			Weng Chunxia	CHN	29.8.92	5		Neubrandenburg	28 May	
60.94		Allison	Randall	JAM	25.5.88	1		Ashland	17 Jun	
60.94		Anita	Márton	HUN	15.1.89	1		Budapest	4 Sep	
60.76		Anna	Jelmini	USA	15.7.90	1		Claremont	12 Jun	
60.73		Shelbi	Vaughan	USA	24.8.94	1	Johnson	Waco	23 Apr	
60.57		Rachel	Varner	USA	20.7.83	1		Claremont	11 Jun	
		(50)								
60.54		Katelyn	Daniels	USA	11.4.95	5	NCAA	Eugene	11 Jun	
60.51		Dragana	Tomasevic	SRB	4.6.82	Q	EC	Amsterdam	6 Jul	
60.48		Eliska	Stanková	CZE	11.11.84	1		Kolín	12 Jun	
60.46		Natalya	Shirobokova	RUS	18.1.94	1-22		Adler	12 May	
60.31		Joanna	Wisniewska	POL	24.5.72	1	Skol	Cetniewo	12 Jul	
60.27		Taryn	Gollshewsky	AUS	18.5.93	1		Perth	28 Sep	
60.11		Veronika	Domjan	SLO	3.9.96	Q	EC	Amsterdam	6 Jul	
60.09		Summer	Pierson	USA	3.9.78	4		Salinas	29 May	
59.88		Jessica	Maroszek	USA	26.2.92	1		Lawrence	11 Jun	
59.80		Karen	Gallardo	CHI	6.3.84	1		Santiago de Chile	8 Apr	
		(60)								
59.80		Stefania	Strumillo	ITA	14.10.89	Q	EC	Amsterdam	6 Jul	
59.76		Hrisoúla	Anagnostopoúlou	GRE	27.8.91	1	BalkC	Pitesti	25 Jun	
59.64		Andressa	de Morais	BRA	21.12.90	2		Santiago de Chile	8 Apr	
59.53		Svetlana	Saykina	RUS	10.7.85	5		Adler	12 May	
59.45		Rosalía	Vázquez	CUB	11.10.95	Q	NC	La Habana	17 Mar	
59.42		Te Rina	Keenan	NZL	29.9.90	4		Los Angeles	14 Apr	
59.39		Krishna	Poonia	IND	5.5.82	2		Claremont	11 Jun	
59.36		Lidia	Augustyniak	POL	14.5.94	2cB	Werfer	Halle	21 May	

DISCUS

Mark	Name		Nat	Born	Pos	Meet	Venue	Date	
59.28	Maggie	Ewen	USA	23.9.94	6		Chula Vista	21	Apr
59.03	Gleneve	Grange	JAM	6.7.95	1	NC	Kingston	1	Jul
(70)									
58.94	Gia	Lewis-Smallwood	USA	1.4.79	1		St.Louis	2	Apr
58.87	Rachel	Longfors	USA	6.6.83	7	NC	Eugene	2	Jul
58.75	Zaneta	Glanc	POL	11.3.83	2	NC	Bydgoszcz	25	Jun
58.72	Mariah	Garcia	USA	26.12.93	1		Norman	23	Apr
58.53	Kimberley	Mulhall	AUS	9.1.91	9		La Jolla	22	Apr
58.43		Yang Fei	CHN	20.7.87	1	NC	Tianjin	16	Sep
58.30	Kristina	Rakocevic	MNE-J	13.6.98	1-j		Split	16	Apr
58.30		Xie Yuchen	CHN	12.5.96	2		Quanzhou	17	Jul
58.25	Jeré	Summers	USA	21.5.87	11		La Jolla	22	Apr
58.09	Alexandra	Emilianov	MDA-Y	19.9.99	1	EY	Tbilisi	15	Jul
(80)									
58.05	Daria	Zabawska	POL	16.4.95	2-22	Werfer	Halle	22	May
58.03	Julie	Hartwig	GER	30.6.94	6cB	Werfer	Halle	21	May
57.93	Danniel	Thomas	JAM	11.11.92	1		Akron	7	May
57.93	Sarah	Thornton	USA	29.8.86	1		Peabody	25	Jun
57.91	Agnes	Esser	CAN	22.8.95	2q	NCAA-W	Lawrence	28	May
57.79	Rocío	Comba	ARG	14.7.87	1		Río Tercero	18	Feb
57.76		Liang Yan	CHN	2.1.95	2	NGP	Taiyuan	21	May
57.71	Becky	Famurewa	USA	24.2.94	1		Lexington	7	May
57.54	Siositina	Hakeai	NZL	1.3.94	1		Auckland (NS)	4	Jun
57.52	Alex	Collatz	USA	25.5.93	6		Los Angeles	14	Apr
(90)									
57.47		Tan Jian	CHN	20.1.88	7	NGP	Chengdu	11	Apr
57.26	Trecey	Hoover	USA	11.1.88	1		Texas	17	Jun
57.15	Viktoriya	Klochko	UKR	2.9.92	1	NCp	Kirovohrad	25	May
57.12	Lidiane	Cansian	BRA	8.1.92	14		La Jolla	22	Apr
56.95	Elena	Bruckner	USA-J	14.4.98	1		San Jose	22	Apr
56.91	Suzanne	Kragbé	CIV	22.12.81	1		Toulouse	8	May
56.86	Ischke	Senekal	RSA	8.1.93	1	NC	Stellenbosch	16	Apr
56.85	Raven	Saunders	USA	15.5.96	1		Tuscaloosa	19	Mar
56.85	Salla	Sipponen	FIN	13.3.95	1		Ikaalinen	31	May
56.83	Marike	Steinacker	GER	4.3.92	6		Schönebeck	3	Jun
(100)									

Mark	First	Last	Nat	Born	Date1		Mark	First	Last	Nat	Born	Date2
56.80	Valentina	Aniballi	ITA	19.4.84	25 May		54.83	Kätlin	Tollasson	EST	4.6.93	21 May
56.75	Nikki	Okwelogu	NGR	5.5.95	24 Jun		54.74	Giada	Andreutti	ITA	16.2.95	1 May
56.74	Corinne	Nugter	NED	28.3.92	11 Jul		54.72	Shanice	Love	JAM-J	9.6.97	28 Apr
56.63	Laura	Bobek	USA	16.2.91	28 May		54.69	Alissa	Rausch	USA	.92	4 May
56.48	Samantha	Hall	JAM	19.4.93	9 Apr		54.68A	Madison	Pachner	USA	.94	23 Apr
56.46	Alexa	Evans	USA	27.11.93	28 May		54.68	Anastasiya	Vityugova	RUS-J	13.3.97	28 Jun
56.43		Gu Siyu	CHN	11.2.93	13 May		54.65	Anastasiya	Kashtonova	BLR	14.1.89	9 Apr
56.30	Julia	Viberg	SWE	8.1.92	22 Apr		54.64	Laura	Bordignon	ITA	26.3.81	5 Jun
56.28	Natalina	Capoferri	ITA	6.11.92	25 May		54.63		Li Tsai-Yi	TPE	3.12.89	20 May
56.24	Eden	Francis	GBR	19.10.88	26 Jun		54.62	Paula	Ferrándiz	ESP	4.1.96	28 May
56.19	Alena	Belyakova	RUS-J	21.12.98	28 Jun		54.61	Izabela	da Silva	BRA	2.8.95	1 Jul
56.18	Veronika	Watzek	AUT	13.8.85	30 Jul		54.60	Kree	Clark	USA	.94	5 May
56.14	Yekaterina	Burmistrova	RUS	18.8.90	20 Feb		54.53	Jontavia	Dykes	USA	95	27 May
56.11	Olha	Abramchuk	UKR	12.4.91	30 Apr		54.43	Chioma	Onyekwere	NGR	28.6.94	15 May
56.09	Tatyana	Zhuravlyova	RUS	27.5.89	14 May		54.38	Katrine	Bebe	DEN	27.1.91	11 Jun
56.04	Corina	Cox	USA	5.1.95	19 Mar		54.37	Krisztina	Váradi	HUN	21.10.93	24 Sep
56.04	Katarzyna	Mos	POL	20.12.94	8 May		54.33	Ulrike	Giesa	GER	16.8.84	16 Apr
56.02	Sofia	Larsson	SWE	22.7.88	6 Jul		54.32	Stamatía	Skarvéli	GRE	17.8.95	21 Apr
56.01	Kirsty	Law	GBR	11.10.86	22 Apr		54.30	Rosalina	Álvarez	CUB-J	3.1.97	13 May
55.99	Annelies	Peetroons	BEL	4.5.87	21 May		54.28	Kirsty	Williams	AUS-J	13.1.97	19 Nov
55.94	Andrea	Alarcón	ESP	3.12.94	21 May		54.25	Cion	Hicks	USA	14.10.94	2 Apr
55.82	Adriana	Brown	USA	15.5.96	22 Apr		54.25	Kamalpreet	Kaur	IND	4.3.96	30 Sep
55.77	Micaela	Hazlewood	USA	18.6.95	27 May		54.24	Katelyn	Weimerskirch	USA	28.2.94	6 May
55.73	Navjeet	Kaur Dhillon	IND	6.3.95	24 Apr		54.22	Ayumi	Sakaguchi	JPN	31.8.89	21 May
55.65	Sasha-Ann	Lebert	JAM	8.3.93	27 May		54.20	Jessica	Woodard	USA	4.2.95	15 May
55.52A	Johana	Martínez	COL	9.9.86	8 Apr		54.20	Katri	Hirvonen	FIN	25.6.90	22 Jun
55.46	Rachel	Dincoff	USA	24.12.93	2 Apr		54.18	Nia	Henderson	USA	5.11.94	27 May
55.45	Amber	Monroe	USA	14.10.93	7 May		54.08	Kayla	Hopkins	USA	23.4.96	14 May
55.30	Dasha	Tsema	USA	10.8.94	25 Jun		54.05	Rechelle	Bessard	USA	22.12.92	2 Apr
55.29	Julia	Bremser	GER	27.4.82	4 Jun		54.04	Sylvia	Galarza	PUR	17.9.85	27 May
55.14	Lloydricia	Cameron	USA	8.4.96	22 Apr		54.03	Haley	Teel	USA	20.6.96	1 May
55.05	Clare	Fitzgerald	IRL	12.9.91	29 May		54.02	Androniki	Lada	CYP	19.4.91	14 May
55.02	Rachel	Andres	CAN	21.4.87	12 Jun		53.96	Julia	Agawu	GHA	20.4.91	14 May
55.00	Heavin	Warner	USA	4.3.93	9 Apr		53.95	Ginger	Jarchow	USA	.94	30 Apr
54.99	Tanja	Komulainen	FIN	2.3.80	25 Jun		53.94	Sabine	Rumpf	GER	18.3.83	4 Jun
54.98	Rachel	Alesi	USA	25.10.94	28 May		53.91	Melissa	Ausman	USA	.95	30 Apr
54.96	Brianna	Cueva	USA	6.6.95	13 May		53.90	Raqurra	Ishmar	USA	3.2.93	13 May
54.93	Sandeep	Kumari	IND	10.12.92	29 Apr		53.88	Kiana	Phelps	USA-J	22.7.97	24 Jun
54.85		Li Shanshan	CHN	6.1.92	7 Apr		53.86	Majesty	Tutson	USA	2.5.91	23 Apr

WOMEN 2016

488 HAMMER

Mark			Name		Nat	Born	Pos	Meet	Venue		Date
53.84		Julia	Ritter		GER-J	13.5.98	19	Jul	53.72	Josephine Schaefer USA-Y 10.4.99	24 Jun

JUNIORS
(180)

See main list for top 3 juniors. 10 performances by 4 women to 54.80. Additional marks and further juniors:

Mark	Name		Nat	Born	Pos	Meet	Venue	Date
Rakocevic	56.36	1 WJ Bydgoszcz	21 Jul	55.48	1		Sremska Mitrovica	26 Mar
Emilianov	55.69	1 Balk-y Krusevac	2 Jul	55.14	1		RoulC Pitesti	4 Jun
Bruckner	55.19	1 Mountain View	23 Mar	54.81	1		NC-j Clovis	24 Jun
56.19	Alena	Belyakova	RUS	21.12.98	1	NC-j	Kazan	28 Jun
54.72	Shanice	Love	JAM-	9.6.97	1	PennR	Philadelphia	28 Apr
54.68	Anastasiya	Vityugova	RUS	13.3.97	2	NC-j	Kazan	28 Jun
54.30	Rosalina	Álvarez	CUB	3.1.97	2		La Habana	13 May
54.28	Kirsty	Williams	AUS-	13.1.97	1		Brisbane	19 Nov
53.88	Kiana	Phelps	USA-	22.7.97	2	NC-j	Clovis	24 Jun
53.84	Julia	Ritter (10)	GER	13.5.98	1q	WJ	Bydgoszcz	19 Jul
53.72	Josephine	Schaefer	USA-Y	10.4.99	3	NC-j	Clovis	24 Jun
53.63	Nanaka	Kori	JPN	2.5.97	1		Kurume	17 Sep
53.41	CeCilya	Johnson	USA	4.3.97	2		Orlando	13 May
53.37	Alyssa	Wilson	USA-Y	20.2.99	1		Bayville	12 May
52.87	Karolina	Urban	POL	18.10.98	1		Torun	15 Jul
52.73	Serena	Brown	BAH	15.9.98	4	WJ	Bydgoszcz	21 Jul
52.68		Sun Kangping	CHN-Y	7.3.97	Q	WJ	Bydgoszcz	19 Jul
52.54	Norma	Cunigan	USA	25.6.97	2	NCAA-II	Bradenton	27 May
52.53	Ailén	Armada	ARG	3.10.98	6	WJ	Bydgoszcz	21 Jul
52.33	Helena	Leveelahti (20)	FIN	30.9.99	1	ECCp-B	Leiria	17 Sep

HAMMER

Mark				Name		Nat	Born	Pos	Meet	Venue		Date
82.98			Anita	Wlodarczyk		POL	8.8.85	1	Skol	Warszawa		28 Aug
							79.68	80.31	81.77	82.98	81.27	x
	82.29	1	OG	Rio de Janeiro	14 Aug	76.35	80.40	82.29	x	81.74	79.60	
	80.26	1		Cetniewo	12 Jul	79.58	79.67	79.62	x	80.26	79.39	
	79.61	1	Kuso	Szczecin	18 Jun	77.17	79.61	x	76.58	77.56	76.14	
	79.48	1	Werfer	Halle	21 May	76.40	79.48	x	79.04	78.80	78.90	
	79.45	1		Forbach	29 May	78.10	78.29	79.45	x	77.33	78.27	
	78.69	1	NC	Bydgoszcz	26 Jun	76.38	77.52	76.45	78.69	76.92	x	
	78.54	1	GS	Ostrava	19 May	71.55	77.42	78.54	77.43	77.32	76.98	
	78.14	1	EC	Amsterdam	8 Jul	72.82	75.73	77.11	77.65	78.12	78.14	
	78.10	1	Gyulai	Székesfehérvár	18 Jul	74.23	75.46	76.84	78.10	76.51	x	
	77.70	1	PTS	Samorín	4 Jun	x	74.09	77.70	73.87	x	x	
	76.93	Q	OG	Rio de Janeiro	12 Aug	76.93						
	76.61	1		Montreuil-sois-Bois	7 Jun	x	74.03	72.74	76.61	73.71	75.81	
	73.94	Q	EC	Amsterdam	6 Jul	65.79	73.94					
76.75				Zhang Wenxiu		CHN	22.3.86	2	OG	Rio de Janeiro		15 Aug
							75.06	74.04	76.19	74.65	76.75	70.93
	75.58	1		Beijing	18 May	70.89	73.43	72.15	75.58	74.88	69.24	
75.77			Betty	Heidler		GER	14.10.83	2	EC	Amsterdam		8 Jul
							71.27	73.19	75.77	71.31	73.64	74.35
	75.46	1		Berlin	4 Jun	71.84	72.62	73.33	75.46	73.57	x	
	75.32	1	NC	Kassel	18 Jun	73.35	74.91	75.32	74.98	75.08	74.24	
	74.00	1		Borkum	11 Sep							
	73.71	4	OG	Rio de Janeiro	15 Aug	71.38	69.24	69.84	72.71	73.71	x	
74.54			Sophie	Hitchon		GBR	11.7.91	3	OG	Rio de Janeiro		15 Aug
							x	73.29	71.73	72.28	72.89	74.54
74.50				Wang Zheng		CHN	14.12.87	1	NGP	Chengdu		10 Apr
	73.80	2	GS	Ostrava	19 May	68.28	73.80	x	68.53	71.82	71.58	
74.21			Zalina	Marghieva		MDA	5.2.88	1	NC-w	Chisinau		6 Feb
							x	69.70	x	74.21	x	73.02
	73.89	1		BalkC Pitesti	26 Jun	71.70	73.89	x	x	x	72.59	
72.81												
74.03			Amber	Campbell		USA	5.6.81	1	NC	Eugene		6 Jul
							x	66.78	69.93	72.02	70.33	74.03
	73.61	1	MSR	Norwalk	14 Apr	72.15	71.30	70.46	72.70	72.31	73.61	
73.87			Hanna	Skydan		AZE	14.5.92	2		Montreuil-sois-Bois		7 Jun
							x	71.14	70.79	73.38	73.87	73.39
	73.83	3	EC	Amsterdam	8 Jul	x	71.07	73.83	72.20	73.69	69.89	
			(30/8)									
73.09			Gwen	Berry #		USA	29.6.89	2	NC	Eugene		6 Jul
73.09			DeAnna	Price		USA	8.6.93	3	NC	Eugene		6 Jul
			(10)									
73.07			Oksana	Menkova		BLR	28.3.82	1	NCp	Brest		21 May
72.98			Joanna	Fiodorow		POL	4.3.89	1		Bialystok		1 Jun
72.78			Hanna	Malyshik		BLR	4.2.94	1		Lappeenranta		27 Aug

HAMMER

Mark	Name		Nat	Born	Pos	Meet	Venue	Date	
72.74	Malwina	Kopron	POL	16.11.94	2		Bialystok	1	Jun
72.47	Katerina	Safránková	CZE	8.6.89	1		Kolín	12	Jun
72.41	Rosa	Rodríguez	VEN	2.7.86	Q	OG	Rio de Janeiro	12	Aug
72.34	Martina	Hrasnová	SVK	21.3.83	1	NC	Banská Bystrica	25	Jun
72.23	Iryna	Klymets	UKR	4.10.94	1	NC-w	Mukachevo	12	Feb
72.16	Alexandra	Tavernier	FRA	13.12.93	1		Bruay-la- Buissière	17	Jun
72.09	Heather (20)	Steacy	CAN	14.4.88	1		Tempe	9	Apr
72.07	Anna	Bulgakova	RUS	17.1.88	1		Adler	12	May
71.90	Amanda	Bingson	USA	20.2.90	1		Clermont	14	May
71.78	Kathrin	Klaas	GER	6.2.84	2		Fränkisch-Crumbach	15	May
71.48	Daina	Levy	JAM	27.5.93	1		Lawrence	25	Jun
71.41	Marina	Nikisenko	MDA	28.6.86	3	NC-w	Chisinau	6	Feb
71.21	Tugçe	Sahutoglu	TUR	1.5.88	1		Mersin	24	May
71.10	Yirisleyidi L.	Ford	CUB	18.8.91	1	Barr	La Habana	27	May
71.10	Jeneva	Stevens	USA	28.10.89	1		Chula Vista	28	May
71.08	Kıvilcim	Salman	TUR	27.3.92	1		Mersin	14	Feb
71.06	Nataliya (30)	Zolotuhina	UKR	4.1.85	3	NC	Tiraspol	28	May
71.00	Iryna	Novozhylova	UKR	7.1.86	1	NC	Lutsk	16	Jun
70.99	Tracey	Andersson	SWE	5.12.84	1		Bottnaryd	19	Jun
70.98	Charlene	Woitha	GER	21.8.93	1		Zeulenroda	24	Jun
70.81	Éva	Orbán	HUN	29.11.84	1		Veszprém	14	Jun
70.75	Oksana	Kondratyeva	RUS	22.11.85	2		Sochi	26	May
70.75	Julia	Ratcliffe	NZL	14.7.93	1		London	9	Jul
70.52	Berta	Castells	ESP	24.1.84	1		Manresa	16	Jun
70.50	Maggie	Ewen	USA	23.9.94	2q	NCAA-W	Lawrence	27	May
70.43	Yelena	Soboleva	BLR	11.5.93	2	NC	Grodno	24	Jun
69.73	Yelizaveta (40)	Tsareva	RUS	15.3.93	1	NC-w	Adler	19	Feb
69.69	Réka	Gyurátz	HUN	31.5.96	1		Szombathely	8	Jun
69.65		Liu Tingting	CHN	29.1.90	1	NGP	Shaoxing	15	Apr
69.65	Jillian	Weir	CAN	9.2.93	1		Tucson	21	May
69.62	Britney	Henry	USA	17.10.84	1		Chula Vista	18	Jun
69.48	Veronika	Kanuchová	SVK	19.4.93	1		Gainesville	22	Apr
69.43	Marinda	Petersson	SWE	3.2.95	1		Helsingborg	12	Jun
69.40	Yelena	Krechik	BLR	20.7.87	2	Klim	Minsk	9	Jun
69.33	Heavin	Warner	USA	4.3.93	1	NCAA-II	Bradenton	26	May
69.21	Jenny	Dahlgren	ARG	27.8.84	1		Buenos Aires	16	Jul
69.20	Anastasiya (50)	Kolomoyets	BLR	15.7.94			Minsk	9	Apr
69.15	Merja	Korpela	FIN	15.5.81	1		Kurikka	11	Jun
69.14	Sultana	Frizell	CAN	24.10.84	2	NC	Edmonton	9	Jul
69.06	Laura	Redondo	ESP	3.7.88	1		Pamplona	21	May
69.01	Tereza	Králová	CZE	22.10.89	1		Brno	15	Jun
68.98	Ayamey	Medina	CUB-J	21.2.98	2	Barr	La Habana	27	May
68.97	Gulfiya	Agafonova	RUS	4.6.82	1	Znam	Zhukovskiy	4	Jun
68.71	Anna Maria	Orel	EST	11.12.96	1		Tallinn	10	Dec
68.59	Laëtitia	Bambara	BUR	30.3.84	3		Sotteville-lès-Rouen	18	Jul
68.56		Yan Ni	CHN	7.2.93	2	NGP	Shaoxing	15	Apr
68.56	Alyona (60)	Shamotina	UKR	27.12.95	1		Kirovohrad	24	Jul
68.52	Carolin	Paesler	GER	16.12.90	1		Leichlingen	2	Jul
68.47	Natalya	Polyakova	RUS	9.12.90	2	Znam	Zhukovskiy	4	Jun
68.35	Amy	Sène	SEN	6.4.85	1	AfCh	Durban	22	Jun
68.33	Aubrey	Baxter	USA	7.11.85	1		Sioux City	16	Apr
68.26	Alena	Lysenko	RUS	3.2.88	2	NC-w	Adler	19	Feb
68.18	Fruzsina	Fertig	HUN	2.9.93	2		Veszprém	14	Jun
68.15	Barbara	Spiler	SLO	2.1.92	1		Novo Mesto	1	Jul
68.02	Brooke	Pleger	USA	21.6.92	1	Owens	Columbus	23	Apr
67.86	Beatrice Nedberge	Llano	NOR-J	14.12.97	1		Bergen (Fana)	10	Jul
67.48	Jessica (70)	Ramsey	USA	26.7.91	3	MSR	Norwalk	14	Apr
67.40	Inga	Linna	FIN	21.2.95	1		Helsinki	16	May
67.33	Viktoriya	Holda	UKR-J	5.2.97	1J		Kirovgrad	21	Apr
67.32	Silvia	Salis	ITA	17.9.85	1		Genova	6	May
67.30	Jolien	Boumkwo	BEL	27.8.93	1	NC	Bruxelles	26	Jun
67.13	Sarah	Holt	GBR	17.4.87	3cB	Werfer	Halle	21	May
67.11	Katarzyna	Furmanek	POL	19.2.96	1		Kielce	13	May
66.91	Ida	Storm	SWE	26.12.91	1		Salinas	17	Apr
66.89	Cintia	Gergelics	HUN	16.11.91	2		Szombathely	8	Jun

HAMMER

Mark	Name		Nat	Born	Pos	Meet	Venue	Date
66.86	Nikola	Lomnická	SVK	16.9.88	8	GS	Ostrava	19 May
66.85	Lauren	Stuart	CAN	16.11.91	2		Long Beach	15 Apr
(80)								
66.81	Julia	Reedy	USA	27.1.93	1		Tempe	18 Mar
66.79	Akane	Watanabe	JPN	13.8.91	1		Fukuroi	3 May
66.79	Alina	Duran	USA	28.3.90	3		Tucson	21 May
66.68	Iliána	Korosídou	GRE	14.1.95	4	BalkC	Pitesti	26 Jun
66.57	Alina	Kostrova	BLR	2.3.90	5	NCp	Brest	21 May
66.44	Jade	Grace	USA	22.9.88	1	Bush	Norwalk	4 Jun
66.44	Susen	Küster	GER	27.7.94	1		Halle	13 Jul
66.38	Anastasiya	Maslova	BLR-Y	16.10.97	5	NC	Grodno	24 Jun
66.26	Bianca	Ghelber-Perie	ROU	1.6.90	6	BalkC	Pitesti	26 Jun
66.20	Lara	Nielsen	AUS	19.12.92	1		Adelaide	20 Feb
(90)								
66.13	Amy	Haapanen	USA	23.3.84	11	NC	Eugene	6 Jul
66.09	Eleni	Larsson	SWE	4.4.93	3		Bottnaryd	19 Jun
66.05	Laura	Igaune	LAT	2.10.88	1		Rome	26 Mar
66.05	Shelby	Ashe	USA	13.3.93	2		Athens	30 Apr
65.96	Sofiya	Palkina	RUS-J	9.6.98	1-j		Cheboksary	30 May
65.96	Camille	Sainte-Luce	FRA	18.4.96	2		Bruay La Buissière	17 Jun
65.82	Emily	Hunsucker	USA	20.4.91	1		Air Force Academy	6 May
65.77	Daniela	Manz	GER	19.9.86	1		Leichlingen	16 Apr
65.77	Johanna	Salmela	FIN	6.11.90	2		Orimattila	28 Jul
65.75	Elisa	Palmieri	ITA	18.9.83	1	NC-w	Lucca	20 Feb
(100)								
65.75	Alex	Hulley	AUS-J	24.7.97	1		Sydney (C)	29 May
65.67	Ashley	Jenkins	USA	10.12.93	14 May			
65.61	Sara	Savatovic	SRB	5.10.93	9 Jun			
65.60	Monique	Griffiths	USA	10.8.94	14 Apr			
65.50	Brooke	Andersen	USA	23.8.95	18 Mar			
65.50		Wang Lu	CHN	22.12.91	15 Apr			
65.48	Bianca	Lazar	ROU	24.2.93	26 Jun			
65.47	Kati	Ojaloo	EST	31.1.90	21 May			
65.46	Vanessa	Sterckendries	BEL	15.9.95	11 Jun			
65.30	Caressa	Sims	USA	7.3.86	25 Jun			
65.25	Kayla	Padgett	USA	.93	1 Apr			
65.21	Marthaline	Cooper	LBR	10.11.94	9 Jun			
65.13	Rachel	Hunter	GBR	30.8.93	16 Jul			
65.12	Nakel	McClinton	USA	3.1.94	23 Jun			
64.99	Laura	Schroeder	USA	.93	13 May			
64.95	Johana	Moreno	COL	15.4.85	30 May			
64.93	Ariannis	Vichy	CUB	18.5.89	19 Feb			
64.90	Mariana	Marcelino	BRA	16.7.92	30 Jun			
64.86	Micaela	Mariani	ITA	11.2.88	20 Feb			
64.86	Taylor	Bush	USA	26.11.89	9 Apr			
64.85	Audrey	Ciofani	FRA	13.3.96	8 May			
64.83	Nicole	Zihlmann	SUI	30.7.86	28 Aug			
64.75	Crystal	Bourque	USA	7.1.89	18 Jun			
64.74	Carys	Parry	GBR	24.7.81	11 Jun			
64.65	Iryna	Sekachyova	UKR	21.7.76	16 Jun			
64.65	Anna Paula	Pereira	BRA	7.8.86	19 Jun			
64.64	Trude	Raad	NOR	27.4.90	5 Jun			
64.63	Krista	Tervo	FIN-J	15.11.97	21 Jul			
64.59	Suvi	Koskinen	FIN-J	24.4.97	28 Dec			
64.55	Becky	Famurewa	USA	24.2.94	22 Apr			
64.46	Francesca	Massobrio	ITA	9.7.93	21 May			
64.37	Masumi	Aya	JPN	1.1.80	24 Jun			
64.35	Natalya	Pospelova	RUS	28.6.96	16 Jul			
64.28	Osarumen	Odeh	ESP	15.11.95	25 Jun			
64.28	Mona	Holm Solberg	NOR	5.8.83	29 Jul			
64.23	Tatyana	Kachegina	RUS	6.2.89	19 Feb			
64.17	Nina	Volkova	RUS	26.8.84	12 May			
64.14	Jocelyn	Williams	USA	23.1.91	2 Apr			
64.14	Wendy	Koolhaas	NED	2.1.80	15 May			
64.06	Carly	Fehringer	USA	9.11.91	26 Jun			
63.99	Sophie	Gimmler	GER	18.3.96	15 May			
63.92	Lisa	Wilson	USA	29.3.88	25 Jun			
63.82	Hitomi	Katsuyama	JPN	21.5.94	23 Jul			
63.47	Anastasiya	Borodulina	RUS-J	7.11.98	20 Feb			
63.43		Li Yumao	CHN	28.3.93	6 Apr			
63.30	Lyndsey	Thorpe	USA	5.11.92	9 Jun			
63.28		Zong Dan	CHN	19.1.95	10 Apr			
63.27		Zhao Fan	CHN-J	26.3.97	20 May			
63.20	Sarah	Bensaad	TUN	27.1.87	6 Jul			
63.19	Jermisha	Frazier	USA	.93	17 Mar			
63.18	Haley	Showalter	USA-J	3.6.97	6 May			
63.17	Jenni	Penttilä	FIN	9.3.91	23 Apr			
63.02	Venessa	Pfeifer	GER	26.7.94	24 Jul			
63.00	Anna	Zayanchkovskaya	BLR	9.7.96	24 Jun			
62.99	Viktoriya	Sadova	RUS	18.3.93	19 Feb			
62.98	Maria Barbaño	Acevedo	ESP	14.5.94	25 Jun			
62.93	Casey	Kraychir	USA	2.3.91	9 Apr			
62.91	Christina	Jones	GBR	5.4.90	22 May			
62.78	Soukana	Zakkour	MAR	13.10.93	30 Apr			
62.66	Kristin	Smith	USA	23.12.87	30 Apr			
62.65		Luo Na	CHN	8.10.93	15 Apr			
62.62	Susan	McKelvie	GBR	15.6.85	16 Jul			
62.58	Galina	Mityayeva	CAN	29.4.91	25 Jun			
62.57		Xu Xinying	CHN-J	17.2.97	20 May			
62.52	Celina	Julin	DEN	12.8.94	8 May			
62.51	Katja	Vangsnes	NOR	16.11.91	4 May			
62.51	Jessika	Guéhaseim	FRA	23.8.89	22 May			
62.50	Diana	Nusupbekova	KAZ	25.5.92	25 May			
62.48	Viktoriya	Sakhno	UKR-J	18.12.97	25 Jun			
62.44	Sara	Fantini	ITA-J	16.9.97	10 Sep			
62.42	Yelizaveta	Sukhanova	UKR	22.1.96	21 Apr			
62.33	Maci	Bingham	USA	30.12.92	15 Apr			
62.32	Cynthia	Watt	USA	8.12.93	1 Apr			
62.29	Louisa	James	GBR	5.7.94	20 Aug			
62.26	Krista	Chauvin	USA	17.1.92	22 Apr			
62.22	Marcela	Solano	CHI	27.3.86	8 Apr			
62.18	Mayra	Gaviria	COL-J	22.5.97	23 Jul			
62.12	Marika	Kaczmarek	POL	25.4.96	18 Jun			
62.12	Josefin	Berg	SWE	27.12.85	5 Mar			
62.12		Shang Ningyu	CHN-J	26.5.98	18 May			
62.12	Lucy	Marshall	GBR	28.11.81	9 Jul			
62.10	Anastasiya	Mazurina	BLR	21.2.93	23 Jan			
62.08	Zeliha	Uzunbilek	TUR	10.6.91	1 May			
62.07	Joy	McArthur	USA-Y	5.7.99	25 Jun			
62.04		Park Hee-sun	KOR	21.12.92	1 May			
62.01	Annette	Echikunwoke	USA	29.7.96	9 Jun			
61.94	Ashley	Bryant	USA	.94	18 May			
61.91	Kaytlyn	Coleman	USA	2.8.93	13 May			
61.91	Luz Dary	Muñoz	COL	11.11.88	26 Jun			
61.88	Karolina	Pedersen	SWE	16.4.87	26 Aug			
61.85	Meagan	McKee	USA	6.12.91	23 Apr			
61.82	Valeria	Chiliquinga	ECU	27.2.91	27 Mar			
61.81	Sarita	Prakash Singh	IND	26.10.89	28 Apr			
61.80	Krystal	Alnas	USA	.95	7 May			
61.67	Kelsey	Card	USA	20.8.92	13 May			
61.63	Sarah	Tolson	USA	1.5.93	18 Mar			
61.63	Anna	Grigoryeva	RUS-J	14.8.98	16 Jun			
61.62	Zouina	Bouzebra	ALG	3.10.90	22 Jun			
61.61	Anamari	Kozul	CRO	20.1.96	21 May			
61.61	Pavla	Kuklová	CZE	1.11.96	19 Jun			
(200)								

Mark	Name		Nat	Born	Pos	Meet	Venue	Date
Drugs disqualification								
76.31	Gwen	Berry #	USA	29.6.89	(1)		San Diego	21 May
				x	72.06	76.31	x x	71.71

JUNIORS

See main list for top 6 juniors. 11 performances by 6 women to 65.40. Additional marks and further juniors:

Mark	Name			Nat	Born	Pos	Meet	Venue	Date
Llano	67.26	2	Potchefstroom	20 Jan	66.24	1		Mannheim	25 jun
	66.56	1	Bergen (Fana)	8 May	65.48	1	NC	Askøy	29 Jul
Maslova	65.92	1J Klim	Minsk	9 Jun					
64.63	Krista		Tervo	FIN	15.11.97	Q	WJ	Bydgoszcz	21 Jul
64.59	Suvi		Koskinen	FIN	24.4.97	1		Kurikka	28 Dec
63.47	Anastasiya		Borodulina	RUS	7.11.98	2	NC-wj	Adler	20 Feb
63.27			Zhao Fan (10)	CHN	26.3.97	3	NGP	Taiyuan	20 May
63.18	Haley		Showalter	USA	3.6.97	1		Madison	6 May
62.57			Xu Xinying	CHN	17.2.97	4	NGP	Taiyuan	20 May
62.48	Viktoriya		Sakhno	UKR	18.12.97	1		Kyiv	25 Jun
62.44	Sara		Fantini	ITA	16.9.97	1		Caorle	10 Sep
62.18	Mayra		Gaviria	COL-J	22.5.97	5	WJ	Bydgoszcz	23 Jul
62.12			Shang Ningyu	CHN-J	26.5.98	9		Beijing	18 May
62.07	Joy		McArthur	USA-Y	5.7.99	1	NC-j	Clovis	25 Jun
61.63	Anna		Grigoryeva	RUS	14.8.98	1		Moskva	16 Jun
61.39	Deniz		Yaylaci	TUR	17.7.98	3		Mersin	24 May
61.37	Frida		Bååth (20)	SWE	5.7.97			Umeå	18 May

JAVELIN

Mark	Name				Nat	Born	Pos	Meet	Venue	Date
67.30		Vera		Rebrik	RUS	25.2.89	1	NC-w	Adler	19 Feb
						60.35	67.40	p	p p	p
	66.77	1	Znam	Zhukovskiy		4 Jun	60.63	62.02	66.77 x x	60.90
	66.03	1		Moskva		28 Jul	66.03	64.16	62.62 63.18	
	64.80	1		Adler		13 May	62.00	61.70	61.75 x x	64.80
67.11		Maria		Andrejczyk	POL	9.3.96	Q	OG	Rio de Janeiro	16 Aug
							67.11			
	64.78	4	OG	Rio de Janeiro		18 Aug	61.92	59.25	60.23 59.31 64.78	63.69
66.87		Barbora		Spotáková	CZE	30.6.81	1	NC	Tábor	19 Jun
							66.87	x	p 59.38 63.04	60.50
	66.06	1		Kolín		4 Aug	?	?	? ? ?	66.06
	64.80	3	OG	Rio de Janeiro		18 Aug	60.16	63.73	x 61.25 64.80	x
	64.65	Q	OG	Rio de Janeiro		16 Aug	62.50	64.65		
	64.48	2	Athl	Lausanne		25 Aug	62.76	62.31	62.56 x 64.48	x
66.41		Christin		Hussong	GER	17.4.94	1	NC	Kassel	19 Jun
							62.39	66.41	57.24 x x	58.30
66.34		Tatyana		Kholodovich	BLR	21.6.91	1	EC	Amsterdam	9 Jul
							61.82	66.34	62.91 65.79 62.94	60.71
	65.10	1	NC-w	Minsk IStaiki)		14 Feb	63.88	60.50	65.10 x x	x
	64.60	5	OG	Rio de Janeiro		18 Aug	62.68	60.24	64.60 60.49 63.52	64.24
	64.54	1	NCp	Brest		20 May	64.54	61.93	x x 61.96	59.62
66.18		Sara		Kolak	CRO	22.6.95	1	OG	Rio de Janeiro	18 Aug
							60.89	62.95	63.00 66.18 x	59.42
66.18		Madara		Palameika	LAT	18.6.87	1	VD	Bruxelles	9 Sep
							66.18	60.52	x 60.70 x	63.17
	65.68	1	DL	Birmimgham		5 Jun	65.06	64.01	x 59.96 65.68	64.61
	65.29	1	Athl	Lausanne		25 Aug	55.49	64.13	62.29 x 64.12	65.29
	64.76	1		Rabat		22 May	61.94	58.37	64.76 60.92 x	x
65.64				Liu Shiying	CHN	24.9.93	1	NGP	Shaoxing	16 Apr
							65.62	64.51	x 61.62 62.82	63.53
65.25		Linda		Stahl	GER	2.10.85	2	EC	Amsterdam	9 Jul
							60.40	60.80	59.19 59.30 x	65.25
65.14		Sunette		Viljoen (10)	RSA	6.1.83	1	DL	Doha	6 May
							65.14	64.56	64.82 59.97 63.11	63.95
	64.92	2	OG	Rio de Janeiro		18 Aug	64.92	61.04	x 63.00 x	x
64.96		Christina		Obergföll	GER	22.8.81	1	Werfer	Halle	21 May
							x	62.03	58.24 64.96 60.09	x
64.37		Kathryn		Mitchell	AUS	10.7.82	1		Melbourne	5 Mar
							60.33	x	60.55 57.62 59.97	64.37
	64.37	1		Beijing		18 May	x	61.81	64.09 64.37 60.33	p
	64.36	6	OG	Rio de Janeiro		18 May	x	64.36	x x 62.20	63.02
	(30/12)									
64.04				Lu Huihui	CHN	26.6.89	7	OG	Rio de Janeiro	18 Aug
63.84A		Flor Denis		Ruiz	COL	24.1.91	1		Cali	25 Jun
63.65		Liina		Laasma	EST	13.1.92	2		Rabat	22 May
63.54		Matilde		Andraud	FRA	28.4.89	2	Werfer	Halle	21 May

492 JAVELIN

Mark	Name		Nat	Born	Pos	Meet	Venue	Date	
63.20	Katharina	Molitor	GER	8.11.83	4	EC	Amsterdam	9	Jul
62.89		Li Lingwei	CHN	26.1.89	1		Pihtipudas	3	Jul
62.82	Kateryna	Derun	UKR	24.9.93	1		Kyiv	5	May
62.78	Sinta	Ozolina/Sprudzane	LAT	26.2.88	1		Rīga	31	May
	(20)								
62.59	Liz	Gleadle	CAN	5.12.88	1		Kawasaki	8	May
62.19	Maggie	Malone	USA	30.12.93	1	NCAA	Eugene	9	Jun
62.13	Yuki	Ebihara	JPN	28.10.85	2		Kawasaki	8	May
62.13	Heidi	Nokelainen	FIN	30.9.90	1		Lappeenranta	27	Aug
62.10	Tatyana	Korzh	BLR	17.3.93	1		Minsk	1	Jun
62.09	Lina	Müze	LAT	4.12.92	2		Valmiera	10	Jun
62.02	Hanna	Hatsko-Fedusova	UKR	3.10.90	1		Kyiv	25	Jun
61.86	Kara	Winger	USA	10.4.86	3	VD	Bruxelles	9	Sep
61.70	Laila	Silva	BRA	30.7.82	Q	NC	São Bernardo do Campo	1	Jul
61.56		Zhang Li	CHN	17.1.89	1	NGPF	Chongqing	18	Jun
	(30)								
61.48	Marcelina	Witek	POL	2.6.95	1		Zlocieniec	30	Apr
61.42	Anna	Wessman	SWE	9.10.89	1	vFIN	Tampere	3	Sep
61.38	Haruka	Kitaguchi	JPN-J	16.3.98	3		Kawasaki	8	May
61.37	Ásdís	Hjálmsdóttir	ISL	28.10.85	3	Odlozil	Praha	6	Jun
61.32	Liveta	Jasiunaite	LTU	26.7.94	1		Kaunas	21	May
61.27	Brittany	Borman	USA	1.7.89	5	DL	Doha	6	May
61.20	Hannah	Carson	USA	26.1.93	2	NCAA	Eugene	9	Jun
61.03	Martina	Ratej	SLO	2.11.81	1		Velenje	31	Aug
60.86	Risa	Miyashita	JPN	26.4.84	1		Osaka	24	Sep
60.70	Jenni	Kangas	FIN	3.7.92	1		Heinola	18	Aug
	(40)								
60.37	Coralys	Ortiz	PUR	16.4.85	1		Gurabo	27	Feb
60.01	Annu	Rani	IND	29.8.92	1	NC	Lucknow	29	Sep
59.68	Ariana	Ince	USA	14.3.89	1		Tucson	21	May
59.55	Mariya	Abakumova	RUS	15.1.86	2	NC-w	Adler	19	Feb
59.50	Anete	Kocina	LAT	5.2.96	3		Valmiera	10	Jun
59.45	Suman	Devi	IND	15.7.85	1	SAsG	Guwahati	11	Feb
59.41	Sanni	Utriainen	FIN	5.2.91	1		Vantaa	28	May
59.39	Réka	Szilágyi	HUN	19.1.96	1		Bar	1	May
59.33	Sigrid	Borge	NOR	3.12.95	1-22	ECp-w	Arad	12	Mar
59.19		Zhu Dandan	CHN	1.3.94	2	NGP	Chengdu	10	Apr
	(50)								
59.16	Sofi	Flink	SWE	8.7.95	2		Kuortane	25	Jun
59.02	Kelsey-Lee	Roberts	AUS	21.9.91	1		Canberra	20	Feb
58.98		Yang Xinli	CHN	7.2.88	3	NC	Tianjin	15	Sep
58.95	Eda	Tugsuz	TUR-J	1.3.97	1		Mersin	23	May
58.86	Oona	Sormunen	FIN	2.8.89	1		Lahti	14	Jul
58.81	Avione	Allgood	USA	14.12.93	1	Big 12	Fort Worth	15	May
58.79	Goldie	Sayers	GBR	16.7.82	1		Austin	7	May
58.78		Du Xiaowei	CHN	11.8.87	4	NC	Tianjin	15	Sep
58.72	Abigail	Gómez	MEX	30.1.91	1		Claremont	9	Apr
58.65	Kim	Hamilton	USA	28.11.85	Q	NC	Eugene	7	Jul
	(60)								
58.53	Tetyana	Fetiskina	UKR	11.9.94	2		Kyiv	5	May
58.31	Krista	Woodward	CAN	22.11.84	1		Langley	19	Jun
58.21	Marina	Saito	JPN	15.10.95	1		Kumagaya	4	Sep
58.18	Nikola	Ogrodníková	CZE	18.8.90	1		Ústí Nad Orlicí	4	Sep
57.86	Jarmila	Jurkovicová	CZE	9.2.81	7	Odlozil	Praha	6	Jun
57.85	Alexia	Kogut Kubiak	FRA	22.1.88	1		Aix-en-Provence	8	May
57.83	Irena	Sedivá	CZE	19.1.92	2	FlaR	Gainesville	1	Apr
57.81	Marija	Vucenovic	SRB	3.4.93	2	SEC	Tuscaloosa	13	May
57.81	Alexie	Alais	FRA	9.10.94	1		Grenoble	15	Jun
57.67	Yevgeniya	Ananchenko	RUS	7.11.92	2	NC	Cheboksary	23	Jun
	(70)								
57.59	Klaudia	Maruszewska	POL-J	28.8.97	1	WJ	Bydgoszcz	20	Jul
57.56	Indre	Jakubaityte	LTU	24.1.76	1		Alicante	24	Apr
57.50		Kim Kyung-ae	KOR	5.3.88	1	NC	Hwaseong	4	Jun
57.45	Mariya	Safonova	RUS	28.10.94	3	NC	Cheboksary	23	Jun
57.44	Joanna	Blair	GBR	1.3.86	1	NC	Birmingham	26	Jun
57.40	Fabienne	Schönig	GER-J	27.7.97	1		Wipperfürth	1	May
57.34	Lidia	Parada	ESP	11.6.93	15q	EC	Amsterdam	7	Jul
57.32		Su Lingdan	CHN-J	12.1.97	1	Asi-J	Ho Chi Minh	4	Jun
57.32	Jo-Ané	van Dyk	RSA-J	3.10.97	2	WJ	Bydgoszcz	20	Jul
57.20	Kim	Mickle	AUS	28.12.84	22q	OG	Rio de Janeiro	16	Aug
	(80)								

JAVELIN – PENTATHLON – HEPTATHLON

Mark	Name		Nat	Born	Pos	Meet	Venue	Date	
57.09	Yulenmis	Aguilar	CUB	3.8.96	1	NACAC	San Salvador	17	Jul
57.06	Audrey	Malone	USA	16.6.95	3	NCAA	Eugene	9	Jun
57.02	Edivania	Araújo	BRA	27.8.95	Q	NC	São Bernardo do Campo	1	Jul
56.99	Annabella	Bogdán	HUN	7.4.92	7	ECp-w	Arad	12	Mar
56.98	Sarah	Leidl	GER	5.3.87	1	Bayer	Erding	17	Jul
56.92	H.L.Dilhani	Lekamge	SRI	14.1.87	1		Diyagama	14	Aug
56.91	Jessie	Merckle	USA	13.7.94	1		High Point	1	Apr
56.88	Sofía	Ifantídou	GRE	5.1.85	1H		Firenze	30	Apr
56.86	Zahra	Bani	ITA	31.12.79	1		Pavia	1	May
56.79	Hiroko	Takigawa	JPN	25.7.94	1		Hiratsuka	12	Jun
	(90)								
56.73	Poonam	Rani	IND	6.6.90	2	NC	Lucknow	29	Sep
56.64	Marta	Kakol	POL	25.2.92	3	Szelest	Warszawa	21	May
56.57	Yuka	Sato	JPN	21.7.92	1		Nara	2	Apr
56.56	Sara	Jemai	ITA	12.4.92	2		Pavia	1	May
56.48	Mahiro	Osa	JPN-Y	26.11.99	1		Okayama	30	Jul
56.40	Anna	Tarasyuk	BLR-J	30.10.97	Q	WJ	Bydgoszcz	19	Jul
56.35	Nicolle	Murphy	USA	19.10.94	5	NC	Eugene	9	Jul
56.24	Eleonora	Bacciotti	ITA	13.12.89	1	NC	Rieti	26	Jun
56.21	Margaux	Nicollin	FRA	1.5.95	2	Med-23	Radès	4	Jun
56.19	Nikol	Tabacková	CZE-J	24.1.98	4	WJ	Bydgoszcz	20	Jul
	(100)								
56.17	Shiori	Toma	JPN	7.2.96	17 Sep	54.42	Nuttha	Nacharn	THA	4.6.90	13 Jan
56.07	Luziana	Tomé	BRA	1.8.85	1 Jul	54.42	Elisabeth	Höglund	SWE	19.2.90	28 Aug
56.03	Allison	Updike	USA	16.10.92	28 May	54.36	Marisleisys	Duarthe	CUB-Y	17.9.00	29 May
55.97	Jucilene	de Lima	BRA	14.9.90	14 Jun	54.30	Lisanne	Schol	NED	22.6.91	11 Jun
55.94	Kiho	Kuze	JPN	28.3.95	20 May	54.18	Bethany	Drake	USA	10.10.93	28 May
55.93	Laura	Ikauniece-Admidina	LAT	31.5.92	13 Aug	54.17	Daniella	Nisimura	BRA	26.3.94	5 Jun
55.90	Jelena	Jaakkola	FIN	7.3.89	28 Jun	54.15		Chang Chunfeng	CHN	4.5.88	10 Apr
55.88	Mackenzie	Little	AUS	22.12.96	1 Apr	54.15	Estefany	Chacón	VEN-J	1.11.97	7 May
55.87		Peng Juanhong	CHN	8.8.93	10 Apr	54.12	Kateryna	Retiva-Dovhenko	UKR	10.2.89	18 Jun
55.87	Lilian	Seibert	BRA	23.7.89	16 May	54.08	Anikó	Ormay	HUN	22.1.91	18 Jul
55.82	Elizabeth	Herrs	USA	20.12.93	15 May	54.06		He Daixian	CHN	1.9.94	13 May
55.81		Suh Hae-an	KOR	1.7.85	3 Jul	53.90	Séphora	Bissoly	FRA	6.11.81	24 Jun
55.76	Anouk	Vetter	NED	4.2.93	9 Jul	53.86	Angéla	Moravcsik	HUN	13.5.96	30 Jul
55.74	Ai	Yamauchi	JPN	6.12.94	19 Oct	53.85	Panayióta	Touloumtzí	GRE	26.9.86	14 May
55.72	Nadeeka	Lakmali	SRI	18.9.81	14 Aug	53.83	Andrea	Lindenthaler	AUT	7.9.87	8 May
55.53	Tsugumi	Okabayashi	JPN-J	19.7.98	9 Oct	53.80	Sharmila	Kumari	IND	2.3.95	2 Jul
55.43	Kato	Van Den Brulle	BEL	29.10.96	6 Aug	53.72	Nicoleta	Anghelescu	ROU	13.1.92	25 Jun
55.39	Sarah	Firestone	USA	16.2.95	21 Apr	53.67	Brittni	Wolczyk	CAN-J	10.9.97	17 Jun
55.37		Chen Jiajia	CHN-J	14.10.98	16 Apr	53.67	Violène	Granger	FRA	18.7.94	24 Jun
55.35		Chang Chu	TPE-J	11.9.97	20 Jul	53.66	Charlotte	Müller	GER	14.9.93	19 Jun
55.34	Kseniya	Zybina	RUS	1.2.89	19 Feb	53.65	Luz Mariana	Castro	MEX-J	23.1.97	5 Jun
55.30	Viktoriya	Sudarushkina	RUS	2.9.90	13 May	53.61	Yelizaveta	Gorbachova	RUS	12.7.89	19 Feb
55.30	Gundega	Griva	LAT	8.4.91	19 Jun	53.61	Melissa	Dupré	BEL	5.11.86	21 Ma
55.24	Eva	Vivod	SLO	7.8.94	9 Apr	53.60A	Odalis	Romero	PUR	20.3.94	23 Apr
55.15	Riko	Nishimura	JPN	1.11.93	2 Jul	53.55	Desirée	Schwarz	GER	24.4.92	5 Jun
55.11	Nadja-Marie	Pasternack	SUI	4.7.96	22 May	53.52	Kelechi	Nwanaga	NGR-J	24.12.97	8 Jul
55.04	Rebekah	Wales	USA	2.10.95	13 May	53.46	Miho	Nakajima	JPN	26.7.94	3 Sep
54.99	Paola	Padovan	ITA	4.12.95	4 Jun	53.43		Han Hyo-hee	KOR	3.5.86	21 Apr
54.97	Lyubov	Zhatkina	RUS	30.3.90	19 Feb	53.39	Melissa	Fraser	CAN	26.5.89	30 Apr
54.97	Katie	Reichert	USA	22.8.93	17 Jun	53.38	Géraldine	Ruckstuhl	SUI-J	24.2.98	20 Jul
54.96	Sophia	Rivera	USA-J	17.10.98	18 Apr	53.37	Katarina	Gasparovic	CRO	12.9.94	22 May
54.96	Dana	Bergrath	GER	24.4.94	30 Apr	53.36	Haruka	Matoba	JPN	24.4.87	22 May
54.96	Hitomi	Sukenaga	JPN	4.5.88	22 May	53.34	Estefania	López	ESP	10.7.94	4 Jun
54.89	Mikako	Yamashita	JPN-J	3.5.97	20 Jul	53.34	Saara	Lipsanen	FIN	13.9.95	22 Jul
54.88	Pascaline	Adanhouegbe	BEN	19.10.95	25 Jun	53.22		Lee Hye-rim	KOR	6.3.89	3 May
54.81		Yu Yuzhen	CHN-J	5.3.98	6 Apr	53.19	Tori	Peeters	NZL	17.5.94	21 Oct
54.77	Marija	Bogavac	MNE	31.7.96	18 Mar	53.13A	Megan	Wilke	RSA	23.8.95	8 Mar
54.75	Arantxa	Moreno	ESP	16.1.95	12 Mar	53.13	Nafissatou	Thiam	BEL	19.8.94	13 Aug
54.72	Nora Aïda	Bicet	ESP	29.10.77	28 Sep	53.08	Fawn	Miller	USA	10.5.92	1 Apr
54.65	Yuka	Kuwazoe	JPN-Y	.99	10 Jul	53.08	Tamara	Yevdokymova	UKR	6.11.94	24 Jul
54.64		Jin Pingping	CHN	28.8.93	13 May	53.07	Mari-Liis	Tulev	EST	6.4.95	12 Mar
54.62	María Paz	Ríos	CHI	13.10.89	19 Feb	53.07	Carolina	Visca	ITA-Y	31.5.00	26 Jun
54.62	Rafaela	Gonçalves	BRA	27.11.91	2 Jul	53.03	Mizuki	Murakami	JPN	3.5.91	2 May
54.59	Berivan	Sakir	TUR	22.9.93	23 May		(188)				
54.44	Mirell	Luik	EST-J	3.1.97	10 Jan						

JUNIORS

See main list for top 9 juniors. 11 performances by 6 women to 57.24. Additional marks and further juniors:

Kitaguchi	60.84	1	Nanbu Sapporo		10 Jul				
Tugsuz	58.13	Q	EC	Amsterdam	7 Jul	57.40	2	ECCp Mersin	28 May
	57.77	Q	WJ	Bydgoszcz	19 Jul	57.24	1	NC Mersin	16 May
55.53	Tsugumi		Okabayashi (10)	JPN-J	19.7.98	1		Kitakami	9 Oct
55.37			Chen Jiajia	CHN	14.10.98	5	NGP	Shaoxing	16 Apr
55.35			Chang Chu	TPE	11.9.97	5	WJ	Bydgoszcz	20 Jul

WOMEN 2016

JAVELIN – PENTATHLON

Mark	Name		Nat	Born	Pos	Meet	Venue	Date	
54.96	Sophia	Rivera	USA	17.10.98	1		Brentwood	18 Apr
54.89	Mikako	Yamashita	JPN-	3.5.97	6	WJ	Bydgoszcz	20 Jul
54.81		Yu Yuzhen	CHN	5.3.98	5	NGP	Chengdu	6 Apr
54.65	Yuka	Kuwazoe	JPN-Y	.99	1		Rifu	10 Jul
54.44	Mirell	Luik	EST	3.1.97	6		Valmiera	10 Jun
54.36	Marisleisys	Duarthe	CUB-Y	17.9.00	1	Barr	La Habana	29 Ma
54.15	Estefany	Chacón	VEN	1.11.97	1	NC-j	Barquisimeto	7 Ma
53.67	Brittni	Wolczyk (20)	CAN	10.9.97	5	Jerome	Burnaby	17 Jun

INDOOR PENTATHLON

Mark	Name		Nat	Born	Pos	Meet	Venue	Date
4881	Brianne	Theisen-Eaton	CAN	18.12.88	1	WI	Portland	18 Mar
	8.04 1.85 13.70 6.42 2:09.99							
4847	Anastasiya	Mokhnyuk	UKR	1.1.91	2	WI	Portland	18 Mar
	8.11 1.85 15.01 6.66 2:23.19							
4770	Alina	Fyodorova	UKR	31.7.89	3	WI	Portland	18 Mar
	8.27 1.85 15.44 6.33 2:20.42							
4745		Mokhnyuk			1		Zaporizhzhya	27 Jan
	8.20 1.82 14.58 6.24 2:16.69							
4703	Kendell	Williams	USA	14.6.95	1	NCAA	Birmingham, AL	11 Mar
	8.09 1.86 13.55 6.35 2:20.47							
4688	Claudia	Rath	GER	25.4.86	1		Tallinn	14 Feb
	8.45 1.81 12.85 6.40 2:09.19							
4688		Fyodorova			1	NC	Sumy	25 Feb
	8.48 1.79 15.97 6.18 2:16.63							
4678	Nafissatou	Thiam	BEL	19.8.94	1	NC	Gent	7 Feb
	8.49 1.91 14.60 6.23 2:22.84							
4661	Barbara	Nwaba	USA	18.1.89	4	WI	Portland	18 Mar
	8.43 1.82 15.00 5.84 2:10.07							
4656	Györgyi	Zsivoczky-Farkas	HUN	13.2.85	5	WI	Portland	18 Mar
	8.56 1.85 14.54 6.28 2:18.48							
4643	Akela	Jones	BAR	22.4.95	1		Manhattan	22 Jan
	8.25 1.85 12.99 6.64 2:25.63							
4535	Ulyana	Aleksandrova	RUS	1.1.91	1	NC	Smolensk	19 Feb
	8.57 1.90 12.79 6.27 2:23.25							
	(12/10)							
4519	Morgan	Lake	GBR-J	12.5.97	1	v2N-23	Salamanca	20 Feb
	8.63 1.93 12.97 5.89 2:18.53							
4506	Katerina	Cachová	CZE	26.2.90	1	NC	Praha	13 Feb
	8.30 1.84 11.67 6.28 2:18.78							
4482	Lyubov	Tkach	RUS	18.2.93	2	NC	Smolensk	19 Feb
	9.07 1.81 14.86 6.03 2:15.52							
4470	Yana	Maksimova	BLR	9.1.89	1	NC	Gomel	17 Feb
	8.92 1.86 14.27 5.91 2:17.70							
4457	Taliyah	Brooks	USA	8.2.95	2		Fayetteville	29 Jan
	8.18 1.78 11.40 6.35 2:19.06							
4444	Amalie Hammild	Juel	NOR	17.4.94	1		Seattle	26 Feb
	8.48 1.78 11.07 6.03 2:06.88							
4434	Mariya	Gromysheva	RUS	10.1.90	1	NC	Volgograd	20 Jan
	8.63 1.74 13.37 6.42 2:21.05							
4425	Eliska	Klucinová	CZE	14.4.88	1	v3N	Reims	30 Jan
	8.85 1.83 14.22 6.02 2:21.49							
4400	Karolina	Tyminska	POL	4.10.84	1	NC	Torun	5 Mar
	8.50 1.69 14.00 6.10 2:16.84							
4393	Jess	Lehman	USA	17.1.93	1	Big 10	Geneva	26 Feb
	8.75 1.67 13.98 6.03 2:10.33							
	(20)							
4392	Georgia	Ellenwood	CAN	5.8.95	2	Big 10	Geneva	26 Feb
	8.61 1.82 12.50 5.90 2:15.70							
4380A	Makeba	Alcide	LCA	24.2.90	1		Albuquerque	5 Feb
	8.42 1.77 13.20 5.96 2:19.78							
4373	Lisa	Maihöfer	GER-J	28.10.98	1	NC-j	Hamburg	31 Jan
	8.70 1.87 11.52 6.28 2:24.28							
4371	Payton	Stumbaugh	USA	29.11.95	5	NCAA	Birmingham, AL	11 Mar
	8.10 1.74 12.14 5.97 2:18.01							
4369	Michelle	Zeltner	SUI	22.12.91	2		Tallinn	14 Feb
	8.63 1.81 13.83 5.84 2:21.40							
4363	Annie	Kunz	USA	16.2.93	1		College Station	5 Feb
	8.51 1.81 12.78 5.94 2:20.78							
4354	Alina	Shukh	UKR-Y	12.2.99	2		Zaporizhzhya	27 Jan
	9.08 1.82 13.45 5.94 2:16.63							

HEPTATHLON

Mark	Name			Nat	Born	Pos	Meet	Venue	Date	
4347	Celina		Leffler	GER	9.4.96	1	NC	Hamburg	31 Jan	
	8.50	1.69	14.35 6.09		2:22.19					
4341	Aleksandra		Butvina	RUS	14.2.86	3	NC	Smolensk	19 Feb	
	8.78	1.75	14.36 5.76		2:16.34					
4336	Alex		Gochenour	USA	17.2.93	6	NCAA	Birmingham, AL	11 Mar	
	8.38	1.71	12.65 5.95		2:15.38					
(30)										
4322	Daryna		Sloboda	UKR	19.6.95	2	NC	Sumy	25 Feb	
	8.87	1.76	13.17 6.03		2:17.38					
4320	Lisa		Linnell	SWE	30.4.91	1		Sandnes	21 Feb	
	8.67	1.72	12.62 5.96		2:12.95					
4292	Hanna		Gorodskaya	BLR	31.1.93	1		Minsk	28 Jan	
	8.77	1.87	12.22 5.90		2:23.91					
4292	Vanessa		Spínola	BRA	5.3.90	3		Tallinn	14 Feb	
	8.81	1.75	13.62 5.87		2:18.25					
4291	Austra		Skujyte	LTU	12.8.79	4		Tallinn	14 Feb	
	8.86	1.78	16.12 5.84		2:32.52					
4285	Kaylon		Eppinger	USA	17.9.89	2	NC	Crete	27 Feb	
	8.18	1.74	13.12 5.70		2:21.73					
4282	Karli		Johonnot	USA	21.8.93	1		Chapel Hill	21 Jan	
	8.65	1.80	13.21 5.82		2:22.95					
4268	Xenia		Rahn	GER	9.3.91	7	NCAA	Birmingham, AL	11 Mar	
	8.42	1.68	13.00 6.07		2:21.34					
4260	Ivona		Dadic	AUT	29.12.93	5		Tallinn	14 Feb	
	8.83	1.75	13.32 5.98		2:21.30					
4250	Lecabela		Quaresma	POR	26.12.89	1	NC	Aubière	27 Feb	
	8.39	1.67	13.27 5.87		2:19.11					
(40)										
4245	Beatrice		Puiu	ROU	1.1.86	1	NC	Bucuresti	30 Jan	
	8.58	1.74	14.32 5.92		2:29.26					
4226	Clairwin		Dameus	USA	12.6.94	8	NCAA	Birmingham, AL	11 Mar	
	8.29	1.59	12.04 6.36		2:20.84					
4225	Chari		Hawkins	USA	21.5.91	3	NC	Crete	27 Feb	
	8.36	1.74	12.52 5.78		2:22.08					
4224	Yekaterina		Voronina	UZB	16.2.92	1	AsC	Doha	21 Feb	
	9.00	1.81	13.57 5.85		2:25.20					
4222	Lindsay		Schwartz	USA	23.4.90	4	NC	Crete	27 Feb	
	8.65	1.74	13.00 5.79		2:20.10					
4219	Tatum		Souza	USA	20.4.92	5	NC	Crete	27 Feb	
	8.49	1.71	14.40 5.45		2:19.83					
4218	Leigha		Brown	USA	19.9.94	9	NCAA	Birmingham, AL	11 Mar	
	8.64	1.71	13.11 5.57		2:13.87					
4215	Jaclyn		Siefring	USA	.96	1		Akron	26 Feb	
	8.67	1.66	12.74 6.05		2:17.79					
4214	Jessica		Taylor	GBR	27.6.88	3	v3N	Reims	30 Jan	
	8.47	1.68	12.39 5.98		2:19.54					
4208	Anna		Maiwald	GER	21.7.90	2	NC	Hamburg	31 Jan	
	8.48	1.72	13.06 5.68		2:19.95					
(50)										
4208	Anaëlle		Nyabeu Djapa	FRA	15.9.92	2	NC	Aubière	27 Feb	
	8.37	1.67	12.84 5.89		2:20.96					

HEPTATHLON

Mark	Name			Nat	Born	Pos	Meet	Venue	Date
6810	Nafissatou		Thiam	BEL	19.8.94	1	OG	Rio de Janeiro	13 Aug
	13.56/0.3	1.98	14.91 25.10/-0.7		6.58/-0.5	53.13		2:16.54	
6775	Jessica		Ennis-Hill	GBR	28.1.86	2	OG	Rio de Janeiro	13 Aug
	12.84/0.0	1.89	13.86 23.49/-0.1		6.34/-1.2	46.06		2:09.07	
6765	Brianne		Theisen-Eaton	CAN	18.12.88	1	Hypo	Götzis	29 May
	12.93/0.5	1.83	13.71 23.33/1.3		6.56/0.2	47.74		2:10.98	
6733			Ennis-Hill			1		Ratingen	26 Jun
	13.13/-0.8	1.84	14.29 23.36/-0.3		6.63/1.2	44.37		2:11.46	
6653			Theisen-Eaton			3	OG	Rio de Janeiro	13 Aug
	13.18/0.0	1.86	13.45 24.18/-0.1		6.48/0.3	47.36		2:09.50	
6626	Anouk		Vetter	NED	4.2.93	1	EC	Amsterdam	9 Jul
	13.29/-0.7	1.74	15.69 23.89		6.38w/2.9	55.76		2:21.50	
6622	Laura		Ikauniece-Admidina	LAT	31.5.92	2	Hypo	Götzis	29 May
	13.07/0.5	1.83	13.00 23.64/1.3		6.16/-0.1	54.83		2:14.77	
6617			Ikauniece-Admidina			4	OG	Rio de Janeiro	13 Aug
	13.33/0.3	1.77	13.52 23.76/-0.1		6.12/-0.5	55.93		2:09.43	
6557	Carolin		Schäfer	GER	5.12.91	3	Hypo	Götzis	29 May
	13.26/0.5	1.80	14.33 23.37/1.0		6.31/0.2	48.20		2:17.02	

496 HEPTATHLON

Mark	Name		Nat	Born	Pos	Meet	Venue	Date
6540		Schäfer			5	OG	Rio de Janeiro	13 Aug
	13.12/0.0	1.83 14.57 23.99/-0.1		6.20/0.6		47.99	2:16.52	
6523	Katarina	Johnson-Thompson	GBR	9.1.93	6	OG	Rio de Janeiro	13 Aug
	13.48/-0.3	1.98 11.68 23.26/-0.1		6.51/0.9		36.36	2:10.47	
6494	Barbara	Nwaba	USA	18.1.89	1	NC	Eugene	10 Jul
	13.49/0.0	1.82 13.77 23.76/0.0		6.23/1.5		43.48	2:07.13	
6491		Thiam			4	Hypo	Götzis	29 May
	13.63/0.3	1.89 15.04 25.09/0.1		6.26/-0.6		48.61	2:17.28	
6481	Yorgelis	Rodríguez	CUB	25.1.95	7	OG	Rio de Janeiro	13 Aug
	13.61/-0.3	1.86 13.69 24.26/0.0		6.25/-0.1		48.89	2:14.65	
6476		Schäfer			2		Ratingen	26 Jun
	13.48/-0.8	1.75 14.56 23.78/-0.3		6.27/0.6		50.73	2:16.93	
6458	Antoinette	Nana Djimou (10)	FRA	2.8.85	2	EC	Amsterdam	9 Jul
	13.26/-0.7	1.71 16.17 24.92/-0.7		6.31/0.4		51.72	2:19.33	
6442	Györgyi	Zsivoczky-Farkas	HUN	13.2.85	8	OG	Rio de Janeiro	13 Aug
	13.79/-0.2	1.86 14.39 25.38/-0.7		6.31/0.1		48.07	2:11.76	
6423	Heather	Miller Koch	USA	30.3.87	2	NC	Eugene	10 Jul
	13.47/0.0	1.73 12.72 23.64/0.0		6.19/0.6		41.23	2:07.32	
6408	Ivona	Dadic	AUT	29.12.93	3	EC	Amsterdam	9 Jul
	13.83/1.2	1.77 14.10 24.11		6.32/0.6		47.92	2:12.83	
6402	Kendell	Williams	USA	14.6.95	3	NC	Eugene	10 Jul
	12.99/-0.1	1.84 12.95 23.67/-1.6		6.20/0.2		42.21	2:15.31	
6401	Jennifer	Oeser	GER	29.11.83	9	OG	Rio de Janeiro	13 Aug
	13.69/0.3	1.86 14.28 24.99/0.4		6.19/-0.7		47.22	2:13.82	
6394		Vetter			10	OG	Rio de Janeiro	13 Aug
	13.47/-0.3	1.77 14.78 23.93/0.0		6.10/0.0		48.42	2:17.71	
6385	Sharon	Day-Monroe	USA	9.6.85	4	NC	Eugene	10 Jul
	13.31/0.0	1.76 15.62 24.32/0.0		6.05/0.9		44.90	2:09.41	
6383		Nana Djimou			11	OG	Rio de Janeiro	13 Aug
	13.37/0.0	1.77 14.88 25.07/0.4		6.43/-1.6		48.76	2:20.36	
6377	Nadine	Broersen	NED	29.4.90	1	Décastar	Talence	18 Sep
	13.60w/2.2	1.81 13.56 25.23/1.8		6.38/1.7		51.77	2:17.64	
6373		Rodríguez			1	NC	La Habana	19 Mar
	13.61/2.2	1.87 13.19 24.35/0.9		6.24/0.7		45.83	2:15.73	
6328	Katerina	Cachová	CZE	26.2.90	1		Kladno	11 Jun
	13.16/-0.4	1.82 12.96 24.12/1.4		5.99/0.2		45.11	2:13.18	
6326	Chantae	McMillan	USA	1.5.88	5	NC	Eugene	10 Jul
	13.33/-0.2	1.78 13.50 24.77/-0.9		6.10/1.3		49.45	2:14.46	
6310	Claudia	Rath	GER	25.4.86	3	Décastar	Talence	18 Sep
	13.59w/2.1 (30/20)	1.72 12.59 24.09/0.9		6.50/1.4		43.65	2:09.06	
6307	Akela	Jones	BAR	22.4.95	1	MSR	Azusa	14 Apr
	13.36/1.5	1.95 13.64 23.28/1.9		6.12/0.4		38.97	2:28.70	
6270A	Evelis	Aguilar	COL	3.1.93	1		Cali	26 Jun
	13.56w/2.3	1.71 13.25 23.76w/3.5		6.06/-0.3		45.98	2:10.08	
6266	Xénia	Krizsán	HUN	13.1.93	4	EC	Amsterdam	9 Jul
	13.53/1.2	1.74 13.93 25.05/-0.7		6.13/0.9		47.38	2:11.18	
6190	Nadine	Visser	NED	9.2.95	19	OG	Rio de Janeiro	13 Aug
	13.02/0.0	1.68 12.84 24.34/-0.7		6.35/0.5		42.48	2:14.47	
6188	Vanessa	Spínola	BRA	5.3.90	1	NC	São Bernardo do Campo	1 Jul
	14.23/-1.1	1.81 13.07 24.16/0.0		6.15/-2.1		45.83	2:16.01	
6182	Eliska	Klucinová	CZE	14.4.88	11	Hypo	Götzis	29 May
	13.94/0.2	1.77 15.21 24.41/0.1		6.25/0.4		40.51	2:19.30	
6170	Erica	Bougard	USA	26.7.93	1	SEC	Tuscaloosa	13 May
	13.38/0.1	1.84 12.15 23.72/0.7		6.11/-2.1		37.24	2:14.67	
6153	Uhunoma	Osazuwa	NGR	23.11.87	1	AfCh	Durban	25 Jun
	13.32/1.4	1.83 12.87 24.19		6.24/0.0		36.30	2:17.50	
6124A	Alysbeth	Félix	PUR	7.3.93	2		Cali	26 Jun
	13.48w/2.3	1.83 11.52 24.31w/3.5		6.28/0.5		38.83	2:14.98	
6099	Alina	Shukh	UKR-Y	12.2.99	1	NC	Lutsk	19 Jun
	14.72/0.1 (40)	1.92 12.94 26.85/1.0		6.15/0.0		51.52	2:17.68	
6098	Lindsay	Lettow	USA	6.6.90	2	vGER	Fayetteville	30 Jul
	13.47/1.2	1.73 12.74 24.57/0.6		6.11/1.9		43.34	2:14.43	
6089	Quintunya	Chapman	USA	7.1.93	6	NC	Eugene	10 Jul
	13.68/-0.2	1.60 14.61 24.32/-1.6		6.10/1.2		46.35	2:16.30	
6088	Lilli	Schwarzkopf	GER	28.8.83	14	Hypo	Götzis	29 May
	13.92/0.2	1.77 14.56 25.89/-0.2		5.90/-1.8		49.20	2:17.72	
6086	Hanna	Kasyanova	UKR	24.4.83	15	Hypo	Götzis	29 May
	13.39/1.1	1.74 13.78 24.65/0.1		5.82/-1.0		46.61	2:19.63	

HEPTATHLON

Mark	Name		Nat	Born	Pos	Meet	Venue	Date	
6076	Yana	Maksimova	BLR	9.1.89	2		Kladno	11	Jun
	14.25/0.9	1.88 14.25	26.00/-2.7	5.72/0.5		43.38	2:11.17		
6075	Karolina	Tyminska	POL	4.10.84	3		Kladno	11	Jun
	13.70/-0.4	1.67 14.00	24.08/1.4	5.99/0.9		40.13	2:10.81		
6068	Jessica	Flax	USA	4.9.90	2	MSR	Azusa	14	Apr
	13.20/1.5	1.71 13.69	24.26w/2.8	5.86w/2.1		39.69	2:13.81		
6051	Veronica	Torr	NZL	17.5.87	1		Brisbane	10	Jan
	13.61/-0.9	1.76 13.24	24.68/-0.6	6.22/-1.8		43.85	2:23.90		
6050	Verena	Preiner	AUT	1.2.95	7	EC	Amsterdam	9	Jul
	13.94/-0.9	1.71 13.51	24.64	5.68/-0.4		48.31	2:12.03		
6038	Annie	Kunz	USA	16.2.93	8	NC	Eugene	10	Jul
	13.56/-0.2	1.75 13.58	24.52/0.6	6.02/1.0		38.72	2:15.58		
	(50)								
6036	Lindsay	Schwartz	USA	23.4.90	9	NC	Eugene	10	Jul
	13.55/0.0	1.67 13.24	24.06/0.0	5.88/0.3		41.62	2:15.97		
6025	Sofía	Ifantídou	GRE	5.1.85	8	EC	Amsterdam	9	Jul
	13.79/1.2	1.65 13.23	26.08/0.2	6.04/0.6		56.36	2:18.59		
6024	Ellen	Sprunger	SUI	5.8.86	17	Hypo	Götzis	29	May
	13.45/1.5	1.71 12.82	23.34/1.3	5.95/0.3		38.61	2:17.03		
6022	Yusleidys	Mendieta	CUB	17.2.94	2	NC	La Habana	19	Mar
	13.50/0.0	1.72 13.86	23.63/0.6	6.09/-2.2		44.40	2:32.50		
6021	Yekaterina	Netsvetayeva	BLR	26.6.89	9	EC	Amsterdam	9	Jul
	14.20/1.2	1.71 14.82	25.61/-0.7	5.91w/3.2		46.36	2:13.72		
6020	Anna	Maiwald	GER	21.7.90	10	EC	Amsterdam	9	Jul
	13.54/1.2	1.68 13.73	24.38	5.93/1.3		41.87	2:14.92		
6011	Amalie Hammild	Iuel	NOR	17.4.94	1	Pac-12	Seattle	8	May
	13.81/-0.7	1.84 11.63	23.41/0.0	5.89/-1.1		29.51	2:06.34		
6010	Michelle	Zeltner	SUI	22.12.91	11	EC	Amsterdam	9	Jul
	13.93/-0.9	1.77 14.49	24.80/-0.7	6.10w/2.9		35.54	2:15.38		
5991	Taliyah	Brooks	USA	8.2.95	1	TexR	Austin	31	Mar
	13.16w/2.9	1.78 11.44	24.47w/3.1	6.21w/2.1		36.85	2:17.66		
5990	Allison	Reaser	USA	9.9.92	3	MSR	Azusa	14	Apr
	13.67/1.0	1.68 12.36	24.15/1.5	6.11/0.0		40.84	2:13.31		
	(50)								
5987	Portia	Bing	NZL	17.4.93	2		Firenze	30	Apr
	14.06/1.7	1.72 13.14	24.97/1.4	5.97/-0.5		43.87	2:12.47		
5985(w)	Payton	Stumbaugh	USA	29.11.95	2	TexR	Austin	31	Mar
	13.20w/2.9	1.69 11.52	23.76w/3.1	6.13/1.7		39.54	2:16.79		
5985	Austra	Skujyte	LTU	12.8.79	20	Hypo	Götzis	29	May
	14.34/0.6	1.77 16.13	26.22/-0.2	5.86/0.0		47.77	2:23.72		
5977	Kiani	Profit	USA	18.2.90	3		Santa Barbara	2	Apr
	13.79/-0.7	1.69 11.77	24.21/-0.5	5.93/0.0		42.17	2:08.77		
5970	Mariya	Gromysheva	RUS	10.1.90	1	NC	Cheboksary	22	Jun
	13.82/0.0	1.75 11.82	24.54	6.34/2.0		40.37	2:18.68		
5962	Alex	Gochenour	USA	17.2.93	4	NCAA	Eugene	11	Jun
	13.32/1.7	1.72 13.13	24.57/0.2	6.06w/3.1		37.70	2:18.14		
5960	Sarah	Lagger	AUT-Y	3.9.99	1	WJ	Bydgoszcz	22	Jul
	14.25/0.6	1.77 13.09	24.93/1.4	5.95/-0.8		43.65	2:15.99		
5956	Chari	Hawkins	USA	21.5.91	4		Santa Barbara	2	Apr
	13.30/-0.7	1.78 11.84	24.73/-0.5	6.04/0.3		36.74	2:15.01		
5952	Chelsea	Eades	USA	21.8.89	1		Chula Vista	29	May
	13.15/0.3	1.69 11.83	24.32/0.9	6.32w/2.6		35.19	2:15.65		
5952	Marthe	Koala	BUR	8.3.94	2	AfCh	Durban	25	Jun
	13.27/1.4	1.77 12.40	24.56	5.90/0.5		40.75	2:21.00		
	(60)								
5951	Tiffeny	Parker	USA	8.6.88	1		Dallas	5	Jun
	13.62/0.2	1.78 13.48	24.96w/2.2	6.07w/3.4		44.97	2:30.85		
5951	Morgan	Lake	GBR-J	12.5.97	6		Kladno	11	Jun
	14.42/1.1	1.91 12.83	25.64/1.7	6.04/0.2		40.08	2:19.06		
5948	Tatum	Souza	USA	20.4.92	4	MSR	Azusa	14	Apr
	13.72/0.7	1.74 13.53	24.99/1.5	5.76/1.7		41.42	2:14.23		
5944	Jessica	Zelinka	CAN	3.9.81	22	Hypo	Götzis	29	May
	13.36/0.5	1.62 13.54	24.44/0.1	5.77/-0.3		43.73	2:14.97		
5935	Georgia	Ellenwood	CAN	5.8.95	5	NCAA	Eugene	11	Jun
	13.81/1.4	1.75 12.36	24.60/0.2	6.11/0.4		39.67	2:17.29		
5925	Adriana	Rodríguez	CUB-Y	12.7.99	2	WJ	Bydgoszcz	22	Jul
	13.69/1.7	1.80 12.65	23.95/1.4	5.96/-1.6		37.36	2:23.27		
5918	Breanna	Leslie	USA	11.8.91	5	MSR	Azusa	14	Apr
	13.37/1.5	1.65 12.13	24.20/1.9	5.89/1.9		40.80	2:12.88		
5917	Jess	Lehman	USA	17.1.93	6	MSR	Azusa	14	Apr
	14.36/0.7	1.74 12.60	25.08w/2.8	5.77/0.0		46.54	2:12.17		

HEPTATHLON – 4 x 100 METRES

Mark	Name		Nat	Born	Pos	Meet	Venue	Date	
5913(w)	Jessica	Taylor	GBR	27.6.88	1	Eng Ch	Bedford	15 May	
	13.94w/3.1	1.66 12.63	23.67w/2.2	6.18w/2.4		37.28	2:15.62		
5890	Beatrice	Puiu	ROU	1.1.86	1	BalkC	Pitesti	26 Jun	
	14.26/-1.3	1.83 14.37	26.32/-1.5	6.00/0.0		41.78	2:22.25		
	(70)								
5886A	Ana Camila	Pirelli	PAR	10.1.89	3		Cali	26 Jun	
	13.38w/2.3	1.65 13.85	24.74w/3.5	5.57/-0.8		44.54	2:17.85		
5882	Megu	Hemphill	JPN	23.5.96	1	NC	Nagano	12 Jun	
	13.43/1.7	1.68 11.23	25.29/1.4	5.95/0.5		47.84	2:16.63		
5881	Hanne	Maudens	BEL-J	12.3.97	3	WJ	Bydgoszcz	22 Jul	
	14.75/1.0	1.77 11.49	24.58/1.4	6.34/0.3		40.29	2:15.70		
5877	Ida	Marcussen	NOR	1.11.87	9	Décastar	Talence	18 Sep	
	14.29/1.8	1.69 12.51	26.02/1.5	5.94/1.0		48.69	2:11.65		
5870	Nia	Ali	USA	23.10.88	3		Azusa	14 Apr	
	13.14/-0.6	1.81 12.28	24.45w/2.4	5.69/1.4		37.67	2:23.32		
5862	Lisa	Linnell	SWE	30.4.91	1		Marburg	22 May	
	14.66/-0.2	1.77 12.19	25.19/-0.9	6.09/0.6		41.18	2:12.79		
5852w	Makeba	Alcide	LCA	24.2.90	1	NC	Vieux-Fort	26 Jun	
	13.64w/3.5	1.82 12.91	24.46w/3.6	5.86w/2.9		36.15	2:24.78		
5851	Noor	Vidts	BEL	30.5.96	4		Firenze	30 Apr	
	13.98/1.8	1.78 12.93	24.83/1.5	5.93/-0.6		34.60	2:14.51		
5849	Yekaterina	Voronina	UZB	16.2.92	7		Kladno	11 Jun	
	14.89/-1.4	1.76 13.53	25.67/-2.7	5.81/-0.8		48.16	2:17.39		
5848	Judith	Nagy	ROU	14.9.89	5		Ratingen	26 Jun	
	14.11/-1.2	1.66 12.02	24.70/-0.2	6.26/0.4		43.24	2:18.65		
	(80)								
5842	Caroline	Klein	GER	4.3.96	1	NC-23	Kienbaum	14 Aug	
	13.68/0.3	1.75 12.64	25.08/-0.7	6.07/0.4		40.54	2:23.99		
5840	Bianca	Salming	SWE-J	22.11.98	4	WJ	Bydgoszcz	22 Jul	
	14.62/1.0	1.83 13.29	26.13/1.2	5.81/-0.1		44.39	2:17.69		
5835	Géraldine	Ruckstuhl	SUI-J	24.2.98	1	NC-j	Hochdorf	25 Sep	
	14.28/-0.7	1.75 13.41	25.25/-0.2	5.54/-0.1		51.63	2:25.02		
5833	Tamara	de Souza	BRA	8.9.93	1		São Bernardo do Campo	20 Mar	
	14.20/0.7	1.77 14.49	24.90	5.99/1.4		40.68	2:29.96		
5833	Paige	Knodle	USA	15.8.93	8	NCAA	Eugene	11 Jun	
	13.50/1.4	1.66 10.48	24.63/0.2	6.05/1.3		45.10	2:16.98		
5829	Ashtin	Zamzow	USA	13.8.96	4	TexR	Austin	31 Mar	
	13.80w/3.4	1.69 11.56	24.91w/3.9	5.73/-0.5		50.65	2:20.86		
5822	Caroline	Agnou	SUI	26.5.96	1	NC	Hochdorf	25 Sep	
	14.35/-0.1	1.63 13.53	24.99/0.4	6.07/0.1		45.84	2:20.24		
5808	Giovana	Cavaleti	BRA	13.1.89	2	NC	São Bernardo do Campo	1 Jul	
	14.13/-1.1	1.72 13.42	24.53/0.0	6.11/0.5		35.27	2:19.94		
5805	Alina	Fyodorova	UKR	31.7.89	9		Kladno	11 Jun	
	14.07/0.9	1.76 14.82	25.16/1.7	5.93/0.6		34.63	2:22.08		
5802	Lecabela	Quaresma	POR	26.12.89	1	NC	Maia	26 Jun	
	13.54w/3.1	1.64 14.29	25.34/0.8	5.97/-1.3		35.06	2:14.95		
	(90)								
5781	Jessamyn	Sauceda	MEX	22.5.89	5	TexR	Austin	31 Mar	
	14.21w/2.9	1.69 12.20	24.78w/3.8	6.24w/2.1		40.04	2:20.46		
5777(w)	Katie	Stainton	GBR	8.1.95	2	Eng Ch	Bedford	15 May	
	14.02w/3.1	1.75 11.42	24.25w/2.2	5.96w/2.5		38.45	2:19.50		
5777	Mari	Klaup	EST	27.2.90	24	Hypo	Götzis	29 May	
	13.94/0.3	1.80 12.74	25.94/-0.2	5.49/0.3		47.32	2:22.11		
5768	Amber	Metoyer	USA	7.9.83	8	MSR	Azusa	14 Apr	
	14.11/0.7	1.71 14.07	25.12w/2.8	5.82/0.1		41.62	2:24.02		
5768	Anaëlle	Nyabeu Djapa	FRA	15.9.92	3		Arona	5 Jun	
	13.78/-0.3	1.68 13.16	25.13/-1.1	5.99/0.7		36.96	2:17.37		
5766	Izabela	Mikolajczyk	POL	4.9.90	2		Hexham	10 Jul	
	14.12/1.6	1.75 11.61	24.45w/3.8	6.12/0.6		39.94	2:24.53		
5765	Mareike	Arndt	GER	29.1.92	1	NC	Kienbaum	14 Aug	
	13.73/1.2	1.60 14.08	24.45/-1.7	5.78/0.2		39.53	2:19.11		
5751	Yuki	Yamasaki	JPN	6.6.92	1		Nagasaki	22 May	
	14.05/0.2	1.69 11.84	24.52/-1.2	5.74/-2.3		43.66	2:18.29		
5735	Melissa-Maree	Farrington	AUS	28.5.95	1	ACC	Tallahassee	14 May	
	13.40/0.5	1.70 11.16	24.88/-0.3	5.88/0.8		40.51	2:20.16		
5735	Laura	Arteil	FRA	9.10.93	2	NC	Angers	25 Jun	
	14.30/0.7	1.60 13.69	25.09w/2.1	5.97/1.3		41.85	2:16.73		
	(100)								
5730	Elizabeth	Dadzie	GHA	21.3.93	25 Jun	5723	Lovisa	Östervall	SWE-J 9.3.97 22 Jul
5729	Clairwin	Dameus	USA	12.6.94	7 Apr	5715	Daryna	Sloboda	UKR 19.6.95 30 Apr
5724	Sami	Spenner	USA	21.3.91	10 Jul	5709	Odile	Ahouanwanou	BEN 5.1.91 25 Jun

HEPTATHLON – 4 x 100 METRES

Mark	Name		Nat	Born								

Mark	Name		Nat			Mark	Name		Nat		
5707	Jutta	Heikkinen	FIN	27.10.94	12 Jun	5547	Alysha	Burnett	AUS-J	4.1.97	2 Apr
5706	Purnima	Hembram	IND	10.7.93	29 Apr	5545	Elizabeth	Morland	IRL-J	3.3.98	29 May
5693	Natasha	Jackson	CAN	10.6.89	18 Jun	5542	Christina	Kiffe	GER	2.5.92	22 May
5685(w)	Estefanía	Fortes	ESP	25.4.87	26 Jun	5541A	Erika	McLeod	USA	17.5.95	12 May
5682	Louisa	Grauvogel	GER	28.9.96	22 May	5541	Yekaterina	Bolshova	RUS	4.2.88	22 Jun
5677	Leigha	Brown	USA	19.9.94	11 Jun	5541	Hertta	Heikkinen	FIN	27.10.94	28 Aug
5676	Grete	Sadeiko	EST	29.5.93	31 Mar	5540	Lisa	Maihöfer	GER-J	28.10.98	22 Jul
5668	Eri	Utsunomiya	JPN	11.4.93	1 May	5539	Elisa	Pineau	FRA-J	26.10.98	22 Jul
5667	Valérie	Reggel	SUI	3.1.87	9 Jul	5538w	Aaron	Howell	USA	3.10.95	14 May
5666	Karin	Strametz	AUT-J	18.4.98	22 May	5538	Vanessa	Grimm	GER-J	22.4.97	14 Aug
5658	Nada	Cheroudi	TUN	20.11.87	17 Mar	5537	Kiara	Reddingius	AUS	2.1.92	29 Sep
5657	Crystiane Tereza Barroso		BRA	26.8.88	1 Jul	5530	Madison	Hansen	USA	4.11.93	8 May
5648	Jo	Rowland	GBR	29.12.89	19 Jun	5528	Abrianna	Torres	USA	3.1.93	14 Apr
5643		Wang Qingling	CHN	14.1.93	17 Apr	5525	Emma	Oosterwegel	NED-J	29.6.98	15 May
5641	Andrea	Medina	ESP	26.4.96	24 Jul	5522	Fiorella	Chiappe	ARG	1.1.96	30 Mar
5639	Nina	Schultz	CAN-J	12.11.98	22 Jul	5522	Paola	Sarabia	ESP-J	23.5.98	5 Jun
5632	Marisa	De Aniceto	FRA	11.11.86	30 Apr	5509	Sarah	Chauchard	FRA	13.3.91	28 Apr
5627(w)	Jaclyn	Siefring	USA	.96	31 Mar	5508	Nicole	Wadden	CAN	.93	12 May
5626	Sandra	Jacmaire	FRA	4.1.91	25 Jun	5506	Emily	Godwin	USA	16.4.95	23 Apr
5625	Weronika	Grzelak	POL-J	19.3.97	8 May	5504	Kaymarie	Jones	JAM	3.3.90	30 Apr
5622	Hanna	Gorodskaya	BLR	31.1.93	25 Jun	5504	Anna-Lena	Obermaier	GER	10.7.96	14 Aug
5621	Yanira	Soto	ESP	21.8.88	5 Jun	5499	Margarita	Korneychuk	RUS	21.2.95	17 Jul
5615	Lucia	Mokrásová	SVK	27.3.94	31 Mar	5498	Kristina	Korolyova	RUS	6.11.90	9 Sep
5611	Lucija	Cvitanovic	CRO	17.9.91	13 May	5495	Kelsey	Herman	USA	15.6.96	13 May
5611	Silvia	Mrotzek	GER	7.5.90	22 May	5493	Carmen	Ramos	ESP-J	18.6.98	8 May
5604	Mariya	Pavlova	RUS	21.5.96	22 Jun	5493	Amanda Marie Grefstad Frøynes		NOR-J	13.9.98	22 Jul
5602	Alina	Korotchenko	RUS	24.7.94	22 Jun	5492	Maria	Huntington	FIN-J	13.3.97	29 May
5600	Xenia	Rahn	GER	9.3.91	12 Jun	5487	Saga	Kivekäs	FIN-J	6.5.97	28 Aug
5600	Sophie	Hamann	GER	12.8.96	14 Aug	5484	Frida	Thorsås	NOR	31.1.94	13 May
5597	Chie	Kiriyama	JPN	2.8.91	12 Jun	5483	Estefania	García	DOM	22.2.91	12 Jun
5594	Carly	Loeffel	USA	20.8.92	14 May	5482	Marijke	Esselink	NED-Y	22.6.99	11 Jun
5591	Esther	Turpin	FRA	29.4.96	25 Jun	5471	Natalie	Thompson	USA	30.9.93	14 May
5590	Yelena	Yermolina	RUS	2.2.89	22 Jun	5460	Anouk	Forafo	FRA	23.10.85	11 Jun
5586	Madelaine	Buttinger	CAN	3.11.89	14 Apr	5486	Riko	Nishimura	JPN	1.11.93	4 Sep
5582	Moe	Sasegbon	NGR	16.9.91	19 Jun	5451	Aleksandra	Butvina	RUS	14.2.86	9 Sep
5580	Alyssa	Thompson	USA	25.9.94	8 May	5447	Gavyn	Yetter	USA		16 Mar
5580	Jessica	Rautelin	FIN-J	16.1.97	28 Aug	5442	Kendall	Gustafson	USA	30.3.95	14 Apr
5577	Emma	Fitzgerald	USA-J	1.7.97	22 Jul	5442	Stanislava	Lajcáková	SVK	20.4.96	22 May
5572	Sophie	Stanwell	AUS	8.6.91	1 Apr	5442	Lea	Menzel	GER	10.1.96	30 Jul
5569	Riley	Cooks	USA	.94	25 Mar	5430	Sandra	Böll	DEN	6.11.94	31 Jul
5569	Teddi	Maslowski	USA	6.8.93	14 Apr	5428	Casidhe	Simmons	AUS	6.2.95	1 Apr
5568	Katarína	Kustárová	SVK	23.3.95	22 May	5428	Shelby	Bozner	USA		27 May
5567	Yelena	Molodchinina	RUS	16.4.91	22 May	5427	Taylor	Morgan	USA	21.6.94	8 May
5564	Liz	Harper	USA	1.5.95	8 May	5423	Sarah	Graham	USA	9.8.93	7 Apr
5561	Marion	Milan	FRA	5.1.95	25 Jun	5421	Iryna	Rofe-Beketova	UKR-J	18.9.98	24 Jul
5555	Houda Mohamed Atef		EGY	11.5.95	25 Jun	5418	Lisa	Steinlage	GER	22.6.93	14 Aug
5553	Rachael	McIntosh	CAN	17.1.91	14 Apr		(200)				
5552	Jessica	Green	USA	1.8.94	12 May	5411	Mareike	Rösing	GER-Y	31.12.99	22 May
						5408	Simone	Mrotzek	GER	7.5.90	22 May

Best at low altitude

6263	Evelis		Aguilar		COL	3.1.93	15	OG	Rio de Janeiro		13 Aug
	13.84/-0.2	1.72	13.30	23.90/0/9		5.83/1.1		42.70	2:13.26		
6003	Alysbeth		Félix		PUR	7.3.93	5		Kladno		11 Jun
	13.67/-0.4	1.79	11.66	24.49/1.4		6.20/0.9		37.49	2:14.01		
5748	Ana Camila		Pirelli		PAR	10.1.89	3	IbAm	Rio de Janeiro		16 May
	13.55/0.3	1.57	13.75	24.91/0.5		5.43/0.0		43.80	2:13.65		

JUNIORS

See main list for top 7 juniors. 10 performances by 8 women to 5700. Additional marks and further juniors:

Lagger	5776	25		Götzis			29 May				
Maudens	5709	8		Firenze			30 Apr				
5723	Lovisa		Östervall		SWE	9.3.97	5	WJ	Bydgoszcz		22 Jul
	13.97/1.7	1.80	10.39	24.88/1.4		6.09/-0.5		36.90	2:19.94		
5666	Karin		Strametz		AUT	18.4.98	1		Marburg		22 May
	14.23/-1.3	1.71	10.50	25.27/-1.1		6.15/0.9		39.28	2:15.93		
5639	Nina		Schultz (10)		CAN	12.11.98	6	WJ	Bydgoszcz		22 Jul
	14.13/1.7	1.77	11.53	24.79w/2.6		5.57/-0.4		42.84	2:24.74		
5625	Weronika		Grzelak		POL	19.3.97	1		Wroclaw		8 May
	14.64/0.9	1.80	11.48	25.44/0.6		6.18/0.1		37.77	2:25.30		
5580	Jessica		Rautelin		FIN	16.1.97	1	NC-j	Joensuu		28 Aug
	14.11w/3.1	1.66	12.64	24.99W/4.1		5.65/0.0		37.07	2:17.08		
5577	Emma		Fitzgerald		USA	1.7.97	8	WJ	Bydgoszcz		22 Jul
	14.36/0.6	1.71	10.47	25.68/1.2		5.74/-0.6		50.63	2:25.23		
5547	Alysha		Burnett		AUS	4.1.97	1	NC-j	Sydney		2 Apr
	15.02/-0.4	1.79	12.60	25.82/1.6		5.76/-0.4		48.71	2:36.26		
5545	Elizabeth		Morland		IRL	3.3.98	1	NC-j	Dublin		29 May
	13.92/0.6	1.70	10.53	24.95/0.6		5.75w/2.3		39.84	2:21.22		

WOMEN 2016

500   HEPTATHLON – 4 x 100 METRES

Mark	Name		Nat	Born	Pos	Meet	Venue	Date	
5540	Lisa	Maihöfer	GER	28.10.98	9	WJ	Bydgoszcz	22	Jul
	14.33/1.0	1.80 11.08 24.95w/2.6		5.79/-2.2		34.72	2:22.75		
5539	Elisa	Pineau	FRA	26.10.98	10	WJ	Bydgoszcz	22	Jul
	14.89/1.0	1.77 13.23 25.72/1.2		5.96/-0.3		35.94	2:25.56		
5538	Vanessa	Grimm	GER	22.4.97	1	NC-j	Kienbaum	14	Aug
	14.91/0.9	1.71 12.26 25.05/0.0		5.68/0.0		42.27	2:22.24		
5525	Emma	Oosterwegel	NED	29.6.98	1	NC-j	Alphen aan den Rijn	15	May
	14.46w/2.1	1.72 10.97 25.86/0.8		5.56/1.4		49.31	2:24.33		
5522	Paola	Sarabia (20)	ESP	23.5.98	1		Arona	5	Jun
	14.65/0.0	1.77 10.51 25.54/-1.4		5.94/0.0		36.38	2:17.11		

4 X 100 METRES RELAY

Mark	Nat	Names	Pos	Meet	Venue	Date	
41.01	USA	Bartoletta, Felix, Gardner, Bowie	1	OG	Rio de Janeiro	19	Aug
41.36	JAM	C.Williams, Thompson, Campbell-Brown, Fraser-Pryce	2	OG	Rio de Janeiro	19	Aug
41.62	GER	Pinto, Mayer, Lückenkemper, Haase	1		Mannheim	29	Jul
41.65	JAM	C.Williams, Thompson, Facey, Campbell-Brown	1	WK	Zürich	1	Sep
41.77	USA	Bartoletta, Felix, Gardner, Akinosun	1h3	OG	Rio de Janeiro	18	Aug
41.77	GBR	Philip, Henry, Asher-Smith, Neita	3	OG	Rio de Janeiro	19	Aug
41.79	JAM	Facey, Forbes, Campbell-Brown, Fraser-Pryce	1h1	OG	Rio de Janeiro	18	Aug
41.81	GBR	Philip, Henry, Asher-Smith, Neita	1	DL	London (OS)	22	Jul
41.93	GBR	Philip, Henry, Asher-Smith, Neita	2h1	OG	Rio de Janeiro	18	Aug
42.00	GER	Pinto, Mayer, Lückenkemper, Haase	1		Regensburg	5	Jun
42.04	NED	Samuel, Schippers, van Schagen, Sedney	1	EC	Amsterdam	10	Jul
42.10	GER	Pinto, Mayer, Lückenkemper, Haase	4	OG	Rio de Janeiro	19	Aug
42.12	TTO	Hackett, Ahye, Baptiste, St.Fort	5	OG	Rio de Janeiro	19	Aug
42.18	GER	Pinto, Mayer, Lückenkemper, Haase	1h2	OG	Rio de Janeiro	18	Aug
42.36	UKR	Povh, Pohrebnyak, Ryemyen, Bryzgina	6	OG	Rio de Janeiro	19	Aug
42.45	GBR	Philip, Asher-Smith, B Williams, Neita	2	EC	Amsterdam	10	Jul
42.48	GER	Pinto, Mayer, Lückenkemper, Haase	3	EC	Amsterdam	10	Jul
42.49	UKR	Povh, Pohrebnyak, Ryemyen, Bryzgina	3h1	OG	Rio de Janeiro	18	Aug
42.55	NGR	Asumnu, Okagbare, Madu, Osazuwa	2h2	OG	Rio de Janeiro	18	Aug
42.59	BRA	Farias, A C Silva, Venâncio, R Santos	2	DL	London (OS)	22	Jul
		(20 performances by teams from 9 nations)					
42.65	CHN	Yuan Qiqi, Wei Yongli, Ge Manqi, Liang Xiaojing	1		Beijing	18	May
42.67	GHA	Owusu-Agyapong, Acheampong, Gyaman, Amponsah	1		Cape Coast	8	Jul
42.70	CAN	Jacques, Emmanuel, George, Bingham	4h1	OG	Rio de Janeiro	18	Aug
42.84	FRA	Gnafoua, Distel-Bonnet, Paré, Akakpo	3	DL	London (OS)	22	Jul
42.87	SUI	Del Ponte, Atcho, E.Sprunger, Kora	2h1	EC	Amsterdam	9	Jul
42.92	KAZ	Kashafutdinova, Zyabkina, Rakhmanova, Safronova	1		Almaty	4	Jul
43.24	POL	Forkasiewicz, Popowicz-Drabala, Kielbasinska, Swoboda	7	EC	Amsterdam	10	Jul
43.28	ITA	Draisci, Hooper, Amidei, Alloh	3		Genève	11	Jun
43.28	CIV	Ziketh, Ta Lou, Gouenon, Gaha	2		Cape Coast	8	Jul
43.42	IND	Joseph, Jyothi, Nanda, Chand (20)	2		Almaty	4	Jul
43.43	PUR	Cruz, Morales, Cancel, Rodriguez	1		Road Town	3	Jul
43.45	IVB	Kelly, Harrigan, Malone, King	1		Road Town	3	Jul
43.61A	COL	Padilla, Rivera, Obregon, Palacios	1		Medellín	10	Jul
43.65	BAH	Seymour, Gaither, Lanece, Strachan	2h1		Nassau	10	Jul
43.66	RSA	Mamatu, Conley, Thomas, Horn	1	AfCh	Durban	24	Jun
43.81	JPN	Doi, Ichikawa, Seko, Fukushima	2		Beijing	18	May
43.87	CYP	O.Fotopoulou, Papaioannou, F.Fotopoulou, Artymata	5h1	EC	Amsterdam	9	Jul
43.94	VEN	Purica, Vargas, Villalobos, Soto	3	IbAm	Rio de Janeiro	16	May
44.14	ESP	M I Pérez, Jacob, E García, Lara	5h2	EC	Amsterdam	9	Jul
44.27	SWE	Östlund, Killander, Eurenius, P Nilsson (20)	6h1	EC	Amsterdam	9	Jul

444.29	IRL	9 Jul	44.51	GRE	25 Jun	44.65	SVK	4 Jun	45.02	RUS	20 Jul	45.09	CHI	16 May
44.34	HUN	9 Jul	44.54A	DOM	30 Apr	44.85	POR	17 Jun	45.04	NZL	22 Jan	45.12	FIN	4 Sep
44.39	AUS	20 Feb	44.63	CUB	29 Apr	44.99	CZE	20 May	45.05	NOR	1 Sep	45.22	TPE	2 May
												45.23	THA-J	5 Jun

Mixed nationalities
42.22   Gainesville (Henry GBR, Schippers NED, Onuora GBR, Bartoletta USA) 1   Gainesville   22 Apr
Best at low altitude
44.13   COL   Idrobo, Palacios, Obregon, Rivera   5   IbAm   Rio de Janeiro   16 May

JUNIORS

Mark	Nat	Names	Pos	Meet	Venue	Date	
43.69	USA	Tia Jones, T Bennett, K Harris, C Hill	1	WJ	Bydgoszcz	23	Jul
43.82	FRA	Murcia, Leduc, Peltier, Raffai	2	WJ	Bydgoszcz	23	Jul
44.18	GER	Fehm, Kwadwo, Frommann, Butzek	3	WJ	Bydgoszcz	23	Jul
44.30	JAM	Hines, Moody, Reid, Burton	1	Carifta	St. George	27	Mar
44.55	POL	Adamek, Kotwila, Pietrzak, Swoboda	3h2	WJ	Bydgoszcz	22	Jul
44.56	GBR	Brier, McLennaghan, Agyapong, Marrs	2		Mannheim	25	Jun

4x100m – 4x200m – 4 x 400m RELAY

Mark		Name	Nat	Born	Pos	Meet	Venue	Date	
44.72	NED				1		Leiden	11	Jun
44.82	IRL	Scott, Mawdsley, Akpe-Moses, Neville			5	WJ	Bydgoszcz	23	Jul
44.95	ITA	Dosso, Bonicalza, Niotta, Oki			6	GGala	Roma	2	Jun
44.99	ESP	Verdú, Petrirena, Sevilla, Gómez			6	WJ	Bydgoszcz	23	Jul

4 X 200 METRES RELAY

1:30.56	Pure Athletics Bowie, K Brown, Townsend all USA, Shaunae Miller BAH	1	FlaR	Gainesville	2	Apr
1:31.17	USA McGrone, Whitney, Duncan, C Jones	1	PennR	Philadelphia	30	Apr
1:31.30	Louisiana State Un USA Harvey, Johnson, Misher, Martin	1	TexR	Austin	2	Apr
1:31.34	JAM McLaughlin-Whilby, Stewart, Segree, Le-Roy	2	PennR	Philadelphia	30	Apr
1:31.49	Star Athletics Ahouré CIV, Whitney. McGrone, Love	2	FlaR	Gainesville	2	Apr

4 X 400 METRES RELAY

3:19.06	USA	Okolo 50.3, Hastings 49.2, Francis 49.82, Felix 49.66	1	OG	Rio de Janeiro	20	Aug
3:20.34	JAM	McPherson 50.6, McLaughlin-Whilby 49.6, Jackson 49.47, Williams-Mills 50.82	2	OG	Rio de Janeiro	20	Aug
3:21.42	USA	Okolo 50.7, Ellis-Watson 50.4, McCorory 49.68, Francis 50.53	1h1	OG	Rio de Janeiro	19	Aug
3:22.38	JAM	Day 51.4, McLaughlin-Whilby 49.9, Gordon 50.49, Williams-Mills 50.58	1h2 OG		Rio de Janeiro	19	Aug
3:24.54	UKR	Logvynenko 52.2, Bibik 50.9, Melnyk 51.36, Zemlyak 50.02	2h1	OG	Rio de Janeiro	19	Aug
3:24.81	GBR	Diamond 51.7, Onuora 50.3, Massey 51.43, Ohuruogu 51.34	2h2	OG	Rio de Janeiro	19	Aug
3:24.94	CAN	Muir 51.3, A Brown 50.8, Montcalm 51.94, Watson 50.75	3h2	OG	Rio de Janeiro	19	Aug
3:25.05	GBR	Diamond 51.8e, Onuora 50.7e, Doyle 50.99, Bundy-Davies 51.42	1	EC	Amsterdam	10	Jul
3:25.16	ITA	Chigbolu 52.1, Spacca 51.3, Folorunso 51.44, Grenot 50.18	4h2	OG	Rio de Janeiro	19	Aug
3:25.34	POL	Holub 51.7, Wyciszkiewicz 50.9, Baumgart 51.37, Swiety 51.28	3h1	OG	Rio de Janeiro	19	Aug
3:25.48	USA	(Un. of Arkansas) Birch, Harper, Dobbins, C Watson 50.04	1h2	NCAA-W	Lawrence	28	May
3:25.71	AUS	Thornton 51.7, Rubie 51.1, Sargent-Jones 51.79, Mitchell 50.97	4h1	OG	Rio de Janeiro	19	Aug
3:25.88	GBR	Doyle 52.5, Onuora 51.4, Diamond 51.15, Ohuruogu 50.72	3	OG	Rio de Janeiro	20	Aug
3:25.96	FRA	Anacharsis 52.6e, Ntiamoh 51.5e, Gayot 51.82, Guei 49.92	2	EC	Amsterdam	10	Jul
3:26.02	GER	Müller 52.1, Möhlenkamp 50.9, Hoffmann 52.8, Spelmeyer 50.83	5h2	OG	Rio de Janeiro	19	Aug
3:26.18	FRA	Anacharsis 52.4, Ntiamoah 52.2, Gayot 51.76, Guei 49.76	5h1	OG	Rio de Janeiro	19	Aug
3:26.28	USA	(Un. of Florida) Reynolds, Jefferson, Barnett, C Francis	1	FlaR	Gainesville FL	2	Apr
3:26.36	BAH	L Clarke 52.4, Strachan 51.9, Cox 50.91, Amertil 51.07	6h2	OG	Rio de Janeiro	19	Aug
3:26.42	GBR	Doyle 51.3e, Adeoye 51.5e, Massey 51.40, Bundy-Davies 52.07	1h1	EC	Amsterdam	9	Jul
3:26.43	CAN	Muir 52.0, A Brown 51.1, Montcalm 52.74, Watson 50.56	4	OG	Rio de Janeiro	20	Aug
	(20 performances by teams from 11 nations)							
3:26.98	NED	Ghafoor 52.4, Lisanne de Witte 51.0, van Leuveren 50.99, Laura de Witte 52.49	6h1	OG	Rio de Janeiro	19	Aug
3:27.88	IND	Sheoran, Luka, Poovamma, Thomas	1		Bengaluru	10	Jul
3:28.49	RSA	Griesel, Nel, Palframan, Semenya	1	AfCh	Durban	26	Jun
3:29.08	ROU	Pastor 52.7e, Ionita 52.6e, Belgyan 51.99, Miklos 51.71	4h2	EC	Amsterdam	9	Jul
3:29.94	NGR	Omotoso, George, Ajayi, P George	2	AfCh	Durban	26	Jun
3:30.11	CUB	Veitía 52.8, Casanova 52.3, R Gómez 52.31, Bonne 52.66	8h2	OG	Rio de Janeiro	19	Aug
3:30.21	KEN	Shikanda, Maiyo, Thomas, Wambui	3	AfCh	Durban	26	Jun
3:30.27	BRA	J Sousa 53.9, Coutinho 51.2, L de Souza 51.91, J de Lima 54.11	8h1	OG	Rio de Janeiro	19	Aug
3:30.37	TTO	Bellille, Selvon, McKnight, Dom.WIlliams	2		Nassau	10	Jul
	(20)							
3:30.91	JPN	Aoyama, Ishizuka, Ichikawa, Kira	1		Osaka	10	Jul
3:31.23	BLR	Kyevich 53.4e, Yurenya 53.7e, Khairullina 52.21, I Usovich 51.85	4h1	EC	Amsterdam	9	Jul
3:31.54	BOT	Botlogetswe, Jele, Galefele, Seleka	4	AfCh	Durban	26	Jun
3:31.66	SVK	Salgovicová 53.9e, Stuková 53.3e, Bezeková 52.63, Putalová 51.73	5h1	EC	Amsterdam	9	Jul
3:31.66	GRE	Daláka 54.2e, A Vasilíou 51.9e, Mourtá 51.19	6h2	EC	Amsterdam	9	Jul
3:31.73	NOR	Hauge 53.3e, Jensen 52.6e, Hansen 53.53, Kloster 52.59	6h1	EC	Amsterdam	9	Jul
3:32.48	POR	Mentai 54.6e, Martins 53.1e, Azevedo 51.44, Évora 53.23	7h1	EC	Amsterdam	9	Jul
3:33.57	ESP	Bueno 53.8e, Bokesa 51.8e, Camblor 53.96, Ussía 53.89	7h2	EC	Amsterdam	9	Jul
3:33.93	CHN	Pan Gaoqin, Wang Huan, Huang Yan, Cheng Chong	1		Kimchun	3	Jul
3:34.02	IRL	Denny 53.5e, Healy 52.7e, Bromell 52.82, McCallion	8h2	EC	Amsterdam	9	Jul
	(30)							

3:34.96 BEL	18 Jun	3:37.38 FIN	18 Jun	3:37.72 TUR	25 Jun	3:39.30 DOM	8 Apr	3:39.75A COL	24 Apr
3:36.38 CZE	23 Jul	3:37.62 RUS	20 Jul	3:38.89 SRI	11 Feb	3:39.73 SWE	4 Sep		

Mixed nationalities

3:25.59	USA (Un.of Texas) C Gordon JAM, Golden, Ariel Jones, Okolo 49.86	2h2	NCAA-W	Lawrence	28	May
3:36.68	Enka SC (TUR) B Ylldirim, Razor ROU, E Ylldirim, Lalova-Collio BUL	1		Mersin	24	May

JUNIORS

3:29.11	USA	L Irby 53.7, A Cockrell 50.9, K Winters 52.04, S Watson 52.47	1	WJ	Bydgoszcz	24	Jul
3:31.01	JAM	Kalawan 53.2, James 51.2, S-A Williams 54.69, Bromfield 51.92	2	WJ	Bydgoszcz	24	Jul
3:32.25	CAN	Santiago 53.6, Best 53.7, McDonald 52.84, Tachinski 52.11	3	WJ	Bydgoszcz	24	Jul
3:32.63	GER	Demes 54.2, Richter 52.6, Reinert 54.07, N Mergenthaler 51.76	4	WJ	Bydgoszcz	24	Jul
3:33.95	UKR	Kachur, Bryzhina, Stavnycha, Koba 51.92	5	WJ	Bydgoszcz	24	Jul

WOMEN 2016

RELAYS – 3000m – 5000m – 10,000 METRES WALK

Mark	Name		Nat	Born	Pos	Meet	Venue	Date	
3:36.38	CZE	Vondrová, Kruoparová, Slavíková, Seidlová			5h1	WJ	Bydgoszcz	23	Jul
3:36.95	POL	Martyna, Lozowska, Weglarz, Karzmarek			6	WJ	Bydgoszcz	24	Jul
3:37.67	JPN	(H.Osaja Unv.(			1		Okayama	2	Aug
3:37.83	AUS	Thornton, Cason, Blakey, Billings			6h1	WJ	Bydgoszcz	23	Jul
3:38.23	ITA	Mangione, Troiani, Putti, Folorunso			2h2	WJ	Bydgoszcz	23	Jul
3:41.36	IVB	Lacey, De Freitas, Moses, Wraner			1		Clermont	28	May

4 X 100 METRES HURDLES

Mark	Name				Pos	Meet	Venue	Date	
53.21	Louisiana State Un (Phillips, Brisco, Chase CAN, G Gordon JAM)				1		Baton Rouge	30	Apr
53.77	Florida All Stars				1	FlaR	Gainesville	2	Apr

3000 METRES WALK

Mark	Name	Surname	Nat	Born	Pos	Meet	Venue	Date	
11:50.30	Marina	Pandakova	RUS	1.3.89	1		Moskva	28	Jul
12:00.10	Svetlana	Vasilyeva	RUS	24.7.92	2		Moskva	28	Jul
12:05.91	Mariya	Ponomaryova	RUS	18.6.95	3		Moskva	28	Jul
12:06.05	Raquel	González	ESP	16.11.89	1		Mataró	6	Jul
12:21.0+	Eleonora	Giorgi	ITA	14.9.89	1	in 5k	Milano	22	Apr
12:23.42	Taika	Nummi	FIN-J	12.10.97	1		Espoo	6	Jun
12:24.70	Bethan	Davies	GBR	7.11.90	1		Cardiff	11	Jun
12:28.97	Sofiya	Brodatskaya	RUS	4.10.95	4		Moskva	28	Jul
12:29.00	María José	Poves	ESP	16.3.78	2		Mataró	6	Jul
12:36.32	Emilie	Menuet	FRA	27.11.91	1		Blois	22	May

Indoors

12:20.77	Brigita	Virbalyte-Dimsiene	LTU	1.2.85	1		Vilnius	30	Jan
12:25.23	Ana	Cabecinha	POR	29.4.84	1	NC	Pombal	20	Feb
12:33.75	Maria	Michta-Coffey	USA	23.6.86	1	NC	Portland	12	Mar
12:34.51	Neringa	Aidietyte	LTU	5.6.83	2		Vilnius	30	Jan
12:35.17	Emilie	Menuet	FRA	27.11.91	1		Eaubonne	24	Jan

5000 METRES WALK

Mark	Name		Surname	Nat	Born		Pos	Meet	Venue	Date	
20:31.46	Eleonora		Giorgi	ITA	14.9.89		1		Milano	22	Apr
21:02.78			Giorgi				1		Trento	26	Jul
21:09.04	Raquel		González	ESP	16.11.89		1		Barcelona (S)	30	Jun
21:09.24			R González				1		Alcobendas	18	Jun
21:14.85+			R González				1	in 10kW	Gijón	23	Jul
21:19.3	María José		Poves	ESP	16.3.78		1		Castellón	11	Jun
21:19.46	Bekki		Smith	AUS	25.11.86		1		Melbourne	5	Mar
21:19.55	Regan		Lamble	AUS	14.10.91		2		Milano	22	Apr
21:21.00	Kumiko		Okada	JPN	17.10.91		1		Kumagaya	21	May
21:22.91			Poves				2		Alcobendas	18	Jun
21:31.09	Julia		Takacs	ESP	29.6.89		3		Alcobendas	18	Jun
21:39.03	Katie	Hayward	AUS-Y	23.7.00	23 Oct		21:44.82	Tanya	Holliday	AUS	21.9.88	5 Mar
21:39.9	Agnese	Pastare	LAT	27.10.88	11 Jun		21:46.96	Ai	Michiguchi	JPN	3.6.88	11 Jul
21:40.45	Valentina	Trapletti	ITA	12.7.85	24 Sep		21:49.27	Chahinez	Nasri	TUN	3.6.96	8 Jun
21:40.71	Mária	Pérez	ESP	29.4.96	18 Jun		21:51.63	Inês	Henriques	POR	1.5.80	18 Jun
							21:51.91	Emilie	Menuet	FRA	27.11.91	25 Jun

Indoors

20:15.6	Yelena	Lashmanova	RUS	9.4.92	1		Saransk	30	Dec
20:23.2	Yekaterina	Medvedyeva	RUS	29.3.94	2		Saransk	30	Dec
20:48.9	Sofiya	Brodatskaya	RUS	4.10.95	3		Saransk	30	Dec
21:31.9	Olga	Shargina	RUS	24.7.96	1-j		Chelyabinsk	6	Jan
21:46.21	Irina	Kashina	UKR	27.9.91	1		Sumy	19	Dec

JUNIORS

21:39.03	Katie	Hayward	AUS-Y	23.7.00	1		Brisbane	23	Oct
21:40.871	N.Sch	Canberra		2 Dec					
22:14.52	Nanako	Fujii	JPN-Y	7.5.99	2		Kitakami	10	Dec
22:14.94	Teresa	Zurek	GER	29.7.98	1	NC	Bülhertal	11	Jun
22:18.94	Taika	Nummi	FIN	12.10.97	1	NC-j	Lappeenranta	5	Aug

10 KILOMETRES WALK

See also 10km times in 20k list below

Mark	Name	Surname	Nat	Born	Pos	Meet	Venue	Date	
41:59	Marina	Pandakova	RUS	1.3.89	1		Podolsk	8	May
42:14.12t	Raquel	González	ESP	16.11.89	1	NC	Gijón	23	Jul
42:35.69	Beatriz	Pascual	ESP	9.5.82	2	NC	Gijón	23	Jul
42:38	Nadezhda	Sergeyeva	RUS	6.11.94	2		Podolsk	8	May
42:55.85	Déspina	Zapounídou	GRE	5.10.85	1		Dráma	23	Apr
43:13		R González			1		Viladecans	24	Jan
43:22		Pascual			2		Viladecans	24	Jan
43:29.57t	Ana	Cabecinha	POR	29.4.84	1	NC	Maia	25	Jun

10 KILOMETRES WALK

Mark	Name		Nat	Born	Pos	Meet	Venue	Date	
43:32+	Svetlana	Vasilyeva	RUS	24.7.92	1=	in 10k	Cheboksary	25	Jun
43:48.08t	Bekki	Smith	AUS	25.11.86	1	NC	Sydney	1	Apr
43:51+	Eleonora	Giorgi	ITA	14.9.89	3	in 20k	Roma	7	May
43:52.80t	Inês	Henriques	POR	1.5.80	1		Vagos	19	Mar
43:54		Qieyang Shenjie			1		Suzhou	28	Sep
43:55.70t	Julia	Takacs	ESP	29.6.89	3	NC	Gijón	23	Jul
(14/11)									
44:07+		Yang Jiayu	CHN	18.2.96	8	in 20k	Roma	7	May
44:07+	Alyona	Khramova	RUS	18.8.93	5=	in 20k	Cheboksary	25	Jun
44:08	Nadiya	Borovska	UKR	25.2.81	1		Lutsk	26	Jun
44:09+	Maria	Michta-Coffey	USA	23.6.86	1	in 20k	St. Louis	3	Apr
44:09.84t	Kumiko	Okada	JPN	17.10.91	1		Isahaya	11	Dec
44:13.83t	Mária	Pérez	ESP	29.4.96	4	NC	Gijón	23	Jul
44:18+		Nie Jingjing	CHN	1.3.88	10	in 20k	Roma	7	May
44:25		Ma Yiming	CHN-J	10.9.97	1-j	NGP	Taicang	23	Apr
44:29		Ma Zhenxia	CHN-J	1.8.98	1-j	NGP	Huangshan	5	Mar
44:30		Zhang Lifang	CHN-J	6.12.97	2-j	NGP	Huangshan	5	Mar
(20)									
44:33		Wang Yingliu	CHN	1.3.92	2r2		Suzhou	28	Sep
44:33.87t	Tanya	Holliday	AUS	21.9.88	2	NC	Sydney	1	Apr
44:34.60 t	Rachel	Seaman	CAN	14.1.86	1		San Diego	2	Jan
44:38	Monika	Vaiciukeviciute	LTU	3.4.96	1		Grodno	8	Oct
44:41		Ma Li	CHN-Y	15.1.00	3-j	NGP	Huangshan	5	Mar
44:41	Valentina	Trapletti	ITA	12.7.85			Rieti	26	Jun
44:41.8	Grace Njue	Wanjiru	KEN	10.1.79	1		Thika	5	Mar
44:49		Yang Liujing	CHN-J	22.8.98	4-j	NGP	Huangshan	5	Mar
44:50		Cun Hailu	CHN-J	15.8.97	5-j	NGP	Huangshan	5	Mar
44:52		Yin Hang	CHN-J	7.2.97	2-j	NGP	Taicang	23	Apr
(30)									
44:55	Sae	Matsumoto	JPN	15.5.93	1		Tokyo	1	Jan
44:55.51t	Laura	García-Caro	ESP	16.4.95	1	Med-23	Radès	4	Jun
44:56	Mária	Czaková	SVK	2.10.88			Olomouc	25	Mar
44:59	Bethan	Davies	GBR	7.11.90	1	Eng Ch	Coventry	6	Mar
44:59+	Mirna	Ortiz	GUA	28.2.87		in 20k	Dudince	19	Mar
45:01	Mária	Gáliková	SVK	21.8.80			Borský Mikuláš	14	May
45:01	Taika	Nummi	FIN-J	12.10.97	1	NC-j	Turku	12	Jun
45:02	Chahinez	Nasri	TUN	3.6.96	1-j		La Coruña	28	May
45:03.0t	Olga	Yeliseyeva	RUS-J	6.9.98	1	NC-wj	Sochi	28	Feb
45:05.0t	Yana	Smerdova	RUS-J	7.2.98	2	NC-wj	Sochi	28	Feb
(40)									
45:05.09t	Mariya	Losinova	RUS-J	2.3.97	1	NC-j	Cheboksary	25	Jun
45:06.15t	Viktória	Madarász	HUN	12.5.85	1		Székesfehérvár	11	Sep
45:12		Xue Ke	CHN-J	14.3.98	1-j	NGP	Shangrao	8	Apr
45:16.26A	Erika	Morales	MEX		1		Tlaxcala	18	Dec
45:23.85t	Noemi	Stella	ITA-J	2.2.97	2	WJ	Bydgoszcz	19	Jul
45:24		Xiao Han	CHN-J	12.11.98	6-j	NGP	Huangshan	5	Mar
45:26	Lidia	Sánchez-Puebla	ESP	17.7.96	2		Getafe	18	Nov
45:27+	Olga	Shargina	RUS	24.7.96		in 20k	Cheboksary	25	Jun
45:28	Valeria	Ortuño	MEX-J	27.5.98	3	WCp-j	Roma	7	May
45:30+	Paola	Pérez	ECU	21.12.89		in 20k	Roma	7	May
(50)									
45:33	Yana	Smerdova	RUS		3		Mis	8	May
45:33	Brigita	Virbalyte-Dimsiene	LTU	1.2.85	1		Druskininkai	10	Sep
45:33.69t	Yehualye	Belete	ETH-J	31.7.98	3	WJ	Bydgoszcz	19	Jul
45:38.20A	Alegna	González	MEX-J	.97	2		Tlaxcala	18	Dec
45:40.57 t	Miranda	Melville	USA	20.3.89	2		San Diego	2	Jan
45:44		Li Leilei	CHN	18.8.89	7r2		Suzhou	28	Sep
45:44.53t	Ainhoa	Pinedo	ESP	17.2.83	7	NC	Gijón	23	Jul
45:48+	Anastasiya	Yatsevich	BLR	18.1.85	9	Apr	46:07+	Violaine	Averous	FRA	15.3.85	7	May
45:48		Ge Sangzhuoma	CHN-J	16.7.98	8	Sep	46:08+	Alana	Barber	NZL	8.7.87	20	Mar
45:51.27t		Jiang Shanshan	CHN-J	28.2.97	19	Jul	46:08.91t	Maria	Larios	ESP	29.10.92	23	Jul
45:54	Tamara	Havrylyuk	UKR	14.12.95	26	Jun	46:10+		Nguyen Thi Thanh Phuc	VIE	12.8.90	20	Mar
45:54	Yuliya	Turova	RUS-J	9.6.97	3	Sep	46:11		Ji Yefang	CHN	4.3.96	28	Sep
45:55+	Aynalem	Eshetu	ETH	5.2.92	7	May	46:13.44t	Edna	Barros	POR	18.12.96	25	Jun
45:59+	Susana	Feitor	POR	28.1.75	19	Mar	46:15+	Olena	Shumkina	UKR	24.1.88	7	May
46:02		Mao Yanxue	CHN	15.2.94	28	Sep	46:15.24t	Karla	Jaramillo	ECU-J	21.1.97	19	Jul
46:02.41A	Gabriela	González	MEX	10.4.91	18	Dec	46:17		Xiao Xianghua	CHN-J	19.2.97	8	Sep
46:02.60A	Andrea	Martínez	MEX	4.5.88	18	Dec	46:18,91t	Amandine	Marcou	FRA	26.4.92	6	Nov
46:03.44t	Daniela	Cardoso	POR	15.12.91	15	May	46:19.49t	Yukiho	Mizoguchi	JPN-J	6.12.97	19	Jul
46:04+	Monika	Kapera	POL	15.2.90	19	Mar	46:20+	Kristina	Saltanovic	LTU	20.2.75	9	Apr
46:04		Yang Weiwei	CHN-Y	3.8.99	9	Sep	46:20	Olena	Mizernyuk	UKR	23.11.95	26	Jun
46:05.07A	Vivian	Castillo	MEX-J	10.6.98	18	Dec	46:20.5t	Kseniya	Buldygina	RUS-J	20.9.98	28	Feb

WOMEN 2016

10 – 20 KILOMETRES WALK

Mark		Name		Nat	Born	Pos	Meet	Venue		Date
46:20.69t	Agnieszka	Szwarnóg		POL	28.12.86	28 May		46:24.71t Evelin Inga	PER-J 16.4.98	19 Jul
46:22.0t	Lana	Ryazanova		RUS-J	11.8.98	28 Feb		46:25.69tAPaola Pérez	ECU 21.12.89	26 Mar
46:22.71t	Rachelle	De Orbeta		PUR-Y	27.3.00	19 Jul		46:26.0t Darya Melenteva	RUS-J 7.4.98	28 Feb
46:23.72t	Amanda	Cano		ESP	19.8.94	23 Jul		46:29 Zoe Hunt	AUS-J 4.12.97	21 Feb
46:24	Anastasiya	Kalashnikova		RUS-J	29.6.97	3 Sep		46:29 Lucie Pelantová	CZE 7.5.86	10 Jun

Best track times

45:01.32t	Érica		de Sena	BRA	3.5.85	1	IbAm	Rio de Janeiro	15 May
45:18.45t			Ma Zhenxia	CHN-J	1.8.98	1	WJ	Bydgoszcz	19 Jul
45:26.88t	Chiaki		Asada	JPN	21.1.91	2		Osaka	24 Sep
45:28.58t	María José		Poves	ESP	16.3.78	5	NC	Gijón	23 Jul
45:31.76t	Masumi		Fuchise	JPN	2.9.86	3		Osaka	24 Sep
45:44.33t	Valeria		Ortuño	MEX-J	27.5.98	4	WJ	Bydgoszcz	19 Jul
45:54.90t	Chahinez	Nasri	TUN	3.6.96	4 Jun	46:18.67t Lidia	Sánchez-Puebla	ESP	17.7.96	4 Jun
45:57.22t	Rena	Goto	JPN	6.9.95	11 Jun	46:19.97t Ai	Michiguchi	JPN	3.6.88	24 Sep
46:04.74t	Taika	Nummi	FIN-J	12.10.97	19 Jul	46:22.43A Valeria	Ortuño	MEX-J	27.5.98	18 Dec

JUNIORS

See main list for top 17 juniors. 10 performances by 10 women to 45:05. Further juniors:

45:48		Ge Sangzhuoma	CHN	16.7.98	2-j	NGP	Huhehaote	8 Sep
45:51.27t		Jiang Shanshan	CHN	28.2.97	5	WJ	Bydgoszcz	19 Jul
45:54	Yuliya	Turova	RUS	9.6.97	1-j		Kostroma	3 Sep

Best track

| 46:04.74t | Taika | Nummi | FIN | 12.10.97 | 6 | WJ | Bydgoszcz | 19 Jul |
| 46:22.43A | Valeria | Ortuño | MEX | 27.5.98 | 4 | | Tlaxcala | 18 Dec |

20 KILOMETRES WALK

20k	10k		Name	Nat	Born	Pos	Meet	Venue	Date
1:24:58	43:32	Yelena	Lashmanova	RUS	9.4.92	1	NC	Cheboksary	25 Jun
1:25:54		Olga	Kaniskina	RUS	19.1.85	1	NC-w	Sochi	27 Feb
1:25:56			Liu Hong	CHN	12.5.87	1	OT	Huangshan	6 Mar
1:26:17	43:51	María Guadalupe	González	MEX	9.1.89	1	WCp	Roma	7 May
1:26:40		Yekaterina	Medvedyeva	RUS	29.3.94	2	NC-w	Sochi	27 Feb
1:26:45	44:07		Medvedyeva			2	NC	Cheboksary	25 Jun
1:26:46	44:07	Mariya	Ponomaryova	RUS	18.6.95	3	NC	Cheboksary	25 Jun
1:26:47	44:07	Klavdiya	Afanasyeva	RUS	15.1.96	4	NC	Cheboksary	25 Jun
1:26:49	43:51		Qieyang Shenjie	CHN	11.11.90	2	WCp	Roma	7 May
1:27:18		Marina	Pandakova	RUS	1.3.89	3	NC-w	Sochi	27 Feb
1:27:18	43:56	Érica	de Sena (10)	BRA	3.5.85	3	WCp	Roma	7 May
1:27:52	44:18		Qieyang Shenjie			1		Rio Maior	9 Apr
1:27:58		Svetlana	Vasilyeva	RUS	24.7.92	4	NC-w	Sochi	27 Feb
1:27:58			Afanasyeva			5	NC-w	Sochi	27 Feb
1:27:59	44:03		Pandakova			5	NC	Cheboksary	25 Jun
1:28:03	43:56	Elisa	Rigaudo	ITA	17.6.80	4	WCp	Roma	7 May
1:28:05	44:58	Eleonora	Giorgi	ITA	14.9.89	1		Dudince	19 Mar
1:28:07			Lu Xiuzhi	CHN	26.10.93	2	OT	Huangshan	6 Mar
1:28:12			Yang Jiayu	CHN	18.2.96	3	OT	Huangshan	6 Mar
1:28:16			Qieyang Shenjie			4	OT	Huangshan	6 Mar
1:28:20	44:21		Giorgi			2		Rio Maior	9 Apr
1:28:21	44:29		Wang Na	CHN	29.5.95	1		Nomi	20 Mar
1:28:22	44:59		de Sena			2		Dudince	19 Mar
1:28:30	44:26		Qieyang Shenjie			1		La Coruña	28 May
1:28:31	45:00		Rigaudo			3		Rio Maior	9 Apr
1:28:35	45:24		Liu Hong			1	OG	Rio de Janeiro	19 Aug
1:28:36	44:07		Lu Xiuzhi			5	WCp	Roma	7 May
1:28:37	45:24		M G Gonzalez			2	OG	Rio de Janeiro	19 Aug
1:28:40	45:01		de Sena			4		Rio Maior	9 Apr
1:28:40	44:33	Ana	Cabecinha (30/17)	POR	29.4.84	6	WCp	Roma	7 May
1:28:43	44:28		Liang Rui	CHN	18.6.94	2	1 AsiC	Nomi	20 Mar
1:29:00	44:33	Inês	Henriques	POR	1.5.80	8	WCp	Roma	7 May
1:29:01	44:35	Raquel	González (20)	ESP	16.11.89	9	WCp	Roma	7 May
1:29:03	45:24	Antonella	Palmisano	ITA	6.8.91	4	OG	Rio de Janeiro	19 Aug
1:29:27	45:02	Beatriz	Pascual	ESP	9.5.82	1	NC	Motril	28 Feb
1:29:30	44:59	Mirna	Ortiz	GUA	28.2.87	4		La Coruña	28 May
1:29:31	44:54	Sandra	Arenas	COL	17.9.93	10	WCp	Roma	7 May
1:29:33	44:33	Regan	Lamble	AUS	14.10.91	11	WCp	Roma	7 May
1:29:35		Déspina	Zapounídou	GRE	5.10.85	1	NC	Mégara	27 Mar
1:29:35	45:20	Alejandra	Ortega	MEX	8.7.94	1		Podébrady	9 Apr
1:29:38	43:59	Kimberley	García	PER	19.10.93	12	WCp	Roma	7 May

20 KILOMETRES WALK

Mark		Name		Nat	Born	Pos	Meet	Venue	Date	
1:29:38			Nie Jingjing	CHN	1.3.88	2	NGP	Huhehaote	9	Sep
1:29:40	44:25	Kumiko	Okada	JPN	17.10.91	1	NC	Kobe	21	Feb
		(30)								
1:29:47	44:53	Julia	Takacs	ESP	29.6.89	13	WCp	Roma	7	May
1:29:49	44:07	Bekki	Smith	AUS	25.11.86	14	WCp	Roma	7	May
1:29:53			Ni Yuanyuan	CHN	6.4.95	4	NGP	Huhehaote	9	Sep
1:29:56	44:34	Tanya	Holliday	AUS	21.9.88	15	WCp	Roma	7	May
1:29:57		Nadezhda	Sergeyeva	RUS	6.11.94	6	NC-w	Sochi	27	Feb
1:30:05		Tatyana	Mineyeva	RUS	10.8.90	7	NC-w	Sochi	27	Feb
1:30:21	45:00	Anezka	Drahotová	CZE	22.7.95	6		Dudince	19	Mar
1:30:27	44:57	Agnieszka	Dygacz	POL	18.7.85	1		Naumburg	22	May
1:30:33	45:15	Ángela	Castro	BOL	21.2.93	17	WCp	Roma	7	May
1:30:34	44:34	Inna	Kashyna	UKR	27.9.91	18	WCp	Roma	7	May
		(40)								
1:30:36	45:20	Paulina	Buziak	POL	16.12.86	2		Podébrady	9	Apr
1:30:43		Grace Njue	Wanjiru	KEN	10.1.79	1	AfCh	Durban	26	Jun
1:30:44	45:00	Chiaki	Asada	JPN	21.1.91	4		Nomi	20	Mar
1:30:47	45:23	Viktória	Madarász	HUN	12.5.85	1	NC	Békéscsaba	30	Apr
1:30:48	45:03	Brigita	Virbalyte-Dimsiene	LTU	1.2.85	8		Rio Maior	9	Apr
1:30:49	45:00	Maria	Michta-Coffey	USA	23.6.86	5		Nomi	20	Mar
1:30:50	45:20	Agnieszka	Szwarnóg	POL	28.12.86	3		Podébrady	9	Apr
1:30:51			Wang Yingliu	CHN	1.3.92	1		Taicang	23	Apr
1:30:52	45:20	Mária	Gáliková	SVK	21.8.80	4		Podébrady	9	Apr
1:30:52	45:34	Maritza Rafaela	Poncio	GUA	3.12.94	2		Alytus	10	Jun
		(50)								
1:30:56	45:34	Antigóni	Drisbióti	GRE	21.3.84	3		Alytus	10	Jun
1:30:56			Hou Yongbo	CHN	15.9.94	5	NGP	Huhehaote	9	Sep
1:31:00	45:01	Rena	Goto	JPN	6.9.95	6		Nomi	20	Mar
1:31:10	45:01	María José	Poves	ESP	16.3.78	9		La Coruña	28	May
1:31:18			Yang Mingxia	CHN	13.1.90	6	NGP	Huhehaote	9	Sep
1:31:20	45:27	Neringa	Aidietyte	LTU	5.6.83	7		Dudince	19	Mar
1:31:28	45:33	Valentina	Trapletti	ITA	12.7.85	4		Alytus	10	Jun
1:31:31	45:08	María Guadalupe	Sánchez	MEX	4.8.95	10		La Coruña	28	May
1:31:32	44:42	Nadiya	Borovska	UKR	25.2.81	20	WCp	Roma	7	May
1:31:33	45:53	Rachel	Tallent	AUS	20.2.93	1	Oce Ch	Adelaide	21	Feb
		(60)								
1:31:38	45:46	Emilie	Menuet	FRA	27.11.91	12		La Coruña	28	May
1:31:42	45:50	Miranda	Melville	USA	20.3.89	7		Nomi	20	Mar
1:31:45	45:02	Masumi	Fuchise	JPN	2.9.86	8		Nomi	20	Mar
1:31:46			La Mao	CHN	17.12.96	7	NGP	Huhehaote	9	Sep
1:31:51	44:38	Ai	Michiguchi	JPN	3.6.88	9		Nomi	20	Mar
1:31:52	44:59	Sandra	Galvis	COL	28.6.86	9		Dudince	19	Mar
1:31:53		Anastasiya	Yatsevich	BLR	18.1.85	1	NCp	Brest	2	Apr
1:31:58		Yehualye	Beletew	ETH-J	31.7.98	2	AfCh	Durban	26	Jun
1:32:02			Ji Yefang	CHN	4.3.96	7	OT	Huangshan	6	Mar
1:32:02		Sofiya	Brodatskaya	RUS	4.10.95	1-22		Kostroma	3	Sep
		(70)								
1:32:18			He Qin	CHN	23.3.92	2	NGP	Shangrao	8	Apr
1:32:19			Xie Lijuan	CHN	14.5.93	2		Taicang	23	Apr
1:32:22		Olga	Shargina	RUS	24.7.96	2-22		Kostroma	3	Sep
1:32:36	45:53	Katarzyna	Golba	POL	21.12.89	6		Podébrady	9	Apr
1:32:39		Natalya	Tarasova	RUS	7.5.92	8	NC-w	Sochi	27	Feb
1:32:39			Li Leilei	CHN	18.8.89	9	NGP	Huhehaote	9	Sep
1:32:42		Tamara	Havrylyuk	UKR	14.12.95	1	NC	Sumy	11	Jun
1:32:45	45:28	Yeseida	Carrillo	COL	22.10.93	15		La Coruña	28	May
1:32:48	46:23	Alana	Barber	NZL	8.7.87	25	WCp	Roma	7	May
1:32:52	46:07	Ainhoa	Pinedo	ESP	17.2.83	1		Cáceres	20	Mar
		(80)								
1:32:54	45:57	Claudia	Stef	ROU	25.2.78	10		Dudince	19	Mar
1:32:54	46:14	Arabelly	Orjuela	COL	24.7.88	17		La Coruña	28	May
1:32:57			Yang Lei	CHN	29.11.95	1	NGP	Taicang	23	Apr
1:32:59		Nadezhda	Mokeyeva	RUS	10.1.96	7	NC	Cheboksary	25	Jun
1:33:04	45:48	Mária	Czaková	SVK	2.10.88	7		Podébrady	9	Apr
1:33:05		Alina	Tsviliy	UKR	18.9.94	2	NC	Sumy	11	Jun
1:33:15	45:25	Wendy	Cornejo	BOL	7.1.93	27	WCp	Roma	7	May
1:33:20	46:13	Jéssica	Hancco	PER	10.9.95	28	WCp	Roma	7	May
1:33:23	45:44	Claire	Tallent	AUS	7.6.81	2		Naumburg	22	May
1:33:23			Sun Huanhuan	CHN	15.3.90	2	NGP	Changbaishan	4	Jun
		(90)								
1:33:24		Laura	García-Caro	ESP	16.4.95	10		Rio Maior	9	Apr
1:33:25		Paola	Pérez	ECU	21.12.89	1	NCp	Sucua	5	Mar

WOMEN 2016

20 KILOMETRES WALK

Mark		Name		Nat	Born	Pos	Meet	Venue	Date	
1:33:25		Olena	Mizernyuk	UKR	23.11.95	3	NC	Sumy	11	Jun
1:33:30		Sibilla	Di Vincenzo	ITA	22.1.83	1	NC	Cassino	20	Mar
1:33:32		Monika	Kapera	POL	15.2.90	8		Podébrady	9	Apr
1:33:32	45:27	Jeon Yong-eun		KOR	24.5.88	31	WCp	Roma	7	May
1:33:34		Susana	Feitor	POR	28.1.75	2	NC	Batalha	28	Feb
1:33:39	45:56	Nicole	Colombi	ITA	29.12.95	9		Podébrady	9	Apr
1:33:41		Li Ping		CHN	7.1.94	10	OT	Huangshan	6	Mar
1:33:41	46:08	Gabriela (100)	González	MEX	10.4.91	17		La Coruña	28	May
1:33:43		Wang Yalan		CHN	19.2.93	9 Sep				
1:33:44		Mária	Pérez	ESP	29.4.96	20 Mar				
1:33:45	45:48	Stephanie Stigwood		AUS	21.10.90	21 Feb				
1:33:46		Daniela	Cardoso	POR	15.12.91	28 Feb				
1:33:47		Panayióta	Tsinopoúlou	GRE	16.10.90	7 May				
1:33:48		Bethan	Davies	GBR	7.11.90	5 Jun				
1:33:53	45:56	Lee Jung-eun		KOR	13.9.94	20 Mar				
1:33:58	45:48	Laura	Polli	SUI	7.9.83	9 Apr				
1:33:59		Violaine	Averous	FRA	15.3.85	13 Mar				
1:34:00		Monika	Vaiciukeviciute	LTU	3.4.96	9 Apr				
1:34:01		Mariavittoria Becchetti		ITA	12.12.94	9 Apr				
1:34:06		Mao Yanxue		CHN	15.2.94	9 Sep				
1:34:07		Ana	Rodean	ROU	23.6.84	20 Mar				
1:34:13		Alyona	Khramova	RUS	18.8.93	27 Feb				
1:34:14	46:20	Kristina	Saltanovic	LTU	20.2.75	9 Apr				
1:34:14		Ma Faying		CHN	30.8.93	9 Sep				
1:34:21	46:24	Kaori	Kawagoe	JPN	30.5.95	21 Feb				
1:34:21		Yang Peili		CHN	7.8.94	9 Sep				
1:34:21		Zhang Xuhong		CHN	2.1.94	9 Sep				
1:34:25		Magaly	Bonilla	ECU	8.2.92	7 May				
1:34:25		Yin Hang		CHN-J	7.2.97	9 Sep				
1:34:29	46:24	Rei	Inoue	JPN	23.7.91	21 Feb				
1:34:31	46:29	Halyna	Yakovchuk	UKR	21.2.92	9 Apr				
1:34:33		Regina	Rykova	KAZ	19.12.91	20 Mar				
1:34:35		Chahinez Nasri		TUN	3.6.96	13 Mar				
1:34:37		Polina	Repina	KAZ	29.6.90	28 May				
1:34:41		Tang Caihong		CHN	29.4.96	23 Apr				
1:34:47	46:05	Lee Da-seul		KOR	8.11.96	20 Mar				
1:34:47		Sae	Matsumoto	JPN	15.5.93	20 Mar				
1:34:47		Andrea	Martínez	MEX	4.5.88	28 May				
1:34:48		Chen Chen		CHN	25.8.95	23 Apr				
1:34:49		Anél	Oosthuizen	RSA	22.4.95	9 Apr				
1:34:49		Katarzyna Zdzieblo		POL	28.11.96	16 Apr				
1:34:49	46:29	Lucie	Pelantová	CZE	7.5.86	10 Jun				
1:34:50		Mayra Carolina Herrera		GUA	20.12.88	9 Apr				
1:34:50	45:40	Askale	Tiksa	ETH	21.7.94	7 May				
1:34:51		Agnese	Pastare	LAT	27.10.88	19 Mar				
1:34:51		Mariya	Filyuk	UKR	14.10.95	11 Jun				
1:34:53		Khushbir Kaur		IND	9.7.93	27 Feb				
1:34:59		Nadezda	Dorozhuk	BLR	23.1.90	2 Apr				
1:34:59		Kristina	Mikhaylova	RUS	16.10.92	25 Jun				
1:35:07	46:30	Janeth	Guamán	ECU	15.1.88	7 May				
1:35:08		Lizbeth	Silva	MEX	30.9.89	23 Apr				
1:35:10		Barbara	Kovács	HUN	26.7.93	19 Mar				
1:35:10		Viktoryia	Rashchupkina	BLR	23.5.95	23 Jun				
1:35:13		Diana	Aydosova	KAZ	5.5.95	9 Apr				
1:35:28		Valentyna Myronchuk		UKR	10.8.94	7 May				
1:35:30		Zhao Huimin		CHN	12.10.93	6 Mar				
1:35:33		Olena	Shumkina	UKR	24.1.88	6 Mar				
1:35:33		Zivile	Vaiciukeviciute	LTU	3.4.96	19 Mar				
1:35:33		Rita	Récsei	HUN	30.1.96	30 Apr				
1:35:37		Marina	Ignatova	RUS	6.6.95	27 Feb				
1:35:45		Lidia	Sánchez-Puebla	ESP	17.7.96	20 Mar				
1:35:45		Andreea	Arsine	ROU	14.9.88	9 Apr				
1:35:50		Gabriela	Cornejo	ECU	11.4.89	3 Apr				
1:35:53		Gao Ni		CHN	14.9.91	9 Sep				
1:35:54		Florida	Miniyanova	KAZ	1.7.92	4 Jul				
1:35:56		Maria	Larios	ESP	29.10.92	28 May				
1:35:57		Sapna		IND	2.1.88	20 Mar				
1:36:00		Stefany	Coronado	BOL	16.9.96	28 May				
1:36:01		Mihaela	Acatrinei	ROU	27.2.95	20 Mar				
1:36:05		Anastasiya Rarovskaya		BLR	12.11.96	23 Jun				
1:36:12		Zhao Qianyuan		CHN	11.3.95	6 Mar				
1:36:14		Nozomi	Yagi	JPN	4.11.94	21 Feb				
1:36:19		Zhang Xin		CHN	17.8.89	9 Sep				
1:36:23		Claudia	Balderrama	BOL	13.11.83	10 Jun				
1:36:25		Remi	Okubo	JPN	22.2.95	21 Feb				
1:36:25		Emilia	Lehmeyer	GER-J	11.4.97	8 Oct				
1:36:27		Yesenia	Miranda	ESA	26.3.94	7 May				
1:36:34		Zhao Wenli		CHN	11.12.96	8 Apr				
1:36:40		Valeria	Ortuño	MEX-J	27.5.98	22 May				
1:36:43	45:34	Yukiho	La Mao	JPN-J	6.12.97	21 Feb				
1:36:43				CHN	7.6.96	9 Sep				
1:36:49		Jessica	Ching Siu Nga	HKG	11.2.87	22 May				
1:36:52		Ekateríni	Theodoropoúlou	GRE	1.12.93	27 Mar				
1:36:58		Mar	Juárez	ESP	27.9.93	28 May				
1:36:59		Amanda	Cano	ESP	19.8.94	28 May				
1:37:02		Xu Liqin		CHN	6.2.90	9 Sep				
1:37:14		Mizuka	Takayama	JPN	21.11.96	23 Oct				
1:37:18		Mylène	Ortiz	FRA	15.2.79	13 Mar				
1:37:19		Dong	Genmiao	CHN	16.7.94	9 Sep				
1:37:23		Amandine	Marcou	FRA	26.4.92	13 Mar				
1:37:28		Anastasiya Taushkanova		RUS	25.3.96	25 Jun				
1:37:31		Li Qiuye		CHN	2.12.93	23 Apr				
1:37:31		Chiaki	Yamato	JPN	20.11.90	23 Oct				
1:37:32		Zhu Kunyu		CHN	14.5.96	23 Apr				
1:37:40		Mihaela	Puscasu	ROU	22.1.95	20 Mar				
1:37:40		Cisiane	Lopes	BRA	17.2.83	3 Apr				
1:37:40		Mara	Ribeiro	POR	11.5.95	9 Apr				
1:37:42		Serena	Sonoda	JPN	.96	20 Mar				
1:37:42		Erin	Gray	USA	15.5.85	3 Apr				
1:37:42		Zhang Yan		CHN-J	3.1.97	9 Sep				
1:37:53		Wang Lixue		CHN	15.12.96	9 Sep				
1:37:55		Anastasiya Chernova		RUS	16.4.96	27 Feb				
1:37:57		Anett	Torma	HUN	2.4.84	30 Apr				
1:37:58		Evaggelía	Xinoú	GRE	22.11.81	10 Jun				
1:37:59		Jamy	Franco	GUA	1.7.91	28 May				
1:38:00		Lucie (198)	Auffret	FRA	6.7.88	13 Mar				

Best track time
1:36:48.6A Sandra Arenas COL 17.9.93 23 Apr

JUNIORS

Mark		Name		Nat	Born	Pos	Meet	Venue	Date	
1:34:25		Yin Hang		CHN	7.2.97	16	NGP	Huhehaote	9	Sep
1:36:25		Emilia	Lehmeyer	GER	11.4.97	1		Andernach	8	Oct
1:36:40		Valeria	Ortuño	MEX	27.5.98	6		Naumburg	22	May
1:36:43	45:34	Yukiho	Mizoguchi	JPN-	6.12.97	9	NC	Kobe	21	Feb
1:37:42		Zhang Yan		CHN	3.1.97	29	NGP	Huhehaote	9	Sep
1:38:59		Giada Francesca	Ciabinbi	ITA	8.6.97	1	NC-j	Cassino	20	Mar
1:39:14		Teresa	Zurek	GER	29.7.98	2		Andernach	8	Oct
1:39:25		Saskia	Feige	GER	13.8.97	3		Andernach	8	Oct

Drugs disqualification
| 1:25:59 | | Liu Hong # | | | | (1) | WCp | Roma | 7 | May |
| 1:27:43 | | Liu Hong # | | | | (1) | | La Coruña | 28 | May |

25/30 KILOMETRES WALK

| 1:56:12 | 2:19:43 | Eleonora | Giorgi | ITA | 14.9.89 | 1 | | Catania | 31 | Jan |

50 KILOMETRES WALK

Mark		Name	Nat	Born	Pos	Meet	Venue	Date	
4:34:01		Zhou Kang	CHN	24.12.89	1	NGP	Huangshan	6	Mar
4:38:56		Wang Dan	CHN	11.1.95	2	NGP	Huangshan	6	Mar
4:39:09	Kseniya	Radko	UKR	18.8.94	1	NC	Ivano-Frankivsk	16	Oct
4:42:15	Erin	Talcott	USA	21.5.78	1		Timaru	13	Nov
4:44:35	Vasylyna	Vitovshchyk	UKR	30.4.90	2	NC	Ivano-Frankivsk	16	Oct
4:46:50		Wang Lixue	CHN	15.12.96	1	NGP	Huhehaote	10	Sep
4:47:28		Li Maocuo	CHN	20.10.92	2	NGP	Huhehaote	10	Sep
4:47:59		Xia Kaili	CHN	16.3.96	3	NGP	Huhehaote	10	Sep
4:48:12		Ma Lingyu	CHN	6.1.95	3	NGP	Huangshan	6	Mar
4:49:54		Ma Faying	CHN	30.8.93	1	NGP	Changbaishan	5	Jun
4:55:34		Zhu Chunyan	CHN	3.6.92	4	NGP	Huhehaote	10	Sep
4:56:44		Yang Shuqing	CHN	30.8.96	5	NGP	Huhehaote	10	Sep
5:00:02		Guo Runfeng	CHN	9.5.95	4	NGP	Changbaishan	5	Jun

ALL-TIME WORLD INDOOR SPRINT LISTS – MEN

60 METRES

Mark	Name		Nat	Born	Pos	Meet	Venue	Date	
6.39	Maurice	Greene	USA	23.7.74	1rA		Madrid	3 Feb	98
6.41	Andre	Cason	USA	20.1.69	1		Madrid	14 Feb	92
6.42	Dwain	Chambers ¶	GBR	5.4.78	1s2	El	Torino	7 Mar	09
6.43	Tim	Harden ¶	USA	27.1.74	2	WI	Maebashi	7 Mar	99
6.44	Asafa	Powell	JAM	23.11.82	1h5	WI	Portland	18 Mar	16
6.45	Bruny	Surin	CAN	12.7.67	1		Liévin	13 Feb	93
6.45A	Leonard	Myles-Mills	GHA	5.9.73	1	WAC	Air Force Academy	20 Feb	99
6.45A	Terrence	Trammell	USA	23.11.78	1		Pocatello	17 Feb	01
6.45	Justin	Gatlin ¶	USA	10.2.82	1	NC	Boston	1 Mar	03
6.45	Ronald	Pognon	FRA	16.11.82	1		Karlsruhe	13 Feb	05
6.45A	Trell	Kimmons ¶	USA	13.7.85	1	NC	Albuquerque	26 Feb	12
6.45A	Ronnie	Baker	USA	15.10.93	1	NC	Albuquerque	5 Mar	17
6.45	Christian	Coleman	USA	6.3.96	1	NCAA	College Station	11 Mar	17
6.46	Jon	Drummond	USA	9.9.68	2rA	Spark	Stuttgart	1 Feb	98
6.46A	Marcus	Brunson	USA	24.4.78	1		Flagstaff	30 Jan	99
6.46	Jason	Gardener	GBR	17.9.75	3	WI	Maebashi	7 Mar	99
6.46	Tim	Montgomery ¶	USA	28.1.75	2	WI	Lisboa	11 Mar	01
6.46	Leonard	Scott	USA	19.1.80	1		Liévin	26 Feb	05
6.47	Linford	Christie ¶	GBR	2.4.60	1		Liévin	19 Jan	95
6.47	Shawn	Crawford	USA	14.1.78	1	NC	Boston (R)	28 Feb	04
6.47	Dwight	Phillips	USA	1.10.77	1		Madrid	24 Feb	05
6.47	Lerone	Clarke	JAM	12.6.81	1	GP	Birmingham	18 Feb	12
6.47	James	Dasaolu	GBR	5.9.87	1h2	GP	Birmingham	15 Feb	14
6.47	Kim	Collins	SKN	5.4.76	1	Pedros	Lódz	17 Feb	15
6.47	Trayvon	Bromell	USA	10.7.95	1	WI	Portland	18 Mar	16
6.48	eight men								

60 METRES HURDLES

Mark	Name		Nat	Born	Pos	Meet	Venue	Date	
7.30	Colin	Jackson	GBR	18.2.67	1		Sindelfingen	6 Mar	94
7.33	Dayron	Robles	CUB	19.11.86	1		Düsseldorf	8 Feb	08
7.36r?	Greg	Foster	USA	4.8.58	1	Sunk	Los Angeles	6 Jan	87
7.42					1		San Sebastián	15 Mar	91
7.36	Allen	Johnson	USA	1.3.71	1	WI	Budapest	6 Mar	04
7.36	Terrence	Trammell	USA	23.11.78	2	WI	Doha	14 Mar	10
7.37	Roger	Kingdom	USA	26.8.62	1		Pireás	8 Mar	89
7.37	Anier	García	CUB	9.3.76	1		Pireás	9 Feb	00
7.37	Tony	Dees	USA	6.8.63	1		Chemnitz	18 Feb	00
7.37	David	Oliver	USA	24.4.82	1	Spark	Stuttgart	5 Feb	11
7.38	Mark	Crear	USA	2.10.68	1		Sindelfingen	8 Mar	98
7.38	Reggie	Torian	USA	22.4.75	1	NC	Atlanta	27 Feb	99
7.40A	Dexter	Faulk	USA	14.4.84	1h3	NC	Albuquerque	25 Feb	12
7.41	Courtney	Hawkins	USA	11.7.67	2	WI	Barcelona	12 Mar	95
7.41	Falk	Balzer	GER	14.12.73	1h2		Chemnitz	29 Jan	99
7.41		Liu Xiang	CHN	13.7.83	1	GP	Birmingham	18 Feb	12
7.41	Dimitri	Bascou	FRA	20.7.87	1	ISTAF	Berlin	13 Feb	16
7.41	Omar	McLeod	JAM	25.4.94	1	WI	Portland	20 Mar	16
7.42	Igor	Kazanov	LAT	24.9.63	1		Moskva	25 Feb	89
7.42	Anthony	Jarrett	GBR	13.8.68	2		Liévin	19 Feb	95
7.42	Ladji	Doucouré	FRA	28.3.83	1		Liévin	26 Feb	05
7.43	Duane	Ross	USA	5.12.72	1	NC	Atlanta	28 Feb	98
7.43A	Aries	Merritt	USA	24.7.85	1	NC	Albuquerque	26 Feb	12

Mark	Name		Nat	Born	Pos	Meet	Venue	Date
7.43	Andrew	Pozzi	GBR	15.5.92	1		Birmingham	18 Feb 17
7.44	Mark	McKoy	CAN	10.10.61	1		Sindelfingen	3 Mar 91
7.44	Elmar	Lichtenegger	AUT	25.5.74	2	EI	Wien	2 Mar 02
7.44	Larry	Wade ¶	USA	22.11.74	2	Tyson	Fayetteville	15 Feb 03
7.44	Yevgeniy	Borisov	RUS	7.3.84	1	EICp	Moskva	16 Feb 08
7.44	Petr	Svoboda	CZE	10.10.84	1	NC	Praha (Stro)	27 Feb 10
7.45	four men							

WOMEN – 60 METRES

Mark	Name		Nat	Born	Pos	Meet	Venue	Date
6.92	Irina	Privalova	RUS	12.11.68	1		Madrid	11 Feb 93
6.95	Gail	Devers	USA	19.11.66	1	WI	Toronto	12 Mar 93
6.95	Marion	Jones ¶	USA	12.10.75	1		Maebashi	7 Mar 98
6.96	Merlene	Ottey	JAM	10.5.60	1		Madrid	14 Feb 92
6.96	Ekateríni	Thánou	GRE	1.2.75	1	WI	Maebashi	7 Mar 99
6.97	Laverne	Jones-Ferrette #	ISV	16.9.81	1	Spark	Stuttgart	6 Feb 10
6.98	Shelly-Ann	Fraser-Pryce	JAM	27.12.86	1	WI	Sopot	9 Mar 14
.98	Elaine	Thompson	JAM	28.6.92	1		Birmingham	18 Feb 17
6.99	Murielle	Ahouré	CIV	23.8.87	1	GP	Birmingham	16 Feb 13
7.00	Nelli	Cooman	NED	6.6.64	1	EI	Madrid	23 Feb 86
7.00	Veronica	Campbell-Brown	JAM	15.5.82	1	WI	Doha	14 Mar 10
7.00	Dafne	Schippers	NED	15.6.92	1	ISTAF	Berlin	13 Feb 16
7.00	Barbara	Pierre	USA	28.4.87	1	NC	Portland	12 Mar 16
7.01	Savatheda	Fynes	BAH	17.10.74	2s1	WI	Maebashi	7 Mar 99
7.01	Me'Lisa	Barber	USA	4.10.80	1	WI	Mosvka	10 Mar 06
7.01	Lauryn	Williams	USA	4.10.80	2	WI	Mosvka	10 Mar 06
7.02	Gwen	Torrence	USA	12.6.65	1	Mill	New York	2 Feb 96
7.02	Christy	Opara-Thompson ¶	NGR	2.5.70	2		Gent	12 Feb 97
7.02	Chioma	Ajunwa ¶	NGR	25.12.70	1		Liévin	22 Feb 98
7.02	Philomenah	Mensah	CAN	11.5.75	1h2	WI	Maebashi	7 Mar 99
7.02A	Carmelita	Jeter	USA	24.11.79	1	NC	Albuquerque	28 Feb 10
7.02	Tianna	Madison/Bartoletta	USA	30.8.85	1		Fayetteville	11 Feb 12
7.03	Anelia	Nuneva	BUL	30.6.62	2s1	EI	Liévin	22 Feb 87
7.04	Marita	Koch	GDR	18.2.57	1	NC	Senftenberg	16 Feb 85
7.04	Silke	Möller'	GDR	20.6.64	1s1	EI	Budapest	6 Mar 88
7.04	Carlette	Guidry	USA	4.9.68	2	NC	Atlanta	4 Mar 95
7.04	Petya	Pendareva	BUL	20.1.71	1s1	WI	Lisboa	11 Mar 01
7.04	Mariya	Bolikova	RUS	23.5.77	1		Samara	4 Feb 06
7.05	Chandra	Sturrup	BAH	12.9.71	1	WI	Lisboa	11 Mar 01

60 METRES HURDLES

Mark	Name		Nat	Born	Pos	Meet	Venue	Date
7.68	Susanna	Kallur	SWE	16.2.81	1		Karlsruhe	10 Feb 08
7.69	Lyudmila	Narozhilenko ¶	RUS/SWE	21.4.64	1	NC	Chelyabinsk	4 Feb 90
7.72	Lolo	Jones	USA	5.8.82	1	WI	Doha	13 Mar 10
7.73	Cornelia	Oschkenat'	GDR	29.10.61	1		Wien	25 Feb 89
7.73	Sally	Pearson	AUS	19.9.86	1	WI	Istanbul	10 Mar 12
7.74	Yordanka	Donkova	BUL	28.9.61	1	NC	Sofia	14 Feb 87
7.74	Michelle	Freeman	JAM	5.5.69	1		Madrid	3 Feb 98
7.74	Gail	Devers	USA	19.11.66	1h1	NC	Boston	1 Mar 03
7.74A	Kendra	Harrison	USA	18.9.92	1h2	NC	Albuquerque	5 Mar 17
7.75					1		Lexington	21 Jan 17
7.75	Bettine	Jahn	GDR	3.8.58	1	EI	Budapest	5 Mar 83
7.75	Perdita	Felicien	CAN	29.8.80	1	WI	Budapest	7 Mar 04
7.76	Gloria	Siebert'	GDR	13.1.64	1		Sindelfingen	5 Feb 88
7.76	Brianna	Rollins	USA	18.8.91	1	NC	Portland	12 Mar 16
7.77	Zofia	Bielczyk	POL	22.9.58	1	EI	Sindelfingen	1 Mar 80
7.78	Brigita	Bukovec	SLO	21.5.70	1		Stuttgart	7 Feb 99
7.79A	Kellie	Wells	USA	16.7.82	1	NC	Albuquerque	27 Feb 11
7.79	Pamela	Dutkiewicz	GER	28.9.91	1	NC	Leipzig	18 Feb 17
7.80	Carolin	Nytra	GER	26.2.85	1	EI	Paris (B)	4 Mar 11
7.80	Tiffany	Porter	USA/GBR	13.11.87	2	EI	Paris (B)	4 Mar 11
7.80A	Nia	Ali	USA	23.10.88	1	NC	Albuquerque	23 Feb 14
7.81	Jackie	Joyner-Kersee	USA	3.3.62	1		Fairfax	5 Feb 89
7.82	Yelizaveta	Chernyshova	RUS	26.1.58	1	WI	Budapest	5 Mar 89
7.82	Monique	Ewanje-Epée	FRA	11.7.67	1	6N	Paris	23 Feb 91
7.82	Glory	Alozie	ESP	30.12.77	1h1		Madrid	16 Feb 99
7.82	Olga	Shishigina ¶	KZK	23.12.68	1		Liévin	21 Feb 99
7.82	Linda	Ferga-Khodadin	FRA	24.12.76	3	WI	Budapest	7 Mar 04
7.82	Priscilla	Lopes-Schliep	CAN	26.8.82	1	Spark	Stuttgart	6 Feb 10
7.82A	Janay	DeLoach	USA	12.10.85	2	NC	Albuquerque	23 Feb 14
7.82	Christina	Manning	USA	29.5.90	1		Athlone	15 Feb 17
7.82A	Jasmin	Stowers	USA	23.9.91	2	NC	Albuquerque	5 Mar 17

MEN'S INDEX 2016

Athletes included are those ranked in the top 100s at standard (World Championships) events (plus shorter lists for 1000m, 1M, 2000m and 3000m). Those with detailed biographical profiles are indicated in first column by:
* in this year's Annual, ^ featured in a previous year's Annual.

Name		Nat	Born	Ht/Wt	Event	2016 Mark	Pre-2016 Best
Abadía	Antonio	ESP	2.7.90	180/72	1500	3:37.24	3:41.68- 12
					5000	13:12.68	13:26.98- 15
Abate	Emanuele	ITA	8.7.85	190/78	110h	13.54	13.28- 12
Abbas	Ali Khamis	BRN	30.6.95	185/75	400	44.36	45.65- 13
Abbas	Mohammad Nasser	QAT	.96		400	45.59A	46.78- 13
Abda	Harun	USA	1.1.90	178/64	800	1:45.77	1:45.55- 14
Abdallah	Abubaker Haydar	QAT	28.8.96	181/68	800	1:45.28	1:47.06- 15
Abdelrahman ¶	Ihab	EGY	1.5.89	194/96	JT	81.51, 87.37 drugs dq	89.21- 14
Abdi	Bashir	BEL	10.2.89	168/59	5000	13:14.92	13:06.10- 15
					10k	28:01.49	27:36.40- 14
Abdullah	Bilal	USA	6.10.93	185/75	LJ	7.98i	7.65i, 7.45- 15
Abele	Arthur	GER	30.7.86	184/80	Dec	8605	8477- 14
Abera	Melaku	ETH	20.4.94	177/61	Mar	2:09:27	-0-
Abera	Tesfaye	ETH	31.3.92	192/68	Mar	2:04:24	2:09:46- 15
Abinet	Abiyot	ETH	10.5.89	170/52	10k	27:45.04	-0-
Abraham	Tadesse	SUI	12.8.82	178/61	Mar	2:06:40	2:07:45- 13
Abramchuk	Mikhail	BLR	15.11.92	192/110	SP	20.18i, 20.13	19.88- 14
Abromavicius	Aleksas	LTU	6.12.84	197/115	DT	62.59	63.32- 10
Adamczyk	Patryk	POL	5.1.94	188/76	400h	49.72	50.89- 13
Adams	Antoine	SKN	31.8.88	180/79	100	10.18, 10.08w	10.01, 10.00w- 13
Adams	Antoine	SKN	31.8.88	180/79	200	20.38	20.08- 14
Adams	Lyukman	RUS	24.9.88	194/87	TJ	17.15	17.53- 12
Adams	Spencer	USA	10.9.89	188/84	110h	13.44	13.33- 14, 13.24w- 13
Addisie	Birhanu	ETH	13.9.95		Mar	2:09:27	2:10:20- 14
Addison	Jonathan	USA	27.2.95	176/73	LJ	8.17i, 7.92	7.88i, 7.87, 7.99w- 15
Adhana	Gebretsadik	ETH	16.7.92	158/50	Mar	2:08:17	2:06:21- 12
Adkins	Bradley	USA	30.12.93	190/79	HJ	2.29i, 2.26	2.29i, 2.25- 15
Adola	Guye	ETH	20.10.90	175/54	10k	27:09.78	-0-
Afonin	Maksim	RUS	6.1.92	184/115	SP	20.96	20.06- 15
Aghasyan	Levon	ARM	19.1.95	191/76	TJ	16.85A,16.49	16.33A- 12,16.19i- 15,16.17- 13
Agrusti	Andrea	ITA	30.8.95		50kW	3:56:17	4:09:11- 15
Ahmed	Mohammed	CAN	5.1.91	175/61	3000	7:40.11i	7:54.22i- 14
					5000	13:01.74	13:10.00- 15
Ahmed Hassan	Mustafa Amr	EGY	16.12.95	184/130	SP	20.19	20.57- 15
Aikines-Aryeetey	Harry	GBR	29.8.88	180/87	100	10.08, 10.02w	10.08- 13
Akimenko	Mikhail	RUS	6.12.95		HJ	2.28	2.24- 14
Akins	Tyrone	NGR	6.1.86	180/79	110h	13.55	13.25- 08, 13.2w- 10
Al-Dawoodi	Sultan Mubarak	KSA	16.6.77	180/110	DT	65.52	65.08- 12
Al-Garni ¶	Mohamed	QAT	2.7.92	178/66	1500	3:36.35i	3:34.61- 11
					3000	7:39.23i	7:46.17i- 12
Al-Harthi	Barakat	OMA	15.6.88	172/64	100	10.05	10.16, 10.05w- 15
Al-Hayrani	Jamal	QAT	26.5.93	175/61	800	1:46.22	1:46.16- 15
Al-Hebshi	Sultan	KSA	23.2.83	185/103	SP	19.81	21.13- 09
Al-Mandeel	Abdulaziz	KUW	22.5.89	175/66	110h	13.51	13.49- 14, 13.32w- 15
Al-Masrahi ¶	Youssef	KSA	31.12.87	176/76	400	45.51 drugs dq	43.93- 15
Al-Yoha	Yacoub	KUW	31.1.93	185/70	110h	13.55	13.58, 13.37w- 15
Alamirew	Yenew	ETH	27.5.90	175/57	3000	7:40.24i	7:27.26- 11
					5000	13:04.29	12:48.77- 12
Alberto	Dominik	SUI	28.4.92	182/80	PV	5.55	5.20- 14
Alcalá	Marc	ESP	7.11.94	175/69	1500	3:36.93	3:38.42- 15
Alejandro	Eric	PUR	15.4.86	180/70	400h	49.16	49.07- 14
Alexander	Colby	USA	13.6.91	183/64	1500	3:34.88	3:36.56- 15
					1M	3:54.94	3:59.19- 15
Ali	Ahmed	SUD	15.11.93	180/80	200	20.16	20.46- 15
Alic	Hamza	BIH	20.1.79	186/127	SP	20.57	20.73- 13
Alkana	Antonio	RSA	12.4.90	185/77	110h	13.28	13.32- 15
Allen	Devon	USA	12.12.94	183/84	110h	13.03	13.16- 14
Allen	Lavon	USA	26.11.90	184/79	LJ	8.05	7.75i, 7.72, 7.86w- 15
Allen	Nathon	JAM	28.10.95	178/68	400	45.39	45.30- 15
Álvarez	Alberto	MEX	8.3.91	189/72	TJ	16.99	16.63- 14
Alves	Higor	BRA	23.2.94	181/75	LJ	8.19	8.18- 14
Aman	Mohamed	ETH	10.1.94	169/55	800	1:44.70	1:42.37- 13
Amare	Hailemariyam	ETH-J	22.2.97	165/50	3kSt	8:21.10	8:24.19- 15
Amb	Kim	SWE	31.7.90	180/85	JT	84.50	84.61- 13
Amdouni	Mourad	FRA	21.1.88	175/60	1500	3:35.58	3:34.05- 15
					3000	7:47.70i	7:37.50- 09
					5000	13:22.64	13:14.19- 09

MEN'S INDEX

Name		Nat	Born	Ht/Wt	Event	2016 Mark	Pre-2016 Best
Amezcua	Luis Alberto	ESP	1.5.92	183/67	20kW	1:21:39	1:22:03- 15
Amos	Nijel	BOT	15.3.94	179/60	800	1:44.66	1:41.73- 12
Ampomah	John	GHA	11.7.90	187/90	JT	83.09	82.94- 15
Anas	Mohammed	IND	17.9.94	176/64	400	45.40	46.66- 15
Anastasákis	Mihaíl	GRE	3.12.94	183/103	HT	77.08	73.23- 15
Anderson	Jeshua	USA	22.6.89	187/84	400h	48.88	47.93- 11
Anderson	Nick	USA	28.4.95	186/77	110h	13.60, 13.59w	13.60- 15
Andrade	Jordin	CPV	5.5.92	183/73	400h	49.26	49.24- 15
Andrews	Robby	USA	29.3.91	177/68	800	1:46.06	1:44.71- 11
1500	3:34.88		3:34.78- 12		1M	3:53.16i	3:57.15- 15
Andreyev	Leonid	UZB	6.10.83	188/82	Dec	8250 doubtful	7879- 14
Andriyanov	Nikita	RUS	7.2.90	183/73	400h	49.73	49.62- 11
Andújar	Daniel	ESP	14.5.94	183/78	800	1:45.61	1:46.78-14
Anic	Lazar	SRB	14.12.91	188/78	LJ	7.98	7.60, 7.62w- 15
Anishchenkov	Nikita	RUS	25.7.92	188/80	HJ	2.25	2.30- 15
Anne	Mame-Ibra	FRA	7.11.89	184/70	400	45.39	45.26- 15
Anou	Abderrahmane	ALG	29.1.91	172/60	1500	3:38.11	3:35.2- 11
Antonelli	Michele	ITA	23.5.94	177/64	50kW	3:53:08	4:04:06- 15
Aouad	Zouhair	BRN	7.4.89	175/69	3000	7:45.80	8:05.19- 13
					5000	13:14.16	13:26.19- 15
Apak	Esref	TUR	3.1.82	186/105	HT	76.45	81.45- 05
Appier	Garrett	USA	15.10.92	197/114	SP	20.79	19.55i, 18.54- 15
Arai	Hirooki	JPN	18.5.88	179/61	20kW	1:19:54	1:20:35- 15
					50kW	3:41:24	3:40:20- 15
Arai	Ryohei	JPN	23.6.91	183/96	JT	84.54	86.83- 14
Araptany	Jacob	UGA	11.2.92	168/58	3kSt	8:21.53	8:14.48- 12
de Araújo	Luiz Alberto	BRA	27.9.87	190/90	Dec	8315	8276- 12
Araya	Edward	CHI	14.2.86	177/58	50kW	3:58:54A	4:00:31A- 13
Araya	Yerko	CHI	14.2.86	174/59	20kW	1:21:26	1:20:47.2t- 11
Arcilla	Francisco	ESP	14.1.84	171/62	20kW	1:21:21	1:22:23- 13
					50kW	3:55:06	3:58:00- 14
Arents	Mareks	LAT	6.8.86	190/85	PV	5.70	5.65- 15
Arévalo	Eider	COL	9.3.93	165/58	20kW	1:20:47	1:19:45- 13
Arikan	Polat Kemboi	TUR	12.12.90	173/62	10k	27:35.50	27:38.81- 12
Arita	Stephen	KEN	26.6.88	165/54	10k	27:59.0A	27:55.17A- 15
					HMar	61:15	60:52- 15
Arnaudov	Tsanko	POR	14.3.92	192/118	SP	20.59	21.06- 15
Arnold	Mike	USA	13.8.90	190/84	PV	5.77Ai, 5.56	5.72A- 15, 5.70- 15
Arrhenius	Leif	SWE	15.7.86	192/120	SP	20.00i, 20.00	20.50- 13
					DT	62.50A	64.46- 11
Arrhenius	Niklas	SWE	10.9.82	192/125	DT	66.02A	66.22- 11
de Arriba	Álvaro	ESP	2.6.94	180/65	800	1:45.93	1:47.42 -14
Arroyo	Andrés	PUR	7.6.95	171/61	800	1:45.78	1:46.49- 15
Art	Arnaud	BEL	28.1.93	185/83	PV	5.61i, 5.60	5.65- 15
Arteaga	Mauricio	ECU	8.8.88	173/65	20kW	1:21:08	1:21:46- 14
Arzandeh	Mohammad	IRI	30.10.87	180/76	LJ	8.16	8.17- 12
Asaoka	Mitsunori	JPN	11.1.93	162/50	10k	27:59.72	28:26.56- 15
Ash	Ronnie	USA	2.7.88	188/86	110h	13.18	12.99- 14, 12.98w- 10
Ashmeade	Nickel	JAM	7.4.90	184/87	100	9.94	9.90- 13
					200	20.07	19.85- 12
Atanasov	Zlatozar	BUL	12.12.89	191/77	TJ	16.71	17.09- 13
Atnafu	Yitayal	ETH	20.1.93	172/55	Mar	2:08:53	-0-
Augustyn	Rafal	POL	14.5.84	178/71	50kW	3:43:22	3:43:55- 15
Auzeil	Bastien	FRA	22.10.89	190/82	Dec	8191	8147- 15
Avila	Eric	USA	3.10.89	176/64	1500	3:36.37	3:41.29- 14
Awad	Thomas	USA	27.5.94	173/61	1500	3:37.75	3:40.68- 15
Awotunde	Josh	NGR	12.6.95	188/107	SP	20.11	18.57- 15
Ayalew	Aweke	BRN	23.2.93	182/64	5000	13:18.15	13:05.00- 13
Ayeko	Thomas	UGA	10.2.92	168/58	10k	27:57.3A	27:40.96- 13
					HMar	60:26	61:12- 15
Ayele	Abayneh	ETH	4.11.87	175/57	10k	27:35.83	27:57.51- 15
HMar	59:59		61:43- 13		Mar	2:06:45	2:07:16- 15
Ayouni	Abdessalem	TUN	16.5.94	187/79	800	1:45.98	1:47.72- 14
Bába	Jaroslav	CZE	2.9.84	196/82	HJ	2.28i, 2.26	2.37i, 2.36- 05
Babayev	Nazim	AZE-J	8.10.97	185/70	TJ	16.83	17.04- 15
Babineaux	Ricky	USA	14.12.90	184/75	400h	48.88	51.63- 14
Bachir	Youssouf Hiss	DJI	87	178/70	3000	7:43.44i	7:48.32i- 14, 7:50.96- 13
Bäck	Kristian	FIN	18.7.96	193/83	LJ	7.95, 7.96w	7.50, 7.61w- 15
Baden	Joel	AUS	1.2.96	190/70	HJ	2.29	2.29- 14
Badji	Ndiss Kaba	SEN	21.9.83	192/79	LJ	7.90, 8.13w	8.32- 09
Baeten	Stijn	BEL	3.6.94	171/57	1500	3:38.05	3:44.49- 15

MEN'S INDEX

Name		Nat	Born	Ht/Wt	Event	2016 Mark	Pre-2016 Best
Bagio	José Alessandro	BRA	16.4.81	172/63	20kW	1:22:15	1:21:37.9t- 04
Bahner	Austin	USA	7.7.91	188/81	Dec	7776	7847w, 7744- 13
Bailey	Aldrich	USA	6.2.94	183/70	200	20.44	20.30, 20.16w- 15
					400	45.42	45.19- 12
Bailey	Daniel	ANT	9.9.86	173/70	100	10.09	9.91- 09
Bailey	Oshane	JAM	9.8.89	168/64	100	10.13	10.11- 10, 10.06w- 12
					200	20.42	20.66- 14
Bailey	Tavis	USA	6.1.92	190/134	DT	65.82	64.51- 14
Bailey-Cole	Kemar	JAM	10.1.92	195/86	100	10.00	9.92- 15
Baji	Balázs	HUN	9.6.89	192/84	110h	13.28	13.29- 14
Baker	Chris	GBR	2.2.91	197/84	HJ	2.36i, 2.29	2.28i, 2.27- 14
Baker	Ronnie	USA	15.10.93	178/73	100	10.09, 9.95w	10.05, 9.94w- 15
Bakharev	Viktor	RUS	5.5.94	184/70	3kSt	8:25.34	8:32.45- 15
Bakosi	Péter	HUN	23.6.93		HJ	2.26	2.23- 14
Balla	Abdulrahman Musaeb	QAT	19.3.89	175/60	800	1:45.93i	1:43.82- 15
Balner	Michal	CZE	12.9.82	193/78	PV	5.70i, 5.66	5.82- 15
Balnuweit	Erik	GER	21.9.88	189/75	110h	13.56	13.44, 13.32w-13
Baloyes	Bernardo	COL	6.1.94	177/66	200	20.42A,20.60	20.43,20.35Aw- 14, 20.37A- 15
Baltaci	Özkan	TUR	13.2.94	187/111	HT	75.77	72.89- 14
Baltadoúros	Dimítrios	GRE	1.10.89	180/70	TJ	16.64	16.60- 15
Bamoussa	Abdoullah	ITA	2.6.86	170/59	3kSt	8:32.54	8:41.12- 15
Baniótis	Konstadínos	GRE	6.11.86	202/80	HJ	2.33i, 2.25	2.34- 13
Bannister ¶	Jarrod	AUS	3.10.84	190/100	JT	78.29	89.02- 08
Banzeruk	Ivan	UKR	9.2.90	177/65	50kW	3:51:57	3:44:49- 14
Barannikov	Oleksandr	UKR-J	23.1.97	189/75	HJ	2.26	2.21- 15
Barber	Shawnacy	CAN	27.5.94	190/82	PV	6.00Ai, 5.91	5.93- 15
Barnes	Emre Zafer	TUR	7.11.88	178/73	100	10.12	10.14- 13
Barnes	Will	PUR	17.3.94	188/77	110h	13.41	13.56- 15
Barr	Thomas	IRL	24.7.92	183/73	400h	47.97	48.65- 15
Barras	Romain	FRA	1.8.80	193/84	Dec	8007	8453- 10
Barroilhet	Gonzalo	CHI	19.8.86	196/96	Dec	7711	8065- 12
de Barros	Bruno	BRA	7.1.87	178/70	100	10.28, 10.12w	10.16 -09
					200	20.50, 20.38w	20.16- 11
Barry	Trevor	BAH	14.6.83	190/77	HJ	2.29	2.32- 11
Barshim	Mutaz Essa	QAT	24.6.91	192/70	HJ	2.40	2.43- 14
Barsoton	Leonard	KEN	21.10.94	166/56	10k	27:31.86	27:20.74- 14
Bárta	Marek	CZE	8.12.92	194/110	DT	61.38	60.15- 15
Bascou	Dimitri	FRA	20.7.87	182/79	110h	13.12, 13.05w	13.16- 15
Bashan	Nikolay	RUS	18.11.92	182/95	HT	72.61	72.04- 15
Bastien	Steve	USA	4.3.94	183/76	Dec	7917	6823w- 13
Bates	KeAndre	USA	24.5.96	181/75	LJ	8.11, 8.32w	8.02i, 7.73, 7.97w- 15
					TJ	16.63, 16.73w	16.42i- 15, 15.70- 13
Batzávalis	Paraskevás	GRE	25.11.94	185/100	JT	85.95	81.04- 15
Bayer	Andrew	USA	3.2.90	180/60	1M	3:55.46	3:52.90- 13
3000	7:45.24, 7:42.33i		7:43.84- 13		3kSt	8:16.11	8:18.08- 15
Bayer	Maximilian	GER	5.12.90	181/73	110h	13.43	13.70- 15, 13.63w-14
Beach	Curtis	USA	22.7.90	183/75	400h	49.87	51.67- 15
					Dec	7728	8083- 11
Bednarek	Sylwester	POL	28.4.89	198/75	HJ	2.30	2.32- 09
Bédrani	Djilali	FRA	1.10.93	179/59	3kSt	8:28.34	8:40.6- 15
Bekele	Kenenisa	ETH	13.6.82	162/54	HMar	61:11+	60:09- 13
					Mar	2:03:03	2:05:04- 14
Belcher	Chris	USA	29.1.94	175/75	100	10.07	10.27 -14
					200	20.39	21.40- 14, 21.11w- 15
Belferrar	Mohamed Amine	ALG	6.2.91	180/69	800	1:45.01	1:46.07- 13
Bell	Dylan	USA	21.7.93	195/85	PV	5.70A	5.50Ai, 5.35A- 14
Bell	Javere	JAM	20.9.92	184/73	400	45.51	45.08- 13
Belo	Francisco	POR	27.3.91	193/120	SP	19.58	18.64i- 12, 18.45- 13
Bélocian	Wilhem	FRA	22.6.95	178/78	110h	13.25, 13.15w	13.28- 15
Benard	Chris	USA	4.4.90	190/79	TJ	17.21	17.10- 14
Bencosme de Leon	José	ITA	16.5.92	187/77	400h	49.76	49.33- 12
Benedetti	Giordano	ITA	22.5.89	189/68	800	1:46.41	1:44.67- 13
Benitz	Timo	GER	24.12.91	170/56	1500	3:36.40	3:34.94- 14
Benjamin	Rai	ANT-J	27.7.97	191/77	400h	49.82	49.97- 15
Benmahdi	Khalid	ALG	22.10.88	180/68	800	1:46.21	1:46.06- 15
Bennett	Chris	GBR	17.12.89	188/115	HT	76.45	74.66- 15
Bennett	LaRon	USA	25.11.82	183/75	400h	49.82	48.74- 05
Benyahia	Amor	TUN	1.7.85	176/54	3kSt	8:20.72	8:14.05- 13
Berian	Boris	USA	19.12.92	180/73	800	1:44.20	1:43.34- 15
Berihu	Solomon	ETH-Y	22.10.99?		5000	13:12.67	
Berry	Michael	USA	10.12.91	184/73	400	45.18	44.75- 12

512 MEN'S INDEX

Name		Nat	Born	Ht/Wt	Event	2016 Mark		Pre-2016 Best
Bertemes	Bob	LUX	24.5.93	187/118	SP	20.14		20.56i, 19.87- 15
Bertolini	Roberto	ITA	9.10.85	187/100	JT	81.05		80.97- 15
Bertrand	Jean-Pierre	FRA	5.11.92	180/71	LJ	8.03		7.80- 15
Beshr	Anas	EGY	19.7.93	188/77	400	45.40		45.59A, 45.60- 14
Bett	Bernard	KEN	4.1.93		HMar	60:36		60:43- 15
Bett	Emmanuel	KEN	30.3.83	170/55	10k	27:53.05		26:51.16- 12
Bett	Kipyegon	KEN-J	2.1.98	182/70	800	1:43.76		1:44.55A- 15
Bett	Nicholas	KEN	20.12.96	172/52	3kSt	8:10.07		8:19.26- 15
Bett	Nicholas	KEN	14.6.92	186/77	400h	48.01		47.79- 15
Beukes	Eben	RSA	9.3.90	183/75	PV	5.60A		5.30A- 13
Beyo	Chala	ETH	18.1.96	174/57	3kSt	8:17.84		8:25.45- 14
Beznits	Pavlo	UKR-J	17.6.97	200/80	TJ	16.55		16.05, 16.31w- 15
Bianchetti	Sebastiano	ITA	20.1.96	188/125	SP	19.78		18.77i, 18.63- 15
Bigot ¶	Quentin	FRA	1.12.92	179/95	HT	76.10		78.58- 14
Bilderback	Zack	USA	27.8.93	193/80	400	45.27i, 46.05		45.53- 15
Bile	Ahmed	USA	21.9.93	183/68	1500	3:37.73		3:40.72- 15
Bilodeau	Mathieu	CAN	27.11.83	185/73	50kW	3:53:56		3:59:48- 14
Bird-Smith	Dane	AUS	15.7.92	178/66	20kW	1:19:37		1:20:05- 15
Birech	Jairus	KEN	14.12.92	167/56	3kSt	8:03.90		7:58.41- 14
Birega	Selemon	ETH-Y	20.1.00	173/59	5000	13:21.21		
Birgen	Bethwel	KEN	6.8.88	178/64	1500	3:33.94		3:30.77- 13
1M	3:55.41i	3:50.42- 13	3000	7:32.48		7:37.15- 13	5000	13:04.66 13:50.6A- 13
Birkinhead	Damien	AUS	8.4.93	190/130	SP	21.21		20.40- 15
Bishop	Alex	USA	17.5.91	175/75	PV	5.52		5.45i-14, 5.40- 13
Biwott	Robert	KEN	28.1.96	180/68	800	1:45.84		1:43.56- 15
1000	2:13.89			-0-	1500	3:33.05		3:30.10- 15
Biwott	Stanley	KEN	21.4.86	176/60	HMar	60:40		58:56- 13
					Mar	2:03:51		2:04:55- 14
Blair-Sanford	Donald	ISR	5.2.87	193/84	400	45.26		45.04- 15
Blake	Yohan	JAM	26.12.89	181/79	100	9.93		9.69- 12
					200	20.13		19.26- 11
Blankenship	Ben	USA	15.12.89	173/61	1500	3:34.26		3:35.48, 3:35.28i- 15
1M	3:53.83	3:54.10- 11, 3:53.13i- 15			3000	7:44.96i		7:38.08- 15
Blankenship	Jake	USA	15.3.94	183/79	PV	5.72i, 5.65		5.80- 15
Bledman	Keston	TTO	8.3.88	183/75	100	10.07		9.86, 9.85w- 12
Blocki	Adrian	POL	11.4.90	173/63	50kW	3:47:16		3:49:11- 15
Blocki	Damian	POL	28.4.89	180/65	50kW	3:54:26		3:51:32- 13
Bockarie	Solomon	NED	18.5.87	170/64	100	10.13		10.29, 10.28w- 15
					200	20.37		20.81- 15
Bogatyrev	Pyotr	RUS	11.3.91		20kW	1:21:50		1:20:18- 11
Boirie	Baptiste	FRA	26.12.92	171/65	PV	5.60i, 5.60		5.50- 12
Bol	Peter	AUS	22.2.94	168/57	800	1:45.41		1:46.51- 15
Bolt	Usain	JAM	21.8.86	196/88	100	9.81		9.58- 09
					200	19.78		19.19--09
Bondarenko	Artyom	BLR	19.6.91	187/78	TJ	16.90		16.26, 16.74nwi- 15
Bondarenko	Bogdan	UKR	30.8.89	197/80	HJ	2.37		2.42- 14
Bonevacia	Liemarvin	NED	5.4.89	180/81	400	45.03		44.72- 15
Bonfim	Caio	BRA	19.3.91	170/58	20kW	1:19:42		1:20:28- 14
					50kW	3:47:02		4:02:20- 14
Bonvecchio	Norbert	ITA	14.8.85	181/80	JT	79.21		80.37- 14
Bor	Emmanuel	KEN	14.4.88		HMar	61:04		61:06- 15
Bor	Hillary	USA	22.11.89	168/57	3kSt	8:13.68		8:32.41- 13
Bore	Ambrose	KEN	8.8.95		5000	13:20.39		13:23.80- 15
Boreysha	Pavel	BLR	16.2.91	193/105	HT	78.60		77.03- 15
Borichevskiy	Konstantin	BLR	29.5.90	191/87	LJ	8.01, 8.08w		8.17, 8.22w- 15
Borlée	Dylan	BEL	20.9.92	190/77	400	45.61		45.57- 15
Borlée	Jonathan	BEL	22.2.88	180/70	400	45.34		44.43- 12
Borlée	Kévin	BEL	22.2.88	180/71	400	45.17		44.56- 12
Bortolato	Marco	ITA	11.2.94	189/107	HT	72.17		70.85- 15
Bortoluzzi	Jérôme	FRA	20.5.82	180/111	HT	75.13		78.26- 12
Bosse	Pierre-Ambroise	FRA	11.5.92	185/68	800	1:43.41		1:42:53- 14
Bosworth	Tom	GBR	17.1.90	184/54	20kW	1:20:13		1:22:20- 14
Bouchicha	Hichem	ALG	19.5.89	183/70	3kSt	8:23.51		8:20.11- 13
Boulama	Mohammed	MAR	31.12.93	183/68	3kSt	8:31.05		8:21.62- 13
Bouqantar	Soufiyan	MAR	30.8.93	173/54	3000	7:46.37, 7:45.15i		7:43.43- 14
					5000	13:21.70		13:19.59- 12
Bouraada	Larbi	ALG	10.5.88	187/84	Dec	8521		8461- 15
Bowness	James	GBR	26.11.91	185/73	800	1:45.96		1:47.49- 15
Boyce	Brendan	IRL	15.10.86	183/70	50kW	3:53:59		3:48:55- 15
Boyce	Lutalo	USA	11.8.91	178/75	LJ	7.91i, 7.95w		7.87- 15
Bracy	Marvin	USA	15.12.93	175/74	100	9.94		9.93- 15

MEN'S INDEX

Name		Nat	Born	Ht/Wt	Event	2016 Mark	Pre-2016 Best
Bragg	Adam	USA	18.4.93	184/75	PV	5.65i, 5.53	5.43i, 5.42- 15
Bramble	Daniel	GBR	14.10.90	178/76	LJ	8.14i, 8.00	8.21- 15
Brannen	Nathan	CAN	8.9.82	175/59	1500	3:36.84	3:34.22- 12
					1M	3:55.31	3:52.63- 09
Brathwaite	Shane	BAR	8.2.90	182/75	110h	13.51	13.21- 15
Braun	Pieter	NED	21.1.93	182/80	Dec	8058	8197- 15
Bravo	Alberth	VEN	29.8.87	198/85	400	45.53	45.21A- 14, 45.26- 15
Braz da Silva	Thiago	BRA	16.12.93	193/84	PV	6.03	5.92- 15
Brazier	Donavan	USA-J	15.4.97	188/73	800	1:43.55	1:47.55- 15
Brembach	Nils	GER	23.2.93	184/68	20kW	1:20:58	1:21:21- 15
Brenes	Nery	CRC	25.9.85	174/62	200	20.20	20.49A -14, 20.3- 08
Brenes	Nery	CRC	25.9.85	174/62	400	44.60	44.65A- 11, 44.84- 10
Briggs	Kemonie	USA	21.5.96	188/77	LJ	7.98w	
Brits	Stefan	RSA	19.1.92	185/73	LJ	8.22	8.05- 13
Broeders	Ben	BEL	21.6.95	178/75	PV	5.61	5.35- 15
Bromell	Trayvon	USA	10.7.95	175/71	100	9.84	9.84, 9.76w- 15
					200	20.30	20.03, 19.86w- 15
Brondyke	Kurtis	USA	24.1.89	198/93	Dec	7795	7613- 14, 7689w- 15
Brookins	Ronald	USA	5.7.89	185/75	110h	13.49, 13.35w	13.42- 11
Brooks	Lance	USA	1.1.84	198/123	DT	63.63	65.15- 12
Brown	Aaron	CAN	27.5.92	185/79	100	9.96, 9.95w	10.05, 10.01w- 13
					200	20.00	20.16, 20.02w- 14
Brown	Chris	BAH	15.10.78	178/68	400	45.56	44.40- 08
Brown	Izaiah	USA-J	1.1.97	186/77	400	45.27	46.40- 15
Brown	Kemarley	JAM/BRN	20.7.92	180/72	100	10.03	9.93 -14
Brown	Rodney	USA	21.5.93	183/109	DT	66.00	65.04- 15
Brown	Tony	USA	13.7.95	183/88	110h	13.71, 13.52w	13.92- 15
Bruchet	Lucas	CAN	23.2.91	175/60	5000	13:24.10	13:29.79- 15
Brugger	Mathias	GER	6.8.92	192/93	Dec	7886	8009- 15
Bruintjies	Henricho	RSA	16.7.93	179/72	100	10.11, 9.89w	9.97- 15
Bryan	Christoffe	JAM	26.4.96	193/75	HJ	2.25i, 2.25	2.28i- 15, 2.24- 14
Bryant	Ashley	GBR	17.5.91	180/82	Dec	8056	8070- 13
Brylinski	Robert	POL	2.4.91	188/78	400h	49.88	50.47- 14
Brzozowski	Artur	POL	18.12.88	173/67	20kW	1:22:11	1:22:16- 13
Bube	Andreas	DEN	13.7.87	178/65	800	1:45.87	1:44.89- 12
Bubeník	Matús	SVK	14.11.89	197/78	HJ	2.30i, 2.24	2.31i, 2.29- 15
Budza	Sergiy	UKR	6.12.84	180/75	50kW	3:53:22	3:47:36- 13
Bühler	Matthias	GER	2.9.86	189/74	110h	13.44	13.34- 12, 13.20w- 14
Bukowiecki	Konrad	POL-J	17.3.97	191/129	SP	21.14	20.78- 15
Bulanov	Aleksandr	RUS	26.12.89	193/120	SP	19.56i, 19.24	19.92i ,19.81-13
Bultheel	Michaël	BEL	30.6.86	189/81	400h	49.27	49.04- 15
Burton	Tom	GBR	29.10.88	178/68	400h	49.62	49.36- 15
Busendich	Ishmael	KEN	7.7.91		Mar	2:08:20	2:08:25- 14
Bussotti (Neves)	João	ITA	10.5.93	180/60	1500	3:37.90	3:40.75- 15
Bustos	David	ESP	25.8.90	182/65	1500	3:36.14	3:34.77- 12
Butchart	Andrew	GBR	14.10.91	173/61	3000	7:45.00	8:09.59i- 15, 8:11.13- 14
					5000	13:08.61	13:29.49- 15
Butenko	Viktor	RUS	10.3.93	196/116	DT	65.17	65.97- 13
Butler	Quentin	USA	18.9.92	175/70	100	10.06	9.96- 15
Bychkov	Igor	ESP	7.3.87	189/80	PV	5.53i, 5.51	5.65- 13
Cabral	Donn	USA	12.12.89	175/60	3000	7:47.18i	7:51.47i- 14, 7:53.48- 12
					3kSt	8:20.72	8:13.37- 15
Cabral	Johnathan	CAN	31.12.92	193/82	110h	13.35	13.37, 13.22w- 15
Cáceres	Eusebio	ESP	10.9.91	176/69	LJ	8.02A, 7.94	8.37- 13
Cadée	Erik	NED	15.2.84	201/120	DT	64.24, 65.48dh	67.30- 12
Cadogan	Levi	BAR	8.11.95	171/68	200	20.45	20.67- 14
Caesa	Leslie	CUB-J	14.1.97	179/61	TJ	16.54, 17.15w	16.48, 16.83w- 15
Cai Zelin		CHN	11.4.91	172/55	20kW	1:19:26	1:18:47- 12
Cakss	Gatis	LAT	13.6.95	184/93	JT	78.45	80.06- 15
Caldwell	Chris	USA	6.4.94	188/88	110h	13.59	13.56- 15
Callahan	Peter	USA/BEL	1.6.91	183/68	1500	3:37.87	3:37.88- 15
Camara	Alyn	GER	31.3.89	195/85	LJ	8.21	8.29- 13
Cambridge	Aska	JPN	31.5.93	180/76	100	10.10	10.21- 14
Campbell	Kemoy	JAM	14.1.91	165/57	3000	7:40.79i	7:46.95i- 13
Campbell	Taylor	GBR	30.6.96	191/95	HT	72.70	69.39- 15
Campener	Corentin	BEL	5.10.90	175.64	LJ	7.94, 8.05w	7.82- 15
Campion	Kevin	FRA	23.5.88	183/63	20kW	1:20:45	1:20:39- 14
Can	Yavuz	TUR	23.2.87	181/70	400	45.51	45.65- 15
Cann	Luke	AUS	17.7.94	183/90	JT	80.27	79.36- 14
Cantero	Bryan	FRA	28.4.91	178/64	1500	3:37.03	3:36.08- 14
Cantwell	Christian	USA	30.9.80	193/154	SP	19.72	22.54- 04

514 MEN'S INDEX

Name		Nat	Born	Ht/Wt	Event	2016 Mark			Pre-2016 Best
Cao Shuo		CHN	8.10.91	183/69	TJ	17.13			17.35- 12
Caporaso	Teodorico	ITA	14.9.87	166/60	50kW	3:48:29			3:51:44- 15
Carbin	Darius	USA-J	4.3.98		HJ	2.25			2.16- 15
Carnes	Brandon	USA	6.3.95	175/73	100	10.06w			10.24, 10.10w -15
Carson	Hamish	NZL	1.11.88	181/66	1500	3:36.25			3:38.04 -12
Carter	Chris	USA	11.3.89	186/80	TJ	17.18			17.15Ai, 17.09- 14
Carter	Deuce	JAM	28.9.90	182/75	110h	13.20			13.49A- 15, 13.53- 13
Carvalho	Florian	FRA	9.3.89	182/69	1500	3:35.29			3:33.47- 13
Carvalho	Jefferson	BRA	13.9.90		Dec	7958u			7394- 15
Casañas	Frank	ESP	18.10.78	187/115	DT	65.32			67.91- 08
Castillo	Maurys Surel	ESP	19.10.84	182/60	1500	3:36.41			3:35.03- 12
Castro	Luis Joel	PUR	28.1.91	195/72	HJ	2.29			2.26- 14
Cato	Roxroy	JAM	1.5.88	183/76	400h	48.56			48.48- 14
Cedenio	Machel	TTO	6.9.95	183/70	400	44.01			44.36- 15
Centrowitz	Matthew	USA	18.10.89	176/61	1000	2:16.67			2:17.00i- 15
1500	3:34.09	3:30.40- 15		1M	3:50.63i		3:50.53- 14	3000	7:40.74i	7:46.19i- 12
Chalyy	Timofey	RUS	7.4.94	190/79	400h	48.57			48.69- 14
Chambers	Dwain	GBR	5.4.78	180/83	100	10.26, 10.11w			9.97- 99, 9.87dq- 02
Chambers	Marcus	USA	3.11.94	178/75	400	45.27			44.95- 15
Chan Ming Tai		HKG	30.1.95	175/65	LJ	8.12			7.89- 15
Chani	Hassan	BRN	5.5.88	171/55	10k	27:56.48			28:11.46- 15
Chapelle	Axel	FRA	24.4.95	180/79	PV	5.65			5.55- 14
Charfreitag	Libor	SVK	11.9.77	191/117	HT	74.47			81.81- 03
Chatbi ¶	Jamal	ITA	30.4.84	178/62	5000	13:22.53			13:27.08- 13
					3kSt	8:21.92			8:08.86- 09
Chávez	Arturo	PER	12.1.90	190/76	HJ	2.31A			2.25- 13
Chebet	Evans Kiplagat	KEN	10.11.88		HMar	61:11+			
					Mar	2:05:31			2:07:46- 14
Chebet	Wilson	KEN	12.7.85	174/59	Mar	2:08:19			2:05:27- 11
Chebii	Collins	KEN-J	.97		3kSt	8:32.10			8:51.54- 12
Chebii	Ezekiel	KEN	3.1.91		Mar	2:06:07			2:07:18- 15
Cheboi	Collins	KEN	25.9.87	175/64	1500	3:35.74			3:30.34- 15
2000	4:59.5+e		5:00.30- 12		3000	7:45.32			7:51.41- 10
Chelanga	Samuel	USA	23.2.85	168/57	10K	27:54.57			27:08.39- 10
Chelimo	Paul	USA	27.10.90	171/57	3000	7:37.98			7:49.87- 12
					5000	13:03.90			13:21.89- 12
Chemlal	Jaouad	MAR	11.4.94	177/59	3kSt	8:31.87			8:19.22- 13
Chemlany	Stephen	KEN	9.8.82	175/64	Mar	2:07:37			2:06:24- 14
Chen Ding		CHN	5.8.92	180/62	20kW	1:19:32			1:17:40- 12
Cheng Min		CHN	6.7.91		50kW	3:58:38			4:00:48- 14
Chepkok	Vincent	KEN	5.7.88	174/60	10K	27:54.99			26:51.68- 12
Chepkwony	Frankline	KEN	15.6.84		Mar	2:06:51			2:06:11- 12
Cheprot	Simon	KEN	2.7.93	183/62	HMar	60:12			59:20- 13
Cheptegei	Joshua	UGA	12.9.96	179/61	1500	3:37.82			
5000	13:00.60		13:28.50A- 15		10k	27:10.06			27:27.57- 15
Cheroben	Abreham	BRN	11.10.92	174/58	10k	27:31.86			-0-
					HMar	60:35			58:48- 14
Cherono	Lawrence	KEN	7.8.88		Mar	2:07:24			2:09:39- 15
Cherry	Michael	USA	23.3.95	186/75	400	44.81			45.37- 14
Cheruiyot	Ferguson	KEN	30.11.89	183/73	800	1:43.43			1:42.84- 14
Cheruiyot	Timothy	KEN	20.11.95	178/64	1500	3:31.34			3:34.86A- 15
					1M	3:53.17			3:55.80- 15
Chesani	Silvano	ITA	17.7.88	190/75	HJ	2.30i, 2.22			2.33i, 2.31 -13
Chesebe	Abednego	KEN	20.6.82	174/62	1500	3:37.82A			3:35.02A- 12
Cheserek	Edward	KEN	2.2.94	168/57	3000	7:40.51i			7:47.20i- 14
Chiaraviglio	Germán	ARG	16.4.87	192/77	PV	5.70			5.75- 15
Chihuán	Pavel	PER	19.1.86	170/70	50kW	3:58:32			3:56:35- 14
Chizhikov	Dmitriy	RUS	6.12.93	194/85	TJ	16.85i, 16.78			17.20- 15
Chmielak	Hubert	POL	19.6.89	188/88	JT	80.42			82.58- 14
Chocho	Andrés	ECU	4.11.83	167/67	20kW	1:20:07			1:20:23.8t- 14
					50kW	3:42:57A			3:46:00- 15
Choge	Augustine	KEN	21.1.87	162/53	3000	7:43.00, 7:39.23i			7:28.00i, 7:28.76- 11
10k	28:22.8A		29:06.5A- 02		HMar	60:01			-0-
Choge	Raymond	KEN	.88		Mar	2:08:39			
Chopra	Neeraj	IND-J	24.12.97	184/80	JT	86.48			81.04- 15
Chumba	Dickson	KEN	27.10.86	167/50	Mar	2:07:34			2:04:32- 14
Chumo	Rodgers Kemoi	KEN-J	3.3.97	165/49	5000	13:18.98			13:28.62- 15
Chumo	Victor	KEN	1.1.87	175/59	5000	13:13.07			13:12.67- 12
Churkor	Patrick	KEN	17.2.91	177/58	3kSt	8:28.45			8:25.54- 15
Churylo	Andrey	BLR	19.5.93	190/72	HJ	2.30i, 2.22			2.30- 14
Cienfuegos	Javier	ESP	15.7.90	193/134	HT	76.37			76.71- 13

MEN'S INDEX 515

Name		Nat	Born	Ht/Wt	Event	2016 Mark	Pre-2016 Best
Cisneros	Omar	CUB	19.11.89	186/80	400h	49.36	47.93- 13
Clarke	Andre	JAM	6.6.92	185/75	400h	49.64	49.87- 15
Clarke	Everton	JAM	24.12.92	172/70	100	10.08	10.21- 13
					200	20.45	20.51- 14
Clarke	Jordan	USA	10.7.90	193/125	SP	21.11	21.49- 15
Clarke	Lawrence	GBR	12.3.90	187/78	110h	13.42	13.31, 13.14w- 12
Clavier	Jérôme	FRA	3.5.83	185/73	PV	5.77i	5.81i- 11, 5.75- 08
Claye	Will	USA	13.6.91	180/68	LJ	8.14, 8.42w	8.29- 11
					TJ	17.76	17.75- 14
Clement	Kerron	USA	31.10.85	188/84	400h	47.73	47.24- 05
Clemons	Kyle	USA	27.8.90	181/73	400	44.79	44.84- 15
Cobbo	Guilherme	BRA	1.10.87	185/65	HJ	2.25	2.28- 12
Cochrane	Michael	NZL	13.8.91	188/82	400h	49.86	49.58- 15
Coertzen	Willem	RSA	30.12.82	186/80	Dec	7879	8398- 15
Coleman	Christian	USA	6.3.96	175/73	100	9.95	10.18, 10.16w- 15
Coleman	Christian	USA	6.3.96	178/73	200	20.26	20.61- 15
Collie-Minns	Latario	BAH	10.3.94	173/64	TJ	16.97	17.18, 17.25w- 15
Collins	Kyle	USA	9.9.94	183/77	400	45.33	46.16- 15
Collins	LeShon	USA	11.12.93	179/73	200	20.43	21.05, 21.00w- 15
Collins	Kim	SKN	5.4.76	175/64	100	9.93	9.96- 14, 9.92w- 03
Colomo	Javier	ESP	26.3.94	180/62	110h	13.58, 13.56w	13.73- 15
Colwick	Jason	USA	25.1.88	182/77	PV	5.67i, 5.55	5.72- 09
Comick	Jace	USA-J	10.7.98	185/70	100	10.09Aw	
Compaoré	Benjamin	FRA	5.8.87	189/86	LJ	8.02	7.87- 12
					TJ	17.09i, 16.76	17.48- 14
Constantino	Gabriel	BRA	9.2.95	186/77	110h	13.50	13.75- 15
Contreras	Yidiel	ESP	27.11.92	186/73	110h	13.45	13.35- 15
Cooper	Mitch	AUS	2.6.95	196/115	DT	62.56	58.19- 15
Cooper	Tyrese	USA-Y	21.3.00	183/75	400	45.23	46.44- 15
Coover	Jeff	USA	1.12.87	185/77	PV	5.62i, 5.57	5.68i- 15, 5.60- 13
Copeland	Leslie	FIJ	23.4.88	186/94	JT	81.76	80.45- 11
Copello	Alexis	ex-CUB	12.8.85	185/80	TJ	16.99i,16.98	17.68A- 11, 17.65,17.69w- 09
Copello	Yasmani	TUR	15.4.87	196/86	400h	47.92	48.46- 15
Corbett	Marquise	USA		93 183/70	LJ	7.97w	7.59- 15
Corréa	Harold	FRA	26.6.88	190/78	TJ	17.08, 17.11w	16.94i, 16.92- 13
Cota	Mario	MEX	11.9.90	188/115	DT	63.35	61.63- 14
Cotter	Dylan	RSA	23.8.91	188/73	LJ	8.16A	7.87A- 13
Cotton	Kenzo	USA	13.5.96	185/87	100	10.07	10.36, 10.32w- 15
					200	20.35	20.82- 15
Cotton	Terrel	USA	19.7.88	182/73	200	20.45	20.16- 15
Couto	Kurt	MOZ	14.5.85	180/67	400h	49.74	49.02- 12
Cowart	Donnie	USA	24.10.85	170/60	3kSt	8:23.38	8:26.38- 11
Cowley	Rhydian	AUS	4.1.91	181/65	20kW	1:22:07	1:23:27- 15
Craddock	Omar	USA	26.4.91	178/79	TJ	17.16, 17.42w	17.53- 15
Cranston	Kyle	AUS	3.9.92		Dec	7703	7629- 15
Crawford	Graham	USA	29.12.92	180/64	1500	3:37.08	3:38.49- 15
Cray	Eric	PHI	6.11.88	176/73	400h	48.98	49.12- 15
Cremona	Orazio	RSA	1.7.89	192/130	SP	20.05	20.63- 14
Crittenden	Freddie	USA	3.8.94	183/73	110h	13.48, 13.43w	13.62- 15
Cronje	Johan	RSA	13.4.82	182/69	1500	3:37.49	3:31.93- 13
Crouser	Ryan	USA	18.12.92	201/127	SP	22.52	21.39- 14
Culson	Javier	PUR	25.7.84	198/79	400h	48.46	47.72- 10
Culver	Trey	USA	18.7.96	193/75	HJ	2.26	2.17- 15
Cunningham	Logan	USA	30.5.91	183/80	PV	5.71, 5.80dh	5.70- 14
Cunningham	Randall	USA	4.1.96	196/84	HJ	2.26i, 2.25	2.24- 15
Cunningham	Ricardo	JAM	3.10.80	183/78	400h	49.66	-0-
Cutts	Luke	GBR	13.2.88	192/82	PV	5.70i, 5.61	5.83i- 14, 5.70- 13
Czykier	Damian	POL	10.8.92	186/73	110h	13.32, 13.13w	13.68- 14
D'Hoedt	Jeroen	BEL	10.1.90	182/59	3kSt	8:31.54	8:30.03- 15
Dacres	Fedrick	JAM	28.2.94	191/97	DT	68.02	66.75- 14
Dahm	Tobias	GER	23.5.87	203/117	SP	20.56i, 20.42	19.97i- 15, 19.96- 13
Dahmani	Samir	FRA	3.4.91	183/65	800	1:44.07	1:45.62- 15
Dairokuno	Shuho	JPN	23.12.92	168/51	10k	27:54.75	27:46.55- 15
Dasaolu	James	GBR	5.9.87	180/75	100	10.10, 9.93w	9.91- 13
Davide	Kléberson	BRA	20.7.85	175/67	800	1:45.79	1:44.21- 11
Davies	Jonathan	GBR	28.10.94		5000	13:23.94	13:43.74- 15
Davis	Paul	USA	11.9.90	190/97	SP	19.90	21.05- 13
Dayarathne	Waruna Lakshan	SRI	14.5.88		JT	78.52	77.39- 15
Days	Braheme	USA	18.1.95	185/136	SP	20.21	19.61- 15
de Beer	Gerhard	RSA	5.7.94	201/131	DT	61.97	59.60- 12
de Deus	Eduardo	BRA	8.10.95		110h	13.56	13.80- 15

MEN'S INDEX

Name		Nat	Born	Ht/Wt	Event	2016 Mark	Pre-2016 Best
De Grasse	Andre	CAN	10.11.94	180/73	100	9.91	9.92, 9.75w- 15
					200	19.80	19.88, 19.58w- 15
de Jager	Shaun	RSA	28.6.91	186/68	400	45.70A, 45.90	45.66A, 45.74- 14
De Luca	Marco	ITA	12.5.81	188/69	20kW	1:22:01	1:22:13- 15
					50kW	3:44:47	3:45:25- 14
Dean	Genki	JPN	30.12.91	182/88	JT	79.59	84.28- 12
Debela	Dejene	ETH	.94	180/62	3000	7:44.96	7:43.94- 15
Debjani	Ismael	BEL	25.9.90	175/61	1500	3:35.62	3:42.11- 15
DeChant	Matt	USA	31.5.89	195/115	SP	19.56	19.82i- 11, 19.74- 15
Dechase	Chala	ETH	13.6.84	167/52	Mar	2:09:19	2:06:33- 10
Dedewo	Paul	NGR/USA	5.6.91	185/73	400	45.67	45.41- 15
Deksisa	Solomon	ETH	11.3.94	170/55	Mar	2:06:22	-0-
del Carmen	Stanly	DOM	20.9.95	172/68	200	20.46, 20.26w	21.12, 20.69Aw- 15
del Real	Diego	MEX	6.3.94	185/103	HT	77.49	72.66- 15
Delaney	Arthur	USA	23.6.93	180/75	100	10.11w	10.24- 12
					200	20.49, 20.23w	20.52- 14
Demelash	Yigrem	ETH	28.1.94	167/52	5000	13:05.64	13:03.30- 12
10k	26:51.11		26:57.56- 12		HMar	59:48	-0-
Demps	Jeff	USA	8.1.90	175/77	100	10.06	10.01- 08, 9.96w- 10
Dendy	Marquis	USA	17.11.92	190/75	LJ	8.42	8.39, 8.68w- 15
Denmukhametov	Artyom	RUS	15.5.93	184/73	400	45.71	46.31- 15
Denny	Matthew	AUS	2.6.96	195/115	DT	65.37	62.58- 15
Dergachev	Yuriy	KAZ	8.11.94	187/65	HJ	2.26i, 2.23	2.28- 14
Derrick	Chris	USA	17.10.90	180/64	10k	27:38.69	27:31.38- 12
Desalu	Eseosa	ITA	19.2.94	179/69	200	20.31	20.55- 14
Desisa	Lelisa	ETH	14.1.90	170/52	HMar	60:37	59:30- 11
Dewhurst	Ian	AUS	13.11.90	185/73	400h	49.76	49.52- 14
Dheeb	Ahmed Mohamed	QAT	29.9.85	195/113	DT	61.49	63.70. 64.56dq- 10
Díaz	Andy	CUB	25.12.95	180/68	TJ	16.80	16.81- 15
Díaz	Carlos Martín	CHI	9.7.93	174/58	1500	3:37.82	3:37.86- 15
Díaz	José Ignacio	ESP	22.11.79	168/53	50kW	3:51:10	3:51:09- 05
Dilla	Karsten	GER	17.7.89	189/80	PV	5.70	5.73i, 5.72- 11
Dimitrov	Rumen	BUL	19.9.86	175/77	TJ	16.59i, 16.46	16.87- 15
Diniz	Yohann	FRA	1.1.78	185/69	50kW	3:37:48	3:32:33- 14
Dirieh	Djamal Abdi	DJI-J	.97	170/60	5000	13:21.50	
Distelberger	Dominik	AUT	16.3.90	182/77	Dec	8175	8168- 14
Dix	Walter	USA	31.1.86	178/84	100	10.03	9.88- 10, 9.80w- 08
					200	20.14	19.53- 11
Djouhan	Lolassonn	FRA	18.5.91	188/118	DT	61.95	61.70- 13
Dmitrik	Aleksey	RUS	12.4.84	191/69	HJ	2.28i, 2.26	2.40i- 14, 2.36- 11
Dmytrenko	Ruslan	UKR	22.3.86	180/62	20kW	1:20:33	1:18:37- 15
Dobek	Patryk	POL	13.2.94	183/75	400h	49.01	48.40- 15
Dodson	Jeremy	SAM	30.8.87	184/75	200	20.44A, 20.47, 20.20w	
							20.27A- 14, 20.31- 15, 20.07w- 11
Dohmann	Carl	GER	18.5.90	182/62	20kW	1:21:26	1:21:42- 14
					50kW	3:47:57	3:50:12- 15
Dolezal	Jan	CZE	6.6.96		Dec	7730	7260- 15
Dolezal	Riley	USA	16.11.85	188/100	JT	80.42	83.50- 13
Dolve	Eirik Greibrokk	NOR	5.5.95	185/80	PV	5.66	5.50- 15
Domingos	Wágner	BRA	23.6.83	183/126	HT	78.63	75.47- 14
Donato	Fabrizio	ITA	14.8.76	189/82	TJ	16.93	17.73i- 11, 17.60- 00, 17.63w- 12
Dong Bin		CHN	22.11.88	179/67	TJ	17.58	17.38- 12
Donisan ¶	Mihai	ROU	24.7.88	193/74	HJ	2.26i/ 2.23 drugs dq, 2.22i 2.32i- 14, 2.31- 13	
Donnelly	Sean	USA	1.4.93	183/107	HT	74.35	66.01- 14
Doris	Troy	GUY	12.4.89	174/73	TJ	17.18	16.85- 14
Douglas	Nathan	GBR	4.12.82	183/71	TJ	16.58	17.64- 05
Doukkana	Rabie	MAR	6.12.87	168/57	1500	3:38.19	3:37.81- 14
Douma	Richard	NED	17.4.93	184/67	1500	3:35.77	3:39.71- 15
Douvalídis	Konstadínos	GRE	10.3.87	184/78	110h	13.38, 13.37w	13.33- 15
Downing	Quincy	USA	16.1.93	185/75	400h	49.32	49.63- 15
Drack	Jonathan	MRI	6.11.88	184/77	LJ	7.98w	7.80, 7.84w- 15
					TJ	16.67i, 16.66	16.96, 17.05w- 15
Drouin	Derek	CAN	6.3.90	195/80	HJ	2.38	2.40- 14
Drummond	Braxton	USA	1.7.94	183/74	LJ	8.10	8.02i- 15, 7.66, 7.75w- 14
Dry	Mark	GBR	11.10.87	184/110	HT	76.26	76.93- 15
Dryhol ¶	Oleksandr	ISR	25.4.66	183/104	HT	77.70	79.42- 12
Dubitskiy	Oleg	BLR	14.10.90	184/100	HT	75.74	76.67- 15
Dubler	Cedric	AUS	13.1.95	190/82	Dec	8114	7197- 15
Duckworth	Tim	GBR	18.6.96	185/80	Dec	7709	7156- 15
Dudarov	Gleb	BLR	17.10.96	196/107	HT	72.86	-0-
Dudas	Mihail	SRB	1.11.89	182/85	Dec	8174	8275- 13

Name		Nat	Born	Ht/Wt	Event	2016 Mark	Pre-2016 Best
Dukes	Dedric	USA	2.4.92	180/70	100	10.13	10.18, 10.17w- 15
					200	20.41, 20.14w	19.97- 14, 19.86w- 15
Dulhanty	Chris	CAN	6.4.92	183/66	3kSt	8:31.02	8:33.76- 15
Dumitrache	Marius	ROU	15.6.89		HJ	2.26i, 2.20	2.27i, 2.27- 12
Dunbar	Colin	USA	27.6.88	190/115	HT	72.59	73.56- 15
Dunbar	Trevor	USA	29.4.91	180/70	3000	7:43.33i	7:45.09- 14
Dunfee	Evan	CAN	28.9.90	186/68	20kW	1:20:34	1:20:13- 14
					50kW	3:41:38	3:43:45- 15
Dunkley	Fitzroy	JAM	20.5.93	188/75	400	45.06	45.78- 15
Duquemin	Zane	GBR	23.9.91	185/110	DT	62.28	63.46- 12
Dutamby	Stuart	FRA	24.4.94	176/74	100	10.12	10.42, 10.40w- 14
Dutch	Johnny	USA	20.1.89	180/82	400h	48.10	47.63- 10
Dutra de Oliveira	Augusto	BRA	16.7.90	180/70	PV	5.70	5.82- 13
Dwyer	Rasheed	JAM	29.1.89	188/80	100	10.10, 10.08w	10.16- 15
Eaton	Ashton	USA	21.1.88	186/86	400	45.63	45.00- 15
					110h 13.48 13.35- 11,13.34w- 12	LJ 8.08i, 8.01, 8.09w	8.23- 12 Dec 8893	9045- 15
Eaton	Jarret	USA	24.6.89	183/82	110h	13.25	13.41, 13.40w- 15
Eaves	Max	GBR	31.5.88	186/84	PV	5.64i, 5.57	5.62- 14
Echevarría	Juan Miguel	CUB-J	11.8.98	185/71	LJ	7.96, 8.15w	8.05- 15
Echols	Dondre	USA	6.7.93	178/77	110h	13.54, 13.35w	13.46- 15
Edie	Sadeekie	JAM	28.10.93		LJ	7.97i	7.65- 15
Edoburun	Ojie	GBR	2.6.96	183/77	100	10.19, 10.02w	10.16, 10.15w- 14
Edoki	Fabian	NGR-J	30.3.98	188/73	LJ	7.91A, 8.02Aw	
Edris	Muktar	ETH	14.1.94	172/57	3000	7:33.28	7:46.0- 14
					5000	12:59.43	12:54.83- 14
Edward	Alonso	PAN	8.12.89	183/73	200	19.92	19.81- 09
Efekoro	Oghenakpobo	NGR	15.7.96	190/138	SP	19.57	17.75- 15
Ektov	Yevgeniy	KAZ	1.9.86	187/76	TJ	16.55i	17.22- 12
El Abbassi	El Hassan	BRN	13.4.84	171/54	5000	13:19.36	13:33.95- 14
					10k	27:47.29	27:25.02- 15
El Aziz	Mustapha	MAR	24.12.85	175/60	HMar	59:29	61:05- 15
El Bakkali	Soufiane	MAR	7.1.96	188/70	3kSt	8:14.35	8:27.79- 15
El Guesse	Abdellatif	MAR	27.2.93	186/68	800	1:45.87	1:45.78- 15
El Kaam	Fouad	MAR	27.5.88	177/62	1500	3:34.96	3:33.71- 13
El-Seify	Ashraf Amjad	QAT	20.2.95	183/100	HT	78.19	78.04- 15
Elemba	Franck	CGO	21.7.90	200/115	SP	21.20	20.25- 15
Ellington	James	GBR	6.9.85	180/75	100	10.04, 9.96w	10.13- 14, 10.10w- 15
					200	20.31	20.42- 13
Ellis	Burkheart	BAR	18.9.92	175/64	200	20.36	20.65- 13
Ellis	Nigel	JAM-J	8.8.97	186/77	200	20.40	21.07- 15
Emanuel	Lee	GBR	24.1.85	178/64	1500	3:36.29	3:35.66i, 3:36.35- 15
					1M	3:55.43	3:54.30i- 14, 3:54.75- 13
Emilianov	Ivan	MDA	19.2.77	202/160	SP	20.80	20.64- 11
Enekwechi	Chukwuebuka	USA	28.1.93	181/107	SP	20.37	19.46- 15
Engelbrecht	Jaco	RSA	8.3.87	200/125	SP	20.00	20.45- 15
Engels	Craig	USA	1.5.94	187/73	800	1:46.03	1:46.13- 15
					1500	3:37.66	3:40.28- 15
English	Mark	IRL	18.3.93	187/76	800	1:45.36	1:44.84- 13
Erewa	Robin	GER	24.6.91	184/77	200	20.40	20.46- 14
Erickson	Chris	AUS	1.12.81	175/62	50kW	3:48:40	3:49:33- 14
Erins	Edgars	LAT	18.6.86	191/87	Dec	7643	8312- 11
Ernest	Aaron	USA	8.11.93	183/75	200	20.45	20.22, 20.11w- 15
Essalhi	Younès	MAR	20.2.93	181/68	1500	3:36.19	3:35.52- 13
	3000 7:46.24		7:49.21- 14		5000	13:17.32	13:16.07- 13
Eto	Takashi	JPN	5.2.91	183/67	HJ	2.29	2.28- 14
Evans	Andrew	USA	25.1.91	198/110	DT	65.41	66.37- 14
Évora	Nelson	POR	20.4.84	181/70	TJ	17.03	17.74- 07, 17.82w- 09
Ezzine	Hamid	MAR	5.10.83	174/60	3kSt	8:19.31	8:09.72- 07
Fajdek	Pawel	POL	4.6.89	186/118	HT	82.47	83.93- 15
Falloni	Simone	ITA	26.9.91	187/110	HT	73.78	73.29- 15
Fang Hongzhen		CHN	6.3.96		50kW	4:02:01	-0-
Farah	Mohamed	GBR	23.3.83	171/65	1500	3:31.74	3:28.81- 13
	3000 7:32.62		7:33.1+i, 7:34.66- 15		5000	12:59.29	12:53.11- 11
	10k 26:53.71		26:46.57- 11		HMar	59:59	59:22dh, 59:32- 15
Farnosov	Andrey	RUS	9.7.80	182/66	3kSt	8:26.36	8:21.95- 11
Farquhar	Stuart	NZL	15.3.82	187/98	JT	83.93	86.31- 12
Farrell	Thomas	GBR	23.3.91	174/61	3000	7:42.47i	7:47.54i, 7:57.2- 14
Fasasi	Kunle	NGR	23.6.96	183/75	400	45.43	46.21- 14
Fassinotti	Marco	ITA	29.4.89	190/71	HJ	2.35i, 2.29	2.34i- 14, 2.33- 15
Fauble	Scott	USA	5.11.91	175/61	10k	28:00.43	28:43.70- 14
Fearon	Joel	GBR	11.10.88	175/77	100	9.96	10.10- 13

518 MEN'S INDEX

Name		Nat	Born	Ht/Wt	Event	2016 Mark	Pre-2016 Best
Fedaczynski	Rafal	POL	3.12.80	168/61	20kW	1:21:47	1:20:18- 14
					50kW	3:48:42	3:46:05- 11
Felix	Alphonce	TAN	14.2.92		Mar	2:09:19	2:12:01- 15
Felix	Kurt	GRN	4.7.88	190/88	Dec	8323	8302- 15
Ferlic	Mason	USA	5.8.93	188/68	3kSt	8:21.57	8:35.45- 15
Fernández	Jorge	CUB	2.10.87	190/100	DT	65.30	66.50- 14
Fernández	Sergio	ESP	1.4.93	188/70	400h	48.87	49.90- 14
Ferreira	Diogo	POR	30.7.90	175/77	PV	5.55	5.67- 14
Fifa	Illias	ESP	16.5.89	174/55	5000	13:11.83	13:05.61- 15
Fikadu	Dawit	ETH	95		5000	13:23.03	13:43.31- 14
Filip	Scott	USA	28.1.95	188/85	Dec	7876	7045w- 14
Filippídis	Konstadinos	GRE	26.11.86	188/73	PV	5.84i, 5.72	5.91- 15
Finley	Mason	USA	7.10.90	203/150	DT	66.72	64.80A- 15
Firfirica	Alin Alexandru	ROU	3.11.95	196/108	DT	65.03	61.04- 15
Fisher	Andrew	JAM/BRN	15.12.91	168/64	100	10.07	9.94- 15
Florant	Fabian	NED	1.2.83	176/73	TJ	16.92	16.75i- 12, 16.65- 09, 16.85w- 13
Florez-Studer	Alex	SUI	11.5.71		50kW	4:02:37	4:07:36- 12
Floriani	Yuri	ITA	25.12.81	180/64	3kSt	8:30.03	8:22.62- 12
Fofana	Hassane	ITA	28.4.92	184/78	110h	13.52	13.55- 14
Fontenot	Ryan	USA	4.5.86	188/75	110h	13.48, 13.40w	13.44- 13, 13.39w -12
Forbes	Damar	JAM	18.9.90	185/77	LJ	8.23	8.25, 8.35w- 13
Forbes	Ronald	CAY	5.4.85	192/86	110h	13.36	13.47- 15, 13.24w- 11
Forte	Julian	JAM	1.7.93	186/73	100	10.05, 9.94w	10.03- 14, 9.98w- 13
					200	19.97	20.04- 15
Forte	Simone	ITA	20.1.96	180/68	TJ	16.62i	16.24- 15
Fortes	Marco	POR	26.9.82	189/139	SP	19.93	21.02- 12
Forys	Craig	USA	13.7.89	176/64	3kSt	8:27.19	8:24.09- 14
Francis	Javon	JAM	14.12.94	183/73	400	44.77	44.50- 15
Francis	Miguel	ANT	28.2.95	186/75	200	19.88, 19.67 irr	20.05, 19.76dt- 15
Frater	Michael	JAM	6.10.82	170/67	100	10.04	9.88, 9.86w- 11
Frayne	Henry	AUS	14.4.90	187/72	LJ	8.16	8.27- 12
Frederick	Norris	USA	17.2.86	183/79	LJ	8.04	8.12i- 08, 8.10- 11
Fredericks	Cornel	RSA	3.3.90	178/70	400h	49.75	48.14- 11
Freeman	Josh	USA	22.8.94	193/134	SP	20.06i, 19.92	20.15- 15
French	Cameron	NZL	17.5.92	180/73	400h	49.87	49.72- 15
Friday	Trentavis	USA	5.6.95	188/75	100	10.13	10.00- 14
					200	20.46, 20.33w	20.33, 20.03w- 14
Fringeli	Jonas	SUI	12.1.88	187/85	Dec	7862	7829- 12
Frydrych	Petr	CZE	13.1.88	198/99	JT	84.10	88.23- 10
Fryman	Andy	USA	3.2.85	188/130	HT	73.33	73.90- 14
Fu Haitao		CHN	1.11.93		TJ	16.69	16.79- 15
Fujisawa	Isamu	JPN	12.10.87	165/53	20kW	1:18:45	1:19:08- 15
Fujiwara	Takeshi	JPN	5.8.85	175/64	400	45.44A	45.99A- 12
Furtula	Danijel	MNE	31.7.92	195/115	DT	63.85	64.60- 13
Futch	Eric	USA	25.4.93	175/70	400h	48.91	49.45- 15
Fyodorov	Aleksey	RUS	25.5.91	184/73	TJ	17.02	17.42- 15
Gachaga	Morris Munene	KEN	7.4.95		HMar	60:35	61:32- 15
Gado	Ruben	FRA	13.12.93	180/73	Dec	7720	7610- 15
Gag	Andrei	ROU	7.4.91	195/118	SP	21.06	20.96- 15
Gaisah	Ignisious	NED	20.6.83	185/75	LJ	8.00	8.43, 8.51w- 06
Gakémé	Antoine	BDI	24.12.91	170/57	800	1:45.24	1:44.09- 15
Galeta	Kristo	EST	9.4.83	190/94	SP	19.78	19.16i- 15, 19.15- 13
Galvan	Matteo	ITA	24.8.88	182/78	400	45.12	45.35- 13
Ganapathi	Krishnan	IND	29.6.89	173/76	20kW	1:21:41	1:22:41- 14
Gao Xinglong		CHN	12.3.94	181/65	LJ	8.23	8.34- 15
Garcia	Samuel	ESP	4.12.91	194/84	400	45.65	45.50- 14
García	Diego	ESP	19.1.96	174/60	20kW	1:21:36	1:21:45- 15
García	Jesús Ángel	ESP	17.10.69	172/64	50kW	3:54:29	3:39:54- 97
García	Yordani	CUB	21.11.88	193/88	Dec	8068	8496- 09
Gardiner	Daniel	GBR	25.6.90	181/73	LJ	7.96	7.78i, 7.70- 15, 7.80w- 14
Gardiner	Steven	BAH	12.9.95	188/75	400	44.46	44.27- 15
Gardner	Jonathan	USA	10.12.91	180/77	TJ	16.53	16.45i- 15, 16.15- 14
Garrett	Richard	USA	21.12.90	186/118	SP	20.06	20.35- 14
Garrido	Iván	COL	25.1.94		20kW	1:21:35	1:21:39- 15
Gaspar	José Luis	CUB	25.8.95	188/72	400h	49.17	49.67A- 15, 49.88- 14
Gastaldi	Román	ARG	25.9.89	187/86	Dec	7695	7826A- 11, 7882w- 15
Gathimba	Samuel	KEN	26.10.87		20kW	1:19:24	1:23:12A- 15
Gatlin	Justin	USA	10.2.82	185/79	100	9.80	9.74- 15
					200	19.75	19.57- 15
Gaul	Florian	GER	21.9.91	182/78	PV	5.77	5.53- 15
Gavriilidis	Nikólaos	GRE	15.3.95	191/107	HT	72.02	61.40- 13

Name		Nat	Born	Ht/Wt	Event	2016 Mark	Pre-2016 Best
Gay	Tyson	USA	9.8.82	180/73	100	9.97	9.69- 09, 9.68w- 08
					200	20.16	19.58- 09
Gaye	Demish	JAM	20.1.93	188/77	400	45.30	46.15- 15
Gdula	Lukás	CZE	6.12.91	178/65	50kW	3:54:29	3:59:03- 15
Geay	Gabriel	TAN	10.9.96		10k	28:04.98	28:41.9- 15
Gebremedhin	Mekonnen	ETH	11.10.88	180/64	1500	3:35.50	3:31.45- 12
Gebremeskel	Dejen	ETH	24.11.89	178/53	3000	7:38.03i, 7:50.98	7:34.14i- 12, 7:45.9- 10
					5000	12:59.89	12:46.81- 12
Gebrhiwet	Hagos	ETH	11.5.94	167/65	3000	7:30.45	7:30.36- 13
					5000	13:00.20	12:47.53- 12
Gebrselassie	Leul	ETH	20.9.93	170/55	3000	7:44.50i	7:53.58- 14
5000	13:13.88		13:14.59- 14		10k	27:19.71	27:22.89- 15
Geffrouais	Florian	FRA	5.12.88	183/78	Dec	8073	8164- 14
Geist	Jordan	USA-J	21.7.98	188/113	SP	20.82i	-0-
Gelant	Elroy	RSA	25.8.86	174/55	5000	13:04.88	13:15.87- 13
Gemili	Adam	GBR	6.10.93	178/73	100	10.11	9.97- 15
					200	19.97	19.98- 14
Genest	Alexandre	CAN	30.6.86	178/63	3kSt	8:30.25	8:19.33- 11
Geng Yudong		CHN	13.6.94		50kW	4:00:50	4:16:07- 15
George	Aaron	USA	2.8.95		LJ	7.99w	7.87i- 15, 7.68w- 14
George	Winston	GUY	19.5.87	174/66	200	20.53, 20.42w	20.59- 13, 20.4- 14
Geraghty	Peter	USA	11.6.91	183/73	PV	5.60i, 5.45, 5.56irr	5.64- 15
Geremew	Mosinet	ETH	12.2.92	174/57	HMar	60:43	59:11- 14
Gertleyn	Ivan	RUS	25.9.87	184/75	PV	5.60	5.70- 15
Getachew	Limenih	ETH	30.4.90		Mar	2:08:48	2:06:49- 14
Getahun	Birhan	ETH	5.9.91	181/64	3kSt	8:21.30	8:17.36- 11
Gezahegn	Kelkile	ETH	.91		Mar	2:08:56	-0-
Gföhler	Benjamin	SUI	27.1.94	178/	LJ	8.13	7.93- 15
Ghalenouei	Peyman	IRI	29.1.92	190/96	HT	77.18	73.07- 15
Ghazal	Majed El Dein	SYR	21.4.87	193/72	HJ	2.36	2.31- 15
Ghebregergish	Yohannes	ERI	11.1.94		HMar	60:21	61:42- 15
Ghebreslassie	Ghirmay	ERI	14.11.95		Mar	2:07:46	2:07:47- 15
Ghuys	Bram	BEL	14.2.93	192/71	HJ	2.25	2.24- 14
Gibson	Jeffery	BAH	15.8.90	186/79	400h	48.96	48.17- 15
Giehl	Tobias	GER	25.7.91	185/73	400h	49.48	49.75- 12
Giesting	Chris	USA	10.12.92	191/80	400	45.69	45.53- 14
Giles	Elliot	GBR	26.5.94	173/64	800	1:45.54	1:47.55- 15
Gill	Jacko	NZL	20.12.94	190/118	SP	20.83	20.75- 15
Gillespie	Cravon	USA	31.7.96	175/66	100	10.21, 10.04w	10.45- 15
					200	20.20	21.11- 15
Girma	Tesfaye	ETH	.95		3kSt	8:16.14	
Gittens	Ramon	BAR	20.7.87	180/77	100	10.03	10.02- 13, 10.01Aw- 15
					200	20.42	20.44- 14
Giupponi	Matteo	ITA	8.10.88	190/70	20kW	1:20:27	1:20:58- 12
					50kW	3:52:27	3:49:52- 15
Givans	Senoj-Jay	JAM	30.12.93	178/73	100	9.96	10.03- 15, 9.90w- 14
Glass	Najee	USA	12.6.94	183/73	400	44.79	44.79- 14
Gniki Gisamoda	Emanuel	TAN	18.5.88		HMar	60:47	
Golabek	Rob	USA	27.4.89	178/116	SP	19.96i	19.75- 12
Gomes	Hélio	POR	27.12.84	191/73	1500	3:37.74	3:37.50- 13
Gomes da Silva	Aldemir	BRA	8.6.92	179/67	200	20.32	20.32- 14
Gómez	Iñaki	CAN	16.1.88	172/58	20kW	1:19:20	1:20:18- 14
Gómez	Joaquín	ARG	14.10.96		HT	71.50	67.98- 14
Gómez	Pedro	MEX	31.12.90	175/64	20kW	1:20:05	1:21:38- 13
					50kW	3:53:23	-0-
Gomis	Kafétien	FRA	23.3.80	183/67	LJ	8.23i, 8.05	8.26- 15
González	Andy	CUB	17.10.87	183/70	800	1:46.04	1:45.3- 08, 1:45.40- 10
González	Erwin	MEX	7.2.94		20kW	1:21:54	1:22:36- 14
Goodwin	Marquise	USA	19.11.90	177/83	LJ	8.45	8.33- 12, 8.37w- 15
Gordon	Lalonde	TTO	25.11.88	188/83	200	20.39w	20.26- 13
					400	44.69	44.52- 12
Gorokhov	Georgiy	RUS	20.4.93	183/75	PV	5.70i, 5.65	5.65- 15
Gotch	Jarvis	USA	25.3.92	185/73	LJ	8.24, 8.35w	8.12i- 15, 8.09A, 8.18Aw- 13
Grabarz	Robbie	GBR	3.10.87	192/87	HJ	2.33i, 2.33	2.37- 12
Grace	Bobby	USA	10.10.90	193/118	SP	20.18	20.51- 15
Grant	Robert	USA	31.1.96	180/76	400h	49.36	51.16- 14
Gray	Nick	USA-J	2.6.97	181/66	200	20.45	21.09- 15
Green	Jack	GBR	6.10.91	187/82	400h	48.96	48.60- 12
Green	Jeremiah	USA	9.2.94	173/70	TJ	16.68i, 16.25	16.29i- 14, 16.50w- 15
Greene	Cejhae	ANT	6.10.95	174/68	100	10.01	10.25- 15, 10.20w- 14
Gregorek	John	USA	7.12.91	178/61	1500	3:36.04	3:40.89- 15
					1M	3:55.27	3:57.47i- 15

MEN'S INDEX

Name		Nat	Born	Ht/Wt	Event	2016 Mark	Pre-2016 Best
Gregory	Ben	GBR	21.11.90	184/82	Dec	7882	7725- 14
Gregson	Ryan	AUS	26.4.90	184/68	1500	3:32.13	3:31.06- 10
1M	3:52.59		3:52.24- 10		3000	7:44.90	7:49.53- 11
Greguric	Matija	CRO	17.9.96	187/90	HT	72.24	69.13- 15
Grethen	Charel	LUX	22.6.92	180/68	800	1:46.44	1:47.22- 14
Grice	Charlie	GBR	7.11.93	182/68	800	1:45.53	1:47.00- 14
1500	3:33.60		3:35.29- 15		1M	3:52.64	3:54.61- 13
Griffith	Adrian	BAH	11.11.84	178/75	100	10.11, 10.02w	10.14, 10.03w- 14
Griva	Janis Svens	LAT	23.4.93		JT	79.36	77.34- 15
Grobler	Johannes	RSA-J	6.8.97	176/79	JT	80.59	69.38- 15
Gruber	Hendrik	GER	28.9.86	192/82	PV	5.61	5.75i- 13, 5.70- 10
Grzeszczuk	Lukasz	POL	3.3.90	189/95	JT	83.60	84.77- 14
Gudnason	Gudni Valur	ISL	11.10.95	198/115	DT	61.85	63.50- 15
Gudzius	Andrius	LTU	14.2.91	200/130	DT	65.18, 67.96dh	66.11- 14
Guliyev	Ramil	TUR	29.5.90	187/73	100	10.07	10.08- 09
					200	20.09	19.88- 15
Guo Jinqi		CHN	21.9.92		HJ	2.25	2.24- 12
Gurr	James	AUS	20.12.83	180/68	800	1:46.09	1:46.45- 14
Haapala	Eero	FIN	10.7.89	193/87	LJ	7.95A, 7.94, 7.99Aw	8.11i, 7.90- 13
Haatainen	Harri	FIN	5.1.78	186/85	JT	80.32	86.63- 01
Habte	Abraham	ERI	14.7.96		10k	27:53.38	-0-
Hadadi	Ehsan	IRI	21.1.85	193/125	DT	63.61	69.32- 08
Hadis	Abadi	ETH-J	6.11.97	170/63	5000	13:02.49	13:13.17- 15
(Embaye)					10k	26:57.88	
Haftu	Fikadu	ETH	21.2.94		HMar	61:02	61:50- 14
Hague	Adam	GBR-J	29.8.97	188/73	PV	5.53i	5.60- 15
Haileselassie	Yemane	ERI-J	21.2.98	175/57	3kSt	8:22.52	8:32.05- 15
Haitengi	Roger	NAM	12.9.83	184/80	TJ	16.78A,16.48	16.57A- 14,16.74w- 10,16.40- 15
Haji	Yasin	ETH	22.1.96	168/52	3000	7:42.18i	7:41.74- 15
					5000	13:19.50	13:10.67- 15
Halász	Bence	HUN-J	4.8.97	188/86	HT	73.97	69.80- 15
Halim	Muhammad	ISV	26.10.86	193/84	TJ	16.99	16.70i, 16.53 -10, 16.66w -08
Hall	Arman	USA	12.2.94	188/77	200	20.34, 20.33w	20.40- 14
					400	44.82	44.82- 13
Hall-Thompson	Elijah	USA	22.8.94	174/68	200	20.37A	20.60- 13
Hamada	Mohamed Ahmed	EGY	22.10.92	176/64	800	1:45.25	1:44.98- 12
Hamann	Lars	GER	4.4.89	187/88	JT	85.79	84.26- 15
Hamman	Le Roux	RSA	6.1.92	186/69	400h	49.24A, 49.60	50.08- 15
Hamza	Mohamed	EGY	30.8.96	189/115	SP	20.32	19.78- 15
Han Yucheng		CHN	16.12.78	177/59	50kW	3:42:43	3:36:20- 05
Hanekom	Lindsay	RSA	15.5.93	176/65	400h	49.03A, 49.81	50.00- 15
Hann	Mamadou Kassé	FRA	10.10.86	189/79	400h	49.15	48.50- 13
Hannes	Pieter Jan	BEL	30.10.92	186/72	1500	3:35.38	3:34.49- 14
Hansson	Anders	SWE	10.3.92	177/67	50kW	4:01:23A	4:03:20- 15
Hara	Shota	JPN	18.7.92	180/75	200	20.33	20.41- 14
Haratyk	Michael	POL	10.4.92	194/136	SP	21.35i, 21.23	20.10i- 15, 19.95- 14
Hardy	Mike	USA	13.1.90	183/64	3kSt	8:32.55	8:41.44- 15
Harmse	Chris	RSA	31.5.73	184/118	HT	73.32	80.63- 05
Haroun	Abdelilah	QAT-J	.97	178/73	400	44.81	44.27- 15
Harradine	Benn	AUS	14.10.82	198/115	DT	62.20	68.20- 13
Harrell	Jason	USA	10.1.91	188/109	DT	62.12	61.74- 15
Harris	Aleec	USA	31.10.90	185/77	110h	13.43, 13.32w	13.11- 15
Harris	Isaiah	USA	18.10.96	178/73	800	1:45.76	1:49.63- 15
Harris	Tremaine	CAN	10.2.92	181/79	200	20.40w	20.22A- 12, 20.53- 13
Härstedt	Axel	SWE	28.2.87	197/130	DT	66.03	64.72- 15
Hart	Yanick	JAM	10.1.93	183/79	110h	13.58	13.68- 15
Hartfield	Mike	USA	29.3.90	190/77	LJ	8.34, 8.39w	8.27, 8.42w- 15
Harting	Christoph	GER	4.10.90	207/120	DT	68.37	67.93- 15
Harting	Robert	GER	18.10.84	201/127	DT	68.04	70.66- 12
Hartmann	Alex	AUS	7.3.93	188/80	200	20.45	20.59- 15
Harvey	Jak Ali	TUR	5.4.89	182/73	100	9.92A, 10.03	10.01- 15
Hasegawa	Daigo	JPN	27.2.90	173/60	TJ	16.88	16.49- 15
Hasegawa	Kohei	JPN	1.1.90	184/102	JT	81.55	76.75- 14
Hassi	Juuso	FIN	4.4.93	185/79	Dec	7734	7569- 14
Hathat	Yassine	ALG	30.7.91	180/68	800	1:44.81	1:45.79- 15
Haukenes	Håvard	NOR	22.4.90	180/68	50kW	3:46:33	3:56:38- 12
Heath	Garrett	USA	3.11.85	178/65	1M	3:55.10i	3:53.15- 13
1500	3:38.48i	3:34.12- 13		3000	7:41.26i	7:37.40i- 14, 7:37.97- 15	5000 13:23.06 13:16.31- 15
Heffernan	Robert	IRL	20.2.78	173/55	50kW	3:43:55	3:37:54- 12
Heinle	Fabian	GER	14.5.94	189/73	LJ	8.01, 8.11w	7.91- 13
Helcelet	Adam Sebastian	CZE	27.10.91	187/86	Dec	8291	8252- 13

Name		Nat	Born	Ht/Wt	Event	2016 Mark	Pre-2016 Best
Helebrandt	Máté	HUN	12.1.89	174/60	50kW	3:53:54	-0-
Henderson	Jeff	USA	19.2.89	178/82	LJ	8.38, 8.59w	8.52, 8.54w- 15
Henderson	Khalil	USA	18.11.94	188/75	200	20.43, 20.20w	20.29- 15
Henriksen	Eivind	NOR	14.9.90	191/116	HT	74.97	75.57- 12
Hernandez	Hector	PUR	25.9.94	173/61	800	1:46.15	1:47.73- 14
Hernández	Osviel	CUB	31.5.89	179/76	TJ	16.50, 16.88w	17.49- 12
Herrera	José Carlos	MEX	5.2.86	187/77	200	20.17	20.35- 14, 20.33A- 15
Hess	Max	GER	13.7.96	185/75	TJ	17.20	16.55- 14
Hesselbjerg	Ole	DEN	23.4.90	183/70	3kSt	8:30.51	8:33.22- 15
Hester	Tevin	USA	10.1.94	170/66	100	10.22, 9.99w	10.05, 9.87w- 15
					200	20.13	20.14- 15
Hicks	Antwon	NGR	12.3.83	187/79	110h	13.27	13.09- 08
Hightower	Dakarai	USA	15.7.94	183/68	HJ	2.25	2.24- 14
Hill	Darrell	USA	17.8.93	193/135	SP	21.63	20.86- 15
Hill	Devon	USA	26.10.89	185/75	110h	13.44, 13.33w	13.35- 12, 13.32w- 13
Hill	Ryan	USA	31.1.90	176/60	1500	3:35.59	3:37.10- 14
3000	7:30.93		7:34.87i, 7:38.64- 14		5000	13:15.59	13:05.69- 15
Hinds	Chadic	JAM	11.8.92	183/70	100	10.12	10.32- 15
Hlaselo	Dumisani	RSA	8.6.89	168/56	1500	3:36.65	3:36.36- 15
Hlavan	Igor	UKR	25.9.90	172/62	20kW	1:21:55	1:19:59- 14
					50kW	3:44:02	3:40:39- 13
Hoffa	Reese	USA	8.10.77	181/133	SP	21.02i, 20.83	22.43- 07
Hoffmann	Karol	POL	1.6.89	197/80	TJ	17.16	17.09- 12
Hofmann	Andreas	GER	16.12.91	195/108	JT	85.42	86.14- 15
Hogan #	Victor	RSA	25.7.89	198/108	DT	64.04, 67.62 drugs dq	65.33- 13
Hollis	Mark	USA	1.12.84	190/84	PV	5.71A	5.83- 14
Holmes	Timothy "TJ"	USA	2.7.95	182/73	400h	49.31	49.90- 14
Holusa	Jakub	CZE	20.2.88	183/72	1500	3:33.36	3:34.26- 15
Holzdeppe	Raphael	GER	28.9.89	181/78	PV	5.84i, 5.70	5.94- 15
Hondrokoukis	Dimitrios	CYP	26.1.88	193/72	HJ	2.26	2.33i- 12, 2.32- 11
Honeycutt	Josh	USA	7.3.89	182/73	TJ	16.78, 16.81w	16.83- 14
Hooper (Hou Yubo)	Ted	TPE	31.1.91	173/66	LJ	8.05, 8.15w	8.08- 15
Hortelano	Bruno	ESP	18.9.91	181/72	100	10.06	10.27A, 10.36- 12
					200	20.12	20.47- 13
Horvat	Ivan	CRO	17.8.93	188/77	PV	5.70	5.70- 15
Hostetler	Cyrus	USA	8.8.86	190/95	JT	83.83	83.16- 09
Hough	Nick	AUS	20.10.93	191/86	110h	13.56	13.42- 15
Houston	Scott	USA	11.6.90	193/79	PV	5.65, 5.70 irr	5.65- 15
Howard	Julian	GER	3.4.89	176/75	LJ	8.03i	8.07, 8.13w- 13
Howell	Renard	USA/JAM	3.3.95	188/82	200	20.15	20.62- 14, 20.46w- 15
Hrechkovskyy	Andrey	UKR	30.8.93	174/55	50kW	3:53:04	3:49:06- 14
Huang Bokai		CHN	26.9.96	183/75	PV	5.75i, 5.60	5.50- 15
Huang Changzhou		CHN	20.8.94	183/66	LJ	8.21i, 8.12	8.17- 15
Huang Shih-Feng		TPE	2.3.92	181/88	JT	83.82	82.11- 13
Hudgins	Brandon	USA	14.1.87	178/64	1500	3:38.20	3:42.88- 15
Hudi	Ákos	HUN	10.8.91	185/95	HT	73.09	76.93- 13
Hudson-Smith	Matthew	GBR	26.10.94	192/79	400	44.48	44.75- 14
Hughes	Matt	CAN	3.8.89	180/64	3kSt	8:20.63	8:11.64- 13
Hughes	Zharnel	GBR	13.7.95	190/79	100	10.10	10.12- 14
Huling	Dan	USA	16.7.83	185/70	3kSt	8:18.58	8:13.29- 10
Humphreys	Sam	USA	12.9.90	201/115	JT	78.77	83.14- 13
Hunegnaw	Fentahun	ETH			HMar	61:21	60:10- 15
Hunter	Myles	USA	16.8.95	180/73	110h	13.70, 13.60w	13.96- 14, 13.80w- 15
Hussein	Kariem	SUI	1.4.89	190/77	400h	48.87	48.45- 15
Huszák	János	HUN	5.2.92	197/118	DT	64.89	61.30- 15
Hutchison	Je'Von	USA	4.5.92	188/77	400	45.70	45.71- 14
Hyde	Jaheel	JAM-J	2.2.97	180/73	400h	48.81	49.01- 14
Hyman	Kemar	CAY	11.10.89	178/74	100	10.12, 10.05w	9.95- 12, 9.85Aw- 15
Ibadin	Edose	USA	27.2.93	172/64	800	1:46.31	1:48.37- 14
Ibáñez	Anatole	SWE	14.11.85	177/69	20kW	1:20:54	1:22:36- 12
Ibargüen	Arley	COL	4.12.82	182/85	JT	81.23A	81.07- 09
Ibrahim	Mohamed Ismail	DJI-J	.97	173/55	3kSt	8:23.77	8:24.58- 15
Ibrahimov	Hayle	AZE	18.1.90	168/58	3000	7:37.76	7:34.57- 13
					5000	13:13.92	13:09.17- 14
Ichida	Takashi	JPN	16.6.92	163/48	10k	27:53.59	28:17.09- 15
Iguider	Abdelaati	MAR	25.3.87	170/52	1500	3:31.40	3:28.79- 15
1M	3:51.96		3:49.09- 14		2000	4:59.20+	
3000	7:30.09		7:34.92i- 13, 7:34.99- 14		5000	13:08.61	12:59.25- 15
Iizuka	Shota	JPN	25.6.91	185/80	200	20.11	20.21- 13
Ikonnikov ¶	Kirill	RUS	5.3.84	187/115	HT	76.26	80.71- 12
Ilyichev	Ivan	RUS	14.10.86		HJ	2.25i	2.30i- 14, 2.26- 08

MEN'S INDEX

Name		Nat	Born	Ht/Wt	Event	2016 Mark			Pre-2016 Best
Ingebrigtsen	Filip	NOR	20.4.93	187/75	1000	2:16.95			-0-
					1500	3:32.43			3:38.76- 13
Ingebrigtsen	Henrik	NOR	24.2.91	180/69	1500	3:34.57			3:31.46- 14
					1M	3:53.19			3:50.72- 14
Ioannou	Kyriakos	CYP	26.7.84	193/66	HJ	2.32i, 2.29			2.35- 07
Irabaruta	Olivier	BDI	25.8.90	171/61	5000	13:17.98			13:23.44- 14
					10k	27:55.92			28:39.26- 14
Irfan	Kolothum Thodi	IND	8.2.90	172/55	20kW	1:22:15			1:20:21- 12
Iribarne	Roger	CUB	2.1.96	183/68	110h	13.53			13.80w- 14
Isene	Ola Stunes	NOR	29.1.95	193/106	DT	61.36			59.97- 15
Ishikawa	Kazuyoshi	JPN	6.11.82	178/70	TJ	16.77			16.98- 04
Ishikawa	Suehiro	JPN	27.9.79	169/56	Mar	2:09:25			2:09:10- 13
Israel	Märt	EST	23.9.83	190/119	DT	61.53			66.98- 11
Ivakin	Anton	RUS	3.2.91	178/73	PV	5.55i			5.65i- 13, 5.65- 14
Ivanov	Aleksandr	RUS	25.4.93	182/68	20kW	1:22:25			1:19:45- 14
Ivanov	Georgi	BUL	13.3.85	187/130	SP	20.62			21.09- 13
Ivanov	Ivan	KAZ	3.1.92	202/144	SP	19.63			19.47- 12
Ivanov	Tihomir	BUL	11.7.94	198/77	HJ	2.29			2.28- 14
Ivanytskyy	Vasyl	UKR	29.1.91	186/80	Dec	7683			7651- 14
Ivanyuk	Ilya	RUS	9.3.93	183/75	HJ	2.25i, 2.21			2.30- 15
Ivashko	Pavel	RUS	16.11.94	185/75	400	45.71			45.25- 15
Jaakkola	Aleksi	FIN-J	17.11.97	192/117	HT	73.77			67.10- 15
Jackson	Bershawn	USA	8.5.83	173/69	400h	49.04			47.30- 05
Jacobs	Lamont Marcell	ITA	26.9.94	188/79	LJ	7.95, 8.48w			8.03i- 15, 7.68- 13
Jager	Evan	USA	8.3.89	186/66	1M	3:54.21			3:53.33- 14
	3000	7:40.10i	7:35.16- 12		5000	13:16.86	13:02.40- 13	3kSt	8:04.01	8:00.45- 15
Jagers	Phillip	USA	12.8.95	183/95	DT	62.71			57.33- 15
Jagers	Reggie	USA	13.8.94	185/100	DT	61.64			61.00- 15
Jagor	Jaak-Heinrich	EST	11.5.90	190/80	400h	49.65			49.37- 15
James	Kirani	GRN	1.9.92	185/74	400	43.76			43.74- 14
Jammeh	Adama	GAM	10.6.93	184/79	200	20.45			20.59- 14
Janet	Roberto	CUB	29.8.86	187/106	HT	76.52			78.02- 15
Janezic	Luka	SLO	14.11.95	192/83	400	45.07			45.28- 15
Jasinski	Daniel	GER	5.8.89	207/125	DT	67.16			65.98- 14
Jasper	Martin	GER	6.1.89	193/89	TJ	16.55			16.37- 14
Jaszczuk	Tomasz	POL	9.3.92	195/83	LJ	8.00			8.15- 14
Jayasiri	W.P.Amila	SRI	24.1.94		LJ	8.15			7.86- 14
Jelonek	Jakub	POL	7.7.85	184/71	20kW	1:21:38			1:21:05- 12
Jenkins	Devin	USA	16.2.94	183/75	200	20.39			20.72, 20.13w- 14
Jenkins	Eric	USA	24.11.91	170/61	1500	3:35.94			3:38.98- 15
	3000	7:39.43i	7:41.79- 15		5000	13:24.33	13:07.33- 15	10k	27:48.02	28:59.13- 15
Jensen	Curtis	USA	1.11.90	193/130	SP	20.11			20.33- 14
de Jesús	Mikael Antonio	BRA-J	19.8.97	183/70	400h	49.62			50.96Ax- 15
Jeylan	Ibrahim	ETH	12.6.89	168/57	5000	13:03.22			13:09.16- 13
					10k	26:58.75			27:02.81- 06
Jiang Fan		CHN	16.9.89	188/75	110h	13.61			13.47- 11
Jiang Jie		CHN	25.10.94		20kW	1:22:19			1:22:32- 13
Jílek	Jaroslav	CZE	22.10.89	183/85	JT	83.19			81.45- 15
Jin Min-sub		KOR	2.9.92	185/77	PV	5.60			5.65- 14
Jock	Charles	USA	23.11.89	188/73	800	1:45.48			1:44.67- 11
John	Alexander	GER	3.5.86	185/77	110h	13.38			13.35- 09
Johnson	Brandon	USA	6.3.85	175/68	800	1:46.12			1:43.84- 13
Johnson	Jinson	IND	15.3.91	180/68	800	1:45.98			1:47.58- 15
Johnson	Kibwé	USA	17.7.81	189/108	HT	75.11			80.31- 11
Johnson	Shawn	USA	11.1.94	190/79	TJ	16.58, 16.85w			15.94, 16.21w -15
Jones	Alwyn	AUS	28.2.85	189/72	TJ	16.59			16.83- 09
Jones	Avion	USA	31.1.94	190/75	HJ	2.31			2.25- 14
Jones	Jonathan	USA	23.4.91	183/127	SP	20.82i, 20.36			20.92- 15
Jonsson	Hilmar Örn	ISL	6.5.96	181/100	HT	72.12			69.79- 15
Jordán	Jonay	ESP	12.5.91	192/83	Dec	7639			7543- 12
Jørgensen	Rasmus	DEN	23.1.89	180/75	PV	5.62			5.65- 13
Joseph	Stanley	FRA	24.10.91	181/66	PV	5.75			5.62i- 13, 5.55- 12
Julião	Ronald	BRA	16.6.85	194/113	DT	62.87			65.55- 13
Julmis	Jeffrey	HAI	6.1.87	183/80	110h	13.47			13.50, 13.38w- 11
Junghannß	Karl	GER	6.4.96	178/59	50kW	3:52:46			
Juska	Radek	CZE	8.3.93	195/82	LJ	8.11			8.15- 15
Kaazouzi	Brahim	MAR	15.6.90	179/62	1500	3:35.76			3:38.48- 14
					3000	7:46.58			7:49.73- 15
Kafia	Louhab	ALG	24.2.87	192/77	TJ	16.74			16.76- 15
Kamais	Paul	KEN	24.10.96	178/62	5000	13:17.50			13:21.52- 15

Name		Nat	Born	Ht/Wt	Event	2016 Mark	Pre-2016 Best
Kamworor	Geoffrey	KEN	28.11.92	168/54	5000	12:59.98	13:12.23- 11
10k	27:31.94		26:52.65- 15		HMar	59:10	58:54- 13
Kanda	Luka	KEN	.87		Mar	2:07:21	2:07:20- 15
Kandie	Felix	KEN	10.4.87	178/62	HMar	60:04	60:42- 15
					Mar	2:06:25	2:07:07- 15
Kanervo	Jussi	FIN	1.2.93	180/63	400h	49.87	49.66- 15
Kangas	Arttu	FIN	13.7.93	186/108	SP	20.30	20.09i, 19.79- 15
Kangogo	Albert	KEN	16.8.87		HMar	59:29	62:44- 15
Kangogo	Cornelius	KEN	31.12.93	186/62	5000	13:10.80	13:11.14- 14
Kanter	Gerd	EST	6.5.79	196/125	DT	65.27	73.38- 06
Kapsís	Nikólaos	GRE	5.12.91	181/67	LJ	8.00	7.72- 15
Karaca	Askin	TUR	20.10.90	176/70	TJ	16.63	16.51- 13
Karailiev	Momchil	BUL	21.5.82	188/75	TJ	16.81	17.41- 09
Karakolis	Evan	CAN	30.3.94	183/90	JT	79.30	75.09- 15
Karális	Emmanouil	GRE-Y	20.10.99	183/75	PV	5.55	5.25- 15
Kariuki	Simon	KEN	13.2.92	171/54	10k	27:53.50	-0-
Karlström	Perseus	SWE	2.5.90	184/73	20kW	1:19:11	1:21:54- 14
Karoki	Bidan	KEN	21.8.90	169/53	10k	27:07.30	26:52.36- 14
					HMar	59:32	59:14- 15
Karvinen	Joni	FIN	7.2.94	196/100	JT	80.04	75.24- 14
Kasyanov	Oleksiy	UKR	26.8.85	191/87	Dec	8077	8479- 09
Kato	Nobuya	JPN	16.4.95	185/72	400	45.71	45.69- 13
Katsuki	Hayato	JPN	28.11.90	168/58	50kW	3:52:07	3:59:03- 15
Kawamoto	Sho	JPN	1.3.93	175/68	800	1:45.97	1:45.75 -14
Kawasaki	Kazuya	JPN	2.9.92	180/78	Dec	7665	7679- 15
Kawauchi	Yuki	JPN	5.3.87	172/59	Mar	2:09:01	2:08:14- 13
Kaya	Ali	TUR	20.4.94	171/55	HMar	60:16	61:21- 15
Kaya	Aras	TUR	4.4.94	171/55	3kSt	8:29.91	8:50.74- 14
Kazmirek	Kai	GER	28.1.91	189/91	Dec	8580	8471- 14
Kebenei	Stanley	USA	6.11.89	174/61	3kSt	8:18.52	8:23.93- 15
Kedi	Aman	ETH	16.9.94	173/59	1500	3:37.63	3:36.73- 15
Kehr	Gabriel	CHI	3.9.96		HT	71.33	64.65- 15
Keiner	Sebastian	GER	22.8.89	183/65	1500	3:37.62	3:36.46- 15
Kejelcha	Yomif	ETH-J	1.8.97	186/58	3000	7:28.19	7:36.28- 14
					5000	13:03.29	12:53.98- 15
Keller	Levi	USA	30.1.86	183/82	PV	5.61	5.52- 12
Kemboi	Edward	KEN	12.12.91	170/57	800	1:46.24	1:45.58- 15
Kemboi	Elijah	KEN	10.9.84		Mar	2:09:24	2:07:34- 13
Kemboi	Ezekiel	KEN	25.5.82	175/62	3kSt	8:14.19, 8:08.47dq	7:55.76- 11
Kemboi	Hillary	KEN	.86		3kSt	8:29.0A	8:22.26- 14
Kemboi	Lawrence	KEN	15.6.93	170/57	3kSt	8:17.79	8:18.51- 15
Kemboi	Clement	KEN	1.2.92	180/65	3kSt	8:10.65	8:12.68- 15
Kemper	Deante	USA	27.3.93	181/70	HJ	2.27Ai	2.24i- 15, 2.23- 14
Kendagor	Jacob	KEN	24.8.84	158/50	HMar	61:11+	59:36- 13
					Mar	2:08:56	2:07:47- 15
Kende	Yetwale	ETH	10.1.91	170/57	10k	27:58.22	28:42.3A- 11
Kendricks	Sam	USA	7.9.92	189/79	PV	5.92	5.86Ai, 5.82- 15
Kerio	Reuben	KEN	.94		Mar	2:09:05	-0-
Kerley	Fred	USA	7.5.95	193/91	400	45.10	46.38- 14
Kerr	Ian	BAH	1.5.96	180/73	100	10.12w	10.61, 10.39w- 15
Keter	Emmanuel	KEN	.80		Mar	2:08:47	2:15:17- 14
Keter	Kenneth	KEN	4.8.96		HMar	59:48	62:29- 15
Kgosiemang	Kabelo Mmono	BOT	7.1.86	188/74	HJ	2.25A	2.34A- 08, 2.30- 06
Khodjayev	Sukhrob	UZB	21.5.93	186/105	HT	71.50	78.22- 15
Khorava	Bachana	GEO	15.3.93	172/67	LJ	8.25i, 8.02	8.01- 15
Khoua	Mohcine	MAR-J	26.7.98		LJ	7.86, 7.97w	7.52-15
Khudyakov	Aleksey	RUS	31.3.95		DT	62.23	61.25- 15
Kibet	Alex	KEN	20.10.90	172/52	3kSt	8:18.28	8:28.41- 15
Kibet	Raymond	KEN	4.2.96	188/80	400	45.60A	45.39A, 45.66- 15
Kibet	Stephen	KEN	9.11.86	172/55	HMar	59:27	58:54- 12
Kibet	Vincent	KEN	6.5.91	170/57	1500	3:33.56	3:31.96 -14
1M	3:52.71		3:52.15- 14		3000	7:44.87i	7:58.9- 14
Kibichy	Edwin	KEN	2.4.92	183/73	3kSt	8:30.71	8:33.78- 15
Kibitok	Amos	KEN	4.4.94		3kSt	8:32.20	8:50.74- 14
Kibiwot	Abraham	KEN	4.6.96	175/55	3kSt	8:09.25	8:22.10- 15
Kibor	William	KEN	10.1.85		HMar	61:21	60:51- 14
Kibrab	Awet Niftalem	ERI	9.5.95		5000	13:22.90	13:43.48- 15
Kidder	Brannon	USA	18.11.93	183/66	800	1:46.22	1:45.58- 15
Kifle	Aron	ERI-J	20.2.98		5000	13:13.39	13:17.62- 15
					10k	27:26.20	28:18.44- 15
Kifle	Goitom	ERI	3.12.93	178/60	10k	27:37.65	27:32.00- 13
					HMar	60:49	60:20- 14

524   MEN'S INDEX

Name		Nat	Born	Ht/Wt	Event	2016 Mark			Pre-2016 Best
Kigen	Nobert	KEN	24.1.93		HMar	59:42			60:35- 15
Kigen	Norbert	KEN	24.1.93		Mar	2:09:19			2:09:25- 15
Kiiskilä	Jani	FIN	28.12.89	180/81	JT	78.41			77.83- 14
Kilty	Richard	GBR	2.9.89	184/79	100	10.01, 9.92w			10.05- 15
Kim Duk-hyung		KOR	8.12.85	180/70	LJ	8.22, 8.23w			8.20, 8.41w- 09
					TJ	16.45, 16.57w			17.10- 09
Kim Hyun-sub		KOR	31.5.85	175/53	20kW	1:21:44			1:19:13- 15
					50kW	4:01:06			-0-
Kimani	Bernard	KEN	10.9.93	172/54	10k	27:50.81			27:36.60- 14
					HMar	60:41			60:05- 15
Kimeli	Isaac	BEL	9.3.94	175/59	1500	3:37.79			3:39.73- 15
Kimitei	Wilfred	KEN	11.3.85	172/57	10k	27:54.2A			-0-
Kimurer	Joel	KEN	21.1.88		Mar	2:08:07			2:07:48- 13
Kimutai	Marius	KEN	.89	167/57	Mar	2:05:47			2:09:14- 15
Kimutai	Philip	KEN	10.9.83	170/60	Mar	2:09:19			2:06:07- 11
King	David	GBR	13.6.94	187/79	110h	13.54			13.69, 13.61w- 15
King	Devin	USA	12.3.96	185/75	PV	5.70			5.50- 14
King	Dominic	GBR	30.5.83	179/60	50kW	3:55:48			3:59:22- 15
King	Kyree	USA	9.7.94	181/68	200	20.63, 20.37w			20.51- 15
Kingori	Cyrus	KEN-J	5.1.97	174/54	10k	28:01.76			28:13.81- 15
Kinnunen	Jarkko	FIN	19.1.84	187/69	50kW	3:50:40			3:46:25- 12
Kinyor	Job	KEN	2.9.90	176/68	800	1:46.1A			1:43.76- 12
Kipchirchir	Shadrack	USA	22.2.89	175/60	5000	13:18.52			13:37.68- 14
					10k	27:58.32			27:36.79- 14
Kipchirchir	Victor	KEN	5.12.87		Mar	2:07:39			2:09:13- 12
Kipchoge	Cosmas Jairus	KEN	21.3.86	176/63	HMar	61:02			60:23- 15
Kipchoge	Eliud	KEN	5.11.84	167/52	HMar	59:44			59:25- 12
					Mar	2:03:05			2:04:00- 15
Kipchumba	Hillary	KEN	25.11.92		Mar	2:08:23			2:10:02- 10
Kipkemoi	Daniel	KEN	5.7.96	170/52	10k	27:58.32			27:53.19- 15
Kipkemoi	Kenneth	KEN	2.8.84	165/54	10k	27:52.1A			26:52.65- 12
					HMar	60:05			59:01- 14
Kipketer	Alfred	KEN	26.12.96	169/61	800	1:42.87			1:43.95 -14
Kipketer	Gideon	KEN	10.11.92	178/57	Mar	2:08.35			2:08:14- 12
Kipkoech	John	KEN	29.12.91	160/52	3000	7:42.69			7:32.72- 10
					5000	13:18.17			12:49.50- 12
Kipkoech	Nicholas	KEN	22.10.92	168/57	800	1:43.37A			1:44.9A- 15
					1000	2:16.68			2:17.16- 12
Kipkorir	Joshua	KEN	.94		HMar	60:24			
Kipkorir	Paul	KEN	.82		HMar	60:57			61:11- 11
Kipkosgei	Fredrick	KEN	13.11.96	170/57	5000	13:15.59			13:23.66- 15
Kipkosgei	Nelson	BRN	9.3.93	170/55	3kSt	8:26.23			8:22.24- 12
Kiplagat	Benjamin	UGA	4.3.89	186/61	3kSt	8:20.35			8:03.81- 10
Kiplagat	Henry	KEN	16.12.82		HMar	60:52			60:01- 12
Kiplagat	Silas	KEN	20.8.89	170/57	1500	3:33.68			3:27.64 -14
					1M	3:53.04			3:47.88- 14
Kiplagat	Thomas	KEN			Mar	2:08:34			2:07:52- 14
Kiplangat	Davis	KEN-J	10.7.98		5000	13:16.35			13:56.0A- 13
Kiplangat	Peter	KEN	6.9.93	186/75	800	1:45.04A			1:46.8A- 10
Kipleting	Phenus	KEN	.89		3kSt	8:21.23			
Kiplimo	Jacob	KEN-Y	14.11.00		5000	13:19.54			
					10k	27:26.68			
Kiplimo	Joash	KEN	.91		3kSt	8:30.14A			8:24.26A- 15
Kiprop	Asbel	KEN	30.6.89	186/70	800	1:44.6A			1:43.15- 11
	1000	2:14.23	2:17.38- 15	1500	3:29.33		3:26.69- 15	1M	3:51.48	3:48.50- 09
Kiprotich	Felix	KEN	.88		Mar	2:06:58			2:06:59- 15
Kiprotich	Geoffrey	KEN-J	23.11.97	178/64	400	45.38			47.79- 13
Kiprotich	Stephen	UGA	27.2.89	172/56	Mar	2:07:46			2:06:33- 15
Kiprugut	Boaz	KEN-J	18.5.98	173/61	800	1:44.64A			1:48.95- 15
Kipruto	Amos	KEN	.92		HMar	61:11			63:03- 15
					Mar	2:08:12			-0-
Kipruto	Brimin	KEN	31.7.85	176/54	3kSt	8:18.79			7:53.64- 11
Kipruto	Conseslus	KEN	8.12.94	171/55	3kSt	8:00.12			8:01.16- 13
Kipruto	Vincent	KEN	13.9.87	172/57	HMar	61:19+			60:19- 15
Kipsang	Asbel	KEN	10.9.93		Mar	2:07:30			2:09:26- 15
Kipsang	Emmanuel	KEN	13.6.91	171/62	5000	13:19.09			13:08.55- 15
	10k	27:22.99		27:59.7A- 13		HMar	60:14			63:55- 13
Kipsang	Wilson	KEN	15.3.82	178/59	HMar	61:11+			58:59- 09
					Mar	2:03:13			2:03:23- 13
Kipserem	Douglas	KEN	87		5000	13:13.35			13:34.92A- 14
Kipserem	Marius	KEN	17.5.88		Mar	2:06:11			2:09:21- 15

Name		Nat	Born	Ht/Wt	Event	2016 Mark	Pre-2016 Best
Kiptanui	Eliud	KEN	6.6.89	169/55	HMar	61:13+	61:24- 11
					Mar	2:07:47	2:05:21- 15
Kiptanui	Erick	KEN	.90	173/62	1500	3:37.73A	
Kiptanui	Mathew	KEN	20.10.94		3000	7:44.16	7:53.14- 15
					5000	13:14.06	-0-
Kiptoo	Edwin Kiprop	KEN	14.8.93		HMar	61:00	59:26- 15
Kiptum	Abraham	KEN	.89		HMar	59:36	
Kiptum	Barnabas	KEN	8.10.86	173/64	Mar	2:09:21	2:10:29- 14
Kipyatich	Abraham	KEN	10.5.93		HMar	60:16	60:03- 15
Kipyego	Barnabas	KEN	12.6.95	176/57	3kSt	8:09.13	8:17.03- 14
Kipyego	Barselius	KEN	23.7.93		HMar	59:15	60:51- 15
Kipyego	Bernard	KEN	16.7.86	160/50	Mar	2:06:45	2:06:19- 15
Kipyego	Edwin	KEN	16.11.90		HMar	60:27	59:30- 15
Kipyegon	Vincent	KEN-J	31.12.98	167/54	3kSt	8:22.7A	8:41.7A- 15
Kipyeko	Kennedy	KEN	12.12.90		HMar	61:21	60:39- 15
Kirchler	Hannes	ITA	22.12.78	191/113	DT	64.97	65.01- 07
Kiriazis	Ioánnis	GRE	19.1.96	192/84	JT	87.14	78.41- 15
Kirongo	Sammy	KEN	4.2.94	176/62	800	1:45.6A	1:45.3A- 14, 1:45.38 -14
Kirt	Magnus	EST	10.4.90	192/89	JT	84.47	86.65- 15
Kiru	Kyrylo	UKR	6.5.96	180/65	PV	5.55	4.90i- 14, 4.90- 15
Kirui	Abel	KEN	4.6.82	177/62	Mar	2:08:06	2:05:04- 09
Kirui	Amos	KEN-J	9.2.98	169/54	3kSt	8:20.43	8:51.0A- 15
Kirui	Geoffrey	KEN	16.2.93	158/50	Mar	2:06:27	-0-
Kirui	Peter	KEN	2.1.88	179/64	HMar	59:50	59:22- 14
					Mar	2:08:12	2:06:31- 11
Kiryu	Yoshihide	JPN	15.12.95	175/69	100	10.01	10.01- 13, 9.87w- 15
Kiselkov	Fyodor	RUS	3.6.95		LJ	7.97	7.85- 15
					TJ	16.58	16.50- 15
Kishimoto	Takayuki	JPN	6.5.90	171/61	400h	49.89	48.41- 12
Kishoyan	Alphas	KEN	12.10.94	164/60	400	44.96A	44.75A, 45.81- 15
Kitajima	Hisanori	JPN	16.10.84	170/55	Mar	2:09:16	2:12:28- 15
Kitilit	Jonathan	KEN	24.4.94	171/61	800	1:43.05	1:45.0A- 15
					1000	2:13.95	2:15.78- 15
Kitonyi	Daniel	KEN	12.1.94	163/51	10k	27:49.89	28:02.79- 13
Kitum	Silas	KEN	25.5.90	167/52	3kSt	8:32.63	8:12.17- 11
Kitum	Timothy	KEN	20.11.94	172/60	800	1:44.51A	1:42.53- 12
Kitwara	Sammy	KEN	26.11.86	177/54	Mar	2:05:45	2:04:28- 14
					HMar	59:47	58:47- 11
Kivuva	Jackson	KEN	11.8.88	172/59	800	1:44.0A	1:43.72- 10
Kiyeng	David	KEN	22.4.83		Mar	2:08:58	2:06:26- 09
Kniya	Younès	MAR	15.8.95		3kSt	8:30.85	8:29.7- 15
Kobayashi	Kai	JPN	28.2.93	164/52	20kW	1:19:57	1:19:12- 15
					50kW	3:42:08	-0-
Koblov	Dmitriy	KAZ	30.11.92	186/78	400h	49.39	49.40- 14
Koech	Edwin	KEN	15.5.83		HMar	61:16	59:54- 15
					Mar	2:09:07	2:09:04- 14
Koech	Gilbert Yegon	KEN	6.8.88		Mar	2:08:04	2:06:18- 09
Koech	Haron	KEN	27.1.90	188/79	400h	48.49	49.38- 15
Koech	Isiah	KEN	19.12.93	178/60	3000	7:42.53i	7:30.43- 12
					5000	13:08.34	12:48.64- 12
Koech	John	BRN	23.8.95	174/59	3kSt	8:09.62	8:14.75- 15
Koech	Paul Kipsiele	KEN	10.11.81	168/57	3000	7:45.09i	7:32.78i- 10, 7:33.93- 05
5000	13:23.10	13:02.69i- 12, 13:05.18- 10			3kSt	8:08.32	7:54.31- 12
Koffi	Hua Wilfried	CIV	24.9.89	186/80	100	10.01	10.05- 14
Koffi Hua	Wilfried	CIV	24.9.89	186/80	200	20.35w	20.25- 14
Kogo	Micah	KEN	3.6.86	170/60	Mar	2:08:03	2:06:56- 13
Kolasinac	Asmir	SRB	15.10.84	186/137	SP	20.96	21.58- 15
Kolomoyets	Sergey	BLR	11.8.89	191/110	HT	76.00	77.52- 11
Komon	Leonard Patrick	KEN	10.1.88	175/52	HMar	60:48	59:14- 14
Kondratyev	Roman	RUS	15.5.95	183/77	Dec	7940	7752- 15
Konishi	Yuta	JPN	31.7.90	182/70	400h	49.44	49.41- 11
Konstantinou	Vasilios	CYP	13.9.92	173/60	HJ	2.28i, 2.25	2.20- 14
Kopeykin	Vasiliy	RUS	9.3.88	176/73	LJ	8.22	8.00- 13, 8.13w- 15
Koppelaar	Rutger	NED	1.5.93	187/73	PV	5.53	5.52- 14
Korir	Japhet	KEN	30.6.93	168/55	HMar	61:00	
Korir	Laban	KEN	30.12.85		Mar	2:05:54	2:06:05- 11
Korir	Leonard	KEN/USA	10.12.86	173/61	10k	27:35.65	27:29.40- 11
Korir	Mark	KEN	10.1.85	175/59	Mar	2:06:48	2:05:49- 15
Korir	Nicholas	KEN	18.11.90		HMar	59:50	62:40- 10
Korir	Ronald	KEN	.91		Mar	2:09:01	2:07:29- 14
Korir	Sammy	KEN	29.9.85		Mar	2:08:19	2:08:05- 14

526 MEN'S INDEX

Name		Nat	Born	Ht/Wt	Event	2016 Mark	Pre-2016 Best
Korir Kimining	Shadrack	KEN	10.2.96	170/54	HMar	60:53	-0-
Korolyov	Aleksey	RUS	5.4.82	190/118	HT	73.83	79.36- 08
Korotovskiy	Yevgeniy	RUS	21.6.92	184/102	HT	74.46	72.16- 14
Kosecki	Matthew	USA	1.7.91	188/125	DT	61.91	59.95- 14
Kosencha	Leonard	KEN	21.8.94	174/60	800	1:45.4A	1:43.40- 12
Kosgei	Kiprono	KEN	85		400h	49.22A	49.84A, 51.18- 15
Kosgei	Martin	KEN	.89		Mar	2:07:22	2:09:50- 15
Kosgei	Samuel Kiplimo	KEN	20.1.86	173/55	Mar	2:06:53	2:07:07- 15
Kosimbei	Nicholas	KEN	1.10.96		5000	13:17.08	13:51.0A- 14
					10k	27:02.59	28:37.58A- 14
Kostoglídis	Konstadínos-Ioánnis	GRE	10.8.90	181/101	HT	75.10	71.16- 15
Kosynskyy	Dmytro	UKR	31.3.89	200/105	JT	84.08	83.39- 11
Kotut	Cyprian	KEN	.92		HMar	61:04	59:12- 14
					Mar	2:07:11	2:08:55- 15
Kotze	Jan-Louw	RSA	18.3.94	185/100	DT	62.11	59.72- 15
Koumi	Sadam	SUD	6.4.94	173/68	400	45.67	45.41- 15
Kovacs	Joe	USA	28.6.89	181/132	SP	22.13	22.56- 15
Kövágó	Zoltán	HUN	10.4.79	204/127	DT	67.13	69.95- 06
Kovalenko	Nazar	UKR	9.2.89	178/68	20kW	1:21:21	1:19:46- 14
Kovals	Ainars	LAT	21.11.81	192/105	JT	79.02	86.64- 08
Kowal	Yoann	FRA	28.5.87	172/58	3000	7:45.11	7:44.26i- 12, 7:54.31- 15
					3kSt	8:16.21	8:12.53- 13
Kownatke	Rafal	POL	24.3.85	189/133	SP	20.37i, 19.72	20.13- 13
Kozlov	Vladimir	BLR	20.4.85	183/87	JT	79.34	82.86- 12
Kranjc	Matija	SLO	12.6.84	181/81	JT	81.13	80.46- 14
Krauss	Simon	FRA	12.2.92	182/75	110h	13.53, 13.45w	13.51- 14, 13.41w- 13
Kruger	A.G.	USA	18.2.79	193/118	HT	75.32	79.26- 04
Krukowski	Marcin	POL	14.6.92	182/92	JT	84.74	85.20- 15
Krymarenko	Yuriy	UKR	11.8.83	187/65	HJ	2.27	2.34i- 07, 2.34- 13
Kszczot	Adam	POL	2.9.89	178/64	800	1:43.76	1:43.30- 11
Kucera	Martin	SVK	10.5.90	193/74	400h	49.08	49.79 -13
Kucmín	Antón	SVK	7.6.84	180/64	20kW	1:20:43	1:21:59- 14
Kudlicka	Jan	CZE	29.4.88	184/76	PV	5.83 5.80i- 14,5.76,5.83exdh- 13,5.81ex- 11	
Kudryavtsev	Denis	RUS	13.4.92	187/77	400h	49.43	48.05- 15
Kulayev	Aleksey	RUS	7.5.94		SP	19.94	18.67- 15
Kuma	Abera	ETH	31.8.90	160/50	Mar	2:07:48	2:05:56- 14
Kumar	Amit	IND	18.9.92		JT	79.14	77.50- 15
Kumar Sangwan	Sandeep	IND	16.12.86	183/68	20kW	1:20:44	1:22:16- 15
Kupers	Thijmen	NED	4.10.91	180/65	800	1:45.23	1:45.28 -15
					1000	2:17.02i	-0-
Kupper	Martin	EST	31.5.89	198/119	DT	66.61	66.67- 15
Kurong	Moses	UGA	7.7.94		10k	27:27.43	28:31.80 -13
Kuznetsov	Viktor	UKR	17.7.86	194/82	LJ	8.05	8.11i- 10, 8.10- 12, 8.25w- 06
Kwambai	Robert Kipkorir	KEN	22.11.85		Mar	2:08:03	2:08:18- 15
Kwemboi	Gilbert	KEN-J	3.10.97	178/61	1500	3:33.71	3:40.47- 15
Kwemoi	Rodgers Chumo	KEN-J	3.3.97		10k	27:25.23	
Kwemoi	Ronald	KEN	19.9.95	180/68	1500	3:30.49	3:28.81 -14
5000	13:27.77		13:16.14- 15		10k	27:33.94	-0-
Kynard	Eric	USA	3.2.91	193/86	HJ	2.35	2.37- 13
Laanmäe	Tanel	EST	29.9.89	183/94	JT	85.04	83.82- 15
Laari	Sampson	GHA	3.3.93	170/61	800	1:46.44	1:51.48- 15
Labutov	Yevgeniy	KAZ	17.11.84	194/120	DT	60.23, 65.94 doubtful	59.06- 13
Lagat	Alfers	KEN	7.8.86		HMar	61:11+	60:33- 15
					Mar	2:08:28	2:06:48- 15
Lagat	Bernard	USA	12.12.74	174/61	3000	7:43.63, 7:41.25i	7:29.00- 10
5000	13:06.78		12:53.60- 11		10k	27:49.35	-0-
Lagat	Cosmas	KEN	.95		Mar	2:08:14	2:08:33- 14
Lagat	Justus	KEN	20.5.96	168/55	3kSt	8:22.5A	8:26.37- 15
Lagat	Peter	KEN	26.5.92		5000	13:18.78	14:08.3A- 14
Lahoulou	Abdelmalik	ALG	7.5.92	180/70	400h	48.62	48.67- 15
Laidig	Torben	GER	13.3.94	187/82	PV	5.62i, 5.60	5.45i, 5.42- 14
Laine	Samyr	HAI	17.7.84	188/82	TJ	16.64	17.39A, 17.45w- 09, 17.36- 13
Lalang	Lawi	KEN	15.6.91	170/58	3000	7:45.07i	7:36.44- 14
Lambert	James "JC"	USA	12.4.90	186/107	HT	71.94	72.49- 15
Lambrughi	Mario	ITA	5.2.92	184/75	400h	49.35	50.20- 15
Lancashire	Tom	GBR	2.7.85	179/63	1500	3:37.47	3:33.96- 10
Landon	Kyle	USA	16.10.94	193/77	HJ	2.26	2.21i- 15, 2.20- 14
Lang	Simon	GER	16.8.95	186/92	HT	72.61	69.70- 15
Langat	Betwell	KEN	20.11.96		TJ	16.55A	15.82A- 14
Langat	Leonard	KEN	7.8.90	175/58	HMar	59:18	59:52- 11
Langton-Burnell	Benjamin	NZL	10.7.92	183/82	JT	79.80	77.97- 15

Name		Nat	Born	Ht/Wt	Event	2016 Mark	Pre-2016 Best
Lapierre	Fabrice	AUS	17.10.83	179/66	LJ	8.31, 8.36w	8.40, 8.78w- 10
Laptev	Sergey	RUS	7.2.91	176/70	TJ	16.73	16.63- 11
Lasa	Emiliano	URU	25.1.90	180/75	LJ	8.16	8.09, 8.17w- 15
Lattin	Amere	USA-J	17.2.97	188/79	110h	13.59	-0-
Lauro	Germán	ARG	2.4.84	185/127	SP	20.29i, 20.10	21.26- 13
Lavillenie	Renaud	FRA	18.9.86	177/69	PV	6.03i, 5.98	6.16i- 14, 6.05- 15
Lavillenie	Valentin	FRA	16.7.91	170/65	PV	5.71	5.80i, 5.70- 15
Lawrence	Desmond	USA	19.12.91	178/77	100	10.08	10.24, 10.12w- 14
Lawson	Jarrion	USA	6.5.94	188/75	100	10.07, 10.01w	10.04, 9.90w- 15
200	20.17				LJ	8.58	8.39Ai- 14, 8.34, 8.36w- 15
				20.86- 15			
Leandersson	Jonas	SWE	26.1.91	176/61	1500	3:36.92	3:39.37- 14
Lebioda	Piotr	POL	28.5.92	187/85	JT	78.56	76.01- 15
Ledama	Wesley	KEN-Y	2.7.99	173/57	5000	13:23.34	
Lee	BeeJay	USA	5.3.93	168/72	100	10.09, 10.08w	9.99, 9.94w- 15
					200	20.23	20.11- 15
Lee	Dexter	JAM	18.1.91	186/77	100	10.14	10.06- 11
Lee Yun-chul		KOR	28.3.82	188/110	HT	72.55	72.98- 13
Legesse	Berhanu	ETH	11.9.94	168/55	HMar	60:40	59:20- 15
Lehata	Mosito	LES	8.4.89	177/69	100	10.12, 10.04w	10.11- 15
Lehto	Jesse	FIN	12.2.93	180/85	HT	73.09	72.31- 15
Lehtola	Sampo	FIN	10.5.89	188/82	JT	81.88	83.77- 11
Lelièvre	Jérémy	FRA	8.2.91	186/80	Dec	7807	7911- 12
Lemaitre	Christophe	FRA	11.6.90	189/74	100	10.07	9.92- 11
					200	20.01	19.80- 11
Lemi Berhanu	Hayle	ETH	13.9.94	172/56	Mar	2:04:33	2:05:28- 15
Lemiso	Thomas	KEN		95	800	1:46.36	1:49.1A- 13
Lemma	Sisay	ETH	12.12.90		HMar	61:11+	61:11+- 14
					Mar	2:05:16	2:06:26- 15
Lendore	Deon	TTO	28.10.92	179/75	400	45.31	44.36- 14
Lepage	Pierce	CAN	22.1.96		Dec	8027	-0-
Leptikov	Viktor	KAZ	2.7.87	196/80	400h	49.78	49.79- 12
Lescay	Yoandys	CUB	5.1.94	181/77	400	45.00	45.13A- 15, 45.29- 13
Leslie	Cory	USA	24.10.89	175/60	1500	3:37.67+i	3:34.93- 13
1M	3:53.87i		3:53.44- 14		3kSt	8:19.12	8:20.08- 13
Lesnoy	Aleksandr	RUS	28.7.88	194/116	SP	21.03	21.40- 14
Letnicov	Vladimir	MDA	7.10.81	178/70	TJ	16.86	17.06- 02
Letting	Vincent	KEN	16.6.93	171/60	1500	3:35.12	3:36.61A- 12
Levins	Cameron	CAN	28.3.89	181/68	3000	7:45.44i	7:41.59i- 14
Levy	Ronald	JAM	30.10.92	181/73	100	10.10w	10.48- 12
					110h	13.50	13.63- 15
Lewandowski	Marcin	POL	13.6.87	180/64	800	1:43.73	1:43.72- 15
1000	2:14.30		2:15.76- 11		1500	3:37.69	3:37.37i, 3:38.19- 14
Lewin	Teivaskie	JAM	27.12.91	183/73	110h	13.68, 13.59w	13.84- 14
Lewis	Romel	JAM	28.1.88	178/75	400h	49.32	50.63A- 12
Lewis	Steve	GBR	20.5.86	191/83	PV	5.60	5.82- 12
Leyver Ojeda	José	MEX	12.11.85	164/52	50kW	3:50:40	3:49:16A- 11
Li Chengbin		CHN	22.2.90		LJ	7.99i	7.94- 14, 7.96w-13
Li Jinzhe		CHN	1.9.89	188/64	LJ	8.04	8.47- 14
Li Tianlei		CHN	13.3.95	173/63	20kW	1:21:39	1:20:57- 15
Lihrman	Michael	USA	6.12.91	196/114	HT	73.70	75.29- 15
Liipola	Henri	FIN	24.4.94	188/105	HT	72.12	64.94- 15
Likhanov	Yevgeniy	RUS	10.1.95	187/82	Dec	7856	7869- 15
Lilesa	Feyisa	ETH	1.2.90	158/50	HMar	60:45	59:22- 12
					Mar	2:06:56	2:04:52- 12
Limo	Remmy	KEN	3.2.88	173/55	5000	13:15.94	-0-
					HMar	60:06	-0-
Lin Hung-Min		TPE	7.9.90	177/73	LJ	8.04	7.86- 12, 7.95w- 14
Lincoln	Scott	GBR	7.5.93	184/114	SP	19.59	18.54- 15
Lingua	Marco	ITA	4.6.78	176/118	HT	76.03	79.97- 08
Linke	Christopher	GER	24.10.88	191/66	20kW	1:19:19	1:20:37- 15
Lisek	Piotr	POL	16.8.92	188/85	PV	5.77i, 5.75	5.90i- 15, 5.82- 14
Litanyuk	Valeriy	UKR	2.4.94		50kW	3:58:33	4:31:00- 15
Litvinov	Sergey	RUS	27.1.86	185/110	HT	77.67	80.98- 12
Liu Jian		CHN	19.5.95		50kW	3:47:51	3:56:25- 15
Liu Ruihai		CHN	23.12.96		TJ	16.71i, 16.37	16.13- 15
Liu Yang		CHN	29.10.86	190/110	SP	19.68	19.77- 13
Livermore	Jason	JAM	25.4.88	178/77	100	10.03	10.05 -14, 10.01Aw- 15
Locke	Dentarius	USA	12.12.89	170/68	100	10.12, 10.10w	9.96, 9.91w- 13
Lokomwa	Thomas	KEN	26.12.87		HMar	60:56	60:33- 15
Lomnicky	Marcel	SVK	6.7.87	177/106	HT	77.48	79.16- 14
Lomong	Lopez	USA	1.1.85	178/67	3000	7:43.01i	7:39.81- 14

Name		Nat	Born	Ht/Wt	Event	2016 Mark	Pre-2016 Best
London	Wilbert	USA-J	17.8.97	183/68	400	45.27	45.96- 15
Longosiwa	Thomas	KEN	14.1.82	175/57	3000	7:41.31	7:30.09- 09
					5000	13:01.69	12:49.04- 12
Lonyangata	Paul	KEN	12.12.92	170/55	HMar	60:11	59:53- 12
López	Francisco Javier	ESP	29.12.89	181/70	110h	13.56w	13.62- 15
López	Kevin	ESP	12.6.90	172/60	800	1:45.61	1:43.74- 12
López	Luis Fernando	COL	3.6.79	173/60	20kW	1:21:32	1:20:03- 09
López	Miguel Ángel	ESP	3.7.88	181/70	20kW	1:20:34	1:19:14- 15
					50kW	3:53:52	-0-
López	Yeimer	CUB	20.8.82	184/73	800	1:45.75	1:43.07- 08
López Menjivar	Luis	ESA	18.1.94		50kW	4:01:59A	-0-
Lovett	Eddie	ISV	25.6.92	181/73	110h	13.39	13.31A- 15, 13.39, 13.29w- 13
Loxsom	Casimir	USA	17.3.91	183/64	800	1:45.93	1:44.92- 15
Loyanae	Wilson	KEN	20.11.88		Mar	2:05:13	2:05:37- 12
Lu Yang		CHN	9.1.96		110h	13.60	13.81- 15
Ludolph	Sören	GER	25.2.88	180/68	800	1:46.43	1:44.80- 12
Lukás	Marek	CZE	16.7.91	180/75	Dec	7903	7892- 15
Lukyanenko	Artem	RUS	30.1.90	193/84	Dec	8055	8177- 13
Lukyanenko	Yevgeniy	RUS	23.1.85	190/80	PV	5.65i, 5.55	6.01- 08
Lukyanov	Denis	RUS	11.7.89	190/115	HT	75.92	79.61- 13
Lukyanov	Ivan	RUS	31.1.81	178/67	3kSt	8:30.38	8:18.97- 08
Lundy	John	USA	15.3.92	188/84	200	20.70, 20.34w	20.67- 15
Luo Dongpo		CHN	23.6.95		50kW	3:59:10	3:56:46- 15
Luron	Kevin	FRA	8.11.91	184/80	TJ	16.53, 16.89w	16.63, 16.83w- 15
Lyadusov	Konstantin	RUS	2.3.88	190/125	SP	20.88i, 20.62	20.57- 15
Lyakhovich	Aleksandr	BLR	4.7.89	171/65	20kW	1:21:14	1:21:49- 15
Lyles	Noah	USA-J	18.7.97	182/73	100	10.16, 9.9, 10.08w	10.14, 10.07w-15
					200	20.09, 230.10w	20.18- 15
Lysenko	Danyil	RUS-J	19.5.97	192/73	HJ	2.31i, 2.30	2.24- 14
Lyzhin	Pavel	BLR	24.3.81	189/110	SP	20.70i, 19.91	21.21- 10
Ma Qun		CHN	8.2.94		JT	78.82	79.39- 15
Maartens	Hendrik	RSA	24.5.96	183/75	200	20.51A, 20.0Aw	21.07- 15
Mägi	Rasmus	EST	4.5.92	188/74	400h	48.40	48.54- 14
Magour	Ahmed Bader	QAT	3.3.96	190/90	JT	84.74	77.88- 15
Magut	James	KEN	20.7.90	180/64	1500	3:35.18	3:30.61- 14
Maheswary	Renjith	IND	30.1.86	177/72	TJ	17.30	17.07- 10, 17.19w-07
Mahmoud	Hassan Mohamed	EGY	10.2.84	188/110	HT	78.39	78.21- 15
Mahoney	Travis	USA	25.7.90	175/61	3kSt	8:25.44	8:27.08- 15
Maiau	Raihau	PYF	1.8.92	184/77	LJ	8.02i, 7.91w	7.99i, 7.98, 8.14w- 15
Maina	Johana	KEN	24.12.90	170/54	HMar	61:19	61:29- 15
Maina	John	KEN	14.7.93	179/53	5000	13:16.82	13:24.21- 15
					10k	27:21.97	27:35.54- 15
Maiyo	Duncan	KEN	5.8.90		Mar	2:09:25	2:10:15- 15
Maiyo	Hillary	KEN	2.10.93	174/61	3000	7:44.99	7:39.70- 15
Majdán	Dusan	SVK	8.9.87	180/67	50kW	3:58:25	3:53:26- 14
Majewski	Tomasz	POL	30.8.81	204/140	SP	21.08	21.95- 09
Makau	Nicholas	KEN	15.10.90	176/52	HMar	61:03	62:28- 15
Makau	Patrick	KEN	2.3.85	173/57	Mar	2:08:57	2:03:38- 11
Makhloufi	Taoufik	ALG	29.4.88	181/66	800	1:42.61	1:43.53 -14
1500	3:31.35		3:28.75- 15 1M	3:52.24	3:52.16- 14		
Makhrosenko	Zakhar	BLR	10.10.91	182/105	HT	77.41	76.08- 13
Makopane	Rantso	RSA	8.8.94	178/61	3kSt	8:31.72	8:45.12- 14
Makwala	Isaac	BOT	29.9.86	183/79	200	20.42A	19.96, 19.7A- 14
					400	44.85	43.72- 15
Malachowski	Piotr	POL	7.6.83	194/135	DT	68.15	71.84- 13
Mallett	Aaron	USA	26.9.94	188/79	110h	13.48	13.59, 13.40w- 15
Malykhin	Vladyslav	UKR-J	15.1.98	184/76	PV	5.55	5.30- 15
Mamba	Alberto	MOZ	9.10.94	175/64	800	1:46.32	1:46.5- 15, 1:46.68 -14
Manangoi	Elijah	KEN	5.1.93	181/65	800	1:45.1A	1:47.40- 15
1000	2:17.09i	-0-	1500	3:31.19	3:29.67- 15	1M	3:52.04	-0-
Manenti	Davide	ITA	16.4.89	178/80	200	20.44	20.60- 13
Manga	Aurel	FRA	24.7.92	188/75	110h	13.33, 13.25w	13.69- 14
Mannio	Ari	FIN	23.7.87	185/104	JT	81.38	86.82- 15
Mansilla	Humberto	CHI	22.5.96	180/100	HT	72.67	71.01- 15
Manyonga	Luvo	RSA	18.11.91	185/65	LJ	8.48	8.26- 11
Manzano	Leonel	USA	12.9.84	165/57	1500	3:36.62	3:30.98- 14
Marcell	Jan	CZE	4.6.85	197/111	SP	19.74	20.93- 14
					DT	61.68	66.00- 11
Mardare	Adrian	MDA	20.6.95	194/92	JT	78.48	75.60- 15
Marghiev	Serghei	MDA	6.11.92	194/96	HT	78.48	78.72- 15
Markies	Bas	NED	24.7.84	183/70	Dec	7794	7514- 14

Name		Nat	Born	Ht/Wt	Event	2016 Mark	Pre-2016 Best
Markovic	Martin	CRO	13.1.96	190/110	DT	62.01	62.43- 15
Marofit	Mourad	MAR	26.1.82	178/62	HMar	59:33	61:43- 06
Márquez	Dayron	COL	11.6.83	181/93	JT	82.39A	80.61A- 12, 82.20Au- 08
Marschall	Kurtis	AUS-J	25.4.97	188/78	PV	5.70	5.42- 15
Martin	Cory	USA	22.5.85	196/125	SP	20.40	22.10- 10
Martin	Romain	FRA	12.7.88	198/86	Dec	7860	8104 -14
Martín	Álvaro	ESP	18.6.94	181/62	20kW	1:19:36	1:20:19- 15
Martina	Churandy	NED	3.7.84	178/75	100	10.01	9.91- 9, 9.76Aw- 06
					200	19.81	19.85- 12
Martinez	Yancarlos	DOM	8.7.92	167/61	100	10.15, 10.11w	10.14- 15
					200	20.19	20.22- 15
Martínez	Guillermo	CUB	28.6.81	185/106	JT	81.49	87.20A- 11
Martínez	Jorge Alejandro	MEX	25.10.90		20kW	1:20:51	1:27:17A- 13
					50kW	3:51:11A	3:55:21A- 15
Martínez	José Ernesto	CUB	1.1.91	175/73	TJ	16.40, 16.55w	16.78- 15
Martínez	Lázaro	CUB-J	3.11.97	192/83	TJ	17.06	17.24- 14
Martínez	Lois Maikel	ESP	3.6.81	185/90	DT	66.96	67.45- 05
Martinot Lagarde	Pascal	FRA	22.9.91	190/80	110h	13.12	12.95- 14
Martinot Lagarde	Thomas	FRA	7.2.88	186/78	110h	13.61, 13.55w	13.26- 13
Martins	Danylo	BRA	21.11.92		LJ	8.08	7.88- 14
Martinsen	Andreas	DEN	17.7.90	190/82	110h	13.65, 13.59w	13.55- 15
Martos	Sebastián	ESP	20.6.89	178/63	3kSt	8:19.33	8:18.31- 14
Martynyuk	Andriy	UKR	25.9.90	184/110	HT	74.90	77.70- 12
Maruo	Satoshi	JPN	28.11.91		20kW	1:20:14	1:19:42- 15
					50kW	4:02:36	
Masai	Gilbert	KEN	20.5.81		HMar	59:31	59:57- 12
Masilo	Boitumelo	BOT	5.8.95	173/64	800	1:45.87	1:46.80- 15
Maslák	Pavel	CZE	21.2.91	176/67	400	45.06	44.79- 14
Mason	Michael	CAN	30.9.86	188/67	HJ	2.29	2.33- 15
Mason	Tyler	JAM	15.1.95	183/73	110h	13.46	13.32A, 13.39- 15
Massó	Maykel	CUB-Y	8.5.99	176/65	LJ	8.28	8.12- 15
Masuno	Genta	JPN	24.5.93	182/76	110h	13.59, 13.51w	13.58- 14
Matadi	Emmanuel	LBR	15.4.91	183/85	100	10.14, 9.97w	10.35- 14, 10.19w- 15
					200	20.44	20.54- 15
Mätas	Risto	EST	30.4.84	189/91	JT	83.09	83.48- 13
Mathews	Luke	AUS	21.6.95	188/75	800	1:45.16	1:47.60- 15
					1500	3:35.99	3:40.58- 15
Mathieu	Michael	BAH	24.6.83	180/78	400	45.42	45.00- 15
Matsunaga	Daisuke	JPN	24.3.95	174/60	20kW	1:18:53	1:19:08- 15
Matsushita	Yuki	JPN	9.9.91	176/64	400h	49.10	49.14- 15
Matthews	Julian	NZL	21.7.88	178/66	1500	3:36.14	3:37.37- 15
Matthews	Peter	JAM	13.11.89	189/77	400	45.36	44.69- 15
Mattis	Sam	USA	19.3.94	185/100	DT	67.45	62.48- 15
Matusevicius	Edis	LTU	30.6.96	184/79	JT	81.28	78.82- 15
Maxwell	Elbert	USA	20.10.92		LJ	8.04w	7.67- 15
Mayer	Kevin	FRA	10.2.92	186/77	Dec	8834	8521- 14
Mazur	Vladyslav	UKR	21.11.96	173/64	LJ	7.96	7.87- 15
Mbugua	Bernard Nganga	KEN	17.1.85	178/59	3kSt	8:30.87	8:05.88- 11
McBride	Brandon	CAN	15.6.94	195/75	800	1:43.95	1:45.35- 14
McBride	Bryan	USA	10.12.91	188/77	HJ	2.26Ai, 2.24	2.30- 15
McClain	Remontay	USA	21.9.92	188/85	100	10.14, 10.04w	10.07, 9.82w- 15
McClain	Terrell	USA	10.11.95	196/88	LJ	7.95	7.63- 15
McCullough	Conor	USA	31.1.91	186/102	HT	74.79	77.20- 14
McDonald	Jonia	JAM	16.12.89	190/77	400	45.61	45.63- 15
McDonald	Rusheen	JAM	17.8.92	175/73	400	45.22	43.93- 15
McEntee	Sam	AUS	3.2.92	190/75	5000	13:20.72	13:50.51- 15
McFarlane	Javier	PER	21.10.91	186/78	110h	13.52A, 13.55, 13.31Aw	13.57, 13.51Aw- 14
McFarlane	Jorge	PER	20.2.88	176/70	110h	13.53A, 13.57, 13.48Aw	13.53- 14, 13.5- 13
McGorty	Sean	USA	8.3.95	187/72	1M	3:53.95i	3:59.34i - 15
McLaughlin	Taylor	USA-J	2.8.97	183/75	400h	49.45	50.20- 15
McLean	Sean	USA	23.3.92	185/79	100	10.08	10.01- 15
					200	20.24	20.37- 15
McLeod	Omar	JAM	25.4.94	180/73	100	9.99	
					110h	12.98	12.97- 15
McMaster	Kyron	IVB-J	3.1.97	187/79	400h	49.56	50.16- 15
McNamara	Jordan	USA	7.3.87	178/64	1500	3:38.07	3:34.00- 13
McNeill	David	AUS	6.10.86	175/59	5000	13:23.87	13:18.60- 12
					10k	27:51.71	27:45.01- 15
McQuay	Tony	USA	16.4.90	180/70	400	44.24	44.40- 13
McRae	Trey	USA	12.7.93	190/79	HJ	2.25	2.22- 15

530　MEN'S INDEX

Name		Nat	Born	Ht/Wt	Event	2016 Mark	Pre-2016 Best
Mead	Hassan	USA	28.8.89	174/61	1500	3:37.65	3:38.72- 14
3000	7:38.85i		7:46.18- 13		5000	13:04.17	13:02.80- 14
Mechaal	Adel	ESP	5.12.90	184/67	1500	3:35.24	3:36.55- 15
3000	7:39.51	7:46.92i, 7:52.16- 15			5000	13:15.40	14:10.59- 15
Medhin	Teklemariam	ERI	24.6.89	178/57	10k	27:42.34	27:16.69- 12
Megersa	Tujuba	ETH	15.10.87		Mar	2:09:28	2:09:54- 15
Meité	Ben Youssef	CIV	11.11.86	179/70	100	9.96, 9.95w	10.04- 15
Mejias	Reinier	CUB	22.9.90	178/98	HT	72.56	75.98- 13
Mekashaw	Kassa	ETH	19.3.84	167/54	10k	27:43.55	27:38.93- 14
Mekhissi-Benabbad	Mahiedine	FRA	15.3.85	190/75	3kSt	8:08.15	8:00.09- 13
Mekonnen	Tsegaye	ETH	15.6.95	174/56	Mar	2:04:46	2:04:32- 13
Melich	Lukáš	CZE	16.9.80	186/110	HT	75.97	80.28- 13
Melly	Edwin	KEN	23.4.94	178/60	800	1:45.20	1:43.81- 12
Melo	Aleksandro	BRA	26.9.95	179/56	LJ	7.92, 8.06w	8.12- 15
					TJ	16.53	16.28- 15
Mena	Reynier	CUB	21.11.96	174/79	200	20.41	20.32- 15
Menaldo	Kévin	FRA	12.7.92	176/66	PV	5.80	5.81- 15
Mendieta	José Ángel	CUB	16.10.91	187/84	Dec	7680	7967h- 13
Menga	Aleixo Platini	GER	29.9.87	179/76	200	20.27	20.33- 12
Mengich	Richard	KEN	3.4.89	185/68	HMar	59:35	59:59- 15
Mengistu	Asefa	ETH	18.1.85		Mar	2:08:41	2:19:40- 14
Mengistu	Azmeraw	ETH	15.9.92	166/52	10k	27:40.76	27:33.82- 15
					HMar	61:17	60:48- 15
Menjo	Josephat	KEN	20.8.79	168/50	5000	13:20.51	12:55.95- 10
Merber	Kyle	USA	19.11.90	180/64	1500	3:35.83	3:34.54- 15
					1M	3:54.57	3:54.76- 14
Merga	Imane	ETH	15.10.88	174/61	5000	13:06.25	12:53.58- 10
					10k	27:27.33	26:48.35- 11
Merritt	Aries	USA	24.7.85	182/70	110h	13.22	12.80- 12
Merritt	LaShawn	USA	27.6.86	188/82	200	19.74	19.98- 07, 19.80w- 08
					400	43.85	43.65- 15
Mertzanídis-Despotéris	Mihaíl	GRE	21.8.87	186/70	LJ	7.95	8.05- 10
Merzougui	Abdelaziz	ESP	30.8.91	177/62	3kSt	8:26.15	8:18.03- 12
Mesic	Kemal	BIH	4.8.85	196/110	SP	20.74	20.71- 15
Messaoudi	Ali	ALG	13.10.95	178/63	3kSt	8:27.99	8:36.23- 15
Mezones	Freddy	VEN	24.9.87	176/68	400	45.55	45.53- 15
Mihaljevic	Filip	CRO	31.7.94	201/113	SP	20.87i, 20.71	20.16- 15
					DT	62.43	63.11- 15
Mikhou	Sadik	BRN	25.7.90	174/61	1500	3:32.30	3:33.31- 13
					3000	7:39.02	-0-
Mikos	Mateusz	POL	10.4.87	196/107	SP	20.18	20.06- 15
Milanov	Philip	BEL	6.7.91	191/118	DT	67.26, 68.44dh	66.90- 15
Mileusnic	Dejan	BIH	16.11.91	183/84	JT	81.63	80.40- 14
Miller	Ashinia	JAM	6.6.93	189/100	SP	20.06i, 20.02	20.31i, 19.84- 15
Miller	Brunson	USA	10.2.91	183/77	400	45.63	45.86- 13
Miller	Nick	GBR	1.5.93	188/112	HT	76.93	77.55- 15
Millington	Ross	GBR	19.9.89	173/58	10k	27:55.06	-0-
Milliron	Jeff	USA	18.1.92	193/118	DT	61.52	57.50- 15
Milne	Taylor	CAN	14.6.81	180/66	3kSt	8:26.97	8:19.90- 15
Minemura	Kota	JPN	22.12.92	176/63	LJ	7.95	7.94- 14, 8.08w- 15
Minshin ¶	Ildar	RUS	5.2.85	172/63	3kSt	8:25.84 drugs dq	8:17.74- 11
Minzie	Jevaughn	JAM	20.7.95	173/66	100	10.02	10.16, 10.14w- 14
Misans	Elvijs	LAT	8.4.89	190/77	LJ	8.08	8.05- 14
					TJ	16.77	16.58- 11
Mitchell	Curtis	USA	11.3.89	188/79	200	20.37	19.97- 13
Mitchell-Blake	Nethaneel	GBR	2.4.94	186/75	100	10.09	10.42- 14, 10.40w- 13
					200	19.95	20.62- 13
Miticov	Andrei	MDA	15.11.86	183/70	HJ	2.25	2.24- 07
Mitskov	Maksim	BLR	1.12.95		HT	71.84	67.84- 15
Miyao	Kotaro	JPN	12.7.91	172/72	400h	49.67	50.56- 14
Modin	Mitch	USA	12.4.95	190/84	Dec	7785	7578- 15
Mogi	Keijiro	JPN	21.10.95	168/52	HMar	60:54	63:11- 15
Mohammed	Abdullah Abkar	KSA-J	.97	172/73	100	10.04	10.45- 15
					200	20.29w	21.08- 15
Mokoena	Khotso	RSA	6.3.85	190/73	TJ	16.77	17.35- 14
Mokoka	Stephen	RSA	31.1.85	156/50	5000	13:23.66	13:11.44- 15
					10k	27:48.84	27:40.73- 12
Molmy	Darien	FRA	2.10.88	175/63	50kW	3:59:35	
Montaña	José Leonardo	COL	21.3.92	168/61	50kW	3:52:48A	-0-
Montgomery	Kahmari	USA-J	16.8.97	175/66	400	45.13	46.24- 15
Moore	Darien	USA	10.6.91	185/105	SP	20.33	19.31- 14

MEN'S INDEX 531

Name		Nat	Born	Ht/Wt	Event	2016 Mark	Pre-2016 Best
Moore	Isaiah	USA	12.6.96	183/79	110h	13.68, 13.54w	13.72- 15
Moore	Jordan	USA	13.12.93	190/101	110h	13.53	13.47- 15
Morain	Moriba	TTO	8.10.92	177/70	100	10.09w	10.22- 12
Morgan	Jason	JAM	6.10.82	186/114	DT	63.11	68.19- 15
Morgan	Ricky	USA	7.1.96	175/70	400	45.54	46.51- 15
Morgunov	Timur	RUS	12.10.96	188/77	PV	5.80i, 5.60	5.50- 15
Morioka	Koichiro	JPN	2.4.85	184/64	50kW	3:58:59	3:43:14- 12
Moro	Yasuhiro	JPN	21.12.94	180/70	LJ	7.80, 7.96w	7.84- 14, 7.86w- 15
Mörö	Oskari	FIN	31.1.93	181/66	400h	49.04	49.08- 14
Morris	Joe	USA	4.10.89	180/68	100	10.15, 10.09w	10.19, 9.98w- 15
					200	20.61, 20.39w	20.43- 15
Morse	Brett	GBR	11.2.89	191/114	DT	63.08	66.84- 13
Morse	Mikese	USA	30.10.87	185/73	LJ	7.94	7.90i- 09, 7.89, 8.08w- 14
Morton	Amaechi	NGR	30.10.89	187/77	400h	49.77	48.79- 12
Mosby	Correion	USA	31.1.96	180/70	200	20.29A	21.13w- 14
Moses	Nathaniel	USA	1.4.90	183/100	DT	64.49	61.81- 14
Moss	Miller	USA	14.3.88	193/86	Dec	7822	7996- 11
Mouhyadin	Abdi Waiss	DJI	3.7.96	168/52	1500	3:34.55	3:36.09- 15
Mousavi	Kaveh	IRI	27.5.85	196/105	HT	77.40	75.26- 11
Mozia	Stephen	NGR	16.8.93	190/114	SP	21.76	20.79i, 20.46- 14
					DT	62.20	62.80- 14
Mudrov	Ilya	RUS	17.11.91	190/79	PV	5.80	5.78i- 15, 5.70- 14
Mudrov	Sergey	RUS	8.9.90	190/79	HJ	2.27i	2.35i- 13, 2.31- 12
Mulabegovic	Nedzad	CRO	4.2.81	190/120	SP	20.01	20.67- 14
Mullett	Rob	GBR	31.7.87	183/68	3kSt	8:22.42	8:31.32- 15
Münch	Markus	GER	13.6.86	207/130	DT	66.78	66.87- 11
Mundell	Marc	RSA	7.7.83	189/86	50kW	3:56:12	3:54:12- 10
Muneria	Charles	KEN	10.2.96		5000	13:23.79	
					10k	27:57.07A	27:54.6A- 15
Mungara	Kenneth	KEN	7.9.73	170/52	Mar	2:08:38	2:07:36- 11
Munyai	Clarence	RSA-J	20.2.98	176/66	200	20.36A, 20.40, 20.33Aw	20.77A- 15
Murakami	Yukifumi	JPN	23.12.79	186/102	JT	81.81	85.96- 13
Murasky	JC	USA	6.2.93	203/123	SP	20.21	20.16- 15
Murayama	Kota	JPN	23.2.93	174/54	10k	27:44.39	27:29.69- 15
Murillo	Jhon Fredy	COL	13.7.84	183/84	TJ	17.09	16.58, 16.82Aw- 13
Murphy	Clayton	USA	26.2.95	182/68	800	1:42.93	1:45.59- 15
	1500	3:36.23		3:40.69- 15	1M	3:57.11i	4:00.30i- 15
Musaab	Adam Ali	QAT	17.4.95	167/54	1500	3:36.67	3:42.23- 14
Musagala	Ronald	UGA	16.12.92	176/61	800	1:46.35	1:45.27- 14
					1500	3:36.23	3:35.02- 15
Mutai	Abel	KEN	2.10.88	172/73	3kSt	8:16.84	8:01.67- 12
Mutai	Emmanuel	KEN	12.10.84	168/54	HMar	61:15+	59:52- 11
Mutai	Jeremiah	KEN	27.12.92	173/60	800	1:45.25	1:43.9A- 13
Mutai	Laban	KEN	.85		Mar	2:09:16	2:08:01- 12
Muthoni	Simon	KEN	27.2.95		HMar	61:19	63:07- 15
Mutiso	Alexander	KEN	10.9.96		5000	13:21.90	13:30.76- 15
	10k	27:39.25		27:56.87- 15	HMar	60:59	
Mutunga	William	KEN	17.9.93	178/70	400h	49.74A	49.43- 15
Mvumuvre	Gabriel	ZIM	23.4.88	172/75	100	10.14	9.98- 13
Mwaka	Patrick	KEN	2.11.92	165/45	10k	27:41.28	27:33.14- 11
Mwangangi	John	KEN	1.11.90	179/64	Mar	2:08:31	2:06:13- 15
Mwangi	Samuel	KEN-J	19.9.97	169/51	10k	27:45.27	27:50.93- 15
Nabokov	Dmitriy	BLR	20.1.96	186/69	HJ	2.29i, 2.24	2.25- 15
Nadeem	Arshad	PAK-J	2.1.97		JT	78.33	70.46- 15
Nakamura	Akihiko	JPN	23.10.90	181/74	Dec	8180	8043- 15
Nakano	Naoya	JPN	3.7.94		400h	49.51	50.55- 15
Nakatani	Keisuke	JPN	12.1.95	176/58	HMar	61:21	-0-
Nápoles	Cristian Atanay	CUB-J	27.11.98	180/80	TJ	16.92	16.45- 15
Narisada	Shunsuke	JPN	11.7.93		LJ	7.88, 8.02w	7.75- 15
Nava	Horacio	MEX	20.1.82	175/62	20kW	1:20:56	1:22:04- 12
					50kW	3:47:44	3:42:51- 14
Nazarov	Dilshod	TJK	6.5.82	187/115	HT	78.87	80.71- 13
Ndiaye	Amadou	SEN	6.12.92	180/71	400h	49.41	49.61- 14
Ndiku	Caleb	KEN	9.10.92	183/68	3000	7:39.82i	7:30.99- 12
					5000	13:12.25	12:59.17- 14
Ndiku	Jonathan	KEN	18.9.91	173/60	5000	13:15.32	13:11.99- 09
					10k	27:11.23	27:37.72- 09
Ndirangu	Charles	KEN	8.2.93	170/50	HMar	61:00	60:18- 15
Ndirangu	Joseph Macharia	KEN	9.9.94	168/49	5000	13:23.43	13:31.55- 14
					10k	27:57.57	27:59.11- 13
Ndiwa	Mang'ata	KEN	12.12.87	175/60	5000	13:16.85	13:05.02- 09

532 MEN'S INDEX

Name		Nat	Born	Ht/Wt	Event	2016 Mark	Pre-2016 Best
Ndorobo	Peter	KEN	11.8.93		HMar	60:13	61:38- 15
Ndungu	Charles	KEN	20.2.96	168/53	10k	27:57.36	28:10.05- 15
Nebebew	Birhan	ETH	14.8.94	172/55	10k	27:27.30	27:14.34- 13
Nedow	Tim	CAN	16.10.90	198/125	SP	21.33i, 20.88	20.98- 14
Neledva	Taras	UKR	7.6.92	190/70	LJ	8.07, 8.11w	7.90- 13
Nellum	Bryshon	USA	1.5.89	183/79	400	45.50	44.65- 15
Nelson	Adam	USA	7.7.75	183/115	SP	20.48	22.51 -02
Nesterenko	Maksim	BLR	1.9.92	193/82	TJ	16.85	16.66i, 16.59- 15
Nesterenko	Mykyta	UKR	15.4.91	208/115	DT	66.23	65.31- 08
Newman	Calesio	USA	20.8.86	172/66	100	10.13	10.04- 15, 9.96w- 14
					200	20.47, 20.31w	20.28, 20.17w- 12
Ngatia	Hiram	KEN	1.1.96	171/56	10k	27:30.75	27:41.74- 15
Ngeno	Alfred	KEN-J	2.5.97	170/52	5000	13:19.38	13:22.04- 15
Ngeno	Ernest	KEN	20.5.95		Mar	2:07:49	2:07:57- 15
Ngetich	Cleophas	KEN	12.11.95		10k	27:53.30	-0-
Ngetich	Hillary	KEN	15.9.95	171/57	1500	3:32.97	3:35.40, 3:35.26i- 15
					3000	7:45.22	7:52.92- 15
Nichipor	Aleksey	BLR	10.4.93		SP	19.75	19.08- 15
Nilsen	Chris	USA-J	13.1.98	196/84	PV	5.60	5.18- 15
Nilsson	Marcus	SWE	3.5.91	185/90	Dec	7942	8104(w)- 13
Nipperess	James	AUS	21.5.90	180/64	3kSt	8:32.59	8:34.64- 14
Niskala	Pyry	FIN	6.11.90	191/105	DT	61.58	61.17- 15
Niu Wenbin		CHN	20.1.91		50kW	3:48:32	3:51:00- 15
Nizhegorodov	Denis	RUS	26.7.80	180/61	50kW	3:44:47	3:34:14- 08
Njuguna	David	KEN	6.9.89	176/60	10k	27:49.57	28:35.03- 15
Nkhasa	Namakoe	LES	10.1.94		5000	13:21.68	
					10k	28:06.33	29:16.49- 13
Noguchi	Naoto	JPN	27.5.94		400h	49.77	50.06- 15
Norman	Michael	USA-J	3.12.97	183/73	200	20.14, 20.06w	20.24- 15
					400	45.51	45.19- 15
Norwood	Vernon	USA	10.4.92	187/77	400	45.00	44.44- 15
Novac	Alexandru	ROU-J	24.3.97		JT	78.66	73.71- 15
Novák	Martin	CZE	5.10.92	196/115	SP	19.59	19.70- 15
Nowak	Tim	GER	13.8.95	183/78	Dec	7838	7827- 15
Nowicki	Wojciech	POL	22.2.89	196/112	HT	78.36	78.71- 15
Nozawa	Keisuke	JPN	7.6.91	175/62	400h	48.62	49.08- 15
Nuguse	Mamiyo	ETH	13.2.82	180/58	10k	27:24.85	-0-
Nyairo	Dominic	KEN-J	22.8.97	167/49	10k	27:56.47	28:11.49- 15
					HMar	60:50	-0-
Nyakora	Teressa	ETH	26.2.95	171/54	5000	13:23.66	13:33.58- 15
					10k	27:42.75	27:38.93- 15
Nyamadi	Atsu	GHA	1.6.94	190/85	Dec	7800	7567- 15
Nyangau	Mike Mokamba	KEN	28.8.94	171/75	200	20.38A	20.48A, 20.51, 20.2A- 15
Nychyporchuk	Oleksandr	UKR	14.4.92	185/86	JT	79.88	81.80- 15
Nykyforov	Sergiy	UKR	6.2.94	195/85	LJ	8.11, 8.28w	7.78i, 7.75- 15
O'Farrill	Yordan	CUB	9.2.93	185/77	110h	13.51, 13.46w	13.19, 12.9- 14
O'Hare	Chris	GBR	23.11.90	174/60	1500	3:35.37	3:34.83- 15
					1M	3:52.91i	3:52.98i- 13, 3:56.35- 15
O'Neal	Matthew	USA	10.6.94	185/74	TJ	16.92, 17.01w	16.44i, 16.37- 15
Oates	Tray	USA	14.3.95	186/79	PV	5.65	5.30- 15
Obiena	Ernest John	PHI	17.11.95	190/68	PV	5.55	5.45- 15
Ocampo	David	MEX	14.2.92		JT	79.84	77.24A- 14
Occin	Louis-Grégory	FRA	2.6.89	170/69	TJ	16.70	16.61, 16.63w- 15
Odriozola	Mikel	ESP	25.5.73	180/62	50kW	3:54:21	3:41:47- 05
Oduduru	Divine	NGR	7.10.96	175/70	200	20.34	20.45- 15, 20.34w- 14
Odujobi	Gabriel	GBR	15.7.87	183/79	110h	13.57w	14.04, 13.94w- 15
Ogita	Hiroki	JPN	30.12.87	186/80	PV	5.70	5.70- 13
Ogunlewe	Seye	NGR	30.8.91	183/82	100	10.12	10.19- 15
Ogunode	Femi Seun	QAT	15.5.91	183/79	100	9.91	9.91- 15
					200	20.10	19.97- 15
Oiglane	Janek	EST	25.4.94	182/78	Dec	7762	7945- 15
Oikawa	Fumitaka	JPN	5.4.95		20kW	1:20:55	1:22:06- 14
Oishi	Minato	JPN	19.5.88	162/48	10k	27:48.56	28:04.65- 15
Ojala	Aleksi	FIN	9.12.92	180/62	50kW	3:46:25	3:57:14- 15
Ojiaku	Kevin	ITA	20.4.89		LJ	7.88, 7.97w	7.91i, 7.90- 13
Oke	Tosin	NGR	1.10.80	178/77	TJ	17.13	17.23- 12
Okuma	Takeshi	JPN	14.12.83		50kW	3:59:30	3:55:06- 15
Okutu	Jean Marie	ESP	4.8.88	179/68	LJ	8.17A, 7.95	8.04A- 15, 8.01- 14, 8.05w- 12
Olamigoke	Olu	NGR	19.9.90	178/68	TJ	16.70	16.98- 15
Oleitiptip	Alex	KEN	22.9.82	176/58	HMar	60:33	59:28- 15
Oleszczuk	Kacper	POL	15.5.94	182/78	JT	80.97	82.29- 15

MEN'S INDEX

Name		Nat	Born	Ht/Wt	Event	2016 Mark	Pre-2016 Best
Oliva	Pablo	ESP	15.10.96	169/55	50kW	4:00:31	-0-
de Oliveira	Júlio César	BRA	4.2.86	185/97	JT	81.56	83.67- 15
de Oliveira	Pedro	BRA	17.2.92	188/85	400	45.64	45.52- 12
Oliver	David	USA	24.4.82	188/93	110h	13.09	12.89- 10
Olmedo	Manuel	ESP	17.5.83	179/60	800	1:46.37	1:44.56- 11
Omelko	Rafal	POL	16.1.89	195/75	400	45.14	45.66- 14
Omoregie	David	GBR	1.11.95	185/84	110h	13.24	13.50- 15
Omullo	Ezequiel	KEN			Mar	2:08:55	2:09:19- 15
Omuro	Hideki	JPN	25.7.90	180/67	110h	13.52, 13.47w	13.54- 12
Öncel	Emin	TUR-J	1.5.97	186/100	JT	79.42	75.65- 15
Ondoro	Dominic	KEN		.88	Mar	2:08:51	2:09:06- 14
Onnen	Eike	GER	3.8.82	194/83	HJ	2.32	2.34- 07
Opiny	Leonard	UGA			400	45.66A	46.38- 15
Oprea	Marian	ROU	6.6.82	190/80	TJ	16.82i	17.81- 05
Ortega	Mauricio	COL	4.8.94	184/102	DT	65.84, 67.45dh	64.47A- 15
Ortega	Orlando	ESP	29.7.91	185/70	110h	13.04	12.94- 15
Orth	Florian	GER	24.7.89	181/64	5000	13:23.67	13:29.63- 15
Ortíz	Ricardo	MEX	7.2.95		20kW	1:21:45	-0-
Osako	Suguru	JPN	23.5.91	170/53	10k	27:50.27	27:38.31- 13
Osewski	Bartosz	POL	20.3.91	194/104	JT	80.38	83.89- 12
Osman	Abrar	ERI	1.1.94	173/55	5000	13:04.12	13:14.00- 15
					HMar	60:58	60:39- 15
Osmanoglu	Seref	TUR	2.1.89	176/58	TJ	16.85	17.72- 11
Ostos	Luis	PER	9.12.92	160/50	10k	27:54.80	28:43.10- 15
Otterling	Andreas	SWE	25.5.86	183/80	LJ	8.12i	8.06, 8.13w- 15, 8.03- 12
Outzen	Matthew	AUS	12.10.87	185/100	JT	79.71	81.80- 15
Özbilen	Kaan Kigen	TUR	15.1.86	170/54	Mar	2:06:10	2:06:59- 14
Paech	Carlo	GER	18.12.92	190/84	PV	5.77i	5.80- 15
Paes	Lutimar	BRA	14.12.88	179/70	800	1:45.42	1:45.32- 11
Pahapill	Mikk	EST	18.7.83	197/83	Dec	7814	8398- 11
Pai Long		CHN	8.10.89		HJ	2.28	2.28- 12
Palma	Ever	MEX	18.3.92	176/66	20kW	1:19:38	1:21:02 -11
Palma	Isaac	MEX	26.10.90	174/59	20kW	1:20:54	1:21:13- 13
Palmer	Desmond	USA	30.7.95	196/84	400h	49.66	49.41- 15
Palomeque	Diego	COL	5.12.93	176/68	100	10.23A, 10.28, 10.07Aw	10.22A, 10.11Aw- 15
200	20.66A 20.50A, 20.70w- 15, 20.99- 12				400	45.25A, 45.86	45.62A, 46.36- 12
Papamihaíl	Aléxandros	GRE	18.9.88	178/63	20kW	1:21:33	1:21:12- 15
					50kW	3:59:21	3:49:56- 12
Parchment	Hansle	JAM	17.6.90	196/90	110h	13.10	12.94- 14
Parellis	Apostolos	CYP	24.7.85	186/110	DT	65.69	65.36- 12
Park Chil-sung		KOR	8.7.82	173/61	50kW	3:52:26	3:45:55- 12
Parks	Nicholas	USA	19.11.93	176/75	400	45.71	48.03- 15
Pars	Krisztián	HUN	18.2.82	188/113	HT	77.38	82.69- 14
Partanen	Veli-Matti	FIN	28.10.91	178/62	50kW	3:54:02	3:49:02- 15
Pásztor	Bence	HUN	5.2.95	186/95	HT	73.45	75.74- 15
Pathirana	Dhanuka Liyana	SRI	25.6.93		LJ	7.94	7.70- 15
Patsoukákis	Dimítrios	GRE	18.3.87	180/70	PV	5.60i, 5.45	5.62- 14
Paul	Jithin	IND	13.3.90	178/68	400h	49.79	50.41- 14
Peacock	Hamish	AUS	15.10.90	186/96	JT	84.39	83.31- 15
Peltomäki	Sami	FIN	11.1.91	180/87	JT	79.02	80.36- 14
Peña	José Gregorio	VEN	12.1.87	163/60	3kSt	8:26.36	8:20.87- 15
Pender	Barry	IRL	2.4.90	192/75	HJ	2.26i, 2.20	2.20i, 2.18- 15
Pépiot	Valentin	FRA	6.7.91	185/66	3kSt	8:30.28	8:42.74- 12
Percy	Nick	GBR	5.12.94	190/105	DT	63.38	58.61- 14
Pérez	Luis	PUR	6.1.95	183/75	400	45.69	46.33- 15
Perinchief	Jah-Nhai	BER-J	31.12.97	190/68	HJ	2.26	2.15A- 15
Perlaza	Jhon	COL	26.8.94	180/60	400	45.45A, 45.81	45.96- 14
Pesic	Darko	MNE	30.11.92	189/89	Dec	7827	7636- 13
Pestano	Mario	ESP	8.4.78	195/120	DT	61.51	69.50- 08
Peters	Anderson	GRN-J	21.10.97	187/84	JT	79.65	74.20- 15
Pettersson	Simon	SWE	3.1.94	198/105	DT	63.10	60.25- 15
Pezer	Mesud	BIH	27.8.94	198/120	SP	20.58	19.99- 15
Philibert-Thiboutot	Charles	CAN	31.12.90	176/62	1500	3:34.24	3:34.23- 15
					1M	3:55.25	3:54.52- 15
Phillips	Isa	JAM	22.4.84	193/84	400h	49.31	48.05- 09
Phiri	Gerald	ZAM	6.10.88	184/80	100	10.08	10.03- 14, 10.00w- 13
Phora	Thapelo	RSA	21.11.91	183/77	400	45.64A	45.91A- 15
Pienaar	Roelf	RSA	23.12.93	183/76	LJ	7.93, 8.08w	8.01, 8.13w- 15
Pierson	Sam	USA	7.4.88	180/75	PV	5.62A	5.55Ai, 5.40- 15
Pinder	Demetrius	BAH	13.2.89	178/70	200	20.45	20.23- 12
Pineda	Omar	MEX	2.12.94	172/60	20kW	1:19:20	1:24:54- 15

MEN'S INDEX

Name		Nat	Born	Ht/Wt	Event	2016 Mark	Pre-2016 Best
Pintado	Brian	ECU	29.7.95	168/57	20kW	1:21:49	1:23:35- 15
Piskunov	Hlib	UKR-J	25.11.98	182/96	HT	71.53	-0-
Pitkämäki	Tero	FIN	19.12.82	195/92	JT	86.13	91.53- 05
Pittomvils	Niels	BEL	18.7.92	198/88	Dec	8051	8049- 15
Plesko	Nejc	SLO	9.10.92	186/97	HT	73.51	73.63- 15
Pless	David	USA	19.11.90	191/109	SP	20.37	19.83- 15
Plotnitskiy	Dmitriy	BLR	26.8.88	189/80	TJ	16.90	16.91- 10
Pohle	Hagen	GER	5.3.92	177/64	20kW	1:19:58	1:21:29- 14
Polyanskiy	Sergey	RUS	29.10.89	180/75	LJ	7.96i	8.20- 15
Pontvianne	Jean Marc	FRA	6.8.94	170/60	TJ	16.75	16.81- 15
Pope	Mitchell	USA	21.1.84	196/150	SP	20.28	20.59- 08
Porter	Garland	USA	10.2.82	193/118	HT	71.77	72.99- 11
Porter	Jeff	USA	27.11.85	183/84	110h	13.21	13.08- 12
Portilla	Jhoanis	CUB	24.7.90	182/76	110h	13.51	13.30- 15, 13.1w- 11
Posekany	Lukás	CZE	30.12.92	183/79	PV	5.55	5.41- 14
Poska	Domantas	LTU	10.1.96	199/107	DT	62.47	58.32- 15
Powell	Asafa	JAM	23.11.82	190/88	100	9.92	9.72- 08
					200	20.45	19.90- 06
Powlen	Bryan	USA	3.12.87	193/120	DT	61.57	62.81- 14
Pozdnyakov	Anatoliy	RUS	1.2.87	184/101	HT	73.11	79.06- 13
Pozzi	Andrew	GBR	15.5.92	186/79	110h	13.19	13.34- 12
Prader	John	USA	10.2.91	178/73	PV	5.65	5.67- 13
Prásil	Ladislav	CZE	17.5.90	198/125	SP	20.19	21.47- 13
Prescod	Reece	GBR	29.2.96	193/75	100	10.04	10.71- 14
					200	20.38	20.70- 15
Pretorius	Friedrich	RSA	4.8.95	187/84	Dec	7780	7764- 15
Pronkin	Valeriy	RUS	15.6.94	195/115	HT	75.39	76.80- 15
Protsenko	Andriy	UKR	20.5.88	194/80	HJ	2.33	2.40- 14
Prüfer	Clemens	GER-J	13.8.97	198/113	DT	61.62	55.24- 15
Przybylko	Mateusz	GER	9.3.92	194/72	HJ	2.29i, 2.29	2.30- 15
Pujats	Pauls	LAT	6.8.91	187/83	PV	5.70i, 5.60	5.55- 15
Pullen	Clive	JAM	18.10.94	175/73	TJ	16.90	15.92- 12, 16.27w- 15
Pyatnytsya	Oleksandr	UKR	14.7.85	187/95	JT	83.28	86.12- 12
Quérin	Gaël	FRA	26.6.87	182/76	Dec	8114	8194- 14
Quinlee	Ralph	TTO	2.3.91	180/68	100	10.08w	10.46- 15
Quispe	Ronald	BOL	5.3.89	164/57	50kW	4:02:00	4:11:22- 13
Quiyuch	Jaime	GUA	24.4.88	178/59	50kW	3:53:01	3:50:33A- 11
Quow	Renny	TTO	25.8.87	170/66	400	45.54	44.53- 09
Raffin	Melvin	FRA-J	9.8.98	183/65	TJ	16.47, 16.93w	15.81i, 15.62- 15
Rahmouni	Miloud	ALG	13.12.83	175/70	400h	49.65	49.24- 15
Rajiv	Arokia	IND	22.5.91	172/64	400	45.47	45.57- 15
Ranasinghe	R.M.Sumedha	SRI	10.2.91	182/82	JT	80.25	83.04- 15
Randhawa	Nauraj Singh	MAS	27.1.92	193/68	HJ	2.29	2.22- 15
Regassa	Tilahun	ETH	18.1.90	170/54	Mar	2:08:11	2:05:27- 12
Reheda	Serhiy	UKR	6.2.94	190/100	HT	73.58	71.86- 15
Reid	Julian	GBR	23.9.88	186/77	TJ	16.76, 16.96w	16.98, 17.10w- 09
Remes	Tommi	FIN	20.1.94	183/98	HT	72.55	70.05- 15
Rendón	James	COL	7.7.85	155/55	20kW	1:21:35	1:21:13.6t- 11
					50kW	4:00:31	3:47:41- 14
Renner	Robert	SLO	8.3.94	182/75	PV	5.65	5.70- 15
Reus	Julian	GER	29.4.88	177/73	100	10.01	10.05- 14, 10.00w- 13
					200	20.39, 20.23w	20.36- 13
Reuther	Marc	GER	23.6.96	190/77	800	1:46.19	1:47.98- 15
Revé	Ernesto	CUB	26.2.92	182/70	TJ	16.91	17.58- 14
Rew	Quentin	NZL	16.7.84	175/63	20kW	1:21:54	1:22:11- 14
					50kW	3:49:32	3:48:48- 15
Richards	O'Dayne	JAM	14.12.88	178/117	SP	20.82	21.69- 15
Richardson	Jason	USA	4.4.86	186/73	110h	13.28	12.98- 12
Riekmann	Jonathan	BRA	20.8.87	172/59	50kW	3:55:26	4:04:07A- 11
Rietveld	Pelle	NED	4.2.85	184/75	Dec	7659	8204- 14
Riley	Andrew	JAM	6.9.88	188/80	110h	13.35	13.14- 13
Riley-La Borde	Khai	GBR	8.11.95	183/94	110h	13.60	13.77- 15
Rimmer	Michael	GBR	3.2.86	180/71	800	1:44.93	1:43.89- 10
Ringer	Richard	GER	27.2.89	180/62	3000	7:46.59	7:46.18i- 15, 7:50.99- 14
Rise	Lars Vikan	NOR	23.11.88	184/86	Dec	7925	7942- 11
Riseley	Jeff	AUS	11.11.86	192/74	800	1:45.13	1:44.48- 12
Ristic	Milan	SRB	8.8.91	186/72	110h	13.39	13.50- 15
Ritzenhein	Dathan	USA	30.12.82	170/52	HMar	60:12dh	60:00- 09
Rivas	Yeison	COL	24.9.87	175/64	110h	13.36A	13.73A, 13.91- 15
Rivasz-Tóth	Norbert	HUN	6.5.96	182/86	JT	79.47	73.97- 13
Rivera	Edgar	MEX	13.2.91	191/80	HJ	2.30i, 2.29	2.28- 11

MEN'S INDEX 535

Name		Nat	Born	Ht/Wt	Event	2016 Mark	Pre-2016 Best
Rivera	Luis	MEX	21.6.87	183/79	LJ	8.14	8.46- 13
Rivero	Briander	CUB	23.4.91	189/91	Dec	7709	7321- 14
Roberson	Joel	USA	15.12.93	175/70	400	45.66	46.99- 15
Roberts	Gil	USA	15.3.89	188/81	400	44.65	44.53- 14
Roberts	Kurt	USA	20.2.88	191/127	SP	21.57i, 21.40	21.50i, 21.47- 14
Robertson	Ricky	USA	19.9.90	178/70	HJ	2.29	2.32- 12
Robertson	Zane	NZL	14.11.89	180/65	10k	27:33.67	27:46.82- 15
Robinson	Brett	AUS	8.5.91	173/57	3000	7:44.29i	7:45.97- 15
					5000	13:19.29	13:18.96- 13
Robinson	Byron	USA	16.2.95	175/73	400h	48.65	50.42- 15
Robinson	Jeron	USA	30.4.91	193/73	HJ	2.29Ai, 2.26	2.31- 15
Robinson	Joshua	AUS	4.10.85	187/95	JT	85.11	82.48- 14
Rodger	Sebastian	GBR	29.6.91	181/73	400h	49.29	49.19- 13
Rodgers	Michael	USA	24.4.85	178/73	100	9.97	9.85- 11, 9.80w- 14
					200	20.42	20.24- 09
Rodney	Brendon	CAN	9.4.92	190/84	200	19.96	20.18- 15
Roe	Martin	NOR	1.4.92	187/86	Dec	7855	7875- 15
Rogestedt	Johan	SWE	27.1.93	196/72	1500	3:36.58	3:40.03- 15
Röhler	Thomas	GER	30.9.91	195/86	JT	91.28	89.27- 15
Rolnin	Basile	FRA	21.1.94	194/83	Dec	8087	7679- 15
Romani	Darlan	BRA	9.4.91	183/127	SP	21.02	20.90- 15
Romaniw	Anthony	CAN	15.9.91	178/68	800	1:45.60	1:45.60- 13
Romanov	Andrey	RUS	19.9.94	180/90	HT	74.60	69.62- 15
Rono	Mathew	KEN			800	1:45.88A	
Rono	Philemon	KEN	8.2.91		Mar	2:07:20	2:07:07- 14
Rono	Vincent	KEN	22.12.90	165/55	2000	5:01.75+	5:08.35- 11
					3000	7:43.04i	7:41.18- 10, 7:37.87i- 11
Ronoh	Geoffrey	KEN	29.11.82	182/62	HMar	61:11+	59:45- 14
Rooney	Martyn	GBR	3.4.87	198/78	400	45.04	44.45- 13
Rop	Albert	BRN	17.7.92	176/55	2000	5:01.4+	
	3000	7:32.02		7:35.53- 13	5000	13:04.87	12:51.96- 13
Rosa	Jean	BRA	1.2.90	188/78	TJ	16.67	16.80- 15, 16.82w- 13
Rose	Alex	SAM	7.11.91	188/127	DT	65.74	61.35- 15
Rosenberg	Kristjan	EST	16.5.94		Dec	7907	7668- 15
Rosser	Khallifah	USA	13.7.95	188/73	400h	49.04	49.96- 15
Rossi	Eugenio	SMR	6.3.92	192/72	HJ	2.26	2.27- 15
Rotich	Abraham	BRN	26.6.93	183/64	800	1:45.83	1:43.13- 12
Rotich	Anthony	KEN	.93	174/60	3kSt	8:27.62	8:21.19- 13
Rotich	Daniel	UGA	10.10.92		HMar	60:59	61:45- 14
Rotich	Edwin	KEN	88	168/50	HMar	59:32	59:59- 14
Rotich	Lucas	KEN	16.4.90	171/57	Mar	2:08:53	2:07:17- 15
Roulhac	Brandon	USA	13.12.83	188/73	TJ	16.41, 16.54w	17.26, 17.44w- 09
Rowe	Alex	AUS	8.7.92	183/70	800	1:46.27	1:44.40 -14
Rozani	Jacob	RSA	24.1.88	176/59	800	1:45.38	1:46.91A- 15
Rozporski	Michal	POL	20.12.88	192/120	SP	19.67	19.26- 15
Rudisha	David	KEN	17.12.88	189/73	800	1:42.15	1:40.91- 12
Ruiz	Jorge	COL	17.5.89	167/57	50kW	3:51:42	3:58:23- 15
Rungaru	James	KEN	14.1.93	176.61	10k	27:30.17	27:22.53- 11
Rupp	Galen	USA	8.5.86	180/62	5000	13:20.69	12:58.90- 12
Rupp	Galen	USA	8.5.86	180/62	10k	27:08.92	26:44.36- 14
Rush	Cody	USA	11.11.93	190/77	400	45.52	45.91i- 15, 46.12- 14
Ruskys	Eligijus	LTU	1.12.90	198/115	DT	61.53	63.21- 15
Russell	Alonzo	BAH	8.2.92	183/75	400	45.25	45.65A, 45.71- 15
Rutherford	Greg	GBR	17.11.86	188/84	LJ	8.31, 8.36w	8.51- 14
Ruto	Dominic	KEN	.90		Mar	2:09:28	2:13:35- 15
Rutto	Cyrus	KEN	21.4.92	173/52	5000	13:20.32	13:12.91- 13
Rutto	Eliud	KEN	4.6.88	175/64	800	1:45.59	1:45.37- 14
Ruuskanen	Antti	FIN	21.2.84	189/86	JT	88.23	88.98- 15
Ryzhyy	Roman	UKR	17.1.85	190/73	DT	63.15	61.48- 08
de Sá	Mateus Daniel	BRA	21.11.95	183/73	TJ	16.63	16.47- 14
Safiulin	Ilgizar	RUS	9.12.92	183/64	3kSt	8:25.81	8:18.49- 15
Saïd	Saïd Aden	QAT	.93		800	1:46.25	1:50.94i-15
	1500	3:37.29i		3:40.82- 15	3000	7:44.69i	8:08.01i- 15
Saidy Ndure	Jaysuma	NOR	1.7.84	192/72	200	20.43	19.89- 07
Saito	Takumi	JPN	23.3.93	178/61	20kW	1:19:44	1:20:05- 13
Salazar	Julio César	MEX	8.7.93	176/65	20kW	1:20:24	1:21:43- 15
Saluri	Karl Robert	EST	6.8.93	178/75	Dec	8108	7497- 14
Samaai	Rushwal	RSA	25.9.91	178/73	LJ	8.38, 8.40w	8.38- 15
Sambu	Stephen	KEN	3.7.88	169/55	5000	13:21.14	13:13.74i- 12, 13:25.13- 15
	10k	26:58.25		26:54.61- 14	HMar	61:16	60:41- 13
Samimi	Mahmoud	IRI	18.9.88	190/105	DT	65.00	64.67- 09

MEN'S INDEX

Name		Nat	Born	Ht/Wt	Event	2016 Mark	Pre-2016 Best
Samimi	Mohammed	IRI	29.3.87	188/104	DT	63.81	65.46- 14
Samuelsson	Fredrik	SWE	16.2.95	185/80	Dec	7875	7884- 15
Sánchez	Eder	MEX	21.5.86	176/67	20kW	1:21:31	1:18:34- 08
Sancho	Miguel Ángel	ESP	24.4.90	180/67	HJ	2.26	2.27i- 09, 2.26- 11
Sands	Leevan	BAH	16.8.81	190/73	TJ	16.63	17.59- 08
dos Santos	Felipe Vinícius	BRA	30.7.94	181/80	Dec	7859	8019- 15
Santos	Juander	DOM	7.5.95	188/79	400h	49.43	50.27- 15
Santos	Luguelín	DOM	12.11.92	173/61	400	44.71	44.11- 15
dos Santos	Vitor Hugo	BRA	1.2.96	185/75	100	10.11	10.22, 10.18w- 15
Saquipay	Rolando	ECU	21.7.79	166/57	50kW	3:54:32	3:50:19- 14
Sarantsev	Yevgeniy	RUS	5.8.88	188/85	Dec	8017	8123- 14
Sasinek	Filip	CZE	8.1.96	181/62	800	1:46.42	1:49.79- 14
					1500	3:36.32	3:46.13- 14
Sato	Ryo	JPN	21.7.94	183/61	HJ	2.25	2.22- 15
Savanyú	Péter	HUN	26.6.87	189/103	DT	64.15	60.71 -13
Savola	Elmo	FIN	10.3.95	189/77	Dec	7704	7743- 15
Sawano	Daichi	JPN	16.9.80	183/75	PV	5.75	5.83- 05
Sawyers	Roberto	CRC	17.10.86	189/107	HT	77.15	76.37- 15
Sbaï	Hassanine	TUN	21.1.84	176/60	20kW	1:20:49	1:20:19- 11
Scantling	Garrett	USA	19.5.93	190/86	Dec	8228	8232- 15
Schembri	Fabrizio	ITA	27.1.81	183/74	TJ	16.82i	17.27- 09
Scherbarth	Tobias	GER	17.8.85	195/84	PV	5.75	5.76i- 09, 5.73- 14
Scherfose	Patrick	GER	28.11.91	186/86	Dec	7667	7693- 15
Schuurmans	Jared	USA	20.8.87	198/118	DT	63.92	66.10- 15
Schwazer ¶	Alex	ITA	26.12.84	182/72	20kW	1:20:23dq	1:17:30- 12
Scott	Donald	USA	23.2.92	183/84	TJ	17.02	16.84i, 16.71, 16.83w- 15
Scott	Jeremy	USA	1.5.81	206/93	PV	5.52i	5.82i, 5.75- 09
Scott	Jordan	USA	22.2.88	188/84	PV	5.62	5.72- 12
Scott	Jordan	JAM-J	29.6.97		TJ	16.61w	15.61, 15.78w- 15
Sédécias	Benjamin	FRA	18.1.95	177/78	110h	13.45	14.14, 13.98w- 15
Sedoc	Gregory	NED	16.10.81	179/74	110h	13.48	13.37- 07, 13.1w- 10
Sedyuk	Nikolay	RUS	29.4.88	198/115	DT	64.46	64.72- 08
See	Jeff	USA	6.6.86	186/72	3000	7:46.72i	7:50.23i- 11, 7:51.79- 15
Sefir	Dino	ETH	28.5.88	178/64	Mar	2:08:14	2:04:50- 12
Segura	Omar	MEX	24.3.81	170/57	20kW	1:22:19	1:20:03- 14
Seifert	Bernhard	GER	15.2.93	190/88	JT	79.34	82.42- 13
Seiler	Nathaniel	GER	6.4.96	175/65	50kW	3:58:03	-0-
Sein	Timothy Olodaru	KEN	1.2.88	178/64	800	1:45.48A	1:46.8A- 12
Seliverstov	Pavel	BLR	2.9.96		HJ	2.30	2.17- 15
Selmon	Kenny	USA	27.8.96	188/82	400h	49.31	49.60- 15
Selmouni	Sofiane	FRA	22.9.89	190/73	800	1:46.39	1:45.94 -14
Semenov	Oleksiy	UKR	27.6.82	198/120	DT	65.34	65.96- 12
Semyonov	Dmitriy	RUS	2.8.92	195/77	HJ	2.28i	2.31i- 15, 2.28- 14
Sène	Alioune	FRA	3.2.96	185/69	PV	5.60	5.30- 15
Seppänen	Tuomas	FIN	16.5.86	180/107	HT	76.20	75.31- 11
Sepúlveda	Alfredo	CHI	3.8.93	182/73	400h	49.86	50.55- 15
Seurei	Benson	BRN	27.3.84	172/62	1500	3:35.28	3:31.61- 12
Shablyuyev	Ivan	RUS	17.4.88	189/82	400h	49.32	49.04- 15
Shalin	Pavel	RUS	15.3.87	175/73	LJ	7.96i, 7.95	8.25- 10, 8.33w- 11
Shange	Lebogang	RSA	1.8.90	160/56	20kW	1:20:06	1:21:43- 15
Shankar	Tejaswin	IND-J	21.12.98		HJ	2.26	2.14- 15
Sharipov	Sergey	RUS	14.4.92		50kW	3:46:51	3:57:40- 15
Sharma	Ankit	IND	20.7.92	178/68	LJ	8.19	8.04- 14
Sharman	William	GBR	12.9.84	188/82	110h	13.52	13.16- 14, 12.9w- 10
Shayunov	Yuriy	BLR	22.10.87	189/120	HT	75.74	80.72- 09
Shestopalov	Feliks	RUS	11.3.96		Dec	7835	7614j -15
Sheyko	Georgiy	KAZ	24.8.89	183/70	20kW	1:21:52	1:21:34- 15
Shi Yuhao		CHN-J	26.9.98		LJ	8.30	7.63- 15
Shimelis	Belayneh	ETH	.96		3kSt	8:28.01	
Shiojiri	Kazuya	JPN	8.11.96	170/53	3kSt	8:31.89	8:42.80- 15
Shiroyama	Shotaro	JPN	6.3.95	178/64	LJ	8.01	7.72- 14, 7.87w- 15
Shitara	Yuta	JPN	18.12.91	170/48	10k	27:48.35	27:42.71- 15
Shkurenyov	Ilya	RUS	11.1.91	191/82	Dec	8292	8538- 15
Showler-Davis	Kieran	GBR	14.11.91	180/74	100	10.03w	10.27- 15
Shubenkov	Sergey	RUS	4.10.90	190/75	110h	13.20, 12.7w	12.98- 15
Shumay	Mogos	ERI-J	1.1.97		10k	27:56.98	-0-
Sibanda	Karabo	BOT-J	2.7.98	192/79	400	44.25	45.83- 15
Sicard	Lloyd	USA	31.5.95	178/73	110h	13.61	13.60- 15
Siddhanth	Thingalaya	IND	1.3.91	193/87	110h	13.54, 13.47w	13.65- 12
Sidorov	Maksim	RUS	13.5.86	190/126	SP	20.53i, 19.95	21.51- 12
Siegmeier	Zach	USA	8.1.91	183/77	PV	5.60	5.51- 14

Name		Nat	Born	Ht/Wt	Event	2016 Mark	Pre-2016 Best
Sierra	Omar	COL	10.9.88		50kW	4:00:21A	3:59:08- 14
Sigueni	Hicham	MAR	30.1.93	172/51	3kSt	8:20.53	8:16.54- 15
Sikora	Rafal	POL	17.2.87	187/76	50kW	3:51:18	3:46:16- 11
Silnov	Andrey	RUS	9.9.84	198/83	HJ	2.34	2.38- 08
Silva	Andrés	URU	27.3.86	180/76	400h	49.21	48.65- 14
da Silva	Altobeli	BRA	3.12.90	181/60	3kSt	8:26.30	8:52.6 -11
da Silva	Mauro Vinícius	BRA	26.12.86	183/69	LJ	8.14	8.31- 13
Silva	Talles	BRA	20.8.91	190/78	HJ	2.29	2.28- 15
Simanovich	Denis	BLR	20.4.87	179/58	20kW	1:21:48	1:20:42- 12
Simbine	Akani	RSA	21.9.93	174/67	100	9.89	9.97- 15
					200	20.16	20.23- 15
Simmons	Cale	USA	5.2.91	178/70	PV	5.72A, 5.65	5.61- 13
Simmons	Solomon	USA	26.9.93	196/91	Dec	7936	7862- 15
Simpson	Damarcus	USA	14.7.93	175/68	LJ	8.12	8.02, 8.03w- 15
Singh	Devender	IND	18.12.88	178/92	JT	80.21	79.65- 15
Singh	Devender	IND	5.12.83		20kW	1:20:21	1:21:49- 14
Singh	Gurmeet	IND	1.7.85	172/60	20kW	1:20:29	1:20:22.52t- 12
Singh	Inderjeet	IND	19.4.88	191/125	SP	19.85	20.65- 15
Singh	Malkit	IND	5.10.88		TJ	16.57	16.00- 11
Singh	Om Prakash	IND	11.1.87	198/130	SP	19.59	20.69- 12
Singh	Shivpal	IND	6.7.95		JT	79.77	76.76- 15
Singh	Tejinder Pal	IND	13.11.94	190/120	SP	19.93	19.24- 15
Singh Khaira	Ravinder	IND	19.3.86	192/109	JT	79.04	78.02- 14
Singh Rawat	Manish	IND	5.5.91	174/65	20kW	1:20:26	1:22:50- 15
Sirmais	Zigismunds	LAT	6.5.92	190/96	JT	86.66	86.61- 14
Sitonik	William Malel	KEN	1.3.94	165/52	5000	13:19.89	13:19.83- 13
					10k	26:54.66	27:22.12- 15
Siverio	Simón	ESP	2.8.88	186/79	HJ	2.26	2.26i- 12, 2.25- 10
Skagestad	Sven Martin	NOR	13.1.95	201/118	DT	65.20	61.53- 15
Skarvélis	Nicholas	GRE	2.2.93	185/121	SP	20.61	19.82- 15
Skipper	Greg	USA	26.3.93	193/105	HT	71.39	71.25- 15
Skorobogatko	Aleksandr	RUS	7.8.94	186/78	400h	49.33	49.93- 13
Skyers	Roberto	CUB	12.11.91	187/83	100	10.11	10.17, 10.13w- 15, 9.9dt- 10
					200	20.42	20.02- 15
Sloan	Eric	USA	20.6.94	185/77	TJ	17.03i, 16.24	16.31- 14
Smaïli	Mostafa	MAR-J	9.1.97	172/61	800	1:45.05	1:46.57- 15
Smajlaj	Izmir	ALB	29.3.93	184/75	LJ	8.03	7.78- 14
Smaliós	Jiannis	SWE	17.2.87	192/90	JT	81.89	80.77- 10
Smalling	Shivnarine	JAM	28.9.96	178/75	100	10.08Aw	10.61- 14, 10.26w- 15
Smellie	Gavin	CAN	26.6.86	180/75	200	20.43	20.45- 09, 20.16w- 15
Smelyk	Sergiy	UKR	19.4.87	178/74	100	10.10A	10.21, 10.20w- 15
					200	20.40	20.30- 14
Smikle	Traves	JAM	7.5.92	201/95	DT	63.42	67.12- 12
Smirnov	Valentin	RUS	13.2.86	177/62	1500	3:37.24	3:36.14- 11
Smith	Allan	GBR	6.11.92	198/84	HJ	2.26i, 2.26	2.29i- 15, 2.26- 13
Smith	Calvin	USA	10.12.87	180/75	400	45.61	44.81- 10
Smith	David	PUR	2.5.92	183/73	HJ	2.29	2.24- 10
Smith	Rutger	NED	9.7.81	197/129	DT	63.85	67.77- 11
Smith	Tyrone	BER	7.8.86	183/70	LJ	8.18	8.22- 10
Snyman	Wayne	RSA	8.3.85	177/64	20kW	1:20:46	1:23:42- 15
Soares	Alex	BRA	2.2.95		Dec	7659	7167- 15
Sobchuk	Dmytro	UKR	7.11.95	179/64	50kW	3:58:49	4:23:04- 15
Sobera	Robert	POL	19.1.91	190/77	PV	5.77i, 5.70	5.81i- 15, 5.70, 5.80ex- 14
Soboka	Tafese	ETH	29.9.93	176/60	3kSt	8:17.75	8:25.56- 15
Söderberg	David	FIN	11.8.79	185/100	HT	77.60	78.83- 03
Soi	Edwin	KEN	3.3.86	172/55	3000	7:43.30	7:27.55- 11
					5000	13:03.26	12:51.34- 13
Sokirskiy	Aleksey	RUS	16.3.85	185/108	HT	77.78	78.91- 12
Sokolovs	Igors	LAT	17.8.74	187/110	HT	75.44	80.14- 09
Solis	Daniel	ESP	5.11.96		LJ	7.94A	7.19- 15
Solomon	Duane	USA	28.12.84	191/77	800	1:45.47	1:42.82- 12
Solomon	Jarrin	TTO	11.1.86	173/73	400	45.42	44.98- 14
Solomon	Steven	AUS	16.5.93	186/73	400	45.44	44.97- 12
Sorokin	Dmitriy	RUS	27.9.92	176/73	LJ	7.94i	7.63i- 15, 7.55- 10
					TJ	17.05i, 16.49	17.29- 15
Sorrillo	Rondell	TTO	21.1.86	178/62	100	9.99	10.03- 12, 9.99w- 13
					200	20.27, 20.24w	20.16- 11
Soto	Manuel	COL	28.1.94	174/60	20kW	1:20:36	1:23:22.7t- 14
Souleiman	Ayanleh	DJI	3.12.92	172/60	800	1:43.52	1:42.97- 15
1000	2:13.49		2:15.77- 13		1500	3:31.68	3:29.58 -14
Sousa	João Gabriel	BRA	6.11.84	182/75	PV	5.55	5.61- 13

MEN'S INDEX

Name		Nat	Born	Ht/Wt	Event	2016 Mark	Pre-2016 Best
de Souza	Éder Antônio	BRA	15.10.86	189/85	110h	13.61	13.46- 15
Souza	Hugo	BRA	5.3.87	188/77	400	45.69	45.09- 14
Sowinski	Erik	USA	21.12.89	186/70	800	1:45.35	1:44.58 -14
Speakman	Eric	NZL	29.8.90	172/60	1500	3:37.44	3:42.94- 12
Spearmon	Wallace	USA	24.12.84	190/80	200	20.31	19.65- 06
Sperlich	Martin	GER	28.8.91	189/70	1500	3:37.18	3:37.81- 15
Srp	Miklós	HUN	6.3.93	200/83	50kW	3:57:06	4:01:44- 15
Ståhl	Daniel	SWE	27.8.92	200/145	DT	68.72	66.89- 14
Stamatóyiannis ¶	Mihaíl	GRE	20.5.82	188/112	SP	19.86	20.36i- 10, 20.17- 11
Stanchev	Andriy	UKR	10.7.93	190/75	TJ	16.60	16.02- 15
Stanek	Tomás	CZE	13.6.91	190/127	SP	21.30i, 21.26	20.94i- 15, 20.93- 14
Starc	Brandon	AUS	24.11.93	188/73	HJ	2.29	2.31- 15
Stasek	Martin	CZE	8.4.89	190/127	SP	19.85	20.98- 13
Stathelakos	Konstantinos	CYP	30.12.87	181/105	HT	73.61	75.32- 15
Stauß	René	GER	17.9.87	190/75	Dec	7812	7907- 15
Steen	Roger	USA	17.5.92	185/118	SP	19.97	18.81i, 18.73- 15
Stein	Jake	AUS	17.1.94	186/85	Dec	7643	7601- 14
Stigler	Michael	USA	5.4.92	178/70	400h	49.68	48.44- 15
Stój	Bartlomiej	POL	15.5.96	193/115	DT	64.64	59.76- 15
Storl	David	GER	27.7.90	199/122	SP	21.39	22.20- 15
Strobinders	Rolands	LAT	14.4.92	189/106	JT	81.76	83.37- 15
Strother	Nathan	USA	6.9.95	183/70	400	45.07	45.76- 15
Strzalkowski	Adrian	POL	28.3.90	178/64	LJ	7.95, 8.09w	8.18i, 8.02- 14
Su Bingtian		CHN	29.8.89	172/65	100	10.08, 10.104w	9.99- 15
Suárez	Leonel	CUB	1.9.87	181/76	JT	78.29	77.47- 09
					Dec	8460	8654- 09
Suguimati	Mahau	BRA	13.11.84	184/78	400h	48.96	48.67- 09
Sukharev	Kirill	RUS	24.5.92	183/75	LJ	8.07i	8.13- 14
Sulle	Fabiano	TAN	1.10.94		10k	28:01.53	29:00.0 -14
					HMar	61:19	61:59- 15
Sun Song		CHN	15.12.96		20kW	1:21:51	1:23:56- 13
Sun Zhao		CHN	8.2.90	193/83	HJ	2.27i, 2.27	2.25- 12
Svärd Jacobsson	Melker	SWE	8.1.94	188/78	PV	5.70	5.65i, 5.60- 14
Sviridov	Sergey	RUS	20.10.90	192/85	Dec	8065	8365- 12
Svoboda	Petr	CZE	10.10.84	195/83	110h	13.54	13.27- 10
Svyatokho	Valeriy	BLR	20.7.81	186/112	HT	74.33	81.49- 06
Swiderski	Adrian	POL	26.9.86	188/74	TJ	16.68	16.81- 15
Sykora	Jirí	CZE	20.1.95	184/79	Dec	8121	7927- 14
Szikszai	Róbert	HUN	30.9.94	200/118	DT	63.14	63.20- 14
Tabala	Aleksandr	RUS	23.5.86	186/87	Dec	7740	8070- 12
Tabti	Bilal	ALG	7.6.93	175/60	3kSt	8:20.26	8:21.15- 15
Tacir	Ersin	TUR	1.4.85	170/61	20kW	1:22:19	1:24:34- 15
Tadese	Zersenay	ERI	8.2.82	158/52	10k	27:00.66	26:37.25- 06
					HMar	60:31	58:23- 10
Taftian	Hassan	IRI	4.5.93	178/75	100	10.04	10.10- 15
Taha	Islam Ahmed	EGY	23.7.94		HT	72.41	69.19- 15
Taiwo	Jeremy	USA	15.1.90	196/85	Dec	8425	8303- 15
Takahari	Hiromi	JPN	13.11.87	182/64	HJ	2.26i, 2.26	2.28- 15
Takahashi	Eiki	JPN	19.11.92	175/56	20kW	1:18:26	1:18:03- 15
Takase	Kei	JPN	25.11.88	179/67	200	20.31	20.14, 20.09w- 15
Takayama	Shun-ya	JPN	3.9.94	183/71	110h	13.58	13.76- 15
Takele	Adugna	ETH	26.2.89	170/55	HMar	59:40	60:15- 14
Talam	Festus	KEN	20.10.94		Mar	2:06:26	-0-
Talbot	Danny	GBR	1.5.91	184/73	200	20.25	20.27- 15
Tallent	Jared	AUS	17.10.84	178/60	20kW	1:21:50	1:19:15- 10
					50kW	3:41:16	3:36:53- 12
Tamberi	Gianmarco	ITA	1.6.92	189/71	HJ	2.39	2.37- 15
Tamgho	Teddy	FRA	15.6.89	187/82	TJ	17.15	18.04 -13
Tamire	Getaneh	ETH	.94	171/55	5000	13:05.59	13:13.04- 14
Tanabe	Shotaro	JPN	23.4.94	173/63	400h	49.64	50.14- 15
Tang Gongchen		CHN	24.4.89	185/71	LJ	8.03	8.17- 15
Tanii	Takayuki	JPN	14.2.83	167/57	20kW	1:21:23	1:20:39- 04
					50kW	3:44:12	3:40:19- 14
Tanui	Paul	KEN	22.12.90	172/54	3000	7:46.61	7:46.83+- 15
5000	13:15.22		12:58.69- 15		10k	27:05.64	26:50.63- 11
Taplin	Bralon	GRN	8.5.92	180/73	400	44.38	44.89- 15
Tarabin	Dmitriy	RUS	29.10.91	170/85	JT	81.58	88.84- 13
Tarbei	Willy	KEN-J	30.5.98	180/64	800	1:44.84	1:44.51A- 15
Targan	Yousif Abdalla	SUD	28.9.96	175/57	3kSt	8:31.20	8:33.96- 15
Tarus	Eliud	KEN	3.3.93		HMar	61:11	60:04- 15
Tayala	Matthias	USA	27.4.93	183/100	HT	72.52	73.57- 14

Name		Nat	Born	Ht/Wt	Event	2016 Mark	Pre-2016 Best
Taylor	Christian	USA	18.6.90	190/75	LJ	7.96	8.19- 10
					TJ	17.86	18.21- 15
Taylor	Christopher	JAM-Y	29.9.99	178/70	400	45.66	45.27A, 45.55- 15
Taylor	Hoova	USA	11.6.87	196/73	HJ	2.25	2.23i- 14, 2.21- 13
Taylor	Logan	USA	3.4.86	183/70	110h	13.48, 13.47w	13.56- 15, 13.48w- 14
Taylor	Ronald	USA	13.8.90	182/73	LJ	7.94, 8.04w	8.19- 13
Tebira	Hiroshi	JPN	6.8.92		LJ	8.00w	7.78- 15
Teeters	John	USA	19.5.93	183/82	100	10.00	10.07- 15, 9.91w- 14
Tekele	Adugna	ETH	26.2.89	170/55	10k	27:20.65	27:19.34- 15
Teles	Márcio	BRA	27.1.94	180/68	400h	49.09	50.61- 15
Tentóglou	Miltiádis	GRE-J	18.3.98	187/70	LJ	8.19	7.73- 15
Terentyev	Ilya	RUS	25.1.95	184/100	HT	71.82	67.30- 15
Terezan	Artur Langowski	BRA	8.5.91	183/77	400h	49.86	49.73- 15
Tesfaldet (Amsolom)	Nguse	ERI	10.11.86	180/56	10k	27:30.79	27:28.10- 12
					HMar	60:41	59:39- 14
Tesfay	Simon	ERI	15.3.85		HMar	61:00	61:43- 15
Tesfaye	Homiyu	GER	23.6.93	183/66	1500	3:35.05	3:31.98- 14
Teshome	Birhanu	ETH			Mar	2:09:05	
Teshome	Mesfin	ETH			Mar	2:09:24	-0-
Tewelde	Hizkel	ERI	15.9.86		5000	13:17.24	
					10k	27:30.50	-0-
Thebe	Baboloki	BOT-J	18.3.97	178/68	200	20.21A	20.56A- 15
					400	44.22A, 44.69	-0-
Theiner	Wojciech	POL	25.6.86	187/74	HJ	2.29	2.32- 14
Themen	Jurgen	SUR	26.10.85	172/75	100	10.13	10.38- 12, 10.35w- 14
Thomas	Donald	BAH	1.7.84	190/75	HJ	2.37	2.35- 07
Thomas	Mikel	TTO	23.11.87	182/77	110h	13.40	13.17- 15
Thompson	Curtis	USA	8.2.96	183/102	JT	82.88	75.62- 15
Thompson	Joshua	USA	16.1.93	181/75	110h	13.60, 13.58w	13.55, 13.34w- 14
Thompson	Richard	TTO	7.6.85	187/79	100	9.97	9.82, 9.74w- 14
Thormaehlen	Jacob	USA	13.2.90	193/118	SP	20.51	20.50i, 20.31- 12
Thorne	Benjamin	CAN	19.3.93	180/57	20kW	1:19:55	1:19:57- 15
Thornton	Darien	USA	14.7.94	183/100	HT	73.26	67.41- 15
Tiernan	Patrick	AUS	11.9.94	183/68	5000	13:20.88	13:31.25- 14
					10k	27:59.74	-0-
Tikhon	Ivan	BLR	24.7.76	186/110	HT	80.04	84.51- 08, 86.73dq- 05
Tilahun	Belay	ETH	.95		10k	27:11.83	-0-
Timshin	Sergey	RUS	25.11.92	183/79	Dec	7812	7984- 15
Tindouft	Mohammed	MAR	12.3.93		3kSt	8:30.23	8:52.49- 15
Tinsley	Michael	USA	21.4.84	185/74	400h	48.74	47.70- 13
Tistan	Martin	SVK	12.11.92	173/65	50kW	4:00:43	4:02:26- 15
Toader	Andrei	ROU-J	26.5.97	184/105	SP	20.54	19.11- 15
Tobalina	Carlos	ESP	2.8.85	187/127	SP	20.50i, 20.16	20.32- 14
Tola	Seboka	ETH	10.11.87	172/53	Mar	2:09:20	2:06:17- 12
Tola	Tamirat	ETH	11.8.91	181/59	10k	26:57.33	27:22.64- 15
					HMar	60:06	60:08- 15
Toledo	Braian	ARG	8.9.93	187/100	JT	81.96	83.32- 15
Tolosa	Jigisa	ETH	29.3.90	188/70	3kSt	8:21.33	8:22.9- 15
Tomala	Dawid	POL	27.8.89	182/65	20kW	1:21:50	1:20:30- 13
Tonnesen	Pau Gaspar	ESP	24.10.92	196/89	PV	5.53i	5.30- 15
					Dec	8103	8247- 15
Tontodonati	Federico	ITA	30.10.89	169/55	20kW	1:21:56	1:22:00- 12
					50kW	3:55:17	3:49:27- 15
Tonui	Franklin	KEN	2.8.93	175/60	3kSt	8:30.67	8:45.91- 15
Toompuu	Raigo	EST	17.7.81	188/118	SP	19.82	20.20- 10
Torgvaidze	Lasha	GEO	26.5.93	174/65	TJ	16.87A ?, 16.62i	16.58- 15
Torie	Mike	USA	12.3.86	186/110	DT	61.92	63.12- 13
Tornéus	Michel	SWE	26.5.86	184/70	LJ	8.44A, 8.07, 8.21w	8.30i- 15, 8.22- 12
Toroitich	Timothy	UGA	10.10.91	169/57	10k	28:04.84	27:31.07- 13
Torrence	David	USA/PER	26.11.85	175/61	1500	3:34.95	3:33.23- 13
1M	3:54.99		3:52.01- 12		5000	13:19.42	13:16.53- 12
Torrijos	Pablo	ESP	12.5.92	187/78	TJ	16.89A, 16.71	17.04i- 15, 16.87- 14
Tóth	Matej	SVK	10.2.83	185/72	50kW	3:40:58	3:34:38- 15
Tougane	Jaouad	MAR	10.1.89		5000	13:16.12	13:56.49- 14
Traber	Gregor	GER	2.12.92	189/77	110h	13.21	13.32- 15, 13.23w- 14
Trajkovic	Milan	CYP	17.3.92	187/72	110h	13.31	13.65- 14, 13.5- 13
Tremigliozzi	Stefano	ITA	7.5.85	178/68	LJ	7.94i, 7.91	8.06i, 8.05- 14
Trimble	Jamiel	USA	25.6.95	188/82	200	20.12	21.19i, 20.96w- 15
Trofimov	Pyotr	RUS	28.11.83	174/63	20kW	1:22:06	1:18:28- 13
Trotskiy	Ivan	BLR	27.5.76	171/64	20kW	1:22:25	1:19:40- 03
					50kW	3:53:12	3:46:09- 12

540 MEN'S INDEX

Name		Nat	Born	Ht/Wt	Event	2016 Mark	Pre-2016 Best
True	Ben	USA	29.12.85	183/70	1500	3:36.05	3:40.07- 13
					5000	13:12.67	13:02.74- 14
Tsákonas	Likoúrgos-Stéfanos	GRE	8.3.90	184/67	200	20.21	20.09- 15
Tsákonas	Yeóryios	GRE	22.1.88	190/78	LJ	7.98	8.25- 12
Tsegay	Yemane	ETH	8.4.85		Mar	2:08:48	2:04:48- 12
Tsenov	Mitko	BUL	13.6.93	185/64	3kSt	8:21.34	8:20.87- 14
Tsiámis	Dimítrios	GRE	12.1.82	178/67	TJ	16.77	17.55- 06
Tsirikhov	Soslan	RUS	24.11.84	195/125	SP	20.67	20.76- 11
Tsonov	Georgi	BUL	2.5.93	172/66	TJ	16.67, 16.73w	17.03, 17.11w- 15
Tsuetaki	Hironori	JPN	8.5.93	175/59	3kSt	8:29.78	8:32.89- 15
Tsumba	Tatenda	ZIM	12.11.91	175/73	200	20.44	20.46A, 21.21- 15
Tsyplakov	Daniyil	RUS	29.7.92	190/75	HJ	2.30i, 2.28	2.34i, 2.33- 14
Tucker	Russel	RSA	4.11.90	197/115	DT	64.24A	62.74- 15
Tudor	Macklin	USA	13.6.94	188/109	DT	62.50	61.41- 15
Tuemay	Tsegay	ERI	20.12.95	172/55	5000	13:23.04	13:20.89- 13
Tuka	Amel	BIH	9.1.91	187/77	800	1:44.54	1:42.51- 15
Tulu	Kebede	ETH	.96		HMar	61:11	-0-
Tumuti	Boniface Mucheru	KEN	2.5.92	185/75	400h	47.78	48.29- 15
Turner	James	CAN	4.8.93	183/82	Dec	7776	7773w- 15
Turner	Vernon	USA-J	21.8.98	188/77	HJ	2.25	2.03- 15
Tuwei	Dickson	KEN	31.10.92	180/64	Mar	2:09:27	-0-
Tysse	Erik	NOR	4.12.80	184/59	20kW	1:22:12	1:19:11- 08
Ueno	Kohei	JPN	13.7.94	178/68	400h	49.69	50.80- 15
Uhle	Joseph	USA	14.11.92	185/82	PV	5.72	5.55Ai- 15, 5.51- 13
Uibo	Maicel	EST	27.12.92	188/86	Dec	8315	8356- 15
Ujah	Chijindu	GBR	5.3.94	180/75	100	10.01, 9.97w	9.96- 14
Ujakpor	Mark	ESP	18.1.87	192/80	400h	49.65	50.15A- 15
Ukaoma	Miles	NGR	21.7.92	183/75	400h	49.60	48.84- 15
Ukhov	Ivan	RUS	29.3.86	192/83	HJ	2.35	2.42i, 2.41- 14
Updike	Isaac	USA	21.3.92	180/64	3kSt	8:31.42	8:47.00- 15
Urbanek	Robert	POL	29.4.87	200/120	DT	65.56	66.93- 12
Ureña	Jorge	ESP	8.10.93	178/75	Dec	7985	7983- 15
Ursu ¶	Sergiu	ROU	26.4.80	202/127	DT	62.55	64.74- 10
Ushiro	Keisuke	JPN	24.7.86	196/95	Dec	8160	8308- 14
Vadlejch	Jakub	CZE	10.10.90	190/93	JT	88.02	86.21- 15
Valiyev	Roman	KAZ	27.3.84	190/73	TJ	16.87i, 16.80	17.20- 12
Van Der Plaetsen	Thomas	BEL	24.12.90	188/82	Dec	8332	8255- 13
van Liew	Tim	USA	25.5.90	190/95	JT	79.62	79.49- 15
van Niekerk	Wayde	RSA	15.7.92	183/73	100	9.98A	10.45A- 11, 10.51- 10
	200	20.02				19.94- 15	
					400	43.03	43.48- 15
van Rensburg	Phil-Mar	RSA	23.6.89	188/86	JT	78.88	76.85- 15
van Rensburg	Rynhardt	RSA	23.3.92	184/70	800	1:45.33	1:45.40- 15
van Rooyen	Rocco	RSA	23.12.92	188/93	JT	78.48	85.39- 15
van Zyl	Louis 'L.J'	RSA	20.7.85	186/75	400h	48.67	47.66- 11
Varga	Roland	CRO	22.10.77	196/125	DT	62.64	67.38- 02
Vargas	Richard	VEN	28.12.94	178/70	20kW	1:22:10	1:22:24- 15
Vaughn	Clayton	USA	15.5.92	173/77	100	10.02	9.93- 15
Väyrynen	Henri	FIN	16.10.91	185/75	LJ	8.07A	7.93- 15, 8.05w- 14
Vázquez	Wesley	PUR	27.3.94	184/73	800	1:44.75	1:44.64- 14
Vega	Jesús Tadeo	MEX	23.5.94	179/61	20kW	1:19:20	1:22:10A- 14
Vena	Nick	USA	16.4.93	194/120	SP	19.87i, 19.71	20.39- 14
Venyercsán	Bence	HUN	8.1.96		50kW	4:02:35	-0-
Verburg	David	USA	14.5.91	168/64	400	44.82	44.41- 15
Vesely	Vitezslav	CZE	27.2.83	186/94	JT	84.82	88.34- 12
Vetter	Johannes	GER	26.3.93	188/105	JT	89.57	85.40- 15
Vicars	Derrick	USA	8.5.89	188/114	SP	19.65	20.12i- 13
Vicaut	Jimmy	FRA	27.2.92	188/83	100	9.86	9.86- 15
Victor	Lindon	GRN	28.2.93	191/89	Dec	8446	7429- 14, 7453w- 15
Vides	Jorge Henrique	BRA	24.11.92	190/77	200	20.40	20.38- 14
Vieira	João	POR	20.2.76	174/58	50kW	3:49:05	3:45:17- 12
Villanueva	Claudio	ECU	3.8.88	168/55	50kW	3:58:56	3:50:29- 13
Vinichenko ¶	Igor	RUS	11.4.84	196/119	HT	73.77	80.00- 07
Vivas	Borja	ESP	26.5.84	203/140	SP	20.72	21.07- 14
Vizzoni	Nicola	ITA	4.11.73	193/126	HT	72.74	80.50- 01
Vloon	Menno	NED	11.5.94	177/77	PV	5.58	5.55- 15
Volz	Deakin	USA-J	12.1.97	178/75	PV	5.65	5.47i, 5.38- 15
Volz	Drew	USA	20.11.92	181/75	PV	5.62i	5.48- 14
Vonavka	Tomás	CZE	4.6.90	197/109	DT	63.18	62.10- 14
Vukicevic	Vladimir	NOR	6.5.91	193/83	110h	13.54	13.55- 12
Vynohradov	Yevhen	UKR	30.4.84	195/105	HT	77.15	80.58- 08
Waithe	Shakiel	TTO	10.6.95	201/85	JT	79.53	77.30- 15

MEN'S INDEX

Name		Nat	Born	Ht/Wt	Event	2016 Mark	Pre-2016 Best
Walcott	Keshorn	TTO	2.4.93	188/90	JT	88.68	90.16- 15
Wale	Getnet	ETH-Y	20.7.99	178/60	3kSt	8:22.83	
Walelegn	Amedework	ETH-Y	11.3.99		10k	28:00.14	
Walker	Justin	USA	30.11.90	175/70	100	10.05	10.12, 9.95w- 14
					200	20.26	20.29- 15, 20.13w- 14
Walker	Shaquille	USA	24.6.93	178/70	800	1:44.99	1:45.58- 15
Wallace	Tyler	USA	31.7.90	190/80	PV	5.55	5.50- 11
Wallin	Gabriel	SWE	14.10.81	193/93	JT	82.81	83.23- 13
Walsh	Julian Jrummi	JPN	18.9.96	175/75	400	45.35	45.92- 15
Walsh	Tom	NZL	1.3.92	186/123	SP	22.21	21.62- 15
Walters	Ruebin	TTO	2.4.95	184/70	110h	13.60	13.82, 13.53w- 15
Walton	Cody	USA	14.6.95	188/89	Dec	7620w	7232- 15
Wan Yong		CHN	22.7.87	188/107	HT	71.50	74.74- 15
Wang Jianan		CHN	27.8.96	178/61	LJ	8.24	8.25- 15
Wang Kaihua		CHN	16.2.94		20kW	1:19:51	1:19:49- 15
Wang Qin #		CHN	8.5.94		20kW	1:22:08	1:22:50- 14
					50kW	3:50:16	-0-
Wang Rui		CHN	6.1.96		20kW	1:21:23	-0-
Wang Shizhu		CHN	20.2.89	184/100	HT	72.25	75.20- 13
Wang Yu		CHN	18.8.91	192/73	HJ	2.33	2.33- 13
Wang Zhen		CHN	24.8.91	180/62	20kW	1:19:12	1:17:36- 12
Wang Zhendong		CHN	11.1.91	180/65	50kW	3:41:02	3:47:18- 14
Wangari	James Mwangi	KEN	23.3.94	175/58	5000	13:13.93	13:16.06- 14
10k	27:23.04		27:23.66- 14		HMar	59:07	-0-
Wanjiru	Daniel	KEN	26.5.92	174/58	HMar	59:20	59:51- 15
Wanjiru	Daniel	KEN	26.5.92	174/58	Mar	2:05:21	2:08:18- 14
Ward	Ja'Mari	USA-J	21.7.98	175/68	LJ	7.96	7.63, 7.80i- 15
Warholm	Karsten	NOR	28.2.96	187/78	400h	48.49	51.09- 15
Wariner	Jeremy	USA	31.1.84	183/70	400	45.51	43.45- 07
Warner	Damian	CAN	4.11.89	185/83	100	10.15, 10.09w	10.28- 15
110h	13.42	13.27- 15		LJ	8.04	7.65, 7.68w- 15 Dec 8666	8695- 15
Washington	Adarius	USA	19.10.92	183/73	110h	13.40	13.58- 15
Wasihun	Mule	ETH	20.10.93		HMar	61:11	60:08- 14
					Mar	2:05:44	2:10:57- 15
Waweru	Edward	KEN	3.10.90	178/58	10k	27:40.23	27:13.94- 10
Webb	Ameer	USA	19.3.91	175/75	100	9.94, 9.90w	10.04- 15
					200	19.85	20.02- 15
Weber	Julian	GER	29.8.94	190/94	JT	88.29	81.15- 15
Wei Xubao		CHN	1.2.93		20kW	1:21:46	1:23:09- 13
Weir	Warren	JAM	31.10.89	178/75	100	10.07	10.02- 15
					200	20.32	19.79- 13
Weirich	Victor	USA	25.10.87	188/86	PV	5.55Ai	5.66Ai- 15, 5.60- 14
Weißhaidinger	Lukas	AUT	20.2.92	196/136	DT	66.00	67.24- 15
Weldon	Kole	USA	25.3.92	193/114	DT	62.48	62.05- 14
White-Edwards	Tim	USA	15.7.94	181/82	TJ	16.57	16.49A- 13, 16.45- 14
Whiting	Ryan	USA	24.11.86	191/134	SP	21.06	22.28- 13
Whyte	Annsert	JAM	10.4.87	185/75	400h	48.07	48.58- 14
Wieland	Luca	GER	7.12.94	185/82	Dec	7784w	7635- 15
Wierig	Martin	GER	10.6.87	202/127	DT	67.60	68.33- 12
Wiesiolek	Pawel	POL	13.8.91	194/84	Dec	8095	8140- 15
Wightman	Jake	GBR	11.7.94	173/60	1500	3:36.64	3:35.49- 14
					1M	3:54.20	3:57.80- 15
Williams	Brian	USA	18.12.94	188/109	DT	63.23	52.37- 15
Williams	Delano	GBR	23.12.93	183/72	400	45.50	45.42- 15
Williams	Devon	USA	17.1.94	190/84	Dec	8116	7341- 15
Williams	Harrison	USA	7.3.96	190/82	Dec	8032	7806- 15
Williams	Isaac	USA	30.11.93	188/80	110h	13.43	13.56, 13.31w- 15
Williams	Kendal	USA	23.9.95	180/73	100	10.06, 10.04w	10.07, 9.98w- 15
					200	20.31, 20.11w	20.26- 15
Williams	Rhys	GBR	27.2.84	185/73	400h	49.22	48.84- 13
Willis	Nick	NZL	25.4.83	183/68	1500	3:34.29	3:29.66- 15
					1M	3:52.26, 3:51.06i	3:49.83- 14
Wilson	Jamal	BAH	1.9.88	188/68	HJ	2.31, 2.30	2.28- 13
Wilson	Jerome	JAM	10.9.91		LJ	7.95w	7.82- 14, 7.83A, 8.02w- 12
Wilson	Ryan	USA	19.12.80	188/81	110h	13.54	13.02- 07
Winder	Luke	USA	2.8.95	185/75	PV	5.52i, 5.51	5.45- 15
Windle	Drew	USA	22.7.92	183/73	800	1:45.65	1:46.52i, 1:46.91- 14
Winger	Russ	USA	2.8.84	191/120	DT	63.47	66.04- 11
Winkler	Rudy	USA	6.12.94	186/102	HT	76.76	70.36- 15
Winter	Chris	CAN	22.7.86	188/75	3kSt	8:27.18	8:26.55- 15
Wirkkala	Teemu	FIN	14.1.84	187/85	JT	81.16	87.23- 09

542   MEN'S INDEX

Name		Nat	Born	Ht/Wt	Event	2016 Mark	Pre-2016 Best
Woepse	Mike	USA	29.5.91	185/79	PV	5.65	5.62- 14
Wojciechowski	Pawel	POL	6.6.89	190/81	PV	5.84i, 5.71	5.91- 11
Wolde	Dawit	ETH	19.5.91	169/54	1500	3:33.98	3:33.82- 12
1M	3:54.02i, 3:55.80		3:54.51- 13		3000	7:41.69i	7:42.65- 11
Wolfle	Chase	USA	9.10.92	185/84	PV	5.65	5.56- 14
Wolken	Kale	USA	13.9.93	188/86	Dec	7830	7416- 14
Wolski	Allan	BRA	18.1.90	185/110	HT	71.69	73.52- 15
Woo Sang-hyuk		KOR	23.4.96	187/66	HJ	2.29	2.24- 14
Woodruff	Ben	USA	9.5.89	183/91	JT	80.86	78.67- 15
Woodson	Markesh	USA	6.9.93	168/64	100	10.05	10.18, 10.11w -13
Wote	Aman	ETH	18.4.84	181/64	1500	3:34.58	3:29.91- 14
					1M	3:53.23	3:48.60- 14
Wright	Alex	IRL	19.12.90	173/64	20kW	1:21:56	1:22:09- 15
					50kW	3:48:31	3:51:28- 14
Wright	Chad	JAM	25.3.91	188/110	DT	64.45	65.03- 15
Wright	Dontavius	USA	3.1.94	178/68	400	45.12	45.92- 15
Wrobel	David	GER	13.2.91	195/125	DT	63.51, 64.93 dh	62.72- 14
Wu Qianlong		CHN	30.1.90	176/62	50kW	3:57:02	3:47:35- 15
Wu Ruiting		CHN	29.11.95		TJ	16.60	16.83 -15
Wyatt	Audie	USA	30.4.96	190/84	PV	5.65, 5.70 dh	5.50- 15
Wyatt	Vincent	USA	18.10.92	190/84	110h	13.60	13.60, 13.55w- 14
Wynne	Henry	USA	18.4.95	186/75	1500	3:38.05	3:41.19- 15
Xie Wenjun		CHN	11.7.90	188/77	110h	13.34	13.23- 14
Xie Zhenye		CHN	17.8.93	185/80	100	10.08	10.25- 15, 10.24w- 14
Xu Faguang		CHN	17.5.87	178/69	50kW	3:48:07	3:42:20- 11
Xu Xiaolong		CHN	20.12.92	185/70	TJ	16.65	16.93- 15
Xue Changrui		CHN	31.5.91	183/60	PV	5.81i, 5.75	5.80- 14
Yacoub Salem	Mohamed	BRN	1.3.96	175/68	200	20.19	20.71- 15
Yakovenko	Dmytro	UKR	17.9.92	191/72	HJ	2.26	2.30- 15
Yakushev	Maksim	RUS	15.3.92		3kSt	8:26.21	8:34.75- 15
Yamagata	Ryota	JPN	10.6.92	177/70	100	10.03	10.07- 12, 10.04w- 13
Yamakawa	Natsuki	JPN	24.7.95		LJ	8.00	7.81- 15
Yamamoto	Ryoma	JPN	14.7.95	179/64	TJ	16.68	16.28- 14
Yamamoto	Seito	JPN	11.3.92	181/70	PV	5.77Ai, 5.63	5.75- 13
Yamanishi	Toshikazu	JPN	15.2.96	164/53	20kW	1:20:50	1:21:20- 15
Yamashita	Kohei	JPN	6.9.94	179/69	TJ	16.85	16.06- 15
Yáñez	Eure	VEN	20.5.93	194/77	HJ	2.26	2.27- 14
Yang Wei-Ting		TPE	22.9.94		110h	13.61	13.78- 15
Yao Jie		CHN	21.9.90	188/85	PV	5.70	5.65- 15
Yator	Vincent	KEN	11.7.89	172/55	10k	27:25.94	27:33.45A- 15
Yaurivilca	Paolo César	PER	23.4.96	169/62	20kW	1:21:49	-0-
Yazawa	Wataru	JPN	2.7.91	179/73	110h	13.47	13.59- 13
Yego	Hillary	KEN	2.4.92	178/60	3kSt	8:15.10	8:03.57- 13
Yego	Julius	KEN	4.1.89	175/90	JT	88.24	92.72- 15
Yego	Solomon Kirwa	KEN	10.5.87	175/58	HMar	58:44	60:04- 15
					Mar	2:08:31	-0-
Yegon	Geoffrey	KEN	28.8.88		HMar	59:44	-0-
Yemataw	Birhanu	BRN	27.2.96	167/54	3000	7:44.29	8:19.51- 15
					5000	13:09.26	13:39.65- 15
Yemelyanov ¶	Stanislav	RUS	23.10.90	175/62	20kW	1:21:57	1:19:43- 10, 1:18:29dq- 12
Yoon Seung-hyun		KOR	1.6.94	194/74	HJ	2.25i, 2,24	2.32- 15
Yorks	Izaic	USA	17.4.94	174/64	1500	3:37.74	3:42.01- 15
					1M	3:53.89i	3:57.81i- 15
Yoshida	Kazuaki	JPN	31.8.87	180/73	400h	49.78	49.45- 09
Younes Idris	Ali Mohamed	SUD	15.9.89	191/75	HJ	2.25i	2.28i- 14, 2.28- 15
Young	Alex	USA	1.9.94	188/105	HT	72.47	66.50- 15
Young	Isiah	USA	5.1.90	183/75	100	10.03	9.99- 13, 9.82w- 15
					200	20.24	19.86- 13, 19.75w- 15
Young	Jason	USA	27.5.81	185/127	DT	65.67	69.90- 10
Yousif	Rabah	GBR	11.12.86	183/75	400	45.45	44.54- 15
Yu Wei		CHN	11.9.87	180/60	50kW	3:42:54	3:45:21- 15
Yurchenko	Aleksandr	RUS	30.7.92		TJ	16.54	16.81i- 15, 16.67- 13
Zakalnytskyy	Maryan	UKR	19.8.94	180/65	50kW	3:56:30	3:57:18- 15
Zaleski	Yevgeniy	BLR	18.7.93	167/57	20kW	1:22:18	1:25:06- 13
Zalewski	Karol	POL	7.8.93	189/86	200	20.26	20.41- 13
Zalewski	Krystian	POL	11.4.89	185/67	3kSt	8:19.91	8:16.20- 14
Zango	Fabrice	BUR	25.6.93	180/75	TJ	16.81, 16.84w	16.76- 15
Zawude	Tebalu	ETH	2.11.87	184/65	10k	27:25.10	27:20.54- 15
Zayas	Luis	CUB-J	7.6.97		HJ	2.27	2.18-14
Zaytsev	Ivan	UZB	7.11.88	190/98	JT	83.03	85.03- 12
Zaza	Wellington	LBR	20.1.95	175/70	110h	13.75, 13.59w	14.00- 14, 13.86w- 15

MEN'S INDEX

Name		Nat	Born	Ht/Wt	Event	2016 Mark	Pre-2016 Best
Zeghdane	Issam	ALG	9.3.93		3kSt	8:31.48	8:59.92- 12
Zeng Qingcun		CHN	3.4.95		20kW	1:22:19	1:26:08- 15
Zenker	Stephan	GER	18.11.91	178/75	LJ	7.97w	7.71- 15
Zepeda	Omar	MEX	8.7.77	177/68	50kW	3:45:28A	3:47:35- 14
Zerrifi	Abdelhamid	ALG	20.6.86	170/57	3kSt	8:28.14	8:25.96- 13
Zhang Guowei		CHN	4.6.91	200/77	HJ	2.33	2.38- 15
Zhang Hang		CHN	28.10.91		50kW	3:43:31	3:50:01- 15
Zhang Honglin		CHN	12.1.94	188/82	110h	13.59	13.53- 15
Zhang Kuo		CHN	12.12.89		50kW	4:00:11	3:58:47- 15
Zhang Lin		CHN	11.11.93	175/55	50kW	3:48:23	3:44:39- 15
Zhang Yaoguang		CHN	21.6.93		LJ	8.09i, 8.01	7.99- 13, 8.01w- 15
Zhao Qinggang		CHN	24.7.85	184/93	JT	80.42	89.15- 14
Zhelyabin	Dmitry	RUS	20.5.90	187/75	PV	5.60	5.65- 12
Zhong Peifeng		CHN-J	3.3.97	174/61	LJ	8.11	7.59- 15
Zhu Yaming		CHN	4.5.94		TJ	16.97	15.52- 15
Ziani	Mohamed	MAR	.93		HMar	61:21	62:50- 15
Ziegler	Alexander	GER	7.7.87	180/98	HT	73.22	76.29- 14
Ziemek	Zach	USA	23.2.93	190/77	Dec	8413	8107- 15
Zienasellassie	Futsum	USA	16.12.92	176/59	10k	27:52.70	28:35.76- 15
Zoghlami	Osama	ITA	19.6.94	182/58	3kSt	8:32.20	8:37.11- 15
Zunic	Stipe	CRO	13.12.90	188/115	SP	20.70	21.11i- 15, 20.68- 14

WOMEN'S INDEX 2016

Athletes included are those ranked in the top 100s at standard (Olympics and Worlds) events (plus shorter lists for 1000m, 1M, 2000m and 3000m). Those with detailed biographical profiles are indicated in first column by: * in this year's Annual, ^ featured in a previous year's Annual

Name		Nat	Born	Ht/Wt	Event	2016 Mark	Pre-2016 Best
Ababel	Yeshaneh	ETH	10.6.90	157/42	5000	14:41.58	15:17.05- 12
					HMar	67:52	69:00- 11
					10000	30:54.12	30:35.91- 13
Abakumova	Mariya	RUS	15.1.86	178/85	JT	59.55	71.99- 11
Abe	Yukari	JPN	21.8.89	154/48	5000	15:22.29	15:33.25- 13
Abramchuk	Alena	BLR	14.2.88	182/95	SP	18.02i, 17.82	19.24- 13
Abrams	Aliyah	GUY-J	3.4.97	163/53	400	52.04	53.10- 15
Abuova	Dilyara	KAZ	6.1.94	172/52	TJ	13.61	13.60- 15
Achola	Janet	UGA	26.6.88	162/50	1500	4:08.11	4:05.52- 12
Adams	Valerie	NZL	6.10.84	193/120	SP	20.42	21.24- 11
Adamu	Birtukan	ETH	29.4.92	164/49	3kSt	9:35.97	9:20.37- 11
Adanech	Feyisa	ETH-J	23.1.98	160/48	1500	4:05.22	
Adekoya	Kemi	BRN	16.1.93	168/57	400	50.72	50.86- 15
					400h	54.87	54.12- 15
Afanasyeva	Klavdiya	RUS	15.1.96		20kW	1:26:47	
Afework	Abebech	ETH	11.12.90	152/42	Mar	2:24:27	2:23:33- 15
Aga	Ruti	ETH	16.1.94		HMar	68:07	
					Mar	2:24:41	
Agafonova	Gulfiya	RUS	4.6.82	173/84	HT	68.97	77.26- 06
Agai	Margaret	KEN	10.6.88	154/44	HMar	70:28	69:57- 15
					Mar	2:26:20	2:23:28- 13
Agirre	Naroa	ESP	15.5.79	177/64	PV	4.40	4.56i- 07, 4.51- 14
Agnou	Caroline	SUI	26.5.96	171/65	Hep	5822	6123- 15
Aguilar	Evelis	COL	3.1.93	173/64	Hep	6270A, 6263	5930- 15
Aguilar	Yulenmis	CUB	3.8.96	167/70	JT	57.09	63.86- 15
Ahbe	Kelsie	CAN	6.7.91	170/63	PV	4.55	4.50- 15
Ahouré	Murielle	CIV	23.8.87	167/57	100	10.78	10.81- 15
					200	22.52	22.24- 13
Ahye	Michelle-Lee	TTO	10.4.92	168/59	100	10.90	10.85- 14
					200	22.25	22.77- 14
Aidietyte	Neringa	LTU	5.6.83	177/64	20kW	1:31:20	1:29:01- 14
Aiyabei	Valary	KEN	8.6.91		HMar	69:33	
					Mar	2:24:48	2:30:19- 14
Akakpo	Stella	FRA	28.2.94	166/60	100	11.17	11.24, 11.21w- 14
Akdag	Meryem	TUR	5.8.92	171/51	5000	15:24.60, 15:19.27i	15:42.30- 15
					3kSt	9:36.54	9:57.62- 15
Akinosun	Morolake	USA	17.5.94	163/61	100	10.95	11.04- 14, 10.94w- 15
					200	22.54	22.52- 15, 22.17w- 14
Akkaoui	Malika	MAR	25.12.87	160/46	800	1:59.93	1:57.64- 13
					1500	4:07.42	4:04.49- 15
Akpana Assa	Nadia	NOR	22.12.95	176/57	LJ	6.53	6.48- 15
Aksyonova	Kseniya	RUS	14.1.88	177/60	400	51.74	49.92- 10
Aksyonova	Natalya	RUS-J	6.6.97		HJ	1.92	1.88- 15
Alais	Alexie	FRA	9.10.94	168/68	JT	57.81	56.30- 14
Alami	Salima	MAR	29.12.83	167/53	3kSt	9:44.83	9:20.64- 15

WOMEN'S INDEX

Name		Nat	Born	Ht/Wt	Event	2016 Mark	Pre-2016 Best
Alamirew	Enatnesg	ETH	.95		5000	15:22.56	15:45.76- 14
Alcide	Makeba	LCA	24.2.90	175/62	Hep	5852w	6050- 13
Aldama	Yamilé	GBR	14.8.72	173/62	TJ	13.74	15.29- 03
Aleksandrova	Dina	RUS	9.8.92		1000	2:36.07	2:47.25i- 15
Aleksandrova	Ulyana	RUS	1.1.91	182/63	HJ	1.90i	1.90i, 1.89- 15
Alekseyeva	Natalya	RUS	27.5.86		TJ	13.96i, 13.36, 13.65w	14.08i, 13.93- 15
Alemu	Habitam	ETH-J	9.7.97	171/52	800	1:58.99	2:01.27- 15
Alexander	Ayanna	TTO	20.7.82	172/65	TJ	14.10	14.40- 14
Alexander	Kineke	VIN	21.2.86	178/65	400	51.40	51.23, 50.8- 14
Alexoúli	Háido	GRE	29.3.91	179/59	LJ	6.78	6.69- 15
Ali	Nia	USA	23.10.88	170/64	100h	12.55	12.48- 13
					Hep	5870	5824- 09
Allgood	Avione	USA	14.12.93	165/	JT	58.81	57.63- 14
Allman	Valarie	USA	23.2.95	183/70	DT	61.42	57.48- 15
Almanza	Rose Mary	CUB	13.7.92	166/53	800	1:58.49	1:57.70- 15
Álvarez	Raquel	ESP	13.6.83	174/61	HJ	1.90i, 1.84	1.89- 11
Amata	Doreen	NGR	6.5.88	185/55	HJ	1.95	1.95- 08
Amponsah	Janet	GHA	12.4.93	167/52	200	22.99	23.04- 15
Amusan	Tobi	NGR-J	23.4.97	164/52	100h	12.83A, 12.91, 12.79w	13.11- 15
Anacharsis	Phara	FRA	17.12.83	177/60	400h	55.84	55.94- 13
Anagnostopoúlou	Hrisoúla	GRE	27.8.91	176/79	DT	59.76	61.40- 15
Ananchenko	Yevgeniya	RUS	7.11.92	178/73	JT	57.67	60.54- 15
Anderson	Alex	USA	28.1.87	175/60	100	11.19, 10.97w	10.91- 13, 10.88w- 12
					200	22.75, 22.53w	22.60- 09
Andersson	Tracey	SWE	5.12.84	167/87	HT	70.99	70.82- 13
Ando	Yuka	JPN	16.3.94	160/43	10000	31:58.71	32:07.37- 15
					HMar	70:10	69:51- 15
Andraud	Matilde	FRA	28.4.89	172/68	JT	63.54	60.67- 15
Andrejczyk	Maria	POL	9.3.96	174/77	JT	67.11	62.11- 15
Andrews	Jessica	GBR	1.10.92	168/52	5000	15:24.02	16:19.66- 14
(-Martin)					10000	31:35.92	-0-
Angelsen	Tonje	NOR	17.1.90	179/62	HJ	1.93	1.97- 12
Ankiewicz	Emilia	POL	22.11.90	178/64	400h	55.89	56.55- 15
Ansa	Woynshet	ETH	9.4.96	158/42	3kSt	9:37.85	9:53.92- 15
Aoki	Sayaka	JPN	15.12.86	163/51	400h	56.85	55.94- 08
Apine	Madara	LAT	2.3.89		TJ	13.43, 13.79w	13.68- 15
Aragon	Christina	USA-J	17.6.97	161/48	1500	4:08.71	4:16.36- 15
Araújo	Edivania	BRA	27.8.95		JT	57.02	55.16- 15
Arcanjo	Geisa	BRA	19.9.91	180/92	SP	18.27	19.02- 12
Arenas	Sandra	COL	17.9.93	160/50	20kW	1:29:31	1:30:18- 14
Aristarkhova	Natalya	RUS	31.10.89	163/46	3kSt	9:42.49	9:30.64- 13
Arkhipova	Tatyana	RUS	8.4.83	160/53	Mar	2:28:34	2:23:29- 12
Arndt	Mareike	GER	29.1.92		Hep	5765	5709- 14
Arrafi	Rabab	MAR	12.1.91	177/64	800	2:01.49	1:58.55- 15
					1500	4:03.95	4:02.71- 14
Arrieta	Olatz	ESP	1.12.90	176/60	LJ	6.61A, 6.37	6.34- 13
Arteil	Laura	FRA	9.10.93	171/60	Hep	5735	5812- 14
Arusei	Peninah	KEN	23.2.79	165/51	HMar	69:08	67:48- 10
Arzamasova	Marina	BLR	17.12.87	173/57	800	1:58.36	1:57.54- 15
Arzhakova	Yelena	RUS	8.9.89	167/52	800	2:01.17	1:59.35i,1:59.56- 11,1:57.67dq- 12
Asada	Chiaki	JPN	21.1.91		20kW	1:30:44	1:31:28- 15
Asanova	Natalya	UZB	29.11.89	174/62	400h	56.33	56.13- 12
Asefa	Sutume	ETH	.94	153/42	HMar	70:17+	68:47- 15
					Mar	2:24:00	
Asenjo	Sabina	ESP	3.8.86	181/95	DT	61.89	61.36- 15
Ashe	Shelby	USA	13.3.93	173/88	HT	66.05	68.12- 12
Asher-Smith	Dina	GBR	4.12.95	165/55	100	11.07	10.99- 15
					200	22.31	22.07- 15
Ashley	Whitney	USA	18.2.89	176/90	SP	17.62i	17.22i, 17.00- 14
					DT	64.62	64.80- 15
Assani Issouf	Jeanine	FRA	17.8.92	169/57	TJ	14.40	14.24- 15
Assefa	Meskerem	ETH	20.9.85	155/43	HMar	69:39	69:10- 14
Assefa	Sofia	ETH	14.11.87	171/58	3kSt	9:13.09	9:09.00- 12
Assefa	Tigist	ETH	28.3.94	168/53	800	2:00.21	1:59.24- 14
Asumnu	Gloria	NGR	22.5.85	163/52	100	11.24	11.03- 08
Atkins	Joanna	USA	31.1.89	180/64	100	11.09, 10.99w	11.02- 14
					200	22.40	22.27, 22.19w- 15
Augustyniak	Lidia	POL	14.5.94	178/84	DT	59.36	55.67- 15
Avdeyeva	Anna	RUS	6.4.85	171/100	SP	17.67	20.07- 09
Avery	Kate	GBR	10.10.91	175/50	10000	32:11.84	31:41.44- 15
Ayalew	Hiwot	ETH	6.3.90	173/51	3kSt	9:35.09	9:09.61- 12

WOMEN'S INDEX

Name		Nat	Born	Ht/Wt	Event	2016 Mark		Pre-2016 Best
Ayalew	Wude	ETH	4.7.87	150/44	HMar	69:23		67:58- 09
					Mar	2:27:08		2:57:47- 14
Ayana	Almaz	ETH	21.11.91	165/50	2000	5:36.80+		5:35.10+- 15
3000	8:23.11	8:22.22- 15		5000	14:12.59		14:14.32- 15	10000	29:17.45	-0-
Ayele	Gebeyanesh	ETH	1.5.95		HMar	70:21		
Azevedo	Cátia	POR	9.3.94	170/50	400	51.63		52.61- 14
Baak	Bianca	NED	25.1.92	174/56	400h	56.34		56.75- 13
Babar	Lalita	IND	2.6.89	160/58	3kSt	9:19.76		9:27.86- 15
Babsek	Sasa	SLO	27.3.92	172/65	TJ	13.67, 13.81w		13.70- 15
Bacciotti	Eleonora	ITA	13.12.89	178/68	JT	56.24		54.57- 15
Bahta	Meraf	SWE	24.6.89	177/51	1500	4:02.62		4:01.34- 14
1M	4:25.26			3000	8:43.08		8:57.06- 14	5000	14:49.95	14:59.49- 14
Baisden	Kendall	USA	5.3.95	176/61	400	52.09		50.46- 14
Baker	Olivia	USA	12.6.96	163/52	800	2:01.02		2:04.00- 15
Balkwill	Kelsey	CAN	19.9.92	175/62	400h	56.81		
Balta	Ksenija	EST	1.11.86	168/53	LJ	6.79		6.87i- 09, 6.87- 10
Baluyeva	Natalya	RUS	.92		HJ	1.88i		? was this Kushnir?
Bambara	Laëtitia	BUR	30.3.84	180/75	HT	68.59		68.53- 11
Bamgbose	Margaret	NGR	19.10.93	162/52	400	51.11		51.37- 15
Bani	Zahra	ITA	31.12.79	173/71	JT	56.86		62.75- 05
Bânova	Andriana	BUL	1.5.87	178/64	TJ	13.85		14.34- 11
Baptiste	Kelly-Ann	TTO	14.10.86	168/58	100	11.04		10.83- 13
					200	22.73		22.36- 13, 22.33w- 12
Barber	Alana	NZL	8.7.87	163/52	20kW	1:32:48		1:32:50- 15
Barber	Jade	USA	4.4.93	170/64	100h	13.00		12.85- 15
Barber	Kaila	USA	4.4.93	163/54	100h	12.91		13.48- 15, 13.47w- 14
					400h	55.53		56.96- 14
Barber	Me'Lisa	USA	4.10.80	160/53	100	11.25		10.95- 07, 10.87w- 05
Barber	Mikele	USA	4.10.80	160/50	100	11.10		11.02- 07, 10.96w- 11
Barbosa	Vera	POR	13.1.89	168/56	400h	56.20		55.22- 12
Barnett	Tara-Sue	JAM	9.10.93	178/81	DT	61.28		58.55- 15
Barrios	Yarelis	CUB	12.7.83	172/98	DT	62.50		68.03- 12
Barsosio	Agnes	KEN	5.8.82	159/44	Mar	2:24:59		2:24:03- 13
Bartoletta	Tianna	USA	30.8.85	168/60	100	10.78		10.85- 12
					LJ	7.17		7.14- 15
Bass	Gina	GAM	3.5.95	164/52	200	22.92		24.13- 15
Bauer	Katharina	GER	12.6.90	179/68	PV	4.40		4.65- 15
Baumann	Jackie	GER	24.8.95	172/57	400h	56.19		56.62- 15
Bauschke	Melanie	GER	14.7.88	178/62	LJ	6.70, 6.90w		6.83- 09
Baxter	Aubrey	USA	7.11.85	173/84	HT	68.33		70.90- 12
Bazolo	Lorène	POR	4.5.83	170/53	100	11.21		11.41- 15
Beahan	Brianna	AUS	1.11.91	168/57	100h	13.03		13.18- 15
Beans	Kaitlyn	USA	21.4.95		TJ	13.38		13.18- 14
Beard	Jessica	USA	8.1.89	168/57	200	22.94, 22.85w		22.81- 13
					400	51.76		50.56- 09
Beckles	Kierre	BAR	21.5.90	176/61	100h	12.93		12.88- 15
Beesley	Meghan	GBR	15.11.89	167/63	400h	55.43		54.52- 15
Beitia	Ruth	ESP	1.4.79	192/71	HJ	1.98i, 1.98		2.02- 07
Bekele	Ashete	ETH	17.4.88	169/52	Mar	2:25:50		2:23:43- 15
Bekele	Tadelech	ETH	11.4.91	154/40	10000	30:54.61		33:30.7- 15
HMar	69:08			68:38- 13	Mar	2:26:31		2:22:51- 15
Bekh	Maryna	UKR	18.7.95	172/63	LJ	6.93		6.78- 13
Belachew	Agrie	ETH-Y	20.1.99	163/50	3kSt	9:37.17		
Belanovich	Yekaterina	BLR	14.1.91	173/64	400h	55.59		56.36- 15, 56.16dq- 10
Belbiod	Romaissa	ALG	28.2.91	178/65	LJ	6.56		6.49- 15
Belete	Mimi	BRN	9.6.88	169/55	3000	8:51.00		8:30.00- 14
Beletew	Yehualye	ETH-J	31.7.98	165/52	20kW	1:31:58		1:47:33- 14
Belibasáki	María	GRE	19.6.91	174/54	100	11.22w		11.34- 12
Bell	Alexandra	GBR	4.11.92	166/55	800	2:00.53		2:01.82- 15
Belle	Tia Adana	BAR	16.6.96	178.59	400h	55.82		57.45- 15
Bellille	Janeil	TTO	18.6.89	172/60	400h	56.06		55.41- 14
Bendrat	Stephanie	AUT	5.3.91		100h	13.11, 13.04w		13.38- 15
Bengtsson	Angelica	SWE	8.7.93	163/51	PV	4.66i, 4.65		4.70- 15
Bennett	Taylor	USA-J	15.1.97	170/61	200	22.71		23.46- 15
Beriso	Amane	ETH	13.10.91	163/60	HMar	70:17+		68:43- 15
					Mar	2:20:48		
Bernard	Maria	CAN	6.4.93	165/53	3kSt	9:44.81		9:53.71- 15
Berry #	Gwen	USA	29.6.89	176/80	HT	73.09, 76.31dq		73.81- 13
Bettiche	Amina	ALG	14.12.87	165/55	3kSt	9:46.49		9:29.20- 14
Bian Ka		CHN	5.1.93	182/115	SP	18.36		18.71- 15
Bibik	Olha	UKR	5.2.90	178/64	400	51.69		52.66- 15

546 WOMEN'S INDEX

Name		Nat	Born	Ht/Wt	Event	2016 Mark	Pre-2016 Best
Bielawska	Martyna	POL	15.11.90	175/58	TJ	13.70i	13.97- 11
Billaud	Cindy	FRA	11.3.86	165/59	100h	12.83	12.56- 14
Bing	Portia	NZL	17.4.93	179/65	Hep	5987	6102- 15
Bingham	Khamica	CAN	15.6.94	163/58	100	11.37, 11.21w	11.13- 15
Bingson	Amanda	USA	20.2.90	170/89	HT	71.90	75.73- 13
Birch	Damajahnee	USA-J	29.1.97	161/55	400h	56.46	
Biryukova	Svetlana	RUS	1.4.91	180/72	LJ	6.71	6.98i- 14, 6.72, 6.85w- 12
					TJ	14.08	13.68- 11
Bishop	Melissa	CAN	5.8.88	173/57	800	1:57.02	1:57.52- 15
Bisibori	Ruth	KEN	2.1.88	170/55	3kSt	9:44.5A	9:13.16- 09
Blaase	Chelsea	USA	10.4.94	165/52	10000	32:08.39	32:28.39- 15
Black	Symone	USA	26.10.95	158/50	400h	56.03	56.76- 15
Blackburn	Paige	USA	5.3.90	180/82	DT	61.16	57.39- 13
Blair	Joanna	GBR	1.3.86		JT	57.44	54.57- 15
Blocker	Jasmine	USA	9.6.92	170/57	400	51.66	53.60- 15
Blundell	Jenny	AUS	9.5.94	164/49	1500	4:04.62	4:12.00- 14
Bobocea	Claudia	ROU	11.6.92	176/53	800	2:01.49	2:04.17- 14
					1500	4:08.64	4:12.41- 15
Bobocel	Ancuta	ROU	3.10.87	163/52	3kSt	9:40.87	9:25.70- 12
Boekelman	Melissa	NED	11.5.89	177/66	SP	18.36	18.17- 10
Bogdán	Annabella	HUN	7.4.92		JT	56.99	55.95- 15
Bolton	Aliphine	KEN	5.4.89	163/50	10000	31:54.20	32:07.20- 13
Bondarenko	Yelizaveta	RUS-Y	1.7.99		PV	4.40i, 4.30	4.20- 15
Boons	Eefje	NED	18.7.94	176/68	100h	13.07	13.09- 15
Borel	Cleopatra	TTO	10.3.79	168/93	SP	18.78	19.48i- 04, 19.42- 11
Borge	Sigrid	NOR	3.12.95	181/82	JT	59.33	55.72- 15
Borges	Fernanda Raquel	BRA	26.7.88	165/65	DT	62.74	64.01- 14
Borisevich	Darya	BLR	6.4.90		1500	4:08.95	4:11.80- 15
Borman	Brittany	USA	1.7.89	183/77	JT	61.27	64.75- 15
Borovska	Nadiya	UKR	25.2.81	163/50	20kW	1:31:32	1:30:03- 12
Borys	Paulina	POL-J	14.5.98	181/60	HJ	1.87i	1.82- 14
Boslak	Vanessa	FRA	11.6.82	170/57	PV	4.60i	4.70- 06
Bouchard	Marie	FRA	7.12.93	168/53	3kSt	9:45.69	10:07.19- 15
Bougard	Erica	USA	26.7.93	168/57	100h	13.04	12.99- 15
	HJ	1.88		1.88- 15	Hep	6170	6288- 15
Boumkwo	Jolien	BEL	27.8.93	171/77	SP	17.09	16.47- 15
					HT	67.30	66.92- 14
Bowie	Tori	USA	27.8.90	175/61	100	10.78, 10.74w	10.80- 14, 10.72w- 15
					200	21.99	22.18- 14
Boyd	Alana	AUS	10.5.84	171/61	PV	4.81	4.76- 12
Boyer	Zibby	USA	23.9.92	170/58	HJ	1.90i, 1.90	1.88- 15
Bradshaw	Holly	GBR	2.11.91	175/68	PV	4.76i, 4.70	4.87i- 12, 4.71- 12
Brewer	Ciarra	USA	12.3.93	158/52	TJ	13.99	14.01i- 15, 13.91- 14
Brisco	Mikiah	USA	14.7.96	165/54	100	11.24, 11.13w	11.31, 11.24w- 15
					100h	13.10, 13.02w	
Brissett	Chanel	USA-Y	10.8.99	164/54	100h	12.95	
Brits	Maryke	RSA	25.2.94	169/57	LJ	6.56A, 6.54	6.20- 15
Britton	Evonne	USA	10.10.91	173/59	100h	12.78	13.03, 12.92w- 15
Brockington	Tyler	USA	6.2.94	171/57	400h	56.45	56.65- 14
Brodatskaya	Sofiya	RUS	4.10.95		20kW	1:32:02	1:32:02- 15
Broersen	Nadine	NED	29.4.90	171/62	Hep	6377	6539- 14
Bromfield	Junelle	JAM-J	8.2.98	176/59	400	51.74	53.09- 15
Brooks	Taliyah	USA	8.2.95	176/60	Hep	5991	5717- 15
Brooks	Tia	USA	2.8.90	183/109	SP	19.73	19.22i- 13, 19.00- 15
Brost	Leslie	USA	28.9.89	163/57	PV	4.50i, 4.42	4.51- 15
Brown	Aaliyah	USA	6.1.95	173/60	100	11.37, 11.26w	11.08- 15
Brown	Alicia	CAN	21.1.90	168/54	400	51.84	52.08- 13
Brown	Felicia	USA	27.10.93	168/57	100	11.25	11.44, 11.31w- 15
					200	22.19	22.76- 15
Brown	Kristen	USA	26.5.92	167/57	PV	4.70	4.28- 15
Brown	Stephanie	USA	29.7.91	163/50	1500	4:09.16	4:07.55- 15
					1M	4:29.06	4:50.12- 09
Brown	T'erea	USA	24.10.89	178/59	400h	55.30	54.21- 12
Brown	Felicia	USA	27.10.93	168/57	200	22.26	22.76- 15
Brown Trafton	Stephanie	USA	1.12.79	193/102	DT	63.09	67.74- 12
Bruce	Stephanie	USA	14.1.84	167/52	10000	32:14.42	32:24.25- 12
Bruckner	Elena	USA-J	14.4.98		DT	56.95	55.68- 15
Brume	Ese	NGR	20.1.96	167/58	LJ	6.83	6.68- 14
Bryant	Dezerea	USA	27.4.93	157/50	100	11.23w	11.00- 15, 10.96w- 14
Büchel	Selina	SUI	26.7.91	168/58	800	1:58.77	1:57.95- 15
					1500	4:08.95i	4:18.57- 15

WOMEN'S INDEX

Name		Nat	Born	Ht/Wt	Event	2016 Mark	Pre-2016 Best
Buchelgnikova	Marina	RUS	8.2.94		LJ	6.59	6.33- 11
Büchler	Nicole	SUI	17.12.83	162/56	PV	4.80i, 4.78	4.71- 15
Buckley	Landria	USA	2.7.88	160/59	400h	56.45	56.15- 13
Buckman	Zoe	AUS	21.12.88	172/55	1500	4:03.22	4:04.09- 14
Bugakova	Alyona	RUS-J	24.4.97		SP	17.94	16.98- 15
Bul Thi Thu Thuo		VIE	29.4.92	162/53	LJ	6.59	6.65- 15
Bulgakova	Anna	RUS	17.1.88	173/90	HT	72.07	76.17- 13
Bulo	Shuru	ETH-J	27.6.98	161/48	3000	8:51.04	9:01.12- 15
Bulo	Shuru	ETH-J	27.6.98	161/48	5000	15:13.07	
Bunch	Dani	USA	16.5.91	178/95	SP	18.87i, 18.18	18.89- 15
Bundy-Davies	Seren	GBR	30.12.94	171/59	400	51.26	51.48- 15
Burchell	Remona	JAM	15.9.91	166/52	100	11.24, 11.16w	11.03, 10.95w- 14
Burghardt	Alexandra	GER	28.4.94	181/67	100	11.34, 11.18w	11.32- 15
Burka	Gelete	ETH	23.1.86	165/45	3000	8:28.49	8:25.92- 06
			5000 14:52.4+14:31.20- 07		10000	30:26.66 30:49.68- 15	HMar 69:32 71:10- 13
Burks	Quanesha	USA	15.3.95	160/55	LJ	6.80i, 6.77	6.93A, 6.84, 6.91w- 14
Burmistrova	Yekaterina	RUS	18.8.90		SP	17.02	16.51- 14
Burton	Rushelle	JAM-J	4.12.97	175/61	100h	12.87	
Bush	Nicole	USA	4.4.86	159/50	3kSt	9:39.84	9:24.59- 14
Busienei	Selah	KEN	27.12.91	177/57	1500	4:06.28A	4:07.58- 15
					3000	8:42.01	8:54.15- 15
Butterworth	Alycia	CAN	1.10.92		3kSt	9:41.26	10:08.64- 14
Butts	Ty	USA	10.6.90	179/60	HJ	1.89	1.91- 14
Buziak	Paulina	POL	16.12.86	168/52	20kW	1:30:36	1:29:41- 14
Caballero	Denia	CUB	13.1.90	175/73	DT	67.62	70.65- 15
Cabecinha	Ana	POR	29.4.84	168/52	20kW	1:28:40	1:27:46- 08
Cachová	Katerina	CZE	26.2.90	173/63	100h	13.05	13.31- 15
					Hep	6328	6123- 11
Caldwell	Kayla	USA	19.6.91	163/57	PV	4.46i, 4.35	4.50i- 15, 4.40A- 13
Calvert	Schillonie	JAM	27.7.88	166/57	100	11.19	11.05- 11
Calvin	Clémence	FRA	17.5.90	166/55	10000	32:06.23	31:52.86- 14
Camacho-Quinn	Jasmine	USA/PUR	21.8.96	180/73	200	22.87, 22.70w	24.22- 14
					100h	12.69, 12.54w	13.37- 14
Camarena-Williams	Jill	USA	2.3.82	180/91	SP	18.99	20.18- 11
Cameron	Lloydricia	USA	8.4.96		SP	17.06	15.74i, 15.72- 15
Campbell	Amber	USA	5.6.81	170/91	HT	74.03	73.61- 14
Campbell	Simoya	JAM	1.3.94	167/54	800	2:01.12	1:59.26- 15
Campbell-Brown	Veronica	JAM	15.5.82	163/61	100	10.83	10.76- 11
					200	22.29	21.74- 08
Can	Yasemin	TUR	11.12.96	166/49	3000	8:48.8+	
			5000 14:37.61		15:39.90- 15	10000	30:26.41	32:42.31- 15
Cansian	Lidiane	BRA	8.1.92		DT	57.12	56.77- 14
Caravelli	Marzia	ITA	23.10.81	177/63	400h	55.69	56.63- 15
Card	Kelsey	USA	20.8.92	178/115	SP	18.56	17.96- 15
					DT	63.52	60.16- 15
Carmichael	Carolina	USA	28.4.94	165/52	PV	4.44	4.50- 15
Carrillo	Yeseida	COL	22.10.93	168/52	20kW	1:32:45	1:36:57- 14
Carson	Hannah	USA	26.1.93	160/66	DT	61.97	54.98- 15
					JT	61.20	59.57- 15
Carter	Destiny	USA	.93	168/52	100	11.35, 11.11w	11.70- 14, 11.28w- 15
					200	22.97, 22.41w	23.74, 23.24w- 14
Carter	Kori	USA	3.6.92	165/57	400h	54.47	53.21- 13
Carter	Michelle	USA	12.10.85	175/110	SP	20.63	20.24- 13
de Carvalho	Tatiele	BRA	22.11.89	156/50	10000	32:09.14	33:19.43- 15
Casetta	Belén	ARG	26.9.94	163/50	3kSt	9:42.93	9:57.1- 15
Castells	Berta	ESP	24.1.84	174/73	HT	70.52	69.59- 12
Castlin	Kristi	USA	7.7.88	170/75	100h	12.50	12.56, 12.48w- 12
Castro	Ángela	BOL	21.2.93	160/54	20kW	1:30:33	1:35:58- 13
Caswell	Cassie	USA	3.7.94		SP	16.96i, 16.64	14.86i, 14.82- 15
Cavaleti	Giovana	BRA	13.1.89	181/70	Hep	5808	5760- 15
Cavin	Aisha	USA	3.12.92	168/55	200	23.01, 22.84w	22.86- 15
Cérival	Jessica	FRA	20.1.82	185/120	SP	17.47	17.99i- 11, 17.87- 09
Cernjul	Marusa	SLO	30.6.92	177/56	HJ	1.93	1.86- 15
Cestonaro	Ottavia	ITA	12.1.95	176/68	LJ	6.57w	6.30- 15
Chaboudez	Aurélie	FRA	9.5.93	173/60	400h	56.53	55.51- 15
Chambers	Kendra	USA	11.9.90	161/48	800	2:00.76	2:01.93- 15
Chand	Dutee	IND	3.2.96	160/50	100	11.33, 11.24dt	11.62- 13
Chapman	Quintunya	USA	7.1.93	173/66	Hep	6089	6147- 15
Charley	Simone	USA	4.2.95		TJ	13.77	13.32- 15
Chase	Chanice	CAN	6.8.93	173/61	100h	12.94, 12.90w	12.95- 15
					400h	54.94	56.27- 14

548 WOMEN'S INDEX

Name		Nat	Born	Ht/Wt	Event	2016 Mark		Pre-2016 Best
Chebet	Risper	KEN	6.6.92		HMar	69:24		70:43- 15
					Mar	2:27:23		
Chebet	Sandra Felis	KEN-J	20.1.98	160/45	1500	4:08.36A		4:17.5A- 15
Chebet	Winny	KEN	20.12.90	165/50	800	1:59.88		1:59.30- 13
					1500	4:02.66		4:16.0A- 12
Cheever	Jamie	USA	28.2.87	175/55	3kSt	9:37.12		9:29.13- 13
Chekwel	Juliet	UGA	25.5.90	165/52	5000	15:20.15		15:43.47- 14
					10000	31:37.99		32:20.95- 15
Chelimo	Edith	KEN	16.7.86		HMar	69:45A		71:22- 11
Chelimo	Rose	BRN	12.7.89	162/45	HMar	68:08		68:22- 15
					Mar	2:24:14		-0-
Chemtai	Esther	KEN	4.6.88		Mar	2:28:37		2:30:32- 15
Chemutai	Peruth	UGA-Y	10.7.99	165/50	3kSt	9:31.03		10:19.93- 15
Chen Mudan		CHN	4.10.93		TJ	13.91i, 13.76		13.77i, 13.72- 12
Chen Ting		CHN-J	28.8.97		TJ	13.85		
Chen Yang		CHN	10.7.91	180/97	DT	63.61		61.16- 15
Chen Yanzhen		CHN			TJ	13.74		
Chepchirchir	Sarah	KEN	27.7.84	165/49	HMar	67:52		68:07- 11
					Mar	2:24:13		-0-
Chepkirui	Joyce	KEN	20.8.88	152/48	HMar	67:41		66:19- 14
Chepkirui	Sheila	KEN	27.12.90	162/48	5000	15:05.45		
Chepkoech	Beatrice	KEN	6.7.91	171/57	3kSt	9:10.86		10:41.3A- 11
Chepkurui	Caroline	KEN	12.3.90	169/52	3kSt	9:28.81		9:34.15- 15
Chepkurui	Lydia	KEN	23.8.84	171/52	3kSt	9:22.81		9:12.55- 13
Chepkwemoi	Nancy	KEN	8.10.93	162/48	1500	4:05.22		4:03.09- 15
1M	4:30.67		4:28.66- 15		3000	8:49.06i		8:56.52- 12
Chepngeno	Jackline	KEN	16.1.93	164/48	10000	31:27.00		32:08.12A- 15
Chepngetich	Rosefline	KEN-J	17.6.97	166/55	3kSt	9:35.22		9:25.91- 15
Cheptai	Irene	KEN	4.2.92	160/45	5000	14:43.42		14:50.99- 13
					10000	31:15.38		
Cherono	Elizeba	NED	6.6.88		10000	32:15.53		
Cherono	Gladys	KEN	12.5.83	166/50	HMar	66:07		66:38- 15
Chorono	Mercy	KEN	7.5.91	168/54	2000	c.5:40.0+		5:35.68- 10
3000	8:26.36		8:21.14- 14		5000	14:33.95		14:34.10- 15
Cherono	Priscah	KEN	27.6.80	160/47	Mar	2:27:41		2:31:34- 15
Cherotich	Fancy	KEN	10.8.90		3kSt	9:45.31		9:28.04- 13
Cheruiyot	Lucy	KEN-J	4.1.97		HMar	68:17		72:41A- 15
Cheruiyot	Vivian	KEN	11.9.83	155/38	3000	8:31.86		8:28.66- 07
5000	14:26.17	14:20.87- 11		10000	29:32.53	30:30.44- 12	HMar	67:54dh	-0-
Chesang	Agnes	KEN	1.4.86	171/53	3kSt	9:27.22		9:34.33- 13
Chesang	Stella	UGA	1.12.96	161/47	5000	15:10.30		15:25.01- 15
Chesebe	Sylvia	KEN	17.5.87	167/52	800	2:00.96A		2:00.76A- 13
Chesire	Gladys	KEN	20.2.93	162/47	10000	32:17.35A		31:36.87- 15
					HMar	66:57		68:36- 15
Chespol	Celphine	KEN-Y	23.3.99	163/48	3kSt	9:24.73		10:18.3- 15
Chesser	Rena	USA	17.5.83	163/52	3kSt	9:40.49		9:59.99- 12
Cheyech	Filomena	KEN	5.7.82	168/49	HMar	70:05		67:39- 13
					Mar	2:23:18		2:22:44- 14
Chicherova	Anna	RUS	22.7.82	180/57	HJ	1.98		2.07- 11
Chigbolu	Maria Benedicta	ITA	27.7.89	172/53	400	52.01		51.67- 15
Chumachenko	Yuliya	UKR	2.10.94	185/65	HJ	1.93i, 1.89		1.92- 15
Chumba	Eunice	BRN	23.5.93	160/46	HMar	68:04		70:46- 14
					Mar	2:25:00		2:33:12- 15
Cichocka	Angelika	POL	15.3.88	169/54	800	1:58.97		1:59.55- 15
1000	2:34.84	2:36.50- 15		1500	4:03.25	4:03.06- 15	1M	4:25.39	4:49.59- 09
Clark	Megan	USA	10.6.94	167/57	PV	4.63		4.50- 15
Claude-Boxberger	Ophélie	FRA	18.10.88	169/54	3kSt	9:34.96		9:35.56- 15
Claxton	Grace	PUR	19.8.93	167/52	400h	55.85		58.51- 15
Clay	Raven	USA	5.10.90	168/59	100h	12.93		13.05A- 12, 13.10, 12.94w- 15
Clayton	Rushell	JAM	18.10.92	175/61	400h	56.42		56.29- 15
Cliff	Rachel	CAN	1.4.88	163/47	5000	15:23.94mx, 15:28.60		15:33.15- 15
					10000	32:21.98		32:54.70- 15
Clute	Sydney	USA	15.11.93		PV	4.42		4.20- 15
Coburn	Emma	USA	19.10.90	173/55	1500	4:06.92		4:05.10- 15
					3kSt	9:07.63		9:11.42- 14
Cockrell	Anna	USA-J	28.8.97	178/64	400h	55.20		56.67- 15
Collatz	Alex	USA	25.5.93	173/77	DT	57.52		57.82- 15
Colombi	Nicole	ITA	29.12.95		20kW	1:33:39		1:38:50- 15
Comba	Rocío	ARG	14.7.87	175/78	DT	57.79		62.77- 13
Coneo	Muriel	COL	15.3.87	160/49	1500	4:06.99		4:08.31- 15
					3kSt	9:43.16		9:53.1- 15

WOMEN'S INDEX 549

Name		Nat	Born	Ht/Wt	Event	2016 Mark	Pre-2016 Best
Conley	Alyssa	RSA	27.4.91	172/60	100	11.23	11.60- 13
					200	22.84	23.46- 13
Conley	Kim	USA	14.3.86	160/49	1M	4:27.88i	4:24.54i- 14, 4:27.23- 12
					5000	15:10.62, 15:09.31i	15:08.61- 14
Contion	Maeva	FRA	31.5.92	167/55	400h	56.05	56.03- 15
Cooks	Alexis	USA	11.9.93		SP	17.29i	16.79- 15
Cornejo	Wendy	BOL	7.1.93	162/53	20kW	1:33:15	1:34:12- 15
Correa	Carmelita	MEX	5.12.88	170/56	PV	4.41Ai, 4.35A	4.20A- 15
Costa	Keila	BRA	6.2.83	170/62	LJ	6.56	6.88- 07
					TJ	14.02	14.58- 13
Costa	Susana	POR	22.9.84	178/65	TJ	14.34	14.32- 15
Costello	Liz	USA	23.2.88	160/45	10000	31:43.79	32:01.79- 15
Cotten	Jen	CAN	14.10.87	173/60	400h	56.84	56.86- 14
Courtney	Melissa	GBR	30.8.93	170/54	1500	4:07.55	4:09.74- 15
Coutinho	Geisa	BRA	1.6.80	161/55	400	51.54	51.08- 11
Coward	Jackie	USA	5.11.89	167/55	100h	12.68	12.73- 14, 12.67w- 13
Cox	Carmiesha	BAH	16.5.95	168/55	200	23.16, 22.75w	23.33- 15
Cox	Melia	USA	23.11.92	268/55	100h	13.12, 13.01w	13.24, 13.17w- 15
Craft	Shanice	GER	15.5.93	185/89	SP	17.41	17.75- 14
					DT	64.62	65.88- 14
Cragg	Amy	USA	21.1.84	163/46	Mar	2:28:20	2:27:03- 11
Crawford	Ginnie	USA	7.9.83	178/63	100h	12.81	12.45- 07
Crew	Brittany	CAN	3.6.94	178/111	SP	18.06	17.27- 15
Cunliffe	Hannah	USA	9.1.96	169/57	100	10.99	11.58- 13
					200	22.49	23.44, 23.10Aw- 13
Cunningham	Vashti	USA-J	18.1.98	185/66	HJ	1.99i, 1.97	1.96- 15
Czaková	Mária	SVK	2.10.88	165/60	20kW	1:33:04	1:32:23- 15
Czuth	Réka	HUN	27.6.94	174/59	HJ	1.87i	1.80i- 12, 1.80- 13
D'Agostino	Abbey	USA	25.5.92	159/48	3000	8:51.88	8:51.91i- 14, 8:58.39- 15
					5000	15:14.04	15:03.85- 15
Dacheva	Petia	BUL	10.3.85	168/52	TJ	13.83i	14.45- 10
Dadic	Ivona	AUT	29.12.93	183/60	Hep	6408	6151- 15
Dahlgren	Jenny	ARG	27.8.84	180/110	HT	69.21	73.74- 10
Dahlström	Malin	SWE	26.8.89	171/60	PV	4.40	4.55- 15
Daniels	Katelyn	USA	11.4.95		DT	60.54	59.06- 15
Daniels	Teahna	USA-J	27.3.97	165/55	100	11.21	11.24, 11.15w- 15
Danois	Maeva	FRA	10.3.93	165/53	3kSt	9:40.19	9:40.89- 15
Daska	Mamitu	ETH	16.10.83	164/45	HMar	70:18+	66:28- 15
					Mar	2:25:27	2:21:59- 11
Daunay	Christelle	FRA	5.12.74	163/43	HMar	69:58	68:34- 10
Dauwens	Axelle	BEL	1.12.90	171/62	400h	55.68	55.56- 14
David	Yanis	FRA-J	12.12.97	169/62	TJ	13.50i, 13.44, 13.64w	13.65- 15
Davis	Jessica	USA	31.10.92	178/61	100	11.32, 11.26w	11.19- 11
Davis	Tiana	USA	12.8.89	168/57	100h	12.96	13.09, 12.96w- 15
Davis-White	Kali	JAM	24.10.94	170/64	100	11.26, 11.18w	11.45- 12
					200	22.86, 22.66w	23.05- 13
Day	Christine	JAM	23.8.86	168/51	400	50.29	50.14- 15
Day-Monroe	Sharon	USA	9.6.85	175/70	Hep	6385	6550- 13
De Coninck	Nenah	BEL	2.9.96	171/57	400h	56.27	57.19- 15
de Jesus	Claudine	BRA	9.9.94		TJ	13.71	13.70- 15
Defar	Meseret	ETH	19.11.83	155/42	3000	8:30.83i	8:23.72i- 07, 8:24.66- 06
					5000	15:06.96	14:12.88- 08
Degefa	Biruktayit	ETH	29.9.90	157/40	Mar	2:26:07	2:23:51- 15
Degefa	Worknesh	ETH	28.10.90		HMar	66:14	67:14- 15
Degefu	Beyenu	ETH-Y	12.7.99	162/45	3000	8:41.76	
Dekebo	Muliye	ETH-J	13.3.98		HMar	69:52	74:40- 15
Del Buono	Federica	ITA	12.12.94	164/48	1500	4:08.94	4:05.32- 14
					1M	4:28.13	
Delasa	Sechale	ETH	20.9.91		Mar	2:28:43	2:26:27- 12
DeLoach	Janay	USA	12.10.85	165/59	100h	12.88	12.84- 15
					LJ	6.93	7.03, 7.15w- 12
Demas	Danielle	USA	28.8.93	165/55	100h	12.97	13.03- 15
Demidenko	Natalya	RUS	7.8.93	175/62	PV	4.40i	4.50i- 15, 4.40- 11
Demireva	Mirela	BUL	28.9.89	180/58	HJ	1.97	1.95- 12
Demise	Shure	ETH	21.1.96	168/54	10000	32:14.25	32:54.1A- 15
					Mar	2:25:04	2:20:59- 15
Demsew	Dihihinet	ETH	15.9.84		HMar	70:13	72:02- 10
Deng Linuo		CHN	16.3.92	165/44	TJ	13.64	13.92- 13
Dereje	Roza	ETH			Mar	2:26:18	
Dereli	Emel	TUR	25.2.96	181/110	SP	18.57	18.40- 15
Derkach	Dariya	ITA	27.3.93	167/56	TJ	14.15	13.92- 13

WOMEN'S INDEX

Name		Nat	Born	Ht/Wt	Event	2016 Mark	Pre-2016 Best
Derun	Kateryna	UKR	24.9.93	168/71	JT	62.82	61.90- 15
Desalegn	Betlhem	UAE	13.11.91	164/42	1500	4:03.70	4:05.13- 13
					3000	8:44.59i	8:46.54i- 14, 8:53.75- 15
Detsuk	Kseniya	BLR	23.4.86	177/56	TJ	13.90i, 13.82	14.76, 14.81w- 12
Devi	Suman	IND	15.7.85	164/65	JT	59.45	57.15- 15
Di Vincenzo	Sibilla	ITA	22.1.83	173/50	20kW	1:33:30	1:32:10- 10
Diago	Sahily	CUB	26.8.95	168/49	800	1:58.84A	1:57.74- 14
Diallo	Rouguy	FRA	5.2.95	168/52	TJ	14.16i, 13.94	14.20, 14.44w- 14
Diamond	Emily	GBR	11.6.91	173/57	400	51.23	51.95- 14
Dibaba	Birhane	ETH	11.9.93	159/44	HMar	67:47	69:34dh- 14
					Mar	2:23:16	2:22:30- 14
Dibaba	Genzebe	ETH	8.2.91	168/52	1500	3:57.31+, 3:56.46+i	3:50.07- 15
1M	4:14.30, 4:13.31i		4:22.2e- 14		2000	c.5:39i+	5:27.40- 14
					3000	8:31.84, 8:22.50i	8:16.60i, 8:26.21- 14
Dibaba	Mare	ETH	20.10.89	152/40	HMar	67:55	67:13- 10
					Mar	2:24:09	2:19:52- 12
Dibaba	Tirunesh	ETH	1.10.85	155/44	5000	14:41.73	14:11.15- 08
10000	29:42.56		29:54.66- 08		HMar	68:04dh	66:56- 13
Dicks	Natasha	USA	6.7.95		TJ	13.60	12.68- 14
Dida	Dera	ETH	26.10.96	155/42	3000	8:48.31	8:57.00- 15
					5000	14:42.84	15:28.81- 15
Diriba	Buze	ETH	9.2.94	160/43	10000	31:38.61	31:33.27- 15
Diro	Etenesh	ETH	10.5.91	169/47	3000	8:38.32	9:00.39- 11
5000	14:33.30		15:19.77- 12		3kSt	9:16.87	9:14.07- 12
Domjan	Veronika	SLO	3.9.96	178/94	DT	60.11	56.63- 15
Dong Yangzi		CHN	22.10.92		SP	16.96i, 16.80	17.03i- 15, 16.56- 14
Dongmo	Auriole	CMR	3.8.90	173/95	SP	17.92	17.64- 15
Donohue	Erin	USA	8.5.83	173/66	1M	4:29.07i	4:26.48- 08
Doyle	Eilidh	GBR	20.2.87	172/59	400h	54.09	54.22- 13
Drahotová	Anezka	CZE	22.7.95	183/63	20kW	1:30:21	1:26:53- 15
Drisbióti	Antigóni	GRE	21.3.84	162/52	20kW	1:30:56	1:33:42- 13
Du Xiaowei		CHN	11.8.87	180/72	JT	58.78	61.89- 12
Dubitskaya	Alyona	BLR	25.1.90	182/77	SP	18.78	19.03- 14
Ducó	Natalia	CHI	31.1.89	177/95	SP	18.19	18.80- 12
Duncan	Alexis	USA-J	16.8.98	159/55	100h	12.93	13.33- 14, 13.25w- 15
Duncan	Kimberlyn	USA	2.8.91	173/59	100	11.11	10.96, 10.94w- 12
Duncan	Melissa	AUS	30.1.90	170/55	1500	4:06.93i, 4:09.70	4:05.56- 15
Duran	Alina	USA	28.3.90		HT	66.79	64.64- 15
Dusanova	Nadezhda	UZB	17.11.87	174/56	HJ	1.94	1.96i- 09, 1.95- 12
Dutkiewicz	Pamela	GER	28.9.91	168/58	100h	12.85	12.95- 14
Dygacz	Agnieszka	POL	18.7.85	160/51	20kW	1:30:27	1:28:58- 14
Eades	Chelsea	USA	21.8.89	168/61	100h	13.09, 13.02w	12.78- 12
					Hep	5952	5999- 13
Ealey	Chase	USA	20.7.94	178/84	SP	18.46	17.39- 15
Ebihara	Yuki	JPN	28.10.85	164/68	JT	62.13	63.80- 15
Eccleston	Amanda	USA	18.6.90	160/50	1500	4:03.25	4:08.08- 14
					1M	4:25.64	4:29.06- 15
Eckhardt	Neele	GER	2.7.92	166/49	TJ	13.93	13.67, 13.98w- 14
Edao	Bontu	BRN-J	12.12.97		5000	15:25.12	
Edesa	Worknesh	ETH	11.9.92		Mar	2:24:04	
Efraimson	Alexa	USA-J	20.2.97	170/57	800	2:00.99	2:01.11- 15
1500	4:06.38		4:03.39- 15		1M	4:27.39	4:42.41- 12
Eid Naser	Salwa	BRN-J	23.5.98	168/54	400	50.88	51.39- 15
Ekarare	Helen	KEN-Y	3.3.99	167/46	5000	15:12.89	
Eke	Nadia	GHA	11.1.93		TJ	13.82	13.40, 13.46w- 15
Ektova	Irina	KAZ	8.1.87	172/63	TJ	13.91	14.32- 15
Ektova	Yekaterina	KAZ	30.8.92	169/59	TJ	14.16	13.84- 13
Elbe	Jenny	GER	18.4.90	180/60	TJ	14.28	14.20- 14, 14.38w- 15
Ellenwood	Georgia	CAN	5.8.95	170/63	Hep	5935	5786- 15
Ellis	Kendall	USA	8.3.96	173/59	400	51.82	52.32- 15
Ellis-Watson	Taylor	USA	6.5.93	183/64	200	22.48	22.93- 15
					400	50.25	51.18- 15
Elvemo	Yngvild	NOR	28.5.90	167/52	800	2:01.77	2:02.87- 15
Embaye	Axumawit	ETH	18.10.94	160/50	1500	4:03.05	4:02.35- 14
					1M	4:27.75i, 4:29.59	4:23.50i, 4:26.84-15
Emerson	Niamh	GBR-Y	22.4.99		HJ	1.89	1.82- 15
Emilianov	Alexandra	MDA-Y	19.9.99		DT	58.09	52.78- 15
Emmanuel	Crystal	CAN	27.11.91	170/59	100	11.26, 11.18w	11.27- 15, 11.16w- 13
					200	22.80	22.89- 13, 22.83w- 15
England	Hannah	GBR	6.3.87	177/54	800	2:01.34	1:59.66- 12
					1500	4:07.78	4:01.89- 11

WOMEN'S INDEX

Name		Nat	Born	Ht/Wt	Event	2016 Mark		Pre-2016 Best
Ennaoui	Sofia	POL	30.8.95	158/40	800	2:00.34		2:00.11- 15
1000	2:35.15		2:41.06mx- 13		1500	4:01.00		4:04.26- 15
1M	4:25.34		4:27.32- 15		3000	8:49.07i		8:53.22i- 15, 8:59.44- 14
Ennis-Hill	Jessica	GBR	28.1.86	164/57	100h	12.76		12.54- 12
HJ	1.89	1.95- 07	LJ	6.63	6.51- 10, 6.54w- 07	Hep	6775	6955- 12
Epps	Christina	USA	20.6.91	175/63	TJ	14.17		14.09- 15
Eriksson	Sandra	FIN	4.6.89	163/48	3kSt	9:31.88		9:24.70- 14
Eshete	Shitaye	BRN	21.5.90	164/51	Mar	2:25:36		-0-
Espinoza	Ahymará	VEN	28.5.85	180/99	SP	18.19		18.15- 13
Esquivel	Ximena	MEX-J	22.8.97		HJ	1.90A		1.86A- 15
Esser	Agnes	CAN	22.8.95	183/86	DT	57.91		54.38- 15
Eutsey	Ebony	USA	3.5.92	166/55	400	51.39		52.07- 12
Evans	Gayon	JAM	15.1.90	158/50	100	11.24		11.37- 11
Ewen	Maggie	USA	23.9.94	178/79	SP	16.85i, 16.82		16.57i- 14, 16.33- 15
DT	59.28		57.44- 15	HT	70.50	60.54- 15		
Eykens	Renée	BEL	8.6.96	170/54	800	2:00.00		2:02.55- 15
Facey	Simone	JAM	7.5.85	162/53	100	11.00 11.09-14,11.0-04,	10.95A- 08,	11.04w-15
Facey	Simone	JAM	7.5.85	162/53	200	22.50		22.25- 08
Famurewa	Becky	USA	24.2.94	180/86	DT	57.71		57.13- 15
Fantu	Taye	ETH-Y	29.3.99		1500	4:05.84		
Farmer	Erin	USA	11.8.95	183/105	SP	17.80		15.57- 15
Farquharson	Gabrielle	USA	12.12.92	170/57	200	23.07, 22.91w		23.62- 14
					LJ	6.54		6.36i- 15, 6.18, 6.23w- 14
Farrington	Melissa-Maree	AUS	28.5.95		Hep	5735		5300- 12
Fatherly	Rachel	USA	20.4.94	180/86	SP	17.27i, 16.96		17.15- 15
Fazlitdinova	Gulshat	RUS	28.8.92	165/48	5000	15:25.37		15:18.88- 15
Fédronic	Justine	FRA	11.5.91	168/54	800	1:59.86		2:00.41- 14
Feitor	Susana	POR	28.1.75	160/52	20kW	1:33:34		1:27:55- 01
Felix	Allyson	USA	18.11.85	168/57	200	22.02		21.69- 12
					400	49.51		49.26- 15
Félix	Alysbeth	PUR	7.3.93	171/59	Hep	6124A, 6003		5810- 15
Félix	Dulce	POR	23.10.82	165/53	10000	31:19.03		31:30.90- 09
Feng Bin		CHN	3.4.94	184/95	DT	65.14		62.07- 15
Fente	Birtukan	ETH	18.6.89	166/50	3kSt	9:42.64		9:24.91- 15
Fernández	Nuria	ESP	16.8.76	170/57	5000	15:24.17		15:31.02- 14
Ferrando	Cristina	ESP	12.1.92	175/59	HJ	1.87i, 1.87		1.88- 15
Fertig	Fruzsina	HUN	2.9.93	175/80	HT	68.18		68.62- 15
Fetiskina	Tetyana	UKR	11.9.94	172/63	JT	58.53		57.30- 13
Fiack	Marion	FRA	13.10.92	170/60	PV	4.38i, 4.20		4.71i- 15, 4.55- 14
Finn	Erin	USA	19.11.94	160/52	5000	15:23.16i		15:26.08- 14
					10000	31:51.84		32:41.65- 14
Finn	Michele	IRL	16.12.89	160/52	3kSt	9:43.19		9:43.34- 15
Fiodorow	Joanna	POL	4.3.89	169/89	HT	72.98		74.39- 14
Fischer	Julia	GER	1.4.90	192/95	DT	68.49		66.46- 14
Flanagan	Shalane	USA	8.7.81	165/50	Mar	2:25:26		2:21:14- 14
Flax	Jessica	USA	4.9.90		Hep	6068		5826- 12
Flink	Sofi	SWE	8.7.95	168/71	JT	59.16		61.96- 13
Folorunso	Ayomide	ITA	17.10.96	170/55	400h	55.50		57.19- 15
Fontanive	Petra	SUI	10.10.88	170/60	400h	56.48		56.09- 15
Forbes	Sashalee	JAM	10.5.96	160/55	100	11.17		11.55- 14
Ford	Yirisleyidi L.	CUB	18.8.91	168/69	HT	71.10		72.40- 15
Fougberg	Charlotta	SWE	19.6.85	165/51	3kSt	9:30.11		9:23.96- 14
Francis	Claudia	USA	14.11.93	165/55	400	51.55		52.51- 15
					400h	55.55		
Francis	Phyllis	USA	4.5.92	178/61	200	22.50		22.70- 15
					400	49.94		50.50- 15
Franek	Bridget	USA	8.11.87	160/50	3kSt	9:33.51		9:29.53- 12
Franklin	Alexis	USA	9.10.93	161/52	400h	55.28		56.55- 14
Franklin	Autumne	USA	20.7.94	162/54	400h	54.65		56.65- 14
Franklin	Tori	USA	7.10.92		TJ	13.66i		13.56i, 13.49- 14
Fraser-Pryce	Shelly-Ann	JAM	27.12.86	160/52	100	10.86		10.70- 12
Frederick	Priscilla	ANT	14.2.89	178/68	HJ	1.90i, 1.89		1.91- 15
Freeman	Der'Renae	USA	15.4.94		LJ	6.54, 6.70w		6.40, 6.59w- 15
Freeman	Octavious	USA	20.4.92	169/57	100	11.14, 11.05w		10.87- 13
Frerichs	Courtney	USA	18.1.93	171/53	3kSt	9:20.92		9:31.36- 15
Fricker	McKayla	USA	19.4.92	167/52	800	2:01.29		2:00.81- 15
Friedrich	Ariane	GER	10.1.84	178/59	HJ	1.88i		2.06- 09
Frizell	Sultana	CAN	24.10.84	183/110	HT	69.14		75.73- 14
Fuchise	Masumi	JPN	2.9.86	161/51	20kW	1:31:45		1:28:03- 09
Fukushi	Kayoko	JPN	25.3.82	160/47	HMar	70:28+		67:26- 06
					Mar	2:22:17		2:24:21- 13

WOMEN'S INDEX

Name		Nat	Born	Ht/Wt	Event	2016 Mark	Pre-2016 Best
Fukushima	Chisato	JPN	27.6.88	166/50	200	22.88	22.89- 10
Funderburk	Kala	USA	14.9.92	174/59	400	52.00	51.09- 15
Furlani	Erika	ITA	2.1.96	174/51	HJ	1.91	1.87- 14
Furmanek	Katarzyna	POL	19.2.96	174/76	HT	67.11	64.83- 15
Fyodorova	Alina	UKR	31.7.89	175/70	Hep	5805	6278- 15
Gaines	Jessie	USA	12.8.90	164/52	LJ	6.52	6.55- 14
Gaither	Tynia	BAH	16.3.93	158/50	100	11.19, 11.08w	11.27- 15, 11.23w- 14
					200	22.54	22.88, 22.80w- 14
Galais	Jennifer	FRA	7.3.92	169/59	100	11.25	11.40- 14
Galiart	Rianna	NED	22.11.85	168/56	PV	4.40i, 4.35	4.40- 15
Gáliková	Mária	SVK	21.8.80	161/55	20kW	1:30:52	1:31:42- 15
Gallagher	Kerri	USA	31.5.89	169/52	1500	4:08.53+i	4:03.56- 15
1M	4:26.18i		4:30.24- 15		3000	8:56.52i	9:07.39i- 14, 9:32.61- 15
Gallardo	Karen	CHI	6.3.84	175/95	DT	59.80	61.10- 15
Galvis	Sandra	COL	28.6.86	165/60	20kW	1:31:52	1:31:15- 15
Gambetta	Sara	GER	18.2.93	183/70	SP	17.95	17.26- 15
Ganeyeva	Vera	RUS	6.11.88	172/87	DT	61.86	64.30- 13
Gao Yang		CHN	1.3.93	178/110	SP	19.20	19.04- 15
Garcia	Asa	USA-J	15.5.97		TJ	13.38	12.94- 15
Garcia	Mariah	USA	26.12.93		DT	58.72	55.39- 13
Garcia	Stephanie	USA	3.5.88	168/52	1500	4:06.80	4:05.39- 15
1M	4:28.47i		4:28.84- 15		3000	8:53.20i	8:58.09- 14
5000	15:16.56		15:19.50- 15		3kSt	9:19.48	9:23.48- 15
García	Claudia	ESP	30.9.92	169/54	HJ	1.88i, 1.87	1.90i, 1.89- 15
García	Kimberley	PER	19.10.93	167/44	20kW	1:29:38	1:29:44- 14
García-Caro	Laura	ESP	16.4.95	165/56	20kW	1:33:24	1:29:32- 15
Gardner	English	USA	22.4.92	162/50	100	10.74	10.79, 10.76w- 15
Gardzielewska	Urszula	POL	21.7.88	178/55	HJ	1.93i, 1.86	1.92i, 1.89- 15
Gashaw	Tigist	BRN	25.12.96	172/54	1500	4:06.53	4:05.58- 15
					3000	8:48.60	
Gause	Diamond	USA	4.4.94	160/55	200	23.28, 22.93w	23.51- 14, 23.21w- 15
Gebre	Trihas	ESP	29.4.90	163/46	10000	32:09.67	32:03.39- 13
Gebrekidan	Hiwot	ETH	11.5.95		HMar	68:00	
Gebreselassie	Goytatom	ETH	15.1.95	152/42	3000	8:50.8+	8:45.05i- 15, 8:57.23- 14
5000	15:00.21		14:57.33- 15		10000	31:14.52	31:51.42- 13
Gebreslasea	Letebrhan	ETH	29.10.90	155/40	Mar	2:26:15	2:25:24- 15
Gebru	Azmera	ETH	5.5.92	160/45	5000	15:24.27	14:58.23- 12
Gega	Luiza	ALB	5.11.88	166/56	1500	4:06.89i	4:02.63- 15
3000	8:53.78		9:09.74- 12		3kSt	9:28.52	9:54.72- 11
Geleto	Fate Tola	ETH/GER	22.10.87		HMar	69:51	69:38- 10
					Mar	2:25:42	2:25:14- 12
Genemo	Shuko	ETH	.95		Mar	2:24:31	2:27:29- 15
Geng Shuang		CHN	9.7.93		SP	18.06i, 17.87	17.16- 15
George	Patience	NGR	25.11.91	176/61	400	51.06	50.71- 15
George	Phylicia	CAN	16.11.87	178/65	100	11.26, 11.14w	11.25- 12
					100h	12.74, 12.67w	12.65- 12
Gergel	Melissa	USA	24.4.89	170/62	PV	4.41i, 4.31	4.53i, 4.50- 15
Gergelics	Cintia	HUN	16.11.91		HT	66.89	65.92- 15
German	Elvira	BLR-J	19.6.97	168/54	100h	12.85	13.20, 13.15w- 15
Getachew	Bezunesh	ETH-J	.97	164/48	5000	15:16.98	15:25.20- 15
Geubelle	Andrea	USA	21.6.91	165/57	LJ	6.57i	6.69i- 13, 6.59, 6.70w- 15
					TJ	14.15	14.18i, 13.85- 13, 14.17w- 12
Ghee	Lauryn	USA-J	30.10.98	172/57	200	22.97	24.02- 15
Ghelber-Perie	Bianca	ROU	1.6.90	170/70	HT	66.26	73.52- 10
Gholston	Alexandra	USA	1.3.95	170/55	400	52.11	52.31- 15
Ghribi	Habiba	TUN	9.4.84	170/57	3kSt	9:18.71	9:05.36- 15
Gibson	Dannielle	BAH	5.4.96		TJ	13.54, 13.63w	13.05- 15
Gidey	Letesenbet	ETH-J	20.3.98	163/48	3000	8:53.3+	9:04.64A- 15
					5000	14:45.63	15:39.83- 15
Gierisch	Kristin	GER	20.8.90	178/59	TJ	14.31	14.46i, 14.38, 14.46w- 15
Giorgi	Eleonora	ITA	14.9.89	163/52	20kW	1:28:05	1:26:17- 15
Gipson	Whitney	USA	20.9.90	168/57	LJ	6.72, 6.84w	6.97- 12
Gizaw	Melkam	ETH	17.9.90	163/48	Mar	2:24:28	2:25:42- 15
Glanc	Zaneta	POL	11.3.83	186/93	DT	58.75	65.34- 12
Gleadle	Liz	CAN	5.12.88	183/95	JT	62.59	64.83- 15
Gnafoua	Floriane	FRA	30.1.96	158/60	100	11.19	11.69, 11.55w- 14
Gobena	Amane	ETH	1.9.82	163/48	HMar	69:51	68:16- 09
					Mar	2:21:51	2:23:30- 15
Gochenour	Alex	USA	17.2.93	181/70	100h	12.98	13.15- 15
					Hep	5962	6027w, 5892- 15
Godfay	Afera	ETH	25.9.91	156/42	HMar	68:32	69:51- 15

WOMEN'S INDEX 553

Name		Nat	Born	Ht/Wt	Event	2016 Mark	Pre-2016 Best
Golba	Katarzyna	POL	21.12.89	160/52	20kW	1:32:36	1:32:32- 15
Gollshewsky	Taryn	AUS	18.5.93	184/80	DT	60.27	58.24- 14
Gómez	Abigail	MEX	30.1.91	164/69	JT	58.72	59.26A- 15
Gomis	Sandra	FRA	21.11.83	165/53	100h	12.79	12.89- 12
Gong Lijiao		CHN	24.1.89	174/110	SP	20.43	20.35- 09
Gonska	Nadine	GER	23.1.90	168/58	100	11.43, 11.21w	11.53- 14
					200	22.79	23.27, 23.09w- 14
González	Gabriela	MEX	10.4.91		20kW	1:33:41	1:40:00- 14
González	María Guadalupe	MEX	9.1.89	162/48	20kW	1:26:17	1:28:48- 14
González	Raquel	ESP	16.11.89	176/55	20kW	1:29:01	1:28:36- 14
Gordeyeva	Irina	RUS	9.10.86	185/55	HJ	1.94i, 1.94	2.04- 12
Gordon	Chris-Ann	JAM	18.9.94	164/52	400	51.02	51.39- 14
Gordon	Daeshon	JAM	8.11.96	168/60	100h	12.99w	12.97- 15
Gorodskaya	Hanna	BLR	31.1.93		HJ	1.88	1.90- 15
Gosa	Dalilah Abdelkadir	BRN-J	27.6.98	159/42	3000	8:46.42	
	1500	4:09.58		4:13.35A- 15		5000	15:10.79	
Goto	Rena	JPN	6.9.95	160/47	20kW	1:31:00	1:35:06- 15
Goule	Natoya	JAM	30.3.91	160/50	800	1:59.38	1:59.63- 15
Grace	Jade	USA	22.9.88	178/84	HT	66.44	62.48- 15
Grace	Kate	USA	24.10.88	173/55	800	1:58.28	1:59.47- 13
	1500	4:05.65		4:07.35- 14		1M	4:28.30i	4:28.79i- 13
Grange	Gleneve	JAM	6.7.95	170/75	DT	59.03	58.04- 15
Graumann	Jossie	GER	18.3.94	175/58	HJ	1.90	1.86- 15
Gray	Alia	USA	12.11.88	160/52	10000	31:59.23	32:29.06- 15
Gray	Kianna	USA	30.12.96	171/57	100	11.20, 11.12w	11.73- 15
Gray	Kianna	USA	30.12.96	171/57	200	22.79, 22.58w	24.09- 14
Green	Emma	SWE	8.12.84	180/62	HJ	1.90	2.01- 10
Grenot	Libania	ITA	12.7.83	175/61	200	22.56	22.85, 22.45w- 12
					400	50.43	50.30- 09
Gromysheva	Mariya	RUS	10.1.90		Hep	5970	5885- 12
Grøvdal	Karoline Bjerkeli	NOR	14.6.90	167/52	1500	4:09.03	4:11.21- 15
1M	4:26.23				3000	8:39.47	8:52.83- 15
5000	14:57.53		15:15.18- 15		10000	31:14.07	
Grove	Emily	USA	22.5.93	168/61	PV	4.50i, 4.50	4.51Ai- 14, 4.32- 12
Grunewald	Gabe	USA	25.6.86	168/55	5000	15:19.50	15:19.01- 15
Guba	Paulina	POL	14.5.91	180/90	SP	18.63i, 17.74	17.95- 15
Gudeta	Netsanet	ETH	12.2.91	162/45	10000	30:36.75	31:06.53- 15
					HMar	68:01	67:31- 15
Gudmundsdóttir	Arna Stefania	ISL	1.9.95	175/59	400h	56.08	57.60- 15
Guei	Floria	FRA	2.5.90	166/53	200	23.00	23.39i- 14, 23.60- 12, 23.06w- 15
					400	50.84	50.89- 15
Guerrero	Esther	ESP	7.2.90	169/60	800	2:01.20	2:01.43- 15
Guillaume	Ilionis	FRA-J	13.1.98	179/69	TJ	13.46	13.11- 15
Guillon-Romarin	Ninon	FRA	15.4.95	163/53	PV	4.40	4.35- 15
Guillory	Briana	USA-J	21.11.97	165/57	200	22.95	23.99- 15
Gulyayeva	Aleksandra	RUS	30.4.94	173/59	800	2:00.24	2:09.44- 13
Gumenyuk	Irina	RUS	6.1.88	176/59	TJ	13.78i, 13.76, 14.05w	14.58- 13
Gunnarsson	Lisa	SWE-Y	20.8.99	171/57	PV	4.50	4.25- 15
Guo Tianqian		CHN	1.6.95	180/110	SP	18.24	18.59- 15
Gusarova	Inessa	RUS	29.10.95		1000	2:36.67	
Guster	Elexis	USA	7.7.94	171/60	400	51.85	52.19- 15
Gutermuth	Sophie	USA	2.11.92		PV	4.41i, 4.32	4.35- 15
Gutzmore	Sineade	GBR	9.10.86		TJ	13.70	13.54- 15
Gyurátz	Réka	HUN	31.5.96	175/70	HT	69.69	70.39- 15
Haapanen	Amy	USA	23.3.84	172/79	HT	66.13	70.63- 12
Haase	Rebekka	GER	2.1.93	170/53	100	11.22, 10.98w	11.21- 15
Hackett	Semoy	TTO	27.11.88	173/70	100	11.07	11.10, 11.04dq- 12, 10.98w- 11
					200	22.61	22.51A- 15, 22.55- 12, 22.14w- 11
Hackworth	Kenyattia	USA	15.9.93	168/55	LJ	6.81	6.50- 15
Hailey	Nnenya	USA	23.2.94	165/54	100h	12.96	13.48- 14
					400h	54.98	56.43- 15
Hailu	Meseret	ETH	12.9.90	168/54	Mar	2:26:26	2:21:09- 12
Hakeai	Siositina	NZL	1.3.94	182/105	DT	57.54	59.81- 15
Hall	Kate	USA-J	12.1.97		LJ	6.54i, 6.53, 6.59w	6.83- 15
Hall	Linden	AUS	29.6.91	167/51	1500	4:01.78	4:10.41- 15
Hall	Marielle	USA	28.1.92	160/52	3000	8:54.70i	8:54.48- 15
5000	15:13.66, 15:06.05i		15:06.45- 15		10000	31:37.45	
Hall	Sara	USA	15.4.83	163/48	HMar	70:07	70:49- 15
Hall-Pritchett	Patricia	JAM	16.10.82	165/58	400	51.64	50.71- 12
Hamblin	Nikki	NZL	20.5.88	165/52	1500	4:07.18	4:04.82- 11
Hamilton	Kim	USA	28.11.85	170/70	JT	58.65	59.05- 15

554 WOMEN'S INDEX

Name		Nat	Born	Ht/Wt	Event	2016 Mark	Pre-2016 Best
Hancco	Jéssica	PER	10.9.95	153/44	20kW	1:33:20	1:36:14.0t- 15
Hargrove	Monica	USA	30.12.82	173/58	400	51.72	50.39- 09
Haroye	Alemitu	ETH	9.5.95	160/44	5000	14:43.58	14:43.28- 15
Harper Nelson	Dawn	USA	13.5.84	168/61	100h	12.65	12.37- 12
Harrigan	Tahesia	IVB	15.2.82	157/54	100	11.25	11.13, 11.02w- 06, 10.89wdq- 11
Harrison	Kendra	USA	18.9.92	163/52	200	23.00	23.69- 15, 23.47w- 14
					100h	12.20	12.50, 12.46w- 15
Harrison	Queen	USA	10.9.88	170/60	100h	12.57, 12.54w	12.43- 13
Hartwig	Julie	GER	30.6.94	188/75	DT	58.03	54.55- 13
Harvey	Rushell	USA	9.9.95	170/59	100	11.33, 11.26w	11.62- 14, 11.44w- 15
Hasay	Jordan	USA	21.9.91	163/45	10000	31:58.33	31:39.67- 14
Hassan	Sifan	NED	1.1.93	170/49	800	2:00.27	1:58.50- 15
1500	3:57.13				3:56.05- 15	1M	4:25.50	4:18.20- 15
Hastings	Natasha	USA	23.7.86	173/63	200	22.57	22.61- 07, 22.55w- 14
					400	49.90	49.84- 07
Hatsko-Fedusova	Hanna	UKR	3.10.90	174/73	JT	62.02	67.29- 14
Hatton	Lucy	GBR	8.11.94	168/62	100h	13.18, 13.05w	12.84- 15
Havrylyuk	Tamara	UKR	14.12.95		20kW	1:32:42	
Hawi	Alemitu	ETH	14.11.96	168/52	3000	8:52.08	8:51.23- 15
					5000	15:10.13	15:10.46- 14
Hawkins	Chari	USA	21.5.91	170/57	Hep	5956	5750- 15
Haye-Smith	Yanique	JAM	22.3.90	170/55	400h	56.17	57.32- 12
Hayes	Quanera	USA	7.3.92	172/59	100	11.27	11.83- 15
200	22.89		23.29, 22.81w- 15		400	49.91	50.84- 15
He Qin		CHN	23.3.92		20kW	1:32:18	1:27:42- 13
Hechavarría	Zurian	CUB	10.8.95	164/58	400h	56.34A, 57.17	55.97- 15
Heidler	Betty	GER	14.10.83	175/80	HT	75.77	79.42- 11
Heinig	Katharina	GER	22.8.89		Mar	2:28:34	2:33:56- 14
Hejnová	Zuzana	CZE	19.12.86	170/54	400h	53.92	52.83- 13
Hemphill	Megu	JPN	23.5.96	167/57	Hep	5882	5678- 15
Henderson	Ashley	USA	4.12.95	168/59	100	11.21, 10.96w	11.64- 15
					200	22.64, 22.44w	24.12- 14
Henderson/Gailliard	Nia	USA	5.11.94	168/93	SP	17.67	17.21- 15
Henriques	Inês	POR	1.5.80	156/48	20kW	1:29:00	1:29:30- 13
Henry	Britney	USA	17.10.84	178/84	HT	69.62	71.27- 10
Henry	Chloé	BEL	5.3.87	170/58	PV	4.40	4.42- 15
Henry	Desiree	GBR	26.8.95	172/60	100	11.06	11.11- 15, 11.04w- 14
					200	22.46	22.94- 15
Herashchenko	Iryna	UKR	10.3.95	181/68	HJ	1.94	1.95i- 14, 1.94- 15
Hering	Christina	GER	9.10.94	185/62	800	2:00.37	1:59.54- 15
Hernández	Margarita	MEX	3.12.85	150/46	10000	32:11.04	32:36.29- 15
Herunga	Tjipekapora	NAM	1.1.88	167/51	400	52.03	51.24A- 12, 51.51- 15
Hicks	Cion	USA	14.10.94	178/	SP	17.39i, 17/09	16.69- 15
Higginson	Ashley	USA	17.3.89	167/52	1500	4:08.13	4:11.82- 13
1M	4:30.16i, 4:33.90		4:32.31i, 4:32.32- 15		3kSt	9:29.77	9:27.59- 14
Hilali	Siham	MAR	2.5.86	161/58	1500	4:07.39	4:01.33- 11
Hildebrand	Nadine	GER	20.9.87	158/51	100h	12.64	12.71- 14
Hill	Candace	USA-Y	11.2.99	175/59	100	11.07	10.98- 15
					200	22.76, 22.38w	22.43A, 23.05- 15
Hill	Deanna	USA	13.4.96	168/55	100	11.21	11.41- 15
					200	22.60	22.88- 15
Hillman	Christina	USA	6.10.93	178/84	SP	17.93i, 17.69	18.15i- 14, 17.73- 14
Hills	Madeline	AUS	15.5.87	174/53	1500	4:06.47	4:13.30- 15
5000	15:04.05				15:11.17- 15	3kSt	9:20.38	9:21.56- 15
Hingst	Carolin	GER	18.9.80	174/60	PV	4.40	4.72- 10
Hinriksdóttir	Aníta	ISL	13.1.96	161/50	800	2:00.14	2:00.49- 13
Hitchcock	Precious	USA	.95	172/59	200	23.18, 22.92w	
Hitchon	Sophie	GBR	11.7.91	170/75	HT	74.54	73.86- 15
Hixson	Kristen	USA	1.7.92	170/60	PV	4.65i, 4.65	4.50- 14
Hjálmsdóttir	Ásdís	ISL	28.10.85	175/65	JT	61.37	62.77- 12
Hofmann	Franziska	GER	27.3.94	175/69	100h	13.02, 13.00w	12.87- 14
Holda	Viktoriya	UKR-J	5.2.97	168/	HT	67.33	57.77- 15
Holder	Montayla	USA	7.2.94	160/52	400h	56.70	57.81- 14
Holder	Nikkita	CAN	7.5.87	170/59	100h	12.92, 12.86w	12.80- 12
Holliday	Becky	USA	12.3.80	160/	PV	4.39i, 4.32	4.65i, 4.60- 15
Holliday	Tanya	AUS	21.9.88	167/52	20kW	1:29:56	1:31:28- 12
Holodnaya	Olha	UKR	14.11.91	183/95	SP	18.45	18.72- 13
Holt	Sarah	GBR	17.4.87	185/80	HT	67.13	68.97- 15
Holub	Malgorzata	POL	30.10.92	168/56	400	51.67	51.74- 15
Hooper	Gloria	ITA	3.3.92	175/63	200	22.89	22.92- 15
Hoover	Trecey	USA	11.1.88	195/105	DT	57.26	58.76- 12

WOMEN'S INDEX

Name		Nat	Born	Ht/Wt	Event	2016 Mark		Pre-2016 Best
Hori	Yuka	JPN	13.6.96	155/40	5000	15:23.53		
Horie	Misato	JPN	10.3.87	168/49	Mar	2:26:40		2:27:57- 14
Horn	Carina	RSA	9.3.89	169/56	100	11.07		11.06- 15
Hou Yongbo		CHN	15.9.94		20kW	1:30:56		1:28:30- 15
Houlihan	Shelby	USA	8.2.93	160/54	800	2:01.56		2:01.12- 14
1500	4:03.39				4:09.62- 15			
					5000	15:06.14		15:49.72- 15
Howard	Marisa	USA	9.8.92	160/53	3kSt	9:42.94		9:37.84- 15
Howell	Jacklyn	USA	3.10.96	160/52	100h	12.90, 12.87w		13.07- 15
Hrasnová	Martina	SVK	21.3.83	177/88	HT	72.34		76.90- 09
Hrivnák Klocová	Lucia	SVK	20.11.83	171/58	800	2:00.57		1:58.51- 08
					1500	4:07.96		4:02.99- 12
Hrubá	Michaela	CZE-J	21.2.98	182/62	HJ	1.95i, 1.93		1.91- 14
Hryshutyna	Krystyna	UKR	21.3.92	176/59	LJ	6.71		6.81- 15
Huang Yan		CHN	12.1.96		400h	56.48		57.44- 14
Huddle	Molly	USA	31.8.84	163/48	5000	14:48.14		14:42.64- 14
10000	30:13.17 30:47.59- 14			HMar	67:41	68:31- 15	Mar 2:28:13	-0-
Hughes	Amber	USA	23.8.94		TJ	13.50		12.90- 15
Hulley	Alex	AUS-J	24.7.97		HT	65.75		63.65- 15
Hunsucker	Emily	USA	20.4.91	168/	HT	65.82		64.91- 14
Hussong	Christin	GER	17.4.94	187/82	JT	66.41		65.92- 15
Hutson	Kylie	USA	27.11.87	165/57	PV	4.70		4.75Ai, 4.70- 13
Hyacinthe	Kimberly	CAN	28.3.89	179/62	200	23.02, 22.88w		22.78- 13, 22.56w- 15
Hyder	Jasmine	USA	25.8.88	168/54	400h	56.49		55.22- 11
Hynne	Hedda	NOR	13.3.90	172/57	800	2:00.94		2:02.24- 14
Ibargüen	Caterine	COL	12.2.84	181/65	TJ	15.17		15.31- 14
Ichiyama	Mao	JPN-J	29.5.97	157/42	10000	32:15.73		
Ifantídou	Sofía	GRE	5.1.85	164/53	JT	56.88		57.50- 15
					Hep	6025		6113- 15
Igaune	Laura	LAT	2.10.88	170/70	HT	66.05		68.94- 12
Ikauniece-Admidina	Laura	LAT	31.5.92	179/60	100h	13.07		13.21- 15
					Hep	6622		6516- 15
Iljustsenko	Anna	EST	12.10.85	168/49	HJ	1.90		1.96- 11
Ince	Ariana	USA	14.3.89	180/75	JT	59.68		59.84- 15
Infeld	Emily	USA	21.3.90	163/48	5000	15:13.87, 15:00.91i		15:07.18- 15
					10000	31:26.94		31:38.71- 15
Inglese	Veronica	ITA	22.11.90	161/45	5000	15:22.45		16:02.72- 12
10000	31:37.43				32:25.76- 14		HMar	70:57- 14
Inoue	Ai	JPN	13.1.90	158/44	10000	32:07.56		32:39.04- 15
Insaeng	Subenrat	THA	10.2.94	183/105	DT	61.12		60.09- 15
Irby	Lynna	USA-J	6.12.98	168/55	400	51.39		51.79A, 53.36- 15
Irozuru	Abigail	GBR	3.1.90	170/61	LJ	6.62A		6.80- 12
Ishii	Hisami	JPN	10.8.95	161/47	10000	31:48.24		
					HMar	70:09		
Ishizuka	Haruko	JPN-J	2.6.97	161/53	400h	56.75		57.09- 15
Isinbayeva	Yelena	RUS	3.6.82	174/66	PV	4.90		5.06- 09
Ito	Mai	JPN	23.5.84	156/41	HMar	70:27		69:57- 15
Itoya	Juliet	ESP	17.8.86	174/63	LJ	6.79		6.64- 14
Iuel	Amalie Hammild	NOR	17.4.94	180/59	400h	55.79		55.92- 15
					Hep	6011		5610- 15
Ivancevic	Andrea	CRO	21.8.84	167/59	100h	12.90, 12.88w		12.87- 15
Ivanova	Viktoriya	RUS	21.11.91		3kSt	9:42.83		9:40.78- 14
Ivonina	Yekaterina	RUS	14.6.94	164/52	3kSt	9:24.66		9:36.79- 15
Iwade	Reia	JPN	8.12.94	154/42	Mar	2:24:38		2:27:21- 14
Jabore	Tigist	ETH	.93		HMar	69:16		
Jackson	Shericka	JAM	15.7.94	174/59	200	22.95, 22.86w		22.84- 13
					400	49.83		49.99- 15
Jaensch	Chelsea	AUS	6.1.85	163/56	LJ	6.70		6.63, 6.74w- 15
Jagaciak Michalska	Anna	POL	10.2.90	176/68	LJ	6.55		6.74- 10
					TJ	14.33, 14.40w		14.25- 11
Jakubaityte	Indre	LTU	24.1.76	177/70	JT	57.56		63.65- 07
James	Tiffany	JAM-J	31.1.97	160/52	400	51.32		53.21- 14
Jameson	Tameka	NGR	11.8.89	168/54	400h	56.44		55.73- 10
Jarder	Erica	SWE	2.4.86	173/59	LJ	6.60A, 6.53i, 6.49, 6.53w	6.71i- 13, 6.70- 15	
Jasiunaite	Liveta	LTU	26.7.94	174/68	JT	61.32		56.10- 12
Jean	Mulern	USA	25.9.92	165/50	100h	13.01		13.25- 13
Jebet	Ruth	BRN	17.11.96	165/49	3000	8:47.24i		9:09.8A- 13
					3kSt	8:52.78		9:20.55- 14
Jebet	Sarah	KEN	.88		Mar	2:27:07		2:31:09- 14
Jefferson	Kyra	USA	23.9.94	165/57	100	11.17		11.72, 11.66w- 10
200	22.56				22.24- 15		400	52.11	51.50- 15
Jelagat	Viola	KEN	20.4.92		HMar	70:24		69:27- 15

WOMEN'S INDEX

Name		Nat	Born	Ht/Wt	Event	2016 Mark	Pre-2016 Best
Jele	Lydia	BOT	22.6.90	172/54	400	51.50A, 52.14	52.57- 15
Jelela	Korene	ETH	18.1.87	165/50	Mar	2:27:06	2:22:43- 11
Jelmini	Anna	USA	15.7.90	176/86	DT	60.76	60.80- 10
Jemai	Sara	ITA	12.4.92	178/65	JT	56.56	57.20- 15
Jemison	Breana	USA	11.12/93	178/93	SP	17.36	16.54- 15
Jenneke	Michelle	AUS	23.6.93	172/67	100h	12.93	12.82- 15
Jeon Yong-eun		KOR	24.5.88	157/43	20kW	1:33:32	1:30:35- 15
Jepchirchir	Peres	KEN	27.9.93	153/40	HMar	66:39	67:17- 15
Jepchumba	Violah	KEN	23.10.90	172/52	HMar	65:51	69:30- 15
Jepkemoi	Hyvin	KEN	13.1.92	156/45	3kSt	9:00.01	9:10.15- 15
Jepkesho	Visiline	KEN	30.12.89	160/45	HMar	69:43	70:53- 14
					Mar	2:25:53	2:24:44- 15
Jepkirui Kirwa	Eunice	BRN	20.5.84	165/52	HMar	68:06	68:31- 14
					Mar	2:22:40	2:21:41- 12
Jepkorir	Winnie	KEN	10.6.90		Mar	2:28:46	2:27:57- 14
Jepkosgei	Joyciline	KEN	8.12.93	156/42	10000	31:28.28	
					HMar	69:07	74:06- 15
Jepkosgei	Nelly	KEN	14.7.91	164/53	800	2:00.7A	1:59.40- 13
					1500	4:04.26	4:08.10- 11
Jeptoo	Priscah	KEN	26.6.84	165/49	HMar	67:55dh	65:45- 13
Jeptoo	Priscah	KEN	26.6.84	165/49	Mar	2:25:57	2:20:14- 12
Jerez	Caridad	ESP	23.1.91	170/57	100h	12.99	12.94- 15
Jerotich	Emily	KEN	.86	165/48	800	2:00.0A	
Jeter	Carmelita	USA	24.11.79	163/63	100	11.16	10.64- 09
Ji Yefang		CHN	4.3.96		20kW	1:32:02	1:31:06- 14
Jiang Yanfei		CHN	5.7.92	172/54	LJ	6.61i, 6.39	6.57- 14
Jimma Eticha	Fantu	ETH	11.9.87		Mar	2:26:53	2:26:14- 15
Jimoh	Funmi	USA	29.5.84	173/64	LJ	6.76	6.96- 09
John	Deborah	TTO	10.4.90		100h	13.07	13.24- 13
Johnson	Alaysha	USA	20.7.96	160/52	100h	12.96	13.84- 12
Johnson	Brandee'	USA-J	3.4.98	163/52	400h	56.16	57.47- 15
Johnson	Felisha	USA	24.7.89	186/127	SP	19.26	19.18- 14
Johnson	Jessie	USA	21.11.93		PV	4.43	4.35- 15
Johnson	Kortnei	USA-J	11.8.97	165/52	100	11.27, 11.13w	11.51- 14, 11.26w- 15
					200	22.78, 22.67w	23.94- 13, 23.39w- 15
Johnson	LaTessa	USA-J	13.4.97	165/52	200	22.80, 22.75w	23.79- 14
Johnson	Lauren	USA	4.5.87	170/52	800	2:01.59	2:02.02- 15
	1500	4:05.29		4:04.17- 15	1M	4:25.04	4:33.00- 14	
Johnson-Thompson Katarina		GBR	9.1.93	183/70	200	22.79	22.89- 14
HJ	1.981.97i- 15, 1.90- 14			LJ	6.84	6.93i- 15, 6.92- 14	Hep 6523 6682- 14
Johny	Mayookha	IND	9.4.88	171/55	TJ	14.09A, 14.00i, 13.85	14.11- 11
Jones	Akela	BAR	22.4.95	186/77	100h	12.94	13.10- 15
HJ	1.98i, 1.95 1.91- 15			LJ	6.80i, 6.75	6.64i, 6.60- 15	Hep 6307 6371(w)- 15
Jones	Ariel	USA	18.7.95	165/52	400h	56.55	57.08- 15
Jones	Cambrya	USA	20.9.90	171/64	200	22.80, 22.76w	22.72- 12
Jones	Tenaya	USA	22.3.89	162/53	100h	12.99	12.72, 12.68Aw- 15
Jones	Tia	USA-Y	8.9.00	163/52	100h	12.84	13.45, 13.08w- 15
Jover	María del Mar	ESP	21.4.88	167/56	LJ	6.56, 6.68w	6.78A, 6.59- 14, 6.78w- 13
Joye	Hannah	AUS	4.1.96	177/63	HJ	1.87	1.92- 15
Józwik	Joanna	POL	30.1.91	168/53	800	1:57.37	1:58.35- 15
					1000	2:34.93	2:35.57- 15
Jung Hye-lim		KOR	1.7.87	167/52	100h	13.04, 12.86w	13.06- 12
Jungfleisch	Marie-Laurence	GER	7.10.90	181/68	HJ	2.00	1.99- 15
Jupiter	Ka'lynn	USA	12.1.95	168/57	400h	56.63	58.55- 15
Jurkovicová	Jarmila	CZE	9.2.81	172/78	JT	57.86	62.60- 06
Kabange	Mupopo	ZAM	21.9.92	170/57	400	51.04A, 51.35	50.22- 15
Kajan	Selma	AUS	30.7.91	169/52	800	2:01.27	2:01.96- 14
Kakol	Marta	POL	25.2.92	178/78	JT	56.64	58.43- 15
Kalawan	Shannon	JAM-J	25.11.97	168/52	400h	56.29	58.93- 15
Kalina	Anastasiya	RUS	16.2.94	162/50	800	2:01.80	2:02.06- 15
	1000	2:37.09				1500	4:05.67	4:07.37- 15
Kallur	Susanna	SWE	16.2.81	170/62	100h	12.91	12.49- 07
Kambundji	Mujinga	SUI	17.6.92	168/59	100	11.14	11.07- 15
					200	22.78	22.64- 15
Kamilos	Jessica	USA	3.8.93	158/42	3kSt	9:41.28	9:49.25- 14
Kampf	Heather	USA	19.1.87	162/53	800	2:00.55	2:00.04- 13
	1500	4:04.46		4:04.50- 15	1M	4:27.23	4:30.37- 15
Kamulu	Pauline	KEN	16.4.95	154/40	10000	31:56.70	34:03.7A- 06
Kangas	Jenni	FIN	3.7.92	178/74	JT	60.70	56.56- 15
Kaniskina	Olga	RUS	19.1.85	161/45	20kW	1:25:54	1:24:56- 09
Kanuchová	Veronika	SVK	19.4.93	170/69	HT	69.48	65.77- 15

Name		Nat	Born	Ht/Wt	Event	2016 Mark	Pre-2016 Best
Kapera	Monika	POL	15.2.90	170/54	20kW	1:33:32	1:32:29- 15
Karabulut	Elif	TUR	8.8.91	170/55	3kSt	9:46.17	9:48.48- 15
Karimi	Lucy	KEN	9.10.86		HMar	68:43	71:33- 15
					Mar	2:24:46	2:27:08- 15
Karol	Yuliya	BLR	26.6.91	162/57	800	2:01.09	2:03.40- 15
Kashyna	Inna	UKR	27.9.91	162/49	20kW	1:30:34	1:30:17- 14
Kasyanova	Hanna	UKR	24.4.83	178/67	Hep	6086	6586- 13
Käther	Nadja	GER	29.9.88	178/62	LJ	6.63, 6.64w	6.66- 10
Kato	Asami	JPN	12.10.90	156/38	HMar	70:30	70:21- 13
Kato	Misaki	JPN	15.6.91	155/40	5000	15:23.98	15:35.21- 15
					10000	31:59.72	32:05.87- 14
Kaur	Manpreet	IND	6.7.90	170/79	SP	17.94	17.96- 15
Kaya	Özlem	TUR	20.4.90	160/49	3kSt	9:32.03	9:30.23- 15
Kaysarova	Regina	KAZ	7.4.93	182/64	HJ	1.88	1.85- 15
Kebede	Aberu	ETH	12.9.86	163/50	HMar	69:27+	67:39- 09
					Mar	2:20:45	2:20:30- 12
Keenan	Te Rina	NZL	29.9.90	180/84	DT	59.42	60.78- 15
Keitany	Mary	KEN	18.1.82	158/45	HMar	68:53	65:39dh- 14, 66:02- 15
					Mar	2:24:26	2:18:37- 12
Kenzel	Alina	GER-J	10.8.97	183/78	SP	17.58	16.13- 15
Kessely	Haoua	FRA	2.2.88	173/66	LJ	6.58	6.55- 11
Kguriatukei (Kihara)	Rael	KEN	4.4.84		HMar	70:19	69:29- 14
					Mar	2:27:53	2:25:23- 11
Khamidova	Sitora	UZB	12.5.89	166/50	10000	31:57.77	32:12.54- 14
Kholodovich	Tatyana	BLR	21.6.91	181/83	JT	66.34	63.61- 14
Kibalnikova	Valentina	UZB	16.10.90	176/54	100h	13.00	13.12- 14
Kibet	Betty	KEN-Y	3.4.00	164/50	3kSt	9:38.27	10:18.7- 15
Kibiwot	Viola	KEN	22.12.83	167/50	3000	8:34.50	8:24.41- 14
					5000	14:29.50	14:33.48- 13
Kielbasinska	Anna	POL	26.6.90	170/55	200	22.95	22.94- 15
Kikuchi	Risa	JPN	5.2.90	165/47	10000	32:21.20	33:25.08- 12
Kikuchi	Yuko	JPN	8.6.92	165/47	10000	32:17.66	33:46.87- 14
Kilel	Caroline	KEN	21.3.81	172/54	Mar	2:27:39	2:22:34- 13
Kim Hye-gyong		PRK	9.3.93	153/42	Mar	2:28:36	2:27:05- 14
Kim Hye-song		PRK	9.3.93	153/43	Mar	2:28:36	2:27:58- 14
Kim Ji-hyang		PRK	26.9.95		Mar	2:28:06	2:32:17- 15
Kim Kyung-ae		KOR	5.3.88	163/62	JT	57.50	58.77- 15
Kimanzi	Grace	KEN	1.3.92	161/48	5000	15:16.44	15:17.43- 13
Kimura	Ayako	JPN	11.6.88	168/53	100h	13.22, 13.04w	13.03- 13
Kimura	Tomoko	JPN	12.11.94	154/43	5000	15:18.08	15:44.02- 10
Kinsey	Erika	SWE	10.3.88	185/68	HJ	1.93i, 1.90	1.97- 15
Kipkemboi	Gladys	KEN	15.10.86	158/48	3kSt	9:26.36	9:13.22- 10
Kipkemboi	Margaret Chelimo	KEN	9.2.93	162/45	3000	8:37.54	
					5000	14:47.24	15:28.6A- 15
Kipketer Jepkorir	Valentine	KEN	5.1.93	150/40	HMar	69:05A	68:21- 11
					Mar	2:23:41	2:23:02- 13
Kipkirui	Caroline	KEN	26.5.94	162/47	10000	31:16.38	
Kipkoech	Pascalia	KEN	22.12.88	153/42	HMar	67:58	67:17- 12
Kiplagat	Edna	KEN	15.11.79	171/54	HMar	70:31+	67:41- 12
					Mar	2:22:36	2:19:50- 12
Kiplagat	Florence	KEN	27.2.87	155/42	HMar	69:19	65:09- 15
					Mar	2:21:32	2:19:44- 11
Kipp	Shalaya	USA	19.8.90	170/58	3kSt	9:28.72	9:35.73- 12
Kiprono	Leah	KEN	15.4.80		Mar	2:27:39	2:36:55- 15
Kiprop	Helah	KEN	7.4.85	164/48	HMar	68:11	67:39- 13
					Mar	2:21:27	2:24:03- 15
Kiprop	Nancy	KEN	.79		Mar	2:25:13	2:27:34- 15
Kipyego	Sally	KEN	19.12.85	168/52	5000	14:43.98	14:30.42- 11
HMar	69:53		68:31- 14	Mar	2:28:01		
Kipyegon	Faith	KEN	10.1.94	157/42	1500	3:56.41	3:56.98- 13
					1M	4:18.60	4:16.71-15
Kipyokei	Diana Chemtai	KEN	.94		HMar	68:38	
Kiriakopoúlou	Nikoléta	GRE	21.3.86	167/56	PV	4.81i, 4.75	4.83- 15
Kirichenko	Irina	RUS	18.5.87		SP	18.35i, 17.93	17.82- 15
Kirui	Purity	KEN	13.8.91	162/47	3kSt	9:22.47	9:17.74- 15
Kisa	Janet	KEN	5.3.92	160/48	2000	5:41.4+	5:45.9- 14
3000	8:28.33			8:32.66- 14	5000	14:38.70	14:52.59- 14
Kitaguchi	Haruka	JPN-J	16.3.98	178/80	JT	61.38	58.90- 15
Kitur	Bornes	KEN	.88		HMar	70:00	70:32- 14
Kiyeng	Judy	KEN	.94	160/45	1500	4:05.45A	4:11.46- 15
					1M	4:29.29	

WOMEN'S INDEX

Name		Nat	Born	Ht/Wt	Event	2016 Mark	Pre-2016 Best
Kiyota	Mao	JPN	12.9.93	153/44	10000	32:05.05	31:44.79- 15
					Mar	2:24:32	
Kizaki	Ryoko	JPN	21.6.85	157/44	Mar	2:28:49	2:23:34- 13
Klaas	Kathrin	GER	6.2.84	168/72	HT	71.78	76.05- 12
Klaup	Mari	EST	27.2.90	180/58	Hep	5777	6023(w)- 15
Klein	Caroline	GER	4.3.96		Hep	5842	5362- 13
Klein	Hanna	GER	6.4.93	172/55	1500	4:08.56	4:09.91- 15
Klishina	Darya	RUS	15.1.91	180/57	LJ	6.84	7.05- 15
Klochko	Viktoriya	UKR	2.9.92	187/115	DT	57.15	58.01- 15
Klosterhalfen	Konstanze	GER-J	18.2.97	169/52	800	2:01.55	2:06.42- 15
	1500	4:06.91	4:09.58- 15	3000	8:46.74	8:53.21mx- 15	5000 15:16.98
Klucinová	Eliska	CZE	14.4.88	177/69	Hep	6182	6460- 14
Klymets	Iryna	UKR	4.10.94	168/70	HT	72.23	65.21- 15
Knäsche	Anjuli	GER	18.10.93	169/61	PV	4.55	4.45- 13
Knibb	Kellion	JAM	25.12.93	193/93	DT	61.44	61.34- 14
Knodle	Paige	USA	15.8.93		Hep	5833	5681- 14
Knoroz	Polina	RUS-Y	20.7.99		PV	4.35	4.10- 15
Koala	Marthe	BUR	8.3.94	177/69	Hep	5952	5852- 15
Kocina	Anete	LAT	5.2.96	176/65	JT	59.50	60.01- 15
Kock	Maren	GER	22.6.90	173/55	5000	15:24.73	15:22.75mx- 14
Kogut Kubiak	Alexia	FRA	22.1.88	169/68	JT	57.85	57.10- 11
Kohlmann	Fabienne	GER	6.11.89	170/57	800	2:00.49	1:58.34- 15
Kolak	Sara	CRO	22.6.95	170/74	JT	66.18	57.79- 13
Kolb	Viktoryia	BLR	26.10.93	182/90	SP	17.33	17.47- 15
Kolbo	Natasha	USA	5.4.92	168/	PV	4.35	4.23- 14
Koleczek	Karolina	POL	15.1.93	169/49	100h	13.03, 13.01w	12.91, 12.87w- 15
Kolesnychenko	Olena	UKR	3.6.93	172/58	400h	55.48	56.55- 14
Kolokithá	Efthimía	GRE	9.7.87	168/55	LJ	6.66	6.61- 14
Kolomoyets	Anastasiya	BLR	15.7.94		HT	69.20	67.37- 15
Kondratyeva	Oksana	RUS	22.11.85	180/80	HT	70.75	77.13- 13
Koneva	Yekaterina	RUS	25.9.88	169/55	LJ	6.70i, 6.49	6.82i- 15, 6.70, 6.80w- 11
					TJ	14.42	15.04- 15
Kononova	Yevgeniya	RUS	28.9.89	175/53	HJ	1.87i	1.92- 13
Konstants	Irina	RUS	1.3.90		TJ	13.47	14.11- 14
Kopron	Malwina	POL	16.11.94	170/63	HT	72.74	71.27- 15
Koren	Petra	SLO	30.7.93		TJ	13.82	13.24- 15
Koressel	Allie	USA	2.3.91	168/57	PV	4.46	4.32- 15
Kornuta	Anna	UKR	10.11.88	168/57	LJ	6.70	6.72- 13
Korobkina	Yelena	RUS	25.11.90	163/47	1500	4:06.75	4:05.18- 13
Korolyova	Kristina	RUS	6.11.90	183/68	HJ	1.91i, 1.88	1.91- 15
Korosídou	Iliána	GRE	14.1.95	175/72	HT	66.68	66.47- 15
Korpela	Merja	FIN	15.5.81	170/75	HT	69.15	69.56- 09
Korzh	Tatyana	BLR	17.3.93	175/75	JT	62.10	56.74- 15
Kosgei	Brigid	KEN	.94		Mar	2:24:45	2:47:59- 15
Kosolapova	Valentina	RUS-J	11.7.97		TJ	13.37, 13.74w	13.43- 15
Koster	Maureen	NED	3.7.92	175/56	1500	4:03.84	3:59.79- 15
	3000	8:48.46		9:23.20- 11	5000	15:07.20	15:07.73- 15
Kostrova	Alina	BLR	2.3.90	181/79	HT	66.57	70.31- 12
Koubaa	Sanaa	GER	6.1.85	168/58	3kSt	9:35.15	9:43.08- 12
Koudelová	Lucie	CZE	6.7.94	170/64	100h	13.12, 13.05w	13.15- 14, 13.12w- 15
Kowal	Matylda	POL	11.1.89	165/54	3kSt	9:35.13	9:39.87- 12
Kowalska	Katarzyna	POL	7.4.85	177/55	HMar	70:06	71:27- 11
Kragbé	Suzanne	CIV	22.12.81	179/92	DT	56.91	59.61- 14
Králová	Tereza	CZE	22.10.89	175/85	HT	69.01	70.21- 13
Kramer	Regine	GER	5.4.93	168/59	PV	4.40	4.26- 14
Krasnova	Angelina	RUS	7.2.91	168/55	PV	4.66i, 4.50	4.70- 13
Krause	Gesa Felicitas	GER	3.8.92	167/55	1500	4:06.99	4:11.03- 15
	3000	8:49.43i		9:00.25i, 9:02.04- 15	3kSt	9:18.41	9:19.25- 15
Krebs	Denise	GER	27.6.87	157/48	1500	4:08.14	4:06.01- 12
Krechik	Yelena	BLR	20.7.87	174/73	HT	69.40	72.06- 15
Krivoshapka	Antonina	RUS	21.7.87	168/60	400	50.70	49.16- 12
Krizsán	Xénia	HUN	13.1.93	171/62	Hep	6266	6322- 15
Kromah	Mariam	LBR	1.1.94	163/52	400	52.11	53.00- 15
Kropivko	Yekaterina	RUS-J	13.6.97		TJ	13.40	
Krumpoch	Megan	USA	31.8.92	170/54	800	2:01.75	2:03.82- 14
Krylova	Anna	RUS	3.10.85		TJ	13.93	14.40- 12
Kubokura	Satomi	JPN	27.4.82	161/52	400h	56.14	55.34- 11
Kuchina	Mariya	RUS	14.1.93	182/60	HJ	2.00	2.01i- 14, 2.01- 15
Kudzelich	Svetlana	BLR	7.5.87	170/52	3000	8:54.51	8:46.83- 15
					3kSt	9:32.93	9:27.95- 14

WOMEN'S INDEX

Name		Nat	Born	Ht/Wt	Event	2016 Mark	Pre-2016 Best
Kuijken	Susan	NED	8.7.86	170/54	3000	8:46.88	8:36.08- 14
5000	15:00.69		15:04.36- 13		10000	31:32.43	31:31.97- 15
Kulyatina	Alla	RUS	9.6.90	157/45	10000	32:12.70	32:52.27- 15
Kuma	Dibaba	ETH	14.9.96		HMar	69:21	
Kunova	Vera	RUS	2.4.90		SP	17.22i, 15.98	17.48- 15
Kunz	Annie	USA	16.2.93	183/70	Hep	6038	5442- 13
Kuria	Mary	KEN	29.11.87	157/48	1500	4:04.13	4:03.18- 12
Küster	Susen	GER	27.7.94	165/69	HT	66.44	64.00- 15
Kuwahara	Sayaka	JPN	8.3.93	162/45	Mar	2:25:09	
Kwasniewska	Michalina	POL	22.10.91	185/63	HJ	1.88i, 1.86	1.83- 13
Kylypko	Marina	UKR	10.11.95	165/58	PV	4.65	4.30- 15
La Mao		CHN	17.12.96		20kW	1:31:46	
Laasma	Liina	EST	13.1.92	178/77	JT	63.65	63.17- 14
Labiche	Lissa	SEY	18.2.93	172/52	HJ	1.89i, 1.87	1.92- 15
LaCaze	Genevieve	AUS	4.8.89	164/53	3000	8:52.28	9:11.6- 14
5000	15:06.67		16:05.60- 15		3kSt	9:14.28	9:33.19- 14
LaFond	Thea	DMA	5.4.94	173/65	TJ	13.61i, 13.41, 13.70w	13.35, 13.60Aw- 15
Lagat	Violah	KEN	13.3.89	165/49	1500	4:06.00	4:04.10- 15
					1M	4:28.82	4:29.43- 14
Lagger	Sarah	AUT-Y	3.9.99	174/60	Hep	5960	
Lahti	Sarah	SWE	18.2.95	177/57	1500	4:08.91	4:17.20- 15
3000	8:50.97	9:26.02- 13		5000	15:10.76	16:19.58- 14	10000	31:28.43
Laing	Kimberley	JAM	8.1.89	167/55	100h	13.07	12.89, 12.71w- 15
Lake	Morgan	GBR-J	12.5.97	178/64	HJ	1.94	1.94- 14
					Hep	5951	6148- 14
Lally	Jade	GBR	30.3.87	183/81	DT	65.10	60.76- 11
Lalonde	Geneviève	CAN	5.9.91	167/47	3kSt	9:30.24	9:35.69- 15
Lalova-Collio	Ivet	BUL	18.5.84	168/55	100	11.11	10.77- 04
					200	22.42	22.32- 15
Lamble	Regan	AUS	14.10.91	174/55	20kW	1:29:33	1:30:08- 12
Lamote	Renelle	FRA	26.12.93	168/57	800	1:58.01	1:58.86- 15
Landázuri	Narcisa	ECU	25.11.92	167/52	100	11.26A,11.27,11.0A	11.30A,11.48,11.33w- 15
Landwehr	Katie	USA	23.1.93	168/54	3kSt	9:41.22	10:07.24- 15
Lang	Salome	SUI-J	18.11.97		HJ	1.87i, 1.86	1.83- 14
Lansiquot	Imani	GBR-J	17.12.97	170/59	100	11.17	11.56- 15
Larsson	Eleni	SWE	4.4.93	186/100	HT	66.09	68.76- 15
Lashmanova	Yelena	RUS	9.4.92	170/48	20kW	1:24:58	1:25:02- 12
Latham	Viershanie	USA	1.8.95		TJ	13.60	13.05- 15
Lawrence	Mel	USA	29.8.89	162/52	3kSt	9:36.35	9:40.98- 09
Lawrence	Shadae	JAM	31.12.95	173/84	DT	61.18	48.66- 15
Lawson	LeKeisha	USA	3.6.87	168/57	100	11.07	11.06- 15
					200	22.98	22.99, 22.88w- 15
Le-Roy	Anastasia	JAM	11.9.87	172/57	200	22.85	23.08- 08
					400	52.00	50.84- 14
Lebedeva	Lyudmila	RUS	23.5.90	165/48	3kSt	9:46.73	9:36.56- 15
Legesse	Meseret	ETH	28.8.87		Mar	2:26:08	2:26:15- 13
Lehman	Jess	USA	17.1.93	173/61	Hep	5917	6014- 15
Leidl	Sarah	GER	5.3.87	173/65	JT	56.98	56.89- 15
Lekamge	H.L.Dilhani	SRI	14.1.87		JT	56.92	56.37- 15
Lekepana	Perendis	KEN	4.8.91		HMar	69:49	70:53- 14
LeLeux	Morgann	USA	14.11.92	170/62	PV	4.60	4.50i- 13, 4.44- 12
Lema	Marta	ETH	30.12.90		HMar	67:58	76:58- 15
Lema	Marta	ETH	30.12.90		Mar	2:24:32	2:25:59- 15
Lemus	Sandra	COL	1.1.89	170/102	SP	17.04	18.03- 13
Leonard	Alison	GBR	17.3.90	168/56	800	2:00.52	2:00.08- 14
					1500	4:08.96mx,4:09.59	4:09.73mx- 14,4:13.23- 15
Leontyuk	Yuliya	BLR	31.1.84	185/80	SP	18.92	19.79- 08
Leslie	Breanna	USA	11.8.91	172/61	Hep	5918	5893- 14
Lesueur	Éloyse	FRA	15.7.88	179/65	LJ	6.57	6.92- 14, 7.04w- 12
Lettow	Lindsay	USA	6.6.90	175/62	Hep	6098	6023- 15
Levchenko	Yuliya	UKR-J	28.11.97	179/60	HJ	1.95	1.92- 15
Levy	Daina	JAM	27.5.93	165/98	HT	71.48	69.01- 15
Levy	Jura	JAM	4.11.90	157/50	100	11.25, 11.11w	11.10, 11.07w- 11
Lewetegn	Sintayehu	ETH	9.5.96	161/48	5000	15:06.49	15:25.78- 15
Lewis	Yvette	PAN	16.3.85	173/62	100h	13.13, 13.02w	12.67- 13
Lewis-Smallwood	Gia	USA	1.4.79	183/93	DT	58.94	69.17- 14
Li Leilei		CHN	18.8.89	160/46	20kW	1:32:39	1:31:49- 15
Li Ling		CHN	6.7.89	180/65	PV	4.70i, 4.63	4.66- 15
Li Lingwei		CHN	26.1.89	174/52	JT	62.89	65.11- 12
Li Ping		CHN	7.1.94		20kW	1:33:41	1:33:39- 15
Li Xiaohong		CHN	8.1.95	162/48	TJ	13.73	14.20- 15

560   WOMEN'S INDEX

Name		Nat	Born	Ht/Wt	Event	2016 Mark	Pre-2016 Best
Li Yanmei		CHN	6.2.90	171/56	TJ	13.64	14.35- 13
Liang Rui		CHN	18.6.94		20kW	1:28:43	1:29:22- 15
Liang Yan		CHN	2.1.95		DT	57.76	62.01- 13
Liashenko	Valentina	GEO	30.1.81	176/63	HJ	1.90	1.92- 15
Licwinko	Kamila	POL	22.3.86	184/65	HJ	1.99	2.02i, 1.99- 15
de Lima	Jaílma	BRA	31.12.86	174/65	400	51.99	51.66- 11
Limo	Cynthia	KEN	18.12.89	167/52	HMar	66:04	67:02- 15
Linden	Desiree	USA	26.7.83	157/44	Mar	2:26:08	2:22:38dh- 11, 2:25:55- 12
Lindh	Lovisa	SWE	9.7.91	169/56	800	1:59.41	2:01.73- 14
					1000	2:36.04	2:40.17- 15
Linkiewicz	Joanna	POL	2.5.90	172/55	400h	55.25	55.62- 15
Linna	Inga	FIN	21.2.95	172/72	HT	67.40	68.25- 15
Linnell	Lisa	SWE	30.4.91	175/66	Hep	5862	5888- 13
Lipsey	Charlene	USA	16.7.91	168/57	800	2:00.65	2:00.60- 15
Little	Shamier	USA	20.3.95	163/52	400	51.74i	51.06- 14
					400h	53.51	53.74- 15
Liu Hong		CHN	12.5.87	161/48	20kW	1:25:56	1:24:38- 15
Liu Jingyi		CHN	27.10.94		HJ	1.90	1.84- 14
Liu Ruihuan		CHN	29.6.92		10000	32:15.40	31:56.80- 13
					Mar	2:26:13	2:28:35- 15
Liu Shiying		CHN	24.9.93	179/76	JT	65.64	62.77- 15
Liu Tingting		CHN	29.1.90	178/87	HT	69.65	73.06- 14
Liu Xiangrong		CHN	6.6.88	185/119	SP	17.98	19.24- 12
Llano	Beatrice Nedberge	NOR-J	14.12.97	169/90	HT	67.86	67.05- 15
Lloyd	Cassandra	USA	27.1.90	163/54	100h	12.86	12.90- 13
Lobe	Ricarda	GER	13.4.94	165/52	100h	13.01, 13.00w	13.22- 15
Lomnická	Nikola	SVK	16.9.88	166/70	HT	66.86	71.58- 14
Longfors	Rachel	USA	6.6.83	183/82	DT	58.87	59.67- 14
López	Yaniuvis	CUB	1.2.86	180/71	SP	18.67	18.81- 09
Lotout	Marion	FRA	19.11.89	165/54	PV	4.36i, 4.30	4.60- 13
Love	Alexis	USA	24.4.91	168/57	100	11.29, 11.25w	11.28- 12
					200	22.63	23.03- 12, 22.98w- 15
Løvnes	Ingeborg	NOR	5.9.92	165/52	3kSt	9:43.97	9:48.89- 15
Lowe	Chaunté	USA	12.1.84	175/60	HJ	2.01	2.05- 10
Lu Huihui		CHN	26.6.89	171/68	JT	64.04	66.13- 15
Lu Xiaoxin		CHN	22.2.89	184/90	DT	62.76	63.27- 13
Lu Xiuzhi		CHN	26.10.93	167/52	20kW	1:28:07	1:25:12- 15
Lückenkemper	Gina	GER	21.11.96	170/58	100	11.04	11.25- 15
					200	22.67	23.04, 22.41w- 15
Ludlow	Molly	USA	4.8.87	173/59	800	1:57.68	1:58.68- 15
Luka	Tintu	IND	26.4.89	164/51	800	2:00.58	1:59.17- 10
Lunyova	Anna	UKR	1.10.91	175/59	LJ	6.73	6.61- 15
Lupu	Nataliya	UKR	4.11.87	172/62	800	1:59.70	1:58.46- 12
Luzolo	Maryse	GER	13.3.95	169/54	LJ	6.59	6.47i, 6.45- 13
Lyakhova	Olha	UKR	18.3.92	174/57	800	2:00.32	1:58.64- 15
Lysenko	Alena	RUS	3.2.88		HT	68.26	69.01- 14
Machado	Maíla Paula	BRA	22.1.81	167/62	100h	12.99	12.86- 04
Mackey	Katie	USA	12.11.87	165/53	800	2:01.47	2:01.20- 15
1500	4:06.33	4:03.81- 15	1M	4:25.48		4:27.78- 14	3000	8:46.58	8:52.99- 15
Mackey	Katie	USA	12.11.87	165/53	5000	15:18.60	15:04.74- 14
Madarász	Viktória	HUN	12.5.85	153/46	20kW	1:30:47	1:30:57- 14
Madu	Jennifer	USA	23.9.94	160/52	100	11.27	11.16, 11.12w- 15
Mageean	Ciara	IRL	12.3.92	168/56	800	2:00.79	2:02.31- 11
1500	4:01.46		4:06.49- 15		1M	4:28.40i	4:30.64- 15
Magnani	Margherita	ITA	26.2.87	161/45	1500	4:07.91	4:06.05- 14
Maihöfer	Lisa	GER-J	28.10.98		HJ	1.87i	1.84- 15
Maiwald	Anna	GER	21.7.90	176/62	Hep	6020	6111- 15
Maiyo	Maureen	KEN	28.5.85	167/59	400h	56.12	56.65A- 15
Majester	Kat	USA	22.5.87	173/59	PV	4.50	4.51Ai- 14, 4.40- 12
Májková	Lucie	CZE	9.7.88	182/66	TJ	13.93	13.80- 15, 13.85w- 14
Majors	Felecia	USA	2.12.95	168/57	200	22.85	23.21i, 23.36w- 14, 23.40- 15
					400	51.29	52.65i, 52.67- 14
Mäkelä	Kristiina	FIN	20.11.92	184/71	TJ	14.24	14.20i, 14.06- 15
Måkestad Bovim	Ingvill	NOR	7.8.81	172/59	1500	4:05.35	4:02.20- 10
Mäki	Kristiina	CZE	22.9.91	170/50	1500	4:08.68	4:12.52- 15
Maksimova	Yana	BLR	9.1.89	182/70	HJ	1.90	1.95i- 15, 1.91- 12
					Hep	6076	6198- 12
Malácová	Romana	CZE	15.5.87	164/57	PV	4.62i, 4.55	4.50- 14
Malavisi	Sonia	ITA	31.10.94	173/67	PV	4.51	4.42- 13
Malone	Audrey	USA	16.6.95	178/75	JT	57.06	47.97- 15
Malone	Chantel	IVB	2.12.91	175/62	LJ	6.66	6.69A- 15,6.65i- 11,6.65- 13,6.66w- 12

WOMEN'S INDEX 561

Name		Nat	Born	Ht/Wt	Event	2016 Mark	Pre-2016 Best
Malone	Maggie	USA	30.12.93	173/77	JT	62.19	55.37- 14
Maltseva	Yuliya	RUS	30.11.90	187/84	DT	63.27	63.48- 15
Malyshik	Hanna	BLR	4.2.94	175/90	HT	72.78	67.53- 14
Mamina	Alena	RUS	30.5.90	168/58	400	51.50	51.17- 13
Mamo	Meskerem	ETH			5000	15:18.06	
Mamona	Patrícia	POR	21.11.88	168/53	TJ	14.65	14.52- 12
Mann	Brittany	USA	16.4.94	173/89	SP	17.49	17.40i, 17.25- 15
Manning	Christina	USA	29.5.90	163/54	100h	12.87, 12.67w	12.68- 12
Manning	Crystal	USA	15.4.86	173/64	TJ	13.94	13.96- 10
Manz	Daniela	GER	19.9.86	160/70	HT	65.77	66.42- 14
Marchant	Lanni	CAN	11.4.84	155/45	10000	32:04.21	31:46.94- 15
Marcussen	Ida	NOR	1.11.87	173/67	Hep	5877	6226- 07
Maresová	Oldriska	CZE	14.10.86	187/67	HJ	1.87i	1.92i, 1.91- 15
Marghieva	Zalina	MDA	5.2.88	174/90	HT	74.21	73.97- 15
Marie-Nély	Nathalie	FRA	24.11.86	175/66	TJ	14.03	14.03- 12, 14.18w- 11
Maroszek	Jessica	USA	26.2.92	175/91	DT	59.88	61.21- 15
Marshall	Tonea	USA-J	17.12.98	178/75	100h	13.04	13.44, 13.12w- 15
Marten	Isabella	GER	12.5.96		TJ	13.35	13.22- 14
Martin	Jada	USA	8.6.95	170/55	100	11.40, 11.24w	11.34, 11.27w- 15
					200	22.60, 22.41w	22.76- 15
Martín	Diana	ESP	1.4.81	162/50	3kSt	9:41.23	9:30.70- 14
Martinez	Brenda	USA	8.9.87	163/52	800	1:59.64	1:57.91- 13
					1500	4:03.57	4:00.94- 13
Martins	Eliane	BRA	26.5.86	160/49	LJ	6.72	6.68, 6.73w- 15
Martins	Valdiléia	BRA	19.9.89	180/68	HJ	1.88	1.86- 13
Márton	Anita	HUN	15.1.89	171/84	SP	19.87	19.48- 15
					DT	60.94	59.27- 14
Maruszewska	Klaudia	POL-J	28.8.97	180/72	JT	57.59	50.43- 15
Masai	Linet	KEN	5.12.89	170/55	10000	32:02.48	30:26.50- 08
					HMar	69:33	71:45- 14
Masai	Magdalene	KEN	4.4.93	160/48	HMar	67:31	
Mashinistova	Yelena	RUS	29.3.94		LJ	6.52	6.67- 15
					TJ	13.38, 13.65w	13.03, 13.26w- 14
Maslova	Anastasiya	BLR-Y	16.10.97		HT	66.38	63.20- 15
Maslova	Darya	KGZ	6.5.95	170/50	10000	31:36.90	32:14.33- 15
Matsuda	Mizuki	JPN	31.5.95	158/46	10000	31:59.12	32:12.25- 15
					HMar	70:25	72:54- 15
Matsuzaki	Riko	JPN	24.12.92	157/44	10000	31:55.26	31:44.86- 15
Matthews	Bria	USA-J	22.7.97		TJ	13.73	13.25- 15
Matusinska	Tina	POL	12.7.88	161/52	400h	56.66	55.87- 12
Maudens	Hanne	BEL-J	12.3.97		Hep	5881	5720- 15
Mavrodieva	Radoslava	BUL	13.3.87	178/86	SP	18.27	18.67- 13
Mayer	Lisa	GER	2.5.96	171/57	100	11.25, 11.04w	11.31- 15
					200	22.86	23.29- 15
Mazina	Margarita	RUS	7.7.95		HJ	1.88i	1.88- 15
Mazuronak	Olga	BLR	14.4.89	165/49	Mar	2:23:54	2:25:36- 15
McCartney	Eliza	NZL	11.12.96	179/65	PV	4.80	4.64- 15
McColgan	Eilish	GBR	25.11.90	176/59	1500	4:03.74	4:09.67- 13
3000	8:43.27		8:47.79- 13				
					5000	15:05.00	15:44.62- 12
McCormack	Fionnuala	IRL	24.9.84	158/45	10000	31:30.74	31:29.22- 12
McCorory	Francena	USA	20.10.88	170/60	400	50.23	49.48- 15
McCoy	Rachel	USA	1.8.95	180/70	HJ	1.93	1.88- 14
McDermott	Nicola	AUS	28.12.96	186/63	HJ	1.88	1.88- 15
McDonald	Sarah	GBR	2.8.93	167/50	800	2:01.10	2:05.69- 13
					1500	4:07.18	4:17.13- 13
McGee	Cory	USA	29.5.92	168/52	1500	4:07.34	4:06.67- 13
					1M	4:28.55	4:32.1- 15, 4:32.10i- 13
McGhee	Brianna	USA	8.11.93	168/55	100h	12.88	13.24, 13.12w- 15
McGowan	Brittany	AUS	24.4.91	163/49	800	2:01.63	2:01.26- 14
McGrone	Candyce	USA	24.3.89	168/59	100	11.13, 11.06w	11.00, 10.91w- 15
					200	23.01, 22.98w	22.01- 15
McKinna	Sophie	GBR	31.8.94	173/95	SP	17.14	17.12- 13
McKnight	Sparkle	TTO	21.12.91	165/55	400h	56.23	55.41- 15
McLaughlin	Madison	USA	14.11.96		SP	16.98	15.94- 15
McLaughlin	Sydney	USA-Y	7.8.99	176/59	400	51.87, 51.84i	52.59- 15
					400h	54.15	55.28- 15
McLaughlin-Whilby	Anneisha	JAM	6.1.86	170/66	200	22.78	22.54- 11
					400	51.03	51.89- 12
McMahon	Christine	IRL	6.7.92	167/55	400h	56.06	56.97- 14
McMillan	Chantae	USA	1.5.88	173/69	Hep	6326	6188- 12
McMillan	Lilla	USA	31.8.94	163/52	200	23.00	23.50- 15
					400	51.38	51.86- 15

WOMEN'S INDEX

Name		Nat	Born	Ht/Wt	Event	2016 Mark	Pre-2016 Best
McPherson	Inika	USA	29.9.86	163/55	HJ	1.94	1.96, 2.00dq- 14
McPherson	Stephenie Ann	JAM	25.11.88	168/55	400	50.04	49.92- 13
McQueen	Darrielle	USA	29.5.96		TJ	13.61i	12.86i, 12.72- 15
McReynolds	Tiffani	USA	4.12.91	153/50	100h	12.88, 12.76w	12.77- 14, 12.70w- 15
Meadows	Jennifer	GBR	17.4.81	156/48	800	2:00.74	1:57.93- 09
Meadows	Tawanna	USA	4.8.86	168/55	100	11.13	11.11- 14
Medeiros	Keely	BRA	30.4.87	180/100	SP	17.36	17.58- 14
Medina	Ayamey	CUB-J	21.2.98	164/53	HT	68.98	60.81- 15
Medvedyeva	Yekaterina	RUS	29.3.94		20kW	1:26:40	1:29:32- 15
Meijer	Michaela	SWE	30.7.93	172/63	PV	4.62	4.55- 15
Mekasha	Dinknesh	ETH	11.9.85	160/48	HMar	70:21+	73:19- 15
					Mar	2:28:11	2:23:12- 15
Mekonen	Tigist	BRN-J	7.7.97	171/70	3kSt	9:31.84	9:20.65- 15
Mekuria	Aberu	ETH	24.12.83		Mar	2:27:41	2:25:30- 15
Melchor	Inés	PER	30.8.86	158/55	10000	32:10.99	31:56.62- 15
					Mar	2:27:40	2:26:48- 14
Melese	Yebrqual	ETH	18.4.90	164/55	HMar	70:18+	68:21- 15
					Mar	2:24:49	2:23:23- 15
Melis Mey	Karin	TUR	31.5.84	173/57	LJ	6.85A, 6.62	6.93- 07
Melkamu	Meselech	ETH	27.4.85	158/48	HMar	70:18+	68:05- 13
					Mar	2:21:54	2:21:01- 12
Melnyk	Bohdana	UKR	25.10.94	174/62	LJ	6.52, 6.58w	6.45- 15
Melnyk	Tetyana	UKR	2.4.95	184/60	400	51.92	
Melville	Miranda	USA	20.3.89	160/54	20kW	1:31:42	1:33:11- 14
Mendieta	Yusleidys	CUB	17.2.94	180/66	Hep	6022	6024- 13
Meng Qianqian		CHN	6.1.91	178/85	SP	17.80	18.31- 11
Mengistu	Meseret	ETH	6.3.90	161/47	Mar	2:25:56	2:23:26- 15
Menkova	Oksana	BLR	28.3.82	186/85	HT	73.07	78.69- 12
Menuet	Emilie	FRA	27.11.91	155/44	20kW	1:31:38	1:32:20- 15
Merckle	Jessie	USA	13.7.94		JT	56.91	53.94- 14
Mergia	Aselefech	ETH	23.1.85	168/51	Mar	2:23:57	2:19:31- 12
Merlano	Briggitte	COL	29.4.82	174/65	100h	12.94A, 12.94, 12.85w	12.89- 11
Metoyer	Amber	USA	7.9.83		Hep	5768	5478- 15
Michiguchi	Ai	JPN	3.6.88	159/53	20kW	1:31:51	1:32:34- 15
Michta-Coffey	Maria	USA	23.6.86	165/51	20kW	1:30:49	1:30:49- 14
Mickle	Kim	AUS	28.12.84	168/70	JT	57.20	66.83- 14
Mihambo	Malaika	GER	3.2.94	170/52	LJ	6.95	6.90- 14
Mikhina	Elina	KAZ	16.7.94	170/55	400	52.09	52.94- 14
Mikolajczyk	Izabela	POL	4.9.90	177/60	Hep	5766	5968- 12
Miller	Jade	USA	13.1.95	168/57	400h	55.75	56.22- 14
Miller	Shaunae	BAH	15.4.94	185/69	100	11.19	11.40- 14
					400	49.44	49.67- 15
200	22.05		22.14- 15				
Miller Koch	Heather	USA	30.3.87	176/63	LJ	6.55	6.26- 12
					Hep	6423	6274- 15
Minenko	Hanna	ISR	25.9.89	178/61	TJ	14.68	14.78- 15
Mineyeva	Tatyana	RUS	10.8.90		20kW	1:30:05	1:28:09- 11
Mironchik-Ivanova	Anastasiya	BLR	13.4.89	171/54	LJ	6.84i	7.08, 7.22w- 12
					TJ	13.75i	14.29- 11
Misher	Rachel	USA-J	4.2.97	163/54	200	23.17, 22.94w	24.82- 15
Misochenko	Anna	RUS	15.4.92		LJ	6.76i, 6.69	6.58- 15
Mitchell	A'Keyla	USA	25.11.95	173/60	200	22.94	22.95, 22.84w- 15
Mitchell	Kathryn	AUS	10.7.82	168/72	JT	64.37	66.10- 14
Mitchell	Morgan	AUS	3.10.94	177/64	400	51.25	52.22- 14
Mitchell	Victoria	AUS	25.4.82	164/48	3kSt	9:39.40	9:30.84- 06
Mix	Lindsey	CAN	14.1.89		PV	4.35	4.25- 15
Miyashita	Risa	JPN	26.4.84	171/71	JT	60.86	60.08- 11
Miyata	Kanayo	JPN	12.10.90	159/45	10000	32:14.40	32:51.07- 11
Mizernyuk	Olena	UKR	23.11.95	172/53	20kW	1:33:25	1:49:50- 15
Mjåland	Trine	NOR	30.6.90	161/54	800	2:01.73	2:01.69- 15
Mnatsakanova	Tatyana	RUS	25.5.83	181/64	HJ	1.91i	1.95- 11
Moerman	Christie	CAN	5.10.86	172/62	100h	13.30,12.96w	
							13.21, 13.00w-13, 13.14A, 12.91Aw- 15
Mögenburg	Katarina	NOR	16.6.91	191/65	HJ	1.88i, 1.87	1.90- 15
Moges	Betelhem	ETH	3.5.91	157/42	Mar	2:26:11	2:24:29- 15
Moguenara	Sosthene	GER	17.10.89	182/68	LJ	7.16	7.04- 13
Moh	Clarisse	FRA	6.12.86	163/54	800	2:01.65	2:01.43- 13
Mohamed	Bezuayehu	ETH	4.1.96	160/50	3kSt	9:44.93	9:36.72- 15
Mokeyeva	Nadezhda	RUS	10.1.96		20kW	1:32:59	
Mokhnyuk	Anastasiya	UKR	1.1.91	175/67	LJ	6.66i	6.62i, 6.57- 13
Moline	Georganne	USA	6.3.90	178/59	400h	53.97	53.72- 13
Molitor	Katharina	GER	8.11.83	182/76	JT	63.20	67.69- 15

WOMEN'S INDEX 563

Name		Nat	Born	Ht/Wt	Event	2016 Mark	Pre-2016 Best
Møller	Anna Emilie	DEN-J	28.7.97	166/52	3000	8:47.83	9:10.30- 15
					3kSt	9:32.68	10:09.58- 15
Momanyi	Grace	KEN	3.3.82	170/48	Mar	2:28:28	2:32:16- 15
Montaner	Concepción	ESP	14.1.81	170/56	LJ	6.88A	6.92- 05
Montaño	Alysia	USA	23.4.86	170/61	800	2:00.20	1:57.34- 10
Montcalm	Noelle	CAN	3.4.88	166/53	400h	55.83	55.81- 14
Moraes	Fabiana	BRA	5.6.86	170/56	100h	12.91	12.98- 14
de Morais	Andressa	BRA	21.12.90	178/100	DT	59.64	64.21- 12
Morales	Celiangely	PUR	2.11.85	164/65	200	23.00	23.03A, 23.34- 15
Moreira	Sara	POR	17.10.85	168/51	HMar	70:17	69:18- 15
Morgan	Monique	JAM	14.10.85	168/60	100h	12.80	12.84- 15
Mori	Chikako	JPN	25.11.92	159/43	3kSt	9:45.27	9:58.98- 14
Morita	Kaori	JPN	19.9.95	160/44	5000	15:21.31	15:37.63- 14
Morris	Sandi	USA	8.7.92	174/65	PV	5.00	4.76- 15
Morrison	Ebony	USA	28.12.94	165/57	100h	12.76	13.06- 14
Morrison	Natasha	JAM	17.11.92	170/57	100	11.27	10.96- 15
Moser	Angelica	SUI-J	9.10.97	168/63	PV	4.57	4.41- 15
Moser	Treniere	USA	27.10.81	159/50	1500	4:07.04	4:02.85- 13
Muhammad	Dalilah	USA	7.2.90	170/62	400h	52.88	53.83- 13
Muir	Carline	CAN	1.10.87	173/65	400	51.05	51.55- 08, 51.1- 14
Muir	Jody Ann	JAM	1.1.91	165/55	400	52.08	52.00- 12
Muir	Laura	GBR	9.5.93	162/54	800	2:00.57	2:00.42- 15
	1500	3:55.22			3:58.66- 15	1M	4:19.12	
Mukasheva	Margarita	KAZ	4.1.86	165/50	800	2:00.46	1:58.96- 13
Mulhall	Kimberley	AUS	9.1.91		DT	58.53	57.24- 11
Müller	Laura	GER	11.12.95	172/57	200	22.81	23.49- 15
					400	51.69	52.33- 15
Müller	Nadine	GER	21.11.85	193/90	DT	66.84	68.89- 12
Mullina	Olga	RUS	1.8.92	166/60	PV	4.65	4.60i, 4.55- 15
Munehisa	Yuki	JPN-J	15.12.97		10000	31:58.46	
Murer	Fabiana	BRA	16.3.81	172/64	PV	4.87	4.85- 11
Murphy	Kate	USA-Y	15.8.99	163/45	1500	4:07.21	4:16.98- 15
Murphy	Nicolle	USA	19.10.94		JT	56.35	53.58- 14
Murto	Wilma	FIN-J	11.6.98	180/62	PV	4.71i, 4.52	4.45i, 4.30- 15
Muscaro	Carly	USA	18.5.95	164/54	400	51.17	51.83- 15
Mustar	Eva	SLO	30.9.96		TJ	13.78	13.32- 14
Muzaric	Valentina	CRO	23.7.92	178/86	SP	17.37	17.89i- 14, 17.52- 13
Müze	Lina	LAT	4.12.92	182/75	JT	62.09	61.97- 13
Mwangi	Ann	KEN	8.12.88	172/51	5000	15:17.43	15:05.34- 09
Myers	Tamara	BAH	27.7.93		TJ	13.60, 13.77w	13.41, 13.78Aw, 13.57w- 15
Nabeshima	Rina	JPN	16.12.93	160/46	5000	15:22.34	15:31.85- 14
Nageotte	Katie	USA	30.6.91	168/59	PV	4.63i, 4.60	4.55- 15
Nagovitsyna	Yelena	RUS	7.12.82	169/55	10000	32:14.43	32:02.99- 13
Nagy	Judith	ROU	14.9.89	171/58	Hep	5848	5973- 12
Nakaayi	Halimah	UGA	16.10.94	160/55	800	1:59.78	2:04.91- 12
Nakamura	Moeno	JPN	21.3.90	167/47	10000	31:57.92	
Nalyanya	Eglay	KEN	28.5.96	166/50	800	2:00.98A	2:05.2A- 15
Nana Djimou	Antoinette	FRA	2.8.85	174/69	Hep	6458	6576- 12
Nanyondo	Winnie	UGA	23.8.93	164/48	800	2:00.57	1:58.63- 14
Nawowuna	Alice Aprot	KEN	2.1.94	174/55	3000	8:44.7+	8:53.55- 14
	5000	14:39.56		15:16.74- 10		10000	29:53.51	31:24.18- 15
Neena	Narayanan V.	IND	2.5.91		LJ	6.66	6.39- 15
Neita	Daryll	GBR	29.8.96	172/61	100	11.23	11.40- 15
Nel	Wenda	RSA	30.7.88	169/52	400h	54.47	54.37- 15
Nelson	Ashleigh	GBR	20.2.91	175/69	100	11.19	11.19, 11.15w- 14
					200	22.96	23.25- 13, 23.22w- 14
Nelson	Ella	AUS	10.5.94	169/58	200	22.50	23.04- 15
Nelvis	Sharika	USA	10.5.90	178/64	100h	12.60	12.34- 15
Netsvetayeva	Yekaterina	BLR	26.6.89	174/64	Hep	6021	6121- 14
Nettey	Christabel	CAN	2.6.91	162/59	LJ	6.75, 6.88w	6.99- 15
Neuenschwander	Maja	SUI	13.2.80	168/55	Mar	2:27:36	2:26:49- 15
Newell	Anicka	CAN	5.8.93	176/64	PV	4.50	4.28- 15
Newman	Alysha	CAN	29.6.94	175/63	PV	4.61	4.41- 14
Neziri	Nooralotta	FIN	9.11.92	174/60	100h	12.81	12.98- 14, 12.94w- 15
Ngugi	Mercy Wacera	KEN	17.12.88	155/	HMar	66:29	67:44- 14
Ni Yuanyuan		CHN	6.4.95		20kW	1:29:53	1:31:36- 15
Nicollin	Margaux	FRA	1.5.95	185/72	JT	56.21	59.73- 15
Nidbaykina	Darya	RUS	26.12.94		TJ	13.72i, 13.64, 13.67w	13.70- 15
Nie Jingjing		CHN	1.3.88	168/45	20kW	1:29:38	1:27:51- 15
Nielsen	Lara	AUS	19.12.92	168/80	HT	66.20	66.37- 15
Nikisenko	Marina	MDA	28.6.86	185/85	HT	71.41	72.53- 15

WOMEN'S INDEX

Name		Nat	Born	Ht/Wt	Event	2016 Mark	Pre-2016 Best
Nikitsina	Aleksandra	BLR	12.9.93		TJ	13.69	13.44- 15
Nikkanen	Minna	FIN	9.4.88	169/53	PV	4.61i, 4.55	4.60i- 11, 4.60- 15
Nikolayeva	Iryna	UKR	20.1.84	170/58	TJ	13.63	13.93- 13, 13.97w- 14
Nikolenko	Svetlana	RUS	26.9.91		HJ	1.88i, 1.88	1.87- 15
Nishihara	Kasumi	JPN	1.3.89	162/47	10000	32:07.77	31:53.69- 14
Nishimwe	Beatha	RWA-J	1.12.98	159/48	1500	4:08.75	4:17.37- 15
Niyonsaba	Francine	BDI	5.5.93	161/56	800	1:56.24	1:56.59- 12
Njeru	Pauline Wanjiku	KEN	.88		HMar	69:52	69:06- 14
Nokelainen	Heidi	FIN	30.9.90	170/68	JT	62.13	59.86- 15
Norman	Breana	USA	14.9.92	174/63	100h	13.07	13.35- 14
Novozhylova	Iryna	UKR	7.1.86	175/90	HT	71.00	74.10- 12
Novy	Tera	USA	10.2.94	183/84	DT	61.10	59.12- 15
Ntshingila	Patience	RSA	26.8.89	175/65	TJ	13.90A	13.89A, 13.55- 12
Nugent	Leah	JAM	23.11.92	173/66	400h	54.45	55.63- 15
Nukuri	Diane	BDI	1.12.84	175/54	10000	31:28.69	32:29.14- 13
					HMar	69:23	69:12- 13
Numata	Michi	JPN	6.5.89	155/45	Mar	2:27:27	
Nwaba	Barbara	USA	18.1.89	175/64	HJ	1.90	1.87- 12
					Hep	6494	6500- 15
Nyabeu Djapa	Anaëlle	FRA	15.9.92	174/63	Hep	5768	5817- 14
Nyambura	Virginia	KEN	20.7.93	165/48	3kSt	9:18.95	9:13.85- 15
Nyaruai	Veronica	KEN	29.10.89	165/43	HMar	68:06	73:55- 11
Nygård	Sanna	FIN	22.3.88	176/60	TJ	13.63i	13.73- 15
Nyirarukundo	Salomé	RWA-J	20.12.97	156/42	10000	31:45.82	
Nzisa	Winfredah	KEN-J	30.5.97		1500	4:09.25	4:11.23A- 15
O'Brien	Becky	USA	30.4.90	173/86	SP	17.48	18.34i, 18.21- 15
O'Connell	Jessica	CAN	10.2.89	158/48	5000	15:07.72	15:06.44- 15
O'Connor	Leah	USA	30.8.92	171/55	3kSt	9:18.85	9:31.03- 15
O'Flaherty	Kerry	IRL	15.7.81	167/52	3kSt	9:45.35	9:42.61- 15
Obergföll	Christina	GER	22.8.81	175/78	JT	64.96	70.20- 07
Obiri	Hellen	KEN	13.12.89	155/45	1500	3:59.34	3:57.05- 14
	2000	5:40.89+	5:37.7+- 14	3000	8:24.27	8:20.68- 14	5000 14:25.78 15:49.7A- 13
Obleshchuk	Halyna	UKR	23.2.89	177/94	SP	18.13	19.40- 14
Ochichi	sabella	KEN	28.10.79	162/48	HMar	69:08	68:38- 01
Odiong	Edidiong Ofonime	BRN-J	13.3.97	168/60	200	22.74	23.56, 22.98w- 15
Oeser	Jennifer	GER	29.11.83	176/65	Hep	6401	6683- 10
Ofili	Cindy	GBR	5.8.94	172/60	100h	12.63	12.60- 15
Ogoegbunam	Amaka	NGR	3.3.90	168/60	400h	56.65	55.46- 14
Ogrodníková	Nikola	CZE	18.8.90	175/73	JT	58.18	60.04- 14
Ohara	Rei	JPN	10.8.90	165/47	HMar	70:04	69:17- 15
					Mar	2:23:20	3:05:21- 15
Ohuruogu	Christine	GBR	17.5.84	175/70	400	51.05	49.41- 13
Okada	Kumiko	JPN	17.10.91	158/47	20kW	1:29:40	1:29:46- 15
Okagbare	Blessing	NGR	9.10.88	180/68	100	11.02, 10.92w	10.79, 10.75w- 13
200	22.58			22.23- 14	LJ	6.73	7.00, 7.14w- 13
Okolo	Courtney	USA	15.3.94	168/54	200	22.79i	22.93- 15
					400	49.71	50.03- 14
Okoro	Chinwe	NGR	20.6.89	184/84	DT	61.58	59.79- 14
Okpala	Nneka	NZL	27.4.88	175/63	TJ	13.91	13.65- 15
Okparaebo	Ezinne	NOR	3.3.88	164/56	100	11.27, 11.26w	11.10- 12, 11.0- 15
Okuneva	Oksana	UKR	14.3.90	175/61	HJ	1.97	1.98- 14
Okwelogu	Nikki	NGR	5.5.95	173/100	SP	17.91	17.32- 15
Olishevska	Yuliya	UKR	2.2.89	165/58	400	51.70	51.68- 12
Oliver	Imani	USA	7.3.93	165/59	TJ	14.02	13.21- 15
Oliver	Javianne	USA	26.12.94	155/52	100	11.29, 11.16w	11.53- 15
Oliver	Lucy	NZL	18.11.88	168/63	5000	15:20.13	15:21.08- 13
Oljira	Belaynesh	ETH	26.6.90	165/49	3000	8:38.55	8:40.73- 10
5000	14:42.57			14:58.16- 10	10000	30:50.25	30:26.70- 12
Omotoso	Omolara	NGR	25.5.93	152/50	400	51.58	51.28- 12
Onishi	Misaki	JPN	24.2.85	164/46	5000	15:19.37	15:16.82- 15
Onnen	Imke	GER	17.8.94	190/66	HJ	1.87i	1.89- 15
Onofre	Marta	POR	28.1.91	171/65	PV	4.51i, 4.38	4.36- 15
Onuora	Anyika	GBR	28.10.84	175/69	400	51.47	50.87- 15
Orbán	Éva	HUN	29.11.84	173/75	HT	70.81	73.44- 13
Orel	Anna Maria	EST	11.12.96	171/70	HT	68.71	62.32- 15
Orji	Keturah	USA	5.3.96	166/61	LJ	6.62	6.63- 15
					TJ	14.71	14.15- 15
Orjuela	Arabelly	COL	24.7.88	150/43	20kW	1:32:54	1:32:48.7t- 11
Ortega	Alejandra	MEX	8.7.94	164/56	20kW	1:29:35	1:31:04- 15
Ortiz	Coralys	PUR	16.4.85	178/61	JT	60.37	58.20A- 14
Ortiz	Mirna	GUA	28.2.87	158/44	20kW	1:29:30	1:28:32- 13

WOMEN'S INDEX 565

Name		Nat	Born	Ht/Wt	Event	2016 Mark	Pre-2016 Best
Osa	Mahiro	JPN-Y	26.11.99	173/62	JT	56.48	
Osazuwa	Uhunoma	NGR	23.11.87	178/65	HJ	1.87	1.87- 15
					Hep	6153	6106- 15
Osika	Shannon	USA	15.6.93		1500	4:09.08	4:14.26- 15
					1M	4:28.45	4:39.72- 13
Oskan-Clarke	Shelayna	GBR	20.1.90	167/54	800	1:59.45	1:58.86- 15
Ostrander	Allie	USA	24.12.96	158/45	3000	8:54.27i	
					5000	15:24.74, 15:21.85i	
Ovchinnikova	Mariya	KAZ-J	19.10.98	152/34	TJ	13.60, 13.67w	13.11- 15
Owens	Bridgette	USA	14.3.92	163/52	100h	12.94	12.71- 12, 12.62w- 14
Owers	Torie	NZL/USA	6.3.94	170/80	SP	17.50	16.93- 15
Owusu-Agyapong	Flings	GHA	16.10.88	168/55	100	11.26	11.39- 13, 11.16w- 15
Ozolina/Sprudzane	Sinta	LAT	26.2.88	186/72	JT	62.78	64.38- 13
Paesler	Carolin	GER	16.12.90	167/72	HT	68.52	70.76- 14
Pagano	Sarah	USA	23.7.91	160/47	10000	32:16.03	32:45.46- 15
Palacios	Eliecit	COL	15.8.87	175/64	100	11.21A, 11.48, 11.1A	11.37A- 13, 11.40- 14
Palameika	Madara	LAT	18.6.87	185/76	JT	66.18	66.15- 14
Palkina	Sofiya	RUS-J	9.6.98		HT	65.96	59.89- 14
Palmieri	Elisa	ITA	18.9.83	169/85	HT	65.75	67.33- 11
Palmisano	Antonella	ITA	6.8.91	166/49	20kW	1:29:03	1:27:51- 14
Palsyte	Airine	LTU	13.7.92	186/62	HJ	1.97i, 1.96	1.98- 14
Panaet	Elena	ROU	5.6.93		3kSt	9:42.39	9:52.14- 15
Panagi	Nektaria	CYP	20.3.90	165/48	LJ	6.59	6.62- 15
Pandakova	Marina	RUS	1.3.89		20kW	1:27:18	1:25:03- 15
Panova	Yelena	RUS	2.3.87	185/95	DT	62.60	63.22- 15
Panturoiu	Elena	ROU	24.2.95	170/57	TJ	14.33	14.13- 15, 14.20w- 14
Papahrístou	Paraskeví	GRE	17.4.89	170/53	LJ	6.56	6.60- 12
					TJ	14.73	14.72- 11, 14.77w- 12
Papaioannou	Ramona	CYP	15.6.89	170/63	100	11.25	11.36, 11.29w- 15
Papp	Krisztina	HUN	17.12.82	170/54	10000	32:19.15	31:46.47- 10
Páppas	Alexi	GRE	28.3.90	165/49	10000	31:36.16	32:02.22- 15
Papps	Sophie	GBR	6.10.94	177/65	100	11.27	11.47- 12, 11.39wmx- 15
Paquette	Lauren	USA	27.6.86	163/45	5000	15:14.45	
Parada	Lidia	ESP	11.6.93	174/70	JT	57.34	59.03- 15
Parker	Tiffeny	USA	8.6.88	170/60	Hep	5951	5734(w)- 15
Parnov	Liz	AUS	9.5.94	164/37	PV	4.40	4.50- 12
Parnov	Vicky	AUS	24.10.90	175/62	PV	4.40	4.40- 07
Pascual	Beatriz	ESP	9.5.82	163/53	20kW	1:29:27	1:27:44- 08
Patrignelli	Megan	USA	22.6.92	163/52	3kSt	9:43.37	10:03.82- 14
Patterson	Eleanor	AUS	22.5.96	182/66	HJ	1.93	1.96- 15
Patterson	Elizabeth	USA	9.6.88	183/65	HJ	1.93i	1.95i- 09, 1.91- 10
Patterson	Liz	USA	9.6.88	183/65	HJ	1.93	
Pavey	Jo	GBR	20.9.73	163/51	5000	15:24.74	14:39.96- 06
					10000	31:33.44	30:53.20- 12
Payne	Demi	USA	30.9.91	182/65	PV	4.90i. 4.45	4.75i, 4.71- 15
Payne	Kymber	USA	4.6.96	168/54	400h	56.38	58.14- 15
Payton	Malaina	USA	16.10.91		LJ	6.53	6.44- 13, 6.56w- 12
Peake	Sally	GBR	8.2.86	164/57	PV	4.40	4.42i- 12, 4.40- 14
Pearson	Sally	AUS	19.9.86	166/60	100h	13.14, 12.92w	12.28- 11
Pease	Sarah	USA	9.11.87	166/52	3kSt	9:40.94	9:46.66- 15
Pedersen	Isabelle	NOR	27.1.92	168/54	100h	12.86	12.86- 15
Pedroso	Yadisleidy	ITA	28.1.87	168/51	400h	55.78	54.54- 13
Peinado	Robeilys	VEN-J	26.11.97	168/62	PV	4.56	4.60- 15
Peiponen	Johanna	FIN	18.12.90	162/44	10000	31:42.9	32:51.04- 15
Pejchalová	Lada	CZE-J	15.11.98		HJ	1.90	1.85- 15
Peleteiro	Ana	ESP	2.12.95	171/52	TJ	13.91i, 13.55	14.17- 12
Pen Freitas	Marta	POR	31.7.93	153/46	1500	4:06.54	4:10.98- 15
Pena	Tori	IRL	30.7.87	167/57	PV	4.52	4.60- 13
Pennella	Giulia	ITA	27.10.89	169/53	100h	13.04	13.03- 14
Penney	Jessica	AUS	21.12.87		LJ	6.60	6.54- 14
Peoples	Kearsten	USA	20.12.91	183/105	SP	17.89	18.22- 12
Pereira	Solange Andreia	ESP	12.12.89	168/49	1500	4:08.29	4:11.33- 14
Pérez	Paola	ECU	21.12.89	148/55	20kW	1:33:25	1:31:53- 15
Pérez	Yaimí	CUB	29.5.91	174/78	DT	68.86	67.13- 15
Perkovic	Sandra	CRO	21.6.90	183/80	DT	70.88	71.08- 14
Perry	Alexis	USA	8.8.94	170/57	100h	12.90, 12.87w	13.16, 13.14w- 15
					LJ	6.66	6.45- 14
Pesirídou	Elisávet	GRE	12.2.92	174/55	100h	12.93	13.27- 14
Petersen	Sara Slott	DEN	9.4.87	171/57	400h	53.55	53.99- 15
Petersson	Marinda	SWE	3.2.95	165/74	HT	69.43	65.67- 15
Petrillose	Kaitlin	USA	10.12.92	168/57	PV	4.50	4.60Ai, 4.50- 14

566 WOMEN'S INDEX

Name		Nat	Born	Ht/Wt	Event	2016 Mark	Pre-2016 Best
Petrova	Gabriela	BUL	29.6.92	167/61	TJ	14.32i, 13.92	14.66.14.85w- 15
Petty	Angela	NZL	16.8.91	164/55	800	2:00.62	1:59.06- 15
					1500	4:07.83	4:08.54- 15
Philip	Asha	GBR	25.10.90	163/54	100	11.16	11.10- 15
Pidluzhnaya	Yuliya	RUS	1.10.88	180/63	LJ	6.75i, 6.65	6.87- 15
Pierdevara	Florina	ROU	29.3.90	172/51	800	2:01.23	2:00.91- 15
Pierre	Barbara	USA	28.4.87	175/60	100	11.07, 11.01w	10.85- 13
Pierson	Summer	USA	3.9.78	180/84	DT	60.09	61.23- 15, 61.25dh- 09
Pilipenko	Anastasiya	KAZ	13.9.86	174/55	100h	12.87	12.69- 12
Pimenova	Iryna	UKR	19.12.88	172/60	TJ	13.74	13.64- 13
Pinedo	Ainhoa	ESP	17.2.83	171/60	20kW	1:32:52	1:31:58- 15
Pinto	Tatjana	GER	2.7.92	170/56	100	11.00	11.19- 12, 11.07w- 15
Pirelli	Ana Camila	PAR	10.1.89	175/70	Hep	5886A, 5748	5733- 13
Planell	Diamara	PUR	16.2.93	180/67	PV	4.50	4.35i, 4.30- 15
Pleger	Brooke	USA	21.6.92	171/77	HT	68.02	69.72- 15
Plis	Renata	POL	5.2.85	165/51	1500	4:05.40	4:03.50- 11
3000	8:50.75i		8:39.18- 14		5000	15:23.19	15:18.75- 14
Plotitsyna	Hanna	UKR	1.1.87	182/65	100h	13.02	12.93- 14, 12.91w- 13
Pluim	Femke	NED	10.5.94	180/62	PV	4.50i, 4.45	4.55- 15
Podolskaya	Anastasiya	RUS	18.8.90		SP	17.74i, 17.70	17.97i- 15, 17.71- 14
Podominick	Liz	USA	5.12.84	188/86	DT	61.67	63.87- 15
Pohrebnyak	Nataliya	UKR	19.2.88	171/62	100	11.11	11.09- 15
					200	22.64	22.75- 15
Polk	Tori	USA	21.9.83	173/62	LJ	6.68, 6.77w	6.75- 11, 6.80w- 13
Polyakova	Natalya	RUS	9.12.90		HT	68.47	70.04- 14
Poncio	Maritza Rafaela	GUA	3.12.94		20kW	1:30:52	1:33:14- 14
Ponomaryova	Mariya	RUS	18.6.95		20kW	1:26:46	1:27:17- 15
Pooley	Isobel	GBR	21.12.92	191/70	HJ	1.93i, 1.88	1.97- 15
Poonia	Krishna	IND	5.5.82	182/80	DT	59.39	64.76- 12
Poplavskaya	Yekaterina	BLR	7.5.87	172/60	100h	12.88	12.91- 12
Porter	Chanice	JAM	25.5.94	170/	HJ	1.87i	1.84- 15
					LJ	6.67	6.58- 12
Porter	Kiara	USA	22.10.93	158/52	400	52.10	51.42- 15
Porter	Tiffany	GBR	13.11.87	172/62	100h	12.70	12.51- 14, 12.47w- 12
Potter	Beth	GBR	27.12.91	168/48	3000	8:53.94mx	8:58.01mx-14, 9:15.76- 09
5000	15:28.32		15:36.49- 15		10000	32:03.45	32:33.36- 14
Pousse	Pauline	FRA	17.9.87	184/84	DT	62.68	59.93- 15
Povea	Liadagmis	CUB	6.2.96	165/61	TJ	14.56	14.08- 15
Poves	María José	ESP	16.3.78	167/52	20kW	1:31:10	1:28:15- 12
Povh	Olesya	UKR	18.10.87	169/63	100	11.21	11.08- 12, 11.0- 14
Powell	Micha	CAN	12.1.95	168/55	400	51.97	53.36- 15
Prandini	Jenna	USA	20.11.92	172/59	100	10.95, 10.81w	10.92, 10.90w- 15
					200	22.39	22.20, 22.18w- 15
Praught	Aisha	JAM	14.12.89	173/55	3kSt	9:31.75	9:34.69- 14
Preiner	Verena	AUT	1.2.95	177/64	Hep	6050	5840- 15
Pressley	Maya	USA	1.2.91	175/60	HJ	1.90	1.92- 13
Price	Candice	USA	26.10.85	170/62	100h	12.75	12.71- 08
Price	Chanelle	USA	22.8.90	166/53	800	2:00.80	1:59.10- 15
Price	Kylie	USA	1.10.93	178/64	LJ	6.54, 6.66w	6.52, 6.55w- 13
Price	DeAnna	USA	8.6.93	173/99	HT	73.09	72.30- 15
Prinsloo	Lynique	RSA	30.3.91	165/54	LJ	6.78A, 6.59	6.81- 13
Proctor	Shara	GBR	16.9.88	174/56	LJ	6.91i, 6.80	7.07- 15
Profit	Kiani	USA	18.2.90	163/55	Hep	5977	6133- 13
Prokopenko	Viktoriya	RUS	17.4.91	174/60	TJ	14.28	14.41i- 13, 14.35- 12
Prouse	Charlotte	CAN-J	9.2.97	165/50	3kSt	9:44.62	10:12.44- 15
Provalinskaya-Korolchik Yanina		BLR	26.12.76	186/87	SP	18.52	20.61- 01
Pryshchepa	Nataliya	UKR	11.9.94	163/50	800	1:58.60	2:04.47- 12
Ptácníková	Jirina	CZE	20.5.86	175/69	PV	4.66i, 4.65	4.76- 13
Ptashkina	Tetyana	UKR	10.1.93	183/63	TJ	13.68i	14.08- 15
Pudenz	Kristin	GER	9.2.93	180/92	DT	61.01	62.61- 15
Puiu	Beatrice	ROU	1.1.86		Hep	5890	5814- 13
Punia-Antil	Seema	IND	27.7.83	179/85	DT	62.62	64.84- 04
Puzakova	Anastasiya	BLR	12.12.93	161/45	3kSt	9:42.91	9:58.29- 15
Qieyang Shenjie		CHN	11.11.90	160/50	20kW	1:26:49	1:25:16- 12
Quach Thi Lan		VIE	18.10.95	173/54	400h	56.67	
Quaresma	Lecabela	POR	26.12.89	172/67	Hep	5802	5792- 15
Quick	Elizabeth	USA	14.11.94		PV	4.35i	4.14- 15
Quigley	Colleen	USA	20.11.92	173/59	3kSt	9:20.00	9:24.92- 15
Radoslav	Taysia	CAN	17.9.96	173/60	400h	56.48	57.87- 15
Radzivil	Svetlana	UZB	17.1.87	184/61	HJ	1.95	1.97- 12
Rajabi	Leyla	IRI	18.4.83	185/95	SP	17.34	18.18- 13

WOMEN'S INDEX

Name		Nat	Born	Ht/Wt	Event	2016 Mark	Pre-2016 Best
Rakocevic	Kristina	MNE-J	13.6.98	189/79	DT	58.30	53.91- 15
Ramsey	Jessica	USA	26.7.91	165/85	SP	18.28i, 17.74	18.42- 15
					HT	67.48	69.47- 15
Randall	Allison	JAM	25.5.88	180/95	DT	60.94	61.21- 12
Rani	Annu	IND	29.8.92	165/63	JT	60.01	59.53- 14
Rani	Poonam	IND	6.6.90		JT	56.73	52.73- 15
Rao Fan		CHN	1.1.96		TJ	13.61i, 13.56	13.41- 14
Rard-Reuse	Clélia	SUI	1.8.88	171/58	100h	12.87	13.19- 12
Ratcliffe	Julia	NZL	14.7.93	171/66	HT	70.75	70.28- 14
Ratej	Martina	SLO	2.11.81	178/69	JT	61.03	67.16- 10
Rath	Claudia	GER	25.4.86	175/65	LJ	6.62	6.73, 6.84w- 15
(Salman-Rath)					Hep	6310	6462- 13
Reaser	Allison	USA	9.9.92	171/61	Hep	5990	5917- 14
Rebrik	Vera	RUS	25.2.89	176/65	JT	67.30	66.86- 12
Redondo	Laura	ESP	3.7.88	165/80	HT	69.06	69.59- 13
Reedy	Julia	USA	27.1.93	178/	HT	66.81	64.41- 15
Reese	Brittney	USA	9.9.86	173/64	LJ	7.31	7.25- 13
Rehberg	Maya	GER	28.4.94	170/58	3kSt	9:39.18	9:49.88- 15
Reid	Sheila	CAN	2.8.89	166/52	1500	4:03.96	4:02.96- 13
1M	4:27.57i		4:27.02i- 13, 4:37.46- 15		3000	8:56.50i	8:44.02- 13
dos Reis	Jéssica Carolina	BRA	17.3.93	160/50	LJ	6.69	6.66- 14
Reynolds	Robin	USA	22.2.94	162/50	400	51.84	51.36- 14
Rhodes	Annie	USA	13.5.95	173/64	PV	4.45	4.38- 15
Ribalta	Yosleivis	CUB	2.5.90	183/74	TJ	13.73w	14.61- 11
Ribeiro Costa	Joana	BRA	15.8.81	174/60	PV	4.50	4.40- 07
Riddick	Monique	USA	8.11.89	168/84	SP	17.73	17.57- 15
Rigaudo	Elisa	ITA	17.6.80	168/56	20kW	1:28:03	1:27:12- 08
Rionoripo	Purity	KEN	10.6.93	165/48	HMar	70:30+	68:29- 15
					Mar	2:24:47	2:25:09- 15
Rivas	Ányela	COL	13.8.89	180/82	SP	17.29	17.53- 12
Rivera	Evelin	COL-J	8.12.97	157/54	100	11.20A	11.53- 15
Roberson	Daye Shon	USA	3.7.95	167/52	200	22.65	23.22- 15
					400	51.42	51.37- 15
Roberson	Savannah	USA	15.1.96	169/55	200	22.98w	24.61- 15
Robert-Michon	Mélina	FRA	18.7.79	180/85	DT	66.73	66.28- 13
Roberts	Kelsey-Lee	AUS	21.9.91	175/70	JT	59.02	63.92- 14
Rocha	Carla Salomé	POR	25.4.90	158/48	10000	32:05.82	32:19.98- 14
Rodrigues	Irina	POR	5.2.91	182/81	DT	63.96	63.25- 15
Rodríguez	Adriana	CUB-Y	12.7.99	172/64	Hep	5925	
Rodríguez	Déborah	URU	2.12.92	174/61	400h	56.79	56.30- 15
Rodríguez	Rosa	VEN	2.7.86	180/85	HT	72.41	73.64- 13
Rodríguez	Yorgelis	CUB	25.1.95	173/66	HJ	1.87	1.86- 15
					Hep	6481	6332- 15
Rodríguez	Zudikey	MEX	14.3.87	168/56	400h	56.42A, 56.89	
Roesler	Laura	USA	19.12.91	168/54	800	2:00.15	1:59.04- 14
Rogers	Natosha	USA	7.5.91	164/48	10000	32:06.82	31:59.21- 12
Rogers	Raevyn	USA	7.9.96	171/64	800	2:00.59	1:59.71- 15
Rojas	Yulimar	VEN	21.10.95	189/75	TJ	15.02	14.20, 14.37w- 15
Roleder	Cindy	GER	21.8.89	178/68	100h	12.62	12.59- 15
Rolland	Megan	USA	30.8.88	173/57	3kSt	9:35.31	9:53.81- 15
Rollins	Brianna	USA	18.8.91	164/55	100h	12.34	12.26- 15
Roloff	Annika	GER	10.3.91	166/54	PV	4.60	4.45Ai- 14, 4.45- 15
Romanova	Aleksandra	KAZ	26.12.90	168/58	400h	55.95	56.26- 12
Romero	Marisol	MEX	26.11.83	155/48	10000	32:13.17	31:46.43- 13
Rono	Janet	KEN	8.12.88	172/58	Mar	2:27:23	2:26:03- 14
Roos	Fanny	SWE	2.1.95	173/78	SP	17.58	17.05- 15
Rosa	Chiara	ITA	28.1.83	178/95	SP	17.90i, 17.52	19.15- 09
Rosado	Rita	MEX	17.8.90		TJ	13.60	12.90- 15
Roslova	Taisya	BLR	7.2.92		HJ	1.86	
Rosolová	Denisa	CZE	21.8.86	175/63	400h	56.36	54.24- 12
Ross	Kortney	USA	26.7.92	180/64	PV	4.43	4.15- 15
Rossit	Desirée	ITA	19.3.94	181/53	HJ	1.97	1.91i, 1.89- 15
Rotaru	Alina	ROU	5.6.93	175/54	LJ	6.67	6.75- 15
Rotich	Lydia	KEN	8.8.88	158/45	3kSt	9:23.49	9:18.03- 10
Rotich	Naomi	KEN	.94		HMar	70:28	
Rotich Chepkosgei	Pamela	KEN	.84		Mar	2:28:06	2:30:25- 15
Rowbury	Shannon	USA	19.9.84	165/52	800	1:59.97	2:00.03- 15
1500	3:57.78		3:56.29- 15		1M	4:24.39i	4:20.34- 08
3000	8:51.2+		8:29.93- 14		5000	14:38.92	14:48.68- 14
Rubie	Anneliese	AUS	22.4.92	172/56	400	51.92	51.69- 15
Ruckstuhl	Géraldine	SUI-J	24.2.98		Hep	5835	-0-

568 WOMEN'S INDEX

Name		Nat	Born	Ht/Wt	Event	2016 Mark	Pre-2016 Best
Rudakova	Vera	RUS	20.3.92	175/57	400h	54.48	55.55- 15
Rüh	Anna	GER	17.6.93	186/78	SP	17.68i, 17.20	17.08- 15
					DT	64.08	66.14- 15
Ruiz	Flor Denis	COL	24.1.91	171/67	JT	63.84A	63.80- 14
Ruiz	Úrsula	ESP	11.8.83	170/83	SP	17.31i, 17.24	17.99- 12
Rushin	Jill	USA	18.7.91	183/93	SP	17.63	17.72- 15
Russell	Alexandra	GBR	27.3.90		TJ	13.40	13.05- 15
Russell	Janeive	JAM	14.11.93	175/63	400	51.17	51.49- 14
					400h	53.96	54.64- 15
Ryan	Marshay	USA	4.2.95		TJ	13.38, 13.68w	13.60- 14
Rypakova	Olga	KAZ	30.11.84	183/62	TJ	14.74	15.25- 10
Ryzih	Lisa	GER	27.9.88	179/59	PV	4.73	4.72i- 15, 4.71- 14
Sado	Besu	ETH	12.1.96	172/56	1500	3:59.47	4:00.65- 15
Saeed	Alia Mohammed	UAE	18.5.91	164/53	3000	8:48.62i	8:48.27i- 14, 8:55.40- 15
					10000	31:10.25	31:51.86- 14
Safonova	Mariya	RUS	28.10.94		JT	57.45	53.25- 14
Safránková	Katerina	CZE	8.6.89	191/105	HT	72.47	71.16- 12
Safronova	Olga	KAZ	5.11.91	171/62	100	11.09	11.12- 12
					200	22.95	22.85- 14
Sagnia	Khaddi	SWE	20.4.94	173/63	LJ	6.74	6.78- 15
Sahalinirina	Eliane	MAD	20.3.82	155/43	3kSt	9:44.50	9:47.57- 12
Sahutoglu	Tugçe	TUR	1.5.88	180/120	HT	71.21	74.17- 12
Saina	Betsy	KEN	30.6.88	163/48	5000	14:44.67	14:39.49- 14
					10000	30:07.78	30:57.30- 14
Sainte-Luce	Camille	FRA	18.4.96	180/84	HT	65.96	62.80- 15
Saito	Marina	JPN	15.10.95	164/64	JT	58.21	57.90- 15
Saladukha	Olha	UKR	4.6.83	175/55	TJ	14.40	14.99- 12, 15.06w- 11
Salaski	Tamara	SRB	16.10.88	166/54	400	51.89	53.21- 14
Salis	Silvia	ITA	17.9.85	179/74	HT	67.32	71.93- 11
Salman	Kıvılcım	TUR	27.3.92	167/80	HT	71.08	72.55- 12
Salmela	Johanna	FIN	6.11.90	172/76	HT	65.77	65.83- 15
Salming	Bianca	SWE-J	22.11.98		Hep	5840	
Samuel	Jamile	NED	24.4.92	168/57	200	22.83	22.72- 14
Samuel	Laura	GBR	19.2.91	165/68	TJ	14.09	14.09- 14
Sananès	Deborah	FRA	26.10.95	171/52	400	51.75	52.09- 15
Sánchez	María Guadalupe	MEX	4.8.95	165/48	20kW	1:31:31	1:42:23- 15
Sánchez	Marjorie	CUB	3.10.85		TJ	13.52	12.75- 15
Sandblom	Linda	FIN	18.10.89	176/62	HJ	1.93	1.89- 13
Sanders	Shayla	USA	6.1.94	168/55	100	11.13	11.20, 11.12w- 14
					200	22.77	23.25- 14
Sandu	Cristina	ROU	4.3.90	172/58	TJ	13.94, 14.10w	13.99- 14
Santiusti	Yusneysi	ITA	24.12.84	161/48	800	2:00.04	1:58.53- 12
dos Santos	Juliana Paula	BRA	12.7.83	158/53	3kSt	9:38.63	9:55.92- 15
Santos	Rosângela	BRA	20.12.90	165/55	100	11.23	11.04, 11.01w- 15
Sapa	Tanya	USA	13.6.95		SP	16.96	15.24- 13
Sarrapio	Patricia	ESP	16.11.82	168/58	TJ	14.16A, 13.84i, 13.84	14.10- 10, 14.30w- 12
Sato	Yuka	JPN	21.7.92	161/68	JT	56.57	59.22- 12
Sauceda	Jessamyn	MEX	22.5.89	173/60	Hep	5781	5786- 15
Saunders	Raven	USA	15.5.96	166/108	SP	19.35	18.62i, 18.35- 15
					DT	56.85	51.21- 15
Saunders	Sha'Keela	USA	18.12.93	168/59	LJ	6.89	6.75- 15
Savchenko	Anastasiya	RUS	15.11.89	175/65	PV	4.40	4.73- 13
Savigne	Yargelis	CUB	13.11.84	168/59	TJ	14.09, 14.19w	15.28- 07
Sawyers	Jazmin	GBR	21.5.94	167/52	LJ	6.75, 6.86w	6.71- 15
Saxer Sibears	Mary	USA	21.6.87	169/57	PV	4.71Ai, 4.43	4.71Ai- 14, 4.70- 13
Sayers	Goldie	GBR	16.7.82	172/67	JT	58.79	66.17- 12
Saykina	Svetlana	RUS	10.7.85	177/82	DT	59.53	63.42- 08
Schäfer	Carolin	GER	5.12.91	178/66	Hep	6557	6547- 15
Scheper	Jeannelle	LCA	21.11.94	175/60	HJ	1.91	1.96- 15
Scherl	Anja	GER	12.4.86	160/48	Mar	2:27:50	2:36:31- 15
Schippers	Dafne	NED	15.6.92	179/68	100	10.83	10.81- 15
					200	21.86	21.63- 15
Schlumpf	Fabienne	SUI	17.11.90	183/62	3kSt	9:30.54	9:37.81- 14
Schneider	Rachel	USA	18.7.91	168/52	1500	4:07.84	4:06.90- 15
					1M	4:28.50i, 4:31.72	4:30.62i, 4:31.04- 15
Schönig	Fabienne	GER-J	27.7.97	170/60	JT	57.40	53.33- 14
Schwanitz	Christina	GER	24.12.85	180/103	SP	20.17	20.77- 15
Schwartz	Lindsay	USA	23.4.90	178/64	Hep	6036	5998- 15
Schwarzkopf	Lilli	GER	28.8.83	174/63	Hep	6088	6649- 12
Scott	Dominique	RSA	24.6.92	160/50	3000	8:46.65	9:02.33i- 14, 9:45.28- 09
	5000	15:25.10			15:32.55- 15		
					10000	31:51.47	32:11.60- 15

WOMEN'S INDEX

Name		Nat	Born	Ht/Wt	Event	2016 Mark	Pre-2016 Best
Sears	Ja'nia	USA	15.4.93	168/55	LJ	6.63	6.37i- 13, 6.27- 14
Seboka	Mulu	ETH	24.9.84	158/45	HMar	70:18+	69:11- 15
					Mar	2:24:24	2:21:56- 15
Seccafien	Andrea	CAN	27.8.90	152/46	5000	15:17.81	15:52.06- 14
Sedivá	Irena	CZE	19.1.92	173/70	JT	57.83	59.89- 15
Sedova	Yelena	RUS	1.3.90	170/55	10000	32:13.44	32:48.60- 13
See	Heidi	AUS	9.7.89	168/52	1500	4:08.45	4:08.15- 15
Segree	Audrea	JAM	5.10.90	160/52	100	11.30, 11.21w	11.44- 14
					200	22.89	23.34- 15, 23.15Aw- 14
Seidel	Molly	USA	12.7.94	165/47	5000	15:15.21i	15:48.31i, 15:52.41- 15
Sekine	Hanami	JPN	26.2.96	156/43	5000	15:24.74	15:37.94- 14
					10000	31:22.92	32:12.54- 15
Selvon	Kai	TTO	13.4.92	165/59	200	22.88	22.85- 12, 22.65w- 13
Semashko	Veronika	RUS	17.10.90	172/57	LJ	6.71i	6.79- 13
					TJ	13.71i	14.50- 12
Semenova	Nataliya	UKR	7.7.82	178/85	DT	62.93	64.70- 08
Semenya	Caster	RSA	7.1.91	170/64	400	50.40	52.54- 11
800	1:55.28		1:55.45- 09		1500	4:01.99	4:08.01- 09
de Sena	Érica	BRA	3.5.85	168/55	20kW	1:27:18	1:29:37- 15
Sendriute	Zinaida	LTU	20.12.84	188/89	DT	61.89	65.97- 13
Sène	Amy	SEN	6.4.85	175/80	HT	68.35	69.70- 14
Senekal	Ischke	RSA	8.1.93	175/110	DT	56.86	51.18- 15
Sergeyeva	Nadezhda	RUS	6.11.94		20kW	1:29:57	1:32:13- 15
Setterington	Nicole	CAN	18.4.95	168/57	100h	12.98	13.43- 14
Seyaum	Dawit	ETH	27.7.96	161/49	1500	3:58.09	3:59.53- 14
Seymour	Katia	USA-J	3.10.97	164/50	100	11.26A	11.86- 15
Seymour	Kiah	USA	11.1.94	178/64	400h	54.67	55.88- 14
Seymour	Pedrya	BAH	29.5.95	166/57	100h	12.64	
Shamotina	Alyona	UKR	27.12.95	178/87	HT	68.56	68.96- 15
Shargina	Olga	RUS	24.7.96		20kW	1:32:22	
Sharp	Lynsey	GBR	11.7.90	175/60	800	1:57.69	1:57.71- 15
Shatalova	Mariya	UKR	3.3.89	169/56	3kSt	9:30.89	9:36.87- 15
Shchagina	Anna	RUS	7.12.91	166/54	800	2:01.62	2:01.07- 13
1000	2:34.90				1500	4:07.74	4:01.46- 15
Shell	Mackenzie	USA-J	6.1.97		PV	4.41	4.19- 15
Sheoran	Nirmala	IND	15.7.95	166/52	400	51.48	53.94- 13
Shimizu	Miho	JPN	13.5.90	158/52	HMar	69:41	
Shimura	Hitomi	JPN	8.11.90	167/53	100h	13.10, 13.06w	13.02- 13
Shirobokova	Natalya	RUS	18.1.94		DT	60.46	58.53- 15
Shkurat	Oksana	UKR	30.7.93	170/50	100h	12.96	13.48- 14
Shone	Guteni	ETH	17.11.91	166/50	HMar	70:23	68:31- 14
Shukh	Alina	UKR-Y	12.2.99	175/60	HJ	1.92	1.78- 15
					Hep	6099	
Shulgina	Mariya	BLR	14.8.89		HJ	1.86	
Shutkova	Veronika	BLR	26.5.86	171/51	LJ	6.55	7.01- 12
Shvydkina	Tatyana	RUS	8.5.90	171/62	PV	4.35i	4.50i, 4.45- 15
Shynyzbekova	Aygerim	KAZ	1.7.92	173/63	100h	12.98	13.63- 15
Sichala	Kumeshi	ETH	.95		Mar	2:28:43	2:30:56- 15
Sidi Madane	Fadwa	MAR	20.11.94	162/50	3kSt	9:32.94	9:27.87- 15
Sidorova	Anzhelika	RUS	28.6.91	170/52	PV	4.85	4.80i, 4.79- 15
Sifuentes	Nicole	CAN	30.6.86	173/57	1500	4:03.97	4:04.65- 13
1M	4:27.93i		4:28.97i- 14, 4:31.98- 11		3000	8:46.25	8:56.80i- 12, 9:22.73- 07
Sigurdardóttir	Hafdís	ISL	12.2.87	174/64	LJ	6.62	6.56- 15, 6.72w- 14
Silhanová	Rebeka	CZE	22.3.95	174/59	PV	4.40	4.35- 14
da Silva	Karla	BRA	12.11.84	168/58	PV	4.35	4.53- 13
Silva	Laila	BRA	30.7.82	180/80	JT	61.70	60.33- 14
da Silva	Tânia	BRA	17.12.86	178/59	TJ	13.96	14.11- 07
da Silva	Tatiane Raquel	BRA	10.6.90	162/49	3kSt	9:46.86	9:56.8- 15
Silva	Yarisley	CUB	1.6.87	169/68	PV	4.84	4.91- 15
Silva #	Ana Cláudia	BRA	6.11.88	168/55	100	11.14A, 11.27	11.01, 10.96w- 15
Silvander	Anna	SWE	22.6.93	174/61	1000	2:37.78	2:42.84- 15
Simic	Ana	CRO	5.5.90	177/58	HJ	1.96	1.99- 14
Simmonds	Megan	JAM	18.3.94	159/48	100h	12.79	12.91- 15
Simpson	Jenny	USA	23.8.86	165/50	1500	3:58.19	3:57.22- 14
Sin Yong-sun		PRK	20.5.90		Mar	2:28:48	2:31:31- 15
Sinclair	Kenia	JAM	14.7.80	167/54	800	2:00.81	1:57.88- 06
Sindelar	Jamie	USA	.93		SP	16.99	16.87i- 15, 16.46- 14
Singh	Sudha	IND	25.6.86	163/52	3kSt	9:26.55	9:35.64- 14
Sinkler	April	USA	1.9.89	170/57	TJ	13.83	13.89- 13
Sipponen	Salla	FIN	13.3.95	178/73	DT	56.85	54.56- 15
Sisson	Emily	USA	12.10.91	165/47	5000	15:24.83	15:12.22i, 15:25.84- 15

WOMEN'S INDEX

Name		Nat	Born	Ht/Wt	Event	2016 Mark	Pre-2016 Best
Sivkova	Kristina	RUS-J	28.2.97	165/54	100	11.22	11.31- 14
Skoog	Sofie	SWE	7.6.90	181/65	HJ	1.94i, 1.94	1.92- 15
Skujyte	Austra	LTU	12.8.79	188/82	Hep	5985	6599- 12
Skydan	Hanna	AZE	14.5.92	183/114	HT	73.87	74.21- 12
Slattery	Sara	USA	2.10.81	173/52	10000	32:13.03	31:57.94- 06
Smets	Fanny	BEL	21.4.86	173/59	PV	4.40	4.40- 13
Smietanka	Justyna	POL	24.9.94	178/60	PV	4.40	4.20- 15
Smirnova	Yevgeniya	RUS	16.3.91		SP	16.99	17.49- 15
Smith	Amina	USA	10.1.92	175.59	HJ	1.91	1.87- 14
Smith	Bekki	AUS	25.11.86	165/46	20kW	1:29:49	1:30:24- 15
Smith	Brittany	USA	25.3.91	178/89	SP	18.94	19.01i, 18.96- 15
Smith	Courtney	USA	1.5.96	160/45	10000	32:08.32	34:53.67- 15
Smith	Megan	USA	31.3.93		SP	17.21	16.62- 15
Smith	Rochene	JAM	.95	170/57	100	11.22Aw	11.73, 11.18w- 15
Smith	Toni	USA	13.10.84		TJ	13.60, 13.67w	13.99- 08, 14.02w- 10
Snow/Goodwin	Morgan	USA	26.7.93	161/52	100h	12.86	12.78- 15
Soares	Núbia	BRA	26.3.96	176/52	TJ	14.17	14.22- 14
Soboleva	Yelena	BLR	11.5.93	180/96	HT	70.43	72.86- 15
Sogbesan	Ekundayo	USA	29.3.92	170/57	400	52.01	53.56- 12
Sokolenko	Yekaterina	RUS	13.9.92	164/50	3kSt	9:29.02	9:25.77- 15
Sokolova	Yekaterina	RUS	16.12.95		1500	4:06.96	4:09.15- 15
Sokolova	Yelena	RUS	23.7.86	170/61	LJ	6.59	7.07- 12
Solomon	Shalonda	USA	19.12.85	169/56	100	11.16, 11/05w	10.90- 10
					200	22.63, 22.58w	22.15- 11
Solovyova	Yevgeniya	RUS	28.6.86	185/90	SP	18.50	18.71i- 12, 18.03- 12
Song Jiayuan		CHN-J	15.9.97		SP	17.56	15.91- 15
Sormunen	Oona	FIN	2.8.89	165/72	JT	58.86	60.56- 13
Soto	Nercely	VEN	23.8.90	169/55	200	22.88	22.53- 12
de Souza	Tamara	BRA	8.9.93	185/76	Hep	5833	5962- 14
Souza	Tatum	USA	20.4.92	175/66	Hep	5948	5771(w)- 15
Sow	Rougui	FRA	7.6.95	170/58	LJ	6.58	6.24, 6.35w- 15
Spanovic	Ivana	SRB	10.5.90	176/65	LJ	7.10	7.02- 15
Spelmeyer	Ruth Sophia	GER	19.9.90	175/57	400	51.43	52.04- 15
Spencer	Ashley	USA	8.6.93	168/54	400	51.09	50.28- 13
					400h	53.72	56.32- 13
Spencer	Kaliese	JAM	6.5.87	175/63	400h	55.02	52.79- 11
Spencer	Levern	LCA	23.6.84	180/54	HJ	1.96	1.98- 10
Spiegelburg	Silke	GER	17.3.86	173/64	PV	4.56i, 4.50	4.82- 12
Spiler	Barbara	SLO	2.1.92	184/79	HT	68.15	71.25- 12
Spill	Tanja	GER	16.12.95	167/52	800	2:01.63	2:06.41- 15
Spínola	Vanessa	BRA	5.3.90	178/68	Hep	6188	6103- 15
Spotáková	Barbora	CZE	30.6.81	182/80	JT	66.87	72.28- 08
Sprunger	Ellen	SUI	5.8.86	172/62	200	22.89	23.26- 14
					Hep	6024	6124- 12
Sprunger	Léa	SUI	5.3.90	183/69	200	22.38	23.08- 12
					400h	54.92	55.60- 15
St.Fort	Khalifa	TTO-J	13.2.98	168/52	100	11.16	11.19A, 11.31- 15
Stafford	Gabriela	CAN	13.9.95	165/53	1500	4:06.53	4:07.44- 15
1M	4:29.07i		4:32.8- 15		3000	8:54.87i	9:13.10- 14
Stahl	Linda	GER	2.10.85	174/72	JT	65.25	67.32- 14
Stainton	Katie	GBR	8.1.95		Hep	5777(w)	5356- 14
Stanciu	Daniela	ROU	15.10.87	175/57	HJ	1.93i	1.94- 14
Stanková	Eliska	CZE	11.11.84	181/82	DT	60.48	59.34- 14
Steacy	Heather	CAN	14.4.88	175/73	HT	72.09	72.16- 12
Stef	Claudia	ROU	25.2.78	160/48	20kW	1:32:54	1:27:41- 04
Stefanídi	Ekateríni	GRE	4.2.90	172/63	PV	4.90i, 4.86	4.77Ai- 15, 4.71- 14
Stefanowicz	Monika	POL	15.5.80	163/49	Mar	2:28:26	2:29:28- 15
Steinacker	Marike	GER	4.3.92	184/80	DT	56.83	59.03- 15
Steiner Bennett	April	USA	22.4.80	175/61	PV	4.55	4.63- 08
Stellingwerff	Hilary	CAN	7.8.81	160/48	1500	4:05.61	4:05.08- 12
Stepanova	Yekaterina	RUS	24.7.94		HJ	1.88	1.86i- 12, 1.84- 15
Stepter	Jaide	USA	25.4.94	173/64	400	50.91	52.89i- 15
					400h	54.95	55.83- 15
Stetsyuk	Tatyana	RUS	27.8.92	174/62	PV	4.35i	4.40- 14
Stevens	Dani	AUS	26.5.88	182/82	DT	67.77	67.99- 14
Stevens	Deajah	USA	19.5.95	172/60	100	11.18, 11.04w	11.53- 15
					200	22.25	23.18- 15
Stevens	Jeneva	USA	28.10.89	178/102	SP	19.11	19.10i- 12, 18.84- 15
					HT	71.10	74.77- 13
Stewart	Chastity	USA	2.5.93	175/61	100h	13.03	13.39- 13

Name		Nat	Born	Ht/Wt	Event	2016 Mark	Pre-2016 Best
Stewart	Kerron	JAM	16.4.84	175/61	100	11.19	10.75- 09
					200	22.99, 22.69w	21.99- 08
Stiverne	Aiyanna	CAN	20.2.95	168/55	400	52.08	52.43- 15
Stolz	Xenia	GER	14.1.89	174/58	LJ	6.63i, 6.56	6.74- 15
Storey	Lora	AUS	19.10.89	170/54	800	2:01.67	2:05.84- 15
Storm	Ida	SWE	26.12.91	189/90	HT	66.91	69.13- 14
Stowers	Jasmin	USA	23.9.91	175/64	100h	12.55	12.35- 15
Strachan	Anthonique	BAH	22.8.93	168/57	200	22.96	22.32- 13
Strati	Laura	ITA	3.10.90	171/58	LJ	6.59	6.37, 6.43w- 15
Stratton	Brooke	AUS	12.7.93	168/58	LJ	7.05	6.73- 15
Stratulat	Natalia	MDA	24.7.87	178/82	DT	61.85	62.13- 12
Strokova	Yekaterina	RUS	17.12.89	184/80	DT	65.26	65.78- 14
Strumillo	Stefania	ITA	14.10.89	182/81	DT	59.80	58.22- 15
Strutz	Martina	GER	4.11.81	160/53	PV	4.70	4.80- 11
Stuart	Bianca	BAH	17.5.88	168/52	LJ	6.52, 6.76w	6.83- 15, 6.91w- 11
Stuart	Lauren	CAN	16.11.91	168/79	HT	66.85	67.56- 15
Stumbaugh	Payton	USA	29.11.95	194/73	100h	12.83	13.74- 15
					Hep	5985(w)	5422- 15
Stuy	Hrystyna	UKR	3.2.88	168/60	100	11.24	11.24- 14
Su Lingdan		CHN-J	12.1.97		JT	57.32	53.13- 14
Su Xinyue		CHN	8.11.91	179/70	DT	65.59	64.27- 15
Suhr	Jenn	USA	5.2.82	180/64	PV	5.03i, 4.82	5.02Ai- 13, 4.92- 08
Sujew	Diana	GER	2.11.90	166/52	1500	4:07.40	4:05.62- 13
Sum	Eunice	KEN	2.9.88	172/53	800	1:57.47	1:56.99- 15
Sumgong	Jemima Jelagat	KEN	21.12.84	158/45	HMar	66:58	68:32- 14
					Mar	2:22:58	2:20:41- 14
Summers	Jeré	USA	21.5.87	172/84	DT	58.25	59.59- 12
Sun Huanhuan		CHN	15.3.90	161/50	20kW	1:33:33	1:27:36- 13
Sunang	Marestella	PHI	20.2.81	164/53	LJ	6.72	6.71- 11
Sussmann	Jana	GER	12.10.90	166/47	3kSt	9:41.05	9:43.28- 11
Sutej	Tina	SLO	7.11.88	173/58	PV	4.56	4.71i- 14, 4.61- 11
Sutherland	Sara	USA	31.1.92	175/66	1500	4:06.43	4:11.06- 15
Suttie	Taryn	CAN	7.12.90	182/95	SP	17.88	17.61- 15
Suzuki	Ayuko	JPN	8.10.91	154/38	5000	15:24.47	15:08.29- 15
					10000	31:18.16	31:48.18- 15
Sviridova ¶	Olesya	RUS	28.10.89	176/94	SP	17.87i, 17.73, 18.66 dq	19.72- 12
Swiety	Justyna	POL	3.12.92	170/56	400	51.62	52.13i- 14, 52.22- 13
Swoboda	Ewa	POL-J	26.7.97	164/55	100	11.12, 11.10w	11.24. 11.21w- 15
Szabó	Barbara	HUN	17.2.90	175/59	HJ	1.90	1.94- 15
Szilágyi	Réka	HUN	19.1.96		JT	59.39	55.91- 15
Szwarnóg	Agnieszka	POL	28.12.86	167/59	20kW	1:30:50	1:30:56- 12
Ta Lou	Marie Josée	CIV	18.11.88	159/57	100	10.86	11.02, 10.95w- 15
					200	22.21	22.56- 15
Tabacková	Nikol	CZE-J	24.1.98		JT	56.19	52.80- 15
Tadesse	Feyse	ETH	19.11.88	167/53	Mar	2:25:03	2:20:27- 14
Takacs	Julia	ESP	29.6.89	171/53	20kW	1:29:47	1:28:44- 13
Takamizawa	Anju	JPN	6.3.96	165/51	3kSt	9:44.22	9:53.72- 15
Takashima	Yuka	JPN	12.5.88	153/40	10000	31:35.76	31:37.32- 15
Takechi	Shiho	JPN	18.8.90	159/44	10000	32:20.94	32:26.38- 15
					Mar	2:25:29	2:31:18- 15
Takenaka	Risa	JPN	6.1.90	159/41	HMar	70:27+	70:10- 14
Takigawa	Hiroko	JPN	25.7.94	155/55	JT	56.79	54.94- 13
Talay	Alina	BLR	14.5.89	164/54	100h	12.63	12.66- 15
Tallent	Claire	AUS	7.6.81	163/50	20kW	1:33:23	1:28:53- 12
Tallent	Rachel	AUS	20.2.93	167/54	20kW	1:31:33	1:34:16- 15
Tan Jian		CHN	20.1.88	179/80	DT	57.47	64.45- 12
Tanaka	Tomomi	JPN	25.1.88	154/40	Mar	2:23:19	2:26:05- 14
Tanimoto	Mizuki	JPN	18.12.94	151/40	10000	32:18.44	34:05.26- 15
Tanui	Norah	KEN	2.10.95	157/45	3kSt	9:25.07	9:45.1A- 11
Tanui	Angela	KEN	27.7.92	155/42	HMar	67:16	68:41- 15
Tarasova	Irina	RUS	15.4.87	183/110	SP	18.78	19.35- 12
Tarasova	Natalya	RUS	7.5.92		20kW	1:32:39	1:30:19- 13
Tarasyuk	Anna	BLR-J	30.10.97		JT	56.40	52.62- 14
Tarmoh	Jeneba	USA	27.9.89	167/59	100	11.29, 11.26w	10.93- 15
					200	22.81	22.23- 15, 22.06w- 14
Tate	Cassandra	USA	11.9.90	174/64	400h	54.47	54.01- 15
Tavares	Maria Eleonor	POR	24.9.85	164/55	PV	4.50	4.50- 11
Tavernier	Alexandra	FRA	13.12.93	170/82	HT	72.16	74.39- 15
Taylor	Jessica	GBR	27.6.88	172/63	Hep	5913(w)	5826- 14
Taylor	Kellyn	USA	22.7.86	167/52	5000	15:22.10	15:21.93- 14
					10000	31:40.70	32:29.88- 15

WOMEN'S INDEX

Name		Nat	Born	Ht/Wt	Event	2016 Mark	Pre-2016 Best
Tebo	Jessica	USA	8.4.88	162/48	5000	15:21.88	15:18.17- 14
Teferi	Senbere	ETH	3.5.95	159/45	3000	8:45.1+	8:34.32- 15
5000	14:29.82		14:36.44- 15		10000	30:40.59	
Tejeda	Gladys	PER	30.9.85	162/46	HMar	70:14	71:24- 14
Telushkina	Mariya	KAZ	3.4.94	178/90	DT	61.20	53.45- 15
Tenorio	Ángela	ECU	27.1.96	167/59	100	11.13	10.99- 15
					200	22.94	22.84A, 22.86, 22.59w- 15
Terlecki	Josephine	GER	17.2.86	182/78	SP	17.41	18.87- 12
Terzic	Amela	SRB	2.1.93	169/51	800	2:00.99	1:59.90- 15
					1500	4:05.53	4:04.77- 15
Tesfay	Fotyen	ETH-J	17.2.98	160/40	3000	8:47.46	
Tesfay	Haftamnesh	ETH	28.4.94	162/48	3000	8:40.80	8:55.19- 15
					5000	15:10.85	15:20.52- 15
Theisen-Eaton	Brianne	CAN	18.12.88	180/64	100h	12.93	12.98- 15
LJ	6.56		6.72- 15		Hep	6765	6808- 15
Thiam	Nafissatou	BEL	19.8.94	184/69	HJ	1.98	1.97- 14
LJ	6.58		6.43- 15		Hep	6810	6508- 14
Thipe	Tsholofelo	RSA	9.12.86	153/55	400	51.96A	51.15- 09
Thomas	Charlene	GBR	6.5.82	166/52	1500	4:05.98	4:03.74- 13
Thomas	Danniel	JAM	11.11.92	166/89	SP	17.60	17.76- 15
					DT	57.93	59.38- 14
Thomas	Gabrielle	USA	7.12.96	170/57	200	22.47, 22.37w	
Thomas	Maureen	KEN-J	29.12.97	163/52	400	52.09	52.73A- 15
Thomas	Reyare	TTO	23.11.87	168/60	100	11.22	11.22- 15, 11.16w- 14
					200	22.72	22.82- 15, 22.57w- 14
Thomas	Shanieka	JAM	2.2.92	182/84	TJ	14.57	14.23A- 15, 14.15- 13
Thompson	Brenessa	GUY	22.7.96	163/52	100	11.14	11.60, 11.34w- 14
					200	22.99	23.91- 14
Thompson	Elaine	JAM	28.6.92	169/57	100	10.70	10.84- 15
					200	21.78	21.66- 15
Thompson	Turquoise	USA	31.7.91	178/66	400h	55.22	54.99- 13
Thornton	Jess	AUS-J	12.4.98	170/59	400	52.05	52.50- 14
Thornton	Sarah	USA	29.8.86	174/79	DT	57.93	56.55- 15
Thweatt	Laura	USA	17.12.88	168/52	5000	15:26.28	15:04.98- 14
					10000	31:52.94	32:15.51- 13
Tikhonova	Olesya	RUS	28.1.90		TJ	13.89i,13.61,13.92w	13.98- 15,14.11w- 14
Tilahun	Yenenesh	ETH	.94		10000	32:17.38	
Tima	Ana José	DOM	10.10.89	168/56	TJ	14.22	14.03A, 13.80, 14.21Aw- 15
Timmers	Zoe	AUS	25.5.89	176/56	HJ	1.87	1.87- 09
Tirop	Agnes	KEN	23.10.95	159/44	3000	8:46.38	8:39.13- 13
					5000	15:02.67	14:50.36- 13
Titimets	Anna	UKR	5.3.89	173/62	400h	55.00	54.56- 14
Tkachuk	Anastasiya	UKR	20.4.93	168/57	800	2:01.22	2:00.21- 15
					1000	2:37.48	2:40.97- 10
Tkachuk	Viktoriya	UKR	8.11.94	178/69	400h	55.32	56.25- 15
Tkhakur	Santa	RUS	23.4.93	160/50	800	2:01.21	2:06.49- 15
					1000	2:36.89	
Todd	Jasmine	USA	23.12.93	165/55	100	11.20	10.92, 10.86w- 15
Tollesa	Gulume	ETH	11.9.92	155/42	HMar	68:40	69:28- 14
					Mar	2:26:14	2:23:12- 15
Toma	Carmen	ROU	28.3.89	168/50	TJ	13.94i	14.29- 09, 14.56w- 13
Tomasevic	Dragana	SRB	4.6.82	175/80	DT	60.51	63.63- 06
Torr	Veronica	NZL	17.5.87	175/61	Hep	6051	5837- 12
Townsend	Tiffany	USA	14.6.89	163/50	100	11.11, 11.03w	11.08- 15
					200	22.63, 22.38w	22.26- 13
Tracey	Adelle	GBR	27.5.93	164/54	800	2:00.04	2:01.10- 15
Tracey	Nikita	JAM	18.9.90	173/63	400h	56.21	55.18- 14
Tracey	Ristananna	JAM	9.5.92	173/68	400h	54.15	54.52- 13
Tran Hue Hoa		VIE	8.8.91	170/55	TJ	13.63	14.12- 13
Trapletti	Valentina	ITA	12.7.85	172/56	20kW	1:31:28	1:31:44- 15
Treacy	Sara	IRL	22.6.89	168/59	3kSt	9:39.41	9:44.14- 15
Treasure	Alyx	CAN	15.5.92	181/	HJ	1.94	1.89- 15
Treviño	Ivonne	MEX	8.3.89	170/65	LJ	6.70	6.30- 11
Troest	Stina	DEN	17.1.94	169/57	400h	56.00	55.56- 15
Trost	Alessia	ITA	8.3.93	188/68	HJ	1.95i, 1.94	2.00i, 1.98- 13
Trotter	Deedee	USA	8.12.82	178/60	400	51.75	49.64- 07
Trybanska-Stronska	Malgorzata	POL	21.6.81	177/59	TJ	13.80	14.44- 10
Tsareva	Yelizaveta	RUS	15.3.93	177/82	HT	69.73	71.35- 15
Tsegay	Gudaf	ETH-J	23.1.97	163/50	800	1:59.77	
1500	4:00.18		4:02.83- 14		1M	4:24.98i	4:26.84i- 15

Name		Nat	Born	Ht/Wt	Event	2016 Mark	Pre-2016 Best
Tsegaye	Tirfi	ETH	25.11.84	165/54	HMar	70:17+	67:42- 12
					Mar	2:19:41	2:20:18- 14
Tsviliy	Alina	UKR	18.9.94	155/43	20kW	1:33:05	1:38:48- 15
Tsyhotska	Ruslana	UKR	23.3.86	165/56	TJ	14.41	14.53- 12
Tufa	Mestawat	ETH	14.9.83	157/45	HMar	70:17+	68:48- 10
					Mar	2:26:34	2:26:20- 13
Tufa	Tigist	ETH	26.1.87	155/40	Mar	2:23:03	2:21:52- 14
Tugsuz	Eda	TUR-J	1.3.97	172/70	JT	58.95	56.52- 15
Tully	Nicole	USA	30.10.86	156/45	5000	15:04.08	15:05.58- 15
Tusa	Rahma	ETH	.93		Mar	2:28:49	2:33:57- 15
Twell	Stephanie	GBR	17.8.89	168/54	1500	4:06.20	4:02.54- 10
	3000	8:40.98	8:42.75mx- 10, 8:50.89- 08		5000	14:59.00	14:54.08- 10
Twiss	Erica	USA	17.6.92	169/57	400h	56.50	57.19- 15
Tyminska	Karolina	POL	4.10.84	176/64	Hep	6075	6544- 11
Uceny	Morgan	USA	10.3.85	168/57	1500	4:03.94	4:00.06- 11
					1M	4:27.99i, 4:33.72	4:29.39i- 15, 4:29.61- 14
Uehara	Miyuki	JPN	22.11.95	154/39	5000	15:23.41	15:21.40- 15
					10000	31:38.80	32:16.66- 15
Ugen	Lorraine	GBR	22.8.91	178/64	LJ	6.93i, 6.80, 6.82w	6.92, 6.96w- 15
Uloga	Svetlana	RUS	23.11.86	162/55	800	1:59.88	2:01.35- 14
					1000	2:37.53	2:40.00- 15
Umehara	Satsuki	JPN	22.5.94	157/46	400h	56.79	
Urbaniak	Lena	GER	31.10.92	175/95	SP	18.32i, 18.02	18.00- 15
Urbanik	Danuta	POL	24.12.89	167/58	1000	2:38.00	2:38.71- 13
					1500	4:06.58	4:07.95- 14
Urrutia	Yosiri	COL	26.6.86	175/61	TJ	14.08A, 13.95	14.58- 14
Utriainen	Sanni	FIN	5.2.91	170/64	JT	59.41	63.03- 15
Utura	Sule	ETH	8.2.90	169/50	10000	32:08.02	30:55.50- 13
Uusimäki	Hilla	FIN	12.6.96	174/54	400h	56.33	58.55- 14
Vallet	Marine	FRA	9.9.93	174/54	HJ	1.88	1.83- 14
Van Accom	Sofie	BEL	7.6.89		1500	4:07.30	4:10.45- 14
van Dyk	Jo-Ané	RSA-J	3.10.97		JT	57.32	51.59- 15
Van Hessche	Hanne	BEL	5.7.91	180/60	HJ	1.87i, 1.85	1.88i- 13, 1.87- 09
van Leuveren	Nicky	NED	25.5.90	165/55	400	52.02	52.04- 15
van Schagen	Tessa	NED	2.2.94	168/64	200	22.86	23.36- 14, 23.35w- 15
VanBuren	Cleo	USA	1.5.86	175/60	100	11.47, 11.24w	11.10- 06
Vargas	Nedian	VEN	5.9.94	160/48	100	11.42, 11.0A	11.43A- 14, 11.33w- 15
Varner	Rachel	USA	20.7.83	176/82	DT	60.57	59.06- 14
Vasilíou	Iríni	GRE	18.3.90	168/57	400	52.12	53.50- 15
Vasilyeva	Svetlana	RUS	24.7.92		20kW	1:27:58	1:25:04- 15
Vaskovskaya	Irina	BLR	2.4.91	179/65	TJ	14.23i, 14.19	13.91- 15
Vastenburg	Jip	NED	21.3.94	181/59	10000	32:04.00	31:35.48- 15
Vaughan	Shelbi	USA	24.8.94	183/127	DT	60.73	64.52- 15
Vázquez	Rosalía	CUB	11.10.95	175/75	DT	59.45	57.39- 15
Veale	Marie	USA	17.11.94	178/61	200	22.98	23.29- 15
Veiga	Evelise	POR	3.3.96		TJ	13.41	12.83- 15
Veitía	Lisneidy	CUB	29.4.94	169/57	400	52.06	51.72A- 14, 52.25- 15
					800	1:58.93	
Velazco	Davisleidis L.	CUB-Y	4.9.99	170/60	TJ	14.08	13.23- 15
Veldáková	Dana	SVK	3.6.81	182/68	TJ	14.11	14.51- 08, 14.59w- 10
Veldáková	Jana	SVK	3.6.81	177/59	LJ	6.75	6.72- 08, 6.88w- 10
Velmyakina	Olga	RUS	3.8.92		TJ	13.65	13.21- 14
Velvere	Liga	LAT	10.2.90	171/59	400h	56.85	56.77- 15
Venâncio	Kauiza	BRA	11.6.87	164/58	200	22.93	23.29- 14
Verstegen	Sanne	NED	10.11.85	168/53	800	1:59.29	2:00.55- 14
Vessey	Maggie	USA	23.12.81	170/58	800	2:00.82	1:57.84- 09
Vetter	Anouk	NED	4.2.93	177/62	Hep	6626	6458- 15
Viart	Saily	CUB	10.9.95	169/97	SP	17.94	17.50- 15
Vidts	Noor	BEL	30.5.96		Hep	5851	5652- 15
Viljoen	Sunette	RSA	6.1.83	170/73	JT	65.14	69.35- 12
Virbalyte-Dimsiene	Brigita	LTU	1.2.85	165/50	20kW	1:30:48	1:30:20- 15
Visser	Nadine	NED	9.2.95	175/63	100h	12.89	12.81- 15
					Hep	6190	6467- 15
Vita	Claudine	GER	19.9.96	177/66	SP	17.90	17.13- 15
					DT	62.77	62.31- 15
Viuf	Katy	USA	23.5.87	175/61	PV	4.51i, 4.40	4.50- 12
Vlasic	Blanka	CRO	8.11.83	192/75	HJ	1.97	2.08- 09
Vlasova	Natalya	RUS	19.7.88	164/48	3kSt	9:31.95	9:34.16- 14
Voronina	Yekaterina	UZB	16.2.92	175/65	Hep	5849	5912- 14
Vovk	Olga	RUS	13.2.93		3kSt	9:33.70	9:52.85- 15
Vucenovic	Marija	SRB	3.4.93	172/70	JT	57.81	57.12- 12

574 WOMEN'S INDEX

Name		Nat	Born	Ht/Wt	Event	2016 Mark	Pre-2016 Best
Vukovic	Marija	MNE	21.1.92	194/69	HJ	1.95	1.91- 10
Vyatkina	Natalya	BLR	10.2.87	176/50	TJ	14.22	14.40- 13
Wairimu	Susan	KEN	11.10.92	160/40	5000	15:25.95	15:20.49- 13
Waite	Lennie	GBR	4.5.86	172/59	3kSt	9:35.91	9:40.39- 15
Waithera	Mariam	KEN	23.12.96	169/49	5000	15:20.94	15:32.53- 15
Walker	Sonikqua	JAM	24.9.94	173/61	400	51.93	51.53- 15
Wallace	Sasha	USA	21.9.95	175/64	100h	12.95, 12.81w	13.00- 15
Wallader	Rachel	GBR	1.9.89	180/87	SP	17.53	17.42- 15
Wambui	Margaret	KEN	15.9.95	171/57	400	51.39A, 51.97	
					800	1:56.89	2:00.49- 14
Wang Chunyu		CHN	17.1.95	175/55	800	1:59.93	2:01.34- 11
Wang Huan		CHN	21.9.94	168/54	400h	56.44	57.16- 14
Wang Na		CHN	29.5.95		20kW	1:28:21	1:30:19- 15
Wang Wupin		CHN	18.1.91		TJ	13.91i, 13.73	14.10- 15
Wang Yang		CHN	14.2.89	185/65	HJ	1.88i, 1.88	1.92- 12
Wang Yingliu		CHN	1.3.92		20kW	1:30:51	1:30:20- 15
Wang Zheng		CHN	14.12.87	175/105	HT	74.50	77.68- 14
Wanjiru	Grace Njue	KEN	10.1.79	1564/45	20kW	1:30:43	1:35:05- 13
Wanjiru	Maryanne	KEN	.86		HMar	70:13	71:11- 13
Wanjiru	Rosemary	KEN	9.12.94	159/44	5000	15:15.14	15:15.42- 15
Wanjugu	Felista	KEN	18.2.90	160/44	5000	15:19.47	15:02.28- 08
10000	32:04.11		34:07.90- 15		HMar	70:02	69:36- 13
Ward	Abby	GBR-Y	19.4.99	185/	HJ	1.89i, 1.86	1.80i- 15, 1.78- 14
Warner	Heavin	USA	4.3.93	180/86	HT	69.33	67.24- 15
Warren	McKenzie	USA	3.12.93		SP	17.26	15.52i- 12, 15.30- 15
Washington	Ariana	USA	4.9.96	175/59	100	11.01, 10.95w	11.22- 14, 11.18Aw- 13
					200	22.21	22.96- 14
Watanabe	Akane	JPN	13.8.91	173/75	HT	66.79	64.92- 15
Watson	Sage	CAN	20.6.94	175/62	400	52.01	52.68A- 13, 52.97- 15
					400h	54.82	55.97- 15
Weeks	Lexi	USA	20.11.96	167/60	PV	4.70	4.46irr, 4.35i, 4.32- 15
Weeks	Tori	USA	20.11.96		PV	4.40i, 4.40	4.37i, 4.29A- 15
Wei Yongli		CHN	11.10.91	166/54	100	11.24	11.27- 15
Weightman	Laura	GBR	1.7.91	172/58	1500	4:02.66	4:00.17- 14
Weightman	Lisa	AUS	16.1.79	157/44	Mar	2:27:35	2:26:05- 13
Weir	Jillian	CAN	9.2.93	177/78	HT	69.65	67.43- 14
Welling	Tara	USA	14.6.89	162/45	10000	32:02.80	32:09.15- 12
					HMar	70:25	
Wellings	Eloise	AUS	9.11.82	167/44	5000	15:01.59	14:54.11- 06
10000	31:14.94		31:41.31- 11		HMar	69:29	69:56- 15
Wells	Lauren	AUS	3.8.88	179/86	400h	55.23	55.08- 13
Wells	Sarah	CAN	10.11.89	163/56	400h	56.45	55.65- 13
Weng Chunxia		CHN	29.8.92		DT	61.01	62.20- 15
Werner	Elienor	SWE-J	5.5.98	174/56	PV	4.35i	4.26A- 15
Wertman	Cassie	USA	14.6.93		SP	17.68i, 17.20	17.26- 14
Wessman	Anna	SWE	9.10.89	164/70	JT	61.42	58.34- 15
Wester	Alexandra	GER	21.3.94	173/59	LJ	6.95i, 6.79, 7.00w	6.59- 15
White	Mandy	USA	23.10.88	170/60	100	11.28, 11.11w	11.07- 13
White	Shelbi	USA	3.7.96	173/59	100	11.21	11.45- 15
Whitehorn	Kaitlin	USA	16.8.94		HJ	1.89	1.79- 15
Whitney	Kaylin	USA-J	9.3.98	167/57	100	11.17, 11.15w	11.10- 14, 11.01w- 15
					200	22.84	22.47- 15
Whittle	Laura	GBR	27.6.85	169/55	3000	8:51.48	8:50.37- 09
					5000	15:08.58	15:20.92- 14
Whyte	Angela	CAN	22.5.80	170/56	100h	12.85, 12.81w	12.63- 07, 12.52w- 13
Whyte	Rhonda	JAM	6.11.90	170/55	400h	55.58	56.72- 15
Williams	Alisha	USA	5.2.82	167/52	5000	15:23.11	15:09.73- 15
Williams	Chrishuna	USA	31.3.93	161/54	400	52.13	52.43- 14
					800	1:59.59	2:01.61- 15
Williams	Christania	JAM	17.10.94	165/63	100	10.96	11.11- 15
Williams	Danielle	JAM	14.9.92	168/59	100h	12.77, 12.55w	12.57- 15
Williams	Jodie	GBR	28.9.93	174/65	200	22.69	22.46- 14
Williams	Kendell	USA	14.6.95	173/64	100h	12.83	12.87- 14
HJ	1.87i		1.88Ai, 1.83- 14		Hep	6402	6223- 15
Williams	Kimberly	JAM	3.11.88	169/66	TJ	14.56, 14.66w	14.62, 14.78w- 13
Williams	Lauren Rain	USA-Y	25.7.99	170/57	100	11.39, 11.17w	11.37- 15
					200	22.80, 22.44w	22.90A, 23.16, 22.68w- 15
Williams	Sada	BAR-J	1.12.97	178/63	200	22.61	23.43- 14
					400	52.07	52.39- 15
Williams	Shermaine	JAM	4.2.90	174/62	100h	12.86	12.78, 12.65w- 12
Williams	Tiffany	USA	5.2.83	158/57	400h	56.06	53.28- 07

Name		Nat	Born	Ht/Wt	Event	2016 Mark	Pre-2016 Best
Williams-Mills	Novlene	JAM	26.4.82	170/57	400	50.64	49.63- 06
Williamson	Kimberly	JAM	2.10.93	168/57	HJ	1.88	1.90- 15
Wilson	Ajee'	USA	8.5.94	169/55	800	1:59.44	1:57.67- 14
Wilson	Alyssa	USA-Y	20.2.99		SP	17.00i, 17.99	16.58i, 15.20- 15
Wilson	Nickiesha	JAM	28.7.86	174/66	100h	12.89	12.79- 09, 12.63w- 08
Wimbley	Shakima	USA	23.4.95	178/61	200	22.56	22.43- 15
					400	50.90	50.84- 15
Winger	Kara	USA	10.4.86	183/86	JT	61.86	66.67- 10
Winters	Dani	USA	18.2.93	182/91	SP	17.97i, 17.39	17.75- 15
Wisniewska	Joanna	POL	24.5.72	178/84	DT	60.31	63.97- 99
Witek	Marcelina	POL	2.6.95	168/58	JT	61.48	61.24- 14
Withrow	Melinda	USA	30.10.84	165/52	PV	4.55Ai, 4.50	4.60- 15
Wlodarczyk	Anita	POL	8.8.85	178/94	HT	82.98	81.08- 15
Wodaj	Etaferahu	ETH	.89		HMar	70:35+	71:22- 15
Wodak	Natasha	CAN	17.12.81	160/45	10000	31:53.14	31:41.59- 15
Woitha	Charlene	GER	21.8.93	178/77	HT	70.98	68.05- 15
Woodall	Kenya	USA	17.7.94	169/60	400	51.83	51.78- 15
Woodard	Jessica	USA	4.2.95	178/	SP	17.88	15.75i, 15.51- 15
Woodward	Krista	CAN	22.11.84	163/59	JT	58.31	60.15- 13
Wright	Phoebe	USA	30.8.88	170/57	800	2:01.03	1:58.22- 10
Wu Shuijiao		CHN	19.6.91	161/53	100h	13.02	12.72- 14
Wyciszkiewicz	Patrycja	POL	8.1.94	169/50	400	52.02	51.31- 15
Xie Lijuan		CHN	14.5.93		20kW	1:32:19	1:29:14- 15
Xie Yuchen		CHN	12.5.96	179/79	DT	58.30	57.08- 15
Xu Xiaoling		CHN	13.5.92		LJ	6.66i	6.63- 12
Yada	Mikuni	JPN-Y	29.10.99		5000	15:25.87	
Yakoltsevich	Irina	BLR	26.1.93	165/55	PV	4.51	4.25- 15
Yalew	Genet	ETH	31.12.92	156/42	3000	8:49.6+	9:01.75- 10
	5000 14:51.04 14:48.43- 12				10000	30:37.38 31:08.82- 15	HMar 66:26 68:12- 15
Yamasaki	Yuki	JPN	6.6.95	165/57	Hep	5751	5173- 15
Yan Ni		CHN	7.2.93	176/62	HT	68.56	66.25- 15
Yang Fei		CHN	20.7.87	186/90	DT	58.43	60.43- 12
Yang Jiayu		CHN	18.2.96		20kW	1:28:12	1:36:50- 15
Yang Lei		CHN	29.11.95		20kW	1:32:57	1:35:43- 13
Yang Mingxia		CHN	13.1.90	163/44	20kW	1:31:18	1:28:56- 08
Yang Xinli		CHN	7.2.88		JT	58.98	61.92- 15
Yang Yanbo		CHN	9.3.90		DT	61.37	63.32- 12
Yanovska	Olena	UKR	15.2.90	171/61	100h	13.00	13.32- 11
Yarigo	Noélie	BEN	26.12.85	167/56	800	1:59.12	2:00.51- 14
Yaryshkina	Aleksandra	RUS	10.6.94		HJ	1.88i, 1.84	1.88- 13
Yator	Gladys	KEN	8.8.92		HMar	68:39	70:46- 15
Yatsevich	Anastasiya	BLR	18.1.85	158/48	20kW	1:31:53	1:29:30- 11
Yermachenkova	Tatyana	RUS-J	9.9.98			1.87i	
Yevdokimova	Natalya	RUS	7.9.93		TJ	13.86	13.88- 15
Yokoe	Risa	JPN	12.10.94	164/40	5000	15:18.11	15:33.77- 15
Yüksel	Burcu	TUR	3.5.90	182/58	HJ	1.87i, 1.86	1.94- 11
Zabara	Olesya	RUS	6.10.82	165/56	TJ	13.91	14.54i- 08, 14.50- 06
Zabawska	Daria	POL	16.4.95	185/92	DT	58.05	60.23- 15
Zagré	Anne	BEL	13.3.90	176/69	100h	12.78	12.71- 15
Zakharutkina	Mariya	RUS	14.8.96		PV	4.35	4.20i, 4.10- 15
Zaldívar	Liuba M.	CUB	5.4.93		TJ	14.51A, 13.92, 14.03w	14.20- 13
Zamzow	Ashtin	USA	13.8.96		Hep	5829	5482- 15
Zapounídou	Déspina	GRE	5.10.85	166/55	20kW	1:29:35	1:31:08- 12
Zelinka	Jessica	CAN	3.9.81	172/62	Hep	5944	6599A, 6480- 12
Zeltner	Michelle	SUI	22.12.91	184/72	Hep	6010	5824- 15
Zemlyak	Olha	UKR	16.1.90	165/55	400	50.75	51.00- 14
Zhang Li		CHN	17.1.89	174/65	JT	61.56	65.47- 14
Zhang Wenxiu		CHN	22.3.86	182/108	HT	76.75	77.33- 14
Zhang Xinyan		CHN	9.2.94	170/55	3kSt	9:28.54	9:46.82- 15
Zhao Jing		CHN	9.7.88	168/55	1500	4:09.28	4:10.67- 11
Zheng Xingjuan		CHN	20.3.89	184/60	HJ	1.90	1.96- 14
Zhu Dandan		CHN	1.3.94		JT	59.19	57.56- 15
Zolotuhina	Nataliya	UKR	4.1.85	180/79	HT	71.06	72.22- 11
Zongo-Filet	Amy	FRA	4.10.80	165/51	TJ	13.88	14.08i- 09, 14.03- 08, 14.16w- 12
Zsivoczky-Farkas	Györgyi	HUN	13.2.85	170/58	HJ	1.87	1.86- 14
					Hep	6442	6389- 15
Zubkovska	Oksana	UKR	15.7.81	175/62	LJ	6.70	6.71- 07
Zuykevich	Yelena	RUS	26.2.90		400h	56.75	57.18- 15
Zyabkina	Viktoriya	KAZ	4.9.92	170/55	100	11.27, 11.15dt	11.19- 15
					200	22.66	22.77- 15
Zyryanova	Valeriya	RUS	12.8.90		SP	17.67	17.30- 14

WORLD INDOOR LISTS 2017 – MEN

Note: including some marks from December 2016 (*), # Oversized track (over 200m)

60 METRES

Mark	First	Last	Nat	DOB	Pos	Meet	Venue	Date
6.45A	Ronnie	Baker	USA	15.10.93	1	NC	Albuquerque	5 Mar
6.46					1		Torun	10 Feb
6.45	Christian	Coleman	USA	6.3.96	1	NCAA	College Station	11 Mar
6.51	Kendal	Williams	USA	23.9.95	1		Clemson	17 Feb
6.52	Kim	Collins	SKN	5.4.76	1		Mondeville	4 Feb
6.53	Yunier	Pérez	CUB	16.2.85	1		Lódz	16 Feb
6.53	Cameron	Burrell	USA	11.9.94	2h1	NCAA	College Station	10 Mar
6.54	Richard	Kilty	GBR	2.9.89	1	EI	Beograd	4 Mar
6.54A	LeShon	Collins	USA	11.12.93	2	NC	Albuquerque	5 Mar
6.56	Chijindu	Ujah	GBR	5.3.94	2		Torun	10 Feb
6.56	Sean	Safo-Antwi	GHA	31.10.90	1		Athlone	15 Feb
6.56	Ryan	Shields	JAM	12.5.83	2		Lódz	16 Feb
6.56	Jaylen	Bacon	USA	5.8.96	3	NCAA	College Station	11 Mar
6.57	Everton	Clarke	JAM	24.12.92	3		Düsseldorf	1 Feb
6.57	James	Dasaolu	GBR	5.9.87	1	ISTAF	Berlin	10 Feb
6.57	Andrew	Robertson	GBR	17.12.90	1	NC	Sheffield	11 Feb
6.57	Andrew	Fisher	BRN	15.12.91	1		Ostrava	14 Feb
6.57	Warren	Fraser	BAH	8.7.91	2		Clemson	17 Feb
6.57A	Desmond	Lawrence	USA	19.12.91	1h2	NC	Albuquerque	5 Mar
6.57	Kyree	King	USA	9.7.94	3h1	NCAA	College Station	10 Mar
6.58	Christophe	Lemaitre	FRA	11.6.90	1r1		Tignes	5 Jan
6.58	Riak	Reese	USA	23.11.94	1		Akron	4 Feb
6.58A	Ameer	Webb	USA	19.3.89	1		Flagstaff	4 Feb
6.58	Ján	Volko	SVK	2.11.96	2	EI	Beograd	4 Mar
6.58	Joseph	Dewar	GBR	27.1.96	1		Eton	5 Mar
6.59	Rafael	Scott	USA		1		Nashville	21 Jan
6.59	Brandon	Carnes	USA	6.3.95	1		Iowa City	21 Jan
6.59	Hakim	Montgomery	USA	23.6.97	1h2		Clemson	27 Jan
6.59	Kyle	de Escofet	GBR	4.10.96	2h1		Mondeville	4 Feb
6.59	Darryl	Haraway	USA	19.3.97	1		Fayetteville	10 Feb
6.59	Theo	Etienne	GBR	3.9.96	2	NC	Sheffield	11 Feb
6.59	Julian	Forte	JAM	1.7.93	5		Birmingham	18 Feb
6.59	Senoj-Jay	Givans	JAM	30.12.93	1	Big12	Ames	25 Feb
6.59	Mario	Burke	BAR	18.3.97	1		Birmingham AL	25 Feb
6.59A	Dentarius	Locke	USA	12.12.89	2h2	NC	Albuquerque	5 Mar
6.60	Giovanni	Cellario	ITA	22.11.94	14 Jan		6.61	Omar	McLeod	JAM	25.4.94	17 Feb
6.60	Massimiliano	Ferraro	ITA	6.2.91	21 Jan		6.61	Yang Yang		CHN	26.6.93	19 Feb
6.60A	Shavez	Hart	BAH	6.9.92	4 Feb		6.61A	Quentin	Butler	USA	18.9.92	5 Mar
6.60	D'Angelo	Cherry	USA	1.8.90	15 Feb		6.61A	Tevin	Hester	USA	10.1.94	5 Mar
6.60	Ramon	Gittens	BAR	20.7.87	15 Feb		6.61	Kenzo	Cotton	USA	13.5.96	10 Mar
6.60	Eric	Cray	PHI	6.11.88	16 Feb		6.62	Michael	Rodgers	USA	24.4.85	8 Feb
6.60A	HuaWilfried	Koffi	CIV	12.10.89	17 Feb		6.62	Reece	Prescod	GBR	29.2.96	10 Feb
6.60		Mi Hong	CHN	8.7.93	23 Feb		6.62	Dwain	Chambers	GBR	5.4.78	11 Feb
6.60	Odean	Skeen	JAM	28.8.94	25 Feb		6.62	Clayton	Vaughn	USA	15.5.92	11 Feb
6.60A	Cordero	Gray	USA	9.5.89	5 Mar		6.62	Gao Ze		CHN	20.10.94	19 Feb
6.60A	Marqueze	Washington	USA	29.9.93	5 Mar		6.62	Solomon	Bockarie	NED	18.5.87	24 Feb
6.60	Mobolade	Ajomale	CAN	31.8.95	11 Mar		6.62	Keitavious	Walter	LCA	16.4.96	3 Mar
							6.62A	Blake	Smith	USA	28.5.93	5 Mar

200 METRES

Mark	First	Last	Nat	DOB	Pos	Meet	Venue	Date
20.11	Christian	Coleman	USA	6.3.96	1r1	NCAA	College Station	11 Mar
20.31	Jereem	Richards	TTO	13.1.94	1r2	NCAA	College Station	11 Mar
20.36	Just'N	Thymes	USA	24.1.94	2r2	NCAA	College Station	11 Mar
20.48	Omar	McLeod	JAM	26.4.94	1r5		Fayetteville	17 Feb
20.49	Lalonde	Gordon	TTO	25.11.88	1		Boston (Allston)	28 Jan
20.49	Nethaneel	Mitchell-Blake	GBR	2.4.94	1r2	Tyson	Fayetteville	11 Feb
20.49	Rondell	Sorrillo	TTO	21.1.86	2r1	Tyson	Fayetteville	11 Feb
20.52	Robin	Erewa	GER	24.6.91	1	NC	Leipzig	19 Feb
20.56	Marqueze	Washington	USA	29.9.93	2r5		Fayetteville	17 Feb
20.57	Cameron	Williams	USA	11.9.95	1		Boston (Allston)	19 Feb
20.57	Pavel	Maslák	CZE	21.2.91	1	NC	Praha (Stromovka)	26 Feb
20.58	Fred	Kerley	USA	7.5.95	1rB		Fayetteville	27 Jan
20.59	Christopher	Belcher	USA	29.1.94	1		Boston (Allston)	26 Feb
20.65	Kenzo	Cotton	USA	13.5.96	10 Mar			
20.67	Ncincihli	Titi	RSA	15.12.93	11 Feb		20.69	Maxwell	Willis	USA-J	2.9.98	11 Mar
20.67A	Jamiel	Trimble	USA	25.6.95	25 Feb		20.71	Elijah	Hall-Thompson	USA	22.8.94	21 Jan
20.69	Wallace	Spearmon	USA	24.12.84	11 Feb		20.71	Josh	Washington	USA	25.8.95	27 Jan
20.58#	Nick	Gray	USA	2.6.97	1	Big10	Geneva	25 Feb

300 METRES

Mark	First	Last	Nat	DOB	Pos	Meet	Venue	Date
31.87A	Noah	Lyles	USA	18.7.97	1r2	NC	Albuquerque	4 Mar
32.67					1		Boston (Roxbury)	28 Jan

WORLD INDOOR LISTS 2017   577

Mark	First	Last	Nat	DOB	Pos	Meet	Venue	Date
31.92A	Paul	Dedewo	USA	5.6.91	2r2	NC	Albuquerque	4 Mar
31.97	Bralon	Taplin	GRN	8.5.92	1		Ostrava	14 Feb
32.19	Pavel	Maslák	CZE	21.2.91	2		Ostrava	14 Feb
32.37	Lalonde	Gordon	TTO	25.11.88	1		New York (Armory)	4 Feb
32.46A	Dontavius	Wright	USA	3.1.94	1h3	NC	Albuquerque	4 Mar
32.63A	Brycen	Spratling	USA	10.3.92	1r1	NC	Albuquerque	4 Mar
32.73	Rafal	Omelko	POL	16.1.89	3		Ostrava	14 Feb
32.79A	Amir	James	USA	7.12.95	4 Mar	32.87	Tyrese Cooper USA-Y 21.3.00	4 Feb
32.80	Grant	Holloway	USA	19.11.97	7 Jan	32.97A	John Lundy USA 15.3.92	4 Mar

400 METRES

Mark	First	Last	Nat	DOB	Pos	Meet	Venue	Date
44.85	Fred	Kerley	USA	7.5.95	1r2	NCAA	College Station	11 Mar
45.19	Bralon	Taplin	GRN	8.5.92	1		Madrid	24 Feb
45.57	Kunle	Fasasi	NGR	23.6.96	2h1	NCAA	College Station	10 Mar
45.63	Marqueze	Washington	USA	29.9.93	1r2	Tyson	Fayetteville	10 Feb
45.64	Michael	Cherry	USA	23.3.95	1r1	NCAA	College Station	11 Mar
45.68	My'Lik	Kerley	USA	6.6.96	3h1	NCAA	College Station	10 Mar
45.77	Pavel	Maslák	CZE	21.2.91	1	EI	Beograd	4 Mar
45.80	Luguelín	Santos	DOM	12.11.92	2		Madrid	24 Feb
45.92	Óscar	Husillos	ESP	18.7.93	1	NC	Salamanca	19 Feb
45.96	Karsten	Warholm	NOR	28.2.96	1	NC	Ulsteinvik	4 Feb
46.01	Tyrese	Cooper	USA-Y	21.3.00	10 Feb	46.14	Lalonde Gordon TTO 25.11.88	28 Jan
46.01	Eric	Janise	USA	3.9.93	10 Mar	46.16	Obie Igbowke USA 28.1.97	10 Feb
46.02	Steven	Gayle	JAM	19.3.94	11 Mar	46.16	Eric Futch USA 25.4.93	11 Mar
46.08	Rafal	Omelko	POL	16.1.89	4 Mar	46.23	Lucas Búa ESP 12.1.94	18 Feb

Oversized track

Mark	First	Last	Nat	DOB	Pos	Meet	Venue	Date
45.32	Izaiah	Brown	USA	1.1.97	1	Big10	Geneva	25 Feb
45.43	Akeem	Bloomfield	JAM	10.11.97	2r1	SEC	Nashville	25 Feb
45.59	Sean	Bailey	JAM	15.7.97	1	JUCO	Pittsburg	4 Mar
45.73A	Paul	Dedewo	USA	5.6.91	1		Flagstaff	17 Feb
45.73	Obie	Igbowke	USA	28.1.97	1r2	SEC	Nashville	25 Feb
45.75	Mar'yea	Harris	USA	24.11.97	2	Big10	Geneva	25 Feb
45.80A	Dontavius	Wright	USA	3.1.94	2		Flagstaff	17 Feb
45.87	Tyler	Terry	USA		2	JUCO	Pittsburg	4 Mar

500 METRES

Mark	First	Last	Nat	DOB	Pos	Meet	Venue	Date
1:00.11	Vernon	Norwood	USA	10.4.92	1	Mill	New York (Armory)	11 Feb
1:00.90	Brycen	Spratling	USA	10.3.92	11 Feb	1:01.17	Bershawn Jackson USA 8.5.83	11 Feb
1:00.99	Pavel	Maslák	CZE	21.2.91	17 Jan	1:01.47	Chris Giesting USA 10.12.92	11 Feb

600 METRES

Mark	First	Last	Nat	DOB	Pos	Meet	Venue	Date
1:14.91	Casimir	Loxsom	USA	17.3.91	1		State College	28 Jan
1:14.96	Isaiah	Harris	USA	18.10.96	2		State College	28 Jan
1:14.97A	Emmanuel	Korir	KEN	15.6.95	1		Albuquerque	20 Jan
1:15.07A	Erik	Sowinski	USA	21.11.89	1	NC	Albuquerque	5 Mar
1:15.39A	Shaquille	Walker	USA	24.6.93	5 Mar	1:15.96A	Christopher Giesting USA 10.12.92	5 Mar
1:15.86A	Russell	Dinkins	USA	27.6.89	5 Mar	1:16.10	Kyle Langford GBR 2.2.96	15 Feb
1:15.88	Daniel	Kuhn	USA	11.8.95	27 Jan	1:16.10A	Donavan Brazier USA 15.4.97	5 Mar

Oversized track

Mark	First	Last	Nat	DOB	Pos	Meet	Venue	Date
1:15.23	Daniel	Kuhn	USA	11.8.95	1	Big10	Geneva	25 Feb
1:15.55	Nate	Roese	USA	19.9.94	25 Feb	1:15.99	Anthony Johnson USA 20.10.94	25 Feb

800 METRES

Mark	First	Last	Nat	DOB	Pos	Meet	Venue	Date
1:46.13	Casimir	Loxsom	USA	17.3.91	1		Birmingham	18 Feb
1:46.17	Adam	Kszczot	POL	2.9.89	1		Düsseldorf	1 Feb
1:46.23#	Patrick	Joseph	USA	7.9.95	1	ACC	Notre Dame	25 Feb
1:46.34	Nicholas	Kipkoech	KEN	22.12.92	1		Torun	10 Feb
1:46.42#	Daniel	Kuhn	USA	11.8.95	1		Notre Dame	4 Feb
1:46.42#	Drew	Piazza	USA	28.1.95	2	ACC	Notre Dame	25 Feb
1:46.44#	Joseph	White	USA	16.11.95	1		Ames	11 Feb
1:46.50#	Emmanuel	Korir	KEN	15.6.95	1		Nashville	14 Jan
1:46.58	Kevin	López	ESP	12.6.90	2		Sabadell	7 Feb
1:46.59	Amel	Tuka	BIH	9.1.91	2		Birmingham	18 Feb
1:46.65#	Isaiah	Harris	USA	18.10.96	1		Lexington	21 Jan
1:46.70#	Eliud	Rutto	KEN	4.6.94	2		Ames	11 Feb
1:46.71#	Robert	Heppenstall	CAN	28.2.97	25 Feb			
1:46.79	Kyle	Langford	GBR	2.2.96	18 Feb	1:47.18#	Andres Arroyo PUR 7.6.95	25 Feb
1:46.80	Erik	Sowinski	USA	21.11.89	4 Feb		1:47.25	28 Jan
1:46.86	Andreas	Kramer	SWE	13.4.97	3 Mar	1:47.19	Andreas Bube DEN 13.7.87	4 Feb
1:46.90A	Michael	Saruni	KEN		4 Feb	1:47.21	Thijmen Kupers NED 4.10.91	3 Mar
1:47.00	Guy	Learmonth	GBR	20.4.92	18 Feb	1:47.22#	Clayton Murphy USA 26.2.95	17 Feb
1:47.02	Andrew	Osagie	GBR	19.2.88	18 Feb	1:47.32#	Avery Bartlett USA 8.2.97	25 Feb
1:47.11	Mateusz	Borwkowski	POL	2.4.97	10 Feb	1:47.33#	Carter Lilly USA 19.10.95	4 Feb
1:47.13	Mostafa	Smaïli	MAR	9.1.97	24 Feb	1:47.34#	Blair Henderson USA 4.10.94	11 Feb
1:47.16	Daniel	Andújar	ESP	14.5.94	7 Feb	1:47.46#	Abraham Alvarado USA 4.8.95	11 Feb
1:47.17	Donavan	Brazier	USA	15.4.97	18 Feb			

1000 METRES
2:18.60A	Clayton		Murphy	USA	26.2.95	1	NC	Albuquerque	5 Mar
2:19.10A	Brannon		Kidder	USA	18.11.93	2	NC	Albuquerque	5 Mar

1500 METRES
3:36.42	Ben		Blankenship	USA	15.12.89	1		Birmingham	18 Feb
3:36.50	Ryan		Gregson	AUS	26.4.90	2		Birmingham	18 Feb
3:37.01+	Edward		Cheserek	KEN	2.2.94	1	in 1M	Boston (Allston)	26 Feb
3:37.32	Bethwel		Birgen	KEN	6.8.88	3		Birmingham	18 Feb
3:37.58+	Andrew		Butchart	GBR	14.10.91	1	in 1M	New York (Armory)	4 Feb
3:37.62	Elijah		Manangoi	KEN	5.1.93	1		Düsseldorf	1 Feb
3:37.69	Kalle		Berglund	SWE	11.3.96	4		Birmingham	18 Feb
3:37.76+	John		Gregorek	USA	7.12.91	2	in 1M	Boston (Allston)	26 Feb
3:37.83+	Kyle		Merber	USA	19.11.90	3	in 1M	Boston (Allston)	26 Feb
3:38.04+	Ford		Palmer	USA	6.10.90	4	in 1M	Boston (Allston)	26 Feb
3:38.19	Hillary		Ngetich	KEN	15.9.95	5		Birmingham	18 Feb
3:38.24	Marcin		Lewandowski	POL	13.6.87	2		Torun	10 Feb
3:38.27+	Christian		Soratos	USA	26.9.92	1rB	in 1M	New York (Armory)	11 Feb
3:38.33	Silas		Kiplagat	KEN	20.8.89	3		Torun	10 Feb
3:38.41	Vincent	Kibet	KEN	6.5.91	10 Feb	3:39.36+	Charles	Philibert-Thiboutot	CAN 31.12.90	11 Feb
3:38.44	Eric	Jenkins	USA	24.11.91	11 Feb	3:39.51	Vladimir	Nikitin	RUS 5.8.92	21 Feb
3:38.52	Tom	Lancashire	GBR	2.7.85	18 Feb	3:39.72	Garrett	Heath	USA 3.11.85	18 Feb
3:39.25+	Clayton	Murphy	USA	26.2.95	11 Feb	3:39.79	David	Torrence	PER 26.11.85	4 Feb

1 MILE
3:52.01	Edward		Cheserek	KEN	2.2.94	1		Boston (Allston)	26 Feb
3:52.22	Kyle		Merber	USA	19.11.90	2		Boston (Allston)	26 Feb
3:53.15	Johnny		Gregorek	USA	7.12.91	3		Boston (Allston)	26 Feb
3:53.23	Eric		Jenkins	USA	24.11.91	1	Mill	New York (Armory)	11 Feb
3:54.23	Andrew		Butchart	GBR	14.10.91	1		New York (Armory)	4 Feb
3:54.23	Christian		Soratos	USA	26.9.92	1rB	Mill	New York (Armory)	11 Feb
3:54.31	Clayton		Murphy	USA	26.2.95	2	Mill	New York (Armory)	11 Feb
3:54.92	Ford		Palmer	USA	6.10.90	4		Boston (Allston)	26 Feb
3:55.33	Charles		Philibert-Thiboutot	CAN	31.12.90	4	Mill	New York (Armory)	11 Feb
3:55.78	Matthew	Centrowitz	USA	18.10.89	28 Jan	3:56.80	Drew	Hunter	USA 5.9.97	11 Feb
3:55.99	Colby	Alexander	USA	13.6.91	11 Feb	3:56.89#	Joshua	Thompson	USA 9.5.93	11 Feb
3:56.09	Vincent	Kibet	KEN	6.5.91	28 Jan	3:57.04	Robert	Andrews	USA 29.3.91	11 Feb
3:56.49	Ryan	Gregson	AUS	26.4.90	15 Feb	3:57.24	Jake	Wightman	GBR 11.7.94	28 Jan
3:56.55#	Lopez	Lomong	USA	1.1.85	11 Feb	3:57.31	Ben	True	USA 29.12.85	28 Jan
3:56.55#	Evan	Jager	USA	8.3.89	11 Feb	3:57.39	Adam	Palamar	CAN 12.3.94	28 Jan

3000 METRES
7:40.80+	Ryan		Hill	USA	31.1.90	1	in 2M	New York (Armory)	11 Feb
7:40.96+	Ben		True	USA	29.12.85	2	in 2M	New York (Armory)	11 Feb
7:41.05+	Andrew		Butchart	GBR	14.10.91	3	in 2M	New York (Armory)	11 Feb
7:41.13+	Mohammed		Ahmed	CAN	5.1.91	4	in 2M	New York (Armory)	11 Feb
7:42.29	Paul		Chelimo	USA	27.10.90	1		Boston (Roxbury)	28 Jan
7:43.04	Hagos		Gebrhiwet	ETH	11.5.94	3		Boston (Roxbury)	28 Jan
7:44.26	Eric		Jenkins	USA	24.11.91	4		Boston (Roxbury)	28 Jan
7:44.55	Mourad		Amdouni	FRA	21.1.88	1		Metz	12 Feb
7:44.65	Vladimir		Nikitin	RUS	5.8.92	1	Winter	Moskva	5 Feb
7:44.73	Hillary		Ngetich	KEN	15.9.95	1		Düsseldorf	1 Feb
7:44.95	Mekonnen		Gebremedhin	ETH	11.10.88	2		Metz	12 Feb
7:45.01+	Lawi		Lalang	KEN	15.6.91	5	in 2M	New York (Armory)	11 Feb
7:45.28+	Garrett		Heath	USA	3.11.85	6	in 2M	New York (Armory)	11 Feb
7:45.69+	Matthew		Centrowitz	USA	18.10.89	6	in 2M	New York (Armory)	11 Feb
7:45.71#	Colby		Gilbert	USA	17.3.95	1		Seattle	28 Jan
7:46.06	Dejen		Gebremeskel	ETH	24.11.89	6		Boston (Roxbury)	28 Jan
7:46.22#	Charles		Philibert-Thiboutot	CAN	31.12.90	2		Seattle	28 Jan
7:46.85	Edward		Cheserek	KEN	2.2.94	1		New York (Armory)	28 Jan
7:47.18#	Nathan	Brannen	CAN	8.9.82	28 Jan	7:49.08+	Ben	Blankenship	USA 15.12.89	11 Feb
7:47.57#	Marc	Scott	GBR	21.12.93	11 Feb	7:49.29	Lee	Emanuel	GBR 24.1.85	4 Feb
7:47.66	Dawit	Wolde	ETH	19.5.91	1 Feb	7:49.39	Kyle	Merber	USA 19.11.90	28 Jan
7:47.82#	Justyn	Knight	CAN	19.7.96	11 Feb	7:49.46	Morgan	Pearson	USA 22.9.93	4 Feb
7:48.39	Adel	Mechaal	ESP	5.12.90	7 Feb	7:49.52#	Martin	Hehir	USA 19.12.92	11 Feb
7:48.39	Hayle	Ibrahimov	AZE	18.1.90	12 Feb	7:49.76#	Clayton	Young	USA	28 Jan
						7:49.93	John	Gregorek	USA 7.12.91	28 Jan

2 MILES
8:11.33	Ben		True	USA	29.12.85	1	Mill	New York (Armory)	11 Feb
8:11.56	Ryan		Hill	USA	31.1.90	2	Mill	New York (Armory)	11 Feb
8:12.63	Andrew		Butchart	GBR	14.10.91	3	Mill	New York (Armory)	11 Feb
8:13.16	Mohammed		Ahmed	CAN	5.1.91	4	Mill	New York (Armory)	11 Feb
8:18.70	Lawi		Lalang	KEN	15.6.91	5	Mill	New York (Armory)	11 Feb
8:19.61	Garrett		Heath	USA	3.11.85	6	Mill	New York (Armory)	11 Feb
8:21.07	Matthew		Centrowitz	USA	18.10.89	7	Mill	New York (Armory)	11 Feb

5000 METRES

Mark	First	Last	Nat	DOB	Pos	Venue	Date
13:04.60	Mohammed	Ahmed	CAN	5.1.91	1	Boston (Allston)	26 Feb
13:05.85	Eric	Jenkins	USA	24.11.91	2	Boston (Allston)	26 Feb
13:06.74	Ben	True	USA	29.12.85	3	Boston (Allston)	26 Feb
13:07.61	Ryan	Hill	USA	31.1.90	4	Boston (Allston)	26 Feb
13:09.16	Mohamed	Farah	GBR	23.3.83	1	Birmingham	18 Feb
13:09.43	Albert	Rop	BRN	17.7.92	2	Birmingham	18 Feb
13:10.60	Soufiane	El Bakkali	MAR	7.1.96	3	Birmingham	18 Feb
13:11.18	Mourad	Amdouni	FRA	21.1.88	4	Birmingham	18 Feb
13:12.22	Woody	Kincaid	USA	21.9.92	5	Boston (Allston)	26 Feb
13:12.27	Lopez	Lomong	USA	1.1.85	6	Boston (Allston)	26 Feb
13:14.45	Kemoy	Campbell	JAM	14.1.91	7	Boston (Allston)	26 Feb
13:19.35	Chris	Derrick	USA	17.10.90	8	Boston (Allston)	26 Feb
13:23.99	Yemaneberhan	Crippa	ITA	15.10.96	5	Birmingham	18 Feb

60 METRES HURDLES

Mark	First	Last	Nat	DOB	Pos	Meet	Venue	Date
7.43	Andrew	Pozzi	GBR	15.5.92	1		Birmingham	18 Feb
7.46	Omar	McLeod	JAM	25.4/94	1	Mill	New York (Armory)	11 Feb
7.48	Orlando	Ortega	ESP	29.7.91	1		Torun	10 Feb
7.51	Dimitri	Bascou	FRA	20.7.87	2		Düsseldorf	1 Feb
7.51	Pascal	Martinot-Lagarde	FRA	22.9.91	1		Paris	8 Feb
7.51A	Aries	Merritt	USA	24.7.85	1	NC	Albuquerque	5 Mar
7.53	Garfield	Darien	FRA	22.12.87	3		Düsseldorf	1 Feb
7.53	Balázs	Baji	HUN	9.6.89	1	NC	Budapest (BH)	19 Feb
7.53	Aurel	Manga	FRA	24.7.92	2	NC	Bordeaux	19 Feb
7.53	Petr	Svoboda	CZE	10.10.84	3	EI	Beograd	3 Mar
7.54A	Aleec	Harris	USA	31.10.90	2	NC	Albuquerque	5 Mar
7.56					2	Mill	New York (Armory)	11 Feb
7.56	Milan	Trajkovic	CYP	17.3.92	1h2	EI	Beograd	3 Mar
7.57	Edward	Lovett	ISV	25.6.92	3	Mill	New York (Armory)	11 Feb
7.58	Grant	Holloway	USA	19.11.97	1	Tyson	Fayetteville	10 Feb
7.59A	Jarret	Eaton	USA	24.6.89	3	NC	Albuquerque	5 Mar
7.61	Chad	Zallow	USA	25.4.97	1		New York (Armory)	4 Feb
7.61	Spencer	Adams	USA	10.9.89	5	Mill	New York (Armory)	11 Feb
7.62	Erik	Balnuweit	GER	21.9.88	1	NC	Leipzig	18 Feb
7.63	David	Omoregie	GBR	1.11.95	2		Cardiff	28 Jan
7.63	Michael	Dickson	USA	25.1.97	1		Winston-Salem	4 Feb
7.63	David	King	GBR	13.6.94	2		Birmingham	18 Feb
7.63	Aaron	Mallett	USA	26.9.94	1	Big10	Geneva	25 Feb
7.65	Konstantin	Shabanov	RUS	17.11.89	22 Jan			
7.65	Freddie	Crittenden	USA	3.8.94	24 Feb			
7.65	Damian	Czykier	POL	10.8.92	3 Mar			
7.66	Dondre	Echols	USA	6.7.93	12 Feb			
7.66	Xie	Wenjun	CHN	11.7.90	28 Feb			
7.67	Simon	Krauss	FRA	12.2.92	19 Feb			
7.68	Wilhem	Belocian	FRA	22.6.95	12 Feb			
7.68	Greggmar	Swift	BAR	16.2.91	18 Feb			
7.68	Andreas	Martinsen	DEN	17.7.90	3 Mar			
7.69	Benjamin	Sedécias	FRA	18.1.95	31 Jan			
7.69A	Chris	Caldwell	USA	6.4.94	3 Feb			
7.69	Yidiel	Contreras	ESP	27.11.92	4 Feb			
7.69	Maximilian	Bayer	GER	5.12.90	18 Feb			
7.69	David	Kendziera	USA	9.9.94	25 Feb			
7.69	Nicholas	Anderson	USA	28.4.95	10 Mar			
7.70	Thingalaya	Siddhanth	IND	1.3.91	14 Jan			
7.70	Terence	Somerville	USA	5.11.89	18 Feb			

HIGH JUMP

Mark	First	Last	Nat	DOB	Pos	Meet	Venue	Date
2.35*	Ivan	Ukhov	RUS	29.3.86	1		Yekaterinburg	29 Dec
2.32					1	NC	Moskva	20 Feb
2.33	Danyil	Lysenko	RUS	19.5.97	1	Winter	Moskva	5 Feb
2.33	Sylwester	Bednarek	POL	28.4.89	1=		Banská Bystrica	8 Feb
2.33	Derek	Drouin	CAN	6.3.90	1=		Banská Bystrica	8 Feb
2.32	Pavel	Seliverstov	BLR	2.9.96	1		Trinec	11 Feb
2.31	Ilya	Ivanyuk	RUS	9.3.93	3	Winter	Moskva	5 Feb
2.31	Donald	Thomas	BAH	1.7.84	4		Banská Bystrica	8 Feb
2.31	Erik	Kynard	USA	3.2.91	1		Birmingham	18 Feb
2.30	Edgar	Rivera	MEX	13.2.91	2		Hustopece	4 Feb
2.30	JaCorian	Duffield	USA	2.9.92	1	Tyson	Fayetteville	11 Feb
2.30	Nikita	Anishchenkov	RUS	25.7.92	3	NC	Moskva	20 Feb
2.30	Robbie	Grabarz	GBR	3.10.87	2	EI	Beograd	5 Mar
2.28	Mateusz	Przybylko	GER	9.3.92	2		Karlsruhe	4 Feb
2.28	Dmitriy	Semyonov	RUS	2.8.92	4	Winter	Moskva	5 Feb
2.28	Lukáš	Beer	SVK	23.8.89	5		Banská Bystrica	8 Feb
2.28	Tikhomir	Ivanov	BUL	11.7.94	8		Banská Bystrica	8 Feb
2.28	Sun	Zhao	CHN	8.2.90	1		Xianlin	23 Feb
2.28	Matús	Bubeník	SVK	14.11.89	Q	EI	Beograd	4 Mar
2.28	Silvano	Chesani	ITA	17.7.88	Q	EI	Beograd	4 Mar
2.27	Jamal	Wilson	BAH	1.9.88	3		Trinec	11 Feb
2.27	Michael	Mason	CAN	30.9.86	2	Mill	New York (Armory)	11 Feb
2.27	Randall	Cunningham	USA	4.1.96	1		Seattle	25 Feb
2.26	Janick	Klausen	DEN	3.4.93	25 Jan			

WORLD INDOOR LISTS 2017

2.26A	Bradley	Adkins	USA	30.12.93	3 Feb		2.25	Clayton	Brown	JAM	8.12.96	7 Jan
2.26	Chris	Kandu	GBR	10.9.95	4 Feb		2.25	Aleksey	Dmitrik	RUS	12.4.84	11 Jan
2.26	Konstadinos	Baniótis	GRE	6.11.86	4 Feb		2.25	Allex	Austin	USA		28 Jan
2.26	Allan	Smith	GBR	6.11.92	4 Feb		2.25	Christian	Falocchi	ITA	30.1.97	4 Feb
2.26	Naoto	Tobe	JPN	31.3.92	4 Feb		2.25	Miguel ángel	Sancho	ESP	24.4.90	5 Feb
2.26	Martin	Heindl	CZE	2.6.92	25 Feb		2.25	Fabian	Delryd	SWE	15.10.96	11 Feb
2.26	Trey	Culver	USA	18.7.96	11 Mar		2.25	Rauvydas	Stanys	LTU	3.2.87	23 Feb
2.26	Kyle	Landon	USA	16.10.94	11 Mar		2.25	Vasilios	Konstantinou	CYP	13.9.92	25 Feb

POLE VAULT

6.00	Piotr	Lisek	POL	16.8.92	1		Potsdam		4 Feb
5.86	Thiago	Braz da Silva	BRA	16.12.93	1vcA		Rouen		28 Jan
5.85	Konstadinos	Filippídis	GRE	26.11.86	2	EI	Beograd		3 Mar
5.85	Pawel	Wojciechowski	POL	6.6.89	3	EI	Beograd		3 Mar
5.85A	Sam	Kendricks	USA	7.9.92	1	NC	Albuquerque		4 Mar
5.83	Shawnacy	Barber	CAN	27.5.94	1		Clermont-Ferrand		5 Feb
5.82	Armand	Duplantis	SWE-J	10.11.99	1		New York (Armory)		11 Mar
5.80	Timur	Morgunov	RUS	12.10.96	1		Chelyabinsk		11 Jan
5.80	Jan	Kudlicka	CZE	29.4.88	4	EI	Beograd		3 Mar
5.80	Raphael	Holzdeppe	GER	28.9.89	5	EI	Beograd		3 Mar
5.80	Axel	Chapelle	FRA	24.4.95	6	EI	Beograd		3 Mar
5.78	Kévin	Menaldo	FRA	12.7.92	1	NC	Bordeaux		19 Feb
5.76	Ivan	Horvat	CRO	17.8.93	1	BalkC	Beograd		25 Feb
5.71	Renaud	Lavillenie	FRA	18.9.86	6		Clermont-Ferrand		5 Feb
5.70	Georgiy	Gorokhov	RUS	20.4.93	2		Chelyabinsk		11 Jan
5.70	Ilya	Mudrov	RUS	17.11.91	1		Moskva		18 Jan
5.70A	Victor	Weirich	USA	25.10.87	1		Air Force Academy		21 Jan
5.70	Chris	Nilsen	USA-J	13.1.98	1	Tyson	Fayetteville		10 Feb
5.70	Dmitriy	Zhelyabin	RUS	20.5.90	1=		Sankt-Peterburg		14 Feb
5.70	Andrew	Irwin	USA	23.1.93	1		Fayetteville		17 Feb
5.70	Emmanouil	Karális	GRE-J	20.10.99	2	NC	Piréas		19 Feb
5.70		Xue Changrui	CHN	31.5.91	1		Xianlin		23 Feb
5.66	Deakin	Volz	USA	12.1.97	1		Blacksburg		18 Feb
5.65	Rutger	Koppelaar	NED	1.5.93	1		Vught		22 Jan
5.65	Stanley	Joseph	FRA	24.10.91	2		Praha		21 Feb
5.65	Menno	Vloon	NED	11.5.94	2		Zweibrücken		25 Feb
5.65	Malte	Mohr	GER	24.7.86	3		Zweibrücken		25 Feb
5.65A	Kyle	Pater	USA	24.12.94	1	MWC	Albuquerque		25 Feb
5.65A	Logan	Cunningham	USA	30.5.91	2	NC	Albuquerque		4 Mar
5.65A	Chris	Pillow	USA	8.7.93	3	NC	Albuquerque		4 Mar
5.63		Huang Bokai	CHN	26.9.96	1		Nevers		21 Jan
5.63	Danyil	Kotov	RUS	14.11.95	1	Winter	Moskva		4 Feb
5.63	Karsten	Dilla	GER	17.7.89	3		Potsdam		4 Feb
5.61*	Arnaud	Art	BEL	28.1.93	1		Rennes		17 Dec
5.61	Valentin	Lavillenie	FRA	16.7.91	9		Clermont-Ferrand		5 Feb
5.61	Nikandros	Stylianou	CYP	22.8.89	3	BalkC	Beograd		25 Feb
5.60	Florian	Gaul	GER	21.9.91	1		Sindelfingen		21 Jan
5.60	Jeff	Coover	USA	1.12.87	1		Cedar Falls		27 Jan
5.60	Ivan	Gertleyn	RUS	25.9.87	2	NC	Moskva		20 Feb
5.60	Adrián	Vallés	ESP	16.3.95	1		Birmingham AL		24 Feb
5.60	Marek	Arents	LAT	6.8.86	8=	EI	Beograd		3 Mar
5.60A	Scott	Houston	USA	11.6.90	4	NC	Albuquerque		4 Mar
5.56	Baptiste	Boirie	FRA	26.12.92	4 Feb		5.51	Devin	King	USA	12.3.96	22 Feb
5.55A	Michael	Arnold	USA	13.8.90	13 Jan		5.51	Robert	Renner	SLO	8.3.94	25 Feb
5.55	Eirik Greibrokk	Dolve	NOR	5.5.95	11 Feb		5.50	Adam	Hague	GBR	29.8.97	8 Jan
5.55	Urho	Kujanpää	FIN	18.5.97	19 Feb		5.50	Anatoliy	Bednyuk	RUS	30.1.89	11 Jan
5.55	Dimítrios	Patsoukákis	GRE	18.3.87	19 Feb		5.50	Masaki	Ejima	JPN-J	6.3.99	14 Jan
5.55	Torben	Laidig	GER	13.3.94	25 Feb		5.50A	Cale	Simmons	USA	5.2.91	21 Jan
5.55	Dominik	Alberto	SUI	28.4.92	25 Feb		5.50	Jérôme	Clavier	FRA	3.5.83	28 Jan
5.55A	Max	Babits	USA	30.5.92	4 Mar		5.50	Mateusz	Jerzy	POL	29.3.95	4 Feb
5.55A	Chase	Brannon	USA	8.2.91	4 Mar		5.50	Nate	Richartz	USA	2.11.94	10 Feb
5.55	Audie	Wyatt	USA	30.4.96	10 Mar		5.50	Drew	Volz	USA	20.11.92	10 Feb
5.54	Emile	Denecker	FRA	28.3.92	14 Jan		5.50	Karol	Pawlik	POL	17.3.94	11 Feb
5.54	Jake	Albright	USA	22.12.93	21 Jan		5.50	Barrett	Poth	USA	18.4.96	11 Feb
5.54	Diogo	Ferreira	POR	30.7.90	11 Feb		5.50	Ilya	Prosvirin	RUS	28.2.95	14 Feb
5.53	Alexandre	Feger	FRA	22.1.90	6 Jan		5.50		Yang Yansheng	CHN	5.1.88	23 Feb
5.53	Alioune	Sène	FRA	3.2.96	21 Jan		5.50	Dídac	Salas	ESP	19.5.93	23 Feb
5.51	Levi	Keller	USA	30.1.86	28 Jan		5.50	Vladyslav	Malykhin	UKR-J	15.1.98	25 Feb
5.51	Nikólaos	Nerántzis	GRE-J	13.3.98	12 Feb		5.50	Bo Kanda	Lita Baehre	GER-J	29.4.99	25 Feb
5.51	Matthew	Ludwig	USA	5.7.96	17 Feb		5.50	Timothy	Ehrhardt	USA	16.3.95	10 Mar

LONG JUMP

8.21	Artyom	Primak	RUS	14.1.93	1	NC	Moskva		21 Feb
8.18	Serhiy	Nykyforov	UKR	6.2.94	Q	EI	Beograd		3 Mar
8.17	Julian	Harvey	USA	17.6.95	1		Charleston		24 Feb
8.16		Zhang Yaoguang	CHN	21.6.93	1		Xianlin		27 Feb

WORLD INDOOR LISTS 2017   581

8.13		Huang	Changzhou	CHN	20.8.94	1		Xianlin	23 Feb
8.11	Fyodor	Kiselkov		RUS	3.6.95	2	NC	Moskva	21 Feb
8.08	Jean-Pierre	Bertrand		FRA	5.11.92	1		Tignes	3 Jan
8.08	Izmir	Smajlaj		ALB	29.3.93	1	EI	Beograd	4 Mar
8.08	Michel	Tornéus		SWE	26.5.86	2	EI	Beograd	4 Mar
8.07	Lamont Marcell	Jacobs		ITA	26.9.94	1	NC-23	Ancona	4 Feb
8.05	Grant	Holloway		USA	19.11.97	1		Blacksburg	21 Jan
8.05	Khotso	Mokoena		RSA	6.3.85	1		Karlsruhe	4 Feb
8.05	Filippo	Randazzo		ITA	27.4.96	2	NC	Ancona	18 Feb
8.04	KeAndre	Bates		USA	24.5.96	1	SEC	Nashville	25 Feb
8.01	Damarcus	Simpson		USA	14.7.93	1		New York (Armory)	28 Jan
8.01	Andrew	Howe		ITA	12.5.85	3	NC	Ancona	18 Feb
8.01	Maksim	Kolesnikov		RUS	28.2.91	3	NC	Moskva	21 Feb
7.98	Aleksandr	Petrov		RUS	9.8.86	1		Moskva	10 Jan
7.98	Eusebio	Cáceres		ESP	10.9.91	1	NC	Salamanca	18 Feb
7.98		Shi Yuhao		CHN-J	26.9.98	3		Xianlin	23 Feb
7.98	Lazar	Anic		SRB	14.12.91	Q	EI	Beograd	3 Mar
7.98	Tomasz	Jaszczuk		POL	9.3.92	4	EI	Beograd	4 Mar
7.97	Julian	Howard	GER	3.4.89	4 Feb	7.91	Marcos	Chuva	POR 8.8.89 12 Feb
7.94	Andre	Dorsey	USA	11.3.93	11 Feb	7.89A	Terrell	McClain	USA 10.11.95 10 Feb
7.93	Kevin	Ojiaku	ITA	20.4.89	18 Feb	7.89	Charles	Brown	USA 28.5.97 24 Feb
7.93	Travonn	White	USA	3.6.95	25 Feb	7.89	Will	Williams	USA 31.1.95 10 Mar
7.93A	La'Derrick	Ward	USA	28.12.92	4 Mar	7.88	Anatoliy	Ryapolov	RUS 31.1.97 11 Feb
7.92	Elvijs	Misans	LAT	8.4.89	29 Jan	7.88	Christopher	Ullmann	SUI 21.8.93 18 Feb
7.92	Kirill	Sukharev	RUS	24.5.92	21 Feb				

TRIPLE JUMP

17.52	Max	Hess		GER	13.7.96	Q	EI	Beograd	3 Mar
17.20	Lyukman	Adams		RUS	24.9.88	1	NC	Moskva	20 Feb
17.20	Melvin	Raffin		FRA-J	9.8.98	Q	EI	Beograd	3 Mar
17.20	Nelson	Évora		POR	20.4.84	1	EI	Beograd	5 Mar
17.19	Clive	Pullen		JAM	18.10.94	1	Tyson	Fayetteville	11 Feb
17.13	Jean-Marc	Pontvianne		FRA	8.8.94	1	NC	Bordeaux	19 Feb
17.13	Fabrizio	Donato		ITA	14.8.76	2	EI	Beograd	5 Mar
17.12		Dong Bin		CHN	22.11.88	1		Xianlin	24 Feb
17.10	Alexis	Copello		CUB	12.8.85	1		Madrid	24 Feb
17.10A	Chris	Carter		USA	11.3.89	1	NC	Albuquerque	5 Mar
17.02	Elvijs	Misans		LAT	8.4.89	4	EI	Beograd	5 Mar
16.99A	Donald	Scott		USA	23.2.92	2	NC	Albuquerque	5 Mar
16.95	Dmitriy	Chizhikov		RUS	6.12.93	2	NC	Moskva	20 Feb
16.94	Aleksandr	Yurchenko		RUS	30.7.92	1	Winter	Moskva	5 Feb
16.94		Wu Ruiting		CHN	29.11.95	2		Xianlin	24 Feb
16.94	Harold	Corréa		FRA	26.6.88	2		Madrid	24 Feb
16.91A	Josh	Honeycutt		USA	7.3.89	3	NC	Albuquerque	5 Mar
16.86		Fang Yaoqing		CHN	20.4.96	1		Xianlin	28 Feb
16.84	Simo	Lipsanen		FIN	13.9.95	7	EI	Beograd	5 Mar
16.81	KeAndre	Bates		USA	24.5.96	1	SEC	Nashville	24 Feb
16.78	Georgi	Tsonov		BUL	2.5.93	8	EI	Beograd	5 Mar
16.77	Pablo	Torrijos		ESP	12.5.92	Q	EI	Beograd	3 Mar
16.72	Kevin	Luron		FRA	8.11.91	2	NC	Bordeaux	19 Feb
16.72		Zhu Yaming		CHN	4.5.94	2		Xianlin	28 Feb
16.70A	Matthew	O'Neal		USA	10.6.94	4	NC	Albuquerque	5 Mar
16.69		Cao Shuo		CHN	8.10.91	3		Xianlin	28 Feb
16.68		Xu Xiaolong		CHN	20.12.92	3		Xianlin	24 Feb
16.66		Lu Zhiwei		CHN	4.4.96	4		Xianlin	28 Feb
16.62	Benjamin	Compaoré		FRA	5.8.87	3	NC	Bordeaux	19 Feb
16.59	Levon	Aghasyan	ARM	19.1.95	18 Feb	16.49	Daniele	Cavazzani	ITA 4.12.92 19 Feb
16.59	Yoann	Rapinier	FRA	29.9.89	19 Feb	16.49	O'Brien	Wasome	JAM 24.1.97 11 Mar
16.58	Clayton	Brown	JAM	8.12.96	24 Feb	16.42	Karol	Hoffmann	POL 1.6.89 10 Feb
16.56	Hayden	McClain	USA	8.10.95	11 Feb	16.42	Mike	Sandle	USA 10.6.92 25 Feb
16.54A	Felix	Obi	USA	15.6.94	5 Mar	16.41	Daniele	Greco	ITA 1.3.89 19 Feb
16.53	Nathan	Fox	GBR	21.10.90	11 Feb	16.40	Tosin	Oke	NGR 1.10.80 14 Jan
16.53	Adtian	Swiderski	POL	26.9.86	11 Feb	16.40	Tomás	Veszelka	SVK 9.7.95 19 Feb
16.51	Fabrice	Zango	BUR	25.6.93	3 Jan				

SHOT

21.97	Konrad	Bukowiecki		POL	17.3.97	1	EI	Beograd	4 Mar
21.43	Tomás	Stanek		CZE	13.6.91	2	EI	Beograd	4 Mar
21.37	David	Storl		GER	27.7.90	1		Rochlitz	5 Feb
21.30	Mostafa Amr	Ahmed Hassan		EGY	16.12.95	1	MWC	Albuquerque	25 Feb
21.09	Maksim	Afonin		RUS	16.1.92	1	NC	Moskva	20 Feb
21.08	Tsanko	Arnaudov		POR	14.3.92	4	EI	Beograd	4 Mar
21.04	Stipe	Zunic		CRO	13.12.90	5	EI	Beograd	4 Mar
20.87	Asmir	Kolasinac		SRB	15.10.84	1		Beograd	18 Feb
20.86	Franck	Elemba		CGO	21.7.90	1		Madrid	24 Feb

WORLD INDOOR LISTS 2017

Mark	First	Last	Nat	DOB	Pos	Meet	Venue	Date
20.84	Ladislav	Prásil	CZE	17.5.90	1	NC	Praha (Stromovka)	26 Feb
20.82*	Jordan	Geist	USA	21.7.98	1		Greensburg	22 Dec
20.80	Aleksandr	Lesnoy	RUS	17.7.88	2		Sankt-Peterburg	14 Feb
20.78	Darien	Moore	USA	10.6.91	1	NC	Albuquerque	4 Mar
20.68	Michal	Haratyk	POL	10.4.92	4		Potsdam	8 Feb
20.63	Bob	Bertemes	LUX	24.5.93	1		Metz	4 Feb
20.53	Jonathan	Jones	USA	23.4.91	2	NC	Albuquerque	4 Mar
20.47	Jared	Kern	USA	10.6.95	1		Nashville	11 Feb
20.41	Borja	Vivas	ESP	26.5.84	1		Sabadell	7 Feb
20.38	Josh	Freeman	USA	22.8.94	1		Charleston	17 Feb
20.37	Mesud	Pezer	BIH	27.8.94	1		Istanbul	17 Feb
20.35	Francisco	Belo	POR	27.3.91	1		Jamor	4 Feb
20.32	Jakub	Szyszkowski	POL	21.8.91	1		Torun	22 Jan
20.32	Chukwuewuka	Enekwechi	USA	28.1.93	1		Notre Dame	4 Feb
20.32	Carlos	Tobalina	ESP	2.8.85	1	NC	Salamanca	18 Feb
20.31	David	Pless	USA	19.11.90	3	NC	Albuquerque	4 Mar
20.23	Curtis	Jensen	USA	1.11.90	1		Oshkosh	18 Feb
20.22	Mihail	Stamatóyiannis	GRE	20.5.82	1	NC	Piréas	18 Feb
20.18	Arttu	Kangas	FIN	13.7.93	1	NC	Jyvaskyla	19 Feb
20.16	Darrell	Hill	USA	17.8.93	4	NC	Albuquerque	4 Mar
20.11	Rafal	Kownatke	POL	24.3.85	3	NC	Torun	19 Feb
19.99	Mikalai	Abramchuk	BLR	22.9.92	4	Mar		
19.98	Frédéric	Dagée	FRA	11.12.92	28	Jan		
19.97	Aleksey	Nichipor	BLR	10.4.93	18	Feb		
19.97	Filip	Mihaljevic	CRO	31.7.94	25	Feb		
19.89	Nick	Vena	USA	16.4.93	14	Jan		
19.88	Konstantin	Lyadusov	RUS	2.3.88	20	Feb		
19.88	Denzel	Comenentia	NED	25.11.95	10	Mar		
19.87	Roger	Steen	USA	17.5.92	4	Mar		
19.85	Nicolai	Ceban	MDA	4.2.95	26	Jan		
19.84	Oghenakpobo	Efekoro	USA	15.7.96	10	Mar		
19.82	Andrei	Gag	ROU	7.4.91	12	Feb		
19.81	Georgi	Ivanov	BUL	13.3.85	3	Feb		
19.80	Dotun	Ogundeji	USA	24.2.96	25	Feb		
19.79	Willie	Morrison	USA	23.11.96	25	Feb		
19.76	Timothy	Nedow	CAN	16.10.90	18	Feb		
19.76	Nicholas	Demaline	USA	1.3.96	25	Feb		
19.75	Matt	Katnik	USA	10.10.96	25	Feb		
19.67	Mateusz	Mikos	POL	10.4.87	19	Feb		

Mark	First	Last	Nat	DOB	Pos	Meet	Venue	Date
19.66	Josh	Awotunde	NGR	12.6.95	10	Mar		
19.60	Daniel	Ståhl	SWE	27.8.92	11	Feb		
19.55	Ashinia	Miller	JAM	6.6.93	7	Jan		
19.54	Coy	Blair	USA	10.6.94	26	Feb		
19.53	Aaron	Castle	USA	7.10.93	17	Feb		
19.52	Sebastiano	Bianchetti	ITA	20.1.96	9	Feb		
19.50	Sarunas	Banevicius	LTU	20.11.91	17	Feb		
19.48	Dennis	Lewke	GER	23.7.93	8	Feb		
19.48		Liu Yang	CHN	29.10.86	19	Feb		
19.46	Daniele	Secci	ITA	9.3.92	9	Feb		
19.44	Patrick	Cronie	NED	5.11.89	18	Feb		
19.42	Maksim	Sidorov	RUS	13.5.86	5	Feb		
19.39	Bodo	Göder	GER	27.6.93	12	Feb		
19.35	Mohamed	Hamza	EGY	30.8.96	28	Jan		
19.30	Ryan	Whiting	USA	24.11.86	4	Mar		
19.25	Martin	Novák	CZE	5.10.92	4	Feb		
19.22	Richard	Chavez	USA	30.7.92	4	Feb		
19.21	Alex	Renner	USA	.94	14	Jan		

DISCUS

Mark	First	Last	Nat	DOB	Pos	Meet	Venue	Date
66.90	Daniel	Ståhl	SWE	27.8.92	1	v3N	Tampere	11 Feb
63.84	Christoph	Harting	GER	4.10.90	1	ISTAF	Berlin	10 Feb
62.67	Martin	Wierig	GER	10.6.87	2	ISTAF	Berlin	10 Feb
62.23	Lukas	Weisshaidinger	AUT	20.2.92	3	ISTAF	Berlin	10 Feb
61.67	Sven Martin	Skagestad	NOR	13.1.95	11 Feb	61.43 Pyry Niskala FIN 6.11.90		18 Feb
61.46	Robert	Urbanek	POL	29.4.87	10 Feb	61.04 Axel Härstedt SWE 28.2.87		4 Mar

WEIGHT

Mark	First	Last	Nat	DOB	Pos	Meet	Venue	Date
24.02	Alexander	Young	USA	1.9.94	1	NC	Albuquerque	5 Mar
23.74	Colin	Dunbar	USA	27.6.88	2	NC	Albuquerque	5 Mar
23.57	Sean	Donnelly	USA	1.4.93	3	NC	Albuquerque	5 Mar
23.56	Johnnie	Jackson	USA	19.9.94	1		Birmingham AL	21 Jan
23.44	Gleb	Dudarov	BLR	17.10.96	1	Tyson	Fayetteville	10 Feb
23.32	Rudy	Winkler	USA	6.12.94	1		State College	3 Feb
23.31	Grant	Cartwright	USA	19.11.94	1	Big10	Geneva	25 Feb
23.06	Daniel	Haugh	USA	3.5.95	1	SEC	Nashville	25 Feb
22.91	Jordan	Young	CAN	21.6.93	1		Cambridge	3 Feb
22.77	Joe	Frye	USA	20.7.88	4	NC	Albuquerque	5 Mar
22.62	Adam	Kelly	USA	6.7.97	2		New York (Armory)	25 Feb
22.59	Andrew	Fryman	USA	3.2.85	5	NC	Albuquerque	5 Mar
22.49	Joe	Ellis	GBR	10.4.96	2	Big10	Geneva	25 Feb
22.30	A.G.	Kruger	USA	18.2.79	11 Feb	22.04 Josh Davis USA 23.9.95		11 Mar
22.25	Alexandros	Poursanidis	CYP	23.1.93	24 Feb	22.01 Reginald Jagers USA 13.8.94		25 Feb
22.23	Riley	Budde	USA	31.5.95	17 Feb	22.01 Luis Rivera USA 2.3.94		5 Mar
22.20	Daniel	Roberts	USA	11.12.94	28 Jan	21.81 Elias Häkansson SWE 29.2.92		25 Feb
22.11	James	Hubbard	USA	10 Feb	21.70* Jonathan Schertz USA		3 Dec

HEPTATHLON

Total	First	Last	Nat	DOB	Pos	Meet	Venue	Date
6479	Kevin	Mayer	FRA	10.2.92	1	EI	Beograd	5 Mar
	6.95	7.54	15.66	2.10	7.88	5.40	2:41.08	
6249	Jorge	Ureña	ESP	8.10.93	1	v4N	Praha (Stromovka)	29 Jan
	6.91	7.62	13.96	2.04	7.85	5.00	2:40.06	
6188	Adam Sebastian	Helcelet	CZE	27.10.91	1		Praha (Stromovka)	12 Feb
	6.99	7.58	14.78	2.05	7.94	5.10	2:48.31	

WORLD INDOOR LISTS 2017

Score	First	Last	Nat	DOB	Pos	Meet	Venue	Date
6177	Devon	Williams	USA	17.1.94	1	NCAA	College Station	11 Mar
	6.88	7.83 14.11		1.95 7.75		4.76	2:41.26	
6165	Tim	Duckworth	GBR	18.6.96	2	NCAA	College Station	11 Mar
	6.77	7.77 13.09		2.16 8.10		5.26	3:04.24	
6089#*	Luca	Wieland	GER	7.12.94	1		Brookings	3 Dec
	6.92	7.46 14.83		2.10 8.23		4.80	2:46.39	
6063	Dominik	Distelberger	AUT	16.3.90	4	EI	Beograd	5 Mar
	6.94	7.38 13.55		1.98 7.80		5.10	2:42.32	
6051	Karl Robert	Saluri	EST	6.8.93	3	NCAA	College Station	11 Mar
	6.79	7.58 14.41		1.86 8.33		4.96	2:36.92	
6015	Fredrik	Samuelsson	SWE	16.2.95	5	EI	Beograd	5 Mar
	7.06	7.40 14.24		2.01 8.18		5.00	2:42.97	
5996	Hunter	Price	USA	28.8.94	4	NCAA	College Station	11 Mar
	6.94	7.30 13.27		2.04 8.01		4.66	2:37.99	
5986	Kristjan	Rosenberg	EST	16.5.94	1		Tallinn	4 Feb
	7.01	7.25 13.62		2.13 8.37		4.87	2:42.96	
5985	Jirí	Sykora	CZE	20.1.95	2		Praha (Stromovka)	12 Feb
	6.99	7.53 14.85		1.96 8.01		4.80	2:48.40	
5984	Mathias	Brugger	GER	6.8.92	1	NC	Hamburg	29 Jan
	7.09	7.30 14.63		1.97 8.22		5.00	2:40.62	
5984	Darko	Pesic	MNE	30.11.92	5	EI	Beograd	5 Mar
	7.22	7.12 16.08		2.01 7.99		4.70	2:38.23	
5976	Lindon	Victor	GRN	28.2.93	5	NCAA	College Station	11 Mar
	6.99	7.23 16.55		2.07 8.43		4.76	2:51.14	
5975	Ashley	Bryant	GBR	17.5.91	2	v4N	Praha (Stromovka)	29 Jan
	7.08	7.79 14.32		1.98 8.10		4.90	2:40.84	
5970	Harrison	Williams	USA	7.3.96	6	NCAA	College Station	11 Mar
	7.02	7.03 13.34		1.95 8.23		5.36	2:39.45	
5966	Niels	Pittomvils	BEL	18.7.92	1		Gent	5 Feb
	7.21	7.09 13.66		1.99 8.10		5.40	2:44.11	
5962	Pavel	Rudnev	RUS	26.10.92	1	NC	Smolensk	16 Feb
	7.09	7.20 12.88		2.05 8.24		5.20	2:42.60	
5902	Maxime	Maugein	FRA	27.9.92	1	NC	Bordeaux	19 Feb
	7.10	7.12 14.03		2.00 8.12		4.75	2:38.14	
5879	Marek	Lukás	CZE	16.7.91	3		Praha (Stromovka)	12 Feb
	7.06	7.11 14.91		1.93 8.09		4.90	2:45.33	
5875	Yevgeniy	Likhanov	RUS	10.10.95	2	NC	Smolensk	16 Feb
	7.14	7.38 14.59		2.08 8.24		4.70	2:51.19	
5858	Jérémy	Lelièvre	FRA	8.2.91	2	NC	Bordeaux	19 Feb
	6.98	7.31 14.87		1.94 8.31		4.45	2:37.75	
5843#	Steven	Bastien	USA	4.3.94	1		Akron	4 Feb
	6.84	7.33 13.00		1.93 8.17		4.75	2:43.98	
5841	Simone	Cairoli	ITA	12.9.90	12	EI	Beograd	5 Mar
	7.04	7.55 12.21		2.04 8.31		4.70	2:40.14	
5834	Benjamin	Gregory	GBR	21.11.90	1		Glasgow	5 Mar
	7.29	7.30 13.22		1.99 8.22		4.97	2:40.92	
5833	Florian	Geffrouais	FRA	5.12.88	3	NC	Bordeaux	19 Feb
	7.12	6.92 15.36		1.91 8.32		4.85	2:38.09	
5832	Liam	Ramsay	GBR	18.11.92	1		Sheffield	8 Jan
	7.00	7.21 13.58		2.05 8.28		4.41	2:38.86	

Score	First	Last	Nat	DOB	Date		Score	First	Last	Nat	DOB	Date
5824	Bas	Markies	NED	24.7.84	5 Feb		5786	Jonathan	Wells	USA	18.4.96	11 Mar
5820	Vasyl	Ivanytskyy	UKR	29.1.91	18 Feb		5780	Artem	Lukyanenko	RUS	30.1.90	16 Feb
5817#	Steele	Wasik	USA	8.12.95	25 Feb		5778	Yevgeniy	Sarantsev	RUS	5.2.88	19 Jan
5815	Tim	Nowak	GER	13.8.95	29 Jan		5770	John	Seals	USA	22.10.95	19 Feb
5814	Roman	Kondratyev	RUS	15.5.95	16 Feb		5760	Ruben	Gado	FRA	13.12.93	19 Feb
5813	Hunter	Veith	USA	14.1.95	26 Feb		5756	Austin	Jamerson	USA	16.3.95	26 Feb
5804#	Wolf	Mahler	USA	26.9.94	25 Feb		5747#	Mitch	Modin	USA	12.4.95	25 Feb
	5791				11 Mar		5738A	Japheth	Cato	USA	25.12.90	4 Mar

3000 METRES WALK

Time	First	Last	Nat	DOB	Pos	Meet	Venue	Date
11:15.15	Alex	Wright	IRL	19.12.90	1		Abbotstown	5 Feb
11:16.43+	Tom	Bosworth	GBR	17.1.90	1	in 5k	Sheffield	12 Feb

5000 METRES WALK

Time	First	Last	Nat	DOB	Pos	Meet	Venue	Date
18:39.47	Tom	Bosworth	GBR	17.1.90	1	NC	Sheffield	12 Feb
18:50.70	Alex	Wright	IRL	19.12.90	1	NC	Dublin	18 Feb
18:59.06	Francesco	Fortunato	ITA	13.12.94	1	NC	Ancona	18 Feb
19:00.4*	Sergey	Shirobokov	RUS-J	16.2.99	1		Saransk	30 Dec
19:08.82	Christopher	Linke	GER	24.10.88	1	NC	Erfurt	5 Mar
19:12.98	Aléxandros	Papamihaíl	GRE	18.9.88	1	NC	Piréas	18 Feb

10000 METRES WALK

Time	First	Last	Nat	DOB	Pos	Meet	Venue	Date
39:40.97	Aleksandr	Lyakovich	BLR	4.7.89	1	NC	Mogilyov	18 Feb

WORLD INDOOR LISTS 2017 – WOMEN

60 METRES

Time	First Name	Last Name	Nat	DOB	Pos	Meet	Venue	Date
6.98	Elaine	Thompson	JAM	28.6.92	1		Birmingham	18 Feb
7.06	Asha	Philip	GBR	25.10.90	1	EI	Beograd	5 Mar
7.07A	Hannah	Cunliffe	USA	9.1.96	1		Albuquerque	11 Feb
7.13					1h1	NCAA	College Station	10 Mar
7.08A	Morolake	Akinosun	USA	17.5.94	1	NC	Albuquerque	5 Mar
7.10	Olesya	Povh	UKR	18.10.87	2	EI	Beograd	5 Mar
7.10	Ewa	Swoboda	POL	26.7.97	3	EI	Beograd	5 Mar
7.11	Barbara	Pierre	USA	28.4.87	1h1		Toruń	10 Feb
7.11A	Dezerea	Bryant	USA	27.4.93	2	NC	Albuquerque	5 Mar
7.12					1	Mill	New York (Armory)	11 Feb
7.13	Dina	Asher-Smith	GBR	4.12.95	1h1		Karlsruhe	4 Feb
7.13	Ezinne	Okparaebo	NOR	3.3.88	2		Toruń	10 Feb
7.14	Rebekka	Haase	GER	2.1.93	1		Erfurt	27 Jan
7.14	Gayon	Evans	JAM	15.1.90	1		Karlsruhe	4 Feb
7.14	Gina	Lückenkemper	GER	21.11.96	1	NC	Leipzig	18 Feb
7.14	Marie Josée	Ta Lou	CIV	18.11.88	1h2	NC	Bordeaux	18 Feb
7.14	Javianne	Oliver	USA	26.12.94	1h2	NCAA	College Station	10 Mar
7.15A	LeKeisha	Lawson	USA	3.6.87	3	NC	Albuquerque	5 Mar
7.20					1		Athlone	15 Feb
7.16	Stella	Akakpo	FRA	28.2.94	1		Reims	31 Jan
7.16	Mujinga	Kambundji	SUI	17.6.92	4	EI	Beograd	5 Mar
7.17	English	Gardner	USA	22.4.92	1		Boston (Roxbury)	28 Jan
7.17A	Ashley	Henderson	USA	4.12.95	1	MWC	Albuquerque	25 Feb
7.18					3h1	NCAA	College Station	10 Mar
7.17	Deajah	Stevens	USA	19.5.95	2h1	NCAA	College Station	10 Mar
7.18A	Schillonie	Calvert-Powell	JAM	27.7.88	1		Flagstaff	17 Feb
7.18	Tatjana	Pinto	GER	2.7.92	1s2	NC	Leipzig	18 Feb
7.18	Christania	Williams	JAM	17.10.94	3		Birmingham	18 Feb
7.18	Lisa	Mayer	GER	2.5.96	3	NC	Leipzig	18 Feb
7.18	Aleia	Hobbs	USA	24.2.96	1	SEC	Nashville	25 Feb
7.19	Mikiah	Brisco	USA	14.7.96	1		Fayetteville	28 Jan
7.19	Alexandra	Burghardt	GER	28.4.94	4	NC	Leipzig	18 Feb
7.20	Kristina	Sivkova	RUS	28.2.97	1		Sankt-Peterburg	14 Feb
7.20	Andrea	Purica	VEN	29.11.95	2		Ostrava	14 Feb
7.20A	Destiny	Smith-Barnett	USA	26.7.96	1h4	MWC	Albuquerque	24 Feb
7.20		Liang Xiaojing	CHN	7.4.97	1rA		Xianlin	27 Feb
7.20	Floriane	Gnafoua	FRA	30.1.96	7	EI	Beograd	5 Mar
7.20	Ariana	Washington	USA	4.9.96	3	NCAA	College Station	11 Mar
7.21	Teahna	Daniels	USA	27.3.97	21 Jan			
7.21	Kristina	Timanovskaya	BLR	19.1.96	18 Feb			
7.21A	Mikele	Barber	USA	4.10.80	5 Mar			
7.21	Quanesha	Burks	USA	15.3.95	10 Mar			
7.21	Kortnei	Johnson	USA	11.8.97	10 Mar			
7.22	Stephanie	Kalu	NGR	5.8.93	10 Feb			
7.22	Jessica	Young-Warren	USA	6.4.87	14 Feb			
7.22	Jura	Levy	JAM	4.11.90	16 Feb			
7.22		Yuan Qiqi	CHN	26.10.95	27 Feb			
7.24	Crystal	Emmanuel	CAN	27.11.91	18 Feb			
7.25	Chantal	Butzek	GER	25.2.97	10 Feb			
7.25A	Makenzie	Dunmore	USA	7.10.97	11 Feb			
7.25	Tawanna	Meadows	USA	4.8.86	12 Feb			
7.25A	Jerayah	Davis	USA	15.4.96	24 Feb			
7.26	Yasmin	Kwadwo	GER	9.11.90	27 Jan			
7.26	Remona	Burchell	JAM	15.9.91	28 Jan			
7.26	Kianna	Gray	USA	30.12.96	3 Feb			
7.26	Deanna	Hill	USA	13.4.96	10 Feb			
7.26		Wei Yongli	CHN	11.10.91	11 Feb			
7.26	Flings	Owusu-Agyapong	GHA	16.10.88	15 Feb			
7.26	Anna	Bongiorni	ITA	15.9.93	19 Feb			
7.26	Cassondra	Hall	USA	23.9.97	24 Feb			
7.26	Jada	Martin	USA	8.6.95	24 Feb			
7.26	Devynne	Charlton	BAH	26.11.95	25 Feb			

200 METRES

Time	First Name	Last Name	Nat	DOB	Pos	Meet	Venue	Date
22.42	Ariana	Washington	USA	4.9.96	1r2	NCAA	College Station	11 Mar
22.53	Hannah	Cunliffe	USA	9.1.96	2r2	NCAA	College Station	11 Mar
22.54	Deanna	Hill	USA	13.4.96	3r2	NCAA	College Station	11 Mar
22.65	Deajah	Stevens	USA	19.5.95	1r1		New York (Armory)	28 Jan
22.77	Rebekka	Haase	GER	2.1.93	1	NC	Leipzig	19 Feb
22.81A	Ashley	Henderson	USA	4.12.95	1r2	MWC	Albuquerque	25 Feb
22.83					1r1	NCAA	College Station	11 Mar
22.85	Jada	Martin	USA	8.6.95	1h2	NCAA	College Station	10 Mar
22.86	Brittany	Brown	USA	18.4.95	2h2	NCAA	College Station	10 Mar
22.88	Gabrielle	Thomas	USA	4.7.97	1		New York (Armory)	26 Feb
22.94	Ashley	Spencer	USA	8.6.93	1		Lincoln	4 Feb
22.94	Diamond	Spaulding	USA	29.9.96	3h1	NCAA	College Station	10 Mar
22.97	Kendall	Ellis	USA	8.3.96	2r1	Tyson	Fayetteville	11 Feb
22.98	Léa	Sprunger	SUI	5.3.90	1	NC	Magglingen	19 Feb
23.00	Taylor	Bennett	USA	15.1.97	1	Tyson	Fayetteville	11 Feb
23.00	Danyel	White	USA-J	10.2.98	4h1	NCAA	College Station	10 Mar
23.13	Anna	Kielbasinska	POL	26.6.90	19 Feb			
23.14	Jasmine	Camacho-Quinn	PUR	21.8.96	11 Feb			
23.15	Phyllis	Francis	USA	4.5.92	18 Feb			
23.18	Candyce	McGrone	USA	24.3.89	6 Feb			
23.19	Lara	Matheis	GER	2.8.92	19 Feb			
23.21	Ama	Pipi	GBR	26.11.95	10 Mar			
23.22	Kori	Carter	USA	3.6.92	11 Feb			
23.22	Sabrina	Hadley	USA	1.1.95	10 Mar			

Time	First	Last	Nat	DOB	Pos	Meet	Venue	Date
23.25	Kianna	Gray	USA	30.12.96				11 Feb
23.26	Kortnei	Johnson	USA	11.8.97				11 Feb
23.26	Kamaria	Brown	USA	21.12.92				18 Feb
23.27	Khristina	Khorosheva	RUS	5.4.93				20 Jan

Oversized track

Time	First	Last	Nat	DOB	Pos	Meet	Venue	Date
22.79	Brittany	Brown	USA	18.4.95	1h5	Big10	Geneva	24 Feb
22.83	Shakima	Wimbley	USA	23.4.95	1	ACC	Notre Dame	25 Feb
22.92	Jada	Martin	USA	8.6.95	1r1	SEC	Nashville	25 Feb
23.17	Kianna	Gray	USA	30.12.96				
				20 Jan	23.19	Ama	Pipi	GBR	26.11.95	25 Feb

300 METRES

Time	First	Last	Nat	DOB	Pos	Meet	Venue	Date
35.71	Quanera	Hayes	USA	7.3.92	1		Clemson	7 Jan
35.71	Shaunae	Miller-Uibo	BAH	15.4.94	1	Mill	New York (Armory)	11 Feb
36.15A	Phyllis	Francis	USA	4.5.92	1r2	NC	Albuquerque	4 Mar
36.18A	Joanna	Atkins	USA	31.1.89	2r2	NC	Albuquerque	4 Mar
36.27	Ashley	Spencer	USA	8.6.93	2	Mill	New York (Armory)	11 Feb
36.56A	Candace	Hill	USA-J	11.2.99	1r1	NC	Albuquerque	4 Mar
36.86					2		Clemson	7 Jan
36.72	Shakima	Wimbley	USA	23.4.95	1		Blacksburg	13 Jan
36.82	Sydney	McLaughlin	USA-J	7.8.99	17 Feb	36.87A	Robin	Reynolds	USA	22.2.94	4 Mar
36.87	Courtney	Okolo	USA	15.3.94	28 Jan	36.88	Natasha	Hastings	USA	23.7.86	11 Feb
36.87A	Jessica	Beard	USA	8.1.89	4 Mar	36.92	Rebekka	Haase	GER	2.1.93	27 Jan

400 METRES

Time	First	Last	Nat	DOB	Pos	Meet	Venue	Date
51.07	Shakima	Wimbley	USA	23.4.95	1r2	NCAA	College Station	11 Mar
51.07	Kendall	Ellis	USA	8.3.96	2r2	NCAA	College Station	11 Mar
51.46	Léa	Sprunger	SUI	5.3.90	1		Magglingen	5 Feb
51.61	Sydney	McLaughlin	USA-J	7.8.99	1		New York (Armory)	12 Mar
51.71	Chris-Ann	Gordon	JAM	18.9.94	1r2	Tyson	Fayetteville	10 Feb
51.77	Zuzana	Hejnová	CZE	19.12.86	1		Birmingham	18 Feb
51.78	Carly	Muscaro	USA	18.5.95	1	NCAA II	Birmingham AL	11 Mar
51.84	Sage	Watson	CAN	20.6.94	1r1	NCAA	College Station	11 Mar
51.86	Eilidh	Doyle	GBR	20.2.87	1		Wien	28 Jan
51.90	Laviai	Nielsen	GBR	13.3.96	2		Birmingham	18 Feb
51.90	Floria	Guei	FRA	2.5.90	1	El	Beograd	4 Mar
51.93	Daina	Harper	USA	26.6.95	2r1	NCAA	College Station	11 Mar
52.02	Chrishuna	Williams	USA	31.3.93	2r2	Tyson	Fayetteville	10 Feb
52.07	Sharrika	Barnett	USA	16.4.97	1		Fayetteville	28 Jan
52.09	Olha	Zemlyak	UKR	26.1.90	2rA		Metz	12 Feb
52.09	Justyna	Swiety	POL	3.12.92	1	NC	Torun	19 Feb
52.11	Shamier	Little	USA	20.3.95	3		Birmingham	18 Feb
52.13	Tovea	Jenkins	JAM	27.10.92	2	NCAA II	Birmingham AL	11 Mar
52.17	Iga	Baumgart	POL	11.4.89	1		Torun	10 Feb
52.23	Alexandra	Gholston	USA	1.3.95	3r1	NCAA	College Station	11 Mar
52.43	Lisanne	de Witte	NED	10.9.92	27 Jan	52.60	Malgorzata	Holub	POL	30.10.92	19 Feb
52.45	Cameron	Pettigrew	USA	17.4.95	10 Feb	52.64	Grace	Claxton	PUR	19.8.93	26 Feb
52.51	Patrycja	Wyciszkiewicz	POL	8.1.94	18 Feb	52.65	Sparkle	McKnight	TTO	21.12.91	10 Feb
52.52	Yekaterina	Renzhina	RUS	18.10.94	5 Feb	52.66	Brittny	Ellis	USA	1.9.97	10 Feb
52.54	Leticia	de Souza	BRA	6.5.96	10 Feb	52.67	Zola	Golden	USA	20.6.97	10 Mar

Oversized track

Time	First	Last	Nat	DOB	Pos	Meet	Venue	Date
51.77	Daina	Harper	USA	26.6.95	1h2	SEC	Nashville	24 Feb
52.11	Zola	Golden	USA	20.6.97	2	Big12	Ames	25 Feb
52.19	Brittny	Ellis	USA	1.9.97	2	ACC	Notre Dame	25 Feb

Time	First	Last	Nat	DOB	Pos	Meet	Venue	Date
1:07.34	Courtney	Okolo	USA	15.3.94	1	Mill	New York (Armory)	11 Feb
1:08.40	Sage	Watson	CAN	20.6.94	1r3		New York (Armory)	3 Feb
1:09.05	Carly	Muscaro	USA	18.5.95	4 Feb	1:09.63	Ajee'	Wilson	USA	8.5.94	14 Jan
1:09.55	Alysia	Montaño	USA	23.4.86	11 Feb	1:09.66	Dalilah	Muhammad	USA	7.2.90	11 Feb

600 METRES

Time	First	Last	Nat	DOB	Pos	Meet	Venue	Date
1:23.84A	Ajee'	Wilson	USA	8.5.94	1	NC	Albuquerque	5 Mar
1:24.48					1		New York (Armory)	4 Feb
1:24.00A	Courtney	Okolo	USA	15.3.94	2	NC	Albuquerque	5 Mar
1:25.21					1		Lincoln	4 Feb
1:25.35	Natoya	Goule	JAM	30.3.91	1		Clemson	17 Feb
1:25.46A	Kendra	Chambers	USA	11.9.90	3	NC	Albuquerque	5 Mar
1:25.89	Marilyn	Okoro	GBR	23.9.84	2		Clemson	28 Jan
1:26.54A	Olicia	Williams	USA	26.2.94	4	NC	Albuquerque	5 Mar
1:26.74	Cecilia	Barowski	USA	7.12.92	2		New York (Armory)	4 Feb
1:26.97#	Raevyn	Rogers	USA	7.9.96	14 Jan	1:27.38A	McKayla	Fricker	USA	19.4.92	4 Mar
1:27.13	Samantha	Watson	USA-J	10.11.99	4 Feb	1:27.39	Hanna	Green	USA	16.10.94	18 Feb
1:27.16	Lynsey	Sharp	GBR	11.7.90	4 Feb	1:27.40+	Joanna	Józwik	POL	30.1.91	10 Feb

800 METRES

Time	First	Last	Nat	DOB	Pos	Meet	Venue	Date
1:58.27	Ajee'	Wilson	USA	8.5.94	1	Mill	New York (Armory)	11 Feb
1:58.64	Charlene	Lipsey	USA	16.7.91	2	Mill	New York (Armory)	11 Feb
1:59.29	Joanna	Józwik	POL	30.1.91	1		Torun	10 Feb

WORLD INDOOR LISTS 2017

Time	First	Last	Nat	DOB	Pos	Rnd	Venue	Date
2:00.18mx	Selina	Büchel	SUI	26.7.91	1mx		St.Gallen	12 Feb
2:00.38					1	El	Beograd	5 Mar
2:00.39	Shelayna	Oskan-Clarke	GBR	20.1.90	2	El	Beograd	5 Mar
2:00.55+	Laura	Muir	GBR	9.5.93	1	in 1000	Birmingham	18 Feb
2:00.62+	Genzebe	Dibaba	ETH	8.2.91	1	in 1000	Madrid	24 Feb
2:00.69	Jazmine	Fray	USA	6.6.97	1		Clemson	11 Feb
2:00.91	Malika	Akkaoui	MAR	25.12.87	1		Metz	12 Feb
2:00.92	Olha	Lyakhova	UKR	18.3.92	2		Metz	12 Feb
2:01.09	Raevyn	Rogers	USA	7.9.96	1	NCAA	College Station	11 Mar
2:01.14	Lynsey	Sharp	GBR	11.7.90	3	Mill	New York (Armory)	11 Feb
2:01.18	Anita	Hinriksdóttir	ISL	13.1.96	1		Reykjavik	4 Feb
2:01.36	Justine	Fédronic	FRA	11.5.91	4	Mill	New York (Armory)	11 Feb
2:01.37	Lovisa	Lindh	SWE	9.7.91	4	El	Beograd	5 Mar
2:01.40	Aleksandra	Gulyayeva	RUS	30.4.94	1		Yaroslavl	23 Feb
2:01.42	Melissa	Bishop	CAN	5.8.88	1		Athlone	15 Feb
2:01.42#	Shea	Collinsworth	USA	19.2.95	1		Ames	11 Feb
2:02.35					3	NCAA	College Station	11 Mar
2:01.52	Cecilia	Barowski	USA	7.12.92	5	Mill	New York (Armory)	11 Feb
2:01.55	Hedda	Hynne	NOR	13.3.90	2		Reykjavik	4 Feb
2:01.55+	Esther	Guerrero	ESP	7.2.90	2	in 1000	Madrid	24 Feb
2:01.57	Anastasiya	Tkachuk	UKR	20.4.93	3		Metz	12 Feb
2:01.78	Samantha	Watson	USA	10.11.99	6	Mill	New York (Armory)	11 Feb
2:01.83	Sanne	Verstegen	NED	10.11.85	1	NC	Apeldoorn	12 Feb
2:01.98	Marina	Arzamasova	BLR	17.12.87	3		Karlsruhe	4 Feb
2:02.00	Tigist	Ketema	ETH-J	15.9.98	1		Sabadell	7 Feb
2:02.13	Hanna	Green	USA	16.10.94	11 Mar			
2:02.18	Liga	Velvere	LAT	10.2.90	15 Feb			
2:02.20	Cory	McGee	USA	29.5.92	27 Jan			
2:02.22	Megan	Krumpoch	USA	31.8.92	27 Jan			
2:02.28	Tatyana	Markelova	RUS	19.12.88	13 Jan			
2:02.29#	Kate	Grace	USA	24.10.88	28 Jan			
2:02.38	Habitam	Alemu	ETH	9.7.97	28 Jan			
2:02.43	Yekaterina	Kupina	RUS	2.2.86	20 Jan			
2:02.53	Svetlana	Uloga	RUS	1.3.86	20 Feb			
2:02.54	Anna	Silvander	SWE	22.6.93	27 Jan			
2:02.58	Clarisse	Moh	FRA	6.12.86	12 Feb			
2:02.60	Yelena	Kotulskaya	RUS	8.8.88	20 Feb			
2:02.71	Diana	Mezuliáníková	CZE	10.4.92	28 Jan			
2:02.74#	Stina	Troest	DEN	17.1.94	11 Feb			
2:02.93					5 Mar			
2:02.89#	Aaliyah	Miller	USA-J	28.8.98	11 Feb			
2:02.97	Lenka	Masná	CZE	22.4.85	28 Jan			
2:02.97	Siofra	Cleirigh-Buttner	IRL	21.7.95	28 Jan			

1000 METRES

Time	First	Last	Nat	DOB	Pos	Rnd	Venue	Date
2:31.93	Laura	Muir	GBR	9.5.93	1		Birmingham	18 Feb
2:33.06	Genzebe	Dibaba	ETH	8.2.91	1		Madrid	24 Feb
2:36.97	Kate	Grace	USA	24.10.88	2		Birmingham	18 Feb
2:37.97A	Charlene	Lipsey	USA	16.7.91	1	NC	Albuquerque	5 Mar
2:38.05	Gudaf	Tsegay	ETH	23.1.97	2		Madrid	24 Feb
2:38.19	Darya	Borisevich	BLR	6.4.90	3		Madrid	24 Feb
2:38.33A	Lauren	Johnson	USA	4.5.87	2	NC	Albuquerque	5 Mar
2:38.55	Axumawit	Embaye	ETH	18.10.94	4		Madrid	24 Feb
2:38.72	Sanne	Verstegen	NED	10.11.85	18 Feb			
2:39.47	Zoe	Buckman	AUS	21.12.88	18 Feb			
2:39.53	Sarah	McDonald	GBR	2.8.93	18 Feb			
2:39.76	Aleksandra	Gulyayeva	RUS	30.4.94	6 Jan			

1500 METRES

Time	First	Last	Nat	DOB	Pos	Rnd	Venue	Date
3:58.80	Genzebe	Dibaba	ETH	8.2.91	1		Torun	10 Feb
4:02.39	Laura	Muir	GBR	9.5.93	1	El	Beograd	4 Mar
4:03.05+	Sifan	Hassan	NED	1.1.93	1	in 1M	New York (Armory)	11 Feb
4:04.45	Konstanze	Klosterhalfen	GER	18.2.97	2	El	Beograd	4 Mar
4:04.56+	Shannon	Rowbury	USA	19.9.84	2	in 1M	New York (Armory)	11 Feb
4:04.86+	Kate	Grace	USA	24.10.88	3	in 1M	New York (Armory)	11 Feb
4:04.95	Axumawit	Embaye	ETH	18.10.94	2		Torun	10 Feb
4:06.40	Meraf	Bahta	SWE	24.6.89	3		Torun	10 Feb
4:06.59	Sofia	Ennaoui	POL	30.8.95	4		Torun	10 Feb
4:06.66	Luiza	Gega	ALB	5.11.88	1		Istanbul	17 Feb
4:07.47	Aleksandra	Gulyayeva	RUS	30.4.94	1	Winter	Moskva	5 Feb
4:08.15	Yelena	Korobkina	RUS	25.11.90	2	Winter	Moskva	5 Feb
4:08.19	Claudia	Bobocea	ROU	11.6.92	1		Athlone	15 Feb
4:08.50	Anna	Shchagina	RUS	7.12.91	3	Winter	Moskva	5 Feb
4:08.56	Taye	Fantu	ETH-J	29.3.99	3		Ostrava	14 Feb
4:08.76	Rababe	Arrafi	MAR	12.1.91	4		Ostrava	14 Feb
4:08.97	Anastasiya	Kalina	RUS	16.2.94	4	Winter	Moskva	5 Feb
4:09.17	Basu	Sado	ETH	12.1.96	5		Torun	10 Feb
4:09.48	Renata	Plis	POL	5.2.85	5		Ostrava	14 Feb
4:09.95	Meryem	Akdag	TUR	5.8.92	2		Istanbul	17 Feb
4:10.04	Simona	Vrzalová	CZE	7.4.88	14 Feb			
4:10.35+	Nicole	Sifuentes	CAN	30.6.86	11 Feb			
4:10.35	Amela	Terzic	SRB	2.1.93	3 Mar			
4:10.90+	Dominique	Scott	RSA	24.6.92	11 Feb			
4:11.00+	Kaela	Edwards	USA	8.12.93	11 Feb			
4:11.12+	Alexa	Efraimson	USA	20.2.97	11 Feb			
4:11.18	Zoe	Buckman	AUS	21.12.88	15 Feb			
4:11.43+	Heather	Kampf	USA	19.1.87	11 Feb			
4:11.45	Winny	Chebet	KEN	20.12.90	14 Feb			
4:11.53	Diana	Mezuliáníková	CZE	10.4.92	14 Feb			
4:11.54	Yasemin	Can	TUR	11.12.96	17 Feb			
4:11.62	Sarah	McDonald	GBR	2.8.93	15 Feb			
4:11.73	Katarzyna	Broniatowska	POL	22.2.90	10 Feb			
4:11.77	Linn	Nilsson	SWE	15.10.90	15 Feb			

WORLD INDOOR LISTS 2017   587

4:11.93+	Leah	O'Connor	USA	30.8.92	11 Feb	4:12.47+	Kate	Van Buskirk	CAN	9.6.87	4 Feb
4:12.24+	Charlene	Lipsey	USA	16.7.91	4 Feb	4:12.52	Darya	Borisevich	BLR	6.4.90	3 Mar
4:12.35+	Elinor	Purrier	USA	20.2.95	11 Feb	4:12.55	Özlem	Kaya	TUR	20.4.90	17 Feb
4:12.46	Ciara	Mageean	IRL	12.3.92	15 Feb	4:13.19	Geneviene	LaCaze	AUS	4.8.89	15 Feb

1 MILE

4:19.89	Sifan	Hassan	NED	1.1.93	1	Mill	New York (Armory)	11 Feb
4:21.3+e	Genzebe	Dibaba	ETH	8.2.91	1	in 2000	Sabadell	7 Feb
4:22.93	Kate	Grace	USA	24.10.88	2	Mill	New York (Armory)	11 Feb
4:23.05	Shannon	Rowbury	USA	19.9.84	3	Mill	New York (Armory)	11 Feb
4:24.16	Shelby	Houlihan	USA	8.2.93	1		Boston (Allston)	10 Feb
4:24.88	Colleen	Quigley	USA	20.11.92	2		Boston (Allston)	10 Feb
4:25.62	Rachel	Schneider	USA	18.7.91	3		Boston (Allston)	10 Feb
4:27.27#	Brie	Felnagle	USA	9.12.86	1		Seattle	28 Jan
4:28.39	Heather	Kampf	USA	19.1.87	4	Mill	New York (Armory)	11 Feb
4:28.47	Dominique	Scott	RSA	24.6.92	5	Mill	New York (Armory)	11 Feb
4:28.75	Kaela	Edwards	USA	8.12.93	6	Mill	New York (Armory)	11 Feb
4:29.27	Nicole	Sifuentes	CAN	30.6.86	7	Mill	New York (Armory)	11 Feb
4:29.44	Elinor	Purrier	USA	20.2.95	8	Mill	New York (Armory)	11 Feb
4:29.54	Alexa	Efraimson	USA	20.2.97	9	Mill	New York (Armory)	11 Feb

4:30.03	Cory	McGee	USA	29.5.92	4 Feb	4:32.06	Sarah	McDonald	GBR	2.8.93	21 Jan
4:30.13	Charlene	Lipsey	USA	16.7.91	4 Feb	4:32.18	Anna	Shchagina	RUS	7.12.91	14 Feb
4:30.14	Kate	Van Buskirk	CAN	9.7.87	21 Jan	4:32.35	Kerri	Gallagher	USA	31.5.89	21 Jan
4:31.19	Aleksandra	Gulyayeva	RUS	30.4.94	21 Jan	4:32.41	Stephanie	Garcia	USA	3.5.88	4 Feb
4:31.24	Karisa	Nelson	USA	12.6.96	11 Mar	4:32.55#	Danae	Rivers	USA-J	3.2.98	11 Feb
4:32.02	Megan	Krumpoch	USA	31.8.92	10 Feb	4:32.73	Anastasiya	Kalina	RUS	16.2.94	21 Jan

2000 METRES

5:23.75	Genzebe	Dibaba	ETH	8.2.91	1		Sabadell	7 Feb
5:40.57+	Hellen	Obiri	KEN	13.12.89	1	in 3000	Karlsruhe	4 Feb
5:41.5+	Laura	Muir	GBR	9.5.93	2	in 3000	Karlsruhe	4 Feb
5:44.42	Aleksandra	Gulyayeva	RUS	30.4.94	1		Moskva	10 Jan

3000 METRES

8:26.41	Laura	Muir	GBR	9.5.93	1		Karlsruhe	4 Feb
8:28.41	Hellen	Obiri	KEN	13.12.89	1		Birmingham	18 Feb
8:30.76	Sifan	Hassan	NED	1.1.93	2		Birmingham	18 Feb
8:37.65	Dawit	Seyaum	ETH	27.7.96	3		Birmingham	18 Feb
8:41.94	Shannon	Rowbury	USA	19.9.84	3		Boston (Roxbury)	28 Jan
8:43.00	Meraf	Bahta	SWE	24.6.89	4		Birmingham	18 Feb
8:43.02	Eilish	McColgan	GBR	25.11.90	5		Birmingham	18 Feb
8:43.46	Yasemin	Can	TUR	11.12.96	2	El	Beograd	5 Mar
8:44.63	Maureen	Koster	NED	3.7.92	5		Birmingham	18 Feb
8:45.29	Sofia	Ennaoui	POL	30.8.95	7		Birmingham	18 Feb
8:45.81	Geneviene	LaCaze	AUS	4.8.89	8		Birmingham	18 Feb
8:45.95	Stephanie	Twell	GBR	17.8.89	10		Birmingham	18 Feb
8:47.26#	Kate	Grace	USA	24.10.88	1		Seattle	14 Jan
8:49.52	Axumawit	Embaye	ETH	18.10.94	3		Karlsruhe	4 Feb
8:50.36	Taye	Fantu	ETH-J	29.3.99	1		Eaubonne	10 Feb
8:50.74	Gudaf	Tsegay	ETH	23.1.97	2		Eaubonne	10 Feb
8:51.27	Heather	Kampf	USA	19.1.87	1		New York (Armory)	4 Feb
8:51.58	Claudia	Bobocea	ROU	11.6.92	5		Karlsruhe	4 Feb
8:51.75	Konstanze	Klosterhalfen	GER	18.2.97	6		Karlsruhe	4 Feb
8:52.08	Kate	Van Buskirk	CAN	9.7.87	1	Mill	New York (Armory)	11 Feb

8:52.35#	Brie	Felnagle	USA	9.12.86	14 Jan	8:55.83	Violah	Lagat	KEN	13.3.89	11 Feb
8:52.53	Luiza	Gega	ALB	5.11.88	10 Feb	8:56.13	Gesa Felicitas	Krause	GER	3.8.92	19 Feb
8:53.48	Stephanie	Garcia	USA	3.5.88	11 Feb	8:56.14#	Leah	O'Connor	USA	30.8.92	14 Jan
8:53.55	Nicole	Sifuentes	CAN	30.6.86	28 Jan	8:56.19	Giulia	Viola	ITA	24.4.91	5 Mar
8:53.56	Alina	Reh	GBR	23.5.97	19 Feb	8:56.52	Shannon	Osika	USA	15.6.93	11 Feb
8:54.06	Dominique	Scott	RSA	24.6.92	28 Jan	8:56.88	Feyisa	Adanech	ETH-J	23.1.98	4 Feb
8:54.61	Tori	Gerlach	USA	2.6.94	11 Feb	8:57.24	Emily	Lipari	USA	19.11.92	4 Feb
8:54.71#	Lauren	Paquette	USA	27.6.86	14 Jan	8:57.65	Birtukan	Fente	ETH	18.6.89	18 Feb
8:55.20	Ana	Lozano	ESP	22.2.91	5 Mar	8:57.86	Hanna	Klein	GER	6.4.93	19 Feb
8:55.21	Charlotta	Fougberg	SWE	19.6.85	3 Mar	8:57.87mx	Cory	McGee	USA	29.5.92	31 Dec

5000 METRES

14:49.12	Laura	Muir	GBR	9.5.93	1		Glasgow		4 Jan
15:01.64	Molly	Huddle	USA	31.8.84	1		Boston (Allston)		26 Feb
15:02.10	Emily	Sisson	USA	12.10.91	2		Boston (Allston)		26 Feb
15:19.14	Karissa	Schweizer	USA	4.5.96	1	NCAA	College Station		10 Mar
15:27.36	Erin	Finn	USA	19.11.94	2	NCAA	College Station		10 Mar
15:28.89#	Katherine	Receveur	USA	19.1.96	1	Big10	Geneva		25 Feb
15:28.99#	Tessa	Barrett	USA	9.2.96	2	Big10	Geneva		25 Feb
15:29.83	Anna	Rohrer	USA-J	27.2.98	3	NCAA	College Station		10 Mar

60 METRES HURDLES

Mark	First	Last	Nat	DOB	Pos	Meet	Venue	Date
7.74A	Kendra	Harrison	USA	18.9.92	1h2	NC	Albuquerque	5 Mar
7.75					1		Lexington	21 Jan
7.79	Pamela	Dutkiewicz	GER	28.9.91	1	NC	Leipzig	18 Feb
7.82	Christina	Manning	USA	29.5.90	1		Athlone	15 Feb
7.82A	Jasmin	Stowers	USA	23.9.91	2	NC	Albuquerque	5 Mar
7.99					2		Toruń	7 Feb
7.84	Cindy	Roleder	GER	21.8.89	2	NC	Leipzig	18 Feb
7.86	Alina	Talay	BLR	14.5.89	1s1	EI	Beograd	3 Mar
7.87A	Sharika	Nelvis	USA	10.5.90	2h1	NC	Albuquerque	5 Mar
7.87	Sasha	Wallace	USA	21.9.95	1h1	NCAA	College Station	10 Mar
7.91	Sally	Pearson	AUS	19.9.86	2h1		Karlsruhe	4 Feb
7.92	Hanna	Plotitsyna	UKR	1.1.87	2s1	EI	Beograd	3 Mar
7.92	Nadine	Visser	NED	9.2.95	2h2	EI	Beograd	3 Mar
7.93	Phylicia	George	CAN	16.11.87	1		Łódź	16 Feb
7.93	Devynne	Charlton	BAH	26.11.95	2	NCAA	College Station	11 Mar
7.95A	Jacquelyne	Coward	USA	5.11.89	3h2	NC	Albuquerque	5 Mar
7.97					2		Val de Reuil	6 Feb
7.96	Leah	Nugent	USA	23.11.92	2		Lexington	21 Jan
7.96	Cindy	Ofili	GBR	5.8.91	5		Karlsruhe	4 Feb
7.96	Andrea	Ivancevic	CRO	21.8.84	1		Toruń	10 Feb
7.97	Pedrya	Seymour	BAH	29.5.95	3	NCAA	College Station	11 Mar
7.98	Isabelle	Pedersen	NOR	27.1.92	2h2		Karlsruhe	4 Feb
7.98A	Tobi	Amusan	NGR	23.4.97	1h2		Albuquerque	10 Mar
8.00					3h1	NCAA	College Station	10 Mar
7.98	Mikiah	Brisco	USA	14.7.96	1	Tyson	Fayetteville	10 Feb
7.98	Anne	Zagré	BEL	13.3.90	1		Metz	12 Feb
7.98	Anna	Cockrell	USA	28.8.97	2h1	NCAA	College Station	10 Mar
7.99	Ricarda	Lobe	GER	13.4.94	3	NC	Leipzig	18 Feb
8.00	Tiffany	McReynolds	USA	4.12.91	2		Łódź	16 Feb
8.00	Klaudia	Siciarz	POL-J	15.3.98	1	NC	Toruń	18 Feb
8.01A	Alaysh'a	Johnson	USA	.96				11 Feb
8.05								10 Mar
8.02	Jasmine	Camacho-Quinn	PUR	21.8.96				25 Feb
8.02	Rushelle	Burton	JAM	4.12.97				11 Mar
8.03	Janay	DeLoach	USA	12.10.85				11 Feb
8.03	Sharona	Bakker	NED	12.4.90				16 Feb
8.03	Kendell	Williams	USA	14.6.95				10 Mar
8.04	Anastasiya	Nikolayeva	RUS	24.9.95				14 Feb
8.04	Elisávet	Pesirídou	GRE	12.2.92				19 Feb
8.04A	Evonne	Britton	USA	10.10.91				5 Mar
8.05	Vanessa	Clerveaux	USA	17.6.94				25 Feb
8.06	Ivana	Loncarek	CRO	8.4.91				10 Feb
8.06	Susanna	Kallur	SWE	16.2.81				11 Feb
8.06A	Lorenda	Holston	USA	15.8.95				11 Feb
8.06	Lindsay	Lindley	NGR	6.10.89				12 Feb
8.07	Karolina	Koleczek	POL	15.1.93				18 Feb
8.07	Megan	Simmonds	JAM	18.3.94				18 Feb
8.08	Dior	Hall	USA	2.1.96				10 Feb
8.08	Nooralotta	Neziri	FIN	9.11.92				19 Feb
8.08	Raven	Clay	USA	5.10.90				16 Feb
8.09	Danielle	Williams	JAM	14.9.92				17 Feb
8.10	Jade	Barber	USA	4.4.93				4 Feb
8.10A	Kaila	Barber	USA	4.4.93				5 Mar

HIGH JUMP

Mark	First	Last	Nat	DOB	Pos	Meet	Venue	Date
2.03	Mariya	Kuchina	RUS	14.1.93	1	NC	Moskva	21 Feb
2.01	Airine	Palsyte	LTU	13.7.92	1	EI	Beograd	4 Mar
1.98	Ruth	Beitia	ESP	1.4.79	1		Madrid	24 Feb
1.97	Kamila	Licwinko	POL	22.3.86	1		Łódź	16 Feb
1.96	Nafissatou	Thiam	BEL	19.8.94	1P	EI	Beograd	3 Mar
1.96A	Vashti	Cunningham	USA-J	18.1.98	1	NC	Albuquerque	5 Mar
1.94	Oksana	Okuneva	UKR	14.3.90	1	NC	Sumy	18 Feb
1.94	Yuliya	Levchenko	UKR	28.11.97	3	EI	Beograd	4 Mar
1.93	Iryna	Herashchenko	UKR	10.3.95	1		Banská Bystrica	8 Feb
1.93	Madeline	Fagan	USA	4.6.96	1	NCAA	College Station	10 Mar
1.92	Jossie	Graumann	GER	18.3.94	1		Unna	22 Jan
1.92	Ana	Simic	CRO	5.5.90	2		Cottbus	25 Jan
1.92	Morgan	Lake	GBR	12.5.97	1		Hustopece	4 Feb
1.92	Sofie	Skoog	SWE	7.6.90	1	v3N	Tampere	11 Feb
1.92	Marie-Laurence	Jungfleisch	GER	7.10.90	1	NC	Leipzig	19 Feb
1.92	Michaela	Hrubá	CZE-J	21.2.98	6	EI	Beograd	4 Mar
1.91	Svetlana	Nikolenko	RUS	26.9.91	2		Chelyabinsk	11 Jan
1.91	Linda	Sandblom	FIN	18.10.89	1	NC	Jyvaskyla	19 Feb
1.91	Kristina	Korolyova	RUS	6.11.90	2	NC	Moskva	21 Feb
1.91	Natalya	Aksenova	RUS	6.6.97	3	NC	Moskva	21 Feb
1.91	Svetlana	Shkolina	RUS	9.3.86	4	NC	Moskva	21 Feb
1.91		Zheng Xingjuan	CHN	20.3.89	1		Xianlin	28 Feb
1.90	Tatiana	Goúsin	GRE	26.1.94	7	Jan	1.89	Alyxandria	Treasure	CAN	15.5.92	8 Feb
1.90	Yuliya	Chumachenko	UKR	2.10.94	10	Jan	1.89	Lavern	Spencer	LCA	23.6.84	8 Feb
1.90	Erika	Furlani	ITA	2.1.96	5	Feb	1.89	Doreen	Amata	NGR	6.5.88	8 Feb
1.90	Stacey	Destin	USA	7.11.96	10	Mar	1.89	Bethan	Partridge	GBR	11.7.90	11 Feb
1.90	Logan	Boss	USA	4.8.97	10	Mar	1.89	Mariya	Zhodzik	BLR	19.1.97	18 Feb
1.89	Marija	Vukovic	MNE	21.1.92	25	Jan	1.89	Yekaterina	Krasovskiy	AUT	13.7.84	19 Feb
1.89	Emma	Green	SWE	8.12.84	28	Jan	1.88*	Natalya	Baluyeva	RUS	24.12.92	24 Dec
1.89	Serena	Capponcelli	ITA	24.1.89	29	Jan	1.88*	Aleksandra	Yaryshkina	RUS	10.6.94	24 Dec
1.89	Alina	Shukh	UKR-J	12.2.99	4	Feb	1.88	Marina	Smolyakova	RUS	12.6.89	15 Jan

WORLD INDOOR LISTS 2017

1.88	Yekaterina	Stepanova	RUS	24.7.94	15 Jan		1.88	Prisca	Duvernay	FRA	26.5.91	28 Jan
1.88	Laura	Gröll	GER-J	11.4.98	21 Jan		1.88	Inika	McPherson	USA	29.9.86	16 Feb
1.88	Katarina	Mögenburg	NOR	16.6.91	22 Jan		1.88	Irina	Ilyeva	RUS	22.12.89	21 Feb
1.88	Karina	Taranda	BLR-J	10.2.99	25 Jan		1.88	Yevgeniya	Kononova	RUS	28.9.89	21 Feb
							1.88	Eleonora	Omoregie	ITA	22.5.96	24 Feb

POLE VAULT

4.85	Ekaterini	Stefanídi	GRE	4.2.90	1	EI	Beograd	4 Mar
4.81	Jennifer	Suhr	USA	5.2.82	1		Kent	14 Jan
4.75	Elizaveta	Ryzih	GER	27.9.88	2	EI	Beograd	4 Mar
4.72	Sandi	Morris	USA	8.7.92	1		Düsseldorf	1 Feb
4.70	Anzhelika	Sidorova	RUS	28.6.91	1		Novocheboksarsk	14 Jan
4.70	Eliza	McCartney	NZL	11.12.96	1		Auckland	22 Feb
4.66	Wilma	Murto	FIN-J	11.6.98	1		Tignes	6 Jan
4.65	Alysha	Newman	CAN	29.6.94	1		Toronto	21 Jan
4.65A	Katie	Nageotte	USA	30.6.91	2	NC	Albuquerque	5 Mar
4.65A	Mary	Saxer Sibears	USA	21.6.87	3	NC	Albuquerque	5 Mar
4.61	Nicole	Büchler	SUI	17.12.83	3		Clermont-Ferrand	5 Feb
4.60	Olga	Mullina	RUS	1.8.92	2	NC	Moskva	5 Feb
4.60	Lexi	Weeks	USA	20.11.96	1		Fayetteville	17 Feb
4.60	Angelica	Bengtsson	SWE	8.7.93	1	NC	Växjö	25 Feb
4.60A	Kortney	Ross	USA	26.7.92	4	NC	Albuquerque	5 Mar
4.57	Tori	Weeks	USA	20.11.96	1	SEC	Nashville	24 Feb
4.56	Morgann	LeLeux	USA	14.11.92	1		Baton Rouge	17 Feb
4.55	Megan	Clark	USA	10.6.94	1		Seattle	28 Jan
4.55	Minna	Nikkanen	FIN	9.4.88	2		Karlsruhe	4 Feb
4.55	Maryna	Kylypko	UKR	10.11.95	1		Metz	12 Feb
4.55	Michaela	Meijer	SWE	30.7.93	2	NC	Växjö	25 Feb
4.55	Lisa	Gunnarsson	SWE	20.8.99	6=	EI	Beograd	4 Mar
4.55A	Kristen	Brown	USA	26.5.92	5	NC	Albuquerque	5 Mar
4.51	Annika	Roloff	GER	10.3.91	1		Potsdam	3 Feb
4.51	Romana	Maláčová	CZE	15.5.87	4		Clermont-Ferrand	5 Feb
4.51	Kristen	Hixson	USA	1.7.92	1		Allendale	10 Feb
4.50	Angelina	Krasnova	RUS	7.2.91	3		Novocheboksarsk	14 Jan
4.50	Irina	Yakoltsevich	BLR	26.1.93	1		Eaubonne	10 Feb
4.50	Polina	Knoroz	RUS-J	20.7.99	4	NC	Moskva	19 Feb
4.49	Olivia	Gruver	USA	29.7.97	24 Feb		4.40	Alayna	Lutkovskaya	RUS	15.3.96	10 Feb
4.45A	Allison	Koressel	USA	2.3.91	21 Jan		4.40		Li Ling	CHN	6.7.89	20 Feb
4.45	Anicka	Newell	CAN	5.8.93	11 Feb		4.40	Amalie	Svábiková	CZE-J	22.11.99	26 Feb
4.45	Emily	Grove	USA	22.5.93	17 Feb		4.40	Angelica	Moser	SUI	9.10.97	4 Mar
4.45	Tina	Sutej	SLO	7.11.88	25 Feb		4.40A	Jacqueline	Williams	USA	13.11.94	5 Mar
4.45	Lakan	Taylor	USA	21.6.95	11 Mar		4.40	Lucy	Bryan	GBR	22.5.95	11 Mar
4.45	Annie	Rhodes	USA	13.5.95	11 Mar		4.38		Xu Huiqin	CHN	4.9.93	21 Jan
4.43	Anjuli	Knäsche	GER	18.10.93	25 Feb		4.36	Jade	Ive	GBR	22.1.92	19 Feb
4.42	Kally	Long	USA	28.8.95	14 Jan		4.35	Kayla	Caldwell	USA	19.6.91	3 Feb
4.41	Marion	Lotout	FRA	19.11.89	6 Jan		4.35	Alina	McDonald	USA	26.8.97	11 Feb
4.40	Mariya	Zakharutkina	RUS	14.8.96	11 Jan		4.35	Desiree	Freier	USA	24.7.96	11 Feb
4.40	Marta	Onofre	POR	28.1.91	25 Jan		4.35	Maria Eleonor	Tavares	POR	24.9.85	18 Feb
4.40	Victoria	von Eynatten	GER	7.10.91	4 Feb		4.35	Nikol	Jiroutová	CZE	30.3.92	26 Feb
4.40	Tatyana	Shvydkina	RUS	8.5.90	7 Feb		4.34	Fanny	Smets	BEL	21.4.86	25 Feb

LONG JUMP

7.24	Ivana	Spanovic	SRB	10.5.90	1	EI	Beograd	5 Mar
6.97	Lorraine	Ugen	GBR	22.8.91	2	EI	Beograd	5 Mar
6.94	Claudia	Salman-Rath	GER	25.4.86	3	EI	Beograd	5 Mar
6.90	Sha'Keela	Saunders	USA	18.12.93	1	NCAA	College Station	10 Mar
6.84	Darya	Klishina	RUS	15.1.91	4	EI	Beograd	5 Mar
6.79	Ksenja	Balta	EST	1.11.86	5	EI	Beograd	5 Mar
6.76	Quanesha	Burks	USA	15.3.95	2	SEC	Nashville	25 Feb
6.72	Keturah	Orji	USA	5.3.96	3	SEC	Nashville	25 Feb
6.71	Alexandra	Wester	GER	21.3.94	3	ISTAF	Berlin	10 Feb
6.71	Jazmin	Sawyers	GBR	21.5.94	2		Birmingham	18 Feb
6.71	Maryna	Bekh	UKR	18.7.95	Q	EI	Beograd	4 Mar
6.69	Katarina	Johnson-Thompson	GBR	9.1.93	2	NC	Sheffield	12 Feb
6.68	Tara	Davis	USA-J	20.5.99	1		Frisco	11 Feb
6.67	Chantel	Malone	IVB	2.12.91	4	ISTAF	Berlin	10 Feb
6.59	Marina	Buchelnikova	RUS	8.2.94	2	Winter	Moskva	5 Feb
6.59	Laura	Strati	ITA	3.10.90	1	NC	Ancona	18 Feb
6.57	Heather	Arneton	FRA-Y	27.7.02	1		Eaubonne	15 Jan
6.56	Yariagnis	Argüelles	CUB	18.4.84	1		Madrid	2 Feb
6.56	Maryse	Luzolo	GER	13.3.95	5	ISTAF	Berlin	10 Feb
6.56	Angela	Morosanu	ROU	26.7.86	1	NC	Bucuresti	19 Feb
6.55		Zhou Xiaoxue	CHN	19.6.92	1		Xianlin	27 Feb
6.53	Jhoanmy	Luque	VEN	20.12.95	24 Feb		6.51		Lu Minjia	CHN	29.12.92	27 Feb
6.52	Kendell	Williams	USA	14.6.95	21 Jan		6.51		Xu Xiaoling	CHN	13.5.92	27 Feb
6.51	Juliet	Itoya	ESP	17.8.86	18 Feb		6.50	Melanie	Bauschke	GER	14.7.88	10 Feb

TRIPLE JUMP

Mark	First	Last	Nat	DOB	Pos	Rd	Venue	Date
14.79	Yulimar	Rojas	VEN	21.10.95	1		Madrid	28 Jan
14.37	Kristin	Gierisch	GER	20.8.90	1	EI	Beograd	4 Mar
14.33	Elena	Panturoiu	ROU	24.2.95	1		Bucuresti	4 Feb
14.32	Keturah	Orji	USA	5.3.96	1	SEC	Nashville	24 Feb
14.32	Patricia	Mamona	POR	21.11.88	2	EI	Beograd	4 Mar
14.27	Jenny	Elbe	GER	18.4.90	Q	EI	Beograd	3 Mar
14.24	Paraskeví	Papahrístou	GRE	17.4.89	3	EI	Beograd	4 Mar
14.20	Ana	Peleteiro	ESP	2.12.95	Q	EI	Beograd	3 Mar
14.18	Kristiina	Mäkelä	FIN	20.11.92	Q	EI	Beograd	3 Mar
14.15	Anna	Jagaciak-Michalska	POL	10.2.90	Q	EI	Beograd	3 Mar
14.09	Neele	Eckhardt	GER	2.7.92	2		Düsseldorf	1 Feb
14.05	Darya	Derkach	ITA	27.3.93	1	NC	Ancona	19 Feb
14.02	Olha	Saladukha	UKR	4.6.83	1	NC	Sumy	19 Feb
14.02	Irina	Gumenyuk	RUS	6.1.88	1	NC	Moskva	21 Feb
14.01	Jeanine	Assani Issouf	FRA	17.8.92	1		Eaubonne	10 Feb
14.00	Viktoriy	Prokopenko	RUS	17.4.91	2	NC	Moskva	21 Feb
13.99	Susana	Costa	POR	22.9.84	7	EI	Beograd	4 Mar
13.94	Irina	Vaskovskaya	BLR	2.4.91	1		Mogilyov	21 Jan
13.93	Yanis	David	FRA	12.12.97	1	Tyson	Fayetteville	11 Feb
13.93		Rao Fan	CHN	1.1.96	1		Xianlin	28 Feb
13.89	Anna	Krylova	RUS	3.10.85	4	Feb		
13.86	Cristina	Bujin	ROU	12.4.88	18	Feb		
13.86A	Tori	Franklin	USA	7.10.92	5	Mar		
13.83	Aiga	Grabuste	LAT	24.3.88	9	Feb		
13.83		Chen Ting	CHN	28.8.97	24	Feb		
13.76		Deng Linuo	CHN	16.3.92	28	Feb		
13.75	Shardia	Lawrence	JAM	31.12.95	11	Feb		
13.72	Dana	Veldáková	SVK	3.6.81	3	Mar		
13.70	Lucie	Májková	CZE	9.7.88	17	Jan		
13.69	Violetta	Skvortsova	BLR	15.4.98	18	Feb		
13.66	Natalya	Yevdokimova	RUS	7.9.93	4	Feb		
13.66	Irina	Ektova	KAZ	8.1.87	11	Feb		
13.65	Jhoanmy	Luque	VEN	20.12.95	25	Feb		
13.64	Athanasía	Pérra	GRE	2.2.83	19	Feb		

SHOT

Mark	First	Last	Nat	DOB	Pos	Rd	Venue	Date
19.56	Raven	Saunders	USA	15.5.96	1	NCAA	College Station	10 Mar
19.28	Anita	Márton	HUN	15.1.89	1	EI	Beograd	3 Mar
19.03A	Michelle	Carter	USA	12.10.85	1	NC	Albuquerque	5 Mar
18.72	Felisha	Johnson	USA	24.7.89	1		Indianapolis	11 Feb
18.54	Jeneva	Stevens	USA	28.10.89	1		Birmingham AL	21 Jan
18.50	Christina	Schwanitz	GER	24.12.85	1	NC	Leipzig	18 Feb
18.45	Dani	Bunch	USA	16.5.91	1		Notre Dame	18 Feb
18.40	Danniel	Thomas	JAM	11.11.92	2	NCAA	College Station	10 Mar
18.39	Yuliya	Leontyuk	BLR	31.3.84	1		Minsk	11 Feb
18.36	Radoslava	Mavrodieva	BUL	13.3.87	2	EI	Beograd	3 Mar
18.29	Brittany	Smith	USA	25.3.91	2	NC	Albuquerque	5 Mar
18.13	Alyona	Dubitskaya	BLR	25.1.90	Q	EI	Beograd	3 Mar
18.13	Fanny	Roos	SWE	2.1.95	4	EI	Beograd	3 Mar
18.12	Maggie	Ewen	USA	23.9.94	1		Albuquerque	11 Feb
18.09	Claudine	Vita	GER	19.9.96	5	EI	Beograd	3 Mar
18.00	Emel	Dereli	TUR	25.2.96	1		Izmir	11 Feb
18.00	Paulina	Guba	POL	14.5.90	6	EI	Beograd	3 Mar
17.93	Brittany	Crew	CAN	3.6.94	1		State College	18 Feb
17.89		Bian Ka	CHN	5.1.93	1		Beijing	20 Feb
17.85	Yevgeniya	Solovyova	RUS	28.6.86	1	NC	Moskva	20 Feb
17.80	Erin	Farmer	USA	11.8.95	1		Bloomington IN	21 Jan
17.78	Brittany	Mann	USA	16.4.94	10	Mar		
17.76	Jessica	Cérival	FRA	20.1.82	3	Mar		
17.70	Kelsey	Card	USA	20.8.92	17	Feb		
17.68	Alina	Kenzel	GER	10.8.97	5	Feb		
17.65	Valeriya	Zyryanova	RUS	12.8.90	4	Feb		
17.62	McKenzie	Warren	USA	3.12.93	11	Feb		
17.60	Chase	Ealey	USA	20.7.94	5	Mar		
17.58		Liu Xiangrong	CHN	6.6.88	20	Feb		
17.57	Christina	Hillman	USA	6.10.93	5	Mar		
17.55	Jessica	Woodard	USA	4.2.95	10	Feb		
17.54	Melissa	Boekelman	NED	11.5.89	11	Feb		
17.51	Alyssa	Wilson	USA	20.2.99	28	Feb		
17.50	Viktoriya	Kolb	BLR	26.10.93	25	Jan		
17.50	Emmonie	Henderson	USA	5.11.94	10	Mar		
17.47	Lloydricia	Cameron	USA	8.4.96	20	Jan		
17.47	Monique	Riddick	USA	8.11.89	25	Feb		
17.45	Noora	Salem Jassem	BRN	27.11.96	4	Feb		
17.43	Rachel	Wallader	GBR	1.9.89	11	Feb		
17.37	Austra	Skujyte	LTU	12.8.79	3	Mar		
17.35	Cion	Hicks	USA	14.10.94	11	Feb		
17.34	Josephine	Terlecki	GER	17.2.86	12	Feb		
17.33	Alyona	Bugakova	RUS	15.4.97	11	Feb		
17.33		Geng Shuang	CHN	9.7.93	20	Feb		
17.31	Janeah	Stewart	USA	21.7.96	24	Feb		
17.30	Dimitriana	Surdu	MDA	12.5.94	25	Feb		
17.23	Rachel	Fatherly	USA	20.4.94	29	Jan		
17.21	Anna	Avdeyeva	RUS	6.4.85	20	Feb		
17.20	Vera	Kunova	RUS	2.4.90	4	Feb		

WEIGHT

Mark	First	Last	Nat	DOB	Pos	Rd	Venue	Date
25.60	Gwen	Berry	USA	29.6.89	1	NC	Albuquerque	4 Mar
24.30	DeAnna	Price	USA	8.6.93	2	NC	Albuquerque	4 Mar
24.22	Felisha	Johnson	USA	24.7.89	3	NC	Albuquerque	4 Mar

WORLD INDOOR LISTS 2017   591

24.04	Jessica	Ramsey	USA	26.7.91	4	NC	Albuquerque		4 Mar
23.73	Ida	Storm	SWE	26.12.91	1		Malmö		15 Feb
23.65	Jeneva	Stevens	USA	28.10.89	1		Birmingham AL		21 Jan
23.61	Sultana	Frizell	CAN	24.10.84	1		Anderson		25 Feb
23.48	Amber	Campbell	USA	5.6.81	5	NC	Albuquerque		4 Mar
23.18	Janeah	Stewart	USA	21.7.96	1	SEC	Nashville		25 Feb
22.69	Annette	Echikunwoke	USA	29.7.96	1		Birmingham AL		24 Feb
22.53	LaPorscha	Wells	USA	25.10.94	1		Birmingham AL		22 Jan
22.38	Kaitlyn	Long	USA	25.4.96	1		Mankato		24 Feb
22.10*	Amanda	Bingson	USA	20.2.90	1		College Station		10 Dec
22.01	Dolly	Nyemah	USA	9.5.93	1		Notre Dame		23 Feb
21.89*	Mel	Herl	USA	14.2.94	9 Dec	21.73	Sade	Olatoye	USA	25.1.97	17 Feb
21.81	Janee'	Kassanavoid	USA	19.1.95	17 Feb	21.67A	Raven	Saunders	USA	15.5.96	3 Feb
21.76	Shelby	Ashe	USA	13.3.93	27 Jan	21.66A	Brooke	Andersen	USA	23.8.95	17 Feb
21.74	Victoria	Merriweather	USA	2.1.95	11 Mar	21.60	Banke	Oginni	USA	8.5.96	21 Jan

PENTATHLON

4870	Nafissatou	Thiam	BEL	19.8.94	1	EI	Beograd		3 Mar
	8.23	1.96	15.29	6.37	2:24.44				
4767	Ivona	Dadic	AUT	29.12.93	2	EI	Beograd		3 Mar
	8.45	1.87	13.93	6.41	2:14.13				
4723	Györgyi	Zsivoczky-Farkas	HUN	13.2.85	3	EI	Beograd		3 Mar
	8.47	1.81	14.95	6.38	2:15.86				
4686#	Kendell	Williams	USA	14.6.95	1	SEC	Nashville		25 Feb
	8.04	1.84	12.66	6.49	2:19.65				
4682					1	NCAA	College Station		10 Mar
	8.03	1.78	12.96	6.43	2:15.61				
4631	Xénia	Krizsán	HUN	13.1.93	4	EI	Beograd		3 Mar
	8.30	1.81	14.24	6.09	2:15.08				
4582	Nadine	Broersen	NED	29.4.90	5	EI	Beograd		3 Mar
	8.42	1.81	14.59	6.19	2:20.63				
4580	Taliyah	Brooks	USA	8.2.95	2	NCAA	College Station		10 Mar
	8.13	1.84	11.97	6.33	2:22.39				
4558A	Erica	Bougard	USA	26.7.93	1	NC	Albuquerque		3 Mar
	8.21	1.87	11.97	6.18	2:18.41				
4550	Alina	Shukh	UKR-J	12.2.99	1		Zaporizhzhya		27 Jan
	8.85	1.88	14.27	6.04	2:17.69				
4486	Verena	Preiner	AUT	1.2.95	1		Linz		15 Jan
	8.65	1.72	14.21	6.06	2:11.21				
4473	Lecabela	Quaresma	POR	26.12.89	1	NC	Bordeaux		18 Feb
	8.54	1.76	14.29	6.06	2:17.60				
4452	Yana	Maksimova	BLR	9.1.89	1		Mogilyov		25 Jan
	8.94	1.85	14.71	5.93	2:20.29				
4428	Nadine	Visser	NED	9.2.95	1	NC	Apeldoorn		5 Feb
	8.01	1.68	13.61	6.18	2:21.90				
4409	Lucie	Slanicková	SVK	8.11.88	9	EI	Beograd		3 Mar
	8.60	1.78	11.30	6.35	2:15.40				
4404A	Sharon	Day-Monroe	USA	9.6.85	2	NC	Albuquerque		3 Mar
	8.56	1.75	14.44	5.85	2:17.55				
4389	Bianca	Salming	SWE-J	22.11.98	10	EI	Beograd		3 Mar
	8.87	1.81	13.59	5.67	2:11.44				
4379#	Leigha	Brown	USA	19.9.94	3	SEC	Nashville		25 Feb
	8.41	1.75	13.05	5.91	2:16.41				
4377	4257				3		Fayetteville		27 Jan
		Shukh			11	EI	Beograd		3 Mar
	8.99	1.84	13.22	5.90	2:16.29				
4376#	Barbara	Nwaba	USA	18.1.89	1		Seattle		27 Jan
	8.50	1.82	13.93	5.38	2:14.33				
4367	Mariya	Pavlova	RUS	21.5.96	1	NC	Smolensk		15 Feb
	8.62	1.84	12.95	5.90	2:21.47				
4340	Nina	Schultz	CAN-J	12.11.98	10 Mar	4278	Kelsey	Herman	USA	15.6.96	27 Jan
4319	Michelle	Atherley	USA	9.12.95	10 Mar	4256	Esther	Turpin	FRA	29.4.96	4 Feb
4309	Elena	Panturoiu	ROU	24.2.95	11 Feb	4248	Odile	Ahouanwanou	BEN	5.1.91	18 Feb
4302	Caroline	Agnou	SUI	26.5.96	5 Feb	4221	Géraldine	Ruckstuhl	SUI-J	24.2.98	5 Feb
4301	Laura	Arteil	FRA	9.10.93	3 Mar	4211A	Sami	Spenner	USA	21.3.91	3 Mar
4297	Noor	Vidts	BEL	30.5.96	5 Feb	4210	Mareike	Arndt	GER	29.1.92	29 Jan
4291A	Brittany	Howell	USA	1.9.92	3 Feb	4204#	Jaclyn	Siefring	USA	.96	3 Feb
4284	Hanna	Gorodskaya	BLR	31.1.93	25 Jan						

12:08.83	Antonella	Palmisano	ITA	6.8.91	1	NC	Ancona		18 Feb

3000 METRES WALK

5000 METRES WALK

20:15.6*	Yelena	Lashmanova	RUS	9.4.92	1		Saransk		30 Dec
20:23.2*	Yekaterina	Medvedeva	RUS	29.3.94	2		Saransk		30 Dec
20:48.9*	Sofiya	Brodatskaya	RUS	4.10.95	3		Saransk		30 Dec

LATE AMENDMENTS

p.5 Olympics: LJ: 2. Luvo Manyonga
p..34: Recent Marriages: Maren Kock GER & Florian Orth GER 25.3.17
  Name changes: Eva Strogies GER now Meisolle
  Transfer of Allegiance: Miguel Francis ANT to GBR

p.63 **European Youth ~Championships:** Placing/Medal table leaders

Nat.	G	S	B	Points
GER	4	4	2	136
GBR	5	4	4	131.5
FRA	3	2	2	97
ESP	-	4	4	96
ITA	3	3	3	89.25
FIN	2	-	5	84
POL	1	2	2	75
ROU	2	1	3	56
SWE	1	2	1	56
BEL	1	2	1	53
GRE	3	1	1	50.5
UKR	2	-	1	50
BLR	1	3	1	47
SUI	2	-	-	44
TUR	1	2	1	42

30 nations won medals (22 gold)

Drugs bans

Further RUS cancelled results from 2012 Olympic Games
Women: Viktoriya Valyukevich (8th TJ), Mariya Bespalova (8th HT) and Gulfiya Khanafeyeva–Agafonova (13th HT qual)
Jemima Sumgong Jelagat KEN was reported to have failed an out-of-competition trest in February 2017 – an investigation is pending.

Obituary

p. 92: CAMPAGNER: b. 11 Oct 1920 Schio
p. 100 Witold KRUPINSKI (Poland) b. 2 Aug 1945 Skierniewice

Records

W20 PV: 5.90 Armand Duplantis SWE Austin 1 Apr 2017
W, Afr, Com: Road 10k, 15k, 20k, HMar: 30:04, 45:37, 1:01:25, 1:04.52 Joyciline Jepkosgei KEN at Praha 1 Apr 2017

IAAF World Indoor Tour 2017

Düsseldorf, Karlsruhe, Boston, Stockholm and Birmingham. Another (outside Europe) to be added for 2018.
Winners, who gained a 'wild card' for the 2018 World Indoor Championships.
Men: 400m: Pavel Maslák CZE, 1500m: Bethwel Birgen KEN, 60mh: Orlando Ortega ESP, HJ: Donald Thomas BAH, LJ: Khotso Mokoena RSA. Women: 60m: Gayon Evans JAM, 800m: Joanna Józwik POL, 3000m: Hellen Obiri KEN, PV: Nicole Büchler, TJ: Patricia Mamona POR, SP: Anita Márton.